I0822210

Dictionary of
Louisiana French

Senior Editor
Albert Valdman

Associate Editor
Kevin J. Rottet

Assistant Editors
Barry Jean Ancelet
Richard Guidry
Thomas A. Klingler
Amanda LaFleur
Tamara Lindner
Michael D. Picone
Dominique Ryon

Dictionary of Louisiana French

As Spoken in Cajun, Creole, and American Indian Communities

UPM

University Press of Mississippi / *Jackson*

This publication is funded under a grant from the Louisiana Endowment for the Humanities, the state affiliate of the National Endowment for the Humanities.

Publication of this book is also made possible in part by grants from the College of Arts and Sciences at Indiana University and the School of Liberal Arts at Tulane University.

Further support has been provided by the Cultural Services of the French Embassy and the Consulate General of France in New Orleans.

Liberté • Égalité • Fraternité

RÉPUBLIQUE FRANÇAISE

www.upress.state.ms.us

The University Press of Mississippi is a member of the Association of American University Presses.

Manufactured in the United States of America

First printing 2010

∞

Library of Congress Cataloging-in-Publication Data

Dictionary of Louisiana French : as spoken in Cajun, Creole, and American Indian communities / Albert Valdman, senior editor ; Kevin J. Rottet, associate editor.

p. cm.

Includes bibliographical references and index.

ISBN 978-1-60473-403-4 (cloth : alk. paper) 1. French language—Dialects—Louisiana—Dictionaries. 2. French language—Louisiana—History. I. Valdman, Albert. II. Rottet, Kevin J. (Kevin James)

PC3680.U7L728 2009

447'.976303—dc22 2009015211

British Library Cataloging-in-Publication Data available

In memory of Richard Guidry

When we remember Richard Guidry, it is tempting to recall the African proverb that says "when an elder dies, a library burns down." His vast knowledge of Louisiana French language, culture, geography, history, flora, and fauna was phenomenal, and it is certain that much was lost with his untimely passing in July 2008. Even today, when a question in any of these domains comes up, our first natural reflex is still to respond, "Let's call Richard!" Fortunately for us all, during his lifetime Richard generously shared his knowledge and love of French Louisiana with everyone who would listen. His stories, annotated maps, lists, emails, lectures, and dinner conversations touched the lives of people from many walks of life. And so, even though the vast library that was Richard Guidry is no longer with us, he saw to it that much of the wealth of his knowledge would be entrusted to a new generation. That was the kind of defender and steward of his culture that Richard was. The value of his contributions as a co-author of this dictionary is immeasurable, and so it is with gratitude and affection that we dedicate this work to his memory.

Contents

Acknowledgments

This dictionary was prepared under terms of two research grants from the National Endowment for the Humanities, Grant numbers PA-23298-99 and PA-24087-02, whose support is gratefully acknowledged. Matching support was also provided by Indiana University, the University of Louisiana at Lafayette, Louisiana State University, the University of Alabama, and the University of Wisconsin–Whitewater.

When there is a big job to be done in south Louisiana, it is often accomplished through a social cooperative effort that we call a *coup de main*. This term usually refers to the coming together of many friends, family, and neighbors in order to bring in a harvest quickly before a hurricane, to butcher a hog and consume the meat before it spoils, or in more modern times, to raise funds to help out a sick person with medical bills. This sharing of the load is also a way of turning tough times into good times. Therefore, we believe *coup de main* is also the appropriate term to describe the many hands that came together over the past ten years to bring this work to fruition.

First and foremost, we are deeply grateful to the numerous Louisiana French speakers who shared with us the riches of their cultural and linguistic heritage during the fieldwork sessions and other informal occasions. They spent countless hours answering our questions, granting our requests for yet more details, and even at times contacting us, leaving messages about words or phrases on answering machines and in emails. The fresh coffee, slices of pie, and good humor that they offered so graciously along with their time were *lagniappe*. It is with regret that we have decided not to list all of these informants, who number in the hundreds, for fear of inadvertently leaving some out. We hope, however, that they will be proud and gratified to read their words in the pages that follow.

One of the primary objectives of the team of authors was to insure that those Franco-Louisianans who are invested in or interested in their ancestral speech have access to this dictionary. That this more-than-900-page work is readily affordable was made possible by publication subsidies from the College of Arts and Sciences of Indiana University, the School of Liberal Arts at Tulane University, the Louisiana Endowment for the Humanities, and the *Festivals Acadiens et Créoles*. Our thanks also go to the Cultural Services of the French Embassy, and in particular to the Consulate General of France in New Orleans, for supporting the project by agreeing to purchase a significant number of copies of the dictionary for distribution to Louisiana schools. The tedious task of producing the reverse index that makes it possible to access information about particular words or expressions by means of English was undertaken generously and cheerfully by Dr. Marvin Moody, a former member of the Department of French and Italian at Indiana University who serves as pro bono informatics consultant for the Creole Institute.

A deep debt of gratitude is owed to Deborah Piston-Hatlen who, as program coordinator of the Creole Institute, oversaw various aspects of the preparation of the Louisiana French Dictionary Project. In addition to drafting funding proposals, coordinating the team, supervising research assistants, and filing and classifying the copious materials, she also managed the planning and production of the interactive CD-ROM, *A la découverte du français cadien à travers la parole/Discovering Cajun French through the Spoken Word*. David Rojas, a native Louisianan, served as informatics consultant during crucial stages of the project.

We are grateful to the Center for Acadian and Creole Folklore at the University of Louisiana at Lafayette, whose archives provided field recordings and transcriptions used extensively in our project. We also extend thanks to Debbie Clifton, Dana David, Elizabeth Landry, Luc Guglielmi, Lydwine Lafontaine, Monicque Larrocque, Katy Miller, and Helena Putnam, of the University of Louisiana at Lafayette, who assisted in the collection of data in the field and the transcription of material. Graduate students in various linguistic programs at Indiana

University—Bruce Anderson, Lisa Klueppel, Joe Price, Tristan Purvis, and Don Reindl—also provided research assistance during various stages of this project. Tristan's careful attention to detail was particularly appreciated in the editing of the dictionary. In Acadiana, Rocky McKeon and Brenda Mounier were keen word detectives who contributed new entries and provided important feedback to the editors by patiently responding to queries about forms and usage, and checking them with relatives and friends. At Tulane University, Katie Carmichael and Nathalie Dajko checked phonetic transcriptions in the final editing stages.

We also owe a large debt to Audrey Babineaux-George, who currently resides in Houma. The interest of the project director, Albert Valdman, in the linguistic situation of south Louisiana dates back more than forty years to a serendipitous meeting with Audrey who, at that time, served as foreign language consultant for the Louisiana Department of Education. To demonstrate that Louisiana French was still widely spoken, she invited Valdman to speak at the annual meeting of the Louisiana Foreign Language Teachers Association. With the assistance of the late Hosea Phillips, Professor of French at the University of Southwestern Louisiana (later renamed the University of Louisiana at Lafayette) and author of an early description of the French of Evangeline Parish, she introduced Valdman to many fluent speakers of the language as well as to James Domengeaux as the latter was launching CODOFIL (Council for the Development of French in Louisiana). Many years later, Audrey Babineaux-George facilitated Kevin Rottet's extensive fieldwork in Lafourche and Terrebonne parishes by providing contacts with French-speaking Cajun and American Indian communities. Cheril Eden and Reggie and Yvonne Dupre also deserve special mention for their extensive help to Rottet in making contacts with Cajun French speakers over the years, as well as their personal friendship.

The idea for this dictionary emerged in the 1980s during a meeting between Albert Valdman, Barry Ancelet, and David Barry, current dean of the College of Arts and Sciences at the University of Louisiana at Lafayette. Ancelet and Barry had reached the conclusion that only by the use of emerging informatics could a proper lexical inventory of Louisiana French be undertaken. That decade saw the publication of three lexical studies of Louisiana French, those of Father Jules Daigle (the most extensive), Patrick Griolet, and Maguy Lavaud-Grassin, whose seminal contributions to the present undertaking are recognized in the preface. These works challenged and motivated us to invest ourselves in a more comprehensive documentation of the lexical inventory of French in Louisiana, which financial support from the NEH and the universities mentioned, along with the assistance of many other hands and minds, made possible.

The great English lexicographer Samuel Johnson characterized members of that profession as "harmless drudges." Indeed, preparing a dictionary is a long-term endeavor, requiring heavy time commitments on the part of its authors and great forbearance on the part of the members of their families. It is told that the wife of an early English lexicographer, Thomas Cooper, grew so "irreconcilably angry with him sitting-up late at night so, compiling his dictionary" that she sneaked into his study, gathered the fruit of his labor, and threw it into the fire. We were fortunate that our spouses or partners and children showed more forbearance. For almost a decade, they remained unwavering in their support, agreeing to unburden us of household and other responsibilities so that we could continue to be harmless drudges. To them we owe the greatest debt of all.

Preface

The *Dictionary of Louisiana French: As Spoken in Cajun, Creole, and American Indian Communities* is the capstone of a long-term collaborative project whose objective has been to document all French-related varieties in Louisiana. The salient features of this project are its collaborative nature and the inclusion of outreach components. It has served as a catalyst in establishing communication among scholars working on French-related speech varieties in Louisiana. These efforts have already yielded significant results. In addition to the *Dictionary of Louisiana Creole*, the first major inventory of the vocabulary for that language, they have led to the publication of a state-of-the-art collective volume, *French and Creole in Louisiana*, and have facilitated, on the part of Louisiana-based scholars, a more robust contribution to published overviews of all varieties of North American French, such as *Le français en Amérique du Nord: État présent*. The outreach objectives of the project were partially fulfilled by the preparation and distribution of a CD-ROM, *Discovering Cajun French through the spoken word /A la découverte du français cadien à travers la parole*. This product made it possible to disseminate part of the results of the research to a very broad public, including the francophone Louisianans who had served as consultants during the fieldwork. This very complex and sophisticated CD-ROM not only provides 150 pages of representative texts accompanied by oral samples, but it incorporates lexical search software that provides access to a 3,000 word lexicon. It also contains a concordance for that lexicon and makes it possible for the user to locate each occurrence of the individual items in the texts. Another important outreach contribution of the project is the continuing Louisiana contribution to an international database, the *Banque de données lexicographiques panfrancophone* (BDLP). The BDLP is a collaborative project sponsored by the Agence universitaire de la Francophonie that makes available freely, on-line, the differential vocabulary of more than a dozen regions where French is either the everyday or official language. This vocabulary, specific to each region, consists of lexical items that are either absent from Standard French or whose form or semantic range differs from corresponding items of that variety of the language.

Louisiana became a French colony in 1682 when Cavalier de la Salle and his French Canadian exploration team reached the mouth of the Mississippi River. La Salle immediately turned around and said, "Je prends possession de toute la terre vidée par ce fleuve au nom de Louis XIV, roi de France et de Navarre" and named that vast territory *Louisiane*. With that apparently simple pronouncement, the French theoretically came into possession of the entire Mississippi River basin. In practice, developing colonial Louisiana proved to be considerably more difficult, and it was only the southernmost part of the territory that attracted a large concentration of French settlers. This critical demographic mass carried French language and culture into the 21st century.

South Louisiana is culturally, historically, and linguistically connected to the French-speaking world, but it would be an over-simplification to think of it as a homogenous linguistic region. The varieties of French spoken in Louisiana today have their origins in several distinct waves of immigration. During the French colonial period (1699–1762), colonists from different parts of France and from Quebec insured that the language of the colony would be marked by numerous dialectal features, many of which have endured to the present. The modest social origins of most of the colonists, along with their limited access to education, meant that French in Louisiana would be further distinguished from Standard French by its incorporation of many features typical of the informal spoken style usually referred to as *français populaire* ('Folk French'). A second significant wave of francophone immigration occurred between 1764 and 1785, when the Spanish authorities, who had assumed control of the colony in 1762, welcomed approximately 3,000 Acadian exiles after their expulsion from their homeland in present-day

Nova Scotia by the British in 1755. The Acadians brought with them their own variety of French, which had strong roots in the dialects of western France. Finally, during the first half of the nineteenth century, Louisiana's flourishing plantation economy attracted thousands of new French speakers from the former colony of Saint Domingue (present-day Haiti) and from France. Many of these new arrivals were highly educated, and along with Louisiana's own wealthy planter class, they were largely responsible for the presence in Louisiana of what may be called Plantation Society French, a variety closely resembling Standard French.

Plantation Society French has all but disappeared today, but the French of the Acadians and the French of the earlier colonial period eventually merged and now live on in what may be considered a single language showing significant regional variation. Today, this type of French is most commonly referred to as 'Cajun' (*cadien* in the local spelling). However, because the French of the Acadians (the term from which *cadien* and 'Cajun' derive) is only one of its sources, and because it is spoken not only by people who call themselves Cajun but also by many Creoles of color and American Indians, we prefer the broader and more neutral label *Louisiana French*.

The presence of Louisiana Creole adds to the complexity of the linguistic situation of South Louisiana. Although much of its vocabulary overlaps with that of Louisiana French, major differences in grammatical structure make it an autonomous language. For example, tense and aspect are not expressed by endings but by short forms preceding a usually invariable verb stem: *pé* or *apé* for the progressive aspect, *mo apé chanté* 'I'm singing'; *va* for the future, *to va chanté* 'you'll sing'; *sé* for the conditional, *yé sé chanté* 'they would sing'. The term 'Creole' as used in South Louisiana is quite ambiguous, for it refers to ethnic groups as well as to the language. Historically, the term referred to people born in the Louisiana colony but whose origins lay in Europe or Africa. The label was thus applied to the descendants of the original French (and, later, Spanish) colonists as well as to Louisianans of African descent. The term also came to designate the large mixed-race population of Louisiana, many of whom were Free People of Color (*Gens de couleur libres*); the members of this group often owned land and were highly educated and cultured. Although the term was also eventually applied to the Louisiana Creole language, it is important to understand that there is not always clear overlap between those who identify themselves as Creoles ethnically and those who speak Louisiana Creole. While there are whites, blacks, and Creoles of color who self-identify as Creole and who speak that language, there are also many members of each group who call themselves Creole but speak either Louisiana French or no variety of French at all.

French was the language of everyday life and government in Louisiana into the 19th century. But the Louisiana Purchase in 1803 and statehood in 1812 placed serious pressure on French Louisiana to conform to the language and culture of the United States. French Creoles understood that their future was necessarily going to be American and they assimilated into the American mainstream. It was not until the arrival of Anglo-Americans, farmers from the Midwest in the late 19th century and oil workers and developers from Texas, Oklahoma, and Pennsylvania in the early 20th century, that the geographically and socially isolated Cajuns followed on the road to assimilation. Also, at that time, Theodore Roosevelt's battle cry, "One nation, one people, one language!", thundered across the land. It induced a quest for national unity that suppressed regional diversity across the country. Free public education was eventually made available throughout the state, but, beginning in 1916, mandatory English language education was imposed in the southern part of the state in a well-meaning effort to bring the French-speaking Cajuns into the American mainstream. As a result, Cajun children were punished for speaking the language of their parents in school, often by teachers with the same last names as the students. Several generations of young Cajun pupils soon associated their native language and culture with social stigmatization; speaking local French was considered something well-raised people did not do in public.

In the late 1940s, the tide began to turn. Soldiers in France during World War II had discovered that the language and culture they had been told to forget made them invaluable as interpreters. After the war, returning GIs sank into the hot bath of their own culture. The glowing embers of the Cajun cultural revival were fanned by local political leaders who used the 1955 bicentennial of the Acadian exile as a rallying point for the revitalization of ethnic pride. The message of 1955 was that the Cajuns had survived the worst; their culture and language were injured but alive. In 1968, after the U.S. Congress passed the Bilingual Education Act, the state of Louisiana officially fostered the movement with the creation of the Council for the Development of French in Louisiana (CODOFIL), appointing former U.S. Congressman James Domengeaux its chairman. The message of 1968 was that it was officially all right to be a francophone in public again. But the movement was not without problems. CODOFIL found itself faced with the monumental task of creating a quality French language education program from scratch. Its mandate as a state agency covered the entire state. For these reasons, CODOFIL was forced to water its wine and pressed only for the teaching of Standard French as a second language in elementary schools. A dearth of native-born French teachers compounded the problem, and CODOFIL opted to import 'international brigades', teachers from France, Belgium, and Québec as a stopgap. This, along with a broad program of cultural exchanges, brought the Louisiana French experiment to the attention of the Francophone world. Meanwhile, activists on the home front felt that the indigenous language and culture were once again forced into the shadows as many Cajuns dutifully echoed past criticisms, apologizing that their language was "not the real French, just broken-down Cajun French."

But conversely, francophone Louisianans no longer felt alone. For their own reasons, France, Belgium, and Québec became interested in fanning the fires of self-preservation along the bayous. They invested significantly to create a life-support system in the hopes that French culture and language might ultimately survive and even thrive in South Louisiana. Along with money and teachers have come hordes of tourists eager to visit this long-lost, long-forgotten 'exotic' place where, against all odds, French has somehow survived in the belly of the beast. This contact has shown the Cajuns, Creoles, and francophone American Indians that, contrary to their childhood lessons, their French works just fine to communicate with folks who speak 'real' French.

Prior to the *Dictionary of Louisiana French: As Spoken in Cajun, Creole, and American Indian Communities,* no inventory of the vocabulary resources of Louisiana French was available that could be considered comparable in scope and thoroughness to the *Dictionary of Louisiana Creole*. To be sure, the vocabulary of Louisiana French has received considerable attention from native Louisiana scholars, beginning with Fortier's 1881 article "The Acadians in Louisiana and their dialect," and continuing especially in the 1930's with book-length studies: Read's 1931 *Louisiana French* and Ditchy's 1932 *Les Acadiens louisianais et leur parler*. Later in that decade, and continuing into the 1940's, professors of French at Louisiana State University had graduate students devote MA theses to the preparation of differential lexicons of the speech of individual parishes. These were inventories of words not found in Standard French, that is, local lexical particularities, such as *éloise* (also spelled *élouase* and *alouez*) 'lightning', as compared to Standard French *foudre*; words that are pronounced differently, such as *seau* 'bucket' [sjo], as compared to Standard French [so]; and words whose meaning differs, such as *grenier* (also pronounced *grénier, grinier*) which, in addition to the shared senses 'attic, garret', also means 'ceiling' and 'hay loft' in Louisiana French.

In recent years, more extensive vocabulary inventories have been produced; two that contain lexical particularities are Griolet's 1986 *Mots de Louisiane : Études lexicales d'une francophonie* and Lavaud-Grassin's 1988 unpublished *Particularités lexicales du parler cadjin en Louisiane (Etats-Unis): Enquête, dictionnaire et documentation bibliographique*, a four-volume doctoral dissertation presented at the University of Paris III (Sorbonne Nouvelle). More notable is Daigle's 1984 bilingual dictionary, *A Dictionary of the Cajun Language*, that aims to present the total vocabulary available to speakers of Louisiana French. Father Daigle, a native Louisiana French speaker, set himself objectives that were more than simply descriptive. Aware that the language was being lost, he aimed to document the language in it 'purest' state—as it was spoken prior to World War I—as well as to include words from Standard French not used by speakers of Louisiana French. The pedagogical objective of the Daigle dictionary is reflected by the fact that the English-Cajun part is three times as large as the Cajun-English part, 429 versus 165 pages, respectively.

We acknowledge our debt to our precursors, especially to Father Daigle, and it is by standing on their shoulders that we are able to produce a work that extends the range and the wealth of knowledge about the lexical resources of Louisiana French. Unlike Daigle's work, the *Dictionary of Louisiana French: As Spoken in Cajun, Creole, and American Indian Communities* is properly descriptive in nature. Its purpose is to provide an inventory of the vocabulary of Louisiana French reflecting the speech of the period from 1930 to today. Its great strength is its empirical nature, a feature that makes it a reliable reflection of current usage. A representative set of Louisiana French-speaking communities were selected consisting of 24 areas and 124 communities within five broad regions of south Louisiana: (1) the coastal marshes (Terrebonne, Lafourche, St. Mary parishes); (2) regions along the banks of the Mississippi river (Plaquemines, St. Charles, St. John, St. James, Ascension, West Baton Rouge, Pointe Coupee parishes); (3) the central area (St. Martin, Assumption, Iberia, Lafayette parishes); (4) the north (Avoyelles, Evangeline, St. Landry parishes); (5) the western prairie (Acadia, Cameron, Calcasieu, Jefferson Davis, Vermilion parishes). Interviews were conducted with at least five persons in each of the 24 areas by members of the project team, some assisted by graduate students who were fluent speakers of Louisiana French. Data from the fieldwork were transcribed, prepared for automatic computerized analysis, and stored in a database. Follow-up fieldwork, using an elicitation protocol that included a 100-item questionnaire and visual aids, was then conducted to complement the data and to verify items listed in the existing lexical inventories. The verification phase also included a vetting of all entries by the three editors who are native Cajuns and who have brought to the project their intimate knowledge of Louisiana French as well as their commitment to maintain the language as a medium for the expression of the South Louisiana cultural heritage.

In addition to the data collected from fieldwork conducted in the twenty-first-century, the *Dictionary of Louisiana French: As Spoken in Cajun, Creole, and American Indian Communities* contains material compiled from existing inventories and written texts published after 1930 and from recordings and oral corpora from that period. The importance and usefulness of broadening our sources beyond material collected by direct elicitation from current speakers is illustrated by the case of the word *pirogue*, which describes a type of Cajun canoe still in use today. The examination of previous inventories revealed the existence of two derivatives of *pirogue*: *piroguer* 'to transport in a pirogue' and *piroguée* 'the contents of a pirogue', as in *une piroguée de poissons* 'a pirogueful of fish'. Knowledge of the existence of these derivatives led us to discover their still widespread use and to another word that had not been previously attested, *pirogueur* 'someone who travels in a pirogue'. This case demonstrates that the language still provides speakers with the potential of creating new words by resorting to internal processes such as derivation.

The *Dictionary of Louisiana French: As Spoken in Cajun, Creole, and American Indian Communities* will be of great interest to scholars from various disciplines. It will be of interest to scholars concerned with issues of language contact because of the significant effect of English on the vocabulary of Louisiana French. Specialists of the French language will find it very useful because the language serves as a sort of repository for words and usages that have disappeared from present-day Standard French. However, the primary readership we aim for are those Louisianans who, considering Louisiana French as a basic cultural asset and as a fundamental component of their heritage, wish to acquire or extend their knowledge of its lexical resources. Such knowledge is essential for all activities designed to maintain and widen its use. Those who are attempting to create a local written norm and to produce written texts need to know which terms are currently used by fluent speakers and which terms are part of the inherited cultural heritage. These lexical resources of Louisiana French are also of great importance to teachers and to developers of pedagogical material who attempt to adapt Standard French to local culture and to revalorize and invigorate the local vernacular linguistic varieties. Because not all potential users of this dictionary are familiar with Standard French or fluent speakers of Louisiana French, we have provided English glosses (equivalents) for the entries, subentries, and illustrative examples. In addition, the dictionary contains a reverse English-French index that makes it possible for users to find the Louisiana French equivalents of English terms.

A User's Guide to the Dictionary

This section provides a general guide to the organization of the dictionary article (i.e., a headword and all materials subsumed under it). A representative article will first be presented with the various parts labeled. This presentational diagram will be followed by an explanation of certain elements that are not exemplified in the sample article or that require additional information.

Guide to the Article

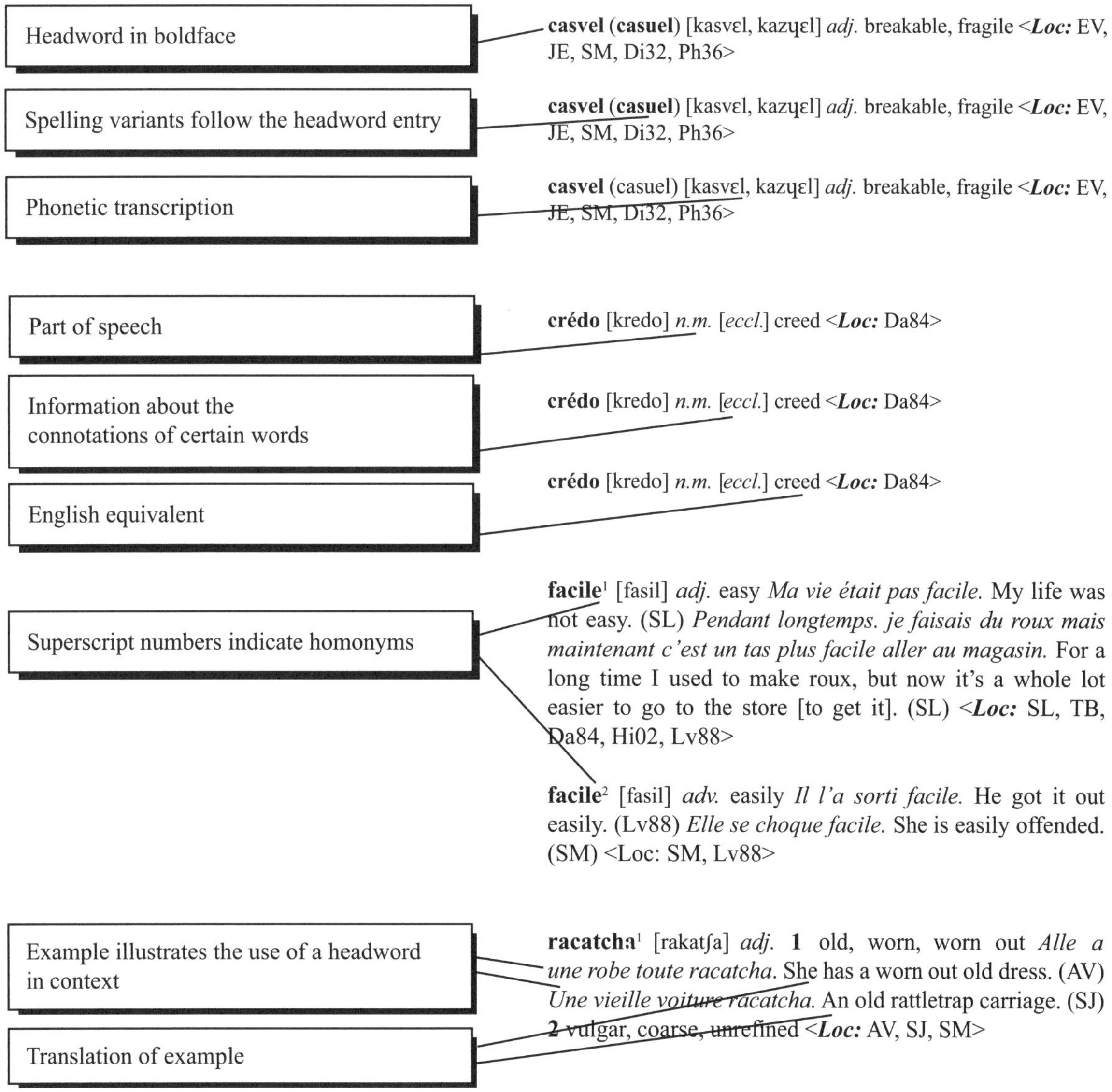

Headword in boldface

casvel (**casuel**) [kasvɛl, kazɥɛl] *adj.* breakable, fragile <***Loc:*** EV, JE, SM, Di32, Ph36>

Spelling variants follow the headword entry

casvel (**casuel**) [kasvɛl, kazɥɛl] *adj.* breakable, fragile <***Loc:*** EV, JE, SM, Di32, Ph36>

Phonetic transcription

casvel (casuel) [kasvɛl, kazɥɛl] *adj.* breakable, fragile <***Loc:*** EV, JE, SM, Di32, Ph36>

Part of speech

crédo [kredo] *n.m.* [*eccl.*] creed <***Loc:*** Da84>

Information about the connotations of certain words

crédo [kredo] *n.m.* [*eccl.*] creed <***Loc:*** Da84>

English equivalent

crédo [kredo] *n.m.* [*eccl.*] creed <***Loc:*** Da84>

Superscript numbers indicate homonyms

facile[1] [fasil] *adj.* easy *Ma vie était pas facile.* My life was not easy. (SL) *Pendant longtemps. je faisais du roux mais maintenant c'est un tas plus facile aller au magasin.* For a long time I used to make roux, but now it's a whole lot easier to go to the store [to get it]. (SL) <***Loc:*** SL, TB, Da84, Hi02, Lv88>

facile[2] [fasil] *adv.* easily *Il l'a sorti facile.* He got it out easily. (Lv88) *Elle se choque facile.* She is easily offended. (SM) <Loc: SM, Lv88>

Example illustrates the use of a headword in context

Translation of example

racatcha[1] [rakatʃa] *adj.* **1** old, worn, worn out *Alle a une robe toute racatcha.* She has a worn out old dress. (AV) *Une vieille voiture racatcha.* An old rattletrap carriage. (SJ) **2** vulgar, coarse, unrefined <***Loc:*** AV, SJ, SM>

Roman numerals distinguish among syntactic roles of verbs (transitive, intransitive, pronominal)

forger [fɔrʒe] **I** *v.tr.* **1** to forge, fabricate, counterfeit, falsify *Forger un document.* To forge a document. (Lv88) **2** to invent, make up *Ça, je ne l'ai pas forgé du tout, c'était vrai.* I did not make it up at all, it was true. (Lv88) **II se forger** *v.pron.* **1** to be forged (of metal) **Le fer se forge bien.* The iron is easy to forge. (Da84) **2** to make up, invent (a story) *C'est pas la vérité. Il s'a forgé cette histoire.* That's not the truth. He made up that story. (VM) <***Loc:*** EV, IB, SB, SL, VM, Da84, Di32, Gr86, Lv88, Ph36>

Arabic numbers indicate the various meanings of a headword

forger [fɔrʒe] **I** *v.tr.* **1** to forge, fabricate, counterfeit, falsify *Forger un document.* To forge a document. (Lv88) **2** to invent, make up *Ça, je ne l'ai pas forgé du tout, c'était vrai.* I did not make it up at all, it was true. (Lv88) **II se forger** *v.pron.* **1** to be forged (of metal) **Le fer se forge bien.* The iron is easy to forge. (Da84) **2** to make up, invent (a story) *C'est pas la vérité. Il s'a forgé cette histoire.* That's not the truth. He made up that story. (VM) <***Loc:*** EV, IB, SB, SL, VM, Da84, Di32, Gr86, Lv88, Ph36>

Subentries are set off by a diamond

fale (falle) [fal] *n.f.* 1 crop, craw, maw (of a bird) **2** set stomach (of a person or animal) ◊ **•avoir la fale basse** to be hungry *J'ai la fale basse.* I'm hungry. (Gu00) <Gu00> **•avoir la fale creuse** to be hungry (LA) **•avoir la fale pleine** to have eaten enough, be full <LA, La99> <***Loc:*** AV, EV, IB, JD, LA, SB, SJ, SL, SM, TB, VM, Da84, Di32, Fa77, Gu00, La99, Lv88, Re31>

Each individual subentry is set off by a bullet

fale (falle) [fal] *n.f.* 1 crop, craw, maw (of a bird) **2** set stomach (of a person or animal) ◊ **•avoir la fale basse** to be hungry *J'ai la fale basse.* I'm hungry. (Gu00) <Gu00> **•avoir la fale creuse** to be hungry (LA) **•avoir la fale pleine** to have eaten enough, be full <LA, La99> <***Loc:*** AV, EV, IB, JD, LA, SB, SJ, SL, SM, TB, VM, Da84, Di32, Fa77, Gu00, La99, Lv88, Re31>

English equivalent of subentry

fale (falle) [fal] *n.f.* 1 crop, craw, maw (of a bird) **2** set stomach (of a person or animal) ◊ **•avoir la fale basse** to be hungry *J'ai la fale basse.* I'm hungry. (Gu00) <Gu00> **•avoir la fale creuse** to be hungry (LA) **•avoir la fale pleine** to have eaten enough, be full <LA, La99> <***Loc:*** AV, EV, IB, JD, LA, SB, SJ, SL, SM, TB, VM, Da84, Di32, Fa77, Gu00, La99, Lv88, Re31>

Example illustrates the use of a subentry in context

Translation of example

Code for source of subentry

fricasser [frikase] *v.tr.* to stew (i.e. browning meat in fat then simmering in liquid) ◊ **•s'en fricasser** to be indifferent, be unconcerned *Eh bien, je m'en fricasse.* Well, it doesn't matter to time. (IB) <IB, Di32> <***Loc:*** IB, Da84, Di32>

Asterisk indicates an example from a published source

Code for source of example

List of parishes and textual sources where the headword was found

naître [nɛt(r)] (*p.p.* **éné** [ɛ̃ne], **né** [ne]) *v.intr.* to be born **Il a été né et élevé dans le petit village de Mire.* He was born and raised in the little town of Mire. (LA, An94) *Il y a des petits bébés qui naît qui a pas de bras et qui a pas de mains.* There are some babies who are born who don't have any arms and who don't have any hands. (EV) ◊ **•premier né** firstborn, eldest <Da84> <***Loc:*** AC, AV, EV, LA, TB, An94, Da84>

Detailed discussion of the content and structure of entries

Orthography

Beginning in the late nineteenth century and continuing to the present day, a number of Louisiana writers, poets, playwrights, and teachers have produced various kinds of texts written in Louisiana French. The spellings found in their work are highly variable, in part because they had in mind different kinds of readers with diverse backgrounds and needs. A few writers opted for folk phonetic spellings based on English pronunciation conventions, in an attempt to render the sounds of Louisiana French interpretable for people comfortable reading English but not French. A noteworthy example is James Faulk's *Cajun French I* textbook published in 1977. Compare the following sentence from Faulk with the way the same sentence would look in something much closer to International French (often called Standard French) spelling:

> Sh-kone paw ākoñ sah pahr.
>
> *Je connais pas équand ça part.*
>
> 'I don't know when they're leaving.'

The majority of writers and teachers have not followed Faulk in using a phonetically based system. Instead, affirming that Louisiana French is, after all, a kind of French, they have sought to follow French orthographic conventions to one degree or another. The results have varied from a purely International French spelling to a heavily modified one—sometimes called *eye-dialect*—that seeks to represent nearly every feature of the local pronunciation when this differs from the standard. By way of illustration, consider the following sentence from Richard Guidry's *C'est p'us pareil* (1982), first in eye-dialect and then in an orthography much closer to that of International French:

> *J'sus assez larguée d'a'tend' parler d'not' magnière de parler à nous-aut', j'pourrais rej'ter.*
>
> *Je suis assez larguée d'attendre parler de notre manière de parler à nous-autres, je pourrais rejeter.*
>
> 'I am so tired of hearing people talk about our way of speaking, I could throw up.'

The eye-dialect version gives much more information about local pronunciation but is harder for learners of French or French speakers not from Louisiana to read.

The editorial team of this dictionary affirms the uniqueness and importance of the local varieties of French in Louisiana, but we also recognize the value of links with the larger French-speaking world. Therefore we opted to use a spelling system that would enable people who read International French to also read Louisiana French without much difficulty, and vice versa. This means that for headwords, and for all previously unpublished material, we have used spellings that are as close to International French as possible. However, we were also conscious of a need to help readers work their way through texts written in Louisiana French, and therefore noteworthy local spellings are given as variant spellings of headwords and in illustrative example sentences quoted from published texts, as described in more detail below.

If in our orthography we have consciously preferred the norms of International French, this is not true of our handling of the grammar. We have preserved without alteration the grammar of our Louisiana French sources, never adding words that were not actually uttered or changing those that were. Thus the reader will see *J'ai pas mangé* 'I didn't eat' where International French would have *Je n'ai pas mangé*, *Faut que je vas* 'I have to go' for standard *Il faut que j'y aille*, or *Je m'ai couché* 'I went to bed' for standard *Je me suis couché*.

Perhaps the most vexing grammatical issue that bears directly on spelling is the representation of agreements between subjects, verbs, and past participles. The reader should note that some Louisiana French authors write *eusse all**aient*** 'they went' and *la tarte que j'ai mang**ée*** 'the pie that I ate' because such agreements, even though inaudible, are present in written International French, whereas others write *eusse all**ait*** and *la tarte que j'ai mang**é***, preferring not to represent agreements for which the spoken language provides no evidence. Likewise, some write *vous-autres vas*, *vous-autres fais* while others use *vous-autres va* and *vous-autres fait*. When we quote published texts (indicated by an asterisk before the example) we do not alter the writer's choices, and users of our dictionary should not be surprised to find variation in such examples. However, when presenting unpublished material or any new material of our own, we have implemented the following policies. First and most importantly, we do not represent agreements when these would suggest a pronunciation that was not actually used. For instance, we do not write *la robe que j'ai fai**te*** 'the dress that I made' (instead of '*…fait*') or *eusse fini**ssent*** 'they finish' (instead of *finit*) unless the speaker actually said [fɛt] or [finis]. But whenever an audible agreement was present, we transcribe accordingly (thus, the combinations [i puvɔ̃], [i pœv] and [i pø] would be transcribed as *ils pouvont*, *ils peuvent*, *ils peut* respectively). Secondly, we use third person singular verb forms with the subject pronoun *vous-autres* (e.g. *vous-autres va*). Finally, in the third person plural, we follow International French conventions in writing silent agreement endings with plural noun subjects and with the pronoun *ils* (thus, *les hommes faisaient* and *ils faisaient*). With the pronouns *ça*, *eux-autres*, *eux* and *eusse*, however, we have opted not to add silent plural endings to the verb. This is because, unlike verb forms occurring with *ils* where audible endings are common, audible endings are rarely heard with *ça*, *eux-autres*, *eux* and *eusse*, which suggests that for most speakers these pronouns take an unmarked (or third person singular) verb form. We follow this principle as well in cases where the endings would be inaudible, thus *eusse faisait*, *ça mangeait*, *eux-autres pouvait*.

In a small number of cases we have departed from International French spelling conventions in order to represent audible grammatical distinctions that are important in Louisiana French but are not part of International French spelling. Two examples include the distinction between *plus* 'more' and *p'us* or *pus* 'no more, no longer' (e.g. *j'en veux plus* 'I want some more' and *j'en veux pus* 'I don't want any more') and *elle* 'her (disjunctive pronoun)' versus *alle / al / a* 'she (subject pronoun)' (e.g., *Jean a parlé avec elle* 'John spoke with her' versus *Alle a parlé avec Jean* 'She spoke with John'). Even in these cases, variation will be encountered, with some writers using only the standard spellings *elle* and *plus*. Our purpose in writing this dictionary is not to attempt to resolve every possible orthographic question but rather to offer a portrait of spoken and written Louisiana French in all its fullness and variety.

When we quote material from published sources, we generally retain the published spellings intact. This will be discussed further in the section on illustrative examples. However, in the case of material drawn from Father Daigle's (1984) published dictionary, we have corrected occasional inadvertent misspellings such as his **citronier** for **citronnier** 'lemon tree'.

Headwords

The headword presents the primary spelling of a word and the one that the reader will use to locate an entry in the dictionary.

In keeping with our stated policy on orthography, we have generally spelled headwords in a way that is close to or identical with the International French spelling of the same word when that spelling is a reasonable representation of the Louisiana French word. However, when the Louisiana French word generally or always occurs in a form that differs markedly from the standard, we have opted for a more faithful local spelling for the headword. Thus, in our entry for the verb 'to hear' we use the spelling **attendre** as the headword, as in the example sentence above quoted from Guidry (1982), though we do list the standard spelling **entendre** as a variant. Spelling variants are listed after the headword, in parentheses and in boldface, as follows:

attendre (**entendre**)
cacasser (**carcasser**, **cagasser**)

The word **cacasser** is an example of a headword that does not occur in International French at all.

A common type of variation in Louisiana French affects many words that start with a vowel sound. These words are often pronounced as though they started with an initial consonant. In order to help readers familiar with International French locate these words in the dictionary, we set off these variable initial sounds with a hyphen, and we use the variant without the initial sound as our primary spelling (for purposes of the headword), as follows:

acre (**z-acre**)
arbre (**l-arbre, z-arbre**)

The reader should understand that **un acre** 'an acre' may also be found as **un z-acre**, and that **un arbre** 'a tree' may also be encountered as **un l-arbre** or **un z-arbre**.

Unless the form is irregular, a feminine form that is derived from a masculine adjective or noun is not spelled out in full; the feminine ending is given after a hyphen, in both the spelling and the pronunciation field (phonetic transcription):

cobi, **-e** [kobi]
cochon, **-onne** [koʃɔ̃, -ɔ̃n]

cochonnier, **-ière** [koʃɔ̃je, -jær]
coléreux, **-euse** [kolerø, -øz]

Thus, the feminine forms of each of these are **cobie** [kobi], **cochonne** [koʃɔ̃n], **cochonnière** [koʃɔ̃jær], and **coléreuse** [kolerøz]. In cases such as **cobie**, the feminine ending is a matter of spelling only and has no effect on the Louisiana French pronunciation, but in the last three cases above, the feminine pronunciation is different from the masculine. Our policy in such cases is to list actually attested feminine endings, but also to indicate feminine endings considered usual or at least unsurprising by our native speaking informants.

When a headword is spelled in SMALLCAPS, this indicates that the word is of English origin and that it does not have a consistent or usual spelling in Louisiana French other than the English spelling, e.g., CAN, CHALK, CHECK, CHUNK. The pronunciation of such words may vary from a fully English pronunciation to a more or less Louisiana French pronunciation. There is, in fact, a wide variety of English dialects spoken in the regions inhabited by speakers of Louisiana French, including Cajun English, Southern American English, New Orleans area Yat, African American Vernacular English, and Standard American. Deeming it the most neutral, Standard American is used as the basis for English pronunciations in this dictionary. In some cases a word spelled in smallcaps is not a fully English spelling either, e.g., CLEAVE, which means '(meat) cleaver'. Sometimes both an English-style spelling and a French one are found, and in such cases we give both, e.g., **COAL OIL** (**coloïe**).

In general, we have not included proper names such as place names or personal names. To do justice to these areas would require a separate dictionary.

Homonyms

Homonyms, or different words spelled the same way, are presented in separate dictionary entries. The reader is alerted to the fact that there are multiple headwords with the same spelling by the use of superscript numbers, as follows:

cabaner[1] to camp
cabaner[2] to dent, crush

cabri[1] goat
cabri[2] navel, belly button

In our decisions about whether a word such as **cabaner** should be treated as a single word with multiple meanings (polysemy), or as two different words that happen to be pronounced alike (homonymy), we have been guided less by etymology (word origins) than by modern meanings. Thus, there is no apparent link between the meanings 'to camp' and 'to crush' for **cabaner**, so we have opted to present these as homonyms and to treat them in separate entries.

Pronunciation

Pronunciations are given using the International Phonetic Alphabet. For a complete table of pronunciation symbols used, see the Pronunciation Guide.

When spelling variants correspond to different pronunciations, these are given in the same order when possible. Thus, for **cacasser** the reader will see the following:

cacasser (**carcasser**, **cagasser**) [kakase, karkase, kagase]

This indicates that, in principle, the first spelling, **cacasser**, corresponds to the first pronunciation [kakase]; the second spelling, **carcasser**, corresponds to the second pronunciation [karkase], and so on. In many entries, variant pronunciations that we have recorded in speech are not assigned a specific orthography. In other words, there may be more pronunciations than spellings for a given word. It is common for a language to be more variable in its spoken than in its written form.

In noting pronunciations, we were forced to make a number of decisions about what level of detail and variation to include and what to leave out. In the interest of space, we decided not to indicate certain high frequency variant pronunciations when these are systematic and easy to identify. Please see the Pronunciation Guide for more information.

Parts of speech

Most of the labels for parts of speech have purely conventional meanings and require no special comment here. A few brief comments are, however, in order.

Every noun in Louisiana French has grammatical gender, meaning that it belongs either to the class of nouns considered masculine, or to those considered feminine, and this information is noted with *n.m.* or *n.f.* as the part of speech. A number of nouns are attested with variable gender, masculine for some speakers and feminine for others, and such nouns are marked as *n.m./f.*. A noun whose gender changes to reflect the biological sex of the person it refers to is simply marked *n.*, as for instance **nageur, -euse**, which indicates that a male swimmer is called a **nageur** and a female swimmer is a **nageuse**.

Some verbs are exclusively transitive, intransitive, or pronominal, whereas other verbs may allow two or all three of these uses. In such cases, the different uses are separated with Roman numerals within the entry. For instance:

macorner (amacorner, mancorner) [makɔrne, mɑ̃kɔrne, markone, amakɔrne] **I** *v.tr.* **1** to yoke [...] **2** to attach, join (two things) together [...] **II** *v.intr.* to live together (without benefit of marriage) [...] **III se macorner** *v.pron.* to live with (a romantic partner) without benefit of marriage [...]

In this example we see that transitive uses of the verb **macorner** (those that take a direct object), intransitive uses (those that do not take a direct object), and pronominal uses (those whose infinitive begins with the pronoun **se**) are all three documented. They are presented after Roman numerals I, II, and III respectively.

Some verbs are marked with the label *invar.,* which stands for "invariable." Such verbs behave differently from most Louisiana French verbs in that they do not take personal endings for tense, mood or aspect. However, it should be noted that many such verbs can be heard with the endings of the *imparfait* (e.g., *–ais, -ais, -ait, -aient*), and the reader should not be surprised to see such apparent exceptions to the otherwise robust claim that such verbs are "invariable."

Usage comments

Occasionally an entry is flagged with an italicized usage note in square brackets, placed immediately before the relevant definition, to alert the reader that the word or phrase is not neutral but may cause surprise, amusement, or even offense if used in the wrong context. Some examples of entries with usage codes follow:

baba[2] [baba] *n.m.* [*baby talk*] water

bambara [bãbara] *adj.* [*offensive*] carefree, indifferent (often with respect to one's appearance)

bèbe [bɛb, be^ib] *n.* **1** baby **2** [*term of endearment*] babe, baby

In other cases, a usage comment may supply additional grammatical information about the word. This kind of information is italicized and in parentheses. For example:

ça[1] [sa] *pron.* **1** *(in impersonal expr.)* it *Ça fait chaud.* It's hot. (SM) *Ça mouille dehors.* It's raining outside. (SM)

Here we learn that the pronoun **ça** 'it' can be used in impersonal expressions such as those referring to the weather.

Definitions and equivalents

In this dictionary, as in bilingual dictionaries in general, the definitions are usually English translation equivalents of the Louisiana French headword. For words with multiple meanings, the various definitions are numbered and presented in an order that reflects their logical connections to one another and that broadly follows their frequency, with more frequent uses listed before less frequent ones.

In cases in which the English equivalent is not well known or is a cultural reference that might be unfamiliar to many readers, we provide a longer description in addition to the shorter translation equivalent. For instance:

chasse-galerie *n.f.* (in folk culture) "wild hunt," a mysterious racket, din, or chorus that passes through the night sky, often interpreted as an omen

charivari *n.m.* charivari, noisy serenade held by surprise and at night for a newlywed couple who are unconventional in some way, usu. because one of them is marrying for the second time (the couple are traditionally expected to invite the serenaders inside and offer them food and drink)

Some definitions are accompanied by a "delimiter" in parentheses to narrow down the interpretation. For instance, the parenthetical "(of a chain)" tells the reader just what kind of 'link' is intended in this definition:

maille [maj] *n.f.* **1** link (of a chain), knot (of mesh), stitch (in knitting)

In the case of the names of flora and fauna (plant names and names of wildlife), we have given English common names, occasionally with a comment to help clarify the intended referent, and also local names when these names differ from general American English names.

cache-cache *n.m.* yellow nut grass, chufa, earth almond

congre (congue) *n.m.* amphiuma (aquatic salamander known variously as congo eel, conger eel, or congo snake)

We have not attempted to provide scientific names of flora and fauna.

Illustrative or contextual examples

Illustrative examples are sentences or parts of sentences presented to show the headword in use in a natural context. In general we have attempted to illustrate each word, and each sense of a word, with at least one example. In the case of short, high frequency grammatical words such as **il**, **elle**, **avec**, and **avoir**, we often give numerous examples to illustrate a variety of contexts and uses. One use of illustrative examples is to reveal the grammatical frame in which a word occurs. Consider the following examples, taken from the articles **payer** and **penser** respectively:

> *Ç'a payé pour la glacière, et les éventails, et l'estricité, ç'a payé pour tout.* They paid for the refrigerator, and the fans, and the electricity, they paid for everything. (TB)

> *Je vas penser à quelque chose.* I will think of something. (SM)

The first example shows that the verb **payer** can take the preposition **pour** before its complement in Louisiana French, and the second example shows that the verb **penser** takes a complement preceded by **à**.

A second important function of illustrative examples is that they often reveal collocations, or frequent and useful combinations of words. Consider these examples from the article **jour**:

> *Il passait tous les jours après pedler son pain.* He passed by every day peddling his bread. (LA)

> *Ce gros vent l'autre jour a manqué d'arracher la porte de dessus les pentures.* That strong wind the other day nearly tore the door off its hinges. (VM)

Here we see two collocations involving **jour** 'day', namely **tous les jours** 'every day' and **l'autre jour** 'the other day'. Because these phrases are relatively transparent, they are not treated as entries or subentries, but it is nonetheless useful for the student of Louisiana French to be aware of them.

Our examples are drawn from several different kinds of sources that fall into two large groups, namely examples quoted from published sources and those drawn from unpublished materials. The source of each example is indicated in parentheses after its English translation. The following example shows how we present a quote from a published text:

> **Dans einne foule, l'monne [=monde] s'poussaille.* In a crowd, people push each other. (EV, Ph36)

This example is preceded by an asterisk and followed by the code "(EV, Ph36)", which indicates that the example is quoted from a published work on Evangeline Parish, namely the 1936 book by Hosea Phillips. The asterisk is used to alert the reader to the fact that, because the example is from a published source, we have retained the original published spelling unaltered. However, some words in such examples may not correspond to the spellings we use elsewhere in this dictionary. In such cases, we give our spelling in brackets, preceded by an equals sign (=). Thus, in this example, the spelling 'monne' is followed by the more conventional spelling **monde**, which is the spelling we have used for the headword.

Examples drawn from unpublished materials are of several types and are not preceded by an asterisk, which means we have freely altered their spellings to conform to our orthography as needed. For instance, we often quote song lyrics:

> *Ta mère puis ton père.* Your mother and your father. (ch: *Là-bas chez Moreau*)

The code "ch" tells the reader that this example is drawn from the lyrics to a song (ch = chanson 'song'), in this case one entitled "*Là-bas chez Moreau*". (Some song lyrics are of course published, but most exist in multiple variations, and the version we quote is not always available in print).

We also drew examples, like the following, from plays in the Théâtre Cadien (ThCa) series. This example is taken from a play entitled "*La douce réunion*":

> *Tu pourrais passer voir ta Tante Vivian et ta cousine Marie à Washington en ervenant.* You could stop by to see your Aunt Vivian and your cousin Marie in Washington on your way back. (ThCa: *La douce réunion*)

When preceded by an asterisk, Théâtre Cadien examples are drawn from a written version of the plays, frequently the collection edited by May G. Waggoner (1999) entitled *Une fantaisie collective*. When the asterisk is absent, as above, this indicates that we have drawn the example from a live performance; the version of the text in that case is not available in print.

Finally, consider this example from the entry **macaquerie**:

> *Il a fait des macaqueries quand son papa est parti.* He got into mischief when his dad was gone. (SM)

The code "(SM)" indicates that the example is from Saint Martin Parish. When no further information is given, as in this example, the illustrative sentence is from our unpublished materials, generally our own fieldwork with fluent speakers of Louisiana French, though it may also be from an unpublished master's or doctoral thesis. Finally, in cases in which we were unable to find a suitable illustrative example in our existing sources, we asked a fluent native speaker to construct a sentence to show the word used in context.

Subentries

Subentries are given in boldface type after a bullet. Here are two examples of subentries, the first from the entry **macaquerie**, and the second from the entry **machine**:

> **•faire des macaqueries** to be mischievous *Il a fait des macaqueries quand son papa est parti.* He got into mischief when his dad was gone. (SM) <SM, Lv88>

> **•machine à coudre** sewing machine <JE, Da84>

Each subentry is structured more or less like a regular dictionary entry, generally with its own examples and sources. For instance, the subentry **faire des macaqueries** consists of the following parts: the subheadword (**faire des macaqueries**); the English translation equivalent "to be mischievous"; an illustrative sentence showing this expression in use in a natural context; the English translation of this sentence; a code in parentheses identifying the source of the sentence (in this case, our unpublished materials from Saint Martin Parish, coded SM); and finally a Location field, in angled brackets, listing all of the places where we have found this expression (in this case, Saint Martin Parish and the unpublished 1988 doctoral thesis by Maguy Lavaud-Grassin, coded Lv88).

We usually do not give a pronunciation for subentries, because in the normal case the pronunciation of each word in the subentry can be determined by looking up the individual words in the subentry, if desired. Subentries generally are not labeled for part of speech, either, because the subentry either belongs to the same part of speech as the headword (e.g., **machine à coudre** is a feminine noun, just like **machine**), or the subentry is simply a multiple-word expression (e.g., **faire des macaqueries** is a verbal expression using the verb **faire** and the noun **macaqueries**).

Some subentries vary in form. Consider the following:

> **•magasin de {à} foin** ***a*** hay barn ***b*** barn <AV, IB, TB>

> **•seconde {deuxième} main** used, secondhand *Il l'a achetée seconde main.* He bought it used. (IB) <IB, LA, TB, Lv88>

> **•malade comme un carencro {chien}** very sick <VM, La99>

Variants presented in curved brackets may be used instead of the preceding word or words. Thus, for "barn", one may encounter **magasin de foin** or **magasin à foin**. A "secondhand (car)" may be called either "(un char) **seconde main**" or "(un char) **deuxième main**." Lastly, the idiomatic expression for someone who is very sick may take the form **malade comme un carencro** or **malade comme un chien**.

When a subentry has more than one meaning, the various senses are indicated with italicized and bolded lowercase letters of the alphabet. Thus, for **magasin de foin**, above, two senses are given, 'hay barn' and 'barn', labelled ***a*** and ***b*** respectively.

Subentries that begin with the headword of the entry in which they are found are listed first, in alphabetical order, followed by those in which the headword is not the first word of the subentry. Thus, in the entry **maison** 'house', the subentries **maison à chien** 'doghouse' and **maison d'école** 'schoolhouse' are listed before the subentry **à la maison** 'at home', because the latter does not start with the word **maison**.

Locations

At the end of each entry, in angled brackets, is a list of location codes preceded by the abbreviation "***Loc:***". These location codes indicate in which parishes and written texts we have found the headword in question. The reader should not necessarily infer that the word is not used in other parishes or texts besides those listed; it simply means that we did not record the word in such places. Consider the entry for **cabanage**:

> **cabanage** [kabɑ̃naʒ] *n.m./f.* **1** hut, cabin (for hunters or fishermen) **2** slave quarters (on a plantation) **3** campsite <***Loc:*** SL, Di32, Lv88>

The Location field for this entry informs the reader that we have found the word **cabanage** in three sources: our unpublished materials from Saint Landry Parish (SL), and two written works, namely Ditchy 1932 (coded Di32) and Lavaud-Grassin 1988 (coded Lv88).

The Location field for a subentry is also presented in angled brackets, but without the abbreviation "***Loc:***":

> **•faire des macaqueries** to be mischievous *Il a fait des macaqueries quand son papa est parti.* He got into mischief when his dad was gone. (SM) <SM, Lv88>

As for all illustrative examples, the source code in parentheses indicates the source of the example sentence; the codes in angled brackets identify all of the places where the subentry has been found. In other words, location codes in parentheses refer to the source of *examples*, and location codes in angled brackets refer to the sources of *headwords*.

Index

The body of the dictionary is unidirectional (Louisiana French to English), which means that it is designed to go from a French word or expression to an English equivalent, but not to go in the reverse direction (English to Louisiana French). However, many readers may want to use the dictionary to find out how a particular English notion would be expressed in Louisiana French, and to this end we have prepared an English-to-French index to the dictionary that can be found at the end of this volume.

To show how the index works, part of the index entry for **talk** is given here:

> **talk** *v.* causer, charlanter, charrer, converser, jabloter, parler **talk about** parler de {dessus / après / pour} **talk deliriously** déparler **talk endlessly** parler à l'en plus finir, radoter **talk excessively** bagueuler, battre sa gueule, cacasser **talk excitedly** faire des (grands) hélas

This entry tells the reader that among the words for 'to talk' in Louisiana French, one finds **causer**, **charlanter**, **charrer**, **converser**, **jabloter**, and **parler**. These broad equivalents are listed in alphabetical order, not in order of frequency or appropriateness for any particular use. It is important to understand that an index is not the same thing as a dictionary. The reader who wants to know how to say 'to talk' in Louisiana French can look up **talk** in the index, but finding this list of translation equivalents is only the first step. The next and equally important step is to explore the French words given by looking them up in the body of the dictionary until the best choice is found for a particular use. The reader will then see that **parler** is the most neutral way to express 'to talk' in most uses. It occurs last in the indexed list of synonyms merely because of its position in the alphabet.

The purpose of the index is thus merely to direct the reader to particular articles in the body of the dictionary for more information. The index is not intended as an English-to-French dictionary.

References List

Allain, M., & Ancelet, B. J. (Eds.). (1981). *Littérature française de la Louisiane: Anthologie*. Bedford, NH: National Materials Development Center for French.

Ancelet, B. (1977). *Je su's sûrement pas ein conteur de contes mais... Oral literature of French Louisiana*. Unpublished master's thesis, Indiana University, Bloomington.

Ancelet, B. J. (Ed.). (1980). *Cris sur le bayou: Naissance d'une poésie acadienne en Louisiane*. Montréal, Québec: Éditions Intermède.

Ancelet, B. J. (Ed.). (1983). *Acadie tropicale*. Lafayette, LA: USL Éditions da la Nouvelle Acadie.

Ancelet, B. J. (1994). *Cajun and Creole folktales: The French oral tradition of south Louisiana*. Jackson: University Press of Mississippi.

Ancelet, B. J., & Morgan, E. (1984). *Musiciens Cadiens et Créoles / The makers of Cajun music*. Austin: University of Texas Press.

Arceneaux, J. (1982). *On va les embêter*. Typewritten text.

Arceneaux, J. (1994). *Je suis cadien*. New York: Cross-Cultural Communications.

Arceneaux, J. (1998). *Suite du loup: Poèmes, chansons, et autres textes*. Moncton, NB: Éditions Perce-Neige.

Babin, L. (1937). *A glossary of the French spoken on Grand Isle*. Unpublished master's thesis, Louisiana State University, Baton Rouge.

Babington, M., & Atwood, E. B. (1961). Lexical usage in southern Louisiana. *Publications of the American Dialect Society, 36*, 1–24.

Barnhill, V. L. (1950). *A linguistic atlas type investigation in southwestern Louisiana*. Unpublished master's thesis, Tulane University, New Orleans, Louisiana.

Bernard, L. M. (1933). *A study of Louisiana French in Lafayette Parish*. Unpublished master's thesis, Louisiana State University, Baton Rouge.

Bossu, J.-B. (1980). *Nouveaux voyages en Louisiane, 1751–1768*. Paris: Aubier-Montaigne.

Boudreaux, A. M. (1969). *A profile study of the folklore and idiomatic expressions of the French language of the Kaplan area in Vermillon*. Unpublished master's thesis, University of Southwestern Louisiana, Lafayette.

Boudreaux, A.-M. (1975). Jokes of Vermilion Parish. *Louisiana Folklore Miscellany, 3(4)*, 85–97.

Brandon, E. (1955). *Mœurs et langue de la paroisse Vermillon en Louisiane*. Unpublished doctoral dissertation, Laval University, Quebec.

Breton, R. J.-L. (1979). *Géographie du français et de la francité en Louisiane*. Québec: Centre International de Recherche sur le Bilinguisme.

Broussard, M.-J. (1945). *The Creole and French of Lafayette, Louisiana: A comparative study*. Unpublished master's thesis, Atlanta University, Atlanta, GA.

Bruce, C., & Gipson, J. (2002). *Cajun French-English English-Cajun French: Dictionary & phrasebook*. New York: Hippocrene Books, Inc.

Calais, G. D. (1968). *The Acadian French of the Parks (St. Martin Parish), Louisiana area*. Unpublished master's thesis, University of Southwestern Louisiana, Lafayette.

Castille, J. (1983). *Moi, Jeanne Castille, de Louisiane*. Paris: Luneau-Ascot Éditeurs.

Chaudoir, C. C. (1937). *A study of the grammar of the Avoyelles French dialect*. Unpublished master's thesis, Louisiana State University, Baton Rouge.

Cheramie, D. (1997). *Lait à mère*. Moncton, NB: Éditions d'Acadie.

Claudel, C. (1948). *A study of Louisiana French folktales in Avoyelles Parish*. Unpublished master's thesis, University of North Carolina, Chapel Hill.

Clifton, D. J. (1975). *La conspiration, la variation et la stabilité linguistique: Le cas des consonnes affriquées aux parlers français de la Louisiane*. Unpublished master's thesis, Ohio State University, Columbus.

Clifton, D. (1999). *À cette heure la louve*. Moncton, NB: Éditions Perce-Neige.

Coco, E. R. (1933). *An etymological glossary of the variants from Standard French used in Avoyelles Parish*. Unpublished master's thesis, Louisiana State University, Baton Rouge.

Comeaux, E., & Meaux, K. (1980). *The Best of Bec Doux: World's only Cajun comic strip*. Baton Rouge: Blue Elf.

Conwell, M. J., & Juilland, A. (1963). *Louisiana French grammar*. The Hague: Mouton.

Daigle, A. T. (1934). *Folklore and etymological glossary of the variants from Standard French in Jefferson Davis Parish*. Unpublished master's thesis, Louisiana State University, Baton Rouge.

Daigle, J. O. (1984). *A dictionary of the Cajun language*. Ann Arbor: Edwards Brothers.

Daigle, J. (1992). *Cajun self-taught*. Chelsea, MI: Book Crafters [also published at Ville Platte: Soileau Publications].

De Blanc, B. F. (1935). *A glossary of variants from Standard French found in St. Martin Parish, Louisiana*. Unpublished master's thesis, Louisiana State University, Baton Rouge.

Ditchy, J. (1932). *Les Acadiens louisianais et leur parler*. Paris: E. Droz.

Doucet, C. J. (1970). *The Acadian French of Lafayette, Louisiana*. Unpublished master's thesis, University of Southwestern Louisiana, Lafayette.

Doucet, C. (1985). *La charrue*. Lafayette, LA: USL Éditions de la Nouvelle Acadie.

Dugas, A. M. (1935). *A glossary of the variants from Standard French used in the Parish of Saint James*. Unpublished master's thesis, Louisiana State University, Baton Rouge.

Farella, P. (1976). *Étude du dialecte acadien à partir d'enregistrements faits dans différentes paroisses du sud-ouest de la Louisiane*. Unpublished master's thesis, Université de Provence (Aix-Marseille I).

Faulk, J. D. (1977). *Cajun French I*. Abbeville, LA: Cajun Press.

Granier, E. L. (1939). *A glossary of the French spoken in St. John Parish*. Unpublished master's thesis, Louisiana State University, Baton Rouge.

Gravelles, M. U. de. (1979). *Mille misères: Laissant le bon temps rouler en Louisiane*. Projet Louisiane, n°5, March. Quebec: Laval University.

Griolet, P. (1982). *Les Acadiens de Louisiane à travers leurs récits: Étude de littérature spontanée*. Unpublished doctoral dissertation, Paris IV.

Griolet, P. (1986). *Mots de Louisiane: Étude lexicale d'une Francophonie*. Paris: L'Harmattan.

Guidry, R. (1982). *C'est p'us pareil*. Lafayette: Center for Louisiana Studies.

Guidry, R. (1993). *La cuisine louisianaise*. Lafayette, LA: CODOFIL.

Guidry, R. (2000). Unpublished collection of manuscripts.

Guilbeau, J. (1936). *A glossary of variants from Standard French in Lafourche Parish*. Unpublished master's thesis, Louisiana State University, Baton Rouge.

Guilbeau, J. (1950). *The French spoken in Lafourche Parish, Louisiana*. Unpublished doctoral dissertation, University of North Carolina, Chapel Hill.

Guilbeau, J. (1972). Folklore and the Louisiana French lexicon. *Louisiana Review, 1(1)*, 45–54.

Hamlett, J. A. (1954). *The folklore of the French-speaking negro of Evangeline Parish*. Unpublished master's thesis, Louisiana State University, Baton Rouge.

Hickman, F. M. (1940). *The French speech of Jefferson Parish*. Unpublished master's thesis, Louisiana State University, Baton Rouge.

Holmes, W. C. (1990). *Flore Louisiane: An ethno-botanical study of French-speaking Louisiana*. Lafayette: Center for Louisiana Studies.

Howard, Jr., C. A. (1975). *A comparative study of the grammar of Acadian and Cajun narratives*. Unpublished master's thesis, Georgetown University, Washington, DC.

Hurst, H. (1953). *A glossary of the French spoken in St. Charles Parish*. Unpublished master's thesis, Louisiana State University, Baton Rouge.

Iseringhausen, F. J. (1956). *A glossary of the French spoken in Church Point, Acadia Parish, Louisiana*. Unpublished master's thesis, Louisiana State University, Baton Rouge.

Jannisse, H., & Whatley, R. P. (1978). *Conversational Cajun French 1*. Baton Rouge: Chicot Press.

Jeansonne, S. L. (1938). *A glossary of words that vary from Standard-French in Avoyelles Parish*. Unpublished master's thesis, Louisiana State University, Baton Rouge.

Lafleur, A. (1999). *Tonnerre mes chiens*. Ville Platte: Renouveau.

Lanclos, D. (1975). Two Acadian-French Tales. *Revue de Louisiane, 4(2)*, 55–56.

Landreneau, R. L. (1989). *The Cajun French Language*. Atlanta: Chicot Press.

Larousse, P. (1961). *Larousse du xxe siècle* (P. Augé, Ed.). Paris: Librairie Larousse.

Lavaud-Grassin, M. (1988). *Particularités lexicales du parler cadjin en Louisiane (États-Unis)*. Unpublished doctoral dissertation, University of Paris III.

Loupe, S. R. (1932). *Acadian folklore of "La Côte Française."* Unpublished master's thesis, Louisiana State University, Baton Rouge.

Melançon, D. A. (1964). *French folklore in Terrebonne Parish*. Unpublished master's thesis, Louisiana State University, Baton Rouge.

Montgomery, E. (1946). *A glossary of variants from Standard French in Vermilion Parish, Louisiana*. Unpublished master's thesis, Louisiana State University, Baton Rouge.

Nelson, S. F. K. (1965). *A phonetic study of the French spoken in Reserve, St. John the Baptist Parish, Louisiana*. Unpublished master's thesis, Louisiana State University, Baton Rouge.

Olivier, L. (1937). *A glossary of variants from Standard French in St. Landry Parish.* Unpublished master's thesis, Louisiana State University, Baton Rouge.

Oukada, L. (1977). *A linguistic study with descriptive analysis of Lafourche Parish dialect.* Unpublished master's thesis, Louisiana State University, Baton Rouge.

Parr, U. M. (1940). *A glossary of the variants from Standard French in Terrebonne Parish with an appendix of popular beliefs, superstitions, medicine, and cooking recipes.* Unpublished master's thesis, Louisiana State University, Baton Rouge.

Patin, P. (1976). *A lexicon of Breaux Bridge, Louisiana.* Unpublished master's thesis, University of Texas at Austin.

Pellerin, E. (1937). *La langue française en Louisiane.* Unpublished master's thesis, McGill University, Montreal, Quebec.

Perrin du Lac, F. M. (1805). *Voyages dans les deux Louisianes, et chez les nations sauvages du Missouri, par les États-Unis, l'Ohio et les provinces qui le bordent en 1801, 1802 et 1803.* Lyon: Bruyset aîné et Buynand.

Phillips, H. (1935). *A glossary of the variants from Standard French used in Evangeline Parish.* Unpublished master's thesis, Louisiana State University, Baton Rouge.

Phillips, H. (1936). *Étude du parler de la paroisse Evangéline.* Paris: Droz.

Pirkle, M. N. B. (1935). *Variants from Standard-French common to the dialects of Lafayette Parish and Canada.* Unpublished master's thesis, Louisiana State University, Baton Rouge.

Rantero, J. (1981). *Étude du français cajun de la paroisse Vermillon de Louisiane.* Unpublished master's thesis, Université de Rouen, France.

Read, W. A. (1939). A score of Louisiana-French words. *Zeitschrift für französische Sprache und Literatur, 63,* 41–64.

Read, W. A. (1963). *Louisiana French* (Rev. ed.). Baton Rouge: Louisiana State University Press. (Original work published 1931).

Reed, R. (1976). *Lâche pas la patate: Portrait des Acadiens de la Louisiane.* Montreal: Parti Pris.

Richard, Z. (1985). *Voyage de nuit.* Lafayette, LA: Center for Louisiana Studies.

Richard, Z. (1997). *Faire récolte: Poésie.* Moncton, NB: Éditions Perce-Neige.

Saltzman, J. D. (1957). *A phonetic study of the French spoken in Saltzman Settlement, Vermilion Parish, Louisiana.* Unpublished master's thesis, Louisiana State University, Baton Rouge.

Saucier, C. (1956). *Traditions de la paroisse des Avoyelles en Louisiane.* Memoirs of the American Folklore Society, Vol. 47. Philadelphia: MAFS.

Soileau, J. (1975). Proverbs and proverbial locutions of the St. Martinville area. *Louisiana Folklore Miscellany, 3(4),* 29–34.

Sullivan, M. A. (1977). *A phonological analysis of the French of the Swords, Louisiana, area.* Unpublished master's thesis, Louisiana State University, Baton Rouge.

Tentchoff, D. (1977). *Speech in a Louisiana Cajun community.* Unpublished doctoral dissertation, Case Western Reserve University.

Trahan, L. M. (1936). *Etymological glossary of the variants from Standard French in Assumption Parish.* Unpublished master's thesis, Louisiana State University, Baton Rouge.

Trappey, M. M. (1940). *The French of Iberia Parish.* Unpublished master's thesis, Louisiana State University, Baton Rouge.

Viator, A. B. (1935). *A glossary of neologisms, loan-words and variants from Standard French in the Parish of St. John the Baptist.* Unpublished master's thesis, Louisiana State University, Baton Rouge.

Voorhies, E. T. (1949). *A glossary of variants from Standard French in St. Martin's Parish, Louisiana followed by some of the folklore of the parish.* Unpublished master's thesis, Louisiana State University, Baton Rouge.

Waggoner, M. (1999). *Une fantaisie collective: Anthologie du drame louisianais cadien.* Lafayette, LA: Center for Louisiana Studies.

Whatley, R. P. (1983). *Du chicot: A collection of essays.* Baton Rouge: Chicot Press.

Whitfield, I. T. (1969). *Louisiana French folk songs.* New York: Dover Publications.

Radio stations

KAJN. Crowley, Acadia Parish, LA. 1560 AM.*

KEUN. Eunice and Mamou, St. Landry Parish, LA. 1490 AM.*

KPEL. Lafayette, Lafayette Parish, LA. 1420 AM.*

KROF. Abbeville, Vermillon Parish, LA. 960 AM, 105 FM.*

KRVS. Lafayette, Lafayette Parish, LA.*

KSIG. Crowley, Acadia Parish, LA. 1450 AM.*

KSLO. Opelousas, St. Landry Parish, LA. 1230 AM.*

KVPI. Ville Platte, Evangeline Parish, LA. 1050 AM, 93.5 FM.*

Periodicals

La Gazette des Acadiens.

Louisiane.

List of Source Codes for Published Examples

Al81	Allain & Ancelet 1981
An77	Ancelet 1977
An83	Ancelet 1983
An84	Ancelet & Morgan 1984
An94	Ancelet 1994
Ar82	Arceneaux 1982
Ar98	Arceneaux 1998
Bo80	Bossu 1980
Ca83	Castille 1983
Co63	Conwell & Juilland 1963
Co80	Comeaux & Meaux 1980
Da84	Daigle 1984
Da92	Daigle 1992
De85	Desmarais 1985
Di32	Ditchy 1932
Fa77	Faulk 1977
Gr82	Griolet 1982
Gr86	Griolet 1986
Gu82	Guidry 1982
Gu00	Guidry 2000
Hi02	Bruce & Gipson 2002
Ho90	Holmes 1990
La89	Landreneau 1989
La99	Lafleur 1999
Lv88	Lavaud-Grassin 1988
LGA	La Gazette des Acadiens
Pe37	Pellerin 1937
Ph36	Phillips 1936
Re31	Read 1931
Re39	Read 1939
Re63	Read 1963
Re76	Reed 1976
St95	Stabler 1995
ThCa	Théâtre Cadien
Wh69	Whitfield 1969
Wh83	Whatley 1983

List of Parish Codes

AC	Acadia
AL	Allen
AN	Ascension
AS	Assumption
AV	Avoyelles
CL	Calcasieu
CM	Cameron
EV	Evangeline
IB	Iberia
IV	Iberville
JE	Jefferson
JD	Jefferson Davis
LA	Lafayette
LF	Lafourche
LI	Livingston
PQ	Plaquemines
PC	Pointe Coupée
SD	Saint Bernard
SC	Saint Charles
SJ	Saint James
SB	Saint John the Baptist
SL	Saint Landry
SM	Saint Martin
SY	Saint Mary
ST	Saint Tammany
TB	Terrebonne
VM	Vermilion
WB	West Baton Rouge

List of Abbreviations Used in the Dictionary

adj.	adjective, adjectival
adj.dem.	demonstrative adjective
adj.f.	feminine adjective
adj.invar.	invariable adjective
adj.m.	masculine adjective
adj.poss.	possessive adjective
adv.	adverb, adverbial
adv.interrog.	interrogative adverb
art.	article
art.def.	definite article
art.indef.	indefinite article
art.part.	partitive article
dir.obj.	direct object
f.sing.	feminine singular
ind.obj.	indirect object
aux.	auxiliary
conj.	conjunction
def.	definite
dem.	demonstrative
eccl.	ecclesiastical
emph.	emphatic
exclam.	exclamation
expr.	expression
f.	feminine
f.pl.	feminine plural
impers.	impersonal
indef.	indefinite
interj.	interjection
interrog.	interrogative
intr.	intransitive
invar.	invariable
m.	masculine
m./f.pl.	masculine and feminine plural
m.pl.	masculine plural
m.sing.	masculine singular
n.	noun [gender varies according to the biological sex of the referent, e.g. *un nageur, une nageuse*.]
neg.	negative
n.f.pl.	feminine plural noun
n.m./f.	feminine and/or masculine noun [gender varies in the usage of different regions and/or speakers]
n.m.pl.	masculine plural noun
n.pl.	plural noun
n.prop.	proper noun
obj. of prep.	object of preposition
occ.	occasionally
pej.	pejorative
pers.	person, personal
pl.	plural
poss.	possessive
p.p.	past participle
prep.	preposition
pron.	pronoun, pronominal
pron.dem.	demonstrative pronoun
pron.indef.	indefinite pronoun
pron.interrog.	interrogative pronoun
pron.pers.	personal pronoun
pron.poss.	possessive pronoun
pron.rel.	relative pronoun
prop.	proper
refl.	reflexive
rel.	relative
sing.	singular
s.o.	someone
s.t.	something
subj.	subject

tonic	tonic
tr.	transitive
usu.	usually
v.	verb, verbal
v.aux.	auxiliary verb
v.cop.	copular verb
v.intr.	intransitive verb
v.pron.	pronominal verb
v.intr.invar.	invariable intransitive verb
v.tr.	transitive verb
v.tr.invar.	invariable transitive verb
vulg.	vulgar

Pronunciation Guide

Phonetic Symbols used in the Dictionary

IPA	Transcription	Louisiana word	English equivalent
a	[taba]	tabac	'tobacco'
e	[taʃe]	tacher	'to stain, spot, soil'
ɛ	[turtrɛl]	tourterelle	'dove'
i	[tapi]	tapis	'carpet, rug'
o	[toro]	taureau	'bull'
ɔ	[tɔrku]	torcou	'wryneck woodpecker'
u	[tusaje]	toussailler	'to cough'
y	[tyrlyt]	turlutte	'fight, loud noise'
ø	[turnkø]	tourne-queue	'mosquito larva'
œ	[tafjatœr]	tafiateur	'drunkard'
ɔ̃	[tɔ̃be]	tomber	'to fall'
ɑ̃	[tɑ̃buje]	tambouiller	'to cook'
ɛ̃	[topɛ̃]	taupin	'burly, large, strong man'
œ̃	[lœ̃di]	lundi	'Monday'
ỹ	[prỹje]	prunier	'plum tree'
ĩ	[opĩjɔ̃]	opinion	'opinion, idea'
ə	[tə]	te (t')	'you'
æ	[tær]	terre	'earth, world'
j	[tojas]	toyasse	'weak coffee'
ɥ	[tradɥir]	traduire	'to translate'
w	[turnwa]	tournoi	'tournament, match'
b	[tablo]	tableau	'blackboard'
k	[takinri]	taquinerie	'teasing'
ʃ	[tirvaʃ]	tire-vache	'milking-pail'
d	[tɑ̃di]	tandis	'while'
f	[fisɛl]	ficelle	'twine, string'
g	[figyr]	figure	'figure, number'
ɲ	[tiɲɔ̃]	tignon	'turban, headscarf'
ŋ	[tʃuflɑ̃ŋ]	tchouflangue	'small, cheap business'
h	[haʃ]	hache	'ax'
ʒ	[tiraʒ]	tirage	'milking (of cows)'
l	[tolerɑ̃s]	tolérance	'toleration, endurance'

IPA	Transcription	Louisiana word	English equivalent
m	[tɔ̃m]	tombe	'tomb, grave'
n	[tɔ̃niba]	tonibas	'my goodness'
tʃ	[tʃarabo]	tcharabo	'rifle'
dʒ	[badʒo]	badjo	'uneducated person'
p	[tape]	taper	'to slap, strike, hit'
r	[tarif]	tarif	'tariff, charge, tax'
s	[tas]	tasse	'cup'
t	[tatine]	tatiner	'to dabble'
v	[truv]	trouve	'discovery'
z	[trezɔr]	trésor	'treasure'

Additional sounds occurring in words of English origin

IPA	Transcription	Louisiana word	English equivalent
ɑ	[pɑɹk]	PARK	'to park'
ɪ	[mɪsteɪk]	MISTAKE	'mistake'
ʌ	[blʌf]	BLUFF	'bluff, deception'
ɔɪ	[bigbɔɪ]	BIG BOY	'bigshot'
aʊ	[blækaʊt]	BLACKOUT	'to black out'
aɪ	[blaɪn(d)]	BLIND	'blind'
eɪ	[meɪl]	MAIL	'mail'
oʊ	[broʊk]	BROKE	'broke, penniless'
iɪ	[mɪsdiɪl]	MISDEAL	'misdeal (in cards)
ɹ	[paɹti]	PARTY	'party'

Pronunciation notes

We summarize here some of the salient characteristics of Louisiana French pronunciation, focusing in particular on features that distinguish it from the pronunciation of Standard French.

Vowels

On the whole, the vowels of Louisiana French are not substantially different from their Standard French counterparts. However, it is noteworthy that Louisiana French often preserves the nasal vowel [œ̃] (pronounced with the lips slightly rounded) as in *lundi* 'Monday' [lœ̃di], which in the French of Paris and other parts of France has largely been replaced by [ɛ̃] (pronounced with the lips spread). Though [œ̃] may be merging with [ɛ̃] in Louisiana as well—variable pronunciations may be encountered for many words (*défunt* 'deceased' [defœ̃]/[defɛ̃], *lundi* [lœ̃di]/[lɛ̃di], *un livre* 'a book' [œ̃liv]/[ɛ̃liv], *Lejeune* [ləʒœ̃n]/[ləʒɛ̃n])—most speakers of Louisiana French still make use of the contrast between [œ̃] and [ɛ̃] to maintain a distinction between certain pairs of words, such as *brin* 'bit, small quantity' [brɛ̃] and *brun* 'brown, light complected' [brœ̃], whereas Parisians tend to pronounce both as [brɛ̃]. Another distinguishing feature of Louisiana French is the widespread nasalization of the vowels [a], [e], [ɛ], [œ], [o], [ɔ] and, less frequently, of [i], [y], and [u] when they occur before a nasal consonant: *femme* 'woman' [fam] > [fɑ̃m], [fɔ̃m]; *chêne* 'oak tree' [ʃɛn] > [ʃɛ̃n]; *pomme* 'apple' [pɔm] > [pɔ̃m]. As the example of *femme* 'woman' [fɑ̃m], [fɔ̃m] illustrates, the nasal vowels [ɑ̃] and [ɔ̃] are often conflated in Louisiana French, with words that in Standard French are pronounced with [ɑ̃] frequently being realized with a vowel more closely resembling [ɔ̃]: *ensemble* 'together' [ɔ̃sɔ̃m], *campagne* 'country' [kɔ̃pɔ̃j]. We transcribe such words only with [ɑ̃] ([ɑ̃sɑ̃m], [kɑ̃pɑ̃j]), but the reader should be aware that they may often hear them pronounced with [ɔ̃], as well.

A few remarks are also in order regarding the oral (non-nasal) vowels. When it occurs before [r], especially at the end of a word or before another consonant, the vowel [ɛ] of Louisiana French frequently lowers. The degree of lowering varies. The vowel [æ], which is similar to the sound of the vowel in the English word *cat*, is most commonly heard. However, some speakers will lower further to the vowel [a], as in the English exclamation *ah*. Examples include *frère* 'brother' [frɛr] > [frær] > [frar] and *personne* 'no one' [pɛrsɔn] > [pærsɔ̃n] > [parsɔ̃n]. The low back vowel [ɑ], which is intermediate in quality between the vowels of the English words *father* and *caught*, is much more common in Louisiana French than in Standard French, appearing regularly in words such as *avalasse* 'downpour' [ɑvɑlɑs], *mal* 'bad, badly' [mɑl], and especially after [w]: *moi* 'me' [mwɑ]; *loi* 'law' [lwɑ]; *croire* 'to believe' [krwɑr]. However, since there are no words that can be distinguished purely on the basis of being pronounced with [ɑ] vs. [a], and since both vowels may potentially be heard in the same word, we use [a] to represent both, except in the case of English loanwords such as *park* [pɑɹk]. Lowering of high rounded vowels—front [y] and back [u]—to mid rounded vowels [ø] and [o] respectively is sometimes encountered. Lowering occurs most commonly before [r], but for the back rounded high vowel [u], it is not uncommon in other contexts as well: *pure* 'pure' [pyr] > [pør]; *ouragan* 'hurricane' [uragɑ̃] > [oragɑ̃]; *oublier* 'to forget' [ublije] > [oblije]. Finally, the front rounded vowels of Standard French are sometimes unrounded, so that [y] becomes [i], [ø] becomes [e], and, [œ] becomes [ɛ]. Perhaps the most common example of this is the second person singular subject pronoun *tu* 'you' [ty], which is frequently pronounced *ti* [ti].

Consonants and Glides

Louisiana French possesses all of the consonants and glides found in Standard French. However, the palatal nasal consonant [ɲ], as in *tignon* 'turban, headscarf' [tiɲɔ̃], is rare, and when it occurs between two vowels it is generally replaced by the palatal glide [j]. The trace of the nasal consonant usually remains in the form of a nasalized preceding vowel, however, and often the glide is nasalized, as well: *saigner* 'to bleed' [sɛ̃j̃e]. Similarly, the alveolar nasal [n], if followed directly by a palatal glide [j], will sometimes be replaced by nasalization of the preceding vowel, with possible nasalization of the glide as well: *panier* 'basket' [panje] > [pɑ̃j̃e]; *manière* 'manner' [manjɛr] > [mɑ̃j̃ær]; *opinion* 'opinion' [opinjɔ̃] > [opĩj̃ɔ̃]; *prunier* 'plum tree' [prynje] > [prỹj̃e]. In the case of [vw] clusters, the presence of the labio-velar glide [w] may lead to loss of the preceding labio-dental fricative consonsant [v]: *savoir* 'to know' [savwar] > [sawar]; *voisin* 'neighbor' [vwazɛ̃] > [wazɛ̃]; *voilà* 'there is, there are' [vwala] > [wala].

Louisiana French possesses three consonants not found in Standard French, though all three were present in the French of France at earlier stages. One is the glottal fricative [h] (the consonant in English *home*), as in *honte* 'shame' [hɔ̃t] or *haler* 'to pull, to haul' [hale]. The other two are the palatal affricates [tʃ] (the consonant in English *church*) and [dʒ] (the consonant in English *judge*), as in *tcharabo* 'rifle' [tʃarabo] and *badjo* 'uneducated person' [badʒo]. Often the occurrence of [tʃ] and [dʒ] results from the consonants [t] and [d] appearing directly before the palatal glides—whether unrounded [j] or rounded [ɥ]—or directly before the vowels [i], [y], [e], or [ø], as in *tiens!* 'Here!', pronounced [tjɛ̃] or [tʃɛ̃], and *diable* 'devil', pronounced [djab] or [dʒab]. However, in some words, such as *tcharabo* and *badjo*, noted above, the pronunciation with [tʃ] or [dʒ] is the only one possible and cannot be explained by the contact of [t] or [d] with the following sound.

One consonant that has notably different pronunciations in Louisiana and Standard French is the one represented by the letter *r* and, in our dictionary, by the IPA symbol [r]. Whereas in Standard French this consonant is velar, meaning that it is realized by a constriction formed between the back (or root) of the tongue and the soft palate, in Louisiana it is most often apical, meaning that it is realized as a light tap of the tip (or apex) of the tongue against the alveolar ridge located just behind the upper incisors. While not typical of Standard French pronunciation, the [r] of Louisiana is found in many parts of the French-speaking world, including among some speakers in Quebec, Acadia, Francophone Africa, and even in rural parts of France. A notable feature of [r] in Louisiana is its weakening in word-final position after a vowel, which can sometimes result in its being dropped altogether. Most often, however, a trace of the [r] remains in the lengthening of the preceding vowel. Thus the word *frère* 'brother' may be pronounced [frær], [fræ:] (where ':' represents a lengthening of the vowel), or [fræ]. In our transcriptions, we note only the form with a fully pronounced [r].

The reduction of clusters of consonants at the end of words is a hallmark feature of Louisiana French pronunciation. While also typical of informal spoken French in France and other parts of the Francophone world, in Louisiana such simplification is common in all registers and can be said to be nearly categorical. It is most systematic in the case of the liquids [l] and [r] occurring after another consonant, as in *table* 'table' [tab] and *quatre* 'four' [kat]. These consonants are virtually never pronounced in this context unless they are followed by a word beginning with a vowel, as in *quatre ans* 'four years' [katrɑ̃]. Consonant cluster reduction also affects other consonants, however, as in *masque* 'mask' [mas] and *insecte* 'insect' [ɛ̃sɛk].

Another feature of pronunciation that is not unknown in informal registers of French elsewhere in the world but is nearly systematic in Louisiana is the change of the consonants [b] and [d] to [m] and [n], respectively, when they occur in word-final position after a nasal vowel. This frequently occurs when [b] and [d] find themselves in word-final position due to the dropping of [l] or [r], as described above: *ensemble* 'together' [ɑ̃sɑ̃bl] > [ɑ̃sɑ̃b] > [ɑ̃sɑ̃m], *descendre* 'to get down, go down' [desɑ̃dr] > [desɑ̃d] > [desɑ̃n].

Some aspects of pronunciation vary according to region. Perhaps the most striking example of this is the variable pronunciation of the voiced palatal fricative [ʒ] (and, less often, of [ʃ], [z], and [s]) as [h] in Terrebonne and Lafourche parishes: *jamais* 'never' [ʒɑ̃me], [hɑ̃me]; *j'ai mangé* [ʒemɑ̃ʒe], [hemɑ̃he]. Another example of regional variation is the frequent assibilation of [t] and [d]—such that they are pronounced with a following slight [s] or [z] respectively—before the high front vowels [i] and [y] and before the palatal glides [j] and [ɥ]: *petit* 'little' [pətˢi], *il dit* 'he says' [idᶻi]. This phenomenon, which is typical of Québécois French, is in Louisiana restricted to Evangeline and neighboring parishes. We do not note such regional variants in our transcriptions.

An aspect of pronunciation that appears to be strongly linked to ethnicity is the variable realization of the palatal fricative consonants [ʒ] or [ʃ] as alveolar fricative consonants [z] or [s] respectively: *chez* 'at someone's home or place' [ʃe] > [se]; *changer* 'to change' [ʃɑ̃ʒe] > [ʃɑ̃ze]. This is especially salient when it occurs as a feature of the first person singular subject pronoun *je*: *je mange* 'I eat' [ʒ(ə)mɑ̃ʒ] > [z(ə)mɑ̃ʒ], *je connais* 'I know' [ʃkɔ̃ne] > [skɔ̃ne]. The variants [z] and [s] seem to be especially common among black, Creole of color, and Indian speakers. We do not note them in our transcriptions.

A final feature of pronunciation that merits comment involves the vowel [ə], which switches places with a preceding consonant (a process known as metathesis) in certain contexts, but especially in the words *je* 'I' and *le* 'the' (masculine singular), and in the prefix *re-*: *je mange* 'I eat' [ʒəmɑ̃ʒ], [əʒmɑ̃ʒ], *recevoir* 'to receive, to get' [rəsəvwar], [ərsəvwar].

Dictionary of Louisiana French

a, a' ♦see **alle**

à [a] (*contractions:* **à** + *art.def.* **le** = **au** [o], **à** + *art.def.pl.* **les** = **aux** [o, oz]) *prep.* **1** to *C'est du monde païen. Eusse va pas à l'église.* They are heathens. They don't go to church. (LF) **J'ai su par après que Henri avait été renvoyé en France, à une place nommée Belle Ile.* I found out afterward that Henri had been sent to France, to a place called Belle Ile. (An98) *Quand on a déménagé* BACK *au village.* When we moved back to the city. (IB) *On va au* SWIMMING POOL. We go to the swimming pool. (TB) **2** at *Il y avait une file de monde au* PICTURE SHOW. There was a line of people at the movies. (EV) *Il s'a trouvé à l'autre bout du lac sans pagaille pour son bateau.* He found himself at the other end of the lake without a paddle for his boat. (Gu00) *J'ai été passer une semaine à leur maison.* I went to spend a week at their home. (TB) **3** in *Labourer au milieu du clos.* Plowing in the middle of the field. (LA) *Sa fête qu'eusse avait fêté, là-bas c'est au parc l'autre bord.* His birthday that they celebrated, that was in the park on the other side. (TB) *Je fréquente pas assez souvent les affaires à Eunice.* I don't go to the events in Eunice very often. (LA) **4** at, in (a time) *Venez à bonne heure.* Come early. (Lv88) *À soir.* In the evening. (Lv88) **A la brune.* At dusk. (Da84) *Je débauchais à midi.* I used to get off work at noon. (LF) *Ils se sont fiancés au printemps.* They became engaged in the spring. (LA) **5** at the rate of, per **A la journée.* By the day. (Da84) **A la livre.* By the pound. (Da84) **6** at a distance of *A quatre-vingts arpents d'ici.* Eighty acres from here. (VM) **A dix miles à la ronde.* For 10 miles around. (Da84) **7** *(with indirect object)* to *J'ai ramassé deux plats d'haricots pour donner à mes deux belles-sœurs.* I gathered two plates of beans to give to my two sisters-in-law. (LF) *Il voulait me passer ses traitements et tout parce que il avait personne d'autre qui voulait, et il voulait le passer à quelqu'un.* He wanted to pass his treatments on to me and all because there was no one else who wanted them, and he wanted to hand them on to somebody. (SJ) **8** of, belonging to *Le char à Tom.* Tom's car. (Lv88) *La femme à Edouard, elle avait déménagé.* Edward's wife, she had moved out. (SL) **9** son of, wife of, etc. (used to distinguish a person with a common first name) *Louis à Thomas.* Louis, son of Thomas. (Lv88) *Mary à Burton.* Burton's wife, Mary. (EV) **12** for, intended for *Je pêche juste des cages à écrevisses et de temps en temps je vas pêcher des lignes, des* TROTLINE. I only use crawfish traps for fishing and from time to time I use trotlines. (SM) **9** to, in order to *On use des fusils à chasser.* We use guns to hunt. (JE) **10** by, with (an instrument, technique, or means) *Les cannes, c'était chargé à la main ça.* Cane was loaded by hand. (TB) *On pourrait peut-être aller se promener à la pagaille.* Maybe we could go for a ride paddling [in a pirogue]. (LF) **11** with **Un homme à barbe blanche.* A white-bearded man. (Da84) **Café au lait.* Coffee with milk. (Da84) *Fusil à six coups.* Six-shooter. (Da84) <***Loc:*** EV, IB, JE, LA, LF, SJ, SL, SM, TB, VM, An94, An98, Da84, Hi02, Lv88>

abaisser [abese] **I** *v.tr.* **1** to lower (e.g. one's judgment, one's opinion) *Mon opinion de lui a été abaissée.* My opinion of him has been lowered. (EV) **2** to humiliate, degrade *Il a abaissé sa femme devant tout le monde.* He humiliated his wife in front of everyone. (VM) **II s'abaisser** *v.pron.* to lower o.s., humble o.s. **C'était pas bien s'appeler créole. Plutôt que d'te relever, tu t'abaissais.* It wasn't good to call yourself Creole. Rather than raising yourself, you lowered yourself. (Gr86) <***Loc:*** EV, VM, Da84, Gr86>

abaissir (s') [abesir] *v.pron.* to lower one's dignity or moral standing *Tu t'abaissis quand tu dis ça.* You lower yourself when you say that. (AV) <***Loc:*** AV>

abajoue[1] [abaʒu] *n.f.* cheek pouch <***Loc:*** Da84, Lv88>

abajoue[2] ♦see **bajoue**

abalourdir [abalurdir] *v.tr.* to bore, weary, tire *Il m'abalourdit avec ses sottises.* He bores me with his nonsense. (Lv88) <***Loc:*** Da84, Lv88>

abandon [abɑ̃dɔ̃, ɑ̃bɑ̃dɑ̃] *n.m.* abandonment, destitution, ruin *Ça va à l'abandon.* That is going to ruin. (JE) <***Loc:*** JE, Da84>

abandonner [abɑ̃dɔ̃ne, ɑ̃bɑ̃dɔ̃ne] **I** *v.tr.* **1** to abandon, desert *Une petite maison que mon défunt pape avait abandonnée.* A little house that my late father had abandoned. (TB) **2** to give up, renounce *Mais eux-autres voulait abandonner les juges de paix et les constables parce que c'est tout* OUTDATED. But they wanted to give up justices of the peace and constables because that was all outdated. (LF) **3** to quit, stop, cease *Il a abandonné travailler.* He quit work. (Lv88) **II** *v.intr.* to quit, stop, cease *Il a abandonné de boire.* He stopped drinking. (JE) **III s'abandonner** *v.pron.* to neglect o.s., let o.s. go to pot *Depuis que son mari est mort, elle s'a abandonné.* Since her husband's death, she let herself go to pot. (VM) ◊ **•s'abandonner à** to yield to, give in to, give o.s. up to *Il s'a abandonné à la boisson.* He gave in to drinking. (LA) <LA> <***Loc:*** JE, LA, LF, SL, TB, VM, Da84, Lv88, Wh83>

abasourdir [abasurdir] *v.tr.* to stun, astound, stupefy *La nouvelle de sa mort m'a abasourdi.* The news of his death stunned me. (VM) <***Loc:*** VM, Da84>

abâtardi, -e (**bâtardi, -e**) [abatardi, batardi] *adj.* **1** hybrid (of plants) *Du maïs abâtardi.* Hybrid corn. (Lv88) **2** crossbred, mongrel, of mixed breed *Un chien abâtardi.* A mixed-breed dog, a mongrel. (Lv88) **3** [*offensive*] mixed blood, half-breed, bastardized (of people) **Des abâtardis Mexicains, noirs et blancs.* Mixed-blood Mexicans, black and white. (Gr82) *Mes neveux sont bâtardis américains.* My nephews are mixed-race Americans. (VM) **4** bastardized, mixed (of languages) *Un français abâtardi avec l'anglais.* A French mixed with English. (Lv88) <***Loc:*** AV, IB, IV, SB, SM, VM, Da84, Gr82, Lv88>

abâtardir (**bâtardir**) [abatardir, batardir] **I** *v.tr.* **1** to hybridize, cross-breed (two varieties of some species) *Abâtardir une bourrique et un étalon donne un mulet créole.* Mixing a jenny and a stallion produces a creole mule. (VM) **2** to bastardize, mix (races, blood, languages) **II s'abâtardir** *v.pron.* to be bastardized, be mongrelized *J'ai peur qu'il va s'abâtardir avec ce monde-là.* I'm afraid he's going to get bastardized by those people. (VM) <***Loc:*** IB, SM, TB, VM, Da84, Lv88>

abâtardissage [abatardisaʒ] *n.m.* bastardization, bastardizing, mongrelizing <***Loc:*** EV, LA, VM>

abâtardissement [abatardismɑ̃] *n.m.* bastardization, bastardizing, mongrelizing <***Loc:*** Da84>

abat-jour (**bajou, bajour**) [abaʒur, baʒu, baʒur] *n.m.* **1** shutter, outside blind **2** blind, Venetian blind **3** shade, window shade <***Loc:*** Lv88>

abattage [abataʒ] *n.m.* **1** felling, cutting down (of a tree) **2** cutting or flattening (of grass, etc.) **3** slaughter (of an animal) <***Loc:*** Da84>

abatteur, -euse [abatœr, -øz] *n.* **1** one who fells trees, lumberjack **2** slaughterer <***Loc:*** Da84>

abattre [abat(r)] *v.tr.* **1** to fell, chop down (a tree) *Il a travaillé sur des* PULLBOATS, *il abattait des gros cypres dans les cyprières en arrière de Lac Verret.* He worked on tugboats, he felled big cypress trees behind Lake Verret. (AS) **2** to knock down *Le coup de temps a abattu ma barrière et tout mes bêtes ont sorti.* The bad weather knocked my fence down and all my cattle got out. (VM) **3** to beat down *On a été obligé d'abattre les joncs plats pour arriver à l'écore.* We had to beat down the cattails to reach the bank. (VM) **4** to demolish (a building) **5** to kill *David a abattu le géant dans la vieille histoire.* David killed the giant in the old story. (LA) **6** to eliminate, get rid of *Moi je peux t'abattre un mal de tête, ou un mal dans le dos, ou les coliques pour les enfants.* I can get rid of a headache for you, or a backache, or children's colic. (LF) **7** to humble, dishearten, discourage *Avec beaucoup de mots, il a abattu cet homme.* With many words, he humbled that man. (LA) <***Loc:*** AS, IV, LA, LF, TB, VM, Da84>

abattu, -e [abaty] *adj.* **1** haggard-looking **2** plagued, vexed, afflicted *Il est abattu par la fièvre.* He is plagued by fever. (SM) *Il est abattu de la migraine.* He is plagued by migraines. (VM) <***Loc:*** SM, VM, Da84>

abbé [abe] *n.m.* [*eccl.*] priest, abbot <***Loc:*** Da84>

abbesse [abɛs] *n.f.* [*eccl.*] abbess <***Loc:*** Da84>

abcès [apse] *n.m.* abscess <***Loc:*** Da84, Lv88>

abeille [abɛj] *n.f.* honeybee <***Loc:*** IB, Da84>

abîmé, -e (**abûmé**) [abime, abyme] *adj.* **1** badly damaged, ruined *Fourniture abîmée.* Damaged furniture. (LA) **2** in poor health, broken with age or illness *Il est tellement abîmé, j'ai manqué pas le reconnaître.* He's so worn out, I almost didn't recognize him. (SM) *La maladie l'a laissé abîmé.* The sickness left him ruined. (Lv88) **3** exhausted, worn out **Tu ressembles abîmé. —Mais, il dit, j'ai travaillé toute la journée.* You look exhausted. —But, he says, I worked all day long. (An94) <***Loc:*** LA, SM, VM, An94, Da84, Lv88>

abîmer (**abûmer**) [abime, abyme] **I** *v.tr.* **1** to damage badly, ruin *J'ai abîmé la chaudière de ma mère en battant dessus avec une grosse cuiller.* I ruined my mother's pot beating it with a big spoon. (VM) **2** to beat, beat up **Papa m'a abîmé d' coups.* Dad beat me. (EV, Ph36) **3** to abuse, mistreat *Il abîmait son cheval.* He would abuse his horse. (Lv88) **4** to exhaust, tire out *L'ouvrage dans le bois m'a abîmé.* Working in the woods exhausted me. (LA) **II s'abîmer** *v.pron.* **1** to injure o.s., hurt o.s. *Il s'est abîmé avec le couteau.* He hurt himself with the knife. (Lv88) **2** to decline in health, deteriorate, waste away *Ça fait pitié de voir comme il est après s'abîmer.* It's a pity to see how he is wasting away. (VM) <***Loc:*** AV, EV, LA, LF, SB, SL, SM, VM, Da84, Lv88, Ph36>

abnormal [abnɔrmal] *adj.* abnormal <***Loc:*** AV, SJ>

aboëtte (**boëtte**) [abwɛt, abwat, bwat, bwɛt] *n.f.* bait *Quelle sorte d'aboëtte t'as usée pour attraper tous ces patassas?* What kind of bait did you use to catch all those perch? (VM) <***Loc:*** TB, VM, Gu00, Lv88>

aboëtter (**boëtter**) [abwete, abwate, bwete, bwate] *v.tr.* to bait *Tu aboëttes tes pièges avec du poisson.* You bait your traps with fish. (Lv88) <***Loc:*** TB, VM, Gu00, Lv88>

aboiement [abwɑ̃mɑ̃] *n.m.* howl, howling <***Loc:*** EV, LA, VM>

abolir [abolir] *v.tr.* to abolish, repeal, do away with *Ça dit que Abraham Lincoln a aboli l'esclavage.* They say that Abraham Lincoln abolished slavery. (VM) <***Loc:*** VM, Da84>

abominable [abɔ̃minab(l)] *adj.* **1** abominable, terrible *Tous les affaires qui se passent en Irak c'est abominable.* All the things happening in Iraq are abominable. (LA) **2** large, huge, enormous *Une bâtisse abominable.* A huge building. (Lv88) *Une quantité abominable de pacanes.* An enormous quantity of pecans. (Lv88) <***Loc:*** JE, LA, LF, Da84, Lv88>

abomination [abɔ̃minasjɔ̃] *n.f.* abomination, horror <***Loc:*** Da84>

abominer [abɔ̃mine] *v.tr.* **1** to beat, whip *C'était un mauvais bougre; il abominait ses chevaux.* He was a mean guy, he used to beat his horses. (Lv88) **2** to annoy, bother *Elle* *s'adonne pas avec personne et elle abomine son père tous les jours.* She doesn't get along with anyone and she annoys her father every day. (Lv88) **3** to detest, hate *Il était rendu à abominer les vieux.* He had gotten to the point of hating the old folks. (LA) <***Loc:*** AS, AV, LA, SJ, SL, Da84, La99, Lv88>

abondance [abɔ̃dɑ̃s] *n.f.* abundance <***Loc:*** Da84>

abondant, -e [abɔ̃dɑ̃, -ɑ̃t] *adj.* abundant, plentiful, numerous *Les pluies de l'été n'étaient pas abondantes.* The summer rains were not plentiful. (LA) <***Loc:*** LA, Da84>

abonner [abɔ̃ne] **I** *v.tr.* to subscribe *Elle a abonné son père à la gazette d'Abbeville. She* subscribed her father to the Abbeville newspaper. (LA) **II s'abonner** *v.pron.* to become a subscriber, subscribe (to a magazine, etc.) *Je m'abonne à la gazette.* I subscribe to the newspaper. (LA) <***Loc:*** LA, Da84>

abonnesir ♦see **abonnir**

abonnir (abonnesir) [abɔ̃nir, abɔ̃nzir] **I** *v.tr.* to improve, make better *Ils auront du mal à abonnir ces enfants.* They're going to have a hard time making those kids better. (LA) **II s'abonnir** *v.pron.* to become or be made better, improve *Ton mari va s'abonnir.* Your husband will get better. (LA) <***Loc:*** LA, Da84>

abordage [abɔrdaʒ] *n.m.* **1** collision, wreck **2** confrontation <***Loc:*** Da84>

aborder (border) [abɔrde, bɔrde] *v.tr.* **1** to collide with, run into, bump, hit, strike *Son char a abordé le mien juste devant la grocerie.* His car ran into mine right in front of the grocery store. (Lv88) *Le char a abordé le 'tit garçon et l'a tué.* The car hit the little boy and killed him. (Guoo) **2** to come up to, approach, accost *J'ai abordé ma tante pour cinq piastres.* I approached my aunt [to ask] for five dollars. (SM) *Il a pas aimé la manière que tu l'as abordé.* He didn't like the way you accosted him. (EV) **3** to board, get on, get in (a vehicle) *Aborde mon char, ça va mouiller fort.* Get into my car, it's going to rain hard. (Lv88) *Il a abordé le train pour aller à New York.* He boarded the train for New York. (SB) **4** to land (e.g. a boat) *Aborder un bateau.* To land a boat. (VM) **II** *v.intr.* **1** to come up, approach, come near *Aborde pas icitte.* Don't come near here. (Lv88) **Il aborde pas d'la maison.* He doesn't come near the house. (EV, Ph36) **2** to run into each other, bump into each other, collide *Deux chars vont aborder.* Two cars will collide. (VM) **III s'aborder** *v.pron.* to run into each other, bump into each other, collide *Allons dire on va passer moi et toi, on s'aborde sans vouloir.* Let's say you and I are going by, we collide accidentally. (VM) ◊ **•aborder contre** to run into *Il a abordé contre un arbre.* He ran into a tree. (SL) <SL> **•s'aborder contre** to bump into **Je m'ai abordé contre la porte.* I bumped into the door. (Da84) <Da84> **•border la terre** to land, dock *On a resté six ans sur mer sans pouvoir border la terre.* We were six years at sea without being able to land. (IB, ch: *Six ans sur mer*) <IB> <***Loc:*** AV, EV, IB, JD, LA, LF, SB, SL, SM, TB, VM, Da84, Guoo, Hi02, Lv88, Ph36>

abouer [abuwe] *v.intr.* to get bogged down in mud *Tu peux aller près du fond. Mais tu vas trop près du fond il aboue, il va dans la boue.* You can go close to the bottom. But if you get too close to the bottom it gets caught in the mud. (TB) <***Loc:*** TB>

abouler [abule] *v.tr.* to carry *Il aboule son argent dans un sac.* He carries his money in a bag. (AV) <***Loc:*** AV>

aboutage [abutaʒ] *n.m./f.* addition, annex (to a building) *L'aboutage à cette maison est bien construit.* The addition on this house is well built. (AV) <***Loc:*** AV, SJ, Lv88>

abouter [abute] **I** *v.tr.* **1** to join end to end *Ils ont eu besoin d'abouter les derniers soliveaux pour finir.* They had to join the last beams to finish the job. (LA) **2** to add, add on (a room to a house) *Nous-autres va abouter une 'tite cuisine en arrière de la maison.* We're going to add on a little kitchen in the back of the house. (Lv88) *Il a abouté une cuisine à sa maison.* He added a kitchen onto his house. (SJ) **II** *v.intr.* to be adjacent *Mon clos aboute à la terre de l'église.* My field is adjacent to the church's land. (Lv88) <***Loc:*** AV, LA, SB, SJ, SL, Da84, Lv88>

aboutir [abutir] *v.intr.* **1** to come to a head, burst (e.g. of a boil) *L'abcès va aboutir.* The abscess is at the point of bursting. (Lv88) *Le clou est après aboutir.* The boil is coming to a head. (Lv88) **2** to succeed *Il a abouti à faire ça.* He succeeded in doing that. (LF) **3** to become, end up *Il veut aboutir en gouverneur.* He wants to become governor. (VM) ◊ **•aboutir en bien** to come out well, fare well <Lv88> **•aboutir en mal** to come to a bad end, fare poorly <Da84, Lv88> **•aboutir en rien** to come to nought, fail completely *Tout le travail qu'il a fait, ça a tout abouti en rien.* All the work he did, it all came to nought. (LA) <LA, Da84> <***Loc:*** IB, LA, LF, VM, Da84, Lv88>

aboutissage [abutisaʒ] *n.f.* **1** coming to a head **2** result, outcome, ending <***Loc:*** EV, LA, VM>

aboyer [abwaje] *v.intr.* to howl (of hounds) <***Loc:*** EV, LA, VM>

abréger [abreʒe] *v.tr.* **1** to shorten, make shorter *Elle a abrégé sa jupe entre la maison et le bal.* She shortened her skirt between the house and the dancehall. (LA) **2** to abridge <***Loc:*** LA, Da84>

abreuvoir [abrøvwar] *n.f.* watering trough <***Loc:*** AV, SJ, Lv88>

abreyer ♦see **abrier**

abri [abri] *n.m.* shelter, refuge ◊ **•se mettre à l'abri** to take shelter *Le vent est après s'élever. On devrait peut-être se mettre à l'abri.* The wind is coming up. Maybe we should take shelter. (LA) <LA, VM, Da84> <***Loc:*** EV, LA, Da84>

abricot [abriko] *n.m.* **1** apricot **2** strange or eccentric individual, 'nut', 'odd bird' *Il y a des abricots qui font les mardis-gras.* There are some nuts who dress up like Mardi Gras. (Lv88) <***Loc:*** AV, LA, SB, SJ, Da84, La99, Lv88>

abricotier [abrikotje] *n.m.* 1 apricot tree 2 strange or eccentric individual, 'nut', 'odd bird' <*Loc:* AV, SJ, Da84, Lv88>

abrié (abriée) [abrije] *adj.* dressed warmly against the elements, dressed in layers *Asteur, les enfants sont bien abriés à l'école.* These days, children are warmly dressed for the cold at school. (Lv88) <*Loc:* Lv88>

abrier (abreyer) [abrije, abreje] **I** *v.tr.* 1 to dress warmly, dress with layers *Asteur, les enfants sont bien abriés à l'école.* These days, children are well dressed for the cold at school. (Lv88) 2 to cover with blankets *Abrie bien les enfants. Il va faire froid à soir.* Cover the kids well. It will be cold tonight. (LA) 3 to shelter, cover for protection (esp. a seed or young plant) *Clet' est après abrier les jardinages à cause de l'orage.* Clet' is covering the plants because of the storm. (Lv88)) 4 to shelter, bring into or under a shelter *Tu devrais abreyer ce cheval dans un pareil temps.* You should get this horse under shelter in such weather. (SB) **II s'abrier** *v.pron.* 1 to get dressed (esp. as protection against inclement weather) *Il s'est abrié chaudement à matin pour la pêche.* He dressed warmly this morning for fishing. (Lv88) 2 to cover o.s., cover up *L'hiver j'aime m'abrier avec un tas de couvertes.* In winter I like to cover myself with a pile of blankets. (Guoo) <*Loc:* AV, LA, LF, SB, SJ, SL, TB, VM, Guoo, Lv88>

abrogation [abrogasjɔ̃] *n.f.* 1 abrogation 2 repeal (of a law) <*Loc:* Da84>

abroquer [abroke] *v.tr.* to chip, break a chip off of, nick *Il a abroqué sa hache.* He chipped his axe. (AV) <*Loc:* AV>

absence [apsɑ̃s] *n.f.* absence, lack ◊ **•dans mon absence** in my absence <Da84> <*Loc:* Da84>

absinthe [apsɛ̃t] *n.f.* 1 bitterweed *La vache a pâturé dans les absinthes, c'est pour ça que le lait est haigre.* The cow grazed in the bitterweed, that's why the milk is bitter. (VM) 2 absinthe, wormwood 3 absinthe liqueur 4 anisette <*Loc:* SL, SM, VM, Da84, Lv88>

absolu, -e [apsɔly] *adj.* absolute, complete *La vérité absolue.* The absolute truth. (LA) <*Loc:* LA, Da84>

absolument [apsɔlymɑ̃] *adv.* absolutely, completely, entirely *T'as envie de venir manger à soir? —Absolument.* Do you want to come over to eat tonight? —Absolutely. (LA) <*Loc:* LA, VM, Da84, Fa77>

absolution [apsɔlysjɔ̃] *n.f.* [*eccl.*] absolution, remission, forgiveness (of sin) <*Loc:* Da84, Fa77>

absoudre [apsud(r)] *v.tr.* to absolve, forgive, pardon, exonerate *Je t'absous de tous tes péchés.* I absolve you of all your sins. (LA) <*Loc:* LA, Da84>

abstenir (s') [apstənir] *v.pron.* 1 to abstain, refrain *J'ai promis de m'abstenir de la boisson pour Carême.* I promised to abstain from alcohol for Lent. (LA) 2 to fast (from food or drink) <*Loc:* LA, Da84>

abstinence [apstinɑ̃s] *n.f.* [*eccl.*] 1 abstinence 2 fasting ◊ **•faire abstinence de** to abstain from <Da84> <*Loc:* Da84>

abstinent, -e [apstinɑ̃, -ɑ̃t] *adj.* [*eccl.*] 1 abstaining, abstinent 2 fasting <*Loc:* Da84>

abûmé ♦see **abîmé**

abûmer ♦see **abîmer**

abus [aby] *n.m.* abuse, misuse ◊ **•faire abus de** to indulge freely in, overindulge in *Il fait abus de la boisson.* He overindulges with alcohol. (LA) <LA> **•faire un abus (à qqn)** to impose (on s.o.) *Je vas partir, je veux pas faire un abus.* I'm going to leave, I don't want to overstay my welcome. (Lv88) *Je sais que c'est un grand abus je te fais.* I know it's a big imposition I'm making on you. (VM) <VM, Lv88> <*Loc:* LA, SM, VM, Da84, Lv88>

abuser [abyze] **I** *v.tr.* 1 to abuse, mistreat *Il abusait son cheval.* He abused his horse. (Lv88) 2 to insult *Il a abusé la police.* He insulted the police officer. (Lv88) **II** *v.intr.* to take advantage, impose *Je veux pas rester chez eux; je me sens comme si je suis après abuser dessus eux-autres.* I don't want to stay at their house; I feel like I'm taking advantage of them. (Lv88) *Parce que je suis généreux, tout le monde abuse sur moi.* Because I'm generous, everyone takes advantage of me. (SM) *Ces enfants abusent dessus leur mère. Elle est tout le temps après cuire pour eusse.* Those kids take advantage of their mother. She is always cooking for them. (VM) **III s'abuser** *v.pron.* to masturbate *S'il arrête pas de s'abuser, il va pousser des poils dans les mains.* If he doesn't stop masturbating, he will grow hair in his hands. (VM) <*Loc:* SM, VM, Da84, Lv88>

abuseur, -euse [abyzœr, -øz] *adj.* parasitic, sponging (of a person) *Alle est assez abuseuse.* She's pretty parasitic <*Loc:* VM>

abusif (abusive) [abyzif, abyziv] *adj.* 1 abusive, excessive 2 insulting *Il a usé des gestes abusives.* He used insulting gestures. (Lv88) <*Loc:* VM, Da84, Lv88>

abuter ♦see **buter**

abutter (arbutter) [abyte, ærbyre, ærbyte] *v.tr.* to support, stay, stake, prop up *Il a abutté son figuier.* He staked his fig tree. (Lv88) <*Loc:* SL, TB, Lv88>

acacia (agacia, arcacia) [agasia, akasja, arkasja, arkɑ̃sja] *n.m.* 1 acacia 2 honey locust tree 3 flowering black locust tree <*Loc:* AC, LA, VM, Guoo, Lv88>

académie [akadẽmi] *n.f.* academy <*Loc:* Da84>

acadiac (acajac, à cajac) [akadʒak] *adv.* astride, astraddle *Elle est acajac sur la chaise.* She is astride the chair. (Lv88) *Il était assis acadiac sur la chaise.* He was straddling the chair. (LA) *Monter (un cheval) à cajac.* To straddle (a horse). (SM) <*Loc:* LA, VM, Lv88>

Acadiana [akadjɑ̃na, akadʒjɑ̃na] *n.m.* Acadiana (official designation of the francophone parishes of Louisiana) <*Loc:* LA>

Acadie [akadi] *n.f.* 1 Acadia Parish *Mon vieux grand-père devenait de quèque part dans l'Acadie, à l'entour de Morse, de l'Anse Couche-couche ou de la Pointe Lyons.*

My grandfather came from somewhere in Acadia Parish, around Morse, l'Anse Couche-couche or Point Lyons. (VM) **2** Acadia <***Loc:*** AC, EV, VM, Hi02>

acadien[1], -ienne [akadʒɛ̃, -dʒɛ̃n, -djɛ̃n] *adj.* **1** Acadian, of or pertaining to any of the francophone people of Acadia (modern Nova Scotia) or their modern descendants **2** Louisiana Acadian, Cajun **Le cadeau qui ravit les petits Acadiens: un sac de caniques.* The gift that thrilled the young Acadians: a sack of marbles. (SM) *La Côte des Acadiens.* The Acadian Coast. (Lv88) <***Loc:*** SM, Hi02, Lv88>

acadien[2] [akadʒɛ̃, akadjɛ̃] *n.m.* language of the Acadians, Acadian French <***Loc:*** LA, VM, Lv88>

Acadien[3], -ienne [akadʒɛ̃, -dʒɛ̃n, -djɛ̃n] *n.* Acadian *Et ç'a tout amené les Acadiens ici.* They all brought the Acadians here. (LF) *Chaque hiver les canards et oies refont le voyage de nos ancêtres les Acadiens exilés.* Every winter the ducks and the geese redo the voyage of our exiled Acadian ancestors. (ThCa: *Mille misères*) *Là, t'as l'Acadien qu'a arrivé. Parce que dans le conte qu'ils ont pour le Grand Dérangement, ils l'ont dispersé de la Nouvelle Écosse, il est venu ici.* Then there is the Acadian who arrived. Because in the tale they have about the exile, they dispersed him from Nova Scotia, he came here. (SM) <***Loc:*** LF, SM, Da84, Gr82, Gr86, Hi02, ThCa>

acajac ♦see **acadiac**

acajou (**arcajou**) [arkaʒu] *n.m./f.* **1** mahogany *Cette table est en arcajou.* This table is made of mahogany. (TB) **2** cashew nut <***Loc:*** SB, TB, VM, Da84, Lv88>

accablant, -e [akablɑ̃, -ɑ̃t] *adj.* stuffy, oppressive **La chaleur est accablante.* The heat is oppressive. (Da84) <***Loc:*** Da84>

accablé [akable] *adj.* sunken, dark (of the eyes) <***Loc:*** Fa77>

accabler [akable] *v.tr.* to overcome, overwhelm, oppress (esp. with heat) *Elle était accablée par la chaleur dans sa cuisine.* She was overwhelmed by the heat in her kitchen. (LA) <***Loc:*** LA, Da84>

accalmir [akalmir] **I** *v.tr.* to calm *On va essayer d'accalmir les enfants, mais ils sont beaucoup excités.* We'll try to calm the children, but they are very excited. (LA) **II** *v.intr.* to calm down, fall calm *Le train est après accalmir.* The noise is calming down. (Lv88) **III s'accalmir** *v.pron.* to calm down, fall calm *La mer est après s'accalmir.* The sea is calming down. (JE) <***Loc:*** JE, LA, LF, Lv88>

accaparer [akapare] **I** *v.tr.* to seize, get hold of, take possession of *Il a accaparé le livre de Jean.* He took Jean's book. (LA) **II s'accaparer** *v.pron.* to seize for o.s., take over, take possession *Ma tante s'a accaparé de la terre de son mari.* My aunt took possession of her husband's land. (LA) <***Loc:*** LA, Da84>

accent [aksɑ̃] *n.m.* accent <***Loc:*** LF, Da84>

acceptable [aksɛptab(l), absɛptab(l)] *adj.* acceptable *On était pas acceptable de la société du monde si on était ça qu'on appelle des "petits Cadiens."* We were not acceptable in society if we were what they call "little Cajuns." (TB) ◊ •**pas moindrement acceptable** not in the least acceptable <Da84> <***Loc:*** TB, Da84>

acceptance [aksɛptɑ̃s] *n.f.* acceptance **On est tout cajain [=cadien] par acceptance de la culture, les coutumes et la langue françaises.* We are all Cajun here by acceptance of the French culture, customs and language. (Gr86) <***Loc:*** Gr86>

acceptation [aksɛptasjɔ̃] *n.f.* acceptance <***Loc:*** Da84>

accepter [aksɛpte] *v.tr.* to accept *Et il faulait qu'on parle comme les autres dans Amérique. Dans ce temps-là c'était généralement accepté que ça c'est la manière que ça devrait être.* And we had to talk like everyone else in America. In those days it was generally accepted that that was how it was supposed to be. (TB) **Et ils l'ont accepté.* And they accepted him. (LA, An94) <***Loc:*** AV, LA, SJ, TB, An94, Da84, Hi02>

accès [aksɛ, akse] *n.m.* access, admittance <***Loc:*** Da84>

accident [aksidɑ̃] *n.f.* accident, mishap *J'ai eu un accident dedans mon jardin.* I had an accident in my garden. (EV) ◊ •**par accident** accidentally, by accident *Il a pété par accident au milieu de la grand'messe.* He farted by accident during High Mass. (LA) <LA, Da84> <***Loc:*** AC, AV, EV, LA, SM, VM, Da84, Gu82, Lv88, Wh83>

accointance [akwɛ̃tɑ̃s] *n.f.* **1** acquaintance, familiarity (with people) *L'accointance du monde de l'huile est bien utile.* It is very useful to know people who work in the oil business. (Lv88) **2** acquaintance, person whom one knows *Il a des accointances dans le collège.* He has acquaintances at the university. (Lv88) <***Loc:*** Lv88>

accointer[1] [akwɛ̃te] *v.tr.* **1** to corner, drive into a corner *Je vas lui parler et je vas l'accointer.* I'm going to talk him into a corner. (Lv88) **2** to put (a child) in the corner as punishment *La maîtresse m'avait accointé parce que je parlais français.* The teacher put me in the corner because I was speaking French. (Lv88) <***Loc:*** IB, Lv88>

accointer[2] (s') [akwɛ̃te] *v.pron.* **1** to meet (for the first time) *On s'a accointé au Bayou Lafourche.* We met at Bayou Lafourche. (Lv88) **2** to get acquainted *A s'accointe vite avec le monde.* She gets acquainted with people quickly. (TB) <***Loc:*** TB, Lv88>

accolé, -e [akole] *adj.* living together (without benefit of marriage) *Ils étaient accolés depuis des années.* They were living together for years. (LA) <***Loc:*** LA, LF, La99>

accoler (s') [akole] *v.pron.* to live together (without benefit of marriage) *Elle s'est accolée avec son ami longtemps passé.* She moved in with her boyfriend a long time ago. (Lv88) <***Loc:*** Lv88>

accommodation [akɔ̃modasjɔ̃] *n.f.* accommodation <***Loc:*** Da84>

accommodations [akɔ̃modasjɔ̃] *n.f.pl.* accommodations *Il a* *trouvé de bonnes accommodations à l'hôtel.* He got good accommodations at the hotel. (Lv88) <*Loc:* Lv88>

accommoder (**acmoder**) [akmode, akɔ̃mode] **I** *v.tr.* **1** to accommodate, provide lodging for *Reste avec nous-autres, je peux t'acmoder à soir et on va parler.* Stay with us, I can put you up for the night and we'll talk. (Lv88) **2** to accommodate, oblige *On a pour accommoder le monde d'alentour ici pour essayer de s'adonner.* We have to accommodate the people around here to try to get along. (AS) **3** to clean (fish or fowl) for cooking *Elle est après acmoder les poissons.* She is cleaning the fish. (JE) *Il faut tu connais accommoder le lapin avant le cuire.* You have to know how to clean the rabbit before you cook it. (Lv88) **4** to season, add flavor to (food) *Acmode bien la viande, j'aime ça piqué aux ails.* Season the meat well, I like it stuffed with garlic. (VM) **5** to fix, prepare, dress (food) *Tu peux accommoder la salade si tu veux.* You can prepare the salad, if you like. (Lv88) **II s'accommoder** *v.pron.* to accommodate o.s., adapt o.s. *Il peut pas s'accommoder à la nouvelle heure.* He can't adapt to the time change [to daylight savings time]. (LA) <*Loc:* AS, JE, LA, TB, VM, TB, Da84, Lv88>

accompagner [akɔ̃pɑ̃je] *v.tr.* **1** to accompany, play a musical accompaniment to *Ils avaient eu Gilroy Giselin pour jouer du violon et Sylvain Canavaise l'avait accompagné avec un tambour.* They had Gilroy Giselin to play the fiddle and Sylvain Canavaise accompanied with the drum. (AV) **2** to accompany, go along with as a companion <*Loc:* AV, Da84>

accompagneur [akɔ̃pɑ̃jœr] *n.* companion, one who accompanies or walks with another <*Loc:* AV, IB, SJ>

accomplet [akɔ̃ple] *n.m.* feat, accomplishment **Deux Américains sont posés [...] et ont marché sur la lune [...]. Certainement un grand accomplet.* Two Americans landed and walked on the moon. Certainly a big accomplishment. (Gr86) <*Loc:* Gr86>

accomplir [akɔ̃plir] *v.tr.* **1** to carry out, perform, accomplish **2** to complete, finish *Il a accompli son HOMEWORK.* He completed his homework. (AV) <*Loc:* AC, AV, Da84>

accomplissement [akɔ̃plismɑ̃] *n.m.* accomplishment *Y en a qu'est des gens de grands accomplissements qui travaillent à la tête des banques ou des affaires comme des bonnes positions, des ingénieurs et tout.* There are some who are people of great accomplishments, who work at the head of banks or things like good positions, engineers and all. (TB) <*Loc:* TB, Da84>

acconnaître [akɔ̃nɛt(r)] *v.tr.* ◊ **•faire acconnaître** ***a*** to make known *Le gouverneur a fait acconnaître la loi.* The governor made the law publicly known. (EV) ***b*** to inform, tell *Je lui ai bien fait acconnaître ça j'ai pensé de son frère.* I really let him know what I thought of his brother. (VM) <EV, LF, VM> <*Loc:* EV, LF, VM>

accord [akɔr] *n.m.* accord, agreement ◊ **•être d'accord** to agree *Oui, la place que moi, je voudrais mourir, c'est dans les bras de mon petit bébé, demander pardon pour ça j'ai fait, là je serais d'accord de m'en aller dans Grand Gueydan.* Oh, the place where I'd like to die, is in the arms of my baby. To ask forgiveness for what I've done, then I'd agree to leave and go to Gueydan. (ch: *Reno waltz*) <LA, VM> <*Loc:* VM, Da84>

accordant[1], **-e** [akɔrdɑ̃, -ɑ̃t] *adj.* **1** compatible **Ils sont accordants.* They get along, they are compatible. (Da84) **2** accommodating, amiable, pleasant *Alle, alle est vaillante, mais le vieux est pas accordant.* She's nice, but the old man is not very pleasant. (VM) <*Loc:* VM, Da84, Lv88>

accordant[2] [akɔrdɑ̃] *prep.* **1** according to *Accordant le TELEVISION, il va faire frette à soir.* According to the television, it's going to be cold tonight. (Lv88) **2** in keeping with, in conformity with *Il faut que vous êtes accordant la loi.* You have to be in conformity with the law. (TB) <*Loc:* TB, Da84, Gr86, Lv88>

accordement [akɔrdmɑ̃] *n.m.* **1** betrothal, engagement *L'accordement a été célébré à Lafayette.* The engagement was celebrated in Lafayette. (Lv88) **2** accord, agreement *Il y a pas d'accordement entre eux depuis ça.* There's not been accord between them since then. (VM) **3** act of reconciling <*Loc:* VM, Lv88>

accordéon (**accordion**) [akɔrdeɔ̃, akadeɔ̃, akɔrdjɔ̃, akɔrdejɔ̃] *n.m./f.* accordion (particularly the diatonic accordion used in Louisiana) ◊ **•accordéon français** diatonic accordion <Lv88> <*Loc:* AC, AV, EV, JE, SL, SM, Da84, Hi02, Lv88>

accorder [akɔrde] **I** *v.tr.* **1** to grant, give, concede *Il lui a accordé les droits d'huile pour le morceau derrière le magasin.* He granted him the oil rights for the land behind the barn. (LA) **2** to reconcile *Ils vont jamais accorder les Meche et les Melançon.* They will never reconcile the Meches and the Melançons. (LA) **3** to match, match up (e.g. clothing) *Accorder du linge.* To match clothing. (LA) **4** to tune (a guitar) *C'est malheureux comment les oreilles ça se gâte, sus les petites machines comme ça-là icitte pour accorder la guitare.* It's terrible how your ears get spoiled when you use little machines like this to tune the guitar. (TB) **II s'accorder** *v.pron.* **1** to agree with one another **2** to get along with each other *Il est bien vaillant et on s'accorde bien.* He's quite nice and we get along well. (Lv88) *Et le monde s'accordait presque aussi bien ou mieux qu'asteur.* And people got along almost as well or better than now. (TB) **3** to correspond, match *Hé, ta chemise s'accorde pas du tout avec tes culottes.* Hey, your shirt doesn't match your pants at all. (LA) <*Loc:* EV, IB, LA, LF, SL, SM, TB, An94, Da84, Gr86, Hi02, Lv88>

accordion ♦see **accordéon**

accordioniste [akɔrdjɔ̃nis(t)] *n.* accordion player <*Loc:* Hi02>

accoster [akɔste] *v.intr.* to draw alongside shore (of a boat) *Higgin d'en ville, a fait ces bateaux-là qu'a accosté, le monde débarquait à la terre dedans.* Higgins of New Orleans made those boats which came up along shore, the people landed. (LF) <*Loc:* LF, Da84>

accotement [akɔtmɑ̃] *n.f.* support <*Loc:* Di32, Lv88>

accouchage [akuʃaʒ] *n.m./f.* childbirth, delivery (of a newborn) <*Loc:* IB, SJ, Lv88>

accouchée [akuʃe] *n.f.* woman confined for childbirth <*Loc:* Da84>

accouchement [akuʃmɑ̃] *n.m./f.* childbirth, delivery (of a newborn) ◊ **•fausse accouchement** miscarriage <Da84> <*Loc:* Da84>

accoucher [akuʃe] **I** *v.tr.* to give birth to, deliver *Quand j'ai accouché mon premier enfant, j'ai crié à tout les saints.* When I delivered my first-born, I shouted out to all the saints. (LA) **II** *v.intr.* to give birth *Une femme accouche.* A woman gives birth. (SJ) <*Loc:* LA, SJ, Da84>

accoucheuse [akuʃøz] *n.f.* midwife <*Loc:* EV, Da84>

accoupler [akuple] **I** *v.tr.* **1** to couple, join in pairs **2** to mate *Accoupler une jument et un bourriquet pour faire un mulet américan.* To mate a mare and a jackass to produce an American mule. (VM) **3** to yoke *Accoupler deux mulets pour faire l'ouvrage plus vite.* To yoke two mules to do the work faster. (LA) **II s'accoupler** *v.pron.* **1** to pair up, couple, become a couple *Ils se sont accouplés il y a deux ans.* They got together [i.e. became a couple] two years ago. (Lv88) **2** to copulate, mate *Les chiens s'ont accouplé droit là dans la cour devant Mame et tous les enfants.* The dogs mated right there in the yard in front of Mama and the all the kids. (LA) **3** to live together (without benefit of marriage) *Ça s'a accouplé pour un an avant de se marier.* They lived together for a year before marrying. (LA) <*Loc:* LA, LF, VM, Da84, La99, Lv88>

accourcir [akursir] **I** *v.tr.* to shorten, make shorter *J'ai accourci le pantalon aujourd'hui.* I shortened the pants today. (LA) **II s'accourcir** *v.pron.* to become shorter, shrink *J'ai lavé les pantalons et ça s'a accourci.* I washed the pants and they shrank. (LA) <*Loc:* LA, Da84, Lv88>

accoutré, -e [akutre] *adj.* ◊ **•mal accoutré** crudely or absurdly dressed *J'aurais honte d'aller au village mal accoutré comme ça.* I'd be embarrassed to go to town tackily dressed like that. (VM) <VM> <*Loc:* VM, Da84>

accoutumance [akutymɑ̃s] *n.f.* habit, custom, usage <*Loc:* Da84>

accoutumer [akutyme] **I** *v.tr.* to accustom, cause to get used to *Il fallait que j'accoutume mon cheval à traverser les ponts en bois.* I had to accustom my horse to crossing wooden bridges. (LA) **II s'accoutumer** *v.pron.* to become accustomed to, get used to *J'accoutume pas de me lever tard depuis que j'ai* RETIRE. I haven't gotten used to getting up late since I retired. (LA) <*Loc:* LA, Da84>

accouvage ♦see **couvage**

accouver ♦see **couver**

accroc[1] **(écroc)** [akro, ekro, akrɔk] *n.m.* **1** tusk (of an elephant, a wild boar, etc.) **2** tear, rip *Là, tu l'as fait un vilain accroc dans ton capot.* There you made a nasty tear in your overcoat. (TB) <*Loc:* TB, VM>

accroc[2] [akro] *n.m.* **1** simpleton **2** smart aleck <*Loc:* AV>

accroc[3] [akro] *n.* ◊ **•coup d'accroc** stroke of luck *Il a frappé la balle; c'était un coup d'accroc.* He hit the ball; it was a stroke of luck. (LF) <LF> <*Loc:* LF>

accrochage [akroʃaʒ] *n.m.* **1** hooking, catching, hanging **2** skirmish, altercation <*Loc:* Da84>

accroche [akrɔʃ] *n.m.* hook *Pends-lé sur l'accroche en arrière la porte.* Hang it on the hook behind the door. (VM) <*Loc:* VM>

accroche-cœur [akrɔʃkœr] *n.m.* **1** trim, gingerbreading (on a house) *Des accroche-cœurs sur une maison.* Trim on a house. (SJ) **2** any fancy decoration that can be hung on the wall *J'avais un accroche-cœur fait d'un panier qui pendait sur un clou.* I had a fancy decoration made from a basket hanging on a nail. (IB) **3** impediment, obstacle, hindrance *Avoir des accroche-cœurs dans son chemin.* To have obstacles in one's path. (SJ) <*Loc:* AV, IB, SJ>

accrocher [akroʃe] **I** *v.tr.* **1** to hang, hang up (on a hook) *J'avais acheté du manger pour mes chats [...] Et pour pas que les chats le gaspillent sur la terre, je l'avais accroché où les chats pouvaient pas monter.* I had bought cat food. And so that the cats wouldn't waste it on the ground, I had hung it where the cats couldn't climb up. (TB) **2** to hitch, hitch up (a mule, etc.) *Ils prenaient une corde, tu l'amarrais sur le bateau, et là tu halais le bateau. Tu pouvais prendre un mulet ou un cheval et l'accrocher et là haler le bateau doucement.* They took a rope, you tied it onto the boat, and then you hauled the boat. You could get a mule or a horse and hitch it up and pull the boat slowly. (LF) **3** to latch, hook, fasten with a hook *Accroche bien la porte et quitte-les pas entrer.* Latch the door firmly and don't let them in. (VM) **II** *v.intr.* to hook, attach (to) *Une cigale de nuit [...] ça sort et ça accroche sur le bois et là eusse sort de l'écale, comme une crabe ou une chevrette.* A seven-year locust, it comes out and it hooks onto a tree and then they come out of their shell, like a crab or a shrimp. (LF) **III s'accrocher** *v.pron.* **1** to get hooked, get caught (on s.t.) *Et quelque manière il s'a accroché une de ces vignes-là qui poussent sur la plaille. Le vieux s'a accroché, ç'a commencé à tomber et il a fait ça.* And somehow he caught one of those vines that grow on the beach. The old guy got caught, he started to fall and he went like that. (LF) **2** to tangle with s.o. or each other *Ils s'ont accroché après le bal.* They tangled after the dance. (LA) **3** to steal, snatch for o.s. *S'accrocher un souvenir.* To steal a souvenir. (SJ) ◊ **•accroché après** attached to, hooked to *Le palonnier est accroché après la charrue.* The swing bar is attached to the plow. (LA) <LA> <***Loc:*** AC, AV, EV, IB, LA, LF, SB, SJ, SL, SM, VM, Da84>

accrochi, -e [akroʃi] *adj.* hooked *Quand le sabot dépasse en haut, il est accrochi.* When the hoof grows over, it is hooked. (VM) <***Loc:*** VM>

accrochoire [akroʃwar] *n.f.* hook, peg, nail (on which s.t. can be hung) *Ce clou fait une bonne accrochoire.* This nail makes a good place to hang things. (IB) <***Loc:*** AV, IB, SJ>

accroire [akrwar] *v.intr.* ◊ **•faire accroire** ***a*** to convince, make (s.o.) believe *C'est mieux pour toi d'être naturel plutôt que faire accroire tu peux faire quelque chose.* It's better for you to act naturally than to convince people that you can do anything. (Lv88) *Il va te faire accroire toute qualité de choses.* He'll make you believe all sorts of things. (Lv88) ***b*** to pretend, make believe, play at *On va faire accroire que c'est ta catin.* We'll pretend it's your doll. (LA) *Il fait accroire qu'il est riche, mais lui il est pas riche.* He pretends he is rich, but he isn't rich. (LA) *J'embrasse mon oreiller des fois, ça fait z'accoire que ça serait toi.* I kiss my pillow sometimes and make believe it's you. (Lv88) <LA, SL, An94, Lv88> <***Loc:*** LA, SL, An94, Da84, Gr86, Lv88>

accroires [akrwar] *n.m.pl.* lies, unfulfilled promises *Ne fais pas des accroires, tu peux parler comme nous-autres.* Don't tell lies, you can talk like us. (Lv88) *Oh! 'tite fille, mais rappelle-toi, bébé les accroires, chère, toi tu m'as faits.* Oh girl, remember the lies you told me, baby. (Lv88) <***Loc:*** Gr86, Lv88>

accroupi, -e [akrupi] *adj.* squatting, crouched, crouching *Ils étiont accroupis devant le feu.* They were crouched in front of the fire. (EV) <***Loc:*** EV, LA, Da84>

accroupiller (s') [akrupije] *v.pron.* to squat, crouch *Il va s'accroupiller sur la terre.* He is going to squat on the ground. (JE) <***Loc:*** JE, LF, Lv88>

accroupir (s') [akrupir] *v.pron.* to squat, crouch *Il s'est accroupi pour travailler dans le jardin.* He squatted down to work in the garden. (LA) <***Loc:*** LA, Da84, Fa77>

acculer ♦see **aculer**

acculoire (aculoir, aquiloire) [akilwar, akulwar, akylwar] *n.m./f.* breeching (part of a harness) <***Loc:*** AV, EV, IB, SB, SL, SM, TB, Lv88, Ph36>

accusation [akyzasjɔ̃] *n.f.* accusation, charge <***Loc:*** Da84>

accusé, -e [akyze] *n.* accused, defendant <***Loc:*** Da84>

accuser [akyze] **I** *v.tr.* to accuse, charge, blame *Il a accusé le voisin d'avoir volé son cochon.* He accused the neighbor of stealing his pig. (LA) **II s'accuser** *v.pron.* [*eccl.*] to accuse o.s., confess, own up to, admit guilt *Père, je m'accuse d'avoir juré.* Father, I confess to having cursed. (LA) <***Loc:*** LA, Da84>

accuseur, -euse [akyzœr, -øz] *n.* accuser <***Loc:*** LA, SM, Lv88>

acertainer [asærtɛ̃ne] *v.tr.* **1** to assure, declare, certify *J'ai acertainé que j'ai pas cassé la porte.* I declared that I didn't break the door. (Lv88) **2** to verify, assess *Le député va venir pour acertainer le dommage.* The deputy is going to come to assess the damage. (Lv88) <***Loc:*** SL, Di32, Lv88>

achalage (enchalage) [ɑ̃ʃalaʒ] *n.m.* surplus clothing that causes the wearer to feel too warm <***Loc:*** AV>

achalant, -e [aʃalɑ̃, -ɑ̃t] *adj.* **1** stiflingly hot, uncomfortably warm *Le temps devient achalant.* The weather is getting stiflingly hot. (Lv88) **2** annoying, irritating *Ce bougre est achalant.* This guy is annoying. (Lv88) <***Loc:*** Da84, Lv88>

achalé, -e (enchalé, -e) [aʃale, ɑ̃ʃale] *adj.* **1** excessively warm or hot, suffering from the heat, overheated *Le petit était achalé à force de jouer fort.* The child was overheated from playing so hard. (EV) **2** overwhelmed, heavily oppressed (by fate, by troubles, etc.) **3** annoyed, irritated, angry *Je suis assez achalé.* I'm pretty angry. (VM) <***Loc:*** AV, EV, IB, SL, SM, VM, Gr86, Lv88, Ph36>

achaler (enchaler) [aʃale, ɑ̃ʃale] *v.tr.* **1** to make uncomfortably warm or hot, overheat *Le soleil l'a achalé.* The sun on him was oppressive. (Lv88) *Cette ouvrage m'achale.* This work is making me overheated. (Lv88) *Enchaler un enfant.* To put too much clothing on a child. (SJ) **2** to annoy, irritate, anger *Va-t'en là-bas, tu m'achales.* Go over there, you are annoying me. (VM) *Sors de là, tu m'achales.* Move, you make me uncomfortable. (VM) *Elle m'achale, elle est tout le temps après babiller.* She gets on my nerves, she's always grumbling. (Lv88) **3** to bore, weary, tire <***Loc:*** AV, EV, SJ, TB, VM, Da84, Lv88, Ph36>

achat [aʃa] *n.m.* **1** purchase **2** purchasing, buying ◊ **•achat à crédit** purchase on credit <Da84> <***Loc:*** Da84>

ache [aʃ] *interj.* exclamation used to indicate disgust or irritation <***Loc:*** SM, Lv88>

achécher ♦see **chesser**

acheter (ageter) [aʃte, aʒte] **I** *v.tr.* **1** to buy, purchase *Il avait de la viande qu'était tout arrangée, et il vendait ça, le monde achetait ça là par petits paquets.* He had meat that was all prepared, and he sold it, people bought it in small packages. (TB) *C'est beaucoup plus aisé asteur, aller au magasin, t'achètes ça tout fait déjà.* It's much easier now, just go to the store, and you buy it ready-made. (AV) **2** to bribe *Acheter un politicien.* To buy a politician's favors. (LA) *Il a acheté des voix.* He bought votes through bribery. (LA) **II s'acheter** *v.pron.* to buy for o.s. *Je m'ai acheté un char.* I bought myself a car. (AC) *Il travaillait pour lui-même. Il s'est acheté une petite place là.* He worked for himself. He bought himself a little place, there. (EV) ◊ **•acheter à crédit** to buy on credit *Il achète tout à credit.* He buys everything on credit. (LA) <LA, Da84> **•acheter à la tchiquette** to buy very little (of s.t.) at a time <LA, SM, Lv88> **•acheter à l'œil** ***a*** to buy on a whim, buy hastily and without thorough examination *Acheter une bête à l'œil.* To buy a cow on a whim. (Lv88) <Lv88> **•acheter au CASH** to pay cash *J'achète pas à credit,* *tout ça j'achète au* CASH. I don't buy with credit, all of that I pay in cash. (VM) <VM> **•acheter au poids** to buy by weight <Da84> **•acheter avec** to buy from, patronize *Mon mari achetait ça avec son vieux oncle.* My husband used to buy that from his old uncle. (SL) *J'agète pus avec lui. Il est trop chérant.* I don't buy from him anymore, he's too expensive. (SM) <EV, SL, SM, VM> **•acheter en détail** to buy retail <Da84> **•acheter en gros** to buy wholesale <Da84> **•s'acheter un beau parterre** to take a bad fall *Je m'ai acheté un beau parterre quand j'ai tombé dans ma cour. T'aurais dû me voir tomber sur mon gros derrière.* I took a bad fall when I fell in my yard. You should have seen me fall on my big behind! (Guoo) <Guoo> <***Loc:*** AC, AV, EV, IB, JE, LA, LF, SL, SM, TB, VM, An94, Da84, Guoo, Gu82, Lv88, Wh83>

acheteur, -euse [aʃtœr, -øz] *n.m.* buyer, purchaser *Son père était un acheteur de riz.* His father was a rice buyer. (VM) *Acheteur de bêtes.* Cattle buyer. (VM) <***Loc:*** TB, VM, Da84>

achevaler [aʃ(ə)vale] *v.tr.* to straddle (a horse) *Il arrive achevalé.* He arrives on horseback. (AV) <***Loc:*** AV, Da84>

achever [aʃ(ə)ve] **I** *v.tr.* **1** to accomplish, complete, conclude, finish (a job, a task, etc.) **2** to finish off, do in, kill *Achever un canard.* To finish off a duck. (VM) **II** *v.intr.* to finish up *Le monde prendait à couper. Et le soir quand ils achèvent,* WELL *mon père comptait les compas.* The people began to cut [the sugarcane]. And in the evening when they finished, well, my father counted the "compas." (AS) <***Loc:*** AS, VM, Da84>

acide[1] [asid] *adj.* acid, acidic *Les tomates sont trop acides pour mon estomac.* Tomatos are too acidic for my stomach. (LA) <***Loc:*** LA, Da84>

acide[2] [asid] *n.m.* acid ◊ **•acide carbolique** carbolic acid <Da84> **•acide de batterie** battery acid <LA> **•acide de citron** citric acid *Là j'ai mis d'autres "*VITAMINS*" et d'autres "*MINERALS*" et aussi j'ai mis de l'acide de citron pour aider à l'estomac et j'ai mis de l'alcool aussi.* Then I added other vitamins and minerals and I also added citric acid for the stomach, and I put in some alcohol too. (ThCa: *Messieurs, mesdames*) <ThCa> <***Loc:*** IB, LA, TB, Da84, Fa77, ThCa>

acidité [asidite] *n.f.* acidity <***Loc:*** Da84>

acier [asje] *n.m.* **1** steel **2** tool steel <***Loc:*** LF, Da84, Fa77>

acler ♦see **encler**

açmine ♦see **assimine**

açminier ♦see **assiminier**

acmoder ♦see **accommoder**

acœurant, -e (**écœurant, -e**) [akørɑ̃, -ɑ̃t, ekørɑ̃, -ɑ̃t] *adj.* excessively rich or sweet (of food) *Alle avait fait une poutine avec du* SWEETENED CONDENSED MILK, *et c'était écœurant.* She had made a pudding with sweetened condensed milk, and it was sickeningly sweet. (LA) <***Loc:*** LA, Da84>

acœurer (**écœurer, encœurer, rancœurer**) [akøre, ekøre, ɑ̃køre, ɑ̃tʃøre, rɑ̃køre, rɑ̃tʃøre] *v.tr.* to nauseate, disgust, sicken *J'ai mangé trop de gâteau et ça m'a écœuré.* I ate too much cake and it made me sick. (LA) *C'était trop doux, ça m'a encœuré.* It was too sweet, it disgusted me. (Lv88) <***Loc:*** LA, VM, Da84, Lv88>

acolyte [akolit] *n.m.* altar boy, acolyte <***Loc:*** VM, Da84>

acompte [akɔ̃t] *n.m./f.* **1** installment, partial payment **2** bank account *Y'a proche plus d'argent dans mon acompte.* There is almost no more money in my account. (Lv88) **3** charge account (at a store) *Avoir un acompte à un magasin.* To have a charge account at a store. (SJ) *Mets ça sur mon acompte.* Charge this to my account. (AV) **4** discount *On lui a donné une bonne acompte sur le capot.* They gave him a good discount on the coat. (Lv88) <***Loc:*** AV, LA, SB, SJ, Da84, Lv88>

aconseiller ♦see **conseiller**

aconter ♦see **raconter**

acquittance [akitɑ̃s] *n.f.* acquittal, discharge, payment (of a debt) <***Loc:*** Da84>

acquittement [akitmɑ̃] *n.m.* acquittal, discharge, payment (of a debt) <***Loc:*** Da84>

acquitter [akite] **I** *v.tr.* to pay off (a debt) *J'ai acquitté l'hypothèque sus ma maison. Asteur c'est pour moi et le Bon Dieu.* I paid off the mortgage on my house. Now it's for me and the Good Lord. (LA) **II s'acquitter** *v.pron.* to acquit o.s., pay off *Il s'a acquitté de ses dettes.* He paid off his debts. (VM) <***Loc:*** LA, VM, Da84>

acre (**z-acre**) [ak(r), ark, zak(r)] *n.m./f.* acre <***Loc:*** AC, EV, SM, TB, VM, Da84, Fa77, Gr86, Lv88>

âcre ♦see **hâcre**

ACT (**acter**) [ak(t), æk(t), akte] *v.intr.* to act, peform in a theatrical role *Elle a acté dans le festival l'an passé.* She acted at the festival last year. (Lv88) *Moi j'ai* ACT *dans deux* MOVIE *que Glen a fait.* I acted in two movies that Glen made. (LF) <***Loc:*** EV, JE, LF, Di32, Lv88, Ph36>

acte [ak, akt, ækt] *n.m.* action, act, deed ◊ **•acte de charité** charitable deed, act of charity <Da84> **•acte de contrition** act of contrition <TB> <***Loc:*** EV, TB, Da84, Fa77, Lv88>

acter ♦see **ACT**

acteur, -euse [aktœr, -øz] *n.* **1** *(m.)* actor **2** *(f.)* actress <***Loc:*** AV, IB, SB, SJ, Da84, Lv88>

actif (**active**) [aktif, aktiv] *adj.* active, busy *Alle a tellement de l'énergie et alle est tellement actif.* She has so much energy and she is so active. (LF) <***Loc:*** AV, LF, Da84>

action [aksjɔ̃] *n.f.* action, activity <***Loc:*** Da84>

actionner [aksjɔ̃ne] *v.tr.* to jiggle *Actionner la serrure de la porte.* To jiggle the door lock. (VM) <***Loc:*** VM>

activité [aktivite] *n.f.* activity <***Loc:*** Da84>

actrice [aktris] *n.f.* actress <***Loc:*** Da84>

aculer (**acculer**) [akyle] *v.tr.* to tread down, wear down the heel of *J'ai aculé mes souliers.* I have worn down the heels of my shoes. (JE) <***Loc:*** JE, LF>

aculoire ♦see **acculoire**

adaptable [adaptab(l)] *adj.* adaptable, adjustable *C'est du monde adaptable. Ils sont pas difficiles du tout.* They are adaptable people. They are not picky at all. (LA) <***Loc:*** LA, Da84>

adapter [adapte] **I** *v.tr.* to adapt, adjust, fit *Il a eu pour adapter le morceau pour pouvoir le tourner dans la place entre la machine et le mur.* He had to adapt the piece to be able to turn it in the space between the motor and the wall. (LA) **II s'adapter** *v.pron.* to adapt o.s. to, conform, fit *Il va s'adapter ou il faudra qu'il s'en va.* He is going to conform, or he will have to leave. (LA) <***Loc:*** LA, Da84>

addicter (s') [adikte] *v.pron.* to get addicted to, get hooked on *Et hier on a été ramener les bébés. On était juste après s'addicter avec les enfants.* And yesterday we went to take the babies back. We were just getting hooked on the kids. (LF) <***Loc:*** LF>

addition [adisjɔ̃] *n.f.* **1** addition, adding **2** addition, annex (to a building) <***Loc:*** EV, Da84, Lv88>

additionner [adisjɔ̃ne] *v.tr.* **1** to add, put in *Il additionnait tout le temps quelque chose après "Bouki et Lapin"; ça fait, il faisait le conte tout le temps un peu plus long.* He always added something to "Bouki and Lapin" stories; so, he made the story a little longer every time. (Lv88) **2** to add, add on (a room to a house) *Quand j'avais 12 ans, mon père a additionné une chambre à bains sur notre maison.* When I was twelve years old, my father added a bathroom to our house. (VM) **3** to add, add up, calculate (a sum) *Additionne mon compte pour voir combien je te dois.* Calculate my account to see how much I owe you. (VM) <***Loc:*** VM, Da84, Lv88>

adieu [adʒø, adjø] *interj.* good-bye, farewell <***Loc:*** LA, Da84>

admettable [admetab] *adj.* admittable, admissible *C'était un menteur connu, ça fait le juge a déclaré que son témoignage était pas admettable.* He was a known liar, so the judge declared that his testimony was not admissible. (LA) <***Loc:*** EV, LA, SM, VM, Lv88, Ph36>

admettre [admet(r)] *v.tr.* **1** to admit, concede, own up to, acknowledge *Il peut pas admettre qu'il est* WRONG. He can't admit that he is wrong. (LA) **2** to let in, admit, allow to enter *Ils voulaient pas l'admettre dans la salle après le tour qu'il avait fait la semaine d'avant.* They didn't want to admit him into the dance hall after the trouble he had caused the week before. (VM) <***Loc:*** LA, VM, Da84, Wh83>

administration [administrasjɔ̃] *n.f.* **1** administration, management **2** act of administering <***Loc:*** Da84, Fa77>

admirable[1] [admirab(l)] *adj.* admirable, marvelous, wonderful *Ils avaient une relation admirable.* They had an admirable relationship. (LA) <***Loc:*** LA, Da84, Fa77>

admirable[2] [admirab(l)] *n.f.* verbena <***Loc:*** VM>

admirer [admire] **I** *v.tr.* to admire **Tout quelqu'un l'admirait. Eux espéraient il arrive toute différente place, des soirées de familles ou dans des magasins, tout quelque chose.* Everyone admired him. They waited for him to arrive in various places, at evening family gatherings, in stores, everything. (LA, An94) **II s'admirer** *v.pron.* to admire o.s. or each other *Ils étaient plantés là après s'admirer quand le bus a parti.* They were standing there admiring each other when the bus left. (LA) <***Loc:*** LA, An94, Da84>

admissible [admisib(l)] *adj.* admissible <***Loc:*** Da84>

admission [admisjɔ̃] *n.f.* **1** admission of guilt *L'admission est pas facile.* Admitting guilt is not easy. (Lv88) **2** admission (into a house, party, etc.) **3** admission fee *L'admission est cinq piasses.* Admission is five dollars. (Lv88) <***Loc:*** Da84, Lv88>

adonnance [adɔ̃nɑ̃s] *n.f.* **1** chance, coincidence *C'est une adonnance de les avoir trouvés là.* It's a coincidence to have found them there. (AV) *Des chevreuils c'était une adonnance, parce que y avait assez de monde qui les avait chassés il y a plus un tas qui restait là.* Deer were a real coincidence, because there were so many people who had hunted them, there weren't very many left anymore. (TB) **2** agreement *On vit en bonne adonnance.* We live in good agreement. (Lv88) ◊ **•par adonnance** by chance, by coincidence *C'est par adonnance j'ai trouvé mon mari.* It was by chance that I found [i.e. met] my husband. (Lv88) <EV, VM, Da84, Lv88, Ph36> <***Loc:*** AV, IB, EV, JE, LA, LF, SB, SL, SM, TB, VM, Da84, Gr86, Lv88, Ph36>

adonner [adɔ̃ne] **I** *v.intr. (in impersonal expr.)* to happen, happen by chance *Il m'a adonné à faire ça.* It happened that I was doing that. (VM) **II s'adonner** *v.pron.* **1** to fit together *Les morceaux s'adonnent.* The pieces fit together. (LA) **2** to match, go with, correspond *Le capot s'adonne pas avec ta chemise.* The jacket doesn't go with your shirt. (Lv88) **3** to get along with each other *On s'adonne comme deux frères.* We get along like two brothers. (Lv88) *On a pour accommoder le monde d'alentour ici pour essayer de s'adonner.* We have to accommodate the people around here to try to get along. (AS) **4** to get used to *Il va s'adonner.* He will get used to it. (Lv88) **5** to happen, happen by chance *Je m'ai adonné à le rejoindre au village.* I happened to meet him in town. (VM) *Je m'adonne à pas avoir d'argent ici.* It happens that I don't have any money here. (IB) **6** *(in impersonal expr.)* to happen, happen by chance, just so happen *Là, un soir, ça s'adonnait qu'on avait une petite soirée et Louella m'a demandé pour* *que je chante "Grand Texas."* Then, one evening, it just so happened that we had a little gathering and Louella asked me to sing "Grand Texas." (VM, An84) *On parlait de Marie et il s'a adonné qu'elle était après entrer.* We were talking about Mary and it so happened that she was coming in. (IB) *Ça s'est adonné qu'ils sont venus au même temps.* It happened that they came at the same time. (AV) ◊ **•s'adonner bien** ***a*** to come at an opportune time, come at just the right time *Tu t'adonnes bien pour manger.* You've come just in time to eat. (LF) ***b*** *(in impersonal expr.)* to be convenient, timely, proper *Ça va s'adonner bien qu'il vient à soir.* It will be good timing for him to come tonight. (LA) <LA, LF> **•s'adonner comme chien et chat** to not get along, quarrel habitually <La99> **•s'adonner mal** *(in impersonal expr.)* to happen at a bad time, be inconvenient *Tu viens le voir? Ça s'adonne mal, il est pas là.* You've come to see him? It turns out that, unfortunately, he's not here. (Lv88) <Lv88> <***Loc:*** AS, AV, EV, IB, JE, LA, LF, SL, SM, TB, VM, An84, Da84, Gr86, La99, Lv88, Ph36>

adopter [adopte] **I** *v.tr.* **1** to adopt (a child) *Alle a pas eu d'enfants pour elle-même. Alle en a adopté une.* She hasn't had any children of her own. She adopted one. (TB) **2** to adopt, take as one's own (e.g. customs) *D'autre monde étranger a venu dans la Louisiane aussi, mais à mesure que ça venait, ça adoptait la culture et la langue des Acadiens.* Other foreigners came into Louisiana also, but as they came, they adopted the culture and the language of the Acadians. (VM) **3** to pass (a resolution, a law, etc.) *Ils ont adopté la loi contre les fumeurs.* They passed the law against the smokers. (LA) **II s'adopter** *v.pron.* to live together (without benefit of marriage) *Asteur, il y a un tas de jeunes qui s'adoptent.* These days a lot of young people live together without getting married. (Lv88) <***Loc:*** AV, IB, LA, TB, VM, Da84, La99, Lv88, Wh83>

adoption [adɔpsjɔ̃] *n.f.* adoption <***Loc:*** Da84>

adorable [adɔrab(l)] *adj.* adorable *Cet enfant était adorable quand il était plus jeune.* That child was adorable when he was younger. (VM) <***Loc:*** LA, VM, Da84>

adorateur [adoratœr] *n.m.* adorer, worshipper <***Loc:*** Da84>

adoration [adorasjɔ̃] *n.f.* adoration, worship <***Loc:*** Da84>

adorer [adore] *v.tr.* to adore, worship *Parce que on dirait c'était le plus joli et c'est celui là j'adorais le plus.* Because it seemed he was the best looking one and he was the one I adored the most. (EV) <***Loc:*** EV, Da84, Fa77>

adorner [adɔrne] *v.tr.* to adorn <***Loc:*** Fa77>

adoucir [adusir, ɑ̃dusir] **I** *v.tr.* **1** to sweeten *Passe-moi 'oir le sucrier que je peuve adoucir mon café.* Pass me the sugar bowl so I can sweeten my coffee. (VM) **2** to tame, gentle, domesticate *Il est après adoucir le cheval farouche.* He is taming the wild horse. (VM) **3** to coax, flatter, seduce *Adoucir une fille.* To seduce a girl. (Gr86) **4** to slow down, moderate *Adoucir la marche.* Walk more slowly. (Lv88) **II s'adoucir** *v.pron.* **1** to become sweet *Si tu ramasses des figues trop de bonheur, ça va mûrir, mais ça va pas s'adoucir.* If you pick figs too early, they will ripen, but they will not get sweet. (VM) **2** to become tame, become gentle *Les chats s'adoucissent vite.* Cats become tame quickly. (Lv88) <***Loc:*** AC, AV, EV, IB, JE, LA, LF, SB, SM, TB, VM, Da84, Gr86, Lv88>

adoucissage [adusisaʒ] *n.m.* **1** sweetening **2** taming, gentling, domesticating <***Loc:*** Da84>

adoucissant, -e [adusisɑ̃, -ɑ̃t] *adj.* **1** sweetening **2** taming **3** soothing *Une voix adoucissante.* A soothing voice. (EV) <***Loc:*** EV, Da84>

adoucissement [adusismɑ̃] *n.m.* **1** sweetening **2** taming, gentling, domesticating <***Loc:*** Da84>

adresse[1] [adrɛs, adres] *n.f.* skill, dexterity, cleverness *Je me moque de ces juges et tous ces bonnets carrés. Fille par son adresse, son amant-z-est sauvé.* I don't care about these judges and all of these square hats. The girl by her cleverness has saved her lover. (PQ, ch: *Quand la belle entendit dire*) <***Loc:*** EV, PQ, Da84, Lv88>

adresse[2] [adrɛs, adres] *n.f.* address *Et là quand vous va partir, si vous veut* KEEP IN TOUCH *avec nous-autres, vous prend l'adresse et écrire des postillons.* And then when you leave, if you want to keep in touch with us, take the address and write letters. (LF) *Il a été à la mauvaise adresse.* He went to the wrong address. (EV) <***Loc:*** EV, LF, SL, TB, Da84>

adresse[3] [adrɛs, adres] *n.m./f.* speech, address, talk *Le maire a fait une adresse au monde présent.* The mayor gave a speech to the people who were there. (EV) <***Loc:*** EV, IB, SB, SM, VM, Da84>

adresser[1] [adrese] *v.tr.* to address (a letter) *Elle a adressé la lettre à son garçon qu'était dans l'armée.* She addressed the letter to her son who was in the army. (LA) <***Loc:*** AV, LA, Da84>

adresser[2] [adrese] **I** *v.tr.* **1** to address, speak to *Pour quelque raison on adressait les animaux en anglais.* For some reason we addressed animals in English. (LF) **2** to make an address or speech to *Je viens adresser vous-autres pour vous expliquer les choses qui se passont dedans le gouvernement.* I've come to give a speech to explain the things that are going on in the government to you. (VM) *Il a adressé les gradués.* He addressed the graduates. (SM) **II s'adresser** *v.pron.* **1** to address, speak to *Je m'adresse pas à toi.* I'm not talking to you. (VM) **2** to be of concern to *Ça qui arrive dans cette maison, ça s'adresse pas à toi!* What happens in this house is not your concern. (VM) ◊ **•adresser la parole à qqn** to address, speak to s.o. *Il a sorti par la porte de devant sans jamais adresser la parole aux hommes qui le guettaient dessus la galerie.* He went out through the front door without saying a word to the men who were watching him on the porch. (AC) <AC, Da84> <***Loc:*** AC, LF, SB, SM, TB, VM, Da84, Lv88>

adrigaillé, -e [adrigaje] *adj.* dressed in poor taste, dressed tackily *Mais garde donc comment il est adrigaillé!* Just look at his getup! (VM) <***Loc:*** VM>

adrigailler (s') [adrigaje] *v.pron.* to dress o.s. in poor taste, dress tackily *Il s'habillait pas avec du linge qui était raisonnable… une chemise abîmée qu'avait un morceau déchiré. Il est après s'adrigailler.* He didn't dress in reasonable clothes . . . a soiled shirt that had a piece torn out. He is dressing tackily. (VM) <***Loc:*** VM>

adroit (**adroite**) [adrwa, adrwɔit, adrwɛt, adrwat] *adj.* **1** skillful, clever *C'est un homme bien adroit.* He's a clever man. (SM) **2** handy, capable (with tools) *Moi j'étais adroite là-dedans.* I was quite handy at that. (EV) <***Loc:*** AV, EV, SL, SM, TB, VM, Da84>

adroitir ♦see **droitir**

adultère [adyltær] *n.m.* adultery **Commettre l'adultère.* To commit adultery. (Da84) <***Loc:*** Da84>

ADVERTISEMENT ♦see **avertissement**

adviner ♦see **deviner**

advineur ♦see **devineur**

adviser ♦see **aviser**

aéroplane (**AIRPLANE**) [eroplin, ɛɹəple^{l}n, aeroplɛ̃n] *n.m.* airplane <***Loc:*** LF, VM, SL, Da84, Lv88>

affaiblir (**affeublir**) [afeblir, aføblir] **I** *v.tr.* to weaken, lessen *Les fièvres l'ont bien affaibli.* The fevers really weakened him. (SM) *Alle était tellement affaiblie et alle avait tellement maigri, la pauvre bête, jusqu'à alle caracolait.* She was so weakened and she had become so thin, poor thing, that she was stumbling. (AV) **II s'affaiblir** *v.pron.* **1** to weaken, become weak or weaker *Elle s'affaiblit d'un jour à l'autre.* She is growing weaker from one day to the next. (LA) **2** to grow dim (of a light) *La lumière de la lampe était après s'affaiblir quand il a arrivé à grand galop.* The lamp light was growing dim, when he arrived a full gallop. (LA) <***Loc:*** AV, LA, SL, SM, TB, Da84>

affaiblissant, -e [afeblisɑ̃] *adj.* weakening, debilitating *Une maladie affaiblissante.* A debilitating illness. (LA) <***Loc:*** LA, Da84>

affaiblissement [afeblismɑ̃] *n.m.* weakening <***Loc:*** Da84>

affaire [afær] *n.m./f.* **1** affair, concern, matter **C'était si dur que j'aurais pas honte de dire si j'avais perdu ma belle dans l'affaire.* It was so hard that I wouldn't be ashamed to say that I had lost my sweetheart in the affair. (An02) **Les affaires se brassent mal.* Things are rough. (Da84) **2** thing *Tu veux me faire croire que t'as pas entendu parler des plaques, bougre? C'est une affaire en cire avec des petites traces dessus.* You want me to believe you've never heard of records, buddy? It's a thing made out of wax with little grooves on it. (ThCa: *Martin Weber*) *Un outil faisait trois différentes des affaires.* The same tool would be used for three different things. (AC) *Deux affaires que j'aime pas faire, c'est éplucher une volaille, et mettre du gaz dans mon char.* Two things I don't like to do are to pluck a chicken and to put gas in my car. (LF) **3** business **Il y avait pas d'eau là-bas sur la lune, quand ils ont arrivé, mais Mayo a fait de l'eau! Mayo travaillait pour l'affaire d'eau.* There was no water over there on the moon when they got there, but Mayo produced water. He worked for the waterworks. (EV, An94) **Mon défunt papa et la défunte maman étaient intéressés dans l'affaire de musique.* My late father and mother were interested in the music business. (EV, JD, An94) **4** genitals (male or female) **Ça fait, il a arraché l'affaire, il a* WEE-WEE *dessus le manche de sa hache.* So he took out his thing [i.e. penis], he peed on the handle of his ax. (EV, An94) ◊ **•affaire de chevrette {de DRILL / de nutria / de piège / de pêche / de trôle / d'huile (etc.)}** shrimp / oil drilling / nutria / trapping / fishing / trawling / oil (etc.) business *Et l'affaire d'huile avait retombé vilain, ça fait j'étais pris avec deux mille* SHARE, *j'avais payé treize milles.* And the oil business had fallen badly, so I was stuck with two thousand shares, I had paid thirteen thousand. (TB) *Y avait assez d'argent à faire dans l'affaire de* DRILL *que t'avais pas de besoin d'avoir une éducation pour faire une bonne vie.* There was enough money to be made in the oil drilling business that you didn't need to have an education to make a good living. (TB) <TB> **•avoir pas d'affaire à (faire qqch)** to have no business (doing s.t.) *Eux-autres valait pas dix sous parce qu'ils aviont pas d'affaire à quitter leur pauvre petite fille toute seule.* They weren't worth ten cents because they had no business leaving their poor little girl all alone. (EV) *Il avait pas d'affaire à aller.* He had no business going. (Lv88) <EV, Lv88> **•avoir affaire (avec)** to have dealings (with) *Je joins toujours de ce monde là que j'avais affaire avec pendant des années.* I still meet with some of the people that I dealt with for many years. (SL) **Tu as pas d'affaire ici.* You have no business here. (Da84) <SL, Da84, Lv88> **•belle affaire!** ***a*** the hell, you say! I don't believe you! ***b*** [*ironic*] big deal! *Belle affaire, cette bande de capons.* Big deal, that gang of cowards! (ThCa: *Martin Weber*) <ThCa> **•ça c'est une affaire, oui!** that's a hell of a thing! <Da84> **•ça va faire l'affaire** it will do the trick, it will do the job <Da84> **•c'est pas de tes affaires** it's none of your business, it doesn't concern you <Da84> **•comment les affaires?** how's it going? <SM, Gu00> **•être grosse affaire** to be friendly, be close, have a close relationship *Petit Pete et puis Pérat étaient grosse affaire.* Little Pete and Pérat were real close. (LA) <LA, SL, An94> **•être une affaire** to be a difficult thing (to do) *C'est une affaire, écrire une thèse.* Writing a thesis is difficult. (AV) <AV> **•grosse affaire** big deal *Quand -t- on se préparait pour faire une boucherie nous-autres ça c'était une grosse affaire.* When we got ready to do a butchering, that was a big deal. (AC)

Grosse affaire! Big deal! (Da84) <AC, Da84> **•les affaires se brassent mal** things are rough, times are hard <Da84> **•pas d'affaire!** nothing doing, no deal <Da84> **•pas grande affaire** not much *Je connais pas grande affaire à la pêche.* I don't know much about fishing. (Lv88) *Je me rappelle pas grande affaire de ça.* I don't remember much about that. (SM) <SM, Lv88> **•s'occuper de ses affaires** to mind one's own business <LA, Da84> **•toute qualité d'affaires** all kinds of things, all sorts of things *Il faisait toute qualité d'affaires.* He was involved in all kinds of things. (Lv88) <JE, TB, Lv88> <***Loc:*** AC, AS, AV, EV, IB, IV, JD, JE, LA, LF, PQ, SL, SM, TB, VM, An94, An02, Da84, Hi02, Lv88, Ph36, Re63, ThCa, Wh83>

affamé, -e [afɑ̃me] *adj.* famished, starving *Il a quitté sa femme et ses enfants qu'étiont affamés.* He left his wife and his children who were starving. (VM) <***Loc:*** VM>

affamer [afɑ̃me] **I** *v.tr.* to cause to be hungry, make hungry *Passer tout la journée à haler une seine, ça m'a affamé. J'aurais pu manger la jument et son poulain.* Spending the whole day hauling a seine made me very hungry. I could've eaten a mare and her colt. (LA) **II** *v.intr.* to be hungry *Quand il a revenu de l'ouvrage, ses chiens étaient affamés.* When he returned from work, his dogs were famished. (LA) <***Loc:*** LA, Da84>

affecter [afɛkte] *v.tr.* to affect, influence *Mon "bill" a affecté cent mille voteurs et peut-être plus.* My bill affected a hundred thousand voters and perhaps more. (ThCa: *Messieurs, mesdames*) <***Loc:*** AC, EV, Da84, ThCa>

affection [afɛksjɔ̃] *n.f.* affection, fondness <***Loc:*** Da84>

affermir [afærmir] *v.tr.* harden, strengthen *Ça va pas mouiller demain; ça va aider à affermir ton ciment.* It won't rain tomorrow; that's going to help to harden your concrete. (LA) <***Loc:*** LA, Da84>

affeublir ♦see **affaiblir**

affichage [afiʃaʒ] *n.m.* advertising <***Loc:*** Da84>

affiche [afiʃ] *n.f.* **1** advertisement, sign board **2** poster **3** public notice <***Loc:*** JE, Da84, Lv88>

afficher [afiʃe] **I** *v.tr.* **1** to advertise **Le vieux homme affichait juste avec des petits* SIGNS *desur le bord du chemin qui donnait des directions à sa maison.* The old man advertised just with little signs on the side of the road which gave directions to his house. (Wh83) **2** to give notice of **3** to post (land) in order to prevent trespassing *Si t'as pas affiché ta terre, le monde va peut-être toujours chasser dessus.* If you haven't posted your land, people still might hunt on it. (VM) **II s'afficher** *v.pron.* to make a show of o.s., draw attention to o.s. *Depuis il va chez Red, il s'habille pour s'afficher.* Since he's been going to Red's [health club], he dresses to show off. (LA) <***Loc:*** AV, LA, VM, Da84, Hi02, Wh83>

afficheur [afiʃœr] *n.m.* advertiser <***Loc:*** Da84, Lv88>

affidavit [afidavi, afidavit] *n.m.* affidavit <***Loc:*** JE, LF, SL, SM, Da84, Lv88>

affier (s') [afje] *v.pron.* to trust *Je peux pas m'affier à elle.* I can't trust her. (TB) <***Loc:*** TB, Lv88>

affilage (enfilage) [afilaʒ, ɑ̃filaʒ] *n.m.* sharpening (of a cutting edge) <***Loc:*** Da84>

affilé[1]**, -e (enfilé, -e)** [afile, ɑ̃file] *adj.* **1** sharp, sharpened (of a cutting edge) *Je peux pas couper ce papier. Mon couteau est pas affilé.* I can't cut this paper. My knife isn't sharp. (VM) **2** sharp, cunning, crafty *C'est pas la personne la plus affilée de la bande.* He's not the sharpest one of the gang. (LA) <***Loc:*** LA, VM, Da84, La99>

affilé[2]**, -e** [afile] *adj.* in succession, at a stretch, in a line *Les vaches étaient tout affilées dans le chute pour être médecinées.* The cows were lined up in the chute to be medicated. (LA) <***Loc:*** LA>

affilée (filée) [afile, file] *n.f.* line, file, row, succession *Une affilée de soldats.* A line of soldiers. (Lv88) *Une filée de monde.* A line of people. (EV) ◊ **•à l'affilée / à la filée** in a row <VM, Da84> <***Loc:*** EV, VM, Da84, Lv88>

affiler (filer, enfiler, effiler) [afile, file, ɑ̃file, efile] *v.tr.* to sharpen (a cutting edge) *Ça tu uses pour affiler des couteaux.* This is to be used for sharpening knives. (AV) *Une meule pour filer des couteaux, des haches.* A grindstone to sharpen knives, axes. (AC) *Mon couteau est assez affilé il est rasant.* My knife is so well sharpened that it's razor sharp. (LA) <***Loc:*** AC, AV, LA, TB, VM, Da84, Fa77, Hi02, Lv88>

affileur [afilœr] *n.m.* sharpener, one who sharpens <***Loc:*** VM, Da84>

affileuse [afiløz] *n.f.* sharpener, tool for sharpening <***Loc:*** VM, Da84>

affiquiaux ♦see **affûtiaux**

affirmative [afirmativ] *adj.* affirmative *Sa réponse était affirmative.* Her response was affirmative. (EV) <***Loc:*** EV, Da84>

affirmer [afirme] *v.tr.* to assert, affirm, declare *Alle a affirmé ça que j'y ai dit.* She affirmed what I told him. (EV) <***Loc:*** EV, Da84>

affitiaux ♦see **affûtiaux**

afflétrir [afletrir] **I** *v.tr.* to flatten **II** *v.intr.* to wilt <***Loc:*** Fa77>

affliction [afliksjɔ̃] *n.f.* affliction *Il peut pas travailler parce qu'il a une affliction.* He can't work because he has an affliction. (EV) <***Loc:*** EV, Da84, Lv88>

afflictionné, -e [afliksjɔ̃ne] *adj.* afflicted, deformed, handicapped *Pauvre bête, il est afflictionné terrible.* Poor thing, he's terribly afflicted. (VM) <***Loc:*** VM, Lv88>

affligé, -e [afliʒe] *adj.* **1** crippled, handicapped *Elle est beaucoup affligée, elle a des béquilles pour marcher.* She's quite handicapped, she walks with crutches. (Lv88) *Il est affligé depuis la guerre.* He's been crippled since the war. (SM) *Elle est affligée des pieds.* Her feet are crippled. (LF) **2** deformed *Le bébé est né affligé.* The baby was born deformed. (VM) **3** badly dressed <***Loc:*** AV, IB, JE, LA, LF, SB, SL, SM, TB, VM, Da84, Lv88>

affliger [afliʒe] **I** *v.tr.* **1** to cripple, maim *Il frappe tout le temps son cheval, ça va l'affliger.* He hits his horse all the time, that's going to maim it. (Lv88) **2** to afflict, torment, trouble *La mort de son père quand il était jeune l'a affligé pour la balance de sa vie.* The death of his father when he was young left him troubled for the rest of his life. (LA) **II s'affliger** *v.pron.* to dress o.s. in poor taste <***Loc:*** JE, LA, LF, SL, SM, Da84, Lv88>

affoler (**affolir**) [afole, afolir] **I** *v.tr.* to aggravate, frustrate, drive (s.o.) crazy *Cette personne est après m'affoler avec son cassement de tête.* This person is driving me crazy with his harping. (EV) **II s'affoler** *v.pron.* to become aggravated, become frustrated *Je m'affole dans ces meetings avec les professeurs d'espagnol!* I get so frustrated in those meetings with the Spanish teachers! (VM) <***Loc:*** EV, IB, VM, Da84, Gr86, Lv88, Ph36>

affolir ♦see **affoler**

AFFORD [əfɔɹd] *v.tr.invar.* to afford *J'ai pas acheté de char, parce que je pouvais pas l'AFFORD.* I didn't buy a car because I couldn't afford it. (VM) *Et eux, tu pouvais AFFORD d'engager pour repousser le bateau BACK à l'eau.* And those people, you could afford to hire them to push the boat back in the water. (JE) <***Loc:*** JE, VM, Hi02>

affranchir [afrɑ̃ʃir] *v.tr.* **1** to free, set free, emancipate *Il a affranchi ses esclaves avant la guerre.* He set his slaves free before the war. (SM) **2** to clear, pass by, pass under or over without coming in contact *Ce bateau va pas affranchir le bas du pont.* This boat will not clear the bottom of the bridge. (VM) <***Loc:*** SM, VM, Da84>

affreusement [afrøzmɑ̃] *adv.* terribly, dreadfully, very, extremely **Il est affreusement malade.* He is very sick. (Da84) <***Loc:*** SM, Da84>

affreux[1]**, -euse** [afrø, -øz] *adj.* **1** horrible, frightful, terrible *Et ça c'est la colère qu'il avait, cher! Il avait une colère affreux.* And that's the anger he had, dear! He had a terrible anger. (TB) **2** very numerous *Une quantité affreuse.* A huge quantity. (Lv88) *Y avait du monde affreux au village samedi.* There were lots of people in town on Saturday. (VM) <***Loc:*** EV, SL, SM, TB, VM, Da84, Lv88, Ph36>

affreux[2] [afrø] *adv.* to a great extent, terribly, very much, very *Il aime affreux la sauce piquante.* He very much likes hot sauce. (Lv88) *J'ai rencontré un jeune homme, c'est intéressant affreux. Il vient de Shreveport.* I met a young man, this is really interesting. He's from Shreveport. (VM) *Il fait chaud affreux.* It's terribly hot. (EV) <***Loc:*** EV, SM, VM, Gr86, Lv88>

affront [afrɔ̃] *n.m.* affront, insult, snub, slight *Marche plus loin, ti m'fais affront.* Go farther away, you're offending me. (TB) <***Loc:*** TB, Da84, Lv88>

affronter [afrɔ̃te] *v.tr.* **1** to affront, insult, offend, snub *Ça va pas vous affronter si je mets la chaudière sur la table?* It won't offend you if I put the pot on the table, will it? (Lv88) *Elle affrontait tout quelqu'un* She insulted everyone. (Lv88) **2** to confront, face *Il m'a affronté avec ces questions.* He confronted me with these questions. (EV) **3** to sexually molest *Monsieur N. a affronté ses filles.* Mister N. molested his daughters. (VM) <***Loc:*** EV, IB, SM, VM, Da84, Lv88>

affût [afy] ◊ **•homme d'affût** artful, crafty, sly man <Lv88> <***Loc:*** Lv88>

affûtiaux (**affiquiaux, affitiaux**) [afytjo, afikjo, afitjo] *n.m.pl.* **1** baubles, shoddy decorations **2** small tools <***Loc:*** Lv88>

afistoler ♦see **rafistoler**

africain, -e [afrikɛ̃, -ɛ̃n] *adj.* African *La calinda était une danse africaine.* The calinda was an African dance. (LA) <***Loc:*** LA, Hi02>

Afrique [afrik] *n.f.* Africa <***Loc:*** SL, Hi02>

agaçant, -e [agasɑ̃, -ɑ̃t] *adj.* **1** annoying, irritating *Ton chien est bien agaçant. Tu devrais faire quelque chose avec.* Your dog is really annoying. You should do something with it. (LA) **2** worrisome <***Loc:*** LA, Da84>

agacer (**engacer**) [agase, ɑ̃gase] *v.tr.* **1** to provoke, annoy, irritate *Arrête de m'agacer! Tu m'agaces tout le temps!* Stop annoying me! You irritate me all the time! (EV) **2** to tease *Elle a engacé le petit garçon et il est parti.* She teased the little boy and he left. (SB) **3** to worry <***Loc:*** EV, SB, SM, Da84>

agacerie [agasri] *n.f.* annoyance, irritation <***Loc:*** Da84>

agaceur, -euse [agasœr, -øz] *n.* trouble-maker <***Loc:*** EV>

agacia ♦see **acacia**

agauche ♦see **gauche**

âge [aʒ] *n.m./f.* **1** age *Mon grand-père a vi jusqu'à l'âge de cent trois ans.* My grandfather lived until the age of 103. (LF) *Alle a la même âge que son mari.* She is the same age as her husband. (TB) **2** period, epoch ◊ **•avoir un bon âge** to be elderly, be of ripe age <Da84> **•bel {belle} âge** ***a*** long time *Il y a belle âge qu'il est parti.* It's been a long time since he left. (Lv88) ***b*** good or ripe age <Da84, La99, Lv88> **•d'âge** old, aged *Une femme d'âge.* An old woman. (SM) *C'est un homme d'âge.* He's an old man. (SM) <SM, Lv88> **•en âge** of legal age *Il est en âge de voter.* He is of voting age. (JE) *Il est en âge de se marier.* He's old enough to marry. (LA) *Venir en âge.* To turn the age of legal adulthood. (SJ) <JE, LA, SJ, SM> **•grand-âge** a long time *Jean a grand-âge pour faire son ouvrage.* John has a long time to do his work. (AV) <AV> **•hors d'âge** very old, extremely old *Il était déjà hors d'âge quand il a eu son cancer.* He was already extremely old when he got cancer. (EV) <LA, SM, La99, Lv88> <***Loc:*** AC, AV, EV, IV, JE, LA, LF, SJ, SL, SM, TB, VM, Da84, Fa77, Hi02, La99, Lv88>

âgé, -e [aʒe] *adj.* aged, elderly, old *Il est trop âgé pour faire l'amour.* He is too old to make love. (EV) <***Loc:*** EV, Da84, Fa77, Hi02>

agence [aʒɑ̃s] *n.f.* agency <***Loc:*** SL, Da84>

agenclé, -e [aʒɑ̃kle] *adj.* ◊ **•mal agenclé** badly dressed *T'as* *vu comment il était mal agenclé?* Did you see how badly dressed he was? (SB) <SB> <***Loc:*** SB>

agent [aʒɑ̃] *n.m.* agent, representative ◊ **•agent de la paroisse** county agent <VM> **•agent de poste** postmaster <SM> **•agent de tickettes {gare}** station agent <SM> <***Loc:*** SM, VM, Da84, Fa77>

ageter ♦see **acheter**

aggraver ♦see **engraver**

agile [aʒil] *adj.* agile, supple *Lui, il est agile pour son âge.* He's agile for his age. (EV) <***Loc:*** EV, Da84>

agilité [aʒilite] *n.f.* agility, suppleness <***Loc:*** Da84>

agir [aʒir] **I** *v.intr.* **1** to act, take action *C'est exactement pourquoi il faut agir asteur.* That's exactly why we have to act now. (ThCa: *Mille misères*) *Il est gommeux; il veut pas agir.* He is slow and awkward. He doesn't want to get things done. (EV) **2** to behave **3** to have an effect (as a medicine) **II s'agir** *v.pron. (in impersonal expr.)* to be the question, have to do with **I s'agit de...* The question is . . . (Da84) <***Loc:*** EV, Da84, ThCa>

agitation [aʒitasjɔ̃] *n.f.* agitation, disturbance, commotion <***Loc:*** Da84>

agité, -e [aʒite] *adj.* agitated, excited, fretful *Il a venu beaucoup agité quand il a attendu la nouvelle.* He became very agitated when he heard the news. (EV) <***Loc:*** EV, Da84>

agiter [aʒite] **I** *v.intr.* **1** to function, act *Mon cœur agite pas bien, c'est pour ça le docteur m'a donné cette médecine.* My heart doesn't function well, that's why the doctor gave me this medecine. (VM) **2** to excite, stimulate *Juste te regarder, ça m'agite le "cœur" assez je peux pas souffler.* Just looking at you excites my heart so much that I can hardly breathe. (ThCa: *Le charivari*) *T'as jamais vu comment la pleine lune agite les enfants*? Have you ever seen how the full moon excites children? (VM) **3** to go fast, step on the gas *Il a agité après il a viré.* He stepped on the gas after he turned around. (VM) **II s'agiter** *v.pron.* to be agitated, be excited, become nervous <***Loc:*** VM, Da84, ThCa>

agneau [ɑ̃ɲo, ɑ̃jo] *n.m.* lamb <***Loc:*** Da84>

agonie [agɔ̃ni] *n.f.* agony, anguish ◊ **•agonie de la mort** death throes, death agony <Da84> <***Loc:*** Da84>

agoniser[1] [agɔ̃nize] *v.tr.* **1** to insult, verbally abuse, bawl out *Agoniser quelqu'un de sottises.* To shower someone with abusive language. (Lv88) *La femme a agonisé son mari quand elle l'a vu avec une autre femme.* The woman heaped insults on her husband when she saw him with another woman. (SM) **2** to vex, aggravate *Si sa femme arrête pas de l'agoniser, il va la quitter un jour.* If his wife doesn't stop aggravating him, he's going to leave her one day. (LA) <***Loc:*** AV, IB, LA, SB, SJ, SL, SM, La99, Lv88>

agoniser[2] [agɔ̃nize] *v.intr.* to suffer, be in agony *Il a beaucoup agonisé avant de mourir.* He suffered a lot before dying. (VM) <***Loc:*** SM, VM, Da84, Lv88>

agrafe (**z-agrafe**) [agraf, zagraf] *n.f.* **1** fastener, clasp **2** snap **3** hook and eye closure <***Loc:*** SB, Da84>

agrafer [agrafe] *v.tr.* to fasten with a clasp, hook *Agrafe ma robe.* Hook my dress. (VM) <***Loc:*** VM, Da84>

agrandir ♦see **égrandir**

agrandissement see **égrandissement**

agrapper [agrape] *v.tr.* to swipe, snatch, pilfer **Il a agrapé tout l'argent.* He swiped all the money. (EV, Ph36) *Jean agrape toutes les pacanes si on le guette pas.* John steals all the pecans if we don't watch him. (IB) <***Loc:*** EV, IB, Lv88, Ph36>

agréable [agreab(l), agrejab(l)] *adj.* agreeable, pleasant, nice *Sa femme est beaucoup agréable.* His wife is very pleasant. (EV) <***Loc:*** EV, Da84, Lv88>

agrément [agremɑ̃] *n.m./f.* **1** pleasure, joy, delight, fun *J'ai pas eu d'agrément à Mamou.* I didn't have any fun in Mamou. (EV) **On avait de l'agrément et on apprenait beaucoup.* We had fun and we learned a lot. (Gu82) **2** peace, quiet *On n'a pas d'agrément avec ces enfants-là.* We have no peace with these children. (Lv88) *Il y a d'agrément ici.* There is quiet here. (JE) <***Loc:*** EV, JE, LA, LF, SM, VM, Da84, Gu82, Hi02, Lv88>

agrès [agrɛ, agre] *n.m.pl.* **1** riggings, fittings (for a horse or draft animal) *Je peux nommer les agrès que ça usait pour travailler avec les animaux.* I can name the rigs they used to work with animals. (LA) **2** harness, harnessing **3** tools, equipment **4** clothes, clothing ◊ **•agrès de noces** wedding garments and accessories <IB, SJ> <***Loc:*** AC, IB, LA, SJ, SL, VM, Da84, Gr86, Lv88>

agricher ♦see **engrucher**

agricole [agrikol] *adj.* agricultural, farm-related *Et là, dans quarante-huit j'ai commencé travailler pour un coopératif qui fait des prêts agricoles.* And then in forty-eight, I started working for a cooperative that makes farm loans. (SL) <***Loc:*** SL>

agriculture [agrikyltyr] *n.f.* agriculture <***Loc:*** SL, Da84>

agriculturiste [agrikyltyris(t)] *n.* farmer **Mon père était agriculturiste. Il élevait des bêtes à corne, des cochons et des chevaux dans les bois.* My father was a farmer, he raised cattle, pigs, and horses in the woods. (Gr86) <***Loc:*** Gr86>

agriffer ♦see **agripper**

agripper (**agriffer**) [agripe, agrife] **I** *v.tr.* **1** to grip, grasp, grab *Il a agrippé la branche pour pas tomber.* He grabbed the branch to avoid falling. (LA) **2** to climb *Le chat a agrippé l'arbre et ça peut pas descendre.* The cat climbed the tree and it can't get down. (VM) **II s'agripper** *v.pron.* to grab, grasp, cling *Il avait juste assez de temps pour s'agripper après la barrière avant que la grosse lame a frappé.* He had just enough time to grab onto the gunwale before the big wave hit. (LA) <***Loc:*** LA, VM, Da84, Hi02>

agrisser ♦see **engrucher**

agrouer (s') [agrue] *v.pron.* to squat or crouch (of a hen who protects her chicks in this way) <***Loc:*** Di32, Lv88>

agrucher, agrusser ♦see **engrucher**

ah [a] *interj.* ah!, oh! <***Loc:*** Da84>

ahonter ♦see **éhonter**

aide[1] [ɛd] *n.f.* help, aid, assistance *Et finalement, j'aimerais remercier ma femme pour son aide.* And finally, I'd like to thank my wife for her help. (EV) <***Loc:*** AC, EV, LF, Da84>

aide[2] [ɛd] *n.m./f.* helper, aid, assistant <***Loc:*** Da84>

aider [ede, ajide] **I** *v.intr.* **1** to help, aid, assist *Il aide à Martha un tas un tas dans la maison.* He helps Martha a whole lot in the house. (EV) *C'était moi tout le temps qui avais pour y aider à faire n'importe qui il avait pour faire.* I was always the one who had to help him to do anything he had to do. (EV) **2** to avoid, help, keep from (doing s.t.) *Il peut pas aider de faire le couillon.* He can't help acting like a fool. (VM) **II s'aider** *v.pron.* to help o.s. or each other *Le monde s'aidait un à l'autre dans ce temps là.* People helped each other in those days. (TB) <***Loc:*** AC, AV, EV, LA, TB, VM, Da84, Lv88>

aideur, -euse [edœr, -øz] *n.* helper, aid, assistant *J'a commencé dans la cuisine [...] à aider les cuiseurs. Eusse, ça appelait ça un* FLUNKY *mais c'était un aideur pour un* COOK, A COOK'S HELPER*, un aideur de cuiseur.* I started in the kitchen helping the cooks. They called it a flunky but it was a cook's helper. (TB) <***Loc:*** TB>

aïe[1] ♦see **yaïe**

aïe[2]**, aïe-aïe** ♦see **ayayaie**

aigle [ɛg(l), æg(l)] *n.m.* eagle ◊ **•aigle à tête blanche** American eagle, bald eagle <Re31> <***Loc:*** SL, Da84, Re31>

aiglon [eglɔ̃] *n.m.* **1** eagle **2** Cooper's hawk <***Loc:*** AV, TB, Lv88, Re31>

aigre ♦see **haigre**

aigrette [egrɛt] *n.m./f.* egret (any of several white herons of Louisiana, esp. the snowy egret) ◊ **•aigrette à vaches** cattle egret <Gu00> **•aigrette blanche** snowy egret <TB> **•aigrette bleue** blue egret <Re31> **•aigrette câille** Louisiana heron, blue crane <Re31> **•aigrette noire** American egret <TB> <***Loc:*** AV, IV, TB, SB, Da84, Gr86, Gu00, Lv88, Hi02, Re31>

aigreur ♦see **haigreur**

aigrir ♦see **haigrir**

aigrissement ♦see **haigrissement**

aiguille[1] [egɥij, egwij] *n.f.* **1** needle **2** hypodermic needle *Faut je prends un* SHOT *tous les jours. [...] Moi je peux pas arranger ces aiguilles, je vois pas assez bien pour mettre la médecine dans l'aiguille.* I have to take a shot every day. I can't prepare the needles, I don't see well enough to put the medicine in the needle. (TB) **3** hand (of a clock) **4** steeple (of a church) ◊ **•aiguille à fil** sewing needle <AV> **•aiguille à mailler** needle for making mesh (for nets) <LF> <***Loc:*** AV, JE, LA, LF, SL, TB, Da84>

aiguille[2] [ɛgɥij, egwij] *n.f.* needlefish <***Loc:*** JE>

aiguisage [egɥizaʒ] *n.m.* sharpening <***Loc:*** Da84>

aiguiser [egɥize] *v.tr.* to sharpen **J'ai été chercher la meule pour aiguiser le couteau.* I went to get the grinding stone to sharpen the knife. (LA, An94) <***Loc:*** IB, LA, An94, Da84>

ail (**z-ail, lail**) [aj, zaj] *n.m./f.* garlic *Tu mets des ails dans ton gombo?* Do you put garlic in your gumbo? (VM) <***Loc:*** AC, CL, IB, SM, TB, VM, Da84, Hi02, Lv88>

aile (**z-aile**) [ɛl, zɛl, zel] *n.f.* **1** wing (of a bird, insect, etc.) *Une z-aile de poule.* A chicken wing. (Lv88) **2** wing (of a building, a trawl net, etc.) *Elle est née dans l'autre aile de l'hôpital.* She was born in the other wing of the hospital. (VM) ◊ **•z-aile bleue** blue-winged teal <check loc in db> **•z-aile pointue** duck hawk, peregrine falcon <Lv88> **•z-aile rond(e)** ***a*** Cooper's hawk ***b*** chicken hawk <JE, Lv88> **•z-aile rouge** redwing blackbird <Lv88> **•z-aile vert** green-winged teal <TB> **•prendre des ailes** to take flight *Et allons dire que c'était pas trop une belle ouragan, ça. Il a venté, et le magasin à maïs là, moi je croyais qu'il allait prendre des ailes et puis s'en aller là-dedans.* And let's say that it wasn't a very nice hurricane. There was wind, and the corn barn, I thought it was going to take flight and head off. (TB) <TB> <***Loc:*** TB, LA, LF, SM, VM, Da84, Lv88>

ailleurs (**alieurs**) [aljɔr, aljœr] *adv.* elsewhere *C'est pas comme ça ailleurs. Lafayette, Eunice, Mamou, Ville Platte, c'est pas comme ça.* It's not like that in other places. Lafayette, Eunice, Mamou, Ville Platte, it's not like that. (SM) *Y a plus que la moitié qui venait d'ailleurs, il voulait tout les mettre que c'était cèze-là qu'étaient élevés sauvage.* More than half of them came from elsewhere; he wanted to claim that all of them had been raised wild. (TB) ◊ **•ailleurs de** instead of *Alieurs d'aller il a resté.* Instead of going he stayed. (JE) <JE> <***Loc:*** AC, JE, SM, TB, Da84, Lv88>

aimable [ɛ̃mab(l)] *adj.* amiable, likeable, pleasant *La vie est belle et si aimable dans les campagnes de la Louisiane.* Life is beautiful and so pleasant in the Louisiana countryside. (Lv88, ch: *Dans les campagnes de la Louisiane*) <***Loc:*** Da84, Gr86, Lv88>

aimant [ɛ̃mɑ̃] *n.m.* magnet <***Loc:*** Da84>

aimer [ɛ̃me] **I** *v.tr.* **1** to love **Et Petit Poucet était plus* SMART *que les autres et il était aimé plus par le papa et la maman.* And Tom Thumb was smarter than the others and he was loved more by his father and his mother. (LA, An94) **Il aimait jusqu'à la nature, les arbres, les fleurs, la terre. Il avait un grand sentiment pour tout ce qui existait.* He even loved nature, trees, flowers, the earth. He had great affection for everything that existed. (EV, An94) **2** to like *Tu devrais voir comme il aime ça.* You should see how he likes that. (VM) *Ils aimeraient que je reconsidère ma position.* They would like me to reconsider my position. (LA) *Son père aime pas quand elle le reprend comme ça.* His father doesn't like it when she corrects him like that. (LA) *J'ai assayé déjà mais j'ai pas aimé les cigares.* I have tried before but I did not like cigars. (AC) *C'est une place qu'est bien tranquille icitte sur le bayou, tout chacun se connaît, c'est une place qu'est aimée.* It's a place that is very quiet here on the bayou, everyone knows each other, it's a place that is well liked. (LF) **II** *v.intr.* to like *Elle aime à encharger les enfants de travailler.* She likes to order the children to work. (SB) *Elle aime à serrer.* She likes to economize. (AV) **III s'aimer** *v.pron.* to love o.s. or each other *On va s'aimer pour la balance de la vie.* We'll love each other for the rest of our lives. (LF) ◊ **•aimer à la folerie** to love like crazy *Il aimait ça à la folerie.* He loved it like crazy. (Lv88) <Lv88> **•aimer comme cochon aime la boue {la lavure / le maïs}** to like very much <La99> **•aimer la bouteille** to be a heavy drinker <Da84> **•aimer mieux** to prefer, like more *Je veux pas* INTERRUPT *mais tu bois du café? Ou tu veux un* COKE *plutôt, qui-ce t'aimerais mieux?* I don't want to interrupt, but do you drink coffee? Or would you rather have a coke, what would you prefer? (LF) <LF> <***Loc:*** AC, AV, EV, IB, IV, LA, LF, SB, SL, SM, TB, VM, An94, Da84, Guoo, Hi02, La99, Lv88, Wh83>

ain ♦see **hein**

aîné, -e [ɛ̃ne] *adj.* elder, eldest, first born *C'est quel des deux qu'est l'aîné?* Which of the two is the oldest? (LA) <***Loc:*** EV, LA, Da84>

aingue [ɛ̃ŋ] *n.f.* groin *Il a des glandes dans ses aingues.* He has [swollen] glands in his groin. (VM) <***Loc:*** VM>

ainsi [ɛ̃si] *adv.* so, thus, in this way *Cette chaise placée ainsi dans le salon fait un effet bœuf.* That chair placed that way in the living room looks great. (Pe37) ◊ **•ainsi de suite** and so forth <VM, Da84> **•ainsi que** as well as *Tapez, tapez, tambours, trompettes ainsi que violons.* Strike, strike drums, trumpets as well as violins. (PQ, ch: *La belle et le capitaine*) <PQ, Da84> **•ainsi soit-il** amen <TB, Da84> **•pour ainsi dire** so to speak <Da84> <***Loc:*** JE, PQ, SM, TB, Da84, Pe37>

air[1] [ær] *n.m./f.* **1** air *L'air est bonne et fraîche.* The air is good and fresh. (SL) *C'est pas lui qui t'a donné ce rhume. C'est dans l'air.* He's not the one who gave you that cold. It's in the air. (VM) *Là j'ai pris ces gros* INNERTUBES, *j'ai mis de l'air dedans.* Then I took those big innertubes, I put air in them. (TB) **2** expression, appearance, air, look **Avoir l'air bête.* To seem crazy. (Da84) **Avoir l'air fâché.* To appear angry. (Da84) **3** tune **Et son père jouait proche tous les mêmes airs avant lui.* And his father played almost all the same tunes before him. (EV, An84) ◊ **•air de vent** weathervane <VM> **•à l'air** bare, uncovered *Alle avait les bras à l'air.* She had bare arms. (TB) <TB> **•air froide** air conditioning *Ça c'est ça qu'ils appelont* A CANELOADER. *[...] On loadait les cannes, dans le vieux temps avec ça ici. [...] Y a de l'air froide dedans.* That's what they call a caneloader. We would load the cane, in the old days, with this. It has air conditioning. (AS) <AS> **•avoir des faux airs avec** to resemble, look like *Je trouve que t'as des faux airs avec ma sœur.* I find that you resemble my sister. (SM) <SM> **•courant d'air** draft, air current <Da84> **•en l'air** ***a*** up in the air *Asteur tu pousses un bouton et la drague s'en vient en l'air.* Now you push the button and the net goes up in the air. (JE) ***b*** up *Lever le chassis en l'air.* To raise the window sash. (SJ) *Avant que je mets 200 ou 250 dollars pour tiendre mes culottes en l'air je vas prendre une corde. Je vas prendre une ceinture.* Before I spend $200 or $250 to hold my pants up, I'll get a rope. I'll get a belt. (TB) ***c*** high, high up *Mets-les en l'air.* Put them high up. (AV) ***d*** upstairs *Il a monté en l'air.* He went upstairs. (JE) ***e*** fickle *Une femme en l'air.* A fickle woman. (Lv88) <AV, JE, LF, SJ, TB, Lv88> **•en l'air de** on top of *C'est en l'air du* WARDROBE. It's on top of the wardrobe. (Lv88) <Lv88> **•en pleine air** outdoors, in the open air *Je veux rester ici en pleine air.* I want to stay right here in the open air. (AV) <AV> **•l'air du temps** ***a*** high up, in the air **Il a volé dans l'air du temps.* It flew way up high. (Da84) ***b*** the sky <Da84> **•sur {dessus} l'air** on the air, on the radio *Le petit brin qu'eux-autres met sur l'air. Y en a pas beaucoup.* The little bit that they put on the air. There isn't much. (TB) *Je l'ai déjà conté sur l'air.* I already told it on the radio. (Lv88) *Il aimerait être dessus l'air avec nous-autres.* He would like to be on the air with us. (LA) <LA, TB, Lv88> <***Loc:*** AS, AV, EV, JE, LA, PQ, SB, SJ, SL, SM, TB, VM, Da84, Guoo, Lv88>

air[2] [ær] *n.m.* condition of having red, itchy eyes (e.g. due to allergies) *Le persil fait un bon traitement pour l'air. L'air, c'est quand t'as les yeux rouges, qui brûlent et te démangent un tas.* Parsley is a good treatment for eye irritation. That's when you have red eyes that burn and itch a lot. (VM) <***Loc:*** VM>

aircotien ♦see **herbe coquin**

airer [ere] *v.tr.* to ventilate, air out *Dans les premiers jours du printemps, on mettait nos matelas dessus la galerie pour les airer.* During the first days of spring, we would put our mattresses out on the porch to air them out. (VM) <***Loc:*** EV, IB, VM, Lv88, Ph36>

AIRPLANE ♦see **aéroplane**

aise [ɛz] *n.f.* **1** ease, convenience **2** comfort ◊ **•en aise** easy *Si moi je connais eusse le connaît, moi je vas plus les parler en français parce que c'est plusse en aise, tu connais, c'est plus aisé.* If I know they know it, I'll more likely speak French to them because it's easier, you know. (TB) <TB> **•être à son aise** ***a*** to be at one's ease ***b*** to have things easy, have an easy time of it *On était pas à notre aise.* We didn't have things easy. (SM) <SM, Da84> **•mal à son aise** ill at ease, uncomfortable <Da84> **•se mettre à son aise** to make o.s. comfortable *Il a rentré dans la maison et il s'a mis à son* *aise.* He went into the house and he made himself comfortable. (LA) <LA> <***Loc:*** LA, SM, TB, Da84>

aisé[1]**, -e** [eze] *adj.* easy *C'est beaucoup plus aisé asteur, aller au magasin, t'achètes ça tout fait déjà.* It's much easier now, just go to the store, and you buy it already all made. (AV) <***Loc:*** AC, AV, SL, TB, VM, Da84, Lv88, Hi02>

aisé[2] [eze] *adv.* **1** slowly *Va aisé avec ça. Laisse pas ça tomber.* Go slowly with that. Don't drop it. (SM) **2** easily **T'es en erreur si tu crois de te débarrasser de moi aussi aisé que ça.* You are mistaken if you think you can get rid of me so easily. (ThCa: *Le charivari*) **3** carefully *Aisé! Tu vas l'aborder.* Careful! You're going to hit it! (VM) <***Loc:*** AC, SM, TB, VM, Lv88, ThCa>

aisément [ezemɑ̃] *adv.* easily *Si quelqu'un aurait voulu prendre avantage de nous-autres, eux-autres aurait pu aisément faire ça.* If someone had wanted to take advantage of us, they could easily have done that. (TB) <***Loc:*** TB, Da84>

aises [ɛz] *n.m.pl.* arrangement, layout (of a house) *Alle connaît pas encore les aises de la maison.* She doesn't know the layout of the house yet. (VM) <***Loc:*** VM>

ajamber ♦see **enjamber**

ajoupa [aʒupa] *n.m./f.* **1** perch, roost **2** bird cage **3** ramshackle cabin, hut *Eusse reste dans une ajoupa qu'il a fait.* They live in a hut that he made. (LF) <***Loc:*** LF, Di32, Lv88>

ajouquer (**jouquer**) [aʒuke, ʒuke] *v.tr.* to yoke *Jouquer des bœufs.* To yoke oxen. (LA) <***Loc:*** LA, Da84, Lv88>

ajoutement [aʒutmɑ̃] *n.m./f.* addition (to a building) *Il a fait un ajoutement à sa maison.* He put an addition on his house. (SB) *La maison est encore trop petite même avec l'ajoutement.* The house is still too small even with the addition. (IB) <***Loc:*** EV, IB, SB, SL, SM, TB, VM, Lv88, Ph36>

ajouter [aʒute] *v.tr.* to add, add on *Ajouter une quille sur un bateau.* To add a keel on a boat. (VM) <***Loc:*** SM, VM, Da84>

ajustage [aʒystaʒ] *n.m.* adjustment, adjusting <***Loc:*** Da84>

ajustement [aʒystmɑ̃] *n.m.* **1** adjustment **2** settlement, arrangement <***Loc:*** Da84>

ajuster [aʒyste] **I** *v.tr.* **1** to adjust *Je vas aux Opelousas pour ajuster mes lunettes.* I go to Opelousas to adjust my glasses. (SL) **2** to regulate, set (a clock) *On a pour ajuster les pendules deux fois par an pour la nouvelle heure et la vieille heure.* We have to set our clocks twice a year for the new time and the old time. (LA) **3** to settle (accounts or differences) *Ajuster un compte.* To settle an account. (VM) **II s'ajuster** *v.pron.* to adjust o.s., adjust one's clothes *Ajustez vous-autres. On va vous prendre en portrait.* Straighten up your clothes. They're going to take your picture. (VM) <***Loc:*** LA, SL, VM, Da84>

ajusteur [aʒystœr] *n.m.* adjuster (of insurance, etc.) <***Loc:*** Da84>

al ♦see **alle**

alarme [alarm] *n.f.* **1** alarm **2** fright, state of alarm <***Loc:*** Da84>

alastique ♦see **élastique**

alcohol ♦see **alcool**

alcool (**alcohol, arcahol**) [alkɔl, alkohɔl, arkaɔl, arkohɔl] *n.m./f.* alcohol *Quand ça arrivait chez eux-autres, il faulait que ça se lave avec l'alcohol pour pas amener la maladie.* When they got home, they had to wash with alcohol so as to not bring in the disease. (TB) *Ça sent l'arcahol.* That smells like alcohol. (JE) ◊ **•alcool de bois** sap *En printemps l'alcool de bois monte.* In spring the sap rises. (JE) <JE> <***Loc:*** AV, JE, LF, SB, SJ, TB, Da84, Lv88>

alègne ♦see **alêne**

alêne (**alène, alègne**) [alɛ̃n, alɛ̃j] *n.f.* **1** awl **2** stringer hook *L'alêne a cassé au bout de la corde et j'ai perdu tous mes poissons.* The hook on the end of the stringer broke and I lost all my fish. (VM) **3** fishhook *Il pêche avec des grosses alènes.* He fishes with big hooks. (SB) <***Loc:*** AC, AV, IB, SB, SJ, VM, Da84, Lv88>

alentir [alɑ̃tir] **I** *v.tr.* to slow, make slow *Il a alenti son cheval en arrivant en avant de chez sa belle.* He slowed his horse down as he arrived in front of his girlfriend's house. (LA) **II** *v.intr.* to become slow *Quand on est vieux, on est bien alenti.* When one is old, one becomes quite slow. (Lv88) <***Loc:*** LA, Lv88>

alentour (**à l'entour**) [alɑ̃tur] *adv.* near, nearby, around *Quand on était jeune on parlait pas français à l'école. Non. On parlait si les maîtresses étaient pas alentour.* When we were young we didn't speak French in school. We spoke it if the teachers weren't around. (TB) **Eine bande d'hommes était planté à l'entour après brocanter des contes de chasse.* A group of men were standing around swapping hunting stories. (Wh83) ◊ **•alentour (de) / à l'entour (de)** around, near *Elle alle a été élevée un peu en haut de là où mon j'a été élevé, alentour de l'église St. Joseph.* She was raised a little bit above where I was raised, around St. Joseph Church. (TB) *Il a alentour de cinquante ans.* He's about fifty (years old). (SM) *Il reste alentour St. Martin.* He lives near St. Martin. (SM) *J'ai vu tous les chandelles allumées à l'entour de ton cercueil.* I saw candles lit around your coffin. (Lv88, ch: *J'ai passé devant ta porte*) *J'ai alentour trente vaches.* I have around thirty cows. (SL) *Il vient d'à l'entour de Mamou.* He comes from around Mamou. (Lv88) <IB, SL, SM, TB, Lv88> <***Loc:*** AC, AV, EV, IB, SL, SM, TB, VM, Da84, Hi02, Lv88, Wh83>

alentour [alɑ̃tur] *n.m.* ◊ **•dans l'alentour de / dans les alentours de** approximately, around, about *J'avais dans l'alentour de cent poulets.* I had approximately one hundred chickens. (IB) *Elle a dans les alentours de dix-huit ans.* She is about eighteen years old. (JE) <IB, JE> <***Loc:*** IB, JE>

alentours [alɑ̃tur] *n.m.pl.* neighborhood, environs **Dans les* *alentours.* In the neighborhood. (Da84) <*Loc:* LF, TB, Da84, Hi02, Lv88>

alfafa ♦see **alfalfa**

alfalfa (**alfafa**) [alfafa] *n.m./f.* alfalfa <*Loc:* LA, TB, Da84, Fa77>

alieurs ♦see **ailleurs**

alignement (**enlignement**) [aliɲəmɑ̃, ɑ̃liɲəmɑ̃] *n.m.* alignment, aligning <*Loc:* Da84>

aligner (**enligner**) [aliɲe, ɑ̃liɲe] **I** *v.tr.* to align, line up, put in line *On enlignait les machines dans les bateaux. Enligner ça veut dire qu'on mettait les machines en plan avec le* SHAFT *et les* PROPELLER, *follait que tout ça soye en ligne pour bien que ça travaille.* We lined up the motors in the boats. Lining up means we put the motors even with the shaft and the propeller, it all had to be lined up so that it would work well. (LF) **II s'aligner** *v.pron.* to line up, get into line *Il s'a enligné derrière les autres wagons pour vendre son coton.* He got in line behind the other wagons to sell his cotton. (LA) <*Loc:* LA, LF, VM, Da84, Lv88>

aliment [alimɑ̃] *n.m.* food, nourishment <*Loc:* Da84>

alingé, -e [alɛ̃ʒe] *adj.* possessing a large wardrobe, well dressed *C'est une femme bien alingée.* She's a woman with a wide choice of clothes. (VM) <*Loc:* VM, Lv88>

alisier [alizje] *n.m.* blackhaw <*Loc:* Da84, Lv88, Re31>

alison ♦see **alizon**

alizon, -e (**alison, -nne**) [alizɔ̃, -ɔ̃n] *adj.* brindled, reddish brown or yellowish brown, often with darker spots *J'avais une belle grosse vache alisonne dans ma savane, mais le gros chien alison à mon voisin a attaqué ma vache et l'a tuée.* I had a beautiful, large brindle cow in my field, but my neighbor's big spotted dog attacked my cow and killed it. (Guoo) <*Loc:* SM, VM, Guoo, Lv88>

ALL RIGHT[1] [ɔlraɪt, ɔraɪt] *adj.* satisfactory, well **Là c'est comme si c'était* ALL RIGHT, *parce que là on était chez nous-autres, là.* Then, it was as if it was all right, because we were at home then. (EV, An84) <*Loc:* EV, An84, Da84>

ALL RIGHT[2] [ɔlraɪt, ɔraɪt] *interj.* all right, O.K. <*Loc:* EV, Da84>

alle (**a, a', al, elle, e'**) [al, a, *occ.* ɛl, ɛ] *pron.pers.f. (subj.)* she, it *A va pas venir, alle est malade.* She's not going to come, she's sick. (Lv88) *Alle a fait ça.* She did that. (VM) *Elle tend son linge sur l'herbe.* She spreads her clothes on the grass. (SB) *Elle tenait la maison et cuisait à dîner pour nous-autres, elle lavait notre linge.* She kept the house and cooked dinner for us, she washed our clothes. (IB) <*Loc:* IB, LF, SB, SM, TB, VM, Lv88>

allée [ale] *n.f.* **1** alley, side road, path **2** aisle, passage between rows of seats or pews **3** turnrow, headland (strip of uncultivated land at the end or side of a field where a plow can turn) ◊ •**allée de clos** turnrow, headland <EV, JD> <*Loc:* EV, JD, SL, VM, Da84, Lv88>

allège (**alliège, lège, à lège**) [alɛʒ, aljɛʒ] *adj.* **1** without cargo, empty *Le chaland est allège.* The flat-boat is light. (JE) **L'wagon est revenu lège; Pape avait vendu ses balles de coton.* The wagon came back empty; Dad had sold his bales of cotton. (EV, Ph36) **2** empty-handed *Je vais à la grocerie allège.* I'm going to the grocery store empty-handed. (SM) *Il est parti chargé mais il est revenu à lège.* He left with a load but came back empty-handed. (SL) <*Loc:* EV, JE, LF, SL, SM, VM, Lv88, Ph36>

alléger (**allégir**) [aleʒe, aleʒir] *v.tr.* **1** to lighten (a load) *Il aura pour allégir son voyage de riz. Ça va casser le pont.* He'll have to lighten his load of rice. It'll break the bridge. (VM) **2** to alleviate, relieve *La médecine que sa mère lui a donnée a manière commencé à allégir son mal de tête.* The medicine that his mother gave him sort of started to relieve his headache. (LA) <*Loc:* LA, VM, Da84>

allégir ♦see **alléger**

alléluia [aleluja] *interj.* [*eccl.*] alleluia <*Loc:* Da84>

Allemagne [almɑ̃j, almɑ̃] *n.f.* Germany *J'étais quatre fois dans l'Allemagne so je peux comprendre un petit brin d'allemand.* I've been to Germany four times, so I can understand a little bit of German. (TB) <*Loc:* LA, LF, TB, Hi02>

allemand[1], **-e** [almɑ̃, -ɑ̃d] *adj.* German *Dans mon chemin rencontre trois garçons allemands.* In my path I meet three German boys. (ch: *Dans mon chemin rencontre*) <*Loc:* Da84, Hi02>

allemand[2] [almɑ̃] *n.m.* German, the German language <*Loc:* Da84, Hi02>

Allemand[3], **-e** [almɑ̃, -ɑ̃d] *n.* German *Sa famille c'est des Allemands. Quand les Allemands a venu ici à la Louisiane. Son dernier nom c'est Hoffpauir.* Her family, they're Germans. When the Germans came here to Louisiana. Her last name is Hoffpauir. (TB) <*Loc:* IB, LF, SB, TB, VM, Fa77, Lv88>

aller[1] [ale] (*p.p.* **été** [ete]) **I** *v.intr.* **1** to go *Le jeune monde, t'as du tracas à les faire aller à l'église. Les enfants veut pus aller à l'église.* Young people, you have trouble making them go to church. Young people no longer want to go to church. (LF) **Aller à la chasse, à la messe.* To go on a hunt, to go to mass. (Da84) **Aller et venir.* To come and go. (Da84) **Aller à cheval.* To go on horseback. (Da84) **Aller en bateau.* To go by boat. (Da84) **2** to be (of any state of affairs, esp. health) *Ça va bien?* Are you okay?/Is everything all right? (TB) *Ça va bien.* I'm okay./Everything is fine. (TB) *Ça va mal.* I'm not well./I'm not feeling well. (TB) *Et ça va pire en pire.* And it's getting worse and worse. (TB) *Il dit, "ça va bien." Il dit, "Ma femme a eu un gros garçon."* He said, "Things are going well." He said, "my wife had a big baby boy." (EV) **Comment ça va?* How are you?/How's it going? (Da84) **3** to suit, fit **Ça me va.* That suits me. (Da84) **Ce linge te va bien.* That clothing suits you well, looks good on you. (Da84) **Est-ce que ça vous va?* Does that suit you? (Da84) **II s'en aller** *v.pron.* to go away, leave, depart *Il reste pas là, il s'en va lui.* He's not staying there, he's leaving. (JE) *On s'en va pendant une ouragan.* We get out when there is a hurricane. (JE) *Va-t-en, tu bats la berloque.* Get out of here, you are crazy. (JE) *Va-t-en!* Go away! (VM) **Allez-vous-en!* Get away from here! (Da84) *Et je croyais pas qu'il allait s'en aller à* GERMANY. And I didn't think he was going to leave for Germany. (TB) *Y en a t'a resté mais y en a ti s'en a été.* There were some who stayed and some who got out [after the hurricane]. (JE) ◊ **•aller à pied** to walk <EV, Da84> **•aller après** to go after, go get, fetch *Sa fille est malade, ça fait il va après le docteur.* His daughter is sick, so he goes to get the doctor. (EV) <AC, EV, Da84> **•aller aux caïmans {crabes / écureuils / mûres (etc.)}** to go alligator hunting / crabbing / squirrel hunting / blackberry picking (etc.) *Si un de nous allait aux écureuils, il aurait tué huit, dix écureuils.* If one of us went squirrel hunting, he'd kill eight, ten squirrels. (SL) *Aller aux mûres.* To go blackberry picking. (EV) <EV, LF, SL> **•aller avec** to court, date, go steady with *Je vas avec Marie.* I am courting Marie. (SM) <SM> **•aller chercher** to go after, go get, fetch *Peut-être que moi je vas les chercher si vous-autres veut rester ici.* Maybe I'll go get them if you all want to stay here. (TB) <JE, LA, LF, SJ, SL, TB, VM, An94, Da84, Lv88> **•s'en aille!** cry used to make dogs go away <SM> **•va donc!** go on! (expression of disbelief) <La99> <***Loc:*** AC, AV, EV, IB, JE, LA, LF, SB, SJ, SL, SM, TB, VM, An94, Da84, Hi02, La99, Lv88, Ph36, Wh83>

aller[2] [ale] *v.aux. (for future tense)* to be going to *Tu penses que ça va venir?* Do you think they're going to come? (EV) *Pour même, je vais le faire.* Nevertheless, I'm going to do it. (VM) *Je vais pousser route. C'est tard.* I'm going to leave. It's late. (SM) *Je suis pas un musicien professional mais je vais te jouer quelque chose.* I'm not a professional musician, but I'll play you something. (VM) *Si tu travailles dur, tu vas prospérer.* If you work hard, you will prosper. (LA) *Je parie que tu regardes à ça et tu vas le comprendre bien, huh?* I bet you look at that and you'll understand it well, huh? (TB) *On va plumer le bœuf quand ça fait froid.* We will skin the ox when it gets cold. (VM) *Tu ferais mieux de bien planner ton affaire ou ça va te coûter une fortune.* You'd better plan your thing well or it'll cost you a fortune. (LA) *"Quand ça me prend," je dis, "on dirait je vas mourir."* "When it [the pain] comes," I said, "it's as if I'm going to die." (EV) *Les enfants sont trop animés à soir. Ils vont jamais s'endormir.* The children are too lively tonight. They'll never get to sleep. (VM) <***Loc:*** AC, AV, EV, IB, JE, LA, LF, SB, SJ, SL, SM, TB, VM, An94, Da84, Hi02, La99, Lv88>

alliance [aljɑ̃s] *n.f.* **1** alliance **2** wedding ring ◊ **•par alliance** by marriage **Être parent par alliance.* To be related by marriage. (Da84) **Mon cousin par alliance.* My cousin by marriage. (Da84) <***Loc:*** TB, An94, Da84, Fa77>

allianté, -e [aljɑ̃te, arjɑ̃te] *adj.* ◊ **•mal allianté** badly dressed, shabbily dressed *L'homme était mal allianté.* The man was badly dressed. (SB) <SB> <***Loc:*** SB>

alliège ♦see **allège**

alligateur ♦see **alligator**

alligator (alligateur) [aligatɔr, aligatœr] *n.m.* alligator <***Loc:*** AC, TB, Da84, Lv88>

allô [alo] *interj.* hello <***Loc:*** Da84>

allonge (élonge) [alɔ̃ʒ, elɔ̃ʒ] *n.f. (occ. m.)* **1** addition, extension, annex (to a house or building) *Il a fait une allonge à la cuisine.* He added on to his kitchen. (SB) **2** additional clause (of a will) ***Loc:*** AV, EV, IB, SB, SJ, SL, SM, VM, Da84, Lv88, Ph36>

allongement [alɔ̃ʒmɑ̃] *n.m.* **1** lengthening **2** extension, addition <***Loc:*** Da84>

allonger (élonger) [alɔ̃ʒe, elɔ̃ʒe] **I** *v.tr.* **1** to lengthen, extend **2** to stretch, stretch out *Tu vois ces jeunes petits bougres, comment eux élongent leurs soufflets, leurs accordéons vont pas durer.* You see those young guys, how they stretch out the bellows, their accordions aren't going to last. (LA) **3** to build on to, add on to (a house, etc.) *On va allonger la maison.* They're going to build an annex on the house. (IB) **II s'allonger** *v.pron.* **1** to stretch o.s. out, lie down *Je me suis allongé après dîner.* I laid down after dinner. (SM) *Il s'a élongé dans le lit.* He stretched out in the bed. (VM) *Il faut que je m'élonge un élan avant de laver les vaisselles.* I have to lie down a moment before I wash the dishes. (TB) **I s'est élongé su l'lit.* He stretched out on the bed. (EV, Ph36) **2** to stretch (one's muscles) *En se levant il s'élonge.* When he gets up he stretches. (LF) **3** to extend (of rope) *Le câble s'élonge d'un char à l'autre.* The rope extends from one car to the other. (LA) ◊ **•allonger la main** to stretch out one's hand <Da84> <***Loc:*** AC, AV, JD, LA, LF, SM, TB, VM, Da84, Lv88>

allongir [alɔ̃ʒir] *v.tr.* to lengthen, extend *La porte a besoin d'être allongie.* The door needs to be lengthened. (SB) <***Loc:*** SB>

allons [alɔ̃, anɔ̃] *v.* **1** let's go **Allons.* Let's go. (Da84) *Allons chez l'autre voisin.* Let's go to the other neighbor's house. (Lv88, ch: *Chanson du Mardi-Gras*) *Allons nous-en.* Let's go. (VM) **2** *(imperative auxiliary)* let's *Allons parler français, allons faire affaire en français.* Let's speak French, let's do business in French. (Lv88) *Allons s'en aller.* Let's go home. (VM) *Allons aller au* CAMP *pour l'hiver pour camper.* Let's go to the camp to spend the winter. (LF) *Et allons dire que c'était pas trop une belle ouragan, ça.* And let's say that it wasn't a very nice hurricane. (TB) *Allons s'aviser sur cette affaire.* Let's get some sense of direction in this matter. (Lv88) <***Loc:*** AS, EV, JD, JE, LA, LF, SM, TB, VM, An94, Da84, Lv88, Wh69>

alloquer [aloke] *v.tr.* to allocate, apportion, portion out *Alloquer des droits d'huile.* To allocate mineral rights. (LA) <***Loc:*** LA, Da84>

allume-feu [alymfø] *n.m.* kindling, tinder <***Loc:*** VM, Da84>

allumer [alyme] **I** *v.tr.* **1** to light (a lamp, fire, cigarette, etc.) *Si vous allumez une cigarette, je vas vous dire* WELL, *vous pouvez rester mais la cigarette va en-dehors.* If you light a cigarette I will tell you, well you can stay, but the cigarette goes outside. (TB) *Ça a été allumer les réchauds dans l'église, pour la messe, préparer pour la messe.* They went to light the heaters in the church for mass, to prepare for mass. (TB) **2** to turn on (a stove, an electric light, etc.) *Va allumer les lumières. J'ai peur de rentrer dans le noir.* Go turn on the lights in the house. I'm afraid to go in there in the dark. (LA) **II s'allumer** *v.pron.* to ignite *Le bois est trop trempe pour s'allumer.* The wood is too wet to ignite. (LA) <***Loc:*** AV, EV, LA, SL, SM, TB, VM, Da84, Fa77, Hi02, Wh69>

allumette [alymɛt] *n.f.* match *Tu tirais une allumette.* You would strike a match. (SM) *C'est pas toi qu'as fait les allumettes!* You're not the one who invented matches! (insult for someone arrogant or not very intelligent) (La99) <***Loc:*** LA, SL, SM, TB, VM, An94, Da84, Fa77, Hi02, La99>

allure [alyr] *n.f.* **1** sense *Des fois eusse dit des affaires en anglais qu'a pas d'allure non plus, enfin, ça c'est ça, ça revient toujours au même.* Sometimes they say things in English that don't make sense either, well, that's the way it is, it always boils down to the same thing. (TB) *Ça fait pas d'allure.* It doesn't make any sense. (TB) *Ç'a pas d'allure faire ça.* That's not a good idea. It doesn't make any sense to do that. (Lv88) **2** appearance, look *Ça c'est une allure que t'as avec cette robe.* That's quite a look you've got with that dress. (TB) **3** *(pl.)* happenings, goings on *T'as vu les allures?* Have you seen what's going on? (SB) <***Loc:*** LF, SB, TB, Lv88>

almanach (**almanaque, armana, armanach, arménac**) [almɑ̃nak, armɑ̃na, armɛ̃na, armɛ̃nak, armɑ̃nak, armənak] *n.m./f.* **1** calendar *Le bougre d'assurance donnait des arménacs. Et là, on le disait, "Equand tu vas nous donner notre compteur de mois?" C'est ça que c'était, ça compte la journée du mois et tout.* The insurance man used to give calendars. And then we would say to him, "When are you going to give us our calendar?" That's what it was, it counts the day of the month and all. (LF) **2** almanac <***Loc:*** AV, LF, SM, TB, VM, Da84, La99, Lv88>

almanaque ♦see **almanach**

alochon [alɔʃɔ̃, alɔ̃ʃɔ̃] *n.m.* tooth of a gear-wheel, cog <***Loc:*** Di32, Lv88>

aloise ♦see **éloise**

alombre ♦see **ombre**

alors [alɔrs, alɔr] *adv.* so, thus, then **"Mais," elle dit, "je veux vous-autres me laisses parler un élan." Alors ils ont dit, "Tu peux dire tout ce que tu veux."* "But," she said," I want you to let me speak for a while." Then, they said, "You can say whatever you like." (An94) *Et là, la racine de cette herbe là c'était rouge et c'était bien bon à manger pour les canards et les oies. Alors eusse fouillait ça à peu près comme un des cochons après chercher pour du manger dans la boue.* And the root of that grass was red and it was very good to eat for ducks and geese. So they would dig it up about like a pig digging for food in the mud. (TB) *Ils m'a pas invité, alors j'ai pas été.* They didn't invite me so I wasn't there. (SM) **C'est compris, alors!* It's understood, then! (Da84) <***Loc:*** AC, AV, EV, JE, LA, LF, PQ, SB, SJ, SL, SM, TB, VM, An94, Da84, Lv88>

alouase [alwaz] *n.m.* aloe <***Loc:*** VM>

alouète ♦see **luette**

alouette [alwet] *n.f.* field lark <***Loc:*** SM, Da84>

alouèze ♦see **éloise**

alourdir [alurdir] *v.tr.* to make heavy, add weight to *Tout ce linge trempe a alourdi son sac.* All those wet clothes made his bag heavy. (LA) <***Loc:*** LA, Da84>

alphabet [alfabe, alfabɛt] *n.m./f.* alphabet *Je connais l'alphabet.* I know the alphabet. (JE) <***Loc:*** JE, LF, SL, Da84, Lv88>

altère (**artère**) [altær, artær] *n.f. (occ. m.)* **1** artery *Son pied saigne parce qu'il s'est coupé une altère.* His foot is bleeding because he cut an artery. (SB) **2** main highway, traffic artery <***Loc:*** AV, JE, LA, LF, SB, SJ, SL, SM, TB, Lv88, Da84>

altéré, -e [altere] *adj.* thirsty *Tu parles d'altéré, Jack! J'étais à la crève de soif!* Talk about thirsty, Jack! I was dying of thirst! (LA) <***Loc:*** LA, Da84>

altérer [altere] *v.tr.* to make thirsty, provoke thirst in *Plus je bois, plus je bois, plus le vin m'altère.* The more I drink, the more I drink, the more the wine makes me thirsty. (IB, ch: *Mes amis, je suis gris*) <***Loc:*** IB, Da84>

althéa [altea] *n.f.* althea, rose of Sharon <***Loc:*** Da84>

altière (**artière**) [altjær, artjær] *n.f.* garter <***Loc:*** EV, IB, SB, SM, Gr86, Lv88, Ph36>

altitude [altityd] *n.f.* altitude, height <***Loc:*** Da84>

aluminium [lymiəm, alyminɔ̃m] *n.m.* aluminum <***Loc:*** SM, TB, Da84>

alun [alœ̃, alɛ̃] *n.m./f.* alum <***Loc:*** AV, SJ, TB, Da84>

alvée ♦see **levée**

amacornage ♦see **macornage**

amacorner ♦see **macorner**

amalgame [ɑ̃malgɑ̃m] *n.f.* mixture <***Loc:*** SB>

amanché ♦see **emmanché**

amanchement ♦see **emmanchement**

amancher ♦see **emmancher**

amande [ɑ̃mɑ̃d] *n.* **1** almond **2** kernel at the center of a peach pit *Y a du monde qui mange l'amande au milieu d'un noyau de pêche.* There are people who eat the kernel at the center of a peach pit. (VM) <***Loc:*** VM>

amant, -e [ɑ̃mɑ̃, -ɑ̃t] *n.* **1** lover, sweetheart **2** *(m.)* boyfriend **3** *(f.)* girlfriend <***Loc:*** Da84>

amaricain ♦see **américain**

Amaricain ♦see **Américain**

amarinage [ɑ̃marinaʒ] *n.m.* marinating, seasoning <*Loc:* Da84>

amariné, -e [ɑ̃marine] *adj.* marinated, seasoned *Des grillades amarinées.* Marinated pieces of meat. (EV) *Mmm! J'aime ça. C'est bon des grillades amarinées!* Mmm, I like that. Marinated strips of meat are good! (VM) <*Loc:* EV, LA, VM, Da84, Gu00, Lv88>

amariner [ɑ̃marine] *v.tr.* **1** to marinate, season *Amariner de la viande de cochon.* To marinate pork. (SL) **2** to pickle, preserve in vinegar or salt *Amariner des BEANS.* To preserve beans. (JE) *Amariner des cocombres.* To pickle cucumbers. (LF) *Amariner du poisson.* To preserve fish in salt. (LF) **3** to preserve in fat *Amariner une saucisse.* To preserve a sausage [in the fat in which it was cooked]. (SJ) <*Loc:* AV, IB, JE, LF, SJ, SL, TB, VM, Da84, Lv88>

amarrage [ɑ̃maraʒ] *n.m.* **1** tying, lashing, knotting *Il pourra jamais défaire cet amarrage.* He will never be able to undo all of that knotting. (SL) **2** tie, rope **3** living together (without benefit of marriage) <*Loc:* SL, Da84, Lv88>

amarre [ɑ̃mar] *n.f.* rope, tie, string, length of cord or material used to tie s.t. ◊ **•amarre de soulier** shoelace <TB, Lv88> <*Loc:* EV, SJ, SL, TB, Da84, Lv88>

amarrer (emmarrer) [ɑ̃mare] **I** *v.tr.* **1** to tie, bind, fasten, attach *Il a amarré les cordes de son soulier.* He tied the laces of his shoe. (VM) *J'ai amarré la vache su la barrière.* I tied the cow to the fence. (SM) *Mais c'est pour amarrer cette affaire-là, faut tu l'attrapes.* But it's to attach that thing there, you have to get it. (AL) **2** to moor (a boat) *Quand on amarrait le bateau, l'eau était tout le temps pardessus.* When we moored the boat, the water was still over the top. (TB) **3** to harness, put a halter on *Il y a des vaches—la seule manière tu peux les adoucir— il faut tu les donnes à manger et les amarrer et les brosser jusqu'à que tu... ils vont venir à s'adoucir.* There are some cows—the only way you can break them—you have to feed them and harness them and brush them until you ... they'll come around and become docile. (VM) **4** to arrange, set up, negotiate the terms of (a match, race, etc.) *Ils ont amarré une course avec quelqu'un d'autre.* They set up a race with someone else. (EV) **II s'amarrer** *v.pron.* to become overcast (of the weather) *Le temps s'amarre.* The weather is becoming overcast. (Lv88) ◊ **•amarrer ses chiens avec des saucisses** to be abundantly wealthy so that one can afford excess and foolishness <La99> **•amarrer une date** to set a date <Hi02> **•s'amarrer le cœur** to be brave <La99> <*Loc:* AL, AV, EV, IB, JE, LA, LF, SL, SM, TB, VM, An94, Da84, Gu00, Hi02, La99, Lv88, Re31>

amarreur, -euse [ɑ̃marœr, -øz] *n.* person who binds or bundles (esp. sugar cane) <*Loc:* TB, Lv88>

amasser [ɑ̃mase] **I** *v.tr.* to amass, heap up, hoard (e.g. money) **II s'amasser** *v.pron.* **1** to amass or accumulate (for o.s.) *Il s'a amassé une fortune en vendant sa terre pour passer le nouveau chemin.* He amassed a fortune by selling his land to make the new road. (VM) **2** to huddle *Les bêtes s'amassent dans le coin de la savane quand il fait mauvais.* The cattle huddle in the corner of the pasture when the weather gets bad. (VM) <*Loc:* VM, Da84>

ambassadeur [ɑ̃basadœr] *n.m.* ambassador <*Loc:* Da84>

ambitieux, -euse [ɑ̃bisjø, -øz] *adj.* ambitious *Fais attention. Il est ambitieux.* Be careful. He's ambitious. (LA) <*Loc:* LA, Da84>

ambition [ɑ̃bisjɔ̃] *n.f.* ambition *Pauvre bête! Son mari a pas d'ambition. Il travaille pas.* Poor thing! Her husband doesn't have any ambition. He doesn't work. (VM) <*Loc:* LA, VM, Da84>

ambitionner [ɑ̃bisjɔ̃ne] **I** *v.tr.* to encourage **II** *v.intr.* to be ambitious, be eager *Tu ambitionnes de trop. Tu me rends nerveuse.* You are overly eager. You make me nervous. (LA) **III s'ambitionner** *v.pron.* **1** to become enthused or eager, take a keen interest *Il s'ambitionne à son ouvrage.* He's very interested in his work. (LF) **S'ambitionner de finir.* To be eager to finish (Da84) **2** to labor hard, make an effort *Il s'ambitionne bien mais il ne finit pas.* He strives hard but he does not finish. (JE) ◊ **•ambitionner dessus qqn** to abuse, take advantage of s.o. *Le bourgeois ambitionne dessus son travaillant.* The landowner is taking advantage of his laborer. (VM) <VM> **•ambitionner pour** to desire strongly, hanker after *Il ambitionne pour son RETIREMENT.* He strongly desires his retirement. (VM) <VM> <*Loc:* JE, LA, LF, SM, VM, Da84>

ambitionneux, -euse [ɑ̃bisjɔ̃nø, -øz] *adj.* ambitious *Elle s'a marié avec un jeune gens beaucoup ambitionneux.* She married a very ambitious young man. (SL) <*Loc:* SL>

ambulance [ɑ̃bylɑ̃s] *n.f.* ambulance <*Loc:* AC, LA, TB, VM, Da84>

âme [ɑ̃m] *n.f.* soul, spirit *Il est mort asteur, que le Bon Dieu ait pitié de son âme.* He's dead now, may God have mercy on his soul. (TB) <*Loc:* SJ, TB, Da84, Hi02>

amédaille, amédale ♦see **amygdale**

amen [ɑ̃mɛ̃n] *interj.* [*eccl.*] amen <*Loc:* Da84>

amenant ♦see **avenant**

amendable [ɑ̃mɑ̃dab(l)] *adj.* amendable <*Loc:* Da84>

amendement [ɑ̃mɑ̃dmɑ̃, ɑ̃mɑ̃nmɑ̃] *n.m.* amendment <*Loc:* Da84>

amender [ɑ̃mɑ̃de] *v.tr.* to amend *Amender la constitution.* To amend the constitution. (VM) <*Loc:* VM, Da84>

amener [ɑ̃mne] **I** *v.tr.* **1** to bring *J'ai amené de la viande.* I brought some meat. (TB) *T'as amené tes en-tout-cas?* Did you bring your emergency provisions? (VM) *Je vas chercher les outils et les amener ici.* I'm going to get the tools and bring them here. (LF) **Ça qui m'a amené à venir rester ici à Basile, c'était la musique.* What brought me to come and live here in Basile was music. (EV, VM, An84)

Quand ça arrivait chez eux-autres, il faulait que ça se lave avec l'alcohol pour pas amener la maladie. When they got home, they had to wash with alcohol so as to not bring in the disease. (TB) **2** to take, transport (s.o. or s.t. somewhere) *On les amenait tout partout parce qu'eusse avait pas de char.* We took them everywhere because they didn't have a car. (TB) *Ce bougre-là était pas balancé. Ils ont eu pour l'amener à Pineville.* That fellow was mentally unstable. They had to take him to Pineville [State Mental Hospital]. (LA) **3** to lead (an animal) **Amener un cheval.* To lead a horse. (Da84) **4** to lead (a life) **Amener une bonne vie.* To lead a good life. (Da84) **II s'amener** *v.pron.* **1** to take along, bring along (for o.s.) *Ça s'amenait du pain aussi mais si le pain venait à moisir,* WELL, *eux-autres avait ces gâteaux-là à manger.* They brought along bread too, but if the bread got moldy, well, they had those cakes to eat. (TB) **2** to approach, draw near *Ça avait été averti par le* WEATHER BUREAU *de la ville qu'il y avait du mauvais temps qui s'amenait.* They had been warned by the city weather bureau that there was bad weather approaching. (LF) **3** to arrive, show up *Le vieux s'amenait sur la plaille.* The old man arrived on the beach. (LF) **4** to bring o.s. (to do s.t.) ◊ **•amener du tracas** to bring trouble, cause trouble, make trouble <Da84> **•amener qqn au bercail** to make s.o. obey, make s.o. give in <AV, La99> **•amener (un enfant) au monde** to bring (a child) into the world *Alle était morte avant qu'alle soye amenée au monde.* She was dead before she was brought into the world. (LF) <LF, Da84> **•amener un tapage {du train}** to carry on a racket, make noise **Quand elle s'a réveillée, il y avait un moqueur qu'était après amener du train côté de sa fenêtre.* When she awoke, there was a mockingbird that was making a racket next to her window. (LA, An94) <LA, An94, Da84> **•est-ce que t'amènes la pluie?** expression used to greet a visitor one hasn't seen for a long time <La99> <***Loc:*** AC, AV, EV, LA, LF, SL, SM, TB, VM, An84, An94, Da84, Hi02, La99, Lv88, Ph36>

amenotter [ɑ̃mɔnote, ɑ̃mɛ̃note] *v.tr.* to handcuff *La loi l'a amenotté.* The police arrested him. (Lv88) ◊ **•être amenotté** to have one's hands tied, be restricted *La police de l'État est amenotée asteur, a peut pas rien faire.* The State Police has its hands tied right now, they can't do anything. (Lv88) <Lv88> <***Loc:*** JE, LF, SM, VM, Lv88>

amer, amère [ɑ̃mær] *adj.* bitter *Les chalottes, [...] tu peux pas user plein de ça pour cuire parce que c'est trop amer.* Shallots, you can't use too many of them because they're too bitter. (LF) ◊ **•amer comme du fiel** very bitter <EV, La99> <***Loc:*** EV, LF, SM, TB, VM, Da84, La99, Re31, Wh83>

américain[1]**, -e** (**amaricain, -e**) [ɑ̃merikɛ̃, ɑ̃marikɛ̃, -ɛ̃n] *adj.* **1** American *Mais cher, c'est l'argent, eux-autres voulait l'argent américain.* But dear, it's the money, they wanted American money. (TB) **2** English, pertaining to the English language *Non,* MICROWAVE *en français aussi. Ça je dis, c'est tout des mots américains qu'on a.* No, [we say] microwave in French too. That's what I'm saying, we have a lot of English words [in our French]. (LF) **3** Anglophone, English-speaking *Mon père disait que les nègres créoles travaillaient mieux que les nègres amaricains.* My father used to say that creole blacks worked better than Anglo blacks. (VM) <***Loc:*** IB, LA, LF, TB, VM, An84, Da84, Gu00, Hi02, Wh83>

américain[2] [ɑ̃merikɛ̃, merikɛ̃] *n.m.* English, the English language *Quand nous-autres a eu l'école icite... le Grand Bayou là... nos mères et nos pères... maîtresses d'école voulaient qu'on parle l'américain.* When we had school here [at] Grand Bayou, our mothers and fathers, schoolteachers wanted us to speak American [i.e. English]. (PQ) <***Loc:*** PQ, Hi02>

Américain[3]**, -e** (**Amaricain, -e, Méricain, -e**) [ɑ̃merikɛ̃, ɑ̃marikɛ̃, merikɛ̃, -ɛ̃n] *n.* **1** American *Les soldats anglais se battaient avec les Américains dans la deuxième guerre.* English soldiers fought with the Americans in the Second World War. (LA) **2** Anglo, English speaker who is not of French descent *C'est plutôt des Américains qui restent dans le nord de la Louisiane.* It's mostly English-speakers who live in the north of Louisiana. (SM) *Un tas d'Américains ont venu autour de Crowley et, avec quelques Cadiens, ont fait une grosse affaire avec le riz.* A lot of Anglos settled around Crowley and, with some Cajuns, they did very well in the rice business. (VM) <***Loc:*** AV, LA, LF, PQ, SM, TB, VM, Da84, Gu00, Hi02, Lv88>

américaniser [ɑ̃merikɑ̃nize] **I** *v.tr.* to Americanize *Mon gendre est après essayer d'américaniser ma fille.* My son-in-law is trying to Americanize my daughter. (LA) **II s'américaniser** *v.pron.* to become Americanized *Les Cadiens de Lafayette sont après s'américaniser.* The Cajuns of Lafayette are becoming Americanized. (LA) <***Loc:*** LA, Da84>

Amérique [ɑ̃merik] *n.f.* America <***Loc:*** AC, EV, SM, TB, Hi02, Da84>

ameublir [ɑ̃møblir] *v.tr.* to loosen, make friable, make mellow, soften (soil) *Passe le rateau pour ameublir la terre avant de planter tes fèves plates.* Rake to loosen the soil before planting your butter beans. (VM) <***Loc:*** VM, Da84>

ami, -e [ɑ̃mi] *n.* friend **Bon ami.* Good friend. (Da84) *Chers amis.* Dear friends. (ThCa: *Messieurs, mesdames*) ◊ **•être bon ami** to be good friends *On est bon ami avec Madame Wilma.* We are good friends with Madame Wilma. (TB) <TB> **•faire ami** ***a*** to make friends *J'ai fait ami avec l'étranger.* I made friends with the stranger. (LA) ***b*** to be reconciled, settle differences *J'aime Paul. On a fait ami encore.* I love Paul. We've reconciled. (SM) <LA, SM> **•refaire ami** to be reconciled *On était fâché mais on a refait ami.* We were on the outs but we've reconciled. (LA) <LA> <***Loc:*** AC, AV, EV, IB, JD, JE, LA, LF, SL, SM, TB, VM, An94, Da84, Gu00, Lv88, ThCa, Wh83>

amiable [ɑ̃mjab(l)] *adj.* friendly, amiable *On va faire ça à* *l'amiable.* We'll do that on a friendly basis. (VM) <***Loc:*** VM, Da84>

amicable [ãmikab(l)] *adj.* friendly, amicable, kind *Des voisins beaucoup amicables.* Very nice neighbors. (LA) <***Loc:*** LA, SB, Lv88>

amicablement [ãmikabləmã, ãmikabmã] *adv.* in a friendly way, amicably *On vit amicablement avec les voisins.* We live amicably with our neighbors. (EV) <***Loc:*** AV, EV, IB, SB, SJ, SL, SM, Da84, Di32, Lv88, Re31>

amidon [ãmidɔ̃] *n.m.* starch <***Loc:*** Da84>

amidonnage [ãmidɔ̃naʒ] *n.m.* starching <***Loc:*** Da84>

amidonner [ãmidɔ̃ne] *v.tr.* to starch *J'aime pas ça quand on amidonne mes chemises.* I don't like it when my shirts are starched. (SM) <***Loc:*** EV, LA, SM, Da84>

amijoler ♦see **emmioler**

amiliée ♦see **amille**

amille (amiliée) [ãmij, ãmilje] *n.f.* female friend <***Loc:*** VM>

amincir [ãmɛ̃sir] *v.tr.* **1** to slim down, thin, thin out **Amincir une planche.* To thin out a board. (Da84) **2** to make (one) appear thinner *Cette robe t'amincit.* That dress makes you look thinner. (VM) <***Loc:*** VM, Da84>

amincissement [ãmɛ̃sismã] *n.m.* thinning, slimming <***Loc:*** Da84>

amioler ♦see **emmioler**

amioleur ♦see **emmioleur**

amise [ãmiz] *n.f.* female friend *Mon amise qu'est canadien, elle montre le français à les enfants au Bayou Bœuf.* My friend who is Canadian, she teaches French to children in Bayou Bœuf. (LF) <***Loc:*** EV, IB, LF, SB, SM, VM, Lv88, Ph36>

amitié [ãmitje, ãmitʃe] *n.f.* **1** friendship, affection **2** love *Notre amitié était si fort, si doux et pur comme de l'or. Ça qui me donne autant chagrin, je vas jamais te voir encore.* Our love was so strong, so sweet and as pure as gold. What makes me so sad is that I'm never going to see you again. (ch: *La valse d'amitié*) <***Loc:*** Da84, Fa77, Gr86, Lv88>

ammonia (armoniac) [ãmɔ̃nja, ãmɔ̃njak] *n.f.* ammonia <***Loc:*** LA, SM, Da84, Lv88>

ammunition [ãmynisjɔ̃, ãmɔ̃nisjɔ̃] *n.f.* ammunition <***Loc:*** AV, IB, SJ, SL, VM, Da84, Lv88>

amoindrir [ãmwɛ̃drir] **I** *v.tr.* to diminish, decrease, lessen *Il était après essayer d'amoindrir sa honte.* He was trying to lessen her shame. (LA) **II s'amoindrir** *v.pron.* to decrease, diminish *Son tracas s'amoindrissait pas.* His troubles were not diminishing. (LA) <***Loc:*** LA, Da84>

amollesir ♦see **amollir**

amollir (amollesir, amolzir) [ãmolir, ãmolzir] **I** *v.tr.* to soften *Il faut que t'amollis le fer avant de le travailler.* You have to soften iron before working it. (LA) **II s'amollir** *v.pron.* **1** to soften, weaken, relent *Quand il a vu son garçon arriver, son cœur s'a amolli.* When he saw his son arrive, his heart softened. (LA) **2** to get better, become milder (of the weather) *Le temps s'amolzit.* The weather is getting better. (Lv88) <***Loc:*** AV, LA, SL, SM, Da84, Lv88, Re31>

amolzir ♦see **amollir**

amortie [ãmorti] *n.f.* part of a river with no current <***Loc:*** Lv88>

amortir [ãmɔrtir] *v.tr.* **1** to amortize (a debt) **2** to deaden (pain) *Le docteur lui a donné des médecines pour amortir son mal.* The doctor gave him some medicine to deaden the pain. (VM) **3** to break (a fall) *Une chance qu'il y avait ce gros morceau caltron pour amortir le coup quand j'ai tombé de mon grenier!* Luckily, there was that big piece of cardboard to break my fall when I fell from the attic! (VM) **II s'amortir** *v.pron.* to weaken, lose strength *L'ouragan est après s'amortir.* The hurricane is weakening. (VM) <***Loc:*** VM, Da84>

amour [ãmur] *n.m./f.* love, affection ◊ **•amour-de-maman** hand-sewn wedding outfit made for one's daughter <Lv88> **•amour-propre** self-love <Da84> **•en amour** in love *Et cette femme là, alle aimait mon oncle. Alle avait tombé en amour.* And that woman, she loved my uncle. She had fallen in love. (TB) <AV, JE, LF, SB, SM, TB, Gr86, Lv88, Re31> **•faire des amours à** to make love to <Da84> **•faire l'amour (à)** ***a*** to court, woo *J'ai rencontré une jolie brune, j'ai commencé à lui faire l'amour.* I met a pretty brunette, I started to court her. (Lv88) ***b*** to make love (to), have sex (with) **Ils ont fait l'amour un bout de temps.* They made love for a while. (EV, An94) *Il est trop âgé pour faire l'amour.* He is too old to make love. (EV) <EV, SB, An94, Hi02, Lv88> **•pour l'amour de Dieu / pour l'amour du Bon Dieu** for the love of God, for God's sake (expression of imploring, exasperation, sometimes astonishment) *J'ai eu assez peur quand on a été dans ce bateau-là, pour l'amour de Dieu!* I got so scared when we got into that boat, for the love of God! (TB) <LA, TB, La99> <***Loc:*** AC, AV, EV, IB, JE, LA, SB, SM, TB, VM, An94, Da84, Gr86, Hi02, La99, Lv88, Re31>

amouraché, -e [ãmuraʃe] *adj.* in love *Il est amouraché d'elle.* He is in love with her. (AV) <***Loc:*** AV>

amouracher (s') [ãmuraʃe] *v.pron.* **1** to become infatuated, fall madly in love *Il s'a amouraché de mémère. Et il aurait voulu marier mémère.* He fell in love with Grandmother. And he wanted to marry Grandmother. (TB) **2** to have an affair *Et là son mari, lui il a un autre job, peut-être lui il travaille la nuit. Ça fait ça se voit pas plein. Ça fait là ça s'amourache. Et puis, le tracas.* And then her husband, he has another job, maybe he works at night. So they don't see each other much. So they have little love affairs. And then, trouble. (TB) <***Loc:*** AV, TB, Da84>

amoureux, -euse[1] [ãmurø, -øz] *adj.* in love, enamored **Elle a vu qu'elle était amoureuse.* She saw that she was in love. (EV, An94) ◊ **•amoureux comme une puce** ***a*** womanizing ***b*** deeply in love <EV, La99> **•amoureux comme un paon**

womanizing, philandering <AC, La99> <***Loc:*** AC, EV, An94, Da84, La99>

amoureux, -euse[2] [ɑ̃murø, -øz] *n.* lover, sweetheart <***Loc:*** Da84>

ampas [ɑ̃pa] *n.m./f.pl.* lampas (inflammation of a horse's palate) <***Loc:*** SL, SM, Lv88>

ampoule (**z-ampoule**) [ɑ̃pul, zɑ̃pul] *n.f.* blister <***Loc:*** AV, LF, SB, Da84>

ampoulé, -e [ɑ̃pule] *adj.* blistered *Ma main est toute ampoulée, j'ai trop pioché.* My hand is all blistered, I dug too much. (Lv88) <***Loc:*** Da84, Lv88>

ampouler [ɑ̃pule] **I** *v.tr.* to blister *Tout cet ouvrage à la pelle a ampoulé mes mains.* All that work with a shovel has blistered my hands. (LA) *Là où son soulier frottait ça a ampoulé son pied.* Where his shoe rubbed, it caused a blister on his foot. (VM) **II s'ampouler** *v.pron.* to get blistered *J'ai pas l'habitude de travailler à la pelle comme ça, et je m'ai bien ampoulé.* I'm not used to working with a shovel like that, and I got all blistered. (LA) ◊ **•faire ampouler** to cause to blister *Les brûlures font ampouler la peau.* Burns make the skin blister. (SL) <SL> <***Loc:*** LA, SL, VM, Da84>

amputation [ɑ̃pytasjɔ̃] *n.f.* amputation <***Loc:*** Da84>

amputer [ɑ̃pyte] *v.tr.* to amputate, cut off *Ils ont eu pour lui amputer un pied à cause de la maladie du sucre.* They had to amputate one of his feet because of his diabetes. (LA) <***Loc:*** LA, Da84>

amusant, -e [ɑ̃mɥzɑ̃, -ɑ̃t] *adj.* **1** fun *C'est presqu'on peut pas appeler ça un job, parce que c'est tellement amusant pêcher des écrevisses, c'est presqu'un plaisir.* It's almost like we can't call it a job, because it is so much fun to catch crawfish, that it's almost a pleasure. (SM) **2** funny *Je l'ai pas trouvé amusant du tout.* I didn't find him funny at all. (LA) <***Loc:*** LA, SM, Da84>

amusement [ɑ̃myzmɑ̃] *n.m.* amusement, entertainment, fun *Il y a pas d'amusement pour le jeune monde par icitte.* There's no entertainment for young people around here. (Lv88) <***Loc:*** EV, LA, SB, SM, Da84, Lv88>

amuser [ɑ̃myze] **I** *v.tr.* to amuse, entertain **Je calcule, je suis autant que l'homme qu'est après travailler à la shove, ou le mécanicien, ou n'importe quel autre métier, parce que je fais mon devoir chez moi, et la musique amuse tout le monde.* I figure, I'm as good as the man who is working with a shovel, or the mechanic or any other job, because I do my work at home, and music entertains everyone. (VM, An84) **II s'amuser** *v.pron.* to have fun, have a good time, enjoy or amuse o.s. or each other **Amuse-toi bien.* Have a good time. (Da84) *On va aller dans le bois, et on va s'amuser.* We're going to go into the woods and we're going to have some fun. (LA) *Je m'ai bien amusé avec ça.* I had great fun with that. (EV) <***Loc:*** AC, EV, LA, VM, An84, Da84, Hi02, St95>

amusette [ɑ̃myzɛt] *n.f.* amusement, plaything *Jeunes filles de la campagne, mariez-vous-autres jamais. Une fille, c'est une amusette...* Young girls of the countryside, never marry. A girl is a plaything . . . (AC, ch: *Jeunes filles de la campagne*) <***Loc:*** AC>

amydaille ♦see **amygdale**

amygdale (**amédaille, amédale, amydaille**) [ɑ̃medaj, ɑ̃medal, ɑ̃midal, ɑ̃midaj] *n.f.* tonsil *J'ai fait couper mes amédailles.* I had my tonsils removed. (JE) <***Loc:*** AL, AV, EV, IB, JE, SB, SL, SM, TB, Da84, Hi02, Lv88>

an [ɑ̃] *n.m.* year **Tous les dix ans.* Every ten years. (Da84) **Dix fois par an.* Ten times a year. (Da84) *Mon grand-père a vi jusqu'à l'âge de cent trois ans.* My grandfather lived to the age of 103. (LF) ◊ **•avoir dix {vingt, etc.} ans** to be ten (twenty, etc.) years old *Quand j'avais 19 ans, on s'a marié.* When I was 19, we got married. (LF) <AC, EV, IB, JE, LF, SM, TB, VM, An84, Lv88> **•faire dix {vingt, etc.} ans** to turn ten (twenty, etc.) years old *Alle va faire 87 ans dans janvier.* She'll turn 87 years old in January. (LF) <LF> <***Loc:*** AC, AV, EV, IB, IV, JD, JE, LA, LF, PQ, SB, SL, SM, TB, VM, An84, Da84, Gu00, Hi02, Lv88, Re31, Wh83>

analyser [ɑ̃nalize] *v.tr.* to analyze *Le docteur a analysé les résultats de mon test.* The docteur analyzed the results of my test. (VM) <***Loc:*** VM, Da84>

ananas (**z-ananas**) [ɑ̃nɑ̃na, zɑ̃nɑ̃na] *n.m.* pineapple <***Loc:*** LA, SB, VM, Da84, Fa77>

anatomie [ɑ̃natɔ̃mi] *n.f.* anatomy <***Loc:*** Da84>

ancêtre [ɑ̃sɛt(r)] *n.m.* ancestor, forefather, forebear *Tu connais quoi-ce c'est des ancêtres, nègre? C'est ton vieux monde de longtemps passé.* Do you know what ancestors are, man? They are your people from long ago. (VM) <***Loc:*** VM, Da84, Hi02, Lv88>

ancien, -ienne [ɑ̃sjɛ̃, -ɛ̃n] *adj.* old, ancient *Sa maison est ancienne. Elle a plus que cent ans.* Her house is ancient. It is more than 100 years old. (VM) <***Loc:*** VM, Da84>

anciennement [ɑ̃sijɛ̃mɑ̃, ɑ̃sjɛ̃nmɑ̃] *adv.* formerly, previously, in olden times *Anciennement, il y avait pas de réfrigérateurs.* Formerly, there were no refrigerators. (SL) <***Loc:*** SL, Da84>

andain (**ondain**) [ɑ̃dɛ̃] *n.m.* mowed hay left lying in rows before it is gathered <***Loc:*** TB>

andouille [ɑ̃duj] *n.f.* **1** andouille (type of pork sausage made of the large intestine of a hog) **2** tripe sausage, chitterling *Il y avait des andouilles, mais il y avait pas de viande dedans. C'était des tripes dans la tripe.* There was tripe sausage, but there wasn't any meat in it. It was tripes in the tripe. (EV) **3** foolish person *Fais pas ça, espèce d'andouille.* Don't do that, you fool. (LA) <***Loc:*** AV, EV, LA, SB, SM, TB, VM, Da84, Hi02, Lv88>

âne [ɑ̃n] *n.* **1** *(m.)* ass, jackass, donkey **2** *(f.)* jenny, she-ass ◊ **•faire l'âne pour avoir l'avoine {le foin}** to act foolish in order to reap profit <AV, SB, La99> <***Loc:*** AV, SB, Da84, La99>

ange [ɑ̃ʒ] *n.m.* angel ◊ **•ange gardien** guardian angel <Da84> <***Loc:*** SL, Da84, Hi02>

angélus [ɑ̃ʒelys] *n.m.* [*eccl.*] angelus <***Loc:*** Da84>

angine (**anjouine**) [ɑ̃ʒin, ɔ̃ʒwin] *n.f.* angina *On a perdu un petit frère à six ans avec une angine.* We lost a little brother who was six, he died of an angina. (SM) <***Loc:*** SM, VM, Da84>

anglais[1], **-e** [ɑ̃gle, ɑ̃glɛz] *adj.* English *Les soldats anglais se battaient avec les Américains dans la deuxième guerre.* English soldiers fought with the Americans in the Second World War. (LA) <***Loc:*** LA, VM, Da84, Hi02>

anglais[2] (**n-anglais**) [ɑ̃gle, nɑ̃gle, lɑ̃gle] *n.m.* English, the English language *Quand j'étais à l'école il a faulu que j'apprends à parler le n-anglais.* When I was at school I had to learn to speak English. (LF) **Jean Sot avait été à l'école pour apprendre l'anglais.* Jean Sot had gone to school to learn English. (EV, An94) <***Loc:*** AC, AV, EV, LA, LF, PQ, SM, TB, An94, Hi02, Lv88>

Anglais[3], **-e** [ɑ̃gle, ɑ̃glɛz, nɑ̃gle] *n.* **1** English speaker, Anglophone **Mon père était 'anglais': sa famille venait de l'Etat de Maine.* My father was an anglophone; his family came from the state of Maine. (Gr86) *Malgré les 'Anglais' (je rappelle que nous appelons ainsi les Américains, nos compatriotes), toujours plus nombreux.* In spite of the 'English' (I remember that that's what we called the Americans, our countrymen), always more numerous. (SM) **2** English person <***Loc:*** PQ, SM, Da84, Gr86, Hi02, Lv88>

angle [ɑ̃ŋ, ɑ̃g(l)] *n.m.* angle <***Loc:*** Da84>

Angleterre [ɑ̃glətær] *n.f.* England <***Loc:*** Da84>

anguille [ɑ̃gij, lɑ̃gij] *n.m./f.* eel <***Loc:*** AL, SL, SM, VM, Da84, Gu00>

angulaire [ɑ̃gylær] *adj.* angular *Il cherche une pierre angulaire pour le coin.* He's looking for an angular stone for the corner. (LA) <***Loc:*** LA, Da84>

anhonter ♦see **éhonter**

aniée ♦see **araignée**

animal (**animau**) [ɑ̃nimal, ɑ̃nimo] *n.m./f.* **1** domestic animal *Une bride c'est pour un animau que tu vas monter dessus.* A bridle is for an animal that you are going to ride. (LA) **Il y avait une grosse animal qu'était crevée.* There was a large animal that was dead. (LA, An94) *Essayer d'observer la différence que il y a parmi les animals et parmi le monde.* Try to observe the difference between animals and people. (EV) **2** cow, bovine *Habitudement c'était la panse de bête, d'animau.* Usually it [la panse] referred to the stomach of a bovine (LF) **3** *(pl.)* farm animals, livestock (usu. cattle) *Les animaux ont froid dans l'hiver.* The livestock is cold in the winter. (SM) **4** brute, brutish person *Arrête de maltraiter ta femme, animal!* Stop mistreating your wife, you brute! (VM) <***Loc:*** AC, AV, EV, IB, LA, LF, SB, SJ, SL, SM, TB, VM, An94, Da84, Lv88>

animau ♦see **animal**

animé, -e [ɑ̃nime] *adj.* **1** lively, spry, animated, spirited, zestful *Les enfants sont trop animés à soir. Ils vont jamais s'endormir.* The children are too lively tonight. They'll never get to sleep. (VM) **2** enamored or taken (with), very fond (of) *Elle est animée de lui.* She likes him very much. (JE) <***Loc:*** JE, VM, Da84, Hi02>

animer [ɑ̃nime] **I** *v.tr.* to animate, excite, enliven, arouse *La boisson l'anime.* Alcohol makes him lively. (VM) **II s'animer** *v.pron.* to become lively, be excited *Elle boit et s'anime, et quand elle revient le soir, elle, elle est pas contente.* She drinks and she becomes lively, and when she returns home at night, she's not happy. (EV, ch: *Je me suis marié*) <***Loc:*** EV, VM, Da84>

anis [ɑ̃ni] *n.m.* anise ◊ **•anis sauvage** Yankee weed <SB> **•anis marron** cypress weed, dog fennel <Ho90> <***Loc:*** SB, Da84, Ho90>

anisette [ɑ̃nizɛt] *n.f.* anisette <***Loc:*** SM, VM, Da84>

anjouine ♦see **angine**

anneau [ɑ̃no] *n.m.* **1** ring **2** ring placed in the nose of a pig to prevent it from digging *Je t'ai demandé en grâce pour mettre des anneaux. Tu les as pas mis. Et j'ai dit ils sont après fouiller mon clos.* I asked you nicely to put rings [in your pigs' snouts]. You didn't put them in. And I said they are digging up my field. (SL) **3** ring, part of rigging on halter **4** link ◊ **•anneau de chaîne** chain link <Da84> <***Loc:*** EV, SL, VM, An84, Da84, Fa77>

année [ɑ̃ne] *n.f.* year **D'une année à l'autre.* From one year to the other. (Da84) **Il y a des années de ça.* It's been years since then. (Da84) **Des années passées.* Years ago. (Da84) **Les années passées.* Years gone by. (Da84) *Et ça pour des années et des années c'est comme si ça voulait pas te montrer le français.* And then for years and years it seemed as if they didn't want to teach you French. (JD) **Ça fait, la première année, ils ont planté des patates, juste des patates.* So the first year they planted potatoes, just potatoes. (SM, An94) ◊ **•l'année passée** last year <Da84> **•l'année prochaine / l'année qui vient** next year <Da84> **•cette année** this year <JE, TB, Da84> **•des années** many years ago *J'ai chassé déjà, mais des années j'ai arrêté chasser.* I've already hunted, but many years ago I stopped hunting. (SL) <SL> <***Loc:*** AC, EV, JD, JE, LA, LF, SL, SM, TB, VM, An94, Da84, Hi02, Lv88>

annexer [ɑ̃nɛkse] *v.tr.* to annex *Ils vont annexer mon voisinage dans le village.* They're going to annex my neighborhood into the town. (VM) <***Loc:*** VM, Da84>

anniversaire [ɑ̃niværsær] *n.m.* anniversary <***Loc:*** Da84, Fa77, Hi02>

annonce [ɑ̃nɔ̃s] *n.f.* announcement, published announcement <***Loc:*** Da84>

annoncement [ɑ̃nɔ̃smɑ̃] *n.m.* announcement <***Loc:*** EV, An94, Da84, Gr86, Hi02>

annoncer [ɑ̃nɔ̃se] **I** *v.tr.* to announce **Annonce au monde, si ça voit cette vache-là, c'est pour moi.* Announce to the people, if they see that cow, it's mine. (EV, An94) **II s'annoncer** *v.pron.* to announce one's candidacy (in a political race) **Y a un p'tit jeune homme qui s'a annoncé contre toi dans la gazette.* There's a young man who said he would run against you in the newspaper. (Gr86) <***Loc:*** AC, EV, SL, VM, An94, Da84, Gr86, Hi02>

annonceur[1] [ɑ̃nɔ̃sœr] *n.m.* announcer <***Loc:*** Da84>

annonceur[2] [ɑ̃nɔ̃sœr] *n.m.* plover <***Loc:*** EV, LA, Ph36>

annuel, -lle [ɑ̃nɥɛl] *adj.* annual, yearly *Un paiement annuel.* An annual payment. (EV) <***Loc:*** EV, Da84>

annulement [ɑ̃nylmɑ̃] *n.m.* **1** annulment (of a marriage) **2** repeal (of a law) <***Loc:*** Da84>

annuler [ɑ̃nyle] *v.tr.* **1** to annul *Il a intercédé auprès de l'évêque pour annuler le mariage.* He pleaded with the bishop to annul the marriage. (LA) **2** to cancel, void **Ça fait, un a gagné une bataille de chiens. L'autre a gagné une bataille de gaïmes. Ils ont resté annulés, mais ça s'aimait pas.* So one won a dog fight. The other won a cockfight. They cancelled each other, but they didn't like each other. (LA, An94) <***Loc:*** LA, An94, Da84>

anreingné ♦see **araignée**

anse [ɑ̃s] *n.m./f.* **1** bail, semicircular handle (of a cooking pot, lantern, etc.) **À force la chaudière était grande, les deux hommes qu'étaient après mettre les anses chaque bord s'entendaient pas, leurs coups de marteau sur la chaudière.* The pot was so big, the two men who were attaching the handles on each side couldn't hear each other, their hammer blows on the pot. (EV, An94) **2** hook used to hang a cooking pot by its handles over the fire *Il y avait deux anses pour sortir la chaudière du feu.* There were two hooks to take the pot out of the fire. (LA) **3** curve, turn (in a road) *Y a une anse dans le chemin un mille d'ici.* There's a turn in the road one mile from here. (SM) **4** bay, arm of a prairie extending into a woods, area of land partially enclosed by woodland and opening onto a prairie *Moi, je connais on peut avoir un temps, c'est là-bas à l'Anse aux Pailles.* I know we can have a time, there in Straw Cove. (EV, ch: *L'Anse aux pailles*) **5** cove, small inlet *Ils s'ont mis à l'abri dans la petite anse l'autre bord de la pointe.* They sought shelter in the little cove on the other side of the point. (VM) <***Loc:*** AC, EV, IB, LA, SL, SM, TB, VM, An94, Da84, Gr86, Gu00, Hi02, Lv88>

anserine liane [ɑ̃sərin ljɑ̃n] *n.f.* eardrop vine <***Loc:*** Ho90>

ansieux ♦see **anxieux**

anthrasse ♦see **anthrax**

anthrax (anthrasse) [ɑ̃traks, ɑ̃tras, ɑ̃tɔrs] *n.f. (occ. m.)* **1** anthrax **2** carbuncle *J'ai une anthrasse sur mon bras.* I have a carbuncle on my arm. (SL) <***Loc:*** AV, IB, SB, SJ, SL, VM, Da84>

anticipation [ɑ̃tisipasjɔ̃] *n.f.* anticipation <***Loc:*** Da84>

anticiper [ɑ̃tisipe] *v.tr.* to anticipate, expect *Il aurait pas pu anticiper la colère de son voisin.* He could not have anticipated the anger of his neighbor. (LA) <***Loc:*** LA, Da84>

antiquité [ɑ̃tikite] *n.f.* old objet of little value *Cette chaise est plus bonne. Va la mettre avec les antiquités dans le grenier.* This chair is no longer any good. Go put it with the old furniture in the attic. (SL) <***Loc:*** SL>

antiseptique[1] [ɑ̃tisɛptik, ɑ̃tizɛpti] *adj.* antiseptic *Les couteaux étaient pas du tout antiseptiques.* The knives were not at all antiseptic. (LA) <***Loc:*** LA, Da84>

antiseptique[2] [ɑ̃tisɛptik, ɑ̃tizɛpti] *n.f.* antiseptic *De l'antiseptique c'est bon pour ça.* Antiseptic is good for that. (TB) <***Loc:*** TB, Da84>

anvalage ♦see **envalage**

anvalement ♦see **envalement**

anvaler ♦see **envaler**

anxiété [ɑ̃ksjete] *n.f.* anxiety, uneasiness <***Loc:*** Da84>

anxieux, -ieuse (ansieux, -ieuse) [ɑ̃ksjø, -øz, ɑ̃sjø, -øz] *adj.* **1** anxious, uneasy, worried *Son mari était pas encore revenu de la chasse et elle commençait d'être un peu anxieuse de le voir arriver.* Her husband was not yet back from hunting and she was beginning to be anxious to see him return. (LA) **2** eager, anxious **Et le père était anxieux de voir les progrès que son chien aurait eu fait.* And the father was anxious to see the progress that his dog would have made. (LA, An94) <***Loc:*** LA, SM, TB, An94, Da84, Lv88>

août [au] *n.m.* August <***Loc:*** AC, EV, IB, JE, LA, LF, PQ, SL, SM, TB, Da84, Hi02, Lv88, Ph36>

apairer [apere] *v.tr.* to couple, join in a pair *Ces chevals-là sont bien apairés.* Those horses are well paired. (Lv88) <***Loc:*** Lv88>

apaisement [apɛzmɑ̃] *n.m.* **1** appeasement, pacifying **2** quieting <***Loc:*** Da84>

apaiser [apeze] **I** *v.tr.* **1** to appease *Tenez, ma mère, prenez son enfant. Présentez-lui pour l'apaiser.* Here, my mother, take his child. Present it to him to appease him. (PQ, ch: *Sainte Catherine*) **2** to quiet, calm *Il a brûlé des rameaux pour apaiser le mauvais temps.* He burned some palms to calm the bad weather. (VM) **3** to alleviate (suffering) *Le docteur lui a donné des médecines pour apaiser son mal.* The doctor gave him some medicine to alleviate his suffering. (VM) **II s'apaiser** *v.pron.* to calm down *Le mauvais temps est après s'apaiser.* The bad weather is calming down. (VM) <***Loc:*** PQ, VM, Da84>

aparcevance ♦see **apercevance**

aparçoir ♦see **apercevoir**

apénaire [apɛ̃nær] *n.f.* sweet potato leaf *Dans le vieux temps on faisait cuire les apénaires.* In the old days we cooked sweet potato leaves. (TB) <***Loc:*** TB>

apercevable [apærsəvab(l)] *adj.* noticeable, perceptible, perceivable *Le trou dans sa chemise était proche pas apercevable.* The hole in his shirt was hardly noticeable. (LA) <***Loc:*** LA, Da84>

apercevance (**aparcevance**) [apærsəvɑ̃s] *n.f.* **1** view, sight, perception **À la première aparcevance, il' avont couri tout leur vie.* At first sight, they had run all their lives. (Gu82) **2** sign, indication *Regarde woir si tu wois quelqu'apercevance pour on peut se trouver de l'ouvrage.* Look and see if you see any indication that we can find work. (VM) **3** foreboding, misgiving, premonition *Il avait une apercevance que quelque chose va arriver.* He had a premonition that something was going to happen. (Lv88) ◊ **•faire son apercevance** to make one's appearance *Il a fait son apercevance mais il a pas visité longtemps.* He made his appearance but didn't stay long. (Lv88) <Lv88> <***Loc:*** Da84, Gu82, Hi02, Lv88>

apercevoir (**aperçoir**, **aparçoir**) [apærsəvwar, apærswar] **I** *v.tr.* to notice, see, perceive **Alors, ils ont fouillé, jusqu'à ils ont aperçu que c'était un cocodril.* So they dug until they noticed that it was an alligator. (EV, An94) **II s'apercevoir** *v.pron.* **1** to notice, realize, become aware **Ein jour j'm'ai aperçue que le lait que Pierre rentrait était bleu.* One day I noticed that the milk that Pierre was bringing in was blueish. (Gu82) *Il s'a aperçu trop tard que l'eau montait.* He realized too late that the water was rising. (LA) **2** to discover, find out **Mais le marié s'est aperçu du fer dans le lit, et il connaissait pas quoi c'était.* But the husband discovered the iron in the bed and he didn't know what it was. (LA, An94) <***Loc:*** AC, AV, EV, IB, LA, SL, SM, TB, VM, An94, Da84, Gu82, Hi02, Lv88>

aperçoir ♦see **apercevoir**

à-peu-près [apøpre, apøprɛ] *n.m.* **1** approximation *C'était beaucoup triste comment ils étiont malades, et il y avait pas de docteur, pas moyen d'avoir le docteur. Fallait aller après des médecines et dire quoi tu connaissais et le docteur envoyait sur un à-peu-près.* It was very sad how sick they were, and there was no doctor, no way to get the doctor. You had to go after the medicines and tell the doctor what you knew and he would send it based on an approximation. (AC) **2** common sense *Quand il parle de ça qu'il veut faire avec sa vie il a pas beaucoup d'à-peu-près.* When he talks about what he wants to do with his life, he doesn't have much common sense. (AC) ◊ **•avoir un à-peu-près** to have a feeling, have a notion <EV, La99> <***Loc:*** AC, EV, Da84, La99>

aplangir ♦see **aplanir**

aplangissement ♦see **aplanissement**

aplanir (**aplangir**) [aplɑ̃nir, aplɑ̃ʒir] *v.tr.* to level, flatten, smooth out *Aplanir la couverte.* To smooth out the covers. (LA) <***Loc:*** LA, Da84, Lv88>

aplanissement (**aplangissement**) [aplɑ̃nismɑ̃, aplɑ̃ʒismɑ̃] *n.m.* leveling, smoothing, planing <***Loc:*** Da84>

aplatir [aplatir] **I** *v.tr.* **1** to flatten *Ils aplatissont trop leurs boulettes.* They flatten their patties too much. (VM) **2** to floor, knock flat on the ground *Il lui a sacré un coup de poing et il l'a aplati.* He hit him and he knocked him to the floor. (LA) **3** to squash *Il a aplati le ravert.* He squashed the roach. (LA) **II s'aplatir** *v.pron.* to flatten o.s. out *La souris s'a aplati pour passer dans le trou.* The mouse flattened itself to go into the hole. (LA) <***Loc:*** LA, VM, Da84>

aplatissage [aplatisaʒ] *n.m.* flattening <***Loc:*** Da84>

aplomb[1] (**à plomb, d'aplomb**) [aplɔ̃, daplɔ̃] *adj.* **1** perpendicular, straight, plumb *Garde 'oir si la chaise est bien aplomb.* Look and see if the chair is straight. (Lv88) *Ils étaient après travailler à mettre les poteaux d'aplomb.* They were working to put the posts perpendicular. (LA) *J'ai mis le* BOOKCASE *aplomb.* I straightened the bookcase. (SM) *Quand tu commences une maison, il faut tu mets tes murs d'aplomb.* When you begin a house, you have to plumb your walls. (LA) *Le mur est pas d'aplomb.* The wall is out of plumb. (LA) **2** adroit, dexterous, skillful *Les garçons LeDoux sont bien d'aplomb à cheval.* The LeDoux boys are very adroit on horseback. (VM) **3** self-assured, composed *C'est un bougre aplomb.* He's a composed fellow. (LA) <***Loc:*** LA, SM, VM, Da84, Lv88>

aplomb[2] [aplɔ̃] *n.m.* **1** perpendicularity **2** adroitness, dexterity, skillfulness *Leur mère a un tas d'aplomb à cheval aussi.* Their mother has a lot of adroitness on horseback as well. (VM) **3** composure, self-assurance, self-confidence *Il a pas d'aplomb.* He doesn't have any self-assurance. (VM) <***Loc:*** LA, VM, Da84, Fa77>

apocalypse [apokalips] *n.f.* [*eccl.*] apocalypse <***Loc:*** Da84>

apoigner ♦see **empoigner**

apoplexie [apoplɛksi] *n.f.* apoplexy, stroke <***Loc:*** Da84>

apostasie [apostazi] *n.f.* [*eccl.*] apostasy <***Loc:*** Da84>

apostat [aposta] *n.* [*eccl.*] apostate <***Loc:*** Da84>

apostolat [apostola] *n.m.* [*eccl.*] apostolate <***Loc:*** Da84>

apostolique [apostolik] *adj.* [*eccl.*] apostolic <***Loc:*** Da84>

apostrophe[1] [apostrof] *n.m.* slap, rap, tap ◊ **•mettre un apostrophe à qqn** to slap s.o. <SJ, La99> <***Loc:*** AV, SJ, La99, Lv88>

apostrophe[2] [apostrɔf] *n.m.* boring, uninteresting person *Je l'aime pas. C'est rien qu'un apostrophe.* I don't like him. He's nothing but a wet blanket. (SM) *Un drôle d'apostrophe.* A queer fellow. (SJ) <***Loc:*** AS, AV, LA, SC, SJ, SM, La99, Lv88>

apostropher (**apostrophier**) [apostrofe, apostrofje] *v.tr.* **1** to slap, rap, tap **2** to insult, address in a desultory or insolent manner <***Loc:*** Lv88>

apostrophier ♦see **apostropher**

apostume ♦see **postume**

apothécaire [apotekær, apotikær] *n.m.* **1** druggist, pharmacist *Défunt Pépère Filosie était pas juste un traiteur. Il était un apothécaire aussi.* Grandpa Filosie wasn't just a faith healer. He was also an apothecary. (VM) **2** drugstore, pharmacy *Il a été à l'apothécaire chercher la médecine.* He went to the drugstore to get the medecine. (TB) <***Loc:*** TB, VM, Da84>

apotiquer ♦see **hypothéquer**

apôtre [apot] *n.m.* [*eccl.*] apostle <***Loc:*** VM, Da84>

apparages ♦see **parages**

apparaître [aparɛt(r)] *v.intr.* to appear *Ça dit qu'il avait apparu à côté du lit de la vieille juste au même moment que le* RIG *a capoté.* They say that he appeared next to the old lady's bed just at the same time as the rig was flipping over. (LA) <***Loc:*** LA, Da84>

apparemment [aparɑ̃mɑ̃] *adv.* apparently *Apparemment c'est ça qu'il voulait. Il a sûr demandé pour.* Apparently that's what he wanted. He sure asked for it. (LA) <***Loc:*** LA>

apparence [aparɑ̃s] *n.f.* appearance, semblance ◊ **•avoir pas d'apparence** to be unlikely, not make sense **Y a pas d'apparence qu'on a été sortir dans un pareil temps.* It is unlikely that he left at the same time. (ThCa: *Le charivari*) *Ça pas d'apparence quoi tu dis.* What you say does not make sense. (Lv88) <Lv88> <***Loc:*** Da84, Lv88, ThCa>

apparenté, -e [aparɑ̃te] *adj.* related *Je suis sûr qu'on est apparenté quelque sorte de manière, mais je connais pas comment.* I'm sure we are related somehow, but I'm not sure how. (LA) <***Loc:*** LA, Da84>

appartement [apartəmɑ̃] *n.m.* apartment <***Loc:*** IB, IV, LF, TB, Da84, Fa77>

appartenir [apartənir] **I** *v.tr.* to own *Le bougre qu'appartenait le bateau s'appelait Joe.* The guy who owned the boat was named Joe. (TB) **II** *v.intr.* to belong *C'était la pharmacie qu'appartient au défunt Monsieur Manouvrier.* It was the pharmacy that belongs to the late Mr. Manouvrier. (JD) **Appartenir ici.* To belong here, fit here. (Da84) <***Loc:*** JD, LA, TB, Da84, La99>

appât [apa, apat] *n.m.* bait, lure *Mais y a un monsieur qui quitte des appâts vivants dans ses cages pour empoigner des truites et les poissons rouges et les plies.* There's a gentleman who leaves live bait in his box traps for catching trout and redfish and flounder. (TB) <***Loc:*** AV, JE, PQ, SM, TB, Da84, Hi02>

appâter [apate] *v.tr.* to bait *Ça l'appâte avec des* SOYBEAN CHIP *ou des affaires comme ça.* They bait it with soybean chip or things like that. (SM) <***Loc:*** SM>

appauvrir [apovrir] *v.tr.* to impoverish *Le gamblage était après l'appauvrir.* Gambling was impoverishing him. (VM) <***Loc:*** VM, Da84>

appeau [apo] *n.m.* decoy, bird decoy *Mon défunt père avait des beaux appeaux de zoies, mais quand y avait un gros brouillard, tu pouvais user des gazettes.* My late father had beautiful goose decoys, but when it was really foggy you could use newspapers. (VM) <***Loc:*** LF, TB, VM, Gu00>

appel [apɛl] *n.m.* **1** call, summons **2** appeal **Cour d'appel.* Court of appeal. (Da84) <***Loc:*** Da84>

appeler [ap(ə)le] **I** *v.tr.* **1** to call, summon **Appeler les enfants.* To summon the children. (Da84) **2** to call, phone, telephone *Ça m'appelle pour tout quelque chose.* They call me for everything. (IB) **3** to call, name *Moi j'appelle ça voler, parce que quand tu prends quelque chose et pas demander, c'est pas voler ça?* I call that stealing, because when you take something without asking, isn't that stealing? (TB) *Ma mère était énée dedans la Paroisse Terrebonne dedans la communauté qu'on appelle le Bayou du Large.* My mother was born in Terrebonne Parish in the community we call Bayou du Large. (TB) **II** *v.intr.* to call, call out **Il a été à la maison et il a appelé. La maîtresse de la maison a sorti.* He went to the house and called out. The lady of the house came out. (LA, An94) **III s'appeler** *v.pron.* to be called, be named **Il s'appelle Joseph.* He is called Joseph. His name is Joseph. (Da84) ◊ **•appeler des {les} noms** to call bad names, tease *Il m'a appelé des noms, alors je l'ai pété un œil.* He called me bad names so I gave him a black eye. (JE) <JE, LF, SL, SM> **•appeler sur {dessus}** ***a*** to appeal to, call upon ***b*** to call on *La maitresse appelait dessus moi quand elle croyait que je savais pas la bonne réponse.* The teacher called on me when she thought that I didn't know the right answer. (VM) <VM> <***Loc:*** AC, AV, EV, IB, IV, JE, LA, LF, SJ, SL, SM, TB, VM, An94, Da84, Gu00, Hi02, Lv88, Wh83>

appeleur [aplœr] *n.m.* **1** duck call *On mettait les appeaux à l'eau, et là j'ai toujours mon appeleur.* We would set out the duck decoys in the water, and I still have my duck call. (TB) **2** caller (of ducks during a hunt) *Mais j'ai été un grand appeleur parce que tous les autres garçons de mon même âge avec moi, ils amenaient pas de monsieur là ou l'autre monsieur. Il allait là avec son fusil qu'il appelait les canards.* But I was a great duck caller because all the other boys of my age, they didn't accompany this or that gentleman. He would take his gun and call ducks. (TB) <***Loc:*** TB>

appendésie ♦see **appendicite**

appendice [apɑ̃dis] *n.m.* **1** appendix **2** appendage <***Loc:*** LA, Da84>

appendicite (**appendésie, appendicitis**, **pénésie**) [apɑ̃dizit, apɛ̃disid, apɑ̃dezi, pɑ̃dezi, pɛ̃nezi, apɑ̃disitis, apɛ̃disitis, epɑ̃disajtis, pɛ̃desaid] *n.m/f.* appendicitis <***Loc:*** EV, SB, SM, VM, Da84, Lv88, Ph36>

appendicitis ♦see **appendicite**

appétissant, -e [apetisɑ̃, -ɑ̃t] *adj.* appetizing, tasty, tempting *Ce gâteau est pas beaucoup appétissant.* That cake is not very appetizing. (LA) <***Loc:*** LA, Da84>

appétit [apeti] *n.m./f.* appetite, craving, hunger **Appétit vorace.* Ravenous appetite. (Da84) **Bon appétit!* Enjoy your meal! (Da84) **Manque d'appétit.* Lack of appetite. (Da84) <***Loc:*** Da84, Lv88>

applaudir [aplodir] **I** *v.tr.* to applaud, approve, praise **On était si fier de notre culture de voir le monde de tout partout comme ça applaudir la musique que nous-autres, on les amenait de la Louisiane.* We were so proud of our culture to see the people from all over like that applauding the music that we were bringing them from Louisiana. (VM, An84) **II** *v.intr.* to applaud, clap *Le bougre a fait son beau discours et personne a applaudi.* The fellow gave his great speech and no one applauded. (LA) <*Loc:* LA, VM, An84, Da84>

applaudissement [aplodismɑ̃] *n.m.* applause, clapping <*Loc:* Da84>

applicable [aplikab(l)] *adj.* applicable, suitable *C'est pas applicable dans notre cas à nous-autres, ça.* That's not applicable in our case. (VM) <*Loc:* VM, Da84>

applicage [aplikaʒ] *n.m.* **1** application (of a method) **2** applying (of a remedy) <*Loc:* Da84>

applicant [aplikɑ̃] *n.m.* applicant *Il n-avait un tas d'applicants pour ce job.* There were a lot of applicants for this job. (Lv88) <*Loc:* EV, IB, SB, SM, TB, Da84, Lv88, Ph36>

application [aplikasjɔ̃] *n.f.* **1** application *L'application d'une loi.* The application of a law. (EV) **2** application form, application (e.g. for a job) *Il a rempli une application pour travailler chez Halliburton.* He filled out an application to work for Halliburton. (LA) ◊ **•faire (une) application** to make an application, apply for *Il a fait application pour un nouveau automobile.* He filled out an application for a new car. (SM) *Elle a fait une application pour* WELFARE. She applied for welfare. (Lv88) <SM, Lv88> **•mettre une application** to submit an application *J'ai mis une application et j'ai été engagé.* I put in an application and I was hired. (Lv88) <Lv88> **•sur application** on request *Il l'a reçu sur application.* He got it on request. (TB) <TB> <*Loc:* AV, EV, IB, JE, LA, LF, SL, SM, TB, Da84, Gr86, Lv88, Ph36>

appliqué [aplike] *n.m.* trimming <*Loc:* Da84>

appliquer [aplike] **I** *v.tr.* to apply, employ, make use of *Quand je vas gradué, je vas essayer d'appliquer les principes que j'ai appris au collège.* When I graduate, I'll try to make use of the principles that I learned in college. (VM) **II** *v.intr.* to apply (for a job, a loan, etc.) *J'ai appliqué pour ma licence.* I applied for my driver's license. (Lv88) **III s'appliquer** *v.pron.* to apply o.s., make an effort *Il est pas après s'appliquer comme il devrait.* He is not making an effort like he should. (LA) <*Loc:* EV, LA, VM, Da84, Lv88, Ph36>

appointement [apwɛ̃tmɑ̃] *n.m./f.* **1** appointment, nomination, naming to a position *Il a reçu son appointement à LSU ce matin.* He was named to the position at LSU this morning. (SM) **2** appointment, meeting *J'ai un appointement à cinq heures.* I have an appointment at five o'clock. (SM) <*Loc:* AV, EV, IB, LF, SB, SJ, SL, SM, TB, Da84, Lv88, Ph36>

appointer [apwɛ̃te, apwɔ̃te] **I** *v.tr.* **1** to appoint, name *Il a été appointé constable.* He was named constable. (SM) **2** to appoint, choose *La semaine appointée pour faire boucherie.* The appointed week for having a "boucherie." (EV) **II s'appointer** *v.pron.* to appoint o.s. *Il s'a appointé lui-même constable.* He appointed himself keeper of the peace. (LA) <*Loc:* EV, IB, LA, LF, SB, SL, SM, TB, Da84, Lv88, Ph36>

appointir [apwɛ̃tir] *v.tr.* to sharpen to a point, make pointed **Appointir un crayon.* To sharpen a pencil. (Da84) *Appointir un poteau.* To sharpen a stake. (Lv88) <*Loc:* EV, Da84, Lv88, Ph36>

apportailler [apɔrtaje] *v.tr.* to bring back and forth, bring frequently *Il est toujours après apportailler des chiens ici.* He's always bringing dogs here. (IB) <*Loc:* IB>

apporter [apɔrte] *v.tr.* to bring, carry **Il a dit ça, qu'il avait apporté de la boisson pour eux boire.* He said this, that he had brought liquor for them to drink. (SL, An94) <*Loc:* EV, LA, SB, SJ, SL, TB, An94, Da84, Lv88>

apporteur [apɔrtœr] *n.m.* pallbearer <*Loc:* LA>

apportionner [apɔrsjɔne] *v.tr.* to apportion, portion out, allocate *Tout la terre de vieux M. Sonnier avait déjà été apportionnée avant sa mort, mais la famille a eu mille misères quand même après.* All of old man Sonnier's land had already been portioned out before his death, but the family had lots of trouble afterwards anyway. (LA) <*Loc:* LA, Da84>

appréciation [apresjasjɔ̃] *n.f.* **1** appreciation **2** estimation <*Loc:* Da84>

apprécier [apresje] *v.tr.* to appreciate, value, esteem *Mais tout ça qui sort, il apprécie ça si quelqu'un y demande* TO GET INVOLVED IN IT. But everything new, he appreciates it if someone asks him to get involved in it. (LF) *N'importe quoi vous-autres pourrait faire, ça serait beaucoup apprécié.* Anything you all could do would be greatly appreciated. (LA) <*Loc:* EV, LA, LF, TB, VM, An94, Da84>

appréhenter [apreɑ̃te] *v.tr.* to expect with anxiety, fear *J'appréhente la nuit.* I fear the night. (JE) <*Loc:* JE, LF>

apprendre [aprɑ̃n, aprɑ̃d(r)] *v.tr.* **1** to learn *Il faulait que j'apprends leur langage pour être capable de faire mon job.* I had to learn their language to be able to do my job. (TB) *La fièvre forte, ç'a brûlé la cervelle, c'est tellement forte que ç'a détruit... ça fait ils pouvaient pas apprendre comme avant.* The high fever, that burned their brains, it was so high that it destroyed . . . so they couldn't learn like before. (SJ) **2** to teach **Ça va t'apprendre.* That will teach you. (Da84) *Viens ici. Je vas t'apprendre à amarrer tes souliers.* Come here. I'll teach you to tie your shoes. (LA) ◊ **•apprendre à** to learn how to **Apprendre à lire.* To learn to read. (Da84) <LA, LF, PQ, SM, An84, Da84, Wh83> **•apprendre par cœur** to learn by heart *J'ai appris tout mes leçons par cœur.* I learned all my lessons by heart. (LA) <LA, Da84> **•apprendre par cœur comme un perroquet** to learn quickly, learn easily <La99> <*Loc:* AC, AV, EV, IB, LA, LF, PQ, SJ, SL,

SM, TB, VM, An94, Da84, Gu82, Hi02, La99, Lv88, Wh83>

apprenti [aprɑ̃ti] *n.* apprentice *Le forgeron a eu de la misère à se trouver un apprenti.* The blacksmith had trouble finding an apprentice. (LA) <***Loc:*** LA, Da84, Fa77>

apprentissage [aprɑ̃tisaʒ] *n.m.* apprenticeship <***Loc:*** Da84>

appresser (s') [aprese] *v.pron.* to hurry, hurry up, make haste *Si tu t'appresses-toi pas, le transfer va passer.* If you don't make haste, the school bus is going to go by. (VM) <***Loc:*** VM>

apprêtement [aprɛtmɑ̃] *n.m.* product of workmanship (e.g. cooking, sewing, or other craft) *Voilà le bel apprêtement que j'ai fait pour le petit.* Look at the nice thing [toy, sweater, etc.] that I made for the little one. (VM) <***Loc:*** VM>

apprivoisable [aprivwazab(l)] *adj.* tameable, able to be domesticated *Ces jeunes poulains sont pas apprivoisables.* Those young colts are untameable. (LA) <***Loc:*** LA, Da84>

apprivoisement [aprivwazmɑ̃] *n.m.* taming, domesticating <***Loc:*** Da84>

apprivoiser [aprivwaze] **I** *v.tr.* to tame, domesticate *Je crois pas que ces chats vont se laisser apprivoiser.* I don't know if those cats will allow themselves to be domesticated. (LA) **II s'apprivoiser** *v.pron.* to become tame *Le chat voulait juste pas s'apprivoiser.* The cat just would not become tame. (LA) <***Loc:*** LA, VM, Da84>

approchable [aproʃab(l)] *adj.* approchable, accessible *Les oies sont pas approchables. Ils sont trop loin de la levée.* The geese are not approchable. They are too far from the levee. (VM) <***Loc:*** VM, Da84>

approchant[1] [aproʃɑ̃] *adv.* nearly, about, almost *C'est possible que c'était approchant comme ça, mais soixante ans passés je me rappelle pas qui-ce qu'allait de l'avant.* It's possible that it was almost like that, but 60 years ago I don't remember what went on. (TB) *Trois garçons, mais elle a eu approchant sept à huit filles.* Three boys, but she had about seven or eight girls. (PQ) ◊ **•en approchant** almost, nearly *C'est en approchant le même prix.* It's almost the same price. (VM) *C'est en approchant la même affaire.* It's almost the same thing. (VM) <VM, Da84> <***Loc:*** LF, PQ, TB, VM, Da84, Lv88>

approchant[2] [aproʃɑ̃] *n.m.* ◊ **•dans un approchant** about, more or less *Combien t'as pris d'écrevisses à soir? —50 livres, dans un approchant.* How much crawfish did you catch in the evening? —50 pounds, more or less. (Lv88) <Lv88> <***Loc:*** Lv88>

approché [aproʃe] *prep.* near, close, next to *Le* CHUCK *est sur l'épaule approché du cou, au ras du cou.* The chuck [cut of meat] is on the shoulder, next to the neck, right next to the neck. (VM) <***Loc:*** VM>

approcher [aproʃe] **I** *v.tr.* to approach, draw near to, come near *Il a décidé de les approcher.* He decided to approach them. (Lv88) *Ça approche midi.* It will soon be noon. (Lv88) **Ça fait, Bouki a parti. En peu de temps, il approchait l'ours.* So Bouki left. Shortly, he was approaching the bear. (SM, An94) **II** *v.intr.* to approach, draw near, come near *Il a approché tout doucement et il les a attendu après parler.* He approached slowly and he heard them talking. (LA) **III s'approcher** *v.pron.* to approach, come near **La fête s'approche.* The feast is near. (Da84) **Une fois, il y avait une femme qui était après laver des tripes de cochon au bord d'un bayou et un chien étrange s'approchait d'elle et elle dit, "Tu veux passer! Tu veux passer!" parce qu'elle en avait peur.* Once there was a woman who was washing pork tripe next to a bayou and a strange dog came up to her and she said, "You go away! You go away!" because she was afraid of it. (VM, An94) <***Loc:*** EV, IV, LA, SM, VM, An94, Da84, Lv88>

appropriation [apropriasjɔ̃] *n.m./f.* appropriation *On a reçu l'appropriation hier.* We received the appropriation yesterday. (SM) <***Loc:*** SM, Da84, Lv88>

approprier [aproprije] **I** *v.tr.* to appropriate *Le gouvernement a approprié de l'argent pour les chemins.* The government appropriated money for the roads. (SM) *Il a approprié la terre et mis une barrière.* He appropriated the land and put up a fence. (Lv88) **II s'approprier** *v.pron.* to take for o.s., take possession *Le village va s'approprier de ma terre.* The town will take possession of my land. (LA) <***Loc:*** IB, LA, SL, SM, TB, Da84, Lv88>

approuver [apruve] *v.tr.* **1** to approve, approve of, consent to, agree to *Il fait G. se fâcher* THOUGH. *Il devrait pas faire ça, parce qu'elle a le sang haut. Et ça j'approuve pas ça.* He makes G. mad though. He shouldn't do that, because she has high blood pressure. And I don't approve of that. (TB) **2** to confirm, ratify, authorize **Il avait tout le temps un [homme] avec lui pour approuver ça il tuait.* He always had a man with him to ratify [confirm] what he killed. (LA, An94) **3** to pass (a law) *La législature va jamais approuver une loi contre les batailles de guimes.* The legislature will never pass a law against cockfighting. (LA) <***Loc:*** LA, TB, An94, Da84>

approvisionnement [aprovizjɔnmɑ̃] *n.m.* provision, supply, stock <***Loc:*** Da84>

approvisionner [aprovizjɔne] **I** *v.tr.* to supply, stock *Il avait bien approvisionné sa cuisine.* He had stocked his kitchen well. (LA) **II s'approvisionner** *v.pron.* to supply o.s., stock up *C'est du monde qui s'approvisionne bien pour l'hiver.* They are people who supply themselves well for the winter. (VM) <***Loc:*** LA, VM, Da84>

appui [apɥi] *n.m.* support, prop, brace <***Loc:*** Da84>

appuyer [apɥije, apyje] **I** *v.tr.* to support, prop, lean **Il a vu le petit garçon se mettre à genoux sur l'autre bord du lit, et appuyer sa tête sur le bord du lit comme si qu'il était après prier avec beaucoup de piété.* He saw the little boy get on his knees on the other side of the bed and lean his head on the edge of the bed as though he were praying with much fervor. (LA, An94) **II s'appuyer** *v.pron.* to prop o.s., lean *Il s'a appuyé contre un poteau pour espérer que sa femme sort du magasin.* He leaned against a post to wait for his wife to come out of the store. (LA) ◊ **•s'appuyer l'estomac** to eat, satisfy one's hunger, satiate o.s. <VM, Lv88> <***Loc:*** LA, SM, VM, An94, Da84>

après[1] [apre, aprɛ] *adv.* **1** after, afterward, thereafter *Une heure après, le prêtre a arrivé.* An hour afterward, the priest arrived. (TB) *Et eusse mettait les cabris là-dedans, les cabris mangeaient les herbes, tu vois, on avait pas besoin de les couper au sabre après.* And they put the goats in there, the goats ate the grass, you see, we didn't need to cut it with a scythe afterwards. (TB) **Quelques années après.* A few years later. (LA, An94) **Quelque temps après, il a revenu* BACK. Some time later, he came back. (SM, An94) **Doris Léon (D. L.) Ménard a appris à jouer la guitare à 16 ans et six mois après a joué son premier bal au Palombo Club dans Abbeville.* Doris Leon (D.L.) Menard learned how to play the guitar when he was 16 and six months later played his first dance at the Palombo Club in Abbeville. (Wh83) *Ils ont fait un test trois mois après pour voir si ça avait travaillé.* They did a test three months later to see if it had worked. (VM) **2** then, next *Après tu les enterres en dessous une dégouttière.* Then you bury them under a gutter. (TB) *En premier c'était tout des* DERRICKS *boulonnés. Eux-autres montait ça* PIECE BY PIECE ALL THE WAY TO THE TOP. *Et eux-autres serrait les boulons et après ils ont venu avec des* JACKKNIFE. At first it was all derricks that were bolted together. They took it up piece by piece all the way to the top. And they tightened the bolts and later they came along with jackknives. (LF) ◊ **•d'après** next, following **Ça fait, l'année d'après, ils ont planté du maïs.* So the next year, they planted corn. (SM, An94) *Il a daté son chèque pour la semaine d'après.* He dated his check for the following week. (LA) *J'ai eu dix-sept ans dans décembre et je m'ai marié dans août d'après.* I turned seventeen in December and I got married the following August. (EV) *Le samedi d'après, un autre aurait tué son veau et il aurait séparé la viande parmi les autres, c'étiont comme un groupe.* The following Saturday, another one would kill his calf and he would divide the meat among the other ones, they were like a group. (AC) <AC, EV, LA, SL, SM, An94> **•par après** after, afterwards **Il savait que Joe l'aurait bûché par après.* He knew that Joe would have beat him afterwards. (LA, An84) <LA, An84> <***Loc:*** AC, EV, LA, SL, SM, TB, VM, An84, An94, Lv88, Wh83>

après[2] [apre, aprɛ] *prep.* **1** after *Après la messe on a été manger chez Larry.* After mass we went to eat at Larry's. (TB) **Ils estiont contents avec lui après ça.* They were happy with him after that. (LA, An94) **2** about, concerning *Je rêve après des choses que je vas faire.* I dream about things that I'm going to do. (TB) *Eh ben, aie pas peur on va pas parler après toi en arrière de ton dos, parce qu'on a pas été élevé comme ça.* Well, don't be scared that we will talk about you behind your back, because we weren't raised like that. (TB) **3** at, with (doing s.t.) *J'étais bon après ça.* I was good at that. (AC) **4** attached to, on *Il y avait deux sangles après la selle.* There were two cinch straps attached to the saddle. (EV) *J'ai mis les pentures après mes portes.* I put the hinges on my doors. (TB) **5** in *La clef est après la porte.* The key is in the door. (LA) ◊ **•après (que)** after *Drette après que les bessons étaient énés.* Right after the twins were born. (TB) *Après que le bateau était fini eusse le mettait à l'eau.* After the boat was finished they put it in the water. (LF) **Après il était couché, il était pas satisfait.* After he was in bed, he wasn't satisfied. (LA, An94) *Après sa femme a mouru, il s'a démoralisé.* After his wife died, he became desolate. (VM) <EV, IV, LA, LF, TB, An94, Da84, Wh83> **•d'après** according to, in the opinion of **D'après moi, l'ours était après courir manière vite.* As I see it, the bear was running pretty fast. (SM, An94) **Il a dépris le lapin d'après le* TAR MAN. He set the rabbit free, according to the tar man. (An77) <LA, SL, SM, VM, An77, An94> <***Loc:*** AC, AV, EV, IB, JE, LA, LF, SB, SL, SM, TB, VM, An94, Da84, Gu00, Hi02, Lv88, Wh83>

après[3] [aprɛ, apre] *prep.* in the process of *Mon garçon [...] est dans le Texas asteur après arpenter.* My son is surveying in Texas now. (TB) *Là j'ai lavé mon linge que j'avais à ce matin sur le dos, il est tout propre, là il est pendu après sécher.* I washed the clothes that I had on this morning, they're all clean, they're hung up drying. (TB) ◊ **•être après** *(progressive construction)* to be in the act of (doing s.t.) *Il est après couper les herbes.* He is cutting the grass. (Lv88) *C'est pour ça j'ai réussi si bien, j'étais après faire ça réellement je voulais faire.* It is for this reason I succeeded so well, I was doing what I really wanted to do. (SM) *J'ai commencé à aller aux trawls dans 1941. Ça fait qu'il y a longtemps que je suis après jouer avec ce maillage.* I began going trawling in 1941. So I've been playing with that mesh for a long time. (TB) **Quoi il est après faire?* What is he doing? (Da84) <AC, AV, EV, IB, IV, JD, JE, LA, LF, SB, SL, SM, TB, VM, An94, Da84, Gu00, Lv88, Wh83> **•être**

après pour to be about to (do s.t.) *J'étais après pour t'appeler.* I was just about to call you. (EV) <EV> <***Loc:*** AC, AL, AV, EV, IB, IV, JD, JE, LA, LF, SB, SL, SM, TB, VM, An94, Da84, Gu00, Lv88, Wh83>

après-demain [aprɛdmɛ̃] *adv.* the day after tomorrow <***Loc:*** Da84, Fa77>

après-midi[1] [aprɛ̃midi] *n.m./f.* afternoon <***Loc:*** AC, AV, EV, LA, SL, SM, TB, An94, Da84, Wh83>

après-midi[2] [aprɛ̃midi] *adv.* this afternoon *J'avais arrêté chez M. là-bas après-midi. J'ai resté là trois heures de temps.* I had stopped at M's this afternoon. I stayed there three hours. (TB) <***Loc:*** TB, VM, Fa77>

à-propos [apropo] *n.m.* sense of appropriateness, common sense *Il a pas plus d'à-propos qu'une sauterelle dans un parc à dindes.* He does have any more sense of appropriateness than a grasshopper in a turkey pen. (EV) <***Loc:*** EV, Da84>

aquiloire ♦see **acculoire**

arabe[1] (**arabique**) [arab, arabik] *adj.* Arabic, Arabian <***Loc:*** VM, Da84>

Arabe[2] [arab] *n.* Arab *Les Boustany et les Abdalla sont des Arabes.* The Boustanys and the Abdallas are Arabs. (VM) <***Loc:*** VM, Da84>

Arabique[1] [arabik] *n.m.* Arabic, Arabic language <***Loc:*** Da84>

arabique[2] ♦see **arabe**

arable [arab(l)] *adj.* tillable, arable *La terre arable.* Arable land. (LA) <***Loc:*** LA, Da84>

aragne ♦see **araignée**

araignée (**aniée, aragne, argnée, arignée, anreingné, z-aignée, z-araignée**) [arɛ̃je, arœ̃je, ɑ̃je, arɑ̃ɲ, arɲe, ɑ̃nje, arjɛ̃, ɑ̃rje, ɑ̃rɛ̃je, zarɛ̃jɛ̃] *n.m./f.* spider <***Loc:*** IB, IV, JE, LA, LF, PQ, SL, SM, TB, Da84, Fa77, Lv88>

arasement [arazmɑ̃] *n.m.* height of the ceiling, height of a room *Sa maison a juste 12 pieds d'arasement.* His house has ceilings only 12 feet in height. (Lv88) <***Loc:*** SM, Lv88>

arbitraire [arbitrær] *adj.* arbitrary *Une décision arbitraire.* An arbitrary decision. (EV) <***Loc:*** EV, Da84>

arbre (**l-arbre, z-arbre**) [arb(r), larb(r), zarb(r)] *n.m.* tree *Y avait un homme qui venait de la Belgique. Il voulait marcher dans les arbres on appelle, dans les bois.* There was a man who came from Belgium. He wanted to walk in the trees as they call them, in the woods. (TB) ◊ •**arbre à chapelets** chinaberry tree <Lv88> •**arbre à {de} poules** any tree in which chickens roost, in particular the Chinese tallow tree <Ho90> •**arbre à fruit** fruit tree <Da84> •**arbre à gomme** sweetgum tree <Lv88> •**arbre à rameau** magnolia <Lv88> •**arbre de Christmas** Christmas Tree <LF> •**arbre de cipre** eastern red cedar <VM> •**arbre de Noël** Christmas tree <Da84> •**arbre de pommette** crabapple tree <Lv88> •**arbre Saint-Jean** crape myrtle <Lv88> •**arbre (à) volaille** cassava tree, manihot <Da84, Ho90, Lv88, Re31> <***Loc:*** AV, EV, IB, JD, LA, LF, PQ, SB, SL, SM, TB, VM, An94, Da84, Gu00, Hi02, Ho90, Lv88, Re31, Wh83>

arbriquin [arbrikɛ̃] *n.m.* mantlepiece scarf *L'arbriquin a tombé dans le feu.* The mantlepiece scarf fell into the fire. (AV) <***Loc:*** AV>

arbutter ♦see **abutter**

arc [ark] *n.m.* **1** arch **2** bow <***Loc:*** Da84, Lv88>

arcacia ♦see **acacia**

arcahol ♦see **alcool**

arcajou ♦see **acajou**

arce ♦see **as**

arc-en-ciel [arkɑ̃sjɛl] *n.m.* rainbow <***Loc:*** Da84, Fa77>

arcette ♦see **recette**

archange [arkɑ̃ʒ] *n.m.* [*eccl.*] archangel <***Loc:*** Da84>

arche [arʃ] *n.f.* **1** arch **2** ark, Noah's ark <***Loc:*** Da84>

archer [arʃe] *n.m* slingshot **On avait des archers [...] et on tirait [...] des caniques de boue séchée.* We had slingshots and we shot marbles made of dried mud. (Gr82) <***Loc:*** Gr82, Lv88>

archet [arʃe] *n.m.* bow (for playing a musical instrument) <***Loc:*** Hi02>

archevêque [arʃəvɛk] *n.m.* [*eccl.*] archbishop <***Loc:*** Da84>

archigrand [arʃigrɑ̃] *adj.* extremely big, huge <***Loc:*** SM>

architecte [arʃitɛk(t)] *n.m.* architect <***Loc:*** SM, Da84, Hi02>

architecture [arʃitɛktyr] *n.f.* architecture <***Loc:*** Da84, Hi02>

archuter ♦see **rechuter**

arcollant [arkolɑ̃] *n.m.* beggar's lice plant *L'arcolant c'est juste comme une petite feuille plate et ça colle aussi.* Beggar's lice has a flat little leaf and it sticks [to your clothing] also. (TB) <***Loc:*** TB>

arcompter ♦see **recompter**

arconnaître ♦see **reconnaître**

arcoquin ♦see **herbe coquin**

arculer ♦see **reculer**

ardent, -e [ardɑ̃, -ɑ̃t] *adj.* ardent, fervent, burning *Il avait le cœur ardent.* He had a fervent heart. (LA) <***Loc:*** LA, Da84>

ardeur [ardœr] *n.f.* **1** ardor, fervor **2** speed *Il m'a passé à grande ardeur.* He passed me at full speed. (JE) <***Loc:*** JE, LA, LF, SM, Da84, Lv88>

ardoise [ardwaz] *n.f.* **1** slate **2** school slate, writing slate, blackboard **3** cement tile used for facing the exterior of a house <***Loc:*** Da84, Lv88>

arèche ♦see **arête**

arête (**arèche**) [arɛt, arɛʃ] *n.f.* fish bone <***Loc:*** AL, IB, SM, VM, Da84, Lv88>

argent [arʒɑ̃] *n.m./f.* **1** money *L'homme bamboche son argent.* The man squanders his money. (AV) *Le monde qu'avait de l'argent engageait du monde comme ma grand-mère pour aller frotter le linge.* People who had money would hire people like my grandmother to go scrub the linens. (IB) **2** silver *Si tu laisses tes affaires en argent dehors, ça va les ternir.* If you leave your silver things out, it will tarnish them. (LA) *Je te donnerai une robe de noce toute ourlée-z-en fils d'argent.* I'll give you a wedding dress all hemmed in silver thread. (VM, ch: *Le papier d'épingles*) **3** silverware ◊ •**argent blanc** silver money, change <IB> •**argent claire** silver money, change <SJ> •**argent comptant** cash <SJ, TB> •**avoir l'argent tambour battant** to be very wealthy <La99> •**(se) faire de l'argent** to earn money, make money *Moi je suis pas prêt lui dire pour il arrête parce que c'est un job il peut faire et il fait de l'argent avec ça.* I'm not ready to tell him to stop because it's a job that he can do and he makes money with that. (EV) *Alle s'a fait plein de l'argent parce qu'alle allait chanter pour des noces.* She made a lot of money because she used to go sing at weddings. (TB) *Parce que moi, j'étais pauvre, personne voulait pas de moi. Et là, j'ai eu de la chance que moi, je m'ai fait de l'argent.* Because I was poor, nobody wanted me. And then, I was fortunate enough to make some money. (ch: *Quand j'étais pauvre*) <EV, TB> <***Loc:*** AC, AV, EV, IB, JE, LA, LF, SB, SJ, SL, SM, TB, VM, An94, Da84, Gu00, Hi02, La99, Lv88>

argenté, -e [arʒɑ̃te] *adj.* **1** silvered, silverplated, silvery *Elle a servi ça dans une belle assiette argentée.* She served that in a beautiful silvery plate. (LA) **2** rich, wealthy, well-to-do *Il est argenté.* He is rich. (JE) <***Loc:*** AV, JE, LA, LF, Da84, Lv88, Re31>

argenter [arʒɑ̃te] *v.tr.* to silverplate *Argenter une vieille médaille.* To silverplate an old medal. (LA) <***Loc:*** LA, Da84>

argnée ♦see **araignée**

argoneau ♦see **organeau**

argot[1] [argo] *n.m.* slang, jargon **Les Français c'était boucoup gentil mais ça me disait: vous parle argot.* The French were very nice to me but they told me, "You speak slang." (Gr86) <***Loc:*** Gr86>

argot[2] ♦see **ergot**

arguinil [argini] *n.m.* goad, small thorny branch placed under a horse's tail to make it go faster *Il fallait piquer le cheval avec l'arguinil.* We had to poke the horse with the goad. (AV) <***Loc:*** AV>

argument [argymɑ̃] *n.m./f.* **1** argument, quarrel, dispute **2** discussion <***Loc:*** VM, Da84, Lv88>

argumenter [argymɑ̃te] *v.intr.* to argue *L'avocat a argumenté devant le juge.* The lawyer argued before the judge. (VM) <***Loc:*** VM, Da84>

aria, ariasse ♦see **haria**

ariate [arjat] *n.f.* lariat, lasso <***Loc:*** IB>

aridelle ♦see **ridelle**

arien, à-rien ♦see **rien**

arignée ♦see **araignée**

arismétique ♦see **arithmétique**

arithmétique (**arithmitique, arismétique**) [arizmetik, arikmitik, aritmetik] *n.m./f.* arithmetic <***Loc:*** EV, Da84, Ph36>

arithmitique ♦see **arithmétique**

Arkansas [arkɑ̃sa, arkɑ̃sas] *n.pl.* Arkansas *Il reste aux Arkansas.* He lives in Arkansas. (Lv88) <***Loc:*** Lv88, Hi02>

arkansia [arkɑ̃sja] *n.m./f.* black locust, robinia, flowering locust <***Loc:*** VM, Gu00>

armadille ♦see **armadillo**

armadillo (**armadille**) [armadijo, armadij, ɹmədilə] *n.m.* armadillo <***Loc:*** Da84, Gu00, Lv88>

armana, armanach ♦see **almanach**

arme [arm] *n.f.* weapon, arm ◊ •**arme à feu** firearm <Hi02> <***Loc:*** LA, SL, TB, An94, Da84, Hi02>

armée [arme] *n.f.* **1** army, armed forces **2** large group **Une armée de monde.* A large group of people. (Da84) <***Loc:*** EV, IB, LA, SM, TB, VM, An94, Da84, Hi02>

armement [arməmɑ̃] *n.m.* armament, arms <***Loc:*** Da84>

arménac ♦see **almanach**

armer [arme] **I** *v.tr.* to arm, load (a firearm) *Il a pas tiré un seul canard dans la bande parce qu'il avait oublié d'armer son fusil.* He didn't kill one duck in the flight because he had forgotten to load his shotgun. (LA) **Fusil armé.* Loaded gun. (Da84) **II s'armer** *v.pron.* to arm o.s. *Il s'a bien armé avant de sortir de la maison.* He armed himself well before leaving the house. (LA) <***Loc:*** LA, Da84, Fa77>

armeuil [armœj] *n.m.* large bust (of a woman) <***Loc:*** IB>

arminette ♦see **harminette**

armise ♦see **remise**

armistice [armistis] *n.m./f.* armistice *Le onze de Novembre, c'est le jour de l'Armistice.* November eleventh is Armistice day. (VM) <***Loc:*** VM, Da84, Fa77>

armoire [armwar] *n.f.* **1** armoire, wardrobe **2** chest of drawers <***Loc:*** AC, LA, SL, SM, VM, Da84, Hi02, Re31>

armoniac ♦see **ammonia**

armontrance ♦see **remontrance**

arnicroche [arnikrɔʃ] *n.* ◊ •**être à l'arnicroche** to not be in good shape, not be doing well <Lv88> <***Loc:*** Lv88>

arnicrot [arnikro] *n.m.* quirk, idiosyncrasy <***Loc:*** Da84>

aromatique [aromatik] *adj.* aromatic *Du riz aromatique.* Aromatic rice. (LA) <***Loc:*** LA, Da84>

aronce ♦see **éronce**

arouelle [arwɛl] *n.f.* space between a bed and the wall <***Loc:*** AV, JD>

arpent [arpɑ̃] *n.m./f.* arpent, land measure of 36,864 sq. ft. (slightly smaller than an acre) *Un acre est un petit brin plus grand qu'un arpent.* An acre is a tiny bit bigger than an arpent. (TB) <***Loc:*** EV, IB, LF, SL, SM, TB, VM, An94, Da84, Gr86, Hi02, Lv88>

arpentage [arpɑ̃taʒ] *n.m.* surveying <***Loc:*** Da84>

arpenter [arpɑ̃te] *v.tr.* to survey *Il a fait arpenter la terre avant de l'acheter.* He had the land surveyed before buying it. (VM) <***Loc:*** SM, TB, VM, Da84, Fa77>

arpenteur [arpɑ̃tœr] *n.m.* surveyor <***Loc:*** EV, TB, Da84>

arpenteuse [arpɑ̃tøz] *n.f.* surveyor worm, span worm <***Loc:*** Da84>

arrachage [araʃaʒ] *n.m.* **1** pulling out **2** uprooting **3** tearing out <***Loc:*** Da84>

arracher [araʃe, raʃe] **I** *v.tr.* **1** to pull out **C'est un tas d'ouvrage, casser une maison, nettoyer le bois, arracher les clous.* It was a lot of work, tearing down a house, cleaning the wood, pulling out the nails. (EV, An84) *Alle a pris Myrtle par les cheveux, et alle a manqué tout lui arracher les cheveux.* She grabbed Myrtle by the hair, and she nearly pulled out all her hair. (TB) **2** to uproot, pull up by the roots **Et le diable arrachait des arbres, c'était pour desserrer le bois.* And the devil was pulling out trees in order to clear the woods. (AC, An84) **3** to extract, remove *Quand t'allais arracher ses graines, là il était un capon.* When you were going to remove his testicles, then he was a capon. (IB) **4** to tear out, rip out *Ces petits, quand il envale le l'hameçon, et faut que vous arrache l'hameçon là-dedans.* Those little fish, when they swallow the hook you have to tear the hook out. (TB) *Si tu manquais ton clou, t'aurais fait, t'aurais arraché une coche dans ton* CEILING TILE. If you missed the nail, you would make, you would've gouged a nick in your ceiling tile. (SL) **5** to tear off, rip off *Ce gros vent l'autre jour a manqué d'arracher la porte de dessus les pentures.* That strong wind the other day nearly tore the door off its hinges. (VM) *Alle a venu icitte en noir, je te dis. Dessus la route alle a arraché la robe noire et alle a mis une rouge.* She came here dressed in black, I tell you. On the road she tore off the black dress and put on a red one. (TB) *J'ai été dans le lit, j'ai arraché le drap, je l'ai bourré dans le drap comme si qu'il avait froid.* I went to the bed, I tore off the sheet, I wrapped him in the sheet as though he were cold. (TB) **II s'arracher** *v.pron.* **1** to come loose, break away **Tout mon estomac-là, c'est comme si ça voulait s'arracher de dans moi.* All my stomach, it's as though it was trying to break away from inside of me. (VM, An84) **2** to get by, manage *Je suis manière après apprendre à un petit peu à parler l'espagnol mais c'est bien peu parce que je veux pas apprendre ça plus que pour assayer de m'arracher le mieux que je peux.* I am more or less learning a little bit of Spanish but it's very little, because I don't want to learn it any better than to try to get by the best I can. (TB) **3** to take o.s. out of, leave *A 18 ans un enfant peut s'arracher de même de l'école.* At 18 years old a child can take himself out of school. (LF) **4** to remove o.s., get out of (e.g. a situation, a tight spot, the way) *Quand j'ai vu que ce* TRUCK *a passé et que il était parti en bas, eh ben mon je m'ai revenu, j'ai pris* BACK *le pont, ça c'est comme ça que je m'en ai arraché.* When I saw that that truck had passed and that it was headed down the bayou, I came back, I crossed the bridge again, that's how I got out of it. (TB) *Arrache-toi hors de mon chemin.* Get out of my way. (VM) ◊ **•arracher les yeux de la tête** to overcharge for goods, charge exorbitant prices <Da84> **•arracher un trou** to dig out a hole *J'ai arraché mon trou avec un* SLEDGE, *une grosse masse en fer.* I dug out my hole with a sledgehammer. (LF) <LF> <***Loc:*** AC, EV, IB, IV, LA, LF, SL, SM, TB, VM, An84, Da84, Hi02>

arracheur, -euse [araʃœr, raʃœr, -øz] *n.* ◊ **•arracheur de dents** dentist <LA, SM, Da84, Hi02, La99> **•arracheur de piquants** tweezers <JE> <***Loc:*** JE, LA, SM, Da84, Hi02, La99>

arracheux ♦see **racheux**

arrangeable [arɑ̃ʒab(l)] *adj.* reparable *J'ai peur que ton char est pas arrangeable.* I'm afraid your car is not reparable. (LA) <***Loc:*** LA, Da84>

arrangeage [arɑ̃ʒaʒ] *n.f.* fixing, repairing <***Loc:*** SB, Lv88>

arrangeant, -e [arɑ̃ʒɑ̃, -ɑ̃t] *adj.* accommodating *Ça, c'était pas arrangeant pour eux.* That wasn't very accommodating for them. (LA) <***Loc:*** LA, Da84>

arrangement [arɑ̃ʒmɑ̃] *n.m.* **1** repair, repairing, fixing, mending *Il m'a jamais payé pour les arrangements que j'ai faits sur sa maison.* He never paid me for the repairs I did on his house. (VM) **2** arrangement, settlement, agreement *Ils ont fait arrangement.* They made an arrangement. (Lv88) ◊ **•faire {prendre} des arrangements** to make a deal, reach an understanding *Les deux politiciens ont fait des arrangements entre eux.* The two politicians made a deal between themselves. (LA) <LA, Da84> <***Loc:*** AC, LA, VM, Da84, Lv88>

arranger [arɑ̃ʒe] **I** *v.tr.* **1** to repair, fix, mend *Je peux faire la charpente de moi-même. Et j'arrange les machines à la vieille, et les* DRYER, *j'arrange tout ça moi-même.* I can do carpentry by myself. And I fix the wife's machines and the dryer, I fix all that myself. (TB) **2** to adjust *Je faisais mes appeleurs moi-même. Tu peux les acheter mais il faut que t'arranges pour ton souffle à toi.* I used to make my own duck calls. You can buy them but you have to adjust them for your own breath. (TB) **3** to arrange, set in order *Ils ont tout bien arrangé ça.* They set everything in order. (SL) **4** to arrange, set up *Peut-être je peux arranger un* INTERVIEW. *Tu veux que je l'appelle?* Maybe I can set up an interview. Do you want me to call him? (LF) **6** to fix, prepare (a meal) *Mom arrangeait du riz, de la sauce et de la viande.* Mom used to make rice with sauce and meat. (AV) **7** to suit, please, satisfy **Ça, ça m'arrange.* That suits me. (Da84) **8** to castrate, spay (an animal) *J'ai besoin de faire arranger mon chat avant il vient trop grand.* I need to have my cat spayed before he gets too big. (LA) **II s'arranger** *v.pron.* **1** to get fixed up, get ready, prepare o.s. **Il s'arrangeait pour aller en haut.* He arranged his affairs to be on top. (LA, An94) **2** to come to terms (with each other) *Tracasse-toi pas. Ça va s'arranger.* Don't worry. They'll come to terms. (LA) **3** to clear up (of the weather) **Le temps s'arrange.* The weather is clearing up. (Da84) ◊ **•arranger un lit** to make a bed <SL> **•être bien arrangé** to be in good shape (e.g. financially) *Il a* RETIRE*, mais il est joliment bien arrangé.* He is retired, but he's is pretty financially sound. (LA) <LA> <***Loc:*** AC, AV, EV, IB, JE, LA, LF, SL, TB, SM, VM, An94, Da84, Hi02>

arrangeur [arɑ̃ʒœr] *n.m.* repairman ◊ **•arrangeur de souliers** shoemaker, shoe repairman <VM, Fa77> <***Loc:*** IB, SM, VM, Da84, Fa77, Lv88>

arrasse [aras] *n.f.* ◊ **•à grosse arrasse** having feathers along the legs (of chickens) <VM> <***Loc:*** VM>

arrêt [arɛ, are] *n.m.* **1** stop, halt **2** arrest <***Loc:*** Da84>

arrêter [arete] **I** *v.tr.* **1** to stop, halt *Et là ça* LOAD *les cannes dans cette charrette là, et quand le bougre dit que le* LOAD *est plein, il arrête la machine.* And then they load the cane in this wagon, and when the guy says that the load is full, he stops the machine. (AS) *Le gouvernement a essayé de les arrêter, mais ça pouvait pas les empêcher de* BOOTLEG*.* The government tried to stop them, but they couldn't prevent them from selling (whiskey) illegally. (LA) *Je l'ai arrêté propre.* I stopped it right there. (VM) **2** to stop, cease *J'ai chassé déjà, mais des années j'ai arrêté chasser.* I've hunted before, but many years ago I stopped hunting. (SL) *Arrête berdasser.* Stop dilly-dallying. (JE) **3** to arrest **Y a eu in vrai halaillement quand l'officier a arrêté l'garçon.* There was a real fight when the policeman arrested the boy. (EV, Ph36) **II** *v.intr.* **1** to stop, halt, come to a standstill **Il a arrêté pour* CHECK *sa* NET*.* He stopped to check his net. (EV, An94) **Arrête. Je veux te dire quelque chose.* Stop. I want to tell you something. (CL, An94) *J'avais arrêté chez M. là-bas après-midi. J'ai resté là trois heures de temps.* I had stopped at M's this afternoon. I stayed there three hours. (TB) *J'arrête au bord du chemin, j'ai du tracas avec mon char.* I stop on the side of the road, I have problems with my car. (IB) **2** to stop, cease *Y a une semaine j'ai arrêté de fumer.* I quit smoking a week ago. (SM) **Quand le tonnerre a arrêté hier, cet ouragan de tonnerre, il y en avait un drôle de train.* When the thunder stopped yesterday, the thunderstorm, there was a funny noise. (EV, An94) *Arrête de faire le bouffon, tu me fais honte!* Stop acting like a clown! You're embarrassing me! (VM) *S'il arrête pas de s'abuser, il va pousser des poils dans les mains.* If he doesn't stop masturbating, he will grow hair in his hands. (VM) **3** to wait *C'est vrai, mais arrête un peu pour écouter mon côté.* That's true, but wait a bit to hear my side. (SM) **III s'arrêter** *v.pron.* to stop, halt *La pirogue s'arrête aux premiers pièges.* The pirogue stops at the first traps. (Lv88) **Et le monde qui passe s'arrête souvent pour un bout de temps.* And the people who are passing by often stop for a while. (EV, An94) *Il s'a arrêté pour boire de l'eau sur la tournure.* He stopped to drink some water on the turnrow. (IV) <***Loc:*** AC, AS, AV, CL, EV, IV, JD, JE, LA, LF, SL, SM, TB, VM, An94, Da84, Hi02, Lv88, Ph36, Wh83>

arrière (**errière**) [arjær, ærjær] *n.m.* ◊ **•(d')en arrière** back, hind, located in the rear *La porte en errière.* The back door. (Lv88) *Il passe son temps dans la cour en arrière.* He spends his time in the back yard. (SM) *Les deux pattes d'en arrière.* The two back paws. (TB) <AV, LA, LF, SM, TB, VM, An94, Da84, Lv88, La99> **•en arrière *a*** in back, in the back *J'étais en arrière après tirer des cannes d'aluminum.* I was in back shooting at aluminum cans. (LF) *Il s'est assis en arrière avec elle.* He sat in back with her [in the car]. (Lv88) ***b*** behind *Quand on voit les tourbillons, la pluie est pas loin en arrière.* When you see the whirlwinds, the rain can't be far behind. [proverb] (Lv88) ***c*** slow (of a clock) *La pendule est en arrière.* The clock is slow. (Lv88) ***d*** in the past WELL *ça vient de loin d'en arrière, ça vient du vieux temps en avant quand mon père était là.* Well, that comes from long ago, that comes from the old days when my father was around. (AS) <AS, EV, JD, LA, LF, SL, TB, VM, An84, Da84, Gr82, Lv88> **•en arrière (de) *a*** behind *En arrière chez nous.* Behind our house. (Lv88) *Il a caché le char en arrière de sa maison.* He hid the car behind his house. (LA) *Il monte le cheval en arrière de lui.* He mounts the horse behind him. (Lv88) *Mais en arrière de ces cannes-là c'est tout des savanes et le monde a plein des animaux.* But behind that cane it's all grasslands and people have a lot of cattle. (LF) ***b*** behind s.o.'s back, secretly, in secret *Il a fait ça en arrière sa Mom.* He did that behind his mother's back. (Lv88) ***c*** in the back (of) **Il été parti passer son après midi avec ein huitaine d'autres vieux hommes à jouer aux cartes en arrière de la boutique à Edwin Guillory.* He went to spend his afternoon with about eight other men playing cards in the back of Edwin Guillory's shop. (Wh83) <AS, EV, JD, LA, LF, TB, VM, Lv88, Wh83> **•être en arrière** to be behind *Je suis en arrière des mes paiements.* I am behind in my payments. (Lv88) *Il est en arrière de son ouvrage.* He is behind in his work. (Lv88) *On est un petit peu en arrière dessus le job.* We're running a little behind on the job. (LA) <LA, Lv88> **•par en arrière de** from behind *Et tout d'un coup j'ai sentu quelqu'un, quelque chose de venir par en-arrière de mon et me* GRAB *comme ça.* And suddenly I felt someone, something, come up from behind me and grab me like that. (TB) <SL, TB> <***Loc:*** AC, AS, AV, EV, JD, LA, LF, SL, SM, TB, VM, An94, Da84, Gr82, Hi02, La99, Lv88, Wh83>

arrière-grand-mère [arjærgrɑ̃mær] *n.f.* great-grandmother *Ça provient de mon arrière-grand-mère, ça.* That comes from my great grandmother. (VM) <***Loc:*** VM>

arrière-grand-père [arjærgrɑ̃pær] *n.m.* great-grandfather *Mon arrière-grand-père a été décoré durant la guerre des Confédérés.* My great-grandfather was decorated during the Civil War. (VM) <***Loc:*** VM>

arrimer [arime] *v.tr.* to arrange, put in order *Elle avait besoin d'arrimer sa maison.* She needed to put her house in order. (LA) <***Loc:*** LA, Lv88>

arrivée [arive] *n.f.* arrival, coming <***Loc:*** Da84, Lv88>

arriver [arive] *v.intr.* **1** to arrive, come *Une heure après, le prêtre a arrivé.* An hour after, the priest arrived. (TB) **Arriver à la fin.* To come to the end. (Da84) **Arriver au bout.* To reach the end. (Da84) **2** to take place, happen, occur *Je suis content que ç'a arrivé comme ça.* I'm glad it happened that way. (AS) **Ça arrive.* It happens. (Da84) **Ça peut arriver.* It can happen. (Da84) **3** to succeed, manage **Arriver à finir.* To manage to finish. (Da84) ◊ **•arriver sur** to encounter by chance, run into *Je suis arrivée sur Béa quand j'étais* SHOP *à matin au* MALL. I ran into Bea this morning on my way to the Mall to go shopping. (Lv88) <Lv88> <***Loc:*** AC, AS, AV, EV, JD, LA, LF, SB, SJ, SL, SM, TB, VM, An94, Da84, Hi02, Lv88>

arroche [arɔʃ] *n.* spiny pigweed <***Loc:*** Ho90>

arrochon [arɔʃɔ̃] *n.m.* gear (of a car) <***Loc:*** VM>

arrogance [arogɑ̃s] *n.f.* arrogance, pride <***Loc:*** Da84>

arrogant, -e [arogɑ̃, -ɑ̃t] *adj.* arrogant <***Loc:*** Da84>

arrondir [arɔ̃dir] **I** *v.tr.* to round, round off *On a arrondi les bouts de poteaux pour pas que les enfants aient des écharpes.* We rounded off the ends of the posts so that the children would not get splinters. (VM) **II s'arrondir** *v.pron.* to become round or dull *Le bout de la mèche de mon vire-brequin est après s'arrondir.* The tip of my drill bit is getting dull. (VM) <***Loc:*** VM, Da84>

arrosage [arozaʒ] *n.m.* watering, sprinkling <***Loc:*** Da84>

arrosement [arozmɑ̃] *n.m.* watering, sprinkling <***Loc:*** Da84>

arroser [aroze] *v.tr.* to water, irrigate *Mon père est après arroser son jardin.* My father is watering his garden. (LA) <***Loc:*** IV, LA, Da84>

arrosoir [arozwar] *n.m.* **1** watering can **2** lawn sprinkler, garden sprinkler **3** hose nozzle <***Loc:*** AC, LA, Da84>

arscokin ♦see **herbe coquin**

arsouille [arsuj] *n.m./f.* shiftless person *Elle est une arsouille.* She's a shiftless person. (SB) <***Loc:*** SB>

art [ar] *n.m.* art, skill *Filer et frapper au métier, c'est un art qu'est après s'en aller.* Spinning and weaving is an art that is disappearing. (SM) *Sacrer en français est un art chez les Cadiens.* To swear in French is an art for Cajuns. (Lv88) <***Loc:*** SM, Da84, Lv88>

Artaguette [artagɛt] *n.prop.* ◊ **•ça date du temps d'Artaguette** ***a*** it is very old ***b*** that was a long time ago <LA, La99> <***Loc:*** LA, La99>

artère ♦see **altère**

artésien, -ienne [artezjɛ̃, -ɛ̃n] *adj.* artesian *Il y avait un puits artésien ayoù ma grand-mère restait au bord de la mer à Créole.* The was an artesian well on the beach in Creole where my grandmother lived. (VM) <***Loc:*** VM, Da84>

ARTHRITIS [aɹθɹaɪtɪs] *n.m.* arthritis <***Loc:*** Da84>

artichaut [artiʃo, hærtiʃo] *n.m.* artichoke, globe artichoke <***Loc:*** IB, SL, VM, Da84>

article [artik(l)] *n.m.* **1** article, item (of food, clothing, etc.) *J'ai acheté quelques articles de linge.* I bought several articles of clothing. (VM) **2** article *Il y avait un article dans la gazette là-dessus.* There was an article in the newspaper on that. (LA) <***Loc:*** LA, VM, Da84>

artière ♦see **altière**

artifailler (s') [artifaje, atifaje] *v.pron.* to dress o.s. in a strange, gaudy or tacky manner *Elle s'artifaille avec des colliers impossibles et des chapeaux encore plus drôles.* She dresses bizarrely with impossible necklaces and hats that are even funnier. (SM) <***Loc:*** IB, SM>

artifailles (attifailles) [artifaj, atifal, atʃifaj] *n.m./f.pl.* **1** small kitchen utensils **2** trinkets, knick-knacks, bric-a-brac **3** clothes, clothing (esp. if peculiar or strange) *Il a des drôles d'artifailles sur lui.* He's wearing some strange-looking clothes. (SM) **4** rubbish, junk (esp. old metal scraps) *Tu vas tout te salir avec ces artifailles.* You'll get yourself all dirty with that rubbish. (LF) <***Loc:*** EV, IB, LF, SB, SM, VM, Lv88, Ph36>

artifaux [atifo] *n.m.pl.* trinkets, knick-knacks, bric-a-brac <***Loc:*** Lv88>

artillerie [artijri] *n.f.* artillery ◊ **•faire l'artillerie** to make a lot of noise <VM, La99> <***Loc:*** VM, Da84, La99>

artisan [artizɑ̃] *n.m.* **1** artisan, craftsman **2** mechanic <***Loc:*** Da84>

artiste [artis(t)] *n.m./f.* artist <***Loc:*** EV, LA, LF, TB, Da84, Fa77>

aruiner ♦see **ruiner**

arvange ♦see **revenge**

arvanger ♦see **revenger**

as (arce) [as, ars] *n.m.* ace (in cards) ◊ **•as de pic** ace of spades <EV> <***Loc:*** EV, JE, SM, Da84, Fa77>

asbeste (asbestos) [azbɛst, æzbestos] *n.m.* asbestos <***Loc:*** Da84>

asbestos ♦see **asbeste**

ascension [asɑ̃sjɔ̃] *n.f.* [*eccl.*] ascension, ascent **La fête de l'Ascension.* The Feast of the Ascension. (Da84) <***Loc:*** PQ, Da84, Fa77>

ase ♦see **asthme**

asoir ♦see **soir**

asphyxier [asfiksje] **I** *v.tr.* to asphyxiate *Il est mort asphyxié.* He died of asphyxiation. (VM) **II s'asphyxier** *v.pron.* to suffocate *Il était après s'asphyxier au fond du trou quand ils l'ont trouvé.* He was suffocating at the bottom of the hole when they found him. (LA) <***Loc:*** LA, VM, Da84>

aspic[1] [aspik] *n.m.* asp, viper *Des aspics, ça c'est eusse-là qu'a les piquants au bout de la tcheue.* Asps, those are the ones that have stingers on the end of their tail. (LF) <***Loc:*** IB, LF, Da84, Gu00>

aspic[2] [aspik] *n.m.* aspic salad <***Loc:*** Da84, Gu00>

aspiration [aspirasjɔ̃] *n.f.* **1** aspiration, ambition **2** longing, yearning, desire *Il avait des aspirations d'être docteur.* He had a longing to become a doctor. (LA) <***Loc:*** LA, Da84>

aspirer [aspire] *v.tr.* to breathe in, inhale *Il a aspiré de l'eau en nageant.* He breathed in water while swimming. (VM) <***Loc:*** VM, Da84>

aspirine [aspirin] *n.f.* aspirin <***Loc:*** Da84>

assafœtida (**safétida**) [safetida, saktifida, sasafida, særtifida, satyfida] *n.m./f.* asafoetida (herb formerly worn around the neck in a small bag to ward off germs) <***Loc:*** IB, LF, SM, TB, VM, Da84>

assaie ♦see **essai**

assaisonnement [asɛzɔ̃nmɑ̃, asazɔ̃nmɑ̃] *n.m.* seasoning, condiment *Je fais jaunir [...] la viande et je mets des oignons, des piments, des assaisonnements, et là je remets le riz cru, avec l'eau dedans, et, cuis tout ensemble.* [To make a jambalaya] I brown the meat, and I add onions, peppers, seasonings, and I add in the uncooked rice, with water in it, and cook everything together. (SL) <***Loc:*** IV, LA, SL, VM, Da84>

assaisonner (**saisonner**) [asezɔ̃ne, asazɔ̃ne, sezɔ̃ne] *v.tr.* **1** to season, flavor, spice *On hachait la viande fine, fine et là, on l'assaisonnait.* We ground the meat very fine, and then we seasoned it. (AC) *On use le basilic pour saisonner le manger.* We use basil to season food. (TB) *Tu parles de si c'est que c'est assaisonné plein? Non.* Do you mean whether it was heavily seasoned? No. (TB) **2** to spice up, liven up **Plutôt que quitter la musique Américaine dominer dans le Sud de la Louisiane, on prend des chansons populaires, traduit les en Français et quitte des musiciens Cajins assaisonner les aires avec des accordéons et violons.* Rather than letting American music dominate in southern Louisiana, we take popular songs, translate them into French and let Cajun musicians spice up the tunes with accordeons and violins. (Wh83) **3** to incite, start (a fight) *Ça voulait pas que ça danse avec leurs belles. Ça c'est une affaire qui va assaisonner une bataille vite.* They didn't want them [others] to dance with their girlfriends. That's an affair that will quickly start a fight. (SL) <***Loc:*** AC, EV, SL, SM, TB, VM, Da84, Lv88, Wh83>

assapé (**sapé**) [asape] *adj.* packed down *La terre est assapée depuis la pluie.* The soil is packed down since the rain. (LA) *La terre est bien sapée.* The soil is well-packed. (SM) <***Loc:*** LA, SM>

assaper[1] (**saper**) [asape, sape] *v.tr.* **1** to pack down *Je vais assaper le matelas bien avant de le tourner.* I'm going to pack the mattress down well before I turn it over. (IB) **2** to beat, hit, strike, whip *Espère qu'il arrive, je vas l'assaper!* Wait until he gets here, I'm going to beat him! (VM) <***Loc:*** EV, IB, LA, SL, SM, VM, La99, Lv88, Ph36>

assaper[2] (**saper**) [asape, sape] *v.tr.* to soak *Ils ont bien assapé la terre autour de l'arbre et je crois il va prendre.* They soaked the earth around the tree really well and I think it will grow. (Lv88) <***Loc:*** SL, LA, Da84, Lv88>

assassin [asasɛ̃] *n.m.* **1** assassin, murderer **2** assassination, murder *Il dit qu'il était droite là pour l'assassin même.* He says he was right there even for the murder. (TB) <***Loc:*** EV, LA, SM, TB, An94, Da84, Lv88, Ph36>

assassinat [asasina] *n.m.* assassination, murder <***Loc:*** Da84>

assassination [asasinasjɔ̃] *n.f.* assassination, murder <***Loc:*** SB, Lv88>

assassiner [asasine] *v.tr.* to assassinate, murder *Les deux frères Blanc ont assassiné Martin Begnaud.* The two Blanc brothers murdered Martin Begnaud. (VM) <***Loc:*** VM, Da84>

assassineur, -euse [asasinœr, -øz] *n.* **1** assassin, murderer **2** one who destroys *Un assassineur de réputation.* A person who destroys another's reputation. (Lv88) <***Loc:*** SM, Lv88>

assaut [aso] *n.m.* **1** attack *Il a attrapé un assaut cet hiver, il est pas fort un tas.* He had an attack during the winter, he's not very strong. (Lv88) **2** assault *Il est accusé d'assaut.* He was accused of assault. (Lv88) <***Loc:*** Da84, Lv88>

assavoir [asawar] *v.tr.* ◊ •**faire assavoir** to make known, broadcast (information) *Il a fait assavoir de ses nouvelles.* He made his news known. (Lv88) <AV, Lv88> <***Loc:*** AV, Lv88>

assayer ♦see **essayer**

assécher ♦see **chesser**

assemblage [asɑ̃blaʒ] *n.m.* **1** assembly, gathering **2** assemblage, assembling **3** mixture, mix *Un rôti, c'est des gratons, du boudin..., un assemblage de viande. Chacun avait sa part.* A "rôti" [from a "boucherie"], it's cracklings, boudin . . . , a mixture of meat. Everyone got his share. (SL) <***Loc:*** SL, Da84>

assemblée [asɑ̃ble] *n.f.* assembly, meeting, gathering (of people) *On a fait une belle assemblée pour Christmas.* We had a nice family Christmas party. (Lv88) <***Loc:*** Da84, Gr86, Lv88>

assembler [asɑ̃ble] **I** *v.tr.* to gather, assemble, bring together *Il a assemblé ses hommes dans l'anse avant d'aller chercher pour le prisonnier.* He gathered his men in the cove before going to look for the prisoner. (LA) **II s'assembler** *v.pron.* to meet, assemble, gather *Les hommes du voisinage s'assemblaient sur la galerie pour parler de la politique, du temps, ou de la récolte.* The men of the neighborhood gathered on the porch to talk about politics, the weather, or the crops. (VM) <***Loc:*** LA, VM, Da84>

asseminier ♦see **assiminier**

assent [asɑ̃] *n.m.* assent, agreement *Être d'assent.* To consent. (Lv88) <***Loc:*** Lv88>

asseoir (**assir, assoyer**) [aswar, asir, aswaye] **I** *v.tr.* to seat, place in seats *La maîtresse a assis les enfants chacun à sa place.* The teacher seated the children each in his place. (LA) *Quand une poule avait éclore ses petits poulets, euh, tu voulais que cette poule commence à pondre aussi vite* *que tu peux. Tu l'assirais elle dedans un baril d'eau.* When a hen had hatched her chicks, uh, you wanted that hen to start laying as quickly as possible. You would seat her in a barrel of water. (IV) **II** *v.intr.* to sit, sit down, be seated *J'ai assis auprès de lui à l'église.* I sat next to him at church. (SM) *La terre éioù-ce qu'on est assis ici était une terre de famille.* The land where we're seated here was a family property. (LF) **Tout d'un coup, la femme s'est levée assis dans le lit, puis elle a commencé à crier.* All of a sudden, the woman sat up in bed and then she started yelling. (EV, An94) **III s'asseoir** *v.pron.* **1** to seat o.s., sit down, be seated **Et le vieux s'a assis dans le banc en avant.* And the old man sat down on the bench in front. (EV, An94) *Va t'assir.* Go sit down. (JE) *Les hommes s'assisaient au ras du feu.* The men sat close to the fire. (Lv88) *Assisez-vous.* Have a seat. (SM) *Il vient s'asseoir là avec nous-autres.* He'll come over to sit with us. (PQ) *Assoyez-vous.* Have a seat there. (SM) *Il va s'assoyer.* He's going to sit down. (IB) *Assis-toi, assisez-vous.* Sit down. (SM) **2** to perch (of a bird) *Il y avait une grive qui s'avait assis dessus la barrière.* There was a robin that had perched on the fence. (LA) <***Loc:*** AC, EV, IB, IV, JE, LA, LF, PQ, SB, SM, TB, VM, An94, Da84, Hi02, Lv88, Ph36>

assessement [asɛsmɑ̃] *n.m.* assessment <***Loc:*** Da84>

assesser [asɛse, asese] *v.tr.* **1** to assess *Dans le vieux temps, comme eux-autres assessait la propriété, un assesseur, eux-autres assessait les maisons par leur montant des chambres qu'eux-autres avait.* In the old days, when they assessed the property, an assessor, they would assess houses by the number of rooms they had. (LF) **2** to tax *Il est assessé fort asteure.* He's really being taxed now. (Lv88) <***Loc:*** LF, SM, Da84, Lv88>

assesseur [asesœr] *n.m.* assessor (parish official who evaluates property for purposes of taxation) <***Loc:*** EV, LF, SM, Da84, Gr86, Lv88, Ph36>

assez [ase] *adv.* **1** enough **Ça, c'est assez.* That's enough. (Da84) **Assez!* Enough! (Da84) **Assez pour jeter aux cochons.* Enough to throw [some] to the hogs. (Da84) *Il a figuré qu'il avait pas assez de temps le soir.* He figured he didn't have enough time in the evening. (LF) **2** very *Il est assez entêté.* He is very stubborn. (Lv88) **3** so *J'ai eu assez peur, y avait assez des gros coups de tonnerre que j'ai allumé la chandelle et je l'ai mis sur la petite table-là, parce que moi je peux pas coucher dans le noir.* I was so afraid, there were so many big claps of thunder that I lit the candle and put it on the little table there, because I can't sleep in the dark. (TB) *Pauvre bête, alle était assez maigre.* Poor thing, she was so skinny. (Lv88) ◊ **•assez de** so much, so many *On avait assez des pacanes, des pistaches, les rats nous ont infestés* We had so many pecans and peanuts, the rats infested our supply. (Lv88) <Lv88> <***Loc:*** AC, AV, EV, IV, JE, LA, LF, SL, TB, VM, Da84, Hi02, Lv88>

assiette [asjɛt, asijɛt] *n.f.* **1** plate **2** record ◊ **•assiette à gâteau(x)** ***a*** cake pan ***b*** pie pan <EV, LA> **•assiette creuse** soup bowl <Da84> **•assiette plate** dinner plate <Da84> <***Loc:*** EV, JE, LA, SL, Da84, Lv88>

assiettée [asjete] *n.f.* plateful <***Loc:*** LF, Da84>

assignement [asiɲmɑ̃] *n.m.* assignment (in school) **J'ai commencé à donner des assignements aux élèves.* I started giving the pupils assignments. (Gr86) <***Loc:*** Gr86>

assigner [asiɲe] *v.tr.* to assign, allot *Et de New York City j'ai été assigné sur un navire, un aircraft carrier.* And from New York City I was assigned to a ship, an aircraft carrier. (TB) <***Loc:*** TB, Da84>

assimine (açmine) [asimin, asmin] *n.f.* pawpaw fruit <***Loc:*** Da84, Lv88, Re31>

assiminier (asseminier, açminier) [asimĩje, asmĩje] *n.m.* pawpaw tree <***Loc:*** Da84, Lv88, Re31>

assir ♦see **asseoir**

assistance [asistɑ̃s] *n.f.* **1** assistance, aid, help *Tu peux plus avoir de l'assistance asteur.* You can't get any more aid these days. (Lv88) **2** attendance, presence *L'assistance à l'école était pas obligée quand moi j'étais petit.* Attendance at school was not obligatory when I was young. (Lv88) <***Loc:*** IB, Da84, Hi02, Lv88>

assistant, -e [asistɑ̃, -ɑ̃t] *n.* assistant, aid, helper <***Loc:*** LF, Da84>

assister [asiste] **I** *v.tr.* to assist, aid, help, help out *Ils ont fait un bénéfit pour assister la famille.* They put on a benefit to help the family. (LA) **II** *v.intr.* to attend *Les plus près parents, tels que le père et la mère, le mari ou la femme, assistaient pas à l'enterrement.* The closest relatives, such as the father and the mother, the husband or the wife, did not attend the funeral. (VM) **III s'assister** *v.pron.* to help each other *Le monde s'assiste p'us beaucoup.* People don't help each other much anymore. (Lv88) <***Loc:*** LA, VM, Da84, Fa77, Gr86, Lv88>

association [asosjasjɔ̃] *n.f.* association, society, partnership <***Loc:*** Da84>

associé, -e [asosje] *n.* associate, partner *Ses associés sont des brigands.* His associates are rowdy. (IB) <***Loc:*** IB, Da84, Lv88>

associer [asosje] **I** *v.tr.* to associate, connect **Jean Sot était fier et bien associé avec la nature.* Jean Sot was proud and well connected with nature. (EV, An94) **II s'associer** *v.pron.* to associate o.s., join *Et les quatre classes-là, c'était des classes qui s'associaient pas avec un et l'autre.* And the four classes, they were classes that did not associate with one another. (SM) <***Loc:*** EV, SM, An94, Da84>

assodié, -e [asodje] *adj.* bent, inclined, crouched *Il est toujours assodié là auprès du feu.* He's always crouched over there by the fire. (VM) <***Loc:*** VM>

assogné, -e [asɔ̃je] *adj.* quiet, still, silent *T'es bien assogné-là dans ton coin.* You are pretty quiet over there in your corner. (VM) <***Loc:*** VM>

assoiffé, -e [aswafe] *adj.* thirsty *Les enfants sont rentrés assoiffés.* The children came in thirsty. (VM) <***Loc:*** SM, VM>

assolement [asolmɑ̃] *n.m.* underpinning (of a building), sills <***Loc:*** Da84>

assolider (**solider**) [asolide, solide] *v.tr.* to strengthen, reinforce, fortify *Bois ça, chère, ça va t'assolider.* Drink this, dear, it will give you strength. (VM) *J'ai fait une cheminée de briques qu'a solidé ma maison.* I made a brick chimney that reinforced my house. (SM) *Tu feras mieux de solider cette engruchade.* You had better reinforce that roost. (TB) <***Loc:*** EV, IB, SB, SM, TB, VM, Da84, Lv88, Ph36>

assommer [asɔ̃me] *v.tr.* **1** to beat mercilessly, beat up severely *Viens ici, je veux t'assommer.* Come here, I want to beat you up. (LA) **2** to bore *Le prêtre nous a assommé avec son prône dimanche passé.* The priest bored us with his sermon last Sunday. (LA) <***Loc:*** LA, Da84, La99>

assommoir [asɔ̃mwar] *n.m.* one who bores or tires others with tedious conversation <***Loc:*** JD, La99>

assomption [asɔ̃psjɔ̃] *n.f.* [*eccl.*] Assumption, Feast of the Assumption (traditional Cajun holiday) <***Loc:*** Da84, Fa77>

assortement ♦see **assortiment**

assorti, -e [asɔrti] *adj.* assorted, mixed, varied *Il y avait des bonbons assortis dans la vitrine.* There were some assorted candies in the window. (LA) <***Loc:*** LA, Da84>

assortiment (**assortement**) [asɔrtimɑ̃, asɔrtəmɑ̃] *n.m.* assortment <***Loc:*** Da84>

assortir (**assorter**) [asɔrtir, asɔrte] *v.tr.* to sort, sort out *On va assortir le linge avant de le mettre sur les tablettes.* We're going to sort the clothes before putting them on the shelves. (VM) <***Loc:*** VM, Da84>

assourdir [asurdir] *v.tr.* to deafen *Les canons les avaient assourdis.* The cannons had deafened them. (LA) <***Loc:*** LA, Da84>

assourdissant, -e [asurdisɑ̃, -ɑ̃t] *adj.* deafening *La musique aujourd'hui est assourdissante.* Music today is deafening. (VM) <***Loc:*** VM, Da84>

assoyer ♦see **asseoir**

assujetti, -e [asyʒeti] *adj.* **1** subject, liable (to) *Asteur, il est assujetti à une attaque de cœur.* Now he's running the risk of a heart attack. (Lv88) **2** obliged, obligated, required (to) *Il était assujetti d'aller à Viet Nam.* He had to go to Vietnam. (Lv88) <***Loc:*** Da84, Lv88>

assumer [asyme] *v.tr.* to assume, take on *Assumer ses responsabilités.* To assume one's responsibilities. (VM) <***Loc:*** VM, Da84>

assurable [asyrab(l)] *adj.* insurable *Son garçon a eu tellement de* WRECKS *qu'il est pus assurable.* His son had so many wrecks that he is no longer insurable. (LA) <***Loc:*** LA, Da84>

assurance (**ensurance**) [asyrɑ̃s, ɑ̃syrɑ̃s] *n.f.* **1** insurance **Policie d'assurance.* Insurance policy. (Da84) **Compagnie d'assurance.* Insurance company. (Da84) *Si l'ouragan prend ta maison, t'as de l'ensurance pour te rebâtir encore.* If the hurricane takes your house, you've got insurance to rebuild again. (TB) **2** assurance, certainty, boldness (of character) <***Loc:*** AC, EV, TB, Da84>

assuré[1], -e [asyre] *adj.* **1** confident *Un homme assuré.* A confident man. (VM) **2** sure, certain *Oh, oui, c'est assuré.* Oh yes, that's for sure. (TB) <***Loc:*** TB, VM, Da84>

assuré[2], -e [asyre] *n.* insured party <***Loc:*** Da84>

assuré[3] [asyre] *adv.* to be sure, certainly *Oh oui, assuré. Oh oui. Ça a été les meilleures chanteuses a été notre famille à nous-autres icitte.* Oh yes, to be sure. Oh yes. They were the best singers, our family here. (PQ) <***Loc:*** PQ>

assurément [asyremɑ̃] *adv.* assuredly, surely, certainly, of course *C'est lui que j'ai vu hier soir avec ta fille. Oh oui, assurément.* He's the one I saw with your daughter last night. Oh yes, surely. (LA) *Plus Clomaire buvait et traînait, plus elle badgeulait; et assurément, aussitôt qu'elle badgeulait, lui il retournait au village se soûler encore.* The more Clomaire drank and dragged the streets, the more she nagged, and of course, as soon as she started nagging, he would go back to town and get drunk again. (ThCa: *Le charivari*) <***Loc:*** LA, Da84, Fa77, ThCa>

assurer [asyre] **I** *v.tr.* **1** to insure *Il peut pas* AFFORD *d'assurer son char.* He can't afford to insure his car. (LA) **2** to assure, guarantee **II s'assurer** *v.pron.* to make sure, be assured, be convinced *Je voulais m'assurer que t'avais attendu les nouvelles.* I wanted to make sure that you heard the news. (VM) <***Loc:*** LA, VM, Da84, Fa77>

assureur [asyrœr] *n.m.* insurer <***Loc:*** Da84>

astacot [astako] *adv.* in this way, like so, thus *Nous avons fait ça astacot.* We did it like so. (SB) <***Loc:*** SB>

asteur (**asteure, à c'te heure**) [astœr] *adv.* **1** now, right now *Asteure, j'vas essayer d'écrire à vous en cadjin.* Now I'm going to try to write to you in Cajun. (Lv88) *Asteure, lâche!* Now, let go! (JE) *Alle après cuire asteur-là.* She's cooking right now. (JE) **2** at present, these days, nowadays **A c'te heure je reste à Basile.* I'm living in Basile these days. (Gr86) *Les affaires de cinq sous d'habitude, c'est trente sous asteur.* Things that were usually five cents are thirty cents these days. (SL) <***Loc:*** AC, AV, EV, JD, JE, LA, LF, SB, SL, SM, TB, VM, An84, Da84, Gr86, Hi02, Lv88>

asteure ♦see **asteur**

asthma ♦see **asthme**

asthme (**ase, asthma**) [az, asm, azma] *n.m.* asthma <***Loc:*** TB, Da84>

astique ♦see **élastique**

astronome [astrɔ̃nɔ̃m] *n.m.* **1** astronomer **2** prophet, soothsayer <***Loc:*** LA, SB, Da84>

atacalpa [atakalpa, altakapa, altapa] *n.m.* catalpa tree <***Loc:*** LA, TB, Lv88>

atelier [atəlje] *n.m.* workshop, shop <***Loc:*** Da84>

atlantique [atlɑ̃tik] *n.* Atlantic ocean <***Loc:*** Da84>

atout [atu] *n.m.* **1** trump **2** trump card <***Loc:*** Da84, Fa77>

attabler (s') [atable] *v.pron.* to prepare o.s. for a difficult or unpleasant task, get down to business *C'était mon garçon qui payait tous mes* BILLS, *mais il m'a dit "Mame, il faut t'attabler, parce que moi, je peux pus le faire."* It was my son who paid all my bills, but he told me "Mom, you'll have to get yourself ready, because I'm not going to be able to do it anymore." (LA) <***Loc:*** LA>

attachage [ataʃaʒ] *n.m.* attaching, nailing, pinning <***Loc:*** Da84>

attache [ataʃ] *n.f.* attachment, fastening <***Loc:*** Da84>

attachement [ataʃmɑ̃] *n.m.* attachment, affection, fondness <***Loc:*** Da84>

attacher [ataʃe] **I** *v.tr.* **1** to attach *Attache ça bien avant ça tombe par terre.* Attach that well before it falls to the ground. (LA) **2** to nail, fasten with nails *Ça mettait des perches à travers, sur les chevrons, puis ça les attachait.* They put the roofing slats across, on the rafters, then they nailed them down. (SL) **3** to pin, attach with a pin **Il faut t'attaches ça sur ta chemise une autre fois.* You must pin it to your shirt the next time. (EV, An94) **II** *v.intr.* to become attached *J'ai perdu le soulier et le cap et je donnerais bien de l'argent pour toujours de l'avoir parce que c'était ma maman qui m'avait sauvé ça. Elle avait attaché à ça et me sauvait ça.* I lost the shoe and the cap and I would give a lot of money to still have them because it was my mother who had saved them for me. She had become attached to them and was saving them for me. (AV) **III s'attacher** *v.pron.* to become attached, become fond of *Il s'a attaché après ce petit chien.* He became very fond of that little dog. (VM) <***Loc:*** AC, AV, EV, LA, SL, TB, VM, An94, Da84>

attaque [atak] *n.f.* **1** attack, assault **2** fit, convulsion, attack ◊ **•attaque de cœur** heart attack <EV, An94, Da84, Hi02, Lv88> **•attaque de maladie** attack, bout of sickness <Da84, Lv88> <***Loc:*** EV, TB, An94, Da84, Hi02, Lv88>

attaquer[1] [atake] **I** *v.tr.* to attack, assault *Et il a follu qu'il tue, la serpent l'aurait attaqué.* And he had to kill it, the snake would have attacked him. (LF) **Mais, j"ai peur que ces maringouins m'attaquent encore.* But I'm afraid that those mosquitoes will attack me again. (EV, An94) **II s'attaquer** *v.pron.* to attack each other *Le monde de ces deux voisinages, ça s'attaquait tout les deux ou trois semaines.* The people from those two neighborhoods, they would attack each other every two or three weeks. (LA) <***Loc:*** AV, EV, LA, LF, SM, TB, An94, Da84, Gu00, Lv88>

attaquer[2] [atake] *v.tr.* to latch with a slide-bolt <***Loc:*** Lv88>

attaqueur [atakœr] *n.m.* attacker <***Loc:*** Da84>

atteindre [atɛ̃d(r)] *v.tr.* to reach, attain, arrive at *Une fois que l'eau avait atteint la maison, c'était trop tard pour partir.* Once the water had reached the house, it was too late to leave. (LA) <***Loc:*** LA, Da84>

attelage [atlaʒ, ɑ̃tlaʒ] *n.m./f.* **1** 'rig' comprising a horse and vehicle **2** rigging, harness *Il a mis l'attelage sur le cheval.* He put the harness on the horse. (LF) <***Loc:*** JE, LF, SL, SM, Da84, Lv88>

attelé, -e [atle] *adj.* equipped *Cet habitant est bien attelé.* That farmer is well-equipped. (SM) <***Loc:*** SM, Lv88>

atteler [atle] **I** *v.tr.* to hitch, harness (a horse to a vehicle) **Il s'a préparé un* HACK *et il a attelé un de ses chevaux dessus.* He prepared a hack for himself and he hitched one of his horses to it. (SL, An94) **II s'atteler** *v.pron.* to get hold of **S'atteler après un cable.* To get hold of a rope (and pull). (Da84) <***Loc:*** AC, EV, LA, SL, An94, Da84>

attelle[1] [atɛl] *n.f. (usu.pl.)* harnessing, harness rigging *Je connais tous les morceaux de les attelles pour atteler un cheval ou un mulet dessus le wagon.* I know all the pieces of the harness rigging to hitch up a horse or a mule to a wagon. (AC) <***Loc:*** AC, EV, Ph36>

attelle[2] [atɛl] *n.m./f.* wood shaving <***Loc:*** Lv88>

attendant[1]**, -e** [atɑ̃dɑ̃, -ɑ̃t] *n.* attendant *Leurs attendants vont venir et pomper la gazoline pour vous. T'as pas besoin de sortir de ton automobile.* Their attendants will come and pump the gas for you. You don't need to get out of your car. (EV) <***Loc:*** EV, Da84>

attendant[2] [atɑ̃dɑ̃] ◊ **•en attendant** meanwhile, till then, until then <Da84> <***Loc:*** Da84>

attendre[1] [atɑ̃n, atɑ̃, atɑ̃d(r)] **I** *v.tr.* to await, wait for, expect *Pour causer des amours, je suis encore trop jeune. Attendez-moi un an, vous serez mon amant.* To speak of love, I am too young yet. Wait one year for me, you will be my lover. (IB, ch: *Je m'ai fait une maitresse*) **II** *v.intr.* to wait **Il dit, "Attends, maman," il dit, "je vas te montrer."* He says, "Wait, mama," he says, "I'll show you." (LA, An94) **III s'attendre** *v.pron.* to expect <***Loc:*** EV, IB, LA, An94, Da84>

attendre[2] **(entendre)** [atɑ̃n, atɑ̃, atɑ̃d(r)] **I** *v.tr.* to hear *J'ai attendu ça sur le radio aujourd'hui.* I heard it on the radio today. (IB) *J'ai attendu que tu pars demain.* I heard you were leaving tomorrow. (SM) *Il avait attendu quoi c'était ça.* He had heard before what it was. (AC) *La dernière fois on a attendu de lui.* The last time we heard from him. (Lv88) **II** *v.intr.* to hear *J'avais tracas avec une oreille, je pouvais pas attendre.* I had problems with one ear, I could not hear. (SM) **III s'attendre** *v.pron.* to hear each other **À force la chaudière était grande, les deux hommes qu'étaient après mettre les anses chaque bord s'entendaient pas, leurs coups de marteau sur la chaudière.* The pot was so big, the two men who were attaching the handles on each side couldn't hear each other, their hammer blows on the pot. (EV, An94) ◊ **•attendre clair** to have a keen ear <VM, Lv88> **•attendre dur** to be hard of hearing **Et le vieux s'a assis dans le banc en avant. Il entendait beaucoup dur.* And the old man sat in the front pew. He was very hard of hearing. (EV, An94) <EV, An94> **•attendre haut** to be hard of hearing *Alle* *attendait haut.* She was hard of hearing. (LF) <LF> **•attendre parler de** to hear of, hear about *J'ai attendu parler de ça.* I have heard about this. (AC) <AC> <***Loc:*** AC, AV, EV, IB, JE, LA, LF, SL, SM, TB, VM, An94, Hi02, Lv88>

attendrir (tendzir) [atɑ̃drir, tɑ̃dzir] *v.tr.* to tenderize, soften *J'ai cuit c'te daube pour trois heures de temps. J'ai jamais pu la tendzir.* I cooked that roast for three hours. I never could tenderize it. (VM) <***Loc:*** VM, Da84>

attendu (entendu) [atɑ̃dy, ɑ̃tɑ̃dy] *adj.* understood, agreed *C'était entendu que les deux hommes s'auraient joint le lendemain matin.* It was understood that the two men would meet the next morning. (LA) ◊ **•bien attendu** of course *T'as faim? Mais, bien entendu!* Are you hungry? Well, of course! (LA) <LA, Da84> <***Loc:*** LA, Da84>

attenir [atənir] *v.intr.* to touch, adjoin, be contiguous *Sa maison attient à la mienne.* His house adjoins mine. (LA) <***Loc:*** LA, Da84>

attention [atɑ̃sjɔ̃, ɑ̃tɑ̃sjɔ̃, tɑ̃sjɔ̃] *n.f.* attention, heed, notice ◊ **•faire attention *a*** to pay attention, look out *Fait attention!* Pay attention! (SM) ***b*** to be careful *Et si les lapins avaient la fièvre là là, faulait tu fais attention quand tu les arranges.* And if the rabbits had the fever, you had to be careful when you prepared them. (TB) <SM, TB> <***Loc:*** EV, LF, SB, SL, SM, TB, VM, Da84, Hi02>

attentionné, -e [atɑ̃sjɔ̃ne] *adj.* **1** attentive, considerate *Elle est bien attentionnée pour ses enfants.* She is very attentive to her children. (VM) **2** careful *Il est bien attentionné quand il prend le bateau avec les petits.* He's very careful when he takes the boat out with the children. (VM) <***Loc:*** VM, Da84>

attiché ♦see **entiché**

atticher ♦see **enticher**

attiédir [atjedir] *v.tr.* to warm slightly, make lukewarm *Il s'a levé deux ou trois fois dans la nuit pour attiédir une bouteille pour le bébé.* He got up two or three times during the night to warm a bottle for the baby. (LA) <***Loc:*** LA, Da84>

attifailles ♦see **artifailles**

attiner (tiner) [atine, tine] *v.tr.* **1** to provoke, nag **2** to pick on, tease *Oh tout le temps il l'attinait tu vois? Ça fait qu'elle alle aimait parler français et les disputer en français et tout pour les faire rire, tu connais.* Oh he always teased her, you see? So she liked to speak French and scold them in French and all to make them laugh, you know. (LF) *Eux-autres aiment tiner le chat.* They like to tease the cat. (TB) <***Loc:*** JE, LF, SM, TB, Da84, Fa77, Lv88>

attineur, -euse [atinœr, -øz] *n.* **1** nag **2** tease, teaser *Il a tout le temps était beaucoup attineur.* He has always been a teaser. (LA) <***Loc:*** LA, Da84, Lv88>

attirailler [atiraje] *v.tr.* to attract, draw *La viande est tout après attirailler les mouches.* The meat is attracting flies. (TB) <***Loc:*** TB>

attirant, -e [atirɑ̃, -ɑ̃t] *adj.* enticing, attractive *Je suis pas attirante avec mes cheveux gris.* I'm not attractive with my gray hair. (VM) <***Loc:*** VM, Da84>

attirer [atire] *v.tr.* to attract, entice, lure, draw **Il aimait voir tout d'autres choses aussi, mais toujours, à chaque place, c'était le cimetière qui l'attirait.* He liked to see everything else, too, but always, in every place, it was the cemetery that attracted him. (LA, An94) <***Loc:*** LA, An94, Da84>

attisée [atize] *n.f.* armful of wood put into a fire <***Loc:*** Lv88>

attiser [atize] *v.tr.* to poke, stir up, stoke (a fire) *Il était après attiser le feu bonne heure le matin.* He was stoking the fire early in the morning. (LA) <***Loc:*** LA, Da84>

attisonner ♦see **tisonner**

attitude [atityd] *n.f.* attitude, disposition <***Loc:*** Da84>

attraction [atraksjɔ̃] *n.f.* **1** attraction **2** attractiveness <***Loc:*** Da84>

attrapage [atrapaʒ] *n.f.* catching, trapping <***Loc:*** Da84>

attrape [atrap] *n.m./f.* **1** trap, snare *Une attrape à souris.* A mousetrap. (Lv88) **2** catch (from hunting or trapping) *C'était pas bon l'hiver passé, j'ai eu proche pas d'attrapes.* Last winter was no good, I hardly caught anything hunting. (Lv88) **3** trap, trick *Je croyais avoir un bon barguine mais c'était juste une attrape.* I thought I was getting a good deal, but I was had. (Lv88) ◊ **•attrape à souris** mousetrap <TB> **•attrape-mouches / attrape à mouches *a*** fly trap ***b*** idiot, nitwit ***c*** bigmouth, chatterbox ***d*** [*pej.*] mouth, 'trap' *Frème ton attrape à mouches.* Shut your trap. (TB) <EV, TB, La99> <***Loc:*** EV, TB, VM, Da84, Hi02, La99, Lv88>

attraper [atrape, trape] **I** *v.tr.* **1** to trap, catch, capture **Si eux le coursaient, il fallait eux l'attrapent.* If they chased him, they would surely trap him. (SL, An94) *Quelle sorte d'aboëtte t'as usée pour attraper tous ces patassas?* What kind of bait did you use to catch all those perch? (VM) **2** to catch (e.g. a ball) *Tire la pelote en l'air, je vas l'attraper.* Throw the ball in the air, I'll catch it. (Gu00) *Tant que ça pouvait attraper la pelote et venir frapper un de vous-autres, ils aviont le devant.* As long as they could catch the ball and come hit one of you, they had the lead. (VM) **3** to grab, seize *La manière qu'elle attrape son bébé par le bras, c'est drôle qu'elle défait pas son épaule.* The way she grabs her baby by the arm, it's surprising that she doesn't dislocate his shoulder. (VM) **Il a été, il a attrapé la carabine. Il lui a donné.* He went, he grabbed his rifle. He gave it to him. (SL, An94) **Il est un peu haut. Je vais essayer de sauter et essayer de l'attraper.* It's a bit high. I will try to jump and try to grab it. (LA, An94) *Il a attrapé mon bras il l'a serré aussi fort qu'il pouvait.* He grabbed my arm and he squeezed it as hard as he could. (LA) **4** to get, fetch *Attrape-moi six escalins en dedans le régistre.* Get me seventy-five cents from the cash register. (VM) *Attrape une chaise et viens nous rejoindre.* Grab a chair and join us. (SM) *Attrape-moi du café.* Get me some coffee. (VM) *Attrape-moi le livre là-bas.* Get me the book over there. (SM) **5** to catch up with, overtake *Il faut on les attrape avant qu'ils arrivent au bois.* We have to catch up with them before they reach the woods. (LA) *Il l'a attrapé en tournant dans le dernier quart de mile.* He overtook him turning into the last quarter-mile. (LA) **6** to entrap, trick **Ça fait, le lendemain matin, il fallait la vieille femme va pour lui ramener ça. Il l'a pas voulu. Il dit, "Non, on va l'attraper."* So the next morning, the old woman goes to take it back to him. He didn't want it. He says, "No, we'll entrap him." (SL, An94) **7** to catch, discover (in the act of doing s.t.) *Si ça nous attrapait parler français dehors, ils avaient des petits* RULER *à peu près un pied, on mettait notre main comme ça et pah! pah!* If we were caught speaking French, they had small rulers around one foot long, we would give our hand like that and whack! whack! (IB) *Sa femme l'a quitté. Elle l'a attrapé après chiennailler.* His wife left him. She caught him sleeping around. (LA) *Je veux bien l'éhonter si je l'attrape après dire du mal de moi.* I want to shame him if I catch him saying bad things about me. (LA) **8** to catch (a cold or other illness) *Alle dit je vas attraper le* FLU. *Non, je dis j'ai été au docteur, eusse m'a piqué dessus chaque bras avec des aiguilles.* She says I'll catch the flu. No, I said I've been to the doctor, they gave me a shot in each arm with needles. (TB) *Il a attrapé un frais.* He caught a cold. (EV) *Il a travaillé dans la pluie et il a attrapé le rhume.* He worked in the rain and he caught a cold. (LA) *Quand j'ai attrapé ce* STROKE *là, j'ai resté trois mois dans l'hôpital.* When I had that stroke, I stayed in the hospital for three months. (TB) **9** to get caught in, get caught by (rain) *J'ai attrapé la pluie en venant ici.* I got caught in the rain coming over here. (SM) **On a attrapé une ratatouille.* We caught a downpour. (Da84) **10** to get, receive *Tu vas attraper une bonne rincée équand tu rentres chez toi.* You're going to get a good thrashing when you get home. (VM) **Quand il était petit, il avait attrapé un coup de pied de cheval.* When he was young, he had received a blow from a horse. (SL, An94) **II s'attraper** *v.pron.* **1** to grab hold of each other *Les petits là alentour d'un* COFFEE TABLE, *les petits juste qui commençaient à s'attraper puis se tenir là.* The children there around a coffee table, the children who were just starting to grab hold and hold themselves up. (EV) **2** to get, fetch (for o.s.) **S'attraper du pain.* To fetch bread for oneself. (Da84) ◊ **•attraper à la pincette** to grab (e.g. the ear) between thumb and forefinger *Alle l'attrape à la pincette, alle le tire par la fenêtre en disant qu'il était soûl.* She pinches his ear and pulls him out the window saying that he was drunk. (TB) <TB> **•attraper du bois** to collect logs to use as firewood *So c'était tous les ans, attraper du bois ils appelaient ça. "On va aller attraper du bois." Et ils avaient ça avec des chaînes, et des* SPIKE *et là plus tard dans le printemps, ils allaient au bord du fleuve et scier le bois et le couper avec une hache et là amener ça dans leur cour pour l'hiver.* So it was every year, catching wood they called it. "We're going to go catch wood." And they did that with chains and spikes and then later in the springtime they would go to the riverside and saw the wood and cut it with an axe and take it to their yard for winter. (SB) <SB> **•attraper du froid** to catch cold *Rentrez. J'ai assez peur que les enfants vont attraper du froid.* Come in. I'm so afraid that the children will catch cold. (LA) <LA, Da84> **•attraper du mal** ***a*** to get hurt *Fais pas ça. J'ai peur que tu vas attraper du mal.* Don't do that. I'm afraid you'll get hurt. (LA) ***b*** to get sick *Elle me mettait couché au ras d'elle pour me tiendre chaud, pour pas j'attrape du mal.* She put me to bed right next to her, to keep me warm so that I wouldn't get sick. (SL) <LA, SL, Da84> **•attraper la fraîche** to take advantage of a cool breeze <SM, VM> **•attraper un coup de lilas** to be afflicted with laziness, be lazy <AC, La99> **•attraper une touche** to get tired, get worn out *Je suis allé à la chasse hier et j'ai attrapé une fameuse touche.* I went hunting last night and I really wore myself out. (SB) <SB, La99> **•se faire attraper** to get o.s. caught *Il va se faire attraper avant ça finit.* He's going to get caught before it's over. (LA) <LA> <***Loc:*** AC, AV, EV, IB, JD, JE, LA, LF, SB, SL, SM, TB, VM, An94, Da84, Gr86, Gu00, Hi02, La99>

attrapeur ♦see **trappeur**

attriquage [atrikaʒ] *n.m./f.* strange clothing, bizarre attire <***Loc:*** LF, Lv88>

attriqué, -e [atrike] *adj.* dressed, dressed up (esp. in a peculiar or tacky way) *Je te dis il est tout attriqué, tu devrais le voir.* He's all dressed up, let me tell you; you should see him. (TB) *Moi je te dis elle est attriquée comme une paillasse.* I'm telling you, she's dressed up like a clown. (SM) *Elle est tout le temps mal attriquée.* She's always dressed in a tacky way. (VM) <***Loc:*** IB, SB, SL, SM, TB, VM>

attriquement [atrikmɑ̃] *n.m./f.* strange clothing, bizarre attire *Quel attriquement! Pourquoi il apprend pas à s'habiller.* What bizarre attire! Why doesn't he learn to dress himself. (SM) <***Loc:*** SM, Lv88>

attriquer [atrike] **I** *v.tr.* to dress in a gaudy, flashy, or tacky way *Pourquoi tu veux attriquer tes enfants comme ça?* Why do you want to dress your children in such a tacky way? (VM) **II s'attriquer** *v.pron.* to dress in a gaudy, flashy or tacky way *Il s'attrique avec le plus drôle de linge.* He dresses up in the funniest clothes. (SM) <***Loc:*** EV, SM, VM, Lv88, Ph36>

au ♦see **à**

aubèle ♦see **aubelle**

aubelle (aubèle) [obɛl] *n.f.* alburnum, sapwood *Eux-autres prenait un cipre, eux-autres ôtait tout l'aubelle qu'eux-autres appelle le bois qui vient au ras de l'écorche, dur, pas comme le cœur du bois.* They used a cypress, they removed all the sapwood as they call the wood that comes around the bark, it's hard, [but] not like the heartwood. (TB) <***Loc:*** TB, Da84, Lv88>

aucun[1], **-e** [okœ̃, okɛ̃, okyn, okœ̃n, okɛ̃n] *adj.* not any, no *Il follait que ça soye bien bien bien soigné pour être sûr que aucun z-essence ou aucun n-huile va pas dans les eaux.* It had to be extremely well kept up to be sure that no gas and no oil would go into the water. (LF) *J'en veux pas aucune qualité.* I don't want any kind. (LF) *Pas aucune femme.* Not any woman. (LF) ◊ **•aucun temps** no time, no time at all *Il va être ici dans aucun temps.* He'll be here in no time. (SM) *Well, ça pas pris aucun temps.* Well, that didn't take any time at all. (Gu82) <SM, Gu82, Lv88> ***<Loc:*** EV, LA, LF, SM, TB, VM, Da84, Gu82, Lv88>

aucun[2], **-e** [okœ̃] *n.* one, someone, person *Et là uh si l'aucun que le bateau est fait pour, il trouvait pas qu'il avait assez de tenture dedans, eh ben ça pouvait le fermer comme ça.* And then if the one that the boat was being made for found that there wasn't enough flair in it, well they could close it like that. (LF) **Il y a des aucuns.* There some people. (Da84) **Il y a des aucunes.* There are some [female] people. (Da84) ***<Loc:*** LF, SB, Da84>

aucun[3], **-e** [okœ̃] *pron.* none, not one, not any *Aucun de eux avait été à l'école.* Not one of them had been to school. (LF) *J'en vois pas aucun.* I don't see a single one. (SB) ***<Loc:*** LF, SB, Da84>

audace [odas] *n.f.* audacity, foolhardiness, nerve, boldness, brashness ◊ **•avec audace** audaciously <Da84> ***<Loc:*** Da84>

audacieux, -euse [odasjø, -øz] *adj.* audacious, bold, presumptuous *Tant qu'à lui, il était purement audacieux.* As for him, he was absolutely audacious. (LA) ***<Loc:*** LA, Da84, Lv88>

audience [odjɑ̃s] *n.f.* audience, spectators, assembly *Il a parlé devant une audience de trois cents personnes.* He spoke to an audience of three hundred people. (SL) ***<Loc:*** EV, IB, SL, SM, Da84, Ph36>

auditeur [oditœr] *n.m.* **1** auditor **2** [*recent*] listener, hearer ***<Loc:*** Da84>

audition [odisjɔ̃] *n.f.* audition, hearing ***<Loc:*** Da84>

aufaîter (**enfaîter**) [ofete, ɑ̃fete] *v.tr.* to fill to the brim, fill to overflowing *Quand t'encannes des figues, il faut aufaîter tes jarres.* When you can figs, you have to fill your jars right to the top. (VM) ***<Loc:*** JE, VM, Da84, Di32>

auge (**orge**) [ɔʒ, ɔrʒ] *n.m./f.* trough (for water or feed) ***<Loc:*** LA, LF, SM, VM, Da84, Lv88>

augmentation [ɔgmɑ̃tasjɔ̃] *n.f.* augmentation, increase, raise (e.g. in salary) ***<Loc:*** Da84>

augmenter [ɔgmɑ̃te] **I** *v.tr.* to augment, increase, raise **II** *v.intr.* to increase, rise *Le riz de plant et les machineries augmentent toujours et on a presque pas rien pour le riz.* The seed rice and the machinery are always increasing [in price] and we get almost nothing for the rice. (VM) **II s'augmenter** *v.pron.* to increase, grow **Le vent s'augmente.* The wind is increasing. (Da84) **Le troupeau s'augmente.* The herd is increasing. (Da84) ***<Loc:*** VM, Da84>

aujourd'hui [oʒɔrdɥɪ, aʒɔrdɥi, aʒurdɥi] *adv.* **1** today **Aujourd'hui en huit jours.* A week from today. (Da84) *On part aujourd'hui.* We are leaving today. (JE) **2** at present, these days, nowadays *Et on s'assisait sur les galeries, y avait pas de trafic qu'il y a aujourd'hui.* And we used to sit out on the porch, there wasn't traffic like there is nowadays. (LF) ◊ **•au jour d'aujourd'hui** today *J'aime parler avec le monde en français jusqu'au jour d'aujourd'hui, tu connais, tous les pêcheurs eusse parle en français.* I like talking to people in French even today, you know, all the fishermen speak French. (LF) <LF> **•jusqu'à jour d'aujourd'hui** until now, until this very day *Jusqu'à jour d'aujourd'hui, j'ai jamais dit à Emas.* Until this very day, I have never told Emas. (AC) <AC> ***<Loc:*** AC, AV, EV, IB, IV, JE, LA, LF, SJ, SL, SM, TB, VM, An94, Da84, Hi02, Lv88, Wh83>

aumône [ɔ̃mɔ̃n] *n.f.* alms, charity ***<Loc:*** Da84>

auparavant (**paravant**) [oparavɑ̃, paravɑ̃] *adv.* previously, formerly, beforehand, before *Oh euh, ben, elle est mort, vous savez. C'est, c'est du vieux monde d'auparavant.* Oh well, she's dead, you know. Those were old people from long ago. (PQ) ◊ **•auparavant de** before *Un beau mais jeune garçon, prends bien l'exemple à prendre sur moi. C'est comme ça vous aurez ça à conserver: C'est d'aller la voir auparavant de s'en aller. Paravant, paravant de s'en aller.* Handsome but young man, take the example from me. That's how you will have this to preserve. Go to see her before leaving. Before, before leaving. (IB, ch: *Le pays des étrangers*) <IB> ***<Loc:*** IB, PQ, Da84>

auprès [oprɛ, opre] *adv.* near, close, close by *Petit bougre, lui, il a été. Il a été auprès. Et il a regardé son père.* The little fellow, him, he went. He went close by. And he looked at his father. (IB) ◊ **•auprès de *a*** near, close to *Tout ceux-là qu'était tout auprès de la levée. Auprès du fleuve.* All of those who were near the levee, near the river. (SJ) ***b*** by, next to *Il est toujours assodié là auprès du feu.* He's always crouched over there by the fire. (VM) *J'ai assis auprès de lui à l'église.* I sat next to him at church. (SM) ***c*** to, with (s.o.) *Il a intercédé auprès de l'évêque pour annuler le mariage.* He pleaded with the bishop to annul the marriage. (LA) <EV, LA, SJ, SM, TB, VM, An94> **•d'auprès** from close, close *On peut le voir mieux d'auprès.* We can see it better from up close. (VM) <VM, Da84> ***<Loc:*** EV, IB, LA, SJ, SL, SM, TB, VM, An94, Da84>

auquel ♦see **quel**

auriculaire [orikylær] *adj.* [*eccl.*] auricular (as in Roman Catholic Church "auricular confession") ***<Loc:*** Da84>

aussi (**aussite, aussitte**) [osi, osit] *adv.* **1** also, too, likewise *Lui aussite il va avec eux.* He's also going with them. (SM) *Ça s'amenait du pain aussi mais si le pain venait à moisir,* WELL *eux-autres avait ces gâteaux-là à manger.* They brought bread too, but if the bread got moldy, well they had those cakes to eat. (TB) *Je vais pas autrement que tu vas aussi.* I'm not going unless you go too. (SM) **2** so **C'est toi qu'après voler ma crème aussi longtemps.* You're the one who's been stealing my cream for so long. (EV, An94) *Il était aussi content!* He was so happy! (EV) *C'est ça qui fait on a autant de petits qui est aussi malheureux.* [Drugs], that's why we have so many children who are so unhappy. (EV) *Aussi loin de ma maison, ça me casse le cœur.* So far from my house, it breaks my heart. (Lv88) ◊ **•aussi bien *a*** as well *Le monde s'accordait aussi bien ou mieux qu'asteur.* People got along as well or better than [they do] now. (TB) ***b*** moreover, besides *On devrait pas être après faire ça, et aussi bien, ton père pourrait arriver.* We shouldn't be doing this, and besides your father might show up. (LA) <LA, TB> **•aussi bien que *a*** as well as **On figurait que c'était pour leur montrer à eux que quand même si on avait pas d'éducation comme eux ils aviont, on pouvait apprendre à jouer de la musique aussi bien que n'importe qui d'autre à l'oreille.* We figured that it was to teach them that even though we didn't have an education like they had, we could learn to play music as well as anyone else by ear. (LA, An84) ***b*** suppose, what if (used to express a probability) **Aussi bien qu'il irait se faire tuer.* Suppose he gets killed. (Da84) <LA, An84, Da84> **•aussi... que / aussi... comme** as . . . as *Aussi gros qu'il est, il danse léger, léger, léger.* As big as he is, he dances very lightly. (LA) *Alle est venue aussi lesse qu'un papillon dans une bol de beurre.* She became as lively as a butterfly in a bowl of butter. (AV) *J'aurais jamais cru que j'aurais été aussi bête que ça!* I would never have thought I could be that stupid. (TB) *Elle a travaillé aussi bien qu'un docteur.* She [the midwife] worked as well as a doctor. (EV) *Il est aussi gros comme moi.* He's as fat as me. (SM) *Ça fait aussi froid comme hier.* It is as cold [today] as yesterday. (Lv88) <AV, EV, LA, SM, TB, An84, Gu82, Lv88, Wh83> <***Loc:*** AC, AV, EV, LA, LF, PQ, SB, SL, SM, TB, VM, An84, An94, Da84, Gu82, Hi02, Lv88, Wh83>

aussitôt [osito] *adv.* at once, immediately *Son frère a arrivé et ils ont parti aussitôt.* His brother arrived and they left immediately. (LA) ◊ **•aussitôt que** as soon as *Les grandes ouragans, aussitôt que le vent calmait, l'eau s'en va.* Big hurricanes, as soon as the wind died down, the water went away. (TB) <TB, Da84> <***Loc:*** LA, TB, Da84>

autant [otɑ̃] *adv.* as much, so much *Toi tu vas pas rire autant, je pense.* You won't laugh as much, I think. (TB) *Tu peux blesser quelqu'un autant avec des paroles qu'avec des coups.* You can injure someone as much with words as with blows. (LA) **Monsieur Johnson, moi, je peux pas dire autant de vous. Je vous trouve pas beau.* Mr. Johnson, I can't say as much about you. I don't find you handsome. (SM, An94) *Il se respecte pas du tout. C'est pour ça qu'il boit autant.* He has no respect for himself. That's why he drinks so much. (LA) ◊ **•autant comme autant** many times *Je l'ai disputé autant comme autant, il le fait quand même.* I've scolded him many times, but he does it all the same. (LF) <LF> **•autant de *a*** as much, so much *On a pas besoin de planter autant de canne.* We don't need to plant as much sugarcane. (AS) *Moi j'ai jamais de ma vie vu autant d'eau.* I've never in my life seen so much water. (TB) ***b*** as many, so many *Je trouve que les Indiens a pas autant de mots que nous-autres.* I find that the Indians don't have as many words as we do. (TB) *Ne pleurez pas autant la belle, ne versez pas autant de larmes.* Don't cry so much, girl, don't shed so many tears. (ch: *La veuve de sept ans*) <AC, EV, IV, LA, SM, TB, VM, An94> **•autant dire** you might as well say *Alle était après mourir, autant dire.* You might as well say she was dying. (TB) <TB> **•autant moins** by so much less <Da84> **•autant que {comme}** as much as **Ça se ressemble autant que deux petits peut se ressembler.* They resemble each other as much as two children can resemble each other. (EV, An94) *La picote, c'est une maladie défigurante, mais pas autant que la lèpre.* Smallpox is a disfiguring disease, but not as much as leprosy. (VM) *Je vaux autant comme toi.* I'm worth as much as you. (SM) <EV, SM, TB, VM, An94, Da84, Lv88> **•autant que pour** as for <Da84> **•autant quitte** just as well **Vaut autant quitte aller.* One might as well as go. (Da84) *Autant quitte que tu sors.* It's just as well that you leave. (LF) *T'as autant quitte aller tout à l'heure.* You would do just as well by going there right away. (Lv88) <LF, SM, Da84, Lv88> **•d'autant plus** so much more, all the more **J'ai toujours les mêmes sentiments qui me fâchaient en 1975, et ça me fâche d'autant plus aujourd'hui.* I still have the same feelings that angered me in 1975, and they anger me that much more today. (LA, An84) <LA, An84, Da84> <***Loc:*** AC, AS, EV, LA, LF, SM, TB, VM, An84, An94, Da84, Hi02, Lv88>

autel [otɛl] *n.f.* altar <***Loc:*** Da84, Hi02, Lv88>

auteur [otœr] *n.m.* **1** author, writer **2** cause, maker **Il en est l'auteur.* He is the cause. (Da84) *C'est toi l'auteur.* It is your fault. (JE) <***Loc:*** JE, LF, Da84>

autographe [otograf] *n.m.* [*recent*] autograph <***Loc:*** Da84>

automatique[1] [otɔ̃matik] *adj.* automatic *Il avait fait ça assez souvent que ça a devenu automatique.* He did that so often that it became automatic. (LA) <***Loc:*** LA, LF, Da84>

automatique[2] [otɔ̃matik] *adv.* automatically *Et y a des bateaux asteur, le dedans c'est fait avec une espèce de ciment, comme un ciment qu'ils mettont là-dedans. Et là ils ont des machines à* FREEZE *pour glacer automatique, so ils dépendont pas sur la glace.* And there are boats today, the inside is made of a kind of cement, like a cement they put in there. And they have freezers to freeze automatically, so they don't depend on ice. (LF) *Les crabes dedans ces* AUTOMATIC TRAPS *là qui attrape automatique là, quand alle rentre alle peut pas ressortir, ils ont crevé dedans juste dans une journée.* The crabs in those traps that trap automatically, when she goes in there she can't get back out, they died in there in just one day. (TB) <***Loc:*** LF, TB>

automne [otɔ̃n] *n.m./f.* autumn, fall <***Loc:*** AC, Da84, Hi02>

automobile (**z-automobile**) [otɔ̃mobil, zɔ̃mobil] *n.m./f.* automobile, car <***Loc:*** AV, EV, LF, SJ, SM, TB, Da84>

autorisation [otorizasjɔ̃] *n.f.* authorization <***Loc:*** Da84>

autoriser [otorize] *v.tr.* to authorize, permit, sanction *Ils l'ont jamais autorisé à faire ça qu'il a fait.* They never authorized him to do what he did. (LA) <***Loc:*** LA, Da84>

autorité [otorite] *n.f.* authority, power ◊ **•les autorités** the authorities <Da84> <***Loc:*** Da84>

autour (**entour**) [otur, ɑ̃tur] *adv.* about, around, hereabout *Y en a pus de chiens autour.* There are no longer many dogs around. (TB) ◊ **•autour (de)** ***a*** around, near, in the vicinity of *Je reste autour de Lafayette.* I live near Lafayette. (SM) **Autour d'ici.* Around here. (Da84) **Autour de la maison.* Around or near the house. (Da84) *Il y avait pas de chemin de fer autour ici.* There was no railway around here. (EV) ***b*** approximately, around *J'ai reçu autour de trois cents piastres aujourd'hui.* I received about three hundred dollars today. (SM) *Il est autour d'onze heures.* It is about eleven o'clock. (JE) **I' sont venus à Mamou entours de 1922.* They came to Mamou around 1922. (Wh83) <EV, JE, SM, Da84, Wh83> <***Loc:*** AV, EV, JE, LA, LF, SB, SL, SM, TB, VM, Da84, Hi02, Lv88, Wh83>

autre [ɔt(r)] *adj.* other **Une autre fois.* Another time. (Da84) **L'autre jour.* The other day. (Da84) **D'une place à l'autre.* From one place to another. (Da84) **Les autres fois.* Olden days. (Da84) **Ni l'un ni l'autre.* Neither one. (Da84) **Qui d'autre?* Who else? (Da84) **Quoi d'autre?* What else? (Da84) **Il y en a d'autres.* There are others. (Da84) *'Coute les enfants ricaner dans l'autre chambre.* Listen to the kids laughing in the other room. (SM) ◊ **•autre part** elsewhere *T'as pour le chercher autre part; il est pas ici dans.* You'll have to look for him elsewhere; he's not here. (VM) <VM> **•autre que** other than, besides **Autre que ça, j'ai vu personne.* Other than that, I saw no one. (Da84) <EV, LF, VM, Da84> **•d'autre** more, additional **Il y en a d'autre.* There's more. (Da84) *Je vais t'en donner d'autre gâteau.* I'm going to give you more cake. (SM) *Ils avont pas assez de riz, donne-y-en d'autre.* They don't have enough rice, give them some more. (VM) *T'en veux d'autre?* Do you want more? (VM) <EV, SM, VM, An94, Da84, Lv88> **•l'un l'autre / l'un à l'autre** one another, each other *Le monde s'aidait l'un à l'autre.* People helped each other. (SL) *On rit après l'un à l'autre.* We laugh at each other. (LF) <LA, LF, SL, SM, VM, Lv88> **•un et l'autre** ***a*** one another, each other *Dessus le bayou je crois que tout chacun est parent. Si on est pas parents, tout chacun connaît un et l'autre et c'est une place qu'est bien tranquille icitte sur le bayou.* On the bayou I think everyone is related. If we're not related, everyone knows each other and it'a a place that's very quiet here on the bayou. (LF) ***b*** somebody, someone *Un et l'autre ramassait un jeune cochon pour une piasse ou deux, et là on met ça en dehors, et on feedait ça, jusqu'à que ça vient bon à tuer.* Someone would pick up a young pig for a dollar or two, and then we put it outside, we fed it until it was good to slaughter. (TB) ***c*** this and that, one thing and the other *Et là y a huit ans que je suis* RETIRE *de ça. Et là asteur là juste je pigoche dans l'un et l'autre.* And it's eight years since I retired from that. And now I just putter in this and that. (TB) <LA, LF, TB> <***Loc:*** AC, AV, EV, IV, LA, LF, PQ, SL, SM, TB, VM, Da84, Hi02, Lv88>

autrefois [otrəfwa, ɔtfwa] *adv.* formerly, in the past *Autrefois, il aurait pas fait ça comme ça.* In the past, he would not have done that that way. (LA) <***Loc:*** LA, TB, Da84>

autrement (**entrement**) [otrəmɑ̃] *adv.* otherwise, or else *Y avait peut-être trois familles qu'avaient un peu d'argent. Autrement tout le reste était pauvre mais ça les faisait pas de différence.* There were perhaps three families who had a little money. Otherwise all the reste were poor, but that didn't make any difference to them. (SB) ◊ **•autrement de {que} ça** otherwise, apart from that *Mais autrement de ça il faut que tu les amènes sur le Bayou Black.* But otherwise you have to take them to Bayou Black. (TB) *Pour la première communion et tout ça on chantait mais autrement que ça non.* We used to sing for the first communion but apart from that no. (IB) *Entrement de ça peut-être le lendemain t'aurais manqué et quelqu'un te courait par-derrière.* Otherwise the next day you might have turned up missing and someone would go after you. (TB) *Entrement que ça, je sais pas comment le monde aurait vi. Mais là, ça a rechangé, par exemple.* Other than that, I don't know how people would have survived. But then, things changed again, for example. (AC) <AC, IB, TB> **•autrement que** unless *Je vais pas autrement que tu vas aussi.* I'm not going unless you go too. (SM) <SM, TB> <***Loc:*** AC, AV, EV, IB, SB, SM, TB, VM, Da84>

autrui [otrɥi] *pron.* [*eccl.*] others, other people <***Loc:*** Da84>

auvent [ovɑ̃] *n.f.* awning <***Loc:*** Da84>

aux ♦see **à**

auxiliaire [oksiljær] *adj.* auxiliary, aiding **Les dames auxiliaires.* Ladies aid society, ladies' auxiliary. (Da84) <***Loc:*** Da84>

avalage see ♦**envalage**

avalasse [avalas, avlas] *n.f.* **1** downpour, deluge, heavy rain *Y a tombé une avalasse hier au soir. Y avait de l'eau dans les rues.* There was a downpour yesterday evening. There was water in the streets. (Gu00) *Il a mouillé une avalasse le soir.* It rained, a deluge, in the evening. (LA) **2** avalanche <***Loc:*** AL, EV, IB, JE, LA, LF, SB, SL, SM, TB, Da84, Fa77, Gu00, Hi02, Lv88, Ph36>

avalement ♦see **envalement**

avaler ♦see **envaler**

avaloire [avalwær] *n.m.* esophagus *Un morceau lui a resté collé dans l'avaloire, ça l'a proche étouffé.* A piece stayed stuck in his esophagus, it almost suffocated him. (VM) <***Loc:*** VM>

avançant, -e [avɑ̃sɑ̃] *adj.* quick, fast *Cette ouvrage est bien avançante.* This work goes really fast. (Lv88) *Ça c'est un bougre bien avançant à l'ouvrage.* That's a guy who's quick at work. (Lv88) <***Loc:*** VM, Lv88>

avance [avɑ̃s] *n.f.* advance, headway, progress ◊ **•d'avance *a*** beforehand, ahead of time *Chère Mam, c'est ca qui me fait plus de peine. De savoir ma mort aussi longtemps d'avance.* Dear Mother, that's what hurts me so. To know my death so far ahead of time. (IB: ch: *Les clefs de la prison*) ***b*** previous *Moi j'ai un garçon d'un mariage d'avance, et là Julia a deux filles d'un mariage d'avance.* I have a son from a previous marriage, and Julia has two daughters from a previous marriage. (TB) <EV, IB, LA, TB> **•en avance** ahead *Il est en avance avec son maïs.* He's ahead with his corn crop. (VM) <SM, VM, Lv88> **•faire des avances** to make advances, make overtures *Il a le toupet de faire des avances à cette pauvre veuve. Il y a juste deux mois que son mari est mort.* He's got some nerve making advances toward that poor widow. It's only been two months since her husband died. (EV) <EV, Da84> **•faire des avances (d'argent)** to advance (money) *Il pouvait pas lui faire une avance, parce qu'il était déjà tellement en dette lui-même.* He couldn't advance him any money because he was in such debt already himself. (LA) <LA> **•faire plus d'avance** to work faster *Elle fait plus d'avance que moi pour casser le gombo.* She is faster than me at harvesting okra. (Lv88) <Lv88> <***Loc:*** EV, IB, LA, SM, TB, VM, Da84, Lv88>

avancé, -e [avɑ̃se] *adj.* ahead, advanced *Je suis avancé dans mon ouvrage.* I am ahead in my work. (Lv88) **La saison est avancée.* It's late in the season. (Da84) **Le jour est avancé.* The day is advanced. (Da84) ◊ **•en avancé** forward *Il a été en avancé.* He went forward. (JE) <JE> <***Loc:*** JE, Da84, Lv88>

avancement [avɑ̃smɑ̃] *n.m.* **1** advancement, advancing **2** promotion <***Loc:*** Da84>

avancer [avɑ̃se, vɑ̃se] **I** *v.tr.* **1** to advance, move forward **Avancer la pendule.* To set the clock ahead. (Da84) *En autres mots t'après avancer ton éducation, et en même temps tu* TEACH*?* In other words, you're advancing your education, and at the same time you teach? (TB) **2** to lend *Il m'a avancé dix piastres.* He lent me ten dollars. (JE) **3** to promote *Il a peur que ça va jamais l'avancer dans son ouvrage.* He is afraid that they will never promote him at his work. (LA) **II** *v.intr.* to advance, move up, move forward **L'ouvrage avance.* The work is progressing. (Da84) *'Vance-woir-toi!* Come forward! (SM) **III s'avancer** *v.pron.* to move ahead, approach **Et toujours, sur sa route, l'après-midi était après s'avancer.* And in any case, on his way, afternoon was approaching. (LA, An94) <***Loc:*** EV, JE, LA, LF, SM, TB, An94, Da84, Wh83>

avant[1] [avɑ̃, ɑ̃vɑ̃] *n.m.* ◊ **•aller de l'avant** to go on (of an event) *So il avait une danse qu'allait de l'avant.* There was a dance going on. (LF) <LF> **•(d')en avant** front, located in front *Le quartier d'en avant pour 17 piasses 95.* The front quarter [of the pig] for 17 dollars and 95 cents. (EV) *Ouvre la vitre d'en avant.* Open the front window. (Lv88) **La cour d'en avant.* The front yard. (Da84) **La chambre d'en avant.* The front room. (Da84) <AC, EV, LF, TB, VM, Da84, Gu00, Lv88, Wh83> **•en avant *a*** ahead *Ayoù il est? Il est loin là-bas en avant.* Where is he? He's way up ahead over there. (LA) *J'ai sorti deux cents piastres en avant.* I came out ahead by two hundred dollars. (LA) *Il va prendre quelques jours off. Ils sont en avant avec le* JOB*.* He's going to take a few days off. They're ahead on the job. (LA) ***b*** fast (of a clock) *La pendule est en avant.* The clock is fast. (Lv88) ***c*** in reserve *J'aime avoir du linge en avant.* I like to have some clothes in reserve. (Lv88) <AS, EV, JE, LA, VM, Lv88> **•en avant de *a*** in front of *Quand on allait coucher le weekend, pour pas on ait froid l'hiver, 'tit Mam mettait un matelas droit en avant de le foyer.* When we went to bed on weekends, so that we would not be cold in the winter, Mom put a mattress right in front of the fireplace. (SL) *Il passait un char en avant de chez lui.* A car was going by in front of his house. (Lv88) ***b*** ahead of *Les Mardi Gras sont pas supposés d'aller en avant du capitaine.* The Mardi Gras runners are not supposed to go ahead of the captain. (LA) <LA, LF, SL, SM, TB, VM, An94, Da84, Gu00, Lv88> **•être de l'avant** to be ahead (e.g. in one's work) *Si vous commencez de matin vous serez de l'avant.* If you begin in the morning you'll be ahead. (SB) <SB, Lv88> <***Loc:*** AC, AS, EV, JE, LA, LF, SB, SL, SM, TB, VM, An94, Da84, Gu00, Lv88, Wh83>

avant[2] [avɑ̃] *prep.* **1** before, ahead of, in advance of **Naturellement, il y a une qu'a été servie avant l'autre.* Naturally, there was one who was served before the other one. (EV, An94) **2** before, till, to (in telling time) *Il est dix minutes avant cinq heures.* It's ten till five. (Lv88) ◊ **•avant de** before **Mon père et mon beau-frère ont resté un soir un arpent avant de rentrer dans la savane à l'écouter passer.* My father and my brother-in-law stayed out one evening before going out into the pasture to listen to him pass over. (SL, An94) <AC, EV, IB, LA, LF, PQ, SB, SL, SM, TB, VM, An94, Gu00, Lv88, Wh83> **•avant (que)** before *Avant il fait son jardin.* Before he plants his garden. (Lv88) *Avant que l'école commence.* Before school starts. (Lv88) **Mais tu resteras dans la caverne. Sors pas avant que je reviens.* But you will stay in the cave. Don't come out before I come back. (IB, An94) <AC, EV, IB, LA, SL, TB, VM, An94, Da84, Lv88> **•avant tout** above all *Avant tout, c'était le moment où les familles se rencontraient et laissaient les jeunes filles sortir parmi* *le monde.* Above all, it was the time when families met and allowed the girls to go out among the community. (VM) <SL, VM, Da84, Lv88> <***Loc:*** AC, EV, IB, LA, LF, PQ, SB, SL, SM, TB, VM, An94, Da84, Guoo, Hi02, Lv88, Wh83>

avantage [avɑ̃taʒ] *n.m.* advantage, benefit ◊ **•prendre avantage de** to take advantage of *Si quelqu'un aurait voulu prendre avantage de nous-autres, eux-autres aurait pu aisément faire ça.* If someone had wanted to take advantage of us, they could easily have done that. (TB) <TB, Da84> **•prendre (l')avantage** to take the advantage *Quand l'autre bougre a tombé, il a pris l'avantage.* When the other fellow fell, he took the advantage. (LA) <EV, LA> <***Loc:*** EV, LA, TB, Da84, Fa77>

avantagé, -e [avɑ̃taʒe] *adj.* lucky *Pauvre bête, il était pas trop avantagé.* Poor thing, he wasn't too lucky. (LA) <***Loc:*** AL, LA>

avantageux, -euse [avɑ̃taʒø, -øz] *adj.* advantageous, favorable *Ce* DEAL *il fait, c'était pas avantageux pour sa famille du tout.* That deal he made was not advantageous at all for his famille. (LA) <***Loc:*** LA, Da84, Fa77>

avant-hier (avant-z-hier) [avɑ̃zjær, avɑ̃jær] *adv.* the day before yesterday *L'autre avant-z-hier.* Three days ago. (LF) *Elle a parti avant-z-hier.* She left day before yesterday. (JE) ◊ **•avant-hier (matin, midi, soir)** day before yesterday (morning, noon, night) <Da84> <***Loc:*** JE, Da84, Hi02>

avant-jour [avɑ̃ʒur] *n.m.* dawn, daybreak **J'm'ai réveillé z'un matin su(r) l'avant-jour.* I woke up one morning at dawn. (Gr86) <***Loc:*** Da84, Gr86, Lv88>

avant-midi [avɑ̃midi] *n.m.* morning, forenoon *Et là après ça, dans l'avant-midi, eux-autres commençait à faire le bouilli.* And after that, in the morning, they started making the boiled meat. (LF) <***Loc:*** AC, EV, LA, LF, SM, VM, Gu82, Lv88>

avant-z-hier ♦see **avant-hier**

avare[1] [avar] *adj.* **1** stingy, tight, avaricious **Et il avait une truie qu'était beaucoup avare.* And he had a sow that was very stingy. (EV, An94) **2** gluttonous **Il est si avare qu'il a mangé tout ça y avait.* He is so gluttonous that he ate everything in sight. (EV, Ph36) <***Loc:*** EV, An94, Da84, Fa77, Ph36>

avare[2] [avar] *n.m.* miser, tightwad <***Loc:*** Da84>

avarice [avaris] *n.f.* avarice, greed, stinginess <***Loc:*** Da84>

avarie [avari] *n.f.* tragedy, terrible event *Y avait une avarie hier au soir au village.* There was a terrible event in the village last night. (VM) <***Loc:*** VM>

avec [avɛk, ave] *prep.* **1** with *Je m'assis dessus la galerie, le monde arrête charrer avec moi.* I sit on my porch, people stop to talk with me. (EV) *Ils vont venir avec du barbecue.* They're going to come with some barbecue. (EV) *Il est parent avec ma femme.* He is related to my wife. (VM) *Il attrape une poule et puis parte avec.* It catches a hen and and takes off with it. (SL) **2** from *Il avait emprunté ça avec un voisin.* He had borrowed that from a neighbor. (Lv88 *J'ai acheté mon char avec Léon.* I bought my car from Leon. (Lv88) ◊ **•avec pas** without *Au commencement les bateaux étaient faits avec pas de machines dedans. Avec une voile, et le pousser.* In the beginning boats were made without engines in them. With a sail, and pushing. (LF) *Et il voulait pas qu'on travaille avec pas de l'assurance dessus. C'était trop risqué.* And he didn't want us to work with no insurance. It was too risky. (TB) <LF, TB> <***Loc:*** AC, AS, AV, EV, JE, LA, LF, PQ, SB, SL, SM, TB, VM, An94, Da84, Guoo, Hi02, Lv88>

avenant, -e (amenant, -e) [avnɑ̃, abnɑ̃, ɑ̃mnɑ̃, -ɑ̃t] *adj.* pleasing, nice, likeable *Tu es si avenant.* You are so agreable. (JE) *On va chez Lorita pour souper. Alle est très avenante, alle nous invite tout le temps.* We're going to Lorita's for supper. She's very nice, she invites us all the time. (LF) <***Loc:*** JE, LF>

avenir [avnir] *n.f.* future ◊ **•à l'avenir** in the future, henceforth *Un jour à l'avenir ma petite va grandir.* One day in the future my daughter will grow. (AV) <AV, Da84> **•avoir une bonne avenir** to have a good future <Da84> <***Loc:*** AV, EV, LA, Da84, Hi02, Lv88>

avent [avɑ̃] *n.m.* Advent (the four weeks preceding Christmas) <***Loc:*** Da84, Fa77>

aventure [avɑ̃tyr] *n.f.* adventure, exploit ◊ **•bonne aventure** fortune <VM, Da84, La99> <***Loc:*** VM, Da84, Fa77, La99>

aventurer [avɑ̃tyre] **I** *v.tr.* to take a chance with, venture, risk *Aventurer de l'argent.* To venture a bet. (LA) **II s'aventurer** *v.pron.* to take a chance, venture, risk *Mon petit chien s'a aventuré dans la savane avec les vaches hier.* My little dog ventured out in the pasture with the cows yesterday. (VM) <***Loc:*** LA, VM, Da84>

avenue [avny] *n.f.* avenue <***Loc:*** Da84, Lv88>

averse [aværs] *n.f.* heavy rain, downpour *Ça a tombé une averse dans l'après-midi.* A heavy rain fell this afternoon. (LA) <***Loc:*** LA, Da84>

avertir [aværtir] *v.tr.* to warn, inform, notify *Ça avait été averti par le* WEATHER BUREAU *de la ville qu'il y avait du mauvais temps qui s'amenait.* They had been warned by the city weather bureau that bad weather was coming. (LF) ◊ **•avertir d'avance** to inform beforehand, forewarn *Ils étaient pus là. Quelqu'un les avait avertis d'avance.* They were no longer there. Someone had forewarned them. (LA) <***Loc:*** AV, EV, LA, LF, Da84, Fa77, Hi02>

avertissement[1] [aværtismɑ̃] *n.m./f.* **1** warning, notification, information **2** premonition *C'est comme un avertissement que quelque chose va arriver. Eh ben deux soirs avant que mon garçon se fait tuer, [...] j'ai eu un avertissement.* It's like a premonition that something is going to happen. Two nights before my son got killed, I had a premonition. (TB) **3** spiritual visit *La femme a eu une avertissement dans la nuit. Son* *mari avait paru à côté de son lit pour lui parler juste après minuit, et c'est exactement l'heure qu'il a été frappé par le char.* The lady had a spiritual visit in the night. Her husband appeared next to her bed to talk to her just after midnight, and that's exactly when he was hit by the car. (LA) <*Loc:* EV, LA, TB, Da84, Lv88>

avertissement[2] (ADVERTISEMENT) [aværtismɑ̃, adværtismɔ̃, advərtaizmənt] *n.m.* advertisement **Des avertissements de terrains à vendre.* Advertisements for land for sale. (Gr86) <*Loc:* EV, LA, SM, TB, Da84, Gr86, Lv88>

aveuglant, -e [avøglɑ̃, -ɑ̃t] *adj.* blinding, dazzling, glaring *Le soleil était positivement aveuglant.* The sun was positively blinding. (LA) <*Loc:* Da84>

aveugle [avœg(l)] *adj.* blind ◊ **•aveugle de naissance** blind from birth <Da84> <*Loc:* Da84, Fa77>

aveugler [avøgle] **I** *v.tr.* to blind **Il lui a ôté les deux yeux. Il l'a aveuglé, l'homme, et il avait la pendule.* He plucked out his two eyes. He blinded him, that man, and he had the clock. (SL, An94) **II s'aveugler** *v.pron.* to blind o.s. *Je m'ai aveuglé en regardant la lampe.* I blinded myself looking at the lamp. (VM) <*Loc:* SL, An94, Da84>

avide [avid] *adj.* avid, eager, greedy *C'est un vrai maquereau. Il est avide des femmes.* He's a real ladies' man. He can't get enough of women. (VM) <*Loc:* VM, Da84>

avidité [avidite] *n.f.* avidity, eagerness, greed <*Loc:* Da84>

avion [avjɔ̃] *n.* [*recent*] airplane <*Loc:* TB>

avirer [avire] *v.intr.* to change course *Le vent l'a fait avirer.* The wind made him change course. (IB) <*Loc:* IB>

avis [avi] *n.m.* **1** advice **2** idea, opinion ◊ **•prendre l'avis** to take advice *Il prend pas l'avis de personne.* He won't take anyone's advice. (EV) <EV, Lv88> <*Loc:* EV, Da84, Lv88>

aviser (**adviser**) [avize, avise, advize] **I** *v.tr.* to give advice to, advise, counsel *J'aviserais pas quelqu'un d'assayer de coucher sur la rue en ville asteur.* I would not advise someone to try to sleep on the street in New Orleans nowadays. (TB) *Il dit: "je t'adviserais," il dit, "lui quitter son nom il est venu avec."* He says, "I'd advise you," he says, "to leave him with the name he came with." (AV) **II s'aviser** *v.pron.* to find out, get information *Allons s'aviser sur cette affaire.* Let's get some sense of direction in this matter. (Lv88) ◊ **•bien avisé** well-advised *Il serait bien avisé d'écouter sa femme.* He would be well advised to listen to his wife. (LA) <LA, Da84> <*Loc:* AV, EV, SM, TB, Da84, Lv88, Ph36>

aviseur [avizœr] *n.m.* advisor, counselor <*Loc:* SB, Lv88>

avisse ♦see **vis**

avisser ♦see **visser**

avocado ♦see **avocat**

avocasser [avokase] *v.tr.* to plead (a case), defend (a position) *Il était toujours après avocasser son cas à deux heures du matin.* He was still pleading his case at two in the morning. (LA) <*Loc:* LA, Lv88>

avocat[1] (**avocado**) [avoka, avokado] *n.m.* avocado <*Loc:* Da84, Hi02>

avocat[2] [avoka] *n.m.* **1** lawyer, counselor, attorney *Quelqu'un m'a dit d'aller voir un avocat.* Someone told me to go see a lawyer. (TB) **2** [*pej.*] know-it-all ◊ **•avocat (de) district** ***a*** district attorney ***b*** know-it-all <JE, Da84> **•avocat général** attorney general *L'avocat général de l'état.* The attorney general of the state. (VM) <VM, Da84> **•ça prend pas un avocat** that's obvious, that's easy to understand. <La99> **•t'es pas proche un avocat** you're not as smart as you think you are <La99> <*Loc:* AV, EV, JE, LF, SM, TB, VM, Da84, Hi02, La99>

avocat[3] [avoka] *n.m.* black-necked stilt <*Loc:* Lv88, Re31>

avoine [avwɛ̃, avwɑ̃, vwɛ̃] *n.f.* oats ◊ **•farine d'avoine** oatmeal <Da84> <*Loc:* IB, JE, LA, SM, Da84, Fa77, La99>

avoir[1] [awar, avwar] *v.tr.* **1** to have, possess, own *J'ai des grosses bombes en fer là là.* I have some big iron pots right there. (TB) *On les amenait tout partout parce qu'eusse avait pas de char.* We took them everywhere because they didn't have a car. (TB) *Alors, j'ai été visiter parmi les fermiers et mesurer la quantité de récolte ils aviont.* So, I would go out to visit the farmers and measure the amount of crop they had. (SL) **2** to be (an age) *J'auras* EIGHTY-FIVE *le premier d'août.* I'll be eighty-five on August first. (SL) ◊ **•avoir chaud / faim / froid / soif** to be hot / hungry / cold / thirsty *Je commence à avoir chaud.* I'm beginning to get hot. (SM) <IB, IV, JD, LA, SJ, SL, SM, TB, VM, An94, Hi02, La99, Lv88, St95> **•avoir assez** to have enough, be fed up <SL, An94, Da84> **•avoir pour** to have to, be obligated to *J'ai pour étudier cet après-midi.* I have to study this afternoon. (SM) *C'était moi tout le temps qui avais pour y aider à faire n'importe qui il avait pour faire.* It was always I who had to help him to do anything he had to do. (EV) *Il a pour aller aujourd'hui.* He has to go today. (LA) *J'ai pour travailler.* I have to work. (SM) <EV, LA, SB, SM, VM, Da84> **•en avoir par dessus la tête** ***a*** to have a large quantity of s.t. *J'en veux pus, j'en ai déjà par dessus la tête.* I don't want anymore, I've already got a lot of them. (LA) ***b*** to have too much (to do) *Je pourras pas aller à soir. J'en ai par dessus la tête.* I won't be able to go tonight. I've got too much to do. (LA) <LA> **•il y a / il n-a** [ija, ja, ina, ena] there is, there are **Il y a personne ici.* There is no one here. (Da84) **Je peux pas l'entendre. Il y a trop de train.* I can't hear him. There's too much noise. (EV, An94) *Il y a pas assez de* PLUGS *dans la cuisine.* There are not enough outlets in the kitchen. (LA) **Il y en a pas.* There is none. (Da84) *Quoi il n-a?* What's the matter? (Gu00) *Qui il n-a?* What's the matter? (Gu00) *Il n-a des bayous qui va tout partout.* There are bayous going everywhere. (SM)

Peut-être il va y avoir un là-bas. There might be one in there. (LF) *L'année passée, il n-a eu une terrible récolte d'écrivisses.* Last year there was an abundant crawfish harvest. (Lv88) *Il y avait pas de publication, il y avait pas de journal, il y avait pas de livres, rien qui était écrit en français avant une vingtaine d'années passées, je pense.* There were no publications, no newspaper, no books written in French before about twenty years ago, I think. (SL) <AC, AV, EV, IV, JE, LA, LF, PQ, SJ, SL, SM, TB, VM, An94, Da84, Gr82, Guoo, Lv88, Ph36, Wh83> **•il y a pas de quoi** you're welcome, don't mention it <Da84> <***Loc:*** AC, AV, EV, IB, IV, JD, JE, LA, LF, PQ, SB, SJ, SL, SM, TB, VM, An94, Da84, Gr82, Guoo, Hio2, La99, Lv88, Ph36, St95, Wh83>

avoir[2] [awar, avwar] *v.aux. (in compound tenses)* to have *Il s'avait mis une petite calotte comme dans le vieux temps.* He had put on a little beanie cap like in the old days. (LA) *Pour pas avoir mouillé plein, on a fait un bon jardin.* For it not having rained much, we've had a good garden. (LF) *Il m'a enchargé de le faire quand il a parti.* He charged me to do it when he left. (TB) **J'ai travaillé toute la journée.* I worked all day. (EV, An94) **T'as déjà vu ces petites-filles là?* Have you ever seen those little girls? (EV, An94) *Il a tiré sur sa pipe.* He drew on his pipe. (LA) *Vous avez ti été là-bas?* Have you ever been there? (SL) **Ils ont dansé chacun son tour avec la même fille.* They each took a turn dancing with the same girl. (SL, An94) *Moi j'étais après prendre des tests la semaine passée, pour supposé j'avais des trous dans mes tripes, le docteur m'avait dit ça.* I was taking tests last week, supposedly I had holes in my intestines, the doctor had told me that. (LF) *Mais alle était paralysée. Alle avait eu un* STROKE. But she was paralyzed. She had had a stroke. (TB) *Mon beau-frère Cliff et mon beau-frère Joe avaient parti marron. Ils avaient échappé mes sœurs. Ils avaient été au bal.* My brother-in-law Cliff and my brother-in-law Joe left without notice. They escaped from my sisters and went to the dance. (AC) <***Loc:*** AC, AV, EV, IB, IV, JD, JE, LA, LF, PQ, SB, SJ, SL, SM, TB, VM, An94, Da84, Gr82, Guoo, Hio2, La99, Lv88, Ph36, St95, Wh83>

avortement [avɔrtəmɑ̃] *n.m.* abortion <***Loc:*** Da84>

avorter [avɔrte] *v.tr.* **1** to abort **2** to miscarry *Elle a avorté son premier enfant.* She miscarried her first child. (LA) ◊ **•avorter un complot** to foil a plot <Da84> <***Loc:*** Da84>

avorton [avɔrtɔ̃] *n.m.* [*pej.*] runt <***Loc:*** LA, VM>

avouer [avwe] *v.tr.* to admit, avow, confess **Il a avoué ses péchés.* He confessed his sins. (Da84) <***Loc:*** Da84>

Avoyelles [avojɛl] *n.f.pl.* Avoyelles Parish <***Loc:*** AV>

avril [avri] *n.m.* April <***Loc:*** LF, TB, Da84, Fa77, Hio2, La99>

ayayaie (aïe, aïe-aïe) [ajajaj] *interj.* oh, ouch *Ayayaie! Tu me fais mal.* Ouch! you are hurting me. (JE) <***Loc:*** IB, JE, SB, SL, SM, TB, Da84>

ayoù (éioù, éyoù, éoù, et-où, évou, ioù, où, y'où) [aju, eju, au, eu, evu, ey, ju, u] *adv.* where *Éyoù Marie?* Where is Marie? (Lv88) *Et le monde a pas d'ouvrage, évoù ils vont prendre l'argent pour guimbler?* People don't have jobs, where are they going to get the money to gamble? (TB) *Je connais pas ayoù il a passé.* I don't know where he went. (VM) **Et-où t'es parti? Éoù t'es parti?* Where are you going? (SM, Da84) **Y'où tu es parti?* Where are you going? (Da84) ◊ **•ayoù ce que / iousque / ousque / oùsque** where *Ousque tu vas?* Where are you going? (SM) **D'oùsque tu viens?* Where do you come from? (Da84) **Ousque vous allez maintenant?* Where are you going now? (Re31) **Il a pris à le retracer en regrichant la trace, ayoù ce qu'il devenait.* He started to retrace the trail, backtracking, in the direction that it [the deer] had come from. (AC, An94) <AC, IV, SM, TB, An94, Da84, Re31> **•là où / là vou** where *On faisait du train tout le tour de la maison là où eux-autres était.* We made noise all around the house where they were. (TB) *Lui, il a été éné droite là la même place là où il reste asteur, il a resté lui toute sa vie droite là.* He was born right there, the same place he lives now, he has lived his whole life right there. (TB) **Y a einne écarrure là-où an peut passer.* There's a square opening there where we can get through. (EV, Ph36) <EV, LF, SL, SM, TB, VM, Gu82, Ph36> **•n'importe ayoù** anywhere, wherever *Un violon, tu peux jouer n'importe éyou.* A violin, you can play it anywhere. (Lv88) *Les Mardi Gras les coursaient n'importe ayoù-ce que qu'eux-autres allait.* The Mardi Gras chased them wherever they went. (LF) *N'importe ayoù-ce tu vas tu peux parler les deux langues, moi je trouve que c'est bien intéressé.* Wherever you go you can speak the two languages, I find that to be very interesting. (TB) <IV, LF, TB, An94, Lv88> <***Loc:*** AC, EV, IV, JE, LA, LF, SB, SJ, SL, SM, TB, VM, An94, Da84, Gu82, Hio2, La99, Lv88, Ph36, Re31, Wh69>

azélia [azelja] *n.m./f.* azalea <***Loc:*** EV, CL, SM, Da84, Fa77, Guoo, Lv88>

B

baba[1] [baba] **I** *v.tr.invar.* [*baby talk*] to drink *Tu veux baba un petit peu de l'eau, cher?* You want to drink a little water, dear? (LA) **II** *v.intr.invar.* [*baby talk*] to drink *Baba pour Mame.* Drink for Mommy. (SM, VM) <***Loc:*** EV, LA, SB, SM, VM, Ph36>

baba[2] [baba] *n.m.* [*baby talk*] water *Donne-moi du baba.* Give me some water. (JE, SM) <***Loc:*** AV, EV, IB, JE, LF, SB, SL, SM, TB, Ph36>

babiche[1] [babiʃ] *n.f.* **1** thong, lash, lace, strap (of leather or rawhide) **2** old, ragged garment *Je dois jeter cette babiche.* I have to throw away that old, ragged thing. (VM) **3** small bits, shards, shavings **4** energy <***Loc:*** AV, EV, SL, TB, VM, Da84, Hi02, La99, Lv88, Ph36>

babiche[2] [babiʃ] *n.f.* **1** mouth *On a foutu ce mulet un coup dans la babiche.* The mule was hit in the mouth. (IB) *Ferme ta babiche.* Shut your mouth. (Lv88) **2** facial expression of displeasure or sulkiness ◊ **•grosse babiche** big mouth <Lv88> **•prendre une babiche** to pout *Il prend une babiche quand sa MOM le babille.* He pouts when his mom scolds him. (Lv88) <Lv88> <***Loc:*** IB, Lv88>

babillage [babijaʒ] *n.m.* scolding, fussing, nagging <***Loc:*** Da84>

babillard, -e [babijar, -jard] *adj.* **1** carping, bad-tempered, grouchy *Je connais pas quoi il y a avec lui aujourd'hui. Il est bien babillard.* I don't know what's wrong with him today. He's particularly grouchy. (LA) **2** fastidious, fussy <***Loc:*** EV, IB, LA, SM, Lv88, Ph36>

babiller [babije] **I** *v.tr.* to scold, reprimand, chide *Il faut tu babilles l'enfant qui fait du désordre.* You must scold the child who makes a mess. (Lv88) **II** *v.intr.* **1** to grumble, be in a bad mood *Elle m'achale, elle est tout le temps après babiller.* She gets on my nerves, she's always grumbling. (Lv88) **2** to be looking for a quarrel <***Loc:*** AV, IB, LA, SB, SL, SM, TB, Da84, Lv88>

babine[1] [babin] *n.f.* **1** lip (esp. hanging lower lip) **2** large lip (of a person or animal) *Quelles babines il a.* What big lips he has. (JE) **3** pout, pouting expression *Sa babine te dit qu'il est pas content.* His pout tells you he's not happy. (SB) ◊ **•babine longue** long face, pout <SM> **•bon à la babine** delicious <Lv88> **•faire une {la} babine / faire des babines *a*** to pout, sulk, show discontentment *C'est pas la peine de faire une babine; tu vas pas aller quand même.* It's no use to pout. You're not going anyway. (LA) ***b*** to be sad or depressed *Il est après faire une babine depuis que son père lui a dit qu'il pouvait pas l'aider.* He's been sad since his father told him that he couldn't help him. (LA) <AV, EV, LA, LF, SM, Da84, La99, Lv88> <***Loc:*** AV, EV, LF, JE, LA, SB, SL, SM, TB, Da84, La99, Lv88>

babine[2] ♦see **bobine**

babinot [babino] *n.m.* big, thick lip <***Loc:*** EV, Ph36>

babiole [babijɔl] *n.f.* trifle, unimportant thing *Ce qu'il dit c'est de la babiole.* What he's saying is unimportant. (SB) <***Loc:*** SB>

babord [babɔr] *n.m.* stern <***Loc.*** La99>

baboune [babun] *n.f.* large stupid-looking face *As-tu jamais vu une baboune comme ça?* Have you ever seen such a stupid-looking face? (JE) ◊ **•faire la baboune** to sulk <SM, Lv88> <***Loc:*** JE, LF, SM, Lv88>

bac[1] [bak] *n.m./f.* **1** wooden tub, washtub **2** bathtub *J'ai baigné dans la bac.* I bathed in the tub. (SM) **3** watering trough, large wooden vat for feeding lifestock ◊ **•bac à bain** bathtub <Gu00> <***Loc:*** IB, SL, SM, TB, VM, Gu00, Lv88>

bac[2] ♦see **barque**

bacalet [bakalɛ, bakale] *n.m.* lazy fellow *Ce Jacques est un vrai bacalet.* Jack is a very lazy fellow. (IB) <***Loc:*** IB>

bacchanale [bakanal, bakini] *n.f.* **1** drunken spree *Le bal a fini en bacchanale.* The dance ended in a drunken spree. (EV) **2** noise, racket, commotion *Tu parles d'une bacchanale ici dedans quand notre HOT WATER TANK a cassé.* Talk about a racket in here when our hot water tank broke. (VM) <***Loc:*** EV, SB, VM, Da84, Gu00>

bachelier [baʃəlje] *n.m.* bachelor, unmarried man <***Loc:*** Lv88>

bacher [baʃe] *v.tr.* to botch *Elle va bacher sa couture.* She is going to botch her sewing. (IB) <***Loc:*** IB>

bachoucta [baʃukta] *n.m.* red dye made from smooth sumac ◊ **•bachoucta d'ouvrage** job done badly or carelessly <SM, Lv88> <***Loc:*** SB, SM, Ho90, Lv88>

BACK[1] [bak, bæk] **I** *v.tr.invar.* to back up, move back *J'ai BACK mon char dans la cour.* I backed my car into the yard. (Lv88) **II** *v.intr.invar.* to back up, move back, reverse direction *Il a BACK quand il m'a vu.* He backed up when he saw me. (VM) <***Loc:*** AV, EV, SL, SM, VM, Da84, Lv88, Ph36>

BACK[2] [bak, bæk] *v.tr.invar.* to back, support *Si il court pour gouverneur, moi, je vas le BACK sûr.* If he runs for governor, I'll definitely back him. (VM) <***Loc:*** VM>

BACK[3] [bæk] *adv.* **1** back *J'ai revenu BACK huit jours plus tard.* I came back eight days later. (Lv88) *La dame est jamais revenue BACK.* The lady never came back. (IB) **2** again, back *Je vas chauffer le thé BACK.* I'm going to reheat the tea. (Lv88) *Dis-moi ça BACK.* Tell me that again. (Lv88) *Et je m'ai jamais ressoûlé BACK.* And I've never gotten drunk again. (LF) *Et elle alle va rouverre BACK pour la chevrette blanc.* And it [the season] will open up again for jumbo shrimp.

(TB) ◊ **•à BACK** back *Je veux le sac à BACK.* I want the bag back. (Lv88) *Ça avait pris longtemps pour tout arranger les trous et le mettre à BACK à l'eau.* It took a long time to repair all the holes and get it [the beached boat] back in the water. (JE) <JE, VM, Lv88> **•faire BACK** to back up *Il a été dans le fossé en faisant BACK.* He went into the ditch while backing up. (LA) *Fais BACK mon char.* Back up my car. (SB) <LA, SB, Da84, Lv88> <*Loc:* AC, EV, IB, JE, LA, LF, SB, SL, TB, VM, Da84, Lv88>

bâclée ♦see **batelée**

bâcler [bakle] *v.tr.* **1** to make a clean sweep, bring to a final conclusion, achieve complete closure *Ils ont tout bâclé l'affaire.* They made a clean sweep of the deal. (VM) **2** to overcome, overpower, beat *La maladie l'avait bâclé.* Illness had overcome him. (EV) **3** to finish hurriedly, do in a slipshod manner ◊ **•bâcler les plats** to eat everything on the table <Da84> <*Loc:* EV, JE, SJ, SL, VM, Da84, La99>

bacon ♦see **béquine**

bacul[1] [baky] *n.m.* large crupper, saddle tie <*Loc:* Lv88>

bacul[2] [baky] *n.m.* **1** swingle-bar, singletree, whiffletree **2** doubletree <*Loc:* AV, SL, TB, Di32>

BAD LUCK (badloque) [badlɔk] *n.m.* bad luck *Il a du BAD LUCK.* He's got bad luck. (Lv88) ◊ **•un BAD LUCK** stroke of bad luck *Il a eu un BAD LUCK, l'ouragan a noyé sa terre.* He had a stroke of bad luck, the hurricane flooded his land. (VM) <VM> <*Loc:* EV, SL, VM, Da84, Lv88, Ph36, Re31>

badaud ♦see **badjo**

badgaileur ♦see **bagueuleur**

badgueuler ♦see **bagueuler**

badiner [badine] *v.intr.* **1** to waste time **2** to joke <*Loc:* LA>

badjo (badaud) [badʒo] *n.m.* **1** person of modest upbringing and little education **2** imaginary being used by parents to frighten children, boogeyman *Si tu dors pas, le vieux badjo va venir te prendre.* If you don't go to sleep, the boogeyman will get you. (SM) <*Loc:* SM>

badloque ♦see **BAD LUCK**

bâdrer [badre] *v.tr.* to annoy, pester, bother *Ils étaient pas bâdrés par ça que leurs voisins avaient essayé de faire.* They weren't bothered by what their neighbors had tried to do. (LA) <*Loc:* IB, LA, Lv88>

bafouer [bafwe] *v.tr.* **1** to baffle, confuse, puzzle, stump *Ça m'a bafoué, la manière qu'il a dit ça.* It baffled me, the way that he said that. (VM) **2** to criticize harshly, slander *Joséphine aime trop à bafouer les autres.* Josephine is too fond of criticizing others. (AV) <*Loc:* AV, IB, SJ, VM, Da84>

bagage [bagaʒ] *n.m.* baggage, luggage <*Loc:* Da84, Fa77>

bagari [bagari] *n.m.* **1** saddle **2** saddle-flap *L'eau était haute. Quand j'étais rendu au milieu du platin, j'étais rendu aux bagaris.* The water was high. When I got to the middle of the low spot, the water was up to my saddle flaps. (AS) **3** *(pl.)* side-whiskers, hair grown long at the ears *Ça fait vilain avec ces bagaris, va te les faire raser.* You look ugly with those side-whiskers, go get them shaved. (VM) <*Loc:* AC, AS, VM>

bagasse [bagas] *n.f.* bagasse (fibrous residue of sugarcane that has been crushed to extract the juice) ◊ **•faire bagasse** to get lost *Va donc faire bagasse.* Get lost. (Lv88) <SM, Lv88> <*Loc:* IB, LA, SM, TB, Da84, Lv88>

bagatelle [bagatɛl] *n.f.* junk, cheap items (collectively) <*Loc:* Da84>

bagoul [bagul] *n.m.* gibberish, incomprehensible speech <*Loc:* EV, Ph36>

bagouler [bagule] *v.intr.* to speak incomprehensibly **A bagoule, j'la comprends pas.* She speaks incomprehensibly, I can't understand her. (EV, Ph36) <*Loc:* EV, Ph36>

bague [bag] *n.f.* ring, band (e.g. wedding ring) ◊ **•bague d'engagement** engagement ring <JE> <*Loc:* JE, LF, SL, SM, Da84, Lv88>

baguette [bagɛt] *n.f.* **1** rod, ramrod **On mettait de la mousse noire et on la foulait, et une fois on l'avait bien foulée avec une baguette, un bâton à peu près long comme ça, on venait et on mettait de la poudre.* We would put black moss and we would pack it, and when we had packed it well with a ram rod, a stick about this long, we'd come and we'd put some powder. (LA, An94) **2** stick ◊ **•baguette de STOVE** iron rod for cleaning a stove <VM> <*Loc:* LA, VM, An94, Da84>

bagueulage (bajeulage) [bagølaʒ, badʒølaʒ] *n.m.* **1** foolish, useless, incessant talk **2** gossip **3** insult <*Loc:* SM, Da84, Lv88>

bagueulard[1]**, -e (bajeulard, -e)** [bagølar, badʒølar, -lard] *adj.* talkative, indiscreet *Tant qu'à lui, il est assez bagueulard, je lui dirais pas rien.* As for him, he is so indiscreet, I wouldn't tell him anything. (LA) <*Loc:* LA, Lv88>

bagueulard[2]**, -e (bajeulard, -e)** [bagølar, badʒølar, -lard] *n.* talker, blabber, talkative person <*Loc:* Da84, Lv88>

bagueuler (bajeuler, badgueuler) [bagøle, badʒøle] *v.intr.* **1** to talk excessively, blabber, babble *Il était assez perdu, il bagueulait comme un fou.* He was so lost, he was babbling like a fool. (LA) **2** to yell, argue, get angry **Plus Clomaire buvait et traînait, plus a' badgueulait.* The more Clomaire drank and hung around, the more she argued. (ThCa: *Le charivari*) **3** to speak contemptuously, utter violent abuse *Il bagueulait tout le temps. Sa femme a eu pour le quitter.* He spoke contemptuously all the time. His wife had to leave him. (LA) <*Loc:* EV, IB, JE, LA, SM, TB, Da84, Lv88, Ph36, ThCa>

bagueuleur, -euse (badgaileur, -euse) [bagølœr, badʒølœr, -øz] *n.* **1** chatterbox, talkative person **2** one who gossips, esp. in a spiteful or malicious manner <*Loc:* AL, SM, Lv88>

bai ♦see **baille**

baie [bɛ, be] *n.f.* bay <*Loc:* TB, Da84, Gu00>

baignage [bẽjaʒ] *n.m.* bathing, soaking <*Loc:* Da84>

baigne ♦see **beigne**

baigner [bẽje] **I** *v.tr.* **1** to bathe *Ils ont pour baigner le bébé une fois par jour.* They have to bathe the baby once a day. (LA) **2** to dip, immerse (an animal) in disinfectant solution *Ça les aurait assemblé là-bas. Il fallait tout ça soit baigné, ça.* They would have gathered them over there. They all had to be dipped. (SL) **II** *v.intr.* to go swimming *Ils allaient baigner dans le bayou Teche.* They used to swim in the bayou Teche. (IB) **III se baigner** *v.pron.* **1** to take a bath, bathe, shower *Il est charpentier, il a pour se baigner après l'ouvrage.* He is a carpenter, he has to take a shower after work. (Lv88) **2** to swim *Et on va jouer à la pelote, passer le temps. Et on finit de jouer à la pelote et on va au SWIMMING POOL et on se baigne dans le POOL.* And we go play ball, pass the time. And we finish playing ball and we go to the swimming pool and we bathe in the pool. (TB) ◊ **•se baigner à la plie** to skinny dip, swim nude <JE> <***Loc:*** EV, IB, JE, LA, SL, SM, TB, Da84, Lv88>

baigneur, -euse [bẽjœr, -øz] *n.* bather <***Loc:*** Da84>

baignoire [bẽjwar] *n.m./f.* **1** bathtub **2** public bath, bathhouse <***Loc:*** AC, EV, IB, IV, JD, JE, LA, LF, SB, SM, TB, VM, Da84, Fa77>

baille[1] (**bai, baye**) [baj] *adj.* **1** blond, golden (of the hair) *Tu vois ce petit garçon tête baille?* You see the little boy with the blond hair? (Guoo) **2** having a golden or tan coat and a white or cream-colored mane and tail (said of palomino horses) *Mon grand-père avait une petite jument baille.* My grandfather had a little palamino horse. (Guoo) *Cheval baille.* Palomino horse. (AV) ◊ **•Baille a couru** it's all over, it's too late now [Baille is the name of a well-known palomino race horse from the Bosco area.] <La99> <***Loc:*** AV, JE, SM, TB, Da84, Guoo, La99, Lv88>

baille[2] [baj] *n.m./f.* **1** bucket, tub, basin *On lavait le linge dans une baille.* We used to do the laundry in a basin. (AV) **2** bathtub **3** foot tub ◊ **•baille à bain {baigner}** bathtub, old-fashioned tub for bathing <AV, EV, JD, SM> **•baille à laver *a*** washtub *On lavait nos crabes et nos écrévisses dans une baille à laver.* We washed off our crabs and crawfish in a washtub. (Guoo) ***b*** bathtub *On se baignait dans une baille à laver.* We washed in a bathtub. (IB) <EV, JE, TB, Da84, Ph36> **•petite baille** foot tub <EV> <***Loc:*** AC, AV, EV, IB, JD, JE, LA, LF, SB, SL, SM, TB, Da84, Guoo, Lv88, Ph36>

bâille [baj] *n.f.* yawn <***Loc:*** AV, SB, SJ>

bâillement [bajmɑ̃] *n.m.* yawning, yawn <***Loc:*** Da84>

bâiller [baje] *v.intr.* to yawn, gape *Ce prêtre me donne envie de bâiller.* That priest makes me feel like yawning. (LA) <***Loc:*** LA, Da84>

bâilleur, -euse [bajœr, -øz] *n.* yawner, gaper <***Loc:*** Da84>

baillonne[1] [bajɔ̃n] *adj.* having a yellow or golden coat (of a cow; by extension, name for a yellow- or golden-colored cow) <***Loc:*** LA, VM>

baillonne[2] [bajɔ̃n] *n.f.* blond person (often a term of endearment) <***Loc:*** Lv88>

bain [bẽ] *n.m.* **1** bath **2** bathtub ◊ **•prendre un bain** to take a bath *Il a pris un bain avant de se coucher.* He took a bath before going to bed. (LA) <LA> <***Loc:*** EV, LA, Da84, Fa77>

baïonnette [bajɔ̃nɛt] *n.f.* **1** bayonet **2** bayonet tree <***Loc:*** Da84, Fa77>

baire ♦see **bère**

baisser [bese] **I** *v.tr.* to lower, let down **Et un soir, chez Esta Hébert, il y avait venu des hommes de Marais-bouleur, des bogheis avec des TOPS baissés.* And one evening, at Esta Hebert's place, there came some men from the Marais-bouleur, buggies with the tops lowered. (LA, An94) **II** *v.intr.* **1** to go down, dwindle *Mon père dit comme ça, il dit, "Euh, j'ai trouvé que le bois de foyer," il dit, "arrière du garage est après baisser joliment vite."* My father said this way, he said, "Uh, I found that the firewood," he said, "behind the garage is dwindling pretty fast." (IB) **2** to lean over **Ça vaut pas baisser et ramasser.* That's not worth leaning over to pick up. (La99) **III se baisser** *v.pron.* **1** to stoop, bend over, bow down *C'était un vieux Marais-bouleur. Il se baissait pas pour personne.* He was an old Marais-bouleur. He didn't bow to anyone. (LA) **2** to become overcast *Le temps était après se baisser.* The weather was getting overcast. (LA) ◊ **•baisser à la course** to start running fast **Ça fait, le bougre, lui, tout à l'heure, le mal au ventre l'a pris, le marié. Ça fait, il a baissé à la course.* So the fellow, after a while, he got a stomach ache, the groom. So he took off running fast. (EV, An94) <EV, An94> **•baisser la tête** to lower one's head *Il avait si honte, il a baissé sa tête.* He was so ashamed, he lowered his head. (LA) <LA, Da84> **•baisser le prix** to reduce the price *S'il baisse pas son prix, personne pourra les acheter.* If he doesn't lower his price, no one will be able to buy them. (LA) <LA, Da84> <***Loc:*** AV, EV, IB, LA, TB, An94, Da84, Hi02, La99, Lv88>

baissière ♦see **bassière**

bajeulage ♦see **bagueulage**

bajeulard ♦see **bagueulard**

bajeuler ♦see **bagueuler**

bajou ♦see **abat-jour**

bajoue (**abajoue**) [baʒu, abaʒu] *n.f.* cheek, chop, jowl <***Loc:*** VM, Da84>

bajour ♦see **abat-jour**

bakerie [bakri] *n.f.* bakery *On a mangé des bons gâteaux de la bakerie.* We ate some good cakes from the bakery. (TB) <***Loc:*** TB>

BAKING (**béquine**) [bekin] *n.m.* baking powder <***Loc:*** TB, Da84>

bal [bal] *n.m.* dance, ball ◊ **•bal de maison *a*** young people's party ***b*** gathering of neighborhood families at one of their houses, in the course of which people of all ages dance. *Dans ce temps-là, ça faisait des bals de maison, y'avait pas de clubs.* In those days, they had house dances, there weren't any clubs. (Lv88) <Lv88> **•bal de noce** wedding ball or dance <Da84> **•bal et bazar et course et bataille** assortment of activities <LA, La99> **•bal masqué** masked ball <Da84> <***Loc:*** AC, EV, LA, SL, VM, Da84, Gu00, Hi02, La99>

balafre[1] [balaf(r)] *n.f.* mouth *Sa balafre est grand.* He has a big mouth. (AV) <***Loc:*** AV, SJ>

balafre[2] [balaf(r)] *n.f.* smear, spot *Une balafre de boue sur sa robe.* A spot of mud on her dress. (IB) <***Loc:*** IB>

balai [balɛ, bale] *n.m.* broom ◊ **•balai acadien {cadien}** broom made of palmetto leaves or coarse prairie grass <JE, Di32> **•balai du ciel** northwest wind that heralds good weather *Le balai du ciel a passé. Il fait beau aujourd'hui.* The northwest wind pushed away the clouds. Today we have a nice weather. (SM) <IB, SM> <***Loc:*** EV, IB, JE, SM, Da84, Di32, La99, Lv88>

balan [balɑ̃] *n.m.* **1** swing **2** pendulum **3** kite **4** equilibrium, balance, balancing *Ga! tu vas perdre ton balan.* Watch out! you're going to lose your balance. (Lv88) *Il a perdu son balan et il a tombé.* He lost his balance and fell. (JE) **5** swinging motion, swaying, rocking *Il a un balan quand il marche.* He sways when he walks. (LF) *Le balan du bateau.* The rocking of the boat. (LF) **6** rhythm *Il tapait du pied pour garder le balan de la musique.* He tapped his foot to keep the rhythm of the music. (Lv88) ◊ **•au {en} balan / sur le {un} balan** undecided, hesitant *Je sais pas quoi faire, je suis sur un balan.* I don't know what to do, I am undecided. (VM) <IB, SB, VM, Lv88> **•être dessus un balan** to be balanced, be equal *Vous-autres est dessus un balan. L'un vaut l'autre.* Y'all are equal. One is as good as the other. (VM) <VM> <***Loc:*** IB, JE, LF, SB, SM, TB, VM, Da84, Lv88, Re31>

balance [balɑ̃s] *n.f.* **1** scale, balance (for weighing) *Là les femmes passent en travers encore pour voir s'il y a peut-être des drigailles, ou les épluches, et après ça ils sont pesés sur la balance.* Then the women go through them again to see if there may be some refuse, or peelings, and after that they're weighed on a scale. (LF) **Maman, tu vas aller chez le Roi demander pour ses balances pour peser mon argent.* Mom, go to the king and ask for his scales to weigh my money. (An94) **2** balance, remainder, left over part *La balance du monde.* The rest of the world. (VM) *On s'a promis de l'amitié pour la balance de la vie.* We promised each other friendship for the rest of our lives. (Lv88) *Ils ont appris la première partie de la chanson, ils ont oublié la balance.* They learned the beginning of the song, they forgot the rest. (Lv88) *On se baignait, se lavait et la balance de la journée, quand j'étais petit, c'était juste jouer.* We bathed and cleaned ourselves and the rest of the day, when I was a small child, was just spent playing. (IB) *Quand le sucre est revendu sur le marché, on reçoit la balance de notre argent.* When the sugar is sold back at the market, we get the rest of our money (IB) **3** swing **Pousse pas la balance trop fort.* Don't push the swing too hard. (EV, Ph36) <***Loc:*** AC, AV, EV, IB, JE, LA, LF, SB, SL, SM, TB, VM, Da84, Hi02, Lv88, Ph36>

balancer [balɑ̃se] **I** *v.tr.* to balance *Il faut balancer la pratique et les méthodes nouvelles.* You have to balance established practices and new methods. (Lv88) **II** *v.intr.* to swing *Tu t'es aperçu comment tes soliveaux là grouillent? Dans le hall, quand le monde danse, le plancher balance comme ça.* Have you noticed how your rafters move? In the hall, when people are dancing, the floor swings like that. (EV) **III se balancer** *v.pron.* **1** to swing *Dans le vieux temps, quand on allait visiter une fille, souvent on se balançait sur la galerie avec le père et la mère droit là avec nous-autres.* In the old days, when we would go to visit a girl, often we would swing on the porch with the father and mother right there with us. (LA) **2** to balance o.s. *Il se balançait dans la pirogue grand debout.* He was balancing himself in the pirogue standing straight up. (LA) ◊ **•pas balancé** mentally unstable *Ce bougre-là était pas balancé. Ils ont eu pour l'amener à Pineville.* That fellow was mentally unstable. They had to take him to Pineville [State Mental Hospital]. (LA) <LA, La99> <***Loc:*** EV, LA, TB, Da84, La99, Lv88>

balancier [balɑ̃sje] *n.m.* pendulum <***Loc:*** Da84>

balancine [balɑ̃sin] *n.f.* **1** see-saw **2** gliding rocking chair <***Loc:*** JE, Lv88>

balayage (baliage) [baljaʒ] *n.m.* sweeping, act of sweeping ◊ **•faire le balayage** to do the sweeping *C'est toi qui fais le balayage aujourd'hui.* You're the one who's going to sweep today. (EV) <EV, Da84> <***Loc:*** EV, SM, TB, Da84, Ph36>

balayer (balier) [baleje, balje, bɔlje] *v.tr.* to sweep *Elle va balayer le plancher.* She is going to sweep the floor. (JE) <***Loc:*** EV, IB, JE, LA, LF, SB, SL, SM, Da84, Hi02, Ph36, Re31>

balayeur, -euse (balieur, -ieuse) [balejœr, baljœr, -jøz] *n.m.* **1** sweeper **2** janitor *Ça c'est le vieux balieur au* PICTURE SHOW. That's the old janitor at the picture show. (SM) <***Loc:*** EV, IB, SB, SM, TB, Da84, Lv88, Ph36>

balayeuse [balejøz] *n.f.* mechanical sweeper <***Loc:*** Da84>

balayures (baliures) [baljyr] *n.f.pl.* sweepings <***Loc:*** JE, Lv88>

balbuter [balbyte] **I** *v.tr.* to scold *Elle a balbuté ce gamin.* She scolded that little boy. (IB) **II** *v.intr.* to stammer, stutter *Il parle pas bien, il balbute.* He doesn't speak well, he stutters. (AV) <***Loc:*** AV, IB, SJ>

BALD HEAD [bɔlhæd] *adj.* bald *Lui, il a pas de cheveux, il est* BALD HEAD. He doesn't have any hair, he's bald. (SL) <***Loc:*** SL, VM>

bale [bal] ◊ **•herbe à bale** loosestrife <Ho90> <***Loc:*** Ho90>

baleine [balɛ̃n] *n.f.* **1** whale *J'en ai vu dans Alaska, des baleines. Des grosses affaires. Des grosses, plein plus gros qu'au large.* I saw some whales in Alaska. Big things. Much bigger than the ones out in the Gulf. (TB) **2** whale bone (as used in umbrellas, corsets, etc.) **3** switch, whip (often a coachwhip) *Qui tu vas frapper avec cette baleine?* Who are you going to strike with that whip? (JE) **4** antenna *Baleine de radio.* Radio antenna. (Lv88) <***Loc:*** EV, JE, LF, SL, SM, VM, Da84, Lv88>

baleiner [balɛ̃ne] *v.tr.* to beat, beat with a switch, whip *Eux-autres m'a baleiné à moi, moi je m'ai fait baleiné. À la palette.* They whipped me, I got myself whipped. With a paddle. (TB) <***Loc:*** JE, LF, SB, SM, TB>

baler [bale] *v.intr.* to go dancing, frequent dances, balls, etc. *Cette demoiselle fait rien que baler.* That girl doesn't do anything but go dancing. (SM) *Il bale tous les soirs.* He goes to dances every night. (IB) <***Loc:*** IB, SM, Da84, Lv88>

bales [bal] *n.f.pl.* vesicular stomatitis (viral disease of horses, cows etc.) <***Loc:*** VM, Lv88>

baleur, -euse [balœr, -øz] *n.* **1** one who frequents dances **2** dancer <***Loc:*** JE, SL, SM, TB, Lv88>

baliage ♦see **balayage**

balier ♦see **balayer**

balieur ♦see **balayeur**

baliures ♦see **balayures**

BALL [bɔl] *n.m.* ball, baseball <***Loc:*** EV, Da84>

balle [bal] *n.f.* **1** bullet, shot *Une carabine, ça tire des balles, un fusil, ça tire des cartouches.* A rifle shoots bullets, a shotgun shoots shotgun shells. (LA) **2** bale (of hay, cotton, etc.) *Ça prenait cinq cents livres de coton pour faire une balle.* It took five hundred pounds of cotton to make a bale. (St83) **3** ball ◊ **•balle de foin** bale of hay **L'affaire va peut-être casser bonne heure dans Septembre si la femme à Fontenot est mordu dessus le coude par ein congo pendant elle est après assayer d'arracher des bales de foin que Aucoin a mit à la geuele du fossé.* The possible flashpoint may come in early September when Fontenot's wife is bitten on the elbow by a water moccasin while trying to pull up bales of hay which Aucoin has placed at the mouth of drainage ditch. (Wh83) **•balle de plomb** lead ball attached along the bottom of a trawl net to serve as a weight <TB> <***Loc:*** AC, EV, JE, LA, TB, Da84, Hi02>

baller [bale] *v.tr.* to bale, put into bales *Baller du foin.* To bale hay. (EV) <***Loc:*** EV, Da84>

ballet [balɛ, bale] *n.f.* ballet <***Loc:*** Da84>

BALLOON [balun] *n.m.* **1** balloon **2** airship, dirigible <***Loc:*** Da84>

balloter ♦see **ballotter**

ballottement [balɔtmɑ̃] *n.m.* oscillation, swinging <***Loc:*** Da84>

ballotter (**balloter**) [balote, barlote] **I** *v.tr.* to jerk, shake up *Ce* RIDE *dans ce vieux char m'a assez ballotté.* The ride in that old car shook me up pretty well. (VM) **II** *v.intr.* **1** to totter, wobble, sway **2** to dangle, swing **3** to bounce around *Les ressorts étaient cassés dessus le vieux boghei et on a ballotté tout le long au village.* The springs on the old buggy were broken and we bounced around all the way to town. (LA) **4** to go well **Ça ballotte.* Things are going well. (EV, Ph36) ◊ **•comment ça ballotte?** how's it going? <SM, La99, Lv88> <***Loc:*** LA, SM, TB, VM, Da84, La99, Lv88>

balloune [balun] *n.f.* short, heavyset woman <***Loc:*** TB>

ballustrade [balystrad] *n.f.* banister, balustrade <***Loc:*** Da84>

baloche [balɔʃ] *n.m.* musical instrument used to keep time **[Les musiciens] usaient les p'tits fers... ou peut-être bien aussi un frottoir à laver l'linge pour avoir un baloche.* The musicians used to use triangles or maybe also a laundry washboard to keep time. (Gr86) <***Loc:*** Gr86>

bambara [bɑ̃bara] *adj.* [*offensive*] carefree, indifferent (often with respect to one's appearance) **Un tit' nègre bambara.* A carefree untidy, little black boy. (Da84) <***Loc:*** Da84, Re31>

bamboche [bɑ̃bɔʃ] *n.f.* drinking spree *Il s'a foutu une bamboche.* He went on a drinking spree. (SM) <***Loc:*** SM>

bambocher (**bombocher, berbocher**) [bɑ̃boʃe, bærboʃe] **I** *v.tr.* to squander *L'homme bamboche son argent.* The man squanders his money. (AV) **II** *v.intr.* to carouse, dissipate (esp. getting drunk or running around) *Tous les samedis, il est parti bambocher.* Every Saturday, he goes out drinking and carousing. (EV) *Quand il était jeune, tout ça il faisait, c'était traînailler les rues et bambocher toute la nuit.* When he was young, all he did was run around in the streets and drink all night long. (LA) <***Loc:*** EV, JE, LA, SJ, SM, TB, Da84, Hi02>

bambocheur (**bombocheur**) [bɑ̃boʃœr, bɑ̃boʃø] *n.m.* **1** dissipater, carouser, woman chaser **2** big drinker, drunkard **3** squanderer <***Loc:*** AV, JE, SJ, SM, VM, Da84, Fa77, Hi02>

bambou [bɑ̃bu] *n.m.* bamboo <***Loc:*** TB, Da84>

bamboula [bɑ̃bula] *n.m./f.* **1** drum made from a joint of bamboo **2** dance performed to the sound of the bamboula drum **3** uproar, disturbance, racket, din **I'z ont fait tant d'bamboula que ch'pouvais pas dormir.* They made such a racket that I couldn't sleep. (EV, Ph36) **4** wild party <***Loc:*** EV, SB, SM, Lv88, Ph36>

banacassa ♦see **casse-banane**

banane [bɑ̃nɑ̃] *n.f.* **1** banana **2** sardine, ladyfish <***Loc:*** JE, LF, SL, TB, Da84, Hi02>

bananier [bɑ̃nɑ̃nje] *n.m.* banana tree <***Loc:*** JE, SL, Da84, Fa77>

banari ♦see **bénéri**

banc [bɑ̃] *n.m.* **1** bench, pew, seat *J'étais assis le quatrième ou le cinquième banc d'en avant.* I was sitting in the fourth or fifth pew from the front. (TB) **2** bank, reef **3** shelf ◊ **•banc d'huîtres** oyster bed <VM> **•banc-vaisselle** shelf at window for washing dishes <TB> <***Loc:*** EV, JE, LF, SL, SM, VM, Da84>

banco [bɑ̃ko] *n.m.* **1** reception for members of a political party, usually the night before an election **2** evening spent with family members or friends **3** banquet, feast **4** gaming event for fundraising purposes **5** diversion, recreation, pastime <*Loc:* SM, Lv88>

BAND [bɛ̃n, bɛ̃d] *n.m.* band, orchestra <*Loc:* AC, EV, JE, LF, SB, SL, SM, Da84, Guoo, Lv88, Ph36>

bandage [bɑ̃daʒ] *n.m.* bandage <*Loc:* Da84>

bande [bɑ̃n, bɑ̃d] *n.m./f.* **1** band of cloth (e.g. bandage) **2** any mechanical belt (e.g. fan belt, conveyor belt) *La bande de mon char est cassée.* My car has a broken belt. (Guoo) **3** band, pack (of animals), flock (of birds), school (of fish) *Une bande de canards.* A flock of ducks. (Lv88) **4** gang, group, band (of people) *C'est pas la personne la plus affilée de la bande.* He's not the sharpest one of the gang. (LA) *Il y a une bande de Marais Bouleurs qui sont après casser le bal chez Gérard Forrestier.* There is a gang of Marais Bouleurs crashing the dance at Gerard Forrestier's place. (TM) **5** crowd <*Loc:* AC, AV, EV, LA, LF, VM, Da84, Guoo, Hio2, Lv88>

bander[1] [bɑ̃de] *v.tr.* to bandage, wrap *Bander les yeux.* To bandage the eyes. (AC) <*Loc:* AC, Da84>

bander[2] [bɑ̃de] *v.intr.* to have an erection *Il pouvait pus bander jusqu'à qu'il a découvert le Viagra.* He could no longer have an erection until he discovered Viagra. (LA) <*Loc:* LA>

bandit [bɑ̃di] *n.m.* bandit, robber <*Loc:* Da84>

bangala [bɑ̃gala] *n.m.* stout stick tipped with iron, formerly used as a walking stick <*Loc:* JE, Di32, Lv88>

banjo [bɑ̃ʒo] *n.m.* banjo <*Loc:* Da84>

bannir [bɑ̃nir] *v.tr.* to exile, expel, banish *La vigilance bannissait les voleurs de vaches au Texas.* The vigilantes banished cattle rustlers to Texas. (VM) <*Loc:* VM, Da84>

bannissement [bɑ̃nismɑ̃] *n.m.* banishment, expulsion, exile <*Loc:* Da84>

banque[1] [bɑ̃k] *n.f.* **1** bank, financial institution **2** money-box <*Loc:* Da84, Hio2, Lv88>

banque[2] [bɑ̃k] *n.f.* bank of a canal or ditch *La banque du fossé est haute.* The bank of the ditch is high. (IB) <*Loc:* IB, JE, Di32, Lv88>

banquer ♦see **banquier**

banqueroute [bɑ̃krut] *n.f.* bankruptcy ◊ **•faire banqueroute** to go bankrupt *Elle va finir par faire banqueroute puis elle va perdre son* TRUCK. She's going to end up going bankrupt and then she will lose her truck. (VM) <VM, Da84, Fa77> <*Loc:* SJ, VM, Da84, Fa77>

banqueroutier [bɑ̃krutje] *n.m.* one who is bankrupt <*Loc:* Da84>

banquet [bɑ̃kɛ, bɑ̃ke] *n.m.* banquet <*Loc:* JE, Da84>

banquette [bɑ̃kɛt, bɑ̃ket] *n.f.* **1** sidewalk, boardwalk (concrete or wooden) *Dans ce temps-là t'aurais pu prendre ton portemonnaie et t'aurais pu te coucher sur la banquette et mettre ton porte-monnaie sur toi et dormir, et personne aurait touché ton porte-monnaie.* In those days you could have taken your wallet and you could have slept on the sidewalk and put your wallet on top of yourself and slept, and no one would have touched your wallet. (TB) **2** flower bed *Madame Broussard faisait des banquettes pour planter ses rosiers.* Mrs. Broussard made flower beds to plant her roses. (Guoo) **Banquette de fleurs.* Flower bed. (Fa77) <*Loc:* AV, EV, IB, JE, LA, LF, SB, SJ, SM, TB, Guoo, Lv88, Ph36, Re31>

banquier (**banquer**) [bɑ̃kje] *n.m.* banker <*Loc:* VM, Da84, Fa77>

bans [bɑ̃] *n.m.pl.* banns (of marriage) <*Loc:* EV, Da84>

baptême [batɛ̃m] *n.m.* baptism ◊ **•avoir son baptême** to do s.t. for the first time *J'ai eu mon baptême dans la politique quand j'avais vingt-six ans.* I had my initiation into politics when I was twenty-six. (EV) <EV, La99> **•ça c'est pas baptême catin** it's a difficult situation, it's not 'fun and games' *C'est pas baptême catin, d'être marié avec un homme qui boit comme ça.* It's not fun being married to a man who drinks like that. (SM) <SM, La99> <*Loc:* EV, IB, SM, Da84, Hio2, La99>

baptiser [batize] *v.tr.* **1** to baptize *Baptiser un bébé.* To baptize a baby. (EV) **2** to dilute, water down (e.g. coffee, wine) *Baptiser son vin.* To dilute one's wine. (EV) **3** to initiate, introduce (s.o. to an activity) *Il connaissait rien pour les chevaux de course, mais là J. l'a baptisé.* He didn't know anything about racehorses, but J. got him started. (EV) <*Loc:* AC, AV, EV, SM, Da84, La99>

baptiseur [batizœr] *n.m.* baptizer <*Loc:* Da84>

baptistaire (**batistaire, batistère**) [batistær] *n.m./f.* **1** baptismal font or room, baptistery **2** baptism record or certificate **Produire son batistaire.* To produce his registry of baptism. (Re31) **3** birth certificate <*Loc:* AV, IB, LA, SB, SJ, SL, SM, TB, Da84, Lv88, Re31>

baptiste[1] [baptis(t), bæptis(t), batis(t)] *adj.* Baptist *Les églises baptistes ont toujours des grosses colonnes devant.* Baptist churches always have big columns out in front. (VM) <*Loc:* TB, VM, Da84, Fa77>

Baptiste[2] [baptis(t), bæptis(t), batis(t)] *n.* Baptist ◊ **•St. Jean Baptiste** St. John the Baptist <Da84> <*Loc:* TB, Da84, Fa77>

baquet [bakɛ, bake] *n.m.* bucket, pail *Va chercher un baquet d'eau.* Go get a bucket of water. (JE) *Eusse dit un "baquet" et nous-autres on dit un "siau."* They say "baquet" and we say "siau." (TB) ◊ **•baquet à boire** pail <EV> <*Loc:* EV, IV, JE, LA, LF, SB, SL, SM, TB, VM, Da84, Fa77, Guoo>

bar (**barre**) [bar] *n.m./f.* **1** bar, saloon, café *Je vais à la bar boire un verre de bière.* I'm going to the bar to drink a glass of beer. (SM) **2** bar, counter **Un monsieur à la barre, qui envoie des* DRINK *à Tine.* A man at the bar, who sends drinks over to Tine. (ThCa: *La table des veuves*) ◊ **•BARROOM** bar, café, barroom <Lv88> <*Loc:* AC, JE, LF, SB, SM, Da84, Hio2, Lv88, ThCa>

baranquer (**barlonquer**) [barɑ̃ke, barlɑ̃ke] *v.intr.* **1** to talk nonsense, talk gibberish, talk unintelligently, not make sense, talk out of one's mind *Tu dois l'attendre baranquer quand il est soûl.* You should hear him babble when he's drunk. (VM) **2** to stagger, reel, falter *Quand il a arrivé à la maison après minuit, il baranquait.* When he arrived home after midnight, he was staggering. (VM) <***Loc:*** LA, SM, VM, La99, Lv88>

baraque (**barraque**) [barak] *n.f.* **1** crude wooden building, esp. a large one **2** anything old, in bad shape or disrepair *Une vieille baraque de voiture, une vieille baraque de femme.* An old car, an old woman (Lv88) <***Loc:*** EV, SM, TB, Da84, Lv88, Ph36>

baratte [barat] *n.f.* **1** churn **2** ice cream freezer <***Loc:*** IB, Da84, Hi02, La99>

barbe [barb] *n.f.* **1** beard, whiskers *Et là Johnny avait la grande barbe comme ça.* And Johnny had a long beard, like this. (TB) **2** barbel (of a catfish), whiskers (of shrimp) *On attrapait ces grosses chevrettes avec un épreuvier. […] Arracher la barbe.* We used to catch jumbo shrimp with a castnet. […] Pulling of the whiskers. (TB) ◊ **•barbe de maïs** corn tassels <Da84> **•barbe espagnole** Spanish moss <IB, JE, Da84, Ho90, Lv88> <***Loc:*** IB, JE, TB, Da84, Hi02, Ho90, Lv88, Re31>

barbecue[1] (**bar-b-que**) [barbəky, bærbiky, barbeky, barbakø] *v.tr.invar.* to barbecue, roast meat over hot coals *Si vous-autres peut venir dimanche, on va barbecue des poulets.* If you all can come Sunday, we'll barbecue some chickens. (LA) <***Loc:*** LA, Da84>

barbecue[2] (**bar-b-que**) [barbəky, bærbiky, barbeky, barbakø] *n.m.* **1** barbecue pit *On a mis des saucisses dessus le barbecue.* We put some sausages on the pit. (EV) **2** meat cooked on a barbecue pit *Le barbecue est paré. Allons manger!* The barbecue is ready. Let's eat! (EV) **3** barbecue, social gathering at which meat is cooked on an outdoor pit *Ils ont donné un barbecue pour la politique.* They hosted a barbecue for the political meeting. (AV) <***Loc:*** AC, AV, EV, SL, SM, TB, VM, Da84>

BARBER ♦see **barbier**

BARBER-SHOP [barbəʃɔp] *n.f.* barbershop <***Loc:*** LF, Da84>

barbeux [barbø] *adj.* bearded (of a man) *Ma fille va se marier avec un grand barbeux. Il devrait bien se raser pour les noces.* My daughter is marrying a bearded fellow. He really should shave for the wedding. (VM) <***Loc:*** EV, IB, LF, SM, TB, VM, Da84, Lv88, Ph36>

barbiche [babiʃ] *n.f.* goatee <***Loc:*** SM>

barbichet [barbiʃɛ, barbiʃe] *n.m.* goatee <***Loc:*** VM>

barbier (**BARBER**) [barbje, barbər] *n.m.* barber *J'ai été à l'école pour barbier.* I went to barber school. (SM) <***Loc:*** JE, SM, Da84, Fa77, Lv88>

barbillon [barbijɔ̃] *n.m.* barbel (of a catfish) <***Loc:*** LF>

barbot [barbo] *n.m.* **1** ink spot **2** beetle, June bug, May bug **3** boisterous, rowdy child <***Loc:*** JE, VM, Da84, Fa77, Lv88>

barbotage [barbotaʒ, barbədaʒ, barbodaʒ] *n.m.* **1** careless, sloppy work **2** chatter, frivolous talk, light-hearted talk <***Loc:*** JE, Da84, Lv88>

barbote [barbɔt] *n.* catfish <***Loc:*** Lv88>

barboter [barbote] **I** *v.tr.* **1** to botch, bungle, mess up, do carelessly, perform in a slipshod manner *J'ai barboté mon ouvrage.* I messed up my work. (SM) **2** to stammer, stutter *Il a barboté ses prières.* He stammered his prayers. (LA) **II** *v.intr.* **1** to stammer, stutter, mumble *Il était assez nerveux, il pouvait pas s'empêcher de barboter.* He was so nervous, he couldn't keep from stammering. (LA) **2** to waste time, piddle around *Tu parles de paresseux. Il est tout le temps après barboter dans la maison.* Talk about lazy. He is always piddling around in the house. (LA) **3** to drink (alcoholic beverages) *Il a barboté toute la nuit.* He was out drinking all night. (Lv88) **III se barboter** *v.pron.* to smear o.s. (with s.t.) *Il s'est barboté la figure avec de la boue.* He smeared mud on his face. (SB) <***Loc:*** EV, IB, LA, SB, SM, Da84, Lv88, Ph36>

barboteur, -euse [barbotœr, -øz] *n.* one who works in a careless or slipshod manner <***Loc:*** SM, Lv88>

barbouillage [barbujaʒ] *n.m.* **1** messy writing or painting, smear, defacement **2** badly-done work **3** mess of any kind *Qui a fait ce barbouillage?* Who made this mess? (JE) <***Loc:*** JE, LF, SM, Da84, Lv88>

barbouiller [barbuje] *v.tr.* **1** to mess up, spoil *L'enfant avait pas de précaution. Il barbouillait tout le temps ses leçons.* The child was careless. He would always mess up his homework. (LA) **2** to smear *La pauvre dame avait trop bu; elle a tout barbouillé son MAKEUP.* The poor woman had drunk too much; she smeared her makeup all over. (LA) ◊ **•barbouiller le cœur** to make sick, upset the stomach **Le peu que j'ai mangé m'a barbouillé le cœur.* The little I ate upset my stomach. (Di32) <Di32> <***Loc:*** LA, TB, Da84, Di32>

barbouilleur, -euse [barbujœr, -øz] *n.m.* one who messes up writing, painting, etc. <***Loc:*** Da84>

bar-b-que ♦see **barbecue**

barbue [barby] *n.f.* channel catfish, blue catfish, blue channel catfish ◊ **•barbue à tête plate** flathead catfish <LF> **•la barbue du bon Dieu** a very good or good-natured person, the 'essence' of goodness <IB, SJ, TX> <***Loc:*** AL, AV, CL, EV, IB, IV, JE, LA, LF, SB, SJ, SL, SM, TB, TX, VM, Da84, Fa77, Gu00, Hi02, Lv88, Re31>

barconcu [barkɔ̃ky] *n.m.* swingle-bar, singletree, whiffletree <***Loc:*** SM>

bardasser ♦see **berdasser**

bardeau [bardo] *n.m.* wood shingle <***Loc:*** AC, EV, LA, LF, SL, Da84, Fa77, Hi02>

barder [barde] **I** *v.tr.* to dodge *Il a bardé la vache avec le char.* He dodged the cow with his car. (AV) **II** *v.intr.* **1** to veer, change course suddenly, swerve *Il a bardé là-bas.* He veered that way. (JE) **2** to flee in order to avoid s.o. *Quand il* *l'a vu après venir dans le chemin, il a bardé.* When he saw him coming down the road, he fled. (VM) <***Loc:*** AV, IB, JE, LF, SB, SJ, VM, Lv88>

barène [barɛ̃n] *n.f.* hopscotch <***Loc:*** JE, Lv88>

bargée [barʒe] *n.f.* **1** load of a barge or boat **2** load of any vehicle <***Loc:*** AV, SJ, Lv88>

barguine [bargin] *n.m./f.* **1** bargain, deal *Moi je vas juste à St. Louis, Missouri, deux cent quatre-vingt-seize. Encore c'est une barguine. On achète un, eux-autres m'a donné un pour quatorze piasses.* I just go to St. Louis, Missouri, $296. Even that's a bargain. You buy one [plane ticket], they give me one for $14. (TB) **2** exchange (in kind), trade *J'ai offert une barguine, je lavais les plats, si elle voulait mettre mes souliers.* I offered her a deal, I would wash the dishes if she would put on my shoes. (VM) ◊ **•bon barguine** good deal *Tu fais un bon barguine avec le service après la vente.* You get a good bargain with service after the sale. (EV) <EV> **•faire (un/une) barguine (avec)** ***a*** to do business (with) *Les bougres qu'avaient les banques et tout, eux-autres voulait pas faire barguine avec les Cadiens.* The guys who had the banks and all, they didn't want to do business with Cajuns. (TB) ***b*** to swap, exchange, barter, trade *On a fait un barguine. Je l'ai donné deux cochons pour une vache.* We made an exchange. I gave him two pigs for a cow. (SM) <SM, TB> <***Loc:*** AV, EV, IB, JE, LA, LF, SB, SL, SM, TB, VM, Da84, Lv88, Ph36>

barguiner [bargine, bargɛ̃ne] *v.tr.* to bargain, barter, exchange *Il aurait barguiné des œufs pour du pain.* He would have exchanged eggs for bread. (SL) **II** *v.intr.* to bargain, haggle *Ils ont barguiné avec le docteur pour qu'il la garde un jour encore.* They bargained with the doctor so that he would keep her for another day. (Lv88) *Toi, tu veux trop barguiner.* You try to bargain too much. (JE) **III se barguiner** *v.pron.* **1** to barter, trade one thing for another *Les voisins s'échangaient des rôtis, ils appelaient ça un rôti, c'est une portion de viande. Le monde se barguinait ça.* Neighbors exchanged meat portions, they called that a "rôti," it's a portion of meat. People traded them among themselves. (VM) **2** to exchange *On se barguinait quelques paroles.* We exchanged a few words. (EV) <***Loc:*** AC, EV, IB, JD, JE, LA, SB, SL, SM, VM, Da84, Hi02, Lv88, Ph36>

barguineur [barginœr] *n.m.* trader, one who bargains or haggles <***Loc:*** AV, JE, SB, SM, Da84, Lv88>

baribara [baribara, bardibarda] *n.m.* **1** stammering, stuttering, sputtering, muttering, mumbling **2** commotion, disturbance, hullabaloo *Quand j'ai arrivé chez Marie, ils aviont le plus grand baribara que j'ai jamais entendu.* When I arrived at Mary's, they had the most commotion I've ever heard. (SL) **3** difficulty, embarrassing circumstances, trouble <***Loc:*** AV, IB, JE, SL, Lv88>

barificoter [barifikote] *v.intr.* to make big, unrealistic plans, be a dreamer <***Loc:*** SM>

barificoteur [barifikotœr] *n.m.* dreamer, one who entertains unrealistic plans <***Loc:*** SM>

baril [bari, barij] *n.m.* **1** barrel **2** dry measure (210 or 220 pounds) *J'ai deux barils de chevrettes.* I have two barrels of shrimp. (JE) **3** forty gallon oil barrel **4** preacher's pulpit ◊ **•baril de lavure** rinse water barrel <LA> <***Loc:*** AC, EV, IV, JE, LA, LF, TB, VM, Da84, Hi02, Lv88>

bariolé, -e [barjole] *adj.* striped *Elle portait une robe bariolée.* She wore a striped dress. (SB) <***Loc:*** SB, SM>

barlander ♦see **berlander**

barlanguer [barlɑ̃ge] *v.intr.* to botch, bungle, do in a slipshod way *Elle barlangue son ouvrage.* She does her work very carelessly. (IB) <***Loc:*** IB>

barligoter [barligote] *v.tr.* to swathe <***Loc:*** JE>

barlonquer ♦see **baranquer**

BARLOW [barlo] *n.m.* pocketknife *Il s'est coupé son doigt avec son* BARLOW*.* He cut his finger with his pocketknife. (AV) <***Loc:*** AV, EV, Lv88, Ph36>

baromètre [barɔ̃mɛt(r)] *n.m.* barometer <***Loc:*** Da84>

baron[1]**, -esse** [barɔ̃, barɔ̃nɛs] *n.* **1** *(m.)* baron **2** *(f.)* baroness <***Loc:*** Da84>

baron[2] [barɔ̃] *n.m.* hummingbird <***Loc:*** Lv88, Re31>

baroque[1] [barɔk] *adj.* **1** foolish, silly *Toute cette famille est manière baroque.* That whole family is sort of foolish. (EV) **2** strange, bizarre *Une histoire baroque.* A bizarre story. (EV) **3** broken, mixed (of speech) *Avec ma mère je parle en français avec elle tout le temps, mais elle alle parle moitié en anglais. On appelle ça baroque, c'est mêlé, quelques mots français, anglais.* With my mother I speak French all the time, but she speaks half in English. We call that broken, it's mixed, some words in French, [others] English. (TB) *Et comme mon garçon qui reste en haut là, tu peux voir, lui il parle plein en français, mais il parle pas comme nous-autres. Tu peux voir qu'il était pas habitué à parler français. T'appelles ça "baroque."* And like my son who lives up the bayou, he speaks French, but he doesn't talk like us. You can tell he was not used to speaking French. They call that "baroque." (TB) <***Loc:*** EV, LF, SB, TB, La99, Lv88>

baroque[2] [barɔk] *adv.* in a broken, mixed way (of speech) *Il comprend tout et il peut dire quelques affaires, mais il parle pas bien en français. C'est pour ça on dit qu'il parle baroque. Parce que il dit quelques mots en anglais et quelques mots en français.* He understands everything and he can say a few things, but he doesn't speak French well. That's why we say he speaks "baroque." Because he says some words in English and some words in French. (LF) <***Loc:*** LF>

barosse [barɔs] *adj.* **1** sluggish, slow, lazy, dull **2** yellow or tan colored (of an animal's coat) **3** gaudy, motley, of many colors **4** spotted, speckled <***Loc:*** EV, JE, SM, Da84, Lv88, Ph36>

barouche[1] [baruʃ, barus] *n.f.* surrey, large two-seat carriage ◊

•barouche à frange fringed surrey <Da84> <***Loc:*** IB, JE, LA, SM, TB, Da84, Fa77, Lv88>

barouche[2] [baruʃ] *n.f.* disagreement, discord ◊ **•faire {avoir} barouche** to break up, have a disagreement <LF, TB, La99> <***Loc:*** LF, TB, La99>

barouette ♦see **berouette**

baroui ♦see **ébaroui**

barque (**bac**) [bark, bak] *n.f.* **1** bark, small boat **2** rowboat made with planks <***Loc:*** IV, TB, Da84>

barrage [baraʒ] *n.m.* **1** blocking **2** locking **3** partition, wall <***Loc:*** VM, Da84>

barrancages [barɑ̃kaʒ] *n.m.pl.* odds and ends *T'es après chercher les barrancages.* You're searching for odds and ends. (VM) <***Loc:*** VM>

barraque ♦see **baraque**

barre[1] [bar, bɔr] *n.f.* **1** bar (of wood, metal, etc.) **2** transversal bar in certain rowboats to which the oars are attached **3** block, chunk *Une barre de fromage.* A chunk of cheese. (SL) **4** striped bass ◊ **•barre à clous** crowbar <VM> **•barre de candi** candy bar <SB, TB, Da84> **•barre de corps** railing, esp. on a porch *Tiens sur la barre de corps.* Hold on to the railing. (JE) <JE, LF, Lv88> **•barre de fer** iron rod <Da84> **•barre de savon** bar of soap <SB, SM, VM> **•barre d'or** goldenrod <TB> **•barre du cou** nape of the neck *Lave ta barre du cou.* Wash the nape of your neck. (JE) <JE, LF, SB, Lv88> **•barre du jour** dawn, daybreak *On a été pêcher à la barre du jour.* We went fishing at daybreak. (TB) <JE, LF, SM, TB, Lv88> **•barre du lit** headboard of a bed <TB> **•à barres** striped *Où t'as pris ce* SUIT *à barres?* Where did you get that striped suit? (JE) <JE, Lv88> <***Loc:*** AC, JE, LF, SB, SL, SM, TB, VM, Da84, Gu00, Hi02, Lv88>

barre[2] [bar] *n.f.* sharp pain, esp. in the head or abdomen *J'ai une barre dans l'estomac.* I have a sharp pain in my chest. (AV) <***Loc:*** IB, SJ, SL, SM>

barre[3] ♦see **bar**

barré, -e [bare] *adj.* **1** striped *J'ai une paire de pantalons barrés.* I have a pair of striped pants. (JE) **2** constipated *Il avait mangé trop de fromage pour les noces et il a resté barré pour deux jours.* He had eaten too much cheese for the wedding, and he remained constipated for two days. (LA) <***Loc:*** JE, LA, LF, SB, SL, SM, TB, VM, Da84, Hi02, Lv88>

barreau [baro] *n.m.* thin, straight cylindrical piece or bar of metal or wood (e.g. rung, spindle, dowel) *Les barreaux de la prison.* The bars of the prison. (VM) <***Loc:*** VM, Da84, Lv88>

barreauté, -e (**barroté, -e**) [barote] *adj.* **1** made of small bars (of wood or metal) *Le dos de la berce est barreauté.* The back of the rocker is made of small bars of wood. (Lv88) **2** striped *Elle porte une robe barreautée rouge et blanc.* She is wearing a red and white striped dress. (SB) *L'étoffe barreautée.* Striped cloth. (LF) **3** cross-barred *On a une galerie barreautée.* We have a cross-barred porch. (SM) <***Loc:*** EV, LA, LF, SB, SM, Da84, Lv88, Ph36>

barreauter (**barroter**) [barote] *v.tr.* to blockade, bar, enclose with bars *J'ai barreauté une cage pour le chaoui.* I made a cage out of bars for the raccoon. (Lv88) <***Loc:*** IB, TB, Lv88>

barré (**barrée**) [bare] *adj.* locked *Il y avait pas une porte de barrée.* There wasn't a locked door. (SL) <***Loc:*** LF, SL, TL>

barrer [bare] *v.tr.* **1** to lock *Barre la porte.* Lock the door. (JE, LF, SM) **2** to close, lock with a bar *Tu peux barrer quelque chose sans te servir d'un cadenas. Mets une barre. C'est là ça vient barré.* You can lock something without using a padlock. Place a bar. Then it is locked. (IB) **3** to fasten with a hook or other means *Il a barré la porte avec une corde.* He fastened the door with a rope. (SM) **4** to block, blockade (a road) *Si tu voulais que ton chemin reste privé, il faulait tu le barres un jour dans l'année.* If you wanted your road to remain private, you had to block it one day each year. (LA) **5** to constipate *Ça l'a barrée, après elle l'avait mangé.* It made her constipated after she ate it. (VM) **II** *v.intr.* to close, end (of a fishing season) *Cette saison-ici-là, elle va barrer dans une autre, je crois que c'est une autre trois semaines.* This [fishing] season, it's going to close in another, I think it's another three weeks. (TB) **III se barrer** *v.pron.* to become locked, lock o.s. **Et ça dit quand il mettait sa main dessus quelque chose, c'était pareil comme un étau. Ça se barrait!* And they say when he would put his hand on something, it was just like a vise. It would become locked. (IB, An94) ◊ **•barrer la bouche** to cause the mouth to pucker (in reaction to a bitter taste) *C'est comme ça ils sont bons, ils sont mous. Si c'est pas mou ça barre la bouche.* That's when they're good, they're soft. If it's not soft it makes your mouth pucker. (TB) <TB, Lv88> <***Loc:*** AC, AV, EV, IB, IV, JE, LA, LF, SB, SJ, SL, SM, TB, VM, An94, Da84, Hi02, Lv88, Ph36, Re31, Wh69>

barrière [barjær] *n.f.* fence, barrier ◊ **•barrière à {de} pieux** board fence (either pickets, upright boards, or horizontal boards) <Da84, Lv88> **•barrière à (fil de fer à) piquants** barbwire fence <Da84, Lv88> **•barrière à fil de fer et à carreau** net fence <Da84> **•barrière en pieux debout** barrier made of boards driven into the ground alongside one another <Lv88> <***Loc:*** EV, IB, LA, LF, SB, SL, SM, TB, Da84, Gu00, Hi02, Lv88>

barrique [barik] *n.f.* **1** large barrel **2** one half of a barrel (sawn in two) used as a washtub, water trough, etc. <***Loc:*** LA, VM, Da84>

barroté ♦see **barreauté**

barroter ♦see **barreauter**

bartelle ♦see **bretelle**

bas[1], **-sse** [ba, bas] *adj.* **1** low *Asteur la terre basse est tout plantée en binnes, en fèves.* Now, the lowland is all planted in beans. (ThCa: *Mille misères*) **2** shallow, of less than average depth *Moi je pêche dans les bayous, mais l'eau est tellement basse, tellement il fait sec que l'eau est pas bonne, et alors un poisson mord pas.* I fish in the bayous, but the water is so low, it's so dry that the (condition of the) water isn't right, and so a fish won't bite. (SL) **3** mean, vile *Un coup bas.* A mean or vile act. (VM) ◊ **•bas-d'eau** pond <JE> **•bas-fond** ***a*** lowland ***b*** pond for washing vegetables <JE, Da84> **•bas-jarret** singletree <JE, Di32> **•bas monde** low-class people <Da84> <***Loc:*** EV, JD, JE, LA, SL, VM, Da84, Di32, Hi02, ThCa>

bas[2] [ba] *n.m.* stocking, sock <***Loc:*** AC, EV, JE, LA, LF, SM, Da84, Gu00, Hi02>

bas[3] [ba] *n.m.* base, bottom, underside ◊ **•bas de (la) porte** threshold *Reste sur le bas de la porte.* Remain in the threshold. (JE) <JE, LF, SM, Lv88> **•bas de pantalon** cuff of trousers <LF, SM> **•bas de rang** furrow, space between cultivated rows <AC, EV> **•bas du STOVE** oven <EV> <***Loc:*** AC, EV, JE, LF, SM, Da84, Lv88>

bas[4] [ba] *adv.* **1** under, beneath, below **2** in a low position, level, space or situation *C'est le whisky qui l'a entraîné si bas.* It's whiskey that dragged him down so low. (LA) **3** softly, quietly *Parle plus bas.* Speak more softly. (LA) ◊ **•en bas** ***a*** under, underneath, beneath, below *Il est couché en bas le lit.* He is sleeping under the bed. (SM) **WELL, je vas mettre mon boghei là, et ma bêtaille en bas de la lumière-là.* Well, I'll put my buggy there and my horse underneath the light there. (SL, An94) **Là, il y en a un qui avait monté après un chaoui et l'autre était en bas.* Then there was one who climbed up after a raccoon and the other was down below. (AC, An94) *En bas ton linge.* Underneath your clothes. (Lv88) ***b*** down **Il courait tout parmi tout le monde, les tables de gâteaux et de manger, et le bougre était couché sur le dos du cochon, avec les culottes en bas!* It was running among the people, the cake tables and the food tables, and the fellow was lying on the back of the pig, with his pants down! (EV, An94) ***c*** upside down *Elle jetait l'eau, elle tournait les bailles en bas.* She would throw out the water and turn the washtubs upside down. (LA) ***d*** downstairs *Dans les vieilles maisons, les vieux dormaient en bas et les jeunes dormaient en haut.* In the old houses, the older folks slept downstairs and the younger ones slept upstairs. (LA) *Il faulait on couche en bas quand ça faisait chaud.* We had to sleep downstairs when it was hot. (VM) ***e*** downstream, down the bayou *Je porte pas grand attention, mais je peux dire quand eux-autres vient d'en bas, et si c'est que ça vient d'en haut, parce que le monde d'en haut parle pas pareil comme eusse d'en bas.* I don't pay much attention, but I can tell when they come up from down the bayou or if they come from up the bayou, because people up the bayou don't talk the same as those from down the bayou. (TB) *Eusse viendait en bas sus les weekends, et aller à la pêche, et là ça s'en va BACK, et eusse restait au camp dessus les weekends.* They came down on weekends and went fishing, then they went back, and they stayed at the camp on weekends. (TB) *Le monde de par en bas parlent pas comme nous autres.* The people from down the bayou don't talk like us. (LF) <AC, LA, LF, SL, SM, TB, VM, An94, Da84, Lv88> **•en bas de** ***a*** under, underneath **En bas d'un arbre.* Under a tree. (Da84) *Il s'a abordé la caloquinte dessus la sole en bas de la maison.* He bumped his head on the beam under the house. (LA) *Il est caché en bas du lit.* It is hidden under the bed. (Lv88) ***b*** in the bottom of *Quand tu vas finir avec la gazette, tu peux me la donner pour la mettre en bas de la cage à pigeons.* When you're finished with the newspaper, you can give it to me to put in the bottom of the pigeon cage. (ThCa: *Messieurs, mesdames*) ***c*** at the bottom, at the foot of **Ça fait qu'elle a descendu en bas de la montagne et elle a trouvé de quoi qui coupait.* So, she went down to the foot of the mountain and she found something that cut. (IV, An94) ***d*** down from **Alors, il a sauté en bas du lit, et puis il a foncé à la cuisine...* So he jumped down from the bed and rushed to the kitchen . . . (EV, An94) <EV, IV, JD, LA, SL, VM, An94, Da84, Lv88, ThCa> **•là-bas** over there **Regarde ce bougre qui vient là-bas-là.* Look at the fellow who is coming over there. (IB, An94) <IB, An94> **•mettre en bas** to set down, to put below or under *Quand ma mère s'a manière levé pour changer le foin dedans des boîtes on mettait en bas la maison pour les poules pondre, Joe Bill, le petit cabri, lui a enfoncé ça dans le derrière.* When my mother kind of got up to change the hay in the boxes we would put under the house for the chickens to lay, Joe Bill, the little goat, he rammed her behind. (IB) <IB, Da84> <***Loc:*** EV, IB, JD, LA, SL, SM, TB, VM, An94, Da84, Hi02, Lv88>

basane [bazɑ̃n] *n.f.* freckle <***Loc:*** Da84, Lv88>

basané, -e [bazɑ̃ne] *adj.* **1** freckled *Il est tout basané.* He is quite freckled. (JE) **2** speckled, spotted *Ça c'est un SPECKLED TROUT. Tu l'appelles une truite grise, alle est grise les deux bords, alle est matachée, basanée les deux bords.* That is a speckled trout. It's called a "truite grise," it's gray on both sides, it's speckled, spotted on both sides. (TB) <***Loc:*** IB, JE, LA, LF, SM, TB, Da84, Hi02, Lv88>

basaneux [bazɑ̃nø] *adj.* freckled *Il est basaneux.* He is freckled. (JE) <***Loc:*** JE, LF>

basanure [bazɑ̃nyr, bazɑ̃nœr] *n.m./f.* freckle <***Loc:*** IB, JE, LF, SM, TB, Lv88>

basculage [baskylaʒ] *n.m.* wrestling match <***Loc:*** SM>

bascule [baskyl] *n.f.* **1** somersault, flip **2** punishment or game in which a person is swung by the arms and legs (and knocked into a hard surface) *Si t'arrêtes pas ça, je vas te passer à la bascule.* If you don't stop that, I am going to give you a beating. (VM) <***Loc:*** SM, VM, Da84, Lv88>

basculer [baskyle] **I** *v.tr.* **1** to turn over, turn upside down, throw from one side to another, *Il a tout basculé le butin.* He turned over all the furniture. (Lv88) **2** to mistreat, upset *L'imbécile, il m'a basculé.* The fool, he upset me. (JE) **II** *v.intr.* to fight, scuffle *Les deux hommes étaient après basculer dans la cour l'autre soir.* The two men were fighting in the yard the other night. (Lv88) **III se basculer** *v.pron.* to fidget *Arrêtez de vous basculer! On arrive à la messe.* Stop fidgeting! We're almost at church (for mass). (VM) <***Loc:*** JE, LF, SM, VM, Da84, Lv88>

base [baz] *n.f.* base, basis, foundation <***Loc:*** Da84>

baser [baze] *v.* ◊ **•baser sur** to base on *Ton* RETIREMENT *est basé sur ton salaire.* Your retirement is based on your salary. (LA) <LA, Da84> **•se baser sur** to base o.s., one's ideas or actions on *Il se base sur ça que sa femme lui a dit.* He is basing his ideas on what his wife told him. (LA) <LA, Da84> <***Loc:*** LA, Da84>

basilique[1] [bazilik, bazelik, bazəlik] *n.m.* basilica <***Loc:*** SL, TB, VM>

basilique[2] [bazilik, bazelik, bazəlik] *n.m.* basil <***Loc:*** SL, TB, VM>

basir [bazir] *v.intr.* to disappear *Tandis que j'étais après parler avec ton mari, t'as basi.* While I was talking with your husband, you disappeared. (Gu00) <***Loc:*** JE, Di32, Gu00, Lv88>

basque [bask] *n.f.* **1** flap or fender of a western saddle **2** very tight-fitting coat <***Loc:*** IB, JE, Di32, Lv88>

basquine [baskin] *n.f.* peculiar or funny dress *Ça, c'est une basquine.* That's a funny-looking dress. (AV) <***Loc:*** AV>

basse [bas] *n.f.* **1** bass drum **2** double bass, string bass <***Loc:*** VM, Hi02>

basse-classe [basklas] *adj.* low, sleazy, of weak morals *Je savais pas qu'il était assez basse-classe pour faire ça.* I didn't know he was low enough to do that. (VM) <***Loc:*** TB, VM, Da84, Fa77>

basse-cour [baskur] *n.f.* **1** chicken yard *Elle avait des poules variées dans sa basse-cour.* She had assorted chickens in her chicken yard. (LA) **2** domestic flock (of miscellaneous fowl) **3** barnyard animals (collectively) <***Loc:*** LA, VM, Da84, Fa77>

basset, -ette [basɛ, -ɛt, base, -et] *adj.* short (of stature) *Cousine Toutoune, elle était bassette, et large comme la glacière, pauvre bête.* Cousin Toutoune, she was short, and as wide as the refrigerator, poor thing. (Lv88) <***Loc:*** AL, LA, SM Da84, Hi02, Lv88>

bassette [basɛt, baset] *adj.f.* short-legged (of a cow; by extension, name given to a short-legged cow) <***Loc:*** Da84, Lv88>

bassière (baissière) [basjær, besjær] *n.f.* **1** low swampy or marshy place, lowland, sink or depression in the land (in which water collects) *Il y a une bassière dans le coin gauche de la cour.* There's a low area in the left corner of the yard. (VM) *J'ai consacré ma bassière pour élever des écrevisses.* I dedicated my lowland to raising crawfish. (VM) **2** swamp **3** flood plain <***Loc:*** EV, IB, JE, SL, SM, VM, Da84, Gu00, Hi02, Lv88, Ph36>

bassin [basɛ̃] *n.m.* **1** any vessel of tin or aluminum, such as a pan, bucket, basin, or bowl **Je les ai mis à tremper dans un bassin de térébenthine.* I put them [tweezers] to soak in a bucket of terebenthine. (ThCa: *Le charivari*) **2** dish, container **3** foot tub, bathtub **4** lavatory **5** low area of land, basin ◊ **•bassin à lait** milk pail <LA> **•bassin à mains / bassin lave mains** washbasin, handbasin <SB, SL, Da84, Lv88> **•bassin à vaisselle** dishpan, washbasin *Attrape le bassin à vaisselle et commence laver la vaisselle.* Get the washbasin and start washing the dishes. (LA) <LA, Gu00> **•bassin bossu {cabossu}** dented or crumpled pan or can <Da84> **•bassin d'école** lunch pail *Le bassin d'école est dans la salle à manger.* The lunch pail is in the dining room. (SL) <SL> **•faire bassin** to be warped or out of line (of wheels) *Les roues du wagon sont après faire bassin.* The wagon wheels are warped. (VM) <VM> **•le bassin de l'Atchafalaya** the Atchafalaya Basin <LA> <***Loc:*** AC, AV, EV, JE, LA, LF, SB, SL, SM, TB, VM, Da84, Gu00, Lv88, ThCa>

bassine [basin] *n.f.* **1** washbowl, washtub, tub *On gardait de l'eau dans une petite bassine pour laver les pieds.* We kept water in a small washtub to wash our feet. (LA) **2** oven *T'attends plus ces mots là, pareil comme une "bassine." Une bassine pour mon, c'est un* OVEN. *Et tu peux l'appeler une "boîte à pain."* You no longer hear those words like a "bassine." A "bassine" for me is an oven. And you can call it a "boîte à pain." (LF) <***Loc:*** LA, LF, TB, VM, Da84>

bassinée [basine] *n.f.* washtub full <***Loc:*** Da84>

bassinet [basinɛ, basine] *n.m.* **1** small tub **2** bassinet <***Loc:*** Da84>

bastringue [bastrɛ̃g, bastrɛ̃ŋ, bastrɛ̃j] *n.m./f.* **1** large, old house *Il reste dans une grosse bastringue.* He lives in a big, old house. (SM) **2** old car, any old vehicle **3** mess, stuff *Toute la bastringue a tombé.* All the stuff fell. (Lv88) **4** triangle, steel triangle used as a percussive instrument **5** percussion, percussive instrument(s) **6** band, group, clique, following *Elle va avec toute sa bastringue.* She goes around with her cliquc. (SB) <***Loc:*** AV, SB, SM, VM, Lv88>

bas-ventre [bavɑ̃t(r)] *n.m.* underbelly <***Loc:*** Da84>

bataclan [bataklɑ̃] *n.m.* shebang, lot, bunch ◊ **•tout le sacré bataclan** the bunch, the whole shebang <Da84> <***Loc:*** LA, Da84>

bataille [bataj] *n.f.* **1** fight, battle, combat **2** card game known as "battle" ◊ **•bataille à coups de chapeau** ***a*** insignificant squabble over trifles ***b*** fight in which no one is hurt <Da84> **•bataille à coups de poing** fistfight <Da84> **•bataille de gaimes** cockfight <Da84> <***Loc:*** AC, EV, SB, SM, TB, Da84, Hi02, Lv88>

batailler (se) [bataje] *v.pron.* to fight repeatedly, fight in play

Ces petits sont toujours après se batailler. Those kids are always fighting playfully. (IB) <***Loc:*** IB>

batailleur[1]**, -euse** [batajœr, -øz] *adj.* pugnacious *On le voyait tout le temps dans les bars. Il était beaucoup batailleur.* We'd always see him in the bars. He was a big fighter. (EV) <***Loc:*** EV, Da84>

batailleur[2]**, -euse** [batajœr, -øz] *n.m.* fighter, scrapper *Le shérif, c'est pour les rôdailleurs, les batailleurs.* The sheriff, he handles the vagrants and the brawlers. (Lv88) <***Loc:*** EV, IV, An94, Da84, Lv88>

bataillon [batajɔ̃] *n.m.* **1** battalion **2** gamecock <***Loc:*** JE, Da84, Lv88>

bâtard[1]**, -e** [batar, -ard] *adj.* mixed, hybrid *Du maïs batard, blanc et jaune.* Hybrid corn, white and yellow. (Lv88) *Février est pas bâtard.* (proverb) February can be as cold as the earlier months of winter. (VM) <***Loc:*** VM, Da84, Lv88>

bâtard[2]**, -e** [batar, -ard] *n.* **1** offspring born out of wedlock, illegitimate child *Ce premier, c'est pas son enfant à elle et lui. C'est un bâtard.* The first one is not their child together. He's a child born out of wedlock. (VM) **2** offspring of mixed blood, mongrel **3** [*offensive*] bastard ◊ **•bâtard sonnette** type of poisonous snake, related to the rattlesnake <EV> <***Loc:*** EV, VM, Da84, Lv88>

bâtard[3] [batar] *n.* dam, dike <***Loc:*** JE>

bâtardi ♦see **abâtardi**

bâtardir ♦see **abâtardir**

bateau [bato] *n.m.* **1** boat, ship **2** flat boat with squared ends, a bit wider in the back than the front, developed to accommodate gasoline engines ◊ **•bateau à fret** freight boat <SJ> **•bateau à pagailles** rowboat <Fa77> **•bateau à vapeur** steamboat <Fa77>_**•bateau à voiles** sailboat <LF, Fa77> **•bateau à-z-huîtres** oyster boat <LF, TB> **•bateau de boue** mudboat <TB> **•bateau de chevrette** shrimp boat <TB> **•bateau de trawl** trawler <TB> **•en {par} bateau** by boat *C'est comme une île, la seule manière tu peux arriver là c'est par bateau.* It's like an island, the only way you can get there is by boat. (TB) <TB> <***Loc:*** JE, LA, LF, SJ, SM, TB, Da84, Fa77, Hi02, Lv88>

batelée (bâclée) [batle, bakle] *n.f.* large group, gang, band *Il y avait une batelée de monde au meeting.* There was quite a crowd at the meeting. (AV) *Alle a une vraie bâclée d'enfants.* She has a big bunch of children. (TB) <***Loc:*** AV, JE, TB, Di32, Lv88>

bâtiment [batimɑ̃] *n.m.* building <***Loc:*** Da84>

bâtir [batir] **I** *v.tr.* **1** to build, construct *On a bâti des bateaux en bois.* We built wooden boats. (JE) *On l'avait bâti une petite maison à deux chambres.* We had built a small house for her with two rooms. (IB) **2** to make, fabricate *On a bâti des cages et puis on a bâti un bateau.* We made cages and we built a boat. (SM) **II se bâtir** *v.pron.* to build o.s. a home *On s'est bâti en 1960.* We built ourselves a house in 1960. (Lv88) *Il s'est bâti en brique un peu plus loin.* He built a brick house a little farther on. (Lv88) ◊ **•se bâtir un magasin** to build o.s. a barn, a store <Da84> <***Loc:*** EV, IB, JE, SM, TB, Da84, Lv88>

batiscan [batiskɑ̃] *interj.* mild oath to express surprise, regret or discontent <***Loc:*** AV>

bâtisse [batis] *n.f.* building, structure *C'était la première bâtisse bâtie pour faire le* HIGH SCHOOL *de la paroisse Ibérie.* It was the first building built for high school in Iberia parish. (IB) <***Loc:*** AV, EV, IB, JE, LF, SB, SL, SM, TB, VM, Da84, Hi02, Lv88>

bâtisseur [batisœr] *n.m.* builder <***Loc:*** Da84>

batistaire, batistère ♦see **baptistaire**

batiste [batis(t)] *n.f.* batiste, cambric cloth <***Loc:*** Da84>

bâton [batɔ̃] *n.m.* **1** stick, rod **Passer à coups de bâton.* To beat with a stick. (Da84) **2** stalk, stem (of a plant) **3** nervure, veins (of a leaf) **4** drumstick (of cooked fowl) **5** praying mantis ◊ **•bâton à {de} lit** bed staff, used to spread the sheets on a bed <JE, LF, SM, Lv88> **•bâton boulon** a stick with a kind of bolt on the end <Lv88> **•bâton de coton** cotton stalk <Da84> **•bâton de pile** pestle <Lv88> **•bâton de vieillesse** a person who can be depended upon for help in one's old age **Celui-là va être mon bâton de vieillesse.* This one is going to be my comfort in my later years. (La99) <La99> **•bâton merdeux** person who is in a very bad humor *Il est comme un bâton merdeux depuis il a perdu son argent.* He's an old grouch since he lost his money. (SM) <SM> **•bâton pilon** drumstick of a cooked fowl <SM> **•bâton pour transmission** gear shift lever <Lv88> **•mettre des bâtons dans la roue {les roues}** to obstruct, impede, hamper, put impediments or obstacles in the way of one's success <Da84, La99> **•prends ça à coups de bâton!** he/she should be beaten! <AC, LA, VM> <***Loc:*** AC, EV, IB, JE, LA, LF, SM, TB, VM, Da84, Hi02 La99, Lv88>

bâtonner [batɔ̃ne] *v.tr.* **1** to beat with a stick, cudgel *Ça mérite de se faire bâtonner.* He deserves to be beaten. (VM) **2** to install the wooden struts in a wall, later to be filled with "bousillage" **3** to put upright bars between the horizontal railings of a banister <***Loc:*** AV, JE, VM, Da84, Di32, Lv88>

battage [bataʒ] *n.m.* **1** pounding, beating **2** threshing (of grain) ◊ **•battage (de) charrue** beating of plowshare to sharpen it <SM> **•battage de riz** threshing of rice <Da84> <***Loc:*** SM, Da84>

batte-feu [batfø] *n.m.* flint and steel (for striking a light) <***Loc:*** JE>

battement [batmɑ̃] *n.m.* **1** clapping (of hands) **2** throbbing, pulsation ◊ **•battement d'ailes** flapping of wings <Da84> **•battement de cœur** heartbeat <Da84> <***Loc:*** Da84>

batterie [batri] *n.f.* **1** battery **2** threshing floor, area for threshing grain **3** collection of large kettles used in the preparation of cane sugar **4** any of the individual kettles used in the preparation of cane sugar, esp. the fourth and last kettle ◊

•batterie de cuisine set of kitchen utensils <Da84, Lv88> <*Loc:* IB, JE, LF, TB, VM, Da84, Lv88>

batteur [batœr] *n.m.* **1** beater (of a mixer or other machine) **2** agitator (of a washing machine) ◊ **•batteur d'œuf** egg-beater <Fa77> <*Loc:* EV, LA, TB, VM, Da84, Fa77>

batteuse [batøz] *n.f.* threshing machine <*Loc:* EV, TB, VM, Da84>

battocher [batoʃe] *v.intr.* to flap in the wind (as clothes on a clothesline) <*Loc:* LF>

battoir [batwar] *n.m.* **1** washboard **2** stick used to beat the washing <*Loc:* AC, IB, LF, VM>

battre [bat(r)] **I** *v.tr.* **1** to beat, hit, strike, beat up **J'ai été chercher bâton pour battre les chiens.* I went to get the stick to beat the dogs. (LA, An94) **2** to strike, beat (clothes or metal) *On battait le linge au bayou pour le laver.* They would beat the laundry at the bayou to wash it. (LA) **3** to shape, break, sharpen by repeated blows *Le forgeron a pas fini de battre la charrue.* The blacksmith has not finished beating the plow. (LA) **4** to thresh *Ils ont déjà commencé à battre le riz.* They have already started to thresh the rice. (LA) **5** to mix with a utensil *Il faut tu bats deux œufs, et là tu les mélanges avec un peu du lait.* You have to beat two eggs and then you mix them with a little milk. (LA) **6** to make fight (e.g. gamecocks) **Ça battait les chiens à Ossun.* They used to fight dogs in Ossun. (An77) *Ça vient de Cuba pour venir battre leurs gaimes icite.* They come from Cuba to fight their gamecocks here. (Lv88) **7** to beat, defeat (in a contest, game, etc.) **Il y avait un qui avait battu l'autre.* There was one who had defeated the other. (AC, An94) **8** to surpass *Ces pommes ne peut pas être battues.* These apples can't be surpassed. (JE) **II** *v.intr.* **1** to beat (of the heart), throb (of the pulse) **Et là, je veux me faire mettre un cœur de caouane bord-là. Tu connais ces caouanes de mer-là, ça vit trois cents années, ça. Ça fait, quand ce maudit va arrêter de battre comme ça-là, j'aurais un petit bouton-là, "Proupe!"* And then, I want to have installed in me a sea-turtle heart on this side. You know, those sea-turtles, they live three hundred years. So when this damned thing will stop beating like that, I'd have a little button there, "Proupe!" (EV, An94) **2** to fight *Ils sont tout le temps parés pour battre.* They are always ready to fight. (SM) *Quand il a voulu battre, j'ai calé.* When he wanted to fight, I backed down. (SM) **III se battre** *v.pron.* to fight *Deux s'accordaient pas, si ça voulait pas s'accorder, ça voulait se battre tout le temps. So tu quittais ces deux là se battre.* Two didn't get along, if they didn't want to get along, they wanted to fight all the time. So you let those two fight. (TB) *Ils s'ont parié que les enfant s'auraient battu avant la fin de la journée.* They bet on whether or not the children would fight before the end of the day. (VM) *Il a fait comme si il voulait se battre, mais il a caillé quand c'était temps pour se battre.* He was acting like he wanted to fight, but he backed down when it was time to fight. (SM) ◊ **•battre la berloque** ***a*** to be in ruins, be dilapidated *La bourouette bat la berloque.* The wheelbarrow is broken down. (LF) ***b*** to talk randomly, exaggerate, be deranged, talk wildly, rave *Je le compends pas. Il est à battre la berloque.* I don't understand him. He's talking crazy. (SM) *Va-t-en, tu bats la berloque.* Get out of here, you are crazy. (JE) <IB, JE, LF, SB, SM, Da84, La99, Lv88> **•battre les yeux** to bat one's eyelids **Quand tu vas voir que je vas plus souffler, et je vas plus parler, et je vas plus battre mes yeux, mes lèvres vont venir noires, je serai morte.* When you see that I will no longer be breathing, and I will no longer be speaking, and I will no longer bat my eyelids, my lips will turn black, I will be dead. (IB, An94) <IB, An94> **•battre sa gueule** to chatter on, talk excessively *Arrête donc de battre ta gueule.* Why don't you stop chattering on. (LA) <LA, La99> **•battre une lame de charrue** to sharpen a plow <Da84> **•se battre aux armes** to fight a duel **Le dimanche matin à dix heures, ils se seraient rencontrés en avant. Ils se seraient battus aux armes.* On Sunday at ten o'clock in the morning, they would meet out in front. They would fight a duel. (SL, An94) <SL, An94> <*Loc:* AC, EV, IB, JE, LA, LF, SB, SL, SM, TB, An77, An94, Da84, Hi02, La99, Lv88>

batture [batyr] *n.f.* **1** flood plain, flat land along a waterway that floods at high tide or seasonally *Si t'après faire route, et ça vient bien platte et y a pas plein de l'eau ça c'est une batture.* If you're travelling along and it gets very flat and there's not much water, that's a flood plain. (LF) **2** small levee, ridge of sand formed along a river *Ça a commencé faire des battures, des* SANDBAR, *ça empêchait l'eau passer. Le sable a tout reposé et ça a fait une petite levée tout au long de ces bayous là.* Sandbars started building up, it prevented the water from going through. The sand would stay there and a levee would appear all along the bayou there. (SM) **3** bald spot (on a man's head) ◊ **•avoir la batture** to be bald <LF> <*Loc:* IB, JE, LF, SJ, SM, TB, Lv88, Re31>

bauche [boʃ] *n.f.* foot-race, run *J'ai fait une bonne bauche dimanche matin.* I had a nice run Sunday morning. (Lv88) <*Loc:* Lv88>

baudette [bodɛt] *n.m.* folding bed <*Loc:* JE, Di32>

baume [bɔ̃m] *n.m.* mint ◊ **•baume (de) sauvage** camphor weed <SB, Ho90> **•baume tranquille** species of mint <EV> <*Loc:* EV, SB, Da84, Ho90>

bavard[1], -e [bavar, -ard] *adj.* talkative, garrulous *Son frère était tellement bavard qu'il pouvait proche te soûler avec son discours.* His brother was so talkative that he could almost intoxicate you with his words. (LA) <*Loc:* LA, Da84>

bavard[2], -e [bavar, -ard] *n.* babbler, prattler, talkative person <*Loc:* Da84>

bavardage [bavardaʒ] *n.m.* babble, prattle <*Loc:* Da84>

bavarder [bavarde] *v.intr.* to babble, prattle, gab *Ils étaient* *juste après bavarder à la manière des vieux.* They were just gabbing like old folks. (LA) <***Loc:*** LA, Da84, Hi02>

bavardeur[1]**, -euse** [bavardœr, -øz] *adj.* talkative, garrulous *Lui, il est bavardeur, mais son frère, tu l'entends proche pas.* He's talkative, but his brother, you almost never hear him. (LA) <***Loc:*** LA, SM, Da84, Lv88>

bavardeur[2]**, -euse** [bavardœr, -øz] *n.* babbler, prattler, talkative person *Il était un bavardeur sans pareil.* He was a bigmouth without equal. (Lv88) <***Loc:*** LA, SM, Da84, Lv88>

bave [bav] *n.f.* drool <***Loc:*** Da84>

baver [bave] *v.intr.* to slobber, slaver, drool *Léon, son mari, va te fondre des gratons qui vont te faire baver.* Leon, her husband, will fry cracklins that will make you drool. (VM) <***Loc:*** VM, Da84, Hi02>

baves [bav] *n.f.pl.* disease of animals <***Loc:*** Lv88>

bavette[1] [bavɛt] *n.f.* baby bib <***Loc:*** Da84>

bavette[2] [bavɛt] *n.f.* vehicle license *J'ai acheté la bavette à Betsie.* I bought a licence for my car Betsy. (SL) <***Loc:*** SL, Lv88>

baveur [bavœr] *adj.* dribbling, drooling <***Loc:*** EV, Ph36>

bavoler [bavole] *v.intr.* to slobber, drool *Il a bavolé dans ma figure.* He slobbered in my face. (VM) <***Loc:*** VM>

baye ♦see **baille**[1]

bayou [baju] *n.m.* bayou, stream *Il reste sur le bayou.* He lives on the bayou. (JE) <***Loc:*** AC, AV, EV, IB, JE, LA, LF, SL, SM, TB, VM, An94, Da84, Gu00, Hi02, Lv88, Ph36>

bazar [bazar] *n.m.* **1** bazaar, fair **2** unaccompanied group singing and dancing event <***Loc:*** JD, VM, Da84, Lv88>

béaba [beaba] *n.m.* alphabet <***Loc:*** JE, Di32>

BEAN [bin] *n.m./f.* bean ◊ **•BEAN blanc** white bean <TB> **•BEAN vert** green bean <JE> <***Loc:*** JE, LF, TB, Lv88>

BEAT (beater) [bit, bite] *v.tr.* to beat, surpass *Il l'a beaté à la course.* He beat him in the race. (Lv88) *Il t'a beaté à l'école.* He beat you at school. (VM) ◊ **•ça me BEAT** beats me, I don't know <Lv88> <***Loc:*** TB, VM, Lv88>

beater ♦see **BEAT**

beau[1]**, belle** [bo, bɛl] *adj.* **1** beautiful, nice, pretty, handsome *Tu parles du joli monde. Lui il est beau garçon et sa sœur, elle est belle fille.* Talk about some beautiful people. He's a handsome boy and his sister is a pretty girl. (LA) **Il est in beau homme.* He's a fine-looking man. (EV, Ph36) *Elle avait des beaux cheveux bouclés.* She had beautiful curly hair. (LA) **2** large, big, fine *C'est son frère qu'a eu le plus beau morceau de terre.* It's his brother who got the finest piece of land. (LA) **3** nice, pleasant, sunny (of the weather) **Il fait beau.* The weather is nice. (Da84) ◊ **•au beau milieu** in the very middle. <Da84> **•j'ai beau dire et j'ai beau faire** no matter what I say or do <Da84> <***Loc:*** EV, LA, TB, VM, Da84, Hi02, La99>

beau[2] [bo] *n.m.* boyfriend, sweetheart *Cette fille a quinze beaux.* That girl has fifteen sweethearts. (SM) ◊ **•faire le beau** to stand or sit on its hind legs by itself (of a dog) <La99> <***Loc:*** JE, LF, SM, Da84, Hi02, La99, Lv88>

beaucoup (boucoup) [boku, buku] *adv.* **1** very *Avec douze piastres et demie, il pouvait pas aller beaucoup loin.* With twelve and a half dollars, he couldn't go very far. (SL) **C'était beaucoup une grosse salle de danse.* It was a very big dance hall. (LA, An94) **Un beaucoup vieux homme.* A very old man. (An77) *On l'a vu il y a pas beaucoup longtemps.* We saw him not very long ago. (IB) *C'est beaucoup mauvais de dire ça.* It's very bad to say that. (SL) **Il avait beaucoup faim.* He was very hungry. (LA, An94) *Ma femme vient avec moi beaucoup souvent.* My wife comes with me very often. (SM) *C'est pas beaucoup bien dit.* It's not very well-said. (SM) **2** much, a lot, a great deal *Il est méchant, tu peux pas beaucoup le* TRUST*, c'est tout.* He is mean, you can't trust him much, that's all. (AS) **Ça coûte beaucoup pour l'éducation à Rover.* It costs a lot for Rover's education. (LA, An94) **Et l'enfant continuissait à rire. Ça tracassait l'homme beaucoup.* And the child continued to laugh. That bothered the man a lot. (LA, An94) **J'apprécierais ça beaucoup, Monsieur.* I would appreciate that a great deal, sir. (EV, An94) **Ça voyait comme une petite lumière, pas beaucoup plus grosse qu'une chandelle.* It looked like a little light, not much bigger than a candle. (VM, An94) **Merci beaucoup, Madame.* Thank you very much, ma'am. (VM, An94) ◊ **•beaucoup de** many, a lot of, a great deal of, much *Et dans ce temps-là ils aviont pas beaucoup des affaires à faire d'autre chose que d'assir et se conter des contes.* And in those days, they didn't have a lot of other things to do than to sit down and tell each other stories. (EV) *Sur la Grande Ile, il y a beaucoup de bec-à-ciseaux.* On Grande Ile there are many black skimmers. (JE) *Il a beaucoup d'argent.* He has a great deal of money. (JE) <EV, JE, LA, An94> <***Loc:*** AC, AS, AV, EV, IB, JE, LF, SL, SM, TB, VM, An77, An94, Da84, Hi02, Lv88, Ph36>

beau-fils [bofis] *n.m.* **1** son-in-law **2** stepson <***Loc:*** Da84>

beau-frère [bofrær] *n.m.* **1** brother-in-law **2** stepbrother <***Loc:*** TB, Da84, Hi02>

beau-père [bopær] *n.m.* **1** father-in-law **2** stepfather <***Loc:*** AC, Da84, Hi02>

beauté [bote] *n.f.* **1** beauty **Signe de beauté.* Beauty mark, mole. (Da84) **2** beautiful woman *Je connais pas si t'as déjà vu sa femme, mais tu parles d'une beauté.* I don't know if you have seen his wife but she is a real beauty. (LA) <***Loc:*** LA, Da84>

beaux-parents [boparɑ̃] *n.m.pl.* **1** parents-in-law, in-laws **2** step-parents <***Loc:*** Da84>

bèbe [bɛb, beᶦb] *n.* **1** baby **2** [*term of endearment*] babe, baby **Ti viens avec mon, bèbe?* Are you coming with me, babe? (EV, Ph36) <***Loc:*** EV, SB, SM, Lv88, Ph36>

bébé [bebe, bibi, bəbe, beb] *n.m.* **1** baby, child, infant **2** youngest child of a family *Notre bébé a quarante ans.* Our youngest child is forty years old. (Lv88) **3** [*term of endearment*] baby *T'avais déjà, cher bébé, un autre que moi. Et t'as promis de rester avec elle.* Baby, you already had someone besides me. And you promised to stay with her. (ch: *Tu m'as fait t'aimer*) ◊ **•un bébé de** one heck of a **Comment tu crois, j'aurais un bébé de barbe, trois cents années.* Don't you think I'd have a grand beard in three hundred years. (EV, An94) <EV, An94> ***<Loc:*** EV, LA, LF, SM, TB, VM, An94, Da84, Lv88>

bébelle (**bébel, bebelle**) [bebɛl, bebel] *n.m./f.* **1** toy, plaything *On avait pas tous ces bébelles qu'ils ont asteur.* We did not have all these toys that they have nowadays. (AC) **L'enfant joue avec ces bébels.* The child is playing with these toys. (EV, Ph36) **2** trinket, knicknack *Des bébelles sur la cheminée.* Gaudy knicknacks (paper flowers, statuettes etc.) on the mantlepiece. (SJ) **3** ornament, decoration, bauble *Jeanne a trop de bébelles sur sa robe.* Jeanne has too many gaudy trimmings on her dress. (AV) *Et dans ce temps-là on allait couper des bois dans la cour pour faire notre* CHRISTMAS TREE*. On avait pas des bébelles comme on a aujourd'hui.* And in those days we would cut down a tree in the yard to make our Christmas tree. We didn't have ornaments like we have today. (LF) ***<Loc:*** AC, EV, IB, JE, LA, LF, SJ, SL, SM, TB, Da84, Lv88, Ph36, Re31>

bébellerie [bebɛlri] *n.f.* trinket, knicknack, curio ***<Loc:*** SM, Lv88>

bébête (**bébette**) [bebɛt, bəbɛt] *n.f.* **1** small dark frog with a white belly, that sings in the evening **2** insect, bug *J'avais pour jeter la farine de maïs, les bebettes l'avaient tout prise.* I had to throw away the cornmeal, the bugs had gotten all into it. (VM) **3** [*baby talk*] animal **4** boogeyman, imaginary creature used to frighten children into behaving *Une bébette c'était quelque chose que le vieux monde disait à un enfant, "Fais pas ça, la bébête va venir te chercher."* The boogeyman was something that old folks would tell a child, "Don't do that or the boogeyman will come and get you." (LF) ◊ **•bébête de marais** rain frog <Da84> ***<Loc:*** JE, LF, VM, Da84, La99, Lv88>

bébette ♦see **bébête**

bébitte ♦see **bibitte**

bec [bɛk, bek] *n.m.* **1** beak, bill *C'est ça qu'un canard fait. Et là des fois la mère va crier, c'est manière embourbé parce qu'alle a de la boue dans le bec. Ça fait pas un son bien clair.* That's what a duck does. And then sometimes the mother will call out, it's kind of muddy because she has mud in her beak. It doesn't make a very clear sound. (TB) **2** mouth, kisser *Ferme ton bec.* Shut up. (LF) *Il aurait écrasé la cigarette dans ton bec.* He would have squashed that cigarette in your mouth. (LA) **3** kiss *J'ai pas besoin d'un bec doux.* I don't need a sweet kiss. (TB) **4** visor, brim (of a cap) *J'ai déchiré le bec de mon* CAP. I tore up the visor of my cap. (SM) ◊ **•bec-à-ciseaux / bec-en-ciseaux** black skimmer <JE, LF, TB, Re31> **•bec-à-lancette** snakebird, anhinga, water turkey <AV, IB, Lv88> **•bec-bleu** lesser scaup <TB> **•bec-croche** white ibis <EV, Da84, Lv88, Re31> **•bec-de-hache** [bɛgdɔʃ] oyster catcher <Lv88, Re31> **•bec-fin** long-nosed or needle-nosed garfish <AV, IB> **•bec-scie** American merganser <TB, Re31> **•blanc-bec** ***a*** greenhorn, novice ***b*** braggart, boastful person <TB, Da84> **•gros-bec** night heron (locally called 'grosbeak') <IV, SB, Da84, Hi02, Lv88> ***<Loc:*** AL, AV, EV, IB, IV, JE, LA, LF, SM, TB, Da84, Hi02, Lv88, Ph36, Re31>

bécasse [bekas, begas] *n.f.* woodcock, snipe ◊ **•bécasse de marais** snipe, black-necked stilt <TB> **•bécasse de nuit** woodcock <IB> ***<Loc:*** IB, TB, Da84>

bécassine [bekasin] *n.f.* snipe ◊ **•bécassine créole** red beans and rice <La99> **•bécassine de mer** red-breasted snipe, dowitcher <Lv88, Re31> **•bécassine des marais** snipe, black-necked stilt <Lv88, Re31> **•bécassine grosse tête {gros-tête}** sandpiper <Lv88, Re31> ***<Loc:*** IB, Da84, La99, Lv88, Re31>

bêche [bɛʃ] *n.f.* spade, type of shovel ***<Loc:*** Da84>

bêcher [beʃe] *v.tr.* to dig, spade *Il était après bêcher la terre ayoù il voulait faire mettre sa banquette.* He was turning the earth where he was going to have his sidewalk put in. (LA) *Tu bêches le jardin avant de faire tes rangs pour planter.* You turn over the dirt in the garden before making your rows for planting. (EV) ***<Loc:*** AC, EV, LA, Da84, Lv88>

bécher (**ébécher**) [beʃe, ebeʃe] **I** *v.tr.* to peck, crack (its eggshell) (said of a chick just prior to hatching) *Le petit poulet a béché l'œuf.* The little chick pecked the egg. (JE) **II** *v.intr.* to hatch *Des petits poulets béchés.* Little hatching chicks. (Lv88) *Des œufs béchés.* Hatched eggs. (Lv88) ***<Loc:*** IB, JE, LF, SJ, SM, Lv88>

bécon ♦see **béquine**

becquer [beke] **I** *v.tr.* **1** to peck **Ils ont des becs croches! Ça peut pas becquer.* They have crooked bills! They cannot peck. (EV, An94) **2** to kiss *Il a becqué sa belle droit là devant tout sa famille.* He kissed his girlfriend right there in front of his whole family. (LA) **II se becquer** *v.pron.* **1** to kiss each other *Dans le vieux temps, ça pouvait pas se becquer comme asteur.* In the old days, they couldn't kiss each other like now. (LA) **2** to preen (of a bird) *L'oiseau se becquait sur la branche.* The bird was preening itself on the branch. (LA) ***<Loc:*** EV, IB, JE, LA, SM, TB, An94, Da84, Lv88, Ph36>

becquetée [bɛkte, bekte] *n.f.* billfull, beakfull ***<Loc:*** LF, Lv88>

becqueter [bɛkte] *v.tr.* to peck, crack (its eggshell) (said of a chick just prior to hatching) *Les poulets avaient juste commencé à becqueter leurs coquilles.* The chicks had just started pecking at their shells. (LA) ***<Loc:*** LA, Da84>

bedaine [bedɛ̃n, bədɛ̃n] *n.f.* big belly, potbelly, paunch ***<Loc:*** LF, TB, Da84>

bedeau [bədo] *n.m.* usher, handyman, beadle (of the church) <*Loc:* Da84>

BEG ♦see **béguer**[1]

bégaiement [begemɑ̃] *n.m.* stammering, stuttering <*Loc:* Da84>

bégayer (**béguer**) [begeje, bege] *v.intr.* to stutter, stammer *Pauvre bête, il bégayait tellement mauvais que il pouvait pas user le phone du tout.* Poor thing, he stuttered so badly that he couldn't use the telephone at all. (LA) <*Loc:* AL, EV, LA, LF, TB, Da84, Lv88>

bégayeur[1], **-euse** [begejœr, -jøz] *adj.* stuttering, stammering <*Loc:* EV, SM, Da84, Lv88, Ph36>

bégayeur[2], **-euse** (**bégueur, -euse**) [begejœr, begœr, -øz] *n.* stutterer, stammerer <*Loc:* AV, JE, SB, SM, TB, Da84, Lv88>

béguer[1] (**BEG**) [bege, bɛg] *v.tr.* to beg *Ils ont bégué pour quelqu'un dans la famille que telle et telle venait nous traiter.* They begged for someone in the family, that one or another would come and treat us. (EV) <*Loc:* EV, JE, Lv88>

béguer[2] ♦see **bégayer**

bégueur[1], **-euse** [begœr, -øz] *n.m.* mendicant, beggar <*Loc:* JE, TB, Lv88>

bégueur[2] ♦see **bégayeur**[2]

beigne (**baigne**) [bɛ̃j] *n.m./f.* fritter, doughnut, deep fried corn or wheat cake <*Loc:* JD, JE, La99, Lv88>

beignet [bɛ̃je, beje] *n.m.* fritter, batter fried in deep fat then sprinkled with sugar <*Loc:* SB, SL, TB, Da84, Fa77>

belette (**blette**) [blɛt, blet] *n.f.* **1** mink **2** weasel <*Loc:* SM, TB, Da84, Fa77, Guoo, Lv88>

Belgique [bɛlʒik] *n.f.* Belgium <*Loc:* AV, TB>

bélier [belje, bœlje] *n.m.* ram <*Loc:* VM, Da84, Fa77>

bella [bela] *n.m.* boar <*Loc:* JE, Di32, Lv88>

belle[1] ♦see **beau**

belle[2] [bɛl] *n.f.* girlfriend, sweetheart ◊ •**belle de jour** morning glory <TB, Guoo> •**belle de nuit** ***a*** night-blooming cereus ***b*** evening primrose ***c*** four o'clock, plant with flowers that open in late afternoon <IB, TB, Da84, Guoo, Ho90, Re31> •**faire (sa) belle** ***a*** to stand up (of a child, before having learned to walk) *Fais belle, mignon.* Stand up, cutie. (VM) ***b*** to sit on its haunches and beg (of a dog) *Fais belle!* Beg! (IB) <IB, VM, Lv88> <*Loc:* IB, JE, LF, SL, SM, TB, VM, Da84, Guoo, Hi02, Ho90, Lv88, Re31>

belle-dame [bɛldɑ̃m] *n.f.* **1** paddlefish **2** spoonbill catfish **3** southern water hemp **4** wench <*Loc:* SB, SL, Guoo, Ho90, Lv88>

Belle-Feuille [bɛlfœj] *n.f.* name commonly given to a cow <*Loc:* JE>

belle-fille [bɛlfij] *n.f.* **1** daughter-in-law **2** stepdaughter <*Loc:* AC, AV, EV, IB, IV, JE, LA, LF, SB, SM, TB, VM, Da84>

Belle-Jasmine [bɛlʒasmin] *n.f.* name commonly given to a cow <*Loc:* JE>

belle-mère [bɛlmær] *n.f.* **1** mother-in-law **2** stepmother **3** hangnail, agnail <*Loc:* EV, SM, Da84, Hi02>

bellesir (se) [bɛlzir] *v.pron.* to become more beautiful or more handsome *Elle s'a bellesie.* She prettied herself up. (Lv88) <*Loc:* Lv88>

bellesivère [bɛlsivær, belzivær] *n.f.* trailing periwinkle <*Loc:* SM, Lv88>

belle-sœur [bɛlsœr] *n.f.* **1** sister-in-law **2** stepsister <*Loc:* AC, EV, LF, TB, Da84, Hi02>

belsamine [bɛlzamin] *n.f.* touch-me-not, balsamine <*Loc:* EV, JE, LF, SB, Lv88, Ph36>

béluette (**berluette**) [belyɛt, belɥɛt, bærlɥɛt] *n.f.* **1** spark, flash, brilliance **2** grain of dust or cinder <*Loc:* JE, Di32, Lv88>

ben [bɛ̃] *interj.* well, well then *Hé ben!* Well then! (EV) *Ben là!* And so! (LA) *Ben mais, va, d'abord.* Well, go on then. (VM) <*Loc:* AV, EV, LA, LF, VM>

bènaise[1] [bɛ̃nɛz] *adj.* happy *Je suis bènaise de te voir.* I am happy to see you. (JE) <*Loc:* JE>

bènaise[2] [bɛ̃nɛz] *n.m.* comfort, ease, contentment <*Loc:* JE, Di32>

bénari ♦see **bénéri**

bendé [bɛ̃de, bɛ̃te] *n.m.* bantam chicken <*Loc:* TB,VM>

béné ♦see **benné**

bénédiction [bɛ̃nediksjɔ̃] *n.f.* benediction, blessing ◊ •**bénédiction de bateau** blessing of the boats (an annual ceremony in shrimping communities) <TB> <*Loc:* TB, VM, Da84, Hi02, La99>

bénée [bɛ̃ne] *adj.f.* ◊ •**poule bénée** Cornish hen <Lv88> <*Loc:* Lv88>

bénéfice [bɛ̃nefis, bɛ̃nifis] *n.m.* **1** gain, profit, benefit *Il a pas fait de bénéfice sur sa vente.* He didn't make any profit on his sale. (LF) **2** benefits, pension, insurance or public assistance *Eux-autres appelle ça, c'est "SOCIAL SERVICE." Ils ont assez du bénéfice, tu connais, pour les enfants qu'a pas de pape, pas de mame.* They call that social service. They have a lot of benefits, you know, for children who don't have a dad or a mom. (TB) **3** fundraiser *On va faire un bénéfice pour l'église.* We're going to put on a fundraiser for the church. (SM) ◊ •**faire du bénéfice** to make a profit (on a sale, etc.) <Da84> <*Loc:* JE, LF, SM, TB, Da84>

bénéficié, -e [bɛ̃nefisje] *n.* beneficiary *Qui c'est tu veux mettre pour tes bénéficiés?* Who do you want to put down as your beneficiaries? (VM) <*Loc:* VM>

bénéficier [bɛ̃nefisje] *v.intr.* to profit, benefit, gain (by) *Il a bénéficié du puits d'huile parce qu'il était dans le POOL.* He benefitted from the oil well because he was in the pool. (LA) <*Loc:* LA, Da84>

bénéri (**bénéris, bénari, banari**) [bɛ̃neri, bɛ̃nari, bɑ̃nari] *n.m.* wren <*Loc:* EV, Lv88, Ph36, Re31>

bénéris ♦see **bénéri**

bengale [bɑ̃gal] *adj.* fierce, mean *Il est un homme bengale.* He's a fierce man. (IB) <*Loc:* IB>

béni, -e (**bénit, -e**) [bẽni, -it] *adj.* blessed, holy *L'eau bénie.* Holy water. (SM) <*Loc:* SM, TB, VM, Da84>

bénir [bẽnir] *v.tr.* to bless *Y avait pas rien du tout, juste le prêtre venait bénir la fosse et c'était tout.* There was nothing at all, just the priest came to bless the grave and that was it. (TB) <*Loc:* TB, Da84, Hi02>

bénit ♦see **béni**

bénitier [bẽnitje] *n.m.* stoup, holy water font <*Loc:* Da84>

benne [bẽn] *n.f.* large reusable container designed to be transported by truck, rail, or ship *Il n-avait une benne et le sel tombait dedans.* There was a large container and the salt would fall into it. (IB) <*Loc:* IB, JD>

benné (**béné**) [bẽne] *n.m.* sesame seed <*Loc:* EV, IB, JD, JE, SM, VM, Da84, Di32, Lv88, Ph36>

bennêt [bẽnɛ, bẽne] *adj.* ◊ •**bennêt pour** crazy about *Quand j'étais petit, j'étais bennêt pour la crème glacée.* When I was young, I was crazy about ice cream. (VM) <VM> <*Loc:* VM>

bentôt ♦see **bientôt**

béquille [bekij] *n.f.* **1** crutch **2** stilt *Les béquilles est yienque bon à casser le cou.* Stilts are only good for breaking your neck. (TB) ◊ •**béquille de vieillesse** person who can be depended upon for help in one's old age <La99> <*Loc:* EV, IB, JE, SB, SL, SM, TB, Da84, La99, Lv88>

béquine[1] (**bacon, bécon**) [bekin, bakɔ̃, bekɔ̃, beˈkən] *n.m./f.* **1** bacon *On ôtait le béquine dans le cochon, on fondait de la graisse, on faisait ça on appelait des "grattons."* We would remove the bacon, melt the fat, and make what we used to call "grattons" [fried pig skins]. (AC) **2** lard <*Loc:* AC, EV, IB, JE, LA, SL, SM, Da84, Lv88, Ph36>

béquine[2] ♦see BAKING

berbocher ♦see **bambocher**

berbocheur ♦see **bambocheur**

bercail [bærkaj] *n.m.* ◊ •**amener au bercail** to make obey, make give in *Dans tous nos querelles alle m'amène au bercail.* In all of our fights she makes me give in. (AV) <AV> <*Loc:* AV>

berce (**berse**) [bærs] *n.f.* **1** rocking chair, rocker **2** crib, cradle **3** rocker, runner (of a crib or rocking chair) <*Loc:* AV, EV, IB, JE, LA, SB, SJ, SL, SM, TB, Da84, Gu00, Hi02, Lv88, Ph36, Re31>

berceau [bærso] *n.m.* **1** cradle (for a baby) **2** arbor, support for vining plants (e.g. beans) ◊ •**berceau de fèves** bean trellis *J'ai un portrait de mon père dans son jardin devant son berceau de fèves.* I have a picture of my father in his garden in front of his bean trellis. (VM) <VM> <*Loc:* AC, VM, Da84>

bercement [bærsmɑ̃] *n.m.* rocking movement <*Loc:* Da84>

bercer [bærse, bœrse] **I** *v.tr.* to rock, swing *Bercer la galance.* To swing the porch swing. (VM) **II** *v.intr.* to rock *Tout ce qu'eux-autres faisait, eux-autres s'assit dessus la galerie et bercait et parlait.* All they did was sit on the porch and rock and talk. (LF) **III se bercer** *v.pron.* to rock o.s. *J'étais après me bercer dans la cuisine quand elle a arrivé.* I was rocking in the kitchen when she arrived. (LA) ◊ •**bercer son âme** to rock contentedly *Elle était dessus la galerie après bercer son âme.* She was on the porch rocking contentedly. (SL) <SL, TB> <*Loc:* EV, LA, LF, SL, TB, VM, Da84>

berceuse [bærsøz, bœrsøz] *n.f.* **1** rocking chair, rocker **2** rocker, blade or runner (curved wooden bottom) of a rocking chair <*Loc:* AC, AV, EV, IB, JE, LF, SM, TB, VM, Da84, Gu00, Hi02, Lv88>

berdas[1] (**beurdas**) [bærda, bœrda] *n.m.* noise, uproar, racket, disturbance *Faire du beurdas.* To make noise. (Lv88) ◊ •**berdi(s)-berda(s)** noise, commotion <EV, Lv88, Ph36> <*Loc:* EV, Lv88, Ph36>

berdas[2] (**beurdas**) [bærda, bœrda] *n.m.* housework, household duties <*Loc:* EV, Lv88, Ph36>

berdassement[1] (**beurdassement**) [bærdasmɑ̃, bœrdasmɑ̃] *n.m.* **1** noise, commotion, disturbance *Les voleurs ont fait un berdassement dans le magasin.* The thieves made quite a disturbance in the store. (AV) **2** noise of moving heavy objects (such as furniture) **3** disorder <*Loc:* AV, EV, JE, Lv88, Ph36>

berdassement[2] (**beurdassement**) [bærdasmɑ̃, bœrdasmɑ̃] *n.m.* **1** small household projects, pottering **2** piddling, wasting time, fiddling around *Il fait jamais arien. J'aime pas le beurdassement.* He never does anything. I don't like wasting time. (SM) **3** waste of time <*Loc:* IB, SM, Da84, Lv88>

berdasser[1] (**bardasser, beurdasser, bredasser**) [bærdase, bœrdase, brədase] **I** *v.tr.* **1** to make noise by shaking or moving around (as furniture) **2** to alter, upset the order or arrangement of (books, etc.) **II** *v.intr.* to make a great deal of noise **III se berdasser** *v.pron.* to rattle around, get jostled around noisily *Et eux-autres met ces chevrettes secs en-dedans et eux-autres prend une machine, et ça tourne doucement. Et eux-autres se bardasse en-dedans.* And they put the dried shrimp inside and they take a motor, and that spins slowly. And they get jostled around in there. (TB) <*Loc:* EV, JE, TB, Hi02, Lv88, Ph36, Re31>

berdasser[2] (**bardasser, beurdasser, bredasser**) [bærdase, bœrdase, brədase] *v.intr.* **1** to do odds and ends, work without pressure, do light work *Il berdassait toujours à l'entour de l'habitation.* He was always doing odds and ends around the house. (Lv88) **2** to do inferior work *C'est mieux que tu travailles pas plutôt que berdasser.* It's better for you not to work at all than to do inferior work. (SL) **3** to waste time, dilly-dally, piddle, fiddle around *Il beurdasse toute la journée.* He piddles around all day. (SM) *Arrête berdasser.* Stop dilly-dallying. (JE) <*Loc:* AV, EV, IB, JE, LA, LF, SJ, SL, SM, TB, Da84, Lv88, Ph36>

berdasseur (**beurdasseur**) [bærdasœr, bœrdasœr] *n.m.* one who fiddles around or wastes time *Bougre-ça-là c'est un foutu beurdasseur.* That guy there, he's a hell of a time-waster. (SM) <*Loc:* SM>

berdassier, -ière [bærdasje, -jær] *n.* one who makes unnecessary noise <*Loc:* JE>

berdouiller [bærduje] **I** *v.tr.* to stammer, stutter **II** *v.intr.* to stammer, stutter <*Loc:* Lv88>

bère (**baire, ber, berre, bers**) [bær] *n.m./f.* mosquito net, mosquito bar <*Loc:* AV, EV, IB, JE, LF, SB, SM, TB, Da84, Lv88, Ph36, Re31>

béret [berɛ, bere] *n.m.* beret <*Loc:* Da84>

berge[1] [bærʒ] *n.f.* stack, haystack <*Loc:* IB, LA, LF, SM, TB, VM, Da84, Gu82, Hi02, Lv88>

berge[2] [bærʒ] *n.f.* barge *J'ai été travailler pour produire l'huile, travailler sur des* TANK *berges, et courir des lignes de tuyaux, et toute espèce d'affaires comme ça.* I went to work producing oil, working on tank barges, and running pipelines, and all kinds of things like that. (TB) <*Loc:* TB, Da84, Hi02>

berger [bærʒe] *n.m.* shepherd <*Loc:* Da84>

bergerie [bærʒri] *n.f.* sheepfold, sheep pen <*Loc:* Da84>

bergo ♦see **bourgo**

bergonner ♦see **bourgonner**

berlader ♦see **berlander**

berlander (**barlander, berlader**) [bærlɑ̃de, bærlade, bærlɑ̃ge] *v.intr.* **1** to hesitate, require persuading **2** to lounge around, loaf, dilly-dally, waste time *Il est après berlander chez son voisin.* He's passing the time at his neighbor's house. (Lv88) *Il va berlader tout le journée.* He is going to dilly-dally all day long. (JE) *Je peux berlander maintenant que j'ai fini mon ouvrage.* I can kill time now that I've finished my work. (IB) **3** to stroll <*Loc:* EV, IB, JE, LF, SB, SM, TB, Lv88, Ph36>

berlingue [bærlɛ̃ŋ] *n.f.* small carriage ◊ •**chiquette et berlingue** ridiculous or absurd-looking couple <SM, La99> <*Loc:* SM, La99>

berloque [bærlɔk] *n.f.* **1** watch, clock (esp. a cheap or old one) **2** trinket, charm <*Loc:* IB, JE, SM, Da84, Lv88>

berluette ♦see **béluette**

bernique[1] [bærnik] *n.f.pl.* spectacles <*Loc:* JE, Di32>

bernique[2] (**bernicle**) [bærnik, bærnik(l)] *adj.* ◊ •**c'est bernique** it's all over, it's too bad, all is lost <La99> <*Loc:* La99>

berouette (**barouette, bérouette, beurouette, birouette, bourouette, brouette**) [bɔrwet, bærwɛt, bærwet, berwet, birwɛt, birwet, bɔrwɛt, burwɛt, burwet] *n.f.* wheelbarrow <*Loc:* AC, AV, IB, JE, LA, LF, SB, SJ, SM, Da84, Hi02, Lv88, Re31>

berouettée [bærwete, burwete] *n.f.* load of a wheelbarrow, wheelbarrowful <*Loc:* LF>

berre ♦see **bère**

berse ♦see **berce**

bertelle ♦see **bretelle**

bervocheur (**berbocheur**) [bærvoʃœr, bærboʃœr] *n.m.* **1** dissipater, carouser, woman chaser **2** drunkard <*Loc*: Di32>

besoin [bezwɛ̃, bezwɑ̃, bɔzɔ̃n, bɔzɔ̃, bwɛ̃] *n.m.* need, necessity ◊ •**avoir besoin (de)** to need *T'as besoin de tourner à droite ici-là.* You need to turn to the right here. (TB) **Un homme qui avait tout ça qu'il avait de besoin.* A man who had everything that he needed. (SL, An94) **Vous-autres as pas besoin de vous tracasser.* You don't need to worry. (LA, An94) <LA, SL, TB, An94> •**avoir de besoin (de)** to need *Ce gros magasin là il vendait tout, ce que quelqu'un avait de besoin dans un gros magasin.* That big store sold everything, whatever someone would need in one big store. (TB) <TB, An94, Da84, Hi02> •**être dans le besoin** to be in need, in distress <Da84> •**être de besoin** to be needed *Oui j'étais de besoin dessus le* FARM *pour la récolte.* Yes, I was needed on the farm for the harvest. (SJ) <SJ> •**faire ses besoins** to void one's bladder or bowels *Il a été faire ses besoins.* He went to the bathroom. (EV) <EV, An94, Da84> <*Loc:* AC, EV, IV, JE, LA, LF, SJ, SL, TB, VM, An94, Da84, Hi02>

beson [bɔzɔ̃] *n.m.* wild bull <*Loc:* JE>

besson[1], **-onne** [bɔsɔ̃, besɔ̃, bezɔ̃, -ɔ̃n] *n.* twin *C'est des petits* TWINS. *Des petits bessons. Ça pesait sept livres et cinq -z-onces chaque quand ils sont énés.* They are little twins. They weighed seven pounds five ounces apiece when they were born. (LF) <*Loc:* EV, IV, JD, JE, LA, LF, SJ, TB, Da84, Lv88>

besson[2] [bɔsɔ̃] *n.m.* "love bug" (i.e. one of the small bugs that fill the air in September and May) <*Loc:* VM>

bêtaille ♦see **bétaille**[2]

bétaille[1] [betaj] *adj.* awful, outrageous *Ça c'est bétaille, quand même.* That's awful, anyway. (VM) <*Loc:* SB, VM, La99, Lv88>

bétaille[2] (**bêtaille**) [betaj] *n.f.* **1** animal, creature *Un piège, ça c'est pour trapper les bétailles.* A trap, that is to catch wild animals. (SM) *Icitte, la corneille et le corbeau, c'est tout la même bétaille.* Around here, the "corneille" and the "corbeau," it's all the same animal. (Lv88) *Ça c'est une belle bétaille, ce taureau.* That's a beautiful animal, that bull. (VM) **Il y a pas de bêtailles qui pèsent seize mille livres. C'est huit tonnes, ça!* There aren't any animals that weigh sixteen thousand pounds. That's eight tons! (EV, An94) **2** cow, bovine, bull **Il avait une belle bêtaille noire.* He had a beautiful black cow. (SL, An94) **3** livestock *Il a de la bétaille.* He has livestock. (VM) *Il faut je vas donner à manger à ma bétaille.* I have to go feed my livestock. (VM) **4** insect, bug, worm *Il y a des bétailles dans le fromage.* There are bugs in the cheese. (SM) **5** beast, monster *Il fait la bétaille avec sa femme et ses enfants.* He acts like a monster with his wife and children. (VM) ◊ •**bétaille à feu** firefly, lightning bug <SL> •**bétaille à mille pattes**

centipede, millipede <SM, TB, VM, Lv88> **•bétaille caille** kind of spirit which changes its shape, usually from dog to pig and vice versa, and frightens people <SM> **•espèce de bétaille!** you beast! <Da84> **•gros bétaille** big man <EV> **•petite bétaille** beetle <LF> <*Loc:* AV, IB, JE, LA, LF, SB, SL, SM, TB, VM, An94, Da84, Hi02, La99, Lv88>

bétaille[3] [betaj] *interj.* damn, darn, hell *Bétaille, ça m'a échappé!* Hell, I can't remember! (VM) <*Loc:* VM>

bétasse [betas] *adj.* stupid, simple-minded, foolish, goofy *Ah! Quel bétasse tu es.* Ah! what a stupid person you are. (JE) *Cet homme est bétasse.* That man is stupid. (SB) <*Loc:* JE, LF, SB, SM, Da84, Re31>

bêtasserie [betasri] *n.f.* nonsense *Il dit toujours des bêtasseries.* He always says foolish things. (SB) <*Loc:* SB>

bête[1] [bɛt, bet] *adj.* **1** foolish, stupid, silly *Quand je pense à ça, des fois, je ris, bonne sœur! J'aurais jamais cru que j'aurais été aussi bête que ça!* When I think of that, sometimes I laugh, good Lord! I would never have thought I could be that stupid. (TB) *C'est des lois qu'est bête, mais c'est comme ça que c'est. Si vous se fait prendre, les* FINE *est mauvais.* They are laws that are dumb, but that's how it is. If you get caught, the fines are stiff. (TB) **2** crazy ◊ **•bête comme une bête à chandelle** crazy as a June bug <Da84> **•bête comme une oie** crazy as a goose <Da84> **•bête à coucher dehors {manger de l'herbe / pincer l'herbe}** very stupid <La99> **•bête comme ses pieds {un bourriquet / un cabri / un cheval / un chou / un poteau de coin / une bête à cornes / une bête à chandelles / une cruche / une djogue / une z'oie / trente-six chous dans un sac}** very stupid <Da84, La99> **•être trop bête pour vider un pot de chambre** to be too stupid to empty a chamber pot <Da84> **•être aussi bête que la lune est haute** to be as stupid as the moon is high <TB, La99> **•faire le bête** to act stupid or foolish *Les enfants, ça c'était juste pour des guémes, ça se mettait des chemises qu'était plus grands pour eux-autres, et ça mettait un chapeau, et là ça mettait de la—du couleur sur leur figure, ça se faisait une moustache, les petits garçons et là ç'allait c'ez les voisins, ça faisait le bête,* THAT MEAN THEY WERE DOING THE STUPID. The children, it was just for games, they would put on shirts that were too big for them, and they would put on a hat, and then they would put makeup on their faces, they made themselves a moustache, the boys, and then they'd go to the neighbors', they acted stupid. (TB) <LF, TB> **•faire son bête** (said of a man) **/ faire sa bête** (said of a woman) to be very foolish <LF> <*Loc:* EV, LF, TB, VM, Da84, Hi02, La99>

bête[2] [bɛt, bet] *n.f.* **1** animal, creature *Équand-ce qu'il avait pas de vent, ils avaient des bêtes, des mulets ou des chevals qui halaient les bateaux sur les bayous.* When there was no wind, they had animals, mules or horses, that hauled the boats on the bayous. (LF) **2** cow, bovine, bull **Un troupeau de bêtes.* A herd of cattle. (Da84) **3** meat, particularly beef and veal *Du jus de bête.* Some beef gravy. (EV) *On mange du cochon et de la bête.* We eat pork and beef. (Lv88) **4** insect, bug ◊ **•bête à Bon Dieu** beetle <LA> **•bête à chandelle** June bug, May beetle **Bête comme une bête à chandelle.* Crazy as a June bug. (Da84) <LA, SL, TB, Da84, Lv88> **•bête à corne *a*** any horned animal ***b*** cow, bovine <TB, Da84> **•bête à feu** firefly <Lv88> **•bête à Guillaume** May bug <AV> **•bête à mille pattes** centipede, millipede <IB, TB> **•bête farouche** wild animal, wild beast <IV, An94, Da84> **•bête puante** skunk, polecat *Ça sent de la bête puante.* It smells like skunk. (JE) <AV, EV, IB, JE, LF, SM, Da84, Hi02, Lv88, Ph36> **•bête rouge** chigger, redbug <EV, IB, JE, LA, SL, SM, TB, Da84, Lv88, Ph36> **•chère {pauvre} petite bête** poor little dear <Da84> **•pauvre bête** poor thing, poor dear, poor fellow *Pauvre bête, alle se lève à cinq heures tous les matins.* Poor thing, she gets up at 5:00 every morning. (LF) *Il est pas blâmable, pauvre bête, pour les misères de sa famille.* He is not blamable, poor fellow, for the ills of his family. (LA) <AC, EV, JE, LA, LF, TB, An94, Da84, Lv88> <*Loc:* AC, AV, EV, IB, JE, LA, LF, SL, SM, TB, VM, An94, Da84, Gu00, Hi02, Lv88, Ph36>

bêtise [betiz] *n.f.* **1** foolishness, silliness, nonsense **2** joke *Il a raconté une bêtise.* He told a joke. (SL) **3** foolish mistake, stupidity **•faire des bêtises** to cut up, play jokes <Da84> **•pas de bêtise!** no kidding! <TB, La99> <*Loc:* LF, SL, SM, TB, An94, Da84, Hi02, La99>

bêtiser [betize] **I** *v.tr.* **1** to kid, tease, banter, speak banteringly or playfully (to or about) *Il était après bêtiser son frère pour la fois qu'il avait essayer de sauter la barrière.* He was kidding his brother about the time he had tried to jump the fence. (LA) **2** to cheat on, run around on *Il était après bêtiser sa femme avec la cousine à John.* He was cheating on his wife with John's cousin. (LA) **II** *v.intr.* **1** to joke, cut up, tell jokes, fool around *Il aimait beaucoup bêtiser et rire et avoir du bon temps.* He liked to fool around and laugh and have a good time. (Lv88) **2** to goof off, play around, esp. instead of working *Je bétise avec les enfants.* I joke around with the children. (VM) **3** to waste time *On a pas bêtisé avec le cadjin du tout, mes enfants parlent bien l'amaricain.* We didn't waste time with Cajun [French] at all, my children speak good American. (Lv88) **4** to frequent, court, fool around with, have an affair with *Il bêtise avec cette femme.* He's courting that lady. (Lv88) **5** to fool with, tamper with, play with in an inappropriate way *Ne bêtise pas avec cette machine.* Don't tamper with this machine. (IB) <*Loc:* AL, AV, EV, IB, JE, LF, SL, SM, TB, VM, Da84, Gr82, Lv88, Ph36>

bêtiseur [betizœr] *n.m.* practical joker <*Loc:* JE, LF, SL, SM, Lv88>

bêtot, bétôt ♦see **bientôt**

betterave [betrav] *n.f.* beet <*Loc:* Da84>

beuglage [bøglaʒ] *n.m.* 1 bellowing, moaning 2 loud sobbing and crying ***<Loc:*** SJ, Da84>

beuglement [bøgləmɑ̃] *n.m.* 1 bellowing, moaning 2 loud sobbing and crying ***<Loc:*** AV, SJ, Da84>

beugler [bøgle] *v.intr.* 1 to moo *Je connais pas quoi il y a avec la vache, mais elle beugle tout le temps.* I don't know what's wrong with the cow, but she moos all the time. (LA) 2 to bellow, low *Il a commencé à rouler le matelas. J'ai commencé à beugler.* He started to roll up the mattress. I started bellowing. (SL) 3 to weep, cry *Elle a beuglé pendant deux heures.* She wept for two hours. (SB) ***<Loc:*** LA, SB, SL, Da84>

beurdas ♦see **berdas**

beurdassement ♦see **berdassement**

beurdasser ♦see **berdasser**

beurdasseur ♦see **berdasseur**

beurgo ♦see **bourgo**

beurgoter ♦see **bourgonner**

beurouette ♦see **berouette**

beurre [bœr] *n.m.* butter ***<Loc:*** AV, IV, JE, SL, TB, Da84, Hi02>

beurrer [børe] *v.tr.* 1 to butter *Et là, tu vas bien beurrer ta poêle avant de mettre ton pain.* And then, you will butter your frying pan well before putting in your bread. (LA) 2 to spread (jam, etc.) on bread *Il a beurré son pain avec de la confiture.* He put jam on his bread. (LF) 3 to seduce, betray, dupe *Je l'ai bien beurré: il va venir asteur.* I really duped him, he's going to come now. (Lv88) **Tu peux pas me beurrer avec ça.* You can't fool me with that. (AC, La99) ***<Loc:*** AC, EV, LA, LF, SM, Da84, La99, Lv88, Ph36>

beurriner [børine] *v.tr.* to soil, besmear *Il beurrine tout avec ses doigts.* He soils everything with his fingers. (LF) ***<Loc:*** LF, TB>

biais[1] [bjɛ, bje] *adj.* slanting, oblique ◊ **•en biais** obliquely, diagonally, across **Couper en biais.* To cut on a bias. (Da84) <Da84> ***<Loc:*** SB, Da84>

biais[2] [bjɛ, bje] *n.m.* 1 bias, slant, angle *Et là tu mets l'étrave, tu donnes le biais que tu veux dans l'étrave.* And then you put on the bow, you put the angle that you want in the bow. (TB) 2 bias tape for sewing ***<Loc:*** TB, VM, Da84>

biaiser [bjeze] *v.intr.* to go obliquely, go across diagonally *Tu vois, sa ligne à lui biaisait à travers le bois, entre mon coin et le pont.* You see, his property line went diagonally across the woods, between my corner and the bridge. (LA) ***<Loc:*** LA, Da84>

biberon (**buberon**) [bibrɔ̃, bybrɔ̃, bybərɔ̃] *n.m./f.* 1 nipple of a baby bottle 2 baby bottle ***<Loc:*** AV, EV, IV, JE, LA, LF, SB, SJ, SM, TB, VM, Da84, Lv88>

bibillote [bibjɔt] *n.f.* nonsense *C'est tout de la bibillote.* That's all nonsense. (SB) ***<Loc:*** SB>

bibite ♦see **bibitte**

bibitte (**bibite, bébitte**) [bibit, bebit] *n.f.* [*vulg.*] penis *Il a une grosse bébitte.* He has a large penis. (JE) ***<Loc:*** JE, SB, SM, Gu00, Hi02, Lv88>

bible [bib(l)] *n.f.* Bible ***<Loc:*** EV, TB, Da84, Hi02>

bibliothèque [bibliotɛk] *n.f.* 1 library 2 bookcase ***<Loc:*** Da84>

biblique [biblik] *adj.* biblical *Cette histoire-là est pas biblique.* That story is not biblical. (LA) ***<Loc:*** LA, Da84>

bic [bik] ◊ **•à bic-à-blanc** out in the open *Le jeune monde a pus de honte. Ils étaient après se tâtonner grand debout à bic-à-blanc droite là devant tout le monde dessus le plancher de danse.* Young people have no shame anymore. They were petting standing up right there on the dance floor in public in front of everyone. (LA) **Il a commencé à annoncer qu'il pouvait pas voir dans le monde qui dans le tonnerre qu'avait fait ce qu'ils avaient fait avec sa bêtaille, droit là, à bic-à-blanc en bas de la lumière.* He started announcing that he couldn't see for the world who in tarnation had done what they had done to his horse, right there in the wide open under the light. (SL, An94) ***<Loc:*** LA, SL, An94>

bichon [biʃɔ̃] *n.m.* fawn ***<Loc:*** VM>

bicler ♦see **bigler**

bicycle [bajsik, bisik] *n.m./f.* bicycle ◊ **•à bicycle** by bicycle *Je venais la voir à bicycle.* I would come to see her by bicycle. (LA) <LA> ***<Loc:*** AV, EV, IB, LA, LF, SB, SM, TB, VM, Da84, Gu00, Lv88, Ph36>

bidet [bidɛ, bide] *n.m.* 1 clumsy, awkward person 2 fat person, fatso 3 good-for-nothing, lazybones, bum *Grand bidet, juste que tu dors et tu manges.* Lazybones, you do nothing but sleep and eat. (LF) ***<Loc:*** AS, LF, SM, Lv88>

bidon [bidɔ̃] *n.m.* 1 top hat 2 derby hat 3 any old hat or cap *Alle a mis son bidon pour aller à la messe.* She put on her old hat to go to mass. (AV) ***<Loc:*** AV, IB, LA, SB, SM, VM, Da84>

bien[1] [bjɛ̃] *adj.* 1 good, fine, satisfying 2 well, in good form, in good health 3 correct, right **Et tu pouvais pas changer son idée. Il était tout le temps, tout le temps bien; jamais, jamais mal.* And you could never change his mind. He was always right; never, ever wrong. (EV, An94) ◊ **•bien bien** very well <Da84> **•assez bien** pretty good, well enough *Au printemps ça a été assez bien.* In the spring, it [the fishing] was pretty good. (SL) <SL> **•c'est bien** okay, that's right <Da84> **•être bien** to be well <Da84> **•faire bien** to do right <Da84> ***<Loc:*** EV, SL, An94, Da84>

bien[2] [bjɛ̃] *n.m.* 1 good *Mais le bien que les écoles d'immersion fait, un principal ou une maîtresse qu'est dédiqué à son job peut pas être contre parce que ça fait trop de bien.* But the good that the immersion schools do, a principal or a teacher who is dedicated to his or her job can't be against them, because they do too much good. (LF) 2 property, possessions *Les vieux l'ont délégué pour s'occuper de leur bien.* The old folks delegated him to take care of their belongings. (LA) ◊ **•faire du bien** to do good *Alle m'a écrit une lettre* *pour me laisser savoir comment beaucoup du bien ça lui avait fait.* She wrote me a letter to let me know how much good it had done her. (LF) <LF, TB, Da84> **•avoir du bien** possess property <Da84> <***Loc:*** LA, LF, TB, Da84, Hi02>

bien[3] (**bin**) [bjẽ, bẽ] *adv.* **1** well *Il a bien mangé.* He ate well. (SM) **2** thoroughly, completely **Et puis il a pris à déboutonner ses culottes avant d'arriver bien.* And he started to unbutton his pants before arriving completely. (EV, An94) **3** very, really *C'est un vieux village, bien vieux.* It's an old village, very old. (SL) **Ça fait qu'un jour, elle a tombé bien malade.* So one day she got very sick. (IV, An94) **Il y avait deux hommes dans le vieux temps qu'étaient riches, bien riches les deux, mais entêtés comme t'as jamais vu de ta vie.* There were two men in the old days who were rich, very rich, both of them, but stubborn like you've never seen in your life. (LA, An94) **4** indeed, definitely **"O," il dit, "j'aurais bien cru que toi, tu pourrais, parce que t'es tout le temps bien; t'es jamais* WRONG." "Oh," he said, "I would have definitely thought that you could, because you're always right, you're never wrong." (EV, An94) **5** carefully, properly, quite, rather **Même, à bien jongler, c'est peut-être pas un péché.* In fact, thinking carefully on it, it is perhaps not a sin. (EV, An94) **6** gladly *J'accepterai bien la clef de ton cœur.* I'd gladly accept the key to your heart. (VM, ch: *Le papier d'épingles*) **7** at least *O, ma campagne, elle a bien duré, o, regarde, elle a duré sept ans.* Oh my campaign lasted at least, oh look, it lasted seven years. (IB, ch: *La veuve de sept ans*) ◊ **•bien que** even though *Il lui a demandé si il aurait voulu prendre un orphelin, et,* AND *[je] pense c'était un peu dur pour décider, bien qu'il avait cinq enfants.* He asked him if he would like to take an orphan, and [I] think it was a bit hard to decide, even though he had five children. (AV) <AV> **•aussi bien *a*** as well *Le monde s'accordait aussi bien ou mieux qu'asteur.* People got along as well or better than [they do] now. (TB) ***b*** moreover, besides *On devrait pas être après faire ça, et aussi bien, ton père pourrait arriver.* We shouldn't be doing this, and besides your father might show up. (LA) <LA, TB> **•aussi bien que *a*** as well as **On figurait que c'était pour leur montrer à eux que quand même si on avait pas d'éducation comme eux ils aviont, on pouvait apprendre à jouer de la musique aussi bien que n'importe qui d'autre à l'oreille.* We figured that it was to teach them that even though we didn't have an education like they had, we could learn to play music as well as anyone else by ear. (LA, An84) ***b*** used to express a probability **Aussi bien qu'il irait se faire tuer.* Suppose he gets killed. (Da84) <LA, An84, Da84> **•eh {et} bien *a*** well, so *"Eh bien," elle dit, "tu peux me montrer le petit garçon qui a fait ça?"* "So," she said, "can you show me the little boy who did that?" (EV) ***b*** oh well *Eh bien, allons!* Oh well, let's go! (JE) <EV, JE, Da84> **•ou bien** or, or else *J'ai pris le char et j'ai* RIDE *les blues jusque ça ou bien le plus loin le char m'amène.* I took the train and I rode the blues until there or else as far as the train would take me. (IB, ch: *J'ai vu Lucille*) <IB, Da84> <***Loc:*** AC, AV, EV, IB, IV, JE, LA, PQ, SL, SM, VM, An84, An94, Da84, Hi02>

bien-aimé, -e [bjẽneme] *n.* beloved, dear **Mon bien-aimé.* My beloved. (Da84) <***Loc:*** Da84>

bien-être [bjẽnɛt(r)] *n.m.* well-being <***Loc:*** Da84>

bienfaiseur ♦see **bienfaiteur**

bienfait [bjẽfɛ, bjẽfe] *n.m.* good deed, good turn, kindness, favor <***Loc:*** Da84>

bienfaiteur (**bienfaiseur**) [bjẽfetœr, bjẽfezœr] *n.m.* benefactor <***Loc:*** Da84>

bienheureux, -euse [bjẽnørø, -øz] *adj.* pleased, happy, fortunate <***Loc:*** Da84>

bientôt (**bentôt, bétôt, bêtot**) [bẽto, beto, betwɔ] *adv.* soon, shortly, before long, presently, in a minute *Espère, il va venir bientôt.* Wait, he'll come soon. (VM) *Tu ferais mieux de te dépêcher, il va arriver bientôt.* You had better hurry, he'll arrive soon. (LA) <***Loc:*** AV, JE, LA, SM, VM, Da84, Di32, Fa77, Hi02>

bière [bjær] *n.f.* beer ◊ **•bière créole** homemade beer made with rice and sugar cane <Lv88> <***Loc:*** AV, EV, Da84, Hi02, Lv88, Re31>

big bog ♦see **BIG BOY**

BIG BOY (**big bog**) [bigbɔɪ, bigbɔg] *n.m.* person of wealth or importance, big shot *Bougre-ça-là a un tas l'argent. C'est un big bog.* That guy has a heap of money. He's a big shot. (SM) <***Loc:*** SL, SM, VM>

bigler (**bicler**) [bigle, bikle, bekle] *v.intr.* **1** to be cross-eyed *Il a un œil qui bicle.* He has an eye that is crossed. (LA) **2** to squint ◊ **•bicler l'œil** to squint <TB, Lv88> <***Loc:*** JE, LA, TB, Lv88>

bigorneau [bigɔrno, bigarno, bigoro] *n.m.* saltwater snail, periwinkle <***Loc:*** JE, LF, TB, Lv88>

bigot, -e [bigo, -ɔt] *adj.* stupid <***Loc:*** TB, Da84, La99>

bigote [bigɔt] *n.f.* dipper, ladle *J'aime avoir une bigote pour servir mon lait.* I like to have a ladle for serving my milk. (TB) <***Loc:*** TB>

bijou [biʒu] *n.m.* gem, jewel <***Loc:*** Da84>

bijouterie [biʒutri] *n.f.* **1** jewelry store **2** jewelry <***Loc:*** LF, Da84, Gu00, Lv88>

bile [bil] *n.f.* bile, gall ◊ **•avoir la bile en mouvement *a*** to have loose bowels ***b*** to be bilious <Da84> <***Loc:*** AV, Da84>

BILL [bil] *n.m.* **1** bill, invoice **2** monetary note, bill **3** sign, poster ◊ **•faire un BILL** to make purchases on credit <Lv88> <***Loc:*** JE, LF, SB, SL, TB, Da84, Lv88>

billard [bijar] *n.m.* billiards, pool <***Loc:*** Da84>

bille [bij] *n.f.* section of a log, heavy piece of wood (before it is split) ◊ **•bille de bois** cut log from a tree (before it is split) <SL> <***Loc:*** SL, Da84>

billet [bijɛ, bije] *n.m.* **1** monetary note, bill **2** promisory note <***Loc:*** LA, TB, Da84, Fa77>

billion [biljɔ̃] *n.m.* billion <*Loc:* Da84>

biloxi [bilɔksi] *n.m.* type of trawler originally built in the town of the same name <*Loc:* Lv88>

binacle [binak(l)] *n.* [*offensive*] halfbreed, person with any combination of white, Native American, and African American blood <*Loc:* TB>

binette [binɛt, binet] *n.f.* 1 face *Il a une drôle de binette.* He has a funny face. (SM) 2 grimace *Elle m'a fait une binette quand j'ai rentré.* She made a face at me when I came in. (IB) <*Loc:* AV, IB, SJ, SM>

bingo[1] [biŋgo] *v.intr.invar.* to play bingo *Allons bingo à soir.* Let's play bingo tonight. (Lv88) <*Loc:* Lv88>

bingo[2] [biŋgo] *n.m.* 1 bingo *Le bingo, ça* ENTERTAIN *le monde.* Bingo, it entertains people. (Lv88) 2 bingo session *Il n-a un bingo à soir à Sainte-Thérèse.* There's bingo tonight at Saint Theresa's. (Lv88) 3 bingo hall *Tu veux visiter le bingo? C'est pas loin.* You want to go to the bingo hall? It's not far. (Lv88) ◊ •**faire bingo** to bingo <Da84> <*Loc:* Da84, Lv88>

biocque, bioque ♦see **biorque**[2]

biorque[1] [bjɔrk, bjɔk] *adj.* stupid, foolish <*Loc:* AS, SM, TB, La99>

biorque[2] (**bioque, biocque**) [bjɔrk, bjɔk] *n.* 1 American bittern (locally called sungazer) 2 moron, airhead, idiot *Elle est bioque.* She's an airhead. (SM) <*Loc:* AS, SM, La99, Lv88>

biorqué, -e (**bioqué, -e**) [bjɔrke, bjɔke] *adj.* mentally deranged *Cette femme-là est bien bioquée.* That lady is mentally deranged. (SM) <*Loc:* SM>

bique [bik] *n.f.* female goat ◊ •**vieille bique** [*pej.*] old woman <TB> <*Loc:* TB>

birebiquin ♦see **virebrequin**

birouette ♦see **berouette**

bisbille [bisbij, bizbiz] *n.f.* quarrel, bickering ◊ •**en bisbille avec qqn** on bad terms with s.o. *Elle était en bisbille avec ses cousines.* She was on bad terms with her cousins. (LA) <LA, SM, La99> <*Loc:* IB, LA, SM, La99>

bisconcoin ♦see **bisquencoin**

biscuit [biskɥi, byskɥi] *n.m.* 1 biscuit 2 biscuit, soda cracker ◊ •**biscuit soda** soda cracker <JE> <*Loc:* EV, JE, SL, TB, VM, Da84, Gu00, Hi02>

bis-en-coin ♦see **bisquencoin**

bisque [bis(k)] *n.m./f.* 1 bisque 2 seafood sauce ◊ •**bisque d'écrevisses** crawfish bisque <Re31> <*Loc:* SJ, Da84, Hi02, Re31>

bisquencoin (**bisconcoin, bis-en-coin, bistencoin**) [biskɑ̃kwɛ̃, bizɑ̃kwɛ̃, bistɑ̃kwɛ̃] *adj.* 1 crooked, askew, out of line *La maison est tout bisconcoin depuis l'ouragan.* The house is all crooked since the hurricane. (SM) 2 diagonal, catercornered *Il a mis le bois bisconcoin.* He put the wood diagonally. (SB) <*Loc:* EV, IB, SB, SL, SM, TB, Lv88, Ph36>

bisquet [biskɛ, biske] *n.* shiner, small silvery fish <*Loc:* JE>

bistencoin ♦see **bisquencoin**

bitaco (**habitaco**) [bitako, abitako] *n.m.* 1 hick, country bumpkin 2 vulgar, ill-mannered person *Il a pas de manières. C'est un vrai bitaco.* He doesn't have any manners. He's a real boor. (SM) 3 fat person, fatso <*Loc:* AV, SM, Lv88>

bite (**bitte**) [bit] *adj.* intoxicated, tipsy, drunk *Pauvre W. il était assez bite, il a* JUMP *dedans la baille qu'eusse bouillait des crabes!* Poor W. was so drunk, he jumped into the tub they were boiling crabs in! (TB) *Ils s'en a venu bites hier au soir.* They showed up drunk last night. (VM) <*Loc:* EV, JE, LA, SB, TB, VM, Lv88, Ph36>

biter [bite] **I** *v.tr.* to get s.o. drunk, give s.o. alcoholic beverages with the purpose of rendering intoxicated *Il l'a bité avec du whiskey hier au soir.* He got him drunk on whisky last night. (Lv88) **II se biter** *v.pron.* to get drunk *On était parti attendre Ti-Don Leboeuf jouer le violon. Et W. se bite, et cher Bon Dieu, nous-autres on s'en a revenu, lui il était après faire le* CIRCLE *dessus le* HUEY P. LONG BRIDGE. We had gone to hear Ti-Don Leboeuf play the violin. And W. gets drunk, and dear God, we all came back, and he was circling around on the Huey P. Long bridge. (TB) <*Loc:* TB, VM, Lv88>

bitte ♦see **bite**

biture [bityr] *n.f.* 1 state of drunkenness *Il s'a donné une bonne biture.* He got himself into a real state of drunkenness. (VM) 2 drinking spree ◊ •**avoir une biture** to be drunk <Lv88> •**faire {prendre / se foutre} une biture** to get drunk, go on a drinking spree *Quelle biture j'ai pris ce matin.* What a drinking spree I went on this morning. (JE) *Il s'a foutu une biture.* He went on a drinking spree. (SM) <JE, SM, La99> <*Loc:* JE, LF, SB, SM, TB, VM, La99, Lv88>

biturier [bityrje] *n.m.* drunkard <*Loc:* JE>

bizarre [bizar] *adj.* bizarre, queer, strange *C'est un enfant bizarre.* That's a strange child. (LA) <*Loc:* LA, Da84>

biznisse ♦see **business**

BLACK EYE [blɛkaj, blækaɪ, blakaj] *n.m.* 1 black eye 2 black-eyed pea <*Loc:* AV, EV, LA, SL, TB, Da84, Lv88, Ph36>

BLACK JOE (**BLACK-JO**) [blækdʒo, blɛkdʒo] *n.m.* molasses, blackstrap molasses <*Loc:* LA, Da84>

BLACK-JO ♦see **BLACK JOE**

BLACKOUT [blækaʊt, blɛkaʊt] *v.intr.invar.* to black out, lose consciousness *Il a bu, il a bu jusqu'à qu'il a* BLACKOUT. He drank and drank until he blacked out. (LA) <*Loc:* LA, Da84>

BLACKTOP[1] [blæktɔp, blaktɔp, blɛktɔp] *v.tr.* to pave *Ils ont* BLACKTOP *le chemin.* They paved the road. (Lv88) <*Loc:* Lv88>

BLACKTOP[2] [blæktɔp, blaktɔp, blɛktɔp] *n.m.* 1 tar, blacktop 2 paved road <*Loc:* Lv88>

blagaillerie [blagajri] *n.f.* foolishness *Ça c'est tout de la blagaillerie.* That's all foolishness. (AV) <*Loc:* AV>

blague [blag] *n.f.* 1 bladder 2 air bladder, swim bladder (of a fish) **3** tobacco pouch **4** penis **5** joke <***Loc:*** AL, AV, EV, IB, JE, LF, SB, SL, SM, Da84, Lv88, Ph36>

blaguer [blage] *v.intr.* to joke, talk silly **Je suis après blaguer avec vous-autres.* I'm joking with you all. (LA, An84) <***Loc:*** LA, An84, Da84>

blagueur [blagœr] *n.m.* jokester **Monsieur Bi-là, lui, c'était un bon blagueur.* Mr. Bi, he was a good jokester. (LA, An94) <***Loc:*** LA, An94, Da84, Fa77>

blâmable [blɑ̃mab(l)] *adj.* blameworthy, blamable *Il est pas blâmable, pauvre bête, pour les misères de sa famille.* He is not blamable, poor fellow, for the ills of his family. (LA) <***Loc:*** LA, Da84>

blâme [blɑ̃m] *n.f.* guilt, blame <***Loc:*** LA, Da84>

blâmer [blɑ̃me] **I** *v.tr.* to blame, censure **Quand le roi a vu ça, lui il a fait tuer son gardien qu'elle avait, et puis il l'a blâmée, elle.* When the king saw that, he had her guardian killed and then he blamed her. (IB, An94) **II se blâmer** *v.pron.* to blame o.s. *Il se blâme lui-même pour ça qu'a arrivé.* He blames himself for what happened. (LA) ◊ **•à blâmer** blamable *C'est toi qu'es à blâmer pour tout le malheur qu'a arrivé.* You are to blame for all the trouble that has happened. (LA) <LA, Da84> <***Loc:*** IB, LA, An94, Da84>

blanc[1], blanche [blɑ̃, blɑ̃ʃ] *adj./n.* white (color) **Quand t'es* GONE *de chez toi, Lilly Mae met une essuie-mains blanche dessus la porte.* When you're gone from home, Lilly Mae puts a white handkerchief on the door. (EV, An94) ◊ **•blanc comme du coton {du lait / la neige / un champignon / un linge}** very white <AV, EV, VM> **•blanc de baleine** parrafin <SM, VM> **•blanc de Paris** plaster of Paris <Da84> **•blanc d'œil** white of the eye <Da84> **•blanc d'œuf** egg white <Da84> **•au blanc *a*** wide open ***b*** exposed, in view, out in the open <SL, VM, An94, Da84> **•se mettre au blanc** to expose o.s. (to danger) *Il aurait pas dû se mettre au blanc comme ça pour si peu.* He should not have exposed himself to danger like that for so little. (LA) <LA, Da84> <***Loc:*** AC, AV, EV, SL, TB, VM, An94, Da84, Hi02, La99>

blanc[2], blanche [blɑ̃, blɑ̃ʃ] *n.* white person ◊ **•gros blanc** upper-class white, large land-holder <Lv88> <***Loc:*** LA, SL, VM, Da84, Lv88>

blanchâtre [blɑ̃ʃat(r)] *adj.* whitish *On était après chercher une maison manière blanchâtre.* We were looking for a kind-of whitish house. (LA) <***Loc:*** LA, TB, Da84>

blanchette [blɑ̃ʃɛt] *adj.f.* predominantly white in color (of a cow; by extension, name given to a black and white cow) *Vache blanchette.* A mostly-white cow. (VM) <***Loc:*** AV, SM, VM>

blancheur [blɑ̃ʃœr] *n.f.* whiteness <***Loc:*** Da84>

blanchir [blɑ̃ʃir] **I** *v.tr.* **1** to whiten, make white **2** to bleach *Elle avait du mal à blanchir son linge.* She had trouble bleaching her clothes. (LA) **3** to whitewash **4** to ice (a cake) *J'ai juste assez de chocolat pour blanchir le gâteau.* I have just enough chocolate to ice the cake. (VM) **II** *v.intr.* to pale, turn white *Quand elle a vu qui c'est qui venait dans la petite manche, elle a blanchi.* When she saw who it was who was coming down the lane, she got pale. (LA) <***Loc:*** LA, TB, VM, Da84>

blanchissage [blɑ̃ʃisaʒ] *n.m.* **1** whitening **2** bleaching **3** whitewashing <***Loc:*** Da84>

blanchissement [blɑ̃ʃismɑ̃] *n.m.* **1** whitening **2** bleaching **3** whitewashing <***Loc:*** Da84>

blanco [blɑ̃ko] *adj.* blond *Elle a marié un blanco de Carencro.* She married a blond from Carencro. (LA) <***Loc:*** LA, Da84>

BLANK [blɛ̃k] *n.m.* blank <***Loc:*** AV, Lv88>

blanque [blɑ̃k] *n.f.* openness, exposure **•à la blanque** exposed, in full view, out in the open <Da84> <***Loc:*** Da84>

blasphème [blasfɛ̃m] *n.f.* blasphemy <***Loc:*** Da84>

blasphémer [blasfɛ̃me] **I** *v.tr.* to blaspheme, curse *Il t'a blasphémé.* He cursed you. (VM) **II** *v.intr.* to blaspheme, curse *C'est soi-disant un péché de blasphémer.* It is supposedly a sin to curse. (LA) <***Loc:*** LA, VM, Da84>

blé [ble] *n.m.* wheat <***Loc:*** Da84, Fa77, Hi02>

blême [blɛ̃m] *adj.* sickly pale, sallow *Richard l'a portée. Elle avait venu chétif, maigre. Elle était blême, sa figure, et puis elle avait perdu un tas de poids.* Richard carried her. She had become worn-looking, thin. Her face was pale and she had lost a lot of weight. (SL) <***Loc:*** SL, Da84>

blêmesir ♦see **blêmir**

blêmir (**blêmesir**) [blɛ̃mir, blɛ̃mzir] *v.intr.* to turn pale *Il a blêmi beaucoup depuis qu'il a tombé malade.* He has turned very pale since he got sick. (LA) <***Loc:*** JE, LA, Da84, Lv88>

blesser [blese] **I** *v.tr.* to wound, injure, hurt, offend *Tu peux blesser quelqu'un autant avec des paroles qu'avec des coups.* You can injure someone as much with words as with blows. (LA) **II se blesser** *v.pron.* to wound o.s., hurt o.s. *Il s'a blessé loin dans le fond des bois. C'est par pure chance que son frère l'a trouvé.* He got hurt deep in the woods. It was pure luck that his brother found him. (LA) <***Loc:*** EV, LA, Da84>

blessure [blesyr] *n.f.* **1** wound, injury **2** hurt, offense **3** blister <***Loc:*** EV, Da84>

blette ♦see **belette**

bleu[1], -e (bleuse) [blø, bløz] *adj./n.* blue (color) *Bleu comme l'indigo.* As blue as indigo. (AV) **Bleu comme le ciel.* As blue as the sky. (La99) *C'est une robe bleuse qu'alle s'a acheté.* What she bought herself is a blue dress. (TB) ◊ **•bleu foncé / gros bleu** dark blue <SM, VM, Da84, Lv88> **•bleu pâle / bleu Sainte Vierge** pale blue <Da84> <***Loc:*** AV, SL, SM, TB, VM, Da84, Hi02, La99, Lv88>

bleu[2], -e [blø] *n.* **1** blueness **2** bluing **3** bruise ◊ **•bleu à laver** bluing <Da84> **•une belle bleue** a big lie <EV, LA, La99> <***Loc:*** AV, EV, JE, LA, SM, Da84, La99>

bleu[3], -e [blø] *n.* person of mixed white and African-American blood *Je connais plusieurs bleus.* I know many people of mixed blood. (JE) <***Loc:*** JE, LF, TB>

bleu[4] [blø] *n.m.* nickel, five-cent coin <***Loc:*** EV, Ph36>

bleuse ♦see **bleu**[1]

bleusir [bløzir] *v.tr.* **1** to blue (by using bluing) *Je bleusis toujours mon linge.* I always blue my laundry. (Lv88) **2** to bruise, make black and blue *Il a bleusi l'œil d'un bon coup de poing.* He blackened that eye with a good punch. (Lv88) <***Loc:*** JE, LA, LF, SM, Da84, Lv88>

bleuzâtre [bløzat(r)] *adj.* bluish *J'ai vu Rose avec sa robe bleuzâtre.* I saw Rose with her bluish dress. (SL) <***Loc:*** LF, SL>

BLIND[1] [blaɪn(d)] *adj.* blind *Elle était BLIND, elle voyait pas.* She was blind, she couldn't see. (AC) <***Loc:*** AC, EV, TB>

BLIND[2] [blaɪn(d)] *n.m.* **1** blind, mini-blind **2** blind, shelter (for concealing hunters) <***Loc:*** LA, Lv88>

bloc (**bloque**) [blɔk] *n.m.* **1** block, butcher's block *Il vend sa viande fraîche coupée sur le bloc.* He sells fresh meat cut on the (butcher's) block. (Lv88) **2** block, support pier under a house *Tu mettais des blocs tout les sept pieds.* You put blocks every seven feet. (SL) **3** block of houses, city block *Et là y a un Rousseau qui reste à peu près deux blocs là-bas.* And there's a Rousseau who lives about two blocks down there. (TB) **4** tide, current <***Loc:*** AV, EV, SL, TB, VM, Da84, Hi02, Lv88, Ph36>

blocage [blokaʒ] *n.m.* blockage, obstruction <***Loc:*** Da84>

bloff (**BLUFF**) [blɔf, blʌf] *n.m.* **1** cheating, duping, deception **2** bluff ◊ **•prendre un bloff** to be tricked <LF, SM, Lv88> <***Loc:*** JE, LF, SL, SM, Da84, Lv88>

bloffer (**bluffer, BLUFF**) [blofe, blɔf] **I** *v.tr.* to dupe, deceive, fool **Lapin, il bluffait tout le temps Bouki.* Lapin was always fooling Bouki. (An94) *Elle voulait me bloffer pour me vendre une autre assurance.* She wanted to deceive me in order to sell me more insurance. (Lv88) *Je vais casser ton cou si tu me bloffes!* I'll break your neck if you deceive me! (SM) **II** *v.intr.* to bluff *Moi, tu connais, j'étais après bloffer.* I was bluffing, you know. (SL) ◊ **•se faire bloffer** to be deceived *Je m'ai fait bluffé une fois, mais ça va pas arriver encore.* I was fooled once, but it won't happen again. (LA) <LA, Da84> <***Loc:*** AV, EV, IB, JE, LA, LF, SB, SL, SM, TB, An94, Da84, Lv88, Ph36>

bloffeur, -euse [blofœr, -øz] *n.* bluffer, deceiver <***Loc:*** AV, JE, LF, SL, SM>

blond, -e [blɔ̃, blɔ̃d] *adj.* blond, fair *Les yeux bleus, les cheveux blonds—elle ressemble pareille comme Mémère.* Blue eyes, blond hair—she looks just like Granny. (AC, ch: *Two-step à Tina*) <***Loc:*** AC, AV, EV, Da84>

blonde [blɔ̃n, blɔ̃d] *n.f.* girlfriend <***Loc:*** JE, Di32, Lv88, Gr86>

blondir [blɔ̃dir] **I** *v.intr.* to grow white or fair *Il a blondi au soleil.* His hair turned blond in the sun. (VM) **II se blondir** *v.pron.* to bleach one's hair *Il s'a blondi juste avant sa graduation.* He bleached his hair just before his graduation. (LA) ◊ **•blondir les cheveux** to bleach hair <Da84> <***Loc:*** LA, VM, Da84>

bloque ♦see **bloc**

bloquer [bloke] **I** *v.tr.* **1** to block, obstruct, stop up, dam *Le gros bougre était après bloquer son chemin.* The big fellow was blocking his way. (LA) **2** to erect struts or supports for construction *On a fini de bloquer le hangar.* We finished erecting supports for the shed. (LA) **3** to build on pillars (e.g. a house) **II se bloquer** *v.pron.* to get blocked up, constipated *Il a mangé trop de fromage et il s'a bloqué.* He ate too much cheese and he got constipated. (LA) <***Loc:*** LA, SB, SL, TB, Da84, Lv88>

blouse [bluz] *n.f.* **1** nightgown *Mets ta blouse et couche-toi.* Put on your nightgown and go to bed. (AV) **2** gown, smock ◊ **•blouse de nuit** nightgown <SM, Da84> **•blouse (volante)** loose dress widely known as a "Mother Hubbard" <TB, Re31> <***Loc:*** AC, AV, EV, IB, JE, LA, SB, SL, SM, TB, VM, Da84, Gu00, Lv88, Re31>

BLUE GRASS [blugræs, bugræs] *n.m.* blue grass, Bermuda grass <***Loc:*** VM, Da84>

BLUFF ♦see **bloff, bloffer**

bluffer ♦see **bloffer**

bo[1] [bo] *v.tr.invar.* [*baby talk*] to kiss *Va bo ta Mom.* Go kiss your mom. (Lv88) <***Loc:*** EV, IB, LF, SB, SL, SM, Lv88, Ph36>

bo[2] [bo] *n.m.* [*baby talk*] kiss *Chère, donne-moi un 'tit bo.* Honey, give me a little kiss. (Lv88) <***Loc:*** AV, Lv88>

BOARD [bɔrd] *n.m.* board, committee, council <***Loc:*** Lv88>

BOAT (**botte**) [bot] *n.m.* **1** boat *Une seine, il faut tu la hales, tu la hales jusqu'à t'arrives au BOAT.* A net, you have to haul it, you haul it until you get to the boat. (JE) **2** toy boat <***Loc:*** JE, LF>

bobèche (**bobette**) [bobɛʃ, bobɛt] *n.m./f.* **1** burner (of a kerosene stove or lamp) **2** device to catch dripping wax of a candle <***Loc:*** AV, VM, Da84>

bobette ♦see **bobèche**

bobine (**babine**) [bobin, babin] *n.f.* bobbin, spool ◊ **•bobine de fil** spool of thread <TB> <***Loc:*** JE, LF, TB, Da84>

bobinette [bobinɛt] *n.m./f.* fine net material used for mosquito bars, veils, etc. <***Loc:*** Da84, Lv88>

bobo[1] [bobo] *adj.* dangerous, vicious *Le loup est bobo.* The wolf is dangerous. (AV) <***Loc:*** AV, SB, SJ>

bobo[2] [bobo] *n.m.* sore, hurt, wound *J'ai un bobo sur ma main.* I have a wound on my hand. (SM) ◊ **•bobo de fièvre** fever blister <EV, TB> **•faire (du) bobo** to hurt, injure *Touche pas ça! Ça va te faire bobo!* Don't touch that! It will hurt you! (SM) <EV, SM, Da84, Ph36> <***Loc:*** EV, IV, SM, TB, Da84, Ph36>

bocal (**bocale**) [bokal] *n.m./f.* **1** glass, drinking glass, goblet **2** canning jar *On a fait de la confiture, cinquante bocales.* We made jam, fifty jars. (LA) <***Loc:*** LA, Da84>

bocale ♦see **bocal**

bocaut ♦see **boucaut**

boétailler ♦see **boitailler**

boëte ♦see **boîte**

boëter ♦see **boiter**

boëtte ♦see **aboëte**

boëtter ♦see **aboëtter**

bœuf [bœf] *n.m.* **1** draft ox **2** bull **3** steer **4** beef *Ça mangeait bien peu du bœuf dans ce temps-là. C'était tout le temps de la viande de cochon.* They ate very little beef in those days. It was always pork. (TB) ◊ **•bœuf de tire** draught ox <Lv88> **•bœuf sauvage** buffalo, American bison <Re31> <***Loc:*** AV, EV, SM, SB, TB, VM, Da84, Gu00, Hi02, Re31>

bœufalo, boffalo ♦see **buffalo**

boghei (**bogui, boguet**) [boge, bogi, bogɛ] *n.m.* **1** buggy, one-seat buggy **2** baby carriage ◊ **•boghei de boue** marsh buggy <TB> **•boghei de plairie** marsh buggy (vehicle invented by the oil industry for traveling across marsh, water, etc.) <LF> **•mettre le bogui avant le cheval** to put the cart before the horse, recount events in the wrong order when telling a story <La99> <***Loc:*** AC, EV, IB, JE, LF, SL, SM, TB, VM, An84, Da84, La99, Lv88>

bogonia [bogɔ̃ja] *n.f.* begonia <***Loc:*** VM>

boguet, bogui ♦see **boghei**

boire [bwar] **I** *v.tr.* to drink *Après la messe on va aller à la maison boire du café.* After mass, we'll go home and drink coffee. (JE) **II** *v.intr.* to drink alcohol *Mais quand ça vient samedi soir, chère, elle boit pareille comme Pépère.* But when Saturday night comes around, honey, she drinks just like Pépère. (AC, ch: *Two-step à Tina*) *Moi, j'ai été au village hier au soir, après boire pour oublier tous mes tracas.* I went to town last night, drinking to forget all my troubles. (ch: *Katherine*) ◊ **•boire à la santé de qqn** to drink to s.o.'s health *Nous allons boire à la santé de notre aimable société.* We're going to drink to the health of our amiable group of friends. (ch: *À l'honneur du patron*) <Da84> **•boire à l'excès** to drink to excess <Da84> **•boire comme si on n'avait pas de fond / boire comme un chien {poisson / tablier / trou}** to drink excessively <AV, VM, La99> **•boire un coup {filet}** to take a swig (of liquor) <Da84> **•boire une goutte** to take a sip *Bois une petite goutte et tu vas te sentir mieux.* Drink a little sip and you'll feel better (EV) <EV, Da84> **•faire boire** to water the animals <Da84> <***Loc:*** AC, AV, EV, JE, TB, VM, Da84, Hi02, La99>

bois [bwa] *n.m.* **1** tree *On a coupé un gros bois, puis là on prenait à scier.* We cut down a big tree, then we took to sawing it. (SL) **2** stick *Il se penche pour attraper un bois pour boucher le trou.* He bends down to pick up a stick to plug the hole. (EV) **3** wood, timber, lumber *C'est fait en bois.* It is made of wood. (AV) **4** forest, woods *On va aller dans le bois.* We are going into the forest. (SM) **5** firewood *Ça le chauffait avec du bois.* They heated it with wood. (AC) ◊ **•bois à linge** clothespin <JE> **•bois blanc** adelia, swamp privet <SB, Ho90, Re31> **•bois-bouton** ***a*** buttonbush ***b*** flowering dogwood <VM, Ho90, Lv88, Re31> **•bois connu {inconnu}** ***a*** hackberry tree, sugarberry tree ***b*** hickory ***c*** catalpa tree <IB, JE, LA, LF, SB, TB, Gu00, Hi02, Ho90, Lv88, Re31> **•bois cornu** species of dogwood <Da84> **•bois d'amourette** ***a*** prickly ash ***b*** honey locust <Lv88> **•bois d'arc** mock orange, osage orange, bodock (tree or wood) <AL, EV, IB, LA, SL, TB, Da84, Ho90, Lv88, Ph36, Re31> **•bois debout** ***a*** standing timber ***b*** land that has not been cleared of its timber <Da84, Re31> **•bois de cèdre** cedar tree <TB> **•bois de cheminée** chimney or fireplace wood <Da84> **•bois de chien** dogwood <CL> **•bois de collier** wooden collar or harness <EV, Lv88, Ph36> **•bois de cogné / bois inconnu** hackberry <IB, Gu00> **•bois de fer** flowering dogwood <Lv88> **•bois de filé** sassafras tree <TB> **•bois de flèche** any species of dogwood (including flowering dogwood, stiff or swamp dogwood, and rough-leaved dogwood) <EV, IB, LA, TB, Da84, Ho90, Lv88, Ph36, Re31> **•bois de foyer {feu}** firewood *On dirait que mon bois de feu est après réduire plus vite que ça devrait.* It seems as if my firewood supply is diminishing faster than it ought to. (IV) <IB, IV> **•bois de fruit** fruit tree <TB> **•bois de gombo** sassafras tree <TB> **•bois de lit en fer** iron bed <SL> **•bois de marais** button-bush (also called button-tree, globe-flower, honey-balls) <TB, Ho90, Re31> **•bois de pin / bois gras** pine tree or wood <IV, JE, TB> **•bois de rameaux** magnolia <TB, Hi02, Lv88> **•bois dérive** driftwood <JE> **•bois de STOVE** stove wood <Da84> **•bois-jaune** tulip tree or yellow poplar <Ho90, Re31> **•bois-malin** trigger of a bird trap <AV, IB, SJ> **•bois massif** rough cut lumber <EV, LA, VM> **•bois puant** catalpa, Samara elm <EV, LA, SL, Gu00, Ho90, Lv88, Ph36> **•bois rose** crape myrtle <EV, SL, Lv88> **•grand bois** ***a*** forest, woods ***b*** broad-leafed tree forest in the center of Louisiana <Gu00, Lv88> **•gros bois** ***a*** rough wood (for construction) ***b*** heavy timber <EV, SL> <***Loc:*** AC, AV, CL, EV, IB, IV, JE, LA, LF, SB, SJ, SL, SM, TB, VM, Da84, Gu00, Hi02, Ho90, Lv88, Ph36, Re31>

boisseau [bwaso] *n.m.* **1** bushel **2** bushel basket <***Loc:*** IB, TB, Da84>

boisson [bwasɔ̃] *n.f.* liquor, booze, alcoholic beverage *Son mari, il cachait sa boisson.* Her husband hid his booze. (TB) *Cet homme ça-là a persécuté sa pauvre famille à cause de la boisson.* That man persecuted his poor family because of alcohol. (VM) **Le poisson sans boisson est poison.* Fish without drink is poison. (Da84) ◊ **•en boisson** ***a*** tipsy ***b*** drunk <SM, Da84, La99, Lv88> <***Loc:*** EV, SM, TB, Da84, Hi02, La99, Lv88>

boisure [bwazyr] *n.f.* **1** wainscot, wainscoting **2** woodwork **3** wooden structure **4** thick foliage, thick shrubbery or woods *Quand tu passes en avant de chez Madame Kelly tu vois pas sa maison à force qu'alle est dans une boisure.* When you pass by Mrs. Kelly's you don't see her house for all the thick foliage. (TB) ◊ •**boisure de cheminée** mantelpiece <AV, SJ> <*Loc:* AV, EV, SJ, TB, VM, Da84, Ph36, Re31>

boitailler (**boétailler**) [bwetaje] *v.intr.* to limp **I boétaille, il a di mal au pied.* He's limping, his foot hurts. (EV, Ph36) <*Loc:* EV, SM, Ph36>

boîte (**boëte**) [bwat, bwɛt, bwet] *n.f. (occas. n.m.)* **1** box **2** chest **3** can ◊ •**boîte à charpente** carpenter's box <EV> •**boîte à malle** mailbox <LF> •**boîte à musique** radio <LF> •**boîte à pain** oven <LF> •**boîte de couleurs** box of crayons <SL> •**boîte de poste** ***a*** post office box ***b*** mailbox <LA, Da84> •**boîte de sardines** can of sardines <Da84> •**boîte en carton** cardboard box <LF, Da84> <*Loc:* AC, AV, EV, IB, JE, LA, LF, SB, SL, SM, TB, Da84, Hi02, Lv88>

boitement [bwatmɑ̃] *n.m.* limping <*Loc:* Da84>

boiter (**boëter**) [bwate, bwete] *v.intr.* **1** to limp *Alle marche, mais alle boite. Et c'est pas comme ça devrait être.* She walks, but she limps. It's not like it's supposed to be. (TB) *Il boëte d'une jambe.* He limps on one leg. (SM) **2** to be lame ◊ •**boiter tout bas** to have a bad limp *Le vieux bonhomme boite tout bas.* The old man has a bad limp. (SM) <SM, Lv88> <*Loc:* AV, SL, SM, TB, Da84, Lv88>

boiterie [bwetri] *n.f.* limping <*Loc:* JE, VM>

boiteur, -euse (**boiteux, -euse**) [bwatœr, bwetœr, bwatø, bwetø, -øz] *n.* one who is lame, one who limps <*Loc:* Da84>

boiteux[1]**, -euse** (**boîteux, -euse**) [bwatø, bwetø, -øz] *adj.* lame, limping <*Loc:* Da84>

boiteux[2] ♦see **boiteur**

boiture [bwatyr] *n.f.* ◊ •**boiture d'encadrement** woodwork around windows and doors <IB> <*Loc:* IB>

bokette [bokɛt] *n.m.* bucket *Je veux un bokette d'eau.* I want a bucket of water. (JE) <*Loc:* JE>

bol [bɔl] *n.f. (occ. n.m.)* **1** bowl *T'as mangé deux grosses bols de couche-couche.* You ate two big bowls of couche-couche. (ThCa: *Le charivari*) **2** washbasin **3** toilet bowl ◊ •**bol à mains** washbasin <JE, Lv88> •**bol de lavabo** washbasin <VM> <*Loc:* AV, EV, JE, LA, LF, SL, TB, VM, Da84, Di32, Fa77, Hi02, Lv88, ThCa>

BOLL-WEEVE [bolwiv] *n.m.* boll weevil <*Loc:* Fa77>

bombardement [bɔ̃bardəmɑ̃] *n.m.* bombardment <*Loc:* Da84>

bombarder [bɔ̃barde] **I** *v.tr.* **1** to bombard, bomb *Les Américains ont bombardé Baghdad.* The Americans bombed Baghdad. (VM) **2** to bombard, assail (with constant questions or requests, etc.) *Les enfants ont bombardé la maîtresse de questions.* The children bombarded the teacher with questions. (VM) **II** *v.intr.* to fuss, grumble *Il bombarde tout le temps.* He grumbles all the time. (JE) <*Loc:* JE, LF, VM, Da84>

bombardier [bɔ̃bardje] *n.m.* bombardier <*Loc:* Da84>

bombe[1] (**bomme**) [bɔ̃b, bɔ̃m, bɑ̃m] *n.f.* **1** kettle **2** saucepan, cooking pot (esp. of cast iron) **3** barrel bung ◊ •**bombe à café** coffeepot <JE> •**bombe à cuire** cooking pot <JE> •**bomme à tcheue raide** large pot with a handle <JE> •**bombe en fer** cast iron pot <TB> <*Loc:* AV, EV, IB, JE, LA, LF, SB, SL, SM, TB, VM, Da84, Lv88, Ph36>

bombe[2] [bɔ̃b] *n.f.* bomb ◊ •**bombe atomique** atomic bomb <Da84> <*Loc:* EV, SM, Da84, Ph36>

bombocher ♦see **bambocher**

bombocheur ♦see **bambocheur**

bôme[1] [bɔ̃m] *n.m.* boom (for lifting objects) <*Loc:* TB>

bôme[2] [bɔ̃m] *n.m./f.* boom, barrier made of floating logs *Dans le bayou il y a une bôme pour tiendre les herbes du bayou.* In the bayou there is a boom to hold back the grasses. (TB) <*Loc:* JE, TB>

bomme ♦see **bombe**

bon, bonne [bɔ̃, bɔ̃n] *adj.* **1** good, nice, fine, kind *Et il était bon, je l'ai donné pas un mauvais cheval, je l'ai donné un bon cheval, tu connais.* And he was nice, I didn't give him a bad horse, I gave him a good horse, you know. (TB) *Ouais, on avait des bêtes pour nous-autres, et on avait des bonnes vaches à lait.* Yeah, we had cattle, and we had good milking cows. (EV) **2** good, well-behaved *Ces petits enfants sont bien bons.* Those little children are quite good (well-behaved). (Lv88) **3** right, correct, appropriate *Je faisais du roux [...] avec de l'huile et de la farine, brassé jusqu'à ce que c'est de la bonne couleur, un peu brun.* I used to make roux with oil and flour, stirred until it's the right color, brownish. (SL) ◊ •**bon cœur** good, goodhearted *Il est bon cœur comme sa mame.* He is goodhearted like his mother. (IB) <EV, IB, Ph36> •**bon comme la vie** very good <LA, La99> •**bon comme son père {un ange}** very good (of a person) <SM, La99> •**pas assez bon pour faire du savon** worthless <La99> •**pas bon** good-for-nothing, fickle person, libertine <Lv88> <*Loc:* EV, IB, JE, LA, SL, SM, Da84, Hi02, La99, Lv88, Ph36>

bon-à-rien (**bonrien**) [bɔ̃arjɛ̃, bɔ̃rjɛ̃, bɔ̃nare, bɑ̃nare] *n.m.* good-for-nothing, loser, scamp *Il est tout le temps soûl. C'est un bon-à-rien.* He's always drunk. He's a worthless fellow. (SM) *Moi, je connais, je suis bonrien, mais je suis bonrien pour moi-même. J'ai jamais fait rien à personne.* Me, I know I'm a a good-for-nothing, but I'm a good-for-nothing to myself. I've never done anything to anyone. (EV) **On nous contait des petits contes de ces trois bonriens.* He told us some short stories about the three good-for-nothings. (Gr82) <*Loc:* EV, LF, SL, SM, Gr82, Lv88>

bonarienté [bɔ̃narjɛ̃te] *n.m.* worthlessness, rascality <*Loc:* VM>

bonasse [bɔ̃nas] *adj.* **1** easy-going, good-natured *Elle était assez bonasse, pauvre bête, elle disait jamais arien si on l'écoutait pas.* She was so easy good-natured, poor thing, she never said anything if we didn't mind her. (EV) **2** simple **3** goody-goody <*Loc:* EV, Da84>

bonbon [bɔ̃bɔ̃] *n.m.* candy, goody ◊ **•bonbon à rhume** cough drop <VM> <***Loc:*** VM, Da84, Hi02>

bon-bout [bɔ̃bu] *n.m.* giant ragweed, bloodweed <***Loc:*** SB>

bond [bɔ̃] *n.m.* leap, jump, bounce <***Loc:*** Da84>

bondir [bɔ̃dir] *v.intr.* to bounce, bound, rebound *Le bougre a bondi de derrière le lit quand il a entendu sa femme arriver.* The fellow bounded from behind the bed when he heard his wife arrive. (LA) <***Loc:*** LA, Da84>

bonheur [bɔ̃nœr] *n.m.* good fortune, prosperity, happiness, success ◊ **•ton bonheur** your sake, your good <Fa77> <***Loc:*** Da84, Fa77, Hi02>

bonhomme [bɔ̃nɔ̃m] *n.m.* **1** man, fellow **Il arrive un bonhomme.* A man is coming. (Da84) **2** any crude representation of a human figure **Il a vu le bonhomme, et a cru que c'était Bouki. "Mais," il dit, "je vas t'installer, Bouki!"* He saw the mannequin and thought that it was Bouki. "Well," he said, "I'll fix you, Bouki!" (SM, An94) **3** scarecrow <***Loc:*** SL, SM, An94, Da84, Lv88>

bonifier [bɔ̃nifje] **I** *v.tr.* to ameliorate, improve, better **II se bonifier** *v.pron.* to improve o.s., better o.s. <***Loc:*** Da84>

bonito [bɔ̃nito] *n.m.* Atlantic bonito <***Loc:*** LF>

bonjour [bɔ̃ʒur] *interj.* good day, good morning, good afternoon, goodbye <***Loc:*** AC, TB, Da84, Fa77>

bonne-à-rienne [bɔ̃narjɛ̃n] *n.f.* good-for-nothing woman, harlot *Elle est juste une bonne-à-rienne.* She is just a harlot. (JE) <***Loc:*** JE, LF, SM>

bonnement [bɔ̃nmɑ̃] *adv.* simply, plainly, merely ◊ **•tout bonnement** once and for all **Allons tout bonnement finir avec ça.* Let's get this over with once and for all. (Da84) <Da84> <***Loc:*** Da84>

bonnet [bɔ̃nɛ, bɔ̃ne] *n.m.* **1** bonnet, sunbonnet **2** cap **3** muzzle placed over a calf's face to keep it from suckling <***Loc:*** LA, Da84, Hi02, Lv88>

bonsoir [bɔ̃swar] *interj.* good evening, good night <***Loc:*** Da84, Fa77>

bonté [bɔ̃te] *n.f.* kindness, goodness ◊ **•avoir (de) la bonté de** to have the kindness to **Avoir la bonté de m'aider.* To have the kindness to help me. (Da84) <Da84> **•bonté ti possible** for goodness sake <Da84> <***Loc:*** Da84>

BOOTLEG[1] [butlɛg] *v.tr.invar.* to bootleg, sell illegally *Le gouvernement a essayé de les arrêter, mais ça pouvait pas les empêcher de* BOOTLEG. The government tried to stop them, but they couldn't prevent them from selling (whiskey) illegally. (LA) <***Loc:*** EV, LA, TB, Lv88, Ph36>

BOOTLEG[2] [butlɛg] *adj.* bootleg, illegal (usu. of whiskey) **Il y a du monde qui faisait le* BOOTLEG *whisky et là d'autres le serraient en haut de leurs greniers, dans leurs maisons, dans leurs magasins.* There are people who made bootleg whiskey and others would store it up in their attics, in their houses, in their barns. (SL, An94) <***Loc:*** LA, SL, An94>

BOOTLEG[3] [butlɛg] *n.m.* bootleg whiskey <***Loc:*** LA, SL, An94>

BOOTLEG[4] **(BOOTLEGGER)** [butlɛg] *n.m.* bootlegger, smuggler <***Loc:*** EV, VM, Ph36>

BOOTLEGGER ♦see **BOOTLEG**

boqueteau [bɔkto] *n.m.* sturdy shoe <***Loc:*** SM>

bord [bɔr] *n.m.* **1** side *On tournait les patates de bord dans la cendre.* We turned the potatoes on their sides in the ashes. (Lv88) **2** line of descent *Mon grand-père sur le bord de mon popa.* My grandfather on my father's side. (Lv88) **3** border (of a forest) **4** shore, edge (of water), riverbank **5** margin (of a page) **6** side, party, affiliation *Il était dans notre faction, mais il a changé de bord.* He was in our faction, but he changed sides. (SM) *Sur quel bord t'as voté?* What side did you vote on? (Lv88) **7** edge ◊ **•bord à droite** starboard <JE> **•bord à gauche** port side **•bord de la mer** seashore <JE, LF, Da84> **•bord du chemin** down the road, along the road, by the roadside <JE> **•bord du lac** lakeshore <Da84> **•bord du nord** north side <Da84> **•bord ici bord là** here and there <Da84> **•bord icite** on this side (of a river, lake, etc.) <Lv88> **•à bord de** on board *Ça donne une place pour mettre ton pied quand tu vas embarquer à bord du bateau.* That makes a place for you to put your foot when you're getting into the boat. (LF) <LF> **•de mon bord** for my part <AV> **•de tous les bords** from all sides, on all sides *L'eau est venue de tous les bords.* Water came from all sides. (SL) <AV, SL, Da84> **•d'un bord à l'autre** from one side to the other <Da84> **•être du même bord** to be on the same side <Da84> **•l'autre bord** ***a*** on the other side *Tu restes l'autre bord du grand bois.* You live on the other side of the big woods. (Lv88) ***b*** the Old World, Europe *Ça qu'a changé ça plein, c'est après la guerre numéro deux quand les hommes a revenu de l'autre bord.* What changed that a lot is after World War II when men came back from Europe. (TB) ***c*** abroad <LF, SL, TB, Hi02, Lv88> <***Loc:*** AC, AV, EV, IB, JE, LA, LF, SL, SM, TB, Da84, Hi02, Lv88, Ph36>

bordage [bɔrdaʒ] *n.f.* edge, margin, border *La bordage du tapis est bleue.* The edge of the rug is blue. (AV) <***Loc:*** AV>

bordeau [bɔrdo] *n.m.* tuna <***Loc:*** Fa77>

bordel[1]**, -elle** [bɔrdɛl] *n.* **1** unpleasant, unkind person **Ç't homme est in bordel.* That man is a bear. (EV, Ph36) **2** *(f.)* woman of ill repute, harlot, whore <***Loc:*** AV, EV, SM, VM, Ph36>

bordel[2] [bɔrdɛl] *n.m.* brothel, whorehouse <***Loc:*** Da84>

bordel[3] [bɔrdɛl] *interj.* damn!, hell! <***Loc:*** EV, SM, Ph36>

bordelation [bɔrdelasjɔ̃] *interj.* shucks! hell! *Bordelation du diable!* Damnation of the devil! (VM) <***Loc:*** VM>

border[1] [bɔrde] **I** *v.tr.* **1** to border, hem (a garment) *Je suis après border ma jupe parce qu'elle était trop longue.* I am hemming my skirt because it was too long. (LA) **2** to border **Et c'était une île qu'avait des cherokees. Ça bordait le chemin.* And it was an island that had cherokee bushes. They bordered the road. (LA, An94) **II** *v.intr.* to border on, be adjacent to **Sa maison borde au chemin.* His house borders on the road. (Da84) <*Loc:* LA, VM, An94, Da84>

border[2] ♦see **aborder**

bordure [bɔrdyr] *n.f.* **1** edge (of a piece of wood, etc.), edging **2** border **3** bank of a stream that has no levee ◊ •**bordure de bois** edge of the woods <Da84> <*Loc:* AV, LF, IB, SB, SJ, TB, Da84, Lv88>

borgne[1] [bɔrɲ] *adj.* blind in one eye *Cet homme avait eu un œil d'arraché dans une bataille avec son voisin. Il a fait le restant de sa vie borgne.* That man had an eye pulled out in a fight with his neighbor. He spent the rest of his life one-eyed. (LA) <*Loc:* LA, Da84>

borgne[2] (**borgnon**) [bɔrɲ, bɔrnjɔ̃] *n.m.* one-eyed man <*Loc:* SM, Da84>

borgnon ♦see **borgne**

borne [bɔrn] *n.f.* boundary mark, bench mark, limit, boundary <*Loc:* Da84>

borné, -e [bɔrne] *adj.* bounded, limited *Il a un peu l'esprit borné.* His vision is a bit limited. (LA) <*Loc:* LA, Da84>

borner [bɔrne] *v.tr.* to set boundary marks, set limits <*Loc:* Da84>

bosale ♦see **bossal**

boscot, -e, -tte [bosko, -ot, -ɔt] *adj.* hunchbacked (of a person) *Elle avait le dos bossu, elle était boscotte.* She had a hunched back, she was a hunchback. (Lv88) <*Loc:* SM, TB, La99, Lv88>

boscoyo (**boscoillot**) [boskojo, buskuju, buskujo] *n.m.* **1** stump, large piece of rough or knotty wood **2** cypress knee, pneumatophore **3** knot on a tree **4** lump *Il a un gros boscoyo sur sa tête où il a été frappé.* He has a big lump on his head where he was hit. (SM) **5** tough old man ◊ •**boscoyo de cipre** cypress knee <Gu00> <*Loc:* AV, EV, IB, LF, SB, SL, SM, TB, VM, Da84, Gu00, Hi02, Ho90, Lv88, Ph36, Re31>

bosquer [boske] *v.tr.* to hit, strike *Il lui en a bosqué un droit au milieu du front.* He knocked him a good one right in the middle of the forehead. (LA) ◊ •**bosquer les œufs** to knock eggs, an Easter tradition <SM> <*Loc:* LA, SM, Lv88>

BOSS (**boss**) [bɔs] *n.m.* boss, employer, owner, headman, foreman, master <*Loc:* AV, EV, JE, LA, LF, SB, SL, SM, TB, Da84, Lv88>

bossal[1] (**bosale, bossale**) [bosal] *n.m.* **1** halter, muzzle **2** hackamore bridle <*Loc:* AV, EV, IB, JE, SB, SJ, SL, SM, TB, Da84, La99, Lv88, Ph36, Re31>

bossal[2] (**bosale, bossale**) [bosal] *n.m.* [*offensive*] black person <*Loc:* Lv88>

bossal[3] [bosal] *n.m.* ◊ •**prendre un bossal** to give o.s. a treat (esp. nice food) <JE, La99> <*Loc:* JE, La99>

bossale ♦see **bossal**

bossard [bosar] *n.m.* muzzle *Il fallu qu'on met un bossard sus notre chien.* We had to put a muzzle on our dog. (TB) <*Loc:* TB>

bosse [bɔs] *n.f.* **1** lump, bit, piece **2** large serving, portion, helping (usu. of food) *Je m'a pris une bonne bosse.* I took a large helping. (TB) **3** bump, swelling **Elle dit, "Ça fait des bosses sur ma tête quand je cogne ma tête sur le plancher et," elle dit, "je suis fâchée."* She said, "It raises bumps on my head when I hit my head on the floor and," she said, "I'm mad." (EV, An94) **4** mons pubis ◊ •**bosse de sucre** lump of sugar <Da84, Lv88> •**se foutre une bosse** to get drunk *Je me suis foutu une bosse carabinée.* I got magnificently drunk. (SM) <SM> <*Loc:* EV, SB, SL, TB, An94, Da84, Lv88>

bosser [bose] *v.tr.* to batter, dent *Il a bossé la pelote.* He battered the ball. (AV) <*Loc:* AV>

bossu, -e [bosy] *adj.* hunchbacked *Il est bossu depuis son accident.* He is hunchbacked since his accident. (LA) <*Loc:* LA, Da84>

boster [boste] **I** *v.tr.* to bust, burst **II** *v.intr.* to bust, burst *Le ballon a bosté avec un grand bruit.* The balloon burst with a loud noise. (SB) *Il a bosté de rire dans sa figure.* He burst out laughing in his face. (TB) <*Loc:* SB, TB>

botte[1] [bɔt] *n.f.* boot ◊ •**botte en élastique {gomme}** rubber boot <LA, Da84> <*Loc:* EV, LA, SL, SM, TB, VM, Da84, Hi02>

botte[2] [bɔt] *n.f.* **1** bale **2** bundle (of harvested rice) ◊ •**botte de foin** bale of hay <Da84> •**en bottes** said of rice when it shoots out from sides instead of only in one cluster <VM> <*Loc:* EV, VM, Da84>

botte[3] ♦see **BOAT**

botteler [bɔtle] *v.tr.* to bale, bundle *Botteler du papier à gazette.* To bundle newspaper. (LA) <*Loc:* LA, Da84>

bottes [bɔt] *n.m.pl.* bots (a stomach disease of cattle and horses) **Le cheval a les bottes.* The horse has stomach cramps. (Da84) <*Loc:* Da84, Lv88>

botton [botɔ̃] *n.m.* stuffing box <*Loc:* LF>

boubouce [bubus] *n.f.* old-fashioned high-topped shoe <*Loc:* SL>

bouboune [bubun] *n.m.* nipple (of a baby bottle) *L'enfant veut le bouboune.* The baby wants the nipple. (SB) <*Loc:* SB>

boucanage [bukɑ̃naʒ] *n.m.* smoking (of meat, etc.) <*Loc:* Da84>

boucane [bukɑ̃n] *n.f.* smoke *La boucane des cigarettes.* Cigarette smoke. (Lv88) *Brûle pas les herbes. Ça fait trop de boucane.* Don't burn the weeds. It makes too much smoke. (SM) ◊ •**faire (de) la boucane** to make smoke to ward off mosquitoes *On faisait de la boucane pour les maringouins pour être capable s'assir dans la galerie.* We would make smoke for the mosquitos, so we could sit out on the porch. (SL) <SL, Da84, Lv88> •**sacré {cré} boucane** holy smoke <Da84> •**mettre de la boucane en sac** to do a task that serves no purpose <SL, La99> <*Loc:* AC, AV, EV, IB, JE, LA, LF, SB, SL, SM, TB, Da84, Hi02, La99, Lv88, Ph36, Re31>

boucané, -e [bukɑ̃ne] *adj.* **1** smoked (of meat) *Nous-autres,* *on use des saucisses boucanées dans notre gombo.* We use smoked sausages in our gumbo. (EV) **2** hazy, misty, cloudy (of the weather) *Le temps est boucané.* The weather is hazy. (SM) <***Loc:*** EV, SM, TB, Da84, La99, Lv88>

boucanée [bukɑ̃ne] *n.f.* smoking, smoking process for meat *C'était le meilleur bois pour faire les... la boucanée de la viande.* That was the best wood to do the . . . the smoking of the meat. (AC) <***Loc:*** AC>

boucaner [bukɑ̃ne] **I** *v.tr.* **1** to smoke, smoke-dry (meat, tobacco) *On boucane la viande pour la conserver.* We smoke meat to preserve it. (SM) **Boucaner de la viande, du poisson, du tabac.* To smoke-dry meat, fish, tobacco. (Re31) **2** to fumigate *On va boucaner la maison.* We are going to fumigate the house. (JE) *Boucaner les maringouins.* To smoke out mosquitos. (EV) **II** *v.intr.* to smoke *La cheminée boucane quand ça mouille.* The chimney smokes when it rains. (Lv88) <***Loc:*** AC, AV, IB, JE, LF, SB, SL, SM, TB, Hi02, Lv88, Re31>

boucanière [bukɑ̃jær] *n.f.* smokehouse <***Loc:*** AC, AV, EV, IB, SL, SM, Da84, Lv88, Ph36>

boucaut (bocaut) [buko, boko] *n.m.* large barrel, hogshead <***Loc:*** IB, JE, TB, Lv88>

bouchage [buʃaʒ] *n.m.* stoppage, clogging <***Loc:*** Da84>

bouche [buʃ] *n.f.* mouth ◊ **•bouche de la rivière** mouth of the river <TB> **•de bouche** verbal, verbally *Ils avont fait ça de bouche, alors il avait pas rien à montrer.* They did it verbally, so he didn't have anything to show. (VM) <VM> **•faire la bouche couler** to make the mouth water <SL, SM, Lv88> <***Loc:*** EV, SL, SM, TB, VM, Da84, Hi02, Lv88>

bouché, -e [buʃe] *adj.* stopped up, plugged up, stoppered *J'ai le nez bouché depuis une semaine.* I have had a stopped up nose for a week. (LA) <***Loc:*** LA, TB, Da84>

bouchée [buʃe] *n.f.* mouthful (of food) **Il mange des petits pins d'une bouchée, des petits pins haut comme ça-là.* It eats little pine trees in one mouthful, little pine trees about so tall. (EV, An94) <***Loc:*** EV, An94, Da84>

bouchelle (bushel) [buʃɛl] *n.m.* bushel <***Loc:*** AV, Da84, Lv88>

boucher[1] [buʃe] **I** *v.tr.* **1** to stop up, dam, obstruct, plug, fill in *Ils bouchaient les rivières avec des arbres.* They dammed rivers with trees. (Lv88) **2** to shut s.o. up, silence *Je l'ai bouché avec un mot.* I shut him up with one word. (JE) *Il croyait qu'il m'avait bouché, mais je lui ai tapé ça, je te dis.* He thought he had shut me up, but I put him in his place, I'll tell you. (LA) **II se boucher** *v.pron.* **1** to be plugged up *Là si le bateau coulait un petit peu, que la craque s'avait pas bouché, ils prendont du coton exprès, du coton avec du godron dedans.* Then if the boat leaked a little, if the crack hadn't been plugged, they take special cotton, cotton with tar in it. (LF) **2** to shut up, stop talking *Il faudra je me bouche. Il va pas lâcher.* I'll have to shut up. He won't give up. (LA) ◊ **•boucher une dent** to fill a dental cavity <VM> **•boucher un trou** to stop up a hole **Quoi-ce qui bouche le trou?* What's stopping the hole? (AC, An94) <AC, An94, Da84> **•bouche ta gueule** shut up! be quiet! <Da84, La99> **•bouche-trou** ready response, quick retort <SC, La99> <***Loc:*** AC, JE, LA, LF, SC, SL, SM, TB, VM, An94, Da84, La99, Lv88>

boucher[2] [buʃe] *n.m.* butcher <***Loc:*** LF, Da84>

boucherie [buʃ(ə)ri] *n.f.* **1** slaughter, butchering **2** slaughterhouse ◊ **•boucherie de bloque {de quartier}** communal neighborhood slaughter or butchering event <EV, SL> **•boucherie de société** cooperative slaughtering <Da84> **•faire boucherie** to slaughter, butcher *On fait une grosse boucherie, on tue deux cochons et on fait des boudins, des gratons.* We have a big slaughter, we slaughter two pigs and we make boudin and cracklings. (SM) *On a fait boucherie hier. On a tué un cochon de trois cents livres.* We had a butchering yesterday. We slaughtered a three hundred pound hog. (SM) <SM, Da84, Lv88> <***Loc:*** AC, EV, JE, LA, LF, SL, SM, TB, Da84, Hi02, Lv88>

bouchon [buʃɔ̃] *n.m.* **1** stopper, plug **2** bung (in a barrel) **3** cork **4** float, bobber (for fishing) **5** wad (of cotton) ◊ **•le bouchon est après caler** said when s.o. is nodding off to sleep <AC, JE> <***Loc:*** AC, AV, JE, LF, TB, Da84, Hi02, La99>

bouchonner [buʃɔ̃ne] *v.tr.* to botch, bungle, mess up, do poorly **Il a bouchonné l'ouvrage.* He botched the job. (EV, Ph36) <***Loc:*** EV, Ph36>

boucle [buk(l)] *n.f.* **1** buckle **2** lock, curl of hair ◊ **•boucle d'oreille** earring <AV, SM, Da84> <***Loc:*** AV, JE, SM, Da84>

bouclé, -e [bukle] *adj.* curly *Elle avait des beaux cheveux bouclés.* She had beautiful curly hair. (LA) <***Loc:*** LA, Da84>

boucler [bukle] **I** *v.tr.* **1** to buckle *Ma ceinture est bouclée.* My belt is buckled. (LA) **2** to curl (the hair) *Elle se faisait boucler les cheveux tous les quinze jours chez Yvonne.* She would have her hair curled every two weeks at Yvonne's. (LA) **II** *v.intr.* to curl *Ses cheveux ont bouclé après elle avait fini ses traitements.* His hair curled after he finished his treatments. (LA) **III se boucler** *v.pron.* **1** to buckle o.s., one's belt *Il s'a bouclé la ceinture.* He buckled his belt. (LA) **2** to curl one's hair *Elle s'a bouclé les cheveux.* She curled her hair. (LA) <***Loc:*** LA, Da84>

bouclet [buklɛ, bukle] *n.m.* buckle <***Loc:*** SM>

bouclette [buklɛt] *n.f.* small lock, curl (of hair) <***Loc:*** AV, IB, TB, Da84>

boucoup ♦see **beaucoup**

boudard, -euse [budar, -øz] *n.* one who pouts <***Loc:*** LF, SB, SM>

boude [bud] *n.f.* pouting, sulking ◊ **•faire (de) la boude** to pout *Il fait la boude.* He's pouting. (SB) *Il me fait de la boude depuis hier.* He has refused to talk to me since yesterday. (TB) <SB, TB> <***Loc:*** SB, TB>

boudé, -e [bude] *adj.* pouting, sulking *Le petit était tout boudé.*

Son père l'avait puni pour un mois. The child was sulking. His father had punished him for a month. (LA) <***Loc:*** LA, Da84>

bouder [bude] **I** *v.intr.* to pout, sulk *Arrête de bouder et va jouer.* Stop pouting and go play. (EV) **II se bouder** *v.pron.* to act in a pouting manner (towards each other) *Ils se boudent depuis des semaines.* They have been pouting over each other for weeks. (EV) ◊ **•bouder après (qqn)** to act in a pouting manner toward (s.o.) *Lui là-bas c'est pas tout le temps qu'il nous parle, il boude après nous-autres. Il peut rester trois ou quatre mois sans nous parler.* The guy [who lives] down there, he doesn't always talk to us, he refuses to talk to us. He can go three or four months without talking to us. (TB) <TB> <***Loc:*** EV, TB, Da84, Hi02>

bouderie [budri] *n.f.* pouting, sulking <***Loc:*** Da84>

boudière ♦see **boudinière**

boudin [budɛ̃] *n.m.* boudin, type of Cajun sausage made of pork, rice, onions, and seasoning stuffed into a pork intestine or other casing *Le boudin, ils preniont du riz, le foie, et de la viande, ils moulaient ça tout ensemble et ils cuisaient ça un bout de temps.* [To make] boudin, they would take rice, liver, and meat, they would mince it all together and they would cook it for a while. (AV) ◊ **•boudin blanc** rice-based boudin (as opposed to boudin rouge) <Da84, Gu00, Lv88> **•boudin rouge** blood sausage, boudin containing a large quantity of fresh blood *Vous-autres sauvait le sang? Des fois oui, quand on faisait du boudin rouge.* Did you save the blood? Sometimes, yes, when we were making blood sausage. (AC) <AC, Da84> **•faire son boudin** to pout <La99> <***Loc:*** AC, AV, EV, LA, TB, Da84, Gu00, Hi02, La99>

boudinière (**boudière, emboudinière**) [budĩjær, budjær, ɑ̃budĩjær] *n.f.* funnel (traditionally made of a sawed-off cow horn) used to stuff the sausage casing in making boudin *Comment on bourrait les boudins? Avec une boudière, avec une corne de bête.* How did we stuff the boudin? With a "boudière," with a cow horn. (LA) *Une boudinière, c'était un petit entonnoir exprès pour faire le boudin.* A "boudinière" was a little funnel especially for making boudin. (LF) <***Loc:*** AC, IB, LA, LF, VM, Da84>

boudoudoume (**boudoume**) [bududum, budum, budzum, burdum] *interj.* boom, the sound that results when a heavy object falls *Boudoudoume! Il a tombé sur son boudoume.* Boom! He fell on his bottom. (SM) *Boudouboume, il a roulé en bas de l'escalier.* Boom, he came rolling down the stairs. (LF) ◊ **•faire boudouboume** [*baby talk*] to fall down <LF, SM> <***Loc:*** LF, SL, SM>

boudoume[1] [budum] *n.m.* posterior, bottom <***Loc:*** SM>

boudoume[2] ♦see **boudoudoume**

boue [bu] *n.f.* mud, mire <***Loc:*** SL, Da84, Hi02>

bouffée [bufe] *n.f.* ◊ **•bouffée de vent** gust of wind <Lv88> <***Loc:*** Lv88>

bouffir [bufir] *v.intr.* to puff up, swell up (esp. of the face) *Après ses traitements, sa figure était tout bouffie.* After his treatments, his face was all swollen. (VM) <***Loc:*** VM, Da84>

bouffon [bufɔ̃] *n.m.* clown, buffoon ◊ **•faire le bouffon** to clown, clown around, act like a clown *Arrête de faire le bouffon, tu me fais honte!* Stop acting like a clown! You're embarrassing me! (VM) <VM, Da84> <***Loc:*** VM, Da84>

bouffonner [bufɔ̃ne] *v.intr.* to clown, clown around, play the clown *Il est tout le temps après bouffonner. Il peut pas être sérieux.* He is always clowning. He can't be serious. (VM) <***Loc:*** VM, Da84>

bouffonnerie [bufɔ̃nri] *n.f.* buffoonery, clowning <***Loc:*** Da84>

bougali [bugali] *n.m.* [*offensive*] insulting name for an African American, a mulatto, or a Cajun <***Loc:*** Lv88>

bougeon ♦see **bougon**

bougie à feu [buʒiafø] *n.m.* spark plug <***Loc:*** SL>

bougillon [buʒijɔ̃] *n.m.* stub, small piece <***Loc:*** Da84>

bougon (**bougeon**) [bugɔ̃, buʒɔ̃] *n.m.* **1** stunted, badly formed ear of corn, small ear of corn with few grains **2** puny, paltry, rickety person <***Loc:*** SM, Da84, Lv88, Re31>

bougonnement [bugɔ̃nmɑ̃] *n.m.* grumbling <***Loc:*** Da84>

bougonner [bugɔ̃ne] *v.intr.* to grumble, complain *Ça vaut pas la peine bougonner.* It is not worthwhile complaining (JE) <***Loc:*** JE, LF, Da84>

bougonneur, -euse [bugɔ̃nœr, -øz] *n.* grumbler, complainer <***Loc:*** Da84>

bougre [bug(r), buk] *n.m.* man, guy, fellow, chap *C'était un jeune bougre massif.* He was a massive young man. (IB) ◊ **•bon bougre** good fellow *Celui-là, c'est un bon bougre.* He's a good guy. (Gu00) <Da84, Gu00> **•mauvais bougre** bad fellow <Da84> **•petit bougre** ***a*** little fellow ***b*** young fellow <Da84> **•vaillant bougre** nice man, nice fellow <Da84> <***Loc:*** AC, EV, IB, JE, LA, LF, SB, SL, SM, TB, Da84, Gu00, Hi02, Lv88>

bougresse [bugrɛs] *n.f.* young, unmarried woman known for having a 'wild side' <***Loc:*** VM, Da84>

bouillabaisse [bujabɛs] *n.f.* highly seasoned fish stew, bouillabaisse <***Loc:*** LF, Da84, Re31>

bouillage [bujaʒ] *n.m.* boiling *Tu connais quelque chose pour le bouillage des écrevisses?* Do you know anything about boiling crawfish? (VM) *Quand ça vient en bouillage, tu baisses ton feu.* When it starts boiling, you lower your fire. (VM) <***Loc:*** VM, Da84>

bouillant, -e [bujɑ̃, -ɑ̃t] *adj.* **1** boiling, very hot, scalding *Je tue les fromilles avec de l'eau bouillante.* I kill ants with boiling water. (EV) **2** teeming **La place est bouillante avec des rats.* The place is teeming with rats. (Da84) <***Loc:*** EV, Da84>

bouillanter ♦see **ébouillanter**

bouille [buj, boj] *n.f.* **1** cooking pot **2** kettle <***Loc:*** AC, AV, SB>

bouillée [buje] *n.f.* tuft, bundle (of stalks, branches) *Noncle a vingt-cinq bouillées de fèves plattes dans le jardin.* Uncle has twenty-five butter bean plants in his garden. (TB) <***Loc:*** TB, Lv88>

bouilleur [bujœr] *n.m.* ◊ **•bouilleur de sucre** [person] sugar boiler *Les Cubiens c'était les bouilleurs de sucre, et moi j'étais un travaillant pour eux.* The Cubans were sugar boilers, and I was one of their workers. (TB) <TB> <***Loc:*** TB>

bouilli [buji] *n.m./f.* **1** stew made of organ meat, often highly seasoned **2** boiled pork **3** boil ◊ **•bouilli d'écrevisses** crawfish boil <Hi02> <***Loc:*** AC, EV, JD, LF, Da84, Gu00, Hi02, Lv88>

bouillie [buji] *n.f.* pudding, (vanilla) custard *Une tarte à la bouillie.* Custard pie. (Lv88) ◊ **•bouillie au lait** pudding, custard (made of eggs, milk, flour or cornstarch, sugar, and flavoring), often used as filling for sweet dough pies or as food for the sick or convalescent <Lv88> <***Loc:*** EV, SL, VM, Da84, Gu00, Hi02, Lv88>

bouillir [bujir] (*p.p.* **bouilli** [buji], **bouillu** [bujy]) **I** *v.tr.* to boil *Ils bouillissaient la graine du mamou pour faire un thé.* They boiled the seeds of the coral tree to make tea. (Lv88) *Elle bouillait une racine de coton pour faire un thé.* She boiled a cotton root to make tea. (Lv88) *Tu peux les bouillir, les manger bouillies.* You can boil them, eat them boiled. (IB) *Tu bouilles ça jusqu'à ça vient manière mou.* You boil it until it becomes kind of soft. (AV) **II** *v.intr.* to boil *Moi, je me rappelle, la première chose ma mère faisait, elle y vidait de l'eau, brassait ça bien, puis mettait dans une chaudière, comme ça, et bouillir un bon bout de temps.* I remember, the first thing that my mother used to do [when she made a gumbo], she would empty the water into it [the roux], stir it well, and put it in a cooking pot to boil [for] a good long while. (SL) *Tu prendais tes linges quand ils aviont bouillu assez longtemps.* You would take out your clothes after they had boiled long enough. (AC) ◊ **•bouillir à gros bouillons** to boil briskly *La soupe était après bouillir à gros bouillons.* The soup was boiling briskly. (EV) <EV, Da84> **•bouillir de** to be teaming with *Ça bouille du monde là-dedans.* It's packed with people in there. (EV) <EV, Da84> **•ça fait bouillir sa chaudière** that makes him or her very angry <VM, La99> **•faire bouillir** to boil *Tu fais bouillir ton eau avant de mettre les chevrettes.* You boil your water before you put the shrimp in. (EV) <EV, Da84> <***Loc:*** AV, EV, IB, LA, LF, SL, SM, TB, VM, Da84, Hi02, La99, Lv88, Ph36>

bouilliture [bujityr] *n.f.* ◊ **•bouilliture de chevrettes** shrimp boil (a festive gathering at which large quantities of shrimp are boiled and served) *À la bouilliture de chevrettes il a pas beaucoup mangé. C'est parce qu'il est pas supposé de manger trop de chevrettes.* At the shrimp boil he didn't each much. It's because he's not supposed to eat too much shrimp. (TB) <TB> <***Loc:*** TB>

bouilloir [bujwar] *n.m.* boiler, container for boiling liquids *J'étais BOILER FIREMAN—ça chauffait huit gros bouilloirs.* I was a boiler fireman—they would heat eight big boilers. (EV) <***Loc:*** EV>

bouilloire [bujwar] *n.f.* **1** water kettle, kettle for boiling water *Une bouilloire—y'en a qui l'appelle ça des bombes—pour chauffer de l'eau.* A kettle—some people call them "bombes"—for heating water. (AC) **2** steam boiler used for heating houses *Une bouilloire c'est ça ils sert pour la chaleur de la maison. La bouilloire bouille l'eau et là l'eau chaude.* A boiler is what they use for heat in a house. The boiler boils water and then [you've got] hot water. (SB) **3** industrial steam boiler *T'avais des bouilloires dans la sucrerie, c'est avec du STEAM.* There were boilers in the sugar refinery, they ran on steam. (LF) <***Loc:*** AC, AV, EV, IB, IV, JD, LA, LF, SB, TB, VM, Da84, Re31>

bouillon [bujɔ̃] *n.m.* **1** bouillon, broth **2** abnormal discharge of female sex organs **3** semen <***Loc:*** AV, EV, SJ, SM, VM, Da84, Gu00>

bouillonner [bujɔ̃ne] *v.intr.* ◊ **•bouillonner de rage** to be very angry *Il bouillonnait de rage.* He was boiling mad. (VM) <SJ, VM, La99> <***Loc:*** SJ, VM, La99>

Bouki [buki] *n.prop.* Hyena, character who is the counterpart of Rabbit (Lapin) in creole folk tales <***Loc:*** Lv88>

boulaille ♦see **BULL-EYE**[1], **BULL-EYE**[2]

boulailler ♦see **BULL-EYE**[1]

boulanger [bulɑ̃ʒe] *n.m.* baker <***Loc:*** LF, Da84>

boulangerie [bulɑ̃ʒri] *n.f.* bakery or bakery shop ◊ **•les boulangeries se sont battues** there is frost on the ground <La99> <***Loc:*** Da84, Hi02, La99>

boule [bul] *n.f.* ball ◊ **•boule à nana {nénaine}** small mudball placed on a stick and thrown at a distance *Les enfants a sali la maison avec des boules à nana.* The children splattered the house with mudballs. (TB) <TB> **•boule de gomme** ball of gum <Da84> **•boule de neige** snowball <Da84> **•boule de pin** pine cone <Da84> **•boule de tactac** popcorn ball <TB> **•boule de terre** ball of dirt <Da84> **•boule d'olivier** fruit of the tupelo gum tree <Re31> **•avoir une boule sus le cœur** to be heartbroken in love <La99> <***Loc:*** AV, EV, TB, Da84, La99, Re31>

boulé ♦see **boulet**

bouledogue [buldɔg] *n.m.* bulldog <***Loc:*** SL, An94, Da84>

bouledou[1] [buldu] *n.m.* **1** imposing, officious person, one of overbearing disposition **2** bully *Ce gros garçon est rien qu'un bouledou.* That big boy is nothing but a bully. (LF) <***Loc:*** LA, LF, VM>

bouledou[2] ♦see **BULLDOZE, BULLDOZER**

bouledouze ♦see **BULLDOZE**

boulehed [bulɛd] *n.m.* bullhead fish <***Loc:*** JE>

boulet (boulé) [bulɛ, bule] *n.m.* **1** big, strapping man **C'est un boulet d'homme.* He is a big fellow. (Da84) **2** bully *Si quelqu'un disait c'était le boulé du lot, ils auraient été* *chercher n'oncle Joe.* If someone said it was the bully of the bunch, they would have gone to look for Uncle Joe. (SL) <***Loc:*** EV, SL, Da84>

bouleton [bultɔ̃] *n.m.* two-wheeled cart *Il y a une roue de cassée sus le bouleton.* There's a wheel broken on the cart. (TB) <***Loc:*** TB>

boulette [bulɛt] *n.f.* **1** meatball, dumpling, fish patty, croquette, etc. *Y a du monde qu'aime des boulettes de poisson armé, mais moi, j'aime mieux des boulettes de choupique.* Some people like patties of garfish, but I prefer mudfish patties. (Guoo) **2** ace (in a deck of cards) *Il a toujours la boulette de pique.* He always has the ace of spades. (IB) ◊ **•boulette de chevrette** shrimp cake <TB> **•boulette de crabe** crab cake <TB> **•boulette de genou** kneecap *Mes boulettes de genoux me fait mal.* My kneecaps hurt. (TB) <JE, TB, Lv88> <***Loc:*** IB, JE, LF, SM, TB, Da84, Guoo, Lv88>

bouleverse [bulværs] *n.* confusion ◊ **•mettre en bouleverse** to agitate, upset *La nouvelle m'a mis en bouleverse.* The news bowled me over. (Lv88) <Lv88> <***Loc:*** SM, Lv88>

bouleversement [bulværsmɑ̃] *n.m.* overturning, disorder <***Loc:*** Da84>

bouleverser [bulværse] *v.tr.* **1** to overturn, turn topsy-turvy, upset *Il a passé dans le magasin, il a tout bouleversé les balles de foins.* He went into the barn and he turned the bales of hay completely topsy-turvy. (VM) **2** to scold *Son père l'a bien bouleversé.* His father gave him a good scolding. (SB) <***Loc:*** LA, SB, VM, An94, Da84>

bouliner [buline] **I** *v.tr.* to churn up *Le bateau avec sa machine bouline l'eau du lac.* The boat with its motor churns up the water of the lake. (Lv88) **II** *v.intr.* to spin, whirl, turn around in circles *Son bateau boulinait dans la rivière.* His boat was turning in circles in the river. (VM) <***Loc:*** LF, VM, Lv88>

boulon [bulɔ̃] *n.m.* bolt, machine bolt <***Loc:*** AC, EV, JE, LF, TB, Da84>

boulonnage [bulɔ̃naʒ] *n.m.* **1** bolting, assembly of bolts *Le boulonnage dessus la machine est lâche.* The bolting on the motor is loose. (VM) **2** tightening of a bolt <***Loc:*** VM, Da84>

boulonner [bulɔ̃ne] *v.tr.* to bolt, bolt together *Ça ici c'est un* V-BOTTOM, *les courbes sont droites, pas droites, sur un biais, et là un* FLARE *comme ça, et là tu boulonnes les [courbes].* This one is a V-bottom, the ribs are straight, not straight, on an angle, and there's a flare like this, and you bolt down the ribs. (TB) <***Loc:*** LF, TB, Da84>

boulotte [bulɔt] *n.f.* ball ◊ **•boulotte de genou** knee cap <La99> <***Loc:*** La99>

boulotter [bulote] *v.intr.* **1** to work, turn **2** to be thriving, be prosperous, be full of activity *La ville boulotte.* The town is bustling. (AV) ◊ **•Comment ça boulotte?** How are you? How are things? <La99> <***Loc:*** AV, La99>

bouloune [bulun] *n.m.* balloon <***Loc:*** Da84>

boulouque [buluk] *n.m.* any spherical ornament <***Loc:*** SL>

boulvari [bulvari, bulbari] *n.m.* noise, racket, ruckus, din **I'z ont fait un boulvari juchequ'à ch'pouvais pas dôrmir.* They made such a ruckus that I couldn't sleep. (EV, Ph36) <***Loc:*** EV, JE, LF, Ph36>

boum [bum] *interj.* boom ◊ **•aller {faire} boum** [*baby talk*] to fall down *Fais attention, tu vas faire boum.* Be careful, you'll fall. (TB) <TB> <***Loc:*** SB, TB>

boumlala [bumlala] *n.m.* drinking spree, carousal <***Loc:*** LF>

bouqué, -e [buke] *adj.* pouting, sulking, peeved, irritated, angry *Il est bouqué après moi.* He's angry with me. (Lv88) <***Loc:*** Da84, Lv88>

bouquer [buke] **I** *v.intr.* to refuse, back down *Il bouque pas sur l'ouvrage.* He doesn't refuse work. (Lv88) **II se bouquer** *v.pron.* to pout, sulk, get peeved (at), get sore (at) ◊ **•se bouquer après** to refuse to talk to, keep away from <Da84> <***Loc:*** Da84, Lv88>

bouquet [bukɛ, buke] *n.m.* **1** bouquet, bunch of flowers *Bouquet de fleurs.* Bouquet of flowers. (SL) **2** flower *J'ai cassé ce bouquet dans la cour.* I picked this flower in the yard. (VM) **3** flower-bearing plant <***Loc:*** AV, EV, IB, SL, TB, VM, Da84, Lv88, Ph36, Re31>

bouquin [bukɛ̃, bukwɛ̃] *n.m.* goatee <***Loc:*** AV, EV, IB>

bourbé, -e [burbe] *adj.* muddy *Un choupique ça reste dans l'eau douce, et de l'eau bourbée, de la boue.* A mudfish lives in fresh water, and muddy water, mud. (LF) <***Loc:*** LF, SM>

bourber (se) [burbe] *v.pron.* to get muddy *Ils vont tout se bourber là.* They're going to get all muddy down there. (TB) <***Loc:*** TB>

bourbeux, -euse [burbø, -øz] *adj.* muddy *Depuis quelques années, l'eau dans ce bayou est bourbeuse.* Since a few years ago, the water in this bayou is muddy. (SL) <***Loc:*** EV, SL, Da84>

bourbier [burbje] *n.m.* **1** mud hole, mud puddle **2** puddle of water on the floor <***Loc:*** Da84>

bourbière [burbjær] *n.f.* mud hole *Il est tombé dans la bourbière.* He fell in the mud hole. (SB) <***Loc:*** SB>

bourdon [burdɔ̃] *n.m.* **1** bumblebee **2** any of a variety of bees or wasps ◊ **•bourdon de bois / bourdon de la maison** carpenter bee <Da84, Re31> **•bourdon de terre** ***a*** bumblebee that nests in the ground ***b*** green beetle <Da84, Re31> <***Loc:*** AL, IB, JE, LA, LF, SB, Da84, Re31>

bourdonnement (**bourgonnement**) [burdɔ̃nmɑ̃, burgɔ̃nmɑ̃] *n.m.* hum, buzz, humming, buzzing <***Loc:*** JE, LF, Da84>

bourdonner [burdɔ̃ne] **I** *v.tr.* to hum *Il marchait en bourdonnant une petite chanson.* He was walking while humming a little song. (LA) **II** *v.intr.* **1** to hum, buzz *Tu pouvais attendre les mouches à miel après bourdonner d'ici.* You could hear the bees buzzing from here. (LA) **2** to become angry *Il bourdonne beaucoup facile.* He gets mad easily. (AV) <***Loc:*** AV, LA, Da84>

bourgeois [burʒwa] *n.m.* landowner, proprietor, landlord *Quand le prix du coton a baissé, les bourgeois ont déguerpé leurs* *travaillants à la part.* When the price of cotton went down, the landowners evicted their sharecroppers. (VM) <*Loc:* VM, Da84>

bourgeon [burʒɔ̃] *n.m.* sprout, bud, shoot <*Loc:* Da84, Lv88>

bourgeonnement [burʒɔ̃nmɑ̃] *n.m.* budding <*Loc:* Da84>

bourgeonner [burʒɔ̃ne] **I** *v.tr.* to thin out sprouts at the roots of corn stalks *Bourgeonner le maïs.* To thin out the corn sprouts. (SL) **II** *v.intr.* **1** to bud *Les azélias bourgeonnent tard cette année.* The azaleas are budding late this year. (LA) *Les roses sont plus jolies juste après que c'est bourgeonné.* Roses are prettiest just after they are budded. (LA) **2** to sprout *Le maïs est pas encore bourgeonné.* The corn is not yet sprouted. (LA) <*Loc:* LA, SL, Da84>

bourgo (**bergo, beurgo**) [burgo, bɔrgo, bærgo, bœrgo] *n.m.* type of horn traditionally made of a conch shell <*Loc:* JE, SB, TB, Di32, Lv88>

bourgonnement ♦see **bourdonnement**

bourgonner (**bergonner, beurgoter**) [burgɔ̃ne, bærgone, bœrgote, bærgote, burgote, bɔrgote, byrgote] *v.tr.* to blow a conch shell horn *Il a bourgonné longtemps.* He blew the horn for a long time. (JE) *Alle appelle son mari dans le clos en beurgotant.* She calls her husband from the field by blowing a conch shell horn. (IB) <*Loc:* IB, JE, SB, Lv88>

bouri-boura [buribura] *n.m.* hubbub, great noise caused by a lot of people <*Loc:* AV>

bourilleau [burijo] *n.m.* noise, din *C'en est une, un bourilleau que t'emmènes.* You are certainly making a lot of noise. (LF) <*Loc:* LF>

bourlingue [burlɛ̃ŋ, burlɛ̃g] *n.f.* **1** smack, slap **2** mistreatment, abuse **3** scolding *Je l'ai entendu leur donner une bourlingue.* I heard him give them a scolding. (SB) <*Loc:* JE, LF, SB, Lv88>

bourlinguer [burlɛ̃ge, burlɑ̃ge] *v.tr.* **1** to mistreat, abuse *Il a bourlingué l'enfant de coups de pied.* He kicked the child repeatedly. (LF) **2** to scold *Il a bourlingué les enfants.* He scolded the children. (SB) **3** to force s.o. to do s.t. *Les enfants, il faut les bourlinguer pour ils parlent français.* Children, you have to force them to speak French. (Lv88) **4** to plead, beg *Il faut bourlinguer pour l'argent.* You have to beg for money. (IB) <*Loc:* IB, JE, LF, SB, Lv88>

bourouette ♦see **berouette**

bourrage [buraʒ] *n.m.* wadding, packing, tamping, stuffing <*Loc:* Da84>

bourrasque (**bourrasse**) [buras(k)] *n.f.* storm, squall, sudden heavy downpour <*Loc:* AV, IB, JE, LF, SB, SJ, TB>

bourrasse ♦see **bourrasque**

bourrasser [burase] *v.tr.* to mistreat, abuse **Son poupa l'a bourrassé trop, alors il a parti.* His dad mistreated him too much, so he left. (EV, Ph36) *Sa maîtresse d'école le bourrasse tout le temps.* His schoolteacher treats him badly all the time. (IB) <*Loc:* EV, IB, Lv88, Ph36>

bourre[1] [bur] *n.f.* **1** wad (esp. for a gunshell) **2** stuffing (e.g. of a chair) <*Loc:* LA, VM, Da84>

bourre[2] (**bourrée**) [bur, bure] *n.f.* name of a card game (known as 'bourrée' in English) *Il a perdu plus que cent piastres à jouer à la bourre.* He lost over a hundred dollars playing bourrée. (LA) <*Loc:* Da84, Hi02, Lv88>

bourreau [buro] *n.m.* **1** bully, tyrant, tormentor **2** criminal **3** mean, grouchy, ill-tempered person *J'aime pas ce bourreau-là.* I don't like that grouch. (IB) <*Loc:* EV, IB, SM, Da84, La99, Lv88, Ph36>

bourrée ♦see **bourre**

bourrelet [burlɛ, burle] *n.m.* roll, bread roll ◊ •**bourrelet aux mûres** blackberry roll <Re31> <*Loc:* Re31>

bourrer[1] [bure] **I** *v.tr.* **1** to stuff (a turkey, etc.) *Bourrer un dinde.* To stuff a turkey. (Da84) *On prenait les tripes de cochon, là on bourrait ça, on faisait du boudin.* We took the pig intestines, we stuffed them, we made boudin. (TB) *Chez Shucks' à 'Béville, ils servont les meilleures huîtres bourrées.* At Shucks' in Abbeville, they serve the best stuffed oysters. (Gu00) **2** to stuff, pad, upholster *J'aime m'assire dans une chaise bourrée.* I like to sit in an upholstered chair. (JE) **Bourrer un matelas.* To stuff a mattress. (Da84) **3** to tamp, ram, cram *On avait pour bourrer tous ces enfants dans un petit char.* We had to cram all those kids into a little car. (EV) **4** [taxidermy] to stuff *J'ai vu une spatule bourrée.* I saw a stuffed roseate spoonbill duck. (VM) **II se bourrer** *v.pron.* to stuff o.s. with food *Je m'ai bourré hier au soir. J'avais pas faim à ce matin.* I stuffed myself last night. I wasn't hungry this morning. (LA) ◊ •**bourré de** loaded with, full of *J'ai fait ça pour le Jazz Fest. Le Jazz Fest c'est du monde que tu vas jamais revoir, tu peux être bourré de menteries!* I did that [storytelling] for the Jazz Fest. The Jazz Fest is all people you'll never see again, you can be full of lies! (LF) <LF> <*Loc:* AC, EV, JE, LA, LF, SM, TB, VM, Da84, Gu00, Hi02, Lv88>

bourrer[2] (**embourrer**) [bure, ɑ̃bure] *v.tr.* to wrap, wrap up *J'ai été dans le lit, j'ai arraché le drap, je l'ai bourré dans le drap comme si qu'il avait froid.* I went to the bed, I pulled up the sheet, I wrapped him in the sheet as though he were cold. (TB) *Il a embourré les souliers.* He wrapped up the shoes. (LF) <*Loc:* LF, TB>

bourreuse [burøz] *n.f.* funnel (traditionally made of a sawed-off cow horn) used for stuffing sausage casing in making boudin <*Loc:* Da84>

bourrier (**brouillé**) [burje, bruje] *n.m.* **1** speck (in the eye, in water, etc.), foreign matter *Un brouillé dans l'œil.* A speck, cinder in the eye. (LF) **2** trash heap, garbage dump *Va jeter ça au bourrier.* Go throw that in the trash. (Lv88) <*Loc:* AV, LA, LF, SM, TB, Da84, Lv88>

bourrinque [burɛ̃k, burwɛ̃k] *n.f.* cart made from an auto chassis and wheels, buggy <*Loc:* AV>

bourrique[1] [burik] *n.f.* **1** female donkey **2** mule **3** very stubborn person ◊ **•faire la bourrique** to act stupidly or stubbornly <Da84> <***Loc:*** SL, Da84, Hi02, Lv88>

bourrique[2] [burik] *n.f.* navel, belly button <***Loc:*** TB>

bourriquet [burikɛ, burike] *n.m.* **1** donkey, jackass **2** mule <***Loc:*** IB, SL, Da84>

bourru [bury] *adj.* cross, moody, contrary, grouchy <***Loc:*** Da84>

bourrure [buryr] *n.f.* **1** stuffing (in furniture, clothing, etc.) **2** harness collar for a horse or mule <***Loc:*** LA, VM, Da84, Lv88>

bourse [burs] *n.f.* purse, sack of money <***Loc:*** Da84>

boursole [bursɔl] *n.f.* compass, mariner's needle <***Loc:*** AV, IB, SJ>

bousculade [buskylad] *n.f.* **1** overturning **2** jostling, pushing, shoving <***Loc:*** LF, SB, SM, Da84>

bousculailler [buskylaje] *v.tr.* **1** to overturn, upset, disturb *Il va tout bousculailler les meubles.* He's going to upset the furniture completely. (IB) **2** to shock, upset *La nouvelle m'a bousculaillé.* The news shocked me. (IB) <***Loc:*** IB>

bousculer (**busculer**) [buskyle, byskyle] **I** *v.tr.* to overturn, turn topsy-turvy, turn upside down *Il a tout bousculé sa chambre après chercher pour ses souliers noirs.* He turned his room completely upside down looking for his black shoes. (LA) **2** to jostle *Il les a busculés quand il entrait dans la salle.* He jostled them when he came into the hall. (LA) **3** to upset *Ça l'a busculé quand il a entendu cette nouvelle.* It upset him when he heard the news. (LA) **II se bousculer** *v.pron.* to jostle each other *Le monde pouvait pas se bousculer de trop dans ces temps ça dans les salles de danses. Ça voulait se battre.* People couldn't not jostle each other too much in those days in the dance halls. They wanted to fight. (LA) <***Loc:*** JE, LA, SM, Da84>

bousillage [buzijaʒ] *n.m.* **1** act or process of constructing (a wall, a chimney) with a mixture of mud and Spanish moss over a framework of wooden slats **2** mixture of mud and Spanish moss used in the construction of houses and chimneys <***Loc:*** SM, TB, VM, Da84>

bousillé, -e [buzije] *adj.* **1** constructed of bousillage (a mixture of mud and Spanish moss) *La vieille maison avait des murs bousillés.* The old house had bousillage walls. (LA) **2** smeared, streaked, soiled, muddy *T'es tout bousillé avec la boue.* You're all soiled with mud. (SM) *L'eau bousillée du bayou.* The dirty water of the bayou. (Lv88) <***Loc:*** EV, LA, SM, VM, Lv88>

bousiller [buzije] **I** *v.tr.* **1** to construct (a wall, a chimney) with a mixture of mud and Spanish moss over a framework of wooden slats *Ils avaient habitude de bousiller les vieilles maisons.* They used to fill the walls of old houses with a mixture of mud and moss. (LA) **2** to prepare bousillage *On bousillait de la mousse et de la boue pour faire la cheminée.* We prepared a mixture of moss and mud to make the chimney. (Lv88) **3** to dirty, mess up, smear (esp. with mud) *J'ai pour te bousiller la figure.* I need to smear your face [with paint]. (SB) **II se bousiller** *v.pron.* to smear, soil (one's face or clothing) with dirt *Je lui avais dit qu'il s'aurait tout bousillé s'il jouait déhors.* I had told him that he would have gotten all muddy if he played outside. (LA) <***Loc:*** LA, SB, TB, Da84, Lv88>

bousilleux, -euse [buzijø, -øz] *adj.* muddy *Le boghei était tout bousilleux quand ils ont arrivé à la maison après la pluie.* The buggy was all muddy when they arrived home after the rain. (LA) <***Loc:*** LA, VM>

boussole [busɔl, bysɔl, busrɔl] *n.f.* swelling, small bump (e.g. as produced by a mosquito bite) *J'ai des boussolles dans ma tête.* I have some small bumps on my head. (JE) <***Loc:*** JE, LF, SM, Lv88>

bout (**boute**) [bu, but] *n.m.* **1** small amount, bit (of time, distance or quantity) *Espère un bout.* Wait a bit. (VM) *Il reste un petit bout d'icite.* He lives a little way from here. (VM) *Après j'ai resté un bout de temps icite, moi j'ai tout le temps aimé le bois et puis icite c'était le paradis, n'avait presque pas du monde.* After I lived here for a while, I have always liked the woods and here it was paradise, there was almost no one. (SM) *J'ai cuit deux bouts de saucisses.* I cooked two pieces of sausage. (VM) **2** tip, point, end, extremity **Il va gratter avec ses grandes cornes. Ça prend quinze minutes, un petit yinquis, pour voler dessus le bout pour arriver à l'autre bout.* He will scratch with his big horns. It takes fifteen minutes, a little sparrow, to fly from one tip and arrive at the other tip. (EV, An94) *Tu amarres les deux bouts sur un sac.* You tie the two ends to a bag. (AC) *Pirogue [...] les deux boutes est pointu.* Pirogue . . . both ends are pointed. (JE) ◊ **•boute à boute** end to end <Da84> **•à bout** tired, worn out *Cet individu est à bout.* That individual is worn out. (SB) <SB> **•au bout de** at the end of, after (a period of time) *Au bout d'un an et un jour t'es supposé de DRAW du sang.* After one year and one day you are supposed to draw blood (JE) <JE> **•au bout de patience** at the end of one's patience <Da84> **•au bout du câble** at the end of one's rope *Il est au bout du câble.* He's at the end of his rope. (VM) <VM> **•au bout du chemin** at the end of the road <Da84> **•au bout du compte** finally, after all <Da84> **•au boute le boute** it's over with, there's nothing more to talk about <Lv88> **•avoir le boute courte** to have the short end <Da84> **•de bout en blanc** from one end to the other *Il a marché de bout en blanc.* He walked from one end to the other. (LF) <LF> **•d'un boute à l'autre** from one end to the other *Les jeunes il y en a plein que je connais pas, mais tout le monde, je peux te les nommer d'un boute à l'autre de la Pointe.* Young people, there are a lot of them that I don't know, but everyone (else), I can name them for you from one end of Pointe aux Chênes to the other. (TB) <Da84> **•un bon bout de temps** a good (long) while *Moi, je me rappelle, la première chose ma mère faisait, elle* *y vidait de l'eau, brassait ça bien, puis mettait dans une chaudière, comme ça, et bouillir un bon bout de temps.* I remember, the first thing that my mother used to do [when she made a gumbo], she would empty the water into it [the roux], stir it well, and then put it in a cooking pot, like that, to boil a good long while. (SL) <SL, Da84> **•un bon boute** ***a*** a good distance, quite a distance *Il reste un bon bout d'ici.* He lives quite a distance from here. (SM) ***b*** quite a while, rather long time *Il y a un bon bout que je l'attends.* It's been a rather long time that I've been waiting for him. (SM) <SM, Da84> **•un bout** a ways, a distance *Des fois, ils voulaient aller à la maison. Ça me trainait un bout jusqu'à je les tournais.* Sometimes, they [the mules] wanted to go to the house. They would drag me a ways away until I could bring them back. (SL) <SL> <***Loc:*** AC, EV, IB, JE, LA, LF, SB, SL, SM, TB,VM, An94, Da84, La99, Lv88>

boutaille (**boutaillon**) [butaj, butajɔ̃] *n.m.* small piece of anything, scrap *Ramasse ces boutaillons de pieux pour nettoyer la cour.* Pick up those pieces of wood to clean up the yard. (TB) ◊ **•des petits boutailles** little bits of things, odds and ends <Da84> <***Loc:*** TB, Da84>

boutaillon ♦see **boutaille**

bouteille [butɛj] *n.f.* **1** bottle **2** baby bottle **3** flask ◊ **•bouteille de bébé / bouteille à {de} lait** baby bottle <AV, LF, SM, TB, VM> <***Loc:*** AV, EV, JD, JE, LA, LF, SJ, SM, TB, VM, Da84, Hi02>

bouteiller ♦see **embouteiller**

boutique [butik] *n.f.* **1** any store or shop **2** grocery store **3** small specialized retail shop selling clothing, jewelry, crafts or knicknacks *Y a plein du monde de la France qui vient ici à ma boutique pour voir les souvenirs qu'on a de la paroisse, et eux-autres peut pas croire que je parle en français.* There are a lot of people from France who come here to my store to see the souvenirs that I have of the parish, and they can't believe that I speak French. (LF) **4** wardrobe, armoire, closet ◊ **•boutique de bijouterie** jewelry shop <LF> **•boutique de campagne** country store <SL> **•boutique de souliers** shoe shop <LF> **•toute la boutique** the whole shebang <Da84> <***Loc:*** AC, AV, EV, IB, IV, JD, LA, LF, SL, SM, TB, VM, Da84, Hi02, Lv88>

bouton [butɔ̃] *n.m.* **1** button (on clothing) **2** button (on a machine) **3** button (on a diatonic accordion) **4** bud (on a plant) **5** pimple **6** "button," bump on the skin of an alligator ◊ **•bouton d'argent** chrysanthemum <EV, Lv88> **•bouton de col** collar button <Da84> **•bouton de fièvre** fever blister <Da84> **•bouton de fleur** flower bud <Da84> **•bouton de poignet** cuff link <Da84> <***Loc:*** AL, AV, EV, JE, SL, TB, Da84, Hi02, Lv88>

boutonner [butɔne] **I** *v.tr.* to button *Boutonne ta chemise avant de sortir.* Button your shirt before going out. (LA) **II se boutonner** *v.pron.* to button (one's clothing) *Il s'a boutonné puis là il s'a tourné de bord.* He buttoned up and then he turned around. (LA) <***Loc:*** LA, Da84>

boutonnière [butɔ̃jær] *n.f.* **1** buttonhole **2** flower or small cluster of flowers worn on one's coat lapel <***Loc:*** Da84>

bouttine [butin] *n.f.* bootie <***Loc:*** VM>

bouture [butyr] *n.f.* cutting, slip for transplanting or grafting <***Loc:*** Da84>

boxe [bɔks, bɔsk] *n.f.* **1** boxing **2** boxing match <***Loc:*** Da84, Fa77, Lv88>

boxer [bokse, boske] *v.intr.* to box, fight with the fists *Mon père a boxé avec mon oncle à l'école.* My father boxed my uncle at school. (VM) <***Loc:*** VM, Lv88>

boxeur [bɔksœr] *n.m.* boxer <***Loc:*** Da84>

boy (**boyce**) [bɔj, bɔjs] *interj.* on boy!, wow!, gee! **Boy, mais il est fort!* Boy is he strong. (Da84) *Boyce, il pouvait manger des œufs et du* CORNBREAD*!* Boy, could he eat eggs and cornbread! (EV) <***Loc:*** EV, Da84>

boyau [bwajo, bojo] *n.m. (usu. pl.)* intestines, bowels ◊ **•boyau gras** rectum <IB> **•avoir les boyaux malades** to have dysentery or diarrhea <VM> <***Loc:*** IB, VM>

boycde ♦see **boy**

brac ♦see **bric**

bracage [brakaʒ] *n.m.* cocking (of a gun) <***Loc:*** Da84>

BRACE [bɹeⁱs, brɛs] *n.m.* orthopedic brace <***Loc:*** VM>

bracelet [braslɛ, brasle] *n.m.* bracelet <***Loc:*** EV, Da84>

braguer (**braquer**) [brage, brake] *v.intr.* to leave, depart, move *Il a bragué sur un autre bord.* He moved to another side. (VM) <***Loc:*** VM>

braguet [bragɛ, brage] *n.m.* diaper <***Loc:*** AV, IB, LF, SM>

braguette [bragɛt, braget, bradʒɛt] *n.f.* **1** fly, zipper (on trousers) **2** sanitary napkin, pad **3** diaper **4** primrose <***Loc:*** AV, SM, TB, VM, Da84, Re31>

brahma [brɑ̃ma, brɛ̃ma] *n.m.* Brahma (type of cattle) <***Loc:*** VM, Da84>

braillard, -e [brajar, -ard] *n.* cryer, crybaby, one who cries at the least provocation <***Loc:*** SM, Da84>

braille [braj] *n.f.* crying, bawling, weeping <***Loc:*** Da84>

brailler [braje] *v.intr.* to cry, bawl, weep *L'affaire est* GONE*, c'est pas la peine brailler.* It's over, there's no use crying. (AC) *J'ai vu mon pauvre père, il était fait prisonnier, pendant que ma mère, ma belle mère, elle braillait.* I saw my poor father; he was taken prisoner while my mother, my beautiful mother, she cried. (LA) ◊ **•brailler à chaudes larmes {haute tête / haute voix}** ***a*** to cry profusely ***b*** to cry out loud <VM, La99> **•brailler comme un petit bébé** to cry profusely <La99> <***Loc:*** AC, AL, AV, EV, IB, LA, SB, SL, SM, TB, VM, Da84, Hi02, La99, Lv88, Ph36>

braillerie [braj(ə)ri] *n.f.* bawling <***Loc:*** SL>

brailleur, -euse [brajœr, -øz] *n.* cryer, crybaby, one who cries at the least provocation <***Loc:*** AV, IB, SB, SL, SM, TB, Da84>

braise [brɛz] *n.f.* hot coal, ember <***Loc:*** SL, Da84, Hi02>

braiser [breze] *v.tr.* to braise *Braiser de la viande.* To braise meat. (LA) <*Loc:* LA, Da84>

braisier (brésier) [brezje] *n.m.* **1** brazier, live coals **2** quick, clear fire *Un beau brésier de feu.* A nice quick, clear fire. (VM) <*Loc:* SM, VM, Da84>

BRAKE [bɹe^{i}k] *n.m.* brake (e.g. of a car) <*Loc:* Da84, Lv88>

braline [bralin, parlin] *n.f.* ◊ **•mettre à la braline** to bleach clothes by putting them in direct sunlight *Mettre le linge à la braline.* To put the clothes out to bleach in the sun. (SM) <SM, Lv88> <*Loc:* SM, Lv88>

braliner [braline] *v.tr.* to bleach clothes by putting them in direct sunlight *J'ai braliné le linge.* I bleached the clothes in the sun. (SM) ◊ **•braliner au soleil** to bleach s.t. in the sun <SJ> **•braliner au serein** to bleach at night (e.g. silks, because the sunshine would yellow them) <SJ> <*Loc:* SJ, SM, Re31>

brancard [brɑ̃kar] *n.m.* **1** shaft (of a one-horse carriage, a stretcher) **2** either of two long wooden poles by means of which a horse or mule placed between them is harnessed to a buggy **3** temple (of eyeglasses) **4** stock (of cards that have not yet been dealt or played) *Peut-être que l'as de pique est toujours dans le brancard.* Perhaps the ace of spades is still in the remaining deck. (LA) <*Loc:* EV, LA, SL, SM, Da84, Lv88>

branchage [brɑ̃ʃaʒ] *n.m.* branches (collectively) <*Loc:* Da84>

branchailles [brɑ̃ʃaj] *n.f.pl.* branches, boughs <*Loc:* EV, LF, SL, SM, Da84, Lv88, Ph36>

branche [brɑ̃ʃ] *n.f.* **1** branch, limb (of a tree) **2** road or railroad spur **3** lineage, branch (of a family) <*Loc:* AC, AV, EV, TB, Da84, Hi02>

brancher [brɑ̃ʃe] *v.intr.* **1** to branch, branch out, branch off (as a road or stream) *Le chemin branche à droite.* The road branches off to the right. (Lv88) **2** to turn (off a road) *J'ai branché à droite.* I turned right. (SM) <*Loc:* LA, SM, Da84, Lv88>

branchu[1], -e [brɑ̃ʃy] *adj.* forked, branched *Mon copal est branchu à six pieds de la terre.* My gum tree is forked at six feet above the ground. (VM) <*Loc:* VM, Da84, Lv88>

branchu[2] [brɑ̃ʃy] *n.m.* wood duck <*Loc:* AL, IB, LF, SL, SM, TB, VM>

brandy [brɑ̃di, brɛ̃de] *n.m.* brandy <*Loc:* AV, Da84>

branle [brɑ̃l] *n.n.* cradle <*Loc:* AV>

branle-bas [brɑ̃lba] *n.m.* G-string *Il avait juste un petit branle-bas là, pas* MUCH. *Un pauvre petit caneçon, juste pour cacher l'affaire et puis c'est tout.* He just had on a little G-string, not much. A poor little pair of underwear, just to hide his thing and that's it. (TB) <*Loc:* TB>

braque [brak] *adj.* stupid *Il est assez braque, il comprend pas rien.* He's so stupid, he doesn't understand anything. (SM) <*Loc:* AV, SL, SM, TB, La99>

braqué, -e [brake] *adj.* **1** stubborn, headstrong **Mom, t'es joliment tête dure et des fois on arrive pas à comprendre pourquoi t'es si braquée.* Mom, you're really hardheaded and sometimes we can't understand why you're so stubborn. (ThCa: *La Douce Réunion*) **2** crazy, obsessed ◊ **•mal braqué** headed for trouble *Il est mal braqué.* He's headed for trouble. (VM) <VM> <*Loc:* IV, SM, VM, Da84, Lv88, ThCa>

braquer[1] [brake] **I** *v.tr.* to aim, level (a gun) *Il a braqué le fusil.* He aimed the shotgun. (VM) **II** *v.intr.* **1** to stand, place o.s. *Braque pas là.* Don't stand there. (VM) **2** to aim for *Elle est braquée droit pour icite.* She's aimed right for here. (IV) **III se braquer** *v.pron.* to place o.s. in a location *Il s'est braqué devant moi.* He planted himself in front of me. (Lv88) ◊ **•se braquer sur** ***a*** to be obsessed by *Il s'a braqué sur les chevaux de course.* He became obsessed with racehorses. (VM) ***b*** to sit astride *Se braquer sur une chaise.* To sit astride a chair. (LF) <LF, VM, La99> <*Loc:* EV, LF, SL, VM, Da84, La99, Lv88, Ph36>

braquer[2] ♦see **braguer**

braquette [brakɛt] *n.f.* wire staple <*Loc:* VM>

bras [bra] *n.m.* **1** arm **2** branch (of a road or stream) ◊ **•bras de lunette** temple (of eyeglasses) <VM> **•bras de pompe** pump handle <VM> **•bras dessus bras dessous** [bradsi-bradsu] arm in arm, on friendly terms *Ces deux là sont bras dessus bras dessous mais ça va pas durer longtemps.* Those two are on friendly terms but it won't last long. (TB) <TB> **•endessous du bras** armpit <VM> **•être le bras droite** to be very reliable, be one's right hand man, the person one counts on in time of need *C'est mon bras droite; je peux toujours compter dessus lui.* He's my right hand man; I can always count on him. (EV) <EV, Da84, La99> <*Loc:* AV, EV, LA, TB, VM, Da84, Hi02, Lv88>

braser [braze] *v.t.* to braze *Il a fait braser la chaudière.* He had the pot brazed (to repair it). (SM, VM) <*Loc:* SM, VM>

brassage [brasaʒ] *n.m.* stirring, mixing **•brassage de chaudière** stirring of a pot <Da84> <*Loc:* Da84>

brasse [bras] *n.f.* span of both arms fully extended (about 6 feet) ◊ **•à {en} brasse-corps** around the waist, in an embrace *Il l'a tenu à brasse-corps.* He held her by the waist. (JE) *Je l'ai tenu en brasse-corps.* I held her in an embrace. (VM) <EV, JE, LF, VM, Lv88, Ph36> <*Loc:* EV, JE, LF, SM, VM, Da84, Lv88, Ph36>

brassée [brase] *n.f.* armful ◊ **•brassée de bois** armful of wood <Da84> <*Loc:* SL, TB, Da84>

brassement [brasmɑ̃] *n.m.* stirring, mixing <*Loc:* Da84>

brasser [brase] *v.tr.* **1** to stir, mix (ingredients, food, beverages) *Tu mets une* CUP *de farine et une* CUP *de* COOKING OIL *et puis là tu le mets en dedans pour trente minutes et là tu le brasses de temps en temps.* You take a cup of flour and a cup of cooking oil, and then you put it inside for thirty minutes, and then you stir it from time to time. (SM) *Tu brassais ça avec les mains.* You would mix it with your hands. (AC) *Brasser le café.* To stir the coffee. (SM) **2** to beat (e.g. eggs)

3 to fluff up (a cornshuck mattress) **4** to shuffle (cards) *Brasse les cartes avant qu'on joue.* Shuffle the cards before we play. (SM) **5** to be 'up to,' occupied with *Quoi c'est tu brasses là?* What are you doing over there? (VM) **II** *v.intr.* to growl (of the stomach or intestines) *Tes boyaux brassont.* Your intestines are growling. (VM) *Mon ventre brasse.* My stomach is growling. (SM) **III se brasser** *v.pron.* to stir up *Il y a un mauvais temps qui se brasse dans l'est.* There's some bad weather stirring up in the east. (LA) ◊ **•brasser mer et larmes** ***a*** to cause misery and trouble *Ce garçon a brassé mer et larmes pour ses pauvres parents.* That boy has caused no end of grief for his poor parents. (EV) ***b*** to mess things up <EV, La99> **•comment ça se brasse?** how are you? how are things? how's it going ? <La99, Lv88> **•quoi (c'est) qui se brasse (là)?** what's happening? <Lv88> **•va brasser dans tes chaudières** mind your own business <Da84> <***Loc:*** AC, EV, IB, LA, SB, SL, SM, TB, VM, Da84, Hi02, La99, Lv88, Ph36>

brasseur [brasœr] *n.m.* beater ◊ **•brasseur d'œuf** hand-held egg-beater <VM> <***Loc:*** VM>

brassière [brasjær] *n.f.* bra, brassiere <***Loc:*** AV, SM, Da84, Lv88>

brave[1] [brav] *adj.* courageous, brave *T'es brave de travailler toute cette place tout seul.* You're brave to work this whole farm by yourself. (EV) <***Loc:*** EV, Da84, Lv88>

brave[2] [brav] *adv.* confidently **Si t'avais trente-cinq sous pour aller au bal dans ces temps ça-là, tu dansais brave.* If you had thirty-five cents to go to the dance in those days, you danced confidently. (An94) *Deux chevaux et puis tu tenais brave le bord. C'était une charrue ça et puis le cheval hâlait ça.* With two horses, you could be confident about staying on the edge. It was a plow and the horse would pull it. (EV) <***Loc:*** EV, An94>

braver [brave] *v.tr.* to brave, defy, face or face up to (danger) **Tu répondras, c'est Léonise qui brave tout, pour son amant.* You will answer that it is Léonise who braves everything for her lover. (ch: *O donne-moi ton casque, beau cruel*) <***Loc:*** Da84>

braveure [bravœr] *n.m.* **1** bravery, courage **2** gallantry *Toutes les femmes aiment son braveure.* All the women like his gallantry. (AV) <***Loc:*** AV>

brayette [brajɛt] *n.f.* short trousers, knee breeches <***Loc:*** AV, IB>

brazil ♦see **brésil**[1]

BREAST-CHAIN [brɛstʃe'n] *n.m.* breast chain, part of harness used to attach the singletree to the breast yoke <***Loc:*** EV>

BREAST-YOKE [brɛstjok] *n.m.* breast yoke, part of harness used to support the singletree <***Loc:*** EV>

brébis (**brebis**) [brebi] *n.f.* sheep, ewe <***Loc:*** IV, An94, Da84>

brèche [brɛʃ] *n.f.* notch, chip, nick (in a cutting edge) ◊ **•faire brèche** to make a breach or gap (in s.t.) (e.g. shooting at a flock of birds and killing many) <Da84> <***Loc:*** Da84>

brécher [breʃe, brəʃe] *v.tr.* to chip, nick *Il a bréché son égouine sur un clou.* He chipped his saw on a nail. (Lv88) <***Loc:*** EV, Lv88, Ph36>

bréchet (**breuchet**) [breʃɛ, breʃe, brœʃɛ, brœʃe] *n.m.* **1** breast bone of fowl **2** brisket (of beef) *Le bréchet, tu le mets dans un gombo févi.* Brisket, you put it in okra gumbo. (VM) <***Loc:*** VM, Da84, Lv88>

bréchure [breʃyr] *n.f.* **1** breach **2** notch, chip, nick **Il a fait einne grosse bréchure au couteau.* He put a big nick in the knife. (EV, Ph36) <***Loc:*** EV, SM, Lv88, Ph36>

bredasser ♦see **berdasser**

bref [brɛf] *adj.* short, brief, curt *Mon grand-père a tout le temps été bref.* My grandfather was always curt. (VM) <***Loc:*** VM, Da84>

brème[1] [brɛ̃m] *n.f.* eggplant (plant or fruit) <***Loc:*** AV, EV, IB, IV, JE, LF, SL, SM, TB, VM, Da84, Gu00, Hi02, Lv88, Ph36, Re31>

brème[2] [brɛ̃m] *n.m.* perch, any of various spiny-finned freshwater fish <***Loc:*** AL, AV, IB, JE, SM, VM>

brésier ♦see **braisier**

brésil[1] (**brazil**) [brezil, brazil] *n.* brown shrimp, Brazilian shrimp <***Loc:*** LF, TB>

brésil[2] [brezil] *n.m.* cassabanana, curuba, musk cucumber (type of gourd with a curved neck, used to make jam) <***Loc:*** TB>

bretelle (**bartelle, bertelle**) [brətɛl, bretɛl, bartɛl, bərtɛl, brotɛl] *n.m./f. (usu. pl.)* suspenders <***Loc:*** AV, LA, SM, VM, Da84, Lv88>

brèter [brete] *v.tr.* to be 'up to,' occupied with *Qui-ce tu brètes ici?* What are you doing here? (TB) <***Loc:*** TB>

breuchet ♦see **bréchet**

breuquin ♦see **broquin**

bric [brik] *n.* ◊ **•faire à la bric-brac** to do hurriedly, do in a slipshod way *T'es après faire cette couverte à la bric-brac.* You're making that quilt too hurriedly. (TB) <TB> **•de bric et de brac** up and down, here and there, on all sides *Ça se brasse de bric et de brac.* Things are getting stirred up all over the place. (TB) <TB> <***Loc:*** TB>

bricole [brikɔl] *n.f.* **1** shoulder strap used to pull or carry loads **2** breast collar of a harness **3** pair of suspenders *Sa bricole est cassée.* His pair of suspenders is broken. (SL) **4** *(usu. pl.)* suspenders <***Loc:*** AV, SL, Da84, Lv88>

bride [brid] *n.f.* **1** bridle **2** chellitis, a disease comprising sores at the corners of the mouth (once common among school children) ◊ **•(à) (la) bride abattue** at full speed, very rapidly and carelessly *Ce petit garçon courait à la bride abattue.* That little boy was running full speed. (EV) *Il l'a fait bride abattu.* He did it very quickly. (SB) <EV, SB, SM, La99> **•à la bride molle** very rapidly and carelessly <EV, La99> <***Loc:*** AV, EV, LA, SB, SM, VM, Da84, La99>

brider [bride] *v.tr.* **1** to bridle *Brider un cheval.* To bridle a horse. (LA) **2** to restrain (e.g. a horse) *Bride tes enfants.* Control your kids. (VM) <***Loc:*** LA, VM, Da84>

bridon [bridɔ̃] *n.m.* **1** bridle part of a complete harness (usu. equipped with side blinders) **2** bit, the part of a bridle that goes in the mouth of the horse or mule (usu. made of metal) **3** sore at the corner of the mouth <***Loc:*** AV, EV, LA, SL, VM, Da84>

brigand[1]**, -e** [brigɑ̃, -ɑ̃d] *adj.* **1** teasing **Ç'piti garçon est brigand.* That little boy is quite a tease. (EV, Ph36) **2** naughty, mischievous *Le petit garçon est brigand.* The little boy is naughty. (SB) **3** boisterous, restless, unruly, rowdy (of a child) *Elle est tellement brigande, je peux pas faire arien avec elle.* She's so boisterous, I can't do anything with her. (SM) *Les enfants sont trop brigands ensemble.* The children are too rowdy together. (SB) <***Loc:*** AV, EV, SB, SM, TB, Lv88, Ph36>

brigand[2] [brigɑ̃] *n.m.* **1** brigand, ruffian, vandal, robber, outlaw, gangster, pirate **2** mischievous child **3** unmanageable, undisciplined, unruly child ◊ **•les brigands de Lafitte** pirates <Lv88> <***Loc:*** AV, IB, LF, SL, Da84, Lv88>

brigandage [brigɑ̃daʒ] *n.m.* **1** plunder, brigandage, vandalism **2** misbehavior ◊ **•faire des brigandages** to misbehave *Ils s'ont comportés au commencement, mais à la fin ils ont commencé à faire des brigandages.* They behaved themselves at the beginning but at the end they started misbehaving. (SM) <SM> <***Loc:*** SM, Da84>

brigander [brigɑ̃de] *v.intr.* **1** to misbehave, make mischief *Les enfants à ma belle-sœur sont tout le temps après brigander.* My sister's children are always making mischief. (EV) **2** to carry on noisily (usu. said of children) *Les enfants ont brigandé jusqu'à j'étais prèque fou.* The children misbehaved noisily until they almost drove me crazy. (SM) **3** to create a disturbance *Il va brigander toute la nuit.* He'll create a disturbance all night. (SM) <***Loc:*** EV, SL, SM, Da84, Lv88>

brillance [brijɑ̃s] *n.f.* brilliance, brightness <***Loc:*** Da84>

brillant[1]**, -e** [brijɑ̃, -ɑ̃t] *adj.* **1** bright, brightly colored *Pourquoi les mâles brillent, et les femelles est toujours cachées? C'est pour quand y a des œufs, tu peux pas les voir si aisé. Alle est cachée, la couleur la cache. Tu peux voir, tous les femelles est bruns et le mâle est plus brillant.* Why are the males bright, and the females are always hidden? It's so that when there are eggs, you can't see them as easily. She is hidden, the color hides her. You can see, all of the females are brown and the male is brighter. (TB) **2** bright, shiny, shining, glittering, sparkling **Vous-autres vois la lune, comment ce qu'elle est brillante?* Do you see the moon, how it's shining? (IV, An94) **3** made of stainless metal or aluminum *Une chaudière... Il y a des noires et il y a des brillantes.* Cooking pots, there are black ones and there are metal ones. (EV) <***Loc:*** EV, IV, SL, TB, An94, Da84>

brillant[2] [brijɑ̃] *n.m.* **1** tinfoil, silver paper *On a pas de brillant sur des cigarettes asteur.* There's no tinfoil on cigarettes these days. (VM) **2** sequin, shiny metallic decoration for clothing <***Loc:*** VM>

brillantine [brijɑ̃tin] *n.f.* brilliantine <***Loc:*** Da84>

briller [brije] *v.intr.* **1** to shine, sparkle, glitter *La gelée le matin quand le soleil se lève, ça brille.* The frost in the morning sparkles when the sun shines on it. (VM) **2** to be brightly colored (of plumage) *Allons voir, on a le branchu, ça c'est un joli z-oiseau. C'est un mâle. Pourquoi les mâles brillent, et les fumelles est toujours cachées? C'est pour quand y a des œufs, tu peux pas les voir si aisé.* Let's see, we have the wood duck, that's a pretty bird. This is a male. Why are the males bright, and the females are always hidden? It's so that when there are eggs, you can't see them as easily. (TB) <***Loc:*** TB, VM, Da84, Hi02>

brimbale [brɛ̃bal] *n.f.* connecting rod (of a motor vehicle) <***Loc:*** VM>

brin[1] [brɛ̃] *n.m.* **1** blade (of grass) **2** straw (of a broom) ◊ **•brin d'herbe** blade of grass <Da84> **•un petit brin** a little bit *C'est un petit brin trop* NICE *pour moi.* It's a little bit too nice for me. (AC) *Donne-moi un petit brin de whiskey.* Give me a little bit of whiskey. (SM) *Mais il comprend un petit brin.* But he understands a little bit. (SL) *Elle est un petit brin plus vieille que moi.* She's a little bit older than me. (TB) *Il mettait un petit brin de sucre là-dessus.* He would put a little bit of sugar on it. (TB) *Un petit brin meilleur marché.* A little bit cheaper. (Lv88) *Tu payes un petit brin à la fois.* You pay a little at a time. (EV) <AC, EV, LA, SL, SM, TB, An94, Da84, Lv88> <***Loc:*** AC, EV, LA, SB, SL, SM, TB, An94, Da84, Hi02, Lv88>

brin[2] [brɛ̃] *n.m.* gauze, cheesecloth, very thin cloth **On faisait [la moustiquaire] avec du brin qu'on coudait ensemble.* We made the mosquito net with gauze that we sewed together. (Gr82) ◊ **•brin à bère** netting used to make a mosquito bar <TB> <***Loc:*** SB, SL, TB, Gr82>

brindezingues [brɛ̃dzɛ̃g, brɛ̃nzɛ̃ŋ] *n.pl.* ◊ **•aller aux brindezingues** to fall into poverty or decrepitude <Lv88> **•être dans les brindezingues** ***a*** to be drunk ***b*** to be in a bad mood *À matin, il est dans les brindezingues.* He's in a bad mood this morning. (Lv88) <LA, SM, La99, Lv88> **•prendre ses brindezingues** to act in an unbecoming manner, do foolish things <Lv88> <***Loc:*** LA, SM, La99, Lv88>

bringue [brɛ̃g] *n.f.* worthless, good-for-nothing, lazy girl <***Loc:*** TB>

brioche [brijɔʃ] *n.f.* bun, type of bread made with eggs <***Loc:*** Da84>

brique [brik] *n.m./f.* **1** brick **2** crushed brick used to scour floors *De la brique tendre.* Easily crushed brick. (EV) *Pour faire ce bois là venir propre là, fallait qu'on use de la brique. Fallait qu'on frotte de la brique sur le plancher.* To make the wood floors clean, we had to use crushed brick. We had to scrub the floors with crushed brick. (TB) *Dedans ce temps là fallait frobir à la brique. Il y avait pas de* RUG.

In those days we had to scrub with crushed brick. There was no carpet. (EV) ◊ •**brique de savon** bar of soap <EV, TB, VM, Da84> <***Loc:*** EV, SL, TB, VM, Da84>

briqué [brike] *n.* bastard file <***Loc:*** SM>

briquer [brike] *v.tr.* to spread powdered brick on floors to scour and clean them <***Loc:*** Da84>

briquerie [brikri] *n.f.* **1** brick kiln **2** brick-making **3** brickfield <***Loc:*** LF, SM, Lv88>

briquet [brikɛ, brike] *n.m.* rabbit dog <***Loc:*** SB>

briqueter [brikte] *v.tr.* to brick, cover with bricks *Ils ont briqueté sa maison cette semaine.* They bricked her house this week. (VM) <***Loc:*** VM, Da84>

brise [briz] *n.f.* breeze <***Loc:*** TB, Da84>

brise-fer (**brisfaire, brisefert**) [brizfær] *n.m.* one who tends to break things (intentionally or not), 'bull in a china shop' *Il est un vrai brise-fer.* He is a regular bull in a china shop. (JE) <***Loc:*** EV, IB, JE, LF, SB, SM, TB, Da84, Ph36>

brisefert ♦see **brise-fer**

briser [brize] **I** *v.tr.* to shatter, smash, break to pieces, crush **J'ai été chercher la hache pour briser la meule.* I went to get the ax to smash the grindstone. (LA, An94) **II** *v.intr.* to break, shatter *La vitre a brisé en morceaux.* The window shattered into pieces. (LA) <***Loc:*** JE, LA, SM, An94, Da84>

briset [brizɛ, brize] *n.m.* annex (to a house) *Il a bâti un briset à sa maison.* He built an annex to his house. (JE) <***Loc:*** JE, LF>

briseur [brizœr] *n.m.* one who tends to break things (intentionally or not), 'bull in a china shop' <***Loc:*** Da84>

brisfaire ♦see **brise-fer**

brisure [brizyr] *n.f.* break, fragment, crack (as in a brittle substance) <***Loc:*** Da84>

britchet [britʃɛ, britʃe] *n.m.* a vigorous rubbing of the scalp in play or in a fight <***Loc:*** LF>

brocantage [brokɑ̃taʒ] *n.m.* trading, bartering, swapping *Le brocantage des recettes, des remèdes faisait partie des visites des femmes.* Swapping recipes and remedies was part of women's get-togethers. (Lv88) <***Loc:*** Da84, Lv88>

brocanter [brokɑ̃te] **I** *v.tr.* to exchange, swap **Eine bande d'hommes était planté à l'entour après brocanter des contes de chasse.* A group of men were standing around swapping hunting stories. (Wh83) **II** *v.intr.* to trade, barter, swap *Je connais pas si eux aime trop brocanter. Eux veut leur argent.* I don't know if they like to barter too much. They want their money. (LA) <***Loc:*** JE, LA, Da84, Lv88>

brocanteur [brokɑ̃tœr] *n.m.* trader, barterer <***Loc:*** Da84>

broccoli [brokoli] *n.m.* broccoli <***Loc:*** SL, VM, Hi02>

broche [brɔʃ] *n.f.* **1** spit and skewer *Ça faisait cuire de la viande [...] Une broche de fer.* They would cook meat, an iron spit and skewer. (EV) **2** stringer (for fish) *On mettait nos poissons sur une broche avant qu'on avait des glacières.* We would put our fish on a stringer before we had ice chests. (LA) <***Loc:*** EV, LA, Da84>

brochée [broʃe] *n.f.* spitful, stringerful ◊ •**brochée de poissons** stringerful of fish <Da84> <***Loc:*** Da84>

brocher [broʃe] *v.tr.* to knit *Son beau lui a broché un* SWEATER FOR *sa fête.* Her boyfriend knitted her a sweater for her birthday. (LA) <***Loc:*** LA, Lv88>

brodage [brodaʒ] *n.m.* embroidery <***Loc:*** EV, TB, Ph36>

broder [brode] *v.tr.* to embroider *La vieille passait son temps à broder des oreillons pour ses petits-enfants.* The old woman spent her time embroidering pillowcases for her grandchildren. (LA) <***Loc:*** IB, LA, Da84>

broderie [brodri] *n.f.* embroidery <***Loc:*** Da84>

brodeur, -euse [brodœr, -øz] *n.* embroiderer, one who embroiders <***Loc:*** Da84>

brodure [brodyr] *n.f.* embroidery <***Loc:*** JE, LF, Lv88>

broguin ♦see **broquin**

BROKE (**broque**) [broᵘk, brɔk] *adj.* broke, penniless *"Quand un va* RUN BROKE,*" il dit, "les autres va lui prêter."* "When one will run broke," he said, "the others will lend to him." (IB) <***Loc:*** IB, SB, TB, Da84, Lv88>

BROKER [brokœr] *n.m.* broker <***Loc:*** SB>

bronche [brɔ̃ʃ, brɔ̃ʒ] *n.f.* lung, either of the two bronchi or conduits of the lungs <***Loc:*** LF>

bronchite (**bronchue**) [brɔ̃ʃit, brɔ̃ʃy] *n.f.* bronchitis <***Loc:*** VM, Da84>

bronchue ♦see **bronchite**

bronque [brɔ̃k] *adj.* wild (of a horse) *Un cheval bronque.* A wild horse. (AV) <***Loc:*** AV, Lv88>

broque[1] [brɔk] *n.f.* gang ◊ •**tout la broque** the whole gang *Je peux dire j'ai élevé mon frère aussi. J'ai élevé tout la broque.* I can say I raised my brother too. I raised the whole gang. (TB) <TB> <***Loc:*** TB>

broque[2] ♦see BROKE

broquette [brokɛt] *n.f.* tack ◊ •**broquette à doigt** thumbtack <VM> <***Loc:*** VM, Da84>

broquin (**breuquin, broguin**) [brokɛ̃, brøkɛ̃, brogɛ̃] *n.m.* **1** half-boot, ankle-boot, laced boot **2** heavy work shoe <***Loc:*** AV, EV, IB, Lv88, Ph36>

brossage [brosaʒ] *n.m.* brushing <***Loc:*** Da84>

brosse [brɔs] *n.f.* **1** brush **2** paintbrush ◊ •**brosse à cheveux {de tête}** hairbrush <SL, Da84> •**brosse à dents** toothbrush <SL, Da84, Hi02> •**brosse à habits {linge}** clothes brush <SL, Da84> •**brosse à souliers** shoe brush <Da84> <***Loc:*** EV, LA, SL, Da84, Hi02>

brosser [brose] **I** *v.tr.* **1** to brush **Puis dans le temps, le bougre avait un beau cheval. Il avait une belle queue et il brossait ce crin et puis c'était soigné comme tu soignes ton char aujourd'hui.* And in those days, the fellow had a beautiful horse. It had a beautiful tail and he brushed that horse hair and it was cared for like you care for your car today. (SL, An94) **2** to scrub *Mon mari a tout arrangé, il l'a brossé.* My husband cleaned everything, he scrubbed it. (SL) **II se brosser** *v.pron.* to brush o.s. *Compère Chaoui s'a brossé* *avant le bal.* Compère Chaoui brushed himself before the dance. (VM) ◊ **•se brosser les cheveux** to brush one's hair <Da84> **•se brosser les dents** to brush one's teeth **J'ai vu il y avait deux maringouins de Texas qu'étaient après se brosser les dents avec des lattes de mon jardin.* I saw there were two mosquitoes from Texas that were brushing their teeth with pickets from my garden. (EV, An94) <EV, An94> <***Loc:*** EV, SL, VM, An94, Da84>

brosseur [brosœr] *n.m.* ◊ **•brosseur du portrait** touch-up artist *J'ai un bon ami qui travaillait dans les portraits des années passées, tu parles d'un brosseur du portrait, il peignait des portraits aussi.* I have a good friend who worked in photographs years ago, you talk about a touch-up artist, he painted pictures also. (VM) <VM> <***Loc:*** VM>

broucheter [bruʃte] *v.tr.* to work too hurriedly, spoil one's work *Il a tout broucheté ça il faisait.* He spoiled all that he did. (VM) <***Loc:*** VM>

brouette ♦see **berouette**

brouillard [brujar] *n.m.* **1** fog **2** haze, mist **3** blotter <***Loc:*** LA, LF, SB, Da84>

brouillasse [brujas] *n.f.* fog <***Loc:*** TB>

brouille [bruj] *n.f.* **1** misunderstanding, falling out, estrangement **2** trash <***Loc:*** JE, Da84>

brouillé ♦see **bourrier**

brouillé, -e [bruje] *adj.* **1** foggy *Les vitres étaient tout brouillées.* The windows were all foggy. (LA) **2** misty *C'était un temps manière brouillé, bonne heure le matin sur le bord du marais.* The weather was a bit misty, early in the morning on the edge of the swamp. (LA) **3** blurred *Tu peux pas les voir trop bien. Le portrait est manière brouillé.* You can't see them very well. The photograph is kind of blurred. (LA) **4** estranged, not on speaking terms *Ils ont eu une dispute pour une vache qu'avait cassé une barrière, et ils ont resté brouillés pour des années après ça.* They had an argument over a cow that had broken a fence, and they remained estranged for years after that. (LA) <***Loc:*** LA, Da84>

brouiller [bruje] **I** *v.tr.* **1** to fog up *Le temps frais a brouillé le miroir dans le camp.* The cool weather fogged up the mirror in the camp. (LA) **2** to confuse, blur *J'avais bu un peu et ça m'avait manière brouillé l'idée.* I had drunk a bit and it had sort-of blurred my senses. (LA) **3** to cloud up, get cloudy (of water, of vision) **II se brouiller** *v.pron.* **1** to become foggy (of the weather, eyeglasses, etc.) *Ma montre se brouille dans le temps froid.* My watch fogs up in cold weather. (LA) **2** to feud, have a falling out, get at odds (with each other) *Ils s'ont brouillé pour pas plus de tracas que ça.* They fell out for no other reason than that. (LA) <***Loc:*** LA, TB, Da84>

broussailles [brusaj] *n.f.pl.* trash *Ramasser les broussailles dans la cour.* To pick up the trash in the yard. (AV) <***Loc:*** AV>

brozine [brozin] *n.f.* sales tax token <***Loc:*** SL>

bru [bry] *n.f.* daughter-in-law <***Loc:*** VM>

bruit [bry, brɥi] *n.m.* noise, sound, din, racket <***Loc:*** TB, Da84>

brûlable [brylab(l)] *adj.* burnable *Il m'a vendu du bois qu'était pas brûlable.* He sold me some wood that was not burnable. (LA) <***Loc:*** LA, Da84>

brûlage [brylaʒ] *n.m.* burning <***Loc:*** Da84>

brûlant, -e [brylɑ̃, -ɑ̃t] *adj.* burning hot, torrid *Touche pas la grille. C'est toujours brûlant.* Don't touch the grill. It's still hot. (VM) <***Loc:*** VM, Da84>

brûlé [bryle] *n.m.* **1** burning smell, burnt smell **Ça sent le brûlé.* It smells burned. (Da84) **2** burnt part of a wood or forest **3** small natural dike or embankment, esp. in the eastern portion of the Atchafalaya basin **4** clearing in the woods (typically produced by burning) **Ça se fait, il a été dans le brûlé, ayoù il y avait pas d'herbe.* So he went into the burned clearing, where there was no grass. (IB, An94) <***Loc:*** IB, An94, Da84, Lv88>

brûlée [bryle] *n.f.* whipping, thrashing <***Loc:*** SB, La99>

brûlement [brylmɑ̃] *n.m.* heartburn, burning sensation ◊ **•brûlement d'estomac** heartburn <Da84> <***Loc:*** Da84>

brûler [bryle] **I** to burn, scorch, singe *Il faut pas la laisser brûler.* You must not let it [the roux] burn. (SL) **Il est mort en mangeant de la viande de mulet brûlée.* He died from eating burned mule meat. (EV, An94) **2** to irk, annoy, irritate *Ça me brûle.* That irks me. (SM) **II** *v.intr.* to be burned, burn, be on fire **Tu connais quand le feu était bien après brûler, il y avait une grosse buche en arrière, une vieille petite chaudière avec un petit peu du thé de sassafras.* You know, when the fire was burning well, there was a big log in the back, a little old pot with a little bit of sassafras tea. (VM, An84) **III se brûler** *v.pron.* to burn o.s., scorch o.s. *Je m'ai bien brûlé sur la grègue.* I really burned myself on the coffee pot. (LA) ◊ **•brûler la chandelle aux deux bouts** ***a*** to throw away one's fortune ***b*** to have too many things to do, 'burn the candle at both ends' <VM, La99> **•se faire brûler** to get o.s. burned *Il va se faire brûler si il fait pas plus attention.* He's going to get himself burned if he doesn't pay any more attention. (LA) <LA, Da84> <***Loc:*** EV, LA, SL, SM, VM, An84, An94, Da84, Hi02, La99>

brûlis [bryli] *n.m.* **1** remains of a fire **2** land that has been cleared by burning after a harvest <***Loc:*** TB, Da84>

brûlot[1] [brylo] *n.m.* gnat <***Loc:*** LF, SL, SM, TB, Da84, Lv88>

brûlot[2] [brylo] *n.m.* carmelized sugar <***Loc:*** Da84>

brûlure [brylyr] *n.f.* **1** burn **2** scald <***Loc:*** Da84>

brumas [bryma] *n.m.* light rain, drizzle <***Loc:*** LA, VM, Lv88>

brumassant, -e [brymasɑ̃, -ɑ̃t] *adj.* rainy, misty *Un temps brumassant.* Misty weather. (VM) <***Loc:*** VM, Da84>

brumasser [brymase] *v.intr.* to mist, rain lightly on and off, drizzle *Ça brumasse un peu, mais la pluie tombe pas fort.*

It's drizzling a little, but the rain is not coming down hard. (SM) <*Loc:* AV, IB, SM, VM, Da84, Gu00>

brun, -e [brɛ̃, brœ̃, bryn] *adj./n.* brown (color) *Elle s'a acheté un sofa brun.* She bought herself a brown sofa. (EV) ◊ **•faire brun** to get dark (at dusk) *Il commence à faire brun.* It's beginning to get dark. (SM) **Et là, quand nous-autres, on a arrivé à eux, ça commençait juste à faire bien, bien brun.* And then, when we reached them, it was just getting real dark. (LA, An94) <EV, LA, SM, TB, An94, Da84, Ph36> <*Loc:* AV, EV, LA, SL, SM, TB, An94, Da84, Lv88, Ph36>

brunâtre [brynat(r)] *adj.* brownish *Elle avait un capot manière brunâtre.* She had a coat that was kind of brownish. (LA) <*Loc:* LA, Da84>

brune [bryn] *n.f.* **1** dusk **2** brunette, brown-haired woman ◊ **•à la brune** at dusk **Et l'après-midi, proche au soleil-couché, ça revenait à la brune.* And in the afternoon, almost at sunset, they would come back at dusk. (EV, An94) <EV, An94, Da84> **•la brune est arrivée** night has fallen <Da84> <*Loc:* EV, An94, Da84, Lv88>

brunesir [brynzir] **I** *v.intr.* to brown, to make brown *Brunesir de la viande, un roux.* To brown meat, a roux. (Lv88) **II se brunesir** *v.pron.* to tan *Se brunesir dans le soleil.* To tan oneself in the sun. (Lv88) <*Loc:* Lv88>

brunette [brynɛt] *n.f.* brunette, brown-haired woman *Il pouvait choisir de une blonde ou une brunette.* He could choose between a blond and a brunette. (AV) <*Loc:* AV>

brut[1] (**brute**) [bry, bryt] *adj.* **1** not cleaned (of a fish) *Le poisson brut quarante sous, cinquante sous la livre et puis là nettoyé cinq piastres la livre.* The fish which is not cleaned is forty, fifty cents a pound and then cleaned, five dollars a pound. (SM) **2** rude, brutish, coarse, rough *Les Marais Bouleurs étaient bruts.* The men from Marais Bouleur were brutish. (LA) **3** rough, difficult *C'était joliment brute dans ces temps ça.* It was pretty rough in those days. (SL) **4** wild, savage, undomesticated *Il a coreillé le cheval brut.* He corralled the wild horse. (VM) *Les enfants sont bruts.* The children are wild. (VM) <*Loc:* LA, SL, SM, VM, Da84, Hi02>

brut[2] [bry] *n.m.* stupid person <*Loc:* TB>

brut[3] (**brute**) [bry, bryt] *adv.* brutally, coarsely, cruelly, roughly **Ça fait, elle parlait un peu brute.* So she spoke a bit brutally. (LA, An94) <*Loc:* LA, An94>

brutal, -e [brytal] *adj.* rough, cruel, brutal *Cette femme était brutale après ses esclaves.* That woman was cruel to her slaves. (VM) <*Loc:* VM, Da84>

brutaliser [brytalize] *v.tr.* to brutalize, mistreat, bully *Ils étaient après le brutaliser, le pauvre bougre.* They were brutalizing him, the poor fellow. (SL) <*Loc:* SL, Da84>

brutalité [brytalite] *n.f.* brutality, mistreatment, outrage *Ils ont eu pour souffert des brutalités.* They had to suffer outrages. (LA) <*Loc:* LA, Da84>

brute ♦see **brut**

buberon ♦see **biberon**

bûchailler [byʃaje] *v.tr.* **1** to chop, chop at *J'ai bûchaillé quelques billes de bois.* I chopped at a few logs. (VM) **2** to beat, whip (a person) *Ils ont bûchaillé ce pauvre enfant jusqu'à il a quitté la maison.* They beat that poor child until he left home. (LA) <*Loc:* AV, LA, SB, SL, SM, VM, Da84, Lv88>

bûche [byʃ] *n.f.* **1** short section of a log or large branch **2** stupid, dull, heavy person <*Loc:* IV, LA, Da84, La99>

bûchée [byʃe] *n.f.* reprimand, punishment, whipping, beating <*Loc:* EV, SM, Lv88, Ph36>

bûcher[1] [byʃe] **I** *v.tr.* **1** to fell (a tree) **2** to chop (wood) *Ils sont en arrière du magasin après bûcher du bois pour l'hiver.* They're behind the barn chopping wood for the winter. (LA) **3** to beat, beat up, strike, whip *Quand on parlait français, la maîtresse nous bûchait.* When we spoke French, the schoolmistress beat us. (Lv88) *Il était tout le temps après tchincailler ces bougres-là. Et puis ils s'ont mis ensemble et ils l'ont bûché.* He was always teasing those guys. And they got together and they beat him up. (LA) **4** to interrogate *Nous-autres on les bûchait pas.* We did not interrogate them. (IB) **II se bûcher** *v.pron.* to beat each other *Ça se bûchaient tout les samedis soirs jusqu'à que Joe Hanks a arrivé.* They would beat each other up every Saturday night, until Joe Hanks got there. (LA) ◊ **•bûche ça à coups de bâton! / bûche ça avec une chaîne!** I'm so angry about that! <AC, LA, VM, La99> **•le Bon Dieu descend pas pour bûcher** [proverbial] justice is not always immediate, but it will prevail in the end <La99> <*Loc:* AC, AV, EV, IB, LA, SB, SL, SM, VM, Da84, Gr82, Hi02, La99, Lv88, Ph36>

bûcher[2] [byʃe] *n.m.* wood pile <*Loc:* Da84, Lv88>

bûcherie [byʃri] *n.f.* **1** group who cuts wood (often coming together to help s.o. else) **2** whipping **Il a été, il s'a couché de ça-là, de cette bûcherie ils l'aviont fait-là. Et ils l'ont bûché juste parce qu'il jouait de l'accordéon.* He went to bed from there, from that whipping that they gave him. And they whipped him just because he played the accordion. (LA, An94) <*Loc:* LA, An94, Lv88>

bûcheur [byʃœr] *n.m.* **1** woodcutter, lumberjack **2** one who beats others ◊ **•bûcheur de bois** woodcutter <SM, TB> <*Loc:* AV, EV, IB, JE, LF, SL, SM, Da84, Lv88, Ph36>

buffalo[1] (**boffalo**) [byfalo, boflo] *v.tr.invar.* to fool *Il l'a buffalo pour proche tout son argent.* He fooled him for almost all his money. (LA) <*Loc:* EV, LA, Ph36>

buffalo[2] (**bœufalo**) [byfalo, boflo, bofalo, bøfalo] *n.m.* buffalo <*Loc:* EV, JE, LF, SL, SM, TB, Da84, Lv88, Ph36>

buffet [byfɛ, byfe] *n.m.* **1** buffet, sideboard **2** self-service meal, buffet <*Loc:* EV, An94, Da84>

buis [bɥi] *n.m.* hedge, boxwood, privet <*Loc:* Da84>

bulbe [bœlb] *n.m.* bulb, lightbulb <*Loc:* AV, Da84>

BULLDOZE (**bouledou, bouledouze**) [buldoᵘz, buldoz, buldu, bulduz, buduz] *v.tr.invar.* **1** to bulldoze *Ils ont éclairci le terrain, ils ont tout bouledouze les chousses.* They cleared out the land, they bulldozed all the stumps. (VM) **2** to brow-beat, bully, intimidate, tyrannize *Il les a tout bouledous, lui tout seul.* He intimidated them all by himself. (LA) **3** to command, direct, boss *Alle veut bouledou tout quelque chose.* She wants to direct every single thing. (VM) **4** to fool, deceive **I m'a bouledouze ç'coup-là.* He deceived me that time. (EV) <*Loc:* EV, LA, SL, TB, VM, Da84, Lv88, Ph36>

BULLDOZER (**bouledou**) [buldo^{u}zə, buldu] *n.m.* bulldozer <*Loc:* Da84, Lv88>

BULL-EYE[1] (**boulaille, boulailler**) [bulaɪ, bulaj, bulaje] *v.tr. invar.* to hunt at night with the aid of a powerful light *À soir, on va BULL-EYE les guernouilles.* Tonight, we're going to hunt frogs. (Lv88) <*Loc:* LF, Lv88, Re31>

BULL-EYE[2] (**boulaille**) [bulaɪ, bulaj] *n.m.* **1** flashlight **2** bright flashlight or headlamp used for hunting (e.g. bullfrogs) at night <*Loc:* JE, LF, TB, VM, Lv88>

bûmé ♦see **abîmé**

bûmer ♦see **abîmer**

burbuquin ♦see **birebiquin**

bureau [byro] *n.m.* **1** desk, bureau **2** chest of drawers **3** department (in government) <*Loc:* Da84, Lv88>

burgau [byrgo] *n.m.* clam <*Loc:* Da84>

BUS (**bus**) [bʌs, bɔs, bys] *n.m.* bus <*Loc:* AC, LF, SL, TB, Da84, Lv88>

busculer ♦see **bousculer**

bushel ♦see **bouchelle**

business (**biznisse**) [biznɛs, biznis, bisnis] *n.m.* **1** business, occupation, affairs *J'ai du biznisse en ville.* I have some business in town. (JE) **2** business *Et on a fait un après-midi avec du monde qui courait un petit biznisse dans le village.* And we spent an afternoon with people who ran a small business in the village. (TB) **3** business, concern *Ça c'est mon business, pas le tien.* That's my business, not yours. (SM) <*Loc:* EV, JE, LF, SL, SM, TB, VM, Lv88, Ph36>

BUSTER [bos, bostə] *n.m.* double plow <*Loc:* AC, EV>

but [by] *n.m.* **1** objective, target, aim, purpose, goal, mark **Quel est le but?* What's the purpose? (Da84) **2** base (in games or sports, e.g. baseball) *Premier BASE.* First base. (LF) *Deuxième BASE.* Second base. (LF) **3** hunter's blind ◊ **•d'un but en blanc** suddenly <SM> <*Loc:* IB, LA, LF, SM, Da84>

BUT [bʌt, bøt] *conj.* but **On dirait, c'est manière drôle de dire ça, BUT supposé ça a arrivé.* One would say that it is kind of strange, but supposedly it happened. (SL, An94) <*Loc:* JE, SL, TB, An94>

butage [bytaʒ] *n.m.* stumbling <*Loc:* AV, Da84>

buté, -e [byte] *adj.* balky, stubborn <*Loc:* Da84>

buter (**abuter**) [byte, abyte] **I** *v.intr.* **1** to stumble, trip *J'ai buté sur la chaise.* I tripped on the chair. (SM) **2** to meet accidentally, run into *Je pensais pas le voir, mais j'ai buté sur lui au SHOW.* I didn't think I'd see him, but I ran into him at the show. (SM) **II se buter** *v.pron.* to stumble, trip *Il s'est abuté après le chicot.* He stumbled on the stump. (AV) <*Loc:* AV, SM>

butin [bytɛ̃] *n.m.* **1** furniture **2** household belongings (incl. furniture, clothing, etc.) *Quand sa maison a brulé, il a perdu tout son butin.* When his house burned down, he lost all his household belongings. (SM) **3** merchandise, provisions, goods <*Loc:* AV, EV, IB, JE, LF, SB, SJ, SL, SM, TB, Da84, Lv88, Ph36, Re31>

butor [bytɔr] *n.m.* American bittern (locally called sungazer) <*Loc:* Re31>

buttage [bytaʒ] *n.m.* mounding or banking of dirt <*Loc:* Da84>

butte [byt] *n.f.* **1** mound, hill, elevation, high ground **2** pile, heap *Une butte (de) patates, une butte de terre, une butte de rat musqué.* A heap of potatoes, a pile of earth, a muskrat pile. (Lv88) ◊ **•butte à rat / butte de rat musqué** muskrat house <LF, TB, Re31> **•butte de {à} patates** mound of potatoes covered with straw and dirt for winter storage <LF, SL, SM, VM> **•par-dessus les buttes** somewhat, partially *Il comprend le français par-dessus les buttes.* He understands French somewhat. (Lv88) <Lv88> <*Loc:* LF, SL, SM, TB, VM, Da84, Gu00, Hi02, Lv88, Re31>

butter [byte] *v.tr.* to earth up, bank up, store (e.g. potatoes) in mounds **Butter les patates.* To bank up potatoes. (Da84) <*Loc:* Da84>

buvable [byvab(l)] *adj.* drinkable, fit to drink *Le whisky qu'ils nous ont donné était pas buvable.* The whiskey they gave us was not drinkable. (LA) <*Loc:* LA, Da84>

buveur [byvœr] *n.m.* drunkard, heavy drinker ◊ **•buveur de lait** one who does not drink alcohol, 'teetotaler' <La99> <*Loc:* AL, EV, Da84, Hi02, La99>

BYE-BYE [baɪbaɪ, babaj] *interj.* good-bye ◊ **•BYE-BYE le chaland** used to express disappointment when having lost or broken s.t. <Lv88> **•faire BYE-BYE** ***a*** to say bye-bye *Fais BYE-BYE à nonc Joe, cher.* Say bye-bye to Uncle Joe, honey. (SM) ***b*** to greet, wave at *Des fois alle passe dans le char et me fait BYE-BYE.* Sometimes she passes in the car and waves to me. (VM) <SM, VM> <*Loc:* SM, VM, Lv88>

C

ça[1] [sa] *pron.* **1** *(in impersonal expr.)* it *Ça fait chaud.* It's hot. (SM) *Ça mouille dehors.* It's raining outside. (SM) **2** *(subj.)* he, she, it *Alle est avec eusse asteur parce qu'alle est malade un petit peu. so alle couche là. Ça a quatre-vingts-six ans.* She is with them now because she is a bit sick. So, she sleeps over there. She is eighty-six years old. (LF) *La peau sus la chaise s'a tendu à mesure que ça chessait.* The skin on the chair tightened as it dried. (VM) **3** *(subj.)* they *Ça parlait en anglais, et si ça voulait pas les enfants connaît quoi c'était après dire, ça parlait en français.* [Normally] they would speak English, but if they did not want the children to know what they were talking about, they spoke French. (AC) **4** *(obj. of prep.)* him, her, it *Je voudrais pas être marié avec ça. Elle est trop obligeante.* I wouldn't want to be married to her. She is too demanding. (EV) <***Loc:*** AC, AV, EV, LF, SM, TB, VM, Da84, La99, Lv88>

ça[2] [sa] *pron.interrog.* what? *Ça tu dis?* What did you say? (Lv88) *Ça i-n-a?* What's the matter? (SM) *Ça i-n-a avec toi!* What's with you! (SM) *Ça tu veux?* What do you want? (SM) <***Loc:*** SB, SJ, SM, Lv88>

ça[3] [sa, ha] *pron.dem.* this, that **Ça c'est bon.* That's good (Da84) **Ça c'est dur.* That's hard, that's difficult. (Da84) **Ça c'est tout.* That's all. (Da84) *C'est comme ça.* It's like that. (SM) **Combien ça coûte?* How much does it cost? (Da84) **Comment ça se fait?* Why? How come? (Da84) *Y a plus personne qui pêche comme ça là.* No one fishes like that any more. (TB) *Je vas jamais oblier ça tant que je vas vivre.* I won't forget that as long as I live. (TB) ◊ **•ça fait** so, therefore *Ça fait il a dit c'était correct.* So, he said it was correct. (Lv88) *Il a venu, ça fait elle a venu étout.* He came, therefore she came too. (SM) *J'ai ri, ça fait il s'a choqué.* I laughed, consequently he got upset. (VM) <EV, IB, IV, JD, LA, LF, SJ, SL, SM, TB, VM, An94, Gu82, Lv88, Wh83> **•ça-ici(-là) / ça-icitte(-là)** this, this one *Ça ici, t'appelles ça en anglais* PERCH *mais ici on appelle ça patassa.* This one, you call it a perch in English, but down here we call it a patassa. (TB) *Ça-icitte-là, ça ça ramasse pas cent pour cent mais ça ramasse alentour de dans les* NINETY PLUS. This one doesn't yield a hundred percent, but it does yield in the ninety plus range. (AS) <AS, TB> **•ça-là(-là)** that, that one, this, this one *Je me rappelle pas d'avoir vu ça-là.* I don't remember ever seeing that one. (LF) *L'homme ça-là est escran.* That man is crippled. (SM) <LF, SM> **•ça par exemple** that's something!, what the devil! <Da84> **•ça que** that which, what *Donne-moi ça tu m'a promis.* Give me that which you promised me. (SM) *C'est ça que mon père faisait aussi, il piégeait. Il était un piégeur.* That's what my father did also, he went trapping. He was a trapper. (LF) <AC, EV, LA, LF, SM, TB, VM, Gu82, Lv88> **•ça qui** that which, what *Allons dire que t'as nettoyé un poulet, une poule, eh ben ça qui reste c'est les débris.* Let's say you've cleaned a chicken, well, what is left, that's the offal. (LF) <EV, IV, LA, LF, TB, VM, An84> **•ça y est** that's it, it is done, it's finished <Da84> **•à ça oui** now that's enough!, now look here! <Da84> **•c'est ça** that's it **C'est ça puis c'est ça.* That's final, that's it. (Da84) <Da84> **•ci et ça** this and that *Mais ma mémère, ma grand-mère était forte pour ça pour bouillir ci et ça, et c'était une médecine.* But my grandmother was good at boiling this or that to make medicine. (SB) <SB> **•(comment) ça va?** how are you? **Ça va bien.* I am well, okay, etc. (Da84) <TB, VM, Da84, Guoo> **•de ça** ago *Mon popa a* RETIRE *à peu près cinq ans de ça.* My dad retired about five years ago. (LF) *C'était la dernière fois, y a des années de ça asteur.* That was the last time, it was years ago now. (TB) <LF, TB, VM, An94> <***Loc:*** AC, EV, IB, IV, JD, LA, LF, SB, SJ, SL, SM, TB, VM, An84, An94, Da84, Guoo, Gu82, La99, Lv88, Wh83>

cabale [kabal] *n.f.* soliciting, coaxing (for votes, favors, etc.) <***Loc:*** Da84>

cabaler [kabale] **I** *v.tr.* to solicit, coax, attempt to influence (usu. by intrigue or dishonest means) *Faut cabaler le docteur pour il donne des médecines plus douces.* You need to coax the doctor into giving you milder medecine. (Lv88) *Je l'ai cabalé pour venir avec moi.* I coaxed him into coming with me. (Lv88) *Ils ont tellement flatté ma domestique, ils ont réussi à la cabaler.* They so flattered my maid, they succeeded in wooing her away. (SM) **II** *v.intr.* **1** to campaign *Cabaler pour un candidat.* To campaign for a candidate. (EV) **2** to cabal, make use of intrigue and dishonesty in conducting a political campaign *Il a cabalé quand il a couri pour l'office.* He conducted a dishonest campaign when he ran for office. (VM) <***Loc:*** EV, IB, SJ, SM, TB, VM, Da84, Lv88, Ph36>

cabaleur, -euse [kabalœr, -øz] *n.* **1** political candidate who resorts to corrupt campaign methods (such as bribery, rash promises, etc.) **2** schemer, one who makes use of intrigue or deception *J'aime pas voir Irène parler avec ma domestique. C'est une foutue cabaleuse.* I don't like seeing Irene talking to my maid. She is a damned schemer. (SM) <***Loc:*** SM, VM>

cabanage [kabɑ̃naʒ] *n.m./f.* **1** hut, cabin (for hunters or fishermen) **2** slave quarters (on a plantation) **3** campsite <***Loc:*** SL, Di32, Lv88>

cabanasse [kabɑ̃nas] *n.f.* cabin, shack *Il a acheté une vieille cabanasse.* He bought an old shack. (SJ) <***Loc:*** SJ>

cabane [kabɑ̃n] *n.f.* **1** cabin, shack **Cabane à nègre.* Negro shack. (Da84) *Quand mon j'étais garçon, eusse coupait toujours les cannes à la main. Eh ben eusse allait alentour de Opelousas et Lafayette et tout chercher des hommes. Et eusse avait des petites maisons, des petites cabanes manière que eusse restait là dans le temps de la roulaison.* When I was a little boy they still cut sugar cane by hand. And, well, they went around Opelousas and Lafayette and all looking for men. And they would have little houses, little cabins, like, that they lived in during the time of the sugar season. (LF) **2** shed, toolshed *Ça c'est ça que tu fais pour mettre tes* TOOL. *Allons voir dans le* SHED. *Nous-autres on appelle ça une cabane.* That's what you make to store your tools. Let's go look in the shed. We call that a "cabane." (LF) **3** outhouse, outdoor privy ◊ **•cabane à laver** washhouse <TB> **•cabane de chien** kennel <TB> **•cabane sauvage** wigwam <Re31> <*Loc:* AC, AV, EV, LF, SL, TB, VM, Da84, Hi02, Re31>

cabaneau [kabɑ̃no] *n.m./f.* cabin, shack *Cette vieille cabaneau va tomber bétôt.* That old shack will fall down soon. (IB) <*Loc:* IB, JE, LF>

cabaner[1] [kabɑ̃ne] **I** *v.intr.* **1** to camp *Il va cabaner dans son petit camp.* He's going to camp in his little camp. (Lv88) *Tous les soirs, on cabanait autour d'un grand feu.* Every night we camped around a big fire. (Di32) **2** to be confined to one's home (because of illness) *Depuis sa maladie il est cabané.* Since his illness he has been confined to home. (IB) **3** to be a homebody, stay at home *Après que je vas* RETIRE, *je veux pas faire arien. Je veux juste cabaner.* After I retire, I don't want to do anything. I want to just stay home. (LA) *Elle est tout le temps cabanée.* She is always cooped up at home. (JE) **II se cabaner** *v.pron.* to stay at home, shut o.s. in, stay cooped up **I s'cabane tous les dimanches.* He stays at home every Sunday. (EV, Ph36) <*Loc:* AV, EV, IB, JE, LA, SJ, SL, SM, TB, Di32, Lv88, Ph36>

cabaner[2] [kabɑ̃ne] *v.tr.* **1** to dent in, crush *Il a tout cabané son chapeau.* He dented his hat all up. (Lv88) **2** to bend (the ears) in or out with a hat *Ses oreilles étaient cabanées dessous le chapeau.* His ears were bent in underneath the hat. (SM) <*Loc:* JD, LA, SM, Lv88>

cabaret[1] [kabarɛ, kabare] *n.m.* bar, tavern, barroom, saloon *Fréquenter les cabarets.* To frequent bars. (LF) *Il y avait des cabarets qui flottaient dessus le bayou.* There were taverns that floated in the bayou. (LF) <*Loc:* AC, EV, LA, LF, Da84, Hi02, Lv88>

cabaret[2] [kabarɛ, kabare] *n.m.* **1** square baking pan **2** platter, tray <*Loc:* LA>

cabas [kaba] *n.m.* **1** suitcase, travel bag, valise **2** book sack *Il a ses livres dans son cabas.* He has his books in his book sack. (JE) **3** basket <*Loc:* JD, JE, LF, Da84>

cabêche ♦see **caboche**

cabildeau [kabildo] *n.m.* lean-to, shed <*Loc:* Da84>

cabine [kabin] *n.f.* **1** cabin (of a fishing boat) *Et là il faulait qu'on met ça dans un skiff, un bateau avec pas de cabine et pas rien, un gros skiff. Faulait qu'on décoquille ces huîtres.* And then we had to put them in a skiff, a boat with no cabin and nothing, a big skiff. We had to shuck those oysters. (TB) **2** cabin (on a merchant vessel) **3** toilet, bathroom *Et y avait pas de cabine en-dedans, faulait que tu sors en dehors pour user la cabine.* There was no toilet inside, you had to go outside to use the bathroom. (TB) ◊ **•cabine en dehors** outhouse, outdoor privy *Dans ce temps-là c'était des cabines en dehors.* In those days they had outhouses. (TB) <TB> **•aller à la cabine** to go to the bathroom <LF, TB> <*Loc:* JE, LF, SM, TB, Da84>

cabinet [kabinɛ, kabine] *n.m.* **1** cabinet, cupboard **Tit Tone avait attrapé la mauvaise bouteille dans le cabinet dans la baignoire et pour des jours, ça semblait comme s'il avait attrapé ein mauvais coup de soleil dessus sa tête.* 'Tit Tone grabbed the wrong bottle out of the bathroom cabinet, and for days it looked like he had caught a bad sunstroke on his head. (Wh83) *Je sais pas éiou c'est. Ouvre voir ce cabinet-là.* I don't know where it is. Open that cupboard. (TB) *Alle fait une grègue de café. Et le cabinet est plein de tasses craquées, et alle lui sort une tasse craquée.* She makes a pot of coffee. And the cupboard is full of cracked cups, and she gets him out a cracked cup. (LF) **2** small closet (for clothes) **3** toilet, bathroom **Aller au cabinet.* To go to the toilet. (Da84) **4** outhouse, outdoor privy *Ça voulait aller aux cabinets et ça me demandait comment on demandait à la maîtresse d'école et je les disais en français et puis là je me faisais fouetter aussi.* They wanted to go to the toilet and they would ask me how to say it to the teacher and I would tell them in French and I would get whipped too. (AC) <*Loc:* AC, EV, IB, JD, JE, LA, LF, SJ, SM, TB, Da84, Lv88, Re31, Wh83>

cabinette [kabinɛt] *n.f.* small office *Il est dans sa cabinette.* He is in his little office. (SJ) <*Loc:* SJ>

câble [kab(l)] *n.m.* **1** cable, rope *Il mettait des guides en câble.* He put on rope reins. (LA) *Attrape la vache avec le câble.* Catch the cow with the cord. (SM) **2** thick rope used to moor boats *Amarre le bateau avec ce câble.* Tie the boat with that large rope. (JE) **3** cable television *Il y a pas de câble ici, on a une satellite.* There's no cable television here, we have a satellite. (SL) <*Loc:* JD, JE, LA, LF, SL, SM, Da84, Di32, Hi02, Lv88>

caboche (**cabosse, cabêche**) [kabɔʃ, kabɔs, kabɛʃ] *n.f.* head, noggin *Il a une grosse caboche.* He has a big head. (SM) <*Loc:* AV, EV, IB, JD, SJ, SL, SM, TB, Da84, Di32, Lv88, Ph36, Re31>

cabosse ♦see **caboche**

cabosser [kabose] **I** *v.tr.* to dent, bend *J'ai cabossé la boîte.* I dented the box. (SM) *Il a grêlé cet après-midi. Mon char est tout cabossé.* It hailed this afternoon. My car is all dented up. (EV) **II se cabosser** *v.pron.* to get dented *Le siau se cabosse.* The bucket is getting all dented up. (LF) ◊ **•se cabosser la tête** to get a knot on one's head (after banging it) <LF> <***Loc:*** EV, JD, JE, LF, SJ, SM, TB, Da84, Di32>

cabossure [kabosyr] *n.f.* dent *Il y a une cabossure dans la casterole.* There is a dent in the saucepan. (SL) <***Loc:*** AV, SL, Da84, Di32, Lv88>

cabousse [kabus] *n.f.* **1** caboose **2** small addition to the back of a house (often used as a kitchen or office) *Je vas le mettre à coucher dans la cabousse ce soir.* I'll put him up in the back room tonight. (TB) <***Loc:*** TB, Da84, Di32, Lv88>

cabresse [kabrɛs] *n.f.* horsehair rope <***Loc:*** AV, LA, SM, Di32, Lv88, Re31>

cabri[1] [kabri] *n.m.* goat (regardless of age or sex) *Il élève des cabris.* He raises goats. (JE) *Le monde avait des cabris plus pour tiendre les herbes en bas. On mettait trois ou quatre cabris dans la cour d'en avant, c'était parqué, tu vois.* People kept goats mostly to keep the grass low. We put three or four goats in the front yard, it was fenced in, you see. (TB) ◊ **•comment le cabri apporte sa queue?** how are you? how are things? <AV, La99> **•il y a un cabri dans le maïs** said when s.o.'s underpants have crawled up and become stuck between the buttocks <La99> <***Loc:*** AV, IB, JE, LA, LF, SJ, SL, SM, TB, VM, Da84, Gu00, Hi02, La99, Lv88>

cabri[2] [kabri] *n.m.* navel, belly button <***Loc:*** IB>

cac[1] [kɛk] *n.m.* excrement, dung, crap <***Loc:*** SM>

cac[2] ♦see **caca**[1]

caca[1] (**cac**) [kaka, kɛk] *v.intr.invar.* [*baby talk*] to poop *Tu as caca sur le plancher.* You pooped on the floor. (JE) *Le bébe a cac.* The baby pooped. (SM) <***Loc:*** JE, LF, SL, SM>

caca[2] [kaka] *adj.* [*baby talk*] dirty, filthy *Mange pas ça, c'est caca.* Don't eat that, it's dirty. (JD) <***Loc:*** JD>

caca[3] [kaka] *n.f.* excrement, dung, crap *J'ai marché dans la caca de vache.* I stepped in cow dung. (SM) **Caca de poule.* Chicken dung. (Da84) **C'est caca.* This is crap. (Da84) ◊ **•caca matelot** sour grass, sorrel grass <SB> **•caca pour merde** ***a*** one is as bad as the other ***b*** it's over and done with <AC, LA, SL, La99> **•être sous la caca de vache** to not yet be born *Moi, j'étais toujours sous la caca de vache dans ces temps-là.* I still wasn't born yet. (La99) <La99> **•faire caca** to defecate <Da84> <***Loc:*** AC, LA, SL, SM, Da84, Hi02, La99>

cacao [kakao] *n.m.* cocoa <***Loc:*** Da84, Re31>

cacasser (**carcasser, cagasser**) [kakase, karkase, kagase] **I** *v.tr.* to prattle, utter incoherently *Il cacasse quelque chose que je ne comprends pas ni queue ni tête.* He rattles something off that I can't understand head nor tail of. (SJ) **II** *v.intr.* **1** to talk excessively, chatter, jabber **Ça cacasse tout l'temps.* They're always chattering. (EV, Ph36) **2** to cackle, squawk *La poule faisait que cagasser et quand j'ai été voir, elle avait pondu.* The hen was just cackling, and when I went to see she had laid an egg. (TB) *Quand la femelle est après manger, quand alle sort sa tête, alle a peut-être l'eau dans le bec, la boue et du manger, alle peut pas crier beaucoup fort. Alle crie ça différentes manières, on appelle carcasser.* When the female is eating, when she pulls her head out, she may have water in her beak, mud and food, she can't quack very loud. She quacks in different ways, thay call that squawking. (TB) <***Loc:*** EV, SJ, TB, VM, Ph36>

cacatoir [kakatwar] *n.m.* bathroom, restroom *Il est constipé. Il a passé une heure dans le cacatoir.* He's constipated. He spent an hour in the bathroom. (SM) <***Loc:*** SM, Di32>

cacha (**coucha**) [kaʃa, kuʃa, katʃa] *n.m.* cushaw, crookneck squash <***Loc:*** AV, CL, JD, LA, SM, TB, VM, Da84, Ho90, Lv88>

cache [kaʃ] *n.f.* **1** secret hiding place **2** cache, s.t. that is hidden **3** fear *Quand j'ai vu j'étais dans le cimetière à minuit, la cache m'a pris.* When I saw I was in the cemetery at midnight, fear took me over. (SM) ◊ **•avoir la {une} cache** to be in great fear, be very much afraid *J'avais une cache qu'il me trouve dans sa maison.* I was very much afraid that he would find me in his house. (SM) <JE, SM, La99> <***Loc:*** JE, SM, Da84, Di32, La99>

cache-cache [kaʃkaʃ] *n.m.* **1** snipe *On a les cache-caches. Il y a deux qualités—Wilson snipe and Jack snipe.* We have snipes. There are two kinds—Wilson snipe and Jack snipe. (VM) **2** yellow nut grass, chufa, earth almond <***Loc:*** AV, EV, IB, JE, LA, LF, SL, TB, VM, Da84, Ho90, Lv88, Ph36, Re31>

cachembeau ♦see **cachimbo**

cachemire [kaʃmir] *n.m.* cashmere <***Loc:*** Da84>

cacher [kaʃe] **I** *v.tr.* to hide, conceal *Ayoù il cache son argent?* Where does he hide his money? (EV) *J'ai dit, "Fais ça, confesse-toi de tout ça tu as fait et cache pas rien!"* I said, "Do that, confess everything you have done and don't hide anything!" (EV) **II se cacher** *v.pron.* to hide *Il s'a caché derrière le magasin.* He hid behind the store. (EV) ◊ **•cacher-fouet** ***a*** hide the whip (children's game) ***b*** hide-and-seek <AV, IB, SM, VM, Lv88> **•cacher son argent dans des cornes à bœuf** to hide one's money around the house (often due to distrust of banks) <La99> **•cache-cache (bin) la bague** hide-the-ring (parlor game) <SM, VM, Lv88> **•cache-cache Nicolas** hide-and-seek <EV, Ph36> **•cache-est-faite / cache-et-faite / cache-fette / cachez-fête / caché-fête** hide-and-seek *On jouait cache-est-faite assez.* We played hide-and-seek a lot. (IB) *Après le repas, pendant que les tantes faisaient la vaisselle, les enfants jouaient à caché-fête.* After the meal, while the aunts were doing the dishes, the children were playing hide-and-seek. (SM) <AV, IB, LA, SJ, SM, VM, Da84, Hi02, Lv88> **•cache-mouchoir** drop the handkerchief (game) <Da84> **•cache-toi** I don't believe you <TB> **•va te cacher / va te faire cacher à Lafayette** ***a*** go to hell! ***b*** oh, go on!, nonsense!, I don't believe you ***c*** you should be ashamed of yourself ***d*** beat it, get lost, leave me alone <SL, SM, VM, Da84, La99>

<*Loc:* AC, AV, EV, IB, JE, LA, SJ, SL, SM, TB, VM, An94, Da84, Hi02, La99, Lv88, Ph36>

cache-tout [kaʃtu] *n.m.* **1** closet, storeroom **2** cellar <*Loc:* AV>

cachette [kaʃɛt] *n.f.* **1** hiding place *J'ai peur quelqu'un va trouver ma cachette.* I'm afraid someone will find my hiding place. (LA) **2** hide-and-seek **Jouer à la cachette.* To play hide-and-seek. (Da84) ◊ **•à la cachette / en cachette** secretly, in secret, on the sly *Quand on était à l'école, les maîtresses voulaient pas qu'on parle français mais on parlait en français en cachette, parce que c'était plus vite fait.* When we were at school, the teachers didn't want us to speak French, but we spoke French in secret, because it was quicker. (TB) <AC, EV, TB, Da84, Lv88> <*Loc:* AC, EV, LA, TB, Da84, Lv88>

cachimbo (**cachembeau**) [kaʃɛ̃bo, kaʃimbo] *n.m.* smoking pipe (usu. made of clay) <*Loc:* AV, Di32, Re31>

cachot [kaʃo] *n.m.* small prison cell, solitary confinement cell <*Loc:* Da84>

cachoupic [kaʃupik, kaʃupi] *adj.* tacky, countrified *Ce chapeau qu'elle porte est cachoupic.* That hat she's wearing is tacky. (IB) <*Loc:* IB>

cachouque ♦see **catchouque**

cadavre [kadav(r)] *n.m.* corpse, cadaver <*Loc:* Da84>

cadeau [kado] *n.m.* gift, present *Ici c'est pas tout à fait ça qu'on appelle un magasin parce que on a toute qualité de cadeaux.* This is not exactly what we call a store, because we have all kinds of gifts. (LF) <*Loc:* EV, LF, Da84, Hi02>

cadenas (**calenas, carenas**) [kadna, kalna, karna] *n.m.* lock, padlock **Barrer au cadenas.* To padlock. (Da84) *J'ai barré la porte avec un cadenas.* I locked the door with a lock. (JE) <*Loc:* EV, JE, LA, Da84, Ph36, Re31>

cadet, -ette [kadɛ, kade, -ɛt] *n.* second child of a family <*Loc:* IB, SB, SJ, La99>

cadien[1]**, -ienne** (**cadjin, -e**) [kadʒɛ̃, kadjɛ̃, -dʒɛ̃n, -djɛ̃n, -dʒin] *adj.* **1** Cajun, of or pertaining to the francophone people of Louisiana or their speech *C'est un parleur courant du français cadien.* He is a fluent speaker of Cajun French. (Lv88) *Il n-a une connection intéressante entre les noirs et la musique cadienne.* There's an interesting connection between the blacks and Cajun music. (Lv88) *Du bon manger cadien.* Good Cajun food. (EV) *Et Robinson, c'est pas un nom cadien ça!* And Robinson, that's not a Cajun name! (TB) *Les enfants ça a tout été élevé dans des maisons cadiens.* The children were all raised in Cajun households. (TB) **2** [*pej.*] (formerly) in poor taste, tacky *Mon chapeau cadien.* My tacky hat. (VM) *Du linge cadien.* Tacky clothes. (SM) **3** [*pej.*] (formerly) lower class, uneducated and countrified *Des coutumes cadiennes.* Countrified ways. (LF) <*Loc:* EV, LF, SM, TB, Di32, Hi02, Lv88>

cadien[2] (**cadjin**) [kadʒɛ̃, kadjɛ̃] *n.m.* Cajun French *Le monde qu'est par-dessus soixante ans en bas c'est tout du monde qui parle proche juste le cadien.* People who are over 60 down here are all people who speak almost nothing but Cajun. (TB) *Il parle cadien proche comme un bougre de la Louisiane.* He speaks Cajun French almost like a guy from Louisiana. (Lv88) *Moi j'appelle mon langage le cadien, et elle c'était le pur français.* I call my language Cajun, and hers is pure French. (AS) <*Loc:* AS, TB, Lv88>

Cadien[3]**, -ienne** (**Cadjin, -e**) [kadʒɛ̃, kadjɛ̃, -dʒɛ̃n, -djɛ̃n, -dʒin] *n.* **1** Cajun, Louisiana Acadian *Si tu veux un Cadien de la Louisiane, tu fais mieux de connaître comment le manœuvrer.* If you want a Cajun from Louisiana, you'd better know how to handle him. (TB) **Ça qui m'a amené au rock-and-roll, c'est que tous les Cadiens de mon âge aimaient ça quand on était après grandir.* What brought me to rock-and-roll is that all Cajuns my age liked that when we were growing up. (LA, An84) *Moi, je peux pas dire que j'étais élevé un Cadien pauvre à la crève de faim.* I can't say that I grew up as a poor Cajun on the verge of starvation. (JD) *Les petites Cadjines de la Louisiane est les meilleures cuiseuses du pays.* Little Louisiana Cajun girls are the best cooks in the country. (Lv88) **2** person of any origin (generally, but not necessarily, white) who speaks Cajun French **Et' cadjin, c'est eine monyère [=manière] de viv' [=vivre] et de jongler.* Being Cajun, it's a way of living and of thinking. (ThCa: *Mille misères*) **3** [*pej.*] (formerly) lower class or illiterate Francophone of Louisiana ◊ **•Cadien ventre jaune** lazy Cajun <Guoo> <*Loc:* EV, IB, JD, LA, LF, SM, TB, VM, Da84, Di32, Gr86, Guoo, Hi02, Lv88, ThCa>

cadjin, cadjine ♦see **cadien**

Cadjin, Cadjine ♦see **Cadien**

cadran [kadrɑ̃] *n.m.* face of a clock <*Loc:* Da84>

cadre [kad(r)] *n.m.* **1** frame (for pictures, windows, etc.) **2** quilting frame ◊ **•cadre de cheminée** fireplace screen <JD> <*Loc:* JD, SL, Da84>

cadrer[1] (**encadrer**) [kadre, ɑ̃kadre] *v.tr.* **1** to frame *Elle a proche fini de cadrer le portrait.* She's almost finished framing the picture. (LA) *Je vas encadrer son portrait.* I'm going to frame her picture. (LA) **2** to stay, support *Cadrer un puits.* To support a well (by covering its walls with boards so that it doesn't cave in). (Lv88) <*Loc:* JD, LA, Da84, Di32, Lv88>

cadrer[2] ♦see **corder**

cafa [kafa] *n.m.* stomach **Ton cafa doit êt [=être] plein!* Your stomach must be full! (EV, Ph36) <*Loc:* EV, Ph36>

café [kafe] *n.m.* **1** coffee *Faulait que tu grilles le café, et là faulait que tu le moules.* You had to roast the coffee, and then you had to grind it. (TB) *Après la messe on va aller à la maison boire du café.* After mass, we'll go home and drink coffee. (JE) **2** cafe, small restaurant **Pour dix sous ça pouvait acheter eine fille ein hamburger à ein café au boute de la rue.* For ten cents they could buy a girl a hamburger at a restaurant on the corner of the street. (Wh83)

3 bar, barroom, saloon *Je vais au café boire un verre de bière.* I'm going to the bar to drink a glass of beer. (SM) **4** whirligig beetle ◊ **•café (au) brûlot** café brûlot, black coffee flavored with sugar and burning cognac or whisky <JD, Da84, Lv88, Re31> **•café au lait** ***a*** coffee with milk ***b*** drink made of milk poured over carmelized sugar <AV, Da84, Lv88> **•café égoutté** dripped coffee <Da84> **•café fort** black coffee <Da84> **•café grillé** roasted coffee <Da84> **•café minote caïac** wild senna <SB> **•café noir** black coffee <JD, Da84> **•café sauvage** ***a*** indigo plant ***b*** coffeeweed <IB, Da84, Gu00> <***Loc:*** AC, AV, EV, IB, JD, JE, LA, LF, SB, SL, SM, TB, VM, An94, Da84, Di32, Gr86, Gu00, Hi02, Lv88, Re31, Wh83>

cafetière (**cafière**) [kaftjær, kafjær] *n.f.* **1** coffee canister, coffee can, coffee jar **2** coffeepot, pot for serving coffee <***Loc:*** VM, Da84>

cafière ♦see **cafetière**

cagasser ♦see **cacasser**

cafiau [kafjo] *n.m.* weak coffee, watered-down coffee *Donne le bébé du cafiau.* Give the baby some weak coffee. (IB) <***Loc:*** IB>

cafiot [kafjo, kafju] *n.m.* coffee fiend, one who drinks a great deal of coffee *Henri devient cafiot comme son père.* Henry is becoming a coffee fiend like his father. (IB) <***Loc:*** IB, LF, SM>

cage [kaʒ] *n.f.* **1** cage *Quand tu vas finir avec la gazette, tu peux me la donner pour la mettre en bas de la cage à pigeons.* When you're finished with the newspaper, you can give it to me to put in the bottom of the pigeon cage. (ThCa: *Messieurs, mesdames*) **2** protective enclosure around a tree or shrub **3** bird trap, bird snare *On a attrapé des oiseaux dans ces cages.* We caught birds in those bird-traps. (VM) **4** box trap, special type of trap used in seafood fishing *Mais y a un monsieur qui quitte des appâts vivants dans ses cages pour empoigner des truites et les poissons rouges et les plies.* There's a gentleman who leaves live bait in his box traps for catching trout and redfish and southern flounder. (TB) ◊ **•cage à crabe(s)** crab trap *Il y avait une grosse brise, je dis "Tu vas pas aller dans ce bayou et mettre ces cages à crabes là à soir. Tu vas espérer demain."* There was a strong breeze, I said, "You're not going into the bayou and set up those crab traps tonight. You'll wait till tomorrow." (TB) <TB> **•cage à poules** chicken coop <LA> **•cage à z-oiseau** bird cage <LA> <***Loc:*** IB, IV, LA, PQ, SM, TB, VM, Da84, Di32, Lv88, ThCa>

cagée [kaʒe] *n.f.* coopful <***Loc:*** Da84>

cager[1] [kaʒe] *v.tr.* to build a protective enclosure around (a tree or shrub) *Cager un figuier.* To build a protective enclosure around a fig tree. (EV) ◊ **•cager du bois** to pile up wood in the form of a cage <VM> <***Loc:*** EV, VM>

cager[2] [kaʒe] *v.intr.* to agree *Sa lettre a cagé avec ce qu'il a dit.* His letter agreed with what he said. (AV) <***Loc:*** AV>

cageux [kaʒø] *n.m.* flat barge, raft *Le cageux a calé.* The raft sank. (AV) <***Loc:*** AV, Di32>

cagne [kɑ̃j, kɑ̃ŋ] *n.f.* laziness *J'ai rien fait aujourd'hui. La cagne m'avait pris.* I did nothing today. Laziness got a hold of me. (SM) *Il a une cagne abominable.* He is awfully lazy. (JE) *Se tenir une cagne.* To be lazy. (LF) <***Loc:*** JE, LF, SM>

cagou [kagu] *adj.* out of sorts, sickly looking, listless, languid *Alle est toute cagou, alle a pas de courage pour faire arien.* She's so languid, she doesn't have the energy to do anything. (Lv88) *Le petit poulet est cagou.* The little chicken is sickly looking. (SM) **Qui c'est il a, il est si cagou ç'matin? Il a la fièv(re), et il s'ennuye.* What's wrong with him, he looks out of sorts this morning. He's running a fever and he's lonely. (EV, Ph36) <***Loc:*** AV, EV, IB, JE, LA, LF, SJ, SL, SM, TB, Da84, Di32, Hi02, Lv88, Ph36>

cagouette [kagwɛt, kagwet] *n.f. (occ. m.)* **1** back of the neck, nape of the neck *Il l'a attrapé par la cagouette et il l'a garroché dans la rue.* He caught him by the back of the neck and threw him into the street. (VM) **2** head *Mets ton chapeau sur ta cagouette.* Put your hat on your head. (SM) **3** large twist of hair worn at the back of the head *Elle s'est fait une cagouette.* She put her hair up in a twist. (IB) <***Loc:*** AV, IB, JD, LA, LF, SL, SM, TB, VM, Da84, Di32, Lv88>

cahier [kaje] *n.m.* notebook, tablet <***Loc:*** LF, Da84>

caïac (**kaïac**, **kayac**) [kajak] *n.m.* **1** steer **2** bull too old to breed **3** big, powerful fellow, boor, lout *Cette espèce de caïac était tout le temps après chercher à se battre.* That lout was always looking for a fight. (EV) **4** disagreeable, crusty old man ◊ **•vieux caïac** tough old man <Da84> <***Loc:*** EV, IB, LA, SM, Da84, Lv88, Re31>

caïacot (**kaïacot**) [kajako] *n.m.* tough little fellow <***Loc:*** Re31>

caillant [kajɑ̃] *n.m.* clot, coagulation *Il y a sorti des gros caillants de sang.* There were big clots of blood coming out. (VM) <***Loc:*** VM>

caille[1] [kaj] *n.f.* any of various songbirds (incl. the catbird, meadowlark, thrush, and tanager) ◊ **•caille de bois** brown thrasher <LA, Re31> **•caille de clos** field lark <IB> **•caille de laurier** red-eyed vireo <Re31> **•caille de prairie** field lark *Les cailles de prairie chantent.* The field larks are singing. (JE) <JE> **•caille pivelée** speckled thrush, wood thrush <Re31> <***Loc:*** AV, EV, JD, JE, LA, SJ, SL, SM, VM, Da84, Lv88, Ph36, Re31>

caille[2] [kaj] *adj.* **1** spotted, esp. black and white *Caillette était le nom qu'on donnait à une vache caille.* "Caillette" was the name we would give to a spotted cow. (Gu00) *J'ai une vache caille.* I have a white-and-black spotted cow. (SM) **2** multicolored *Une belle couverte caille.* A beautiful blanket of many colors. (Lv88) *Tes caleçons cailles.* Your multicolored underpants. (Lv88) **3** freckled *Sa figure est caille.* His face is freckled. (SM) **4** dull, listless *Elle a les yeux cailles.* Her eyes are dull. (JE) **5** cloudy, overcast *Le temps caille.* Cloudy weather. (LF) <***Loc:*** AV, EV, IB, JD, JE, LA, LF, SJ, SL, SM, TB, Da84, Di32, Gu00, Hi02, Lv88, Ph36, Re31>

caille[3] ♦see **cale**

caillé [kaje] *n.m.* clabber, cottage cheese *La seule manière pour faire du caillé c'était prendre le… mettre ça dedans un bol et met àyou il fait chaud. Là il va* CLABBER*. Là ça prenait ce* CLABBER*, ça le mettait dans un petit sac de farine, quelque chose.* AND IT WOULD DRIP. The only way to make cottage cheese was to take the . . . put it in a bowl and put it where it was warm. Then it will clabber. Then they took that clabber and put it in a little flour sack or something. And it would drip. (VM) ◊ **•caillé-goutté / caillé-égoutté** ***a*** cottage cheese ***b*** cream cheese <LA, SJ, SM, TB, Da84, Lv88> <***Loc:*** JD, LA, SJ, SM, TB, VM, Da84, Hi02, Lv88>

cailleau (caille-eau) [kajo] *n.m.* **1** frogfruit **2** wild sage, lantana <***Loc:*** Ho90>

caille-eau ♦see **cailleau**

caillematchal [kajmatʃal] *adj.* grayish *Le cheval est couleur caillematchal.* The horse is of a grayish color. (AV) <***Loc:*** AV>

caille-molle [kajmɔl] *n.f.* softshell turtle <***Loc:*** Da84, La99>

cailler [kaje] **I** *v.tr.* to cause to clabber, curdle or coagulate (milk, blood, etc.) *Si tu veux cailler ton lait, tu mets du vinaigre dedans.* If you want to clabber your milk, you put vinegar in it. (EV) *Cailler du lait avec du vinaigre.* To clabber milk with vinegar. (EV) **II** *v.intr.* **1** to clabber, curdle, coagulate *Le lait a caillé.* The milk curdled. (EV) **2** to yield, cower, back down *Il a fait comme si il voulait se battre, mais il a caillé quand c'était temps pour se battre.* He was acting like he wanted to fight, but he backed down when it was time to fight. (SM) ◊ **•cailler la botte** to die *Pauvre bête, il a caillé la botte.* Poor fellow, he died. (SB) <SB, La99> <***Loc:*** AV, EV, JE, LA, LF, SB, SM, VM, Da84, La99, Lv88>

caillette[1] [kajɛt] *n.f.* fourth stomach of a ruminant (abomasum) or its lining (rennet) *Tu bouilles ça comme la panse. Là, il y avait la panse, la caillette, le feuillet. La caillette, c'est bon à manger. Y a plus personne qui fait ça.* You boil that like the stomach. There was the stomach, the abomasum, the omasum. The abomasum is good to eat. No one makes that any more. (VM) <***Loc:*** VM, Da84, Re31>

Caillette[2] [kajɛt] *n.f.* name commonly given to a spotted milking cow *Caillette donne pus de lait.* Caillette doesn't give any more milk. (VM) ◊ **•Caillette pourrait perdre son veau là-dedans** the place in question is very messy, disorganized, cluttered <La99> **•faire 'poteau, Caillette' à qqn** to make s.o. obey, force s.o. to give in <AV, La99> **•poteau, Caillette!** ***a*** command to a cow to get in position for milking ***b*** command to a person to get in line, get on board, get with the program <LA> <***Loc:*** AV, EV, IB, JD, LA, SJ, SL, SM, TB, VM, Da84, Di32, La99>

caillibossé ♦see **calibossé**

caillot [kajo] *n.m.* verbena *Mais les caillots sont jolis.* But the verbena are pretty. (TB) <***Loc:*** TB>

caillou [kaju] *n.m.* **1** pebble, small stone, piece of gravel *Arrête jeter ces cailloux-là.* Stop throwing those pebbles. (JE) **2** hard lump **Un caillou de sucre.* A lump of sugar. (Da84) **La terre est tourné en caillou.* The earth is lumpy. (Da84) ◊ **•caillou de sang** blood clot <EV, LA, VM> <***Loc:*** EV, JE, LA, LF, TB, VM, An94, Da84, Hi02>

caïman [kajmɑ̃] *n.m.* alligator *Parce qu'un caïman va faire comme si qu'il est mort, tu vas jamais attraper la queue, il va te jeter à toi à l'eau, peut-être avec ton fusil ou tes* TAG. Because an alligator will play dead, you'll never catch his tail, he'll throw you in the water, maybe with your gun or your tags. (TB) <***Loc:*** JE, LF, SJ, SM, TB, Da84, Gu00, Hi02, La99, Re31>

caine ♦see **CAN**

cainner ♦see **encanner**

cainque ♦see **coinque**

cairson ♦see **tiercent**

caisse [kɛs] *n.f.* **1** box *Soit une caisse ou une boîte.* Either a carton or a box. (JE) **2** wooden crate *On avait une caisse en haut-là pour les poules pondre.* There was a crate up there for the chickens to lay eggs in. (LA) **3** case *Une caisse de bière.* A case of beer. (EV) **4** box trap **5** body of a buggy *Moi, j'étais assis dans la caisse du boghei.* I was sitting in the body of the buggy. (LA) ◊ **•caisse à chevrette** shrimp trap *Mais aussi ça avait des caisses à chevrettes. Des caisses, pour mettre du manger là-dedans comme des morceaux de viande et ils mettaient tous les jours, ils allaient chercher leurs chevrettes.* But they also had shrimp traps. Boxes, to put food in like pieces of meat, they put it out every day and they'd go collect their shrimp. (SJ) <SJ> **•caisse à mouches** beehive <AV> **•caisse en carton** cardboard box. <LF, TB> <***Loc:*** AV, EV, JE, LA, LF, SJ, TB, Da84>

cajac ♦see **acadiac**

cala[1] [kala] *n.m.* **1** sweetened fried rice cake **2** fried bread dough <***Loc:*** SM, TB, Lv88, Re31>

cala[2] [kala] *n.m.* old hat *Elle avait un cala sur sa tête.* She had an ugly old hat on her head. (IB) <***Loc:*** IB, SJ>

calabousse [kalabus] *n.f.* jail (esp. a small jail where people are incarcerated for minor offences such as drunkenness, vagrancy, etc.) <***Loc:*** AV, SM, TB, Da84, Di32, Lv88>

calalou [kalalu] *n.m.* ◊ **•faire manger du calalou (à qqn)** to get even with s.o. <Re31> <***Loc:*** Lv88, Re31>

calamar [kalamar] *n.m.* squid *Les calamars sont bons à manger.* Squid are good to eat. (JE) <***Loc:*** JE, LF, Gu00>

calamité [kalamite] *n.f.* calamity, misfortune <***Loc:*** Da84>

calciner [kalsine] *v.intr.* **1** to congeal, coagulate, clot *Son sang calcine vite.* His blood clots quickly. (JE) **2** to calcify *L'endedans des tuyaux avait calciné à travers les années.* The inside of the pipes had calcified through the years. (LA) *L'eau du puits a calciné dans les tuyaux.* The well water calcified in the pipes. (LA) **3** to crack and peel after hardening (of paint or varnish) *Les vieilles peintures sont calcinées sur le meuble.* The coats of old paint on the furniture are cracked and peeling. (Lv88) <***Loc:*** JE, LA, LF, SM, Lv88>

calcul (**carcul**) [kalkyl, karkyl] *n.m./f.* **1** calculation, figuring *Est-ce que ce carcul est bien?* Is this calculation correct? (JE) **2** arithmetic, computation, counting *Il a étudié la carcul à l'école.* He studied arithmetic at school. (SM) <***Loc:*** JE, SL, SM, TB, Da84, Lv88>

calculer (**carculer**) [kalkyle, karkyle, kalkyre] **I** *v.tr.* to calculate, figure *J'ai une petite* GRANDDAUGHTER *et alle a venu ici un soir, alle pouvait pas calculer un certain problème. Je lui ai donné la main, je l'ai figuré,* BUT *c'était pas comme c'était supposé d'être.* BUT *j'ai sorti avec la même réponse.* I have a little granddaughter and she came here one evening, she couldn't calculate a certain problem. I gave her a hand, I figured it out, but it wasn't like it was supposed to be. But I came out with the same answer. (TB) **II** *v.intr.* **1** to calculate, figure **Je calcule, je suis autant que l'homme qu'est après travailler à la shove, ou le mécanicien, ou n'importe quel autre métier.* I figure that I'm worth as much as the man who works the shovel, or the engineer, or someone who does any other type of work. (VM, An84) *Il faut carculer avant de bâtir la maison.* It is necessary to calculate before building the house. (SM) **2** to reflect (on), ponder *Il carcule sur tout ça qui se passe.* He reflects on everything that happens. (SL) **III se calculer** *v.pron.* to consider o.s. *Il se carcule l'homme le plus heureux du monde.* He considers himself the happiest man in the world. (LF) <***Loc:*** AC, IB, JE, LF, PQ, SB, SL, SM, TB, VM, An84, Da84, Lv88>

cale (**caille**) [kal, kaj] *n.f.* **1** pier, block, pillar, footing (of a building) *Une maison haute sur les cales.* A house built on piers. (VM) **2** hull (of a boat) *Équand-ce qu'il a fini la cale on a été pour le faire enregistrer avec le* COAST GUARD. When he finished the hull we went to have it registered with the Coast Guard. (TB) **3** hold (of a boat) *Ils mettaient de la glace là-dedans et à mesure que ça empoignait la chevrette, eusse mettait ça dans la cale.* They put ice in it, and as they caught shrimp, they put it in the hold. (LF) <***Loc:*** AV, LA, LF, TB, Da84, An94, Gu82, Lv88>

calebasse [kalbas, katbas] *n.f.* **1** gourd **2** head, noggin **Tu vas casser ta calebasse.* You will crack your skull. (Da84) **3** fool, idiot *Ça c'est la grande calebasse!* What a fool! (JD) ◊ **•avoir une calebasse pour sa tête** to be foolish <SB, La99> <***Loc:*** JD, SB, SJ, SM, VM, Da84, Hi02, La99, Lv88>

calèche [kalɛʃ] *n.f.* fancy carriage ◊ **•adieu la calèche!** so much for that! (said of s.t. that falls and breaks) *Il a lâché le marteau! Adieu la calèche!* He dropped the hammer! So much for that! (SM) <SM, Di32, La99, Lv88> <***Loc:*** JD, SM, La99, Da84, Di32, Lv88>

caleçon (**caneçon**) [kalsɔ̃, kɑ̃lsɔ̃, kɑ̃nsɔ̃, kɔ̃nsɑ̃] *n.m. (often pl.)* underpants, undershorts, briefs, panties, drawers *Mettre son caleçon, une paire de caleçons.* To put on underpants, a pair of underpants. (EV) *Tes caleçons cailles.* Your multicolored underpants. (Lv88) <***Loc:*** AV, EV, IB, JE, LA, LF, SB, SL, SM, TB, Da84, Gu00, Lv88, Re31>

calembour [kalɑ̃bur] *n.m.* **1** traditional word game **2** nonsense, bunk *Ça c'est des calembours.* That's a bunch of nonsense. (SL) <***Loc:*** JD, SL, Da84>

calenas ♦see **cadenas**

calendrier [kalɑ̃drije] *n.m.* **1** calendar **2** almanac <***Loc:*** Da84>

caler [kale] **I** *v.tr.* **1** to insert upright, drive down *Il a calé un poteau dans la terre.* He planted a pole into the ground. (SM) **2** to support with blocks, piers, etc. *Caler une maison.* To place a house on blocks or pillars. (VM) *La vieille maison était toujours bien calée.* The old house was still well supported on its piers. (LA) **3** to sink *Et c'est un navire qui a calé son bateau. Et il s'a noyé.* And it's a ship that sank his boat. And he drowned. (TB) **4** to submerge, dunk, immerse *Ça voulait se faire baptiser tout calé dans l'eau.* They [Baptists] wanted to be baptised dunked completely in the water. (Lv88) **5** to soak *J'ai calé le linge dans l'eau un bon boute avant de le laver.* I soaked the laundry in the water for a good while before washing it. (Lv88) **6** to swallow, drink down *Il va caler un petit filet avant de s'en retourner.* He is going to have a drink before going back. (Lv88) **7** to spend, lose *Il a calé toute sa fortune.* He spent his entire fortune. (Lv88) *Il a calé une fortune.* He spent a fortune. (SM) **8** [*vulg.*] to have sex with, screw *Caler une femme.* Have sex with a woman. (Lv88) **II** *v.intr.* **1** to sink *Le char a calé dans la boue après l'avalasse.* The car sank in the mud after the storm. (Lv88) *Le bateau a calé dans le bayou.* The boat sank in the bayou. (SM) *C'était moi et défunt Camel qu'étaient avec le tracteur, calé dans la boue jusqu'à là.* It was me and the late Camel who were with the tractor, sunk in the mud up to there. (LA) **2** to submerge, go under water *Le garçon a calé trois fois, mais il a pas noyé.* The boy went under three times, but he didn't drown. (SM) **3** to get stuck *La roue de la voiture a calé dans la boue.* The wheel of the car got stuck in the mud. (SM) **4** to back down *Quand il a voulu battre, j'ai calé.* When he wanted to fight, I backed down. (SM) **III se caler** *v.pron.* **1** to sink, go deep or far down *Sa famille s'est calée dans la misère.* His family sank into misery. (Lv88) **2** to drink *Il s'a calé un verre d'eau.* He drank a glass of water. (TB) ◊ **•caler au fond** to sink to the bottom <Da84> **•caler le bouchon** ***a*** to disappear ***b*** to back out, give up, run away from a contest <Da84> <***Loc:*** AV, EV, IB, JE, LA, LF, SJ, SL, SM, TB, VM, An94, Da84, Di32, La99, Lv88>

calibarda ♦see **caliberda**

caliberda (**calibarda, galibarda**) [kalibærda, kalibarda, galibarda] *n.m.* clumsy person, klutz *Il ne peut pas faire arien. C'est un grand caliberda.* He can't do anything. He's a big klutz. (SM) ◊ •**à calibarda** astride, astraddle *Il est à calibarda sur le cheval.* He is astride on the horse. (AV) <AV> <***Loc:*** AV, SM>

calibossé[1]**, -e (caillebossé, -e)** [kalibose, kajibose] *adj.* said of one who goes to bed early *Il a tout le temps été calibossé.* He has always been a person who goes to bed early. (LF) <***Loc:*** LF, La99>

calibossé[2]**, -e (caillebossé, -e)** [kalibose, kajibose] *adj.* badly dressed *Une femme calibossée.* A badly dressed woman. (LF) <***Loc:*** LF, VM, La99>

calibrer [kalibre] *v.tr.* to calibrate *Il avait besoin de calibrer ses instruments.* He had to calibrate his instruments. (LA) <***Loc:*** LA, Da84>

calicantuce [kalikɑ̃tys] *n.m.* 1 strawberry shrub, common sweetshrub 2 magnolia fuscata <***Loc:*** IB, Da84>

calicature ♦see **caricature**

calice [kalis] *n.m.* chalice <***Loc:*** Da84>

calicoler ♦see **caracoler**

calicot [kaliko] *n.m.* calico <***Loc:*** Da84>

califourchon [kalifurʃɔ̃] *n.m.* ◊ •**à califourchon** astride, astraddle *Les enfants étiont à califourchon dessus la barrière.* The children were straddling the fence. (EV) <EV> •**aller à califourchon** to ride astride (e.g. a horse) <Da84> <***Loc:*** EV, Da84, Lv88>

calimaçon [kalimasɔ̃, kalimosɔ̃] *n.m.* 1 snail *En France on mange des calimaçons.* In France people eat snails. (JE) 2 small shellfish, univalve seashell 3 whelk <***Loc:*** AV, EV, IB, JE, LF, SJ, SL, SM, TB, Da84, Di32, Hi02, Lv88, Re31>

calimaçonner [kalimasɔ̃ne] *v.intr.* to do things very slowly *Il calimaçonne dans son ouvrage.* He does his work very slowly. (IB) <***Loc:*** IB>

calimatcha ♦see **galimatias**

câlin[1]**, -e** [kalɛ̃, -in] *adj.* lazy **Y'avait du monde qui était mayère câlin, qui travaillait pas.* There were some people who were kind of lazy, who didn't work. (Gr82) <***Loc:*** AV, LA, LF, SJ, SM, TB, Lv88>

câlin[2]**, -e** [kalɛ̃, -in] *n.* idler, lazybones, bum *Il est un câlin.* He is an idler. (JE) *T'es malheureux de ramasser un maudit câlin. Un câlin, ça veut pas travailler.* You're bad off becausc you got yourself a damned bum. A bum, he doesn't want to work. (TB) <***Loc:*** JE, LF, SM, TB, Di32>

calinda (colinda) [kalinda, kolinda] *n.f.* 1 calinda (dance reputedly of African origin) *Allons danser colinda.* Let's dance the calinda. (Lv88, ch) 2 game of stealing bases <***Loc:*** EV, JD, Da84, Lv88, Ph36, Re31>

calmant [kalmɑ̃, kɔ̃mɔ̃] *n.m.* 1 sedative, tranquilizer *J'ai pris un calmant pour bien dormir.* I took a sedative in order to sleep well. (VM) 2 aspirin <***Loc:*** EV, TB, VM, Da84>

calme[1] [kalm, kɑ̃m] *adj.* calm, tranquil, quiet *C'était bien calme, aussi calme que cette table-là est. Et pas de vent du tout.* It [the sea] was very calm, as calm as this table is. And no wind at all. (TB) <***Loc:*** EV, TB, VM, Da84>

calme[2] [kalm, kɑ̃m] *n.m.* 1 sedative, tranquilizer 2 aspirin <***Loc:*** EV, VM, Da84>

calmer [kalme, kɑ̃me] **I** *v.tr.* to calm, calm down *Ça pouvait pas la calmer après qu'elle avait eu la nouvelle pour son mari.* They couldn't calm her down after she received the news about her husband. (LA) *Il essayait de calmer son chien dans le* BLIND. He was trying to calm his dog down in the blind. (LA) **II** *v.intr.* 1 to calm, calm down *Les grandes ouragans, aussitôt que le vent calmait, l'eau s'en va.* Big hurricanes, as soon as the wind died down, the water went away. (TB) 2 to slow down, reduce speed *Tu ferais mieux de calmer. Le chemin est trempe.* You had better slow down. The road is wet. (LA) **III se calmer** *v.pron.* to become calm, calm down *Z-enfants, z-enfants! Calmez vous-autres.* Children, children! Calm down. (ThCa: *La fête à Clomaire*) <***Loc:*** LA, TB, VM, Da84, ThCa>

calocaine ♦see **caloquinte**

calomel [kalomɛl] *n.m.* calomel, mercuric chloride <***Loc:*** SM, Da84>

calomnie [kalɔ̃mni] *n.f.* calumny, slander, defamation <***Loc:*** Da84>

caloque [kalɔk] *n.f.* head, noggin *Sa caloque est dure.* He has a hard head. (AV) <***Loc:*** AV, IB, SJ>

caloquinte (calocaine) [kalokɛ̃t, kalokɛ̃n, kalokɛ̃] *n.f.* 1 small melon 2 head, noggin *Il s'a abordé la caloquinte dessus la sole en bas de la maison.* He bumped his head on the beam under the house. (LA) 3 beanie, skullcap <***Loc:*** AV, IB, LA, SJ, SM, Da84, Lv88>

calotte[1] [kalɔt] *n.f.* 1 beanie, skullcap (as worn by bishops) *Il s'avait mis une petite calotte comme dans le vieux temps.* He had put on a little beanie cap like in the old days. (LA) 2 crown, upper part of a hat (excluding the brim) *Le Marais Bouleur s'a assis sur son chapeau et il a écrasé la calotte.* The guy from Marais Bouleur sat on his hat and crushed the crown. (LA) 3 scalp, skull *Sa calotte est sale.* His scalp is dirty. (IB) *J'ai pus de cheveux sur ma vieille calotte.* I have no more hair on my old skull. (EV) 4 head *Il s'a cogné la calotte.* He hit his head. (LA) <***Loc:*** AS, AV, EV, IB, JD, JE, LA, LF, SM, VM, Da84>

calotte[2] [kalɔt] *n.f.* 1 slap *Je l'ai pété une calotte.* I gave him a slap. (JE) 2 rap on the head with the knuckles ◊ •**foutre une calotte à qqn** to slap s.o., give s.o. a slap *Alle m'a foutu une calotte.* She slapped me. (LF) <LF> <***Loc:*** JE, LF, SJ>

calotter [kalote] *v.tr.* to slap *J'aurais été calotté si j'aurais pas usé le mot de "vous."* I would have been slapped if I didn't use the word "vous." (LF) <***Loc:*** JE, LF>

caltron ♦see **carton**

calvaire [kalvær] *n.m.* [*eccl.*] Calvary <***Loc:*** Da84>

calypson [kalipsɔ̃] *n.m.* bad person, bad egg *Va-t'en, espèce de calypson, va!* Get lost, you bad egg! (TB) <***Loc:*** TB>

camarade [kɑ̃marad] *n.m.* 1 companion, friend, buddy, pal 2 fellow worker, coworker, comrade ◊ •**faire camarades**

a to become friends **I'z ont fait camarades.* They became friends. (EV, Ph36) ***b*** to make up, reconcile, become friends again <EV, SM, Ph36> <***Loc:*** EV, SM, Da84, Hi02, Ph36>

camaraderie [kɑ̃maradri] *n.f.* comaraderie, comradeship, friendship <***Loc:*** Da84>

cambouille (**combouille**) [kɑ̃buj, kɔ̃buj] *n.f.* toe cheese, toe jam, odorous residue between the toes due to uncleanliness <***Loc:*** IB, SL, La99>

cambré, -e [kɑ̃bre] *adj.* **1** bowed *T'as les jambes tellement cambrées que ça fait penser à des bois de colliers.* Your legs are so bowed that you make me think of yokes. (AV) **2** bowlegged *Un enfant cambré.* A bowlegged child. (SJ) <***Loc:*** AV, IB, SJ, SM, Lv88>

cambrure [kɑ̃bryr] *n.f.* curvature, bowing *La cambrure d'un violon.* The curvature of a violin. (VM) <***Loc:*** VM>

cambuse [kɑ̃byz] *n.f.* building, house *Etre toujours dans la cambuse.* To remain cooped up in the house all day. (SJ) <***Loc:*** AV, SJ>

camélia [kɑ̃melja] *n.* **1** *(m.)* camellia shrub, camellia tree **2** *(f.)* camellia flower <***Loc:*** CL, VM, Da84>

caméra [kɑ̃mera] *n.m.* camera <***Loc:*** VM, Da84>

camisole [kɑ̃mizɔl] *n.f.* **1** nightgown **Elle se met une jolie petite camisole frayante.* She puts on a sexy little nightgown. (Gr86) **2** slip (woman's undergarment) <***Loc:*** AV, EV, IB, IV, JD, JE, LF, SJ, SL, SM, TB, VM, Da84, Gr86, Guoo, Lv88>

camoisir ♦see **cramoisir**

camomille ♦see **camomine**

camomine (**camomille**) [kɑ̃mɔ̃min, kɑ̃mɔ̃mij] *n.f.* chamomile ◊ •**camomine sauvage** Santa Maria plant <SB> <***Loc:*** LA, SB, VM>

camouflage [kɑ̃muflaʒ] *n.m.* camouflage, disguise <***Loc:*** Da84>

camp[1] [kɑ̃] *n.m.* **1** slave quarters (on a plantation) **2** workers' quarters, settlement of workers in some industry *Le camp des nègres est à l'autre bord de la grande rue.* The blacks' quarters are on the other side of the large road. (VM) <***Loc:*** SL, VM, Di32>

CAMP[2] [kẽp, kẽmp] *v.intr.invar.* to camp *Y a des places pour CAMP.* There are places to camp. (Lv88) <***Loc:*** Lv88>

CAMP[3] [kẽp, kẽmp] *n.m.* **1** secondary dwelling (traditionally used during seasonal work or, today, for recreational purposes), locally called a "camp" *C'était le monde d'en ville, c'était juste un CAMP, eusse viendait en bas sus les weekends, et aller à la pêche, et là ça s'en va BACK, et eusse restait au CAMP dessus les weekends.* It was people from the city, it was just a camp, they came down on weekends and went fishing, then they went back, and they stayed at the camp on weekends. (TB) **2** modest house, cabin, shack *Il peut te faire un CAMP, si tu veux le marier.* He can make you a modest house, if you want to marry him. (VM) <***Loc:*** IV, JE, LA, TB, VM, An94, Da84, Lv88>

campagnard [kɑ̃pɑ̃jar] *n.m.* country dweller, one who lives in the country <***Loc:*** Da84>

campagne [kɑ̃pɑ̃j] *n.f.* **1** country, countryside *Y'avait une petite école de campagne.* There was a little country school. (AC) **2** campaign, military campaign *Non, j'ai pas fait la campagne de l'Afrique du Nord, Italie seulement.* No, I wasn't involved in the North African campaign, only Italy. (SL) <***Loc:*** AC, EV, IB, LA, SL, SM, TB, VM, Da84, Guoo>

campement [kɑ̃pmɑ̃] *n.m.* camp *La Chênière Caminada, il restait dans un petit campement là.* He lived in a little camp right on Cheniere Caminada. (LF) <***Loc:*** LF>

camper[1] [kɑ̃pe] **I** *v.intr.* **1** to camp **2** to spend the winter (fur trapping season) in one's seasonal home *Un CAMP ça c'est ça que tu vas camper dedans, qu'eusse disait dans le vieux temps "Allons aller au CAMP pour l'hiver pour camper."* A camp is what you go to spend the winter in, as they said in the old days: "Let's go to the camp to spend the winter." (LF) **3** to make a long visit, stay for a long time *Alle a venu et alle a campé.* She came and she stayed for a long time. (VM) *Rester campé.* To stay a long time. (SM) **4** to occupy a position, settle in a spot *Il est campé au ras de la porte.* He is positioned by the door. (SM) *Compère Lapin était campé dans le coin avec une mine de malade.* Compère Lapin was settled in the corner looking sickly. (VM) **5** to lean *Ne campe pas ta tête de ce côté-ci.* Do not lean your head on this side. (IB) **II se camper** *v.pron.* **1** to camp **2** to make a long visit, stay for a long time, overstay one's welcome *Se camper chez quelqu'un.* To overstay one's welcome at someone's house. (Lv88) **3** to position o.s., settle o.s. *Il peut se camper là, et pas grouiller pour des heures.* He can position himself there and not move for hours. (LA) ◊ •**campé comme un as de pique** rooted, stuck in one spot <SB, La99> <***Loc:*** LA, LF, SB, SM, TB, VM, An94, Da84, Di32, La99, Lv88>

camper[2] (**caper**) [kɑ̃pe, kape] *v.tr.* to strike, bump *Il a capé sa tête après la porte.* He struck his head against the door. (AV) *Elle a campé son pied sur cette chaise.* She struck her foot on this chair. (IB) <***Loc:*** AV, IB>

camperie [kɑ̃pri] *n.f.* camping trip *J'ai une liste longue comme ça pour une vieille petite camperie de quatre jours.* I have such a long list for a little old four-day camping trip. (AL) <***Loc:*** AL>

campeur, -euse [kɑ̃pœr, -øz] *n.* one who stays a long time, esp. one who overstays his or her welcome *Cette Marie, elle est une campeuse quand elle vient ici.* That Mary is one who stays a long time when she comes here. (IB) <***Loc:*** IB>

camphier ♦see **camphrier**

camphre [kɑ̃f(r)] *n.m.* camphor <***Loc:*** Da84>

camphré, -e (**tchanfré, -e**) [kɑ̃fre, tʃɑ̃fre] *adj.* **1** camphorated *Whisky camphré.* Camphorated whisky. (VM) **2** intoxicated, inebriated, drunk *Il a bu tellement de bière, il est camphré.* He drank so much beer that he's drunk. (SM) <***Loc:*** SM, TB, VM, Da84, Di32, La99>

camphrer [kɑ̃fre] *v.tr.* to camphorate *Camphrer le linge d'hiver.* To camphorate winter clothes. (EV) *Camphrer la closette.* To camphorate a closet. (EV) <***Loc:*** EV, VM, Da84>

camphrier (camphier) [kɑ̃frije, kɑ̃fje] *n.m.* camphor tree <***Loc:*** VM, Da84, Guoo>

CAN[1] [kæn] *v.tr.invar.* to can *Venez demain, on va* CAN *des haricots de facterie.* Come by tomorrow, we're going to can some stringless beans. (TB) <***Loc:*** LF, SL, TB>

CAN[2] **(caine, canne)** [kæn, kẽn, kɑ̃n] *n.m.* can, tin can *On achetait jamais rien dans les* CANS. We never bought anything in cans. (TB) *Il a un* CAN *de sardines.* He has a can of sardines. (JE) ◊ **•CAN d'aluminum** aluminum can *J'étais en arrière après tirer des* CANS *d'aluminum.* I was out back shooting aluminum cans. (LF) <LF> **•avoir le CAN** to be pregnant <LF> **•en CAN** canned, preserved *Tout ça qui restait pour manger, c'était des figues en* CAN. All that was left to eat were canned figs. (LA) <LA, VM> <***Loc:*** AV, EV, IB, JE, LA, LF, SJ, SL, SM, TB, VM, Da84, Lv88>

Canada [kɑ̃nada] *n.m.* **1** Canada **2** Canada goose <***Loc:*** EV, LF, TB, Da84>

canadien[1]**, -ienne** [kɑ̃nadjẽ, -jẽn] *adj.* Canadian *Une chanson canadienne.* A Canadian song. (LA) *Mon amise qu'est canadien, elle montre le français à les enfants au Bayou Bœuf.* My friend who is Canadian, she teaches French to children in Bayou Bœuf. (LF) <***Loc:*** LA, LF, Hi02>

Canadien[2]**, -ienne** [kɑ̃nadjẽ, -jẽn] *n.* Canadian <***Loc:*** Hi02>

canaille[1] [kɑ̃naj] *adj.* **1** shrewd, tricky *Elle est jolie, elle est petite, elle est canaille.* She's pretty, she's little, she's tricky. (Lv88) **2** mischievous *Ce petit garçon est assez canaille!* This little boy is pretty mischievous. (Guoo) **3** unruly *J'étais assez canaille, quand j'étais dans le cinquième grade dans l'école publique, ça m'a* KICK OUT, *oh oui j'étais pas bon, j'ai cogné la maîtresse, j'ai honte mais elle m'a cogné à moi en premier.* I was rather unruly, when I was in the fifth grade in public school, they kicked me out, oh yes I was bad, I hit the school teacher, I am ashamed but she hit me first. (IB) <***Loc:*** IB, LA, SL, SM, TB, VM, Da84, Di32, Guoo, Hi02, Lv88>

canaille[2] [kɑ̃naj] *n.m./f.* **1** shrewd, clever person *C'est un canaille cet avaocat-là.* That lawyer is a shrewd man. (JD) **2** trickster, prankster, mischievous person, practical joker *Tu ferais mieux le guetter. C'est un fameux canaille.* You'd better watch him. He's a known trickster. (SM) **3** scoundrel, rascal *C'est un vrai canaille ce garçon là.* That guy is a real rascal. (SJ) <***Loc:*** SJ, SM, VM, Da84>

canailler [kɑ̃naje] **I** *v.tr.* to dupe, deceive *Il l'a canaillé, lui s'a fait foutre en dedans.* He duped him, the other guy really got taken. (Lv88) *Il canaille tout le monde.* He deceives everyone. (JE) **II** *v.intr.* to play tricks, make mischief *Il est après canailler à la bar.* He's playing pranks at the bar. (Lv88) <***Loc:*** JE, LF, TB, Da84, Di32, Lv88>

canaillerie [kɑ̃najri] *n.f.* **1** prank, mischievous trick *Les enfants sont pleins de canailleries.* Kids are full of mischievous tricks. (SM) **2** mischief, mischievousness *Un tas de canailleries.* A bunch of mischief. (SM) **3** wickedness, unkind action *Ils en ont ti fait des canailleries quand ils étaient jeunes.* They sure did some bad things when they were young. (LA) **4** deceit *Ça c'est de la canaillerie.* That's deceit. (TB) <***Loc:*** LA, SM, TB, Da84, Di32, Hi02, Lv88>

canal [kɑ̃nal] *n.m.* **1** canal, channel *Les canals donnent dans le bayou.* The canals run into the bayou. (JE) **2** ditch *J'allais pêcher dans les champs, dans à peu près toute qualité de canal.* I used to go fishing in the fields, in nearly any kind of ditch. (LF) <***Loc:*** AV, JE, LA, LF, SB, SJ, SL, SM, TB, VM, Da84, Lv88>

canard, -e [kɑ̃nar, -ard] *n.* duck *Une journée j'attends la pauvre vieille canard qu'était sur le nid, coin coin! Je dis y a quelque chose qui l'a fait déranger.* One day I hear the poor old female duck that was on the nest, quack quack! I said, there's something that has disturbed her. (TB) ◊ **•canard branchu** wood duck <EV, TB, Da84, Ph36, Re31> **•canard de(s) bois** wood duck <EV, IV, LA, Lv88, Re31> **•canard cheval** canvasback duck (locally called horse duck) <TB, Da84, Lv88, Re31> **•canard congo** green-winged teal <Lv88> **•canard des îles *a*** Florida duck ***b*** Texas mottled duck <Re31> **•canard d'été** black duck <TB, Da84> **•canard d'Inde** muscovy duck <EV, IB, LA, TB, Da84, Lv88, Ph36, Re31> **•canard doux** tame duck, domesticated duck <Da84, Lv88> **•canard farouche** wild duck <Da84> **•canard français** mallard duck <EV, IB, IV, JE, LF, SL, SM, TB, Da84, Guoo, Lv88, Ph36, Re31> **•canard français d'été** mottled duck <Lv88> **•canard gris *a*** gadwall ***b*** gray duck <JE, LF, TB> **•canard mulet** mule duck <EV, IB, LA, Da84, Lv88, Re31> **•canard noir *a*** ring-necked duck ***b*** black duck <LF, TB, Lv88, Re31> **•canard noir d'été *a*** Florida duck ***b*** Texas mottled duck <TB, Re31> **•canard noir du nord** northern black mallard <Lv88, Re31> <***Loc:*** AC, AV, EV, IV, JE, LF, SJ, SL, SM, TB, VM, An94, Da84, Guoo, Hi02, Lv88, Re31>

cancan [kɑ̃kɑ̃] *n.m.* **1** mischievous gossip *T'aurais dû entendre ce cancan autour de la table.* You should have heard the gossip around the table. (LA) **2** trouble, confusion *Il fait un tas de cancan.* He makes a lot of trouble. (SM) **3** fiasco *Ça a tout fini dans un sacré cancan.* It all ended in a grand fiasco. (LA) **4** rowdy event *Il y a eu un cancan dans le village hier. La police a venu.* There was a big stir in town last night. The police came. (SL) **5** racket, ruckus **Qui c'est qui fait ç'pareille cancan?* Who's making all that racket? (EV, Ph36) <***Loc:*** EV, LA, SL, SM, VM, Da84, La99, Ph36>

cancanage (coconnage) [kɑ̃kɑ̃naʒ, kokɔ̃naʒ] *n.m. (usu. pl.)* gossip, talk *Depuis que je vas pas au bal je connais pus les coconnages.* Since I don't go to the dances, I don't know the gossip. (VM) <***Loc:*** JD, SM, VM>

cancanailles [kɑ̃kɑ̃naj] *n.f.pl.* gossip *Il ne faut pas croire toutes* *ces cancanailles.* One must not believe all those tales. (IB) <***Loc:*** IB>

cancaner [kɑ̃kɑ̃ne] *v.intr.* **1** to gossip, carry tales *Ces vieux bougres sont tout le temps après cancaner.* Those old men are always gossiping. (LA) **2** to be in conference, have a tête-à-tête *C'est Jean qui veut cancaner avec moi.* John is the one who wants to have a conference with me. (AV) <***Loc:*** AV, LA, SM, Da84>

cancaneur, -euse [kɑ̃kɑ̃nœr, -øz] *n.m.* gossiper *Il connaît tous les affaires du village. C'est un grand cancaneur.* He knows everything that's going on in town. He's a big gossip. (SL) <***Loc:*** IB, SL, Da84>

cancer [kɑ̃sær] *n.m.* cancer *Une bonne chose pour elle, son cancer est traitable.* A good thing for her, her cancer is treatable. (LA) *Des cancers du peau.* Skin cancers. (SM) <***Loc:*** LA, LF, SM, Da84>

cancéreux, -euse [kɑ̃serø, -øz] *adj.* cancerous *Le tumeur était cancéreux.* The tumor was cancerous. (LA) *Son test a revenu, et c'est cancéreux.* His test returned, and it's cancerous. (LA) <***Loc:*** LA, Da84>

candi [kɑ̃di] *n.m.* candy *Un candi de* PEPPERMINT. A peppermint. (Lv88) ◊ **•candi barré** ***a*** candy cane, peppermint candy ***b*** flamboyant person, dandy <EV, VM, Hi02, La99> **•candi de maison** taffy <IB> <***Loc:*** EV, IB, SJ, SL, SM, TB, VM, Da84, Hi02, La99, Lv88, Ph36>

candidat [kɑ̃dida] *n.m.* candidate <***Loc:*** Da84>

candja ♦see **condjo**

candjateur, -euse [kɑ̃dʒatœr, -øz] *n.* one who casts spells *Une candjateuse c'est quelqu'un qui donne des candjas [=condjos].* A "candjateuse" is a woman who casts spells. (TB) <***Loc:*** TB>

caneçon ♦see **caleçon**

caneton [kɑ̃ntɔ̃] *n.m.* duckling, small duck <***Loc:*** JD>

cangrène ♦see **gangrène**

cangrener ♦see **gangrener**

cani-cani [kɑ̃nikɑ̃ni] *interj.* cry for calling ducks <***Loc:*** EV, SM, Lv88, Ph36>

caniche ♦see **canuche**

canicroche [kɑ̃nikrɔʃ] *n.m.* **1** obstacle, impediment, hindrance, hitch *Il y a toujours un canicroche dans l'affaire.* There is always a hitch in the matter. (AV) **2** slip, blunder *J'ai fait un canicroche.* I made a blunder. (Lv88) **3** tomfoolery, monkeyshines ◊ **•faire des canicroches** ***a*** to play a trick, play a practical joke ***b*** to cut silly capers <SJ, Lv88> <***Loc:*** AV, IB, SJ, Lv88>

canique [kɑ̃nik, kɑ̃nij] *n.f.* **1** playing marble **Le cadeau qui ravit les petits Acadiens: un sac de caniques.* The gift that thrilled the young Acadians: a sack of marbles. (SM) *Nous-autres on jouait à caniques, on jouait ça tous les jours avec les caniques.* We used to play marbles, we played with marbles every day. (IB) *Il joue aux caniques.* He is playing marbles. (JE) **2** testicle *Il a été frappé dans les caniques.* He was hit in the testicles. (LA) ◊ **•canique de l'œil** eyeball *La branche l'a coupé droit sur la canique de l'œil.* The branch cut him right on the eyeball. (LA) <LA, SM> <***Loc:*** AC, AV, EV, IB, JD, JE, LA, SJ, SL, SM, TB, Da84, Di32, La99, Lv88, Ph36>

cannage [kẽnaʒ, kɑ̃naʒ] *n.m.* canned goods *J'ai mangé du cannage.* I ate some canned goods. (JE) *Nous va à la grocerie, nous achète des cannages, de l'eau. [...] Des cannages de manger qui va pas gâter.* We go to the grocery store, we buy cans, water. Cans of food that will not spoil. (SM) <***Loc:*** JE, LF, SM, Lv88>

canne[1] [kɑ̃n] *n.f.* **1** reed, cattail *Il s'a caché dans les cannes à côté du bayou.* He hid in the reeds along the bayou. (LA) **2** sugar cane *Il élevait des cannes lui aussi. Il était proche sûr le plus gros fermier des cannes.* He raised cane also. He was almost certainly the biggest cane farmer. (LA) **3** drinking straw *Tu veux une canne pour ta limonade?* Do you want a straw for your lemonade? (EV) **4** walking stick, cane *Et le vieux, ç'a venu qu'il pouvait presque plus marcher. Il amenait sa petite canne pointue.* And the old guy, it got so that he could hardly walk. He would bring his little pointed cane. (LF) ◊ **•canne à fuseau** wild cane reed, bamboo <VM, Lv88> **•canne farouche** wild cane reed, bamboo <AV, SL, Lv88> **•canne à pêche {pêcher}** ***a*** fishing pole ***b*** wild cane reed, bamboo <Da84, Hi02> **•canne à sucre** sugar cane <IB, Da84, Hi02> **•canne au cochon** big cordgrass <Ho90> **•canne de cochon** quill cane <VM> **•canne de maïs** corn stalks <VM, Da84> **•canne des cochons** hog cane, marsh grass <Re54> **•canne-goutte** eye dropper <LA> **•canne marronne** wild cane reed, bamboo <IB, SJ> **•canne sauvage** wild cane reed, bamboo <IB> **•canne terre haute** wild cane reed, bamboo <SJ> <***Loc:*** AC, AS, CL, EV, IB, IV, JD, JE, LA, LF, SJ, SL, SM, TB, VM, Da84, Hi02, Lv88>

canne[2] see CAN

cannelle[1] [kɑ̃nɛl] *adj.* cinnamon-colored *J'avais un vieux petit cheval cannelle.* I had a little old cinnamon-colored horse. (Lv88) <***Loc:*** AV, IB, EV, LF, SJ, An84, Da84, Lv88>

cannelle[2] [kɑ̃nɛl] *n.m./f.* cinnamon *Du pain perdu, c'est encore du vieux pain et c'est passé dans l'œuf et avant de le cuire c'est de l'œuf et de la cannelle. Et là tu mets ça dedans un poêlon et puis tu chauffes sur les deux bords. On appelle ça du pain perdu.* French toast, that too is made with old bread and you dip it in egg, and before cooking it it's egg and cinnamon. And you put it in a frying pan and then you heat it on both sides. They call that 'lost bread.' (LF) <***Loc:*** AV, LF, SM, Da84, Lv88>

cannelle[3] [kɑ̃nɛl] *n.* ◊ **•en cannelles** to pieces, to bits *J'ai cassé ce vase en cannelles.* I broke that vase to bits. (Pe37) *Le chat a mis le livre en cannelles.* The cat tore the book to shreds. (SM) <SM, Lv88, Pe37> <***Loc:*** SM, Lv88, Pe37>

canner ♦see **encanner**

cannerie [kænri, kɑ̃nri] *n.f.* cannery <***Loc:*** Fa77, Lv88>

cannette [kɑ̃nɛt] *n.f.* cane reed *Il a besoin une cannette pour faire un pétard.* He needs a cane reed to make a firecracker. (SJ) <***Loc:*** SJ>

canneur, -euse [kɑ̃nœr, -øz] *n.* canner, one who cans <***Loc:*** LA>

cannibale [kɑ̃nibal] *n.m.* cannibal <***Loc:*** LF, Da84, Re31>

canon [kɑ̃nɔ̃] *n.m.* **1** cannon **2** leg (of a pair of pants) ◊ **•canon de fusil** gun barrel <Da84> <***Loc:*** EV, JE, SM, Da84, Ph36>

canoniser [kɑ̃nɔ̃nize] *v.tr.* to canonize *Ils sont après essayer de faire canoniser la petite fille de Richard.* They are trying to have the little girl from Richard canonized. (LA) <***Loc:*** LA, Da84>

canonner [kɑ̃nɔ̃ne] *v.tr.* to beat, pelt *Ils l'ont canonné à coups de pierre.* They pelted him with stones. (JD) <***Loc:*** JD>

canot ♦see **canotte**

canotte (**canot**) [kɑ̃nɔt] *n.m./f.* **1** any of various fishing boats with a round bottom *C'est toujours une canotte si le fond est rond. Si le fond est plat, c'est un skiff.* It's always a "canotte" if the bottom is round. If the bottom is flat, it's a skiff. (JE) **2** lugger, Louisiana lugger *Un canotte a des courbes rondes. Tous les courbes est coupées rondes.* A lugger has round ribs. All the ribs are cut round. (TB) *Canotte, ça c'est un vieux bateau des vieux temps. Il y en a plus plein de ça. Un canotte, un vieux bateau avec le fond rond.* Lugger, that's an old boat from the old days. There aren't many of those left. A lugger, it's an old boat with a round bottom. (TB) <***Loc:*** JE, LF, TB, Lv88>

cant [kɑ̃] *n.m.* narrow side, edge (of a board, etc.) *Poser un livre sur le cant.* Set a book on its edge. (Lv88) <***Loc:*** Di32, Lv88>

cantaque [kɑ̃tak] *n.m.* smilax <***Loc:*** Re31>

cantier ♦see **quantier**

cantique[1] [kɑ̃ntik] *n.f.* gambling joint, club for playing cards *Il y avait un qu'avait été tué dans une petite cantique pas loin là. Il était après jouer aux cartes.* There was one who got killed in a little gambling joint not far away. He was playing cards. (SL) <***Loc:*** SL>

cantique[2] [kɑ̃ntik] *n.m.* hymn, canticle <***Loc:*** TB, Da84>

canton [kɑ̃tɔ̃] *n.m.* neighborhood, section of town *Dans mon canton.* In my neighborhood. (SJ) <***Loc:*** LA, SJ>

canuche (**caniche**) [kɑ̃nyʃ, kɑ̃niʃ] *n.m./f.* **1** reed, small bamboo *Les cannes, c'est fait de canuche...tu sais, ils appelaient des bamboos.* Cane, it's made of reeds . . . you know, they call them bamboo. (IV) **2** switch grass <***Loc:*** EV, IB, IV, TB, Di32, Guoo, Lv88, Ph36, Re31>

canulant, -e [kɑ̃nylɑ̃, -ɑ̃t] *adj.* boring, tiresome *Il est vaillant mais un peu canulant.* He's nice but a bit boring. (SM) <***Loc:*** SM>

canule [kɑ̃nyl] *n.f.* boring, tiresome person (usu. one who talks incessantly) <***Loc:*** SM>

canuler [kɑ̃nyle] *v.tr.* to bore, be tiresome to <***Loc:*** SM>

caouane (**caouenne**) [kawɑ̃n, kawɛ̃n, kajwɛ̃n] *n.m./f.* **1** alligator snapping turtle, (freshwater) loggerhead snapping turtle **2** head, noggin **3** stubborn person, hardheaded person **4** big, slow, dowdy woman **5** [*vulg.*] female genitals ◊ **•caouenne galeuse** common snapping turtle <EV> **•caouenne à trois rangs** alligator snapping turtle, (freshwater) loggerhead snapping turtle <EV> <***Loc:*** AC, AV, EV, IB, IV, JD, JE, LA, LF, SJ, SM, TB, VM, Da84, Guoo, La99, Lv88, Re31>

caouenne ♦see **caouane**

caouitchouc ♦see **caoutchouc**

caoutchouc (**caouitchouc**) [kautʃu, kaotʃu, kawitʃu] *n.m.* **1** rubber (esp. hard rubber) *Ces* TIRES *sont faits de caoutchouc.* These tires are made of rubber. (JE) **2** plastic, celluloid *Le caouitchouc c'était, que je me rappelle, c'est un plastique noir, ça qu'ils faisont les plaques à* PHONOGRAPH *avec.* Celluloid was, as I remember, it's a black plastic, what they made phonograph records with. (LF) **3** isinglass <***Loc:*** EV, JE, LF, SM, VM, Da84, Ph36>

CAP[1] [kæp, kɛp, kap] *v.tr.invar.* **1** to cap, put a cap on (a bottle) *Et on cappait les bouteilles.* And we used to cap the bottles [of homemade root beer]. (LF) **2** to stop up, obstruct *J'ai* CAP *le tuyau.* I plugged up the pipe. (Lv88) <***Loc:*** LF, Lv88>

CAP[2] [kæp, kɛp, kap] *n.m.* **1** cap, baseball cap *Y avait son* CAP *d'ôté de sa tête.* He had his cap off his head. (TB) **2** bottle cap *Il sauve les* CAPS *pour mettre dans son* DRIVEWAY. He saves bottle caps to put in his driveway. (LA) **3** pistol cap *Il s'a brûlé les doigts en jouant avec des* CAPS. He burned his fingers playing with caps. (LA) <***Loc:*** AV, EV, JD, LA, LF, SJ, SL, SM, TB,VM, Da84, Di32, Lv88, Ph36>

capable [kapab(l)] *adj.* **1** able, capable *Je me rappelle pas de pas être capable parler français.* I don't remember ever not being able to speak French. (SL) *Il faulait que j'apprends leur langage pour être capable de faire mon job.* I had to learn their language to be able to do my job. (TB) *On faisait de la boucane pour les maringouins pour être capable s'assir dans la galerie.* We would make smoke for the mosquitos, so we could sit out on the porch. (SL) **2** likely *Il est capable d'aller.* He's likely to go. (IB) <***Loc:*** EV, IB, JD, SJ, SL, TB, Da84, Lv88>

capacité [kapasite] *n.f.* capacity, ability <***Loc:*** Da84>

cap-cap ♦see **cape-cape**

capahu [kapay, kapary] *n.m.* capaiba *Après, tu mets une goutte de capahu.* Then you put in a drop of capaiba. (TB) <***Loc:*** TB>

cape [kap] *n.f.* cape, cloak, mantle <***Loc:*** Da84>

cape-cape (**cap-cap**, **kap-kap**) [kapkap] *n.m./f.* **1** big black beetle **2** snipe **3** green-backed heron, little green heron **4** American bittern (locally called sungazer) **5** tightrope walker *Équand on était petit, nos parents nous amenaient au cirque. Et le monde qui marchait sur les cordes là, on appelait ça des cape-capes.* When we were small, our parents took us to the circus. And the people who walked on tightropes there, we called them "cap-caps." (LF) **6** ignorant, uneducated, insignificant or foolish person *Boy! Ca c'est un cape-cape oui!* Boy! He's a real fool! (JD) **7** uneducated, illiterate speech **Il parle cap-cap.* He speaks an uneducated dialect. (Re31) ◊ **•cap-cap doré** least bittern <Re31> <***Loc:*** AC, EV, FL, IB, JD, LA, LF, SB, SJ, SL, SM, TB,VM, Da84, La99, Lv88, Ph36, Re31>

caper ♦see **camper**[2]

capichon ♦see **capuchon**

capillaire [kapilar] *n.m.* maidenhair <***Loc:*** Fa77>

capitaine [kapitɛ̃n] *n.m.* **1** captain (of a boat) *J'ai travaillé sus des* TUG*. Ici c'est ma licence de capitaine de bateau.* I worked on tugboats. Here is my boat captain's license. (TB) **2** captain, team leader (esp. for Mardi Gras games) **3** head, leader, one who outperforms one's peers *Il est le capitaine de la classe.* He is at the head of his class. (AV) ◊ **•Capitaine Souris** captain, team leader (of Mardi Gras festivities) *Les enfants ont galopé à la barrière pour voir la Dorothée et le capitaine Souris.* The children ran to the fence to see the Mardi Gras queen and king. (SL) <SL> <***Loc:*** AV, SL, SM, TB, Lv88>

capital, -e [kapital] *adj.* capital, principal **Les septs péchés capitaux.* The seven capital sins. (Da84) <***Loc:*** Da84>

capitale [kapital] *n.f.* **1** capital (of a state) **2** capitol building <***Loc:*** VM, Da84>

capitaliste [kapitalist] *n.m.* capitalist <***Loc:*** Da84>

capon, -onne [kapɔ̃, -ɔ̃n] *n.* fearful person, coward *Il faut pas tu sois un capon pour être un shérif.* You mustn't be a coward to be a sheriff. (Lv88) *Bande de capons.* Bunch of cowards. (Lv88) ◊ **•capon comme un mouton** as cowardly as a sheep <Lv88> <***Loc:*** IB, IV, JE, SL, SM, Da84, Guoo, Lv88>

caponner [kapɔ̃ne] *v.intr.* to act cowardly, back down (from a challenge) *Il a caponné, il a pas sorti.* He backed down, he didn't go out. (Lv88) <***Loc:*** Da84, Lv88>

caporal [kaporal] *n.m.* **1** corporal **2** red-winged blackbird <***Loc:*** Da84, Re31>

capot [kapo] *n.m.* **1** coat, overcoat *Ça c'est pour accrocher le linge, les capots et les chapeaux.* This is to hang clothes, coats and hats. (AC) **2** jacket ◊ **•capot à pluie** raincoat <SL> **•capot ciré** raincoat <AV, EV, IB, JD, SJ, SM, TB, Da84, Ph36> **•gros capot** overcoat, heavy coat <Da84> <***Loc:*** AC, AV, EV, IB, JD, JE, LA, LF, SJ, SL, SM, VM, Da84, Di32, Guoo, Ph36>

capotage [kapotaʒ] *n.m.* **1** rolling over (e.g. of a car) *Il y a eu un capotage dessus le chemin de l'Anse Bleue.* There was a rollover on the L'Anse Bleue Road. (LA) **2** somersault **3** overthrow, upset *Un capotage dans les éléctions.* An upset in the elections. (Lv88) **4** commotion <***Loc:*** LA, Lv88>

capote[1] [kapɔt] *n.f.* prophylactic, condom <***Loc:*** JE, SM, VM>

capote[2] [kapɔt] *n.f.* fall, tumble <***Loc:*** JD>

capoter [kapote] **I** *v.tr.* **1** to turn over *Le Vendredi Saint [...], les lames des charrues sont capotées la tête en bas.* On Good Friday the blades of the plows are turned upside down. (SM) *Ça c'est pour* CHOP*, après que t'as capoté ta terre, tu la tapes.* That's for chopping, after you've turned the ground over, you strike it. (LF) **2** to knock down, knock over, topple *Il a capoté le panier de z-œufs.* He knocked over the basket of eggs. (Lv88) *La malaria capote le monde.* Malaria fells people. (Lv88) **Capotez pas la maison!* Don't overturn the house [with your unruliness]! (TB, La99) **3** to dump, pour *Et là ça tombe tout dans ces bogheis et par différentes* SIZE*, juste la viande de chevrette. Alle est tout épluchée. Une fois qu'eusse tombe là-dedans on les met l'autre boutte et on les capote dans une autre* TANK *avec de l'eau.* And they all fall into these buggies by different sizes, just the shrimp meat. It's completely peeled. Once they fall in there we put them down at the other end and we dump them into another tank of water. (LF) **II** *v.intr.* **1** to roll over, flip over *La voiture a capoté en sortant de la cour.* The car flipped over while leaving the yard. (SM) **2** to topple over, fall down **3** to capsize *Son bateau a capoté.* His boat capsized. (JE) **4** to recline *Des sièges qui capotent.* Reclining seats. (Lv88) <***Loc:*** AV, EV, IB, JE, LA, LF, SL, SM, TB, Da84, Di32, La99, Lv88>

caprice [kapris] *n.m.* caprice, whim, impulse *Avoir ses caprices.* To have one's capricious ways, moods. (AV) *Faire quelque chose par caprice.* To do something on a whim. (AV) *Il a rebouqué quand je lui ai dit ça que je pensais de ses caprices.* He backed down when I told him what I thought of his fancies. (VM) <***Loc:*** AV, VM, Da84>

capricieux, -ieuse [kaprisjø, -øz] *adj.* capricious, impulsive, full of whims *Un enfant capricieux.* A capricious child. (AV) <***Loc:*** AV, Da84>

capsule [kapsyl] *n.f.* **1** capsule (of medicine) **2** cap, firing cap <***Loc:*** SM, Da84>

captivité [kaptivite] *n.f.* captivity, bondage <***Loc:*** Da84>

capuchon (capichon) [kapyʃɔ̃, kapiʃɔ̃] *n.m.* **1** tall, pointed hat (esp. as worn by a costumed Mardi Gras runner) *Quand les Mardi Gras ont arrivé, tu pouvais voir des douzaines de capuchons qui sortaient du wagon.* When the Mardi Gras participants arrived, you could see dozens of pointed caps sticking out of the wagon. (LA) **2** nightcap *Il couche avec un capichon.* He goes to bed with a nightcap. (JE) **3** skull cap **4** old hat or cap <***Loc:*** AV, IB, JE, LA, SJ, SL, SM, TB, Da84, Lv88>

caquiche ♦see **caquisse**

caquisse (caquiche) [kakis, kakiʃ] *n.f.* baby tooth, milk tooth <***Loc:*** LF, SM, VM, Lv88>

car [kar] *conj.* because *Fais courir tes paroles avec ce prisonnier car les messieurs de la justice ne tarderont pas longtemps.* Convey your words by means of this prisoner because the men of the court will not tarry long. (PQ, ch: *Quand la belle entendit dire*) <*Loc:* PQ, Da84>

çar ♦see **celui**

carabas [karaba, karabas] *n.m.* ugly hat <*Loc:* AV, Re31>

carabine [karabin] *n.f.* rifle, carbine *Asteur c'est avec des couteaux, des fusils, des carabines.* Nowadays it's with knives, guns, rifles. (TB) <*Loc:* EV, LF, TB, Da84>

carabiné, -e [karabine] *adj.* 1 splendid, excellent, first-class, magnificent **Dîner carabiné.* Fine dinner. (Da84) 2 extravagant, excessive *Je me suis foutu une bosse carabinée.* I got magnificently drunk. (SM) *Il a attrapé une pile carabinée.* He caught a really large quantity. (SM) <*Loc:* AV, IB, SB, SJ, SM, TB, Da84, La99, Re31>

caracoler (**calicoler**) [karakole, kalikole] *v.intr.* 1 to stagger, totter, wobble *Je faisais comme si j'étais saoûl. Je prenais à caracoler.* I acted like I was drunk. I began to stagger. (SL) 2 to stick with, unload s.t. undesirable on *Il m'a caracolé ce vieux tabac.* He stuck me with this old tobacco. (IB) <*Loc:* AV, IB, JD, LA, SL, SJ, SM, TB, Da84, Di32>

caractère [karaktær] *n.m.* 1 character, disposition, personality *Il a un tas le caractère à son papa.* He has very much the character of his dad. (SM) 2 extravagant or original person, character *Ça c'est un caractère.* He's a character. (Lv88) <*Loc:* SM, Da84, Lv88>

caractéristique [karakteristik] *n.f.* characteristic <*Loc:* Da84>

carafe [karaf] *n.f.* 1 carafe, decanter 2 water bottle <*Loc:* Da84>

caragne (**carangue**) [karɑ̃j] *n.m.* any of several carangid fish, including the Amberjack and the Crevalle jack <*Loc:* TB, Re31>

caramel [karɑ̃mɛl] *n.m.* 1 caramel, toffee 2 browned sugar <*Loc:* Da84>

caramboler [karɑ̃bole] *v.tr.* to push violently *Il m'a carambolé.* He pushed me violently. (JE) <*Loc:* JE, LF>

carangue ♦see **caragne**

caravane [karavɑ̃n] *n.f.* sojourn, stay *Passer une caravane c'ez quelqu'un.* To stay at someone's house. (LF) *Partir en caravane.* To head off to someone's house for a stay. (LF) *Alle a venu sus une caravane.* She came to spend a few days. (TB) <*Loc:* LF, TB>

carbolique [karbolik] *adj.* carbolic ◊ •**(acide) carbolique** carbolic acid <Da84> •**boule de carbolique** mothball <Lv88> <*Loc:* Da84, Lv88>

carbone [karbɔ̃n] *n.f.* carbuncle, boil <*Loc:* LF>

carcailler [karkaje] *v.intr.* to clown around, cut up, act foolish *Arrête carcailler.* Stop clowning around. (SL) <*Loc:* SL>

carcan [karkɑ̃] *n.m.* triangular wooden collar put around the neck of an animal to stop it from breaking through a fence ◊ •**faire le carcan** to carry s.o. on one's shoulders *Jean est trop lourd pour faire le carcan.* John is too heavy to be carried on the shoulders. (IB) <IB> <*Loc:* IB, LA, SL, SM, TB, Da84, Di32>

carcasse [karkas] *n.f.* 1 carcass, dead body *Quand ce char m'a frappée, j'ai livré ma carcasse au diable.* When that car hit me, I thought I was a goner. (VM) 2 chassis (of a motor vehicle) *La carcasse d'un char, une carcasse rouillée.* The chassis of a car, a rusted chassis. (VM) <*Loc:* AV, VM, Da84>

carcasser ♦see **cacasser**

carcul ♦see **calcul**

carculer ♦see **calculer**

carculeur [karkylœr] *n.m.* 1 mathematician 2 one who calculates numbers *Il est un bon carculeur.* He's good with figures. (TB) <*Loc:* SM, TB, Lv88>

carde (**écarde**) [kard, ekard] *n.f.* card (tool used to comb wool, cotton, etc.) <*Loc:* JD, SJ, TB, Da84>

carder (**écarder**) [karde, ekarde] *v.tr.* 1 to card, comb or brush (cotton, wool, etc.) *Elle est après écarder le coton pour faire des couverts.* She's carding cotton to make blankets. (VM) **Carder la laine.* To card wool. (Da84) 2 to beat, whip, thrash <*Loc:* AV, JD, SJ, SL, TB, VM, Da84, Lv88>

cardinal[1]**, -e** [kardinal] *adj.* [*eccl.*] main, principal, cardinal *Un péché cardinal.* A cardinal sin. (VM) <*Loc:* VM, Da84>

cardinal[2] [kardinal] (*pl.* **cardinals** [kardinal], **cardinaux** [kardino]) *n.m.* cardinal (in the Roman Catholic Church) *Les cardinals de Rome.* The Cardinals of Rome. (VM) <*Loc:* LA, LF, VM, Da84>

cardinal[3] ♦see **cardinau**

cardinau (**cardinal**) [kardino, kardinal] *n.m.* cardinal, redbird *Un nic de cardinal, une plume de cardinal.* A cardinal's nest, a cardinal's feather. (EV) *Rouge comme un cardinau.* Red as a cardinal. (Lv88) *Le cardinau est un joli z-oiseau.* The cardinal is a pretty bird. (JE) <*Loc:* AV, EV, IB, JD, JE, LA, LF, SJ, SL, SM, TB, Da84, Lv88, Re31>

cardon [kardɔ̃] *n.m.* 1 small spool of wool or cotton 2 piece of cotton or wool that has been carded (to be used between the two layers of cloth in a quilt) <*Loc:* JD, SM, VM, Lv88>

Carême [karɛ̃m] *n.m.* Lent ◊ •**faire le Carême** to keep Lent, observe Lent <Da84> <*Loc:* LF, Da84>

carenas ♦see **cadenas**

carencro [karɑ̃kro] *n.m.* 1 turkey buzzard 2 carrion crow 3 black vulture 4 [*offensive*] black person ◊ •**carencro tête-rouge** turkey buzzard <Lv88, Re31> •**carencro tête noire** black vulture <Re31> •**carencro de mer** man-o'-war bird, frigate bird <Re31> •**carencro-vole** children's game <Lv88> •**comme des carencros autour d'une charogne** like vultures around carrion (in reference to a large number, usu. of people, ready to take advantage of a bad situation) <AC, La99> •**'tit carencro** love bug <VM> <*Loc:* AC, AV, EV, IB, JD, JE, LA, SJ, SL, SM, TB, VM, Da84, Di32, Gu00, La99, Lv88, Ph36>

caresse [karɛs] *n.f.* 1 caress 2 hug, embrace 3 kiss <*Loc:* Da84>

caresser [karese] **I** *v.tr.* to caress, fondle, pet **Elle a commencé à la caresser jusqu'à qu'elle a rentré.* She started petting it [a deer] until it came in. (IB, An94) **Nathan s'est* *advancé [=avancé] et a embrassé Jeanette en arrière de l'oreille. Elle a jigaillé et Nathan l'a bien caressé.* Nathan leaned over and kissed her behind the ear. She squirmed and Nathan sweetly caressed her. (Wh83) **II se caresser** *v.pron.* **1** to caress each other, fondle each other **2** to hug each other *Ça s'aimait assez, ça se caressait tous les après-midi quand le frère rentrait de l'école.* They loved each other so much, they would hug each other every afternoon when the brother would get home from school. (EV) <*Loc:* EV, IB, TB, An94, Da84, Wh83>

caret [karɛ, kare] *n.m.* **1** mud turtle **2** diamond-back terrapin <*Loc:* Re40>

cargaison [kargezɔ̃, kargesɔ̃] *n.f.* wagonload *J'ai une cargaison de bois pour toi.* I have a wagonload of wood for you. (SM) <*Loc:* SM, Re31>

cargué, -e [karge] *adj.* sway-backed *L'homme est cargué.* The man is sway-backed. (LF) <*Loc:* LF>

carguer [karge] **I** *v.intr.* to lean, lean back *Cargue pas trop. Tu vas tomber.* Don't lean back too far. You'll fall. (SM) **II se carguer** *v.pron.* **1** to lean, lean back **I s'est cargué conte la porte.* He leaned against the door. (EV, Ph36) **2** to recline, sit back comfortably *Il va se carguer dans cette chaise toute la matinée.* (IB) *Elle se cargue dans la chaise.* She reclines comfortably in the chair. (JE) **3** to rear (of a horse) ◊ **•être cargué** to be seated comfortably *J'étais cargué dans une chaise.* I was comfortably seated in a chair. (JE) <JE, LF> **•être cargué dans une place** to be left in the lurch somewhere <SJ> <*Loc:* EV, IB, JD, JE, LA, LF, SJ, SL, SM, Ph36>

caricature (**calicature**) [karikatyr, kalikatyr] *n.f.* caricature, grotesque effigy <*Loc:* SM, Da84>

carlet ♦see **carrelet**

carmagnole [karmɑ̃jol, karmɑ̃jo] *n.f.* ◊ **•danser la carmagnole** to suffer through a difficult experience, be in a bad fix *J'ai dansé la carmagnole au dentiste.* I had quite an ordeal at the dentist's. (SM) <SM, Lv88> <*Loc:* SM, Lv88>

carnage [karnaʒ] *n.m.* **1** noise, racket, hubbub, disturbance **Les officiers du bateau [...] voulaient pas que les Acadiens [fassent] trop du train et du carnage.* The officers of the boat didn't want the Acadians to make too much trouble and noise. (Gr82) **2** malicious mischief (esp. vandalism or stealing) <*Loc:* JE, LA, LF, SL, SM, TB, Da84, Di32, Gr82, La99, Lv88>

carnager [karnaʒe] *v.intr.* **1** to act destructively, engage in malicious mischief, make a mess *Les chaouis ont carnagé tout partout dans le clos.* The raccoons plundered everything all over the field. (Lv88) *Les enfants sont après carnager dans la maison.* The kids are making a mess in the house. (Lv88) **2** to make a racket, play noisily *Les enfants sont toujours après carnager.* Kids are always making a racket. (EV) <*Loc:* EV, LA, SM, Da84, Di32, Lv88>

carnageries [karnaʒri] *n.f.pl.* **1** vandalism, destructiveness **2** boisterousness, carrying on *Jimmy a arrêté ses carnageries quand il s'a marié.* Jimmy stopped his carrying on when he got married. (VM) <*Loc:* VM>

carnageur, -euse (**carnageux, -euse**) [karnaʒœr, karnaʒø, -øz] *n.* **1** vandal *C'est des carnageurs qu'ont tout cassé les vitres à l'école.* Some vandals broke all the windows at the school. (LA) **2** disorderly, boisterous person (or animal), troublemaker *Il est juste un carnageur. Il va défaire tout.* He is just a troublemaker. He will upset everything. (LA) **2** child who makes a lot of noise while playing <*Loc:* LA, SM, Da84, Di32, Lv88>

carnageux ♦see **carnageur**

carnassier[1] [karnasje] *v.tr.* to wreak havoc with, pillage, ruin *Les sacrés chiens avont tout carnassié mon jardin.* The damn dogs tore my garden all up. (VM) <*Loc:* VM>

carnassier[2], **-ière** (**carnassieux, -ieuse**) [karnasje, -jær, karnasjø, -jøz] *adj.* **1** destructive *Le bébé est d'âge où il est carnassieux.* The baby is of an age when he is destructive. (VM) **2** mischievous *Un enfant carnassier.* A mischievous child. (AV) **3** boisterous, rambunctious, noisy (esp. of children) **4** vicious, mean *Des chiens carnassiers.* Vicious dogs. (LA) <*Loc:* AV, IB, LA, SJ, SM, VM, Lv88>

carnassière [karnasjær] *n.f.* game bag, hunting bag <*Loc:* IV, An94>

carnassieux ♦see **carnassier**[2]

carnaval [karnaval] *n.m.* **1** Carnival, Mardi Gras celebration *John et Frank sont partis au carnaval samedi.* John and Frank are going to the Mardi Gras on Saturday. (LA) **2** fair, carnival (esp. a street fair or church fair) *Carnaval d'église.* Church fair. (LA) ◊ **•faire un carnaval** to make noise, cause an uproar <AV, SJ> <*Loc:* AV, LA, SJ, Da84>

carotte [karɔt, karot] *n.f.* **1** carrot **2** plug or twist of chewing tobacco *Dans le vieux temps, le monde se faisait des carottes de périque pour chiquer dans l'année.* In the old days, people would make themselves twists of "périque" [tobacco] to chew throughout the year. (LA) *Une carotte de tabac.* A twist of tobacco. (SM) <*Loc:* AC, JD, JE, LA, SM, TB, Da84, La99>

carotter [karote] *v.tr.* **1** to roll very tightly (as tobacco) *Carotter un bébé dans une couverte.* Roll a baby tightly in a blanket. (Lv88) **2** to confine *Je suis carottée dans ma maison.* I'm confined to my house. (Lv88) <*Loc:* Lv88>

carouk ♦see **carouque**

carouque (**carouk**) [karuk] *n.f.* red-breasted snipe <*Loc:* Lv88, Re31>

carpe [karp] *n.f.* **1** carp **2** buffalo fish ◊ **•carpe blanche** white carp <Lv88> **•carpe bleue** blue carp <Lv88> **•carpe jaune** yellow carp <Lv88> <*Loc:* EV, IB, IV, SL, SM, TB, An94, Da84, Gu00, Lv88>

carpiche [karpiʃ] *n.f.* somersault *Prendre une carpiche.* To turn a somersault. (AV) <*Loc:* AV, Re31>

carré[1], **-e** [kare] *adj.* **1** square *Le derrière du bateau est plutôt carré plutôt que pointu.* The back of the boat is square rather than pointed. (LF) **Sosthène lui voulait user des* *clous carrés.* Sosthène wanted to use square nails. (Gu82) **2** square (of units measuring area) *Il y a une place, là, il y a un mile carré de terre.* There's a place, there, there is one square mile of land. (LA) <***Loc:*** LA, LF, Da84, Gu82, Lv88>

carré[2] [kare] *n.m.* **1** square **2** square, block (of land) **3** frame, framework (of a house) *On employait des feuilles, on se faisait une maison. Y a un carré dessus la terre.* We used to use leaves, we would make ourselves a [play] house. There's a frame [built] on the ground. (JE) ◊ **•carré de lit** bed frame <Da84> **•carré de maison** basic frame of a house <Da84> <***Loc:*** EV, JD, JE, TB, Da84, Lv88>

carreau [karo] *n.m.* **1** plot or patch of land in a field **2** small piece or scrap of cloth, patch (esp. as used in quiltmaking) *On peut faire des quilts avec des carreaux.* You can make quilts out of scraps. (SM) **3** window pane **4** diamond (in cards) **5** block *Eusse faisait des glacières avec du bois. Et tu pouvais mettre [...] un carreau de glace à peut-être, 25, 30, 35 livres. Tu pouvais mettre ton lait avec la glace, il restait frais.* They made refrigerators out of wood. And you could put in a block of ice maybe 25, 30, 35 pounds. You could put your milk with the ice, it stayed cool. (LF) ◊ **•carreau de chassis** window pane <LF> <***Loc:*** EV, IB, JD, LF, SL, SM, Da84, Fa77, Lv88, Ph36>

carreauté, -e [karote, karode, karjote] *adj.* checkered *Une étoffe carreautée.* Checkered cloth. (VM) <***Loc:*** AV, IB, SJ, VM, Lv88>

carrelet (**carlet**) [karlɛ, karle, karəle] *n.m.* (*occ. f.*) **1** dipnet *Un carlet c'est quelque chose que t'as un manche dessus, t'attrapes quelque chose avec.* A dipnet, it's something that's got a handle on it, you catch something with it. (JE) *Il a attrapé un carrelet plein.* He caught a dipnet full. (JE) **2** hoopnet *Ça fait, le poisson vient pour l'odeur, ça rentre dans le carlet et ça peut pas sortir.* So, the fish comes for the smell, it goes in the hoopnet and it can not get out from it. (SM) **3** cast net, throw net **4** crab cage *Là asteur il y a des carlets carrés et là, là avec des trous de chaque côté et les crabes rentrent dedans, et [on] met un appât.* Now there are square-shaped crab cages with holes on each side and the crabs go inside, and you put in bait. (PQ) **5** game bag, hunting bag *J'arrive à ce piège là, y a un loutre vivant dedans, ça me vaut 50 piastres. [...] Je l'ai mis dans le carrelet, dans le sac.* I arrive at that trap, there's a live otter in it, it's worth $50 to me. I put it in the game bag, in the sack. (TB) <***Loc:*** AV, IB, JE, PQ, SJ, SM, TB, Da84>

carreleter (**carreléter**) [karlete] *v.tr.* to fish with a square net, cast net or dipnet *Carreleter des écrevisses.* To fish for crawfish with a square net. (Lv88) *On a été carreléter hier.* We went crawfishing [with nets] yesterday. (SM) <***Loc:*** SM, Lv88>

carrément [karemɑ̃] *adv.* **1** immediately, straightaway, right away **Il a parti carrément.* He left at once. (Da84) *Dessus le télévision quand eusse commence à montrer une serpent, je vas changer de station. Carrément.* On TV when they start to show a snake I'll change the channel. Immediately. (TB) *Il voulait se marier tout carrément.* He wanted to get married right away. (EV) **2** completely, outright, downright *Les enfants sont carrément fiévreux juste avant les fêtes.* The children are downright excited just before the holidays. (LA) **3** directly, straightforwardly *Je lui ai dit tout carrément.* I told him quite directly. (SJ) <***Loc:*** EV, JD, LA, SJ, SM, TB, Da84>

carrencaouai [karɑ̃kawe] *n.m.* cannibal, savage *La vieille fait peur aux enfants avec des carrencaouais aux gros écrocs.* The old lady scares the children with stories of cannibals with big tusks. (VM) <***Loc:*** VM>

carrick [karik] *n.m.* baby's cloak <***Loc:*** LF>

carrière [karjær] *n.m.* roasting pan <***Loc:*** AV>

carriole [karjɔl] *n.f.* two-wheeled horse-drawn buggy *Dans ce temps que moi je suis après parler asteur-là, ben c'était, ça prendait oh peut-être 45 minutes, pour sûr, parce que ces vieilles carrioles, ça faisait pas route trop vite.* In the days that I'm talking about now, well, it took about 45 minutes, for sure, because those old two-wheeled buggies, they didn't travel very fast. (TB) <***Loc:*** LA, TB, Da84>

carrisser [karise] *v.tr.* **1** to shrug (the shoulders) **Il a carrissé ses épaules quand j'i ai demandé de faire ça.* He shrugged his shoulders when I asked him to do that. (EV, Ph36) **2** to open (the eyes) wide **Il a carrissé les yeux quand il a attendu ça.* He opened his eyes really wide when he heard that. (EV, Ph36) <***Loc:*** EV, Ph36>

carrosse [karɔs] *n.f.* high class carriage, fancy carriage <***Loc:*** Da84>

carrousel [karuzɛl] *n.m.* merry-go-round <***Loc:*** Da84>

carte [kart] *n.f.* **1** card *Chaque cinq piasses que t'achètes [...] eusse te donne un petit* STAMP *et dès que t'as 50 piasses de complet dessus ta carte tu peux t'acheter cinq morceaux de vaisselle pour deux piasses.* For every five dollars worth you buy they give you a little stamp, and when you've filled $50 on your card you can buy five pieces of dishware for two dollars. (LF) **2** playing card *Un jeu de cartes.* A game or deck of cards. (EV) *Brasser les cartes.* Shuffle the cards. (EV) **3** greeting card *J'ai acheté une belle carte, et j'ai écrit un* CHECK *de cinquante piasses, quand il a gradué pour être docteur.* I bought a nice card, and I wrote a check for fifty dollars when he graduated to become a doctor. (TB) **4** map *Ça se trouve pas dessus tous les cartes.* It can't be found on all the maps. (SL) ◊ **•carte postale** postcard <Da84> **•carte de Christmas** Christmas card *On yeux a déjà envoyé une carte de Chrismusse et quelque chose comme ça.* We've sent them Christmas cards and things like that. (TB) <TB> <***Loc:*** EV, JE, LF, SL, SM, TB, Da84, La99>

carton (**caltron, cartron**) [kartrɔ̃, kaltrɔ̃, kaltɔ̃, katrɔ̃] *n.m.* **1** cardboard **2** cardboard box, carton *Il lui a envoyé un carton* *plein de bonbons.* He sent her a cardboard box full of candy. (LA) ◊ **•en carton** cardboard, made of cardboard *Je peux avoir cette boîte en caltron?* Can I have that cardboard box? (TB) *Caisse en carton.* Cardboard box. (LF) <LF, TB> <***Loc:*** AC, AV, IB, JE, LA, LF, SB, SJ, SL, SM, TB, VM, Da84, Lv88>

cartouche [kartuʃ] *n.f.* cartridge, shell, gun shell <***Loc:*** LA, TB, Da84>

cartron ♦see **carton**

carvelle [karvɛl] *n.m./f.* spike, large nail <***Loc:*** EV, SL, Da84, Lv88>

cas [ka] *n.m.* **1** case, set of circumstances *Il y a pas trop de cas comme ça.* There aren't too many cases like that. (SB) *Dans mon cas, être un autre* FOLKSINGER *américain, c'était pas grand'chose.* In my case, being another American folksinger didn't amount to much. (LA, An84) **2** case, legal case *Ils ont jugé son cas la semaine passée.* They tried his case last week. (LA) **Son opponent a présenté son cas avec plein de vigueur.* His opponent presented his case with much vigor. (Gr82) ◊ **•dans ce cas-là** in that case <Da84> **•dans tous les cas *a*** in any case, under any circumstances ***b*** at any rate, regardless <VM, Da84> **•en cas que** in case, if *Je peux le faire en cas que vous voulez.* I can do it if you want. (SJ) <SJ> **•en tout cas *a*** in case, just in case **J'ai porté de l'eau en tout cas.* I brought water in case of need. (Da84) ***b*** in any case, at any rate <Da84> **•en tout cas (que)** in case, in the event (that) *C'est pour ça que mon j'ai un* ANSWERING SERVICE, *en tout cas qu'eusse m'appelle et que je suis pas là.* That's why I have an answering service, in case they call me and I'm not there. (LF) *Allons cuire un gombo en tout cas que Patrick veut rester souper.* Let's cook a gumbo in case Patrick wants to stay for supper. (VM) **T'as pour avoir assez de quoi, quand tu vas te rencontrer une dame, en tout cas tu te décides de te marier, peut-être pas longtemps après.* You have to have enough means, when you are going to meet a lady, in case you decide to get married, maybe not long afterwards. (SL, An94) <LF, SL, VM, An94, Da84> **•par cas que** in case that *Par cas que je la vois, je la dirai.* If I see her I shall tell her. (JE) <JE, LF> <***Loc:*** EV, IV, JD, JE, LA, LF, SB, SJ, VM, An84, An94, Da84, Gr82>

casaque [kazak] *n.* coat, overgarment <***Loc:*** La99>

casaquin [kazakɛ̃] *n.m.* head, noggin <***Loc:*** SM, La99>

casbergau ♦see **casburgot**

casburgot (**casse-burgau, casbergau**) [kasbyrgo, kasbærgo, kasbirgo, kasbrigo, kalbrəgu] *n.m.* **1** freshwater drum, goofish, gaspergou *Je crois qu'un casburgot est plus à l'eau fraîche comme un* CARP. I think a gaspergou is more in fresh water like a carp. (LF) **2** common sheepshead fish ◊ **•casbergau d'eau salée** sheepshead fish <VM> <***Loc:*** AV, EV, IB, IV, JD, JE, LA, LF, SJ, SL, SM, TB, Da84, Guoo, Lv88, Ph36, Re31>

CASH[1] [kaʃ, kæʃ, kɛʃ] *v.tr.invar.* to cash *J'ai pour aller à la banque* CASH *son* CHECK *du* RELIEF. I have to go to the bank to cash his relief check. (VM) <***Loc:*** VM>

CASH[2] [kaʃ, kæʃ, kɛʃ] *n.m.* cash *Hâle du* CASH. Bring some cash. (Lv88) **Avoir du* CASH. To have cash. (Da84) **Payer* CASH. To pay cash. (Da84, Lv88) *Acheter du* CASH. To pay cash. (Lv88) *Tu peux pas amener du* CASH? You can't bring cash? (SL) *Je l'ai acheté au* CASH. I paid cash for it. (TB) <***Loc:*** AV, EV, SL, TB, VM, Da84, Lv88, Ph36>

casino [kazino, kasino] *n.m.* **1** casino **2** card game of casino <***Loc:*** Da84, Lv88>

caspulaire ♦see **scapulaire**

casque [kas(k)] *n.m.* cap, baseball cap ◊ **•casque à bec** baseball cap <Lv88> <***Loc:*** IB, LF, SL, TB, VM, Da84, Lv88>

casquette [kaskɛt] *n.f.* cap, baseball cap <***Loc:*** VM, Da84>

cassable [kasab(l)] *adj.* breakable *De la vaisselle cassable.* Breakable dishes. (LA) <***Loc:*** LA>

cassage [kasaʒ] *n.m.* **1** breaking, breakage *Il y avait pas un tas de cassage après le bal.* There wasn't much breakage after the dance. (LA) **2** harvesting (esp. of corn or grains that must be cut or pulled from a stalk) *Le cassage va être bonne heure cette année.* The harvest will be early this year. (SM) **Cassage de maïs.* Harvesting of corn. (Da84) <***Loc:*** JD, LA, SM, Da84, Lv88>

cassailler [kasaje] *v.tr.* to break into bits *Il va tout cassailler ma vaisselle.* He is going to break my china to bits. (IB) <***Loc:*** AV, IB>

cassant, -e [kasɑ̃, -ɑ̃t] *adj.* fragile, breakable *Touche pas ça, c'est cassant.* Don't touch that, it's breakable. (LA) <***Loc:*** LA, Da84>

casse[1] [kas] *n.m.* baking pan *Je suis après mettre mes biscuits dans le casse.* I'm putting my biscuits in the baking pan. (IB) *Mes casses à pain sont trop grands. Il faut que je m'achète d'autres.* My bread pans are too big. I need to buy some more. (TB) <***Loc:*** IB, SJ, TB>

casse[2] [kas] *n.f.* home *Aller à la casse.* To go home. (AV) <***Loc:*** AV>

cassé, -e [kase] *adj.* **1** broken *Ouais, mon cœur est tout cassé depuis toi, t'as quitté.* Yes, my heart is completely broken since you left. (ch: *Comment je vas faire*) **2** broke, penniless *On est tout le temps cassé, mais on est tout le temps content.* We're always broke, but we're always happy. (Lv88) **3** extremely well dressed *T'es cassé cet après-midi!* You are extremely well dressed this afternoon! (SM) ◊ **•cassé à la maille** ruined, penniless, financially devasted <SL, SM, La99, Lv88> **•cassé à la souche {chousse}** completely broke, financially ruined <SL, La99> <***Loc:*** AC, EV, IB, LA, LF, SL, SM, TB, Da84, Guoo, La99, Lv88>

casse-babine [kasbabin] *n.f.* harmonica <***Loc:*** SM>

casse-banane (**banacassa**) [kasbɑ̃nɑ̃n, bɑ̃nakasa] *n.f.* cassabanana, curuba, musk cucumber (type of gourd with a curved neck, used to make jam) <***Loc:*** EV, IB, Lv88>

casse-brise [kasbriz] *n.* one who tends to break things <***Loc:*** JE, LF>

casse-burgau ♦see **casburgot**

casse-cou [kasku] *n.m.* **1** dangerous place (e.g. a sharp curve in the road) noted for leading to injuries **2** dangerous game, dangerous undertaking <***Loc:*** JD, Da84>

cassée [kase] *n.f.* breaking, change (in the weather) ◊ •**cassée du temps** clearing up of the weather <LF, La99> <***Loc:*** LF, La99>

cassement [kasmɑ̃] *n.m.* breaking, breaking up *Tu parles d'un cassement de vaisselle, cher!* You talk about a breaking up of dishes, dear! (LA) ◊ •**cassement de tête** harping, nagging *Cette personne est après m'affoler avec son cassement de tête.* This person is driving me crazy with his harping. (EV) <EV> <***Loc:*** EV, LA>

casse-noix [kasnwa] *n.m.* nutcracker <***Loc:*** Da84>

casse-pacane [kaspakɑ̃n] *n.m.* nutcracker *On casse des pacanes avec un casse-pacane.* One cracks pecans with a nutcracker. (JE) <***Loc:*** JE>

casser [kase] **I** *v.tr.* **1** to break *Je vais casser ton cou si tu me bloffes!* I'll break your neck if you deceive me! (SM) **2** to demolish, tear down (a house, etc.) *Eusse a cassé cette maison-là, eusse a bâti une autre maison plus en arrière.* They tore down that house, they built another house further back. (TB) **3** to harvest, pick (fruit, flowers, vegetables, esp. those growing on a stalk) *Tous les ans, on casse les cannes à l'automne.* Every year, we harvest the sugar cane in autumn. (Lv88) **4** to break (ground) *Ils ont cassé la terre pour le nouveau presbytère.* They broke ground for the new rectory. (EV) **5** to break, make change for (a banknote) *Asteur tu peux casser des billets de cent piasses partout.* These days you can get change for a hundred dollar bill anywhere. (Lv88) **6** to infringe, break, violate (e.g. a principle, law, vow, promise) *Ils ont pris un cardinal qu'était pas italien pour casser la tradition.* They got a cardinal who wasn't Italian, to break with tradition. (Lv88) *Casse pas ta promesse.* Don't break your promise. (ThCa: *Grosbecs*) *Le prêtre a pas le droit de casser la loi de l'État.* The priest does not have the right to break the State's laws. (Lv88) **7** to enter without an invitation or permission, crash (a ceremony, a party) *Ils ont rentré en-dans-là, le bal, ils ont cassé le bal.* They went in there, the dance, they crashed the dance. (An77) **II** *v.intr.* **1** to break, burst *Quand le tank a cassé, ça pissait de l'eau tout partout.* When the tank broke, it was spurting water everywhere. (LA) **Il a mangé jusqu'à son ventre était au moment de casser.* He ate until his stomach was about to burst. (EV, An94) **2** to break down (of a car, etc.) *Et des fois on est en route, je dis à ma femme, "Oh* LORD, *le char va casser."* And sometimes we're on the road, I'll say to my wife, "Oh Lord, the car is going to break down." (LF) **3** to end (of a ceremony, meeting, etc.) *Le bal casse à une heure.* The dance ends at one o'clock. (Lv88) **4** to break out (of a war, a fight) *C'est alors la guerre a cassé.* Then the war broke out. (Lv88) **III se casser** *v.pron.* **1** to break (a limb, etc.) *Alle se sent pas bien? Alle s'avait cassé le cou déjà, hein?* She doesn't feel well? She has broken her neck before, hasn't she? (TB) **2** to break up, clear up (of the weather) *Le temps est après se casser.* The weather is clearing up. (Da84) **3** to break (of the day) *Le jour était après se casser quand il s'a levé.* The day was breaking when he got up. (Lv88) **4** to dress up, get dressed up ◊ •**casser égal** to break even <Hi02> •**casser en cannelles** to break to pieces *J'ai cassé ce vase en cannelles.* I broke that vase to bits. (Pe37) <Pe37> •**casser en douelles** to tear to pieces, smash *L'oragan a tout cassé la maison en douelles.* The storm tore the house all to pieces. (VM) <VM> •**casser la bande** to end a friendship <LF> •**casser la paille *a*** to break up (a friendship or marriage) *Ça m'a fait de la peine quand ils ont cassé la paille.* It made me sad when they broke up. (LA) ***b*** to sever relations *J'ai cassé la paille avec mon assurance.* I severed relations with my insurance company. (LA) <LA, SL, Da84, La99, Lv88> •**casser la patte** to break up a relationship or marriage <AC> •**casser la pipe** to die, croak <JD, SL, Da84, La99> •**casser la vaisselle *a*** to break up (of a couple or household) *Ils ont cassé la vaisselle juste deux mois après la noce.* They broke up just two months after their wedding. (EV) ***b*** to fall down, have a nasty fall *Il a manqué un pas sur l'escalier et il a cassé la vaisselle.* He missed a step on the stairs and fell down. (LA) ***c*** to do a cannonball dive <AC, EV, LA, LF, La99> •**casser le cœur (à qqn)** to break (s.o.'s) heart *J'ai cassé ton petit cœur doux.* I broke your sweet little heart. (TB) <TB, Lv88> •**casser le ménage *a*** to break up a household or marriage ***b*** to become separated <Da84> •**casser le petit bâton** to break a promise not to indulge in something <SL, La99> •**casser sa pénitence** to break a Lenten promise <VM> •**casser un œil (à qqn)** to give s.o. a black eye *Il va te casser un œil.* He is going to give you a black eye. (JE) <JE> •**pas casser la rate** to not work, be lazy in one's work <EV, La99> •**se casser (à) la maille** to spend everything *Il s'a cassé la maille pendant les fêtes.* He spent everything during the holidays. (LA) <LA, Lv88> •**se casser en deux** to strive hard (to do s.t.), break one's back (doing s.t.) *Elle s'a cassé en deux pour finir avant qu'ils arrivent.* She tried hard to finish before they arrived. (LA) <LA, SL, La99> •**se casser le cou *a*** to break one's neck *Il s'a cassé le cou dans l'accident.* He broke his neck in the accident. (LA) ***b*** to get married *Si il fait pas attention, il va se casser le cou.* If he's not careful, he's going to end up married. (LA) <LA, TB, VM, Da84, La99> <***Loc:*** AC, AV, EV, JD, JE, LA, LF, SB, SJ, SL, SM, TB, VM, An77, An94, Da84, Hi02, La99, Lv88, ThCa, Wh83>

casserole (**casterole**) [kasrɔl, kastrɔl] *n.f. (occ. m.)* **1** saucepan, stewpan, long-handled cooking pot *Donne-moi la* *casterole.* Give me the saucepan. (JE) **2** casserole dish *Un casserole, tu peux mettre ça dans l'oven et tu cuis ton manger dedans.* A casserole dish, you can put it in the oven and you cook your food in it. (JD) **3** casserole **4** tea kettle <***Loc:*** AV, EV, JD, JE, LF, SB, SJ, SL, SM, TB, VM, Da84, Lv88>

casse-tête [kastɛt] *n.m.* **1** hatchet, small axe *Et ça c'est un vieux casse-tête. Le manche sur ça aussite a dépéri, la vieillesse je pense. Et je devrais toujours les amancher, mettre d'autres manches dessus.* And that's an old hatchet. The handle on that has rotted too, old age I guess. I ought to put a new handle on them. (LF) **2** puzzle <***Loc:*** AV, IB, IV, JD, JE, LF, SJ, SL, SM, TB, An94, Da84, Lv88, Re31>

casse-tout [kastu] *n.m.* child that breaks everything <***Loc:*** Lv88>

cassette [kasɛt] *n.f.* cassette <***Loc:*** EV, TB>

casseur, -euse [kasœr, -øz] *n.* harvester, picker (person who gathers a crop) *Paul est un casseur de maïs.* Paul is a corn-picker. (SM) ◊ **•casseur de bal** troublemaker, hoodlum who breaks up dances by starting fights <EV, Lv88> **•casseur de portes ouvertes *a*** braggart ***b*** one who makes a big show of doing s.t. that is not really difficult ***c*** rough, brutish person who uses excessive force <La99> <***Loc:*** EV, SM, La99, Lv88>

cassine [kasin] *n.f.* small isolated house in the prairie <***Loc:*** Da84>

cassinier [kasinje] *n.m.* yaupon <***Loc:*** Da84, Re31>

cassure [kasyr] *n.f.* break, crack, fracture *Le docteur a pas corrigé bien la cassure.* The doctor didn't set the break well. (VM) <***Loc:*** VM, Da84>

casterole ♦see **casserole**

castile [kastil] *n.* ◊ **•avoir castile avec qqn** to quarrel with s.o. <AV, La99> <***Loc:*** AV, La99>

castor [kastɔr] *n.m.* **1** beaver **2** whirligig beetle <***Loc:*** LF, VM, Da84, Gu00, Lv88, Re31>

castronier ♦see **gastronia**

casuel ♦see **casvel**

casvel (casuel) [kasvɛl, kazɥɛl] *adj.* breakable, fragile <***Loc:*** EV, JE, SM, Di32, Ph36>

catachrèse [katakrɛs] *n.f.* old gossiper *Je peux pas m'affier à elle. C'est rien qu'une catachrèse.* I can't trust her. She's just an old gossip. (TB) <***Loc:*** TB>

catafal (catalfaque) [katafal, katalfak] *n.m.* catafalque <***Loc:*** SM>

catalfaque ♦see **catafal**

catalique [katalik] *n.f.* blister beetle, Spanish fly <***Loc:*** Da84>

catalogne [kɑ̃talɔ̃ɲ, katalɔ̃n, kɑ̃talɔ̃j] *n.f.* rug made of strips (usu. cut from used cloth) <***Loc:*** JE, Di32, Lv88>

catalogue [katalɔg] *n.m.* catalog, list <***Loc:*** Da84>

catalpa [katalpa] *n.m.* catalpa <***Loc:*** Da84, Gu00>

cataplâme ♦see **cataplasme**

cataplasme (cataplâme, cataplasse) [kataplɑ̃m, kataplas] *n.m.* **1** cataplasm, poultice *Il a un cataplasse sur son épaule.* He has a cataplasm on his shoulder. (JE) **2** excessively large serving of food *Un grand cataplasse de riz.* A huge helping of rice. (IB) **3** reprimand, scolding **4** pest, person who hangs around unwelcome **5** awkward and slow-moving person *Tu parles d'un cataplasme! Il est assez doucement!* What a slow-moving person! He's pretty sluggish! (VM) <***Loc:*** AV, IB, JD, JE, LA, LF, SJ, SL, SM, TB, VM, Da84, La99, Lv88, Re31>

cataplasse ♦see **cataplasme**

cataracte [katarak(t)] *n.f.* cataract *Ils ont ôté les cataractes.* They took out the cataracts. (EV) <***Loc:*** EV, Da84>

catastrophe [katastrɔf] *n.f.* catastrophe <***Loc:*** Da84>

catchouelle ♦see **tchacouelle**

catchouque[1] [katʃuk] *adj.* **1** tacky, gaudy (in dress and appearance) *Il est vaillant, mais trop catchouque.* He is nice, but too tacky. (SM) **2** out of style <***Loc:*** JD, SM, Pe37>

catchouque[2] **(cachouque)** [katʃuk] *n.f.* dowdy woman **Une vieille cachouque.* A dowdy old woman. (Re31) <***Loc:*** Re31>

catéchisme (catéchisse) [kateʃis] *n.m.* **1** catechism, catechetical instruction *On était à plusieurs qui restait entour ici-là, qu'allait au catéchisme là, apprendre les prières.* There were several of us who lived around here, who went to catechism to learn the prayers. (TB) **2** long story *Il m'a foutu tout un catéchisse.* He told me a whole long story. (SM) **3** scolding, stern talking-to <***Loc:*** AC, AL, AV, EV, IB, JE, LA, LF, SJ, SL, SM, TB, Da84, Lv88, Re31>

catéchisse ♦see **catéchisme**

cathédrale [katedral] *n.f.* cathedral <***Loc:*** LA>

catherine [katrin] *n.f.* ◊ **•il y a pas de catherine** there's no ifs, ands or buts, there's no two ways about it **Il y a pas de catherine, il faut.* There's no ifs, ands or buts, it must be. (Da84) <JD, Da84> <***Loc:*** JD, Da84>

catholique[1] [katolik] *adj.* Catholic *Je te garantis, n'importe quelle église, ça pourrait être catholique ou une autre, si ça serait en français, y a plein du monde qui vadrait.* I guarantee you, any church, be it Catholic or something else, if it was in French, there are a lot of people who would go. (LF) ◊ **•être pas (trop) catholique** to not be well, not feel well *Jean est pas trop catholique aujourd'hui.* John isn't well today. (SL) <SL> <***Loc:*** AC, EV, LA, LF, SL, SM, TB, VM, An94, Da84, La99, Lv88, Re38, Wh83>

Catholique[2] [katolik] *n.* Catholic **Nous-autres, on est tous des Catholiques ici.* We're all Catholics here. (EV, An94) ◊ **•Catholique à gros grain *a*** non-practicing Catholic, Catholic who ignores many rules of the church ***b*** a very fervent or fanatical Catholic ***c*** hypocritical Catholic who makes a show of observing liturgical rites but does not behave morally <VM, Da84, La99, Lv88> <***Loc:*** AC, EV, LA, LF, TB, VM, An94, Da84, La99, Lv88, Wh83>

catin [katɛ̃] *n.f.* **1** doll *Mes sœurs avaient des catins comme ça* *faits à la main.* My sisters had dolls like that, handmade. (AC) **2** dear, sweetheart (referring to a little girl) *Chère 'tite catin.* Dear little sweetheart. (Lv88) *La mère était là avec sa catin.* The mother was there with her little sweetheart. (SM) **3** corn silk, young ear of corn as it begins to silken *Le maïs est en catin.* The corn is in the silk stage. (VM) ◊ **•catin à viser** baby doll (children's game) <Da84> **•catin de l'ours** teddy bear, stuffed bear <SL> **•ça c'est pas baptême catin** it's a difficult situation, it's not fun and games *C'est pas baptême catin, d'être marié avec un homme qui boit comme ça.* It's not fun being married to a man who drinks like that. (SM) <SM, La99> <***Loc:*** AC, AV, EV, JE, LA, LF, SJ, SL, SM, TB, VM, Da84, Gu00, Hi02, La99, Lv88, Ph36, Re31, Wh69>

catiner [katine] **I** *v.tr.* to pamper, spoil, indulge *Ma sœur est trop catinée, son mari fait tout à la maison.* My sister is too spoiled, her husband does everything around the house. (Lv88) **II** *v.intr.* to play with dolls *Les 'tites filles sont tout le temps après catiner.* Little girls are always playing with dolls. (VM) *Mes 'tites filles catinent tout le temps.* My little girls play with dolls all the time. (SM) **III se catiner** *v.pron.* to pamper o.s., take it easy *J'ai juste envie de me catiner aujourd'hui.* I just feel like pampering myself today. (VM) <***Loc:*** JD, SM, VM, Da84, Lv88>

catogan [katogɑ̃] *n.m.* bun, roll, twist, or knot of hair worn at the back of the head <***Loc:*** EV>

catouche [katuʃ] *n.f.* prostitute <***Loc:*** JD>

cauchemar [koʃmar] *n.m.* nightmare <***Loc:*** AL>

caucus [kokys] *n.m.* caucus <***Loc:*** SM, Lv88>

causade [kozad] *n.f.* conversation, talk, chat *La causade est belle, mais c'est l'heure de s'en aller.* The conversation is nice, but it's time to go. (VM) <***Loc:*** VM, Da84>

causard, -e [kozar, -ard] *n.* one who talks a lot *Avec le caractère qu'il a, Dudley est causard et il connaît quoi dire pour obtenir l'information qu'il en a besoin.* With his character, Dudley is a talker and he knows what to say to get the information he needs. (ThCa: *Messieurs, mesdames*) <***Loc:*** SM, Lv88, ThCa>

cause [koz] *n.f.* **1** cause, origin **2** reason, cause *J'ai jamais donné de causes pour ça. Si quelqu'un lui donnait une cause, ouais, il avait sa colère.* I never gave a reason for that. If someone gave him a reason, yes, he had his temper. (AC) **3** cause (set of principles or purposes) **C'était une autre cause révolutionnaire que j'allais embrasser, mais cette fois, c'était beaucoup plus important parce que ça me touchait directement.* It was another revolutionary cause that I would embrace, but this time it was more important because it concerned me directly. (LA, An84) ◊ **•à cause de** because of, on account of *Clet' est après abrier les jardinages à cause de l'orage.* Clet' is covering the vegetables because of the storm. (Lv88) <Lv88> **•à cause que** because, since *A cause que t'es comme ça, on va avoir du mal à s'adonner.* Because you're like this, we're going to have trouble getting along. (LA) <LA, Da84> <***Loc:*** AC, EV, LA, An84, Da84, Lv88>

causer[1] [koze] *v.intr.* **1** to chat, converse, talk *Et nous-autres on dit "On va aller causer avec les voisins."* And we say, "We're going to go chat with the neighbors." (LF) *En causant avec Marie, j'ai su que son père avait mouri.* While talking to Mary, I discovered that her father had died. (VM) **2** to speak *Ma fille cause pas un mot en français.* My daughter doesn't speak a word of French. (SM) <***Loc:*** LA, LF, SM, TB, VM, Da84>

causer[2] [koze] *v.tr.* to cause, be the cause of **Ça a dû causer un divorce.* That must have caused a divorce. (An94) *Le vent a causé un débâcle dans le village.* The wind caused a building to collapse in the village. (AV) <***Loc:*** AV, IB, An94, Da84>

causerie [kozri] *n.f.* chat, conversation, talk *C'était une belle soirée. La causerie a duré jusqu'à minuit.* It was a nice evening. The conversation went on until midnight. (LA) <***Loc:*** LA, Da84>

causeur, -euse [kozœr, -øz] *n.* talker, big talker <***Loc:*** Da84>

causionner [kozjɔ̃ne] *v.tr.* to occasion, cause, produce *T'as causionné un tas de tracas à ta maman.* You caused a heap of trouble for your mother. (SM) <***Loc:*** SM, TB, Lv88>

caustique[1] [kostik] *adj.* caustic *Fais attention. C'est caustique. Ça va te brûler.* Be careful. It's caustic. It will burn you. (VM) <***Loc:*** VM, Da84>

caustique[2] [kostik] *n.m.* lye *On a usé du caustique pour déboucher les tuyaux.* We used lye to unclog the pipes. (VM) <***Loc:*** VM>

cautériser [koterize] *v.tr.* to burn, cauterize <***Loc:*** Da84>

caution [kosjɔ̃] *n.f.* guarantee, bail <***Loc:*** Da84>

cautionnement [kosjɔ̃nmɑ̃] *n.m.* act of bailing <***Loc:*** VM, Da84>

cautionner [kosjɔ̃ne] *v.tr.* **1** to put up bail for, bail out **2** to vouch for, underwrite, co-sign a loan for *Je peux pas t'aider. Je peux pas te cautionner pas pour cinq sous, pas pour rien.* I can't help you. I can't underwrite you for five cents, not for anything. (EV) <***Loc:*** EV, Da84>

cavache [kavaʃ] *n.m.* coward *Espèce de cavache, t'as peur.* You coward, you're afraid. (LF) <***Loc:*** LF>

cavaillade [kavajad, kavaljad] *n.f.* **1** cavalcade, group of riders on horseback **2** drove, band (of moving horses or mules) <***Loc:*** AV, IB, LF, SB, SJ, SL, Da84, Lv88>

cavalier [kavalje] *n.m.* **1** horseman, cowboy, one who works cattle on horseback **2** horse rider, jockey **3** knight *O non, non, non, franc cavalier, ma femme est trop fidèle à moi.* Oh no, no, no, honest knight, my wife is too faithful to me. (PQ, ch: *O Catherine, vaillante Catherine*) **4** sweetheart, beau, suitor **5** straight clothespin <***Loc:*** PQ, SL, SM, VM, Da84>

cave [kav] *n.f.* **1** cellar **2** pantry *Mes groceries sont dans la* *cave.* My groceries are in the pantry. (IB) <***Loc:*** IB, TB, Da84>

caveau [kavo] *n.m.* burial vault *Le monde lave les caveaux, eux-autres peinture, et ça nettoye les herbes entour, et là ça amène des nouvelles fleurs. C'est proche comme un* MEMORIAL. People wash the vaults, they paint, and they clean away the grass, and then they bring new flowers. It's almost like a memorial. (TB) <***Loc:*** TB>

caverne [kaværn] *n.f.* cave, cavern <***Loc:*** Da84>

cavité [kavite] *n.f.* cavity <***Loc:*** Da84>

cayenne [kajɛ̃n] *n.m.* cayenne, cayenne pepper <***Loc:*** Da84>

ce[1]**, cette** (*m.sing.* **ce** [s(ə)], *m.sing. before a vowel* **cet, c't, ç't, este** [st, stə, ɛst], *f.sing.* **cette, c't', steu, ç'té, est'** [sɛt, stə, ste, ɛst], *m./f.pl.* **ces** [se], *m./f.pl. before a vowel* **ces** [sez]) *adj.dem.* this, that, these, those *Ce voyage va être juste une fatique, j'ai pas envie d'aller.* This trip is going to be just a tiresome thing, I don't want to go. (VM) *Este gâteau est pas beaucoup appétissant.* That cake is not very appetizing. (LA) *C'est foutant quand même que je peux pas finir cet été.* It's disappointing that I can't finish this summer. (SM) *Va tremper cette serviette pour moi.* Go wet this towel for me. (LF) *On a attrapé des oiseaux dans ces cages.* We caught birds in those bird traps. (VM) ◊ **•(à) ce matin** this morning <Da84> **•cette année (c't' année / est'année)** this year <Da84> **•cet après-midi** this afternoon <Da84> <***Loc:*** AC, AV, EV, IB, IV, JE, LA, LF, SB, SL, SM, TB, VM, An84, An94, Da84, Di32, Gr86, Guoo, Lv88>

ce[2] [s(ə)] *pron.dem.* ◊ **•ce qui** *(subj.)* what, that which *J'ai récordé tout ce qui s'a passé jusqu'à la fin.* I recorded everything that happened until the end. (Lv88) **Tu sais que je sais que tout ce qui se fait là, que c'est toute des menteries.* You know that I know that everything that's going on there, that it's all lies. (IV, An94) <IV, An94, Lv88> **•ce que** *(obj.)* what, that which *C'est une tristesse je pense, ce que le gouvernment faisait.* It's a shame, I think, what the government was doing. (TB) **Il voulait demander à sa mère ce que c'était cet outil, pour travailler le jardin.* He wanted to ask his mother what was that tool for working in the garden. (LA, An94) <LA, TB, An94> <***Loc:*** AC, EV, IV, JE, LA, TB, An94, Lv88>

ceci [səsi] *pron.dem.* this ◊ **•comme ceci** like this, this way <Da84> <***Loc:*** Da84>

céder [sede] **I** *v.tr.* to cede, yield **II** *v.intr.* to give in, yield *C'est pas la peine tu le pousses. Il va jamais céder.* It's no use that you push him. He'll never yield. (VM) <***Loc:*** VM, Da84>

cèdre [sɛd(r)] *n.m.* cedar (esp. white cedar) *Mais le meilleur bois pour faire l'appeleur c'est du bambou que tu pêches avec ou du cèdre.* But the best wood for making a duck call is bamboo that you fish with, or cedar. (TB) ◊ **•cèdre rouge** Eastern red cedar <EV, Ho90> <***Loc:*** EV, LF, SB, TB, Da84, Guoo, Ho90>

ceiling [siliŋ] *n.m.* **1** ceiling, soffit **2** tongue and groove lumber (for constructing inside walls and ceilings of houses) <***Loc:*** EV, LF, SL, VM, Da84, Guoo, Lv88, Ph36>

ceinture [sɛ̃tyr] *n.f.* **1** belt *Alle vend des ceintures, alle fait toute qualité d'affaires avec les peaux.* She sells belts, she makes all kinds of things with the skin. (TB) **2** girdle *Elle aura pour s'acheter une ceinture pour les fêtes.* She's going to have to buy herself a girdle for the holidays. (LA) **3** sash *Ils aviont donné des ceintures à tous les filles dans la compétition.* They had given sashes to all the girls in the competition. (EV) **4** midriff, waist *Elle a amarré la corde autour de sa ceinture.* She tied the rope around her waist. (LA) **5** shingles, herpes zoster *J'avais ça qu'on appelle la ceinture. So j'ai été au docteur. Des toutes petites taches, tu pourrais proche pas dire qui c'était.* I had what they call shingles. So, I went to the doctor. Little tiny spots, you almost couldn't tell what it was. (TB) ◊ **•à {en} pleine ceinture** in full pregnancy <TB, VM, La99> **•en ceinture** pregnant *La grosse femme est en ceinture.* The big woman is pregnant. (SM) <JE, SB, SM, VM, La99> <***Loc:*** AV, EV, IV, JE, LA, SL, SM, TB, VM, An94, Da84, Gr86, La99>

cela [s(ə)la] *pron.dem.* this, that *Moi j'use jamais cela.* I never use that. (LF) <***Loc:*** LF, SL, An94, Da84>

célébrant [selebrɑ̃] *n.m.* celebrant <***Loc:*** Da84>

célébration [selebrasjɔ̃] *n.f.* celebration *Mais là, la Journée de Pâques, ça c'était une grosse célébration.* But then, Easter Sunday was a big celebration. (TB) <***Loc:*** TB>

célèbre [selɛb(r)] *adj.* celebrated, famous *C'était une famille célèbre.* They were a famous family. (SM) <***Loc:*** SM, Da84>

célébrer [selebre] **I** *v.tr.* to celebrate (a feast, marriage, birthday, etc.) *On va célébrer notre cinquantième anniversaire de mariage cette année.* We're going to celebrate our fiftieth wedding anniversary this year. (LA) **II** *v.intr.* to celebrate *Et quand les fêtes arriviont... il pouvait pas célébrer plus qu'il faisait d'habitude.* And when the holidays came . . . he couldn't celebrate any more than he usually did. (ThCa: *Le charivari*) *Quand quelqu'un gagne, il aime célébrer avec tous ses amis.* When somebody wins, he likes to celebrate with all his friends. (Lv88) <***Loc:*** LA, Da84, Lv88, ThCa, Wh83>

céleri (**célérie, célerie**) [sɛlri, selri, seleri] *n.m./f.* celery <***Loc:*** SB, SM, TB, Da84>

celle ♦see **celui**

celui, celle (*m.sing.* **celui, çui, çu, cil, cilui, c't'i** [səlɥi, sɥi, sy, sil, silɥi, sti], *f.sing.* **celle, c'telle, cette, çar, la celle, cil, ceute** [sɛl, stɛl, sɛt, sar, lasɛl, sil, søt], *m./f.pl.* **ceux, ceusses, ceuz, ceuzes, cèzes, les ceux** [sø, søs, søz, sɛz, lesø]) *pron.dem.* this (one), that (one), these, those, the one, the ones ◊ **•celui-ci / celui-ici** this one <VM> **•celui-là / celui-là-là / celui-là-ici** that one, this one **Tu parles d'un beau coco, celui-là!* Talk about a character, that one! (EV, La99) *C'est celui-là j'adorais le plus.* He's the one I loved the most. (EV) **Çar-là ch'parle pour.* The one I'm talking about.

(Ph36) **T'as entendu cil-là pour le Cadien.* You heard the one about the Cajun. (IB, An94) *Ça fait, il a ramassé cil-là qu'avait pas de petit bonnet.* So he picked up the one who didn't have a little nightcap. (LA, An94) *Celle-là voulait être une* NURSE. She wanted to be a nurse. (SB) *Madame Arile, cette-là qui m'a* TEACH *mon catéchisme en français, elle, elle contait des contes pour Compère Bouki et Compère Lapin.* Mrs. Arile, the one who taught me my catechism in French, she would tell stories about Brer Bouki and Brer Rabbit. (SL) <EV, LF, SB, SL, TB, VM, Ph36> **•ceux-là / ceux-là-là / ceux-là-ici / ceux-ici** those, these *Les plus forts et ceux-là qu'est auprès d'elle va manger mais les autres va rien avoir.* The strongest and those that are near her will eat, but the others will get nothing. (TB) *Y a un Bon Dieu dans le ciel. Cèzes-là qui vole là, ils vont payer pour.* There is a God in heaven. Those who steal will pay for it. (TB) *Cèzes-là-là, ces chênes là, on a planté ça ici.* These here, these oak trees, we planted them. (TB) *Tes garçons? Ceusses-là me donnent jamais du tracas.* Your boys? Those [guys] never give me any trouble. (LF) *Les musiciens écrit des chansons, de les femmes, celles-là qu'a quitté. Ils vont jamais jongler à s'apercevoir, de les femmes, celles-là qu'a resté.* Musicians write songs about women, those who left. They never think to notice the women, those who stayed. (Ch: *Les bonnes femmes*) <LF, SB, SL, TB, Gu00, La99, Ph36> <***Loc:*** EV, IB, JD, LA, LF, SB, SL, SM, TB, An94, Da84, Gu00, Hi02, La99, Lv88, Ph36>

cendre [sɑ̃n, sɑ̃d(r)] *n.f.* ash, ashes, cinder <***Loc:*** EV, LF, SM, TB, Da84, Lv88>

cendrier [sɑ̃drije] *n.m.* ashtray, ash receptacle <***Loc:*** Da84>

cenelle [snɛl] *n.f.* haw, berry of the hawthorn tree <***Loc:*** TB, Da84, Lv88>

cenellier [snɛlje] *n.m.* **1** hawthorn, haw tree **2** winterberry tree **3** crabapple <***Loc:*** EV, SL, TB, VM, Da84, Fa77, Ho90, Lv88, Ph36, Re31>

cent [sɑ̃] (*before a consonant* [sɑ̃], *before a vowel* [sɑ̃t, sɑ̃z]) *adj./n.m.* hundred, one hundred *Y a une église qu'est plus que cent -z- ans, une belle église.* There's a church that's more than a hundred years old, a beautiful church. (LF) *L'oragan Audrey a tué au ras de cinq cents personnes.* Hurricane Audrey killed nearly five hundred people. (Lv88) *Mon grand-père a vi jusqu'à l'âge de cent trois ans.* My grandfather lived until the age of 103. (LF) ◊ **•du cent** percent *Je dirais peut-être un bon cinquante du cent du monde jusqu'à oh peut-être 1960, eusse travaillait tout sur l'eau.* I would say maybe a good fifty percent of people until maybe 1960 worked on the water. (LF) <LF, TB> **•pour cent** percent *Ça-icitte-là, ça ça ramasse pas cent pour cent mais ça ramasse alentour de dans les* NINETY PLUS. This one doesn't yield a hundred percent, but it does yield in the ninety plus range. (AS) <AS> <***Loc:*** AC, AS, AV, EV, IB, LF, SB, SL, SM, TB, VM, An94, Da84, Lv88>

centaine [sɑ̃tɛ̃n] *n.f.* about a hundred **Ils étaient à peu près une cinquantaine, ou une centaine.* They were at about fifty, or about a hundred. (VM, An94) <***Loc:*** VM, An94, Da84>

centième [sɑ̃tjɛ̃m] *adj.* one hundredth *Ils sont après avoir un gros* SALE *pour leur centième anniversaire.* They're having a big sale for their one-hundredth anniversary. (LA) <***Loc:*** LA, Da84>

central [sɑ̃tral] *adj.* central, main, principal *Ils vont déménager dans le bâtiment central.* They're going to move into the central building. (LA) <***Loc:*** LA, Da84>

centraliser [sɑ̃tralize] *v.tr.* to centralize, center *Asteur, tout quelque chose est centralisé à Abbéville.* Now, everything is centralized in Abbeville. (VM) <***Loc:*** VM, Da84>

centre [sɑ̃t(r)] *n.m.* center, middle <***Loc:*** LF, Da84>

centrer [sɑ̃tre] *v.tr.* to center, place in center *Le portrait est pas centré dessus le mur.* The picture is not centered on the wall. (VM) <***Loc:*** VM, Da84>

cependant [ɛspɑ̃dɑ̃] *adv.* **1** nevertheless, however, yet *Ils auraient dû faire ça pour Wal-Mart. Cependant, il y a des Wal-Mart au Texas.* They should have done that for Wal-Mart. However, there are Wal-Marts in Texas. (ThCa: *La douce réunion*) **2** perhaps *Mais mes filles, je croyais de voir samedi prochain pour la réunion. Vous-autres s'a pas trompé de la date, cependant?* But girls, I thought I would see you next Saturday for the reunion. You didn't get the date mixed up perhaps? (EV) <***Loc:*** EV, Da84, ThCa>

cerclage [særklaʒ] *n.m.* encircling, circling <***Loc:*** Da84>

cercle [særk(l), sark(l)] *n.m.* **1** circle *T'amarres ta corde sur le côté du bateau, là tu jettes ça à l'eau. Et là tu fais route avec le bateau, tu hales ça un cercle.* You tie your rope on the side of the boat, then you throw it [the dragnet] into the water. And then you set off in the boat, and you pull that into a circle. (TB) **2** metal ring, hoop (e.g. the one that holds together a wooden barrel, or the metal ring around a wagon wheel) ◊ **•faire un cercle** to make a circle (referring to a particular technique used in shrimp fishing) *Et ça empoignait la chevrette avec des filets, les Cadiens appellent ça une seine. Et ça se mettait à l'eau et eusse halait la seine et eusse faisait un cercle pour entasser les chevrettes pour les ramasser.* And they would catch shrimp with nets, the Cajuns call it a seine. And they would get in the water and they pulled the net and they made a circle to collect the shrimp to gather them up. (LF) <LF> **•semicercle *a*** semicircle ***b*** semicircular <Da84> <***Loc:*** AC, LF, TB, Da84>

cercler [særkle] *v.tr.* **1** to circle, encircle **2** to ring, girdle (a tree) <***Loc:*** Da84>

cercueil [særkœj] *n.m.* coffin <***Loc:*** IB, SL, SM, TB, Da84>

cérémonie [serɛ̃mɔ̃ni] *n.f.* ceremony <***Loc:*** Da84>

cerf-volant [særvolɑ̃] *n.m.* **1** kite, paper kite **2** restless or flighty person, one who is always moving around *Il est un cerf-volant quand il entre dans la maison.* He becomes very restless when he enters the house. (IB) ◊ **•faire cerf-volant**

to go from place to place <SM> <***Loc:*** IB, SJ, SM, Da84, Lv88>

cerne [særn] *n.* feeding coop for baby chicks <***Loc:*** IB, SL>

cerné [særne] *adj.* ◊ **•avoir les yeux cernés** to have rings under one's eyes, have bags under one's eyes <VM> <***Loc:*** VM>

cerner (**encerner**) [særne, ɑ̃særne] *v.tr.* **1** to corner, hem in *Je l'ai cerné hier avant qu'il m'a vu.* Yesterday I cornered him before he saw me. (SM) **2** to surround *Je vais encerner la plaie avec de l'iode.* I'm going to surround the wound with iodine. (IB) **3** to ring, girdle (a tree) *Encerner un arbre.* To girdle a tree. (SJ) <***Loc:*** IB, SJ, SM, Da84>

cerni, -e (**sani, -e**) [særni, sarni, sani] *adj.* damned, darned *J'aime pas ce cerni homme.* I don't like that damned guy. (IB) **Cerni coquin.* Damn crook. (Da84) **Ç'sani homme veut pas nous laisser passer.* That damn guy doesn't want to let us through. (EV, Ph36) *J'ai propté ma maison hier. Alle était assez sale que ça m'a pris toute la cernie journée.* I cleaned the house yesterday. It was so dirty that it took me the whole darned day. (Gu00) <***Loc:*** EV, IB, SM, Da84, Gu00, Ph36>

certain, -e [særtɛ̃, -ɛ̃n] *adj.* **1** certain, sure *C'est un remède certain.* It's a sure remedy. (SM) **2** particular, certain, given *Les enfants se rassemblaient en une certaine place.* The children gathered in a certain place. (LF) *Il a rencontré une certaine femme et ils sont séparés.* He met a certain lady and they got separated. (EV) <***Loc:*** EV, IB, LA, LF, TB, SL, SM, An84, Da84>

certainement [særtɛ̃nmɑ̃, særtɛlmɑ̃] *adv.* certainly, surely *T'as envie partir? Mais certainement!* Do you feel like leaving? Well, certainly! (LA) <***Loc:*** AV, IB, LA, SJ, Da84, Gr86>

certaineté (**certainté**) [særtɛ̃nte] *n.f.* certainty, sure thing *C'est une certaineté.* It's a sure thing. (SM) <***Loc:*** SM, Da84>

certainté ♦see **certaineté**

certificat [særtifika] *n.m.* certificate ◊ **•certificat de mortalité** death certificate <Lv88> <***Loc:*** EV, SM, TB, Da84, Lv88>

certification [særtifikasjɔ̃] *n.f.* certification <***Loc:*** Da84>

certifier [særtifje] *v.tr.* to certify, attest, guarantee *Ils ont besoin de certifier que la terre leur appartient.* They have to certify that the land is theirs. (LA) <***Loc:*** LA, Da84>

certifis [særtifi] *n.m.* salsify, vegetable oyster <***Loc:*** JE, TB, Di32>

certitude [særtityd] *n.f.* certitude, certainty <***Loc:*** Da84>

cerveau [særvo] *n.m.* **1** sinus cavity, sinuses *Il est rouge, et c'est mauvais pour la santé ça, le son de scie, ça brûle dans le cerveau.* It's red, and it's bad for your health, the sawdust [from the Spanish cedar], it burns in your sinuses. (LF) *J'ai le cerveau bouché.* I'm congested. (VM) **2** nostril *Il a une graine de maïs dans son cerveau.* He has a kernel of corn in his nostril. (SL) <***Loc:*** LF, SL, VM, Da84>

cervelle [særvɛl, sarvɛl] *n.f.* **1** brain **2** brains (consumed as food) *La cervelle, ils cuisont ça seule. La cervelle de bœuf. J'ai jamais mangé la cervelle de cochon mais la cervelle de bœuf c'est comme des huîtres dès que tu le fris.* The brains, they cook that by itself. Beef brains. I've never eaten pork brains but beef brains, it's like oysters once you fry it. (LF) <***Loc:*** AV, EV, LF, SJ, TB, Da84, Hi02, Wh83>

ces ♦see **ce**

cessation [sesasjɔ̃] *n.f.* cessation, discontinuation, stoppage <***Loc:*** Da84>

cesse [sɛs] *n.f.* ending, end ◊ **•sans cesse** without end, never ending *Parler sans cesse, se lamenter sans cesse.* To talk to no end, complain without end. (SL) <SL> <***Loc:*** SL, Da84>

cesser [sese] *v.tr.* to cease, stop, discontinue *Cessez ce train, z-enfants.* Stop that noise, children. (VM) <***Loc:*** VM, Da84>

cet, cette ♦see **ce**

cette ♦see **celui**

ceusses, ceute, ceux ♦see **celui**

cez ♦see **chez**

cèzes ♦see **celui**

chabec [ʃabɛk] *n.m.* boat <***Loc:*** AV, LF, Re31>

chabouillure, chaboulure ♦see **échauboulure**

chabraque [ʃabrak] *n.f.* **1** big, usu. delapidated or poorly constructed building *Il reste dans une vieille chabraque.* He lives in a big, old, delapidated house. (SM) **2** old car, jalopy **3** anything old, in bad shape or in disrepair *Une chabraque de machine.* A run-down old machine. (Lv88) *Cette chabraque ne vaut pas cinq sous.* That rickety old thing is not worth a nickel. (IB) <***Loc:*** IB, JD, LA, SM, TB, Da84, Lv88>

chacaça [ʃakasa] *n.m.* shock absorber *Les chacaças de mon char sont cassés.* The shock absorbers on my car are broken. (SL) <***Loc:*** SL>

chacot [ʃako] *n.m.* sharpener ◊ **•chacot à crayon** pencil sharpener <LA> <***Loc:*** LA>

chacote [ʃakɔt] *n.f.* wood shaving (as of a pencil that has been sharpened) <***Loc:*** JD>

chacoter [ʃakote] **I** *v.tr.* **1** to chip, chop *J'étais après chacoter des bûches quand il m'a appelé.* I was chopping some logs when he called me. (LA) **2** to whittle *Mon grand-père m'a chacoté un moc à canards.* My grandfather whittled me a duck call. (Gu00) *Il chacote tout le temps.* He's always whittling. (LF) **3** to sharpen (e.g. a pencil) *Chacoter un crayon.* To sharpen a pencil. (LA) **II** *v.intr.* to hack at *Allons jouer le Perrodin Two-Step. Il y en a qui essaient de chacoter là-dessus.* Let's play the Perrodin Two-Step. There are some [musicians] who try to hack at that one [on the violin]. (JD) <***Loc:*** IB, JD, JE, LA, LF, SM, TB, VM, Da84, Fa77, Gu00, Lv88>

chacta[1] [ʃakta] *adj.* **1** irritable, mean *Moi je joue pas avec lui. Il est trop chacta.* Me, I don't play with him. He's too irritable. (SM) **2** stingy *Jean est chacta avec son argent.* John is tight with his money. (IB) **3** [*pej.*] inferior **Une cabine chacta.* An inferior cabin. (Re31) **Un cheval chacta.* A runted, undersized horse. (Re31) <***Loc:*** IB, SM, Re31>

chacta[2] [ʃakta] *n.m.* **1** midget horse, Shetland pony **2** runted or undersized animal (esp. a horse) **3** [*pej.*] runt, midget, half-pint <***Loc:*** EV, IB, SM, Da84, Lv88, Ph36>

chacun, -e [ʃakɛ̃, -ɛ̃n, ʃakœ̃, -yn] *pron.indef.* each, each one *Et ils ontvaient chacun une saquée, une avait une saquée de haricots de rame et l'autre avait une saquée de fèves plates.* And they each had a sackful, one had a sackful of pole beans, and the other had a sackful of butter beans. (TB) *Il, il nous a foutu chacune une raclée, chère, parce qu'on a pas resté là.* He gave us each a slap because we didn't stay there. (EV) *A chacun son mauvais goût.* To each his bad taste (i.e. to each his own). (EV) ◊ **•chacun (à) son tour** to each his turn, each in turn *Anciennement, il y avait pas de réfrigerateur. Moi, je me rappelle, on avait--je pense partout dans la Louisiane--on appelait des boucheries de quartier, éyou il y avait tant de familles qui se mettaient ensemble, et tous les samedis, ils tuaient un veau, chacun à son tour.* Formerly, there were no refrigerators. I remember, they had--I guess everywhere in Louisiana--they were called neighborhood slaughtering co-ops, where a certain number of families got together every Saturday, they would kill a calf, each in turn. (SL) <SL, An94> **•chacun pour lui-même** each one for himself <Da84> **•tout chacun** everyone *Tout chacun avait sa modèle pour faire un bateau.* Everyone had his own design for making a boat. (LF) *Dessus le bayou je crois que tout chacun est parent. Si on est pas parents, tout chacun connaît un et l'autre et c'est une place qu'est bien tranquille icitte sur le bayou.* On the bayou I think everyone is related. If we're not related, everyone knows each other and it'a a place that's very quiet here on the bayou. (LF) <AC, EV, LF, Lv88> <***Loc:*** AC, EV, IB, JD, LA, LF, SB, SL, TB, VM, An94, Da84, Gr86, Lv88, Wh83>

chadègue (**chadigue**) [ʃadɛg, ʃadig] *n.f.* grapefruit <***Loc:*** LF, Re38>

chadigue ♦see **chadègue**

chadron ♦see **chardon**

chafaud ♦see **échafaud**

chaganon ♦see **chaouinon**

chagrin[1] [ʃagrɛ̃] *adj.* sad, unhappy, grieved *Il était chagrin après la mort de son chien.* He was sad after his dog died. (EV) <***Loc:*** EV, Da84>

chagrin[2] [ʃagrɛ̃] *n.m.* sadness, sorrow, grief, heartache *Il est mort du chagrin. Il a perdu quelqu'un qu'il s'avait habitué avec, tu connais. Il pouvait pas vivre sans lui.* He died of heartache. He lost someone he had grown accustomed to, you know. He couldn't live without him. (LF) <***Loc:*** AC, IB, LF, SM, VM, Da84, La99>

chagrinant, -e [ʃagrinɑ̃, -ɑ̃t] *adj.* **1** saddening, heartbreaking *Quelle triste nouvelle. C'est chagrinant.* What sad news. It's heartbreaking. (VM) **2** distressing <***Loc:*** JD, VM, Da84, Fa77>

chagriner [ʃagrine] **I** *v.tr.* to grieve, sadden *Ça me chagrine de te voir partir.* It saddens me to see you leave. (LA) **2** to concern, distress **Boy, je connais pas pour ce record-ça-là. Ça me chagrine d'aller le faire.* Boy, I don't know about that record. It concerns me to go and cut it. (VM, An84) **II se chagriner** *v.pron.* **1** to fret, grieve *Chagrine-toi pas, bèbe. Il vaulait pas la peine.* Don't grieve, baby. He wasn't worth it. (EV) **2** to become angry, be peeved *Il s'a chagriné avec moi.* He got angry with me. (SM) <***Loc:*** EV, SM, VM, An84, Da84>

chaîne [ʃɛ̃n] *n.f.* **1** chain **2** wool or thread carried by a shuttle (in weaving), threads that cross the warp in a fabric <***Loc:*** AC, LA, LF, SB, SL, SM, TB, VM, An94, Da84>

chaintre (**chaîntre**) [ʃɛ̃t(r)] *n.m./f.* **1** uncultivated area around a field *Tout le long de la chaintre, il n-avait des 'tites maisons pour les travaillants sur la plantation.* All along the uncultivated area around the field, there were little houses for the workers on the plantation. (Lv88) **2** turnrow, headland (strip of uncultivated land at the end or side of a field where a plow can turn) *Tu peux pas tourner dans les rangs. Il fallait ça soyait au bout ayoù tu tournes. Et tu laissais ça peut-être un 15, 20 pieds de large. C'est ça tu appelles un chaîntre.* You can't turn [the plow] in the rows. It had to be at the end that you would turn. And you left that about 15 or 20 feet wide. That's what you call a turnrow. (VM) **3** road along a fence (used by a farmer) <***Loc:*** AC, AV, IB, JD, LA, SM, VM, Da84, Lv88>

chair [ʃær] *n.f.* **1** flesh, meat *Les Français ont nommé ça "sac-à-lait": la chair est très blanche.* The French named that [crappie] "sack-of-milk": the flesh is very white. (SL) **2** flesh, meat, pulp (e.g. of fruit) *Oh ouais, les gros melons avec la chair jaune. Ça, c'est bâtardé.* Oh yes, the big melons with yellow meat. That's a hybrid. (IV) <***Loc:*** IV, LF, SL, Da84>

chaire [ʃær] *n.f.* pulpit <***Loc:*** Da84>

chaise [ʃɛz, ʃɛ3, ʃe3, sɛz] *n.f.* chair, seat **Chaise qui se recargue.* Reclining chair. (Fa77) ◊ **•chaise à roues** wheelchair *Il a resté malade longtemps dans la chaise à roues.* He was sick for a long time in the wheelchair. (TB) <TB> **•chaise bourrée** ***a*** armchair ***b*** upholstered chair <JE, LA, Gu00> **•prendre une chaise** to sit, have a seat *Prends une chaise.* Have a seat. (VM) <EV, VM, Da84> <***Loc:*** AL, AV, EV, IB, JE, LA, LF, SJ, SL, SM, TB, VM, Da84, Fa77, Gu00, La99, Lv88, Ph36>

chaland [ʃalɑ̃] *n.m.* **1** flat-bottomed rowboat **2** barge <***Loc:*** AV, IB, IV, JE, LF, SJ, SM, TB, Da84, Lv88>

châle (**charle**) [ʃal, ʃarl] *n.m.* shawl <***Loc:*** SB, Da84, Fa77>

châlet [ʃalɛ, ʃale] *n.m.* country home <***Loc:*** Da84>

chaleur [ʃalœr] *n.f.* heat, warmth *C'est un mulet qu'a été elevé ici qui habitué de le climette, de la chaleur de de l'humidité.* It's a mule that was raised here and that is used to the climate, the heat and the humidity. (LF) ◊ **•en chaleur** in heat (i.e. sexual arousal of an animal) *Fais attention de fermer* *la porte de cour. Ma chienne est en chaleur.* Be careful to close the yard gate. My [female] dog is in heat. (LA) <LA> <***Loc:*** LA, LF, SB, TB, VM, Da84, Fa77>

CHALK [tʃɔk] *n.m.* chalk <***Loc:*** SM, VM>

chalote ♦see **échalote**

chaloupe [ʃalup] *n.f.* rowboat <***Loc:*** Da84>

chamaie ♦see **chamois**

chamaille [ʃãmaj] *n.f.* quarrel, squabble, fuss, fight *Ils ont eu une grande chamaille.* They had a big fuss. (SM) <***Loc:*** LA, LF, SJ, SL, SM>

chamailler [ʃãmaje] **I** *v.tr.* **1** to bother, tease, annoy, pick on *Il avait habitude de chamailler ce pauvre homme tous les samedis soirs.* He used to pick on that poor man every Saturday night. (SL) **2** to scold *Le professeur l'a chamaillé.* The teacher scolded him. (AV) **II** *v.intr.* to squabble, bicker, wrangle, fuss *Il est tout le temps après chamailler comme un enfant.* He is always bickering like a kid. (LA) **III se chamailler** *v.pron.* to squabble, bicker, wrangle, fuss with each other *C'est vaillant quand il n-a de la compagnie ou quelque chose, mais là après ça, quand c'est juste eux-autres, ça se chamaille.* They are nice [with each other] when they have company or something, but afterwards, when it's just them, they bicker. (AV) <***Loc:*** AV, LA, SL, TB, Da84>

chamaillerie [ʃãmajri] *n.f.* quarrel, squabble, fuss, fight <***Loc:*** Da84>

chamanderie ♦see **tchamanderie**

chamandeur ♦see **tchamandeur**

chambouhourra ♦see **tchampourra**

chambranler (**chambranner, chambreler**) [ʃãbrãle, ʃãbrãne, ʃãbrəle] **I** *v.tr.* to shake, cause to shake *Le vent chambrelle le bois.* The wind shakes the tree. (IB) *Le vent chambranne toute la maison.* The wind makes the whole house shake. (Lv88) **II** *v.intr.* to shake *Il avait tellement peur qu'il chambranlait.* He was so scared he was shaking. (SJ) *Le vent a fait chambranner le magasin à maïs.* The wind caused the corn crib to shake. (IB) <***Loc:*** AV, IB, SJ, Lv88>

chambranner ♦see **chambranler**

chambre [ʃãm, ʃãb(r)] *n.f.* room *Ma maison a sept chambres: un salon, une cuisine, une salle à manger, une chambre à bain, et deux chambres à coucher.* My house has seven rooms: a living room, a kitchen, a dining room, a bathroom, and two bedrooms. (Guo0) ◊ **•chambre à bain(s)** bathroom *L'eau venait d'une grosse citerne dans les chambres à bain.* The water came from a big cistern into the bathrooms. (EV) *Je peux user la chambre à bains?* May I use the bathroom? (Lv88) <AC, EV, IB, JE, LA, LF, SM, TB, Fa77, Guo0, Lv88> **•chambre à coucher** bedroom <EV, JE, LF, TB, Da84, Fa77, Guo0> **•chambre à lit** bedroom <LF, TB, Lv88> **•chambre de classe** classroom <Lv88> **•chambre de cour** courtroom <Lv88> **•chambre de devant** living room, front room <Da84, Guo0, Lv88> **•chambre en avant** living room, front room <AC> <***Loc:*** AC, AV, EV, IB, JE, LA, LF, SJ, SM, TB, Da84, Fa77, Guo0, Lv88>

chambrelant, -e [ʃãbrəlã, -ãt] *adj.* shaky, unsteady *Le lit est chambrelant.* The bed is unsteady. (IB) <***Loc:*** IB>

chambreler ♦see **chambranler**

chameau [ʃãmo] *n.m.* camel <***Loc:*** SL, Da84, Fa77>

chamois (**chamaie**) [ʃãmwa, ʃãmɛ, ʃãme] *n.m.* chamois, shammy <***Loc:*** Da84>

chamonder ♦see **quémander**

chamondeur ♦see **quémandeur**

champ [ʃã] *n.m.* **1** field *Une savane, ça c'est éioù-ce qu'eusse mettrait des animaux, des vaches. Un champ c'est éioù tu vas planter ton maïs ou tes cannes à sucre.* A pasture is where they put their cattle. A field is where you plant your corn or your sugar cane. (LF) **2** lot, parcel of land *Un champ, ça c'est une pièce dans le clos.* A lot, that's a piece of the field. (Lv88) ◊ **•champ de bataille** battlefield <Fa77> **•champ de canne** sugar cane field *Mais dans ce temps-là les champs de canne allait dans des 40 et 60 arpents de profond du chemin.* But in those days the cane fields went back 40 or 60 arpents deep from the road. (TB) <LF, TB> **•champ d'huile** oil field *Et quand moi j'a été à l'ouvrage dans les champs d'huile, j'a été à l'ouvrage comme un Cadien.* And when I went to work in the oil fields, I went to work as a Cajun. (TB) <TB> <***Loc:*** LF, TB, Fa77, Lv88>

CHAMP [tʃæmp] *n.m.* champ, champion <***Loc:*** Da84>

champagne[1] [ʃãpãɲ, ʃãpãj] *n.m.* champagne, sparkling wine <***Loc:*** Da84>

champagne[2] [ʃãpãɲ, ʃãpãj] *n.m.* **1** basket or container with a capacity of 1/3 barrel, or 70 lbs., used in the seafood fishing industry (originally made of palmetto, later of iron or plastic) **2** the quantity of oysters, shrimp, etc. held by such a basket <***Loc:*** LF>

champignon [ʃãpiɲɔ̃, ʃãpĩjɔ̃] *n.m.* **1** mushroom **2** mold, fungus *Le riz était plein de champignons.* The rice was full of mold. (TB) **3** jerk, bastard, asshole <***Loc:*** AV, SL, TB, Da84, Fa77>

champion [ʃãpjɔ̃] *n.m.* champion <***Loc:*** Da84>

champoura ♦see **tchampoura**

chance [ʃãs] *n.f.* **1** chance, risk *Tu peux prendre la chance de perdre toute ta maison, tout ça que t'as.* You can take a chance on losing your home, everything you own [if you stay during a hurricane]. (JE) **2** luck *J'ai eu plein de la chance parce que j'ai appris vite, tous les jobs que je prendais j'apprendais ça vite.* I was very lucky because I learned fast, all the jobs that I took I learned quickly. (TB) **3** opportunity *Ils faisaient de la misère au pitit chaque fois qu'ils ont eu de la chance.* They teased the little one every time they had the opportunity. (Lv88) ◊ **•chance à** thanks to *Chance à elle.* Thanks to her. (Fa77) <Fa77> **•avoir autant de chance qu'un rat dans un tuyau de pipe** to be unlucky <La99> **•avoir la chance de** to have the chance to, have the opportunity to *J'ai eu la chance de charrer avec elle.* I had the opportunity to talk to her. (SL) *J'ai la chance d'aller en ville.* I have the opportunity to go into the city. (IB) <IB, SL> **•avoir pas plus de chance qu'une sauterelle dans un parc de dindes** to be very unlucky <La99> **•avoir (une) chance** to have a chance, have an opportunity *Peut-être j'aurais une chance de le voir.* Maybe I would have the opportunity to see him. (SM) *Comme ça j'aurai chance d'aller là-bas.* That way I'll have an opportunity to go over there. (VM) <SM, VM> **•bonne chance** good luck <EV, LF, Da84> **•prendre une chance / prendre des {ses} chances** to take a chance, take a risk *Je vas prendre une chance, si vous voulez, que le Vieux Diable me mange.* If you want me to, I'll take the risk of the Old Devil eating me up. (LA) *Je vas plus prendre des chances.* I'm not going to take any more chances. (JE) <JE, LA, Lv88> **•une chance (que) / chance** it's a good thing that, luckily *Une chance qu'il a plu: mes fèves étaient tout secs.* It's a good thing that it rained: my beans were quite dry. (Lv88) *Chance, il t'a pas vu.* Luckily, he didn't see you. (VM) *Une chance il avait ce chien-là. Il lui a mordu la croix de sa carabine-là, ah ben mais les dents se sont gravées dedans.* Lucky he had that dog. He bit the stock of his rifle, and his teeth left a mark in it. (EV) <EV, VM, Lv88> ***<Loc:*** AC, EV, IB, JE, LA, LF, SB, SL, SM, TB, VM, Da84, La99, Lv88, Ph36, Re76>

chanceux, -euse [ʃɑ̃sø, -øz] *adj.* lucky, fortunate *Et quelqu'un qu'était assez chanceux d'avoir un char pouvait aller à Houma et ces places-là.* And someone who was lucky enough to have a car could go to Houma and those places. (TB) *Ouais, tu vois, j'ai été plus chanceuse que elle.* Yes, you see, I was luckier than her. (EV) *J'ai été chanceux durant ma vie.* I have been lucky in my life. (IB) ***<Loc:*** AC, EV, IB, TB, Da84, Fa77>

chanceusement [ʃɑ̃søzmɑ̃] *adv.* luckily ***<Loc:*** Fa77>

chancre [ʃɑ̃k(r)] *n.m.* 1 cancer 2 ulcer ***<Loc:*** Da84>

chandelier [ʃɑ̃dəlje, ʃɑ̃dilje] *n.m.* candlestick, candle holder ***<Loc:*** LA, Da84, Fa77>

chandelle [ʃɑ̃dɛl] *n.f.* candle (of wax or tallow) ◊ **•chandelle de glace** icicle <AV, LA, SM, Da84, Fa77, La99> ***<Loc:*** AV, IB, LA, SM, TB, Da84, Fa77, La99, Lv88>

chandilier [ʃɑ̃dilje] *n.m.* support, reinforcement added under a weak part in a floor ***<Loc:*** VM>

change [ʃɑ̃ʒ] *n.m.* 1 change (e.g. of clothes) **T'avais justement un bon change de bon linge. Si tu te battais, t'allais le déchirer, salir, et tout ça.* You had just one good change of clothes. If you fought, you would tear it, dirty it, and all that. (IV, An94) 2 change (coins or money) *Est-ce que t'as du change pour cinq piastres?* Do you have change for five dollars? (SM) ◊ **•change de linge** change of clothing *J'ai mis deux ou trois changes de linge en dedans.* I put two or three changes of clothes in it. (EV) <EV, IV, An94, Da84> **•faire du change** to make change <Da84> ***<Loc:*** EV, IV, SM, An94, Da84, Lv88>

changeable [ʃɑ̃ʒab(l)] *adj.* changeable, fickle, inconstant *Il a l'idée beaucoup changeable.* His opinion is very inconstant. (LA) ***<Loc:*** LA, Da84>

changeage [ʃɑ̃ʒaʒ] *n.m.* exchange, changing *Ils sont en grand changeage de chevaux.* They are in the middle of changing horses. (SB) ***<Loc:*** SB>

changeailler [ʃɑ̃ʒaje] **I** *v.tr.* to change (esp. often or capriciously) *Il changeaillait son idée tous les deux minutes.* He would change his mind every two minutes. (LA) **II** *v.intr.* to change often or capriciously, change back and forth in a fickle way ***<Loc:*** IB, LA, Da84>

changeant, -e [ʃɑ̃ʒɑ̃, -ɑ̃t] *adj.* changeable, inconstant, fickle *Le temps est changeant.* The weather is changeable. (VM) ***<Loc:*** VM, Da84>

changement [ʃɑ̃ʒmɑ̃] *n.m.* change, variation ◊ **•changement d'age** menopause <SM> **•changement de vie** menopause *Elle après avoir son changement de vie.* She's having her menopause. (SM) <SM, Da84, Lv88> ***<Loc:*** EV, SM, Da84, Lv88, Ph36>

changeotage [ʃɑ̃ʒɔtaʒ] *n.m.* exchange, swap *C'était un fameux changeotage.* That was a fine exchange. (IB) ***<Loc:*** AV, IB, SJ>

changeoter [ʃɑ̃ʒɔte] **I** *v.tr.* 1 to exchange, swap, barter *Il est tout le temps après changeoter une affaire pour une autre.* He is always exchanging one thing for another. (VM) 2 to change (esp. often or capriciously) *Elle est toujours à changeoter son idée.* She's always changing her mind. (AV) **II** *v.intr.* to change often or capriciously, change back and forth in a fickle way *T'es trop journalier, tu changeotes de trop.* You're too moody, you change too often. (VM) ***<Loc:*** AV, IB, SJ, VM, Da84, Lv88>

changeoteur [ʃɑ̃ʒɔtœr] *n.m.* instable person, changeable person ***<Loc:*** JD, Lv88>

changer [ʃɑ̃ʒe, ʃɑ̃ze] **I** *v.tr.* 1 to change, alter *Ça qu'a changé ça plein, c'est après la guerre luméro deux quand les hommes a revenu de l'autre bord.* What changed that a lot, is after WWII when men came back from Europe (lit. the other side). (TB) *Là ils ont changé la ligne deux ou trois fois depuis ça.* Then they've changed the [property] line two or three times since then. (TB) 2 to change, replace, exchange *Changer une couche.* To change a diaper. (LF) *Dessus le télévision quand eusse commence à montrer une serpent, je vas changer de station.* On TV when they start to show a snake I'll change the channel. (TB) *Ces nouvelles bandes en élastique, ça s'use tellement vite qu'il faut que tu les changes tous les ans.* Those new rubber belts wear out so fast that you have to change them every year. (VM) **II** *v.intr.* to change, become different **Mais mon ennui pour des jours Cajins poudrait être quec'chose qui dur eine quarantaine d'années si les affaires changent pas et les jeunes commencent pas à apprendre à parler la langue Cajine.* But my longing for the Cajun days could be something which lasts forty odd years if things don't change and young people don't start learning the Cajun language. (Wh83) **III se changer** *v.pron.* to change one's clothes, change *Il faudra je me change avant d'aller à la messe.* I'll have to change my clothes before going to Mass. (LA) ◊ **•changer de bord** to change sides *Le prêtre dit, "Allons changer de bord alors."* The priest said, "Let's change sides then." (AS, ch: *Rivière*) <AS> **•changer de place** to change places *Ils ont changé de place.* They changed places. (EV) <EV> **•changer de vie** to go through menopause *Alle est toujours malade depuis qu'alle est après changer de vie.* She's always sick since she's been going through menopause. (VM) <SM, VM> **•changer les mots** to translate *Là M. de Québec a attendu ça, il dit, boy t'as une bonne chanson, mais il dit je peux pas jouer ça dans le collège, il dit, faut que tu fais ça en français. Et je dis, regarde, changer les mots d'une chanson c'est pas aisé non.* Then M. from Quebec heard that, he says, boy you've got a good song, but he says, I can't play that in the college, it has to be in French. And I say, look, translating a song is not easy. (TB) <TB> **•changer son fusil d'épaule** to change one's opinions <La99> **•changer son idée** to change one's mind *J'ai changé mon idée en faisant mon paquet.* I changed my mind while packing my bags. (AC, ch: *Valse de la belle*) <AC, EV, An94> **•être changé** to be dressed *Il est pas changé.* He's not dressed. (SL) <SL> ***<Loc:*** AC, AS, AV, EV, IB, LA, LF, SL, SM, TB, VM, An94, Da84, La99, Wh83>

changeur [ʃɑ̃ʒœr] *n.m.* ◊ **•changeur de chevaux** person who engages in the practice of exchanging one horse for another, horse swapper <SM, Re31> ***<Loc:*** SM, Re31>

chanson [ʃɑ̃sɔ̃, ʃɑ̃ʃɔ̃] *n.f.* song ◊ **•faire des chansons** to write songs, compose songs *J'ai arrêté de faire des chansons parce que j'ai plus un tas de temps, les moustiques me tracasse et je suis manière malade, tu vois?* I've stopped composing songs because I don't have a lot of time anymore, and the mosquitoes bother me and I'm somewhat sick, you see? (TB) <TB> ***<Loc:*** AC, AV, EV, LA, PQ, SM, TB, VM, Da84, Lv88, Wh83>

chansonnette [ʃɑ̃sɔ̃nɛt] *n.f.* short song, little ditty ***<Loc:*** Da84>

chant [ʃɑ̃] *n.m.* **1** chant **2** melody, song **3** singing ***<Loc:*** Da84>

chantage [ʃɑ̃taʒ] *n.m.* singing, song *Le chantage n'était rien de fameux.* The song wasn't anything great. (SB) ***<Loc:*** SB>

chantailler [ʃɑ̃taje] *v.intr.* to sing intermittently ***<Loc:*** IB>

chanter [ʃɑ̃te] **I** *v.tr.* to sing (a song) **II** *v.intr.* **1** to sing *Je chante aussi bien comme toi.* I sing as well as you. (SM) *On va faire un* CHOIR, *il dit, juste pour tes filles, parce que cher Bon Dieu, ça c'est des filles qui peut chanter!* We'll put together a choir, he says, just for the girls, because dear God, those are some girls who can sing! (TB) **2** to sing, produce its customary call (of an insect or bird, e.g. chirp, cackle, crow, coo) **La poule qui chante première, c'est elle qui a pondu.* The hen that cackles first is the one that laid the egg. (Da84) ◊ **•chanter comme un carencro** to sing badly <La99> **•chanter dans la tribune** to sing in the choir-loft <Da84> **•chanter des midis à quatorze heures** ***a*** to tell a cock and bull story, exaggerate, say things that cannot be true ***b*** to tell a long story, talk on and on <AV, EV, Da84, La99> ***<Loc:*** AC, AV, EV, IB, JE, LA, LF, PQ, SL, SM, TB, VM, An84, An94, Da84, La99, Wh83>

chante-galerie ♦see **chasse-galerie**

chanterie [ʃɑ̃tri] *n.f.* singing ***<Loc:*** JD>

chanteur, -euse [ʃɑ̃tœr, -øz] *n.* singer ***<Loc:*** EV, LF, PQ, Gr86, Da84>

chantillon ♦see **échantillon**

chantonnier [ʃɑ̃tɔ̃nje] *v.intr.* **1** to hum **2** to sing softly and repeatedly ***<Loc:*** SJ>

chaoui [ʃawi, ʃawe] *n.m.* raccoon ◊ **•chaoui cyprière** dark-furred raccoon that lives in cypress swamps <Re31> ***<Loc:*** AL, AV, EV, IB, LA, LF, SB, SL, SM, TB, Da84, Gu00, Lv88, Ph36, Re31>

chaouanon ♦see **chaouinon**

chaouinon (**chaouanon**, **chaganon**) [ʃawinɔ̃, ʃwɛ̃nɔ̃, ʃawɑ̃nɑ̃, ʃawɑ̃nɔ̃, ʃawɑ̃nɔ̃t, ʃagɑ̃nɔ̃] *n.m.* bob-tailed chicken, shawnee chicken ***<Loc:*** IB, SJ, SM, Lv88, Re31>

chapeau [ʃapo] *n.m.* **1** hat **2** cradle cap (form of seborrhea that occurs on the heads of infants) **3** snuff, charred part of lamp wick ◊ **•chapeau de laine** felt hat <Da84> **•chapeau de paille** straw hat *Pour travailler dans les clos ça mettait les chapeaux de paille.* They would wear straw hats to work in the fields. (AC) <AC, Da84> **•chapeau de St. Jacques** red amaryllis <VM> ***<Loc:*** AC, AV, EV, JE, LA, LF, SL, SM, TB, VM, An94, Da84, Fa77, Lv88, Pe37>

chapelain [ʃaplɛ̃] *n.m.* chaplain ***<Loc:*** Da84>

chapelet [ʃaplɛ, ʃaple] *n.m.* rosary, prayer beads *Il dit son chapelet tous les matins en français.* He says his rosary every morning in French. (LF) ◊ **•chapelet bénit** blessed rosary beads <Da84> **•faire un chapelet à qqn** ***a*** to tell s.o. off ***b*** to scold s.o. *Il m'a fait un chapelet quand j'ai rentré tard.* He gave me a scolding when I came in late. (EV) <EV, La99> ***<Loc:*** EV, LF, SL, SM, VM, Da84, Fa77, La99, Lv88>

chapelle [ʃapɛl] *n.f.* chapel ***<Loc:*** EV, IB, IV, LF, Da84, Fa77>

chaperon[1] [ʃaprɔ̃] *n.m.* chaperone ***<Loc:*** EV, VM, Da84>

chaperon[2] ♦see **chapon**

chapitre [ʃapit(r)] *n.m.* chapter ◊ **•en faire tout un chapitre** to talk endlessly about s.t., rattle on and on about s.t. <JD> ***<Loc:*** JD, Da84>

chapon (**chaperon**) [ʃapɔ̃, ʃaprɔ̃] *n.m.* capon, castrated cockerel ***<Loc:*** VM, Da84, Fa77>

chaponner [ʃapɔ̃ne] *v.tr.* to caponize, castrate *Penche-toi pas trop près de cette tortue cocodril, tu vas te faire chaponner.* Don't bend over too close to that alligator snapping turtle, you will get yourself castrated. (VM) ***<Loc:*** VM, Da84>

chapper ♦see **échapper**

chaque[1] [ʃak] *adj.* each, every *Chaque hiver les canards et oies* *refont le voyage de nos ancêtres les Acadiens exilés.* Every winter the ducks and the geese redo the voyage of our exiled Acadian ancesters. (ThCa: *Mille misères*) *Chaque bête avait un TAG sur le dos.* Each animal had a tag on its back. (VM) *Tu me fais du mal chaque fois je te regarde, ma vilaine.* You hurt me every time I look at you, you rascal. (ch: *Madame Atchen*) *Il faut pas que tu retailles les arbres chaque année.* You mustn't reprune the trees every year. (LA) *Des petites rosettes pour mettre dessus chaque côté de le MANTLE. Pour le SHOWER samedi.* Little rosettes to put on each side of the mantle. For the shower Saturday. (TB) <***Loc:*** AC, AS, AV, EV, LA, LF, SL, SM, TB, Da84, ThCa, Wh83>

chaque[2] [ʃak] *pron.* each, each one *C'est des petits TWINS. Des petits bessons. Ça pesait sept livres et cinq -z- onces chaque quand ils sont énés.* They are little twins. They weighed seven pounds five ounces each when they were born. (LF) *Et les quatre classes là, c'était des classes qui s'associaient pas avec un et l'autre. Chaque avait son petit clique.* And the four [social] classes, they were classes that did not associate with each other. Each one had their little clique. (SM) Et là quand le candi était cuit dans la cheminée ça prendait une cuillère, je suppose, ça mettait ça dans chaque de les pailles. And when the candy was cooked in the fireplace, they took a spoon, I suppose, they put it in each of the cornhusks. (TB) <***Loc:*** LF, SM, TB>

chaque[3]**, chaqué** ♦see **tchac**

chaquer ♦see **tchaquer**

char [ʃar, ʃau] *n.m.* **1** car, automobile *Je vas rentrer dans le char.* I'm going to get in the car. (JE) **2** train *Il prend le char pour aller chez lui.* He's taking the train to go home. (SB) **3** car, coach (of a train) ◊ **•char à bagages** baggage car <TB, Fa77, Re31> **•char-à-banc** ***a*** four-wheel cart (with seats) *Iry Lejeune s'en venait dans son char-à-banc, lui et sa femme.* Iry Lejeune used to come in his four-wheel cart, he and his wife. (LA) ***b*** 'beater,' old junky car <IB, LA, Da84> **•char-à-bras** hand-propelled railroad cart <Da84> **•char à fret** ***a*** freight train ***b*** freight car (of a train) <LA, LF, SL, SM, Lv88> **•char à l'électricité** streetcar, tram <LF, SM> **•char à passagers** ***a*** passenger train ***b*** passenger car (of a train) <LA, SB, SM, VM, Fa77, Lv88> **•char à vapeur** train <LF, Hi02> **•char de chemin de fer** train <LA> **•char de haleine** train <VM> **•char électrique** streetcar, tram <SL> **•en {par} char** by car *Je vais en ville en char.* I'm going to town by car. (SM) *Leeville est pas loin, d'icitte-là en bateau dans quarante-cinq minutes. Et par char ça prend une heure et demie.* Leeville is not far, [you can go] from here to there by boat in 45 minutes. And by car it takes an hour and a half. (TB) <SM, TB, Da84> **•gros char** train **Ca fait, on monte sur le gros char ici un matin, et puis on a été en Ville.* So we got on the train here one morning, and then we went to New Orleans. (An84) *Son mari, c'est un bougre qui guide les gros chars.* Her husband is a fellow who conducts trains. (Lv88) <An84, Lv88> <***Loc:*** AC, AV, EV, IB, JE, LA, SB, SL, SM, TB, VM, An94, Da84, Gu00, Hi02, Lv88, Ph36, Re31>

charabouche [ʃarabuʃ] *n.m.* dummy locomotive *Le charabouche a passé derrière la maison avec des cannes.* The dummy locomotive went by behind the house with a load of cane. (TB) <***Loc:*** TB>

charade[1] [ʃarad] *n.f.* charade <***Loc:*** Da84>

charade[2] (**charage**) [ʃarad, ʃaraʒ] *n.f.* **1** conversation, chat *Elle est toujours dans une charade avec quelqu'un.* She is always in a chitchat with someone. (IB) **Il a eu einne charade avec Sam.* He had a chat with Sam. (EV, Ph36) *C'était une charade amicable.* It was a friendly chat. (SL) **2** talking, idle talk, prattle **3** *(pl.)* gossip **J'ai commencé à croire c'est des charades.* I began to think it was gossip. (An77) **4** trouble *Il y a pas eu de charade, il s'est rentourné.* There wasn't any trouble, he came back. (EV) <***Loc:*** AV, EV, IB, JD, SL, SM, VM, An77, Da84, Lv88, Ph36>

charader [ʃarade] *v.intr.* to talk a lot, prattle, chatter *Les 'tites filles sont après charader.* The little girls are chattering. (VM) <***Loc:*** AV, IB, SB, SJ, VM, Lv88>

charage ♦see **charade**

charaque [ʃarak] *n.m.* senseless talk, idle talk <***Loc:*** TB>

charara ♦see **tcharara**

charbon [ʃærbɔ̃, ʃarbɔ̃] *n.m.* **1** coal, charcoal *Y avait pas d'électricité, et eusse se chauffait avec des gros réchauds à bois ou avec du charbon.* There was no electricity, and they heated their houses with big wood stoves or with coal. (TB) **2** anthrax **3** black rot (in plants) **4** Cajun card game in which the winner of a hand makes a black mark on the face of the loser of the hand using a burnt cork from a wine bottle <***Loc:*** IB, TB, Da84>

charbonnier [ʃarbɔ̃je] *n.m.* coalman, one who makes charcoal ◊ **•charbonnier est maître chez lui** a man is master of his own house, a man's house is his castle <Da84> <***Loc:*** Da84>

charcher ♦see **chercher**

chardon (**chadron, chardron, chaudron**) [ʃardrɔ̃, ʃodrɔ̃] *n.m.* thistle <***Loc:*** LF, SB, SL, SM, TB, Da84, Hi02, Lv88, Re31, ThCa>

chardron ♦see **chardon**

charge [ʃarʒ] *n.m./f.* **1** load *Une charge de coton.* A load of cotton. (LA) **2** charge, accusation, indictment, complaint *Il a été condamné à deux ans dessus une charge de...* He was sentenced to two years on a charge of . . . (EV) *Il a fait un charge contre moi.* He made a complaint against me. (VM) *Follait que le juge de paix décide s'il va faire une charge, si c'était sérieux.* The justice of the peace had to decide if he was going to bring charges, if it was serious. (LF) ◊ **•avoir charge de** to have charge of, be in charge of *Un de les bougres qu'a charge de ça c'est W.* One of the guys who has charge of that is W. (LF) <LF> **•en charge de** in charge of *C'est moi qu'étais en charge de bâtir ce bateau-là.* I'm the one who was in charge of building this boat. (TB) <LF, TB> **•faire {mettre} une charge contre** to make or bring a charge against *Le juge de paix, fait des charges contre du monde. Il faut que le juge de paix fait la charge.* The justice of the peace makes charges against people. The justice of the peace has to bring the charge. (LF) **Je suis parti asteur mettre une charge contre lui.* I'm going right now to bring a charge against him. (SL, An94) <LF, SL, VM, An94, Da84> **•prendre charge** to take charge *Martin Weber était un homme qui pouvait prendre charge d'une salle.* Martin Weber was a man who take charge of a dance hall. (LA) <LA, Da84> <***Loc:*** EV, LA, LF, SL, TB, VM, An94, Da84, Lv88>

chargé, -e [ʃarʒe] *n.m.* official ◊ **•chargé d'affaires** government official <Da84> <***Loc:*** Da84>

charger [ʃarʒe] **I** *v.tr.* **1** to charge, bill (s.o. for goods or services) **Là, Guillory a chargé Hébert $327 pour faire le job.* Then, Guillory charged Hébert $327 to do the job. (Wh83) *Je charge pas le monde, le monde donne un petit quelque chose. Ça qu'eusse veut.* I don't charge people, people give a little something. Whatever they want. (TB) **2** to charge, bill (a fee) *J'ai été à l'hôpital et ils ont chargé cent et quelques piastres.* I went to the hospital and they charged one hundred and something dollars. (IB) *Tu vas charger ça dessus mon compte.* You'll charge that to my account. (Lv88) *On charge l'entrée du terrain du jeu.* We charge admission to the field [for sports]. (Lv88) **3** to bring a charge against, accuse *Ils les ont chargé hier pour avoir tué M. Begnaud.* They charged them yesterday for the murder of Mr. Begnaud. (LA) **4** to charge (with an obligation) *Marcus, tu as plus de responsabilité que tu crois, parce que Grandma Douce te charge avec l'obligation la plus lourde.* Marcus, you have more responsibility than you think because Grandma Douce is giving you the most difficult task. (ThCa: *La douce réunion*) **5** to load (a gun) *Le fusil était pas chargé.* The shotgun was not loaded. (EV) **6** to load (goods) into a vehicle *Ça chargeait le riz dessus les bateaux.* They would load the rice onto the boats. (EV) **7** to charge (e.g. a battery) **II** *v.intr.* to charge, collect a fee *Mais je chargeais pas, ça me demandait combien ça me devait.* But I didn't charge, they would ask me how much they owed me. (LF) **Ils étaient chauds après moi parce que je chargeais trop bon marché.* They were mad at me because my fee was too low. (An84) **III se charger** *v.pron.* **1** to become overcast **Le temps se charge.* The sky is overcast. (Da84) **2** to assume charge, take responsibility *Il s'a chargé de tuer le cochon cette année.* He took responsibility for killing the pig this year. (VM) <VM, Da84> <***Loc:*** AC, EV, IB, LA, LF, SB, SM, TB, VM, An84, Da84, Lv88, ThCa>

charier ♦see **charrier**

chariot [ʃarjo] *n.m.* float (made by children using boxes, colored paper and candles, and paraded through the streets at night in imitation of New Orleans Mardi Gras parades) <***Loc:*** SM>

charitable [ʃaritab(l), ʃeritab(l)] *adj.* charitable, kind *C'est du monde bien charitable, mais ça va pas à la messe.* They are very charitable people, but they don't go to Mass. (VM) <***Loc:*** EV, LF, TB, VM, Da84>

charité (**chérité**) [ʃarite, ʃerite] *n.f.* **1** charity *Je joue avec un* BAND *de cadien. […] Et c'est mon le chanteur. Tout partout en autour d'ici. Plutôt pour la charité.* I play in a Cajun band. And I'm the singer. [We play] all around here. It's mostly for charity. (LF) **2** alms **3** charity, charitable organization ◊ **•faire la charité** to give alms <Da84> <***Loc:*** LF, TB, VM, Da84>

charivari [ʃarivari, ʃaribari] *n.m.* charivari, noisy serenade held by surprise at night for a newlywed couple who are unconventional in some way, usu. because one of them is marrying for the second time (the couple are traditionally expected to invite the serenaders inside and offer them food and drink) *Quand quelqu'un se marie et sa femme est mort et il se marie encore et là ils donnent un charivari, c'est beaucoup du train.* When someone gets married and his wife is dead and he marries again, then they give him a charivari, it is a lot of noise. (AV) <***Loc:*** AV, EV, IB, LF, SB, SJ, SL, SM, TB, Da84, Ph36, ThCa>

charlanter (**écharlanter**) [ʃarlɑ̃te, eʃarlɑ̃te] **I** *v.tr.* to talk to, chatter at, jabber at **Il avait jamais essayé à sortir, parce que son père, il continuait à l'écharlanter.* He never tried to go out, because his father continued to chatter to him. (SL, An94) **II** *v.intr.* to chatter, jabber, prattle *Ces deux femmes charlantent beaucoup.* Those two women jabber on and on. (AV) <***Loc:*** AV, SB, SL, SM, An94>

charlatan [ʃarlatɑ̃] *n.m.* charlatan, quack, fake professional <***Loc:*** Da84>

charle ♦see **châle**

charlotte[1] [ʃarlɔt] *n.f.* larva of a tiger beetle <***Loc:*** Re31>

charlotte[2] ♦see **échalote**

charmant, -e [ʃarmɑ̃, -ɑ̃t] *adj.* **1** charming, pleasant, agreeable *C'est une fille bien charmante.* That's a truly charming girl. (LA) **2** magical, enchanted *Tout un beau soir en me promenant oh tout du long du petit bois charmant.* One fine evening while strolling through the little magical woods. (IB, ch: *Tout un beau soir en me promenant*) <***Loc:*** IB, LA, Da84>

charme [ʃarm] *n.m.* charm <***Loc:*** Da84>

charmer [ʃarme, ʃærme] *v.tr.* **1** to charm, fascinate, delight *Celui là qui était tout sec, il se met à nous charmer, parler de la chasse et parler de ça et parler de l'autre, mais tout en anglais.* The one who was dry, he started to charm us, talking about hunting and talking about this and that, but all in English. (JD) 2 to charm, entrance, hyponotize, bewitch *Le chat a charmé le serpent.* The cat entranced the snake. (VM) <***Loc:*** JD, JE, LA, VM, Da84>

charmille [ʃarmij] *n.f.* planer tree, water elm <***Loc:*** Ho90, Lv88, Re31>

charnu, -e [ʃarny] *adj.* fleshy, plump *Elle était bien charnue après les fêtes.* She was rather plump after the holidays. (LA) <***Loc:*** LA, Da84>

charogne [ʃarɔ̃j] *n.f.* carrion, carcass of an animal *Ils étaient autour de lui comme des carencros autour d'une charogne.* They crowded around him like vultures around a carcass. (AC) <***Loc:*** AC, LA, Da84>

charpente [ʃarpɑ̃t, ʃærpɑ̃t] *n.f.* carpentry *Il travaille la charpente.* He works in carpentry. (Lv88) *Et mon j'ai travaillé à toute qualité de z-affaires, travaillé à la charpente, bâti des bateaux.* And I've done all kinds of work, I've worked in carpentry, built boats. (TB) ◊ **•faire la charpente** to do carpentry, practice carpentry *Il a fait la charpente toute sa vie.* He practiced carpentry his whole life. (TB) <TB> <***Loc:*** EV, LA, LF, SL, SM, TB, An84, Da84, Lv88>

charpenter [ʃarpɑ̃te] **I** *v.tr.* to trim, cut (a piece of wood) down to size *Charpenter une sole.* To trim a beam. (VM) **II** *v.intr.* to carpenter, practice carpentry *Il a habitude de charpenter, mais il fait pus ça depuis qu'il a tombé de l'échafaud.* He used to carpenter, but he no longer does that since he fell from the scaffold. (LA) <***Loc:*** LA, TB, VM, Da84>

charpenteur [ʃarpɑ̃tœr] *n.m.* carpenter *Après avoir fini de charpenter, le charpenteur a brûlé les ripes.* After he finished the carpentry job, the carpenter burned the wood shavings. (TB) <***Loc:*** TB, Lv88>

charpentier [ʃarpɑ̃tje] *n.m.* carpenter <***Loc:*** IB, LA, LF, SL, SM, Da84, Fa77, Lv88>

charpiller ♦see **écharpiller**

charrant, -e [ʃarɑ̃, -ɑ̃t] *adj.* 1 affable, kindly 2 talkative, garrulous *Quoi il y a avec toi. T'es bien charrant aujourd'hui.* What's the matter with you, you're very talkative today. (VM) <***Loc:*** VM, Lv88>

charré ♦see **charrette**

charrer [ʃare] *v.intr.* to talk, chat, converse, make conversation *À la sortie de l'église, ça va charrer avec l'un, charrer avec l'autre.* Leaving the church, they'll talk to one, talk to the other. (Lv88) *Allons charrer pour le K & B Grocery.* Let's talk about the K & B Grocery. (EV) <***Loc:*** AV, EV, LA, SL, SM, TB, Da84, Guoo, Lv88, Ph36, Re31>

charretée (**chartée**) [ʃarte, ʃarjete] *n.f.* 1 load, cartload, wagonful *Une charretée de foin, de bois.* A load of hay, of wood. (VM) 2 a great deal, plenty *La femme a une charretée d'enfants.* The woman has oodles of children. (LF) ◊ **•par charretée / à la charretée** a great deal, plenty *On a ramassé des giraumons par charretée cette année.* We picked plenty of pumpkins this year. (VM) <SB, VM, La99> <***Loc:*** JD, LF, SB, SM, VM, Da84, La99>

charreter [ʃarte] *v.tr.* to transport **Il a charreté l'bois.* He transported the wood. (EV, Ph36) <***Loc:*** EV, Ph36>

charretil ♦see **chartil**

charrette (**charré**) [ʃarɛt, ʃare] *n.f.* 1 two-wheeled cart *Un wagon a quatre roues. Il était plus grand qu'une charrette. Une charrette avait juste deux roues.* A wagon has four wheels. It was bigger than a cart. A cart had just two wheels. (EV) 2 buggy ◊ **•charrette à bœufs** ox cart <Da84> **•charrette à bras** handcart, pushcart <Da84> <***Loc:*** AS, EV, LA, LF, TB, VM, Da84, Fa77, Guoo>

charreur[1]**, -euse** [ʃarœr, -øz] *adj.* talkative, garrulous *Mon oncle était beaucoup charreur.* My uncle was very talkative. (LA) <***Loc:*** JD, LA, SM, VM, Da84, Lv88>

charreur[2]**, -euse** [ʃarœr, -øz] *n.* talker, talkative person *Un grand charreur.* A big talker. (SL) <***Loc:*** JD, SL>

charrier (**charier**) [ʃarje] *v.tr.* to carry, transport, move *On a eu pour charrier nos sacs d'écrevisses l'autre bord de la rivière.* We had to carry our sacks of crawfish to the other side of the river. (AS) <***Loc:*** AS, SL, TB, Da84, Fa77>

charroyage [ʃarwajaʒ] *n.m.* transportation <***Loc:*** Lv88>

charroyer (**charvoyer**) [ʃaroje, ʃarwaje, ʃarvwaje] *v.tr.* to carry, transport, move *Ce pauvre monde ont eu pour charroyer tout leur butin pour des mois après que leur vieille grand-mère a manqué.* Those poor people had to carry all of their belongings from place to place for months after their old grandmother died. (LA) *Elle charroïe sa poupée partout où elle va.* She carries her doll with her everywhere she goes. (SM) <***Loc:*** LA, SM, Lv88>

charrue [ʃary] *n.f.* plow ◊ **•charrue double** double plow, lister plow, middlebuster plow <EV, SJ> <***Loc:*** EV, LA, LF, SJ, SM, TB, Da84, Fa77>

chartée ♦see **charretée**

charteur [ʃartœr] *n.m.* charter, charter flight <***Loc:*** SL>

chartil (**charretil**) [ʃarti] *n.m.* cab, bed (of a truck, wagon, etc.) *Ils étaient après galoper leurs chevaux avec Roy rebondissant dans le chartil du wagon.* They were galloping their horses with Roy bouncing around in the bed of the wagon. (VM) <***Loc:*** JD, LA, SM, VM, Da84, Guoo>

charvoyer ♦see **charroyer**

chas [ʃa] *n.m.* eye of a needle <***Loc:*** TB>

chasse [ʃas] *n.f.* 1 hunt, chase 2 hunting season *La chasse ouvre le premier samedi en octobre tous les ans, et là ça ferme la fin de février.* The hunting season starts the first Saturday of October each year, and it closes at the end of February. (SM) ◊ **•aller à la chasse** to go on a hunt, go hunting *Mais mon grand-père il a tout le temps fait la pêche et il a été à la chasse pour à peu près trente, trente-cinq ou quarante ans de sa vie.* But my grandfather always went fishing and he went hunting for thirty, thirty-five or forty years of his life. (LF) <LA, LF, SM, Da84, La99> **•faire la chasse** to hunt **Un jour, le petit garçon dit à sa mère, il était parti faire la chasse dans le bois.* One day, the little boy said to his mother that he was going to hunt in the woods. (LA, An94) <IV, LA, An94, Da84> **•on envoye pas un chien à la chasse à coups de bâton** you can't force someone against his will <Da84> <***Loc:*** EV, IV, JD, LA, LF, SM, TB, An94, Da84, La99, Wh83>

chasse-femme (**chaste-femme**) [ʃasfɑ̃m, ʃazfɑ̃m] *n.f.* midwife <***Loc:*** IB, SB, SJ, SL, SM, Da84, Lv88>

chasse-galerie (**chante-galerie**) [ʃasgalri, ʃasgarli, ʃɑ̃tgalri, ʃɑ̃tgarli, ʃɑ̃garli] *n.f.* (in folk culture) "wild hunt," a mysterious racket, din, or chorus that passes through the night sky, often interpreted as an omen **La chasse-galerie, c'est un homme qui avait été à la messe dimanche matin, tu connais.* The wild hunt is a man who had gone to Mass on Sunday morning, you know. (SM, An94) *La chante-galerie a laissé un bouquet tomber sur ma galerie.* The wild hunt dropped a bouquet on my porch. (SL) <***Loc:*** LF, SL, SM, An94, Lv88>

chasse-mouche [ʃasmuʃ, saʃmuʃ] *n.f.* **1** flyswatter **2** fly repellant <***Loc:*** TB, Da84>

chassepareille (**sassepareille**) [ʃasparɛj, ʃasparej, sasparej, ʃærʃparɛj] *n.f. (occ. m.)* **1** sarsaparilla **2** French mulberry <***Loc:*** AV, EV, IB, LA, LF, SJ, SM, TB, Da84, Ho90, Lv88, Ph36, Re31>

chasser [ʃase, ʃaʃe] **I** *v.tr.* **1** to chase away, chase out, expel *Et le monde du Marais Bouleur avait venu pour chasser ceux là de la Pointe Noire. Et la bataille a pris.* And the people from Marais Bouleur had come to chase away those from La Pointe Noire. And the fight started. (AC) **2** to hunt *Moi j'ai l'habitude de chasser des coyotes et des renards.* I have the habit of hunting for prairie wolves and foxes. (IB) **II** *v.intr.* to hunt *J'ai chassé déjà, mais des années j'ai arrêté chasser.* I've hunted before, but many years ago I stopped hunting. (SL) *On use des fusils à chasser.* We use guns to hunt. (JE) ◊ **•chasser au flambeau** to hunt at night with a light <VM> <***Loc:*** AC, EV, IB, IV, JE, LF, SL, SM, TB, VM, An94, Da84, Guoo, Lv88>

chasseur [ʃasœr] *n.m.* hunter <***Loc:*** LA, LF, TB, Da84, Fa77>

châssis (**chassis**) [ʃasi] *n.m.* **1** window *Ça fait mon j'étais après bercer G., et j'ai vu la figure d'un homme au chassis! Les rideaux se fermaient pas, il y avait comme une craque. Et j'ai vu la tête d'un homme.* I was rocking G., and I saw a man's face in the window. The curtains did not close, there was like a crack. And I saw a man's head. (TB) *Baisse le chassis.* Close the window. (SM) **2** window sash *Lever le chassis en l'air.* To raise the window sash. (SJ) **3** window pane *Il a cassé le châssis.* He broke the window pane. (SB) <***Loc:*** AV, EV, IB, IV, JD, JE, LA, LF, SB, SJ, SL, SM, TB, VM, Da84, Fa77, Gu82, Lv88, Ph36, Re31>

chaste [ʃas(t)] *adj.* [*eccl.*] chaste, pure, moral <***Loc:*** VM, Da84>

chaste-femme ♦see **chasse-femme**

chasteté [ʃastəte] *n.f.* chastity, purity <***Loc:*** Da84>

chat[1] [ʃa] *n.m.* **1** cat **2** male cat, tomcat **3** raccoon ◊ **•chat échaudé craint l'eau froide** once fooled, twice shy <Da84> **•chat sauvage** bobcat <Guoo> **•gros chat** big shot, important person <Da84> <***Loc:*** AC, AV, EV, IB, LA, LF, SB, SL, SM, TB, VM, An94, Da84, Guoo, Hi02, Lv88, Re31>

chat[2] [ʃa] *interj.* scat (cry used to chase away cats) <***Loc:*** LA, SL, SM, Da84>

châtaignier [ʃatɛ̃je] *n.m.* **1** chestnut tree **2** planer tree, water elm <***Loc:*** LA, Da84, Ho90, Re31>

châtain[1] (**châtin, -e**) [ʃatɛ̃, -in] *adj.* auburn, brown, brownish, chestnut (of the hair) <***Loc:*** SM, VM, Da84, Lv88>

châtain[2] (**châtin, -e**) [ʃatɛ̃, -in] *n.* person with auburn or chestnut-colored hair *Y'a des blondes, des petites brunes, des châtines, des têtes brunes.* There are blondes, little brown-haired girls, auburn-haired girls, dark-haired girls. (Lv88) *Elle est châtine. C'est une châtin.* She has auburn-colored hair. (SM) <***Loc:*** EV, SM, VM, Da84, Lv88, Ph36>

château [ʃato] *n.m.* **1** castle **On va rentrer dans le château.* We're going to go back into the castle. (IV, An94) **2** large fine house, palace, mansion **3** cloud, large cloud bank *Des châteaux blancs sur soleil levant, on aura la pluie.* White clouds in the rising sun, we will have rain. (proverb) (Lv88) *Un gros château noir.* A large black cloud. (SL) ◊ **•château de pluie** large cloud (cumulonimbus) that brings rain <Guoo> <***Loc:*** IV, SL, VM, An94, Da84, Guoo, Lv88>

chat-huant [ʃaɥɑ̃] *n.m.* screech owl <***Loc:*** Re31>

châtin ♦see **châtain**

Châtine [ʃatin] *n.f.* name commonly given to a light brown cow <***Loc:*** JD, SL, SM>

chatouillant, -e [ʃatujɑ̃, -ɑ̃t] *adj.* tickling, funny, laughable *Ça, c'est réellement chatouillant. Ça me donne envie de rire.* That is really funny. It makes me feel like laughing. (LA) <***Loc:*** LA, Da84>

chatouillement [ʃatujmɑ̃] *n.m.* tickling, act of tickling <***Loc:*** Da84>

chatouiller [ʃatuje] *v.tr.* to tickle *Quand j'étais petit, mes frères me chatouillaient tout le temps.* When I was little, my brothers used to tickle me all the time. (LA) <***Loc:*** EV, LA, Da84, Ph36>

chatouilleux, -euse [ʃatujø, -øz] *adj.* ticklish *Ma sœur est pas du tout chatouilleuse.* My sister is not at all ticklish. (LA) <***Loc:*** LA, Da84>

châtrer [ʃatre] *v.tr.* to castrate *Châtrer des veaux pour les faire engraisser.* To castrate calves to fatten them. (LA) <***Loc:*** LA, Da84>

chatte[1] [ʃat] *n.f.* **1** female cat **2** highly sexed girl **3** naughty, disobedient girl *Hé, ma petite chatte, fais pas ça!* Hey, naughty little girl, don't do that. (SM) <***Loc:*** AV, SM, Da84, La99>

chatte[2] [ʃat] *n.f.* tag (children's game) *Jouer à la chatte.* To play tag. (LF) <***Loc:*** LF>

chatterie [ʃatri] *n.f.* coquetry, flirting <***Loc:*** JD>

chat-tigre (**chat-tigré**) [ʃatig(r), ʃatigre] *n.m.* **1** ocelot, bobcat

2 cougar, puma <***Loc:*** EV, SB, SM, TB, Da84, Fa77, Gu00, Ph36, Re31>

chauboulure ♦see **échauboulure**

chaud[1], **-e** [ʃo, -d] *adj.* **1** hot *L'eau quède [c'est] ni chaud ni glacé.* Lukewarm water is neither hot nor cold. (JE) *C'est pas assez chaud assez longtemps.* It's not hot long enough. (SL) *Des journées chaudes et doucementes.* Hot, slow days. (Lv88) **2** angry, mad *Tu parles d'un bougre qu'était chaud, mais il était chaud.* You wanna talk about a guy who was mad, this guy was mad! (SL) **Ils étaient chauds après moi parce que je chargeais trop bon marché.* They were mad at me because my fee was too low. (An84) **3** very expensive *Ça coûte chaud.* It's very expensive. (Lv88) <***Loc:*** AC, AV, EV, JD, JE, LF, SB, SL, TB, VM, An84, Da84, Gu82, Lv88, Re31, Wh69>

chaud[2] [ʃo] *n.m.* **1** heat, warmth **2** warm weather *Je crois ça prend vingt-deux mois de chaud.* I think it takes twenty-two months of [continuous] warm weather [to grow]. (SL) ◊ **•avoir chaud** to be hot *Alle peut pas rester trop au* STOVE. *Elle peut pas avoir trop chaud.* She can't stay near the stove. She's not supposed to get too hot. (TB) <SM, TB> **•faire chaud** to be hot (of the weather) *On avait juste un éventail comme ça pour t'éventer avec ta main, et il faisait chaud pareil comme il fait ici asteur.* We just had a little fan for fanning yourself by hand like that, and it was hot just like it is here now. (LF) <LA, LF, SM, TB, VM, Lv88> <***Loc:*** LA, LF, SL, SM, TB, VM, Da84, Lv88>

chaudement [ʃodmɑ̃] *adv.* warmly *Z-enfants, habillez-vous-autres chaudement. Il fait froid dehors aujourd'hui.* Children, dress yourselves warmly. It's cold outside today. (LA) **S'habiller chaudement.* To dress warmly. (Da84) <***Loc:*** LA, Da84, Lv88>

chaude-pisse (**chausse-pisse**) [ʃodpis, ʃospis] *n.f.* gonorrhea <***Loc:*** EV, LA, VM>

chaudière [ʃodjær, ʃodʒær] *n.f.* **1** any cooking pot or kettle, esp. of cast iron *Ma mère cuisait avec une chaudière en fer et ma grand-mère aussi.* My mother used to cook with a black iron skillet, my grand-mother too. (AC) **Il avait sûr la chaudière là-bas chez lui. La chaudière en fer-là.* He surely had the kettle over there at his house. The iron kettle. (LA, An94) **2** old-fashioned cooking pot with legs and a handle ◊ **•chaudière à frire** frying pan <LA, SL> **•chaudière à laver** large cauldron formerly used for washing clothes <SM> **•chaudière à queue** ***a*** saucepan, long-handled cooking pot ***b*** pressure cooker <AL, VM> **•chaudière d'eau** double boiler <AL> **•chaudière en fer** cast-iron cooking pot <SB> **•chaudière noire** cast-iron cooking pot <AC, LA, SL, An94> **•faire chaudière** ***a*** to stop, during a fishing or hunting excursion, in order to prepare a meal ***b*** to camp, halt overnight <JE, La99, Lv88> **•faire chaudière ensemble** to get married <JE, SM, TB, La99> <***Loc:*** AC, AL, AV, EV, IB, IV, JD, JE, LA, LF, SB, SL, SM, TB, VM, An94, Da84, Gu00, La99, Lv88>

chaudièrée (**chaudiérée**) [ʃodjere, ʃodjəre] *n.f.* potful *J'ai mis proche une chaudiérée de sucre dans ces figues.* I put almost a potful of sugar in these figs. (VM) *J'ai fait une chaudiérée de couche-couche.* I made a potful of couche-couche. (SM) <***Loc:*** AC, AV, EV, IB, JD, LA, SJ, SL, SM, TB, VM, Da84, Lv88>

chaudin [ʃodɛ̃] *n.m.* **1** stuffed and baked pig's stomach (a Cajun delicacy) **2** pig's intestine *Le chaudin, c'est le z-intestin du cochon.* The "chaudin" is the intestine of the pig. (SM) ◊ **•chaudin bourré** stuffed and baked pig's stomach *Le chaudin bourrée est bien bon.* Stuffed stomach is really good. (VM) <IV, VM, Lv88> <***Loc:*** AC, EV, IB, IV, JD, LA, LF, SM, TB, VM, Da84, Lv88>

chaud-l'eau ♦see **cholo**

chaudron[1] [ʃodrɔ̃, ʃødrɔ̃] *n.m.* **1** cauldron (formerly used to make syrup, boil clothing, etc.) **2** bucket *Le chaudron a tombé dans le puits.* The bucket fell into the well. (AV) <***Loc:*** AV, VM, Da84>

chaudron[2] ♦see **chardon**

chauffage [ʃofaʒ] *n.m.* **1** heating **2** combustible material used for heating (e.g. wood) <***Loc:*** Da84, Lv88>

chauffe [ʃɔf] *n.f.* **1** heating **2** severe reprimand ◊ **•foutre une chauffe** to scold, to bawl out *Son papa lui a foutu une chauffe la semaine passée pour cette même chose.* His father bawled him out last week for exactly the same thing. (SB) <SB, SJ, Da84, La99, Lv88> <***Loc:*** JD, SB, SJ, Da84, La99, Lv88>

chauffer [ʃofe] **I** *v.tr.* **1** to heat, heat up *J'ai faim, il dit. Chauffe les crabes, il dit, pour que je mange.* I'm hungry, he says. Heat up the crabs, he says, for me to eat. (TB) *Ça aurait chauffé tout la maison.* That would have heated the whole house. (SL) **2** to rebuke, reprimand, scold *Je l'ai bin chauffé pour ça il avait fait.* I reprimanded him well for what he had done. (VM) **II** *v.intr. (in impersonal expr.)* to be difficult, be a strain *Dans ces temps-là, ça chauffait pour toi sortir avec une fille tout seul.* In those days it was difficult for you to go out with a girl all alone. (EV) *Ç'a chauffé, mais j'ai finalement fini.* It was difficult, but I finally finished. (SM) *Ça chauffe pour faire une vie maintenant.* It's difficult to make a living these days. (SM) *Ç'a chauffé, il a manqué mourir.* Things were rough, he almost died. (Lv88) *Ça chauffe.* Things are tough. (SM) *Ça va chauffer pour finir aujourd'hui.* It will be tough to finish today. (LA) **III se chauffer** *v.pron.* **1** to warm o.s., heat one's residence *Et eux-autres se chauffait au* COAL-OIL *aussi, eux-autres avait un stove à* COAL-OIL. They used kerosene for heating too, they had a kerosene stove. (TB) **2** to become angry, get mad *Je voyais qu'il était après se chauffer, ça fait j'ai fendu l'air.* I saw that he was getting angry, so I got out of there quickly. (EV) <***Loc:*** AC, AV, EV, JD, LA, LF, SB, SJ, SL, SM, TB, VM, Da84, La99, Lv88>

chauffeur [ʃofœr] *n.m.* **1** one who fires a boiler or furnace **2** driver (of a car, truck, etc.) <***Loc:*** Da84, Fa77>

chaume [ʃɔ̃m] *n.m.* rice stubble *Y a du monde qui brûle leur chaume pour empêcher le riz rouge de reprendre.* There are people who burn their rice stubble to prevent the red rice from growing back. (VM) <***Loc:*** VM, Guoo>

chaurice ♦see **tchaurisse**

chausse-pisse ♦see **chaude-pisse**

chausser [ʃose] **I** *v.tr.* **1** to put on footwear (e.g. stockings, socks, shoes) **Dans le chemin, ils ont fait rencontre d'un petit bonhomme, un pied chaussé, l'autre nu.* On the road, they met a little man, one foot shod and the other bare. (VM, ch: *Madame Gallien*) **2** to provide footwear for, furnish with footwear *Eusse étaient assez pauvres qu'eusse pouvaient pas chausser leurs enfants.* They were so poor that they could not furnish their children with shoes. (VM) **3** to bank up, reinforce, bring dirt up around (plants) **II se chausser** *v.pron.* to put on or wear footwear *Mon grandpère se chaussait jamais avec des souliers en cuir.* My grandfather never wore leather shoes. (LA) <***Loc:*** JD, LA, VM, Da84>

chaussette [ʃosɛt, ʃoʃɛt] *n.f.* **1** sock **2** woman's or child's sock <***Loc:*** AC, AV, EV, IB, JE, LA, LF, SB, SJ, SL, SM, TB, VM, Da84>

chausson [ʃosɔ̃] *n.m.* **1** sock **2** man's sock *Pape avait des chaussons, et nous-autres on avait des chaussettes.* Daddy had socks ["chaussons"], and the rest of us had "chaussettes." (SB) **3** heavy sock *Chausson, c'est plus épais, en hiver...* A heavy sock, it's thicker, for winter . . . (JE) <***Loc:*** AC, AV, EV, IB, IV, JD, JE, LA, LF, SB, SM, TB, VM, Da84, Guoo, Lv88, Ph36>

chaussure [ʃosyr] *n.m.* shoe *Il était tellement pauvre, il avait pas des chaussures.* He was so poor, he didn't have shoes. (LA) <***Loc:*** EV, LA, Da84>

chauter [ʃote] *v.tr.* to whitewash with lime *Ils ont chauté le devant de la maison comme dans le vieux temps.* They whitewashed the front of the house with lime like in the old days. (LA) <***Loc:*** LA, Da84>

chauvage ♦see **sauvage**

chauve [ʃov] *adj.* bald, hairless **Tête chauve.* Bald head. (Da84) <***Loc:*** Da84>

chauvelle ♦see **shovel**

chauveler ♦see **shoveler**

chauve-souris [ʃovsuri, ʃɔfsuri] *n.f.* bat ♦cf **souris-chaude** <***Loc:*** SB, Da84>

chaux [ʃo] *n.f.* lime *On a fait un plancher en terre. Mettre ça là, piler ça. C'était tout fait à la main. Ils venaient là et mettre de la chaux.* We made a dirt floor. We put it down, packed it down. It was all made by hand. They came along and put down lime. (LF) *Ils mettaient de la chaux pour pas ça pue.* They put lime so that it does not stink. (IB) <***Loc:*** IB, LF, VM, Da84>

chavirer [ʃavire] *v.tr.* **1** to upend, turn over, capsize *La grosse lame a chaviré notre petit bateau.* The big wave capsized our little boat. (LA) **2** to cause to waver *Quand j'ai vu ça, ça m'a chaviré.* When I saw that, it caused me to waver. (LA) <***Loc:*** LA, Da84>

chécher ♦see **chesser**

chécheresse ♦see **chesseresse**

chécheuse ♦see **chesseuse**

CHECK[1] (**chèque, tchèque**) [tʃɛk] *n.m.* check *Il m'a donné un CHECK de cent piastres.* He gave me a check for a hundred dollars. (SB) ◊ **•chèque à trous** social security check <LF> <***Loc:*** AC, EV, LF, SB, SM, TB, VM, Da84, Hio2, Lv88, Ph36>

CHECK[2] (**checker, tchéquer**) [tʃɛk, tʃeke] *v.tr.* **1** to check, examine, inspect *Il faut tu CHECK ton portrait voir il n'y a pas de DEFECTS dessus.* You have to check your picture to make sure there are no defects on it. (VM) *Il y a deux ou trois habitants, ils vont voir--checker leur marque de bête.* There are two or three farmers, they go check their cattle brand. (VM) *Et là après ça j'ai un job pompeur. C'est moi qui tchéquait les TANKS tous les jours.* And after that I got a job as a gager. I checked the tanks every day. (LF) *Tchèque mon HOMEWORK pour moi.* Check my homework for me. (SM) **2** to check in (e.g. luggage, a coat) **Jeune homme, ici, on marche pas avec des chapeaux sur la tête. Tu vas aller les faire CHECK.* Young man, here, we don't walk around with hats on our head. You're going to go and check them in. (LA, An94) **J'ai CHECK mes bagages.* I checked my bags. (EV, Ph36) ◊ **•CHECK sur** to check on *Les NURSE et tout a commencé à venir et CHECK sur elle.* The nurses and all started to come and check on her. (TB) <TB> <***Loc:*** EV, JD, LA, LF, SM, TB, VM, An94, Lv88, Ph36>

checker ♦see **CHECK**

CHEEK ♦see **tchique**

chef [ʃɛf] *n.m.* **1** chief, leader **2** head cook ◊ **•être en chef** to be in charge, be the leader <Da84> <***Loc:*** Da84>

chemin [ʃmɛ̃] *n.m.* **1** road **Dans le chemin, ils ont fait rencontre d'un petit bonhomme, un pied chaussé, l'autre nu.* On the road, they met a little man, one foot shod and the other bare. (VM, ch: *Madame Gallien*) **2** highway *Le chemin 90.* Highway 90. (Lv88) **3** path, way ◊ **•chemin de charrette** turnrow, headland (strip of uncultivated land at the end or side of a field where a plow can turn) *Un chemin de charrette. THAT WAS A HEADLAND dedans le champ de canne ou dans le champ de maïs ou n'importe qui.* A "chemin de charrette" was what we called a headland in the canefield or the cornfield or whatever. (LF) <LF> **•chemin de fer** railroad *C'était quelque chose qu'était usé pour dégrossir du bois et pour faire les CROSSTIES, les TIES sur le chemin de fer.* That was something that was used to whittle down wood to make the crossties, the ties on the railroad. (LF) <EV, LF> **•chemin de godron** asphalt road <VM> **•chemin de (la) Croix** Way of the Cross *On allait tous les vendredis au Chemin de la Croix.* Every Friday [during Lent] we went on the Way of the Cross. (LF) <LF, TB, Da84> **•chemin de scie** path of a saw <Da84> **•chemin de travers(e)** *a* turnrow, headland ***b*** crossroad <AV, IB, SJ> **•aller les deux chemins** to pace, rack *Ce cheval-là aime pas aller d'aplomb, il va toujours les deux chemins.* That horse does not like to trot, it always paces. (VM) <VM> **•dans son chemin** in one's way *Tu mets une lumière sur ta tête le soir, un demi-mille autour s'il y a rien qui est dans ton chemin, tu vas voir son œil. Ça brille comme une chandelle.* You put a light on your head at night, a half mile around if there's nothing in your way you'll see his [i.e. the alligator's] eye. It shines like a candle. (TB) <TB> **•grand chemin** highway, main road *J'ai parti dans les grands chemins.* I left on the main roads. (Lv88) <Lv88> **•pas aller les quatre chemins** to do or say s.t. without hesitating or waffling, not beat around the bush *Quand il avait quelque chose pour faire, il allait pas les quatre chemins.* When he had something to do, he did it without hesitating. (LA) <AV, LA, La99> **•prendre le chemin** to hit the road, set out on the road *J'ai pris le chemin. Je connaissais à peu près ayoù il restait, mon frère.* I set out on the road. I knew pretty much where he lived, my brother. (EV) <EV, LF, Da84> **•prendre le mauvais chemin** to take the wrong road *On est perdu. J'ai peur qu'on a pris le mauvais chemin.* We're lost. I'm afraid that we've taken the wrong road. (LA) <LA> ***<Loc:*** AV, EV, IB, JE, LA, LF, SL, SM, TB, VM, An94, Da84, Guoo, La99, Lv88>

cheminée (**chuminée, chunée**) [ʃ(ə)mine, ʃimine, ʃimne, ʃymine, ʃyne, ʃymne] *n.f.* **1** chimney *Tu connais cette vieille maison en bas, avec la cheminée en brique? Y a un canard qui descend tous les jours dedans ça.* Do you know that old house down the bayou, with the brick chimney? There's a duck that goes down in there every day. (TB) **2** fireplace **3** mantlepiece *La pendule est sur la cheminée.* The clock is on the mantlepiece. (AV) **4** lamp glass, lamp globe ◊ **•cheminée bousillée** chimney built of mud and Spanish moss, or sometimes straw <Re38> **•cheminée de lampe** lamp glass, lamp globe <Da84> ***<Loc:*** AC, EV, AV, LA, LF, SB, SJ, SM, TB, VM, Da84, La99, Lv88>

chemise [ʃmiz, ʃmiʒ, ʃẽmiʒ, ʃəmil, ʃmin] *n.f.* shirt ◊ **•chemise de dessous *a*** camisole ***b*** man's undershirt <LA, SM, Fa77, Guoo> **•chemise de laine** wool shirt <Da84> **•chemise de nuit** night shirt <Da84> **•chemise de peau** undershirt <Lv88> ***<Loc:*** AV, EV, IB, JE, LA, SB, SL, SM, TB, VM, An94, Da84, Fa77, Guoo, La99, Lv88>

chenaille [ʃnaj] *n.f.* mosquito hawk, dragonfly ***<Loc:*** SB>

chenal [ʃnal] *n.m.* **1** deep water stream, channel *Le chenal est creux.* The stream is deep. (VM) *Si tu vas dans la rivière il faut que tu restes dedans le chenal. C'est le plus creux dedans un bayou ou une rivière.* If you go in the river you have to stay in the channel. It's the deepest part of a bayou or a river. (LF) **2** cleared area for passage (e.g. through a woods) ***<Loc:*** LF, TB, VM>

chenaleux [ʃənalø] *adj.* elegant ***<Loc:*** SL>

chêne [ʃẽn] *n.m.* oak *C'est faite avec du chêne.* It's made of oak. (SM) ◊ **•chêne à vache** swamp chestnut oak, cow oak <Fa77> **•chêne blanc** southern live oak, white oak <Da84, Fa77> **•chêne gris** water oak *Les chênes gris perd les feuilles en hiver.* Water oaks lose their leaves in winter. (TB) <TB> **•chêne poison** poison oak <Fa77> **•chêne rouge** red oak <Fa77, Guoo> **•chêne vert** southern live oak, white oak <LA, LF, SM, Da84, Guoo, Re31> ***<Loc:*** AC, JD, JE, LA, LF, SL, SM, TB, Da84, Fa77, Guoo, Re31>

chêneau[1] [ʃẽno] *n.m.* oak grove ***<Loc:*** Fa77>

chêneau[2] [ʃẽno] *n.f.* (*usu. pl.*) cane brake (in a swamp) *Ils sont après chasser dans les chêneaux.* They are hunting in the cane breaks. (IB) ***<Loc:*** IB>

chênerie [ʃẽnri] *n.f.* oak grove ***<Loc:*** VM>

chenet [ʃənɛ, ʃəne] *n.m.* andiron, firedog ***<Loc:*** Da84>

chênière [ʃẽnjær] *n.f.* **1** oak grove *C'est pour ça qu'eusse appelle ça ici là "chênière" parce que c'était rien que des chênes.* That's why they call it a "chênière" here, because it's nothing but oak trees. (JE) **2** row of planted oak trees **3** grove or stand of oak trees in an otherwise treeless swamp ***<Loc:*** JE, LF, TB, Da84, Guoo, Lv88, Re31>

chenille [ʃ(ə)nij] *n.f.* **1** caterpillar **2** snail ◊ **•chenille brûlante** green caterpillar <VM> ***<Loc:*** EV, IV, SL, SM, Da84, Fa77>

chenu [ʃny, ʃnyk] *n.m.* elegant ◊ **•être du chenu** to be very fine, be extraordinary *C'est du chenu, cette robe.* That is a very fine dress. (LF) <LF> ***<Loc:*** LF>

chéquailler ♦see **tchincailler**

chèque ♦see **CHECK**

cher[1], **chère** [ʃær] *adj.* **1** dear, beloved *Cher ami.* Dear friend. (Da84) *Cher vieux Pape, il était assez bon pour nous-autres.* Dear old Dad, he was pretty good to us. (EV) *Chère petite fille.* Dear little girl. (EV) **2** expensive, costly **Les marchandises sont chères.* The merchandise is costly. (Da84) ◊ **•chère 'tite bête** poor little thing <Da84> **•cher 'tit nègre** precious little fellow <Da84> ***<Loc:*** EV, IB, LA, PQ, SL, SM, TB, VM, An94, Da84, Gu82, La99, Lv88>

cher[2], **chère** [ʃær] *n.* [*term of endearment*] dear, honey, hon *Qui tu veux, cher?* What do you want, dear? (EV) *Quoi il y a, cher?* What's wrong, dear? What is it, dear? (EV) *Comment ça va, chère.* How's it going, honey? (Lv88) ◊ **•c'est un 'cher' ici, 'cher' la-bàs** saying that describes a couple who make a show of affection in public, but who fight frequently in private <La99> **•mon cher** my dear <Da84> ***<Loc:*** AC, AV, EV, IB, LA, SL, SM, TB, VM, An94, Da84, La99, Lv88>

chérant, -e [ʃerɑ̃, -ɑ̃t] *adj.* **1** expensive, costly **L'pain est chérant.* The bread is expensive. (EV, Ph36) **2** overpriced, unduly expensive *J'aimerai acheter avec lui, mais il est si chérant!* I'd like to buy from him, but he's so expensive! (SM) ***<Loc:*** IB, JD, LA, SL, SM, TB, VM, Da84, Fa77, Lv88, Re31>

chercer ♦see **gercer**

chercher (**charcher**, **cherser**) [ʃærʃe, ʃærse, særʃe] **I** *v.tr.* to seek, look for, search for *Il traversait et retraversait le bayou en cherchant son canard qu'avait tombé loin du BLIND.* He crossed and recrossed the bayou looking for his duck that had fallen far from the blind. (LA) **A cette époque-là, je pense qu'on cherchait une identité.* At that time, I think we were seeking an identity. (LA, An84) **II** *v.intr.* **1** to search, make a search, look around *Ils ont cherché tout partout, mais ils ont jamais trouvé la clé.* They looked all over the place, but they never found the key. (EV) *Je cherche dans ces parages pour mon chien.* I'm looking in this neighborhood for my dog. (IB) **2** to seek (to do s.t.), be out (to do s.t.) *Chercher à manger.* Look for something to eat. (EV) *Cette espèce de caïac était tout le temps après chercher à se battre.* That lout was always looking for a fight. (EV) **III se chercher** *v.pron.* to look for each other ◊ **•chercher à pied et à cheval** to search extensively and exhaustively, search high and low <La99> **•chercher après** to look for *J'ai été chercher après elle.* I went to look for her. (SL) <SL> **•chercher chique** to look for trouble <JD> **•chercher pour** to look for *Il les a quitté rentrer, il a été à son DESK, il a fouillé, il savait éyoù-ce qu'il l'avait mais il a fouillé un peu, il dit "Ça c'est ça que vous-autres cherche pour?"* He let them come in and he went to his desk, he knew where he had put it but he dug around a bit, and he said, "Is this what you are looking for?" (LF) <LA, LF, SM, TB, VM, Lv88> **•chercher querelle** to be looking for a quarrel, pick a quarrel <Da84> **•chercher (une) chique** to look for trouble *Tant qu'à cil-là, il est tout après chercher une chique.* As for that one, he's always looking for trouble. (LA) <LA, Lv88> **•aller chercher** to go get, fetch *Va chercher pour un couteau.* Go get a knife. (Da84) *Il dit que pépère Hilaire allait chercher ses groceries.* He said that granddad Hilaire used to go get his groceries. (LF) ♦cf **hâcher**[2] <JE, LA, LF, SJ, SL, TB, VM, An94, Da84, Guoo, Lv88> <JE, LA, LF, SJ, SL, TB, An94, Da84, Lv88> ***<Loc:*** AC, AV, EV, IB, JD, JE, LA, LF, SB, SJ, SL, SM, TB, VM, An84, An94, Da84, Guoo, La99, Lv88, Re31>

chéri, -e [ʃeri] *adj.* cherished, beloved ◊ **•mon chéri** my dear <Da84> ***<Loc:*** Da84>

chérir [ʃerir] *v.tr.* to cherish, love tenderly, value greatly *Je vous promets de chérir votre fille pour la balance de notre vie.* I promise you that I will cherish your daughter for the rest of our lives. (VM) ***<Loc:*** VM, Da84>

chérité ♦see **charité**

cherokee ♦see **chéroquis**

chéroquis (**cherokee**) [ʃeroki, tʃeroki] *n.m.* **1** Cherokee Indian **2** Cherokee rose **3** Chickasaw rose bush **4** wild rose ***<Loc:*** CL, SM, VM, Da84, Lv88>

cherser ♦see **chercher**

chessage (**séchage**) [ʃesaʒ] *n.m./f.* drying *Un des plus mauvais tracas, c'est le séchage des marais.* One of the biggest problems is the drying of the marshes. (LA) ***<Loc:*** LA, Da84>

chesse (**sèche**) [ʃɛs] *n.f.* drying ◊ **•mettre à la sèche** to set out to dry <Da84> ***<Loc:*** Da84>

chesser (**sécher, assécher, achécher, chécher**) [ʃese, aseʃe, aʃeʃe, ʃeʃe] **I** *v.tr.* **1** to dry **Sécher son linge.* To dry one's clothes. (Da84) *Eux-autres plantaient des BEANS blancs, et eux-autres séchait ça.* They planted white beans, and they dried them. (TB) *On les séchait et on les mettait dans des bouilloires pour brûler, pour faire des STEAM, pour courir le moulin.* They [the "bagasses"] were dried and burned and used to produce steam to run the mill. (IB) **2** to drain *Ils ont eu pour sécher le vivier pour tuer les mauvaises herbes là dedans.* They had to drain the pond to kill the weeds in there. (LA) **II** *v.intr.* **1** to dry, dry out *Le linge peut pas assécher.* The laundry can't dry. (Lv88) *Quand il est chessé, on le passe avec le wagon, on ramasse tout BACK.* When it is dry, we pick it up with the wagon, we take it all back. (SM) **2** to drain *La pièce a pas séché assez pour planter.* The field has not drained enough to plant. (LA) **III se sécher** *v.pron.* to dry off, dry o.s. *Chesse-toi avant de sortir de la chambe à bain.* Dry yourself off before coming out of the bathroom. (LA) ◊ **•faire chesser** to dry out, cause to dry *Des grosses feuilles, tu faisais chesser ça à l'abri du temps.* Large leaves, you would dry them sheltered from the weather. (AC) <AC> **•mettre à sécher** to set out to dry, hang out to dry *Elle mettait ça à chesser dessus la citerne.* She would put it to dry on the cistern. (SL) <SL, Da84> ***<Loc:*** AC, AV, IB, LA, LF, SB, SL, SM, TB, VM, Da84, Lv88>

chesseresse (**chécheresse, sécheresse**) [ʃes(ə)rɛs, ʃesrɛs, sɛsərɛs, ʃeʃrɛs] *n.f.* drought, dry spell *J'ai peur qu'on aura une chécheresse cet été.* I'm afraid we will have a drought this summer. (SM) ***<Loc:*** AC, AV, IB, JE, LF, SB, SL, SM, TB, An94, Da84, Lv88>

chesseuse (**chécheuse, sécheuse**) [ʃesøz, ʃeʃøz] *n.f.* **1** dryer *Eux-autres allume ces chesseuses, et l'eau chesse les chevrettes.* They turn on the dryers, and the water [i.e. the steam] dries the shrimp. (TB) **2** electric clothes dryer ***<Loc:*** TB, Da84, Fa77, Lv88>

chéti, -e (**chétif**, **chétite**) [ʃeti, ʃetit] *adj.* **1** sickly, unhealthy looking, weak, feeble, not well *Richard l'a portée. Elle avait venu chétif, maigre. Elle était blême, sa figure et puis elle avait perdu un tas de poids.* Richard carried her. She had become worn-looking, thin. Her face was pale and she had lost a lot of weight. (SL) *Je me sens chéti.* I feel weak. (Lv88) **2** bad, bad tasting, spoiled *Du café chéti.* Bad-tasting coffee. (Lv88) **Ça goûte chéti.* It tastes bad. (Da84) *Quelque chose est dégoûtant ou chétif parce qu'il a tourné.* Something is disgusting or spoiled because it has turned. (AC) **3** morally bad, despicable *Il est pas trop vaillant, il est manière chétif.* He's not very nice, he is fairly bad. (VM) **4** meager, shabby, poor, bad *La récolte pourrait être* *meilleure, elle pourrait être plus chétie.* The harvest could be better, it could be poorer. (Lv88) ◊ **•du chéti monde** bad people *Oh, c'est du chétif monde. Si c'est du pas bon monde, ça veut pas s'accorder.* Oh, they're bad people. If it's not good people, they won't get along. (VM) <VM> <***Loc:*** AC, AV, EV, IB, JD, LA, LF, SB, SJ, SL, SM, TB, VM, Da84, Fa77, Lv88, Ph36, Re31>

chétif ♦see **chéti**

chétiment [ʃetimɑ̃] *adv.* meanly, badly, poorly *Il m'a chétiment réçu.* He received me poorly. (SM) <***Loc:*** SM, Da84>

chétite ♦see **chéti**

cheu ♦see **cho**

cheue ♦see **queue**

cheuve ♦see **shove**

cheval [ʃəval, ʃval, ʃfal, ʃwal] (*pl.* **chevals** [ʃval], *occ.* **chevaux** [ʃvo]) *n.m.* **1** horse **2** sawhorse, trestle *Mets la planche sur le cheval et mesure-la.* Put the board on the sawhorse and measure it. (SL) ◊ **•cheval bai** bay horse <Da84> **•cheval-carotte / cheval-carosse** lubber grasshopper (black grasshopper with an orange stripe) <JE, LF, TB> **•cheval créole** nonthoroughbred horse <Lv88> **•cheval de bataille** hard worker <LA> **•cheval de course** race horse <VM, Da84> **•cheval de {du} diable / cheval-diable *a*** praying mantis ***b*** lubber grasshopper (black grasshopper with an orange stripe) *Cheval-diable, ça s'appelle le diable parce qu'il est noir.* Lubber grasshopper (lit. devil horse), it's called devil because it's black. (PQ) ***c*** dragonfly, mosquito hawk <EV, PQ, SL, SM, TB, Da84, Lv88, Ph36, Re31> **•cheval de mer** seahorse <VM, Fa77> **•cheval de selle** saddle horse <Da84> **•cheval de tire** draft horse <Di32, Gu86, Lv88> **•cheval donné, regarde pas la bride** don't look a gift horse in the mouth <SM> **•cheval habillé (en zinc)** rough, ill-mannered person <SM, La99> **•cheval normand** draft horse <Fa77> **•cheval rétif** balky horse <Da84> **•cheval rosse** sluggish horse <Da84> **•cheval traître** horse that is liable to kick <Da84> **•aller à cheval** to go on horseback <Da84> **•mettre un cheval à l'herbe** to put a horse to pasture <Da84> **•quand on a pas de cheval on monte mulet** one has to make do with what one has <SM> <***Loc:*** AC, AV, EV, IB, JE, PQ, SB, SL, SM, TB, VM, Da84, Di32, Gu86, La99, Lv88, Re31>

chevalement [ʃfalmɑ̃] *n.m.* **1** scaffolding **2** rig *Y'a un grand chevalement drète-là, mais ça va être un trou sec.* There is a big rig right there, but it is going to be an unproductive drilling. (Lv88) <***Loc:*** Lv88>

chevalet [ʃfalɛ, ʃfale] *n.m.* **1** sawhorse, trestle **2** andiron, firedog **3** small grasshopper <***Loc:*** LF, TB>

chevalier [ʃfalje] *n.m.* **1** knight **2** sawhorse ◊ **•chevalier de batture** spotted sandpiper <Re31> **•Chevalier de Colombus** Knight of Columbus <Da84> **•Chevalier de Nuit** Night Rider (member of a white supremacist group after the Civil War) <IB> <***Loc:*** AC, IB, Da84, Lv88, Re31>

chevaux ♦see **cheval**

chevelle ♦see **shovel**

chevelure [ʃəvlyr] *n.f.* head of hair ◊ **•chevelure de Vénus *a*** cypress vine, Indian pink ***b*** maidenhair fern <Da84> <***Loc:*** Da84, Re31>

cheveu [ʃfø] *n.m. (usu. pl.)* **1** hair (on the head) *Ma grand-mère avait jamais coupé ses cheveux.* My grandmother had never cut her hair. (IB) *Alle a pris Myrtle par les cheveux.* She grabbed Myrtle by the hair. (TB) *Mes cheveux sont pleins de peau morte.* My hair is full of dandruff. (SM) **Ses cheveux sont tous chien-fou.* Her hair is disheveled. (La99) **2** hair (of an animal) *On grattait le cochon pour ôter tous les cheveux.* We would scrape the pig to remove all the hair. (AC) *C'est pour couper les cheveux des mulets.* It is for cutting the mule's hair. (AC) ◊ **•être venu un cheveu de sa mort** to come a hair from death, come very close to dying <La99> **•grands cheveux** long hair *Tu connais Jésus a des grands cheveux.* You know, Jesus has long hair. (TB) <TB> <***Loc:*** AC, AV, EV, IB, JD, LA, LF, SL, SM, TB, VM, An94, Da84, Gu00, Hi02, La99>

cheville (**chuille**) [ʃəvij, ʃfij, ʃwij, ʃɥij, tʃwij] *n.f.* **1** ankle *Elle a foulé sa cheville quand elle a tombé hier.* She twisted her ankle when she fell yesterday. (LA) **2** plug, stopper, bung *Quand ils ont ôté la cheville, ils ont vu que le vin avait haigri.* When they removed the bung, they saw that the wine had soured. (LA) *Un baril bouché à la cheville.* A barrel plugged with a bung. (LA) **3** peg, dowel **Pepère Gustave voulait que Sosthène attache les chevrons et les poteaux ensemb' avec des chevilles de bois, mais Sosthène lui voulait user des clous carrés.* Pepère Gustave wanted Sosthène to attach the rafters with wooden pegs, but Sosthène wanted to use square nails. (Gu82) ◊ **•cheville de {du} pied** ankle *Je m'ai refoulé la cheville de pied en sortant de la maison un matin quand je m'en allais au Bâton Rouge.* I sprained my ankle leaving the house when I was leaving for Baton Rouge. (VM) <VM, Da84, Fa77> <***Loc:*** EV, IB, LA, LF, SM, TB, VM, Da84, Gu82, Hi02, Lv88>

chèvrefeuille [ʃɛvrəfœj, ʃovrəfœj, ʃøvrøfœj] *n.m.* honeysuckle ◊ **•chèvrefeuille de France** bush honeysuckle <Re31> <***Loc:*** AV, CL, SM, VM, Da84, Fa77, Re31>

chevrette [ʃəvrɛt, ʃəvret, ʃevrɛt, ʃærvɛt] *n.f.* shrimp ◊ **•chevrette Alphonse** crane fly (gray fly that dances up and down in groups and that smells like shrimp when it dies) <SB> **•chevrette blanche** white shrimp, jumbo shrimp <PQ, TB> **•chevrette BROWN** brown shrimp <TB> **•chevrette du fleuve** river shrimp *Mais les chevrettes du fleuve est différents, le goût est plus doux, il a un goût différent. C'est pas aussi fort que l'autre.* But the river shrimp are different, the taste is sweeter, it has a different taste. It's not as strong as the other one. (SJ) <SJ> **•chevrette du lac** lake shrimp <SJ> **•chevrette grise** brown shrimp <PQ> **•chevrette sec** dried shrimp <TB> **•chevrette verte *a*** raw shrimp *Mais* *avec 210 livres de chevrettes vertes, de chevrettes fraîches, eux-autres sort avec entre 30 et 33 livres de chevrettes secs.* But with 210 pounds of raw shrimp, fresh shrimp, they end up with between 30 and 33 pounds of dried shrimp. (TB) ***b*** fresh shrimp <TB, VM> <***Loc:*** AV, EV, IB, IV, JE, LA, LF, PQ, SB, SJ, SL, SM, TB, VM, Da84, Gu00, Lv88, Ph36, Re31>

chevreuil [ʃəvrœj] *n.m.* deer (esp. white-tailed deer) <***Loc:*** AL, AV, EV, IB, IV, SL, TB, VM, An94, Da84, Gu00, Lv88, Ph36>

chevron [ʃəvrɔ̃, ʃovrɔ̃] *n.m.* rafter *Les chevrons tiennent la couverture.* The rafters hold the roof. (AV) ◊ **•chevron de vallée** valley rafter <SM> <***Loc:*** AC, AV, EV, LA, SL, SM, Da84, Gu82, Lv88, Ph36>

chez (**cez, c'ez**) [ʃe, se, ʃø, sø] *prep.* to, at, at the house of *Moi, j'allais souvent chez Pépère.* I used to go often to Pépère's. (EV) <***Loc:*** AC, AV, EV, IB, JD, JE, LA, LF, PQ, SB, SL, SM, TB, VM, An94, Da84, Di32, Gu00, La99, Lv88, Wh83>

chia [ʃja] *interj.* oh heck, oh shucks <***Loc:*** Da84>

chiasse [ʃjas] *n.f.* diarrhea <***Loc:*** LF, Hi02>

chibaigne [ʃibɛ̃j] *n.f.* ◊ **•toute la chibaigne** the whole crowd, the whole gang *Toute la chibaigne était là.* The whole gang was there. (LF) <***Loc:*** LF, SL>

chicai ♦see **chiquet**

chicailler (**chiquailler**) [ʃikaje] *v.tr.* to chew *Il était après chiquailler de la vieille viande boucanée.* He was chewing on some old smoked meat. (LA) ◊ **•se chicailler un temps** to have a good time <AV> <***Loc:*** AV, IB, LA, Lv88>

chicaire[1] [ʃikær] *n.m.* pen, enclosure in which calves are kept separated from cows <***Loc:*** JE, VM, Di32>

chicaire[2] (**chiquet**) [ʃikær, ʃikɛ, ʃike, ʃige] *interj.* **1** cry used to call a calf into the pen **2** cry used to chase away a calf *Chiquet! Chiquet, toi!* Git! Git, you! (SM) <***Loc:*** JD, LA, SL, SM, Da84, Di32>

chicane [ʃikɑ̃n] *n.f.* **1** chicanery, deceitful act **2** fight, quarrel, argument **La chicane a pris, i' se sont quittés.* The fight began, they broke up. (An77) ◊ **•avoir chicane** to have trouble, have a dispute *Ils ont eu chicane. Il l'a fait sortir avec ça.* They had a fight. He made him take it outside. (EV) <EV> <***Loc:*** EV, SL, SM, VM, An77, An94, Da84, Lv88>

chicaner [ʃikɑ̃ne] **I** *v.tr.* to quibble with, haggle with *Ils nous ont chicané pour le morceau de terre.* They quibbled with us over the piece of property. (LA) **2** to argue with, bicker with *Il me chicane tout le temps.* He argues with me all the time. (LA) **II se chicaner** *v.pron.* to quibble, bicker, fuss *Gilbert et sa femme se chicanent tout le temps.* Gilbert and his wife quibble all the time. (EV) <***Loc:*** EV, LA, Da84, Hi02, Lv88>

chicanerie [ʃikɑ̃nri] *n.f.* chicanery <***Loc:*** Da84>

chiche[1] (**chisse**) [ʃiʃ, ʃis] *adj.* stingy, tight, miserly, avaricious *Il était pas chisse. Un disait "donne-moi un gâteau, Bob," et Bob a tout donné ses gâteaux.* He was not stingy. One would say, "Give me a cookie, Bob," and Bob ended up giving away all his cookies. (LF) <***Loc:*** AL, IB, LA, LF, SL, SM, TB, VM, Da84, Hi02, Lv88>

chiche[2] (**chisse**) [ʃiʃ, ʃis] *n.m.* tightwad, miser <***Loc:*** EV, Da84>

chicheresse (**chisseresse**) [ʃiʃrɛs, ʃisrɛs] *n.f.* stinginess, miserliness, avarice, parsimony <***Loc:*** SM, Lv88>

chicheté (**chisseté**) [ʃiʃte, ʃiste] *n.f.* stinginess, miserliness, avarice, parsimony *La chisseté l'a rendu fou.* Avarice made him crazy. (SM) <***Loc:*** EV, JD, LA, LF, SL, SM, Da84, Lv88, Ph36>

chichetesse (**chissetesse**) [ʃiʃtɛs, ʃistɛs, ʃistes] *n.f.* stinginess, miserliness, avarice, parsimony *Il a fait ça par chissetesse.* He did it out of stinginess. (VM) <***Loc:*** SM, VM, Lv88>

chichicois [ʃiʃikwa] *n.m.* rattle, shaker made of a gourd filled with seeds (used as a musical instrument) <***Loc:*** Di32, Lv88>

chicoré [ʃikore] *n.m.* chicory <***Loc:*** LF>

chicot [ʃiko] *n.m.* **1** stubble (left by crops that have been cut, such as sugarcane or rice), ratoon *Y a du monde qui brûle leur chicot pour empêcher le riz rouge de reprendre.* There are people who burn their rice stubble to prevent the red rice from coming back. (Gu00) **2** stump (of a felled tree) *Il s'est assis sur le gros chicot de cipre là-bas.* He sat down on the big cypress stump over there. (Gu00) **3** whisker, beard stubble *Arrête de frotter tes vieux chicots sur ma figure ça me lime.* Stop rubbing your old stubble on my face, it's scratching me. (Gu00) **4** stock, lineage, ancestry *Entremariage, ça arrivait plein parce que dans ma famille, j'ai le* FAMILY TREE, *ça revient tout jusqu'à ça vient* BACK *au même chicot.* Intermarriage, it happened a lot because in my family, I have the family tree, they all go back to the same stock. (SJ) ◊ **•chicot de canne** sugar cane stubble <Da84> **•chicot de cipre** cypress knee <AV> **•chicot de dent** broken-off tooth <Da84> **•chicots de riz** rice stubble <VM> **•faire chicot** to stand by o.s. (said of a child unable to walk yet) <AV, IB> **•premier / deuxième / troisième chicot** first-, second-, third-year sugarcane stubble <SJ> <***Loc:*** AV, EV, JD, LA, SB, SJ, SL, SM, VM, Da84, Gu00, Hi02, Lv88, Wh83>

chicoter [ʃikote] **I** *v.tr.* **1** to whittle *Chicoter un morceau de bois.* To whittle a piece of wood. (Re31) **2** to nibble, bite at **3** to eat away, erode *Les lames des bateaux ont chicoté l'écore du bayou.* The wake of the boats ate away at the banks of the bayou. (VM) **4** to harrass, annoy, irritate **II** *v.intr.* **1** to nibble **L'poisson chicotte [=chicote].* The fish is nibbling. (EV, Ph36) **2** to eat away, wear away *Le bateau était après chicoter après le pont.* The boat was eating away at the bridge. (LA) **3** to argue, disagree, wrangle over trifles *Il est tout le temps après chicoter avec moi.* He's always arguing with me. (SM) ◊ **•chicoter pour du tracas** to be looking for trouble, be looking for a fight *Il est après chicoter pour du* *tracas.* He is looking for a scuffle. (Lv88) <Lv88> <***Loc:*** EV, IB, LA, SM, VM, Da84, Lv88, Ph36, Re31>

chien[1]**, -ienne** [ʃjɛ̃, ʃijɛ̃, -jɛ̃n] *n.* dog *Joue pas avec la chienne. Elle va te mordre. Elle est en saison.* Don't play with the dog. She'll bite you. She's in heat. (SM) ◊ **•chien à canard** retriever <LF> **•chien à lapins** rabbit dog, beagle *On avait des chiens à lapins. On aurait tué peut-être huit, dix lapins en allant là-bas.* We had rabbit dogs. We would kill maybe eight, ten rabbits when going down there. (SL) <SL> **•chien alison** brindle cattle dog <VM> **•chien basset** basset hound <Da84> **•chien de chasse** hunting dog <Da84> **•chien de fusil** gun hammer and trigger <Da84> **•chien de garde** watchdog <Da84> **•chien de terre** ***a*** mole cricket ***b*** salamander ***c*** groundhog <JD, TB, Da84, Gu00, Hi02> **•chien enragé** mad dog <EV, Da84, La99> **•chien farouche** ***a*** wild dog ***b*** coydog <AL> **•chien-fou** tousled, disheveled *Ses cheveux sont tous chien-fou.* Her hair is disheveled. <La99> **•chien-loup** ***a*** wolfdog ***b*** werewolf <LF> **•chien mord chien** it takes one to know one, birds of a feather flock together <La99> **•chien qui va à la chasse perd sa place** if you leave, s.o. else will usurp your place, you snooze you lose <La99> **•chien salé** great goodness! good heavens! <JD, Da84> **•chien taïaut** bloodhound <Da84> **•bon chien tient de race** like father like son, a chip off the old block <SM, Da84> **•chaque chien a son jour** every dog has his day <Da84> **•être pas plus chien que boule** to be as good as anyone else <La99> **•faire manger du chien enragé** to make s.o. angry <VM, La99> **•gros chien** ***a*** rich person ***b*** important person, big shot *C'est un gros chien depuis il a un puits d'huile.* He's a big shot since he got an oil well. (SM) <SM, Da84, Lv88> **•je lui garde chien de ma chienne** said of s.o. who has harmed you and against whom you seek revenge <SM> **•on envoye pas un chien à la chasse à coups de bâton** you can't force s.o. against his will <Da84> **•pauvre vieux chien** poor devil <Da84> **•vieux chien** [*term of endearment*] man, buddy, old friend <Da84> <***Loc:*** AC, AL, AV, EV, IB, IV, JD, JE, LA, LF, SL, SM, TB, VM, An94, Da84, Gu00, Hi02, La99, Lv88>

chien[2] [ʃjɛ̃] *n.m.* black-necked stilt <***Loc:*** Re31>

chiendent (chien-dent) [ʃjɛ̃dɑ̃] *n.m.* **1** switch grass, couch grass, bermuda grass **2** crabgrass **3** tall paspalum, dallis grass <***Loc:*** LA, LF, SB, SL, TB, Da84, Re31>

chiennailler [ʃjɛ̃naje] *v.intr.* to sleep around, engage readily or frequently in casual sex **Il a chiennaillé tout la nuit, il a bu et il a couru avec les femmes.* He whored around all night, he drank, and he ran around with women. (EV, Ph36) *Sa femme l'a quitté. Elle l'a attrapé après chiennailler.* His wife left him. She caught him sleeping around. (LA) <***Loc:*** EV, SM, LA, Lv88, Ph36>

chiennailleur, -euse [ʃjɛ̃najœr, -øz] *n.* **1** *(m.)* woman-chaser, womanizer, playboy **2** *(f.)* man-chaser, loose woman <***Loc:*** Lv88>

chienne[1] ♦see **chien**

chienne[2] [ʃjɛ̃n] *n.f.* whore, slut <***Loc:*** AC>

chienner [ʃjɛ̃ne] *v.intr.* **1** to sleep around, engage readily or frequently in casual sex *Il a arrêté de chienner quand il s'a marié.* He stopped sleeping around when he got married. (LA) **2** to debauch, dissipate, sow wild oats *T'as assez chienné hier au soir?* Did you dissipate enough last night? (VM) <***Loc:*** LA, VM, Da84>

chiennerie [ʃjɛ̃nri] *n.f.* debauchery, dissipation, dissoluteness <***Loc:*** JD, LF, SM, Lv88>

chier [ʃie] *v.intr.* to defecate, shit *Chier dans sa culotte.* To shit one's pants. (EV) ◊ **•chier sa crotte de noces** to give a great effort to do something and not succeed <EV, SL, La99> **•chier sur le palonnier** to make a big mistake, fail in one's effort <La99> **•ça chie dans le même sac** they are two of a kind, they are equally bad <VM, La99> <***Loc:*** AS, EV, IB, SL, VM, Da84, Hi02, La99>

chierie [ʃiri] *n.f.* **1** diarrhea **2** riffraff, scum, lowlives **Tout ç'te chierie vaut pas rien.* All of that riffraff isn't worth much. (EV, Ph36) <***Loc:*** EV, SM, Ph36>

chiffon [ʃifɔ̃] *n.m.* **1** chiffon fabric **2** rag, torn piece of cloth **3** cluster, wad, bundle *Tu frèmes la gaffe, ça attrape un chiffon.* You close the tongs, it grabs a cluster [of oysters]. (VM) *Marion Marcotte, quand il voulait bourrer son fusil pour tirer la z-oie, il a pris un chiffon de mousse, il l'a bien tapée, la musquette.* Marion Marcotte, when he wanted to stuff his shotgun to shoot the goose, he took a wad of moss, he tapped it well, the musket. (VM) ◊ **•chiffon de pain** chunk of bread <LF, SM> <***Loc:*** LF, SM, VM, Da84, Lv88>

chiffonner [ʃifɔ̃ne] *v.tr.* **1** to rumple, wrinkle *Assieds-toi pas encore, tu vas chiffonner ta robe de Pâques.* Don't sit yet, you'll wrinkle your Easter dress. (VM) **2** to shuffle (cards) *Pourtant, j'avais bien chiffonné les cartes.* Yet I had shuffled the cards well. (LA) <***Loc:*** LA, VM, Da84>

chiffonnier [ʃifɔ̃je] *n.m.* chifforobe, dresser with drawers and hanging space <***Loc:*** Da84>

chiffonnière [ʃifɔ̃jær] *n.f.* dresser <***Loc:*** Da84>

chiffonnerie [ʃifɔ̃nri] *n.f.* rags *Tout il y avait dans la vieille boîte, c'était des vieilles chiffonneries.* All that was in the old box was old rags. (LA) <***Loc:*** LA, Da84>

chiffre [ʃif(r)] *n.m.* number <***Loc:*** Da84>

chigneux, -euse [ʃiɲø, ʃĩjø, -øz] *adj.* complaining, whining *Ces enfants sont assez chigneux, ils sont jamais satisfaits.* Those kids are pretty whiny, they're never satisfied. (VM) <***Loc:*** VM>

chignon ♦see **tignon**

chimère [ʃimær] *n.f.* foolish idea ◊ **•être en chimère** to be in a bad mood, be looking for a fight <Lv88, Re31> <***Loc:*** SL, Lv88, Re31>

chinane [ʃinɑ̃n] *n.f.* sweetheart <***Loc:*** Re38>

chincaillerie ♦see **quincaillerie**

chine ♦see **tchine**

chiner ♦see **échiner**

chingding [ʃiŋdiŋ] *n.m.* dance *Il y aura un chingding samedi soir.* (SB) <***Loc:*** AV, SB>

chinois[1], **-e** [ʃinwa, -waz] *adj.* Chinese <***Loc:*** LF, Da84, Lv88>

Chinois[2], **-e** [ʃinwa, -waz] *n.* Chinese person *Les Chinois a venu à la Louisiane.* The Chinese came to Louisiana. (LF) *Les Japonais et les Chineaux s'imitent un tas.* The Japanese and the Chinese look a lot alike. (VM) <***Loc:*** LF, VM, Da84, Fa77>

chiper ♦see **tchiper**

chipote [ʃipɔt] *n.f.* quarrel <***Loc:*** SJ>

chipoter (se) [ʃipote] *v.pron.* to quarrel, bicker *Les deux filles se sont chipotées hier matin.* The two girls quarreled yesterday morning. (SB) <***Loc:*** SB>

chipoteur, -euse [ʃipotœr, -øz] *n.* **1** nitpicker, one who quarrels over trivial matters *Il est bien un chipoteur de se fâcher pour ça.* He sure is a nitpicker to get upset about that. (IB) **2** tattler, tattletale, talebearer *La chipoteuse venait souvent chez moi.* The tattler often came to my house. (SB) <***Loc:*** AV, IB, SB, SJ>

chiquailler ♦see **chicailler**

chique [ʃik] *n.f.* **1** chew, plug, wad (of tobacco) *Il me donnait une petite chique tous les temps en temps.* He would give me a small chew once in a while. (AC) **2** mouthful **I mange vite et à grandes chiques.* He eats fast and by big mouthfuls. (EV, Ph36) **3** cud (of ruminants) **4** veiled insult, subtly disparaging remark, dig *C'était une vraie chique.* That was a real dig. (IB) *Mettre une chique à quelqu'un.* To make a subtle dig at someone. (SJ) **5** sugar teat, piece of cloth soaked in milk and sugar given to an infant as a pacifier <***Loc:*** AC, AV, EV, IB, JE, LA, SJ, SL, SM, VM, Da84, Hi02, La99, Lv88, Ph36>

chiquenailler [ʃiknaje] *v.tr.* to cut unevenly, hack up *Alle a tout chiquenaillé ce morceau d'étoffe.* She hacked up this piece of cloth. (TB) <***Loc:*** TB>

chiquer [ʃike] **I** *v.tr.* **1** to chew *Ils ont chiqué de la gomme jusqu'à ils ont fait une grosse pelote.* They chewed gum until they made a big ball. (EV) **2** to deceive *Il s'est bien fait chiquer.* He was deceived. (Lv88) **II** *v.intr.* to chew tobacco *Le vieux monde chiquait.* Old people would chew tobacco. (LA) ◊ **•chiquer du vieux linge** to complain incessantly *Il est trop tard pour chiquer du vieux linge.* It's too late to complain. (EV) <EV, SL, La99> **•chiquer poteau** to be disregarded, be left out on a limb *Pauvre bête, elle l'a laissé à chiquer poteau pour les fêtes.* Poor thing, she left him out on a limb for the holidays. (LA) <LA, SM> **•faire chiquer poteaux à qqn** to beat s.o. in competition <JE, La99> <***Loc:*** AC, AL, AV, EV, JE, LA, SL, SM, TB, Da84, La99, Lv88>

chiquet ♦see **chicaire**

chiquette [ʃikɛt] *n.* ◊ **•chiquette et berlingue** ridiculous or absurd-looking couple <SM, La99> <***Loc:*** SM, La99>

chiqueur, -euse [ʃikœr, -øz] *n.* one who chews tobacco ◊ **•chiqueur de lavettes grasses** stupid person <La99> <***Loc:*** Da84, La99>

chire ♦see **chiure**

chirurgien (**cirugien, cirurgien, sirugien, sirurgien**) [ʃiryrʒjɛ̃, siryrʒɛ̃] *n.m.* surgeon <***Loc:*** IB, Da84, Lv88, Re31>

chirvauché, -e [ʃirvoʃe] *adj.* crooked, bent *Il est tout chirvauché.* He is all crooked. (LF) <***Loc:*** LF>

chisse ♦see **chiche**

chisseresse ♦see **chicheresse**

chisseté ♦see **chicheté**

chissetesse ♦see **chichetesse**

chiure (**chire**) [ʃjyr, ʃir] *n.f.* excrement (esp. of insects) ◊ **•chiure de mouche** fly speck <Da84> <***Loc:*** Da84>

chloroforme [klorofɔrm] *n.m.* chloroform <***Loc:*** Da84>

cho (**cheu**) [tʃo, tʃu] *interj.* cry for calling cows or pigs <***Loc:*** EV, SM, Lv88, Ph36>

choc ♦see **tchac**

chocatif (**chocative**) [ʃokatif, ʃokativ] *adj.* touchy, irritable, quick to anger *Tu peux pas y parler de politique du tout. Il est trop chocatif.* You can't talk to him at all about politics. He gets angry too easily. (VM) *Il est vaillant, mais il est chocatif quand il a pas mangé.* He's nice but he's irritable when he hasn't eaten. (EV) <***Loc:*** EV, SM, VM, Lv88>

chocative ♦see **chocatif**

chock-a-block ♦see **tchoque-à-bloque**

chocolat [ʃokola, ʃakola] *n.m.* chocolate <***Loc:*** SJ, Da84>

chocolatière [ʃokolatjær] *n.f.* marsh hawk, prairie hawk <***Loc:*** Re31>

chœur [kœr] *n.m.* choir, sanctuary <***Loc:*** Da84>

choge ♦see **chose**

choisir [ʃwazir, ʃwɛzir] *v.tr.* to choose, select, pick out *[Eusse] a déjà été choisir un* SET *[...] pour amener dans leur maison, c'est un beau* SET *de vaisselle.* They've already gone to pick out a set to take to their home, it's a lovely set of dishes. (LF) <***Loc:*** AC, AV, EV, LF, VM, Da84>

choix [ʃwa] *n.m.* choice <***Loc:*** Da84>

CHOKE [tʃok] *n.m.* **1** choke, bore (of a gun) *Il s'avait fait mettre un* CHOKE *pour tirer les z-oies.* He had a choke installed to shoot geese. (LA) **2** choke of a motor <***Loc:*** LA, Da84>

choléra [kolera] *n.m.* **1** cholera **2** loose bowels <***Loc:*** EV, LA, VM, Da84>

cholo (**chaud-l'eau**) [ʃolo] *n.m.* weak coffee, watered-down coffee <***Loc:*** TB, La99>

chopine (**tchopine**) [ʃopin, ʃupin, tʃopin] *n.f.* **1** tin cup, dipper *Apporte-moi une chopine d'eau.* Bring me a dipperful of water. (SB) *La tchopine a tombé dans la citerne.* The water dipper fell into the cistern. (AV) **2** small or medium-sized metal cooking container or its contents **3** drinking cup made of a small gourd <***Loc:*** AV, IB, JE, SB, SJ, SM, Re38>

choppe ♦see **SHOP**

choquant, -e [ʃokɑ̃, -ɑ̃t] *adj.* **1** offensive, shocking *C'est* *choquant de l'attendre parler comme ça à sa mère.* It's shocking to hear him talk to his mother like that. (LA) **2** angering, provoking to anger **3** annoying, unpleasant, displeasing <***Loc:*** LA, Da84>

choque[1] ♦see **tchoc**

choque[2] [ʃɔk] *n.f.* bun, roll, twist, or knot of hair worn at the back of the head *Sa choque est bien arrangée, hein?* Her knot is well arranged, isn't it? (IB) <***Loc:*** IB>

choque-à-bloque ♦see **tchoque-à-bloque**

choquer [ʃoke] **I** *v.tr.* **1** to offend *Je fais beaucoup attention à quoi je dis à quelqu'un et je veux pas choquer quelqu'un.* I pay a lot of attention to what I say to a person and I don't want to offend someone. (EV) **2** to anger **Ça, ça m'a choqué!* That made me angry! (Da84) *Équand on parle en français et que mes petits-enfants sont là, eux-autres ça les choque. Parce que eux-autres peut pas comprendre ça qu'on dit, et des fois eux-autres croit on après dire de quoi après eux-autres.* When we're speaking French and my grandchildren are there, that makes them mad. Because they can't understand what we're saying, and sometimes they think we're talking about them. (TB) **3** to annoy, displease *Il se vantait toujours à mon cousin et ça le choquait, il aimait pa ça.* He would always brag to my cousin and that annoyed him, he didn't like it. (Lv88) **II se choquer** *v.pron.* **1** to get angry, mad, upset *Je me choque facilement.* I am easily angered. (SM) **2** to take offense, be offended *Elle se choque facile.* She feels easily offended. (SM) ◊ **•choqué au fiel** very angry *Quand il les a vus ensemble, il était choqué au fiel.* When he saw them together, he was very angry. (LA) <LA, La99> **•être choqué après {avec} qqn** to be angry at s.o. *Je suis choqué avec lui.* I'm angry with him. (SM) <SM> <***Loc:*** EV, LA, LF, SM, TB, VM, Da84, La99, Lv88>

chorus ♦see **corusse**

chose[1] **(choge)** [ʃoz, ʃɔʒ, ʃɔʃ] *n.f.* thing **C'est une bonne chose.* It's a good thing. (Da84) *Les choses étaient un tas plus bon marché dans ce temps-là.* Things were a lot less expensive in those days. (IB) *I-n-a qui dit une chose, i-n-a d'autres qui dit d'autres choses, on connaît qui ils veut dire parce que c'est tout proche pareil.* Some people say one thing and some others something else, but we know what they both mean because it is almost the same. (AV) *C'est la même chose.* It's the same thing. (AV) ◊ **•avoir quatre cent cinquante mille choses à faire** to have a million things to do *Moi je peux jamais m'assir après dîner, j'ai tout le temps quatre cent cinquante mille choses à faire.* I can never sit down after dinner, I always have a million things to do. (TB) <TB> **•pas grand'chose** not much <LA, Da84> **•toute chose** all, everything <Da84> **•tout quelque chose** everything <EV, IB, JD, LA, VM, An94, Da84, Gu82, Hi02> <***Loc:*** AC, AV, EV, IB, JD, JE, LA, LF, SL, TB, VM, An94, Da84, Gu82, Hi02, Lv88, Wh83>

chose[2] [ʃɔz, ʃɔʒ, ʃɔʃ] *n.m.* **1** person whose name does not come to mind, 'what's-his-name' *Tu connais chose, comment il s'appelle?* You know 'who-z-it,' what's his name? (SM, VM) **2** whatchamacallit, thingamajig *Ça c'est une espèce de bois de pin qu'a été traité avec du chose pour pas que l'eau embêche le bois.* That's a kind of pine wood that was treated with something to keep water from harming the wood. (LF) <***Loc:*** LF, SM, VM, Lv88>

chou[1] [ʃu] *n.m.* **1** cabbage **2** [*term of endearment*] darling **Cher 'tit chou.* Dear little darling. (Da84) ◊ **•chou vert** borecole, curled kale <TB, Re31> **•choux de Bruxelles** Brussels sprouts <Da84> <***Loc:*** LA, SL, VM, Da84, Lv88, Re31>

chou[2] **(chu)** [ʃu, ʃy] *interj.* "shoo", cry used to call or drive away pigs, dogs, chickens, etc. *Chou! Chou!* Shoo! shoo! (VM) <***Loc:*** AV, LA, SB, SJ, SL, SM, TB, VM, Re31>

chouboulure ♦see **échauboulure**

chouce, chouche ♦see **chousse**

chouchou [ʃuʃu] *n.m.* **1** firecracker that does not explode, dud **2** missed opportunity <***Loc:*** EV, LA, VM, Da84>

chouchoute [ʃuʃut] *n.f.* [*term of endearment*] little girl, dear, sweetheart *Mame m'appelait tout le temps chouchoute.* Mom always called me 'chouchoute.' (TB) <***Loc:*** TB>

chou-crème [ʃukrɛ̃m] cream puff <***Loc:*** IB, LA, Lv88>

choucroute [ʃukrut] *n.m./f.* **1** sauerkraut **2** cole slaw <***Loc:*** EV, Da84, Lv88, Ph36>

choué [ʃue] *interj.* cry used for chasing away pigs <***Loc:*** EV, Ph36>

choui [tʃui] *interj.* cry used for calling pigs <***Loc:*** SM>

chouche [ʃuʃ] *interj.* cry used to chase away chickens <***Loc:*** SB>

chouer ♦see **échouer**

chouette [ʃwɛt] *n.f.* screech owl, hoot owl ◊ **•ma petite chouette** *(ironic term of endearment) Ma maudite petite chouette.* You little son-of-a-gun. (Lv88) <Lv88> <***Loc:*** IB, SB, TB, VM, Da84, Fa77, Lv88, Re31>

chou-fleur [ʃuflœr] *n.m.* cauliflower <***Loc:*** SL, VM, Da84>

chou-gras [ʃugra] *n.m.* pokeberry, pokeweed <***Loc:*** AV, EV, IB, SB, SL, TB, VM, Da84, Lv88, Ph35, Re31>

chouiner ♦see **chouriner**

chouinque [ʃwɛ̃k] *n.m.* large amount, great many *Il a un chouinque de crayons.* He has a great many pencils. (LF) <***Loc:*** LF>

chouler [ʃule] *v.tr.* to coax, try to persuade *Je l'ai choulé pendant des heures.* I tried to persuade him for hours. (SB) <***Loc:*** SB>

chou-navet [ʃunavɛ, ʃunave] *n.m.* **1** kohlrabi **2** horseradish <***Loc:*** JD, Da84>

choupèque [ʃupɛk] *n.m.* home-made moccassin <***Loc:*** VM>

choupique [ʃupik] *n.m.* bowfin, mudfish, grindle, cypress trout *Un choupique ça reste dans l'eau douce, et de l'eau bourbée, de la boue. C'est pas un bon poisson. C'est pas trop mangé.* A bowfin lives in fresh water, and muddy water, mud. It's not a good fish. It's not eaten much. (LF) <***Loc:*** AC, AL, AV, EV, IB, IV, JE, LF, SB, SL, SM, TB, VM, Da84, Fa77, Guoo, Lv88, Ph36, Re31>

chouquechi [ʃukʃi] *n.m.* cushaw, crookneck squash <***Loc:*** AV, Lv88, Re31>

chourice ♦see **tchaurisse**

chouriner (**chouiner, suriner**) [ʃurine, ʃwine, syrine] *v.tr.* to coax, try to persuade *Quand il veut quelque chose, il me chourine jusqu'à je lui donne.* When he wants something, he coaxes me until I give it to him. (Lv88) <***Loc:*** Lv88>

chourouque [ʃuruk] *n.m.* tobacco <***Loc:*** SM>

chousse (**chouce, chouche, souche**) [ʃus, ʃuʃ, ʃos] *n.f.* **1** stump *J'ai eu mille misères à arracher cette grosse chousse de chêne vert.* I had a ton of problems pulling out that big live oak stump. (VM) **2** stock, ancestry *C'est tout parents. Ça vient back tout à ces mêmes chousses.* They're all relatives. They all go back to the same stock. (TB) ◊ **•chouce de miel** beehive <JE, La99> <***Loc:*** AC, AV, IB, IV, JE, LA, LF, SJ, SL, TB, VM, TB, Da84, Guoo, La99, Lv88>

chrétien[1], **-ienne** [kretjɛ̃, -jɛ̃n] *adj.* Christian *Une fête chrétienne.* A Christian holiday. (LA) *C'est un homme beaucoup chrétien.* He is very Christian man. (LA) <***Loc:*** AS, LA, Da84, Fa77>

chrétien[2] [kretjɛ̃] *n.m.* **1** Christian **2** individual, person, soul *Il restait pus un chrétien dans la paroisse après l'ouragan.* Not a soul was left in the parish after the hurricane. (LA) *Il restait pas un chrétien après le bal.* There wasn't a soul left after the dance. (LA) <***Loc:*** LA, VM, Da84, Lv88>

Chrismisse, Chrismeusse, Chrissmusse ♦see **Christmas**

Chrisquine ♦see **Christine**

Christ [krist] *n.m.* Christ <***Loc:*** TB, Da84>

christianisme [kristjɑ̃nism] *n.m.* Christianity <***Loc:*** Da84>

christianité [kristjɑ̃nite] *n.f.* Christianity <***Loc:*** Da84>

christine (**chrisquine**) [kristin, kriskin, kriʃtin] *n.f.* **1** *(prop.)* Santa Claus, Father Christmas *La Christine apportait les jouets.* Santa Claus would bring toys. (Lv88) *Et on savait que la Christine allait venir, et là le matin tout pouvait pas espérer pour nous réveiller pour voir s'il y avait des présents en-dessous du bois.* And we knew that Santa Claus would come, and then in the morning everyone couldn't wait to wake up to see if there were presents under the tree. (LF) **2** *(prop.)* (in folklore) a character whom children believed would visit on New Year's Eve to reward good children with candy *La Christine, ça c'était pour le Jour de l'An. La Christine, c'était la femme à Papa Noël. Alle amenait des candis et toute espèce de petites affaires, mais si t'étais méchant, que t'écoutais pas, alle t'amenait des oignons ou des patates.* The 'Christine' was for New Year's Day. The Christine was Santa Claus' wife. She brought candy and all sorts of little things, but if you were bad, if you didn't listen, she brought you onions or potatoes. (LF) **3** masked Carnaval reveller **4** boogeyman, ghost *Il y avait une christine dans la vieille maison.* There was a ghost in the old house. (AV) *La christine va t'attraper.* The ghost will get you. (SB) <***Loc:*** AV, IB, LF, SB, SJ, SL, TB, VM, Fa77, Lv88>

Christmas (**Chrismisse, Chrismusse, Chrismeusse**) [krismis, krismys, krismœs] *n.m.* Christmas <***Loc:*** EV, IB, LF, SB, TB, VM, Da84, Gu82, Hi02, Lv88, Ph36, Wh83>

chrome [krɔ̃m] *n.m.* chrome <***Loc:*** Da84>

chronique [krɔ̃nik] *adj.* chronic *Une maladie chronique.* A chronic illness. (VM) <***Loc:*** VM, Da84>

chrysanthème [krezɑ̃tɛ̃m] *n.f.* chrysanthemum <***Loc:*** SB>

chu[1] ♦see **chou**[2]

chu[2] ♦see **tchu**

chuchotement [ʃyʃɔtmɑ̃] *n.m.* whispering <***Loc:*** Da84>

chuchoter [ʃyʃote] *v.intr.* to whisper *Elle a chuchoté dans mon oreille.* She whispered in my ear. (LA) <***Loc:*** Da84>

chuille ♦see **cheville**

chuminée, chunée ♦see **cheminée**

CHUNK (**tchonque**) [tʃɔ̃k, tʃœ̃k] *n.m.* large piece, chunk *Il pouvait pas apporter le gros* CHUNK *de bois.* He couldn't carry the big chunk of wood. (SB) <***Loc:*** EV, SB, Ph36>

chuter [ʃyte, ʃute] *v.intr.* **1** to fall *Tu vas chuter là, vieux, t'es pas tout le temps jeune, non!* You're going to fall there, pal, you're not all that young any more! (TB) **2** to relapse, have a relapse, fall sick again *Il a eu le flu, et il a chuté.* He had the flu, and he relapsed. (AV) <***Loc:*** AV, JD, TB>

ci ♦see **ça**[3]

ciblème (**siblème, cibline**) [siblɛ̃m, siblin, siblim] *n.m./f.* squash (variously or regionally referring to the yellow, patty pan, scalloped, summer, or acorn squash) <***Loc:*** AL, AV, CL, EV, JE, LF, SL, SM, TB, VM, Da84, Lv88, Ph36>

cibline ♦see **ciblème**

ciboire [sibwar] *n.m.* ciborium <***Loc:*** Da84>

cicatrice [sikatris] *n.f.* **1** scar **2** scab <***Loc:*** EV, VM, Da84>

cicatriser [sikatrize] *v.intr.* **1** to scar **2** to form a scab *Il avait un bobo qui voulait pas cicatriser.* He had a sore that didn't want to form a scab. (LA) *Son bobo commence à cicatriser.* His wound is scabbing over. (LA) <***Loc:*** LA, Da84>

ciel [sjɛl, sjel] *n.m.* **1** sky *Le vent a éclairci le ciel.* The wind cleared the sky. (LA) **2** heaven *Qui a créé la terre et le ciel?* Who created the earth and the heavens? (LA) *Y a un Bon Dieu dans le ciel.* There is a God in heaven. (TB) ◊ **•ciel de lit** bed canopy, tester <Da84> <***Loc:*** AC, LA, PQ, SM, TB, VM, Da84, La99, Lv88>

cigale (**cigare**) [sigal, sigar, sinigal] *n.m./f.* **1** cicada, locust *Une cigale, ça commence avec un ver dans la terre, une larve.* A cicada begins his life as a worm in the ground, a grub worm. (AV) **2** grasshopper **3** dragonfly, mosquito hawk **4** ultralight airplane ◊ **•cigale à chêne** ***a*** cicada ***b*** seven-year locust *On appelle ça des cigales à chêne. Parce que habitudement tu trouves ça dans les chênes verts, et dans l'été quand il fait plein plein chaud tu peux les attendre chanter. La chaleur les fait leur corps trembler.* We call them oak cicadas. Because usually you find them in live oaks, and in summer when it's really hot you can hear them singing. The heat makes their bodies tremble. (LF) <LF> **•cigale à {de} bois** cicada, seventeen-year locust <AC, LA, Da84, Guoo> **•cigale anglaise {zi-zi}** species of cicada or locust that makes a rasping sound <Re31> **•cigale chanteuse** cicada <LF> **•cigale de nuit** cicada *Une cigale de nuit [...]. C'est une bétaille qui reste dans la terre pour longtemps, des années de temps. Et là ça sort et ça accroche sur le bois et là eusse sort de l'écale.* A seven-year locust It's an insect that lives in the ground for a long time, years at a time. And then it comes out and it hooks onto a tree and then they come out of their shell. (LF) <LF, TB> <***Loc:*** AC, AV, EV, IB, IV, JE, LA, LF, SB, SJ, SL, SM, TB, VM, Da84, Guoo, Lv88, Re31>

cigalère ♦see **cigalière**

cigalière (**cigalère**) [sigaljær, sigalær] *n.f.* tobacco pouch (formerly made from a bladder) <***Loc:*** IB, SM, TB, Lv88>

cigare[1] [sigar] *n.m.* cigar <***Loc:*** AC, EV, LA, SL, An84, An94, Da84>

cigare[2] ♦see **cigale**

cigarette (**cigaritte**) [sigarɛt, sigarit] *n.f.* cigarette <***Loc:*** AC, AV, IB, LA, LF, SB, SL, TB, VM, Da84, Lv88>

cigaritte ♦see **cigarette**

cil ♦see **celui**

ciller ♦see **siller**

cilui ♦see **celui**

ciment [simɑ̃] *n.m.* **1** cement **2** concrete **3** sidewalk *Marcher sur le ciment.* To walk on the sidewalk. (SJ) <***Loc:*** AV, IB, JE, LF, SB, SJ, SL, TB, Da84>

cimenter [simɑ̃te] *v.tr.* to cement *Quand il y avait un mort, ça fouillait un trou et puis ça cimentait ça.* When there was a dead person, they would dig a hole and cement it. (SL) <***Loc:*** SL, Da84>

cimetière (**cimitière**) [simitjær] *n.m.* graveyard, cemetery <***Loc:*** AC, AV, EV, IB, LA, SL, SM, TB, VM, Da84, Re31>

cimitière ♦see **cimetière**

cingle [sɛ̃ɲ, sɛ̃g(l)] *n.m.* cinch strap <***Loc:*** EV>

cingler [sɛ̃gle] *v.tr.* to cinch a saddle onto (a horse) *Tu voulais cingler ton cheval.* You wanted to cinch the saddle on your horse. (EV) <***Loc:*** EV>

cinq [sɛ̃k] (*before a consonant* [sɛ̃k, sɛ̃], *before a vowel* [sɛ̃k, sɛ̃z]) *adj./n.m.* five *L'admission est cinq piasses.* Admission is five dollars. (Lv88) *J'ai un appointement à cinq heures.* I have an appointment at five o'clock. (SM) *Le nouveau de lune est le cinq de mars.* The new moon is March 5. (TB) <***Loc:*** AC, AV, EV, IB, LF, SB, SJ, SL, SM, TB, An94, Da84, Gr86, La99, Lv88, Wh83>

cinq-sous[1] [sɛ̃su] *n.f.* dwarf rose <***Loc:*** VM>

cinq-sous[2] [sɛ̃su] *n.m.* nickel, five-cent coin *Un jour il demande à mame pour un cinq-sous pour aller s'acheter des gâteaux.* One day he asks mother for a nickel to go buy himself some cookies. (LF) <***Loc:*** EV, TB, LF, TB, Lv88>

cinquantaine [sɛ̃kɑ̃tɛ̃n] *n.f.* about fifty *Quand tu partais avec un voyage d'hommes là tu pouvais mettre une cinquantaine d'hommes dans le bateau.* When you set off with a load of men, you could put about 50 men in the boat. (LF) <***Loc:*** LF, TB, VM, An94, Da84>

cinquante [sɛ̃kɑ̃t] *adj./n.m.* fifty *Je dirais peut-être un bon cinquante du cent du monde jusqu'à oh peut-être 1960, eusse travaillait tout sur l'eau.* I would say a good fifty percent of the people until oh about 1960 worked on the water. (LF) <***Loc:*** AC, AS, EV, LF, SL, SM, TB, VM, An94, Da84>

cinquantième [sɛ̃kɑ̃tjɛ̃m] *adj.* fiftieth *Leur cinquantième anniversaire de mariage.* Their fiftieth wedding anniversary. (EV) <***Loc:*** EV, LA, Da84>

cinquième [sɛ̃kjɛ̃m] *adj.* fifth *C'est une belle place, nous-autres on a été sur le cinquième plancher, c'est un hôtel et un restaurant.* It's a lovely place, we were on the fifth floor, it's a hotel and a restaurant. (TB) ◊ **•cinquième roue** fifth wheel (of horse-drawn vehicles) <Da84> <***Loc:*** AV, EV, IB, LF, TB, Da84, Lv88>

cipre (**cypre**) [sip(r)] *n.m.* **1** any of various species of cypress, including the bald, red, and American cypress *Il y a du bois de cypre qu'est rouge, mais cela, ce cypre-là, c'est ça qu'on appelle le cypre de gros-bec, c'est pas des vieux vieux cypres.* There is cypress wood that's red, but this cypress is what we call "gros-bec" cypress, it's not really old cypress. (LF) **2** Eastern red cedar ◊ **•cipre frisé** choice grain of cypress <Lv88> **•cipre piqué** pecky cypress *J'ai usé des planches de cipre piqué pour mon plafonnage.* I used pecky cypress to cover my walls. (VM) <VM> **•cipre rouge** Eastern red cedar <AV> <***Loc:*** AS, AV, IB, IV, LA, LF, SL, SM, TB, VM, Da84, Guoo, Lv88, Re31>

ciprière (**cyprière**) [siprijær] *n.f.* **1** cypress grove, cypress swamp *Pour notre maison, on a sorti les arbres dedans la cyprière, du cypre et on a scié ça et on a bâti notre maison presque pour arien.* For our house, we removed trees from the swamp, cypress wood, we sawed it and built our house for almost nothing. (SM) **2** swamp <***Loc:*** AS, AV, IB, IV, LA, LF, SB, SM, TB, VM, Da84, Guoo, Re31>

cirage [siraʒ] *n.m.* waxing, act of waxing <***Loc:*** Da84>

circasienne [sirkasjɛ̃n] *n.f.* showgirl <***Loc:*** Da84>

circoncision [sirkɔ̃sizjɔ̃] *n.f.* [*eccl.*] circumcision <***Loc:*** Da84>

circonstance [sirkɔ̃stɑ̃s] *n.f.* circumstance *A la dernière circonstance.* The last time it happened. (LA) <***Loc:*** LA, Da84>

circulaire[1] [sirkylær, syrkylær] *adj.* circular <***Loc:*** LF>

circulaire[2] [sirkylær, syrkylær] *n.m.* gore (in dressmaking) *Une jupe à circulaires.* A skirt with gores. (VM) <***Loc:*** VM>

circulation [sirkylasjɔ̃, syrkylasjɔ̃] *n.f.* circulation *Le docteur a expliqué la circulation du sang.* The doctor explained blood circulation. (SM) <***Loc:*** LF, SL, SM, TB, Da84>

circuler [sirkyle, syrkyle] **I** *v.tr.* to circulate (news, etc.) *Va* *circuler la nouvelle.* Go spread the news. (VM) **II** *v.intr.* **1** to circulate *L'air circule pas dans la maison.* The air isn't circulating in the house. (VM) *Son sang circule pas bien.* His blood doesn't circulate well. (VM) **2** to form a circle *Les chiens alisons circulaient autour du troupeau.* The brindle cattle dogs circled around the herd. (VM) <***Loc:*** LF, SL, TB, VM, Da84>

cire [sir] *n.f.* **1** wax **2** inflammation of the edge of the eyelid ◊ **•cire rouge** red geranium <VM> <***Loc:*** AV, SM, VM, Da84, Lv88, Re31>

cirer [sire] *v.tr.* to wax *Cirer ses souliers, ses bottes.* To wax one's shoes, one's boots. (EV) <***Loc:*** EV, VM, Da84>

cirier [sirje] *n.f.* **1** cedarbird, cedar waxwing **2** wax myrtle **3** bayberry, small waxberry <***Loc:*** EV, SL, TB, Lv88, Ph36, Re31>

ciroper [sirope] *v.tr.* to wax (nautical equipment, e.g. ropes, tarpaulins) <***Loc:*** LF>

ciroüène [sirwɛ̃n] *n.f.* porous plaster <***Loc:*** SM>

cirque [sirk] *n.m.* circus <***Loc:*** AC, LF, Da84>

cirugien, cirurgien ♦see **chirurgien**

cisaille [sizaj] *n.f.* shears, tin shears <***Loc:*** Da84>

cisailler [sizaje] *v.tr.* to cut unskillfully, hack *Il a tout cisaillé mes cheveux.* He hacked up my hair. (LA) *Son mari a tout cisaillé l'étoffe.* Her husband hacked at the cloth. (LA) <***Loc:*** IB, LA, VM>

ciseau [sizo] *n.m.* **1** chisel **2** *(often pl.)* scissors, pair of scissors *Avec un ciseau.* With scissors. (SM) *Paire de ciseaux.* Pair of scissors. (Da84) *Des ciseaux pour couper le maillage.* Scissors to cut the netting. (TB) ◊ **•ciseau à bois** wood chisel *N'importe qui tu veux faire un trou dans ça tu uses un ciseau à bois.* Any kind of hole you want to make, you use a wood chisel. (SM) <EV, SM> **•ciseau à froid** cold chisel <Da84> <***Loc:*** AV, EV, JE, SL, SM, TB, Da84>

citation [sitasjɔ̃] *n.f.* citation <***Loc:*** Da84>

cité [site] *n.f.* city, town <***Loc:*** Da84>

citer [site] *v.tr.* **1** to cite, quote *L'avocat a cité la loi 714.* The lawyer cited Act 714. (VM) *Son nom a été cité dans le contrat.* He was named in the contract. (VM) **2** to make an appointment, set a time for an engagement *Nous avions cité d'aller à trois heures.* We made an appointment to go at three o'clock. (VM) *Le dentiste m'avait cité onze heures.* The dentist set the time for eleven o'clock. (VM) <***Loc:*** VM, Da84>

citerne [sitærn, sitɛ̃n] *n.f.* cistern (rain water reservoir) *On avait de l'eau parce que j'avais une citerne.* We had water because I had a cistern. (EV) <***Loc:*** AV, EV, LA, LF, SL, SM, TB, VM, Da84, Lv88>

citoyen, -enne [sitwajɛ̃, -ɛ̃n] *n.* **1** citizen *J'ai rencontré plusieurs citoyens de la France.* I met several citizens of France. (Lv88) **2** *(pl.)* people *C'est nous-autres les citoyens qu'est connus comme les Cadiens.* We are the people known as Cajuns. (Lv88) <***Loc:*** Da84, Lv88>

citron [sitrɔ̃] *n.m.* **1** citron tree **2** lemon **3** creeping cucumber, melonette (locally known as "smellin' melon") <***Loc:*** CL, SM, VM, Lv88, Da84>

citronnelle [sitrɔ̃nɛl] *n.f.* **1** citronella **2** lemongrass <***Loc:*** Da84, Ho90>

citronnier [sitrɔ̃je] *n.m.* citron plant <***Loc:*** Da84>

citrouille [sitruj] *n.f.* pumpkin <***Loc:*** Ho90>

cive [siv] *n.f.* drinking straw <***Loc:*** VM>

civette [sivɛt] *n.f.* skunk, polecat, civet cat <***Loc:*** Da84>

civil, -e [sivil] *adj.* civil, well mannered, polite, considerate *Le juge a demandé au monde de rester civil durant le procès.* The judge asked the people to remain civil during the trial. (LA) <***Loc:*** LA, LF, Da84>

civilisation [sivilizasjɔ̃] *n.f.* civilization <***Loc:*** Da84>

civilisé, -e [sivilize] *adj.* civilized, polite *Comporte-toi comme du monde civilisé!* Act like civilized people! (VM) <***Loc:*** VM, Da84>

civiliser [sivilize] *v.tr.* to civilize *C'est Martin Weber qu'a civilisé les Marais Bouleur.* Martin Weber civilized the Marais Bouleur. (EV) <***Loc:*** EV, Da84>

civilité [sivilite] *n.f.* civility, courtesy, politeness <***Loc:*** Da84>

civique [sivik] *adj.* civic *Le Centre Civique de Lac Charles.* The Lake Charles Civic Center. (VM) <***Loc:*** VM, Da84>

clac (claque) [klak] *onom.* clack <***Loc:*** Da84>

claion ♦see **clayon**

clair[1], -e [klær] *adj.* **1** clear, transparent *Quand l'eau est claire dans le bayou, la pêche est bonne pour les sacalaits.* When the water is clear in the bayou, it is good for fishing white perch. (VM, Gu00) **2** plain, clear, obvious *C'est clair qu'elle l'aime pas.* It's obvious that she doesn't like him. (LA) **3** bright, light, well lit *Et là, tu prépares pas des portraits dans une chambre claire comme ça non. Il faut tu soyes dans le noir.* And you don't develop the pictures in a lit room like this, no, you have to be in the dark. (VM) **4** scarce, sparse, rare *Y a plus de monde qui piègent asteur, ça met les bêtes plus claires.* There are more people trapping now, it makes animals scarcer. (Lv88) **5** thin (of a liquid) *Avec ce test, si mon sang est clair.* With this test, if my blood is thin. (VM) **6** unfertilized (of an egg) *Oeuf clair.* Unfertilized egg. (LF) **7** impotent *Homme clair.* Impotent man. (LF) ◊ **•clair comme de l'eau trouble {de la boue} / clair comme du jus de tabac {chique}** clear as mud (i.e. unclear) <EV, La99> **•clair comme le jour {un miroir}** as clear as day (i.e. very clear) <EV, VM, Da84, La99> **•faire claire** to be light, be daylight *J'avais fini de bouillir avant il faisait clair.* I had finished boiling before it was light. (SL) <SL> <***Loc:*** AC, EV, LA, SL, SM, TB, VM, Da84, Gu00, La99, Lv88>

clair[2] [klær] *n.m.* light, brightness, shine ◊ **•clair de lune** moonlight *La lune était claire, la lune était pleine, et il faisait clair de lune.* The moon was bright, the moon was full, and it was a moonlit night. (LF) <EV, LF, Da84, Gu00>

•être dans le clair to be in the clear *Pour si eusse t'attrapes après pêcher, faut que tu les montres ça, t'es dans le clair. Si t'as pas ça, t'es dans le noir.* Because if they catch you fishing, you have to show them that, you're in the clear. If you don't have that, you're in trouble. (TB) <TB> **•mettre au clair** to bring out into the open <Da84> <***Loc:*** EV, LF, TB, Da84, Guoo>

clair[3] [klær] *n.m.* clearing in the woods or in a marsh <***Loc:*** Guoo>

clair[4] [klær] *adv.* clearly *Mais ça il se rappelait bien clair.* But he remembered that clearly. (Lv88) ◊ **•tout à clair** clearly, plainly, distinctly *La leçon est écrite tout à clair.* The lesson is written clearly. (SB) <SB, TB, VM, Lv88, Re31> <***Loc:*** SB, TB, VM, Lv88, Re31>

clairement [klærmɑ̃] *adv.* clearly, obviously, evidently <***Loc:*** Da84>

clairiasse [klærjas] *n.f.* weak coffee, watered-down coffee <***Loc:*** SM>

clairté ♦see **clarté**

clajeux [klaʒø] *n.m.* poison-flag, water-flag <***Loc:*** AV, Re31>

clamer [klɑ̃me] *v.tr.* **1** to claim *Il clame ça qu'est pour lui.* He claims what is his. (Lv88) **2** to claim, maintain *Eusse clame que ça a un goût comme la poule frit.* They claim it tastes like fried chicken. (TB) <***Loc:*** TB, Da84, Fa77, Lv88>

clan ♦see **klan**

claque ♦see **clac**

claquée [klake] *n.f.* a series of blows or slaps <***Loc:*** JD>

claquer [klake] *v.intr.* **1** to clack, make a clacking sound *Nos dents claquaient, nos genoux claquaient à force qu'on avait froid.* Our teeth were clacking, our knees were clacking, we were so cold. (JD) **2** to snap, come to a head (of a situation) *J'ai resté assis, je savais que il y avait quelque chose qu'allait claquer. Je pouvais le voir dans la figure.* I remained seated, I knew something was going to snap. I could see it in his face. (TB) ◊ **•claquer son fouet** to crack one's whip, snap one's whip <Da84> <***Loc:*** JD, TB, Da84>

clarifier [klarifje] *v.tr.* to clarify *Laisse-moi clarifier ça je viens de dire.* Let me clarify what I just said. (LA) <***Loc:*** LA, Da84>

clarifieuse [klariføz] *n.f.* clarifying tank (in a sugar refinery) *Le vin de canne est passé dans une clarifieuse pour retirer la marc dedans le vin de canne.* The cane juice is passed through a clarifying tank to remove the dregs. (TB) <***Loc:*** TB>

clarinette [klarinɛt, klɛrinɛt, klɛrinet] *n.f.* clarinet <***Loc:*** SM, VM>

clarté (**clairté**) [klarte, klærte] *n.f.* **1** light *Et là j'ai vu une clarté brillante entre ces deux plants-là.* And then I saw a bright light between those two plants. (TB) *Tu es dans ma clarté et je peux pas lire.* You're in my light and I can't read. (AV) **2** daytime, sunlight ◊ **•à la clarté** in the light <Da84> **•clarté du jour** light of day, daylight <LF> <***Loc:*** AV, IB, JD, LA, LF, SJ, TB, Da84, Lv88>

classe [klas] *n.f.* **1** class, type, order **2** class (group or cohort of pupils or students) *Alle est la meilleure espeleure de la classe.* She is the best speller in the class. (AV) *Le pauvre maître d'école pouvait pas seulement gouverner sa classe.* The poor schoolteacher could not even control his class. (LA) **3** class, course *Eux-autres avait commencé à faire une classe français.* They had started doing a French class. (TB) **4** classroom *Le maître d'école a gambadé à travers de la classe comme un jeune chevreuil.* The teacher romped across the classroom like a young deer. (VM) ◊ **•faire classe** to teach school *Elle fait classe de dix heures à midi.* She teaches from ten to noon. (SB) <SB> <***Loc:*** AV, LA, SB, TB, VM, Da84>

classer [klase] **I** *v.tr.* to class, classify, arrange in order *Si le marchand gagnait assez d'argent, il montait une deuxième charrette, puis une troisième, et il était classé selon la quantité de ses charrettes.* If the merchant earned enough money, he set up a second wagon, then a third, and he was classed according to the quality of his wagons. (VM) **II se classer** *v.pron.* to class o.s, classify o.s. *Il se classait parmi les plus forts de la place.* He classed himself among the strongest of the place. (LA) <***Loc:*** LA, VM, Da84>

clavicule [klavikyl, klavityl] *n.f.* **1** clavicle, collarbone *La petite fille a déplacé sa clavicule.* The little girl dislocated her collarbone. (VM) **2** shoulder blade <***Loc:*** VM, Da84>

clayon (**cléon, claion**) [klɛjɔ̃, kleɔ̃] *n.m.* **1** gate (in a fence), small yard gate **2** large farm gate *Détourner les bêtes avant qu'ils arrivent au clayon ouvert.* To turn the cattle back before they get to the open gate. (VM) <***Loc:*** SL, SM, VM, Da84, Guoo>

clé ♦see **clef**

CLEAVE [kliv] *n.* meat cleaver <***Loc:*** JE>

cléclette [kleklɛt] *n.f.* curl, permanent wave (in the hair) *Alle s'est fait mettre des cléclettes.* She got a permanent. (AV) <***Loc:*** AV>

clef (**clé**) [kle] *n.f.* **1** key **2** wrench **3** key, tonality (in music) *Mon vas apprendre mes clés et tout ça et commencer avec la musique.* I'll start with my kcys and all and start learning music. (TB) ◊ **•clef anglaise** ***a*** monkey wrench ***b*** wrench <AC, Da84> **•mettre en clef** to lock *Il a mis la porte en clef.* He locked the door. (AV) <AV> <***Loc:*** AC, AV, EV, LA, LF, SL, TB, VM, Da84>

clématis [klematis] *n.m.* clematis <***Loc:*** Lv88>

cléon ♦see **clayon**

clergé [klærʒe] *n.m.* clergy <***Loc:*** Da84>

cléter [klete] *v.tr.* to lock *J'ai clété la porte.* I locked the door. (EV, Ph36) <***Loc:*** EV, IB, Ph36>

cliché [kliʃe] *n.m.* trite saying, cliché <***Loc:*** Da84>

cliclique (**cli-clique**) [kliklik] *n.m.* sparrow hawk <***Loc:*** AV, IB, Lv88, Re31>

client [klijã] *n.m.* client, customer <***Loc:*** SM, Da84>

clientèle [klijãtɛl] *n.f.* clientele, practice <***Loc:*** Da84>

climat (**climette**) [klima, klimɛt] *n.m.* climate *Dans le vieux temps y avait des mulets créoles. C'est un mulet qu'a été elevé ici qui habitué de le climette, de la chaleur, de l'humidité.* In the old days there were Creole mules. That's a mule that was raised here and is used to the climate, to the heat and the humidity. (LF) <***Loc:*** LF, Da84>

clin [klɛ̃] *n.m.* **1** wink **2** decline ◊ **•clin de lune** waning of the moon <Da84> **•clin d'œil** wink *La vie a passé tellement vite, ça semble comme un clin d'œil.* Life passed so fast, it seems like the blink of an eye. (IB) **Dans un clin d'œil.* Quick as a wink. (Da84) <IB, Da84> <***Loc:*** IB, Da84>

clinique [klinik] *n.f.* clinic <***Loc:*** SB, Da84>

clips [klips] *n.m.* clippers *Le barbier rase en avant et passe le clips en arrière.* The barber shaves in the front and uses the clippers in the back. (VM) <***Loc:*** VM>

clique [klik] *n.f.* clique, group <***Loc:*** Da84>

clivier [klivje] *n.m.* tool used to insert wooden pegs in construction <***Loc:*** EV>

cloasser ♦see **closser**

cloche [klɔʃ] *n.f.* **1** bell *Comme la cloche sonnait nous-autres vadait dehors pour jouer.* When the bell rang we would go outside to play. (TB) **2** doorbell *Eusse vient cogner à la porte ou eusse sonne la cloche.* They come knock on the door or they ring the doorbell. (TB) **3** blister **4** domed cover **5** jingle bell, small ornamental bell (as on a costume) **6** bee hive ◊ **•cloche d'eau** blister *La brûlure a fait une cloche d'eau.* The burn caused a blister. (Lv88) <Fa77, Lv88> <***Loc:*** AL, EV, SM, TB, An94, Da84, Fa77, Lv88>

clocher[1] [kloʃe] *v.intr.* to blister *Il s'a brûlé au soleil et ça a cloché.* He got sunburned and it blistered. (VM) <***Loc:*** JD, LA, LF, SB, SM, VM, Da84, Lv88>

clocher[2] ♦see **closser**

clocher[3] [kloʃe] *n.m.* steeple, belfry <***Loc:*** Da84>

cloison (**croison**) [klwazɔ̃, krwazɔ̃] *n.f.* partition, dividing wall (in a house) *Ils ont ôté la croison entre les deux chambres devant.* They removed the dividing wall between the two front rooms. (AV) <***Loc:*** AV, IB, SJ, SL, TB, Da84, Re31>

clos[1], **-e** [klo, -oz] *adj.* **1** enclosed, closed **2** sealed *Ma maison était pas bien close avant que je change mes chassis.* My house was not well sealed before I changed my windows. (LA) <***Loc:*** LA, Da84>

clos[2] [klo] *n.m.* field *J'ai travaillé dans les clos pour cinquante sous par jour.* I worked in the fields for fifty cents a day. (VM) ◊ **•clos de maïs** cornfield, patch of corn <Da84> **•clos de patates** potato field <Lv88> **•clos de riz** rice field <LA, VM, Gu00, Lv88> **•clos d'huile** oilfield <SL, Gr86, Lv88> <***Loc:*** AC, AV, LA, SB, SL, SM, VM, Da84, Gr86, Gu00, Lv88>

closette [klozɛt] *n.f.* closet *Le chat a attrapé une souris dans la closette.* The cat caught a mouse in the closet. (AV) <***Loc:*** AV, Lv88>

closser (**cloasser**, **clocher**, **crosser**, **crousser**) [klose, klwase, kloʃe, krose, kruse] *v.intr.* to cackle (esp. of a hen that has laid an egg) *La poule a pondu, alle est après clocher.* The hen laid an egg, she's cackling. (VM) <***Loc:*** SL, SM, VM>

clôture [klotyr] *n.f.* enclosure, closing <***Loc:*** Da84>

clou [klu] *n.m.* **1** nail, peg **Pepère Gustave voulait que Sosthène attache les chevrons et les poteaux ensemb' avec des chevilles de bois, mais Sosthène lui voulait user des clous carrés.* Pepère Gustave wanted Sosthène to attach the rafters with wooden pegs, but Sosthène wanted to use square nails. (Gu82) **2** skin eruption (boil, pimple, sty) *Alle était après nettoyer un NUTRIA et ça lui a pissé dessus. Ouais! Alle avait eu comme des clous dans le nez. Alle était bien malade avec ça.* She was cleaning a nutria and it pissed on her. Yeah! She had like boils in her nose. She was quite sick with that. (TB) ◊ **•clou de girofle** whole clove <Da84, VM> **•clou de marteau** nail <EV, SL> <***Loc:*** EV, JE, LA, LF, SL, SM, TB, VM, An84, Da84, Gu00, Gu82, Lv88>

clouage [kluaʒ] *n.m.* act of nailing <***Loc:*** Da84>

clou-clou ♦see **clouclouque**

clouclouque (**clou-clou, clouk-clouk**) [klukluk, kluku] *n.m.* greater yellow-legs <***Loc:*** IB, Re31>

clouer (**clouver**) [klue, kluve] *v.tr.* to nail *Papa a été, il a tout clouvé les fenêtres et les portes de ma chambre à coucher.* Papa went and he nailed shut all the windows and doors of my bedroom. (EV) <***Loc:*** EV, LF, SB, TB, Da84>

clouk-clouk ♦see **clouclouque**

clouver ♦see **clouer**

CLUB [klʌb] *n.m.* **1** club, nightclub *Mon je suis l'homme qu'a rouvert le BARROOM ici. Et tu pouvais amener ta femme et ton mari et boire quelques DRINK et danser. J'ai couru un petit CLUB sept ans.* I'm the man who opened the barroom here. You could bring your wife or your husband and have a few drinks and dance. I ran a little club for seven years. (LF) **2** club, association *Il était membre d'un CLUB des éleveurs de bêtes.* He was a member of a cattlemen's club. (LA) <***Loc:*** LA, LF, Da84, Lv88>

clystère (**crystère, cristère**) [klistær, kristær] *n.m.* **1** enema **2** douche <***Loc:*** SB, SL, SM, Da84, Lv88>

co (**cope**) [ko, kop] *interj.* cry used to call a horse <***Loc:*** SM>

COAL OIL (**coloïe**) [kolɔj] *n.m.* coal oil, kerosene *Et là t'avais un STOVE à COAL OIL pour cuire.* And then you had a kerosene stove for cooking. (Lv88) <***Loc:*** AV, TB, Gr86, Lv88>

coloïe ♦see **COAL OIL**

cobalt [kobalt] *n.m.* cobalt <***Loc:*** TB>

cobbe [kɔb] *n.m.* snap hook <***Loc:*** VM>

cobi, -e [kobi] *adj.* **1** bent, twisted, crooked *Mon dos est tout cobi.* My back is all crooked. (Lv88) **2** dented *Le char a capoté, il est tout cobi asteur.* The car flipped over, it's all dented up now. (Lv88) <***Loc:*** AC, LF, SM, Da84, Lv88>

cobiche [kobiʃ] *n.f.* nick, dent (in a metal object) <***Loc:*** JD>

cobir [kobir] *v.tr.* **1** to bend, twist, make crooked *Cobir un tuyau.* To bend a pipe. (VM) **2** to dent *Il a tout cobi son char dans le* WRECK. He completely dented his car in the wreck. (LA) <***Loc:*** JD, LA, VM, Da84, Lv88>

cobissure [kobisyr] *n.f.* **1** bend **2** dent <***Loc:*** Da84>

cocagne [kokɑ̃j] *n.* drunkard <***Loc:*** LF, SM>

cocarde [kokar(d), kokar(t)] *n.f.* **1** ribbon *Quelle belle cocarde rouge!* What a fine red ribbon! (TB) **2** bow (tied from a ribbon) <***Loc:*** LF, TB>

cochage ♦see **corsage**

coche [kɔʃ, kɔrʃ] *n.f.* **1** nick, gouge *Si tu manquais ton clou, t'aurais arraché une coche dans ton* CEILING TILE. If you missed the nail, you would've gouged a nick in your ceiling tile. (SL) **2** slot, notch *Faire une coche dans le bois.* To make a notch in the wood. (EV) ◊ **•faire une coche mal taillée** to be mistaken, make a big mistake <AC, JE, La99, Lv88> <***Loc:*** AC, EV, JE, SL, TB, VM, Da84, La99>

cocher[1] [koʃe] *v.tr.* to notch, nick *Le constable a coché son bâton pour chaque bataille.* The bouncer notched his stick for each fight. (LA) <***Loc:*** LA, Da84>

cocher[2] [koʃe] *n.m.* driver of a carriage or car, coachman <***Loc:*** Da84>

cochère [koʃær] *adj.* ◊ **•porte cochère** carport <Da84> <***Loc:*** Da84>

cochon[1], **-onne** [koʃɔ̃, -ɔ̃n] *adj.* **1** dirty (of a word, joke, etc.) *T'aurais manière dit un mot cochon, puis là la fille t'aurait foutu un coup de tape sur la gueule.* You would have said a dirty word and then the girl would have given you a slap on the mouth. (LA) **WELL, les petits contes cochons, tu connais, on racontait pas ça quand il y avait des filles, tu connais, parce que dans ces temps-ça, c'était un tas plus suspect qu'asteur.* Well, the little dirty jokes, you know, we didn't tell them when there were girls, you know, because in those days, people were a lot more easily offended than now. (LA, An94) **2** nasty, filthy (of a person) *Elle est une femme cochonne qui garde des vilaines manières.* She's a filthy woman who has nasty habits. (SL) <***Loc:*** LA, SL, An94, Da84, Lv88>

cochon[2] [koʃɔ̃, kɔ̃ʃɔ̃] *n.m.* **1** pig, hog *J'ai mis un cochon à l'engrais.* I fattened up a pig. (LA) **2** pork *Tout nous-autres, on se mettait à la table, et on avait du riz, et du cochon avec de la viande frit, pour déjeuner.* All of us, we sat down at the table, and we had rice, and pork with fried meat for lunch. (LF) *Un rôti de cochon.* A pork roast. (TB) **3** dirty, untidy man **4** scup, southern porgy ◊ **•cochon de garde** wild boar <TB> **•cochon de lait** ***a*** suckling pig ***b*** social gathering at which a suckling pig is roasted <AV, Da84> **•cochon farouche** wild boar <AV, Lv88> **•cochon guinée** guinea pig <IB> **•faire le cochon de Saint Antoine** to roam around from place to place <TB, La99> **•petit cochon tonquin** very short, fat pig <SM> <***Loc:*** AC, AV, EV, IB, IV, JE, LA, LF, SJ, SL, SM, TB, VM, An94, Da84, Gu00, La99, Lv88, Ph36, Re31>

cochon[3] [koʃɔ̃] *adv.* indecently, in a vulgar way *Chien était dans la salle après danser cochon.* Chien [a nickname] was in the dancehall dancing in a vulgar manner. (LA) <***Loc:*** LA>

cochondrie ♦see **cochonnerie**

cochonne[1] ♦see **cochon**

cochonne[2] [koʃɔ̃n] *n.f.* filthy woman <***Loc:*** SB>

cochonner [koʃɔ̃ne] *v.tr.* to dirty, spoil, mess up *On l'avait engagé pour peinturer la chambre, mais il a tout cochonné l'affaire.* We had hired him to paint the room, but he made a big mess of it. (EV) <***Loc:*** EV, LA, Da84>

cochonnerie (**cochondrie**) [koʃɔ̃nri, koʃɔ̃dri] *n.f.* **1** immoral or indecent act, sordid deed *Elle l'a divorcé par rapport à ses cochonneries.* She divorced him because of the nasty things he had done. (EV) *Il fait ses cochonneries avec une capote.* He does his dirty work with a prophylactic. (JE) **2** nastiness, filth **3** pigsty, pigpen **4** piece of work done poorly or in a slipshod manner *C'est la cochondrie que vous avez fait.* This work you've done is garbage. (SB) **5** worthless thing, piece of junk or trash *Il a gaspillé son argent sur des cochondries.* He spent his money on garbage. (IB) ◊ **•dire des cochonneries** to say nasty things, tell dirty jokes <Da84> **•faire des cochonneries** to do nasty things <Da84> <***Loc:*** EV, IB, JE, LA, SB, SL, SM, Da84, Ph36, Wh83>

cochonneur [koʃɔ̃nœr] *n.m.* one who does bad or sloppy work <***Loc:*** Lv88>

cochonnier[1], **-ière** [koʃɔ̃je, -jær] *adj.* dirty, slovenly <***Loc:*** Re38>

cochonnier[2] [koʃɔ̃je] *n.m.* pigsty, pigpen <***Loc:*** LA, SB, Lv88, Re38>

cochonnière[1] ♦see **cochonnier**[1]

cochonnière[2] [koʃɔ̃jær] *n.f.* pigsty, pigpen <***Loc:*** Re38>

cochotte [koʃɔt] *n.f.* zucchini, courgette <***Loc:*** SM>

coco [koko] *n.m.* **1** coconut **2** head **3** [*baby talk*] egg **4** cocograss, nut grass (type of weed) *Il faut arracher tout ce coco là.* We need to pull up all of that nutgrass. (TB) **5** cacao **6** chocolate **7** *(ironic or affectionate term for a person) Espèce de coco, viens me béquer.* You little rascal, come here and give me a kiss. (TB) ◊ **•beau coco** unusual character, nut, oddball, weirdo **Tu parles d'un beau coco, celui-là!* Talk about a character, that one! (EV, La99) <EV, La99> <***Loc:*** AC, EV, IB, LA, LF, SB, SM, TB, VM, Da84, La99, Lv88, Ph36>

cocobanane [kokobɑ̃nɑ̃n] *n.f.* cassabanana, curuba, musk cucumber (type of gourd with a curved neck, used to make jam) <***Loc:*** IB>

cocodaine ♦see **cocodinde**

cocodinde (**cocodaine**) [kokodɛ̃d, kokodɛ̃n] *n.m.* *(occ. f.)* freckle *Sa figure est pleine de cocodaines.* Her face is full of freckles. (AV) <***Loc:*** AV, IB, SB, SL, SM, TB, Lv88>

cocodrie (**crocodril, crocodile**) [kokodri, kokodril] *n.m.* **1** alligator *Vous-autres a déjà vu un cocodrie?* Have you ever seen an alligator? (AC) **2** crocodile *Nous-autres on a des alligators icitte, les cocodries peut-être dans la Floride mais pas icitte.* We have alligators here, crocodiles can be found in Florida but not here. (AC) **3** fool, ass *Cette espèce de cocodrie, je l'aime pas.* That ass, I don't like him. (IB) <***Loc:*** AC, AV, EV, IB, IV, JD, LA, LF, SB, SL, SM, TB, VM, Da84, Guoo, Lv88, Ph36>

cocombre (**concombre**) [kokɔ̃m, kokɔ̃b(r)] *n.m.* cucumber ◊ **•cocombre-sent-bon** creeping cucumber, melonette (locally known as "smellin' melon") <EV> **•cocombre zombi** horse nettle <SB> <***Loc:*** AC, AV, CL, EV, IB, JE, LA, LF, SL, SM, TB, VM, Da84, Re31>

coconnage ♦see **cancanage**

cocotte [kokɔt] *n.f.* **1** hen **2** [*vulg.*] female genitals <***Loc:*** EV, LF, SB, SM, Da84, Guoo, La99, Lv88, Ph36, Re31>

cocu [kotʃy] *n.m.* cuckold <***Loc:*** LF>

codache [kodaʃ] *adj.* foolish <***Loc:*** SJ>

cœur [kœr, tʃœr, kɔr] *n.m.* **1** heart *Battement de cœur.* Heartbeat. (Da84) *Mais t'es la seule mon cœur désire.* But you are the only one my heart desires. (ch: *La valse du bambocheur*) **2** heart (in a deck of cards) **3** core, center **4** (*in fig. uses*) stomach **Le peu que j'ai mangé m'a barbouillé le cœur.* The little I ate upset my stomach. (Di32) **5** courage ◊ **•cœur de poule** one who is sensitive to physical pain <JD> **•cœur noir** base person, despicable person <La99> **•à contre cœur** unwillingly, reluctantly *Il a été, mais à contre cœur.* He went, but unwillingly. (LA) <LA> **•avoir le cœur gros {gros cœur}** ***a*** to have a heavy heart, be sad ***b*** to be on the verge of tears <Da84, La99> **•avoir le cœur sur ses bras** to wear one's heart on one's sleeve *Et p'is c'est trop de tristesse, mon j'ai le cœur sur mes bras quand je vois tous ces enfants là, tu sais.* And then it's too sad, I have my heart on my sleeve when I see all those children there, you know. (TB) <TB> **•avoir le cœur tendre** to be tenderhearted <Da84> **•avoir (qqch) sur le cœur** to be chagrined by s.t., have s.t. bothering one <La99> **•avoir un cœur de poisson** to be a weakling <Lv88> **•avoir un cœur de poule** to be timid <Lv88> **•avoir (un) cœur de roi** to be good natured <Lv88> **•avoir un cœur lourd** ***a*** to have a heavy heart, be sad ***b*** to be on the verge of tears <La99> **•avoir un cœur noir** to be wicked, be bad <Lv88> **•casser le cœur** to break one's heart <Da84, Lv88> **•(de) bon cœur** kind, good, good hearted, generous *Il est bon cœur.* He is generous. (Lv88) *Elle est bon cœur. Elle ferait n'importe quoi pour toi.* She's kind. She would do anything for you. (SM) <SM, Da84, Lv88> **•de bon cœur** willingly, gladly, with a good heart <Da84> **•de tout mon cœur** with all my heart <Da84> **•faire le gros cœur à** to sadden, distress *Ça m'a fait gros cœur. Je jonglais,* OH, MY GOD*! C'est là Nell sera enterrée!* It made me sad. I thought, Oh, my God! That's where Nell will be buried! (SL) <SL> **•j'ai pas le cœur** I don't have the heart <Da84> **•sans cœur** heartless <Da84> **•sans-cœur** hard pitiless person <SB, La99> <***Loc:*** IB, JD, JE, LA, SB, SL, SM, TB, VM, Da84, La99, Lv88>

cofaire ♦see **quoi faire**

coffre [kɔf(r)] *n.m.* **1** coffer, chest, box *Eusse a levé un gros coffre de ce trou-là avec des cordes et des chaînes et tout.* They lifted a large chest from that hole with ropes and chains and all. (LF) **2** coffin *Ma mame et ma sœur, une de mes sœurs, les deux est mortes dans une journée à l'hôpital. Les deux a été enterrées dans le même coffre.* My mother and my sister, one of my sisters, they died the same day at the hospital. The two of them were both buried in the same coffin. (TB) <***Loc:*** LF, TB, Da84>

coffre-fort [kofrəfɔr, kɔ̃fləfɔr] *n.m.* safe, strong-box <***Loc:*** LF, SJ, Da84>

coffrer [kofre] *v.tr.* **1** to gore *Un taureau l'a coffré.* A bull gored him. (VM) **2** to spur *Le guème m'a coffré la jambe quand j'ai rentré dans la basse-cour.* The rooster spurred me in the leg when I went into the chicken yard. (VM) **3** to claw, scratch with the claws *Ce chat a bien coffré mon chien.* That cat really clawed my dog. (IB) **4** to stab *Il a coffré l'homme avec son* BARLOW. He stabbed the man with his knife. (AV) **5** to hit, strike *Il l'a coffré d'un coup de bâton.* He dealt him a blow with a stick. (LF) <***Loc:*** AV, EV, IB, LF, SJ, SM, VM, Da84, Lv88, Ph36>

cognac [kɔ̃jak] *n.m.* cognac, brandy <***Loc:*** Da84>

cogner [kɔ̃je] **I** *v.tr.* **1** to hit, strike *J'étais assez canaille, quand j'étais dans le cinquième grade dans l'école publique, ça m'a* KICK OUT*, oh oui j'étais pas bon, j'ai cogné la maîtresse, j'ai honte mais elle m'a cogné à moi en premier.* I was rather unruly, when I was in the fifth grade in public school, they kick me out, oh yes I was bad, I hit the school teacher, I am ashamed but she hit me first. (IB) **2** to run into, bump into *La seule chose qui m'a arrêté, un jour j'avais été assez bas, j'ai cogné un chicot.* The only thing that stopped me, one day I had been so low, I ran into a tree stump. (SL) *Il m'a jusqu'à cogné avec son coude, il m'a pas reconnu.* He even bumped me with his elbow, but he didn't recognize me. (VM) **II** *v.intr.* **1** to knock *Eusse vient cogner à la porte ou eusse sonne la cloche.* They come knock on the door or they ring the doorbell. (TB) **2** to bump, strike (into, against) *Il a cogné son char contre un arbre.* He bumped his car into a tree. (LA) **III se cogner** *v.pron.* **1** to hit o.s. **Et puis il se cognait l'estomac, tu connais, comme s'il avait devenu un taureau tout du coup.* And then he was beating his chest, you know, as though he had become a bull all of a sudden. (SL, An94) *Quand il s'a cogné, il s'a fait un beau nocoillot.* When he struck himself he made himself quite a bump. (IB) **2** to knock o.s., bump o.s. *Il s'a cogné la hanche contre le comptoir.* He hit his hip against the counter. (EV) ◊ **•cogner des clous** to nod off while avoiding sleep <La99> **•cogner qqn comme une bol de merde** to hit s.o. like a ton of bricks (i.e. to become suddenly apparent to s.o., usu.

said of an important idea or realization) <La99> **•cogner un bon somme** to take a good nap <SM> <***Loc:*** AC, AV, EV, IB, LA, SB, SL, SM, TB, VM, An94, Da84, Gu00, La99, Lv88>

cohéritier [koeritje] *n.m.* co-heir <***Loc:*** Da84>

coiffage [kwafaʒ] *n.m.* hairdo, coiffure, manner of styling the hair <***Loc:*** JD>

coiffé, -e [kwafe] *adj.* **1** coiffed, having a type of hairdo *Elle est toujours bien coiffée.* She's always got a nice hairdo. (EV) **2** having a veil or caul on one's face at birth *Elle est née coiffée.* She was born with a veil. (SL) <***Loc:*** EV, SL>_

coiffer [kwafe] *v.tr.* to cover the head *Il faut que tu sois coiffée avant de rentrer dans l'église.* You have to have your head covered before going into church. (VM) <***Loc:*** VM, Da84>

coiffeur, -euse [kwafœr, -øz] *n.* hairdresser <***Loc:*** Da84>

coiffure [kwafyr] *n.f.* **1** hairdo, coiffure, manner of styling the hair **2** headpiece <***Loc:*** Da84>

coin[1] [kwɛ̃] *n.m.* **1** corner *Alle va aller pendre sa robe là dans le coin là dans sa chambre.* She'll go hang her dress there in the corner of her room. (TB) **2** wedge used to split wood *Si ça voulait fendre quelque chose, ça mettait un coin, ça appelait, mettait un coin dedans. Ça partait, ça le cognait avec une masse.* If they wanted to split something, they would put a wedge, it was called putting in a wedge. They started, they would hit it with a sledgehammer. (SL) **3** brace *Coin de guet.* Corner brace. (VM) ◊ **•coin de fer** wedge used to split wood <SL> **•en coin** cater-cornered, diagonal <VM> <***Loc:*** EV, IB, LA, SL, TB, VM, An94, Da84>

coin[2] ♦see **coinque**

coincement [kwɛ̃smɑ̃] *n.m.* wedging, jamming <***Loc:*** Da84>

coincer [kwɛ̃se] **I** *v.tr.* **1** to wedge, jam, bind **2** to corner *Je pouvais pas m'empêcher d'y parler. Il m'avait de coincé dans l'allée.* I could not avoid talking to him. He had me cornered in the aisle. (VM) **3** to garnish (one's wages) *BUT ils ont passé une loi pour aller par-derrière des papes ou les mames. Si la mame laisse l'enfant à la valdrague et qu'alle a un job, ils vont coincer ton CHECK. T'appelles ça GARNISH ici.* But they passed a law for going after the dads or the moms. If the mom leaves the child abandoned and she has a job, they'll hold back your check. They call that a garnish here. (TB) **II se coincer** *v.pron.* to get (o.s. or one's finger, etc.) jammed or caught *Se coincer un doigt.* To get one's finger jammed or caught. (EV) <***Loc:*** EV, IV, LA, TB, VM, Da84>

coinque (cainque, coin) [kwɛ̃k, kɛ̃k, kwɛ̃] *onom.* quack ◊ **•pas dire coinque** to say nothing, not say a word <EV, IB, SM, VM, Ph36> <***Loc:*** EV, IB, SM, TB, VM, Ph36>

coinquer [kwɛ̃ke] *v.intr.* ◊ **•pas coinquer** *(used only in the negative)* to not utter a word *Elle coinque pas quand il vient.* She doesn't say a word when he comes. (IB) <IB> <***Loc:*** IB>

cointer [kwɛ̃te] *v.tr.* **1** to put (a child) in the corner (as a punishment) **2** to lean, prop **J'ai cointé la chaise contre la porte pou pas a s'ouvre.* I leaned the chair against the door so it wouldn't open. (EV, Ph36) <***Loc:*** EV, Lv88, Ph36>

col [kɔl] *n.m.* collar <***Loc:*** Da84>

colère [kolær] *n.f.* **1** temper *Tu vas jamais jouer avec Milton. Il a trop une mauvaise colère et toi aussi.* You will never play with Milton. He has too much of a bad temper and so do you. (SL) *Et ça c'est la colère qu'il avait, cher! Il avait une colère affreux.* And that's the kind of temper he had, my dear! He had a terrible temper. (TB) **2** anger *Alle partait en colère de la table, parce qu'alle aimait pas le manger que je lui ai cuit.* She used to leave the table angry, because she didn't like the food I cooked for her. (TB) *Il aurait pas pu anticiper la colère de son voisin.* He could not have anticipated the anger of his neighbor. (LA) ◊ **•avoir une colère prime** to have a bad temper <VM> **•prendre une colère** to get angry <Da84> <***Loc:*** LA, PQ, SL, TB, VM, Da84, Lv88>

coléreux, -euse [kolerø, -øz] *adj.* prone to anger, hot-tempered *Elle savait pas qu'il était coléreux comme ça quand elle l'a marié.* She didn't know he was so hot-tempered when she married him. (LA) <***Loc:*** LA, Da84>

colibri [kolibri] *n.m.* **1** hummingbird **2** killdeer <***Loc:*** IB, JD, Da84, Re31>

colidor ♦see **corridor**

colinda ♦see **calinda**

colique [kolik] *n.f.* colic *Le bébé a les coliques.* The baby has colic. (EV) <***Loc:*** EV, LF, Da84>

collage [kolaʒ] *n.m.* gluing, act of gluing <***Loc:*** Da84>

collant, -e [kolɑ̃, -ɑ̃t] *adj.* **1** sticky, gluey, tacky *Je m'en rappelle de ça, c'était collant collant.* I remember that, it [the chinaball tree] was really sticky. (TB) **2** clingy, needy, possessive *Je sors pus avec elle parce qu'elle est trop collante.* I don't go out with her any more because she is too clingy. (VM) <***Loc:*** TB, VM, Da84>

collanter [kolɑ̃te] *v.tr.* to make sticky *Le candi a collanté ses mains.* The candy made his hands sticky. (SL) <***Loc:*** SL>

collation [kolasjɔ̃] *n.f.* **1** collation, light meal, snack between meals **2** reception (esp. for a wedding) *On allait se marier à l'église mais on revenait BACK, et la noce, la collation et tout ça c'était tout dans la cour.* We would go get married in church, but we came back, and the reception and all that was in the courtyard. (TB) <***Loc:*** TB, Da84>

colle [kɔl] *n.f.* **1** glue, paste *C'est une espèce de comme une colle qu'était pour boucher la tête des clous pour les empêcher de rouiller.* It was a sort of, like a glue that was to cover the heads of nails to prevent them from rusting. (LF) **2** label **3** cake made of brown sugar or molasses and nuts **4** lecture, scolding, stern talking-to *J'y ai foutu une colle.* I really gave it to him. (JD) <***Loc:*** JD, LA, VM, Da84, Lv88, Re31>

collé[1], **-e** [kole] *adj.* stuck *Il était trempe; ses cheveux étaient* *collés à sa tête.* He was wet; his hair was stuck to his head. (JD) ◊ **•collé comme un sangsue** stuck like a leech (refers to a guest who won't leave or an acquaintance who is a pest) *Il était collé comme un sangsue. Je croyais qu'il allait jamais partir.* He was stuck like a leech. I thought he would never leave. (EV) <EV, VM, La99> <***Loc:*** EV, JD, LA, VM, Da84, La99, Lv88>

collé[2] [kole] *adv.* near, very close *Je te vois dans ses bras après danser si collé.* I see you in his arms, dancing so close. (Lv88, ch: *Allons danser Colinda*) ◊ **•collé à {après / de}** next to, near *J'ai été élevée collé à l'eglise.* I was raised near the church. (Lv88) *C'était collé après la barrière.* It was next to the fence. (SM) *L'église est tout collée d'ici.* The church is very near here. (SM) <SM, Lv88> **•à collé de** adjacent to, next door to *Ils restont à collé de la maison.* They live right next to our house. (LA) <LA, Da84> <***Loc:*** LA, SM, Da84, Lv88>

collecter [kolɛkte, kolekte] *v.tr.* **1** to gather, collect (usu. money) *Il a collecté deux mille piastres.* He raised two thousand dollars. (Lv88) *Le monde qui étudie notre héritage essaie aujourd'hui de collecter des contes des vieux raconteurs avant qu'ils disparaissont.* The people who study our heritage try today to collect stories from the old storytellers before they are gone. (VM) **2** to collect, receive as payment *À la fin de la semaine, tu collectais neuf piastres et quelque chose, je crois que c'était, et tu pouvais aller au bal un soir ou deux avec ça.* At the end of the week you collected nine dollars and change, I think it was, and you could go to the dance a night or two with that. (TB) **II** *v.intr.* to collect payments *Il collecte pour le magasin.* He's a bill collector for the store. (IB) <***Loc:*** EV, IB, LF, SB, SJ, SL, SM, TB, VM, Da84, Lv88, Ph36>

collecteur [kolɛktœr, kolektœr] *n.m.* **1** collector **2** tax collector <***Loc:*** SM, TB, Da84, Lv88>

collection [kolɛksjɔ̃, koleksjɔ̃] *n.f.* collection (of money) *Faire une collection pour les pauvres.* To take up a collection for the poor. (SJ) <***Loc:*** IB, SB, SJ, SM, TB, Da84, Lv88>

collège [kolɛʒ] *n.m.* **1** college, university *Il est au collège, il est dans sa troisième année de collège à Shreveport, Centenary.* He's in college, he's in his third year of college in Shreveport, Centenary. (VM) **2** college or university studies *Il a fait son collège dessus le G.I. BILL.* He did his university studies on the G.I. Bill. (EV) **3** official body (e.g. college of cardinals) <***Loc:*** EV, TB, VM, Da84>

coller [kole] **I** *v.tr.* **1** to glue, stick with glue *Coller deux morceaux de papier ensemble.* To glue two pieces of paper together. (EV) **2** to stick, place *Mon mari a pris un oignon, et il l'a coupé en deux, et il l'a frotté dessus le bobo [...], et après qu'il a fait ça avec les deux morceaux d'oignon, il les a collé back ensemble.* My husband took an onion, he cut it in two, and he rubbed it on the wound, and after he did that with the two pieces of onion he stuck them back together. (TB) **3** to get hold of, get one's hands on *Si Jean te colle, il va te punir.* If John gets his hands on you he'll punish you. (LF) **4** to catch (s.o. doing s.t.) *Ils l'ont collé après voler des chevaux.* They caught him stealing horses. (LA) *Nous-autres on pouvait pas parler français du temps qu'on était à l'école, on été punis si on était collé à parler français.* We couldn't speak French while we were at school, we were punished if we were caught speaking French. (LF) **II** *v.intr.* to stick *Quand vous brassez un roux pour faire le gombo... il n'y a rien qui colle là-bas.* When you stir a roux to make gumbo . . . there's nothing that sticks there. (SL) **III se coller** *v.pron.* **1** to embrace, draw each other close *Eurgarde pas, ils se collont à cette heure.* Don't look, they're being close right now. (VM) **2** to stick, cling *Il s'a collé après moi et il m'a pas laissé tranquille toute la soirée.* He clung to me and didn't leave me alone the entire evening. (EV) **3** to stay *Il s'est collé là longtemps.* He stayed there a long time. (AV) ◊ **•coller à {après}** to adjoin, be adjoining *Mon jardin colle au sien.* My garden adjoins his. (SM) *L'école était collée après l'église.* The school adjoined the church. (Lv88) <SL, SM, VM, Lv88> **•coller une tape** to slap *Il m'a collé une tape.* He slapped me. (AV) <AV, TB> **•se coller sur** to be intimate with, associate with *Les autres enfants allont pas vouloir se coller sur toi avec ce darte-là.* The other children won't want to associate with you, with that skin disease. (VM) <VM> **•se coller un temps** to have a good time *On s'a collé un temps hier au soir. Bruce était après jouer.* We had a great time last night. Bruce was playing. (AV) <AV> **•se faire coller** to get caught (doing s.t.) *Dans le Canal Yankee le* SPEED LIMIT *est 30 miles a l'heure. Et si tu te fais coller à aller plus, tu vas te faire donner un* FINE. In Canal Yankee [i.e. Golden Meadow] the speed limit is 30 miles an hour. And if you get caught going faster, you'll be given a fine. (LF) <AV, LF, La99> <***Loc:*** AV, EV, LA, LF, SL, SM, TB, VM, Da84, La99, Lv88>

colletailler (**coltailler**) [koltaje] *v.intr.* to wrestle *Arrêtez de colletailler.* Stop wrestling. (Lv88) <***Loc:*** EV, LA, SL, SM, Lv88, Ph36>

collier [kolje] *n.m.* **1** necklace **2** collar (part of a harness) **3** ring around the neck (on certain ducks) **4** Wilson plover ◊ **•collier en bois** wooden collar <EV> **•collier en cuir** leather collar <EV> <***Loc:*** EV, SL, SM, TB, Da84, Lv88>

colline [kolin] *n.f.* hill <***Loc:*** Da84, Gu00>

colon [kolɔ̃] *n.m.* colonist, settler <***Loc:*** Da84>

colonel [kolɔ̃nɛl] *n.m.* colonel <***Loc:*** Da84>

coloniser [kolɔ̃nize] *v.tr.* to colonize *Coloniser un pays, coloniser un territoire.* To colonize a country, colonize a territory. (EV) <***Loc:*** EV, Da84>

colonnade [kolɔ̃nad] *n.f.* colonade <***Loc:*** Da84>

colonne [kolɔ̃n] *n.f.* **1** column, pillar *Les églises baptistes ont toujours des grosses colonnes devant.* Baptist churches always have big columns out in front. (VM) **2** column, linear formation *Une colonne de soldats.* A column of soldiers. (VM) **3** bedpost **4** tornado *J'ai déjà été pris avec une colonne quand on était après pêcher sur de l'eau. Elle a formé sur l'eau, elle a monté sur la terre, oh on avait peur.* I have been caught by a tornado while fishing on the water. It started from the water and then went on the ground, we were scared. (IB) **5** storm *Ça dit des colonnes mais c'est pour une bourrasque.* They say "colonnes" but it means a heavy downpour. (TB) <***Loc:*** AC, IB, IV, LA, LF, TB, VM, Da84, Guoo, Lv88>

colosse [kolɔs] *n.* **1** *(m.)* giant, colossus, huge and strong man or animal **C'était un colosse d'homme.* He was a giant of a man. (Da84) **2** *(f.)* very big woman *Une grosse colosse.* A very fat woman. (SL) <***Loc:*** SL, VM, Da84>

coltailler ♦see **colletailler**

coma [kɔ̃ma] *n.m.* coma <***Loc:*** Da84>

combat [kɔ̃ba] *n.m.* combat, strife, fight, struggle ◊ **•combat de la mort** death struggle <Da84> <***Loc:*** Da84>

combien[1] [kɔ̃bjɛ̃, kɔ̃bɛ̃, kobe, kobɛ̃, kɔ̃mjɛ̃] *adv.* how much, how many *Combien ça coûte, ça?* How much does that cost? (SM) *J'ai vu je sais pas combien de vaches dans le clos.* I saw I don't know how many cows in the field. (SM) <***Loc:*** AV, EV, LA, LF, SL, SM, TB, VM, An84, Da84, Lv88>

combien[2] [kɔ̃bjɛ̃, kɔ̃bɛ̃, kobe, kobɛ̃, kɔ̃mjɛ̃] *n.m.* date *Qué combien du mois c'est aujourd'hui?* What's the date today? (TB) *Le combien on est aujourd'hui, hein?* What's the date today? (JD) <***Loc:*** JD, TB>

combinaison [kɔ̃binezɔ̃, kɔ̃mynezɔ̃] *n.f.* **1** combination *La combinaison d'un coffre-fort.* The combination of a safe. (SJ) **2** scheme, plot <***Loc:*** AV, SJ, Da84>

combiner [kɔ̃bine] **I** *v.tr.* to plan, scheme, plot *Quoi c'est que vous-autres est après combiner là-bas?* What are you cooking up over there? (VM) **II se combiner** *v.pron.* to scheme, plot *Je suis après me combiner une manière de faire une cage à lapin.* I'm trying to think up a way to make a rabbit cage. (VM) <***Loc:*** VM, Da84>

comble [kɔ̃m, kɔ̃b(l)] *n.m.* top ◊ **•de fond en comble** from bottom to top <Da84> <***Loc:*** Da84>

combler [kɔ̃ble] *v.tr.* to fill up, fill to overflowing <***Loc:*** Da84>

combouille ♦see **cambouille**

comète [kɔ̃mɛt] *n.f.* comet, shooting star <***Loc:*** JD, Da84>

comique [kɔ̃mik] *adj.* comical, funny *Une histoire comique.* A comical story. (LA) <***Loc:*** LA, Da84>

comité [kɔ̃mite] *n.m.* committee, board ◊ **•comité d'église** church board of trustees <Da84> **•comité de vigilance** vigilance committee <JD, Da84> <***Loc:*** JD, LF, Da84>

commandant [kɔ̃mɑ̃dɑ̃] *n.m.* commander, commandant *Le commandant du Poste des Attakapas, c'était un Fusilier.* The commandant of the Attakapas Post was a Fusilier. (SM) <***Loc:*** SM, Da84>

commande [kɔ̃mɑ̃d] *n.f.* order (for merchandise) *Ils ont fait une commande pour de la graine de coton.* They made an order for cottonseed. (LA) <***Loc:*** LA, Da84>

commandement [kɔ̃mɑ̃dmɑ̃] *n.m.* commandment, order, rule ◊ **•Les Dix Commandements** The Ten Commandments <LF> <***Loc:*** LF, Da84>

commander [kɔ̃mɑ̃de] *v.tr.* to order (goods) *Commander du linge.* To order clothes. (VM) <***Loc:*** SM, VM, Da84>

comme[1] [kɔ̃m] *adv.* **1** like, as *Des gaffes à main c'était comme deux râteaux qu'avait un boulon dessus.* Oyster tongs were like two rakes that had a bolt on them. (LF) **2** how, how much *Tu vois comme je t'aime?* Do you see how I love you? (EV) **3** when *Comme le monde est venu je suis parti.* When everyone came I left. (SM) *Viens comme tu peux.* Come when you can. (SM) **4** like, for example, for instance *Aussitte le monde de Marksville et tout ça, la Paroisse de Avoyelles, y a des différentes mots. Comme une "chaudière," on appelle ça "une bombe."* Also people of Marksville and all that, Avoyelles Parish, there are different words. For example, [what they call] a "chaudière," we call that a "bombe." (TB) ◊ **•comme ça** ***a*** so *Comme ça, je vois t'as un nouveau job?* So, I see you have a new job? (SM) ***b*** pregnant <SM, La99> **•comme ci, comme ça** ***a*** this way and that ***b*** so-so <Da84> **•comme de fait** sure enough *Alle a jamais rappelé. Alle m'a fait ça une fois à moi. J'ai pensé entre moi-même, je vas te rappeler à toi. Et là comme de fait, alle a appelé, alle dit je vas te rappeler plus tard.* She never called back. She did that to me once. I thought to myself, I'll call you back. And then, sure enough, she called, and she said I'll call you back later. (TB) <TB> **•comme de juste** obviously, naturally, as it should be <Da84> **•comme des patates et des puces** like two peas in a pod (referring to people or things that go together naturally) <SL, La99> **•comme le fil en aiguille** very well, very smoothly <La99> **•comme si** as if *Comme si il va venir asteur.* As if he's going to come now. (LA) *Notre cousin de Béville nous dédaigne comme si il se croit plus que nous-autres.* Our cousin in Abbeville looks down on us as if he thinks he's better than we are. (VM) <EV, IV, LA, LF, SL, SM, TB, VM, An94, Da84, La99> **•comme tout** very, extremely, exceedingly *Il est laid comme tout!* He's ugly as anything! (SM) <IB, JE, SM, TB, VM, Da84> **•comme une plume** very well, very smoothly **Danser comme une plume.* To dance very well. (AC, La99) <AC, SM, La99> **•comme un papier de musique** ***a*** very well, very smoothly ***b*** very smooth <La99> **•c'est comme ça** it's like that, it's this way <Da84> **•c'est comme le feu et l'eau / c'est comme chat et chien** they're always quarreling <La99> **•c'est comme Saint Roch et son chien / c'est comme cul et coton de maïs** these two people are always together <La99> <***Loc:*** AC, AL, AS, EV, IB, IV, JD, JE, LA, LF, SJ, SL, SM, TB, VM, An84, An94, Da84, Guoo, La99, Lv88, Wh83>

comme[2] [kɔ̃m] *conj.* ◊ **•aussi... comme** as... as *Je chante aussi bien comme toi.* I sing as well as you. (SM) *Je vois ça* *aussi bien comme si c'était hier.* I see it as well as if it were yesterday. (Lv88) <SM, An84, Lv88> **•pareil comme** like, just as *Ça c'est pareil comme lui.* That's just like him. (SM) <IB, LA, LF, SL, SM, TB, VM, An94, Lv88> <***Loc:*** IB, LA, LF, SL, SM, TB, VM, An84, An94, Lv88>

commémorer [kɔ̃mɛ̃more] *v.tr.* to commemorate *Ils ont fait ça pour commémorer les soldats.* They did that to commemorate the soldiers. (LA) <***Loc:*** LA, Da84>

commencement [kɔ̃mɑ̃smɑ̃] *n.m.* beginning, start *Ils s'ont comportés au commencement, mais à la fin ils ont commencé à faire des brigandages.* They behaved themselves at the beginning, but at the end they started misbehaving. (SM) <***Loc:*** LF, SM, TB, VM, Da84>

commencer [kɔ̃mɑ̃se] **I** *v.tr.* to begin, start *Quand tu commences une maison, il faut tu mets tes murs d'aplomb.* When you begin a house, you have to plumb your walls. (LA) *Et là, dans quarante-huit j'ai commencé travailler pour un coopératif qui fait des prêts agricoles.* And then in forty-eight, I started working for a cooperative that makes farm loans. (SL) **II** *v.intr.* to begin, start *Il commence à faire un peu trop chaud pour travailler sur ça.* It's starting to be a little too hot to work on that. (LF) *Si vous commencez de matin vous serez de l'avant.* If you begin this morning you'll be ahead. (SB) *Une cigale, ça commence avec un ver dans la terre, une larve.* A cicada begins his life as a worm in the ground, a grub worm. (AV) *Avant que l'école commence.* Before school starts. (Lv88) <***Loc:*** AV, EV, IB, IV, LA, LF, SB, SL, SM, TB, VM, An84, An94, Da84, Gr86, Guoo, Lv88, Wh83>

comment [kɔ̃mɑ̃] *adv.* **1** how *Comment les affaires? Comment la famille?* How's business? How's the family? (EV) *Comment tu t'as fait mal?* How did you hurt yourself? (EV) **2** how, how much, in what way *Tu sais pas comment il l'aime.* You don't know how he loves her. (SM) *On va doucir notre café. Comment doux tu l'aimes?* We're going to sweeten our coffee. How sweet do you like it? (LF) *Comment grand il est?* How tall is he? (SM) ◊ **•comment (ça) se fait** why, how come *Comment ça se fait t'as pas été?* Why weren't you there? (SM) <AV, SM, Da84> **•comment ça se peut** how can it be <Da84> **•comment ça va?** how are you? <Da84> **•comment c'est / comment les cannes sont / comment les haricots?** how are you? how are things? <La99> **•comment longtemps** how long <Da84> **•comment tu crois?** how do you like that! how about that! <EV, La99> **•comment vous êtes?** how are you? *Bonjour, bonjour, comment vous êtes?* Hello, how are you? (PQ) <PQ> <***Loc:*** AC, AV, EV, IB, IV, LA, LF, PQ, SL, SM, TB, VM, An94, Da84, La99, Wh83>

commérage [kɔ̃meraʒ] *n.m.* commotion, bustle, hubbub, goings on *Il y avait un tas de commérage chez nous avant la noce à Marie.* There was a lot of commotion at our place before Marie's wedding. (IB) <***Loc:*** IB>

commerçant [kɔ̃mærsɑ̃] *n.m.* trader, tradesman <***Loc:*** Da84>

commerce [kɔ̃mærs] *n.m.* **1** commerce, trade **2** commotion, bustle, hubbub, goings on **Il y a un commerce qui va là.* There is something going on there. (Da84) <***Loc:*** IB, Da84>

commercial [kɔ̃mærsjal] *adj.* commercial **On a fait un 45 tours avec La Louisianne, quelque chose qui était soi-disant aussi commercial que du* SLICED BREAD, *mais qui a jamais vendu.* We made a 45 with La Louisianne, something that was supposed to be as commercial as sliced bread but that never sold. (LA, An94) <***Loc:*** LA, An94, Da84>

commettre [kɔ̃mɛt(r)] *v.tr.* to commit, perpetrate *Il a commis un grand péché.* He committed a huge sin. (LA) <***Loc:*** LA, Da84>

commier ♦see **communier**

commion ♦see **communion**

commis [kɔ̃mi] *n.* clerk, salesperson, employee in a shop ◊ **•commis de jour** registrar, clerk of the court <Lv88> **•commis voyageur** ***a*** travelling salesman ***b*** sales representative *J'ai vendu du whisky, j'étais commis voyageur.* I sold whisky, I was sales representative. (IB) <IB> <***Loc:*** IB, SJ, TB, Da84, Fa77, Lv88>

commission [kɔ̃misjɔ̃] *n.f.* **1** message (implying an instruction or order) *Il m'avait envoyé une commission par Nonc Derbes. Il voulait me rencontrer.* He had sent me a message through Uncle Derbes. He wanted to meet me. (EV) **2** errand *J'ai pour faire d'autres commissions avant de rentrer.* I have to do some other errands before going home. (EV) **3** *(usu. pl.)* groceries, provisions *Qui-ce qu'a été au magasin acheter les commissions?* Who went to the store to buy groceries? (LF) **4** profit, commission (made in a deal) *Quand il vend un char il fait une grosse commission.* When he sells a car he makes a big commission. (VM) **5** power, authority, warrant *S'il a une commission, le député shérif peut courser quelqu'un n'importe éoù.* If he has a warrant, the deputy sheriff can chase somebody anywhere. (Lv88) **6** commission, administrative board ◊ **•commission scolaire** school board <Lv88> **•être en commission** to be running errands *Elle est pas là asteur. Elle est en commission.* She's not here right now. She's running errands. (LA) <LA> **•faire une commission** ***a*** to carry a message ***b*** to run an errand <Da84, Wh83> <***Loc:*** EV, LA, LF, SM, VM, Da84, Lv88, Wh83>

commissionnaire [kɔ̃misjɔ̃nær] *n.m.* **1** commissioner **2** agent, messenger *Et ça fait il y a un marchand qui passait vendre, un commissionnaire, t'appelais ça, vendre les grosseries dans les boutiques, tu connais.* And so, there's a merchant who came by to sell, an agent, you'd call that, to sell groceries in the stores, you know. (PQ) **3** poll worker <***Loc:*** EV, LA, PQ, VM, Da84>

commissionner [kɔ̃misjɔ̃ne] *v.tr.* to commission, authorize, charge *Ils m'ont commissioné d'aller dire au monde qu'il* *fallait sortir pour l'ouragan.* They authorized me to go tell the people to get out for the hurricane. (VM) <***Loc:*** VM, Da84>

commode[1] [kɔ̃mɔd] *adj.* **1** convenient, handy **2** suitable, appropriate *Chaque fois qu'elle venait ici elle amenait son chien. C'était donc pas commode.* Every time she came here she brought her dog. It was not appropriate. (VM) <***Loc:*** LF, VM, Da84>

commode[2] [kɔ̃mɔd, ekɔ̃mɔd] *n.f.* **1** toilet, commode *J'ai débouché la commode.* I unclogged the toilet. **(EV) 2** restroom, bathroom, toilet **3** outhouse **4** chest of drawers ◊ **•aller à la commode** to go to the bathroom, use the bathroom <AS, TB> <***Loc:*** AC, AS, EV, LA, LF, SB, SL, SM, TB, Da84, Gu00, Lv88>

commotion [kɔ̃mosjɔ̃] *n.f.* commotion, disturbance <***Loc:*** Da84>

commun, -e [kɔ̃mœ̃, -yn] *adj.* **1** common, usual, ordinary *Les termes de* BUSHEL *et tout ça c'était pas quelque chose qu'était commun.* Terms like bushel and all that were not common. (LF) **2** gross, crude *Arrête de faire ça. C'est commun.* Stop doing that. It's crude. (LA) ◊ **•en commun** in common *Les deux frères avaient pas un tas en commun.* The two brothers didn't have a lot in common. (LA) <LA, Da84> <***Loc:*** LA, LF, Da84>

communauté [kɔ̃mynote, kɔ̃mynite] *n.f.* **1** community *J'étais éné sur le bayou de Petit Caillou dans la communauté de Chauvin.* I was born on Bayou Petit Caillou in the community of Chauvin. (TB) **2** community (of property, as in marriage) **3** religious order or society <***Loc:*** SL, TB, Da84>

commune [kɔ̃myn] *n.f.* **1** town **2** group, community <***Loc:*** SL, Da84>

communicant [kɔ̃mynikɑ̃] *n.m.* [*eccl.*] communicant <***Loc:*** Da84>

communication [kɔ̃mynikasjɔ̃] *n.f.* communication, message <***Loc:*** Da84>

communier (**commier**) [kɔ̃mynje, kɔ̃mije, kɔ̃mĩje] **I** *v.tr.* to administer the sacrament of communion to **II** *v.intr.* to receive the sacrament, receive communion, take communion *Et là dessus le Dimanche de Pâques, tout le monde s'habillait avec les chapeaux et les belles robes et les* SUITS *pour les hommes, et tout allait à l'église et communier.* And then on Easter Sunday, everyone dressed up in hats and nice dresses and suits for men, and everyone went to church to take communion. (LF) <***Loc:*** LF, SL, SM, TB, VM, Da84, Lv88>

communion (**commion**) [kɔ̃mĩjɔ̃] *n.f.* communion *J'ai été à la messe de cinq heures et demie pour prendre communion.* I went to church for the 5:30 mass to take communion. (TB) ◊ **•faire sa première commion** to make one's first communion <Da84> <***Loc:*** LF, SL, SM, TB, VM, Da84>

communiquer [kɔ̃mynike] *v.tr.* to communicate *On communiquait sur le* SHORTWAVE, *sur le radio,* FM FREQUENCY, *on parlait en français sur l'air.* We used to communicate on the shortwave radio, FM frequency, we spoke in French on the air. (TB) <***Loc:*** LA, TB, Da84>

communiste[1] [kɔ̃mynis(t)] *adj.* communist **Le monde va croire c'est des aéroplanes communistes. Ça va les* SHOOT DOWN. People will think that they are communist airplanes. They will shoot them down. (EV, An94) <***Loc:*** EV, An94, Da84>

communiste[2] [kɔ̃mynis(t)] *n.* communist <***Loc:*** EV, An94, Da84>

compagnie [kɔ̃pɑ̃ji, kɔ̃paji, kɑ̃pɑ̃ji] *n.f.* **1** company, business, partnership **2** group of guests, company, visitors, callers *Elle se casse en deux quand elle a de la compagnie.* She bends over backwards when she has company. (Lv88) **3** attendance, group of people attending a wake *Elle a une belle compagnie pour son âge. Tu connais, à 90 ans, il reste pus beaucoup de son monde.* She has a fine attendance at her wake for her age. You know, at 90 years old, there aren't many of her people left. (LA) **4** company (in the military) *Eux, ils étaient dans l'Afrique du Nord, à Sicile, mais quand moi j'ai joint la compagnie, c'était le régiment... en Italie.* They were in North Africa, in Sicily, but when I joined the company, it was the regiment [that was] in Italy. (SL) ◊ **•compagnie d'assurances** insurance company <LF, TB, VM> **•compagnie d'huile** oil company <LF, SM, TB, Gr86> <***Loc:*** AV, EV, IB, JE, LA, LF, SL, SM, TB, VM, Da84, Gr86, Lv88>

compagnon [kɔ̃pɑ̃jɔ̃] *n.m.* companion, associate, comrade, buddy <***Loc:*** VM, Da84>

comparable [kɔ̃parab(l)] *adj.* comparable *Les deux chevaux étaient pas comparables.* The two horses were not comparable. (VM) <***Loc:*** LA, VM, Da84>

comparaison [kɔ̃parezɔ̃] *n.f.* comparison <***Loc:*** Da84>

comparer [kɔ̃pare] *v.tr.* to compare *Tu peux pas comparer les deux bateaux. Cil-là vaut pas rien du tout.* You can't compare the two boats. That one isn't worth anything at all. (LA) <***Loc:*** LA, Da84>

compartement [kɔ̃partəmɑ̃] *n.m.* compartment, section <***Loc:*** Da84>

compas [kɔ̃pa] *n.m.* **1** compass **2** calipers **3** measurement, six feet in length, used to quantify the amount of sugar cane that a worker in the field had cut *Un compas c'est six pieds. Et tous les jours le monde prendait à couper. Et le soir quand ils achèvent,* WELL, *mon père comptait les compas. Y en a qu'était plus que d'autres, et ceux-là qu'étaient moins,* BUT *c'était tout marqué dans des livres avec leurs noms. X a coupé tant de compas et toi t'en as coupé tant.* A "compas" is six feet. And every day, people would start cutting. And in the evening when they finished my father counted the "compas." Some had more than others, and others had less, but it was all written down in books with their names. X cut so much cane, and you cut so much. (AS) <***Loc:*** AS, Da84>

compassion [kɔ̃pasjɔ̃] *n.f.* **1** compassion, mercy, pity **2** great effort *Ça prend de la compassion pour se préparer.* It takes a lot of effort to get oneself ready. (SM) **3** mess, disorder *Qué compassion il y a icite.* What a mess there is here. (SM) <***Loc:*** EV, SM, Da84, Ph36>

compatissant, -e [kɔ̃patisɑ̃, -ɑ̃t] *adj.* compassionate, sympathetic *On est tout compatissant avec le monde qu'a été affecté par le raz de marée dedans Sri Lanka.* We are all sympathetic with the people who were affected by the tidal wave in Sri Lanka. (VM) <***Loc:*** VM, Da84>

compensation [kɔ̃pɑ̃sasjɔ̃] *n.f.* compensation, reward <***Loc:*** Da84>

compenser [kɔ̃pɑ̃se] *v.tr.* **1** to compensate, reward **2** to compensate, make up for *Le Bon Dieu va te compenser pour ça t'as fait.* The Good Lord will repay you for what you did. (ThCa: *La table des veuves*) <***Loc:*** Da84, ThCa>

compère-loriot [kɔ̃pærlorjo] *n.m.* sty (on the eye) <***Loc:*** Da84>

compétent, -e [kɔ̃petɑ̃, -ɑ̃t] *adj.* competent, capable, able *Engage pas cil-là. Il est pas compétent.* Don't hire that one. He's not competent. (LA) <***Loc:*** LA, Da84>

compétition [kɔ̃petisjɔ̃] *n.f.* **1** competition **An [=On] aura d'la compétition, l'aut magasin est ouvert.* We'll have competition, the other store is open. (EV, Ph36) **2** rivalry *Les deux écoles ont une compétition.* The two schools have a rivalry. (Lv88) ◊ **•faire compétition avec** to compete with, be in competition with *Il fait competition avec moi.* He's in competition with me. (SM) <SM> <***Loc:*** EV, SM, Da84, Lv88, Ph36>

complaindre [kɔ̃plɛ̃n, kɔ̃plɛ̃d(r)] *v.tr.* to complain *Et je peux pas complaindre. J'ai tout le temps été* RECOGNIZE *avec le monde plus vieux que moi.* And I can't complain. I've always been respected by people older than me. (LF) <***Loc:*** LF>

complainte [kɔ̃plɛ̃t] *n.f.* sad or tragic ballad <***Loc:*** EV, LA, VM, Da84>

complaisance [kɔ̃plezɑ̃s] *n.f.* complacency, satisfaction, agreeableness <***Loc:*** Da84>

complaisant, -e [kɔ̃plezɑ̃, -ɑ̃t] *adj.* obliging, accommodating, agreeable, pleasant *C'est pas dur du tout de s'adonner avec lui. Il est beaucoup complaisant.* It's not at all hard to get along with him. He's very accommodating. (LA) <***Loc:*** LA, Da84>

complet (**complète**) [kɔ̃plɛ, kɔ̃ple, kɔ̃plɛt] *adj.* **1** complete, whole, entire **2** full, filled *Si t'achètes cinq piastres de groceries avec eux, [...] eusse te donne un petit* STAMP *et dès que t'as 50 piastres de complet dessus ta carte tu peux t'acheter cinq morceaux de vaisselle pour deux piastres.* If you buy five dollars worth of groceries from them, they give you a little stamp, and when you have 50 dollars filled on your card you can buy five pieces of dishes for two dollars. (LF) <***Loc:*** LF, Da84>

complètement [kɔ̃plɛtmɑ̃] *adv.* completely, wholly, entirely *C'est complètement différent.* That's completely different. (LF) <***Loc:*** LF, Da84>

compléter [kɔ̃plete] *v.tr.* to complete, finish, achieve *Il a jamais complété son collège.* He never finished college. (EV) <***Loc:*** EV, Da84>

complétion [kɔ̃plesjɔ̃] *n.f.* end, completion *J'attends la complétion du pont avant d'essayer de traverser la rivière.* I'm waiting for the completion of the bridge before trying to cross the river. (SM) <***Loc:*** SM, Lv88>

complexion [kɔ̃plɛksjɔ̃, kɔ̃pleksjɔ̃] *n.f.* complexion *Une belle complexion.* A beautiful complexion. (EV) <***Loc:*** AV, EV, Da84, Lv88>

complication [kɔ̃plikasjɔ̃] *n.f.* complication <***Loc:*** Da84>

compliment [kɔ̃plimɑ̃] *n.m.* **1** compliment *Il a donné un compliment à Marie.* He gave Marie a compliment. (LF) **2** harsh criticism *Il a donné un compliment à Marie.* He criticized Marie quite harshly. (LF) <***Loc:*** LF, Da84>

complimenter [kɔ̃plimɑ̃te] **I** *v.tr.* **1** to compliment *Ils l'ont complimenté pour ça il avait fait.* They complimented him for what he had done. (LA) **2** to criticize harshly **II se complimenter** *v.pron.* to compliment each other *C'est trop de bonne heure pour commencer de se complimenter.* It's too early to start complimenting ourselves. (LA) <***Loc:*** LA, LF, Da84>

compliqué, -e [kɔ̃plike] *adj.* complicated *Je connais pas quoi c'est qu'on va faire, mais ça va d'être compliqué.* I don't know what we're going to do, but it's going to be complicated. (LA) <***Loc:*** LA, Da84>

compliquer [kɔ̃plike] **I** *v.tr.* to complicate *Si son garçon commence à travailler, ça va compliquer sa vie à elle.* If her son starts working, that's going to complicate her life. (LA) **II se compliquer** *v.pron.* to become complicated *Les affaires va se compliquer asteur.* Things are going to get complicated now. (EV) <***Loc:*** EV, LA, Da84>

complot [kɔ̃plo] *n.m.* plot, conspiracy <***Loc:*** Da84>

comploter [kɔ̃plote] *v.tr.* **1** to plot, conspire *Ces deux là-là, je suis sûr qu'ils sont après comploter quelque chose.* Those two, I'm sure they're plotting something. (VM) **2** to come up with, make up, cook up (a story) *Mama et* UNCLE HEALY *et peut-être* UNCLE ANDREW *s'a comploté un* STORY. Mama and Uncle Healy and maybe Uncle Andrew conspired and hatched a story. (SL) <***Loc:*** LA, SL, VM, Da84>

comporte [kɔ̃pɔrt] *n.f.* behavior, conduct <***Loc:*** Da84>

comporter (se) [kɔ̃pɔrte] *v.pron.* to behave, conduct o.s. **Je suis partie à la chasse et faut vous-autres se comportes bien. Faut vous soies pas canaille, faut pas vous-autres vas trop loin.* I'm going hunting and you must behave yourselves. You mustn't be naughty, you mustn't go too far. (LA, An94) <***Loc:*** LA, An94, Da84>

composer [kɔ̃poze] *v.tr.* **1** to compose *Je l'ai pas écrit, je peux pas écrire, c'est moi qui l'a composé.* I didn't write it, I can't write, I'm the one who composed it. (TB) **2** to make, construct **Et je m'ai fait un violon moi-même. Je m'ai composé ça avec une boîte de cigares.* And I made myself a violin. I built it with a cigar box. (LA, An84) <***Loc:*** LA, TB, An84, Da84>

composition [kɔ̃pozisjɔ̃] *n.f.* composition <***Loc:*** Da84>

compotier [kɔ̃potje] *n.m.* pot or jar from which syrup or honey is served <***Loc:*** JD, Da84>

compréhension [kɔ̃preɑ̃sjɔ̃] *n.f.* comprehension, understanding <***Loc:*** Da84>

comprenable [kɔ̃prənab(l)] *adj.* **1** comprehensible, understandable *C'était pas comprenable pour quelqu'un comme nous-autres venir d'ici en bas dans une campagne d'icitte et aller d'une place comme ça.* It wasn't understandable for someone like us who came from down here in the country here, to go to a place like that. (TB) **2** conceivable, plausible *Ça c'est bien comprenable quand-même.* It's conceivable, anyway. (VM) *Une histoire bien comprenable.* A plausible story. (SJ) <***Loc:*** AV, IB, LF, SB, SJ, SL, SM, TB, VM, Da84, Lv88>

comprendre [kɔ̃prɑ̃n, kɔ̃prɑ̃d(r)] *v.tr.* **1** to understand *C'est un différent langage* BUT *le second jour j'étais habitué à leur langage et j'ai pas eu de tracas pour les comprendre.* It's a different language but the second day I was used to their language and I had no trouble understanding them. (AS) **Je comprends exactement qui tu veux dire.* I understand exactly what you mean. (EV, An94) **Ils ont compris qu'il y avait quelque chose de drôle.* They understood that something was funny. (EV, An94) **2** to include, comprise **II se comprendre** *v.pron.* **1** to understand o.s. or each other *Si je suis avec un de mes amis français de mon âge, plein souvent on parle français. On se comprend mieux.* If I'm with one of my French-speaking friends of my age, very often we speak French. We understand each other better. (LF) **2** to be lucid, be focused **Il était surpris de ça et il se comprenait pas bien.* He was surprised by that and he was confused. (EV, An94) **3** to come to an agreement, settle **Ça va réfléchir. Vous-autres vas se comprendre plus tard.* They'll think it over. You'll settle things later. (SL, An94) <***Loc:*** AC, AS, EV, IB, LA, LF, SL, SM, TB, VM, An94, Da84, Lv88, Ph36>

comprenure [kɔ̃prənyr] *n.f.* comprehension, understanding *Quand même si qu'eux-autres a jamais eu d'école, eux-autres avait une comprenure de faire des affaires, de bâtir de quoi.* Even if they had never had any schooling, they had an understanding about how to do things, to build things. (TB) *Un enfant qui a beaucoup de comprenure.* An intelligent child. (SJ) *Il a pas beaucoup de comprenure de notre mayère.* He doesn't understand much about our way of life. (Lv88) ◊ **•pas avoir sa bonne comprenure** ***a*** to not be in one's right mind ***b*** to be mentally deficient, be mentally handicapped <Da84> <***Loc:*** AV, EV, IB, LA, LF, SL, SM, TB, Da84, Lv88, Ph36>

compresse [kɔ̃prɛs] *n.f.* cotton press <***Loc:*** EV, LA, VM, Da84>

compris, -e [kɔ̃pri, -iz] *adj.* **1** understood **C'est compris, alors!* It's understood, then! (Da84) **2** included *C'est tout compris dans le prix.* It's all included in the price. (VM) ◊ **•mal compris** misunderstood <Da84> <***Loc:*** VM, Da84>

compte [kɔ̃t] *n.m.* account, record, count *On a perdu compte de ça.* We've lost count of that. (TB) <***Loc:*** TB, Da84>

compter [kɔ̃te] **I** *v.tr.* **1** to count *À la Grande Passe qu'on appelle, tu perds un cent pieds de terre presque tous les ans depuis qu'eusse a compté ça.* At Grande Passe as they call it, you lose a hundred feet of land every year [by erosion] ever since they started counting that. (TB) **2** to include *Il faut payer le* BILL *d'électricité. C'est sans compter tous les autres* BILLS *au bout de mois.* You've got to pay the electricity bill. That's not including all the other bills at the end of the month. (VM) **II** *v.intr.* **1** to count, matter, be of importance **Ça compte pas.* It doesn't count. (Da84) *Il y avait des batailles qui comptaient, que ça tirait.* There were battles that were important, where they fired. (EV) **2** to rely, count (on) *Je connais qu'on peut compter sur lui si ça va plus mal.* I know we can rely on him if things get worse. (LA) **III se compter** *v.pron.* to reckon, consider o.s. **Je me compte chanceux.* I consider myself lucky. (Da84) ◊ **•compter plus z-herbes** to no longer amount to anything, no longer count as important *Si tu poussais pas le tien, t'étais marqué, ouais. Toi, tu comptais plus z-herbe dedans le voisinage.* If you didn't grow your own, you were blacklisted, yes. You weren't worth anything in the neighborhood. (SL) <SL> **•compter quelque chose** to matter, be worthwhile *Tu penses ça va compter quelque chose.* You think that's worth something. (VM) <VM> **•ça compte pas plus qu'un pet dans un ouragan {la poussière}** that is of little value <AC, JE, La99> <***Loc:*** AC, EV, JE, LA, SL, TB, VM, Da84, La99>

compteur[1] [kɔ̃tœr] *n.m.* ◊ **•compteur de mois** calendar *Le bougre d'assurance donnait des arménacs. Et là, on le disait "Equand tu vas nous donner notre compteur de mois?" C'est ça que c'était, ça compte la journée du mois et tout.* The insurance man used to give calendars. And then we would say to him, "When are you going to give us our calendar?" That's what it was, it counted the day of the month and all. (LF) <LF> <***Loc:*** LF>

compteur[2]**, -euse** [kɔ̃tœr, -øz] *n.* census taker *Il semble que la compteuse a pris le mauvais chemin par accident et elle a arrivé devant ma cabane à moi.* It seems that the census taker took the wrong road by accident and she arrived in front of my cabin. (ThCa: *Mille misères*) <***Loc:*** ThCa>

comptième ♦see **quantième**

comptine [kɔ̃tin] *n.f.* nursery rhyme *Mon père récitait souvent des petites comptines.* My father would often recite little rhymes. (VM) <***Loc:*** VM, Gu00>

comptoir [kɔ̃twar] *n.m.* **1** counter (in a store or house) **2** bar, counter (in a barroom) <***Loc:*** SM, Da84>

concentré, -e [kɔ̃sɑ̃tre] *adj.* concentrated, condensed **Lait concentré.* Condensed milk. (Da84) <***Loc:*** Da84>

concentrer [kɔ̃sɑ̃tre] **I** *v.tr.* to concentrate *Les patassas sont concentrés au pied des cipres.* The bream are concentrated at the foot of the cypress trees. (LA) **II se concentrer** *v.pron.* to become concentrated, concentrate (one's efforts) on *Je souhaite qu'il va se concentrer sur son école asteur qu'il a cassé la paille avec sa belle.* I hope he's going to concentrate on his schooling now that he's broken up with his girlfriend. (LA) <***Loc:*** LA, Da84>

conception [kɔ̃sɛpsjɔ̃] *n.f.* [*eccl.*] conception (of a child) ◊ **•immaculée conception** immaculate conception <Da84> <***Loc:*** Da84>

concernant [kɔ̃særnɑ̃] *adj.* concerning, in regard to *Je veux te parler concernant le* PIPELINE *que ça veut passer sus notre terre.* I want to talk to you about the pipeline they want to run on our land. (VM) <***Loc:*** VM, Da84>

concerner [kɔ̃særne] *v.tr.* to concern **Ça me concerne pas.* It doesn't concern me. (Da84) <***Loc:*** Da84>

concert [kɔ̃sær] *n.m.* concert <***Loc:*** Da84>

concession [kɔ̃sesjɔ̃] *n.f.* **1** concession, grant (of land) **2** allotment <***Loc:*** Da84>

concevable [kɔ̃səvab(l)] *adj.* conceivable, plausible *On dirait c'est pas concevable, ça.* That seems inconceivable. (VM) <***Loc:*** VM, Da84>

concevoir [kɔ̃səvwar] *v.tr.* **1** to conceive, conceive of (an idea, a plan, etc.) *C'est dur à concevoir.* That's hard to imagine. (LA) **2** to conceive (a child), become pregnant with <***Loc:*** LA, Da84>

conclure [kɔ̃klyr] *v.tr.* to conclude, bring to an end *Ils ont jamais conclu leur affaire. Il est mort avant.* They never concluded their business deal. He died beforehand. (LA) <***Loc:*** LA, Da84>

conclusion [kɔ̃klyzjɔ̃] *n.f.* conclusion <***Loc:*** Da84>

concombre ♦see **cocombre**

concourir [kɔ̃kurir] *v.intr.* to agree with, concur *Je concours dans votre opinion.* I agree with your opinion. (SM) <***Loc:*** SM>

concubinage [kɔ̃kybinaʒ] *n.m.* [*eccl.*] concubinage <***Loc:*** Da84>

concurrence [kɔ̃kyrɑ̃s] *n.f.* competition ◊ **•faire concurrence (avec)** to compete, vie (with) <Da84> <***Loc:*** Da84>

condamnable [kɔ̃dɑ̃nab(l)] *adj.* condemnable, blameable, terrible *C'est condamnable ça ils ont fait.* It's terrible what they did. (VM) <***Loc:*** VM, Da84>

condamnation [kɔ̃dɑ̃nasjɔ̃] *n.f.* condemnation <***Loc:*** Da84>

condamner [kɔ̃dɑ̃ne] **I** *v.tr.* **1** to condemn *Condamner quelqu'un à la mort, à la prison.* To condemn someone to death, to prison. (LA) **2** to censure **II se condamner** *v.pron.* to condemn or blame o.s. *Condamne-toi pas. C'était pas de ta faute.* Don't condemn yourself. It wasn't your fault. (VM) <***Loc:*** LA, VM, Da84>

condition [kɔ̃disjɔ̃] *n.f.* condition, state ◊ **•à condition que** on condition that *Je te donne ce petit chien à condition que c'est toi qui le soigne.* I'm giving you this little dog on the condition that you're the one who takes care of him. (VM) <VM, Da84> **•sans condition** without condition *Il m'ont loué la terre sans condition.* They leased the land to me without condition. (LA) <LA, Da84> **•sous condition que** on condition that *Mon oncle a fait un testament qui laissait sa terre au dernier vivant, sous condition qu'il ait pas d'enfants.* My uncle made a will that left his land to the last remaining survivor on condition that he have no children. (LA) *Je lui ai dit qu'il pouvait emprunter ma pelle sous condition qu'il la ramène propre.* I told him that he could borrow my shovel on the condition that he bring it back clean. (VM) <LA, VM, Da84> <***Loc:*** LA, VM, Da84>

conditionnel, -elle [kɔ̃disjɔ̃nɛl] *adj.* conditional *Sa promesse est conditionnelle.* His promise is conditional. (VM) <***Loc:*** VM, Da84>

condjo[1] (**conja, candja, conjo, coundja**) [kɔ̃dʒo, kɔ̃ʒa, kɑ̃dʒa, kɑ̃dʒja, kɔ̃dʒa, kɔ̃ʒo, kundʒa] *n.m.* spell, magical charm, jinx, curse *Il guérissait les malades avec ses prières et ses conjos--avec bon succès.* He cured the sick with his prayers and his spells--with good success. (ThCa: *Mille misères*) *Il y a du monde qui croit dans les condjas.* There are people who believe in spells. (TB) *Alle m'a passé un coundja.* She put a spell on me. (Lv88) ◊ **•faire un condjo contre** to cast a spell on, jinx *Il avait peur que quelqu'un avait fait un condjo contre lui.* He was afraid that someone had cast a spell on him. (LA) <LA, Da84> **•mettre un condjo sur** to cast a spell on, jinx *Tu pourrais demander à la vieille pour mettre un conjo sur lui.* You could ask the old lady to put a spell on him. (LA) <LA, Da84> <***Loc:*** EV, LA, LF, SJ, SL, Da84, Lv88, Ph36, ThCa>

condjo[2] (**conja, candja, conjo, coundja**) [kɔ̃dʒo, kɔ̃ʒa, kɑ̃dʒa, kɔ̃dʒa, kɔ̃ʒo, kundʒa] *v.tr.invar.* to put a spell on <***Loc:*** SJ>

conducteur [kɔ̃dyktœr] *n.m.* conductor, driver <***Loc:*** Da84>

conduire [kɔ̃dɥir] **I** *v.tr.* **1** to drive (a car, tractor, etc.) *Et c'était nommé par le nom, toi tu me disais à mon, Je veux le numéro 15, pour* DRIVE*, pour conduire.* And they would call it by its name, you would tell me, I want the number 15 to drive. (TB) **2** to lead, conduct **3** to carry out, conduct, perform (a task, one's work) *Y avait quelqu'uns de les police qui travaillait avec mon qui parlait français. Et on parlait français parmi nous-autres. Mais on conduisait tout notre ouvrage en anglais.* There were some of the police who spoke French. We would speak French together. But we carried out all our work in English. (LF) **II se conduire** *v.pron.* **1** to steer o.s. *Tu connais quand c'est que tu perds ton balan, ton équilibre, c'est ça j'empoigne des fois. [...] Si je peux, je touche quelque chose pour me conduire droite.* You know, when you lose your balance, that's what I get sometimes. If I can, I touch something to steer myself straight. (TB) **2** to behave, conduct o.s. **Il dit à Bouki, "Asteur, Bouki, tu vas te conduire." Et il dit, "Je veux pas tu fais un cochon avec toi-même!"* He said to Bouki, "Now, Bouki, you are going to behave yourself." And he said, "I don't want you to make a pig of yourself!" (EV, An94) <***Loc:*** EV, LF, TB, An94, Da84, Gr86>

conduite [kɔ̃dɥit] *n.f.* behavior, conduct <***Loc:*** Da84>

confédération [kɔ̃federasjɔ̃] *n.f.* confederation <***Loc:*** Da84>

confédéré[1], **-e** [kɔ̃federe] *adj.* confederate *La Guerre confédérée.* The Civil war. (VM) <***Loc:*** VM, Da84>

confédéré[2] [kɔ̃federe] *n.m.* Confederate (soldier) <***Loc:*** LF, SM, Da84>

conférence [kɔ̃ferɑ̃s] *n.f.* **1** conference **2** discussion <***Loc:*** LF, Da84>

confesse [kɔ̃fɛs] *n.f.* confession **Aller à la confesse.* To go to confession. (Da84) <***Loc:*** Da84>

confesser [kɔ̃fese] **I** *v.tr.* **1** to confess *Confesser un crime, confesser un péché.* To confess to a crime, to confess a sin. (EV) **Père, je veux confesser mes péchés.* Father, I want to confess my sins. (EV, An94) **2** to hear the confession of and grant absolution to (of a priest) **Le prêtre les a confessés.* The priest heard their confession. (EV) **II** *v.intr.* to confess, make the sacrament of confession **Un homme va confesser au prêtre.* A man goes to confess to the priest. (EV, An94) *Il faulait que ça confesse au prêtre pour être sûr qu'eux-autres soye paré pour prendre les sacrements de le mariage.* They had to confess to the priest to be sure they were ready to take the sacrament of marriage. (TB) **III se confesser** *v.pron.* to confess one's sin or guilt, go to confession **Il a été se confesser au prêtre.* He went to confess his sins to the priest. (An94) ◊ **•le confesse à Dieu** Act of Contrition (Catholic prayer of penitence) <TB> <***Loc:*** EV, TB, An94, Da84>

confesseur [kɔ̃fesœr] *n.m.* confessor (priest) <***Loc:*** Da84>

confession [kɔ̃fesjɔ̃] *n.f.* **1** confession **Aller à la confession.* To go to confession. (Da84) **2** prayer of confession *Tous les soirs il s'assisait sur ses genoux là à son lit avant qu'il se couche, et j'aimais l'attendre dire la confession, le Confiteor, tu connais.* Every evening he knelt down at his bed before he retired for the night, and I liked to hear him say his prayer of confession, the Confiteor, you know. (TB) <***Loc:*** TB, VM, Da84>

confessional [kɔ̃fesjɔ̃nal] *n.m.* confessional <***Loc:*** Da84>

confiance [kɔ̃fjɑ̃s] *n.f.* confidence, faith, trust *J'ai pas trop confiance en la Croix Rouge.* I don't have much faith in the Red Cross. (IB) <***Loc:*** IB, TB, Da84>

confier [kɔ̃fje] **I** *v.tr.* to entrust *Je lui ai confié mon étalon et il l'a ramené tout mordu par la jument.* I entrusted my stallion to him and he brought him back all bitten up by the mare. (LA) **II se confier** *v.pron.* to entrust o.s. *On va se confier au Bon Dieu.* We'll entrust ourselves to God. (LA) <***Loc:*** LA, Da84>

confirmation [kɔ̃firmasjɔ̃] *n.f.* **1** confirmation, ratification, sanction **2** sacrament of Confirmation (in the Catholic Church) <***Loc:*** Da84>

confirmer [kɔ̃firme] **I** *v.tr.* **1** to confirm, ratify *Je lui ai confirmé la nouvelle que le Pape était mort.* I confirmed the news that the Pope was dead. (VM) **2** to confirm (in the Catholic Church) *Tout mes enfants sont communiés et confirmés.* All of my children have made their First Communion and have been confirmed. (VM) **II** *v.intr.* to be confirmed, receive the sacrament of Confirmation *On veut te remercier pour nous avoir montré le catéchisme. On a fait notre première communion, et on a confirmé dimanche.* We want to thank you for teaching us catechism. We did our First Communion, and we were confirmed on Sunday. (TB) <***Loc:*** TB, VM, Da84>

confisquer [kɔ̃fiske] *v.tr.* to confiscate, seize *Ils ont confisqué son whisky et puis ils l'ont mis au forçat pour trois mois.* They confiscated his whiskey and then they put him in jail for three months. (EV) <***Loc:*** EV, Da84>

confiture [kɔ̃fityr] *n.f.* jam, jelly, preserves ◊ **•confiture aux mûres** berry preserves <Da84> **•confiture de figues** fig jam <TB> <***Loc:*** LA, LF, SM, TB, VM, Da84>

confondre [kɔ̃fɔ̃n, kɔ̃fɔ̃d(r)] *v.tr.* to confound, confuse *Je confonds toujours les deux bessonnes, les petites Héberts.* I always confuse the two little Hebert twins. (VM) <***Loc:*** VM, Da84>

conforme [kɔ̃fɔrm] *adj.* conforming (to), in conformity (with) *Tu peux dire ça tu veux, mais c'est pas conforme à la loi.* You can say what you want, but that's not conforming to the law. (VM) <***Loc:*** VM, Da84>

conformer (se) [kɔ̃fɔrme] *v.pron.* to conform, comply *Depuis qu'elle est mariée, elle a eu pour se conformer à leurs manières.* Since her marriage, she has had to conform to their ways. (VM) <***Loc:*** VM, Da84>

confort [kɔ̃fɔr] *n.m.* comfort <***Loc:*** Da84>

confortable [kɔ̃fɔrtab(l)] *adj.* comfortable *T'étais assez fatiqué, faulait que ça soye confortable.* You were tired enough that it had to be comfortable. (LF) <***Loc:*** LF, Da84>

conforter [kɔ̃fɔrte] *v.tr.* **1** to comfort, console *Il a essayé de conforter sa mère après l'accident mais il a pas pu.* He tried to console his mother after the accident but he could not. (LA) **2** to strengthen, fortify <***Loc:*** AV, LA, SM>

confrère [kɔ̃frær] *n.m.* confrere, colleague <***Loc:*** Da84>

confronter [kɔ̃frɔ̃te] *v.tr.* to confront, face *J'ai idée de le confronter au bal à soir.* I intend to confront him at the dance tonight. (LA) <***Loc:*** LA, Da84>

confusion [kɔ̃fyzjɔ̃] *n.f.* confusion, disorder <***Loc:*** Da84>

congéror [kɔ̃dʒerɔr] *n.m.* clove *Aline, je veux une boîte de congérors.* Aline, I want a box of cloves. (SL) <***Loc:*** SL>

congesté, -e [kɔ̃ʒɛste] *adj.* congested *J'ai passé le printemps* *tout congesté.* I spent the entire spring congested. (LA) <***Loc:*** LA, Da84>

congestion [kɔ̃ʒɛstjɔ̃] *n.f.* congestion <***Loc:*** Da84>

congo[1] [kɔ̃go] *adj.* dark black ◊ **•nègre congo** [*pej.*] very dark person of color <EV, LA, VM> <***Loc:*** EV, LA, VM, Da84>

congo[2] [kɔ̃go, kɑ̃go] *n.m.* **1** congo (dance formerly performed by Louisiana African-Americans) **2** [*offensive*] black person <***Loc:*** AV, EV, Lv88, Ph36>

congo[3] [kɔ̃go, kɑ̃go] *n.m.* **1** water mocassin, cottonmouth **2** amphiuma (aquatic salamander known variously as congo eel, conger eel, or congo snake) **3** green-winged teal ◊ **•congo à tête plate / serpent congo** water mocassin, cottonmouth <LF, Da84> **•faire le congo** to pretend to be sleeping <La99> **•petit congo** green-winged teal <JE> <***Loc:*** AV, EV, IB, JE, LF, SL, SM, TB, VM, La99, Lv88, Ph36, Re31>

congratulation [kɔ̃gratylasjɔ̃] *n.f.* congratulation <***Loc:*** Da84>

congre (**congue, corne**) [kɔ̃ŋ, kɔ̃g(r), kɔrn] *n.m.* amphiuma (aquatic salamander known variously as congo eel, conger eel, or congo snake) <***Loc:*** SM, Da84>

congrégation [kɔ̃gregasjɔ̃] *n.f.* congregation, assembly <***Loc:*** Da84>

congrène ♦see **gangrène**

congrener ♦see **gangrener**

congrès [kɔ̃grɛ, kɔ̃gre] *n.m.* congress <***Loc:*** Da84>

congri [kɔ̃gri] *n.m.* highly seasoned dish of rice, beans, and meat <***Loc:*** Lv88, Re31>

congue ♦see **congre**

conja ♦see **condjo**

conjecture [kɔ̃ʒɛktyr] *n.f.* conjecture, supposition <***Loc:*** Da84>

conjo ♦see **condjo**

conjugal [kɔ̃ʒygal] *adj.* [*eccl.*] conjugal <***Loc:*** Da84>

connaissance [kɔ̃nesɑ̃s] *n.f.* **1** knowledge **2** acquaintance **3** consciousness *La medecine l'a fait perdre connaissance.* The medicine made him lose consciousness. (AC) ◊ **•à {de} ma connaissance** to my knowledge, as far as I know *Pas de ma connaissance asteur, non.* Not as far as I know, no. (TB) <TB> **•en connaissance** in one's right mind *Alle est morte en connaissance. Mais alle était paralysée. Alle avait eu un* STROKE. She died in her right mind. But she was paralyzed. She had had a stroke. (TB) <TB> **•en pleine connaissance** fully conscious <Da84> **•sans connaissance** unconscious *Quand j'ai arrivé à toi, belle, T'étais sans connaissance, belle.* When I got to you, my sweet, you were unconscious (ch: *Belle*) <Da84> **•faire la connaissance (de)** to get acquainted (with), make the acquaintance (of) *Ça a commencé quand j'ai pris le job de vendre l'assurance d'enterrement pour le TBA et j'ai fait la connaissance de Cousin Dud.* It started when I took the job of selling funeral insurance for the TBA and I met Cousin Dud. (ThCa: *Messieurs, mesdames*) <LA, Da84, ThCa> <***Loc:*** AC, LA, TB, Da84, ThCa>

connaisseur, -euse [kɔ̃nesœr, -øz] *n.* expert <***Loc:*** Da84>

connaître [kɔ̃nɛt(r), kɔ̃net(r)] **I** *v.tr.* **1** to know (a person, a place, etc.) *J'ai prétendu que je le connaissais pas.* I pretended that I didn't know him. (SM) *Tu connais un bon restaurant pas loin d'ici?* Do you know of a good restaurant not too far from here? (EV) **2** to know (a fact) *Je connais que vous-autres est après parler de nous-autres parce que vous avez parlé en français.* I know that you are talking about us because you were speaking French. (SL) *Je connais pas quoi c'est tu veux dire.* I don't know what you mean. (Gu00) *J'ai connu que c'était quelqu'un t'était avec le diable.* I found out that it ["lougarou"] was someone who was with the devil. (JE) **3** to know how (to do s.t.) *Je connais pas bien cuire.* I don't know how to cook very well. (Lv88) *Je connais lire et je connais compter.* I know how to read and I know how to count. (SM) **II se connaître** *v.pron.* to know each other, be acquainted *C'est une place qu'est bien tranquille icitte sur le bayou, tout chacun se connaît.* This is a place that is very quiet here on the bayou, everyone knows each other. (LF) ◊ **•connaître comment** to know how *Je connais comment faire le pain mais j'ai perdu l'habitude.*I know how to make bread but I've lost the habit. (IB) <EV, IB, LA, LF, TB> **•connaître la tune *a*** to know what's happening ***b*** to have the knack for <VM, Lv88> **•connaître où cabri porte la queue *a*** to know how far one can go (in an affair, a discussion) ***b*** to know what to believe <Lv88> **•connaître ses oignons** to be very knowledgeable, esp. in one's business or specialty <La99> **•donner à connaître** to let s.o. know *Il lui a donné à connaître qu'il faulait partir avant que les autres arrivent.* He let him know that it was necessary to leave before the others got there. (LA) <LA, Da84> **•laisser connaître** to send a message, send news, let s.o. know *Ça fait, j'ai dit à mon garçon, "Si jamais tu veux t'essayer, laisse-moi connaître."* So, I said to my son, "If ever you want to try yourself [with me], let me know." (LA) <LA, Da84> **•tu {vous} connais / vous connaissez** you know, you see *Il y a des fois, on plantait ça dans le clos, tu connais.* There are times, we would plant that in the field, you know. (SL) <AC, EV, IV, LA, LF, PQ, SL, SM, TB, An94> <***Loc:*** AC, EV, IB, IV, JD, JE, LA, LF, PQ, SB, SL, SM, TB, VM, An94, Da84, Gu00, Lv88, Wh83>

connecter [kɔ̃nɛkte] *v.tr.* **1** to connect, couple, link *Là éiou vous reste asteur-là, ça c'est le boutte de le bayou, ça c'est le boutte de Terrebonne. C'est tout connecté ensemble.* Where you're staying right now is the end of the bayou, it's the end of Terrebonne. It's all connected together. (TB) **2** to connect (gas or electricity) *Ça va venir connecter mon gaz demain.* They're going to come and connect my gas line tomorrow. (EV) ◊ **•connecté avec** associated with, involved in, connected to *Il est connecté avec la banque.* He's associated with the bank. (SM) *Il est connecté avec cette bande de crapules.* He's involved with that bunch of losers. (VM) *Les traiteurs, c'est toujours connecté avec la religion.* Traiteurs, they are always involved with religion. (Lv88) <SM, VM, Lv88> <***Loc:*** EV, SM, TB, VM, Da84, Lv88>

connexion [kɔ̃nɛksjɔ̃, kɔ̃neksjɔ̃] *n.f.* **1** connection, link *Il n-a une connection intéressante entre les noirs et la musique cadienne.* There's an interesting connection between the blacks and Cajun music. (Lv88) **2** plug **3** connection, connecting conveyance (e.g. bus, train) *T'as une connexion avec le bus à sept heures.* You have a connection with the 7 o'clock bus. (Lv88) <***Loc:*** EV, SM, VM, Da84, Lv88, Ph36>

connu [kɔ̃ny] ◊ **•bois connu {inconnu}** hackberry tree, sugarberry tree <IB, SB> <***Loc:*** IB, SB>

consacrer [kɔ̃sakre] **I** *v.tr.* to consecrate, dedicate *J'ai consacré ma bassière pour élever des écrevisses.* I dedicated my lowland to raising crawfish. (VM) **II se consacrer** *v.pron.* to dedicate o.s. (e.g. to God) *Il s'a consacré à sa famille après une jeunesse de bamboche.* He dedicated himself to his family after a youth spent in debauchery. (LA) <***Loc:*** LA, VM, Da84>

conscience [kɔ̃sjɑ̃s] *n.f.* conscience ◊ **•en conscience** my goodness! gracious! *Mais, en conscience, t'en as fait assez!* But, gracious, you've done enough! (SM) <SM, VM> <***Loc:*** SM, VM, Da84>

conscription [kɔ̃skripsjɔ̃] *n.f.* conscription <***Loc:*** Da84>

conscrit [kɔ̃skri] *n.m.* conscript <***Loc:*** Da84>

conseil [kɔ̃sɛj] *n.m.* **1** advice, counsel **2** council, board **3** law counsel, lawyer <***Loc:*** Da84>

conseiller (aconseiller) [kɔ̃seje, akɔ̃seje] *v.tr.* to counsel, advise *Sur ta fête, je t'aconseille de te sauver. On your birthday,* I advise you to get out of here. (ThCa: *Mille misères*) <***Loc:*** Da84, ThCa>

conseilleur [kɔ̃sejœr] *n.m.* counselor, advisor <***Loc:*** Da84>

consentant, -e [kɔ̃sɑ̃tɑ̃, -ɑ̃t] *adj.* consenting, willing *Son père était pas consentant qu'ils mariont.* His father did not consent to their marriage. (VM) <***Loc:*** VM, Da84>

consentement [kɔ̃sɑ̃tmɑ̃] *n.m.* consent, willingness, agreement <***Loc:*** Da84>

consenter ♦see **consentir**

consentieux, -ieuse [kɔ̃sɑ̃sjø, -jøz] *adj.* agreeable, pleasant *C'était du monde consentieux.* They were agreeable people. (VM) <***Loc:*** VM>

consentir (consenter) [kɔ̃sɑ̃tir, kɔ̃sɑ̃te] **I** *v.tr.* to consent, agree *Je comprends pas comment vous-autres a cru que le prêtre aurait consenté qu'un Méthodiste se marie dans l'église Catholique.* I don't understand how you all thought that the priest would consent to a Methodist marrying in the Catholic Church. (ThCa: *La dernière quilte*) **II** *v.intr.* to consent, agree <***Loc:*** Da84, ThCa>

conséquence [kɔ̃sekɑ̃s] *n.f.* **1** consequence, result **2** importance, consequence ◊ **•par conséquence** as a result, hence, therefore <Da84> <***Loc:*** Da84>

conséquent, -e [kɔ̃sekɑ̃, -ɑ̃t] *adj.* considerable, substantial *Il a une habitation assez conséquente.* He has a rather considerable plantation. (SM) *Une fortune conséquente.* A substantial fortune. (SM) <***Loc:*** EV, SM, VM, Da84, Ph36>

conserve[1] [kɔ̃sær(v)] *n.f.* **1** preserves **2** canned tomato paste <***Loc:*** VM, Da84>

conserve[2] [kɔ̃sær(v)] *n.f. (usu. pl.)* **1** sunglasses *Le soleil était assez fort que y a fallu que je me mets des conserves sus les yeux.* The sun was so strong that I had to put on sunglasses. (Guoo) **2** goggles *Conserves à poussière.* Dust-goggles (VM) <***Loc:*** VM, Guoo>

conserver [kɔ̃særve] **I** *v.tr.* **1** to preserve, conserve *Le tasso, c'est la viande séchée à la fumée, qui la conserve.* Tasso is meat that is smoked while it's dried, to preserve it. (SL) **2** to save *Le jeune monde aujourd'hui connaît pas conserver pour un autre jour. Ça dépense tout ce que ç'a.* Young people today don't know how to save for another day. They spend everything they have. (LF) **II se conserver** *v.pron.* to keep, be preserved (of food) *Et là eux-autres mettait ça dans des barils, et ça se conservait, c'était salé pareil comme du poisson salé.* And then they put it in barrels, and it kept, it was salted just like salted fish. (TB) <***Loc:*** LF, SB, SL, TB, Da84, Guoo, Wh83>

considérable [kɔ̃siderab(l)] *adj.* considerable, significant *Il avait une propriété qu'était joliment considérable dans le temps.* He had property that was pretty considerable in that time. (LA) <***Loc:*** LA, Da84>

considération [kɔ̃siderasjɔ̃] *n.f.* consideration, regard, respect <***Loc:*** Da84>

considérer [kɔ̃sidere] **I** *v.tr.* **1** to consider, ponder, think about *Considérer une idée, considérer une proposition.* To ponder an idea, consider a proposition. (EV) **2** to consider, regard as **La conversation en sortant du cimitière est souvent pour ceux-là qu'est pas venus, parceque c'est considéré dérespectable, pareil comme pas faire tes Pâques.* The conversation when leaving the cemetery is often about those who didn't come, because it's considered disrespectful, just like not observing Easter. (Wh83) **II se considérer** *v.pron.* to consider o.s. *Ils se considèrent mariés parce que ça reste ensemble depuis six ans.* They consider themselves married because they've lived together for six years. (EV) <***Loc:*** EV, SJ, VM, An84, Da84>

consistance [kɔ̃sistɑ̃s] *n.f.* consistency <***Loc:*** Da84>

consistant, -e [kɔ̃sistɑ̃, -ɑ̃t] *adj.* substantial, nourishing (of food) *Il faut tu manges quelque chose de consistant.* You have to eat something substantial. (VM) <***Loc:*** VM, Da84>

consister [kɔ̃siste] *v.intr.* to consist (of), be composed (of) *Ça consiste en quoi, ça?* That consists of what? (LA) <***Loc:*** LA, Da84>

consolable [kɔ̃solab(l)] *adj.* consolable <***Loc:*** Da84>

consolant, -e [kɔ̃solɑ̃, -ɑ̃t] *adj.* consoling, comforting *Son mari était pas beaucoup consolant après l'enterrement.* Her husband was not very consoling after the funeral. (LA) <***Loc:*** LA, Da84>

consolation [kɔ̃solasjɔ̃] *n.f.* consolation, comfort <***Loc:*** Da84>

consoler [kɔ̃sole] **I** *v.tr.* to console, comfort *C'est son frère qui l'a consolé après qu'il a entendu la nouvelle.* It's his brother who consoled him after he heard the news. (LA) **II se consoler** *v.pron.* to console o.s., find solace *Il pouvait juste pas se consoler après la mort de son père.* He just couldn't console himself after the death of his father. (LA) <***Loc:*** LA, Da84>

consomption [kɔ̃sɔ̃psjɔ̃] *n.f.* consumption, tuberculosis <***Loc:*** Da84>

constable [kɔ̃stab(l)] *n.m.* **1** constable, police officer **2** chief of police **3** town marshall **4** bouncer *Le constable a coché son bâton pour chaque bataille.* The bouncer notched his stick for each fight. (LA) <***Loc:*** LA, LF, VM, Da84, Lv88>

constamment [kɔ̃stɑ̃mɑ̃] *adv.* constantly, continually *On t'en donne constamment.* We're constantly giving to you. (VM) <***Loc:*** VM, Da84>

constance [kɔ̃stɑ̃s] *n.f.* constancy, fidelity <***Loc:*** Da84>

constipation [kɔ̃stipasjɔ̃] *n.f.* constipation <***Loc:*** Da84>

constipé, -e [kɔ̃stipe] *adj.* constipated *J'ai resté constipé pour trois jours après les fêtes.* I was constipated for three days after the holidays. (LA) <***Loc:*** LA, Da84>

constiper [kɔ̃stipe] *v.tr.* to constipate *Il peut pas manger le fromage parce que ça le constipe.* He can't eat cheese because it constipates him. (LA) <***Loc:*** LA, Da84>

constituant [kɔ̃stitɥɑ̃] *n.m.* constituent <***Loc:*** Da84>

constitution [kɔ̃stitysjɔ̃] *n.f.* constitution <***Loc:*** Da84>

constructeur [kɔ̃stryktœr] *n.m.* constructor, builder <***Loc:*** Da84>

construction [kɔ̃stryksjɔ̃] *n.f.* construction, building <***Loc:*** Da84>

constructive [kɔ̃stryktiv] *adj.* constructive *Il aurait pu faire plus pour se venger, mais ça aurait pas été constructive.* He could have done more to get even, but it wouldn't have been constructive. (LA) <***Loc:*** LA, Da84>

construire [kɔ̃strɥir] *v.tr.* to construct, build *Souvent ça mettait le corps sur une simple table construite avec deux ou trois planches placées sur un support.* Often they would put the body on a simple table built with two or three planks placed on a supporting foundation. (VM) <***Loc:*** VM, Da84, Gr82>

consultant [kɔ̃syltɑ̃] *n.* consultant, advisor <***Loc:*** Da84>

consultation [kɔ̃syltasjɔ̃] *n.f.* consultation <***Loc:*** Da84>

consulte [kɔ̃sylt] *n.f.* consultation *J'ai eu une consulte avec le docteur.* I had a consultation with the doctor. (SM) <***Loc:*** SM, Da84, Lv88>

consulter [kɔ̃sylte] *v.tr.* to consult **Ça fait, elle avait été consulter sa grand-mère.* So she had gone to consult her grandmother. (LA, An94) <***Loc:*** LA, An94, Da84>

contact [kɔ̃tak(t)] *n.m.* contact **Comment est-ce que mes enfants pourraient s'identifier avec une culture folklorique qui n'a jamais quitté le dix-septième siecle? Une culture illettrée en français à quatre-vingt-dix-neuf pour cent qui n'a jamais fondé d'écoles, qui n'a aucun contact avec l'extérieur de ses villages?* How could my children identify with a folkloric culture that has never left the seventeeth century? A culture which is ninety-nine percent illiterate in French, which never founded schools, which has no contact with the world outside its villages? (ThCa: *Mille misères*) <***Loc:*** Da84, ThCa>

contacter [kɔ̃takte] *v.tr.* to contact, touch *Ils l'ont contacté à la maison pour lui dire qu'il avait perdu son père.* They contacted him at home to tell him that his father had passed away. (LA) <***Loc:*** LA, Da84>

contagieux, -ieuse [kɔ̃taʒjø, -jøz] *adj.* contagious, infectious *Une maladie contagieuse.* A contagious illness. (LA) <***Loc:*** LA, Da84>

contamination [kɔ̃tɑ̃minasjɔ̃] *n.f.* contamination, pollution <***Loc:*** Da84>

contaminer [kɔ̃tɑ̃mine] *v.tr.* to contaminate, pollute *L'eau dans le vivier à côté du puits d'huile était contaminé.* The water in the pond next to the oil well was contaminated. (LA) <***Loc:*** LA, Da84>

conte [kɔ̃t] *n.m.* **1** story, tale *Et je t'avais déjà conté pour le conte de mon popa, huh?* And I've already told you the story about my dad, huh? (TB) **2** falsehood, tall tale *Y en a plein qui vous conteraient des contes mais ils vont pas dire que c'est des contes. Ils va assayer de vous faire croire que c'est la verité mais c'est des contes.* There are a lot of people who will tell you tales but they won't say that they're tales. They'll try to get you to believe it's the truth but they're falsehoods. (TB) ◊ **•conte cochon** dirty story <Da84, Lv88> **•faires des contes** to tell a falsehood <La99> <***Loc:*** EV, LA, LF, SL, SM, TB, VM, An94, Da84, Gr82, La99, Lv88, Wh83>

contempler [kɔ̃tɑ̃ple] *v.tr.* to contemplate, consider, think about *Il passe proche tout sont temps à contempler la nature.* He spends almost all his time contemplating nature. (LA) <***Loc:*** LA, Da84>

contenir (**contiendre**) [kɔ̃tnir, kɔ̃tʃjɛ̃n, kɔ̃tʃjɛ̃d(r)] **I** *v.tr.* to hold, contain *Combien de galons ça contient?* How many gallons does it contain? (LA) **II se contenir** *v.pron.* to contain o.s., restrain o.s. *Quand il a vu les cadeaux, il pouvait pus se contenir.* When he saw the presents, he could no longer contain himself. (LA) <***Loc:*** LA, Da84>

content, -e [kɔ̃tɑ̃, -ɑ̃t] *adj.* **1** happy, glad *Alle a venu taper à la porte. Tu parles d'un homme qu'était content, c'était moi!* She came to knock at the door. Talk about a man who was happy, I was! (LF) *Content de t'avoir rencontré.* Happy to have met you. (TB) **2** satisfied, content *Il a étudié un petit peu à collège comme moi, mais [...] faulait étudier de trop et je pense que j'étais content avec mes C's.* He studied it a little in college like me, but you had to study too much, and I think I was satisfied with my C's. (LF) <***Loc:*** AC, AL, AS, EV, IB, LA, LF, SM, TB, An94, Da84, Gu82, Lv88>

contentement [kɔ̃tɑ̃tmɑ̃] *n.m.* contentment, satisfaction ◊ **•à son contentement** to satiety, as much as one wishes, to one's heart's desire *Les poules mangeaient du maïs à leur contentement.* The chickens would eat as much corn as they wished. (Lv88) <Lv88> <***Loc:*** Da84, Lv88>

contenter [kɔ̃tɑ̃te] **I** *v.tr.* to please, satisfy, gratify *Ils s'ont séparé parce qu'il pouvait pas la contenter.* They separated because he could not satisfy her. (LA) **II se contenter** *v.pron.* to be pleased, be satisfied *Je m'ai contenté de le voir faire son mieux.* I was satisfied to see him do his best. (LA) <***Loc:*** LA, Da84>

contenu [kɔ̃tny] *n.m.* content <***Loc:*** Da84>

conter [kɔ̃te] **I** *v.tr.* to tell, relate, narrate *Faut que je conte à Barry la première année qu'on a décidé de planter des affaires dans le clos.* I have to tell Barry about the first year that we decided to plant things in the field. (AC) **II** *v.intr.* to tell, relate, narrate *Et je t'avais déjà conté pour le conte de mon popa, huh?* And I've already told you the story about my dad, huh? (TB) ◊ **•conter des contes {histoires}** to tell stories, tell tales *C'est tout du monde qu'aime avoir du fonne, et qu'aime conter des contes.* They're all people who like to have fun, and to tell stories. (LF) <EV, LF, An94> **•conter des menteries** to tell lies, fib *Et il dit, "Papa connaît pas lire." Et [...] et la petite fille croyait qu'il était après lui conter des menteries.* And he told her, "Grandpa doesn't know how to read." And the little girl though he was pulling her leg. (TB) <TB> <***Loc:*** AC, EV, LA, LF, SL, TB, An94, Da84, Gr82, Gr86>

contestable [kɔ̃tɛstab(l)] *adj.* contestable, debatable *L'élection était pas contestable.* The election was not contestable. (LA) <***Loc:*** LA, Da84>

contester [kɔ̃tɛste] *v.tr.* to contest *Sa belle-famille a contesté le testament.* His in-laws contested the will. (LA) <***Loc:*** LA, Da84>

conteur [kɔ̃tœr] *n.m.* storyteller ◊ **•conteur de contes** storyteller <Da84> **•conteur de menteries** liar, fibber, teller of tall tales <Da84> <***Loc:*** EV, An94, Da84>

contiendre ♦see **contenir**

continuation [kɔ̃tinɥasjɔ̃] *n.f.* continuation, continuance <***Loc:*** Da84>

continué [kɔ̃tinɥe] *adv.* continually *Il me dit, comment tu peux dire la même histoire, la même continué, mais je te dis, ils l'ont pas attendu.* He tells me, how can you tell the same story, the same one continually, but I say, they haven't heard it. (TB) <***Loc:*** TB>

continuer [kɔ̃tinɥe] **I** *v.tr.* to continue, extend *Ils ont continué le chemin jusqu'à la terre des écoles.* They continued the road up to the school board property. (LA) **II** *v.intr.* to continue, go on *Et en temps perdu, plein souvent j'ai continué à lire son livre et a étudier moi-même.* And in my free time, quite often I've gone on reading his book and studying it myself. (LF) **III se continuer** *v.pron.* to continue, go on *Ça s'a continué jusqu'à Dieu sait quelle heure.* It went on until God knows what time. (VM) <***Loc:*** LA, LF, SL, TB, VM, An94, Da84, Wh83>

contour [kɔ̃tur] *n.m.* contour, outline *La levée d'un clos de riz suit les contours de la terre.* The rice field levee follows the contour of the land. (LA) <***Loc:*** LA, Da84>

contracter [kɔ̃trakte] **I** *v.tr.* **1** to contract, enter into by contract (e.g. a marriage) **2** to contract, incur, acquire (e.g. a debt, a disease) *Ils ont contracté un paiment pour la dette.* They contracted a payment plan for the debt. (VM) **3** to contract, hire work done on contract *Cette maison ici, oui. J'ai contracté ça mon-même.* This house here, yes. I contracted it myself. (TB) **II** *v.intr.* to make a contract, make a sale *Il a contracté à six piasses l'acre.* He made a contract for six dollars an acre. (Lv88) <***Loc:*** TB, VM, Da84, Lv88>

contracteur [kɔ̃traktœr] *n.m.* contractor <***Loc:*** LF, SM, Da84, Lv88>

contradiction [kɔ̃tradiksjɔ̃] *n.f.* contradiction <***Loc:*** Da84>

contraïr ♦see **contrarier**

contraire [kɔ̃trær] *n.m.* the contrary, the other way around *Je croyais qu'elle voulait le divorce mais c'est le contraire.* I thought she wanted the divorce, but it's the other way around. (EV) ◊ **•au contraire** on the contrary *Il dit qu'il dit tout le temps la vérité, mais au contraire, il mentit souvent.* He says he always tells the truth, but, on the contrary, he often lies. (LA) <LA> **•au contraire de** contrary to *Au contraire de ça que le monde dit, c'est pas un bon restaurant.* Contrary to what everyone says, it's not a good restaurant. (EV) <EV> <***Loc:*** EV, LA, VM, Da84>

contrariant, -e [kɔ̃trarjɑ̃, -ɑ̃t] *adj.* contrary, uncooperative, ornery *C'est un enfant contrariant, il aime jamais ça qu'on fait pour lui.* He's an ornery child, he never likes anything you do for him. (EV) <***Loc:*** EV, SL, Da84>

contrarier (contraïr) [kɔ̃trarje, kɔ̃trair] **I** *v.tr.* to oppose, contradict *Il a juste fait ça pour contrarier sa femme.* He just did that to contradict his wife. (LA) *Contrariez-moi pas.* Don't oppose me. (VM) **II se contrarier** *v.pron.* **1** to contradict o.s. or each other **2** to disagree, fuss, argue *Ça m'étonne pas qu'ils sont séparés. Ça se contrariaient tout le temps.* I'm not surprised that they are separated. They were always in disagreement. (LA) <***Loc:*** LA, VM, Da84>

contrarieux, -euse [kɔ̃trajø, -øz] *adj.* contrary <***Loc:*** Fa77>

contrariété [kɔ̃trarjete] *n.f.* contrariness, contradiction <***Loc:*** Da84>

contrat [kɔ̃tra] *n.m.* **1** contract, agreement **2** promissory note <***Loc:*** LA, LF, TB, VM, Da84>

contre[1] [kɔ̃t(r)] *adv.* against, in opposition *Mais le bien que* *les écoles d'immersion fait, un principal ou une maîtresse qu'est dédiqué à son job peut pas être contre parce que ça fait trop de bien.* But the good that the immersion schools do, a principal or a teacher can't be against them because they do too much good. (LF) <*Loc:* LF>

contre[2] [kɔ̃t(r)] *prep.* **1** against, up against, in contact with *Il s'a appuyé contre un poteau pour espérer que sa femme sort du magasin.* He leaned against a post to wait for his wife to come out of the store. (LA) *Pendant l'ouragan Audrey toutes qualités d'affaires s'ont ramassé contre la levée du* INTERCOSTAL. During hurricane Audrey, all kinds of things got piled up against the Intercostal levee. (VM) **2** against, opposed to *Y avait un prêtre au commencement de la* WORLD WAR *II. [...] Il était après* RADIO *des messages à des sous-marins contre l'Allemagne.* There was a priest at the start of WWII. He was radioing messages to submarines against Germany. (LF) *Et s'il y avait une bataille, c'était un contre un. C'était pas des maudits gangs comme t'as asteur.* And if there was a fight, it was one against one. There weren't these damned gangs like you have now. (TB) <*Loc:* AV, EV, LA, LF, SL, SM, TB, VM, An94, Da84, Gr82, La99, Lv88>

contrecoup [kɔ̃trəku] *n.m.* counterblow <Da84>

contredire [kɔ̃trədir] **I** *v.tr.* to contradict, oppose, gainsay *Viens pas me contredire, je connais bien ça que je suis après parler pour.* Don't contradict me, I know what I'm talking about. (EV) **II se contredire** *v.pron.* to contradict o.s. or each other *Ça peut pas parler sans se contredire.* They can't talk without contradicting each other. (LA) <*Loc:* EV, LA, Da84>

contremarche [kɔ̃trəmarʃ] *n.f.* riser (of a step) <*Loc:* Da84>

contremarque [kɔ̃trəmark] *n.m.* countermark <*Loc:* Da84>

contrepoids [kɔ̃trəpwa] *n.m.* counterbalance, counterweight <*Loc:* Da84>

contrepoint (**contrepointe**) [kɔ̃trəpwɛ̃(t)] *n.m.* **1** counterpoint **2** alternation **Ils ont amarré les deux chevaux sur deux poteaux côte à côte et ils ont commencé à danser au bal, mais eux étaient en contrepointe.* They tied the two horses on two posts side by side and they started dancing at the ball, but they were in alternation [to check on the horses]. (SL, An94) <*Loc:* SL, An94, Da84>

contrepoison [kɔ̃trəpwazɔ̃] *n.m.* antidote <*Loc:* Da84>

contresigne [kɔ̃trəsiɲ] *n.m.* countersign <*Loc:* Da84>

contribuer [kɔ̃tribɥe] *v.tr.* to contribute *Elle a propté des canards qu'avaient été vendus et c'est ça qu'a contribué à son crime.* She cleaned some ducks that had been sold and that's what contributed to her crime. (VM) <*Loc:* VM, Da84>

contribution [kɔ̃tribysjɔ̃] *n.f.* contribution <*Loc:* Da84>

contrôlable [kɔ̃trolab(l)] *adj.* controllable *Je pense que les esprits étaient pas contrôlables ce soir-ça.* I suppose that the spirits were not controllable that night. (SM) <*Loc:* SB, SM, Da84>

contrôle [kɔ̃trol] *n.m.* control <*Loc:* Da84>

contrôler [kɔ̃trole] **I** *v.tr.* **1** to control *On peut pas contrôler les terroristes parce qu'ils sont fous.* You can't control terrorists because they are crazy. (EV) **2** to govern *Contrôler sa famille.* To govern one's family. (VM) **3** to force *J'ai pas voulu, mais alle m'a contrôlé.* I didn't want to, but she forced me. (VM) **4** to rape *Le garçon l'a contrôlée.* The boy raped her. (VM) **II se contrôler** *v.pron.* to control o.s. *Il était assez fâché qu'il pouvait pus se contrôler.* He was so mad that he couldn't control himself. (LA) <*Loc:* EV, LA, VM, Da84>

convenable [kɔ̃vnab(l)] *adj.* suitable, proper, fitting, fit *Cette maison est pas convenable pour une famille avec des petits enfants.* This house is not suitable for a family with small children. (EV) <*Loc:* EV, Da84>

convenance [kɔ̃vnɑ̃s] *n.f.* agreement <*Loc:* Da84>

convénience [kɔ̃vɛ̃njɑ̃s] *n.f.* convenience <*Loc:* Da84>

convenir [kɔ̃vnir] **I** *v.tr.* to agree **Ça fait, ils ont convenu qu'ils auraient élevé des petits cochons.* So they agreed that they would raise little pigs. (IV, An94) **II** *v.intr.* **1** to agree, be in accord **2** to be proper, be suitable *C'est dommage. Ça lui convient pas de faire comme ça.* It's too bad. It isn't becoming of him to act like that. (LA) *Ça durait pas et ça convenait pas pour des bals ordinaires.* It [the fabric] didn't last and it wasn't appropriate for regular dances. (EV) <*Loc:* EV, IB, IV, LA, An94, Da84>

convention [kɔ̃vɑ̃sjɔ̃] *n.f.* **1** convention **2** treaty <*Loc:* Da84>

convenu [kɔ̃vny] *adj.* agreed *C'est convenu que on va se rencontrer à trois heures.* It's agreed that we will meet at three o'clock. (LA) <*Loc:* LA, Da84>

conversation [kɔ̃værsasjɔ̃] *n.f.* conversation, talk <*Loc:* LF, SL, TB, VM, Da84, Wh83>

converser [kɔ̃værse] *v.intr.* to converse, talk *Comme eux-autres veut, s'ils voulont parler français on va assayer de converser avec en français.* As they like, if they want to speak French we try to converse in French. (TB) <*Loc:* TB, Da84>

conversion [kɔ̃værsjɔ̃] *n.f.* conversion <*Loc:* Da84>

converti, -e [kɔ̃værti] *n.* convert <*Loc:* Da84>

convertir [kɔ̃værtir] **I** *v.tr.* to convert *Ceux là qui passent visiter le monde, tu connais, c'était après essayer de le convertir.* The ones who go around visiting people, you know, they were trying to convert him. (LA) **II se convertir** *v.pron.* to convert, be converted *Le jeune Américain s'a converti catholique pour marier la petite fille à René Dugas de Vatican.* The young Anglo-American had converted to become Catholic in order to marry the daughter of René Dugas of Vatican. (LA) <*Loc:* LA, Da84>

convict [kɔ̃vik(t)] *n.m.* convict <*Loc:* AV, SB, SL, Da84, Lv88>

conviction [kɔ̃viksjɔ̃] *n.f.* **1** conviction, certainty **2** conviction, condemnation (by a court, by proof) <*Loc:* Da84, Lv88>

convocation [kɔ̃vokasjɔ̃] *n.f.* convocation <*Loc:* Da84>

convoquer [kɔ̃voke] *v.tr.* to convoke, convene *On a convoqué toute la famille pour décider quoi faire avec la maison de Pepère.* We convened the entire family to decide what to do with Pepère's house. (EV) <*Loc:* EV, Da84>

COOK [kuk] *n.* cook <*Loc:* AV, SB, TB>

cooler (**cool**) [kulɛ, kul] *n.m.* cooler, ice chest *J'ai oblié de mettre de l'eau dans le cooler.* I forgot to put water in the cooler. (TB) <*Loc:* LF, TB>

COONASS [kunas] *n.m.* [*pej.*] coonass, insulting nickname for a Cajun (used by Anglophones) <*Loc:* Lv88>

coopératif [kooperatif] *n.m.* cooperative <*Loc:* SL>

coopération [kooperasjɔ̃] *n.f.* cooperation <*Loc:* Da84>

copaille ♦see **copal**

copain, copine [kopɛ̃, kopin] *n.* friend, companion <*Loc:* JD>

copal (**copaille**) [kopal, kopaj] *n.m./f.* **1** sweet gum tree *Quand on voulait aller à l'ombrage, on allait en bas le copal.* When we wanted to go in the shade, we would go under the sweet gum tree. (SL) **2** any of various species of gum tree <*Loc:* AV, IB, LA, SL, SM, TB, VM, Da84, Guoo, Lv88, Re31>

cope[1] ♦see **CUP**

cope[2] ♦see **co**

copeau ♦see **écopeau**

copie [kopi] *n.f.* **1** copy, duplicate **2** copy, issue <*Loc:* SM, Da84, Lv88>

copier [kopje] *v.tr.* **1** to copy, duplicate **2** to imitate, copy ◊ **•copier dessus** to copy, copy after **Ça fait, les Cadiens ont copié dessus eux-autres.* So the Cajuns copied after them. (EV, An94) <EV, An94> <*Loc:* EV, An94, Da84>

copine ♦see **copain**

copropriétaire [koproprietær] *n.m.* joint owner, co-owner <*Loc:* Da84>

coq [kɔk] *n.m.* rooster, cock *"Ouais, mais," il dit, "si t'as remarqué, le coq change de poule à chaque coup."* "Yes, but," he says, "if you noticed, the rooster changes hens each time." (AS) <*Loc:* AS, AV, IB, IV, PQ, SB, Da84>

coquage [kokaʒ] *n.m.* [*vulg.*] sexual intercourse <*Loc:* TB>

coquaillerie [kokajri] *n.f.* indecent act or utterance *Faire des coquailleries.* To do indecent things. (SM) *Dire des coquailleries.* To say indecent things. (LF) <*Loc:* LF, SM>

coqueluche [koklyʃ] *n.f.* whooping cough <*Loc:* LA, Da84>

coquer [koke] **I** *v.tr.* [*vulg.*] to have sex with *Il est après coquer la femme du voisin.* He was having sex with the neighbor's wife. (LA) **II** *v.intr.* [*vulg.*] to have sex *Mon père récitait souvent cette petite comptine: "J'ai jamais fait fortune comme j'ai déjà coqué, le ventre au clair de lune, le derrière au fossé."* My father used to recite this little rhyme: "I have never been as fortunate as I have been laid, belly in the moonlight and butt in the ditch." (Guoo) <*Loc:* LA, SB, SM, TB, Guoo, Lv88>

coqueret [kokrɛ, kokre] *n.m.* ground cherry <*Loc:* Ho90>

coquette [kokɛt] *n.f.* flirt, coquette <*Loc:* Da84>

coquille (**cotchille**) [kokij, kotʃij] *n.f.* **1** shell (of an egg, a nut, etc.) **2** seashell, shell (of a mollusk) **3** stub of the stem on a gourd-like plant (squash, melon, pumpkin, etc.) *Ote la cotchille du giraumon.* Take the stem off the pumpkin. (EV) ◊ **•coquille de mer** seashell <LF> **•coquille d'huître** oyster shell <TB, Da84> **•coquille d'œuf** eggshell <Da84> <*Loc:* EV, JE, LA, LF, SB, TB, Da84>

coquin [kokɛ̃] *n.m.* crook, thief *Je crois que Jean est un coquin.* I think John is a thief. (SB) ◊ **•un coquin de** ***a*** enormous, huge *J'ai trouvé un coquin de rat de bois dans mon grenier.* I found a huge opossum in my attic. (SM) *Un coquin de bateau.* An enormous boat. (SB) ***b*** strong, burly **Un coquin de nègre.* A big, burly black man. (Da84) ***c*** *(used to intensify or qualify another noun) Altère, c'était un coquin de grand et gros homme.* Altère was one heck of a big, heavyset man. (EV) <EV, SM, Da84> <*Loc:* EV, LF, SB, SL, SM, Da84>

coquiner [kokine] *v.tr.* to deceive, dupe, trick (for one's own gain) *J'ai coquiné le voisin pour sa faucheuse.* I stole my neighbor's mower. (VM) *Il m'a bien coquiné avec ses chères belles promesses.* He deceived me with his impressive promises. (VM) <*Loc:* JD, VM, Da84, Lv88>

coquinerie [kokinri] *n.f.* thievery, stealing, pilfering <*Loc:* Da84>

cor [kɔr] *n.m.* corn, clavus (esp. on toes) *Elle avait des durillons et des cors sur les orteils qui semblaient à des nœuds de bois gras.* She had calluses and corns on her toes that ressembled knots of long-leaf pine. (AV) <*Loc:* AV, Da84, Fa77>

corail[1] (**corral**) [koraj, koral] *n.m./f.* yard, enclosure, pen (for pigs, cattle, etc.) *Ça mettait les bêtes dans un corail.* They would put the cattle in a cattle pen. (EV) <*Loc:* AV, EV, SB, SM, TB, VM, Lv88, Ph36, Re31>

corail[2] [koraj] *n.m.* salvia (any of various plants of the sage family) <*Loc:* VM>

corasse [koras] *n.f.* **1** scab (of a sore) **2** leather covering of a saddle <*Loc:* VM>

corbeau [kɔrbo] *n.m.* **1** crow **2** [*offensive*] dark-skinned black man <*Loc:* EV, SB, SM, Da84, La99, Lv88, Ph36>

corbeille [kɔrbɛj] *n.f.* basket <*Loc:* Da84>

corbier [kɔrbje] *v.tr.* to cram, stuff, pack full *Corbier une chambre de meubles.* To fill a room full of furniture. (SJ) <*Loc:* AV, SJ>

corbigeau [kɔrbiʒo] *n.* long-billed curlew (type of shore bird) <*Loc:* EV, LA, VM, Re31>

corbillard [kɔrbijar, kɔrbojar] *n.m.* hearse <*Loc:* LF, VM, Da84>

corbin (**corbu**) [kɔrbɛ̃, kɔrby] *adj.* hooked (of a nose), crooked *Un nez corbin.* A hooked nose. (Lv88) <*Loc:* Lv88>

corbu ♦see **corbin**

corchage ♦see **corsage**

corcher ♦see **écorcher**

corcobiage (**corcobillage**) [kɔrkobjaʒ, kɔrkobijaʒ] *n.m.* **1** bucking (of an untamed horse) **2** jumping around *Il a fait* *les petits arrêter ce corcobiage.* He made the children stop their jumping around. (IB) ◊ •**faire des corcobiages** to misbehave, cut capers *Les enfants ont fait des corcobiages quand leur maman était pas là.* The children misbehaved when their mother wasn't around. (SM) <SM> <***Loc:*** AV, IB, SB, SL, SM, Da84, Lv88>

corcobier ♦see **corcobiller**

corcobillage ♦see **corcobiage**

corcobiller (**courcoubier, corcobier**) [kɔrkobje, kurkubje, korkobije] *v.intr.* **1** to buck (of a horse) *Il y avait des chevaux, tu pouvais pas aller mettre ça en arrière. Il aurait corcobié.* There were horses, you couldn't go put that on their backs. It would've bucked. (EV) *Corcobiller comme un cheval.* To buck like a horse. (LA) **2** to jump, jump around *Le docteur va le faire corcobier quand il lui coupera le doigt.* The doctor will make him jump when he cuts his finger. (SB) *Les enfants ont corcobié assez en haut qu'ils ont cassé la grosse sole du milieu.* The children jumped around so much up there that they broke the big center beam. (LA) *Les 'tits sont après courcoubier sur le lit.* The little ones are jumping around on the bed. (Lv88) <***Loc:*** AV, EV, LA, SB, SL, SM, VM, Da84, Lv88, La99, Ph36>

cordage [kɔrdaʒ] *n.m.* cordage, cords, strings *Quand il a été pour ramasser sa palangre, tout son cordage était mêlé.* When he went to pick up his trotline, his cordage was all tangled. (VM) <***Loc:*** VM, Da84>

corde[1] [kɔrd] *n.f.* **1** rope *Équand on était petits, nos parents nous amenait au cirque. Et le monde qui marchait sur les cordes là, on appelait ça des capecapes.* When we were little, our parents took us to the circus. And the people that walked on those ropes, we used to call them "capecapes." (LF) **2** string, cord, twine **3** string (of a fiddle, guitar, etc.) *Mon s'a commencé sus la guitare à six cordes.* I started on a six string guitar. (TB) *L'archet, ça gratte sur les cordes.* The bow scratches across the strings [on the fiddle]. (ch: *Bon rêve*) **4** *(usu. pl.)* sandal ◊ •**corde à linge** clothesline <LA, Da84, Fa77> •**corde à marchand** store twine <Da84> •**corde à sauter** jump rope <Da84> •**corde à soulier** shoelace, shoestring <TB, Da84, Fa77, Lv88> •**corde échappée** ***a*** animal that has been deliberately lost and is wandering the streets ***b*** unintelligent person <SL, La99> <***Loc:*** AC, LA, LF, SL, TB, Da84, Guoo, La99, Lv88>

corde[2] [kɔrd] *n.f.* cord (of wood), measure of cut and split firewood **Corde de bois.* Rank of wood, cord of wood. (Da84) <***Loc:*** AC, LA, LF, SL, TB, Da84, Guoo, La99, Lv88>

cordé, -e [kɔrde] *adj.* **1** corded, stacked (as wood) *Du bois cordé.* Stacked wood. (EV) **2** packed, jammed, crowded *La chambre est cordée de tes affaires.* The room is jammed with your stuff. (VM) *C'était cordé de monde.* It was full of people. (Lv88) <***Loc:*** EV, VM, Da84, Lv88>

cordeau [kɔrdo] *n.m.* **1** cable, thick rope **2** *(pl.)* reins, leather reins <***Loc:*** SM, Lv88, Re31>

cordelle [kɔrdɛl] *n.f.* **1** cordelle (heavy rope formerly used for towing boats or barges along bayous, etc., often by horses or mules walking along a path that ran beside the bayou) **2** clothesline <***Loc:*** LF, SB>

corder (**cadrer**) [kɔrde, kadre] **I** *v.tr.* **1** to stack, pile, line up *On cordait les saucisses dans des jarres.* We stacked up sausages in jars. (Lv88) **2** to stack, cord (firewood, usu. to cure and dry) *Il avait le foyer. Il l'aurait cordé plein de bois jusqu'à en haut.* He had the hearth. He would stack it full of firewood up to the top. (SL) *Quatre cordes dans la journée. Tu les sciais, et coupais, fendu et cordé.* Four cords in a day. You would saw them, and cut them, split and corded. (SL) **3** to cram, stuff, pack full *On a cordé la chambre avec des drigailles.* We crammed the room full of your junk. (IB) **4** to roll, roll up, coil *Il faudra corder le HOSE.* The hose will have to be rolled up. (LA) **II se corder** *v.pron.* to line up *Tout quelqu'un se cordait pour acheter du gaz.* Everyone lined up to buy gas. (EV) <***Loc:*** EV, IB, LA, SB, SL, SM, TB, Da84, Lv88>

cordial [kɔrdjal] *adj.* cordial, friendly <***Loc:*** Da84>

cordon [kɔrdɔ̃] *n.m.* **1** string, strand **2** shoelace **3** chimes (of a boat frame) ◊ •**cordon bleu** blue cord (used as a symbol of dedication of a child to the Virgin Mary)<Da84> <***Loc:*** IB, LF, Da84>

cordonnier [kɔrdɔ̃je] *n.m.* shoemaker, shoe repairman <***Loc:*** Da84>

coriance [kɔrjɑ̃s] *n.f.* coriander *Graine de coriance.* Coriander seed. (TB) *Thé de coriance.* Coriander tea. (TB) <***Loc:*** TB>

cormoran [kɔrmorɑ̃, kalmɔrɔ̃] *n.m.* cormorant <***Loc:*** JE, SB, Da84, Fa77, Lv88>

cornailler [kɔrnaje] *v.tr.* to butt, strike with the horns <***Loc:*** JD, LA>

cornard [kɔrnar] *n.m.* jimson weed <***Loc:*** EV, IB, TB, Guoo, Lv88, Ph36, Re31>

corne[1] [kɔrn] *n.f.* **1** horn (of a cow or other animal) **2** horn (musical instrument) **3** horn (of a car or other vehicle) **4** corn, clavus ◊ •**corne creuse** 'hollow horn' (malady believed by farmers to afflict cattle) <VM> •**corne de mouton** corkscrew <Lv88> •**corne de vache** rutabaga <Lv88> •**corne grecque** okra <Lv88> <***Loc:*** EV, LA, TB, VM, An77, An94, Da84, La99, Lv88>

corne[2] ♦see **congre**

corneille [kɔrnɛj, kɔrnej] *n.f.* crow ◊ •**corneille fouetteur** bee martin, kingbird <Re31> <***Loc:*** AV, LA, SB, SL, SM, VM, Da84, Lv88, Re31>

corner [kɔrne] **I** *v.tr.* to sound, honk, blow (a horn) *Corner la corne.* To honk the horn. (TB) **II** *v.intr.* to blow a horn, honk *Quand j'ai attendu le char corner, je savais il y avait quelque chose de mauvais qui était arrivé.* When I heard the car honk its horn, I knew something bad had happened. (EV) <***Loc:*** EV, TB, Da84>

cornet [kɔrnɛ, kɔrne] *n.f.* **1** cornet, bugle, musical horn **2** horn (of a car or other vehicle) *J'avais cru que j'avais entendu un cornet de char.* I thought I had heard a car horn. (VM) **3** horn, amplifying device **4** duck call *Le cornet fait le train d'un canard.* The duck call makes the sound of a duck. (Lv88) ◊ •**cornet de crème** ice cream cone <AV, IB> <***Loc:*** AV, IB, SL, VM, Da84, Lv88>

corniche (**cornuche**) [kɔrniʃ, kɔrnyʃ] *n.f.* **1** cornice, ledge, mantel, mantelpiece *Mets-lé sus la cornuche.* Put it on the mantelpiece. (TB) **2** eaves *Quand mes parents étaient jeunes, ils pendiont les canards sur la corniche de la maison.* When my parents were young, they hung ducks from the eaves of the house. (VM) <***Loc:*** LA, LF, SL, TB, VM, Da84, Lv88>

cornichon [kɔrniʃɔ̃] *n.m.* pickle ◊ •**en cornichons** pickled **Ça aimait les navets, ce monde-là, et particulièrement quand ils étiont en cornichons avec du vinaigre.* They liked turnips, those people, and particularly when they were pickled in vinegar. (EV, An94) <EV, An94> <***Loc:*** EV, IB, An94, Da84>

cornoyo [kɔrnojo] *n.m.* **1** 'it' (in children's games) **2** old, decrepit person **Vieux Deville c'est in [=un] vrai côrnôyau, i peut proche pus marcher.* Old Deville is old and decrepit, he can hardly walk any more. (EV, Ph36) <***Loc:*** EV, Da84, Ph36>

cornuche ♦see **corniche**

coronaire [kɔrɔ̃nær, kɔrɔ̃nœr] *n.m.* coroner <***Loc:*** SM, Da84>

coroneur ♦see **coronaire**

corporation [kɔrporasjɔ̃] *n.f.* **1** corporation, company **2** incorporated area of a town **3** civil corporation <***Loc:*** SM, Da84>

corporé, -e [kɔrpore] *adj.* ◊ •**bien corporé *a*** well built, shapely **Mon grand plaisir à moi, c'est... d'observer comment bien corporés les jeunes filles sont!* A great pleasure of mine is . . . to see how well made the girls are! (Gr82) ***b*** large, stout *Elle est bien corporée.* She's stout. (SM) <SM, Gr82> <***Loc:*** LA, SM, Gr82, Lv88>

corporel[1], **-elle** [kɔrporɛl] *adj.* corporal, bodily *Une punition corporelle.* A corporal punishment. (LA) <***Loc:*** LA, Da84>

corporel[2] [kɔrpɔrɛl] *n.m.* carburetor <***Loc:*** LF>

corporence [kɔrpɔrɑ̃s] *n.f.* corpulence <***Loc:*** JD>

corps [kɔr] *n.m.* **1** body *Il n'y a ni médecin ni chirurgien qui peut remettre mon corps en sain.* There is no doctor or surgeon to make my body healthy once again. (PQ, ch: *Sainte Catherine*) *Le corps [du rabot], je crois que c'est à peu près dix ou douze pouces.* The body [of the planer], I think it's about ten or twelve inches long. (JE) **2** corpse *Un corps s'a ramassé au Lac Arthur.* A corpse ended up deposited at Lake Arthur. (VM) **3** trunk (of a tree) ◊ •**corps relâché** loose bowels <Da84> •**faire du corps** to gain weight *Rose a fait du corps.* Rose has gained weight. (IB) <IB> •**vieux corps** [*term of endearment*] old fellow, buddy, friend <Da84> <***Loc:*** EV, IB, JE, LF, PQ, SM, TB, VM, Da84, La99, Lv88>

corrailler (**correiller**) [koraje, koreje] *v.tr.* to pen up, drive or lead (an animal) into a pen *Ils ont eu pour corailler les taures.* They had to pen up the heifers. (LA) <***Loc:*** LA, VM>

corral ♦see **corail**

correct [korɛk(t)] *adj.* **1** correct, right *C'est pas correct parce que t'as pas bien écrit mon nom.* It's not correct because you didn't spell my name right. (EV) **2** okay, all right *J'avais perdu mes lunettes, mais c'est correct, je les ai trouvées.* I had lost my glasses but it's okay, I found them. (EV) *Tout quelque chose est correct asteur.* Everything is all right now. (EV) **3** right, in proper working condition *Sa mémoire est pas tout à fait correct.* His memory isn't quite right. (AS) ◊ •**c'est correct** it's all right <Lv88> <***Loc:*** AS, EV, VM, An94, Da84, Lv88>

correctement [korɛkt(ə)mɑ̃] *adv.* correctly *Si tu vas pas le faire correctement, laisse ça tranquille.* If you're not going to do it correctly, leave it alone. (EV) <***Loc:*** EV, Da84>

correcter [korɛkte] *v.tr.* **1** to correct *Il a correcté son erreur.* He corrected his error. (LA) **2** to correct, grade (school papers) **Correcter les devoirs.* To correct papers. (EV, Ph36) **3** to discipline *Je vas correcter l'enfant.* I'm going to discipline the child. (IB) <***Loc:*** EV, IB, SL, SM, Da84, Lv88, Ph36>

correction [korɛksjɔ̃] *n.f.* **1** correction **2** correction, punishment <***Loc:*** Da84>

correiller ♦see **corrailler**

correspondance [korɛspɔ̃dɑ̃s] *n.f.* correspondence, exchange of letters <***Loc:*** Da84>

correspondant, -e [korɛspɔ̃dɑ̃, -ɑ̃t] *n.* correspondant <***Loc:*** Da84>

correspondre [korɛspɔ̃n, korɛspɔ̃d(r)] *v.intr.* **1** to correspond, match, harmonize *Ça correspond pas à ça je croyais.* That doesn't correspond to what I thought. (LA) **2** to correspond, exchange letters *Mes grandes tantes avaient l'habitude de correspondre avec leur parenté qu'avait resté en France.* My great aunts were in the habit of corresponding with the members of their family who had remained in France. (LA) <***Loc:*** LA, Da84>

corridor (**colidor**) [koridɔr, kolidɔr] *n.m.* corridor, hallway *J'aime pas une maison qu'a un colidor.* I don't like a house that has a hallway. (TB) <***Loc:*** SB, SL, SM, TB, VM, Da84, Lv88>

corriger [koriʒe] **I** *v.tr.* **1** to set (a broken bone), put (a broken or dislocated bone) back in position *Le docteur a pas corrigé bien la cassure.* The doctor didn't set the break well. (VM) **2** to correct *Tu devrais corriger ça avec ton frère. Tu devrais pas rester brouillé après lui.* You should make amends with your brother. You shouldn't stay on the outs with him. (VM) **3** to discipline *Il faut que tu corriges tes enfants quand ils faisont mal.* You have to discipline your children when they do wrong. (VM) *Garçons à marier, prenez exemple sur moi.*

Corrigez bien vos femmes. Boys who are marrying, follow my example. Be sure to discipline your wives. (VM, ch: *Je me suis marié*) **II se corriger** *v.pron.* **1** to correct o.s. **2** to mend one's ways *Je m'ai corrigé. Je bois pus comme avant.* I have mended my ways. I don't drink like I used to. (VM) <***Loc:*** TB, VM, Da84>

corrupter [korypte] *v.tr.* to corrupt *Mais c'est malheureux que le système d'école est tellement sale, c'est corrupté par le diable. Ça les enseigne que eux-autres vient des bétailles.* But it's awful how the school system is so dirty, it's corrupted by the devil. They teach them that they come from animals. (LF) <***Loc:*** LF>

corruption [korypsjɔ̃] *n.f.* corruption <***Loc:*** Da84>

corsade ♦see **cossarde**

corsage (**corchage, cochage**) [kɔrʃaʒ, koʃaʒ] *n.m.* **1** blouse **2** corsage, bodice (of a dress) **3** corsage (of flowers) ◊ **•corsage de dessous** brassiere <Fa77, Guoo> <***Loc:*** EV, LA, SL, VM, Da84, Fa77, Guoo, Lv88>

corselette [kɔrslɛt] *n.f.* band or girdle of elastic material (for exerting pressure on some part of the body) <***Loc:*** VM>

corset [kɔrsɛ, kɔrse] *n.m.* **1** corset **2** girdle <***Loc:*** Da84>

cortège [kɔrtɛʒ] *n.m.* **1** cortege, procession **2** cortege, retinue <***Loc:*** Da84>

corusse (**korusse, chorus**) [korys, kurys] *n.m.* **1** cock, rooster **2** gamecock *Et ça enfilait les éperons sur les corusses pour se battre, et le dernier corusse en vie c'est lui qui gagnait.* And they strung spurs on the roosters for fighting, and the last rooster alive was the winner. (LF) <***Loc:*** AV, IB, IV, JE, LF, SB, SJ, SM, TB, VM, Lv88, Re31>

cosmétique [kɔsmetik] *n.m.* **1** cosmetic **2** oily black crayon used by African-Americans to straighten the hair or beard <***Loc:*** VM, Da84>

cossarde (**corsade, coissarde**) [kosard, kɔrsad, kwasard] *n.f.* **1** any of various hawks **2** sparrow hawk, American kestrel **3** duck hawk, peregrine falcon **4** prairie hawk **5** red-tailed hawk **6** marsh hawk, harrier <***Loc:*** IB, TB, VM, Guoo, Lv88, Re31>

costume [kɔstym] *n.m.* **1** costume *Un costume de Mardi Gras.* A Mardi Gras costume. (LA) **2** uniform dress *Un costume de soldat.* A soldier's uniform. (VM) <***Loc:*** LA, VM, Da84>

cotchille ♦see **coquille**

côte[1] [kot] *n.f.* rib **Quand je vas mourir (j'ai fait mon* WILL *l'autre jour), je veux ça prend rien que ma tête. Et les côtes, que ça donne ça aux chiens.* When I die (I made my will the other day), I want them to take nothing but my head. And the ribs, they can give those to the dogs. (EV, An94) *Côtes de cochon.* Pork ribs. (Fa77) ◊ **•côte à côte** even, parallel, side by side *Ils ont amarré les deux chevaux sur deux poteaux côte à côte.* They tied the two horses on two posts that were side by side. (SL, An94) <SL, An94, Da84> **•avoir les côtes en long** to be lazy <SM, TB, Da84, La99, Re31> <***Loc:*** EV, SL, SM, TB, An94, Da84, Fa77, La99, Re31>

côte[2] [kot] *n.f.* **1** coast **Au long de la côte.* Along the coast. (Da84) **2** group of farms or houses, settlement of a particular community or ethnic group (often used in toponyms) *La Côte des Acadiens.* The Acadian Coast. (Lv88) *La Côte des Allemands.* The German Coast. (Lv88) *Cette partie ici,* CUTOFF*, c'était appelé la Côte Blanche.* This area here, Cutoff, it used to be called the White Coast. (LF) **3** neighborhood *Je reste au ras de ma famille, on reste tout ensemble dans la même côte, dans le même voisinage.* I live near my family, we all live together in the same neighborhood. (LF) *Il est quelque part dans la côte.* He is somewhere in the neighborhood. (TB) **4** hill ◊ **•faire la côte** to canvass a neighborhood *Alle a fait la côte pour le* FAIR*.* She canvassed the neighborhood for the fair. (TB) <TB> <***Loc:*** AV, EV, JE, LF, SL, TB, VM, An94, Da84, Guoo, La99, Lv88>

côté[1] [kote] *n.m.* side *T'amarres ta corde sur le côté du bateau, là tu jettes ça à l'eau.* You tie the rope onto the side of the boat, then you throw it in the water. (TB) *Le mal anglais m'a laissé un placard sus le côté.* The shingles left me with a big spot on my side. (VM) ◊ **•à côté** apart, aside, on the side *Je vendais de l'assurance à côté.* I sold insurance on the side. (LF) <LF> **•(à) côté de** ***a*** beside, next to *Il s'a caché dans les cannes à côté du bayou.* He hid in the reeds beside the bayou. (LA) *Ça a arrivé côté de la ville, dans la rivière.* That happened near the city, in the river. (TB) ***b*** near, close to *Rester côté de la maison.* To stay near the house. (Da84) *Ça a arrivé côté de la ville, dans la rivière.* That happened near the city, in the river. (TB) ***c*** at the house of *Venez côté de chez moi.* Come over to my house. (Da84) ***d*** out of, away from *Y avait personne qui nous voulait, c'était tout des criminels. Ils nous ont chassé côté de* NOVA SCOTIA*.* No one wanted us, they were all criminals. They chased us out of Nova Scotia. (TB) ***e*** about, approximately *Il a reçu côté de dix piastres.* He got about ten dollars. (VM) <AC, LA, TB, VM, An94, Da84> **•mettre de côté** to put aside, put away *Hormis que c'est un job que l'homme a et qu'il faut qu'il travaille [...], mais à part de ça on travaille pas cette journée-là, on met cette journée-là de côté.* Unless it's a job that a man has where he must work, but otherwise we don't work on that day, we put that day aside. (TB) <TB> **•se mettre à côté** to keep away, stay away <Da84> **•sur le côté de** beside, next to *J'étais sur le côté d'eux.* I was beside them. (LA) <LA> <***Loc:*** LA, LF, SJ, TB, Da84>

côté[2] [kote] *prep.* **1** beside, next to *On reste côté pape.* We live next door to dad. (SM) **2** at the house of *Hier après-midi on a été là-bas côté sa mame.* Yesterday afternoon we went down to his mother's. (TB) *T'as été côté Dovie?* Have you been to Dovie's? (TB) **3** from *Je vais emprunter l'argent côté mon frère.* I'm going to borrow money from my brother. (Lv88) **4** toward, to *Viens côté moi.* Come to me. (SB) <***Loc:*** AC, LA, SM, TB, VM, Lv88, An94, Da84>

côteau [koto] *n.m.* **1** hill, mound, ridge **2** land that doesn't flood

3 elevated land in a swamp <*Loc:* SM, Da84, Guoo, La99, Lv88>

côteiller ♦see **courtiller**

côtelette [kɔtlɛt] *n.f.* cutlet, chop ◊ **•côtelette de cochon** pork chop <VM> <*Loc:* VM, Da84>

cotillon [kotijɔ̃] *n.m.* 1 dance 2 dress <*Loc:* Da84>

côtiller ♦see **courtiller**

côtiser ♦see **courtiser**

côtisot ♦see **courtisaud**

coton[1] [kotɔ̃] *n.m.* 1 cotton plant 2 cotton, cotton cloth ◊ **•coton à tapisser** cheesecloth <VM> **•coton baille** pale, unbleached cotton <Lv88> **•coton jaune** yellow cotton *Et dans le vieux temps eux-autres faisait les draps avec du coton jaune.* And in the old days they made sheets with yellow cotton. (TB) <LA, TB, Lv88> <*Loc:* CL, EV, IB, JE, LA, LF, SL, SM, TB, VM, Da84, Guoo, La99, Lv88>

coton[2] [kotɔ̃] *n.m.* stem, stalk *Le coton de la feuille a cassé.* The stem of the leaf broke. (AV) ◊ **•coton-maïs** corncob *Le monde sauvait tout quelque chose. Ça sauvait les coton-maïs après c'était érobé.* People saved everything. They saved the corncobs after they were shucked. (SL) <AV, EV, IB, SJ, SL, SM, TB, VM> <*Loc:* AV, EV, IB, SJ, SL, SM, TB, VM>

cotonnade [kotɔ̃nad] *n.f.* 1 cheap cotton cloth, homespun cloth *Y'a pas de fin de cotonnade.* There isn't any fine homespun cotton cloth. (Lv88) 2 cotton goods <*Loc:* CL, SB, Da84, Lv88>

cotonnerie [kotɔ̃nri] *n.f.* cotton storage shed, cotton seed storage shed <*Loc:* LA>

cotonnier [kotɔ̃je] *n.m.* 1 cottonwood tree 2 sycamore 3 buttonwood <*Loc:* AV, EV, LA, SB, SL, TB, Da84, Guoo, Lv88, Ph36, Re31>

cou [ku] *n.m.* 1 neck *Je vais casser ton cou si tu me bloffes!* I'll break your neck if you deceive me! (SM) 2 neck (of a bottle) ◊ **•cou-blanc** semipalmated plover <Lv88> **•cou-collier** ring-necked plover <Lv88> **•cou-rouge** [*pej.*] redneck, Anglophone not of Cajun ethnicity <AV, IB, LA, Da84, La99, Lv88> <*Loc:* AV, EV, IB, JE, LA, SM, TB, VM, An94, Da84, La99, Lv88, Wh83>

couac [kwak] *n.m.* American bittern (locally called sungazer) <*Loc:* LF, Lv88, Re31>

couac-soleil (couac-à-soleil) [kwaksolɛj, kwakasolɛj] *n.m.* 1 American bittern (locally called sungazer) 2 worthless man, bum *Sa fille reste avec un couac-soleil, un homme qui vaut pas rien.* Her daughter lives with a worthless bum, a man who's no good. (TB) <*Loc:* LF, TB>

couarte (couarte) [kwart] *n.m./f.* 1 bullwhip, short whip made of plaited thongs *Il a cassé la couarte sur le dos de l'animal.* He broke the whip on the back of the animal. (SL) 2 riding crop ◊ **•avoir la couarte sus l'épaule** to be ready to leave <EV, Ph36> <*Loc:* EV, SL, SM, VM, Lv88, Ph36>

couarter (couetter) [kwarte] *v.tr.* to whip (with a braided whip or riding crop) *Son cheval était si loin en avant qu'il a jamais eu pour le couetter.* His horse was so far in front that he never had to whip it. (LA) <*Loc:* LA, SM, Lv88>

coucha ♦see **cacha**

couchant, -e [kuʃɑ̃, -ɑ̃t] *adj.* setting **Le soleil couchant.* The setting sun. The sunset. (Da84) <*Loc:* Da84>

couche [kuʃ] *n.f.* 1 confinement (for childbirth) 2 delivery (of an infant) 3 diaper 4 coat of paint 5 layer *Tu venais là et tu mettais une couche de* DELAMITE. You came there and you put down a layer of dynamite. (LF) ◊ **•fausse-couche *a*** miscarriage ***b*** abortion <Da84> <*Loc:* IB, IV, JE, LA, LF, SB, SL, SM, TB, VM, An94, Da84>

couche-couche [kuʃkuʃ] *n.f.* 1 steamed, moist cornmeal eaten as a cereal 2 fried corn meal mush (corn meal dough sweetened with sugar, fried brown, and served with milk) ◊ **•couche-couche caillé *a*** 'curds and whey' (dish made of couche-couche served with curdled milk or cream) ***b*** name of a children's game <CL> <*Loc:* CL, EV, LA, SM, VM, Da84, Guoo, Lv88>

couchée [kuʃe] *n.f.* setting (of the sun) **La couchée du soleil.* The setting of the sun. (Da84) <*Loc:* Da84>

coucher [kuʃe] **I** *v.tr.* 1 to put to bed *Il a eu pour coucher ses vaches dedans le bois ce soir là.* He had to bed down his cattle in the woods that night. (LA) 2 to flatten (grass, cane, etc.) *On commence à couper les cannes grandes avec ces nouvelles autres machines qu'on a là, un* TWO-ROW *machine alle coupe deux rangs à la fois, alle couche les cannes par terre.* We're starting to cut the tall sugarcane with these other new machines, a two-row machine cuts two rows at once, it flattens the cane. (AS) 3 to hunt *On allait avec des chiens coucher des lapins.* We used to go with dogs to hunt for rabbits. (IB) **II** *v.intr.* to sleep, spend the night *Et là si les garçons couchaient en l'air, c'était une garçonnière eusse appelait ça. Parce que les garçons couchent en l'air et les filles couchent en bas.* And then if the boys slept upstairs they called it a "garçonnière." Boys sleep upstairs and girls sleep down below. (LF) **III se coucher** *v.pron.* 1 to go to bed *Le monde avait l'habitude que tous les voisins et tout après souper, eusse se rencontrait tout à une maison, eusse faisait tout la veillée là, jusqu'à c'était l'heure que tout tchéqu'un va se coucher.* People used to meet with all their neighbors after supper, they would all meet at a house, they visited all evening, until it was time for everyone to go to bed. (LF) 2 to sleep *Dans les Philippines, tout le monde se couche par terre.* In the Philippines, everyone sleeps on the ground. (VM) ◊ **•coucher au poignet** to wrist wrestle, arm wrestle <LA, Da84> **•coucher au serein** to stay out all night, esp. after carousing <La99> **•se coucher avec les poules** to go to bed early <Da84> **•se coucher tout rond** to go to bed with all one's clothes on <VM, Da84> **•va te coucher *a*** I don't believe you ***b*** you should be ashamed of yourself ***c*** go away and leave me alone ***d*** go to hell! <La99> <*Loc:* AS, AV, EV, IB, JE, LA, LF, SL, SM, TB, VM, An94, Da84, Guoo, La99, Wh83>

couchette [kuʃɛt] *n.f.* camp bed, cot <***Loc:*** TB>

coucou[1] [kuku] *adj.* **1** stupid, ridiculous, idiotic *Ça c'est coucou.* That's idiotic. (Lv88) **2** crazy, insane <***Loc:*** LA, SB, Lv88>

coucou[2] [kuku] *n.m.* **1** cuckoo bird **2** wood thrush **3** nut, nutty person, wacko <***Loc:*** IB, Da84, Re31>

coucoua [kukuwa] *n.m.* owl *J'ai tué un coucoua hier soir.* I killed an owl last night. (AV) <***Loc:*** AV>

coucounne [kukun] *n.m.* cocoon <***Loc:*** Da84>

cou-croche (**coucroche**) [kukrɔʃ] *n.m.* cushaw, crookneck squash <***Loc:*** IB, Ho90, Re31>

coudage ♦see **cousage**

coude [kud, kut] *n.m./f.* **1** elbow **2** bend (in a road, etc.) **3** elbow in a pipe ◊ **•foutre un coup de coude** to elbow, jab with an elbow <Da84> <***Loc:*** TB, VM, Da84>

coudeuse (**coudrieuse**) [kudøz, kudrijøz] *n.f.* **1** dressmaker, seamstress **2** sewing machine <***Loc:*** Lv88>

coudpiéter ♦see **coupdepieter**

coudre (**couser**) [kud(r), kuze] (*p.p.* **coudu** [kudy], **cousu** [kusy]) **I** *v.tr.* to sew *Elle cousera le pantalon avant demain.* She'll sew the pants before tomorrow. (SB) *Asteur ça coude ça avec du plastique.* Nowadays, they sew it with plastic. (SM) **II** *v.intr.* to sew *Quand alle était plus jeune alle avait bitude de coudre.* When she was younger, she used to sew. (JE) *J'ai cousu un tas pour les enfants.* I used to sew extensively for the kids. (IB) ◊ **•coudre à la main** to sew by hand *Tu coudais ça à la main ou avec une machine jusqu'à que tu en ayes assez grand pour couvert un lit.* You sewed it by hand or with a machine until you had it big enough to cover a bed. (TB) <TB> **•coudre au doigt** to sew by hand <Lv88> <***Loc:*** AC, AV, EV, IB, JE, SB, SM, TB, VM, Da84, Lv88>

coudrieuse ♦see **coudeuse**

couenne [kwɑ̃n, kwɛ̃n] *n.f.* **1** pig skin, pork rind *Ils bouillont, ils faisont de la gelée et des boudins. Ils bouillont de la viande de cochon, de la couenne, cœur.* They boil it, they make head cheese and boudin. They boil pork meat, pig skin, the heart. (LF) **2** skin, hide *Il va massacrer sa couenne.* He'll tan his hide [i.e. give him a good beating]. (TB) <***Loc:*** AV, IB, LF, SB, TB, Da84>

couétil [kweti, koti, kwiti] *n.m.* mattress cover, mattress ticking <***Loc:*** IB, TB, Lv88>

couétir [kwetir] **I** *v.tr.* to warp, cause to warp *L'eau haute a tout couéti mon plancher.* The flood warped my floor. (VM) **II** *v.intr.* to warp, become warped *Mon plancher a tout couéti.* My floor got all warped. (VM) <***Loc:*** VM>

couette[1] [kwɛt, kwet] *n.f.* braid of hair <***Loc:*** EV, IB, JD, LA, SL, SM, TB, Da84, Ph36, Re31>

couette[2] [kwɛt, kwet] *n.f.* ticking, covering (of a mattress or pillow) ◊ **•couette de matelas** mattress ticking <JD, Da84> **•couette d'oreiller** pillow ticking <JD, Da84> <***Loc:*** IB, JD, LA, SM, TB, Da84, Lv88, Re31>

couette[3] ♦see **couarte**

couetter[1] [kwete] *v.tr.* to braid (hair) *Sa sœur a passé une bonne partie de l'après-midi à couetter ses cheveux.* Her sister spent much of the afternoon braiding her hair. (LA) <***Loc:*** LA, Da84>

couetter[2] ♦see **couarter**

couille [kuj] *n.f.* testicle <***Loc:*** SM, Da84>

couillon[1], **-onne** [kujɔ̃, -ɔ̃n] *adj.* stupid, foolish *Tu dois croire que je suis couillon pour de même!* You must think I'm really stupid! (TB) ◊ **•couillon comme la lune {un bourriquet / un cheval}** stupid, foolish <La99> <***Loc:*** IB, LA, LF, SL, SM, TB, Gu00, La99, Lv88>

couillon[2], **-onne** [kujɔ̃, -ɔ̃n] *n.* **1** nut, joker, funny person **2** simpleton, imbecile, idiot, nitwit *Je vas vous dire de quoi, je sais pas si vous va me croire ou me prendre pour un couillon.* I'm going to tell you something, I don't know if you'll believe me or take me for an imbecile. (LF) ◊ **•couillon d'eau douce** simpleton, imbecile, idiot, nitwit (lit. "freshwater idiot") <La99> **•faire son couillon** ***a*** to show off ***b*** to mess around, horse around *C'est une disgrace la manière qu'ils font leur couillon dans l'église.* It's a disgrace the way they horse around in the church. (SM) <SM, Lv88> <***Loc:*** AV, IB, JE, LA, LF, SB, SM, VM, Da84, Gu82, La99, Lv88>

couillonade [kujɔ̃nad] *n.f.* **1** joke, cutting up, joking *Tu t'ennuies pas, c'est toujours après dire quelque couillonnade.* You don't get bored, you're always telling some joke. (Lv88) **2** stupid thing, foolish thing, bit of foolishness or nonsense *Jean a fait une couillonade quand il s'a marié.* Jean did a really stupid thing when he got married [by getting married]. (SM) *Dire des couillonades.* To say foolish things. (AV) **3** cheating, fooling around (with s.o. other than one's spouse) *Sa femme est placée avec un Sabine de en bas du Petit Caillou. [...] C. savait pas qu'il y avait ces couillonades après aller.* His wife is shacked up with a Sabine from down in Little Caillou. C. didn't know that that fooling around was going on. (TB) <***Loc:*** AV, LA, SB, SM, TB, Da84, Lv88>

couillonner [kujɔ̃ne] **I** *v.tr.* to deceive, dupe, cheat, swindle, fool *Il l'a couillonné pour cent piastres.* He cheated him out of a hundred dollars. (AS) **II** *v.intr.* to clown around, fool around, cut up *Tu devrais bien arrêter de couillonner.* You ought to stop fooling around. (LA) ◊ **•couillonner avec** ***a*** to tamper with, fool around with *Couillonne pas avec mes livres.* Don't fool with my books. (LF) ***b*** to bother, mess around with *Couillonne pas avec moi.* Don't mess around with me. Don't bother me. (SM) ***c*** to cheat, fool around with (s.o. other than one's spouse) *Il est après couillonner avec la femme d'un autre.* He's fooling around with another man's wife. (LF) <***Loc:*** AS, IB, LA, LF, SB, SL, SM, TB, Da84, Lv88>

couillonnerie [kujɔ̃nri] *n.f.* clowning, joking, cutting up <***Loc:*** Da84>

couilte ♦see **quilt**

couilter ♦see **quilter**

couique [kwik] *n.m.* lazy, unambitious person <***Loc:*** SM>

coulage [kulaʒ] *n.m.* straining (of a liquid) <***Loc:*** Da84>

coulant, -e [kulɑ̃, -ɑ̃t] *adj.* flowing *Ils ont trouvé de l'eau coulante derrière le magasin.* They found flowing water behind the barn. (LA) <***Loc:*** LA, Da84>

coulante [kulɑ̃t] *n.f.* gonorrhea <***Loc:*** VM>

coulée [kule] *n.f.* **1** stream, brook, creek, rivulet *L'homme a attrapé des poissons dans la coulée.* The man caught some fish in the stream. (SB) **2** coulee, gully, ravine **3** lowland where rainwater collects and stands <***Loc:*** AC, AV, EV, IB, LA, LF, SB, SJ, SM, Da84, Guoo, Lv88, Ph36>

couler [kule] **I** *v.tr.* **1** to drain, strain *Elle aurait coulé son jus pour voir s'il n'avait pas des petits morceaux de feuilles.* She would strain her juice to see if there were not any small pieces of leaves. (SL) **2** to pour *Couler de l'eau dans le verre.* To pour water into the glass. (LF) **II** *v.intr.* **1** to flow, run *Et là tu vois là-bas, j'ai un trou dans le* TANK *et là il coule, tu vois le tuyau en-dessous là?* And you see over there, I have a hole in the tank, and it flows, you see the tube down there? (TB) **2** to leak out, drain out **Tu connais, quand tu mets onze gallons d'eau dans ton chapeau, puis tu le mets sur ta tête, mais ça tient la tête froide, tu connais, mais l'eau coule des fois, s'il est pas bien serré.* You know, when you put eleven gallons of water in your hat, and you put it on your head, it keeps your head cool, you know, but the water leaks sometimes, if it's not really tight. (EV, An94) **3** to leak, drip *La couverture coule.* The roof is leaking. (SM) ◊ **•couler le café** to drip coffee <Da84, Lv88> **•coule-macaroni** colander <TB> <***Loc:*** AC, EV, IB, IV, LA, LF, SL, SM, TB, An94, Da84, Lv88>

couleur [kulœr] *n.f.* **1** color *Je faisais du roux [...] avec de l'huile et de la farine, brassé jusqu'à ce que c'est de la bonne couleur, un peu brun.* I used to make roux with oil and flour, stirred until it's the right color, brownish. (SL) *Sa couleur est pas bonne depuis sa maladie.* His [skin] color is not good since his illness. (EV) **2** dye *Il a commencé à mettre de la couleur dans ses cheveux.* He started putting dye in his hair. (VM) **3** colored person, black person **Ma p'tite fille est maîtresse d'école. Elle a des pitits blancs et des pitites couleurs.* My granddaughter is a school teacher. She has little whites and little blacks. (Gr82) *Cimetière de couleurs.* Cemetery for black people. (SM) **4** makeup, color *Là ça mettait de la couleur sur leur figure.* Then they would put makeup on their faces. (TB) **5** *(usu. pl.)* watercolor paints ◊ **•la couleur** colored people, esp. African-Americans *L'aut' bord, c'est tout la couleur.* On the other side of the street, there is nothing but blacks. (Lv88) <Da84, Lv88> <***Loc:*** AV, EV, LF, SL, TB, VM, Da84, Gu82, Lv88>

couleurer [kulœre] **I** *v.tr.* to color *L'enfant a couleuré mon livre.* The child colored my book. (SM) **II se couleurer** *v.pron.* to dye (one's hair) *Mon j'étais après me* DYE *les cheveux à dix-neuf ans. J'avais les cheveux blancs déjà. Et j'ai arrêté de me les couleurer après que D. est née.* I was dyeing my hair at nineteen. I already had white hair. And I stopped dyeing it after D. was born. (TB) <***Loc:*** SL, SM, TB, Lv88>

couleuvre (**coulève**) [kulɛv] *n.f.* garter snake, grass snake <***Loc:*** EV, SL, Guoo, Lv88, Ph36>

coulève ♦see **couleuvre**

couline [kulin] *n.f.* **1** stream **2** pond <***Loc:*** TB>

coulisse [kulis] *n.f.* groove, runner (as of a sliding door) <***Loc:*** SL>

couloir (**couloire, écouloir**) [kulwar, ekulwar] *n.m.* colander, strainer, sieve *J'ai faim, il dit. Chauffe les crabes, il dit, pour que je mange. Ça fait que j'ai pris une bombe, j'ai mis le couloir dessus avec les crabes dedans, et p'is je les ai rechauffés.* I'm hungry, he says. Heat up the crabs, he says, for me to eat. So I took a cooking pot, I put the strainer on it with the crabs inside, and I heated them up. (TB) <***Loc:*** AL, AV, EV, IB, JE, LA, LF, SJ, SM, TB, VM, Da84, Lv88>

couloire ♦see **couloir**

coundja ♦see **condjo**

counoute [kunut] *n.f.* penis <***Loc:*** SB>

coup [ku] *n.m.* **1** blow, strike, hit *Sacrer un coup de main.* To strike with the hand. (Lv88) **2** time, occasion *Dis-lui après quand il a venu ici pour Christmas, le premier coup que tu l'as rencontré.* Tell him about the time when he came here for Christmas, the first time that you met him. (TB) **3** practical joke *Et là, elle m'a foutu le coup, je lavais les plats toujours et je mets mes souliers moi-même.* And then she played the practical joke on me, I still had to wash the plates and put on my shoes myself. (VM) **4** drink, shot (of liquor) ◊ **•coup d'accroc** stroke of luck *Il a frappé la balle; c'était un coup d'accroc.* He hit the ball; it was a stroke of luck. (LF) <LF, SB> **•coup de bâton** blow with a stick <TB, Da84> **•coup de bec** peck (of a bird) <Da84> **•coup de chance** stroke of luck <Da84> **•coup de colère** fit of anger <LA, Da84> **•coup de force** feat of strength <Da84> **•coup de fusil** gunshot <SM, TB, VM, Lv88> **•coup de grâce** finishing blow <Da84> **•coup de main *a*** assistance, help, helping hand *Tu peux me donner un coup de main demain?* Can you give me a hand tomorrow? (LA) ***b*** neighborhood cooperative effort *Vieux M. Sonnier était trop malade pour rentrer son maïs, ça fait ses voisins ont fait un coup de main pour l'aider.* Old Mr. Sonnier was too sick to harvest his corn, so his neighbors got together to do it for him. (LA) <AV, LA, Da84, La99> **•coup de malin** sly trick, clever ruse <TB> **•coup de midi** stroke of noon <Da84> **•coup de nord** cold wave, usu. violent with much rain <SM> **•coup de pied** kick <LF, SL, An94, Da84> **•coup de poing** punch <AV, LA, LF, SM, TB, Lv88> **•coup de sifflet** whistle <Da84> **•coup de soleil *a*** sunburn ***b*** sunstroke <TB, Guoo> **•coup de tape** slap <EV, LA, An94, Gu82, Lv88> **•coup d'état** coup d'état <Da84> **•coup de temps** bad weather, storm <VM, Da84, Guoo, Lv88> **•coup de tonnerre** thunder clap

<TB> **•coup de vent** ***a*** sudden gust of wind ***b*** sudden storm <LA, Da84> **•coup d'œil** glimpse <Da84> **•coup mortel** mortal blow <Da84> **•à chaque coup** each time *À chaque coup je vois la fille à Annette, dit "TELL MR. MANUEL I WANT TO SEE HIM."* Each time I see Annette's daughter [she] says, "tell Mr. Manuel I want to see him." (EV) *"Ouais, mais," il dit, "si t'as remarqué, le coq change de poule à chaque coup."* "Yes, but," he says, "if you noticed, the rooster changes hens each time." (AS) <AS, EV, TB> **•à coup sûr** with certainty <VM, Da84> **•avoir un bon coup de fourchette** to be a big eater, be a glutton <VM, La99> **•avoir un coup de lune** to be in a contrary mood <SB, La99> **•d'un coup** at a time, at one time *On prend un siau et on rouvre les huîtres. Et des fois on mange la motchié de le sac d'un coup!* We get a bucket and we open the oysters. And sometimes we eat half of the bag at one time! (TB) <TB> **•faire les quatre cents coups** ***a*** to cut up, act mischievously, raise all kinds of hell ***b*** to make a lot of noise ***c*** to do all sorts of things <Da84, La99> **•faire un beau {bon} coup** ***a*** to strike it lucky ***b*** to make a good deal <Da84> **•faire un gros coup** to make a big deal <Da84> **•faire un mauvais coup** to make a bad deal <Da84> **•foutre des coups (à qqn)** to beat (s.o.) up <Da84> **•petit coup de grandeur** something done as a 'show-off' act <La99> **•prendre ça à coups de bâton** to be so angry <La99> **•sur le coup de (minuit)** on the stroke of (midnight) <SM> **•tout d'un coup** suddenly, all of a sudden <AV, EV, JE, LA, SM, TB, An94, Da84> **•un coup que** once, when *Un coup qu'il a fait son idée, il la change pas.* Once he has made up his mind, he does not change it. (JD) <JD, TB, Da84, Lv88> ***<Loc:*** AV, EV, IB, JD, JE, LA, LF, SB, SL, SM, TB, VM, Da84, Gu00, Gu82, La99, Lv88>

coupable [kupab(l)] *adj.* guilty, at fault *Tu te sens pas coupable?* Don't you feel guilty? (VM) ***<Loc:*** VM, Da84>

coupacher [kupaʃe] *v.tr.* to cut up, cut to pieces *Ils ont tout coupaché ma robe.* They cut my dress all to pieces. (SL) ***<Loc:*** SL>

coupage [kupaʒ] *n.m.* cutting ◊ **•coupage de canne** cane cutting, cane harvest <Da84> ***<Loc:*** Da84>

coupailler [kupaje] *v.tr.* to cut up, chop up, hack up *Le petit garçon a coupaillé mon livre.* The little boy cut up my book. (SM) ***<Loc:*** AV, IB, JD, LF, SB, SL, SM, TB, Da84>

coupant, -e [kupɑ̃, -ɑ̃t] *adj.* sharp, cutting *Les feuilles des lames d'épée sont coupantes comme un couteau.* The leaves of cut grass are as sharp as a knife. (VM) ***<Loc:*** VM, Da84>

coupdepiéter (**coudpiéter**) [kutpjete, kudpjete] *v.tr.* to kick *Il était après coupdepiéter un CAN quand son RIDE a arrivé.* He was kicking a can when his ride arrived. (LA) ***<Loc:*** JD, LA, SB, Da84, Lv88>

coupe[1] [kup] *n.f.* **1** cut **2** cut or opening in land or in a levee for drainage *Si je veux noyer mon clos, il faut que je bouche les coupes.* If I want to flood my field, I have to plug up the openings in the levee. (VM) ◊ **•coupe (de cheveux)** haircut <EV, Hi02> **•avoir la coupe de figure de (qqn)** to resemble (s.o.) *Il a la coupe de figure de son pape.* He resembles his father. (TB) <TB> ***<Loc:*** EV, VM, Da84, Gu00, Hi02, Lv88>

coupe[2] [kup] *n.f.* cup ***<Loc:*** Da84>

coupe-paille [kuppaj] *n.m.* lawnmower ***<Loc:*** Re31>

couper [kupe] **I** *v.tr.* **1** to cut *On commence à couper les cannes grandes avec ces nouvelles autres machines.* We're starting to cut the tall sugarcane with these other new machines. (AS) *Il a coupé son pied creux.* He cut his foot deeply. (SM) *Asteur le monde s'aide toujours mais il y en a plein qu'essaye de te couper la gorge.* Nowadays people still help each other, but there are many who try to cut your throat. (TB) *Tu te mettais sus les genoux à quatre pattes pour couper les herbes avec ça.* You got down on all fours to cut the grass with that. (TB) *Des ciseaux pour couper le maillage.* Scissors to cut the netting. (TB) *Tu te faisais une robe, tu ramassais tous les retailles. Et là tu coupais ça une certaine manière que ça allait FIT ensemble.* You made yourself a dress, you gathered up all the scraps of cloth. And then you cut them a certain way so they'd fit together. (TB) **2** to cut off *Y a deux jeunes garçons qui s'a fait tuer là, couper la tête.* There are two boys who got killed there, they got their heads cut off. (TB) **Le Ta-Taille ça dit est ein gros bétaille qui ressemble manière comme ein ravert. Il vient après la nuit et coupe les orteils des petits méchants.* The "Ta-Taille" is said to be a giant creature that resembles a cockroach. It comes after dark and cuts off the toes of mean children. (Wh83) **3** to cut down *J'ai coupé de la fardoche.* I cut some underbrush. (VM) *Ça c'est ça qu'on appelait un passe-partout pour couper des arbres, pour couper le bois pour la cheminée ou le STOVE.* This is what was called a two-handled saw, to cut down trees to be used as firewood in the chimney or in the stove. (AC) **4** to cut, carve *On lui a acheté un gâteau et un cadeau. Et lui a coupé son gâteau là-bas.* We bought him a cake and a gift. And he cut his cake down there. (TB) *Le filet c'est quand tu prends le filet KNIFE et puis tu le coupes et tu ôtes tous les os dessus le poisson.* The fillet is when you take the fillet knife and then you cut and remove all the bones from the fish. (SM) **5** to stab *Ils ont coupé Doudou, mais c'est Black eux voulait couper.* They stabbed Doudou, but it's Black they wanted to stab. (LA) **6** to clip, cut *Il faut que tu coupes les ongles de tes enfants pour pas que ça se graffigne.* You have to cut your children's nails so that they don't scratch themselves. (LA) **7** to castrate *Couper un veau, un poulain.* To castrate a calf, a colt. (EV) **8** to diminish, reduce *Allons couper les prix dessus les chars neufs.* Let's cut the prices on new cars. (EV) **II** *v.intr.* **1** to cut, be sharp **Le couteau coupe bien.* The knife cuts well. (Da84) **2** to pause *Allons couper un moment.* Let's pause for a moment. (LF) **3** to cut in, break in *C'est un* VERSE *en anglais et là il coupe en français.* It's a verse in English and then he cuts in in French. (LF) **4** to trump (in card games) *J'ai joué mon as de cœur, mais il a coupé avec un cinq de pique.* I played my ace of hearts, but he trumped with a five of spades. (LA) *Il pouvait pas couper parce qu'il faulait fournir en piques.* He couldn't trump because he had to follow suit in spades. (LA) **III se couper** *v.pron.* **1** to cut o.s. *Il s'a coupé le doigt en faisant boucherie.* He cut his finger doing a butchering. (EV) *Tu vas te couper si tu fais pas attention.* You're going to cut yourself if you aren't careful. (EV) *Je m'ai coupé au vif avec ce poignard.* I cut myself to the quick with that butcher knife. (VM) **2** to be cut **Les cannes se coupent bien.* The cane is easy to cut. (Da84) **3** to step in animal feces (esp. a cow patty) *Hé, quelqu'un s'a coupé. Regardez vos souliers.* Hey, I think somebody stepped in a cow patty. Check your shoes. (LA) ◊ **•couper au raccourci** to take a shortcut <Da84> **•couper avec une hache à deux taillants** to be very critical of others, criticize incessantly <EV, La99> **•couper carré** to slice completely, cut completely <Da84> **•couper court** to cut short, shorten *On parle vite et on a des petits mots et des fois on coupe les affaires un petit peu court, tu connais?* We talk fast and we have little words, and sometimes we cut things a bit short, you know? (LF) <LF> **•couper en avant (de qqn)** to cut ahead (of s.o. waiting in line) *Il y avait quinze minutes que j'espérais pour voir le docteur et il a coupé en avant de moi.* I had been waiting to see the doctor for fifteen minutes and he cut in front of me. (VM) <VM> **•couper en travers** to cut across *Couper en travers du clos.* To cut across the field. (VM) <VM> **•couper la conversation {le discours}** to interrupt, cut into a conversation *C'est comme ça que les Cadiens est, ça* INTERRUPT. *Ça coupe la conversation de l'autre.* That's what Cajuns are like, they interrupt. They cut into each other's conversation. (TB) <TB> **•couper les gages** to cut wages <SL, SM, TB, Lv88> **•couper les herbes** to cut the grass, mow the lawn *J'ai dit que t'étais apres couper les herbes, il dit "Laisse-lé travailler, laisse-lé faire son ouvrage."* I said that you were out cutting the grass, and he said, "Let him work, let him do his work." (TB) <AC, SM, TB> **•couper le sifflet (à qqn)** to cut (s.o.) short, shut (s.o.) up *Ça, ça lui a coupé le sifflet.* That shut him up. (Da84) <Da84> **•couper le souffle (à qqn)** to take (s.o.'s) breath away *Il m'a cogné si fort dans le dos, ça m'a coupé le souffle.* He hit me so hard in the back that it took my breath away. (VM) <VM> **•couper le vin** to dilute the wine *Quand j'étais petit, ma grand-mère coupait notre vin avec de l'eau.* When I was little, my grandmother used to dilute our wine with water. (VM) <SM, VM, Da84> **•couper l'herbe à qqn** to take away s.o.'s chance of succeeding <AV, La99> **•couper ses dents** to cut teeth (of a baby) <SL> **•couper une fraîche** to 'cut out', get the hell out, go quickly (to move so quickly that one's passage creates a breeze) *Je te dis, il a coupé une fraîche.* I'm telling you, he cut out. (VM) *Il a coupé une fraîche.* He came by very quickly. (VM) <VM> **•ça coupe comme une jambe de chien / ça coupe comme la jambe à {de} ma grand-mère / ça coupe aussi bien que mon doigt** it doesn't cut, it is not very sharp <La99> **•ça coupe comme la langue de ma grand-mère** it is very sharp <VM, La99> <***Loc:*** AC, AS, AV, EV, IV, LA, LF, SL, SM, TB, VM, An94, Da84, Gu00, La99, Lv88, Wh83>

coupeur [kupœr] *n.m.* cutter <***Loc:*** Da84>

coupeuse [kupøz] *n.f.* harvesting machine, combine (for rice, wheat, etc.) ◊ **•coupeuse à {de} cannes** cane cutting machine <LA, Lv88> **•coupeuse de riz** rice cutting machine <Lv88> **•coupeuse d'herbes** lawnmower <Lv88> <***Loc:*** EV, LA, SL, Da84, Lv88>

couple [kup(l)] *n.f.* couple, pair <***Loc:*** Da84>

couplet [kuplɛ, kuple] *n.m.* **1** hinge *Il y a un couplet de la porte qui est* cassé. One of the hinges on the door is broken. (AV) **2** couplet <***Loc:*** AV, EV, SJ, VM, Da84>

coupon [kupɔ̃] *n.m.* coupon <***Loc:*** Da84>

coupure [kupyr, kupœr] *n.f.* cut, incision **Quand on marqué [=marquait] ein cochon, it fallait traiter la coupeur [=coupure].* When we branded a hog, you had to treat the cut. (Wh83) <***Loc:*** LF, TB, Da84, Wh83>

cour[1] [kur] *n.f.* **1** yard, courtyard *On achetait pas des fleurs, c'était tout le temps des fleurs qui poussaient dans la cour.* We did not buy flowers, there were always flowers growing in the yard. (IB) **2** court (of law) ◊ **•cour d'appel** court of appeal <Da84> **•cour d'école** schoolyard, school playground <TB> **•cour de magasin** barnyard <VM, Da84> **•cour (d')en arrière** back yard <LF, SM, TB, Da84> **•cour (de) devant {(d')en avant}** front yard <LF, TB, Da84, Gu00> **•cour d'état** state court <LF> **•aller en cour** to go to court *Faudrait j'alle en cour faire serment.* I have to go testify in court. (Lv88) <Lv88> **•mettre en cour / mettre devant la cour** to bring to court, sue, file suit against <SM, Da84, Lv88> <***Loc:*** AC, AV, EV, IB, LA, LF, PQ, SB, TB, VM, Da84, Fa77, Gu00, Lv88, Wh83>

cour[2] [kur] *n.f.* courtship ◊ **•faire la cour à** to court, woo *Il a juste dit ça parce qu'il veut te faire la cour.* He just said that because he'd like to go out with you. (EV) <EV> <***Loc:*** EV>

courage [kuraʒ] *n.m.* **1** will, spirit, heart *Il faut avoir du courage pour travailler.* You've got to have will to work. (TB) **Tu vas arriver de l'enterrement, tu vas t'assir dans ta berceuse. T'as pas le courage de te déchanger. T'as le chagrin sur ton idée.* You'll arrive from the funeral, you'll sit in your rocker. You just don't feel up to changing clothes. You have sadness on your mind. (ch: *C'est juste les anges qu'après pleurer*) **2** courage, daring, bravery *Il y en a du monde qui disait que Huey est un homme de courage et il va se battre pour aider quelqu'un qu'a besoin.* There are those who said that Huey is a man of courage and that he's going to fight to help someone in need. (ThCa: *Messieurs, mesdames*) ◊ •**prendre courage** to take heart *La vieille m'a quitté avec les petits enfants. Prenez courage, alle va s'en revenir.* The old lady left me with the small children. Take heart, she'll come back. (LF) <LF, TB> <***Loc:*** LA, LF, SM, TB, VM, Da84, Lv88, ThCa>

courageux, -euse [kuraʒø, -øz] *adj.* courageous, brave *Comme ca, on sera sûr que vous-autres ne vas pas essayer quelque chose de courageux.* That way, we'll be sure that you're not going to try to do anything too brave. (ThCa: *Martin Weber*) *On est fier, nous-aut', que l'écrevisse est le symbole des Cadiens par rapport que c'est l'animal le plus courageux dedans le monde.* We are proud that the crawfish is the symbol of the Cajuns because it is the bravest animal in the world. (ThCa: *Mille misères*) <***Loc:*** Da84, ThCa>

courailler ♦see **coursailler**

couraillerie ♦see **coursaillerie**

courailleur ♦see **coursailleur**

couramment [kurɑ̃mɑ̃] *adv.* **1** fluently **2** easily *J'apprenais mon cathéchisse couramment.* I learned my catechism easily. (AC) <***Loc:*** AC, Da84>

courant[1], **-e** [kurɑ̃, -ɑ̃t] *adj.* **1** current, present *C'est courant.* That's current [i.e. everyone knows that]. (VM) **2** fluent *C'est un parleur courant du français cadien.* He is a fluent speaker of Cajun French. (Lv88) ◊ •**au courant** up to date, informed *Delta est morte. T'étais pas au courant?* Delta died. You hadn't heard? (VM) <VM, Da84> <***Loc:*** VM, Da84>

courant[2] [kurɑ̃] *n.m.* current, tide *Ça qui va nager, ça qui va venir en descendant ce courant-là va faire se prendre dans le carrelet.* What swims down with that current [i.e. the fish] is going to be caught in the dip net. (SM) ◊ •**courant d'air** draft <Da84> •**courant électrique** electric current <Da84> <***Loc:*** LF, SB, SM, TB, Da84>

courbe [kurb, kob] *n.f.* rib of a boat <***Loc:*** JE, LF, TB, VM>

courbé, -e [kurbe] *adj.* bent, stooped, curved, twisted *Tête courbée.* Bowed head. (VM) <***Loc:*** VM, Da84>

courber (se) [kurbe] *v.pron.* to be submissive *Il se courbe devant son père.* He is submissive to his father. (VM) <***Loc:*** VM>

courcoubier ♦see **corcobiller**

coureur [kurœr] *n.m.* **1** runner **Ça se fait, quand le pistolet a craqué, le Grand Sauvage a parti loin devant le coureur à Jean l'Ours.* So when the gun fired, the Grand Sauvage took off far in front of Jean l'Ours' runner. (EV, An94) **2** race horse ◊ •**coureur de Mardi Gras** Mardi Gras runner (one who goes from house to house, disguised and often on horseback, on Fat Tuesday) *Et les plus grands se fait courser, [...] les Mardi Gras couraient. C'est pour ça qu'ils disont les coureurs de Mardi Gras. Les Mardi Gras les coursaient n'importe aiou-ce que qu'eux-autres allait.* And the oldest ones [children] got themselves chased, the Mardi Gras revelers were running [after them]. That's why they're called Mardi Gras runners. The Mardi Gras revelers would chase them wherever they went. (LF) <LF> <***Loc:*** EV, LF, VM, An94, Da84, Fa77>

coureuse [kurøz] *n.f.* **1** blue racer snake *On a les serpents bleues, les* BLUE RUNNER *en anglais, des coureuses, eusse va vite vite.* We have the blue snakes, the 'blue runners' (i.e. blue racers) in English, they go quite fast. (TB) **2** streetwalker, prostitute **3** boy-crazy girl <***Loc:*** TB, VM, Da84>

courgette [kurʒɛt] *n.f.* courgette, zucchini <***Loc:*** SL>

courimavini ♦see **courivini**

courir [kurir] (*p.p.* **couri** [kuri], **couru** [kury]) **I** *v.tr.* **1** to run, race (horses, cars, etc.) **Courir les chevaux.* To run race horses. (Da84) *Ça courait les chevals chez 'Tit Maurice.* They raced horses at 'Tit Maurice's place. (Lv88) *Ça court des chars icite.* They race cars here. (Lv88) **2** to run, operate *Les* MODEL *T, tu pouvais les courir avec du whisky.* Model T's, you could run them on whiskey. (SL) *Je le cours bas tout le temps.* I always run it [the air conditioning] on low. (TB) **3** to drive, pilot, steer *Je connais courir un char.* I know how to drive a car. (VM) *Mais je courais un bateau là, j'étais pilote d'un bateau.* But I ran a boat, I was a boat captain. (TB) **4** to run, direct, administer, manage (a business, etc.) *Quand j'avais que 23 ans je courais une compagnie déjà et asteur c'est pour moi la compagnie.* When I was only 23 I was already running a company and now the company belongs to me. (TB) *Il court une petite grocerie.* He runs a little grocery store. (VM) **II** *v.intr.* **1** to run, race **Courir vite.* To run fast. (Da84) *Et là ces bateaux venait là, [...] et là les soldats couraient à terre.* And then those boats came and the soldiers would run onto the land. (LF) **2** to run around, roam *Ça courait en bétaille, tu voyais les bétailles mais tu connaissais pas qui c'était.* They ran around as an animal, you saw the animals but you didn't know who it was. (TB) **3** to run, be a candidate (for political office) **Courir pour gouverneur.* To run for governor. (Da84) *Mon cousin court pour sénateur.* My cousin is running for senator. (Guoo) **4** to work, run, operate, function *La machine court au gaz.* The machine runs on gas. (Lv88) *Ma montre court plus.* My watch doesn't work anymore. (Lv88) **5** to run, extend (of an event, a season, etc.) *La saison d'écrevisses court en travers de septembre et d'octobre.* Crawfish season runs through September and October. (Lv88) **6** to run, vary (in size, price, etc.) within a specified range *Sur les bateaux eusse va casser les plus grandes chevrettes qui court de dix, quinze, à* THIRTY-ONE, THIRTY-FIVE *eusse va casser.* On the boat they'll break the heads off the biggest shrimp that run from 10, 15 to 31, 35 [to the pound], they break those. (LF) ◊ •**courir après (qqn)** to run after (s.o.) *Et il dit, "si t'arrêtes pas de courir après ma femme," il dit, "la prochaine fois je vas te tuer, ouais!"* And he says, "If you don't stop running after my wife, next time I'm going to kill you, yeah!" (JD) <JD> **•courir la chance** to take a chance *Achète pas une maison dans ce voisinage-là. Tu cours la chance de te faire noyer.* Don't buy a house in that neighborhood. You're taking a chance of getting flooded. (VM) <VM, Da84> **•courir Mardi Gras** to take part in a costumed Mardi Gras run *T'es assez grand pour courir Mardi Gras cette année.* You're big enough to do the Mardi Gras run this year. (VM) <SL, VM> **•courir rougarou** to roam the roads at night as a werewolf (because one has been placed under a curse) *Il dit, "Il y a un an que je suis après courir rougarou. Il dit "Je suis assez content que tu m'as délivré."* He said, "I've been a werewolf for a year now." He said, "I am so glad that you saved me [by breaking the spell]." (TB) *Et eux-autres dit qu'il courait rougarou, lui. Le jour il dort, et le soir il rôde les chemins.* And they say that he roamed the roads at night. In the day he sleeps, and in the evening he prowls the streets. (TB) <TB> **•courir un risque** to run the risk *Je vas pas laisser mes enfants tout seuls là-bas. Ils courent trop de risques avec leur grand-père qui les soigne pas.* I'm not going to leave my children alone over there. They run too many risks with their grandfather who doesn't take care of them. (EV) <EV, Da84> **•faire courir** to race (horses) *Je suis un coursier; je fais courir mes chevaux à Evangeline Downs.* I'm a racehorse breeder; I run my horses at Evangeline Downs. (VM) <VM> <***Loc:*** AS, EV, JD, IB, LA, LF, PQ, SL, SM, TB, VM, An94, Da84, Guoo, La99, Lv88>

courivini (**courimavini**) [kurivini, kurimavini] *n.m.* Louisiana Creole, esp. as spoken in the vicinity of St. Martinville *Je peux pas comprendre cet homme, c'est le courimavini qu'il parle.* I can't understand that man, he speaks that "courimavini." (VM) <***Loc:*** VM>

couronne [kurɔ̃n] *n.f.* **1** crown **2** wreath **3** bridal veil assembly with wreath attached *Amène ta robe et amène ta couronne, on se marie demain matin au Texas.* Bring your dress and bring your veil, we'll marry tomorrow morning in Texas. (ch: *Brasse donc le couche-couche*) ◊ **•couronne de chêne** bunch of mistletoe <Re31> **•couronne de mariée** bridal wreath plant <EV, IB, VM, Da84, Ph36> <***Loc:*** EV, IB, VM, Da84, Ph36, Re31>

couronner [kurɔ̃ne] *v.tr.* to crown *C'est aujourd'hui que ma tête est couronnée, et que mon cœur est orné d'un bouquet.* Today my head is crowned, and my heart is decorated with a bouquet. (VM, ch: *Adieu, la fleur de jeunesse*) <***Loc:*** VM, Da84>

courpion ♦see **croupion**

courrier [kurje] *n.m.* courrier, messenger <***Loc:*** Da84>

courroie [kurwa] *n.f.* strap ◊ **•courroie d'étrieux** stirrup strap <VM> <***Loc:*** VM>

cours[1] [kur] *n.m.* **1** course, flow (of a waterway) **Il y en a qui ont regriché le cour [=cours], pour retrouver l'Acadie devenue Nova Scotia* There were some who went against the current to get back to Acadia, which had become Nova Scotia. (Ar82) **2** tract, path **3** orbit <***Loc:*** Ar82, Da84>

cours[2] [kur] *n.m.* class, course *Un enfant qui fait le détestable, quand il écoute pas, il est dans le cours, et il t'ecoute pas, il est détestable.* A child who is willfully disobedient, when he doesn't listen, he's in the class and he doesn't listen to you, he's incorrigible. (VM) <***Loc:*** VM>

coursailler (**courailler**) [kursaje, kuraje] **I** *v.tr.* **1** to run after, chase, pursue *À Gheens y en a qui se masque, ils faisont leur parade, là les jeunes garçons coursaillent les jeunes filles. Et si ça les empoigne, ça va les tailler avec leur baleine.* In Gheens there are some people who put on masks, they have their parade, then the young boys chase the young girls. And if they catch them, they'll whip them with their switch. (LF) **2** to chase (women or men), philander with *Il coursaille les femmes.* He chases women. (LF) **II** *v.intr.* **1** to dissipate, chase women or men, debauch, philander *Le Bon Dieu va te damner à l'enfer si t'arrêtes pas de coursailler comme tu fais.* God is going to damn you to hell if you don't stop running around like you do. (VM) *Il coursaille avec les femmes.* He runs around with women. (SL) **2** to run around, gallivant *Arrête donc de coursailler; tu brûles trop de gaz.* Stop running around; you burn too much gas. (VM) ◊ **•courailler les rues** to run the roads, gad about, gallivant *Ça fait rien que courailler les rues de matin au soir, ces trois petits là.* Those three kids do nothing but run the roads from morning till evening. (TB) <TB> <***Loc:*** AV, EV, IB, LA, LF, SB, SM, TB, VM, Da84, Lv88, Ph36>

coursaillère [kursajær] *n.f.* whip <***Loc:*** SM>

coursaillerie (**couraillerie**) [kursajri, kurajri] *n.f.* philandering, debauchery, dissipation *C'est dommage qu'il passe son temps en coursaillerie.* It's too bad that he spends his time at debauchery. (SM) <***Loc:*** EV, SM, Lv88, Ph36>

coursailleur, -euse (**courailleur, -euse**) [kursajœr, kurajœr, -jøz] *n.* **1** *(m.)* woman-chaser, womanizer, playboy, philanderer **Surtout pas un homme comme Adam, un vieux garçon, un coursailleur.* Especially not a man like Adam, an old bachelor, a philanderer. (ThCa: *La table des veuves*) **2** *(f.)* man-chaser, loose woman **3** *(f.)* streetwalker, prostitute <***Loc:*** EV, LA, SB, SM, Da84, Lv88, Ph36, ThCa>

course [kurs] *n.f.* **1** running **2** race *On a pas reviré à notre maison, on a* GO HEAD *aller aux courses.* We didn't turn back toward our house. We continued on to the races. (EV) *Ça a tourné que Louis a pas pu finir la course avec son frère.* It turned out that Louis could not finish the race with his brother. (LA) **3** course, racecourse **4** chase, pursuit *Je l'ai foutu une course.* I gave him quite a chase. (SM) **5** errand *Je courais des courses pour aller délivrer des groceries à le différente monde.* I ran errands to go deliver groceries to different people. (TB) ◊ **•course de chevaux** horse race *Là, ils avaient des courses le dimanche après-midi, des courses de chevaux là.* They had races there on Sunday afternoon, horse races. (EV) <EV, TB> **•à la course** running, by running *Et là tu viens à la course et tu fais le tour de ce baril-là.* And then you come running up and you go all the way around that barrel. (LF) <LF, TB> **•à la pleine course** at full speed, at a dead run *Le cheval s'en allait à la pleine course. Il a pas pu l'arrêter.* The horse was going at full speed. He couldn't stop it. (EV) <EV, SL, An94> **•faire la course** to run <VM> **•faire une course** to run a race <Da84> **•faire une petite course** to take a short trip <Da84> **•prendre la course** to take off running, run off *Oh elle a manqué de mourir, moi j'a pris la course, mon. J'ai eu assez peur, mon j'ai parti.* Oh, she nearly died, I took off running. I was so scared, I got out of there. (TB) <TB> <***Loc:*** EV, LA, LF, SL, SM, TB, VM, An94, Da84, Hi02, Lv88, Wh83>

courser [kurse] **I** *v.tr.* **1** to run after, chase, pursue *Il coursait sa sœur avec un bâton.* He was chasing his sister with a stick. (Lv88) *Les Mardi Gras les coursaient n'importe ayoù-ce que qu'eux-autres allait.* The Mardi Gras chased them wherever they went. (LF) **2** to race, race with *Je vais le courser pour avoir la gazette.* I am going to race him to get the paper. (Lv88) **3** to chase (women or men), philander with *Je savais pas que t'avais commencé à courser les femmes aussite.* I didn't know you had also started chasing women. (ThCa: *La table des veuves*) **4** to chase off, run off *Oh si alle a un nique avec des œufs [...] Alle va assayer de te courser, tu connais, te faire sortir d'au ras de le nique.* Oh, if she has a nest with eggs, she'll try to chase you off, you know, make you get away from the nest. (TB) **5** to hunt with dogs *Il a coursé les lapins.* He hunted rabbits with hunting dogs. (SB) **II** *v.intr.* to dissipate, chase women or men, debauch, philander *Il est tout le temps après courser.* He's always chasing women. (SM) ◊ **•courser après** to pursue, chase *Ça m'étonne pas qu'alle l'a eu. Alle était tout le temps après courser après lui.* It doesn't surprise me that she caught him. She was always chasing after him. (JD) <JD> <***Loc:*** EV, IB, IV, JD, LA, LF, SL, SM, TB, VM, Da84, Gu82, Lv88, Ph36, ThCa>

courseur, -euse [kursœr, -øz] *n.* **1** *(m.)* woman-chaser, womanizer, playboy, philanderer **2** *(f.)* man-chaser, loose woman <***Loc:*** LF, SM, Lv88>

coursier [kursje] *n.m.* **1** breeder or trainer of racehorses *Je suis un coursier; je fais courir mes chevaux à Evangeline Downs.* I'm a racehorse breeder; I run my horses at Evangeline Downs. (VM) **2** person who is passionate about horse racing, race fan <***Loc:*** VM, Da84, Lv88>

court, -e [kur, -t] *adj.* **1** short, brief, quick **Quand j'ai vu ça, j'ai jonglé le plus court je peux faire, c'est ôter la bride du cheval et rester en haut.* When I saw that, I thought, the quickest thing I can do is to take the bridle off the horse and stay on. (SL, An94) **2** short (in height or length) *Il a tiré la courte paille.* He drew the short straw. (IB) ◊ **•court sur pattes** short in stature *J'ai toujours été courte sur pattes.* I was always short in stature. (TB) <TB> **•être à court** to be short (of money, food, etc.) *Elle était tout le temps là pour nous aider quand on était à court de quelque chose.* She was always there to help us when we were short of something. (EV) *La paille de riz, c'était pas bon, bon, bon, mais quand le manger était à court ça l'aimait, ça. Les vaches mangeaient ça un tas.* Rice straw wasn't really the best, but when food was in short supply, they liked that. Cows ate that a lot. (EV) <EV, Da84> <***Loc:*** AC, AL, EV, IB, LF, SB, SL, TB, VM, An94, Da84, Gr86, Lv88>

courtaud [kurto] *adj.* short, dumpy (of a person) *Elle a marié un petit homme courtaud.* She married a short, squat man. (VM) <***Loc:*** VM, Da84>

courtbouillon [kurbujɔ̃] *n.m.* fish stew eaten with rice <***Loc:*** AL, LA, SB, SM, TB, VM, Da84, Gu00, Lv88, Re31>

courtepaille [kurtəpaj] *n.f.* lots *Il a tiré la courte paille.* He drew the short straw. (IB) <***Loc:*** IB, Da84>

courtepointe [kurtpwɛ̃t, kurtəpwɛ̃t, kurtdəpwɑ̃t] *n.f.* bedspread <***Loc:*** EV, IB, JD, LA, SL, SM, TB, Da84, Lv88, Ph36>

courtiller (côtiller, côteiller) [kotije, koteje] *v.tr.* to court, woo *Côteiller une belle fille.* To court a pretty girl. (SJ) <***Loc:*** AV, SB, SJ>

courtisaud (côtisot) [kotizo] *n.m.* ladies' man <***Loc:*** VM>

courtise [kurtiz] *n.f.* courting, courtship <***Loc:*** Da84>

courtiser (côtiser) [kurtize, kotize] *v.tr.* to court, woo, give amourous attention to *Son fils a côtisé ma fille pour deux années.* His son courted my daughter for two years. (VM) **Il y avait deux garçons qui courtisaient la même fille, et c'était deux hommes qui étaient grosse affaire.* There were two boys who were courting the same girl, and they were two men who were close. (SL, An94) <***Loc:*** SL, VM, An94, Da84, Lv88>

courtiseur [kurtizœr] *n.m.* one who courts, suitor <***Loc:*** Da84>

cousage (coudage) [kuzaʒ] *n.m.* sewing <***Loc:*** TB>

couser ♦see **coudre**

couseur, -euse [kuzœr, -øz] *n.* sewer <***Loc:*** Da84>

cousin[1]**, -e** [kuzɛ̃, -in] *n.* cousin *Cette femme-là est ma sœur et cette femme-là est ma cousine.* This lady is my sister and that lady is my cousin. (JE) ◊ **•cousin germain** first cousin <VM, Da84> **•cousin par alliance** cousin through marriage <Da84> **•premier {deuxième / troisième (etc.)} cousin** first / second / third (etc.) cousin <SL, TB, Lv88> <***Loc:*** JE, SJ, SL, SM, TB, VM, Da84, Lv88>

cousin[2] [kuzɛ̃] *n.m.* mosquito <***Loc:*** Da84>

coussin [kusɛ̃] *n.m.* **1** cushion, pad, seat cushion **2** pillow *Si on met un morceau de gâteau de noces sous son coussin on va rêver à çu-là qu'on va marier.* If you put a piece of wedding cake under your pillow, you'll dream of the one you're going to marry. (TB) <***Loc:*** TB, Da84>

cousure [kuzyr] *n.f.* **1** suture **2** seam **3** stitch <***Loc:*** Da84>

coût [ku] *n.m.* price, cost *J'ai arrêté de faire du coton à cause du coût de la graine qui montait.* I stopped raising cotton because the cost of seed was rising. (VM) <***Loc:*** VM>

coûtance [kutɑ̃s] *n.f.* price, cost <***Loc:*** JD>

coûtant [kutɑ̃] *adj.* ◊ **•au prix coûtant** wholesale *Il vend ça au prix coûtant.* He sells that at wholesale. (VM) <VM> <***Loc:*** VM, Da84>

couteau [kuto] *n.m.* **1** knife **2** dagger ◊ **•couteau à {de} canne** cane knife <JD, SM, VM, Da84, Lv88, Re31> **•couteau à deux manches** draw knife, two-handled draw knife (used in carpentry, boatbuilding) <LF, SB, Da84> **•couteau à deux tranchants** ***a*** double-edged sword ***b*** hypocrite, two-faced person <La99> **•couteau à z-huîtres** oyster knife <LF> **•couteau de boucherie** butcher knife <Fa77> **•couteau de galfat** caulking knife <LF> **•couteau de poche** pocketknife <Da84> **•couteau de table** table knife <Da84> **•couteau rond** round knife (used in boatbuilding) <LF> **•être à couteaux tirés** to be at dagger's point <Da84> **•grand couteau** butcher knife <Da84> **•petit couteau** worthless person who thinks a lot of himself <EV, La99> <***Loc:*** AC, AV, EV, IB, JD, JE, LA, SB, SL, SM, TB, VM, An94, Da84, La99, Lv88, Ph36, Re31>

couter ♦see **écouter**

coûter [kute] *v.tr.* to cost *Un bateau comme ça va vous coûter 300 ou 400 piasses.* A boat like that will cost you $300 or $400. (LF) ◊ **•coûter les yeux de la tête** to cost a fortune *J'aimerais aller, mais ça me coûterait les yeux de la tête.* I'd like to go, but it would cost me a fortune. (LA) <LA> **•coûte qui coûte** cost what it may, at any cost <Da84> <***Loc:*** EV, LA, LF, SL, SM, TB, VM, An94, Da84, Lv88, St95>

coûteux, -euse [kutø, -øz] *adj.* costly, expensive *Cette qualité de char là est joliment coûteuse.* That kind of car is pretty expensive. (LA) <***Loc:*** LA, Da84>

coutume [kutym] *n.f.* custom, habit *Et si un homme et sa femme s'accordaient pas,* WELL, *ça c'était eux-autres coutume à rester ensemble. Et ça boudait, ça se parlait pas, [...] mais y avait jamais de divorce.* If a man and a woman didn't get along, well, it was their custom to stay together. They sulked, they didn't talk to each other, but there was never divorce. (TB) ◊ **•avoir (la) coutume (de)** to be in the habit (of) *J'ai coutume pêcher des hameçons mais depuis les* POND *à poissons, ils ont commencé farmer les* CATFISH. I am used to fishing with hooks but because of the fishing ponds, they have started to farm catfish. (SM) <SM> **•selon la coutume** according to the custom <Da84> <***Loc:*** IB, SM, TB, Da84, Wh83>

couture [kutyr] *n.f.* **1** needlework, sewing **2** sewn seam **3** stitch <***Loc:*** LF, SL, TB, Da84>

couturier, -ière [kutyrje, -jær] *n.* dressmaker, tailor <***Loc:*** SM, Da84>

couturieuse [kutyrjøz] *n.f.* **1** seamstress **2** dressmaker <***Loc:*** AV, JD, SM, TB>

couvage (accouvage) [kuvaʒ, akuvaʒ] *n.m.* incubating, hatching <***Loc:*** Da84>

couvarte ♦see **couverte**

couvasse [kuvas] *n.f.* setting hen, broody hen <***Loc:*** EV, IB, Ph36>

couvée [kuve] *n.f.* setting of eggs, clutch <***Loc:*** Da84>

couvent [kuvɑ̃] *n.m.* convent, nunnery *Ma chère sœur, reconsole-toi. Papa te mettra au couvent.* My dear sister, console yourself. Papa will place you in a convent. (IB, ch: *Une fille de quatorze ans*) <***Loc:*** IB, SL, Da84>

couver (accouver) [kuve, akuve] **I** *v.tr.* to incubate, sit on (eggs) *Dans un temps j'élevais des canards pour avoir du plaisir. Alors on quittait les femelles couver leurs œufs et les serpents les mangeaient sur la terre.* At one time I raised ducks for fun. So we would let the females sit on their eggs and the snakes would eat them on the ground. (TB) **II** *v.intr.* to brood, sit on eggs *La z-oie va siller après toi, si alle est après couver.* The goose will hiss at you if she is brooding. (VM) ◊ **•couver un rhume** to be catching a cold <TB, La99> <***Loc:*** EV, IB, TB, VM, An94, Da84, La99>

couverre (couvrir) [kuvær, kuvrir] **I** *v.tr.* **1** to cover *Oublie pas de couverre ton persil avec un sac de pite après que tu l'as semé.* Don't forget to cover your parsley with a bag of peat after you've sown it. (Guoo) **Elle a tout couvert le whiskey, mais là ça a éteint la flamme.* She covered the whiskey completely, but then it extinguished the flame. (SM, An94) **2** to roof *Ils ont couvert leur maison avec des bardeaux, comme dans le vieux temps.* They roofed their house with shingles, like in the old days. (LA) **II se couverre** *v.pron.* **1** to cover o.s. *Il s'avait couvert de sable à Holly Beach croyant que ça aurait guéri ses rheumatismes.* He covered himself with sand at Holly Beach thinking that it would cure his arthritis. (LA) **2** to become overcast, become cloudy (of the weather) **Le temps se couvre.* The weather is getting cloudy. (Da84) <***Loc:*** LA, SM, TB, VM, An94, Da84, Guoo, Lv88>

couvert[1], -e [kuvær, -ært] *adj.* **1** covered **Couvert de fruits.* Covered with fruits. (Da84) **2** overcast, cloudy *Le temps est couvert.* The sky is overcast. (LA, TB) <***Loc:*** LA, TB, Da84>

couvert[2] [kuvær] *n.m.* **1** cover, lid, cap (of a pot, cup, container, etc.) *Eux-autres cuisait la viande de cochon, et eux-autres mettait ça en jarres avec un couvert, et ça se gardait longtemps.* They cooked the pork, and they put it in jars with a lid, and it kept for a long time. (TB) **2** cover (of a book, piece of furniture, etc.) **3** blanket *Elle est après écarder le coton pour faire des couverts.* She's carding cotton to make blankets. (VM) **4** place setting (at a table) ◊ **•couvert de bouteille** bottlecap <LA> **•couvert de table** tablecloth <SL> <***Loc:*** AC, EV, LA, LF, SL, SM, TB, VM, Da84, Guoo, Lv88, Ph36>

couverte (couvarte) [kuvært, kuvart] *n.f.* bed cover (e.g. blanket, quilt, bedspread) *Une belle couverte caille.* A beautiful blanket of many colors. (Lv88) *Carotter un bébé dans une couverte.* Roll a baby tightly in a blanket. (Lv88) ◊ **•couverte de pays** hand-woven blanket <Lv88> **•couverte piquée** quilt <Guoo> <***Loc:*** AC, AV, EV, IB, LA, LF, SB, SL, SM, TB, VM, Da84, Guoo, Lv88, Ph36, Re31>

couverture [kuværtyr] *n.f.* **1** roof, roofing **La colonne avait enlevé la couverture du poulailler.* The tornado had taken the roof off the chicken coop. (ThCa: *Le charivari*) *La couverture coule.* The roof leaks. (AV) **2** covering, cover ◊ **•couverture d'oreiller** pillowcase, pillow slip <SB> <***Loc:*** AC, AV, EV, IB, IV, JE, LA, LF, SB, SM, TB, VM, Da84, Guoo, Lv88, ThCa>

couveuse [kuvøz] *n.f.* **1** setting hen, broody hen **2** incubator *J'ai perdu une paire de bessons. J'étais pas tout à fait rendue. Il y avait pas de couveuses dans ces temps-ça.* I lost a pair of twins. I wasn't completely delivered. There weren't any incubators in those days. (VM) <***Loc:*** EV, LA, VM, An94, Da84>

couvre-joint [kuvrəʒwɛ̃] *n.m.* bat, batten, lath (used on board and batten construction) <***Loc:*** Da84>

couvreur [kuvrœr] *n.m.* roofer <***Loc:*** Da84>

couvrir ♦see **couverre**

coyoche [kojɔʃ] *n.f.* head **Quand je vas mourir (j'ai fait mon* WILL *l'autre jour), je veux ça prend rien que ma tête. Et les côtes, que ça donne ça aux chiens. Je vas aller chez Simon-là, je veux il me donne une de ces petites boîtes à souliers-là. Je vas mettre ma coyoche en dedans-là, rien qu'avec assez pour une petite cravate.* When I die (I made my will the other day), I want them to take nothing but my head. And the ribs, they can give those to the dogs. I'm going to go to Simon's, I want him to give me one those little shoe boxes. I'm going to put my head inside, nothing but just enough for a little tie. (EV, An94) <***Loc:*** EV, An94>

coyote [kajut] *n.m.* coyote, prairie wolf *Moi j'ai l'habitude de chasser des coyotes et des renards.* I have the habit of hunting prairie wolves and foxes. (IB) <***Loc:*** AL, IB, Guoo>

crabe [krab, krap] *n.m./f.* **1** crab **2** crab louse, crab ◊ **•crabe (a) dormi** sleeping crab <PQ> **•crabe à paquet** sponge crab *Mais là après qu'il a de les œufs il tient ça dans le paquet. La crabe à paquet.* But after it has eggs it holds them in a cluster under the abdominal apron. A sponge crab it's called. (TB) <TB> **•crabe bleue** Atlantic blue crab <PQ> <TB> **•crabe molle {moute}** soft-shell crab <PQ, TB, Lv88> **•aller aux crabes** to go crabbing <LF> <***Loc:*** PQ, SL, SM, TB, VM, Da84, Guoo, Lv88>

crac [krak] *onom.* crack <***Loc:*** Da84>

crachailler [kraʃaje] *v.intr.* to spit here and there, spit repeatedly *Il était après crachailler tout partout.* He was spitting all around. (LA) <***Loc:*** LA, Da84>

crachat [kraʃa] *n.m.* spit, saliva <***Loc:*** VM, Da84, La99>

crachement [kraʃmɑ̃] *n.m.* spitting <***Loc:*** Da84>

cracher [kraʃe] *v.intr.* to spit *Et tu voyais que le pauvre bête avait tombé dans le bayou parce qu'il était après tousser et cracher et tout quelque chose.* And you could see that the poor fellow had fallen into the bayou because he was coughing and spititng and everything. (JD) ◊ **•cracher dans le feu** to do s.t. useless, waste one's time <AC, LA, La99> **•crache dans l'air, ça tombe sur le (bout du) nez** if you speak ill of others, it comes back to haunt you <La99> **•il crache pas dans la bouteille** he is a heavy drinker <La99> <***Loc:*** AC, JD, LA, TB, VM, Da84, La99>

crachis [kraʃi] *n.m.* spittle, matter that has been spit up <***Loc:*** JD>

crachoir [kraʃwar] *n.m.* spittoon <***Loc:*** AC, Da84>

crack (**CRACK**) [krɛk, krak, kræk] *adj.* crazy, nuts, bonkers *Il fait toujours comme si il est crack.* He always acts like he's crazy. (SB) *Son oncle a tout le temps été manière* CRACK. His uncle was always somewhat crazy. (LA) <***Loc:*** EV, LA, SB, SL, SM, TB, Lv88, Ph36>

craie [krɛ, kre] *n.f.* chalk <***Loc:*** Da84>

craignant (**craindant**) [krɛ̃jɑ̃, krɛ̃dɑ̃] *adj.* fearful, afraid *Les enfants sont pus craignants asteur comme ils étaient dans le temps.* Children are no longer fearful like they were in the old days. (LA) <***Loc:*** LA, Da84, Lv88>

craindant ♦see **craignant**

craindre [krɛ̃n, krɛ̃d(r)] *v.tr.* to fear, be afraid of, dread *Son père l'a mis dans une tour, craint que son cher amant lui fasse la cour.* Her father placed her in a tower, [he] fears that her lover courts her. (PQ, ch : *C'était une fille de quinze ans*) <***Loc:*** PQ, Da84>

crainte [krɛ̃t] *n.f.* fear, dread <***Loc:*** Da84>

craintif (**craintive**) [krɛ̃tif, krɛ̃tiv] *adj.* **1** meek, timid *Notre papa était beaucoup sévère dessus nous-autres, ça fait on a tout le temps été craintif.* Our father was very strict with us, so we have always been timid. (EV) **2** fearful, afraid *Son chien était trop craintif pour amener à la chasse.* His dog was too fearful to be taken out hunting. (LA) <***Loc:*** EV, LA, Da84>

craintive ♦see **craintif**

crâlant [kralɑ̃] *adj.* crunchy, crisp *Je vas te faire fondre des gratons bien crâlants.* I'm going to melt you some crunchy cracklins. (Lv88) <***Loc:*** Fa77, Lv88>

crâlement [kralmɑ̃] *n.m.* crackling, creaking, popping <***Loc:*** VM>

crâler [krale] *v.intr.* **1** to crack, crackle, crunch *Tu pouvais entendre ses os après crâler.* You could hear his bones cracking. (LA) **2** to pop, explode, burst open *J'aimais le son du tac-tac qui crâlait dans le foyer.* I loved the sound of popcorn popping in the hearth. (LA) <***Loc:*** LA, VM, Lv88>

crâleur [kralœr] *n.m.* ◊ **•crâleur d'os** chiropractor <Fa77, Lv88> <***Loc:*** Fa77, Lv88>

cramoisir (**camoisir**) [krɑ̃mwazir, kɑ̃mwazir] *v.intr.* to mildew (esp. of clothing) *Laisse du linge trop longtemps dans une armoire et il va camoisir.* Leave clothing in an armoire too long and it will mildew. (SM) *Mon* SUIT *de l'année passée est tout cramoisi.* My suit from last year is all mildewed. (SM) <***Loc:*** SM, Di32>

crampe[1] [krɑ̃p] *n.f.* cramp ◊ **•crampe d'estomac *a*** stomach cramp ***b*** stomachache <Da84> <***Loc:*** AC, SM, TB, Da84, Lv88>

crampe[2] [krɑ̃p] *n.f.* staple *Cil-là c'est pour des barrières, ça attachait les fils avec des crampes.* This one was for fences, they would tie the wire with staples. (AC) <***Loc:*** AC, IB, LA, SL, TB, Da84, Lv88>

crampeux, -euse [krɑ̃pø, -øz] *adj.* subject to cramps, afflicted with cramps *Il a travaillé dans son jardin hier et il est tout crampeux.* He worked in his garden yesterday and he is afflicted with cramps. (LA) <***Loc:*** IB, LA, SM, Da84, Lv88>

cramponner [krɑ̃pɔ̃ne] **I** *v.tr.* to grab hold of, hold fast **II se cramponner** *v.pron.* to cling to, hold fast *Il s'a cramponné après le poteau pour pas que le vent le prend.* He clung to the post so that the wind wouldn't carry him off. (VM) <***Loc:*** VM, Da84>

crâne [krɑ̃n] *n.m.* cranium, skull <***Loc:*** Da84>

crapaud [krapo] *n.m.* **1** toad *Saute, crapaud, ta queue va brûler.* Jump, toad, you tail will burn. (ch: *Saute, crapaud*) **2** toadfish **3** dried mucus from the nose, booger *T'as un gros crapaud qui pend de ton nez.* You've got a big booger hanging on your nose. (SM) **4** carbuncle, boil **5** short, stumpy man ◊ **•crapaud de nez** dried mucus from the nose, booger <La99> **•crapaud volant** bullbat, nighthawk <Re31> <***Loc:*** AV, IB, JD, LA, LF, SJ, SL, SM, TB, VM, Da84, Gu00, La99, Lv88>

crapule [krapyl] *n.f.* **1** low-class person, rascal, low-life *Cet homme est une crapule.* That man is a rascal. (SJ) **2** dirty, low-class people *Ça c'est de la p'us basse crapule.* Those are some of the lowest disagreeable people. (VM) **3** trash, junk <***Loc:*** AV, EV, IB, SJ, SM, VM, Da84, Ph36>

craque [krak] *n.f.* crack, crevice, break *Y'a une craque dans le verre qu'a été capoté par terre.* There's a crack in the glass that was knocked onto the floor. (Lv88) <***Loc:*** AV, EV, IB, LF, SM, TB, VM, An94, Da84, Lv88, Ph36>

craqué, -e [krake] *adj.* **1** cracked, split, broken *Ça ici, j'ai fait ça, ça c'est du cèdre. Tu vois ça semble qu'il a été verni et qu'il est craqué et tout. Ça semble il a été verni, c'est pas vrai non.* I made this one; it's [made with] cedar wood. You see it looks like it was varnished and that it's cracked and all. It looks varnished, but it's not. (TB) **2** cracked, nutty, crazy *Ses enfants sont tout manière craqués.* His children are all a bit nutty. (LA) <***Loc:*** AV, IB, LA, LF, SB, TB, Da84, Lv88>

craque-bine [krakbin] *adj.* stupid, silly *Alle est bien craque-bine.* She's quite silly. (TB) <***Loc:*** TB>

craquelin [kraklɛ̃] *n.m.* runt horse <***Loc:*** JD, Da84>

craquer [krake] **I** *v.tr.* **1** to crack, split, break *Il a pas cassé le vase, mais il l'a craqué.* He didn't break the vase but he cracked it. (SM) **2** to chap *Le froid avait tout craqué ses lèvres.* The cold had chapped his lips. (LA) **3** to strike (a match) **"Mais," je dis, "l'imbécil," je dis, "il a craqué une allumette," je dis, "le feu a pris dans le barril."* "Well," I said, "the idiot," I said, "he struck a match," I said, "the fire started in the barrel." (SL, An94) **4** to shoot **Il dit qu'il a craqué une balle, il avait un .38.* He said that he shot a bullet, he had a .38. (IV, An94) **II** *v.intr.* **1** to crack, split, break *À fur et à mesure qu'il traversait la glace, ça craquait derrière lui.* As he gradually went across the ice, it was cracking behind him. (LA) **2** to crack, crackle, snap *Il a resté si longtemps sur le plancher, quand-ce qu'ils l'ont enlevé j'ai attendu ses os craquer.* He stayed on the floor so long that when they moved him, I could hear his bones cracking. (TB) **3** to fire, go off (of a gun) **Ça se fait, quand le pistolet a craqué, le Grand Sauvage a parti loin devant le coureur à Jean l'Ours.* So when the gun fired, the Grand Sauvage took off far in front of Jean l'Ours' runner. (EV, An94) **4** to joke, cut up *Elle craque avec ses amis.* She cuts up with her friends. (SB) **5** to give out, succomb *Il a eu tellement des malheurs qu'il a venu à craquer.* He had so much misery that he finally gave out. (LA) **6** to die *Il a craqué hier soir.* He gave up the ghost last night. (SB) ◊ **•craquer du vent** to pass wind <Da84> **•craquer une farce** to crack a joke *Il pouvait pas s'empêcher de craquer des farces, même à l'enterrement.* He couldn't keep himself from telling jokes, even at the funeral. (LA) <LA, Da84, Lv88> **•craquer une tape** to hit, strike *Je vais te craquer une tape.* I'm going to hit you. (SB) <SB> **•ça craque pas fort** that is of little value, it's not worth much <SM, La99> <***Loc:*** EV, IB, IV, LA, LF, SB, SL, SM, TB, An94, Da84, La99, Lv88>

craquette [krakɛt, kraket] *n.m./f.* **1** cracker **2** soda cracker <***Loc:*** IB, LA, LF, SB, SL, SM, TB, VM, Da84, Lv88>

craqueur [krakœr] *n.m.* ◊ **•craqueur d'os** chiropractor <Da84, Lv88> <***Loc:*** Da84, Lv88>

crasé [kraze] *n.m.* party *Ils ont eu un gros crasé chez Nonc Paul hier soir.* They had a big party at Uncle Paul's last night. (SM) <***Loc:*** SM>

craser ♦see **écraser**

crasse[1] [kras] *adj.* crass, gross **Ignorance crasse.* Crass ignorance. (Da84) <***Loc:*** Da84>

crasse[2] [kras] *n.f.* **1** dirt, filth, crud **2** dirty trick, lowdown act *C'est une crasse qu'il m'a fait.* It's a dirty trick, what he did to me. (JD) **3** dirty, low-class people *Je m'associe pas avec ça. C'est la crasse même.* I don't associate with them. That's trash itself. (SM) **Ça c'est de la crasse.* That person is scum. (La99) <***Loc:*** EV, JD, SM, Da84, La99, Lv88, Ph36>

crasseux, -euse [krasø, -øz] *adj.* dirty, filthy, cruddy *Reste dehors, tes souliers sont tout crasseux.* Stay outside, your shoes are all filthy. (LA) <***Loc:*** LA, Da84>

cravate [kravat] *n.f.* necktie, tie <***Loc:*** AC, EV, LA, SM, An94, Da84, Lv88>

crayon [krejɔ̃, krijɔ̃] *n.m.* **1** pencil **2** crayon **3** needlefish ◊ **•crayon à {de / en} couleur** colored pencil <LF> <***Loc:*** AV, LA, LF, SL, SM, TB, VM, Da84>

cré ♦see **sacré**

créateur [kreatœr] *n.m.* creator, inventor <***Loc:*** Da84>

création [kreasjɔ̃] *n.f.* **1** creation **2** the world <***Loc:*** Da84>

créature [kreatyr] *n.f.* **1** creature **2** young woman *Une belle créature.* A lovely young woman. (SL) **3** nonbeliever, person of no religious faith *C'est une créature, ça va pas à l'église.* That's a nonbeliever, who doesn't go to church. (VM) <***Loc:*** SL, VM, Da84>

crébisse ♦see **écrevisse**

crèche [krɛʃ] *n.f.* **1** crib **2** manger **3** nativity scene, crèche **4** hay rack <***Loc:*** LA, Da84, Fa77>

crédit [kredi] *n.m.* credit *J'ai jamais acheté à crédit.* I've never bought on credit. (SM) ◊ **•avoir du crédit** to have credit <Da84> <***Loc:*** LA, SM, TB, Da84>

créditer [kredite] *v.tr.* to credit *Le marchand a crédité une selle à tous les hommes pour essayer de trouver qui en avait acheté une sans la marquer.* The store owner credited a saddle to each man's account to try to find who had bought one without signing for it. (LA) <***Loc:*** LA, Da84>

créditeur [kreditœr] *n.m.* creditor <***Loc:*** SM, Da84>

crédo [kredo] *n.m.* [*eccl.*] creed <***Loc:*** Da84>

crédule [kredyl] *adj.* credulous *Dans cette famille, il y en pas un tas qu'est crédule.* In that family, there aren't many who are credulous. (VM) <***Loc:*** VM, Da84>

créer [kree] *v.tr.* [*eccl.*] to create, make, invent *Qui a créé la terre et le ciel?* Who created the earth and the heavens? (LA) <***Loc:*** LA, Da84>

crème [krɛ̃m] *n.m./f.* **1** cream *Et puis le beurre prendait à se faire et ça se séparait et c'était le gras du crème.* And then the butter would start to form and the fat of the cream would separate. (AC) **2** ice cream *Il veut voir si tu veux avoir une crème.* He wants to know if you want to have an ice cream. (TB) ◊ **•crème à la glace / crème glacée** ice cream <LA, SB, SM, TB, VM, Da84, Fa77, Lv88> **•crème battue** whipped cream <Fa77> **•crème de lait** liquid coffee creamer <LF> **•crème de sabotière** homemade ice cream <SL> **•crème de tartre** cream of tartar <TB, Fa77> **•crème pour les dents** toothpaste <LA> <***Loc:*** AC, EV, JD, LA, LF, SB, SL, TB, VM, An94, Da84, Fa77, Lv88, Re31, Wh83>

crèmerie [krɛ̃mri] *n.f.* creamery <***Loc:*** Da84>

crémeux, -euse [krɛ̃mø, -øz] *adj.* creamy *Quand ton sucre et ton beurre viennent crémeux, là tu mets ta farine.* When your sugar and butter get creamy, then you put in your flour. (VM) <***Loc:*** VM, Da84>

crémier [krɛ̃mje] *n.m.* creamer, cream pitcher <***Loc:*** Fa77>

crémière [krɛ̃mjær] *n.f.* creamer, cream pitcher <***Loc:*** LA>

créneure [krɛ̃nœr] *n.f.* head *Il a la créneure dure.* He has a hard head. (AV) <***Loc:*** AV>

créole[1] [kreɔl] *adj.* **1** Creole, pertaining to Creole language or culture *Ça c'est un mot créole.* That's a Creole word. (LA) *L'hospitalité créole.* Creole hospitality. (SJ) *Tu serais intéressé dans aller manger du manger créole, cadien?* Would you be interested in going to eat Creole or Cajun food? (SJ) **2** Creole, native to Louisiana, grown or produced in Louisiana *Mon père élevait des bêtes, mais c'était juste des bêtes créoles, ça ça voulait dire qu'il avait pas une race particulière.* My father raised cattle, but they were just native [Louisiana] cattle, that meant that they weren't any particular breed. (VM) *Des oignons créoles.* Creole onions (i.e. locally grown in Louisiana). (SJ) *Dans le vieux temps y avait des mulets créoles. C'est un mulet qu'a été elevé ici qui habitué de le climette, de la chaleur, de l'humidité.* In the old days there were Creole mules. That's a mule that was raised here and is used to the climate, to the heat and the humidity. (LF) ◊ **•à la créole** Creole-style *Courtbouillon à la créole.* Creole-style redfish stew. (Re31) *Casburgot à la créole.* Creole-style sheepshead. (Re31) <Re31> <***Loc:*** EV, LA, LF, SJ, VM, Da84, Gu00, La99, Lv88, Re31>

créole[2] [kreɔl] *n.m.* **1** Louisiana Creole, Creole language of Louisiana *Les jeunes [noirs], là ils aiment plus parler français. Les vieux noirs parlaient presque tous le patois, le créole.* The young [blacks], they don't like to speak French anymore. The old blacks almost all used to speak patois, creole. (SL) **2** creole, creolized language *Je connais des noirs dont la parlure a gardé beaucoup de ressemblance avec le créole d'Haïti.* I know blacks whose language has maintained a lot of resemblance with Haitian Creole. (SM) <***Loc:*** SL, SM, VM, Gu00, Lv88>

Créole[3] [kreɔl] *n.* **1** Creole, descendant of original French or Spanish colonists of Louisiana **2** Creole, black person who speaks French or Creole *La plupart des Nègres ici sont créoles.* Most of the blacks here are Creoles. (Lv88) **3** any Louisianan who speaks a local variety of French *On est tous des Créoles icitte à ce matin.* Everyone here this morning is Creole. (Gu00) *On a parlé français toute la journée avec ce monde. C'était des Créoles pareil comme nous-autres.* We spoke French with those people all day long. They were Creoles just like us. (VM) ◊ **•Créole de couleur** person of mixed race with a light complexion <Da84> <***Loc:*** AV, LA, SM, VM, Da84, Gu00, Lv88>

crèpe [krɛp] *n.m.* dried mucus from the nose, booger <***Loc:*** SM>

crêpe [krɛp] *n.f.* **1** crepe (cloth) **2** crepe paper **3** crepe, thin pancake **4** fritter ◊ **•va aux crèpes!** get lost! <EV, Ph36> <***Loc:*** EV, SM, TB, Da84, Ph36>

crêque ♦see **crête**

cresson [kresɔ̃] *n.m.* **1** cress, watercress **2** peppergrass **3** chickweed <***Loc:*** SM, Da84, Ho90>

crête (**crêque**) [krɛt, krɛk] *n.f.* comb, crest (of fowl) ◊ **•crête de coq** coxcomb, celosia <SM> **•crête de corusse** coxcomb, celosia <LF, TB> **•crête de guime** coxcomb, celosia *La crête de guime était une des fleurs qu'on mettait dessus les tombes pour la Toussaint.* Coxcomb was one of the flowers we used to put on the tombs for All Saints' Day. (VM) <IB, VM> <***Loc:*** IB, LF, SM, TB, VM, Da84, Lv88>

crêté, -e [krete] *adj.* crested *Les petits poulets sont pas encore crêtés.* The chicks are not yet crested. (VM) <***Loc:*** VM, Da84>

crêter [krete] *v.intr.* to form a crest *Les poulets sont juste après crêter asteur.* The chicks are just now forming crests. (VM) <***Loc:*** VM>

cretonne [krətɔ̃n] *n.f.* cretonne, heavy fabric <***Loc:*** Da84>

creusement [krøzmɑ̃] *n.m.* hollow, deepened area <***Loc:*** Da84>

creuser [krøze] *v.tr.* **1** to deepen *Ils ont besoin de creuser le fossé.* They need to deepen the ditch. (LA) **2** to dig out *Creuser une coulée.* To dig out a coulee. (EV) **3** to hollow out *Un* SPOKESHAVER *c'était une petite outil avec une lame dessus. Et tu halais, si tu voulais creuser ou quelque chose, un* SPOKESHAVER *on appelait ça.* A spokeshaver is a small tool with a blade on it. And you would pull, if you wanted to hollow something out, a spokeshaver they called it. (TB) <***Loc:*** EV, LA, TB, Da84>

creuseur [krøzœr] *n.f.* **1** depth *Quoi c'est la creuseur au bayou?* What's the depth of the bayou? (VM) **2** height of a shovel or spade (used as a measure of depth) *J'ai fouillé trois creuseurs pour enterrer le chien.* I dug three spades deep to bury the dog. (VM) <***Loc:*** SM, VM, Da84, Lv88>

creusir [krøzir] *v.tr.* to deepen *Ton trou est pas assez creux. Il faudra tu le creusis.* Your hole is not deep enough. You will have to deepen it. (VM) <***Loc:*** VM>

creux[1], -euse [krø, -øz] *adj.* **1** deep *Si tu vas dans la rivière il faut que tu restes dedans le chenal. C'est le plus creux dedans un bayou ou une rivière.* If you go in the river you have to stay in the channel. It's the deepest part of a bayou or a river. (LF) **2** empty, hollow **Estomac creuse.* Empty stomach. (Da84) <***Loc:*** AC, LA, LF, SL, SM, TB, VM, An94, Da84, Lv88>

creux[2] [krø] *adv.* deeply *Il a coupé son pied creux.* He cut his foot deeply. (SM) <***Loc:*** SM>

creux-creux [krøkrø] *n.m.* medium-sized frog found along ditches <***Loc:*** LF>

crevasse (crévasse) [krəvas, krevas] *n.f.* **1** crevice, fissure, crack (esp. in a levee or dike) *Si y a une crevasse a Morganza, on va avoir la grande eau ici.* If there's a break in the levee at Morganza, we will have a flood here. (SM) **2** flood caused by a break in a levee *Et on faisait du maïs, et on faisait des cannes. Mais les levées a cassé. Et là ç'a* FLOOD, *tout l'eau a rentré. Et là ils l'ont pas repompé. Alors ça c'est une crévasse.* And we raised corn, and we raised sugar cane. But the levees broke. And it flooded, all the water came in. And they didn't pump it back out. So that's what we call a flood. (LF) **3** lowland, low-lying area susceptible to flooding <***Loc:*** EV, LF, SB, SJ, SM, An94, Da84, Lv88, Ph36>

crévasse[1] (crevasson) [krevas, krəvasɔ̃] *n.m.* sickly person or animal *Pauvre espèce de crévasse.* Poor, sickly thing. (VM) *Se marier avec un crevasson.* To marry someone who is unwell. (SJ) <***Loc:*** AV, SJ, VM>

crévasse[2] ♦see **crevasse**

crévasson ♦see **crévasse[1]**

crévation [krevasjɔ̃] *n.f.* dying ◊ **•faire sa crévation** to die *La bête a fait sa crévation.* The animal died. (VM) <VM> <***Loc:*** EV, VM, Da84, Ph36>

crevé, -e [krəve] *adj.* dead *Il y avait un chien crevé au bord du chemin.* There was dead dog on the side of the road. (LA) <***Loc:*** LA, An94, Da84>

crève [krɛv] *n.f.* ◊ **•être à la crève** to be dying or about to die, be at death's door *Moi, je peux pas dire que j'étais élevé un Cadien pauvre à la crève de faim parce que il n-a un tas de mes amis, ça l-aime dire ça, mais pour moi c'était pas le cas.* I can't say that I grew up as a poor Cajun on the verge of starvation because a lot of my friends like to say that, but for me that wasn't the case. (JD) <JD, LA, Da84> <***Loc:*** JD, Da84>

crève-faim [krɛvfɛ̃] *n.m.* **1** one who is starving **2** one who is always hungry <***Loc:*** SB, Da84>

crever (créver) [krəve, kreve] **I** *v.tr.* to pierce, gouge (an eye) *Quelqu'un y a crevé un œil avec une fourche.* Someone gouged his eye with a pitchfork. (VM) **II** *v.intr.* to die *Asteur, tu crèverais comme un rat.* Now you would die like a rat. (SL) *Il a crevé hier soir.* He died last night. (SM) ◊ **•crever de faim** to die of hunger, starve to death *Tu vas crever de faim dans l'Atchafalaya.* You're going to starve to death in the Atchafalaya. (SM) <SM> **•crever de rire** to die of laughter <Da84> **•crever le cœur à qqn** to break s.o.'s heart, move s.o. to sadness *Ça m'a crevé le cœur assez que j'ai pleuré.* That broke my heart so much that I cried. (TB) <TB> **•ça crève les yeux** that's obvious <AV, La99> <***Loc:*** AL, AV, EV, IB, SB, SL, SM, TB, VM, Da84, La99, Lv88, Ph36>

cri [kri] *n.m.* cry, scream, yell <***Loc:*** EV, LA, LF, TB, Da84, Ph36>

criaillement [kriajmɑ̃] *n.m.* repeated yelling or shouting <***Loc:*** Da84>

criailler [kriaje] *v.intr.* to cry, yell, shout (esp. repeatedly or annoyingly) *Arrêtez de criailler!* Stop yelling! (EV) <***Loc:*** EV, Da84>

criant, -e [kriɑ̃, -ɑ̃t] *adj.* crying **Dos brillant et ventre criant.* Shiny back and crying belly [said of people who dress fancily but have little to eat]. (Da84) <***Loc:*** Da84>

criard[1], -e [kriar, -ard] *adj.* **1** noisy, loud *Des oiseaux criards.* Loud birds. (VM) **2** overly colorful or decorative, tacky *Une chemise criarde.* A loud shirt. (VM) <***Loc:*** VM, Da84>

criard[2], -e [kriar, -ard] *n.* one who yells <***Loc:*** Da84>

crible [krib(l)] *n.m.* strainer, colander, sieve <***Loc:*** TB, Lv88>

criblé, -e [krible] *adj.* **1** riddled, full of holes *Un mur criblé.* A wall riddled with holes. (EV) **2** full (of), infested (with) *Sa* *tête était criblée de poux.* His head was infested with lice. (SM) **3** overwhelmed *Criblé de dettes.* Overwhelmed with debts. (VM) <***Loc:*** EV, LF, SM, VM, Da84>

cribler [krible] *v.tr.* to riddle, pierce full of holes *Garde comment les bétailles ont criblé les feuilles de mon* HIBISCUS*!* Look at how the insects chewed holes in the leaves of my hibiscus! (EV) <***Loc:*** EV, Da84>

crichet ♦see **criquet**

cricheter ♦see **critcher**

criée [krije] *n.f.* ◊ **•criée des cannes** backwoods *Ça m'a pris trois ans d'expérimenter avec un vieux sauvage dans la criée des cannes avant on a pu trouver les ingrédients pour perfectionner ce tonique du Hasitall.* It took me three years of experimentation with an old Indian in the backwoods before we were able to find the ingredients to perfect this Hasitall tonic. (AV) <AV> <***Loc:*** AV>

crier [krije] **I** *v.tr.* to cry out, yell, shout *J'ai passé devant ta porte, j'ai crié "bye-bye, ma belle!"* I passed in front of your door, I cried out "bye-bye, my sweetheart!" (ch: *J'ai passé devant ta porte) Il m'a crié* LOOK OUT *quand j'étais après traverser la grande rue.* He yelled at me to look out when I was crossing the main street. (VM) **II** *v.intr.* **1** to scream, yell, holler *Ma femme a crié quand j'ai marché sur son orteil.* My wife screamed when I stepped on her toe. (AV) *Et il m'a crié dessus.* And he yelled at me. (TB) **2** to call out, cry (of a bird, etc.) *C'est ça qu'un canard fait. Et là des fois la mère va crier, c'est manière embourbé parce qu'alle a de la boue dans le bec. Ça fait pas un son bien clair.* That's what a duck does. And then sometimes the mother will call out, it's kind of muddy because she has mud in her beak. It doesn't make a clear sound. (TB) **3** to cry, weep *Alle a beaucoup crié à l'enterrement.* She wept a lot at the funeral. (AV) ◊ **•crier après (qqn)** ***a*** to call out to, call out for (s.o.) *Ils criaient après nous-autres tard le soir.* They called out for us at night. (SL) *Quand-ce qu'on criait après une vache au lieu de dire "Passez!" on disait, on criait "*GO THERE*!"* When we shouted at a cow, instead of saying "Passez!" we would say "Go there!" (LF) ***b*** to yell at, shout at (s.o.) *Il a venu assez fâché qu'il criait après moi.* He became so angry that he was yelling at me. (VM) <LF, SL, VM> **•crier un cri en l'air** to cry out *J'ai crié un cri en l'air, j'ai dit "Daddy!"* I cried out, I said, "Daddy!" (TB) <TB> <***Loc:*** AC, AV, EV, IB, LA, LF, SB, SL, SM, TB, VM, An94, Da84, Lv88>

crieur [krijœr] *n.m.* **1** one who yells or shouts **2** auctioneer **3** bailiff *Le crieur amène les criminels en avant de la cour.* The bailiff brings the criminals before the court. (Lv88) ◊ **•crieur de cour** bailiff <Lv88> <***Loc:*** Da84, Lv88>

crignasse (tignasse) [krẽjas, tiɲas, tĩjas] *n.f.* **1** mane **2** head of hair, esp. one that is untidy or unkempt *Alle doit faire quelque chose avec cette crignasse-là.* She's got to do something with that unkempt hair. (VM) **•avoir sa crignasse en lutine** to have one's hair all matted up <SJ> <***Loc:*** AV, EV, IB, LA, LF, SB, SJ, SM, TB, VM, Lv88, Ph36>

crime [krim] *n.m.* **1** crime, offense **2** injustice, offense *J'ai du regret pour tous les crimes je t'ai faits.* I regret all the injustices I've done you. (Lv88) <***Loc:*** EV, IB, LF, PQ, VM, Da84, Lv88>

crimer [krime] *v.tr.* **1** to beat, beat up **N'appelez jamais une femme "une taïaute." C'est criminel et les chances sont qu'elle va te crimer aussi.* Never call a woman a "taïaute." It's terrible and chances are she'll beat you, too. (Re76) **2** to treat cruelly *Ça a défendu les batailles de guime, c'est crimer les bétailles.* Cockfights are prohibited, it treats the animals cruelly. (Lv88) <***Loc:*** Da84, Lv88, Re76>

criminel[1]**, -elle** [kriminɛl, krẽminɛl] *adj.* **1** criminal *Faire des affaires criminelles.* To do criminal things. (EV) **2** cruel, hateful *Un homme criminel.* A cruel man. (VM) **3** harmful *Ça ça c'est un* CATFISH*. Mais ça vient joliment gros. Et alle est bonne à manger, elle, mais alle a toujours des piquants mais ils sont pas si criminels que le mâchoiron.* That's a catfish. But that one gets quite big. And it's good to eat, it still has spines but they're not as harmful as [the spines on] the gafftopsail catfish. (TB) <***Loc:*** EV, LF, TB, VM, Da84, Lv88>

criminel[2]**, -elle** [kriminɛl, krẽminɛl] *n.* **1** criminal *Le crieur amène les criminels en avant de la cour.* The bailiff brings the criminals before the court. (Lv88) **2** terrible, cruel person **Quoi je t'ai fait malheureuse? Quoi je t'ai fait criminelle?* What did I do to you, miserable woman? What did I do to you, cruel one? (LA, Wh69) *Trop petite et trop mignonne pour faire ta criminelle.* Too small and too cute to play the cruel one. (Wh69) <***Loc:*** IV, LA, TB, An94, Lv88, Wh69>

crin [krẽ] *n.m.* **1** coarse animal hair (e.g. of a pig, of a horse's mane or tail) *Et ça tenait la* THE BLADE *et le manche et ça pouvait couper ça tu vois, les crins dessus la peau du cochon.* And they held the blade and the handle and they could cut them off, you see, the hairs on the pig skin. (LF) **2** mane ◊ **•avoir du crin** to have self-confidence, possess self-assurance <SJ> **•avoir le crin raide** ***a*** to be very angry ***b*** to be defiant of authority <EV, SJ, La99> <***Loc:*** EV, LF, SB, SJ, SL, VM, An94, Da84, Fa77, La99, Lv88>

crinière [krĩjær] *n.f.* mane <***Loc:*** Da84>

criote [krijɔt] *n.f.* **1** mess, disorder **Qué criote y a ici!* What a mess there is here! (EV, Ph36) **2** lowlives, scum **C'est jusse d'la criote tout ça.* They're just a bunch of scum. (EV, Ph36) <***Loc:*** EV, Ph36>

criquet (critchet, crichet) [krikɛ, krike, kritʃe, kriʃe] *n.m.* **1** cricket **2** grasshopper <***Loc:*** AV, JE, LA, LF, SB, SM, TB, Da84, Re31>

criquette[1] [krikɛt] *n.m./f.* cricket <***Loc:*** IB, JE, LA, LF, SB, SM, TB, Re31>

criquette[2] [krikɛt] *n.f.* [*term of endearment*] little girl <***Loc:*** VM>

crise [kriz] *n.f.* **1** crisis **2** convulsion, seizure *Adam, ça dit, il prend des "ECLIPSES" avec son "EPICLEPSY." Tu connais? Mais, il prend des crises.* Adam, they say he has "eclipses" with his "epiclepsy," you know? He has seizures. (ThCa: *La Table des Veuves*) **3** fit, tantrum *Couper une crise, faire une crise.* To have a tantrum, have a fit. (VM) <***Loc:*** LA, VM, Da84, ThCa>

cristal [kristal] *n.m.* **1** crystal, cut glass **2** translucent glass marble <***Loc:*** VM, Da84>

cristère ♦see **clystère**

critché [kritʃe] *n.m.* rubbing of the knuckles on s.o.'s head <***Loc:*** TB>

critcher (**cricheter, crochetiller, croustiller**) [kritʃe, kriʃte, krɔʃtije, krustije] *v.tr.* to grit, grind (one's teeth) *Ça fait critcher les dents.* That makes you grit your teeth. (VM) <***Loc:*** IB, TB, VM, Lv88>

critchet ♦see **criquet**

critiquer [kritike] *v.tr.* to criticize, find fault with *Il est tout le temps après me critiquer parce que je vote démocrate.* He's always criticizing me because I vote Democrat. (VM) <***Loc:*** IB, VM, Da84>

croc [kro] *n.m.* hook, barb *Un aspic c'était une serpent qu'avait comme un croc sur sa queue.* A viper was a snake that had something like a barb on its tail. (VM) <***Loc:*** VM>

croche[1] (**croiche**) [krɔʃ, krwaʃ] *adj.* **1** crooked, bent *Le chemin qui passe en avant de chez moi est assez croche que je me perds dessus.* The road that passes in front of my house is so crooked that I get lost on it. (Guoo) *Regarde voir ce panier là, il est manière croche.* Look at that basket, it's somewhat crooked. (TB) **2** bent, stooped *Le dos de la vieille femme est croche.* The old woman's back is bent. (SM) *Il marche tout croche.* He walks all crooked. (Lv88) **3** crossed (of the eyes) *Les yeux croiches.* Crossed eyes. (AL) **4** dishonest, crooked *Le monde croche de la politique.* The dishonest [crooked] world of politics. (Lv88) *Il est croche en bizinisse.* He's crooked in business. (Lv88) **5** wrong, bad, incorrect (of language) *Mon père, asteur, il comprend et il peut parler en anglais, mais c'est manière croche.* My father now can understand and speak English, but it's sort of incorrect. (LA) *Mon français est tout croche.* My French is all wrong. (Lv88) ◊ **•croche comme un baril de serpents {d'hameçons}** crooked as a barrel of snakes, very crooked, very corrupt *J'ai jamais vu un politicien qu'était pas croche comme un baril de serpents.* I never saw a politician who wasn't crooked as a barrel of snakes. (Guoo) <LA, VM, LF, Guoo, La99> **•aller croche** to become dishonest, become disreputable, go astray *C'est dur pour les politiciens de pas aller croche.* It's hard for politicians to not become dishonest. (VM) <SM, VM, Lv88> <***Loc:*** AL, EV, LA, LF, SL, SM, TB, VM, An94, Da84, Guoo, La99, Lv88>

croche[2] [krɔʃ] *n.m./f.* **1** bend, curve (in a road, bar, etc.) *Y a une croche dans le chemin.* There's a bend in the path. (VM) **2** crookedness, underhanded work *Y a de la croche là-dedans.* There's some crookedness in it. (VM) **3** swindler, cheat, crook *Méfie-toi de ce croche.* Do not trust that swindler. (LF) **4** ibis ◊ **•avoir une croche (d')accrochée** to be in a bad mood <La99> <***Loc:*** LA, LF, SM, TB, VM, Da84, La99, Lv88>

croche[3] [krɔʃ] *adv.* ◊ **•parler croche** to speak incorrectly *L'enfant parle croche.* The child speaks incorrectly. (IB) <IB, LA> <***Loc:*** IB, LA>

crocher [krɔʃe] *v.tr.* **1** to hook, catch with a hook *Il a croché un poisson sans s'apercevoir.* He hooked a fish without noticing. (SL) **2** to crochet *Ma grand-mère m'a croché un gilet.* My grandmother crocheted me a vest. (EV) <***Loc:*** EV, SL, Da84, Lv88>

crochet [krɔʃe] *n.m.* **1** hook **2** latch *Mettre le crochet sur la porte.* To latch the door. (SJ) **3** tusk **4** crochet, crocheting <***Loc:*** AC, AV, SJ, SM, Da84, La99, Lv88>

crochetiller ♦see **critcher**

crochette [krɔʃɛt] *n.f.* ◊ **•marcher à la crochette** to walk together holding each other by the waist <EV, Ph36> <***Loc:*** EV, Ph36>

crochi ♦see **crochu**

crochir [krɔʃir] **I** *v.tr.* **1** to bend *Crochir le genou.* Bend one's knee. (Lv88) *Crochir une barre de fer.* Bend an iron rod. (Lv88) *Tu l'as crochi, ga'.* You bent it, look. (VM) *J'ai crochi la vis.* I bent the screw. (SM) **2** to warp **3** to tread down (the heel or sole of a shoe) **II** *v.intr.* **1** to bend *Durant le mauvais temps les deux bois crochissaient. Ils étaient lourds et le vent était froid.* During the storm the two trees bent. They were heavy and the wind was cold. (TB) **2** to curve *Le chemin crochit juste avant le bois.* The road curves just before the woods. (LA) **III se crochir** *v.pron.* to become bent or warped *Ma table s'a crochi au soleil.* My table warped in the sun. (VM) <***Loc:*** JD, LA, LF, SL, SM, TB, VM, Da84, Lv88>

crochu, -e (**crochi, -e**) [krɔʃy, krɔʃi] *adj.* crooked, bent *Le nez crochu.* Crooked nose. (EV) <***Loc:*** EV, Da84>

croquemitaine [krɔkmitɛ̃n] *n.m.* boogeyman, imaginary being used to frighten children *Alle dit qu'alle a rouvert le baril, y avait un croquemitaine là-dedans. C'est une bétaille avec des grandes pattes.* She said that she opened the barrel, and there was a bogeyman in there. It was a creature with big paws. (TB) <***Loc:*** SM, TB>

crocodile, crocodril ♦see **cocodrie**

crocro [krokro, krokrɔk] *n.m.* **1** old plowshoe **2** old shoe <***Loc:*** IB, LA, SB, SM, TB, Re31>

croiche ♦see **croche**[1]

croire [krwar] **I** *v.tr.* **1** to believe *Tu me crois pas?* You don't believe me? (AC) *Il faut pas croire ses menteries.* You should not believe his lies. (EV) **2** to think *Je crois que son dernier nom était Ouarnet.* I think his last name was Ouarnet. (TB) **II** *v.intr.* to believe, have faith *Je peux pas croire!*

I can't believe! (EV) **Il faut croire.* One must believe, one is led to believe. (Da84) **III se croire** *v.pron.* **1** to think of o.s., consider o.s. *Ça parlait pas comme nous-autres, ça se croyait plus smarts.* They did not speak like us, they thought they were smarter. (IB) **2** to be proud, be vain, think too highly of o.s. *Ça se croit de trop, ça veut pas parler français.* They think too much of themselves, they don't want to speak French. (TB) *J'aime pas le monde qui se croit.* I don't like people who think too highly of themselves. (SM) ◊ **•Comment tu crois?** How do you like that? <EV, An94> **•le crois en Dieu** the Apostle's Creed <Da84> **•s'en croire** to be haughty, vain *Il s'en croit, lui.* He's haughty, that guy. (VM) <VM> **•tu crois (que) t'as de la barbe et des crochets** you are impudent <La99> **•tu crois (que) t'es maître et majeur** you think you are behaving like an adult, but you are being foolish or impudent <La99> <***Loc:*** AC, AV, EV, IB, JE, LA, LF, SB, SL, SM, TB,VM, An77, An94, Da84, Gu82, La99, Lv88, St95, Wh83>

crois-sein [krwasɛ̃] *n.m.* swollen gland under the arm <***Loc:*** TB>

croisée [krwaze] *n.f.* crossing, intersection (of roads, etc.) <***Loc:*** Da84>

croiser [krwaze] **I** *v.tr.* **1** to cross, traverse **Ils auront croisé le pont pour aller l'autre bord.* They would have crossed the bridge to go to the other side. (An94) **2** to cross, overlap **Et le vieux homme était assis sur la galerie avec sa jambe croisée.* And the old man was sitting on the porch with his legs crossed. (SL, An94) **3** to make the sign of the cross over **Mais le prêtre s'a mis à les croiser.* But the priest began making the sign of the cross over them. (EV, An94) **4** to partition, divide into rooms *Il a pas encore croisé la maison, mais on va faire quatre chambres.* He hasn't partitioned the house yet, but we are going to make four rooms. (VM) **5** to interbreed, crossbreed *Vous croisez une femelle bourriquet avec un cheval, ça fait un mulet.* You interbreed a she-ass with a horse and you get a mule. (IB) **II se croiser** *v.pron.* **1** to cross each other, pass by each other (e.g. on the road) **Et Kossuth était* GONE *à sa boucherie, et Johnny était* GONE *à la sienne. Et ils se sont croisés là-là.* And Kossuth was going to his butchery, and Johnny was gone to his. And they crossed each other right there. (EV, An94) **2** to thwart each other ◊ **•croiser avec** to encounter, happen upon *J'ai croisé avec lui au village.* I encountered him in town. (VM) <VM> <***Loc:*** EV, IB, SL, SM, VM, An94, Da84, Lv88>

croison[1] [krwazɔ̃] *n.f.* crossing <***Loc:*** Da84, Lv88>

croison[2] ♦see **cloison**

croix [krwa] *n.f.* **1** cross **2** rein bar (on a wagon or buggy) **3** stock (of a gun) *Une chance il avait ce chien-là. Il lui a mordu la croix de sa carabine-là, ah ben mais les dents se sont gravées dedans.* Lucky he had that dog. He bit the stock of his rifle, and his teeth left a mark in it. (EV) ◊ **•Croix Rouge** Red Cross <IB> **•faire la croix *a*** to make the sign of the cross *Dire des prières et puis eux-autres faisait des croix.* To say prayers and then they'd make the sign of the cross. (LF) ***b*** to swear not to do s.t. again *Je fais la croix. Je vais jamais parler avec lui encore.* Cross my heart. I'll never speak to him again. (SM) <LA, LF, SM, La99> <***Loc:*** IB, LA, LF, SM, TB, VM, Da84, La99>

cropillon, cropion ♦see **croupion**

croquant[1]**, -e** [krokɑ̃, -ɑ̃t] *adj.* crisp, crackling, crunchy *Les gratons étaient bien croquants.* The pork rinds were crunchy. (LA) <***Loc:*** LA, Da84>

croquant[2] [krokɑ̃] *n.m.* cartilage <***Loc:*** EV, LA, VM>

croquecignole (croquignole, croquesignole) [krɔksĩjɔl, krokĩjɔl, grosĩjɔl] *n.m./f.* doughnut, cake doughnut *La maîtresse bien souvent avait des grands plateaux de patates douces qu'elle avait cuit d'avance, et des fois des grands plateaux de croquesignoles.* The mistress of the house very often had big platters of sweet potatoes that she had cooked ahead of time, and sometimes big trays of cake doughnuts. (EV) <***Loc:*** AV, EV, IB, LF, SL, SM, TB, VM, Da84, Lv88>

croquer [kroke] *v.tr.* to crunch, crack (e.g., nuts, ice) with one's teeth *Croquer de la glace.* To chew ice. (EV) <***Loc:*** EV, Da84>

croquesignole, croquignole ♦see **croquecignole**

croquetter [krokete] *v.intr.* to hatch *Les oeufs ont bien croquetté.* The eggs hatched well. (AV) <***Loc:*** AV>

crosser ♦see **closser**

CROSS-TIE [krɔstaj] *n.f.* cross-tie <***Loc:*** TB>

crotte [krɔt] *n.f.* **1** hard, rounded animal droppings (rabbit, sheep, etc.) **2** turd, piece of feces *Les crottes de bébé sont trop dures quand tu y donnes du riz.* Babies' bowel movements are too hard when you give them rice. (EV) **3** obnoxious or ill-tempered person *Vieille crotte!* Old biddy! (VM) ◊ **•crotte-au-cul** constipation <AV> **•crotte de poule *a*** chicken dropping ***b*** jelly bean <Da84> <***Loc:*** AV, EV, VM, Da84, La99>

crotté, -e [krote] *adj.* kinky (of the hair) *Les nègres ont les cheveux crottés.* Black people have kinky hair. (SM) <***Loc:*** LF, SB, SM, VM>

crotter (croûter) [krote, krute] *v.tr.* to encrust with filth *Ils ont tout croûté le lavabo avec leurs mains sales.* They encrusted the washbasin with their filthy hands. (SL) *Ses souliers étaient tout crottés.* His shoes were encrusted with filth. (VM) <***Loc:*** SL, VM, Da84>

crottin [krotɛ̃] *n.m.* turd, piece of feces *Il a fait un gros crottin.* He made a big turd. (SB) ◊ **•en crottins** dirty, filthy *Tes cheveux sont en crottins.* Your hair is dirty. (SB) <***Loc:*** SB>

crouler ♦see **écrouler**

croup [krup] *n.f.* croup (disease) <***Loc:*** Da84>

croupe [krup] *n.f.* **1** rump, buttock **2** croup, hindquarters of a horse <***Loc:*** EV, Da84>

croupière (**écroupière**) [krupjær, ekrupjær] *n.f.* crupper strap, strap that keeps the tail of a horse up <***Loc:*** IB, Da84>

croupion (**cropion, courpion**) [kropjɔ̃, kropijɔ̃, kurpjɔ̃] *n.m.* rump, derriere, butt (of a human or animal) *Il a tombé sur son courpion.* He fell on his behind. (AV) <***Loc:*** AV, LF, VM, Da84, Re31>

crousser ♦see **closser**

croustiller ♦see **critcher**

crouston [krustɔ̃, kruʃtɔ̃] *n.m.* **1** heel, end of a loaf of bread **2** piece of bread (esp. pointed end of French bread) **3** crumb <***Loc:*** AV, IB, LF, SB, SJ, SL, SM, TB, Da84, Lv88>

croûte [krut] *n.f.* **1** crust (of bread, a pie, etc.) *Ma sœur mange jamais la croûte de son pain.* My sister never eats the crust of her bread. (LA) **2** scab (of a sore) *Ecorcher la croûte d'un bobo.* To tear off the scab of a lesion (VM) **3** heel, end of a loaf of bread <***Loc:*** LA, SM, VM, Da84>

croûter ♦see **crotter**

croûteux, -euse [krutø, -øz] *adj.* **1** crusty (of food) *Du pain croûteux.* Crusty bread. (LA) **2** scabby (of a sore) *Son bobo était tout croûteux.* His sore was scabby. (LA) ◊ **•vieux croûteux** crusty old man <Da84> <***Loc:*** LA, Da84>

croûton [krutɔ̃] *n.m.* crouton, dried piece of bread (esp. the end piece) ◊ **•vieux croûton** [*pej.*] old man <TB> <***Loc:*** TB, Da84>

CROWBAR (**gros-bar**) [krobar, grobar] *n.m.* crowbar <***Loc:*** EV, SL, TB, VM, Da84, Fa77, Lv88, Ph36>

croyable [krwajab(l)] *adj.* believable, credible *C'est pas croyable, cette histoire!* It's not believable, that story! (EV) <***Loc:*** EV, Da84>

croyance [krwajɑ̃s] *n.f.* **1** belief *Ç'a venu qu'après la guerre t'as eu plein du différent de monde, différent de religions. Pas dire que c'est mauvais, ça a des différentes croyances.* It happened that after the war you had a lot of different people, different religions. That's not to say that it's bad, they have different beliefs. (LF) **2** faith *Avec la croyance que t'as dedans moi, il dit, eh bien je pourras te guérir.* With the faith that you have in me, he said, well, I will be able to heal you. (LF) **3** opinion <***Loc:*** LF, TB, Da84>

croyant, -e [krwajɑ̃, -ɑ̃t] *n.* [*eccl.*] believer <***Loc:*** TB, Da84>

cru, -e, -te [kry, kryt] *adj.* raw *C'est la viande crute.* It's raw meat. (LA) **Viandre crute.* Raw meat. (Da84) *Riz cru.* Uncooked rice. (SL) <***Loc:*** LA, LF, SL, VM, Da84, Lv88>

cruauté [kryote] *n.f.* cruelty, cruel act <***Loc:*** Da84>

cruche [kryʃ] *n.f.* jar, jug <***Loc:*** TB, Da84>

crucifier [krysifje, krysyfje] *v.tr.* **1** to crucify *Il y avait un bon homme dans l'histoire et ils l'ont crucifié.* There was one good man in the story and they crucified him. (VM) **2** to maltreat, punish *Ils l'avont crucifié à faire pitié.* They punished him enough to inspire pity. (VM) <***Loc:*** VM, Da84>

crucifix [krysifi, krysyfi] *n.m.* crucifix <***Loc:*** SL, Da84>

crucifixion [krysifiksjɔ̃] *n.f.* crucifixion <***Loc:*** Da84>

crudité [krydite] *n.f.* **1** crudity, coarseness **2** raw food <***Loc:*** Da84>

cruel, -elle [kryɛl] *adj.* **1** cruel *Calmez votre colère, sachez que la justice pour sûr met sur le ciel un crime aussi cruel.* Calm your anger, know that justice surely places in the hands of heaven a crime so cruel. (PQ, ch: *Le jour de l'Ascension*) **2** awful, disturbing *C'est une rue cruelle, le monde est toujours après passer.* That's an awful street, people are always going by. (VM) <***Loc:*** VM, Da84>

cruellement [kryɛlmɑ̃] *adv.* cruelly *Ils l'ont fouetté cruellement.* They whipped him cruelly. (VM) <***Loc:*** VM, Da84>

crystère ♦see **clystère**

c'telle, c't'i ♦see **celui**

cu ♦see **tchu**

çu ♦see **celui**

cuartil ♦see **quarti**

cueillette [køjɛt, tʃøjɛt] *n.f.* harvest <***Loc:*** Lv88>

cueillir [køjir] *v.tr.* to pick, gather *Il avait juste les fruits qu'eusse cueillait et des citernes eusse ramassait de l'eau qu'eusse avait comme ça.* They just had the fruits that they picked and cisterns, that's how they collected their water. (TB) <***Loc:*** TB>

çui ♦see **celui**

cuillère [kɥiljær, kyjær, kijær, tʃijær, tʃyjær, kyljær, kyrijær, krɥjær] *n.f.* spoon ◊ **•cuillère à café** coffee spoon <Fa77> **•cuillère à lait** ***a*** ladle ***b*** serving spoon <AC, LA, Fa77> **•cuillère à manger** soup spoon, tablespoon <LA> **•cuillère à soulier** shoe-horn <IB, Lv88> **•cuillère à soupe** ladle <LA> **•cuillère à table** soup spoon, tablespoon <Fa77, Lv88> **•cuillère à thé** teaspoon <Da84, Fa77, Wh83> **•cuillères à mésure** measuring spoons <LA> **•grand cuillère** tablespoon <Da84> <***Loc:*** AC, AV, IB, JD, JE, LA, LF, SB, SL, SM, TB, VM, Da84, Fa77, Lv88, Wh83>

cuillerée [kɥijere, kyljare] *n.f.* spoonful ◊ **•grande cuillerée** tablespoonful <Da84> **•petite cuillerée** teaspoonful <Da84> <***Loc:*** EV, Da84, Fa77>

cuir [kɥir] *n.m.* leather <***Loc:*** AC, EV, LA, Da84>

cuirage ♦see **curage**

cuire [kɥir] **I** *v.tr.* to cook *J'ai cuit une bonne sauce piquante pour le souper.* I cooked a good spicy sauce for dinner. (Lv88) **II** *v.intr.* to cook, do the cooking *Je fais pas de recettes, je cuis comme mère cuisait juste.* I don't do recipes, I just cook like mother cooked. (SL) **III se cuire** *v.pron.* **1** to be cooked *Tu peux pas faire un bon gombo avec des jeunes poulets. Ça se cuit trop vite.* You can't make a good gumbo with young pullets. They cook too quickly. (VM) **2** to cook for o.s. **Se cuire à manger.* Cook oneself something to eat. (Da84) ◊ **•faire cuire** to cook <EV, Da84> <***Loc:*** AC, AL, AV, EV, IB, JD, JE, LA, LF, SL, SM, TB, VM, Da84, Guoo, Lv88>

cuiseur, -euse [kɥizœr, -øz] *n.* cook *J'ai un garçon qui demeure icitte, qu'est marié et sa femme est une bonne cuiseuse aussi.* I have a son who lives here, he is married and his wife is a good cook too. (IB) <***Loc:*** IB, TB, Lv88>

cuisine (**cusine**) [kɥizin, kyzin, kuzin] *n.f.* kitchen *Nous-autres* *va abouter une 'tite cuisine en arrière de la maison.* We're going to add on a little kitchen in the back of the house. (Lv88) ◊ •**faire la cuisine** to cook, do the cooking <Da84> <***Loc:*** AV, EV, IB, JE, LA, SB, SJ, SM, TB, VM, An94, Da84, Fa77, Gu00, Lv88>

cuisinier, -ière [kyzinje, -jær] *n.* cook <***Loc:*** SM, VM, Da84, Fa77>

cuisse [kɥis] *n.f.* **1** thigh **2** leg **3** hindquarter ◊ •**cuisse de poule** drumstick <Da84> •**cuisses cailles a passé** nothing has been going right <La99> •**cuisses de ouaouaron** frogs' legs <Fa77> •**gros de cuisse** the thigh of fowl <Da84> <***Loc:*** AC, EV, JE, LF, SB, TB, VM, Da84, Hi02, La99>

cuissière [kɥisjær, kwisjær] *n.f.* trouser leg <***Loc:*** VM>

cuite [kɥit, kyit] *n.f.* **1** thick cane syrup drawn just before the syrup crystallizes into sugar **2** feast *On aurait tué peut-être huit, dix lapins en allant là-bas. Et s'aurait fait une grosse cuite, bien mangé.* We would kill maybe eight or ten rabbits when we went over there. We would make a big feast for ourselves, eat well. (SL) **3** exhaustion, fatigue *Ce travail lui a donné une fameuse cuite.* That work made him really exhausted. (SB) ◊ •**se foutre une cuite** to get drunk, go on a bender *Il s'a foutu une cuite* AND A HALF *hier soir.* He went on a bender and a half last night. (SM) <SM, La99> •**(se) prendre une cuite** to get drunk, go on a bender *Il s'a pris une sacrée cuite hier au soir.* He got really drunk last night. (LA) <LA, La99> <***Loc:*** AV, IB, LA, SB, SL, SM, TB, Da84, La99, Lv88, Re31>

cuiture [kɥityr] *n.f.* cookery, cooking <***Loc:*** Da84>

cuivre [kɥiv, kwiv] *n.m.* **1** copper **2** brass *Il m'a vendu cette bague pour de l'or, mais c'est bien du cuivre.* He sold me this ring as gold, but it's brass. (VM) <***Loc:*** SB, TB, VM, Da84>

cuivré, -e [kɥivre, kwivre] *adj.* coppered, coppery *Des chaudières cuivrées.* Coppered pots. (LA) <***Loc:*** LA, Da84>

cul ♦see **tchu**

culbute [kylbyt] *n.f.* **1** flip, somersault *Il a fait une culbute.* He did a somersault. (VM) **2** mess, great disorder *Ma maison est tout en culbute.* My house is all a mess. (Lv88) ◊ •**faire la culbute** to give birth, be delivered of child *Marie a fait la culbute ce matin.* Marie had her baby this morning. (IB) <IB> <***Loc:*** IB, JE, SM, VM, Da84, La99, Lv88>

culbuter [kylbyte] **I** *v.tr.* **1** to flip, upend *Il a culbuté l'autre bougre quand il essayé de rentrer dans la salle.* He flipped the other guy when he was trying to come back into the dance hall. (LA) **2** to mess up, make a mess of *Elle a tout culbuté sa chambre en cherchant pour la boîte.* She completely turned her room upside down while searching for the box. (LA) **II** *v.intr.* to do a somersault *Le petit a culbuté en sautant par dessus le fossé.* The kid did a somersault while jumping over the ditch. (LA) <***Loc:*** LA, Da84, Lv88>

culer ♦see **reculer**

culotte[1] [kylot, kylɔt] *n.f. (often pl.)* trousers, pants *Il a déchiré sa culotte en ribandelles.* He tore his pants to shreds. (SM) *Les femmes portaient pas des culottes comme on en porte asteur, c'était plus des robes.* Women did not wear pants as they do today, they wore more dresses. (AC) ◊ •**culotte(s) courte(s)** shorts <SL> <***Loc:*** AC, AV, EV, LA, LF, SB, SL, SM, TB, VM, An94, Da84, Lv88, Ph36, Wh69>

culotte[2] [kylot, kylɔt] *n.m./f.* pied-billed grebe <***Loc:*** AV, Re31>

cultivable [kyltivab(l)] *adj.* arable *Il y avait pas la moitié de la terre qu'était cultivable.* Less than half of the land was arable. (LA) <***Loc:*** LA, Da84>

cultivage [kyltivaʒ] *n.m.* cultivation *Le cultivage se fait dans le printemps.* Cultivation is in spring. (Lv88) <***Loc:*** Da84, Lv88>

cultivateur [kyltivatœr] *n.m.* **1** cultivator (machine) **2** farmer, one who cultivates <***Loc:*** SM, Da84>

cultiver [kyltive] *v.tr.* **1** to cultivate, till *Ça, c'était du monde qui connaissait comment cultiver la terre.* They were people who knew how to cultivate the land. (LA) **2** to cultivate, foster **Cultiver l'amitié.* To foster friendship. (Da84) <***Loc:*** LA, Da84>

cultiveur [kyltivœr] *n.m.* farmer, planter <***Loc:*** SM, TB, Lv88>

culture [kyltyr] *n.f.* **1** culture *D'autre monde étranger a venu dans la Louisiane aussi, mais à mesure que ça venait, ça adoptait la culture et la langue des Acadiens.* Other foreigners came into Louisiana also, but as they came, they adopted the culture and the language of the Acadians. (VM) **On était si fier de notre culture de voir le monde de tout partout comme ça applaudir la musique que nous-autres, on les amenait de la Louisiane.* We were so proud of our culture to see the people from all over like that applauding the music that we were bringing them from Louisiana. (VM, An84) **2** cultivation <***Loc:*** VM, An84, Da84, Gr86, Wh83>

cumuler [kymyle] *v.tr.* to accumulate *J'ai cumulé de quoi dans ma vie, mais j'ai travaillé pour.* I accumulated much in my life, but I worked for it. (VM) <***Loc:*** VM, Da84>

CUP (cope) [kɔp] *n.m./f.* **1** cup **2** dipper ◊ •**cope de café** coffee cup <SM> <***Loc:*** IB, LF, SB, SM, VM, Lv88>

curage (cuirage) [kyraʒ, kyras, kɥiraʒ] *n.m.* water pepper, smartweed <***Loc:*** AV, IB, LA, SB, TB, VM, Da84, Lv88, Re31>

curatif, -ive [kyratif, -iv] *adj.* curative, healing *C'est curatif, du thé de mamou.* Mamou tea is curative. (VM) <***Loc:*** VM, Da84>

curative [kyrativ] *n.m.* curative, remedy <***Loc:*** Da84>

curder ♦see **curer**

cure [kyr] *n.f.* charge, care <***Loc:*** Da84>

curé [kyre] *n.m.* pastor, rector, priest <***Loc:*** Da84>

cure-dent (écurdent) [kyrdɑ̃, ekyrdɑ̃] *n.m.* toothpick <***Loc:*** VM, Da84>

curer (curder) [kyre, kyrde] **I** *v.tr.* to pick, clean by picking

Curer une pipe. To clean a pipe. (EV) **II se curer** *v.pron.* to pick o.s. clean *Il s'a bien curé après qu'il a sorti du magasin de foin.* He picked himself clean after coming out of the hay barn. (LA) ◊ **•se curer les dents** to pick one's teeth <Da84> <***Loc:*** EV, LA, Da84>

curieusité ♦see **curiosité**

curieux, -ieuse [kyrjø, -øz] *adj.* **1** curious **Elles estiont curieux de voir et ils avaient jamais vu des HAMBURGERS.* There were curious to see, and they had never seen hamburgers. (EV, An94) **Je serais curieux d'avoir vingt ans.* I would be interested to be twenty years old [again]. (EV, An84) **2** nosy *Il est curieux comme un pot de chambre.* He is as nosy as a chamber pot. (VM) **3** strange, odd, curious **Je trouvais emasse [=en masse] de les traitments curieux et des fois je doubtais [=doutais] si ça aurait travailler.* I found many of the treatments strange and sometimes I doubted whether they would work. (Wh83) <***Loc:*** EV, SL, TB, VM, An84, An94, Da84, Wh83>

curiosité (**curieusité**) [kyrjøzite] *n.f.* **1** curiosity, inquisitiveness **2** object of curiosity <***Loc:*** LA, SM, VM, Da84>

cusine ♦see **cuisine**

cuve [kyv, kyb] *n.m.* cistern (large round tank made of cypress wood, formerly built next to houses to collect rainwater) <***Loc:*** IB, LF, SB, TB, Re31>

cuvette [kyvɛt] *n.f.* handbasin <***Loc:*** Da84>

cyclone [siklɔ̃n, siglɔ̃n] *n.m./f.* **1** tornado **2** hurricane <***Loc:*** IV, JE, LF, TB, Da84>

cygne [siɲ] *n.m.* swan, whistling swan <***Loc:*** Da84, Re31>

cylindre [silɛ̃n, silɛ̃d(r)] *n.f.* cylinder <***Loc:*** SM, TB, Da84>

cypre ♦see **cipre**

cyprès [siprɛ, sipre] *n.m.* **1** red cedar **2** eastern brown cedar <***Loc:*** SB, SL, SM, Da84, Gu00, Lv88, Re31>

cyprière ♦see **ciprière**

cyst [sis] *n.m.* cyst <***Loc:*** TB>

D

d'abord [dabɔr] *adv.* **1** first, first of all *Tu dois d'abord figurer la distance.* First you have to calculate the distance. (Lv88) **2** in that case, then, and so **Moi, je travaille dur. Allons se coucher d'abord. On va se lever beau matin.* I work hard. Let's go to bed, in that case. We'll get up early in the morning. (EV, An94) ◊ **•d'abord que** ***a*** provided that *Tu peux venir, d'abord que tu sois tranquille.* You can come, provided that you are quiet. (LF) ***b*** because, since **D'abord que c'est plus à la mode, ça danse pas la valse, le deux-pas, le Jitterbug, ou le Contredanse Cajin, éspécialment pas en publique.* Since it's no longer stylish, they don't dance the Cajun waltz, two-step, jitterbug, or Contredanse, especially not in public. (Wh83) **D'abord que ti veux pas, j'le fera pas.* Since you don't want me to, I won't do it. (EV, Ph36) <EV, JE, LF, Di32, Ph36, Wh83> <*Loc:* AC, AV, EV, JE, LF, An94, Da84, Di32, Hi02, Lv88, Ph36, Wh83>

d'aplomb ♦see **aplomb**

dada [dada, dadal] *n.m.* [*baby talk*] horse <*Loc:* JE, SM>

DAGO ♦see **dégo**

daigner [dẽje] *v.intr.* to deign, condescend *Je peux pas croire qu'il a daigné de me parler.* I can't believe he deigned to speak to me. (VM) <*Loc:* VM, Da84>

daigué [dege] *n.m.* pond *Les canards sont dans le daigué.* The ducks are in the pond. (AV) <*Loc:* AV>

dais [dɛ] *n.m.* canopy <*Loc:* Da84>

dalle [dal] *n.f.* **1** rain spout **2** roof gutter *La pelote a tombé dans la dalle.* The ball fell into the gutter. (AV) **3** roof valley (descending metal strip where sections adjoin) <*Loc:* AV, IB, SB, SJ, SL, SM, TB, VM, Da84, Lv88>

DAM [dɛm, dɛ̃m] *n.m.* dike, dam, embankment, causeway <*Loc:* Lv88>

damas [dɑ̃mas] *n.m.* damask cloth <*Loc:* AV, IB, SJ, Da84>

dame [dɑ̃m] *n.f.* **1** lady **2** wife **La dame du maire.* The mayor's wife. (Re31) **3** queen (in a deck of cards) ◊ **•aller à dame** to ride side-saddle <Da84> **•Notre Dame** Our Lady, the Virgin Mary <Da84> <*Loc:* AV, JE, IB, SJ, SM, Da84, Hi02, Re31>

dame-jeanne [dɑ̃mʒɑ̃n] *n.f.* **1** demijohn *La dame-jeanne est pleine de whisky.* The demijohn is full of whisky. (AV) **2** crock, large earthen jar *Va dans l'office me chercher de la viande salée dans la dame-jeanne.* Go into the pantry to get me some salted meat from the crock. (TB) <*Loc:* AV, IB, LF, TB, Da84>

damnation [dɔ̃nasjɔ̃, dɑ̃nasjɔ̃] *n.f.* **1** damnation, perdition **2** trouble, difficulty, annoyance *Ça me fait trop de damnation.* That's too much trouble for me. (VM) <*Loc:* EV, SM, VM, Da84, Ph36>

damné, -e [dɑ̃ne] *adj.* **1** damned *Y a pas moyen de le sauver, lui. Il est damné.* That guy is beyond saving. He is damned. (VM) **2** mischievous, full of mischief *Mon frère est damné. Y a rien à son épreuve.* My brother is so full of mischief, there is nothing he won't do. (VM) ◊ **•les damnés** the damned <Da84> **•vieux damné** old mischief-maker <Da84> <*Loc:* VM, Da84, Hi02>

damner [dɑ̃ne] **I** *v.tr.* to damn *Le Bon Dieu va te damner à l'enfer si t'arrêtes pas de coursailler comme tu fais.* God is going to damn you to hell if you don't stop running around like you do. (VM) **II se damner** *v.pron.* to curse o.s., doom o.s. *Il s'a damné à l'enfer quand il a volé la terre à sa sœur.* He doomed himself to hell when he stole his sister's land. (VM) <*Loc:* VM, Da84>

dandine [dɑ̃din] *n.f.* beating, whipping, thrashing **Pape m'a donné einne dandine.* Dad gave me a sound thrashing. (EV, Ph36) <*Loc:* EV, IB, Ph36>

dandiner [dɑ̃dine] *v.intr.* to dilly-dally, procrastinate, waste time *Arrête de dandiner. On sera tard.* Stop wasting time. We'll be late. (VM) <*Loc:* AV, SJ, VM, Da84>

danger [dɑ̃ʒe] *n.m.* danger, risk, hazard, peril *Y a pas autant de danger icitte que dans les villages.* There's not as much danger here as in the towns. (TB) <*Loc:* TB, Da84>

dangereusement [dɑ̃ʒrøzmɑ̃] *adv.* dangerously, hazardously, perilously <*Loc:* Da84>

dangereux, -euse [dɑ̃ʒərø, -øz] *adj.* dangerous *Il y [...] a une qualité de petit serpent on appelle un couleuvre. C'est pas dangereux.* There's one kind of little snake we call a "couleuvre." It's not dangerous. (SL) *Essaie de te retiendre. C'est un bougre dangereux.* Try to hold yourself back. He is a dangerous fellow. (LA) <*Loc:* SL, Da84>

dans [dɑ̃] *prep.* **1** in, inside *Une cigale, ça commence avec un ver dans la terre, une larve.* A cicada begins his life as a worm in the ground, a grub worm. (AV) *Il garde une topette dans sa poche tout le temps.* He keeps a flask in his pocket all the time. (SM) *J'ai tisonné le feu dans la cheminée.* I stirred the fire in the fireplace. (AV) *Malgré qu'il s'a détruit, il a été enterré dans de la terre sacrée.* Even though he committed suicide, he was buried in sacred ground. (LA) **Il s'est caché dans le coin de la boutique.* He hid in the corner of the store. (EV, An94) *Dans le bayou y a une bôme pour tiendre les herbes du bayou.* In the bayou there is a boom to hold back the grasses. (TB) *Et là j'appelais tout le monde pour que ça vient travailler dans la facterie.* And I called all those people to have them come to work in the factory. (TB) **Ils étaient à la chasse dans le bois.* They were hunting in the woods. (SM, An94) **2** into, in **Lapin, je voulais te brûler, mais je veux te jeter dans les éronces-là!* Rabbit, I wanted to burn you, but I want to throw you into the briars. (SM, An94) **Oublie pas aussi de mettre sel et persil dans le gumbo.* Also don't forget to put salt and parsley in the gumbo. (EV, An94) *Il a calé un poteau dans la terre.* He planted a pole into the ground. (SM) *Elle s'est tirée dans mes bras.* She thew herself into my arms. (Lv88) **Tu vides du café dans du lait, ça le tourne marron, mais marron blanc.* You pour coffee into some milk, it turns it brown, light brown. (LA, An94) **Dans ma famille on a jamais eu besoin de 'garder dans ein liv' pour sa'oir dans quel sens le vent soufflait.* In my family we have never needed to look in a book to know which way the wind was blowing. (ThCa: *Mille misères*) **3** during, in *Ma fête est dans février.* My birthday is in February. (SL) *J'ai couru dans 1952, et j'ai gagné et j'ai resté trois termes de quatre ans. Douze ans. Et là j'ai* GIVE UP *ça, et je travaillais dans l'office d'assesseur.* I ran in 1952, and I won, and I stayed for three four-year terms. Twelve years. And then I gave that up and I worked in the assessor's office. (LF) *Dans le vieux temps, ça torquait le périque pour faire des torquettes.* In the old days, they would twist the perique tobacco into rolls. (LA) *Dans ce temps là, tu connais, les affaires étaient* TIGHT. In those days, you know, there was not much money. (EV) *Il faut je me lève tôt le matin dans l'hiver.* I have to get up early in the morning during the wintertime. (LA) *Il a fait des mauvais tours dans sa vie.* He pulled off some malicious pranks in his life. (LA) **4** among *Y a personne dans vous-autres qui veut aller?* There's no one among you who wants to go? (VM, Lv88) *Y a trois dans eux qui restent avec nous.* There are three of them live who with us. (SM) *Il y avait personne dans ses enfants qui voulait 'i aider tellement il avait été méchant pour leur défunte mère.* There was nobody among his children who wanted to help him, [because] he had been so mean to their late mother. (VM) **5** to, in (with cardinal directions) **Et eux battaient ces chiens-là chez Monsieur Norbert Lormand à Ossun, trois milles dans le nord de Scott, trois milles au nord de le* TRIANGLE CLUB. And they fought those dogs at Mr. Norbert Lormand's in Ossun, three miles north of Scott, three miles north of the Triangle Club. (LA, An94) *À Charenton, dans le nord du lac Charenton, il y avait ce vieux Indien qui s'appelait Jim.* In Charenton, to the north of Lake Charenton, there was this old Indian named Jim. (SM, An94) *Ouais, ça venait d'une certaine place. Ça venait de dans le nord de nous-autres.* Yeah, they came from a certain place. They came from [a place] to the north of us. (LA, An94) *Il était parti dans l'ouest.* He departed to the west. (EV, An94) **6** out of, from *J'ai ôté la lancette dans mon doigt.* I took the stinger out of my finger. (SL) ◊ **•dans moi {toi, eux, etc.}** to me, to you, to them, etc. **Dans eux, quand même si je parlais français, chanter français c'était un différent langage.* To them, even if I were speaking French, singing in French, it was a different language. (VM, An84) *Dans toi, quoi tu crois ça va faire?* To you, what do you think that will do? (LA) *Dans lui, il est expert dans tout lui.* According to him, he is an expert in everything. (VM) <LA, VM, An84> <***Loc:*** AC, AV, EV, IV, LA, LF, SL, SM, TB, VM, An84, An94, Da84, Hi02, Lv88, ThCa, Wh83>

dansailler [dɑ̃saje] *v.intr.* to dance about <***Loc:*** IB, JE>

danse [dɑ̃s] *n.f.* **1** dance **Tous les temps en temps on jouait pour une danse en quelque part.* Every now and then we played at a dance somewhere. (An84) **2** song or musical number (live or recorded) to accompany dancing *Ça, c'est la plus belle danse que Paul Daigle a fait.* That's the most beautiful dance that Paul Daigle recorded. (LA) ◊ **•danse carrée** square dance <Hi02> **•danse masquée** masked dance <Da84> **•danse ronde** round dance, play-party dance, figured dance <SM, Hi02, Lv88> **•ronde de danses** a series of five dances, traditionally played in order: waltz, polka, waltz in two, two-step, mazurka <Lv88> <***Loc:*** AC, EV, IB, LA, SL, SM, VM, An84, An94, Da84, Hi02, Lv88>

danser [dɑ̃se] *v.intr.* to dance **Danser avec elle, c'est comme traîner une herse dans les grandes herbes.* Dancing with her is like dragging a harrow through tall grass (i.e. she can't follow). (La99) ◊ **•danser comme un dinde dans la cendre chaude** to be in a peck of trouble <Da84> **•danser comme une plume** to dance well, dance smoothly <AC, La99> **•danser la carmagnole** to suffer through a difficult experience, be in a bad fix *J'ai dansé la carmagnole au dentiste.* I had quite an ordeal at the dentist's. (SM) <SM, Lv88> **•danser la quadrille** to square dance <Da84> **•danser la queue raide** to dance very energetically, 'cut a rug' <IB, SM, La99> **•danser une valse** to waltz, dance a waltz <Da84> **•faire danser** to give trouble, make trouble (for s.o.) *Cet enfant m'a fait danser toute la nuit.* That child gave me trouble all night. (SL) <SL> <***Loc:*** AC, AV, EV, IB, LA, SL, SM, TB, VM, An94, Da84, Hi02, La99, Lv88>

danseur, -euse [dɑ̃sœr, -øz] *n.m.* dancer *J'étais bonne danseuse.* I was a good dancer. (EV) <***Loc:*** AC, EV, VM>

dard [dar] *n.m.* **1** stinger (of an insect) *Le bourdon, quand il te pique, il garde son dard.* The bumblebee, when it stings you, it keeps its stinger. (AL) **2** dart **3** sharp or pointed instrument **4** wiseguy, smooth fellow <***Loc:*** AL, AV, Da84>

darder [darde] **I** *v.tr.* to harpoon, spear, stick with a pointed instrument *Darder les poissons.* To spear fish. (Lv88) *Déluc Hébert était après darder des poissons armés dans le mèche quand il a trouvé la croix.* Déluc Hébert was spearing garfish in the marsh when he found the cross. (VM) **II se darder** *v.pron.* to dart out, lunge, throw o.s., hurl o.s. *J'ai pas pu le manquer. Il s'a dardé devant le char.* I couldn't avoid him. He darted out in front of the car. (VM) <***Loc:*** LF, SM, VM, Da84, Lv88>

dardon [dardɔ̃] *n.m.* **1** thorn, barb *Il s'est planté un dardon dans le pied.* He got a thorn in his foot. (AV) **2** stinger (of an insect) *Le dardon d'une mouche à miel.* The stinger of a bee. (SJ) **3** dart <***Loc:*** AV, IB, SJ>

dardre, darte ♦see **dartre**

darter [darte] *v.tr.* to sting *Quand elle va te darter, il reste lui et elle crève.* When she stings you, it [the stinger] stays in and she dies. (AL) <***Loc:*** AL>

dartre (**darte, dardre**) [dart(r), dard(r)] *n.f.* **1** mole (on the skin), wart, birthmark **2** skin disease, herpes **3** ringworm *L'oncle à ma maman traitait pour des dardres.* My mother's uncle treated for ringworm. (SB) <***Loc:*** SB, TB, Da84, Lv88>

DASHBOARD [dæʃbɔɹd] *n.m.* dashboard <***Loc:*** AV, Lv88>

date [dat] *n.f.* date <***Loc:*** EV, Da84, Hi02>

dater [date] *v.tr.* to date (a letter, an event, etc.) *Il a daté son chèque pour la semaine d'après.* He dated his check for a week later. (LA) ◊ **•ça date de l'an quarante *a*** it is very old ***b*** that happened a long time ago <LA, La99> <***Loc:*** LA, Da84, La99>

datte [dat] *n.f.* date, fruit of the date palm <***Loc:*** Da84>

daube [dob, dɔb] *n.f.* any of several dishes prepared from the hindquarter of an animal, such as a roast, stew or casserole *Dis au boucher de m'envoyer une bon daube.* Tell the butcher to send me a good roast. (VM) *Une daube, c'est un morceau de cochon comme la fesse de le cochon. On pique ça à l'ail et puis là tu cuis ça dessus le* STOVE *dans une chaudière ou bien dans le* OVEN *tu peux cuire les deux manières.* A roast, it's a piece of pork like the buttock of the pig. We stuff it with garlic and then you cook it in a pot over the stove or in the oven, you can do it both ways. (SM) <***Loc:*** JE, SM, TB, VM, Da84, Hi02, Lv88>

dauber [dobe] *v.tr.* to stuff (for cooking) *On les daube, les bréchets.* You stuff briskets. (VM) <***Loc:*** VM>

dauiaut [dojo] *n.m.* boor, person with unrefined or uncouth tastes *Tu peux reconnaître ce dauiaut par son linge.* You can recognize that boor by his clothes. (LF) <***Loc:*** LF>

dauphin [dofɛ̃] *n.* **1** dolphin **2** dolphinfish <***Loc:*** SL>

davantage [davɑ̃taʒ] *adv.* **1** more **J'en ai davantage.* I have more. (Da84) **2** further, longer <***Loc:*** Da84>

de[1] [də] (*contractions:* **de +** *art.def.* **le = du** [dy], **de +** *art.def. pl.* **les = des** [de, dez]) *prep.* **1** of **Une pincée de sucre.* A pinch of sugar. (Da84) *Dans la clarté du soleil.* In the light of the sun. (ch: *J'ai fait une grosse erreur*) *Durant le temps de les fêtes.* During the holidays. (IB) *Achète ça pour un de les enfants.* Buy that for one of the children. (IB) *Si t'aurais pas écouté tous les conseils des autres.* If you hadn't listened to the advice of others. (ch: *Jolie blonde*) **2** of, belonging to *J'ai fini de te voir [...] sur la terre du Bon Dieu.* I will no longer see you on the Good Lord's earth. (ch: *Blues de la prison*) **Il a échappé avec le drap et l'alliance de la femme.* He escaped with the woman's sheet and wedding ring. (An94) **Il a passé à côté des lits de ses enfants.* He passed next to his children's beds. (LA, An94) **3** made of *Confiture de figues.* Fig jelly. (EV) **4** from, of **Il a sorti de la grosserie avec ses cinq sous dans la poche.* He walked out of the grocery store with his five cents in his pocket. (An94) *Jeunes gens de la campagne, mariez vous-autres jamais.* Young men from the country, don't ever get married. (ch: *Jeunes gens de la campagne*) *L'eau était à peu près comme ça de le haut de la levée.* The water was about that far from the top of the levee. (SB) **5** by *Un poème de Deborah Clifton.* A poem by Deborah Clifton. (EV) **6** about *Ils parlont de cette-là qu'a quitté, mais jamais de cette-là qu'a resté.* They talk about the one who left, but never about the one who stayed. (ch: *Les bonnes femmes*) *Tu peux nous dire l'histoire de comment t'as commencé.* You can tell us the story about how you started [with that]. (VM) **T'as jamais pas entendu parler d'un feu follet?* You never heard of a will-o'-the-wisp? (An94) *Souvent ils nous ont renconté des histoires, des contes du vieux temps.* Often they told us stories, stories about the old days. (LA) ◊ **•de près, de loin** from near and far <Da84> **•de trop** too much *(Je parle) pas de trop en anglais* I don't speak English too much (LF) <LF> **•de ça** ago *Et ça c'est à peu près peut-être dix ans de ça qu'eusse a fait ça.* And it was about ten years ago that they did that. (LF) <LF> <***Loc:*** EV, IB, LA, LF, SB, SM, An94>

de[2] (**du, de la, de l'**) (*m.sing.* **du** [dy], *f.sing.* **de la** [d(ə)la], *m./f. sing. before a vowel* **de l'** [d(ə)l], *with negation* **de, d'** [d(ə), d]) *art. part.* **1** some **On délaye de la farine et on fond du sucre.* We dissolve flour and we melt sugar. (Da84) **Et il était après chercher pour trouver du manger.* And he was looking for some food. (LA, An94) **Il a dit ça, qu'il avait apporté de la boisson pour eux boire.* He said that he had brought some drinks for them to drink. (SL, An94) **2** *(with negation)* any *Eux-autres avait pas de place à rester.* They did not have any place to stay. (TB) *Lui, il a pas de cheveux.* He doesn't have any hair. (SL) **Il y a pas de bêtailles qui pèsent seize mille livres. C'est huit tonnes, ça!* There aren't any animals that weigh sixteen thousand pounds. That's eight tons! (EV, An94) **Il y a pas de doute.* There's no doubt. (SM, An94) **Il y avait pas d'eau là-bas sur la lune.* There was no water over there on the moon. (EV, An94) *Il y a pas d'accordement entre eux depuis ça.* There's not been accord between them since then. (VM) *Asteur il n-a plus du monde.* Now there's no longer anybody. (SM) <***Loc:*** LA, SL, SM, An94, Da84>

dé [de] *n.m.* **1** die, one of a pair of dice **2** thimble <***Loc:*** JE, LA, Da84>

DEAL [dil] *n.m.* deal, bargain *Il a le bon* DEAL *pour vous-autres.* He has a good deal for you. (EV) <***Loc:*** EV, Lv88>

débâcle [debak(l)] *n.m./f.* **1** debacle, rout, clean sweep **2** collapse *Le vent a causé un débâcle dans le village.* The wind caused a building to collapse in the village. (AV) <*Loc:* AV, SJ, Da84>

débagager [debagaʒe] *v.intr.* to move on, head off, move away *Ça va pas durer bien longtemps. Il va bien vite débagager là.* It won't last long. He'll move on soon. (TB) <*Loc:* JE, TB>

déballage [debalaʒ] *n.m.* 1 unpacking 2 unbaling <*Loc:* Da84>

déballer [debale] *v.tr.* 1 to unpack *Il a déballé le wagon.* He unpacked the wagon. (LA) 2 to unbale *On déballait le foin pour donner à les animaux.* We unbaled the hay to give to the animals. (IB) <*Loc:* IB, LA, Da84>

débander [debɑ̃de] *v.intr.* to lose one's erection *Quand j'ai vu ma mère rentrer, j'ai vite débandé.* When I saw my mother come in, I quickly lost my erection. (LA) <*Loc:* LA, VM>

débarbouillage [debarbujaʒ] *n.m.* 1 washing, cleaning 2 clearing away (of confusion), clearing (of the mind) <*Loc:* Da84>

débarbouiller [debarbuje] **I** *v.tr.* 1 to wash *Elle avait besoin de bien débarbouiller le bébé quand il a rentré de dehors.* She had to wash the baby well when he came in from outside. (LA) 2 to clear (the mind) *Ce petit somme m'a débarbouillé l'esprit.* That little nap cleared my mind. (VM) **II se débarbouiller** *v.pron.* 1 to wash o.s. *Va te débarbouiller avant de t'assir à la table.* Go wash up before sitting at the table. (LA) 2 to clear (one's mind) *En dormant, il s'a débarbouillé l'esprit.* By sleeping, he cleared his mind. (VM) <*Loc:* LA, VM, Da84>

débarque [debark] *n.f.* 1 disembarking (from a vehicle) 2 landing place *Quand ils ont arrivé à la débarque ils ont tout débarqué.* When they got to the landing place they unloaded everything. (TB) <*Loc:* TB, Da84>

débarquement [debarkmɑ̃] *n.m.* 1 disembarking, getting off of or out of (a vehicle or boat) 2 unloading (of effects or merchandise) <*Loc:* EV, SM, Da84, Lv88, Ph36>

débarquer [debarke] **I** *v.tr.* to unload (effects or merchandise) from a vehicle or boat *Dans l'affaire de pêche on a ouvert une place à nous-autres-mêmes pour débarquer la chevrette.* In the fishing business we opened a place of our own for unloading shrimp. (TB) *Va débarquer les groceries.* Go unload the groceries. (Lv88) **II** *v.intr.* 1 to disembark, get off of or out of (a vehicle or boat) *Quand le char a arrivé en ville j'ai débarqué.* When the car arrived in town I got out. (VM) *Higgin d'en ville a fait ces bateaux-là qu'a accosté, le monde débarquait à la terre dedans, ça sortait pour la guerre.* Higgins in New Orleans made those boats which came up along shore, the people got out on dry land, they came out for the war. (LF) 2 to turn off, get off (of a bridge, a road, etc.) *Tu débarques de l'overpass et tu vas peut-être un demi mille.* You get off of the overpass and you go maybe a half mile. (LF) <*Loc:* AV, EV, IB, LF, SB, SJ, SL, SM, TB, VM, Da84, Lv88, Ph36>

débarras [debara] *n.m.* riddance <*Loc:* Da84>

débarrasser [debarase] **I** *v.tr.* to clear off, clear out *Il a aidé à débarrasser la table après le souper.* He helped clear the table after supper. (LA) **II** *v.intr.* to get rid of *J'aimerais bien débarrasser de ça.* I would really like to get rid of that. (IB) **III se débarrasser** *v.pron.* 1 to get rid of *Je voudrais me débarrasser de ces voisins que j'ai à Gueydan.* I would like to get rid of those neighbors that I have in Gueydan. (VM) 2 to get by, manage *[Je parle] pas de trop en anglais mais assez pour me débarrasser, tu vois.* I don't speak too much English but enough to get by, you see. (LF) <*Loc:* EV, LA, LF, TB, VM, Da84>

débarrer [debare] *v.tr.* to unlock, unlatch, open *Débarre la porte et quitte-lé rentrer.* Unlock the door and let them in. (VM) <*Loc:* AC, EV, IB, LF, SL, SM, TB, VM, Da84, Lv88, Ph36>

débat [deba] *n.m.* struggle, strife <*Loc:* Da84>

débâtir [debatir] *v.tr.* to tear down, demolish *Il voulait le terrain mais pas la maison, ça fait il l'a débâtie.* He wanted the lot but not the house, so he tore it down. (LA) <*Loc:* LA, Da84>

débattement [debatmɑ̃] *n.m.* struggle, effort *Il marche avec un débattement.* He walks with an effort. (AV) <*Loc:* AV, EV, SM, Ph36>

débattre [debat(r)] **I** *v.intr.* 1 to struggle, put up a fight *C'est une femme qu'a débattu dans sa vie.* That's a woman who struggled in her life. (VM) 2 to undertake, do *Quand on faisait boucherie, c'est toi qui débattais tout l'affaire.* When we had a boucherie, you were the one who undertook the whole thing. (LA) **II se débattre** *v.pron.* 1 to struggle, fight *Il s'a débattu avec este poisson-là pour une bonne demi-heure avant de pouvoir l'emmener dans le bateau.* He struggled with that fish for a good half hour before being able to bring it to the boat. (LA) 2 to get by, manage *Mes grands-mères dessus les deux bords pouvait manière se débattre mais eux-autres pouvait pas s'expliquer en anglais.* My grandmothers on both sides could more or less get by, but they couldn't communicate in English. (TB) ◊ **•débattre comme un chat dans l'eau bénie** to fight furiously, squirm <LF, La99> **•se débattre comme le diable dans de l'eau bénite {un bénitier}** ***a*** to fight furiously, squirm ***b*** to struggle to get out of a bad situation <LA, SM, TB, La99> <*Loc:* EV, LA, LF, SM, TB, VM, Da84, La99>

débauchage [deboʃaʒ] *n.m.* 1 debauchery, drunkenness *Il passe son temps en débauchage.* He spends his time on debauchery. (SM) 2 mess, messy job *Les ouvriers ont fait un débauchage dans ma cuisine.* The carpenters made a mess in my kitchen. (LA) 3 leaving work (for the day) <*Loc:* JE, LA, SM, Lv88>

débauche [deboʃ] *n.f.* 1 debauchery, drunkenness 2 leaving work (for the day) *Il a arrivé à l'heure de débauche.* It got to be quitting time. (TB) ◊ **•se mettre à la débauche** to drink to excess <SM> <*Loc:* SM, TB, Da84>

débauché, -e [deboʃe] *n.* heavy drinker <***Loc:*** SM>

débaucher [deboʃe] **I** *v.tr.* to debauch, corrupt *C'est ça la femme qu'a débauché ce jeune garçon.* That's the woman who corrupted that young boy. (LA) **II** *v.intr.* **1** to drink excessively **2** to get off, finish (school, work, etc.) for the day *Je débauche pas d'école jusqu'à deux heures et demie.* I don't get out of school until two thirty. (LF) **Les hommes ont débauché à quatre heures.* The men got off work at four o'clock. (EV, Ph36) **3** to have the day off, be off work *Mais je travaillais pas le samedi-là. On débauchait.* But I didn't work on Saturdays. We were off. (LF) **III se débaucher** *v.pron.* to become corrupt, go astray *J'étais sûr qu'alle s'aurait débauché quand alle a rencontré cet homme-là.* I was sure she would go astray when she met that man. (VM) <***Loc:*** EV, IB, LA, LF, SB, TB, VM, Da84, Ph36>

débaucheur [deboʃœr] *n.m.* debaucher, corrupter (of others) *Débaucheur de filles.* Seducer of young women (AV) <***Loc:*** AV, Da84>

déberner [debærne] **I** *v.tr.* to clean, clean up (esp. by wiping off excrement, mud, or smeared substances) *J'ai déberné l'enfant.* I cleaned up the child. (SM) **II se déberner** *v.pron.* **1** to clean o.s. up *Va te déberner!* Go clean up! (EV) **2** to get o.s. out of a difficult situation <***Loc:*** EV, SL, SM, Lv88>

débile [debil] *adj.* weak, feeble, debilitated *Le pauvre vieux bougre était rendu débile.* The poor old fellow had become feeble. (LA) <***Loc:*** LA, Da84>

débilité [debilite] *n.f.* debility, weakness <***Loc:*** Da84>

débine [debin] *n.f.* state of misery *Il a pris une débine depuis il a eu ces malchances.* He has become miserable since he had that stroke of bad luck. (SB) <***Loc:*** SB>

débité ♦see **député**

débiter[1] [debite, debrite] *v.tr.* **1** to cut up, carve up *Débiter un morceau de bois.* To cut up a piece of wood. (AV) **2** to parcel out cuts of meat from, cut (a slaughtered animal) into pieces *Débiter une bête.* To cut a cow carcass in pieces. (IB) <***Loc:*** AV, EV, IB, Da84>

débiter[2] [debite] *v.tr.* to debit, subtract *Débiter un compte de banque.* To debit a bank account. (EV) <***Loc:*** EV, Da84>

déblocage [deblokaʒ] *n.m.* unblocking, unclogging <***Loc:*** Da84>

débloquement [deblɔkmɑ̃] *n.m.* unblocking, unclogging <***Loc:*** Da84>

débloquer [debloke] **I** *v.tr.* to unblock, unclog, open *Débloquer le chemin.* To unblock the road. (EV) **II se débloquer** *v.pron.* to have a bowel movement after being constipated *Enfin il s'est débloqué.* He finally had a bowel movement. (SL) <***Loc:*** AV, EV, SL, Da84>

déboiser [debwaze] *v.tr.* to clear of trees and brush. *Déboiser une pièce.* To clear a plot of land. (SL) <***Loc:*** SL>

débord [debɔr] *n.m.* overflow, overflowing <***Loc:*** AV, Da84>

débordage [debɔrdaʒ] *n.m.* overflow, overflowing <***Loc:*** AV, Da84>

débordement [debɔrdmɑ̃] *n.m.* overflow, overflowing <***Loc:*** AV, Da84>

déborder [debɔrde] *v.intr.* to overflow, run over *La chaudière a commencé à faire de la bouillie, ça a commencé à déborder, tomber par terre.* The pot started to boil, it started to overflow and spill onto the ground. (SM) *Un siau débordé.* An overflowing pail. (AV) ◊ **•à déborder** overflowing <Da84> <***Loc:*** AV, SM, Da84>

déboucher [debuʃe] *v.tr.* **1** to open **Quand le paquet a arrivé, j'ai débouché la boîte.* When the package arrived, I opened the box. (An84) **2** to uncork *Déboucher une bouteille.* To uncork a bottle. (SL) **3** to unclog, unstop *J'ai debouché la commode.* I unclogged the toilet. (EV) **4** to clear *Cette médecine va déboucher ses poumons.* This medicine will clear her lungs. (SL) <***Loc:*** EV, SL, An84, Da84, Lv88>

déboucler [debukle] *v.tr.* **1** to unbuckle (a belt, etc.) *Déboucler une ceinture.* To unbuckle a belt. (AV) **2** to uncurl (hair) *La pluie a débouclé mes cheveux.* The rain uncurled my hair. (SL) <***Loc:*** AV, SL, Da84>

déboulage [debulaʒ] *n.m.* sliding, caving in, crumbling <***Loc:*** AV, Da84>

déboulement [debulmɑ̃] *n.m.* sliding, caving in, crumbling ◊ **•déboulement de terre** landslide <Da84> <***Loc:*** AV, Da84>

débouler [debule] **I** *v.tr.* **1** to dump, dump out *J'ai déboulé les mirlitons du bassin sur la galerie.* I dumped the mirlitons out of the basin onto the porch. (Lv88) **2** to tumble down, roll down *J'ai déboulé l'escalier.* I tumbled down the stairs. (SM) **II** *v.intr.* **1** to slide down, cave in **La terre a déboulé.* The dirt caved in. (Da84) **2** to roll down, tumble down *Le baril a déboulé.* The barrel rolled down. (Lv88) *Il a déboulé en bas des escaliers.* He tumbled to the bottom of the stairs. (EV) **3** to tumble out, spill out, *Les affaires dans ta closette, ça va tout débouler.* The things in your closet are all going to spill out. (AV) <***Loc:*** AV, EV, SB, SM, TB, Da84, Lv88>

déboulir [debulir] *v.intr.* to spill out, roll out, tumble out *Il y a eu une grosse bataille et tous les musiciens ont débouli comme des pelotes.* There was a big fight and all the musicians [at the dance] came spilling out like balls. (AV) <***Loc:*** AV>

déboulis [debuli] *n.m.* **1** debris, refuse, rubbish **2** rush, madhouse (of people, esp. holiday shoppers) *C'était un seul déboulis chez Kress.* It was a complete madhouse at Kress'. (AV) <***Loc:*** AV, VM, Lv88>

déboulonner [debulɔ̃ne] *v.tr.* to unbolt *On va déboulonner le manche de la charrue.* We're going to unbolt the handle of the plow. (IB) <***Loc:*** IB, Da84>

débouquer [debuke] **I** *v.intr.* **1** to emerge, appear, come out from behind s.t. *Quand elle a débouqué du poteau, je l'ai vue.* When she came from behind the post, I saw her. (LF) **2** to cheer up **3** to reconcile, be reconciled after a quarrel **II**

se débouquer *v.pron.* **1** to cheer up, get over a pouting spell **2** to be reconciled after a quarrel <***Loc:*** IB, LF, Lv88>

débourbage [deburbaʒ] *n.m.* **1** clearing off, washing away of mud **2** act of pulling out of the mud <***Loc:*** Da84>

débourber [deburbe] **I** *v.tr.* to free from mud, pull from the mud **Débourber la voiture* To free the buggy from the mud. (Da84) **II se débourber** *v.pron.* to get free from mud *J'ai tombé dans un trou de cocodrie quand j'étais petit, et j'ai manqué de jamais de m'en débourber.* I fell into an alligator hole when I was little, and I almost never got out of there. (VM) <***Loc:*** VM, Da84>

débourrer [debure] *v.tr.* **1** to remove the wadding from (a shotgun shell) **2** to unclog *Débourrer un moulin.* To unclog a mill. (SL) <***Loc:*** SL, VM, Da84>

déboursement [debursmɑ̃] *n.m.* disbursement, expenditure <***Loc:*** Da84>

débourser [deburse] *v.tr.* to disburse, pay out *Les banques ont déboursé un tas d'argent après l'eau haute de '27.* The banks paid out lots of money after the flood of '27. (VM) <***Loc:*** VM, Da84>

débousiller [debuzije] **I** *v.tr.* to clean mud off of *Il a débousillé le mur avec le tuyau.* He cleaned the mud off the wall with the hose. (Lv88) **II** *v.intr.* to become cleaner, become clearer *Je vas laisser tout ça débousiller et je crois ça va aller.* I'm going to let all of that clear up and I think it will be okay. (Lv88) <***Loc:*** Lv88>

debout[1] (**deboute**) [dəbu, dəbut] *adj.* **1** standing, upright *Tu es debout dans l'eau là avec une seine.* You stand up there in the water with a dragnet. (SM) **2** up and awake, out of bed *J'ai appelé la voisine, et j'ai dis "T'es deboute?"* I called the neighbor, and I said, "Are you up?" (TB) <***Loc:*** EV, SM, TB, VM, Da84, Lv88>

debout[2] (**deboute**) [dəbu, dəbut] *adv.* in an upright position ◊ **•grand debout** fully upright *Je marchais grand debout, j'avais pas besoin de me pencher.* I could stand straight up, I didn't need to bend over (EV) <EV> <***Loc:*** EV, TB, VM, Da84, Hi02, Lv88>

déboutonner [debutɔ̃ne] **I** *v.tr.* to unbutton *Déboutonner sa robe.* To unbutton one's dress. (EV) **II se déboutonner** *v.pron.* to unbutton one's clothes *Mon petit garçon peut se déboutonner tout seul.* My little boy can unbutton himself all by himself. (EV) <***Loc:*** EV, An94, Da84>

débrancher [debrɑ̃ʃe] **I** *v.tr.* to prune, cut branches off *Débrancher un arbre.* To prune a tree. (IB) **II se débrancher** *v.pron.* to get out from among branches *Il s'est débranché de l'arbre.* He came down out of the tree. (AV) <***Loc:*** AV, IB, Da84>

débraquer [debrake] *v.tr.* to uncock (a gun) *Débraque ton fusil, je le reconnais.* Uncock your gun, I recognize him. (LA) <***Loc:*** LA, Da84>

débris [debri] *n.m.* **1** innards, giblets, various edible organs (of a slaughtered animal) *Le débris comptait pas dans le dévisage.* The innards didn't count for divvying up (at a "boucherie"). (SL) *On a une bonne sauce de débris pour dîner.* We've got a good organ meat stew for dinner. (VM) **2** offal, entrails, inedible waste parts (of a slaughtered animal) *Allons dire que tu vas éplucher des chevrettes chez toi, et là jeter les débris à l'eau.* Let's say that you're going to peel shrimp at home, and then throw the refuse into the water. (LF) *Toute la partie dedans ils appelaient ça des débris. Ça qu'était pas pour manger.* All of the insides [of the slaughtered pig] they called "débris." That which wasn't for eating. (SJ) **3** inedible or waste parts of a plant *Ou plucher quelque chose d'autre, des patates ou n'importe qui, tu connais, tu vas jeter les débris à l'eau.* Or to peel something else, potatoes or whatever, you know, you'll throw the refuse into the water. (LF) **4** rubbish, debris, trash ◊ **•débris du cochon** traditional dish of pork giblets in sauce <Lv88> <***Loc:*** AC, AV, EV, IB, IV, LA, LF, SJ, SL, SM, VM, Da84, Gu00, Lv88>

débriter [debrite] *v.tr.* to gut and dress (an animal, esp. fowl) *Débriter une poule.* To gut a hen. (SL) <***Loc:*** SL, VM>

débrocher [debroʃe] *v.tr.* **1** to take off of a spit *Il a débroché la daube.* He took the roast off the spit. (LA) **2** to take off of a stringer, unstring (fish) *Il a débroché un hourra de patassas.* He unstrung a big bunch of bream. (LA) <***Loc:*** LA, Da84>

débrouiller [debruje] **I** *v.tr.* to clear (e.g. glass) of frost or fog *Débrouiller une vitre.* To clear the frost off a windowpane. (LA) **II** *v.intr.* to make up, quit feuding *Les deux ça là, ils ont tout le temps été brouillés, là ils ont décidé de débrouiller.* Those two were always feuding. Now, they decided to make up. (IB) **III se débrouiller** *v.pron.* **1** to clear (one's mind) *Il s'a débrouillé l'esprit.* He cleared his mind. (LA) **2** to make up, quit feuding *Mon grand-père et son beau-frère s'ont jamais débrouillés de leur vie.* My grandfather and his brother-in-law never ended their feud during their lifetimes. (LA) <***Loc:*** IB, LA, Da84>

début [deby] *n.m.* **1** beginning, outset **2** debut, first appearance <***Loc:*** AC, EV, Da84>

débutant, -e [debytɑ̃, -ɑ̃t] *n.* beginner <***Loc:*** Da84>

décacher [dekaʃe] *v.tr.* to off-bar, bar off (move soil from either side of a row of plants, leaving the plant roots in a high narrow bed) <***Loc:*** EV, Ph36>

décacheter [dekaʃte] *v.tr.* to unseal (a letter or package) *J'ai décacheté ma lettre.* I opened my letter. (AV) <***Loc:*** AV, Da84>

décade [dekad] *n.f.* **1** decade **2** group of ten <***Loc:*** Da84>

décalogue [dekalɔg] *n.m.* the Ten Commandments, decalog <***Loc:*** Da84>

décamper (**décomper**) [dekɑ̃pe, dekɔ̃pe] *v.intr.* **1** to leave *A quelle heure on va décamper?* What time are we going to head out? (LA) **2** to move out *Ils ont décampé de chez eux-autres.* They moved out of their house. (AV) <***Loc:*** AV, LA, Da84>

décaniller [dekɑ̃nije] **I** *v.tr.* to drive off, chase away *J'ai décanillé le couveuse.* I chased away the setting hen. (VM) **II** *v.intr.* to move, relocate, change residences *La famille a décanillé au Pont Breaux.* The family moved to Breaux Bridge. (Lv88) **III se décaniller** *v.pron.* to move o.s., get out of the way *Décanille-toi, je vas balayer.* Move it, I'm going to sweep. (VM) <***Loc:*** VM, Lv88>

décarabiné, -e [dekarabine] *adj.* unrestrained, extravagant *Un dîner décarabiné.* An extravagant meal. (LA) ◊ **•à tout décarabiné** unrestrainedly, with all one's might *Il a travaillé à tout décarabiné.* He worked with all his might. (LF) <LF, La99> <***Loc:*** LA, LF, La99>

décarcaner [dekarkɑ̃ne, dekargɑ̃ne, degargɑ̃ne] *v.tr.* **1** to remove a wooden collar from (an ox, a cow) *L'homme a décarcané le bœuf parce qu'il passait pus dans la barrière.* The man removed the collar from the ox because it no longer tried to get through the fence. (TB) **2** to take off or unbutton a collar <***Loc:*** JE, TB>

décembre [desɑ̃m, desɑ̃b(r)] *n.m.* December <***Loc:*** AC, EV, TB, Da84, Hi02>

décence (**décenceté**) [desɑ̃s, desɑ̃ste] *n.f.* decency <***Loc:*** Da84>

décenceté ♦see **décence**

décent, -e [desɑ̃, -ɑ̃t] *adj.* decent, becoming *C'est pas décent, ça il fait.* What he does is not decent. (AV) <***Loc:*** AV, Da84>

déception [desɛpsjɔ̃] *n.f.* deceit, deception <***Loc:*** AV, Da84>

déchaîné, -e [deʃɛ̃ne] *adj.* **1** unchained *On a pas le droit d'avoir des chiens déchaînés dans le village.* One cannot have an unchained dog in town. (LA) **2** without restraint, unruly, wild *Une petite fille déchaînée.* An unruly little girl. (SL) **3** determined, unrelenting, unswerving **Etre déchaîné à son ouvrage.* To be totally involved in or dedicated to one's work. (Da84) <***Loc:*** LA, SL, Da84>

déchaîner [deʃɛ̃ne] **I** *v.tr.* to unchain *Déchaîner un chien.* To unchain a dog. (AV) **II se déchaîner** *v.pron.* to work tirelessly *Il s'a déchaîné pour finir notre cuisine.* He worked tirelessly to finish our kitchen. (VM) <***Loc:*** AV, VM, Da84>

déchanger [deʃɑ̃ʒe] **I** *v.tr.* to change the clothes of *Déchanger les enfants pour la messe.* To change the children's clothes for Mass. (EV) **II se déchanger** *v.pron.* to change one's clothes *Je vas me déchanger asteur.* I'm going to change clothes now. (AV) <***Loc:*** AV, EV>

décharge [deʃarʒ] *n.f.* **1** unloading **2** discharge (of a gun) **3** semen <***Loc:*** LF, SM, Da84>

déchargeage [deʃarʒaʒ, deʃaraʒ] *n.m.* unloading *Ç'a mis trois heures pour le déchargeage de coton.* They spent three hours on the unloading of cotton. (AV) <***Loc:*** AV, JE, SB, Da84>

déchargement [deʃarʒmɑ̃] *n.m.* unloading <***Loc:*** Da84>

décharger [deʃarʒe] **I** *v.tr.* **1** to unload *Ils ont déchargé le TRUCK.* They unloaded the truck. (EV) **2** to liberate, release, discharge (from the military, from prison, etc.) *Le juge a déchargé l'accusé.* The judge liberated the accused. (SM) *Ça c'est après j'ai été déchargé dans le service.* That was after I was discharged from the service. (TB) **3** to fire, release from employment, let go, lay off, dismiss *J'ai déchargé mon serviteur.* I fired my servant. (SM) *Il a été chercher son argent, il était déchargé, tu connais.* He went to get his money, he was fired, you know. (Lv88) **4** to discharge, fire (a gun) *Décharger un fusil.* To discharge a shotgun. (IB) **II se décharger** *v.pron.* to go off, discharge, fire (of a gun) *Quand son fusil a tombé par terre, il s'a déchargé.* When his gun fell down, it went off. (VM) <VM> <***Loc:*** EV, IB, SM, TB, VM, Da84, Lv88>

déchausser [deʃose] *v.tr.* **1** to remove footwear from *Il a pas seulement déchaussé son petit avant de le mettre couché.* He didn't even take off his child's shoes before putting him to bed. (LA) **2** to remove top dirt from (plants) *Il a déchaussé ses cannes pour pouvoir piocher.* He removed the top dirt from his sugar cane in order to be able to hoe. (SM) **II se déchausser** *v.pron.* to remove one's footwear *Il a pas pris le temps de se déchausser, il était assez largué.* He didn't even take the time to take his shoes off, he was so tired. (LA) <***Loc:*** AV, LA, SM, Da84>

déchécher ♦see **déchesser**

déchemin ♦see **deux-chemin**

déchessant (**desséchant**) [deʃesɑ̃, deseʃɑ̃] *n.m.* drying agent *Ça use cette poudre pour un déchessant.* They use that powder as a drying agent. (LA) <***Loc:*** LA, Da84>

déchesser (**déchécher, dessécher**) [deʃese, deʃeʃe, deseʃe] **I** *v.tr.* to dry, dry up, dry out, parch *Le soleil a déchéché mon jardin.* The sun dried out my garden. (VM) **II** *v.intr.* **1** to dry, dry out, dry up *Mon jardin a déchessé.* My garden dried up. (AV) **2** to wither, atrophy *On dirait il a déchéché depuis la dernière fois je l'ai vu.* You'd think he had withered up since the last time I saw him. (SM) *Ses membres aviont tout déchéché.* His extremities had all atrophied. (VM) <***Loc:*** AV, LF, SL, SM, TB, VM, Lv88>

déchiffrable [deʃifrab(l)] *adj.* decipherable <***Loc:*** Da84>

déchiffrage [deʃifraʒ] *n.m.* deciphering <***Loc:*** Da84>

déchiffrer [deʃifre] *v.tr.* to decipher, figure out *Ça pouvait pas déchiffrer pour qui la terre était.* They couldn't figure out to whom the land belonged. (VM) <***Loc:*** VM, Da84>

déchiquenailler [deʃiknaje] *v.tr.* to tear, cut up, slash *Déchiquenailler du linge.* To tear one's clothes. (LF) *Déchiquenailler la chair.* To slash up the flesh. (LF) <***Loc:*** LF>

déchirage [deʃiraʒ] *n.m.* tearing, ripping (of cloth or clothing) <***Loc:*** Da84, Wh83>

déchirailler [deʃiraje] *v.tr.* to shred **Son plan c'est de le mettre dessus la terre juste avant Tchou Flang coupe les herbes pour que le papier peut être déchiraillé par la fourcheuse [=faucheuse].* His plan is to put them on the lawn just before

Tchou Flang cuts the grass so the paper can be shredded by the lawnmower. (Wh83) <*Loc:* Wh83>

déchirer [deʃire] **I** *v.tr.* **1** to tear, tear up, tear off (e.g. clothes) *Et là ça prenait des morceaux qu'ils déchirait des draps dessus le lit. Et ça déchirait pour le mettre autour.* And then they would take pieces that they had torn off of the sheets on the bed. And they tore them up to put around [the splint]. (SB) *T'as revenu ce matin, ta robe était tout déchirée.* You got home this morning, your dress was all torn up. (ch: *Ma négresse*) **2** to pull down, tear down (a structure) *On a déchiré des vieux vieux maisons.* We pulled down some really old homes. (IB) **II se déchirer** *v.pron.* to tear one's clothing **Je m'ai déchiré la culotte.* I tore my pants. (Da84) ◊ **•déchirer la couverture {couverte} (en deux)** to break up, separate (of a couple) *Ils vont bien vite déchirer la couverte là.* They'll be breaking up soon. (TB) <JE, TB, VM, La99, Lv88> **•déchirer le gingas *a*** to stretch the truth, exaggerate badly ***b*** to tell a falsehood <Da84, La99> <*Loc:* AL, IB, SB, JE, TB, VM, Da84, La99, Lv88>

déchirure [deʃiryr] *n.f.* tear, rip <*Loc:* Da84>

déchousser [deʃose] *v.tr.* to uproot (a tree) <*Loc:* IB>

décidé, -e [deside] *adj.* **1** decided *C'est décidé, et ben. Ça sera le samedi après Thanksgiving.* It's decided, then. It'll be the Saturday after Thanksgiving. (ThCa: *La douce réunion*) **2** determined, resolved *Un couillon bien decidé.* A person who is determined to do something stupid. (VM) <*Loc:* VM, Da84, ThCa>

décider [deside] **I** *v.tr.* to decide, settle *Quand même, mais faudra décider ça ensemble.* Anyway, we'll have to decide that together. (ThCa: *La fête à Clomaire*) **II** *v.intr.* to decide, make a decision *Il avait décidé tout de suite.* He had decided right away. (AV) *Mais là, pauvre Selena, elle se sentait assez fautive d'avoir brûlé l'argent à Alphonse, qu'elle a décidé de s'en aller au Texas avec lui.* But then poor Selena felt so bad about having burned Alphonse's money that she decided to go to Texas with him. (ThCa: *La dernière quilte*) **III se décider** *v.pron.* to decide, make up one's mind **T'as pour avoir assez de quoi, quand tu vas te rencontrer une dame, en tout cas tu te décides de te marier.* You have to have something for when you meet a lady, in case you make up your mind to get married. (An94) *Tôt ou tard, il faudrait il se décide.* Sooner or later, he'll have to make up his mind. (LA) *Et une journée on s'a décidé de commencer à faire des tartes, des tartes à la patate douce.* And one day we decided to start making pies, sweet potato pies. (TB) <*Loc:* AV, EV, LA, TB, An94, Da84, Hi02, ThCa>

décirer [desire] *v.tr.* to unwax, remove wax from *Décirer le plancher.* To unwax, remove wax from the floor. (VM) <*Loc:* VM, Da84>

décision [desizjɔ̃] *n.f.* decision <*Loc:* Da84, Hi02>

déclaration [deklarasjɔ̃] *n.f.* declaration, avowal, statement **•Déclaration d'indépendance** the Declaration of Independence <Da84> <*Loc:* Da84>

déclarer [deklare, deklere] **I** *v.tr.* **1** to declare, proclaim *Ils ont déclaré la guerre.* They declared war. (IB) **2** to denounce *Elle a déclaré le voleur.* She denounced the thief. (LA) **3** to admit, acknowledge *Il a déclaré qu'il était coupable.* He admitted that he was guilty. (IB) **II** *v.intr.* to become officially engaged *Quand une fille et un garçon déclaraient, ça, ça voulait dire ils aviont demandé la permission du père et de la mère de la fille pour se marier.* When a girl and boy declared, that meant that they had asked the permission of the father and mother of the girl to get married. (EV) **III se déclarer** *v.pron.* **1** to state one's mind or intention **Se déclarer coupable.* To admit to one's guilt. (Da84) **2** to be declared, be announced **Justement quand elle était mariée, la guerre s'a déclarée pour son mari.* Just when she got married, war was declared, and her husband had to go. (IV, An94) <*Loc:* EV, IB, IV, LA, TB, An94, Da84, Lv88>

décler [dekle] *v.tr.* to unlock <*Loc:* EV, Ph36>

déclin [deklɛ̃] *n.m.* **1** decline **2** waning, ebb (of the moon) *La lune est en déclin.* The moon is waning. (VM) *Le déclin de la lune, c'est le contraire du profitant de la lune.* The waning moon is the opposite of the waxing moon. (VM) <*Loc:* VM, Da84>

décliner [dekline] *v.intr.* **1** to decline, weaken, worsen *O, c'est la petite Anna-z-à Mogène Meaux, qui s'en va-t-en déclinant.* Oh, it's little Anna, Mogène Meaux's daughter, who's wasting away. (VM, ch: *La petite Anna*) **2** to wane (of the moon) *Il fallait pas mettre les œufs à couver parce que la lune était après décliner.* You weren't supposed to put the eggs to be set upon, because the moon was waning. (IB) <*Loc:* IB, VM, Da84>

déclouer (**déclouter, déclouver**) [deklue, deklute, deklote, dekluve] **I** *v.tr.* to unnail *Déclouer une planche.* To unnail a plank. (IB) **II** *v.intr.* to become unnailed, become loose **Il a arrivé droit dessous le milieu du plancher. Il y avait une planche qu'était déclouée.* He got right under the middle of the floor. There was a plank that was unnailed. (An94) **III se déclouer** *v.pron.* to become unnailed *Après l'eau haute, le plancher était après se déclouer.* After the flood, the flooring was becoming unnailed. (VM) <*Loc:* IB, JE, LF, TB, VM, An94, Da84>

déclouter, déclouver ♦see **déclouer**

décoction [dekɔksjɔ̃] *n.f.* **1** mixture, concoction **2** beating, whipping *Il a foutu une décoction à l'homme.* He gave the man a beating. (LF) <*Loc:* LF, SB, Da84>

décoctionner [dekoksjɔ̃ne] *v.tr.* to stun *Il l'a décoctionné d'un coup de poing.* He stunned him with a punch. (LF) <*Loc:* LF>

décoiffer [dekwafe] **I** *v.tr.* **1** to disarrange or mess up the hair of *Le vent l'a décoiffé.* The wind messed up his hair. (VM) **2** to remove a head covering from *Décoiffer un bébé.* To remove a baby's bonnet. (EV) **II se décoiffer** *v.pron.* **1** to get one's hair messed up, have one's hair get disarranged *Il s'a décoiffé dans le boghei.* His hair was messed up in the buggy. (LA) **2** to remove one's head covering *Il s'a pas décoiffé quand il a rentré dans la salle de danse.* He didn't remove his hat when he entered the dance hall. (VM) <*Loc:* EV, LA, VM, Da84>

décoincer [dekwɛ̃se] **I** *v.tr.* to unwedge, free, unbind, loosen *On a manqué de jamais décoincer le sofa de la porte quand on était après assayer de la sortir de la maison.* We almost never got the sofa loose from the door when we were trying to get it out of the house. (VM) **II se décoincer** *v.pron.* to get o.s. out, free o.s. *J'ai eu de la misère à me décoincer d'entre la chaise et la table.* I had trouble getting myself out from between the chair and the table. (VM) <*Loc:* VM, Da84>

décoller [dekole] **I** *v.tr.* **1** to unglue, unstick, disjoin, detach *Et là, ils vont mettre un plancher là, qu'ils pourrait marcher dessus, pour pas que tu marches dessus le fond, parce que ça va décoller le— détacher le plancher si tu marches sur le fond.* And then they will put in a deck there that they can walk on, so that you don't walk on the bottom [of the boat], because that'll detach the flooring if you walk on the bottom. (LF) **2** to dislodge (congestion) *Y a rien de mieux que du thé de mamou pour décoller un rhume.* There's nothing better than mamou tea to clear up a cold. (VM) **3** to lay bare the roots of (a plant) **II** *v.intr.* to separate, come apart *Les deux planches a décollé.* The two boards came apart. (IB) **III se décoller** *v.pron.* **1** to unglue o.s., become unglued *Lapin pouvait pus se décoller.* Rabbit could no longer unglue himself. (LA) **2** to separate, disengage physically from each other *Ils s'avont décollé vite quand le vieux a rentré.* They disengaged [from their embrace] quickly when the old man came home. (VM) <*Loc:* IB, LF, SJ, VM, Da84>

décolletage [dekɔltaʒ] *n.m.* **1** baring of the neck, shoulders, etc. **2** low neckline *J'aime pas cette robe avec le décolletage.* I don't like that dress with the low neckline. (VM) <*Loc:* VM, Da84>

décolleté, -e [dekɔlte] *adj.* low-cut, having a low neckline *Ma bru aime trop porter des robes décolletées.* My daughter-in-law is too fond of wearing low-cut dresses. (VM) <*Loc:* VM, Da84>

décolleter [dekɔlte] **I** *v.tr.* to expose the neck and shoulders of **II se décolleter** *v.pron.* to bare one's neck and shoulders *Alle va se décolleter pour attirer de l'attention au bal.* She is going to bare her neck and shoulders to attract attention at the dance. (LA) <*Loc:* LA, Da84>

décolorer (**découleurer**) [dekolore dekulœre] **I** *v.tr.* to discolor, remove dye or color from, cause to fade *Le soleil a décoloré sa robe.* The sun faded her dress. (LA) **II** *v.intr.* to fade, lose color *Je vas laver à la main, ce linge découleure un tas.* I'm going to wash by hand, this clothing fades a lot. (Lv88) **III se décolorer** *v.pron.* to fade, lose color, become discolored *J'ai lavé cette robe juste une fois et alle s'a découleuré.* I washed that dress just once and it faded. (LA) <*Loc:* JE, LA, SL, Da84, Lv88>

décombouiller [dekɔ̃buje] *v.tr.* **1** to remove scum from *Il a eu pour décombouiller son cheval avant de le mettre dans l'écurie.* He had to remove the scum from his horse before putting it in the stall. (LA) **2** to clean *Il a décombouillé l'office.* He cleaned the office. (SL) <*Loc:* LA, SL, La99>

décomper ♦see **décamper**

décomposer [dekɔ̃poze] *v.tr.* to cause to decompose *La chaleur a décomposé la charogne.* The heat caused the corpse to decompose. (LA) <*Loc:* LA, Da84>

décompter [dekɔ̃te] *v.tr.* to give up on, give up hope for (a sick person) *Le docteur l'a décompté.* The doctor gave up hope for him. (VM) **Le malade est décompté.* There is no hope for the sick person. (Da84) *Alle avait guéri une petite fille qui était décomptée.* She had cured a little girl who was given up for dead. (IV) <*Loc:* IV, LF, SL, SM, TB, VM, Da84, Lv88>

déconnecter [dekɔ̃nɛkte] *v.tr.* to unplug, disconnect *Vas déconnecter l'éventail si c'est trop frète.* Go unplug the fan if it's too cold. (Lv88) <*Loc:* JE, Lv88>

déconseiller [dekɔ̃seje] *v.tr.* to dissuade, advise (s.o.) against *Sa mère a essayé de la déconseiller de se marier avec ce bougre-là.* Her mother tried to dissuade her from getting married to that fellow. (VM) <*Loc:* VM, Da84>

décoquiller [dekokije, dekotʃije] *v.tr.* **1** to remove (a shellfish) from its shell *Follait qu'on décoquille ces huîtres. Follait séparer les huîtres de les coquilles, tu connais.* We had to shuck those oysters. We had to separate the oysters from the shells, you know. (TB) **2** to clean the shells of oysters by removing parasitic shell growths *T'avais des coquilles dessus les huîtres qu'était pas bon, il follait que ça soye décoquillé.* You'd have shells on the oysters that weren't good, they had to be cleaned off. (LF) <*Loc:* LF, TB, VM>

décoration [dekorasjɔ̃] *n.f.* decoration *À peu près une semaine avant Christmas, on aime aller se promener pour voir les décorations.* About a week before Christmas, we like to go out walking to see the decorations. (VM) <*Loc:* VM, Da84>

décorder [dekɔrde] *v.tr.* **1** to take apart a pile (of corded wood) *Les enfants s'amusent à décorder le bois que j'ai déjà cordé.* The kids have fun messing up the wood that I've already arranged in cords. (VM) **2** to take off of a clothesline *Elle a eu pour décorder son linge parce que la pluie s'en venait.* She had to take her clothes off the clothesline because the rain was approaching. (LA) <*Loc:* LA, VM, Lv88>

décorer [dekore] **I** *v.tr.* **1** to decorate *T'aimes la manière j'ai décoré ça?* Do you like the way I decorated this? (ThCa: *La dernière quilte*) *Venez veiller demain au soir. On va décorer la maison pour les noces.* Come visit tomorrow night. We are going to decorate the house for the wedding. (VM) *La maison est tout décorée pour Christmas.* The house is all decorated for Christmas. (VM) **2** to decorate, confer an honor upon *Mon arrière-grand-père a été décoré durant la guerre des Confédérés.* My great-grandfather was decorated during the Civil War. (VM) **II se décorer** *v.pron.* to decorate o.s. *Elle s'a décoré avec les colliers de sa première femme.* She decorated herself with the necklaces of his first wife. (LA) <***Loc:*** LA, VM, Da84, ThCa>

décorner (écorner) [dekɔrne, ekɔrne] *v.tr.* to dehorn (an animal) *Avec les nouvelles races de vaches asteur, t'as pus besoin de les décorner.* With the new breeds of [polled] cattle nowadays, you don't have to dehorn them anymore. (VM) *Écorner un boeuf.* To dehorn a bull. (LA) **Un vent à décorner un bœuf.* A very strong wind, wind strong enough to pull the horns off an ox. (La99) <***Loc:*** LA, VM, Da84, La99>

découcher [dekuʃe] *v.intr.* **1** to sleep away from home *J'aime pas découcher. J'aime trop mon lit.* I don't like to sleep away from home. I like my own bed too much. (VM) **2** to commit adultery *Son mari découche un tas depuis qu'elle a eu son bébé.* Her husband sleeps around a lot since she had her baby. (VM) <***Loc:*** VM, Da84>

découder ♦see **découdre**

découdre (découder) [dekud(r), dekude] (*p.p.* **décousu** [dekuzy], **découdu** [dekudy]) **I** *v.tr.* to unsew, rip (a seam) *Découdre une robe.* To unsew a dress. (IB) **II** *v.intr.* to become unsewn *Regarde! Ton bas de robe est découdu.* Look! The hem of your dress is unsewn. (VM) **III se découdre** *v.pron.* to become unsewn *Mon ourlet s'a tout décousu.* My hem came completely undone. (EV) <***Loc:*** AV, EV, IB, JE, VM, Da84, Lv88>

découler [dekule] *v.intr.* to flow, trickle, run *Tout le whisky a découlé du baril.* All of the whiskey trickled out of the barrel. (SL) <***Loc:*** SL, Da84>

découleurer ♦see **décolorer**

découpage [dekupaʒ] *n.m.* cut-out, carving, cutting <***Loc:*** Da84>

découpailler [dekupaje] *v.tr.* **1** to cut up, cut to pieces *J'ai découpaillé la viande dessus les os.* I cut the meat off the bone in small pieces. (TB) **2** to chop in an irregular or careless fashion *Il a tout découpaillé le gâteau jusqu'à c'était pus présentable.* He cut up the cake so carelessly that it was no longer presentable. (LA) <***Loc:*** AV, IB, LA, LF, SB, SM, TB, Da84, Lv88>

découper [dekupe] *v.tr.* **1** to cut off *Je me souviens que les voisins sont venus nous dire que Papa avait perdu son bras. La machine l'avait découpé.* I remember that the neighbors came to tell us that Papa had lost his arm. The machine had cut it off. (ThCa: *Mille misères*) **2** to trim, carve, cut out *Mon pape se levait pour la couper. Lui il connaissait comment la découper.* My father would get up to cut it [meat] up. He knew how to trim it. (TB) <***Loc:*** TB, Da84, ThCa>

découpeur [dekupœr] *n.m.* trawl net maker <***Loc:*** TB>

découpler [dekuple] *v.tr.* to uncouple *Ils ont découplé le locomotive des chars à fret.* They uncoupled the locomotive from the freight cars. (VM) <***Loc:*** IB, VM, Da84>

décourageant, -e [dekuraʒɑ̃, -ɑ̃t] *adj.* discouraging *Une nouvelle décourageante.* Discouraging news. (EV) <***Loc:*** EV, Da84, Wh83>

découragement [dekuraʒmɑ̃] *n.m.* discouragement <***Loc:*** Da84>

décourager [dekuraʒe] **I** *v.tr.* to discourage *Ses parents voulaient pas qu'elle s'en va aussi loin, surtout sa mémère. Ils ont essayé de la décourager.* Her parents didn't want her to go so far away, especially not her grandma. They tried to discourage her. (ThCa: *La dernière quilte*) **II se décourager** *v.pron.* to become discouraged, give up, lose heart *Je m'ai découragé et j'ai été travaillé à la mine à AVERY ISLAND.* I became discouraged and went to work in the mine at Avery Island. (IB) <***Loc:*** IB, Da84, ThCa>

découvasser [dekuvase] *v.tr.* to remove (a setting hen) from its nest, break (a hen) of sitting *Il faut fermer une poule dans une cage pour la découvasser.* You have to lock a hen in a cage to break her from sitting. (IB) <***Loc:*** IB, SJ, Lv88>

découver [dekuve] *v.tr.* **1** to remove (a setting hen) from its nest, break (a hen) of sitting *Quand on avait trop de poules pour couver, là ils prenaient ça ils avaient pas besoin et mettaient dans un COOP pour une semaine pour les découver.* When they had too many hens to set, then they took the ones they didn't need and put them in a coop for a week to get them to stop setting. (IB) **2** to get (s.o.) out of the house, induce (s.o.) to leave the house *On pouvait pas la découver après son garçon est mort.* We couldn't get her out of the house after her son died. (EV) <***Loc:*** EV, IB, SB, SL, TB VM VM, Da84, Lv88>

découverre (découvrir, découvert) [dekuvɛr, dekuvrir, dekuvɛrt] (*p.p.* **découvert** [dekuvær], **découvri** [dekuvri]) **I** *v.tr.* **1** to discover, find out, learn **Il découvre quelqu'un avait coupé la queue de son cheval. Il s'a imaginé que c'était son partner qui lui avait fait ça.* He finds out that someone had cut off his horse's tail He figured that it was his buddy who had done that to him. (An94) **2** to uncover **Ses trois filles et sa femme étaient dans la maison, et ils ont rentré dans la maison fouillasser en dedans, capoter les matelas et tout quelque chose pour le découvrir, voir s'il était peut-être pas caché en dedans-là.* His three daughters and his wife were in the house, and they went in the house digging around inside, turning over mattresses and everything to find him, to see if perhaps he wasn't hidden in there. (An94) **3** to unroof, remove the roof from *Ils ont détouré la maison avant de la découverte.* They removed the weatherboarding from the house before unroofing it.

(TB) **II se découvrir** *v.pron.* to bare o.s., uncover one's body *Il s'avait découvert dans la nuit parce qu'il faisait tellement chaud dans la maison.* He had uncovered himself during the night because it was so hot in the house. (LA) <*Loc:* LA, TB, An94, Da84, Hi02>

découvert ♦see **découverre**

découverte [dekuvært] *n.f.* discovery, find **Il a fait une découverte.* He made a discovery. (Da84) <*Loc:* Da84>

décoxer [dekokse] *v.tr.* to strike on the head *Je l'ai décoxé.* I hit him on the head. (SL) <*Loc:* SL>

décramponner [dekrɑ̃pɔ̃ne] *v.tr.* to cause to let go, loosen one's grip, loosen one's hold *Il avait assez peur, on pouvait pas le décramponner.* He was so scared, we couldn't make him let go. (EV) <*Loc:* EV, Da84>

décrasser [dekrase] **I** *v.tr.* to clean, clean up, remove crud, dirt, or filth *T'as pour décrasser une chauvelle ou une charrue.* You have to remove the dirt from a shovel or plow. (IB) **II se décrasser** *v.pron.* to wash up, clean o.s. up, clean o.s. of filth *On était assez sale, ça nous a pris deux bains pour se décrasser.* We were so dirty, it took two baths to clean ourselves up. (LA) <*Loc:* IB, LA, Da84>

décrocher[1] [dekroʃe] **I** *v.tr.* **1** to unhook, take down from a hook *Décrocher le portrait du mur.* To unhook the picture from the wall. (IB) **2** to unlatch *Décroche la porte.* Unlatch the door. (VM) **3** to separate, pull apart (people who are fighting) *Il a décroché les deux garçons qui se battaient.* He separated the two boys who were fighting. (LF) **II se décrocher** *v.pron.* **1** to unhook o.s. *Le poisson va se décrocher.* The fish is going to unhook itself. (SM) **2** to remove for o.s. *Là, je m'ai décroché ma cigarette de Bull Durham de derrière mon oreille et je l'ai allumée.* Then, I removed my Bull Durham cigarette from behind my ear and I lit it. (AV) <*Loc:* AV, IB, LF, SM, VM, Da84, Hi02>

décrocher[2] ♦see **décrochir**

décrochir (décrocher) [dekroʃir, dekroʃe] *v.tr.* to make straight, straighten out *Décrocher des clous.* To straighten nails. (VM) <*Loc:* IB, VM, Da84, Lv88>

décrotter [dekrote] **I** *v.tr.* to remove dirt from, clean away mud or filth from *Ils ont couru dans la boue, ça fait il a fallu décrotter son cheval après la course.* They ran in the mud, so he had to wash the mud off his horse after the race. (LA) **II se décrotter** *v.pron.* to wash up, clean o.s. up, clean o.s. of mud or filth *Je vais me décrotter dans la bac.* I'm going to wash up in the bathtub. (SM) <*Loc:* LA, SM>

décroûter (écroûter) [dekrute, ekrute] **I** *v.tr.* **1** to remove the crust from *Décroûter du pain.* To remove the crust from bread. (VM) **2** to remove a scab from *Arrête de te gratter, tu vas décroûter ton bobo.* Stop scratching yourself, you'll remove the scab from your sore. (VM) **3** to wash up, clean up *Il faudra que je te décroûte avant que tu rentres dans la maison.* I'll have to clean you up before you come into the house. (LA) **II se décroûter** *v.pron.* to wash o.s., tidy up *T'as besoin de te décroûter avant de rentrer dans la maison.* You need to clean up before coming into the house. (LA) *J'ai pour m'habiller et m'écroûter manière avant je peux aller avec vous-autres.* I have to get dressed and tidy up a bit before I can go with you. (VM) *J'avais pour me décroûter manière.* I had to wash up a bit. (VM) <*Loc:* LA, VM, Da84>

déculotté, -e [dekylote, dekilote] *adj.* **1** pantless *Ces pauvres bébés sont à moitié déculottés.* Those poor babies are almost pantless. (LA) **2** untucked (of a shirt) *Ta queue de chemise est déculottée.* Your shirttail is untucked. (LA) *L'homme déculotté.* The man with his shirttail out. (LF) <*Loc:* LA, LF, Da84, Lv88>

déculotter [dekylote] **I** *v.tr.* **1** to remove the pants of *Les enfants étaient après se battre et Pierre a déculotté Paul.* The kids were fighting and Peter pulled Paul's pants off. (VM) **2** to pull out the shirttail of **II se déculotter** *v.pron.* to remove one's pants *Il a commencé à se déculotter dans le* DRIVEWAY. He started taking off his pants in the driveway. (LA) <*Loc:* LA, LF, VM, Da84>

dédaignable [dedɛ̃jab(l)] *adj.* nasty, disgusting *Je peux pas manger ça, c'est dédaignable!* I can't eat that; it's disgusting! (EV) <*Loc:* EV, VM>

dédaigner [dedɛ̃je] *v.tr.* to disdain, scorn *Notre cousin de Béville nous dédaigne comme si il se croit plus que nous-autres.* Our cousin in Abbeville looks down on us as if he thinks he's better than us. (VM) <*Loc:* VM, Da84>

dédain [dedɛ̃] *n.m.* disdain, scorn, disgust **J'ai rien que du dédain pour lui.* I have nothing but scorn for him. (Da84) ◊ •**avoir dédain de** to have an aversion to, be repulsed by *Là j'avais déjà dédain de ça, ça fait ça aurait été malaisé de me décider de mettre ça dans ma bouche.* I was already disgusted by that, so it would have been hard for me to decide to put it in my mouth. (LA) <LA> <*Loc:* LA, Da84>

dedans[1] **(endedans)** [dədɑ̃, ɑ̃dədɑ̃] *n.m.* **1** inside, interior *Les charpentiers ont fini le dehors de la maison, mais il ont toujours pas fini le dedans.* The carpenters have finished the exterior of the house, but they still haven't completed the interior. (VM) **2** insides, innards (of an animal) *Il n-a un tas du monde qui dit du cowboy stew pour parler des dedans de bête.* There are lots of people who say "cowboy stew" to refer to the insides of an animal. (Gu00) *On l'éventrait, on ôtait tout l'endedans.* We gutted it, we took out all the insides. (AC) <*Loc:* AC, LF, SL, VM, Gu00>

dedans[2] [dədɑ̃] *adv.* in, inside *Et là tu secouais la jarre comme ça là. Tu mettais un petit brin du sel dedans.* And then you would shake the jar like this. You put a little bit of salt inside. (TB) *Eusse a été pour prendre leurs portraits à mettre sur la gazette, et le vieux dit qu'eux-autres a oublié de mettre le film dedans, so y a pas un portrait qu'a sorti.* They went to have their pictures taken for the newspaper, and the old man said they forgot to put the film in, so not one picture came out. (TB) <*Loc:* AV, EV, SL, TB>

dedans[3] [dədã] *prep.* **1** in, inside *On est dedans la misère icitte.* We are [living] in misery here. (VM) *Ils sont dedans la pauvreté.* They are [living] in poverty. (SM) *Quand l'électricité a manqué pour l'ouragan, ça a tout déglacé ça on avait dedans le* FREEZE. When the electricity went off during the hurricane, it thawed everything we had in the freezer. (LA) **2** during, in *Je vais dedans mai.* I'm going in May. (SM) *J'ai fait mon devoir dedans le passé.* I did my work in the past. (VM) *Dedans ma vie j'ai jamais volé un sou.* In my life, I've never stolen a penny. (VM) *Dedans ce temps là fallait frobir à la brique.* In those days, we had to clean the floors with powdered brick. (EV) **3** after, in (an amount of time) *Les nouvelles du temps dedans juste cinq minutes.* The weather report [will be] in just five minutes. (EV) ◊ **•en dedans** in, inside *Il est en dedans la maison.* He is inside the house. (VM) *Il est en dedans le bayou.* He is in the bayou. (SM) **Et vous-autres vas juste mettre la chaudière-là sur le feu, qu'a rien en dedans, et vous-autres vas cogner avec les petits bâtons au bord de la chaudière.* And you all are just going to put that pot on the fire, which has nothing in it, and you're going to hit the side of the pot with the little sticks. (An94) **Ils ont chessé la mer. Ils l'ont tout plantée en riz en dedans.* They dried up the sea. They planted it entirely in rice in there. (An94) *Elle a été fermée en dedans de la maison.* She was shut up in the house. (SB) <SB, SM, VM, An94> **•ici dedans** in here *Quand j'ai rentré dans la boutique à René, j'ai vu ce malfaiteur Bradley Meaux qui était assis dessus le bout du comptoir. Quand j'ai paru dans la porte il dit, "Gardez-donc qui les chats ont traîné ici dedans."* When I went into René's store, I saw that troublemaker Bradley Meaux who was sitting on the end of the counter. When I appeared in the door, he said, "Well, look what the cats dragged in here." (AV) <AV> **•là dedans *a*** in there **Là, Geneviève était là dedans. Elle a sorti.* Geneviève was in there. She came out. (An94) ***b*** in that, about that *Je suis joliment savant là-dedans.* I'm quite knowledgeable about that. (TB) <TB, An94> **•par endedans** from the inside *La chousse d'arbre est pourrite par endedans.* The tree stump is rotten from the inside. (VM) <VM> <***Loc:*** AC, EV, IV, LA, SB, SL, SM, TB, VM, An94, Da84, Hi02, Lv88>

dédication [dedikasjɔ̃] *n.f.* dedication (esp. of a church) <***Loc:*** Da84>

dédier [dedje] **I** *v.tr.* to dedicate, devote **Dédier, vouer un enfant à la Sainte Vierge* To dedicate a child to the Holy Virgin. (Da84) **II se dédier** *v.pron.* to devote o.s., dedicate o.s. *Alle s'a dédié à la Sainte Vierge après la maladie de son garçon.* She devoted herself to the Virgin Mary after her son's illness. (LA) <***Loc:*** LA, Da84>

dédiqué, -e [dedike] *adj.* dedicated *Mais le bien que les écoles d'immersion fait, un principal ou une maîtresse qu'est dédiqué à son job peut pas être contre parce que ça fait trop de bien.* But the good that immersion schools do, a principal or a schoolteacher who is dedicated to his job cannot be against it because it does too much good. (LF) <***Loc:*** LF>

dédire [dedir] **I** *v.tr.* to contradict, gainsay *Arrête donc de me dédire.* Stop contradicting me. (LA) **II se dédire** *v.pron.* to contradict o.s. *Il était après se dédire lui-même.* He was contradicting himself. (LA) <***Loc:*** LA, Da84>

dédommage [dedɔ̃maʒ] *n.m.* damage, harm *La pluie a fait un grand dédommage aux récoltiers.* The rain did great damage to the farmers. (VM) <***Loc:*** AV, EV, JE, SM, VM, Da84, Lv88, Ph36>

dédommager [dedɔ̃maʒe] *v.tr.* to damage, harm *Tu devrais voir tout ça le vent a dédommagé.* You should see everything the wind tore up. (VM) <***Loc:*** EV, SM, VM, Da84, Lv88, Ph36>

dédoubler [deduble] *v.tr.* to take out the lining (of a garment) *Dédoubler un capot.* To remove the lining of a coat. (EV) <***Loc:*** EV, Da84>

déduire [dedɥir] *v.tr.* to infer, deduce *Il pouvait pas déduire qui a volé son maïs.* He couldn't deduce who stole his corn. (LA) <***Loc:*** LA, Da84>

DEEP FREEZE [dipfɹiz] *n.m.* freezer <***Loc:*** Lv88>

défâcher (se) [defaʃe] *v.pron.* to get over one's anger *Y a une élan que je l'ai pas vu. Je me demande si il s'a défâché depuis la dernière fois que je l'ai vu?* I haven't seen him for a while. I wonder if he's gotten over his anger since the last time I saw him. (VM) <***Loc:*** VM, Da84>

défaillance [defajɑ̃s] *n.f.* **1** faintness, weakness **2** swoon, fainting spell <***Loc:*** Da84>

défaire [defær] **I** *v.tr.* **1** to undo, untie *Ils preniont ça [les tripes], ils les defaisiont, c'était tout ensemble, ils prenaient un couteau, ils les vidiont.* They would take the tripes, they would untie them, they were all [tied up] together, they would take a knife, they would empty them. (AV) **2** to take apart, pull apart, disassemble *Je peux défaire une machine et tout secouer les morceaux d'un* CAN *de cinq gallons et là les remettre à* BACK. I can take a machine apart and shake all the pieces up in a five-gallon can and then put them back together. (TB) **3** to dislocate (a joint) *La manière qu'elle attrape son bébé par le bras, c'est drôle qu'elle défait pas son épaule.* The way she grabs her baby by the arm, it's surprising that she doesn't dislocate his shoulder. (VM) **4** to tear down *Asteur ils voulont défaire ma vieille maison et m'en rebâtir une neuve.* Now they want to tear down my old house and build me a new one. (VM) **5** to get rid of, do away with *Eux-autres voulait défaire le langage.* They wanted to get rid of the [French] language. (TB) **6** to upset, disconcert, crush the spirits of *Tu m'as tout défait quand tu m'as dit ça.* You really upset me when you told me that. (VM) **II se défaire** *v.pron.* **1** to do away with, get rid of, rid oneself of *J'ai jamais étudié le français à l'école, non, [...] Quand moi j'ai été élevé, eux-autres était après assayer de* *se défaire du français.* I've never studied French in school, no, when I was raised they were trying to get rid of French. (TB) **2** to come undone *Quand j'ai hâlé la petite corde, le* HOSE *s'a défait.* When I pulled the little string, the hose came undone. (SL) **3** to dislocate (a joint, one's back, etc.) *Il s'a défait la hanche.* He dislocated his hip. (VM) *Se défaire le dos.* To dislocate one's back. (Da84) <***Loc:*** AV, EV, LF, SL, SM, TB, VM, Da84, Lv88, Wh83>

défaufiler [defofile] *v.tr.* to untack, unbaste (a hem, a garment) *Asteur j'ai fini la robe, je vas la défaufiler.* Now that I've finished the dress, I will unbaste it. (VM) <***Loc:*** VM, Da84>

défaut [defo] *n.m.* defect, flaw, fault *Tu vas trouver des défauts dans du* PLYWOOD *comme ça souvent.* You'll often find flaws in plywood like that. (LF) <***Loc:*** LF, Da84>

défectif, -ive [defektif, -iv] *adj.* defective *Il m'a vendu un moulin à viande qu'était défectif.* He sold me a meat grinder that was defective. (VM) <***Loc:*** VM, Da84>

défendeur [defɑ̃dœr] *n.m.* defender <***Loc:*** EV, Da84, Ph36>

défendre [defɑ̃n, defɑ̃d(r)] **I** *v.tr.* to defend, protect **II** *v.intr.* **1** to forbid, prohibit *Le gouvernement fédéral nous défend de tuer les cocodris.* The federal government prohibits us from killing alligators. (ThCa: *Mille misères*) **2** to challenge, dare *Tu dis c'est facile, je te défends de le faire.* You say it's easy, I dare you to do it. (VM) **III se défendre** *v.pron.* **1** to defend o.s., fight back **Et là, elle lui a donné des fusils, deux fusils. Elle dit, "Si t'es jamais gêné, défends-toi!"* So then, she gave him shotguns, two shotguns. She said, "If anyone ever bothers you, then fight back!" (VM, An94) **2** to hold one's own *Petit Poucet était un enfant beaucoup smart et il observait tout et il pouvait se défendre avec les plus vieux.* Petit Poucet was a very smart child and he observed everything and he could hold his own with the older children. (LA) **3** to get by, manage *Je lui ai envoyé assez d'argent pour qu'il se défend.* I sent him enough money so that he can get by. (VM) *Comment ça va? Je me défends.* How's it going? I'm managing. (VM) *Il peut se défendre en anglais.* He can manage in English. (VM) *Ça se défend là-bas?* Things going all right over there? (VM) <***Loc:*** AC, EV, LA, VM, An94, Da84, ThCa>

défendu, -e [defɑ̃dy] *adj.* illegal, forbidden, against the law *C'est défendu [...] parce que ça croit que tu fais trop un gaspillage dans les petits poissons.* It's illegal [to fish there] because they think that you waste too many of the small fish. (LF) <***Loc:*** LF>

défense [defɑ̃s] *n.f.* defense ◊ •**défense d'éléphant** elephant's tusk <VM> •**sans défense** helpless *Pauvre bête, elle était sans défense, elle était manière doucement.* Poor thing, she was helpless, she was kind of retarded. (EV) <EV, Da84> <***Loc:*** EV, VM, Da84>

déferrer [defere] *v.tr.* to unshoe (a horse) *Il faut que tu déferres un cheval avant de le referrer, mais pas pour un poulain que t'as jamais ferré avant.* You have to unshoe a horse before reshoeing it, but not a colt that you've never shod before. (VM) <***Loc:*** VM, Da84>

défi [defi] *n.m.* defiance, challenge <***Loc:*** Da84>

déficeler (se) [defisle] *v.pron.* to take off one's good clothes *Va te déficeler.* Go take off your good clothes. (SL) <***Loc:*** SL>

défier [defie] *v.tr.* **1** to defy, dare, challenge **Je te défie!* I dare you! (Da84) **2** to brave (a danger) <***Loc:*** Da84>

défiger [defiʒe] **I** *v.tr.* to melt, cause to melt *Quand il fait froid, le sirop est figé. Il faut que tu le défiges avant de t'en servir.* When it's cold, syrup is stiff. You have to melt it before using it. (VM) **II** *v.intr.* to melt *Le fromage de tête va défiger si tu le laisses sur le comptoir.* The head cheese will melt if you leave it out on the counter. (LA) <***Loc:*** LA, VM, Da84>

défigurant, -e [defigyrɑ̃, -ɑ̃t] *adj.* disfiguring *La picote, c'est une maladie défigurante, mais pas autant que la lèpre.* Smallpox is a disfiguring disease, but not as much as leprosy. (VM) <***Loc:*** VM, Da84>

défiguré, -e [defigyre, defygyre] *adj.* **1** disfigured *Il a eu un accident de char et il a sorti tout défiguré.* He had a car accident and he was completely disfigured. (VM) **2** forlorn-looking, of mournful aspect *Il est défiguré depuis la mort de son ami.* He is forlorn since the death of his friend. (SM) <***Loc:*** SM, VM, Da84>

défigurer [defigyre, defygyre] **I** *v.tr.* to disfigure, mar the appearance of *L'accident l'a défiguré.* The accident disfigured him. (LA) **II se défigurer** *v.pron.* to make a face, grimace *C'est pas la peine tu te défigures comme ça. Tu vas faire comme je te dis de faire.* There's no need to twist your face up like that. You're going to do what I tell you to do. (VM) <***Loc:*** LA, VM, Da84>

défilé [defile] *n.f.* line (of people or objects), succession, file <***Loc:*** Da84>

défiler [defile] **I** *v.tr.* **1** to unroll (string, yarn, etc.) *Le chat avait tout défilé sa laine.* The cat had completely unrolled her yarn. (LA) **2** to unthread *Tu peux défiler ton aiguille. On va pas finir la robe à soir.* You can unthread your needle. We won't finish the dress tonight. (LA) **II** *v.intr.* **1** to wear away, wear out, wear thin *C'est plus servable, cette robe, garde comme ça a défilé.* It's no longer good for anything, this dress, look how it has worn thin. (VM) **2** to come apart, unravel, fray *C'est pour couper, pour pas ça défile.* It's used to cut, so that it doesn't fray. (SM) <***Loc:*** LA, SM, VM, Lv88>

défiloper (se) [defilope, defiloke] *v.pron.* to become threadbare, become tattered *Ça se défilope tout. C'est pus servable.* It's becoming all threadbare. It's no longer usable. (VM) *Le bas de ma robe est tout défilopé.* The bottom of my dress is all tattered. (TB) <***Loc:*** JE, TB, VM>

définiment (définitement) [definimɑ̃, definitmɑ̃] *adv.* definitely *Oh oui, définitement.* Oh yes, definitely. (TB) <***Loc:*** TB, Da84>

définitif (**définitive**) [definitif, definitiv] *adj.* definite, exact, final *Ses plans de vacances sont pas définitifs encore.* His vacation plans are not yet definite. (VM) <***Loc:*** VM, Da84>

définition [definisjɔ̃] *n.f.* definition <***Loc:*** Da84>

définitive ♦see **définitif**

défint ♦see **défunt**

défonçage [defɔ̃saʒ] *n.m.* **1** breaking down (e.g. a door) **2** breaking in, breaking into (a house) <***Loc:*** Da84>

défoncer [defɔ̃se] **I** *v.tr.* to break down, break open, smash in *Il a défoncé la porte pour rentrer.* He broke down the door to get in. (VM) *Ils ont défoncé le plancher.* They broke through the floor. (LA) **II** *v.intr.* **1** to break in (for a burglary) *Ils ont défoncé chez Jean hier soir.* They broke into Jean's house last night. (SM) **2** to break open, burst open **Le baril a défoncé.* The barrel broke open. (Da84) <***Loc:*** AV, EV, EB, SB, SM, TB, VM, Da84, Hi02, Ph36>

défonceur [defɔ̃sœr] *n.m.* ◊ **•défonceur d'une porte ouverte / défonceur de porte(s) ouverte(s)** ***a*** one who brags or exaggerates wildly, braggart ***b*** one who makes a big show of s.t. that is not really difficult ***c*** politician who attacks non-existent issues ***d*** big talker and little doer ***e*** rough, brutish person, one who uses excessive force <SM, Da84, La99> <***Loc:*** SM, TB, Da84, La99>

déformation [defɔrmasjɔ̃] *n.f.* deformation, malformation <***Loc:*** Da84>

déformer [defɔrme] *v.tr.* to deform, distort, misshape *Sa maladie l'avait tout déformé.* His illness had completely deformed him. (EV) *Pauvre garçon! Il est tout déformé depuis la guerre.* Poor guy! He's all deformed since the war. (SM) <***Loc:*** EV, LA, SM, Da84>

défourner [defurne] *v.tr.* to remove from the oven *Défourner le pain.* To take the bread out of the oven. (VM) <***Loc:*** VM>

défraîchi (**défréchis**) [defreʃi, defriʃi] *n.m.* **1** cleared land (as for cultivation) *J'ai fait un défréchis pour faire mon jardin.* I made a clearing for my garden. (VM) **2** clearing, clear patch (in a forest) <***Loc:*** JE, SB, SM, VM>

défraîchir (**défréchir, défricheter, défricher**) [defreʃir, defriʃte, defryʃte, defriʃe] *v.tr.* **1** to deforest, clear (land, e.g. for cultivation) *Je veux pas vendre ce morceau de terre. Mon pauvre mari a travaillé si dur, il l'avait nettoyé, il l'avait défraîchi, il ôtait tous les petits arbres en dedans, puis il l'avait paré pour faire récolte.* I don't want to sell this piece of land. My poor husband worked so hard [on it], he had cleaned it up, he had cleared it out, he took out all the little trees in it, then he had gotten it ready for harvesting. (SL) **Ein Cadien, c'est comme ein chêne qui peut pas êt' deraciné. Il a défriché ein désert et fondé son pays.* A Cajun is like an oak that cannot be uprooted. He has cleared a piece of land and founded his country. (ThCa: *Mille misères*) **2** to clear out weeds or underbrush from *Ils sont après défréchir le bord du fossé.* They're clearing the edge of the ditch. (VM) **3** to clean out (a drawer, a house, etc.) *Elle a défricheté son tiroir.* She cleaned out her drawer. (IB) <***Loc:*** AV, EV, IB, SB, SJ, SL, SM, VM, Da84, Lv88, Ph36>

défraîchissage [defreʃisaʒ] *n.m.* deforesting, clearing (of land, e.g. for cultivation) <***Loc:*** Da84>

défraîchissement [defreʃismɑ̃] *n.m.* **1** deforestation, clearing (of land, e.g. for cultivation) **2** piece of land that has been cleared <***Loc:*** IB, SB, SL>

défréchir ♦see **défraîchir**

défréchis ♦see **défraîchi**

défricheter ♦see **défraîchir**

défroncer [defrɔ̃se] *v.tr.* **1** to unpleat, remove pleats or gathers (of a garment) *Défroncer une jupe de robe.* To ungather the skirt of a dress. (VM) **2** to unwrinkle, iron out wrinkles from *Elle a eu pour défroncer sa chemise avant qu'il pouvait sortir.* She had to unwrinkle his shirt before he could go out. (LA) ◊ **•défroncer le front** to unknit one's brow *Tu ferais mieux de défroncer ce front droit asteur, mon petit.* You had better unknit that brow right now, son. (LA) <LA, Da84> <***Loc:*** LA, VM, Da84>

défropter [defrɔpte] *v.tr.* **1** to ruin, mess up, break up, damage *Ils ont tout défropté la maison.* They completely messed up the house. (LA) **2** to undo, take apart *J'ai tout défropté ça.* I took that all apart. (VM) <***Loc:*** LA, VM, Lv88>

défroqueter [defrokte, defrɔkte] *v.tr.* **1** to ruin, mess up, damage *J'ai eu un accident et j'ai tout défroqueté mon char.* I had an accident and I completely ruined my car. (LA) **2** to hurt, injure, mess up *Je vas te défroqueter à coup de poings.* I'm going to mess you up with my fists. (SM) <***Loc:*** LA, SL, SM, Lv88>

défunt[1], **-e** (**défint, -e**) [defɛ̃, -ɛ̃t] *adj.* late, deceased, defunct, (dearly) departed **Mon défunt père.* My late father. (Da84) *C'est défunt Amédée qui a fait cette maison.* It's the late Amédée who built this house. (Lv88) *Il a déshonoré sa défunte femme quand il s'a remarié deux mois plus tard.* He dishonored his late wife when he remarried two months later. (VM) *Prier pour l'âme du défunt.* To pray for the soul of the departed. (SJ) *J'ai rêvé à défint Jean hier soir.* I dreamed of departed Jean last night. (SM) <***Loc:*** AC, AV, EV, LA, SL, SM, TB, VM, Da84, Hi02, Lv88>

défunt[2], **-e** (**défint, -e**) [defɛ̃, -ɛ̃t] *n.* the deceased, the departed ◊ **•son défunt / sa défunte** deceased mate or spouse *Alle est triste, alle sort d'enterrer son défint.* She's sad, she's just come from burying her deceased husband. (VM) <VM> <***Loc:*** IB, LF, SB, SL, VM, Da84>

dégabiller [degabije] *v.tr.* to tear off (clothes) *Dégabiller le linge de quelqu'un.* To tear someone's clothes off. (LF) <***Loc:*** LF>

dégagé, -e [degaʒe] *adj.* **1** free, unrestrained *Un chien dégagé.* An unrestrained dog. (VM) **2** cheerful, gay, animated *Une conversation dégagée.* An animated conversation. (VM) <***Loc:*** VM, Da84>

dégager [degaʒe] **I** *v.tr.* to extricate, free *Ça nous a pris un bon* *bout de temps pour dégager la glacière de la porte.* It took us a good while to free the icebox from the door. (LA) **II se dégager** *v.pron.* **1** to free o.s. *Il a réussi à se dégager de là avant que son père arrive.* He succeeded in getting himself out of there before his father returned. (LA) **2** to get out, get out quickly *Alle se dégageait, alle se halait à côté de sa tour éyou on prendait notre chevrette.* She got herself out of there and hurried over to the side of her tower where we used to catch our shrimp. (LF) **3** to hurry *Il s'est dégagé pour arriver à l'heure.* He hurried to arrive on time. (AV) <***Loc:*** AV, LA, LF, TB, Da84>

dégaine [degɛ̃n, dedʒɛ̃n] *n.m./f.* **1** slovenliness, sloppiness (of appearance) *Sa dégaine l'empêche de trouver un mari.* Her slovenliness prevents her from finding a husband. (VM) **2** awkwardness, strangeness (of dress, gait, etc.) *Il a une dégaine pour marcher.* He has an awkward gait. (LF) ◊ **•être en dégaine** to be improperly dressed, not neatly or well dressed *Quand ils sont venus j'étais en dégaine.* When they came I wasn't properly dressed. (SM) <SM> <***Loc:*** LF, SM, VM, Lv88>

dégainé, -e [degɛ̃ne, dedʒɛ̃ne, degɛ̃je] *adj.* **1** badly dressed, shabbily dressed, of neglected appearance *Tu vas pas être choquée? Je suis toute dégainée à ce matin.* You won't be upset? I'm really badly dressed this morning. (Lv88) **2** dressed in poor taste *Il était tout le temps tout dégainé. Je lui ai dit qu'il aurait jamais eu une belle comme ça.* He was always poorly dressed. I told him he'd never get a girlfriend like that. (LA) **3** ragged, tattered (of clothing) *Son* SUIT *était tout dégainé.* His suit was all ragged. (LA) <***Loc:*** LA, SL, SM, VM, Lv88>

dégainer [degɛ̃ne] *v.tr.* **1** to hand over *Dégainer l'argent.* To hand over the money. (LF) **2** to take off, shed (an article of clothing) *Dégainer les pantalons.* To take off one's pants. (LF) <***Loc:*** LF>

déganter [degɑ̃te] **I** *v.tr.* to unglove *Déganter un enfant.* To remove a child's gloves. (VM) **II se déganter** *v.pron.* to remove one's gloves *Dans le temps, une dame se dégantait pas en public.* In the old days, a lady did not remove her gloves in public. (LA) <***Loc:*** LA, VM, Da84>

dégarnir [degarnir] *v.tr.* to remove ornaments or decorations from *Dégarnir l'arbre de Noël.* To remove the ornaments from the Christmas tree. (VM) <***Loc:*** VM, Da84>

dégât [dega] *n.m.* damage, havoc, mess ◊ **•faire du dégât** to cause damage, make a mess <Da84> <***Loc:*** Da84, Hi02>

dégâter [degate] **I** *v.tr.* to unspoil (e.g. a child) *Ils auront du mal à dégâter cet enfant là.* They are going to have a hard time unspoiling that child. (LA) **II se dégâter** *v.pron.* to become unspoiled *Cet enfant va jamais se dégâter.* That child will never get unspoiled. (LA) <***Loc:*** LA, Da84>

dégelée [deʒəle] *n.f.* drubbing, thrashing, beating *Je l'ai donné une dégelée de coups de bâton.* I gave him a thrashing with a stick. (SL) <***Loc:*** SL>

dégeler [deʒəle] **I** *v.tr.* **1** to thaw, thaw out *Demande ta mère si elle veut que je dégèle de la viande pour cuire ce soir.* Ask your mother if she wants me to thaw out some meat to cook tonight. (LA) **2** to defrost, de-ice *J'ai eu pour dégeler ma vitre avant de partir pour aller à l'ouvrage.* I had to defrost my windshield before leaving for work. (LA) <***Loc:*** LA, Da84>

dégêner (se) [deʒɛ̃ne] *v.pron.* to get over one's shyness *Il est timide. Il met du temps à se dégêner.* He is timid. It takes him a while to get over his shyness. (VM) <***Loc:*** VM>

dégénérer [deʒɛ̃nere] *v.intr.* to degenerate, deteriorate, worsen *Cette conversation a dégénéré en bataille.* That conversation degenerated into a fight. (VM) <***Loc:*** VM, Da84>

dégérer ♦see **digérer**

dégirage [deʒiraʒ] *n.m.* digestion **Faire ein thé pour des crampes d'éstomac et pour aider le dégirage.* To make tea for stomach cramps and to help digestion. (Wh83) <***Loc:*** Wh83>

dégirer ♦see **digérer**

déglacer [deglase] *v.tr.* **1** to thaw, thaw out *Quand l'électricité a manqué pour l'ouragan, ça a tout déglacé ça on avait dedans le* FREEZE. When the electricity went off during the hurricane, it thawed everything we had in the freezer. (LA) **2** to defrost, de-ice (e.g. a freezer) *Dans le temps, il faulait déglacer le* FREEZE *tous les mois.* In the old days, you had to defrost the freezer every month. (LA) <***Loc:*** EV, LA, TB, Da84>

dégo, -ote (DAGO) [dego, -ɔt] *n.* American of Italian origin (not necessarily pejorative) *Ma fille s'a marié avec un Dégo.* My daughter married an Italian-American. (VM) <***Loc:*** EV, LF, SB, SL, SM, TB, VM, Lv88, Ph36>

dégobillage [degobijaʒ] *n.m.* vomit <***Loc:*** IB, SJ>

dégobiller [degobije] *v.tr.* to whittle down, eat away *Elle a laissé la daube sur la table, et ils ont fini par tout la dégobiller.* She left the roast on the table, and they eventually ate it away. (VM) <***Loc:*** VM, Da84>

dégommer [degɔ̃me] *v.tr.* to remove gum or any gummy substance from *Tu parles qu'il a eu du tracas pour dégommer sa machine.* He really had trouble removing the gum from his motor. (LA) <***Loc:*** LA, Da84>

dégonfler [degɔ̃fle] *v.tr.* **1** to reduce swelling *Un morceau de viande froide est supposé de dégonfler un* BLACK EYE. A piece of cold meat is supposed to reduce the swelling of a black eye. (LA) **2** to deflate, let air out of *Ils ont passé et tout dégonflé ses* TIRES. They went by and completely deflated his tires. (LA) **Nagok traitait ein cheval gonflé par lui donner juste du foin sec à manger ou par emmarer ein petit morceaux de bois en travers de sa geuele [=gueule] pour le tchein [=tiendre] ouvert pour le faire rôter et l'aider a dégonfler.* Nagok treated a bloated horse by giving it only dry hay to eat or by tying a small piece of wood through his mouth to keep it open and make him belch and help him deflate. (Wh83) <***Loc:*** LA, Da84, Wh83>

dégorger [degɔrʒe] *v.tr.* to disgorge, remove (an obstruction) (from the throat, a pipe, a tube, etc.) *Il a dégorgé une canique du tuyau.* He removed a marble from the pipe. (LA) <***Loc:*** LA, Da84>

dégoter [degote] **I** *v.tr.* to unstop, unclog, free of a blockage *Dégoter une tondeuse, une machine à coudre.* To free up a sheep shear, a sewing machine. (Lv88) **II se dégoter** *v.pron.* **1** to become unclogged **2** to clear, unclog one's throat *Donne-moi de l'eau, j'ai besoin de me dégoter.* Give me some water, I need to unclog my throat. (LA) <***Loc:*** LA, Da84, Lv88>

dégourdir [degurdir] **I** *v.tr.* to limber up, eliminate numbness or stiffness from *Des fois quand je me lève, ça me prend quelques minutes pour dégourdir mes vieilles jambes.* Sometimes when I get up, it takes me a few minutes to wake up my old legs. (LA) **II** *v.intr.* to limber up **Si les garçons pouvaient trouver 85¢ ça pouvait s'acheter ein jog de vin muscatel et dégourdir pour danser.* If the boys could find 85¢ they could buy a jug of muscatel wine and limber up for a dance. (Wh83) **III se dégourdir** *v.pron.* to limber up *Espère une minute. Ça va me prendre quelque temps pour me dégourdir.* Wait a minute. It'll take me a while to limber up. (LA) <***Loc:*** LA, Da84, Wh83>

dégoût [degu] *n.m.* disgust, distate <***Loc:*** Da84>

dégoûtant, -e [degutɑ̃, -ɑ̃t] *adj.* disgusting, repulsive, distasteful *Fais pas ça. C'est dégoûtant.* Don't do that. It's disgusting. (LA) <***Loc:*** LA, Da84>

dégoûtation [degutasjɔ̃] *n.f.* cause of displeasure, source of disgust *Ça c'est une dégoûtation.* That's a disgusting thing. (VM) <***Loc:*** VM>

dégoûté, -e [degute] *adj.* disgusted, fed up, no longer interested *Il est dégoûté, il veut pus les voir du tout.* He's disgusted, he doesn't want to see them any more. (LA) <***Loc:*** LA, Da84>

dégoûter [degute] **I** *v.tr.* **1** to disgust, cause aversion *Tout ce qui me dégoûte d'eusses, eusse portent un 'tit soulier numero neuf.* The only thing that disgusts me about them, they wear a little number nine shoe. (AC, ch: *Les filles à N-Oncle Hilaire*) *Ça prendait le sang de le cochon et eux-autres cuisait ça quelque qualité de manière, mon j'en ai jamais mangé parce que ça m'a dégoûté.* They used to take the blood of the pig and they cooked it in some way, I never ate it because it disgusted me. (LF) **2** to change s.o.'s mind, persuade s.o. against *Alle m'a dégoûté et je vas pas le faire.* She changed my mind and I'm not going to do it. (TB) **II se dégoûter** *v.pron.* **1** to be fed up, be disgusted *Je me dégoûte de la politique depuis ce bougre a rentré.* I'm fed up with politics since that guy was elected. (LA) **2** to change one's mind *Il devait se marier, mais il s'est dégoûté.* He was supposed to get married, but he changed his mind. (Lv88) <***Loc:*** AC, JE, LA, LF, SM, TB, Da84, Lv88>

dégouttation [degutasjɔ̃] *n.f.* drip, dripping, leak, trickle <***Loc:*** JE>

dégouttement [degutmɑ̃] *n.m.* drip, leak, trickle <***Loc:*** Da84>

dégoutter [degute] *v.intr.* to drip, trickle *Ça va glacer à soir. Il faudrait quitter les robinets dégoutter.* It's going to freeze tonight. We'll have to let the faucets drip. (LA) <***Loc:*** LA, Da84>

dégouttière [degutjær] *n.f.* gutter *Après tu les enterres en dessous une dégouttière.* Then you bury them under a gutter. (TB) <***Loc:*** TB>

dégraboter [degrabote] *v.tr.* to remove (seeds) from a pod *Pour planter les graines de fleurs il a fallu que nous les dégrabote.* To plant the flower seeds we had to remove them from the pod. (TB) <***Loc:*** TB>

dégradant, -e [degradɑ̃, -ɑ̃t] *adj.* degrading, debasing *Nettoyer des fossés, c'est dégradant.* Cleaning ditches is degrading. (VM) <***Loc:*** VM, Da84>

dégradation [degradasjɔ̃] *n.f.* degradation <***Loc:*** Da84>

dégrader [degrade] **I** *v.tr.* **1** to disgrace *Il a dégradé sa famille.* He disgraced his family. (LA) **2** to wear away, damage, erode, wash away *Ça va dégrader la pierre si elle est sec.* It is going to damage the stone if it is dry. (AC) *La terre est dégradée un tas icitte.* The land is eroded quite a bit here. (VM) **3** to abandon, desert, leave behind on purpose *Il a dégradé le chien dans le bois.* He abandoned the dog in the woods. (LF) **II** *v.intr.* to degrade *Le premier coton était bon, mais depuis ça s'en va en dégradant.* The first cotton was good, but it has degraded since then. (VM) **III se dégrader** *v.pron.* to degrade, debase, disgrace o.s. *Arrête de faire ça, tu te dégrades.* Stop doing that, you're disgracing yourself. (LA) <***Loc:*** AC, JE, LA, LF, VM, Da84>

dégrafer [degrafe] *v.tr.* to unclasp, unhook, unsnap, unfasten *Dégrafe voir ma robe. Mon épaule me fait mal.* Unclasp my dress. My shoulder hurts. (LA) <***Loc:*** LA, Da84>

dégraisser (**dégrasser**) [degrese, degrase] *v.tr.* to degrease, remove fat or grease from *Tout le monde, les femmes et les hommes, ça allait en dehors et ça commençait à couper la viande et là eux-autres dégrassait la viande et eux-autres prendait les morceaux de gras et ça coupait ça dans des petits carreaux.* Everyone, the women and the men, went outside and they began cutting the meat up and then they removed the fat and they took the pieces of fat and cut them up in small squares [to make crackling]. (LF) <***Loc:*** LF, Da84>

degré [dəgre] *n.m.* degree, grade, stage <***Loc:*** Da84>

dégréement [degremɑ̃] *n.m.* dismantling, taking apart, disassembling <***Loc:*** VM>

dégréer (**dégreiller, dégreyer, dégréyer**) [degree, degreje] **I** *v.tr.* **1** to dismantle, disassemble *J'ai pour dégréer le lit pour le peinturer.* I have to disassemble the bed to paint it. (VM) **2** to unrig *On aura pour dégréer le wagon après la saison de coton.* We'll have to unrig the wagon after cotton season. (LA) **3** to clear (the table) *Laisse ça. Les enfants vont dégréer* *la table.* Leave that alone. The children will clear the table. (LA) **4** to clear out, strip of furnishings and decorations *Ils ont tout dégréé la maison à Mam après qu'elle est morte.* They cleared my mother's house out after she died. (VM) *Il faut dégreyer la chambre pour la papiéter.* We have to take all the furniture out of the room to wallpaper it. (IB) **5** to rob, strip clean, deprive of goods or property *Sa femme l'a dégréé avec le divorce.* His wife cleaned him out with the divorce. (VM) **6** to strip *Il l'a dégréyée de tout son linge.* He stripped her of all her clothes. (LF) **II se dégréer** *v.pron.* **1** to get rid of *Il a eu pour se dégréer de son bateau après son STROKE.* He had to get rid of his boat after his stroke. (LA) **2** to get undressed *Dégrée-toi dehors. Tu vas pas rentrer dans la maison plein de boue comme ça.* Undress outside. You're not going to come in the house full of mud like that. (LA) ◊ **•dégréer Saint Paul pour gréer Saint Pierre** to take a button from one dress to put on another <TB, La99> **•dégreer Saint-Pierre pour gréer Saint-Paul** to rob Peter to pay Paul (i.e. to take funds or materials from where they are needed in order to use them elsewhere) <Da84, La99, Lv88> <***Loc:*** AV, EV, IB, LF, LA, SL, SM, TB, VM, Da84, Lv88, Ph36, Re31>

dégreiller ♦see **dégréer**

dégreyer, dégréyer ♦see **dégréer**

dégringolage [degrɛ̃golaʒ] *n.m.* tumbling, tumbling down *J'ai entendu un grand dégringolage.* I heard a loud sound of someone tumbling. (SB) <***Loc:*** SB>

dégringole [degrɛ̃gol] *n.f.* deterioration, ruin ◊ **•aller à la dégringole** to go to pot, become run down <Da84> <***Loc:*** Da84>

dégringoler [degrɛ̃gole] *v.intr.* to deteriorate, go to ruin, break down, go to pot *Leur place est après dégringoler depuis le vieux est mort.* Their place is going to ruin since the old fellow died. (LA) <***Loc:*** LA, Da84>

dégrossir [degrosir] **I** *v.tr.* to whittle down, reduce (in size) *C'était quelque chose qu'était usé pour dégrossir du bois et pour faire les CROSSTIES, les TIES sur le chemin de fer.* That was something that was used to whittle down wood and to make the crossties, the ties on the railroad. (LF) **II** *v.intr.* to shrink, reduce in size *Ma femme a dégrossi, mais pas moi.* My wife lost weight, but I didn't. (LA) <***Loc:*** LA, LF, Da84>

dégrouler [degrule] *v.intr.* **1** to tumble down **2** to go from bad to worse, go to the dogs *La banque a dégroulé en rien.* The bank went to the dogs in no time. (AV) <***Loc:*** AV, JE>

dégrucher (**dégricher**) [degryʃe, degriʃe] **I** *v.tr.* **1** to descend, climb down, scramble down *Le chat a dégriché le poteau.* The cat descended the pole. (SM) **2** to set down, put down, lay down *Il a dégruché son fusil.* He laid down his gun. (TB) **II** *v.intr.* to descend, climb down, scramble down *Il a dégruché de l'arbre.* He scrambled down out of the tree. (VM) <***Loc:*** AV, JE, SM, TB, VM, Da84>

déguélinié ♦see **déguénillé**

déguénillé, -e (**déguélinié, -e, éguenillé, -e**) [degɛ̃nije, deginije, degənije, deglĩje, egønije, eginije] *adj.* **1** untidy, poorly groomed, dressed in rags *Ces enfants étaient tout le temps tout déguénillés.* Those kids were always dressed in rags. (VM) **2** dressed in poor taste *Tu vas pas à l'église déguénillé comme ça.* You don't go to church dressed poorly like that. (LA) <***Loc:*** AV, IB, LA, SJ, SL, SM, VM, Da84>

déguerper [degærpe] *v.tr.* to evict, turn out (a tenant) *Quand le prix du coton a baissé, les bourgeois ont déguerpé leurs travaillants à la part.* When the price of cotton went down, the landowners evicted their sharecroppers. (VM) <***Loc:*** SM, VM>

déguiser [degize] **I** *v.tr.* to disguise *Il y en a qui déguisent jusqu'à leurs chevaux pour Mardi Gras.* There are some who even disguise their horses for Mardi Gras. (LA) **II se déguiser** *v.pron.* to disguise o.s. *Il avait habitude se déguiser comme une vieille femme.* He used to disguise himself as an old woman. (LA) <***Loc:*** LA, Da84>

déhaler (se) [deale] *v.pron.* to ease, slip, crawl silently in or out *Il se déhale dans la maison.* He slips quietly into the house. (LF) <***Loc:*** LF>

déhancher (se) [dehɑ̃ʃe] *v.pron.* to dislocate one's hip *Il s'a proche déhanché au bal.* He almost dislocated his hip at the dance. (LA) <***Loc:*** LA, Da84>

dehors[1] [dejɔr, deɔr, dihɔr, dijɔr, diɔr, djɔr] *n.m.* outside *Le couteau rond à deux manches était plutôt pour le dedans, et le couteau à deux manches était plutôt pour le dehors.* The round two-handled drawknife was mostly for the inside, and and the [regular] two-handled drawknife was for the outside. (LF) *Les charpentiers ont fini le dehors de la maison, mais il ont toujours pas fini le dedans.* The carpenters have finished the exterior of the house, but they still haven't completed the interior. (VM) <***Loc:*** LF, VM>

dehors[2] [dejɔr, deɔr, dihɔr, dijɔr, diɔr, djɔr] *adv.* outside, outdoors *On jouait dehors un tas quand on était petit.* We used to play outside a lot when we were young. (AC) *Si ça nous attrapait parler français dehors, ils avaient des petits RULER à peu près un pied, on mettait notre main comme ça et pah! pah!* If we were caught speaking French outside, they had small rulers about one foot long, we would [have to] put our hand like that and bam! bam! (IB) ◊ **•aller dehors *a*** to go outside **Ça fait, lui, il va dehors.* So he goes outside. (SL, An94) ***b*** to go to the outhouse or toilet *Il y a pas de chambre à bain au camp. Il faut ça va déhors.* There's no bathroom at the camp. They have to do their business outside. (LA) <AV, LA, SL, An94, Da84> **•en dehors *a*** outside *Elle est en dehors la maison.* She is outside the house. (SM) *Allez jouer en dehors!* Go play outside! (TB) *Moi je veux aller fumer en dehors, tu vas y tiendre compagnie un élan?* I'm going to go smoke outside, are you going to keep him company for a spell? (TB) ***b*** out *Et on avait un bateau de trawl, eusse trawlait et pêchait des huîtres avec,* *on restait cinq, six jours en dehors.* And we had a trawl boat, they would trawl and fish oysters with it. We would stay out five or six days. (TB) <IV, SM, TB, VM, An94, Da84, La99> **•en dehors de** besides, except for, other than *Il connaît pas arien en dehors de ça.* He doesn't know anything besides that. (SM) <SM> **•mettre (qqn) dehors** to kick out, throw out, eject, expel *Il a fait tellement de tracas, ils ont eu pour le mettre dehors.* He caused so much trouble, they had to throw him out. (LA) <LA, Da84> <***Loc:*** AC, IB, IV, LA, LF, SL, SM, TB, VM, An94, Da84, Hi02, Lv88>

dehors[3] [dejɔr, deɔr, dihɔr, dijɔr, diɔr, djɔr] *prep.* **1** off, off of *La maison a flotté dehors des bloques.* The house floated off of its blocks. (SL) **2** except for, besides *Déhors ça, je connais arien* Aside from that, I know nothing. (VM) <***Loc:*** SL, VM>

déjà [deʒa, dʒa] *adv.* **1** already, previously *Il pouvait pas lui faire une avance, parce qu'il était déjà tellement en dette lui-même.* He couldn't advance him any money because he was already in such debt himself. (LA) *J'ai tous mes patrons de fait mesurés sus vos robes il y a déjà quelques jours.* I have all my patterns done, measured on your dresses several days ago already. (AC) **2** ever **Félix pouvait mentire comme personne d'autre que j'ai déjà connu.* Felix could lie like no one else I've ever known. (Wh83) **3** *(phrase-final discourse marker)* anyway, after all, again *Et-où j'ai mis ça déjà?* Where did I put that, anyway? (VM) <***Loc:*** AC, LA, VM, An94, Da84, Hi02, Wh83>

déjeuner[1] [deʒœ̃ne] *v.intr.* to eat breakfast *On a déjeuné, puis on est parti à l'ouvrage.* We ate breakfast, then we left for work. (EV) <***Loc:*** EV, LA, Da84>

déjeuner[2] [deʒœ̃ne] *n.m.* breakfast <***Loc:*** IB, SL, TB, Da84, Hi02>

déjointer [deʒwɛ̃te, deʒwɑ̃te] **I** *v.tr.* **1** to dislocate (a joint) *Quand alle a tombé, ça lui a déjointé la hanche.* When she fell, it dislocated her hip. (VM) **2** to cut apart at the joint (e.g. meat or poultry) *Il a déjointé une douzaine de poules pour le gombo de Mardi Gras.* He disjointed a dozen chickens for the Mardi Gras gumbo. (LA) **II se déjointer** *v.pron.* to dislocate (one's elbow, etc.) *En tombant en bas du lit il s'a déjointé le coude du bras.* He dislocated his elbow by falling out of bed. (TB) <***Loc:*** AV, EV, IB, LA, LF, SB, SJ, SL, SM, TB, VM, Da84, Lv88, Ph36>

déjouquer [deʒuke] **I** *v.tr.* **1** to remove (a hen) from its roost *On a déjouqué les poules pour les mettre à l'abri dans le poulailler.* We got the chickens off their roosts to put them safely in the chicken coop. (VM) **2** to unharness, unyoke *Déjouquer un bœuf d'une charrette.* To unharness an ox from a cart. (VM) **II** *v.intr.* to get off the roost (of a hen) <***Loc:*** JE, VM, Lv88>

délacer [delase] *v.tr.* to unlace, untie (shoes, etc.) *Délacer les souliers.* To untie shoes. (VM) <***Loc:*** VM, Da84>

délâcher [delaʃe] *v.tr.* to relieve, empty the bowels of **La seul manière pour le délâcher c'est pour que la femme déchire ein morceau de son* SLIP *et elle l'attache dessus le lange du petit.* The only way to relieve it [the baby's bowels] is for the woman to tear a piece of her slip off and pin it to the baby's diaper. (Wh83) <***Loc:*** Wh83>

délaissé, -e [delese] *n.* **1** one who has been abandoned by a partner or loved one *Quand moi et la belle, on s'a marié j'ai fait des choses j'aurais pas dû. Aujourd'hui je suis un délaissé.* When my girl and I got married, I did some things that I shouldn't have. Today I am an abandoned one. (ch: *La vie je croyais je voulais*) **2** one who is divorced or separated <***Loc:*** LF, SL, SM, VM, Lv88>

délaisser [delese] **I** *v.tr.* **1** to abandon, desert, forsake (esp. wife or children) *Il a délaissé sa femme et ses enfants.* He abandoned his wife and his children. (LA) **2** to divorce **II se délaisser** *v.pron.* to separate, split up, divorce *Ils se sont délaissés l'année passée.* They separated last year. (VM) <***Loc:*** LA, LF, SM, VM, Da84, Lv88>

délasser [delase] *v.tr.* to remove a lasso from *Délasse le veau, j'ai fini de le marquer.* Remove the lasso from the calf, I've finished branding it. (VM) <***Loc:*** VM>

délayer (délier) [deleje, delje] *v.tr.* **1** to dilute, thin *Il faut délier la pâte avec d'autre eau.* You have to thin the dough with more water. (Lv88) **2** to dissolve **On délaye de la farine et on fond du sucre, de la graisse.* We dissolve flour and we melt sugar, fat. (Da84) **Ça déliait du candi dûr [...] dans du whiskey.* They would dissolve hard candy in whisky. (Wh83) <***Loc:*** EV, IB, SL, SM, VM, Da84, Lv88, Ph36, Wh83>

délégation [delegasjɔ̃] *n.f.* delegation <***Loc:*** Da84>

délégué [delege] *n.m.* delegate <***Loc:*** Da84>

déléguer [delege] *v.tr.* to delegate, authorize *Les vieux l'ont délégué pour s'occuper de leur bien.* The old folks delegated him to take care of their belongings. (LA) <***Loc:*** LA, Da84>

délibération [deliberasjɔ̃] *n.f.* deliberation <***Loc:*** Da84>

délibérer [delibere] *v.intr.* to deliberate *Le jury a délibéré longtemps après le procès.* The jury deliberated a long time after the trial. (LA) <***Loc:*** LA, Da84>

délicat, -e [delika, -at] *adj.* **1** delicate, sensitive *Alle dit aussi que son cinquième mari Clopha était tout le temps après se plaindre avec du mal dans l'estomac, que il avait l'estomac tellement délicat jusqu'à le docteur a eu pour le mettre à la diète.* She also says that her fifth husband Clopha was always complaining about stomachaches and that his stomach was so delicate that the doctor had to put him on a diet. (AV) **2** fussy, hard to please <***Loc:*** AV, Da84, Hi02>

délicatesse[1] [delikatɛs] *n.f.* delicacy, refinement, sensitivity ◊ **•avoir pas de délicatesse** to lack refinement, be crude or ill-mannered *Et c'était pas qu'il avait pas de délicatesse, c'était juste qu'il avait manière peur qu'il aurait fait* *quelque chose de pas bien et qu'il aurait eu honte.* And it wasn't that he was ill-mannered, it was just that he was kind of scared he'd do something that wasn't correct and that he would be embarrassed. (ThCa: *La fête à Clomaire*) <Da84> <***Loc:*** Da84>

délicatesse[2] [delikatɛs] *n.f.* **1** delicacy, treat, choice food item **2** delicatessen <***Loc:*** Da84>

délice [delis] *n.m.* delight, pleasure <***Loc:*** Da84>

délicieux, -euse [delisjø, -jøz] *adj.* delicious *Des pêches délicieuses.* Delicious peaches. (EV) <***Loc:*** EV, Da84>

délier ♦see **délayer**

délire (**délure**) [delir, delyr] *n.m.* delirium ◊ **•être dans le délire** to be delirious <Da84> <***Loc:*** JE, Da84>

délivrage [delivraʒ] *n.m.* delivery (of a baby) **Pour faire le délivrage du petit plus aisé, c'était advisé de mettre eine hache endessous du lit avec la pointe levé.* To make the delivery of a baby easier, it was recommended to put an ax under the bed with its blade pointed up. (Wh83) <***Loc:*** Wh83>

délivrance [delivrɑ̃s] *n.f.* deliverance, release <***Loc:*** Da84>

délivrée [delivre] *n.f.* delivery <***Loc:*** Da84>

délivrer [delivre, delivere] **I** *v.tr.* **1** to deliver *Le postillon délivre la malle l'après-midi.* The postman delivers the mail in the afternoon. (Lv88) **2** to serve (papers) *Il délivrait les papiers, faisait des* ARRESTS, *ça qu'un constable faisait.* He served papers, made arrests, whatever a constable did. (LF) **3** to help give birth to, deliver (a baby) *La grand-mère à mon papa, elle était une traiteuse et elle délivrait des enfants.* My dad's grandmother, she was a treater and she used to deliver babies. (SB) **4** to set free, deliver from oppression *J'aimerais que tu viens délivrer mon corps, je veux plus être avec le diable.* I want you to come and deliver my body, I no longer want to be with the devil. (LF) **II se délivrer** *v.pron.* to surrender, give o.s. up, deliver o.s. (e.g. to authorities) *Il va jamais se délivrer, lui, il est trop maudit.* He will never give himself up, he's too mean. (LA) <***Loc:*** AC, IB, LA, LF, SB, SL, SM, VM, Da84, Lv88>

délogement [delɔʒmɑ̃] *n.m.* move, relocation, change of residence *Et j'ai été éné dans 1914 drète à un mille et demi de ma maison. J'ai juste fait ce délogement-là.* And I was born in 1914 just a mile and a half from my house. I've just made that move. (TB) <***Loc:*** TB, Da84>

déloger [deloʒe] **I** *v.tr.* to force out, evict *Il a eu pour déloger ses locataires à force qu'ils étaient sales.* He had to evict his renters because they were dirty. (VM) **II** *v.intr.* **1** to move, change residences *Et dans 1966 on a délogé de la Pointe aux Chênes, on a venu ici.* And in 1966 we moved from Pointe aux Chênes, we came here. (TB) *On a délogé ici, j'ai bâti une petite maison voisin icitte là.* We moved here, I built a small house next door to this one. (TB) **2** to leave home, go away *Il avait habitude de déloger pour l'été.* He used to leave home for the summer. (LA) **III se déloger** *v.pron.* to move away *On s'a délogé de là.* We moved away from there. (VM) <***Loc:*** LA, TB, VM, Da84>

déluge [delyʒ] *n.m.* **1** deluge, flood **2** very heavy rain <***Loc:*** Da84>

délure ♦see **délire**

déluré, -e [delyre] *adj.* up-to-date, wise, smart *C'était du monde déluré.* They were people who were in the know. (VM) <***Loc:*** SM, VM, Da84>

démaçonner [demasɔ̃ne] *v.tr.* to tear down masonry *Je vas démaçonner votre cheminée pour vous-autres si vous me donne mon manger tous les jours.* I'll tear down your chimney for you if you give me my food every day. (TB) <***Loc:*** TB>

demain [dəmɛ̃] *adv.* tomorrow *Tracasse-toi pas. Ça va se désenfler avant demain.* Don't worry. That will be less swollen before tomorrow. (LA) *Demain, je vas à un encan de bêtes aux Opélousas.* Tomorrow I'm going to a livestock auction in Opelousas. (Lv88) *Il a déterminé de finir demain.* He decided to finish tomorrow. (LA) *Donne le mot à Coon qu'on va commencer à couper du riz demain, s'il mouille pas.* Pass the word on to Coon that we'll start cutting rice tomorrow if it doesn't rain. (VM) *J'ai pour laver le linge demain.* I have to do laundry tomorrow. (SM) **Je vais espérer à demain.* I'll wait until tomorrow. (Da84) ◊ **•demain après-midi** tomorrow afternoon <Da84> **•demain (au) soir** tomorrow evening, tomorrow night *Si l'occasion se présente, je vas retourner demain au soir.* If I get a chance, I'm going back again tomorrow night. (AC, ch: *J'ai été z-au bal*) <AC, Da84> **•demain en huit jours** a week from tomorrow <Da84> **•demain matin** tomorrow morning <Da84> **•après demain** day after tomorrow <Da84> <***Loc:*** AC, EV, IV, LA, SM, TB, VM, An94, Da84, Hi02, Lv88, Wh83>

démain ♦see **désamain**

démancher [demɑ̃ʃe] **I** *v.tr.* **1** to loosen or remove a handle from (a tool) *Il a travaillé tellement dur, il a démanché son marteau.* He worked so hard, he loosened the handle on his hammer. (LA) **2** to loosen, disconnect, disassemble (a fitting) *Ils ont eu de la misère à démancher le robinet.* They had lots of trouble disconnecting the faucet. (VM) **3** to dismantle, take apart *Il a démanché sa bicyclette.* He took apart his bicycle. (SB) **4** to dislocate, pull out of joint *La pauvre malheureuse a démanché une hanche.* The poor unfortunate lady dislocated a hip. (VM) **II se démancher** *v.pron.* **1** to come loose (from a handle) *La pelle s'a démanché dans ses mains.* The shovel handle came loose in his hands. (LA) **2** to wear out, cause to fall apart *Rose va se démancher les souliers.* Rose is going to wear out her shoes. (IB) <***Loc:*** IB, LA, SB, TB, VM, Da84, Lv88>

demandant[1], **-e** [dəmɑ̃dɑ̃, -ɑ̃t] *adj.* begging, insistent *Les enfants sont assez demandants.* Kids are pretty insistent. (VM) <***Loc:*** VM, Da84>

demandant[2], **-e** [dəmɑ̃dɑ̃, -ɑ̃t] *n.m./f.* **1** one who asks or solicits **Il y en a pas assez pour les demandants.* There is not enough for those asking. (Da84) **2** customer *Le magasin a pas assez pour les demandants.* The store doesn't have enough for the customers. (VM) <***Loc:*** SB, VM, Da84>

demande [dəmɑ̃d] *n.f.* **1** request **2** question **3** demand ◊ **•en demande** in demand *Et un homme s'habituait à faire quelque chose comme ça et après ça il était en demande.* And a man would get used to doing something like that, and after that he was in demand. (LF) <LF> <***Loc:*** LF, Da84>

demander [dəmɑ̃de] **I** *v.tr.* **1** to ask for, request **C'est ça la valse qui t'après jouer le soir où je l'ai demandée.* That's the waltz that was playing the night that I asked for her hand. (ch: *La valse du malchanceux*) **2** to question, inquire **Elle dit à Monsieur Viator, elle lui a demandé voir combien est-ce qu'il vendait ses œufs.* She said to Mr. Viator, she asked him how much he sold his eggs for. (IV, An94) **3** to require, demand *Ça demande un tas de patience, montrer l'école.* It requires a lot of patience to teach school. (VM) **II se demander** *v.pron.* to ask o.s., wonder *Je me demande quoi c'est le pauvre monde est après faire.* I wonder what the poor people are doing. (LA) ◊ **•demander la charité** to ask for charity, beg *Les Mardi Gras [...] ça passe une fois par an demander la charité.* The Mardi Gras revelers come by once a year to ask for charity. (ch: *La danse de Mardi gras*) <ch> **•demander pardon** ***a*** to ask forgiveness ***b*** to apologize <SL, Da84> **•demander pour** to ask for *Pour traiter un coup de soleil le traiteur demande pour un bassin.* To treat sunstroke the treater asks for a washbasin. (TB) <TB> <***Loc:*** IV, LA, TB, VM, An94, Da84, Hi02>

démangeaison [demɑ̃ʒezɔ̃] *n.f.* itch ◊ **•prendre des démangeaisons** to get itches **Je peux pas* STAND *la messe! Je prends des démangeaisons et je trouve le temps long et tout ce qu'on fait c'est se lever, se mettre à genoux et chanter des chansons.* I can't stand mass. I get itches and I get bored and all we do is get up, kneel, and sing songs. (Wh83) <Wh83> <***Loc:*** Da84, Wh83>

démanger [demɑ̃ʒe] *v.tr.* to itch **Ça me démange.* It itches. (Da84) <***Loc:*** Da84, Wh83>

démarche [demarʃ] *n.f.* process, procedure, step ◊ **•faire des démarches** to initiate a process, start, take steps *Elle a fait des démarches pour se désembrouiller avec sa sœur.* She took steps to break the feud with her sister. (VM) <AV, VM, Da84, La99> <***Loc:*** AC, AV, VM, Da84, La99>

démarié, **-e** [demarje] *n.* **1** *(m.)* man separated from his wife **2** *(f.)* woman separated from her husband <***Loc:*** VM>

démarier [demarje] **I** *v.tr.* to divorce *Je t'ai marié, je peux te démarier.* I married you, I can divorce you. (VM) **II se démarier** *v.pron.* to divorce, break marriage bonds *On est comme quatrièmes cousins. Et là,* WELL, *asteur ça fait pas rien, je suis marié, et je vas pas aller me démarier parce qu'on est parents!* We are like fourth cousins. And, well, now it doesn't make any difference, I'm married, and I'm not going to go get unmarried just because we're related! (LF) <***Loc:*** LF, VM, Da84>

démarrer [demare] *v.tr.* **1** to unfasten, loosen, untie *Ça fait si chaud il a démarré sa cravate.* It was so hot that he loosened his tie. (Lv88) **2** to untie, undo a knot in *Je peux pas démarrer le cable.* I can't untie the rope. (VM) **3** to unhitch *J'ai démarré la vache.* I unhitched the cow. (SM) <***Loc:*** AV, EV, IB, LF, SB, SJ, SL, SM, TB, VM, Da84, Lv88, Ph36, Re31>

démasquer [demaske] *v.tr.* to unmask, expose *Démasquer un Mardi Gras.* To unmask a Mardi Gras participant. (LA) **II se démasquer** *v.pron.* to take off one's mask *Le monde s'habillait, ça se masquait. Là ça prendait le chemin et ça faisait le Mardi Gras toute la journée, et là ça se démasquait le soir à minuit, le Mercredi des Cendres.* People got dressed up, they put on masks. Then they took to the roads and ran Mardi Gras all day, and then in the evening they took off their masks at midnight, Ash Wednesday. (LF) <***Loc:*** LA, LF, Da84>

démêlage [demelaʒ] *n.m.* untangling, sorting <***Loc:*** Da84>

démêlée [demele] *n.f.* conflict, fray <***Loc:*** LF>

démêler [demele] **I** *v.tr.* **1** to untangle *Je vas jamais démêler ma ligne.* I'll never untangle my line. (LA) **2** to sort out, separate *Elle a eu de la misère à démêler ses petits enfants.* She had lots of trouble sorting out her grandchildren. (VM) **3** to mix *Des beignets c'est la même farine, la même pâte que tu démêles pour faire le pain.* Beignets use the same flour, the same dough that you mix to make bread. (TB) **II se démêler** *v.pron.* **1** to untangle o.s., extricate o.s. *J'ai manqué de jamais m'en démêler.* I was almost unable to ever untangle myself. (VM) **2** to get by, manage *Je parle bien en anglais, vous connais, je veux dire assez pour me démêler,* GET BY. I speak English well, you know, I mean enough to get by. (LF) <***Loc:*** LA, LF, TB, VM, Da84>

démêloir [demɛlwar, demɛ̃nwar] *n.m.* comb, large-toothed comb *Le démêloir est bien propre.* The comb is quite clean. (AV) <***Loc:*** AV>

démembré, **-e** [demɑ̃bre] *adj.* maimed, crippled, lame *Il est démembré de sa jambe.* He is lame in one leg. (VM) <***Loc:*** VM>

démembrement [demɑ̃brəmɑ̃] *n.m.* dismemberment <***Loc:*** Da84>

déménagement [demɛ̃naʒmɑ̃] *n.m.* moving, relocation <***Loc:*** Da84>

déménager [demɛ̃naʒe, demaʒe] **I** *v.tr.* to move (a domicile, business, building) *Ils ont déménagé la halle l'autre bord du chemin.* They moved the slaughterhouse across the street. (LA) **II** *v.intr.* to move, relocate, change residences *Je m'ai marié et là j'ai déménagé à Baton Rouge et dans ce temps-ça je restais là, j'avais un char.* I got married and then I moved to Baton Rouge, and in those days I lived there, I had a car. (IB) <***Loc:*** IB, LA, SB, TB, Da84>

démenti [demɑ̃ti] *n.m.* denial, contradiction <***Loc:*** Da84>

démentir [demɑ̃tir] **I** *v.tr.* to deny, contradict, belie *Il est tout le temps après me démentir.* He is always contradicting me. (VM) **II se démentir** *v.pron.* to contradict o.s. *Ce gros menteur, il se démentit lui-même.* That big liar, he contradicts himself. (VM) <***Loc:*** VM, Da84>

démerder (se) [demærde] *v.pron.* **1** to rid o.s. (of), get rid (of) *Elle s'a démerdé de son mari soûlard.* She got rid of her drunkard of a husband. (VM) **2** to extricate o.s. (from), get o.s. out (of) *Il s'a bien démerdé de son tracas.* He really got out of trouble. (LA) *T'as réussi de t'en démerder?* Did you manage to get out of that situation? (VM) **3** to get by, manage *Il commence à bien se démerder avec son* COMPUTER. He's beginning to get by well with his computer. (VM) <***Loc:*** LA, VM, Hi02>

démesuré, -e [deməzyre] *adj.* excessive, out of proportion, unchecked, uncontrolled *Quand il boit, il a une colère démesurée.* When he drinks, he has an excessive temper. (VM) <***Loc:*** VM, Da84>

démettre (se) [demɛt(r)] *v.pron.* **1** to get rid of, cast off *Ça m'embarrasse, mais je peux pas me démettre de ça.* It embarrasses me, but I can't get rid of it. (VM) **2** to do without *Je pourrais jamais me démettre de ça, ça me fait tant de bien.* I could never do without it, it does me so much good. (VM) <***Loc:*** VM>

demeure [dəmœr] *n.f.* abode, home, dwelling ◊ **•à demeure** permanently, always, continually *Il reste là à demeure.* He lives there permanently. (LF) <LF, SM> <***Loc:*** LF, SM, Da84>

demeurer [dəmøre] *v.intr.* to live, reside *Elle demeure plus avec nous-autres depuis elle est mariée, mais elle est tout le temps là pour nous-autres.* She does not live with us anymore since she got married, but she is always there for us. (IB) *Ils demeuraient pas icitte, ils restaient au Texas.* They didn't live here, they lived in Texas. (IB) <***Loc:*** IB, Da84>

demi[1] [dəmi] *adj.* half ◊ **•demi-douzaine** half dozen <Da84> **•demi-frère** half brother ***b*** stepbrother <TB, Da84> **•demi-heure** half hour <Da84> **•demi-journée** half day <Da84> **•demi-sœur** ***a*** half sister ***b*** stepsister <TB, Da84> **•demi-tasse** demitasse, small cup (for coffee) <Da84> <***Loc:*** LF, TB, Da84>

demi[2] [dəmi] *n.m.* **1** half *Ils ont travaillé sur un demi.* They worked on halves (for a half share). (VM) **2** short pants *C'était tout des* SHORT PANTS. *Et là quand tu venais un certain âge, tu mettais tes, ça te mettait, t'appelais ça comme un demi. Eh ben t'étais un petit misérable. Et mon je trouvais que ça me fitterait pas.* [All the young boys] wore short pants. And then when you reached a certain age, you put on your, they gave you, it was called a "demi." And you were quite miserable. I found that it didn't fit me. (LF) <***Loc:*** JE, LF, VM>

démocrate [demokrat] *n.* Democrat, member of the Democratic party <***Loc:*** Da84>

demoiselle[1] [dəmwazɛl] *n.f.* **1** girl, miss, young lady *Il va courtiser sa demoiselle.* He's going to court his lady. (Lv88) **2** daughter <***Loc:*** AV, JE, SB, SJ, SL, SM, Da84, Lv88, Re31>

demoiselle[2] ♦see **moiselle**

démolir [demolir] *v.tr.* to demolish *Ils ont démoli la vieille école.* They demolished the old school. (VM) <***Loc:*** VM, Da84>

démon [demɔ̃] *n.m.* **1** the Devil, Satan **2** demon, devil <***Loc:*** Da84>

démonté, -e [demɔ̃te] *adj.* unwound, wound down **La pendule est démontée.* The clock is unwound. (Da84) <***Loc:*** Da84>

démonter [demɔ̃te] **I** *v.tr.* **1** to dismantle, take apart **Démonter une machine.* To take apart, dismantle a motor. (Da84) **2** to tear down **Démonter une maison.* To tear down a house. (Da84) **II se démonter** *v.pron.* to run down, unwind itself (of a timepiece) *Ma montre s'a démonté.* My watch wound down. (VM) <***Loc:*** VM, Da84>

démoraliser [demoralize] **I** *v.tr* to demoralize *Quand il a perdu son job, ça l'a démoralisé.* When he lost his job, it demoralized him. (VM) **II se démoraliser** *v.pron.* to become upset, become desolate *Après sa femme a mouru, il s'a démoralisé.* After his wife died, he became desolate. (VM) <***Loc:*** VM, Da84>

démoyé, -e [demwaje] *adj.* coming loose, coming apart, falling apart *La roue était démoyée* The wheel was coming loose. (VM) *La chaise était démoyée.* The chair was falling apart. (VM) <***Loc:*** VM>

dempuis ♦see **depuis**

dengué [dɛ̃ge] *n.m./f.* **1** dengue fever, dengue **2** type of flu <***Loc:*** LF, SM, Da84, Lv88>

dénicher [deniʃe e] *v.tr.* to remove from a nest *Dénicher une poule.* To remove a hen from the nest. (LA) <***Loc:*** LA, Da84>

dénier [denje] *v.tr.* to deny **On a besoin d'arrêter de dénier notre héritage et commencer eine bataille pour sauver notre manière de parler français.* We need to stop denying our heritage and start a battle to save our way of speaking French. (Wh83) <***Loc:*** Wh83>

déniquer [denike] **I** *v.tr.* **1** to take out of a nest, remove from a nest *J'ai eu de la peine à déniquer la poule pour avoir les œufs.* I had trouble removing the hen from the nest to get the eggs. (VM) **2** to remove from a comfortable place or situation *J'ai pas voulu déniquer les enfants à ce matin. Il faisait trop froid.* I didn't want to get the kids up this morning. It was too cold. (LA) **3** to force or cause to move out *Ça m'a pris un temps pour les déniquer de là.* It took me a while to get them to move out of there. (VM) **II se déniquer** *v.pron.*

to move o.s., get out of the way *Dénique-toi, j'ai pour faire le lit.* Move, I've got to make the bed. (VM) <***Loc:*** EV, IB, JE, LA, SL, SM, TB, VM, Da84, Lv88, Ph36>

déniveler [denivəle] *v.tr.* to make unlevel *L'ouragan a dénivelé ma maison.* The hurricane made my house unlevel. (VM) <***Loc:*** VM, Da84>

dénoncer [denɔ̃se] *v.tr.* to denounce *Le témoin l'a dénoncé devant le juge. The* witness denounced him before the judge. (VM) <***Loc:*** VM, Da84>

dénouer [denue] *v.tr.* to untangle, unravel *Mam a dénoué mes cheveux.* Mama untangled my hair. (VM) <***Loc:*** VM, Da84>

dent [dɑ̃] *n.f.* **1** tooth **2** fang **3** cog (in a gear) ◊ **•dent creux** tooth with a cavity <VM> **•dent de herse** harrow tooth, harrow tine <EV> **•dent de sagesse** wisdom tooth <Da84> **•dent d'œil** eyetooth <VM> **•dents fausses {postiches} / fausses dents** false teeth <IB, Da84> **•avoir une dent contre qqn** to hold s.t. against, have a grudge against s.o. <AV, La99> <***Loc:*** AV, IB, LF, SB, SL, TB, VM, Da84, Hi02, La99>

dentelle [dɑ̃tɛl] *n.f.* lace <***Loc:*** Da84, Wh83>

dentelure [dɑ̃tlyr] *n.f.* set of teeth *Alle a une jolie dentelure.* She has a nice set of teeth. (AV) <***Loc:*** AV, SJ>

dentisse ♦see **dentiste**

dentiste (dentisse) [dɑ̃tis(t)] *n.m.* dentist <***Loc:*** LF, SM, VM, Da84, Hi02, Lv88, Re31>

dépareillé, -e [depareje] *adj.* **1** unpaired, unmatched, mismatched, forming an incomplete set **2** of many colors or designs *Alle a choisi des étoffes pour faire une couverte tout dépareillée.* She chose pieces of fabric to make a motley quilt. (TB) <***Loc:*** SM, TB, Da84>

déparler [deparle] *v.intr.* to talk deliriously, rave, talk nonsense *Pendant il avait la fièvre il déparlait.* While he had the fever, he was talking deliriously. (SM) <***Loc:*** AV, EV, LF, SB, SJ, SL, SM, TB, VM, Da84, Lv88, Ph36>

départ [depar] *n.m.* departure <***Loc:*** Da84>

département [departəmɑ̃] *n.m.* department **Le CIA, le Département de l'Etat ou le Kremlin.* The CIA, the State Department, or the Kremlin. (Wh83) <***Loc:*** Da84, Wh83>

départir [departir] *v.intr.* to depart, go away, leave *Il départ de bonne heure.* He leaves early. (SB) <***Loc:*** JE, SB>

dépassé [depase] *adj.* past, after *Quand-même il est dépassé quatre heures, je l'espère toujours.* Although it's after four o'clock, I'm still waiting for him. (VM) *Juste dépassé l'hôpital.* Just past the hospital. (EV) <***Loc:*** EV, VM>

dépasser [depase] *v.tr.* **1** to pass, go by *Avant tu dépasses le chemin de l'île, en allant là-bas.* Before you pass the road to the island, going down that way. (TB) **2** to go beyond, exceed **Dépasser la limite.* To exceed the limit. (Da84) **II** *v.intr.* to show, stick out (e.g. of an undergarment) *Ta jupe dépasse.* Your slip is showing. (VM) <***Loc:*** TB, VM, Da84>

dépêche [depɛʃ] *n.f.* hurry ◊ **•à la dépêche** in a hurry <Da84> <***Loc:*** Da84>

dépêcher [depeʃe] **I** *v.tr.* to hurry *Sa mère était après essayer de le dépêcher, mais il dormait debout.* His mother was trying to hurry him, but he was sleeping standing up. (LA) **II se dépêcher** *v.pron.* to hurry up **Ça fait, quand ils ont donné son* STEAK, *il s'est dépêché à manger vite.* So, when they gave him his steak, he hurried up to eat quickly. (EV, An94) ◊ **•dépêche-toi!** hurry up! <Da84> <***Loc:*** EV, LA, An94, Da84, Hi02>

dépeigner [depẽje] *v.tr.* to uncomb, dishevel, disarrange the hair of *Le coup de vent l'a tout dépeigné.* The gust of wind messed up his hair. (LA) <***Loc:*** LA, LF, Da84, Re31>

dépeindre [depɛ̃n, depɛ̃d(r)] *v.tr.* to describe, picture **Il dit, "J'ai perdu une vache." Et il dépeint la vache, à qui elle ressemblait.* He says, "I lost a cow." And he describes the cow, what it looked like. (EV, An94) <***Loc:*** EV, An94, Da84>

dépendable [depɑ̃dab(l)] *adj.* dependable, worthy of trust *Ces deux là sont pas du tout dépendables.* Those two are not at all dependable. (LA) <***Loc:*** LA, Lv88>

dépendance [depɑ̃dɑ̃s] *n.f.* dependence <***Loc:*** Da84>

dépendant [depɑ̃dɑ̃] *adj.* dependent, depending *Je connais pas si je vas aller, c'est dépendant qui sera là avec nous-autres.* I don't know if I'm going, it's dependent on who will be there with us. (LA) **Il avait ein homme qui s'est rebouté dessur et il l'a cassé ou tchué [=tué], en dépendant comment tu le regardes.* A man stumbled over it and broke it or killed it, depending on how you look at it. (Wh83) <***Loc:*** LA, Da84, Wh83>

dépendeur [depɑ̃dœr] *n.m.* one who unhooks s.t. ◊ **•dépendeur d'andouille** one who does work that requires little effort <La99> <***Loc:*** La99>

dépendre [depɑ̃n, depɑ̃d(r)] *v.intr.* to depend *Ça dépend.* It depends. (Lv88) *Il n-a un tas du monde qui dépend de ça pour leur vie.* There are a lot of people who depend on that for a living. (SM) ◊ **•dépendre dessus {sur}** ***a*** to depend on, rely on, count on **On peut dépendre sur lui.* One can count on him. (Re31) *Ça se soûle trop, tu peux pas dépendre dessus eux-autres.* They get drunk too much, you can't depend on them. (Lv88) ***b*** to be dependent on *Si un homme avait un garçon, et il faisait récolte, et il dépendait dessus son garçon à faire récolte, il a* DEFER, *il a pas été.* If a man had a son, and he did farming, and he depended on his son for farming, he got a deferment, he didn't go [to war]. (LF) <IB, LF, SM, Lv88> <***Loc:*** AV, EV, IB, LF, SL, SM, TB, Da84, Lv88, Ph36, Re31>

dépense [depɑ̃s] *n.f.* **1** pantry *Quand on pouvait venir de l'école et mame était pas là, on allait dans la dépense [...] on se cassait un grand bout de saucisse.* When we could come back from school and Mom wasn't there, we would go into the pantry. We would break off a big piece of sausage for ourselves. (AC) **2** small room or building used as a pantry, mudroom, laundry room, etc. **3** consumption, use *Je fais des tomates juste pour ma dépense.* I grow tomatoes just for my own use. (Lv88) **4** expense **Ein bon jardin peut diminuer les dépenses de manger.* A good garden can reduce eating expenses. (Wh83) ◊ **•faire des dépenses** to incur expenses <Da84> <***Loc:*** AC, AV, EV, LA, SB, VM, Da84, Hi02, Lv88, Ph36, Re31, Wh83>

dépenser [depɑ̃se] *v.tr.* **1** to consume, use, use up *J'ai dépensé toutes les patates.* I used up all the potatoes. (Lv88) **2** to spend (money) **Et si t'avais une belle, t'aurais pas aimé dépenser le dix sous-là sur une autre, tu connais.* And if you had a girlfriend, you wouldn't like to spend that ten cents on another, you know. (VM, An84) <***Loc:*** VM, An84, Da84, Hi02, Lv88>

dépenseur ♦see **dépensier**

dépensier (**dépenseur**) [depɑ̃sje, depɑ̃sœr] *adj.* spendthrift, wasteful <***Loc:*** Da84>

dépérir [deperir] *v.intr.* **1** to perish, waste away, wither *Si je m'aurais pas occupé de mon figuier cette année, il aurait dépéri.* If I had not taken care of my fig tree this year, it would have withered. (LA) **2** to rot, deteriorate *Et ça c'est un vieux casse-tête. Le manche sur ça aussite a dépéri, la vieillesse je pense.* And that's an old hatchet. The handle on that has rotted too, old age I guess. (LF) <***Loc:*** LA, LF, Da84>

dépétrir [depetrir] *v.tr.* to disentengle *Le poisson armé s'a dépétri de la seine.* The garfish untangled itself from the seine net. (VM) <***Loc:*** VM>

dépicoter [depikote] *v.tr.* to clean by picking out foreign particles (from rice, beans, etc.) *Quand ça mouillait, ça passait les après-midi à dépicoter les fèves.* When it rained, they spent the afternoons picking the particles out of the beans. (LA) <***Loc:*** LA, Lv88>

depis ♦see **dépit**

dépit (**depis**) [depi, dəpi] *n.m.* **1** bad condition, ruined or worsened state **2** depression, state of being depressed *Le dépit l'a pris.* He got depressed. (VM) ◊ **•être au dépit** to be in bad condition (physical or moral) *Il est au dépit.* He is in bad shape. (VM) <VM, Lv88> **•prendre un dépit / tomber en dépit** to go into a depression **Ein jour il a pris ein dépit et il a decidé de se détruire.* One day he got into a depression and decided to commit suicide. (Wh83) <Wh83> **•s'en aller au dépit** to go to pot, go to ruin, get worse <Da84, Lv88> <***Loc:*** VM, Da84, Lv88, Wh83>

déplacer [deplase] *v.tr.* **1** to misplace, displace **Confiance déplacée.* Misplaced confidence. (Da84) **2** to dislocate *La petite fille a déplacé sa clavicule.* The little girl dislocated her collarbone. (VM) <***Loc:*** SM, VM, Da84>

déplaire [deplær] *v.intr.* to displease, offend *Il faisait tout ce qu'il pouvait faire pour pas déplaire à Mame.* He did all he could to avoid displeasing Mama. (EV) <***Loc:*** EV, Da84>

déplaisant, -e [deplezɑ̃, -ɑ̃t] *adj.* unpleasant, disagreeable *C'était pas déplaisant, ça.* That wasn't at all unpleasant. (VM) <***Loc:*** VM, Da84>

déplanchonner [deplɑ̃ʃɔ̃ne] *v.tr.* to remove flooring from *Mon cousin est après déplanchonner ma galerie asteur.* My cousin is removing the flooring from my porch right now. (VM) <***Loc:*** VM>

déplisser [deplise] *v.tr.* **1** to unpleat, remove pleats from (a garment) **2** to unwrinkle *Il pourra pas déplisser son linge avant l'heure pour la messe.* He won't be able to unwrinkle his clothes in time for Mass. (LA) <***Loc:*** LA, Da84>

déployer [deplwɑje, depleje] *v.tr.* to unfold, unbend *Il avait pas fini de déployer le papier quand il a compris quoi ça voulait.* He had not finished unfolding the paper when he understood what they wanted. (LA) <***Loc:*** JE, LA, TB, Da84, Lv88>

déplumer (**éplumer**) [deplyme, eplyme] **I** *v.tr.* **1** to pluck feathers from *Il a éplumé sa poule.* He plucked his chicken. (SM) **2** to skin (e.g. one's knee) *Il a déplumé la peau de son bras.* He skinned his arm. (SM) **II** *v.intr.* **1** to shed hair or skin *Tu déplumes où tu as été brulé du soleil.* You are peeling where you were sunburnt. (VM) **2** to peel (of the skin) *Sa peau a déplumé dans le soleil.* His skin peeled in the sun. (LF) <***Loc:*** EV, LF, SM, VM, Da84, Ph36>

dépoitraillé, -e [depwatraje, depotraje] *adj.* with chest exposed, shirtless or having one's shirt unbuttoned *Tu vas pas t'assire à table tout dépoitraillé comme ça.* You're not going to sit at the table with your chest all exposed like that. (VM) <***Loc:*** VM>

dépoitrailler [depwatraje, depotraje] **I** *v.tr.* to bare the chest of (by removing or unbuttoning the shirt) *Je l'ai dépoitraillé.* I exposed his chest. (SL) **II se dépoitrailler** *v.pron.* to expose the chest or breast, go shirtless *Jean se dépotraille tout le temps.* Jean goes shirtless all the time. (SM) <***Loc:*** SL, SM>

déportation [depɔrtasjɔ̃] *n.f.* deportation **Les homards et les Cadiens aviont resté ensemb' en paix des siec' de temps jusqu'à la déportation.* Lobsters and Cajuns had lived together in peace for centuries until the deportation. (Wh83) <***Loc:*** Da84, Wh83>

déporter [dipɔrte] *v.tr.* to deport, banish *Ils ont une liste de tout le monde qu'a été déporté de d'là, et eux-autres a échappé dans différentes parties de les États-Unis.* They have a list of everyone who was deported from there, and they escaped to different parts of the United States. (TB) <***Loc:*** TB, Da84>

déposer [depoze] *v.tr.* **1** to put down, lay down *A l'heure du service, ils transportont le corps à l'église et ensuite au cimetière où il est déposé dans la fosse sous un lit de fleurs.* At the time of the service, they will transport the body to the church and then to the cemetery where it is laid in the grave underneath a bed of flowers. (VM) **2** to depose, take a deposition from *Déposer quelqu'un en cour.* To depose someone in court. (LA) <***Loc:*** LA, VM, Da84>

déposition [depozisjɔ̃] *n.f.* deposition, testimony <***Loc:*** Da84>

dépôt [depo, dipo] *n.m.* **1** wharf, pier, landing-stage **2** depot, railroad station, terminus *Mon ami va descendre du char au dépot à Ibéria.* My friend is getting off the train at the station in [New] Iberia. (SM) **3** abscess, pus pocket <***Loc:*** AV, EV, IB, JE, LF, SB, SL, SM, TB, VM, Da84, Lv88, Ph36>

dépouiller [depuje] **I** *v.tr.* to strip, rob *Avant qu'il s'a aperçu de quelque chose, ils l'avaient tout dépouillé.* Before he noticed anything, they had robbed him of everything. (LA) **II se dépouiller** *v.pron.* to strip, undress o.s. *O mon cher frère, me laisseras-tu noyer? —Non, non, ma sœur, je suis à me dépouiller.* Oh my dear brother, will you let me drown? —No, no, my sister, I am undressing. (VM, ch: *Le pont de Nantes*) <***Loc:*** LA, VM, Da84>

déprécier [depresje] *v.tr.* to depreciate, lose value *Quand ils ont coupé le chêne devant la maison, ça a déprécié sa valeur.* When they cut down the oak in front of the house, it depreciated its value. (VM) <***Loc:*** VM, Da84>

déprendre [deprɑ̃n, deprɑ̃d(r)] **I** *v.tr.* **1** to loose, set free, liberate, release (an animal from a trap) **Il a dépris le lapin d'après le* TAR MAN. He set the rabbit free, according to the tar man. (An77) *Y'a pas à déprendre, des fois il se coupe la patte.* There's nothing to retrieve, sometimes it [the animal caught in the trap] cuts its foot off. (Lv88) **2** to undo, disengage (a trap) *C'est dur à déprendre les pièges.* It's hard to disengage traps. (Lv88) **II se déprendre** *v.pron.* to get loose, free o.s. *Lapin pouvait pas se déprendre.* Rabbit could not get free. (LA) <***Loc:*** LA, An77, Da84, Lv88>

dépression [diprɛsjɔ̃] *n.f.* **1** economic depression **2** the Great Depression *Ça c'était dans le temps de la dépression et tout ça-là, y avait pas un cinq sous dans le vaisseau.* That was in the time of the Depression and all, there wasn't a nickel in the jar. (TB) <***Loc:*** TB, Da84>

depuis (**dempuis, depus**) [depi, dɑ̃pɥi, dɑ̃py, dəpy] *prep.* since, from, for (an amount of time) GOODBYE *la jolie fille. Tu m'as promis de me marier depuis le temps que t'étais petite.* Goodbye pretty girl. You promised to marry me since the time you were a child. (TB, ch) *Il a triplé sa rente de coton depuis l'année passée.* He tripled his cotton profits since last year. (VM) *Depuis deux semaines il est couché avec ça.* For two weeks he's been in bed with that [illness]. (VM) *J'ai le nez bouché depuis une semaine.* I've had a stopped-up nose for a week. (LA) ◊ **•depuis** (**que**) ***a*** since *Il est bien pour vivre depuis on a trouvé l'huile sur sa terre.* He's well off since oil was found on his land. (SM) *Il a blêmi beaucoup depuis qu'il a tombé malade.* He has turned very pale since he got sick. (LA) ***b*** because *Depus toi tu restes, moi je vas rester aussite.* Because you're staying, I'll stay too. (VM) *Depuis que je vas pas au bal je connais pus les coconnages.* Since I don't go to the dances, I don't know the gossip. (VM) <IB, LA, SB, SL, SM, TB, VM> <***Loc:*** EV, IB, IV, LA, LF, SB, SL, SM, TB, VM, An94, Da84, Hi02>

député (**débité**) [depyte, debite] *n.m.* deputy <***Loc:*** LF, VM, Da84, Lv88>

déraciner [derasine] *v.tr.* to uproot *Ils ont eu mille misères à déraciner les arbres à poule.* They had a hard time uprooting the Chinese tallow trees. (LA) **Ein Cadien, c'est comme ein chêne qui peut pas êt' deraciné. Il a défriché ein désert et fondé son pays.* A Cajun is like an oak that cannot be uprooted. He has cleared a piece of land and founded his country. (ThCa: *Mille misères*) <***Loc:*** LA, Da84, ThCa>

déraillement [derajmɑ̃] *n.m.* derailment <***Loc:*** Da84>

dérailler (**déreiller**) [deraje, dereje] *v.intr.* to derail, run off track *Le char a déreillé au ras de Cade.* The train derailed near Cade. (SM) <***Loc:*** SM, VM, Da84>

déralinguer [deralɛ̃ge] *v.tr.* to tear, put (a net) out of working order *La seine a été déralinguée quand l'homme l'a accrochée dans le fond de la mer.* The fishing net got torn when the man got it caught on the sea floor. (TB) <***Loc:*** TB>

dérangement [derɑ̃ʒmɑ̃] *n.m.* **1** diarrhea, loose bowels *Il avait mangé trop de figues et ça lui avait donné un mauvais dérangement.* He had eaten too many figs and it had given him a terrible case of diarrhea. (LA) **2** disturbance, bother, annoyance *Le constable aurait pas manqué le plus petit dérangement dans la place.* The bouncer would not have missed the least disturbance in the place. (LA) **3** expulsion from Acadia, exodus *Ils n'ont pas pris part dans le dérangement.* They didn't take part in the exodus [from Acadia]. (SL) ◊ **•le Grand Dérangement** the forcible expulsion of the French-origin population in Acadia (now Nova Scotia) by the English in 1755 <Hi02, Lv88> <***Loc:*** LA, SL, Da84, Hi02, Lv88>

déranger [derɑ̃ʒe] **I** *v.tr.* to disturb, bother, annoy *Quand il arrivait dans les petites heures de la nuit, ça dérangeait toute la famille.* When he came in during the wee hours of the morning, it would disturb the whole family. (LA) **II se déranger** *v.pron.* **1** to take the trouble, go to the bother (of doing s.t.) *Dérange-toi pas. Je vas le faire moi-même.* Don't bother. I'll do it myself. (LA) **2** to throw o.s. out of place, get out of kilter, dislocate a part of one's body *Alle vient qu'alle se dérange des fois après se baisser le bras, quelque chose comme ça. Et ça dérange le bébé, eh ben je traite pour ça et ça vient à* BACK *droite en place.* It happens that she [a pregnant woman] throws herself out of place sometimes while lowering her arm, something like that. And that moves the baby out of position, and I treat for that and it goes back in place. (TB) **3** to take leave of one's senses (e.g. under the influence of alcohol) *Moi je m'ai jamais soûlé de ma vie. [...] Quand tu vas te déranger tu connais p'us qui t'après faire, tu connais p'us qui tu dis.* I've never gotten drunk in my life. When you take leave of your senses you don't know what you're doing, you don't know what you're saying. (TB) ◊ •**déranger le corps** to cause diarrhea *Quand je mange trop de figues, ça me dérange le corps.* When I eat too many figs, it gives me diarrhea. (VM) <VM> <***Loc:*** LA, TB, VM, Da84, Lv88>

dérater [derate] *v.tr.* to tear up, rend, damage *Les chiens avont dératé la cour.* The dogs have torn up the yard. (VM) <***Loc:*** VM>

dérégler [deregle] *v.tr.* to upset the accurate and proper function of (a mechanism) *Le fil s'a arraché et ça a déréglé ma machine.* The wire came loose and it put my motor out of time. (VM) <***Loc:*** VM, Da84>

déreiller ♦see **dérailler**

dérêner [derẽne] *v.tr.* to loosen the reins of, slacken the reins of *Dérêne les chevaux et quitte-les boire.* Loosen the horses' reins and let them drink. (VM) <***Loc:*** IB, JE, SB, TB, VM>

dérespectable [derespɛktab(l)] *adj.* disrespectful **La conversation en sortant du cimitière est souvent pour ceux-là qu'est pas venus, parceque c'est considéré dérespectable, pareil comme pas faire tes Pâques.* The conversation when leaving the cemetery is often about those who didn't come, because it's considered disrespectful, just like not observing Easter. (Wh83) <***Loc:*** Wh83>

dérider [deride] *v.tr.* to smooth out wrinkles in the skin of *Le Botox lui a déridé la figure.* Botox unwrinkled his face. (VM) <***Loc:*** VM, Da84>

dérive [deriv] *adj.* ◊ •**bois dérive** driftwood <JE> <***Loc:*** JE>

dériver [derive] *v.intr.* to be weak, lack strength <***Loc:*** Pe37>

dernier, -ière[1] [dærnje, darnje, -jær] *adj.* **1** last, final, ultimate **Il dit, "Fini. Et c'est la dernière fois."* He says, "Finished. And it's the last time." (SM, An94) *Il l'a attrapé en tournant dans le dernier quart de mile.* He overtook him turning into the last quarter-mile. (LA) **Quand on a jeté le dernier caillou de terre-là, Boulé a sauté à côté.* When he threw the last stone, Boulé jumped aside. (EV, An94) **2** last, most recent *Et là depuis les dernières années, 15, 20 ans, ils ont commencé à faire des masques qui représentent toute espèce de chose, le président, ou des macaques.* And then in the last 15 or 20 years, they've begun making masks that look like all sorts of things, the president, or monkeys. (LF) **3** last in rank, lowest *Il a tout le temps été dernier dans sa classe.* He was always last in his class. (EV) <***Loc:*** EV, LA, LF, SM, TB, An94, Da84, Hi02>

dernier, -ière[2] [dærnje, darnje, -jær] *n.* last one **Il y avait une famille, ils avaient plusieurs enfants et le dernier, ils appelaient Petit Poucet.* There was a family, they had several children and the last one, they called Petit Poucet. (LA, An94) ◊ •**avant-dernier** second to last, next to last *On a été élevé à six et moi j'étais l'avant-dernière.* Six of us were raised together and I was the second to last. (LF) <LF> •**en dernier** in the end **En dernier, il avait une grosse CROSS-TIE.* In the end, he had a big cross-tie. (EV, An94) <EV, An94> <***Loc:*** EV, LA, LF, An94, Da84, Hi02>

dernièrement [dærnjærmɑ̃] *adv.* lately, recently, of late *Si ta machine casse, tu vas rester là-dedans. Là dernièrement ils ont des RADIO et tu peux appeler.* If your motor breaks [in your boat], you'll stay in there. Now lately they have radios and you can call [for help]. (TB) **Po-Pop, est-ce que t'a pas attendu les nouvelles dernièrement?* Grandpa, haven't you been keeping up with the news lately? (Wh83) <***Loc:*** EV, TB, Da84, Wh83>

dérober ♦see **érober**

dérocher [deroʃe] *v.tr.* to remove fragments (such as pieces of wood, brick, gravel, etc.) from <***Loc:*** VM>

déroller ♦see **dérouler**

dérouillement [derujmɑ̃] *n.m.* rust removal <***Loc:*** Da84>

dérouiller [deruje] *v.tr.* to remove rust from *Il aura du mal à dérouiller ces vieilles charrues.* He's going to have a hard time removing the rust from those old plows. (LA) <***Loc:*** LA, Da84>

dérouler (**déroller**) [derule, derole] **I** *v.tr.* to unroll *Il a déroulé le nouveau fil au long de la vieille barrière.* He unrolled the new wire along the old fence. (VM) **II se dérouler** *v.pron.* to become unrolled **Le rouleau s'a déroulé.* The roll came unrolled. (Da84) <***Loc:*** VM, Da84>

dérouter [derute] *v.tr.* to disappoint, disconcert *Ça me déroute quand je te trouve pas là.* It disconcerts me when I don't find you there. (VM) <***Loc:*** VM>

derrick [derik, derek, derɛk] *n.m.* **1** derrick, (offshore) oil drilling derrick *Les compagnies à l'huile a commencé à venir et ça a amené tous ces gros derricks là.* The oil companies began arriving and they brought all those big derricks. (TB) **2** derrick, hoisting apparatus for weighing and loading sugar cane *Il a halé ses cannes au derrick.* He hauled his cane to the derrick. (VM) <***Loc:*** JE, LA, SL, SM, TB, VM, Lv88>

derrière[1] [dærjær, dærijær] *n.m.* **1** behind, derriere, back side, rump, back end *Il t'a piqué dans le derrière?* He [the rooster] pecked you in the behind? (TB) **Le derrière de le premier joint du pouce.* The back of the first knuckle of the thumb. (Wh83) **2** stern ◊ •**derrière du bateau** back of a boat *Le derrière du bateau est plutôt carré plutôt que pointu.* The back of the boat is square rather than pointed. (LF) <LF, TB> <***Loc:*** JE, LF, TB, Da84, Lv88, Wh83>

derrière[2] [dærjær, dærijær] *prep.* behind, in back of *Il gardait ses chevaux derrière la maison de son beau-père.* He kept his horses behind his father-in-law's house. (LA) ◊ •**aller par derrière qqn** to go after s.o. *Et si l'homme qu'était marié s'en allait et qu'il a assayé de pas supporter sa famille, les hommes de la campagne allaient par derrière lui.* And if the man who was married went off and tried to not support his family, the men of the countryside went after him. (TB) <TB> **•être derrière qqn** ***a*** to torment or nag s.o. ***b*** to be out to get s.o. **Ils sont derrière Jesse parce qu'il sort avec la belle de ce bougre.* They're after Jesse because he's going out with that guy's girlfriend. (LA, An84) <AV, IB, LA, An84, La99> <***Loc:*** AV, EV, IB, LA, TB, An84, Da84, Hi02, La99>

dès (**drès**) [de, dre] *prep.* as early as, as soon as *On l'a fait drès le lendemain.* We did it as early as the next day. (TB) ◊ **•dès que / desque / drès que** ***a*** when *Mais faut que tu fais attention dès que tu vas parler avec son pape.* But you have to be careful when you talk to his dad. (LF) *Dès que j'avais huit ans mon père nous a tout déménagés en bas du bayou.* When I was eight my father moved us all down the bayou. (LF) **Ça fait, dès que le bougre a regardé, tous les autres étaient* GONE. *Ça fait, il a* GONE *aussi.* So, when the guy looked, all the others were gone. So he left too. (SM, An94) ***b*** as soon as **Il va venir desqu'il aura fini.* He will come as soon as he is through. (Da84) *Drès qu'il l'a bu, il a tombé malade.* As soon as he drank it, he fell sick. (VM) **Ils ont commencé à fouiller. Et dès qu'ils ont fouillé un bout, il y avait un gros bœuf qui s'en venait en travers de le bois avec la flamme qui lui sortait du nez.* They started to dig. And as soon as they dug a bit, there was a big bull that came from across the woods with flames coming out of his nose. (SM, An94) ***c*** from the time, from the moment *Dès que nous-autres on a commencé l'école on parlait juste français.* From the time we started school we spoke only French. (LF) ***d*** as long as *C'est magnifique à rester ici dès qu'y a pas d'ouragan, mais dès qu'il y a des ouragans c'est pas trop* NICE. It's wonderful to live here as long as there are no hurricanes, but as soon as there are hurricanes it's not too nice. (JE) ***e*** until *Et le vent venait ça sifflait, et là ç'a pas pu connaître comment dès que la clarté du jour s'a fait le lendemain le dommage que ça ç'avait fait.* And the wind came, it was blowing, and they couldn't know until daylight broke the next day the damage it had done. (LF) <EV, IB, JE, LF, SM, TB, VM, An94, Da84, Ph36> <***Loc:*** EV, IB, JE, LF, SM, TB, VM, An94, Da84, Ph36>

désabrier [dezabrije] **I** *v.tr.* to uncover, expose *Elle a désabrié son petit parce qu'elle trouvait qu'il faisait chaud.* She uncovered her child because she found that it was hot. (LA) **II se désabrier** *v.pron.* to uncover oneself *Il s'a désabrié au milieu de la nuit.* He uncovered himself in the middle of the night. (LA) <***Loc:*** JE, LA, Lv88>

désaccord [dezakɔr] *n.m.* disagreement, discord <***Loc:*** Da84>

désaccorder [dezakɔrde] **I** *v.tr.* to untune *Quand il a échappé son violon, ça l'a tout désaccordé.* When he dropped his violin, it untuned it. (LA) **II** *v.intr.* to disagree, be at variance *C'était deux frères, mais c'était proche tout le temps désaccordé.* They were two brothers, but they were nearly always in disagreement. (LA) <***Loc:*** LA, Da84>

désagréable [dezagreab(l)] *adj.* unpleasant, disagreeable, distasteful *C'était un homme qu'était jamais, jamais désagréable.* He was a man who was never disagreeable. (LA) <***Loc:*** LA, Da84>

désagrément [dezagremɑ̃] *n.m.* **1** unpleasantness, disagreeableness **2** nuisance <***Loc:*** Da84>

désamain (**démain**) [dezɑ̃mɛ̃, demɛ̃] *n.m./f.* ◊ **•à (la) désamain / à la démain / au désamain** inconvenient *C'est trop à la desamain pour me rendre là.* It's too inconvenient for me to get over there. (VM) *Tout quelque chose est à la desamain dans la campagne.* Everything is inconvenient in the country. (VM) *Cette tablette est à désamain tant elle est haute.* That shelf is so high that it is unhandy. (IB) <IB, LF, SL, SM, TB, VM, Da84, Lv88, Pe37> <***Loc:*** IB, LF, SL, SM, TB, VM, Da84, Lv88, Pe37>

désappointement [dezapwɛ̃tmɑ̃] *n.m.* disappointment <***Loc:*** Da84>

désappointer [dezapwɛ̃te] *v.tr.* to disappoint *J'étais pas intéressé d'aller, et là, ma maman aurait été beaucoup désappointée.* I was not interested in going, and besides, my mother would've been very disappointed. (AV) <***Loc:*** AV, Da84, Hi02, Lv88>

désarmer [dezarme] *v.tr.* **1** to disarm *Il a désarmé son voisin avant qu'il se tire lui-même.* He disarmed his neighbor before he shot himself. (VM) **2** to uncock (a gun) <***Loc:*** VM, Da84>

désastre [dezast(r)] *n.m.* disaster <***Loc:*** Da84>

désatisfaction (**dissatisfaction**) [desatisfaksjɔ̃, disatisfaksjɔ] *n.f.* dissatisfaction <***Loc:*** Da84>

désatteler ♦see **dételer**

désavantage [dezavɑ̃taʒ] *n.m.* disadvantage, drawback <***Loc:*** Da84>

descendant [desɑ̃dɑ̃] *n.m.* descendant <***Loc:*** Da84, Wh83>

descendre [desɑ̃n, desɑ̃d(r)] **I** *v.tr.* **1** to take down *Après qu'on aura nettoyé la chasse, on va te les descendre.* After we clean the game we killed, we'll take them [the trunks] down for you. (ThCa: *La douce réunion*) **2** to go down, come down (a hill, a river, stairs, etc.) **J'était après descendre les éscaliers.* I was coming down the stairs. (Wh83) **Y z'ont dû [...] descend' le Mississipi dedans des 'tits bateaux.* They had to descend the Mississippi in small boats. (ThCa: *Mille misères*) **II** *v.intr.* **1** to descend, go down *Tu connais cette vieille maison en bas, avec la cheminée en brique? Y a un canard qui descend tous les jours dedans ça.* Do you know that old house down the bayou, with the brick chimney? There's a duck that goes down in it every day. (TB) **Au lieu de descendre, il a pris à monter.* Instead of going down [the trail], he began to go up. (AC, An94) **Ça fait qu'y z'ont descendu jusqu'à la Nouvelle Acadie, la Louisiane.* So they came down to New Acadia, Louisiana. (Wh83) **2** to get off, to get out (of a vehicle) *Quand on a descendu du grand char à Crowley un tireur de portraits a fait un* SNAPSHOT *de* *nous-autres ensemble et il l'a donné à Huey Long.* When we got out of the train in Crowley, a photographer took a snapshot of us together and he gave it to Huey Long. (ThCa: *Messieurs, mesdames*) **3** to be descended from (an ancestor) *Il descend des Mouton de Lafayette.* He comes from the Moutons from Lafayette. (LA) <***Loc:*** AC, JD, SL, TB, An94, Da84, ThCa, Wh83>

descente [desɑ̃t] *n.f.* **1** descent, downward slope **2** hernia <***Loc:*** SM, VM, Da84, Lv88>

description [deskripsjɔ̃] *n.f.* description <***Loc:*** Da84>

désembrouiller (se) [dezɑ̃bruje] *v.pron.* to end a feud *Elle a fait des démarches pour se désembrouiller avec sa sœur.* She took steps to break the feud with her sister. (VM) <***Loc:*** AV, VM, Da84, La99>

désempêtrer [dezɑ̃petre] *v.tr.* to disentengle, remove hobbles *Va désempétrer le cheval. On a besoin de partir.* Go remove the hobbles from the horse. We have to leave. (LA) <***Loc:*** LA, Da84>

désenferger [dezɑ̃færʒe] *v.tr.* to unfetter (a horse) *Jean-Sot a oublié de désenferger son cheval avant de monter.* Jean-Sot forgot to unfetter his horse before mounting. (LA) <***Loc:*** JE, LA, VM>

désenfler [dezɑ̃fle] **I** *v.tr.* to reduce the swelling of *Mets de la glace, ça va désenfler ta figure.* Put some ice on that, it will reduce the swelling on your face. (VM) **II se désenfler** *v.pron.* to become less swollen *Tracasse-toi pas. Ça va se désenfler avant demain.* Don't worry. That will be less swollen before tomorrow. (LA) <***Loc:*** LA, VM, Da84>

désennuyer [dezɑ̃nɥije] *v.tr.* to amuse, cheer up *Bien merci d'avoir eu venu. Votre visite m'a bien désennuyé.* Thanks for coming. Your visit has really cheered me up. (LA) <***Loc:*** LA, VM, Da84>

désenterrer [dezɑ̃tere] *v.tr.* to unearth, exhume, dig up *Ils ont eu pour désenterrer mon père pour examiner son corps.* They had to exhume my father to examine his body. (VM) <***Loc:*** SM, TB, VM>

désentortiller [dezɑ̃tɔrtije] *v.tr.* to untangle, unravel, untwist *Désentortiller un fil autour d'un poteau.* To unravel a wire around a post. (VM) <***Loc:*** VM, Da84>

déserage [dezeraʒ, deseraʒ] *n.m.* clearing (of land, e.g. for cultivation) <***Loc:*** JE, VM, Lv88>

déserer (**desserrer**) [dezere, desere, dereze, deleze] *v.tr.* **1** to clear (land, e.g. for cultivation) *Ils ont déséré un tas de bois.* They cleared a lot of forest. (Lv88) **Petit Jean s'avait engagé avec un géant. Le vieux diable, on l'appelait. Et le diable arrachait des arbres, c'était pour desserrer le bois.* Petit Jean had hired a giant, the old devil, they called him. And the devil pulled up trees, it was to clear the woods. (An94) **2** to remove (weeds, etc.) from land intended for cultivation **C'est plutot le temps pour labourer, piocher et amortir des bois et désserrer des grands herbes.* It is rather the time to plow, hoe, and deaden trees and clear out weeds. (Wh83) <***Loc:*** EV, IB, JE, SM, TB, VM, An94, Da84, Lv88, Ph36, Wh83>

déséreur [dezerœr] *n.m.* **1** one who clears land **2** woodcutter, woodsman <***Loc:*** SM, VM, Lv88>

désert[1]**, -e** [dezær, -ært] *adj.* cleared (of trees, underbrush, etc.) *Un terrain désert.* A cleared lot. (SL) <***Loc:*** Da84>

désert[2] [dezær] *n.m.* **1** cleared land **Ein Cadien, c'est comme ein chêne qui peut pas êt' deraciné. Il a défriché ein désert et fondé son pays.* A Cajun is like an oak that cannot be uprooted. He has cleared a piece of land and founded his country. (ThCa: *Mille misères*) **2** desert **3** wilderness **Le voyage a été dur pour nos ancêt's. Y z'ont dû traverser des déserts, se batt' avec les sauvages et descend' le Missississipi dedans des 'tits bateaux pour arriver icitte à la fin.* The journey was hard for our ancestors. They had to cross wildernesses, fight with Indians, and descend the Mississippi in small boats to finally end up here. (ThCa: *Mille misères*) <***Loc:*** EV, JE, VM, Da84, Lv88, Ph36, ThCa>

déserter [dezærte] *v.tr.* to desert, forsake, abandon *Son mari l'a désertée.* Her husband abandoned her. (VM) <***Loc:*** VM, Da84>

déserteur [dezærtœr] *n.m.* deserter <***Loc:*** Da84>

déserver [dezærve] *v.tr.* to deserve, merit *Il déserve un prix pour ça.* He deserves an award for that. (SB) <***Loc:*** SB>

désespérance [dezesperɑ̃s] *n.f.* despair <***Loc:*** Da84>

désespérer ♦see **désespoirer**

désespoir [dezespwar] *n.m.* despair <***Loc:*** Da84>

désespoiré, -e [dezespware] *adj.* despairing, without hope *Alle était si désespoirée ça faisait pitié de la voir.* She was so despairing that it was pitiful to see her. (VM) <***Loc:*** VM>

désespoirer (**désespérer**) [dezespware, dezespere] **I** *v.tr.* to cause to lose hope *Ça l'a désespoiré quand il a perdu son job.* It caused him to lose hope when he lost his job. (VM) **II** *v.intr.* to despair, lose hope <***Loc:*** VM, Da84>

déshabiller [dezabije] **I** *v.tr.* to undress, remove clothing from *La petite fille a déshabillé ses catins.* The little girl undressed her dolls. (EV) **II se déshabiller** *v.pron.* to undress o.s., strip, disrobe **L'enfant et l'homme a parti pour aller à leur chambre, et tout naturellement, l'enfant s'est déshabillé et mis son linge de nuit plus vite que l'homme.* The child and the man left to go to their room and, naturally, the child undressed himself and put on his nightclothes faster than the man. (EV, An94) <***Loc:*** EV, An94, Da84, Hi02>

déshabituer [dezabitɥe] **I** *v.tr.* to break (s.o.) of a habit *Faudra je déshabitue mon bébé de sucer son pouce.* I'll have to break my child's habit of sucking her thumb. (VM) **II se déshabituer** *v.pron.* to break one's habit *Je m'ai déshabitué de boire du café.* I broke my coffee habit. (VM) <***Loc:*** VM, Da84>

déshériter [dezerite] *v.tr.* to disinherit *Dans la Louisiane, tu peux pas déshériter tes enfants.* In Louisiana, you can't disinherit your children. (VM) <***Loc:*** VM, Da84>

déshonneur [dezɔ̃nœr] *n.m.* dishonor, shame, disgrace *Alle a commencé à rire après lui et à dire que, oh, c'était un déshonneur de ça qu'il était après faire.* She began to laugh at him and to say that, oh, what he was doing was a disgrace. (TB) <***Loc:*** TB, Da84>

déshonorer [dezɔ̃nore] *v.tr.* to dishonor, disgrace *Il a déshonoré sa défunte femme quand il s'a remarié deux mois plus tard.* He dishonored his late wife when he remarried two months later. (VM) <***Loc:*** VM, Da84>

désigner [dezĩje, deziɲe] *v.tr.* **1** to point out **2** to designate *Le vieux m'a désigné moi pour m'occuper de ses affaires.* The old fellow designated me to take care of his affairs. (VM) <***Loc:*** VM, Da84>

désinfectant [dezɛ̃fɛktɑ̃] *n.m.* disinfectant <***Loc:*** Da84>

désinfecter [dezɛ̃fɛkte] *v.tr.* to disinfect, purify *Le docteur a désinfecté la cicatrice avec du* DR. TICHENOR'S. The doctor disinfected the scar with some Dr. Tichenor's. (VM) <***Loc:*** VM, Da84>

désintéressement [dezɛ̃terɛsmɑ̃] *n.m.* disinterestedness <***Loc:*** Da84>

désir [dezir] *n.m.* desire, wish, longing *C'est mon désir d'aller, et mon espoir.* It's my desire to go, and my hope. (LF) <***Loc:*** LF, Da84>

désirer [dezire] *v.tr.* to desire, wish for, long for *Mais t'es la seule mon cœur désire.* But you are the only one my heart desires. (ch: *La valse du bambocheur*) <***Loc:*** Da84>

DESK [dɛs(k)] *n.m.* desk, writing table <***Loc:*** EV, SB, Ph36>

désobéir [dezobeir] *v.intr.* to disobey *Ma fille Hélène, elle m'a désobéi.* My daughter Hélène, she disobeyed me. (VM, ch: *Au pont de Nantes*) <***Loc:*** VM, Da84>

désobéissant, -e [dezobeisɑ̃, -ɑ̃t] *adj.* disobedient *Un enfant désobéissant.* A disobedient child. (VM) <***Loc:*** VM, Da84>

désoccuper [dezokype] *v.tr.* to disturb, interrupt (s.o. at work) *Je veux pas te désoccuper de ton ouvrage, continue avec ça t'étais après faire.* I don't want to interrupt your work, continue with what you were doing. (VM) <***Loc:*** VM>

désolation [dezolasjɔ̃] *n.f.* grief, desolation, affliction <***Loc:*** Da84>

désolé, -e [dezole] *adj.* heartbroken, grief-stricken, inconsolable, desolate *Quand son mari est mort, ça l'a laissée désolée.* When her husband died, it left her grief-stricken. (VM) <***Loc:*** VM, Da84>

désoler (se) [dezole] *v.pron.* **1** to weep profusely, be brokenhearted, be inconsolable *O, quand la belle a entendu ça, elle se mit à se désoler. —Ne pleurez pas autant la belle, ne versez pas autant de larmes.* Oh, when the beautiful girl heard that, she began to weep of a broken heart. —Don't cry so much, girl, don't shed so many tears. (IB, ch: *La veuve de sept ans*) **2** to burst into tears *Elle s'est désolée quand sa maman l'a babillée.* She burst into tears when her mom scolded her. (SM) <***Loc:*** IB, LF, SL, SM, Da84, Lv88>

désordeur, -euse [dezɔrdœr, -øz] *n.* troublemaker <***Loc:*** VM>

désordre [dezɔrd(r)] *n.m.* disorder, confusion, disturbance, disarray ◊ **•faire du {un} désordre *a*** to make a mess *Les enfants ont fait un sacré désordre dans la chambre en arrière.* The kids made a heck of mess in the back room. (LA) ***b*** to cause trouble, discord (between people) *Quand la petite fille s'est mariée avec ce bougre-ça là, ça a fait du désordre dans la famille.* When the little girl married that fellow there, it caused discord in the family. (LA) <LA> <***Loc:*** LA, Da84>

désorganisé, -e [dezɔrgɑ̃nize] *adj.* disorganized *Il est beaucoup désorganisé dans son ouvrage.* He is very disorganized in his work. (VM) <***Loc:*** VM, Da84>

désosser [dezose] *v.tr.* to debone *Désosser une poule.* To debone a chicken. (VM) <***Loc:*** VM, Da84>

dessaim [desɛ̃] *n.m.* swarm, crowd *Un dessaim de mouches à miel.* A swarm of bees. (Lv88) <***Loc:*** IB, SJ, TB, VM, Lv88>

dessaler [desale] *v.tr.* to remove salt *Dessaler de la morue, du petit salé.* To remove salt from cod, salted meat. (VM) <***Loc:*** VM, Da84>

dessangler [desɑ̃gle] *v.tr.* to ungirth (a horse) *Dessangler un cheval.* To ungirth a horse. (LA) <***Loc:*** LA, Da84>

dessatisfait, -e [desatisfɛ, desatisfe, -ɛt] *adj.* dissatisfied *Quand j'ai laissé, j'étais bien dessatisfait avec.* When I quit, I was quite disappointed with it. (VM) <***Loc:*** SM, VM>

desse [dɛs] *n.m.* lamp burner <***Loc:*** VM>

desséchant ♦see **déchessant**

dessèchement [desɛʃmɑ̃] *n.m.* **1** marshland that has been reclaimed by draining **2** waterwheel used for draining land to be reclaimed <***Loc:*** SJ>

dessécher ♦see **déchesser**

dessein [desɛ̃] *n.m.* design, plan, intention <***Loc:*** Da84>

desseller [desele, desle] **I** *v.tr.* to unsaddle **Il a descendu. Il a désellé son cheval.* He got down. He unsaddled his horse. (SL, An94) **II se desseller** *v.pron.* to roll up one's sleeves, remove articles of clothing (to get ready for a fight) *Quitte-moi me desseller.* Let me roll up my sleeves. (VM) <***Loc:*** JE, SL, VM, An94, Da84, Di32>

desserrer[1] [desere] *v.tr.* to loosen, untighten *Desserrer un boulon.* To loosen a bolt. (VM) <***Loc:*** VM, An94, Da84>

desserrer[2] ♦see **désérer**

dessert [desær] *n.m.* **1** dessert **2** wedding reception **Un gros mariage, tu connais, des autres fois passées, ça faisait le dessert dehors sous les arbres, l'été.* For a big wedding, you know, in the old days, they would have the reception outside under the trees in the summer. (EV, An94) <***Loc:*** EV, An94, Da84, Hi02>

desservir [desærvir] *v.tr.* to clear (the table) **Desservir la table.* To clear off the table. (LA, Da84) <***Loc:*** LA, Da84>

dessin [desɛ̃] *n.m.* design, drawing, plan *C'est pour ça que je t'avais fait cette robe-là pour le baptême à Belle. T'avais* *pas le temps de coudre, Ada, t'étais trop occupée. Et, je savais que t'aurais aimé ce petit dessin rose.* That's why I made you that dress for Belle's baptism. You didn't have the time to sew, Ada, you were too busy. And I knew you would like that little rose design. (ThCa: *La dernière quilte*) <***Loc:*** Da84, ThCa>

dessouder [desude] **I** *v.tr.* to unsolder *Dessouder des tuyaux.* To unsolder pipes. (VM) **II se dessouder** *v.pron.* to become unsoldered *Un tuyau qui s'a dessoudé.* A pipe that came unsoldered. (VM) <***Loc:*** VM, Da84>

dessoûler [desule] **I** *v.tr.* to sober up, cause to sober up *Il faudra qu'on le dessoûle avant de le ramener à la maison.* We have to sober him up before we take him home. (LA) **II se dessoûler** *v.pron.* to sober up *Je m'ai vite dessoûlé quand mon char a rentré dans le fossé.* I sobered up quickly when my car went into the ditch. (VM) <***Loc:*** LA, VM, Da84>

dessour ♦see **dessous**

dessous[1] **(dessour)** [dəsu, dsu, tsu, dsur] *n.m.* bottom, underside <***Loc:*** Da84, Hi02>

dessous[2] **(dessour)** [dəsu, dsu, tsu, dsur] *prep.* under, below, beneath, underneath **Dessous la table.* Under the table. (Da84, Lv88) ◊ **•au-dessous** underneath <Da84> **•en dessous (de)** under, underneath *Il est assis en-dessous l'arbre là-bas.* He is sitting under the tree over there. (Lv88) *J'étais un boss. Et j'avais des hommes en dessour de mon.* I was a boss. And I had men under me. (LF) *Et l'eau a commencé de monter en dessous de mon camp.* And the water started rising underneath my camp. (JE) <JE, LF, Lv88> **•en-dessous *a*** under, below, beneath, underneath *Et le bateau est monté là-dessus, il est nettoyé en-dessour et il est peinturé.* And the boat is mounted up there, it is cleaned underneath and it is painted. (LF) ***b*** hypocritical, two-faced ***c*** sneaky, underhanded, deceitful *Il faut tu guettes cet enfant. Il est en-dessous, il va malfaire en cachette.* You've got to watch that child. He is sneaky, he will do wrong secretly. (VM) <IB, JE, LF, SM, TB, VM, Da84> **•par en-dessous** sneaky, michievous, deceitful, hypocritical, underhanded *Je pourrais jamais me fier à quelqu'un comme ça; il est par en-dessous.* I could never trust someone like that; he's underhanded. (EV) <EV, JE, SL, TB, Da84, La99> <***Loc:*** EV, JE, LF, SL, SM, TB, VM, Da84, Hi02, La99, Lv88>

dessur ♦see **dessus**

dessus[1] [dəsy, dsy, tsy] *n.m.* top, upper part **Propter le dessus de la table.* To clean the table top. (Da84) **•prendre le dessus** to get the upper hand <Da84> <***Loc:*** Da84, Hi02>

dessus[2] [dəsy, dsy, tsy] *adv.* **1** on *Et là, ils vont mettre un plancher là qu'ils pourrait marcher dessus.* And then they will put in a deck there that they can walk on. (LF) **2** turned on (of an appliance) *On avait pas besoin d'avoir ça dessus.* We didn't need to have that [the TV] on. (TB) <***Loc:*** LF, TB, Da84>

dessus[3] **(dessur)** [dəsy, dsy, tsy, dɛsyr] *prep.* **1** on, upon *Ils dorment dessus la paille.* They sleep on straw. (VM) **Je voudrais que tu reviens [...] coucher ta chère tête dessus mon épaule.* I want you to come back [and] lay your dear head on my shoulder. (ch: *La valse de Cajun*) *Il a des têtes de chevreuils dessus les murs de sa maison.* He has [mounted] deer heads on the walls of his house. (Lv88) *J'ai un oncle, il a toujours travaillé dessus les habitations.* I have an uncle, he has always worked on plantations. (IV) *Mon grand-père travaillait dessus les barges qui fouillaient le* WHISKEY BAY CHANNEL. My grandfather used to work on the barges that dredged the Whiskey Bay Channel. (SM) *Je l'ai vu dessus la galerie.* I saw him on the porch. (SM) *Quand on était monté dessus le transfer c'était pareil comme on était gone là-bas en ville.* When we had gotten on the bus, it was just like as if we had gone to town. (SL) *Ça met du plastique dessus ce fil pour empêcher ce fil de rouiller, parce que ça rouille vite.* They put plastic on this wire to prevent this wire from rustinsg because it rusts fast. (SM) *On va nous mettre une autre taxe dessus le dos.* They are going to put another tax on our backs. (VM) *Tu peux pas dépendre dessus eux-autres.* You cannot depend on them. (Lv88) **2** on, at **Dessus la veille de Chrismise.* On Christmas Eve. (Wh83) *Il est dessus un vacance.* He is on vacation. (Lv88) **3** on, about, regarding *Il a des idées fortes dessus la politique.* He has strong ideas regarding politics. (Lv88) ◊ **•au-dessus (de)** more than, over *Pour au-dessus trois semaines.* For more than three weeks. (Lv88) *Ils ont au-dessus trente ans d'expérience.* They have more than thirty years of experience. (EV) *Alle coûte au-dessus de huit cent mille piastres.* It costs more than eight hundred thousand dollars. (TB) <EV, TB, Lv88> **•en dessus** over, on top, above *Là, on venait et on mettait nos postes ou notre plomb, n'importe quoi on voulait mettre par en dessus ça.* Then we came and we put our buckshot or our shot, whatever we wanted to put on top of that. (LA, An94) <LA, An94, Da84> **•par-dessus** more than, over *Le monde qu'est par-dessus soixante ans en bas c'est tout du monde qui parle proche juste le cadien.* People who are over 60 down here are all people who speak almost nothing but Cajun. (TB) <TB> <***Loc:*** EV, IV, JE, LA, SB, SL, SM, TB, VM, An94, Da84, Hi02, Lv88, Wh83>

destinée [destine] *n.f.* destiny, fate <***Loc:*** Da84>

destructif, -ive [destryktif, -iv] *adj.* destructive *Ces enfants ça-là sont assez destructifs, j'aime pas les voir arriver.* Those kids are so destructive. I don't like to see them come here. (LA) <***Loc:*** LA, Da84>

destruction [destryksjɔ̃] *n.f.* destruction <***Loc:*** Da84>

détacher [detaʃe] **I** *v.tr.* to unnail, detach, unpin, unfasten *Il avait pour détacher un tas des clous sur le gros bois.* He had to unnail lots of nails on the rough wood. (LA) *Détacher une planche, la couverture.* To unnail a board, to unfasten the roof. (VM) **II se détacher** *v.pron.* to come loose, get loose *Il y a une voliche qui s'a détaché.* There is a piece of siding that came loose. (LA) <***Loc:*** LA, LF, VM, Da84>

détail [detaj] *n.m.* detail **Expliquer les détails.* To explain the details. (Da84) ◊ **•en détail** retail *Les groceries étaient en détail et en gros barils.* Groceries were in retail (small quantities) and in large barrels (wholesale). (VM) <VM> <***Loc:*** VM, Da84, Wh83>

détailler [detaje] *v.tr.* **1** to cut piece by piece, cut into pieces, cut up *Détailler l'étoffe.* To cut the fabric piece by piece. (LA) *Détailler un veau.* To cut up a calf (for distribution). (VM) **2** to carve down, whittle down *Allons dire que t'étais après faire un bateau, et que t'avais plein du bois* ROUGH *et que tu voulais le détailler un peu pour l'amener plus près.* Let's say you were making a boat, and you had a lot of rough wood and you wanted to carve it down a little to bring it in to a closer fit. (LF) **3** to divide, separate *L'intérieur de cette maison est mal détaillé.* The inside of this house is poorly divided. (Lv88) **4** to sort *Il a détaillé les bonbons dans la boutique.* He sorted the candies in the store. (LA) **5** to detail, set out the details **Madame, je suis Monsieur Romain Weber et j'avais détaillé une bataille à l'arme avec votre mari, et j'ai mon fusil asteur-là.* Madame, I am Romain Weber and I had set out the details for an armed duel with your husband, and I have my shotgun now. (LA, An94) **6** to describe or recount in detail *Il m'a tout détaillé sa soirée.* He recounted his whole evening in detail to me. (LA) <***Loc:*** LA, LF, VM, An94, Da84, Lv88>

détamer [detɑ̃me] **I** *v.tr.* to discolor, tarnish, damage (a surface or coating) *J'ai monté la mèche trop haut en dessous de ma chaudière et ça a détamé le grenit.* I put the burner on too high under my pot and it damaged the enamel. (VM) *Le chlore a détamé sa robe.* The chlorine discolored her dress. (Lv88) **II** *v.intr.* to become worn, faded, discolored, or tarnished *Le fond du bassin a détamé.* The bottom of the pan lost its enamel. (VM) *Les fourchettes en argent sont tout détamées.* The plating of the silver forks is completely wearing off. (LF) *Le portrait est détamé.* The picture is faded. (Lv88) <***Loc:*** LF, SL, SM, VM, Da84, Lv88>

détaquer [detake] *v.tr.* to unhook, unlatch *Il a détaqué la porte pour les laisser rentrer.* He unlocked the door to let them in. (LA) <***Loc:*** LA, LF, SL, SM, Lv88>

détarder [detarde] *v.tr.* to retard, delay *Il m'a assez détardé dans mon ouvrage.* He delayed me quite a bit in my work. (TB) <***Loc:*** JE, TB, Lv88>

détasser [detase] *v.tr.* to spread, scatter (e.g. a pile) *Il l'a tout détassé et j'avais pour le ramasser.* He scattered it all and I had to pick it up. (VM) *Mon frère a tout détassé mes cordes de bois.* My brother completely scattered my cords of wood. (LA) <***Loc:*** LA, TB, VM, Lv88>

détecter [detɛkte] *v.tr.* to detect, find *Ils ont détecté un trou dans le tuyau de gaz.* They found a hole in the gas line. (LA) <***Loc:*** LA, Da84>

détectif ♦see **détective**

détection [detɛksjɔ̃] *n.f.* detection <***Loc:*** Da84>

détective (**détectif, ditective**) [detɛktif, detɛktiv, detektiv, ditɛktiv, ditektiv] *n.m.* detective **Boy, quand ça voyait les détectifs, les Revenues. God dog, ça épaillait partout.* Boy, when they saw the detectives, the Revenuers. God dog, they scattered everywhere. (SL, An94) <***Loc:*** IB, SB, SL, SM, TB, An94, Da84>

déteindre [detɛ̃n, detɛ̃d(r)] (*p.p.* **déteint** [detɛ̃], **déteindu** [detɛ̃dy]) **I** *v.tr.* to cause to lose color, fade, discolor, bleach *Le* BLEACH *a tout déteint sa robe de dimanche.* The bleach faded her Sunday dress. (LA) **II** *v.intr.* to fade, lose color *Sa chemise avait tout déteint.* His shirt had completely faded. (LA) **III se déteindre** *v.pron.* to fade, discolor *L'étoffe s'a déteint quand je l'ai lavée.* The material got discolored when I washed it. (EV) <***Loc:*** EV, LA, Da84>

dételage [detəlaʒ] *n.m.* unhitching, unharnessing <***Loc:*** Da84>

dételer (**désatteler**) [detəle, dezatle] *v.tr.* to unharness, unhitch **Il a mis ses chevaux dans l'hangar. Il a dételé son wagon.* He put his horses in the shed. He unhitched his wagon. (SL, An94) *On a désattelé les mulets à midi.* We unhitched the mules at noon. (TB) ◊ **•dételer le wagon au milieu du marais / dételer le mulet des rangs** to give up in the middle of an undertaking <AC, LA, SL, La99> <***Loc:*** AC, LA, SL, SM, TB, An94, Da84, La99, Lv88>

détendre [detɑ̃n, detɑ̃d(r)] **I** *v.tr.* to slacken, loosen (a cord or rope) *Laisse pas ton câble détendre. Le veau va s'échapper.* Don't let your rope slacken. The calf will get away. (VM) *Détends le fil pour qu'on peuve le rouler.* Loosen the string so we can roll it. (VM) **II se détendre** *v.pron.* to slacken, become loose *Quand ta corde à linge se détend, tu la lèves avec un grand bâton au milieu.* When your clothesline slackens, you raise it with a big stick in the middle. (VM) <***Loc:*** VM, Da84>

détermination [detærminasjɔ̃] *n.f.* determination, firmness <***Loc:*** Da84>

déterminé, -e [detærmine] *adj.* determined, resolved *Ils étaient déterminés de rester dans la salle.* They were determined to stay in the dance hall. (LA) <***Loc:*** LA, Da84>

déterminer [detærmine] *v.intr.* to decide, resolve, determine *Il a déterminé de finir demain.* He decided to finish tomorrow. (LA) *Ils ont déterminé de vendre leur pièce.* They resolved to sell their piece of land. (LA) <***Loc:*** LA, Da84>

déterrer [detere] *v.tr.* to dig up, unearth, disinter *Il faudrait qu'il les déterre de dans le cimetière.* He would have to exhume them from the cemetery. (LA) *Ils ont déterré le trésor.* They dug up the treasure. (LA) <***Loc:*** LA, VM, Da84>

détervioler [detærvjole] *v.tr.* to stun (with a blow) *Il l'a détervíolé d'un coup de poing.* He stunned him with a blow. (LF) <***Loc:*** LF>

détestable [detestab(l)] *adj.* **1** detestable, hateful, horrible

Ces deux là étaient haïssables et détestables. Those two were hateful and detestable. (LA) **2** incorrigible ◊ **•faire le détestable** to be willfully disobedient, behave defiantly *Un enfant qui fait le détestable, quand il écoute pas, il est dans le cours, et il t'écoute pas, il est détestable.* A child who is willfully disobedient, when he doesn't listen, he's in the class and he doesn't listen to you, he's incorrigible. (VM) <VM> <*Loc:* LA, VM, Da84>

détester [deteste] *v.tr.* to detest, hate *Tout le voisinage le détestait.* The whole neighborhood hated him. (LA) <*Loc:* LA, Da84>

détordre [detɔrd(r)] **I** *v.tr.* to untwist, unravel *Il était après avoir du mal à détordre son cable.* He was having trouble unraveling his rope. (LA) **II se détordre** *v.pron.* to unravel, become unravelled or untwisted *La vieille cabresse s'avait tout détordu.* The old horse-hair rope had come completely unravelled. (LA) <*Loc:* LA, Da84>

détortiller [detɔrtije] **I** *v.tr.* to untwist, unravel *Elle avait pour détortiller les vieux fils avant de les réuser.* She had to unravel the old threads before reusing them. (LA) **II se détortiller** *v.pron.* to unravel, become untwisted or unravelled *C'est un miracle. Le fil s'a détortillé tout seul.* It's a miracle. The string unravelled all by itself. (LA) <*Loc:* LA, Da84>

détour [detur] *n.m.* **1** detour, roundabout way **Faire un détour.* To take a detour. (Da84) **2** wrenching (of the back) *Je m'ai fait un détour quand j'ai tombé.* I wrenched my back when I fell. (VM) ◊ **•détour de reins** strained back <JE, LF> <*Loc:* JE, LF, VM, Da84>

détourer [deture] *v.tr.* **1** to remove ground cover or mulch from (a plant) *Détourer les fraises.* To remove straw from around strawberry plants. (VM) **2** to remove weatherboarding *Détourer la maison après l'hiver.* To remove skirting from [around the bottom of] the house after winter. (LA) *Ils ont détouré la maison avant de la découverte.* They removed the weatherboarding from the house before unroofing it. (TB) <*Loc:* LA, SL, TB, VM, Da84, Lv88>

détourne [deturn] *n.f.* detour *Ils ont fait une grande détourne auprès de ma maison.* They took a big detour near my house. (TB) <*Loc:* TB>

détourner [deturne] *v.tr.* **1** to head off, divert, ward off *Détourner les bêtes avant qu'ils arrivent au clayon ouvert.* To turn the cattle back before they get to the open gate. (VM) **2** to avert, parry (a blow) *Détourner un coup.* To avert a blow. (LA) **3** to treat effectively, cure (an illness) *Si tu détournes pas l'ulcère, ça va tourner cancer.* If you don't treat the ulcer, it will turn into cancer. (VM) <*Loc:* LA, VM, Da84>

détravouiller [detravuje] *v.tr.* to unwind *Le petit chat a tout détravouillé mon fil.* The kitten completely unwound my string. (VM) <*Loc:* VM>

détremper [detrɑ̃pe] *v.tr.* to moisten *Elle a détrempé son front pour essayer de baisser sa fièvre.* She moistened his forehead as an attempt to lower his fever. (LA) <*Loc:* LA>

détriment [detrimɑ̃] *n.m.* injury, detriment <*Loc:* Da84>

détrousser [detruse] *v.tr.* **1** to unroll (rolled-up sleeves, pants, etc.) *Il a détroussé ses manches.* He unrolled his sleeves. (LA) **2** to let down, unhem (e.g. a dress) <*Loc:* LA, Da84>

détruire [detrɥir] **I** *v.tr.* to destroy, exterminate **Et il a dit qu'il fallait que deux hommes, qu'il fallait qu'ils vont la prendre à onze heures le soir et puis aller la tuer, la détruire.* And he said that two men had to go and get her at eleven o'clock at night and then go and kill her, exterminate her. (IV, An94) **II se détruire** *v.pron.* to commit suicide *Sa sœur s'a détruit. Elle avait été malade depuis des années.* Her sister committed suicide. She had been sick for years. (LA) *Malgré qu'il s'a détruit, il a été enterré dans de la terre sacrée.* Even though he committed suicide, he was buried in sacred ground. (LA) <*Loc:* IV, LA, TB, An94, Da84, Wh83>

dette [dɛt] *n.f.* debt <*Loc:* AC, SJ, Da84>

detteur [detœr] *n.m.* debtor *Ça c'est un de mes detteurs.* That's someone who owes me money. (SM) <*Loc:* JE, SM, Da84>

deuil [dœj] *n.m.* mourning ◊ **•en deuil** in mourning *À cinq minutes pour minuit tout le monde était en deuil, parce que là on commençait le Carême.* At five minutes till midnight everyone was in mourning, because then we were starting Lent. (TB) <EV, TB, Da84> **•en gros deuil** in deep mourning <Da84> **•demi-deuil** partial mourning <EV, LA, Wh83> <*Loc:* EV, LA, TB, Da84, Wh83>

deux [dø] *adj./n.m.* two *Pour deux heures.* For two hours. (SL) **Le deux avril.* April second. (Da84) *Je débauche pas d'école jusqu'à deux heures et demi.* I don't get out of school until two thirty. (LF) **Pareil comme deux gouttes d'eau.* Alike as two drops of water. (Da84) ◊ **•deux par deux** two by two, in pairs <Da84> **•deux-par-quatre** two-by-four, wooden stud *C'était fait avec un deux-par-quatre, deux pouces d'épais et quatre pouces de large.* That was made with a two-by-four, two inches thick and four inches wide. (LF) <LF, Lv88> **•à deux doigts** very close **A deux doigts de sa mort.* Very close to death. (AV, La99) <AV, La99> **•en deux** bent over, bent in two *Il marche tout en deux parce qu'il souffre beaucoup.* He walks bent over because he is suffering. (SB) *Il s'a mis en deux tellement qu'il avait des douleurs.* He was bent double because he was in so much pain. (TB) <SB, TB, Lv88> **•les deux** both *Mes grands-mères dessus les deux bords.* My grandmothers on both sides. (TB) *Tu cuis ça dessus le* STOVE *dans une chaudière ou bien dans le* OVEN, *tu peux cuire les deux manières.* You cook it in a pot over the stove or in the oven, you can do it both ways. (SM) <LA, SM, TB, An94, Da84> **•se mettre {se casser} en deux** to strive hard, make excessive efforts *Elle se casse en deux quand elle a de la compagnie.* She bends over backwards when she has company. (Lv88) *Elle* *s'a cassé en deux pour finir avant qu'ils arrivent.* She tried hard to finish before they arrived. (LA) <LA, La99, Lv88> <***Loc:*** AC, AV, EV, IB, LA, LF, SB, SL, SM, TB, VM, An94, Da84, Hi02, La99, Lv88>

deux-chemin (**déchemin**) [døʃəmɛ̃] *n.m.* pacing, pace, rack (a form of trotting) ◊ **•aller le {à} deux-chemin** to pace, rack *Sa petite jument pouvait aller à deux-chemin jusqu'à Carencro.* His little mare could pace all the way to Carencro. (LA) *Ce cheval va le déchemin.* This horse is pacing. (SL) <LA, SL, Da84> <***Loc:*** LA, SL, Da84>

deuxième [døzjɛ̃m] *adj./n.* second **La deuxième fois, il a dit, "Quand je vas revenir la troisième fois, ça sera pas joli!"* The second time, he said, "When I come back a third time, it won't be pretty!" (LA, An94) **Ça fait, l'autre est venue, la deuxième est venue.* So the other one came, the second one came. (EV, An94) *Nonc Alphé, le deuxième de mes frères.* Uncle Alphé, the second of my brothers. (VM) *Henry, ça c'est la deuxième bonne idée t'as eu aujourd'hui.* Henry, that's the second good idea you've had today. (LA) ◊ **•deuxième {seconde} main** used, secondhand *Un char deuxième main.* A secondhand car. (LA) <IB, LA, TB, Lv88> <***Loc:*** EV, LA, LF, TB, VM, An94, Da84>

deuxièmement [døzjɛ̃mmɑ̃] *adv.* secondly, in the second place *Premièrement, elle est folle et deuxièmement elle est pas vaillante.* In the first place, she's crazy, secondly she's not nice. (LA) <***Loc:*** LA, Da84>

deux-pas [døpa] *n.m.* two-step **D'abord que c'est plus à la mode, ça danse pas la valse, le deux-pas, le Jitterbug ou le Contredanse Cajin, éspécialment pas en publique.* Since it's no longer stylish, they don't dance the Cajun waltz, two-step, jitterbug or Contredanse, especially not in public. (Wh83) <***Loc:*** Wh83>

dévaldrade ♦see **dévaldrague**

dévaldrague (**dévaldrade**) [devaldrag, devaldrad] *n.f.* **1** slovenly or unkempt appearance *Garde voir la dévaldrague de cet homme.* Look at how slovenly that man looks. (LF) **2** disrepair, neglected condition **Cette maison s'en va à la dévaldrade.* That house is falling into disrepair. (Pe37) <***Loc:*** LF, Pe37>

dévaliser [devalize] *v.tr.* to turn topsy-turvy, make a mess of *Alle a dévalisé toute la chambre.* She turned the room upside down. (AV) <***Loc:*** AV, IB, SJ>

devant[1] (**d'vent**) [dəvɑ̃, dvɑ̃] *n.m.* **1** front, front part, fore *Laisse quelqu'un qui peut courir prendre le devant.* Let someone who can run take the fore. (AS) *Ça peinturait le devant de leurs maisons* WHITEWASH, *blanc, ça pouvait pas* AFFORD *la peinture.* They whitewashed the front of their houses, they couldn't afford paint. (LF) **2** bow, foredeck, stem (of a boat) *Ça c'est un chaland parce que c'est plat et le devant est carré.* It's a flatboat because it's flat and the bow is square. (JE) ◊ **•devant de jambe** shin <SM> **•avoir le devant** to be in the lead (in a game or competition) *Tant que ça pouvait attraper la pelote et venir frapper un de vous-autres, ils aviont le devant.* As long as they could catch the ball and come hit one of you, they had the lead. (VM) <VM> <***Loc:*** IB, JE, LA, LF, SM, TB, VM, Da84, Gu00>

devant[2] [dəvɑ̃, dvɑ̃] *prep.* in front of, before **Ça se fait, quand le pistolet a craqué, le Grand Sauvage a parti loin devant le coureur à Jean l'Ours.* So when the gun shot, the Grand Sauvage took off far in front of Jean l'Ours' runner. (EV, An94) ◊ **•devant derrière** backwards **Père, tourne ce col et puis ton capot, vire-le devant derrière.* Father, turn that collar and your coat, turn it around backwards. (IV, An94) <IV, An94> **•au-devant** in front of, forward <Da84> **•par devant** from in front *Essaie de l'approcher par devant.* Try to approach him from in front. (LA) <LA, Da84> <***Loc:*** EV, IV, LA, TB, An94, Da84, Hi02>

devanture [dəvɑ̃tyr] *n.f.* **1** front, front part (of a house, etc.) **2** frontage (of a lot) <***Loc:*** Da84, Lv88>

dévaporé, -e [devapore] *adj.* ragged, tattered *Les enfants vont tout dévaporés.* The children run around all ragged. (VM) <***Loc:*** VM>

dévastation [devastasjɔ̃] *n.f.* devastation, havoc, ravaging <***Loc:*** Da84>

dévaster [devaste] *v.tr.* to devastate, ravage, wreak havoc on *Le mauvais temps a dévasté son jardin.* The bad weather devastated his garden. (LA) *Cette chaise est tout dévastée.* That chair is in ruins. (TB) <***Loc:*** LA, TB, Da84>

dévastre [devast(r)] *n.m.* damage, devastation *La pluie a fait du dévastre.* The rain did some damage. (Lv88) *Un des dévastres l'ouragan a occasionnés.* One of the kinds of damage the hurricane caused. (Lv88, ch: *L'ouragan Audrey*) <***Loc:*** Lv88>

développé, -e [devlope] *adj.* ◊ **•pas bien développé** ***a*** not very intelligent ***b*** mentally retarded *Cet enfant, pauvre bête, il est pas bien développé.* That kid, poor thing, he's retarded. (AC) <AC, La99> <***Loc:*** AC, LA, La99>

développement [devlɔpmɑ̃] *n.m.* development, growth, progress <***Loc:*** Da84>

développer [devlope] **I** *v.tr.* **1** to develop **Si tu trouves le* GEOMETRICAL FORMULA *qu'il faut, tu peux développer le* DESIGN *d'un violon.* If you find the right geometrical formula, you can develop the design of a violin. (VM, An84) *Son idée est pas encore développée là-dessus.* His opinion is not yet developed on that issue. (LA) **2** to unfold *Développer un drap.* To unfold a sheet. (LA) **3** to unwrap (a package) *T'aurais dû voir ces enfants après essayer de développer ces paquets.* You should have seen those children trying to unwrap those packages. (LA) **II se développer** *v.pron.* **1** to grow, develop, expand, spread *Un ouragan est après se développer dans le Golfe.* A hurricane is developping in the Gulf. (VM) **2** to become unwrapped *Le paquet s'a développé dans la malle.* The package got unwrapped in the mail. (EV) <***Loc:*** EV, LA, VM, An84, Da84>

devenir [dəvnir, dvənir] *v.intr.* **1** to become **Il est devenu fou.* He went crazy. (Da84) **2** to originate, come from *La croyance dans le Bon Dieu et savoir éyou tu deviens est bien important pour une personne.* Belief in God and knowing where you come from are very important for a person. (TB) *Je deviens de Raceland, c'est une petite place à peu près quinze milles de la ville de Thibodaux.* I come from Raceland, it's a little place about 15 miles from the city of Thibodaux. (LF) *Ces terres l'avont devenu de son père.* This land came to him from his father. (VM) **3** to happen to, become of *Quoi ce qu'en deviendra de moi?* What will become of me? (IB, ch: *La veuve de sept ans*) <***Loc:*** IB, LF, TB, VM, Da84, Hi02>

dévergondé, -e [deværgɔ̃de] *adj.* **1** shameless *Les jeunes sont tout dévergondés asteur.* Young people are all shameless nowadays. (VM) **2** untidy, messed up *Si tu peux croire, elle va à la messe tout dévergondée comme ça.* If you can believe it, she goes to Mass all shabbily dressed like that. (VM) **3** profligate *Il était tout dévergondé avant de se marier.* He was very profligate before he got married. (VM) <***Loc:*** VM, Da84>

dévideur [devidœr] *n.m.* thread winder (on a sewing machine) <***Loc:*** VM>

dévinade ♦see **dévinage**

dévinage (**dévinade**) [devinaʒ, devinad] *n.m.* riddle, guessing game *Les dévinades étaient intéressantes.* The riddles were interesting. (AV) <***Loc:*** AV, VM>

dévinail [dəvinaj] *n.m.* puzzle, riddle, conundrum ◊ •**dévine-dévinail** opening formula used in telling a riddle *Dévine-dévinail qui ce que j'ai dans la main.* Guess what I have in my hand. (LF) <LF> <***Loc:*** LF, SM, TB>

deviner (**adviner**) [dəvine, devine, advine] *v.tr.* **1** to guess *Devine-voir quoi c'est.* Guess what it is. (VM) *Faut que tu devines qui-ce qu'alle après te dire!* You have to guess what she's telling you! (TB) **2** to predict *Ça fait, comme vous-autres a pu deviner, Clomaire et Madeleine ont venu à se quitter.* So as you all could have predicted, Clomaire and Madeleine ended up separating. (ThCa: *Le charivari*) <***Loc:*** AV, SM, TB, VM, Da84, ThCa>

devineur (**advineur**) [dəvinœr, advinœr] *n.m.* **1** mystic, clairvoyant, fortune-teller *Tit Jean était un devineur.* Tit Jean was a fortune-teller. (VM) **2** diviner, dowser, one who searches for underground water with a divining rod **3** divining rod, dowsing rod <***Loc:*** LA, VM, Lv88>

devinette [devinɛt] *n.f.* riddle, guessing game <***Loc:*** AV, Da84>

dévirer [devire] **I** *v.tr.* to cause s.o. to change his or her mind *Je l'ai déviré d'une calotte.* I changed his mind with a slap. (TB) **II** *v.intr.* to turn aside, deviate *Il dévire de sa route.* He deviates from his route. (SB) <***Loc:*** SB, TB>

dévisage [devizaʒ] *n.m.* division into portions or shares, divvying up *Le débris comptait pas dans le dévisage.* The organs didn't count in the divvying up [of the animal carcass]. (SL) <***Loc:*** SL, VM>

dévissage [devisaʒ] *n.m.* unscrewing <***Loc:*** Da84>

dévisser [devise] **I** *v.tr.* to unscrew, unbolt **Quand quelqu'un voulait quelque chose, ça dévissait le petit comme un robinet, tu connais. Ça mettait son quart ou son pint, et puis il l'avissait.* When someone wanted something [moonshine], he'd unscrew the little, like, spigot, you know. He'd put his quart or pint bottle, then he'd screw it back. (LA, An94) **II se dévisser** *v.pron.* to become unscrewed, become unbolted, come loose *Il avait une voiture, une bonne voiture. Et il allait peut-être 30, 40 milles à l'heure. Peut-être moins. Là il a une roue qui s'a dévissé.* He had a car, a good car. And he would go 30 or 40 miles per hour. Perhaps less. Then he had a wheel that came unbolted. (TB) <***Loc:*** LA, TB, An94, Da84>

dévoilement [devwalmɑ̃] *n.m.* unveiling, disclosure, exposing <***Loc:*** Da84>

dévoiler [devwale] **I** *v.tr.* to unveil, disclose, expose, reveal **Je vas te donner de la munition pour tu te défends, mais dévoile-moi jamais!* I'm going to give you ammunition so that you can defend yourself, but don't ever expose me! (LA, An94) **II se dévoiler** *v.pron.* to reveal o.s., expose one's intentions, give o.s. away *Il s'a dévoilé quand il s'a mis à rire.* He gave himself away when he started laughing. (EV) <***Loc:*** EV, LA, An94, Da84>

devoir[1] (**doir**) [dəwar, dwar, dwɑ̃r] *v.tr.* **1** to owe *Il va me doir une piasse.* He will owe me a dollar. (SM) *Tu mérites une belle réunion de famille, Grandma Douce. On te doit ça.* You deserve a nice family reunion, Grandma Douce. We owe you that. (ThCa: *La douce réunion*) *C'est pas la peine de deviner combien tu me dois. C'est mesurable.* There's no need to guess how much you owe me. It's a measurable quantity. (LA) *"Et tant qu'à toi, mon fils de putain," il dit, "si tu me paies pas cet argent ça tu me dois," et il dit, "si t'arrêtes pas de courir après ma femme," il dit, "la prochaine fois je vas te tuer, ouais!"* "And as for you, you son-of-a-bitch," he says, "if you don't pay me the money you owe me," and he says, "if you don't stop chasing after my wife," he says, "the next time I will kill you!" (JD) **2** to have to, must, be obliged to *Tu vas ayoù tu veux, tu vas mourir ayoù tu dois.* You go where you want to, you're going to die where you must. (ch: *La nouvelle d'un étranger*) *C'est quelque chose j'aurais dû te dire longtemps passé.* It's something I should have told you a long time ago. (ch: *I don't want you anymore*) **Je dois aller.* I have to go. (Da84) **Je devrais aller.* I ought to go. (Da84) *Tu devrais parler en anglais et tu devrais parler en français.* You should speak English and you should speak French. (SL) **3** *(hypothesis, speculation)* must *Alle doit être malade, alle est tout masquée.* She must be sick, she is all covered with liver spots. (VM) *Tu dois être après perdre ton petit brin d'esprit que t'as!* You must be losing the little bit of sense that you have! (AV) *Tu dois croire que je suis couillon pour de même!* You must think I'm really stupid! (TB) ◊ **•il doit à Dieu et ses saints** he is heavily in debt <La99> <***Loc:*** AV, JD, LA, LF, SB, SL, SM, TB, VM, Da84, Hi02, La99, Lv88, ThCa>

devoir[2] [dəvwar] *n.m.* duty, obligation, job, chore ◊ **•faire son devoir** to do one's duty *J'ai fait mon devoir dedans le passé.* I did my duty in the past. (VM) <VM, Da84> <***Loc:*** VM, Da84>

dévorer [devore] *v.tr.* **1** to devour, eat ravenously, gobble up *Ce chien, il fait comme si il pourrait te dévorer.* That dog acts as if he could devour you. (VM) **2** to eat up (with affection) *Cet enfant, il est assez mignon, je pourrais le dévorer.* That child is so cute I could eat him up. (LA) <***Loc:*** LA, VM, Da84>

dévotion [devosjɔ̃] *n.f.* **1** devotion, fervor **2** religious practice, spiritual service (prayers, etc.) *Faire ses dévotions durant Carême.* To do one's devotions during Lent. (VM) <***Loc:*** VM, Da84>

dévouement [devumɑ̃] *n.m.* devotion, devotedness <***Loc:*** Da84>

dévouer [devwe] **I** *v.tr.* **1** to dedicate *Dévouer un enfant à la Sainte Vierge.* To dedicate a child to the Holy Virgin. (LA) **2** to devote, give (time, effort, etc.) *J'ai dévoué tous mes dimanches pour passer la journée avec ma grand-mère.* I devoted every Sunday to spend the day with my grandmother. (VM) **II se dévouer** *v.pron.* to devote o.s. *Se dévouer à son ouvrage.* To devote oneself to one's work. (VM) <***Loc:*** LA, VM, Da84>

diabète [djabɛt] *n.f.* diabetes <***Loc:*** Da84>

diable (diaboul) [diab(l), dijab(l), djab(l), dʒab(l), dʒɔb(l), dʒawb(l), dʒabul] *n.m.* **1** devil, demon *C'est des vrais petits diables, ces enfants là. Si c'est brigand!* Those kids are real devils. Are they rowdy! (TB) **2** the Devil, Satan *Le vieux diable te met des mauvaises affaires dans le chemin, faut que tu passes dessus.* The Devil puts bad things in your way, you have to get through them. (LF) *Mais c'est malheureux que le système d'école est tellement sale, c'est corrupté par le diable. Ça les enseigne que eux-autres vient des bétailles.* But it's awful how the school system is so dirty, it's corrupted by the devil. They teach them that they come from animals. (LF) **3** hand truck, cart used for hauling heavy object *Ils ont halé les logues avec le diable.* They hauled logs with the hand truck. (AV) **4** praying mantis **5** devilfish ◊ **•au diable la boutique** *(expr. of exasperation)* **a** I give up ***b*** I'm leaving, I'm out of here <LF, SM> **•avoir le diable au corps** to be mischievous, be hyperactive (esp. of a child) *Il a le diable au corps, lui. Il peut pas rester tranquille cinq minutes.* He's got the devil in him, that one. He can't stay still for five minutes. (EV) <EV, La99> **•faire le diable à quatre** to raise hell, cut up <Da84> **•faire (le) diable et son train** to make much effort *Je vas faire le diable et son train pour être là avant sept heures.* I'm going to do my level best to be there before seven o'clock. (EV) <EV, SM, La99> **•(là-bas) au diable bouilli** in a distant and unknown place, in some God-forsaken place *C'est une petite place là-bas au diable bouilli, mais tu peux pas manger des meilleures écrevisses que ça que tu vas manger là-bas.* It's a little place out in the boondocks, but you cannot eat better crawfish than those you'll eat there. (LA) <LA, SM, Da84, La99> **•le diable et son train** devilment <Da84> **•le diable s'en a mêlé** all hell broke loose <Da84> **•que diable (est ça)!** what the devil! <Da84> **•un diable dans un bénitier** said of a child who struggles or fights, especially in a sedate environment <La99> <***Loc:*** AC, AV, EV, JE, LA, LF, PQ, SB, SL, SM, TB, VM, An94, Da84, Hi02, La99, Lv88, Re31>

diablement [dijabləmɑ̃] *adv.* extremely, awfully *Avoir diablement faim.* To be extremely hungry. (SJ) *Il va diablement vite.* He goes awfully fast. (SB) <***Loc:*** SB, SJ>

diablesse [djablɛs] *n.f.* she-devil, shrew, evil woman <***Loc:*** Da84>

diabolique [djabolik] *adj.* diabolical, devilish <***Loc:*** Da84>

diaboul ♦see **diable**

diacre [djak(r)] *n.m.* deacon <***Loc:*** Da84>

dialecte [djalɛk(t)] *n.m.* dialect <***Loc:*** Da84>

dialogue [djalɔg] *n.m.* dialogue <***Loc:*** Da84>

diamant [diamɑ̃, djɑ̃mɑ̃] *n.m.* **1** diamond **2** diamond (suit of cards) <***Loc:*** JE, Da84>

diamètre [diamɛt(r), djamɛt(r)] *n.m.* diameter *C'est une cylindre à peu près de [...] cinq pieds de diamètre.* That's a cylinder about five feet in diameter. (TB) <***Loc:*** LF, TB, Da84>

diarrhée ♦see **djarette**

dicriche [dikriʃ] *n.m.* person with long hair *Espèce de dicriche, les cheveux va te tomber dans les yeux.* You long-hair, your hair will get in your eyes. (LF) <***Loc:*** LF>

dicter [dikte] *v.tr.* to dictate *Dicter un testament.* To dictate one's testament. (LA) <***Loc:*** LA, Da84>

dictionnaire [diksjɔ̃nær] *n.m.* dictionary <***Loc:*** PQ, Da84>

dicton (ditant, dit-on) [ditɔ̃, ditɑ̃] *n.m.* **1** saying, maxim **Le vieux ditant.* The old saying. (Da84) **2** account, version, side of the story *Le dicton était que...* The story about what happened was . . . (Lv88) ◊ **•(ça) c'est son dicton** that's his/her side of the story *Moi, je sais pas si c'est vrai, mais c'est son dicton.* I don't know if it's true, but that's how he tells it. (VM) <VM, Lv88> <***Loc:***VM, Da84, Lv88>

diète [dʒɛt] *n.f.* diet *Faire la diète, être sur une diète.* To be on a diet. (Lv88) <***Loc:*** AV, Da84, Hi02, Lv88>

dieu [djø, dʒjø, dʒø] *n.m.* **1** God **2** god, deity ◊ **•le Bon Dieu** God, the Good Lord *Le Bon Dieu a été bon pour mon.* God has been good to me. (LF) <EV, IV, JE, LA, LF, SB, SL, SM, TB, An94, Hi02> **•Bon Dieu seigneur {saignable}** expression of surprise or dismay <La99> <***Loc:*** AC, AV,

EV, IV, JE, LA, LF, SB, SL, SM, TB, VM, An94, Da84, Hi02, La99>

différence [diferɑ̃s] *n.f.* **1** difference **Ya eine grande différence entr' ein Amaricain qui prétend de parler français comme ein Parisien et ein Cadien qui est français et qui parle son langage comme le Bon Djeu l'a ordonné.* There's a big difference between an American who claims to speak French like a Parisian and a Cajun who speaks his language like the Good Lord ordained. (ThCa: *Mille misères*) **2** difference in age, height, size, etc. *Ma dernière fille, elle a quarante-huit ans, [...] et J. a quarante-quatre lui, ça fait quatre ans de différence.* My last daughter, she's 48, and J. is 44, that makes four years difference in age. (EV) ◊ **•avoir de la différence** to not get along *Lui et son papa ont tout le temps eu de la différence.* He and his father have always quarreled. (EV) <EV> **•faire une différence** to make a difference *Quelle différence ça fait?* What difference does it make? (ThCa: *Martin Weber*) <AC, EV> <***Loc:*** AV, EV, SL, TB, Da84, ThCa>

différent[1]**, -e** [diferɑ̃, -ɑ̃t] *adj.* **1** different **L'enfant a parti, il a été au collège beaucoup loin, dans un état différent que il restait.* The child left, he went to college far away, in a different state from the one he lived in. (LA, An94) *L'école quand mon j'allais c'est différent qu'asteur.* When I went to school it was different than now. (TB) *Qui-ce qu'y a de différent entre un caveau et une tombe?* What's the difference between a "caveau" and a "tombe"? (TB) **2** apart (in age) *Phillip et moi a trois ans de différent.* Phillip and I are three years apart. (TB) ◊ **•différent de** different, various *Il y a peut-être un peu de différent de mots et de manières mais il y a des différents de manières à parler français en France même.* Maybe there are a few different words and manners but there are different ways of speaking French in France, too. (SL) *Oh, il y a toujours des traiteurs. Il y en a alentour dans différents de bayous.* Oh, there are still folk healers. There are some around in the different bayous. (TB) *Dans le maïs, il y a des chenilles, différent de qualités de chenilles.* In the corn, there are caterpillars, different kinds of caterpillars. (SL) <SL, TB> <***Loc:*** AC, AV, EV, IB, IV, LA, LF, SL, SM, TB, An94, Da84, Lv88, Wh83>

différent[2] [diferɑ̃] *adv.* differently *Des saucisses, du boudin [...] c'est fait différent. Faut que tu mets différents d'affaires dedans.* Sausage and boudin are made differently. You have to put different things in them. (TB) <***Loc:*** AC, TB>

difficile [difisil, defisil] *adj.* **1** difficult, hard *Mais quèquefois les règlements étiont difficiles à suire.* But sometimes the rules were hard to follow. (ThCa: *Mille misères*) **2** fussy, particular, finicky, picky *Mais moi je mange pas ça. Je suis difficile!* But I don't eat that. I'm finicky! (LF) **3** fault-finding, critical *Je pourrais pas vivre avec un homme comme ça. Il est bien trop difficile avec ses enfants.* I couldn't live with a man like that. He's really too critical of his children. (EV) <***Loc:*** EV, LF, Da84, Hi02, ThCa>

difficulté [difikylte, difigylte] *n.f.* **1** difficulty, obstacle *C'est là éioù-ce que j'ai eu plein de difficultés, avec la grammaire.* That's where I had a lot of trouble, with the grammar. (LF) **2** misunderstanding, fuss, trouble (between people) *J'ai eu une difficulté avec lui.* I had a misunderstanding with him. (VM) <***Loc:*** LF, VM, Da84>

digérer (**dégérer, dégirer**) [diʒere, deʒere, deʒire] **I** *v.tr.* to digest *Tu vois, depuis mon opération, j'ai du mal à digérer du gras.* You see, since my operation, I have a hard time digesting fatty foods. (LA) **II** *v.intr.* to digest *J'ai du tracas avec mon fiel. Mon manger dégire pas.* I have trouble with my gall bladder. My food doesn't digest. (VM) <***Loc:*** LA, TB, VM, Da84, Lv88, ThCa>

digestion [diʒestjɔ̃] *n.f.* digestion <***Loc:*** Da84>

digne [diɲ] *adj.* worthy, deserving *Je voudrais que ma fille ait un mari qui serait digne d'elle.* I would like my daughter to have a husband who would be worthy of her. (VM) <***Loc:*** VM, Da84>

dignitaire [diɲitær, dĩjitær] *n.m.* dignitary <***Loc:*** Da84>

dignité [diɲite, dĩjite] *n.f.* dignity <***Loc:*** Da84>

digue [dig] *n.f.* **1** dike **2** dam **3** rain reservoir dug in the ground (often as a watering hole for livestock) <***Loc:*** VM, Da84>

dilemme [dilɛ̃m] *n.m.* dilemma **Mais pauvre Freddy a toujours le dilèmme de gaspiller assez du papier pour forcer le moulin à papier de rouvrir et rengager son oncle.* But poor Freddy always has the dilemma of wasting enough paper to force the paper mill to reopen and rehire his uncle. (Wh83) <***Loc:*** Wh83>

diligence [diliʒɑ̃s] *n.f.* **1** diligence, care **2** stagecoach *Les autres fois la diligence amenait la malle à Gueydan.* The stagecoach used to bring the mail to Gueydan. (VM) <***Loc:*** VM, Da84>

dimanche [dimɑ̃ʃ] *n.m.* Sunday <***Loc:*** EV, LA, SL, SM, An94, Da84, Hi02>

DIME [daɪm] *n.m./f.* dime, ten cent coin <***Loc:*** Lv88>

diminuer [diminɥe] *v.intr.* to diminish, decrease *Un chasseur avait le droit de 25. S'il y en avait deux dans le bateau t'avais le droit de 50 canards. Et là ç'a venu que ça a diminué et diminué.* A hunter had the right to 25. If there were two of you in the boat you had the right to 50 ducks. And then it gradually decreased and decreased. (TB) *Après que les jeunes étaient revenus du service, le français a commencé à diminuer un peu.* After young people came back from the service, French [in Louisiana] started receding a bit. (TB) <***Loc:*** TB, Da84>

dinde (**d'inde**) [dɛ̃d, dɛ̃n, dɛ̃] *n.* **1** *(m.)* male turkey, tom turkey **2** *(f.)* turkey-hen, female turkey **3** silly person, fool, imbecile *Espèce de dinde, tu peux faire mieux que ça.* Silly goose, you can do better than that. (TB) <***Loc:*** AV, IB, JE, LF, SB, SM, TB, Da84, Lv88>

dindon [dẽdɔ̃] *n.m.* male turkey, tom turkey, gobbler <Da84>

dîner[1] [dine] **I** *v.tr.* to eat for dinner, have for dinner *Quoi t'as dîné dimanche au soir?* What did you have for dinner Sunday night? (VM) **II** *v.intr.* **1** to eat the noon meal, have lunch **Un bout de temps, mais là, c'est que c'était rendu à midi. L'homme voulait s'en aller dîner, lâcher pour aller dîner.* A little while later it had gotten to be noon. The man wanted to go eat lunch, to get off to go eat lunch. (SL, An94) *Quand la maîtresse d'école les mettait à genoux dedans le* CLOAK ROOM*, là l'avant-midi là, t'avais pas de dîner pour toi dîner.* When the teacher put them on their knees in the cloak room, the whole morning, you wouldn't have any lunch to eat. (EV) *On va dîner ensemble à midi.* We'll have lunch together at noon. (LA) **2** to dine, eat dinner <***Loc:*** AV, EV, LA, SL, VM, An94, Da84, Lv88>

dîner[2] [dine] *n.m.* **1** lunch, the noon meal *On faisait des biscuits pour nous-autres emmener pour notre dîner.* We made biscuits that we could bring for lunch. (IB) **2** dinner <***Loc:*** EV, IB, SL, TB, Da84, Hi02, Lv88>

diocèse [djosɛz] *n.f.* diocese <***Loc:*** Da84>

dip [dip] *n.f.* dipping vat for livestock <***Loc:*** VM>

DIP [dip] *v.tr.invar.* to dip (livestock) *Ils ont* DIP *les veaux.* They dipped the calves. (EV) <***Loc:*** EV, VM>

diphtérie [difteri] *n.f.* diphteria <***Loc:*** Da84>

diplôme [diplɔ̃m] *n.m.* diploma <***Loc:*** Da84>

dire [dir] **I** *v.tr.* to say, tell **Monsieur Johnson, moi, je peux pas dire autant de vous. Je vous trouve pas beau.* Mr. Johnson, I can't say as much about you. I don't find you handsome. (SM, An94) *Mon je peux dire qu'alle est en famille.* I can tell she's pregnant. (LF) **Dis pas rien.* Say nothing. (Da84) *Tu t'ennuies pas, t'es toujours après dire quelque couillonnade.* You don't get bored, you're always telling some joke. (Lv88) *Dire des prières et puis eux-autres faisait des croix.* To say prayers and they they'd make the sign of the cross. (LF) *Tous les soirs il s'assisait sur ses genoux là à son lit avant qu'il se couche, et j'aimais l'attendre dire la confession, le Confiteor, tu connais.* Every evening he knelt down at his bed before he retired for the night, and I liked to hear him say his prayer of confession, the Confiteor, you know. (TB) *Tu peux dire la même histoire.* You can tell the same story. (TB) *Je vas vous dire de quoi, je sais pas si vous va me croire ou me prendre pour un couillon.* I'm going to tell you something, I don't know if you'll believe me or take me for an imbecile. (LF) *Ça parlait en anglais, et si ça voulait pas les enfants connaît quoi c'était après dire, ça parlait en français.* (Normally) they would speak English but if they did not want the children to know what they were talking about, they spoke French. (AC) *J'avais ça qu'on appelle la ceinture. So j'ai été au docteur. Des toutes petites taches, tu pourrais proche pas dire qui c'était.* I had what they call shingles. So I went to the doctor. Little tiny spots, you almost couldn't tell what it was. (TB) ◊ **•dire des bêtises {farces}** to crack jokes, talk silly *Il aime dire des bêtises.* He likes to tell jokes. (EV) <EV, Da84> **•dire des cochonneries {saletés / saloperies}** to say nasty things, tell dirty stories or coarse jokes *Arrête de dire des saletés devant les enfants!* Stop telling those dirty jokes in front of the children! (EV) <EV, Da84> **•dire en taille douce** to speak diplomatically <Lv88> **•dire (le) bonjour** to greet, say hello <Da84> **•dire qqch après qqn** to say s.t. about s.o. *"Crache en l'air, tombe sur le nez." Si tu dis quelque chose après quelqu'un là,* WELL *plus tard, ça te tombe* BACK *sur le nez.* "Spit in the air, it falls on your nose." If you say something about someone then, well, later on it falls back on you (lit. on your nose). (TB) *Des fois eux-autres croit on après dire de quoi après eux-autres.* Sometimes they think we're talking about them. (TB) <TB> **•dire ses prières** to say one's prayers <Da84> **•dire sur** to tell on, tattle <Da84> **•dire une décade {dizaine}** to say a rosary decade <Da84> **•se dire en {entre} soi-même** to say to oneself *Je m'ai dit entre moi-même, ce gros couillon va se faire tuer.* I thought to myself, that big fool is going to get himself killed. (VM) <VM, Da84> **•avoir pour dire** to have s.t. to say <Da84> **•ça dit** it is said, they say <Da84> **•ça va sans dire** it goes without saying <Da84> **•c'est-à-dire** that is to say, in other words <Da84> **•c'est juste pour dire** it's just to say, just for the record *C'est juste pour dire, mais il a jamais venu hier au soir.* It's just to say, but he never showed up last night. (EV) <EV, Da84> **•comme dit l'autre {le bougre}** as they say, as the saying goes *Il a bien mérité de se trouver avec une femme comme ça. Comme dit le bougre, l'un vaut l'autre et l'autre vaut rien.* He deserves to end up with a woman like that. As they say, one is as good as the other and the other is worthless. (EV) <EV, LA, SL, SM, VM, Da84> **•faire dire** to send word, announce, let it be known *Faire dire aujourd'hui, que j'après m'en aller.* Let it be known today that I'm going away. (ch: *Blues de la prison*) <Da84> **•on dirait** it seems, one would say *Et je dis, "Quand ça me prend," je dis, "on dirait je vas mourir."* And I say, "When it hits me," I say, "you'd think I was dying." (EV) **Il dit, "Quoi ce qu'il y a, maman? On dirait que t'es jongleuse."* He says, "What's the matter, Mom? You seem pensive." (An94) <EV, An94, Da84> **•pas dire coinque {pacane}** to say nothing, not say a word *Il m'a vu, mais il m'a pas dit pacane.* He saw me, but he didn't say a word to me. (SM) <SM, VM, Lv88> **•pour bien {ainsi} dire** to tell the truth *Pour bien dire, j'ai pas d'idée.* To tell you the truth, I have no idea. (LA) <LA, Da84> **•quoi {qui} ça dit?** What do you say? What's new? <LF, TB, La99> **•tu me dis pas** you don't say! <Da84> **•(vaut) autant dire** one might as well say *Alle était après mourir, autant dire.* You might as well say she was dying. (TB) <TB, Da84> <***Loc:*** EV, LA, LF, SL, SM, TB, VM, An94, Da84, Hi02, La99, Lv88>

direct [dirɛk(t)] *adj.* direct, straight *Richard est beaucoup direct.* Richard is very direct. (LA) ◊ **•en direct** live (broadcast) *Je faisais une émission en français le samedi matin pour deux heures de temps en direct, avec de la musique et de la publicité.* I used to do a live two-hour broadcast on Saturday morning, with music and advertising. (SL) <SL> <***Loc*** LA, SL, Da84>

directement [dirɛktəmɑ̃] *adv.* **1** at once, immediately **Je veux savoir ayoù il reste directement.* I want to know immediately where he lives. (SL, An94) **2** directly, expressly *Tibeb s'a assis directement en face de Monsieur Gaston et Ophilia s'a assis à la gauche de Tibeb.* Tibeb sat directly across from Mister Gaston and Ophilia sat on Tibeb's left. (ThCa: *Le charivari*) <***Loc:*** LA, SL, An84, An94, Da84>

directer [dirɛkte] *v.tr.* to direct, give directions, guide *Il a directé le trafic durant la parade.* He directed traffic during the parade. (LA) <***Loc:*** LA, Da84, Hi02>

directeur [dirɛktœr] *n.m.* director, manager <***Loc:*** Da84>

direction [dirɛksjɔ̃, direksjɔ̃] *n.f.* **1** direction *Il m'a dirigé dans la mauvaise direction.* He steered me in the wrong direction. (VM) **2** *(usu. pl.)* directions (to a place) **Le vieux homme affichait juste avec des petits signs desur le bord du chemin qui donnait des directions à sa maison.* The old man advertised simply with small signs on his side of the highway which gave directions to his house. (Wh83) **3** instruction, direction, rule *Il a pris le remède, mais il a pas suivi la direction.* He took the medecine, but he didn't follow the instructions. (SM) **4** behavior *Il a une bonne direction, on croirait jamais qu'il est le fils à ce bon-à-rien.* He has good behavior, one would never believe that he's the son of that good-for-nothing. (VM) <***Loc:*** EV, IB, SL, SM, VM, Da84, Hi02, Lv88, Wh83>

directive [dirɛktiv] *n.m.* rule, directive, direction <***Loc:*** Da84>

directoire [dirɛktwar] *n.m.* directory <***Loc:*** Da84>

diriger [diriʒe, deriʒe] **I** *v.tr.* to direct, steer, conduct *Il m'a dirigé dans la mauvaise direction.* He steered me in the wrong direction. (VM) **II se diriger** *v.pron.* to head for, move toward *Je m'ai dirigé en allant à la Baie Mallette.* I headed for Mallard Bay. (VM) <***Loc:*** VM, Da84>

disable [dizab(l)] *adj.* suitable, decorous, proper, correct *C'est pas disable, ça.* That's not proper. (VM) <***Loc:*** VM, Lv88>

disbander [disbɑ̃de] *v.tr.* to disband, disperse *Après le* SHOW *ils s'ont tous disbandés.* After the show they all dispersed. (TB) <***Loc:*** IB, JE, TB>

disciple [disip(l)] *n.m.* **1** disciple **2** one of the twelve apostles <***Loc:*** Da84>

discompte (**DISCOUNT**) [diskɔ̃t] *n.m./f.* discount *Il m'a donné un bon discompte sur le char.* He gave me a good discount on the car. (Lv88) <***Loc:*** JE, SL, SM, TB, VM, Da84, Lv88>

discompter [diskɔ̃te, dɛskɔ̃te] *v.tr.* to discount, give a discount *Le vieux bougre avait discompté son jardinage parce que c'était tard dans la journée.* The old fellow had offered a discount on his vegetables because it was late in the day. (LA) <***Loc:*** JE, LA, LF, SL, TB, VM, Lv88>

discorde (**discord**) [diskɔrd, diskɔr] *n.m.* discord, disagreement, quarrel, trouble <***Loc:*** Da84, Lv88>

DISCOUNT ♦see **discompte**

discours [diskur] *n.m.* **1** discourse, conversation *Quand la belle a entendu ce discours, elle a monté dans sa chaumière.* When the maiden heard that conversation, she went up into her cottage. (IB, ch: *Une fille de quatorze ans*) *Il s'a emmêlé dans le discours.* He butted into the conversation. (AC) **2** story *Il m'a conté plusieurs des discours de qui-ce qui lui avait arrivé, les grandes fièvres, et les grandes ouragans.* He told me several stories of what had happened to him, the great fevers, and the big hurricanes. (LF) <***Loc:*** AC, IB, LF, Da84>

discussion [diskysjɔ̃] *n.f.* discussion <***Loc:*** Da84>

discutable [diskytab(l)] *adj.* debatable, contestable *Ç'a l'air que c'était quelque chose qu'était pas discutable dans la famille.* It seems that was something that was not debatable in the family. (LA) <***Loc:*** LA, Da84>

discuter [diskyte, deskyte] *v.tr.* to discuss **On a discuté entre nous-autres.* We discussed among ourselves. (LA, An84) <***Loc:*** LA, TB, An84, Da84>

diseur [dizœr] *n.m.* teller *Mon grand-père, c'était un diseur de contes.* My grandfather was a teller of jokes. (LA) ◊ **•diseur de menteries** liar <Da84> <***Loc:*** LA, Da84>

disgrace [disgras, disgrɛs] *n.f.* disgrace, shame *C'est une disgrace la manière qu'ils font leur couillon dans l'église.* It's a disgrace the way they horse around in the church. (SM) <***Loc:*** JE, SM, VM, Da84, Lv88>

disgracieux, -euse [disgrasjø, -øz] *adj.* shameful, disgraceful *La manière qu'il s'est comporté est disgracieux.* The way he acted is shameful. (SM) *Cette chose est disgracieuse.* That thing is shameful. (IB) <***Loc:*** IB, JE, SM>

disparaître [disparɛt(r)] *v.intr.* **1** to disappear, vanish **Les bêtes qu'allaient pour manger, elles auront disparu.* The cows that went to eat, they would disappear. (EV, An94) *Ils ont trouvé la petite fille qui était disparue.* They found the missing girl. (EV) **2** to die *Le monde qui étudie notre héritage essaie aujourd'hui de collecter des contes des vieux raconteurs avant qu'ils disparaissont.* The people who study our heritage try today to collect stories from the old storytellers before they are gone. (VM) <***Loc:*** EV, VM, An94, Da84>

dispense [dispɑ̃s, dispɑ̃] *n.f.* dispensation, exemption (from an ecclesiastical vow, rule, or proscription) *Jimmy a eu une dispense de l'église pour se marier avec une baptiste.* Jimmy got a dispensation from the Church to marry a Baptist. (VM) <***Loc:*** VM, Da84>

dispenser [dispɑ̃se] **I** *v.tr.* to dispense, exempt *Ils l'avaient dispensé de ses obligations.* They had dispensed him of his obligations. (LA) **II se dispenser** *v.pron.* **1** to do without *Je m'ai dispensé d'avoir ça.* I did without having that. (VM) **2** to get rid (of) *J'ai marié un ouvrier, moi qui étais si vaillante fille. Mais c'était de m'en dispenser sans attraper des reproches.* I married a carpenter, I who was a such a nice girl. But it was a matter of how to get rid of him without being blamed. (VM, ch: *J'ai marié un ouvrier*) <VM> <***Loc:*** LA, VM, Da84>

disperser [dispærse] *v.tr.* to disperse, scatter *Là, t'as l'Acadien qu'a arrivé. Parce que dans le conte qu'ils ont pour le Grand Dérangement, ils l'ont dispersé de la Nouvelle Écosse, il est venu ici.* Then there is the Acadian who arrived. Because in the tale they have about the exile, they dispersed him from Nova Scotia, he came here. (SM) <***Loc:*** SM, Da84>

dispersion [dispærsjɔ̃] *n.f.* dispersion, scattering <***Loc:*** Da84>

dispose [dispoz] *n.f.* disposal ◊ **•à votre dispose** at your disposal, at your service <Da84> <***Loc:*** Da84>

disposé, -e [dispoze] *adj.* disposed, inclined *Après leur dispute, il était pas du tout disposé à les aider.* After their dispute, he was not at all disposed to help them. (LA) ◊ **•être bien disposé** to be well disposed <Da84> <***Loc:*** LA, Da84>

disposer [dispoze] *v.tr.* to dispose, arrange, prepare *Disposer des fleurs sur un cercueil.* To arrange flowers on a coffin. (VM) ◊ **•l'homme propose et Dieu dispose** man proposes and God disposes <Da84> <***Loc:*** VM, Da84>

disposition [dispozisjɔ̃] *n.f.* **1** mental disposition, mood, frame of mind *Il a une mauvaise disposition.* He has a bad disposition. (EV) **2** arrangement *La disposition de la salle pour le bal de noces.* The arrangement of the room for the wedding ball. (VM) <***Loc:*** EV, VM, Da84, Wh83>

disputable [dispytab(l)] *adj.* disputable, debatable, doubtful *Sa ligne était pas disputable.* His property line was not disputable. (LA) <***Loc:*** LA, Da84>

disputage [dispytaʒ] *n.m.* scolding **Aussi vite que Paw Paw attendait de cette vilaine manière, le disputage commencait encore.* As soon as Paw Paw heard about this naughtiness, the scolding would commence again. (Wh83) <***Loc:*** Wh83>

disputailler (se) [dispytaje] *v.pron.* to wrangle, quarrel, squabble, bicker with one another *Ça se disputaillait depuis des mois.* They had been bickering among themselves for months. (LA) <***Loc:*** LA, TB, Da84>

dispute [dispyt] *n.f.* dispute, fuss, quarrel, argument <***Loc:*** Da84>

disputer [dispyte] **I** *v.tr.* to scold, reprimand *WELL moi je peux pas me rappeler que j'étais puni mais eux-autres te disputaient.* Well, I can't remember being punished but they would scold you. (LF) *Je l'ai bien disputé pour ça il a fait.* I really scolded him for what he did. (VM) *Quand j'ai pas rentré le linge à l'heure, Mame m'a disputé parce que le serein avait tombé dessus.* When I didn't take the laundry in on time, Mom fussed at me because the night mist had gotten on it. (VM) **II se disputer** *v.pron.* to fuss at, argue with each other *Moi et ma fille on est tout le temps après se disputer par rapport à lui.* My daughter and I are always fussing at each other on account of him. (TB) <***Loc:*** AV, EV, IB, LF, SL, TB, VM, Da84, Lv88>

disputeur [dispytœr] *n.m.* one who wrangles, disputes, fusses <***Loc:*** Da84>

disqualifier [diskwalifje] *v.tr.* to disqualify **Si quec'ein était frappé par la plotte, il était disqualifié pour le restant de le jeu.* If someone was hit by the ball, he was disqualified for the rest of the game. (Wh83) <***Loc:*** Wh83>

disque [dis(k)] *n.m.* **1** disk harrow (implement for preparing a field for planting) **2** record *Papa Cairo, il a récordé un deuxième disque.* Papa Cairo, he cut a second record. (SL) <***Loc:*** SL, Da84>

dissoudre (se) [disud(r)] *v.refl.* to dissolve, break apart **Après ça, le groupe s'est dissolu à cause des problèmes personnels occasionnés par le manque de travail pour le groupe.* After that, the group broke up because of personal problems caused by the lack of work for the group. (LA, An84) <***Loc:*** LA, An84>

distance [distɑ̃s] *n.f.* distance *Sœur Anne, sœur Anne, quoi vois-tu dans la distance?* Sister Anne, Sister Anne, what do you see in the distance? (VM) ◊ **•toutes les distances** every so often **Et toutes les distances, il lâchait une pierre.* And every so often, he would drop a rock. (LA, An94) <LA, An94> <***Loc:*** LA, VM, An94, Da84, Hi02, Lv88>

distiller [distile] *v.tr.* to distill *Distiller du whisky.* To distill whisky. (VM) <***Loc:*** VM, Da84>

distinction [distɛ̃ksjɔ̃] *n.f.* **1** distinction **2** honor ◊ **•faire une distinction** to make a distinction, treat differently *Il fait une distinction entre ses deux enfants.* He treats his two children differently. (VM) <VM> <***Loc:*** VM, Da84>

distinguer [distɛ̃ge] **I** *v.tr.* to distinguish, make a distinction between **Ça peut pas se ressembler plus que ça se ressemble. Enfin, leur mère et leur père peut pas les distinguer.* They can't resemble each other more than they do. In fact, their mother and their father can't distinguish them. (EV, An94) **II se distinguer** *v.pron.* to distinguish o.s., become well known *Mon frère s'a distingué dans la politique.* My brother distinguished himself in politics. (EV) <***Loc:*** EV, An94, Da84, Hi02>

distraction [distraksjɔ̃] *n.f.* distraction, diversion <***Loc:*** Da84>

distribuer [distribɥe] *v.tr.* to distribute, divvy up, parcel out *Ils ont distribué les carabines parmi ceux-là qui restaient.* They distributed the rifles among those who were left. (LA) <***Loc:*** LA, Da84>

distribution [distribysjɔ̃] *n.f.* distribution, division <***Loc:*** Da84>

district [distrik(t)] *n.m.* **1** district (electoral, school, etc.) within a parish or municipality **2** geographic area or region **3** neighborhood <***Loc:*** SM, Da84, Lv88>

dit, -e [di, dit] *n.* aforesaid, aforementioned one **Le dit ou la dite.* The aforesaid man or the aforesaid woman. (Da84) <***Loc:*** Da84>

ditant ♦see **dicton**

ditective ♦see **détective**

dit-on ♦see **dicton**

divan [divɑ̃] *n.m.* divan <***Loc:*** Da84>

divé ♦see **duveté**

diversité [diværsite] *n.f.* diversity, variety <***Loc:*** Da84>

divertir [diværtir] **I** *v.tr.* to amuse, entertain *C'est comme ça qu'il avait habitude de divertir ses enfants.* That's how he used to amuse his children. (LA) **II se divertir** *v.pron.* to amuse o.s., have fun **Allons à la cantine [...] boire et bien rire, et bien se divertir.* Let's go to the cantine to drink and laugh hard and have a real good time. (ch: *Si j'aurais des ailes*) <***Loc:*** LA, Da84>

divertissement [diværtismɑ̃] *n.m.* diversion, amusement, recreation, fun <***Loc:*** Da84>

divinité [divinite] *n.f.* divinity, deity <***Loc:*** Da84>

divisable [divizab(l)] *adj.* divisible *C'est divisable par quatre.* It's divisible by four. (LA) <***Loc:*** EV, LA, Lv88, Ph36>

diviser [divize, devize] **I** *v.tr.* **1** to divide, partition *Ils ont divisé la terre entre les trois frères.* They divided up the land between the three brothers. (LA) **2** to share *Divise ton gâteau avec ton frère.* Share your cake with your brother. (VM) **II se diviser** *v.pron.* to divide, split, break up *Quarante-neuf piastres se divisent pas égal.* Forty-nine dollars does not divide up evenly. (VM) <***Loc:*** LA, SM, VM, Da84>

division [divizjɔ̃] *n.f.* division, partition <***Loc:*** Da84>

divorce [divɔrs] *n.m.* divorce, separation ◊ **•être en divorce** to be quarrelous, be on bad terms or at odds (esp. spouses) **Ils sont toujours en divorce.* They are always quarrelling. (VM) <VM, La99> <***Loc:*** JE, VM, Da84, La99>

divorcé[1]**, -e** [divɔrse] *adj.* **1** divorced *Je suis divorcé depuis 1995.* I've been divorced since 1995. (EV) **2** at odds, not on speaking terms *On est divorcés, nous-autres, on parle plus.* We're at odds, we are, we're no longer speaking. (VM) <***Loc:*** EV, VM, Da84>

divorcé[2]**, -e** [divɔrse] *n.* **1** *(m.)* divorced man **2** *(f.)* divorced woman <***Loc:*** LF, Da84>

divorcer [divɔrse] **I** *v.tr.* to divorce **Elle a divorcé Pascal.* She divorced Pascal. (EV, An94) **II se divorcer** *v.pron.* **1** to divorce each other *Ils s'ont divorcés.* They divorced each other. (VM) **2** to get divorced *A s'a divorcée l'année dernière.* She got a divorce last year. (LA) <***Loc:*** EV, LA, VM, An94, Da84>

dix [dis] (*before a consonant* [di], *before a vowel* [diz]) *adj./n.m.* ten *Moi j'ai travaillé dix ans avec un homme qui connaissait pas parler français du tout du tout, un bougre du Texas.* I worked for ten years with a man who didn't know how to speak French at all, a guy from Texas. (TB) ◊ **•les Dix Commandements** the Ten Commandments <Da84> <***Loc:*** AC, EV, LA, LF, TB, VM, Da84, Hi02>

dix-huit [dizɥit] *adj./n.m.* eighteen *Quand j'avais dix-huit ans je m'ai marié.* When I was eighteen years old, I got married. (AC) <***Loc:*** AC, EV, TB, Da84>

dix-huitième [dizɥitjɛ̃m] *adj./n.* eighteenth <***Loc:*** Da84>

dixième [dizjɛ̃m] *adj./n.* tenth *Je suis après te dire pour la dixième fois.* I'm telling you for the tenth time. (LA) *Trois milles et trois dixièmes.* Three and three-tenths miles. (TB) <***Loc:*** EV, LA, TB, Da84>

dix-neuf [diznœf] *adj./n.m.* nineteen *Ça c'était en dix-neuf cent seize.* That was in nineteen hundred and sixteen. (AC) <***Loc:*** AC, AV, EV, VM, Da84>

dix-neuvième [diznœvjɛ̃m] *adj./n.* nineteenth <***Loc:*** Da84>

dix-sept [disɛt] *adj./n.m.* seventeen *J'ai eu dix-sept ans dans décembre et je m'ai marié dans août d'après.* I turned seventeen in December and I got married the following August. (EV) <***Loc:*** AC, EV, TB, Da84>

dix-septième [disetjɛ̃m] *adj./n.* seventeenth **Ce n'est pas au vingtième siècle que les Acadiens quitteront le dix-septième.* It won't be in the twentieth century that Cajuns leave the seventeenth. (ThCa: *Mille misères*) <***Loc:*** Da84, ThCa>

dix-sous [disu] *n.m.* dime, ten-cent coin <***Loc:*** Da84>

dizaine [dizɛ̃n] *n.f.* quantity of about ten *Une dizaine de monde.* About ten people. (TB) <***Loc:*** TB, VM, Da84>

djarette (diarrhée) [dʒarɛt, djare] *n.f.* diarrhea, loose bowels <***Loc:*** VM, Da84>

djeule ♦see **gueule**

djog ♦see **JUG**

docile [dosil] *adj.* docile, gentle, tame *Tracasse-toi pas, c'est un chien docile.* Don't worry, it's a gentle dog. (VM) <***Loc:*** VM, Da84>

docteur [dɔktœr, doktœr] *n.m.* doctor, physician ◊ **•docteur d'animaux** veterinarian <LF> **•le docteur après la mort!** too late! <La99> <***Loc:*** AC, AV, EV, IB, LF, SL, SM, TB, Da84, Hi02, La99>

doctrine [dɔktrin] *n.f.* doctrine, teaching <***Loc:*** Da84>

document [dokymɑ̃] *n.m.* document, certificate *Eusse avait lit dedans un document que à cette place-là, à ce gros saule, qu'il avait du trésor d'enterré.* They had read in a document that in that place, at that big willow, that there was a treasure buried. (LF) <***Loc:*** LF, Da84>

documentaire [dokymɑ̃tær] *n.m.* documentary *Ils ont fait un documentaire sus le Mardi Gras à Mamou.* They did a documentary on the Mamou Mardi Gras. (EV) <***Loc:*** EV, Da84>

documenter [dokymɑ̃te] *v.tr.* to document, furnish proof, write down *Il faut que ça soit documenté à la maison de cour.* That has to be documented at the courthouse. (VM) <***Loc:*** VM, Da84>

dodo [dodo] *n.m.* [*baby talk*] sleep ◊ **•faire dodo** [*baby talk*] to go to sleep *Fais dodo, le 'tit bébé.* Go to sleep, little baby. (SM) <SM, Da84, Lv88> <***Loc:*** AV, SM, Da84, Lv88>

doignon [dwɑ̃jɔ̃] *n.m.* finger bandage, fingerstall (protective finger covering) <***Loc:*** IB, JE, SL, SM, VM, Lv88>

doigt [dwa] *n.m.* **1** finger *Il s'est coupé son doigt avec son* BARLOW*.* He cut his finger with his pocketknife. (AV) **2** approximative unit of measure *Un doigt de monde étranger qu'a venu, ç'a commencé à mener l'école en anglais.* A handful of outsiders came, they started conducting school in English. (TB) ◊ **•doigt annulaire** ring finger <Da84> **•doigt torchant** index finger <VM> **•à deux doigts de sa mort** very close to death <AV, La99> **•avoir des grands doigts** to be prone to stealing <EV, La99> **•un doigt d'épais {d'épaisseur}** the thickness of a finger <Da84> **•un doigt de whiskey** finger (i.e. small amount) of whiskey <Da84> <***Loc:*** AV, EV, TB, VM, Da84, Hi02, La99>

doir ♦see **devoir**

domaine [dɔ̃mɛ̃n] *n.m.* land, domain ◊ **•être domaine** said of landed property that has been expropriated by the state *La terre qui colle à ma place est domaine.* The land next to my place has become subject to imminent domain. (VM) <VM> <***Loc:*** VM>

domboune [dɔ̃bun] *n.f.* big woman *C'est une grosse domboune ça qui passe dans le chemin public.* That's a big woman going by on the public road. (TB) <***Loc:*** TB>

domestique [dɔ̃mestik] *n.* **1** house servant, domestic **2** *(f.)* maid <***Loc:*** Da84>

domicile [dɔ̃misil] *n.m.* domicile, home, residence <***Loc:*** Da84>

domination [dɔ̃minasjɔ̃] *n.f.* domination, rule <***Loc:*** Da84>

dominer [dɔ̃mine] *v.tr.* to dominate, rule, control **Plutôt que quitter la musique Américaine dominer dans le Sud de la Louisiane, on prend des chansons populaires, traduit les en Français et quitte des musiciens Cajins assaisonner les aires avec des accordéons et violons.* Rather than letting American music dominate in southern Louisiana, we take popular songs, translate them into French and let Cajun musicians spice up the tunes with accordeons and violins. (Wh83) <***Loc:*** Da84, Wh83>

dominicale [dɔ̃minikal] *adj.* *[eccl.]* **1** pertaining to God **2** pertaining to Sunday *Le prêtre a fait sa visite dominicale.* The priest made his Sunday visit. (VM) <***Loc:*** VM, Da84>

domino [dɔ̃mino] *n.m. (usu. pl.)* domino <***Loc:*** Da84>

dommage [dɔ̃maʒ] *n.m. (often pl.)* damage, loss, harm *Les ouragans était dangereux dans ce temps ça là. Y a eu des dommages de la levée.* Hurricanes were dangerous in those days. There was damage to the levee. (SB) ◊ **•c'est dommage** it's too bad, it's a pity <Da84, Hi02> **•faire du dommage** to damage, do damage *L'ouragan [...] nous a fait du dommage.* The hurricane did us some damage. (TB) <TB, Da84> <***Loc:*** LF, SB, TB, Da84, Hi02>

dommager [dɔ̃maʒe] *v.tr.* to damage, harm, break *Le vent avait dommagé la couverture.* The wind had damaged the roof. (LA) <***Loc:*** LA, Da84, Hi02, Lv88>

dompte [dɔ̃t] *adj.* tame, broken, docile *Le cheval est pas dompte, attention!* The horse isn't broken, watch out! (VM) <***Loc:*** VM>

dompter [dɔ̃te] *(p.p.* **dompté** [dɔ̃te], **dompte** [dɔ̃t]*)* *v.tr.* to tame, gentle, domesticate, break (a horse) *Il a dompte le cheval.* He tamed the horse. (LF) *Tu peux pas le dompter, tu peux pas l'adoucir, tu peux pas le* TRAIN. You can't subdue him [that horse], you can't gentle him, you can't train him. (VM) <***Loc:*** LA, LF, VM, Da84>

dompteur [dɔ̃tœr] *n.m.* trainer (of horses) **Aux grandes courses à Mamou, Jim et mon a demandé à ein de les dompteurs de l'information dessus son cheval.* At the races in Mamou, Jim and I asked one of the trainers some information about his horse. (Wh83) <***Loc:*** Wh83>

don [dɔ̃] *n.m.* gift, present, donation <***Loc:*** Da84>

DON'T-CARE [dɔ̃kær] *n.m.* independent person <***Loc:*** EV, Ph36>

donation [dɔ̃nasjɔ̃] *n.f.* donation, gift, offering <***Loc:*** Da84>

donc [dɔ̃k] *conj.* **1** therefore, so, then, hence **Jolie blonde, 'gardez donc quoi t'as fait, tu m'as quitté pour t'en aller.* Pretty blond, so look at what you've done, you left me to go away. (ch: *Jolie blonde*) **2** though **Et ils nous ont pas attrapés. Hé, j'avais peur, donc.* And they didn't catch us. Hey, but I was scared, though. (SL, An94) ◊ **•r'garde mais donc!** well, I'll say! <Hi02> <***Loc:*** AC, EV, SL, An94, Da84, Hi02>

donnailler [dɔ̃naje] *v.tr.* to give here and there, give to various people, give repeatedly *Il donnaille son argent partout.* He gives out money here and there. (IB) *Ça fait on a commencé à donner ça au monde du tour, les tartes à la patate qu'on avait, on était* PROUD *de ça qu'on connaissait faire, so on a donnaillé ça au monde du tour.* So we started giving that to the people around here, the potato pies we had, we were proud of what we knew how to do, so we gave them to people around here. (TB) <***Loc:*** IB, TB>

donner [dɔ̃ne] **I** *v.tr.* **1** to give *Donne-moi ça tu m'as promis.* Give me that which you promised me. (SM) *Donnez-moi ça vous m'avez dit.* Give me that which you said (you would give me). (Lv88) **Donne-moi la.* Give it to me. (Da84) **2** to present, show **Tu peux me donner le chemin* BACK TO *Mamou?* Can you show me the road back to Mamou? (EV, An94) **3** to grant **Les autres quand ça a venu temps, le Bon Dieu a voulu, Il a donné une pluie à eux-autres, ça a fait des épis de maïs.* The others, when the time came and the Good Lord wanted to, He granted a rain to them, and they grew some ears of corn. (SL, An94) **4** to provide, produce, furnish *Mais c'était tout le temps des cochons qu'étaient gros comme moi, proche. Et ça donnait un tas de la graisse.* But it was always pigs that were almost as fat as me. And that provided a lot of fat. (LA) **Ça lui donnait un bon bout à marcher d'une à l'autre.* He had a long way to walk from one to the other. (IV, An94) *Ça y donne un tas d'écrevisses* *à nettoyer.* That gives him a lot of crawfish to clean. (VM) **II** *v.intr.* **1** to bear fruit *Les pacaniers donnent tous les deux ans.* Pecan trees bear every two years. (LA) **2** to shine (of the sun) **Le soleil donne sur la galerie.* The sun shines on the porch. (Da84) ◊ **•donner à boire** to give a drink <Da84> **•donner à comprendre** to make (s.o.) understand *Il m'a donné à comprendre qu'il m'aurait pas payé.* He made me understand that he was not going to pay me. (LA) <LA, Da84> **•donner à connaître** to let (s.o.) know *Il lui a donné à connaître qu'il faulait partir avant que les autres arrivent.* He let him know that it was necessary to leave before the others got there. (LA) <LA, Da84> **•donner à manger** to feed *Ils pouvaient donner à manger à leurs enfants, y avait des écoles.* They could feed their kids, there were schools. (SB) <SB, Da84> **•donner à téter** to nurse <Da84> **•donner au large** to head for the open (sea, etc.) *Le bateau était après donner au large.* The boat was headed out to sea. (EV) <EV, Da84> **•donner de la confiture aux cochons** to throw pearls before swine, match up s.o. of quality with s.o. much less worthy or attractive <La99> **•donner de la place** to make room <Da84> **•donner des coups** to beat up <Da84> **•donner des faux airs (à qqn)** to resemble, look like (s.o.) *On se donne des faux airs dans la famille.* We resemble each other in the family. (VM) <SM, VM> **•donner du crédit** to extend credit <Da84> **•donner du plaisir** to please, give pleasure <Da84> **•donner du tracas** to give trouble <Da84> **•donner du {un} retour** ***a*** to give s.t. in return ***b*** to render a profit *Les vaches Brahmas me donnent un meilleur retour que les Angus.* Brahma cattle are more profitable for me than Angus. (VM) <VM, Da84> **•donner justice** to give justice <Da84> **•donner la liberté** to free, give freedom <Da84> **•donner la moitié** to give one-half *Madame Richard nettoyait des oies pour ma mère, mais il fallait que Mame y donne la moitié.* Mrs. Richard cleaned wild geese for my mother on halves; Mom had to give her half the geese. (VM) <VM, Da84> **•donner la tête vers** to head for or towards **Donner la tête vers la ville.* To head for the city. (Da84) <Da84> **•donner la {une} main** to help, lend a hand *Donne-moi la main, R.* Give me a hand, R. (TB) *Si un projet est commencé, tout chacun donne la main.* If a project is started, everybody helps out. (Lv88) *On travaillait le jardin et lui, il donnait la main.* We were working in the garden, and he lent a hand. (Lv88) <TB, Lv88> **•donner le bon exemple** to give a good example <Da84> **•donner le chemin** ***a*** to yield the road or way, make way *Il était braqué là. Il voulait pas donner le chemin.* He was planted there. He would not yield the way. (LA) ***b*** to show the way **Tu peux me donner le chemin back to Mamou?* Can you show me the way back to Mamou? (EV, An94) <EV, LA, An94, Da84> **•donner le mot** to pass the word or news *Donne le mot à Coon qu'on va commencer à couper du riz demain, s'il mouille pas.* Pass the word on to Coon that we'll start cutting rice tomorrow if it doesn't rain. (VM) <VM, Da84> **•donner le pouvoir** to confer power, authorize <Da84> **•donner notice** to give notice *Mon frère a donné notice qu'il va courir pour maire dans la prochaine élection.* My brother gave notice that he is going to run for mayor in the next election. (VM) <VM, Da84> **•donner réponse** to give an answer, reply <Da84> **•donner sa parole** to give one's word, promise <Da84> **•donner satisfaction** to satisfy, make amends, give satisfaction *J'aime pas mon job, ça payait les BILLS, mais ça me donnait pas satisfaction.* I don't like my job, it paid the bills, but it didn't give me any satisfaction. (VM) <VM, Da84> **•donner son {un} capot (à qqn)** (said of a woman) to spurn, reject, or break up with a suitor *Elle m'a donné mon capot et j'ai braillé.* She rejected me and I cried. (EV) <EV, JE, SL, La99> **•donner sur** ***a*** to face **La maison donne sur le nord.* The house faces north. (Da84) ***b*** [time] to be nearing, be almost **Donner sur midi.* To be almost noon. (Da84) <Da84> **•donner un BLACK-EYE** to give a black eye <Da84> **•donner un cataplasme (à qqn)** to scold s.o., tell s.o. off <La99> **•donner un coup de balai** to hit with a broom <Da84> **•donner un coup de main** to help, lend a helping hand, provide assistance *Tu peux me donner un coup de main avec ma barrière?* Can you give me a hand with my fence? (EV) <EV, Da84, La99> **•donner un coup d'épaule** to help <Da84> **•donner une charade** to have a conversation <Lv88> **•donner une jambette** to trip someone <Lv88> **•donner une partance (à qqn)** to help someone start a venture <TB, La99> **•donner une pourgale** to frighten <Da84> **•donner une pousse** to give a push <Da84> **•donner une reprise** to give a second chance <Da84> **•donner une volée** to give a good whipping <Da84> **•donner un pied (à qqn)** to give s.o. an advantage, a 'leg up' <AV, La99> **•se donner crédit** to give oneself credit <Da84> **•se donner de la misère** to take the trouble *Elle s'a donné de la misère pour faire ce gros dîner et t'as proche pas mangé.* She took the trouble to make that big dinner and you hardly ate. (VM) <VM, Da84> **•se donner de la peine** to do (s.t.) with care <Da84> **•se donner des airs** to put on airs <Da84> **•se donner du tracas** to take the trouble <Da84> **•se donner la main** to shake hands *Après la bataille, ils ont refusé de se donner la main.* After the fight, they refused to shake hands. (LA) *On avait pas l'habitude de se donner la main durant la messe comme on fait asteur.* We didn't used to shake each other's hands during mass like they do now. (EV) <EV, LA, Da84> **•se donner la peine** to take the trouble, make an effort *Il se donne même plus la peine de faire comme si il l'aimait.* He doesn't even make an effort to pretend that he liked her. (LA) <LA, Da84> **•se donner le trouble** to take the trouble <Da84> **•se donner une bosse** to satisfy a desire, indulge a passion (drinking, eating, dancing, etc. to one's heart's content) **Ah! quelle bosse j'm'sommes donnés hier à la noce* *à Zoséphine.* (SM, Wh69) <SM, Lv88, Wh69> **•se donner une touche** to get tired, get worn out, wear o.s. out <SB, La99> **•ça donne une semaine {un mois / deux jours} que** a week, a month, two days ago *Ça donne deux ans qu'il est élevé. Il est dessus des blocs de dix-huit pouces.* It [the house] has been raised for two years now. It's sitting on eighteen inch blocks. (TB) *Combien ça donne de temps qu'on est ensemble?* How long have we been together? (LF) <LF, TB> <***Loc:*** AV, EV, IV, JE, LA, LF, SB, SL, SM, TB, VM, An94, Da84, Hi02, La99, Lv88>

donneur, -euse [dɔ̃nœr, -øz] *adj.* generous *Il a tout le temps été donneur.* He has always been generous. (LA) <***Loc:*** LA, Lv88>

donquin ♦see **tonquin**

dont [dɔ̃] *pron.* [*rare*] whose, of whom, about whom, of which, about which *Je connais des Noirs dont la parlure a gardé beaucoup de ressemblance avec le créole d'Haïti.* I know blacks whose language has maintained a lot of resemblance with Haitian Creole. (SM) **La chose dont (de laquelle) je t'ai parlé.* The thing I talked to you about. (Da84) <***Loc:*** SM, Da84>

dope [dop] *n.m.* dope, drug *Je savais qu'il s'aurait raccroché dessus ce dope-là.* I knew he'd get hooked on that dope stuff again. (LA) <***Loc:*** EV, LA, Da84>

doper [dope] **I** *v.tr.* to dope, give dope to *Doper un cheval.* To dope a horse. (VM) **II se doper** *v.pron.* to take dope, get doped up *Il va mourir jeune. Il est tout le temps après se doper.* He's going to die young. He's always getting doped up. (EV) <***Loc:*** EV, VM, Da84>

dorer [dore] *v.tr.* to gild, cover in gold *Dorer une petite boîte.* To gild a little box. (LA) <***Loc:*** LA, Da84>

dormailler [dɔrmaje, dormaje] *v.intr.* **1** to drowse, doze *Durant le prône du prêtre, il dormaillait.* During the priest's sermon, he was dozing off. (VM) **2** to sleep badly, sleep fitfully *J'ai juste manière dormaillé hier au soir.* I only slept fitfully last night. (LA) <***Loc:*** EV, LA, TB, VM, Lv88, Ph36>

dormeur [dɔrmœr] *n.m.* sea snipe, red-breasted snipe <***Loc:*** Re31>

dormeuse [dɔrmøz] *n.f.* **1** chaise longue **2** pendant earring set with a solitaire diamond <***Loc:*** SM, VM>

dorminique [dɔrminik] *n.m.* sleepy person, sleepy-head *Réveille-toi, espèce de dorminique.* Wake up, you sleepy-head! (VM) <***Loc:*** VM>

dormir [dɔrmir] *v.intr.* to sleep, slumber *Je pouvais pas dormir le soir, mais asteur je peux dormir avec n'importe qui.* I couldn't sleep at night, but now I can sleep with anybody. (ThCa: *Messieurs, mesdames*) ◊ **•dormir comme un caïman {un congo / une caille molle}** to sleep soundly <EV, SM, La99> **•dormir comme une bûche** to sleep well <La99> **•dormir debout** to be very tired, asleep on one's feet *Pauvre bête, elle était assez lasse qu'elle dormait debout!* Poor thing, she was so tired that she was asleep on her feet. (EV) <EV, La99> **•dormir sur un rôti** to sleep on the job, fall asleep at the switch <Re31> **•en dormant** while asleep <Da84> <***Loc:*** AL, EV, LA, SL, SM, Da84, Hi02, La99, Re31, ThCa>

Dorothée [dorote] *n.prop.* name of the carnaval queen, wife of Captain Mouse *Les enfants ont galopé à la barrière pour voir la Dorothée et le capitaine Souris.* The children ran to the fence to see the Mardi Gras queen and king. (SL) <***Loc:*** SL, Lv88>

dortoir [dɔrtwar] *n.m.* dormitory <***Loc:*** Da84>

dorure [doryr] *n.f.* **1** piece of jewelry *T'as des dorures dans les doigts.* You've got jewelry on your fingers. (TB) **2** gold ornament <***Loc:*** AV, LF, SB, SL, SM, TB, Da84, Lv88>

dos [do] *n.m.* back *Le dos de la vieille femme est croche.* The old woman's back is bent. (SM) *Il s'a fait haler un nerf dedans le dos-là. Pour deux jours ça lui a fait mal.* He pulled a muscle in his back. It hurt him for two days. (TB) ◊ **•dos brillant et ventre criant** said of a person who spends much on clothing and little on food <Da84> **•dos-fond** swayback **J'avais un vieux petit cheval dos-fond cannelle.* I had a little old swayback cinnamon-colored horse. (EV, An84) <EV, An84> **•dans le dos** behind one's back, in secret **Rover était après dire quoi t'avais fait, dans le dos à Maman.* Rover was telling what you did behind Mother's back. (LA, An94) <LA, An94> **•être à dos** to be on bad terms in a relationship <La99> **•gros dos** rich or important person <La99> <***Loc:*** EV, IV, JE, LA, LF, SM, TB, VM, An94, Da84, Hi02, La99, Lv88>

dosage [dozaʒ] *n.m.* dosage <***Loc:*** Da84>

dose [doz] *n.f.* dose <***Loc:*** Da84>

dos-gris [dogri] *n.* **1** ring-necked duck **2** lesser scaup duck <***Loc:*** JE, LF, TB, VM, Lv88>

dossier [dosje] *n.m.* **1** back (of a seat, chair, etc.) **2** file, record **3** person's background <***Loc:*** Da84>

dossière [dosjær] *n.f.* **1** padding used under a saddle **2** backband of a harness <***Loc:*** LA, Da84>

doube [dub] *n.m./f.* stave *T'auras pas assez des doubes.* You won't have enough staves. (SB) <***Loc:*** SB>

doublage [dublaʒ] *n.m.* lining (of clothing) <***Loc:*** Da84>

double[1] [dub(l)] *adj.* **1** double, twice as much *Il est plus gros, il est proche double la grosseur de ça-là.* It's bigger, it's almost double the size of that one. (TB) **2** double-faced **Le lendemain, son père l'a envoyé en wagon encore pour chercher une charrue qu'il avait oubliée dans le clos, une grosse charrue double.* The next day, his father sent him in the wagon again to look for a plow that he had forgotten in the field, a big middle-buster plow. (An94) *Une herse double.* A double harrow. (AV) *Un chassis double.* A double-faced window. (LA) <***Loc:*** AV, LA, TB, An94, Da84>

double[2] [dub(l)] *n.m.* **1** double, twice (the quantity or quality) **2** duplicate, replica **3** double (of a person) <***Loc:*** Da84>

doublement [dubləmɑ̃] *adv.* doubly <***Loc:*** Da84>

doubler [duble] **I** *v.tr.* **1** to line, add lining to (clothing, etc.) *Doubler un capot.* To line a coat. (EV) **2** to whip, give a thrashing to, beat up **II se doubler** *v.pron.* to double up (e.g. in pain) *Memère s'a doublé avec des crampes.* Memère doubled up with cramps. (EV) <***Loc:*** EV, JE, SL, VM, Da84>

doubleur [dublœr] *n.m.* lining *J'ai pas de doubleur dans mon capot.* I don't have lining in my coat. (VM) <***Loc:*** VM>

doublure [dublyr] *n.f.* **1** lining (of clothing) **2** padding <***Loc:*** SL, Da84>

doucement[1]**, -e** [dusmɑ̃, -ɑ̃t] *adj.* **1** slow, slow-moving, sluggish *Ça prend du temps pour tisser, c'est bien doucement* Weaving takes time, it's pretty slow. (Lv88) *Des journées chaudes et doucementes.* Hot, slow days. (Lv88) *Il était gros, et grand, fort, mais pas vite, doucement.* He was big, and tall, strong, but not fast, slow. (SL) **Doucement comme la melasse en janvier.* Slow as molasses in January. (AC, La99) **2** lazy *J'étais manière doucement quand j'étais petite.* I was kind of lazy when I was little. (EV) <***Loc:*** AC, EV, LF, SB, SL, SM, TB, VM, Da84, La99, Lv88, Ph36>

doucement[2] [dusmɑ̃] *adv.* **1** slowly *Des fois si ça venait trop vite, follait que je les arrête, les faire aller plus doucement.* Sometimes if they were driving too fast, I had to stop them, make them go more slowly. (TB) *Ça levait doucement, pas comme le* YEAST *de asteur que on achète.* It rose slowly, not like the yeast that we buy now. (SL) **2** softly, gently *Fais doucement quand tu flattes le chat.* Do it gently when you pet the cat. (EV) **3** quietly *Il a commencé chercher et il les a trouvés au magasin, et il a approché tout doucement et il les a attendu après parler.* He started looking and he found them in the barn, and he approached quietly and heard them talking. (LA) ◊ **•doucement!** slow down! <JE> **•doucement comme la lune {un colimaçon / une crabe / une merde / une tortue / Christmas}** very slowly <AC, EV, LF, VM, La99, Lv88> **•tout doucement** slowly, little by little <EV, LA, An84, Da84> <***Loc:*** AC, EV, LA, LF, JE, SB, SL, SM, TB, VM, An84, Da84, Hi02, La99, Lv88, Ph36>

doucer [duse] *v.tr.* to sweeten *Il douce son café trop.* He sweetens his coffee too much. (SB) <***Loc:*** SB>

douceur [dusœr] *n.f.* **1** sweetness, kindness, gentleness **2** *(often pl.)* sweets, confections, candy, sweet things *Il peut plus avoir beaucoup de douceurs et tout ça.* He can not eat sweet things anymore. (IB) *La douceur est engraissante.* Sweets are fattening. (EV) <***Loc:*** IB, Da84>

douche [duʃ] *n.f.* **1** douche **2** enema <***Loc:*** Da84>

doucine [dusin] *n.f.* razor strap <***Loc:*** JE, VM>

doucir ♦ see **adoucir**

dou-dou[1] [dudu] *v.intr.invar.* *[baby talk]* to poop <***Loc:*** SM>

dou-dou[2] [dudu] *n.m.* *[baby talk]* doo-doo, poop, poo <***Loc:*** SM>

doudouces [dudus] *n.f.pl.* candy *J'aime les doudouces rouges.* I like red candy. (SB) <***Loc:*** SB>

douelle [dwɛl, dwal] *n.f.* **1** barrel stave, siding, lath *Il va te manquer deux douelles de six pieds.* You'll be short two six-foot staves. (SB) **2** mason's trowel <***Loc:*** SB, TB, VM, Da84>

douille [duj] *n.f.* **1** beating, whipping, thrashing *Je l'ai foutu une douille.* I gave him a beating. (SM) **2** physical punishment, spanking <***Loc:*** JE, LF, SL, SM, VM, Lv88>

douillet (douillette) [duje, dujɛt] *adj.* **1** weak, sickly *Un enfant douillet.* A sickly child. (EV) **Çt'homme est douillette, i peut pas travailler.* That man is sickly, he can't work. (EV, Ph36) **2** delicate, sensitive, squeamish *Il est trop douillet pour propter des oies.* He's too squeamish to clean geese. (VM) **3** slow *Ça c'est douillette, hourra donc.* That's slow, so hurry up. (VM) **4** plush, cozy, comfy **Sans même de quitter leurs chaises douillettes à Washington, D.C. y pouvont nous empêcher de gongner eine vie honnête en Louisiane.* Without even leaving their comfy chairs in Washington, D.C. they can keep us from earning an honest living in Louisiana. (ThCa: *Mille misères*) <***Loc:*** EV, LF, SM, VM, Lv88, Ph36, ThCa>

douleur [dulœr] *n.f.* **1** pain, suffering, ache *Dis-moi quelque chose Dud; ton Happy Day Headache Powder, ça t'a pas aidé avec tes douleurs?* Tell me something, Dud; your Happy Day Headache Powder, didn't it help with your pains? (ThCa: Messieurs, mesdames) *J'ai une douleur dans mon dos.* I've got a backache. (VM) **2** sorrow, grief <***Loc:*** EV, VM, Da84, Hi02, ThCa>

douleureux, -euse [dulurø, -øz] *adj.* suffering, in pain *Tu connais que proche toutes les femmes ont du tracas avec la maladie de femme tous les mois. Cette maladie les rend douleureuses et nerveuses. Quand elles sont pas gaillardes, elles sont* HELL*, ouais!* You know that almost all women have problems with their monthly 'illness.' That illness leaves them in pain and nervous. When they're out of sorts, they are hell, yeah! (ThCa: *Messieurs, mesdames*) <***Loc:*** ThCa>

doutable [dutab(l)] *adj.* doubtful, questionable, uncertain, unsure *C'est doutable s'il a seulement une éducation du quatrième livre.* It's doubtful if he even has a fourth-grade education. (Lv88) <***Loc:*** AV, EV, IB, JE, SB, SL, SM, TB, VM, Da84, Lv88, Ph36>

doutance [dutɑ̃s] *n.f.* doubt, uncertainty, suspicion *J'ai des doutances là-dessus.* I have doubts about it. (VM) *J'ai des doutances qu'il va venir.* I have doubts that he will come. (SM) <***Loc:*** AV, JE, LF, SB, SM, VM, Da84, Lv88, Re31>

doute [dut] *n.f.* doubt, uncertainty, suspicion, distrust **Il y a pas de doute.* There's no doubt. (SM, An94) <***Loc:*** SM, An94, Da84>

douter [dute] **I** *v.intr.* to doubt *Il doutait qu'un homme avec des prêcheurs méthodistes dans sa famille serait d'accord d'élever ses enfants catholiques.* He doubted that a man with Methodist preachers in his family would agree to raise his children Catholic. (ThCa: La dernière quilte) **Je trouvais* *emasse [=en masse] de les traitments curieux et des fois je doubtais [=doutais] si ça aurait travailler.* I found many of the treatments strange and sometimes I doubted whether they would work. (Wh83) **III se douter** *v.pron.* to suspect **Je m'en doutais de ça.* I suspected that. (Da84) *Je me doutais qu'il aurait venu.* I figured he would come. (VM) <***Loc:*** LA, VM, Da84, ThCa, Wh83>

doux[1], **douce** [du, dus, dos] *adj.* **1** sweet, sweetened *Moi, j'aime mon café bien doux.* I like my coffee really sweet. (Gu00) *On avait de la limonade douce.* We had sweetened lemonade. (EV) **2** tame, gentle (of an animal) *J'étais après charcher un petit chacta bien doux pour mon petit enfant.* I was looking for a nice, gentle little pony for my grandchild. (Gu00) *Attention, le chat est pas doux, il va te grafigner.* Be careful, the cat is not tame, he will scratch you. (VM) **3** fresh, not salt (of water) **Eau douce.* Fresh water. (Da84) *D'eau salée. D'eau douce.* Salt water. Fresh water. (TB) ◊ **•doux comme (le doux dans) le miel *a*** very sweet *Son bec il est doux comme le doux dans le miel.* Her kiss is as sweet as the sweetness of honey. (ch: *La veuve du Lac Bleu*) ***b*** very gentle <AC, La99> <***Loc:*** AC, AV, EV, IB, SM, TB, VM, Da84, Gu00, Hi02, La99, Lv88>

doux[2] [du] *n.m.* sweets *On faisait des pénitences des fois qu'on allait pas manger du doux du Carème.* We would do penance sometimes by not eating sweets during Lent. (TB) *Tu vas t'engraisser si tu manges trop du doux.* You will be become fat if you eat too many sweets. (LA) <***Loc:*** LA, TB>

douzaine [duzɛ̃n] *n.f.* dozen *Il y avait une douzaine dans la boîte.* There were a dozen in the box. (EV) ◊ **•demi-douzaine** half dozen *Peut-être tu ramassais peut-être une douzaine, des fois une demi-douzaine.* Perhaps you gathered about a dozen, sometimes a half dozen [oysters]. (LF) <LF, Da84> <***Loc:*** EV, LF, Da84, Hi02>

douze [duz] *adj./n.m.* twelve *Eusse a eu douze enfants, et nous-autres on était à trois, so on est à quinze dans la famille.* They had twelve children, and there were three of us, so we're a family of fifteen. (TB) <***Loc:*** AC, AV, EV, JE, SL, TB, Da84>

douzième [duzjɛ̃m] *adj./n.* twelfth *Leur douzième enfant est mort du cancer.* Their twelfth child died of cancer. (EV) <***Loc:*** EV, Da84>

dradon ♦see **édredon**

DRAG [dɹæg] *n.m.* drag, puff (on a cigarette) <***Loc:*** Da84>

dragée [draʒe] *n.m./f.* candy (of any type) **Les pitits aiment les dragées.* Children like candy. (EV, Ph36) *Les enfants qui étaient rassis ont eu chacun une dragée.* The children who were reseated each got a hard candy. (LA) <***Loc:*** EV, IB, LA, Ph36>

DRAG-LINE [dɹæglaɪn] *n.m.* dragline, dredge <***Loc:*** Da84>

dragon [dragɔ̃] *n.m.* dragon <***Loc:*** Da84>

drague [drag] *n.f.* **1** dragnet, type of fishing net *Une ligne ça on use pour traverser un bayou, on appelle ça une drague. Ça prend un bord du bayou et ça va l'autre bout.* A line used across a bayou, we call that a dragnet. It goes from one side of the bayou to the other side. (SM) **2** oyster dredge *Ç'a venu trop creux pour [une gaffe]. Et après ça j'ai été avec une petite drague. Et t'amarres la drague sur le côté du bateau.* It got too deep to use oyster tongs. And after that I went with a small oyster dredge. You attach the dredge to the side of the boat. (TB) **3** trotline ◊ **•drague à main** hand-held oyster dredge <TB> <***Loc:*** AL, EV, JE, SM, TB, Re31>

DRAIN (**drine**) [dɹein, drin] *n.m.* **1** drain **2** drain pipe <***Loc:*** TB, Da84, Lv88>

drainer [drɛ̃ne] *v.tr.* to drain *Et le petit Bayou de la Pointe était un de ces petits bayous naturels. Ça drainait à la mer.* And the little bayou in Pointe aux Chênes was one of those natural little bayous. It drained into the sea. (TB) <***Loc:*** TB>

drap [dra] *n.m.* **1** sheet, bedsheet *Et dans le vieux temps eux-autres faisait les draps avec du coton jaune.* And in the old days, they made bedsheets with yellow cotton. (TB) **2** broadcloth ◊ **•drap à maringoins** mosquito net, mosquito bar <SB> <***Loc:*** AL, EV, SB, SL, TB, An94, Da84, Hi02>

drapeau [drapo] *n.m.* diaper <***Loc:*** LA, VM, Da84, Hi02, Lv88>

DRAW [dɹɔ] *v.tr.invar.* to draw (a pension) *Alle est sus ma pension, sus mon* SOCIAL SECURITY. *Alle a pas payé assez, elle, pour* DRAW *le sien.* She's on my pension, on my social security. She didn't pay in enough to draw her own. (TB) <***Loc:*** AV, TB, Lv88>

drès ♦see **dès**

dresser [drese] **I** *v.tr.* **1** to stand up straight, erect, raise *Il a dressé le poteau de coin.* He stood up the corner post. (LA) *Ça lui a dressé les cheveux sur la tête.* It made his hair stand up. (VM) *On avait dressé le petit cabri dessus une manne.* We had stood up the little goat on a big basket. (LA) **2** to straighten *Dresser un clou.* To straighten a nail. (SM) **3** to set (the table) *Les petits dressaient la table.* The children set the table. (VM) **4** to train (an animal) *C'est Monsieur Eugène Broussard qui dressait les chiens à mon père.* It was Mister Eugene Broussard who trained my father's dogs. (Gu00) **II se dresser** *v.pron.* to straighten up (one's body) *Les vaches s'ont dressé quand le chien a rentré dans le parc.* The cows straightened up when the dog came into the corral. (VM) <***Loc:*** LA, SL, SM, VM, Da84, Gu00>

dressir [dresir] *v.tr.* to straighten, straighten out *Mon grand-père dressissait les vieux clous croches pour les réuser.* My grandfather would straighten out old crooked nails to reuse them. (Gu00) **Avant la messe de Toussaint, les fleurs dessus les fosses est dressi.* Before the All Saints' Day Mass, the flowers on the tombs are straightened. (Wh83) <***Loc:*** VM, Gu00, Wh83>

drète ♦see **droite**

drètier ♦see **droitier**

drigaille [drigaj] *n.m./f.* **1** leftover part, remaining portion *Je faisais du savon de pays avec tous les débris du cochon, tous les drigailles.* I made country soap with all the scraps of the pig, all the leftovers. (Lv88) **2** debris, garbage, trash, junk, rubbish *Sa maison est plein de drigailles.* His house is full of junk. (VM) *Ça, c'est de la drigaille.* That's a lot of worthless trash. (Lv88) **3** worthless person or animal **4** person of low class, trash *Ça c'est de la drigaille!* They're trash. (SM) **5** annoying person *Va-t'en, drigaille.* Get out of here, pest. (VM) <***Loc:*** LF, SB, SM, TB, VM, Da84, Hi02, La99, Lv88>

DRILL[1] [dɹɪl, drɪl] *v.tr.* **1** to drill, bore *Et c'était moi qui m'occupais pour* DRILL *ça. T'avais une petite machine pour* DRILL, *aller et tirer le* DELAMITE, *il follait qu'on va cent pieds dans le fond pour tirer.* I was the one responsible for drilling. You had a little machine to drill, go down and set off the dynamite, we had to go 100 feet down to blast. (LF) *Et là après ça ils drillont ça qu'ils voulont, mais ils allont jusqu'à quinze milles pieds. Y a des puits qu'a été plus creux que ça. Et ça dépend qui-ce qu'ils tapont.* And after that they drill what they want to, but they go down as far as fifteen thousand feet. There are wells that that have gone deeper than that. It depends what they hit. (LF) **2** to drill (e.g. troops) *Le sergeant nous a* DRILL *durant des heures et des heures et des heures.* The sergeant drilled us for hours and hours and hours. (VM) <***Loc:*** LF, SB, VM, Lv88>

DRILL[2] [dɹɪl, drɪl] *n.m.* **1** drill, drill-bit **2** practice, drill (e.g. military exercise) <***Loc:*** JE, LF, Da84, Lv88>

drilleur [drilœr] *n.m.* driller, borer ◊ •**drilleur d'huile** oil driller <Lv88> <***Loc:*** Lv88>

DRINK [dɹiŋk, dɹɛ̃k] *n.m.* alcoholic drink *Okay, la femme qui est en famille, c'est ça la raison il y a autant de petits qui naît pas comme il faut, eux-autres ça va, ça prend le* DOPE, *ça prend le* DRINK *de whiskey, et euh... ça ça rôdaille tout la nuit.* Okay, the woman who is pregnant, that's the reason there are so many children who are born with birth defects, they take drugs, they drink whiskey, they go out all night. (EV) *Un monsieur à la barre, qui envoie des* DRINK *à Tine.* A man at the bar, who sends drinks over to Tine. (ThCa: *La table des veuves*) <***Loc:*** EV, SB, Lv88, Ph36, ThCa>

DRIVE[1] (**drive**) [dɹajv, drajv] *n.m.* drive <***Loc:*** Da84, Lv88>

DRIVE[2] [dɹajv, drajv] **I** *v.tr.invar.* to drive *Tu connais pas* DRIVE *le char?* You don't know how to drive the car? (VM) *Je drivais mon* TRUCK *ou je drivais mon gros char.* I would drive my truck or my big car. (LF) **II** *v.intr.* to drive *J'ai* DRIVE *en Ville avec les enfants.* I drove to town with the children. (Lv88) <***Loc:*** EV, LF, VM, Da84, Hi02, Lv88>

drogue[1] [drɔg] *n.m.* drug, dope <***Loc***, Da84, Hi02>

drogue[2] [drɔg] *n.m.* textile, cloth *Va m'acheter de la drogue.* Go buy me some cloth. (VM) <***Loc:*** JE, VM, Da84>

droit[1] [drwɑ, drwɔt, drwɛt] *n.m.* right ◊ •**droit de la terre** lease on land *Il garde un droit de la terre pour deux ans encore.* He has a lease on the land for two more years. (VM) <VM> •**avoir le droit** to have the right *Un pêcheur qui fait ça pour le plaisir, il a pas le droit de vendre des poissons.* A fisherman who does it for pleasure, he doesn't have the right to sell any fish. (TB) <EV, TB, Da84> <***Loc:*** AC, EV, TB, VM, Da84>

droit[2] ♦see **droite**

droite[1] (**drète, drouète**) [drwat, drɔt, dret, drɛt, drwɛt] *adj.* **1** right *Il s'a cassé le bras droite.* He broke his right arm. (TB) *Le soulier droite.* The right shoe. (AV) **2** straight *Ils juste mettent ça drète.* They just set it straight. (SM) **3** direct *Prendre le chemin le plus droite.* To take the most direct route. (VM) **4** upright, honest, true, just, fair (of character) *Un homme droite.* An honest man. (EV) <***Loc:*** AV, EV, SB, SM, TB, VM, Da84, Hi02, Lv88, Wh83>

droite[2] (**drète, drouète**) [drwat, drɔt, dret, drɛt, drwɛt] *n.f.* right, right-hand side ◊ •**à la droite** to the right *Vire à la droite.* Turn right. (JE) *Il faut que tu tournes à la droite.* You have to turn right. (LF) *L'œil, tu vois, à la droite là, il est fermé.* The eye, you see, on the right, it's closed. (VM) <JE, LF, VM, Da84> •**à droite** on the right, to the right *Assieds-toi sur le bateau, à droite là.* Have a seat on the boat, over on the right. (PQ) <AC, PQ, TB> <***Loc:*** AC, EV, JE, LF, PQ, SB, TB, VM, Da84, Hi02>

droite[3] (**droit, drète, drouète**) [drwat, drɔt, dret, drɛt, drwɛt] *adv.* **1** straight, straight ahead, straight to *Va drète pour un mille.* Go straight for one mile. (SM) *J'ai été drète chez lui.* I went straight to his place. (AC) **2** exactly, directly *Droite dans Eunice.* Right in Eunice. (SL) *Sa maison est droite à côté.* His house is right next door. (IB) **Droite dans le milieu.* Right smack in the middle. (Da84) **3** immediately, promptly *Droit à midi je vas partir.* Precisely at noon I will leave. (Lv88) **4** in closest proximity (e.g. right before, just after, around) *Droite avant 9 heures.* Just before 9 o'clock. (SL) *Droite après, un petit message.* Right after [this], a short message. (SL) *Et j'ai été éné dans 1914 drète à un mille et demi de ma maison.* And I was born in 1914 just a mile and a half from my house. (TB) ◊ •**droite asteur** right now <Da84> •**droite au ras de** right in middle of *Droite au ras de 1000 piastres.* Right around 1000 dollars. (SL) <SL, Wh83> •**droite devant** right in front <Da84> •**droite en arrière** right behind <Da84> •**droite ici** right here <LF, JE, Da84> •**droite là** right there *Je l'ai mis droite là.* I put it right there. (SM, VM) **Alors ce jeune homme, un joli jeune homme, il a embourbé droit là dans une petite manche.* So that young man, a cute young man, he got bogged down right there in a small lane. (EV, An94) <AC, EV, LA, SM, VM, An94, Da84> •**tout droite** ***a*** straight ahead ***b*** instantly, immediately, at once *Deux étaient tués tout droite.* Two were killed instantly. (LA) <LA, Da84> <***Loc:*** AC, EV, IB,

JE, LA, LF, SL, SM, TB, VM, An94, Da84, Hi02, Lv88, Wh83>

droitement [drwatmɑ̃, drwɛtmɑ̃, drɛtmɑ̃] *adv.* **1** directly, immediately **2** rightly, justly, honestly <***Loc:*** Da84, Lv88>

droitier (**drètier**) [dretje] *n.m.* horse on the right in a draft team <***Loc:*** VM>

droitir ♦see **adroitir**

droiture [drwatyr] *n.f.* **1** straightness (of a line, of character) **2** justice, rightness <***Loc:*** Da84>

drôle [drol] *adj.* unusual, odd, strange, funny *Ça qu'est drôle dans les Robichaux ici, y a tous les Robichaux qu'il y a dans la Paroisse Lafourche, j'ai pas de famille.* What's funny about the Robichaux is, of all the Robichaux there are in Lafourche Parish, I don't have any relatives. (LF) *Si quelqu'un qui est manière drôle qui a envie de danser, dansez avec.* If someone kind of weird feels like dancing, dance with him. (EV) *La manière qu'il se représentait, c'est pas drôle que le monde l'aimait pas.* Given the way he represented himself, it's no wonder that people didn't like him. (LA) ◊ **•faire drôle *a*** to give an odd impression, look strange or bizarre *Il fait drôle.* He looks strange, he's weird. (SL, Lv88) ***b*** to have a peculiar sensation, experience a strange agitation *Ça m'a fait sûr drôle quand je t'ai vu.* That really struck me as strange when I saw you. (VM) *Ça m'a fait assez drôle de l'attendre.* It had quite a funny effect on me to hear it. (LF) *Ça fait drôle dans mon oreille.* I have a strange sensation in my ear. (SM) <LF, SL, SM, VM, Lv88> **•drôle de** funny, strange, odd, weird **C'est une drôle d'affaire* That's a strange thing. (Da84) *Ça a encore un drôle de français. C'est pas comme nous-autres non plus.* They have a funny French. It's not like ours either. (TB) **Ça dit qu'ils ont vu du drôle de monde et encore des plus drôle de choses.* They said they saw strange people and even stranger things. (Wh83) <TB, Da84, Hi02, Wh83> <***Loc:*** EV, LF, SL, SM, TB, VM, Da84, Hi02, Lv88, Wh83>

drouète ♦see **droite**

dru [dry] *adj.* thick, dense, teeming **Dru comme les cheveux sur la tête.* As thick as hair on the head. (Da84) <***Loc:*** Da84>

drum [drɔ̃m] *n.m.* large cylindrical container (e.g., oil barrel, metal drum) *Je l'appelais quand on cassait les têtes, il venait avec des drums de cinquante-cinq gallons, et il venait ramasser les têtes. Il amenait ça dans son* PICK-UP TRUCK, *il amenait ça là et c'est ça qu'il feedait à les tortues.* I called him whenever we broke the [fish] heads off, he came with 55-gallon drums, and he came to get the heads. He took them away in his pickup truck, and that's what he fed to his turtles. (LF) <***Loc:*** LF, SL, TB, Lv88>

dû[1] [dy] *adj.* expected, due **Il est dû de venir.* He is due to come. (Da84) <***Loc:*** Da84>

dû[2] (**due**) [dy] *n.m.* **1** right, due **C'est son dû.* That's his right. (Da84) **2** *(usu. pl.)* dues, respects **Payer leurs dues de cimitières.* To pay their cemetery dues. (Wh83) <***Loc:*** Da84, Wh83>

dubois ♦see **bois**

due ♦see **dû**

duel [dɥɛl] *n.m.* duel <***Loc:***Da84>

dull [dœl] *adj.* calm, quiet, dull (of business) **Les affaires sont dulls.* Business is quiet. (EV, Ph36) <***Loc:*** AV, EV, SL, Ph36>

dumer [dyme] *v.intr.* to moult, shed skin *Les serpents dument.* Snakes shed their skin. (Lv88) <***Loc:*** JE, Lv88>

duplicité [dyplisite] *n.f.* duplicity, deceit <***Loc:*** Da84>

dur[1], **-e** [dyr] *adj.* **1** hard *Ce bois était assez dur, ça a édenté ma scie.* That wood was so hard, it broke the teeth on my saw. (VM) **Mom, t'es joliment tête dure et des fois on arrive pas à comprendre pourquoi t'es si braquée.* Mom, you're really hardheaded and sometimes we can't understand why you're so stubborn. (ThCa: *La douce réunion*) **2** tough, difficult *J'étais né dans 1929. C'était un temps de dépression, c'était des temps durs.* I was born in 1929. It was a time of depression, it was hard times. (AC) *C'est dur à moi d'expliquer ça.* It's difficult for me to explain that. (VM) *Le cipre est dur à trouver mais les vieilles maisons étaient faites avec ça.* Cypress is hard to find but old houses were made with it. (IB) **2** hard-hearted, unkind, strict *C'était un homme dur. Il fouettait ses enfants pour arien.* He was a hard man. He whipped his children for nothing. (EV) ◊ **•dur comme du caïac** tough and fibrous (of meat, as from an old steer or bull) *La viande est dure comme du caïac.* The meat is as tough as an old bull. (SM) <SM> **•dur comme du caillou {du fer / la brique / la pierre}** very hard <TB, VM, La99> <***Loc:*** AC, EV, IB, SB, SL, SM, TB, VM, Da84, Hi02, La99, ThCa>

dur[2] [dyr] *adv.* hard *Alle après assayer dur d'apprendre le français.* She's trying hard to learn French. (TB) *Il a travaillé tellement dur, il a démanché son marteau.* He worked so hard, he loosened the handle on his hammer. (LA) ◊ **•prendre dur** to take s.t. hard, be badly distressed by s.t. *Mon j'ai pris ça dur. Y avait juste trois mois qu'il était mort.* I took that hard. It had only been three months since he had died. (TB) <TB> <***Loc:*** LA, TB>

durabilité [dyrabilite] *n.f.* durability <***Loc:*** Da84>

durable [dyrab(l)] *adj.* durable, lasting, solid *Le cipre, c'est un bois durable.* Cypress is a durable wood. (LA) <***Loc:*** LA, Da84>

durance [dyrɑ̃s] *n.f.* duration *La durance de la saison de pluie a été remarquée par tous.* The duration of the rainy season was noticed by everyone. (TB) <***Loc:*** JE, TB>

durant [dyrɑ̃] *prep.* during *Y a plein plein du monde qu'est noyé dans le fleuve là, durant le temps que moi j'ai vi.* There are lots and lots of people who drowned in the river, during the time that I've lived. (SB) <***Loc:*** EV, LA, SB, VM, Da84>

durcir [dyrsir] **I** *v.tr.* to harden, toughen *La chesseresse durcit la terre.* The drought makes the ground hard. (EV) **II** *v.pron.* to harden, become hard *T'as laissé le riz dans la chaudière et ça s'a durci.* You left the rice in the pot and it hardened. (VM) <***Loc:*** EV, VM, Da84>

durcissement [dyrsismɑ̃] *n.m.* hardening, toughening <***Loc:*** Da84>

durée [dyre] *n.f.* **1** duration, time span **2** life (of a machine, etc.) <***Loc:*** Da84>

durer [dyre] *v.intr.* **1** to last (a period of time) **Le meeting a duré trop longtemps* The meeting lasted too long. (Da84) *Alle est morte en connaissance. Mais alle était paralysée. Alle avait eu un* STROKE. *Alle a duré deux semaines.* She died conscious. But she was paralyzed. She had had a stroke. She lasted two weeks. (TB) **2** to endure, last *Pour durer, c'est le meilleur bois qu'il y a c'est le cipre.* To last, cypress is the best wood there is. (LF) *Faulait saler la viande pour la faire durer plus longtemps.* It was necessary to salt the meat to make it last longer. (IB) ◊ **•le temps dure (à qqn de faire qqch)** one is impatient, anxious, in a hurry (to do s.t.) **Le temps me dure de vous voir.* I am anxious to see you. (Da84) *Le temps lui dure tout le temps.* He's always in a rush. (Lv88) *Le temps me dure d'aller à la maison.* I'm anxious to get home. (Lv88) <Da84, Lv88> **•(ne) pouvoir plus durer** to be unable to wait any longer *Je voudrais bien qu'il se dépêche. Je peux plus durer.* I really wish he'd hurry. I can't wait any longer. (TB) <TB> <***Loc:*** AC, IB, LF, TB, Da84, Lv88>

dureté [dyrte] *n.f.* hardness, toughness ◊ **•faire des duretés à** to treat harshly, cruelly *La maîtresse a fait des duretés à la pauvre élève.* The teacher treated the poor student harshly. (VM) <VM> <***Loc:*** VM, Da84>

durillon [dyrijɔ̃] *n.m.* corn, callus, hard lump on or under the skin <***Loc:*** AV, Da84, Hi02>

duvet [dyve] *n.m.* **1** down (of a duck or goose) *Duvet de zoie.* Goose down. (VM) **2** soft, fuzzy fur of young animals *Le duvet sur un petit chat.* The fuzzy fur of a kitten. (VM) **3** fine hair on the body of humans *Le duvet sur le bras du petit garçon.* The fuzz on the little boy's arm. (VM) *Il se croit grand, garde le duvet qu'il a sur la lèvre de dessus.* He thinks he's grown up, look at the peach fuzz on his upper lip. (VM) **4** peach fuzz *Le duvet d'une pêche.* Peach fuzz. (VM) **5** dust bunny, dust ball *Quand ils ont halé le lit, t'aurais dû voir le duvet qu'il y avait en-dessous.* When the moved the bed, you should've seen the dust bunnies that were under there. (EV) <***Loc:*** EV, LA, VM, Da84>

duveté, -e (**divé, -e**) [dyvte, dive] *adj.* downy, fuzzy, hairy *Un bras duveté.* A downy arm. (EV) <***Loc:*** EV, Da84>

dynamite [dinɑ̃mit] *n.f.* dynamite <***Loc:*** Da84>

dynamo [dinɑ̃mo] *n.m.* dynamo <***Loc:*** Da84>

dyspépsie [dispepsi] *n.f.* dyspepsia <***Loc:*** Da84>

dyspéptique [dispeptik] *adj.* dyspeptic <***Loc:*** Da84>

E

e' ♦see **alle**

eau [o, lo] *n.f.* water ◊ •**eau bénite {bénie}** holy water <LF, SM, Da84, La99> •**eau de Saint-Jean** midsummer's day dew (traditionally used to treat eye conditions) <Di32, Lv88> •**eau de serein** ***a*** dew gathered for washing the eyes ***b*** water intentionally left out at night and later used for washing the eyes <VM, Gr86, Lv88> •**eau de source** spring water <Da84> •**eau douce** fresh (not salt) water <JE, LF, SL, TB, La99> •**eau fraîche** ***a*** fresh (not salt) water ***b*** cool water, cold water *Ils s'arrêtaient souvent pour boire de l'eau fraîche.* They stopped often to drink cool water (LA) <LA, LF, TB, Da84> •**eau haute** flood *Je vais jamais oublier l'eau haute de 1927.* I will never forget the flood of 1927. (SM) <LA, SM, TB, VM, Lv88> •**eau morte** stagnant water <Da84> •**eau salée {saumâtre}** salt water <SL, TB, VM, Da84> •**eau grasse / eaux grasses** dishwater <SM, VM, Hi02> •**faire {tomber} de l'eau** to pee, urinate *Il était après tomber de l'eau en arrière du magasin.* He was urinating behind the barn. (LA) <LA, Da84, La99> •**grande eau** ***a*** flood *Pour la grande eau, il y avait huit pieds d'eau dans la maison.* During the flood there were eight feet of water in the house. (SL) ***b*** the Great Flood of 1927 <SL, SM, Da84, Lv88> •**mettre de l'eau dans les veines à qqn** to take someone down a peg or two <VM> •**mettre de l'eau dans son vin** to calm down, temper one's remarks (esp. when angry) <La99> <***Loc:*** AC, AV, EV, IV, JE, LA, LF, SB, SL, SM, TB, VM, An94, Da84, Gu00, Hi02, La99, Lv88>

ébahi [ebai] *adj.* dizzy, weak *En marchant dans ce soleil j'ai devenu ébahi.* While walking in this hot sun I became dizzy. (TB) <***Loc:*** TB>

ébarbicher [ebarbiʃe] *v.tr.* to tear into strips *Ils ont ébarbiché sa chemise.* They tore his shirt into strips. (AV) <***Loc:*** AV>

ébarbouiller ♦see **embarbouiller**

ébarouer ♦see **ébarouir**

ébaroui, -e (**baroui, -e**) [ebarwi, barwi] *adj.* shaky, weak *Alle était tout ébarouie après l'accident.* She was shaky after the accident. (LA) <***Loc:*** LA, Lv88>

ébarouir (**ébarouer**) [ebarwir, ebarwe] *v.tr.* to stun, startle *J'ai peur que ça va l'ébarouir quand il va avoir la nouvelle.* I'm afraid it will stun him when he hears the news. (LA) *J'ai resté ébaroui.* I remained stunned. (VM) <***Loc:*** IB, LA, VM>

ébécher ♦see **bécher**

éblouir [ebluir] *v.tr.* to blind, dazzle *Quand il a vu tout l'argent, ça l'a ébloui.* When he saw all the money, it dazzled him. (LA) <***Loc:*** LA, Da84>

éblouissant, -e [ebluisɑ̃, -ɑ̃t] *adj.* blinding, dazzling **Lumière éblouissante.* Blinding light. <Da84> <***Loc:*** Da84>

éblouissement [ebluismɑ̃] *n.m.* blinding, dazzlement <***Loc:*** Da84>

éborgner [ebɔrɲe] **I** *v.tr.* to put out an eye of, blind *Une branche a manqué de m'éborgner.* A branch almost put my eye out. (VM) **II s'éborgner** *v.pron.* to blind o.s., put out one's eye *Sa femme s'a accroché un hameçon dans l'œil et elle s'a éborgné.* His wife caught a fishhook in her eye and blinded herself. (LA) <***Loc:*** LA, VM, Da84>

ébouriflage [eburiflaʒ] *n.f.* **1** messing up of the hair **2** dishevelment, unkemptness <***Loc:*** LF, SM>

ébourifflé, -e [eburifle, burifle] *adj.* **1** disheveled, untidy, ruffled (of hair) *Quand il s'a levé, ses cheveux étaient tout ébourifflés.* When he got up, his hair was all ruffled. (LA) **2** having disheveled hair *L'homme ébourifflé.* The disheveled man. (LF) **3** wild with excitement *Ils sont arrivés tout ébourrifflés.* They arrived all wild with excitement. (SB) <***Loc:*** AV, JD, LA, LF, SB, SM, TB, Da84, Re31>

ébouriffler [eburifle] **I** *v.tr.* to mess up the hair of, dishevel the hair of *Le vent l'a ébourifflé dès qu'il a sorti dehors.* The wind messed up his hair as soon as he went outside. (LA) **II s'ébouriffler** *v.pron.* to mess up one's hair, dishevel o.s. *Je m'ai tout ébourifflé en travaillant dans la cour.* I disheveled my hair while working in the yard. (VM) <***Loc:*** AV, EV, LA, LF, VM, Da84, Lv88, Ph36>

ébranchage [ebrɑ̃ʃaʒ] *n.m.* pruning, trimming, cutting off branches <***Loc:*** Da84>

ébrancher [ebrɑ̃ʃe] *v.tr.* to prune, trim, cut off or strip the branches of (a tree) *J'ai ébranché le gros pacanier.* I trimmed the branches of the big pecan tree. (VM) <***Loc:*** LA, VM, Da84>

ébrécher [ebreʃe] *v.tr.* to nick, dull (an edge) *Tu vas ébrécher ton couteau si tu l'uses contre quelque chose qu'est plus dur.* You'll nick your knife if you use it against something that is harder [than it]. (LA) <***Loc:*** JD, LA, Da84>

ébrousseter [ebruste] **I** *v.tr.* to dust *Alle est après ébrousseter la chambre.* She is dusting the room. (VM) **II s'ébrousseter** *v.pron.* to skin, scratch *Il s'a ébrousseté le bras.* He skinned his arm. (VM) <***Loc:*** VM>

ebsèpe ♦see **excepté**

écaille ♦see **écale**

écale (**écaille, écalle**) [ekal, ekaj] *n.m./f.* **1** scale (of a fish) **2** shell (of a crab, shrimp, etc.) **3** carapace, turtle shell **4** shell, pod, chaff (of nuts, beans, grains, etc.) **5** eggshell **6** chip, morsel, piece ◊ •**écale de poisson** scale of a fish <LF> •**écale de riz** rice chaff <Da84> •**écale de tortue** turtle shell <LF> <***Loc:*** AC, AV, IB, JD, LA, LF, SB, SL, SM, TB, VM, Da84, Lv88>

écaler[1] [ekale] **I** *v.tr.* **1** to scale (a fish) **2** to shell, husk, peel (of nuts, beans, etc.) **Ecaler du riz.* To mill rice (remove husks and bran). (Da84) **3** to clean carefully *Jean va écaler le plancher.* John will painstakingly clean the floor. (IB) **II s'écaler** *v.pron.* **1** to be scaled *Des petits patassas, ça s'écale bien.* Small bream can be scaled easily. (LA) **2** to be shucked, husked, peeled (of nuts, beans, etc.) <***Loc:*** IB, LA, VM, Da84, Lv88>

écaler[2] [ekale, ãkale] **I** *v.tr.* to put to soak *Ecaler le linge.* To soak the clothes (in a kettle of boiling water). (SJ) **II** *v.intr.* to sink *Le bateau écale dans l'eau.* The boat sinks in the water. (SB) <***Loc:*** AV, JE, SB, SJ> :

écaille ♦see **écalle**

écarde ♦see **carde**

écarder ♦see **carder**

écarderie [ekardri] *n.f.* meeting of women for the purpose of carding cotton or wool <***Loc:*** VM, Lv88>

écardon [ekardɔ̃] *n.m.* bat of carded wool or cotton (about four inches wide and eight inches long) ready for spinning <***Loc:*** AV, IB, JD, SB, SJ, VM, Gr86, Lv88>

écarlate [ekarlat] *n.m.* ◊ **•rouge comme un écarlate** scarlet-colored <AV, SJ> <***Loc:*** AV, SJ>

écarrure [ekaryr] *n.f.* **1** square opening **Y a einne écarrure là-où an [=on] peut passer.* There's a square opening there where we can get through. (EV, Ph36) **2** the width of a person's back as measured across the shoulders <***Loc:*** EV, IB, LA, LF, Ph36>

écart [ekar, eskar, ekær] *n.m.* swerve, swerving, side-stepping **Faire un écart.* To bolt, side-step. (Da84) <***Loc:*** JD, LF, Da84>

écartage [ekartaʒ] *n.m./f.* **1** spreading (e.g. of the legs) **2** straying <***Loc:*** LF, SM, Lv88>

écarté, -e [ekarte] *adj.* **1** lost, misplaced *Il a commencé son garage avec des outils écartés qu'il avait trouvés dans un fossé.* He started his garage with some lost tools that he found in a ditch. (LA) **2** stray (of an animal) *Je vois pas pour qui ce cheval écarté peut être.* I don't see whose stray horse this could be. (VM) **3** scatterbrained *Elle est manière écartée aujourd'hui; ça doit être sa journée fraque.* She is sort of scatterbrained today; it must be her crazy day. (LA) <***Loc:*** JD, LA, SB, VM, Da84>

écartement [ekartmɑ̃] *n.m.* **1** straying **2** separation <***Loc:*** Da84>

écarter [ekarte] **I** *v.tr.* **1** to misplace, lose *J'ai écarté mes lunettes.* I misplaced my glasses (Lv88) **2** to disperse, scatter **II s'écarter** *v.pron.* to stray, wander away, get lost *Le petit s'a écarté de sa famille dans le grand magasin.* The child strayed from his family in the big department store. (LA) <***Loc:*** LA, VM, Da84, Lv88>

écartillage [ekartijaʒ] *n.f.* spreading (of the legs) <***Loc:*** LF>

écartiller [ekartije] **I** *v.tr.* to spread (the legs) *Ce n'est pas gentil pour une jeune fille d'écartiller ses jambes comme ça.* It is not nice for a young girl to spread her legs like that. (IB) **II s'écartiller** *v.pron.* to stray, get lost *Le pauvre petit s'a écartillé dans le bois.* The poor child got lost in the woods. (VM) <***Loc:*** IB, VM>

écclesiastique [eklezjastik] *n.m.* ecclesiastic, churchman <***Loc:*** Da84>

écervelé, -e [esærvəle] *adj.* foolish, scatterbrained *Quoi il y a avec toi, t'es écervelé? Tu fais pas attention à ça tu fais.* What's the matter with you, are you scatterbrained? You're not paying attention to what you're doing. (LA) <***Loc:*** LA, Da84>

échafaud (chafaud) [eʃafo, ʃafo] *n.m.* **1** scaffold, scaffolding **2** flower trellis, vine trellis <***Loc:*** VM, Da84>

échafaudage [eʃafodaʒ] *n.m.* scaffolding <***Loc:*** Da84>

échafauder [eʃafode] *v.intr.* to scaffold, erect a scaffold *Ils ont eu pour passer deux jours à échafauder avant de commencer à mettre les briques.* They had to spend two days erecting the scaffolding before they could start laying bricks. (LA) <***Loc:*** LA, Da84>

échalote (chalote, charlotte) [eʃalɔt, eʃarlɔt, ʃalɔt, ʃarlɔt] *n.f.* **1** shallot **2** small onion **3** multiplier onion **4** onion top <***Loc:*** AC, AV, LF, SB, TB, VM, Da84>

échange [eʃɑ̃ʒ] *n.m.* **1** exchange **Ça fait, eux s'avaient rendu joliment une mauvaise échange.* So, they had made a rather bad exchange. (SL, An94) **2** change (coins or money) *T'as de l'échange pour une piasse?* Do you have change for a dollar? (Lv88) **Asteur on rend vingt sous pour ton échange.* Today they give twenty cents for your change. (TB, Gr86) ◊ **•faire (de) l'échange** to make change *J'ai juste un billet de vingt. Tu pourrais faire de l'échange pour moi?* I only have a twenty dollar bill. Could you make change for me? (LA) <LA, SM, Da84, Lv88> <***Loc:*** LA, SL, SM, TB, An94, Da84, Gr86, Lv88>

échanger [eʃɑ̃ʒe] **I** *v.tr.* **1** to exchange, swap, barter *Le commis-voyageur a échangé du pain pour du lait et des œufs.* The traveling salesman exchanged bread for milk and eggs. (LA) **2** to change, replace, exchange *Va échanger ton linge, t'es pas propre.* Go change your clothes, you're not clean. (JD) *Il y a tellement de trous dedans, tellement de vers dedans que il faut que la planche soye échangée.* There are so many holes in them, so many worms in them that the board has to be replaced. (LF) **3** to change, give change for (money) *Est-ce que tu peux échanger un billet de dix piastres pour moi?* Can you change a ten-dollar bill for me? (SM) **II s'échanger** *v.pron.* to barter, exchange (with each other) *Quand un dansait avec la fille, l'autre dansait avec quelqu'un d'autre. Ça fait, eux s'échangeait ça toute la nuit.* When one would dance with the girl, the other would dance with someone else. So they exchanged them between themselves all night long. (SL) <***Loc:*** EV, IB, JD, LA, LF, SL, SM, Da84, Ph36>

échantillon (**chantillon**) [eʃɑ̃tijɔ̃, ʃɑ̃tijɔ̃] *n.m.* sample <***Loc:*** AV, IB, SB, SJ, SM, Da84, Lv88>

échape ♦see **échappe**

échappade [eʃapad] *n.f.* escapade <***Loc:*** Da84>

échappatoire [eʃapatwar] *n.f.* **1** evasion **2** refuge **3** place or means of escape (e.g. from work or trouble) <***Loc:*** Da84>

échappe[1] (**échape**) [eʃap] *n.f.* **1** escape **2** blunder, mistake, slip *C'est une échappe, il a pas voulu faire ça.* That's a mistake, he didn't intend to do that. (LF) <***Loc:*** LF, SM, VM, Da84>

échappe[2] (**échape, écharpe**) [eʃap, eʃarp] *n.f.* splinter *Je me suis planté une échappe dans le pied.* I got a splinter in my foot. (Lv88) <***Loc:*** AV, LA, SB, SJ, SM, TB, VM, Re31, Lv88>

échapper (**chapper**) [eʃape, ʃape] **I** *v.tr.* **1** to let slip, let go, drop *J'ai échappé le chassis sur mes doigts.* I dropped the window on my fingers. (Lv88) *Quand il a échappé son violon, ça l'a tout désaccordé.* When he dropped his violin, it put it completely out of tune. (LA) **2** to escape, escape from *Tu pourras pas échapper ça.* You can't get out of it. (Lv88) *Ils avaient échappé mes sœurs.* They had escaped from my sisters. (AC) **3** to release *Tu mettais la semence là-dedans et tu plantais dans la terre et quand tu ouvrais ça échappait une graine à la fois.* You would put the seed in there and plant it in the soil, and when you opened [it], it would release one seed at a time (AC) **II** *v.intr.* **1** to escape, flee, run away, get loose **2** to slip (from one's grasp, one's memory) *Le vase l'a échappé.* The vase slipped from her grasp. (SM) *Bétaille, ça m'a échappé!* Hell, I can't remember! (VM) **3** to fall *Il a échappé d'en haut.* He fell from up there. (VM) **III s'échapper** *v.pron.* to escape, get away *Quand j'ai tiré, André s'a échappé.* When I shot, André escaped. (SL) ◊ •**échapper une mauvaise parole** to let slip a bad word <Da84> <***Loc:*** AC, EV, IB, JD, LA, LF, SB, SL, SM, TB, VM, An94, Da84, Gr86, Lv88, La99>

écharde [eʃard] *n.f.* splinter <***Loc:*** Hi02>

écharlanter ♦see **charlanter**

écharpe[1] [eʃarp] *n.f.* sash, girdle *Une écharpe autour de la taille.* A sash tied at the waist. (SJ) <***Loc:*** SJ>

écharpe[2] ♦see **échappe**

écharpiller (**charpiller**) [eʃarpije, ʃarpije] **I** *v.tr.* **1** to break, cut, or chop into pieces *Je vais écharpiller un petit brin de viande bouillie pour le petit.* I'm going to cut up a little bit of boiled meat for the baby. (Lv88) **2** to gash, hack **3** to tear to pieces, pull to shreds *Le bébé a écharpillé les fleurs sur le plancher.* The baby pulled the flowers apart on the floor. (TB) **4** to take apart, unravel *Je vais écharpiller l'étoffe.* I'm going to unravel the cloth. (IB) **5** to whittle *Jean écharpille le bâton.* John is whittling the stick. (IB) **II s'écharpiller** *v.pron.* to be cut into very small pieces, be crushed, be reduced to fragments *Des pacanes, ça s'écharpille facilement.* Pecans break into pieces easily. (LA) <***Loc:*** EV, IB, JD, LA, SB, SM, Da84, Gr86, Lv88>

échasse [eʃas] *n.f.* stilt <***Loc:*** Da84>

échauboulure (**chauboulure, chouboulure, chaboulure, chabouillure**) [eʃobulyr, ʃobulyr, ʃubulyr, ʃabulyr, ʃabujyr] *n.f. (usu. pl.)* heat rash, hives, prickly heat ◊ •**si c'est pas les maringouins, c'est les chouboulures** if it's not one thing, it's another <La99> <***Loc:*** EV, LA, SM, Da84, Hi02, La99, Lv88>

échaudage [eʃodaʒ] *n.m.* scalding, blanching <***Loc:*** Da84>

échaudement [eʃodmɑ̃] *n.m.* scalding, blanching <***Loc:*** Da84>

échauder [eʃode, ʃode] **I** *v.tr.* **1** to scald, blanch *Il fallait tuer les cochons et les échauder, les gratter jusqu'à qu'ils étiont blancs, blancs, blancs.* You had to kill the pigs and scald them, then scrape them until they were very white. (AC) **2** to pour boiling water over *Échauder du thé.* Pour boiling water on tea. (Lv88) **3** to heat *Moi, je l'échaudais dans un baril.* I heated it in a barrel. (AC) **II** *v.intr.* to wilt or die from too much moisture (of plants) *Le maïs a échaudé après l'eau haute.* The corn wilted after the flood. (LA) **III s'échauder** *v.pron.* to scald o.s. *Elle s'a échaudée en faisant le café.* She scalded herself while making coffee. (LA) <***Loc:*** AC, EV, LA, SL, SM, Da84, Lv88, La99>

échauffé, -e [eʃofe] *adj.* **1** overheated *Il était tout manière échauffé après la course.* He was pretty overheated after the race. (LA) **2** chafed, having an irritation of the skin *Je suis échauffé à l'endessous du bras.* I have an irritation on the underneath part of my arm. (VM) <***Loc:*** LA, SM, VM, Da84>

échauffer [eʃofe] **I** *v.tr.* to chafe, irritate *Les couches mouillées ont échauffé le bébé.* The wet diapers irritated the baby. (SM) **II** *v.intr.* to overheat, become overheated *La machine a échauffé après juste quelques miles.* The motor became overheated after only a few miles. (LA) **III s'échauffer** *v.pron.* to get overheated *Il s'a échauffé après jouer la pelote toute la journée.* He got overheated playing baseball all day long. (LA) <***Loc:*** LA, SM, VM, Da84>

échauffure [eʃofyr] *n.f.* prickly heat, heat rash <***Loc:*** Da84>

échelle [eʃɛl] *n.f.* ladder ◊ •**échelle-double** step-ladder <Da84> <***Loc:*** AV, LA, Da84>

échelon [eʃ(ə)lɔ̃] *n.m.* soup bone, ham bone <***Loc:*** EV>

échenillage [eʃ(ə)nijaʒ] *n.m.* act of destroying caterpillars (in crops) <***Loc:*** Da84>

écheniller [eʃ(ə)nije] *v.tr.* to get rid of caterpillars from *On a pour écheniller les pacaniers chaque année.* We have to get rid of the catepillars in our pecan trees every year. (SL) <***Loc:*** SL, Da84>

écherpiller [eʃærpije] *v.tr.* to remove sticks, leaves, etc. from moss to prepare it for use <***Loc:*** VM>

échevelage [eʃəvlaʒ, eʃfəlaʒ] *n.m.* **1** tearing hair out, scalping *Il a eu un bon échevelage dans la bagarre.* He took a good scalping in the fight. (Lv88) **2** dishevelment, mussing (of hair) <***Loc:*** LF, SM, Lv88>

échevelé, -e [eʃəvle, eʃfəle] *adj.* disheveled *Ses cheveux étaient* *tout échevelés quand elle a rentré.* Her hair was disheveled when she came in. (LA) <***Loc:*** LA, Da84>

écheveler [eʃəvle, eʃfəle] *v.tr.* to mess up the hair of, dishevel the hair of *Un coup de vent l'a bien échevelé.* A gust of wind really messed up his hair. (LA) <***Loc:*** LA, Da84, Lv88>

échiné, -e (**échigné, -e**) [eʃine, eʃiɲe] *adj.* tired, haggard, worn out *Il était échiné après le* TRAIL RIDE. He was worn out after the trail ride. (LA) <***Loc:*** LA, TB, Da84>

échiner (**chiner**) [eʃine,] **I** *v.tr.* to wear out, tire out *Une grande journée après piocher le coton m'a bien échiné.* A long day of hoeing cotton really wore me out. (LA) *On est après le chiner d'ouvrage.* They are tiring him out with work. (IB) **II s'échiner** *v.pron.* to tire o.s. *Je m'ai échiné à travailler dans mon jardin.* I wore myself out working in my garden. (LA) <***Loc:*** IB, LA, Da84>

écho [eko] *n.m.* echo <***Loc:*** Da84>

échoppe ♦see **SHOP**

échouer (**chouer**) [eʃwe, ʃwe] **I** *v.intr.* **1** to fail, be unsuccessful *Il a essayé de courir un business pour lui même, mais il avait échoué dans rien de temps.* He tried to run his own business, but he failed in no time. (LA) **II s'échouer** *v.pron.* to strand, run aground *Quand tu rentres avec un gros bateau, soyez sûr de rester dans le chenal pour pas s'échouer.* When you're coming in with a big boat, be sure to stay in the channel so you don't run aground. (LF) *On s'est choué sur un vieux log avec le chaland.* We ran aground on an old log with the rowboat. (AV) <***Loc:*** LA, LF, Da84>

échouerie [eʃuri] *n.f.* mess, disaster *Il a fait une échouerie dans les gâteaux.* He made quite a mess of the cakes. (LF) <***Loc:*** JD, LF>

éclabousser [eklabuse] *v.intr.* **1** to shatter, burst *Le verre a éclaboussé tout partout quand je l'ai échappé sur le plancher.* The glass shattered all over when I dropped it on the floor. (LA) **2** to splash *Le bébé a éclaboussé dans la baignoire.* The baby splashed in the bathtub. (VM) <***Loc:*** LA, VM, Da84>

éclair (**z-éclair**) [eklær, zeklær] *n.m.* **1** lightning, flash of lightning **2** eclair, oblong cream puff (pastry) ◊ **•éclair du jour** dawn, daybreak <TB> <***Loc:*** AV, EV, IB, IV, JD, JE, LA, LF, SJ, SM, TB, VM, Da84>

éclairage [eklæraʒ] *n.m.* lighting, illumination <***Loc:*** Da84>

éclaircie [eklærsi] *n.f.* **1** rift (in the clouds) **2** clearing (in a forest or crop) ◊ **•éclaircie du jour** dawn, daybreak *L'éclaircie du jour arrive.* Dawn arrives. (VM) <VM, Lv88> <***Loc:*** VM, Da84, Lv88, Re31>

éclaircir [eklærsir] **I** *v.tr.* **1** to clear *Le vent a éclairci le ciel.* The wind cleared the sky. (LA) **2** to clear, remove growth from (land) *Ils ont éclairci leur bois pour laisser les vaches aller là-dedans.* They cleared their woods in order to release their cows there. (LA) *Ils ont tout éclairci la terre de leur grand-mère.* They cleared their grandmother's land completely. (TB) **3** to thin out (a liquid) *Et puis là, ils donnent du médicine pour éclaircir le sang.* And then they give medecine to thin the blood. (VM) **II s'éclaircir** *v.pron.* to clear up, become clear **Le temps est après s'éclaircir.* The weather is clearing up. (Da84) <***Loc:*** LA, TB, VM, Da84>

éclairé, -e [eklere] *adj.* lit, lighted, illuminated *Asteur que le driveway est bien éclairé, j'ai pus peur de marcher au chemin pour chercher la gazette.* Now that the driveway is well lit, I'm not afraid to walk to the road to get the newspaper. (LA) <***Loc:*** LA, Da84>

éclairer [eklere] **I** *v.tr.* to light, illuminate *Il a éclairé sa galerie pour les fêtes.* He lighted his porch for the holidays. (LA) **II s'éclairer** *v.pron.* to provide light for o.s. **Il s'éclaire avec une lampe.* He uses a lamp for light. (Da84) <***Loc:*** LA, Da84>

éclairissage [eklerisaʒ] *n.f.* clearing, thinning out (of plants) <***Loc:*** Da84>

éclairissement [eklerismɑ̃] *n.m.* clearing up (of a problem, of the weather, etc.) <***Loc:*** Da84>

éclapoutir (**écrapoutir**) [eklaputir, ekraputir] *v.intr.* to overturn, be knocked down *Sa bol de couche-couche a éclapouti par terre.* Her bowl of couche-couche was overturned on the floor. (VM) <***Loc:*** VM, Lv88>

éclat [ekla] *n.m.* **1** clap (of thunder) **2** burst (e.g. of laughter) **Éclat de rire.* Burst of laughter. (Da84) **3** wood chip, wood shaving, piece of kindling *Les éclats vont commencer un bon feu.* The kindling will start a good fire. (SB) <***Loc:*** SB, TB, VM, Da84>

éclatant, -e [eklatɑ̃, - ɑ̃t] *adj.* glittering, brilliant, shining, sparkling *Le collier que je lui ai acheté était éclatant.* The necklace I bought her was brilliant. (LA) <***Loc:*** LA, Da84>

éclater [eklate] **I** *v.tr.* to cause to burst, explode or pop *J'ai éclaté du maïs pour les enfants.* I popped some corn for the kids. (Lv88) **II** *v.intr.* to burst, explode, pop *Le melon a éclaté.* The melon burst. (LA) **III s'éclater** *v.pron.* to burst **S'éclater de rire.* To burst into laughter. (Da84) <***Loc:*** LA, Da84, Gr86, Lv88>

éclipse [eklip, iklips] *n.m./f.* eclipse <***Loc:*** EV, SB, SM, VM, Da84>

éclore [eklɔr] (*p.p.* **éclos** [eklo]) **I** *v.tr.* to hatch *C. est après espérer pour quand ses poules vont éclore leurs œufs.* C. is waiting until her chickens hatch their eggs. (LA) **II** *v.intr.* to hatch *Les œufs étaient tout éclos déjà quand la couveuse a manqué.* The eggs were all hatched when the laying hen went missing. (LA) *Quand les œufs étaient éclos, les petites tortues vaulaient vingt-cinq sous pour une petite tortue.* When the eggs had hatched, the baby turtles were worth 25 cents apiece. (LF) <***Loc:*** IV, LA, LF, TB, Da84>

écluse [eklyʒ] *n.f.* **1** lock (as in a canal) **2** dock, dock bit <***Loc:*** IV, TB>

écœurant ♦see **acœurant**

écœurer ♦see **acœurer**

école [ekɔl] *n.f.* **1** school, school building *C'était une bonne* *école [...] une bâtisse de trois étages, alle est toujours là. T'avais tous les grades dans une école.* It was a good school, a three story building, it's still there. You had all the grades in one school. (LF) **2** school *Avant que l'école commence.* Before school starts. (Lv88) *Quand j'étais à l'école il a faulu que j'apprends à parler le n-anglais.* When I was at school I had to learn to speak English. (LF) **3** schooling, education *Son école le qualifie pas pour faire ça.* His education doesn't qualify him to do that. (LA) ◊ **•école américain** English-language school *On avait l'école ici mais... l'école américain, c'est pas français.* We had school here but... American [English-language] school, it's not French. (PQ) <PQ> **•école d'immersion** immersion school *Les enfants fait tellement mieux dans les écoles d'immersion. Et en même temps eusse après apprendre un autre langage. Et nous-autres on a commencé ça pour assayer de sauver notre héritage et on voit le bien que ça fait.* Children do so much better in immersion schools. And at the same time they're learning another language. We started that to try to save our heritage, and we see the good that it does. (LF) <LF> **•école publique** public school *Je connais qu'eux-autres montre le français dans les écoles publiques.* I know that they teach French in the public schools. (LF) <IB, LF, Da84> **•aller à l'école** to go to school, attend school *[On] indique les enfants en français asteur. [...] Asteur tous les enfants qui va à l'école, ils parlent français.* They teach the children in French now. Now all the children who go to school speak French. (PQ) <PQ> **•faire l'école** ***a*** to teach school ***b*** to teach, give lessons *Pour deux ou trois ans de suite j'ai fait l'école à les infirmières.* For two or three years in a row I taught the nurses. (LF) <LA, LF, TB> <***Loc:*** AC, AV, EV, IB, LA, LF, PQ, SB, SJ, SL, SM, TB, VM, An94, Da84, Gr82, Gr86, Hi02, Lv88, Wh83>

écolier [ekolje] *n.m.* pupil, student <***Loc:*** Da84, Gr86>

écolome (économe) [ekolɔ̃m, ekɔ̃nɔ̃m, ekolɔ̃b] *n.m.* overseer, foreman, manager on a plantation *L'écolome donnait les ordres à les travaillants sur l'habitation.* The overseer gave the orders to the workers on the plantation. (Lv88) <***Loc:*** IB, SB, SJ, TB, Da84, Lv88>

économe ♦see **écolome**

économie [ekɔ̃nɔ̃mi] *n.f.* **1** economy **2** thrift, economy <***Loc:*** Da84>

économiser [ekɔ̃nɔ̃mize] *v.intr.* **1** to save money *Ils ont économisé pour se faire une maison.* They saved to be able to make themselves a house. (LA) **2** to economize, be thrifty <***Loc:*** LA, Da84>

économiseur [ekɔ̃nɔ̃mizœr] *n.m.* economiser <***Loc:*** Da84>

écopeau (écoupeau, copeau) [ekopo, ekupo, kopo] *n.m.* wood chip, wood shaving, piece of kindling <***Loc:*** AV, IB, JD, LA, LF, SB, SJ, SM, TB, Da84, Gr86, Hi02, Lv88, Re31>

écorce (écorche) [ekɔrs , ekɔrʃ] *n.f.* **1** bark (of a tree) *L'écorche de l'arbre est cassée.* The tree bark is broken. (SB) **2** hull, shell, peeling, rind **3** carapace, shell (of a turtle) *Une écorce de caouène.* Turtle shell. (Lv88) <***Loc:*** JD, LF, SB, TB, VM, Da84, Gr86, Lv88>

écorche ♦see **écorce**

écorchement [ekɔrʃmɑ̃] *n.m.* **1** skinning (of an animal) **2** peeling, hulling, debarking <***Loc:*** Da84>

écorcher (corcher) [ekɔrʃe, kɔrʃe] **I** *v.tr.* **1** to flay, skin (an animal) *On aurait fait un feu, puis on aurait écorché un lapin, puis on l'aurait cuit sur le feu là.* We would make a fire, then we would skin a rabbit, then we would cook it on the fire. (SL) **2** to peel, hull, debark *Écorcher un arbre.* To debark a tree. (LA) **3** to graze, scrape, scratch slightly *Corcher un meuble, la vaisselle, la main.* Scratch a piece of furniture, the dishes, your hand. (Lv88) *J'ai juste* WAX *le plancher. Traîne pas ça dessus; tu vas l'écorcher!* I just waxed the floor. Don't drag that on it; you'll scratch it! (LA) *Un genou écorché.* A skinned knee. (LA) **4** to scuff *On avait peur de le perdre dans tout un tas de monde, on marchait si près qu'on a tout écorché ses talons de souliers.* We were afraid of losing him in so many people, we were walking so close that we completely scuffed the heels of his shoes. (EV) **II s'écorcher** *v.pron.* to skin o.s., scratch, scrape (one's skin) *Je m'ai écorché le pied dessus le bord du lit.* I scraped my foot on the side of the bed. (EV) <***Loc:*** EV, LA, LF, SL, SM, TB, Da84, Lv88>

écorcheur [ekɔrʃœr] *n.m.* skinner, one who skins alligators <***Loc:*** TB>

écorder [ekɔrde] *v.tr.* to cord (wood) *Il écorde du bois tous les jours.* He cords wood every day. (SB) <***Loc:*** SB>

écore [ekɔr] *n.f. (occ. m.)* **1** bank (of a lake, river, bayou, etc.) **Un jour, ils estiont après pêcher dessus l'écore du bayou.* One day, they were fishing on the bank of the bayou. (EV, An94) **2** shore *Un tas des bateaux de Cuba ont frappé les écores des Etats-Unis.* A lot of boats from Cuba hit the shores of the United States. (Lv88) **3** escarpment, high ground not subject to flooding that borders a stream, river, swamp or other body of water **Lorsque l'on a passé les écores à Prud-homme, il n'y a plus d'écueils dans le Fleuve Mississippi.* As soon as you've passed the escarpment at Prudhomme, there are no more reefs in the Mississippi. (Bo80) ◊ **•être en bas l'écore** to be on the bank <Lv88> <***Loc:*** AC, AV, EV, IB, LA, LF, SB, SJ, SM, VM, An94, Da84, Gu00, Hi02, Lv88, Ph36>

écornifler (s') [ekɔrnifle] *v.pron.* to scratch, scrape, skin **J'm'ai écornifflé la main.* I scraped my hand. (EV, Ph36) *Je me suis écornifflé la main sur cette épingle.* I scratched my hand with that needle. (IB) <***Loc:*** EV, IB, Ph36>

écorner ♦see **décorner**

écosser [ekose] *v.tr.* to shell *Écosser des fèves.* To shell beans. (LA) <***Loc:*** LA>

écouenner [ekwɛ̃ne, ekwɑ̃ne] *v.tr.* **1** to skin, remove the outer skin from (ham or pork) *Il a écouenné sa viande avant de* *la manger.* He removed the skin from his meat before eating it. (IB) **Il a écouenné la vianne [=viande] de cochon.* He skinned the pork. (EV, Ph36) **2** to deshell, remove the shell from (e.g. a turtle) *Écouenner une tortue.* To deshell a turtle. (EV) **3** to beat, defeat *Si tu joues avec moi je vais t'écouenner.* If you play with me I'll beat you. (IB) <***Loc:*** EV, IB, SM, Lv88, Ph36>

écouiller [ekuje] *v.tr.* to injure the testicles of <***Loc:*** LF>

écouloir ♦see **couloir**

écoupeau ♦see **écopeau**

écourter [ekurte] *v.tr.* to shorten, cut short *Ils ont écourté leur chasse quand il a commencé à mouiller.* They cut short their hunt when it started to rain. (LA) <***Loc:*** LA, Da84>

écouter (**couter**) [ekute, akute, kute] **I** *v.tr.* **1** to listen to *Si t'aurais pas écouté tous les conseils des autres.* If you hadn't listened to the advice of others. (ch: *Jolie blonde*) **Couter son père.* To listen to one's father. (Da84) *Il coute sa maman.* He listens to his mother. (SM) *Écoute donc ça!* Will you listen to that! (EV, LA, Da84) **2** to obey *C'est la grand-mère qui le soigne, mais il l'écoute pas.* It's the grandmother who takes care of him, but he doesn't obey her. (EV) *Un enfant qui fait le détestable, il t'écoute pas, il est détestable.* A child who is willfully disobedient, he doesn't mind you, he's incorrigible. (VM) **II** *v.intr.* **1** to listen *J'ai écouté, mais j'ai pas entendu.* I listened, but I didn't hear. (SM) *Il me dit, comment tu peux dire la même histoire, la même continué, mais je te dis, ils l'ont pas attendu. S'ils m'ont attendu ils veut pas écouter, ils s'en va.* He tells me, how can you tell the same story, the same one continually, but I tell you, they haven't heard it. If they've heard me [tell it], they won't want to listen, they'll leave. (TB) *Écoute voir!* Listen! listen up! (EV, LA, VM) **2** to obey *Son père lui a dit mille fois de pas faire ça, mais il a pas écouté.* His father told him a thousand times to do that, but he didn't obey. (LA) <***Loc:*** AC, AV, EV, LA, LF, SL, SM, TB, VM, An94, Da84, Gu82, Hi02, Lv88>

écouteur [ekutœr] *n.m.* listener *Une chanson demandée par un écouteur.* A song requested by a listener. (LA) <***Loc:*** LA, Da84, Lv88>

écramouiller [ekrɑ̃muje, ekrɔ̃mwale] *v.tr.* to crush, smash *Il a écramouillé les œufs.* He smashed the eggs. (LF) <***Loc:*** LF, TB>

écran [ekrɑ̃] *n.m.* screen <***Loc:*** Da84>

écrapoutir ♦see **éclapoutir**

écrasant, -e [ekrazɑ̃, -ɑ̃t] *adj.* **1** crushing *Le poids écrasant du mur qu'a tombé durant la colonne a tué la pauvre femme qu'était pris en-dessous.* The crushing weight of the wall that fell during the tornado killed the poor woman who was trapped underneath it. (VM) *Le poids était écrasant.* The weight was crushing. (LA) **2** excessive, overbearing *Ses manières étaient écrasantes.* His behavior was overbearing. (VM) <***Loc:*** LA, VM, Da84>

écrasement [ekrazmɑ̃] *n.m.* crushing, squashing <***Loc:*** Da84>

écraser (**craser**) [kraze, ekraze] *v.tr.* **1** to crush, squash, mash *La canne est écrasée pour ôter le jus.* The sugarcane is crushed in order to extract the juice. (IB) *Pommes de terre écrasées.* Mashed potatoes. (IB) *Un ravert écrasé.* A smashed roach. (EV) *Un char écrasé.* A smashed up car. (EV) **2** to speak critically of, put down *Arrête de me parler comme ça! T'es tout le temps après m'écraser!* Stop talking to me like that! You're always putting me down! (EV) **II** *v.intr.* to become sickly, fail in health *Elle écrase parce qu'elle travaille trop.* She is getting sickly because she works too much. (SB) **III s'écraser** *v.pron.* to fail in health, lose one's health *Le vieux garçon est à s'écraser.* The old boy is losing is health. (AV) ◊ **•écraser la mûre (pour)** to have an abundance (of) *Ma belle-fille a eu des bessons et ma fille est après espérer un bébé dans le mois qui vient. On est après écraser la mûre pour les petits-enfants.* My daughter-in-law had twins and my daughter is expecting a baby next month. We have an abundance of grandchildren. (VM) <VM, La99> <***Loc:*** AV, EV, IB, LA, SB, SL, SM, TB, VM, Da84, Hi02, La99>

écrémage [ekrɛ̃maʒ] *n.m.* skimming, removing cream from <***Loc:*** Da84>

écrémer[1] [ekrɛ̃me] *v.tr.* **1** to skim, remove cream from (milk) *Nous-autres, on écrémait le lait, on avait une glacière, on mettait ça dans des gros bidons sur de la glace pour tenir ça froid.* We skimmed the milk, we had an icebox, we put that in large cans on ice to keep it [the cream] cold. (IB) **2** to skim floating matter from the surface of (a liquid) *Asteur que je fais mon roux sans graisse, j'ai pus besoin d'écrémer mon gombo.* Now that I make my roux without grease, I no longer need to skim my gumbo. (VM) <***Loc:*** EV, IB, LA, VM, Da84>

écrémer[2] **(s')** ♦see **excrémer (s')**

écrémeuse [ekrɛ̃møz] *n.f.* cream separator <***Loc:*** Da84>

écrevisse (**écrivisse, écruvisse, crébisse**) [ekrəvis, ekrevis, ekrivis, ekribis, ekrebis, ekryvis, krəvis, krebis] *n.m.* crawfish, crayfish **On est fier, nous-aut', que l'écrivisse est le symbole des Cadjins par rapport que c'est l'animal le plus courageux dedans le monde.* We're proud that the crawfish is the symbol of the Cajuns because it's the bravest animal in the world. (ThCa: *Mille misères*) <***Loc:*** AC, EV, LA, SB, SM, TB, VM, Da84, Gu00, Hi02, La99, Lv88, ThCa, Wh83>

écrire [ekrir] **I** *v.tr.* to write *Alle m'a écrit une lettre.* She wrote me a letter. (LF) *Écrire son nom.* To write one's name. (EV) *Moi, j'sus icitte pour écrire une description de chaque article et indiquer le nom de la personne qui va le recevoir. C'est tout.* I'm here to write down a description of each article and indicate the name of the person who's going to receive it. That's all. (ThCa: *La douce réunion*) **II** *v.intr.* to write *Pushkin, lui, il écrisait mieux en français qu'en russien.* Pushkin wrote better in French than in Russian.

(EV) *Il faut pas tu parles en français... tu peux apprendre mieux à lire et écrire... ils avaient raison pour ça.* You can't speak French [at school] . . . you can learn better to read and write [in English] . . . they were right about that. (PQ) **III s'écrire** *v.pron.* to write to each other *On va s'écrire souvent.* We'll write each other often. (LA) <***Loc:*** AC, AV, EV, LA, LF, PQ, SL, SM, TB, Da84, Hi02, Lv88, ThCa>

écrit [ekri] *n.m. (usu. pl.)* writing, written work *Les écrits de Sidonie de la Houssaye.* The written works of Sidonie de la Houssaye. (EV) <***Loc:*** EV, Da84>

écritage [ekritaʒ] *n.m.* writing *Il a fait son écritage à lui-même.* He made up his own writing system. (LF) <***Loc:*** LF>

écriture [ekrityr] *n.f.* writing, handwriting ◊ **•Les Saintes Ecritures** The Holy Scriptures <Da84> **•tablette d'écriture** writing tablet **Pour acheter plus des tablettes d'écriture.* To buy more writing tablets. (Wh83) <Wh83> <***Loc:*** LA, Da84, Wh83>

écrivain [ekrivɛ̃] *n.m.* writer, author <***Loc:*** Da84, Hi02>

écroc ♦see **accroc**

écroulement [ekrulmɑ̃] *n.m.* collapse, breakdown, falling apart <***Loc:*** Da84>

écrouler (**crouler**) [ekrule, krule] **I** *v.intr.* to break down, fall apart, collapse *La bâtisse a écroulé.* The building collapsed. (EV) *Le magasin a écroulé.* The barn collapsed. (SM) **II s'écrouler** *v.pron.* to collapse, cave in, break down *Leur maison s'a écroulé.* Their house collapsed. (VM) <***Loc:*** EV, SM, VM, Da84>

écroupière ♦see **croupière**

écroutage [ekrutaʒ] *n.m.* scraping, scratching, skinning (of a sore) <***Loc:*** Da84>

écrouter [ekrute] *v.tr.* **1** to scrape, scratch, skin **2** to peel a scab from *Il a écrouté son bobo.* He peeled the scab off of his sore. (EV) <***Loc:*** EV, LA>

écruvisse ♦see **écrevisse**

écuisser[1] [ekwise] *v.tr.* to brown *On usait tout le temps pour écuisser un* ROAST. We used all the time to brown a roast. (SL) <***Loc:*** SL>

écuisser[2] [ekɥise] *v.tr.* **1** to spread the thighs of **2** to split apart by pulling on the legs of *Arrête ça, tu vas l'écuisser.* Stop that, you'll split him in two. (LF) <***Loc:*** LF>

écumage [ekymaʒ] *n.m.* **1** skimming, removing foam **2** foaming <***Loc:*** Da84>

écume [ekœ̃m, ekym] *n.f.* **1** foam, froth, scum *Quand tu fais un gombo, et ta viande part à bouillir, ça monte une écume en haut. Il faut tu ôtes ça.* When you make a gumbo, and your meat starts to boil, it makes a froth on the top. You have to take that off. (EV) **2** bubble *Tu vois, j'ai une pompe icitte-là, et là tu* SET *ton eau avec le valve et tu peux mettre la pression que tu veux, tu vois, il faut mettre la pression là-bas pour de l'air. Tu vois tout ces écumes là?* You see, I have a pump here, and you set your water with the valve, and you can put it at the pressure you want, you see, you have to set the pressure over there, for air. You see all of these bubbles? (TB) <***Loc:*** EV, TB, VM, Da84>

écumer [ekyme] *v.tr.* to skim (a liquid) *Quand tu fais cuire du vin de canne pour faire du sirop, il faut t'écumes ça.* When you cook cane juice to make syrup, you have to skim that. (VM) <***Loc:*** VM, Da84>

écurdent ♦see **cure-dent**

écurder [ekyrde] **I** *v.tr.* to pick (one's teeth) *Écurder ses dents.* To pick one's teeth. (Lv88) **II s'écurder** *v.pron.* to pick one's teeth *Il a eu pour s'écurder après qu'il a mangé du tac-tac.* He had to pick his teeth after he ate popcorn. (LA) <***Loc:*** LA, Da84, Lv88>

écureuil [ekyrœj, kyrœj, kyrøj] *n.m.* squirrel *On a pas eu le dîner d'écureuils parce que lui, il mangeait pas de viande dans Carême.* We didn't have the squirrel dinner, because he wasn't eating meat during Lent. (EV) ◊ **•écureuil volant** flying squirrel <VM> <***Loc:*** AL, EV, IV, JD, LA, SL, SM, TB, VM, Da84, Gu00, Hi02, Lv88>

écurie [ekyri, ekyry] *n.f.* **1** stable (for horses, cows, etc.) **2** stall (in a stable) <***Loc:*** EV, IV, JE, LA, LF, SB, TB, Da84, Hi02>

eczéma [ekzima] *n.m./f.* eczema <***Loc:*** VM, Da84>

édenté, -e [edɑ̃te] *adj.* toothless *Une herse édentée.* A toothless harrow. (VM) <***Loc:*** VM, Da84>

édenter [edɑ̃te] *v.tr.* to break the teeth of *Ce bois était assez dur, ça a édenté ma scie.* That wood was so hard, it broke all the teeth on my saw. (VM) <***Loc:*** VM, Da84>

édification [edifikasjɔ̃] *n.f.* edification, inspiration <***Loc:*** Da84>

édifice [edifis] *n.m.* building, edifice <***Loc:*** Da84>

édit [edi] *n.m.* edict <***Loc:*** Da84>

éditer [edite] *v.tr.* **1** to edit, prepare (a document) *L'évêque a édité une lettre pour faire lire dimanche à la messe.* The bishop prepared a letter to be read Sunday at Mass. (LA) **2** to publish <***Loc:*** LA, Da84>

édradon [edradɔ̃, dradɔ̃] *n.m.* **1** eiderdown comforter **2** quilted bedspread, quilt <***Loc:*** IB>

éditeur [editœr] *n.m.* editor <***Loc:*** Da84>

éducation [edykasjɔ̃, ɛ̃dykasjɔ̃] *n.f.* education, schooling, training <***Loc:*** AC, EV, LA, LF, SL, TB, An84, An94, Da84, Lv88>

éduquer [edyke, ɛ̃dyke] *v.tr.* to educate *On t'a envoyé à l'école pour te faire éduquer.* We sent you to school to be educated. (EV) <***Loc:*** EV, JD, SM, Da84, Lv88>

effacé, -e [efase] *adj.* pale, drained of color *Elle était tout effacée quand elle est arrivée ici.* She was pale when she arrived here. (EV) <***Loc:*** EV>

effacer [efase] *v.tr.* to erase, efface *Effacer un péché.* To erase a sin. (LA) ◊ **•effacer un rêve** to quit having a dream because the dream's event has happened in reality (LA) <LA> <***Loc:*** LA, Da84>

effaceur [efasœr] *n.m.* eraser <***Loc:*** VM, Da84>

effaçure [efasyr] *n.m.* erasure, erasing <***Loc:*** Da84>

effardé -e [efarde] *adj.* unduly excited, agitated, giggly *Quoi il y a avec elle? Elle est tout effardée aujourd'hui.* What's wrong with her? She's all agitated today. (AC) <***Loc:*** AC>

effarder (s') [efarde] *v.pron.* to flutter about in the dust *La poule était après s'effarder.* The hen was fluttering about in the dust. (EV) <***Loc:*** EV, Lv88>

effaré, -e [efare] *adj.* **1** wild, savage *Le chat est effaré.* The cat is wild. (SB) **2** wild, unkempt *Avoir la chevelure toute effarée.* To have a wild head of hair. (SJ) <***Loc:*** SB, SJ>

effarouchant, -e [efaruʃɑ̃, -ɑ̃t] *adj.* frightening *Ils ont fait un bonhomme effarouchant pour Halloween.* They made a frightening human figure for Halloween. (LA) <***Loc:*** LA, Da84>

effarouché -é [efaruʃe] *adj.* **1** frightened *Quoi faire tu ressembles si effarouché?* Why do you look so frightened? (EV) **2** disheveled, in disorder *Ses cheveux étaient effarouchés.* His hair was disheveled. (AC) <***Loc:*** AC, EV, Da84>

effaroucher [efaruʃe] **I** *v.tr.* to frighten, scare *Il a effarouché le chevreuil.* He frightened the deer. (EV) **II s'effaroucher** *v.pron.* to be frightened *Les vaches s'ont effarouché quand ça a commencé à tonner.* The cows became frightened when it started to thunder. (LA) <***Loc:*** EV, LA, Da84>

effet [efɛ, efe] *n.m.* result, effect, consequence ◊ **•en effet** sure, sure enough <Da84> **•faire effet** to produce results, be effective (of medicines, treatments, etc.) *Il m'a dit que cette médecine-là fait effet.* He told me that that medecine is effective. (VM) <VM, Da84> **•faire un effet** to have an effect <Da84> **•faire un effet bœuf** to look great *Cette chaise placée ainsi dans le salon fait un effet bœuf.* That chair placed that way in the living room looks great. (Pe37) *Ce chapeau fait un effet bœuf avec cette robe.* This hat with looks great with that dress. (Pe37) <Pe37> **•prendre effet** to take effect, go into effect *L'assurance va prendre effet le mois qui vient.* The insurance will take effect next month. (EV) <EV> <***Loc:*** EV, VM, Da84, Pe37>

effeuillage [eføjaʒ] *n.m.* **1** defoliation, falling of leaves **2** shucking (of corn) <***Loc:*** Da84>

effeuiller [eføje] **I** *v.tr.* **1** to defoliate, strip leaves off of *Le gros vent a effeuillé les arbres.* The strong wind stripped the leaves off the trees. (EV) **2** to shuck, husk (corn) *Elle effeuille le maïs avant de le dégrainer.* She husks the corn before removing the kernels. (IB) **II s'effeuiller** *v.pron.* to shed leaves *Mon pacanier s'a effeuillé bonne heure cette année.* My pecan tree shed its leaves early this year. (LA) <***Loc:*** EV, IB, LA, Da84>

effile [efil] *n.m.* knife sharpener <***Loc:*** VM>

effiloper (s') [efilope] *v.pron.* to unravel, become unraveled <***Loc:*** TB>

effiler ♦see **affiler**

efflanqué, -e [eflɑ̃ke] *adj.* **1** skinny, emaciated *C'est un grand éflanqué.* He's a tall skinny fellow. (VM) **2** exhausted, worn out <***Loc:*** VM, Hi02, Pe37>

effleurage [eflørаʒ] *n.m.* leveling, evening up, making flush (boards, etc.) <***Loc:*** Da84>

effleurer ♦see **affleurer**

effort [efɔr] *n.m.* **1** effort **Alors, il a ouvert la jarre de beurre et il a commencé à graisser les crevasses dans un effort d'essayer de les guérir.* So, he opened the jar of butter and he started to grease the cracks in an effort to try to heal them. (EV, An94) **2** hernia *Son effort était venu assez mauvais qu'il a eu pour se faire opérer.* His hernia had gotten so bad that he had to have an operation. (EV) <***Loc:*** EV, An94>

effrayant, -e [efrejɑ̃, -ɑ̃t] *adj.* frightening, appalling, scary *Madame Grands Doigts est effrayante.* Madame Grands Doigts is scary. (EV) <***Loc:*** EV, Da84>

effrayer (effroyer) [efreje, efrɔje] **I** *v.tr.* to frighten, terrify *Il a effrayé ses enfants avec ses histoires de loup-garou.* He scared his children with his werewolf stories. (EV) **II s'effrayer** *v.pron.* to be frightened *Effrayez-vous-autres pas.* Don't be frightened. (LA) <***Loc:*** EV, LA, Da84, Hi02>

effronté, -e (fronté, -é) [efrɔ̃te, frɔ̃te] *adj.* shameless, brazen, impudent, nervy **Il est manière effronté pour un bougre qu'a un business.* He's kind of nervy for a fellow with a business. (ThCa: *La table des veuves*) ◊ **•faire l'effronté** to act sassy, behave impolitely *Fais pas l'effronté avec moi, mon petit vaurien.* Don't act sassy with me, you little good-for-nothing. (LA) <LA, Da84> <***Loc:*** LA, Da84, Lv88, ThCa>

effrontément [efrɔ̃temɑ̃] *adv.* brazenly, impudently <***Loc:*** Da84>

effronterie [efrɔ̃təri] *n.f.* effrontery, impudence, nerve, gall **Il a eu l'effronterie de me dire...* He had the gall to tell me . . . (Da84) <***Loc:*** LA, VM, Da84>

effroyable [efrwajab(l)] *adj.* frightful **J'ai toujours respecté les temps solonnels. Je vas aux baptêmes et aux enterrements de la parenté. Mais ces rites me causent eine angoisse effroyab'e.* I've always respected solemn occasions. I go to baptisms and funerals of relatives. But these rites always cause me a frightful anguish. (ThCa: *Mille misères*) **Les jeunes d'asteur, i' faisont des erreurs effroyab' qu'i' faiseriont pas si il' écouterions les vieux.* Young people today, they make frightful errors that they wouldn't make if they listened to their elders. (Gu82) <***Loc:*** Gu82, ThCa>

effroyer ♦see **effrayer**

éflier ♦see **néfrier**

égal[1]**, -e** [egal] *adj.* **1** equal *Les deux paniers sont égals. Prends cil-là tu veux.* The two baskets are equal. Take the one you like. (LA) **La Toussaint est célébrée avec eine vénération et intensité égale avec Chrismise.* All Saints' is celebrated with a veneration and an intensity equal to Christmas. (Wh83) **2** even, smooth *Il a passé le râteau pour mettre la terre tout égale.* He raked over to make the soil all even. (EV) *Ça avait l'habitude d'être égal, plat.* It [the washboard] was usually even, flat. (VM) **3** even, steady *C'est juste un petit rhume, mais il faut je reste égale ou je vas rechuter.* It's just a little cold, but I have to stay steady [in temperature] or I'll relapse. (AC) ◊ **•ça m'est égal** it's okay by me <Da84> **•mal égal** uneven <Da84> **•part et part égal** share and share alike <Da84> <***Loc:*** AC, EV, LA, VM, Da84, Lv88, Wh83>

égal[2] [egal] *n.* equal <***Loc:*** Da84, Hi02>

égal[3] [egal] *adv.* evenly, equally *Quarante-neuf piastres se divisent pas égal.* Forty-nine dollars does not divide up evenly. (VM) <***Loc:*** VM>

égaler [egale] *v.tr.* to level, smooth, make even *Il va égaler la terre avec une herse.* He will level the ground with a harrow. (IB) <***Loc:*** AV, IB, Da84, Lv88>

égalir [egalir] *v.tr.* **1** to equalize, make equal *Il faudra égalir les comptes après l'enterrement.* We'll have to equalize the accounts after the funeral. (LA) **2** to level, smooth, make even *On aura pour égalir notre terrain avant de commencer à bâtir.* We are going to have to level our lot before beginning to build. (LA) **3** to plane *Il a égali ses petites planches pour se faire une table.* He planed his small planks to make himself a table. (LA) <***Loc:*** EV, JD, LA, LF, SB, SJ, SL, TB, Lv88>

égaliser [egalize] *v.tr.* **1** to equalize, make equal *Les deux frères ont égalisé leur bien.* The two brothers equalized their possessions. (LA) **2** to level, smooth, make even *Il a égalisé son terrain en vue de se faire une maison.* He leveled his lot in view of building a house. (VM) *La petite manche qui va à la vieille maison devient raboteux après quelques années, et tout les temps en temps, il faut l'égaliser.* The lane that goes to the old house gets rough after a few years and every now and then, it must be graded. (LA) <***Loc:*** LA, VM, Da84>

égalité [egalite] *n.f.* **1** equality **2** evenness <***Loc:*** Da84>

égaré, -e [egare] *adj.* **1** haggard-looking, gaunt, sickly looking *Une bétaille égarée.* A sickly-looking animal. (Lv88) **2** confused *Il a l'air égaré.* He seems confused. (SM) **3** simple-minded (of a person) *Il a toujours été un petit peu égaré.* He's always been a bit simple-minded. (VM) **4** senile *Alle est bien smatte, BUT alle est après venir égarée un petit brin.* She is quite smart, but she's getting a bit senile. (TB) ◊ **•avoir les yeux égarés** to appear tired **Il a les yeux égarés.* He looks tired. (EV, Ph36) <EV, Ph36> <***Loc:*** EV, SM, TB, Lv88, Ph36>

égarer [egare] **I** *v.tr.* **1** to mislead, lead astray *Fais attention de pas le laisser t'égarer.* Be careful not to let him lead you astray. (LA) **2** to lose, cause to be lost *Alle dit si n-a une d'égaré, alle dit, ça me fait de la peine de dire, mais c'est toi qui l'as égaré.* She said if one of them is missing, I'm sorry to say it, but it's you who lost it. (TB) **II s'égarer** *v.pron.* to go astray, get lost *Il s'a égaré dans les mèches.* He got lost in the marsh. (LA) <***Loc:*** LA, TB, Da84>

égaron [egarɔ̃] *n.m.* stallion, stud horse <***Loc:*** AV>

eggnog [ɛgnɔg] *n.m.* eggnog <***Loc:*** EV, Ph36>

église [egliz] *n.f.* church <***Loc:*** AC, EV, IB, LA, LF, SL, SM, TB, VM, An94, Da84, Hi02, La99, Lv88, Wh83>

égoïne ♦see **égouine**

égorgé, -e [egɔrʒe] *adj.* hoarse *Il est égorgé d'avoir crié.* He is hoarse from shouting. (LF) <***Loc:*** LF>

égorger [egɔrʒe] *v.tr.* to cut the throat of *Il était après égorger le cochon quand son voisin a arrivé; il pouvait pas arrêter.* He was cutting the pig's throat when his neighbor arrived; he couldn't stop. (LA) <***Loc:*** LA, Da84>

égosillé, -e [egozije] *adj.* choking, having s.t. caught in the throat *T'es égosillé?* Are you choking? (VM) <***Loc:*** VM>

égosser [egose] *v.tr.* to remove (cotton) from the bolls after these have been gathered whole and brought into the barn *Il faut égosser le coton avant de faire une balle.* One must separate the cotton from the bolls before making a bale. (LA) <***Loc:*** AV, LA, VM, Da84>

égosserie [egosri] *n.f.* social gathering for the purpose of removing cotton from the bolls after these have been gathered and brought into the barn <***Loc:*** VM, Gr86>

égouine (**égoïne**) [egwin, esgwin] *n.f.* handsaw <***Loc:*** EV, IV, LA, SL, SM, TB, VM, Da84, Gr86, Lv88>

égourbes [egurb] *n.f.pl.* glanders *Le mulet a les égourbes.* The mule has glanders. (TB) <***Loc:*** TB>

égout [egu] *n.m.* **1** drain, drainage **2** drainage ditch *J'ai fouillé un bon égout pour chesser cette terre.* I dug a good drainage ditch to dry out this land. (Lv88) *Il y avait un fossé d'égout là.* There was a drainage ditch there. (EV) **3** eye-dropper <***Loc:*** EV, VM, Da84, Lv88>

égouttage [egutaʒ] *n.m./f.* **1** drainage *Ils avaient à faire des égouttages après la pluie.* They had to work on drainage after the rain. (SB) **2** dripping (of coffee, cream cheese, etc.) ◊ **•égouttage d'eau** sewer, drain <Da84> <***Loc:*** LF, SB, Da84>

égoutter [egute] *v.tr.* **1** to drain (land) *Il a eu pour égoutter les cinq z-acres à côté du bois avant de faire récolte en arrière-là.* He had to drain the five acres next to the woods before planting back there. (LA) **2** to drain by dripping *Ça accrochait tout ça là, ça le laissait égoutter une journée ou deux.* They would hang all of that [smoked meat] there, they would let it drip for a day or two. (EV) **3** to drip (e.g. coffee, clabber for cottage cheese) *Égoutter le café.* To drip coffee. (Lv88) **Café égoutté.* Dripped coffee. (Da84) *Elle avait habitude d'égoutter son caillé dans un sac pendu sur une branche de lilas.* She used to drip her clabber in a sack hanging from a chinaberry tree branch. (LA) **Caillé égoutté.* Cottage cheese, curds. (Da84) <***Loc:*** AC, EV, LA, TB, Da84, Lv88>

égraboter [egrabote] *v.tr.* to remove pod pieces (from harvested cotton) *Quand on était petit, Papa nous mettait à égraboter le coton.* When we were young, Papa would have us pick out the pod pieces from the harvested cotton. (LA) <*Loc:* LA, Lv88>

égrafigner ♦see **grafigner**

égrafignure ♦see **grafignure**

égrainage ♦see **égrenage**

égrainer ♦see **égrener**

égraineuse ♦see **égreneuse**

égrandir (**agrandir**) [egrɑ̃dir, agrɑ̃dir] **I** *v.tr.* **1** to enlarge, make bigger **Il avait eine 'tite hache. Il a égrandi le trou.* He had a little axe. He enlarged the hole. (An77) **2** to add on to (a building) *C'était la même maison mais on l'a égrandi après.* It's the same house but we added on to it afterwards. (TB) **II** *v.intr.* to enlarge, get bigger *À mesure que l'eau coulait à travers, le trou égrandissait.* As the water flowed through, the hole got bigger. (LA) **III s'égrandir** *v.pron.* **1** to add on to one's house, build larger quarters for o.s. *Ils auront besoin de s'égrandir après que le bébé va arriver.* They will have to add on to their house after the baby arrives. (LA) **2** to enlarge, get bigger *L'ouragan s'a égrandi depuis hier.* The hurrricane became larger since yesterday. (LA) <*Loc:* AV, EV, IB, LA, LF, SB, SJ, SM, TB, VM, An77, An94, Da84, Lv88, Ph36>

égrandissement (**agrandissement**) [egrɑ̃dismɑ̃, agrɑ̃dismɑ̃] *n.m.* **1** enlargement **2** extension, adding on <*Loc:* Da84>

égrandisseur [egrɑ̃disœr] *n.m.* enlarger *C'est pour égrandir un portrait. C'est un égrandisseur.* It's to enlarge a picture. It's an enlarger. (VM) <*Loc:* VM>

égrimille ♦see **grémille**

égrémiller ♦see **grémiller**

égrenage (**égrainage**) [egrɛ̃naʒ] *n.m.* **1** shelling (of beans, etc.) **2** saying of the rosary beads <*Loc:* Da84>

égrener (**égrainer, gréner**) [egrɛ̃ne, grɛ̃ne] **I** *v.tr.* **1** to shell (beans, peas, etc.) *Et le pape à C. me disait qu'il yeux donnait de l'argent, cinq ou dix sous, pour aller égrener du maïs.* And C's dad told me he used to give them money, five or ten cents, to go shell corn. (TB) *Gréner le maïs, les fèves.* To shell the corn, the beans. (Lv88) **2** to remove grains (of corn) *Ça sauvait les coton-maïs après c'était égrainé.* They saved the corn cobs after the grains had been removed from the corn. (SL) **3** to grind (e.g. coffee, meat) *Gréner du café.* To grind coffee. (JE) *Ça a grainé la viande hier.* They ground the meat yesterday. (LF) **4** to smash, break to pieces *Il a égrainé le verre.* He smashed the glass to pieces. (LF) **II s'égrainer** *v.pron.* to be shelled **Le maïs s'égraine bien.* The corn shells easily. (Da84) ◊ **•égrainer le chapelet** to say the beads, say the rosary <Da84> <*Loc:* EV, JD, JE, SB, SL, TB, Da84, Lv88>

égreneuse (**égraineuse**) [egrɛ̃nøz] *n.f.* mechanical sheller <*Loc:* LF, Da84>

égrenoir [egrɛ̃nwar] *n.m.* mechanical sheller <*Loc:* AV>

égreyer ♦see **gréer**

égricher ♦see **regricher**

égrimille ♦see **grémille**

égrimiller ♦see **grémiller**

éguenillé ♦see **déguénillé**

éguincher (s') [egɛ̃ʃe] *v.pron.* to dress up *Alle s'a tout éguinchée pour le bal.* She got all dressed up for the ball. (VM) <*Loc:* VM>

éhancher [ehɑ̃ʃe] **I** *v.tr.* to dislocate or break the hip of *Il était assez mauvais danseur qu'il a proche éhanché sa femme.* He was such a terrible dancer that he nearly dislocated his wife's hip. (LA) **II s'éhancher** *v.pron.* to sprain, dislocate or break one's hip *Il s'a proche éhanché quand il a tombé dans le fossé.* He almost broke a hip when he fell in the ditch. (LA) <*Loc:* LA, Da84>

éhonter (**ahonter, anhonter, honter**) [ehɔ̃te, eɔ̃te, aɔ̃te, ahɔ̃te, ɑ̃ɔ̃te, ɑ̃hɔ̃te, ɔ̃te, hɔ̃te] *v.tr.* **1** to shame, disgrace, dishonor *Il a ahonté sa famille.* He disgraced his family. (Lv88) *Alle a ahonté sa pauvre mère.* She shamed her poor mother. (VM) **2** to humiliate, put to shame *Je veux bien l'éhonter si je l'attrape après dire du mal de moi.* I want to shame him if I catch him saying bad things about me. (LA) *Je l'ai ahonté devant tout le monde.* I humiliated him in front of everyone. (SL) <*Loc:* AV, EV, IB, LA, SL, SM, Da84, Lv88, Ph36>

ein, eine, einne ♦see **un**

éioù ♦see **ayoù**

éjamber ♦see **enjamber**

éjarer (s') (**éjarrer**) [eʒare] *v.pron.* to spread one's legs *Il s'a flanqué dans la chaise et puis il s'a éjaré.* He flopped down in the chair and then he spread his legs. (VM) **•être éjarré / se tenir éjarré** to have one's legs spread (Lv88) <*Loc:* JD, LA, VM, Da84, Lv88>

éjarrer ♦see **éjarer**

éjointer [eʒwɛ̃te] *v.tr.* to dislocate *Elle a éjointé son épaule dans le* WRECK. She dislocated her shoulder in the wreck. (VM) <*Loc:* VM>

élan [elɑ̃] *n.m./f.* **1** period of time, a while *Espère un élan.* Wait a while. (LA) *Pour un élan, pour les jeunes, si tu parlais français c'était comme t'es un* SECOND GRADE CITIZEN. For some time, for the young generation, if you spoke French you were considered a second class citizen. (IB) **2** verve, spirit ◊ **•dans un (tit) élan** in a moment *Je vas vous montrer ça dans un élan comment c'est facile.* I'll show you in a moment just how easy it is. (VM) <LA, VM> **•un bon élan** a good while, quite a while *Il y a un bon élan je l'ai pas vu.* I haven't seen him in a good while. (Lv88) <Lv88> <*Loc:* AC, IB, JD, LA, LF, SB, SM, TB, VM, Da84, Guoo, Lv88>

élance [elɑ̃s] *n.f.* thrust, blow, shot *Ça était une jolie élance.* That was a good shot. (VM) <*Loc:* VM>

élargir [elarʒir] **I** *v.tr.* **1** to widen, make wider *Ils ont élargi le chemin en avant de chez nous-autres.* They widened the road in front of our house. (LA) **2** to enlarge, expand **Tout les ans il faisait ein plus grand jardin et il enlargissiait son* *engard [=hangar]*. Every year he made a bigger garden and he expanded his barn. (Wh83) **II s'élargir** *v.pron.* to widen, become wider **La rivière s'élargit.* The river is becoming wider. (Da84) <***Loc:*** LA, Da84, Wh83>

élargissement [elarʒismɑ̃] *n.m.* **1** widening, broadening **2** enlarging <***Loc:*** Da84>

élasticité [elastisite] *n.f.* elasticity <***Loc:*** Da84>

élastique[1] [elastik, alastik] *adj.* elastic, springy *Une corde élastique.* An elastic string. (LA) <***Loc:*** LA, Da84>

élastique[2] (**alastique, astique, lastique**) [elastik, alastik, astik, lastik] *n.m./f.* **1** rubber *Des bottes en lastique.* Rubber boots. (Lv88) *Des pelotes en lastique.* Rubber bullets. (Lv88) *Tape-le avec cette astique.* Hit him with that rubber. (JE) **2** rubber band **3** preserving jar rubber <***Loc:*** EV, JE, LA, SL, TB, VM, Da84, Lv88>

électer [elɛkte, elekte] *v.tr.* to elect *Je suis un politicien. Moi j'ai été électé il y a seize ans déjà.* I'm a politician. I was elected 16 years ago already. (TB) <***Loc:*** LF, SM, TB, VM, Gr86, Lv88>

élection [elɛksjɔ̃] *n.f.* election <***Loc:*** LA, Da84, Hi02, Lv88>

électorat [elɛktora] *n.m.* electorate <***Loc:*** Da84>

électricien [elɛktrisjɛ̃] *n.m.* electrician <***Loc:*** Da84>

électricité (**élestricité, escricité, estrécité**) [elɛktrisite, eletrisite, eskrisite, estrisite, ɛkstrisite, estresite, etrisite, ɛktrisite, ektrisite] *n.m./f.* **1** electricity **2** lightning *T'es habitué à l'escricité, toi.* You are used to lightning. (VM) <***Loc:*** AC, EV, IB, JE, LA, LF, SL, SM, TB, VM, Da84, Hi02>

électrifier [elɛktrifje] *v.tr.* to electrify *Électrifier une barrière.* To electrify a fence. (LA) <***Loc:*** LA, Da84>

électrique (**élestrique**) [elɛktrik, elestrik, alɛktrik, ilɛktrik] *adj.* electric, electrical *Ils ont tous des outils, des nouvelles outils, ils ont tout des* WOOD PLANER *électriques asteur, ils ont des grosses scies électriques.* They all have tools, new tools, they all have electric wood planers now, they have big electric saws. (LF) <***Loc:*** AV, LF, SB, Da84, Hi02>

électrocution [elɛktrokysjɔ̃] *n.f.* electrocution <***Loc:*** Da84>

élégance [elegɑ̃s] *n.f.* elegance <***Loc:*** Da84>

élégant, -e [elegɑ̃, -ɑ̃t] *adj.* elegant *Il a un capot élégant.* He has an elegant coat. (LA) <***Loc:*** LA, Da84>

élément [elemɑ̃] *n.m.* **1** element, component **2** *(pl.)* elements, weather *Et ce vieux monde eusse pouvait prendre une planche et pouvait voir si c'est qu'il y avait trop d'aubelle, et ça fait que ça allait pas durer si c'est qu'eusse mettait ça au, à les éléments, tu connais dans le temps, ç'allait pourrir.* And oldtimers could take a board and they could see whether it had too much sapwood, so that it wouldn't last if they put it in the elements, you know in the weather, it would rot. (TB) <***Loc:*** TB, Da84>

élémentaire [elemɑ̃tær] *adj.* elementary *Il a pas fini l'école élémentaire.* He did not finish elementary school. (LA) <***Loc:*** LA, Da84>

élemi ♦see **ennemi**

éléphant [elefɑ̃, alefɑ̃] *n.m.* elephant <***Loc:*** SL, VM, Da84>

élestricité ♦see **électricité**

élestrique ♦see **électrique**

élevage [el(ə)vaʒ] *n.m.* **1** breeding, raising (of livestock) **2** cultivation, raising (of crops) <***Loc:*** LA, Da84>

élévateur [elevatœr] *n.m.* **1** elevator **2** lift, hoist <***Loc:*** LF, SB, SM, Da84, Lv88>

élévation [elevasjɔ̃] *n.f.* elevation, rise <***Loc:*** Da84>

élève[1] [elɛv, eløv] *n.m./f.* pupil, student <***Loc:*** Da84>

élève[2] [elɛv, eløv] *n.f.* brood, clutch (of eggs, baby birds) *Les canards a venu rares. Et là quand il y a plein des canards, de bonnes élèves, là la limite est plus grande.* Ducks have gotten rare. And then when there are a lot of ducks, good broods, then the limit is higher. (TB) <***Loc:*** SM, TB>

élevée [ɛl(ə)ve] *n.f.* levee <***Loc:*** EV>

élever [ɛl(ə)ve] **I** *v.tr.* **1** to raise, lift up **Et elle a élevé son* BUN. *Quand elle l'a élevé, elle l'a vite rebaissé.* And she raised up [the top part of] her [hot dog] bun. When she raised it, she quickly lowered it. (EV, An94) **2** to raise up, elevate (e.g. land) *Je trouve son terrain est élevé haut.* I find that his lot is raised high. (LA) **3** to raise, cultivate, grow (crops) *On élève plus le coton dans le sud à cause du weevil.* We don't grow cotton in the south anymore because of weevils. (Lv88) **4** to rear, raise (a child, an animal, etc.) *C'est ma grand-mère qui m'a élevé.* My grandmother raised me. (IB) **5** to erect *Ils ont élevé le poteau.* They erected the post. (LA) **II** *v.intr.* to grow *Mon maïs s'a fait prendre par le froid. Je crois pas il va élever. Si il élève, ça sera un miracle.* My corn got the cold. I don't think it will grow. If it grows, that will be a miracle. (LA) **III s'élever** *v.pron.* to rise **Quand il est venu au ras de lui, le hibou a voulu s'élever.* When he came near it, the owl tried to rise. (EV, An94) ◊ **•élever des bêtes** to raise livestock *J'ai été élever des bêtes, un peu.* I used to raise livestock, a little. (SL) <SL> **•élevé sur du vin haigue** lively, energetic <Gr86> **•bien élevé** polite, well mannered *Cet enfant est sûr bien élevé.* That child is surely well raised. (LA) <LA, Da84> **•mal élevé** impolite, rude *Va t'en, espèce de mal élevé.* Go away, you rude thing, you. (EV) <EV, Da84> <***Loc:*** AC, AV, EV, IB, IV, LA, LF, SL, TB, An94, Da84, Gr86, Hi02, Lv88, Wh83>

éleveur [ɛl(ə)vœr] *n.m.* **1** one who breeds or raises animals, breeder **2** one who grows or cultivates crops *Éleveur de coton.* Grower of cotton. (LA) <***Loc:*** LA, TB, Da84>

éleveuse [ɛl(ə)vøz] *n.f.* **1** brooder, brood-hen **2** mare <***Loc:*** Da84>

élimination [eliminasjɔ̃] *n.f.* elimination <***Loc:*** Da84>

éliminer [elimine] *v.tr.* to eliminate, remove *Il va essayer d'éliminer ses cousins de leur part.* He'll try to eliminate his cousins from their share [in the inheritance]. (LA) <***Loc:*** LA, Da84>

élingué, -e [elɛ̃ge] *adj.* thin, slender, lanky, lean *Ils sont des grands élingués, ses fils.* They are really lanky people, his sons. (VM) *Un veau élingué.* A rangy calf. (SJ) <***Loc:*** AV, IB, LF, SB, SJ, SM, VM, Lv88>

élinguer [elɛ̃ge] *v.tr.* **1** to pull the legs off of **2** to beat *Si il te met la main dessur, il va t'élinguer.* If he catches you, he'll beat you. (LF) <***Loc:*** LF>

élire (**élure**) [elir, elyr] (*p.p.* **élu** [ely]) *v.tr.* to elect **On a élu un gouverneur.* We elected a governor. (Da84) <***Loc:*** LA, Da84>

élite [elit] *n.f.* elite <***Loc:*** Da84>

elle[1] ♦see **alle**

elle[2] [ɛl, el] *pron.pers.f.* **1** *(obj. of prep.)* her *Avec ma mère je parle en français avec elle tout le temps, mais elle alle parle moitié en anglais.* With my mother I speak French all the time, but she speaks half in English. (TB) *Elle me mettait couché au ras d'elle pour me tiendre chaud.* She laid me down next to her to keep me warm. (SL) **Et là, il lui a dit qu'il fallait pas qu'elle se tracasse, qu'il allait parler au roi pour la soigner, pour prendre cas d'elle.* Then, he told her that she shouldn't worry, that he would speak to the king to care for her, to take up her case. (IV, An94) *Une bonne chose pour elle, son cancer est traitable.* A good thing for her, her cancer is treatable. (LA) *Tous ses enfants à elle parle français.* All of her children speak French. (LF) *Et là j'ai acheté ça-là avec elle.* I bought all of that from her. (TB) **2** *(tonic)* she, her *Ça c'est elle qu'il faulait qui fait ça.* She's the one who had to do that. (TB) *Des fois elle et moi on va parler en anglais.* Sometimes, she and I will speak English together. (TB) *Elle, alle a trawlé 17 ans avec moi. Sur le bateau.* She went trawling with me for 17 years. On the boat. (TB) *Je crois pas qu'alle parle français, elle.* I don't think she speaks French, her. (TB) ◊ **•elle qui {que}** the one who, the one that *La seule qui parle français c'est Sherry, elle qui reste dans le* TRAILER. The only one who can speak French is Sherry, the one who lives in the trailer. (TB) <TB> <***Loc:*** AC, EV, IV, LA, LF, SL, SM, TB, VM, An94, Da84, Hi02, La99, Lv88>

éloigner [elwɑ̃je, elwɛ̃je] **I** *v.tr.* to place at a distance, put far away *Il a éloigné ses fusils pour pus les voir.* He put away his guns so that he would no longer see them. (LA) **II s'éloigner** *v.pron.* **1** to withdraw, distance o.s., go away *J'aimerais m'éloigner d'ici.* I'd like to leave here. (EV) **2** to get lost, stray, go astray *Je me rappelle ils s'ont éloignés et on a eu pour aller les chercher.* I remember they got lost and we had to go look for them. (EV) *Ils ont joué et ils se sont éloignés de leur nid.* They played and they strayed from their nest. (LA) <***Loc:*** AC, EV, LA, VM, Da84, Hi02>

éloise (**aloise, alouèze, éloize, élouèse**) [elwaz, alwɛz, elwɛz] *n.m./f.* **1** lightning *Il y a des alouezes dans le sud.* There's lightning in the south. (SM) **2** lightning bolt **Miséricorde! Y parle cont' les prêt's. Le Bon Djeu va te frapper avec eine éloise.* Heavens! He's talking badly about priests. The Good Lord is going to strike you with a lightning bolt! (ThCa: *Mille misères*) **3** heat lightning **4** sheet lightning <***Loc:*** AC, IB, SL, SM, VM, Fa77, Gu00, Hi02, Lv88, ThCa>

éloiser [elwaze, lwaze] *v.intr.* to lighten (of lightning) *C'était après éloiser, ça fait on a rentré.* It was lightening, so we came in. (VM) <***Loc:*** VM>

éloize ♦see **éloise**

élonge ♦see **allonge**

élonger ♦see **allonger**

élongir [elɔ̃ʒir] *v.tr.* **1** to lengthen, extend *Je vas élongir l'hangar.* I'm going to lengthen the barn wing. (LA) *Il faudra qu'on hente ces deux-par-quatre pour élongir la couverture.* We'll have to butt these two-by-fours together to extend the roof. (VM) **2** to stretch out <***Loc:*** LA, SB, VM, Fa77>

éloquence [elokɑ̃s] *n.f.* eloquence <***Loc:*** Da84>

éloquent, -e [elokɑ̃, -ɑ̃t] *adj.* eloquent <***Loc:*** Da84>

élouèse ♦see **éloise**

élure ♦see **élire**

émanciper (**imanciper**) [emɑ̃sipe, imɑ̃sipe] *v.tr.* to emancipate, set free *Il a émancipé son garçon.* He emancipated his son. (AV) *Son garçon a demandé pour être imancipé.* His son requested to be emancipated. (LA) <***Loc:*** AV, LA, Da84>

émasculer [emaskyle] **I** *v.tr.* to emasculate, castrate **II s'émasculer** *v.pron.* to emasculate o.s., castrate o.s. <***Loc:*** Da84>

emballage [ɑ̃balaʒ] *n.m.* **1** baling (of hay, etc.) **2** packing, packaging <***Loc:*** Da84>

emballer [ɑ̃bale] **I** *v.tr.* **1** to bale (hay) *Pour les vaches et les chevaux, ça emballait ça, ça faisait des balles de foin pour les bétails.* For the cows and the horses they would bale that [the rice straw], they would make bales of hay for the animals. (EV) **2** to pack, package **II s'emballer** *v.pron.* to be baled **Le foin s'emballe bien.* The hay is easily baled. (Da84) <***Loc:*** EV, LA, Da84>

emballeuse [ɑ̃baløz] *n.f.* baler, baling machine (for hay, straw) <***Loc:*** EV, LA, An94, Lv88>

embarbouiller (**ébarbouiller**) [ɑ̃barbuje, ebarbuje] *v.tr.* to muddy, besmear with mud or dirt *Il a tout ébarbouillé ses souliers neufs.* He got his new shoes all muddy. (EV) *Il avait la figure tout ébarbouillée.* His face was all smeared with dirt. (EV) <***Loc:*** EV, Da84>

embarcation [ɑ̃barkasjɔ] *n.f.* **1** vehicle, means of transportation (except animals) *Je voudrais aller, mais j'ai pas d'embarcation.* I'd like to go, but I don't have transportation. (SM) **Qué sorte d'embarcation t'as? J'ai in bouget.* What kind of transportation do you have? I have a buggy. (EV, Ph36) **2** embarkation, embarking **3** shipment <***Loc:*** AV, EV, IB, LA, SB, SJ, SM, VM, Da84, Gr86, Hi02, Lv88, Ph36>

embarquer [ɑ̃barke] **I** *v.tr.* to bring into or onto a boat *Je le ferme et embarque ça dans le bateau.* I close it and bring it into the boat. (TB) **II** *v.intr.* to board, get into a vehicle *Kossuth a embarqué dans le char-là, et il l'a* CRANK. Kossuth got into the car there, and he cranked it up. (EV) *Si toi, t'embarques à bord, vieux, je dis, moi, je vas t'arranger à toi.* If you get on board, buddy, I said, I'll take care of you. (LF) **III s'embarquer** *v.pron.* to embark, get on, board a vehicle *Embarque-toi vite.* Get in quickly. (IB) <***Loc:*** AC, AV, EV, IB, LA, LF, SJ, SM, TB, VM, Da84, Gu00, Hi02, Lv88, Ph36>

embarras [ɑ̃bara] *n.m.* **1** trouble, difficulty **Un veau c'est un embarras, faut que tu te défais de ça parce que si tu gardes ça, ça coûte pour nourrir.* A calf is a lot of trouble, you have to get rid of it because, if you keep it, it costs money to feed it. (St95) **2** obstruction (esp. vegetation and tree trunks that clog a waterway) ◊ **•faire des embarras** to give trouble *Il fait tout le temps des embarras à ses parents.* He's always giving his parents trouble. (LA) <LA, Da84> <***Loc:*** EV, LA, SL, An94, Da84, Fa77, Lv88, St95>

embarrassant, -e [ɑ̃barasɑ̃, -ɑ̃t] *adj.* **1** troublesome, bothersome *Quand elle vient se promener et elle reste trop longtemps, c'est embarrassant.* When she comes for a visit and stays too long, it's a bother. (EV) **2** embarrassing *Quand elle a quitté, c'était bien embarrassant pour toute la famille.* When she left, it was embarrassing for all the family. (LA) <***Loc:*** EV, LA, Da84, Fa77>

embarrassé, -e [ɑ̃barase] *adj.* **1** troubled, bothered, inconvenienced *Je suis trop embarrassée avec la noce à ma fille pour jongler à ça.* I am too troubled by my daughter's wedding to think about that. (EV) **D'abord qu'elle est embarrassée de l'acheter tout elle-même, elle envoye Flang et Freddy après chaqu'un ein gallon.* Since she is too overburdened to buy it herself, she sends Flang and Freddy after a gallon each. (Wh83) **2** embarrassed *Il était embarrassé avec le* SUIT *à bain de sa fille.* He was embarrassed about his daughter's bathing suit. (VM) <***Loc:*** EV, VM, Da84, Fa77, Wh83>

embarrassement [ɑ̃barasmɑ̃] *n.m.* a lot of trouble <***Loc:*** EV, LA>

embarrasser [ɑ̃barase] **I** *v.tr.* **1** to bother, cause trouble for, inconvenience *Les maringouins t'auraient pas embarrassé.* The mosquitos wouldn't have bothered you. (SL) *Pourquoi Marie l'embarrasse pour faire enterrer la ligne?* Why does Marie bother him to make him bury the line? (SL) **2** to embarrass *Tu vas m'embarrasser comme ça devant tout le monde?* Are you going to embarrass me like that in front of everyone? (EV) **II s'embarrasser** *v.pron.* **1** to take the trouble *Embarrasse-toi pas avec ca.* Don't trouble yourself with that. (VM) **2** to get o.s. deeply involved *Il s'a embarrassé dans la politique.* He got mixed up in politics. (LA) <***Loc:*** EV, LA, SL, VM, An84, Da84, Fa77>

embarrateur[1], **-euse** [ɑ̃baratœr, -øz] *adj.* **1** foolish, silly **2** troublesome, annoying <***Loc:*** TB>

embarrateur[2], **-euse** [ɑ̃baratœr, -øz] *n.* **1** one who annoys, pesters or makes trouble **2** big talker, braggart <***Loc:*** AV, LF, Lv88>

embarrer [ɑ̃bare] *v.tr.* to lock <***Loc:*** TB>

embaucher [ɑ̃boʃe] *v.intr.* to go to work, begin working (for the day) *Il embauche à six heures et débauche à sept heures.* He starts working at six o'clock and stops at seven. (LF) <***Loc:*** LF, SB, TB>

embaumer [ɑ̃bɔ̃me] *v.tr.* to embalm *Ils vont l'embaumer cet après-midi et ils vont ouvert le* FUNERAL HOME *à six heures.* They are going to embalm him this afternoon, and they will open the funeral home at six o'clock. (LA) <***Loc:*** LA, Da84>

embaumeur [ɑ̃bɔ̃mœr] *n.m.* embalmer <***Loc:*** SM, Da84>

embêcher [ɑ̃beʃe] *v.tr.* to damage *Ça c'est une espèce de bois de pin qu'a été traité avec du chose pour le faire, pour pas que l'eau embêche le bois.* That's a kind of pine wood that was treated with something to make it, to keep water from harming the wood. (LF) <***Loc:*** LF>

embellir [ɑ̃belir] *v.tr.* to embellish, beautify *Embellir une robe.* To embellish a dress. (EV) <***Loc:*** EV, Da84>

embellissement [ɑ̃belismɑ̃] *n.m.* embellishment, beautification, adornment <***Loc:*** Da84>

emberlificoter [ɑ̃bærlifikote] *v.tr.* to embarrass *Il pouvait pas s'empêcher d'emberlificoter sa femme au bal.* He couldn't help but embarrass his wife at the dance. (LA) <***Loc:*** LA, SM>

emberner [ɑ̃bærne, ɑ̃bœrne] **I** *v.tr.* to besmear, soil *Mon* TRAILER *est tout emberné avec la boue.* My trailer is all covered with mud. (Lv88) **Il a tout emberné son* SUIT. He got his suit all dirty. (EV, Ph36) *Il a emberné sa robe de graisse.* He besmeared her dress with grease. (LF) *J'emberne mes mains avec du sirop.* I get my hands dirty with syrup. (SB) **II s'emberner** *v.pron.* **1** to besmear o.s. (with an unpleasant substance), soil o.s. *Le bébé s'avait tout emberné et il fallait le laver.* The baby had soiled himself and we had to wash him. (EV) **2** to become entangled, get o.s. deeply involved (in an unpleasant affair) *S'emberner dans la politique.* To become entangled in politics. (EV) <***Loc:*** AV, EV, IB, LA, LF, SB, SM, TB, VM, Da84, Lv88, Ph36>

embêtant, -e [ɑ̃betɑ̃, -ɑ̃t] *adj.* **1** annoying *Qui c'est ce train? C'est donc embêtant.* What's that noise? It certainly is aggravating. (EV) **2** boring <***Loc:*** EV, Da84>

embêtation [ɑ̃betasjɔ̃] *n.f.* **1** bother, annoyance *C'est une embêtation avoir pour écrire mon thesis encore.* It's a bother to have to write my thesis again. (SM) **2** trick, deception *J'ai payé ça trop cher. C'est une embêtation qu'il m'a fait.* I paid too much for that. He deceived me. (VM) <***Loc:*** SM, VM>

embêté, -e [ɑ̃bete] *n.* idiot <***Loc:*** JE>

embêtement [ɑ̃bɛtmɑ̃] *n.m.* **1** annoyance, nuisance, bother **2** deceit, fraud <***Loc:*** Da84>

embêter [ɑ̃bete] **I** *v.tr.* **1** to bother, annoy *Je peux t'embêter un petit brin?* Can I bother you a bit? (TB) *Ça m'embête pas, le n-anglais m'embête pas du tout.* That doesn't bother me, English doesn't trouble me at all. (TB) **2** to deceive, fool, trick *Laisse-toi pas embêter.* Don't let yourself be fooled. (VM) **Se faire embêter.* To allow o.s. to be cheated or tricked. (Da84) **3** to 'knock up,' impregnate *Il a embêté la fille, et il avait pour se marier avec.* He knocked up the girl and he had to marry her. (VM) *Une fille embêtée.* A pregnant girl. (Gr86) **II s'embêter** *v.pron.* **1** to be bothered, be annoyed **2** to bother, mess around (with) *Je tire pas des cartes, non. C'est pas de quoi que je m'embête de ça.* I don't do card readings, no. That's not something I bother with. (TB) <***Loc:*** AC, AV, EV, JD, SM, TB, VM, Da84, Gr86, Hi02, La99, Lv88, Ph36>

embeurrer [ɑ̃børe] *v.tr.* to 'butter up,' flatter for personal gain *J'ai bien embeurré ma mère pour elle me laisse être dans le PEP SQUAD.* I really buttered up my mother so she would let me be in the pep squad. (EV) <***Loc:*** EV, LA, La99>

embeurriner [ɑ̃børine] *v.tr.* to besmear, soil <***Loc:*** LF>

emblème [ɑ̃blɛ̃m] *n.m.* emblem, symbol, badge <***Loc:*** Da84>

emboîtement [ɑ̃bwɛtmɑ̃] *n.m.* encasing, boxing <***Loc:*** Da84>

emboîter [ɑ̃bwete] *v.tr.* to box, put into a box, encase *Ils ont emboîté leur vaisselle pour aller passer la semaine à Holly Beach.* They put their dishes in a box to go spend a week in Holly Beach. (EV) <***Loc:*** EV, Da84>

embosser [ɑ̃bose] *v.tr.* **1** to raise a bump, cause a lump *Il l'a embossé dans le front.* He hit him, producing a bump on his forehead. (VM) **2** to emboss *Embosser du papier à lettre.* To emboss stationary. (LA) <***Loc:*** LA, VM, Da84>

emboucher (**emboufter**) [ɑ̃buʃe, ɑ̃bufte] *v.tr.* to fill, seal, plug (a crack, a hole) *Il est là après emboucher un trou dans le plancher du salle à manger.* He's there filling a hole in the floor of the dining room. (TB) *On a tout embouſté les craques de la maison avec du papier.* We plugged all the cracks in the house with paper. (TB) <***Loc:*** TB>

embouchure [ɑ̃buʃyr] *n.f.* **1** stoppage, clogging **2** confluence where a bayou joins a river <***Loc:*** EV, Da84, Ph36>

emboudinière ♦see **boudinière**

emboulage [ɑ̃bulaʒ] *n.m.* quarrel *Ça va aboutir dans un emboulage.* That is going to end in a quarrel. (IB) <***Loc:*** IB>

embourbé, -e [ɑ̃burbe] *adj.* **1** muddy *Quand-ce qu'on a arrivé, il y avait de la boue, je dis "Va pas dans le CAMP avec ces bottes embourbées là."* When we got there, there was mud, I said "Don't go into the camp with those muddy boots." (TB) **2** stuck in the mud *Il était embourbé et il pouvait pus sortir.* He was stuck in the mud and he couldn't get out by himself. (EV) ◊ **•être embourbé dans** to be deeply involved in *Là, il s'a trouvé embourbé dans une vilaine affaire.* Then he found himself involved in an ugly affair. (EV) <EV> <***Loc:*** EV, SM, TB, Da84, Fa77>

embourber [ɑ̃burbe] **I** *v.tr.* **1** to muddy, cover with mud *Il a bien embourbé son char quand il a passé à travers le bois.* He really muddied his car when he went through the woods. (LA) **2** to stick in the mire or mud **3** to involve (in some trouble) *Il a embourbé son frère dans cette affaire, et les deux ont été pris.* He involved his brother in this mess, and they both were caught. (LA) **II** *v.intr.* to stick in the mire, bog down, get stuck in the mud *On allait en wagon, on embourbait des fois aussi.* We would go in the wagon, sometimes we would also get stuck in the mud. (EV) **III s'embourber** *v.pron.* **1** to bog down, get stuck in the mud *Ça s'embourbait entre Jennings et Elton, le chemin était si mauvais.* They would get stuck in the mud between Jennings and Elton, the road was so bad. (EV) **2** to get o.s. muddy *Il s'avait bien embourbé en travaillant dans les clos.* He got covered in mud working in the fields. (EV) <***Loc:*** EV, JD, LA, LF, Da84, Fa77, Lv88>

embourrer ♦see **bourrer**

embouteillage [ɑ̃butejaʒ] *n.m.* **1** bottling **2** bottleneck, traffic jam <***Loc:*** Da84>

embouteiller (**bouteiller**) [ɑ̃buteje, buteje] *v.tr.* to bottle, fill a bottle with *Il faulait tu fais attention comment t'embouteillais la bière.* You had to be careful how you bottled beer. (LA) <***Loc:*** LA, Da84>

embrassade [ɑ̃brasad] *n.f.* **1** kiss **2** embrace, hug <***Loc:*** Da84>

embrassement [ɑ̃brasmɑ̃] *n.m.* **1** kissing **2** embracing, hugging <***Loc:*** Da84>

embrasser [ɑ̃brase] **I** *v.tr.* **1** to kiss *Viens embrasser Memère avant elle part!* Come kiss Memère before she leaves! (LA) **2** to embrace, hug *Elle l'a embrassé fort fort avant il part pour la guerre.* She hugged him tightly before he left for the war. (LA) **II s'embrasser** *v.pron.* **1** to kiss each other *Ça s'embrassait à chaque fois que ça se voyait.* They kissed each time they saw each other. (EV) **2** to embrace each other, hug each other <***Loc:*** AC, EV, LA, Da84, Fa77, Hi02>

embrochement [ɑ̃brɔʃmɑ̃] *n.m.* **1** skewering (of meat for cooking) **2** stringing (of fish on a stringer) <***Loc:*** Da84>

embrocher [ɑ̃brɔʃe] *v.tr.* **1** to skewer, put on a spit *Embrocher une daube.* To put a roast on a spit. (LA) **2** to string, put on a stringer *Quand t'as pas une glacière, tu peux embrocher tes poissons comme dans le vieux temps.* When you don't have an ice chest, you can string your fish like in the old days. (LA) <***Loc:*** LA, Da84>

embrouille [ɑ̃bruj] *n.f.* entanglement, confusion, muddle *Il est dans une embrouille.* He's in a muddle. (IB) <***Loc:*** IB, VM>

embrouillé, -e [ɑ̃bruje] *adj.* **1** blurry *Avoir la vue embrouillée.* To have blurry vision. (LA) **2** hazy, misty, foggy *Le temps embrouillé.* Foggy weather. (LF) **3** cloudy *Un temps embrouillé.* Cloudy weather. (LA) <***Loc:*** LA, LF, SM, Lv88>

embrouiller [ɑ̃bruje] **I** *v.tr.* **1** to fog up, make foggy (e.g. a mirror, glass) *La vapeur a embrouillé mes lunettes.* The vapor fogged up my glasses. (VM) **2** to dazzle, blind *Le soleil m'embrouille.* The sun is blinding me. (VM) **II s'embrouiller** *v.pron.* **1** to become foggy, fog up *J'ai peur que le temps va s'embrouiller avant qu'on arrive au camp.* I'm afraid the weather will fog up before we arrive at the camp. (LA) **2** to become angry, get mad *Il s'embrouille quand il pense à ça.* He gets mad when he thinks about that. (SB) <***Loc:*** AV, LA, SB, VM, Da84, Lv88>

embuscade [ɑ̃byskad] *n.f.* ambush ◊ **•faire l'embuscade** to lie in ambush *J'amenais des monsieurs de la Nouvelle Orléans chasser des canards. J'ai commencé à 13 et 15 ans, pagailler la pirogue, faire l'embuscade, se cacher.* I used to take men from New Orleans to hunt ducks. I started at 13 or 15 years old, paddling the pirogue, lying in ambush, hiding. (TB) <TB> <***Loc:*** TB>

embutter [ɑ̃byte] *v.tr.* **1** to mound, make a mound of (for storage) *Il manquait de la place dans la pataterie, ça fait il a embutté ses patates dans le clos et il les a couvert avec de la paille.* There was no more room in the potato shed, so he piled his potatoes in the field and covered them with straw. (VM) **2** to put into a silo <***Loc:*** VM, Lv88>

émécher [emeʃe] *v.tr.* to cut or trim the wick of (a candle, etc.) *Peux-tu émécher cette lampe pour moi?* Can you trim the wick of that lamp for me? (IB) <***Loc:*** EV, IB, Ph36>

émecter [emɛkte] *v.tr.* to beat up, injure *Il a émecté le petit garçon.* He injured the little boy. (LF) <***Loc:*** LF>

émerillon [emərijɔ̃] *n.m.* sparrow hawk <***Loc:*** Re31>

émigration [emigrasjɔ̃] *n.f.* emigration <***Loc:*** Da84>

émigré, -e [emigre] *n.* emigrant, refugee <***Loc:*** Da84>

émioler ♦see **émœller**

émissaire [emisær] *n.m.* emissary, envoy <***Loc:*** Da84>

émission [emisjɔ̃, emisijɔ̃] *n.f.* program, broadcast <***Loc:*** SL>

emmanché[1], **-e (amanché, -e)** [ɑ̃mɑ̃ʃe] *adj.* **1** *(m.)* to be well endowed (of a man) *Ce bougre est bien amanché.* That fellow is well hung. (JE) **2** wealthy **Bien amanché.* Wealthy. (La99) <***Loc:*** JE, LF, SM, La99>

emmanché[2], **-e (amanché, -e)** [ɑ̃mɑ̃ʃe] *adj.* living together (without benefit of marriage) *Ils sont amanchés.* They are living together (without being married). (JE) <***Loc:*** JE, LF, SM>

emmanchement (amanchement) [ɑ̃mɑ̃ʃmɑ̃] *n.m./f.* living together (without benefit of marriage) <***Loc:*** JE, LF, Lv88>

emmancher (amancher) [ɑ̃mɑ̃ʃe] **I** *v.tr.* **1** to put a handle on (a tool), fit with a handle *J'ai pour amancher mon marteau. Il a du jeu dedans.* I have to fix the handle on my hammer. It's loose. (VM) **2** to put together, assemble, fit together *Il a amanché les tuyaux.* He fitted the pipes. (JE) *Ça a amanché un char.* They put together a car. (TB) *Tu vas emmancher les deux morceaux ensemble.* You're going to put the two pieces together. (Lv88) **3** to rig up, cobble together *Ils ont eu pour amancher la machine jusqu'à ils rentrent à l'habitation.* They had to rig up a repair for the tractor until they got back to the farm house. (VM) **4** to have the advantage over, have the upper hand (in a discussion or dispute) *L'autre bougre l'a vite amanché.* The other guy quickly got the upper hand. (Lv88) **5** to arrange (e.g. a game of cards, a cockfight, a sporting event) *Ils ont emmanché une partie de pelote pour dimanche après-midi.* They arranged a baseball game for Sunday afternoon. (LA) **II s'emmancher** *v.pron.* **1** to live together (without benefit of marriage) *Ces petits enfants se sont emmanchés.* Those young kids moved in together (without getting married). (Lv88) *Le jeune monde s'amanche plus asteur.* Young people live together without being married more often these days. (Lv88) *On va s'amancher.* We are going to move in together. (JE) **2** to get married, get hitched *Ils s'ont emmanchés au Texas.* They got hitched in Texas. (LA) **3** to get along *Il s'est emmanché avec le shérif.* He got along with the sherrif. (Lv88) ◊ **•emmancher une tape** to slap, strike *Alle lui a emmanché une tape en pleine figure.* She slapped him square in the face. (AV) <AV> <***Loc:*** AC, AV, JE, LF, SB, SM, TB, VM, Da84, La99, Lv88>

emmanchure [ɑ̃mɑ̃ʃyr] *n.f.* complicated affair *C'était une mauvaise emmanchure.* That was a horribly complicated mess. (SB) <***Loc:*** SB>

emmarrer ♦see **amarrer**

emmêlement [ɑ̃mɛl(ə)mɑ̃] *n.m.* entanglement <***Loc:*** Da84>

emmêler [ɑ̃mele] **I** *v.tr.* to tangle, entangle *J'ai emmêlé mes cordes à souliers.* I tangled my shoelaces. (AC) **II s'emmêler** *v.pron.* **1** to get tangled up, get entangled *Avec ces linettes là, ça s'emmêle pas.* With these small fishing lines, they do not get tangled up. (SM) **2** to butt in *Il s'a emmelé dans le discours.* He butted into the conversation. (AC) **3** to get confused, be confused, be mixed up *Eusse s'a emmêlé avec ça, j'sais pas quo'faire* BUT *eusse a tout le temps été emmêlés avec ça.* They've gotten confused about that, I don't know why but they've always been mixed up about that. (TB) ◊ **•être emmêlé dans** to be involved in *Je suis emmêlé dans la politique.* I'm involved in politics. (TB) <TB> <***Loc:*** AC, SM, TB, Da84>

emmené, -e [ɑ̃m(ə)ne] *adj.* **1** (well-, ill-) behaved *Bien-emmené, mal-emmené.* Well-behaved, badly-behaved. (VM) *Elle est mieux emmenée que sa sœur.* She is more well-behaved than her sister. (VM) **2** (well-, badly) conducted *Le bal était mal emmené hier au soir.* The dance was badly conducted last night. (VM) <***Loc:*** VM>

emmener [ɑ̃m(ə)ne] **I** *v.tr.* **1** to lead away, carry away **2** to bring *Il a emmené ce vieux lit au* CAMP. He took that old bed to the camp. (EV) *Emmène-moi mon livre.* Bring me my book. (SM) **II** *v.intr.* to conduct o.s. in a rowdy or noisy way, carry on *Je pense qu'on a emmené au bal hier soir.* I think there was much carrying on at the dance last night. (IB) <***Loc:*** AC, EV, IB, SM, TB, VM, Da84, Hi02>

emmerdant, -e [ɑ̃mærdɑ̃, -ɑ̃t] *adj.* troublesome, annoying *T'es donc emmerdant, toi!* You are really annoying! (VM) <***Loc:*** VM, Da84>

emmerder [ɑ̃mærde] **I** *v.tr.* **1** to soil, besmear with excrement *Il a emmerdé ses culottes.* He soiled his pants with excrement. (LA) **2** to bother, annoy, pester **Viens pas m'emmerder.*

Don't come bother me. (Da84) **II s'emmerder** *v.pron.* to soil o.s., besmear o.s. with excrement *Il s'avait bien emmerdé.* He had really soiled himself. (LA) <***Loc:*** LA, Da84>

emmicher (**emmicheter**) [ɑ̃miʃe, ɑ̃miʃte] *v.tr.* **1** to worry, torment **2** to bother, annoy *Arrête de m'emmicher avec ça!* Stop bothering me with that! (AC) *Va-t'en, tu m'emmiches avec tout tes bêtises.* Go away, you're bothering me with all your foolishness. (JD) ◊ **•s'emmicher avec** to worry about, have worries over ***b*** to bother, fool with <Lv88, SM> <***Loc:*** AC, JD, SM, Lv88>

emmicheter[1] [ɑ̃miʃte] **I** *v.tr.* to soil, besmear with excrement or some unpleasant substance **II s'emmicheter** *v.pron.* to soil o.s., besmear o.s. with excrement or some unpleasant substance *Le bébé s'a tout emmicheté.* The baby smeared itself with excrement. (VM) <***Loc:*** VM>

emmicheter[2] ♦see **emmicher**

emmicheteur, -euse [ɑ̃miʃtœr, -øz] *n.* annoying person, pest <***Loc:*** SM>

emmioler (**amioler, amijoler**) [ɑ̃mjole, ɑ̃miʒole] *v.tr.* **1** to coax, wheedle, seduce, deceive by flattery *Il se laisse emmioler.* He lets himself be deceived by flattery. (VM) **2** to calm, talk to in a soothing way *Il a eu pour emmioler sa petite fille quand elle avait fait un mauvais rêve.* He had to soothe his daughter after she had a bad dream. (EV) <***Loc:*** EV, SL, SM, TB, VM, La99, Lv88>

emmioleur, -euse (**amioleur, -euse**) [ɑ̃mjolœr, -øz] *n.* cajoler, seducer, flatterer <***Loc:*** TB, VM, Lv88>

émœller (**émioler**) [emwale, emjole] *v.tr.* to smash, crush *L'automobile l'a émœllé.* The car crushed him. (LF) <***Loc:*** LF, TB>

émotion [emosjɔ̃] *n.f.* emotion, sentiment <***Loc:*** Da84>

émoussage [emusaʒ] *n.m.* removal of moss (from trees, etc.) <***Loc:*** Da84>

émousser [emuse] *v.tr.* **1** to remove moss (from trees) *Ils ont proche tout émoussé l'Atchafalaya.* They have removed the moss from almost all the trees in the Atchafalaya. (LA) **2** to pull or shake apart strands of (Spanish moss) in order to fluff and clean them **3** to send away in a hurry, chase off *Elle a émoussé sa compagnie.* She sent her guests away in a hurry. (IB) <***Loc:*** AV, IB, JD, LA, SJ, Da84>

émouver [emuve] *v.tr.* **1** to move, change the position of *Aide-moi à émouver cette table.* Help me move this table. (VM) **2** to motivate, invigorate, enliven *Ça va prendre quelque chose d'extra pour l'émouver.* It's going to take something extra to motivate her. (VM) **3** to bring up feelings or emotions of (a past incident) *Émouver le passé.* To bring up memories of the past. (Lv88) *Émouver une vieille chicane.* To revive an old argument. (Lv88) <***Loc:*** JD, VM, Lv88>

émoyer (s') [emwaje] *v.pron.* to inquire *J'ai rencontré Jean hier. Il s'a émoyé de toi.* I ran into John yesterday. He inquired about you. (Gu00) <***Loc:*** VM, Gu00>

empailler [ɑ̃paje] *v.tr.* to encase in wicker *J'ai empaillé la bouteille pour la protecter.* I encased the bottle in wicker to protect it. (VM) <***Loc:*** EV, VM>

empaquetage [ɑ̃paktaʒ] *n.m.* packing, bundling, packaging <***Loc:*** Da84>

empaqueter [ɑ̃pakte] *v.tr.* to pack up *Empaqueter son butin.* To pack up one's household belongings. (VM) <***Loc:*** VM, Da84, Fa77>

emparer (s') [ɑ̃pare] *v.pron.* **1** to take possession of, take over *La banque s'a emparé de ma terre durant la dépression.* The bank took possession of my land during the depression. (VM) **2** to hasten, hurry *Alle s'a emparé de le faire.* She hurried to do it. (VM) <***Loc:*** VM, Da84>

emparquer [ɑ̃parke] *v.tr.* to pen up *Emparquer un cochon.* To pen up a pig. (VM) <***Loc:*** VM, Fa77>

empatter [ɑ̃pate] *v.tr.* to bait (a hook, a line) **J'ai empatté mon hameçon avec la dernière petite lèche rouge.* I baited my line with the last little red earthworm. (Gr86) <***Loc:*** Gr86>

empauvrir [ɑ̃povrir] **I** *v.tr.* to impoverish **II s'empauvrir** *v.pron.* to become impoverished *Je m'ai empauvri à essayer de faire récolte sur la terre de maîche.* I got poor trying to farm marsh land. (VM) <***Loc:*** VM, Da84>

empêche [ɑ̃pɛʃ, ɑ̃peʃ] *n.m.* hindrance, obstacle, impediment *Je vas aller si il n-a pas d'empêche.* I will go if there are no hindrances. (SM) <***Loc:*** SM, VM>

empêchement [ɑ̃pɛʃmɑ̃] *n.m.* hindrance, obstacle **Malgré la difficulté, il a surmonté les empêchements.* Despite the difficulty, he overcame the obstacles. (Wh83) ◊ **•empêchement de famille** birth control <Da84> **•mettre empêchement *a*** to object ***b*** to prevent <Da84> **•mettre un empêchement contre** to put a restraining order on, put a peace bond on *Ils ont mis un empêchement contre lui.* They put a restraining order on him. (VM) <VM> <***Loc:*** VM, Da84, Wh83>

empêcher [ɑ̃peʃe] **I** *v.tr.* to hinder, prevent, stop *Ils mettont des préservatives dans le lait asteur pour l'empêcher de cailler.* They put preservatives in milk now to keep it from curdling. (VM) *Il a empêché l'enfant de tomber dans l'eau.* He stopped the child from falling in the water. (AC) **II s'empêcher** *v.pron.* to refrain, restrain o.s. *Je pouvais pas m'empêcher de pleurer quand ils m'ont dit ça.* I couldn't keep from crying when they told me that. (VM) ◊ **•empêcher la famille** to prevent conception, practice birth control <Da84> <***Loc:*** AC, EV, IV, LA, LF, SM, VM, Da84, Gu00, Hi02>

empereur [ɑ̃prœr] *n.m.* emperor <***Loc:*** Da84>

empester [ɑ̃peste] **I** *v.tr.* to infest, overrun *Les ravets ont empesté la maison.* Cockroaches overran the house. (SM) *Ma maison est empestée de raverts.* My house is infested with roaches. (AC) *La vache est empestée de insectes.* The cow is full of bugs. (SM) **II s'empester** *v.pron.* to contaminate o.s., become infected (with s.t. undesirable) *Rentre pas dans la maison, tu vas t'empester de punaises.* Don't go in the house, you will get infested with bugs. (VM) <*Loc:* AC, LA, SM, VM, Da84, Lv88>

empêtrer [ɑ̃petre] **I** *v.tr.* **1** to entangle, cause to be tangled up *Je faisais pas attention et j'ai empêtré mon cheval dans les éronces.* I wasn't paying attention and I tangled my horse in the briars. (VM) **2** to hobble *Il a eu pour empêtrer son cheval pour l'empêcher de sauter la barrière. C'était soit ça ou le tirer dans le derrière.* He had to hobble his horse to prevent him from jumping the fence. It was that or shoot it in the rear. (VM) **II s'empêtrer** *v.pron.* **1** to get tangled, become entangled *Il s'a empêtré dans les câbles.* He got tangled in the ropes. (LA) **2** to get deeply involved, get in over one's head *Il s'a bien empêtré dans son nouveau business.* He's over his head in his new business. (VM) ◊ **•être empêtré** to be overwhelmed *Elle est empêtrée dans son ouvrage de maison.* She's overwhelmed by her housework. (AC) <AC> <*Loc:* AC, VM, Da84, Lv88>

empiler [ɑ̃pile] *v.tr.* to pile up, stack *Empiler des balles de foin.* To stack bales of hay. (EV) <*Loc:* EV, Da84>

empiloter [ɑ̃pilote] *v.tr.* to pile up, stack *J'ai des boîtes d'empilotées par dessus la tête.* I have boxes piled up over my head. (VM) <*Loc:* VM, Da84>

empire [ɑ̃pir] *n.m.* empire <*Loc:* Da84>

empirer [ɑ̃pire] *v.intr.* to get worse, take a turn for the worse *Les affaires sont après empirer d'une journée à l'autre.* Things are getting worse from one day to another. (LA) <*Loc:* LA, Da84>

emplacement [ɑ̃plasmɑ̃] *n.m.* **1** site, place **2** placement <*Loc:* EV, Da84>

emplate ♦see **emplâtre**

emplâtre[1] (**emplate**) [ɑ̃plat(r)] *adj.* **1** clumsy, awkward and slow *Tant qu'à lui, il est assez emplâtre qu'il a de la misère à mettre ses chaussons le matin.* As for him, he's so clumsy that he has difficulty putting on his socks in the morning. (Gu00) **2** foolish, stupid, lacking common sense *Ti-Jean est un peu emplâtre. Mais il est un vaillant garçon.* Ti-Jean doesn't have much common sense, but he's a nice boy. (ThCa: *La table des veuves*) **3** mentally retarded ◊ **•emplâtre comme du goudron** very awkward <VM, La99> <*Loc:* AC, JD, LA, LF, SB, SM, TB, VM, Da84, Fa77, Gu00, La99, ThCa>

emplâtre[2] (**emplate**) [ɑ̃plat(r)] *n.m./f.* simpleton, moron *Garde voir cet emplâtre.* Look at that simpleton. (LF) <*Loc:* AC, LA, LF, SB, SM, VM, Da84>

emplir [ɑ̃plir] **I** *v.tr.* to fill, fill up *Là j'avais deux barils, je mettais ça en-dedans, et j'avais pompé de l'eau, j'avais empli les deux barils.* Then I had two barrels, I would put that in there, and I had pumped water, I had filled two barrels. (VM) *Il a rempli le* TANK. He filled up the tank. (VM) **II s'emplir** *v.pron.* to fill up, become filled *La citerne va s'emplir vite avec tout cette pluie.* The cistern will fill quickly with all of this rain. (LA) <*Loc:* LA, VM, Da84>

emploi [ɑ̃plwa] *n.m.* employment, occupation <*Loc:* Da84>

employé, -e [ɑ̃plwaje] *n.* employee *Ils ont besoin de plusieurs employés cette semaine pour finir le job.* They need several employees this week to finish the job. (LA) <*Loc:* EV, LA, Da84>

employer [ɑ̃plwaje] *v.tr.* **1** to employ, give employment to *Mon pauvre papa employait personne d'autre, ça fait j'avais pour rester pour travailler.* My poor father didn't hire anybody else, so I had to stay and work. (SJ) **2** to use, employ *On employait des feuilles, on se faisait une maison. Y a un carré dessus la terre.* We used to use leaves, we would make ourselves a [play] house. There's a frame [built] on the ground. (JE) <*Loc:* JE, SJ, Da84>

employeur [ɑ̃plwajœr] *n.m.* employer <*Loc:* Da84>

emplumage [ɑ̃plymaʒ] *n.m.* tarring and feathering <*Loc:* Gr86, Lv88>

empocher [ɑ̃poʃe] *v.tr.* **1** to pocket, put in one's pocket *Il a empoché son couteau avant de rentrer dans la salle de danse.* He put his knife in his pocket before going back into the dance hall. (LA) **2** to take stealthily, steal *J'ai empoché des croquecignoles quand ma mère regardait pas.* I stole some doughnuts when my mother wasn't looking. (VM) <*Loc:* LA, TB, VM, Da84>

empogner ♦see **empoigner**

empoigner (**apoigner, empogner**) [ɑ̃pwɑ̃je, ɑ̃pɔ̃je, pɔ̃je] **I** *v.tr.* **1** to grasp, grab, seize *Il l'a empoigné par la cagouette.* He grabbed him by the nape of the neck. (LA) **2** to catch, capture *Et ça empoignait la chevrette avec des filets, les Cadiens appellent ça une seine.* And they would catch shrimp with nets, the Cajuns call it a seine. (LF) *Et un hiver on a empoigné 8,500 rats musqués.* And one winter we caught 8,500 muskrats. (TB) **3** to catch, contract (a disease) *Sa mame avait la fièvre typhoïde. [...] Et Philippe avait peur qu'alle donne ça à le petit, et qu'elle alle l'empoigne.* His mother had typhoid fever. And Philip was afraid she would give it to the baby, and that she would catch it. (TB) **II s'empoigner** *v.pron.* to grasp each other *Les deux batailleurs se sont empoignés un et l'autre au milieu du grand rond.* The two fighters grabbed each other in the middle of the ring. (LA) ◊ **•empoigner des poissons** to catch fish <LF> **•empoigner un STROKE** to have a stroke *Alle a empoigné un petit* STROKE, *alle peut plus faire arien.* She had a little stroke, she can't do anything any more. (TB) <TB> <*Loc:* AV, JD, LA, LF, TB, Da84, Hi02, Lv88>

empoisonnement [ɑ̃pwazɔ̃nmɑ̃] *n.m.* poisoning <*Loc:* Da84>

empoisonner [ɑ̃pwazɔ̃ne] **I** *v.tr.* **1** to poison *Il a essayé d'empoisonner le chien de son voisin.* He tried to poison his neighbor's dog. (LA) **2** to treat with pesticide or herbicide *Ils empoisonnent les moustiques dans les clos.* They are treating for mosquitos in the field. (Lv88) **II s'empoisonner** *v.pron.* to poison o.s. or each other *Tu ferais mieux d'arrêter de mêler tout ces médecines, tu vas t'empoisonner.* You had better stop mixing all those medications, you're going to poison yourself. (VM) <*Loc:* EV, LA, VM, Da84, Lv88>

emporté, -e [ãpɔrte] *adj.* carried away (with anger, emotion, etc.) *Ils étaient emportés d'entendre la nouvelle que la guerre était finie.* They were carried away with emotion to hear the news that the war was over. (LA) <*Loc:* LA, Da84>

emportement [ãpɔrtmã] *n.m.* outburst of anger or rage <*Loc:* Da84>

emporter [ãpɔrte] **I** *v.tr.* to carry away, remove *Emporte cette corde de bois pour ton foyer. J'en ai pas de besoin.* Carry away this cord of firewood for your fireplace. I don't need it. (VM) **II s'emporter** *v.pron.* to fly into a rage, get carried away *Tracy s'a emporté quand il a su que son gendre avait bûché sa fille.* Tracy flew into a rage when he learned that his son-in-law had beat his daughter. (VM) <*Loc:* VM, Da84>

emprêter (**emprunter**) [ãprete, prete, ãprœ̃te, ãprẽte] *v.tr.* to borrow *Ça c'est eux-autres qui contrôlait qui les Cadiens peut avoir, qui eux-autres pourrait apprendre, combien d'argent eux-autres pourrait emprêter.* They're the ones who controled what Cajuns could have, what they could learn, how much money they could borrow. (TB) *Il a emprété l'argent avec moi.* He borrowed money from me. (SM) *Va emprunter une aiguille à coudre avec Madame Palonier.* Go borrow a sewing needle from Madame Palonier. (EV) <*Loc:* AV, EV, IB, JD, LA, LF, SM, TB, VM, Da84, Hi02, Lv88>

emprisonnement [ãprizɔ̃nmã] *n.m.* imprisonment, custody <*Loc:* Da84>

emprisonner [ãprizɔ̃ne] *v.tr.* to imprison, put in jail, incarcerate *Ça l'a emprisonné pour plus que vingt ans.* They put him in jail for more than twenty years. (LA) <*Loc:* LA, Da84>

emprunt [ãprœ̃] *n.m.* borrowing, loan ◊ •**faire un emprunt** to borrow, get a loan <Da84> <*Loc:* Da84>

emprunter ♦see **emprêter**

emprunteur [ãprœ̃tœr] *n.m.* borrower <*Loc:* Da84>

en[1] [ã] *prep.* **1** in *J'ai du biznisse en ville.* I have some business in town. (JE) *C'est français partout, il y a peut-être un peu de différent de mots et de manières mais il y a des différents de manières à parler français en France même.* It's French everywhere, maybe there are a few different words and ways but there are different ways of speaking French in France too. (SL) *Il a humilié sa femme en sortant avec sa poupoune en public.* He humiliated his wife by going out in public with his mistress. (LA) **D'abord que c'est plus à la mode, ça danse pas la valse, le deux-pas, le Jitterbug ou le Contredanse Cajin, éspécialment pas en publique.* Since it's no longer stylish, they don't dance the Cajun waltz, two-step, jitterbug or Contredanse, especially not in public. (Wh83) **2** to **Il a voyagé de place en place, de ville en ville, et toujours, il avait intérêt de visiter les cimetières.* He traveled from place to place, from town to town, and he was always interested in the cemeteries. (LA, An94) *La première fois que j'ai été en France.* The first time I went to France. (Gu00) **J'ai su par après que Henri avait été renvoyé en France, à une place nommée Belle Ile.* I found out afterward that Henri had been sent to France, to a place called Belle Ile. (An98) *Asteur tu peux aller en Bayou des Allemands dans une heure et demie peut-être, une heure. Mais dans ce temps là, ça peut-être prendait trois heures pour venir à la Pointe.* Now you can go to the Bayou des Allemands in an hour and a half, perhaps, [or] an hour. But in those days it took maybe three hours to come to the Pointe. (TB) **3** in, into (a language) *Sacrer en français est un art chez les Cadiens.* To swear in French is an art for Cajuns. (Lv88) *Ça ici c'est un poisson armé. En anglais c'est* GARFISH. This is a garfish. In English it's called a garfish. (TB) **Plutôt que quitter la musique Américaine dominer dans le Sud de la Louisiane, on prend des chansons populaires, traduit les en Français et quitte des musiciens Cajins assaisonner les aires avec des accordéons et violons.* Rather than letting American music dominate in southern Louisiana, we take popular songs, translate them into French and let Cajun musicians spice up the tunes with accordeons and violins. (Wh83) **4** in, into (a condition, shape, or state) **Couper en biais.* To cut on a bias. (Da84) *Le bal a fini en bacchanale.* The dance ended in a drunken spree. (EV) *La vitre a brisé en morceaux.* The window shattered into pieces. (LA) *Quand ça vient en bouillage, tu baisses ton feu.* When it starts boiling, you lower your fire. (VM) *Il l'a coupé en deux.* He cut it in two. (TB) *Il a fini la course en premier.* He finished first in the race. (EV) **5** in (a month, a year) *On s'est bâti en 1960.* We built ourselves a house in 1960. (Lv88) **6** by, by means of *Leeville est pas loin, d'icitte-là en bateau dans quarante-cinq minutes.* Leeville is not far, [you can go] from here to there by boat in forty-five minutes. (TB) *Je vais en ville en char.* I'm going to town by car. (SM) **7** made of *Un baril en bois.* A wooden barrel. (LF) *Il s'est bâti en brique un peu plus loin.* He built a brick house a little farther on. (Lv88) *Ma grand-mère m'a donné une grosse chaise bourrée en velours.* My grandmother gave me a big stuffed velvet chair. (Gu00) **Botte en élastique.* Rubber boot. (Da84) **8** *(with present participles)* while *Arrête de parler en mangeant.* Stop talking while eating. (LA) *Il a aspiré de l'eau en nageant.* He breathed in water while swimming. (VM) *J'ai attrapé la pluie en venant ici.* I got caught in the rain while coming over here. (SM) *En se levant il s'élonge.* When he gets up he stretches. (LF) ◊ •**en arrière** see **arrière** •**en avant** see **avant** •**en bas** see **bas** •**en dehors** see **dehors** •**en dessous** see **dessous** •**en dessus** see **dessus** •**en haut** see **haut** •**en tout cas** see **cas** •**en travers** see **travers** <*Loc:* AC, AS, AV, EV, IB, IV, JE,

LA, LF, SJ, SL, SM, TB, VM, An94, Da84, Gu00, Hi02, La99, Lv88, Wh83>

en[2] [ɑ̃] *pron.* **1** of him, of her, of it, of them **Il en a pas.* He doesn't have any. (Da84) **Il y en a pas.* There is none [of it]. (Da84) *Asteur ils voulont défaire ma vieille maison et m'en rebâtir une neuve.* Now they want to tear down my old house and build me a new one. (VM) *Alle a pas eu d'enfants pour elle-même. Alle en a adopté une.* She hasn't had any children of her own. She adopted one. (TB) **Une fois, il y avait une femme qui était après laver des tripes de cochon au bord d'un bayou et un chien étrange s'approchait d'elle et elle dit, "Tu veux passer! Tu veux passer!" parce qu'elle en avait peur.* Once there was a woman who was washing pork tripe next to a bayou and a strange dog came up to her and she said, "You go away! You go away!" because she was afraid of it. (VM, An94) **Je vas m'en acheter.* I will buy some of it. (Da84) **Je vas m'en défaire.* I'll get rid of it. (Da84) *Y en a pas beaucoup.* There isn't much. (TB) **2** from it, from there, out of there *J'ai manqué de jamais m'en démêler.* I was almost unable to ever untangle myself. (VM) *J'ai tombé dans un trou de cocodrie quand j'étais petit, et j'ai manqué de jamais de m'en débourber.* I fell into an alligator hole when I was little, and I almost never got out of there. (VM) ◊ **•s'en aller** to leave **Not' peup' s'en va comme eine fleur de chardron emportée par l'ouragan.* Our people are leaving like a thistle flower carried away by a hurricane. (ThCa: *Mille misères*) <EV, IB, JE, LA, SM, TB, VM, ThCa> **•s'en croire** to be haughty *Il s'en croit, lui.* He's haughty, that guy. (VM) <VM> **•s'en revenir / s'en retourner** to come back *La vieille m'a quitté avec les petits enfants. —Prenez courage, alle va s'en revenir.* The old lady left me with the small children. —Take heart, she'll come back. (LF) *On était parti attendre Ti-Don Leboeuf jouer le violon. Et W. se bite, et cher Bon Dieu, nous-autres on s'en a revenu, lui il était après faire le* CIRCLE *dessus le* HUEY P. LONG BRIDGE. We had gone to hear Ti-Don Leboeuf play the violin. And W. gets drunk, and dear God, we all came back, and he was circling around on the Huey P. Long bridge. (TB) *Il va caler un petit filet avant de s'en retourner.* He is going to have a drink before going back. (Lv88) <TB, Lv88> **•s'en venir** to come, show up *Iry Lejeune s'en venait dans son char-à-banc, lui et sa femme.* Iry Lejeune used to come in his four-wheel cart, he and his wife. (LA) *Ils s'en a venu bites hier au soir.* They showed up drunk last night. (VM) <LA, LF, TB, VM, Lv88> <***Loc:*** AC, AS, EV, JD, LA, LF, SL, SM, TB, VM, An94, Da84, Hi02, Lv88, ThCa>

énamelle [ẽnamɛl] *n.f.* enamel <***Loc:*** Da84>

en-avant [ɑ̃navɑ̃] *n.m.* front, forward area **L'en-avant de la maison.* The front of the house. (Da84) <***Loc:*** Da84>

encadrement [ɑ̃kadrəmɑ̃] *n.m./f.* **1** frame, framing (of windows, doors, etc.) **2** jamb <***Loc:*** EV, SL, Da84, Lv88>

encadrer ♦see **cadrer**

encager [ɑ̃kaʒe] *v.tr.* to cage, put in a cage *Encager une chienne en saison.* To enclose a dog in heat in a cage. (VM) <***Loc:*** VM, Da84>

encaille [ɑ̃kaj] *n.f.* oarlock *Il y a des encailles sus le bord des skiffs à ramer pour mettre des rames pour pagayer le bateau.* There are oarlocks on the sides of rowboats to put oars for paddling the boat. (TB) <***Loc:*** TB>

encainner ♦see **encanner**

encaissage [ɑ̃kesaʒ] *n.m.* encasing, caging <***Loc:*** Da84>

encaissement [ɑ̃kɛsmɑ̃] *n.m.* boxing, encasing <***Loc:*** Da84>

encaisser [ɑ̃kese] *v.tr.* to encase, put in a case or box, pack *J'ai encaissé tous ses livres d'école et je les ai mis dans le grenier.* I packed up all her schoolbooks and put them in the attic. (VM) <***Loc:*** VM, Da84>

encan [ɑ̃kɑ̃] *n.m./f.* **1** public sale, auction *Il y avait des encans le mardi, là où ça vendait des bêtes.* There were auctions on Tuesday, where they sold livestock. (VM) **2** auction house, auction barn (usu. for livestock auctions) *On avait pas tout ces bonnes encans on a aujourd'hui.* We didn't have all the nice auction houses that we have now. (EV) ◊ **•mettre à l'encan** to put up for auction <Da84> <***Loc:*** EV, VM, An94, Da84, Lv88>

encanner (**canner, cainner, encainner**) [ɑ̃kɑ̃ne, ɑ̃kẽne, kɑ̃ne, kẽne] *v.tr.* to can, preserve *J'ai encanné des giraumons dans des petites jarres.* I preserved pumpkins in little jars. (Lv88) *On va canner des légumes.* We are going to can some vegetables. (JE) <***Loc:*** JE, LF, VM, Da84, Lv88>

encanneuse [ɑ̃kẽnøz] *n.f.* sterilizer for canning <***Loc:*** Lv88>

encanter [ɑ̃kɑ̃te] *v.tr.* to sell at auction, auction off <***Loc:*** VM, Da84, Lv88>

encanteur [ɑ̃kɑ̃tœr] *n.m.* auctioneer <***Loc:*** Da84, Lv88>

en-cas ♦see **en-tout-cas**

encavé, -e [ɑ̃kave] *adj.* concave, indented, sunken in *Le couvercle était encavé pour mettre des braises.* The cover [of the Dutch oven] was sunken in to allow the placement of hot coals on top. (Lv88) <***Loc:*** Lv88>

encaver [ɑ̃kave] **I** *v.tr.* to push in, dent, crush in *Il s'a assis sus le haut du char, il l'a encavé.* He sat on the top of the car, he dented it. (VM) **II** *v.intr.* to sink, plunge, go deep or far down *Ma bague est trop petite, alle est encavée dans mon doigt.* My ring is too small, it's pressing down into my finger. (TB) <***Loc:*** TB, VM, Lv88>

enceinte [ɑ̃sẽt] *adj.f.* pregnant *Sa femme est enceinte encore.* His wife is pregnant again. (LA) <***Loc:*** LA, Da84, Hi02, Wh83>

encens [ɑ̃sɑ̃] *n.m.* incense <***Loc:*** Da84>

encensement [ɑ̃sɑ̃smɑ̃] *n.m.* incensing <***Loc:*** Da84>

encenser [ɑ̃sɑ̃se] *v.tr.* to incense, perfume with incense *Le prêtre a encensé le cercueil après la messe.* The priest incensed the casket after mass. (LA) <***Loc:*** LA, Da84>

encensoir [ɑ̃sɑ̃swar] *n.m.* censer, thurible <***Loc:*** Da84>

encerclement [ɑ̃særkləmɑ̃] *n.m.* encirclement, surrounding <***Loc:*** Da84>

encercler [ɑ̃særkle] *v.tr.* to encircle, surround *Si tu vas en* *arrière de la savane, on pourra peut-être encercler les bêtes pour les pousser dans le parc.* If you go to the back of the pasture, we might be able to surround the cattle so we can drive them into the pen. (VM) <***Loc:*** VM, Da84>

encerner ♦see **cerner**

enchaînement [ɑ̃ʃɛ̃nmɑ̃] *n.m.* chaining, enchainment <***Loc:*** Da84>

enchaîner [ɑ̃ʃɛ̃ne] *v.tr.* to chain, enchain *Il pouvait enchaîner des centaines de mots ensemble.* He could chain together hundreds of words. (LA) <***Loc:*** LA, Da84>

enchalage ♦see **achalage**

enchalé ♦see **achalé**

enchantement [ɑ̃ʃɑ̃təmɑ̃] *n.m.* delight, enchantment <***Loc:*** Da84>

enchanter [ɑ̃ʃɑ̃te] *v.tr.* to enchant, delight, charm, fascinate *Il parlait et il parlait, et il a fini par l'enchanter.* He talked and talked, and he ended up charming her. (LA) <***Loc:*** LA, An94, Da84>

enchanteur, -euse [ɑ̃ʃɑ̃tœr, -øz] *n.* enchanter, charmer <***Loc:*** Da84>

encharger [ɑ̃ʃarʒe] *v.tr.* to order, charge *Elle aime à encharger les enfants de travailler.* She likes to order the children to work. (SB) *Il m'a enchargé de le faire quand il a parti.* He charged me to do it when he left. (TB) <***Loc:*** SB, TB>

encirer [ɑ̃sire] *v.tr.* to wax, seal or coat with wax *Encirer un pobon.* To seal a jar with wax. (LA) <***Loc:*** Da84>

encler (**enqueler, acler**) [ɑ̃kle, akle] **I** *v.tr.* to lock *J'avais pas coutume acler la porte.* I didn't usually lock the door. (Lv88) *Enquèle la porte avant de te coucher.* Lock the door before you go to bed. (EV) **II** *v.intr.* to lock up *J'ai enclé.* I locked up. (Lv88) ◊ **•encler la maison** to lock the house *Dans le vieux temps, on avait pas besoin d'encler la maison quand on partait.* In the old days, we didn't have to lock the house when we left. (LA) <LA> **•mettre enclé** to lock *Mets la porte enclée.* Lock the door. (AV) <AV> <***Loc:*** AV, IB, EV, LA, SB, SM, Gr82, Lv88>

enclume [ɑ̃klym] *n.f.* anvil <***Loc:*** AV, Da84>

encoche [ɑ̃kɔʃ] *n.f.* notch, groove <***Loc:*** Da84>

encocher [ɑ̃kɔʃe] *v.tr.* to notch, groove *Encocher l'oreille d'un veau.* To notch the ear of a calf. (VM) <***Loc:*** VM, Da84>

encœurer ♦see **acœurer**

encoignure (**enconnure**) [ɑ̃kɔ̃jyr, ɑ̃kɔ̃nyr] *n.f.* **1** angle **2** corner <***Loc:*** SM, Da84>

encombrement [ɑ̃kɔ̃brəmɑ̃] *n.m.* encumbrance, obstruction, clutter <***Loc:*** Da84>

enconnure ♦see **encoignure**

encore [ɑ̃kɔr] *adv.* **1** again *Ils ont parti pour aller au village encore aujourd'hui.* They left to go to town again today. (LA) *Sa femme est enceinte encore.* His wife is pregnant again. (LA) *Je m'ai fait bluffé une fois, mais ça va pas arriver encore.* I was fooled once, but it won't happen again. (LA) *Je venais juste de dressir mon poteau d'antenna après Katrina, quand le vent de Rita l'a recrochi encore.* I had just straightened my antenna pole after Katrina when Rita's winds rebent it. (VM) *Je vas jamais remanger là encore.* I'll never eat there again. (LA) **2** still *Alle a encore des mals dans l'estomac, mais alle a repris du poids, alle a* PICK UP. She still has stomachaches but she has regained some weight, she has picked up. (TB) *Tu vas jeter ça, mais c'est encore servable.* You are going to throw it away, but it is still usable. (VM) *La maison est encore trop petite même avec l'ajoutement.* The house is still too small even with the addition. (IB) **3** more *Ils ont barguiné avec le docteur pour qu'il la garde un jour encore.* They bargained with the doctor so that he would keep her for another day. (Lv88) *Je voudrais rester dans tes bras encore une fois avant de mourir.* I would want to stay in your arms once more before dying. (AC) **4** even *On jouait encore mieux qu'asteur.* We used to play even better than they do today. (SM) **5** even so *Moi je vas juste à St. Louis, Missouri, deux cent quatre-vingt-seize. Encore c'est une barguine. On achète un, eux-autres m'a donné un pour quatorze piasses.* I just go to St. Louis Missouri, $296. Even that's a bargain. We buy one [plane ticket], they gave me one for $14. (TB) ◊ **•encore moins** still less, even less *Elle va manger encore moins demain.* She's going to eat even less tomorrow. (LA) <LA, Da84> **•encore plus** still more, even more *Il est encore plus beau que son frère.* He is even more handsome than his brother. (LA) <EV, LA, SM, TB, Da84, Gu82, Gr86> **•pas encore** not yet *Le maïs est pas encore bourgeonné.* The corn is not yet sprouted. (LA) *Son idée est pas encore développée là-dessus.* His opinion is not yet developed on that issue. (LA) *Les petits poulets sont pas encore crêtés.* The chicks are not yet crested. (VM) *Il a pas encore croisé la maison, mais on va faire quatre chambres.* He hasn't partitioned the house yet, but we are going to make four rooms. (VM) <EV, LA, VM, Da84> <***Loc:*** AC, AV, EV, IV, LA, SL, SM, TB, An94, Da84, Gr82, Gr86, Hi02, Wh83>

encornure [ɑ̃kɔrnyr] *n.f.* horns *La bête a une belle encornure.* The animal has beautiful horns. (VM) <***Loc:*** JE, VM>

encourageant, -e [ɑ̃kuraʒɑ̃, -ɑ̃t] *adj.* encouraging, heartening *On a eu des nouvelles et c'est pas beaucoup encourageant.* We got some news and it's not very encouraging. (SL) <***Loc:*** SL, Da84>

encouragement [ɑ̃kuraʒmɑ̃] *n.m.* encouragement, incentive <***Loc:*** Da84>

encourager [ɑ̃kuraʒe] **I** *v.tr.* **1** to encourage, urge *Il va encourager son frère d'acheter le bœuf.* He's going to encourage his brother to buy the bull. (SL) **2** to encourage, support **II s'encourager** *v.pron.* **1** to take courage, take heart *Encourage-toi. C'est peut-être pas vrai, cette histoire.* Take heart. Maybe that story is not true. (VM) **2** to encourage each other *Après un ouragan, on s'encourage l'un à l'autre.* After a hurricane, we encourage each other. (VM) <***Loc:*** EV, LF, SL, VM, Da84, Wh83>

encrassement [ɑ̃krasmɑ̃] *n.m.* crud, filth <***Loc:*** Da84>

encrasser [ãkrase] **I** *v.tr.* to dirty up, get dirty *Fais attention de pas encrasser tes souliers.* Be careful not to dirty your shoes. (LA) **II s'encrasser** *v.pron.* to get o.s. dirty, get filthy *Il s'a tout encrassé dans le bois.* He got filthy in the woods. (LA) <***Loc:*** LA, Da84>

encre [ãk(r)] *n.f.* ink <***Loc:*** Da84>

encrier [ãkrije] *n.f.* ink well, ink pot <***Loc:*** Da84>

endaler [ãdale] *v.pron.* to get into debt beyond one's means *Jacques s'a bien endalé dans des comptes.* Jack certainly has gotten himself into debt. (IB) <***Loc:*** IB>

endedans ♦see **dedans**

endetté, -e [ãdete] *adj.* indebted, in debt *Ils sont tellement endettés que il faudra il travaille tout sa vie.* They are so much in debt that he will have to work all his life. (LA) <***Loc:*** LA, Da84>

endettement [ãdetmã] *n.m.* indebtedness, debt <***Loc:*** Da84>

endetter [ãdete] **I** *v.tr.* to indebt, bring into debt *Son cheval de course l'a endetté.* His racehorse left him in debt. (VM) **II s'endetter** *v.pron.* to indebt o.s., go into debt *Il a pas voulu s'endetter pour acheter plus grand.* He didn't want to go into debt to buy a bigger place. (SM) <***Loc:*** EV, SM, VM, Da84>

endive [ãdiv] *n.f.* **1** endive **2** chicory <***Loc:*** Da84>

endommagement [ãdɔ̃maʒmã] *n.m.* damage <***Loc:*** Da84>

endommager [ãdɔ̃maʒe] *v.tr.* to damage *L'ouragan a réellement endommagé leur magasin.* The hurricane really damaged their barn. (SL) <***Loc:*** SL, Da84>

endormi, -e [ãdɔrmi] *adj.* sleeping, asleep *Les petits sont endormis. Fais pas de train.* The children are asleep. Don't make any noise. (EV) <***Loc:*** AC, EV, SL, An94, Da84>

endormir [ãdɔrmir] **I** *v.tr.* to put to sleep, induce sleep in *Il a mis toute qualité de boissons, mais tout en espoir pour les endormir.* He put in all sorts of liquors, all in the hopes of putting them to sleep. (SL) **II s'endormir** *v.pron.* **1** to go to sleep *Quand les enfants se sont endormis, il a ôté le bonnet à un et il l'a mis sur sa tête à lui.* When the children went to sleep, he took the bonnet from one and put it on his own head. (LA) **2** to be sleepy *Je m'endors.* I'm sleepy. (LF) **J'm'endors et c'est jusse huit heures.* I'm sleepy and it's only eight o'clock. (EV, Ph36) <***Loc:*** EV, LA, LF, SL, SM, TB, VM, An94, Da84, Hi02, Ph36, Wh83>

endormitoir [ãdɔrmitwar] *n.m.* **1** soporific, anything that induces sleep *Le dinde, c'est un endormitoir. Quand t'en manges, ça t'endort.* Turkey is a soporific. When you eat it, it puts you to sleep. (VM) **2** sleep, sleepiness *Je vas lire ou crocher jusqu'à l'endormitoir me prend.* I am going to read or knit until I get sleepy. (Lv88) ◊ •**avoir l'endormitoir** to be sleepy *T'as l'endormitoir, vas te coucher.* You're sleepy, go to bed. (VM) <JE, VM, Lv88> <***Loc:*** JE, TB, VM, Lv88>

endos [ãdo] *n.m.* dirt thrown to the side of a furrow as the result of plowing, ridge turned up by plow <***Loc:*** VM, Lv88>

endossage [ãdosaʒ] *n.m.* bringing dirt to crops <***Loc:*** Da84>

endossement [ãdɔsmã] *n.m.* endorsement <***Loc:*** Da84>

endosser [ãdose] *v.tr.* **1** to endorse, sign **2** to assume responsibility for, shoulder (e.g. one's burdens) **Endosser sa misère.* To bear one's troubles. (Da84) **3** to bank, bring dirt up to *Endosser la récolte.* To bring dirt to plants. (Da84) **4** to make furrows **J'ai déjà endossé tout ma terre.* I have already made furrows in all my land. (EV, Ph36) <***Loc:*** EV, JD, SM, Da84, Lv88, Ph36>

endosseur [ãdosœr] *n.m.* endorser (of notes) <***Loc:*** Da84>

endoyer [ãdwaje] *v.tr.* to baptize without a church ceremony *Ils ont eu pour endoyer l'enfant, tellement il était malade.* They had to baptize the child themselves, he was so sick. (LA) <***Loc:*** LA, VM, Da84>

endroit (**lendroit**) [ãdrwa, lãdrwa] *n.m.* **1** place, locality *Sur le lendroit.* In the place. (Lv88) **Aller dans un endroit d'un autre.* To go to one place from another. (LA, An94) **2** right side (e.g. of cloth) *Revire ma robe à l'endroit.* Turn my dress right side out. (TB) <***Loc:*** LA, TB, VM, An94, Da84, Lv88>

endurable [ãdyrab(l)] *adj.* endurable, bearable *Il était proche pas endurable.* He was almost unbearable. (SL) <***Loc:*** SL, Da84>

endurance [ãdyrãs] *n.f.* endurance, fortitude <***Loc:*** Da84>

endurant, -e [ãdyrã, -ãt] *adj.* enduring, tolerating, patient **Les marrons veut faire ça qu'est le plus populaire au moment, plutôt que ça qu'est le plus rare et endurant.* The wild ones will do what is most popular at the moment, rather than what is the rarest and most lasting. (Wh83) <***Loc:*** Da84, Wh83>

endurcir [ãdyrsir] **I** *v.tr.* to harden, toughen *Il a perdu sa famille jeune, et ça l'a endurci.* He lost his family while young and it hardened him. (LA) **II s'endurcir** *v.pron.* to become hardened *Là il faut laisser le savon de pays s'endurcir avant de le couper.* Then you have to let the homemade soap harden before cutting it. (VM) <***Loc:*** LA, VM, Da84>

endurcissement [ãdyrsismã] *n.m.* hardening, toughening ◊ •**endurcissement des artères** hardening of the arteries <Da84> <***Loc:*** Da84>

endurer [ãdyre] **I** *v.tr.* to endure, bear, put up with *On peut pas l'endurer, lui, avoir toutes les bonnes choses et d'être aimé plus qu'on est aimé.* We can't put up with him, always having the good things and being loved better than we are loved. (LA) *Il aurait pas enduré ça.* He wouldn't have put up with that. (EV) **II s'endurer** *v.pron.* to put up with each other, tolerate each other *On pouvait plus s'endurer.* We couldn't tolerate each other any more. (Lv88) <***Loc:*** EV, IB, LA, Da84, Hi02, Lv88>

énergie [enærʒi] *n.f.* energy, vigor, strength <***Loc:*** AV, Da84>

énergique [enærʒik] *adj.* energetic, vigorous <***Loc:*** Da84>

énervant, -e [enærvã, -ãt] *adj.* enervating, nerveracking, irritating <***Loc:*** Da84>

énerver [enærve, enærfe] **I** *v.tr.* to unnerve, irritate **II s'énerver** *v.pron.* to become unnerved, become nervous, get irritated <***Loc:*** LA, Da84>

enfaîter ♦see **aufaîter**

enfance [ɑ̃fɑ̃s] *n.f.* infancy, childhood ◊ **•être en enfance** to be in one's second childhood, be senile **La vielle femme était gayarde mais en enfance.* The old woman was healthy but senile. (Wh83) <Wh83> <***Loc:*** LA, VM, Da84, La99, Lv88, Wh83>

enfant [ɑ̃fɑ̃] *n.* **1** child **2** infant, baby **3** offspring, descendant ◊ **•enfant à la traîne** neglected child, uncared-for child <Da84> **•enfant de chien** son of a bitch <Da84> **•enfant de chœur** altar boy <AL> **•enfant de garce** son of a bitch, son-of-a-gun *Quand un enfant fait quelque chose de bien on dit que c'est un enfant de garce.* When a child does something well we say he's a son-of-a-gun. (LF) <LF, TB> **•enfant de monstre** son-of-a-gun <SB, Da84> **•enfant du deuxième lit** child of a second marriage <La99> **•enfant inconnu** illegitimate child <JE, La99> **•enfant prodige** prodigal son <Da84> **•enfant terrible** problem child, incorrigible person <Da84> **•petit-enfant** grandchild <LA, LF, TB, VM, Gu00, Fa77> <***Loc:*** AC, AL, AV, EV, IB, JE, LA, LF, PQ, SB, SL, SM, TB, VM, An94, Da84, Gu00, Hi02, La99, Lv88, Ph36, Wh83>

enfantement [ɑ̃fɑ̃tmɑ̃] *n.m.* childbirth <***Loc:*** Da84>

enfantile (**enfantin**) [ɑ̃fɑ̃til, ɑ̃fɑ̃tɛ̃] *adj.* infantile, childish *Il est assez enfantin, je peux pas travailler avec.* He is so childish, I can't work with [him]. (EV) <***Loc:*** EV, Da84>

enfantin ♦see **enfantile**

enfarge (**enferge**) [ɑ̃farʒ, ɑ̃færʒ] *n.m./f.* **1** shackle, hindrance, impediment **2** hobble (strap or rope used to impede the movement of a horse) <***Loc:*** VM, Lv88>

enfarger (**enferger**) [ɑ̃farʒe, ɑ̃færʒe] *v.tr.* to hobble (a horse) *Cette jument est assez fraque, il faudrait que je l'enfarge.* That mare is so skittish that I'd have to hobble her. (VM) <***Loc:*** AV, SJ, VM>

enfariner [ɑ̃farine] *v.tr.* to flour, sprinkle or dredge with flour *J'ai enfariné le poulet avant de le cuire.* I floured the chicken before cooking it. (VM) <***Loc:*** VM, Da84>

enfaufiler [ɑ̃fofile] **I** *v.tr.* to thread (a needle) *Enfaufiler une aiguille.* To thread a needle. (SL) **II s'enfaufiler** *v.pron.* to mix (with a crowd) *Il s'a enfaufilé parmi le monde et il s'a échappé propre.* He mixed in with the people and he got clean away. (LA) <***Loc:*** LA, SL, Da84>

enfer [ɑ̃fær] *n.m.* hell *Le Bon Dieu va te damner à l'enfer si t'arrêtes pas de coursailler comme tu fais.* God is going to damn you to hell if you don't stop running around like you do. (VM) <***Loc:*** VM, Da84, Hi02, Wh83>

enferge ♦see **enfarge**

enferger ♦see **enfarger**

enfermé, -e (**enfremé, enfrèmé**) [ɑ̃færme, ɑ̃frɛ̃me] *adj.* closed in *Oui ça c'est une pirogue oui. Mais c'est plutôt fait comme ça qu'on appelle un kayak. Il est enfermé pour empêcher l'eau de rentrer en-dedans.* Yes, that's a pirogue. But it's made more like what they call a kayak. It's closed in to prevent water from getting inside. (LF) <***Loc:*** LA, LF>

enfermer [ɑ̃færme, ɑ̃frɛ̃me, færme] *v.tr.* to shut in, lock up *Pendant le froid, il faut enfermer les animaux dans l'hangar.* During cold weather, it is necessary to lock up the animals in the barn. (LA) <***Loc:*** LA, SM, TB, Da84>

enfeuillage [ɑ̃føjaʒ] *n.m.* foliage <***Loc:*** Lv88>

enfilage ♦see **affilage**

enfilé ♦see **affilé**

enfiler[1] (**filer**) [ɑ̃file, file] *v.tr.* **1** to thread (a needle) **2** to string, thread (e.g. beads) *Les enfants ont filé du tac-tac pour mettre sus l'arbre à Chrismeusse.* The children strung popcorn to put on the Christmas tree. (AC) **3** to tie on, strap on *Et ça enfilait les éperons sur les corusses pour se battre, et le dernier corusse en vie c'est lui qui gagnait.* And they strapped spurs on the roosters for fighting, and the last rooster alive was the winner. (LF) **4** to wire for electricity *L'homme est après enfiler la maison.* The man is wiring the house for electricity. (VM) <***Loc:*** EV, LF, SL, VM, Da84, Lv88>

enfiler[2] ♦see **affiler**

enfin [ɑ̃fɛ̃] *adv.* **1** finally, after all, at last *Quand-même elle est partie, sois pas découragé. C'est vendredi enfin. Allons, mais s'amuser.* Even though she's gone, don't be discouraged. It's Friday at last. Let's go have a good time. (ch: *Vendredi enfin*) *Enfin il s'est débloqué.* He finally had a bowel movement. (SL) **2** or rather, to be more exact **Ça fait qu'un jour qu'il voit un chevreuil, une brebis, enfin.* So, one day he sees a deer, or rather a ewe. (IV, An94) **3** as a matter of fact **Ça se ressemble autant que deux petits peut se ressembler. Ça peut pas se ressembler plus que ça se ressemble. Enfin, leur mère et leur père peut pas les distinguer.* They resembled each other as much as two children can look alike. They can't look more alike than they do. As a matter of fact, even their mother and their father can't tell them apart. (EV, An94) **4** well, so *C'était un prêtre qui faisait les messes, enfin la messe était latin, tu connais le* READING *dans la messe?* It was a priest who celebrated the Masses, well the Mass was Latin, you know, the reading in the Mass? (TB) *Ils les aviont jetés dans une grande coulée pas bien loin de é-où ça restait. Ils les ont pas retrouvés avant que ça pouvait pus les reconnaître. Enfin, ça les a reconnus par leurs souliers et leur linge.* They had thrown them into a big coulee not far from where they lived. They didn't find them until they could no longer be recognized. Well, they recognized them by their shoes and their clothes. (AC) **5** in short, in a word **Et tous les samedis tard le soir, mais les bogheis et les cavaliers, ça s'en venait, et ça allait tous au village. C'était tous des blancs, enfin.* And every Saturday late at night, the buggies and riders would come and they were all going to town. It was all white people, you see. (LA, An94) ◊ **•mais enfin!** for heaven's sake! <Da84> **<*Loc:*** AC, EV, IB, IV, LA, SL, TB, VM, An84, An94, Da84>

enflammation [ɑ̃flɑ̃masjɔ̃] *n.f.* inflammation **<*Loc:*** TB>

enflammant, -e [ɑ̃flɑ̃mɑ̃, -ɑ̃t] *adj.* **1** inflammatory *Ses mots étaient bien enflammants.* His words were very inflammatory. (LA) **2** flammable *Des briquettes enflammantes.* Flammable briquettes. (LA) **<*Loc:*** LA>

enflammé, -e [ɑ̃flɑ̃me] *adj.* **1** inflamed (of a sore) *Quand l'ampoule a cassé, je pouvais pas mettre une chaussette dessus parce que c'était tout enflammé.* When the blister burst, I couldn't put on a sock because it was all inflamed. (VM) **2** flaming, on fire *Une maison enflammée.* A house on fire. (VM) **<*Loc:*** VM, Da84, Wh83>

enflammer (se) [ɑ̃flɑ̃me] *v.pron.* to be inflamed *Mon pied s'est bien enflammé.* My foot got very inflamed. (LA) **<*Loc:*** LA, Da84>

enflé, -e [ɑ̃fle] *adj.* **1** swollen, puffed up *J'avais pagaillé cette machine, pis j'étais en famille. Mes pieds étaient enflés.* I had pedaled that machine, and I was pregnant. My feet were swollen. (SL) **2** in a bad mood **<*Loc:*** LF, SL, TB, Da84>

enfler [ɑ̃fle] **I** *v.intr.* to swell *Et j'étais après dompter un cheval un jour et quelque manière je m'ai refoulé la main comme ça. Et ç'a enflé.* I was taming a horse one day and somehow I sprained my hand like that. And it swelled up. (LF) **II s'enfler** *v.pron.* to swell, become swollen *Il a tordu son pied et ça s'a enflé proche le double de sa grosseur.* He twisted his foot and it became swollen to almost twice its normal size. (LA) **<*Loc:*** LA, LF, SL, Da84>

enflure [ɑ̃flyr] *n.f.* swelling ◊ **•enflure blanche** osteomelitis <Da84> **<*Loc:*** TB, VM, Da84>

enfoncement [ɑ̃fɔ̃smɑ̃] *n.m.* driving in, sinking in **<*Loc:*** Da84>

enfoncer [ɑ̃fɔ̃se] **I** *v.tr.* **1** to drive in, push in *Et il a enfoncé la canne dans le dos du loup-garou. Et le loup-garou a disparu parce que il disparaît que si tu fais ça saigner.* He stuck the cane into the werewolf's back. And the werewolf disappeared because he disappears only if you make him bleed. (LF) *Enfoncer des clous.* To drive in nails. (LF) **Il avait le mouchoir juste manière enfoncé dans sa poche.* He had his handkerchief just sort of stuffed into his pocket. (SL, An94) **2** to put in an undesirable place or situation *Eusse m'a enfoncé dans un* WARD *avec tout des vieux hommes qui parlaient français.* They stuck me in a ward with a bunch of old men who spoke French. (TB) **II s'enfoncer** *v.pron.* to sink, go down into *Plus il essayait de sortir de la boue, plus il s'enfonçait dedans.* The more he tried to get out of the mud, the more he sank down into it. (LA) ◊ **•être enfoncé avec** to be stuck with *Je voulais pas t-être enfoncé avec un enfant.* I didn't want to be stuck with a child. (TB) <TB> **<*Loc:*** LA, LF, SL, TB, An94, Da84>

enforcir [ɑ̃fɔrsir] **I** *v.tr.* to strengthen, reinforce *Avec quelques clous, j'ai enforci ma barrière.* With a couple of nails, I reinforced my fence. (LA) **II s'enforcir** *v.pron.* to get stronger, reinforce o.s. **<*Loc:*** LA, Da84>

enformer [ɑ̃fɔrme] *v.tr.* to put (sugar) into casks or barrels **<*Loc:*** VM>

enfourcher [ɑ̃furʃe] *v.tr.* to pierce with a pitchfork, pick up with a pitchfork *Enfourcher du foin.* To pitch hay. (LA) **<*Loc:*** LA, Da84>

enfourner [ɑ̃furne] *v.tr.* **1** to clutter up, encumber **2** to pack, stuff, fill *Il a enfourné son porte-monnaie de l'argent.* He stuffed his wallet with money. (AV) *Il a enfourné le moulin plein de maïs.* He packed the grinder full of corn. (AV) ***Loc:*** AV, Da84>

enfremé, enfrèmé ♦see **enfermé**

engacer ♦see **agacer**

engagé[1]**, -e** [ɑ̃gaʒe] *adj.* engaged (to be married) *Il est engagé. Il va se marier le mois prochain.* He is engaged. He is going to get married next month. (SM) **<*Loc:*** EV, SM, VM, Da84, Gr86, Hi02>

engagé[2]**, -e** [ɑ̃gaʒe] *n.* **1** employee, hired person, hired hand, hired laborer *Il a trois engagés qui travaillent pour lui asteur.* He has three employees working for him now. (EV) **2** sharecropper **<*Loc:*** AC, AV, EV, IB, JD, LA, LF, SB, SJ, SM, TB, VM, Da84, Hi02, Lv88, Ph36>

engagement [ɑ̃gaʒmɑ̃] *n.m.* **1** engagement **2** wages *Combien c'est ton engagement?* How much are your wages? (VM) **<*Loc:*** SB, VM, Da84, Lv88>

engager [ɑ̃gaʒe] **I** *v.tr.* to hire, employ *Il a engagé un homme pour peindre la maison.* He hired a man to paint the house. (SM) **II s'engager** *v.pron.* **1** to hire o.s. out, take employment **Petit Jean s'avait engagé avec un géant.* Petit Jean had hired himself out to a giant. (AC, An94) *C'est sur le* WELFARE*, pourquoi ça irait s'engager?* They are on Welfare, why would they go and get themselves hired on? (Lv88) **2** to become engaged (to be married) **<*Loc:*** AC, EV, IB, JE, LF, SM, TB, An94, Da84, Gr86, Hi02, Lv88, Ph36>

engagère [ɑ̃gaʒær] *n.f.* female employee (usu. a maid) **<*Loc:*** SM, Da84>

engagiste [ɑ̃gaʒist] *n.* hirer, employer **<*Loc:*** Gr86>

engagner [ɑ̃gɑ̃je] *v.tr.* to get the best of, gain the advantage over *Il a bien engagné celui-là.* He certainly got the best of that one. (IB) **<*Loc:*** IB>

engarocher [ɑ̃garoʃe] *v.tr.* to straddle, sit astraddle *Engarocher la barrière.* To straddle the fence. (AV) ◊ **•engarocher un couteau** to stab, stick with a knife *Il lui a engaroché un couteau.* He stuck him with a knife. (AV) **•engarocher une tape** to slap *Il m'a engaroché une tape.* He slapped me. (AV) **<*Loc:*** AV>

engendrer [ɑ̃ʒɑ̃dre] *v.tr.* **1** to breed, raise **2** to engender **<*Loc:*** Da84>

engénieur ♦see **ingénieur**

engin [ɑ̃ʒɛ̃] *n.f.* **1** engine, motor **2** machine **<*Loc:*** Da84>

engloutir [ɑ̃glutir] *v.tr.* **1** to engulf, swallow up **2** to devastate

Ils vont nous engloutir avec toutes ces bombes. They are going to devastate us with all those bombs. (VM) <***Loc:*** VM, Da84>

engommer [ɑ̃gɔ̃me] **I** *v.tr.* to gum up, make sticky *Quand tu coupes du bois de pin, ça va tout engommer ta scie dans rien de temps.* When you cut pine, it will completely gum up your saw in no time. (LA) **II s'engommer** *v.pron.* to become gummy, become sticky *Ma machine à coudre s'est tout engommée.* My sewing machine is all gummed up. (VM) <***Loc:*** LA, VM, Da84>

engorger [ɑ̃gɔrʒe] **I** *v.tr.* to choke up, obstruct, stop up **II s'engorger** *v.pron.* to become choked, become obstructed <***Loc:*** Da84>

engotement [ɑ̃gotmɑ̃] *n.m.* **1** stoppage, stopping up, choking **2** obstruction *J'ai des engotements dans la gorge.* I've got something in my throat. (VM) <***Loc:*** VM, Da84, Lv88>

engoter [ɑ̃gote, ɑ̃gwate] **I** *v.tr.* **1** to choke, choke up, obstruct, clog (a pipe, etc.) *Ses enfants avaient mis la gazette dans sa commode et ça avait tout engoté ses tuyaux.* His children had put the newspaper in his toilet and it had completely clogged his pipes. (LA) **2** to strangle, cause to choke *Ça m'engote quand je mange ça.* It makes me choke when I eat that. (VM) **II s'engoter** *v.pron.* to choke, get choked *Je m'ai engoté dessus mon manger.* I choked on my food. (VM) *C'est trop trempe, la machine à z-herbes s'est engotée.* It's too wet, the lawnmower got choked up. (Lv88) <***Loc:*** IB, LA, LF, SM, TB, VM, Da84, Lv88>

engoulevent [ɑ̃gulvɑ̃] *n.m.* **1** nighthawk, bullbat **2** Florida nighthawk <***Loc:*** Re31>

engourdi, -e [ɑ̃gurdi] *adj.* numb *Ta main est engourdie parce que t'as dormi dessus.* Your hand is numb because you slept on it. (EV) <***Loc:*** EV, Da84>

engourdir [ɑ̃gurdir] **I** *v.tr.* to numb, render numb *Ça a pas fait trop de mal parce que le dentiste avait engourdi ma gencive avant d'arracher la dent.* It didn't hurt too badly because the dentist had numbed my gums before pulling the tooth. (EV) **II s'engourdir** *v.pron.* to get numb **Ma jambe s'a engourdi.* My leg became numb. (Da84) <***Loc:*** EV, Da84>

engourdissant, -e [ɑ̃gurdisɑ̃, -ɑ̃t] *adj.* numbing *Une médecine engourdissante.* A numbing medication. (LA) <***Loc:*** Da84>

engourdissement [ɑ̃gurdismɑ̃] *n.m.* **1** numbness **2** numbing <***Loc:*** Da84>

engrais [ɑ̃gre] *n.m.* ◊ **•mettre à l'engrais** to fatten, fatten up *J'ai mis un cochon à l'engrais.* I fattened up a pig. (LA) <LA, Da84> <***Loc:*** LA, Da84>

engraissant, -e [ɑ̃gresɑ̃, -ɑ̃t] *adj.* fattening *La douceur est engraissante.* Sweets are fattening. (EV) <***Loc:*** EV, Da84>

engraissement [ɑ̃grɛsmɑ̃] *n.m.* fattening, fattening up <***Loc:*** Da84>

engraisser [ɑ̃grese] **I** *v.tr.* to fatten, fatten up *Y avait plein de pâturage, ils les engraissaient encore pour finir la route avant qu'ils arrivaient pour les vendre au marché.* There was a lot of pasture land, they would fatten them [the cows] up to finish out the journey before they arrived at the market to be sold. (SJ) **II** *v.intr.* to grow fat, put on weight *Il doit manger bien ici. Il a engraissé.* He must eat well here. He's put on weight. (SL) **III s'engraisser** *v.pron.* to become fat, fatten up *Tu vas t'engraisser si tu manges trop du doux.* You will be become fat if you eat too many sweets. (LA) <***Loc:*** LA, SJ, SL, Da84>

engravé, -e [ɑ̃grave] *adj.* incurable, irremediable *C'est une maladie engravée.* It is an incurable illness. (VM) <***Loc:*** VM>

engraver[1] [ɑ̃grave] *v.tr.* **2** to engrave *Il a fait engraver son nom sur la tasse.* He had his name engraved on the cup. (IB) **2** to ingrain, ensconce, embed, entrench **La poussière est engravée dans le tapis.* The dust is embedded in the carpet. (Lv88) *Il a la paresse bien engravée.* Laziness is well ingrained in him. (Lv88) *Le gouvernment fédéral est si engravé dans notre système que les maîtres doivent toujours faire des rapports.* The federal government is so entrenched in our system that the leaders always have to make reports. (Lv88) *Je peux pas ôter le clou, c'est engravé là.* I can't remove the nail, it's stuck there. (VM) <***Loc:*** IB, SM, VM, Da84, Lv88>

engraver[2] (**aggraver**) [ɑ̃grave, agrave] **I** *v.tr.* to aggravate, make worse *Va pas aggraver ton cas avec des histoires de loup-garou!* Don't go worsening your argument with werewolf stories! (film: *Chien de Lune*) **II** *v.intr.* to worsen, get worse *La maladie a engravé.* The illness got worse. (Lv88) **III s'engraver** *v.pron.* to worsen, get worse *Sa maladie est après s'engraver, je crois pas qu'il va vivre longtemps.* His illness is getting worse, I don't think he'll live a long time. (VM) <***Loc:*** SM, VM, Da84, Lv88>

engrenage [ɑ̃grənaʒ] *n.m.* gear, cog <***Loc:*** Da84>

engricher ♦see **engrucher**

engruchade [ɑ̃gryʃad] *n.f.* roost *Tu feras mieux de solider cette engruchade.* You'd better strengthen that roost. (TB) <***Loc:*** TB>

engrucher (**engricher, agrucher, agricher, agrusser, agrisser**) [ɑ̃gryʃe, ɑ̃griʃe, agryʃe, agriʃe, agryse, agrise] **I** *v.tr.* **1** to climb, ascend *Il a agriché le poteau.* He climbed the pole. (Lv88) *L'enfant a griché la barrière.* The child climbed over the fence. (VM) **2** to hang, hook, place on a hook *Va m'engrucher ça où je pourrai pas l'empoigner.* Go hang that up somewhere that I won't be able to get it. (TB) **II s'engrucher** *v.pron.* to climb, perch *Jean s'est engruché sur cette échelle.* John perched on that ladder. (IB) **I s'est engruché su la maison.* He climbed on top of the house. (EV, Ph36) <***Loc:*** EV, IB, JD, TB, VM, Di32, Lv88, Ph36>

engueulement [ɑ̃gœlmɑ̃] *n.m.* mouth of a river or bayou <***Loc:*** Gu00>

engueuler[1] [ɑ̃gøle] *v.tr.* to gulp down, swallow hurriedly *Si tu le dépêches, il va engueuler son souper.* If you hurry him, he'll gulp down his supper. (IB) <***Loc:*** IB, Da84>

engueuler[2] [ɑ̃dʒøle] *v.tr.* to scold *Il l'a engueulée quand elle a parlé.* He scolded her when she spoke. (LF) <***Loc:*** LF>

enjamber (**éjamber, ajamber**) [ɑ̃ʒɑ̃be, eʒɑ̃be, aʒɑ̃be, oʒɑ̃be] *v.tr.* **1** to cross by lifting one leg over at a time, step across, step over *Enjamber la barrière.* To cross over the fence. (AV) *Il a enjambé la barrière.* He stepped over the fence. (LA, VM) **2** to straddle *C'est pas rien d'éjamber un cheval comme ça.* It's nothing to straddle a horse like that. (TB) <***Loc:*** AV, IB, LA, TB, VM, Da84, Lv88>

enjarrer [ɑ̃ʒare] *v.tr.* to put into jars *J'ai enjarré des tomates hier et encore aujourd'hui.* I jarred tomatoes yesterday and again today. (TB) <***Loc:*** TB>

enjôler [ɑ̃ʒule] *v.tr.* to flatter *Alle essaye d'enjôler le professeur.* She is trying to flatter the professor. (AV) <***Loc:*** AV, SJ>

enjôleur, -euse [ɑ̃ʒulœr, -øz] *n.* flatterer, deceiver <***Loc:*** SJ>

ENJOY [ɛndʒɔɪ] *v.tr.invar.* to enjoy *On était pauvre, mais on avait* ENJOY *la vie.* We were poor, but we enjoyed life. (SL) <***Loc:*** SL>

enlaidir (**enlaidzir**) [ɑ̃ledir, ɑ̃ledzir] *v.intr.* to become ugly *Il a enlaidzi depuis quéques années.* He has become ugly in the last few years. (SM) <***Loc:*** SM>

enlaidzir ♦see **enlaidir**

enlever [ɑ̃ləve] *v.tr.* **1** to lift, take up, pull up *Après l'ensevelissement, deux personnes enlevaient la paille du lit du mort et allaient la brûler près de la maison.* After the wake, two people took up the straw from the bed of the dead person and went to burn it near the house. (VM) *Mais la mort [...], il a resté si longtemps sus le plancher, quand-ce ils l'ont enlevé j'ai attendu ses os craquer.* But death [...], he stayed on the floor so long that when they picked him up I heard his bones crack. (TB) *Ils ont éternué tellement fort jusqu'à ils ont enlevé le toit de la maison.* They sneezed so hard that they took off the roof of the house. (AV) **2** to abduct, kidnap **Les Marais Bouleurs ont enlevé Marie.* The Marais Bouleurs carried off Marie. (ThCa: *Martin Weber*) **3** to flush (birds) *Mon chien a enlevé les perdrix.* My dog flushed out the quail. (AV) ◊ **•enlever sa soutadaire** to prepare for a fight, roll up one's sleeves <VM> <***Loc:*** AV, EV, SL, VM, Da84, ThCa>

enlignement ♦see **alignement**

enligner ♦see **aligner**

ennemi (**élemi**) [ɛlmi, edmi, elmi] *n.m.* enemy, foe <***Loc:*** EV, LF, SM, TB, VM, Da84, Ph36>

ennui [ɑ̃nɥi] *n.m.* **1** loneliness **Et il a resté un bout de temps, puis là, l'ennui l'a pris. Il était seul.* And he stayed for a while, and then loneliness overwhelmed him. He was alone. (AC, An94) **2** boredom *Il y avait pas rien à faire et l'ennui était après la rendre folle.* There was nothing to do and boredom was driving her crazy. (LA) **3** nostalgia, longing **Mais mon ennui pour des jours Cajins poudrait être quec'chose qui dur eine quarantaine d'années si les affaires changent pas et les jeunes commencent pas à apprendre à parler la langue Cajine.* But my longing for the Cajun days could be something which lasts forty odd years if things don't change and young people don't start learning the Cajun language. (Wh83) <***Loc:*** AC, LA, LF, Da84, Wh83>

ennuyant, -e [ɑ̃nɥijɑ̃, ɑ̃nejɑ̃, -ɑ̃t] *adj.* **1** lonely *Un autre soir ennuyant quand toi, t'es pas là.* Another lonely evening when you're not there. (LA, ch: *Un autre soir ennuyant*) **2** boring, tiresome *C'est ennuyant quand il fait trop froid pour sortir.* It's boring when it's too cold to go out. (VM) <***Loc:*** LA, LF, Da84, Gr86, Hi02, Lv88>

ennuyer (s') [ɑ̃nɥije] *v.pron.* **1** to be lonesome, feel lonely *Il s'ennuie.* He's lonely. (LF) *Je suis moi tout seul dans la chambre, le téléphone à l'oreille. Hello, Nelda, à soir moi, je m'ennuie. Je suis moi seul dedans la chambre après guetter les quatre murs.* I'm all alone in the room, the phone at my ear. Hello, Nelda, I'm lonesome. I'm alone in the room looking at the four walls. (ch: *Hello, Nelda*) **2** to become lonely, get lonesome **"Moi, je veux pas aller là-bas. Je vas m'ennuyer." Il dit, "Je pourras pas rester."* "I can't go [live] over there. I'm going to get lonesome." He said, "I won't be able to stay." (SL, An94) **3** to miss, be lonesome for *Oh, petite fille, je m'ennuie de toi.* Oh, little girl, I miss you. (ch: *Oh, Mam*) *J'avais l'habitude de changer la station quand j'entendais les chansons cadiennes. Moi, je voulais entendre la même musique, pareil comme les Américains. Asteur, je m'ennuie de les vieux Cadiens. C'est souvent je joue leurs disques.* I used to change the station when I heard Cajun songs. I wanted to hear the same music as Americans. Now I miss the old Cajuns. I often play their records. (ch: *Disco et fais-dodo*) <***Loc:*** AC, EV, LA, LF, SL, An94, Da84, Hi02, Lv88>

ennuyeux, -euse [ɑ̃nɥijø, -øz] *adj.* homesick, lonesome *Avant la nuit a pris, il était ennuyeux.* Before night fell, he was homesick. (VM) <***Loc:*** VM>

énormément [enɔrmẽmɑ̃] *adv.* **1** enormously, tremendously *Tu m'as aidé énormément.* You helped me enormously. (LA) **2** many, much, a lot *L'été passé, on a eu énormément des chaleurs.* Last summer, we had a lot of hot spells. (LA) <***Loc:*** LA, Da84>

énormité [enɔrmite] *n.f.* enormity, hugeness <***Loc:*** Da84>

enqueler ♦see **encler**

enquiquinant [ɑ̃kikinɑ̃] *adj.* aggravating *Il est bien enquiquinant, lui!* He's really aggravating! (LA) <***Loc:*** LA, VM>

enquiquiner [ɑ̃kikine, ɑ̃tʃitʃine] *v.tr.* to bother, pester *Il faut pas enquiquiner personne!* Don't bother anyone! (LA) *Elle m'a enquiquiné pour du pain toute la journée.* She pestered me for some bread all day long. (SB) <***Loc:*** LA, LF, SB>

enrabatan [ɑ̃rabatɑ̃] *adv.* included, as well *Tout le monde était là Joseph enrabatan.* Everyone was there including Joseph. (AV) <***Loc:*** AV>

enracinement [ɑ̃rasinmɑ̃] *n.m.* rooting, taking root <***Loc:*** Da84>

enraciner (**raciner**) [ɑ̃rasine, rasine] **I** *v.intr.* to become rooted, take root *Il est bien enraciné dans cette famille.* He is well rooted in that family. (SL) **II s'enraciner** *v.pron.* to take root *Je souhaite que mes rosiers vont s'enraciner dans tout cette chaleur.* I hope my rose bushes will take root in all this heat. (LA) <*Loc:* LA, SL, Da84>

enragé, -e (**ragé, -e**) [ɑ̃raʒe, raʒe] *adj.* **1** rabid *Un chien enragé.* A rabid dog. (EV) *Chien ragé.* Rabid dog. (TB) **2** angry, furious *Il était si enragé qu'il aurait pu m'étrangler.* He was so angry that he could've strangled me. (EV) **3** extremely spicy, hot *Piment enragé.* Hot pepper. (Pe37) <*Loc:* EV, TB, VM, Da84, Hi02, La99, Lv88, Pe37, Re31>

enrageant, -e [ɑ̃raʒɑ̃, -ɑ̃t] *adj.* maddening, irritating, upsetting *C'est enrageant d'avoir à refaire tout ce travail.* It's maddening to have to redo all that work. (EV) <*Loc:* EV, Da84>

enrager [ɑ̃raʒe] **I** *v.tr.* **1** to anger *Tu peux pas enrager cette serpent. Tu l'enrages, il va t'attaquer.* You can't make that snake mad. You anger him, he'll attack you. (LF) **2** to upset *Il m'a enragé.* He upset me. (SL) **II s'enrager** *v.pron.* **1** to fly into a rage, become furious or enraged *Ça va pas aider à rien de t'enrager comme ça.* It won't help anything to get enraged like that. (LA) **2** to get rabies *Faulait guetter les bêtes puantes alentour nos chiens parce que les chiens voulaient les courser mais si elles s'étaient enragées [...] la bête puante c'est celle-là qui peut emmener la rage plus aisée que les autres animaux.* We had to watch for skunks around our dogs because our dogs wanted to chase them, but if they had rabies the skunk is an animal that carries rabies more easily than other animals. (IB) <*Loc:* IB, LA, LF, SL, Da84>

enregistrement [ɑ̃r(ə)ʒistrəmɑ̃] *n.m.* registration, enrollment <*Loc:* Da84>

enregistrer [ɑ̃r(ə)ʒistre] **I** *v.tr.* to register, enlist *Équand-ce qu'il a fini la cale on a été pour le faire enregistrer avec le* COAST GUARD. When he finished the hull we went to have it registered with the Coast Guard. (TB) *Des chevaux enregistrés.* Registered horses. (SM) **II s'enregistrer** *v.pron.* to register o.s., enlist *On s'est enregistré pour voter.* We registered to vote. (SL) <*Loc:* EV, LA, SL, SM, TB, Da84>

enretardé [ɑ̃rətarde] *adj.* late, delayed **S'il n'a pas ein automne trempe, la mamam écrévisse sera averti de ça instinctif durant l'été et elle va pas pondre ses œufs, et ça fera la saison être enretardé.* If there isn't a wet fall, the mother crawfish will instinctively sense this during the summer and she will hold off laying, and that will cause a later season. (Wh83) <*Loc:* Wh83>

enrichir [ɑ̃riʃir] **I** *v.tr.* to enrich, fertilize *Souvent on changeait les récoltes de riz avec le pâturage de bêtes, et les récoltes de coton avec le maïs pour enrichir la terre.* Often they would alternate the rice crop with the pasturing of cows, and the cotton crop with the corn crop to enrich the land. (VM) **II s'enrichir** *v.pron.* **1** to enrich o.s. **2** to get rich, become wealthy <*Loc:* VM, Da84>

enrôlement [ɑ̃rolmɑ̃] *n.m.* enrollment, enlistment <*Loc:* Da84>

enrôler [ɑ̃role] **I** *v.tr.* to enroll, enlist **II s'enrôler** *v.pron.* to enroll o.s., enlist <*Loc:* Da84>

enroué, -e [ɑ̃rwe] *adj.* hoarse **Des fois quand il mouille ou quand il a ein vilain temps, Ma Tchou Flang et Ma Tchou Flette devient enroué de l'appeler, ça fait ça envoie Freddy derrière.* Sometimes when it rains or when there is bad weather, Ma Tchou Flang and Ma Tchou Flette get hoarse from calling him, so they send Freddy after him. (Wh83) <*Loc:* Da84, Wh83>

enrouer [ɑ̃rwe] **I** *v.tr.* to make hoarse *L'opération l'a enrouée.* The operation made her hoarse. (EV) **II s'enrouer** *v.pron.* to grow hoarse *Il s'est enroué en criant.* He got hoarse from yelling. (AV) <*Loc:* AV, EV, Da84>

enrouiller [ɑ̃ruje] **I** *v.tr.* to rust, cause to rust *C'est tout le sel dessus le chemin qui va enrouiller ton char là-bas dans le nord.* It's all the salt on the roads that will rust your car up there in the north. (LA) **II s'enrouiller** *v.pron.* to rust, become rusty *Si tu laisses ton bicycle dehors, ça va s'enrouiller.* If you leave your bicycle outside, it will become rusty. (LA) <*Loc:* LA, Da84>

enrouler [ɑ̃rule] **I** *v.tr.* to roll up, wind, coil *Enrouler la ficelle.* To wind up the string. (SL) **II s'enrouler** *v.pron.* to roll up, curl up *Le chaoui s'a enroulé dans un petit trou pour se cacher.* The raccoon rolled up into a little hole to hide. (EV) <*Loc:* EV, SL, TB, Da84>

enrhumer [ɑ̃ryme] **I** *v.tr.* to give a cold to *Va pas dehors habillé comme ça, ça va t'enrhumer.* Don't go outside dressed like that, it will give you a cold. (LA) **II s'enrhumer** *v.pron.* to catch a cold *Rentre ici-dans et sors de cette pluie. Tu vas t'enrhumer.* Come in here and get out of that rain. You're going to catch a cold. (VM) <*Loc:* LA, VM, Da84>

ensabler [ɑ̃sable] **I** *v.tr.* to sand up, cover with sand **II s'ensabler** *v.pron.* to sand up (as a well or stream), choke with sand <*Loc:* Da84>

ensachage [ɑ̃saʃaʒ] *n.m.* bagging, sacking <*Loc:* Da84>

ensacquer ♦see **ensaquer**

ensaquer (**ensacquer, ensaqueter**) [ɑ̃sake, ɑ̃sakte] *v.tr.* to put into a bag, bag up, sack up *Il a trié les patates et les a ensaquées.* He sorted out the potatoes and put them into bags. (Lv88) **J'ai ensaqueté l'maïs.* I bagged up the rice. (EV, Ph36) <*Loc:* AV, EV, IB, JD, LF, Da84, Gr86, Lv88, Ph36>

ensaqueter ♦see **ensaquer**

enseignant, -e [ɑ̃sɛ̃jɑ̃, -ɑ̃t] *n.* teacher, instructor <*Loc:* Da84>

enseigne [ɑ̃sɛ̃j, ɑ̃sɛ̃ɲ] *n.* sign **Les Anglais voulaient mettre des barrières autour d'beaucoup d'terre et i(ls) mettaient des enseignes: Passez pas ici!* The English wanted to put up fences around a lot of land, and they put up signs: No entry! (Gr86) <*Loc:* Gr86>

enseignement [ɑ̃sẽɲmɑ̃] *n.m.* teaching, education <***Loc:*** Da84>

enseigner [ɑ̃sẽje, ɑ̃sẽɲe] *v.tr.* to teach, instruct <***Loc:*** LF, Da84>

enseigneur [ɑ̃sẽjœr] *n.m.* teacher, instructor **Un p'tit Corsican qu'est v'nu comme enseigneur icite.* A little Corsican who came here as a teacher. (Gr86) <***Loc:*** Gr86>

ensemble[1] [ɑ̃sɑ̃m, ɑ̃sɑ̃b(l)] *adv.* together *Quand il les a vus ensemble, il était choqué au fiel.* When he saw them together, he was very angry. (LA) **On faisait [la moustiquaire] avec du brin qu'on coudait ensemble.* We made the mosquito net with gauze that we sewed together. (Gr82) *Je fais jaunir [...] la viande et je mets des oignons, des piments, des assaisonnements, et là je remets le riz cru, avec l'eau dedans, et, cuis tout ensemble.* [To make a jambalaya] I brown the meat, and I add onions, peppers, seasonings, and I add in the uncooked rice, with water in it, and cook everything together. (SL) ◊ **•se mettre ensemble** ***a*** to unite, associate **On va se mettre tous ensemble pour voter contre.* We are all going to unite to vote against it. (Gr82) ***b*** to gather, get together *Ils se mettent tous ensemble pour discuter comment faire.* They get together to discuss what to do. (Lv88) <AC, LA, SL, TB, An94, Gr82, Gu00, Lv88, Wh83> <***Loc:*** AC, AS, AV, EV, IB, JE, LA, LF, SB, SL, SM, TB, VM, An94, Da84, Gr82, Gu00, Hi02, La99, Lv88, Wh83>

ensemble[2] [ɑ̃sɑ̃m, ɑ̃sɑ̃b(l)] *n.m.* **1** set of clothing **2** suit <***Loc:*** Da84>

ensevelir [ɑ̃səvlir] *v.tr.* to lay out, prepare for burial *Je l'ai-z-enseveli dans une soucoupe, grand Dieu, quel homme, quel petit homme!* I prepared him for burial in a saucer, great God, what a tiny man! (VM, ch: *Quel petit homme*) *Tu vois, vous, votre belle-mère a eu une attaque de cœur, et elle est morte tout d'un coup et elle était ensevelie dans le cercueil et des chandelles allumées autour.* You see, sir, your mother-in-law had a heart attack, and she died suddenly and she was laid out in the coffin with candles lit all around. (EV) <***Loc:*** AC, EV, TB, VM, Da84>

ensevelissement [ɑ̃səvlismɑ̃] *n.m.* wake *Après l'ensevelissement, deux personnes enlevaient la paille du lit du mort et allaient la brûler près de la maison.* After the wake, two people took up the straw from the bed of the dead person and went to burn it near the house. (VM) <***Loc:*** VM>

ensilage [ɑ̃silaʒ] *n.m.* silage <***Loc:*** Da84>

ensouillure [ɑ̃sujyr] *n.f.* **1** mattress covering *Ça dérobait le maïs, et ça ramassait ça dans des sacs. Quand il y avait assez de pailles de maïs eux-autres coudait une ensouillure.* They shucked corn, and they gathered it up in bags. When there were enough cornshucks they sewed a mattress covering. (TB) **2** pillowcase, pillow covering *C'étaient des belles ensouillures d'oreiller qu'alle m'a données.* Those were lovely pillowcases that she gave me. (TB) <***Loc:*** JE, TB, Lv88>

ensuite [ɑ̃sɥit] *adv.* next, then, after that *Elle était la plus vieille, là son frère, ensuite elle, tu connais?* She [her sister] was the oldest, then her brother and then her, you know? (EV) ◊ **•d'ensuite** next, following *Et là l'année d'ensuite on a été piéger à l'Ile Félicité, on a eu dix sous la peau.* And then the next year we went trapping on Felicity Island, we got ten cents per skin. (TB) <TB> **•et ensuite?** what next? <VM> <***Loc:*** EV, TB, VM, Da84>

ensurance ♦see **assurance**

entailler [ɑ̃taje] *v.tr.* to cut, slash <***Loc:*** Da84>

entaller [ɑ̃tale] *v.intr.* to stool out, grow into a clump (of grass, etc.) *Le chiendent a entallé contre la barrière.* The sedge grass grew in clumps against the fence. (LA) <***Loc:*** LA, Da84>

entamer [ɑ̃tɑ̃me] **I** *v.tr.* to begin, start, undertake, launch *Je suis fier d'avoir entamé chez nous, il y a trois ans, la Fête Internationale Acadienne.* I am proud to have launched here, three years ago, the International Acadian Festival. (Lv88) *Entamer une chamaille.* To start an argument. (LA) **II** *v.intr.* to begin, start *Entamer de laver, de cuire.* To begin washing, to begin cooking (Lv88) <***Loc:*** LA, Da84, Lv88>

entassement [ɑ̃tasmɑ̃] *n.m.* heap, pile <***Loc:*** Da84>

entasser [ɑ̃tase] **I** *v.tr.* **1** to heap, pile up, pile together *Et ça se mettait à l'eau et eusse halait la seine et eusse faisait un cercle pour entasser les chevrettes pour les ramasser.* And they would get in the water and they pulled the seine and they made a circle to collect the shrimp to gather them up. (LF) **2** to gather, hoard (money) *Ça sort jamais. Ça reste à la maison, après compter l'argent qu'ils ont entassé.* They never go out. They just stay home counting the money they have hoarded. (LA) **II s'entasser** *v.pron.* to crowd together, pile up *Le fumier s'entassait jusqu'à proche deux pieds de haut dans le magasin durant l'hiver.* The manure would pile up to about two feet high in the barn during the winter. (LA) <***Loc:*** LA, LF, SL, Da84>

entendement [ɑ̃tɑ̃d(ə)mɑ̃] *n.m.* understanding <***Loc:*** Da84>

entendre ♦see **attendre**

entendu ♦see **attendu**

enterrement [ɑ̃tærmɑ̃] *n.m./f.* **1** funeral service, funeral procession *Je vais à l'église pour l'enterrement à pauvre Jacques.* I'm going to the church for poor Jack's funeral service. (SM) **2** burial, interment *Il est tellement oubliard, il va manquer son enterrement.* He is so forgetful, he'll miss his own burial. (LA) <***Loc:*** AC, LA, LF, SL, SM, VM, Da84, Hi02, Lv88>

enterrer [ɑ̃tere] **I** *v.tr.* to bury, inter **Là, un jour, Geneviève est morte. Et ils ont parti l'enterrer.* Then one day, Geneviève died. And they left to bury her. (IV, An94) **II s'enterrer** *v.pron.* **1** to be buried *Dans le vieux temps, le monde s'enterrait en haut de la terre.* In the old days, people were buried above ground. (LA) **2** to bury o.s. or each other <***Loc:*** AC, EV, IV, LA, VM, An94, Da84, Hi02>

entêté, -e [ãtete] *adj.* stubborn, obstinate, determined **Il y avait deux hommes dans le vieux temps qu'étaient riches, bien riches les deux, mais entêtés comme t'as jamais vu de ta vie.* There were two men in the old days who were rich, very rich both of them, but stubborn like you've never seen in your life. (LA, An94) ◊ **•entêté comme un mulet** stubborn as a mule <VM, La99> <***Loc:*** LA,VM, An94, Da84, La99, Lv88>

entêtement [ãtɛtmã] *n.m.* stubbornness, obstinacy, willfulness <***Loc:*** Da84>

entêter [ãtete] **I** *v.tr.* to give a headache to *Drès que j'entre dans une office de docteur l'odeur m'entête.* As soon as I walk into a doctor's office, the smell gives me a headache. (TB) **II s'entêter** *v.pron.* to become obstinate, be stubborn, persist, be determined *Il voulait juste pas aller et il s'a entêté.* He simply did not want to go and he became obstinate. (LA) <***Loc:*** LA, TB, Da84>

entiché, -e (**attiché, -e**) [ãtiʃe, atiʃe] *adj.* **1** infatuated **Il est entiché après elle.* He is infatuated with her. (Da84) **2** very fond (of) *Elle est très attichée de ce mâle.* She is very fond of that fellow. (JE) <***Loc:*** JE, Da84>

entichement [ãtiʃmã] *n.m.* infatuation <***Loc:*** Da84>

enticher (**atticher**) [ãtiʃe, atiʃe] **I** *v.tr.* to incite, provoke *Il est après enticher le chien.* He's provoking the dog. (Lv88) **II s'enticher** *v.pron.* **1** to become infatuated **2** to become greatly attached (to), be very fond (of) *Elle s'a attiché à lui.* She became very fond of him. (JE) <***Loc:*** JE, Da84, Lv88>

entier, -ière [ãtje, -jær] *adj.* whole, entire, full, complete *Ils ont ôté les tapis dans la maison entière.* They took out the carpet in the entire house. (LA) <***Loc:*** LA, TB, Da84>

entièrement (**entièrément**) [ãtjærmã, ãtjeremã] *adv.* wholly, entirely, fully, completely *Ça, c'est entièrément pas vrai.* That is wholly untrue. (LA) <***Loc:*** LA, Da84>

entonner [ãtɔ̃ne] **1** *v.tr.* to funnel, pour (liquid) using a funnel *Ça entonnait le whisky dans des demi-bouteilles.* They would pour the whiskey [by means of a funnel] into half-bottles. (SL) **2** to stuff (e.g. sausage) using a funnel *Entonner du boudin.* To stuff boudin. (EV) <***Loc:*** EV, SL, Da84>

entonnoir [ãtɔ̃nwar, ãtãnwar, etɔ̃nwar] *n.m.* funnel *Une boudinière, c'était un petit entonnoir exprès pour faire le boudin.* A "boudinière" was a little funnel especially for making boudin. (LF) <***Loc:*** IB, JE, LA, LF, VM, Da84>

entortillage [ãtɔrtijaʒ] *n.m.* **1** twisting, tangling **2** winding <***Loc:*** Da84>

entortiller [ãtɔrtije, etɔrtije] **I** *v.tr.* **1** to twist, tangle *Entortiller un câble.* To tangle a rope. (LA) **2** to wind **II s'entortiller** *v.pron.* **1** to get tangled up **2** to wrap o.s. around, coil *La serpent s'avait entortillé autour de ma jambe.* The snake had wrapped itself around my leg. (LA) <***Loc:*** IB, JD, LA, Da84>

entour[1] ♦see **alentour**

entour[2] ♦see **autour**

entourage [ãturaʒ] *n.m.* **1** surroundings, area *Il y avait des grands souris tout dans l'entourage.* There were big mice all over in the area. (EV, SM, ch: *Les tracas de Todd*) **2** *(often pl.)* neighborhood *Tout le monde dans les entourages ici s'appellent Créoles.* Everyone in this neighborhood calls themselves Creoles. (Lv88) *Il reste dans les entourages.* He lives in the neighborhood. (SM) **3** suite, retinue, entourage **4** wall *Le tableau est pendu sur l'entourage.* The picture is hanging on the wall. (SB) **5** fencing, fence **J'ai fait des entourages pou pas les vaches rentrent manger mon maïs.* I put up fences so the cows can't come in and eat my corn. (EV, Ph36) **6** enclosure, pen *Mets la vache dans l'entourage si tu veux pas qu'elle sorte.* Put the cow in the pen if you don't want her to get out. (IB) **7** banking (of crops) <***Loc:*** EV, IB, JE, LF, SB, SM, TB, VM, Da84, Lv88, Ph36>

entourer [ãture] **I** *v.tr.* **1** to surround *Ils ont proche fini d'entourer la maison avec le papier noir.* They've almost finished wrapping the house with a moisture barrier. (LA) **2** to fence in, erect a fence or barrier around, wall in, hem in *J'ai entouré ma cour.* I fenced in my yard. (VM) **3** to go around, pass around *Il a entouré la maison pour voir si vous autres étiont pas là.* He went around the house to see if you were there. (VM) **4** to bank (crops) **Il était après entourer la récolte. Il a arrêté dans le milieu des rangs et il a crié, "Whoa!"* He was banking his crop. He stopped in the middle of the rows and he yelled, "Whoa!" (LA, An94) **II s'entourer** *v.pron.* to surround o.s. (e.g. with bodyguards) *Il s'avait entouré de ses frères et ses cousins.* He had surrounded himself with his brothers and cousins. (LA) <***Loc:*** EV, LA, VM, An94, Da84, Ph36>

en-tout-cas (**en-cas**) [ãtuka, ãka] *n.* emergency provision, anything kept for an emergency *J'avais pas de FLASHLIGHT pour chercher pour mes en-tout-cas dans le TRUNK.* I didn't have a flashlight to look for my emergency stuff in the trunk. (LA) *On va aller à la grosserie acheter des en-tout-cas pour l'ouragan.* We're going to go to the grocery store to buy provisions for the hurricane. (VM) *T'as amené tes en-tout-cas?* Did you bring your emergency provisions? (VM) <***Loc:*** LA, SM, VM>

entrailles [ãtraj] *n.f.pl.* **1** womb *Jésus le Christ de vos entrailles est béni.* Jesus the Christ of your womb is blest. (TB) **2** guts, bowels <***Loc:*** TB, VM, Da84>

entrain[1] [ãtrɛ̃] *n.m.* start, beginning ◊ **•faire des entrains** to make preparations <Da84> **•faire un entrain** to make a start, make a beginning <Da84> <***Loc:*** Da84>

entrain[2] ♦see **train**

entraîner [ãtrɛ̃ne] *v.tr.* **1** to drag along, carry away *Il a eu pour entraîner son wagon jusqu'à la maison.* He had to drag his wagon up to his house. (LA) **2** to lead into evil, drag down *C'est le whisky qui l'a entraîné si bas.* It's whiskey that dragged him down so low. (LA) <***Loc:*** LA, Da84>

entraîneur [ɑ̃trɛ̃nœr] *n.m.* trainer *Un coup de cable aux hanches de la bête faisait comprendre le désir de l'entraîneur.* A flick of the switch on the animal's haunches made it understand what the trainer wanted. (Lv88) <***Loc:*** Lv88>

entrance [ɑ̃trɑ̃s] *n.f.* entrance, admittance (into a hospital) <***Loc:*** SJ>

entr'apercevoir [ɑ̃trapærsəvwar] *v.tr.* to glimpse, catch a glimpse of *Je l'ai juste entr'aperçu en dehors de la salle de danse.* I just caught a glimpse of him outside of the dance hall. (SL) <***Loc:*** SL, Da84>

entre [ɑ̃t(r)] *prep.* between, among **Ils avaient quarante sous dans leurs poches entre eux-autres deux.* They had forty cents in their pockets between the two of them. (SL, An94) *Il a eu pour adapter le morceau pour pouvoir le tourner dans la place entre la machine et le mur.* He had to adapt the piece to be able to turn it in the space between the motor and the wall. (LA) *Mais avec 210 livres de chevrettes vertes, de chevrettes fraîches, eux-autres sort avec entre 30 et 33 livres de chevrettes secs.* But with 210 pounds of raw shrimp, fresh shrimp, they end up with between 30 and 33 pounds of dried shrimp. (TB) ◊ **•entre nous** between us or ourselves *Entre nous, je crois pas qu'il va venir à soir.* Just between you and me, I don't think he's coming tonight. (LA) <LA, Da84> **•entre moi-même {toi-même, nous-mêmes, etc.}** to myself, yourself, ourselves, etc. *J'ai pensé entre moi-même quoi tu crois lui il est après faire?* I thought to myself, what do you think he's doing? (LA) <LA, TB, VM> <***Loc:*** AV, EV, IB, LA, LF, SL, SM, TB, VM, Da84, Hi02, La99>

entrée [ɑ̃tre] *n.f.* entry, entrance, admittance <***Loc:*** EV, Da84, Lv88>

entremariage [ɑ̃trəmarjaʒ] *n.m.* intermarriage <***Loc:*** SJ>

entremêler (s') [ɑ̃trəmele] *v.pron.* to mix, intermingle *Ça s'entremêlait pas beaucoup dans ces temps.* They didn't mix much in those days. (LA) <***Loc:*** LA, Da84>

entrement ♦see **autrement**

entremettre [ɑ̃trəmɛt(r)] *v.tr.* to put between <***Loc:*** Lv88>

entremis [ɑ̃trəmi] *prep.* among, amidst *Entremis ses amis, c'est Paul qu'il peut compter dessus le plus.* Among his friends, it's Paul he can count on the most. (LA) <***Loc:*** IB, LA, Lv88>

entreprendre [ɑ̃trəprɑ̃n, ɑ̃trəprɑ̃d(r)] **I** *v.tr.* to undertake, attempt, try *Je crois qu'il va entreprendre de pêcher des écrevisses cette année.* I think he is going to try crawfishing this year. (AC) **II s'entreprendre** *v.pron.* to be enterprising (in business matters) *Eux-autres avait un petit brin plus d'éducation qu'eux-autres avait avant, et ça connaissait s'entreprendre plein mieux pour faire le business et faire des autres affaires.* They had a little bit more education than they had before, and they knew how to go about things a lot better to conduct business and do other things. (TB) <***Loc:*** AC, TB, Da84>

entrepreneur [ɑ̃trəprənœr] *n.m.* promoter, entrepreneur <***Loc:*** Da84>

entreprise [ɑ̃trəpriz] *n.f.* enterprise, undertaking, effort, try <***Loc:*** Da84>

entrer [ɑ̃tre] *v.intr.* **1** to enter, go in *La vache a entré dans l'écurie.* The cow went into the stall. (LA) **2** to come in *Descendez! Entrez!* Get out of the car! Come in! (LA) <***Loc:*** AV, EV, LA, LF, VM, Da84, Lv88, Gr86>

entretenage [ɑ̃trətənaʒ] *n.f.* darning, mending (of clothing) *Je vas faire son entretenage avant que l'école commence.* I'll do his mending before school starts. (IB) <***Loc:*** IB>

entretenir [ɑ̃trət(ə)nir, ɑ̃tərt(ə)nir, ɑ̃tært(ə)nir] **I** *v.tr.* **1** to keep up, maintain *Alle entretient propre sa maison.* She keeps her house clean. (VM) *Elle avait une maison bien entretenue.* She had a well-kept house. (LA) **2** to harbor, entertain (ideas, thoughts) *Il entretient l'idée qu'alle va revenir.* He entertains the idea that she will return. (LA) **II s'entretenir** *v.pron.* to keep fit, take care of o.s. *Depuis sa femme est* GONE, *il s'entretient pus du tout.* Since his wife left, he doesn't take of himself at all anymore. (LA) <***Loc:*** LA, SM, VM, Da84>

entretenue [ɑ̃trətny] *n.f.* upkeep, maintenance *C'est moins d'entretenue comme ça.* It's less maintenance like that. (LF) <***Loc:*** LF>

entretien [ɑ̃trətjɛ̃] *n.m.* upkeep, maintenance <***Loc:*** Da84>

entretiennement [ɑ̃trətjɛ̃nmɑ̃] *n.m.* upkeep, maintenance <***Loc:*** SJ>

entreturage [ɑ̃trətyraʒ] *n.f.* darning, mending (of clothing) <***Loc:*** SJ>

entreturer [ɑ̃trətyre] *v.tr.* to darn, mend *Elle entreture ses bas.* She is darning her stockings. (SB) <***Loc:*** SB, SJ>

entrevoir [ɑ̃trəvwar] *v.tr.* to glimpse, catch a glimpse of *Je l'ai à peine entrevu avant qu'il a parti.* I barely caught a glimpse of him before he left. (LA) <***Loc:*** LA, Da84>

entrure [ɑ̃tryr] *n.f.* **1** entrance *Alle a fait son entrure quand il regardait pas.* She made her entrance when he wasn't looking. (VM) **2** depth to which a plow share penetrates the soil <***Loc:*** VM>

en-val-en-zèle [ɑ̃valɑ̃zɛl] *adv.* ◊ **•tomber en-val-en-zèle** to fall apart, become delapidated *La barrière est tombée en-val-en-zèle.* The fence fell apart. (TB) <TB> <***Loc:*** TB>

envalage (anvalage, avalage) [ɑ̃valaʒ] *n.m.* swallowing <***Loc:*** Da84>

envalement (anvalement, avalement) [ɑ̃valmɑ̃] *n.m.* swallowing <***Loc:*** Da84>

envaler (anvaler, avaler) [ɑ̃vale] **I** *v.tr.* **1** to swallow *Alle dit que Clopha peut manger des pêches à présent, il envale les noyaux et ça lui fait toujours pas du mal dans l'estomac.* She said that Clopha can eat peaches now, he swallows the pits and it still does not give him a stomachache. (AV) **2** to gulp down, throw down, eat quickly *Il a anvalé son dîner.* He gulped down his dinner. (SM) **II** *v.intr.* to swallow

N'anvale pas si vite. Do not swallow so quickly. (JE) **III s'envaler** *v.pron.* to be swallowed *Ces grosses pillules, ça s'envale mal.* Those big pills are difficult to swallow. (LA) <***Loc:*** AV, EV, IB, JE, LA, LF, SB, SM, TB, VM, Da84, Lv88>

envelimer [ɑ̃vlime] *v.tr.* **1** to irritate *Les herbes avont envelimé son bobo.* The weeds had irritated his injury. (VM) **2** to poison *Mon pauvre chat était tout envelimé.* My poor cat was all poisoned. (TB) <***Loc:*** SB, TB, VM>

enveloppe [ɑ̃vlɔp] *n.f.* **1** envelope **2** wrapper <***Loc:*** Da84>

enveloppement [ɑ̃vlɔpmɑ̃] *n.m.* wrapping, packaging <***Loc:*** Da84>

envelopper [ɑ̃vlope] **I** *v.tr.* to wrap, envelop, encase *Et puis là on aurait mis notre béquine. On l'aurait empaillé. Il l'aurait enveloppé avec du papier.* And then we would put our bacon. We would wrap it. He would wrap it in paper. (EV) *Elle avait une jambe enveloppée.* She had a leg wrapped up. (SL) **II s'envelopper** *v.pron.* to wrap o.s. up *Elle s'avait tout enveloppé dans les draps.* She had completely wrapped herself up in the sheets. (LA) <***Loc:*** EV, LA, SL, TB, Da84, Lv88>

envers[1] **(renvers)** [ɑ̃vær] *n.m.* reverse (side) *Même le renvers de cette étoffe est joli, je trouve.* Even the wrong side of this cloth is pretty, I find. (SB) ◊ **•à l'envers / à renvers *a*** inside out, on the wrong side **Mettre son linge à l'envers.* To put one's clothes on inside out. (Da84) *Sa robe est à renvers.* Her dress is inside out. (TB) ***b*** backwards *Il fait tout quelque chose à l'envers.* He does everything backwards. (SM) <SM, Da84> <***Loc:*** EV, IV, SB, SM, TB, VM, Da84>

envers[2] [ɑ̃vær] *prep.* towards, to **Viens envers moi.* Come towards me. (Da84) <***Loc:*** Da84>

envie [ɑ̃vi] *n.f.* desire, longing, wish **Envie de rire.* Urge to laugh. (Da84) ◊ **•avoir envie de** to wish, desire **Avoir envie de dormir, de rire, etc.* To desire to sleep, laugh, etc. (Da84) *Quand il a rentré dans la maison, elle dit, "Prospère, t'aurais pas envie d'une tasse de café?"* When he went into the house, she said, "Prospère, wouldn't you like a cup of coffee?" (EV) <EV, LA, VM, An77, An94, Da84, Gu82> <***Loc:*** AC, EV, LA, TB, VM, An77, An84, An94, Da84, Gu82, Hi02>

envier [ɑ̃vje] *v.tr.* to envy, begrudge <***Loc:*** Da84>

envieux, -euse [ɑ̃vjø, -jøz] *adj.* **1** jealous **2** envious <***Loc:*** Da84>

environ [ɑ̃virɔ̃, ɑ̃vijɔ̃] *adv.* about, nearly, near **Environ dix.* About ten. (Da84) <***Loc:*** Da84>

environs [ɑ̃vijɔ̃, ɑ̃virɔ̃] *n.m.pl.* **1** surroundings, vicinity **2** neighborhood <***Loc:*** SL, Da84>

envoler (s') [ɑ̃vole] *v.pron.* to fly away *Si je grouille, j'ai peur elle va s'envoler.* If I move, I'm afraid she [the owl] will fly away. (VM, ch: *Le son de la nuit*) <***Loc:*** VM, Da84, Gr86>

envoyage [ɑ̃wɔjaʒ] *n.m.* throw, toss **Le montant de pacanes premièrement envoyé est déterminé avant le jeu commence. Après le premier envoyage, le jeu continue avec chaque joueur après "tirer" des pacanes dans le trou.* The number of pecans initially tossed is determined before the game starts. After the first throw, the game continues with each player "shooting" pecans in the hole. (Wh83) <***Loc:*** Wh83>

envoyer [ɑ̃voje, ɑ̃waje, ɑ̃weje, voje] **I** *v.tr.* **1** to send, transmit **Il a fait une autre lettre pour envoyer au roi.* He prepared another letter to send to the king. (IV, An94) **2** to send off **On envoie pas un chien à la chasse à coups de baton.* One cannot force a dog to hunt. (Da84) **3** to throw, toss *T'envoyes la pelotte.* You throw the ball. (AV) **II s'envoyer** *v.pron.* to throw o.s. *La fille du roi, elle est venue, elle s'est envoyée dedans ses bras.* The king's daughter came, she threw herself into his arms. (EV) ◊ **•envoyer aux fèves** to go to prison <Lv88> **•envoyer chercher** to send for <Da84> **•envoyer dire** to send word *Il a envoyé dire à sa famille que la querelle avait pour finir.* He sent word to his family that the feuding had to stop. (LA) <LA, Da84> **•envoyer qqn à la promenade {à la merde}** to dismiss s.o. rudely, tell s.o. to go to hell *Madame Esta a pas voulu lui en vendre, ça fait il l'a envoyé à la promenade.* Madame Esta didn't want to sell him any, so he told her to go to hell. (LA) <LA, Da84> **•envoyer se cacher / envoyer se faire foutre** to tell s.o. to go to hell <Da84> <***Loc:*** AC, AV, EV, IB, IV, LA, LF, SB, SL, SM, TB, VM, An94, Da84, Hi02, Wh83>

éoù ♦see **ayoù**

épaillage [epajaʒ] *n.m.* **1** scattering, dispersal, spreading **2** disorder, mess *C'était un épaillage quand j'ai rentré.* It was a mess when I came back in. (IB) <***Loc:*** IB, LA, Da84, Lv88>

épaillé, -e [epaje] *adj.* **1** scattered, dispersed *Ses bébelles étaient épaillées partout dans la maison.* His toys were scattered all over the house. (LA) **2** disheveled *Ses cheveux sont tout épaillés.* Her hair is all disheveled. (SM) <***Loc:*** JE, LA, SM, VM, Gu00>

épailler (pailler) [epaje, paje] **I** *v.tr.* **1** to spread *Il a épaillé la nouvelle dans la ville.* He spread the news in the town. (Lv88) **2** to spread out **3** to scatter, disperse *Les petits enfants ont tout épaillé les papiers.* The little children scattered the papers. (SM) *Les clos d'huile épaillés tout partout dans le sud-ouest de la Louisiane.* Oil fields scattered all over southwest Louisiana. (Lv88) **II** *v.intr.* to scatter, disperse *Quand les lapins nous ont vus, ils ont paillé.* When the rabbits saw us, they scattered. (SM) **Boy, quand ça voyait les détectifs, les Revenues, God dog, ça épaillait partout.* Boy, when they saw the detectives, the Revenuers, God dog, they would scatter everywhere. (SL, An94) **III s'épailler** *v.pron.* **1** to spread **Le feu va s'épailler.* The fire will spread. (Da84) **Ça a pas été dix minutes avant les* *rumeurs ont commencé à s'épailler.* It wasn't ten minutes before the rumors started to spread. (Gr86) **2** to scatter, disperse <***Loc:*** AV, EV, IB, LA, LF, SB, SJ, SL, SM, TB, VM, An94, Da84, Gr86, Lv88, Ph36>

épais, -sse [epɛ, epe, epɛs] *adj.* thick, dense *Tu peux pas trouver du cypre de cette épaisseur, ça c'est à peu près le plus épais que tu vas trouver ça.* You can't find cypress wood of that thickness, this is about the thickest you can find it. (LF) *La population dans l'orphelinat était épaisse.* The orphanage was densely populated. (AV) <***Loc:*** AC, AV, EV, JE, LF, SL, TB, VM, Da84>

épaisseur [epesœr] *n.f.* thickness, density <***Loc:*** LF, Da84>

épaissir [epesir] **I** *v.tr.* to thicken *On va laisser la sauce tarir. Ça va l'épaissir.* We'll let the sauce cook down. That'll thicken it. (VM) *Ma grand-mère mettait pas de roux dans son gombo. Elle l'épaississait avec du filé.* My grandmother didn't make her gumbo with a roux. She thickened it with filé. (VM) **II s'épaissir** *v.pron..* to become thicker, become denser *Là tu cuis ça pour à peu près quinze minutes et ça devrait commencer à s'épaissir.* Then you cook that for about fifteen minutes and it should start to thicken. (LA) <***Loc:*** LA, VM, Da84>

épaississement [epesismɑ̃] *n.m.* thickening <***Loc:*** Da84>

éparant [eparɑ̃] *n.m.* clothesline <***Loc:*** VM>

éparer [epare] **I** *v.tr.* **1** to spread out *J'ai éparé mes pistaches dessus une toile au soleil pour les chesser.* I spread my peanuts out on a canvas in the sun to dry them. (VM) **2** to hang out (laundry) to dry *Ça a mouillé après j'ai éparé mon linge.* It rained after I hung out my laundry to dry. (VM) *Éparer du linge sur la corde.* To hang out clothes on the line. (VM) **3** to scatter, disperse *Ma famille est tout éparée dans tout le pays.* My family is scattered all over the country. (SL) **II s'éparer** *v.pron.* to spread *La nouvelle s'épare.* The news is spreading. (VM) <***Loc:*** JD, SL, VM, Da84, Gu00>

épargner [eparɲe] **I** *v.tr.* to save, spare, conserve, economize **II s'épargner** *v.pron.* to save o.s. (trouble, expense, etc.) <***Loc:*** Da84>

éparpillage [eparpijaʒ] *n.m.* **1** scattering, dispersal **2** jumble, mess, disorder *Les livres dans sa chambre était un seul éparpillage.* The books in his room were a big jumble. (AV) <***Loc:*** AV, SB, SJ, Da84>

éparpiller [eparpije] **I** *v.tr.* to scatter, disperse *L'ouragan a éparpillé des feuilles et des branches tout partout.* The hurricane scattered leaves and branches everywhere. (LA) **II** *v.intr.* to spread *Laisse ton cher amour éparpiller.* Let your sweet love spread. (LA, ch) <***Loc:*** LA, Da84>

épaule [epol] *n.f.* shoulder ◊ **•mettre l'épaule à la roue** to get to work, 'put one's shoulder to the grindstone' *Si on veut finir aujourd'hui il faudra mettre l'épaule à la roue.* If we want to finish today, we need to put our shoulder to the grindstone. (EV) <EV, La99> <***Loc:*** AV, EV, IB, JE, LA, TB, VM, Da84, Hi02, La99, Lv88>

épauler [epole] *v.tr.* **1** to shoulder **Épauler un sac de riz.* To shoulder a sack of rice. (Da84) **2** to strike with one's shoulder *J'ai épaulé mon cousin, mais c'était pas par exprès.* I hit my cousin with my shoulder, but it wasn't on purpose. (AV) <***Loc:*** AV, Da84>

épaulette [epolɛt] *n.f.* **1** shoulder strap, shoulder trim **2** shoulder seam <***Loc:*** SL, Da84>

épaulière [epoljær] *n.f.* shoulder (of a garment) *L'épaulière de la chemise est déchirée.* The shoulder of the shirt is torn. (TB) <***Loc:*** IB, TB>

épelage [eplaʒ] *n.f.* spelling <***Loc:*** Da84>

épeler ♦see **espeler**

épelon ♦see **éperon**

épelure (éplure) [eplyr] *n.f.* **1** peel, peeling, paring *J'aime les épelures d'oranges.* I like orange peels. (SM) **2** shell, husk, hull *Oter l'épelure d'einne noisette.* To shell a hazelnut. (VM) <***Loc:*** AV, IB, LA, SJ, SM, VM, Lv88, Re31>

épelurer (éplurer) [eplyre] *v.tr.* **1** to peel *On éplure notres pommes de terre.* We peel our potatoes. (VM) **2** to shell *Éplurer des pois.* To shell peas. (VM) <***Loc:*** VM, Lv88>

éperon (épelon) [eprɔ̃, eplɔ̃] *n.m.* **1** spur (of a horseman) *J'attrape mon cable et mes éperons, pour moi aller voir à mes bêtes.* I grab my rope and my spurs to go see about my cattle. (ch: *La valse du vacher*) **2** spur (of a rooster) **3** spur (used in cockfighting) *Et ça enfilait les éperons sur les corusses pour se battre, et le dernier corusse en vie c'est lui qui gagnait.* And they strapped spurs on the roosters for fighting, and the last rooster alive was the winner. (LF) **4** bunion <***Loc:*** EV, LA, LF, SL, SM, VM, Da84, Hi02>

éperonner [eprɔ̃ne] *v.tr.* to spur *Eperonner un cheval.* To spur a horse. (VM) *Quand le gaime rouge a éperonné le noir dans le cou, ça l'a tué raide.* When the red rooster spurred the black one in the neck, it killed it on the spot. (LA) <***Loc:*** LA, VM, Da84>

épervier (éprevier, épreuvier) [epærvije, eprəvje, eprevje, eprivje] *n.m.* **1** sparrow hawk **2** cast-net, small cast-net *Et là en été dans le temps de les saisons de chevrette il faisait sa vie à pogner les chevrettes avec un épreuvier.* And then in the summer, during shrimp season, he made a living catching shrimp with a castnet. (TB) <***Loc:*** JE, TB, VM, Da84, Hi02, Re31>

épeurer [epøre] *v.tr.* to frighten *Tu m'as épeuré avec ce masque!* You scared me with that mask! (EV) <***Loc:*** EV, Da84>

épi [epi] *n.m.* **1** ear (of any cereal, esp. corn) **2** corn cob ◊ **•épi de maïs** ear of corn <EV, SL, An94, Da84> <***Loc:*** AL, CL, EV, Sl, An94, Da84>

épiauler [epjole] *v.tr.* to beat, whip *Il a épiaulé l'enfant.* He beat the child. (LF) <***Loc:*** LF>

épidémie [epidɛ̃mi, epidimi] *n.f.* epidemic <***Loc:*** AC, SB, SJ, VM, Da84>

épinard [epinar, ɛspinard] *n.m.* spinach <***Loc:*** TB, Da84>

épine [epin, epiŋ] *n.f.* **1** thorn, spine **2** splinter **3** backbone <***Loc:*** SM, Da84>

épineux, -euse [epinø, -øz] *adj.* thorny, prickly, spiny <***Loc:*** Da84>

épingle [epɛ̃j, epɛ̃g(l)] *n.f.* pin ◊ **•épingle à cheveux** hair pin <Da84> **•épingle à couche** safety pin, diaper pin <IB, LA, LF, SM, Da84> **•épingle à linge** ***a*** clothespin, clothes peg ***b*** safety pin, diaper pin <AL, IB, JD, LA, SL, SM, TB, Da84, Re31> **•épingle double** safety pin, diaper pin <Da84> **•épingle droite** straight pin <Da84> **•être sur les épingles** to be excited, be on pins and needles <AC, JE, La99> **•on peut pas y mettre une épingle** there is no more room, the space in question is very crowded <La99> <***Loc:*** AC, AL, IB, JD, JE, LA, LF, SB, SL, SM, TB, Da84, La99, Re31>

épinglette [epɛ̃glɛt, epɛ̃ɲlet] *n.f.* **1** brooch, stick pin **2** tie pin <***Loc:*** EV, LA, LF, SM, VM, Da84, Lv88, Ph36>

épiochon [epjoʃɔ̃] *n.m.* **1** stunted ear of corn **2** runt, undersized person <***Loc:*** JD, LF, TB, VM, Da84, Lv88>

épique [epik] *n.f.* **1** thorn **2** pin <***Loc:*** VM>

épis ♦see **puis**

épisode [epizɔd] *n.f.* episode, happening, event <***Loc:*** Da84>

épitre [epit(r)] *n.f.* epistle, letter <***Loc:*** Da84>

épivardé, -e (pivardé, -e) [epivarde, pivarde] *adj.* **1** flustered **2** stunned, panic-stricken, overwhelmed with fright *Il va pour ramasser un œuf. Il y a une serpent dans le nique et il sort tout épivardé.* He goes to pick up an egg. There's a snake in the nest and he comes out all shook up. (SL) <***Loc:*** SL, Lv88>

épivarder[1] **(pivarder)** [epivarde, pivarde] *v.tr.* to frighten, frighten away *Va épivarder les poules.* Go scare away the chickens. (Lv88) <***Loc:*** JD, LA, Lv88>

épivarder[2] **(s')** [epivarde] *v.pron.* to groom feathers with the beak (of a bird) *Les poules étaient après s'épivarder dans la cour après la pluie.* The chickens were cleaning themselves in the yard after the rain. (LA) <***Loc:*** LA, Lv88>

épluchage [eplyʃaʒ] *n.f.* act of peeling (fruit, etc.) <***Loc:*** Da84>

épluche [eplyʃ] *n.f.* **1** peeling, skin (of a fruit or vegetable) *Le chien mange les épluches de pommes.* The dog eats apple peels. (SM) **2** peel, peeling (of shrimp) *Là les femmes passent en travers encore pour voir s'il y a peut-être des drigailles, ou les épluches, et après ça ils sont pesés sur la balance.* Then the women go through them again to see if there may be some refuse, or peelings, and after that they're weighed on a scale. (LF) <***Loc:*** AC, EV, LA, LF, SB, SM, TB, VM, Da84, Lv88, Ph36>

éplucher (plucher) [eplyʃe, plyʃe] **I** *v.tr.* to peel *Épluchez les pommes de terre.* Peel the potatoes. (IB) *On épluche les chevrettes avec des machines.* We peel the shrimp with machines. (LF) **II s'éplucher** *v.pron.* to be peeled **L'orange s'épluche bien.* The orange peels easily. (Da84) <***Loc:*** EV, IB, LA, LF, SL, SM, TB, VM, Da84, Ph36>

éplumer [eplyme] *v.tr.* **1** to pluck, take the feathers off of *Elle a éplumé la poule.* She plucked the hen. (AV) **2** to rob *On a éplumé Jean.* John was robbed. (IB) <***Loc:*** AV, IB, SB, SJ>

éplure ♦see **épelure**

éplurer ♦see **épelurer**

épointer[1] [epwɑ̃te] (*p.p.* **épointu** [epwɛ̃ty], **épointé** [epwɛ̃te]) *v.tr.* to sharpen, put a point on *Épointer un poteau* To carve a point on the end of a post. (AV) <***Loc:*** AV>

épointer[2] [epwɑ̃te] *v.tr.* to break off a point **Épointer un crayon.* To break the point on a pencil. (Da84) <***Loc:*** Da84>

époitriné, -e [epwatrine] *adj.* suffering from tuberculosis or deep chest congestion *Un enfant époitriné.* A deeply congested child. (EV) <***Loc:*** EV, Lv88>

éponge [epɔ̃ʒ] *n.f.* sponge <***Loc:*** Da84>

éponger [epɔ̃ʒe] *v.tr.* **1** to sponge off, clean, wash *Prends un linge pour éponger l'eau qu'a fouetté sous la porte.* Get a rag to wipe up the water that swept up under the door. (VM) **2** to let rise (of dough) *Éponger une pâte de pain.* To let bread dough rise. (AV) **3** to fluff, plump *Éponger un oreiller.* To fluff a pillow. (AV) <***Loc:*** AV, VM, Da84>

époque [epɔk] *n.f.* era, epoch, period <***Loc:*** LA, An84, Da84>

épouiller [epuje] *v.tr.* **I** to remove lice from *Un macaque après épouiller l'autre macaque et il mange les petits poux.* One monkey is removing lice from the other monkey and he eats the little lice. (AV) **II s'épouiller** *v.pron.* to groom feathers with the beak (of birds) *Le zozo s'épouille.* The bird is cleaning its feathers with its beak. (VM) <***Loc:*** AV, TB, VM>

épouse ♦see **époux**

épouser [epuze] **I** *v.tr.* to marry, wed *C'était trouver ma bien-aimée qui sortait d'être épousée.* It was a matter of finding my beloved who had just gotten married. (IB, ch: *La veuve de sept ans*) **II s'épouser** *v.pron.* to get married, marry each other <***Loc:*** IB, Da84>

époussetage [epustaʒ] *n.m.* dusting <***Loc:*** Da84>

épousseter (épouster) [epuste] *v.tr.* to dust *Va épousseter les tablettes.* Go dust the shelves. (SL) **II s'épousseter** *v.pron.* to dust o.s. off *Il s'a ramassé et il s'a épousseté. He* got himself up and he dusted himself off. (LA) <***Loc:*** LA, SL, Da84>

époussetoir (époussoir) [epustwar, epuswar] *n.m.* **1** feather duster *Il s'est servi d'un époussetoir pour épousseter les meubles.* He used a feather duster to dust the furniture. (SB) **2** dustrag <***Loc:*** AV, IB, LA, SB, SJ, SM, VM, Lv88>

époussier ♦see **époussiérer**

époussiérer (époussier) [epusjere, epusje] **I** *v.tr.* to dust, remove dust from **II s'époussiérer** *v.pron.* to dust oneself off **Le soûlard s'est bien époussié et puis, avec l'aide de deux autres cavaliers, a remonté sa bétaille tout à moitié éreinté.* The drunk dusted himself off, then with the help of two other riders he got back on his animal half exhausted. (Gr86) <*Loc:* Gr86>

époussoir ♦see **époussetoir**

épouster ♦see **épousseter**

époustron [epustrɔ̃, epustɔ̃] *n.m.* duster (formerly made of turkey feathers) <*Loc:* JD, Da84>

épouvantable [epuvɑ̃tab(l)] *adj.* frightening, horrible, terrible *Une affaire épouvantable.* A frightening thing. (EV) <*Loc:* EV, Da84>

épouvantail [epuvɑ̃taj] *n.m.* scarecrow <*Loc:* Da84>

épouvantaille [epuvɑ̃taj] *n.f.* **1** fright, terror **Il y a eu une épouvantaille.* There was a terrifying episode. (Da84) **2** scarecrow <*Loc:* Da84>

épouvanté, -e [epuvɑ̃te] *adj.* **1** frightened, terrified *Tu parles d'une femme épouvantée après l'orage.* Talk about a frightened woman after the storm. (LA) **2** flustered, overexcited *Cette vieille femme est tout le temps épouvantée pour quelque chose.* That old lady is always flustered about something. (SL) <*Loc:* LA, SL, VM, Da84>

épouvante [epuvɑ̃t] *n.f.* fright, terror, fear <*Loc:* Da84>

épouvanter [epuvɑ̃te] **I** *v.tr.* to frighten, scare, scare off *Va épouvanter les oiseaux dans le jardin.* Go scare away the birds in the garden. (VM) **II s'épouvanter** *v.pron.* **1** to become frightened *Il s'a épouvanté; il s'a sauvé.* He got scared; he ran away. (LA) **2** to get flustered, get emotionally worked up *J'ai pas dit grand'chose, mais il s'est épouvanté quand-même.* I hardly said anything, but he got all worked up anyway. (SL) <*Loc:* LA, SL, VM, Da84>

époux, épouse [epu, epuz] *n.* **1** *(m.)* husband, bridegroom, spouse **2** *(f.)* wife, bride, spouse <*Loc:* Da84>

épreuve [eprœv] *n.f.* test, proof, trial *Mon frère est damné. Y a rien à son épreuve.* My brother is so full of mischief, there is nothing he won't do. (VM) ◊ **•avoir rien à son épreuve** ***a*** to have no match, have no equal ***b*** to have nothing one would not do *Il a rien à son épreuve.* There's nothing he wouldn't do. (LF) <LF, Da84> **•faire épreuve** to try out, test *Elle a fait son épreuve avec le gombo.* She tried out the gumbo [recipe]. (SL) <SL, Da84> **•mettre à l'épreuve** to put to the test, test the limits of *Ils ont mis la vieille machine à l'épreuve.* They put the old tractor to the test. (SL) *J'y ai dit de le faire et je l'ai mis à l'épreuve.* I told him to do it and I put him to the test. (VM) <SL, VM, Da84> <*Loc:* EV, LA, LF, SL, VM, Da84>

éprevier, épreuvier ♦see **épervier**

éprouver [epruve] *v.tr.* to test, try, try out *Le tracas qu'il a eu avec sa famille l'a beaucoup éprouvé.* His family troubles really tested him. (VM) <*Loc:* VM, Da84>

épuis ♦see **puis**

épurer [epyre] *v.tr.* **1** to squeeze juice from by crushing or pressing *On a tout épuré les mûres pour en faire une poutine.* We crushed all the blackberries to make a bread pudding. (TB) *Elle épure le limon.* She squeezes the lemon. (IB) **2** to smash, crush *Je l'ai trouvé épuré dans le chemin.* I found it crushed in the road. (SB) **3** to beat violently <*Loc:* IB, LF, SB, SJ, TB>

équand ♦see **quand**

équarrer (**équarrir, équerrer**) [ekare, ekarir, ekere] *v.tr.* to square, make square *Il va équarrer la fondation.* He's going to square the foundation. (AV) <*Loc:* AV, SL, Da84>

équarrir ♦see **équarrer**

équé, équel ♦see **quel**

équerre [ekær] *n.f.* **1** carpenter's square *T'avais une grande équerre de deux pieds.* You had a big two-foot carpenter's square. (SL) **2** right angle (in a road or a piece of land) **Le chemin fait une équerre.* The road makes a right angle. (Da84) <*Loc:* EV, LA, SL, SM, Da84>

équerrer ♦see **équarrer**

équilibre [ekilib(r)] *n.m.* equilibrium, balance <*Loc:* SM, TB, Da84, La99>

équipage [ekipaʒ] *n.m.* **1** equipment, implements, gear **2** battery of pots and boilers used in processing sugar <*Loc:* JE, VM, Da84, Di32>

équipement [ekipmɑ̃] *n.m.* equipment, implements, gear <*Loc:* Da84>

équiper [ekipe] *v.tr.* to equip, outfit *Ils sont bien équipés pour arranger votre char.* They are well equipped to repair your car. (EV) <*Loc:* EV, Da84>

equipollence [ekipolɑ̃s] *n.f.* equivalence <*Loc:* Da84>

érable [erab(l)] *n.m.* maple <*Loc:* CL>

éraillé, -e [eraje] *adj.* **1** ripped **2** unraveled *Son bas de robe était éraillé.* The hem of her dress was unravelled. (SL) **3** tired, worn out, sore *Je suis tout éraillé après ma journée.* I am worn out after my day. (LA) <*Loc:* EV, LA, SL, Lv88, Ph36>

érailler [eraje] *v.tr.* **1** to rip, run (e.g. hosiery) *Elle a éraillé son bas.* She ripped her stocking. (SL) **2** to unravel <*Loc:* SL, Lv88>

érection [erɛksjɔ̃] *n.f.* erection, construction <*Loc:* Da84>

éreinté, -e [erɛ̃te] *adj.* tired out, exhausted *Il a travaillé assez dur qu'il était tout éreinté.* He worked so hard that he was exhausted. (VM) **Le soûlard s'est bien époussié et puis, avec l'aide de deux autres cavaliers, a remonté sa bétaille tout à moitié éreinté.* The drunk dusted himself off, then with the help of two other riders he got back on his animal half exhausted. (Gr86) <*Loc:* VM, Da84, Gr86>

éreinter [erɛ̃te] **I** *v.tr.* **1** to work to excess, tire out *Piocher dans le soleil comme ça c'est après m'éreinter.* Hoeing in the sun like that is killing me. (EV) **2** to break the back of **II s'éreinter** *v.pron.* **1** to work o.s. to excess **2** to hurt or break one's back *Il a tombé par terre et il s'est éreinté.* He fell down and hurt his back. (SL) <*Loc:* EV, SL, VM, Da84>

érésipèle (**erésipère, résipère, résipére, résypère**) [rezipel, erezipær, rezipær, rezypær] *n.m.* erysipelas, Saint Anthony's fire <*Loc:* JD, SM, TB, VM, Da84, Guoo, Lv88>

erésipère ♦see **érésipèle**

erganeau ♦see **organeau**

ergot (**argot**) [ærgo, argo] *n.m./f.* **1** spur (of a rooster), claw (of fowl) *Coupe les argots à ce coq.* Cut the spurs off that rooster. (JE) **2** claw *Le garçon m'a égratigné avec ses grands argots.* The boy scratched me with his big claws. (SB) **3** foot **Ote tes ergots d'là.* Remove your feet from there. (EV, Ph36) **4** hoof **5** derisive term applied to a person <***Loc:*** AV, EV, IB, JE, SB, SM, TB, Da84, La99, Lv88, Ph36>

ergricher ♦see **regricher**

erien ♦see **rien**

éridisseuse [eridisøz] *n.f.* wire stretcher <***Loc:*** Gr86>

érifler [erifle] *v.tr.* to scratch, nick *Il a ériflé mon char.* He scratched my car. (Lv88) *Je m'ai ériflé un morceau de peau.* I nicked a piece of my skin. (VM) <***Loc:*** TB, VM, Lv88>

ériflure [eriflyr] *n.f.* scratch, slight scratch *Cette ériflure est après venir mauvais.* That scratch is getting bad. (TB) <***Loc:*** TB>

ériger [eriʒe] *v.tr.* to erect, build, construct *Ils ont érigé la maison en peu de temps.* They built the house in no time. (SL) <***Loc:*** SL, Da84>

ermite (**hermitte**) [ærmit] *n.m.* hermit <***Loc:*** Da84>

érober (**dérober**) [erobe, derobe] *v.tr.* to shuck, shell *Le maïs était plein de vers quand je l'ai dérobé.* The corn was full of worms when I shucked it. (VM) <***Loc:*** VM, Da84, Lv88>

éronce (**aronce, ronce, erronce**) [erɔ̃s] *n.f. (occ. m.)* **1** bramble, briar, prickle bush, sticker bush *Il l'a fouillé dans les éronces.* He threw him in the sticker bushes. (SL) **2** blackberry bush <***Loc:*** AV, IB, LA, LF, SB, SL, SM, TB, VM, An94, Da84, Gu00, Hi02, Lv88, Re31>

éroncer [erɔ̃se] **I** *v.tr.* to pull brambles from *On a éroncé la levée de canal.* We pulled brambles from the canal levee. (VM) **II s'éroncer** *v.pron.* to get covered with brambles or stickers *Il a été à travers la talle d'éronces et il s'est tout éroncé.* He crossed the bramble bushes and he got covered with brambles. (SL) <***Loc:*** SL, VM, Lv88>

érosion [erozjɔ̃] *n.f.* erosion <***Loc:*** Da84>

errant, -e [erɑ̃, -t] *adj.* wandering, roving, vagrant **Juif errant, c'était un homme riche dans le temps que notre Bon Dieu était sur la terre.* Wandering Jew was a rich man in the time that our Good Lord was on the Earth. (SL, An94) <***Loc:*** SL, An94, Da84>

erreur [erœr] *n.f.* error, mistake *Les étrangers, quand tu fais une erreur eusse connaît pas tes histoires.* Strangers, when you make a mistake, they don't know your stories. (TB) ◊ •**en erreur** mistaken, in error *Il croyait bien faire mais il était en erreur.* He thought he was doing the right thing, but he was mistaken. (LA) <LA, Da84> <***Loc:*** EV, IB, LA, TB, VM, Da84, Gu82, Hi02>

errière ♦see **arrière**

erronce ♦see **éronce**

érussir ♦see **réussir**

escabeau [eskabo] *n.m.* ladder <***Loc:*** SM>

escabie [eskabi] *n.f.* chair (of any kind) <***Loc:*** IB>

escabreux [əskabrø] *adj.* weak, flimsy *C'est joliment escabreux.* [That tree branch] it's really flimsy. (TB) <***Loc:*** TB>

escalier [eskalje] *n.m.* **1** *(often pl.)* steps, stairs, staircase **2** step (of a staircase) *Y avait six escaliers à monter.* There were six stairs to climb. (TB) <***Loc:*** EV, LA, LF, SL, SM, TB Da84, Hi02>

escalin [eskalɛ̃] *n.m.* bit, 12-1/2 cent coin ◊ •**les quatre escalins** soreness from horseback riding <LF> •**six escalins** seventy-five cents *Cinq piastres et six escalins.* Five dollars and seventy-five cents. (Lv88) <Lv88> <***Loc:*** AV, EV, IB, LF, SL, SM, VM, Da84, Hi02, Lv88, Re31>

escamoter [eskɑ̃mote] *v.tr.* to damage, cripple *Il a escamoté mon arbre avec son char.* He damaged my tree with his car. (VM) <***Loc:*** VM, Da84>

escandale ♦see **scandale**

escapade [eskapad] *n.f.* escapade, prank, lark <***Loc:*** Da84>

escaper (s') [eskape] *v.pron.* to escape *Mais le Bon Dieu a voulu qu'eusse a couru à la péniche et ça c'est ça qu'eusse s'a escapé dedans.* But the Good Lord wanted them to run to the boat and that's what they escaped in. (LF) <***Loc:*** LF, TB>

escargot [eskargo] *n.m.* snail <***Loc:*** Da84>

esclavage [esklavaʒ] *n.m.* slavery, bondage <***Loc:*** EV, VM, Da84, Hi02>

esclave [esklav] *n.m.* slave *Les récolteurs était du monde pauvre, eusse pouvait pas avoir des esclaves.* The farmers were poor people, they couldn't keep slaves. (LF) <***Loc:*** LF, SM, VM, Da84, Hi02>

esclopé, -e [esklope] *adj.* **1** suffering, infirm *Seigneur, je suis tout esclopée.* God, I'm suffering. (VM) **2** crippled <***Loc:*** TB, VM>

escloper [esklope] *v.tr.* to cripple <***Loc:*** SJ>

escolter [eskolte] *v.tr.* to get hold of, get one's hands on (s.o. with whom one has a difference to settle) *Si je peux l'escolter, je vas le taper.* If I can get hold of him, I'll hit him. (LF) <***Loc:*** LF>

escorbut (**escourbut**) [eskɔrby, eskurby] *n.m.* **1** scurvy **2** pyorrhea (inflammation of the gum and tooth sockets that leads to loosening of the teeth) <***Loc:*** LF, SL, VM>

escouer ♦see **secouer**

escourbut ♦see **escorbut**

escousse ♦see **secousse**

escouvillon [eskuvijɔ̃] *n.m.* crackbrained person *Espèce d'escouvillon!* You crackbrain! (VM) <***Loc:*** VM>

escrampé, -e [eskrɑ̃pe] *adj.* wobbly **Il y a rien plus dégoûtant que voir une jolie fille ou une belle femme qui marche tout escrampée, tout manière à la façon d'une vache.* There's nothing more disgusting than to see a pretty girl or a beautiful woman who walks all wobbly, just like a cow. (Gr86) <*Loc:* Gr86>

escran (escron, escrant) [eskrɑ̃, eskrɔ̃] *adj.* **1** sick, hurting, suffering, having stiff or sore muscles or joints **Y'a des vieux Acadiens, i(ls) arrivent tout escrans avec des bâtons.* There are old Acadians, they arrive with sore muscles and walking with canes. (Gr82) **2** crippled, lame, disabled *L'homme ça-là est escran.* That man is crippled. (SM) <*Loc:* IB, SM, VM, Gr82, Lv88>

escrant ♦see **escran**

escricité ♦see **électricité**

escrimer[1] [eskrime] **I** *v.tr.* to overwork *Escrimer une femme au travail.* To work a woman to death. (SJ) **II s'escrimer** *v.pron.* to overwork o.s., wear o.s. out *Ils vont s'escrimer à jouer à la pelote.* They're going to wear themselves out playing baseball. (AV) <*Loc:* AV, LF, SJ>

escrimer[2] [eskrime] **I** *v.intr.* to shout very loudly *Elle escrime sur l'enfant.* She's screaming at the child at the top of her voice. (IB) **II s'escrimer** *v.pron.* to shout very loudly *Je m'ai escrimé, ils m'ont pas attendu.* I shouted as loud as I could, but they didn't hear me. (Lv88) <*Loc:* IB, LF, Lv88>

escron ♦see **escran**

espace [espas] *n.m.* **1** space, room **2** gap, space <*Loc:* LF, Da84>

espacer [espase] *v.tr.* to space, leave room between, leave space between *Espacer les poteaux de barrière.* To space the fence posts. (VM) <*Loc:* VM, Da84>

espadron [espadrɔ̃] *n.m.* **1** sawfish **2** swordfish <*Loc:* LF, TB>

Espagne[1] [espɑ̃j] *n.* Spaniard, Spanish person <*Loc:* LF>

Espagne[2] [espɑ̃j, lespɑ̃j] *n.f.* Spain <*Loc:* AV, LF, SL, Hi02>

espagnol[1]**, -e** [espɑ̃jɔl, spɑ̃jol] *adj.* Spanish *Un certain temps la Louisiane était espagnole, et on avait beaucoup des Indiens ici, et alors il y a des certains mots qui vient de l'Espagne.* At a certain period Louisiana was Spanish, and there were lots of Indians here, and so there are some certain words that come from Spain. (SL) <*Loc:* SL, VM, Hi02>

espagnol[2] [espɑ̃jɔl] *n.m.* Spanish, the Spanish language <*Loc:* Hi02>

Espagnol[3]**, -e** [espɑ̃jɔl] *n.* Spaniard, Spanish person <*Loc:* LF, SM, Hi02>

espèce [espɛs] *n.f.* **1** kind, sort, type *Il a ramanché toutes espèces de choses sur toi.* He made up all sorts of things about you. (VM) **Il lui offrait toute espèce de bon manger.* He would offer her all sorts of good food. (IV, An94) **2** *(used to construct insults) *Espèce de fou.* Fool. (Da84) *Tu veux pas te marier avec cette espèce de salope.* You don't to marry that sort of dirty woman. (LA) *Espèce de tchu.* Idiot! (VM) *Fais pas ça, espèce d'andouille.* Don't do that, you fool. (LA) *Va donc te laver, espèce de soudrillonne.* Go wash up, filthy woman. (TB) <*Loc:* AV, IB, IV, SM, TB, An94, Da84>

espécial [espesjal] *adj.* special, particular *On a un livre espécial qu'a été fait par un prêtre nommé Père Daigle. Il a écrit comme une espèce de dictionnaire.* We have a special book that was made by a man named Father Daigle. He wrote like a kind of dictionary. (LF) <*Loc:* EV, LF, VM, Lv88, Ph36>

espécialement [espesjalmɑ̃] *adv.* especially <*Loc:* EV, Ph36>

espeler (espler, épeler) [esple, eple] *v.tr.* to spell *C'est Basile, son nom. Je connais pas comment tu l'espelles.* His name is Basile. I don't know how you spell it. (TB) *Il peut pas seulement espeler son nom.* He can't even spell his name. (LA) <*Loc:* AV, EV, LA, LF, SB, TB, VM, Da84, Hi02, Ph36>

espeleur, -e [esplœr] *n.* speller, one who spells *Alle est la meilleure espeleure de la classe.* She is the best speller in the class. (AV) <*Loc:* AV>

espérance [esperɑ̃s, eperɑ̃s] *n.f.* hope *Je suis chrétien, voilà ma gloire, mon espérance et mon soutien.* I am Christian, here is my glory, my hope, and my sustenance. (AS, ch: *Je suis chrétien*) <*Loc:* AS, Da84>

espérer [espere, epere] **I** *v.tr.* **1** to wait for, await *Je vais t'espérer ce soir.* I'll wait for you tonight. (SM) **2** to hope for *Tout le long d'une allée, elle faisait que pleurer, toujours en espérant Pierrot Grouillet pour se marier.* All along a pathway, she could only weep, always hoping for Pierrot Grouillet to marry. (VM, ch: *Pierrot Grouillet et Mademoiselle Josette*) **3** to expect *L'ouvrage était pas trop dur parce que tout chacun était après espérer un grand, grand barbecue.* The work wasn't too hard because everyone was expecting a very big barbecue. (VM) **4** to assume *J'espère que ça vient de les Indiens.* I assume that it [the word "giraumon"] comes from the Indians. (SL) **II** *v.intr.* to wait *Espère, on va arriver bétôt.* Hang on, we will arrive soon. (VM) **Je vais espérer à demain.* I'll wait until tomorrow. (Da84) *J'ai pris ma retraite à 62. [...] Si j'aurais espéré à 65 j'aurais un peu plus, mais savoir si je l'aurais fait?* I retired at 62. If I had waited till 65 I would have a bit more, but who knows if I would have made it? (TB) *Faulait que tu vas à Westwego pour traverser. Il y avait pas de pont. Faulait que t'espères pour le ferry.* You used to have to go to Westwego to cross. There was no bridge. You had to wait for the ferry. (TB) <*Loc:* AC, AV, EV, IB, LA, LF, SB, SL, SM, TB, VM, An94, Da84, Gr86, Gu00, Hi02, Lv88, Ph36>

espiègle [espjɛg(l)] *adj.* mean, bad, naughty *C'était des enfants espiègles.* They were naughty children. (VM) **J'te demande excuse, missieur, alle dit, j'croyais t'étais jusse un d'ces espiègles-là qui jonglent jusse à une chose.* I beg your pardon, sir, she said, I thought you were one of those naughty fellows that only think of one thing. (Gr86) <*Loc:* VM, Gr86, Lv88>

espingouin [espɛ̃gwɛ̃] *n.m.* **1** penguin **2** simpleton, nitwit, moron <*Loc:* LF>

espion (sipion) [espjɔ̃, sipjɔ̃] *n.m.* spy <*Loc:* EV, Da84, Ph36>

espionnage [espjɔ̃naʒ] *n.m.* **1** espionage, spying **2** snooping <*Loc:* Da84>

espionneur, -euse [espjɔ̃nœr, -øz] *n.m.* **1** spy **2** busybody, snoop <*Loc:* SM, TB, Da84, Lv88>

espler ♦see **espeler**

espoir[1] [espwar] *n.f.* hope *So, c'est mon espoir et mon idée si Dieu veut qu'on peut aller en France cette année en septembre.* So, it's my hope and my idea, if God is willing, that we can go to France this year in September. (LF) *Il a mis toute qualité de boissons, mais tout en espoir pour les endormir.* He put in all sorts of liquors, all in the hopes of putting them to sleep. (SL) ◊ •**avoir espoir (de)** to hope *J'ai espoir de les voir avant trop longtemps.* I hope to see them before too long. (LA) <LA, SM> <*Loc:* LA, LF, SM, Da84, Hi02>

espoir[2] [espwar] *n.* **1** *(m.)* boyfriend, fiancé **2** *(f.)* girlfriend, fiancée <*Loc:* Da84>

esprit [espri] *n.m.* **1** mind **Après mille fois ça commence à pénétrer dans n'importe quel esprit.* After a thousand times, it starts to penetrate into anyone's mind. (*Cris sur le bayou*) *La femme que j'ai prise, elle m'a troublé l'esprit.* The woman I married has troubled my mind. (IB) *Ce petit somme m'a débarbouillé l'esprit.* That little nap cleared my mind. (VM) **2** sense, good sense **Il a pas une once d'esprit.* He hasn't a bit of sense. (Da84) *Pop a perdu tout son esprit. Pour le bébé, il a pas de prix.* Papa has lost his good sense. For the baby, there's no price. (ch: *Bébé (de la famille)*) *Cil-là qu'était supposé d'avoir assez d'esprit et connaître assez pour courir un cheval, il pouvait tourner là.* The one who was supposed to have enough sense and know enough to run a horse, he could turn there. (EV) **3** spirit (of the deceased) *L'esprit à mon défunt père me parle tout le temps, mais j'ai jamais vu son revenant.* My late father's spirit is always with me, but I've never seen his ghost. (VM) *Je pense que les esprits étaient pas contrôlables ce soir-ça.* I suppose that the spirits were not controllable that night. (SM) ◊ •**esprit barosse {rosse}** dull, slow-witted mind <Da84> •**avoir de l'esprit** to have sense, be sensible *Vous avez un vaillant jeune homme qu'a de l'esprit.* You have a handsome young man who is sensible. (EV) •**le Saint Esprit** the Holy Spirit <Da84, Hi02> <*Loc:* EV, IB, IV, LA, SM, VM, An94, Da84, Hi02>

esquelette (squelette) [esk(ə)lɛt, eskelet, eskilɛt] *n.m./f.* **1** skeleton **2** excessively skinny person *Tu dois manger ein tas de couche-couche pour t'engraisser, espèce d'esquelette.* You have to eat a lot of couche-couche to gain weight, you're a real skeleton. (VM) <*Loc:* AV, IB, LA, LF, SB, SJ, SM, TB, VM, Da84, Lv88>

esquif ♦see **skiff**

esquif lafitte ♦see **lafitte**

esquinter [eskẽte] **I** *v.tr.* to beat up, whip *Si tu fais ça encore, je veux t'esquinter.* If you do that again, I mean to beat you up. (LA) **II s'esquinter** *v.pron.* to work hard at something, wear o.s. out *Je m'ai esquinté à travailler.* I exhausted myself working. (SM) *Je m'ai esquinté à le finir.* I wore myself out to finish it. (VM) <*Loc:* LA, SB, SM, TB, VM>

esquiver [eskive] **I** *v.tr.* **1** to avoid, dodge, elude *Esquiver l'ouvrage.* To avoid work. (Lv88) **2** to save, spare *Les petits étaient toujours esquivés.* The children were always spared. (Lv88) **II s'esquiver** *v.pron.* **1** to shirk (a duty, work, etc.) **S'esquiver de l'ouvrage.* To shirk work. (Da84) **2** to get away with *C'est ton zinzin si tu crois tu vas t'esquiver avec ça.* It's your behind if you think you're going to get away with that. (VM) **3** to steal away, disappear *S'esquiver de l'ouvrage, du tracas.* To steal away from work, from trouble. (Lv88) <*Loc:* LA, PQ, VM, Da84, Lv88>

essai (assaie) [ese, asej, asɛj] *n.m./f.* test, try, attempt, trial *Donne un autre coup d'assaie.* Give it another try. (JE) *Prendre à l'assaie, faire une assaie.* To try (s.t.) out, give it a shot. (Lv88) **Prendre à l'essai.* To take on trial, subject to trial. (Da84) <*Loc:* JE, LF, Da84, Lv88>

essayage [esejaʒ] *n.m.* trying, testing <*Loc:* Da84>

essayer (assayer) [eseje, aseje] **I** *v.tr.* to attempt, try *J'ai essayé un ou deux programmes.* I tried one or two programs. (TB) *Oh il y a du monde qui mange ça. Mon j'ai essayé ça mais il y a beaucoup de l'acide, ça te prend un bon estomac pour digérer ça.* Oh, there are people who eat that. I've tried it but it contains a lot of acid, you need a good stomach to digest that. (TB) **II** *v.intr.* to try *J'ai assayé déjà mais j'ai pas aimé les cigares.* I have tried before but I did not like cigars. (AC) *Je vas essayer de le voir.* I'm going to try to see him. (SM) *Ils ont essayé de* KIDNAP *la petite fille, mais ils ont pas pu.* They tried to kidnap the little girl, but they couldn't do it. (LA) **Il m'a inspiré beaucoup et il a essayé de me montrer certaines choses sur l'accordéon que j'essaie encore à faire.* He inspired me very much and he tried to teach me certain things on the accordion that I am still trying to do. (LA, An84) **III s'essayer** *v.pron.* to try o.s. (at), test o.s. (against s.o.) **Laisse-moi m'essayer.* Let me try. (Da84) **Quitte-moi m'essayer.* Let me try. (Da84) *Ça fait, j'ai dit à mon garçon, "Si jamais tu veux t'essayer, laisse-moi connaître."* So, I said to my son, "If ever you want to try yourself [with me], let me know." (LA) <*Loc:* AC, AV, EV, IV, JE, LA, LF, SL, SM, TB, VM, An94, Da84, Hi02, Lv88>

essence [esɑ̃s] *n.f.* **1** flavor *Quelle essence de crème tu veux?* What flavor of ice cream do you want? (VM) **2** extract (for cooking) **3** perfume *Madame Richard se mettait assez d'essence quand alle allait au bal que tu pouvais l'éventer de l'aut' bord de la rue.* Mrs. Richard put on enough perfume when she went to the dance that you could smell her from the other end of the street. (Gu00) **4** gasoline *Il follait que ça soye bien bien bien soigné pour être sûr que aucun z-essence ou aucun huile va pas dans les eaux.* It had to be extremely well kept up to be sure that no gas and no oil would go into the water. (LF) ◊ •**essence de gâteau** vanilla extract *Quand tu vas aller à la grosserie, ramène-moi de l'essence de gâteau.* When you go to the grocery store, bring me back some vanilla extract. (VM) <VM> •**essence de vanille / essence à la vanille** vanilla extract <TB, Da84> <*Loc:* AC, AL, AV, EV, LF, SB, SM, TB, VM, Da84, Gr86, Gu00, Hi02, Lv88, Ph36>

essencer (s') [esɑ̃se] *v.pron.* to put on perfume **Là quand elle a fini, elle s'essence bien [...] elle se frotte avec des essences.* Then when she finished, she puts on her perfume, she rubs herself with perfume. (Gr86) <*Loc:* Gr86>

essieu [esjø] *n.m.* axle <*Loc:* Da84>

essorage [esoraʒ] *n.m.* drying <*Loc:* Da84>

essorant, -e [esorɑ̃, -ɑ̃t] *adj.* drying *Le vent de nord est essorant.* The north wind is a drying wind. (VM) <*Loc:* VM, Da84>

essorer [esore] **I** *v.tr.* to dry, dry out *J'ai une laveuse qui essore bien mon linge.* I have a washer that dries my clothes well. (VM) **II s'essorer** *v.pron.* to dry out <*Loc:* VM, Da84>

essoufflé, -e [esufle] *adj.* out of breath *Il a arrivé à la maison tout essoufflé.* He got home all out of breath. (LA) <*Loc:* LA, Da84>

essoufflement [esufləmɑ̃] *n.m.* breathlessness <*Loc:* Da84>

essouffler [esufle] **I** *v.tr.* to wind, cause to be out of breath *La course m'a essouflé.* The race winded me. (VM) **II s'essoufler** *v.pron.* to become winded, get out of breath *Il s'a essoufflé en galopant.* He got out of breath while running. (LA) <*Loc:* LA, VM, Da84>

essuie [esɥi] *n.m./f.* household cloth (i.e. dish-cloth or cloth for wiping furniture) <*Loc:* JE, SM, Lv88>

essuie-mains [ɛsɥimɛ̃] *n.m.* hand towel, towel <*Loc:* EV, VM, An94, Da84, Gu00>

essuie-pieds [esɥipje] *n.m.* doormat <*Loc:* Da84>

essuie-place [esɥiplas, esɥiplat] *n.m.* **1** floor mop **2** cloth used to scrub the floor **3** doormat, rag left at the door to wipe the feet *J'avais un chien qui volait les essuie-places des voisins.* I had a dog who would steal doormats from the neighbors. (VM) <*Loc:* LA, SM, VM, Da84, Gu00>

essuie-vaisselle [esɥivesɛl] *n.m.* dish towel *Si on échappe un essuie-vaisselle ça veut dire de la compagnie.* If you drop a dish towel, it means you'll have company. (TB) <*Loc:* TB>

essuyage [esɥijaʒ] *n.m.* wiping, drying <*Loc:* Da84>

essuyer [esyje] **I** *v.tr.* to wipe, dry *Ça serait pour essuyer les larmes qui coulent en bas de mes yeux.* It would be to dry the tears that fall from my eyes. (VM, ch: *Je m'ai fait une maîtresse*) **II s'essuyer** *v.pron.* to wipe o.s., dry o.s. **S'essuyer les mains.* To wipe or dry one's hands. (Da84) *Il y avait pas de papier, ça fait il pouvait pas s'essuyer.* There was no paper, so he couldn't wipe himself. (LA) <*Loc:* LA, SM, VM, Da84>

est (es) [ɛs(t)] *n.m.* east <*Loc:* LA, SL, SM, VM, Da84, Hi02, Lv88>

estable ♦see **stable**

estampe [estɑ̃p] *n.f.* stamp, seal *L'estampe de la Louisiane.* The seal of Louisiana. (Lv88) <*Loc:* Lv88>

estamper ♦see **étamper**

estampique[1] (**estompique**) [estɑ̃pik, estɔ̃pik] *n.m./f.* **1** any sudden move or spurt **Ça l'a pris par estampique.* He did this all of a sudden. (Da84) **2** sudden idea or whim, outburst of enthusiasm **Il a pris une estampique.* He got a sudden idea. (Da84) *Quel estampique qui t'a pris tout d'un coup pour faire un gâteau?* What sudden whim made you bake a cake? (SM) **3** great agitation, much ado *A fait pas arien avec toutes ses grandes estampiques.* She doesn't do anything with all of her great ado. (VM) ◊ •**à l'estampique / en estampique** very fast *Il est parti à l'estampique.* He left very quickly. (AV) <AV, EV, Ph36> •**prendre l'estampique / prendre des estampiques** ***a*** to run away *Canelle a pris l'estampique.* Canelle fled. (IB) ***b*** to fly into a rage <IB, VM> •**se prendre un estampique** to decide all at once *Il s'a pris un estampique de faire du bois cette année.* He got a sudden notion to gather wood that year. (Lv88) <Lv88> •**une grande estampique pour rien** much ado about nothing <Lv88> <*Loc:* AV, EV, IB, SM, VM, Da84, Lv88, Ph36>

estampique[2] [estɑ̃pik] *adj.* runaway *Un cheval estampique.* A runaway horse. (AV) *L'estampique a brisé le wagon.* The runaway horse broke the wagon. (AV) <*Loc:* AV>

estatue ♦see **statue**

estaurant, estaurat ♦see **restaurant**

este ♦see **ce**

est-il [eti] *adv.* pardon? what? sorry? (used to ask for a repetition of something one did not hear) *Je vais en ville. —Est-il?* I'm going into town. —What? (IB) <*Loc:* IB>

estimation [estimasjɔ̃] *n.f.* appraisal, estimation <*Loc:* EV, Da84>

estime [estim] *n.f.* esteem, regard <*Loc:* Da84>

estimer [estime] **I** *v.tr.* **1** to estimate, appraise *J'ai estimé que ma récolte aurait dépassé les trente barils cette année.* I estimated that my crop would have surpassed thirty barrels this year. (VM) **2** to esteem *C'est un homme qu'est bien estimé dans son village.* He is a man who is well esteemed in his town. (VM) **II s'estimer** *v.pron.* to esteem o.s. *Il s'estime plus qu'il vaut.* He esteems himself more that he is worth. (LA) <*Loc:* LA, VM, Da84>

estomac [estɔ̃ma] *n.m. (occ. f.)* **1** stomach **2** chest **Et puis il se cognait l'estomac, tu connais, comme s'il avait devenu un taureau tout du coup.* And then he was beating his chest, you know, as though he had become a bull all of a sudden. (SL, An94) **3** woman's breast *Depuis qu'alle a le cancer, alle a un estomac plus gros que l'autre.* Since she had cancer, she has one breast that's larger than the other. (VM) ◊ •**estomac creuse** empty stomach <Da84> •**estomac (de) mulâtre** variety of gingerbread cookie, stage plank cookie

<AV, EV, IB, LF, SB, SJ, SM, TB, VM, La99, Lv88, Ph36, Re31> **•estomac haigre** sour stomach <Da84> **•avoir l'estomac faille** to feel weak because of hunger <SJ> **•mal d'estomac** stomachache <Da84> <***Loc:*** AL, AV, EV, IB, LA, LF, SB, SJ, SL, TB, VM, An94, Da84, Hi02, La99, Lv88, Ph36, Re31>

estompique ♦see **estampique**

estopper [estope] *v.tr.* to darn, mend *Estopper des chaussettes.* To darn socks. (VM) <***Loc:*** LF, VM>

estragon [estragɔ̃] *n.m.* tarragon <***Loc:*** SL, TB, Da84>

estragot [estrago] *n.m.* fool, nitwit, imbecile *Espèce d'estragot! Va-t'en d'ici.* You fool! Get away from here. (TB) <***Loc:*** TB>

estricité ♦see **électricité**

estrier ♦see **étrier**

estronfillau [estrɔ̃fijo] *n.m.* fool, simpleton, moron <***Loc:*** SJ>

estropié, -e [estropje] *adj.* lame, crippled *Il était estropié, le bougre.* He was crippled, the guy. (EV) ◊ **•estropié de la tête / estropié de cervelle** ***a*** crazy, mentally deranged *Il a perdu la carte. Il est estropié de la tête.* He's lost it. He's crazy. (AV) ***b*** stupid, foolish *C'est juste des estropiés de cervelle qui veulent pus parler français.* It's only foolish people who don't want to speak French anymore. (SL) <AV, SL, La99> <***Loc:*** AV, EV, SL, TB, VM, Da84, La99>

estropier [estropje] **I** *v.tr.* to cripple, maim *L'accident l'a estropié.* The accident crippled him. (EV) **II s'estropier** *v.pron.* to cripple o.s., maim o.s. *Il s'a estropié quand il a tombé du cheval.* He crippled himself when he fell from the horse. (LA) <***Loc:*** AV, EV, LA, Da84>

et [ɛ, e] *conj.* and *Elle va nous aider et nous soigner.* She's going to help us and take care of us. (ch: *Le petit cadeau)* ◊ **•et bien** well **Et bien quoi t'es après faire?* Well, what are you doing? (Da84) <LF, JE, TB, VM, Da84> **•et là** and then *Parce que moi, j'étais pauvre, personne voulait pas de moi. Et là, j'ai eu de la chance que moi, je m'ai fait de l'argent.* Because I was pour, nobody wanted me. And then, I was fortunate enough to make some money. (ch: *Quand j'étais pauvre)* **Et là, après ça, il a bien brassé ça tout ensemble.* And then, after that, he stirred it all together well. (EV, An94) <AC, AS, EV, LA, LF, SB, SL, SM, TB, An94, Da84> <***Loc:*** AC, AL, AS, EV, IB, IV, LA, LF, SB, SL, SM, TB, VM, An94, Da84, Hi02, St95, Wh83>

établi [etabli] *n.m./f.* work bench <***Loc:*** EV, LA, VM>

établir [etablir] **I** *v.tr.* **1** to establish *Ils ont établi leur business sur la grand' rue.* They established their business on Main Street. (VM) **2** to prove *Son avocat a établi qu'il était pas là à l'heure qu'alle a été tuée.* His lawyer proved that he was not there at the time that she was killed. (LA) **II s'établir** *v.pron.* **1** to build o.s. a home or business **2** to settle, take up residence *Les premiers Français là, [...] s'ont établis ici comme des planteurs.* The first French, settled here as planters. (SM) *Ils ont venu ici, ils s'ont établis là, Cecilia, Parks, St. Martinville.* They came here and they settled there, [at] Cecilia, Parks, St. Martinville. (SL) <***Loc:*** LA, SL, SM, VM, Da84>

établissement [etablismɑ̃] *n.m.* **1** establishment **2** building, establishing <***Loc:*** Da84>

étage [etaʒ] *n.m./f.* **1** story, floor, level **Une maison à deux étages.* A two-story house. (Da84) *Première étage.* First floor, ground floor. (AV) **2** degree, level *Mon garçon a monté un étage dans le business.* My son advanced a level in business. (Lv88) <***Loc:*** AV, EV, LF, Da84, Hi02, Lv88>

étagère [etaʒær] *n.f.* **1** shelf *Le dictionnaire est sur la première étagère.* The dictionary is on the first shelf. (AV) **2** shelving, set of shelves **3** what-not shelf, étagère <***Loc:*** AV, IB, SJ, Da84>

étain [etɛ̃] *n.f.* aluminum <***Loc:*** SJ>

étaler [etale] **I** *v.tr.* to spread out *Ils ont étalé leur marchandise en arrière du truck.* They spread out their wares in back of the truck. (LA) **II s'étaler** *v.pron.* to spread out *Le petit arbre est après s'étaler.* The little tree is spreading out. (VM) <***Loc:*** LA, VM, Da84>

étalon [etalɔ̃] *n.m.* stallion, stud <***Loc:*** AV, LA, VM, Da84>

étampage [etɑ̃paʒ] *n.m.* stamping, imprinting <***Loc:*** Da84>

étampe [etɑ̃p] *n.f.* **1** stamp, imprint **2** brand, branding iron <***Loc:*** TB, Da84>

étamper (**estamper**) [etɑ̃pe, estɑ̃pe] *v.tr.* **1** to stamp, imprint **2** to print **Etamper une carte.* Print a card. (Lv88) **3** to brand *Estamper une bête.* To brand a cow. (AV) *Ils étamperont les vaches.* They will brand the cattle. (SB) **4** to mark *Le linge est tout estampé.* The laundry is all marked up. (Lv88) <***Loc:*** AV, SB, TB, Da84, Lv88>

état [eta] *n.m.* **1** state (political entity) *La législature de l'état de la Louisiane a passé une loi.* The Louisiana state legislature passed a law. (AV) **2** state, condition **En bon état.* In good shape or condition. (Da84) <***Loc:*** AV, EV, LA, LF, SM, TB, VM, An94, Da84, Hi02, Lv88>

États-Unis [etayni, etazyni] *n.m.pl.* United States <***Loc:*** AV, EV, LF, TB, Da84, Hi02>

étau [eto] *n.m.* vise <***Loc:*** AC, EV, IB, JE, VM, An94, Da84>

été[1] [ete] *n.m./f.* summer, summertime ◊ **•été des Indiens** Indian summer <Lv88> **•en été / dans l'été** in the summer *Et là en été dans le temps de les saisons de chevrette il faisait sa vie à pogner les chevrettes avec un épreuvier.* And then in the summer, during the shrimp season, he made his living fishing for shrimp with a castnet. (TB) *Il piégeait dans l'hiver mais il galfétait les bateaux dans l'été.* He went trapping in winter but he caulked the boats in the summer. (LF) <LA, LF, PQ, SM, TB, VM, Lv88> <***Loc:*** EV, LA, LF, PQ, SM, TB, VM, An94, Da84, Hi02, Lv88, Wh83>

été[2] ♦see **aller**

été[3] ♦see **être**

éteigner [etɛ̃je] *v.tr.* to extinguish, put out (a fire or a light)

Ils ont éteigné la chandelle. They put out the candle. (SM) **J'ai été chercher de l'eau pour éteigner le feu.* I went to look for some water to put out the fire. (LA, An94) <***Loc:*** IB, LA, SM, An94>

éteindre [etẽn, etẽd(r)] (*p.p.* **éteint** [etẽ], **éteindu** [etẽdy]) **I** *v.tr.* **1** to extinguish, put out (a fire or a light) *J'avais éteindu les lumières quand il a rentré.* I had turned off the lights when he got home. (VM) **2** to turn off, shut off (an appliance) *Éteins le TV avant tu sors.* Turn off the television before you go out. (LA) **3** to tamp (dust, powder) *La pluie a éteint la poussière.* The rain tamped the dust. (VM) **II s'éteindre** *v.pron.* to go out, be extinguished **Et l'emballeuse courait toujours. Il dit, "Écoute! Je vas manquer de gaz. […] Et SURE ENOUGH, il a manqué de gaz. Et elle s'est éteint.* And the baler was still running. He said, "Listen! I'm going to run out of gas! And sure enough, he ran out of gas. It died out. (EV, An94) <***Loc:*** EV, LA, LF, SM, TB, VM, An94, Da84>

éteint, -e [etẽ, -ẽt] *adj.* extinguished, out (of a fire) **Et elle a vu la petite fille à elle avec sa chandelle, mais sa chandelle était éteinte.* And she saw the little girl with her candle, but her candle was extinguished. (LA, An94) <***Loc:*** LA, An94, Da84>

étendre [etɑ̃n, etɑ̃d(r)] **I** *v.tr.* **1** to stretch out, spread out **2** to extend, lengthen **3** to set out (a fishing net) *On prendait sa net, sa tremaille, on prendait le lac et on l'étendait.* You took your net, your fishing net, you went out on the lake and set it out. (EV) **Ça se fait, un jour, Prosper venait dedans le bayou et il avait une NET d'étendue droit devant la maison à Petit Lou.* So one day, Prosper was in the bayou and he had a net cast out in front of Petit Lou's house. (EV, An94) **4** to lay out (e.g. with a blow) *Il l'a étendu avec un seul coup de poing.* He laid him out with one blow. (LA) **5** to hang (laundry) out to dry *Il fallait qu'on s'en revient étendre notre linge tard l'après-midi parce qu'on restait une semaine sans laver.* We had to come back and hang out our laundry late in the afternoon because we went a week without washing. (AC) *J'ai eu pour retordre le linge qu'était étendu sur la corde après la pluie.* I had to wring out the clothes on the line again after the rain. (VM) **Ces draps sont trop souples, il faut les étendre au soleil.* These sheets are too wet, they must be hung in the sun. (Di32) **II s'étendre** *v.pron.* to stretch, stretch o.s. out *Etends-toi pas tout partout dans le sofa comme ça.* Don't stretch out all over the sofa like that. (LA) <***Loc:*** AC, EV, LA, VM, An94, Da84, Di32, La99>

étendue [etɑ̃dy] *n.f.* **1** stretch, expanse (of land) **2** extent, scope <***Loc:*** Da84>

éternel, -elle [etærnɛl] *adj.* **1** eternal, endless **2** long-lived, very old (of a person) *Ce shérif est éternel.* That sheriff is eternal [i.e. will never be unseated]. (VM) <***Loc:*** VM, Da84>

éternellement [etærnɛlmɑ̃] *adv.* eternally, forever, endlessly <***Loc:*** Da84>

éternir ♦see **éternuer**

éternité [etærnite, etrẽnite] *n.f.* eternity <***Loc:*** LF, Da84>

éternuement [etærnymɑ̃] *n.m.* sneeze, sneezing <***Loc:*** Da84, Hi02>

éternuer (**éternuir, éternuquer, éternir**) [etærnye, etærnyir, etærnyke, etærnir] (*p.p.* **éternui** [etærnɥi], **éternué** [etærnye]) *v.intr.* to sneeze *J'ai éternui toute la matinée.* I sneezed all morning. (VM) *Ils ont éternué tellement fort jusqu'à ils ont enlevé le toit de la maison.* They sneezed so hard that they took off the roof of the house. (AV) <***Loc:*** AL, AV, EV, SM, VM, Da84, Hi02, Ph36>

éternuir, éternuquer ♦see **éternuer**

éther [etær] *n.m.* ether <***Loc:*** Da84>

étiller ♦see **tiller**

étinceler [etẽs(ə)le] *v.intr.* to sparkle, gleam, spark *Ses yeux étaient après étinceler comme des braises.* Her eyes were sparkling like embers. (LA) <***Loc:*** LA, Da84>

étincelle [etẽsɛl] *n.f.* spark, sparkle <***Loc:*** AV, EV, VM, Da84>

étiquette [etikɛt] *n.f.* etiquette, good manners <***Loc:*** Da84>

étirailler [etiraje] *v.tr.* to shred, tear to pieces *Mon petit chien aime étirailler des Kleenex.* My little dog likes to tear up Kleenex. (VM) <***Loc:*** VM, Da84>

étirer [etire] *v.tr.* to pull tight *Il a étiré sa ceinture.* He tightened his belt. (AV) <***Loc:*** AV>

étoffe [etɔf] *n.f.* cloth, fabric, material <***Loc:*** AC, AV, EV, IB, LA, LF, SB, SL, TB, VM, Da84>

étoile [etwal] *n.f.* star ◊ **•étoile à queue** Big Dipper (constellation) <VM> **•étoile de Bethléhem** star-of-Bethlehem plant <VM> **•étoile de Texas** hibiscus <VM> **•étoile filante** shooting star <Da84> <***Loc:*** JE, VM, Da84, Hi02>

étonnant, -e (**tonnant, -e**) [etɔ̃nɑ̃, tɔ̃nɑ̃, -ɑ̃t] *adj.* astonishing, surprising **D'une manière étonnante.* Surprisingly, in a surprising way. <Da84> <***Loc:*** TB, Da84>

étonnement [etɔ̃nmɑ̃] *n.m.* astonishment, surprise, amazement, wonder <***Loc:*** Da84>

étonner [etɔ̃ne] **I** *v.tr.* to surprise, amaze, astonish *"O mais," il dit, "ça m'étonne pas que ton cheval est après rire depuis quand on est parti de la salle."* "Oh, well," he says, "I'm not surprised that your horse is grinning since we left the dancehall." (SL, An94) **Ça m'étonne.* That surprises me, I am surprised. (Da84) **II s'étonner** *v.pron.* to surprise o.s., be surprised, wonder at, be astonished <***Loc:*** LA, SL, VM, An94, Da84>

étou ♦see **itou**

et-où ♦see **ayoù**

étouffant, -e [etufɑ̃, - ɑ̃t] *adj.* stuffy, suffocating, stifling *Pitié, c'est étouffant ici-dedans.* For pity's sake, it's stuffy in here. (LA) <***Loc:*** LA, Da84>

étouffé, -e [etufe] *adj.* smothered (of food), completely covered *Y a rien que j'aime mieux que de la tortue ventre jaune étouffée avec des oignons.* There's nothing I like better than yellow-bellied turtle smothered with onions. (Guoo) <*Loc:* SM, VM, Da84, Guoo, Hio2>

étouffée [etufe] *n.f.* étouffée, any of various Cajun dishes prepared by braising or smothering the ingredients (meat, seafood, vegetables, or potatoes) in a covered pot with a limited amount of water, and which is usually onion-based (rather than roux-based) ◊ **•étouffée de foie** liver stew <LF> **•étouffée de rognons** kidney stew <LF> **•étouffée de viande** stew <LF> <*Loc:* LF, SL, TB, Da84, Guoo, Hio2>

étouffement [etufmɑ̃] *n.m.* suffocation, smothering, choking <*Loc:* Da84>

étouffer [etufe] **I** *v.tr.* **1** to suffocate, smother, choke *Et moi j'avais le souffle, mais ça m'étouffait.* I had my breath, but it was starting to suffocate me. (TB) **2** to smother, braise, cook in a covered pot with little water *Premièrement, j'étouffe la viande moulue.* First, I smother the ground meat. (Lv88) **II s'étouffer** *v.pron.* to choke ◊ **•s'étouffer à {de} rire** to laugh excessively, laugh heartily, choke with laughter *Il s'a étouffé de rire.* He laughed heartily. (SM) <SB, SM, TB, La99> <*Loc:* EV, LA, LF, SB, SM, TB, VM, Da84, Guoo, La99, Lv88>

étouffeur [etufœr] *n.m.* ◊ **•étouffeur de canards morts** one who overdoes things, one who exaggerates his actions <La99> <*Loc:* La99>

étourdir [eturdir] **I** *v.tr.* **1** to wring the neck of *J'ai étourdi la poule.* I wrung the hen's neck. (VM) **2** to confuse, confound, make dizzy *Marie, tu m'étourdis avec tous ces reproches.* Marie, you make my head spin with all these reproaches. (ThCa: *La douce réunion*) **3** to stun, daze *La nouvelle l'a étourdi.* The news stunned him. (EV) **II s'étourdir** *v.pron.* to knock o.s. out, stun o.s. <*Loc:* EV, VM, Da84, ThCa>

étourdissant, -e [eturdisɑ̃, -ɑ̃t] *adj.* stunning *Un coup étourdissant.* A stunning blow. (LA) <*Loc:* LA, Da84>

étourdissement [eturdismɑ̃] *n.m.* **1** stunning **2** dizziness <*Loc:* Da84>

étourneau [eturno] *n.m.* **1** blackbird **2** red-winged blackbird <*Loc:* SB, Da84>

étrange[1] [etrɑ̃ʒ] *adj.* strange, odd, out of place **Elle connaissait que le vieux diable aurait arrivé plus tard et elle voulait que les enfants soient tous couchés pour quand il serait arrivé pour pas qu'il s'aperçoive qu'il y en avait un d'étrange.* She knew that the old ogre would arrive later and she wanted the children to all be in bed when he arrived so that he wouldn't notice that there was one that was out of place. (LA, An94) <*Loc:* LA, VM, An94, Hio2>

étrange[2] [etrɑ̃ʒ] *n.f.* strangeness ◊ **•à l'étrange** in a strange place or among strangers *Partir à l'étrange* To go to a strange place. (VM) <VM, Da84> <*Loc:* VM, Da84>

étranger[1], **-ère** [etrɑ̃ʒe, -ær] *adj.* foreign, unfamiliar **Et c'était tout du monde un peu étranger à moi.* They were all people who were a bit foreign to me. (VM, An84) <*Loc:* EV, LA, TB, VM, An84, Hio2>

étranger[2], **-ère** [etrɑ̃ʒe, -ær] *n.* stranger, foreigner, outsider *Les étrangers, quand tu fais une erreur eusse connaît pas tes histoires.* Strangers, when you make a mistake, they don't know your stories. (TB) <*Loc:* EV, IB, SM, TB, Da84, Hio2>

étranglement [etrɑ̃gləmɑ̃] *n.m.* strangling, choking, strangulation <*Loc:* Da84>

étrangler [etrɑ̃gle, etrɑ̃ɲe] **I** *v.tr.* to choke, strangle, throttle **Le vieux a essayé d'étrangler son fils.* The old man tried to strangle his son. (EV, An94) *Il était si enragé qu'il aurait pu m'étrangler.* He was so angry that he could've strangled me. (EV) **II** *v.intr.* to choke *Mange pas trop vite, tu vas étrangler.* Don't eat too fast, you'll choke. (LA) **III s'étrangler** *v.pron.* **1** to choke, choke o.s. *Il s'a étranglé sur une arête de patassa.* He choked on a bream bone. (VM) **2** to strangle or choke each other <*Loc:* EV, LA, TB, VM, An94, Da84, Wh83>

étrave [etrav] *n.f.* bow, front of a boat <*Loc:* LF, TB>

être[1] [ɛt(r)] (*p.p.* **été** [ete]) *v.cop.* to be *Moi je suis le premier dans notre famille qu'a eu un char.* I'm the first one in our family who had a car. (TB) *C'est selon aiousque t'es.* It depends on where you are. (LF) *Cet homme-là est plus fort que moi.* That man is stronger than I. (AC, An94) *La saumure était rouge.* The brine was red. (AC) *Les petits ouaouarons commençaient d'être joliment gros.* The little frogs were starting to get pretty big. (LA, An94) *Si tu fais la chasse aux chevreuils, faut que tu sois capable de trouver le manger.* If you hunt deer, you have to be able to find the food. (VM) *Je me rappelle pas de pas être capable parler français.* I don't remember ever not being able to speak French. (SL) *Ils étiont vieux.* They were old. (AC) *C'étiont juste deux frères.* They were only two brothers. (AC) ◊ **•être pour *a*** to belong to *Vingt-cinq* PERCENT *est pour lui.* Twenty-five percent of it is his. (TB) *Quand j'avais que 23 ans je courais une compagnie déjà et asteur c'est pour moi la compagnie.* When I was only 23 I was already running a company and now the company belongs to me. (TB) ***b*** to be about to *Il avait été empoigner ses trawls parce que la trawl était pour commencer.* He had gone to get his trawls because the trawling season was about to begin. (TB) <LF, TB> **•est-ce que** *(sentence-initial interrogative marker) Est-ce que t'as bu ton lait?* Did you drink your milk? (LF) **Est-ce que ça vous va?* Does that suit you? (Da84) <LF, Da84> **•c'est** *(presentative used for emphasis) C'est ma grand-mère qui nous a pris équand-ce que ma mame est morte.* My grandmother is the one who took us when my mother died. (TB) *C'est eusse qui nous a soigné nous-autres trois.* They're the ones who took care of the three of us. (TB) <AC, TB> **•c'est pour ça** that's why *Et c'est pour ça que j'ai continué à parler le français.* And that's why I continued speaking French. (TB) <TB> <*Loc:* AC, EV, IB, JD, JE, LA, LF, SM, TB, VM, An94, Da84>

être[2] [ɛt(r)] (*p.p.* **été** [ete]) *v.aux.* **1** *(in passive constructions)* to be *L'histoire a été terminée.* The story was ended. (AV) *Tous les autres là étaient récordés à la maison.* All of the others [songs] were recorded at the house. (AC) *Le cipre est dur à trouver mais les vieilles maisons étaient faites avec ça.* Cypress is hard to find but old houses were made with it. (IB) *Deux étaient tués tout droite.* Two were killed instantly. (LA) *Malgré qu'il s'a détruit, il a été enterré dans de la terre sacrée.* Even though he committed suicide, he was buried in sacred ground. (LA) *Y'a une craque dans le verre qu'a été capoté par terre.* There's a crack in the glass that was dropped on the floor. (Lv88) *Eh ben, aie pas peur on va pas parler après toi en arrière de ton dos, parce qu'on a pas été élevé comme ça.* Well, don't be scared that we will talk about you behind your back, because we weren't raised like that. (TB) **2** *(occ. used with certain verbs in compound tenses)* to have, be *Je suis énée en dix-neuf cent quatre-vingt.* I was born in 1980. (AC) *Là, elle a tombé malade et elle est morte.* She fell sick and she died. (EV) *Ils sont tous morts petits à naissance.* They all died as babies at birth. (AV) *Et ça fait pour mes noces, j'ai eu beaucoup de la compagnie beaucoup du monde qu'est venu.* And so for my wedding, I had a lot of company, lots of people came. (EV) *Je deviens de Jennings ayoù j'ai été élevé.* I'm from Jennings where I was raised. (JD) *Je suis venu vous demander quelque chose.* I've come to ask you something. (EV) *Il est venu t'à l'heure.* He came a while ago. (SM) *Si ta canique est restée dans le cercle, là t'avais un tracas.* If your marble stayed in the circle, then you were in trouble. (AC) *Son père lui a foutu une trempe quand il est arrivé chez lui.* His father gave him a beating when he got home. (SB) *Sa moman s'est aperçue qui elle était après me dire.* Her mother realized what she was telling me. (EV) *Elle s'est tirée dans mes bras.* She thew herself into my arms. (Lv88) *Tu vois, j'ai une cousine, elle, elle s'est mariée sept fois.* You see, I have a cousin, she got married seven times. (EV) *Elles se sont sauvées dans le clos parce que les vaches farouches les couraient.* They escaped into the field because the wild cows were chasing them. (EV) *Sa grand-mère était partie à Jérusalem.* Her grandmother had departed for Jerusalem. (TB) *On était venus en* STATION WAGON. We had come in a station wagon. (EV) ◊ **•être après** *(progressive construction)* to be in the act of (doing s.t.) **Je suis après chercher le savon. Je m'en avais servi pour me laver les mains tout à l'heure.* I'm looking for the soap. I used it to wash my hands a little while ago. (ThCa: *Le charivari*) *Mon père est après arroser son jardin.* My father is watering his garden. (LA) *Elle est tout le temps après tapocher ses enfants.* She's always slapping her kids around. (VM) *Filer et frapper au métier, c'est un art qu'est après s'en aller.* Spinning and weaving is an art that is disappearing. (SM) *Ta culotte est après pendre si bas que je te vois le tchu.* Your pants are hanging so low that I see your behind. (VM) *C'est pour ça j'ai réussi si bien, j'étais après faire ça réellement je voulais faire.* It is for this reason I succeeded so well, I was doing what I really wanted to do. (SM) *J'étais en arrière après tirer des cannes d'aluminum.* I was in back shooting at aluminum cans. (LF) *La viande est tout après attirailler les mouches.* The meat is attracting flies. (TB) *Je suis manière après apprendre à un petit peu à parler l'espagnol mais c'est bien peu parce que je veux pas apprendre ça plus que pour assayer de m'arracher le mieux que je peux.* I am more or less learning a little bit of Spanish but it's very little, because I don't want to learn it any better than to try to get by the best I can. (TB) **Quoi il est après faire?* What is he doing? (Da84) <AC, AV, EV, IB, IV, JD, JE, LA, LF, SB, SL, SM, TB, VM, An94, Da84, Guoo, Lv88, ThCa, Wh83> **•être après pour** to be about to (do s.t.) *J'étais après pour t'appeler.* I was just about to call you. (EV) <EV> **<*Loc:*** AC, AL, AV, EV, IB, IV, JD, JE, LA, LF, SB, SL, SM, TB, VM, An94, Da84, Guoo, Lv88, ThCa, Wh83>

être[3] [ɛt(r)] *n.m.* being, thing, creature **<*Loc:*** Da84>

étrenne [etrɛ̃n] *n.f.* New Year's gift *Les étrennes ça c'était le vieux monde donnait dans le vieux temps. C'était un cadeau mais c'était ses étrennes [...] pour le jour de l'an.* New Year's gifts, that was [what] the old people gave in the old days. It was a present but it was "étrennes" for New Year's day. (LA) **<*Loc:*** LA, Da84>

étrier[1] [etrije] *v.tr.* **1** to untangle *Viens ici, je vas étrier tes cheveux.* Come here, I'll untangle your hair. (VM) **2** to spread out *Il a étrié la mousse dessus la barrière.* He spread the moss out on the fence. (VM) **<*Loc:*** VM>

étrier[2] (**étrieux, estrier**) [etrije, etryø, etrijø, estrije, estrjø, estryjø, trije] *n.m.* **1** stirrup **2** shaft support (harness) **3** car lock **<*Loc:*** AC, EV, IB, LA, SL, SM, TB, VM, Da84, Lv88>

étrille [etrij] *n.f.* currycomb **<*Loc:*** Da84>

étriller [etrije] *v.tr.* to curry, comb (a horse) *Étriller un cheval.* To currycomb a horse. (AV) **<*Loc:*** AV, SL, Da84>

étriper [etripe] *v.tr.* **1** to gut *Étriper un poulet.* To gut a chicken. (LA) **2** to tear to pieces, rip open *Le chien a étripé le goret.* The dog tore the piglet to pieces. (VM) **3** to beat, whip **<*Loc:*** JD, LF, VM, Da84>

étroit, -e [etrwa, -at] *adj.* narrow *C'était une petite école étroite. Il y avait deux rangées de bancs là.* It was a little narrow schoolhouse. There were two rows of benches there. (EV) **<*Loc:*** EV, VM, Da84>

étron [etrɔ̃] *n.m.* piece of feces, piece of excrement **<*Loc:*** SJ>

étude [etyd] *n.f.* study ◊ **•faire des études** to study <EV, Da84, Ph36> **<*Loc:*** EV, Ph36, Da84>

étudiant, -e [etydjɑ̃, ɑ̃t] *n.* student, scholar **<*Loc:*** Da84, Hi02>

étudier [etydje, etydwe, etydɥije, etylje, tydje] **I** *v.tr.* to study *Etudie bien tes leçons pour demain, la maîtresse va te passer à l'examen.* Study your lessons well for tomorrow, the teacher is going to test you. (VM) **II** *v.intr.* to study *Il a* *étudié beaucoup dur.* He studied very hard. (EV) <***Loc:*** EV, LF, SM, TB, VM, An94, Da84, Gu82, Hi02, Lv88>

eucharistie [økaristi] *n.f.* Eucharist <***Loc:*** Da84>

euchre [juk] *n.m.* euchre (card game) <***Loc:*** Lv88>

eun, eunne ♦see **un**

eurmède ♦see **remède**

Europe [ørɔp, yrɔp] *n.f.* Europe <***Loc:*** SB, SM, VM, Da84, Hi02, Lv88>

européen[1], **-enne** [øropejɛ̃, yropejɛ̃ -ɛ̃n] *adj.* European <***Loc:*** Hi02>

Européen[2], **-enne** [øropejɛ̃, yropejɛ̃, -ɛ̃n] *n.* European <***Loc:*** Hi02, Wh83>

eusse[1] [øs] *adj.poss.* their *C'est ça qu'eusse mettait eusse viande salée dedans.* That's what they put their salted meat in. (TB) <***Loc:*** TB>

eusse[2], **eusses** ♦see **eux**

eux (**eusse, eusses**) [ø, øs, œs] *pron.pers.pl.* **1** *(subj.)* they *Et puis là, eux gardait des braises.* And then they saved the coals. (SL) *Je connaissais du monde de la Nouvelle Ibérie qu'allait à LSU, et eusse restaient au collège, eusse revenaient pour la fin de la semaine.* I used to know some people from New Iberia who went to LSU, and they stayed at the college, they came back for the weekend. (IB) *Eusse a été pour prendre leurs portraits à mettre sur la gazette, et le vieux dit qu'eux-autres a oublié de mettre le film dedans, so y a pas un portrait qu'a sorti.* They went to have their pictures taken for the newspaper, and the old man said they forgot to put the film in, so not one picture came out. (TB) *J'aime parler avec le monde en français jusqu'au jour d'aujourd'hui, tu connais, tous les pêcheurs eusse parle en français.* I like talking to people in French even today, you know, all the fishermen speak French. (LF) *Les Indiens eusse parlent français.* The Indians, they speak French. (Lv88) **Eux avaient peint sa jument verte avec de la peinture.* They had painted his mare green with paint. (SL, An94) *Un mâchoiron jaune comme ça-là, eusse appelle ça un goujon.* A yellow catfish like that is called a "goujon." (LF) **Eux va connaître ayoù me trouver.* They will know where to find me. (LA, An94) **2** *(obj. of prep.)* them *Alle aimait s'assir avec eux et parler en français, ça lui a fait un petit* TAPE *une fois que alle parlait français avec eux.* She liked to sit with them and speak French, they made her a little tape one time where she was speaking French with them. (LF) *Si tu joins quelqu'un qui parle français, tu peux parler avec eusse.* If you meet someone who speaks French, you can talk to them. (Lv88) *Y a trois dans eux qui restent avec nous.* There are three of them live who with us. (SM) **3** *(tonic)* them *Eux, ils étaient dans l'Afrique du Nord, à Sicile, mais quand moi j'ai joint la campagnie, c'était le régiment [...] en Italie.* They were in North Africa, in Sicily, but when I joined the company, it was the regiment [that was] in Italy.' (SL) <***Loc:*** IB, IV, LA, LF, PQ, SL, SM, TB, VM, An94, Lv88, Wh83>

eux-autres [øzot, øzɔt, hɔt] *pron.pers.pl.* **1** *(subj.)* they **Le lendemain matin, eux-autres restaient auprès de leur roi.* The next morning, they stayed near their king. (SL, An94) *Et là j'ai des petits-enfants et eux-autres joue la musique.* And then I have grandchildren and they play music. (LF) *Mes grands-mères dessus les deux bords pouvait manière se débattre mais eux-autres pouvait pas s'expliquer en anglais.* My grandmothers on both sides could more or less get by, but they couldn't communicate in English. (TB) *Eux-autres voulait défaire le langage.* They wanted to get rid of the [French] language. (TB) **2** *(obj. of prep.)* them **Et ils auriont fait un souper pour eux-autres le soir.* And they would have made a dinner for them in the evening. (SL, An94) *Il racontait des histoires à eux-autres.* He was telling them stories. (Lv88) *Ça se soûle trop, tu peux pas dépendre dessus eux-autres.* They get drunk too much, you can't depend on them. (Lv88) **3** *(tonic)* them *Ça c'est eux-autres qui contrôlait qui les Cadiens peut avoir, qui eux-autres pourrait apprendre, combien d'argent eux-autres pourrait emprêter.* They're the ones who controled what Cajuns could have, what they could learn, how much money they could borrow. (TB) <***Loc:*** EV, LF, SB, SL, TB, TB, An94, Lv88, Wh83>

évacuation [evakɥasjɔ̃] *n.f.* evacuation <***Loc:*** Da84>

évacuer [evakɥe] *v.tr.* to evacuate, clear out *Ils ont évacué le village avant l'ouragan.* They evacuated the town before the hurricane. (LA) <***Loc:*** LA, Da84>

évader [evade] **I** *v.tr.* to frighten away, scatter *Il fait de la boucane pour évader les serpents.* He makes smoke to frighten away snakes. (Lv88) **II** *v.intr.* to escape *L'homme a évadé.* The man escaped. (Lv88) **III s'évader** *v.pron.* to escape *Il s'a évadé juste avant les autres ont arrivé.* He escaped just before the others arrived. (LA/VM) <***Loc:*** LA, VM, Da84, Gr86, Lv88>

évangéliser [evɑ̃ʒelize] *v.tr.* to evangelize, teach the gospel to <***Loc:*** Da84>

évangile [evɑ̃ʒil] *n.f.* gospel <***Loc:*** Da84>

évanner (**éventer**) [evɑ̃ne, evɑ̃te] *v.tr.* to winnow *Fallait tout que tu casses les* BEANS *dessus les pieds, et là tu mettais ça dans des sacs. Et là ça tapait ça, là [...] tous les peaux sortaient dessus les* BEANS, *et là eux-autres avait de quoi pour évanner ça.* You had to pick all the beans off the stalks, and you put them in bags. And then you'd beat it, and all the chaff would come off beans, and they had something to winnow them. (TB) <***Loc:*** TB, Pe37>

évanouir [evɑ̃nwir] *v.intr.* **1** to faint, swoon *Elle avait évanoui.* She had fainted. (SL) **2** to evaporate *Le café est assez faible que il va évanouir.* The coffee is so weak that it will evaporate. (LF) **3** to disappear *La lettre a évanoui d'ici.* The letter disappeared from here. (AV) <***Loc:*** AV, IB, LF, SJ, SL, Da84, Lv88>

évanouissement [evɑ̃nwismɑ̃] *n.m.* fainting spell, swoon <***Loc:*** Da84>

évaporer [evapore] **I** *v.tr.* to evaporate, cause to evaporate

Évaporer l'eau de mer pour faire du sel. To evaporate sea water to make salt. (VM) **II** *v.intr.* to evaporate *La rosée avait tout évaporé quand le chasseur a descendu de l'arbre.* The dew had completely evaporated when the hunter came down from the tree. (LA) **III s'évaporer** *v.pron.* to evaporate **L'eau s'a évaporé.* The water evaporated. (Da84) <***Loc:*** LA, VM, Da84>

évargandé, -e (**évargué, -e**) [evargɑ̃de, evarge] *adj.* stupid, silly, foolish <***Loc:*** TB>

évargué ♦see **évargandé**

évasé, -e [evaze] *adj.* flared out (e.g. the shape of a boat) <***Loc:*** TB>

évêché [eveʃe] *n.m.* bishopric, bishop's residence <***Loc:*** Da84>

éveiller [eveje] **I** *v.tr.* to awaken **II s'éveiller** *v.pron.* to wake up <***Loc:*** Da84>

événement [evɛ̃nmɑ̃] *n.m.* event, happening, occurrence <***Loc:*** Da84>

éventail (**ventail**) [evɑ̃taj, vɑ̃taj] *n.m./f.* fan (manual or electric) *Mon père m'a apporté un ventail de France.* My father brought me back a fan from France. (SJ) ◊ **•éventail à electricité** ceiling fan <IB> **•éventail électrique** ***a*** electric fan ***b*** ceiling fan <Hi02> **•en éventail** fan-shaped <Da84> <***Loc:*** EV, IB, LF, SB, SJ, SM, TB, VM, Da84, Gr86, Gu00, Hi02, Lv88>

éventer[1] [evɑ̃te] **I** *v.tr.* **1** to fan *Tante Jeanne suivait son mari pour l'éventer quand il fauchait la cour.* Aunt Jeanne followed her husband to fan him when he mowed the grass. (VM) **2** to smell, get a whiff of, catch the scent of *Et il éventait et s'il éventait une râle, on l'attendait, il courait plus vite.* He would sniff and if he smelled a rail, we heard him, he would run faster. (VM) *Madame Richard se mettait assez d'essence quand alle allait au bal que tu pouvais l'éventer de l'aut' bord de la rue.* Mrs. Richard put on enough perfume when she went to the dance that you could smell her from the other end of the street. (Gu00) **II s'éventer** *v.pron.* to fan o.s. *On avait juste un éventail comme ça pour t'éventer avec ta main, et il faisait chaud pareil comme il fait ici asteur.* We just had a little fan for fanning yourself by hand like that, and it was hot just like it is here now. (LF) <***Loc:*** JD, LF, VM, Da84, Gu00>

éventer[2] ♦see **évanner**

éventrer [evɑ̃tre] *v.tr.* to gut, dress (fish, fowl, etc.) *J'ai de la misère à éventrer les canards. Ça me rend malade.* I have trouble dressing ducks. It makes me sick. (VM) <***Loc:*** AC, EV, VM, Da84>

évêque [evɛk] *n.m.* bishop <***Loc:*** SM, Da84, Hi02, Re31>

évergonne [eværgɔ̃n] *adj.* crippled *Il est évergonne depuis qu'il s'a fait du mal à sa jambe.* He is crippled ever since he hurt his leg. (TB) <***Loc:*** TB>

éviale [evjal] *n.m.* sash <***Loc:*** EV, Ph36>

évianner [evjɑ̃ne] **I** *v.tr.* to tear or mangle the flesh of *C'est pas un bon rapporteur. Il évianne tout le gibier.* He's not a good retriever. He mangles the flesh on the game. (VM) **II s'évianner** *v.pron.* to tear or mangle one's flesh *Il s'a évianné sur la barrière.* He tore himself up on the fence. (LA) <***Loc:*** LA, VM, Da84>

éviction [eviksjɔ̃] *n.f.* eviction, expulsion <***Loc:*** Da84, Lv88>

évidemment [evidɑ̃mɑ̃] *adv.* evidently, obviously **Evidement plaît qu'on la regarde comme eine de les plus grandes économistes national et adviseur de finances, Tchou Flette nous a bien poliement envoyé d'autres suggestions.* Obviously pleased that we regarded her as a leading national economist and financial adviser, Tchou Flette graciously forwarded us further proven suggestions. (Wh83) <***Loc:*** Da84, Wh83>

évidence [evidɑ̃s] *n.f.* evidence, proof <***Loc:*** Da84>

évident, -e [evidɑ̃, -ɑ̃t] *adj.* evident, obvious <***Loc:*** Da84>

éviter [evite] *v.tr.* to avoid, evade, shun <***Loc:*** Da84, Lv88>

évou ♦see **ayoù**

exact[1], **-e** [ɛgzak(t)] *adj.* **1** exact *La quantité exacte.* The exact amount. (LA) **2** correct, accurate, right *On l'appelle le Sud de la Louisiane ou Acadiana, mais c'est pas exact.* We call it southern Louisiana or Acadiana, but that's not quite right. (ThCa: *Mille misères*) <***Loc:*** LA, Da84, ThCa>

exact[2] [ɛgzak(t)] *adv.* exactly <***Loc:*** EV>

exactement [ɛgzaktəmɑ̃] *adv.* exactly, precisely **Je comprends exactement qui tu veux dire.* I understand exactly what you mean. (EV, An94) <***Loc:*** AV, EV, LA, TB, An94, Da84, ThCa>

exactitude [ɛgzaktityd] *n.f.* exactitude, exactness, accuracy <***Loc:*** Da84>

exagération [ɛgzaʒerasjɔ̃] *n.f.* exaggeration <***Loc:*** Da84>

examen [ɛgzɑ̃mɛ̃] *n.m.* examination, test ◊ **•passer à l'examen** ***a*** to examine ***b*** to test, give an exam to *Etudie bien tes leçons pour demain, la maîtresse va te passer à l'examen.* Study your lessons well for tomorrow, the teacher is going to test you. (VM) <SM, VM> **•passer un examen** to take a test <SM, VM> <***Loc:*** SJ, SM, VM, Da84>

examination [ɛgzɑ̃minasjɔ̃] *n.f.* examination *Ils l'ont déterré pour l'examiner encore, faire une meilleure examination.* They dug it up to examine it again, to make a closer examination. (St95) <***Loc:*** St95>

examiner [ɛgzɑ̃mine] **I** *v.tr.* to examine, inspect *Ils ont eu pour désenterrer mon père pour examiner son corps.* They had to exhume my father to examine his body. (VM) **Le hibou était par terre; il était mort. Et ils l'ont examiné.* The owl was on the ground; it was dead. And they examined it. (EV, An94) **II s'examiner** *v.pron.* to examine o.s. **S'examiner la conscience.* To examine one's conscience. (Da84) <***Loc:*** EV, VM, An94, Da84, St95>

exaucer [ɛgzose] *v.tr.* to answer (a prayer) **Ça fait, sa grandmère l'a dit, "Mais, si tu prierais les soirs auprès d'un chêne," elle dit, "ta prière pourrait être exaucée."* So her grandmother told her, "Well, if you were to pray at night next to an oak tree," she says, "your prayer could be answered." (LA, An94) <*Loc:* LA, An94>

excellence [ɛkselɑ̃s] *n.f.* excellence ◊ **•votre excellence** title of a bishop, a governor, etc. <Da84> <*Loc:* Da84>

excepté (**ebsèpe**) [ɛksɛpte, ɛbsɛp, ebsep] *prep.* except, excepting, save *Ils sont tous venus ebsèpe lui.* They all came except him. (SM) *Ils ont parlé avec tout le monde excepté les enfants.* They spoke to everyone except the children. (LA) ◊ **•ebsèpe que** except, save *J'aime toute la famille ebsèpe que lui.* I love all the family except for him. (VM) <VM> **•excepté que** except that **Mais c'est pareil comme Murphy excepté que ti mets ein "Pi" au lieu d'ein M.* But it's just like Murphy except that you put a P instead of an M. (ThCa: *Mille misères*) <Hi02, ThCa> <*Loc:* EV, LA, SM, VM, Da84, Hi02, ThCa>

exception [ɛksɛpsjɔ̃] *n.f.* exception, exclusion <*Loc:* Da84>

excès [ɛkse] *n.m.* excess <*Loc:* Da84>

excitation [eksitasjɔ̃, ɛksitasjɔ̃] *n.f.* excitement *Parle de l'excitation équand alle a venu!* Talk about the excitement when she came! (VM) <*Loc:* IB, SM, VM, Da84>

excité, -e [eksite, ɛksite] *adj.* excited, keyed up *J'étais pas excité à aller dans l'armée mais j'ai calculé j'avais un devoir à faire.* I was not excited to join the army but I thought it was my duty to do so. (IB) <*Loc:* AC, IB, LA, LF, SM, VM, Gr86>

exciter [eksite, ɛksite] **I** *v.tr.* to excite, rouse, stir up *Cette nouvelle m'a tout excité.* The news got me all excited. (VM) **II s'exciter** *v.pron.* to become excited, get stirred up *Il s'a excité quand il a vu sa famille.* He became excited when he saw his family. (LA) <*Loc:* LA, SM, TB, VM, Da84>

exclamation [ɛksklɑ̃masjɔ̃] *n.f.* exclamation <*Loc:* Da84>

excommunier [ɛkskɔ̃mynje] *v.tr.* to excommunicate *L'évèque a dit qu'il l'aurait excommunié s'il arrêtait pas de faire tout ça.* The bishop said that he would excommunicate him if he didn't stop doing that. (LA) <*Loc:* LA, Da84>

excommunication [ɛkskɔ̃mynikasjɔ̃] *n.f.* excommunication <*Loc:* Da84>

excommunion [ɛkskɔ̃mynjɔ̃] *n.f.* excommunication <*Loc:* Da84>

excrément [ɛkskrɛ̃mɑ̃] *n.m.* excrement, feces <*Loc:* Da84>

excrémer (s') (**s'écrémer**) [ɛkskrɛ̃me, ekrɛ̃me] *v.pron.* to clear one's throat (and usually to spit in doing so) *Excuse-moi. J'ai besoin de m'écrémer.* Excuse me. I need to clear my throat. (EV) <*Loc:* EV, VM>

excursion [ɛkskyrsjɔ̃] *n.f.* excursion, trip, outing <*Loc:* SM, Da84>

excusable [ɛkskyzab(l)] *adj.* excusable, pardonable *Vous êtes pas excusable.* You are inexcusable. (EV) <*Loc:* EV>

excuse [ɛskyz, eskyz] *n.f.* **1** excuse **2** alibi <*Loc:* AL, JD, LF, TB, Da84, Gr86>

excuser [ɛkskyze, ɛskyze] **I** *v.tr.* to excuse **Excuse-moi.* Excuse me. (Da84) **II s'excuser** *v.pron.* to excuse o.s., apologize, ask pardon *J'ai jamais rappelé. Là alle a venu s'excuser à moi.* I never called back. Then she came to apologize to me. (TB) <*Loc:* AC, EV, LA, LF, TB, Da84, Gu82>

exécuteur [ɛgzekytœr] *n.m.* executor <*Loc:* Da84>

exécution [ɛgzekysjɔ̃] *n.f.* **1** execution **2** performance, fulfillment (of a sentence, an order, a job, etc.) <*Loc:* Da84>

exemple [ɛgzɑ̃p(l)] *n.m.* example, model ◊ **•ça par exemple!** that's something! that beats everything! <Da84> **•par exemple** ***a*** for example ***b*** but, however *Il a venu juste une fois, lui, par exemple.* However, he came just one time. (SM) <AC, EV, SL, SM, TB> **•pour exemple** for example <SL, Lv88> **•prendre exemple dessus {sur / sus} qqn** to follow s.o.'s example *Garçons à marier, prenez exemple sur moi. Corrigez bien vos femmes.* Boys who are marrying, follow my example. Be sure to discipline your wives. (VM, ch: *Je me suis marié*) <VM, Hi02> <*Loc:* AC, EV, SL, SM, TB, VM, An94, Co63, Da84, Hi02, Lv88>

exempler [ɛgzɑ̃ple] *v.tr.* to serve as an example **Le Bon Dieu, quand Il était sur la terre, c'est pour ça il était là, pour exempler, donner exemple au monde.* The good Lord, when He was on the earth, that's why He was there, to be an example, to serve as an example to people. (SL, An94) <*Loc:* SL, An94>

exempter (**exemptir**) [ɛgzɑ̃te, ɛgzɑ̃tir] *v.tr.* to exempt, free (from a law) *Je suis exempté de payer des taxes sur ma maison parce que je reste dedans.* I am exempted from paying taxes on my house because I live in it. (VM) <*Loc:* EV, VM, Da84>

exempti, -e [ɛgzɑ̃ti] *adj.* exempted, free *Lui, il se croyait exempti de tout les règlements.* Him, he thought himself exempted from all the rules. (LA, VM) <*Loc:* LA, VM, Da84>

exemption [ɛgzɑ̃psjɔ̃] *n.f.* exemption <*Loc:* Da84>

exemptir ♦see **exempter**

exercer [ɛgzærse] **I** *v.tr.* to exercise, practice *Ils ont exercé leur droit de pas parler.* They exercised their right to not speak. (LA) **II s'exercer** *v.pron.* to exercise, practice *Il est après s'exercer au piano.* He is practicing the piano. (VM) <*Loc:* LA, VM, Da84>

exercice [ɛgzærsis] *n.m.* exercise, practice <*Loc:* Da84>

exhausser [ɛgzose] *v.tr.* to exhaust *Ils avont tout exhaussé l'huile.* They had exhausted the supply of oil. (VM) <*Loc:* VM, Da84>

exhibition [ɛgzibisjɔ̃, ɛgzybisjɔ̃] *n.f.* exhibition, showing, display <*Loc:* IB, VM, Da84, Lv88>

exhortation [ɛgzɔrtasjɔ̃] *n.f.* exhortation <*Loc:* Da84>

exhumation [ɛgzymasjɔ̃] *n.f.* exhumation <*Loc:* Da84>

exhumer [ɛgzyme] *v.tr.* to exhume, dig up (a body) *Exhumer un corps.* To exhume a body. (VM) <*Loc:* VM, Da84>

exigeant, -e [ɛgziʒɑ̃, -ɑ̃t] *adj.* exacting, demanding *Tant qu'à elle, alle est assez exigeante que mon frère aura une vie* *difficile.* As for her, she is so demanding that my brother will have a difficult life. (LA) <***Loc:*** LA, Da84>

exigence [ɛgziʒɑ̃s] *n.f.* exigency, demand <***Loc:*** Da84>

exil [ɛgzil] *n.m.* exile, banishment, deportation <***Loc:*** Da84>

exile [ɛgzil] *n.* exile, person in exile **Je suis née Mélina Boudreaux et ma famille a venu du Canada avec les exiles.* I was born Melina Boudreaux and my family came from Canada with the exiles. (Gr86) <***Loc:*** Gr86>

exilé, -e [ɛgzile] *n.* exile, person in exile <***Loc:*** Da84>

exiler [ɛgzile] **I** *v.tr.* to exile, banish *Ils l'ont exilé après qu'il s'a marié cette femme-là.* They banished him after he decided to marry that woman. (LA) **II s'exiler** *v.pron.* **1** to exile o.s. *Alle a été rester loin là-bas; alle s'a exilé de sa famille et ses amis.* She went off to live way out there; she exiled herself from her family and friends. (VM) **2** to slip off unnoticed *Alle s'a exilé de nous-autres.* She slipped off unnoticed by the rest of us. (VM) <***Loc:*** LA, VM, Da84>

existence [ɛgzistɑ̃s] *n.f.* existence, subsistence <***Loc:*** Da84>

exister [ɛgziste] *v.intr.* **1** to exist, be alive **Il aimait jusqu'à la nature, les arbres, les fleurs, la terre. Il avait un grand sentiment pour tout ce qui existait.* He even loved nature, trees, flowers, the earth. He had great affection for everything that existed. (EV, An94) **2** to subsist **Exister sur deux piastres par jour.* To subsist on two dollars a day. (Da84) <***Loc:*** EV, SL, An94, Da84>

exonérer [ɛgzɔ̃nere] *v.tr.* to exonerate *Il a été exonéré d'avoir eu vendu des canards.* He was exonerated of having sold ducks. (VM) <***Loc:*** VM, Da84>

expecter [ɛkspɛkte] *v.tr.* to expect **J'éxpectais ça.* I expected that. (EV, Ph36) *Qu'est-ce qu'on peut expecter de ce crapule-là?* What can you expect from that rascal? (IB) **Il expecte de commencer.* He expects to begin. (Wh83) <***Loc:*** EV, IB, Ph36, Wh83>

expédier [espedje] *v.tr.* to send, ship, send off, dispatch, forward *Ils avont expédié du riz aux Allemands.* They sent rice to the Germans. (VM) <***Loc:*** VM, Da84>

expédition [ɛkspedisjɔ̃] *n.f.* expedition <***Loc:*** Da84>

expérience [ɛksperjɑ̃s] *n.f.* experience <***Loc:*** EV, Da84>

expériencé, -e [ɛksperjɑ̃se] *adj.* experienced *C'est un mécanicien expériencé.* That's an experienced mechanic. (LA) <***Loc:*** LA, Da84>

expériencer [ɛksperjɑ̃se] **I** *v.tr.* to experience *T'as jamais expériencé un ouragan?* Have you ever experienced a hurricane? (VM) **II** *v.intr.* to experiment *On va expériencer là, je suis pas sur le premier va sortir.* We are going to experiment, I'm not on the first that will go. (VM) <***Loc:*** VM>

expériment [ɛksperimɑ̃] *n.m.* experiment <***Loc:*** Da84, Lv88>

expérimentation [ɛksperimɑ̃tasjɔ̃] *n.f.* experimentation, experimenting <***Loc:*** Da84>

expérimenter [ɛksperimɑ̃te] **I** *v.tr.* to test, test out *Expérimenter une recette.* To test a recipe. (EV) **II** *v.intr.* to experiment, test *Eusse était après expérimenter pour trouver de l'huile pour fouiller avec ces* RIG. They were testing to find oil to dig with those rigs. (LF) <***Loc:*** AV, EV, LF, Da84>

expert[1], **-e** [ɛkspær, -ært] *adj.* expert *Dans lui, il est expert dans tout lui.* According to him, he is an expert in everything. (VM) <***Loc:*** VM, Da84>

expert[2], **-e** [ɛkspær, -ært] *n.* expert <***Loc:*** Da84>

expertise [ɛkspærtiz] *n.f.* expertise, skill <***Loc:*** Da84>

expiation [ɛkspjasjɔ̃] *n.f.* expiation (for guilt) <***Loc:*** Da84>

expiration [ɛkspirasjɔ̃] *n.f.* expiration <***Loc:*** Da84>

expirer [ɛkspire] *v.intr.* **1** to exhale *Je peux pus expirer. J'ai pus de souffle.* I can't exhale anymore. I'm out of breath. (VM) **2** to die, expire, breathe one's last breath *Il a expiré, pauvre bête.* He died, poor fellow. (VM) <***Loc:*** VM, Da84>

explicable [ɛksplikab(l)] *adj.* explainable *C'est bien explicable, ça. Je vas te dire comment ça a arrivé.* That's easy to explain. I'll tell you how it happened. (VM) <***Loc:*** VM, Da84>

explication [ɛksplikasjɔ̃, esplikasjɔ̃] *n.f.* explanation <***Loc:*** Da84>

expliquer [ɛksplike, esplike] **I** *v.tr.* to explain *J'avais beaucoup vite appris, mais je pouvais pas expliquer en français quoi ce que je lisais en anglais.* I had learned quickly, but I couldn't explain in French what I read in English. (AC) **II** *v.intr.* to explain *Explique-moi pour la boucherie.* Explain to me about the boucherie. (LA) **III s'expliquer** *v.pron.* **1** to make clear, explain one's meaning *Il s'explique pas bien, lui.* He doesn't make himself clear. (VM) **2** to communicate, articulate *Il a eu un* STROKE *et c'est sa langue, il peut pas s'expliquer.* He had a stroke and it's his tongue, he can't articulate. (TB) ◊ **•expliquer point par point** to explain point by point <Da84> <***Loc:*** AC, EV, LA, SM, TB, VM, Da84, Gu82>

exploration [ɛksplorasjɔ̃] *n.f.* exploration <***Loc:*** Da84>

explorer [ɛksplore] *v.intr.* to explore, investigate *Les Français ont exploré la Louisiane avant* LEWIS AND CLARK. The French explored Louisiana before Lewis and Clark. (VM) <***Loc:*** VM, Da84>

explosion [ɛksplozjɔ̃] *n.f.* explosion, outbreak, outburst <***Loc:*** Da84>

exportation [ɛkspɔrtasjɔ̃] *n.f.* export, exportation <***Loc:*** Da84>

exporter [ɛkspɔrte] *v.tr.* to export *Le vieux Lorrain exportait son bois de cipre à Galveston.* Old man Lorrain exported his cypress wood to Galveston. (VM) <***Loc:*** VM, Da84>

exposé [ɛkspoze] *n.m.* account, explanation <***Loc:*** Da84>

exposer [ɛkspoze] **I** *v.tr.* to expose, exhibit, show *Elle était exposée dans notre église ici pour une journée.* She [her corpse] was exposed in our church here for one day. (SL) **II s'exposer** *v.pron.* **1** to expose o.s. *Défunt Tout s'exposait au monde devant la maison de cour.* The late Tout would expose himself to the people in front of the courthouse. (LA) **2** to be exposed (e.g. to danger) *La garde-malade* *s'a exposé au* FLU. The nurse was exposed to the flu. (VM) <***Loc:*** LA, SL, VM, Da84>

exposition [ɛkspozisjɔ̃] *n.f.* exposition, show <***Loc:*** Da84>

exprès[1] [ɛksprɛ, ɛkspre, esprɛ, espre] *adj.* special, made or intended especially for a given purpose *Nous-autres on appelait ça galféter. Et il y avait des outils d'exprès. On appelait ça un couteau de galfat, c'était un couteau qu'avait une grosse lame large.* We called that caulking. And there were special tools. We called it a caulking knife, it was a knife that had a big wide blade. (LF) *J'étais supposée de frobir, on va dire. Ben fallait je vas écraser ma brique dehors dans [...] un bassin exprès.* Let's say I was supposed to mop. Well, I'd have to crush my brick outside in a basin especially for that purpose. (EV) *Il a des produits exprès [...] qu'il met là-dedans-là pour faire profiter les cocodries plus vite.* He has special tools that he puts in there to make the alligators grow faster. (St95) <***Loc:*** EV, LF, SM, Da84, St95>

exprès[2] [ɛksprɛ, ɛkspre, esprɛ, espre] *adv.* on purpose, expressly, purposely *Le bacon était venu blanc [...] mais là, ça le passait dans de l'eau quède et ça l'accrochait après des barres dans une cabane qu'ils aviont exprès pour boucaner ça.* The bacon got white, then they put it in tepid water and hung it on bars in a shed they had expressly for smoking it. (AC) ◊ **•faire exprès** to do on purpose *Elle a croisé ses guides sans faire exprès.* She crossed her reins without doing it on purpose. (EV) <EV> <***Loc:*** AC, EV, LA, LF, Da84, Lv88>

exprès[3] [ɛksprɛ] *n.* ◊ **•faire un exprès de** to make a point of *Je vas faire un exprès de passer le prendre demain.* I'll make a point of coming to pick it up tomorrow. (EV) <EV, Da84> **•fais pas un exprès** don't go out of your way <AC, EV> **•par exprès** on purpose, intentionally **Il a laissé le robinet ouvert pas par exprès.* He didn't leave the faucet running on purpose. (Lv88) <AV, Da84, Lv88> <***Loc:*** AC, AV, EV, Da84, Lv88>

expressément [ɛkspresemɑ̃] *adv.* expressly *Il a fait ça expressément pour me choquer.* He did that on purpose to make me angry. (VM) <***Loc:*** VM, Da84>

expression [ɛkspresjɔ̃] *n.f.* **1** facial expression **2** expression, figure of speech <***Loc:*** SL, Da84>

expropriation [ɛksproprijasjɔ̃] *n.f.* expropriation <***Loc:*** Da84>

exproprier [ɛksproprije] *v.tr.* to expropriate *La famille nous a exproprié après que les vieux sont morts.* The family expropriated us after the elders died. (LA) <***Loc:*** LA, Da84>

extension [ɛkstɑ̃sjɔ̃] *n.f.* extension, continuation <***Loc:*** Da84>

extermination [ɛkstærminasjɔ̃] *n.f.* extermination <***Loc:*** Da84>

exterminer [ɛkstærmine] *v.tr.* to exterminate, destroy *On va les extérminer dans la partie de pelote.* We will destroy them in the ball game. (LA) <***Loc:*** LA, Da84>

extinction [ɛkstɛ̃ksjɔ̃] *n.f.* extinction <***Loc:*** Da84>

extra[1] [ɛkstra] *adj.* **1** additional, extra *Ça a pas un nom extra, que je sais.* That doesn't have another name that I know of. (VM) **2** supplementary, surplus, extra *Il vendait ça qu'on avait d'extra.* He sold the surplus that we had. (Lv88) **3** fine, especially or particularly good, extraordinary, superior *Cette farine-là coûte cher, mais c'est extra.* That flour is expensive, but it's especially good. (VM) <***Loc:*** EV, TB, VM, Da84, Lv88>

extra[2] [ɛkstra] *adv.* very, extra, extremely *Et ces chauvages là, eux-autres c'était encore plus pauvre que nous-autres on était. Eux-autres était extra-pauvres.* And those Indians, they were even poorer than we were. They were extremely poor. (TB) <***Loc:*** TB, Lv88>

extra[3] [ɛkstra] *n.m.* extra <***Loc:*** Da84>

extraction [ɛkstraksjɔ̃] *n.f.* extraction (e.g. of a tooth) <***Loc:*** Da84>

extraordinaire [ɛkstr(a)ɔrdinær] *adj.* extraordinary, unusual, uncommon *C'était un danseur extraordinaire.* He was an extraordinary dancer. (EV) <***Loc:*** EV, Da84>

extrat [ɛkstra] *n.f.* extract, essence ◊ **•extrat de vanille** vanilla extract <Da84> <***Loc:*** Da84>

extravagance [ɛkstravagɑ̃s] *n.f.* extravagance <***Loc:*** Da84>

extravagué, -e [ɛkstravage, estravage] *adj.* **1** extravagant **2** dazed, bewildered *Extravagué par le coup.* Dazed by the blow. (LF) **3** deranged, crazy, insane **4** scatterbrained, silly <***Loc:*** AV, IB, LF>

extravaguer [estravage] *v.tr.* to beat unmercifully <***Loc:*** SJ>

extrême [ɛkstrɛ̃m] *adj.* extreme, utmost, ultimate *La punition est un peu extrême, tu crois pas.* The punishment was a bit extreme, don't you think. (VM) ◊ **•extrême-onction** extreme unction, last rites, annointing of the sick <Da84> <***Loc:*** VM, Da84>

extrêmement [ɛkstrɛ̃m(ə)mɑ̃] *adv.* extremely **Extrêmement malade.* Very sick. (Da84) <***Loc:*** Da84>

extrémité [ɛktrɛ̃mite, estrinite] *n.f.* extremity, end ◊ **•d'une extrémité à l'autre** from one extremity to the other *Il a pêché la rivière d'une extrémité à l'autre.* He fished the river from one extremity to the other. (VM) <VM, Da84> **•être dans la dernière extrémité** to be in extreme poverty, be in dire straits *Ils sont rendus dans la dernière extrémité.* They are in dire straits. (VM) <VM> <***Loc:*** VM, Da84>

exudation [egzydasjɔ̃] *n.f.* exudation, perspiration <***Loc:*** Da84>

éyoù ♦see **ayoù**

fable [fab(l)] *n.f.* fable, story, tale <*Loc:* Da84>

fabrication [fabrikasjɔ̃] *n.f.* **1** fabrication, manufacture **2** falsehood, forgery, lie <*Loc:* Da84>

fabrique [fabrik] *n.f.* **1** fabric, cloth **2** factory <*Loc:* Da84>

fabriquer [fabrike] **I** *v.tr.* to manufacture, produce *Je fabrique des bateaux.* I make boats. (LF) **II se fabriquer** *v.pron.* to be manufactured, be produced *Il y avait un tas de bateaux là-bas parce que ça se fabriquait dessus le bayou.* There were a lot of boats out there because they were produced on the bayou. (LA) <*Loc:* LA, LF, Da84>

façade [fasad] *n.f.* facade, front <*Loc:* Da84>

face [fas] *n.f.* front, face ◊ **•face de barrière** stretch or length of fence (in one continuous direction) <Da84> **•dans sa face** before one's eyes *Il l'a pris droite dans ma face.* He took it right in front of me. (LA) <LA> **•en face de** across from, opposite *Tibeb s'a assis directement en face de Monsieur Gaston et Ophilia s'a assis à la gauche de Tibeb.* Tibeb sat down directly across from Mr. Gaston and Ophilia sat on Tibeb's left. (ThCa: *Le charivari*) <SM, ThCa> <*Loc:* LA, SM, Da84, ThCa>

fâchant, -e [faʃɑ̃, -ɑ̃t] *adj.* troublesome, unfortunate *C'est fâchant t'as pas pu le voir.* It's unfortunate that you didn't get to see him. (Lv88) <*Loc:* EV, Lv88, Ph36>

fâché, -e [faʃe] *adj.* angry, mad *La femme était fâchée quand son mari a arrivé tard.* The woman was mad when her husband arrived late. (AS) ◊ **•fâché après {avec}** angry with *Il me parle p'us depuis qu'il est fâché après moi.* He doesn't talk to me any more since he's been angry with me. (VM) **Maman sera fâchée après toi!* Mom will be mad at you! (LA, An94) *Je suis fâché avec Jean.* I'm angry with Jean. (SM) <LA, SM, VM, An94> **•fâché comme un chien enragé / fâché comme une dinde {une garce / une guêpe / une hornette / un taureau / un tigre}** very angry <AC, SL, La99> **•être fâché** to be at odds, be on the outs *Les deux voisins étaient fâchés pour un bœuf qu'avait cassé la barrière.* The two neighbors were at odds over an ox that had broken the fence. (LA) <LA> <*Loc:* AC, AL, AS, LA, SL, SM, VM, An94, Da84, Hi02, La99>

fâcher [faʃe] **I** *v.tr.* to anger *Si il boit de trop, il va fâcher sa femme.* If he drinks too much, he will anger his wife. (LA) **Elle dit, "Tu connais, ça me fâche assez," elle dit, "j'ai envie de me revenger."* She says, "You know, it makes me so mad," she says, "I feel like taking revenge." (EV, An94) **II se fâcher** *v.pron.* to get angry, be angry **Je suis plus fâchée que jamais. Plus que ça va, plus je me fâche.* I'm angrier than ever. The more it goes on, the more I get mad. (EV, An94) ◊ **•faire fâcher** to make s.o. angry *Tu vas me faire fâcher.* You're going to make me mad. (LA) <LA> **•se fâcher après** to get angry at *Il s'a jamais fâché après moi.* He has never gotten angry at me. (SL) <SL> <*Loc:* EV, LA, SL, TB, An94, Da84, Gr86, Hi02>

facile[1] [fasil] *adj.* easy *Ma vie était pas facile.* My life was not easy. (SL) *Pendant longtemps je faisais du roux mais maintenant c'est un tas plus facile aller au magasin.* For a long time I used to make roux, but now it's a whole lot easier to go to the store [to get it]. (SL) <*Loc:* SL, TB, Da84, Hi02, Lv88>

facile[2] [fasil] *adv.* easily *Il l'a sorti facile.* He got it out easily. (Lv88) *Elle se choque facile.* She is easily offended. (SM) <*Loc:* SM, Lv88>

facilement [fasilmɑ̃] *adv.* easily *C'était facilement le plus gros poisson qu'il avait jamais attrapé dans le lac.* That was easily the biggest fish he had ever caught in the lake. (LA) **Le carencro plane facilement.* The buzzard glides easily. (Da84) <*Loc:* LA, Da84>

facilité [fasilite] *n.f.* **1** ease, facility **2** convenience *Ils avaient plus de facilité.* It was more convenient for them. (SM) <*Loc:* SM, Da84>

faciliter [fasilite] *v.tr.* to facilitate, make easy or easier *Ils s'arrêtaient souvent pour boire de l'eau fraîche et ça facilitait leur journée de travail.* They stopped often to drink cool water and that made their work day easier. (LA) <*Loc:* LA, Da84>

façon [fasɔ̃] *n.f.* fashion, manner, way ◊ **•en façon de parler** in a manner of speaking <Da84> **•sans façon** without a doubt *Elle se rend sans façon maîtresse de la maison.* She becomes without a doubt mistress of the house. (EV) <EV> <*Loc:* EV, Da84, Fa77>

façonnage [fasɔnaʒ] *n.m.* fashioning, shaping <*Loc:* Da84>

façonner [fasɔ̃ne] *v.tr.* to fashion, make, form *L'écrevisse façonne sa cheminée avec de la boue.* The crawfish makes its chimney out of mud. (VM) <*Loc:* VM, Da84>

facterie (**factrie, factorie, FACTORY**) [faktri, faktɔri] *n.f.* factory *La facterie à chevrette est rouverte dempuis hier.* The shrimp factory has been open since yesterday. (TB) <*Loc:* AV, EV, IB, JD, LF, SL, SM, TB, VM, Da84, Di32, Fa77, Lv88, Ph36>

faction [faksjɔ̃] *n.f.* faction, party, group <*Loc:* Da84, Gr86>

factorie, FACTORY, factrie ♦see **facterie**

facture [faktyr] *n.f.* factory *Je l'ai fait venir de la facture.* I ordered it from the factory. (SL) <*Loc:* LF, SL>

faculté[1] [fakylte] *n.f.* faculty, ability, power <*Loc:* Da84>

faculté[2] [fakylte] *n.f.* faculty (of a school) <*Loc:* Da84>

fadir [fadir] *v.tr.* to weaken *Cette maladie va le fadir beaucoup.* That sickness will really weaken him. (IB) <***Loc:*** IB>

fafa [fafa] *adj.* dim-witted, stupid **Il est fafa comme tout.* He's as dim-witted as anything. (EV, Ph36) <***Loc:*** EV, Ph36>

fagot [fago] *n.m.* bundle of small sticks used for kindling <***Loc:*** Da84>

faible [fɛb(l), feb(l)] *adj.* **1** weak *On travaillait toute la journée, à prendre de la chevrette, là le soir il faulait qu'on vient bouillir ça aux plate-formes. Et mon j'étais faible dans ce temps-là. J'avais de la misère à haler une baille de chevrettes numéro trois.* We worked all day long catching shrimp, and then in the evening we had to come and boil it on the platforms. And I was weak in those days. I had trouble hauling a number three barrel of shrimp. (TB) *Si une muraille est faible, tu peux la fortifier.* If a wall is weak, you can reinforce it. (AV) *Le café est assez faible que il va évanouir.* The coffee is so weak that it will evaporate. (LF) **2** faint, feeble *Il a parlé assez longtemps que sa voix a venu faible.* He spoke so long that his voice became faint. (LA) <***Loc:*** AL, LA, LF, SM, TB, Da84, Hi02>

faiblement [febləmɑ̃] *adv.* weakly, feebly, faintly <***Loc:*** Da84>

faiblesse [feblɛs] *n.f.* weakness *C'est la paresse pas la faiblesse qui l'a empêché de finir son ouvrage.* It's laziness not weakness that prevented him from finishing his work. (VM) ◊ **•avoir des faiblesses** to feel faint, feel weak, dizzy and likely to faint **J'ai des faiblesses quand je me fâche.* I feel faint when I am angry. (EV, An94) <EV, An94> <***Loc:*** EV, VM, An94, Da84, Hi02>

faïence [fajɑ̃s] *n.f.* chinaware, crockery <***Loc:*** Da84>

faignant, -e (fainéant, -e) [fɑ̃jɑ̃, fajɑ̃, fɛ̃jɑ̃, -ɑ̃t] *adj.* good-for-nothing, lazy *Mon oncle était assez fainéant qu'il aurait arrêté de labourer au milieu du clos si quelqu'un passait pour le prendre à la pêche, et il aurait crié à sa femme pour dételer les mulets.* My uncle was so lazy that he would stop plowing in the middle of the field if someone stopped by to take him fishing, and he would yell to his wife to unhitch the mules. (LA) <***Loc:*** IB, LA, LF, VM>

faignanterie (fainéanterie) [fɛ̃jɑ̃tri] *n.f.* worthlessness, laziness <***Loc:*** VM>

FAIL [fɛl, feˈl] *v.intr.invar.* to fail *Il a* FAIL *le quatrième livre.* He failed fourth grade. (LA) <***Loc:*** LA, SB, Lv88>

faillance [fajɑ̃s] *n.f.* ◊ **•tomber en faillance** to go to ruin, go to perdition <JD> <***Loc:*** JD>

faillard, -e [fajar, -ard] *adj.* weak *Il est pas plus faillard aujourd'hui.* He isn't any weaker today. (TB) <***Loc:*** TB>

faille [faj] *adj.* **1** weak *Les uns là là peut pas pincer parce qu'ils sont trop parés pour changer, ils sont failles.* These [crabs] can't pinch because they are too ready to molt, they are weak. (TB) *Le café à C. est bien faille.* C's coffee is really weak. (TB) **2** faint, feeble *Quand j'espère trop longtemps avant de manger, je me sens faille.* If I wait too long before I eat, I feel faint. (Gu00) *J'ai venu faille à l'église.* I fainted in church. (VM) *Il est faille d'avoir couru.* He is weak from running. (LF) <***Loc:*** AV, LA, LF, SB, SL, SM, TB, VM, Da84, Di32, Gu00, Lv88>

faillir [fajir] *v.intr.* to become faint, feel weak, dizzy and likely to faint *Mets-toi à l'ombre si tu veux pas faillir.* Get in the shade if you don't want to become faint. (LA) <***Loc:*** LA, Da84>

faillitude [fajityd] *n.f.* weakness, weak spell, faintness *Plus on buvait, plus on transpirait, plus on était sujet à attraper des faillitudes dans les rangs de coton.* The more we drank, the more we sweated, the more we were at risk of weak spells in the rows of cotton. (Lv88) <***Loc:*** SM, VM, Di32, Lv88>

faillot ♦see **fayot**

faillotte [fajɔt] *adj.* sickly *Je la trouve faillotte.* I find her sickly. (SB) <***Loc:*** SB>

faim [fɛ̃] *n.f.* hunger *La faim nous prenait.* Hunger overwhelmed us. (SL) ◊ **•avoir faim** to be hungry *J'ai faim, il dit. Chauffe les crabes pour que je mange.* I'm hungry, he said. Heat up the crabs for me to eat. (TB) *Elle a pas faim. Elle a picoché dans le manger tout l'avant-midi.* She's not hungry. She was picking at the food all morning. (SM) <LA, SJ, SL, SM, TB, VM, An94, Da84, La99, Wh83> **•avoir faim comme un chien** to be very hungry <La99> **•c'est la faim et la soif** one is as bad as the other <AV, SM, La99> **•la faim m'a pris** I got hungry <Da84> **•la faim et la soif** humorous reference to two poor people who make a couple *La faim et la soif se marient aujourd'hui.* "Hunger" and "thirst" [i.e. two penniless people] are getting married today. (SM) <SM, La99> <***Loc:*** AV, LA, SJ, SL, SM, TB, VM, An94, Da84, Hi02, La99, Wh83>

fainéant ♦see **faignant**

faïouque [fajuk] *n.m.* noise, racket, ruckus **Y avait in [=un] tel faïouque que ch'pouvais pas dôrmir.* There was such a racket that I couldn't sleep. (EV, Ph36) <***Loc:*** EV, Ph36>

FAIR [fɛɹ] *n.m.* fair <***Loc:*** JD, TB, Lv88>

faire [fær] **I** *v.tr.* **1** to make *Des socos, c'est pareil comme un raisin mais c'est différent. Y en a qui fait du vin avec ça.* Muscadine grapes, they're like grapes but they're different. Some people make wine with them. (TB) *La table est fait avec du bois.* The table is made of wood. (IB) **2** to do *Je vas jamais te pardonner pour avoir fait ça.* I will never forgive you for doing that. (TB) *C'est pas de faire ça.* That's not the thing to do. (VM) *C'est une tristesse je pense, ce que le gouvernement faisait.* It's a shame, I think, what the government was doing. (TB) **3** to have, get (s.t. done) *Équand-ce qu'il a fini la cale on a été pour le faire enregistrer avec le* COAST GUARD. When he finished the hull we went to have it registered with the Coast Guard. (TB) **Faire faire une robe.* To have a dress made. (Da84) *J'ai fait haler ma maison icitte.* I had my house moved here. (AC) *Il a fait arpenter la terre avant de l'acheter.* He had the land surveyed before buying it. (VM) **4** to make, have (s.o. or s.t. do s.t.), get (s.o. or s.t. to do s.t.) *Eusse mettait le lait dedans le siau, et ça le mettait dans le puits pour tiendre le lait frais. Comme ça, la chaleur le faisait pas aigrir.* They would put the milk in the bucket, and they put it in the well to keep the milk cool. That way, the heat didn't make it turn sour. (LF) *Le whiskey là et la bière et tout ça, ça boit là, c'est ça qui les fait faire des mauvaises choses.* Whiskey and beer and all that, they drink, that's what makes them do bad things. (EV) *Tu peux les faire manger la viande, mais je crois pas tu peux les faire tuer.* You can make them eat the meat, but I don't think you can get them to kill [the pigs]. (TB) *Des choses le faisaient fâcher, mais s'a jamais fâché après moi.* Some things made him get mad, but he never got mad at me. (AC) *On yeux donnait des patates, ça les faisait venir gras.* We gave them potatoes, that made them get fat. (AC) *Talonner son cheval, ça le fait galoper plus vite.* Spurring one's horse makes it gallop faster. (AV) *Il a bu un petit brin mais pas assez pour nous faire misérer.* He drank a little bit but not enough to make us suffer. (AC) **5** to raise, cultivate, grow, produce *Mon grand-père à Durald là-bas, il faisait du riz.* My grandfather over in Durald grew rice. (EV) **Faire de la récolte.* To raise a crop. (Da84) *Faire jardin.* To raise a garden. (Lv88) *Faire son jardin, faire du maïs, du riz, des cannes.* To cultivate a garden, grow corn, rice, sugar cane (VM) **6** to turn, become (an age) *Je vas faire* EIGHTY-FOUR *le huit de novembre.* I'm going to turn 84 on November 8. (TB) **7** to suit **Ça me fait.* It suits me. (Da84) **8** *(in impersonal expr.)* to be (of the weather) *On avait juste un éventail comme ça pour t'éventer avec ta main, et il faisait chaud pareil comme il fait ici asteur.* We just had a little fan for fanning yourself by hand like that, and it was hot just like it is here now. (LF) *Quand ça faisait froid, on avait juste un foyer et puis un* STOVE. When it was cold, we just had a fireplace and a stove. (IB) **II** *v.intr.* **1** *(in impersonal expr.)* to suffice **Ça peut faire.* It's ok, it can do. (Da84) **Ça va faire.* It will do. (Da84) *La provision de maïs n'est pas forte mais ça fera.* The supply of corn isn't good but it will do. (AV) **Ça y fait.* That does it. (Da84) **2** to defecate *Le 'tit garçon avait tellement peur il a fait dans ses culottes.* The little boy was so scared that he went in his pants [i.e. soiled himself]. (SM) **III se faire** *v.pron.* **1** to make for o.s. **Et je m'ai fait un violon moi-même. Je m'ai composé ça avec une boîte de cigares.* And I made myself a violin. I built it with a cigar box. (LA, An84) *Il s'a fait un* BARBECUE PIT *en pierre.* He built himself a stone barbecue pit. (LA) *On employait des feuilles, on se faisait une maison.* We used to use leaves, we would make ourselves a [play] house. (JE) **2** to make, have, get (s.t. done for or to o.s.) *J'ai été ramasser des socos et je m'ai fait piquer par des guêpes.* I was picking muscadines and I got stung by wasps. (Gu00) *Dans le Canal Yankee le* SPEED LIMIT *est 30 miles àl'heure. Et si tu te fais coller à aller plus, tu vas te faire donner un* FINE. In Canal Yankee [i.e. Golden Meadow] the speed limit is 30 miles an hour. And if you get caught going faster, you'll be given a fine. (LF) *Y a deux jeunes garçons qui s'a fait tuer là, couper la tête.* There are two boys who got killed there, they got their heads cut off. (TB) *Le petit bougre là s'a fait mordre par une serpent deux ans de ça.* The little guy got bit by a snake two years ago. (LF) *Je m'ai fait joliment piquailler en ramassant des mûres.* I got pretty well pricked while picking blackberries. (SL) **Va te faire foutre.* Go to hell. (Da84) **3** to take place, happen, be done *Le cultivage se fait dans le printemps.* Cultivation takes place in spring. (Lv88) **Quand je 'ois que tout quèque choge se fait en amaricain, ça me fait comme si j'sus après enterrer ma parenté et mon peup'.* When I see that everything is done in English, it makes me feel like I'm burying my kin and my people. (ThCa: *Mille misères*) **4** *(in impersonal expr.)* to happen, be **Ça peut se faire.* It could happen, maybe so. (Da84) **Comment ça peut se faire?* How can that be? (Da84) **Comment ça se fait?* Why? How come? (Da84) **5** to break (of day) *La clarté du jour s'a fait.* Daylight broke. (LF) ◊ **•faire avec** to get by with, make do with *Il faudra faire avec ça qu'on a.* We'll have to make do with what we have. (LA) <LA> **•faire belle** to stand by oneself (said of a child unable to walk yet) *C'est ça, fait belle pour papa, chère.* That's it, stand up for Daddy, sweetie. (SM) <SM> **•faire chicot** to stand by o.s. (said of a child unable to walk yet) <AV, IB> **•faire comme si** to make as if, to pretend *Vous fait comme si vous parle pas, mais si j'attrape le palonnier, vous va parler.* You pretend you can't talk, but if I grab the swingletree, you'll talk. (LA) <LA> **•faire (par) exprès** to do on purpose *Il fait exprès de danser avec ma belle.* He is dancing with my girlfriend on purpose. (LA) <LA> **•faire grief** to cause sorrow, be painful *Ça fait grief d'hypothéquer sa place.* It's painful to mortgage one's home. (VM) <VM> **•faire play** to offer no resistance, yield without resistance *T'as fait play.* You offered no resistance. (VM) <VM> **•faire à la six-quatre-deux** to do badly, do poorly, be negligent in doing s.t. <SM, La99> **•faire à tambour battant** to do quickly and not well <SL, La99> **•ça fait** so, then *Ça fait il a dit c'était correct.* Then he said it was correct. (Lv88) <EV, IB, IV, JD, LA, LF, SJ, SL, SM, TB, VM, An94, Gu82, Lv88, Wh83> **•se faire mal** to hurt o.s. *Tu pouvais tomber et te faire mal proche là-dessus.* You could fall and almost get hurt on it. (EV) <EV> <***Loc:*** AC, AL, AV, EV, IB, IV, JD, JE, LA, LF, SJ, SL, SM, TB, VM, An84, An94, Da84, De85, Di32, Gu82, Hi02, La99, Lv88, ThCa, Wh83>

faisable [fəzab(l)] *adj.* feasible, doable *Je connais pas si c'est faisable, mais on va essayer.* I don't know if it's feasible, but we'll try. (LA) <***Loc:*** LA, Da84>

faisage [fəzaʒ] *n.m.* making, doing *Il y a plus eu de trouble pour le tirage de vaches et le faisage de vider le pot.* There's more trouble for the milking of the cows and the emptying of the pots. (EV) <***Loc:*** EV>

faisan [fezɑ̃] *n.m.* pheasant <***Loc:*** Da84>

fais-dodo (fais do-do) [fedodo] *n.m.* traditional Cajun community dance <***Loc:*** AV, IB, JD, SJ, SL, Da84, Fa77, Guoo, Hio2, Lv88, Re31>

faiseur, -euse [fezœr, -øz] *n.* **1** doer, one who acts **Grand parleur et petit faiseur.* All talk and no action. (Da84) **2** maker (of pirogues, of violins, etc.) ◊ **•faiseur de baril** barrel maker <LF> **•faiseur de bateaux** boatbuilder <LF> **•faiseur de maïs** corn farmer <Da84, Lv88> **•faiseur d'embarras** troublemaker <Da84, Lv88> <***Loc:*** LF, Da84, Lv88>

fait [fɛ, fe, fɛt] *n.m.* **1** fact **2** act, deed ◊ **•fait accompli** accomplished fact <Da84> **•au fait** skillful, talented *C'est un homme bien au fait.* He's a very talented man. (SL) <SL> **•comme de fait** [kɔ̃mdəfɛt] in fact, as a matter of fact *Comme de fait, Oviniac était élongé par terre avec une grosse bosse au-dessus de son œil gauche.* As a matter of fact, Oviniac was stretched out on the ground with a large lump above his left eye. (VM) <TB, VM, Da84> <***Loc:*** SL, TB, VM, Da84>

faît [fe, fɛ, fɛt] *n.m.* **1** top *Tu outais les pailles, tu coupais le faît avec un couteau de cannes.* You cut off the outer leaves, you cut off the top [of the cane plant] with a cane knife. (LA) *La nique des 'tits zozos est dans le faît de l'arbre.* The nest of the little birds is in the top of the tree. (VM) **2** peak, summit (of a mountain) *Il a monté jusqu'au faît de la montagne.* He climbed up to the top of the mountain. (SM) **3** roof *Il grimpait sur le faît du magasin et il jouait l'accordéon là.* He would climb up onto the roof of the barn and he would play the accordion there. (EV) **4** crown (of the head) *Il est* BALD *dessus le faît de sa tête.* He is bald on the top of his head. (VM) **5** brim (of a container) **Remplir jusqu'au fait.* To fill to the rim. (Da84) **6** top, surface (of water) *Le faît de l'eau.* The surface of the water. (TB) ◊ **•faît de canne à sucre** top of sugar cane stalk <VM> **•faît d'oignon** onion top *Les chalottes, tu peux pas user plein de ça pour cuire parce que c'est trop amer. Mais les faîts d'oignon, tu peux les user, oui.* Shallots, you can't use a lot of that for cooking because it's too bitter. But the onion tops, you can use them. (LF) <LF> <***Loc:*** AV, EV, IB, LA, LF, SM, TB, VM, Da84, Di32, Fa77, Lv88>

faîtage (faitage) [fetaʒ] *n.m.* **1** treetop **2** ridge row, peak (of a house) <***Loc:*** Da84>

faîter [fete] *v.tr.* to cut off the top of *Il a fait faîter les cannes après qu'il les avait* WINDROW. He cut the tops off the cane after he had windrowed them. (TB) <***Loc:*** TB, Di32>

falbana [falbɑ̃na] *n.f.* frill ◊ **•falbana de** huge, immense *Une falbana de maison.* An extremely large house. (SL) <SL> <***Loc:*** JE, SL, Di32>

falcon [falkɔ̃] *n.m.* falcon <***Loc:*** Fa77>

fale (falle) [fal] *n.f.* **1** crop, craw, maw (of a bird) **2** stomach (of a person or animal) ◊ **•avoir la fale basse** to be hungry *J'ai la fale basse.* I'm hungry. (Guoo) <Guoo> **•avoir la fale creuse** to be hungry <LA> **•avoir la fale pleine** to have eaten enough, be full <LA, La99> <***Loc:*** AV, EV, IB, JD, LA, SB, SJ, SL, SM, TB, VM, Da84, Di32, Fa77, Guoo, La99, Lv88, Re31>

falle ♦see **fale**

falloir (fauloir) [folwar] *v.* (*p.p.* **follu, faulu** [foly]) *(in impersonal expr.)* to have to, be necessary *Il faut qu'un monde s'aide soi-même avant de demander de l'aide aux autres.* A person has to help himself before he asks for help from others. (VM) **Il faut pas lui parler. Il est dans ses ferdaignes.* You mustn't talk to him. He's in a bad mood. (Di32) *Il fallait bien travailler, il faut travailler dans la pêche depuis l'âge de douze ans.* I needed to work, you have to start work in fishing at twelve years old. (PQ) *Quand j'étais jeune, j'ai pas été à l'école, parce qu'il faulait que j'aide mon pape, faire récolte, travailler.* When I was young, I didn't go to school, because I had to help my dad, to farm and work. (TB) *Il a faulu qu'il me ramène à la maison de bonne heure.* He had to take me home early. (TB) **Être comme il faut.* To be as it should. (Da84) **Faire comme il faut.* To do as one should. (Da84) <***Loc:*** AC, EV, IB, IV, JE, LA, LF, PQ, SL, TB, VM, An84, An94, Da84, Di32, Guoo, Hio2, Lv88, Ph36, Wh83>

fameusement [fɑ̃møzmɑ̃] *adv.* **1** famously, excellently, very well *On a fameusement bien réussi.* We really succeeded famously. (VM) **2** much, a great deal *Nous autres, on a fameusement à manger, reste pour dîner.* We have a great deal to eat, stay for dinner. (VM) *Il a fameusement de l'argent.* He has a huge amount of money. (SB) *Il a mouillé fameusement.* It rained a great deal. (IB) <***Loc:*** IB, SB, TB, VM, Da84, Di32>

fameux, -euse [fɑ̃mø, -øz] *adj.* **1** famous, celebrated *Il est fameux, lui. Le monde le connaît partout.* He is famous. People know him everywhere. (VM) **2** [*ironic*] supposed, so-called **C'est un fameux docteur.* That's 'some' doctor. (Da84) ◊ **•pas fameux** not very good *On a été manger chez ma belle-mère hier au soir. C'était pas fameux.* We went to eat at my mother-in-law's house last night. It was not very good. (LA) <LA, TB> <***Loc:*** LA, TB, VM, Da84, Fa77>

familial, -e [fɑ̃miljal] *adj.* familial, pertaining to a family *Faire un devoir familial.* To do a family duty. (VM) <***Loc:*** VM, Da84>

familiarité [fɑ̃miljarite] *n.f.* familiarity <***Loc:*** Da84>

familier, -ière, -ieuse [fɑ̃milje, -jœr, -jøz] *adj.* **1** familiar *Et dans ce temps-là on l'appelait pas* GOLDEN MEADOW, *on l'appelait ça Canal Yankee. Peut-être que t'es familier avec ça.* And in those days we didn't call it Golden Meadow, we called it Canal Yankee. Maybe you're familiar with that. (LF) **2** common, widely known *La motchié de le monde* *ici c'est des Dupre, Naquin, et LeBœuf. Ça c'est les trois noms plus familiers ici.* Half of the people here are Dupres, Naquins and LeBœufs. Those are the three most common surnames here. (TB) **3** intimate, close *C'était deux familles qu'étaient beaucoup familières.* These were two families that knew each other well. (LA) <***Loc:*** LA, LF, TB, VM, Da84, Fa77>

famille [fɑ̃mij] *n.f.* **1** family, kin, relatives **2** family, group of closely related species *Et là des maqueriaux, des* KING MACKEREL AND SPANISH MACKEREL. *C'est tout dans la même famille de maqueriaux.* And there are the mackerels, King mackerel and Spanish mackerel. They're all in the same family of mackerels. (LF) ◊ **•famille de riquiqui** [*humorous*] large family *Voilà la famille de riquiqui.* There's the big family. (SM) <SM> **•en famille** pregnant *Elle est en famille.* She is pregnant. (SM) <AL, EV, IB, LA, LF, SL, SM, VM, Da84, Di32, La99, Lv88> **•être en famille pour** to be pregnant with *J'étais en famille pour M. quand j'ai sorti dans mars. Elle aussi était énée dans juin.* I was pregnant with M. when I went out in March. She also was born in June. (TB) <TB> **•se mettre en famille** to get pregnant <AC> **•venir en famille** to get pregnant *Et là quand j'ai venu en famille je voulais pas rester à Montegut.* And then when I got pregnant I didn't want to stay in Montegut. (TB) <AC, TB> <***Loc:*** AL, EV, IB, LA, LF, SL, SM, TB, VM, An94, Da84, Di32, Hi02, La99, Lv88>

famine [fɑ̃min] *n.f.* famine, scarcity <***Loc:*** Da84>

fanal (**fanau**) [fɑ̃nal, fɑ̃no] *n.m.* **1** lantern **2** headlight (of a carriage, car, boat, etc.) **3** tall, thin and unattractive man <***Loc:*** TB, VM, Da84, Di32>

fanau ♦see **fanal**

fandango [fɑ̃dɑ̃go] *n.f.* fandango dance <***Loc:*** Da84>

fané, -e [fɑ̃ne] *adj.* **1** wilted, withered *Des fleurs fanées.* Withered flowers. (LA) **2** faded *Une robe fanée.* A faded dress. (LA) <***Loc:*** LA, Da84>

faner [fɑ̃ne] *v.intr.* to wilt, wither *Ça faisait si longtemps que ça avait pas mouillé, que les tomates avaient tout fané.* It had been so long since it rained that the tomatoes had all withered. (LA) <***Loc:*** LA, LF, Da84>

fanfaron, -onne [fafarɔ̃, -ɔ̃n] *n.* proud person <***Loc:*** SB>

fanferluche, fanforluche ♦see **fanfreluche**

fanfreluche (**fanferluche**, **fanforluche**, **finfiluche**) [fɑ̃fœrlyʃ, fɑ̃felyʃ, fɑ̃færlyʃ, fɑ̃forlyʃ, fɑ̃firlyʃ, fɛ̃filyʃ, fofærlyʃ] *n.f.* decoration, bauble, frill *Il y a trop de fanferluches sur sa robe.* There are too many baubles on her dress. (SM) ◊ **•faire des fanferluches** to go to great trouble, do more than the usual (e.g. when receiving guests) <Lv88> <***Loc:*** AV, IB, JD, LA, LF, SB, SJ, SL, SM, TB, Lv88, Re31>

fantaisie [fɑ̃tezi] *n.f.* fantasy, imagination ◊ **•en fantaisie** angry, wrathful <VM, Di32> <***Loc:*** VM, Da84, Di32>

fantchon ♦see **fantoche**

fant-de-tchaque [fɑ̃tʃak, fɑ̃tak] *n.* smart aleck, showoff *Il est assez fant-de-tchaque, je peux pas l'endurer.* He is such a showoff, I can't stand him. (TB) <***Loc:*** LF, TB>

fantoche (**fantchon**) [fɑ̃tɔʃ, fɑ̃tʃɔ̃] *n.m.* country man who assumes the pose of urban sophistication *En le voyant je savais qu'il était un fantchon.* When I saw him I knew he was a country boy pretending to be a citydweller. (IB) <***Loc:*** IB, Di32>

faquetaïque [faketaik] *n.f.* little brunette girl <***Loc:*** JD, Re54>

faquin [fakɛ̃, fatʃɛ̃] *adj.* **1** fancy *Mais ça c'est faquin.* Well, that's fancy. (VM) **2** elegantly dressed *T'aurais dû le voir pour le mariage de sa sœur. Il était faquin.* You should have seen him for his sister's wedding. He was elegantly dressed. (VM) **3** vain *C'est un enfant faquin, ça. Il jongle juste à lui-même.* That's a vain child. He thinks only of himself. (VM) ◊ **•faquin comme un paon** proud, vain as a peacock <La99> <***Loc:*** EV, LA, SM, VM, La99, Lv88, Ph36>

far (**farre, fard, fars**) [far] *n.m.* stuffing, rice dressing *Du fars c'est ce qu'on met dans un 'tit cochon farci.* Dressing is what you put in a roast piglet. (SM) *Du fars de dinde.* Turkey giblet dressing. (SJ) <***Loc:*** AV, EV, IB, JD, LA, LF, SJ, SL, SM, TB, VM, Da84, Di32, Gu00, Lv88, Ph36>

faradé ♦see **faraudé**

faraud[1], **-e** [faro, -ɔd] *adj.* **1** well dressed, elegantly dressed **Alle aime être faraud, pauvre bête. Alle achète tout le temps le plus beau et le plus cher.* She likes being elegantly dressed, poor thing. She always buys the most beautiful and the most expensive [things]. (ThCa: *La table des veuves*) *Là il est parti en ville bien faraud dans son habillement de dimanche.* Then he went to town all dressed up in his Sunday clothes. (TB) **2** having pride in one's dress *Il est trop faraud pour mettre ça.* He's too proud of his appearance to wear that. (VM) ◊ **•faraud comme un paon** dressed up like a peacock <Da84, Lv88> <***Loc:*** JD, SB, SM, TB, VM, Da84, Di32, Lv88, ThCa>

faraud[2] [faro] *n.m.* **1** well-dressed person **2** fancy, elegant clothes *C'est pas que je mets du faraud, mais ça que je mets c'est propre.* It's not that I wear fancy clothes, but what I wear is clean. (VM) <***Loc:*** VM, Da84>

faraudé, -e (**faradé, -e**) [farode, farade] *adj.* displaying an excessive elegance *Il était tout faraudé pour aller au bal.* He was really dressed up to go to the dance. (LA) <***Loc:*** LA, Lv88>

farauder [farode] **I** *v.intr.* to sport fine clothes, dress up, dress elegantly *Je pense qu'il faudra farauder pour les noces.* I suppose we'll have to dress up for the wedding. (LA) **II se farauder** *v.pron.* to put on one's Sunday best, dress elegantly *Je n'ai jamais vu une personne aime tant se farauder.* I've never seen anyone who likes to dress so elegantly. (SB) <***Loc:*** JD, LA, SB, VM, Da84, Lv88>

farauderie [farodri] *n.f.* **1** fancy or dressy clothes and accessories *Ça c'est une farauderie!* That is a beautiful outfit!

(SL) **2** pride in one's dress *Alle a de la farauderie. Alle met tout l'argent de son père sur des robes et des chapeaux.* She has a lot of pride in her appearance. She spends all of her father's money on dresses and hats. (VM) ◊ **•en farauderie** decorated elegantly, decked out elegantly *Sa maison est tout le temps en farauderie.* Her house is always decorated elegantly. (VM) <VM> <***Loc:*** EV, IB, SL, SM, VM, Da84, Di32, Lv88, Ph36>

farbana [farbɑ̃na] *n.m.* worthless thing or person *Jette ça, c'est un farbana.* Throw that away, it's a piece of junk. (VM) *C'est un grand farbana, lui.* He's a loser. (VM) <***Loc:*** VM>

farce[1] [fars] *adj.* funny, humorous, comical *Il a raconté une histoire qu'était beaucoup farce.* He told a story that was extremely funny. (LA) <***Loc:*** AV, EV, LA, SB, SJ, VM, Da84, Fa77, Hi02, Lv88>

farce[2] [fars] *n.f.* **1** joke **2** comedy **3** farce ◊ **•faire des farces** to tell jokes <Da84> <***Loc:*** LF, Da84, Fa77, Hi02>

farceur, -euse [farsœr, -øz] *n.m.* **1** jokester, joke teller, comic **2** prankster <***Loc:*** EV, SL, Da84>

farci, -e [farsi] *adj.* **1** roasted, baked **Cochon farci.* Roasted pig. (Da84) *Du fars c'est ce qu'on met dans un 'tit cochon farci.* Dressing is what you put in a roasted piglet. (SM) **2** deep fried in its entirety (of a pig, turkey or duck) **3** stuffed *Un canard farci.* A stuffed duck. (AV) <***Loc:*** AV, SM, VM, Da84>

farcin [farsɛ̃] *n.m.* crud, filth, encrusted dirt <***Loc:*** Da84>

farcir [farsir] *v.tr.* **1** to roast, bake (meat) *Un canard farci, c'était un canard cuit dans le four.* A roasted duck was a duck baked in the oven. (VM) **2** to stuff *Il a farci une poule.* He stuffed a hen. (AV) <***Loc:*** AV, VM, Da84>

fard ♦see **far**

fardeau [fardo] *n.m.* load, burden <***Loc:*** Da84>

fardoche (**ferdoche**, **fordoche**) [fardɔʃ, færdɔʃ, fɔrdɔʃ] *n.f.* **1** underbrush, brushwood *J'ai coupé de la fardoche.* I cut some underbrush. (VM) **2** tall weeds **3** *(pl.)* the sticks, the boondocks, place in the middle of nowhere **Il reste dans les fardoches.* He lives out in the sticks. (Da84) **4** trash, rubbish ◊ **•être dans les fardoches** to have problems, difficulties (esp. financial) <SM, Lv88, Re31> <***Loc:*** EV, LF, SB, SM, TB, VM, Da84, Di32, Lv88, Ph36, Re31>

farine [farin] *n.f.* flour, meal *Je faisais du roux avec de l'huile et de la farine.* I used to make roux with oil and flour. (SL) ◊ **•farine (de) froment** white wheat flour *On fait des biscuits avec la farine froment.* You make biscuits with white flour. (SM) <SM, Fa77> **•farine (de) maïs** cornmeal *On fait la couche-couche avec la farine maïs.* You make couche-couche with cornmeal. (SM) <SM, Fa77> **•farine d'Indien** flour made from green corn <VM> **•farine du diable** ill-gotten wealth *La farine du diable tourne en son.* Ill-gotten gain turns to nothing (lit. the devil's flour turns to sawdust). (VM) <VM> **•farine française** wheat flour <IB, TB, VM, Di32, Lv88> **•au dessus de la farine** rich <La99> <***Loc:*** EV, IB, LA, SL, SM, TB, VM, Da84, Fa77, Hi02, Lv88>

fariner [farine] *v.tr.* to flour, dip in flour, sprinkle with flour or meal *Alle a fariné sa viande avant de la cuire.* She sprinkled her meat with flour before cooking it. (LA) <***Loc:*** LA, Da84>

farineux, -euse [farinø, -øz] *adj.* floured, covered with meal *Heureuse, sucreuse et farineuse bonne année.* Happy new year filled with sugar and flour. (LA) <***Loc:*** LA, Da84>

farmer [farme] *v.tr.* to farm, raise, cultivate *J'ai coutume pêcher des hameçons mais depuis les* POND *à poissons, ils ont commencé farmer les* CATFISH. I am used to fishing with hooks but because of the fishing ponds, they have started to farm catfish. (SM) <***Loc:*** SM>

farmier ♦see **fermier**

farouche [faruʃ] *adj.* **1** wild, uncultivated *Herbe farouche.* Wild grass. (VM) **2** wild, untamed, feral *Nos cochons partaient. Ils allaient dans le bois. Ça restait là. Ça restait farouche.* Our pigs would leave. They would go into the woods. They stayed there. They stayed wild. (SL) **3** very angry *Quand il a perdu sa montre, ça l'a rendu farouche.* When he lost his watch, it made him very angry. (LA) <***Loc:*** AC, AV, EV, LA, SL, VM, Da84, Gu00, Hi02, Lv88>

farre, fars ♦see **far**

fatalité [fatalite] *n.f.* fatality, death <***Loc:*** Da84>

fatigant, -e (**fatiquant, -e**) [fatigɑ̃, fatikɑ̃, -ɑ̃t] *adj.* tiring, fatiguing *L'ouvrage dedans les clos était fatigant.* Work in the fields was tiring. (EV, ch: *Restez, Mom et Pop, restez*) <***Loc:*** EV, Da84>

fatigue (**fatique**) [fatig, fatik] *n.f.* **1** tiredness, weariness, fatigue *Il souffre de la fatigue.* He suffers from fatigue. (SM) *T'as la fatique.* You are tired. (VM) **2** tiresome thing, wearisome thing *Ce voyage va être juste une fatique, j'ai pas envie d'aller.* This trip is going to be just a tiresome thing, I don't want to go. (VM) <***Loc:*** LF, SM, TB, VM, Da84, Di32, Lv88>

fatigué, -e (**fatiqué, -e**) [fatige, fatike] *adj.* tired, weary, fatigued *Quand je suis fatiqué là-dedans je vas dans le jardin.* When I get tired of that I go into the garden. (TB) *T'étais assez fatiqué, follait que ça soye confortable.* You were tired enough, it had to be comfortable. (LF) <***Loc:*** AC, IB, IV, JE, LA, LF, SJ, SL, SM, TB, VM, Da84, Di32, Hi02>

fatiguer (**fatiquer**) [fatige, fatike] **I** *v.tr.* to tire, to make tired, exhaust *L'ouvrage m'a si tellement fatiqué!* The work made me so very tired! (SM) **II se fatiguer** *v.pron.* to tire, get tired *Il s'a endormi dessus la route à force qu'il s'avait fatigué.* He fell asleep driving because he had gotten so tired. (LA) <***Loc:*** LA, LF, SL, SM, TB, VM, Da84, Di32, Hi02, Lv88>

fatiquant ♦see **fatiguant**

fatique ♦see **fatigue**

fatiqué ♦see **fatigué**

fatiquer ♦see **fatiguer**

fatras[1] [fatra] *adj.* **1** worn out, worthless *Un cheval bien fatras.* A worthless old horse. (SJ) **2** weak, delicate *Un enfant fatras.* A delicate child. (AV) <***Loc:*** AV, SJ>

fatras[2] [fatra] *n.m.* **1** junk, worthless thing *Le monde usait pas ce fatras de marijuana et ces affaires comme ça dans le temps.* People did not use that marijuana junk and things like that at that time. (AC) *Des fatras MADE IN JAPAN.* Junk made in Japan. (Lv88) **2** old, worn out tool or machine **3** trash **Il ramassait les fatras pour le village.* He collected the trash for the town. (An84) **4** sweepings *Alle a balié la maison, mais alle a laissé le fatras sur la galerie.* She swept the house but she left the sweepings on the porch. (VM) **5** good-for-nothing person, ne'er-do-well *C'est pas bon à rien, c'est un fatras.* He's not good for anything, he's a ne'er-do-well. (Lv88) **6** riffraff, rabble **Jette tout ç' fatras diors.* Throw all the rabble out. (EV, Ph36) **7** boring or uninteresting person **Dis-mon pas qu' ç' fatras va venir icitte encore.* Don't tell me that old bore is coming here again. (EV, Ph36) <***Loc:*** AC, EV, LA, SM, TB, VM, An84, Da84, Fa77, Hi02, Lv88, Ph36>

fatrouille [fatruj] *n.f.* ◊ **•faire la fatrouille** to keep watch (as for a thief, an enemy) *Jean va faire la fatrouille à soir.* John will keep watch tonight. (IB) <IB> <***Loc:*** IB>

faubourg [fobur] *n.m.* **1** loafer's corner, hangout for loafers **2** [in St. Martinville] 'negro-town' (part of town inhabited by African-Americans) <***Loc:*** SM, VM>

fauces [fɔs] *n.f.pl.* **1** shears *Il est après chercher les fauces pour tondre les moutons.* He's looking for the shears to shear the sheep. (VM) **2** clippers <***Loc:*** VM>

fauchable [foʃab(l)] *adj.* ready for mowing, ready for cutting *Le foin était fauchable au mois d'octobre cette année ici.* The hay was ready to be cut in October this year. (TB) <***Loc:*** TB, Di32>

fauchage [foʃaʒ] *n.m.* mowing **Faire le fauchage.* To do the mowing (Da84) <***Loc:*** Da84>

fauchée [foʃe] *n.f.* amount of grass or hay cut with one swing of the blade or scythe <***Loc:*** AV, SJ>

faucher [foʃe] *v.tr.* to mow, cut *Faucher la cour.* To mow the yard. (LA) <***Loc:*** LA, Da84, Fa77, Hi02, Lv88>

faucheuse [foʃøz, faʃøz] *n.f.* **1** mowing machine **2** lawn mower **Son plan c'est de le mettre dessus la terre juste avant Tchou Flang coupe les herbes pour que le papier peut être déchiraillé par la fourcheuse [=faucheuse].* His plan is to put them on the lawn just before Tchou Flang cuts the grass so the paper can be shredded by the lawnmower. (Wh83) <***Loc:*** EV, LA, SJ, VM, Da84, Fa77, Lv88, Wh83>

faucille [fosij] *n.f.* scythe, sickle *Pour couper le riz, ça passait en premier avec des faucilles, pour faire le tour avant la coupeuse venait passer.* To cut the rice, they would pass through first with sickles, to make the rounds before the combine came through. (SL) <***Loc:*** EV, SL>

faucon [fokɔ̃] *n.m.* hawk <***Loc:*** SL>

faufiler (**fifauler**) [fofile, fifole] **I** *v.tr.* to baste, tack *Faufiler un ourlet.* To baste a hem. (EV) **II se faufiler** *v.pron.* to mix, mingle (with a crowd) *Il s'a faufilé parmi des bons-à-rien et il a rentré dans le tracas.* He was hanging around with some ne'er-do-wells and he got into trouble. (LA) *Il se fifaule partout.* He slips in everywhere. (LF) <***Loc:*** EV, LA, LF, Da84, Lv88>

fauloir ♦see **falloir**

fausse-couche [foskuʃ, fɔskuʃ] *n.f.* miscarriage (of a fetus) <***Loc:*** TB, Da84>

fausse-flèche [fɔsflɛʃ, fosflɛʃ] *n.f.* coupling shaft, coupling pole (of a wagon or carriage) <***Loc:*** SM, Da84>

fausser [fose] **I** *v.tr.* **1** to warp, foul up *J'ai pour aller faire arranger mes lunettes. Ils sont faussés.* I have to go get my eyeglasses fixed. They are out of line. (VM) **2** to falsify *Ils ont faussé les papiers. C'est comme ça qu'ils ont eu la terre.* They falsified the documents. That's how they got the land. (LA) **II se fausser** *v.pron.* to get warped or fouled up ◊ **•fausser son serment** to perjure o.s. <Da84> <***Loc:*** LA, VM, Da84>

fausset (**fosset**) [fosɛ, fose] *n.m.* faucet, tap <***Loc:*** Da84>

fausseté [foste] *n.f.* falsehood, duplicity <***Loc:*** Da84>

faute [fot] *n.f.* **1** fault **C'est ma faute.* It is my fault. (Da84) **C'est pas ma faute.* It is not my fault. (Da84) **2** defect, mistake ◊ **•faute de** (for) lack of *Faute d'argent, j'ai pas acheté ça j'avais de besoin.* For lack of money, I couldn't buy what I needed. (VM) <VM> <***Loc:*** VM, Da84, Fa77>

fauter [fote] **I** *v.tr.* to blame *J'ai fauté Pierre pour ça.* I blamed Pierre for that. (VM) **II** *v.intr.* to err, make a mistake *J'ai fauté quand j'ai volé l'argent.* I erred when I stole the money. (SM) <***Loc:*** SM, VM>

fauteuil [fotœj] *n.m.* **1** armchair **2** rocking chair, rocker <***Loc:*** Da84>

fautif, -ive [fotif, -iv] *adj.* guilty, at fault *Mais là, pauvre Selena, elle se sentait assez fautive d'avoir brûlé l'argent à Alphonse, qu'elle a décidé de s'en aller au Texas avec lui.* But then poor Selena felt so bad about having burned Alphonse's money that she decided to go to Texas with him. (ThCa: *La dernière quilte*) <***Loc:*** ThCa>

faux[1], **fausse** [fo, fos] *adj.* **1** false, fake, artificial *Il a été mis en prison parce qu'il a fait des faux chèques.* He was put in prison because he wrote bad checks. (VM) **Fausse dents.* False teeth. (An94) **2** untrue, fictitious *Il a commencé des faux contes sus sa voisine.* He started telling lies about his neighbor. (VM) **3** empty (of a nutshell or seed pod) *Une pacane fausse (faux).* A pecan that is empty. (VM) *Il y avait un tas des pacanes qui étaient faux.* There were a lot of empty pecans. (VM) *Des grains faux.* Unpollinated [empty] seeds. (VM) <***Loc:*** IB, VM, An94, Da84, Fa77, Hi02>

faux[2] [fo] *n.f.* scythe, sickle <***Loc:*** Da84>

faveur [favœr] *n.f.* favor <***Loc:*** Da84>

favorable [favorab(l)] *adj.* favorable, opportune *Un temps favorable pour la récolte.* Favorable weather for the harvest. (AC) <***Loc:*** AC, Da84>

fayot (faillot) [fajo] *n.m.* white bean <***Loc:*** SB, Ho90, Re31>

fédéral[1], **-e** [federal] *adj.* federal *La seule manière que cette place ici pourrait être sauvée, faudrait que le gouvernement fédéral dépense des millions et des millions de piastres.* The only way this place could be saved, the federal government would have to spend millions and millions of dollars. (TB) <***Loc:*** TB, Da84>

fédéral[2] [federal] *n.m.* federal investigator, FBI agent *Les fédérals l'ont investigué.* The feds investigated him. (EV) <***Loc:*** EV>

fédération [federasjɔ̃] *n.f.* federation, alliance <***Loc:*** Da84>

FEED[1] [fid] *v.tr.* to feed (animals) **Il a sorti son baquet-là pour aller FEED sa truie.* He got out his bucket to go feed his sow. (An77) *Il venait ramasser les têtes (des chevrettes). Il amenait ça dans son PICK-UP TRUCK, et c'est ça qu'il feedait à les tortues.* He came and got the (shrimp) heads. He took them away in his pickup truck, and that's what he fed to his turtles. (LF) ***Loc:*** VM, LF, An77, Lv88>

FEED[2] [fid] *n.m.* feed (for animals) *Le laitereau fait du bon FEED pour les cochons et les lapins blancs.* Milkweed makes good feed for pigs and white rabbits. (TB) <***Loc:*** LF, TB, VM, Lv88>

fêlé, -e [fele] *adj.* **1** cracked, split *J'ai sorti mes verres à vin et il y en a qui est fêlé.* I took out my wine glasses and there's one that's cracked. (VM) **2** cracked, nutty (of a person) *Tu peux jamais dire quoi elle va faire. Elle est manière fêlée.* You can never tell what she's going to do. She's a little nutty. (LA) <***Loc:*** VM, Da84>

fêler [fele] *v.tr.* to crack, break *Il a échappé sa bol, il l'a fêlé.* He dropped his bowl and he broke it. (VM) <***Loc:*** VM, Da84>

félicitation [felisitasjɔ̃] *n.f.* felicitation, congratulation <***Loc:*** Da84>

félicité [felisite] *n.f.* happiness <***Loc:*** Da84>

féliciter [felisite] *v.tr.* to congratulate *Féliciter les mariés.* To congratulate the bride and groom. (EV) <***Loc:*** EV, Da84>

félon [felɔ̃] *n.m.* felon, traitor, outlaw <***Loc:*** Da84>

felouète ♦see **fluet**

fêlure [felyr] *n.f.* crack (in a brittle substance) <***Loc:*** Da84>

femelle[1] **(fumelle)** [fəmel, fymɛl, fymel, fimɛl] *adj.* female *C'était une grosse femelle ourse qui volait son maïs.* It was a big female bear that was stealing his corn. (VM) <***Loc:*** AC, EV, IB, LA, LF, TB, VM, An94, Da84, Hi02>

femelle[2] **(fumelle)** [fəmel, fymɛl, fymel, fimel] *n.f.* **1** female *Pourquoi les mâles brillent et les femelles est toujours cachées? C'est pour quand il y a des œufs, tu peux pas les voir si aisé.* Why are the males brilliantly colored and the females are camouflaged? It's for when there are eggs, you can't see them as easily. (TB) **2** woman, girl *Allons voir les femelles.* Let's go see the girls. (SM) **3** girlfriend, female companion *C'était ma femelle pour moi fréquenter.* That was my girlfriend for me to date. (LF) <***Loc:*** AV, LF, SM, TB, VM, Da84, Hi02, Lv88>

femme [fãm] *n.f.* **1** woman *Cette femme-là est ma sœur et cette femme-là est ma cousine.* That woman is my sister and that woman there is my cousin. (JE) **2** wife **Ses trois filles et sa femme étaient dans la maison.* His three daughters and his wife were in the house. (LA, An94) ◊ **•femme cartée** prostitute who holds a professionnal ID card <IB> **•femme de couleur** colored woman <Da84> **•femme placée** woman who lives with a man, though not married to him <TB, La99> **•femme publique / femme du soir** prostitute <AV, Da84> **•femme sage** midwife <Lv88> **•femme tenue** kept woman <Da84> **•prétende-femme** future wife, bride-to-be <VM> <***Loc:*** AC, AS, AV, EV, IB, IV, JD, JE, LA, LF, PQ, SL, SM, TB, VM, An94, Co80, Da84, Gr86, Gu00, Gu82, La99, Lv88, Wh83>

fendasse [fãdas] *n.f.* split, crack, fissure <***Loc:*** VM>

FENDER [fɛndə, fændə] *n.m./f.* fender, bumper <***Loc:*** EV, VM, An94, Lv88>

fend-gueule [fãdʒœl] *n.m.* harmonica <***Loc:*** IB>

fendre [fãn, fãd(r)] **I** *v.tr.* **1** to chop, split *Ça c'était usé pour fendre le bois. Y avait une grosse lame dessus.* That was used for splitting wood. There was a big blade on it. (LF) **2** to cut open *Quand on voulait les fendre en deux on les pendait.* When we wanted to cut [the pigs] open, we would hang them up. (TB) **3** to crack **4** to rip **II se fendre** *v.pron.* to split, rupture ◊ **•fendre l'air** to make a quick getaway, get away very quickly *Je voyais qu'il était après se chauffer, ça fait j'ai fendu l'air.* I saw that he was getting angry, so I got out of there quickly. (EV) <EV, La99> **•fendre la terre** to break the sod, plow rows (esp. for the first time) *Il a fendu la terre avec la charrue.* He plowed the land with a plow. (SM) <SM> **•se fendre à rire** to burst out laughing *Gaspard s'est fendu à rire.* Gaspard burst out laughing. (EV) <EV, Lv88> **•se fendre la gueule à rire** to laugh heartily *Je m'ai fendu la gueule à rire quand j'ai vu ça.* I laughed heartily when I saw that. (EV) <EV> **•se fendre les côtés à rire** to split one's sides laughing <Da84> <***Loc:*** EV, LF, SL, SM, Da84, La99, Lv88>

fendu, -e [fãdy] *adj.* **1** cracked, split **2** torn **La robe est fendue.* The dress is torn. (Da84) ◊ **•avoir le palais bien fendu** to have a way with words, to have the gift of gab *Il a le palais bien fendu. Tu peux pas rester fâché avec lui.* He has a way with words. You can't stay mad at him. (LA) <LA, Lv88> **•palais fendu** cleft palate <EV> <***Loc:*** EV, LA, Da84, Lv88>

fendure [fãdyr] *n.f.* split, crack *Il y a une fendure dans le mur.* There's a crack in the wall. (Lv88) <***Loc:*** VM, Di32, Lv88>

fenêtre [f(ə)net(r), f(ə)nɛt(r), snɛt(r)] *n.f.* **1** window *Équand mame et mon pape avait de la compagnie, "Allez jouer en dehors!" Mais nous-autres, pour faire le bête et pas les écouter, des fois on se mettait à la porte ou on se mettait au ras de la fenêtre et guetter et écouter.* When mom and dad had company, "Go play outside!" But sometimes to act stupid and not listen to them, we stood near the door or next to the window to watch and listen. (TB) **2** paneless, sashless window (esp. an old-fashioned window with wooden shutters) *Il y avait des fenêtres qu'avaient pas de châssis, juste une porte qui barrait la fenêtre.* There were windows that didn't have any sash, just a door that blocked the window frame. (Lv88) *Une fenêtre c'est une ouvertation, et un chassis c'est avec des vitres dessus.* A "fenêtre" is an opening, and a "chassis" has panes of glass in it. (AS) **3** wooden shutter *Une fenêtre, [...] ça c'est de quoi qu'eusse barre un chassis avec.* A 'fenêtre,' that's what they close a window with. (TB) <***Loc:*** AV, EV, IB, IV, JE, LA, LF, SJ, SL, SM, TB, VM, Da84, Di32, Fa77, Hi02, Lv88>

fente [fɑ̃t] *n.f.* **1** slit (in a dress) **2** crack *Il a mis le coin dans la fente de la bille de bois.* He put the wedge in the crack in the log. (VM) <***Loc:*** VM, Da84>

fer [fær] *n.m.* **1** iron, cast iron *Le* STOVE *est fait avec du fer.* The stove is made of cast iron. (AV) **2** iron, tool for pressing clothes, branding, soldering, etc. **3** horseshoe *Il y en a qui mettait des fers pour aider aux sabots.* Some people put on irons to help the hoofs. (EV) **4** brass knuckles **J'ai parti mon chemin avec la jug au plombeau et le fer à la main.* I went on my way with a jug at the pommel and brass knuckles in my hand. (EV, Gr86) **5** triangle (musical instrument) ◊ **•fer à cheval {chevaux}** horseshoe <Da84> **•fer à repasser** pressing iron, clothing iron <LA, An94, Da84> **•fer à marquer** branding iron <EV, Da84> **•fer à souder** soldering iron <Da84> **•fer volant** scythe <Lv88> **•avoir trop de fers au feu** to have too many irons in the fire <Lv88> **•en fer** made of iron *J'ai des grosses bombes en fer là là.* I have some big iron pots right there. (TB) <TB> **•petit fer / ti-fer** triangle, typically made from bent hay rake tines, used as a percussion instrument to keep time *Ça cognait ces petits fers pour garder le temps derrière l'accordéon et le violon.* They would hit those triangles to keep time with the accordeon and the violin. (EV) <EV> <***Loc:*** AV, EV, LA, LF, JE, SL, SM, TB, VM, An94, Da84, Hi02, Lv88>

ferail (ferraille) [feraj] *n.m./f.* **1** piece of junk iron, scrap iron *De temps en temps on trouve un vieux ferrail d'un vieux essieu de wagon, tu sais, quelque chose qu'eux-autres a dans la terre.* From time to time we find an old piece of scrap iron from an old wagon axle, you know, something in the ground. (TB) **2** brass knuckles **Oh! Les gens de Crowley sont toujours dans chemin avec la jug au plombeau et la ferraille à la poche.* Oh! The people of Crowley are always on the road with their jug on the pommel and brass knuckles in their pocket. (Gr86) <***Loc:*** LA, LF, TB, Da84, Gr86>

fer-blanc [færblɑ̃] *n.m.* **1** any brightly colored rust-resistant metal (esp. galvanized steel, galvanized iron, tin, or aluminum) *Le couteau est fait avec de l'acier et le manche est fait avec du fer-blanc.* The knife is made of tool steel and the handle is made of galvanized metal. (LF) **2** any metal vessel or container (such as a bucket, pail, or pan) *Il amène le lait dans un fer-blanc.* He brings the milk in a metal pail. (SM) **3** potful, panful *Un fer-blanc d'eau.* A panful of water. (SJ) <***Loc:*** AV, EV, IB, JD, LF, SB, SJ, SM, TB, VM, Da84, Di32, Ph36>

ferblanterie [færblɑ̃tri] *n.f.* metal vessels and containers <***Loc:*** Pe37>

ferdaignes ♦see **ferdaines**

ferdaines (feurdaines, ferdaignes) [færdɛ̃n, fœrdɛ̃n] *n.f.pl.* ◊ **•être dans ses feurdaines** to be ill-humored, be in a bad mood *Parle-y pas, il est dans ses feurdaines.* Don't talk to him, he's in a terrible mood. (VM) **Il faut pas lui parler. Il est dans ses ferdaignes. You* mustn't talk to him. He's in a bad mood. (Di32) <VM, Di32, Lv88> <***Loc:*** VM, Di32, Lv88>

ferdiller ♦see **frédiller**

ferdilloux ♦see **frédilleux**

ferdir ♦see **frédir**

ferdoche ♦see **fardoche**

fermage ♦see **fromage**

ferme[1] [færm] *adj.* firm, solid *Sur la terre ferme.* On solid ground. (LA) *Le poisson armé a une chair ferme.* The garfish has a firm flesh. (VM) <***Loc:*** LA, VM, Da84>

ferme[2] [færm, fɔrm] *n.f.* farm ◊ **•ferme de produits** truck farm, vegetable farm, produce farm *Et j'ai acheté des patates douces pour une ferme de produits à Pont Breaux.* And I bought sweet potatoes for a produce farm at Breaux Bridge. (SL) <SL> <***Loc:*** LF, SL, Da84>

ferment[1] [færmɑ̃] *n.m.* leaven, yeast, sourdough <***Loc:*** Da84>

ferment[2] ♦see **ferrement**

fermentation [færmɑ̃tasjɔ̃] *n.f.* fermentation <***Loc:*** Da84>

fermenter [færmɑ̃te] **I** *v.tr.* to ferment *Il faulait tu fermentes ton jus dans un baril.* You had to ferment the juice in a barrel. (SL) **II** *v.intr.* to ferment *Tu mélangeais ça bien, là tu le laissais fermenter pour quelques jours.* You'd mix that well, then you'd let it ferment for a few days. (SL) <***Loc:*** SL, Da84>

fermer (fremer, frémer) [færme, frɛ̃me] **I** *v.tr.* **1** to close, shut *Je vas frémer la porte.* I am going to close the door. (TB) *On avait fermé nos yeux qu'on avait peur du revenant.* We had closed our eyes [because] we were afraid of the ghost. (EV) **2** to enclose *Ils ont fini de fermer la maison.* They finished enclosing the house. (VM) **3** to close, shut down (a business, etc.) *Quand ils ont fait la levée ils ont fermé le* FERRY. When they built the levee they shut down the ferry. (SJ) **4** to put out, switch off, turn off (a light) *Ferme la lumière. C'est l'heure de dormir.* Turn off the light. It's time to sleep. (LA) **II** *v.intr.* **1** to close *Ça rouvre et ça frème là.* It opens and closes there. (AC) **2** to close, end (of a season) *J'ai travaillé jusqu'à la saison ferme là-bas, la saison d'huître.* I worked until the season closed there, oyster season. (TB) **III se fermer** *v.pron.* to close, shut (of a window, blinds, etc.) *Les rideaux se fermaient pas, il y avait comme une craque. Et j'ai vu la tête d'un homme.* The curtains didn't close, there was like a crack. And I saw a man's head. (TB) ◊ **•fermer sa bouche** to stop talking, shut one's mouth, shut up **Ferme ta bouche!* Shut up! (Da84) <Da84> **•fermer son grabot** to stop talking, shut one's mouth <La99> **•ferme ta gueule** shut your trap, shut up <Da84> **•pas fermer l'œil** to not sleep a wink <Da84> <***Loc:*** AC, EV, JE, LA, SJ, SM, TB, VM, Da84, Hi02, La99>

fermeté [færməte] *n.f.* firmness, solidity <***Loc:*** Da84>

fermier (farmier) [færmje, farmje] *n.m.* farmer <***Loc:*** AC, LA, SL, SM, Da84, Fa77>

FERN [fœɹn, fœjn] *n.m.* fern <***Loc:*** EV, TB, VM, Lv88, Ph36>

féroce [feros] *adj.* ferocious, savage, wild *Le chien était rendu féroce.* The dog had become savage. (LA) <***Loc:*** LA, Da84>

ferraille ♦see **ferail**

ferrailler [feraje] *v.intr.* to make a lot of noise, make a racket *Y avait un homme, un soir [...] ses poules étaient après ferrailler.* There was a man, one evening his chickens were making a lot of noise. (Gr86) <***Loc:*** Gr86>

ferré, -e [fere] *adj.* **1** shod (of a horse) *Son cheval était pas ferré.* His horse was not shod. (AC) **2** ironclad *Le bas de la citerne était ferré.* The bottom of the cistern was ironclad. (VM) <***Loc:*** AC, VM, Da84>

ferrée [fere] *n.f.* spade <***Loc:*** Di32, Lv88>

ferrement (ferment) [færmɑ̃] *n.m.* piece of iron <***Loc:*** Da84>

ferrer [fere] *v.tr.* to shoe (a horse) *C'est ça t'appelles ferrer, mettre des fers: mettre les* SHOES *dessous un sabot.* That's what you call shoeing, putting on horseshoes: put the shoes on a hoof. (VM) <***Loc:*** VM, Da84>

ferrie ♦see **FERRY**

FERRY (ferry, ferrie) [feri, fere] *n.m.* ferry *Y avait pas de pont. Follait que t'espères pour le ferry.* There was no bridge. You had to wait for the ferry. (TB) <***Loc:*** EV, JE, SB, SJ, SL, SM, TB, VM, Da84, Lv88, Ph36, Re31>

fertile [færtil] *adj.* fertile, rich *De la terre fertile.* Fertile land. (LA) <***Loc:*** LA, Da84>

fertiliser [færtilize] *v.tr.* to fertilize, enrich (soil, etc.) *On a habitude de fertiliser notre jardin juste avec du fumier.* We usually fertilize our garden only with manure. (LA) <***Loc:*** LA, Da84>

fertilité [færtilite] *n.f.* fertility, fruitfulness <***Loc:*** Da84>

fertillant [fœrtijɑ̃] *adj.* fidgety, frisky <***Loc:*** TB>

fertiller (feurtiller, fertouiller) [færtije, fœrtije, færtuje] *v.intr.* to fidget, wriggle, squirm *Reste tranquille, tout le temps tu feurtilles.* Stay still, you are always fidgeting. (VM) <***Loc:*** JE, VM, Lv88>

fertouiller ♦see **fertiller**

férule [feryl] *n.f.* ferule, sleeve (bearing) <***Loc:*** Da84>

fervent, -e [færvɑ̃, -ɑ̃t] *adj.* fervent, pious <***Loc:*** SM>

ferveur [færvœr] *n.f.* fervor <***Loc:*** Da84>

fesse [fɛs] *n.f.* **1** buttock **2** *(pl.)* butt, rear end, derriere, rump ◊ **•avoir des fesses de moiselle** to have a skinny behind <La99> <***Loc:*** AL, Da84, Hi02, La99>

festin [festɛ̃] *n.m.* feast, banquet <***Loc:*** Da84>

festival [festival] *n.m.* fair, festival <***Loc:*** Hi02>

fête[1] [fɛt] *n.f.* **1** holiday, feast day *J'imagine qu'ils vont rebaisser les prix après les fêtes.* I imagine that they will reduce the prices after the holidays. (LA) **2** birthday *On a six mois de différence, sa fête est le dix de mars et moi c'est le dix de septembre.* We are six months apart, his birthday is the 10th of March and mine is the 10th of September. (IB) ◊ **•fête des dindes** Thanksgiving <> **•fête-Dieu** the feast of Corpus Christi <Da84> **•fête d'obligation** feast day of obligation <Da84> **•fête de naissance** birthday <Da84> **•faire la fête** to celebrate *On a fait la fête hier au soir.* We partied last night. (LA) <LA> **•grande fête** major holiday or holy day <Da84> <***Loc:*** AC, EV, IB, LA, LF, SL, TB, VM, Da84, Hi02, Lv88, Wh83>

fête[2] ♦see **fête-à-cacher**

fête-à-cacher (fête) [fetakaʃe, fɛt] *n.m.* hide-and-seek *Jouer fête.* To play hide-and-seek. (SB) <***Loc:*** LF, SB>

fêter [fete] **I** *v.tr.* to celebrate *Sa fête qu'eusse avait fêté, là-bas c'est au parc l'autre bord.* His birthday that they celebrated, that was in the park on the other side. (TB) **II** *v.intr.* to party *On a bien fêté hier au soir.* We partied last night. (LA) ◊ **•fêter sa fouine** to whore around, sleep around *Quand lui vadait à la mer eh ben ça c'est quand alle fêtait sa fouine.* When he would go off to sea, that's when she would whore around. (TB) <TB> <***Loc:*** LA, TB, Da84>

feu [fø] *n.m.* **1** fire **2** animation, spirit ◊ **•feu d'artifice** fireworks <Da84> **•feu sauvage** impetigo <SM, VM, Fa77, Lv88> **•c'est comme le feu et l'eau** they're always quarreling <La99> **•il y a toujours du feu dans la cheminée** said of a person who is still interested and still active sexually <La99> **•le feu est pris dans la paille jaune {grande paille}** trouble spreads like wild fire <Da84> **•mettre le feu à la paille {poudre}** to start or add to the momentum of a rumor or conflict by one's words <AV, La99> **•prendre en feu** to catch fire, ignite <Da84> <***Loc:*** SL, SM, VM, Da84, Hi02, La99, Lv88>

feu follet (fifolet, fifollet, fufollet) [fifole, fyfole, fofole, tifole] *n.m.* **1** will-o'-the-wisp, ignis fatuus (phosporescent light that hovers and flits over swampy ground at night, often interpreted as an omen) **Et le monde avait une frayeur que si le fufollet aurait tombé sur eux, il les aurait tués.* And the people were terrified that if the will-o'-the-wisp landed on them, it would kill them. (Gr86) **2** ghost, spirit (in voodoo) <***Loc:*** AV, IB, JD, LF, SL, SM, TB, VM, Da84, Gr86, Hi02, Lv88>

feuillage [føjaʒ] *n.m.* **1** foliage **2** leaf <***Loc:*** VM, Da84>

feuille [fœj] *n.f.* **1** leaf (of a plant) *Ça prenait des lilas, des feuilles de lilas, et ça bouillait ça pour faire un thé.* They used to take lilac, lilac leaves, and boil them to make a tea. (SJ) **2** sheet (of paper) **3** sheet (of metal) *Eusse mettait ça sur des morceaux de zinc, des feuilles de zinc, pour chesser. Ça viendait plus chaud là.* They used to put it on pieces of tin, sheets of tin, to dry it. It got hotter that way. (TB) **4** foil (metal, wood, etc.) <***Loc:*** JE, SJ, SL, TB, Da84, Hi02>

feuillet [føje] *n.m.* omasum, manyplies (third compartment of the stomach in ruminants) <***Loc:*** EV, VM>

feurdaines ♦see **ferdaines**

feursaie ♦see **feursie**

feursie (**feursaie**, **feusaie**) [fœrzi, fœrze, føze] *n.m.* bullbat, nighthawk <***Loc:*** JD, Da84, Gr86, Re31>

feurtiller ♦see **fertiller**

feusaie ♦see **feursie**

fève [fɛv, fev, føv] *n.f.* bean, pea (comprises most edible legumes except green beans) *Les z-haricots, si tu les laisses vieux, ils vont faire des fèves dans les épluches.* Beans, if you let them get old, they'll make [more] beans in the husks. (Lv88) ◊ **•fève à la brasse** variety of string bean from 18 inches to 3 feet long <TB, VM> **•fève à vache** cowpea <TB> **•fève (à) z-yeux noir** black-eyed pea <SL, TB, VM> **•fève au cœur noir** black-eyed pea <Hi02> **•fève grise** gray pea <SL> **•fève nombouril noir** black-eyed pea <VM> **•fève blanche** navy bean <SL, VM> **•fève cordée** crowder pea <TB, VM> **•fève de clos** field pea <SM, Hi02> **•fève de foie** kidney bean <AC> **•fève de yard** long green bean <VM> **•fève foulée** dwarf bean, bunch bean <VM> **•fève gourgane** bean *Il a traidé la vache pour trois fèves gourganes.* He traded the cow for three beans. (EV, Gr86) <EV, Di32, Gr86> **•fève marronne** white bean <LF> **•fève nain {nine}** dwarf bean, dwarf pea <SM, VM, Lv88> **•fève platte *a*** lima bean, butter bean ***b*** Christmas bean <EV, LA, SM, TB, Da84, Lv88, Ph36> **•fève platte naine** bush butter bean <Da84> **•fève rouge** red bean <IB, SL, Hi02> <***Loc:*** AC, CL, EV, IB, LA, LF, SL, SM, TB, VM, Da84, Gu00, Hi02, Lv88, Ph36>

févi (**févis**) [fevi] *n.m.* okra *Je mets un tas de févi dans mon gombo-févi. Je mets pas de roux.* I put lots of okra in my okra gumbo. I don't use a roux. (Gu00) <***Loc:*** EV, IB, JD, JE, LF, SB, SL, SM, TB, VM, Da84, Gu00, Lv88, Ph36>

févier [fevje] *n.m.* honey locust tree, false acacia <***Loc:*** Da84, Re31>

févis ♦see **févi**

février [fevrije, føvrije, føvərije] *n.m.* February <***Loc:*** AV, TB, VM, Da84, Fa77, Hi02>

fiable [fjab(l)] *adj.* trustworthy, dependable *Ce cheval est fiable, il va pas vous donner du tracas.* This horse is dependable, he won't give you any trouble. (Lv88) <***Loc:*** LA, SL, SM, TB, VM, Da84, Di32, Gr86, Hi02, Lv88>

fian ♦see **fion**

fiance [fjɑ̃s] *n.f.* engagement (to be married) <***Loc:*** VM>

fiancé[1], **-e** [fjɑ̃se] *adj.* engaged (to marry) *Ils sont fiancés depuis l'été passé.* They have been engaged since last summer. (LA) <***Loc:*** LA, Da84>

fiancé[2], **-e** [fjɑ̃se] *n.* **1** *(m.)* fiancé **2** *(f.)* fiancée <***Loc:*** Da84>

fiancer [fjɑ̃se] **I** *v.tr.* to engage, betroth *Ils ont fiancé leur fille à un vaillant jeune bougre.* They engaged their daughter to a nice young fellow. (LA) **II se fiancer** *v.pron.* to become engaged *Ils se sont fiancés au printemps.* They got engaged in the spring. (LA) <***Loc:*** LA, Da84>

fiander [fjɑ̃de] *v.intr.* to run around, gad about, gallivant *Toi, tu gardes Adèle ici, pour qu'alle va fiander avec toi.* You keep Adèle here so she can go run around with you. (TB) <***Loc:*** TB>

fiasco [fjasko] *n.m.* fiasco, complete failure <***Loc:*** Da84>

fibi [fibi] *n.m.* mischievous or disobedient child *Un fibi, ça veut dire quelqu'un qu'est méchant ou malfaisant.* A "fibi," that means someone who is mean or mischievous. (LF) <***Loc:*** LF>

ficelle [fisɛl] *n.f.* twine, string *C'était une gloire d'avoir des lumières et l'estricité, tu halais sur la ficelle et la lumière venait dessus.* It was a source of pride to have lights and electricity, you pulled on the string and the light came on. (TB) <***Loc:*** JE, TB, Da84, Fa77>

ficher [fiʃe] **I** *v.tr.* **1** to send, drive *Fiche-le dans le derrière du chameau, et puis allons haler.* Drive it into the camel's rear and let's get out of here. (AS) **2** to trump (in a card game) *Je croyais que je l'avais, mais il m'a fiché.* I thought I had him, but he trumped me. (VM) *Fichez l'atout!* Play trump! (SL) **II se ficher** *v.pron.* to not give a darn, not care **Je m'en fiche! Je m'en fichu!* I could care less! (Da84) ◊ **•ficher le {son} camp** to leave **Fiche ton camp!* Get the devil out of here! (Da84) <LF, Da84> <***Loc:*** AS, LF, SL, VM, Da84, Di32, La99, Re31>

fichtre [fiʃ(tr)] *interj.* ◊ **•fichtre non** hell no, certainly not **Ah fichtre non!* Hell no! (Da84) <Da84> **•fichtre oui** hell yes, heck yes *Fichtre oui, j'irai.* Heck yes, I'll go. (SB) <SB> <***Loc:*** JE, SB, Da84, Di32>

fichu[1] [fiʃy] *adj.* beyond hope, ruined, done for *Cet homme est à peu près fichu.* That man is just about done for. (SB) *Je pouvais pas aller parce que je me sentais mal fichu.* I couldn't go because I felt in bad shape. (SB) <***Loc:*** SB>

fichu[2] [fiʃy] *adv.* very *Ça c'est une fichue belle robe.* That's a very beautiful dress. (EV) <***Loc:*** EV>

fiction [fiksjɔ̃] *n.f.* **1** fiction **2** fable <***Loc:*** Da84>

fidèle [fidɛl] *adj.* faithful, trustworthy *O non, non, non, franc cavalier, ma femme est trop fidèle à moi.* Oh no, no, no, honest knight, my wife is too faithful to me. (PQ, ch: *O Catherine*) <***Loc:*** PQ, Da84>

fideleine [fidlɛ̃] *n.f.* gypsy *La fideleine a joué son violon pour nous.* The gypsy played her violin for us. (AV) <***Loc:*** AV, SJ>

fidélité [fidelite] *n.f.* faithfulness, fidelity, loyalty <***Loc:*** Da84>

fiel [fjɛl] *n.m.* **1** gall bladder **2** audacity, nerve, gall *Il aura pas le fiel de faire ça.* He won't have the nerve to do that. (VM) *Il a du fiel pour faire ça.* He's got audacity to do that. (Lv88) <***Loc:*** AL, VM, Da84, Fa77, La99, Lv88>

fier[1] [fje] **I** *v.tr.* to trust, confide, entrust *Il sent pas comme si il peut fier son testament à son frère.* He doesn't feel like he can entrust his will to his brother. (LA) **II se fier** *v.pron.* to trust, rely *Tu peux pas te fier à la gazette.* You cannot trust the newspaper. (IB) <***Loc:*** IB, LA, Da84, Fa77>

fier[2]**, fière** [fjær] *adj.* **1** proud *Il est fier de son garçon, de sa fille.* He is proud of his son, of his daughter. (SM) **2** haughty, vain, boastful, conceited *Elle est fière, elle se croit plus que quelqu'un d'autre.* She is vain, she thinks she is superior to the others. (SM) **3** satisfied, pleased *Je suis bien fier du travail que t'as fait.* I'm very satisfied with the work you have done. (LA) **4** happy, pleased *Je suis fier de faire ta connaissance.* I'm happy to make your acquaintance. (LA) ◊ **•fier comme un paon** very proud, vain <EV, La99> **•avoir fier** to be proud *J'ai fier quoi t'as fait aujourd'hui à l'école.* I am proud of what you did at school today (IB) <IB> <***Loc:*** AC, EV, IB, LA, SM, VM, Fa77, Hi02, La99>

fier[3] [fjær] *n.m.* braggart <***Loc:*** VM>

fiéraud[1] (**fiéroux, -ouse**) [fjero, fjeru, -uz] *adj.* **1** proud **2** vain <***Loc:*** LF, TB, Di32>

fiéraud[2] (**fiérot**) [fjero] *n.m.* haughty, vain, or conceited person <***Loc:*** Da84>

fier-cul [fjærtʃy] *n.m.* braggart <***Loc:*** Lv88>

fièrement [fjærmɑ̃] *adv.* **1** proudly, haughtily *Tante Zème marchait tout le temps fièrement au village.* Aunt Zème always walked proudly to town. (VM) **2** much, many *Nous autres on a fièrement de ça.* We have a lot of that. (VM) <***Loc:*** VM, Da84, Di32, Fa77>

fiérot ♦see **fiéraud**

fiéroux ♦see **fiéraud**

fierté [fjærte] *n.f.* **1** pride **2** vanity, arrogance <***Loc:*** Da84>

fièvre [fjɛv(r)] *n.f.* **1** fever *J'avais un mal de gorge beaucoup mauvais et de la fièvre.* I had a severe sore throat and fever. (AV) **2** excitement *Quand le* BAND *a commencé à jouer, tu parles d'une fièvre dans la place!* When the band started playing, you talk about an excitement in the place! (LA) ◊ **•fièvre à vingt-quatre heures** spinal meningitis, infantile paralysis <VM> **•fièvre d'automne** hay fever, allergies <VM> **•fièvre de foin** hay fever <VM> **•fièvre de lait** undulant fever <VM> **•fièvre de lapin** rabbit fever, tularemia <VM> **•fièvre de pou de bois** tick fever <VM> **•fièvre de rat** typhus <VM> **•fièvre forte** high fever *La fièvre forte, ç'a brûlé la cervelle, c'est tellement forte que ç'a détruit, ça fait ils pouvaient pas apprendre comme avant.* The high fever, that burned their brains, it was so high that it destroyed, so they couldn't learn like before. (SJ) <SJ> **•fièvre jaune** yellow fever *La fièvre jaune, il y a eu une épidémie à la Nouvelle Orléans.* Yellow fever, there was an epidemic in New Orleans. (SJ) <SJ> **•fièvre lente** slight fever **Ça ça donne la fièvre moi je crois, une 'tite fièvre lente, jusque tu peux t'apercevoir assez que t'as froid.* That gives you a fever I think, a slight fever, enough so you realize you're cold. (St95) <St95> **•fièvre longue / longue fièvre *a*** typhoid fever ***b*** malaria <JD, VM, Da84, Lv88> **•fièvre malarienne** malaria <JE> **•fièvre marélia** malaria <Lv88> **•fièvre typhoïde / grande fièvre** typhoid fever *Elle aussi était à l'hôpital mais elle, c'est la fièvre typhoïde on l'appelait. C'est une fièvre que plein du monde qu'est mort avec ça.* She was in the hospital too, but she had typhoid fever as they called it. It was a fever that a lot of people died of. (TB) <TB, VM, Da84, Lv88> **•avoir la fièvre** to have a fever, run a fever <Da84> <***Loc:*** AV, JD, JE, LA, SJ, TB, VM, Da84, Hi02, Lv88, St95>

fiévreux, -euse [fjevrø, -øz] *adj.* **1** feverish *Mon petit était fiévreux pour quelques jours.* My son was feverish for several days. (LA) **2** excited *Les enfants sont carrément fiévreux juste avant les fêtes.* The children are downright excited just before the holidays. (LA) <***Loc:*** LA, Da84>

fifauler ♦see **faufiler**

fiferlin [fifærlɛ̃, fifərlɛ̃, fɛ̃færlɛ̃, fifalɛ̃] *n.m.* trifle, thing of little or no value *Ça vaut pas un fiferlin.* It's not worth one red cent. (TB) <***Loc:*** AV, IB, TB, Di32, Re54>

fifoler [fifole] **I** *v.tr.* to recount in a giddy, senseless way **II** *v.intr.* to talk in a senseless manner *Alle peut te fifoler ça dans un petit moment.* She can rattle on about that for you in a moment. (TB) <***Loc:*** TB>

fifolet, fifollet ♦see **feu follet**

fi-fond-fin-fond ♦see **finfifond**

figer [fiʒe] *v.intr.* to congeal, harden, jell *Tu ramasses du bois, et puis tu fais ton feu. Là, quand il est fini, tu éteins ton feu. Là il fige.* You gather wood, and then you make your fire. Then, when it's finished, you put out your fire. Then it [the soap] hardens. (VM) <***Loc:*** VM, Da84>

FIGHT[1] [faɪt] **I** *v.tr.invar.* to fight *Alle a* FIGHT *ce poisson là pour quarante-cinq minutes je crois.* She fought that fish for forty-five minutes I think. (LF) **II** *v.intr.invar.* to fight *Y a plein qu'est morts et y a plein, je veux dire que ils ont* FIGHT, *mais la fièvre était tellement fort.* There are a lot who died and there are a lot, I mean they fought, but the fever was so strong. (SJ) <***Loc:*** LF, SJ, VM>

FIGHT[2] [faɪt] *n.m./f.* fight <***Loc:*** JE, TB, VM, Di32, Lv88>

figue [fig] *n.f.* **1** fig **2** fig tree ◊ **•figue céleste** common purple fig, Celeste fig <Da84> **•figue de raquette** prickly pear

<Guoo> **•figue-miel** white fig <VM> <***Loc:*** CL, EV, LA, VM, Da84, Guoo>

figuier [figje, fige] *n.m.* fig tree <***Loc:*** IB, LA, SB, SL, SM, VM, Da84, Fa77>

figure[1] [figyr] *n.f.* figure, number *Donne-moi une figure du monde qui reste dans la Louisiane.* Give me the number of people who live in Louisiana. (EV) <***Loc:*** EV, Da84>

figure[2] [figyr, fygyr] *n.f.* **1** face *J'ai jamais pu boire du vin. Ça me soûle tout de suite. Et là ma figure vient rouge rouge rouge rouge.* I've never been able to drink wine. It gets me drunk right away. And then my face gets really, really red. (TB) *Ils l'ont tiré drète devant moi. Ils l'ont tiré dans la figure.* They shot him right in front of me. The shot him in the face. (EV) **2** front, face *Le portrait était par terre, viré en l'air, avec la figure en l'air, et la vitre était tout cassée.* The picture was on the ground, turned upwards, face up, and the glass was all broken. (TB) **3** facial expression (usually negative) *Tu peux changer cette figure droite asteur!* You can change that look on your face right now! (LA) ◊ **•figure à figure** face to face *Figure à figure on peut se comprendre mieux que écouter quelqu'un parler sur un radio ou un television.* Face to face we can understand each other better than listening to someone talk on the radio or the TV. (TB) <TB> **•avoir une figure comme une vache qu'a soif** to grimace, show displeasure or disapproval in one's facial expressions <AC, LA, La99> **•avoir une figure de pot de chambre craquée** to be ugly as sin <Gr86> **•faire figure** to face, face up (to) *Il faudra il faise figure à son tracas. Ça va pas s'en aller tout seul.* He's going to have to face up to his problem. It won't go away by itself. (VM) <VM, Da84> <***Loc:*** AC, EV, LA, LF, SL, SM, TB, VM, An94, Da84, Fa77, Hi02, La99, Lv88, Wh83>

figurer[1] [figyre, fygyre] **I** *v.tr.* **1** to figure, calculate, add up *Il a figuré son bill vite.* He quickly added up his bill. (Lv88) *Figurer le compte.* To find the total amount of the account. (SJ) *Tu dois d'abord figurer la distance.* First you have to calculate the distance. (Lv88) **2** to figure out, discover *Calculer, c'est manière comme des luméros. Mais figurer c'est getting out of a situation.* To calculate, that's like with numbers. But figuring out, that's getting out of a situation. (LF) **3** to decide, conclude *J'ai figuré que je ferais mieux de frèmer ma gueule.* I decided that I'd better shut my mouth. (EV) **4** to believe, suppose, imagine **II se figurer** *v.pron.* to figure, imagine, conclude *Figure-toi, il a pas arrivé avant deux heures du matin!* Imagine, he didn't arrive until two in the morning! (EV) <***Loc:*** AV, EV, IB, LA, LF, SB, SJ, TB, JE, VM, Da84, Fa77, Lv88>

figurer[2] [figyre, fygyre] *v.tr.* to confront *Ce gaillard était après voler mes affaires. J'ai ouvert la porte et je l'ai figuré.* That guy was stealing my stuff. I opened the door and I confronted him. (EV) ◊ **•se figurer avec** to find o.s. face to face with *Il s'a tourné de bord et il s'a figuré avec un gros chien.* He turned around and he found himself face to face with a big dog. (AC) <AC, Wh83> <***Loc:*** AC, EV, Wh83>

fil [fil] *n.m.* **1** thread, yarn **2** wire **3** vine *Ayoù la calebasse est plantée les serpents va pas, et la vigne ou le bois on appelle ça fil de calebasse.* Where the calabash is planted, snakes won't go, and we call the vine or the stalk a calabash vine. (TB) **4** runner (of plants) *Il a coupé tous les fils sus les mûres traînantes.* He cut all the runners on his dewberries. (LA) ◊ **•fil à barrière** fencing wire <Da84> **•fil à {de} carreaux** rectangular-holed wire fencing, hog wire *Le petit cheval a sauté un fossé. Il a resté pris dans un fil à carreaux.* The little horse jumped over a ditch. He got caught in a hog wire. (SL) <SL, Lv88> **•fil à l'électricité** electrical wire <Fa77> **•fil à piquants** barbed wire <IB, LA, VM, Lv88> **•fil à volaille** mesh wire, chicken wire <VM> **•fil d'alton** thin brass or iron tie wire, baling wire <EV, IB, LF, SL, Da84, Fa77, Lv88, Ph36> **•fil d'araignée** spider web <SM, Da84> **•fil de {en} coton** cotton thread <TB> **•fil de fer *a*** wire ***b*** barbed wire *Il s'a fripé contre le fil de fer.* He grazed himself against the barbed wire. (VM) <LA, Da84> **•fil de fer à carreau** rectangular-holed wire fencing, hog wire <Da84> **•fil de fer à piquant** barbed wire <Da84> **•fil de la vierge** *(usu. pl.)* thread of white filament sometimes seen floating in the air in spring <La99> **•fil de téléphone** telephone wire <Da84, Fa77> **•fil du sept {neuf, douze}** thread (of different thicknesses) *Des fils du sept, t'appelles ça. Y a du six, y a du sept, y a du neuf, y a du douze, [...] ça va jusqu'à 100.* Number seven thread, you call it. There's number six, seven, nine, twelve, it goes up to 100. (TB) <TB> **•fil électrique** electric wire <Da84> **•avoir du fil à tordre avec qqn** to have a lot of difficulty dealing with s.o. <La99> **•avoir du fil à retordre avec qqn** to endure hardship because of s.o. <EV, LA, VM> **•comme le fil en aiguille** very well, very smoothly <La99> **•venir (à) un fil de** to come very close to, come within a hair of (doing s.t.) *Il est venu un fil de réussir.* He came within a hair of succeeding. (EV) <EV> <***Loc:*** EV, IB, LA, LF, SL, SM, TB, VM, Da84, Fa77, La99, Lv88, Ph36>

filandrin (flandrin) [filɑ̃drɛ̃, flɑ̃drɛ̃] *n.m.* **1** lean, awkwardly built person **2** lazybones, loafer, bum <***Loc:*** IB, JD, VM, Da84, Di32>

filant, -e [filɑ̃, -ɑ̃t] *adj.* **1** climbing, vining, running (of a plant) *Un rosier filant.* Climbing rosebush. (SM, VM) *Haricots filants.* Runner beans. (Lv88) **2** ropy, stringy **3** slimy *Le gombo févi est filant.* The okra is slimy. (EV) **4** slick, hard to catch (of a criminal) *Il est assez filant que la loi peut pas l'attraper.* He is so slick that the police can't catch him. (EV) <***Loc:*** EV, SM, VM, Da84, Lv88>

filasse [filas] *n.m./f.* **1** corn silk **2** loose thread, hanging thread **3** any stringy material <***Loc:*** AV, JD, SJ, Da84>

file [fil] *n.f.* line *Il y avait une file de monde au picture show.* There was a line of people at the movies. (EV) <***Loc:*** EV>

filé [file] *n.m.* filé, ground sassafras leaves (used as a seasoning and thickening agent in gumbo) <*Loc:* AV, CL, EV, IB, JE, LA, LF, SB, SJ, SL, SM, TB, VM, Da84, Guoo, Hi02, Lv88, Ph36, Re31>

filée ♦see **affilée**

filer[1] [file] **I** *v.tr.* to spin *Filer du coton.* To spin cotton. (EV) **II** *v.intr.* **1** to spin thread, yarn, or string *Elle connaît pas écarder ni filer, mais elle connaît frapper le fil sur le métier.* She doesn't know how to card or spin, but she knows how to weave. (Lv88) **2** to creep, climb (of plants) *Mes mirlitons sont après filer tout partout dessus la galerie.* My vegetable pears are climbing all over the porch. (LA) *Défunte 'Tit-tante disait que c'était dur de piocher le coton quand les liserines prenaient dedans parce que ça file partout.* My late aunt used to say that it was hard to hoe the cotton when the morning glories got into them because they spread everywhere. (Guoo) **3** to get out, scram, beat it **File!* Get out! (Da84) ◊ **•filer un mauvais coton** to be in a bad way (of health or business) <CL> <*Loc:* AC, CL, EV, JD, LA, SM, TB, VM, Da84, Guoo, Lv88>

filer[2] [file] *v.tr.* to fillet *Ma femme va filer les poissons.* My wife will fillet the fish. (SM) <*Loc:* SM>

filer[3] [file] *v.tr.* to add filé to (a gumbo, etc.) *Il a filé son gombo.* He added filé to his gumbo. (EV) <*Loc:* EV>

filer[4] ♦see **affiler**

filer[5] ♦see **enfiler**

filet[1] [filɛ, file] *n.m.* **1** net, netting *Les meuilles, non, ça mord pas, ça, t'empoignes ça avec un filet, avec un épervier.* Mullets, no, they don't bite, you catch them with a net, with a castnet. (TB) **2** bird trap made in the shape of a bow, with horsehair slipknots <*Loc:* LF, TB, Hi02>

filet[2] [filɛ, file] *n.m.* drink, shot (of liquor) *Il a débouché sa bouteille et [...] lui a donné un bon filet de vin.* He opened his bottle and gave him a good little glass of wine. (SL) ◊ **•petit filet** drink *Tu veux boire un 'tit filet avec moi?* Do you want to have a drink with me? (Guoo) <Guoo> **•prendre {boire} un filet** to have a drink *Viens prendre un filet avec nous-autres.* Come have a drink with us. (VM) <*Loc:* AV, EV, IB, JD, LF, SL, SM, VM, Da84, Di32, Guoo, Hi02, Lv88, Ph36>

filet[3] [filɛ, file] *n.m.* fillet, cut of meat or fish *Le filet c'est quand tu prends le filet* KNIFE *et puis tu le coupes et tu ôtes tous les os dessus le poisson.* The fillet is when you take the fillet knife and then you cut and remove all the bones from the fish. (SM) <*Loc:* SM, VM>

filet[4] [filɛ, file] *n.m.* frenum (of the tongue) ◊ **•avoir le filet coupé** to talk without restraint <Da84> <*Loc:* Da84>

filland ♦see **filleul**

fille [fij] *n.f.* **1** girl, female child *Les filles, on aimait jouer avec des poupées, ça c'était notre meilleur passe-temps.* Girls liked to play with dolls, that was our favorite pastime. (SM) **2** daughter *Ils ont renvoyé leur fille quand ils ont trouvé qu'elle était en famille.* They sent their daughter away when they found out she was pregnant. (EV) **3** girl, young (usu. unmarried) woman **Elle était facilement la fille la plus recherchée dans toute la cyprière.* She was easily the most sought after girl in the swamp. (So97) *Ses amis lui ont donné une pousse pour qu'il demande à la fille de danser.* His friends gave him a push to ask the girl to dance. (VM) ◊ **•'tite fille** [*term of endearment*] little girl <Lv88> **•vieille fille** old maid, spinster, woman who has never married <LF, Da84> <*Loc:* LF, JE, Da84, Hi02>

fillette [fijɛt] *n.f.* **1** little girl **2** goddaughter, female godchild <*Loc:* SB, SJ, Da84>

filleu ♦see **filleul**

filleul (**filland, filleu, fillol, fillot**) [fijø, fijɑ̃, fijɔl fijo] *n.m.* godson, male godchild <*Loc:* AV, EV, IB, LF, SM, TB, VM, Da84, Di32, Lv88, Ph36, Re31>

filleule (**filleuse, fillole**) [fijøl, fijøz, fijɔl] *n.f.* goddaughter, female godchild <*Loc:* AV, EV, IB, JD, LF, SM, TB, Da84, Fa77, Lv88, Ph36, Re31>

filleuse[1] [fijøz] *adj.* effeminate, sissified <*Loc:* Fa77>

filleuse[2] ♦see **filleule**

fillol ♦see **filleul**

fillole ♦see **filleule**

fillot ♦see **filleul**

fillotte [fijɔt] *n.f.* little girl <*Loc:* AV, SB, SJ>

film [film] *n.m.* **1** film, roll of film *Quand on développe du film, il n'a pas clareté du tout dans le* DARKROOM. When you develop film, there's no light at all in the darkroom. (VM) **2** film, movie <*Loc:* TB, VM>

filou[1] [filu] *adj.* **1** sly, shrewd, sharp, cunning *Il est filou comme tout, il faut le guetter.* He's sly as anything, you have to watch him. (VM) *Ces souris sont assez filous, ils mangeont et échappont.* Those mice are pretty clever, they eat and escape. (VM) **2** crooked, underhanded *Je ferais jamais affaire avec du monde filou comme ça.* I would never do business with crooked people like that. (VM) **3** thieving, sticky-fingered *Un garçon filou.* A thieving boy. (SJ) ◊ **•filou comme un renard** sly as a fox, very sly <VM, La99> <*Loc:* AV, JD, SJ, VM, Da84, La99>

filou[2] [filu] *n.m.* **1** sly, shrewd, sharp, cunning person *Un fin filou.* A very sly person. (IB) **2** crook **Si quèqu'un a pas d'esprit, pas d'défense, un autre, un malin, un filou comme on dit ici, va prendre l'avantage et l'faire travailler pour rien.* If someone has no wits, no defenses, someone else, a cunning person, a "filou" as we say here, will take advantage of him and make him work for nothing. (Gr86) ◊ **•faire le filou comme un chien basset** ***a*** to do things while trying not to be noticed ***b*** to have a guilty look on one's face <TB, La99> <*Loc:* IB, TB, Da84, La99>

filouterie [filutri] *n.f.* thievery, cheating, trickery <*Loc:* Da84>

fils [fis] ([fi] *in curses*) *n.m.* son *C'est mon premier fils, j'ai trois fils.* He's my first son, I have three sons. (LF) ◊ **•fils de**

chien {garce / putain} / fils de putain de bordel {garce} [*vulg.*] ***a*** son-of-a-bitch ***b*** expression used to show surprise, irritation, or anger <JD, An94, Da84, Gr86, La99> **•fils de monstre {pistache / poteau} / fils de poteau de barrière *a*** son-of-a-gun ***b*** expression used to show surprise, irritation or anger <La99> **•fils unique** only son <Da84> <***Loc:*** JD, LF, TB, An94, Da84, Fa77, Gr86, Hi02, La99, Wh83>

filtration [filtrasjɔ̃] *n.f.* filtration, straining <***Loc:*** Da84>

filtre [filt(r)] *n.m.* filter <***Loc:*** Da84>

filtrer [filtre] *v.tr.* to filter <***Loc:*** Pe37>

fin[1], **fine** [fɛ̃, fin] *adj.* **1** [*sometimes ironic*] fine, first-rate, expert **C'est un fin laboureur.* He's a first-rate plowman. (Di32) **Ça c'est un fin charpentier.* That's a jack-leg carpenter. (Da84) **2** slender, thin *Elle a les cuisses fines.* She has slender thighs. (EV) **3** sharp *Aiguille fine.* Sharp needle. (SL) **Fin comme une aiguille.* Very fine. (La99) **4** delicate, smooth, silky *Une étoffe fine.* Delicate fabric. (SL) **Fin comme de la peau d'un bébé.* Smooth as a baby's skin. (La99) **5** fine, finely ground *Fin comme de la cendre.* Fine as ashes. (EV) **6** fine, lovely *[Une fleur de canne,] quand tu la vois sur la mer de cannes, dans la raie là, c'est fin pour voir.* A sugar cane flower, when you see it in the sea of cane, in the row there, it's lovely to see. (TB) **7** fancy *Arien de fin.* Nothing fancy. (SM) <***Loc:*** EV, SL, SM, TB, An94, Da84, Di32, La99>

fin[2] [fɛ̃] *n.f.* **1** end, conclusion *Ça va être à la fin de janvier, commencement de février.* That will be at the end of January, beginning of February. (TB) **2** objective, purpose *Il a fait ça pour des fins que juste lui, il comprend.* He did that for reasons that only he understands. (LA) ◊ **•à la fin** finally <Fa77> **•à la fin du compte** in the end, after all, finally *Je regardais par-dessus son épaule, et moi je voulais voir qui il était après faire et lui il croyait que j'étais juste curieux, que je voulais voir,* BUT *à la fin du compte ses* CHECK *à lui arrêtait de rentrer.* I watched over his shoulder, I wanted to see what he was doing, and he thought I was just curious, that I wanted to see, but finally, his checks stopped coming in. (TB) <TB> **•fin de semaine** weekend *Ils ont riboté toute la fin de semaine.* They drank all weekend. (LA) *Deux vieux mariés décident d'aller la fin de semaine à Holly Beach.* Two old married people decide to go spend the weekend at Holly Beach. (Gr86) <LA, Gr86> <***Loc:*** EV, LA, SM, TB, VM, An94, Da84, Hi02, La99, Lv88, Wh83>

fin[3] [fɛ̃] *adv.* very, extremely *Ça c'est fin bête.* That's extremely stupid. (VM) <***Loc:*** VM>

final, -e [final] *adj.* final, last, ultimate *Écoute, ma parole est finale.* Listen, my word is final. (EV) <***Loc:*** EV, Da84>

finalement [finalmɑ̃] *adv.* finally, at last *Et finalement, j'aimerais remercier ma femme pour son aide.* And finally, I'd like to thank my wife for her help. (EV) <***Loc:*** EV, Da84>

finance [finɑ̃s] *n.f.* finance <***Loc:*** Da84>

financer [finɑ̃se] *v.tr.* to finance *Il a financé* MY HOUSE. He financed my house. (EV) <***Loc:*** EV, Da84>

financier [finɑ̃sje] *n.m.* financier <***Loc:*** Da84>

finesse [finɛs] *n.f.* **1** finesse, delicacy **2** fineness, thinness **3** shrewdness, craftiness <***Loc:*** Da84>

finfifond (fi-fond-fin-fond, finfond) [fɛ̃fifɔ̃, fifɔ̃fɛ̃fɔ̃, fɛ̃fɔ̃] *n.m.* farthest part, extreme depth (of a field, woods, etc.) *Il s'a perdu dans le finfifond du bois.* He got lost in the deepest depths of the woods. (VM) *Il reste au finfifond de la France.* He lives in the farthest reaches of France. (LF) ◊ **•le finfifond du monde** the boondocks *Ils ont déménagé dans le finfifond du monde.* They moved to the boondocks. (EV) <EV> <***Loc:*** EV, IB, JD, LF, SM, VM, Da84, La99, Lv88, Ph36>

finfiluche ♦see **fanfreluche**

finfond ♦see **finfifond**

fini, -e [fini] *adj.* **1** skillful, top-notch **Un charpentier fini.* A top-notch carpenter. (Da84) **2** proper, delicate, elegant *C'est un mot pas fini.* That's not a proper word. (VM) **3** thin, skinny *Ce pauvre enfant est fini.* That poor child is very thin. (SB) <***Loc:*** SB, VM, Da84>

finiment [finimɑ̃] *adv.* entirely, perfectly, thoroughly *Alle l'a fait finiment.* She did it perfectly. (VM) *C'est finiment bon.* It's perfectly good. (TB) <***Loc:*** JD, TB, VM, Di32>

finir [finir] **I** *v.tr.* to finish, complete *J'ai arrêté dans le dixième pour aller faire l'affaire de pêche, et là après ça j'ai fini la* NIGHT SCHOOL *et j'ai gradué.* I stopped in tenth grade to go into the fishing business, and then after that I finished night school and I graduated. (TB) **II** *v.intr.* **1** to finish, be done *Quand j'empoigne 39 alligateurs j'ai fini pour l'année.* When I've caught 39 alligators, I'm done for the year. (TB) *Et on finit de jouer à la pelote et on va au* SWIMMING POOL *et on se baigne dans le* POOL. And we finish playing baseball and we go to the swimming pool and we take a swim in the pool. (TB) **2** to end, terminate *Après la guerre a fini ils ont revenu ici.* After the war ended they came back here. (LF) ◊ **•finir par** to end up (doing s.t.) *Après tant d'années de chicane, ils ont fini par se divorcer.* After so many years of squabbling, they ended up getting a divorce. (EV) <EV> **•à p'us finir** incessantly, endlessly *Tout d'un coup alle a rentré avec ça. Mais là j'ai commencé à* RAISE HELL *je te dis, à p'us finir.* All of a sudden she came in with him. But then I started to raise hell, I tell you, endlessly. (TB) <TB> **•pour en finir** finally, in conclusion *Mais, pour en finir, j'ai jamais réussi à y parler.* But in conclusion, I never did get to talk to her. (EV) <EV, Da84> <***Loc:*** AC, EV, LA, LF, SJ, TB, VM, Da84, Hi02, Lv88>

finissage [finisaʒ] *n.m.* finishing, final touches <***Loc:*** Da84>

finissement [finismɑ̃] *n.m.* end, conclusion *Tu vas voir au commencement jusqu'au finissement.* You're going to see from beginning to end. (VM) <***Loc:*** VM>

finission ♦see **finition**

finition (finission) [finisjɔ̃] *n.f.* end, conclusion **Ça, c'est la finission du conte.* That's the end of the story. (An77) <***Loc:*** LF, SL, An77, Di32, Hi02, Lv88>

fiole [fjɔl] *n.f.* **1** flask, bottle **2** baby bottle <***Loc:*** EV, Da84>

fion[1] [fjɔ̃] *adj.* finicky, picky *Ces enfants sont trop fions. Ils mangent proche pas rien.* Those children are too finicky. They eat almost nothing. (EV) *C'est un grand fion. Il est jamais satisfait.* He's such a picky person. He's never satisfied. (EV) <***Loc:*** EV>

fion[2] **(fian)** [fjɔ̃, fjɑ̃] *n.m. (usu. pl.)* **1** frill, trimming, decoration *Alle a toujours des fions sur ses robes.* She always has decorations on her dresses. (SM) **2** flourish, unnecessarily showy gesture ◊ **•avoir des fions** to be fussy, be finicky, have idiosyncratic likes or dislikes *Jacques a toujours eu des fions pour son manger.* Jacques has always been difficult about what he eats. (EV) <EV> **•faire {prendre} des fions *a*** to put on frills and fancies ***b*** to put on airs, act prissy ***c*** to take unnecessary pains, make unnecessary efforts *Il fait un tas de fions en se préparant.* He goes to a lot of unnecessary trouble while getting ready. (SM) <SM, Da84, La99> <***Loc:*** EV, IB, LF, SJ, SL, SM, VM, Da84, Di32, La99, Lv88>

fion-fion [fjɔ̃fjɔ̃] *adj.* overly mannered, prissy, finicky *Tu parles de fion-fion! Il mange proche pas rien autre que ça que sa mère y cuit.* Talk about finicky! He eats almost nothing except for what his mother cooks him. (EV) <***Loc:*** EV>

fionner [fjɔ̃ne] *v.intr.* **1** to waste time (doing useless things) *Il est souvent après fionner.* He is often frittering time away. (Lv88) *Il fionne comme il s'habille.* He's wasting his time dressing that way. (SM) **2** to act in a pretentious, haughty or affected way *Elle a venu fionner autour de la maison.* She came to 'pass judgment' around our house. (VM) <***Loc:*** SM, VM, Lv88>

fionneur[1]**, -euse (fionneux, -euse)** [fjɔ̃nœr, fjɔ̃nø, -øz] *adj.* **1** affected *Alle est fionneuse depuis qu'elle est riche.* She has acted affected since she became rich. (IB) **2** particular, affectedly fastidious, hard to please *Il est fionneux. Il aime pas toucher la viande crute, par exemple.* He is particular. He doesn't like to touch raw meat, for example. (VM) <***Loc:*** IB, JD, LF, SL, VM, Lv88>

fionneur[2]**, -euse (fionneux, -euse)** [fjɔ̃nœr, fjɔ̃nø, -øz] *n.* **1** person with affected manners, one who puts on airs **2** one who goes to unnecessary trouble or tries too hard <***Loc:*** IB, SJ, SM, Lv88>

fionneux ♦see **fionneur**

fionnure [fjɔ̃nyr] *n.f.* trimming, decoration, ornament *Alle a plein de fionnures sus sa robe.* She has a lot of decorations on her dress. (TB) <***Loc:*** TB>

fiorella ♦see **fiorelle**

fiorelle (fiorella, fleurella) [fjorɛl, fjorela, fjørela, flørela] *n.m.* dress yoke, round yoke (of a dress or cloak) <***Loc:*** IB, LF, SJ>

fiou-fiou [fjufju] *n.m.* weak coffee **J'aime pas ç' fiou-fiou.* I don't like this weak coffee. (EV, Ph36) <***Loc:*** EV, Ph36>

fiseau ♦see **fuseau**

fissure [fisyr] *n.f.* fissure, crack <***Loc:*** Da84>

fistule [fistyl, fystyl] *n.f.* fistula <***Loc:*** LF, Da84>

FIT[1] **(fiter)** [fit, fite] *v.intr.* to fit *Tu te faisais une robe, tu ramassais tous les retailles. Et là tu coupais ça une certaine manière que ça allait FIT ensemble.* You made yourself a dress, you gathered up all the scraps of cloth. And then you cut them a certain way so they'd fit together. (TB) *Je veux essayer la robe, mais je crois pas elle va me FIT.* I want to try on the dress, but I don't think it will fit me. (Lv88) *Il faut faire fiter cette robe.* We need to have that dress fitted. (Pe37) <***Loc:*** JD, LF, TB, VM, Lv88, Pe37>

FIT[2] [fit] *adj.* **1** fitting, suitable, good *Ces fruits sont pas FIT à manger.* These fruits are not fit to eat. (Lv88) **2** fit, in good health <***Loc:*** Lv88>

FIT[3] [fit] *n.m.* fit *C'est un bon FIT, ce chapeau.* This hat is a good fit. (LF) <***Loc:*** JD, LF>

fiter ♦see **FIT**[1]

fixer [fikse] *v.tr.* **1** to fasten **2** to settle ◊ **•fixer avec les yeux** to fix one's gaze on, stare at *Quand le chevreuil m'a fixé avec les yeux, je l'ai tiré.* When the deer fixed his gaze on me, I shot it. (VM) <VM> <***Loc:*** VM, Da84>

flacon [flakɔ̃] *n.m.* **1** flask, bottle, decanter **2** canning jar, preserve jar *Ma sœur mettait cette viande-là dans des flacons.* My sister put that meat into jars. (AC) <***Loc:*** AC, IB, VM, Da84>

flafla[1] [flafla] *v.intr.invar.* to talk a lot, be full of hot air. *Il reste à flafla.* He's full of hot air. (Lv88) <***Loc:*** EV, SM, Lv88, Ph36>

flafla[2] [flafla] *n.* **1** nonsense, stories often designed to make their teller seem interesting *Il est plein de flafla.* He's full of it. (Lv88) **2** windbag, excessive talker **3** frill *Elle se met toujours des flaflas.* She always wears frills. (IB) <***Loc:*** EV, IB, Lv88, Ph36>

FLAG[1] [flæg, flɛg] *v.tr.* to flag, hail for a ride, make a sign to stop *J'ai embarqué dans le premier char que j'ai FLAG.* I got into the first car that I flagged down. (VM) <***Loc:*** EV, TB, VM, Lv88, Ph36>

FLAG[2] [flæg, flɛg] *n.m.* flag ◊ **•avoir le FLAG** to menstruate <LF, La99> **•avoir le FLAG en l'air** to be eager, be ready to go <EV, La99> <***Loc:*** EV, JD, LF, Da84, Gr86, La99, Lv88, Ph36>

flagosser [flagose] *v.intr.* to be loose fitting *Sa robe y flagossait sus le dos.* Her dress was all baggy in the back. (TB) <***Loc:*** TB>

flailler [flaje, fleje] *v.tr.* **1** to whip *Les maîtresses d'école et les maîtres d'école te flaillaient.* School teachers would whip you. (TB) *Flailler ton derrière.* To whip your behind. (TB) **2** to throw quickly *On flaillait du tac-tac dans le feu, et on prendait des pistaches, on mettait ça dans la cendre chaude.*

We threw popcorn into the fire, and we took peanuts, we put them in the hot ash. (TB) ◊ **•flailler le fouet** to crack the whip <LF> **•flailler le pétard** to explode a firecracker <LF> **•flailler les doigts** to snap one's fingers <TB> **•flailler une tape (à qqn)** to give (s.o.) a slap *Et la femme s'a viré de bord et l'a flaillé une tape dans la figure.* And the woman turned around and gave him a slap in the face. (TB) <TB> <***Loc:*** LF, TB>

flamant [flɑ̃mɑ̃] *n.m.* flamingo <***Loc:*** Da84, Fa77>

flambé, -e [flɑ̃be] *adj.* out of luck *Mes chances sont tout flambées asteur.* My chances are all gone now. (VM) <***Loc:*** SB, VM, La99>

flambeau [flɑ̃bo] *n.m.* **1** torch **2** second kettle in a battery for making cane syrup <***Loc:*** IB, Da84>

flamber (**flammer**) [flɑ̃be, flɑ̃me] **I** *v.tr.* to stare at intently, glare at *Elle était après me flamber après le bal a fini et ça m'a choqué.* She was staring at me after the dance was over and it made me mad. (LA) **II** *v.intr.* **1** to blaze, flare *Le feu a flambé six pieds de haut quand il a jeté les branches dessus.* The fire flared up six feet high when he threw the branches on it. (LA) **2** to glare, flash, sparkle (of the eyes) **3** to fix intently (of the eyes) *Ses yeux étaient après flamber dessus.* His eyes were fixed intently on it. (SL) ◊ **•flamber des {les} yeux *a*** to have a violent, passionate look ***b*** to stare intently *Il était après me flamber des yeux au bal.* He was staring at me violently at the dancehall. (LA) <LA, SM, VM> <***Loc:*** LA, SL, SM, VM, Da84, Di32, La99>

flamme [flɑ̃m] *n.f.* flame, blaze <***Loc:*** SB, Da84, Hi02>

flammer ♦see **flamber**

flânailler [flɑ̃naje] *v.intr.* **1** to stroll *Ils étaient après flânailler dans les bois quand ils ont vu une petite maison.* They were strolling through the woods when they saw a little house. (LA) **2** to loaf, lounge, be idle, be lazy **I travaille pas, i flânaille.* He doesn't work, he loafs. (EV, Ph36) <***Loc:*** AV, EV, LA, Lv88, Ph36>

flanc [flɑ̃] *n.m.* **1** flank, side **2** flank (cut of meat) <***Loc:*** AV, VM, Da84>

flandre [flɑ̃n, flɑ̃d(r)] *n.m.* flounder <***Loc:*** Da84>

flandrin ♦see **filandrin**

flanelle [flɑ̃nɛl] *n.f.* flannel <***Loc:*** Da84, Fa77>

flâner [flɑ̃ne] *v.intr.* **1** to stroll *Il flânait au bord du bois.* He was strolling along the edge of the woods. (LA) **2** to loaf, lounge, be idle, be lazy *Le travail force à cette heure, le monde a pas le temps de flâner.* Work is abundant right now, people don't have time to loaf. (VM) *Ils flânaient au bord du bayou.* They were lounging on the banks of the bayou. (LA) **3** to gad about *Alle est toujours après flâner.* She's always gadding about. (VM) <***Loc:*** LA, VM, Da84>

flâneur, -euse [flɑ̃nœr, -øz] *n.* **1** loafer, bum **2** gadabout <***Loc:*** VM, Da84, Lv88>

flanquer [flɑ̃ke] **I** *v.tr.* to throw, fling *Il a juste flanqué ses livres dessus la table.* He just threw his books on the table. (LA) **II se flanquer** *v.pron.* to throw o.s. **Se flanquer par terre.* To throw oneself down. (Da84) ◊ **•flanquer son camp** to leave, scram, beat it <LF> **•flanquer un coup** to strike, hit, deliver a blow <SB> **•flanquer un coup de fusil** to shoot <Da84> **•flanquer une décoction** to administer a beating *J'ai pour te flanquer une décoction.* I need to give you a beating. (SB) <SB> **•flanquer une pointe** to get drunk <AV, La99> **•flanquer une tape** to slap <Da84> **•en flanquer *a*** to make pretense of doing much ***b*** to talk much about nothing ***c*** to think much of o.s. *Ça c'est un homme qui en flanque.* That's a guy who thinks much of himself. (VM) ***d*** to show off <VM> **•se flanquer des fions** to put on airs, act prissy <IB> **•s'en flanquer une bosse** to eat a great deal <LF> <***Loc:*** EV, IB, JD, LA, LF, SB, VM, Da84, La99>

FLASH-LIGHT [flæʃlait, flɛslait] *n.m.* flashlight <***Loc:*** VM, Da84>

flask ♦see **flasque**

flasque (**flask, flesse**) [flas(k), flɛs(k), flæs(k)] *n.m./f.* flask *J'ai été me chercher un petit flask de whiskey. On avait pas d'argent. Ça fait, il fallait on s'emmène un petit* DRINK *de whiskey.* I went to get a little flask of whiskey. We didn't have any money. So we had to bring a little drink of whiskey along. (SL) <***Loc:*** EV, LF, SL, TB, VM, Ph36>

FLAT[1] [flæt] *adj.* flat (of beer, soda, etc.) *Ma bière a devenu* FLAT *dans le soleil.* My beer got flat in the sun. (LA) <***Loc:*** LA, Da84>

FLAT[2] [flæt] *n.m.* flat tire *Il a jamais eu un* FLAT *sur son bicycle.* He's never had a flat (tire) on his bicycle. (Lv88) <***Loc:*** Da84, Lv88>

FLAT-BOAT [flætbot] *n.m.* flatboat <***Loc:*** VM, Di32>

flatter [flate] **I** *v.tr.* **1** to pet *Fais doucement quand tu flattes le chat.* Do it gently when you pet the cat. (EV) **2** to flatter *Elle va pas laisser son mari la flatter. Elle est trop choquée.* She won't let her husband flatter her. She's too mad. (LA) **II se flatter** *v.pron.* to flatter o.s. or each other *Flatte-toi pas, chère. T'es pas aussi jolie que tu crois.* Don't flatter yourself, dear. You're not as pretty as you think. (LA) <***Loc:*** EV, LA, Da84, Fa77>

flatterie [flatri] *n.f.* flattery <***Loc:*** Da84>

flatteur, -euse [flatœr, øz] *n.* flatterer <***Loc:*** Da84>

flau [flo] *n.m.* **1** scourge, plague **2** flail (for beating grain) <***Loc:*** VM, Di32>

flauber [flobe] *v.tr.* to beat, whip, thrash *Je l'ai bien flaubé pour ça il m'a dit.* I beat him good for what he said to me. (VM) <***Loc:*** VM, Di32>

flèche [flɛʃ] *n.m.* **1** arrow, dart **Droite comme une flèche.* Straight as an arrow. (Da84) **2** shaft, tongue (of a wagon, carriage, etc.) **3** flush (poker hand) **4** singletree, beam, pole, long piece of wood by means of which a pair of horses or mules is attached to a wagon *Sur le wagon, il y avait un grand bois au milieu. Ça c'était une flèche.* On the wagon, there was a big pole in the middle. That was a singletree. (SL) <***Loc:*** EV, SL, Da84, Fa77>

fléchir [fleʃir] **I** *v.tr.* to bend, bow *Il a fléchi la branche.* He bent the branch. (VM) **II** *v.intr.* to bend, bow *Il fléchit devant son père.* He bows before his father. (VM) **2** to give in, submit to authority *Son boss l'a bien disputé et il a fléchi.* His boss fussed at him and he bent. (LA) <***Loc:*** LA, VM, Da84>

flegme [flɛ̃m, flym] *n.m./f.* phlegm, mucus *Il a craché des flegmes.* He spat up mucus. (SL) *Elle a des flegmes qui l'étouffent.* She has chest congestion that makes it hard for her to breathe. (SB) <***Loc:*** EV, LF, SB, SL, SM, Da84, Ph36>

flesse ♦see **flasque**

flète (**flette**) [flɛt] *adj.* wilted, withered, dried up *La rose a venu flète.* The rose got withered. (VM) <***Loc:*** VM, Da84, Di32>

flétrir [fletrir] *v.intr.* to wither, wilt, dry up *La récolte a flétri après plusieurs semaines de sécheresse.* The crop withered after several weeks of drought. (LA) <***Loc:*** LA, Da84>

flette ♦see **flète**

fleur [flœr] *n.f.* **1** flower, bloom **2** choice one, best *La fleur de la bande.* The best of the bunch. (EV) ◊ **•fleur de la famille** the prettiest daughter of the family <La99> **•fleur de la Toussainte** chrysanthemum <VM> **•fleur de lis** seventh daughter of a family <TB, La99> **•faire des fleurs** ***a*** to bloom, produce flowers *L'année passée on a eu une canne qu'a fait des fleurs.* Last year we had a kind of sugarcane that produced flowers. (AS) ***b*** to make s.t. seem better than it is by exaggeration <AS, La99> <***Loc:*** AS, EV, SL, TB, VM, Da84, Hi02, La99>

fleuré, -e [fløre] *adj.* flower-print, having a flowered print *Étoffe fleurée.* Flowered fabric. (VM) <***Loc:*** LA, VM>

fleurella ♦see **fiorelle**

fleuri, -e [fløri] *adj.* blooming, in bloom **Un pêcher fleuri.* A peach tree in bloom. (Da84) <***Loc:*** Da84>

fleurir [flørir] *v.intr.* to bloom, flower, blossom *Mes pêchers étaient juste au moment de fleurir quand on a eu une dernière gelée.* My peach trees were just about to blossom when we got a last frost. (LA) ◊ **•faire fleurir du tac-tac** to pop popcorn <TB, Da84, Lv88> <***Loc:*** LA, TB, Da84, Fa77, Lv88>

fleuve [fløv, flœv] *n.m.* **1** river *Et là lui il allait l'autre bord du fleuve là-bas.* He used to go to the other side of the river. (LF) **2** Mississippi River *Well, les Allemands de* GERMAN COAST*, ils sont venus plus ici de près du fleuve dans Edgard qu'est dans la paroisse Saint Jean Baptiste.* Well, the Germans of the German Coast came here mostly from near the river in Edgard which is in Saint John the Baptist Parish. (SB) **3** flood <***Loc:*** LF, SB, Da84, Gu00, Hi02>

flexibilité [flɛksibilite] *n.f.* flexibility <***Loc:*** Da84>

FLIRT[1] (**flirter**) [flɔɹt, flœrte] *v.intr.* to flirt *Il est toujours après* FLIRT *avec ces filles.* He's always flirting with those girls. (VM) <***Loc:*** EV, VM, Da84, Ph36>

FLIRT[2] [flɔɹt] *n.* flirt <***Loc:*** Da84>

FLOOD[1] [flœd] *v.intr.invar.* to flood *Mais les levées a cassé. Et là ç'a* FLOOD*, tout l'eau a rentré.* But the levees broke. And it flooded, all the water came in. (LF) <***Loc:*** AS, LF, TB>

FLOOD[2] [flœd] *n.f.* flood *Bayou Lafourche [...], ça floodait, et ç'a tout fait cette terre ici. Et asteur l'eau est bloquée, t'as plus ces* FLOODS. Bayou Lafourche, it flooded, and it created all this land here. And nowadays the water is blocked, you don't have those floods any more. (TB) ◊ **•à la FLOOD** flooded *Là ça c'est l'année que la crevasse à Lockport a cassé. Et tout la Galliane, [...] Larose, Côte Blanche, et Lockport était tout à la* FLOOD. That's the year that the levee in Lockport broke. And all of Galliano, Larose, Côte Blanche, and Lockport were all flooded. (LF) <LF> <***Loc:*** LF, TB>

floridien [floridjɛ̃, flodidijɛ̃] *n.m.* large trawler (65 ft. or longer) with a cabin on the prow <***Loc:*** JE, Lv88>

flot [flo] *n.m.* wave <***Loc:*** Da84>

flottage [flotaʒ] *n.m.* floating (of logs, etc.) <***Loc:*** Da84>

flottant [flotɑ̃, flɔ̃tɑ̃] *n.m.* **1** patch of vegetation and humus that has not yet stabilized, in the marshes of the Mississippi delta and the coastal plain **2** voter who can be bought **3** vagabond, drifter <***Loc:*** AV, LF, SJ, SM, Lv88>

flottante [flotɑ̃t] *adj.f.* ◊ **•île flottante** meringue custard dessert <Da84> <***Loc:*** Da84>

flotte [flɔt] *n.m./f.* **1** float (on a line or fishing net) **2** float, parade float *On va orner la flotte pour la parade.* We're going to decorate the float for the parade. (VM) ◊ **•à la flotte** afloat *Après la grande eau, tout était à la flotte.* After the flood, everything was floating around. (Lv88) <JE, LA, Lv88> <***Loc:*** JE, LA, SM, VM, Lv88>

flotter [flote] **I** *v.tr.* to float (logs), transport (logs) by waterway *J'ai flotté des bois quand l'eau venait haute.* I floated logs when the water was high. (IV) **II** *v.intr.* to float, travel by water *Dans le vieux temps quand tu flottais dans les ciprières, ou tu tapais des maringoins, oh! faulait que tu laisses la place.* In the old days when you floated in the cypress swamps, if you ran into mosquitoes, oh!, you had to leave the place. (AS) <***Loc:*** AS, LF, IV, SL, Da84, Di32, Fa77>

flou ♦see **FLU**

flouque [fluk] *n.m.* reversible plow (with two moldboards) <***Loc:*** SM, Lv88>

FLU (**flou**) [flu] *n.m.* influenza, flu <***Loc:*** AC, SJ, TB, VM, Da84, Lv88>

FLUE [flu] *n.m.* stove pipe, chimney flue <***Loc:*** AV, VM>

fluet (**felouète**) [flyɛt, følwɛt] *adj.* thin and weak, sickly <***Loc:*** LA, Fa77>

flûte [flyt] *n.f.* **1** flute **2** champagne glass **3** loaf of French bread **4** harmonica ◊ **•flûte à bouche** harmonica <TB> **•flûte à gueule** harmonica <LF> **•flûte de pain** baguette, loaf of

French bread <LA, SM> <*Loc:* AV, LA, LF, SM, TB, Da84, Gu00>

fluxion [flyksjɔ̃] *n.f.* pneumonia **Il a einne mauvaise fluxion.* He has a bad case of pneumonia. (EV, Ph36) <*Loc:* EV, IB, LF, SM, VM, Da84, Fa77, Lv88, Ph36>

fluxionner [flyksjɔ̃ne] *v.tr.* to treat for pneumonia or for a cold by applying mustard plasters <*Loc:* LF>

FLY-HORSE [flaɪhɔɹs] *n.m.* merry-go-round <*Loc:* Da84>

foi [fwa] *n.f.* faith ◊ **•bonne foi** good faith <Da84> **•ma foi!** well, to be sure! <Da84> **•mauvaise foi** bad faith <Da84> <*Loc:* Da84, Hi02>

foie [fwa] *n.m.* liver ◊ **•foie blanc** lung (of an animal) *Il mange les foies blancs de cochon.* He eats pig lungs. (SL) <SL, SM, TB, VM, Da84, Di32> **•foie gras** liverwurst <Da84> **•foie noir** liver <SM, VM, Di32> **•avoir les foies blancs** to be long-lived (said of a woman who has survived two or more husbands) <JE, La99> <*Loc:* AL, JE, LA, SL, SM, VM, Da84, Di32, Hi02, La99>

foin [fwɛ̃, fwɑ̃, fwɔ̃] *n.m.* hay, fodder *Ils donnaient le foin à les bêtes dans l'hiver.* He gave hay to the animals in winter. (IB) ◊ **•avoir du foin dans ses bottes** to be wealthy <La99> <*Loc:* AV, CL, IB, LF, Da84, La99>

foire [fwar] *n.f.* diarrhea, loose bowels <*Loc:* LA, Da84, Lv88>

foirée [fware] *n.f.* attack of diarrhea, 'the runs' <*Loc:* Da84>

fois [fwa] *n.f.* time, occasion **Deux fois.* Two times. (Da84) **Il est venu pour la troisième fois.* He came for the third time. (Da84) *La prochaine fois.* The next time. (JD) ◊ **•fois après fois** time after time *Je l'ai vu faire ça fois après fois après fois.* I saw him do that time after time after time. (LA) <LA, Da84> **•à la fois** at a time *Eusse nous a montré à parler en anglais. Et là on a appris le français un petit peu à la fois.* They taught us to speak English. And we learned French a little bit at a time. (LF) <AS, EV, LF, An84, Da84> **•(dans) les autres fois** (in) the past, (in) the old days *Il jouait des vieilles valses des autres fois.* He used to play old waltzes from the old days. (Lv88) *Dans les autres fois eux-autres avait ces barils là. Eux-autres mettait leur farine là-dedans.* In the old days they had those barrels. They used to put their flour in them. (TB) <TB, VM, An94, Gu00, Lv88> **•des fois** sometimes *On parle toujours français et anglais. On commence une conversation en français et puis on finit en anglais des fois.* We always speak French and English. We start a conversation in French and we then finish it in English sometimes. (SL) <AC, AS, AV, LF, SL, SM, TB, VM, Da84, Lv88, Wh83> **•des fois et des fois** many times *Ma vieille maman m'a raconté des fois et des fois pour un vieux n-oncle qu'elle avait.* My mother told me many times about an old uncle that she had. (LA) <LA, Da84> **•encore une fois** once more, once again *Je voudrais rester dans tes bras encore une fois avant de mourir.* I would would want to stay in your arms once more before dying. (AC) <AC, Da84> **•mainte et mainte fois** many times, time after time <Da84> **•une autre fois** another time, once again *Comment tu fais pour dire on va avoir le même bateau une autre fois?* How do you know we're going to have the same boat another time? (EV) <EV, Da84> **•une bonne fois** finally, once and for all *Ils ont fini de travailler dans les clos une bonne fois.* They have finished working in the fields once and for all. (SL) <SL, Da84> **•une fois (de) plus** twice as much, twice as many *Quand il a changé de job, il faisait proche une fois de plus qu'il faisait avant.* When he changed jobs, he was making almost twice as much as before. (LA) <LA, Da84> **•une {deux, trois} fois par an {jour, semaine, mois}** once (twice, three times) a year (day, week, month) *Y avait du monde qu'allait communier, qui va à l'église juste une fois par an.* There were people who went to take communion, who go to church just once a year. (LF) <EV, LA, LF, TB, VM, Da84> **•une fois que** once, as soon as *J'ai pas pu tout mettre la-dedans, alors une fois que t'es servi on peut vider l'autre là-dedans.* I couldn't put all of it in there, so once you've helped yourself we'll empty the other one into it. (TB) <TB> <*Loc:* AC, EV, JE, LA, LF, SL, TB, Da84, Hi02, Lv88>

folâtre[1] [folat(r)] *adj.* **1** flighty, unstable, indecisive *Il est pas mature encore, il est tout folâtre.* He's not mature yet, he's quite flighty. (Lv88) **2** coquette, flirtatious <*Loc:* SM, Lv88>

folâtre[2] [folat(r)] *n.f.* wild girl, fast girl *Pas de ces folâtres, une vaillante fille.* Not one of those wild girls, a nice girl. (VM) <*Loc:* VM>

folerie [fɔlri] *n.f.* **1** madness, craziness, foolishness, folly *Un coup de folerie.* Fit of madness. (Lv88) **C'est par pure follerie qu'il a fait ça.* He did that out of sheer madness. (EV, Ph36) **2** joking, silly bantering ◊ **•avoir une (graine de) folerie pour** to be crazy about *Il a une folerie pour les chevaux.* He's crazy for horses. (Lv88) *Le petit Buddy a une graine de folerie pour Ethel, je crois.* Little Buddy is crazy about Ethel, I believe. (TB) <TB, Lv88> <*Loc:* EV, IB, LA, SM, TB, VM, Gr86, Lv88, Ph36>

folie [foli] *n.f.* **1** insanity, madness **2** folly, silliness, craziness <*Loc:* Da84, Hi02>

follement [fɔlmɑ̃] *adv.* foolishly, crazily, madly *Elle était follement en amour avec ce vaurien.* She was madly in love with that ne'er-do-well. (LA) <*Loc:* LA, Da84>

foncé, -e [fɔ̃se] *adj.* dark, deep (of color) **Bleu foncé.* Dark blue, deep blue. (Da84) <*Loc:* Da84>

foncer [fɔ̃se] **I** *v.tr.* to butt, strike, gore (with the horns) *La vache l'a foncé quand il venait la tirer.* The cow butted him when he came to milk her. (Lv88) *Le cabri va te foncer si tu* LOOK OUT *pas.* The goat will butt you if you don't look out. (VM) **II** *v.intr.* to lunge, leap, jump **Il a foncé sur moi.* He lunged at me. (Da84) <*Loc:* EV, IB, JD, LA, LF, SB, SM, TB, VM, Da84, Lv88, Ph36>

fonction [fɔ̃ksjɔ̃] *n.f.* function, duty, job <***Loc:*** Da84>

fond[1]**, -e** [fɔ̃, -n, -d] *adj.* deep *L'eau dans le lac était pas fond.* The water in the lake wasn't deep. (Lv88) *Si tu veux acheter une chaudière, tu veux une chaudière fonde ou une chaudière plate.* If you want to buy a pot, you want a deep pot or a shallow pot. (AV) *Un lac fond.* A deep lake. (AV) <***Loc:*** AV, EV, SB, SL, SM, VM, Di32, Ph36, Lv88>

fond[2] [fɔ̃] *n.m.* **1** bottom, underside *Un skiff, ça a le fond platte, tu vois? Un canotte, ça a le fond rond.* A skiff has a flat bottom, you see? A lugger has a round bottom. (TB) **2** bottom, floor (of a lake, etc.) *Si ta cage touche pas le fond, tu vas pas attraper une écrevisse.* If your cage doesn't touch the bottom, you're not going to catch any crawfish. (SM) **3** bottom, seat (of pants, etc.) *Ça faisait des caneçons avec ça, avec un gros bouledogue dans le fond!* They used to make boxer shorts with that, with a big bulldog on the bottom! (TB) **4** far end, depth **Dans le fond des bois.* Deep in the woods. (Da84) ◊ **•de fond en comble** from top to bottom, from beginning to end <Da84> <***Loc:*** IB, JE, LA, LF, SM, SL, TB, VM, Da84, Hi02, La99>

fondage [fɔ̃daʒ] *n.m.* melting <***Loc:*** Da84>

fondament [fɔ̃dɑ̃mɑ̃] *n.m.* foundation, substructure, underpinning <***Loc:*** Da84>

fondation [fɔ̃dasjɔ̃] *n.f.* foundation (of a drilling platform, a house, etc.) <***Loc:*** JE, Fa77>

fonder [fɔ̃de] **I** *v.tr.* to establish, found, lay the foundation of *Le village a été fondé par un Français, Marcellin Garand.* The town was founded by a Frenchman, Marcellin Garand. (LA) **II se fonder** *v.pron.* to base o.s. (on), rely (on) *T'es après te fonder sur la parole à qui?* You're basing yourself on whose word? (VM) <***Loc:*** LA, VM, Da84>

fonderie [fɔ̃dri] *n.f.* foundry, smelting works, smelting plant <***Loc:*** Da84>

fondre [fɔ̃n, fɔ̃d(r)] **I** *v.tr.* to melt, liquify, dissolve *On fondait la graisse du cochon.* We melted pig fat. (Lv88) **II** *v.intr.* **1** to melt, thaw *Ils avaient des stoves au bois, so ils allaient attraper des bois dans janvier et février quand la neige au nord, la neige fondait.* They had wood stoves, so they would go to 'catch wood' [floating by in the river] in January and February when the snow melted in the north. (SB) **2** to lose weight, grow thin **III se fondre** *v.pron.* to melt, dissolve *Elle s'a fondu dans ses bras.* She melted into his arms. (LA) <***Loc:*** AC, AV, LA, SB, SJ, Da84, Hi02, Lv88>

fonds [fɔ̃] *n.m.* funds, assets, cash <***Loc:*** Da84>

fonne ♦see FUN

fontaine[1] [fɔ̃tɛ̃n] *n.f.* fountain, spring <***Loc:*** SM, Da84>

fontaine[2] [fɔ̃tɛ̃n] *n.f.* soft spot on the top of an infant's head, fontanel <***Loc:*** EV, LF, SL, SM, VM, Lv88>

fonte [fɔ̃t] *n.f.* cast iron <***Loc:*** VM, Da84>

FOOTBALL [futbɔl] *n.m.* football <***Loc:*** Da84>

for [fɔr] *n.m.* roost <***Loc:*** SM, Lv88>

fôrbir ♦see **fourbir**

fôrbissage ♦see **fourbissage**

forçal [fɔrsal] *n.m.* ◊ **•au forçal** by force *On l'a fait faire au forçal.* We made him do it by force. (VM) <VM, Di32> <***Loc:*** VM, Di32>

forçassien ♦see **forcien**

forçat [fɔrsa] *n.m.* prison, penitentiary *Il a été trois ans au forçat.* He served three years in the penitentiary. (VM) <***Loc:*** EV, JD, SM, VM, Da84, Di32, Lv88, Ph36>

forçatien, forçayin ♦see **forcien**

force [fɔrs] *n.f.* force, strength, power, intensity ◊ **•à force de** by dint of, by force of *Tu connais à force de la user ça vient* STRIPPED. You know, by dint of using it, it gets stripped. (TB) <TB> **•à force (que)** so, so much (that) *Je vas jamais l'oublier à force j'ai eu peur.* I'll never forget it, I was so scared. (VM) *Mame tombait par terre à force qu'a braillait.* Mom was crying so hard that she fell down. (EV) *C'est pas sur la carte à force c'est petit.* It's so small it's not on the map. (Lv88) *C'est pas vivable ici, à force il fait chaud.* It's not livable here, it's so hot. (VM) *A force qu'il a travaillé il a réussi.* He worked so hard that he succeeded. (SL) **Force qu'il était gros…*He was so big . . . (Hi02) *A force il a pleuré, je l'ai laissé partir.* He cried so much that I let him leave. (SM) <EV, SL, SM, VM, An94, Hi02, Lv88> **•par force** by force *Le monde de La Chênière voulait pas sortir pour l'ouragan, et ils ont eu pour les faire sortir par force.* The people of Chênière didn't want to leave for the hurricane, and they had to make them leave by force. (VM) <VM, Da84> **•venir en force** to come into force (of a law) *La cour a décidé que la nouvelle loi va pas venir en force.* The court ruled that the new law would not come into force. (VM) <VM, Lv88> <***Loc:*** EV, LF, TB, SL, SM, VM, An94, Da84, Hi02, Lv88>

forcer [fɔrse] **I** *v.tr.* **1** to force, compel, oblige (s.o. to do s.t.) *Ceux-là qui voulaient pas travailler, on les forçait pas à travailler.* Those who didn't want to work were not forced to work. (IB) **2** to increase one's production of (a crop) *Le récolteur forçait sa plante de patates douces d'année en année.* The farmer increased his sweet potato crop from year to year. (TB) **II** *v.intr.* **1** to strain, be difficult *Quand t'es vieux ça force pour marcher.* When you're old, it's difficult to walk. (VM) **2** to be abundant (of work) *Le travail force asteur, le monde a pas le temps de flâner.* Work is abundant right now, people don't have time to loaf. (VM) **3** to increase one's production (of a crop) *Cette année il a forcé sur sa récolte de maïs.* This year he increased his corn yield. (IB) *Si le maïs faisait pas bien il fallait forcer dessus les patates.* If the corn did not yield, we had to increase the potatoes. (VM) **4** to go heavy on, use more than usual *Il fallait forcer dessus la salade parce qu'on avait pas un tas de riz.* We had to go heavy on the salad because we didn't have a lot of rice. (VM) **III se forcer** *v.pron.* to force o.s., oblige o.s., strain *Comme ma belle-fille alle comprend* *pas, so quand elle alle est là il faut qu'on parle en anglais, il faut qu'on se force.* Since my daughter-in-law doesn't understand, when she is there we have to speak English, we have to force ourselves. (TB) *A s'a forcé de laver les chaudières après avoir fini avec les assiettes.* She forced herself to wash the pots after finishing the plates. (TB) ◊ **•être forcé de** to be forced to (do s.t.) *On était pas forcé d'aller à l'école dans ce temps là.* We weren't forced to go to school in those days. (LF) <LF> <***Loc:*** EV, IB, LF, TB, VM, Da84, Fa77>

forcien (forçayin, forçassien, forçatien) [fɔrsjɛ̃, fɔrsajɛ̃, fɔrsasjɛ̃] *n.m.* convict, inmate of a penitentiary *Les forciens ont échappé.* The convicts escaped. (SL) <***Loc:*** SL, VM, Da84, Di32, Lv88>

forçure [fɔrsyr] *n.f.* strain, twist, sprain in the back *Je m'ai donné une forçure.* I strained my back. (VM) <***Loc:*** VM, Di32>

fordoche ♦see **fardoche**

FOREMAN (foreman) [fɔrmɛn] *n.m.* foreman <***Loc:*** EV, TB, Da84, Di32, Pe37, Ph36>

forêt [forɛ, fore] *n.f.* forest, thick woods <***Loc:*** Da84, Hi02>

forge [fɔrʒ] *n.f.* forge, blacksmith shop <***Loc:*** SM, Da84>

forger [fɔrʒe] **I** *v.tr.* **1** to forge, fabricate, counterfeit, falsify *Forger un document.* To forge a document. (Lv88) **2** to invent, make up *Ça, je ne l'ai pas forgé du tout, c'était vrai.* I did not make it up at all, it was true. (Lv88) **II se forger** *v.pron.* **1** to be forged (of metal) **Le fer se forge bien.* The iron is easy to forge. (Da84) **2** to make up, invent (a story) *C'est pas la vérité. Il s'a forgé cette histoire.* That's not the truth. He made up that story. (VM) <***Loc:*** EV, IB, SB, SL, VM, Da84, Di32, Gr86, Lv88, Ph36>

forgeron [fɔrʒərɔ̃, fɔrsərɔ̃] *n.m.* blacksmith <***Loc:*** SB, Da84, Fa77>

forgeur [fɔrʒœr] *n.m.* **1** forger, counterfeiter **2** inventor <***Loc:*** Da84, Lv88>

formage ♦see **fromage**

formance [fɔrmɑ̃s] *n.f.* **1** development *Les fleurs sont en formance.* The flowers are developing. (VM) **2** bud, sprout *La pluie a fait les formances tomber beaucoup.* The rain made many of the buds fall off. (AV) <***Loc:*** AV, VM>

forme [fɔrm] *n.f.* form, shape, figure <***Loc:*** Da84>

former [fɔrme] **I** *v.tr.* to form, conceive, create *Y a deux ans qu'on a formé une organisation des Amis du Français de Lafourche.* Two years ago we formed an organization, the Friends of French in Lafourche. (LF) **II se former** *v.pron.* to take shape, take form, form o.s. **La fleur se forme.* The flower takes form. (Da84) *Et là le lendemain, quand il faisait froid tu passais, tu ramassais tout le par-dessus, c'était comme une crème qui se formait par-dessus. Et tu mettais ça dans une jarre.* And then the next day when it was cold, you went by, you collected the top, there was like a cream that had formed on it. And you would put it in a jar. (TB) ◊ **•bien {tout} formé** completely formed, full grown, mature *L'épi est pas bien formé encore.* The ear is not yet mature. (VM) <VM> <***Loc:*** AC, LF, TB, Da84>

formule [fɔrmyl] *n.f.* formula, recipe <***Loc:*** Da84>

formuler [fɔrmyle] *v.tr.* to formulate, detail, develop **J'avais pas une raison bien formulée dans ma tête.* I didn't have a well-formulated idea in my head. (LA, An84) <***Loc:*** LA, An84, Da84>

fort[1], -e [fɔr, -t] *adj.* **1** strong, powerful *Le courant du fleuve est tellement fort et c'est dangereux.* The current of the river is so strong and it's dangerous. (SB) *Il a une odeur qui est fort.* There is a strong odor. (SM) *Un homme fort.* A strong man. (SM) **2** high (of a fever) *La fièvre forte, ç'a brulé la cervelle, c'est tellement forte que ç'a détruit, ça fait ils pouvait pas apprendre comme avant.* The high fever, that burned their brains, it was so high that it was destructive, so they couldn't learn like before. (SJ) **3** highly seasoned, spicy, peppery *Le manger est fort, il y a trop de piment.* The food is spicy, there is too much pepper. (IB) **4** loud *Le bruit de la musique était trop fort pour le monde parler. Ça couvrait ma voix.* The noise of the music was too loud for people to talk. It covered my voice. (TB) **5** of age, mature **Du moment que j'ai été assez fort pour travailler, je suis après travailler.* From the time I was old enough to work, I've been working. (EV, An84) **6** at the age of reason (six or seven and above) *Quand j'ai été assez fort, c'est probablement dans le temps que j'ai commencé l'école, il m'a dit qui c'est j'étais.* When I was old enough [to understand], probably around the time I started school, he told me who I was. (AV) **7** well-to-do, wealthy *Eusse me donne du jardinage ou des fois comme des chevrettes, des affaires comme ça. Les plus forts, eusse me donne l'argent comme ça.* They give me vegetables or sometimes shrimp, things like that. The most well-to-do simply give me money. (TB) **8** unbelievable, exaggerated, unreal **"Lui, il veut tout le temps dire une plus fort que moi, mais guette, je vas lui en dire une à ce matin qui est plus fort." Il dit, "Il faudra que tu sermentes. Et quand je vas lui dire ça, toi, tu dis que t'as vu ça."* "He always wants to tell a taller one [tale] than me, but watch, I'll tell him one this morning that is taller." He says, "You will have to swear. And when I will tell this to him, you say that you saw it." (IV, An94) ◊ **•fort comme un bœuf {le diable / un éléphant / la mort / un mulet / un cheval}** very strong <La99> **•fort pour** good at, skilled in, adept at *Mais ma mémère, ma grand-mère était forte pour ça pour bouillir ci et ça, et c'était une médecine.* But my grandmother was good at boiling this or that to make medicine. (SB) <SB> **•ça c'est fort (quand même)** that's strange, that's hard to believe <EV, Da84> **•comment fort** how old *Comment fort il était?* How old was he? (EV) <EV> **•pas fort pour** not crazy about, not very fond of *Moi, je suis pas trop fort pour les patates douces.* I'm not too crazy about sweet potatoes.

(EV) <EV> ***<Loc:*** AV, EV, IB, IV, LA, LF, SB, SJ, SL, SM, TB, VM, An84, An94, Da84, Gu00, Hi02, La99, Wh83>

fort[2] [fɔr] *n.m.* fort, fortification ***<Loc:*** Da84>

fort[3] [fɔr] *adv.* **1** strongly, hard *Le vent souffle du nord beaucoup fort, ça va pas être bon pour pêcher.* The wind is blowing quite strong from the north, fishing won't be good. (TB) *Et là, dès que* ROCK AND ROLL *a rentré fort, Colombia a pas renouvelé son contrat.* And then when rock and roll became really popular, Columbia [records] didn't renew his contract. (LF) *Pousse pas la balance trop fort.* Don't push the swing too hard. (EV, Ph36) *J'ai couru fort.* I ran hard. (Gr86) *Elle l'a frappé tellement fort qu'il s'a ployé en deux.* She hit him so hard that he bent over double. (LA) **2** loudly, aloud *Nos parents nous a montré que le soir avant de te coucher que t'allais te mettre d'à genoux, et t'allais dire tes prières et t'allais le dire fort.* Our parents taught us that in the evening before you went to bed, you'd get down on your knees and you'd say your prayers aloud. (TB) *Baisse ta voix! Tu parles trop fort!* Lower your voice! You talk too loud! (EV) **3** very ***<Loc:*** EV, LA, LF, SM, TB, VM, Da84, Gr86, Gu82, Hi02, Lv88, Ph36, Wh83>

fortifiant, -e [fɔrtifjɑ̃, -ɑ̃t] *adj.* fortifying, healthful, strengthening *Cousin Dud vendait des tonics soi-disant fortifiants.* Cousin Dud used to sell tonics that were supposedly fortifying. (VM) ***<Loc:*** VM, Da84>

fortification [fɔrtifikasjɔ̃] *n.f.* fortification ***<Loc:*** Da84>

fortifier [fɔrtifje] **I** *v.tr.* to strengthen, fortify, reinforce *Si une muraille est faible, tu peux la fortifier.* If a wall is weak, you can reinforce it. (AV) **II se fortifier** *v.pron.* to strengthen o.s., grow strong *Il s'a fortifié avec le Hadacol à Cousin Dud.* He strengthened himself with Cousin Dud's Hadacol. (VM) ***<Loc:*** AV, VM, Da84>

fortitude [fɔrtityd] *n.f.* fortitude, strength (e.g. of character) ***<Loc:*** Da84>

fortune [fɔrtyn] *n.f.* **1** fortune **2** chance, luck ◊ **•faire (une) fortune** to get rich, make a fortune *Je vendais de l'assurance à côté. J'avais un* AGENCY *d'assurances. J'aurais dû faire une fortune!* I sold insurance on the side. I had an insurance agency. I should have made a fortune! (LF) <LF> ***<Loc:*** LF, Da84>

fossé [fose] *n.m./f.* ditch, drain, trench *Moi, je nettoyais les fossés après il a labouré. Il fallait nettoyer les fossés avec un cheuve.* I cleaned the ditches after he plowed. I had to clean the ditches with a shovel. (VM) ◊ **•prendre le fossé** to go into a ditch, fall into a ditch *Il avait pris le fossé une fois avec des œufs et il avait tout cassé.* He fell into a ditch one time, with eggs, and he broke them all. (SL) <SL> ***<Loc:*** AC, AV, EV, IB, IV, JD, LA, LF, SB, SL, SM, VM, Da84, Fa77, Hi02>

fosse [fɔs] *n.f.* **1** pit *Mon oncle a fouillé une petite fosse au milieu de la savane parce que ses vaches étaient trop hautes pour son bœuf.* My uncle dug a little pit in the middle of the pasture because his cows were too tall for his bull. (VM) **2** grave *Il y avait pas rien du tout, juste le prêtre venait bénir la fosse et c'était tout.* There was nothing at all, just the priest came to bless the grave and that was it. (TB) *J'ai fait ça, moi, déjà, fouiller des fosses pour enterrer du monde.* I have done that, digging graves to bury people. (AC) ***<Loc:*** AC, JD, TB, VM, Da84, Fa77, Re31>

fosset ♦see **fausset**

fou[1], **folle** [fu, fɔl] *adj.* crazy, insane *On est curieux quand un étranger arrête, tu connais tu peux jamais dire. Le monde est assez fou aujourd'hui, tu connais?* People are curious when a stranger stops, you know you can never tell. People are so crazy today, you know? (TB) ◊ **•fou à baver sus sa chemise / fou à courir les chemins {à manger de l'herbe}** very crazy, totally out of one's mind <La99> **•fou à sept cylindres** very crazy <La99> **•fou comme une banane {un bâton / la lune}** very crazy <La99> **•fou pour** crazy about *Et les petits grognards est fou pour les truites. Pour les truites grises.* And little croakers are crazy about bass. About speckled trout. (TB) <TB> **•à demi {moitié} fou** half crazy *C'était rendu que j'étais à moitié fou avec tout ce monde dans ma maison.* It had gotten to the point that I was half crazy with all those people in my house. (EV) <EV> **•aller {venir} fou** to go crazy *On l'aime beaucoup des huîtres, moi et mon mari. Quand on achète un sac d'huîtres, on va fou avec.* We love oysters, my husband and I. When we buy a sack of oysters we go crazy with them. (TB) <TB> **•pas trop fou de** not too crazy about, not too fond of *Des bougres très fiers d'eux-mêmes et pas trop fous des Cadjins.* Some guys who were very proud of themselves and not too crazy about Cajuns. (Gr86) <Gr86> ***<Loc:*** EV, TB, Da84, Gr86, Hi02, La99>

fou[2] [fu] *n.m.* crazy person, insane person ◊ **•faire le fou** to act crazy *Le monde disait ça à leurs enfants pour les faire rester tranquilles, pour pas que ça fait autant le fou, je pense.* People told that to their children to get them to keep quiet, so they wouldn't act so crazy, I think. (TB) ***<Loc:*** TB, Da84>

fouet (fouette) [fwɛt, fwat] *n.m.* whip, lash ◊ **•fouet à bœuf** bullwhip <SL, TB> **•fouet de boghei** buggy whip <SL> **•fouet de peau** leather whip <LA> ***<Loc:*** AV, IB, LA, LF, SL, TB, VM, An94, Da84, Lv88>

fouette ♦see **fouet**

fouetter [fwete, fwate] *v.tr.* **1** to whip, flog *Tu peux pas parler en français à l'école, ça va te fouetter.* You cannot speak French at school or you will be whipped. (AC) **2** to spank *Je vas te fouetter si tu fais ça encore.* I'm going to spank you if you do that again. (AC) ◊ **•fouetter à quatre piquets** to flog a person whose hands and feet are tied to four pegs in the ground <Da84, Lv88> ***<Loc:*** AC, AV, LF, SB, SL, An94, Da84, Fa77, Lv88, Wh83>

fouetteur [fwetœr] *n.m.* eastern coachwhip snake ***<Loc:*** SL, TB, Lv88, Re31>

fouetteuse [fwetøz] *n.f.* **1** eastern coachwhip snake **2** southern black racer <*Loc:* IB, JD, LF, SL, Da84, Lv88>

foufou [fufu] *n.m.* yellow-rumped warbler <*Loc:* EV>

fouigne ♦see **fouine**

fouillailler [fujaje] *v.intr.* **1** to dig around, rummage around *Arrête de fouillailler dans mes papiers.* Stop digging around in my papers. (AC) **2** to repeatedly and obnoxiously meddle in other people's business *Arrête donc de fouillailler dans mes affaires.* Stop meddling in my business. (LA) <*Loc:* AC, IB, LA, Da84>

fouillailleur [fujajœr] *n.m.* busybody, snoop, nosy person <*Loc:* LA>

fouillard[1], **-e** [fujar, -ard] *adj.* nosy, meddling, prying *Un enfant fouillard.* A little meddler, a child who touches everything. (SJ) <*Loc:* JD, SJ, SM, VM, Da84, Lv88>

fouillard[2], **-e** [fujar, -ard] *n.* **1** busybody, snoop, nosy person *Il est un vrai fouillard.* He's a real snoop. (SB) **2** one fond of rummaging through drawers, closets, etc. *Elle est une fouillarde.* She is always rummaging through things. (IB) <*Loc:* AV, IB, LF, SB, SJ, SL, SM, TB, VM, Da84, Lv88>

fouillarder [fujarde] *v.intr.* to dig around, rummage around *Il était après fouillarder dans mes tiroirs.* He was rummaging around in my drawers. (LA) <*Loc:* AV, LA, SB, VM, Lv88>

fouillasser [fujase] *v.intr.* to search *Ils ont rentré dans la maison fouillasser en dedans, capoter les matelas et tout quelque chose pour le découvrir.* They went into the house searching around in there, turning over mattresses and everything to find him. (LA) <*Loc:* LA>

fouille-fouille [fujfuj] *n.m.* hangnail <*Loc:* VM>

fouille-merde [fujmærd] *n.m.* **1** dung beetle, tumblebug **2** busybody, snoop, nosy person <*Loc:* AC, SM, VM, Da84, La99>

fouille-merder [fujmærde] *v.intr.* to snoop, pry, nose around *Il est tout le temps après fouille-merder dans mes affaires.* He is always snooping around in my things. (LA) <*Loc:* LA>

fouille-merdeur, -euse [fujmærdœr, -øz] *n.* busybody, snoop, nosy person *Tant qu'à lui, c'est rien qu'un fouille-merdeur.* As for him, he's nothing but a busybody. (EV) <*Loc:* EV, LA>

fouille-nez [fujne] *n.m.* busybody, snoop, nosy person *Si il y aurait pas tant de fouille-nez alentours!* If only there weren't so many busybodies around! (TB) <*Loc:* TB>

fouiller [fuje] **I** *v.tr.* **1** to dig *J'ai fait ça, moi, déjà, fouiller des fosses pour enterrer du monde.* I have done that, digging graves to bury people. (AC) **2** to dig up, dig for *Fouiller les patates. Fouiller des pommes de terre.* To dig for potatoes, dig up potatoes. (VM) *Les loirs ont tout fouillé mes pistaches.* The dormice dug up all my peanuts. (Lv88) **3** to dredge *Moi je travaillais sur les* DREDGEBOAT *fouiller des canals et des locations pour aller pour les compagnies d'huile ici.* I worked on the dredgeboats dredging canals and places to go for the oil companies here. (TB) **4** to frisk, pat down, search *Ça les fouillait bien, être sûr que c'était une bataille à coups de poings.* They frisked them right, to make sure that it was a fist fight [i.e. no weapons]. (EV) **II** *v.intr.* **1** to dig *Ça c'est pour fouiller dans la terre.* This is for digging in the soil. (IB) **2** to dig around, rummage around *Il les a quitté rentrer il a été à son desk, il a fouillé, il savait éiou-ce qu'il l'avait mais il a fouillé un peu, il dit "Ça c'est ça que vous-autres cherche pour?"* He let them come in and he went to his desk, he rummaged around, he knew where he had put it but he dug around a bit, and he said, "Is this what you are looking for?" (LF) **3** to snoop, pry, nose around *Arrête de fouiller dans mes affaires.* Stop snooping in my affairs. (LA) ◊ **•fouiller après {pour}** to search for, look for *Fouille après et tu vas le trouver.* Look for it and you will find it. (VM) *Ça c'est mon grand-père, lui il fouillait pour les trésors et tout.* That's [a picture of] my grandfather, he used to dig for treasures and all. (TB) <TB, VM> <*Loc:* AC, EV, IB, LA, LF, SM, TB, VM, Da84, Fa77, Gu00, Hi02, Lv88>

fouille-sable [fujsab(l)] *n.m.* small fish that buries itself in the sand, sand seatrout, white trout *Un fouille-sable est comme un grognard. Mais il est plat. Il ressemble presque pareil comme le grognard, mais il est plus gros, il est plus large.* A sand seatrout is like a croaker. But it's flat. It looks almost like a croaker, but it is bigger, it's wider. (TB) <*Loc:* TB>

fouilleur [fujœr] *n.* **1** digger, one who digs **2** busybody, snoop, nosy person ◊ **•fouilleur de poteau** post hole digger <LA> **•fouilleur de trous** post hole digger <EV> <*Loc:* EV, LA, LF, SL, Lv88>

fouillou (fouyon) [fuju, fujɔ̃] *n.m.* whitlow, infection of the finger or toe around the nail *J'ai eu un fouillou sur mon doigt.* I got an abscess on my finger. (TB) *On peut guérir le fouillou avec cette médecine.* You can cure whitlow with this medecine. (IB) <*Loc:* IB, TB, Di32>

fouine (fouigne) [fwin, fwiŋ] *n.f.* **1** marten, weasel **2** skunk **3** ugly woman **4** woman of loose morals, disreputable woman <*Loc:* JD, LF, SL, TB, VM, Da84, Gr86, Lv88, Re31>

fouiner [fwine, fwẽne] *v.intr.* **1** to flee, run, turn tail *J'ai voulu le battre, mais il a fouiné.* I wanted to beat him up, but he ran. (VM) **2** to lead a dissolute life *Après il a fini l'école, il s'a mis à fouiner et il a perdu proche tous ses amis.* After he finished school, he started leading a dissolute life and lost almost all his friends. (LA) <*Loc:* JD, LA, VM, Di32, Lv88>

foulage [fulaʒ] *n.m.* packing, pressing, tamping <*Loc:* Da84>

foulation [fulasjɔ̃] *n.f.* sprain *J'ai été voir une traiteuse. Et alle m'a traité pour une foulation.* I went to see a healer. And she treated me for a sprain. (TB) <*Loc:* TB>

foule [ful] *n.f.* crowd, multitude *Foule de monde.* Crowd of people. (Fa77) **Dans einne foule l'monne [=monde]* *s'poussaille.* In a crowd, people push each other. (EV, Ph36) <***Loc:*** EV, Da84, Fa77, Ph36>

foulé[1], **-e** [fule] *adj.* **1** crowded, full (of people) *Le monde était foulé au* SHOW *hier au soir.* Everyone was crowded at the show last night. (VM) **2** opaque *C'est foulé, tu peux pas voir à travers.* It's opaque, you can't see through it. (VM) **3** stocky, stout *Un cheval foulé.* A stocky horse. (Lv88) *Cette femme est assez foulée.* That woman is pretty stocky. (VM) <***Loc:*** VM, Lv88>

foulé[2], **-e** [fule] *adj.* crazy, wild *On était des jeunes foulés, ouais!* We were young and crazy people, yes! (TB) <***Loc:*** TB>

fouler [fule] **I** *v.tr.* **1** to pack, pack down, tamp, compact *Là t'avais pour fouler ce coton pour l'emmener au moulin.* You had to pack down the cotton to take it to the mill. (SL) **On mettait de la mousse noire et on la foulait, et une fois on l'avait bien foulée avec une baguette, un bâton à peu près long comme ça, on venait et on mettait de la poudre.* We would put black moss and we would pack it, and when we had packed it well with a ramrod, a stick about this long, we'd come and we'd put some powder. (LA, An94) **2** to hammer, press (metal) *Dans le vieux temps, mon frère avait habitude de fouler du fer chauffé dans sa forge.* In the old days, my brother used to press hot iron in his forge. (LA) **3** to sprain *Je me rappelle pour l'ouragan Hilda, j'avais glissé sur le bateau que je travaillais, j'avais foulé mon pied, et il avait venu enflé.* I remember for Hurricane Hilda, I had slipped on the boat I worked on, I had sprained my ankle, and it had become swollen. (TB) **II** *v.intr.* to trick, dupe, put one over on *On lui a joué une niche. On l'a bien foulé.* We played a practical joke on him. We really put one over on him. (LA) **II se fouler** *v.pron.* **1** to become packed **2** to pack, crowd (into a room) *Le monde s'a foulé dans la cour pour le procès des frères Blanc.* The people packed into the courtroom for the trial of the Blanc brothers. (VM) **3** to sprain (one's foot, ankle, etc.) *Quand tu te foulais un pied, eusse mettait du vinaigre là-dessus. Dans ce temps-là y avait pas de glace et pas rien, tu connais.* When you sprained an ankle, they would put vinegar on it. In those days there was no ice, there was nothing, you know. (TB) ◊ **•fouler sur (qqn)** to trample on, run over, walk all over, oppress *Il a voulu faire du train avec moi, mais je suis un qu'il va pas fouler sur.* He wanted to cause trouble with me, but I'm not one he's going to trample on. (VM) <***Loc:*** LA, SL, TB, VM, An94, Da84, Lv88>

fouleuse [fuløz] *n.f.* compacter (on a haybaler) *La fouleuse a parti. Tu connais, ça qui foulait la balle.* The compacter started. You know, the thing that packs the bale. (EV) <***Loc:*** EV, An94>

foulure [fulyr] *n.f.* sprain *Et quand ça venait pour des foulures et tout, ils venaient là, ils savaient où toucher.* When people would come with a sprain, they [the treaters] would come and they knew where to touch. (SJ) <***Loc:*** SJ, Da84>

four [fur, fɔr] *n.m.* **1** oven *Tous les maisons avaient des fours en terre, eusse avait plein du bois pour chesser et tout.* All of the houses had earthen ovens, they had a lot of wood to dry out and all. (LF) **2** furnace **3** cast iron frying pan **4** Dutch oven *Un four, c'est une chaudière à deux oreilles avec quatre petites pattes courtes et un couvercle.* A Dutch oven, it's a pot that has two handles with four little feet and a lid. (Lv88) **5** burial vault *Son four est fait en brique.* His vault is made of brick. (AV) ◊ **•four à pain** bread oven *Un four à pain c'est une grande chaudière avec trois pattes. Il y a un couvert dessus et on use ça pour cuire du pain.* A bread oven is a big pot with three legs. There's a cover on it and you use it to bake bread. (TB) <TB> **•four de stove** Dutch oven *Après que c'est paré tu le mets dans le four de stove.* After it's ready you put it in the Dutch oven. (TB) <TB> <***Loc:*** AV, EV, LA, LF, SL, TB, Da84, Lv88>

fourbir (**fôrbir, frobir, froubir**) [furbir, fɔrbir, frobir, frubir] *v.tr.* to scrub, clean, wash, mop *On a frobi la cuisine avec des torchons.* We scrubbed the kitchen with rags. (Lv88) *Le plancher peut rester un mois sans froubi du tout.* The floor can go a month without being scrubbed at all. (Lv88) *C'était un plancher en bois, et follait que tu frobis tout ça après que tout le dîner était cuit.* It was a wooden floor, and you had to scrub it after the dinner was all cooked. (TB) <***Loc:*** AV, EV, IB, LF, SB, SL, SM, TB, VM, Hi02, Lv88, Ph36>

fourbissage (**fôrbissage, frobissage, froubissage**) [furbisaʒ, fɔrbisaʒ, frobisaʒ, frubisaʒ] *n.m.* scrubbing, cleaning, mopping <***Loc:*** EV, IB, SL, SM, VM, Da84, Di32, Lv88, Ph36>

fourbisseur, -euse (**frobisseur, froubisseur**) [furbisœr, frobisœr, frubisœr, -øz] *n.* one who scrubs or mops <***Loc:*** SL, SM, Di32>

fourbissoir (**frobissoir**) [furbiswar, frobiswar] *n.m.* brush for scrubbing the floor (formerly made of corn husks nailed to a piece of wood) <***Loc:*** IB, Di32, Lv88>

fourche [furʃ] *n.f.* **1** pitchfork **2** pushpole, forked pole used to advance barges *Le chaland, on use plutôt une fourche, et les pirogues, c'est des pagaïes qu'on use.* With a flat-bottomed boat we use a pushpole, and with pirogues we use paddles. (TB) **3** fork (in a road or tree) *Un bois de flèche avait un tas de fourches.* A wild dogwood had a lot of forks in it. (LA) **4** confluence of two rivers **5** crotch *La fourche du pantalon.* The crotch of the pants. (IB) **6** barrel of a double-barreled shotgun *C'était ces fusils à piston. Il s'a mis à charger les deux fourches.* It was [one of] those open-hammered musket. He began loading both barrels. (LA) ◊ **•fourche à dix dents** ten tined pitchfork <EV> **•fourche à riz** pitchfork for rice <EV, Gr86> <***Loc:*** EV, IB, JD, LA, LF, SB, SM, TB, VM, Da84, Di32, Fa77, Gr86, Lv88, Ph36, Re31>

fourché, -e [furʃe] *adj.* forked, branching *Ils ont campé droit là ayoù le bayou est fourché.* They camped right there where the bayou forks. (LA) <*Loc:* LA, Da84>

fourchée [furʃe] *n.f.* pitchforkful <*Loc:* Da84>

fourcher [furʃe] **I** *v.tr.* to propel (a boat) with a forked push-pole *Ils ont eu pour fourcher le bateau à travers des* LILIES. They had to pole the boat through the lilies. (LA) **II** *v.intr.* **1** to fork, divide, branch, branch off (of a road) **Le chemin fourche.* The road branches off. (Da84) **2** to swerve, turn aside *Il a fourché à gauche quand il a arrivé au bois.* He turned off to the left when he got to the woods. (LA) ◊ •**faire fourcher** to dissuade, cause to deviate *Il va pas me faire fourcher de ça j'ai voulu faire.* He won't dissuade me from what I wanted to do. (VM) <VM> <*Loc:* LA, VM, Da84, Lv88>

fourchette [furʃɛt, fɔrʃɛt, fuʃɛt, fruʃɛt] *n.f.* **1** table fork **2** garden fork, digging fork **3** exit (off a highway) *Plutôt que d'aller en dedans Raceland, quand tu prends* HIGHWAY NINETY, *tu prends la fourchette comme ça.* Rather than going into Raceland, when you take highway 90, you take the exit like that. (TB) **4** bur marigold, swamp marigold ◊ •**fourchette de foin** pitchfork <TB> <*Loc:* AC, AV, EV, IB, JE, LF, SB, SL, SM, TB, VM, Da84>

fourchettée [furʃete] *n.f.* forkful (of food) <*Loc:* Da84>

Fourchien ♦see **Fourchon**

fourchon[1] [furʃɔ̃] *n.m.* crotch <*Loc:* AV, IB, SJ>

Fourchon[2] (**Fourchien**) [fuʃɔ̃, furʃjɛ̃] *n.m.* person from Lafourche Parish *Tu peux dire si c'est un Fourchon.* You can tell if it's someone from Lafourche Parish [from the way they talk]. (TB) <*Loc:* TB, Di32>

fourchu, -e [furʃy] *adj.* forked, branching *Une langue fourchue.* A forked tongue. (LA) **Pied fourchu.* Cloven hoof. (Da84) <*Loc:* LA, Da84>

fourgaille [furgaj] *n.f.* scolding, upbraiding *Je l'ai foutu une fourgaille.* I gave him a good scolding. (SL) <*Loc:* SL>

fourgailler [furgaje] **I** *v.tr.* **1** to scold, upbraid, give a stern talking to, rake over the coals *Je l'ai bien fourgaillé pour ça il a fait.* I really raked him over the coals for what he did. (VM) **2** to frisk, pat down, search *Fourgailler quelqu'un.* To search someone. (AV) **3** to ransack, rummage through (while searching for s.t.) *Il a fourgaillé ma maison pour mes lettres.* He tore my house apart looking for my letters. (SL) **II** *v.intr.* **1** to dig around, rummage around *Il était après fourgailler dans ses tiroirs pour essayer de trouver une paire de chaussettes.* He was rummaging around in his drawers trying to find a pair of socks. (LA) **Pou qui ti fourgailles?* What are you looking for? (EV, Ph36) **2** to snoop, pry, nose around *Il est toujours à fourgailler dans mon tiroir.* He's always nosing around in my drawer. (SB) <*Loc:* EV, IB, LA, LF, SB, SL, SM, TB, VM, Di32, Lv88>

fourgailleur, -euse [furgajœr] *n.m.* busybody, snoop, nosy person <*Loc:* Di32, Lv88>

fourmi (**frémi, fromi, froumi, froumille**) [furmi, frəmi, frɛ̃mi, frɔ̃mi, frumi, frɔ̃mej] *n.m./f.* ant *Les grosses fourmis rouges font des buttes de terre et mordent.* The big red ants make anthills and bite. (Gu00) ◊ •**fromi blanc** termite *C'était un ver, c'est comme un fromi blanc, un* TERMITE. *Ça qu'il fait, il fait des trous dans le bois.* It was a worm, it's like a termite. What it does, it makes holes in the wood. (LF) <*Loc:* AC, AV, JE, LF, SB, SL, SM, TB, VM, Da84, Gu00, Hi02, Lv88>

fourmillière [furmijær] *n.f.* swarm (of ants or other insects) <*Loc:* Da84>

fournaise [furnɛz] *n.f.* ◊ •**manquer un pain dans sa fournaise** to be impatient *Il manque un pain dans ta fournaise.* You're too impatient. (TB) <TB> <*Loc:* TB>

fourneau [furno] *n.m.* **1** oven **2** furnace <*Loc:* Da84, Fa77, Lv88>

fournette [furnɛt] *n.f.* small cast-iron stove (formerly used as a space heater or to heat a clothing iron) *Mon, j'erpasse avec une fournette.* I use a small iron stove when I do the ironing. (TB) <*Loc:* TB>

fourni, -e [furni] *adj.* **1** furnished *Une chambre à coucher complètement fournie.* A completely furnished bedroom. (EV) **2** loaded, heavy (of a fruit-bearing plant) *Les pieds de fèves étaient bien fournis.* The bean plants were loaded with beans. (VM) <*Loc:* EV, VM, Da84>

fournir [furnir] **I** *v.tr.* **1** to furnish *Fournir une maison pour 5000 piasses.* To furnish a house for $5000. (Lv88) **2** to furnish, supply *Si tu travaillais pour cet homme, t'avais tes outils de fournis.* If you worked for that man, you had your tools furnished. (VM) **3** to provide, give, yield *Dans la famille c'est moi qui fournis une place pour que la famille se sauve quand y a un ouragan là.* In the family I'm the one who provides a place for the family to escape to when there is a hurricane. (TB) **II** *v.intr.* **1** to yield, produce **Le coton fournit bien.* The cotton yields well. (Da84) *Le gombo févi a bien fourni cette année.* The okra really produced well this year. (EV) **2** to follow suit (in cards) *Il pouvait pas couper parce qu'il faulait fournir en piques.* He couldn't trump because he had to follow suit in spades. (LA) **III se fournir** *v.pron.* to provide for o.s. *Il s'a bien fourni en bois pour l'hiver.* He provided himself with a good stock of wood for the winter. (LA) <*Loc:* EV, LA, TB, VM, Da84, Fa77, Lv88>

fourniture [furnityr] *n.f.* **1** furniture, furnishings *Ta fourniture, c'est une chose, mais les portraits de ta famille, c'est pas remplaçable.* Your furniture, that's one thing, but family pictures, those are not replaceable. (EV) **2** piece of furniture *Voici les fournitures de la maison.* Here are the pieces of furniture for the house. (IB) <*Loc:* EV, IB, Da84, Fa77, Lv88>

fournu, -e [furny] *adj.* bushy *Le chien j'ai vu avait une queue fournue.* The dog I saw had a bushy tail. (LA) <*Loc:* LA, Da84>

fourrage [furaʒ] *n.m.* fodder, forage, hay <*Loc:* Da84>

fourré, -e [fure] *adj.* furred, furry *Il fait un petit brin d'argent à attraper des petites bétailles fourrées.* He makes a little money trapping small furry animals. (LA) <*Loc:* LA, Da84>

fourreau [furo] *n.m.* **1** sheath, scabbard, slot (for a knife, buggy whip, etc.) **2** finger bandage **3** bonnet, hat **4** pillow-case <*Loc:* IB, LA, VM, Da84>

fourre-nez[1] [furne] *adj.* curious, nosy *Il est beaucoup fourre-nez, il dit, il voudra se fourrer dans les affaires, il voudra vous demander des affaires.* He's very nosy, he said, he wants to get into your business, he will want to ask you things. (AC) <*Loc:* AC, JD, VM, Lv88>

fourre-nez[2] [furne] *n.* busybody, snoop, nosy person **Tracasse-toi pas de moi, espèce de fourre-nez.* Don't worry about me, nosy. (ThCa: *La table des veuves*) <*Loc:* AC, Lv88, ThCa>

fourrer [fure] **I** *v.tr.* **1** to stuff *J'ai fourré mon oreiller avec du coton.* I stuffed my pillow with cotton. (Lv88) **2** to shove, stuff, stick *Dean et l'autre femme a venu avec les têtes de poisson, et il a fourré ça dans le* FREEZER. Dean and the other woman came with the fish heads, and he stuck them in the freezer. (TB) **3** to put on hurriedly or carelessly, throw on (an article of clothing) **Il a attrapé son capot, il l'a fourré l'autre manière.* He grabbed his coat, he threw it on the other way. (IV, An94) **II se fourrer** *v.pron.* **1** to get o.s. (into), enter (e.g. a tight spot) **Il a ôté une des ses bottes et le lapin a venu se fourrer droit dedans sa botte.* He took off one of his boots and the rabbit came and got right into the boot. (IV, An94) **2** to settle, take up residence *Quand il a frappé l'huile ça venait du monde de tout partout qu'a venu se fourrer là pour un job.* When he struck oil, people from everywhere came here for a job. (AC) **3** to intrude *Il vient tout le temps se fourrer ayoù il a pas d'affaire.* He always intrudes where he has no business. (LA) **4** to put on hurriedly or carelessly, throw on (an article of clothing) *Se fourrer un chapeau sur la tête.* To throw a hat on one's head. (SJ) *Il s'a fourré les pantalons à son frère.* He put on his brother's pants. (LF) ◊ **•fourrer le doigt partout** to meddle in the affairs of others <La99> **•fourrer son nez** to stick one's nose in, meddle, butt in **Viens pas fourrer ton nez ici.* Don't come poke your nose around here. (Da84) <Da84> **•être fourré** to be stuck *Icitte là, ça fait quinze ans qu'on est fourré ici.* Here, we've been holed up here for fifteen years. (TB) **Il y'avait des garçons qu'a été fourrés avec des noms de filles commes Audrey, Beverly, Doris, Judy, Lisa et Shirley.* There were boys who were stuck with girls' names like Audrey, Beverly, Doris, Judy, Lisa and Shirlye. (Wh83) <TB, Wh83> <*Loc:* AC, AV, IV, LA, LF, SB, TB, An94, Da84, La99, Lv88, Wh83>

fourre-tout [furtu] *n.m.* catch-all, junk closet <*Loc:* IB>

foutaise[1] [futez, futɛz] *adj.* out-of-sorts *Je me sentais foutaise hier soir.* I felt out of sorts last night. (SM) *Être foutaise, se sentir foutaise.* To be out of sorts, feel out-of-sorts. (VM) <*Loc:* SB, SM, VM, Di32>

foutaise[2] [futez] *n.f.* nonsense, worthless idea or thing *Je peux dire que le CODOFIL c'est de la foutaise.* I can tell you that CODOFIL is a bunch of nonsense. (Gr86) <*Loc:* Di32, Gr86>

foutant [futɑ̃] *adj.* vexing, disappointing, too bad *C'est foutant, j'ai pas pu l'avoir.* It's too bad, I couldn't get it. (Lv88) *C'est foutant quand même que je peux pas finir cet été.* It's disappointing that I can't finish this summer. (SM) *C'est foutant que je peux pas faire ce que je veux.* It's annoying that I can't do what I want. (LF) <*Loc:* JD, LF, SB, SM, Lv88>

foutraille[1] [futraj] *n.f.* **1** trash, refuse *Un tas de foutrailles.* A pile of trash. (SJ) **2** rabble, riffraff **Jette ç'te foutraille déhors.* Throw the rabble out. (EV, Ph36) <*Loc:* AV, EV, IB, SJ, Lv88, Ph36>

foutraille[2] [futraj] *n.* worthless person, good-for-nothing, *Ce foutraille m'ennuie.* That good-for-nothing bores me. (SJ) <*Loc:* AV, SJ>

foutre[1] [fut(r)] **I** *v.tr.* **1** to administer, deal, give (a blow, talking to, etc.) *Je l'ai foutu un coup par en arrière.* I hit him from behind. (SL) **2** to throw, throw down *Ça fait, ils ont tous foutu le sac là et ils ont parti au feu.* So they all threw the sack down there and they took off to the fire. (AC) *J'ai* RIDE *le bicycle, et j'avais bu de la bière* THOUGH. *J'ai tapé le* CYCLONE FENCE *à W. là-bas là, ça m'a foutu par terre.* I rode the bicycle, and I had drunk beer though. I hit W's cyclone fence over there, that threw me to the ground. (TB) **3** to do, make **Quoi ils vouliont foutre avec une pareille grosse chaudière?* What did they want to do with such a big pot? (SL, An94) **Il a décidé de foutre un* TELEPHONE CALL. He decided to make a telephone call. (An94) **II se foutre** *v.pron.* to ridicule, make fun (of) *Il a dit ça pour se foutre de toi.* He said that to poke fun at you. (SM) *On se foutait d'eux-autres.* We made fun of them. (TB) ◊ **•foutre ça à qqn** to beat s.o. up *Foutre ça à Jean.* To beat John up. (LF) <LF> **•en foutre à qqn** to beat s.o. up *En foutre à Jean.* To beat John up. (LF) <LF> **•foutre dedans** ***a*** to cheat ***b*** to betray <Da84, Lv88> **•foutre dehors** to throw (s.o.) out *Y a longtemps que mon j'aurais foutu ça dehors.* I would have thrown him out a long time ago. (TB) <TB> **•foutre en feu** to anger **Eux avaient peint sa jument verte avec de la peinture. Quand il a vu ça, ça l'a foutu en feu, tu vois.* They had painted his mare green with the paint. When he saw that, it angered him, you see. (AC, An94) <AC, An94, La99> **•foutre HELL** to bawl out, rake over the coals <VM> **•foutre le camp** to get out, beat it, go away *Quand le constable a arrivé, tu peux croire qu'ils ont foutu leur camp.* When the constable arrived, you can believe that they got out of there. (LA) <LA, Da84, La99> **•foutre le champ** to get out, beat it, go away <IB> **•foutre le coup à qqn** to screw s.o. over, sock it to s.o. **Le Cadjin va vous foutre le coup dans les calculs et vous doubler le prix.* The Cajun will screw you over in the calculation and will double the price on you. (Gr86) <Gr86> **•foutre le feu (à)** to set fire (to) *Il a foutu le feu à sa maison.* He set fire to his house. (LA) <LA, La99> **•foutre non!** heck no! <IB> **•foutre par terre** to knock over, knock down *Si tu fous un baril par terre, cinq secondes de* PENALTY. *Alors tu peux pas gagner, si tu vois quelqu'un qui fout un baril par terre tu sais qu'il a pas gagné.* If you knock a barrel over, five seconds penalty. So you can't win, if you see someone knock a barrel over you know he hasn't won. (LF) <LF, Da84> **•foutre un coup de pied {coude / poing / tête, etc.}** to deal a blow with the foot (i.e. to kick) / the elbow (i.e. to elbow) / the fist (i.e. to punch) / the head, etc. *Je guette qui-ce que je dis parce que des fois tu peux te foutre un coup de pied dans tes dents à toi-même.* I watch what I say because sometimes you can kick yourself in the teeth. (LF) <LA, LF, Da84, Wh83> **•foutre une calotte à qqn** to give s.o. a slap, slap s.o. *Alle m'a foutu une calotte.* She slapped me. (LF) <LF> **•foutre une jambette à qqn** to trip s.o. <Da84> **•foutre une pourgale (à)** ***a*** to give a good talking-to, bawl out, scold *Et là quand j'ai venu en famille, je voulais pas rester à Montegut parce que à tout moment alle venait et alle me foutait des pourgales, tu connais. Et alle me faisait peur!* And then when I got pregnant, I didn't want to stay in Montegut because she was constantly coming and she would give me a good talking-to, you know. And she scared me! (TB) ***b*** to frighten <TB, Da84> **•se foutre par terre** to fall down *Il s'a foutu par terre en débarquant du char.* He fell down while getting out of the car. (LA) <LA, Da84> **•se foutre une ribotte** to get drunk <Da84> **•s'en foutre (pas mal)** to not give a damn, not care *Je m'en fous pas mal.* I don't give a damn. (VM) *Je m'en fous pas mal quoi tu dis.* I don't care what you say. (LA) <LA, VM, Wh83> **•s'en foutre une bosse** to do s.t. in excess *J'ai été chez Mame, et je m'ai foutu une bosse de gâteau.* I went to Mom's and I pigged out on cake. (SL) *S'en foutre une bosse à danser.* To dance a great deal. (LF) <LF, SL, La99> **•va te faire foutre!** [*vulg.*] go to hell! <Da84> ***<Loc:*** AC, LA, LF, SL, SM, TB, VM, An94, Da84, Gr86, Hi02, La99, Lv88, Wh83>

foutre[2] [fut(r)] *n.m.* ◊ **•pas un foutre** ***a*** not at all, not one bit *Je l'aime pas un foutre.* I don't like him one bit. (VM) ***b*** nothing at all *Il n-a pas un foutre pour faire ici.* There's nothing at all to do here. (SM) *Il fait jamais un foutre.* He never does a damn thing. (SB) <SB, SM, VM, Lv88> ***<Loc:*** SB, SL, SM, VM, Lv88>

foutrement [futrəmɑ̃] *adv.* certainly, sure as hell **Je vois pas qu'il est un sacré foutrement meilleur que le mien.* I don't see that he [the dog] is a damned bit better than mine. (EV, An94) *Il va foutrement pas faire ça.* He is sure as hell not going to do that. (SL) ***<Loc:*** EV, LF, SL, An94, Gr86>

foutu, -e [futy] *adj.* **1** ruined **2** beyond hope, done for *Le docteur dit il est foutu.* The doctor says he's done for. (SM) ◊ **•foutu comme Henri IV sur le Pont Neuf** screwed, without hope <Lv88> ***<Loc:*** IB, LF, SB, SL, SM, TB, Da84, Hi02>

foutumasser [futymase] **I** *v.tr.* to annoy, irritate **Ti m'foutumaces, va-t-en!* You're bugging me, go away! (EV, Ph36) **II** *v.intr.* **1** to fool around, mess around **Arrête de foutumasser avec ça.* Quit fooling with that. (Da84) **Viens pas foutumasser avec moi.* Don't mess with me. (Da84) *J'étais après foutumasser à attraper des poissons dans un chicot à la main.* I was fooling around, catching fish by hand in a stump. (JD) **2** to piddle around, waste time *Il est toujours après foutumasser.* He is always wasting time. (Lv88) *Il a foutumassé presque toute la semaine.* He piddled around nearly all week. (SB) **3** to snoop, pry, nose around *Arrête foutumasser dans mes affaires.* Stop looking through my personal belongings. (LF) ◊ **•foutumasser son temps** to waste one's time <Lv88> ***<Loc:*** EV, JD, LF, SB, SJ, VM, Da84, Lv88, Ph36>

foutûment [futymɑ̃] *adv.* really, certainly, indeed, very much *Il est foutument gros.* He is really fat. (SM) *Être foutûment dans l'embarras.* To be very much in the lurch. (SJ) ◊ **•foutûment oui** yes, indeed <Lv88> ***<Loc:*** AV, JD, SB, SJ, SM, Lv88>

fouyer ♦see **foyer**

fouyon ♦see **fouillou**

foyer (fouyer) [fwaje, fuje] *n.m.* fireplace, hearth *Va t'assir près du foyer un élan.* Go sit by the fireplace for a while. (TB) ***<Loc:*** AV, EV, IB, LA, LF, SB, SL, SM, TB, An94, Da84, Gr86, Lv88, Ph36>

fracas [fraka] *n.m.* fracas, disturbance ***<Loc:*** Da84>

fraction [fraksjɔ̃] *n.f.* fraction, portion, small amount ***<Loc:*** Da84>

fragile [fraʒil] *adj.* **1** fragile, frail, weak, breakable *Fais attention avec ça. C'est fragile.* Be careful with that. It's fragile. (LA) *Il était fragile comme un petit dinde.* He was as fragile as a little turkey. (VM) **2** changeable, unsettled (of the weather) *Le temps est fragile.* The weather is unsettled. (LA) ***<Loc:*** LA, VM, Da84, Fa77>

fragment [fragmɑ̃] *n.m.* fragment, piece ***<Loc:*** Da84>

fragmentation [fragmɑ̃tasjɔ̃] *n.f.* fragmentation ***<Loc:*** Da84>

fragmenter [fragmɑ̃te] *v.intr.* to fragment, break, break to pieces *Elle a échappé le pot, et il a tombé et fragmenté.* She dropped the pot, and it fell and broke to pieces. (LA) ***<Loc:*** LA, Da84>

fraîche[1] ♦see **frais**[1]

fraîche[2] [frɛʃ, freʃ] *n.f.* coolness, cool breeze *Le soir on peut mieux dormir avec la fraîche.* At night you can sleep better with a cool breeze. (Lv88) *Une bonne fraîche est venue.* A nice cool breeze came in. (AV) ◊ **•à la fraîche** in the cool breeze **Se mettre à la fraîche.* To situate oneself so as to take advantage of a cool breeze. (Da84) *S'assir à la fraîche.* To sit in the cool breeze. (LA) <LA, SM, TB, VM, Da84> **•faire une fraîche** to go quickly (i.e. move so quickly that one's passage creates a breeze) *Dans moi, c'était un cocodril qu'a tombé. Tu parles faire une fraîche!* Myself, I think it was an alligator that fell. Talk about getting out of there quickly! (LA) <LA> **•prendre la fraîche** to take advantage of a cool breeze *J'étais assis sur ma berceuse pour prendre la fraîche.* I was sitting on the porch swing to enjoy the cool breeze. (Lv88) <SM, TB, VM, Lv88> <***Loc:*** AV, JD, LA, SB, SM, TB, VM, Da84, Di32, Gr86, Lv88>

fraîchement [freʃmɑ̃] *adv.* newly, recently, freshly *Une gazette fraîchement sortie.* A newly released newspaper. (EV) <***Loc:*** EV, Da84>

fraîcheur [freʃœr] *n.f.* **1** coolness, cool air *Ayoù la fraîcheur après-midi, sur la galerie peut-être?* Where is the cool breeze in the afternoon, maybe on the porch? (VM) *Tout le monde espère les fraîcheurs de l'automne.* Everyone looks forward to the coolness of fall. (LA) **3** aching or sore muscles associated with having a cold <***Loc:*** LA, SJ, VM, Da84>

fraîchir [freʃir] **I** *v.tr.* to cool off, chill *Prends les fraises et mets-les dans le* FRIDGE *pour les fraîchir.* Take the strawberries and put them in the refrigerator to cool them off. (LA) **II se fraîchir** *v.pron.* to cool off, get cooler *Le temps se fraîchit bonne heure dans l'automne.* It gets cool early in the fall. (LA) <***Loc:*** LA, Da84>

fraide ♦see **froide**

frais[1] **(fraîche)** [frɛ, fre, frɛʃ] *adj.* **1** fresh **Des œufs frais.* Fresh eggs. (Da84) *Du bon poisson fraîche.* Good fresh fish. (EV) *Des produits bien fraîches.* Fresh products. (EV) **2** cool *Et l'eau était tout le temps frais dans le fond du puits, c'était pas froid, c'était frais.* And the water was always cool at the bottom of the well, it wasn't cold, it was cool. (TB) *Il fait assez frais que les cannes peut supporter jusqu'à après Christmas.* It's cool enough that the sugarcane can stand it until after Christmas. (AS) **3** cold **Et il faisait frais, frais, frais!* It was really cold! (An94) *Boire une bière fraîche après une journée de travail au soleil, c'est rassasiant.* Drinking a cold beer after a day of work in the sun is very satisfying. (VM) **4** fresh, not salt (of water) *Eau fraîche.* Fresh water. (Da84) ◊ **•frais comme un lapin** energetic, feisty, invigorated, ready to go <La99> <***Loc:*** AC, AS, AV, EV, LA, SM, TB, An94, Da84, Gr86, Hi02, La99, Lv88, Wh83>

frais[2] [frɛ, fre] *n.m.* **1** coolness, freshness **2** cold, common cold *Il a attrapé un frais.* He caught a cold. (EV) <***Loc:*** EV, Da84>

frais[3] [frɛ, fre] *n.m.pl.* expense, cost, charge *Payer les frais des dédommages.* To pay the cost of the damages. (AV) <***Loc:*** AV, Da84, Hi02>

frais[4] [frɛ, fre] *adv.* freshly, newly *Et la maison était propre comme si c'était frais peinturée!* And the house was clean like it was freshly painted! (TB) <***Loc:*** TB>

fraise [frɛz] *n.m./f.* **1** strawberry *Prends les fraises et mets-les dans le* FRIDGE *pour les fraîchir.* Take the strawberries and put them in the refrigerator to cool them off. (LA) **2** strawberry plant <***Loc:*** CL, LA, Da84, Fa77>

framboise [frɑ̃bwaz] *n.f.* raspberry <***Loc:*** CL>

FRAME [fɹeˈm] *n.m.* frame <***Loc:*** AC, VM>

franc[1], **franche** [frɑ̃, frɑ̃ʃ] *adj.* **1** frank, honest **La franche vérité.* The plain truth. (Da84) *O non, non, non, franc cavalier, ma femme est trop fidèle à moi.* Oh no, no, no, honest knight, my wife is too faithful to me. (PQ, ch: *O Catherine, vaillante Catherine*) **2** true, real, veritable *Tant qu'à lui, c'est un franc jureur.* As for him, he's a real curser. (VM) <***Loc:*** PQ, VM, Da84>

franc[2] [frɑ̃] *n.m.* French franc <***Loc:*** Da84>

français[1], **-e** [frɑ̃sɛ, frɑ̃se, -ɛz] *adj.* **1** French *Ma mère chantait des vieilles chansons françaises.* My mother used to sing old French songs. (EV) *Je voulais connaître qui moi j'étais après parler après, chanter après. Et ça c'est comment j'ai appris la langue française.* I wanted to know what I was talking about and singing about. And that's how I learned the French language. (TB) **2** Louisiana French <***Loc:*** EV, TB, Da84, Hi02, Lv88, Wh83>

français[2] [frɑ̃sɛ, frɑ̃se] *n.m.* French, the French language *Je crois pas que sa mère et son père a poussé le français sus lui avant qu'il commence à faire la musique.* I don't think his mother and father starting pushing French on him until he began to play music. (TB) *Je joue de la musique en français.* I play music in French. (TB) ◊ **•français cadien** Cajun French <TB, Wh83> **•le vrai français** 'the real French,' Standard French *Je crois que tu vois quand* CODOFIL *a venu c'était pour montrer les enfants le vrai français.* I think you see that when CODOFIL came it was to teach children the 'real' French. (LF) <LF> <***Loc:*** LF, TB, An94, Da84, Hi02, Lv88, Wh83>

Français[3], **-e** [frɑ̃sɛ, frɑ̃se, -ɛz] *n.* **1** French-speaking Louisianian *On trouve dans la paroisse Calcasieu des places ayoù il n-a des Français.* In Calcasieu Parish you find places where there are French speakers. (Lv88) **2** Frenchman **Les premiers Français là...s'ont établi ici comme des planteurs.* The first French there settled here as planters. (An94) **Mon arrière-grand-père [...] a marié une Française qui était venue en Louisiane pour éduquer ses enfants.* My great-grandfather married a Frenchwoman who had come to Louisiana to raise her children. (Gr86) ◊ **•les vrais Français** 'real' French people (i.e. people from France) *Mais autour de Lafayette et Opelousas et tout là, eux-autres parlait plein comme les vrais Français.* But around Lafayette and Opelousas and all, they talked more like the real French people. (LF) <LF> <***Loc:*** LF, SL, Ca83, An94, Da84, Gr86, Hi02, Lv88, Wh83>

français[4] [frɑ̃sɛ, frɑ̃se] *n.m.* mallard duck <*Loc:* SL>

France [frɑ̃s] *n.f.* France <*Loc:* SM, Da84>

franchement [frɑ̃ʃmɑ̃] *adv.* frankly, truthfully, really *Franchement, tu peux le croire.* Really, you can believe him. (VM) <*Loc:* VM, Da84>

frange [frɑ̃ʒ] *n.f.* fringe, tassel, frill ◊ **•à franges** fringed, tasseled <Da84> <*Loc:* Da84, Fa77>

franger[1] [frɑ̃ʒe] *v.tr.* to fringe, apply fringes *Il a passé des heures à franger son* COSTUME. He spent hours applying fringes to his costume. (EV) <*Loc:* EV, Da84>

franger[2] [frɑ̃ʒe] *v.tr.* to leap over, cross (an obstacle or boundary) quickly or easily *Franger le seuil de la porte.* To cross the threshold in one stride. (SJ) *Il a frangé la barrière comme un cheval.* He leapt over the fence like a horse. (AV) <*Loc:* AV, SJ>

frappage [frapaʒ] *n.m.* **1** knock, knocking, striking **2** weaving **Il(s) avions une autre affaire, ça c'était un métier à frappage pour la "cotonnade."* They had another thing, it was a loom for making homespun. (Gr86) <*Loc:* Da84, Di32, Gr86>

frappe d'abord [frapdabɔr] *n.m./f.* deerfly <*Loc:* LF, TB, Da84, Gr86, Lv88, Re31>

frappé, -e [frape] *adj.* **1** struck, hit, knocked *Il y avait un chien frappé par un char au milieu du chemin.* There was a dog struck by a car in the middle of the road. (LA) **2** mentally deranged ◊ **•frappé de la lune** mentally deranged, moonstruck *Il fait assez drôle depuis que sa femme l'a quitté. On pourrait proche croire qu'il est frappé de la lune.* He acts so strangely since his wife left him. One could almost think that he was mentally deranged. (LA) <LA, La99> **•frappé d'une maladie** struck down with sickness <Da84> <*Loc:* LA, Da84, La99>

frappement [frapmɑ̃] *n.m.* striking, hitting, knocking <*Loc:* Da84>

frapper [frape] **I** *v.tr.* **1** to strike, hit, knock *Il s'endort dès que sa tête frappe l'oreiller.* He falls asleep as soon as his head hits the pillow. (Lv88) **2** to come upon, discover, find, run into (often unexpectedly) *On a frappé l'huile dans le clos.* They struck oil in the field. (Lv88) *Il a frappé une bande de chevreuils.* He ran into a herd of deer [while hunting]. (Lv88) *Des fois le docteur frappe le mal, des fois il frappe pas.* Sometimes the doctor finds the sickness, sometimes he doesn't find it. (Lv88) **3** to occur to s.o. (of an idea) *Quand l'idée me frappe...* When the idea occurs to me . . . (Lv88) **4** to reach, attain, open onto *Le chemin 90 frappe le chemin...* Highway 90 opens onto Highway . . . (Lv88) *Le bus frappe tous les 'tits villages.* The bus hits [i.e. stops at] all the little towns. (Lv88) **5** to engrave, print *Ils ont frappé un livre sur les Indiens.* They printed a book about Indians. (Lv88) **6** to record **J'ai fait frapper des disques.* I had records recorded. (Ca83) **II se frapper** *v.pron.* to strike o.s. or each other *Arrêtez donc de vous frapper comme ça.* Stop hitting each other like that. (LA) ◊ **•frapper à la porte** to knock at the door <Da84> **•frapper au métier** to weave *Elle connaît pas écarder ni filer, mais elle connaît frapper le fil sur le métier.* She doesn't know how to card or spin but she knows how to weave. (Lv88) *J'avais frappé une belle couverte au métier.* I had woven a beautiful blanket. (VM) <VM, Di32, Lv88> **•frapper qqn dans le nom du père** to strike s.o. on the forehead <Da84> **•frapper un nœud** to make a snorting sound when snoring <VM, La99> <*Loc:* AC, LA, VM, Ca83, Da84, Di32, Hi02, La99, Lv88>

fraque[1] [frak] *adj.* **1** high-strung, skittish *Cette jument est assez fraque, il faudrait que je l'enfarge.* That mare is so skittish that I'd have to hobble her. (VM) **2** foolish, silly, crazy *Elle est tout le temps fraque comme ça?* Does she always act so silly? (VM) *Elle est manière écartée aujourd'hui; ça doit être sa journée fraque.* She is sort of scatter-brained today; it must be her crazy day. (LA) <*Loc:* LA, SL, SM, VM, La99>

fraque[2] [frak] *n.f.* silly, foolish, high-strung woman *Vieille fraque!* Old biddy! (AC) <*Loc:* AC>

fraterniser [fratærnize] *v.intr.* to fraternize, associate (with) *Il fraternisait avec eux-autres.* He used to fraternize with them. (AV) <*Loc:* AV, Da84>

fraternité [fratærnite] *n.f.* fraternity, brotherhood <*Loc:* Da84>

fratricide [fratrisid] *n.m.* fratricide <*Loc:* Da84>

fraude [frod] *n.f.* fraud, deceit, dishonesty ◊ **•en fraude** fraudulently <Da84> **•par fraude** fraudulently <Da84> <*Loc:* Da84>

frauder [frode] *v.tr.* to defraud, cheat, deceive *Le bougre a fraudé son ami.* The guy cheated his friend. (AV) *Frauder sa femme.* To cheat on one's wife. (AV) <*Loc:* AV, Da84>

fraudeur [frodœr] *n.m.* swindler, con artist, cheat <*Loc:* Da84>

frayant, -e [frejɑ̃, -ɑ̃t] *adj.* appealing, sexy **Elle se met une jolie petite camisole frayante.* She puts on a sexy little nightgown. (Gr86) <*Loc:* Gr86>

frayeur [frejœr] *n.f.* fear, fright, terror **Et le monde avait une frayeur que le fufollet aurait tombé sur eux, il les aurait tués.* And the people were terrified that if the will-o'-the-wisp landed on them, it would kill them. (Gr86) <*Loc:* Da84, Gr86>

freau [fro] *n.m.* froe (tool to split logs, posts, etc.) <*Loc:* Da84>

frède ♦see **frète**

frédiller (**ferdiller**) [fredije, færdije] *v.intr.* to shiver from the cold *Viens côté de la cheminée, t'es après frédiller.* Come over by the fireplace, you're shivering. (VM) <*Loc:* VM, Di32, Lv88>

frédilleux, -euse (**ferdilloux**) [fredijø, -øz, færdiju] *adj.* cold-natured, sensitive to cold *Je suis frédilleuse comme tout, je me mets six couvertes dessus mon lit.* I'm extremely cold-natured, I put six blankets on my bed. (VM) <***Loc:*** VM, Di32>

frédir (**ferdir**) [fredir, fredzir, færdir] *v.intr.* to become cold or colder, cool off (of the weather) *Ça va frédir ce soir.* It's going to get cold tonight. (SM) *Ça commence à frédir, c'est proche temps pour la roulaison.* It's beginning to get colder, it's almost time for the sugar cane harvest. (VM) <***Loc:*** SM, VM, Di32, Gr86, Lv88>

freeze ♦see **FREEZER**

FREEZER (**freeze**) [fɹizə, fɹiz] *n.m.* **1** freezer **2** ice cream maker *On a fait de la crème à la glace avec le* FREEZER. We made ice cream with the ice cream maker. (AV) <***Loc:*** AV, TB, VM, Lv88>

frégate [fregat] *n.f.* frigate, frigate bird <***Loc:*** JE, Re31>

FREIGHT ♦see **fret**

frein [frɛ̃] *n.m.* **1** restraint, bit, bridle **2** brake <***Loc:*** Da84>

frêle [frɛl] *adj.* frail, fragile, weak *Il était frêle quand il était jeune, mais p'us asteur.* He was frail when he was young, but no longer. (VM) <***Loc:*** Da84>

fremer, frémer ♦see **fermer**

frémi ♦see **fourmi**

frémir [frɛ̃mir] *v.intr.* **1** to be afraid, feel fear or apprehension *Parce que elle alle est vieille, et ce vieux monde regarde toujours le monde d'en dehors, eux-autres frémit qu'il y a quelque chose qui pourrait les arriver.* Because she is old, and those old folks always look at outsiders, they're afraid that something bad might happen to them. (TB) **2** to tremble, shake, quiver *Ça fait froid, ça fait noir, et des fois ça me fait frémir d'être tout seul entre l'amour et l'avenir.* It's cold, it's dark, and sometimes it makes me shiver to be alone between love and the future. (LA, ch: *Entre l'amour et l'avenir*) <***Loc:*** LA, TB, Da84>

frendir [frɑ̃dir] *v.tr.* to cut, slice *Après ça il faut les frendir en quatre.* After that you have to slice them in four. (IB) <***Loc:*** IB>

frêne [frɛ̃n] *n.m.* ash (tree or wood) ◊ **•frêne piquant** prickly ash <JD, TB, Da84> <***Loc:*** AS, IV, JD, SL, TB, Da84, Re31>

fréquentation [frekɑ̃tasjɔ̃] *n.f.* frequentation, frequenting <***Loc:*** Da84>

fréquenter [frekɑ̃te] **I** *v.tr.* **1** to frequent, visit, attend (regularly) *Je fréquente pas assez souvent les affaires à Eunice.* I don't go to the events in Eunice very often. (LA) **2** to frequent, visit, keep company (of) **3** to court, date, go out with, go steady with *La dernière que je l'ai vu, il fréquentait une veuve.* The last time I saw him, he was seeing a widow. (VM) **II se fréquenter** *v.pron.* **1** to visit one another, socialize *On se fréquentait un peu.* We used to see each other a little bit. (IB) **2** to court, date steadily *On s'a fréquenté proche deux ans avant qu'il m'a demandé de le marier.* We courted almost two years before he asked me to marry him. (LA) <***Loc:*** EV, IB, JD, LA, LF, SB, SM, TB, VM, Da84, Ph36, Re31>

frère [fræ̃r] *n.m.* **1** brother *Mon père avait neuf frères et sœurs. Il venait d'une grande famille.* My father had nine brothers and sisters. He came from a big family. (LF) **2** brother (fellow member of certain churches or fraternities) **3** title in addressing certain ministers, Catholic monks or brothers *Ils ont tout fini l'école, les miens, parce qu'ils ont tout été à l'école catholique. Et les garçons étaient avec les frères, et les petites filles étaient avec les sœurs.* They all finished school, my kids, because they all went to Catholic school. And the boys went with the monks, and the little girls went with the nuns. (TB) ◊ **•demi-frère *a*** half brother ***b*** stepbrother <TB, Da84> <***Loc:*** AC, AS, AV, EV, LA, LF, JE, TB, VM, Da84, Hi02>

fressures [fresyr, fresør] *n.f.pl.* internal organs, innards (esp. when used as food) <***Loc:*** AV, EV>

fret (**FREIGHT**) [frɛt, fɹeɪt] *n.m.* **1** freight *C'était pour délivrer les frets que le monde yeux ont donné, ils ont donné leur fret avec les commis de la ville. Et là il le délivrait.* That was to deliver freight that people gave them, they gave their freight to the clerks in the city. And then they would deliver it. (SJ) **2** freight train **3** shipping and handling charges, cost of transportation *J'ai pas assez d'argent pour payer le fret.* I don't have enough money to pay for the shipping and handling. (TB) <***Loc:*** EV, SJ, SM, TB, VM, Di32, Ph36>

frète[1] (**frette, frède**) [frɛt] *adj.* **1** cool, chilly **2** cold *Il fait frète.* It's cold. (Lv88) *L'hiver quand ça fait frette.* In winter when it's cold. (SM) **La bétaille est satisfaite si son ventre est plein, a(lle) boit beaucoup d'eau frède a(lle) dort à l'ombre des chênes.* The animal is satisfied if its stomach is full, it drinks a lot of cold water and it sleeps in the shade of the oaks. (Gr86) ◊ **•avoir frète** to be cold, feel cold *J'ai frète ici dans.* I'm cold in here. (VM) <VM> <***Loc:*** AC, EV, JD, LA, SL, SM, TB, VM, Da84, Gr86, Hi02, Lv88, Re31>

frète[2] [frɛt] *n.m.* cold spell *Un 'tit frète.* A little cold spell. (Lv88) <***Loc:*** Lv88>

frette[1] [frɛt] *n.f.* **1** metal rim (of a wooden wheel) *Là le bois trempait et les frettes revenaient sûrs encore.* The wood would soak and the metal rims would become secure again. (AC) **2** barrel hoop <***Loc:*** AC, Da84>

frette[2] ♦see **frète**[1]

friandise [frijɑ̃diz] *n.f.* **1** sweet, goody, tidbit **2** store-bought or fancy cookie or candy *On avait pas de friandise, mais on mangeait bien.* We didn't have fancy sweets, but we ate well. (SL) <***Loc:*** SL, Da84>

fricadouille [frikaduj] *n.f.* type of stew <***Loc:*** VM>

fricassée [frikase] *n.f.* **1** stew, fricassee (usu. roux-based) *Y a du monde qui met des patates anglaises dans leur fricassée de chevrettes. Nous-autres on met des œufs.* There are people who put potatoes in their shrimp fricassee. We put in eggs. (Gu00) **2** stew (of any kind) *Tu peux mettre n'importe qui. Une fricassée de chevrettes, une fricassée de viande, une* *fricassée de patates. Une fricassée est tout cuit pareil.* You put anything in it. A shrimp stew, a beef stew, a potato stew. Stews are all cooked the same way. (LF) ◊ **•fricassée de cochon** pork organ meat stew <SJ> **•fricassée de la panse** stew made from pork stomach <SJ> **•fricassée de viande** beef stew <LF> <***Loc:*** AV, LF, SJ, SL, SM, TB, VM, Da84, Fa77, Guoo, Hio2, Lv88>

fricasser [frikase] *v.tr.* to stew (i.e. browning meat in fat then simmering in liquid) ◊ **•s'en fricasser** to be indifferent, be unconcerned *Eh bien, je m'en fricasse.* Well, it doesn't matter to me. (IB) <IB, Di32> <***Loc:*** IB, Da84, Di32>

friche ♦see **fritche**

fricot [friko] *n.m.* **1** fried dish (meat or vegetable) **2** stew, ragout **3** supper party, meal with guests *On faisait des grands fricots de poissons frits.* We had big fried fish suppers. (Lv88) <***Loc:*** AC, JD, LA, TB, VM, Da84, Di32, Lv88>

friction [friksjɔ̃] *n.f.* friction, rubbing <***Loc:*** Da84>

frigidaire [friʒidær] *n.m.* refrigerator <***Loc:*** Da84, Guoo>

frigidité [friʒidite] *n.f.* frigidity, coldness <***Loc:*** Da84>

frilant, -e [frilɑ̃, -ɑ̃t] *adj.* chilly, feeling or suffering from the cold **Il est frilant comme tout.* He is susceptible to the cold. (EV, Ph36) <***Loc:*** EV, Ph36>

friler [frile] *v.intr.* to shiver from the cold *J'ai frilé toute la nuit.* I shivered all night. (VM) <***Loc:*** SB, VM, Da84, Lv88>

frileux, -euse [frilø, -øz] *adj.* chilly, feeling or suffering from the cold *J'ai tout le temps été frileux.* I have always suffered from the cold. (LA) <***Loc:*** LA, VM, Da84, Fa77>

frimas (frumas) [frima, fryma] *n.m.* drizzle, light rain <***Loc:*** EV, VM, Ph36>

frimasse [frimas] *n.f.* face, grimace *Ga' [=regarde] comme il fait une frimasse quand il est fâché.* Look how he makes a face when he's angry. (TB) <***Loc:*** TB>

frimasser (frumasser) [frimase, frymase, frumase] *v.intr.* to drizzle *C'est après frimasser.* It's drizzling. (TB) <***Loc:*** IB, TB, VM>

frimousse [frimus] *n.f.* grimace, scowl, frown *Elle a une belle frimousse quand elle se lève.* She's got quite a scowl when she gets up. (LF) ◊ **•faire une frimousse** to grimace, scowl, frown <LA> <***Loc:*** AV, LA, LF, SM, TB, Da84, Fa77>

frimousser [frimuse] *v.intr.* to grimace, scowl, frown *Il a frimoussé quand il t'a vu.* He scowled when he saw you. (LA) <***Loc:*** LA>

fringant, -e [frɛ̃gɑ̃, frɛ̃glɑ̃, -ɑ̃t] *adj.* **1** spirited, frisky (of a horse) *Un cheval fringant.* A frisky horse. (AV) **2** in the habit of running the roads or gadding about *Un jeune gens fringant.* A young man who is always running the roads. (LA) **3** wild, unreserved *C'te fille-là est joliment fringante.* That girl is quite wild. (TB) <***Loc:*** AV, IB, LA, SJ, TB, VM, Da84>

fringue [frɛ̃g] *n.f.* ◊ **•à la fringue** running the roads, gadding about *Alle est partie à la fringue.* She's going out and about. (VM) <VM> <***Loc:*** VM>

fringuer [frɛ̃ge] *v.intr.* **1** to prance, run around, frisk (of a horse) *Regarde le poulain après fringuer dans la savane!* Look at the colt prancing around in the pasture. (EV) **2** to run the roads, gad about *Ayoù t'es parti fringuer?* Where are you going to run the roads? (LA) *Si tu serais pas tout le temps après fringuer, tu pourrais peut-être m'aider.* If you weren't always gadding about, you might be able to help me. (TB) <***Loc:*** EV, IB, JD, LA, SB, SJ, SM, TB, Da84, Lv88>

fripaille [fripaj] *n.f.* rabble, riffraff <***Loc:*** JD>

friper [fripe] **I** *v.tr.* **1** to snatch, swipe, steal *Le chat a fripé la viande du chien.* The cat stole the meat from the dog. (LA) *L'homme a fripé cinquante piastres.* The man swiped fifty dollars. (AV) **2** to devour, eat greedily *Friper le gombo.* Chow the gumbo. (Lv88) **3** to slurp, eat noisily (esp. liquids) *Quand ton gombo est chaud, tu le fripes.* When your gumbo is hot, you slurp it. (VM) *Il fripe son manger.* He slurps his food. (SM) **4** to do hurriedly *Il a fripé son ouvrage.* He did his work hurriedly. (VM) **II se friper** *v.pron.* **1** to lick *Se friper les doigts.* To lick one's fingers. (VM) *Se friper les lèvres.* To lick one's lips. (VM) **2** to scrape or graze one's skin *Il s'a fripé contre le fils de fer.* He grazed himself against the barbed wire. (VM) <***Loc:*** AV, LA, SJ, SL, SM, VM, Da84, Di32, Lv88>

friponnerie [fripɔ̃nri] *n.f.* greed, greediness <***Loc:*** VM>

friponneur, -euse [fripɔ̃nœr, -øz] *adj.* greedy, gluttonous <***Loc:*** VM>

frire [frir] *v.tr.* to fry *C'est ça la cuillère tu uses pour frire ton œuf.* That's the spoon you use to fry your egg. (SL) *Elle les frisait dans un grand poêlon. Elle les frisait, elle les mettait dans un* CROCK JAR*, elle mettait ça tout là, vidait cette graisse chaude là-dessus et ça se conservait.* She browned them [sausages] in a big pan. She would brown them, she put them into a crock, she put all of that, emptied the hot fat on top of them, and that would keep. (AC) ◊ **•faire frire** to fry <Da84> <***Loc:*** LA, SL, TB, Da84, Fa77>

friscata [friskata] *n.m.* banana magnolia <***Loc:*** Guoo>

frisé, -e [frize] *adj.* wrinkled *Tu peux pas sortir comme ça avec ta chemise tout frisée.* You can't go out like that with your shirt all wrinkled. (LA) <***Loc:*** LA, SL>

friser [frize] *v.tr.* to curl, frizz (hair) *Si mes cheveux restaient* NICE *comme toi, je faiserais pas friser les cheveux.* If my hair stayed nice like yours, I wouldn't get it curled. (TB) <***Loc:*** TB>

frisette [frizɛt] *n.f.* curl, small curl <***Loc:*** Da84>

frisson [frisɔ̃] *n.m.* **1** chill *J'ai assez froid, j'ai des frissons partout.* I'm so cold, I have chills all over. (LA) **2** shiver *Alle dit ça te faisait passer les frissons.* She says that gave you the shivers. (LF) <***Loc:*** LA, LF, Da84, Fa77, Hio2>

frissonnement [frisɔ̃nmɑ̃] *n.m.* shivering, shuddering <***Loc:*** Da84>

frissonner [frisɔ̃ne] *v.intr.* to shiver, shudder *Quand j'ai vu la lumière dans le noir, j'ai frissonné.* When I saw the light in the dark, I shivered. (LA) <***Loc:*** LA, Da84>

frit, -e [fri, -t] *adj.* fried *Les* RATTLESNAKE *[...] Moi je l'ai jamais mangé, eusse clame que ça a un goût comme la poule frit.*

Rattlesnakes, I've never eaten that. They claim it tastes like fried chicken. (TB) <*Loc:* TB, Da84, Hi02>

fritche (**friche**) [fritʃ] *n.f.* **1** diarrhea **2** crap, piece of crap, worthless thing **Ça c'est de la friche.* That's crap. (Da84) *Tu vas faire de la fritche avec ça.* You're going to make that unfit for eating. (JD) ◊ **•avoir la fritche** to have diarrhea, have loose bowels <SM> **•faire fritche** to do s.t. too quickly or in a slipshod way, do a shitty job <Da84> <*Loc:* JD, LA, SM, VM, Da84, La99>

friture [frityr] *n.f.* **1** fried food **2** fritter **3** frying <*Loc:* Da84>

frobir ♦see **fourbir**

frobissage ♦see **fourbissage**

frobisseur ♦see **fourbisseur**

frobissoir ♦see **fourbissoir**

froguer [froge] *v.intr.* to go frogging, catch frogs *Ils vont froguer le soir.* They go frogging at night. (TB) ◊ **•se faire froguer** to get into trouble *Tu vas te faire froguer.* You'll get yourself into trouble. (TB) <TB> <*Loc:* TB>

froid[1], -e [frwa, -d] *adj.* cold *Il fait froid/C'est froid.* It's cold. (JE) *La dernière année c'était pas venu froid. À part qu'on a eu un petit peu de la neige au mois de mars.* The last year it didn't get cold. Except that we had a little snow in March. (TB) *C'est pas prudent de mettre les manches courtes quand il fait froid comme ça.* It's not prudent to wear short sleeves when it's cold like that. (VM) <*Loc:* AC, JE, TB, An94, Da84, Hi02>

froid[2] [frwa, fra] *n.m.* cold, coldness *J'ai jamais été dans le nord. Vous-autres a du froid là? Vous-autres a plein du* SNOW*, hein?* I've never been in the north. Do you have cold weather up there? You have a lot of snow, don't you? (TB) *Tu te couches et tu peux passer un gros froid avec ça-ici dessus le dos.* You get in bed and you can make it through very cold weather with that [quilt] on your back. (TB) *Tortille bien le bebé avant de sortir dans le froid.* Wrap the baby up well before going out in the cold. (VM) ◊ **•avoir froid** to be cold *Ce pauvre titisse aura froid cet hiver.* That poor thin man will be cold this winter. (IB) *On était mauve à force on avait froid.* We were so cold that we were mauve. (JD) <IB, JD> **•avoir froid aux yeux** to be afraid <AV, La99> <*Loc:* AV, IB, JD, JE, TB, VM, An94, Da84, Hi02, La99, Wh83>

froide[1] ♦see **froid**

froide[2] (**fraide**) [frwad, frwed] *n.f.* cold one ◊ **•'tite fraide** a cold one (i.e. beer) <Gu00> <*Loc:* Gu00>

fromage (**fermage, formage**) [frɔ̃maʒ, frəmaʒ, fɛrmaʒ, fɔrmaʒ] *n.m.* cheese ◊ **•fromage de cochon** hoghead cheese <Fa77> **•fromage de tête** hoghead cheese <IB, Fa77> **•fromage de tête de cochon** hoghead cheese <Da84> <*Loc:* EV, IB, JD, VM, Da84, Fa77, Lv88>

fromages [frɔ̃maʒ] *n.m.pl.* game played by little girls in which they spin around so quickly that their skirts take the shape of a bell <*Loc:* JD>

froment [frɔ̃mɑ̃] *n.m.* wheat **Farine de froment, pain de froment.* Wheat flour, wheat bread. (Da84) <*Loc:* Da84>

fromi ♦see **fourmi**

froncé, -e [frɔ̃se] *adj.* **1** pleated *Les* UNIFORMS *de Mount Carmel étaient froncés.* The Mount Carmel uniforms were pleated. (LA) **2** creased **3** gathered **4** wrinkled *Sa chemise était tout froncée.* His shirt was all wrinkled. (LA) <*Loc:* LA, Da84>

froncer [frɔ̃se] *v.tr.* **1** to pleat **2** to crease **3** to gather **4** to wrinkle **5** to knit (one's brow) *Il a froncé son front.* He wrinkled his brow. (LA) <*Loc:* LA, Da84>

fronde (**fronne-fronne**) [frɔ̃n, frɔ̃d, frɔ̃nfrɔ̃n] *n.m.* toy, consisting of a button or small piece of wood threaded on a string, which creates a buzzing or whizzing sound when spun in the air *Il a cassé mon fronne-fronne.* He broke my buzzing toy. (SL) <*Loc:* EV, LF, SL, TB>

fronder [frɔ̃de] *v.intr.* to gad about <*Loc:* SL>

fronner [frɔ̃ne] **I** *v.tr.* to rev, increase the noise of (a motor) by accelerating **II** *v.intr.* to whiz by, pass by at great speed *Il a fronné par ici.* He sped through here. (LF) <*Loc:* LA, LF>

front [frɔ̃] *n.m.* forehead, brow *Asteur tu vas là, le prêtre va mettre les cendres dessus ton front.* Nowadays if you go there, the priest will put ashes on your forehead. (LF) *Il a froncé son front.* He wrinkled his brow. (LA) <*Loc:* LA, LF, Da84>

fronté ♦see **effronté**

frontière [frɔ̃tjær] *n.f.* frontier, border <*Loc:* Da84>

frottage [frotaʒ] *n.m.* **1** rubbing **2** massaging **3** stroking **4** friction <*Loc:* Da84>

frottement [frɔtmɑ̃] *n.m.* **1** rubbing **2** massaging **3** stroking **4** friction <*Loc:* Da84>

frotter [frote] **I** *v.tr.* **1** to rub *C'était frotté jusqu'à c'était jaune.* It was rubbed until it was yellow. (SL) **2** to massage *Il aimait se faire frotter les pieds.* He loved to have his feet massaged. (LA) **3** to stroke *Pour le traiter, il faut frotter le front de la main gauche.* To treat it, one must stroke the forehead with the left hand. (VM) **II se frotter** *v.pron.* **1** to rub o.s. **Le chien a venu se frotter sur ses jambes.* The dog came and rubbed itself against his legs. (SM, An94) **2** to stroke o.s. or each other <*Loc:* LA, SL, SM, An94, Da84>

frotteur, -euse [frotœr, -øz] *n.m.* **1** masseur, masseuse **2** one who rubs, buffs or polishes <*Loc:* Da84>

frotteuse [frotøz] *n.f.* washboard, scrubboard <*Loc:* VM, Fa77>

frottoir [frotwar] *n.m.* washboard, scrubboard *Laver ton linge sur le frottoir.* Washing your clothes on the scrubboard. (TB) **[Les musiciens] usaient les p'tits fers… ou peut-être bien aussi un frottoir à laver l'linge pour avoir un baloche.* The musicians used to use triangles or maybe also a laundry washboard to keep the time. (Gr86) <*Loc:* AC, AV, EV, IB, JE, LA, LF, SB, SJ, SL, SM, TB, VM, Da84, Di32, Gr86, Lv88>

froubir ♦see **fourbir**

froubissage ♦see **fourbissage**

froubisseur ♦see **fourbisseur**

frou-frou[1] [frufru] *adj.* **1** silly, irresponsible *Il va jamais trouver à se marier; il est trop frou-frou.* He will never find someone to marry; he is too irresponsible. (LA) **2** given to making a big deal over nothing, given to much fussiness over nothing *Alle est plus frou-frou pour faire quelque chose.* She is fussier about getting something done. (TB) <***Loc:*** LA, TB>

frou-frou[2] [frufru] *n.m.* frill ◊ **•faire des frou-frou** to put on frills <Da84> <***Loc:*** Da84>

froumi, froumille ♦see **fourmi**

fru ♦see **fruit**

fruit (**fru**) [fry] *n.m.* fruit *Des fruits: des figuiers, des pêchers, des pruniers, des poiriers, et des orangers.* The [trees with] fruits: fig trees, peach trees, plum trees, pear trees, and orange trees. (SL) ◊ **•fruits de (la) mer** seafood *Ça se faisait une bonne vie parce que ç'avait tous les fruits de la mer, des poissons, des crabes et de la chevrette.* They made a good life for themselves because they had all the seafood, fish, crabs, and shrimp. (LF) <***Loc:*** LF, SB, SL, TB, Da84, Hi02, Lv88>

fruiter [frɥite] *v.intr.* to bear fruit *Mes figuiers sont déjà après fruiter.* My fig trees are already bearing fruit. (LA) <***Loc:*** LA, Da84>

fruit-stand [fɹutstæn(d), frutstɛ̃n] *n.m.* fruit stand <***Loc:*** EV, TB, Di32, Ph36>

frumas ♦see **frimas**

frumasser ♦see **frimasser**

fumée [fyme] *n.f.* smoke *Le tasso, c'est la viande séchée à la fumée, qui la conserve.* Tasso is meat that is smoked while it's dried, to preserve it. (SL) ◊ **•fumée de midi** heat of the day *Je prends toujours un 'tit somme dans la fumée de midi.* I always take a little nap during the hottest part of the day. (VM) <***Loc:*** SL, VM>

fumelle ♦see **femelle**

fumer[1] [fyme] *v.intr.* to smoke, smoke tobacco *Ils va pas fumer icitte-dedans. Si vous allumez une cigarette je vas vous dire* WELL *vous pouvez rester mais la cigarette va en-dehors.* They won't smoke in here. If you light a cigarette I will tell you, well, you can stay, but the cigarette goes outside. (TB) ◊ **•fumer la pipe** to die <SB, La99> <***Loc:*** AC, LA, SB, TB, VM, Da84, Hi02, La99, Wh83>

fumer[2] (**fumier**) [fyme, fymje] *v.tr.* to fertilize *On a habitude fumer notre clos avec du fumier de parc.* We used to fertilize our fields with manure from the barnyard. (LA) *J'ai fumié mes ferns.* I fertilized my ferns. (TB) <***Loc:*** LA, TB, Da84>

fumerie [fymri] *n.f.* smoking (of tobacco) <***Loc:*** Da84>

fumeur, -euse [fymœr, -øz] *n.* smoker, tobacco smoker <***Loc:*** Da84>

fumier[1] [fymje] *n.m.* **1** manure, animal dung *On a habitude fumer notre clos avec du fumier de parc.* We used to fertilize our fields with manure from the barnyard. (LA) **2** fertilizer <***Loc:*** AC, EV, LA, VM, TB, Da84, Wh83>

fumier[2] ♦see **fumer**

fumière [fymjær] *n.f.* entourage, following **Ga! Jean et sa fumière qu'arrivent.* Look! John and his entourage are arriving. (EV, Ph36) <***Loc:*** EV, Ph36>

fumigation [fymigasjɔ̃] *n.f.* fumigation <***Loc:*** Da84>

fumiguer [fymige] *v.tr.* to fumigate, disinfect *Ils ont eu pour fumiguer son lit après qu'il a déménagé.* They had to fumigate his bed after he moved out. (LA) <***Loc:*** LA, SM, Da84>

FUN (**fonne**) [fɔ̃n, føn, fʌn] *n.m.* fun *Mais c'était assez du* FUN, THOUGH, *d'être élevé Cadien dans ce temps-là.* But it was a lot of fun, though, to be raised Cajun in those days. (TB) *Mardi Gras, c'était du* FUN. Mardi Gras, that was fun. (JE) ◊ **•avoir du FUN** to have fun *Les Cadiens c'est du monde qu'a travaillé dur, et joué dur aussi. C'est tout du monde qu'aime avoir du* FUN, *et qu'aime conter des contes.* Cajuns are people who have worked hard, and played hard too. They're people who like to have fun, and who like to tell stories. (LF) *T'as eu du* FUN *avec T. hier au soir là?* Did you have fun with T. last night? (TB) <LF, TB, VM, Lv88> **•faire FUN de** to make fun of *Temps en temps, je fais* FUN *de lui.* Occasionally I make fun of him (JE) <JE> <***Loc:*** JE, LF, TB, VM, Hi02, Lv88>

fur [fyr] *n.m.* ◊ **•à fur et à mesure** little by little, gradually *A fur et à mesure qu'il traversait la glace, ça craquait derrière lui.* As he gradually went across the ice, it was cracking behind him. (LA) <LA, Da84> <***Loc:*** LA, Da84>

fureter [fyrte] *v.tr.* to ransack *L'officier a fureté la maison.* The officer ransacked the house. (AV) <***Loc:*** AV>

fureur [fyrœr] *n.f.* fury, rage, anger <***Loc:*** Da84>

furvoyante [fyrvwajɑ̃t] *adj.* **•humeur furvoyante** very bad mood <SJ> <***Loc:*** SJ>

fuseau (**fiseau**) [fyzo, fizo] *n.m.* spool, spindle ◊ **•fiseau de fil** spool of thread <Da84> <***Loc:*** AV, EV, IB, JD, SL, TB, VM, Da84, Fa77, Lv88, Ph36>

fusée [fyze] *n.m.* firecracker, roman candle, rocket, flare <***Loc:*** Da84>

fusil [fyzi, fizi] *n.m.* **1** gun *Tirer quelqu'un avec un fusil.* To shoot someone with a gun. (SM) *On use des fusils à chasser.* We use guns to hunt. (JE) **2** shotgun ◊ **•fusil à deux canons** double-barrel shotgun <Da84> **•fusil à piston** open-hammered musket *C'était ces fusils à piston. Il s'a mis à charger les deux fourches.* It was [one of] those open-hammered musket. He began loading both barrels. (LA) **•fusil à six coups** six-shooter, pistol <Da84> <***Loc:*** AV, JE, LA, SM, Da84, Hi02>

fusillade [fyzijad] *n.f.* fusillade <***Loc:*** Da84>

fusillier [fyzije] *n.m.* gunner, sharp shooter <***Loc:*** Da84>

fusion [fyzjɔ̃] *n.f.* fusion <***Loc:*** Da84>

fût de selle [fyd(ə)sɛl] *n.m.* saddle tree <***Loc:*** VM, Di32>

futur [fytyr] *n.m.* future <***Loc:*** Da84>

G

gabardine [gabardin] *n.f.* gabardine <***Loc:*** Da84>

gâcher (**gatcher**) [gaʃe, gatʃe] *v.tr.* to spoil, mess up, botch *Il a tout gâché mon gâteau, espèce de galfa.* He messed up my cake, the greedy guy. (VM) <***Loc:*** VM, Da84>

gâchette (**gazette**) [gaʃɛt, gaʒɛt, gazɛt] *n.f.* trigger (of a gun) <***Loc:*** JE, TB, VM>

gâchiller (**gâchonner**) [gaʃije, gaʃɔ̃ne] *v.tr.* to ruin *Il faut as gachiller le coton.* You mustn't ruin the cotton. (Lv88) *Il n-a tout gachonné l'ouvrage.* He completely ruined the work. (Lv88) <***Loc:*** Lv88>

gâchonner ♦see **gâchiller**

gaffe [gaf] *n.f.* **1** gaff **2** gaffle, metal spur put on fighting cocks *Ça met des gaffes aux gaimes pour la bataille.* They put gaffles on gamecocks for fights. (Lv88) **3** oyster tongs, device for tonging (digging) oysters *On a pêché des huîtres à la gaffe.* We fished for oysters with oyster tongs. (TB) ◊ **•gaffe à main** hand-operated oyster tongs <LF> <***Loc:*** JE, LF, SM, TB, VM, Lv88>

gaffer [gafe] *v.tr.* to grab, grasp, catch hold of *Je l'ai gaffé par le col.* I grabbed him by the collar. (VM) *J'ai gaffé une branche pour pas tomber.* I grabbed a branch in order not to fall. (VM) ◊ **•gaffer des huîtres** to tong oysters using a "gaffe" <JE> <***Loc:*** JE, VM>

gage [gaʒ] *n.m.* **1** wage **2** pledge **3** bet, stake <***Loc:*** Da84>

gager [gaʒe] **I** *v.tr.* to bet, wager *Il va gager dix piasses.* He's going to bet ten dollars. (Lv88) **II** *v.intr.* to bet, wager *Icitte le monde aime gager.* People like betting here. (Lv88) *Tu peux gager sur mon gaime.* You can bet on my gamecock. (Lv88) <***Loc:*** Da84, Lv88>

gageur [gaʒœr] *n.m.* bettor, wagerer <***Loc:*** Da84>

gageure [gaʒyr] *n.f.* bet, wager, stake *Au chassis, le bougre va prendre ta gageure.* The ticket booth employee is going to record your bet. (Lv88) <***Loc:*** Lv88>

gagnable [gɑ̃jab(l)] *adj.* winnable *Ça, c'est une gageure qu'est pas gagnable.* That's a bet that is not winnable. (LA) <***Loc:*** LA, Da84>

gagnant[1], **-e** [gɑ̃jɑ̃, -ɑ̃t] *adj.* winning *Qui c'est qu'a eu le ticket gagnant?* Who got the winning ticket? (LA) <***Loc:*** LA, Da84>

gagnant[2], **-e** [gɑ̃jɑ̃, -ɑ̃t] *n.* winner **On jouait ein tournoi et les deux perdeurs payait chacun ein sous au gagnant.* We played a tournament and the two losers each paid the winner a penny. (Wh83) <***Loc:*** LA, Da84, Wh83>

gagne [gɑ̃j] *n.m./f.* gain, earning <***Loc:*** Da84, Lv88>

gagner [gɑ̃je] **I** *v.tr.* **1** to earn, gain *On veut pas l'argent vous va gagner.* We don't want the money that you will earn. (AC, ch: *Restez, Mom et Pop*) **2** to win, attain in competition *Il avait tout le temps dit qu'il aurait fallu que quelqu'un la gagne pour la marier.* He always said that someone would have to win her in order to marry her. (EV) **3** to catch up with *Je l'ai gagné après qu'on avait couru une demi-heure. Après ça je l'ai dépassé.* I caught up with him after we had run for half an hour. Then I passed him. (VM) **4** to head for *Il a parti d'ici en gagnant au Lac Charles.* He left here headed toward Lake Charles. (VM) **5** to lead to (of a road) *Moi, j'étais sur une allée qui gagnait la même direction qu'eux-autres.* I was on a path that was leading in the same direction as them. (SL) **II** *v.intr.* **1** to win, finish first in a contest *J'aurais presque couru n'importe quelle office dans la paroisse et j'aurais pu gagner.* I could have run for nearly any office in the parish and I would have won. (LF) **2** to gain on (in a race) *La jument baille est après gagner sur l'autre cheval.* The palomino horse is gaining on the other horse. (LA) **3** to gain weight *Les vitamines, ça te fait pas gagner.* Vitamins don't make you gain weight. (Lv88) **III se gagner** *v.pron.* to earn, win (for o.s.) *Il s'a gagné assez d'argent pour s'acheter une petite maison.* He earned enough money to buy himself a little house. (LA) ◊ **•gagner du poids** to gain weight <Da84> **•gagner le sucre** to show oneself as outstanding or superior **Là, t'as gagné le sucre.* You did a great job. (La99) <La99> **•gagner son pain par la sueur de son front** to work hard for a living <La99> **•gagner vers** to head for *Il gagnait vers Pont Breaux quand sa sœur l'a rencontré.* He was heading for Breaux Bridge when his sister met up with him. (LA) <LA, Da84> **•se gagner de l'argent** to earn money <Da84> **•se gagner de quoi** to acquire property or anything of value *Elle essaie de se gagner de quoi pour elle-même.* She's trying to earn something of her own. (LA) <LA, Da84> **•ça me gagne!** that beats me! <Da84> **•en gagner** to recover (after an illness, an accident) *Il était bien malade dimanche au soir, mais il en gagne asteur.* He was quite sick Sunday night, but he's getting better now. (VM) *Il en gagne tous les jours.* His health is improving every day. (SM) <SM, VM, Lv88> <***Loc:*** AC, EV, LA, LF, SL, SM, TB, VM, Da84, Hi02, La99, Lv88, Wh83>

gagneur [gɑ̃jœr] *n.m.* winner <***Loc:*** EV, Wh83>

gai, -e [gɛ, ge] *adj.* happy, merry, gay *Ça a toujours été une personne gaie.* He's always been a happy person. (LA) ◊ **•gai comme un fou** very happy, in a good mood <AV, La99> <***Loc:*** AV, LA, Da84, La99>

gaieté [gete] *n.f.* gaiety, glee, happiness <***Loc:*** Da84>

gaillard[1]**, -e** [gajar, -ard] *adj.* **1** healthy, well, hardy, in good health *J'étais malade, mais je suis gaillard maintenant.* I was sick, but I'm healthy now. (SM) *Il y a pas rien que je connais pas faire, et que je peux pas faire si je serais gaillarde, mais je peux p'us faire ça que j'ai déjà fait.* There is nothing I don't know how to do and that I could not do if I were in good health but I'm no longer able to do what I used to do. (EV) **2** strong *Il était gaillard, il travaillait la charpente aussi fort comme moi.* He was strong, he worked in carpentry as hard as me. (Lv88) **3** having one's menstrual period ◊ **•pas gaillard** generally out of sorts <VM, Lv88> <***Loc:*** AL, EV, SM, VM, Da84, Lv88>

gaillard[2] [gajar] *n.m.* **1** guy, fellow **2** big man, robust fellow ◊ **•grand {gros} gaillard** big fellow *J'aimais des gros gaillards, j'aimais pas me battre avec quelqu'un de petit.* I used to like fighting with big fellows, not small ones. (IB) <IB, Da84> <***Loc:*** IB, Da84>

gaime (guème, guime) [gɛ̃m, gim] *n.m.* rooster *Combien de poules gingas t'as pour chaque guime gingas?* How many speckled hens do you have for each speckled rooster? (VM) ◊ **•guème gaïme / guime gaïme** fighting cock <SM, VM> <***Loc:*** EV, IB, JD, LA, LF, SM, VM, Da84, Hi02, Lv88>

gaïme[1] [gajim, gim] *adj.* bred to fight (of a rooster or chicken), bred to be aggressive for cockfighting *Mon guime gaïme est un tas plus petit que mon guime gingas, mais le gingas peut jamais gagner une bataille.* My fighting cock is a lot smaller than my speckled rooster, but the speckled rooster can never win a fight. (VM) *J'ai une pleine cour de poules gingas, mais j'ai juste un guime gaïme.* I've got a whole yard full of speckled hens, but I only have one fighting cock. (VM) <***Loc:*** SM, VM>

gaïme[2] [gajim, gim] *n.m./f.* fighting cock or hen *Les batailles de gaïmes étaient dans l'été.* Cockfights were in the summer. (Lv88) <***Loc:*** VM, Lv88>

gain [gɛ̃] *n.m.* gain, profit, earning <***Loc:*** Da84>

galance [galɑ̃s] *n.m./f.* swing, esp. one suspended under a porch *Des galances pour se reposer après une grosse ouvrage.* Porch swings for resting after hard work. (AC) <***Loc:*** AC, JE, LA, LF, SM, TB, VM, Da84, Lv88>

galancer [galɑ̃se] **I** *v.tr.* to swing *Il a passé l'après-midi à galancer sa fille.* He spent the afternoon swinging his daughter. (LA) **II** *v.intr.* to swing *La petite fille après galancer sur sa galance.* The little girl swinging on her swing. (SM) **III se galancer** *v.pron.* to swing o.s. *Ils se galancent sur la galerie pour prendre la fraîche.* They swing on the porch to catch the cool air. (Lv88) <***Loc:*** AC, LA, LF, SM, TB, VM, Da84, Lv88>

galand [galɑ̃] *n.m.* flounce *C'est un argoneau en cuivre et tu mets ça sus un baire, vingt-quatre sus le baire, et en avant c'est un galand.* It's a copper ring to put on a mosquito bar, twenty-four on the bar, and in front there is a flounce. (TB) <***Loc:*** TB>

galant de nuit [galɑ̃dənɥi, galɑ̃nɥi] *n.* **1** *(m.)* night-blooming jasmine plant **2** *(f.)* night-blooming jasmine flower <***Loc:*** VM>

galant[1]**, -e** [galɑ̃, -ɑ̃t] *adj.* gallant *Il a toujours été galant avec les filles.* He was always gallant with the girls. (LA) <***Loc:*** LA, Da84>

galant[2] [galɑ̃] *n.m.* gentleman, sir *Ma fille en mariage? Galant, retire-toi. Elle a reçu des gages d'un autre amant que toi.* My daughter in marriage? Sir, withdraw. She has received a pledge from a lover other than yourself. (IB, ch: *Je m'ai fait une maîtresse*) <***Loc:*** IB>

gale [gal] *n.f.* mange, itch *Il a eu la gale de sept ans si mauvais, ça lui a pris huit ans pour la gratter.* He had the seven-year itch so bad that it took him eight years to scratch it (EV) <***Loc:*** EV, LA, LF, Da84, Hi02>

galérage [galeraʒ] *n.m.* planing <***Loc:*** Da84>

galère [galær] *n.m./f.* **1** plane, wood planer **2** large plane with two handles, used to rough down timber ◊ **•galère à électricité** electric wood planer <TB> <***Loc:*** AC, EV, JE, LA, LF, SL, SM, TB, Da84, Lv88>

galérer [galere] *v.tr.* to plane (wood) *Faulait tu galères ton bois toi-même pour être sûr que ça aurait été égal.* You had to plane your wood yourself to make sure that it would be smooth. (LA) ◊ **•galérer les bancs** to be a wallflower at a dance <TB, La99> <***Loc:*** EV, LA, SL, SM, TB, VM, Da84, La99, Lv88>

galerie [galri, galdri, garli] *n.f.* porch, veranda ◊ **•galerie en avant** front porch *Tu vas pas en voir mais y avait plein des maisons qu'avaient leur escalier dessus la galerie en avant.* You won't see any but there used to be a lot of houses that had their staircase on the front porch. (LF) <LF> **•prendre la galerie** to go out on the porch *J'aime prendre la galerie après le souper.* I like to go out on the porch after supper. (Lv88) <Lv88> <***Loc:*** LA, LF, SM, TB,VM, Da84, Hi02, Lv88>

galette [galɛt] *n.f.* **1** cake **2** yeast cake *Là tu mettais une galette. Comme ça, ton pain aurait levé.* Then you would add a yeast cake. That way, your bread would rise. (LA) **3** layer of a cake *J'ai fait un bon gâteau coco à quatre galettes pour le bazar.* I made a great four-layer coconut cake for the bazaar. (VM) **4** thin slice, sliver *Coupe-moi juste une petite galette de gâteau. J'ai pas beaucoup faim.* Cut me just a little sliver of cake. I'm not very hungry. (VM) *Tranche les patates par galettes.* Cut the potatoes into slices. (TB) **5** [*vulg.*] female genitals ◊ **•galette de gomme** stick of gum <LF> **•galette de pain de maïs** tortilla chip <VM> <***Loc:*** LA, LF, TB, VM, Da84, Gu00, Hi02, La99, Lv88>

galeux, -euse [galø, -øz] *adj.* **1** mangy, itchy, scabby *Alle était si galeuse que je pouvais juste pas l'embrasser.* She was so mangy that I couldn't bring myself to hug her. (LA) **2** rough-surfaced, scaly *Un crapaud est galeux, mais une gournouille est unie.* A toad is rough, but a frog is smooth. (VM) **3** filthy, squalid *T'es petite et t'es mignonne mais t'es trop galeuse pour faire ma femme.* You're little and you're cute, but you're too filthy to be my wife. (EV, ch: *T'es petite et t'es mignonne*) <***Loc:*** EV, LA, VM, Da84>

galfa ♦see **galfat**

galfat[1] **(galfa)** [galfa] *adj.* **1** gluttonous **2** inattentive, clumsy *Donne-lui pas ça à faire. Il est trop galfa.* Don't give him that to do. He's too clumsy. (EV) <***Loc:*** EV>

galfat[2] **(galfa)** [galfa] *n.m.* **1** glutton, greedy person *J'avais fait un beau gros gâteau mais ton frère et sa bande de galfats l'ont tout mangé.* I had made a beautiful big cake but your brother and his crowd of gluttons ate the whole thing. (VM) **2** inattentive, clumsy person <***Loc:*** EV, VM, Guoo>

galfétage [galfetaʒ] *n.m.* caulking <***Loc:*** LF>

galféter [galfete] *v.tr.* to caulk *Là ça c'était appelé galféter. Ils prendaient ce coton et ils mettaient ça dans la craque, et ils ont arrêté le bateau de couler comme ça.* That was called caulking. They took that cotton and put it in the crack, they stopped the boat from leaking that way. (LF) <***Loc:*** LF>

galibarda ♦see **caliberda**

galimachas ♦see **galimatias**

galimatias (galimachas, calimatcha) [galimatʃa, kalimatʃa] *n.m.* **1** mess, rubbish **2** confusion, disorder *J'ai jamais vu un pareil galimachas comme la partie hier soir.* I've never seen such disorder as the party last night. (SM) **3** mixture of things **4** dish made of various meats and rice <***Loc:*** JE, SM, VM, Da84, Lv88>

galle [gal] *n.f.* gall (on a tree or plant) <***Loc:*** Da84>

gallon [galɔ̃] *n.m.* gallon <***Loc:*** Da84, Lv88>

galoche [galɔʃ] *n.f.* game of quoits <***Loc:*** VM>

galop [galo] *n.m.* **1** gallop, trot **2** scolding, reprimand, rebuke *Je l'ai foutu un galop!* I gave him a scolding! (SM) *Je l'ai donné un bon galop.* I gave him a good reprimand. (VM) ◊ **•dans un galop** in a short time *Je serai là dans un galop.* I'll be there soon. (VM) <VM> **•grand galop** fast gallop <Da84> **•petit galop** slow gallop, lope <Da84> <***Loc:*** SM, VM, Da84>

galopade [galopad] *n.f.* galloping <***Loc:*** Da84>

galope [gaalɔp] *n.f.* rush ◊ **•à la galope** in a rush *T'as fait ça à la galope, c'est pas propre.* You did that in a rush, it's not clean. (VM) <VM> **•en galope** in heat (of an animal) *Chienne en galope.* Dog in heat. (VM) <VM> <***Loc:*** VM>

galoper [galope] **I** *v.tr.* **1** to run for office, be a candidate for a position *Il a galopé l'élection, mais il a perdu.* He ran in the election, but he lost. (Lv88) **2** to run, manage, tend (a store, a business) *Mon père aussi a galopé une sucrerie.* My father also ran a sugar mill. (Lv88) *Il galope son office lui-même.* He manages his office himself. (SM) **3** to operate, run *Il a commencé à galoper des bateaux sur l'Atchafalaya basin.* He started running boats in the Atchafalaya basin. (Lv88) **4** to pursue, chase, run after *Je l'ai galopé fort, ce petit garçon.* I chased him hard, that little boy. (VM) **II** *v.intr.* **1** to gallop *Le cheval a galopé partout à travers du bois.* The horse galloped all over the woods. (SL) **2** to run *Mon garçon galope vite.* My boy runs fast. (Guoo) **3** to hurry *Galope, je te dis.* Hurry, I'm telling you. (VM) **4** to go, lead (to) *Le chemin galope à Mamou.* The road runs to Mamou. (Lv88) **5** to run, function *Le char galope bien.* The car runs well. (LA) ◊ **•galoper après** to run after *Mon chien était après galoper après un lapin.* My dog was running after a rabbit. (LA) <LA, Da84> **•galoper comme un chat échaudé** to run like a scared cat, run very quickly <SM, La99> **•faire galoper** to manage, run, operate *Il fait galoper son business.* He manages his business. (VM) <VM> <***Loc:*** LA, SL, SM, VM, Da84, Guoo, Hio2, La99, Lv88>

galvaniser [galvɑ̃nize] *v.tr.* to galvanize **Fer galvanisé.* Galvanized iron. (Da84) <***Loc:*** Da84>

gamasin ♦see **magasin**

gambader [gɑ̃bade] *v.intr.* **1** to romp, frisk about *Le maître d'école a gambadé à travers de la classe comme un jeune chevreuil.* The teacher romped across the classroom like a young deer. (VM) **2** to roughhouse, create a ruckus *Les Dartez étaient après gambader dans la salle de danse avec des pieds de gombo.* The Dartez boys were creating a ruckus in the dance hall with okra plants. (VM) <***Loc:*** VM, Da84, Lv88>

gamblage [gɑ̃blaʒ, gɛ̃blaʒ] *n.m.* gambling, betting, gamble **Le gamblage peut continuer tant qu'il y a quelque chose pour gager.* The gambling can continue as long as there's something to bet. (Wh83) <***Loc:*** LF, SM, Da84, Lv88, Wh83>

gambler [gɑ̃ble, gɛ̃ble] **I** *v.tr.* to bet, wager, put up as a stake in gambling *Il a gamblé sa place et il l'a bien perdue.* He wagered his farm and he lost it too. (LA) **II** *v.intr.* **1** to gamble, wager, play a game of chance for stakes, play cards for money *L'Acadien peut gambler sur tout.* The Acadian can gamble on anything. (Lv88) *Et un soir après gambler, j'ai perdu tout mon argent.* And one night while gambling, I lost all my money. (AV, ch: *La rivière rouge*) **2** to take a chance, bet on an uncertain outcome *J'ai gamblé que mon frère m'aurait pas laissé là, et j'avais raison.* I gambled that my brother would not leave me there, and I was right. (LA) <***Loc:*** AV, IV, LA, SM, VM, Da84, Hio2, Lv88>

gambleur, -euse [gɑ̃blœr, gɛ̃blœr, -øz] *n.* gambler <***Loc:*** SM, VM, Da84, Lv88>

game [gɛ̃m] *n.m. (occ. f.)* game *Eusse passait dans les rues pour faire de la boucane pour les moustiques, c'était mauvais des fois. Et eusse allait* SPRAY *alentour de les bancs ayoù le monde s'assisait pour guetter les games.* They would pass in the streets to make smoke because of the mosquitoes, it was bad sometimes. And they would go spray around the benches where people would sit to watch the games.

(LF) *Les jeunes a joué* TAG. *Ça c'était une grosse game.* The young people played tag. That was a popular game. (AV) ◊ **•game de pelote** ball game <Da84, Lv88> <***Loc:*** AV, LF, SM, TB, Da84, Lv88>

gamelle [gɑ̃mɛl, gɑ̃mel] *n.f.* **1** shell, hard covering (of a turtle, shrimp) *La gamelle de la tortue est cassée.* The shell of the turtle is broken. (SM) **2** half of any spherical object (such as a melon) *On a eu chacun une gamelle de melon.* We each had half a melon. (VM) **3** bowl *Une gamelle de chien.* A dog food bowl. (VM) *Une gamelle pour pétrir le pain.* A bowl for kneading bread dough. (VM) <***Loc:*** SM, TB, VM, Da84>

gamin, -e [gɑ̃mɛ̃, -in] *n.* child, kid *Elle a balbuté ce gamin.* She scolded that little boy. (IB) *C'est juste un jeune gamin. Il est trop jeune pour se marier.* He's just a kid. He's too young to get married. (VM) *C'est des gamins qu'ont fait ça. C'est malheureux de les traiter comme du grand monde.* It's kids who did that. It's unfortunate to treat them like adults. (VM) ◊ **•petit(e) gamin(e)** young boy/girl *C'est juste une petite gamine. Elle est trop jeune pour élever un bébé.* She's just a little girl. She's too young to raise a child. (VM) <VM, Da84> <***Loc:*** VM, Da84>

ganache [gɑ̃naʃ] *adj.* unable to stand pain or sickness, weak <***Loc:*** Da84>

gang [gɛ̃ŋ] *n.m.* **1** gang, band (of people) *Un gang de petits.* A large group of children. (VM) **2** large group (of anything) <***Loc:*** SM, TB, VM, Da84, Lv88>

gangrène (**cangrène, congrène**) [gɑ̃grɛ̃n, kɑ̃grɛ̃n] *n.f.* gangrene, infection <***Loc:*** SM, Da84, Lv88>

gangrener (**cangrener, congrener**) [gɑ̃grɛ̃ne, kɑ̃grɛ̃ne] **I** *v.intr.* to become gangrenous, turn into gangrene *Sa jambe avait gangrené et ils ont eu pour la couper.* His leg had become gangrenous and they had to cut it. (LA) **II se gangrener** *v.pron.* to become gangrenous <***Loc:*** JE, LA, Da84, Lv88>

ganif [gɑ̃nif] *n.m.* pocket knife <***Loc:*** VM >

gant [gɑ̃] *n.m.* glove ◊ **•pas mettre des gants** to not mince words, speak directly and plainly (even at the risk of offending another) *Il mettait pas des gants, lui. S'il avait quelque chose à dire, il le disait.* He didn't mince words. If he had something to say, he said it. (LA) <LA, La99> <***Loc:*** LA, SL, SM, Da84, La99>

ganter [gɑ̃te] **I** *v.tr.* to put gloves on *Qui c'est qui va ganter ta chère petite main blanche?* Who is going to glove your dear little white hand? (EV, ch: *Mercredi au soir*) **II se ganter** *v.pron.* to put on gloves *Dans ce temps-là, les femmes se gantaient pour sortir.* In those days, women wore gloves to go out. (LA) <***Loc:*** EV, LA, Da84>

garage [garaʒ] *n.m.* **1** garage **2** garage, mechanic's shop ◊ **•garage postiche** carport <Fa77> <***Loc:*** Da84, Fa77>

garantie [garɑ̃ti] *n.m.* guarantee, warranty <***Loc:*** Da84>

garantir [garɑ̃tir] *v.tr.* to guarantee, vouch for, warrant, assure *Le nom de cette medicine, c'est un tonique on appelle ça Hasitall, et je veux vous garantir et je veux vous avertir mes amis, que du Hasitall c'est bon pour tous les maladies et tous les caprices quelqu'un peut avoir dans la vie.* The name of this medicine, it's a tonic, we call it Hasitall, and I want to guarantee you and I want to announce to you, my friends, that Hasitall is good for all maladies and all caprices that one can have in life. (AV) <***Loc:*** AV, LF, Da84, Hi02>

garaufier ♦see **garofier**

garce [gars] *n.f.* **1** prostitute, whore **2** old hag <***Loc:*** AV, IB, SM, TB, Da84>

garçon [garsɔ̃] *n.m.* **1** boy *Tu parles du joli monde. Lui il est beau garçon et sa sœur, elle est belle fille.* You talk about some beautiful people. He's a handsome boy and his sister is a pretty girl. (LA) **2** son *Elle était mariée avec le garçon à Louis.* She was married to Louis' son. (Lv88) ◊ **•vieux garçon *a*** bachelor ***b*** zinnia ***c*** cornflower, bachelor's button <EV, LF, SL, Da84, Gu00, Lv88> <***Loc:*** EV, JE, LF, SL, SM, Da84, Gu00, Hi02, Lv88>

garçonnière [garsɔ̃jær] *n.f.* bachelor quarters, boys' room, top floor of Acadian house where boys traditionally sleep <***Loc:*** LF, Da84, Gu00, Hi02>

Garde de Côte [gardəkot] *n.f.* Coast Guard <***Loc:*** LF>

garde[1] [gard] *n.f.* **1** care, protection, charge, custody **2** keeping watch, keeping guard **3** guard, guards (collectively) **Le Roi dit qu'il faut tu vas à soir voler son cheval dans l'écurie avec la garde tout le tour.* The king said you have to go tonight to steal his horse with the guards posted all around. (An94) **4** outpost ◊ **•prendre garde** to watch out, be careful **C'est mieux prendre garde que pardon.* Better safe than sorry. (Da84) <Da84> <***Loc:*** LF, IV, An94, Da84>

garde[2] [gard] *n.m.* **1** guard, guardsman **2** guardian, keeper <***Loc:*** LF, SL, Da84>

garde-boue [gardəbu] *n.m.* mud guard <***Loc:*** Da84>

garde-corps [gardəkɔr] *n.m.* railing <***Loc:*** Lv88>

garde-crotte (**garde de crotte**) [gardəkrɔt] *n.m.* dashboard (of a horse-drawn vehicle) <***Loc:*** Da84>

garde-feu [gardəfø] *n.m.* fire guard, fire shield <***Loc:*** Da84>

garde-fou [gardəfu] *n.m.* stair railing, bridge railing *Quand j'ai revenu* BACK, *il était assis sur les garde-fous du pont, je pouvais voir il était beaucoup fatigué.* When I came back he was sitting on the railing of the bridge, I could see he was very tired. (SM) <***Loc:*** SM, Da84>

garde-malade [gardmalad] *n.f.* nurse <***Loc:*** Da84>

garde-manger [gardmɑ̃ʒe, garmɑ̃ʒe] *n.m.* **1** (free-standing) pantry, food-safe **2** kitchen cabinet <***Loc:*** IB, JE, LA, SL, TB, Da84>

garder [garde] **I** *v.tr.* **1** to take care of, look after *Il était après garder les enfants comme il était supposé de faire, et ils ont échappé.* He was looking after the children as he was supposed to do, and they slipped away. (LA) **2** to protect *Et moi, j'ai des vieux parents qu'essaient toujours garder* *la tradition.* And I have old family members who still try to preserve the old tradition. (SM) **3** to preserve, keep (food) *Tu pouvais garder du caillé plus longtemps que du lait.* You could keep clabber longer than milk. (LA) **4** to keep, maintain *Il a ôté son capot, mais il a gardé sa chemise.* He took off his coat, but he kept his shirt on. (LA) *Alle a eu la gale de sept ans tellement mauvais jusqu'à alle l'a gardée huit ans.* She had the seven-year itch so bad that she kept it for eight years. (LF) **II se garder** *v.pron.* to keep o.s. (e.g. clean, proper, lean) *T'as besoin de te garder propre. On va aller voir Tante Eule bien vite.* You need to keep yourself clean. We're going to go see Aunt Eule soon. (LA) <***Loc:*** LA, LF, SM, VM, Da84, Hi02, Lv88>

garder ♦see **regarder**

garde-soleil [gardsolej, garsolɛj, garsolej] *n.m.* **1** American bittern (locally called sungazer) **2** sunbonnet, type of head-covering worn by women in Acadian areas <***Loc:*** AC, IB, JE, LA, LF, SL, SM, VM, Da84, Gu00, Hi02, Lv88>

garde-yeux (**garde de yeux, garde-z-yeux**) [gardzjø, gardəzjø] *n.m.* **1** blinders, blinkers (on a bridle), usually of leather, used to partially shield the vision of a horse or mule **2** any protective eyewear <***Loc:*** AC, LA, SL, SM, VM, Lv88>

gardien [gardjɛ̃] *n.m.* guardian, ward <***Loc:*** Da84>

gare [gar] *n.f.* railroad station, depot <***Loc:*** Da84>

gargaliser (**gargariser, garganiser**) [gargalize, galize, gargarize, gargɑ̃nize] *v.intr.* to gargle *Il s'a brossé les dents et il a bien gargarisé avec du soda.* He brushed his teeth and he gargled well with baking soda [in water]. (LA) <***Loc:*** LA, SM, VM, Da84, Lv88>

gargana ♦see **gargane**

gargand [gargɑ̃] *n.m.* Adam's apple <***Loc:*** Lv88>

gargane (**gargana**) [gargɑ̃n, gargɑ̃na] *n.f.* throat *Ma gargane me fait du mal.* My throat hurts. (SM) <***Loc:*** SM, Da84, Lv88>

garganiser ♦see **gargaliser**

gargotage [gargotaʒ] *n.m.* waste <***Loc:*** Lv88>

gargotant ♦see **gargoton**

gargote [gargɔt] *n.f.* **1** small store or restaurant **2** bad cooking *On a eu de la gargote pour dîner.* We had slop for dinner. (SM) *C'est de la gargote!* It's bad (cooking)! (Lv88) **3** inferior merchandise, junk <***Loc:*** SM, Da84, Lv88>

gargoter [gargote] *v.tr.* to make or do something carelessly, mess up, botch *Elle a gargoté sa robe.* She threw together her dress. (Lv88) *Il a gargoté son ouvrage.* He messed up his work. (SM) <***Loc:*** SM, Lv88>

gargoton (**gargotant**) [gargotɔ̃] *n.m.* **1** throat *Une de mes cousines avait envalé une aiguille et ça 'i a resté pris dans le gargoton.* One of my cousins had swallowed a needle and it stayed stuck in her throat. (Gu00) **2** larynx, Adam's apple **3** windpipe <***Loc:*** SM, VM, Da84, Gu00, Lv88>

gargouiller [garguje] **I** *v.tr.* to work in a slovenly fashion, do poorly *T'as tout gargouillé ça.* You did that really poorly. (VM) **II** *v.intr.* to grumble (of the stomach or intestines) *Mon ventre gargouille.* My stomach is growling. (SM) <***Loc:*** SM, VM>

gariot ♦see **garrion**

garnement [garnəmɑ̃] *n.* bad fellow, 'bad egg' <***Loc:*** Da84>

garnir [garnir] **I** *v.tr.* **1** to adorn, decorate, trim *Sa mère fait faire un beau cerceuil doré, tout à l'entour garni de rubans roses.* His mother had a beautiful gilded coffin made, decorated all around with pink ribbons. (IB, ch: *Au Pont de l'Anse*) **2** to garrison *La ville des Manteau, mon Dieu, qu'elle est si belle. Elle est garnie de tous ces Louisianais et tous ces braves soldats.* The city of Manteau, my God, how it is beautiful. It is garrisoned with all those Louisianians and all those brave soldiers. (EV, ch: *La ville des Manteaux*) **II se garnir** *v.pron.* to adorn o.s. *Elle s'avait garni avec des boucles d'oreilles et des colliers et des bagues et toute sorte d'affaire.* She had adorned herself with earrings and necklaces and rings and all sorts of things. (LA) <***Loc:*** EV, IB, LA, Da84>

garniture [garnityr] *n.f.* **1** decoration **2** trimming **3** furniture <***Loc:*** Da84>

garocher ♦see **garrocher**

garofier (**garaufier**) [garofje, garopje] *n.m.* **1** sweet locust, honey locust, spring locust tree *J'ai passé au ras d'un garofier et ça m'a tout graffigné les bras.* I passed near the spring locust and it scratched my arm all up. (Gu00) **2** thistle, thorn bush <***Loc:*** AC, SM, Da84, Gu00, Hi02, Lv88>

garrion (**gariot**) [garjɔ̃, garjo] *n.m.* stallion <***Loc:*** VM, Lv88>

garrocher (**garocher**) [garoʃe, galoʃe] **I** *v.tr.* **1** to throw, pitch, sling, toss *L'ouragan avait garoché le hangar l'autre bord du chemin.* The hurricane had tossed the shed on the other side of the street. (Lv88) **2** to spend, throw away (money) *Il garoche son argent tout partout.* He throws his money around everywhere. (VM) **II se garrocher** *v.pron.* **1** to throw o.s. *Il s'a garoché à l'eau* He threw himself into the water. (VM) **2** to rush for *Quand il partait, je me garochais dessus le violon.* When he would leave, I would rush for the violin. (Lv88) ◊ •**garrocher ensemble** to throw together, assemble hastily *Il y en a plein qui bâtit des bateaux,* BUT *c'est pas comme ça c'est bâti. Eusse juste garoche ça ensemble.* There are a lot of people who build boats, but not like this one was built. They just throw them together. (TB) <TB> •**garrocher un coup de poing** to throw a punch *Je vas te garocher un coup de poing.* I am going to punch you. (SM) <SM> <***Loc:*** EV, IB, IV, LA, LF, SM, TB, VM, Da84, Gu00, Hi02, Lv88>

garrot [garo] *n.m.* withers <***Loc:*** Da84>

gas ♦see **gaz**

gascon pieds-pus [gaskɔ̃pjepy] *n.m.* low class Frenchman <***Loc:*** SM>

GASOLINE (**gazoline**) [gazolin] *n.f.* gasoline, gas <***Loc:*** Da84, Hi02, Lv88>

gaspareau [gasparo, kasparo] *n.m.* alewife <*Loc:* Lv88>

gaspi ♦see **gaspille**

gaspillage [gaspijaʒ] *n.m.* wasting, squandering, waste <*Loc:* SM, Da84, Lv88>

gaspillard, -e [gaspijar, -ard] *adj.* **1** spendthrift, extravagant *Il faut pas se marier avec un gaspillard.* One should not marry a spendthrift. (LA) **2** wasteful, squandering *Elle est gaspillarde.* She is wasteful. (SM) *Ça c'est gaspillard.* That's wasteful. (VM) <*Loc:* LA, SM, VM, Lv88>

gaspille (**gaspi**) [gaspij, gaspi] *n.m.* wasting, squandering, waste *C'est juste un gaspille tu fais.* It's just waste that you're making. (VM) *Le monde de Des Allemands là-bas, eusse pêche les barbues, et là eusse ramasse la viande et eusse vend les têtes à les pêcheurs à crabes. Et là y a pas de gaspi, tu vois.* The people from Des Allemands, they fish for catfish, and they collect the meat and they sell the heads to crab fishermen. And there's no waste, you see. (TB) <*Loc:* SM, TB, VM, Da84, Lv88>

gaspiller [gaspije] *v.tr.* to waste, squander *On gaspille pas ici.* We don't waste here. (VM) ◊ **•gaspiller de l'argent** to waste money <IB> <*Loc:* IB, VM, Da84, Hi02>

gaspilleur, -euse (**gaspilleux, -euse**) [gaspijœr, gaspijø, -øz] *adj.* wasteful *On est pas gaspilleux avec le riz.* We aren't wasteful with rice. (VM) <*Loc:* VM, Da84>

gaspilleux ♦see **gaspilleur**

gastronia (**castronier**) [gastrɔ̃ja, kastrɔ̃ja, kastrɔ̃je] *n.m.* **1** crape myrtle **2** myrtle tree <*Loc:* SM, TB, Da84, Fa77, Gu00, Lv88>

gatcher ♦see **gâcher**

gâte [gat] *n.m.* gout *C'est une maladie qui vient dans les pieds ça. Ça vient des bosses, et ça fait mal. C'est une maladie qu'est joliment mauvais ça, parce que quand t'attrapes les gâtes, ça ça vient que tu viens* ANEMIC *et tu viens bien malade, tu connais, t'es tout infecté, tu connais tu peux pas travailler, et ça vient des bosses, et c'est mauvais.* It's a disease you get in the feet. You get bumps, and it hurts. It's a disease that's quite bad, because when you get the gout, you become anemic and you get quite sick, you know, it's all infected, you know you can't work, and you get bumps, and that's bad. (TB) <*Loc:* TB>

gâté, -e [gate] *adj.* spoiled **Enfant gâté.* Spoiled child. (Da84) **Chien gâté.* Spoiled dog. (Da84) ◊ **•gâté après (qqn)** emotionally attached to (s.o.) <Da84> **•gâté par (qqn)** spoiled by (s.o.) <Da84> **•faire le gâté** to act like a spoiled child <Lv88> <*Loc:* Da84, Lv88>

gâteau [gato] *n.m.* **1** cake *On a mangé des bons gâteaux de la bakerie.* We ate some good cakes from the bakery. (TB) **2** cookie *Il était pas chisse. Un disait "donne-moi un gâteau, Bob," et Bob a tout donné ses gâteaux.* He was not stingy. One would say, "Give me a cookie, Bob," and Bob ended up giving away all his cookies. (LF) ◊ **•gâteau de mer** hardtack, sea biscuit <LF> **•petit gâteau** ***a*** cookie ***b*** favorite child <Da84, Gu00, Hi02, La99> **•petit gâteau à tasse** cupcake <LF> **•petit gâteau sec** teacake <VM> <*Loc:* LA, LF, SL, TB, VM, Da84, Gu00, Hi02, La99>

gâter [gate] **I** *v.tr.* **1** to spoil, taint, impair *Ça a bien gâté sa réputation quand ils l'ont vu au bal avec la femme à Howard.* It really tainted his reputation when they saw him at the dance with Howard's wife. (LA) **2** to lavish inordinate affection on **Et le papa et la maman pouvaient pas gâter tous les enfants.* And the mother and the father could not lavish affection on all the children. (LA, An94) **3** to do harm to the character by overindulgence *Le veuf a gâté sa nouvelle femme avec trop d'attention.* The widower spoiled his new wife with too much attention. (LA) **4** to dishonor or rape (a virgin) *Il a gâté ma fille.* He dishonored my daughter. (VM) **II** *v.intr.* to rot, become rotten *Ton poisson va gâter, on use la glace mais la glace fond vite.* Your fish is going to rot, we use ice but ice melts fast. (SM) **III se gâter** *v.pron.* **1** to go bad, spoil *Les rats se gâtent, la peau se gâte vite. Et t'as pas de prix sur des mauvais rats.* Muskrats go bad, the skin turns bad quickly. And you don't get any money for bad muskrats. (TB) **2** to change for the worse **Le temps est après se gâter.* The weather is spoiling. (Da84) <*Loc:* LA, SM, TB, VM, An94, Da84, Hi02, Lv88>

gâterie [gatri] *n.f.* spoiling (of children) <*Loc:* Da84>

gauche[1] [gɔʃ] *adj.* left **Il s'a levé debout et il a laché sa main gauche.* He got up and let go [of it] with his left hand. (EV, An84) <*Loc:* EV, SM, An84, Da84, Hi02>

gauche[2] (**agauche**) [gɔʃ, agɔʃ] *adj.* awkward, clumsy **Il est gauche.* He is clumsy or awkward. (Da84) <*Loc:* SB, Da84>

gauche[3] [gɔʃ] *n.f.* left *"Gee" c'était tourner à la droite et "haw" c'était tourner à la gauche.* "Gee" meant "turn right" and "haw" meant "turn left". (EV) <*Loc*: EV, Hi02>

gaucher[1], **-ère** (**gauché, -e**) [goʃe, -ær] *adj.* left-handed *J'ai une cousine qu'est gauchère.* I have a cousin who is left-handed. (SL) <*Loc:* SL, Da84>

gaucher[2] [goʃe] *n.m.* horse on the left in a draft team <*Loc:* VM >

gaucherie [goʃri] *n.f.* **1** awkwardness, clumsiness **2** any awkward or clumsy act or utterance <*Loc:* Da84>

gaucheux, -euse [goʃø, -øz] *n.* left-handed person <*Loc:* Lv88>

gavagner [gavɑ̃je, gavɑ̃ne] **I** *v.tr.* **1** to waste, squander, dissipate (money, property) *Il a gavagné tout son argent.* He squandered all of his money. (VM) **2** to ruin *Il gavagne tout son linge.* He ruins all his clothing. (Lv88) **II** *v.intr.* to hang around, loaf *Il travaille pas. Il gavagne.* He doesn't work. He loafs around. (SM) <*Loc:* SM, VM, Da84, Lv88>

gavagneur [gavɑ̃jœr, gavɑ̃nœr] *n.m.* spendthrift, waster of money, wasteful person <*Loc:* Da84, Lv88>

gavion [gavjɔ̃] *n.m.* craw (of a bird) <*Loc:* VM>

gaz (**gas**) [gaz, gas] *n.m.* **1** natural gas *Ça chauffe leur maison* *avec du gaz.* They heat their house with natural gas. (LA) **2** gasoline *L'huile, ça fait du gaz avec ça.* With oil, they make gas. (AC) **3** flatulence, gas *Les fèves me donnent des gaz.* Beans give me gas. (LA) <***Loc:*** AC, LA, SM, VM, Da84, Hi02, Lv88>

gaze [gaz] *n.f.* gauze <***Loc:*** Da84>

gazette[1] [gazɛt, gazet] *n.f.* newspaper, gazette <***Loc:*** LF, SM, VM, Da84, Hi02, Lv88>

gazette[2] ♦see **gâchette**

gazoline ♦see **GASOLINE**

gazon [gazɔ̃] *n.m.* **1** any lawn grass (e.g. carpet grass, turf) **2** tall grass ◊ **•gros gazon** Dallis grass <LA> **•petit gazon** carpet grass <LA> <***Loc:*** LA, VM, Da84>

geai [ʒɛ, ʒe] *n.m.* **1** jay, jaybird **2** bluejay <***Loc:*** SL, SB, Da84>

géant[1] [ʒeɑ̃] *adj.* gigantic *Un cheval géant.* A gigantic horse. (VM) <***Loc:*** VM, Da84>

géant[2] [ʒeɑ̃] *n.m.* giant <***Loc:*** Da84>

gee (gi) [dʒi] *interj.* used to direct horses to turn right *"Gee" c'était tourner à la droite et "haw" c'était tourner à la gauche.* "Gee" meant "turn right" and "haw" meant "turn left." (EV) <***Loc:*** EV, SM, Da84>

gélatine [ʒelatin] *n.f.* gelatin, jello <***Loc:*** Da84>

gelée [ʒle] *n.f.* **1** frost **Les premiers trois gélée et le troisième brouillard de le printemps.* The first three frosts and the third fog of spring. (Wh83) **2** jelly, gelatin **3** head cheese ◊ **•gelée de cochon** head cheese <LF> <***Loc:*** AC, LF, SL, Da84, Wh83>

geler [dʒele, ʒele] **I** *v.tr.* to freeze *Le vent de l'est, c'est le vent qui gèle les femmes, mais ça glace les hommes aussi.* The east wind is the wind that freezes women, but it freezes men as well. (VM) **II** *v.intr.* **1** to freeze *J'avais un beau oranger là mais il a gelé.* I had a beautiful orange tree there but it froze. (SL) *A peu près une fois dans vingt ans ça gèle ici, mauvais.* About once every twenty years it freezes here hard. (SL) **2** to gel *Et là dès que c'est cuit là, eh ben la viande se retire sur les os. Là ils jetont les os. Là ça gèle avec cette couenne là en-dedans là. Ça gèle, ça vient dur. C'est ça ils appelont de la gelée.* And when it's cooked, the meat comes off the bones. Then they throw away the bones. Then it gels with that pig skin in it. It gels, it gets hard. That's what they call head cheese. (LF) <***Loc:*** IB, LF, SL, VM, Da84>

gémir [ʒẽmir] *v.intr.* **1** to moan, groan *Quoi c'est qui te fait gémir comme un pauvre orphelin?* What makes you moan and groan like a poor orphan? (SL) **2** to grieve, lament <***Loc:*** SL, Da84>

gênant, -e [ʒẽnɑ̃, -ɑ̃t] *adj.* troublesome, embarrassing, annoying *Mangez parce que quand je vas aller chez vous-autres, je vas être plutôt gênant que gêné.* Eat up because when I go to your house, I'll be more troublesome that troubled. (VM) <***Loc:*** VM, Da84>

gencive [ʒɑ̃siv] *n.f.* gingiva, gums *Ça a pas fait trop de mal parce que le dentiste avait engourdi ma gencive avant d'arracher la dent.* It didn't hurt too badly because the dentist had numbed my gums before pulling the tooth. (EV) <***Loc:*** EV, Da84>

gendarme [ʒɑ̃darm] *n.m.* policeman <***Loc:*** Da84>

gendre [ʒɑ̃n, ʒɑ̃d(r)] *n.m.* **1** son-in-law **2** stepson <***Loc:*** IV, LF, SM, TB, Da84>

gêne [ʒẽn] *n.f.* bashfulness, self-consciousness, embarrassment <***Loc:*** Da84>

gêné, -e [ʒẽne] *adj.* **1** bashful, shy *Des fois il est gêné quand-ce qu'il veut parler à quelqu'un.* Sometimes he's bashful when he wants to talk to someone. (LF) **2** embarrassed <***Loc:*** LF, Da84>

généalogie [ʒẽnealoʒi] *n.f.* genealogy <***Loc:*** Da84>

gêner [ʒẽne] **I** *v.tr.* **1** to embarrass *Ça la gênait de parler devant du monde.* It embarrassed her to speak in front of people. (LA) **2** to impede, give trouble **Et il gênait jamais personne. Il avait son affaire, et puis il la faisait.* And he never gave anyone trouble. He had his thing and he did it. (LA, An94) **3** to bother, annoy *Avec nous, elle dit, "Quand vous jetez un mot anglais dans une phrase, ça me gêne."* [When she's] with us, she says, "When you throw an English word into a French sentence, that bothers me." (SL) **II se gêner** *v.pron.* to be bashful, be embarrassed **Gêne-toi pas.* Don't be bashful (Da84) <***Loc:*** LA, SL, An94, Da84, Hi02>

général[1] [ʒẽneral] *adj.* general <***Loc:*** VM, Da84>

général[2] [ʒẽneral] *n.m.* general <***Loc:*** Da84>

généralement [ʒẽneralmɑ̃] *adv.* generally *Dans ce temps-là c'était généralement accepté que ça c'est la manière que ça devrait être.* In those days it was generally accepted that that was how things should be. (TB) <***Loc:*** TB>

génération [ʒẽnerasjɔ̃] *n.f.* generation <***Loc:*** LF, Da84>

générer [ʒẽnere] *v.tr.* to generate, produce *Tu vois, cette nouvelle taxe a généré assez d'argent pour la rente des vieux.* You see, that new tax has generated enough money for the old folks' pension. (VM) <***Loc:*** VM, Da84>

généreux, -euse [ʒẽnerø, -øz] *adj.* generous *C'était un homme qu'était beaucoup généreux, il t'aurait donné sa chemise.* He was a man who was very generous. He would have given you his shirt. (LA) <***Loc:*** LA, Da84>

générosité [ʒẽnerozite] *n.f.* generosity <***Loc:*** Da84>

génie [ʒẽni] *n.m.* genius, talent <***Loc:*** Da84>

genou [ʒnu] *n.m.* knee ◊ **•à genoux** kneeling *Il est à genoux dans le coin.* He is kneeling in the corner. (VM) <VM> **•mettre (qqn) sur {dessus} ses genoux** to make s.o. kneel, put s.o. on his knees *Eusse nous mettait dessus notres genoux si on parlait en français.* They made us kneel if we spoke French [in school]. (TB) <TB> **•se mettre à genoux {d'à genoux / sur les genoux}** to kneel *Nos parents nous a montré que le soir avant de te coucher que t'allais te mettre d'à genoux, et t'allais dire tes prières.* Our parents taught us that in the evening before going to bed, you'd get on your knees and you'd say your prayers. (TB) <TB, Da84> *<Loc:* TB, VM, Da84, Hi02>

genre [ʒɑ̃r] *n.m.* kind, sort, species *<Loc:* Da84>

gens [ʒɑ̃, ʒɑ̃s] *n.* **1** *(sing.)* person *Un gens de couleur.* A colored person. (Lv88) **2** *(pl.)* people, folks *Des gens de Lafayette.* People from Lafayette. (SL) ◊ **•gens de couleur** colored people, people of color <Lv88, Da84> **•gens de couleur libres** freed slaves <Da84> **•gens d'huile / le monde de l'huile** oilworkers <Gr86, Lv88> **•jeune gens** young man *Elle s'a marié avec un jeune gens beaucoup ambitionneux.* She married a very ambitious young man. (SL) <EV, SL, VM> **•les grandes gens** high society <VM> *<Loc:* EV, LF, SL, SM, VM, Da84, Gr86, Lv88>

gentilhomme [ʒɑ̃tijɔ̃m] *n.m.* gentleman *<Loc:* Da84>

GENTLEMAN [dʒentlmən] *n.m.* gentleman *<Loc:* Da84>

génuflexion [ʒɛ̃nyflɛksjɔ̃] *n.f.* genuflection *<Loc:* Da84>

géographie [ʒeografi] *n.f.* geography *<Loc:* Da84>

géologie [ʒeoloʒi] *n.f.* geology *<Loc:* Da84>

gérant [ʒerɑ̃] *n.m.* supervisor, manager *<Loc:* SL>

gerbe [ʒærb] *n.f.* bundle, sheaf *<Loc:* Da84>

gerce [ʒærs] *n.f.* chap, wrinkle *<Loc:* Da84>

gercer (**cherser**) [ʒærse, ʃærse] **I** *v.tr.* to chap *Il a resté des heures dans le vent de nord, à la chasse, et ça a gercé ses lèvres.* He stayed for hours in the north wind, while hunting, and it chapped his lips. (LA) **II** *v.intr.* to chap, be chapped **Alors, il a ouvert la jarre de beurre et il a commencé à graisser les crevasses dans un effort d'essayer de les guérir. Et il pleurait. Il trouvait beaucoup mauvais que la terre était après gercer comme ça.* So, he opened the butter jar and he started applying the butter to the cracks in an effort to heal them. And he was crying. He found it terrible that the earth was chapping like that. (EV, An94) *<Loc*: EV, LA, VM, An94, Da84>

gerçure [ʒærsyr] *n.f.* chap, wrinkle *<Loc:* EV, An94, Da84>

germain, -mine [ʒærmɛ̃, -min] *adj.* first, full (cousin) *Cousin germain.* First cousin or cousin-german. (SM, VM) *Une cousine germine.* A first cousin. (Lv88) *<Loc:* SM, VM, Da84, Lv88>

germe [ʒærm] *n.m.* germ, seed, embryo *<Loc:* Da84>

germer [ʒærme] *v.intr.* to germinate, sprout *Il a planté sa graine trop de bonne heure et le froid l'a empêchée de germer.* He planted his seed too early and the cold prevented it from germinating. (IV) *<Loc:* IV, Da84>

germination [ʒærminasjɔ̃] *n.f.* germination *<Loc:* Da84>

géronium [ʒerɔ̃jœm, ʒirɑ̃mjœm] *n.m.* geranium ◊ **•géronium à la rose** sweet geranium <VM> *<Loc:* VM, Gu00>

géront [ʒerɔ̃] *n.m.* bramble, briar *<Loc:* VM>

gésier (**gigier**) [ʒezje, ʒeʒje, ʒizje, ʒiʒje, ʒyzje] *n.m.* **1** gizzard **2** chicken giblet *<Loc:* LF, SM, VM, Da84, Lv88>

geste [ʒɛs(t)] *n.m.* gesture, sign, motion *<Loc:* Da84>

gester ♦see **gesticuler**

gesteux, -euse [ʒestø, -øz] *adj.* affected in manner or gesture *Lui et son* BOYFRIEND *sont gesteux les deux.* He and his boyfriend are both affected in manner. (VM) *<Loc:* VM>

gesticuler (**gester**) [ʒestikyle, ʒeste] *v.intr.* to make gestures, gesticulate *Il était après gesticuler de loin là-bas l'autre bord de la savane pour essayer de me faire comprendre que c'était l'heure de dîner.* He was gesticulating from way on the other side of the pasture trying to make me understand that it was time to eat. (VM) *<Loc:* VM, Da84>

gi ♦see **gee**

gibier [ʒibje, ʒibe] *n.m.* game (birds or animals) *<Loc:* SL, TB, Da84>

gibote [ʒibɔt] *n.f.* dipper, ladle *Va chercher la gibote pour que je retire la soupe.* Go get the dipper so I can dish out the soup. (TB) *<Loc:* TB>

gigailler [ʒigaje] *v.intr.* to jump, move about *Il était après gigailler comme un jeune cabri.* He was jumping around like a young goat. (EV) *<Loc:* EV, VM, Lv88>

gigier ♦see **gésier**

gigolo [ʒigolo] *n.m.* gigolo *<Loc:* Da84>

gigot [ʒigo] *n.m.* leg of mutton *<Loc:* Da84>

gigue [ʒig] *n.m./f.* jig, dance *<Loc:* Da84, Hi02>

giguer [ʒige, dʒige] *v.intr.* **1** to jig, dance a jig *Ça fait la santé, giguer comme ça.* It makes you healthy, dancing a jig like this. (Lv88) **2** to dance spiritedly, dance vigorously *T'as gigué au bal hier au soir?* Did you dance vigorously at the dance last night? (VM) *<Loc:* SM, VM, Da84, Lv88>

giguler [ʒigyle] **I** *v.tr.* to worry, disturb, cause to worry *L'oragan me gigule.* Storms disturb me. (Lv88) *Cette nouvelle me gigule.* That news worries me. (SM) **II** *v.intr.* to worry *Il gigule tout le temps.* He worries all the time. (Lv88) *<Loc:* SM, Lv88>

gilet [ʒilɛ, ʒile] *n.m.* vest *<Loc:* Da84>

GIN[1] [dʒin] *n.m.* gin *<Loc:* Da84, Lv88>

GIN[2] [dʒin] *n.m.* cotton gin *<Loc:* Da84>

gingas[1] (**gingat**) [ʒɛ̃ga] *adj.* spotted, speckled (black and white, black and gray) *Une poule gingas.* A speckled hen. (Lv88) *<Loc:* SM, VM, Lv88>

gingas[2] (**gingat**) [ʒɛ̃ga] *n.m.* gingham cloth *<Loc:* VM, Da84, Lv88>

gingat ♦see **gingas**

gingembre [ʒɛ̃ʒɑ̃m, ʒɛ̃ʒɑ̃b(r)] *n.m.* ginger *<Loc:* Hi02>

gingue [ʒɛ̃g, dʒɛ̃g] *n.* ◊ **•en gingue** in high spirits *Ils étaient en gingue avant les fêtes.* They were in high spirits before the holidays. (LA) <LA, VM> **•se mettre en gingue** to have fun *On va se mettre en gingue avant qu'ils ont besoin de partir pour l'armée.* We'll have fun before they have to leave for the army. (LA) <LA, Lv88> *<Loc:* LA, VM, Lv88>

ginguer [ʒɛ̃ge, dʒɛ̃ge] *v.intr.* **1** to jump, dance, move about *J'aime pas danser avec lui, il gingue tout partout sur le plancher.* I don't like dancing with him, he jumps around all over the floor. (LA) **2** to gambol, frolic *Le poulain ginguait* *dans le parc.* The colt was gambolling in the corral. (VM) <***Loc:*** LA, VM, Lv88>

gipsie (**gypsie**) [dʒipsi, dʒipse] *n.m./f.* gypsy, bohemian, vagabond, hobo <***Loc:*** Da84, Lv88>

girafe [ʒiraf] *n.f.* giraffe <***Loc:*** Da84>

giration [ʒirasjɔ̃] *n.f.* gyration, pirouette <***Loc:*** Da84 >

giraumon ♦see **giraumont**

giraumont (**giraumon, juraumont**) [ʒirɔ̃mɔ̃, ʒirɑ̃mɔ̃, ʒirɔ̃mɑ̃, ʒirmɔ̃, ʒyrɔ̃mɔ̃] *n.m.* pumpkin ◊ **•giraumont patate / patate juraumont** yellow-fleshed sweet potato <VM, Lv88> <***Loc:*** AC, JE, SL, SM, VM, Da84, Gu00, Hi02, Lv88>

GIRLFRIEND [gəɹlfɹend] *n.f.* girlfriend, sweetheart <***Loc:*** Da84>

girofle [ʒirɔv(l), ʒirɔp, ʒirɔk] *n.m.* clove ◊ **•clou de girofle** whole clove <VM, Da84> <***Loc:*** VM, Da84>

giroflier [ʒiroflije] *n.m.* clove tree <***Loc:*** Da84>

girouette [ʒirwet, ʒirut] *n.f.* **1** weathervane **2** unreliable person <***Loc:*** EV, SM>

glaçant, -e [glasɑ̃, -ɑ̃t] *adj.* freezing, icy *Un temps glaçant.* Freezing weather. (EV) <***Loc:*** EV, Da84>

glace [glas] *n.f.* ice <***Loc:*** LA, Da84, Hi02>

glacé, -e [glase] *adj.* **1** frozen *Un canard tué, plumé et glacé.* A duck killed, plucked and frozen. (Lv88) **2** icy, cold as ice *Faulait je mets ma main par-dessus la sienne, c'était glacée comme tout. Je dis "Claude, t'es malade." Il dit "Je me sens pas bien."* I had to put my hand over his, it was cold as ice. I said, "Claude, you're sick." He said, "I don't feel well." (TB) *Eau glacée.* Cold water. (LF) *L'eau quède, ni chaud ni glacé.* Lukewarm water, neither hot nor cold. (JE) **3** glazed, having a smooth finish *Il avait travaillé assez sur la table qu'elle était glacée.* He had worked so hard on the table that it was glazed. (LA) <***Loc:*** JE, LA, LF, TB, VM, Da84, La99>

glacer [glase] **I** *v.tr.* **1** to freeze *Eux-autres là-bas a des grosses glacières. Ça les glace pas solides, mais ça les met assez froids qu'eusse peut les garder deux trois jours.* Over there they have big refrigerators. They don't freeze them solid, but they get them cold enough that they can keep them two or three days. (TB) **2** to ice, put on ice *Oui, on glaçait notre chevrette et tout.* Yes, we iced our own shrimp and everything. (TB) **II** *v.intr.* to freeze *Des fois la pompe glaçait, fallait l'envelopper.* Sometimes the pump froze, you had to wrap it up. (Lv88) <***Loc:*** AC, LF, TB, Lv88>

glacière [glasjær] *n.f.* **1** refrigerator **2** ice box **3** freezer **4** ice house <***Loc:*** JE, LA, SL, TB, VM, Da84, Gu00, Lv88>

glaie [glɛ, gle] *n.m./f.* wild iris, Louisiana iris <***Loc:*** VM, Gu00, Hi02>

glaine [glɛ̃n] *n.f.* stubble and grass in a field after harvesting, on which livestock is turned out to graze <***Loc:*** VM>

glainer [glɛ̃ne] *v.intr.* to glean, gather what is left by reapers *Les bêtes sont après glainer dans le clos.* The cows are gleaning in the [freshly harvested] field. (VM) <***Loc:*** VM>

glaire [glær] *n.f.* **1** glair, egg white **2** phlegm **3** any thick viscous substance resembling egg white <***Loc:*** Da84>

glaive [glɛv] *n.m.* sword <***Loc:*** Da84>

gland [glɑ̃, glɑ̃n] *n.m.* **1** acorn **2** tassel **3** lash (thong at the end of a whip) ◊ **•gland au bout d'un bâton** person with a long neck and a small face <SM> <***Loc:*** SL, SM, VM, Da84>

glande [glɑ̃, glɑ̃n, glɑ̃d] *n.f.* **1** gland, organ **2** packing gland, stuffing box (on a boat) <***Loc:*** LF, TB, VM, Da84>

glissade [glisad] *n.f.* sliding, slipping, slide <***Loc:*** Da84>

glissant, -e [glisɑ̃ - ɑ̃t] *adj.* slippery *Fais attention! L'écore est glissant.* Be careful! The bank [of the river] is slippery. (VM) <***Loc:*** VM, Da84>

glisser [glise] **I** *v.tr.* to slide, slip *Tu pouvais glisser ça et là tu pouvais coucher là le soir.* You could slide that over and then you could sleep there in the evening. (LF) **II** *v.intr.* to slide, slip *Il voyait que ce char glissait sur les gravailles et qu'il allait d'un bord du chemin à l'autre.* He saw that that car was sliding on the gravel and that it was going from one side of the road to the other. (ThCa: *La fête à Clomaire*) **III se glisser** *v.pron.* to slip into quietly *Il s'a glissé dans le bayou pour pas faire peur aux poissons.* He slipped into the bayou to not scare the fish. (VM) ◊ **•se glisser entre** to get between (people) *Il a essayé de se glisser entre moi et ma belle.* He tried to get between me and my girlfriend. (VM) <VM> <***Loc:*** LF, VM, Da84, ThCa>

globe [glob, glɔb] *n.m.* **1** globe, mantle (of a lantern, a lamp) **2** light bulb ◊ **•globe électrique / globe de lampe** light bulb <Da84> <***Loc:*** IB, LF, SM, TB, VM, Da84, Lv88>

gloire [glwar] *n.f.* **1** glory, fame **2** pride, self-respect *Le monde se sentait comme si qu'eux-autres devrait avoir honte d'eux-autres si eux-autres était Cadiens. Ça fait t'as perdu plein de la gloire d'être Cadien.* People felt like they should be ashamed of themselves if they were Cajun. So you lost a lot of the pride of being Cajun. (TB) **3** source of pride, pleasure or satisfaction *C'était une gloire d'avoir des lumières et l'estricité, tu halais sur la ficelle et la lumière venait dessus.* It was a source of pride to have lights and electricity, you pulled on the string and the light came on. (TB) **4** vainglory, vanity, haughtiness ◊ **•gloire d'Asie** mimosa tree <VM> **•gloire du matin** morning glory vine <VM> <***Loc:*** TB, VM, Da84, Lv88>

glorieuseté [glorjøzte] *n.f.* pride, arrogance, vanity <***Loc:*** VM, Lv88>

glorieux, -euse [glorjø, -øz] *adj.* **1** glorious *Les mystères glorieux.* The glorious mysteries. (VM) **2** proud, vain **C'était un homme, tu connais, qui était glorieux, il voulait se faire accroire mieux que les autres.* He was a man who was very vain, he wanted people to think he was better than everyone else. (SL, An94) <***Loc:*** EV, SL, SM, VM, An94, Da84, Lv88>

glorification [glorifikasjɔ̃] *n.f.* glorification <***Loc:*** Da84>

glorifier [glorifje] *v.tr.* to glorify, honor *Jésus a été glorifié.* Jesus was glorified. (VM) <***Loc:*** VM, Da84>

glou-glou [gluglu] *n.m.* gurgling, bubbling <***Loc:*** Da84>

glue [gly] *n.f.* **1** glue **2** jelly **3** jellyfish ◊ **•glue-qui-brûle** stinging jellyfish <JE> <***Loc:*** JE>

glycine [glisin] *n.f.* wisteria <***Loc:*** CL>

gningnin (**yinyin**) [ɲɛ̃jɛ̃, jɛ̃jɛ̃] *adj.* **1** thin and weak **2** complaining, whining *Ces petits garçons sont assez gningnins.* Those little boys are pretty whiny. (VM) **3** prissy *Elle est gningnin.* She is prissy. (SM) **4** sluggish, slow-moving <***Loc:*** LA, LF, SL, SM, VM>

gnognotte (**yoyotte**) [ɲɔ̃jɔt, jɔ̃jɔt, jojɔt] *n.f.* hogwash, foolishness, nonsense *Je vais pas au meeting. C'est tout de la gnognotte, ça.* I'm not going to the meeting. It's all foolishness. (SM) *Ne croyez pas ça, c'est tout de la yoyotte.* Don't believe that, it's all nonsense. (SB) <***Loc:*** LF, SB, SM, Da84>

gnole [ɲɔl] *n.f.* yawl, small boat <***Loc:*** VM>

go [go] ◊ **•être dessus le mot de go** to be ready and eager to go someplace <EV> <***Loc:*** EV, Da84>

GO AHEAD (**GO HEAD**) [goɛd, gohɛd] *v.intr.invar.* **1** [*imperative*] go ahead **Si tu te sens comme ça,* GO AHEAD. If you feel that way, go ahead. (LA, An94) **2** to continue *On a pas reviré à notre maison, on a* GO HEAD *aller aux courses.* We didn't turn back toward our house. We continued on to the races. (EV) <***Loc:*** EV, LA, VM, An94, Lv88>

GO HEAD ♦see **GO AHEAD**

gobe [gɔb] *n.f.* **1** chunk or slab of wood or stone, esp. the first cut from a log (i.e. soft outer wood plus bark) **2** piece, chunk, slab (esp. one cut or broken off a larger piece) *Une gobe de boue.* A chunk of mud. (VM) *Il s'est ôté une gobe dessus son doigt avec le couteau.* He cut a chunk out of his finger with the knife. (Lv88) **3** mouthful *Il a pris une grosse gobe de riz.* He took a big mouthful of rice. (VM) <***Loc:*** EV, SM, VM, Da84, Lv88>

gobelet [goblɛ, goble] *n.m.* **1** cup, mug, drinking glass, goblet **2** drinking glass with a stem **3** vase <***Loc:*** AC, AV, EV, IV, JD, LA, LF, SB, SL, SM, TB, VM, Da84, Gu00, Hi02, Lv88>

gober [gobe] *v.tr.* **1** to gulp, gulp down, gobble *Le chien a gobé son manger.* The dog gulped down its food. (EV) **2** to hack, remove a piece (from s.t.) *Il faisait attention, mais il a gobé la planche assez mauvais qu'il pouvait p'us l'user.* He was being careful but he hacked such a big chunk out of the board that he could no longer use it. (LA) <***Loc:*** EV, LA, VM, Da84>

gobet [gobɛ, gobe] *n.m.* chunk, big mouthful <***Loc:*** Da84>

goder [gode] *v.tr.* **1** to crease, make a crease in (a garment) **2** to pleat, make tucks in (a garment) *Goder un corsage.* To make tucks in a bodice. (EV) <***Loc:*** EV, Da84>

godet [godɛ, gode] *n.m.* pleat, tuck, dart ◊ **•faire un godet** to make a pleat or tuck *Elle a fait un godet dans sa robe pour la raccourcir.* She put a tuck in her dress to shorten it. (SM) <SM, Da84> <***Loc:*** SM, VM, Da84>

godron ♦see **goudron**

godronner ♦see **goudronner**

godronner ♦see **goudronner**

goéland [gwalɑ̃] *n.m.* **1** seagull **2** tadpole <***Loc:*** JE, VM>

goélette [gwalɛt] *n.f.* fishing boat with a rounded hull <***Loc:*** Lv88>

gogo (**go-go**) [gogo] *n.m.* rear end, butt <***Loc:*** SM, VM, Da84, Lv88>

go-go ♦see **gogo**

gogue [gog, gɔg] *n.f.* stuffed pig stomach <***Loc:*** AV>

goitre [gwat(r)] *n.f.* **1** goiter **2** gout <***Loc:*** SJ, SM, VM, Da84, Fa77, Lv88>

golf [gɔlf] *n.m.* golf <***Loc:*** Da84>

golfe (**gulf**) [gɔlf] *n.m.* **1** gulf **2** Gulf (of Mexico) **•Golfe du Mexique** Gulf of Mexico <TB> <***Loc:*** TB, Da84>

gombo (**gumbo**) [gɔ̃bo, gɑ̃bo] *n.m.* **1** okra *J'ai étouffé une pleine chaudiérée de gombos hier.* I smothered a big pot of okra yesterday. (VM) *Si tu fais un gombo avec des gombos, c'est un gombo févi.* If you make a gumbo with okra, it's a "gumbo févi." (LF) **2** gumbo, soup-like dish made with meat, seafood, or both and with or without okra, served over rice *Ma grand-mère mettait pas de roux dans son gombo. Elle l'épaississait avec du filé.* My grandmother didn't make her gumbo with a roux. She thickened it with filé. (VM) **3** gumbo dinner, dinner featuring gumbo *Vous venez nous rejoindre […] au gumbo ce soir.* You all come join us at the gumbo dinner tonight. (ch: *La danse de Mardi Gras*) **4** gumbo, fine silty soil that forms an unusually sticky mud **5** Louisiana creole language **6** mixture of disparate things, hodgepodge *Oui, la Louisiane c'est un vrai gombo. Y a des Italiens, des Français, des Espagnes, des Allemands, c'est tout du monde qui vient de différents de nationales, mais ils parlont tout le même français.* Yes, Louisiana is a real gumbo. There are Italians, French, Spanish, Germans, they're all people who come from different nationalities, but they all speak the same French. (LF) ◊ **•gombo de fruit de mer** seafood gumbo <SL> **•gombo de jardin** okra <LF> **•gombo de poule {volaille}** chicken gumbo <LF, TB> **•gombo févi *a*** okra (pod and plant) *En Ville ils étouffont pas leur gombo févi avant de le mettre dans leur gombo.* In New Orleans, they don't smother their okra before putting it in their gumbo (Gu00) ***b*** okra gumbo <AV, CL, EV, JE, LA, LF, SL, SM, TB, VM, Da84, Gu00, Hi02> **•gombo filé *a*** okra ***b*** cooked okra ***c*** filé gumbo (i.e. gumbo thickened with filé powder instead of with okra) <IB, LF, PQ, SM, VM, Da84, Lv88> **•gombo z'herbes** gumbo made with greens and cured meat <Lv88> <***Loc:*** AV, CL, EV, IB, IV, JE, LA, LF, PQ, SJ, SL, SM, TB, VM, Da84, Gu00, Hi02, Lv88>

gomme [gɔ̃m] *n.f.* **1** gum, chewing gum *Ils ont chiqué de la gomme jusqu'à ils ont fait une grosse pelote.* They chewed gum until they made a big ball. (EV) **2** rubber ◊ **•gomme de mer** sea gum, black asphaltic lumps found along the beaches of the Louisiana Gulf coast <VM> **•fais-toi pas une gomme avec ça** don't get your hopes up on that, don't rely on this happening <La99> <***Loc:*** EV, IV, VM, Da84, La99, Lv88>

gomme arabique [gɔ̃marabik] *n.f.* gum arabic <***Loc:*** Da84>

gommeux, -euse [gɔ̃mø, -øz] *adj.* **1** sticky, gummy *J'ai échappé du sucre sur le plancher et asteur c'est tout gommeux.* I dropped sugar on the floor and now it's all gummy. (LA) **2** awkward, clumsy and lazy *Il est assez gommeux, il marche dessus ses cordes à souliers.* He is so awkward and lazy that he steps on his shoelaces. (EV) <***Loc:*** EV, LA, La99>

GONE[1] [gɔ̃n] *v.intr.invar.* to leave, go *Il a GONE pour un mois.* He left for a month. (Lv88) *Il va pas GONE, il va juste rester.* He is not going to leave, he is going to stay. (SM) *Good-bye, j'après GONE.* Good-bye, I'm leaving. (SM) *On était GONE là-bas en ville.* We had gone to town. (SL) <***Loc:*** AC, EV, SL, SM, VM, Guoo, Lv88>

GONE[2] [gɔ̃n] *adj.* gone, away, absent *Nous-autres on a resté la maison drette en haut de D., la maison est GONE asteur.* We lived in a house right up from D., the house is gone now. (TB) <***Loc:*** JE, SL, TB, Hi02>

gonelle [gɔ̃nel] *n.f.* side of a flat-bottomed boat <***Loc:*** SM>

gonflage [gɔ̃flaʒ] *n.m.* inflation, swelling <***Loc:*** Da84>

gonfle [gɔ̃f(l)] *adj.* **1** swollen, puffy *Mon pied est gonfle aujourd'hui.* My foot is swollen today. (Lv88) *Tes yeux sont tout gonfles.* Your eyes are all swollen. (SM) *Son pied a venu gonfle.* His foot got swollen. (VM) **2** full *Le bayou est gonfle.* The bayou is full, swollen. (SM) *Le sac est gonfle.* The bag is full. (VM) **3** full (after eating) *Je suis gonfle.* I'm full. (LF) <***Loc:*** LA, LF, SM, VM, Lv88>

gonflé, -e [gɔ̃fle] *adj.* swollen, puffy *Son nez est toujours gonflé depuis son opération.* His nose is still swollen since his operation. (LA) <***Loc:*** LA, Da84>

gonfleau [gɔ̃flo] *n.m.* **1** fritter, doughnut **2** biscuit <***Loc:*** SM, Lv88>

gonfler [gɔ̃fle] **I** *v.tr.* to swell, inflate *J'ai besoin de gonfler mes TIRES.* I need to inflate my tires. (LA) **II** *v.intr.* to swell, inflate *Il a mouillé assez que le bois a gonflé.* It rained so much that the wood swelled up. (TB) **O, avant trente jours, mais ces chères grosses baleines et les porpoises et toute qualité de poissons, ça battait. Et ils ont gonflé dessus l'eau, et puis ça faisait signe avec leurs queues comme ça.* Oh, before 30 days, but those big old whales and the porpoises and all the other kinds of fish were flapping [i.e. beating their tails on the water]. And they would swell up on the water and they would wave their tails like this. (EV, An94) **III se gonfler** *v.pron.* to swell up, puff o.s. up **Il s'est gonflé et il s'est gonflé, et elle a dit, "Gros comme ça?"* He [the frog] puffed himself up and puffed himself up and she [his mother] said "As big as that?" (LA, An94) <***Loc:*** EV, LA, TB, An94, Da84>

gonflure [gɔ̃flyr] *n.m./f.* swelling <***Loc:*** SM, Da84, Lv88>

goret [gorɛ, gore] *n.m.* piglet *Le chien a étripé le goret.* The dog tore the piglet to pieces. (VM) <***Loc:*** VM>

gorge [gɔrʒ] *n.f.* throat ◊ **•grosse-gorge** goiter <VM> <***Loc:*** AL, SM, VM, Da84>

gorgée [gɔrʒe] *n.f.* mouthful, swallow, sip <***Loc:*** Da84>

gorgoyo [gɔrgojo] *n.m.* **1** tadpole, pollywog **2** pot-bellied person **3** little boy <***Loc:*** AV, VM, Da84, Guoo, Hi02, La99, Lv88>

gosier [gozje] *n.m.* throat (usu. of an animal) ◊ **•grand gosier** pelican <Lv88, Wh83> <***Loc:*** Da84, Lv88, Wh83>

gosse [gɔs, gos] *n.m./f.* hull, husk, shell, boll ◊ **•gosse d'ail** clove of garlic <VM, Da84> **•gosse de coton** cotton boll <VM, Da84> **•gosse de pacane** outer hull of pecan nut <VM> <***Loc:*** VM, Da84, Lv88>

gotter [gote] **I** *v.tr.* to choke, apply the choke of (a carburetor) *Il a gotté le tarière de la charette de riz.* He choked the auger of the rice cart. (VM) **II se gotter** *v.pron.* to choke, clog *Quand je travaillais dans la récolte de riz, il fallait tout le temps qu'on faise attention de pas laisser le tarière de la charrette se gotter.* When I harvested the rice, we had to be careful not to let the auger of the cart clog up. (Guoo) <***Loc:*** VM, Guoo>

goudron (godron) [gudrɔ̃, godrɔ̃] *n.m.* **1** tar, coaltar **2** glue **3** any sticky or syrupy material <***Loc:*** LF, VM, Da84>

goudronner (godronner) [gudrɔ̃ne, godrɔ̃ne] *v.tr.* **1** to smear with tar or glue *Il a goudronné la câle de son bateau.* He tarred the hull of his boat. (VM) **2** to pave with asphalt or tar *Ils ont goudronné le chemin devant ma maison.* They put asphalt down on the road in front of my house. (EV) **3** to dirty, soil *Il a revenu tout godronné avec la peinture.* He came back all soiled with paint. (Lv88) **4** to mess up *Il a tout goudronné l'affaire.* He messed up the whole thing. (EV) **II se goudronner** *v.pron.* to smear o.s. with glue, tar, or a similar substance *Quand les moustiques sont mauvais, les bêtes se godronnent dans la terre grasse.* When the mosquitoes are bad, cows smear themselves with wet clay. (VM) <***Loc:*** AV, EV, VM, Da84, La99, Lv88>

gouère[1] [gwær] *adj.* **1** light-colored (of the eyes or complexion) *Des yeux gouères.* Light-colored eyes. (SM, Lv88) **2** very pale blond *J'ai un cousin qui s'a marié avec une Américaine. Tu parles d'une femme qu'est gouère!* I have a cousin who married an American (non-Cajun) woman. Talk about a woman who is pale blonde! (Guoo) <***Loc:*** SM, VM, Guoo, Lv88>

gouère[2] [gwær] *n.* person of weak character <***Loc:*** Lv88>

goujon [guʒɔ̃] *n.m.* **1** flathead catfish (also called yellow catfish, mud catfish) *Un goujon c'est une autre barbue ça.* A mud catfish is another kind of catfish. (TB) **2** bullhead catfish ◊ **•goujon caille** flathead catfish (also called yellow catfish, mud catfish) <AL, EV, Da84, Guoo, Lv88> **•goujon jaune** flathead catfish (also called yellow catfish, mud catfish) <Da84> <***Loc:*** AL, EV, IV, LF, SL, SM, TB, VM, Da84, Guoo, Hi02, Lv88>

goulipiat [gulipja, gulypja] *n.m.* glutton, greedy person, heavy eater <*Loc:* SM, VM, Lv88>

gourde [gurd] *n.f.* dollar coin <*Loc:* SM, Da84, Lv88>

gourgousser [gurguse] *v.intr.* to make throaty noises, growl, mutter *Arrête de gourgousser et parle franc.* Stop muttering and speak clearly. (VM) <*Loc:* VM>

gourmand, -e [gurmɑ̃, -ɑ̃d] *adj.* greedy, gluttonous ◊ **•gourmand comme un chien {cochon}** very greedy <La99> <*Loc:* SL, VM, Da84, La99>

gourmandise [gurmɑ̃diz] *n.f.* gluttony <*Loc:* Da84>

gourme [gurm] *n.* strangles (equine respiratory congestion or infection) <*Loc:* Da84>

gourmer[1] [gurme] *v.intr.* to fawn (over), play up (to) *Ga'-les gourmer après cet homme.* Look at them play up to that man. (VM) <*Loc:* VM>

gourmer[2] **(se)** [gurme] *v.pron.* to get puffed up with anger *Il s'a gourmé comme un ouaouaron quand il a entendu la nouvelle.* He puffed up like a bullfrog when he heard the news. (EV) <*Loc:* AC, EV, La99>

gourmet [gurmɛ, gurme] *n.m.* gourmet <*Loc:* Da84>

gourmette [gurmɛt] *n.f.* curb or restraint for a horse (part of a bridle) <*Loc:* Da84>

gournoter [gurnote] *v.intr.* to waste time, loaf on the job *Arrête de gournoter et fais quelque chose.* Quit wasting time and do something. (SM) <*Loc:* SM>

gournouille ♦see **grenouille**

goût [gu] *n.m.* taste, flavor ◊ **•avoir goût de** to taste like *Le poisson a goût de pétrole maintenant.* The fish tastes like oil now. (Lv88) <Lv88> **•bon goût** good taste <Da84> **•mauvais goût** bad taste <Da84> <*Loc:* Da84, Lv88>

goûtable [gutab(l)] *adj.* delicious, delightful, pleasing *Ça c'est goûtable.* That's delicious. (VM) <*Loc:* VM>

goûtée [gute] *n.f.* little bit, taste **Donne-moi une goûtée.* Give me a taste. (Da84) <*Loc:* Da84>

goûter[1] [gute] **I** *v.tr.* to taste **Ça aimait les navets, ce monde-là, et particulièrement quand ils étiont en cornichons avec du vinaigre. Et lui, il avait jamais goûté ça.* They liked turnips, those people, and particularly when they were in pickles with vinegar. And he had never tasted that. (EV, An94) **II** *v.intr.* **1** to taste **Ça goûte bon.* It tastes good. (Da84) **2** to taste of, have the flavor of *Le poisson goûte l'huile asteur.* The fish tastes like oil now. (Lv88) <*Loc:* EV, An94, Da84, Lv88>

goûter[2] [gute] *n.f.* snack *Quand on arrivait de l'école, Grand-maman Claire nous espérait à la porte avec des patates chaudes dans sa poche de tablier. C'était notre goûter.* When we arrived home from school, Grandma Claire was waiting for us at the door with hot sweet potatoes in her apron pocket. That was our snack. (VM) <*Loc:* VM, Da84>

goutte [gut] *n.f.* **1** drop **Puis alors, elle a lancé un couteau après le chien, puis ça lui a coupé le nez et il a saigné quelques gouttes de sang.* So then, she threw a knife at the dog, and it cut his nose and he bled several drops of blood. (VM, An94) **2** small amount ◊ **•goutte de café** sip of coffee *Donne-moi une petite goutte de café.* Give me a small amount of coffee (i.e. just a taste). (LA) <LA, Da84> <*Loc:* LA, VM, An94, Da84, Hi02>

gouttière [gutjær] *n.f.* **1** drip, leak *Attrape un bassin pour mettre où la gouttière est.* Get a bucket to put where the leak is. (VM) **2** gutter *On avait des barils avec des gouttières en dedans* We had barrels with gutters that went inside (IB) **3** eaves (of a building) <*Loc:* IB, SM, VM, Da84>

gouvernable [guværnab(l)] *adj.* **1** governable, controllable *Leurs enfants sont pas gouvernables. Ils devraient bien les laisser à la maison.* Their children are not controllable. They really ought to leave them at home. (LA) **2** docile *Il s'a marié avec une femme qu'est pas gouvernable du tout.* He married a women who is not at all docile. (LA) <*Loc:* LA, Da84>

gouvernail [guværnaj, guvɛ̃naj] *n.m.* rudder <*Loc:* JE, LF, Da84>

gouvernement [guværnəmɑ̃, guvɑ̃nmɑ̃, guværmɑ̃] *n.m.* **1** government **2** management ◊ **•gouvernement fédéral** federal government <TB> <*Loc:* JE, SL, TB, Da84>

gouverner [guværne] *v.tr.* **1** to govern, rule *Edwards a gouverné la Louisiane pour des années et années.* Edwards governed Louisiana for years and years. (LA) **2** to steer, guide *Ça c'était pour le gouverner, pour le tiendre, pour qu'il va droite parce que avec une voile, s'il était pas tout à fait à le centre du vent ça pourrait te pousser soit d'un bord ou de l'autre.* That [the rudder] was to steer you, to hold it [the boat] so it would go straight, because with a sail, if it wasn't lined up with the wind it could push you to one side or the other. (LF) **3** to control *Le pauvre maître d'école pouvait pas seulement gouverner sa classe.* The poor school teacher could not even control his class. (LA) <*Loc:* LA, LF, Da84>

gouverneur, -euse [guværnœr, -øz] *n.* governor *La gouverneuse a déclaré officiellement qu'on avait été nommé à la commission.* The governor declared officially that we had been named to the commission. (VM) <*Loc:* VM, Da84>

grabat [graba] *n.m.* ◊ **•être au grabat** to be at death's door <*Loc:* VM>

grabon [grabɔ̃] *n.m.* barnacle <*Loc:* LF, Hi02>

grabot [grabo] *n.m.* **1** boll (of cotton) *Le grabot de coton est fermé au printemps, mais s'ouvre en été.* The cotton boll is closed in the spring, but opens up in the summer. (SM) **2** outer hull of pecan **3** [*pej.*] mouth *Si tu veux que quelqu'un répète un secret, tu dis: "Ferme ton grabot."* If you want someone to reveal a secret, you say "Shut your trap." (Guoo) *Son grabot arrête jamais.* He never shuts up. (Lv88) <*Loc:* SM, VM, Da84, Guoo, Hi02, La99, Lv88>

grabotage [grabotaʒ] *n.m.* harvesting of the last cotton (by women and children) <*Loc:* Lv88>

graboter [grabote] **I** *v.tr.* to pick unopened bolls of cotton that remain after the harvest *T'as fini de graboter ce rang-là?* Have you finished picking the bolls on that row? (VM) **II** *v.intr.* to try to eke out an existence on poor land *Ce pauvre monde était rendu à graboter pour leur vie.* Those poor people were eking out a meager living. (LA) <***Loc:*** LA, VM, Da84, Lv88>

graboterie [grabotri] *n.f.* last cotton left in the fields and on plants after the harvest <***Loc:*** SL>

grâce [gras] *n.f.* **1** favor **2** gracefulness, charm **3** grace (of God) ◊ **•grâce à** thanks to *Grâce à la terre que ma grand-mère nous a laissée, on a de l'argent d'huile qui rentre tous les mois.* Thanks to the land that my grandmother left us, we have oil money coming in monthly. (VM) <VM> **•grâce à Dieu** thank God <Da84> **•grâce sanctifiante** sanctifying grace <Da84> **•en grâce** nicely, politely *Je t'ai demandé en grâce pour mettre des anneaux. Tu les as pas mis. Et j'ai dit ils sont après fouiller mon clos.* I asked you nicely to put rings [in your pigs' snouts]. You didn't put them in. And I said they are digging up my field. (SL) <SL> **•faire une belle grâce (à qqn)** to do a good turn or a favor (for s.o.) <La99> <***Loc:*** VM, Da84, La99>

gradation [gradasjɔ̃] *n.f.* gradation, grading <***Loc:*** Da84>

grade [grad] *n.m.* **1** grade (in school) *Mon petit garçon est dans le cinquième grade.* My little boy is in the fifth grade. (Lv88) **2** grade, mark (in a class) *Il a fait un bon grade.* He got a good grade. (Lv88) **3** kind, type *Il y avait différents grades d'Arabes, ceux qui restaient dans les montagnes, ceux qui restaient dans les maisons, mais c'était pauvre, pauvre.* There were different kinds of Arabs, those that lived in the mountains, those that lived in houses, but they were very poor. (VM) **4** grade, rank, degree *Il y a différents grades de patates.* There are different grades of sweet potatoes. (EV) <***Loc:*** EV, TB, VM, Da84, Lv88>

graduation [gradyasjɔ̃] *n.f.* graduation ceremony, commencement exercises *Elle a invité toute la famille pour la graduation à Nancy.* She invited the whole family to Nancy's graduation. (Lv88) <***Loc:*** SM, VM, Da84, Hi02, Lv88>

gradué, -e [gradɥe] *n.* graduate <***Loc:*** Da84, Lv88>

graduer [gradɥe] *v.intr.* to graduate *J'aimais pas l'école, et là mon père me dit, "Il faut que tu gradues," parce que lui avait jamais eu la chance d'aller à l'école.* I didn't like school, and then my father told me, "You have to graduate," because he had never had the chance to go to school. (LF) *J'ai gradué de là, j'ai été à SLI, j'ai été à LSU.* I graduated from there, I went to SLI and LSU. (IB) <***Loc:*** IB, LF, SL, Da84, Hi02, Lv88>

graffigner ♦see **grafigner**

graffignure ♦see **grafignure**

grafigner (**graffigner, égrafigner**) [grafĩje, grafije, egrafĩje, egratĩje] **I** *v.tr.* **1** to scratch *Le chat m'a grafigné.* The cat scratched me. (SM) *Les branches ont tout égrafigné son nouveau char.* The branches scratched up his new car. (LA) *Il coupe les quatre pattes de la tortue pour pas ça nous grafigne.* He cuts all four claws of the turtle so that it won't scratch us. (Lv88) **2** to scrawl, scribble *Il a grafigné ça, je peux pas le lire.* He scrawled that, I can't read it. (VM) **II se grafigner** *v.pron.* to scratch o.s. (on thorns, etc.) *Je m'ai grafigné mauvais dans les éronces.* I scratched myself badly in the briars. (LA) <***Loc:*** AV, IB, JD, LA, SM, TB, VM, Da84, Hi02, Lv88, Re31>

grafignure (**graffignure, égrafignure**) [grafĩjyr, egrafĩjyr, egrafijyr] *n.f.* **1** scratch, scrape, slight wound *Il a une grafignure sur son doigt.* He has a scratch on his finger. (SM) **2** scribblings <***Loc:*** LF, SB, SM, TB, VM, Da84, Hi02, Lv88>

grain [grɛ̃] *n.m.* **1** grain, drop, small piece, particle **2** seed **3** grain, texture (of wood, marble, etc.) **4** cloud, rain cloud *Il semblait comme si qu'il avait du mauvais temps, il avait des grains sur la mer.* It seemed like there was bad weather, there were rain clouds on the sea. (LF) ◊ **•grain de beauté** dimple <VM> **•grain de maïs** kernel of corn <LF> **•grain de pluie** drop of rain <Da84> **•grain de sel** grain of salt <Da84> **•à gros grain** ***a*** barely, in name only *On est des Catholiques à gros grains.* We are Catholics in name only. (VM) ***b*** sparsely *Ça a mouillé à gros grain.* It rained sparsely. (VM) <VM, Da84> **•avoir un grain** to be in a contrary mood <SB, La99> <***Loc:*** LF, SB, VM, Da84, Hi02, La99, Lv88>

grainage [grɛ̃naʒ] *n.m./f.* **1** garden seeds (collectively) **Mais de la grainage ramassée pour planter devrait être ramassée quand la lune est après profiter.* But seeds collected for planting should be gathered when the moon is waxing. (Wh83) **2** balls of grain <***Loc:*** SM, VM, Da84, Lv88, Wh83>

grainasse (**grainassement**) [grɛ̃nas, grɛ̃nasmɑ̃] *n.f.* drizzle <***Loc:*** Lv88>

grainassement ♦see **grainasse**

grainasser [grɛ̃nase, grənase] *v.intr.* to drizzle *Il grainassait hier. C'est pour ça j'ai pas été déhors de la journée.* It was drizzling yesterday; that's why I didn't go out all day. (LA) <***Loc:*** AC, LA, SM, VM, Lv88>

graine [grɛ̃n] *n.f.* **1** seed **2** bean **3** *(pl.)* [*vulg.*] testicles *Quand t'allais arracher ses graines, là il était un capon.* When you removed his testicles, then he was a capon. (IB) ◊ **•graine à voler {vallée}** nelumbo, water chinquapins <VM, Da84, Lv88> **•graine de café** coffee bean <LF, SL> <***Loc:*** IB, LF, SL, TB, VM, Da84, La99, Lv88>

grainer[1] [grɛ̃ne] *v.tr.* to grind *Ça a grainé la viande hier.* They ground the meat yesterday. (LF) <***Loc:*** LF>

grainer[2] [grɛ̃ne] *v.intr.* to drizzle *La pluie graine.* The rain is drizzling. (SM) <***Loc:*** SM, Lv88>

grainette ♦see **rainette**

graissage [gresaʒ] *n.m.* **1** greasing, lubricating **2** fat, any fatty substance *Pour faire le savon, on ramassait des graissages, de la vieille graisse et des gratons, et tout ça qui était gras.* To make soap we'd collect fat, old grease and cracklings, anything that was fatty. (AC) <***Loc:*** AC, Da84>

graisse [gres, grɛs] *n.f.* **1** fat, lard **2** grease **3** oil **4** [*ironic*] greasy gravy *Du riz et de la graisse.* Rice and greasy gravy. (LA) ◊ **•graisse à charette** axle grease <Da84> **•graisse (de) cochon** hog lard for cooking <SL, SM, VM> **•graisse de mouton** mutton suet, tallow <Da84> **•graisse douce** lard for cooking <VM> <***Loc:*** LA, SL, SM, VM, Da84, Hi02>

graisser [grese] **I** *v.tr.* to grease, lubricate **Alors, il a ouvert la jarre de beurre et il a commencé à graisser les crevasses dans un effort d'essayer de les guérir.* So he opened the jar of butter and he began to grease the cracks in an effort to heal them. (EV, An94) **II se graisser** *v.pron.* to grease o.s., apply grease *Il s'a graissé avec du suif de mouton.* He greased himself with sheep tallow. (VM) ◊ **•graisser la main {les poches}** to bribe *Les politiciens travaillent souvent en graissant la main.* Politicians often work on things by bribing. (LA) <LA, Da84, La99> **•graisser ses poches** to cheat <Da84> **•se graisser la patte** ***a*** to bribe ***b*** to accept a bribe *Elle était joliment honnête, mais lui, il avait pas peur de se graisser la patte, lui.* She was pretty honest, but, as for him, he wasn't afraid to accept a bribe. (LA) ***c*** to make a lot of money by questionable means *Je suis sûr qu'il s'avait graissé la patte. Il a jamais travaillé une journée dans sa vie.* I'm sure he made his money by questionable means. He never worked a day in his life. (LA) <LA, La99> <***Loc:*** EV, LA, VM, An94, Da84, Hi02, La99>

graler [grale] *v.tr.* **1** to pop (popcorn) *Viens chez nous-autres à ce soir, on va graler du tac-tac.* Come to our house tonight, we're going to pop some popcorn. (VM) **2** to parch *J'ai gralé des pacanes.* I parched some pecans. (SM) <***Loc:*** SM, VM, Da84>

grammaire [grɑ̃mær] *n.f.* grammar <***Loc:*** LF>

grand[1], **-e** [grɑ̃, -ɑ̃d] *adj.* **1** big, large **Ça allait habitation à habitation, et ça vendait des balais, des grandes affaires que le monde avait de besoin.* They went from farm to farm, and they sold brooms, big things that people needed. (EV, An94) **2** tall *Ma sœur est un tas un tas plus grand que moi.* My sister is a lot taller than me. (SM) *C'était rien que des chênes, c'était grand, c'était gros.* There was nothing but oaks, they were tall, they were big. (JE) **3** long **Elle avait des grands cheveux jaunes, et les yeux bleus.* She had long blond hair and blue eyes. (EV, An94) **4** wide **Et le trou était pas assez grand pour lui passer sa main.* And the hole was not wide enough for him to pass his hand. (EV, An94) **5** great **Laurent et Télismar, c'étaient des grands pêcheurs.* Laurent and Télismar were great fishermen. (EV, An94) **6** important *Il se croyait joliment grand dans la politique.* He thought himself really important in politics. (VM) **7** grown up, of the age of majority *Si je fais ça, je dis, il va venir me chanter des affaires, trouver, et me dire comment je me crois grand.* If I do that, I'm telling you, he will come and tell me stories, find, and tell me how I think I'm grown up. (EV) ◊ **•grande {grand'} rue** main street **Notre band était après jouer sur la grand'rue à Jack's Place.* Our band was playing on Main street at Jack's Place. (LA, An84) <LA, An84, Da84> **•trop grand pour ses culottes** too big for one's britches, arrogant **T'es après venir trop grand pour tes culottes.* You're being arrogant. (La99) <Da84, La99> **•pas grand** ***a*** not much *Il avait pas grand éducation.* He didn't have much education. (SL) *Je faisais pas grand argent.* I didn't make much money. (SL) ***b*** not many *C'est rare tu voyais un char passer. Dans ce temps-là y avait pas grands chars.* It was rare that you'd see a car go by. In those days there weren't many cars. (TB) <SL, TB> <***Loc:*** EV, JE, LA, LF, SL, SM, TB, VM, An94, Da84, Hi02, La99, Lv88>

grand[2], **-e** [grɑ̃, -ɑ̃d] *n.* adult *Dans le vieux temps, dans le temps de mon défunt pape, il y avait un mauvais* FLU, *et dans ce temps-là il y avait peut-être un docteur pour je sais pas combien de grands.* In the old days, in my father's time, there was a bad flu, and in those days there was maybe one doctor for I don't know how many adults. (TB) ◊ **•faire le {son} grand / faire la grande** to act important, show off, act as if one is more important than one really is **Joe est tout le temps après venir se vanter icitte... Il est après m'embarrasser à faire le grand.* Joe always comes here to brag, he is embarrassing me to show off like this (An84) <An84, Lv88> **•faire le grand pour ses culottes** to behave arrogantly <VM, La99> <***Loc:*** EV, JE, LF, SL, SM, TB, VM, An84, Da84, La99, Lv88>

grand[3] [grɑ̃] *adv.* wide **Tout à l'heure, il s'en vient un bougre en travers de la salle qui avait la chemise déboutonnée avec le jabot grand ouvert.* After a while, here comes a fellow across the dancehall with his shirt unbuttoned, with the chest widely bared. (SL, An94) ◊ **•grand debout** standing straight up *Il était grand debout en arrière de la salle.* He was standing straight up in back of the dancehall. (LA) <LA> <***Loc***: LA, SL, An94, Da84>

grand-écaille ♦see **grand-écalle**

grand-écalle (grand-écaille) [grɑ̃tekal, grɑ̃tekaj] *n.f.* tarpon <***Loc:*** TB, Da84>

grandement [grɑ̃nmɑ̃] *adj.* plentiful, in sufficient number *Les mulets étaient pas assez grandements, tu connais, dans ce temps-là. Il y avait pas assez de mulets.* Mules were not plentiful enough, you know, in those days. There were not enough mules. (EV) <***Loc:*** EV>

grandeur [grɑ̃dœr] *n.f.* **1** greatness, magnitude, size **2** height <***Loc:*** Da84>

grandîlier [grɑ̃tilje] *n.* inhabitant of Grand Isle <***Loc:*** JE>

grandir (grandzir) [grɑ̃dir, grɑ̃dzir] *v.intr.* **1** to grow *Le trou grandissait à mesure qu'il essayait de sortir.* The hole grew bigger as he tried to get out. (LA) **2** to grow up **Ça qui* *m'a amené au rock-and-roll, c'est que tous les Cadiens de mon âge aimaient ça quand on était après grandir.* What brought me to rock-and-roll is that all Cajuns my age liked that when we were growing up. (LA, An84) ◊ **•grandir comme un pied de chou** to grow up quickly <LF, La99> <***Loc:*** LA, LF, An84, Da84, La99, Lv88>

grand-maman [grɑ̃mɑ̃mɑ̃] *n.f.* grandmother <Da84>

grand-mère [grɑ̃mær] *n.f.* grandmother ◊ **•grand-grand-mère** great-grandmother <Hi02, Lv88> <***Loc:*** Da84, Hi02, Lv88>

grandpa [grɑ̃pa] *n.m.* grandpa <***Loc:*** LF>

grand-père [grɑ̃pær] *n.m.* grandfather ◊ **•grand-grand-père** great-grandfather <JE, Da84, Lv88> <***Loc:*** JE, LF, TB, Da84, Hi02, Lv88>

grands-parents [grɑ̃parɑ̃] *n.m.pl.* grandparents ◊ **•grands-grands-parents** great-grandparents <LF> <***Loc:*** LF, Da84>

grandzir ♦see **grandir**

granite [grɑ̃nit] *n.m.* granite <***Loc:*** Da84>

graphophone [grafofɔ̃n] *n.m.* record player <***Loc:*** SL>

grapigner ♦see **grappiller**

grapigneur ♦see **grappilleux**

grapilleur ♦see **grappilleux**

grapiner ♦see **grappiller**

grappe [grap] *n.f.* bunch, cluster *Une grosse grappe de fleurs blanches.* A big cluster of white flowers. (TB) ◊ **•grappe de raisin** bunch of grapes <Da84> **•être en grappe** to be headed (of rice) <VM> <***Loc:*** TB, VM, Da84, Hi02>

grappiller (**grapigner**, **grapiner**) [grapije, grapĩje, grapine] *v.tr.* to take, seize, steal *Il a grappillé le dernier morceau de tarte.* He seized the last piece of pie. (LA) <***Loc:*** LA, Lv88>

grappilleux, -euse (**grapilleur**, **-euse, grapigneur, -euse, grapigneux, -euse**) [grapijœr, grapĩjœr, grapĩjø, -øz] *adj.* **1** thieving *Fais attention avec tes affaires. Ils sont joliment grappilleux à l'entour d'ici.* Be careful of your things. They're prone to thievery around here. (LA) **2** biting, sarcastic <***Loc:*** LA, SM, Lv88>

grappin [grapɛ̃] *n.m.* grappling hook ◊ **•mettre le grappin (sur qqn)** to steal from someone <SB, La99> <***Loc:*** SB, La99>

gras[1]**, grasse** [gra, gras] *adj.* **1** fat **Il dit: "Comment ça se fait que t'es tout le temps, tout le temps gras et en bonne condition?"* He says, "Why are you always fat and in good condition?" (EV, An94) **2** greasy, fatty *Le rôti était gras.* The roast was fatty. (EV) *Pour faire le savon, on ramassait des graissages, de la vieille graisse et des grattons, et tout ça qui était gras.* To make soap we'd collect fat, old grease and cracklings, anything that was fatty. (AC) <***Loc:*** AC, AL, EV, An94, Da84, Hi02, La99>

gras[2] [gra] *n.m.* fat (on meat) *Et ça prendait les morceaux de gras et ça coupait ça dans des petits carreaux.* And they took the pieces of fat and cut them up in small squares. (LF) <***Loc:*** LF>

grassel [grasɛl, grase] *n.m.* chewink, towhee, ground robin <***Loc:*** Lv88>

gratification [gratifikasjɔ̃] *n.f.* gratification <***Loc:*** Da84>

gratin [gratɛ̃] *n.m.* partially burned piece of food ◊ **•gratin de riz** crispy, browned or burnt crust along the bottom of a pot of rice <Da84> <***Loc:*** Da84, Hi02>

gratis [gratis] *adv.* free, gratis, at no cost *Après l'ouragan, le gouvernement nous a donné du sucre et de la farine gratis.* After the hurricane, the government gave us sugar and flour for free. (VM) <***Loc:*** VM, Da84>

gratitude [gratityd] *n.f.* gratitude, gratefulness <***Loc:*** Da84>

graton [gratɔ̃] *n.m.* crackling (piece of fried pork rind with some fat attached) *On ôtait la graisse dessus pour faire du graton.* We took the fat off to make cracklings. (AC) *Léon, son mari, va te fondre des gratons qui vont te faire baver.* Leon, her husband, will fry cracklins that will make you drool. (VM) <***Loc:*** AC, SM, VM, Da84, Gu00, Hi02, Lv88>

grattage [grataʒ] *n.m.* scratching, scraping <***Loc:*** Da84>

gratte [grat] *n.f.* **1** scraper **2** rake **3** reprimand (such as a smack, beating or bawling out) *Je vas te foutre une gratte si tu fais pas ça je te dis.* I'm going to give you a smack if you don't do what I tell you. (SM) ◊ **•belle gratte** heck of a thing <Da84> <***Loc:*** SM, VM, Da84, Lv88>

grattelle [gratɛl, gratel] *n.f.* **1** itch, rash **2** scabies **3** chicken pox <***Loc:*** IB, SM, VM, Da84, Lv88>

gratter [grate] **I** *v.tr.* **1** to scratch *Ça fait sentir bien, tu sais... à peu près pareil comme gratter ton dos équand ça démange.* It feels good, you know . . . something like scratching your back when it itches. (VM) **2** to scrape *Il fallait tuer les cochons et les échauder, les gratter jusqu'à qu'ils étiont blancs, blancs, blancs.* You had to kill the pigs and scald them, then scrape them until they were very white. (AC) **3** to strike (a match) *Gratter une allumette.* To strike a match. (VM) **4** to strum, play (an instrument) *Les poulets grattent, en arrière, l'archet, ça gratte sur les cordes.* The chickens scratch, in the back, the bow scratches across the strings [on the fiddle]. (ch: *Bon rêve*) **II** *v.intr.* **1** to scratch **Il a commencé à gratter dessus une montagne, il a fait un VALLEY.* He started to scratch on a mountain, he made a valley. (An94) **2** to work hard, slog, slog away *Tout le monde arrêtait l'école quand t'avais envie. Et si tu voulais pas aller, mon pape m'a dit à moi il me dit si tu veux graduer dans le sixième livre, ben tu vas gratter asteur.* Everyone quit school when they felt like it. And if you didn't want to go, my father told me, he said if you want to graduate from sixth grade, well you're going to work now. (TB) **III se gratter** *v.pron.* to scratch o.s **Le chevreuil était après se gratter l'oreille avec la patte d'en arrière, et il lui a passé la balle dans l'oreille et dans la patte.* The deer was scratching his ear with his back hoof, and he shot the bullet into his ear and his hoof. (An94) *Le monde a commencé à se gratter et éternuer.* People began to scratch themselves and sneeze. (AV) ◊ **•gratter la gorge** to clear one's throat <SM> **•quoi tu grattes ici?** what are you doing here? <Da84> <***Loc:*** AC, AV, EV, SL, SM, TB, VM, An94, Da84, Hi02>

grattes [grat] *n.f.pl.* cultivator <***Loc:*** VM>

gratteur [gratœr] *n.m.* potato peeler <***Loc:*** LA>

gravail (**gravaille, gravel**) [gravaj, gravɛl] (*pl.* **gravails** [gravaj], **graveaux** [gravo]) *n.m.* gravel (including the shells used on roads in the south of Louisiana) *Il s'a obtenu du gravail pour son chemin de la paroisse.* He obtained some gravel for his road from the parish. (VM) *Tu peux pas aller bien vite dessus un chemin de gravails.* You can't go very fast on a gravel road. (VM) *Tu mêles le ciment et du sable et des graveaux ensemble, ça fait tu mets tout en dedans puis là ça tourne, ça mélange.* You mix cement, sand and gravel together, then you put everything inside, and then it turns and mixes together. (AC) <***Loc:*** AC, SM, VM, Da84, Gu00, Hi02, Lv88>

gravaille ♦see **gravail**

grave [grav] *adj.* grave, serious, important *Il a une maladie bien grave.* He has a really serious illness. (VM) <***Loc:*** VM, Da84>

gravel ♦see **gravail**

gravelle [gravɛl] *n.f.* **1** piece of gravel **2** calcified mass in the body, stone (e.g. gallstone, kidney stone) <***Loc:*** Da84>

gravement [gravmɑ̃] *adv.* gravely, seriously <***Loc:*** Da84>

graver [grave] **I** *v.tr.* **1** to engrave, imprint *Graver le nom dessus un tombeau.* To engrave the name on a tomb. (EV) **2** to record (a record) **II se graver** *v.pron.* to be engraved *Une chance il avait ce chien-là. Il lui a mordu la croix de sa carabine-là, ah ben mais les dents se sont gravées dedans.* Lucky he had that dog. He bit the stock of his rifle, and his teeth left a mark in it. (EV) <***Loc:*** EV, Da84>

gravité [gravite] *n.f.* **1** gravity (of earth) **2** seriousness, gravity <***Loc:*** Da84>

gravois [gravwa] *n.m.pl.* gravel *J'ai demandé à la paroisse de mettre des gravois sur mon petit chemin.* I asked the parish to put gravel on my little road. (Gu00) <***Loc:*** EV, TB, SM, Da84, Gu00, Hi02, Lv88>

gravure [gravyr] *n.f.* engraving <***Loc:*** Da84>

gré [gre] *n.m.* will, wish, inclination ◊ **•bon gré, mal gré** willy nilly <Da84> <***Loc:*** Da84>

gréage [greaʒ] *n.m.* equipping, equipment <***Loc:*** Da84>

grèbe [grɛb] *n.f.* grebe <***Loc:*** TB>

grec[1] (**grecque**) [grɛk] *adj.* Greek *Un village grec.* A Greek village. (EV) <***Loc:*** EV, Da84>

grec[2] [grɛk] *n.m.* Greek language <***Loc:*** Da84>

grecque ♦see **grec**

gréement (**agréyement**) [grẽmɑ̃, grejmɑ̃, agrẽmɑ̃] *n.m.* **1** furniture, accoutrements **2** clothes, clothing **3** equipment, collection of materials used for a specific task, occupation, etc. **4** mounting or putting together ◊ **•agréyement de noce** wedding garments and accessories <EV, Ph36> <***Loc:*** EV, VM, Lv88, Ph36>

gréer (**gréyer, agréyer, égreyer**) [greje, agreje, egreje] **I** *v.tr.* **1** to furnish, equip, stock *Ça coûte un tas pour gréyer une maison.* It costs a lot to furnish a house. (VM) *Gréyer une habitation. Gréyer un magasin.* Equip a farm. Stock a store. (VM) **2** to saddle, bridle *Gréyer un cheval.* To saddle a horse. (VM) **3** to dress, outfit completely *J'ai gréyé mes enfants pour l'hiver.* I dressed my children for winter. (SM) **II se gréer** *v.pron.* **1** to obtain clothes or material, equip o.s. *Elle s'a gréyé d'une nouvelle robe.* She obtained a new dress for herself. (VM) **2** to dress, put clothes on **Gréez-vous!* Put clothes on! (Di32) **3** to dress with great care, dress up *Alle s'est gréyée, puis alle a sorti.* She dressed up,then she went out. (Lv88) ◊ **•gréer un soldat** to equip a soldier (with military clothes and equipment) <Di32> **•dégréer Saint-Pierre pour gréer Saint-Paul** to rob Peter to pay Paul <La99, Lv88> <***Loc:*** AV, LA, SJ, SM, VM, Da84, Di32, La99, Lv88>

greffe[1] [grɛf] *n.f.* graft (made on a tree) <***Loc:*** Da84>

greffe[2] [grɛf] *n.m.* clerk of court's office, registry, office of records ◊ **•mettre au greffe** to file in the clerk of court books <Da84> <***Loc:*** Da84>

greffer [grefe] *v.tr.* to graft (plants) *Mon père a essayé de greffer le plaqueminier de sa sœur.* My father tried to graft his sister's persimmon tree. (LA) <***Loc:*** LA, Da84>

greffeur [grefœr] *n.m.* grafter (of plants) <***Loc:*** Da84>

greffier [grefje] *n.m.* clerk of court, recorder <***Loc:*** Da84>

grêgé ♦see **greget**

greget (**grêgé**) [grəʒɛ, grəʒe, greʒɛ, greʒe] *n.m.* ruffle (on clothing), band of cloth added to a dress or skirt to make it longer <***Loc:*** VM>

grègue [grɛg, greg] *n.f.* drip coffeepot, coffeemaker ◊ **•grègue à {de} café** coffeepot <LA, LF> <***Loc:*** AL, EV, JD, JE, LA, LF, SL, SM, TB, VM, Gu00, Hi02, Lv88>

gréguée [grege] *n.f.* potful (of coffee) <***Loc:*** TB>

grêle (**grile**) [grɛl, gril] *n.f.* hail <***Loc:*** AL, Da84>

grêler [grele, grile] *v.intr.* to hail *Il a grêlé cet après-midi. Mon char est tout cabossé.* It hailed this afternoon. My car is all dented up. (EV) <***Loc:*** EV, Da84>

grémil (**grimil**) [grẽmij, grimij] *n.m.* crumb <***Loc:*** SM, Lv88>

grémille (**grimille, égrimille**) [grẽmij, grimij, egrimij] *n.f.* **1** crumb **2** shard, small piece of broken glass or pottery <***Loc:*** VM, Da84, Lv88>

grémiller (**grimiller, égrémiller, égrimiller**) [grẽmije, grimije, egrẽmije, egrimije] **I** *v.tr.* **1** to crumble, break into bits *Faut bien brasser ton couche-couche pour le grémiller.* You have to mix your couche-couche well to crumble it. (Lv88) *Là, il faut tu égrémilles le chocolat presqu'en poudre, puis tu le* *mets dans le bol.* Then, you have to crumble the chocolate almost to a powder, then you put it in the bowl. (LA) **2** to shatter *Il a égrimillé la vitre du chassis.* He shattered the glass of the window. (VM) **II** *v.intr.* to crumble *Là tu mets ça dans le soleil, et là quand c'est chaud chaud là et que ça grémille, tu mets ça dans un moulin, tu moules tout ça.* Then you put that in the sun, and when it's quite hot and it crumbles, you put it in a grinder, you grind it all. (TB) <***Loc:*** EV, IB, JD, LA, SM, TB, VM, Da84, Lv88, Ph36>

grémilleux, -euse [grɛ̃mijø, -jøz] *adj.* **1** crumbly *Un gâteau grémilleux.* A crumbly cake. (VM) **2** pithy, mealy *Cette pomme est grémilleuse.* This apple is mealy. (LA) <***Loc:*** LA, VM, Lv88>

grémillon [grɛ̃mijɔ̃] *n.m.* small crumb *J'ai venu pour du gâteau, mais il y avait que des grémillons.* I came for some cake, but there were only crumbs. (VM) <***Loc:*** VM, Lv88>

grenade [grənad, garnad] *n.f.* **1** pomegranate *Avec les grenades qui levaient farouches dans les éronces, on faisait une limonade.* We made lemonade with the pomegranates growing wild in the brambles. (Lv88) **2** maypop (fruit of the passionflower) **3** grenade ◊ •**grenade à main** hand grenade <Da84> •**grenade française** pomegranate <VM, Lv88> <***Loc:*** SM, VM, Da84, Lv88>

grenadier [grənadje] *n.m.* pomegranate tree, grenadier <***Loc:*** Da84>

gréner ♦see **égrener**

grénier (**grenier, grinier**) [grɛ̃je, grĩje] *n.m.* **1** attic **2** ceiling **3** hay loft **4** garret, loft <***Loc:*** AV, EV, JE, LA, SL, TB, VM, Da84, Gu00, Hi02, Lv88>

grenier ♦see **grénier**

grenit [grɛ̃ni] *n.m.* enamel *J'ai monté la mèche trop haut en dessous de ma chaudière et ça a détamé le grenit.* I put the burner on too high under my pot and it damaged the enamel. (VM) <***Loc:*** TB, VM>

grenouille (**gournouille, guernouille, gueurnouille**) [grənuj, grunuj, gurnuj, gærnuj, gœrnuj] *n.f.* **1** any small green frog (e.g. leopard frog, tree frog) **2** [*vulg.*] female genitals ◊ •**grenouille de bénitier** a woman who volunteers often at chuch <La99> <***Loc:*** SM, TB, VM, Da84, Gu00, Hi02, La99>

grète-boat [grɛtbot] *n.m.* dredge boat <***Loc:*** VM >

grève [grɛv] *n.f.* oysterbed <***Loc:*** TB>

gréyer ♦see **gréer**

gréyeur [grejœr] *n.m.* leathersmith, one who works with leather <***Loc:*** VM>

gréyure [grejyr] *n.f.* equipment, goods *J'ai une bonne gréyure de cheval.* I have good equestrian equipment. (VM) <***Loc:*** VM, Lv88>

gribouille [gribuj] *n.m./f.* **1** simpleton, helpless or defenseless person **2** unpleasant person **3** person of small stature <***Loc:*** Da84, Lv88>

gricher[1] ♦see **grucher**

gricher[2] ♦see **regricher**

grichoux [griʃu] *adj.* ill-tempered, crabby *Espèce de vieux grichoux.* Damn old crabby fellow. (VM) <***Loc:*** VM, Lv88>

grief [grijɛf] *n.* ◊ •**faire grief** to cause sorrow, be painful *Ça fait grief d'hypthéquer sa place.* It's painful to mortgage one's home. (VM) <VM> <***Loc:*** VM>

griffe[1] [grif] *n.m./f.* **1** bird's claw, talon **2** hand, paw *Ote tes griffes dessus.* Get your hands off that. (VM) <***Loc:*** JE, VM, Da84>

griffe[2] [grif] *n.* quadroon, person of mixed race with one black grandparent <***Loc:*** Lv88>

griffer [grife] *v.tr.* **1** to claw, scratch *Le chat m'a griffé le nez.* The cat clawed me on the nose. (LA) **2** to seize with claws or talons *La cossarde a griffé le branchu à la vole.* The hawk seized the wood duck in flight. (VM) <***Loc:*** LA, VM, Da84>

griffien, -ienne (**griffon, -onne**) [grifjɛ̃, -jɛ̃n, grifɔ̃, -ɔ̃n] *n.* quadroon, person of mixed race with one black grandparent <***Loc:*** VM, Lv88>

griffon ♦see **griffien**

grignot ♦see **grillot**

grignotage [grĩjotaʒ] *n.m.* snacking, nibbling <***Loc:*** Da84>

grignote [grĩjɔt, grĩjot] *n.f.* crumb, bit, scrap <***Loc:*** VM, Lv88>

grignoter [grĩjote, grijote] *v.intr.* to nibble *Le patassa a juste grignoté après ma laiche.* The bluegill just nibbled on my worm. (VM) <***Loc:*** VM, Da84>

gri-gri ♦see **gris-gris**

gril [gri, gril] *n.m.* **1** cooking grill **2** grate, grid iron **3** floor for drying cotton <***Loc:*** VM, Da84>

grile ♦see **grêle**

grillade [grijad] *n.f.* **1** slice or cube of meat, often marinated, cut in small pieces for cooking **2** piece of torn flesh *Il s'a erlevé une grillade dans le fil de fer.* He tore off a piece of his own flesh in the wire. (VM) ◊ •**grillade à la chique {Chine}** stomach of an unweaned calf where milk is digested (locally called marigut), considered a delicacy by some <AC, VM> •**grillade amarinée / grillade à la marinée** ***a*** marinated pieces of boneless pork *Les autres fois on coupait les grillades de viande de cochon à peu près grand comme la main pour les amariner. C'était une autre manière de conserver de la viande avant qu'on ait des glacières.* In the past we would cut slices of pork roughly as big as a hand to marinate them. It was another way of preserving meat before we had refrigerators. (Gu00) ***b*** meat sliced and pickled ***c*** sliver of marinated pork <EV, LA, VM, Da84, Gu00, Lv88> •**grillade de cochon** pork cutlet <SJ> <***Loc:*** AC, AV, EV, LA, LF, SJ, SM, TB, VM, Da84, Gu00, Lv88>

grillades [grijad] *n.f.pl.* **1** organ meat stew, cowboy stew **2** pieces of meat that have been marinated, salted and peppered *Des grillades, c'est des morceaux de viande, tu mets ça dans du vinaigre et tous sortes de saisonnements et tu* *quittes ça pour plusieurs jours mariner et là tu cuis ça.* 'Grillades' are pieces of meat, you put them in vinegar and all kind of seasoning and you leave it for a few days marinating, then you cook it. (SM) **3** roasted or grilled slices of pork <***Loc:*** SM>

grillage [grijaʒ] *n.m.* roasting (of coffee beans, etc.) <***Loc:*** VM>

grille [grij] *n.m./f.* **1** screen **2** grill *Touche pas la grille. C'est toujours brûlant.* Don't touch the grill. It's still hot. (VM) <***Loc:*** LF, VM, Da84>

griller [grije, grile] *v.tr.* **1** to toast, roast, grill *Je vas griller le poulet.* I'm going to roast the chicken. (VM) **2** to parch, torrefy *Griller du café.* To roast coffee. (JE) **3** to singe, scorch *Il a grillé sa chemise en repassant son linge.* He scorched his shirt while ironing his clothes. (VM) ◊ **•en griller (de)** to desire intensely **J'en grille d'aller.* I'm very eager to go, I'm dying to go. (Da84) <Da84> <***Loc:*** JE, LA, SM, VM, Da84>

grillot (griot, grignot) [grijo, grĩjo] *n.m.* **1** kernel of dried, unripened corn **2** kernel of unpopped popcorn **3** crumb, small bit or piece (of food, dirt, stone) **4** marble made of agate or a glass imitation of it **5** [*pej.*] person of small stature <***Loc:*** SM, TB, Da84 Lv88>

grimace[1] [grimas] *n.f.* frown, grimace ◊ **•faire une grimace** to make a face *On se fait des grimaces à une et l'autre.* We're making faces at each other. (TB) <TB> <***Loc:*** TB, Da84>

grimace[2] [grimas] *n.f.* fine, gentle, misty rain ◊ **•petite grimace de pluie** a little drizzling <Lv88> <***Loc:*** Da84, Lv88>

grimacer[1] [grimase] *v.intr.* to frown, make faces, grimace *Arrête de grimacer comme ça-là. Si le vent vire au nord, ta figure va rester comme ça.* Stop frowning like that. If the wind shifts to the north, your face will stay like that. (VM) <***Loc:*** VM, Da84>

grimacer[2] [grimase] *v.intr.* to mist, rain lightly on and off, drizzle **Ça grimace.* It is raining lightly. (Da84) <***Loc:*** Da84>

grimil ♦see **grémil**

grimille ♦see **grémille**

grimiller ♦see **grémiller**

grimper [grɛ̃pe] **I** *v.tr.* to mount **Ils la mettont dans le parc avec le mâle. Le mâle l'a grimpée.* They put her in the corral with the male. The male mounted her. (IV, An94) **II** *v.intr.* to climb *Il a grimpé dans le bois.* He climbed into the tree. (TB) *J'étais après grimper dessus un* VINE. I was climbing on a vine. (SL) <***Loc:*** IV, SL, TB, An94, Da84>

grimpeur, -euse [grɛ̃pœr, -øz] *adj.* climbing *Ce bébé était beaucoup grimpeur.* That baby was a real climber. (VM) <***Loc:*** VM, Da84>

grincement ♦see **grinchement**

grincer ♦see **grincher**

grinchement (grincement) [grɛ̃ʃmɑ̃, grɛ̃smɑ̃] *n.m.* **1** gnashing (of teeth) **2** growling <***Loc:*** Da84, Lv88>

grincher (grincer) [grɛ̃ʃe, grɛ̃se] **I** *v.tr.* **1** to gnash, grate (one's teeth) *Il a si tellement froid, il grinche ses dents.* He's so cold, he's gnashing his teeth. (SM) **2** to bare (one's teeth) *Le chien était après grincer ses dents.* The dog was snarling (showing its teeth). (LA) **II** *v.intr.* **1** to growl, snarl *Quand on a vu le chien, il était après grincher, il jappait pas.* When we saw the dog, it was snarling. It wasn't barking. (LA) **2** to squeak, make a grinding sound *Le moyeu de la roue grinchait chaque fois il tournait le coin.* The hub of his wheel squeaked every time he turned the corner. (VM) **3** to grin, snicker, make a squinting, grinning face (usually out of nervousness) *Il grinche comme un imbécile.* He grins like an idiot. (VM) <***Loc:*** AL, LA, SM, TB, VM, Da84, Lv88>

gringoler [grɛ̃gole] *v.intr.* to walk unsteadily, stagger *Il était soûl mort-ivre; il gringolait tout partout dans le chemin.* He was dead drunk; he was staggering all over the road. (LA) <***Loc:*** LA, VM>

grinier ♦see **grénier**

griot ♦see **grillot**

grioter ♦see **grignoter**

gripette [gripɛt] *n.f.* boogeyman <***Loc:*** Lv88>

grippe[1] [grip] *n.f.* grasp, hold ◊ **•grippe et grappe** game in which the players have to catch an object thrown into the middle of their circle <Lv88> <***Loc:*** Da84, Lv88>

grippe[2] [grip] *n.f.* bad cold, flu <***Loc:*** Da84>

gripper [gripe] **I** *v.tr.* to grab, grasp, seize *Tu ferais mieux d'ôter ton argent de la table. Ton frère va le gripper.* You had better remove your money from the table. Your brother will grab it. (VM) **II se gripper** *v.pron.* to catch a hold of *Quand l'eau haute a dévasté la maison, il s'a grippé après ça qui restait du plancher.* When the flood destroyed the house, he caught hold of what was left of the floor. (VM) <***Loc:*** VM, Da84>

gris[1]**, -e** [gri, -z] *adj.* **1** gray-haired *Le vieux bougre était tout gris.* The old man was completely gray-haired. (VM) **2** drunk, tipsy *Mes amis, je suis gris. Remplissez mon verre.* My friends, I am drunk. Refill my glass. (IB) <***Loc:*** IB, SL, VM, Da84, Hi02>

gris[2]**, -e** [gri, -z] *adj./n.* gray (color) *Montez, montez la belle, dessus mon cheval gris.* Climb up, climb, maiden, onto my gray horse. (IB) <***Loc:*** IB, SL, VM, Da84, Hi02>

gris-gris[1] **(gri-gri)** [grigri] *v.tr.invar.* to cast a spell on *Elle m'a gris-gris.* She cast a spell on me. (Lv88) <***Loc:*** Lv88>

gris-gris[2] **(gri-gri)** [grigri] *n.m.* **1** charm, amulet *Le traiteur m'a passé un gris-gris.* The folk healer gave me a charm. (VM) **2** spell, hex **3** evil spirit ◊ **•mettre {faire} un gris-gris** to cast a spell, put a hex on *Et j'avais deux vieilles veuves, deux vieilles femmes qui restaient voisin de mon. Et eux-autres disait tout le temps qu'eux-autres faisait des gris-gris.* And I had two old widows, two old women that lived next door to me. And they always said that they cast spells. (TB) *La vieille traiteuse a mis un gris-gris dessus* *moi.* The old "traiteuse" put a spell on me. (SM) <SM, TB> <***Loc:*** TB, LF, SM, TB, VM, Da84, La99, Lv88>

Grecian bend [griʃinbɛ̃n] *n.* bustle, wire frame or pad formerly worn by women on the back, below the waist to distend the skirts <***Loc:*** SM>

grive [griv] *n.f.* American robin <***Loc:*** SB, SM, VM, Da84, Guoo, Hio2, Lv88>

gro-blo [groblo] *n.m.* card game resembling euchre <***Loc:*** SM>

grocerie ♦see **grosserie**

grocier ♦see **grossier**

grognard[1]**, -euse** (**grognoux, -ouse**) [grɔ̃jar, -øz, grɔ̃ju, -uz] *adj.* grumbling, growling, fussy, cross, ill-natured, ill-tempered, grouchy *Mon petit garçon est grognard quand il se réveille de son somme.* My little boy is grouchy when he wakes from his nap. (VM) <***Loc:*** TB, VM, Da84>

grognard[2] [grɔ̃jar, grɑ̃jar, grĩjard] *n.m.* **1** grumbler, complainer **2** [fish] croaker, Atlantic croaker <***Loc:*** JE, LF, Da84, Guoo, Lv88>

grognement [grɔ̃jmɑ̃] *n.m.* growl, grumbling, snarl <***Loc:*** Da84>

grogner [grɔ̃je] *v.intr.* **1** to groan, snarl *Quand il a ouvert la porte, j'ai grogné.* When he opened the door, I groaned. (SL) **2** to croak, grunt (of a frog, fish) *Le grognard. Tu peux pas l'oublier, parce que la manière qu'il grogne.* A croaker. You can't forget that because of the way he croaks. (TB) **3** to roar, rumble (of thunder) *Que le tonnerre grogne et que la muraille recule. Me voilà par terre du matin au soir.* May thunder rumble and may the wall recede. Here I am on the floor from morning to night. (VM) **4** to grumble, complain *Porte pas de cas de lui, Tit-Paul. Il faut toujours qu'il grogne pour quelque chose.* Don't mind Tit-Paul. He always has to complain about something. (VM) <***Loc:*** JE, SL, TB, VM, Hio2>

grogneur, -euse (**grogneux, -euse**) [grɔ̃jœr, -øz, grɔ̃jø, -øz] *n.* grumbler, complainer <***Loc:*** Da84, Lv88>

grognoux ♦see **grognard**

gronder [grɔ̃de] *v.tr.* to scold, fuss at, reprimand *Tu devrais pas le gronder comme ça. Tu vas le faire brailler.* You shouldn't scold him like that. You'll make him cry. (LA) <***Loc:*** LA, Da84>

gros[1]**, -sse** [gro, -s] *adj.* **1** big, large **Il a emarré la corde dessus eine grosse branche forte et là entour de son cou.* He tied the rope around a big strong branch and then around his neck. (Wh83) **Elle a acheté ein gros bateau neuf pour pêcher.* She bought a big new fishing boat. (Wh83) **2** fat *Il est trop gros. Il devrait perdre quelques livres.* He is too fat. He ought to lose a few pounds. (LA) **3** pregnant *Quand elle était grosse de son troisième enfant...* When she was pregant with her third child . . . (VM) **4** coarse *Du gros gru.* Coarse grits or hominy. (LA) **5** big, important *Ça c'était la plus grosse affaire.* That was the biggest deal. (SL) *Une grosse célébration.* A big celebration. (Lv88) *Un gros bal samedi soir au Legion Hall.* A big dance at the Legion Hall on Saturday night. (EV) **6** deep, profound (in feeling) *En gros deuil.* In deep mourning. (Lv88) **7** dark, intense (of colors) *Gros bleu.* Dark blue. (Lv88) ◊ •**en gros** in bulk, wholesale **Acheter en gros.* To buy in bulk, wholesale. (Da84) <Da84> •**être grosse affaire** to have a close relationship **Il y avait deux garçons qui courtisaient la même fille, et c'était deux hommes qui étaient grosse affaire.* There were two boys who were courting the same girl, and they were two men who were close. (SL, An94) <SL, An94> <***Loc:*** EV, JE, LA, SL, SM, VM, An94, Da84, Hio2, La99, Lv88, Wh83>

gros[2] [gro] *adv.* much, a lot **Oh! cher nègre, je t'aime gros, ouais!* Oh! my dearest, I love you a lot, yeah. (ThCa: *Le charivari*) •**comment gros de** how much? *Comment gros de viande vous voulez?* How much meat do you want? (VM) <VM> <***Loc:*** VM, Hio2, Lv88, ThCa>

gros-bar ♦see **crowbar**

grosbec (**gros-bec**) [grobɛk] *n.m.* night heron (locally called 'grosbeak') <***Loc:*** IV, SB, Da84, Hio2, Lv88>

gros-bec ♦see **grosbec**

grosserie (**grocerie**) [grosri] *n.f.* **1** food store, grocery store **2** *(pl.)* groceries *Il délivrait les groceries dans le village.* He delivered groceries in the village. (Lv88) *Le poisson et les groceries qui va avec.* The fish and the groceries that go with it. (SL) **Un jour, ses parents ont parti aussi à la ville pour acheter des nourritures, grosseries.* One day his parents also went to town to buy food, groceries. (EV, An94) <***Loc:*** AC, EV, IB, LA, SL, SM, VM, An94, Da84, Lv88>

grosseur [grosœr] *n.f.* size *Faut qu'eusse soye une certaine grosseur avant que tu peux les attraper.* They have to be a certain size before you can catch them. (TB) <***Loc:*** LF, TB, VM>

grossier (**grocier**) [grosje, grosœr] *n.m.* **1** grocer **2** bulk retailer, wholesale merchant <***Loc:*** VM, Da84, Lv88>

grossièreté [grosjærte] *n.f.* crudeness, rudeness, vulgarity <***Loc:*** Da84>

grossir [grosir] **I** *v.tr.* to enlarge, swell, make bigger *Tout cette pluie a grossi les viviers.* All this rain has swollen the ponds. (LA) **II** *v.intr.* **1** to enlarge, swell, get bigger *Cet homme-là a réellement grossi depuis qu'il est marié.* That man has really gotten fatter since he's married. (LA) **2** to grow up *Là quand lui il était après grossir c'est tout ce qu'eusse usait. Y avait pas de docteur. Eusse usait juste les traiteurs.* When he was growing up that's all they used. There was no doctor. They only used folk healers. (TB) <***Loc:*** LA, TB, Da84>

grouillement [grujmɑ̃] *n.m.* movement, motion, stir <***Loc:*** Da84>

grouiller [gruje, grije] **I** *v.tr.* to move *Avant je restais drette en haut du magasin-là. Une petite maison que mon défunt pape avait abandonnée, et je l'ai grouillée sur un terrain.*

Before, I lived up the bayou from the store. A little house that my late father had abandoned, and I moved it onto a piece of land. (TB) *Il halait et il grouillait les machineries d'une place à l'autre, dans le temps il y'avait pas un tas des machines au gasoline, c'est ça comme ça il faisait son vie.* He would pull and move the equipment from one place to another, in the past there was not much equipment running with gas, it was how he made a living. (AC) **II** *v.intr.* **1** to move, move around, change position **La vieille maison a jamais grouillé de dessus les cales.* The old house never moved from its pillars. (Gu82) *Ça fait l'écrevisse grouille presque pas.* So the crawfish hardly moves. (SM) **2** to change residence, relocate *Le monde grouillait pas beaucoup vieux temps passé.* People didn't move around much a long time ago. (Lv88) *Ils ont grouillé dans les Avoyelles proche de Bunkie.* They moved to Avoyelles, close to Bunkie. (AV) **3** to exhibit great activity or energy (of a child) *Les enfants peuvent pas rester tranquilles. Ça grouille tout le temps.* Kids can't stay still. They are always moving around. (SM) **4** to hurry *Grouille! Grouille! Regarde, il arrive déjà.* Hurry! Hurry! Look, he's already coming. (LA) **III se grouiller** *v.pron.* **1** to move *Grouille-toi du chemin.* Move out of the way. (LA) **2** to hurry *Grouille-toi.* Hurry up. (VM) ◊ **•grouille ton casaquin {tchu}** hurry up <LA, SM, VM, La99> <***Loc:*** AC, AV, EV, JE, LA, LF, SL, SM, TB, VM, Da84, Gu82, Gu00, Hi02, La99, Lv88>

groupe [grup] *n.f.* **1** group (of people, etc.) **2** clump (of trees, grass, etc.) <***Loc:*** Da84>

gru [gry] *n.m.* grits *Défunte mémère faisait du gru avec le maïs que tu moulais, et alle faisait du bon gru avec ça.* My late grandmother used to make grits with the corn you would grind up, and she made good grits with that. (TB) <***Loc:*** AV, IB, LA, LF, SB, SM, TB, VM, Da84, Gu00, Hi02, Lv88>

grucher (**gricher**) [gryʃe, griʃe] **I** *v.tr.* to climb, shinny (up a tree) *Il était après grucher le bois.* He was climbing the tree. (TB) **II** *v.intr.* to climb *Le chat a griché dans l'arbre quand il a vu le chien.* The cat climbed up into the tree when it saw the dog. (SM) *Je vas gricher, et je vas monter les entourages.* I'll climb, and I'll scale the fences (walls). (TB) <***Loc:*** SM, TB, VM, Da84, Lv88>

grue [gry] *n.f.* whooping crane, crane <***Loc:*** Da84, Gu00>

guème ♦see **gaime**

guenille [gənij, ginij] *n.f.* **1** rag, piece of old cloth **2** trash, unusable pieces of shrimp along with bits of ice in a 210 lb. barrel of shrimp (traditionally, the shrimper was only paid for 200 lbs., under the assumption that 10 lbs. was unusable) <***Loc:*** LF, TB, VM>

guêpe [gɛp] *n.f.* **1** wasp **2** yellow jacket **3** hornet ◊ **•guêpe anglaise** paper wasp *Une guêpe anglaise c'est eusse qui fait des niques en papier. Et là les guêpes noires est eusse qui fait leur nique en boue.* A paper wasp, those are the ones that make nests of paper. And mud daubers are those that make their nests of mud. (LF) <LF, SB> **•guêpe noire** mud dauber, mud wasp <LF> **•guêpe rouge** yellow jacket <Gu00> <***Loc:*** AL, LF, SB, SL, Da84, Gu00, Hi02>

guère [gær] *adv.* hardly *Gèle là, au péril là, mais moi je m'en soucie guère.* Freeze there, in danger there, but I have hardly a care. (IB) ◊ **•pas guère** hardly *J'en ai pas guère.* I hardly have any. (VM) <VM> <***Loc:*** AV, IB, VM>

guérir [gerir] **I** *v.tr.* to heal, cure **Elle avait guéri une petite fille qui était décomptée.* She had cured a little girl who had been considered hopeless. (IV, An94) **II** *v.intr.* to get well *Sa famille avait perdu espoir, mais il a guéri.* His family had lost hope, but he got well. (LA) <***Loc:*** IV, LA, An94, Da84>

guernouille ♦see **grenouille**

guerre [gær] *n.f.* war ◊ **•la Guerre Civile / la Guerre Confédérée / la Guerre des Confédérés** the Civil War <Da84, Lv88> **•la Guerre de Révolution** the Revolutionary War <Da84> **•la Guerre Numéro Deux** World War II <TB, Lv88> **•la Première Guerre mondiale** World War I *Mon père était dans la Première Guerre Mondiale, il a servi d'interprète en France.* My father was in World War I, he served as an interpreter in France. (SL) <SL> **•à la guerre comme à la guerre** it is necessary to do without things sometimes <SM, La99> **•faire la guerre** to make war or fight <Da84> <***Loc:*** EV, SL, SM, TB, Da84, Hi02, La99, Lv88>

guettage [getaʒ] *n.m.* watching **Dans ce temps-là il n'avait pas tout se geuttage [=guettage] de TV comme il n'a aseteur.* In those days there wasn't as much TV watching as there is now. (Wh83) <***Loc:*** Wh83>

guette[1] [gɛt, dʒɛt] *n.f.* **1** hunt at dusk or at night *On va faire une guette à soir.* We are going on a night hunt tonight. (VM) **2** watch, lookout *Je m'ai mis à la guette et quand il a passé, j'ai sauté dessus.* I lay in wait and when he came by, I jumped on him. (VM) ◊ **•aller {partir} à la guette** to go (duck) hunting at dusk or at night *Comment t'as fait pour tuer autant de canards? —J'ai été à la guette. C'était la pleine lune.* How did you manage to kill so many ducks? —I went hunting at night and it was a full moon. (VM) <VM, Da84> **•faire la guette** ***a*** to lie in wait ***b*** to go (duck) hunting at dusk or at night *Faire la passe ou la guette on appelait ça. On allait un élan et les canards sortaient, on les tirait le soir on s'en tuait quelqu'uns.* We called it "faire la passe" or "faire la guette". We would go out for a spell and the ducks would come out, we'd shoot them in the evening and kill a few. (St95) <VM, Lv88, St95> <***Loc:*** EV, VM, Da84, Lv88, St95>

guette[2] [gɛt, dʒɛt] *n.f.* brace, prop, strut <***Loc:*** EV, LA, VM, Da84, Lv88>

guetter [gete, dʒete] **I** *v.tr.* **1** to watch, observe *J'aimais beaucoup la guetter travailler.* I really liked watching her work.

(AC) *À soir, je vas guetter le* TV. I am going to watch TV tonight. (Lv88) *Quand moi je mets le* TELEVISION *dessus je mets le marché. Je guette le marché.* When I put the TV on I watch the stock market. I watch the market. (TB) **2** to take care of, keep an eye on *Je vais guetter les fèves pour toi et les soigner.* I'll keep an eye on the beans for you and take care of them. (Lv88) *Guette le petit garçon pour moi.* Watch the little boy for me. (SM) **3** to look at *Guette la jolie fille là-bas.* Look at the pretty girl over there. (SM) **4** to pay attention to, watch out for, look out for, be careful of *Il faut guetter ça tout le temps, ça t'es après faire.* You have to pay attention all the time to what you are doing. (VM) *Je guette qui-ce que je dis parce que des fois tu peux te foutre un coup de pied dans tes dents à toi-même.* I watch what I say because sometimes you can kick yourself in the teeth. (LF) *Guette, ça va pisser sur toi.* Watch out, it [the frog] will piss on you. (TB) **5** to brace, prop up with a brace **Non, c'est pas moi qu'es si fort que ça. Le mur me guette.* No, I am not as strong as that. The wall braces me. (VM, An94) **II** *v.intr.* **1** to watch, supervise *Il travaille, moi je guette.* He works, I supervise. (Lv88) *Ç'étaient après guetter.* They were keeping an eye out. (AC) **2** to think about, reflect *Guette bien à ça t'as dit.* Think hard about what you said. (VM) **III se guetter** *v.pron.* to pay attention *Guette-toi de pas tomber.* Watch yourself so as not to fall. (LA) ◊ **•guetter comme un détectif** to watch closely <EV, La99> **•s'en guetter** to watch out for *Il a entendu, mais il dit il s'en guettait un peu, mais après un bout de temps, il a* GO AHEAD *à chose.* He heard and he said he would be careful about it, but after a while he just went ahead doing it. (SL) <SL> ***<Loc:*** AC, AL, EV, LA, LF, SL, SM, TB, VM, An94, Da84, Hi02, La99, Lv88>

gueulard, -e [gølar, -ard] *adj.* bawling, crying, whiny *Un enfant gueulard.* A whiny child. (VM) ***<Loc:*** VM, Da84>

gueule (djeule) [gœl, gøl, dʒœl, dʒøl] *n.f.* mouth (esp. of an animal) ◊ **•gueule de loup** snapdragon <VM> **•gueule douce** sweet talker <Lv88> **•gueule rouge** ***a*** one who speaks English but not French ***b*** Yankee, person from the North <SM, La99, Lv88> **•avoir {faire} gueule plate** to pout <SM> **•bouche-gueule** muzzle used for weaning calves or colts, also to restrain plow animals from eating while working in tall crops <Da84> **•grande gueule** ***a*** largemouth bass ***b*** type of sunfish <TB, Da84, Lv88> ***<Loc:*** AC, SM, TB, VM, Da84, Hi02, La99, Lv88, Wh83>

gueulée [gøle, dʒøle] *n.f.* **1** mouthful *Il a mangé quelques gueulées de riz.* He ate a few bites of rice. (SM) **2** loud cry *Il a laissé partir une gueulée.* He let out a loud cry. (VM) ***<Loc:*** SM, VM, Da84, Lv88>

gueuler (jeuler) [gøle, dʒøle] *v.intr.* to cry profusely, bawl, blubber *J'ai jamais vu un bebé à gueuler comme ça.* I've never seen a baby cry like that. (VM) ***<Loc:*** SM, TB, VM, Da84, Lv88>

gueurnouille ♦see **grenouille**

gueux [gø] *n.m.* poor helpless person, ragamuffin ◊ **•gueux-parvenu** upstart, newly rich, vulgar rich <SM> ***<Loc:*** SM, Da84>

guidance [gidɑ̃s] *n.f.* guidance ***<Loc:*** LF>

guide [gid] *n.m./f.* **1** guide **2** rope **3** *(pl.)* reins, harness lines (used to control horses or mules) ***<Loc:*** AC, EV, SL, Da84, Lv88>

guider [gide] *v.tr.* to guide, lead, steer, drive (car, horse, boat, etc.) *Je vais guider le char pour toi.* I'm going to drive the car for you. (Lv88) *Mon plus vieux frère guidait les mulets en avant.* My oldest brother would lead the mules in front. (EV) ***<Loc:*** EV, LF, SM, VM, Da84, Lv88>

guideur, -euse [gidœr, -øz] *n.* guide ***<Loc:*** Lv88>

guignard [gĩjar] *adj.* unlucky *Il est guignard aux cartes.* He is unlucky at cards. (VM) ***<Loc:*** VM>

guignasse [gĩjas, gijas, gijɑ̃s] *n.f.* bad luck *J'ai perdu mon argent! Ça c'est la guignasse!* I lost my money! That's bad luck! (SM) ***<Loc:*** SM, Lv88>

guigne [gĩj] *n.f.* bad luck, jinx, constant misfortune ◊ **•avoir la guigne** to have a run of bad luck, have a jinx <Da84> ***<Loc:*** VM, Da84>

gui-gui [gigi] *n.m.* rustic, uncultured, uncouth, boorish, ignorant person ***<Loc:*** SM, Da84, Lv88>

guiguiches [gigiʃ] *n.pl.* any part of a woman's apparel that hangs or is out of place ***<Loc:*** SM>

guimauve [gimov] *n.f.* **1** marshmallow, hibiscus **2** crimson-eye rose mallow ***<Loc:*** VM, Da84>

guime ♦see **gaime**

guinche [gɛ̃ʃ] *n.m./f.* **1** good-for-nothing, rogue **2** *(f.)* vulgar woman ***<Loc:*** Lv88>

guiné, -e [gine] *adj.* spotted, speckled, flecked *De l'indienne guinée.* Spotted cotton-cloth [from Guinea]. (Lv88) ***<Loc:*** Lv88>

guinee ♦see **guinée**[2]

guinée[1] [gine] *adj.f.* ◊ **•poule guinée** guinea hen <Lv88> ***<Loc:*** Lv88>

guinée[2] **(guinee)** [gine] *n.f.* **1** (inexpensive) flecked cotton-cloth, guinea cloth **2** dotted cloth of navy cotton ***<Loc:*** VM, Da84, Lv88>

guingan [gɛ̃gɑ̃] *n.m.* gingham cloth ***<Loc:*** Da84>

guinguette [gɛ̃gɛt] *n.f.* ◊ **•prendre une guinguette** to become intoxicated <SM, La99, Lv88> ***<Loc:*** SM, La99, Lv88>

guinnegue [ginɛg, gɛ̃nɛg] *n.f.* drinking spree ***<Loc:*** SM>

guitare [gitar] *n.m/f.* guitar ***<Loc:*** SL, Da84, Hi02, Lv88>

gulf ♦see **golfe**

gumbo ♦see **gombo**

gypsie ♦see **gipsie**

H

ha[1] [ha, hɔ] *interj.* 'haw,' used to direct horses to turn left *"Gee" c'était tourner à la droite et "ha" c'était tourner à la gauche.* "Gee" meant "turn right" and "haw" meant "turn left." (EV) <***Loc:*** EV, SB, Da84>

ha[2] [ha, hɔ] *interj.* used to express ignorance, usually accompanied by a shrug of the shoulders *Qui c'est ça? Ha, moi je sais pas.* Who's that? Ha, I don't know. (SM) *Ha, moi, je connais pas.* Ha, me, I don't know. (VM) <***Loc:*** LA, SM, VM>

habile [abil] *adj.* able, capable, skillful, adept *C'était un homme qu'était beaucoup habile.* He was a very capable man. (LA) <***Loc:*** LA, Da84, Hi02>

habilité [abilite] *n.f.* ability, skillfulness <***Loc:*** Da84>

habillé, -e [abije] *adj.* dressed, clothed **Elle a vu plein de petits enfants après faire une marche, et ils étiont tous habillés en blanc, et ils avaient tous des chandelles.* She saw lots of little children taking a walk, and they were all dressed up in white, and they all had candles. (LA, An94) ◊ **•habillé sur le rimpinpin** dressed up smartly <LF> **•bien habillé** well dressed *Le bougre en arrière était tout bien habillé.* The guy in the back was well dressed. (JD) <EV, JD, Da84> <***Loc:*** AV, EV, JD, LA, LF, An94, Da84>

habillement [abijmɑ̃] *n.m.* **1** article of clothing **2** *(pl.)* clothes, clothing *Ça se mettait comme une robe de noces, ou ça mettait des habillements, ça se masquait avec du linge qu'eux-autres avait pas avant, tu connais pour pas que le monde les reconnaît.* They would put on like a wedding dress, or they would put on garments, they would disguise themselves with clothes they didn't have before, you know, so people wouldn't recognize them. (TB) <***Loc:*** TB, Da84, Hi02>

habiller [abije] **I** *v.tr.* to dress, clothe *Il fallait les habiller dans le linge que les voisins nous donnaient pour yeux mettre.* We had to dress them in the clothing that the neighbors gave us for them to wear. (AC) **II s'habiller** *v.pron.* to dress o.s., get dressed, dress up *Hélène s'habille, elle s'est mis-t-à danser.* Hélène dressed up, and she started to dance. (IB, ch: *Au pont de l'anse*) ◊ **•s'habiller en tous les jours** to dress in everyday clothes <Da84> **•s'habiller mardi gras** to dress in poor taste, wear loud colors <Lv88> <***Loc:*** AC, EV, IB, Da84, Hi02, Lv88>

habit [abi] *n.m.* **1** article of clothing **2** costume, garb, uniform **3** suit **Ma femme m'a acheté ein habit neuf pour porter demain au soir.* My wife bought me a new suit to wear tomorrow evening. (Gu82) **4** *(pl.)* clothes <***Loc:*** Da84, Gu82, Hi02>

habitable [abitab(l)] *adj.* habitable, inhabitable, livable *Cette maison est pas habitable.* That house is not habitable. (VM) <***Loc:*** VM, Da84>

habitaco ♦see **bitaco**

habitant (z-habitant) [abitɑ̃, zabitɑ̃] *n.m.* **1** farmer *Lui, il est un habitant de cannes.* He's a sugarcane farmer. (SM) *Le père à 'Tiboy était un habitant dans la Paroisse Acadie. Il plantait du maïs, des patates, du coton, du gombo-févi.* Tiboy's father was a small farmer in Acadia Parish. He grew corn, potatoes, cotton, okra. (Gu00) **2** [*sometimes pej.*] small farmer, subsistence farmer **Maman veut pas que je vas aux noces chez les habitants.* Mother doesn't want me to go to the farmer's wedding. (Di32) **3** rural dweller **4** inhabitant ◊ **•faire l'habitant** to farm, be a farmer <Lv88> <***Loc:*** AV, EV, IB, JD, LA, LF, SB, SL, SM, TB, VM, Da84, Di32, Gu00, Hi02, Lv88, Ph36>

habitation [abitasjɔ̃] *n.f.* **1** farm, plantation, farmstead, ranch *Quand j'étais jeune, j'étais dessus une habitation dans la campagne.* When I was young I used to live on a farm in the countryside. (AC) **2** house, residence *L'habitation était pas bien loin du chemin.* The house wasn't far from the road. (EV) <***Loc:*** AC, EV, IB, IV, LA, SB, SM, TB, VM, An94, Da84, Di32, Hi02, Lv88>

habiter [abite] *v.intr.* to reside, dwell **Le renard était dans le bois où ils habitent et, toujours, il avait beaucoup faim.* The fox was in the woods where they live and, in any case, he was very hungry. (LA, An94) <***Loc:*** AV, LA, TB, An94, Da84, Hi02>

habitude[1] [abityd, abitʃyd, abytyd] *n.f.* **1** habit *"Oh, mais," elle dit, "moi, je vas lui faire passer ça," elle dit, "cette habitude de parier."* "Oh, well," she says, "I am going to cure him of that," she says, "that habit of betting." (AS) *Il a sûr des mauvaises habitudes.* He sure has bad habits. (TB) **2** custom, way, practice *Il y a plus tous ces habitudes de les parents et les enfants aller ensemble.* There are no longer all these customs of parents and children getting together. (LA) ◊ **•avoir habitude (de)** ***a*** used to (do s.t.) *Quand alle était plus jeune alle avait habitude de coudre.* When she was younger, she used to sew. (JE) ***b*** to be accustomed to, be used to *C'est plus le même* SAFETY *qu'on avait habitude d'avoir.* It is no longer the same safety we were accustomed to having. (SL) *J'ai habitude travailler pour une piastre par jour.* I'm used to working for one dollar a day. (EV) <EV, JE, SL> <***Loc:*** AS, AV, EV, JE, LA, SL, SM, TB, Da84, Hi02>

habitude[2] [abityd, abytyd] *adv.* **1** usually, habitually *Habitude, je vas au village le lundi matin.* I usually go to town on Monday morning. (Lv88) **Habitude je suivais les règlements.* Usually I followed the rules. (ThCa: *Mille misères*)

2 formerly, in the past *Habitude on avait TV5; on a p'us.* We used to have TV5; we don't have it anymore. (SL) *C'est plus facile comme habitude.* It is not as easy as it used to be. (SM) *Elle aimait -z- à cuire, habitude. Parce qu'elle alle connaît faire ça aussi.* She used to like to cook. Because she knows how to do that too. (TB) ◊ **•comme (d')habitude** ***a*** as usual **Et il a parti en sifflant comme d'habitude.* And he set off whistling as usual. (EV, An94) ***b*** usually *Comme habitude les sacs de z-oignons tiennent jusqu'à cinquante et quelques livres.* Usually, onion bags hold fifty something pounds. (SM) <EV, LA, SL, SM, An94> **•d'habitude** ***a*** customarily, usually *La façade du magasin avait d'habitude une porte au milieu, une grande fenêtre à chaque bord de la porte et une galerie avec des bancs.* The front of the store usually had a door in the middle, a big window on each side of the door, and a porch with benches. (VM) ***b*** formerly, in the past **Les affaires de cinq sous, d'habitude, c'est trente sous asteur.* Things that cost five cents formerly are thirty cents now. (SL, An94) <LA, SL, TB, VM, An94, Da84> <***Loc:*** AV, LA, SL, SM, TB, VM, An94, Da84, Di32, Lv88, ThCa>

habitudement [abitydmɑ̃, bitydmɑ̃, abytydmɑ̃] *adv.* usually *Oh, six heures, six heures quinze, habitudement il frème.* Oh, six o'clock, six fifteen it usually closes. (LF) *Habitudement t'avais trois hommes qui travaillaient dedans un skiff.* Usually you had three men who worked in a skiff. (LF) <***Loc:*** LF, TB>

habitué[1]**, -e** [abitye, abitʃye] *adj.* accustomed, familiar *On est trop habitué ensemble, moi et toi, pour que je vas à confesse à toi.* We're too familiar, you and I, for me to confess to you. (AS) ◊ **•être habitué avec** ***a*** to be in the habit of, be familiar with, be used to *J'étais pas habitué avec les nouveaux chars, ça fait j'ai manière RETIRE.* I wasn't familiar with the new cars, so I kind of retired. (LA) ***b*** to know very well, be accustomed to the ways of *Je lui dis tout quelque chose, je suis bien habitué avec elle, tu sais.* I tell her everything, I know her well, you know. (VM) <LA, SM, VM, Lv88> <***Loc:*** AS, LA, SM, TB, VM, Da84, Lv88>

habitué[2]**, -e** [abitye, abitʃye] *n.* one who is accustomed <***Loc:*** Da84>

habituel, -elle [abitɥɛl] *adj.* habitual, usual, customary *Elle a arrivé à son heure habituelle.* She arrived at her usual time. (LA) <***Loc:*** LA, Da84>

habituellement [abitɥɛlmɑ̃] *adv.* usually, customarily, habitually <***Loc:*** Da84>

habituer (s') [abitɥe] *v.pron.* to become accustomed, get used to *Et un homme s'habituait à faire quelque chose comme ça et après ça il était en demande.* And a man would get used to doing something like that, and after that he was in demand. (LF) <***Loc:*** AC, AS, LF, Da84>

hache[1] [haʃ] *n.f.* **1** ax **J'ai été chercher la hache pour briser la meule.* I went to get the ax to smash the grindstone. (LA, An94) **2** small ax, hatchet ◊ **•hache à deux taillants** double-edged ax <EV, Lv88> **•hache à main** hatchet <AC> **•hache à parer** ax used for trimming shingles <TB> **•hache à pied** foot ax *Une hache à pied. Et ça c'était usé plein aussite. Le monde a usé ça pour faire leurs pirogues, pour retirer le plus gros du bois.* A foot axe. That was used a lot too. People used that to make their pirogues, to remove the rough areas of the wood. (LF) <LF> **•hache à un taillant** single-edged ax <EV> **•être à la hache** to have no money, be broke <JE, VM, Di32, Lv88> <***Loc:*** AC, EV, JE, LF, SB, SL, TB, VM, Da84, Di32, Hi02, La99, Lv88>

hache[2] [haʃ, aʃ] *interj.* used to indicate disgust <***Loc:*** JE, Di32>

hacher[1] [haʃe, aʃe] *v.tr.* **1** to chop, cut up, mince *Il faulait tu haches ta viande pas trop fin pour faire ces saucisses-là.* You had to chop your meat not too finely to make those sausages. (LA) **2** to beat, whip, beat up *S'il apprend que t'as été là, il va te hacher.* If he finds out you were there, he'll beat you. (VM) *Hacher un cheval à coups de fouet.* To beat a horse with a whip. (SJ) **3** to beat, defeat (in a contest, game, etc.) *Je l'ai haché dans la game de cartes hier soir.* I beat him in the card game last night. (SM) <***Loc:*** AC, AV, EV, IB, JD, LA, SB, SJ, SM, VM, Da84, Hi02, Ph36>

hacher[2] [haʃe, aʃe] *v.tr.* [*regional variant of* **chercher** *used only after* **aller**, **venir**] to get, fetch *On aurait dû aller au magasin hacher un pain français, hein.* We should have gone to the store to get a loaf of French bread. (TB) *J'ai revenu hacher mon fusil.* I came back to get my gun. (TB) <***Loc:*** TB>

hachouiller [haʃuje] *v.tr.* to chop up, hack up <***Loc:*** LA>

HACK (**haque**) [hak, hæk] *n.m.* hack, two-seat buggy *C'est le HACK à Moreau qu'a capoté samedi au soir.* It was Moreau's buggy that flipped over Saturday night. (Lv88) <***Loc:*** AV, EV, SL, VM, Da84, Di32, Gr86, Lv88, Ph36>

hâcre (**âcre**) [hak(r), ak(r)] *adj.* **1** acrid, pungent *Quand j'ai ouvert la glacière, ça sentait hâcre.* When I opened the ice chest, there was an acrid odor. (LA) **2** sour, acidic, tart *Les oranges farouches sont âcres.* Wild oranges are acidic. (Lv88) **3** impure *Sang hâcre.* Impure blood. (VM) <***Loc:*** AV, LA, SM, VM, Lv88>

haie [hɛ, he] *n.f.* hedge, hedgerow ◊ **•haie de chéroquie** Cherokee hedge <Da84> <***Loc:*** Da84>

haigre (**aigre**) [hɛg(r), ɛg(r)] *adj.* sour *Quand la canne est restée sur la terre trop longtemps, la canne va venir aigre.* When the cane stays too long in the soil, the cane will turn sour. (IB) <***Loc:*** AV, IB, JD, LA, LF, SB, SJ, SM, TB, VM, Da84, Di32, Gr86, La99, Lv88>

haigreur (**aigreur**) [hɛgrœr, ɛgrœr, hegryr] *n.f.* sourness <***Loc:*** JD, Da84>

haigrir (**aigrir**) [hegrir, egrir] **I** *v.tr.* to sour, turn or make sour *Si tu laisses ton lait sur le comptoir, ça va le haigrir.* If you leave your milk on the counter, it will render it sour. (LA) **II**

v.intr. to sour, turn sour *Le lait avait pas haigri et le biscuit était toujours mou.* The milk hadn't soured and the biscuit was still soft. (IB) *Le lait va haigrir.* The milk will sour. (LA) <***Loc:*** IB, LA, LF, SM, TB, VM, Da84>

haigrissement (**aigrissement**) [hegrismɑ̃, egrismɑ̃] *n.m.* souring <***Loc:*** Da84>

haillon [hajɔ̃] *n.m.* rag ◊ **•être en haillons** to be dressed in rags <Da84> <***Loc:*** LF, SL, SM, Da84>

haillonné, -e [hajɔ̃ne] *adj.* tattered, torn, frazzled, in rags **Y'en avait un en arrière, plus haillonné que tous les autres.* There was one in the back, more tattered and torn than all the others. (Gr82) *Sa robe est tout haillonnée.* Her dress is all tattered. (VM) <***Loc:*** IB, SJ, VM, Da84, Gr82, Gr86, Lv88>

haillonner [hajɔ̃ne] *v.tr.* to tear up, tatter (clothing) <***Loc:*** Da84>

haillonnerie [hajɔ̃nri] *n.f.* **1** rags (collectively) **2** ragged clothes <***Loc:*** Da84>

haine [hɛ̃n] *n.f.* **1** hate, hatred, dislike **2** feud *Proche tous ces batailles, c'était à cause d'une haine.* Almost all of these fights were because of a feud. (LA) <***Loc:*** LA, Da84, Hi02>

haineux, -euse [hɛ̃nø, -øz] *adj.* full of hate, hating *Du monde haineux.* People full of hate. (VM) <***Loc:*** VM, Da84>

haïr [hajir, hair, hahir, ajir] *v.tr.* to hate, despise, dislike *Je haïssais les cheveux longs.* I hated long hair. (Lv88) *Y'a rien que je hais plus qu'une serpent.* There's nothing I hate more than a snake. (Lv88) *Je hais de dépenser de l'argent.* I hate to spend money. (ThCa: *La table des veuves*) *Il haïssait de partir.* He hated to leave. (Lv88) **Tchou Flette haït le gout de plâtre.* Tchou Flette hates the taste of plaster. (Wh83) <***Loc:*** JD, LF, SB, SL, SM, VM, Da84, Di32, Hi02, Lv88, ThCa, Wh83>

haïssable [haisab(l), heisab(l)] *adj.* **1** hateful, detestable, repulsive *C'était haïssable pour vider ça il y avait dedans, donc.* It was repulsive to empty what there was in there, though. (EV) **2** unkind, spiteful *Cet homme haïssable avait l'habitude de sangler ses enfants.* That unkind man used to beat his children with a strap. (LA) <***Loc:*** EV, LA, SM, TB, VM, Da84, Lv88>

haïsseur [haisœr] *n.m.* one who hates, hater <***Loc:*** Da84>

haïtien, -enne [aisjɛ̃, -ɛ̃n] *adj.* Haitian *A Cecilia, c'est un patois haïtien.* In Cecilia, it's a Haitian patois. (SL) <***Loc:*** SL>

halage [halaʒ] *n.m./f.* hauling, carrying, transport *C'est temps pour commencer le halage de cannes.* It's time to start the hauling of the cane. (SM) ◊ **•halage de riz** rice hauling <VM, Da84> <***Loc:*** EV, JD, LA, SB, SM, TB, VM, Da84, Di32, Gr86, Lv88, Ph36>

halaillage [halajaʒ] *n.m.* fight, argument <***Loc:*** LA, Lv88>

halaillement [halajmɑ̃] *n.m.* **1** fight **Y a eu in vrai halaillement quand l'officier a arrêté l'garçon.* There was a real fight when the policeman arrested the boy. (EV, Ph36) **2** bickering, wrangling, argument *Cette succession a causé un grand halaillement dans la famille.* That succession caused much wrangling in the family. (IB) **3** pushing and pulling *C'était un halaillement au bal, y avait tant de monde.* It was pushing and pulling at the dance, there were so many people. (VM) <***Loc:*** EV, IB, SM, VM, Lv88, Ph36>

halailler [halaje] **I** *v.tr.* to pull, tug (persistently or obnoxiously) *Il était après halailler sur la manche de ma chemise.* He was tugging at the sleeve of my shirt. (LA) **II** *v.intr.* to do hard manual labor *Ça c'est trop halailler.* That's too much hard work. (SL) **III se halailler** *v.pron.* **1** to fight, tussle *Les deux garçons se halaillaient l'un à l'autre.* The two boys tussled with each other. (Lv88) **2** to argue with one another <***Loc:*** EV, IB, JD, LA, SL, SM, Da84, Lv88, Ph36>

halant [halɑ̃] *adj.* difficult, hard, exhausting **Un travail halant.* Hard work. (Di32) <***Loc:*** JE, Di32, Gr86>

haleine [halɛ̃n, alɛ̃n] *n.f.* breath, wind <***Loc:*** Da84, Hi02>

haler [hale] **I** *v.tr.* **1** to pull, haul, tow *Une seine, il faut tu la hales, tu la hales jusqu'à t'arrives au* BOAT. A seine net, you have to haul it, you haul it until you get to the boat. (JE) *Le mulet hale la charrue.* The mule is pulling the plow. (SM) *Je les ai laissé haler leur maison là.* I let them haul their house there. (SL) *Ce pauvre homme croyait qu'il pourrait me haler sur son bord.* This poor man [a politician] thought he could pull me over to his side. (Lv88) *Le char qui hale avec les roues d'en-avant.* Front-wheel drive car. (EV) **2** to transport *Ça halait les petits à l'école en wagonnettes, ça appelait,* COVERED WAGONS, *avec deux chevaux.* They transported the kids to school in covered wagons, with two horses. (EV) **3** to extract (esp. a tooth) *Ça coûtait une piastre pour haler une dent.* It costed a dollar to extract a tooth. (SL) **4** to pull (the trigger of a gun) **[Il] a halé la gagette dessus son pistolet.* He pulled the trigger on his pistol. (Wh83) **5** to strain, pull (a muscle) *Je m'ai halé un muscle.* I pulled a muscle. (VM) **6** to draw (air) *Elle avait un éventail dans le chassis, et puis ça halait l'air.* She had a fan in the window and it drew air. (SL) *Il a halé un grand soupir.* He drew a long sigh. (Lv88) **II** *v.intr.* **1** to pull, tug *Hale pas sur le petit comme ça!* Don't pull on the little one like that! (VM) **2** to work hard *J'ai assez halé dans ma vie, je te garantis.* I've worked plenty hard in my life, I guarantee you. (TB) **Il a fallu haler pour élever ma famille.* I had to work hard to raise my family. (Di32) **3** to be difficult **Ç'a halé pour mettre cette statue debout.* It was difficult to raise this statue. (Di32) **III se haler** *v.pron.* **1** to move, move o.s. *Si tu as froid, hale-toi plus loin de l'éventail.* If you are cold, move farther away from the fan. (Lv88) **2** to scram, beat it *Il s'a halé chez lui.* He left to go home. (VM) **Hale-toi de là!* Get out of there! (Da84) ◊ **•haler dessur** to have a hard time of it *Il a halé dessur pour avoir son argent.* He had a hard time getting his money. (LF) <LF> **•haler ensemble** to work together, pull together <SM> **•haler ses caniques** to beat it, leave in a hurry *Allons haler nos caniques avant ils arrivent.* Let's beat it before they get here. (LA) <LA,

Da84> **•haler ses fesses {ses frètes / son frète}** to leave quickly *Tu ferais mieux de haler tes fesses.* You had better leave quickly. (LA) *Hale ton frète!* Get out! (SM) <AC, AV, LA, SM, La99> **•haler son gratin** to get away quickly, leave abruptly *Il a bien halé son gratin quand j'ai dit ça.* He left abruptly when I said that. (IB) <AV, IB, La99> **•haler un coup** to have sex <SB> **•halez la planche** there's nothing left to say *Quand il dit ça, halez la planche!* When he says that, there's nothing left to say. (IB) <IB> **•se haler à côté** to step aside *Hale-toi à côté pour les laisser passer.* Step aside to let them pass. (LA) <LA, Da84> **•s'en haler de** to manage, get along *Il s'en halera assez bien.* He'll manage pretty well. (VM) <VM, Di32> <***Loc:*** AC, AV, EV, IB, JE, LA, LF, PQ, SB, SJ, SL, SM, VM, Da84, Co80, Di32, Gu00, Hi02, La99, Lv88, Ph36>

haleur [halœr] *n.m.* hauler, driver, delivery man ◊ **•haleur d'argent** ***a*** spendthrift, big spender ***b*** winner at cards <JE, TB, VM, Di32, Gr86> **•haleur d'ouvrage** hard worker <VM, Di32, Gr86, Lv88> <***Loc:*** JE, TB, VM, Di32, Gr86, Lv88>

halicasser [halikase, halekase] *n.m.* **1** turbulence, pandemonium *J'ai jamais vu un pareil halicasser comme ils avaient à la danse hier soir.* I've never seen pandemonium like they had at the dance last night. (SM) **2** celebration, large noisy party <***Loc:*** SB, SM>

HALL [hɔl] *n.m.* **1** hall, hallway *Une fois que j'ai déjeuné je vas marcher le HALL. Tout le HALL en plein, et revenir.* Once I've eaten lunch I walk the hallway. All the way down the hall and back. (TB) **2** vestibule **3** dance hall, ballroom ◊ **•HALL de danse** dance hall <Gr86> <***Loc:*** AV, EV, SB, SL, SM, TB, VM, Da84, Di32, Gr86, Ph36>

halle [hal] *n.f. (often pl.)* **1** meat market *C'était juste tuer pour les halles.* It was just killing for the meat market. (VM) **2** butcher shop *Je m'ai ouvert une halle à Lawtell.* I opened a butcher shop in Lawtell. (EV) <***Loc:*** EV, IB, LA, SM, VM, Da84, Gr86, Lv88>

hallucination [alysinasjɔ̃] *n.f.* hallucination <***Loc:*** Da84>

halocher [haloʃe] *v.tr.* to pull, tug <***Loc:*** JD>

halt [halt] *interj.* halt, stop <***Loc:*** Da84>

hamac [hɑ̃ma] *n.m.* hammock <***Loc:*** Da84>

hameçon (**z-hameçon**) [ɑ̃msɔ̃, ɑ̃msɑ̃, zɑ̃msɔ̃] *n.m.* **1** hook *On mettait l'hameçon au bout pour attraper les petits bétails.* We would put the hook at the end to catch small animals. (AC) **2** fish hook <***Loc:*** AC, AV, EV, JE, SM, TB, Da84, Hi02>

hanche [hɑ̃ʃ] *n.f.* **1** hip *Un coup de cable aux hanches de la bête faisait comprendre le désir de l'entraîneur.* A flick of the switch on the animal's haunches made it understand what the trainer wanted. (Lv88) **2** thigh (of poultry) *Vous-autres voulez la hanche ou l'estomac?* Would you like the thigh or the breast? (Lv88) <***Loc:*** EV, TB, JE, TB, LF, SL, Da84, Lv88>

HANDICAP [hændikæp] *n.m.* handicap <***Loc:*** Da84>

hangar [ɑ̃gar, hɑ̃gar] *n.m./f.* **1** shed, hangar *Un hangar pour les boguets et les barouches.* A shed for the buggies and surreys. (Gr86) **2** barn, shelter for animals *J'ai une grosse hangar en arrière là. Ben là j'ai des écuries dans l'hangar et j'ai du foin aussi et j'ai d'autres affaires.* I have a big barn in the back. I have stables in the barn and I also have hay and other things. (LF) ◊ **•hangar à bateau** boathouse <LF> **•hangar à laver** washhouse <TB> <***Loc:*** EV, IB, JD, JE, LA, LF, SJ, SM, TB, VM, Da84, Gu00, Hi02, Lv88>

hanneton [hɑ̃ntɔ̃] *n.m.* **1** June bug, May bug **2** Japanese beetle <***Loc:*** SB, SM, Da84>

hannir ♦see **hennir**

happer [hape, ape] *v.tr.* to snatch, steal *Il a happé une plaquemine en passant.* He snatched a persimmon in passing. (LA) <***Loc:*** AV, JD, LA, SJ, Da84, Lv88>

haque ♦see **HACK**

harassement [harasmɑ̃] *n.m.* harassment, pestering, harassing <***Loc:*** Da84>

harasser [harase] *v.tr.* **1** to harass, pester, annoy **2** to wear down, fatigue *Les enfants m'ont harassé à l'école aujourd'hui.* The children wore me down at school today. (SM) <***Loc:*** SM, Da84>

hardé [arde] *adj.* ◊ **•œuf hardé** soft-shelled egg <TB, Di32> <***Loc:*** TB, Di32>

hardi, -e [hardi, ardi] *adj.* **1** hardy, strong *Un homme hardi.* A hardy/strong man. (VM) **2** bold *Il est hardi. Il marche tout partout dans la cyprière.* He is bold. He walks all over the swamp. (VM) **3** stingy *Ton frère est trop hardi.* Your brother is too stingy. (SB) <***Loc:*** JE, SB, VM, Da84>

haria ♦see **hariat**

hariat (**haria, aria, ariasse**) [harja, hɑ̃rjɑ̃, arja, arjas] *n.m.* **1** good-for-nothing person *Le monde qui reste auprès de l'école, c'est des harias.* The people who live near the school, they're trash. (SM) **2** *(often pl.)* trash, anything old or beat up *J'ai nettoyé ma grande CLOSET et j'ai porté un tas d'hariats dans le garage.* I cleaned out my big closet and I took a pile of trash into the garage. (Lv88) *C'est un tas d'hariat.* That is a lot of trash. (JE) *Ce capot est un haria.* That coat is an old rag. (IB) **3** bother, row *Quel aria!* What a bother! (SM) <***Loc:*** EV, IB, JD, JE, LA, LF, SB, SJ, SM, TB, Da84, Di32, Lv88>

haricot (**z-haricot, zarico**) [ariko, zariko] *n.m.* **1** bean **2** string bean, snap bean, green bean *On dit pas les haricots verts, on dit les haricots.* We don't say green beans, we say beans. (SL) ◊ **•haricot à brasse** yard-long bean <Da84> **•haricot cire** ***a*** wax bean ***b*** butter bean <JD, Da84> **•haricot de chaland** bush bean <TB> **•haricot de factrie** stringless bean used in canning <TB> **•haricot (de) rame** vining string bean, pole bean <AV, IB, JD, LA, LF, SB, SM, TB, Da84> **•haricot fleur** worthless man <AV> **•haricot nain** bush bean <IB, LA, SB, SM, Da84> **•comment les**

haricots? How are you? How are things? <La99> <***Loc:*** AC, CL, EV, IB, JD, LA, LF, SB, SL, SM, TB, VM, Da84, Gu00, Lv88>

haricoter [arikote] *v.tr.* to do in a slipshod way <***Loc:*** JD>

harminette ♦see **herminette**

harnaché, -e [arnaʃe, arniʃe] *adj.* ◊ **•mal harnaché** ***a*** badly dressed ***b*** in bad shape, in bad condition <SM, Da84> <***Loc:*** SM, Da84>

harnachement [arnaʃmɑ̃] *n.m.* **1** trappings, clothing **2** flashy, gaudy attire **3** harnessing (esp. of poor quality) <***Loc:*** EV, IB, SM, Da84, Ph36>

harnacher [arnaʃe] **I** *v.tr.* **1** to harness *Harnacher un taureau pour l'empêcher de grimper les vaches.* To harness a bull to prevent it from mounting the cows. (VM) **2** to encumber, saddle *Je vois que ta femme t'a harnaché avec les enfants aujourd'hui pour aller au* MALL*.* I see that your wife saddled you with the kids so that she could go to the mall. (LA) **3** to repair or prepare for temporary use, jury-rig *Il va harnacher cette machine.* He's going to jury-rig that machine. (IB) **4** to rig out **II s'harnacher** *v.pron.* to dress o.s. poorly *T'as vu la robe qu'alle s'a harnaché avec aujourd'hui?* Have you seen the dress she's wearing today [how poorly she is dressed]. (VM) <***Loc:*** EV, IB, JD, LA, SM, VM, Da84, Ph36>

harnais (**harnois**) [arnɛ, arne, harne, arnwa, ardɛ̃] *n.m.* **1** harness **2** harness, fittings for horse or mule <***Loc:*** IB, JE, SL, SM, Da84>

harnois ♦see **harnais**

harpe [harp, arp] *n.f.* harp <***Loc:*** TB, Da84>

harpon [harpɔ̃] *n.m.* harpoon <***Loc:*** Da84>

hartchiner [hartʃine, atʃine] **I** *v.tr.* to manhandle, handle roughly *Il hartchine trop ce petit.* He handles that little boy too roughly. (SM) **II se hartchiner** *v.pron.* to fight <***Loc:*** EV, SM, Ph36>

hasard [hazar, azar] *n.m.* hazard, chance, risk ◊ **•d'hasard / par hasard** by chance *Vous avez peut-être pas vu par hasard une petite jument sorrel, queue coupée queue ouvert avec deux poulains derrière?* You wouldn't by chance have seen a little sorrel mare with a cut tail and two foals behind her? (LA, An94) <JE, LA, An94, Da84, Di32> <***Loc:*** JE, LA, An94, Da84, Di32>

hâter (**se**) [hate] *v.pron.* to hurry **Il faudra je me hâte m'en rentourner.* I will have to hurry to return. (EV, An94) <***Loc:*** EV, An94, Da84>

haulier [holje] *n.m.* hame, harness <***Loc:*** VM>

hausse [hos, hɔs] *n.f.* extension, side wall made of boards or other material to increase the carrying capacity of a wagon, truck, or other container *Il y avait trois hausses, à mesure tu foulais, ça levait.* There were three extensions, as you stuffed it, they would extend the side walls upward. (SL) <***Loc:*** SL, VM, Da84, Di32, Lv88>

hausser [hose, hoʃe] **I** *v.tr.* **1** to raise, lift *Une mèche, il faudrait tu la hausses. C'est plus bousilleux.* A lowland, you had to raise it. It was muddier. (VM) **2** to increase, raise **Hausser le prix.* To raise the price. (Da84) **II se hausser** *v.pron.* to lift o.s. up *Mame peut p'us se hausser dans le boghei.* Mama can't lift herself up into the buggy anymore. (VM) <***Loc:*** VM, Da84>

haut[1]**, -e** [ho, hɔt] *adj.* **1** high *L'eau était haute. Quand j'étais rendu au milieu du platin, j'étais rendu aux bagaris.* The water was high. When I got to the middle of the low spot, the water was up to my saddle flaps. (AS) *Notre maison était haute, des cales à peu près tout près de trois pieds.* Our house was up high, [on] blocks about three feet high. (LA, An94) **2** tall, of a certain height *Une bâtisse haute.* A tall building. (TB) **Il mange des petits pins d'une bouchée, des petits pins haut comme ça-là.* It eats little pine trees in one mouthful, little pine trees about so tall. (EV, An94) **Ouais, c'est des maringouins de Texas. Ils sont à peu près six pieds de haut, à peu près deux cents livres.* Yeah, they're mosquitos from Texas. They're about six feet tall, about 200 pounds. (EV, An94) **Les poules et pintales aimaient se jouquer dans cette herbe qui profitait des fois 5 pied de haut.* The chickens and guinea hens liked to roost in this weed that grew up to 5 feet tall sometimes. (Wh83) **3** upper **4** greater than usual or expected *Mon* BLOOD PRESSURE *est toujours haut, il a toujours été comme ça.* My blood pressure is always high, it has always been like that. (IB) <***Loc:*** AS, AV, EV, IB, IV, LA, SM, TB, VM, An94, Da84, Gu00, Hi02, La99, Lv88>

haut[2] [ho] *n.m.* top, highest part *Moi je me rappelle dans 1927 on était tout petit et l'eau était à peu près comme ça de le haut de la levée.* I remember in 1927 we were quite small, and the water was about that far from the top of the levee. (SB) *Je vas essayer de recoller le haut de ton violon avant que t'arrives.* I'll try to reglue the top of your violin before you come. (VM) ◊ **•haut des oignons** green onions, scallions <VM> **•haut du jour** top of the day, from 11 a.m. to 1 p.m. *C'est le haut du jour qu'il fait chaud.* It's at the top of the day that it's hot. (TB) *Sur le haut du jour.* At the hottest time of the day. (Lv88) <AV, SM, TB, Lv88, Re31> <***Loc:*** AV, SB, SM, TB, VM, Hi02, Lv88, Re31>

haut[3] [ho] *adv.* high *Quand ça mouillait les grosses pluies qui montaient haut, on allait pêcher attraper des gros poissons.* When it would rain hard and the water level would rise high, we would go fishing to catch big fish. (AC) *J'ai monté la mèche trop haut en dessous de ma chaudière et ça a détamé le grenit.* I put the burner on too high under my pot and it damaged the enamel. (VM) ◊ **•en haut** ***a*** up, up there *Il était pendu en haut-là.* He was hanging up there. (AC, An94) *Quand il a arrivé en haut, il y avait plus de moutons.* When he got up there, there were no more sheep. (AC, An94) ***b*** on top *Une romaine à viande, c'est la romaine est carrée comme ça. Elle a une petite tablette en haut. Tu mets un bassin et tu pèses ce tu veux.* A meat scale, it's a scale that's about this big of a square. It has a little platform on top. You put a pan [on it] and measure how much you want. (AC) *En bas du baril, tu mettais comme des coton maïs, tu connais,* CORNCOB. *Tu faisais feu. Ça, là boucanait en haut. Et ça boucane la viande.* In the bottom of the barrel you would put corncobs. You'd make a fire. That would smoke the meat at the top. (VM) ***c*** upstairs *Les enfants couchent en haut dans le grenier.* The children sleep upstairs in the attic. (TB) *Dans les vieilles maisons, les vieux dormaient en bas et les jeunes dormaient en haut.* In the old houses, the older folks slept downstairs and the younger ones slept upstairs. (LA) *C'est du monde riche, ils ont une chambre à bain en haut.* They are rich people, they have a bathroom upstairs. (EV) ***d*** upstream, up the bayou *Je porte pas grand attention, mais je peux dire quand eux-autres vient d'en bas, et si c'est que ça vient d'en haut, parce que le monde d'en haut parle pas pareil comme eusse d'en bas.* I don't pay much attention, but I can tell when they come up from down the bayou or if they come from up the bayou, because people up the bayou don't talk the same as those from down the bayou. (TB) <AC, EV, LA, SL, TB, VM, An94> **•en haut (de)** ***a*** on, upon *Lui et petit Edgar Breaux étaient assis en haut la galerie.* He and little Edgar Breaux were seated on the porch. (LA) *Mets-les en haut la table.* Put them on the table. (VM) ***b*** on top of *Ça flotte en haut de l'eau.* It floats on top of the water. (AC) *Il a caché son argent en haut de l'armoire.* He hid his money on top of the armoire. (LA) ***c*** above *Si le monde avait été là, ils auraient tué quelqu'un dans le lit. Juste en haut du lit-là, les balles ont passé.* If people had been there, they would have killed someone in the bed. The bullets passed right there above the bed. (LA, An94) ***d*** up *Mon père a venu acheter un terrain à peu près à dix miles en haut d'ici.* My father came to buy a piece of property about ten miles up from here. (LF) <AC, LA, LF, SL, SM, VM, An94> **•en haut du bayou** up the bayou *Ses petits enfants avait été élevés et ont resté en haut du bayou là-bas.* His children were raised and have lived up the bayou over there. (TB) <TB> **•en haut et en bas** up and down *Tu mets le crème dans une grosse jarre et il y avait un palon dedans, on allait en haut et en bas avec le palon.* You put the cream in a large jar and there was a churning stick inside that you moved up and down. (AC) <AC> **•par en haut** up the parish, northern part of St.Martin Parish (Breaux Bridge, Cecilia, Arnaudville) *Je vais par en haut ce matin.* I'm going up the parish this morning. (SM) <SM> <***Loc:*** AC, EV, LA, SM, TB, VM, An94, Da84, Hi02, Lv88>

hauteur [hotœr] *n.f.* **1** height **2** altitude <***Loc:*** LA, SJ, An94, Da84>

haut-le-corps [holkɔr] *n.m.* **1** ruckus, commotion **Qui c'est qui fait un pareil haut-le-corps?* Who is making such a commotion? (EV, Ph36) **2** scream, yell *J'aime pas entendre ces haut-le-corps le soir.* I don't like hearing that yelling at night. (IB) <***Loc:*** EV, IB, Ph36>

havresac [hɑ̃brəsak] *n.f.* gamebag <***Loc:*** LF>

hé [he] *interj.* **1** word of warning **2** used to call attention **Hé là-bas!* Hey you there! (Da84) <***Loc:*** Da84>

HEADLAND [ɛdlɛ̃, ɛdlɛ̃n, ɛdlɛ̃d, hɛdlɛ̃n] *n.m.* turnrow, headland (strip of uncultivated land at the end or side of a field where a plow can turn) <***Loc:*** LF, SB, SJ>

hébreu [ebrø] *adj.* [*eccl.*] Hebrew, Jewish <***Loc:*** VM, Da84>

hein (ain) [ɛ̃] *interj.* **1** question particle used to reiterate a question or statement (e.g. huh? right? isn't it?) **Ça fait mal, hein?* It hurts, doesn't it? (Da84) *Tu regardes de chaque bord de toi, qui tu vois, juste de l'eau, hein?* You look on either side of you, what do you see, just water, right? (TB) **C'est pas vrai, ça? Hein?* Isn't that true? Isn't it? (SM, An94) **Mais il vit toujours, hein?* But he's still alive, right? (EV, An94) **Il était bien près, hein?* He was really close, wasn't he? (LA, An94) **Ça c'était une histoire, hein?* That was a [good] story, wasn't it? (LA, An94) **Tu t'en rappelles quoi ce qu'on s'a promis, hein?* You remember what we promised each other, don't you? (An94) **2** sorry? pardon? ◊ **•ain-hein** yes <Da84> <***Loc:*** EV, LA, SM, TB, An94, Da84>

hélas [hela, ela] *n.m.* noise **Ç'hélas est assez fort qu'an [=on] peut pas s'attenne [=s'attendre].* That noise is so loud that we can't hear each other. (EV, Ph36) ◊ **•faire des (grands) hélas** ***a*** to exclaim ***b*** to talk excitedly <EV, LA, La99, Lv88> <***Loc:*** EV, LA, SM, La99, Lv88, Ph36>

héler [hele] *v.intr.* **1** to shout, yell, scream *J'ai hélé pour il m'attende.* I shouted loudly so that he would hear me. (Lv88) *Je peux l'entendre héler sur ses enfants de ma maison.* I can hear him yelling at his children from my house. (SB) **2** to cry *Mon petit a hélé toute la nuit.* My little one cried all night. (SM) <***Loc:*** SB, SM, Lv88>

HELICOPTER [helikɔptə] *n.m.* helicopter <***Loc:*** Da84, Lv88>

hem (hém) [hɛ̃m] *interj.* used to call attention <***Loc:*** Da84>

hème [hɛ̃m] *n.m.* hame *Ça passait les guides et les rênes dans les hèmes.* The traces and the reins would go through the hames. (AC) <***Loc:*** AC>

hémorragie [ɛ̃moraʒi] *n.f.* hemorrhage <***Loc:*** TB, Da84>

hémorroïdes (hémorvites) [ɛ̃moroit, ɛ̃moruit ɛ̃mɔrvit] *n.f.pl.* piles, hemorrhoids <***Loc:*** EV, LA, LF, SM, VM, Da84, Lv88, Ph36>

hémorvites ♦see **hémorroïdes**

hennir (hannir) [hɛ̃nir, hɑ̃nir] *v.intr.* **1** to neigh, whinny *Son cheval s'a mis à hannir.* His horse started to whinny. (LA) **2** to giggle *Cesse donc de hennir comme ça.* Quit giggling like that. (VM) <***Loc:*** IB, SM, VM, Da84, Lv88>

henter [hɑ̃te] *v.tr.* to join two pieces of wood end to end *Il faudra qu'on hente ces deux-par-quatre pour élongir la couverture.* We'll have to butt these two-by-fours together to extend the roof. (VM) <***Loc:*** JE, VM, Di32>

henture [hɑ̃tyr] *n.f.* place where two pieces of wood are joined, scarf joint <*Loc:* JE, VM, Di32>

hépatique [epatik] *adj.* hepatic *Du sel hépatique.* Sal Hepatica. (VM) <*Loc:* VM, Da84>

herbages [ærbaʒ] *n.m.pl.* **1** aromatic herbs **2** weeds **3** yard waste (i.e. grass cuttings, pulled weeds, etc.) <*Loc:* SM, VM, Da84, Lv88>

herbailles [ærbaj] *n.f.pl.* **1** aromatic herbs *Mal aux dents, mal d'oreille, mal au ventre, et là il connaissait les tisanes et tout. Il prend les herbailles et il bouillait ça.* Toothache, earache, stomachache, he knew herbal teas and all. He took herbs and boiled them. (TB) **2** weeds *C'est pas souvent qu'elle a autant d'herbailles dans sa cour.* She doesn't often have so many weeds in her yard. (SB) **3** yard waste (i.e. grass cuttings, pulled weeds, etc.) *Les herbailles ont été brûlées.* The grass cuttings have been burned. (TB) <*Loc:* TB, SM, Lv88>

herbe (**z-herbe**) [ærb, zarb, dezarb, zærb, zɛb] *n.f.* **1** (*usu. pl.*) grass **Tchou Flang coupe les herbes.* Tchou Flang cuts the grass. (Wh83) **Pourquoi t'es penché comme ça, Vince? T'as échappé quelque chose dans les herbes?* Why are you bent over like that, Vince? Did you drop something in the grass? (ThCa: *Grosbecs*) **2** herb **3** weed ◊ **•herbe à balai** broomcorn millet <Lv88> **•herbe à bale** loosestrife <Ho90> **•herbe à bâton** ***a*** giant ragweed, bloodweed ***b*** goldenrod <IB, JE, SB> **•herbe à cabri {mouton}** goatweed <SB, SM, VM, Gr86> **•herbe à chenille** Indian heliotrope <SB> **•herbe à chien** Saint-Andrew's cross <Ho90> **•herbe à cocodrie {de batture}** alligator weed <SB, Ho90> **•herbe à crapaud blanche** mistflower <SB> **•herbe à crapaud rouge** creeping spotflower <SB> **•herbe à fer** chestnut grass <SB> **•herbe à houatte** milkweed <Ho90> **•herbe à la puce** poison ivy <AV, IB, JD, JE, LA, LF, SB, SL, SM, TB, VM, Da84, Gr86, Hi02, Ho90, Lv88> **•herbe à malo** lizard's tail, swamp lily <IB, JE, SM, TB, VM, Gr86, Ho90, Lv88> **•herbe amère** bitterweed <Wh83> **•herbe à parasol** pennywort <SB> **•herbe à piquant** pigweed <SB> **•herbe à serpent** Indian mallow, false mallow, Indian hemp <SB, Ho90, Lv88> **•herbe à sureau** elderberry <SB> **•herbe à trois coins** three-cornered grass <TB> **•herbe à trois quarts {écarts}** ***a*** star grass ***b*** crownbeard, Virginia crownbeard, wingstem <IB, JE, SB, TB, Da84, Ho90, Lv88> **•herbe au cœur** yellow water lily <Ho90> **•herbe à vers** ***a*** daisy fleabane ***b*** wormwood <SB, Ho90> **•herbe de marais** swamp grass <VM> **•herbe de Timothée** ***a*** Timothy grass ***b*** meadow foxtail <SB> **•herbe d'huître** smooth cordgrass <Ho90> **•herbe du bayou** water hyacinth, common water lily <TB> **•herbe du {à} sang** giant ragweed, bloodweed <IB, JE, Ho90> **•herbe farouche** weed <Gr39> **•herbe fine / herbe canard gris** pondweed <Ho90> **•herbe honteuse** balsamine, touch-me-not <SB, Lv88> **•herbe mal nommée** creeping spurge <IB, SB> **•herbe ronde** panic grass <SB> **•herbe sainte** absinthe, wormwood <EV, Gr39, Lv88, Ph36> **•herbe tendre** toothcup <SB> **•grandes herbes** weeds <Da84, Lv88> <*Loc:* EV, IB, JE, LA, SB, SM, TB, VM, An94, Da84, Gr39, Gr86, Hi02, Ho90, Lv88, Ph36, ThCa, Wh83>

herbe coquin (**herbe-coquine, herbe à coquin, aircotien, arcoquin, arscokin**) [ærbakokɛ̃, arkotʃɛ̃, ærkotjɛ̃, arkotʃin, arkokɛ̃, arskokɛ̃] *n.m./f.* cocklebur ◊ **•herbe coquin bâtard** small ragweed <SB> <*Loc:* AV, EV, IB, JE, LA, SB, SL, LA, SB, SM, VM, Da84, Di32, Gr86, Ho90, Lv88, Ph36>

herculant [hærkylɑ̃, ærkylɑ̃] *n.m.* hangnail <*Loc:* IB, JE, Di32>

hercule [ærkyl] *n.m.* very strong man, Hercules **Il est un hercule.* He is a very strong man. (Da84) <*Loc:* Da84>

héréditaire [ereditær] *adj.* hereditary *Il y a pas à rien tu peux faire pour ses vilaines manières. C'est héréditaire, ça.* There's nothing you can do about his bad habits. That's hereditary, that. (LA) <*Loc:* LA, Da84>

hérédité [eredite] *n.f.* heredity <*Loc:* Da84>

hérésie [erezi] *n.f.* heresy <*Loc:* Da84>

hérétique [eretik] *n.* [*eccl.*] heretic <*Loc:* Da84>

hérisson [herisɔ̃] *n.* device that separates cotton from its seed <*Loc:* Gr86>

héritage [eritaʒ, haritaʒ] *n.m.* **1** inheritance *Son père l'a laissé un grand héritage.* His father left him a large inheritance. (VM) **2** heritage (cultural and ethnic) *Je crois que c'est une bonne idée pour garder notre héritage, pour eusse montrer comment parler en français.* I think it's a good idea to keep our heritage, for them to teach how to speak French. (LF) **3** genealogy *J'ai un cousin qu'a tracé l'héritage jusqu'à dans le temps que le monde avait pas de derniers noms.* I have a cousin who traced the genealogy back to the time when people didn't have last names. (LF) <*Loc:* LF, VM, Da84, Hi02>

héritance [eritɑ̃s] *n.f.* inheritance <*Loc:* EV, JE, SB, SM, TB, Di32, Lv88, Ph36>

héritation [eritasjɔ̃] *n.f.* inheritance <*Loc:* JE, SM, Di32>

hériter [erite] *v.tr.* to inherit *Il est sûr qu'il va hériter la place à son grand-père.* He's sure that he's going to inherit his grandfather's place. (LA) <*Loc:* LA, Da84, Hi02>

héritier, -ière [eritje, -jær] *n.* heir <*Loc:* Da84>

herminette (**arminette, harminette**) [arminɛt] *n.f.* **1** adze **2** cooper's adze **3** tool to split posts <*Loc:* LF, Da84>

hermitte ♦see **ermite**

hernie [hærni] *n.f.* hernia <*Loc:* Da84>

HERO ♦see **héros**

héroïne [eroin] *n.f.* heroine <*Loc:* Da84>

héron [erɔ̃, herɔ̃] *n.m.* heron ◊ **•héron bleu** blue heron <Gu00> **•héron dos blanc** egret <Lv88, Re63> **•grand héron** great blue heron, great heron <IV, SB, VM> <*Loc:* IB, IV, SB, SM, TB, VM, Da84, Gu00, Hi02, Re63>

héros (**HERO**) [ero, hiɹo] *n.m.* hero <*Loc:* Da84, Hi02>

hersage [hærsaʒ] *n.m.* harrowing <*Loc:* Da84>

herse [hærs] *n.f.* **1** harrow *Une herse, c'était à peu près quatre pieds carrés qu'avait des dents.* A harrow, it was about four square feet that had teeth. (EV) *On mettait deux herses, et puis on les entassait pour les brûler.* We put two harrows, and then we piled them up to burn them. (SL) **2** weeder <*Loc:* EV, SB, SL, VM, Da84>

herser [hærse] *v.tr.* **1** to harrow *Il avait pour herser la pièce avant de planter.* He had to harrow the field before planting. (LA) **2** to beat, whip *Il a hersé le nègre à coups de fouet.* He beat the black man with a whip. (SL) **3** to beat, defeat (in a contest, game, etc.) *Il m'a hersé dans la game de cartes.* He beat me at the card game. (SM) <*Loc:* JD, LA, SB, SL, SM, Da84>

hésitation [ezitasjɔ̃] *n.f.* hesitation, indecision <*Loc:* Da84>

hésiter [ezite] *v.intr.* to hesitate, be undecided *Il aurait jamais hésité d'aider le monde.* He would never hesitate to help people. (LA) <*Loc:* LA, Da84, Hi02>

hêtre [hɛt(r)] *n.m.* beech tree <*Loc:* Hi02>

heure [œr] *n.f.* **1** hour **Il pouvait te raconter des contes qui duraient des heures de temps longs.* He could tell you stories that would last for hours. (SM, An94) **2** time of day **Quelle heure il est? —Dix heures et un quart.* What time is it? —Quarter past ten (ten fifteen). (Da84) **Dix heures dix.* Ten after ten. (Da84) **Dix heures moins dix.* Ten to ten. (Da84) **3** time, moment *C'était l'heure de dîner.* It was time to eat. (VM) ◊ **•(à / de) bonne heure** early *J'ai été à bonne heure remplir mon petit PINT.* I went there early to fill up my my little pint bottle. (SL) *Elle est venue bonne heure.* She came early. (SM) *Il faut se lever bonne heure si tu veux aller à la ville.* You need to get up early if you want to go to New Orleans. (Lv88) *Il a planté sa graine trop de bonne heure et le froid l'a empêchée de germer.* He planted his seed too early and the cold prevented it from germinating. (IV) *C'est plus bonne heure.* It's no longer early. (Lv88) <IV, SL, SM, TB, VM, Da84, Lv88> **•à toutes heures** at all hours <Da84> **•c'est l'heure** it's time <Da84> **•c'est l'heure de voir à couper tes culottes** you are acting too impudent, you need to be put back into your place <La99> **•c'est l'heure qu'on casse le rond** it's time to break up the party or conversation (and go home) <La99> **•c'est l'heure qu'on lève la paille** it's time to go <La99> **•plus de bonne heure** earlier *Tu m'as demandé plus de bonne heure qui on appelait un ALLIGATOR. OKAY, moi j'ai dit un caïman. Ça pourrait être un cocodrie aussite.* You asked me earlier what we called an alligator. Okay, I said it's a "caïman." It could also be a "cocodrie." (TB) <TB> <*Loc:* AC, EV, LF, SL, SM, TB, VM, An94, Da84, Hi02, La99, Lv88>

heureusement [ørøzmɑ̃] *adv.* happily, fortunately *Heureusement que c'est p'us comme ça asteur.* Happily, now it's not that way anymore. (LA) <*Loc:* LA, SM, Da84, Hi02>

heureux, -euse [ørø, yrø, -øz] *adj.* **1** fortunate, lucky, blessed *Il était heureux parce qu'il avait hérité de l'argent.* He was fortunate because he had inherited some money. (VM) **2** happy *Et c'est pas des piastres qui va te faire heureux.* And it's not dollars that will make you happy. (ch: *Valse de la Rivière Rouge*) ◊ **•heureux comme un poisson {les poissons} dans l'eau** very happy <Da84, La99> <*Loc:* JE, VM, Da84, Di32, Hi02, La99>

hibou (z-hibou, l-hibou) [hibu, ibu, zibu, libu] *n.m.* **1** owl **2** sparrow hawk ◊ **•hibou à cornes** great horned owl <IB, JD, TB, Re63> **•hibou de paille** chicken hawk <VM> **•hibou grosse tête** barred owl, night owl, hoot owl <IB, JD, TB, Re63> <*Loc:* IB, JD, SB, SL, SM, TB, VM, Da84, Lv88, Re63>

hickory [hikre, hikore] *n.m.* hickory <*Loc:* Lv88>

hier [ijær, jær] *adv.* yesterday *Ça a grainé la viande hier.* They ground the meat yesterday. (LF) ◊ **•hier (au) soir** last night **J'ai rêvé hier au soir que tu m'avais donné ton cheval.* I dreamed last night that you had given me your horse. (SL, An94) <EV, LA, LF, SL, SM, TB, VM, An94, Da84, Gu00, Lv88> **•hier matin** yesterday morning <Da84> **•hier midi** yesterday noon <Da84> <*Loc:* EV, JE, LA, LF, SL, SM, TB, VM, An94, Da84, Gu00, Hi02, Lv88>

HIGH [haɪ] *v.intr.invar.* to work very hard without stopping *J'ai HIGH toute la journée.* I worked incessantly all day long. (SM) <*Loc:* LA, SM>

hirondelle [irɔ̃dɛl] *n.f.* **1** swallow **2** dragonfly, mosquito hawk **3** purple martin <*Loc:* AC, AV, IB, IV, LF, PQ, SB, SJ, SM, Da84, Lv88>

hisser [hise] **I** *v.tr.* to hoist, raise *Hisser la voile dessus le mât.* To hoist the sail on the mast. (VM) **II se hisser** *v.pron.* to hoist o.s., raise o.s. *J'ai assez de misère à me hisser dans le char.* I have so much trouble hoisting myself into the car. (VM) <*Loc:* VM, Da84>

histoire [istwar] *n.f.* **1** history *L'histoire des Cadjins.* The history of the Cajuns. (LA) *Mon oncle pouvait réciter tout l'histoire de la famille.* My uncle could recite the whole history of the family. (LA) **2** story, tale *Il a pas fini son histoire, il nous a laissé là suspendus.* He didn't finish his story. He left us hanging. (VM) **On dirait, c'est manière drôle de dire ça, BUT supposé ça a arrivé. C'est une histoire vraie.* It seems rather strange to say that, but supposedly it happened. It's a true story. (SL, An94) ◊ **•histoire farce** joke <Hi02> **•faire toute une histoire (de qqch)** to overreact, make a big deal out of s.t. <La99> <*Loc:* LA, SL, SM, VM, An94, Da84, Hi02, La99>

hiver [ivær] *n.m.* winter *Il piégeait tous les hivers.* He went trapping every winter. (TB) ◊ **•dans (l')hiver / en hiver** in winter *Mais son garaufier avait crevé dans l'hiver. Ça fait, il a jamais bourgeonné.* But his honey locust tree died in the winter. So, it never budded. (ThCa: *La dernière quilte*) <IV, PQ, TB, An94, Da84> <*Loc:* IV, LA, PQ, SL, SM, TB, VM, An94, Da84, Gu00, Hi02, ThCa>

ho [ho] *interj.* **1** cry to call a horse **2** cry to stop a horse <***Loc:*** SM>

hoba (**houba, hou ba**) [hoba, huba] *interj.* cry used to drive cattle or chase cattle away <***Loc:*** EV, LA, SL, SM, Da84, Lv88, Ph36>

hobo [obo, hobo] *n.m.* vagabond, hobo, tramp <***Loc:*** LF, SL, VM, Lv88>

hockey [hoke] *n.m.* hockey <***Loc:*** Da84>

hoi [hɔi] *n.m.* badly prepared meal *Ça c'était un hoi qu'alle nous a servi.* That was some slop that she served us. (VM) <***Loc:*** VM>

homard [hɔ̃mar, ɔ̃mar] *n.m.* lobster <***Loc:*** Da84>

hommage [ɔ̃maʒ] *n.m.* homage, honor <***Loc:*** Da84>

homme [ɔ̃m] *n.m.* **1** man *Un rougarou, ça peut être un homme ou une femme.* A werewolf, it can be a man or a woman. (JE) *Quoi les récoltiers allont faire avé les hommes tous partis à l'armée?* What will the farmers do, with all the men gone in the army? (VM) **2** husband **3** boyfriend ◊ **•homme à pipe** plumber <VM> **•homme clair** man not able to produce offspring, sterile man <LF, La99> **•homme d'affaires** businessman <Da84> **•homme d'affût** artful, crafty, sly man <Lv88> **•homme de conséquence** man of importance <Da84> **•homme de couleur** colored man, man of color <LF, Da84> **•homme de paille** ***a*** man who is a bluff, man who pretends to be dangerous but is not ***b*** effeminate man <SM, LA, La99> **•homme invisible** person who has "l'os du chat noir" (the black cat's bone), which according to superstition makes him invisible <VM> **•bel homme** handsome man <Da84> **•être homme** to be a strong, powerful man *Tous ces boulés qui battaient tous les autres, qu'étaient plus hommes que les autres là... C'est pas ça. C'est une qualité d'homme.* All those bullies who beat up all the others, who were more manly than the others . . . It's not that. It's a manly quality. (EV) <EV, LA> **•l'homme qu'a vu l'homme qu'a vu l'ours** the unknown source of a third-hand story or piece of gossip <La99> **•mon homme** [*term of endearment*] my man <Da84> <***Loc:*** AC, AV, EV, IV, JE, LA, LF, SL, SM, TB, VM, An94, Da84, Hi02, La99, Lv88, Wh83>

hongas [hɔ̃ŋa] *n.m.pl.* the blues *J'ai les hongas à ce soir.* I've got the blues tonight. (SM) <***Loc:*** SM>

honnête [ɔ̃nɛt] *adj.* honest, fair, truthful *Tante Besone disait que moi je suis pas honnête. Imagine-toi.* Aunt Besone said I was not honest. Imagine. (ThCa: *Messieurs, mesdames*) <***Loc:*** Da84, Hi02, ThCa>

honnêtement [ɔ̃nɛtmɑ̃] *adv.* honestly, truthfully, fairly <***Loc:*** Da84>

honnêteté [ɔ̃nɛt:e] *n.f.* honesty, integrity <***Loc:*** Da84>

honneur [ɔ̃nœr] *n.m.* honor, integrity, good reputation ◊ **•d'honneur** respectable, honorable *Frank vient d'une bonne famille. C'est du monde d'honneur et bien respecté.* Frank comes from a good family. They're honorable people and well respected. (ThCa: *La dernière quilte*) <ThCa> <***Loc:*** Da84, ThCa>

honorable [ɔ̃norab(l)] *adj.* honorable, respectful *C'est du monde honorable, ça.* They're honorable people. (VM) <***Loc:*** VM, Da84>

honorer [ɔ̃nɔre, ɔ̃nore] **I** *v.tr.* to honor, respect *Il a pas honoré sa promesse.* He did not honor his promise. (VM) **II s'honorer** *v.pron.* **1** to feel honored **2** to honor o.s. *Il s'a pas honoré avec un coup comme ça.* He did not honor himself with an act like that. (LA) <***Loc:*** LA, VM, Da84>

honte [hɔ̃t, ɔ̃t] *n.f.* **1** shame, disgrace, infamy **2** bashfulness, shyness, timidness ◊ **•avoir honte *a*** to be ashamed **J'ai honte.* I am ashamed. (Da84) *Il avait si honte, il a baissé sa tête.* He was so ashamed, he lowered his head. (LA) *J'étais assez canaille, quand j'étais dans le cinquième grade dans l'école publique, ça m'a* KICK OUT, *oh oui j'étais pas bon, j'ai cogné la maîtresse, j'ai honte mais elle m'a cogné à moi en premier.* I was rather unruly, when I was in the fifth grade in public school, they kicked me out, oh yes I was bad, I hit the school teacher, I am ashamed but she hit me first. (IB) ***b*** to be timid, shy, bashful *Il a honte devant le monde.* He is timid in front of people. (SM, VM) ***c*** to be embarrassed *Et la tasse était pas propre. Alle était* SMUDGE. *Et lui il se sert pas, il voulait pas boire le café, il avait honte, il avait zire de la tasse.* And the cup wasn't clean, it was smudged. And he doesn't use it, he didn't want to drink the coffee, he was embarrassed, the cup disgusted him. (LF) <IB, LF, SM, VM, Da84> **•faire honte (à qqn)** to embarrass (s.o.) *Awh, Mom. Tu me fais honte quand tu me flattes devant tout le monde.* Aw, Mom. You embarrass me when you flatter me in front of everyone. (ThCa: *La dernière quilte*) *Arrête de faire le bouffon, tu me fais honte!* Stop acting the clown! You're embarrassing me! (VM) <SL, VM, An94> <***Loc:*** IB, JD, LA, LF, SB, SL, SM, VM, An94, Da84, Hi02, ThCa>

honter ♦see **éhonter**

honteux, -euse [hɔ̃tø, -øz] *adj.* **1** shameful **Ça, c'est honteux.* That's shameful. (Da84) *Je trouvais que c'était honteux d'avoir une taxe si injuste que ça.* I thought it was shameful to have a tax as unjust as that. (ThCa: *Messieurs, mesdames*) **2** timid, bashful, shy *Je crois bien qu'il l'aime mais il va jamais y parler parce qu'il est trop honteux.* I really think he likes her, but he's never going to talk to her because he's too shy. (EV) <***Loc:*** EV, IB, LA, SB, SM, VM, An94, Da84, Hi02, ThCa>

HOP[1] [hap] *adj.* **1** energetic, able, lively *Je me sens pas trop* HOP *aujourd'hui.* I don't feel very lively today. (LA) **2** up to par, of quality *Tu vas pas laisser ta fille sortir avec ce bougre. Il est pas trop* HOP. You're not going to let your daughter go out with that guy. He's not of quality. (LA) *Les patates sont pas* HOP *cette année.* The potato crop is short this year. (SL) <***Loc:*** LA, SL>

hop[2] [hop] *interj.* cry for calling horses <***Loc:*** SB>

hôpital [opital] *n.m./f.* hospital <*Loc:* EV, LA, SM, VM, An94, Da84, Hi02, Lv88>

hoquer [hoke] *v.intr.* to hiccup <*Loc:* IB>

hoquet (**l-hoquet**) [oke, loke] *n.m.* hiccup, hiccups ◊ •**le hoquet de la mort** death gasp or rattle <Da84> <*Loc:* TB, Da84, Pe37>

horizon [orizɔ̃] *n.m.* horizon, skyline <*Loc:* Da84>

horloge [ɔrlɔʒ] *n.f.* clock, timepiece <*Loc:* Da84>

horloger [ɔrloʒe] *n.m.* **1** watchmaker, watch repairman **2** jeweler <*Loc:* Da84>

hormis [ɔrmi, urmi] *prep.* except *Y avait pas de manière que tu pouvais aller là hormis par bateau.* There was no way you could go there except by boat. (TB) ◊ •**hormis que** unless *Alle voudra pas te parler hormis que mon je lui dis que toi tu veux pas lui faire de tort, tu comprends.* She won't want to talk to you unless I tell her that you're not going to do her any harm, you understand. (TB) **Hormis qu'j'sus bien malade, je r'fuse jamais d'aller 'oir mes p'tits.* Unless I am really sick, I never refuse to go see my kids. (Gu82) <TB, Gu82> <*Loc:* EV, IB, LA, LF, TB, Gu82, Lv88>

hornette [hɔrnɛt] *n.f.* hornet <*Loc:* Hi02>

horoscope [oroskɔp] *n.m.* horoscope <*Loc:* Da84>

horreur [orœr] *n.f.* horror, dread, fright <*Loc:* Da84>

horrible [orib(l)] *adj.* horrible, frightful, awful *Son procès fut jugé d'une voix si-z-horrible, car le jeu et la boisson te fait perdre la raison.* The verdict was announced in such a horrible voice because gambling and drinking make you lose your mind. (PQ, ch: *Le jour de l'Ascension*) <*Loc:* PQ, Da84, Hi02>

hors [ɔr, hɔr] *prep.* out of, outside *Arrache-toi hors de mon chemin.* Get out of my way. (VM) ◊ •**hors d'âge** very old, very advanced in age **Ç'te femme est hors d'âge.* That woman is very old. (EV, Ph36) <EV, Ph36> •**hors de moi-même {toi-même etc.}** very nervous <LA, SM> •**hors de prix** very expensive *Cette chemise était hors de prix.* This shirt was very expensive. (VM) <VM> •**hors de service** beyond repair, ruined **Abîmer une machine hors de service.* To ruin a machine. (Da84) <LA, Da84> <*Loc:* EV, LA, SM, VM, Da84, Ph36>

hortense ♦see **hortensia**

hortensia (**hortense**) [ɔrtɑ̃sja, ɔrtɑ̃s] *n.m./f.* hydrangea <*Loc:* EV, Da84, Gu00>

hosanna [hozɑ̃na, ozɑ̃na] *interj.* [*eccl.*] hosanna <*Loc:* Da84>

hostie [osti] *n.f.* host (of communion) <*Loc:* Da84>

hôtel [otɛl] *n.m.* hotel <*Loc:* Da84, Hi02>

hôtellerie [otɛlri] *n.f.* hostelry, inn <*Loc:* Da84>

houba, hou ba ♦see **hoba**

houdou ♦see **voudou**

houppala [upala] *interj.* used when lifting a baby in the air <*Loc*: JD, LF>

hourra[1] [hura] *n.m.* **1** noise, racket **Qui c'est qui fait ç'hourra?* Who's making all that noise? (EV, Ph36) **2** uproar, confusion, fracas *Il y a eu un sacré hourra là-bas hier au soir.* There was a terrible uproar there last night. (VM) *Quand la vieille va au* SHOW, *c'est un vrai hourra à la maison avec les petits.* When the old lady goes to the show, it's a real uproar in the house with the kids. (SM) *Quelle sorte de hourra je suis fourré en dedans?* What kind of fracas have I gotten myself into? (Lv88) **2** large quantity, a lot, a bunch, many *On aurait dû nous tuer un hourra d'écureuils.* We should have killed a bunch of squirrels. (JD) *Ils ont subi un hourra de maladies dernièrement.* They have suffered many illnesses lately. (LA) ◊ •**hourra d'affaires** all sorts of things <Da84> <*Loc:* AV, EV, IB, JD, LA, LF, SB, SJ, SL, SM, TB, VM, Da84, Lv88, Ph36>

hourra[2] [hura, ura] *interj.* **1** hurry up *Hourra, hourra. On va d'être tard.* Hurry, hurry. We're going to be late. (LA) **Hourra!* Hurry up! (Da84) *Hourra! T'es tard.* Quick! You're late. (SM) *Hourra, Cecile, il faut faire vite.* Hurry, Cecile, it must be done quickly. (VM) **2** watch out, pay attention, hey *Hourra toi. Guette qui tu fais.* Hey you. Watch what you're doing. (EV) **3** hooray <*Loc*: AV, EV, JD, LA, SM, VM, Da84>

hourri-hourra [hurihura] *adv.* quickly, in a hurry *Il est venu hourri-hourra.* He came in a hurry. (Lv88) <*Loc:* Lv88>

huche [hyʃ] *n.m.* wood pile *Va sus le huche et hurle-mon un morceau de bois et viens pas ici avec une babine.* Go to the woodpile and get me a piece of wood and don't come back here pouting. (TB) <*Loc:* TB>

hucher [hyʃe] **I** *v.tr.* to call, summon by calling *Huche-lé, je veux y parler.* Call him, I want to talk to him. (TB) **II** *v.intr.* to cry out, call by crying out **Défunte Mam' avait déjà huché après nous aut' plusieurs fois, mais on faisait côme si on l'a'tendait pas.* Late Mom had already called us several times but we acted like we didn't hear her. (Gu82) <*Loc:* JD, TB, Di32, Gu82, Lv88, Pe37>

huile [ɥil, jil, wil] *n.f.* **1** petroleum, crude oil *On a frappé l'huile dans le clos vingt ans passés.* We struck oil in the field twenty years ago. (Lv88) **2** refined petroleum derivative (e.g. machine oil, lubricant oil) **3** any of a variety of oils (e.g. naturally occurring, aromatic, etc.) *Icitte-dedans t'as une huile, une huile espéciale, une huile naturelle qu'empêche l'eau de passer en travers du bois.* In here you've got an oil, a special oil, a natural oil that prevents water from going through the wood. (LF) **4** vegetable oil, cooking oil *Je faisais du roux [...] avec de l'huile et de la farine.* I use to make roux with oil and flour. (SL) ◊ •**huile à cuire** cooking oil <TB, Da84> •**huile à cylindre** cylinder oil <Da84> •**huile à {de} lampe** coal oil, kerosene <LA, SM, VM, Da84> •**huile à purger** castor oil <IB, LA, LF, SB, SL, SM, TB, VM, Da84, Lv88> •**huile de castor** castor oil <VM, Da84, Lv88> •**huile de charbon *a*** petroleum ***b*** coal oil, kerosene <SM, TB, Re31> •**huile de citronnelle** citronella oil <Da84> •**huile de foie de morue** cod liver oil <Da84> **•huile de goudron** pine tar oil <TB> **•huile de lin** linseed oil <Da84> **•huile de palma christi** castor oil <IB> **•huile d'olive** olive oil <Da84> **•huile douce** olive oil <Da84> **•huile fine** olive oil <JE, VM, Di32, Gr86> **•huile frète** gasoline <VM, Gr86> **•sainte huile** holy oil (for anointing the sick) <Da84> <***Loc:*** AC, IB, LA, SB, SL, SM, TB, VM, Da84, Gr86, Hi02, La99, Lv88, Re31>

huiler [ɥile] *v.tr.* to oil, lubricate <***Loc:*** Da84>

huileux, -euse [ɥilø, -øz] *adj.* oily *L'eau du bayou est huileuse depuis qu'ils ont fouillé le puits d'huile.* The bayou water is oily since they dug the oil well. (VM) <***Loc:*** VM, Da84>

huilier [[ɥilje, ɥiljær] *n.m.* oil can, oiler <***Loc:*** IB, Da84>

huit [ɥit] *adj./n.m.* eight *Ma mère était la septième de huit filles.* My mother was the seventh of eight daughters. (EV) *On est le huit aujourd'hui.* Today is the eighth. (VM) <***Loc:*** AV, EV, PQ, SL, SM, TB, VM, Da84, Hi02>

huitaine [ɥitɛ̃n] *n.m.* about eight **Il été parti passer son après midi avec ein huitaine d'autres vieux hommes à jouer aux cartes en arrière de la boutique à Edwin Guillory.* He went to spend his afternoon with about eight other men playing cards in the back of Edwin Guillory's shop. (Wh83) <***Loc:*** Wh83>

huitième [ɥitjɛ̃m] *adj./n.* eighth *Il avait été jusqu'à dedans le huitième et quand il a été dans le* NAVY *là il a fini son école dans le* NAVY. He had gone until the eighth [grade] and then when he was in the navy, he finished school in the navy. (EV) <***Loc:*** AC, EV, LF>

huître (z-huître) [ɥit, zwit, zɥit] *n.f.* oyster <***Loc:*** JE, LA, SL, SM, TB, Da84, Gu00, Hi02, Lv88>

huîtreur (z-huîtreur) [ɥitrœr, zɥitrœr] *n.m.* oyster-grower <***Loc:*** Lv88>

humain [ymɛ̃] *adj.* human **Un être humain.* Human being. (Da84) <***Loc:*** Da84>

humanité [ymɑ̃nite] *n.f.* humanity <***Loc:*** Da84>

humecter [ymɛkte] **I** *v.tr.* to wet, moisten, dampen *Ma grand-mère humectait son linge avant de le repasser.* My grandmother dampened her clothing before ironing it. (VM) **II s'humecter** *v.pron.* to get wet, become damp or moist *Tu laisses du persil s'humecter déhors avec la rosée, et là tu le mets sur tes yeux.* You let parsley become moist with the dew outside, and then you place it on your eyes. (VM) <***Loc:*** EV, VM, Da84>

humeur[1] [ymœr, imœr] *n.f.* mood, humor ◊ **•humeur furvoyante** very bad mood <SJ> **•(de / en) bonne humeur** in a good mood *Il est pas bonne humeur à ce matin.* He's not in a good mood this morning. (SM) <SM, Da84> **•de {en} mauvaise humeur** in a bad mood. *Ils m'ont dit qu'il perce son miroir à coups de balle de pistolet quand il est de mauvaise humeur et se regarde dans le miroir.* They told me he shoots bullet holes in his mirror when he's in a bad mood and sees himself in the mirror. (AV) <AV, VM, Da84> <***Loc:*** AV, SJ, SM, VM, Da84>

humeur[2] [ymœr, imœr] *n.f.* **1** *(pl.)* rash **2** infection, abscess, boil <***Loc:*** EV, SM, TB, VM, Ph36>

humide [ymid] *adj.* humid, damp, moist, wet <***Loc:*** VM, Da84, Hi02>

humidité [ymidite, imidite] *n.f.* **1** humidity **2** moisture **3** dampness, wetness, moistness <***Loc:*** SL, LF, TB, Da84>

humiliant, -e [ymiljɑ̃, -ɑ̃t] *adj.* humiliating *J'ai pas aimé ça qu'il a fait devant tout le monde. C'était humiliant.* I didn't like what he did in front of everyone. It was humiliating. (LA) <***Loc:*** LA, Da84>

humiliation [ymiljɑsjɔ̃] *n.f.* humiliation <***Loc:*** Da84>

humilier [ymilje] **I** *v.tr.* to humiliate *Il a humilié sa femme en sortant avec sa poupoune en public.* He humiliated his wife by going out in public with his mistress. (LA) **II s'humilier** *v.pron.* to humiliate o.s. <***Loc:*** LA, Da84>

humilité [ymilite] *n.f.* humility, meekness <***Loc:*** Da84>

humoriste [ymorist] *n.m.* humorist, comic <***Loc:*** Da84>

huppé, -e [ype] *adj.* tufted, crested *Roger est bien huppé à soir.* Roger has a fine tuft [hairdo] tonight. (LA) <***Loc:*** LA, Da84>

huppe [hyp, høp] *n.f.* **1** comb of a rooster **2** tuft, crest (of feathers, hair) **3** knot of hair at the back of the head **4** pimple mound <***Loc:*** AV, JD, LA, Da84>

hurcher (se) [hyrʃe] *v.pron.* to climb *Policar, hurche-toi sur ce paleron et hurle ton père.* Policar, climb up on that post and call your father. (IB) <***Loc:*** IB>

hurlailler [hyrlaje, hœrlaje] *v.intr.* to howl, yell obnoxiously *Il était après hurlailler comme un chien perdu quand je l'ai trouvé.* He was howling like a lost dog when I found him. (LA) <***Loc:*** LA, Da84>

hurlement [hœrlmɑ̃] *n.m.* **1** howl, yell **2** howling, yelling, shouting <***Loc:*** VM, Da84>

hurler[1] [hœrle, hyrle, høle, hyle, yle] **I** *v.tr.* to call *Il hurle son chien.* He is calling his dog. (AV) *Policar, hurche-toi sur ce paleron et hurle ton père.* Policar, climb up on that post and call your father. (IB) **II** *v.intr.* **1** to howl, bellow *Le chien a hurlé tout la nuit.* The dog howled all night long. (SM) **2** to yell, holler, shout *Il est toujours après hurler sur la radio.* He's always shouting on the radio. (VM) <***Loc:*** AV, IB, JE, SB, SM, VM, Da84>

hurler[2] [yrle] *v.tr.* to bring *Va sus le huche et hurle-mon un morceau de bois et viens pas ici avec une babine.* Go to the woodpile and get me a piece of wood and don't come back here pouting. (TB) <***Loc:*** TB>

hyacinthe [jasɛ̃t] *n.f.* hyacinth <***Loc:*** Lv88>

hydroforme [idrofɔrm] *n.m.* odor of stagnant water *Je sens une odeur d'hydroforme depuis hier.* I've been smelling stagnant water since yesterday. (SL) <***Loc:*** SL>

hydrogène [idroʒɛ̃n] *n.m.* hydrogen <***Loc:*** Da84>

hydrophobie [idrofobi] *n.f.* rabies, hydrophobia <***Loc:*** Da84>

hydropique [idropik] *adj.* dropsical <***Loc:*** SL, Da84>

hydropisie [idropizi] *n.f.* dropsy <***Loc:*** Da84>

hympotiquer ♦see **hypothéquer**

hypnotiser [ipnotize] *v.tr.* to hypnotize *Mon arracheur de dents peut t'hypnotiser ou te donner un SHOT.* My dentist can hypnotize you or give you a shot. (LA) <***Loc:*** LA, Da84>

hypocrisie [ipokrizi] *n.f.* hypocrisy <***Loc:*** Da84>

hypocrite [ipokrit] *n.* hypocrite *Porte pas cas de lui. C'est un pur hypocrite.* Don't pay attention to him. He's a pure hypocrite. (LA) <***Loc:*** LA, Da84>

hypothèque [ipotɛk, ɛ̃potɛk] *n.f.* mortgage <***Loc:*** IB, Da84>

hypothéquer (**apotiquer, hympotiquer, hypotiquer, impotiquer**) [apotike, ɛ̃potike, ɛ̃poteke, ipotike, potike] *v.tr.* to mortgage **J'ai impotiqué mon cheval, belle, pour te sauver la vie, belle.* I have mortgaged my horse in order to save your life, dear. (AC, Wh69) *Ça fait grief d'apotiquer sa place.* It hurts to mortgage your own home. (VM) <***Loc:*** AC, EV, IB, TB, VM, Da84, Lv88, Ph36, Wh69>

hypotiquer ♦see **hypothéquer**

hystérie [isteri] *n.f.* hysteria <***Loc:*** Da84>

hystérique [isterik] *adj.* hysterical *Elle était rendue hystérique. Elle avait des crises proche tous les jours.* She had become hysterical. She had fits nearly every day. (LA) <***Loc:*** LA, Da84>

I

ici[1] **(icite, icitte)** [isi, isit] *adv.* here, over here, around here **Nous-autres, on est tous des Catholiques ici.* We are all Catholics here. (EV, An94) *La seule petite grocerie icitte qui tient des pralines fraîches.* The only little grocery store around here that has fresh pralines. (Lv88) *Mais j'aime ce bayou icitte, y a pas de train ici.* But I like this bayou, there's no trouble here. (TB) ◊ **•ici dans {dedans}** in here, here, in this place *T'as pour le chercher autre part; il est pas ici dans.* You'll have to look for him elsewhere; he's not here. (VM) <SM, VM, Da84> **•ici et là** here and there <Da84> **•d'ici** from here **La maison était à peu près loin comme d'ici à là-bas au* TRUCK*-là.* The house was about as far as from here to over there, to the truck. (LA, An94) *À dix miles en haut d'ici.* Ten miles up the bayou from here. (LF) <LA, LF, TB, An94, Da84> <***Loc:*** AC, AV, EV, IV, JE, LA, PQ, SL, SM, TB, VM, An94, Da84, Gr86, Lv88>

ici[2] **(icite, icitte)** [isi, isit] *dem. (particle used with demonstratives) Ceux-icite veulent pas venir.* These ones don't want to come. (SM) *Ce garçon-icite c'est mon frère.* This boy is my brother. (VM) <***Loc:*** SM, VM>

icite, icitte ♦see **ici**

idéal, -e [ideal] *adj.* ideal, perfect *C'est une place idéale pour faire mon camp.* It's an ideal place to build my camp. (EV) <***Loc:*** EV, Da84>

idée [ide] *n.f.* **1** idea **Tu connais, garçon, c'est peut-être pas une mauvaise idée, ça.* You know, son, maybe that's not a bad idea. (IV, An94) **Tu m'as donné une bonne idée, ouais.* You gave me a good idea, yeah. (An94) *Quelle idée! Je crois qu'il a perdu la carte!* What an idea! I think he's lost his mind! (SM) *Son idée était joliment mal à propos.* His idea was pretty inappropriate. (LA) *Tous ces grandes idées, ça va tout tourner en merde.* All those grand ideas, it will all fall apart. (LA) **2** intention *C'était pas mon idée de commencer à parler de ça.* It was not my intention to start talking about that. (Lv88) **3** mind *N'importe qui-ce que je fais dans mon idée à moi-même, dans ma tête à moi-même, c'est tout fait en français.* Whatever I do in my mind, in my head, it's all done in French. (TB) **Et il y avait un, il avait la tête beaucoup, beaucoup dure. Et tu pouvais pas changer son idée.* And there was one, he had a very hard head. And you couldn't change his mind. (EV, An94) *J'ai eu assez de tracas dedans ma vie à me faire perdre mon idée.* I've had enough trouble in my life to make me lose my mind. (VM) **4** sense, good sense *Elle a beaucoup d'idée.* She has a lot of good sense. (SM) **5** memory *Tu vas garder ça dans ton idée.* You will keep it in your memory. (VM) **6** tiny bit, very little **Juste une idée.* Just a tiny bit. (Da84) *Tu veux du café? Oui, une idée.* Would you like some coffee? Yes, just a little. (SM) ◊ **•avoir idée de** to intend to **J'ai pas idée d'aller.* I do not intend to go. (Da84) *J'ai idée d'aller te voir.* I think I shall go see you. (JD) <JD, Da84, Lv88> **•avoir (une) bonne idée** to be intelligent, be a good thinker *Il a une bonne idée.* He is very smart. (LA) <AV, LA, La99, Lv88> **•faire son idée** to decide, make up one's mind **Mademoiselle, faites votre idée, faites votre paquet, allons à la maison.* Miss, make up your mind, pack up, let's go to the house. (Wh69) *J'ai fait mon idée. Je vais.* I've made up my mind. I'm going. (SM) *Fais ton idée.* Make up your mind. (VM) <SM, VM, Lv88, Wh69> **•pas avoir (son) idée / pas avoir (sa) bonne idée *a*** to be mentally handicapped *L'homme qui reste là-bas a pas tout son idée.* The man who lives over there is mentally handicapped. (SL) ***b*** to be mentally disturbed, not be in one's right mind **Il a pas sa bonne idée.* He's just not all there. (Da84) *Elle a plus trop bonne idée.* She's becoming senile. (Lv88) <SL, Da84, La99, Lv88> **•prendre idée** to get the notion, get the idea (to do s.t.) *S'il aurait pris idée d'aller chez vieux Télus-là, ils s'auront tout sauvé.* If he had taken a notion to go to old man Telus's house, they would have all run away. (EV) <EV> **•se faire une idée** to have an idea, imagine *Et il y avait un grand homme, il était des* DARK HAIR *tu connais, et ça m'a fait penser, c'était pas son pape, mais je m'ai fait une idée que c'était Jésus.* And there was a tall man, he was dark haired you know, and it made me think, it wasn't her father, but I imagined it was Jesus. (TB) <AC, EV, TB, Da84> <***Loc:*** AC, EV, IV, JD, LA, LF, SB, SL, SM, TB, VM, An94, Da84, La99, Lv88, Wh69>

identifier [idɑ̃tifje] *v.tr.* to identify *Ils l'ont faire venir pour identifier le corps.* They had him come to identify the body. (LA) <***Loc:*** LA, Da84>

identité [idɑ̃tite] *n.f.* identity **A cette époque-là, je pense qu'on cherchait une identité. Dans mon* CASE*, être un autre folksinger américain, c'était pas grand'chose.* At the time, I think we were seeking an identity. In my case, being another American folksinger didn't amount to much. (LA, An84) <***Loc:*** LA, An84, Da84>

idiot[1]**, -e** [idjo, idjɔt] *adj.* idiotic, stupid, foolish *Lui là, il est assez idiot pour se faire prendre dans cette piège.* That one, he's idiotic enough to get himself caught in that trap. (LA) **Je doute pas que les maît's d'école t'ont dit eine pareille affaire idiote par rapport que les écoles ont jamais compris la valeur de not' culture.* I don't doubt that schoolteachers told you such an idiotic thing because the schools have never understood the value of our culture. (ThCa: *Mille misères*) <***Loc:*** LA, Da84, ThCa>

idiot[2], -e [idjo, idjɔt] *n.* idiot, imbecile <***Loc:*** Da84>

igname [ĩjɑ̃m] *n.f.* yam, sweet potato <***Loc:*** Ho90>

ignorance [ĩjorɑ̃s] *n.f.* ignorance <***Loc:*** Da84>

ignorant, -e (**ninorant, -e**) [ĩjorɑ̃, inorɑ̃, ninorɑ̃] *adj.* **1** ignorant, lacking education *Ils ont voté comme ça parce que ils sont ignorants.* They voted that way because they are ignorant. (LA) **2** unknowing, unaware *J'étais ignorant de ça.* I was unaware of that. (VM) **3** guiltless, innocent *Pauvres enfants, ils étaient ignorants de tout ça.* Poor kids, they were innocent about all that. (LA) <***Loc:*** LA, VM, Da84>

il [i, il] *(before a consonant* [i], *before a vowel* [il]) *pron.pers. (subj.)* **1** *(m.)* he, it **Il en a pus.* He has no more (Da84) *Il a paniqué quand le bougre a sorti son couteau.* He panicked when the guy took out his knife. (LA) **Il a pas d'idée.* He has no idea (Da84) *Ça qu'il t'a fait est pas pardonnable.* What he did to you is inexcusable. (EV) *Il se parlait tout le temps à lui-même.* He always talked to himself. (LF) *Un caïman, il a des pattes assez grandes.* An alligator, it has rather big feet. (TB) *Là j'ai lavé mon linge que j'avais à ce matin sur le dos, il est tout propre, là il est pendu après sécher.* I washed the clothes that I had on this morning, it's all clean, it's hung up drying. (TB) *Son* TIRE *avait juste une petite piqûre mais il était* FLAT *quand même.* His tire had only a little puncture, but it was flat all the same. (LA) **2** *(f.) locally* she, it *Ma grand-mère elle il va appeler ça-là là un tamis.* My grandmother, she'll call that a tamis. (TB) *Et là je dis à ma femme des fois, "Oh, tu veux pas je te dis," c'est mes manières à parler à ma femme. Alle dit "Ouais," il dit, "dis-mon pour sûr."* And then sometimes I say to my wife, "Oh you don't want me to tell you, " that's my way of talking to my wife. "Yes," she says, "tell me for sure." (TB) *Il est plus vieille que mon.* She's older than me. (PQ) **3** *(in impersonal expr.)* it **Il y en a pas.* There is none. (Da84) *Il y a pas assez de* PLUGS *dans la cuisine.* There are not enough outlets in the kitchen. (LA) **Il pleut.* It's raining. (Da84) *Il faisait froid l'hiver.* It was cold in winter. (Gu00) *Il faisait sec cette année.* It was dry this year. (VM) *Comment ça se fait qu'il fait noir?* Why is it dark? (AC, An94) **Il paraît que...* It seems that . . . (Da84) *Il manquait de la place dans la pataterie.* There was no more room in the potato shed. (VM) *Pour trouver une fille pure, il faut chercher jeune.* To find a chaste girl, it is necessary to search [among the] young. (VM) *Il va avoir du vent et va avoir des éclairs pour vous faire peur.* There will be wind and there will be lightning to scare you. (LF) *Quoi il y a?* What's the matter? (Gu00) *Qui il y a?* What's the matter? (Gu00) **Il y a personne ici.* There is no one here. (Da84) *Asteur il y a un tas de jeunes qui se placent sans se marier.* Today there are a lot of young people who live together without being married. (EV) *L'année passée, il n-a eu une terrible récolte d'écrivisses.* Last year there was an abundant crawfish harvest. (Lv88) <***Loc:*** AC, AV, EV, IB, IV, JD, LA, LF, PQ, SJ, SL, SM, TB, VM, An94, Da84, Gu00, Hi02, Lv88, Ph36, Wh83>

île [il] *n.f.* **1** isle, island **2** grove **En Louisiane, les îles ne sont pas toujours entourées d'eau, elles peuvent surgir de la prairie tremblante ou d'une savane, souvent couronnées de chênes verts.* In Louisiana, islands are not always surrounded with water, they may rise up out of the trembling prairie or from pasture land, often crowned with live oaks. (Al81) *Île de cyprès.* Cypress grove. (SM) ◊ **•île d'arbres** little wooded area in the middle of the prairie <VM> **•île flottante** meringue custard dessert <Da84> <***Loc:*** JD, JE, SM, TB, VM, Da84, Gu00, Lv88>

îlet [ile] *n.m.* city block *Dans mon îlet, plusieurs familles parlent encore le bon français.* On my block, several families still speak good French. (Gr86) *Elle reste deux îlets de l'église.* She lives two blocks from the church. (IB) <***Loc:*** IB, SM, Gr86, Lv88>

îlette [ilet] *n.f.* small island *Il n-a une autre îlette bord du ouest de la Grand'Ile, et c'est dessus la côte de la Paroisse Lafourche.* There is another small island on the west side of Grand Isle, off the coast of Lafourche Parish. (TB) <***Loc:*** TB>

illettré, -e [iletre] *adj.* illiterate **Comment est-ce que mes enfants pourraient s'identifier avec une culture folklorique qui n'a jamais quitté le dix-septième siècle? Une culture illettrée en français à quatre-vingt-dix-neuf pour cent qui n'a jamais fondé d'écoles, qui n'a aucun contact avec l'extérieur de ses villages?* How could my children identify with a folkloric culture that has never left the seventeeth century? A culture which is ninety-nine percent illiterate in French which never founded schools, which has no contact with the world outside its villages? (ThCa: *Mille misères*) <***Loc:*** ThCa>

illustration [ilystrasjɔ̃] *n.f.* **1** illustration **2** example *Je vais te donner une illustration pour te faire comprendre.* I'm going to give you an example to make you understand. (SM) <***Loc:*** SM, VM, Da84, Lv88>

ils [i] *(before a vowel* [il, iz]) *pron.pers.m./f.pl. (subj.)* they **Ils avaient faim et ils avaient soif. Ils étaient après dire comment pauvres ils étaient.* They were hungry and they were thirsty. They were saying how poor they were. (SL, An94) *Ils ont cherché tout partout, mais ils ont jamais trouvé la clé.* They looked all over the place, but they never found the key. (EV) *Ils se considèrent mariés parce que ça reste ensemble depuis six ans.* They consider themselves married because they've been together for six years. (EV) *C'est des poissons qui* MIGRATE *dedans le golfe, ils partont et puis ils suisont le* SHORE. Those are fish that migrate into the gulf, they leave and they follow the shore. (LF) *Comme eux-autres veut, s'ils voulont parler français on va assayer de converser avec en français.* As they like, if they want to speak French we try to converse in French. (TB) *J'ai habitude aller souvent souvent au* NURSING HOME.... *J'ai p'us de z'hommes* CLOSE TO ME THERE. *Mais j'ai trois ou quatre vieilles femmes là. Ils sont contents quand je vas.* I'm used to going very often to the nursing home . . . . I don't have any men close to me there anymore. But I have three or four old women there. They're happy when I go. (EV) <***Loc:*** AC, AV, EV, IB, IV, LA, LF, SB, SJ, SL, SM, TB, VM, An94, Da84, Lv88, Wh83>

image [imaʒ] *n.f.* image, picture (esp. a holy picture) ◊ •**image de communion** small picture of a saint given to a child on the occasion of his or her first communion <SM, VM> <***Loc:*** SM, VM, Da84>

imaginable [imaʒinab(l)] *adj.* imaginable *Il y avait des diamants et de l'or et toute sorte de choses imaginables.* There were diamonds and gold and all sorts of things imaginable. (LA) <***Loc:*** LA, Da84>

imagination [imaʒinasjɔ̃] *n.f.* imagination <***Loc:*** Da84>

imaginer [imaʒine, ɛ̃maʒine] **I** *v.intr.* to imagine, fancy, think up **Mais, c'est sûr une belle pomme, j'imagine.* Well, it's surely a beautiful apple, I imagine. (AC, An94) **II s'imaginer** *v.pron.* **1** to imagine *Il tire les cartes, oh ouais, il dit au monde tout qualité d'affaires, tu vas prendre un grand* TRIP, *il vont venir dans de l'argent, enfin tout espèce de choses qu'il s'imagine.* He does card readings, oh yes, he tells people all kinds of things, you're going to take a big trip, they're going to come into some money, he imagines all kinds of things. (TB) *Imagine-toi qu'y aurait ein taureau, ein lion et eine écrevisse sus ein "*RAIL*" de chemin de fer.* Imagine that there was a bull, a lion, and a crawfish on a railroad rail. (ThCa: *Mille misères*) **2** to fancy o.s. *Il s'imagine un bon danseur.* He fancies himself a good dancer. (EV) <***Loc:*** AC, EV, LA, TB, An94, Da84, Fa77, ThCa>

imanciper ♦see **émanciper**

imbattable [ɛ̃batab(l)] *adj.* unbeatable *Il était imbattable quand il était à jeun.* He was unbeatable when he was sober. (LA) <***Loc:*** LA, Da84>

imbécile[1] [ɛ̃besil] *adj.* foolish, stupid, idiotic *Sois pas imbécile.* Don't be foolish. (LA) <***Loc:*** JE, LA, Da84>

imbécile[2] [ɛ̃besil] *n.m.* imbecile, idiot, fool *Ça c'est une bande de -t- imbéciles!* That's a bunch of idiots! (TB) <***Loc:*** Da84, Fa77, Gr86>

imitation [imitasjɔ̃] *n.f.* imitation <***Loc:*** Da84>

imiter [imite, ɛ̃mite] **I** *v.tr.* to imitate, copy, mimic **J'ai imité le son que j'avais entendu.* I imitated the sound that I had heard. (VM, An84) **II s'imiter** *v.pron.* to resemble one another, look alike *Les Japonais et les Chineaux s'imitent un tas.* The Japanese and the Chinese look a lot alike. (VM) <***Loc:*** SM, VM, An84, Da84>

immaculé, -e [imakyle] *adj.* [*eccl.*] immaculate ◊ •**l'Immaculée Conception** the Immaculate Conception <Da84> <***Loc:*** Da84>

immédiatement [imedjatmɑ̃, imedjɛtmɑ̃] *adv.* immediately, at once, right away *On va aller immédiatement.* We're going immediately. (AV) <***Loc:*** AV, Da84>

immense [imɑ̃s] *adj.* immense, huge <***Loc:*** Da84>

immersion [imærsjɔ̃] *n.f.* immersion, teaching method in which the language to be learned is used as the language of instruction *Mon plus vieux asteur il fait l'école par l'immersion à Lafayette.* My oldest son, he teaches school by immersion in Lafayette now. (LF) <***Loc:*** LF>

immigrant, -e [imigrɑ̃, -ɑ̃t] *n.* immigrant <***Loc:*** Da84>

immigration [imigrasjɔ̃] *n.f.* immigration <***Loc:*** Da84>

immigrer [imigre] *v.intr.* to immigrate *Mon monde à moi a immigré de l'Allemagne.* My people immigrated from Germany. (LA) <***Loc:*** LA, Da84>

immortalité [imɔrtalite] *n.f.* [*eccl.*] immortality <***Loc:*** Da84>

immortel, -elle [imɔrtɛl, ɛ̃mɔrtɛl] *adj.* [*eccl.*] immortal <***Loc:*** Da84, Fa77>

imparfait, -e [ɛ̃parfɛ, ɛ̃parfe, -ɛt] *adj.* imperfect <***Loc:*** Da84, Fa77>

impassable [ɛ̃pasab(l)] *adj.* impassable *Le chemin était impassable à force l'eau était haute.* The road was impassable because the water was so high. (Lv88) <***Loc:*** JD, SM, Da84, Lv88>

impatient, -e [ɛ̃pasjɑ̃, -ɑ̃t] *adj.* impatient <***Loc:*** Da84, Fa77>

impatienté, -e [ɛ̃pasjɑ̃te, epasjɑ̃te] *adj.* **1** impatient **2** tired (of) **La femme était impatientée d'espérer.* The woman was tired of waiting. (An94) <***Loc:*** LF, An94>

impatienter (s') [epasjɑ̃te] *v.pron.* to lose one's patience <***Loc:*** LF>

impatienterie [ɛ̃pasjɑ̃tri] *n.f.* impatience <***Loc:*** JD>

impoli, -e [ɛ̃poli] *adj.* impolite, rude <***Loc:*** Da84, Fa77>

importance [ɛ̃pɔrtɑ̃s] *n.f.* importance, consequence <***Loc:*** Da84>

important, -e [ɛ̃pɔrtɑ̃, -ɑ̃t] *adj.* important, consequential *L'argent c'est pas ça qu'est important dans la vie.* Money is not what's important in life. (ThCa: *La dernière quilte*) **Les autres fois la Semaine Sainte était beaucoup important à les Cajins et c'était observée sérieusement.* Formerly Holy Week was very important to Cajuns and it was observed seriously. (Wh83) **C'était une autre cause révolutionnaire que j'allais embrasser, mais cette fois, c'était beaucoup plus important parce que ça me touchait directement.* It was another revolutionary cause that I would embrace, but this time it was more important because it concerned me directly. (LA, An84) *C'est comme moi là, des fois j'oublie de quoi et je dis c'était pas important, j'en ai déjà de trop en l'air!* That's like me, sometimes I forget something and I say it's not important, I've already got too much going on! (LF) <***Loc:*** EV, LA, LF, An84, Da84, Fa77, ThCa, Wh83>

importer[1] [ɛ̃pɔrte] *v.tr.* to import *Ça importait du vin pour vendre aux Créoles.* They would import wine to sell to the Creoles. (LA) <***Loc:*** LA, Da84>

importer[2] [ɛ̃pɔrte] ◊ **•n'importe** [napɔrt, nɛ̃pɔrt] (*in compound expressions* [napɔrtø, nɛ̃pɔrte]) ***a*** it doesn't matter, never mind *N'importe, il va faire ça il veut quand même.* It doesn't matter, he'll do what he wants to do anyway. (LA) ***b*** either way, in any case, anyway, anyhow *J'ai manqué de mourir dessus mon bicycle en allant chez Henry. Mais n'importe, je pense c'était trois heures et demi quatre heures du matin, j'ai rejoint Henry chez son oncle Amélien.* I almost died on my bike going to Henry's place. But anyway, I think it was three-thirty or four in the morning when I met Henry at his Uncle Amélien's. (JD) *Ils m'ont dit qu'il perce son miroir à coups de balle de pistolet quand il est de mauvaise humeur et se regarde dans le miroir. N'importe, je voulais pas m'ostiner avec un animal comme Bradley Meaux.* They told me he shoots bullet holes in his mirror when he's in a bad mood and sees himself in the mirror. In any case, I didn't want to argue with an animal like Bradley Meaux. (AV) <AV, JD, LA, Da84> **•n'importe ayoù** ***a*** anywhere **Les vaches pouvaient aller n'importe ayoù.* The cows could go anywhere. (IV, An94) ***b*** wherever *N'importe où je peux aller, ça veut tout me courtiser.* Wherever I go, they want to court me. (ch: *Le temps est après finir*) <IV, LF, TB, An94, Da84, Lv88> **•n'importe combien** however many <Da84> **•n'importe comment** ***a*** in any way *On peut faire ça n'importe comment tu veux.* We can do this any way you want. (LA) ***b*** in any case, anyway, anyhow *Je connais pas si c'était un oncle de la famille, ou si c'est juste comme ça qu'eux l'appelaient. Mais n'importe comment, elle le connaissait bien parce que c'est souvent elle allait faire des visites là.* I don't know if he was an uncle of the family or if that was just what they called him, but anyway, she knew him well because she often visited there. (An94) *N'importe comment, la vieille femme a dit que c'était une souris, elle.* Anyway, the old lady said it was a mouse. (SM, An94) <LA, SM, An94, Da84> **•n'importe quand** ***a*** anytime, whenever *N'importe quand tu crois tu voudras venir, ça va faire pour moi.* Anytime you think you want to come, that will be fine with me. (LA) *Tu peux m'appeler n'importe quand.* You can call me anytime. (VM) ***b*** any time, any moment *À n'importe quand il aurait mouillé une grosse, grosse avalassse, une grosse pluie tu connais?* At any time, it would rain a downpour, a big rain, you know? (EV) <EV, LA, VM, Da84> **•n'importe quel** ***a*** either one, whichever one **N'importe quel qui va mourir avant, les deux autres va lui mettre chacun cent piastres dans le cercueil.* Whichever one dies first, the other two will each put a hundred dollars for him in the coffin. (IB, An94) *C'est tout pareil. Tu peux user n'importe équel, selon équel qui sonne mieux équand t'après le dire.* It's all the same. You can use either one, depending on which one sounds better when you're saying it. (TB) ***b*** whichever, any, any one *Je te garantis, n'importe quelle église, ça pourrait être catholique ou une autre, si ça serait en français, y a plein du monde qui vadrait.* I guarantee you, any church, be it Catholic or something else, if it was in French, there are a lot of people who would go. (LF) *C'était le meilleur bois pour faire la boucanée de la viande. Mais n'importe quel bois dur donc faisait de la bonne boucane.* It was the best wood for smoking meat. But any hard wood made good smoke. (AC) *Peut-être t'as quelqu'un qui t'a engagé, t'as fait de la bonne ouvrage, tu vas revenir ici, tu vas pas demander pour n'importe équel, tu vas demander pour çulà que t'es satisfait avec.* Maybe you've got someone who has hired you, you've done good work, you won't ask for just anyone, you'll ask for the one you're satisfied with. (TB) **C'est de quoi pour que n'importe quel père souaye fier.* That's reason enough for any father to be proud. (VM, Gu82) <AC, IB, TB, VM, An84, An94, Da84, Gu82> **•n'importe qui** ***a*** anyone **Et ça me semble, moi, que n'importe qui qui mérite le nom de musicien, c'est ça il faut qu'il faise.* And it seems to me, that anyone who is worthy of the title of musician, that's what he must do. (VM, An84) *N'importe qui aurait pu faire ça.* Anyone could've done that. (EV) *Tu peux demander à n'importe qui alentour là ayoù Orange Grove est.* You can ask anyone around [to find out] where Orange Grove is. (IV) ***b*** anything, whatever **Ils ont des gros melons et n'importe qui est gros là-bas.* They have big melons and anything is big over there. (EV, An94) *Ici, n'importé qui-ce qu'eux-autres peut faire pour te prendre de l'argent eux-autres le fait.* Here, whatever people can do to take your money, they do it. (LF) *L'eau donne plus de tracas que n'importe qui d'autre.* Water causes more trouble than anything else. (SM) *Eusse dit qu'un Cadien va manger n'importe qui qui le mange pas à lui le premier.* They say that a Cajun will eat anything that doesn't eat him first. (LF) *Il a proche n'importe qui t'as besoin.* He's got almost everything that you need. (EV) <EV, IV, LF, SM, VM, An84, An94, Da84> **•n'importe qui temps** whenever *De la mauve. J'en ai bu plein de ça avec défunte mémère. C'était pour te rafraîchir. Tu pouvais boire ça n'importe qui temps.* Mallow. I drank a lot of that with my late grandmother. It was to refresh you. You drink that whenever you wanted. (TB) <TB> **•n'importe quoi** anything, whatever **Il était beaucoup bon traceur, beaucoup, beaucoup bon. Il traçait n'importe quoi.* He was a very good tracker, very, very good. He would track anything. (AC, An94) *Rabourer ou piocher, n'importe quoi, il fallait lui demander quel bord dans la pièce il fallait tu commences.* Plowing or hoeing, anything, you had to ask him what side of the field to start on. (An94) *C'était un forgeron. Il pouvait faire n'importe quoi avec la forge.* He was a blacksmith. He could do anything in a forge. (An94) <AC, An94, Da84> **•peu importe** it's of no importance <Da84> **•qu'importe** whatever, no matter what **Il faut que je me range avec mes frères et sœurs de ma race noire, qu'importe leur langue.*

I have to take my place next to my brothers and sisters of the black race, whatever their language. (ThCa: *Mille misères*) <ThCa> **•ça m'importe pas** it's of no concern to me <Da84> <***Loc:*** AC, AV, EV, IV, JD, LA, LF, SM, TB, VM, An84, An94, Da84, ThCa>

imposer [ẽpoze] *v.tr.* to impose <***Loc:*** Da84, Fa77>

impossible [ẽposib(l)] *adj.* impossible *So, tu dirais que c'était impossible qu'une personne noire pourrait parler [français].* So, you'd think it was impossible that a black person could speak French. (LF) <***Loc:*** LF, Da84>

imposteur [ẽpostœr] *n.m.* imposter <***Loc:*** Da84>

impôt [ẽpo, epo] *n.m.* tax *Et quand il a retourné au Canada, il a follu qu'il paye les impôts dessus trente-sept mille dollars. So, il a follu qu'il emprête l'argent pour payer ses impôts.* And when he went back to Canada, he had to pay taxes on thirty seven thousand dollars. So, he had to borrow the money to pay his taxes. (LF) <***Loc:*** JE, LF>

impotiquer ♦see **hypothéquer**

impression [ẽpresjɔ̃] *n.f.* impression, imprint, mark <***Loc:*** Da84>

impressionnant, -e [ẽpresjɔ̃nɑ̃, -ɑ̃t] *adj.* impressive, striking *La manière qu'ils ont fait leurs noces, c'était beaucoup impressionnant.* The way they did their wedding was really impressive. (LA) <***Loc:*** LA, Da84>

impressionner [ẽpresjɔ̃ne] *v.tr.* to impress, make an impression on *J'étais bien impressionnée à soir avec la manière que* B*EST* M*AN a couri.* I was very impressed tonight with the way Best Man ran. (ThCa: *La table des veuves*) <***Loc:*** Da84, ThCa>

imprimer [ẽprime] *v.tr.* to imprint, print *Ça passait les nouvelles de la mortalité aux parents et aux autres dès que possible par moyen d'invitations imprimées à la main ou bien par l'imprimeur de la gazette.* They would spread the news about the death to family members and others as soon as possible by means of hand printed invitations or by the printer of the newspaper. (VM) <***Loc:*** VM, Da84>

imprimerie [ẽprimri] *n.f.* **1** printing **2** printing shop or plant <***Loc:*** Da84>

imprimeur [ẽprimœr] *n.m.* printer *L'imprimeur de la gazette.* The printer of the newspaper. (VM) <***Loc:*** VM>

improuvement [ẽpruvmɑ̃] *n.m.* improvement *Il a fait des improuvements dessus sa maison.* He made improvements to his house. (SM) *On aperçoit un improuvement dans sa condition.* We notice an improvement in his condition. (Gr86) <***Loc:*** EV, SM, VM, Gr86, Lv88, Ph36>

improuver [ẽpruve] **I** *v.tr.* to improve, make better **Improuver une machine.* To improve a machine. (Da84) **Tous ces changements on improuvé les conditions.* All of these changes have improved conditions. (EV, Ph36) **II** *v.intr.* to improve, get better **Sa santé est improuvée asteur.* His health is better now. (Lv88) <***Loc:*** EV, Da84, Fa77, Gr86, Lv88, Ph36>

imprudence [ẽprydɑ̃s] *n.f.* **1** imprudence, rashness, indiscretion **2** careless or imprudent act *Ecoute tes parents. Fais pas des imprudences.* Listen to your parents. Don't do anything imprudent. (LA) <***Loc:*** LA, Da84>

impur, -e [ẽpyr] *adj.* [*eccl.*] impure, immodest <***Loc:*** Da84>

incapable [ẽkapab(l)] *adj.* incapable <***Loc:*** Da84, Fa77>

inciselage [ẽsizlaʒ] *n.f.* cut, gash, slash *Faire une inciselage à quelqu'un dans le bras avec un couteau.* To make a gash in someone's arm with a knife. (LF) <***Loc:*** LF>

inciseler [ẽsizle] *v.tr.* **1** to make an incision in, cut a slit into *Premier, tu vas inciseler la viande et bien assaisonner.* First, you're going to make an incision in the meat and season it well. (Lv88) **2** to slash, cut *Inciseler quelqu'un d'un coup de couteau.* To slash someone with a knife. (LF) <***Loc:*** LF, SL, Lv88>

includer [ẽklyde] *v.tr.* to include *Les jobs, dans la Paroisse Terrebonne, j'include Houma, tout le sud, eh bien le job est pas comme ç'habitude d'être dans l'État de la Louisiane.* The jobs, in Terrebone Parish, I'm including Houma, all the south, well jobs are not like they used to be in the state of Louisiana. (TB) <***Loc:*** TB>

incomprenable [ẽkɔ̃prənab(l)] *adj.* incomprehensible, unbelievable *L'accident est incomprenable.* The accident is incomprehensible. (SM) *Mais, sûr, c'est bien incomprenable.* Well, sure, it's really unbelievable. (VM) <***Loc:*** AV, EV, IB, JD, SB, SM, VM, Da84, Fa77, Lv88, Ph36>

inconsolable (**inreconsolable**) [ẽkɔ̃solab(l), ẽr(ə)kɔ̃solab(l)] *adj.* unconsolable, disconsolate <***Loc:*** SM, Da84>

incorporer [ẽkɔrpore] *v.tr.* to incorporate *Ils ont incorporé le village, mais ça fait pas grand chose de plus pour nous-autres.* They incorporated the town, but it doesn't do much more for us. (LA) *Le village de Scott est incorporé.* The town of Scott is incorporated. (LA) <***Loc:*** LA, Da84, Lv88>

incrédule [ẽkredyl] *adj.* disobedient, disrespectful <***Loc:*** JE, VM, Da84, Di32>

incroyable [ẽkrwajab(l), ẽkrojab(l)] *adj.* incredible, unbelievable *Et là ces mêmes enfants va parler avec un Français de Haiti. Eusse comprend. Eusse va parler avec quelqu'un de la France ou de Belgique, tous ces places là, et eusse a pas du tout de tracas à changer. Eusse peut changer tout de suite, comme ça. C'est incroyable.* And then these same children will talk with a French speaker from Haiti. They understand. They'll talk with someone from France or Belgium, all of those places, and they have no trouble at all adjusting. They can adjust just like that. It's incredible. (LF) <***Loc:*** LF, SM, Da84>

indépendance [ẽdepɑ̃dɑ̃s] *n.f.* independence <***Loc:*** Da84, Fa77>

indépendant, -e [ẽdepɑ̃dɑ̃, -ɑ̃t] *adj.* independent *Tant qu'à lui, il est joliment indépendant. Tu peux pas lui dire à rien.* As for him, he's pretty independent. You can't tell him a thing.

(LA) *Ouais, il a vu j'avais été manière indépendante.* Yeah, he saw that I was pretty independent. (EV) <***Loc:*** EV, LA, Da84>

index [ɛ̃dɛks] *n.f.* index <***Loc:*** Da84>

indication [ɛ̃dikasjɔ̃] *n.f.* indication, sign, mark <***Loc:*** Da84>

indien[1], **-ienne** (**z-indien, -ienne**) [ɛ̃djɛ̃, zɛ̃djɛ̃, adjɛ̃, -ɛ̃n] *adj.* American Indian, Native American *Un certain temps la Louisiane était espagnole, et on avait beaucoup des Indiens ici, et alors il y a des certains mots qui vient de l'Espagne et il y en a qui est, des certains mots qui est des mots indiens.* [For] a certain period Louisiana was Spanish, and there were lots of Indians here, and so there are certain words that come from Spain and there are certain words which are Indian words. (SL) <***Loc:*** SL, Da84>

Indien[2], **-ienne** (**z-Indien, -ienne**) [ɛ̃djɛ̃, zɛ̃djɛ̃, adjɛ̃, -ɛ̃n] *n.* American Indian, Native American <***Loc:*** EV, IB, IV, JD, JE, LA, LF, SB, SM, TB, VM, Da84, Fa77>

indienne [ɛ̃djɛ̃n] *n.f.* **1** printed calico **2** Indianhead cloth <***Loc:*** Da84>

indigestion [ɛ̃diʒesjɔ̃, ɛ̃dizesjɔ̃] *n.f.* indigestion ◊ **•avoir une indigestion de** to be fed up with <SM, La99> <***Loc:*** SM, VM, Da84, Fa77, La99>

indigne [ɛ̃dĩj] *adj.* **1** bad, terrible **2** mischievous <***Loc:*** TB, Da84>

indigo[1] [ɛ̃digo] *adj./n.* indigo (color) *Elle s'a acheté un nouveau char, manière indigo.* She bought herself a new car, sort-of indigo-colored. (LA) <***Loc:*** LA, Da84>

indigo[2] [ɛ̃digo] *n.m.* **1** indigo weed **2** wild coffee plant <***Loc:*** IB, VM, Da84, Gu00>

indiquer [ɛ̃dike] *v.tr.* to indicate, point out *Ils arrêtaient les pendules pour indiquer qu'elles avaient plus d'heures à marquer pour le défunt.* They stopped the clocks to indicate that they no longer had hours to keep for the deceased [person]. (VM) <***Loc:*** PQ, VM, Da84, Fa77>

indisable [ɛ̃dizab(l)] *adj.* improper, indiscrete **Ç't histoire est indisabe.* That story is unfit to tell. (EV, Ph36) <***Loc:*** EV, Lv88, Ph36>

individu [ɛ̃dividy] *n.m.* individual, person <***Loc:*** LF, Da84>

individuel [ɛ̃dividɥɛl] *n.m.* individual, person <***Loc:*** Lv88>

indulgence [ɛ̃dylʒɑ̃s] *n.f.* [*eccl.*] indulgence <***Loc:*** Da84>

indulgent, -e [ɛ̃dylʒɑ̃, -ɑ̃t] *adj.* indulgent, easy, kind *Ils sont gâtés parce que leur mère était trop indulgente.* They are spoiled because their mother was too indulgent. (LA) <***Loc:*** LA, Da84>

industrie [ɛ̃dystri] *n.f.* industry, skill <***Loc:*** Da84>

industriel[1], **-lle** [ɛ̃dystrijɛl] *adj.* industrial <***Loc:*** Da84>

Industriel[2] [ɛ̃dystrijɛl] *n.prop.* Southwest Louisiana Industrial Institute, eventually renamed University of Louisiana at Lafayette <***Loc:*** SL>

infaillible [ɛ̃fajib(l)] *adj.* infallible *Dieu est infaillible.* God is infallible. (SB) <***Loc:*** SB, Da84>

infanterie [ɛ̃fɑ̃tri] *n.f.* infantry *C'était la trente-quatrième division, infanterie.* It was the thirty-fourth division, infantry. (SL) <***Loc:*** SL>

infecter [ɛ̃fɛkte] *v.tr.* to infect, contaminate *Tu viens* ANEMIC *et tu viens bien malade, tu connais, t'es tout infecté, tu connais tu peux pas travailler, et ça vient des bosses, et c'est mauvais.* You become anemic and you get quite sick, you know, it's all infected, you know you can't work, and you get bumps, and that's bad. (TB) <***Loc:*** TB, Da84>

infection [ɛ̃fɛksjɔ̃] *n.f.* infection, contagion *Et je traite le monde pour le mal de tête, et je les traite pour un coup de soleil, je les traite pour des tumeurs, je les traite pour des* CYSTS, *je les traite pour des infections.* And I treat people for headaches, and I treat them for sunstroke, I treat them for tumors, I treat them for cysts, I treat them for infections. (TB) <***Loc:*** TB, Da84, Fa77>

infernal, -e [ɛ̃færnal] *adj.* [*eccl.*] infernal <***Loc:*** Da84>

infester [ɛ̃fɛste] *v.tr.* to infest *La maison était infestée avec des raverts.* The house was infested with roaches. (LA) <***Loc:*** LA, Da84>

infidélité [ɛ̃fidelite] *n.f.* [*eccl.*] infidelity, disloyalty <***Loc:*** Da84>

infini, -e [ɛ̃fini] *adj.* infinite, endless *Oh, ça prendait des temps infinis pour faire un bateau.* Oh, it took an infinite time to make a boat. (LF) <***Loc:*** LF, Da84>

infirmière [ɛ̃færmjær, ɑ̃farmjær] *n.f.* nurse <***Loc:*** LF>

inflammation [ɛ̃flɑ̃masjɔ̃] *n.f.* inflammation *Alle avait une inflammation des amygdales et la goître.* She had an inflammation of the tonsils and goiter. (AV) <***Loc:*** AV>

influence [ɛ̃flyɑ̃s] *n.f.* influence, power <***Loc:*** Da84>

influencer [ɛ̃flyɑ̃se] *v.tr.* to influence **Mais le musicien qui m'a influencé le plus, c'est sans doute Félix Richard, parce que c'est le seul que je connaissais assez bien pour aller le visiter.* But the musician who influenced me the most is without a doubt Felix Richard, because he is the only one whom I knew well enough to go and visit. (LA, An84) <***Loc:*** LA, An84, Da84>

informalité [ɛ̃fɔrmalite] *n.f.* informality *Je trouve que plusieurs filles ont montré leur informalité.* I find that several girls showed their informality. (SB) <***Loc:*** SB>

information [ɛ̃fɔrmasjɔ̃] *n.f.* **1** information *Avec le caractère qu'il a, Dudley est causard et il connaît quoi dire pour obtenir l'information qu'il en a besoin.* With his character, Dudley is a talker and he knows what to say to get the information he needs. (ThCa: *Messieurs, mesdames*) **2** knowledge **3** news *Il y avait pas tous les informations comme on a maintenant dans ce temps-là.* There wasn't all the news like we have now in those days. (SL) ◊ **•prendre des informations** to get information <Da84> <***Loc:*** EV, SB, SL, Da84, Lv88, Ph36, ThCa>

informé, -e [ɛ̃fɔrme] *adj.* informed, educated *C'est du monde bien informé. Tu peux leur faire confiance.* They are well-educated people. You can trust them. (EV) <***Loc:*** EV, SB, Da84, Lv88>

informer [ɛ̃fɔrme] **I** *v.tr.* to inform *On va espérer jusqu'à à soir pour les informer de la mortalité.* We'll wait until tonight to inform them of the death. (LA) **II s'informer** *v.pron.* to inquire, ask around *Avant de t'engager, de toi, je m'informerai.* Before engaging you, I will make some inquiries. (PQ, ch: *Le jour de l'Ascension*) <***Loc:*** LA, PQ, Da84, Fa77>

informeur [ɛ̃fɔrmœr] *n.m.* informer, one who denounces *On va à l'informeur pour notre information.* We go to the informer for our information. (SB) <***Loc:*** SB, Lv88>

ingénieur (**engénieur**) [ɛ̃ʒɛ̃jœr, ɑ̃ʒɛ̃jœr] *n.m.* **1** engineer *Ce monde smatte, ces ingénieurs, et le* CORPS *de* ENGINEERS, *eux-autres a rapetissé ces rivières là.* Those smart folks, those engineers, and the corps of engineers, they shrank those rivers. (TB) **2** machinist, one who operates heavy machinery **3** engineer, one who operates a locomotive or steamboat engine ◊ •**ingénieur civil** surveyor <LF> <***Loc:*** AV, EV, LF, TB, VM, Da84, Gu82, Lv88, Ph36>

ingrat, -e [ɛ̃gra, -at] *adj.* proud **Il est ingrat d'ses habits.* He is proud of his apparel. (EV, Ph36) <***Loc:*** EV, Ph36>

ingrandjin [ɛ̃grɑ̃dʒɛ̃] *n.m.* **1** scoundrel, rascal, good-for-nothing **2** junk <***Loc:*** EV, SM, Ph36>

ingrédient [ɛ̃gredjɑ̃] *n.m.* ingredient <***Loc:*** AV, SM, TB, Da84>

inguérissable [ɛ̃gerisab(l)] *adj.* incurable <***Loc:*** Da84, Fa77>

injecter [ɛ̃ʒɛkte] *v.tr.* to inject *Ils avaient injecté des assaisonnements dans cette daube.* They had injected seasonings into that roast. (LA) <***Loc:*** LA, Da84>

injection [ɛ̃ʒɛksjɔ̃, ɔ̃ʒɛksjɔ̃] *n.f.* **1** injection **2** douche (for feminine hygiene) <***Loc:*** SM, VM, Da84>

injure [ɛ̃ʒyr] *n.f.* abuse, insult, offense, wrong <***Loc:*** Da84>

injustice [ɛ̃ʒystis] *n.f.* injustice <***Loc:*** Da84>

innocence [inosɑ̃s] *n.f.* innocence <***Loc:*** Da84>

innocent[1], **-e** [inosɑ̃, -ɑ̃t] *adj.* innocent, blameless *Ils l'ont améné en cour, mais le juge l'a trouvé innocent.* They took him to court, but the judge found him innocent. (EV) <***Loc:*** EV, Da84>

innocent[2], **-e** [inosɑ̃, -ɑ̃t] *n.* **1** one who is innocent **2** child **3** retarded person <***Loc:*** Da84>

inquiet, -ète [ɛ̃kjɛ, ɛ̃kje, -ɛt] *adj.* anxious, worried, uneasy *J'étais inquiète parce qu'ils étaient pas encore rentrés.* I was worried because they hadn't gotten back yet. (EV) <***Loc:*** EV, Da84, Lv88>

inquiétant, -e [ɛ̃kjetɑ̃, -ɑ̃t] *adj.* worrisome, alarming, disquieting *C'est une affaire qu'est beaucoup inquiétant.* That's a situation that is very worrisome. (LA) <***Loc:*** LA, Da84>

inquiéter (s') [ɛ̃kjete] *v.pron.* to worry, fret *Il s'inquiétait pour le plus jeune.* He was worried about the youngest one. (EV) <***Loc:*** EV, Da84>

inreconsolable ♦see **inconsolable**

inscription [ɛ̃skripsjɔ̃] *n.f.* inscription <***Loc:*** Da84>

insecte [ɛ̃sɛk(t)] *n.m.* insect, bug *La vache est empestée de insectes.* The cow is full of bugs. (SM) <***Loc:*** SL, SM, Da84, Fa77>

insensible [ɛ̃sɑ̃sib(l)] *adj.* unconscious *Quand on l'a trouvé, il était insensible.* When we found him, he was unconscious. (VM) <***Loc:*** TB, VM, Da84>

inséparable [ɛ̃separab(l)] *adj.* inseparable *Ces deux bougres sont inséparables.* Those two fellows are inseparable. (LA) <***Loc:*** LA, Da84>

insistance [ɛ̃sistɑ̃s] *n.f.* insistence <***Loc:*** Da84>

insister [ɛ̃siste] *v.intr.* to insist *Je voulais pas qu'il me paye pour les canards, mais il a insisté.* I didn't want him to pay me for the ducks, but he insisted. (VM) <***Loc:*** VM, Da84, Fa77>

insolence [ɛ̃solɑ̃s] *n.f.* insolence, rudeness <***Loc:*** Da84>

insolent, -e [ɛ̃solɑ̃, -ɑ̃t] *adj.* insolent, rude *Ce malheureux garçon, tout rempli de boisson, parle à son père comme un insolent.* That unfortunate boy, full of drink, spoke to his father like an insolent person. (PQ, ch: Le jour de l'Ascension) <***Loc:*** PQ, Da84>

insouffrable [ɛ̃sufrab(l)] *adj.* insufferable, unbearable, intolerable <***Loc:*** VM, Da84, Di32>

inspecter [ɛspɛkte, ɛ̃spɛkte] *v.tr.* to inspect, look over, scan *Il inspecte pour le* POLLUTION. He inspects for pollution. (TB) *Et quand-ce que les bateaux, une fois par an il faut que ça soye inspecté par la Garde de Côte. Et il faut que ça soye tout mis en ordre.* And when the boats, once a year they had to be inspected by the Coast Guard. And everything had to be put in order. (LF) <***Loc:*** LF, TB, VM, Da84, Fa77>

inspecteur [ɛ̃spɛktœr, ɛspɛktœr] *n.m.* inspector <***Loc:*** VM, Da84>

inspection [ɛ̃spɛksjɔ̃] *n.f.* inspection, examination <***Loc:*** Da84>

inspiration [ɛ̃spirasjɔ̃] *n.f.* **1** inspiration **2** inhalation <***Loc:*** Da84>

inspirer [ɛ̃spire] *v.tr.* **1** to inspire **Il m'a inspiré beaucoup et il a essayé de me montrer certaines choses sur l'accordéon que j'essaie encore à faire.* He inspired me very much and he tried to teach me certain things on the accordion that I am still trying to do. (LA, An84) **2** to inhale *Je pouvais p'us inspirer à cause de la boucane.* I couldn't inhale anymore because of the smoke. (LA) <***Loc:*** LA, An84, Da84>

installation [ɛ̃stalasjɔ̃] *n.f.* **1** installation *L'installation de sa laveuse était compris dans le prix.* The installation of her washer was included in the price. (VM) **2** partial payment, installment *Il me reste trois installations pour finir de payer mon char.* I have three installments left to pay off my car. (VM) **3** contraption, gadget, set-up *Tu parles d'une installation derrière chez lui.* You talk about a set-up behind his house. (LA) <***Loc:*** LA, VM, Da84>

installement [ɛ̃stalmɑ̃] *n.m.* partial payment, installment <***Loc:*** VM, Di32>

installer [ɛ̃stale] **I** *v.tr.* **1** to install *Ça va prendre à peu près deux heures pour installer la nouvelle machine.* It will take about two hours to install the new motor. (LA) **2** to fix **Il a vu le bonhomme, et a cru que c'était Bouki. "Mais," il dit, "je vas t'installer, Bouki!"* He saw the mannekin and thought that it was Bouki. "Well," he said, "I'll fix you, Bouki!" (SM, An94) **3** to place in office, induct **II s'installer** *v.pron.* **1** to get set up, install o.s. **2** to take a seat *Là, si tu peux croire, il s'installe à la table comme si il y avait eu rien du tout.* Then, if you can believe it, he takes a seat at the table as though nothing had happened. (LA) <***Loc:*** LA, SM, VM, An94, Da84>

instant [ɛ̃stɑ̃] *n.m.* instant, moment ◊ **•à l'instant** this instant, instantly <Da84> **•dans un instant** in a moment <Da84> <***Loc:*** Da84>

instigateur [ɛ̃stigatœr] *n.m.* instigator <***Loc:*** Da84>

instigation [ɛ̃stigasjɔ̃] *n.f.* instigation, incitement <***Loc:*** Da84>

instiguer [ɛ̃stige] *v.tr.* to instigate, incite *C'est qui qu'a instigué la chicane?* Who started the argument? (EV) <***Loc:*** EV, Da84>

instinct [ɛ̃stɛ̃] *n.m.* instinct, tendency <***Loc:*** Da84>

instinctif, -ive [ɛ̃stɛ̃ktif, -iv] *adj.* instinctive *C'est pas quelquechose que t'apprends. C'est instinctive.* It's not something you learn. It's instinctive. (LA) <***Loc:*** LA, Da84>

institution [ɛ̃stitysjɔ̃] *n.f.* institution, institute <***Loc:*** Da84>

instructeur, -trice [ɛ̃stryktœr, -tris] *n.* instructor, teacher **J'ai travaillé comme instructrice, maîtresse d'école, à Homer dans le Nord de la Louisiane.* I worked as a schoolteacher in Homer, in North Louisiana. (SM, Gr86) <***Loc:*** SM, Da84, Gr86>

instruction [ɛ̃stryksjɔ̃] *n.f.* instruction, education <***Loc:*** Da84>

instruire [ɛ̃strɥir] **I** *v.tr.* to teach, instruct, educate *Tout le monde parlait français à la maison, ça fait ils étaient après venir pour -t- être instruit en anglais.* Everyone spoke French at home, so they would come [to school] to be educated in English. (SJ) **II s'instruire** *v.pron.* to educate o.s., get an education *Il a toujours dit à ses enfants comment c'était important de s'instruire.* He always told his children how it was important to get an education. (LA) <***Loc:*** LA, SJ, Da84>

instruit, -e [ɛ̃strɥi, -it, ɛ̃stry] *adj.* educated *Tous leurs enfants étaient instruits; ils avaient tout été à l'école.* All of their children were educated; they had all gone to school. (LA) *Peu instruit.* Poorly educated. (SM) ◊ **•instruit à la pointe des ongles** educated to the fingertips, extremely well educated <LF> <***Loc:*** EV, LA, LF, SM, TB, Da84>

instrument [ɛ̃strymɑ̃, ɛstrɔ̃mɑ̃] *n.m.* **1** instrument *Il avait besoin de calibrer ses instruments.* He had to calibrate his instruments. (LA) *Et les machines à canne qu'un homme pourrait courir et le prix a raugmenté terriblement sur les instruments.* And the canecutters that a man could run, the price went up horribly on the instruments. (AS) **2** musical instrument *Ils pouvont jouer n'importe équé instrument. Ça connaissait pas une note avec une note, [...] mais eux-autres, ça ça jouait tout de la musique.* They can play any instrument. They can't tell one note from another, but they all played music. (LF) **3** tool, means <***Loc:*** AC, AS, LA, LF, VM, Da84>

INSULATE [ɪnsəleˈt] *v.tr.invar.* to insulate *J'ai pas eu le temps pour INSULATE en bas de la maison.* I didn't have time to insulate under the house. (LA) <***Loc:*** LA, Da84>

insulation [ɛ̃sylasjɔ̃] *n.* insulation *Il a eu pour refouler son insulation dans le mur. Ça avait commencé à tomber.* He had to stuff his insulation back into the wall. It had started falling out. (LA) <***Loc:*** LA>

insultant, -e [ɛ̃syltɑ̃, -ɑ̃t] *adj.* insulting *Je vas pas même répondre à des menteries comme ça. C'est insultant.* I will not even respond to lies like that. It's insulting. (LA) <***Loc:*** LA, Da84>

insulte [ɛ̃sylt] *n.f.* insult <***Loc:*** TB, Da84>

insulter [ɛ̃sylte] *v.tr.* to insult *A cette période-là, j'allais jouer chez Fernand Stute, et j'insultais le monde qui me parlait en anglais, qu'ils étaient Cadiens ou pas, ça me faisait pas rien.* At that time, I would go to play at Fernand Stute's place, and I would insult those who would speak to me in English, whether they were Cajuns or not, it made no difference to me. (LA, An84) ◊ **•s'insulter les foies** to abuse one's liver (by drinking too much) <La99> <***Loc:*** AL, LA, TB, An84, Da84, Fa77, La99>

intelligence [ɛ̃teliʒɑ̃s] *n.f.* intelligence, intellect <***Loc:*** Da84>

intelligent, -e [ɛ̃teliʒɑ̃, -ɑ̃t] *adj.* intelligent, smart **Et Petit Poucet, lui, il était beaucoup SMART, comme j'ai déjà dit, et il était intelligent.* And Petit Poucet, he was very smart, as I already said, and he was intelligent. (LA, An94) <***Loc:*** LA, An94, Da84>

intention [ɛ̃tɑ̃sjɔ̃] *n.f.* **1** intention, plan, intent *C'est mon intention à mon de yeux montrer si je peux. BUT les mères et les pères connaît pas, ça fait que je crois pas qu'ils vont connaître grand-chose du français.* It's my intention to teach them [French] if I can. But their parents don't know it, so I don't think they'll end up knowing much French. (LF) **2** mind *Je pense dans les deux langues. Je calcule, et si j'sus après faire une décision, je m'attrape mon-même, dans mon intention à mon-meme, que je pense dans les deux langues. Une ou l'autre, pas les deux en même temps.* I think in both languages. I do arithmetic, and if I'm making a decision, I catch myself, in my mind, thinking in both languages. One or the other, not both at the same time. (LF) <***Loc:*** LA, LF, Da84>

intentionné, -e [ɛ̃tɑ̃sjɔ̃ne] *adj.* intentioned *Ça dit qu'il était bien intentionné, mais je le crois pas.* They say he was well intentioned, but I don't believe it. (LA) <***Loc:*** LA, Da84>

interboler [ɛ̃tærbole] *v.tr.* to confuse, baffle, rattle *Le père m'a interbolé en parlant tant.* The priest rattled me by talking so much. (IB) <***Loc:*** IB, Di32>

interboliser [ɛ̃tærbolize] *v.tr.* to surprise, shock, startle *Je n'aime pas que les enfants viennent m'interboliser quand je travaille.* I don't like the children to come and startle me while I'm working. (SB) *L'homme m'a interbolisé quand il a dit ça.* The man shocked me when he said that. (IB) <***Loc:*** IB, SB, Di32>

intercéder [ɛ̃tærsede] *v.intr.* **1** to plead *Il a intercédé auprès de l'évèque pour annuler le mariage.* He pleaded with the bishop to annul the marriage. (LA) **2** to intercede <***Loc:*** LA, Da84>

Intercoastal [ɪntəko^{u}stl] *n.prop.* Intercoastal Canal <***Loc:*** Da84>

interdiction [ɛ̃tærdiksjɔ̃] *n.f.* interdiction <***Loc:*** Da84>

interdire [ɛ̃tærdir] *v.tr.* to forbid, prohibit *C'était interdit durant Carême de jouer de la musique et de danser.* It was forbidden during Lent to play music and dance. (LA) <***Loc:*** LA, Da84>

interdit [ɛ̃tærdi] *n.* [*eccl.*] interdict <***Loc:*** Da84>

intéressant, -e [ɛ̃teresɑ̃, -ɑ̃t] *adj.* interesting *Les platines sont un tas plus intéressantes parce qu'il y a bien peu de monde qui les fait aujourd'hui.* 'Platines' (i.e., flattened pork sausages) are much more interesting because there are few people who make them today. (VM) <***Loc:*** AC, EV, TB, VM, Da84>

intéressé, -e [ɛ̃terese] *adj.* **1** interested **Et il dit, "Je suis intéressé de connaître où le cimetière."* And he said, "I'm interested in knowing where the cemetery is." (LA, An94) *J'ai jamais été intéressé dans la chasse.* I've never been interested in hunting. (LF) *Tu serais intéressé dans aller manger du manger créole, cadien?* Would you be interested in going to eat creole or cajun food? (SJ) *Et qui t'es -t- intéressé pour?* And what are you interested in? (TB) **2** interesting *N'importe éyou-ce tu vas tu peux parler les deux langues, moi je trouve que c'est bien intéressé.* Wherever you go you can speak the two languages, I find that to be very interesting. (TB) **3** stingy, avaricious *J'achète pas avec lui, il est trop intéressé, il veut juste haler.* I don't buy from him, he's too avaricious, he just wants to rake it in. (VM) <***Loc:*** AC, AV, EV, LA, LF, SJ, TB, VM, An94, Da84>

intéresser [ɛ̃terese] **I** *v.tr.* to interest **C'étaient les choses qui l'intéressaient le plus.* Those were the things that interested him the most. (LA, An94) *Je crois que ça les intéresse pas.* I think that it doesn't interest them. (LF) **II s'intéresser** *v.pron.* to be interested, take interest *Il commence à avoir plusieurs jeunes musiciens comme moi qui s'intéressont à notre vieille musique.* There are beginning to be several young musicians like me who are taking an interest in our music. (VM) <***Loc:*** AV, EV, LA, LF, VM, An94, Da84>

intérêt [ɛ̃tere] *n.m.* **1** interest, concern *Et peut-être que c'est pour ça qu'eux-autres avait perdu intérêt dedans le CODOFIL.* And maybe that's why they had lost interest in CODOFIL. (LF) **2** *(pl.)* interest, interest rates *J'ai vu éyou-ce que vous-autres a tombé votres intérêts et tout ça. Ils ont tombé les intérêts à la France et l'Angleterre.* I saw where you dropped the interest rates and all. They dropped the interest rates in France and England. (TB) ◊ **•avoir intérêt de** to have better (do s.t.) *Il a intérêt de finir son travail aujourd'hui.* He had better finish his work today. (LA) <LA> <***Loc:*** AC, AV, EV, LA, LF, TB, Da84>

intérieur [ɛ̃terjœr] *n.m.* interior <***Loc:*** Da84>

international, -e [ɛ̃tærnasjɔ̃nal] *adj.* international *Le festival international.* The international festival. (LA) <***Loc:*** LA, Da84>

interprète [ɛ̃tærprɛt] *n.m.* interpreter <***Loc:*** SL, Da84>

interpréter [ɛ̃tærprete] *v.tr.* to interpret *Un tas, ça que ça faisait l'autre bord, c'était interpréter pour les officiers.* What a lot of them would do overseas was interpret for the officers. (LA) <***Loc:*** LA, Da84>

interpréteur [ɛ̃tærpretœr, ɔ̃tærpretœr] *n.m.* interpreter <***Loc:*** SB, SM, VM, Da84, Lv88>

intervalle (**intrevalle**) [ɛ̃tærval, ɛ̃trəval] *n.m.* interval ◊ **•dans l'intrevalle / dans les intrevalles** in the meantime <LF> <***Loc:*** LF, Da84, Lv88>

interview [ɛ̃tærvju] *n.f.* interview <***Loc:*** Da84>

intestat, -e [ɛ̃testa, -at] *adj.* intestate **Il est mort intestat.* He died intestate. (Da84) <***Loc:*** Da84>

intestin (**z-intestin**) [ɛ̃testɛ̃, ɔ̃testɛ̃, zɛ̃testɛ̃] *n.m.* intestine, bowel <***Loc:*** SB, SM, Da84, Fa77>

intime [ɛ̃tim] *adj.* intimate, close **Ami intime.* Close friend. (Da84) <***Loc:*** Da84>

intimider [ɛ̃timide] *v.tr.* to intimidate, frighten *Ils ont tout coupé son harnais. Ils essayaient de l'intimider.* They cut up his harnessing. They were trying to intimidate him. (LA) <***Loc:*** LA, Da84>

intrevalle ♦see **intervalle**

intrigué, -e [ɛ̃trige] *adj.* intrigued *Il était intrigué par la fille de son voisin.* He was intrigued by his neighbor's daughter. (LA) <***Loc:*** LA>

introduction [ɛ̃trodyksjɔ̃] *n.f.* introduction <***Loc:*** EV, SM, TB, Da84, Ph36>

introduire [ɛ̃trodɥir] **I** *v.tr.* to introduce, present *Je veux t'introduire ma cousine.* I'd like to introduce my cousin to you. (VM) **II s'introduire** *v.pron.* to introduce o.s. *Il s'a pas introduit en arrivant.* He didn't introduce himself upon arriving. (LA) <***Loc:*** EV, IB, LA, SM, TB, VM, Da84, Lv88, Ph36>

inusable [inyzab(l)] *adj.* durable, lasting, that will not wear out <***Loc:*** VM>

inventaire [ɛ̃vɑ̃tær] *n.m.* inventory, stock <***Loc:*** Da84>

inventer [ɛ̃vɑ̃te] *v.tr.* to invent *S'il y avait de quoi de nouveau qu'était inventé c'était, eux-autres appelait ça comme* *c'était en anglais.* If there was something new that had been invented, they called it like it was in English. (TB) <***Loc:*** TB, Da84>

inventeur [ɛ̃vɑ̃tœr] *adj.* inventive, ingenious *Il est beaucoup inventeur.* He is very inventive. (LA) <***Loc:*** LA, Da84>

invention [ɛ̃vɑ̃sjɔ̃] *n.f.* invention <***Loc:*** Da84>

inventionner [ɛ̃vɑ̃sjɔ̃ne] *v.tr.* **1** to invent *C'est Cousin Dud qu'avait inventionné un tonique.* It's Cousin Dud who had invented a tonic. (VM) **2** to imagine, concoct, fabricate ◊ **•s'inventionner de {à}** to take a notion to (do s.t.) *Il s'a inventionné de le faire.* He took a notion to doing it. (VM) *S'inventionner à faire quelque chose impossible.* To try to do something impossible. (SM) <SM, VM> <***Loc:*** EV, JD, SM, VM, Da84, Lv88, Ph36>

invester [ɛ̃veste] *v.tr.* to invest (money, time, etc.) *J'use les crayons à couleur pour faire des couleurs, ça je l'ai fait avec une plume et là je prends des crayons et je fais les couleurs. Ça me coûte pas rien. Mon j'ai pas d'argent d'investé dans mon* HOBBY. I use the color pencils to make the colors, I did that with a pen and then I take pencils and I add the colors. It doesn't cost me anything. I have no money invested in my hobby. (LF) <***Loc:*** LF, Da84, Gr86, Lv88>

investigation [ɛ̃vestigasjɔ̃] *n.f.* investigation <***Loc:*** Da84>

investiguer [ɛ̃vestige] *v.tr.* to investigate *C'est lui qu'a investigué l'affaire.* He's the one who investigated the affair. (Lv88) *Ils vont envoyer des hommes pour investiguer tout ça.* They will send some men to investigate all of this. (VM) *On va investiguer des feux pour déterminer qui qu'a causé des feux, c'est ça je fais asteur.* We go investigate fires to determine what caused fires, that's what I am doing now. (AV) <***Loc:*** AV, EV, SM, VM, An94, Da84, Lv88, Ph36>

invisible [ɛ̃vizib(l)] *adj.* invisible, unseen *Le Bon Dieu est invisible.* God is invisible. (EV) <***Loc:*** EV, VM, Da84>

invitant, -e [ɛ̃vitɑ̃, -ɑ̃t] *adj.* inviting, appealing *Il faut dire que son dîner était pas trop invitant.* I must say that her dinner was not very appealing. (LA) <***Loc:*** LA, Da84>

invitation [ɛ̃vitasjɔ̃] *n.f.* invitation *Ils ont eu pour réimprimer toutes les invitations à la noce.* They had to reprint all the wedding invitations. (LA) <***Loc:*** LA, VM, Da84>

invité, -e [ɛ̃vite] *n.* guest <***Loc:*** Da84>

inviter [ɛ̃vite] **I** *v.tr.* to invite **Ça se fait, il l'a invité, et le Roi a été.* So, he invited him, and the King went. (EV, An94) **II s'inviter** *v.pron.* to invite each other *Si on avait quelques* FRIEND*, on s'aurait invité à venir à soir.* If we had some friends, we would invite each other to come over in the evening. (EV) <***Loc:*** EV, An94, Da84>

invocation [ɛ̃vokasjɔ̃] *n.f.* [*eccl.*] invocation, prayer <***Loc:*** Da84>

invoquer [ɛ̃voke] *v.tr.* to invoke, appeal to *Ils ont invoqué la Sainte Vierge pour préserver la maison dans le mauvais temps.* They invoked the Blessed Virgin to preserve the house during the bad weather. (VM) <***Loc:*** VM, Da84>

iode ♦see **iodine**

iodine (iode, iote) [jodin, ijɔt, jɔt] *n.m./f.* iodine <***Loc:*** LF, Da84, Lv88>

iote ♦see **iodine**

ioù, iousque ♦see **ayoù**

irrévérence [ireverɑ̃s] *n.f.* [*eccl.*] irreverence, disrespect <***Loc:*** Da84>

irrévérent, -e [ireverɑ̃, -ɑ̃t] *adj.* [*eccl.*] irreverent, without respect <***Loc:*** Da84>

irriter [irite] *v.tr.* **1** to irritate, cause irritation in *Le sel dans les chevrettes a irrité le bobo sur mon doigt.* The salt in the shrimp irritated the sore on my finger. (VM) **2** to irritate, annoy, provoke <***Loc:*** VM, Da84>

isse ♦see **YEAST**

issequèque ♦see **YEASTCAKE**

italien[1], -enne [italjɛ̃, -ɛ̃n] *adj.* Italian *J'ai un* ANCESTOR *qu'était italien.* I have an ancestor who was Italian. (LF) *On est pas sûr s'il est italien ou s'il est français, parce que ils venont de Corsica.* We're not sure if it [the name] is Italian or French, because they come from Corsica. (LF) <***Loc:*** LF>

italien[2] [italjɛ̃] *n.m.* Italian, the Italian language <***Loc:*** LF>

Italien[3], -enne [italjɛ̃, -ɛ̃n] *n.* Italian <***Loc:*** LF>

itou (étou, étout) [itu, etu] *adv.* also, as well, too *Tous les après-midi, après je lâche l'ouvrage à deux heures, tous les après-midi on allait à la chasse, oh ils vit pour ça et moi itou.* Every afternoon, after I finished my work at two o'clock, every afternoon we went hunting, oh they live for hunting and me too. (SM) *Pas juste des Français mais du monde des autres pays qui parle français itou.* Not only French people but people from other countries who speak French too. (SM) *Toi, étou, tu restes icitte.* You, too, you're staying here. (VM) <***Loc:*** EV, SM, TB, VM, Lv88, Ph36>

ivre [iv(r)] *adj.* drunk *Les z-oiseaux mangeaient les petites cerises et puis là ça pouvait p'us voler. Eux étaient ivres.* The birds would eat the little wild cherries and then they could no longer fly. They were drunk. (SL) ◊ **•mort-ivre** dead drunk <VM, Lv88> <***Loc:*** SL, VM, Lv88>

J

j' ♦see **je**

jabloroc [ʒablorɔk] *n.f.* lantern <***Loc:*** SJ, Di32>

jabloter [ʒablote] *v.intr.* to converse, talk *Eh, tu sais, cette petite fille aime jabloter avec les vieux.* Oh, you know, that little girl likes talking with the old folks. (VM) <***Loc:*** VM, Di32>

jabot [ʒabo] *n.m.* **1** bust, bosom, chest **2** jabot, old-fashioned necktie with ruffles (worn in colonial times) **3** shirt front **4** wattle (of a bird) *Nos volailles a tous des beaux jabots.* Our chickens all have fine wattles. (TB) ◊ **•avoir le jabot de travers** to be in a contrary mood <SB, La99> <***Loc:*** SB, SM, TB, Da84, Hi02, La99, Re31>

jaboune [ʒabun] *n.f.* lower jaw <***Loc:*** Da84>

jacasse [ʒakas] *n.f.* gossipy woman <***Loc:*** VM, Di32>

jacasser [ʒakase] *v.intr.* to jabber, gossip *Ces vieilles femmes jacassent tout le temps.* Those old women gossip all the time. (VM) <***Loc:*** VM, Di32>

jacasserie [ʒakasri] *n.f.* gossip <***Loc:*** VM, Di32>

jacinthe d'eau [ʒasẽtdo] *n.f.* water hyacinth <***Loc:*** VM>

JACK[1] [dʒæk] *v.tr.invar.* to jack, lift with a jack *J'ai eu pour JACK mon char droite là dessus le bord du HIGHWAY.* I had to jack my car right there on the side of the highway. (EV) <***Loc:*** EV, Da84>

JACK[2] [dʒæk] *n.m.* **1** fellow, chap **2** stud mule, donkey **3** jack (in a deck of cards) **4** jackstone, jack (used in a game of jacks) **5** jack (for raising heavy objects), car jack ◊ **•JACK-A-DON'T-CARE** [dʒɛkadɔ̃kær] happy-go-lucky person <LF> **•JACK crevalle** jackfish, crevalle jack <LF> <***Loc:*** AV, LF, Da84, Lv88>

JACKET ♦see **jaquette**

jaguar [ʒagwar] *n.m.* jaguar <***Loc:*** Da84>

jais ♦see **jet**

jalon [ʒalɔ̃] *n.m.* staff or rod for surveying or leveling <***Loc:*** Da84>

jalouser [ʒaluze] *v.tr.* to envy, be jealous (of) *Il était grand et fort, la qualité d'homme que j'ai toujours jalousé.* He was tall and strong, the type of man that I always envied. (VM) <***Loc:*** VM, Da84>

jalouserie[1] (**jalousie**) [ʒaluzri, ʒalusi, ʒaluzi] *n.f.* jealousy, envy *Moi je suis pas jaloux, je connais pas la jalouserie.* I'm not jealous, I don't know what jealousy is. (LF) <***Loc:*** EV, LF, SB, SM, VM, Da84, Lv88, Ph36>

jalouserie[2] ♦see **jalousie**[1]

jalousie[1] (**jalouserie**) [ʒalusi, ʒaluzi, ʒaluzri] *n.f.* **1** blind, Venetian blind *Les jalouseries sont peinturées verts.* The blinds are painted green. (TB) **2** type of shutter with adjustable slats (as opposed to fixed-slat shutters that may be used in place of a door or window) <***Loc:*** IB, SB, SM, TB, Da84, Lv88>

jalousie[2] ♦see **jalouserie**[1]

jaloux, -ouse [ʒalu, -uz] *adj.* **1** jealous *Roy aimait pas aller au bal parce qu'il était trop jaloux pour laisser sa femme danser avec un autre homme.* Roy didn't like going to dances because he was too jealous to let his wife dance with another man. (VM) **2** envious *Moi je suis pas un bougre qu'est jaloux, je connais pas qui c'est ça, être jaloux. Je veux pas être jaloux. Parce que si quelqu'un a de quoi, moi je dis "Oh boy, le Bon Dieu était là pour cette personne, pareil comme Il était là pour moi."* I'm not a guy who's envious, I don't know what that is, being envious. I don't want to be envious. Because if someone has something, I say, "Oh boy, God was there for that person, just like He was there for me." (LF) <***Loc:*** AL, LF, VM, Da84, Hi02>

jamais [ʒɑ̃mɛ, ʒɑ̃me, ʒɑ̃mẽ] *adv.* **1** never *J'ai jamais attendu G. parler français.* I've never heard G. speak French. (TB) *Je vas jamais là.* I never go there. (TB) **2** ever *T'as jamais mangé de la viande de chevreuil?* Have you ever eaten deer meat? (EV) ◊ **•jamais de la vie** ***a*** never in (my, his, etc.) life *J'ai jamais été dessus le WELFARE. Jamais de la vie.* I've never been on welfare. Never in my life. (ThCa: *Mille misères*) ***b*** oh no! no way! *Jamais de la vie! Pas une autre guerre!* Oh, no! Not another war! (ThCa: *La dernière quilte*) <Da84, La99, ThCa> **•jamais encore** never again *Il s'a mis à courir et il a jamais encore parlé à Ophilia.* He started running and he never spoke to Ophilia again. (ThCa: *La fête à Clomaire*) <Da84, ThCa> **•mais jamais** well, I declare! *Mais jamais! je peux pas le croire.* Well, I declare! I can't believe it. (VM) *Mais jamais! Je savais pas ça.* Well, I declare! I didn't know that. (SM) <SM, VM, Da84> **•si jamais** if ever *Si jamais il t'arrive quelque chose à toi, Madeleine pourra gagner sa vie.* If anything ever happens to you, Madeleine will be able to earn a living. (ThCa: *Le charivari*) <Da84, ThCa> <***Loc:*** AC, AV, JE, LF, SB, SM, TB, VM, Da84, Hi02, La99, ThCa>

jambage [ʒɑ̃baʒ] *n.m.* doorjamb <***Loc:*** Da84>

jambalaya [dʒɑ̃balaja, ʒɑ̃balaja] *n.m.* **1** jambalaya, Louisiana dish made from raw rice cooked in the broth of meat or seafood (and other seasonings) *Y a le jambalaya d'huîtres, le jambalaya de crabes, le jambalaya de chevrettes et le jambalaya de saucisse.* There's oyster jambalaya, crab jambalaya, shrimp jambalaya and sausage jambalaya. (TB) **2** hodgepodge, jumble, mixture of all sorts of things **3** mess, muddle ◊ **•faire un jambalaya (de)** to make a mess (of) *Ça c'est un jambalaya que ces enfants sont après faire.* That's quite a mess those kids are making. (TB) <TB> <***Loc:*** AV, EV, IB, LF, SB, SJ, SL, SM, TB, VM, Da84, Hi02, Lv88, Ph36, Re31>

jambe [ʒɑ̃b, ʒɑ̃m] *n.f.* **1** leg *T'as les jambes tellement cambrées que ça fait penser à des bois de colliers.* Your legs are so bowed that it makes me think of yokes. (AV) *Les fourmis ont pullulé sur sa jambe quand elle a marché sur le nique.* The ants swarmed on her leg when she stepped on the nest. (VM) **2** shank ◊ **•jambe de lait** thrombophlebitis, varicose veins <VM, La99> **•jambe de liège** wooden leg <EV, LA, VM> **•jambes de quiquisse** very thin legs <Lv88> **•avoir des jambes comme des globes de lampe** ***a*** to have big legs ***b*** to have shapely legs <EV, La99> **•avoir des jambes de baguettes / avoir des jambes comme des baguettes de coton {des baguettes de fusil / des pattes de moqueur}** to have thin legs <EV, La99> **•gras de jambe** calf, back of leg <TB> <***Loc:*** EV, SL, SM, TB, VM, Da84, Hi02, La99, Lv88>

jambée [ʒɑ̃be] *n.f.* stride, span of a step ◊ **•prendre une jambée** to take a stride <Lv88> <***Loc:*** Da84, Lv88>

jamber [ʒɑ̃be] *v.tr.* **1** to step over (an obstacle) **2** to straddle *Cette jeune fille jambe cette haute barrière.* That young girl is straddling the high fence. (SB) <***Loc:*** SB, SM, Lv88>

jambette [ʒɑ̃bɛt] *n.f.* **1** form of tripping, using one's own leg to trip s.o. else *Il m'a foutu une jambette pour me faire tomber, c'est pour ça il a gagné, lui.* He tripped me to make me fall, that's why he won. (VM) **2** wrestling move in which a wrestler places one leg behind his opponent's legs and pulls him backwards to the mat **3** type of step in a fence that allows people to cross over the fence where there is no gate ◊ **•passer une jambette (à qqn)** to con, swindle (s.o.) *J'ai acheté un char avec lui mais il m'a passé une jambette.* I bought a car from him but he swindled me. (LF) <LF> <***Loc:*** LF, SM, VM, Da84, Lv88>

jambon [ʒɑ̃bɔ̃] *n.m.* **1** ham **2** bacon **3** *(pl.)* sideburns, side whiskers *Se raser aux jambons.* To wear muttonchop sideburns. (IB) <***Loc:*** IB, JE, TB, VM, Da84, Di32, Hi02>

jambonneau [ʒɑ̃bɔ̃no] *n.m.* strips of pork loin and fat cooked in a pig's shoulder skin, sliced and served as ham <***Loc:*** IB>

janvier [ʒɑ̃vje] *n.m.* January *À la fin de janvier.* At the end of January. (TB) ◊ **•Petit Bonhomme Janvier** legendary character who brings small gifts to children on New Year's Eve <Da84> <***Loc:*** TB, Da84, Hi02>

Japon[1] [ʒapɔ̃] *n.m.* Japan <***Loc:*** TB, Da84>

Japon[2]**, -ne (Japonais, -e)** [ʒapɔ̃, -ɔ̃n, ʒapɔ̃ne, -ɛz] *n.* Japanese person *Les Japons mangent du poisson cru.* Japanese people eat raw fish. (VM) <***Loc:*** EV, TB, VM, Da84>

japonais, -e [ʒapɔ̃ne, -ɛz] *adj.* Japanese *Il y a un tas de nouveaux restaurants japonais à Lafayette.* There are many new Japanese restaurants in Lafayette. (LA) <***Loc:*** LA, Da84>

Japonais ♦see **Japon**[2]

jappailler [ʒapaje] *v.intr.* **1** to bark, yap, yelp *Un chien qui jappaille.* A yelping dog. (VM) **2** to fuss, complain *Plus Lionel buvait, plus Brune jappaillait. Plus Brune jappaillait, plus Lionel buvait.* The more Lionel drank, the more Brune fussed. The more Brune fussed, the more Lionel would drink. (VM) **3** to chatter <***Loc:*** EV, IB, SM, VM, Lv88, Ph36>

jappement [ʒapmɑ̃] *n.m.* barking, yelping, yapping (of a dog) <***Loc:*** Da84>

japper [ʒape] *v.intr.* **1** to bark, yap, yelp *Les chiens de la voisine ont jappé toute la nuit, on a jamais pu dormir.* The neighbor's dogs barked all night, we never could get to sleep. (Gu00) **2** to chatter <***Loc:*** AV, LF, TB, Da84, Gu00>

jaquer [dʒake, ʒake] *v.tr.* **1** to stick, jab, prick (as with a needle) **I m'a jaqué einne aiguille dans l'bras.* He stuck a needle in my arm. (EV, Ph36) **2** to prod, poke *Jacquer la vache pour la faire passer.* To prod the cow to make it go. (VM) **3** to put, place *Il a jaqué le livre sur la table.* He put the book on the table. (AV) <***Loc:*** AV, EV, SM, TB, VM, Lv88, Ph36>

jaquette (JACKET) [ʒakɛt, dʒækət] *n.f.* jacket, coat <***Loc:*** IB, Da84, Lv88>

jardin [ʒardɛ̃] *n.m.* **1** garden *Grand-maman d'Érath faisait des pâtés avec des gigiers de zoie et de canards et alle les assaisonnait avec du thym qu'alle plantait dans son jardin.* Grandma from Erath made meat pies with goose and duck gizzards that she seasoned with thyme that she planted in her garden. (VM) **2** vegetable garden *C'était le père de ma mère, il avait le plus beau jardin, vous pouviez nourrir la famille avec ça.* It was the father of my mother, he had the most beautiful vegetable garden, you could feed the whole family with it. (IB) ◊ **•faire jardin** to raise a garden, cultivate vegetables *Je vas plus faire jardin.* I'm giving up cultivating vegetables. (TB) <AV, IB, SB, SM, TB, VM, Da84, Lv88> **•faire le jardin** to garden, do the gardening *Et là ils ontvaient des* SEARS ROEBUCK CATALOG *que tu pouvais faire du linge dessus. Eusse donnait du linge ou des outils pour faire le jardin et tout ça.* And they had Sears Roebuck catalogs that you could make clothes from. They offered clothing or tools for gardening and all of that. (LF) <LF> <***Loc:*** AV, IB, LF, SB, SL, SM, TB, VM, Hi02, Da84, Lv88>

jardinage [ʒardinaʒ] *n.m.* *(often pl.)* fresh vegetables, garden produce *Un steak avec deux jardinages.* A steak with two vegetables. (Lv88) *Va voir si on a des jardinages à la grocerie.* Go see if they have fresh vegetables at the grocery. (VM) *Si t'as envie de manger du jardinage, tu peux faire comme lui, plante-toi un jardin.* If you want to eat vegetables, you can do like him, plant yourself a garden. (VM, ch: *Plante-toi un jardin*) <***Loc:*** AV, SM, TB, VM, Da84, Lv88, Re31>

jardinier [ʒardinje] *n.m.* gardener <***Loc:*** Da84>

jardinière [ʒardinjær] *n.f.* flowerpot, flower stand <***Loc:*** Da84>

jargon [ʒargɔ̃] *n.m.* **1** jargon, lingo **2** mumbling, incomprehensible speech **3** noise <***Loc:*** LF, VM, Da84>

jargonner [ʒargɔ̃ne] **I** *v.tr.* to mumble *Il a jargonné quelque chose; j'ai pas rien compris.* He mumbled something; I didn't understand a thing. (VM) **II** *v.intr.* to speak incomprehensibly <***Loc:*** VM, Da84>

jarre [dʒar, ʒar] *n.f.* **1** jar *Tu salais la viande et tu la mettais dans une grosse jarre.* You salted the meat and put it in a large jar. (AV) **2** culvert *Le* POLICE-JURY *s'occupe de fouiller les fossés, mettre les jarres.* The police jury takes care of digging ditches, putting in culverts. (Lv88) ◊ **•jarre en terre** earthen jar <TB> <***Loc:*** AC, AV, SL, SM, TB, VM, Da84, Lv88>

jarrer [ʒare] *v.intr.* to chatter <***Loc:*** LF>

jarret [ʒarɛ, ʒare] *n.m.* **1** thigh (of a person) **2** drumstick (of fowl) **3** ham (of a hog), hind quarter (of beef) **4** shank meat for stew or soup **5** shin bone <***Loc:*** VM, Da84>

jarretière [ʒartjær, ʒɔrtjær] *n.f.* garter ◊ **•jarretière de la Sainte Vierge** ribbon grass, sweetheart grass <LA, VM, La99> <***Loc:*** LA, SM, VM, Da84, La99>

jasmin [ʒasmɛ̃] *n.m./f.* **1** jasmine **2** gardenia, Cape jasmine ◊ **•jasmin de nuit** night-blooming jasmine <Gu00> **•jasmin d'orange** orange jessamine, flowering orange <TB> <***Loc:*** TB, VM, Da84, Gu00, Lv88>

jasmine [ʒasmin] *n.f.* pawpaw <***Loc:*** Ho90, Lv88, Re31>

jasminier [ʒasminje] *n.m.* pawpaw tree <***Loc:*** Ho90, Re31>

jaube ♦see **jobe**

jaunaca [ʒonaka] *n.m.* person with a yellowish-colored face *Espèce de grand jaunaca.* Big yellow-faced person. (TB) <***Loc:*** TB>

jaunâtre [ʒɔ̃nat(r)] *adj.* yellowish *Morve jaunâtre.* Yellowish mucus, phlegm. (EV) <***Loc:*** EV, LF, Da84>

jaune [ʒɔ̃n, ʒɑ̃n] *adj./n.* **1** yellow (color) *Un mâchoiron jaune comme ça-là, eusse appelle ça un goujon.* A yellow catfish like that is called a "goujon." (LF) **2** golden brown (color) *T'as cuit ce poulet dessus le barbecue et ça a sorti jaune, jaune.* You cooked that chicken on the barbecue pit and it came out golden brown. (VM) **3** khaki (color) *Chemise jaune, pantalon jaune.* Khaki shirt, khaki pants. (VM) ◊ **•jaune d'œuf** egg yolk <Da84> <***Loc:*** EV, LF, SJ, SL, TB, VM, An94, Da84, Gu00, Hi02, Lv88>

jaunir (**jaunser**) [ʒɔ̃nir, ʒɔ̃nse] **I** *v.tr.* **1** to paint yellow, dye yellow **2** to yellow, make yellow *Le soleil a jauni la gazette.* The sun yellowed the newspaper. (EV) **II** *v.intr.* to yellow, become yellow, fade *Regarde comment la peinture a jauni!* Look at how the paint has yellowed! (EV) ◊ **•faire jaunir** to brown *Je fais jaunir [...] la viande et je mets des oignons, des piments, des assaisonnements, et là je remets le riz cru, avec l'eau dedans, et, cuis tout ensemble.* I brown the meat, and I put in onions, peppers, seasonings, and I add in the uncooked rice, with water in it, and cook everything together. (SL) <SL> <***Loc:*** EV, SL, TB, VM, Da84>

jaunisse [ʒɔ̃nis] *n.f.* jaundice, yellow jaundice <***Loc:*** Da84>

jaunser ♦see **jaunir**

javion [ʒavjɔ̃] *n.* one who tries unsuccessfully to speak standard French **Famille de javion.* Family of 'wannabe' French speakers. (Da84) <***Loc:*** Da84>

JAW-BREAK [dʒɔbɹeˈk] *n.m.* jawbreaker (large round very hard candy) <***Loc:*** VM>

jazz [dʒaz, dʒæz] *n.m.* jazz ◊ **•JAZZ BAND** [dʒæzbænd] jazz band <Da84> <***Loc:*** Da84>

je (**j'**) [ʒə, əʒ, ʒ, z, s,] *pron.pers.* (*subj.*) I *J'ai tout le temps dit je vas aider l'assesseur, mais moi je veux pas ça. J'ai jamais voulu des grosses offices.* I always said I would help the assessor, but I don't want that. I never wanted big offices. (LF) *Je vais parce que je veux.* I'm going because I want to. (SM) <***Loc:*** AC, AV, EV, IB, JE, LA, LF, SL, SM, TB, VM, An84, An94, Da84, Hi02, Lv88>

jérémiade [ʒerɛ̃mjad] *n.f.* Jeremiad, repeated lamentation <***Loc:*** Da84>

JERSEY [dʒəɹzi] *n.m.* **1** Jersey cow **2** jersey, type of sweater <***Loc:*** Da84>

jésuite[1] [ʒezɥit] *adj.* Jesuit <***Loc:*** Da84>

Jésuite[2] [ʒezɥit] *n.* Jesuit *Aller à l'école chez les Jésuites.* To go to a Jesuit school. (EV) <***Loc:*** EV, Da84>

Jésus-Christ (**Jésus**) [ʒezykri, ʒezy] *n.prop.* Jesus Christ, Jesus <***Loc:*** LF, Da84, Hi02>

jet (**jais**) [ʒɛ, ʒe] *n.m.* jet **Noir comme du jais.* Jet black. (Da84) <***Loc:*** Da84>

jeter [ʃte, ʒete, ʒəte] **I** *v.tr.* **1** to throw, toss *Jette la pelotte!* Throw the ball! (JE) *Avec nous, elle dit, "Quand vous jetez un mot anglais dans une phrase, ça me gêne."* With us, she says, "When you throw an English word into a [French] sentence, that bugs me." (SL) **2** to throw away, discard *Et là dès que c'est cuit là, eh ben la viande se retire sur les os. Là ils jetont les os.* And when it's cooked, well, the meat comes off the bones. Then they throw away the bones. (LF) *Jetez-les!* Throw them away! (JE) **3** to knock over, spill *Il a jeté le bassin de fèves.* He knocked over the bowl of beans. (VM) **4** to cut down, fell (a tree) *Dans le temps, ça aurait jeté un bois avec un passe-partout.* In those days, they would cut down a tree with a cross-cut saw. (IV) **II se jeter** *v.pron.* to throw o.s. *Il s'a jeté dessus le lit en arrivant.* He threw himself on the bed as soon as he arrived. (LA) ◊ **•jeter à côté** to throw out, cast aside *Je vas parler dans la maison de cour, ça va être jeté à côté, crois-moi. Je* HANDLE *mon tracas moi-même. Je connais qui parler avec.* I am going to talk in court, it will be thrown out, believe me. I handle my problems myself. I know who to talk to. (LF) <LF> **•jeter de l'eau** to urinate **Pierre, ça t'ferait pas rien si j'pisserais au boute du bateau? —Moi aussi, j'voudrais j'ter d'l'eau, si ça t'ferait pas rien.* Pierre, do you mind if I piss off the end of the boat ? —I'd also like to urinate, if you don't mind. (Gr86) <Gr86> **•jeter la vue** to glance <Lv88> **•jeter par terre** to throw down <Da84> **•jeter son lait** to spawn (of an oyster) *L'huître jette son lait.* The oyster is spawning. (TB) <TB> **•jeter un coup d'œil** to take a peek, take a quick glance <Da84> **•jeter un cri (en l'air)** to cry out *Elle a jeté un cri en l'air, alle m'a fait assez peur.* She cried out, she gave me such a fright. (TB) <LF, TB> **•se jeter à l'eau pour pas se tremper** to do something foolish that will have worse consequences than the thing one is trying to avoid <La99> **•se jeter par terre** to throw oneself down *Il s'a jeté par terre et il a pris à brailler.* He threw himself down and began to cry. (EV) <EV, Da84> <***Loc:*** AC, EV, IV, JE, LA, LF, SB, SL, SM, TB, VM, Da84, Gr86, Hi02, Lv88, La99>

jeton [ʒətɔ̃, ʃtɔ̃] *n.m.* token, poker chip <***Loc:*** Da84>

jeture [ʃtyr] *n.f.* **1** cotton or wool spun to be woven (the product of a spinning wheel) **2** fabric made of cotton warp and woolen thread <***Loc:*** VM, Lv88>

jeu [ʒø] *n.m.* **1** game *Ils sont après practiquer pour le jeu à ce soir.* They are practicing for the game tonight. (VM) *Un jeu de cartes.* A game of cards. (EV) **2** fun, joke **3** looseness, play (in parts of a machine, etc.) *J'ai pour amancher mon marteau. Il a du jeu dedans.* I have to fix the handle on my hammer. It's loose. (VM) **4** set of harness ◊ **•jeu d'eau** fountain <VM> **•jeu de chien** horseplay <La99> **•le jeu (ne) vaut pas la chandelle** it's not worth the trouble or risk <Da84, La99> <***Loc:*** EV, VM, Da84, La99>

jeudi [ʒødi] *n.m.* Thursday ◊ **•Jeudi Saint** Holy or Maundy Thursday <Da84> <***Loc:*** Da84, Hi02>

jeuler ♦see **gueuler**

jeun [ʒœ̃] *n.m.* ◊ **•à jeun *a*** fasting *Dans ce temps-là, si t'étais à jeun avant de communier, tu pouvais même pas boire de l'eau.* In those days, if you were fasting before communion, you couldn't even drink water. (EV) ***b*** sober, not drinking, 'on the wagon' *Elle disait que Gros était plus dur à endurer quand il était à jeun que quand il était soûl et c'était une belle chose qu'il buvait souvent.* She used to say that Gros was harder to put up with when he was on the wagon than when he was drunk and that it was a good thing he drank often. (ThCa: *Le charivari*) <EV, Da84, La99, ThCa> <***Loc:*** EV, Da84, La99, ThCa>

jeune[1] [ʒœ̃n, ʒɛ̃n] *adj.* young *Et j'ai appris le français joliment jeune.* I learned French quite young. (LF) *Un traiteur du vieux temps te dit si t'es plus jeune que le traiteur, tu peux apprendre la prière.* A treater from the old days tells you, if you're younger than the treater, you can learn the prayer. (LF) <***Loc:*** JE, LF, Da84, Hi02>

jeune[2] [ʒœ̃n, ʒɛ̃n] *n.* young person, youth *Dans les vieilles maisons, les vieux dormaient en bas et les jeunes dormaient en haut.* In the old houses, the older folks slept downstairs and the younger ones slept upstairs. (LA) <***Loc:*** LA, SL, Da84>

jeûne [ʒœ̃n] *n.m.* fast ◊ **•jeûne de Carême** Lenten fast <Da84> <***Loc:*** Da84>

jeûner [ʒœ̃ne] *v.intr.* to fast *Asteur, on jeûne proche pus durant Carême, mais dans le temps, c'était sérieux.* Today, we hardly fast anymore during Lent, but in the old days, it was serious. (LA) <***Loc:*** LA, Da84>

jeunesse [ʒœ̃nɛs, ʒɛ̃nɛs] *n.f.* **1** youth, time of life between childhood and maturity *Il s'a consacré à sa famille après une jeunesse de bamboche.* He dedicated himself to his family after a youth spent in debauchery. (LA) **2** young person, youth **Fillette, jeunesse, mais taisez-vous. Vous n'avez pas encore quinze ans.* Little girl, young girl, be quiet. You are not yet fifteen years old. (IB, ch: *Une fille de quatorze ans*) **3** youth, young people collectively *La jeunesse asteur fait pas ça.* Young people today don't do that. (TB) **4** youthfulness <***Loc:*** IB, LA, TB, Da84, Hi02>

jeunezir [ʒœ̃nzir] *v.intr.* to grow younger, rejuvenate *Il faut je me guette. Je suis p'us après jeunezir.* I have to watch myself. I'm not getting any younger. (LA) *Mais vous jeunezissez toujours.* You always (seem to) get younger. (TB) <***Loc:*** LA, TB, Di32, Lv88>

jigailler [ʒigaje] *v.intr.* to squirm **Nathan s'est advancé [=avancé] et a embrassé Jeanette en arrière de l'oreille. Elle a jigaillé et Nathan l'a bien caressé.* Nathan leaned over and kissed her behind the ear. She squirmed and Nathan sweetly caressed her. (Wh83) <***Loc:*** Wh83>

jiguer [dʒige] *v.intr.* to dance <***Loc:*** EV, Ph36>

job [dʒɔb] *n.m./f.* **1** job, work, employment *J'ai un bon job avec une compagnie d'huile.* I have a good job with an oil company. (SM) **2** duty, task, piece of work **C'est mon job.* It's my duty. (Da84) ◊ **•faire un bon job** to do a good job *T'as fait un bon job avec ta maison.* You did a good job with your house. (SM) <SM, Da84> <***Loc:*** EV, LF, SM, TB, VM, Da84, Hi02, Lv88, Ph36>

jobe (**jaube**) [dʒɔb, ʒɔb] *n.f.* mumps <***Loc:*** AV, IB, LA, SM, VM, Da84, Lv88>

jober [dʒobe] *v.intr.* to work odd jobs, work by the day *Il est après jober plutôt que faire la récolte.* He's doing day labor instead of harvesting. (SM) <***Loc:*** SM, Lv88>

jobeur [dʒobœr] *n.m.* one who does odd jobs <***Loc:*** Pe37>

jogue ♦see **jug**

joie [ʒwa] *n.f.* joy, happiness, gladness ◊ **•joie de vivre** joy of life, zest for living **Ouais, ça c'était eine grand-mère. […] Alle avait la joie de viv'.* Yeah, that was a real grandmother. For her, it was a delight to live. (Gu82) <Gu82, Hi02> <***Loc:*** Da84, Gu82, Hi02>

joignant, -e [ʒwɑ̃jɑ̃, -ɑ̃t] *adj.* touching, adjoining *Les deux bouts joignants.* The two adjoining pieces. (VM) <***Loc:*** VM, Da84>

joindre [ʒwɛ̃n, ʒwɛ̃d(r)] *v.tr.* **1** to join, unite, combine *Il arrivait pas à joindre les deux bouts.* He couldn't join the two ends. (LA) **2** to join, become a member of *Pop a joint les* KNIGHTS OF COLUMBUS. Dad joined the Knights of Columbus. (Lv88) **3** to meet, meet with *Si tu joins quelqu'un qui parle* *français, tu peux parler avec eusse.* If you meet someone who speaks French, you can talk to them. (Lv88) **Tout le monde je joignais me demandait où j'allais.* Everyone I met would ask me where I was going. (Wh69) *Moi, je le joindais chez lui.* I would meet up with him at his house. (AC) **II se joindre** *v.pron.* **1** to gather, assemble, meet **Et il nous faisait le soir se joindre et puis jouer de la musique.* He would have us meet in the evening and then play music. (SL, An84) **C'est ici que le jeune monde [...] s'est joint.* This is where the young people met up. (Wh83) *Le* SCHOOL BOARD *va se joindre à six heures.* The school board will meet at six o'clock. (Lv88) **2** to be adjacent to, adjoin *Proche tous les maisons et les garages se joint asteur.* Almost all houses and garages adjoin now. (VM) <*Loc:* AC, JD, SL, TB, VM, An84, An94, Da84, Hi02, Lv88, Wh69, Wh83>

joint [ʒwɛ̃] *n.m.* **1** joint, seam, lap **2** joint (of the body) *Tu peux subir une attaque de rhumatisse à n'importe quel joint du corps.* You can get a bout of rheumatism in any joint of the body. (Lv88) **3** ankle of a horse <*Loc:* Da84, Lv88>

jointé, -e [ʒwɛ̃te] *adj.* jointed *Les deux soles étaient jointées avec des chevilles.* The two beams were jointed with pegs. (VM) <*Loc:* VM, Da84, Gr86>

jointure [ʒwɛ̃tyr] *n.f.* joint, juncture ◊ **•jointure de canne** internode of sugarcane <AV, IB, SJ> **•jointure du pied** ankle *Pour les rhumatisses on amarre un dix-sous autour de la jointure du pied.* For rheumatism we tie a dime around the ankle. (TB) <TB> <*Loc:* AV, IB, SJ, TB, Da84>

JOKE[1] [dʒoᵘk] *v.intr.invar.* to joke, joke around *Il était toujours après* JOKE. He was always joking around. (Lv88) <*Loc:* Lv88>

JOKE[2] [dʒoᵘk] *n.m.* joke <*Loc:* Da84, Lv88>

joli, -e [ʒoli] *adj.* **1** pretty *Allons voir, on a le branchu, ça c'est un joli z-oiseau.* Let's see, there's the wood duck, that's a pretty bird. (TB) **2** good-looking, cute **Alors ce jeune homme, un joli jeune homme, il a embourbé droit là dans une petite manche.* So that young man, a cute young man, he got bogged down right there in a small lane. (EV, An94) **In [=un] joli homme.* A good-looking man. (EV, Ph36) **3** fine, nice **Il dit, "T'as du joli maïs."* He said, "You have some fine corn." (SL, An94) **4** fair, nice (of the weather) *Il dit, "Allons espérer qu'il fait joli temps pour aller."* He said, "Let's wait until the weather's nice to go." (LA) <*Loc:* EV, LA, SL, TB, An94, Da84, Hi02, Ph36>

joliment [ʒolimɑ̃, ʒulimɑ̃] *adv.* **1** quite, very, really *J'ai des amis qui est joliment malades.* I have friends who are very sick. (SM) *J'ai resté joliment longtemps dans un* WHEELCHAIR. I stayed in a wheelchair for a very long time. (VM) **Joliment bon.* Pretty good. (Da84) **Joliment homme.* Much of a man. (Da84) **2** many, much, a lot, quite a bit **Les écoles nous ont fait joliment plus de mal que de bien.* The schools did us a lot more harm than good. (ThCa: *Mille misères*) *La queue de cocodrie, c'est joliment le même goût avec du poisson armé.* Alligator tail has very much the same taste as garfish. (Lv88) *J'ai fait joliment de l'argent avec des mulets.* I made quite a bit of money with mules. (AC) *Ça coûte joliment mais c'est un bon passe-temps.* It costs a lot but it's a good hobby. (SM) **Joliment du monde.* A good many people. (Da84) <*Loc:* AC, EV, IB, JE, LF, SB, SL, SM, TB, VM, Da84, Hi02, Lv88, ThCa>

jonc [ʒɔ̃] *n.m.* **1** river cane **2** reed, rush, bulrush ◊ **•jonc au trois quarts {à trois écartes}** three-cornered grass (species of bulrush) <VM, Ho90, Lv88> **•jonc coupant** sawgrass <Ho90> **•jonc de chat {au baril} / jonc plat {matelas}** cattail plant <VM, Ho90, Lv88, Re31> **•jonc rond *a*** giant bulrush ***b*** any of various species of rushes <VM, Ho90> <*Loc:* VM, Da84, Gu00, Ho90, Lv88, Re31>

joncière [ʒɔ̃sjær] *n.f.* cattail patch *Pour arriver à ses pièges il fallait qu'il passe en travers de la joncière.* To get to his traps he had to pass through the cattail patch. (TB) <*Loc:* TB, Di32>

jonction [ʒɔ̃ksjɔ̃] *n.f.* junction, juncture <*Loc:* Da84>

jonglage [ʒɔ̃glaʒ] *n.m.* thought, reflection, reverie **Il fallait pas se tracasser d'ein problème de trop, parce que trop de jonglage aurait fondu la cire dans tes oreilles et c'aurait coulé dessus ta cervelle et ça t'aurait rendu fou.* You couldn't worry about a problem too much, because too much thinking would melt your earwax, which would then ooze over your brain and drive you crazy. (Wh83) <*Loc:* Wh83>

jonglailler [ʒɔ̃glaje] **I** *v.tr.* to think about, ponder **II** *v.intr.* to daydream <*Loc:* IB>

jonglement [ʒɔ̃gləmɑ̃] *n.m.* reverie, brooding, fretting ◊ **•faire des jonglements** to brood <Da84> <*Loc:* Da84, Lv88>

jongler [ʒɔ̃gle, ʒɑ̃gle] **I** *v.tr.* to think about, worry about *Ils avaient jonglé Skylab pouvait tomber.* They worried that Skylab could fall. (Lv88) *J'étais après jongler comment longtemps on les avait pas vus.* I was thinking about how long it's been since we've seen them. (EV) *Le monde fait des choses aujourd'hui que le vieux monde peut pas même jongler d'être fait.* People do things now that older people cannot even think of being done. (IB) **II** *v.intr.* **1** to think, meditate, reflect, ponder, worry *Le bougre, il est* TOUGH, *il jongle pas, il se tracasse pas d'arien du tout, tu connais.* The guy, he's tough, he doesn't think, he doesn't worry about anything, you know. (TB) *Quitte-moi jongler.* Let me think. (Lv88) **2** to daydream, dream, indulge in reveries **Ça, c'était juste pour te donner une idée de ça à quoi je jonglais toute la journée.* That was just to give you an idea of what I daydreamed about all day long. (VM, An84) ◊ **•jongler à {après / pour / sur}** to think of, think about *Ça va lui faire jongler à une autre chanson.* That will make him think of another song. (Lv88) *Il est mort il avait soixante-huit ans, pour moi ça semblait vieux, ben si vous jonglez à ça c'est pas vieux.* He died he was sixty-eight, for me it seemed old but, well, if you think of it, it is not old. (IB)

J'ai pas jonglé après ça. I didn't think of that. (SL) *Je vas jongler sur ça.* I'll think about that. (SM) <IB, SL, SM, TB, Lv88> <***Loc:*** AV, EV, IB, IV, JD, JE, LA, LF, SB, SL, SM, TB, VM, Da84, Gu00, Hi02, Lv88, Ph36, Re31>

jonglerie[1] [ʒɔ̃gləri] *n.f.* reverie, daydreaming, deep thought <***Loc:*** VM, Lv88>

jonglerie[2] [ʒɔ̃gləri] *n.f.* farce, trick *On faisait des jongleries sur la galerie, on capotait les chaises.* We played tricks on the porch, we would knock over chairs. (Lv88) <***Loc:*** VM, Lv88>

jongleur[1], **-euse** [ʒɔ̃glœr, -øz] *adj.* dreamy, pensive, musing **Quoi ce qu'il y a, maman? On dirait que t'es jongleuse.* What's the matter, Mama? You seem pensive. (IB, An94) <***Loc:*** IB, An94, Lv88>

jongleur[2], **-euse** [ʒɔ̃glœr, -øz] *n.m.* daydreamer, muser, thinker *Tu veux bien te lever de là, tu vas être un vrai jongleur comme ton pape.* Why don't you get up from there, you're going to be a real daydreamer like your father. (TB) *Il est un fameux jongleur, mais un petit faiseur.* He's a big dreamer, but a little doer. (SB) <***Loc:*** AV, IB, SB, SM, TB, VM, Lv88>

jorée (**joritte**) [ʒore, ʒorit] *n.f.* **1** towhee, chewink **2** wood thrush <***Loc:*** Re31>

joritte ♦see **jorée**

josé [ʒoze, dʒoze] *n.m.* jacket, shirtwaist, overblouse, short housecoat *Mémère porte tout le temps des josés.* Grandma always wears short housecoats. (TB) <***Loc:*** IB, SJ, TB>

jouc (**juc**) [ʒuk, ʒyk] *n.m.* chicken roost or perch <***Loc:*** Lv88>

joue [ʒu] *n.f.* cheek <***Loc:*** Da84, Hi02>

jouer [ʒwe] **I** *v.tr.* **1** to play (a game, a sport) *On a un gang qui joue Pokeno.* We have a bunch of people who play Pokeno. (LF) **Jouer bingo.* To play bingo (Da84) **Jouer le baseball.* To play baseball. (Da84) *Je* FEED *mes poules et mes chiens, et après ça on va jouer des guémes.* I feed my chickens and my dogs, and then we go play games. (TB) **2** to play (music or a musical instrument) *Il joue le violon.* He plays the violin. (TB) *Et là j'ai des petits-enfants et eux-autres joue la musique.* And then I have grandchildren and they play music. (LF) *Il joue le piano.* He plays the piano. (LF) *Je suis pas un musicien professional mais je vais te jouer quelque chose.* I'm not a professional musician, but I'll play you something. (VM) **3** to play (e.g. a tape, a record, the radio) *Il était après jouer le* TAPE. He was playing the tape. (TB) **4** to play (a joke, a trick) *Il est tout le temps après jouer des niches.* He's always playing jokes. (VM) *Jouer un vilain tour.* To play a dirty trick. (EV) **II** *v.intr.* **1** to play, have fun *Les petits font un tchampourra quand ils jouent ensemble.* The kids make a commotion when they play together. (SM) *J'aime pas laisser mes enfants aller jouer là-bas. Ses enfants sont trop téméraires.* I don't like to let my kids go over there to play. His children are too audacious. (EV) **2** to play (a game, a sport) *Jouer à la pelote.* To play baseball. (TB) *Jouer au billard.* To play billiards. (Da84) *Jouer aux dés.* To play dice. (Da84) *Jouer aux caniques.* To play marbles. (TB) *C'est icitte dans 1948 qu'ils ont commencé à jouer au* FOOTBALL *icitte dans le bas de la paroisse, dans le sud de la paroisse.* This is where in 1948 they started to play football here in the southern end of the parish. (LF) *Des fois, on s'aurait mis ensemble, juste des filles, on aurait joué des cartes.* Sometimes, we used to gather, just girls, we used to play cards. (AV) **3** to play (a musical instrument) *Notre grand-père jouait du violon.* Our grandfather played the violin. (LF) *Jouer de la guitare.* To play guitar. (TB) **4** to play (of a song, a tape, etc.) *Ça c'est la valse qu'était après jouer quand on s'a séparé.* That's the waltz that was playing when we broke up. (LA) ◊ **•jouer (à la) madame** to play house *C'était [quand on jouait] à la madame on baliait ça. C'était dans la terre.* It was when we were playing house that we would sweep that up. It was [outside] on the ground. (JE) <JE, Da84> **•jouer la patte de cochon** to play a dirty trick <AV, EV, Da84, La99> <***Loc:*** AV, EV, JE, LA, LF, SM, TB, VM, Da84, La99, Lv88>

joueur [ʒwœr] *n.m.* **1** player *Notre grand-père Hilaire, lui c'était un joueur de violon.* Our grandfather Hilaire was a violin player. (LF) **Le dernier joueur qui restait gagnait.* The last player who remained [in the game] was the winner. (Wh83) **2** performer ◊ **•joueur de musique** musician <TB, Da84> **•joueur de pelote** ball player <Da84> <***Loc:*** LF, SM, TB, Da84, Wh83>

joueuse [ʒwɛz, ʒwøz] *n.f.* **1** taw (large marble used for shooting in the game of marbles) **2** female dancing partner <***Loc:*** SM>

joufflu [ʒufly] *adj.* **1** puffed up in the face *Mon père m'appelait joufflu tout le temps.* My father always called me puffy. (VM) **2** puffed up with pride *Il était tout joufflu avec son nouveau char.* He was puffed up with pride over his new car. (VM) <***Loc:*** VM, Da84>

joug [ʒuk] *n.m.* **1** yoke *Ça mettait un joug sus le cou du bœuf.* They would put a yoke on the ox's neck. (EV) **2** bondage <***Loc:*** EV, VM, Da84>

jouir [ʒwir] *v.intr.* to benefit from, enjoy **Jouir d'une bonne santé.* To have or enjoy good health. (Da84) <***Loc:*** Da84>

jouissance [ʒwisɑ̃s] *n.f.* joy, enjoyment <***Loc:*** Da84>

joujou [ʒuʒu] *n.m.* toy, plaything <***Loc:*** IB, Da84, Wh83>

jouqué, -e [ʒuke] *adj.* living together without benefit of marriage *Il est jouqué avec une femme de l'Anse aux Pailles, mais ils ont pas d'enfants ensemble.* He's living with a woman from l'Anse aux Pailles, but they don't have any children together. (EV) <***Loc:*** EV, La99>

jouquée [ʒuke] *n.f.* collection of roosting fowl *Fais bien attention là. Tire pas dans cette jouquée de volailles.* Be careful there. Don't shoot into that bunch of roosting chickens. (TB) <***Loc:*** JE, TB>

jouquer[1] (**juquer**) [ʒuke, ʒyke] **I** *v.intr.* to roost, perch *Nos poules jouquent dessus la maison.* Our chickens roost on top of the house. (SB) **II se jouquer** *v.pron.* **1** to roost, perch *La poule va se jouquer dessus une branche.* The chicken is going to roost on a branch. (Lv88) **2** to climb **I s'est jouqué su la maison.* He climbed on top of the house. (EV, Ph36) <*Loc:* AV, EV, IB, SB, SM, TB, VM, Lv88, Ph36>

jouquer[2] ♦see **ajouquer**

jouquoir (**juquoir**) [ʒukwar, ʒuʃwar, ʒykwar] *n.m.* chicken roost or perch <*Loc:* EV, LF, SB, SM, TB, VM, Da84, Lv88, Ph36>

jour [ʒur, ʒɔr] *n.m.* **1** day *Il passait tous les jours après pedler son pain.* He passed by every day peddling his bread. (LA) *Ce gros vent l'autre jour a manqué d'arracher la porte de dessus les pentures.* That strong wind the other day nearly tore the door off its hinges. (VM) **2** daytime, daylight *Ça vient en plein jour icitte les ramasser.* They come here and pick them up in broad daylight. (TB) ◊ **•Jour de l'An** New Year's Day <LF, Da84> **•Jour de Noël** Christmas Day <Da84> **•Jour de Pâques** Easter Sunday <Da84, Wh83> **•jour de semaine** weekday *Je me rappelle pas quel jour c'était le premier. C'était un jour de semaine.* I don't remember what day of the week the first was. It was a weekday. (TB) <TB> **•jour ras** slack day (in fishing) <JE> **•au jour** at daybreak, at dawn <Da84> **•au jour d'aujourd'hui** today, these days *J'aime parler avec le monde en français jusqu'au jour d'aujourd'hui, tu connais, tous les pêcheurs eusse parle en français.* I like talking to people in French even today, you know, all the fishermen speak French. (LF) <LF> **•avant-jour** dawn, daybreak *Ils se sont levés sur l'avant-jour pour aller pêcher.* They got up at daybreak to go fishing. (Lv88) <Da84, Lv88> **•beau jour** nice day <Da84> **•de jour en jour** from day to day <Da84> **•d'un jour à l'autre** from day to day, from one day to the next <Da84> **•en plein jour** in broad daylight <Da84> **•faire jour** to be day(light) <Da84> **•grand jour** broad daylight <Da84> **•le jour du jugement** Judgment day *Le Bon Dieu va tout régler le jour du jugement.* The good Lord will settle everything on Judgment day. (VM) <VM> **•le jour est après se faire** day is breaking <Da84> **•quinze jours** two weeks *On jouait là-bas tous les quinze jours.* We played over there every two weeks. (SL) <SL> <*Loc:* AV, JE, LA, LF, SL, SM, TB, VM, Da84, Hi02, Lv88, Re31>

journal [ʒurnal] *n.m.* **1** newspaper **2** journal <*Loc:* SL, Da84, Hi02>

journalier, -ière (**journalieux, -ieuse**) [ʒurnalje, -jær, ʒurnaljø, -jøz] *adj.* **1** changeable, unsteady, fluctuating *J'avais habitude de travailler au moulin, mais l'ouvrage est trop journalieux, ça fait que je m'ai trouvé un job sus les puits d'huile.* I used to work at the mill, but the work is too unsteady, so I found myself a job in the oilfield. (VM) *Elle est en enfance, mais c'est journalieux. Elle a des bons jours et des mauvais jours.* She's senile, but it fluctuates. She has good days and bad days. (VM) **2** moody, subject to mood swings *Il est assez journalier. Tu connais jamais comment tu vas le trouver.* He's so moody, you never know what state you'll find him in. (EV) <*Loc:* EV, TB, VM, Da84, Pe37>

journalieux[1], **-ieuse** [ʒurnaljø, -jøz] *n.* **1** moody person **2** journeyman, day-laborer <*Loc:* Lv88>

journalieux[2] ♦see **journalier**

journée [ʒurne, ʒɔrne] *n.f.* **1** day, duration of a day *J'aurais voulu passer une journée avec cet homme-là qu'il me conte des affaires.* I would have liked to spend a day with that man so he could tell me some stories. (LF) **Faire une journée d'ouvrage.* To do a day's work. (Da84) **2** daytime ◊ **•belle journée** clear day, nice day <Da84> **•toute la journée** the whole day, all day long *Lui, il peut traînailler toute la journée après faire rien du tout.* He can loiter about all day long doing nothing. (LA) *Ça trafique toute la journée dans la salle à manger; ça fait pas de bien de l'nettoyer.* People come and go all day long through the dining room; it does no good to clean it. (TB) <JD, LA, SM, TB, Da84> <*Loc:* LF, Da84, Hi02>

joyeusement [ʒwajøzmɑ̃] *adv.* joyfully, cheerfully *Il chantait joyeusement.* He was singing cheerfully. (VM) <*Loc:* VM, Da84>

joyeuseté [ʒwajøzte] *n.f.* joyfulness, joy <*Loc:* Da84>

joyeux, -euse [ʒwajø, -øz] *adj.* joyful, merry, happy, cheerful **Joyeuse fête!* Happy birthday! (Da84) **Joyeux Noël.* Merry Christmas. (Da84) <*Loc:* Da84>

juc ♦see **jouc**

judiciaire[1] [ʒydisjær] *adj.* judiciary *Une décision judiciaire.* A judiciary decision. (LA) <*Loc:* LA, Da84>

judiciaire[2] [ʒydisjær] *n.* court <*Loc:* Da84>

JUG (**djog, jogue**) [dʒʌg, dʒɔg] *n.f.* jug <*Loc:* EV, IB, SB, SL, SM, TB, VM, Da84, Hi02, Lv88, Ph36>

juge [ʒyʒ] *n.m.* **1** judge **2** justice ◊ **•juge de paix** justice of the peace <LF, Hi02> <*Loc:* LF, Da84, Hi02>

jugement [ʒyʒmɑ̃, ʒyzmɑ̃] *n.m.* **1** judgment *Le Bon Dieu va tout régler le jour du jugement.* The good Lord will settle everything on judgment day. (VM) *Tu vas pas commencer à faire des jugements dessus mon mariage après le mariage que toi t'as eu.* You are not going to start making judgments about my marriage after the marriage that you had. (LA) **2** any official statement by a judge (e.g. judgment, opinion, sentence) *Le juge a prononcé un jugement là-dessus.* The judge pronounced a decision on that. (VM) **3** judgment, discernment, reasoning *Il faut tu uses ton jugement. Il faut tu jongles si c'est une personne blanc ou une personne brun.* You have to use your judgment. You have to think about whether it's a white person or a dark-skinned person. (VM) **4** prejudice *J'ai un jugement contre lui.* I've got a prejudice against him. (VM) ◊ **•jugement du Bon Dieu** final Judgment <VM> <*Loc:* VM, Da84>

juger [ʒyʒe, ʒyze] *v.tr.* **1** to judge *Je suis sûr si moi je juge, l'autre va juger à moi.* I am certain that if I judge [someone], someone is going to judge me. (IB) **2** to try (in court) *Ils ont jugé son cas la semaine passée.* They tried his case last week. (LA) <***Loc:*** IB, LA, Da84>

juif[1]**, -ive** [ʒɥif, dʒɥif, -iv] *adj.* **1** Jewish **2** [*offensive*] stingy, miserly *Etre juif avec son argent.* To be stingy with one's money. (SJ) **Il est trop juif pour nous donner même un bleu.* He's too stingy to give us even a nickel. (EV, Ph36) <***Loc:*** AV, EV, IB, SJ, SM, TB, Da84, Hi02, Lv88, Ph36>

juif[2]**, -ive** [ʒɥif, dʒɥif, -iv] *n.* Jewish person, Jew **•Juif errant** Wandering Jew <Da84> <***Loc:*** Da84, Hi02>

juif-errant (**juif errant**) [ʒɥiferɑ̃, ʒiferɑ̃] *n.m.* **1** wandering jew (perennial herb of the spiderwort family) **2** any bedraggled, forlorn-looking man or boy **3** one who wanders about, vagabond **4** frequent visitor, inopportune guest *Voilà le juif-errant avec son petit paquet.* There's the guy who's always visiting with his pack. (TB) <***Loc:*** SL, TB, VM, Da84, Lv88>

juillet (**juliette, julièle**) [ʒyljɛt, ʒylje, ʒyjɛt, ʒɥijɛt] *n.m.* July *Le sept de juillet.* The seventh of July. (LF) <***Loc:*** AV, IB, LF, SB, SL, SM, TB, VM, Da84, Di32, Gr86, Hi02, Lv88>

juin [ʒwɛ̃, ʒœ̃] *n.m.* June *On s'a marié dans juin.* We got married in June. (TB) <***Loc:*** SB, SL, SM, TB, VM, Da84, Hi02, Lv88>

julièle, juliette ♦see **juillet**

jumeau, -elle [ʒymo, -mɛl] *n.* twin <***Loc:*** AV, EV, IB, JD, LA, SB, SM, Da84>

jument [ʒymɑ̃] *n.f.* female horse, mare ◊ **•jument de brancard** woman of loose morals <SM> <***Loc:*** IB, SM, Da84, Hi02>

JUMPER [dʒʌmpəɹ, dʒɔ̃pa, ʒɔ̃pa] *n.m.* **1** jumper, jumpsuit **2** loose outer jacket <***Loc:*** SL, Da84>

jumper [dʒɔ̃pe] *v.intr.* to jump, give a start *Il a jumpé quand elle lui a mis du vinaigre dans la coupure.* He jumped when she put vinegar in his wound. (LF) <***Loc:*** LF>

JUNK [dʒʌŋk, dʒɔ̃k] *v.tr.invar.* to discard, throw away *Je vas* JUNK *ça.* I'm going to throw that away. (VM) <***Loc:*** VM>

jupe [ʒyp] *n.f.* **1** skirt **2** slip, underskirt *Ta jupe dépasse.* Your slip is showing. (VM) ◊ **•jupe de dessous** petticoat, slip <Da84, Gu00> **•jupe de nuit** nightgown <TB> **•jupe de robe** skirt of a dress <Da84> <***Loc:*** SL, SM, TB, VM, Da84, Gu00, Lv88>

jupon [ʒypɔ̃] *n.m.* petticoat, slip <***Loc:*** SM, Da84>

juquer ♦see **jouquer**

juquoir ♦see **jouquoir**

jurage [ʒyraʒ] *n.m.* curse, profanity, curse word *Equand j'ai travaillé des fois avec mon grand-père, j'en attendais plein des jurages dans français.* When I worked sometimes with my grandfather, I heard a lot of curse words in French. (TB) <***Loc:*** TB>

jurailler [ʒyraje] *v.intr.* to curse *Il était assis dans le coin après bouder et jurailler.* He was sitting in the corner pouting and cursing. (LA) <***Loc:*** LA, Da84>

jurailleur [ʒyrajœr] *n.m.* one who curses habitually <***Loc:*** Da84>

jurard ♦see **jureur**

juraumont ♦see **giraumont**

jurement [ʒyrmɑ̃] *n.m.* curse, profanity, curse word *Les Cadiens sont des spécialistes dans les jurements en français.* Cajuns are specialists in swearing in French. (Lv88) *Un jurement tous les seconds mots elle dit.* A curse word every other word that she says. (Lv88) <***Loc:*** AC, Da84, Hi02, Lv88>

jurer [ʒyre] **I** *v.tr.* **1** to profane *Il jurait toutes sortes de noms sacrés.* He took all kinds of holy names in vain. (Lv88) **2** to curse, swear at *Si vous voulez jurer quelqu'un...* If you want to curse someone . . . (Lv88) **J'suis pas fâché! J't'ai pas juré!* I'm not angry! I didn't curse you! (Gr82) **3** to scold, upbraid *Il va te jurer pour ça.* He's going to yell at you for that. (VM) **II** *v.intr.* to curse, swear, blaspheme *Alors, ça veut dire qu'il faut pas que personne jure ou parle sale devant les dames.* So that means that no one should swear or talk dirty in front of the women. (LA) **III se jurer** *v.pron.* to curse each other *Quand ça vient pour se jurer, il y a pas personne qui peut nous battre.* When it comes to cursing each other, there's no one who can beat us. (Lv88) <***Loc:*** AV, VM, Da84, Gr82, Hi02, Lv88>

jureur (**jurard**) [ʒyrœr, ʒyrar] *n.* one who curses or swears *Tant qu'à lui, c'est un franc jureur.* As for him, he's a real curser. (VM) <***Loc:*** VM, Da84>

jurisdiction [ʒyrisdiksjɔ̃] *n.f.* jurisdiction, authority ♦**cf** autorité <***Loc:*** Da84>

jury [ʒyri] *n.m.* jury **Grand jury.* Grand jury. (Da84) ◊ **•Jury de Police** Police Jury <Da84, Wh83> **•être du jury** to be a juror, be on the jury <Da84> <***Loc:*** Da84, Wh83>

jus [ʒy] *n.m.* **1** juice **Jus de fruit.* Fruit juice. (Da84) **Jus d'orange.* Orange juice. (SM, Da84) **2** sugar cane juice *Le jus était cuit, chauffé jusqu'à qu'il venait en sirop.* The [sugar cane] juice was cooked, heated, until it became a syrup. (LA) **3** broth *T'attrapes ça plein du jus et des morceaux de viande et des saucisses, tu mets ça dans ton plat avec ton riz.* You get it full of sauce and pieces of meat and sausages, you put it on your plate with your rice. (SL) <***Loc:*** LA, SL, Da84, Hi02>

jusque [ʒysk] *prep.* as far as, so far, until *Une mitaine[...] c'est comme un carreau tu plies comme ça là, on va dire, jusque tu peux mettre bien ta main dedans.* A "mitaine," it's like a square that you fold like this, let's say, until you can really put your hand inside. (EV) **Il s'est gonflé et il s'est gonflé jusque tout à l'heure, il a gonflé de trop et il a cassé ouvert et il est mort.* He puffed himself up and he puffed himself up until then, he swelled up too much and he broke open and he died. (LA, An94) ◊ **•jusqu'à** [ʒyska,

ska] ***a*** until *Je débauche pas d'école jusqu'à deux heures et demie.* I don't get out of school until two thirty. (LF) *Alors la terre commence là, ça va jusqu'à la levée là-bas.* So the land starts there, it goes up to the levee over there. (TB) *Restez jusqu'à j'arrive.* Stay until I arrive. (SM) ***b*** up to, as many as *Mon j'ai compté jusqu'à 45 z-œufs dedans.* I've counted as many as 45 eggs in there. (TB) *On avait jusqu'à vingt et quelques piocheurs avec des pioches.* We had up to twenty some people with hoes. (AS) *Des fois ça se couchait jusqu'à quatre dans le même lit!* Sometimes they would sleep as many as four in the same bed! (TB) ***c*** even *Les chaouis [...] eusse va tout manger d'une nuit. Ko, jusqu'à les gras de jambes eusse va manger.* Raccoons, they'll eat everything in one night. Man, they'll even eat your calves. (TB) *Je l'ai jusqu'à ôté dedans le* TRAILER *et l'amener rester ici pour lui cuire son manger et faire pour elle pour qu'alle se soigne mieux.* I even took her out of the trailer and brought her to live here to cook her meals and do for her so she'd take better care of herself. (TB) *Alle vendait son linge jusqu'à.* She even sold her clothes. (TB) *Tu connais, ç'a tiré jusqu'à sur son* TRAILER *et tout?* You know, they even shot at her trailer and all? (TB) <AS, LF, SM, TB, Hi02> **•jusqu'à jour d'aujourd'hui** until now *Jusqu'à jour d'aujourd'hui, j'ai jamais dit à Emas.* Until now, I never told Emas. (AC) <AC> **•jusqu'à que** until *Mais quo'faire tu restes pas jusqu'à qu'il vient?* But why don't you stay until he comes? (TB) <TB> **•jusqu'à tant (que)** until *Je vas espérer jusqu'à tant qu'il vient me prendre.* I'm going to wait until he comes to get me. (VM) *Tu peux rester jusqu'à tant je m'en vas.* You can stay until I leave. (Lv88) <AV, IB, VM, Lv88, Re31> ***<Loc:*** AC, AS, AV, EV, IB, LA, LF, SM, TB,VM, Da84, Hi02, Lv88, Re31>

juste[1] [ʒys, ʒyst, ʒyʃ, yʃ] *adj.* **1** just, fair, right, true *Je trouve son père a pas été juste avec lui quand il a tout donné sa terre à son frère.* I don't think his father was fair with him when he gave all his land to his brother. (VM) **2** tight, narrow *La robe est trop juste pour moi.* The dress is too tight for me. (VM) **3** even, smooth *Le terrain est juste.* The land is even. (VM) ***<Loc:*** IB, LF, VM, Da84, Hi02>

juste[2] [ʒys, ʒyst, ʒyʃ, yʃ] *adv.* **1** just, exactly, precisely *Et ça c'était une job que pas tout le monde pouvait faire parce que follait que ça soye fait juste juste.* That was a job that not everyone could do because it had to be done precisely. (LF) **2** just, just now, moments ago **J'ai juste fini.* I have just finished. (Da84) *Il a juste rentré.* He just came in. (VM) **3** just, only, not more than **J'ai juste pris un piastre.* I took only a dollar. (Da84) *Il a juste cinq sous.* He only has five cents. (VM) *Alle le fait juste quand alle veut.* She does it only when she wants to. (TB) *J'avais juste un frère qu'aurait plus fumé que les autres.* I had only one brother who would smoke more than the others. (AC) ◊ **•juste bien {bon}** just right <Da84> **•juste comme il faut** just right *L'ourlet est juste comme il faut.* The hem is just right. (EV) <EV, Da84> **•comme de juste** obviously, naturally, as it should be <Da84> ***<Loc:*** AC, EV, IB, LF, SJ, TB, VM, Da84, Hi02, Lv88, Ph36>

justement [ʒystəmɑ̃] *adv.* **1** justly, fairly **2** just, just now, moments ago **J'ai justement fini.* I have just finished. (Da84) **3** just, only, simply, merely **J'avais justement mis la bride en haut et puis j'avais amarré après la barrière du camp.* I had just passed the bridle over and I had tied up to the camp fence. (SL, An94) **Il est justement blessé.* He is just wounded [not killed]. (Da84) *Ç'a brûlé le chêne, ç'a brûlé le chêne, ç'a brûlé le chêne je sais pas combien de jours, jusqu'à qu'il restait justement quelques racines qui sortaient de la terre.* They burned the oak, they burned the oak, they burned the oak I don't know how many days, until only some roots were left coming up out of the ground. (LF) *Mais c'était pas des Français de la France, c'était justement des Cadiens qui venait pas, c'était pas de Lafourche, pour sûr.* But they weren't French people from France, they were just Cajuns who didn't come, well they didn't come from Lafourche, for sure. (LF) **4** precisely, exactly, just **Justement quand elle était mariée, la guerre s'a déclarée pour son mari.* Right when she got married, war was declared and her husband was called. (IV, An94) ◊ **•c'est justement** that's it, that's right <VM> ***<Loc:*** IV, LF, SL, TB, VM, An94, Da84>

justesse [ʒystɛs] *n.f.* closeness ***<Loc:*** Da84>

justice [ʒystis] *n.f.* justice, fairness, right ***<Loc:*** Da84, Hi02>

justifiable [ʒystifjab(l)] *adj.* justifiable *C'est pas justifiable, ça il a fait à sa famille.* What he did to his family was not justifiable. (LA) ***<Loc:*** LA, Da84>

justification [ʒystifikasjɔ̃] *n.f.* justification, vindication ***<Loc:*** Da84>

justifier [ʒystifje] **I** *v.tr.* to justify, vindicate *Il peut pas justifier ça qu'il a fait avec moi.* He can't justify what he did to me. (VM) **II se justifier** *v.pron.* to justify or vindicate o.s. *Il peut essayer mais il peut pas se justifier.* He can try, but he can't justify himself. (LA) ***<Loc:*** LA, VM, Da84>

juter [ʒyte] *v.tr.* to juice *Juter un limon.* To juice a lemon. (Lv88) ***<Loc:*** Da84, Lv88>

juteux, -euse [ʒytø, -øz] *adj.* juicy *Les oranges dans l'arbre de mon père sont beaucoup juteuses cette année.* The oranges in my father's tree are really juicy this year. (LA) ***<Loc:*** LA, Da84>

K

kaïac ♦see **caïac**

kaïacot ♦see **caïacot**

kap-kap ♦see **cape-cape**

kayac[1] ♦see **caïac**

kayac[2] ♦see **kayak**

kayak (**kayac**) [kajak] *n.m.* kayak <***Loc:*** VM, Da84>

KEG [kɛg] *n.m.* keg *Un* KEG *de clous.* A keg of nails. (LA) <***Loc:*** LA, Lv88>

kêtch [kɛtʃ] *n.m.* jockey, racehorse rider <***Loc:*** VM>

KHAKI[1] [kæki] *adj./n.* khaki (color) *Il avait des culottes* KHAKI, *manière* TAN. He had on khaki pants, sort of tan. (LA) <***Loc:*** LA, Da84>

KHAKI[2] [kæki] *n.m.* **1** khaki cloth **2** khaki clothing <***Loc:*** Da84>

KIDNAP [kɪdnæp] *v.tr.invar.* to kidnap *Ils ont essayé de* KIDNAP *la petite fille, mais ils ont pas pu.* They tried to kidnap the little girl, but they couldn't do it. (LA) <***Loc:*** LA, Da84>

KIDNAPPER [kɪdnæpə] *n.m.* kidnapper <***Loc:*** Da84>

kidney (**KIDNEY**) [kidnɛ, kɪdni] *n.* kidney *La bière fait bien pour les* KIDNEYS *aussi.* Beer is good for the kidneys, too. (SL) <***Loc:*** AV, EV, JD, SL>

kildi (**kildie**) [kildi] *n.m.* **1** plover, esp. the killdeer **2** hummingbird <***Loc:*** EV, IB, SM, VM, Br55, Da84, Gr86, Lv88, Ph36>

kino [kino] *n.m.* keno, lotto (game of chance) <***Loc:*** IB, SJ, Lv88>

KLAN (**clan**) [klæn, klɑ̃] *n.m.* Klan (i.e. Ku Klux Klan) <***Loc:*** Da84>

klou-klouque [klukluk] *n.m.* **1** Ku Klux Klan **2** Klansman, member of the KKK **3** boogey-man <***Loc:*** SJ, Da84>

KNOCK-OUT[1] [nɑkaʊt] *n.m.* knock-out <***Loc:*** Da84>

KNOCK-OUT[2] [nɑkaʊt] *v.tr.invar.* to knock out *Il l'avait* KNOCK-OUT. He had knocked him out. (LA) <***Loc:*** LA>

kodak [kodak, ko^{u}dæk] *n.m.* **1** Kodak (brand name) **2** any camera <***Loc:*** Da84>

ko [ko…] *interj.* oh! *Ko, jusqu'à les gras de jambes eusse va manger.* Oh, they'll even eat your calves. (TB) <***Loc:*** TB>

korusse ♦see **corusse**

L

l' ♦see **le**

la ♦see **le**

là [la, lɔ, lə] *adv.* **1** there **Il a été. Il s'est posé là.* He went. He landed there. (EV, An94) **2** then *Et à peu près quinze ans après que j'avais commencé à faire l'école c'est là que CODOFIL a venu ici dans la paroisse de Lafourche.* And around 15 years after I had started teaching school, that's when CODOFIL came here to Lafourche Parish. (LF) *Et eux-autres prendait des planches et eux-autres faisait manière comme une banquette et là le monde dansait là-dessus.* And they took boards and they made more or less like a board sidewalk, and then people danced on it. (TB) *La promesse que tu m'avais fait, et là me tourner le dos pour t'en aller rejoindre un autre.* The promise you had made me, and then to turn your back on me to go off with another. (ch: *Evangeline special*) **3** *(intensifier) Alle après cuire asteur-là.* She's cooking right now. (JE) <***Loc:*** EV, JE, LF, An94, Da84, Hi02>

là-bas [laba] *adv.* **1** there, over there **Hé là-bas!* Hey over there! (Da84) **Garde là-bas!* Look over there! (Da84) **Va là-bas.* Go over there. (Da84) *Eux-autres là-bas, ça boit beaucoup du vin.* Over there, they drink a lot of wine. (AV) *On a été dans le Texas là-bas pour pêcher des huîtres.* We were over there in Texas to catch oysters. (TB) **2** down there *Et là y a un Rousseau qui reste à peu près deux blocs là-bas.* And there's a Rousseau who lives about two blocks down there. (TB) <***Loc:*** AC, AV, EV, IV, LA, LF, SL, SM, TB, An94, Da84, Hi02>

labeur [labœr] *n.f.* work, toil <***Loc:*** Da84>

labourage ♦see **rabourage**

labourer ♦see **rabourer**

laboureur ♦see **raboureur**

laboureuse [laburøz] *n.f.* **1** tractor plow **2** disk harrow <***Loc:*** Da84>

laboureux [laburø] *n.m.* laborer <***Loc:*** Re31>

lac [lak] *n.m.* lake ◊ **•Lac Charles** Lake Charles <AC, EV, Hi02> **•Lac Arthur** Lake Arthur <JD> <***Loc:*** AC, EV, JD, SL, SM, TB, An94, Da84, Fa77, Gu00, Hi02>

laçage ♦see **lassage**

lace ♦see **lasse**

lacer ♦see **lasser**

lacet [lasɛ, lase] *n.m.* shoelace, shoestring <***Loc:*** Da84, Hi02>

lâche[1] [laʃ] *adj.* loose, lax *La selle a tombé parce que la cabresse était lâche.* The saddle fell off because the horse-hair rope was loose. (VM) *Le boulonnage dessus la machine est lâche.* The bolting on the motor is loose. (VM) <***Loc:*** VM, Da84>

lâche[2] [laʃ] *adj.* cowardly *Espèce de lâche. T'as pas le courage de lui dire la vérité.* You coward. You don't have the courage to tell him the truth. (LA) <***Loc:*** LA, VM, Da84, Hi02>

lâcher [laʃe] **I** *v.tr.* **1** to loosen, slacken *Il a lâché le cable pour laisser le bœuf respirer un peu.* He loosened the rope to let the bull breathe a little. (LA) **2** to drop, let fall **Toutes les distances, il lâchait une pierre.* Every now and then, he would drop a stone. (LA, An94) **Et un jour, il y a une poule qu'a monté dans la cabane en haut. Elle a lâché un œuf par terre.* And one day, there is a hen that climbed up in the cabin. She let an egg drop on the ground. (EV, An94) **3** to let go of, turn loose, release, unleash **"Mam, si je retourne pas* BACK,*" il dit, "lâche mes chiens."* "Mom, if I don't return," he says, "unleash my dogs." (LA, An94) *Le cheval à mon grand-père était proche tout le temps lâché dans la savane.* My grandfather's horse was almost always let loose in the pasture. (VM) **4** to abandon, give up, let go of *J'ai lâché la boutique.* I let go of the store. (AL) *Oubliez pas le français, il dit. Lâchez pas le français, il dit. Continuissez à montrer à vos enfants le langage en français.* Don't forget French, he said. Don't let go of French, he said. Continue teaching French to your children. (LF) **5** to stop, cease (work, school or other activity) for the day, for the time being, etc. *Quand le soleil se couchait, on lâchait l'ouvrage.* When the sun was setting, we would stop work. (Lv88) **6** to fire, lay off, dismiss, send away *Il est lâché depuis trois mois.* He's been laid off for three months. (Lv88) *Son boss l'a lâché.* His boss fired him. (SM, VM) **7** to perform the last cultivation on (prior to harvest) **Lâcher la récolte.* To 'lay by' the crop. (Da84) **II** *v.intr.* **1** to cease, stop *Il lâche pas de parler.* He never stops talking. (VM) **2** to finish work or school, stop activity (for the day) *Quand je lâchais, je travaillais le soir dans le clos.* When I got off, I would work the field in the evening. (Lv88) *Elle lâche à quatre heures et demie.* She gets off at four thirty. (Lv88) *Ah non, elle dit, c'était trop bonne heure pour lâcher.* Oh no, she says, it was too early to stop working. (SL) ◊ **•lâcher des folies {bêtises}** to say foolish or nonsensical things, speak foolishly, utter nonsense <Da84> **•lâcher la baratte** to give up <La99> **•lâcher la patate** ***a*** to give up **Je peux pus me batt'. J'sus trop largue. Je lâche la patate.* I can't fight any longer. I'm too tired. I'm giving up. (ThCa: *Mille misères*) *Lâche pas la patate!* Don't give up! Hang in there! (La99) ***b*** to mess up <SM, Da84, La99, ThCa> ◊ **•lâcher l'eau** to let water flow (off rice fields) <VM> **•lâcher l'école** to recess school, close school <Da84> **•lâcher les bêtes** to turn the cattle loose <Da84> **•lâcher un pet** to flatulate, break wind, fart

<Da84> <***Loc:*** AL, AV, IB, LA, LF, SL, SM, VM, An94, Da84, Hi02, La99, Lv88, ThCa>

là-dedans [lad(ə)dɑ̃] *adv.* in there, inside *Il y a des caïmans là-dedans asteur là. J'ai jamais vu ça avant.* There are alligators in there now. I never saw that before. (TB) *Mame avait plein des jarres, et c'est là-dedans qu'alle sauvait son jardinage.* Mom had lots of jars, and it was in there that she conserved her vegetables. (TB) *Et il avait quitté du monde rester là-dedans parce que eux-autres avait pas de place à rester.* And he let people stay in there because they did not have any place to stay. (TB) <***Loc:*** EV, IV, TB, VM, An94, Da84, Hi02>

là-dessous [lad(ə)su] *adv.* under there, underneath *Il a été droit à la petite table et il s'a caché là-dessous.* He went straight to the little table and he hid underneath. (LA) <***Loc:*** LA, Da84, Hi02>

là-dessus [lad(ə)sy] *adv.* **1** on there *Tu ramassais des fils d'araignée et tu mettais ça là-dessus pour arrêter le sang.* You would pick up some spider webs and you would put them on there to stop the bleeding. (IV) **2** on it, on that *Il faudra que je refaçonne ce morceau pour ma charrue parce qu'il y a pus personne qui travaille là-dessus.* I'll have to remake that piece for my plow myself from scratch because nobody works on that anymore. (LA) **Se fier là-dessus.* To depend on it. (Da84) <***Loc:*** EV, IV, LA, PQ, TB, Da84, Hi02>

lafitte (**esquif lafitte**) [lafit, ɛskiflafit] *n.m.* Lafitte skiff, a type of trawler 14–50 ft. long with a canvas canopy, designed primarily for fishing inland or along the coast <***Loc:*** Lv88>

lafourchais [lafuʃɛ, lafuʃe] *adj.* of or from Lafourche Parish *Ça, c'est un politicien lafourchais.* That's a politician from Lafourche. (LF) <***Loc:*** LF>

lagniappe [laɲap, lanjap, lɑ̃njap, lɑ̃jap] *n.f.* **1** tip, bonus (money in recognition of service) *Hé toi! Tu veux me faire de la misère, hein? Je crois pas que je vas te donner lagniappe.* Hey you! You want to give me trouble? I don't think I'm going to give you a bonus. (VM) **2** a little something extra received for free (e.g. a small gift made by seller to buyer as a reward, esp. to children) *Dans le vieux temps, on avait toujours lagniappe quand on allait à la grocerie.* In the old days, we always had a little something extra when we went to the grocery store. (LA) **Ç' marchand donne des bonnes lagniappes.* That merchant always gives nice little extras. (EV, Ph36) *Va à ce magasin-là à l'encoignure. Eux-autres donne à lagniappe.* Go to that store on the corner. They give you a little something extra. (TB) **3** windfall, unexpected reward *On voulait juste acheter la terre pour la garder dans la famille, mais on a eu une lagniappe aussi, les droits d'huile.* We only wanted to buy the land to keep it in the family, but we had a windfall too, the oil rights. (LA) <***Loc:*** AV, EV, IB, LA, LF, SB, SL, SM, TB, VM, Da84, Hi02, Lv88, Ph36, Re31>

là-haut [laho, lao] *adv.* **1** up there *Hey, quoi ce que tu fais là-haut?* Hey, what are you doing up there? (LA) **2** upstairs *Il a déjà monté là-haut pour aller se coucher.* He already went upstairs to go to bed. (LA) <***Loc:*** LA, Hi02>

laid (**laide**) [lɛ, le, lɛd, led] *adj.* ugly *Il est laide.* He is ugly. (SB) ◊ **•laid comme un bouki {macaque} / laid comme un coin de banquette {les sept péchés capitaux}** very ugly <AV, VM, La99> <***Loc:*** AV, LA, SB, SM, VM, Da84, La99>

laide ♦see **laid**

laidement [lɛdmɑ̃, ledmɑ̃] *adv.* in an ugly way *Il a fait ça laidement.* He made that in an ugly way. (SM) <***Loc:*** SM, Da84>

laideur [ledœr] *n.f.* ugliness <***Loc:*** Da84>

laidir [ledir] **I** *v.tr.* to make ugly or uglier *Passer l'hiver dehors l'a laidi.* Spending the winter outside has made him uglier. (LA) **II** *v.intr.* to become ugly or uglier *Tu laidis.* You're becoming ugly. (SM) <***Loc:*** LA, SM, Lv88>

laine [lɛ̃n] *n.f.* wool <***Loc:*** Da84, Fa77>

laise [lɛz] *n.f.* width, breadth of cloth <***Loc:*** VM>

laisser [lese] **I** *v.tr.* **1** to let, allow, permit *Ma maman voulait être une* NURSE. *Mais ses parents ont jamais voulu la laisser aller.* My mom wanted to be a nurse. But her parents never wanted to let her go. (SB) *Laisse-moi t'aider avec ça.* Let me help you with that. (LF) *Il faut pas la laisser brûler.* You must not let it [the roux] burn. (SL) *T'envoyais ça dessus le radio dans différentes places pour les laisser savoir équand le navire allait laisser le port et quand il devrait arriver là-bas et qui-ce qu'il y avait dessus le navire.* You sent that out on the radio to different places to let them know when the ship was going to leave the port and when it should arrive there and what there was on the ship. (LF) **2** to leave, leave behind *Ils ont laissé la France dans les seize cents.* They left France in the 1600's. (SB) *Je peux pas laisser mon ouvrage.* I can't leave my work. (SM) *Laisse ça pour moi.* Leave it for me. (SM) **Jolie blonde, tu m'as laissé moi tout seul pour t'en aller chez ta famille.* Pretty blonde, you left me all alone to go back to your family. (ch: *Jolie blonde*) *J'ai laissé chez lui à ce matin.* I left his house this morning. (VM) **3** to leave, bequeath as an inheritance *Equand je sera mort, mon, à qui je peux laisser mes chansons?* When I'm dead, who can I leave my songs to? (ThCa: *Mille misères*) **II se laisser** *v.pron.* **1** to let o.s., allow o.s. (to) **Se laisser aller.* To let oneself go. (Da84) *Se laisser amarrer.* To be tricked. (Lv88) **Se laisser embêter.* To allow oneself to be fooled, duped, or cheated. (Da84) **2** to leave each other, take leave of one another *Les Acadiens sont pas si fous de se laisser sans boire un coup.* The Acadians are not so foolish as to leave each other without having a drink. (VM, ch: *La terre nourrit tout*) ◊ **•laisser à la traîne** to leave lying about <Da84> **•laisser aller la baratte** to give up <La99> **•laisser avoir** to lend *Laisse-moi avoir cinq piasses.* Lend me five dollars. (SM) *Tu peux me laisser avoir ton char pour dimanche?* Could you lend me your car for Sunday? (Lv88) <SM, TB, VM, Lv88> **•laisser faire** ***a*** to let be **C'est une sacrée affaire si je les laisse faire.* That's a hell of a thing, if I let them be. (SL, An94) ***b*** to let s.o. do s.t. *Laisse-le faire.* Let him do it. (IB) <IB, SL, SM, VM, An94, Da84> **•laisser (qqn) en plan** to abandon (a friend) <AV, La99> **•laisser tomber** to let go, drop <Da84> **•laisser tranquille** to let alone, leave be **Et là, cette petite lumière reste. Elle joue avec ce couteau. Là, ça te laisse tranquille.* And then, that little light remains. It plays with the knife. Then it will let you alone. (VM, An94) <VM, An94, Da84> **•laissez un bloque en bas de la maison!** calm down! quiet down! (said to unruly children) <AC, LA, SL, La99> <***Loc:*** AC, AV, IB, LA, LF, SB, SL, SM, TB, VM, An94, Da84, Hi02, La99, Lv88, Re31, ThCa>

lait [lɛ, le, let] *n.m.* milk *Donne-moi un verre de lait.* Give me a glass of milk. (SM) ◊ **•lait bleu** skim milk, low-fat milk *Cèze-là nous-autres on tirait faisait pas un tas de la crème. C'était du lait bleu.* The ones we milked did not produce much cream. It was low-fat milk. (JD) <JD> **•lait caillé** clabbered milk <AV, Da84> **•lait de beurre** buttermilk <Da84> **•lait de magnésie** milk of magnesia <Da84> **•lait égoutté** cottage cheese <TB> **•au lait** on a milk diet <Pe37> **•petit lait** ***a*** whey ***b*** thick milky sap of certain plants such as figs, milkweeds, etc. <LA, Da84> <***Loc:*** AC, AV, EV, IV, JD, LA, LF, SB, SM, TB, An94, Da84, Hi02, Pe37>

laitereau [letro] *n.m.* milkweed, sow thistle *Le laitereau c'est une herbe verte avec des feuilles longues et quand tu les casses, le lait sort dedans. Ça fait du bon* FEED *pour les cochons et les lapins blancs.* Milkweed is a green grass with long leaves and when you break them, the milk comes out. It makes good feed for pigs and rabbits. (TB) <***Loc:*** TB>

laiterie [letri] *n.f.* **1** dairy **2** dairy farm <***Loc:*** LA, Da84, Fa77>

laitier [letje] *n.m.* **1** milker, one whose job is to milk cows **2** milkman <***Loc:*** IB, Da84>

laitière [letjær] *n.f.* **1** milk cow **2** milkmaid <***Loc:*** Da84>

laitue [lety] *n.f.* **1** lettuce **2** wild lettuce (an inedible weed) <***Loc:*** Da84, Fa77, Hi02, Ho90>

laize [lez] *n.f.* **1** crease, pleat *Elle a des laizes sur sa robe.* She has pleats on her dress. (SM) **2** gore, triangular piece of cloth (e.g. in a dress) <***Loc:*** SM>

la-la [lala] *n.m.* term for Creole music *J'aime mieux la vieille musique la-la que le nouveau zydeco.* I prefer the old 'la-la' music than the new zydeco. (LA) <***Loc:*** LA, Hi02>

lambeau ♦see **lambourde**

lambèche (libandèche) [lɑ̃bɛʃ, lɑ̃beʃ, libɑ̃dɛʃ] *n.f.* strip, scrap, shred (of cloth), rag *Son linge est en lambèches.* His clothes are in shreds. (SM) <***Loc:*** SM, TB, VM, Da84, Lv88>

lambin [lɑ̃bɛ̃] *adj.* slow, dawdling <***Loc:*** SM, Da84>

lamboune ♦see **lambourde**

lambourde (lamboune, lambeau) [lɑ̃burd, lɑ̃bun, lɑ̃bo] *n.f.* **1** sill, beam, heavy timber **2** floor joist **3** floor sill, floor beam <***Loc:*** EV, SL, TB, VM, Da84, Fa77>

lame [lɑ̃m] *n.f.* **1** blade (of a knife, plow, etc.) *C'est fait pour ça force pour tiendre la lame.* It's made that way so that it is hard to hold the blade. (AC) **2** wave (on water) *C'est un grand long bateau qui peut prendre les lames.* It's a big long boat that can take waves. (SM) ◊ **•lame de charrue** plowshare, plow blade <EV, Da84> **•lame de feu** tongue of fire <Da84> **•lames d'épée** sawgrass <Ho90> <***Loc:*** AC, EV, JE, LA, SM, An94, Da84, Fa77, Gu00, Hi02, Ho90>

lamentable [lɑ̃mɑ̃tab(l)] *adj.* lamentable, pitiful *C'est lamentable, la manière il traite ses enfants.* It's pitiful the way he treats his children. (EV) <***Loc:*** EV, Da84>

lamentation [lɑ̃mɑ̃tasjɔ̃] *n.f.* lamentation, lament, complaint <***Loc:*** Da84>

lamenter (se) [lɑ̃mɑ̃te] *v.pron.* to lament, moan, gripe, complain *Je crois pas qu'il y a un récoltier qui a pas de la misère à se gagner la vie aujourd'hui. Même les faiseurs de patates se lamentent.* I don't think there is a farmer who doesn't have trouble making a living today. Even the producers of sweet potatoes are complaining. (VM) <***Loc:*** VM, Da84, Hi02>

laminer [lɑ̃mine] *v.tr.* to laminate, splice *J'ai laminé deux deux-par-quatre pour faire un sol.* I laminated two two-by-fours to make a beam. (LA) <***Loc:*** LA, Da84>

lampe [lɑ̃p] *n.f.* **1** lamp, light **2** oil lamp ◊ **•lampe à {de}** COAL OIL oil lamp *Tout le temps que mon j'ai été à l'école, j'ai fait mon* HOMEWORK *à la lumière d'une lampe à coloïe.* All the time that I was in school, I did my homework by the light of a kerosene lamp. (TB) <TB, Lv88> **•lampe à globe** hurricane lamp, kerosene lamp <TB> **•lampe électrique** electric light <Da84> <***Loc:*** EV, JE, SL, TB, Da84, Hi02>

lampogne [lɑ̃pɔ̃j] *n.m./f.* milk left in a cow's udder for the calf after milking <***Loc:*** IB, Lv88>

lancée [lɑ̃se] *n.f.* shooting pain, throbbing pain *J'ai une lancée dans ma jambe.* I have a throbbing pain in my leg. (VM) <***Loc:*** SB, VM>

lancement [lɑ̃smɑ̃] *n.m.* **1** shooting pain, throbbing pain **2** launching, throwing, hurling <***Loc:*** Da84>

lancer [lɑ̃se] **I** *v.tr.* **1** to fling, hurl, throw **Puis alors, elle a lancé un couteau après le chien, puis ça lui a coupé le nez et il a saigné quelques gouttes de sang.* So then, she threw a knife at the dog, and it cut his nose and it bled a few drops of blood. (VM, An94) **2** to drive away, chase off *Lancez les poules de la cour.* Chase the chickens from the yard. (SB) **II** *v.intr.* **1** to shoot (of a pain) *Ça lance dans mon dos depuis que j'ai travaillé dans mon jardin.* I am having shooting pains in my back since I worked in my garden. (LA) **2** to throb (of a wound, sore, etc.) *Ça lance où le docteur m'a injecté.* It's throbbing where the doctor gave me the shot. (SM) **III se lancer** *v.pron.* to leap, dart, fling o.s. *Il s'a lancé derrière la barre quand la pouille a pris.* He leapt behind the bar when the trouble started. (LA) <*Loc:* IB, LA, SB, SL, SM, TB, VM, An94, Da84>

lancette [lɑ̃sɛt, lɑ̃set] *n.f.* stinger (of a wasp, bee, etc.) *J'ai ôté la lancette dans mon doigt.* I took the stinger out of my finger. (SL) <*Loc:* IB, SB, SL, SM, Da84, Lv88>

landrie ♦see **laundry**

landrine [lɑ̃drin] *n.f.* slice of salted meat <*Loc:* Lv88>

langage [lɑ̃gaʒ] *n.m.* **1** language *Le français, c'est mon meilleur langage.* French is my strongest language. (Lv88) *Il n-a différents langages dans l'État de la Louisiane.* There are different languages in the state of Louisiana. (Lv88) *Le langage est pas un tas un tas différent qu'avec ici.* The language is not very very different from the language here. (AC) **2** call, vocalization (of an animal) *Alors l'alligateur est pareil. Il fait plus qu'un langage comme ça, mais ça c'est lui qu'on usait pour les faire ressortir pour les tuer.* And the alligator is like that too. He uses more vocalizations than just that one, but that's the one we would use to get them to come out in order to kill them. (TB) <*Loc:* AC, TB, VM, Da84, Fa77, Hi02, Lv88>

lange (**lante**) [lɑ̃ʒ, lɑ̃t] *n.f.* diaper <*Loc:* AV, EV, JD, LF, SL, VM>

langue [lɑ̃g] *n.f.* **1** tongue *Eusse a savonné sa langue! Et il a pas jamais rejuré après ça.* They soaped his tongue! And he never swore again after that. (TB) **2** language **Tu vois c'est une bonne chose que le monde d'ici peut parler les deux langues, l'anglais et le français.* You see, it's a good thing that people from here can speak the two languages, English and French. (TB) ◊ **•langue affilée** sharp tongue <Da84> **•langue de belle-mère** rattlesnake fern <VM, Lv88> **•langue de {du} bœuf** ***a*** canna lily, type of canna ***b*** arrowhead plant ***c*** pickerelweed <VM, Fa77, Ho90, Lv88> **•langue de femme** sycamore, buttonwood <Ho90> **•langue de serpent** ***a*** adder's-tongue, ribbon fern ***b*** malicious person who speaks badly of others <VM, La99, Lv88> **•langue épais** coated tongue <VM> **•avoir la langue comme une vipère** to be caustic in one's speech <EV, La99> **•avoir la langue trop longue** to talk too much <JD, La99> **•grande langue** gossiper <Da84> **•pas avoir la langue d'amarrée** to be a big talker <La99> **•pas avoir la langue dans la poche** ***a*** to talk a lot ***b*** to not be embarrassed to speak ***c*** to be outspoken <La99> <*Loc:* AL, EV, JD, LF, TB, VM, Da84, Fa77, Gr86, Hi02, Ho90, La99, Lv88, Wh83>

languette [lɑ̃gɛt] *n.f.* tongue of a tongue-and-groove coupling <*Loc:* VM>

languir [lɑ̃gir] *v.intr.* **1** to languish, pine *La belle était après languir pour son beau qui voulait p'us revenir.* The maiden was languishing for her beau who no longer wanted to return. (LA) **2** to cook too long, cook too slowly *Le pain est pas trop bon, ça a tant langui.* The bread isn't so good, it baked much too long. (VM) <*Loc:* LA, VM, Da84, Fa77>

lanière [lɑ̃jær] *n.f.* board (in a fence) <*Loc:* EV, Ph36>

lante ♦see **lange**

lanterne [lɑ̃tærn] *n.f.* lantern <*Loc:* EV, TB, Da84>

laper [lape] *v.tr.* **1** to lap, lap up **2** to eat greedily **L'homme a tout lapé ça y avait su la tabe.* The man scarfed up everything that was on the table. (EV, Ph36) <*Loc:* EV, SM, Ph36>

lapin [lapɛ̃] *n.* **1** *(m.)* rabbit **2** *(m.)* hare **3** *(f.)* female rabbit ◊ **•lapin à queue blanche** cottontail rabbit <Gu00> <*Loc:* EV, SL, SM, TB, An94, Da84, Gu00, Hi02>

Lapin [lapɛ̃] *n.prop.* 'Brer Rabbit,' character who is the counterpart of Bouki (Hyena) in creole folk tales **Là, quand ils travaillaient comme ça-là, Lapin s'avait mis comme un prêtre, tu vois? Il baptisait les enfants.* Then when they worked like that, Rabbit had declared himself a priest, you see? He would baptize children. (SM, An94) <*Loc:* LA, SM, VM, An94>

laquelle ♦see **lequel**

lard [lar] *n.m.* lard, pork fat ◊ **•lard entrelardé** bacon <SB> **•faire du lard** to get fat <SB, La99> <*Loc:* SB, Da84, La99>

largant ♦see **larguant**

large[1] [larʒ] *adj.* large, broad, wide *Des planches larges comme ça [...] à peu près six pouces de large.* Boards this wide, about six inches wide. (EV) *Mais le chemin était pas large, y avait juste pour un passage d'un char.* But the road was not wide, there was just room for the passage of one car. (TB) ◊ **•large comme deux doigts / large comme mes deux fesses** very small or narrow (usu. in reference to a plot of land) *Un morceau de terre large comme mes deux fesses.* A piece of land about as big/wide as my two buttocks. (TB) <TB, La99> <*Loc:* EV, TB, Da84, Hi02, La99>

large[2] [larʒ] *n.m.* **1** open expanse (e.g. the sea, a prairie, a pasture) **2** yard behind a house, away from the road or bayou ◊ **•aller au large** to leave, go away <Lv88> **•au large** ***a*** out to sea, on the open sea *J'étais à peu près dix milles au large dans la mer.* I was about ten miles out to sea. (TB) ***b*** offshore (esp. in the Gulf of Mexico) *Au large là-bas ils drillont dedans mille pieds.* Offshore out there they drill 1000 feet down. (LF) *C'est un bougre d'icitte, qu'est éné et élevé icitte, il pêche au large plein.* He's a guy from here, who was born and raised here, he fishes offshore a lot. (LF) ***c*** out to pasture, in the pasture, on the open prairie or plain *Les bêtes sont au large.* The cows are out to pasture. (VM) ***d*** away, far away *Il est parti au large.* He is gone far away. (EV) <EV, LF, VM, Da84, La99> <*Loc:* EV, LF, SM, TB, VM, Da84, La99, Lv88>

large[3] [larʒ] *adv.* wide, widely **J'en planterais si long et si large, pour en avoir tous mes camarades.* I would plant it [love] so long and so wide, that there would be enough for all my friends. (ThCa: *La dernière quilte*) <*Loc:* VM, ThCa>

largement [larʒmɑ̃] *adv.* largely, fully, amply **Largement logé.* Amply housed. (Da84) <*Loc:* VM, Da84>

largesse [larʒɛs] *n.f.* largess, generosity <*Loc:* Da84>

largeur [larʒœr] *n.f.* width, breadth <*Loc:* Da84>

larguant, -e (largant, -e) [largɑ̃, -ɑ̃t] *adj.* tiring, tiresome, wearisome *C'est largant travailler comme je fais.* It's tiring to work the way I do. (SM) *C'est bien largant de travailler toute la journée.* It's quite wearisome to work all day long. (VM) <*Loc:* SM, VM, Da84>

largue [larg] *adj.* tired, fatigued, weary **Ecoute, je suis largue, hein? On a trop dansé.* Look, I'm tired, okay? We danced too much. (ThCa: *La table des veuves*) **Je peux pus me batt'. J'sus trop largue.* I can't fight. I'm too worn out. (ThCa: *Mille misères*) *Je suis bien largue après tout ce travail.* I'm pretty tired after all that work. (VM) <*Loc:* IB, SM, VM, Da84, Fa77, Guoo, Lv88, ThCa>

largué, -e [large] *adj.* **1** tired, tired out, fatigued, weary *T'es larguée asteur, faut t'arrêtes.* You're tired now, you need to stop. (Lv88) *Après une demi-heure de travailler, il était largué.* After half an hour of working, he was tired out. (SL) **2** fed up **J'sus assez larguée d'a'tend parler d'not' magnière de parler à nous-aut'.* I'm pretty fed up hearing talk about the way we talk. (Gu82) <*Loc:* EV, IB, LA, LF, SL, SM, VM, Da84, Guoo, Hio2, Lv88>

larguer [large] **I** *v.tr.* **1** to tire out, fatigue *J'ai largué l'homme.* I wore out the man. (SM) **2** to let loose *Il a largué ses chiens dans le bois.* He let his dogs loose in the woods. (LA) **3** to turn out (to pasture) *Larguez les mules.* Turn the mules out to pasture. (VM) **4** to let go of, drop *Larguer ça qu'il tenait dans sa main.* To let go of what he held in his hand. (LF) **II** *v.intr.* **1** to be tiring, cause fatigue *L'ouvrage comme ça largue.* That kind of work is tiring. (SM) **2** to get tired *On larguait pas parce qu'on travaillait ensemble.* We didn't get tired because we worked together. (Lv88) **On pouvait l'écouter parler des heures de temps sans larguer.* We could listen to him talk for hours at a time without getting tired. (Gu82) **3** to end the day's work, knock off **III se larguer** *v.pron.* to tire o.s. out, get tired, grow weary *Il s'a largué à couper du bois.* He got tired out from cutting wood. (LA) ◊ •**larguer le renchaussage** to finish 'laying by' the cane crop <SJ> <*Loc:* LA, LF, SJ, SL, SM, VM, Da84, Fa77, Guoo, Gu82, Hio2, Lv88>

larigobil [larigobil] *adv.* in a carefree way *Larigobil, il est parti.* He left in a carefree way. (LF) <*Loc:* LF>

larme [larm, lɑ̃m] *n.f.* tear **Avec les larmes aux yeux.* With tears in one's eyes. (Da84) <*Loc:* Da84, Fa77, Hio2, La99>

lassage (laçage) [lasaʒ] *n.m.* lassoing, roping <*Loc:* Da84>

lassant, -e [lasɑ̃, -ɑ̃t] *adj.* tiring, tiresome *Un travail lassant.* A tiring job. (EV) <*Loc:* EV, Da84>

lasse[1] [las] *adj.* **1** tired, weary *Un jour, j'ai décidé j'aurais vendu tous les bêtes. J'étais lasse et puis c'était dur pour nous-autres.* One day, I decided I would sell all the cows. I was tired and besides it was hard for us. (SL) *Il était beaucoup lasse.* He was very weary. (Lv88) *On va se coucher de bonne heure. Je suis lasse et j'ai travaillé beaucoup aujourd'hui.* We are going to bed early. I'm tired and I worked a lot today. (LA) **2** fed up **Je suis lasse de ça.* I am fed up with that. (Da84) <*Loc:* AC, AL, AV, EV, IB, IV, JD, LA, SB, SL, SM, Da84, Hio2, Lv88>

lasse[2] **(lace, LASSO)** [las, laso, læso^{u}] *n.m.* **1** lasso, lariat *Un lace pour emmarrer les bêtes.* A lasso to tie up the cattle. (Lv88) **2** slip-knot <*Loc:* EV, LF, SB, SL, SM, VM, Da84, Lv88, Ph36>

lasser[1] **(lacer)** [lase] *v.tr.* to lasso, rope *Ils lassont la tête. Et là ils viront le bœuf et là l'autre vient par en-arrière, il lasse les deux pattes d'en arrière.* They lasso the head. And then they spin the ox around and then the other guy comes up from behind, he lassoes the two hind feet. (LF) <*Loc:* EV, LF, SB, SL, SM, VM, Da84, Lv88, Ph36>

lasser[2] **(se)** [lase] *v.pron.* to get tired, grow weary *Je m'ai lassé quand j'ai eu assez d'âge. J'ai pris à me lasser.* I got tired when I got older. I started getting tired. (EV) <*Loc:* EV, Da84>

LASSO[1] [laso, læso^{u}] *v.tr.invar.* to lasso, rope <*Loc:* EV, LF, SB>

LASSO[2] ♦see **lasse**

lastique ♦see **élastique**

latanier (ratanier) [latɑ̃je, ratɑ̃je] *n.m.* palmetto, swamp palm <*Loc:* JE, LF, SL, TB, Da84, Fa77, Guoo, Hio2, Ho90, Lv88, Re31>

latin[1] [latɛ̃] *adj.* Latin *C'était un prêtre qui faisait les messes, enfin la messe était latin, tu connais le* READING *dans la messe?* It was a priest who celebrated the Masses, well the Mass was Latin, you know, the reading in the Mass? (TB) <*Loc:* TB, Da84>

latin[2] [latɛ̃] *n.m.* Latin *Je me rappelle quand la messe était en latin et le prône était en français.* I remember when Mass was in Latin and the sermon was in French. (ThCa: *La douce reunion*) <*Loc:* Da84, ThCa>

lattage [lataʒ] *n.m.* wall <*Loc:* Guoo>

latte [lat] *n.f.* **1** lath, batten (any board or strip of wood 1x4 or less) **2** slat **3** splint for setting a broken arm <*Loc:* EV, SL, TB, Da84>

latter [late] *v.tr.* to splint, put in a splint *Le docteur a latté son bras.* The doctor put his arm in a splint. (TB) <*Loc:* TB>

LAUD ♦see **LORD**

laudanum [lodɑ̃nɔ̃m, lodadɔ̃m, odɑ̃nɔ̃] *n.m.* laudanum <*Loc:* LF, Da84>

laundry (landrie) [lɑ̃dri] *n.m./f.* **1** laundromat *Alle travaille à la laundry.* She works at the laundromat. (VM) **2** laundry, wash *Elle a donné son laundry à un homme de la ville.* She gave her laundry to a man in town. (SB) <*Loc:* LF, SB, SC, VM, Da84, Fa77, Lv88>

laurana [lorɑ̃na] *n.m.* oleander <*Loc:* VM>

laurier [lorje] *n.m.* **1** laurel tree, bay tree **2** bay leaf ◊ •**laurier amande {mande}** cherry laurel tree <Ho90, Re31> •**laurier amandé** wild peach tree <VM> •**laurier blanc**

white oleander <TB> **•laurier doux** sweet bay tree <Ho90, Re31> **•laurier rose** crape myrtle <Ho90, Re31> **•grand laurier** magnolia <VM, Da84> **•petit laurier** ***a*** sweet bay magnolia ***b*** red bay tree <SM, VM, Ho90> <***Loc:*** SB, SL, SM, TB, VM, Da84, Guoo, Ho90, Re31>

lavabo [lavabo] *n.m.* **1** washbasin **2** washstand **3** washing of the priest's hands at mass <***Loc:*** EV, Da84>

lavage [lavaʒ] *n.m.* **1** washing **2** laundry, wash ◊ **•faire le {un / son} lavage** to do laundry *On faisait notre lavage une fois par semaine.* We used to do our laundry once a week. (EV) *Moi j'avais neuf ans là je faisais des lavages pour Mom parce qu'elle pouvait pas.* I was nine years old and I did the laundry for Mom because she couldn't. (EV) <EV, IV, LA> <***Loc:*** AV, EV, IV, LA, SM, Da84, Ph36>

lavailler (se) [lavaje] *v.pron.* to wash o.s. partially, freshen up *Je vais pas prendre un bain. Je vais me lavailler un peu.* I'm not going to take a bath. I'm just going to wash up a bit. (SM) <***Loc:*** SM>

lavane ♦see **lavanée**

lavanée (lavane) [lavɑ̃ne, lavɑ̃n] *adj.* ◊ **•poule lavanée {lavane}** type of dwarf chicken <Lv88> <***Loc:*** Lv88>

lavasse [lavas] *n.f.* unappetizing food *Ça c'était de la belle lavasse cette soupe.* That soup sure was unappetizing. (TB) <***Loc:*** TB>

lavement [lavmɑ̃] *n.m.* **1** washing **2** enema <***Loc:*** Da84>

laver [lave] **I** *v.tr.* **1** to wash, clean **Je vas aller me baigner. Tu vas venir me laver le dos?* I'm going to take a bath. Will you come wash my back? (ThCa: *Le charivari*) **Ein chaoui, c'est cette 'tite bête qui lave ses écrevisses avant de les manger.* A raccoon is that little animal that washes its crawfish before eating them. (ThCa: *Mille misères*) **2** to wash out, wash away, rinse out *Ça lave le* CHEMICAL *qui est dans le papier.* That washes the chemicals out of the paper. (VM) **3** to wash over *Ça lavait les levées.* It washed over the levees. (EV) **II** *v.intr.* to do laundry, do the wash *Il travaillait la journée et moi je lavais et je repassais et je faisais l'ouvrage dans la maison.* He worked during the day and I would wash and iron and do the work in the house. (EV) **III se laver** *v.pron.* **1** to wash o.s. *Quand ça arrivait chez eux-autres, il fallait que ça se lave avec l'*ALCOHOL *pour pas amener la maladie.* When they arrived at the house, they had to wash themselves with alcohol to not bring the sickness. (TB) **2** to erode, be eroded, get washed away *Asteur l'eau rentre et alle sort et il y a assez de courant, ça se lave, ç'après s'en aller.* Now the water comes in and it goes out and there is so much current, it [the land] gets eroded, it's disappearing. (TB) ◊ **•laver la vaisselle** to wash the dishes **Je vas venir quand j'auras fini de laver la vaisselle.* I'll come when I finish washing the dishes. (ThCa: *Le charivari*) <TB, ThCa> **•laver le linge (sale)** to do laundry *J'ai une laveuse qui lave le linge.* I have a washing machine that washes clothes. (TB) <AV, EV, IV, JE, LF, SM, TB, VM> **•se laver la figure** to wash one's face <Da84> **•se laver les mains** to wash one's hands **Je suis après chercher le savon. Je m'en avais servi pour me laver les mains tout à l'heure.* I'm looking for the soap. I used it to wash my hands a little while ago. (ThCa: *Le charivari*) <Da84, ThCa> <***Loc:*** AC, AV, EV, IV, JE, LF, SL, SM, TB, VM, Da84, Hi02, ThCa>

laverie [lavri] *n.f.* **1** act of washing **2** wash house **3** place for washing clothes or dishes (e.g. a laundromat, a laundry room) <***Loc:*** SM, VM, Da84, Gr86>

lavette [lavɛt] *n.f.* **1** dishrag, dishtowel, dishcloth **2** washrag, facecloth **3** wishy-washy person who lets others take advantage of him or her **Il a fait une lavette avec lui.* He made a dishrag out of him. (Da84) <***Loc:*** AC, EV, SL, Da84, Fa77>

laveuse [lavøz] *n.f.* **1** washerwoman *Sa maman est une laveuse.* Her mom is a washerwoman. (SM) **2** washing machine, washer *J'ai une laveuse qui lave le linge.* I have a washing machine that washes clothes. (TB) **3** any washing device *Ça lave le* CHEMICAL *qui est dans le papier. Comme ça il va jamais changer. Il va garder son couleur pour toute votre vie. Il faut je te mette ça dans la laveuse.* That washes out the chemicals that are in the paper. That way it [the photograph] will never change. It will keep its color for life. I have to put it in the washer for you. (VM) ◊ **•laveuse de plats {vaisselle}** dishwasher <TB, Hi02, Lv88> <***Loc:*** AV, LA, LF, SM, TB, VM, Da84, Fa77, Hi02, Lv88>

lavier [lavje] *n.m.* sink, kitchen sink <***Loc:*** Lv88>

lavure [lavyr] *n.f.* **1** dishwater **2** slop (for hogs) *Défunt Monsieur J. L. venait chercher la lavure chez nous-autres pour donner à ses cochons.* The late Mr. J. L. used to come to get the slop from us to give to his hogs. (Guoo) **3** bad coffee **4** bad soup <***Loc:*** EV, LA, SM, TB, VM, Da84, Guoo, La99, Lv88, Ph36>

LAWN [lɔn] *n.m.* lawn, voile (thin or sheer linen or cotton fabric) *L'été je porte que des robes faites du* LAWN. In summer I only wear dresses made of lawn. (VM) <***Loc:*** VM>

LAWN-MOWER [lɔnmo^{u}ɔɹ] *n.m.* lawnmower <***Loc:*** Da84>

LAY-OFF [leˈɔf] **I** *v.tr.invar.* to lay off *Ils m'ont* LAY-OFF *juste avant les fêtes.* They laid me off just before the holidays. (LA) **II** *v.intr.invar.* to take a vacation, stop working temporarily *Il faut je* LAY-OFF *quand le petit est malade.* I have to miss work when the little one is sick. (Lv88) *Il va* LAY-OFF *la semaine qui vient.* He's going to take next week off. (VM) <***Loc:*** LA, VM, Lv88>

le[1] **(l', la, les)** (*m.sing.* **le** [l(ə)], *f.sing.* **la** [la], *m./f.sing. before a vowel* **l'** [l], *m./f.pl.* **les** [le], *m./f.pl. before a vowel* **les** [lez]) *art.def.* **1** the *Le poulain ginguait dans le parc.* The colt was gambolling in the corral. (VM) *La grosse femme est en ceinture.* The big woman is pregnant. (SM) *La maison à Nénaine.* Nénaine's house. (VM) *Dans les vieilles maisons, les vieux dormaient en bas et les jeunes dormaient en haut.*

In the old houses, the older folks slept downstairs and the younger ones slept upstairs. (LA) **2** *(poss.)* his, her, its, my, etc. *Aussi loin de ma maison, ça me casse le cœur.* So far from my house, it breaks my heart. (Lv88) *Alle se sent pas bien? Alle s'avait cassé le cou déjà, hein?* She doesn't feel well? She had broken her neck before, hadn't she? (TB) *Il a jumpé quand elle lui a mis du vinaigre dans la coupure.* He jumped when she put vinegar in his wound. (LF) **3** per, a *Et t'achetais le coloïe à cinq sous le gallon dans ce temps-là.* And you bought kerosene for five cents a gallon in those days. (TB) *Ça se vendait à la livre dans ce temps-là.* That was sold by the pound in the those days. (EV) <*Loc:* EV, LA, LF, SM, TB, VM, Lv88>

le[2] (**la, l', lé, les**) (*m.sing.* **le** [l(ə)], *f.sing.* **la** [la], *m./f.sing. before a vowel* **l'** [l], *m./f.sing. following a verb in the imperative* **lé** [le], *m./f.pl.* **les** [le], *m./f.pl. before a vowel* **les** [lez]) *pron.* **1** *(dir.obj.)* him, her, it, them **Je le vois.* I see him/it. (Da84) **Tu l'aimes, chère?* Do you love him, [my] dear? (ThCa: *La dernière quilte*) *Appelle-lé.* Call her. (IB) *Surfais-lé, tu l'as pas bien fait.* Do it again, you didn't do it right. (TB) **Aye toi du* NUTRIA *et lave-toi-lé propte-toi-lé [...] je va te le cuire.* Get yourself some nutria and wash it for yourself, clean it for yourself, [and] I'll cook it for you. (St95) **Je les vois.* I see them. (Da84) **2** *(ind.obj.) (rare in sing.)* to him, to her, to it, to them *Le Bon Dieu l'a donné un* GIFT. The Good Lord gave him a gift. (TB) *Si tu le donnes du* SLOP, *ta viande va pas être si bonne.* If you give him [the pig] slop, your meat won't be as good. (TB) *Maman les donnait à manger, aux hommes.* Mama would feed the men. (AC) **Tu les offrais ça.* You used to offer them that. (Co63) **On les a donné des exemples.* We gave them some examples. (Co63) *Il va les donner du pain.* He's going to give them some bread. (SL) *Donne-les cinq sous.* Give them a nickel. (IB) *Elle les a taillés dans le dos. Elle les a coupé la peau.* She whipped them on their backs. She broke the skin. (EV) <*Loc:* AC, EV, IB, TB, Co63, Da84, St95, ThCa>

LEADER [li'dəɹ] *n.m.* leader <*Loc:* EV, Da84>

lèche [lɛʃ] *n.f.* earthworm *Si tu pêchais comme la barbue, il y en a plein qui se servaient des lèches, des* WORMS. If you were fishing for catfish, there are plenty of people who used earthworms. (IV) <*Loc:* EV, IB, IV, SM, TB, VM, Da84, Fa77, Gr82, Guoo, Lv88, Ph36>

leçon [ləsɔ̃, lesɔ̃] *n.f.* lesson <*Loc:* LA, LF, VM, Da84, Fa77>

lecture [lɛktyr] *n.f.* **1** reading **2** lecture <*Loc:* Da84>

légal, -e [legal] *adj.* legal, lawful *C'est pas légal, ça ils sont après faire.* It's not legal, what they're doing. (EV) <*Loc:* EV, Da84>

légaliser [legalize] *v.tr.* to legalize *Ils ont légalisé le whisky après quelques années.* They legalized whiskey after a few years. (LA) <*Loc:* LA, Da84>

légalité [legalite] *n.f.* legality <*Loc:* Da84>

lège ♦see **allège**

léger ♦see **légère**[1], **légère**[2]

légère[1] [leʒær] (*occ. m.sing.* **léger** [leʒe], *f.sing.* **légèrte** [leʒært, leʒærd]) *adj.* light *Elle est légère comme une plume.* She is as light as a feather. (LA) *On a mis un drap léger dessus le lit parce qu'il faisait pas trop froid.* We put a light blanket on the bed because it wasn't too cold. (EV) <*Loc:* AC, EV, LA, LF, VM, An77, Da84, La99, Lv88>

légère[2] [leʒær] (*occ.* **léger** [leʒe]) *adv.* lightly *Aussi gros qu'il est, il danse léger, léger, léger.* As big as he is, he dances very lightly. (LA) *Et sa grosse femme danse légère aussi.* And his big wife dances lightly as well. (LA) <*Loc:* LA>

légèreté [leʒærte] *n.f.* lightness <*Loc:* Da84>

légerte ♦see **légère**[1]

légion [leʒjɔ̃] *n.f.* legion <*Loc:* Da84>

législateur [leʒislatœr] *n.m.* legislator <*Loc:* Da84>

législation [leʒislasjɔ̃] *n.f.* law, legislation <*Loc:* Da84>

législature [leʒislatyr, leʒizlatyr] *n.f.* legislature, congress *C'est ça ils faisont dedans la législature.* That's what they do in the legislature. (VM) <*Loc:* AV, VM, Da84, Lv88, Fa77>

légitime[1] [leʒitim] *adj.* legitimate, lawful *Tu vois, c'est pas son garçon légitime.* You see, that's not his legitimate son. (LA) <*Loc:* LA, Da84>

légitime[2] [leʒitim] *n.* **1** *(m.)* legal husband, spouse **2** *(f.)* legal wife, spouse *Prendre quelqu'un pour son légitime / sa légitime.* To take someone as one's lawfully wedded husband / wife. (SJ) <*Loc:* IB, SJ>

légitime[3] [leʒitim] *adv.* legitimately, legally **Et ça trouvait qu'ils étiont pas mariés, c'était pas marié légitime.* And they found that they weren't married, they weren't legally married. (St95) <*Loc:* St95>

léguine[1] [legin] *n.f.* leghorn chicken <*Loc:* VM>

léguine[2] [legin] *n.m.* legging *Je porte tout le temps des léguines l'hiver.* I always wear leggings in the winter. (TB) <*Loc:* TB>

légume [legym] *n.f.* vegetable <*Loc:* JE, Da84, Hi02>

lendemain [lɑ̃dəmɛ̃, lɑ̃nmɛ̃] *n.m.* next day, day after, morrow **Le lendemain.* The next day. (Da84) *Le gouverneur Edwards a proclamé une fête pour le lendemain de Thanksgiving.* Governor Edwards declared a holiday for the day after Thanksgiving. (VM) *Et le lendemain des noces, on a dîné chez ses parents.* And the day after our wedding, we ate lunch at her parents' house. (EV) <*Loc:* AC, EV, IV, LA, LF, TB, VM, An94, Da84>

lendroit ♦see **endroit**

lente [lɑ̃t] *adj.* ◊ •**fièvre lente** slight fever **Ça ça donne la fièvre moi je crois, une 'tite fièvre lente, jusque tu peux t'apercevoir assez que t'as froid.* That gives you a fever I think, just a slight fever, just enough so you can realize that you're cold. (St95) <*Loc:* St95>

lentement [lɑ̃tmɑ̃] *adv.* slowly, sluggishly **Les vols des oiseaux sont comme eine main qui coud lentement mais sans jamais lâcher pour rejoindre les deux parties du peup' cadien que* *le sort a déchiré et séparé par deux mille milles.* The flights of birds are like a hand that sews slowly but without ever stopping to put back together the two parts of the Acadian people that fate has torn apart and separated by 2,000 miles. (ThCa: *Mille misères*) <***Loc:*** TB, Da84, ThCa>

lèpre [lɛp(r)] *n.f.* leprosy <***Loc:*** Da84>

lépreux, -euse [leprø, -øz] *n.* leper <***Loc:*** Da84>

lequel ♦see **quel**

les ♦see **le**

lessi ♦see **lessive**

lessive (**lessi**) [lesiv, lesi] *n.f.* **1** laundry *Je fais toujours ma grosse lessive le lundi matin de bonne heure.* I always do my big load of laundry early on Monday morning. (TB) **2** dirty water (from the washing of clothes or dishes) *Jeter la lessive.* Throw out the washing-water. (VM) ◊ **•faire la lessive** to do the laundry *On a fait la lessive aujourd'hui.* We did the washing today. (LF) <LF> **•faire une lessive** to do a load of laundry <LF> <***Loc:*** LF, TB, VM, Lv88>

leste [lɛs(t)] *adj.* lively, spry, lithe, light, supple in movement *Alle est venue aussi leste qu'un papillon dans une bol de beurre.* She became as lively as a butterfly in a bowl of butter. (AV) <***Loc:*** AV, Hi02>

léthargie [letarʒi, letærʒi] *n.* coma ◊ **•en léthargie** in an unconscious or comatose state *Mon père a resté trois mois en léthargie avant de mourir.* My father was in a coma for three months before he died. (VM) <VM> <***Loc:*** VM>

lettre [lɛt(r)] *n.f.* **1** letter, missive, written message **2** letter (of the alphabet) ◊ **•lettre de passe** pass, permit <JE> <***Loc:*** AC, AV, IV, JE, SL, Da84, Fa77, Hi02>

leur[1] [lœr] (*m./f.pl.* **leurs** [lœr], *before a vowel* **leurs** [lœrz]) *adj.poss.* their **Leur maison.* Their house. (Da84) *Et tout chacun élevait leur viande et leur volaille et tout ça.* And everyone raised their meat and their poultry and all that. (AC) **Quand ils ont arrivé où ce qu'était leur GANG, ils se sont tous rassemblés et ils ont parti, mais la brebis les suivait.* When they arrived where their group was located, they all assembled and they left, but the ewe was following them. (IV, An94) **Ça fait, il l'a soignée pareil comme si elle aurait été une de leurs enfants.* Thus, he took care of her as if she had been one of their children. (IV, An94) <***Loc:*** AC, AV, CL, EV, IV, LA, SL, SM, TB, An94, Da84>

leur[2] [lœr] *pron. (ind.obj.)* to them, for them **Ça fait, ça leur faisait leur vie beaucoup plus facile.* So, that made life much easier for them. (LA, An94) *Moi je leur donnais des petits ROSE BUSH, des petits rosiers là.* I gave them little rose bushes. (EV) <***Loc:*** EV, LA, An94>

levain [ləvɛ̃] *n.m.* **1** leaven, yeast **2** starter **3** sourdough <***Loc:*** SL, Da84>

lève-cul ♦see **lève-queue**

levée (**alvée**) [l(ə)ve, alve] *n.f.* **1** raising, rising, lifting **2** embankment, levee, bank, dike **La levée du fossé.* The bank of the ditch. (Da84) *Quand eux-autres a bâti les levées sur la rivière, tout ce sable qui venait tous les années a arrêté de venir.* When they built levees on the river, all that sand that used to come every year stopped coming. (TB) *Là où il y avait pas assez de terre pour faire une alvée eux-autres faisait des fossés et eusse prendait la terre.* Where there wasn't enough dirt to make a levee they would dig pits and they would take the dirt. (LF) **3** levee in a rice field *Quand t'es récoltier, il faut que tu marches tes levées tous les jours.* If you're a [rice] farmer, you have to walk [along and check] your levees every day. (VM) ◊ **•levée du soleil** sunrise <Da84> <***Loc:*** LF, SL, TB, VM, Da84, Gu00, Hi02>

lève-queue (**lève-cul**) [lɛvkø, lɛvky] *n.m.* mosquito larva, wiggle-tail <***Loc:*** Lv88, Re31>

lever [l(ə)ve, leve] **I** *v.tr.* **1** to raise, lift *À mesure qu'eusse les attrape, eusse lève un DRAG, eusse met sur le DECK, eusse passe en travers, eusse casse les têtes des chevrettes et la balance eusse pousse BACK à l'eau.* As they catch them, they raise a dragline, they put it on the deck, they go through it, they break the heads off the shrimp and the rest they push back into the water. (LF) *Ce piquant-là est aussi poison que le jour que tu le lèves dedans l'eau.* That spine (on the catfish) is as poisonous as the day you lift him from the water. (TB) **2** to flush, force out (a game animal) *Quand il le levait, il fallait il va.* When he flushed it [the bird] out, it [the dog] had to follow. (SL) **II** *v.intr.* **1** to come up (of plants) *Les grenades levaient farouches.* Pomegranates grew wild. (Lv88) **2** to rise *Le YEASTCAKE, c'est trop doucement, c'est pourquoi qu'on faisait ça le soir pour ça lève tout la nuit, et là le matin quand on se levait quelquefois elle aurait fait des beignets.* The yeast is too slow-acting; that's why we made it [the batter] in the evening so that it would rise all night, and then in the morning, when we got up sometimes, she would have [already] made fritters. (SL) **III se lever** *v.pron.* **1** to raise or lift o.s. up, get up *Je me lève.* I get up. (LF, TB) **2** to get up out of bed *Pauvre bête, alle se lève tous les matins à cinq heures.* Poor thing, she gets up every morning at five o'clock. (LF) *Le matin, je me levais à quatre heures, je faisais mon pain de maïs ou mes biscuits ou du MASH, de la bouillie ou du couche-couche [...]. Mais il fallait je me lève tous les matins à quatre heures.* In the morning, I would get up at four o'clock, I'd make my cornbread or my biscuits or mash, custard or cornmeal mush. But I had to get up every morning at four. (EV) **3** to clear up (of the weather) *Le temps va se lever.* The weather is going to clear up. (VM) ◊ **•lever la queue** to make a getaway <SB, La99> **•lever le pied** to leave <AV, La99> **•se lever sur le mauvais pied** ***a*** to get up on the wrong side of the bed ***b*** to start things off badly <AV, EV, La99> <***Loc:*** AV, EV, JE, LF, SB, SL, TB, VM, Da84, Hi02, La99, Lv88>

leveur [l(ə)vœr] *n.m.* ◊ **•leveur de (la) luette** (in folk medicine) healer who lifts the uvula when it has 'fallen' <IB, TB> <***Loc:*** IB, TB>

levier[1] [levje] *n.m.* lever, jack, bar or beam used for leverage <Da84>

levier[2] [levje] ◊ **•père levier** stepfather <Da84> <***Loc:*** Da84>

lèvre [lɛv(r)] *n.f.* lip <***Loc:*** AL, IB, Da84, Fa77>

lézard (**rézard**) [lezar, rezar] *n.m.* lizard <***Loc:*** SB, Da84, Gu00, Fa77>

l-hibou ♦see **hibou**

l-hoquet ♦see **hoquet**

li[1] ♦see **lui**

li[2] [li] *pron.pers. (dir.obj.)* (probably due to influence from Louisiana Creole) him, it *On a venu soigner li et on a jamais quitté.* We came to take care of him and never left. (SM) *Tu vends li toi-même, c'est beaucoup d'ouvrage.* You sell it yourself, it's a lot of work. (SM) <***Loc:*** SM>

liane [lijɑ̃n, ljɑ̃n] *n.f.* vine, creeper, runner *Les patates, ça fait un tas des lianes.* Potatoes make a lot of vines. (Lv88) ◊ **•liane à marteau** morning glory <SB> **•liane à vipère** yellow passionflower <Ho90> **•liane à voico** creeping cucumber <SB> **•liane blanche** wisteria <VM> **•liane de grenade** passionflower, maypop <Ho90> **•liane de mirliton** vegetable pear vine <Ho90, Re31> **•liane de patate** potato vine <TB> **•liane de soco** muscadine <SM, Ho90> **•liane de skine** saw briar <SB> **•liane noire** ***a*** supplejack ***b*** rattan vine, blackjack vine, trelease <TB, Ho90, Re31> **•liane rose** rosa montana <VM> <***Loc:*** EV, SB, SM, TB, VM, An94, Da84, Ho90, Hi02, Lv88, Ph36, Re31>

liard [lijar] *n.m.* **1** southern cottonwood **2** sycamore <***Loc:*** AV, IB, TB, Ho90, Re31>

libandèche ♦see **lambèche**

libération [liberasjɔ̃] *n.f.* liberation, rescue, deliverance <***Loc:*** Da84>

libérer [libere] *v.tr.* to free, liberate *Équand les Américains ont libéré Paris, il y avait une grande fête qu'a duré des jours.* When the Americans liberated Paris, there was a big party that lasted for days. (LA) <***Loc:*** LA, Da84>

liberté [libærte] *n.f.* freedom, liberty <***Loc:*** Da84, Hi02>

librairie [libreri] *n.f.* library <***Loc:*** SB, Da84>

LIBRARY [laɪbɹɛɹi] *n.f.* library <***Loc:*** Lv88>

libre [lib(r)] *adj.* free **Il dit, "Allez voir, allez l'arrêter," il dit. "Il est libre asteur."* He says, "Go see, go arrest him," he says. "He's free now." (LA, An84) *De l'esclavage, lui et son père, quand il est né, son père l'a mis libre.* From slavery, he and his father, when he was born his father set him free. (EV) <***Loc:*** EV, LA, An84, Da84, Fa77, Hi02>

licence [lisɑ̃s] *n.f.* **1** license, permit *Licence de char, licence de chasse, licence de mariage.* Driver's license, hunting license, marriage license. (SM) *Je crois que ça te coûte mille piasses pour une licence.* I think it costs you a thousand dollars for a [hunting] license. (TB) **2** license plate *Il a oublié de changer la licence dessus son vieux char.* He forgot to change the license plate on his old car. (LA) <***Loc:*** AC, EV, LA, LF, SM, TB, VM, Da84, Hi02, Lv88>

lichefrippe [liʃfrip] *n.f.* thin slice, strip, band <***Loc:*** Da84>

licher [liʃe] **I** *v.tr.* **1** to lick *Liche mon doigt.* Lick my finger. (SM) *Caillette a liché son veau.* Caillette licked her calf (teasing reference to slicked-down hair). (VM) **2** to butter up, flatter for one's own gain *Il liche son boss.* He's buttering up his boss. (SM) *Il faut le licher pour avoir un job.* You have to butter him up to get a job. (SL) **II se licher** *v.pron.* to lick o.s. *Le chat était après se licher sur la galerie.* The cat was licking itself on the porch. (LA) ◊ **•se licher les babines** to lick one's lips *Il a commencé à se licher les babines quand il a senti le barbecue.* He started licking his lips when he smelled the barbecue. (LA) <LA, Da84> <***Loc:*** AV, IB, LA, LF, SB, SJ, SL, SM, TB, VM, Da84, Fa77, Hi02, La99, Lv88, Re31>

licherie [liʃri] *n.f.* **1** physical affection **2** gluttony, greediness <***Loc:*** VM, Di32, Lv88>

licheur, -euse [liʃœr, -øz] *n.* flatterer, bootlicker *Ils l'ont pris lui pour le job juste parce qu'il est tellement licheur.* They took him for the job just because he is such a bootlicker. (VM) <***Loc:*** IB, LF, SL, SM, VM, Lv88>

liège [ljɛʒ] *n.m.* **1** cork (tree bark suitable for cork stopper fabrication) *Bouchon de liège.* Cork (bottle stopper). (EV, LA, VM) **2** balsam, light wood *Jambe de liège.* Wooden leg. (EV, LA, VM) <***Loc:*** EV, LA, LF, VM, Da84, Fa77, Hi02>

lier [lje] *v.tr.* to tie, fasten, bind <***Loc:*** Da84>

lieu [ljø] *n.m.* **1** place *Ces affiches donnaient le nom, l'âge et la résidence du mort et le lieu et l'heure du service, d'habitude vingt-quatre heures après la mort.* Those posters gave the name, age and residence of the deceased and the place and time of the service, usually twenty-four hours after the time of death. (VM) **2** outhouse, toilet ◊ **•au lieu (de)** instead of, in place of **Au lieu de descendre, il a pris à monter.* Instead of going down [the trail], he started going up. (AC, An94) *Au lieu nager, essayer nager, je pense il pouvait pas, mais il marchait le... le* BOTTOM. Instead of swimming, trying to swim, I think he couldn't, but he was walking [on] the . . . the bottom. (SL) <AC, SL, An94, Da84> **•avoir lieu** to happen, take place *C'est là ayoù l'accident a eu lieu.* That's where the accident happened. (LA) <LA, Da84> <***Loc:*** AC, EV, LA, SL, VM, An94, Da84, Hi02, Lv88>

lieutenant [ljøtnɑ̃, lutənɑ̃] *n.m.* lieutenant <***Loc:*** Da84>

lièvre [ljɛv(r)] *n.m.* **1** hare **2** rabbit ◊ **•lièvre du Texas** jackrabbit <Gu00> <***Loc:*** Da84, Gu00>

ligne [liŋ, lin, liɲ] *n.f.* **1** line **Ceux-là qui jete la pacane plus proche de la ligne commencent le jeu.* Those who throw the pecan closest to the line begin the game. (Wh83) **2** finish line **En même temps, le Grand Coureur à Jean l'Ours a cassé la ligne, ils estiont moins qu'un demi-pouce de différence, mais il avait gagné.* At the same time, Jean l'Ours' Grand Coureur broke the finish line, they were less than half an inch apart but he had won. (EV, An94) **3** clothesline *Accrocher le linge dessus la ligne.* Hang the laundry on the clothesline. (Lv88) **4** fishing line **Elle a attrapé un* BITE*; c'était une baleine. Elle a commencé à caler, mais elle a jamais voulu lâcher la ligne.* She got a bite; it was a whale. She started to go under, but she would never let go of the line. (EV, An94) **5** trotline *Y en a qui appelle ça une palangue. Y a une ligne sous le côté.* Some people call it a trotline. There's a line on the side. (PQ) **6** pipeline *On changeait des lignes, on faisait des lignes que l'huile flotte dedans.* We used to change pipelines, we laid pipeline that oil floats in. (LF) **7** property line *Tu vois, sa ligne à lui biaisait à travers le bois, entre mon coin et le pont.* You see, his property line went diagonally across the woods, between my corner and the bridge. (LA) *Là ils ont changé la ligne deux ou trois fois depuis ça. Moi j'ai mes piquets chaque boutte.* Then they've changed the property line two or three times since then. But I have my stakes at each end. (TB) **8** electrical line *On a eu pour courir une ligne de la maison jusqu'au poulailler pour mettre une lumière pour les petits poulets.* We had to run an electrical line from the house to the chicken coop to put a light for the chicks. (VM) **9** telephone line *J'ai essayé de t'appeler avant de venir, mais ta ligne était occupée.* I tried to call you before coming, but your line was busy. (EV) *Quand ils ont passé la ligne pour le téléphone, je m'ai fait mettre un* PHONE*.* When they put in the line for the telephone, I got a phone installed. (AC) **10** line, row (of people or objects) *Il n-a une ligne de montres, de cadeaux.* There is a row of watches, of gifts. (EV) **11** line of work or activity *Dans quelle ligne il est? Il travaille pour SLEMCO.* In what line of work is he? He works for SLEMCO [power company]. (LA) ◊ **•ligne à linge** clothesline *Des vieilles maisons avec des lignes à linge en dessous des bois.* Old houses with clotheslines underneath the trees. (JE) <JE> **•ligne à lumière** electric line, power line *Ça fait ç'a commencé à changer les affaires et là les lignes à lumière a venu. L'électricité a venu.* So that started to change things and then the power lines came in. Electricity came in. (TB) <TB> **•ligne à pêche** fishing line <LF> **•ligne de tuyau** pipeline *J'ai été travailler pour produire l'huile, travailler sur des* TANK *berges, et courir des lignes de tuyaux, et toute espèce d'affaires comme ça.* I went to work producing oil, working on tank barges, and running pipelines, and all kinds of things like that. (TB) <TB> **•ligne droite** straight line <Da84> **•c'est pas ma ligne** that's not in my line of work <Lv88> **•en ligne** in line, lined up *Peigner le coton, c'est ôter les grémilles et les saletés, mais carder c'est mettre tous les fils en ligne.* To comb cotton is to take out the impurities, but carding is putting all the fibers in line. (LA) *Le monde a été communier, s'a mis en ligne, tu connais, pour aller communier.* People went up to take communion, [they] got in line, you know, to go celebrate communion. (TB) <LF, TB, Lv88> <***Loc:*** EV, JE, LA, LF, PQ, SL, TB, VM, An94, Da84, Hi02, Lv88, Wh83>

ligneguette (linette) [liŋget, linɛt] *n.f.* set line (small fishing line set on a trotline). *C'est ça les linettes, les cordes amarrées à l'hameçon, des fois on met un petit* SWIVEL *après, pour le poisson quand il se fait prendre, il va tourner.* That's what set lines are, lines tied to a hook, sometimes we put a small swivel on [them] so when the fish bites, it will turn. (SM) <***Loc:*** EV, SM>

lilas [lila] *n.m.* **1** chinaberry tree, chinaball tree **2** lilac *Ça prenait des lilas, des feuilles de lilas, et ça bouillait ça pour faire un thé. Je crois que c'était pour ton* BLADDER*, ta blague.* They would take lilacs, lilac flowers, and they would boil them to make a tea. I think it was for your bladder. (SB) ◊ **•lilas de Perse** chinaball tree <Gu00> **•lilas des Indes** chinaberry tree, chinaball tree <Lv88> **•lilas parasol** chinaberry, chinaball tree with an umbrella-shaped crown *J'aimerais avoir un lilas parasol dans ma cour. Ça donne de la bonne alombre.* I'd like to have a "parasol" chinaberry tree in my yard. It gives really good shade. (Gu00) <VM, Da84, Gu00, Ho90, Lv88> <***Loc:*** AC, EV, IB, LF, SB, SL, SM, VM, Da84, Gu00, Ho90, La99, Lv88, Ph36, Re31>

lilé [lile] *n.f.* water hyacinth <***Loc:*** LF, VM, Lv88>

limage [limaʒ] *n.m.* filing <***Loc:*** Da84>

lime [lim] *n.f.* **1** file **2** knife sharpener, leather sharpening strop ◊ **•lime à trois quarts** three-sided file <EV> **•lime plate** flat file <EV> **•lime-rapé {-râpe}** bastard file (for metal) <EV, Da84> <***Loc:*** EV, JE, LA, VM, Da84, Fa77>

limer [lime] *v.tr.* **1** to file, sharpen *C'était un bougre qu'était beaucoup bon à limer des égoïnes.* He was a fellow who was very good at filing saws. (LA) **2** to chafe *La première fois j'ai monté à bicycle, ça m'a limé.* The first time I rode a bicycle, it chafed me. (LA) <***Loc:*** LA, Da84>

limite [limit] *n.f.* **1** limit, boundary **Ça, c'est la limite!* That's the limit! (Da84) **Il y a une limite dans cette affaire.* There's a limit to this business. (SL, An94) **2** limit, quota *La limite des truites grises [...] c'est vingt-cinq par jour par personne.* The quota on speckled trout is twenty-five per person per day. (TB) *Il dit, "c'est pas la peine, si on a pas tué notre limite asteur, on va jamais la tuer."* He said, "It's not worth it, if we haven't killed our quota by now, we never will." (JD) <***Loc:*** JD, LA, SL, TB, An94, Da84, Fa77, Wh83>

limiter [limite] **I** *v.tr.* **1** to limit *J'ai essayé de limiter les chicanes. J'ai pas invité les M.* I tried to limit the number of fights. I didn't invite any of the M. family. (VM) **Elle est dessus ein* DIET *qui la limite a juste cinq gallons de crème à la glace par jour.* She is on a diet that limits her to just five gallons of ice cream per day. (Wh83) **2** to set a limit on, put a quota on *Il faulait qu'il les limite combien de chevrettes qu'eux-autres pouvait attraper par jour.* He had to give them a quota of how many shrimp they could catch per day. (TB) **II se limiter** *v.pron.* to limit o.s. **Il buvait mais il connaissait de se limiter.* He drank [alcohol] but he knew to limit himself. (EV) <***Loc:*** EV, TB, VM, Da84, Fa77, Wh83>

limon[1] [limɔ̃] *n.m.* **1** lemon *Il y a des orangers dans des places aussi, et des limons.* There are orange trees in some places, and lemons. (SL) **2** lime <***Loc:*** CL, LA, SL, SM, Da84, Fa77, Gu00, Hi02, Lv88>

limon[2] [limɔ̃] *n.m.* cobia, lemonfish <***Loc:*** LF>

limon[3] [limɔ̃] *n.m.* mud, silt, dirt <***Loc:*** Da84>

limon[4] (**vlimon**) [limɔ̃, vlimɔ̃] *n.m.* blue-green algae, a greenish grassy growth appearing on wood or on the ground after a rain <***Loc:*** VM>

limonade [limɔ̃nad] *n.f.* **1** lemonade **2** limeade <***Loc:*** LA, SL, SM, TB, VM, Da84, Fa77, Hi02, Lv88>

limonier [limɔ̃je] *n.m.* **1** lemon tree **2** lime tree <***Loc:*** Da84, Fa77, Lv88>

limousine [limuzin] *n.f.* limousine <***Loc:*** Da84>

lin [lɛ̃] ◊ **•huile de lin** linseed oil <Da84> <***Loc:*** Da84>

linette ♦see **ligneguette**

linge [lɛ̃ʒ] *n.m.* **1** cloth, fabric *Une bande en linge.* A cloth bandage. (Lv88) *Dans ces temps-ça, on gaspillait pas, les sacs à fumier, c'était des sacs en linge.* In the old days, we didn't waste, [even] fertilizer sacks, they were sacks made of cloth. (AC) **2** clothes, clothing *Souvent des fois la femme disait "Il est temps que tu vas t'acheter du linge." J'ai dit "Je vas m'acheter du linge équand-ce que les enfants va avoir tout ce qu'eusse a de besoin du linge."* Often my wife would say, "It's time you go and buy yourself some clothes." I said, "I'll buy myself some clothes when the kids have all the clothes they need." (TB) **3** dirty clothes, laundry *Laver mon linge.* To do my laundry. (VM) **4** sanitary napkin **5** bedding, bed linens *Après ma belle-mère va partir, on va changer le linge dessus son lit.* After my mother-in-law leaves, we'll change the bed linens on her bed. (LA) ◊ **•linge à dormir {de nuit}** nightclothes **L'enfant s'est déshabillé et mis son linge de nuit.* The child undressed and put on his nightclothes. (An77) <SL, An77> **•linge à oreiller** pillowcase <SL> **•linge de corps** clothing *Son linge de corps était pas regardable quand il a sorti de la plairie.* His clothing was not presentable when he came out of the prairie. (TB) <TB> **•linge de coton** cotton cloth, cotton fabric <LF> **•linge de dessous / linge d'en-dessous** underwear, underclothes *Il avait du linge de dessous qui était fait en sac de sucre. Il y avait "100 lbs. Sugar" en arrière là.* He had some underwear made out of a sugar sack. It had "100 lbs. Sugar" [written] on the back. (SL) <AC, SL, Da84, Fa77, Gu00, Lv88> **•linge d'été** summer clothes <Fa77> **•linge d'hiver** winter clothes <Fa77> **•linge de travail / linge d'ouvrage** work clothes (LF) <LF, Lv88> **•se mettre du linge** to put on clothes, get dressed <Da84> **•vieux linge** rag <AL> <***Loc:*** AC, AL, IB, LA, LF, SB, SL, SM, TB, VM, An77, Da84, Fa77, Gu00, Hi02, Lv88>

lingerie [lɛ̃ʒri] *n.f.* lingerie <***Loc:*** Da84>

lingir [lɛ̃ʒir] *v.intr.* to loaf, idle *Il a lingi toute une semaine avant de se mettre à l'œuvre.* He loafed for a week before getting to work. (SB) <***Loc:*** SB>

linguette [lɛ̃gɛt] *n.f.* tall, slender person *T'as déjà vu une pareille linguette?* Have you ever seen such a beanpole? (SL) <***Loc:*** SL>

linteau [lɛ̃to] *n.m.* edge, sill (of a window, a fireplace, etc.) ◊ **•linteau de fenêtre** windowsill <Fa77> **•linteau de porte** threshold <Fa77, Lv88> <***Loc:*** Fa77, Lv88>

lion [ljɔ̃] *n.m.* lion <***Loc:*** TB, Da84, Fa77, Hi02>

liqueur [likœr] *n.f.* **1** liqueur **2** liquor, alcohol <***Loc:*** AC, Da84, Fa77, Lv88>

liquide [likid] *n.m.* liquid ◊ **•en liquide** in liquid form *Tu peux acheter le savon en poudre ou en liquide.* You can buy soap in powder or in liquid. (LA) <LA> <***Loc:*** LA, Da84>

lire [lir] (*p.p.* **li** [li], **lu** [ly]) *v.tr.* to read *On parle en français mais on peut pas lire en français.* We speak French but we cannot read French. (SM) *J'ai li ça dans la gazette.* I read that in the newspaper. (VM) *Quand il a lu cette lettre, il a cru que c'était vrai, lui.* When he read the letter, he thought it was true. (IV) *Et il connaissait quand il fallait il tondre son jardin. Il connaissait pas lire mais il connaissait par la lune.* And he knew when he had to mow his field. He didn't know how to read but he knew according to the stage of the moon. (EV) ◊ **•lire un catéchisse à qqn *a*** to scold, reprimand, lay down the law to s.o. ***b*** to tell s.o. off <SL, Da84, La99> **•lire un chapître à qqn** to scold, reprimand, lay down the law to s.o. <Da84> <***Loc:*** AC, AV, EV, IV, SL, SM, TB, VM, Da84, Hi02, La99, Lv88>

lirette [lirɛt] *n.f.* thick weaving made of strips of used cloth, often used for rugs <***Loc:*** Lv88>

lis[1] (**lys**) [li, lis] *n.m./f.* lily ◊ **•lys blanc** Easter lily <Gu00> **•lys de la Sainte Vierge** Easter lily <VM> **•lys de Saint-Joseph *a*** amaryllis, St. Joseph lily ***b*** Easter lily <VM, Gu00> **•lys jaune** day lily <Gu00> <***Loc:*** VM, Da84, Fa77, Gu00>

lis[2] [li] *n.m.* selvage, list (of material or cloth) <***Loc:*** VM>

lisable [lizab(l)] *adj.* **1** legible *Son écriture est pas lisable.* His writing is not legible. (LA) **2** enjoyable or easy to read, readable *Cette histoire est beaucoup lisable. C'est bon pour les grands et les petites.* This story is very readable. It's good for adults and children. (EV) <***Loc:*** EV, LA, SM, Lv88, Ph36>

liserine (**lisraie, liseron**) [lizrin, lizrɛ, lizre, lizərɔ̃] *n.m./f.* **1** wild morning glory, field bindweed *Défunte 'Tit-tante disait que c'était dur de piocher le coton quand les liserines prenaient dedans parce que ça file partout.* My late aunt used to say that it was hard to hoe the cotton when the morning glories got in it because they spread everywhere. (Gu00) *Si on piochait pas bien notre rang de coton et les liserines prenaient là-dedans, défunt Pap' était pas content.* If we didn't hoe our row of cotton right and the morning glories took over, poor Daddy was not happy. (LA) **2** wild potato vine **3** tare, vetch <***Loc:*** LA, Ho90, Gu00>

liseron ♦see **liserine**

liseur [lizœr] *n.m.* reader <***Loc:*** Da84>

lisière [lizjær] *n.f.* **1** strip *Des lisières de peau.* Strips of leather. (Lv88) **2** edge (of the woods) <***Loc:*** VM, Da84, Lv88>

lisraie ♦see **liserine**

lissage [lisaʒ] *n.m.* smoothing <***Loc:*** Da84>

lissé, -e [lise] *adj.* smooth, sleek, shiny *La table était lissée avec l'âge.* The table was smooth and shiny with age. (LA) <***Loc:*** LA, Da84, Fa77>

lisser [lise] *v.tr.* to smooth, polish, shine *Il a travaillé des jours pour lisser la vieille table.* He worked for days to polish the old table. (LA) ◊ **•lisser le linge** to iron, press clothing <VM> <***Loc:*** LA, VM, Da84>

liste [lis(t)] *n.f.* **1** list **2** roll, sign-up sheet *Ils avont passé avec la liste pour le raffle.* They came by with the [sign-up] list for the raffle. (VM) <***Loc:*** VM, Da84>

lit [li, lit] *n.m.* **1** bed *Des fois ça se couchait jusqu'à quatre dans le même lit!* Sometimes they slept as many as four to a bed! (TB) **2** layer *On mettait un lit de viande, un lit de sauce, et* POTATO SALAD, *des patates.* We would put a layer of meat, a layer of sauce, and potato salad, potatoes. (SL) ◊ **•lit à bébé** baby bed <SL> **•lit à ciel** canopy bed <Da84> **•lit à roulettes** roll-away bed, trundle bed <Da84> **•lit d'eau** waterbed <TB> **•lit double** double bed <VM> **•lit étroit {simple}** single bed, twin bed *Quand on était jeunes, moi et mon frère, on avait chacun un lit simple. Mon père et ma mère couchaient dans un lit double.* When we were young, my brother and I each had a twin bed. My father and mother slept in a double bed. (VM) <AL, VM> **•lit gréyé** made-up bed (with mattress, springs, pillows, linens, etc.) <VM> **•lit qui couche un {deux}** single bed, double bed <SL> **•être au lit** to be sick in bed <Da84> **•mettre au lit** to put s.o. to bed (esp. s.o. who is sick) <Da84> **•prendre le lit** to take sick, become ill <Da84> <***Loc:*** AL, AV, EV, LA, LF, SL, TB, VM, Da84, Hi02>

litage [litaʒ] *n.m.* bedding *Un bon litage, des oreillers et des matelas.* Good bedding, pillows and mattresses. (SL) <***Loc:*** LF, SL, TB, VM, Lv88>

litanie [litɑ̃ni] *n.f.* litany, lengthy repetition or recitation <***Loc:*** Da84>

litre [lit(r)] *n.m.* liter <***Loc:*** Fa77>

littérature [literatyr] *n.f.* **1** literature **2** reading matter <***Loc:*** Da84>

livide [livid] *adj.* livid *Elle était livide de colère.* She was livid with anger. (VM) <***Loc:*** VM, Da84>

livraison [livrezɔ̃] *n.f.* delivery <***Loc:*** Da84>

livre[1] [liv(r)] *n.f.* pound *Ça va remplir un sac de 50 livres de patates.* That will fill a bag with 50 pounds of potatoes. (LF) *Ça prend une livre de beurre.* It takes a pound of butter. (Lv88) ◊ **•à la livre / par livre** by the pound *Ça se vendait à la livre dans ce temps-là.* That was sold by the pound in those days. (EV) <EV, Da84> <***Loc:*** EV, LF, TB, VM, Da84, Hi02, Lv88>

livre[2] [liv(r)] *n.m.* **1** book *Et en temps perdu, plein souvent j'ai continué à lire son livre et à étudier moi-même.* And in my free time, quite often I've continued to read his book and to study on my own. (LF) **2** grade (in school) *Il était au huitième livre quand il a arrêté.* He was in eighth grade when he quit school. (VM) *Il est dans le troisième livre.* He is in the third grade. (Lv88) ◊ **•livre de papiers à cigarette** book of cigarette papers <SM> **•livre de téléphone** phone book *Si tu regardes dans le livre de* TELEPHONE *tu vas voir combien il y en a, c'est une famille que dans la Paroisse Terrebonne y en a plusieurs.* If you look in the phone book you'll see how many there are, it's a family [name] that there's a lot of in Terrebonne Parish. (TB) <TB> **•petit livre** booklet, pamphlet <Da84> <***Loc:*** EV, LA, LF, PQ, SL, SM, TB, VM, Da84, Hi02, Lv88>

livrer [livre] **I** *v.tr.* **1** to cede, give over, hand over **2** to deliver **II se livrer** *v.pron.* to surrender, give o.s. up *Il s'a jamais livré. Ils l'ont tué, lui aussi.* He never surrendered. They killed him, too. (EV) ◊ **•livrer qqn à soi-même** to leave on one's own, leave to one's own devices *Quand leur mère allait à l'ouvrage, elle livrait les enfants à eux-mêmes pour la journée.* When their mother went to work, she left the kids on their own for the day. (VM) <VM> **•livrer sa carcasse au diable** to 'be a goner,' see one's life flash before one's eyes *Quand Dad m'a frappé avec le char, j'ai livré ma carcasse au diable!* When Dad hit me with the car, I saw my life flash before my eyes! (VM) <VM> **•livrer une terre** to cede use of land *Il s'a fait livrer la terre avant de l'acheter.* He had the use of the land turned over to him prior to buying it. (VM) <VM> **•se livrer à *a*** to turn o.s. in *Ça ira mieux pour toi si tu te livres à la police.* It'll go better for you if you turn yourself in to the police. (VM) ***b*** to entrust o.s. to *Je me livre à toi pour lui faire comprendre.* I'll trust you to make him understand. (VM) ***c*** to abandon o.s. to, give o.s. up to (vice, drinking, etc.) *Se livrer à la boisson.* To abandon oneself to drink. (VM) <VM> <***Loc:*** EV, IB, VM, Da84>

livrier [livrije] *n.m.* morning glory <***Loc:*** LA>

lizerée [lizre] *n.f.* drizzle, drizzling rain *Il y a une petite lizerée à ce matin.* There's a little drizzle this morning. (AV) <***Loc:*** AV>

LOAD [loᵘd] *n.m.* load, cargo **Apporte-nous-aut in* LOAD *de bois.* Bring us a load of wood. (EV, Ph36) <***Loc:*** EV, VM, Lv88, Ph36>

LOAF[1] **(loafer)** [loᵘf, lofe] *v.intr.* to loaf, be idle *Il va pas travailler. Il va* LOAF *toute la journée.* He won't work. He'll loaf all day. (VM) <***Loc:*** EV, LF, VM, Da84, Lv88, Ph36>

LOAF[2] [loᵘf] *n.m.* loaf ◊ **•un LOAF de pain** American-style bread (as opposed to French breads) <VM> <***Loc:*** VM>

loafer[1] [lofœr] *n.m.* **1** loafer, casual slip-on shoe **2** lazy person, loafer <***Loc:*** LF, SB, Lv88>

loafer[2] ♦see **LOAF**[1]

lobster **(LOBSTER)** [lɔbstær, lɔbstə, lɑbstəɹ] *n.m.* **1** lobster **2** very large shrimp, prawn <***Loc:*** VM, Lv88>

local, -e [lokal] *adj.* local *C'est juste le monde local qui fréquente cette place.* It's just locals who frequent that place. (EV) <***Loc:*** EV, Da84>

localement [lokalmɑ̃] *adv.* locally *C'est ça je pêche là-là, mais on l'appelle localement sacalait.* That there [crappie] is what I fish, but locally we call it "sacalait." (SL) <***Loc:*** SL>

locataire [lokatær, lokatœr] *n.m.* renter, tenant, lodger *Il a eu pour déloger ses locataires à force qu'ils étaient sales.* He had to evict his renters because they were dirty. (VM) <***Loc:*** SB, VM, Da84>

location [lokasjɔ̃] *n.f.* location, place *Moi je travaillais sur les* DREDGEBOAT *fouiller des canals et des locations pour aller pour les compagnies d'huile ici.* I worked on the dredgeboats digging canals and places to go for the oil companies here. (TB) <***Loc:*** TB, Da84>

loche [lɔʃ] *n.m./f.* minnow, menhaden *Les loches qu'on appelle, c'est un tout petit poisson un loche. On pêche ça, on empoigne ça pour empoigner des gros poissons.* Minnows as we call them, that's a tiny little fish, a minnow. We fish for them, we catch them with our hands in order to catch bigger fish. (TB) *Y a assez de mousse, et t'as ton appât, ta loche reste mêlée dans la mousse et le poisson mord pas.* There's so much moss, and you've got your bait, the minnow stays tangled up in the moss and the fish don't bite. (TB) <***Loc:*** LF, TB>

LOCK [lɔk, lɑk] *n.m. (often pl.)* lock, salt water barrier gate *Ils ont des* LOCKS *au ras de la mer pour empêcher l'eau salée de rentrer durant les chesseresses. Avant l'eau haute de 1940, les* LOCKS *étiont bord icitte de Florence.* They have locks near the Gulf to stop salt water from coming inland during droughts. Before the 1940 flood, the locks were on this side of Florence. (VM) <***Loc:*** VM>

locomotive [lokɔ̃motiv] *n.f.* locomotive <***Loc:*** Da84>

locuste [lokys(t)] *n.f.* **1** locust, grasshopper **2** cicada, 17-year locust <***Loc:*** Da84>

LOG (**logue**) [lɔg, log] *n.m. (occ. f.)* log, felled tree trunk, undressed timber **Ça fait, Petit Jean a entendu ça. Il a sorti. Il s'a attrapé un* LOG *et il l'a mis dans son lit, et puis il s'a fourré quelque part.* So, Little Jean heard that. He went out. He got himself a log and he put it in his bed, and then he hid somewhere. (An94) *Quand on fait tomber un bois, on disait un* LOG. After we cut down a tree, we call it a log. (IV) <***Loc:*** AV, EV, IV, LF, SB, SJ, SL, TB, VM, An94, Da84, Lv88, Ph36>

logeable [lɔʒab(l)] *adj.* fit to live in, habitable, livable *Tu pourras pas rester là. Cette maison est p'us logeable.* You can't live there. That house is not fit to live in anymore. (LA) <***Loc:*** LA, Da84>

logement [lɔʒmɑ̃] *n.m.* lodging, dwelling, accommodation, living quarters <***Loc:*** Da84>

loger [lɔʒe] **I** *v.tr.* to lodge, house *La première année après leurs noces, on les a logés dans une petite maison au ras de chez nous-autres.* The first year after their wedding, we put them up in a little house next to ours. (VM) **II** *v.intr.* to lodge, live, reside *On est logé ici depuis des années.* We've been living here for years. (EV) **III se loger** *v.pron.* to take up lodging, move in, build o.s. lodging **Moi et Deanna, on s'a marié et s'a logé à Nederland et dans rien de temps on avait une belle famille de quatre 'tits enfants.* Deanna and I got married and settled in Nederland and in no time we had a beautiful family of four little children. (ThCa: *La dernière quilte*) <***Loc:*** EV, VM, Da84, Fa77, ThCa>

logue ♦see LOG

loi [lwa] *n.f.* **1** law, civil law, rule **C'est la loi.* It's the law. (Da84) **2** law, piece of legislation *Mais c'est venu un moment après, euh, dix-neuf cent douze que la législature de l'état de la Louisiane a passé une loi en quoi que ils auront plus accepté ça.* But it came a time after that, euh, 1912 when the legislature of the state of Louisiana passed a law according to which they would no longer have accepted that. (AV) **3** the police, 'the law' **La loi m'a ramassé, moi, je suis parti dans la prison.* The police picked me up, I went to prison. (ch: *La porte d'en arrière*) **4** law, jurisprudence *Un vieux livre de loi.* An old law book. (Lv88) *Il est* GONE *étudier la loi.* He has gone to study law. (Lv88) **5** uvula <***Loc:*** AV, TB, VM, Da84, Hi02, Lv88>

loin [lwɛ̃, lwɑ̃] *adv.* far, far away, remote, distant **Combien loin c'est?* How far is it? (Hi02) *Si tu prends le trouble d'aller loin là-bas, tu veux avoir quelque chose pour ramener.* If you take the trouble to go way out there, you want to have something to take back. (LA) ◊ **•loin à loin** far apart **Et si t'avais une belle, t'aurais pas aimé dépenser le dix sous là sur une autre, tu connais. Ça fait, tu dansais manière loin à loin, faire attention jusqu'à* TREAT YOUR LADY. And if you had a girlfriend, you wouldn't have wanted to spend ten cents on another girl, you know. So you would dance kind of far apart, waiting to treat your lady. (VM, An94) <VM, An94, Da84, Lv88> **•loin de** far from **C'est pas loin d'icitte.* It's not far from here. (Hi02) *C'est loin d'être le même papier.* It's far from being the same paper. (VM) <VM, Hi02> **•au loin** far away, in the distance *Au loin là-bas, tu vois, il y a un feu.* In the distance there, you see, there's a fire. (VM) <VM, Da84> **•de loin** from afar *C'est une grande bâtisse. Tu peux la voir de loin.* It's a tall building. You can see it from afar. (EV) <EV, Da84> **•de près, de loin** from near and far <Da84> <***Loc:*** AC, AV, EV, IV, LA, SL, SM, TB, VM, An94, Da84, Hi02, Lv88>

lointain [lwɛ̃tɛ̃] *adj.* distant, remote **Pays lointain.* Far country, remote country. (Da84) <***Loc:*** Da84>

loir [lwar] *n.* dormouse <***Loc:*** Lv88>

lolette [lolɛt] *adj.* foolish, silly <***Loc:*** EV, VM, Ph36>

lolo (**lololle**) [lolo, lolɔl] *n.m.* [*baby talk*] milk *Cher, tu veux du lololle?* My dear, do you want some milk? (SL) <***Loc:*** AV, SL>

lololle[1] **(lolot)** [lolɔl, lolo] *adj.* crazy <*Loc:* EV, VM, Ph36>

lololle[2] ♦see **lolo**

lolot ♦see **lololle**[1]

lombre ♦see **ombre**

long[1], **-ue** [lɔ̃, lɔ̃g] *adj.* long *C'était une robe, allons voir… elle était plein de fleurs en bas, puis longue, plus on l'aimait longue.* It was a dress, let's see . . . it had lots of flowers at the bottom and it was long, we liked it long. (EV) *C'est un grand poisson couleur d'acier, il est long. Et il est mince mince mince.* It's a big steel-colored fish, it's long. And it is extremely thin. (LF) ◊ **•à {au / en / le} long de** along *Moi j'ai cinquante-six ans, et quand-ce que mon j'sutais une petite fille, y avait pas plein du monde à long du bayou qui parlait en anglais, ça parlait tout en français.* I'm 56 years old, and when I was a little girl, there weren't many people along the bayou who spoke English, they all spoke French. (LF) *Le monde se mettait ensemble, deux ou trois, et là ça passait en long du chemin, et mon je me rappelle mes enfants a fait ça déjà, s'habiller au Mardi Gras et passer, aller chez les voisins.* People got together, two or three, and then they went along the road, and I remember my children have done that, get dressed up for Mardi Gras and pass by the neighbors. (TB) *Mais tout le long du chemin, tous les temps en temps il lâchait une petite pierre, une petite pierre pour marquer son chemin.* But all along the road, every once in awhile he'd drop a small stone, a small stone to mark his way. (LA) *On seinait pour les écrevisses au long de la levée.* We seined to catch crawfish along the levee. (SM) *Quand on avait été à la chasse au long du Bayou des Cannes.* When we were hunting along the Bayou des Cannes. (LA) <LA, LF, SM, TB, Da84> **•à la longue** in the long run, in time, eventually *Si t'achètes un vieux char à bon marché, à la longue il te coûte plus cher.* If you buy an old, inexpensive car, in the long run it'll cost you more. (VM) <VM, Da84, Fa77> <*Loc:* CL, EV, LA, LF, SM, TB, VM, An94, Da84, Fa77>

long[2] [lɔ̃] *adv.* long **J'en planterais si long et si large, pour en avoir tous mes camarades.* I would plant it [love] so long and so wide, that there would be enough for all my friends. (ThCa: *La dernière quilte*) <*Loc:* SL, An94, ThCa>

longe [lɔ̃ʒ] *n.f.* sofa *Va t'assir sur la longe.* Go sit down on the sofa. (LF) <*Loc:* LF>

longis [lɔ̃ʒi] *adj.* slow, dull, lifeless, lacking vigor *Le prêtre est longis. Ses messes finit p'us!* The priest is dull and slow. His Masses go on and on! (VM) <*Loc:* VM>

longtemps [lɑ̃tɑ̃, lɔ̃tɑ̃, lotɑ̃] *adv.* a long time **J'avais dit que j'aurais jamais rev'nu. Mais ça a pas été si longtemps, je t'es eu de besoin à mon côté.* I had said I would never come back. But it wasn't such a long time before I needed you at my side. (ch: *J'ai fait une grosse erreur*) *Pendant longtemps je faisais du roux mais maintenant c'est un tas plus facile aller au magasin.* For a long time I used to make roux, but now it's a whole lot easier to go to the store [to get it]. (SL) **Catin, avant trop longtemps moi je te vois 'près t'en rev'nir.* Babe, before too long I see you you coming back. (lyrics: *Duralde Waltz*, I. LeJeune) *Et pas trop longtemps après ils ont amené de l'électricité.* And not too long afterward they brought in electricity. (TB) *Le* FERTILIZER, *ça travaille vite, mais pas pour longtemps.* Fertilizer works fast, but not for long. (Lv88) *Quand j'espère trop longtemps avant de manger, je me sens faille.* If I wait too long before I eat, I feel faint. (Guoo) *La vieille emballeuse est hors de service depuis longtemps.* The old baler has been beyond repair for a long time. (LA) *Je pouvais pas en acheter, pas d'argent pour acheter des souliers. C'est pour ça que mes pieds sont si larges et si plattes. J'ai marché trop longtemps nu-pied.* I couldn't buy any, no money to buy shoes. That's why my feet are so wide and so flat. I walked barefoot too long. (TB) ◊ **•longtemps passé** a long time ago *Je comprends qu'y avait trois Naquin qu'avait venu ici de la France, longtemps passé.* I understand that there were three Naquins who came here from France long ago. (TB) <LA, TB, VM, An94, Lv88> **•aussi longtemps que** as long as <Da84> **•combien longtemps / comment longtemps** how long *Combien longtemps il restait quand il venait pour visiter chez vous?* How long would he stay when he came to visit you? (EV) *Je connais pas comment longtemps, mais c'est pas trop trop longtemps.* I don't know how long, but it wasn't too long. (TB) <TB, VM, An94> **•il y a longtemps** a long time ago **Elle est mort, elle est mort il y a longtemps.* She died, she died a long time ago. (EV) <EV> **•il y a longtemps (que)** for a long time *Ça fait qu'il y a longtemps que je suis après jouer avec ce maillage.* So I've been playing with that mesh for a long time. (TB) *Mais depuis l'âge de douze ans j'ai pris un DECK de cartes, je les ai épaillés, j'ai ramassé, il y a assez longtemps j'ai tiré des cartes.* But since the age of twelve I've taken a deck of cards, I've spread them out, I've gathered them up, I've read cards for quite some time. (LF) <LF, TB> <*Loc:* AC, EV, LA, LF, SL, SM, TB, VM, An94, Da84, Guoo, Lv88>

longuent ♦see **onguent**

longues-jambes [lɔ̃gʒɑ̃m, lɔ̃gʒɑ̃b] *n.m.pl.* long johns <*Loc:* SM>

longueur [lɔ̃gœr] *n.f.* length *La longueur du bateau.* The length of the boat. (LF) <*Loc:* LF, Da84>

longue-vue (longues-vues) [lɔ̃gvy, lɔ̃ŋvy] *n.f. (usu. pl.)* field glasses, binoculars *Il se sert toujours de ses longues-vues.* He always uses his field glasses. (IB) <*Loc:* AV, IB, SM, VM, Da84>

LOOK OUT[1] [lukaut, lukat] *v.intr.invar.* **1** to look at, take notice of *LOOK OUT quoi y'a.* Look what there is. (Lv88) *LOOK OUT les bétailles qu'a entré.* Look at the cows that came in. (Lv88) **2** to be careful, be on the watch, pay attention *Il faut tu LOOK OUT pour les serpents dans la mèche.* You have to be on the watch for the snakes in the swamp. (Lv88) *Tu vas tomber si tu* LOOK OUT *pas.* You're going to fall if you don't pay attention. (VM) <*Loc:* EV, VM, Lv88, Ph36>

LOOK OUT[2] [lʊkaʊt, lukat] *interj.* look out! *T'as vu la femme qu'était avec Pierre au bal? Look out! Ça c'était une belle femme, ouais!* Did you see the woman who was with Pierre at the dance? Look out! That was a really beautiful woman! (VM) *Et tant qu'il y avait le sucre dans la chose, alle aurait mangé là. Il n'avait pas de tracas. Mais quand il n'avait plus de sucre,* LOOK OUT! As long as there was sugar in the thing, she would eat it. There was no trouble. But when there was no more sugar, look out! (EV) <*Loc:* EV, VM>

LOOSE [lu^{n}s] *adj.* **1** loose, slack *Mon soulier est* LOOSE. My shoe is loose. (SM) *La chaîne était* LOOSE. The chain was loose. (AC) **2** loose, at large *Ses bêtes sont* LOOSE. His cows are loose. (VM) <*Loc:* AC, SB, SM, TB, VM, Da84, Lv88>

loque ♦see **LUCK**

loqué, -e [loke] *adj.* well supplied, well fitted out *Elle est bien loquée pour l'année.* She is well fitted out for the year. (IB) <*Loc:* IB>

loquer [loke] *v.tr.* to latch, fasten (doors, etc.) *Loquer les portes.* To latch the doors. (VM) <*Loc:* IB, VM, Da84>

loquet [lokɛ, loke] *n.m.* latch <*Loc:* Da84>

LORD (LAUD) [lɔd] *interj. Oh Laud!* Oh Lord! (VM) <*Loc:* VM, Da84>

lot [lo] *n.m.* **1** lot, portion *J'ai acheté un lot de bois.* I bought a portion of wood. (VM) **2** group, bunch **Un lot de bêtes.* A herd or lot of cattle. (Da84) <*Loc:* VM, Da84>

loterie [lotri] *n.f.* lottery, raffle <*Loc:* Da84>

lotre [lɔt(r)] *adj.poss.* their *Nous-autres on a appris notre manière, eusse a appris de lotre manière, et ça pourrait s'assir là, tous nous-autres, s'assir là et se parler.* We learned our way and they learned their way, and they can all sit down and talk, all of us, sit and talk to each other. (LF) *Faut que ç'achète ces* TAG *là étout pour mettre sur lotre tcheue.* They have to buy those tags and all to put on their [alligators'] tails. (TB) <*Loc:* LF, TB>

lotret ♦see **roitelet**

loucher [luʃe] *v.intr.* to be cross-eyed, look cross-eyed *Il louche.* He's cross-eyed. (VM) *Défunt Jean Trahan a louché jusqu'à l'âge de 17 ans quand il a eu une opération dessus ses yeux.* Poor John Trahan was cross-eyed until he was 17 years old when he had an operation on his eyes. (VM) <*Loc:* VM, Da84>

loucou [luku] *n.m.* mimosa tree <*Loc:* VM>

louer [lwe] **I** *v.tr.* to rent, let, lease *On louait des chambres et des appartements.* We rented rooms and apartments. (IB) **II se louer** *v.pron.* to be for rent **La maison se loue pour dix piastres.* The house rents for ten dollars. (Da84) <*Loc:* EV, IB, Da84, Fa77>

louette ♦see **luette**

lougarou ♦see **loup-garou**

lougre [lug(r)] *n.m.* lugger, small fishing boat with a flat bottom and a small cabin, well-adapted to the shallow waters of the bayous, later replaced by the lafitte and then by the biloxi <*Loc:* Lv88>

louisianais, -e [lwizjɑ̃nɛ, lwizjɑ̃ne, luzjɑ̃nɛ, luzjɑ̃ne, -ɛz] *adj.* from Louisiana, of Louisiana *Les Amies Louisianaises vont jouer au festival.* The Louisiana Friends are going to play at the festival. (LA) <*Loc:* LA, Hi02>

Louisianais, -e [lwizjɑ̃nɛ, lwizjɑ̃ne, luzjɑ̃nɛ, luzjɑ̃ne, -ɛz] *n.* person from Louisiana <*Loc:* Hi02>

Louisiane [lwizjɑ̃n, luzjɑ̃n] *n.f.* Louisiana <*Loc:* JE, LF, TB, Hi02>

loulou[1] [lulu] *n.m.* [*baby talk*] wolf *Le loulou va t'attraper.* The wolf is going to catch you. (SM) <*Loc:* SM, VM>

loulou[2] **(loup)** [lulu, lu] *n.m.* **1** larva of the tiger beetle or pill bug **2** insect, bug <*Loc:* EV, SM, VM, Da84, Ph36, Re31>

loup[1] [lu] *n.m.* wolf ◊ **•loup rouge** red wolf <Gu00> <*Loc:* Da84, Gu00>

loup[2] see **loulou**[2]

loupe [lup] *n.f.* welt, swollen spot on the skin (as from an insect bite or a blow) <*Loc:* SJ, SL, VM, Lv88>

louper [lupe] *v.tr.* **1** to beat, whip *Louper un cheval rétif.* To beat a stubborn horse. (SJ) **2** to provoke or cause bumps or swelling of skin (as insect bites, stings, hives, etc.) *Les fromis m'ont loupé.* The ants bit me. (Lv88) *Nos jambes sont toutes loupées par les froumis.* Our legs are all covered in bites from the ants. (Lv88) **3** to rope *François est après louper les chevaux.* Francis is roping the horses. (IB) <*Loc:* AV, IB, SJ, VM, Lv88>

loup-garou (lougarou, rougarou, warou) [lugaru, rugaru, hugaru, waru] *n.m.* **1** werewolf, weredog, or other man-to-animal transformation of Louisiana folklore *Quand j'étais tout petit ma mère nous faisait peur le soir pour qu'on reste autour de la maison. Alle nous disait que y avait un homme qui tournait rougarou. Et cet individu, tous les soirs, il embrassait sa femme, il disait qu'il allait boire de la bière ou aller au café ou quelque place, et là à moitié route il tournait rougarou puis là il venait faire peur à tout le monde.* When I was young my mother would scare us in the evening so we would stay around the house. She told us that there was a man who changed into a werewolf. This guy, every night he kissed his wife, he said he was going to drink beer or go to the cafe or somewhere, and halfway there he changed into a werewolf and then came to scare people. (LF) *Icitte en bas c'est un homme qui change d'une bétaille, d'un chien, supposé. C'est ça qu'eusse appelle le lougarou.* Down here it's a man who turns into an animal, into a dog, supposedly. That's what they call a "lougarou." (TB) **2** boogeyman, bugaboo, apparition **3** animal or person roaming around at night **4** restless or agitated person or animal ◊ **•en rougarou** in heat, in rut *La vache est en rougarou ce matin.* The cow is in heat this morning. (SB)

<SB, La99> **•faire (le) rougarou** ***a*** to dissipate, carouse, go chasing about at night ***b*** to make a ruckus <SB, La99, Lv88> **•faire son rougarou** to pace the floors at night (due to insomnia) *Il a fait son rougarou toute la nuit.* He was up all night pacing. (LF) <LF> <***Loc:*** JE, LF, SB, SM, TB, Da84, La99, Lv88>

louquer [luke] *v.tr.* to stare at *On louque pas le monde.* We don't stare at people. (TB) <***Loc:*** TB>

lourd, -e [lur, lurd] *adj.* **1** heavy *Le sofa est lourd. Il va d'être dur à manier.* The sofa is heavy. It will be hard to move. (LA) *Un repas lourd.* A heavy meal. (VM) **2** hard, difficult *Marcus, tu as plus de responsabilité que tu crois, parce que Grandma Douce te charge avec l'obligation la plus lourde.* Marcus, you have more responsibility than you think because Grandma Douce is giving you the most difficult task. (ThCa: *La douce réunion*) **3** muggy, humid (of the weather) *Il fait un temps lourd.* The weather is muggy. (EV) **4** cloudy (of the weather) <***Loc:*** AV, EV, IB, LA, VM, Da84, Hi02, ThCa>

loutre [lut(r)] *n.f.* otter *Y a p'us des affaires pour piéger. Tous les rats et les loutres et tout qu'eux-autres était après piéger, il y en a p'us alentour d'ici.* There isn't anything left to trap. All the [musk]rats and otters and everything they used to go trapping, there aren't any more around here. (LF) <***Loc:*** LF, SM, TB, Da84, Gu00, Hi02>

louvre [luv(r)] *n.m.* louver <***Loc:*** VM>

loyal, -e [lwajal] *adj.* loyal, faithful *J'ai tout était loyal à mon candidat.* I have always been loyal to my candidate. (VM) <***Loc:*** VM, Da84>

loyauté [lwajote] *n.f.* loyalty, fidelity, faithfulness <***Loc:*** Da84>

loyer [lwaje] *n.m.* rent <***Loc:*** AV, TB, Da84, Hi02>

lucarne [lykarn] *n.f.* dormer window *La maison à Nénaine là-bas à 'Béville avait une lucarne dans la couverture.* Nénaine's house in Abbeville had a dormer window in the roof. (VM) <***Loc:*** VM, Da84>

lucide [lysid] *adj.* clear, lucid *Son idée est toujours lucide.* His mind is still lucid. (EV) <***Loc:*** EV, Da84>

Lucifer [lysifær] *n.prop.* Lucifer, the devil <***Loc:*** Da84>

LUCK (loque) [lʌk, lɔk, lœk] *n.m.* luck *T'as sûr du loque, toi!* You sure are lucky! (SL) *Il a du loque avec les cartes.* He is lucky at cards. (AV) <***Loc:*** AV, LF, SL, Lv88>

luette (louette, alouète) [lɥɛt, lwɛt, lwet, alwɛt] *n.f.* **1** uvula *Sa luette touche sa langue.* His uvula touches his tongue. (SM) **2** soft palate <***Loc:*** AV, IB, LF, SJ, SM, VM, Da84, Lv88>

lueur [lɥœr] *n.f.* glare <***Loc:*** Fa77>

lui[1] **(li, y)** [lɥi, ly, li, i] *pron.pers. (ind.obj.)* to him, to her, to it *On lui a acheté un gâteau et un cadeau.* We bought him a cake and a gift. (TB) *Donne-li ça pour moi.* Give her that for me. (SM) *Donne-lui mon numéro de téléphone.* Give him my phone number. (LF) *Il lui a demandé si il aurait voulu prendre un orphelin.* He asked him if he would like to take in an orphan. (AV) **Le boeuf lui a fait peur, tellement il était gros.* The bull scared him, it was so big. (LA, An94) *"WELL," il dit, et il lui conte l'affaire.* "Well," he say, and he tells him the story. (IV, An94) <***Loc:*** AV, EV, IV, JE, LA, LF, SL, SM, TB, VM, An94, Da84, Hi02>

lui[2] **(li)** [lɥi, ly, li] *pron.pers.* **1** *(obj. of prep.)* him *Temps en temps, je fais fun de lui.* Occasionally I make fun of him. (JE) *Tu peux pas rester fâché avec lui.* You can't stay mad at him. (LA) *Le magasin est pour lui.* The store is his. (TB) *Alle a commencé à rire après lui.* She began to laugh at him. (TB) **2** *(tonic)* he, him, it *Moi, j'étais élevée à Larose avec cannes, et lui était élevé avec les chevrettes.* Me, I was raised in Larose with sugar cane, and he was raised with shrimp. (JE) *C'est lui qui a bâti ça.* He's the one who built that. (SL) *Il reste pas là, il s'en va lui.* He's not staying. He's going away, he is. (JE) *Lui il parle bien français. Sa femme parle pas français.* He speaks French well. His wife doesn't speak French. (TB) *Mon et lui on cause tout le temps en français.* He and I always chat in French. (TB) **J'en ai plus que lui.* I have more than he has. (Da84) *Mon je les comprends mieux que lui.* I understand them better than he does. (TB) *Il s'a jamais livré. Ils l'ont tué, lui aussi.* He never surrendered. They killed him, too. (EV) <***Loc:*** AV, EV, IV, JE, LA, LF, SL, SM, TB, VM, An94, Da84, Hi02>

lui-même [lɥimɛ̃m] *pron.* himself, itself *Il avait je pense à peu près quarante ans la première maison que il a eu pour lui-même.* He was about 40, I think, [when he got] the first house that he got for himself. (EV) **Ça lui a pris dix-huit mois pour lui la faire, parce qu'il l'a fait proche tout lui-même.* It took him eighteen months to do it, because he did it almost all himself. (EV) <***Loc:*** EV, LF, TB, Hi02>

luméro ♦see **numéro**

lumière [lymjær] *n.f.* **1** light **2** lamp **3** lightbulb **4** flashlight ◊ **•lumière de rue** streetlight <Fa77> **•lumière électrique** electric light <Da84> <***Loc:*** EV, LA, SL, SM, TB, Da84, Fa77, Hi02>

LUNCH [lɔ̃tʃ, lɔ̃ʃ, lɛ̃tʃ, lʌntʃ] *n.m.* **1** lunch (esp. food carried to be eaten away from home) *Il apporte son LUNCH à l'école.* He brings his lunch to school. (VM) **2** sandwich or small meal (that is often purchased) *Tous les vendredis, ça aurait été du LOST BREAD ou ben des LUNCH de pain et de z-œufs.* Every Friday it would be French toast or egg sandwiches. (EV) <***Loc:*** EV, SB, SL, TB, VM, Da84, Lv88, Ph36>

lundi [lɛ̃di, lœ̃di] *n.m.* Monday <***Loc:*** AC, EV, SB, SL, TB, VM, Da84, Hi02>

lune [lyn] *n.f.* **1** moon **2** lunar cycle ◊ **•lune de miel** honeymoon <Hi02> <***Loc:*** EV, IB, IV, SL, An94, Da84, Hi02, La99>

luné, -e [lyne] *adj.* having a white spot or star on the forehead (of an animal) *Une pouliche lunée.* A filly with a star. (EV) <***Loc:*** EV, VM, Lv88>

lunette [lynɛt] *adj.* **1** having a white patch around one eye (of a cow; by extension, name for such a cow) **2** having a star or white mark between the eyes (of a cow; by extension, name for such a cow) <***Loc:*** SL, VM, Da84, Lv88>

lunettes [lynɛt] *n.f.pl.* **1** eyeglasses, spectacles *Peut-être j'aurai besoin de mes lunettes.* Maybe I will need my glasses. (SL) **2** goggles <***Loc:*** SL, SM, VM, An94, Da84, Fa77, Lv88>

luron [lyrɔ̃] *n.m.* imbecile, nitwit *Ça c'est un luron si j'en ai jamais vu un.* That's a nitwit if I've ever seen one. (TB) <***Loc:*** TB>

lutin [lytɛ̃] *n.m.* **1** elf, sprite *Les lutins...Eusse disait que c'était un petit* MIDGET *qui venait se cacher dans le grenier en l'air là.* Sprites, they used to say it was a little midget that came to hide in the attic up there. (TB) **2** ghost, spirit <***Loc:*** TB>

luttailler [lytaje] *v.intr.* to wrestle, scuffle *Les enfants voulaient pas arrêter de luttailler dans leur chambre.* The kids didn't want to quit wrestling in their room. (LA) <***Loc:*** LA, TB, VM, Lv88>

lutte [lyt] *n.f.* **1** wrestling match **2** struggle, contest <***Loc:*** Da84>

lutter [lyte] *v.intr.* **1** to wrestle *Les frères Baillargeon luttaient dessus le TV tous les samedis après-midi.* The Baillargeon brothers wrestled on television every Saturday afternoon. (LA) **2** to fight **Mon nonc', mon professeur Mademoiselle Sénégal m'a dit que je devrais rester à l'école et lutter pour le peuple acadien.* Uncle, my teacher Miss Senegal told me that I should stay in school and fight for the Acadian people. (ThCa: *Mille misères*) <***Loc:*** LA, VM, Da84, Fa77, ThCa>

lutteur [lytœr] *n.m.* wrestler <***Loc:*** Da84>

luxure [lyksyr] *n.f.* lust <***Loc:*** Da84>

LYNCH (**lyncher**) [lɪntʃ, lintʃe] *v.tr.* to lynch *On a lynché le nègre.* They lynched the black man. (SL) <***Loc:*** SL, Da84>

lyncher ♦see **LYNCH**

lys ♦see **lis**

M

ma ♦see **mon**

macaque [makak] *n.m./f.* **1** monkey **2** funny or silly person, clown **3** mischievous person *Ces enfants, c'est de vrais petits macaques.* These kids are real little monkeys (Lv88) **4** ugly, funny-looking person **5** [*pej.*] black person <***Loc:*** AV, LA, LF, SL, SM, VM, Da84, Hi02, Lv88>

macaquerie [makakri] *n.f. (usu. pl.)* **1** monkeyshines, funny antic, cutting up, mischievousness, trickery **2** foolishness, nonsense *Commence pas tes macaqueries.* Don't start your nonsense. (IB) ◊ **•faire des macaqueries** to be mischievous *Il a fait des macaqueries quand son papa est parti.* He got into mischief when his dad was gone. (SM) <SM, Lv88> **•faire des macaqueries dessus qqn** to ape, make fun of s.o. by imitation <SL> <***Loc:*** IB, SL, SM, VM, Da84, Lv88>

macaron ♦see **macaroni**

macaroni (**macaron**) [makarɔ̃ni, makarɔ̃] *n.m.* any pasta (macaroni, spaghetti, etc.) <***Loc:*** LF, TB, Da84>

mâchage [maʃaʒ] *n.m.* mastication, chewing <***Loc:*** SL, SM, VM, Da84, Lv88>

mâchailler ♦see **mâchouiller**

mâchement [maʃmɑ̃] *n.m.* chewing, mastication <***Loc:*** Da84>

mâche-pain (**masse-pain**) [maʃpɛ̃, maspɛ̃] *n.m.* **1** any kind of plain cake without icing (loaf cake, sponge cake, pound cake, ginger cake) **2** layer of a layer cake *On va faire un gâteau avec trois mâche-pains.* We'll make a cake with three layers. (EV) <***Loc:*** AC, EV, JE, SL, SM, Da84, Lv88>

mâcher[1] [maʃe] *v.tr.* to chew, masticate *Mâche pas ta gomme aussi fort.* Don't chew your gum so loud. (EV) ◊ **•mâcher sa chique** to chew one's cud (of a ruminant) <VM> <***Loc:*** EV, VM, Da84, Lv88>

mâcher[2] [maʃe] **I** *v.tr.* **1** to crush, mash *Mâcher une banane.* To mash a banana. (VM) *Mâcher des pommes de terres ou des patates.* To mash potatoes. (VM) **2** to bruise *J'ai échappé le bois et mâché mon pied.* I dropped the wood and bruised my foot. (Lv88) *Ça m'a mâché la main.* It bruised my hand. (VM) **II se mâcher** *v.pron.* to mash (e.g. one's finger) *Se mâcher le doigt.* To mash one's finger. (VM) <***Loc:*** VM, Da84, Lv88>

machette [maʃɛt] *n.f.* machete, heavy-bladed knife used mostly for cutting underbrush <***Loc:*** Da84>

mâchiller ♦see **mâchouiller**

machin [maʃɛ̃] *n.m.* thing, thingamajig <***Loc:*** Da84>

machinalement [maʃinalmɑ̃] *adv.* **1** mechanically, instinctively *Je parle français machinalement.* I speak French instinctively. (Lv88) **2** in a slipshod fashion, carelessly *Son ouvrage est fait tout machinalement.* His work is done carelessly. (Lv88) <***Loc:*** LF, SJ, Da84, Lv88>

machine [maʃin] *n.f.* **1** machine, appliance **2** engine, motor *Ça va prendre à peu près deux heures pour installer la nouvelle machine.* It will take about two hours to install the new motor. (LA) **3** tractor **4** thing, thingamajig *Eh bien, t'as trouvé cette machine-là.* All right, so you found that thing. (VM) ◊ **•machine à canne** canecutter <AS> **•machine à coudre** sewing machine <JE, Da84> **•machine à écrire** typewriter <Da84> **•machine à vapeur** steam engine <Da84> **•machine à z-herbe** lawn mower <LF> **•fait à la machine** machine-made <Da84> <***Loc:*** AC, AS, EV, JE, LF, TB, VM, Da84, Hi02, Lv88>

machinerie [maʃinri] *n.f.* **1** machinery **2** underhand work, scheme, secret plotting *Je connais qu'il y a quelque machinerie là.* I know there is some scheme there. (VM) <***Loc:*** JE, LF, VM, Da84, Lv88>

mâchoire [maʃwar] *n.f.* jaw, jawbone <***Loc:*** Da84>

mâchoiron [maʃwarɔ̃] *n.m.* **1** spotted catfish, Opelousas catfish **2** saltwater catfish, Gafftopsail catfish *Un mâchoiron là, il vient pas gros. Il est un poisson qu'a trois piquants mais ils sont mauvais mauvais, il pique avec.* A gafftopsail catfish doesn't get too big. It's a fish that has three spines that are quite bad, he sticks with them. (TB) **3** yellow catfish, mud catfish ◊ **•mâchoiron de passe** ***a*** channel catfish (freshwater catfish) ***b*** Gafftopsail (saltwater catfish) <LF> <***Loc:*** AL, JE, LF, SL, SM, TB, VM, Gu00, Lv88>

mâchouiller (**mâchailler, mâchiller**) [maʃuje, maʃaje, maʃije] *v.tr.* **1** to chew slowly, with pleasure *Mâchouille pas comme ça, tu peux en avoir un autre si tu l'avales.* Don't keep on chewing like that, you can have another if you swallow it. (VM) **2** to gum, chew with difficulty, chew without or as if without teeth ◊ **•mâchouiller ses mots** to mumble <EV, LA, VM> <***Loc:*** EV, LA, SM, VM, Da84, Lv88>

mâchure [maʃyr] *n.f.* **1** bruise **2** blister <***Loc:*** EV, JE, LA, LF, SM, TB, VM, Lv88>

mâchurer [maʃyre] *v.tr.* to bruise *J'ai le bras mâchuré.* I have a bruised arm. (VM) <***Loc:*** VM, Lv88>

maçon [masɔ̃] *n.m.* mason, bricklayer, brickmason ◊ **•franc-maçon** freemason <Da84> <***Loc:*** LA, Da84>

maçonnage [masɔ̃naʒ] *n.f.* masonry (stonework or brickwork as done by a mason) <***Loc:*** Da84>

maçonne [masɔ̃n] *n.f.* **1** masonry *Il travaille à la maçonne.* He works in masonry. (SM) **2** masonry (stonework or brickwork as done by a mason) *La maçonne des piliers est pas bien fait parce qu'il y a pas assez de ciment dedans.* The masonry of the pillars is not done correctly because there is not enough cement in it. (TB) <***Loc:*** JE, SM, TB, VM, Lv88>

maçonnerie [masɔ̃nri] *n.f.* masonry ◊ **•franc-maçonnerie** freemasonry <Da84> <***Loc:*** Da84>

maçonneur [masɔ̃nœr] *n.m.* mason, bricklayer <***Loc:*** VM, Lv88>

macorenche [makorɛ̃tʃ, mɔ̃kɔrɛ̃tʃ] *n.m.* any big wrench <***Loc:*** TB, VM, Di32>

macornage (**amacornage, mancornage**) [makɔrnaʒ, markɔ̃naʒ, mɔrkɔ̃naʒ, amakɔrnaʒ, mɑ̃kɔrnaʒ] *n.m./f.* **1** coupling, yoking (of animals) **2** living together (without benefit of marriage) *Ils sont dans une amacornage.* They are living together (without being married). (JE) <***Loc:*** JE, LF, SM, VM, Da84, La99, Lv88>

macorne [makɔrn, markɔ̃n, mɔ̃kɔrn] *n.m./f.* **1** tie or leather strap for tying two oxen together by the horns **2** concubine <***Loc:*** JE, SM, VM, Lv88>

macorné, -e [mɑ̃kɔrne] *adj.* living together (without benefit of marriage) *Ils sont pas mariés. Ils sont juste macornés.* They aren't married. They're just living together. (SM) <SM> <***Loc:*** SM, VM>

macorner (**amacorner, mancorner**) [makɔrne, mɑ̃kɔrne, markɔ̃ne, amakɔrne] **I** *v.tr.* **1** to yoke *La terre était assez dure qu'il fallut que je mancorne les deux bœufs ensemble pour haler la charrue.* The ground was so hard that I had to yoke two oxen together to pull the plow. (VM) **2** to attach, join (two things) together *J'ai mancorné les deux deux-par-quatre ensemble parce qu'il me manquait une sole.* I joined two two-by-fours together because I was short a beam. (VM) **II se macorner** *v.pron.* to live together (without benefit of marriage) *Elle va s'amacorner avec lui.* She's going to move in with him. (JE) ◊ **•macorner avec** to live with (a romantic partner) without benefit of marriage *C'est pas son légitime, ça macorne avec.* He is not her husband, he's just living with her. (VM) <VM> <***Loc:*** AV, JE, LF, SL, SM, TB, VM, Da84, La99, Lv88>

macreuse [makrøz] *n.f.* pied-billed grebe <***Loc:*** Lv88, Re31>

macriau ♦see **maquereau**

madame [madɑ̃m] *n.f.* Mrs., madam ◊ **•Madame Grands Doigts** imaginary character in stories designed to frighten children as a way of getting them to obey <SM, Lv88> <***Loc:*** AC, AV, EV, LA, SM, Da84, Hi02, Lv88>

madeleine [madlɛ̃n] *n.f.* stew made of Irish potatoes <***Loc:*** SJ>

mademoiselle [madmwazɛl] *n.f.* **1** miss, maiden, young lady **2** yellowtail fish <***Loc:*** Da84, Hi02, Re63>

madrier [madrije] *n.m.* beam, sill, joist, rafter, heavy timber (used in construction) <***Loc:*** Da84, Hi02>

madrille [madrij] *n.f.* armadillo <***Loc:*** EV, LA, VM>

maganer [magɑ̃ne, margɑ̃ne] *v.tr.* **1** to handle roughly, shake *Je l'ai bien magané.* I gave him a good shake. (VM) **2** to mistreat, abuse *Ce vieux homme magane ses animaux.* That old man mistreats his cattle. (TB) <***Loc:*** JE, LF, TB, VM, Lv88>

maganière [magɑ̃jær] *n.f.* corncrib <***Loc:*** SL>

magasin (**gamasin**) [magazɛ̃, gamazɛ̃] *n.m.* **1** barn *Et t'avais une place pour tirer les vaches aussi pour quand t'allais le matin. C'était tout dans la même hangar, dans le même magasin.* And you had a place for milking the cows too for when you went there in the morning. It was all in the same barn. (LF) **2** storehouse, warehouse *Je mets mon maïs dans un magasin.* I put my corn in a storehouse. (Gu00) **3** store (of any type: supermarket, hardware store, clothing store, etc.) *J'ai jamais eu de retour de cet argent que j'avais investi dans son magasin.* I never had a return on the money I had invested in his store. (EV) *J'avais monté un magasin de linge.* I had started a clothing store. (LF) *Pendant longtemps je faisais du roux mais maintenant c'est un tas plus facile aller au magasin.* For a long time I used to make roux, but now it's a whole lot easier to go to the store (to get it). (SL) **4** shop, boutique ◊ **•magasin à ferraille** hardware store <LF, Lv88> **•magasin de campagne** country store <SL> **•magasin de {à} foin** ***a*** hay barn ***b*** barn <AV, IB, TB> **•magasin de grainage** seed store <Da84> **•magasin de groceries** grocery store, food store <IV, LF, TB> **•magasin de {à} maïs** ***a*** corncrib ***b*** barn <AV, LF, SB, TB, Da84, Lv88> <***Loc:*** AC, AV, EV, IB, IV, JE, LA, LF, SB, SL, SM, TB, VM, Da84, Gu00, Hi02, Lv88>

magasiner [magazine] *v.intr.* to shop, go shopping <***Loc:*** VM, Gr86>

magasinier [magazinje] *n.m.* storekeeper <***Loc:*** SM, VM, Da84, Lv88>

magazine [magazin] *n.f.* magazine <***Loc:*** Da84>

mage [maʒ] *n.m.* [*eccl.*] magus, wise man <***Loc:*** Da84>

magique [maʒik] *adj.* magical **Ein Cadien est ein tas de forces mystérieuses et magiques.* A Cajun is a bunch of mysterious and magic forces. (ThCa: *Mille misères*) <***Loc:*** Da84, ThCa>

magnane [mɑ̃jɑ̃n, maɲɑ̃n] *n.m.* brandy, esp. a drink of brandy taken in the morning **Boire la magnane.* To have one's morning brandy. (Re54) ◊ **•prendre la magnane** to have a drink <JE, Lv88> <***Loc:*** JE, Lv88, Re54>

magnatiser [magnetize] *v.tr.* to hypnotize, magnetize, mesmerize <***Loc:*** Da84>

magnatiseur [magnetizœr] *n.m.* hypnotist <***Loc:*** SJ, Da84>

magnée [mɑ̃je] *n.f.* handful <***Loc:*** VM>

magnésie [mɑ̃nezi] *n.f.* magnesia, Epsom salt *Lait de magnésie.* Milk of magnesia. (VM) <***Loc:*** LF, VM, Da84>

magnifier [maɲifje] *v.tr.* to magnify, enlarge <***Loc:*** Da84>

magnifique [mɑ̃nifik] *adj.* magnificent, wonderful, splendid, fine, great *C'est magnifique à rester ici dès qu'y a pas d'ouragan, mais dès qu'il y a des ouragans c'est pas trop* NICE. It's wonderful to live here when there are no hurricanes, but when there are hurricanes it's not so nice. (JE) *Comment* *les affaires? —Magnifique!* How's business? —Fantastic! (SM) <***Loc:*** EV, JE, LA, SM, VM, Da84, Hi02>

magnifiquement [mɑ̃nifikmɑ̃] *adv.* magnificently, wonderfully, splendidly <***Loc:*** Da84>

magnolia [magnolja] *n.* **1** *(m.)* magnolia tree **2** *(f.)* magnolia flower <***Loc:*** TB, Da84, Gr86, Hi02>

maguiller ♦see **marguiller**

mai [mɛ, me] *n.m.* May <***Loc:*** TB, Da84, Hi02>

maîche ♦see **mèche**[1]

maigre [mɛg(r)] *adj.* **1** skinny, thin *Et alle était tout le temps malade, tout le temps malade, alle a venu maigre maigre. Alle mangeait pas.* And she was sick all the time, sick all the time, she got so skinny. She wasn't eating. (TB) **2** lean, low-fat *La barbue est plus maigre que les goujons et les mâchoirons.* Blue catfish are leaner than yellow catfish and Opelousas catfish. (LA) **3** meatless, prepared without meat ◊ **•maigre comme une aigrette {un pique-bois / un tasso} / maigre comme une vieille vache / maigre comme un manche à balai {un poteau de barrière}** very thin *Il est maigre comme un tasseau.* He is as skinny as a rail. (SB) <AC, EV, LA, SB, SL, SM, La99> **•faire maigre** to abstain from eating meat *Les vendredis et les mercredis de Carême, il faulait faire maigre.* On Fridays and Wednesdays in Lent, we had to abstain from eating meat. (AC) <AC, Da84> <***Loc:*** AC, AL, EV, LA, SL, SM, TB, VM, Da84, Hi02, La99>

maigréchine [megreʃin, megriʃin, megrəʃin] *adj.* thin, skinny, scrawny, puny *Alle a été malade et alle a resté maigréchine.* She was sick and she remained scrawny. (TB) <***Loc:*** JE, SJ, SL, TB, VM, Da84>

maigreur [megrœr] *n.f.* leanness, thinness <***Loc:*** Da84>

maigriller [megrije] *v.intr.* to become very thin *Garde comme il a maigrillé, pauvre bête!* Look how thin he's gotten, poor thing! (AC) <***Loc:*** AC>

maigrir [megrir] *v.intr.* to lose weight, get lean, become thin *Alle était tellement affaiblie et alle avait tellement maigri, la pauvre bête, jusqu'à alle caracolait.* She was so weakened and she had lost so much weight, the poor thing, that she was staggering. (LF) ◊ **•se faire maigrir** to lose weight *Il est après essayer de se faire maigrir.* He's trying to lose weight. (LA) <LA, Da84> <***Loc:*** AV, LA, LF, Da84>

MAIL [meɪl, mɛl] *n.m.* mail <***Loc:*** AC> e[ɪ]

maillage [majaʒ] *n.m.* mesh, netting <***Loc:*** TB>

maille [maj] *n.f.* **1** link (of a chain), knot (of mesh), stitch (in knitting) **2** node, joint, segment (of grass, plant) *Épluche-moi une maille de canne.* Cut a segment of sugar cane for me. (VM) **3** panel of net constituting part of a seine *Le poisson va, il s'enfonce dans la grosse maille, et là il reste pris.* The fish goes, he goes right into the big panel of the net, and he stays stuck there. (JE) **4** rocker, blade, or runner (curved wooden bottom) of a rocking chair ◊ **•maille du dos** vertebra <Lv88> <***Loc:*** EV, JE, TB, VM, Da84, Lv88>

mailler [maje] *v.tr.* to make mesh (for a net) *Là alle prendait son* SHUTTLE, *son aiguille à mailler, alle avait un petit bâton, alle faisait ses nœuds, alle commençait peut-être avec je sais pas combien de tant de nœuds, et là chaque fois qu'alle faisait un tour, mettait une ou deux mailles sur le filet de plus, jusqu'à qu'alle faisait un épervier.* Then she took her shuttle, her needle for making mesh, she had a small stick, she made her knots, she started with I don't know how many knots, and each time she made a circle she put one or two more links of mesh on the net, until she had made a castnet. (LF) <***Loc:*** LF, TB>

maillet [majɛ, maje] *n.m.* **1** mallet **2** type of big sledgehammer <***Loc:*** AC, EV>

mailloche [majɔʃ] *n.f.* unsuccessful biscuit <***Loc:*** VM>

main [mɛ̃] *n.f.* **1** hand **2** paw **3** handwriting ◊ **•à (la) main** ***a*** handy, near-at-hand *Mets ça à la main.* Keep it handy. (VM) *Va, c'est à la main, t'as pas besoin de chercher pour.* Go ahead, it's readily accessible, you don't need to look for it. (VM) *Quand je peux pas dormir, j'ai toujours mon crochet à main.* When I cannot sleep, I always have my crochet handy. (Lv88) ***b*** in mind *J'ai pas ça à la main, je vas dire ça plus tard.* It's not coming to mind, I'll say it later. (Lv88) ***c*** tame, docile, manageable *Le cheval est à la main.* The horse is manageable. (VM) *Ce petit cheval est pas à main du tout.* This little horse isn't docile at all. (Lv88) <VM, Da84, Lv88> **•à toutes mains** skillful, handy *Il est à toutes mains.* He is handy. (Lv88) <Lv88> **•avoir la main pour** to be expert at, adept at *J'ai pas la main pour coudre.* I'm not adept at sewing. (VM) <VM> **•fait à la main** handmade *Follait que ça soye tout fait à la main.* It had to all be done by hand. (LF) <LF, VM, Da84> **•mettre la main** to lend a hand *Si elle a de besoin, son père va mettre la main.* If she needs, her father will lend a hand. (LA) <LA, Da84> **•pleine main** handful *Va me chercher une pleine main de farine.* Go get me a handful of flour. (VM) <VM> **•seconde {deuxième} main** used, secondhand *Il l'a achetée seconde main.* He bought it used. (IB) <IB, LA, TB, Lv88> **•un coup de main** ***a*** a helping hand *Tu peux me donner un coup de main demain?* Can you give me a helping hand tomorrow? (LA) ***b*** a neighborhood cooperative effort *Vieux M. Sonnier était trop malade pour rentrer son maïs, ça fait ses voisins ont fait un coup de main pour l'aider.* Old Mr. Sonnier was too sick to harvest his corn, so his neighbors got together to do it for him. (LA) <LA, Da84, La99> <***Loc:*** AC, EV, IB, JE, LA, SL, TB, VM, Da84, Hi02, La99, Lv88>

mainette [mɛ̃nɛt] *n.f.* little hand <***Loc:*** JE>

maintée [mɛ̃te] *n.f.* handful <***Loc:*** EV, LA, VM, Hi02>

maintenant [mɛ̃tnɑ̃] *adv.* now, nowadays *Pendant longtemps je faisais du roux mais maintenant c'est un tas plus facile aller au magasin.* For a long time I used to make roux, but now it's a whole lot easier to go to the store. (SL) <***Loc:*** IB, SL, TB, Da84, Wh83>

maintien [mɛ̃tjɛ̃] *n.m.* upkeep, maintenance <***Loc:*** Da84>

maire [mær] *n.m.* mayor ◊ **•maire de ville** mayor <Da84> <***Loc:*** Da84>

mais[1] [mɛ, me] *n.* restriction, exception *Quand elle vient, il y tout le temps des mais.* When she comes over, there are always restrictions. (VM) <***Loc:*** VM>

mais[2] [mɛ, me] *conj.* **1** but **Et il sautait et il sautait, mais il venait pas près du raisin, et il s'est découragé.* And he jumped and jumped, but he didn't get close to the grapes and he got discouraged. (LA, An94) **Je suis surement pas un conteur de contes, mais j'ai appris des contes, quand j'étais petit avec mon père et ma mère.* I'm certainly not a storyteller, but I learned some stories, when I was young with my father and my mother. (EV, An94) **Il voulait s'en revenir, mais il pouvait pas, parce qu'il avait pas moyen de sortir.* He wanted to come home, but he couldn't, because he had no way to get out. (AC, An94) **Il a été voir s'il pouvait trouver son chèque mais il était* GONE. He went to see if he could find his check but it was gone. (LA, An94) **Je t'ai pas jamais vue, mais je connais que t'es réellement une belle fille.* I've never seen you, but I know that you are really a beautiful girl. (EV, An94) **Lapin, je voulais te brûler, mais je veux te jeter dans les éronces-là!* Rabbit, I wanted to burn you, but I want to throw you in the briars there! (SM, An94) *On espérait une grosse pluie, mais ç'a juste mouillassé un petit brin.* We were hoping for a big rain, but it just drizzled a little bit. (Gu00) *Il devait se marier, mais il s'est dégoûté.* He was supposed to get married, but he changed his mind. (Lv88) **2** well *"Quoi c'est que tu fais avec ça?" "Mais," il dit, "je mange ça."* "What do you do with that?" "Well," he says, "I eat that." (loc?) **Mais ça, c'est des drôles de noms quand même!* Well, those are strange names indeed! (SM, An94) **•mais jamais** oh, but never <Da84> **•mais là!** well there! <La99> **•mais non** but no <Da84> **•mais oui** but yes <Da84> <***Loc:*** AC, EV, IB, JE, LA, LF, SB, SJ, SL, SM, TB, VM, An94, Da84, Gu00, Hi02, La99, Lv88, Wh83>

maïs [maji, mai] *n.m.* corn, maize ◊ **•maïs dur** feed corn <SL> **•maïs moulé** ground corn <TB> **•maïs sucré** sweet corn <Lv88> **•maïs tendre** ***a*** corn, sweet corn ***b*** roasting corn <CL, EV, SL, Da84, Lv88> **•coton maïs** ***a*** corncob *En bas du baril, tu mettais comme des coton maïs, tu connais,* CORNCOB. *Tu faisais feu. Ça, là boucanait en haut. Et ça boucane la viande.* In the bottom of the barrel you would put corncobs. You'd make a fire. That would smoke the meat above. (VM) ***b*** corn on the stalk <CL, EV, SM, VM, Da84, Lv88> <***Loc:*** AC, CL, EV, SL, SM, TB, VM, Da84, Gu00, Hi02, Lv88>

maison [mezɔ̃] *n.f.* house, home ◊ **•maison à chien** doghouse <SL> **•maison à z-oiseau** birdhouse <LA> **•maison d'arbres** hut <SL> **•maison debout** house with exterior walls built of vertical boards <VM> **•maison d'école** school house <Da84> **•maison de cour** courthouse, court of justice <LF, SL, VM, Da84, Lv88> **•maison de crapaud** mushroom, toadstool <AV, IB, La99> **•maison de putain** whorehouse <Da84> **•maison de santé** nursing home <Lv88> **•maison de SHOW** cinema, movie theater <Lv88> **•maison de vieux** retirement home, old folks' home, nursing home <IB, LA, Lv88> **•à la maison** at home *Après la messe on va aller à la maison boire du café.* After mass, we'll go home and drink coffee. (JE) <JE, Da84> <***Loc:*** AC, AV, EV, IB, JE, LA, LF, SL, TB, VM, Da84, Hi02, La99, Lv88>

maître [mɛt(r)] *n.m.* master, owner, boss ◊ **•maître d'école** school teacher *Il y avait dans les deux, trois cents enfants pour rien qu'un maître d'école.* There were two, three hundred children for just one school teacher. (TB) <EV, TB, Fa77, Hi02> **•maître et majeur** ***a*** at or beyond the age of majority ***b*** old enough to be responsible for one's own actions <La99> **•t'es pas maître ici** you can't tell me what to do <La99> <***Loc:*** EV, PQ, TB, Da84, Fa77, Hi02, La99>

maîtresse [metrɛs] *n.f.* **1** teacher **2** owner **La maîtresse de la maison a sorti.* The lady of the house came out. (LA, An94) **3** mistress ◊ **•maîtresse d'école** ***a*** primary school teacher ***b*** [*pej.*] know-it-all <AC, AV, EV, LF, PQ, Hi02> <***Loc:*** AC, AV, EV, LF, PQ, Da84, Hi02, La99>

majeur[1]**, -e** [maʒœr, maʒɔr] *adj.* **1** great in number, size, or extent *La majeure partie disont ça.* Most people say that. (VM) **2** adult, of legal age *Il est maître et majeur. Il peut faire ce qu'il veut.* He is of legal age. He can do what he wants. (VM) ◊ **•la majeure partie** the greater part, for the most part <Da84> **•la majeure partie du temps** most of the time <Da84> <***Loc:*** VM, Da84, La99>

majeur[2] [maʒœr, maʒɔr] *n.* adult <***Loc:*** Da84>

majorité [maʒɔrite] *n.f.* **1** majority, greatest number or amount *Pas tout le temps,* BUT *la majorité du temps.* Not all of the time, but the majority of the time. (TB) **2** adulthood <***Loc:*** TB, Da84>

mal[1] [mal] *n.m.* **1** bad, wrong **2** pain, sore, ache *Il a des mals tout partout.* He has pains all over. (VM) **3** illness, disease, sickness *Je les traite pour les mals des glandes.* I treat them for gland problems. (TB) **4** evil *Le bien et le mal.* Good and Evil. (LA) ◊ **•mal anglais** ***a*** fistula of withers, saddle sore *Mon cheval avait le mal anglais.* My horse had saddle sores. (LA) ***b*** [disease] shingles <EV, LA, VM, Da84> **•mal au cœur** nausea <SL, Da84> **•mal au {de} ventre** bellyache, stomachache <SL, Da84> **•mal aux dents** toothache <Da84> **•mal aux reins** backache, lower back pain *J'ai coupé des herbes toute la grande journée. Quand je m'ai couché le soir, j'avais mal aux reins si mauvais, je pouvais pas dormir.* I cut grass the whole day long. When I went to bed that night, I had such terrible lower back pain that I couldn't sleep. (EV) *T'as mal aux reins?* Does your back hurt? (LF) <EV, LF, Da84> **•mal blanc** mouth sore in an infant <VM> **•mal de cerveau** sinus trouble <Da84> **•mal de cœur** heart trouble <Da84> **•mal de corne** malady of cows remedied by cutting off the horns <VM> **•mal d'estomac** stomachache, bellyache <Da84> **•mal de gorge** sore throat <Da84> **•mal de lac** quittor, inflammation of the hooves (of horses, etc.) <VM> **•mal de marais** cancerous tumor in horses <VM> **•mal de mer** seasickness <Da84> **•mal de tête** headache <LF, SL, Da84, Hi02> **•mal d'oreille** earache <Da84> **•mau de vénure** sickness that has no apparent cause <VM, Di32> **•à demi mal** half bad <Da84> **•avoir du mal** ***a*** to ache, be sore, hurt *Il voulait pas prendre la médecine. [...] "Pas de ça," il dit. Hier soir, une fois qu'il m'a dit qu'il avait du mal, hier il m'a demandé pour une.* He didn't want to take the medicine. "None of that," he said. Last night, once he told me he was in pain, he asked me for one. (TB) ***b*** to have difficulties, have trouble *J'ai du mal à comprendre pourquoi il aurait fait ça.* I have trouble understanding why he would have done that. (LA) <LA, TB, Da84> **•de mal en pire** from bad to worse *Entre l'ouragan et les maringouins, ça va de mal en pire.* Between the hurricane and the mosquitoes, it's going from bad to worse. (EV) <EV, Da84> **•faire (du) mal** to hurt, pain, ache **Ça fait mal.* It hurts. (Da84) <Da84, Hi02> **•haut mal** epilepsy <Da84> **•se faire (du) mal** to hurt o.s. **Des fois, je tombe par terre et je me fais mal à ma tête.* Sometimes I fall down and I hurt my head. (EV, An94) <EV, An94, Da84> <***Loc:*** EV, LA, LF, SL, TB, VM, An94, Da84, Di32, Hi02, Lv88>

mal[2] [mal] *adv.* **1** badly, wrongly *Si elle est mal chantée, on va la rechanter.* If it is badly sung, we will sing it again. (VM) *Ça va terminer mal.* That's going to end badly. (VM) **2** improperly *Il a mal manié ses affaires.* He handled his affaires improperly. (LA) **3** unfavorably *Leur affaire va mal finir.* Their deal will finish unfavorably. (LA) **4** poorly *J'ai mal dormi hier soir.* I slept poorly (insufficiently) last night. (LA) *On était mal emprovisionné pour l'hiver.* We were poorly provisioned for the winter. (LA) ◊ **•mal à main** ***a*** not handy, out of reach ***b*** hard to control ***c*** disobliging, rather unlikable <IB, JE, Di32, Lv88> **•mal à propos** improper, inappropriate *Je m'ai choqué parce qu'il disait des affaires mal-à-propos.* I got mad because he was saying improper things. (VM) <LA, VM, Da84> **•mal à son aise** ill at ease <Da84> **•mal égal** uneven <Da84> **•mal élevé / malélevé** ill-bred, ill-mannered, impolite, rude *Un enfant mal élevé.* An ill-mannered child. (EV) <EV, Da84> **•mal en train** ***a*** in a bad mood ***b*** fatigued, dejected, out of sorts ***c*** not very bright *T'es sûr mal en train pour pas comprendre ça.* You sure are not very bright for not understanding that. (VM) <VM, Lv88> **•mal fait** poorly done, badly done, badly made *Ils ont mal fait leur affaire.* They made their plans poorly. (LA) <LA, Da84> **•plus mal** worse *Si ça va pas plus mal demain, on pourra finir.* If it doesn't go worse tomorrow, we will be able to finish. (LA) <LA, Da84> <***Loc:*** EV, IB, JE, LA, VM, Da84, Di32, Hi02, Lv88>

malade[1] [malad] *adj.* sick, ill, unhealthy *Et cette femme là, cette fille là alle restait malade toute sa vie.* And that woman, that girl stayed sick all her life. (TB) *Il était malade de son cœur.* He had heart problems. (EV) ◊ **•malade comme un carencro {chien}** very sick <VM, La99> **•se faire {se rendre} malade** to make o.s. sick *Mange pas de trop, tu vas te faire malade.* Don't eat too much, you'll make yourself sick. (LA) <LA, Da84> <***Loc:*** AC, AL, EV, LA, TB, VM, Da84, Hi02, La99>

malade[2] [malad] *n.* sick, ill, unhealthy person ◊ **•faire le malade** to pretend to be sick *Il faisait le malade, mais je l'ai vu à la partie de pelote le même soir.* He was pretending to be sick, but I saw him at the baseball game that same night. (LA) <LA, Da84> <***Loc:*** AC, LA, Da84>

maladie [maladi, maladiz] *n.f.* sickness, illness, disease ◊ **•maladie de cerveau** sinus trouble <Da84> **•maladie de cœur** heart trouble, heart disease <LF, Da84> **•maladie de poitrine** tuberculosis <SM, VM> **•maladie de sang / mauvaise maladie** syphilis <SM, VM, Lv88> **•maladie de {du} sucre** diabetes <AV, LA, VM, Da84, Hi02, Lv88> **•maladie tournante** [disease of animals] sturdy, blind staggers <VM, Lv88> **•maladie d'os** rickets, rachitis <LF, TB, VM> **•maladie de yeux rouges** pinkeye, conjunctivitis <VM> <***Loc:*** AV, LA, LF, SM, TB, VM, Da84, Hi02, Lv88>

maladif, -ive [maladif, -iv] *adj.* unhealthy, sickly *Son dernier petit était beaucoup maladif.* Her last child was very sickly. (LA) <***Loc:*** JE, LA, Da84>

maladroit, -e [maladrwa, -at] *adj.* awkward, clumsy *Pauvre enfant, il était tellement maladroit.* Poor child, he was so clumsy. (LA) <***Loc:*** LA, Da84>

maladvisé, -e [maladvize] *adj.* ill-advised, misled *Ça serait maladvisé de parler trop vite avec la maîtresse.* It would be ill-advised to speak too soon with the teacher. (LA) <***Loc:*** LA, Da84>

malaise [malɛz] *n.m.* discomfort, uneasiness <***Loc:*** Da84>

malaisé, -e [maleze] *adj.* difficult, not easy **La* REEL *était une danse qui était malaisée à danser, puis là, ça prenait des bonnes jambes.* The reel was a dance that was hard to do, and then it took good legs. (EV, An84) ◊ **•être malaisé pour** to be unable to, be at a loss to, find difficult to *Mais je suis malaisé pour vous dire quoi c'est.* But I'm unable to tell you what it is. (VM) <VM> <***Loc:*** EV, SL, VM, An84, Da84>

malajusté, -e[1] [malaʒyste] *adj.* poorly adjusted, badly fitted *Une jupe malajustée.* A poorly fitting skirt. (VM) <***Loc:*** VM, Da84>

malajusté, -e[2] [malaʒyste] *n.* misfit, maladjusted person <***Loc:*** Da84>

malakoff [malakɔf] *n.m.* **1** crinoline **2** hoop skirt <***Loc:*** VM, Lv88>

malaria (maléria) [malarja, malerja, maralja, marelja] *n.f.* malaria <***Loc:*** VM, Da84>

malarienne [malarjɛ̃n] *adj.* ◊ **•fièvre malarienne** malaria <JE> <***Loc:*** JE>

malattriqué, -e [malatrike] *adj.* badly made, shoddy <***Loc:*** Hi02>

malchance [malʃɑ̃s] *n.f.* **1** bad luck, misfortune **2** mishap <***Loc:*** TB, Da84, Lv88>

malchanceux, -euse [malʃɑ̃sø, -øz] *adj.* unlucky, unfortunate *La valse du malchanceux.* The unlucky man's waltz. (ch: *La valse du malchanceux*) <***Loc:*** Da84>

malcommode [malkɔ̃mɔd] *adj.* **1** inconvenient, unpleasant, troublesome *C'est malcommode d'être pauvre, mais c'est pas un déshonneur.* It's inconvenient to be poor, but it's not dishonorable. (Proverbial) **2** uncomfortable *Une chaise malcommode.* An uncomfortable chair. (SJ) <***Loc:*** IB, SJ, Da84>

malcompris [malkɔ̃pri] *n.m.* misunderstanding *C'était tout un malcompris qu'a occasionné la bataille.* It was all a misunderstanding that caused the fight. (AC) <***Loc:*** AC, Da84>

malcontent[1], -e [malkɔ̃tɑ̃, -ɑ̃t] *adj.* unhappy, discontented *Elle était malcontente quand ils ont passé ce chemin devant chez elle.* She was very unhappy when they ran that road in front of her house. (VM) <***Loc:*** VM, Da84>

malcontent[2], -e [malkɔ̃tɑ̃, -ɑ̃t] *n.* discontented person, malcontent <***Loc:*** VM, Da84>

mâle[1] [mal] *adj.* male *Ça, c'est un canard mâle. Il a une tête verte.* That's a male duck. It has a green head. (VM) ◊ **•mâle chat** tomcat <VM> **•mâle z-oie** gander <VM> <***Loc:*** VM, Da84, Lv88>

mâle[2] [mal] *n.m.* male *C'est le mâle qui est le plus beau dans les oiseaux.* In birds, it is the male that is more beautiful. (EV) <***Loc:*** EV, Da84>

malédictieux [malediksjø] *adj.* malicious <***Loc:*** JE>

malédiction [malediksjɔ̃] *n.f.* curse, malediction <***Loc:*** Da84>

malému [malɛ̃my] *adj.* scowling, ill-tempered, ungracious <***Loc:*** JE>

malengueulé, -e [malɑ̃gøle, malɑ̃dʒøle] *adj.* rude, rough, coarse *J'aime pas aller chez eux. C'est du monde malengueulé.* I don't like to go to their house. They are rough people. (LF) <***Loc:*** LF, Lv88>

malentendu [malɑ̃tɑ̃dy] *n.m.* misunderstanding <***Loc:*** Da84>

maléria ♦see **malaria**

malfacteur, malfaicteur ♦see **malfaiteur**

malfaire[1] [malfær] *v.intr.* to do wrong, cut up, raise hell *Ils sont toujours dans les chemins après chercher à malfaire.* They're always in the streets looking to cause trouble. (ch: *Je m'endors*) <***Loc:*** Da84, Hi02>

malfaire[2] ♦see **malfait**

malfaisance [malfəzɑ̃s] *n.f.* mischief, malfeasance <***Loc:*** Da84>

malfaisant[1], -e [malfəzɑ̃, malfezɑ̃, -ɑ̃t] *adj.* mischievous *Un fibi, ça veut dire quelqu'un qu'est méchant ou malfaisant. Il est un fibi.* A fibi, that means someone who is mean or mischievous. A fibi. (LF) <***Loc:*** LF, Da84>

malfaisant[2], -e [malfəzɑ̃, malfezɑ̃, -ɑ̃t] *n.m.* criminal, evildoer *Mais à part de ça y avait pas de malfaisants dans la ville, c'était tout du monde qu'avait été élevé là.* But aside from that, there were no evildoers in the city, it was all people who had been raised there. (TB) <***Loc:*** TB>

malfait (malfaire) [malfe, malfɛ, malfær] *n.m.* evil deed, crime <***Loc:*** JE, VM, Da84, Lv88>

malfaiteur (malfacteur, malfaicteur) [malfɛtœr, malfaktœr, malfɛktœr] *n.m.* evildoer, criminal *Ces malfaicteurs ont revolé ma faucheuse.* Those ne'er-do-wells stole my lawnmower again. (LA) <***Loc:*** JE, VM, Da84, Hi02>

malformé, -e [malfɔrme] *adj.* misshapen, deformed, badly shaped or formed *Son pied a été malformé.* His foot was misshapen. (EV) <***Loc:*** EV, Da84>

malfoutu [malfuty] *adj.* **1** in bad shape, messed up, in a fix, in trouble *On est malfoutu depuis l'ouragan Katrina.* We are in bad shape since Hurricane Katrina. (VM) **2** worn out *Je me sentais malfoutu après mon ouvrage.* I felt worn out after doing my work. (LF) **3** sickly *Elle est malfoutu depuis qu'elle a eu la grippe.* She's sickly since she has had the flu. (VM) <***Loc:*** LF, SL, VM>

malgré [malgre] *prep.* in spite of *Malgré le mauvais temps, on a été pêcher.* In spite of the bad weather, we went fishing. (EV) ◊ **•malgré tout** in spite of it all *Malgré tout, ils sont restés ensemble.* In spite of it all, they stayed together. (EV) <EV, Da84> **•malgré que** even though, although *C'était une bonne vie. Malgré qu'on pouvait pas peut-être sortir des automobiles ou des bogheis mais ils avaient une bonne vie.* It was a good life. Even though people couldn't go out in cars or buggies, they still had a good life. (SB) *Malgré qu'il s'a détruit, il a été enterré dans de la terre sacrée.* Even though he committed suicide, he was buried in sacred ground. (LA) <LA, SB> <***Loc***: EV, LA, SB, Da84, Hi02>

malheur [malœr] *n.m.* **1** unhappiness **2** bad luck, misfortune **3** mishap <***Loc:*** Da84, Hi02>

malheureusement [malørøzmɑ̃] *adv.* unfortunately, unhappily *Malheureusement, on s'a mal compris.* Unfortunately, we misunderstood each other. (LA) <***Loc:*** LA, Da84>

malheureux, -euse [malørø, -øz] *adj.* unhappy, unfortunate *T'es malheureux de ramasser un maudit calin. Un calin, ça veut pas travailler.* You're bad off because you got yourself a damned bum. A bum, he doesn't want to work. (TB) **Pauvre malheureux.* Poor fellow, poor devil. (Da84) <***Loc:*** AC, EV, LA, TB, Da84, Hi02>

malhonnête[1] [malɔ̃nɛt] *adj.* dishonest *Un politicien malhonnête.* A dishonest politician. (VM) <***Loc:*** Da84>

malhonnête[2] [malɔ̃nɛt] *n.* thief <***Loc:*** Da84>

malhonnêtement [malɔ̃nɛtmɑ̃] *adv.* dishonestly <***Loc:*** Da84>

malhonnêteté [malɔ̃nɛtəte] *n.f.* dishonesty <***Loc:*** Da84>

malice [malis] *n.f.* **1** malice, mischief, mischievousness **2** joke, prank, trick ◊ **•faire {jouer} une malice** to play a joke, trick, or prank *Un maudit c'est un farceur. Il joue des malices.* A "maudit" is a joker. He plays jokes. (EV) <EV, LF, Da84> <***Loc:*** EV, LF, Da84, Lv88>

malicieusement [malisjøzmɑ̃] *adv.* maliciously, with evil intent <***Loc:*** Da84>

malicieux[1], **-ieuse** [malisjø, -jøz] *adj.* malicious, mischievous *Bouki est bête et Lapin est malicieux.* Bouki is dumb and Rabbit is mischievous. (VM) <***Loc:*** VM, Da84, Lv88>

malicieux[2], **-ieuse** [malisjø, -jøz] *n.* mischief-maker, mischievous person <***Loc:*** Da84, Lv88>

malin, -e [malɛ̃, -in] *adj.* tricky, shrewd, sharp, sly *Ses frères et ses sœurs sont vaillants, mais lui il est malin.* His brothers and sisters are good people, but he's a sly one. (AC) <***Loc:*** AC, SL, TB, Da84>

malinstruit, -e [malɛ̃strɥi, -it] *adj.* **1** ignorant, uneducated *C'est pas de sa faute. Il est malinstruit.* It's not his fault. He's lacking in education. (VM) **2** rude, ill-mannered, uncouth *Un enfant malinstruit.* An ill-mannered child. (AC) <***Loc:*** AC, JE, VM, Lv88>

malintentionné, -e [malɛ̃tɑ̃sjɔ̃ne] *adj.* ill-intentioned, ill-intended, spiteful, malicious *Une idée malintentionnée qu'alle avait de pas laisser la terre à la famille.* It was an ill-intended idea she had to not leave the land to the family. (VM) <***Loc:*** VM, Da84>

maliton ♦see **mirliton**

maljuger [malʒyʒe] *v.tr.* to misjudge *Je l'ai maljugé. C'est un vaillant bougre.* I misjudged him. He's a good man. (EV) <***Loc:*** EV, Da84>

malle [mal] *n.f.* **1** trunk **2** trunk of a car **3** mail *Le postillon amène la malle à huit heures.* The postman brings the mail at eight o'clock. (Lv88) **4** post office ◊ **•mettre la malle au soleil** to dress to the nines, get dressed up <Lv88> <***Loc:*** IB, VM, Da84, Hi02, Lv88>

mal-nommée [malnɔ̃me] *n.f.* common milkweed <***Loc:*** JE>

malo [malo] ◊ **•herbe à malo** lizard's tail, swamp lily <IB, JE, SM, TB, VM, Gr86, Ho90, Lv88> <***Loc:*** IB, JE, SM, TB, VM, Gr86, Ho90, Lv88>

malouine [malwin, malɥin] *n.f.* boot <***Loc:*** JE>

malpatient, -e [malpasjɑ̃, -ɑ̃t] *adj.* **1** impatient *Elle va jamais finir avec ça. Elle est trop malpatiente.* She'll never finish with that. She's too impatient. (AC) **2** cross, ill-tempered *J'étais assez malpatient avec.* I was rather cross with him. (VM) <***Loc:*** AC, LF, SL, TB, Da84, Lv88>

malpris, -e (mal pris) [malpri, -iz] *adj.* in trouble, caught in a bind **Si quelqu'un voulait se battre avec toi, et toi tu voulais pas, t'étais malpris.* If someone wanted to fight with you and you didn't want to, you were in a bad fix. (LA, An94) *On était dans la Baie Mallette et ça a pris à mouiller. Là, tu parles de mal pris!* We were in Mallard Bay and it started raining. Talk about in a bind! (LA) ◊ **•malpris à** awkward at, having no aptitude for, inept at *Je suis malpris à faire ça.* I have no aptitude for it. (VM) <VM> <***Loc:*** LA, VM, An94, Da84>

malpropre [malprɔp(r)] *adj.* **1** untidy, dirty, unclean *Leur restaurant est malpropre.* Their restaurant is unclean. (EV) **2** vulgar *Langage malpropre.* Vulgar language. (AC) <***Loc:*** AC, EV, Da84>

malpropreté [malproprəte] *n.f.* **1** dirtiness, untidiness **2** immorality <***Loc:*** Da84>

malsain, -e [malsɛ̃, -sɛ̃n] *adj.* unhealthy *Trop de vinaigre, c'est malsain.* Too much vinegar is not good for your health. (EV) <***Loc:*** EV, Da84>

maltraiter [maltrete] *v.tr.* to mistreat, abuse, mishandle *Hé bébé, tu m'as toujours maltraité, En disant que tu m'aimais. Je connais pas quoi moi je vas croire.* Hey, baby, you always mistreated me while telling me you loved me. I don't know what to believe. (ch: *Ça tu dis et ça tu fais sont pas pareils*) **Enfant maltraité.* Battered child. (Da84) <***Loc:*** Da84, Hi02>

malva [malva] *adj.* **1** wicked, bad, vicious **2** cowardly <***Loc:*** JE, VM, Di32>

malveillance [malvejɑ̃s] *n.f.* ill will, malice <***Loc:*** Da84>

maman (mouman) [momɑ̃, mɑ̃mɑ̃, mumɑ̃] *n.f.* mama, mother, mom <***Loc:*** AC, AV, EV, LA, PQ, TB, Da84, Lv88>

mame [mɑ̃m, mɛ̃m] *n.f.* **1** mama, mom **2** madam, Mrs. **Mame Benoît.* Mrs. Benoît. (Da84) ◊ **•vieux-mame** [*term of endearment*] grandmother <SM> <***Loc:*** AC, EV, JE, PQ, SM, TB, VM, Da84, Lv88>

mamelle [mɑ̃mɛl] *n.f.* **1** breast **2** udder <***Loc:*** Da84>

mamelon [mɑ̃mlɔ̃] *n.m.* **1** human nipple **2** teat <***Loc:*** Da84>

mamou [mɑ̃mu] *n.m.* coral bean tree *Ils bouillissaient la graine du mamou pour faire un thé.* They boiled the seeds of the coral tree to make tea. (Lv88) <***Loc:*** SM, VM, Da84, Lv88>

mamselle [mɑ̃mzɛl] *n.f.* **1** miss, young lady **2** dragonfly, mosquito hawk **3** damselfly **4** ladyfish <***Loc:*** LF, SL, Da84, Lv88>

manade [mɑ̃nad] *n.f.* herd of horses, esp. a herd of mares in a pasture guarded by a stallion <***Loc:*** JE, VM, Da84, Lv88>

management ♦see **ménagement**

manager, manageur ♦see **ménageur**

manchac [mɑ̃ʃak] *n.f.* pass, outlet, channel, inlet <***Loc:*** JE>

manche[1] [mɑ̃ʃ] *n.f.* **1** lane, small road, narrow country road between two farms *Les voisins s'observaient passer dans la petite manche.* The neighbors observed each other passing in the little lane. (LA) **Depuis l'âge de quatorze ans, je suis après rouler manche à manche.* Since I was fourteen years old, I've been rambling from one back road to another. (ch: *La valse du bambocheur*) **2** lane, blind path leading only to a house or farm *La petite manche qui va à la vieille maison devient raboteux après quelques années, et tous les temps en temps, il faut l'égaliser.* The lane that goes to the old house gets rough after a few years and every now and then, it must be graded. (LA) **3** dead end, impasse **4** sleeve *J'ai troussé mes manches et j'ai commencé derrière le char.* I rolled up my sleeves and started on the car. (LA) *C'est pas prudent de mettre les manches courtes quand il fait froid comme ça.* It's not prudent to wear short sleeves when it's cold like that. (VM) **5** extension **6** inning *Ils les ont rattrapés dans la dernière manche.* They caught up with them in the last inning. (VM) ◊ **•les quatre manches** crossroads <Lv88> ***<Loc:*** EV, LA, LF, SM, TB, VM, Da84, Hi02, Lv88>

manche[2] [mɑ̃ʃ] *n.m.* **1** handle, stem, grip *On va déboulonner le manche de la charrue.* We're going to unbolt the handle of the plow. (IB) **Ça fait, il a arraché l'affaire, il a* WEE-WEE *dessus le manche de sa hache.* So he took out his thing [i.e. penis], he peed on the handle of his ax. (EV, An94) **2** gun handle **3** lever *Pour haler les manches, tu hales un manche et tu pousses un manche, et l'affaire allait en bas ou l'autre ou n'importe équel.* For pulling levers, you pull a lever and you push a lever and the thing [the tractor] went that way or the other or wherever. (AS) ◊ **•manche à balai** broomstick <Da84> ***<Loc:*** EV, IB, JE, LF, SB, VM, Da84>

mancheur [mɑ̃ʃœr] *n.f.* armhole (of a garment) ***<Loc:*** VM>

mancornage ♦see **macornage**

mangeable [mɑ̃ʒab(l)] *adj.* **1** edible, eatable *La fricassée était trop pimentée, c'était même pas mangeable.* The stew was too peppery, it wasn't even edible. (EV) **2** tasty, palatable *Tu parles de quelque chose qu'est mangeable, c'est ça!* Talk about something tasty, this is it! (VM) ***<Loc:*** EV, VM, Da84>

mangeaille [mɑ̃ʒaj] *n.f.* edibles, food, victuals ***<Loc:*** Da84>

mangeaillé, -e [mɑ̃ʒaje] *adj.* moth-eaten *Mon capot est tout mangeaillé.* My coat is all moth-eaten. (IB) ***<Loc:*** IB>

mangeailler [mɑ̃ʒaje] **I** *v.tr.* to nibble at, pick at, eat on and off *Il mangeaillait son* STEAK, *c'était pas assez cuit.* He picked at his steak, it was not cooked enough. (LA) **II** *v.intr.* to nibble, eat on and off, eat here and there *Plutôt de s'assoir à la table, elle mangeaillait toute la journée.* Rather than sitting down at the table, she nibbled all day long. (AC) *T'es tout le temps après mangeailler.* You're always eating here and there. (VM) ***<Loc:*** AC, LF, TB, VM, Da84, Lv88>

mangeoire [mɑ̃ʒwar] *n.f.* feed trough, manger ***<Loc:*** Da84>

manger[1] [mɑ̃ʒe] **I** *v.tr.* **1** to eat, consume *Allons manger du poisson ce soir.* Let's eat fish tonight. (LF) *Il faut que tu bouilles ça pour à peu près une heure pour cuire les tripes, tu vois. Pour que tu peux manger les tripes.* You have to boil it for about an hour to cook the intestines, you see. So you can eat the intestines. (LF) *J'ai été manger mon* LUNCH *à l'école.* I ate my lunch at school. (TB) *Ils mangeont quatre fois par jour.* They eat four times a day. (VM) **2** to erode *Ça faisait un peu des grosses lames. Ça mangeait ces levées.* It was a little bit like waves, it would eat away the levees. (EV) **II se manger** *v.pron.* to be edible, be for consumption *Ça se mange, cette qualité de poisson?* Is that type of fish edible? (VM) ◊ **•manger à pleine gueule** to eat greedily <EV, La99> **•manger à ventre déboutonné** to eat heartily, greedily <AV, La99> **•manger comme quatre / manger comme un cochon {ours / requin}** to eat a lot, have a large appetite <AV, EV, La99> **•manger de la misère** to have a lot of trouble and hardship in life <SL, La99> **•manger le pain blanc en premier** ***a*** to have the easy life first, usually followed by some hardships ***b*** to take the best of something first without consideration for others <La99> **•manger le poisson d'avril** to be tricked on April Fool's day <La99> **•manger les grillots avec le tactac** to take the good with the bad, make the best of a situation <VM, La99> **•mange de la merde!** eat crap!, go to hell! <Da84> **•être après manger du patassa** to take a long time doing s.t. (refers to the tedious process of picking out the bones of a fish) **Il doit être après manger du patassa.* He's taking a long time. (La99) <La99> **•faire manger de l'avoine (à qqn)** to best (s.o.) in competition <JE, La99> **•se manger de rage** to be angry, be enraged <EV, La99> ***<Loc:*** AC, AV, EV, JE, LF, SB, SL, TB, VM, Da84, Hi02, La99>

manger[2] [mɑ̃ʒe] *n.m.* food, edibles *Du bon manger cadien.* Good cajun food. (EV) ◊ **•manger de mer** seafood <TB> ***<Loc:*** EV, IB, LF, SM, TB, VM, Da84, Lv88>

mangeur, -euse [mɑ̃ʒœr, -øz] *n.* eater ◊ **•mangeur (de) poules / mangeur de poulet** ***a*** sparrow hawk ***b*** hawk <IB, SL, Da84, Lv88> **•mangeur d'ongle** hangnail <JE> **•mangeur {mangeuse} d'œuf(s)** king snake, yellow chicken snake <SL, TB, VM, Gu00, Lv88> **•mangeur maringouins** ***a*** nightjar, goatsucker, nighthawk ***b*** mosquito hawk <IB, SM, Lv88> **•mangeur moqueur** butcher bird <Lv88> ***<Loc:*** IB, JE, SL, SM, TB, VM, Da84, Gu00, Lv88>

manglier [mɑ̃glije] *n.m.* **1** mangrove tree **2** baccharis, sea myrtle *Les mangliers poussent tout partout dans les prairies. Si tu fais un thé avec les feuilles, y a rien de meilleur pour casser la fièvre.* Baccharis grow all over the place in the prairies. If you make a tea with the leaves, there's nothing better to break a fever. (Gu00) ***<Loc:*** VM, Da84, Gu00>

maniable [mɑ̃jab(l), mɛ̃jab(l)] *adj.* workable, manageable, easy to handle (of animals, equipment, people) *Ce cheval est pas maniable.* That horse is not manageable. (LA) ***<Loc:*** JE, LA, VM, Da84>

manier [maje, mɑ̃je] **I** *v.tr.* **1** to move, manipulate *Ça fait quelque temps que je peux plus manier mon bras droit comme il faut, mais ça va un petit brin mieux aujourd'hui.* It's been a while that I can no longer move my arm like I should, but it's a little bit better today. (VM) *Le sofa est lourd. Il va d'être dur à manier.* The sofa is heavy. It will be hard to move. (LA) **2** to operate (a machine), drive (a car) *Il est trop vieux pour manier son char comme avant.* He's too old to drive his car like before. (LA) **3** to handle, manage (an animal) *Il est trop jeune pour manier un cheval comme ça.* He's too young to handle a horse like that. (LA) **4** to handle roughly, rough up *Il l'a bien manié pour avoir mangé ses pommes.* He roughed him up for eating his apples. (LF) **II se manier** *v.pron.* to handle o.s. **Le malade peut pas se manier.* The invalid cannot fend for himself. (Da84) ◊ **•manier la tapette {topette}** ***a*** to drink ***b*** to be a heavy drinker <SB, La99, Lv88> <***Loc:*** EV, LA, LF, SB, VM, Da84, La99, Lv88>

manière[1] **(moyère)** [mɑ̃jær, mɑ̃jœr, majær, mojær] *n.f.* **1** manner, way, style *Le grognard. Tu peux pas l'oublier, parce que la manière qu'il grogne.* A croaker. You can't forget that because of the way he croaks. (TB) *J'aime les attendre parler, je trouvais que c'était joli, la manière qu'eusse parlait.* I like to hear them talk, I found it pretty, the way they talked. (LF) *Ça, c'est la manière des Cadiens.* That's the way of the Cajuns. (Lv88) **2** way, means **Il y a plus d'une manière d'étouffer un chien à part lui donner une saucisse.* There is another way to deal with the situation, 'there's more than one way to skin a cat'. (LF, La99) **3** direction, way *Quand il a mordu, il quittait son bateau aller avec. Aller une manière à l'autre, jusqu'à qu'il l'a fatiqué assez qu'il a pu l'amener.* When it [the tarpon] bit, he let his boat go with it, go one way and then the other, until he tired it out enough that he could bring it in. (TB) **4** *(pl.)* manners ◊ **•avoir des vilaines manières** to have bad manners *Ça dit que j'ai des vilaines manières, mais ayoù tu crois je l'ai appris?* They say I have bad manners, but where do you think I learned them? (AC, ch: *Two step à Tina*) <AC, Da84> **•c'est sa manière** that's his way <Da84> **•dans {d'} une manière** in a way **C'est un joke dans une manière, mais c'est vrai.* It's a joke in a way, but it's true. (IB, An94) <IB, An94, Da84> **•(d')une manière ou une {l'} autre** in one way or another *Il y a joliment de Gisclair dessus le bayou. On est tout parentage une manière ou l'autre.* There are a lot of Gisclairs on the bayou. We're all related in one way or another. (TB) <TB, Da84> **•faire à sa manière** to do it one's own way <Da84> **•quelque manière** somehow *Eux-autres avait les deux langues et eux-autres les a mis ensemble. Et quelque manière il y a le parler cadien.* They had both languages and they put them together. And somehow there's the Cajun language. (LF) *Et j'étais après dompter un cheval un jour et quelque manière je m'ai refoulé la main comme ça. Et ç'a enflé.* I was taming a horse one day and somehow I sprained my hand like that. And it swelled up. (LF) <LF> <***Loc:*** AC, AV, EV, IB, LF, SL, TB, VM, An94, Da84, Gu82, Hi02, La99, Lv88>

manière[2] **(moyère)** [mɑ̃jær, mɑ̃jœr, majær, mojær] *adv.* **1** somewhat, rather, somehow, kind of, a little *Je peux signer mon nom manière.* I can sign my name just barely. (EV) *Un zinzin, ça fait pas de train ça. Ça siffle manière, sssss. Tout ce que t'attends.* A wigeon makes no noise. It kind of whistles, sssss. That's all you hear. (LF) *Tu vois, je suis manière* COLORBLIND. *Vert et bleu ça me ressemble les mêmes.* You see, I'm somewhat colorblind. Green and blue look the same to me. (TB) *Il est moyère paresseux.* He's kind of lazy. (JE, VM) *Alle est manière folle.* She is somewhat crazy. (VM) **2** approximately, nearly *Quand ils étaient manière dix, douze ans.* When they were about ten or twelve years old. (Lv88) **3** more or less *Ça va manière.* It's more or less okay. (Lv88) **4** *(discourse marker)* "like" *Et eusse avait des petites maisons, des petites cabanes manière que eusse restait là dans le temps de la roulaison.* And they would have little houses, little cabins, like, that they lived in during the time of the sugar season. (LF) <***Loc:*** AC, EV, JE, LF, SM, TB, VM, Da84, Hi02, Lv88>

manieur [mɑ̃jœr] *n.m.* handler *Un manieur de bœufs.* A cattle handler. (LA) <***Loc:*** LA, Da84>

manigance [mɑ̃nigɑ̃s] *n.f.* scheme, trick, maneuvering *Il travaille bien, mais il fait trop de manigances.* He's a good worker, but he makes too many schemes. (SM) ◊ **•faire des manigances** to sport around *François et Loulou sont après faire des manigances à Bâton-Rouge.* François and Loulou are sporting around in Baton Rouge. (SL) <SL> <***Loc:*** SL, SM>

maniguette [mɑ̃nigɛt] *n.f.* **1** nutmeg **2** thing, thingamajig <***Loc:*** EV, VM, Lv88>

manila [mɑ̃nila] *n.m.* hemp ◊ **•avoir besoin du manila trempe** to need to be taught a lesson <Lv88> **•un (cable de) manila** very strong rope <Lv88> <***Loc:*** Lv88>

manioc[1] [mɑ̃jɔk] *n.f.* starch, uncooked starch *La laveuse veut de la manioc.* The washerwoman wants starch. (SL) <***Loc:*** LF, SL>

manioc[2] [mɑ̃jɔk] *n.m.* cassava tree <***Loc:*** Da84>

manioler [mɑ̃jole] *v.tr.* to cajole, coax <***Loc:*** JE, Lv88>

manivelle [mɑ̃nivɛl] *n.f.* crank, handle <***Loc:*** SB, La99>

manne [mɑ̃n, mɑ̃j] *n.f.* **1** large woven basket with two handles, traditionally made of split cypress and reeds **2** hamper, large basket **3** bushel basket, bushel <***Loc:*** SL, Da84, Fa77, Lv88>

manœuvrer [mɑ̃nøvre] *v.tr.* **1** to handle, operate, maneuver *T'aurais dû le voir manœuvrer ces sacs de riz. C'est un artiste!* You should have seen him handle those sacks of rice. What an artist! (LA) **2** to manage, run *Bougre-ça là connaît manœuvrer un business.* That guy knows how run a business. (LA) **3** to deal with, handle *Si tu veux un Cadien de la Louisiane, tu fais mieux de connaître comment le manœuvrer.* If you want a Cajun from Louisiana, you'd better know how to handle him. (TB) <***Loc:*** LA, TB, Da84>

manoque [mɑ̃nɔk] *n.f.* **1** handcuff **2** bunch of tobacco leaves layered so as to form a packet that is tied together by a single leaf <***Loc:*** VM, Lv88>

manoquer [mɑ̃noke] *v.tr.* to put handcuffs on *Le sheriff a venu le manoquer.* The sheriff came to handcuff him. (VM) <***Loc:*** VM, Lv88>

manque [mɑ̃k] *n.m./f.* **1** lack, want, failure **Ouais, à cause de le* ARMY CORPS OF ENGINEERS, *ya ein manque d'écrevisses en Louisiane.* Yes, because of the Army Corps of Engineers there is a lack of crawfish in Louisiana. (ThCa: *Mille misères)* **2** gap, bare or barren spot *Y a des manques dans ce rang-ci.* There are gaps in this row. (VM) *Il y a un tas de manques dans les cannes cette année.* There are a lot of barren spots in the sugarcane this year. (Lv88) *Le peintureur a laissé des manques dans le mur.* The painter missed spots on the wall. (VM) ◊ **•manque d'attention** lack of attention, carelessness, inattention <Da84> **•manque de retenue** lack of good manners <Da84> <***Loc:*** VM, Da84, Hi02, Lv88, ThCa>

manquer [mɑ̃ke] **I** *v.tr.* **1** to miss *Il est tellement oubliard, il va manquer son enterrement.* He is so forgetful, he'll miss his own burial. (LA) *T'es après manquer ta chance, mon garçon.* You're missing your chance, my son. (LA) **Manquer le bateau avec le tiquette dans la main.* To miss the boat with the ticket in one's hand (i.e. miss a good opportunity). (SL, La99) *J'ai pas pu le manquer. Il s'a dardé devant le char.* I couldn't miss him. He darted out in front of the car. (VM) *Le constable aurait pas manqué le plus petit dérangement dans la place.* The bouncer would not have missed the least disturbance in the place. (LA) **2** to leave out, omit **Un peut pas manquer l'autre.* One cannot leave the other out. (EV, An84) **3** to run out of, lack *J'ai manqué la gasoline.* I ran out of gasoline. (Lv88) *Dans la chasse, équand tu manques des* TAG, *t'as fini.* In the hunt, when you run out of tags, you're done. (TB) **Il manque pas juste ça.* That's not all that's lacking. (Da84) *Il manquait de la place dans la pataterie, ça fait il a embutté ses patates dans le clos et il les a couverts avec de la paille.* There was no more room in the potato shed, so he piled his potatoes in the field and covered them with straw. (VM) **4** to fail to achieve a goal **Et ils ont pas manqué leur récolte à cause de ça?* And didn't they fail to make their crop because of that? (EV, An94) **5** to feel the lack or loss of *Je manque mon bébé.* I miss my baby. (Lv88) **II** *v.intr.* **1** to be lacking **Et quand tout le beurre a manqué, il s'est vite retourné chez sa mère pour d'autre.* And when all the butter was lacking, he returned quickly to his mother's house for more. (EV, An94) *Il va te manquer deux douelles de six pieds.* You'll be short two six-foot staves. (SB) *Quand l'électricité a manqué pour l'ouragan, ça a tout déglacé ça on avait dedans le* FREEZE. When the electricity went off during the hurricane, it thawed everything we had in the freezer. (LA) **2** to be missing, go missing *Il a manqué la journée d'avant Christmas, et on l'a trouvé le lendemain de Christmas. Les deux étaient noyés.* He went missing the day before Christmas, and we found him the day after Christmas. Both had drowned. (TB) *Les œufs était tout éclos déjà quand la couveuse a manqué.* The eggs were all hatched when the laying hen went missing. (LA) *Entrement de ça peut-être le lendemain t'aurais manqué et quelqu'un te courait par-derrière.* Otherwise the next day you might have turned up missing and someone would go after you. (TB) **3** to misfire (of a gun) *Son pistolet a manqué. C'est la seule raison que j'ai échappé.* His pistol misfired. That's the only reason I got away. (LA) **4** to fail in health *Alle a commencé à manquer l'année passée.* Her health began failing last year. (VM) **5** to die **Si je viendrais à manquer.* If I should die. (Da84) ◊ **•manquer de** to nearly (do s.t.), almost (do s.t.) *Alle a manqué de me faire mourir de peur.* She nearly made me die of fright. (TB) *Il est tellement abîmé, j'ai manqué pas le reconnaître.* He's so worn out, I almost didn't recognize him. (SM) *Eh ben cher, ça ç'a manqué de me tuer.* Well, dear, that nearly killed me. (TB) *J'ai tombé dans un trou de cocodrie quand j'étais petit, et j'ai manqué de jamais de m'en débourber.* I fell into an alligator hole when I was little, and I almost never got out of there. (VM) <SM, TB, VM> **•manquer de souffle** to be out of breath <Da84> **•manquer le coup** to miss the chance <Da84> **•manquer un pain dans sa fournaise** to be impatient *Il manque un pain dans ta fournaise.* You're too impatient. (TB) <TB> <***Loc:*** AC, EV, LA, SL, TB, VM, An84, An94, Da84, Hi02, La99, Lv88>

manteau [mɑ̃to] *n.m.* coat, overcoat <***Loc:*** Da84>

manufacture [mɑ̃nifaktyr] *n.f.* factory <***Loc:*** LF, Da84, Lv88>

manufacturer [mɑ̃nifaktyre] *v.tr.* to manufacture <***Loc:*** Da84, Lv88>

manufactureur [mɑ̃nifaktyrœr] *n.m.* manufacturer <***Loc:*** SJ, Lv88>

maouine [mawin] *n.f.* sweetheart <***Loc:*** SL>

map [map] *n.f.* map *J'ai des maps si vous veux voir ça, comment c'est. Je vas pogner les maps.* I have maps if you want to see how it is. I'll go get the maps. (TB) <***Loc:*** EV, TB, Lv88, Ph36>

mappée (mappure) [mape, mapyr] *n.* powder puff <***Loc:*** JE>

mappure ♦see **mappée**

maquechou (maque-choux) [makʃu, masku] *n.m.* **1** smothered corn (a dish made of young corn, onions, and tomatoes) *Du maquechou, c'est du maïs étouffé.* "Maquechou" is smothered corn. (Gu00) **2** young, tender corn (cut off the cob), fried in a small amount of fat, then simmered <***Loc:*** SM, TB, VM, Da84, Gu00, Hi02, Lv88>

maquemose [makmoz] *v.tr.invar.* **1** to fool, deceive **Jean l'a maquemose dans ç't affaire.* Jean tricked him in that deal. (EV, Ph36) **2** to seduce **Il a maquemose la fille.* He seduced the girl. (EV, Ph36) **3** to hit, strike **J'l'ai maquemose au dessus de l'œil.* I hit him above the eye. (EV, Ph36) <***Loc:*** EV, Ph36>

maquemousser [makmuse] *v.tr.* to arrange in a somewhat illicit way *Ils ont maquemoussé l'affaire.* They arranged the affair fraudulently. (EV) <***Loc:*** EV>

maquereau[1] (**macriau, maquerillot**) [makro, makrijo] *n.m.* **1** mackerel **2** yellow mackerel ◊ **•gros macriau** king mackerel <LF> <***Loc:*** LF, Da84, Re31, Re63>

maquereau[2] (**macriau, maquerillot**) [makro, makrijo] *n.m.* **1** lover **2** common-law mate, concubine **3** ladies' man *C'est un vrai maquereau. Il est avide des femmes.* He's a real ladies' man. He can't get enough of women. (VM) **4** man who lives with another man's wife <***Loc:*** JE, TB, VM, Da84, Gu00, La99, Lv88>

maquerillot ♦see **maquereau**

maquignon ♦see **maquillon**

maquignonnage [makĩjɔ̃naʒ] *n.m.* bustle, hubbub, confusion *Quel maquignonnage pour rien!* What a bustle over nothing! (IB) <***Loc:*** IB>

maquignonner ♦see **maquillonner**

maquillon (**maquignon**) [makijɔ̃, makĩjɔ̃] *n.m.* **1** horse breeder or trainer **2** broncobuster *C'étaient des maquillons, c'était ceux qui domptaient les chevaux.* They were broncobusters, they're the ones who broke the horses to the saddle. (AC) **3** jockey **4** good horseman **5** clothes pin *Je veux cinq sous de maquignons.* I want a nickel's worth of clothes pins. (IB) ◊ **•maquignon cordelle / maquignon à cheval** clothespin <SJ, SM> <***Loc:*** AC, IB, SJ, SL, SM, VM, Da84, Lv88, Re31>

maquillonner (**maquignonner**) [makijɔ̃ne, makĩjɔ̃ne] *v.tr.* **1** to ride (a horse) **2** to jockey **3** to saddle-break (an untamed horse or bronco) <***Loc:*** Da84>

maraille [maraj] *n.f.* piece of land that has sunk <***Loc:*** TB>

marais [marɛ, mare] *n.m.* **1** marsh, swamp **2** pond, shallow pond, pool **3** low area near a bayou, head waters of a bayou where water flows very slowly **4** a depression used for growing rice (on the Louisiana prairies) <***Loc:*** EV, SB, SM, TB, VM, Da84, Gu00, Hi02, Lv88>

marbre [marb(r)] *n.m./f.* **1** marble **2** heavy, granite-like playing marble <***Loc:*** JE, VM, Da84, Lv88>

marbré, -e [marbre] *adj.* marbleized, veined *L'étoffe était marbrée.* The fabric was marbleized. (EV) <***Loc:*** EV, Da84>

marc [mar] *n.m. (occ. f.)* **1** coffee grounds *Ça fait qu'alle va, alle jette les marcs à café en arrière du* STOVE *et alle fait une grègue de café.* So she goes and throws the coffee grounds behind the stove and she makes a pot of coffee. (LF) **2** dregs *Le vin de canne est passé dans une clarifieuse pour retirer la marc dedans le vin de canne.* The cane juice is passed through a clarifying tank to remove the dregs. (TB) <***Loc:*** LF, TB, Da84>

marcaillage [markajaʒ] *n.m.* grafitti <***Loc:*** Lv88>

marcailler ♦see **marquailler**

marchage [marʃaʒ] *n.m.* walking *Et mon beau-frère dit qu'il attendait du potin, du traillail dans la nuit, plein du marchage qu'était fait...* And my brother-in-law said he heard some noise, some racket at night, a lot of walking going on . . . (LF) <***Loc:*** LF>

marchailler [marʃaje] *v.intr.* **1** to walk around, mill around, stroll *On va aller marchailler dans le* MALL. We'll go walk around in the mall. (EV) **2** to pace back and forth <***Loc:*** EV, LA, SM, VM, Da84, Lv88>

marchand, -e [marʃɑ̃, -ɑ̃d] *n.* dealer, shopkeeper, seller, merchant ◊ **•marchand (à) charrette** peddler <VM, Lv88> **•marchand (de) paquet** pack merchant <Da84, Lv88> <***Loc:*** SL, SM, TB, VM, Da84, Hi02, Lv88>

marchander [marʃɑ̃de] *v.tr.* to price (goods) *J'ai pas acheté, j'ai juste marchandé aujourd'hui.* I didn't buy [anything], I just priced [things] today. (Lv88) <***Loc:*** Da84, Lv88>

marchanderie [marʃɑ̃dri] *n.f.* merchandise *S'il faut qu'il va chercher un morceau de marchanderie en ville ou à Houma, c'est lui qui fait ça aussi.* If he has to go get a piece of merchandise in the city or in Houma, he's the one who does that too. (LF) <***Loc:*** LF>

marchandise [marʃɑ̃diz] *n.f.* merchandise, goods, wares ◊ **•marchandises sèches {secs}** ***a*** dry goods (e.g. fabric, sewing supplies) ***b*** dry-goods store <JE, Lv88> **•de marchandise** retail *J'ai travaillé dans une boutique de marchandise.* I worked in a retail store. (SL) <SL> <***Loc:*** JE, SL, SM, TB, Da84, Lv88>

marche [marʃ] *n.f.* **1** walk, stroll **2** gait **3** march **4** step (of a staircase) **Escalier à six marches.* Six-step staircase. (Da84) ◊ **•faire {prendre} une marche** to go for a walk <LA, VM> <***Loc:*** LA, VM, Da84, Lv88>

marché [marʃe] *n.m.* **1** market, marketplace **2** stock market ◊ **•(à) bon marché** cheap, inexpensive *J'ai trouvé un tas des affaires qui étaient bon marché.* I found a lot of things that were inexpensive. (EV) *Il pouvait acheter ça bien bon marché dans le temps. Il pouvait acheter les quatre-vingt-sept acres de terres pour dix-huit cent piastres.* He could buy it at a good price back then. He could buy the eighty-seven acres of land for eighteen hundred dollars. (EV) <EV, IB, Da84> **•au marché** at a bargain *J'ai acheté ça au marché.* I bought that for a bargain [price]. (VM) <VM> **•être en marché** to be in the process of making a deal *On est en marché pour acheter la terre.* We're in the process of negotiating to buy the land. (LA) <LA, Da84> **•faire marché** to make a deal, strike a bargain *Tu crois qu'on pourra faire marché?* Do you think we can make a deal? (LA) <LA, Da84> **•par-dessus le marché** over and above, to boot *Marie-toi pas avec ça. Il est pauvre et par dessus le marché il est bête.* Don't marry him. He's poor and he's stupid to boot. (LA) <LA, Da84> <***Loc:*** AC, EV, IB, LA, SM, TB, VM, Da84, Lv88>

marche-pied [marʃpje, marʃəpje] *n.m.* **1** passage, foot-path (e.g. a board over a ditch) **2** running board, platform where people step to board a buggy, carriage, train, etc. **3** footstool <***Loc:*** VM, Lv88>

marcher [marʃe] *v.intr.* **1** to walk *Il marchait pour s'en revenir et je l'attendais siffler avec son sifflet de loin, loin.* He was walking back and I heard him whistling with his whistle from far far away. (AC) *Le danseur qu'était après danser avec la fille là, lui là, et ben, ils marchiont. Ça arrêtait pas là causer debout là comme ça là. Ça marchait alentour du hall.* The dancer that was dancing with the girl there, well, they were walking. They wouldn't stop and talk while standing. They were walking around the hall. (VM) **2** to step, tread *Marcher dessus un clou.* To step on a nail. (EV) **3** to advance, go ahead *Hourra! Marche!* Get going! (VM) **4** to fare **Comment ça marche?* How are you faring? (Da84) **5** to work, run, function *Ça marche mal, ce chemin.* This road is not good. (VM) ◊ **•marcher démanché** to walk with arms swinging <VM> **•marcher en macreuse** to waddle <Lv88> <***Loc:*** AC, AV, EV, JE, LA, SL, TB, VM, Da84, Hi02, Lv88>

marchette [marʃɛt] *n.f.* **1** foot pedal **2** accelerator pedal **3** sewing machine treadle **4** carriage step **5** rocker, blade, or runner (curved wooden bottom) of a rocking chair *Y a du monde qui dit marchette de berceuse et d'autres qui dit roulette de berceuse.* There are some people who say 'marchette' and others who say 'roulette' (for the runners of a rocking chair). (TB) **6** tripping device on a trap <***Loc:*** LF, SL, TB, VM, Da84, Lv88>

marcheur [marʃœr] *n.m.* walker, pedestrian <***Loc:*** Da84>

mardi [mardi] *n.m.* Tuesday <***Loc:*** EV, Da84, Hi02>

mardi gras[1] [mardigra] *adj.* in bad taste, tacky, gaudy *Une robe mardi gras.* A tacky dress. (Lv88) <***Loc:*** IB, Lv88>

Mardi Gras[2] [mardigra] *n.m.* **1** Shrove Tuesday, Mardi Gras **2** masked person who is celebrating Mardi Gras *Les Mardi Gras vous remercient bien de votre bonne volonté.* The Mardi Gras participants thank you very much for your good will. (EV, ch: *Chanson de Mardi Gras*) **3** badly dressed person, one dressed in a gaudy or tacky way **4** woman wearing too much make-up <***Loc:*** EV, SL, VM, Da84, Hi02, Lv88>

mare [mar] *n.f.* area in a salt marsh governed by the tides <***Loc:*** Gu00>

marécage [marekaʒ] *n.m.* cypress swamp <***Loc:*** LF, TB>

marécages [marekaʒ] *n.m.pl.* seafood *Nous-autres on dit pas 'les fruits de mer', on dit 'les marécages'.* We don't say 'fruits de mer', we say 'marécages' (for seafood). (LF) <***Loc:*** LF, TB>

marée [mare] *n.f.* **1** tide *Quand la marée a baissé, la marée va monter.* When the tide has gone out, the tide will come back in. (LF) **2** flood ◊ **•haute marée** high tide <Da84> <***Loc:*** LF, SM, Da84, Hi02>

marélia [marelja] *adj.* ◊ **•fièvre marélia** malaria <Lv88> <***Loc:*** Lv88>

marenne [marɛ̃n] *n.* hopscotch <***Loc:*** JE>

margarine [mardʒarin] *n.f.* margarine <***Loc:*** Da84>

margot [margo] *n.m.* **1** slip of a plant, layer or division of any plant for propagation **2** germ, embryo ◊ **•margot de patate** short length of potato vine used to grow a new potato plant <EV, Da84> <***Loc:*** EV, VM, Da84, Lv88>

margotter (**margoter**) [margote] *v.tr.* to divide, transplant plants for propagation (esp. bulblets, vines, etc.) by layering or by planting slips *Je margote mes oignons. J'en ai margoté icitte-là. Je les coupe. Là je plante juste le bas là. Je les margotte.* I transplant my onions. I have placed some starter plants here. I cut them, then I just plant the bottom. I transplant them. (VM) *Margoter des patates.* To divide potato plants. (VM) <***Loc:*** IB, SJ, VM, Da84, Lv88>

marguerite [margrit, margərit] *n.f.* **1** daisy **2** chrysanthemum ◊ **•avoir la marguerite** to menstruate <VM> <***Loc:*** VM, Da84, Fa77>

marguiller (**maguiller**) [margije, magije] *n.m.* [*eccl.*] churchwarden <***Loc:*** Da84>

mari [mari] *n.m.* husband ◊ **•prétend-mari** future husband <VM> **•qui prend mari, prend pays** a woman who marries must accomodate herself to her husband's habits, family, etc. <La99> <***Loc:*** AC, AV, EV, IV, TB, VM, Da84, La99>

mariage [marjaʒ] *n.m.* marriage, wedding <***Loc:*** AC, EV, Da84>

marichal [mariʃal] *n.m.* veterinarian for horses (esp. racehorses) <***Loc:*** JE, VM, Di32, Lv88>

marié, -e [marje] *n.* **1** *(m.)* groom **2** *(f.)* bride <***Loc:*** EV, LA, VM, Da84>

marier [marje] **I** *v.tr.* **1** to marry, wed *Il a marié la fille à notre voisin.* He married our neighbor's daughter. (Lv88) *J'ai demandé à le vieux pour la marier, il m'a dit non.* I have asked her father to marry her, he told me no. (AV) **2** to marry, perform the marriage ceremony of *Le prêtre qu'a marié notre garçon.* The priest who married our son. (Lv88) **3** to join (pieces of wood in construction) *Il fallait tu les maries ensemble. Il fallait tu coupes un* NOTCH *dedans.* You had to join them together. You had to cut a notch in it. (SL) **II** *v.intr.* to get married *La première année on a marié, on a resté à Catahoula.* The first year we were married, we lived in Catahoula. (SM) **III se marier** *v.pron.* to get married *C'est trop triste quand quelqu'un se marie à un garçon qu'est pas bon.* It's too sad when someone marries a boy who's no good. (TB) *La mère voulait que sa fille se marie avec ce petit bougre, mais à l'opposé son père voulait pas.* The mother wanted her daughter to marry that little fellow, but on the contrary, the father did not. (VM) ◊ **•bon à marier** handy, adept, efficient (esp. with manual tasks) <La99> <***Loc:*** AC, AV, EV, IV, SL, SM, TB, VM, Da84, Hi02, Lv88>

marinade [marinad] *n.f.* marinade, pickling solution <***Loc:*** Da84>

marinage ♦see **amarinage**

mariner ♦see **amariner**

maringouin [marɛ̃gwɛ̃, marɑ̃gwɑ̃, maragwɛ̃, marɑ̃gwɛ̃,

maregwɛ̃] *n.m.* mosquito <***Loc:*** EV, IB, JD, JE, LA, LF, SL, SM, TB, VM, Da84, Gu00, Hi02, Lv88>

marionnette[1] [marjɔ̃nɛt] *n.f.* **1** buffle-head duck **2** butter pea lima bean <***Loc:*** EV, LA, VM, Lv88>

marionnette[2] [marjɔ̃nɛt] *n.f.* puppet, marionette <***Loc:*** Da84>

marmaille [marmaj] *n.f.* brats, rowdy children (collectively) <***Loc:*** Da84>

marmalade [marmalad] *n.f.* marmalade, jelly, preserves <***Loc:*** Da84>

marmite [marmit] *n.f.* **1** cooking pot **2** crowd, rabble *Ga' donc cette marmite.* Look at that crowd. (VM) <***Loc:*** VM, Da84>

marquablement [makabləmɑ̃] *adv.* doubtless, without doubt <***Loc:*** JE>

marquailler (marcailler) [markaje] *v.tr.* to mark up, scribble on, disfigure by marks *Les petits a marquaillé tous les plafonnages.* Ths kids marked up all the walls. (EV) <***Loc:*** EV, JE, SL, Da84>

marque [mark] *n.f.* **1** mark **2** mark, stamp, brand (to show approval or ownership) *Il faut que tu mets ta marque. Les* GAMEWARDEN, *le* STATE, *il faut tu mets un tag dessus ta cage avec ton numéro de licence.* You have to put your mark on there. The gamewardens, the state, require that you put a tag on your crab traps with your license number. (TB) **3** sign, indication (e.g. to show direction, provide information) **4** grade (in a class) **5** scar *Il l'a cogné. Il l'avait bien fendu ça. Il a crevé avec la marque.* He hit it. He had really split it. He still had the scar when he died. (EV) <***Loc:*** EV, SJ, TB, Da84, Hi02, Lv88>

marqué, -e [marke] *adj.* **1** marked, branded *Une vache marquée.* A branded cow. (LA) **2** marked, blacklisted *Si tu poussais pas le tien, t'étais marqué, ouais.* If you were not pushing your own, you were blacklisted, yeah. (SL) <***Loc:*** LA, SL, Da84>

marquer [marke] *v.tr.* **1** to mark *Je vas marquer sur l'armanach le jour de ta fête.* I am going to write down on the calendar the date of your birthday. (AC) **2** to brand, mark (an animal) for identification *Ça marquait [les cochons] sur les oreilles.* They marked the pigs on their ears. (SL) **3** to mark, cause to have a birthmark *Le monde disait que ça aurait marqué ton enfant si tu mangeais pas ça t'avais envie.* People used to say that it would give your child a birthmark if you didn't eat what you had a craving for [while pregnant]. (EV) **4** to mark, show (time) *Ils arrêtaient les pendules pour indiquer qu'elles avaient plus d'heures à marquer pour le défunt.* They stopped the clocks to indicate that they no longer had hours to keep for the deceased [person]. (VM) **5** to castrate (a bull calf) *On a des veaux à vendre à l'encan et ils sont tous marqués.* We have bull calves to sell at auction and they are all castrated. (LA) <***Loc:*** AC, EV, LA, SL, VM, Da84>

marraine [marɛ̃n] *n.f.* godmother <***Loc:*** Da84, Hi02>

marron[1]**, -onne** [marɔ̃, -ɔ̃n] *adj.* **1** wild, undomesticated *Du riz marron. Un cochon marron.* Wild rice. Wild pig. (VM) **2** gone back to the wild, feral *Un chien marron.* A feral dog. (LA) **3** fugitive, runaway *Le petit est marron.* The child is a runaway. (EV) <***Loc:*** AC, EV, TB, VM, Da84, Gu00, Lv88>

marron[2]**, -onne** [marɔ̃, -ɔ̃n] *adj./n.* brown *Char marron.* Brown car. (VM) *Tu vides du café dans du lait, ça le tourne marron, mais marron blanc.* You pour coffee into some milk, it turns it brown, light brown. (LA) <***Loc:*** LA, VM, Gu00>

marron[3] [marɔ̃] *n.m.* fugitive, runaway <***Loc:*** Lv88>

marronnage [marɔ̃naʒ] *n.m.* desertion, flight, running away <***Loc:*** JE, VM, Lv88>

marronner [marɔ̃ne] *v.intr.* **1** to flee, escape, run away *Guette-lé bien. J'ai peur il va marronner.* Keep an eye on him. I'm afraid he's going to run away. (LA) **2** to run around *Les enfants à Elise sont tout le temps après marronner dans le voisinage.* Elise's children are always running around in the neighborhood. (VM) **3** to thieve, steal things *Ils vont la nuit marronner dans les habitations.* They go and steal in the homes at night. (Di32) <***Loc:*** JE, LA, VM, Di32, Lv88>

marronneur [marɔ̃nœr] *n.m.* runaway, fugitive, deserter <***Loc:*** JE, VM, Lv88>

mars [mars] *n.m.* March <***Loc:*** AC, Da84, Hi02>

marsouin [marswɛ̃, maswɛ̃] *n.m.* porpoise <***Loc:*** JE, VM, Gu00>

marteau [marto, mato] *n.m.* **1** hammer *Il a travaillé tellement dur, il a démanché son marteau.* He worked so hard, he loosened the handle on his hammer. (LA) **2** gun hammer **3** striker for triangle <***Loc:*** EV, JE, LA, LF, SL, Da84, Hi02>

martinet [martinɛ, martine] *n.m.* any of a variety of swallows or martins <***Loc:*** JE>

martingale [martɛ̃gal] *n.f.* martingale <***Loc:*** Da84>

martin-pêcheur ♦see **martin-plongeur**

martin-plongeur (martin-pêcheur) [martɛ̃plɔ̃ʒœr, martɛ̃peʃœr] *n.m.* kingfisher, king martin <***Loc:*** IB, JE, Da84, Lv88>

martyr[1] [martir] *n.m.* martyr <***Loc:*** Da84>

martyr[2] [martir] *n.m.* **1** martyrdom **2** act of cruelty *C'est un martyr, ça qu'il a fait à sa mère.* What he did to his mother is an act of cruelty. (AC) <***Loc:*** AC, Da84>

martyriser [martirize] *v.tr.* **1** [*eccl.*] to martyr **2** to torment, torture *Cet homme-là a martyrisé sa femme assez qu'elle l'a quitté.* That man tormented his wife so much that she left him. (LA) <***Loc:*** LA, Da84>

mascarade [maskarad] *n.f.* masquerade, masking <***Loc:*** Da84>

masque [mas(k)]] *n.m./f.* **1** mask *Tu m'as épeuré avec ce masque!* You scared me with that mask! (EV) **2** hood **3** blinders **4** blindfold **5** masked person <***Loc:*** EV, SL, VM, Da84, Hi02, Lv88>

masqué, -e [maske] *adj.* **1** masked, concealed, blindfolded *Tous les Mardi Gras étaient masqués dans ces temps ça.* All the Mardi Gras were masked in those days. (LA) **2** covered with liver spots, afflicted with chloasma *Alle doit être malade, alle est tout masquée.* She must be sick, she is all covered with liver spots. (VM) <***Loc:*** LA, VM, Da84>

masquer [maske] **I** *v.tr.* to mask, conceal *Elle a poussé la chaise contre le mur pour masquer le trou.* She pushed the chair against the wall to conceal the hole. (VM) **II se masquer** *v.pron.* to put on a mask, wear a mask *Le monde s'habillait, ça se masquait. Là ça prendait le chemin et ça faisait le Mardi gras toute la journée, et là ça se démasquait le soir à minuit, le Mercredi des Cendres.* People got dressed up, they put on masks. Then they took to the roads and ran Mardi Gras all day, and then in the evening they took off their masks at midnight, Ash Wednesday. (LF) ◊ **•masquer les yeux** to blindfold *J'y ai masqué les yeux.* I blindfolded him. (VM) <VM, Da84> <***Loc:*** LF, TB, VM, Da84>

massacre [masak(r)] *n.m.* **1** massacre, slaughter **2** disfigurement **3** whole lot, bunch, large quantity **Il a attrapé un massacre de poissons.* He caught a lot of fish. (Da84) <***Loc:*** Da84>

massacrer [masakre] **I** *v.tr.* **1** to massacre, slaughter *Comment la chasse? —On les a massacrés.* How was the hunt? —We slaughtered them. (LA) **2** to ruin, damage, make a mess of *Tu vas massacrer tes souliers dans la boue.* You'll ruin your shoes in the mud. (Lv88) *Les rats allont massacrer ça.* The rats are going to ruin it. (VM) *Le froid a massacré les pacaniers.* The cold badly damaged the pecan trees. (Lv88) *J'ai tout massacré mon rôti.* I completely ruined my roast [by cooking it too long]. (Lv88) **3** to beat, beat up *Ils s'ont rencontrés le dimanche après-midi et D. B. l'a massacré.* They met up on Sunday afternoon and D. B. beat him up. (LA) *Ils l'ont massacré jusqu'à qu'il était pus reconnaissable.* They beat him up until he was no longer recognizable. (LA) **4** to disfigure *Il a été tout massacré dans cet accident.* He was all disfigured in that accident. (Lv88) *Il est tout massacré depuis sa maladie.* He's all disfigured since his illness. (Lv88) *Ses genoux étaient tout massacrés par la rhumatisme.* His knees were all disfigured by rheumatism. (Lv88) **II se massacrer** *v.pron.* to hurt o.s. badly, mangle o.s. ◊ **•massacrer la couenne** to give s.o. a beating <TB, La99> <***Loc:*** LA, SL, TB, VM, Da84, La99, Lv88>

massage [masaʒ] *n.m.* massage <***Loc:*** Da84>

masse [mas] *n.f.* **1** mass, pile, heap **2** sledgehammer *Une grosse masse en fer.* A big iron sledgehammer. (LF) **3** maul carved out of a solid piece of wood *Là ils ont pris à se servir des* SLEDGE *affaires qui avaient un manche en bois. C'était un tas meilleur qu'une masse.* Then they started using those sledge things that had wooden handles. It was a lot better than a maul. (EV) ◊ **•en masse** a lot *Ils se parlaient entre eux-autres en français en masse.* They used to talk to each other in French a lot. (AV) **Je faisais de l'argent en masse.* I was making a lot of money. (EV, An84) <AV, EV, An84> **•en masse de** many, much, a lot *Il y avait en masse du monde au festival.* There were a lot of people at the festival. (AV) *Ils faisaient tout le temps un jardin, ils avaient en masse des légumes et si n'avait pas des légumes fraîches, ils avaient des légumes glacées, dans le* FREEZER. They always had a vegetable garden, they had plenty of vegetables, and if there weren't any fresh vegetables, they had frozen vegetables, in the freezer. (AV) *Il a mangé en masse du pain.* He ate a lot of bread. (AV) <AV, EV, SL, An84, Da84, Lv88, Wh83> **•il y en a en masse et en pile** there's a whole lot of it <Da84> <***Loc:*** AV, EV, LF, SL, TB, VM, An84, Da84, Lv88, Wh83>

masse-cuite [maskɥit] *n.f.* crystallized sugarcane syrup <***Loc:*** VM>

masse-pain ♦see **mâche-pain**

masser [mase] *v.tr.* to drive (a stake or post) into the ground *Masser des poteaux, on cognait pour caler les poteaux dans la terre.* Driving posts, we would strike to sink the posts into the ground. (EV) <***Loc:*** EV, Da84>

massicot [masiko] *n.m.* ragweed <***Loc:*** SL, TB, Ho90, Re31>

massif (**massive**) [masif, masiv] *adj.* **1** big, strong *Un homme massif.* A huge, strong man. (LA) **2** sturdy, solid, heavy *Un sofa massif.* A sturdy sofa. (VM) **3** rough cut *Les bateaux qu'étaient faits pour les huîtres, ben eux ils avaient pas de trou pour mettre les produits dedans. Le plancher était massif, il avait pas de trou dedans.* The boats that were made for oyster fishing, well, they didn't have a hole to put the products in. The deck was rough cut, there was no hole in it. (LF) <***Loc:*** LA, LF, VM, Da84>

mastic [mastik] *n.m.* putty, mastic <***Loc:*** Da84>

mastoc [mastɔk] *n.m./f.* large mosquito hawk <***Loc:*** SB, SJ>

masturbation [mastyrbasjɔ̃] *n.f.* masturbation <***Loc:*** Da84>

mât [ma] *n.m.* mast *Hisser la voile dessus le mât.* To hoist the sail on the mast. (VM) <***Loc:*** LF, VM>

mataché, -e [mataʃe] *adj.* spotted, speckled *Des gros tigres matachés—plutôt des léopards.* Large spotted tigers, or rather leopards. (Lv88) *Les grives ont des œufs matachés.* Robins have speckled eggs. (VM) *Ça c'est un* SPECKLED TROUT. *Tu l'appelles une truite grise, alle est grise les deux bords, alle est matachée, basanée les deux bords.* That is a speckled trout. It's called a truite grise, it's gray on both sides, it's speckled, spotted on both sides. (TB) <***Loc:*** JE, LF, TB, VM, Lv88>

matacher [mataʃe] *v.tr.* to spot, speckle <***Loc:*** Lv88>

MATCH [mætʃ] *n.m.* **1** match, contest **2** equal **Il a trouvé son* MATCH. He met his match. (Da84) <***Loc:*** Da84>

matelas [matla] *n.m.* **1** mattress, pad *Là ça faisait des matelas avec la paille.* They used to make mattresses with corn shucks. (SL) **2** windrow (of sugarcane) ◊ **•matelas de coton**

cotton mattress <TB, Da84> •**matelas de mousse** moss mattress <Da84> •**matelas de paille {paillasse}** straw mattress, shuck mattress <Da84> •**matelas de plume** feather mattress <Da84> •**mettre les cannes en matelas** to windrow cane <Da84> <***Loc:*** SL, TB, Da84, Hi02>

matelot [matlo] *n.m.* sailor <***Loc:*** SJ>

matelote [matlɔt] *n.f.* old-fashioned child's blouse to which trousers are buttoned <***Loc:*** IB, SM>

mâter [mate] **I** *v.tr.* **1** to stand s.t. up straight *On a eu de la misère à mâter le poteau de coin.* We had trouble righting the corner post. (LA) **2** to upend, prop up (e.g. a boat or board against a wall) *Il a mâté son bateau dans la cour après la saison.* He propped up his boat in the yard after the season. (LA) **II** *v.intr.* to rear (of a horse) *Mon cheval a mâté et j'ai tombé.* My horse reared and I fell. (SL) **III se mâter** *v.pron.* **1** to prance, stand *Le chien s'a mâté sur la barrière.* The dog stood up against the fence. (Lv88) **2** to rear (of a horse) *Le cheval s'a mâté.* The horse reared up. (VM) ◊ •**se mâter contre** to react, protest, rebel against *Après que son père a mouri, le jeune bougre s'a mâté contre sa famille.* After his father died, the young man rebelled against his family. (LA) <LA, VM, Lv88> <***Loc:*** LA, SL, VM, Da84, Lv88>

matériaux [materjo] *n.m.pl.* materials, building materials <***Loc:*** Da84>

matérielle [materjel] *n.f.* material, stock, lumber <***Loc:*** Da84>

maternité [matærnite] *n.f.* maternity, motherhood <***Loc:*** Da84>

mathématique [matematik] *n.f.* mathematics, arithmetic <***Loc:*** Da84>

matière [matjær] *n.f.* **1** matter, substance, material, stuff **Il y a de la matière dans son œil.* There's something in his eye. (Da84) **2** pus *Ça a fait sortir la matière du clou.* It made the pus come out of the blister. (VM) <***Loc:*** SL, VM, Da84, Lv88>

matin [matɛ̃] *n.m.* morning ◊ •**à (ce) matin / ce matin** this morning *Il s'est abrié chaudement à matin pour la pêche.* He dressed warmly this morning for fishing. (Lv88) *T'es pas venue à matin.* You didn't come this morning. (Lv88) *À ce matin j'ai repassé un tas de linge.* This morning I ironed a pile of laundry. (VM) *Il fait manière frais ce matin.* It's a bit cold this morning. (AC) <AC, AV, EV, SM, TB, VM, Da84, Lv88> •**de bon matin** early, in the morning *Faut qu'alle soye là-bas de bon matin pour prendre ses tests pour son sang.* She has to be there early to get her blood tests. (TB) <TB, Da84> <***Loc:*** AC, AV, EV, LA, LF, SM, TB, VM, Da84, Gu00, Hi02, Lv88>

matinal, -e [matinal] *adj.* early, early rising *J'ai jamais été matinal, moi. J'aime trop dormir.* I have never been early to rise. I like to sleep too much. (LA) <***Loc:*** LA, Da84>

matinée [matine] *n.f.* **1** morning, forenoon **2** afternoon show ◊ •**faire la grasse matinée** to sleep late <La99> <***Loc:*** Da84, Hi02, La99>

matou [matu] *n.m.* **1** tomcat **2** tomcatting man <***Loc:*** Da84, Hi02>

matrice [matris] *n.f.* **1** matrix **2** womb <***Loc:*** Da84>

mâtrissage [matrisaʒ] *n.m.* mastery **La première priorité est le mâtrissage de la langue Cajine.* The first priority is mastery of the Cajun language. (Wh83) <***Loc:*** Wh83>

mature [matyr] *adj.* ripe, mature *Il est pas mature encore, il va pas se tenir à son job.* He isn't mature yet, he will not stick with his job. (Lv88) <***Loc:*** Lv88>

maturité [matyrite] *n.f.* maturity, adulthood <***Loc:*** Da84>

maudiceté [modisəte] *n.f.* badness, evil, meanness <***Loc:*** VM>

maudire [modir] *v.tr.* to curse, damn *Ça va pas faire aucun bien à personne de le maudire comme ça.* It won't do anyone any good to curse him like that. (LA) <***Loc:*** LA, Da84>

maudit[1], -e [modi , -it] *adj.* **1** damned, cursed *Et s'il y avait une bataille, un contre un, eh ben c'est ça que c'était, un contre un. C'était pas des maudits gangs comme t'as asteur.* And if there was a fight, one against one, well that's how it was, one against one. There weren't these damned gangs like you have now. (TB) *Cette maudit affaire a tombé.* That damned thing fell. (TB) **2** bad, evil, mean **Ça, c'est un maudit chien.* That's a mean dog. (Da84) *Il y avait du monde qu'était maudit.* There were people who were mean. (EV) **3** annoying, insufferable *Il est assez maudit!* He's pretty annoying! (Lv88) *C'est lui le plus maudit de la famille.* He's the most insufferable of the family. (Lv88) *Ça c'est maudit.* That's annoying. (SM) **4** bad, mischievous *Les enfants sont maudits, tu sais.* Children are mischievous, you know. (VM) ◊ •**maudit comme une gale** as bad as the mange <SL, La99> •**maudit comme un péché mortel** very ugly <EV, La99> <***Loc:*** AC, AV, EV, LF, SB, SL, SM, TB, VM, Da84, Hi02, La99, Lv88>

maudit[2], -e [modi, -it] *n.* **1** bad, mean, or evil person or thing, son-of-a-gun **Ça fait, quand ce maudit va arrêter de battre comme ça-là, j'aurais un petit bouton-là.* So, when that son-of-a-gun will stop beating like that, I'll have a little button. (EV, An94) **2** rascal, joker, mischievous person *Mon maudit!* You sly dog! (often used among card players when someone makes a good play) (EV) <***Loc:*** AV, EV, IB, LA, SL, An94, Da84, La99>

maudit[3] [modi] *interj.* damn! *On jure pas un vrai tas, mais mon je jure en français des fois: "Maudit!" et "Enfant de garce!"* We don't swear a whole lot, but I swear in French sometimes: "Damn!" and "Son of a bitch!" (TB) <***Loc:*** LF, TB, Lv88>

mauditerie [moditri] *n.f.* badness, evil, meanness <***Loc:*** Da84>

mauvais[1], -e [movɛ, move, -ɛz] *adj.* **1** bad **"Mais," il dit, "tu connais, garçon, c'est peut-être pas une mauvaise idée,* *ça.*" "Well," he says, "you know, son, that may not be a bad idea." (IB, An94) *Malgré le mauvais temps, on a été pêcher.* In spite of the bad weather, we went fishing. (EV) *Il a eu pour emmioler sa petite fille quand elle avait fait un mauvais rêve.* He had to soothe his daughter after she had a bad dream. (EV) *Tu jongles pas que il y a quelqu'un qui peut t'emmener une mauvaise nouvelle.* You don't think that someone could bring you bad news. (VM, ch: *La nouvelle d'un étranger*) *Quand une mouche à miel le piquait c'était mauvais, mauvais, mauvais.* When a bee stung him, it was bad, bad, bad. (IB) **2** evil, wicked **Tu connais, c'est pas que je suis une mauvaise femme.* You know, it's not that I'm an evil woman. (EV, An94) **3** mean *Son chien est pas mauvais.* His dog is not mean. (Lv88) **4** malicious *Il a fait des mauvais tours dans sa vie.* He pulled off some malicious pranks in his life. (LA) **5** wrong, incorrect *Il a été à la mauvaise adresse.* He went to the wrong address. (EV) *Il avait mis son soulier sur le mauvais pied.* He had put his shoe on the wrong foot. (LA) ◊ **•mauvaise comme une guêpe** mean as a wasp or hornet <Da84, La99> **•mauvais comme une puce {la gale} / mauvais comme un {une} serpent à sonnette** very bad <EV, TB, La99> **•mauvaise langue** gossip <LF, SL> **•mauvaise mine** bad look, bad appearance <Da84> **•mauvaises affaires** bad things *Il y avait un tas des mauvaises affaires qu'étaient après aller.* There were lots of bad things that were going on. (LA) <LA, Da84> **•mauvais goût** bad taste <Da84> **•mauvais temps** bad weather <Da84> **•de mauvaise paye** not paying one's debts <LF, SL> **•faire mauvais** to be bad weather <Da84> <***Loc:*** AC, EV, IB, IV, JE, LA, LF, SB, SL, SM, TB, VM, An94, Da84, Hi02, La99, Lv88>

mauvais[2] [movɛ, move] *adv.* in a bad, mean way **Il dit ça montait sur la barrière et ça jappait mauvais.* He says they climbed up on the fence and they barked in a mean way. (SL, An94) <***Loc:*** SL, An94>

mauvaiseté [movɛzte, movɛste] *n.f.* **1** evil, wickedness, meanness *Il l'a fait par mauvaiseté.* He did it out of meanness. (VM) **2** one hair that sticks up and refuses to lie in place <***Loc:*** JE, LF, TB, VM, Da84, Lv88>

mauve[1] [mov] *adj./n.* mauve (color) *On était mauve à force on avait froid.* We were so cold that we were mauve. (JD) <***Loc:*** JD>

mauve[2] [mov] *n.f.* mallow *De la mauve. J'en ai bu plein de ça avec défunte mémère. C'était pour te rafraîchir. Tu pouvais boire ça n'importe qui temps.* Mallow. I drank a lot of that with my late grandmother. It was to refresh you. You drink that whenever you wanted. (TB) <***Loc:*** TB>

mayonnaise [majɔ̃nɛz] *n.f.* mayonnaise <***Loc:*** Da84>

mazette [mazet] *adj.* clumsy <***Loc:*** SM>

mazulka ♦see **mazurka**

mazurka (mazulka) [mazyrka, mazylka] *n.f.* mazurka (type of 6/8 dance) <***Loc:*** Da84>

me [mə] *pron.pers.* **1** *(dir.obj.)* me **Et là, quand je jongle à Lilly Mae, comment gros ça me fâche!* And then, when I think of Lilly Mae, how it angers me so. (EV, An94) *T'aurais dû me voir tomber sur mon gros derrière!* You should have seen me fall on my big behind! (Guoo) *Tu me rends nerveuse.* You make me nervous. (LA) *Et tout d'un coup j'ai sentu quelqu'un, quelque chose de venir par en-arrière de mon et me* GRAB *comme ça.* And suddenly I felt someone, something, come up from behind me and grab me like that. (TB) **Ça me va.* That suits me. (Da84) *Arrête de m'agacer! Tu m'agaces tout le temps!* Stop annoying me. You irritate me all the time! (EV) *Ça m'appelle pour tout quelque chose.* They call me for everything. (IB) **2** *(ind. obj.)* me, to me **Tu vas me donner ça.* You will give me that. (Da84) *Ça qui me donne autant chagrin, je vas jamais te voir encore.* What makes me so sad is that I'm never going to see you again. (ch: *La valse d'amitié*) *C'était ma maman qui m'avait sauvé ça. Elle avait attaché à ça et me sauvait ça.* It was my mother who had saved them for me. She had become attached to them and was saving them for me. (AV) *Mon coeur agite pas bien, c'est pour ça le docteur m'a donné cette médecine.* My heart doesn't function well, that's why the doctor gave me this medecine. (VM) *Il m'a avancé dix piastres.* He lent me ten dollars. (JE) *Il m'a fait des mortels, des misères.* He was nasty to me. (VM) **3** *(refl.)* myself *Je m'ai bien amusé avec ça.* I had great fun with that. (EV) **Faudra je vas me coucher.* I'll have to go to bed. (EV, An94) *Je veux pas rester chez eux; je me sens comme si je suis après abuser dessus eux-autres.* I don't want to stay at their house; I feel like I'm taking advantage of them. (Lv88) *Je me suis allongé après dîner.* I laid down after dinner. (SM) <***Loc:*** AC, AV, EV, IV, JE, LA, SL, TB, VM, An84, An94, Hi02, Da84>

MEAN[1] [min] *v.tr.invar.* to mean **Tu* MEAN *ça?* You mean that? (Da84) *Mon père appelait ça un caragne. Caragne, je sais pas qui ça veut* MEAN. My father used to call that a caragne. I don't know what that means. (TB) <***Loc:*** JE, TB, VM, Da84, Lv88>

MEAN[2] [min] *adj.* mean, wicked, malicious *Ça c'est mauvais, c'est* MEAN *comme tout.* That's bad, it's mean as anything. (VM) <***Loc:*** SM, VM>

mécanicien [mekɑ̃nisjɛ̃] *n.m.* mechanic <***Loc:*** Da84, Hi02>

mécanique [mekɑ̃nik] *n.f.* mechanics, mechanic work **Moi, j'ai appris tout ça je connais à travers de mon papa. La charpente et la mécanique, et tout ça.* I learned all that I know from my father. Carpentry and mechanic work, and all that. (LA, An84) *Il se connaît bien dans la mécanique.* He knows a lot about mechanics. (VM) <***Loc:*** LA, VM, An84, Da84>

méchanceté [meʃɑ̃ste] *n.f.* wickedness, badness, evil <***Loc:*** Da84>

méchant[1], **-e** [meʃɑ̃, -ɑ̃t] *adj.* **1** bad, nasty *Quand t'avais du* *méchant temps, tu protégeais les chassis, tu fermais les fenêtres.* When there was bad weather, you would protect the windows, you would close the shutters. (AV) **2** wicked, evil, malicious, mean *Le serpent à sonnette c'est le plus méchant il n-a dans la Louisiane.* The rattlesnake is the most vicious [snake] in Louisiana. (AV) **3** mischievous *Les enfants sont assez méchants aujourd'hui.* The children are so mischievous today. (LA) **4** wrong *Ça c'est le méchant morceau pour l'automobile.* This is the wrong piece for the car. (AV) **5** thin, skinny *Une méchante vache.* A thin cow. (EV) **6** terribly good *C'était un méchant joueur d'accordéon.* He was a terribly good accordion player. (EV) ◊ **•méchant comme une guêpe** mean as a wasp <AV, La99> <***Loc:*** AC, AV, EV, IB, LA, LF, SB, SM, TB, Da84, Hi02, La99>

méchant[2], -e [meʃɑ̃, -ɑ̃t] *n.* wicked, evil, bad, malicious person or thing <***Loc:*** Da84>

méchant[3] [meʃɑ̃] *adv.* extremely, very *Il a une méchant grosse tête.* He has a heck of a big head. (EV) <***Loc:*** EV>

mèche[1] (**maîche**) [mɛʃ] *n.m./f.* **1** marsh, treeless swamp *La mèche n'a pas d'arbres. C'est juste de l'eau.* The marsh doesn't have any trees. It's just water. (VM) **2** area off of Highway 14 between Kaplan and Gueydan in Vermilion Parish *Le monde entre Kaplan et Gueydan reste au mèche.* People between Kaplan and Gueydan live in the marsh. (VM) ◊ **•maîche tremblant** trembling marsh (floating mat of vegetation on water or mud) *Pour arriver au* BLIND, *il fallait traverser du maîche tremblant.* To get to the blind, you had to cross a trembling marsh. (LA) <LA> **•grande mèche** sea marsh <Da84> <***Loc:*** IB, LA, LF, SL, SM, VM, Da84, Gu00, Hi02, Lv88>

mèche[2] [mɛʃ] *n.m./f.* **1** lock (of hair) *Quand ça avait les oppressions, [...], ça allait à un arbre et ça te coupait une mèche de cheveux et ça mettait ça dans l'arbre.* When they had asthma, they would go to a tree and they would cut a lock of your hair and they would put it in the tree. (EV) **2** leather tip of a whip **3** wick (of a lamp, candle, etc.) **4** fuse *Ça lachait un dynamite dans le trou avec un grand mèche.* They would throw dynamite with a long fuse into the hole. (EV) **6** burner rack **6** bit, drill **7** core of an abcess or boil *Mame va arracher la mèche demain.* Mom is going to pull out the core tomorrow. (VM) ◊ **•mèche en bois** drill bit for wood <JE> **•mèche en fer** drill bit for metal <JE> **•mèche-terrière** ground auger <VM> <***Loc:*** EV, JE, LF, VM, Da84>

médaille [medaj] *n.f.* medal <***Loc:*** Da84>

médecin [medsɛ̃] *n.m.* doctor, physician **Le médecin après la mort c'est trop tard.* After death, it's too late for the doctor. (Da84) <***Loc:*** Da84>

médecinal ♦see **médicinal**

médecine [mɛtsin, medsin] *n.f.* medicine, medication, remedy *Ça, c'est de la médecine que je prends, j'ai eu un petit* STROKE. That's the medecine that I take, I had a little stroke. (VM) <***Loc:*** AC, AV, EV, JE, LA, TB, VM, Da84, Hi02, Lv88>

médeciner [medsine, metsine] **I** *v.tr.* **1** to medicate, treat with medicine *Le bébé avait une forte fièvre et j'ai commencé à le médeciner.* The baby had a high fever and I started to medicate him. (Lv88) **2** to treat, spray (plants, livestock, etc.) *J'ai médeciné l'arbre.* I sprayed the tree. (VM) *Les vaches étaient tout affilées dans le chute pour être médecinées.* The cows were lined up in the chute to be medicated. (LA) **II se médeciner** *v.pron.* to take medicine, medicate o.s. *Il a eu pour se médeciner le restant de sa vie après son opération.* He had to take medicine for the rest of his life after his operation. (LA) <***Loc:*** LA, VM, Da84, Lv88>

médical, -e [medikal] *adj.* medical *Vos frais médicals.* Your medical expenses. (VM) <***Loc:*** VM, Da84>

médicament [medikamɑ̃] *n.m.* medicine, medicament, remedy <***Loc:*** Da84>

médicinal (**médecinal**) [medsinal] *adj.* medicinal, having healing properties *La racine de cette herbe-là est médicinal.* The root of that plant is medicinal. (VM) <***Loc:*** VM, Da84>

médire [medir] *v.intr.* to gossip about, talk bad about **Médire sur les autres.* To talk evil of, gossip about others. (Da84) <***Loc:*** Da84>

méditation [meditasjɔ̃] *n.f.* meditation <***Loc:*** Da84>

meeting [mitin, mitiŋ] *n.m.* meeting, assembly, gathering <***Loc:*** EV, TB, Da84, Lv88, Ph36>

méfiance [mefjɑ̃s] *n.f.* mistrust, distrust <***Loc:*** Da84>

méfiant, -e [mefjɑ̃, -ɑ̃t] *adj.* suspicious, unbelieving *Moi, je suis méfiante avec son conte.* I don't believe her story. (EV) <***Loc:*** EV>

méfier (se) [mefje] *v.pron.* to distrust, suspect, be on one's guard *Tu ferais mieux de te méfier de ce monde ça!* You'd better beware of those people. (AC) <***Loc:*** AC, Da84>

meilleur, -e [mejœr] *adj.* **1** better *La récolte pourrait être meilleure, elle pourrait être plus chétie.* The harvest could be better, it could be poorer. (Lv88) *Un* SKIMMERNET *est meilleur, tu peux travailler ça le jour ou le soir.* A skimmernet is better, you can work that during the day or the evening. (TB) *Il dit cèze-là que t'attrapes est beaucoup meilleurs que cèze-là qu'est faits dans un parc, qu'est faits dans une cage.* He says that those that you catch are a lot better than those that come from a breeding tank, that are made in a cage. (TB) **2** favorite *Les filles, on aimait jouer avec des poupées, ça c'était notre meilleur passe-temps.* Girls liked to play with dolls, that was our favorite pastime. (SM) **3** *(superlative; used with art.def.)* the best *Le meilleur buveur du pays.* The best drinker in the land. (ch: *Mon bon vieux mari*) *Allons les vérifier pour voir qui c'est le meilleur.* Let's compare them to see which one is the best. (VM) **Le meilleur des deux.* The best one of the two. (Da84) *Alle est la meilleure espeleure de la classe.* She is the best speller in the class. (AV) *Ma mère fait les meilleures poutines aux mûres t'as jamais mangées.* My mother makes the best blackberry dumplings you've ever eaten. (VM) <***Loc:*** AC, EV, LA, PQ, SL, TB, An94, Da84, Hi02>

mêlailler [melaje] **I** *v.tr.* **1** to mix, mix up *J'ai mêlaillé mes affaires dans mon tiroir.* I mixed up my things in my drawer. (SM) **2** to mix up, jumble, disorganize *Les petits ont tout mêlaillé mes papiers.* The children mixed my papers all up. (EV) **II se mêlailler** *v.pron.* **1** to mix with, keep company with **Ce bon à rien vient se mêlailler avec le bon monde.* That good-for-nothing comes and mixes with the good people. (Da84) **2** to quarrel *Ils vont se mêlailler bien vite là.* They'll be arguing soon. (TB) <***Loc:*** EV, SL, SM, TB, VM, Da84, Lv88>

mélanage [melɑ̃naʒ] *n.m.* mix-up, mess *C'est le plus gros mélanage!* It's the biggest mess! (EV) <***Loc***: EV>

mélange [melaʒ, melɑ̃ʒ] *n.m.* mixture, jumble <***Loc:*** AC, Da84, Hi02>

mélanger [melɑ̃ʒe] *v.tr.* to mix, blend *Il a mélangé les œufs et la farine dans la même bol.* He mixed the eggs and flour in the same bowl. (LA) <***Loc:*** LA, Da84, Hi02>

melasse [məlas, mlas] *n.m.* **1** molasses **2** syrup <***Loc:*** SJ, Da84, Lv88>

mêlé, -e [mele] *n.* mulatto <***Loc:*** Lv88>

mêlée [mele] *n.f.* melee, fracas, free-for-all fight <***Loc:*** Da84>

mêler (méler) [mele] **I** *v.tr.* **1** to mix, blend *C'est pour mêler le ciment.* It is to mix the cement. (AC) *Alors, y'a quelque chose en-dedans et alle est après, ça-là, après mêler quelque chose avec et elle va le mouler.* There is something in there and then she is mixing it with something and then she is going to grind it. (JE) **2** to intermingle, tangle up *Mêler le fil.* To tangle up the thread. (AC) **3** to confuse *Il m'a mêlé dans mes affaires. Il aurait pas dû dire arien.* He mixed me up in the way I was doing things. He shouldn't have said anything. (LA) **II se mêler** *v.pron.* to mix, mingle *Quand ça se mêlait, le tracas prenait. Ça se battait beaucoup souvent.* When they got together, there was trouble. They fought very often. (AC) ◊ **•mêler son grain de sel** to interfere, meddle, stick one's nose in other people's affairs <Da84> **•se mêler dans** to interfere in, get mixed up with, butt in *Il se mêle dans tous les affaires de sa belle-famille.* He gets mixed up in all of his in-laws' business. (EV) <EV, Da84> **•mêlé dans** tangled up in *Y'a assez de mousse, et t'as ton appât, ta loche reste mêlée dans la mousse et le poisson mord pas.* There's so much moss, and you've got your bait, the minnow stays tangled up in the moss and the fish don't bite. (TB) <TB> <***Loc:*** AC, AV, EV, JE, LA, SL, TB, Da84, Lv88>

méli-mélange [melimelɑ̃ʒ, melimelaʒ] *n.m.* **1** disorder, mess, jumble, hodge-podge *C'est un vrai méli-mélange dans sa chambre.* It's a real mess in his room. (SM) **2** misunderstanding *Tout ça a causé un méli-mélange entre ces deux.* All that caused a misunderstanding between those two. (IB) <***Loc:*** IB, SJ, SL, SM, VM, Da84, Lv88>

mélodie [melodi] *n.f.* melody, tune <***Loc:*** Da84>

mélodieux, -ieuse [melodjø, -jøz] *adj.* melodious, tuneful <***Loc:*** Da84>

melon [mlɔ̃, məlɔ̃, məlɑ̃] *n.m.* **1** melon **2** watermelon ◊ **•melon d'eau** ***a*** watermelon ***b*** cantaloupe <AC, AL, IB, IV, LF, SL, SM, TB, VM, Da84, Hi02> **•melon doux** ***a*** watermelon ***b*** honeydew melon <LF, SM, TB, Da84> **•melon (en) français / melon de France** ***a*** cantaloupe ***b*** muskmelon <AV, EV, IB, IV, JD, JE, LA, LF, SB, SL, SM, TB, VM, Da84, Hi02, Lv88> **•melon musqué** ***a*** muskmelon ***b*** cantaloupe <LF> **•melon sent-bon** creeping cucumber, melonette (locally known as "smellin' melon") <SJ> **•melon vert** watermelon <TB> <***Loc:*** AC, AL, AV, CL, EV, IB, IV, JD, JE, LA, LF, SB, SL, SM, TB, VM, Da84, Hi02, Lv88>

mêlzir [mɛlzir] *v.tr.* to mix <***Loc:*** VM>

membrane [mɑ̃brɑ̃n] *n.f.* membrane, skin <***Loc:*** Da84>

membre [mɑ̃m, mɑ̃b(r)] *n.m.* **1** limb, member (of the body) **2** member of a group or society ◊ **•membre de conseil (du village)** alderman <VM> **•membre du Congrès** congressman <Fa77> **•membre du jury** member of the jury, juror <Da84> <***Loc:*** VM, Da84, Fa77>

membré, -e [mɑ̃bre] *adj.* built (of one's physique) ◊ **•bien membré** well built, muscular *Un homme bien membré.* A muscular, well-built man. (AC) <AC> **•membré comme une tortue de rosée** husky, muscular <EV, La99> <***Loc:*** AC, EV, La99>

même[1] [mɛ̃m, mœ̃m] *adj.* **1** same **C'est tout la même chose.* It's all the same thing. (Da84) **J'ai toujours les mêmes sentiments qui me fachaient en 1975, et ça me fache d'autant plus aujourd'hui.* I still have the same feelings that angered me in 1975, and they anger me that much more today. (LA, An84) **Ils ont dansé chacun son tour avec la même fille.* They each took a turn dancing with the same girl. (SL, An94) **2** very, exact, very same **C'est ça même.* That's the very thing. (Da84) **Y tire son existence même de ses traditions, de son langage, de sa musique d'accordéon et de son Djeu.* He draws his very existence from his traditions, his language, his accordeon music and his God. (Wh83) **3** itself *Les familles de Robichaux dans la Paroisse Lafourche y en a pas une qu'est parent* EXCEPT *la famille même.* The families of Robichaux in Lafourche Parish, there isn't one that's related except the family itself. (LF) *Je m'associe pas avec ça. C'est la crasse même.* I don't associate with them. That's trash itself. (SM) *Et on a un joli parc sur la Grand'Ile même.* And there's a nice park right on Grand Isle itself. (LF) ◊ **•le même / la même / les mêmes** the same (one, thing, person, etc.) *Eusse parle un bon français [...]. C'est aisé à comprendre mais c'est pas le même.* They speak a good French. It's easy to understand but it's not the same. (TB) *Tu vois, je suis manière* COLORBLIND. *Vert et bleu ça me ressemble les mêmes.* You see, I'm somewhat colorblind. Green and blue look the same to me. (TB) <LF, TB,

Da84> <***Loc:*** AC, AV, EV, LA, LF, SB, SJ, SL, TB, VM, An84, An94, Da84, Hi02, Wh83>

même[2] [mɛ̃m, mœ̃m] *adv.* even *Même avec ça il a fait, il mérite pas d'aller en prison.* Even with what he did, he doesn't deserve to go to prison. (EV) *La fricassée était trop pimentée, c'était même pas mangeable.* The stew was too peppery, it wasn't even edible. (EV) *Je vas pas même répondre à des menteries comme ça. C'est insultant.* I will not even respond to lies like that. It's insulting. (LA) *Il pouvait pas s'empêcher de craquer des farces, même à l'enterrement.* He couldn't keep himself from telling jokes, even at the funeral. (LA) ◊ **•être à même de choisir** to be free to choose, have the choice <Da84> **•pour (de) même** ***a*** really, truly *Je l'ai fâché pour même.* I really made him angry. (Lv88) *Tu dois croire que je suis couillon pour de même!* You must think I'm really stupid! (TB) *J. dit, "Mam tu m'as proche fait peur des garçons pour même!"* J. said, "Mom, you really almost made me afraid of boys!" (EV) **Là, on a commencé à jouer pour même, moi et lui. On a pris à jouer tout partout.* Then we started playing seriously, me and him. We began to play all over the place. (An84) ***b*** however, nevertheless *Pour même, je vais le faire.* Nevertheless, I'm going to do it. (VM) <EV, IB, SJ, TB, VM, An84, Lv88> <***Loc:*** EV, LA, LF, SM, TB, An84, Da84, Lv88>

mémère [mɛ̃mær] *n.f.* grandmother <***Loc:*** EV, SB, SM, TB, VM, Da84, Lv88>

mémoire[1] [mɛ̃mwar] *n.f.* memory, remembrance <***Loc:*** EV, Da84, Hi02, Lv88>

mémoire[2] [mɛ̃mwar] *n.m.* memoir, written account of one's life <***Loc:*** Da84>

mémorable [mɛ̃morab(l)] *adj.* memorable *Une noce mémorable.* A memorable wedding. (EV) <***Loc:*** EV, Da84>

menaçant, -e [mənasɑ̃, -ɑ̃t] *adj.* threatening, menacing (of weather, words) *Un temps menaçant.* Threatening weather. (LA) <***Loc:*** LA, Da84>

menace [mənas] *n.f.* threat, menace <***Loc:*** Da84>

menacer [mənase] *v.tr.* to threaten, menace *Sa femme le menace de prendre les enfants et de partir à Port Arthur s'il arrête pas de boire.* His wife is threatening to take the kids and leave for Port Arthur if he doesn't quit drinking. (VM) <***Loc:*** VM, Da84>

ménage [mɛ̃naʒ] *n.m.* **1** housekeeping **2** household, married couple **3** furniture ◊ **•faire le ménage** to clean house <Hi02> **•faire un bon ménage** to live a happy family life, get along as man and wife <Da84> <***Loc:*** AC, EV, SJ, SM, TB, Da84, Hi02, Lv88>

ménagement (**management**) [mɛ̃naʒmɑ̃, mɑ̃nɛʒmɑ̃, mɛ̃nærʒmɑ̃] *n.m.* **1** management **2** economy, thrift *Il y a pas de ménagement là du tout. Eux-autres dépense tout, tout!* There's no thrift there at all. They spend everything! (TB) <***Loc:*** IB, TB, VM, Di32, Lv88>

ménager [mɛ̃naʒe, mɛ̃nærʒe] **I** *v.tr.* to manage, handle *Si Carter ménage bien son affaire, il va être président.* If Carter manages his affairs well, he will be president. (Lv88) **II** *v.intr.* to be frugal, economize, save money *Ça va tout gaspiller. Ça connaît plus ménager, les jeunes mondes.* They waste everything. Young people don't know how to economize. (TB) **III se ménager** *v.pron.* **1** to spare o.s., save one's energies *Faut que tu te ménages; tu joues à la pelote demain.* You have to rest up; you're playing ball tomorrow. (LA) **2** to organize one's resources efficiently *S'il veut aller au collège il faudra qu'il se ménage.* If he wants to go to college he'll have to manage his resources. (LA) <***Loc:*** EV, LA, TB, VM, Da84, Lv88>

ménagère [mɛ̃naʒær] *n.f.* **1** housekeeper **2** female manager <***Loc:*** Da84>

ménagerie [mɛ̃naʒri] *n.f.* **1** menagerie **2** housekeeping, home management *La ménagerie de la maison est laissée à Marie.* The management of the house is left to Mary. (SJ) <***Loc:*** JE, SJ, Da84>

ménageur (**manager, manageur**) [mɛ̃naʒœr, mɑ̃nɛʒœr, mɑ̃nɛʒø] *n.m.* manager *Il était le ménageur pour l'habitation.* He was the plantation manager. (SB) <***Loc:*** LF, SB, TB, VM, Da84, Lv88>

mendianité [mɑ̃djɑ̃nite] *n.f.* beggary, begging <***Loc:*** JE>

mendianer [mɑ̃djɑ̃ne] *v.tr.* to beg, beg persistently <***Loc:*** SM, VM>

mener [məne, mne] **I** *v.tr.* **1** to bring, guide, lead **2** to conduct, carry out *Un doigt de monde étranger qu'a venu, ç'a commencé à mener l'école en anglais. Ça fait y avait pus d'école en français après.* A handful of foreigners came, they started conducting school in English. So there was no more school in French after that. (TB) **II** *v.intr.* to carry on, misbehave *Mon mari est après mener aujourd'hui parce que notre gendre a pas ramassé ses outils.* My husband is carrying on today because our son-in-law didn't bring back his tools. (LA) ◊ **•mener la {une} vie** to lead a life *Manoune, j'sus assez vieille pour me défendre moi-même et, tracasse-toi pas, j'mène la vie comme je la veux.* Manoune, I'm old enough to get along on my own and, don't worry, I lead my life the way I want to. (ThCa: *La douce réunion*) <Da84, ThCa> <***Loc:*** LA, TB, Da84, ThCa>

menfoutbin[1] [mɑ̃fubɛ̃] *adj.* careless ◊ **•à la menfoutbin** carelessly <AV> <***Loc:*** AV>

menfoutbin[2] [mɑ̃fubɛ̃] *n.m.* lackadaisical, carefree person <***Loc:*** IB, SJ>

menir ♦see **venir**

menoir [mɛ̃nwar] *n.m.* carriage shaft <***Loc:*** JE>

ménopause [mɛ̃nopoz] *n.m.* menopause <***Loc:*** Da84>

ménotte [mɛ̃nɔt] *n.f.* long mitten without fingers (for protecting hands and arms) <***Loc:*** VM>

menotte [mənɔt] *n.f.* handcuff <***Loc:*** JE, Da84>

mensonge [mɑ̃sɔ̃ʒ] *n.m.* lie, fib <***Loc:*** An94, Da84>

menterie (**mentrie**) [mɑ̃tri] *n.m./f.* **1** lie, fib, falsehood *T'as* *fini de conter tes menteries?* Are you finished telling lies? (ThCa: *Le charivari*) **2** joking, exaggeration, tall tale ◊ **•menterie blanche** white lie <Da84> **•grosse menterie** big lie <Da84> <***Loc:*** AL, LA, LF, SM, TB, VM, Da84, Hi02, Lv88, ThCa>

menteur, -euse [mɑ̃tœr, -øz] *n.* liar, prevaricator ◊ **•être menteur comme un arracheur de dents** to lie through one's teeth <Da84> <***Loc:*** TB, Da84>

menthe [mɑ̃t] *n.f.* mint <***Loc:*** SL, Da84>

mention [mɑ̃sjɔ̃] *n.f.* mention ◊ **•faire mention** to make mention <Da84> <***Loc:*** Da84>

mentionner [mɑ̃sjɔ̃ne] *v.tr.* to mention, name **Ça a venu que je pouvais plus entendre le nom de "La porte d'en arrière" mentionné du tout.* It got to where I could no longer bear to hear the name of "*La porte d'en arrière*" mentioned at all. (VM, An94) <***Loc:*** VM, An94, Da84>

mentir [mɑ̃tir] *v.intr.* to lie, fib, tell lies *Il dit qu'il dit tout le temps la vérité, mais au contraire, il mentit souvent.* He says he always tells the truth, but, on the contrary, he often lies. (LA) **Quand il mentissait, il fallait tout le temps lui haler sur sa queue de capot.* When he would lie, one always had to pull on his coattail. (LA, An94) ◊ **•mentir comme un arracheur de dents / mentir comme un dentiste** to lie through one's teeth <Da84, La99> <***Loc:*** LA, An94, Da84, Hi02, La99>

menton [mɑ̃tɔ̃, matɔ̃] *n.m.* chin <***Loc:*** TB, Da84>

mentonnière [mɑ̃tɔ̃jær, motɔ̃jær] *n.f.* goatee <***Loc:*** IB, JE, LF>

mentrie ♦see **menterie**

mépris [mepri] *n.m.* **1** criticism **2** slander, gossip, back-biting *Il a dit du mépris dessus ma mère.* He said slanderous things about my mother. (VM) <***Loc:*** VM, Da84, Hi02, Lv88>

méprisable [meprizab(l)] *adj.* reproachable, deserving of criticism or blame *C'est pas lui mais son frère qu'est méprisable dans cette affaire.* It's not he but his brother who is deserving of blame in this matter. (LA) <***Loc:*** LA, Da84>

méprisant, -e [meprizɑ̃, -ɑ̃t] *adj.* critical, given to gossip or criticism *Elle est méprisante. Elle va parler derrière ton dos.* She is given to gossip. She will talk behind your back. (LA) <***Loc:*** LA, Da84>

méprisard, -e [meprizar, -ard] *adj.* contemptuous, derisive, scornful, critical <***Loc:*** LF>

mépriser [meprize] **I** *v.tr.* **1** to criticize, find fault with *Mondale a pas arrêté de mépriser Reagan.* Mondale did not stop criticizing Reagan. (Lv88) **2** to slander, gossip about, speak badly of *Alle est toujours après mépriser mes amis.* She is always speaking badly of my friends. (VM) **II** *v.intr.* **1** to criticize, find fault *Tout ça il fait c'est mépriser.* All he does is criticize. (LA) **2** to gossip maliciously *Tu connais dans quel mois les femmes méprisent le moins? Dans février, parce qu'il y a moins de jours.* Do you know in which month women gossip the least? February, because there are fewer days. (Lv88) <***Loc:*** LA, LF, SL, VM, Da84, Hi02, Lv88>

mépriseur, -euse [meprizœr, -øz] *adj.* critical, prone to slanderous or scandalous talk *Elle est beaucoup mépriseuse. Je peux pas la* STAND! She's so critical. I can't stand her! (LA) <***Loc:*** LA, LF, Da84, Lv88>

mer[1] [mær] *n.f.* sea, ocean, any large body of water ◊ **•la grande mer *a*** the ocean ***b*** the Gulf of Mexico <TB, Lv88> <***Loc:*** TB, Da84, Hi02, Lv88>

mer[2] [mær] *n.m.* froth, foam, scum *Sur la batture du bayou il y avait beaucoup du mer.* On the batture there was a lot of foam. (TB) <***Loc:*** TB, Di32>

merci [mærsi] *n.m.* **1** thank you **2** mercy ◊ **•merci beaucoup** thank you very much <Da84> **•merci bien** many thanks <Da84, Lv88> **•merci Bon Dieu** thank God *J'ai jonglé par après mais on a jamais miséré, merci Bon Dieu pour ça.* I thought about it later but we never suffered, thank God for that. (AC) <AC, EV, Da84, La99, Lv88> **•bien merci** many thanks, thanks a lot *Mais bien merci!* Well thanks a lot! (TB) <TB, Da84> **•c'est pas merci** it's not free or cheap *Il voudrait un nouveau char, mais c'est pas merci.* He would like a new car, but it's not cheap. (LA) <LA, Da84> **•être à le merci de** to be at the mercy of <Da84> **•grand merci** many thanks <Da84> <***Loc:*** AC, EV, LA, TB, Da84, Hi02, La99, Lv88>

mercredi[1] [mærkrədi, mækrədi, mekrədi, mœrkredi] *n.m.* Wednesday ◊ **•Mercredi des Cendres** Ash Wednesday <LF, Da84> <***Loc:*** EV, IB, LF, SM, VM, Da84, Hi02, La99>

mercredi[2] [mærkrədi, mækrədi, mekrədi, mœrkredi] *interj.* euphemism for "merde" <***Loc:*** EV, IB, LF, SM, VM, Da84, Hi02, La99>

mercure [mærkyr] *n.m.* mercury, quicksilver <***Loc:*** Da84>

merdailler [mærdaje] *v.intr.* to piddle around, waste time *Arrête donc de merdailler là-bas et viens faire quelque chose.* Stop piddling around over there and come do something. (LA) <***Loc:*** LA>

merdasser [mærdase] *v.intr.* to stir up trouble *C'est pas beurdasser qu'il est après faire, c'est merdasser.* It's not just wasting time that he's doing, he's stirring up trouble. (VM) <***Loc:*** VM>

merde [mærd] *n.f.* [*vulg.*] shit, crap **Ça, c'est de la merde.* That's bullshit. (Da84) ◊ **•merde en bouteille** deceitful act <Da84> **•ça c'est (de la) merde chez Pierre** now trouble has really begun <La99> **•là, la merde est pris** now the trouble has begun <La99> **•pas valoir une merde** to not be worth a crap <Da84> **•va à la merde** go to hell! <La99> <***Loc:*** AV, Da84, Hi02, La99>

merdeux, -euse [mærdø, -øz] *adj.* **1** dirty, shitty *Ses pantalons étaient tout merdeux.* His pants were all shitty. (LA) **2** obnoxious *Mon espèce de petit merdeux!* You obnoxious little kid! (LA) <***Loc:*** LA, Da84>

mère [mær] *n.f.* **1** mother **2** mother superior ◊ •**mère patate** seed potato <Da84> <*Loc:* AC, EV, IV, LA, SL, TB, VM, Da84, Hi02>

Méricain ♦see **Américain**

meringue [mərɛ̃g] *n.* meringue <*Loc:* Da84>

merise [mriz] *n.f.* **1** black cherry **2** wild cherry <*Loc:* VM, Da84>

merisier [mərizje] *n.m.* black cherry tree <*Loc:* Da84, Fa77, Ho90>

mérite [merit] *n.m.* merit, value, worth *On connaît que les sauvages ont un gros mérite dans l'Amérique.* We know that Indians have great merit in America. (EV, ch: *Indien sur le chicot*) <*Loc:* EV, Da84>

mériter [merite] *v.tr.* to merit, deserve, earn *Pour l'amour de Dieu, quoi c'est j'ai fait au bon Dieu pour mériter ça!* For the love of God, what did I do to God to deserve this! (ThCa: *La table des veuves*) ◊ •**mériter de** to deserve, be deserving of *Même avec ça il a fait, il mérite pas d'aller en prison.* Even with what he did, he doesn't deserve to go to prison. (EV) <EV> <*Loc:* EV, Da84, Hi02, ThCa>

merle [mærl] *n.m.* blackbird <*Loc:* Da84>

merliton ♦see **mirliton**

merrain [merɛ̃] *n.m.* roof stave, large wood shingle <*Loc:* EV, IB, SL, TB, Da84, Gu00, Lv88>

merveille [mærvɛj] *n.f.* marvel, wonder, prodigy <*Loc:* Da84>

merveilleux, -euse [mærvejø, -øz] *adj.* marvelous, wonderful, great *Son souper était merveilleux.* Her supper was marvelous. (LA) <*Loc:* LA, Da84>

mes ♦see **mon**

mesdames ♦see **madame**

mesdemoiselles ♦see **mademoiselle**

message [mesaʒ] *n.m.* message <*Loc:* LF, Da84>

messager [mesaʒe] *n.m.* messenger <*Loc:* Da84>

messe [mɛs] *n.f.* Mass ◊ •**messe basse** low Mass, unsung Mass <Da84> •**messe blanche {sec}** prayers, singing, reading, etc. offered by lay people in lieu of actual Mass <JE, Da84, Di32> •**messe noire** irreverent parody of the Catholic Mass <EV> •**grande messe** high Mass <Da84> <*Loc:* EV, JE, SL, TB, Da84, Di32, Hi02, La99, Wh83>

messieurs ♦see **monsieur**

mesurable [məzyrab(l)] *adj.* measurable *C'est pas la peine de deviner combien tu me dois. C'est mesurable.* You don't have to guess how much you owe me. It's a measurable quantity. (LA) <*Loc:* LA, Da84>

mesure[1] [məzyr, mezyr, myzyr] *n.f.* **1** dimension, extent, measure, gauge, size **2** measurement **3** yardstick, ruler **4** measuring tape **5** measuring spoon **6** measuring cup ◊ •**à mesure** little by little *Coupées à la main, les pailles étaient ôtées à mesure.* Cut by hand, straws were removed as fast as they were cut. (IB) <IB> •**à mesure que** as *A mesure qu'il grossit, il commence à avoir la couleur dans la patte, la dernière patte.* As it grows, it starts to get the color in its leg, its hind leg. (TB) <LF, TB> <*Loc:* EV, IB, JE, LF, SL, SM, TB, VM, Da84>

mesure[2] [məzyr, mezyr, myzyr] *n.f.* legislative bill *La mesure pour la taxe est dans le sénat.* The legislative bill for taxation is in the senate. (VM) <*Loc:* VM, Check DB>

mesurement [mezyrmɑ̃] *n.m.* measurement, measuring <*Loc:* Da84>

mesurer [mezyre, myzyre] *v.tr.* to measure *Alors, j'ai été visiter parmi les fermiers et mesurer la quantité de récolte ils aviont.* So, I would go out to visit the farmers and measure the amount of crop they had. (SL) <*Loc:* LF, SL, SM, VM, Da84>

métal [metal] *n.m.* metal <*Loc:* Da84>

méthodiste [metodis(t)] *adj.* Methodist *Ils s'ont mariés dans une église méthodiste.* They were married in a Methodist church. (LA) <*Loc:* LA, Da84, Hi02>

métier [metje] *n.m.* **1** trade, profession, job *Mon père avait un métier, il était un laitier, il tirait des vaches.* My father had a trade, he was a milker, he milked cows. (IB) **2** hand loom, spinning wheel ◊ •**faire le métier** to spin, weave <Fa77> •**fait au métier** homespun <Da84> <*Loc:* IB, LA, SL, Da84, Fa77>

mettable [metab(l)] *adj.* wearable, fit to wear *Ce pantalon est pas mettable. Il est plein de trous.* These pants are not wearable. They're full of holes. (VM) <*Loc:* VM, Da84>

mettre [mɛt(r)] **I** *v.tr.* **1** to put *J'aime pas mettre cette médecine sus mes bobos parce qu'elle est piquante.* I don't like to put that medicine on my sores because it stings. (LA) *Tu plantes ça et là après t'arraches ça, et puis tu mets ça à chesser en dehors. Des pistaches.* You plant them and then you dig them up, and you set them outside to dry. Peanuts. (TB) *Ma grand-mère mettait pas de roux dans son gombo. Elle l'épaississait avec du filé.* My grandmother didn't make her gumbo with a roux. She thickened it with filé. (VM) *Si t'as pas de coton, tu peux mettre un sac de pite dans ta quilt.* If you don't have any cotton, you can put a jute sack in your quilt. (Lv88) *Et après ça, que tout ça c'était fini, ben là ils mettont le plancher ou le* DECK *sur le bateau.* And after that, when it was all done, they put the deck on the boat. (LF) *On les mettait dans des bouilloires pour brûler, pour faire des* STEAM, *pour courir le moulin.* They were burned and used to produce steam to run the mill. (IB) *Ils mettont des préservatives dans le lait asteur pour l'empêcher de cailler.* They put preservatives in milk now to keep it from curdling. (VM) *Je me rappelle de ma grand-mère, elle prendait des gazettes pour mettre sur le mur pour* WALLPAPER*, elle faisait ça.* I remember my grand-mother, she took newspapers to put up on the wall for wallpaper, she did that. (IB) *Ça peut pas tout mettre dans un* MUSEUM*. Comment ça va présenter une guerre dans un* MUSEUM*?* They can't put everything in a museum. How are they going to present a war in a museum?

(LF) *Mets ton linge sale dans le panier.* Put your dirty clothes in the hamper. (LA) **Mets pas ton doigt entre l'arbre et l'écorce!* [proverb] Don't get mixed up in other people's marital problems! (La99) **2** to put in, add *On faisait une fricassée de volaille et puis là on mettait des poutines en dans-là.* We would make a chicken fricassee and put dumplings in it. (LA) *Tu fais bouillir ton eau avant de mettre les chevrettes.* You boil your water before you put the shrimp in. (EV) *Et là, tu vas bien beurrer ta poêle avant de mettre ton pain.* And then, you will butter your frying pan before putting in your bread. (LA) *Je fais jaunir [...] la viande et je mets des oignons, des piments, des assaisonnements, et là je remets le riz cru, avec l'eau dedans, et cuis tout ensemble.* I brown the meat, and I put in onions, peppers, seasonings, and I add in the uncooked rice, with water in it, and cook everything together. (SL) *Ça poppait le tactac premier. Tu mettais ça dans une bombe et tu poppais ton tactac avec de la graisse.* They popped the popcorn first. You would put that in a cooking pot and you popped your popcorn with grease. (TB) **3** to put on, wear *C'est pas prudent de mettre les manches courtes quand il fait froid comme ça.* It's not prudent to wear short sleeves when it's cold like that. (VM) **Ses jambes étaient sûr grosses comme mon cigare, mais il mettait du quatorze dans les souliers.* His legs were surely as big as my cigar, but he wore a size fourteen shoe. (EV, An94) *Mets ta blouse et couche-toi.* Put on your nightgown and go to bed. (AV) **4** to turn on *Il a mis le RADIO dans le char.* He turned on the radio in the car. (LA) *Je mets la pendule, le temps sur la pendule. Et puis, à quand je le mets dans le développement, je hale les manches. Quand la pendule arrive, elle va sonner.* I set the timer. Then when I put [the film] in the developer, I pull the handles of the timer. When the timer is finished, it rings. (VM) *Mets l'AIR CONDITION. Je suis après suer.* Turn on the air conditioning. I'm sweating. (VM) **5** to spend (an amount of time or money) *Elle met deux heures à se pimponner avant d'aller au bal.* She spends two hours primping before going to the dance. (VM) *Avant que je mets 200 ou 250 dollars pour tiendre mes culottes en l'air je vas prendre une corde. Je vas prendre une ceinture.* Before I spend $200 or $250 to hold my pants up, I'll get a rope. I'll get a belt. (TB) **6** to cause to be or become *Le monde a tout aujourd'hui. C'est ça qui nous met paresseux!* People have everything today. That's what makes us lazy! (TB) **II se mettre** *v.pron.* **1** to put on o.s. *Mme Richard se mettait assez d'essence quand alle allait au bal que tu pouvais l'éventer de l'aut' bord de la rue.* Mrs. Richard put on enough perfume when she went to the dance that you could smell her from the other end of the street. (Gu00) **2** to put o.s., place o.s., go *Tracasse-toi pas. Il va se mettre en arrière.* Don't worry. He'll go in the back. (LA) *Le prêtre se met à la porte de l'église pour rencontrer les partants.* The priest goes to the door of the church to meet the departing worshippers. (VM) *On se met par piquets épaillés dans le bois pour chasser.* We spread out by groups in the woods for hunting. (Lv88) *Et ça empoignait la chevrette avec des filets, les Cadiens appellent ça une seine. Et ça se mettait à l'eau et eusse halait la seine et eusse faisait un cercle pour entasser les chevrettes pour les ramasser.* And they would catch shrimp with nets, the Cajuns call it a seine. And they would get in the water and they pulled the seine and they made a circle to collect the shrimp to gather them up. (LF) **3** to become (a profession) *Elle avait été au couvent pour se mettre sœur.* She had gone to the convent to become a nun. (SL) ◊ **•mettre (à) coucher / mettre au lit** to put to bed *Si t'arrêtes pas tout ce train, je vas vous mettre à coucher.* If you don't stop making all that noise, I'll put you all to bed. (LA) *Excuse-moi, il faudra je mets les enfants au lit.* Excuse me, I have to put the children to bed. (LA) <LA, Da84> **•mettre à genoux** to make s.o. kneel *L'école c'était en anglais, eux-autres te disait de pas parler français dans l'école. Eux-autres te mettait à genoux si c'est que tu parlais français dans l'école.* School was in English, they told you not to speak French in the school. They put you on your knees if you spoke French in school. (TB) <TB> **•mettre à la porte** to kick out *Si ça se conformait pas, le constable les mettait à la porte.* If they didn't behave, the bouncer would kick them out. (LA) <LA> **•mettre de côté** to put aside, set aside *On travaille pas cette journée-là, on met cette journée-là de côté.* We don't work that day, we set that day aside. (TB) <TB, Da84> **•mettre dedans** to cheat, fool, swindle <Da84> **•mettre du fond de la malle** to get dressed up, put on one's fine clothes <VM, La99> **•mettre en ordre** to put in order *Et quand-ce que les bateaux, une fois par an il faut que ça soye inspecté par la Garde de Côte. Et il faut que ça soye tout mis en ordre.* And when the boats, once a year they have to be inspected by the Coast Guard. And everything has to be put in order. (LF) <LF> **•mettre ON** to turn on *Mets le radio ON.* Turn the radio on. (Lv88) <Lv88> **•mettre par terre** to remove chicks from nest or incubator twenty-four hours after hatching *J'ai mis par terre une centaine de poulets proche.* I removed nearly a hundred chicks from the incubator. (VM) <VM> **•mettre son nez dans son bol** to interfere <TB, La99> **•mettre une charge contre qqn** to press legal charges against s.o. **Je suis parti asteur mettre une charge contre lui.* I'm going right now to bring a charge against him. (SL, An94) <SL, An94> **•mettons {mettant} que** what if, supposing that *Mettant qu'il arrive pas. Quoi c'est qu'on va faire?* What if he doesn't arrive. What are we going to do? (LA) <LA, Da84> **•se mettre à** to begin to *J'aurais pas dû faire ça do, mais je pouvais plus STAND, je m'ai mis à rire.* I shouldn't have done that though, but I couldn't take it any more, I started to laugh. (LF) <LF> **•se mettre à l'ouvrage** to go to work *On s'a plaint assez. C'est l'heure de se mettre* *à l'ouvrage.* We've complained enough. It's time to get to work. (LA) <LA, Da84> **•se mettre à rien faire** to go to do nothing <Da84> **•se mettre bon pour** to assume responsibility, stand good for <Da84> **•se mettre de travers** to become cross <Da84> **•se mettre en colère** to get angry <Da84> **•se mettre ensemble** to get together **Tout les familles se mettaient ensemble pour faire des boucheries tout les semaines.* All the families would get together to have communal butcheries every week. (LA, An94) *Ma mère se mettait ensemble avec les femmes du voisinage pour piquer des couiltes.* My mother got together with the women of the neighborhood to quilt. (Guoo) <LA, An94, Da84, Guoo> **•s'en mettre à** to indulge in, do to excess <LF> **•allons s'y mettre** let's start, let's go to work <Da84> **•se faire mettre dedans** to get o.s. cheated <Da84> **•se laisser mettre dedans** to allow o.s. to be cheated <Da84> <***Loc:*** AC, AV, EV, IB, LA, LF, SJ, SL, SM, TB, VM, An94, Da84, Hio2, La99>

meuble [mœb(l)] *n.m.* piece of furniture <***Loc:*** Da84, Fa77>

meubler [møble] *v.tr.* to furnish *Je la loue plus cher parce qu'elle est meublée.* I rent it [the house] for more because it is furnished. (VM) <***Loc:*** VM, Da84>

meublier [møblije] *n.m.* furniture maker, cabinet maker <***Loc:*** JE, VM>

meuille [mœj, møj] *n.m./f.* **1** [fish] mullet, striped mullet **2** mudfish ◊ **•meuille noir** Atlantic croaker <TB> <***Loc:*** JE, LF, SM, TB, VM, Guoo, Lv88>

meule [møl] *n.f.* grindstone, whet stone ◊ **•meule douce** fine-grain sharpening stone <LA> <***Loc:*** AC, EV, LA, Da84, Fa77>

meurizon [mørizɔ̃] *n.m./f.* ripening, maturity, maturation <***Loc:*** JE, VM, Di32>

meurtre [mœrt(r)] *n.m.* murder, killing <***Loc:*** Da84, Hio2>

meurzir [mœrzir, mozir] *v.intr.* to ripen <***Loc:*** JE, VM, Di32>

mexicain[1], -aine [mɛksikɛ̃, -ɛ̃n] *adj.* Mexican <***Loc:*** TB>

Mexicain[2], -aine [mɛksikɛ̃, -ɛ̃n] *n.* Mexican *J'ai une grande-petite-fille qu'est mariée avec un Mexicain.* I have a great-granddaughter who married a Mexican. (TB) <***Loc:*** TB>

mexicain[3] [mɛksikɛ̃, masikɛ̃, mesikɛ̃, mærsikɛ̃] *n.m.* **1** balsam apple **2** balsam pear **3** fulvous tree duck <***Loc:*** IB, TB, Re31>

mi- [mi] *prefix* half, semi, mid ◊ **•mi-carême** ***a*** Mid-Lent ***b*** evil spirit in the form of an old hag whose name is used to frighten children into behaving <JE, Da84> **•mi-jour** mid-day <Da84> **•mi-quarante** mid-forties *Ça c'était dans les années quarante, peut-être quarante-huit, quarante-six, mi-quarante.* That was in the forties, maybe forty-eight, forty-six, mid-forties. (SL) <SL> **•en mi-route** midway <Da84> <***Loc:*** JE, SL, Da84>

mi ♦see **mil**

mialement [mjalmɑ̃] *n.m.* **1** mewing, caterwauling **2** cajolery, coaxing, wheedling <***Loc:*** VM, Lv88>

mialer ♦see **miauler**

miaou [mjau] *n.m.* meow, mew <***Loc:*** Da84>

miauler (**mialer**) [mjole, mjale] **I** *v.tr.* to cajole, coax, wheedle *Laisse-toi pas mialer.* Don't let yourself be coaxed. (VM) **II** *v.intr.* to mew, meow, caterwaul *Le matou est après mialer.* The tomcat is mewing. (VM) <***Loc:*** IB, LF, SL, VM, Da84, Lv88>

miche[1] [miʃ] *n.f.* loaf of French bread <***Loc:*** LF, TB, Da84>

miche[2] [miʃ] *n.f.* crap ◊ **•ah, la miche!** the devil! (VM) <VM> <***Loc:*** VM, Da84, Guoo>

michouéron [miʃwerɔ̃] *n.m.* garfish <***Loc:*** SL>

micmac [mikmak] *n.* **1** scheming, intrigue, dishonesty *Il y a du micmac dans cette affaire.* There is some underhand work in this business. (Re63) **2** grimace, (strange) face *Il lui a fait des micmacs dans le dos.* He made faces at her when her back was turned. (LF) <***Loc:*** EV, IB, LF, SL, La99, Ph36, Re63>

micoine (**micouène**) [mikwɑ̃n, mikwɛ̃n] *n.f.* **1** large spoon, large wooden spoon **2** spoon-billed duck, northern shoveler <***Loc:*** JE, LF, TB, VM, Guoo, Lv88, Re31>

micouène ♦see **micoine**

microphone [mikrofɔ̃n] *n.m.* microphone <***Loc:*** Da84>

midi [midi] *n.m.* noon, midday ◊ **•midi à quatorze (heures)** tiresome chattering *Il m'a emmené un midi à quatorze heures.* He wearied me with his chattering. (LF) <LF, VM, La99> **•avant-midi** morning, forenoon *Et là après ça, dans l'avant-midi, eux-autres commençait à faire le bouilli, ça appelait ça "le bouilli."* And after that, in the morning, they started making the boiled meat, they call it "bouilli." (LF) <AC, EV, LA, LF, SM, VM, Gu82, Lv88> **•grand midi** high noon <Da84> <***Loc:*** AC, AV, EV, LF, TB, VM, Da84, Hio2, La99>

mie[1] [mi] *n.f.* soft inside part of bread, cake, etc. <***Loc:*** Da84>

mie[2] ♦see **mil**

miel [mjɛl] *n.m.* honey <***Loc:*** AC, AL, AV, EV, IB, JE, LA, LF, SB, SM, VM, Da84, Guoo, Hio2, La99, Lv88>

mielleux, -euse [mjelø, -øz] *adj.* honeyed, sweet *Elle est mielleuse, mais tu peux pas te fier à elle.* She's sweet, but you cannot trust her. (VM) <***Loc:*** VM, Da84>

mien, mienne [mjɛ̃, mjɛ̃n] *pron.poss.* mine *Mon père avait des belles de nuit jaunes dans sa cour. Les miennes sont toutes rouges.* My father had yellow four o'clocks in his yard. Mine are all red. (Guoo) <***Loc:*** LF, TB, Da84, Guoo, Hio2>

miette [mjɛt] *n.f.* soft inside part of bread, the part that is not crust *J'aime pas la croûte, je mange que la miette.* I don't like the crust, I only eat the white part (of the bread). (VM) ◊ **•pas une miette** not at all <Re63> <***Loc:*** VM, Re63>

mieux[1] [mjø] *adv.* **1** better *Il fait ça mieux que moi.* He does it better than me. (VM) **Il vaudrait mieux.* It would be better. (Da84) **C'est mieux prendre garde que pardon.* Better safe than sorry. (Da84) *Si je suis avec un de mes amis français de* *mon âge, plein souvent on parle français. On se comprend mieux.* If I'm with one of my French-speaking friends of my age, very often we speak French. We understand each other better. (LF) *Et le monde s'accordait presque aussi bien ou mieux qu'asteur.* And people got along almost as well or better than now. (TB) *On peut le voir mieux d'auprès.* We can see it better from up close. (VM) *C'est mieux pour toi d'être naturel plutôt que faire accroire tu peux faire quelque chose.* It's better for you to act naturally than to convince yourself that you can do anything. (Lv88) *Pourtant, il a assez de savoir pour connaître mieux.* Yet he has enough knowledge to know better. (LA) *Bois une petite goutte et tu vas te sentir mieux.* Drink a little sip and you'll feel better (EV) *Y a rien de mieux que du thé de mamou pour décoller un rhume.* There's nothing better than mamou tea to clear up a cold. (VM) *Il lui a rendu mieux qu'il a eu.* He gave him back better than he got. (LA) **2** more *Il gagne mieux que cent piasses.* He makes more than a hundred dollars. (Lv88) **Mieux que trois heures.* More than three hours. (Da84) **3** *(superlative; used with art.def.)* the best *Je suis manière après apprendre à un petit peu à parler l'espagnol mais c'est bien peu parce que je veux pas apprendre ça plus que pour assayer de m'arracher le mieux que je peux.* I am more or less learning a little bit of Spanish but it's very little, because I don't want to learn it any better than to try to get by the best I can. (TB) *J'avais arrangé la patte de la chaise le mieux je pouvais mais elle a refendu.* I had fixed the chair leg the best I could, but it split again. (LA) ◊ **•mieux que ça et les prêtres seraient jaloux / mieux que ça serait de la gourmandise {une bêtise}** things are going very well <La99> **•aller {être} mieux** to be better, be getting better *Mais, pour faire l'affaire aller mieux j'ai emmené un chèque du TBA pour mille piastres pour payer les dépenses d'enterrement pour Tante Besone.* Well, to make things go better, I brought a thousand dollar check from the TBA to pay for Aunt Besone's funeral expenses. (ThCa: *Messieurs, mesdames*) <Da84, ThCa> **•beaucoup mieux / un tas mieux** much better *On avait occasion de communiquer avec nos parents plus qu'à présent. Ah ouais ça se connaissait beaucoup mieux.* We had occasion to communicate with our parents more than now. Oh yes, they knew each other a lot better. (LA) *J'ai coupé les herbes, ça regarde un tas mieux asteur.* I cut the grass, it looks a lot better now. (Lv88) <LA, Da84, Lv88> **•je ferais mieux / tu ferais mieux / il ferait mieux, etc.** I had better, you had better, he had better, etc. *Peut-être tu ferais mieux de t'asseoir là. Il y a moins de vent pour déranger tes cheveux.* Maybe you'd do better to sit there. There's less wind to mess up your hairdo. (ThCa: *La table des veuves*) *Tu ferais mieux de défroncer ce front droit asteur, mon petit.* You had better unknit that brow right now, son. (LA) *Tu ferais mieux le guetter. C'est un fameux canaille.* You'd better watch him. He's a known trickster. (SM) *J'ai figuré que je ferais mieux de frèmer ma gueule.* I decided that I'd better shut my mouth. (EV) <EV, LA, SM, Da84, ThCa> **•tant mieux** so much the better *Il dit qu'il veut pas aller. Mais tant mieux. On a pas besoin de lui quand même.* He says he doesn't want to go. Well, so much the better. We don't need him anyway. (LA) *Tant mieux, tu vas venir avec mon.* So much the better, you're coming with me. (AV) <AV, LA, Da84> <*Loc:* AC, EV, LA, LF, SM, TB, VM, Da84, Gu00, Hi02, La99, Lv88, ThCa>

mieux [mjø] *n.m.* ◊ **•faire son mieux** to do one's best *Je m'ai contenté de le voir faire son mieux.* I was satisfied to see him do his best. (LA) <LA> <*Loc:* LA, TB>

migaillière [migajær] *n.f.* placket (in a dress) <*Loc:* VM>

mignon, -onne [mijɔ̃, -jɔ̃n] *adj.* cute and small *La petite fille est mignonne.* The little girl is cute. (VM) *T'es petite et t'es mignonne mais t'es trop galeuse pour faire ma femme.* You're little and you're cute, but you're too filthy to be my wife. (EV, ch: *T'es petite et t'es mignonne*) <*Loc:* EV, SM, VM, Da84, Hi02>

migraine [migrɛ̃n] *n.f.* migraine, headache *Il est abattu de la migraine.* He is plagued by migraines. (VM) <*Loc:* AV, IB, VM, Da84, Hi02>

mil (mi, mie) [mi] *n.m.* millet, straw *On élevait du mil pour faire des balais.* We grew millet to make brooms. (Lv88) ◊ **•mie de balai** broom straw <Da84> <*Loc:* IB, Da84, Lv88>

millage [milaʒ] *n.m.* mileage *Des petits chars qui donnent un bon millage.* Little cars that get good mileage. (Lv88) <*Loc:* Da84, Lv88>

mile ♦see **mille**

milice [milis] *n.f.* militia, national guard <*Loc:* Da84>

milieu [miljø, myljø] *n.m.* middle, center *Deux sœurs plus vieilles, et un frère plus jeune. Je suis dans le milieu.* Two older sisters, and a younger brother. I'm in the middle. (LF) ◊ **•au beau milieu / droite dans le milieu** right in the middle <Da84> **•au milieu** in the middle <Hi02> <*Loc:* LF, SL, Da84, Hi02>

militaire[1] [militær] *adj.* military *Il a fini son service militaire.* He finished his military service. (LA) <*Loc:* LA, Da84>

militaire[2] [militær] *n.m.* military, army, (armed) service *Pendant la guerre, j'étais chez ma mère aux Opelousas, pendant il était dans le militaire.* During the war, I stayed at my mother's home in Opelousas, while he was in the army. (SL) <*Loc:* SL, Da84>

militant, -e [militɑ̃, -ɑ̃t] *adj.* militant, combative <*Loc:* Da84>

mille[1] **(mile)** [mil] *n.m.* mile **Trois milles dans le nord de Scott.* Three miles north of Scott. (LA, An94) *Il y a une place, là, il y a un mile carré de terre.* There's a place, there, there is one square mile of land. (LA) ◊ **•milles à l'heure** miles per hour <TB> **•demi-mille** half mile <TB> <*Loc:* EV, IV, LA, SL, TB, An94, Da84, Hi02>

mille[2] [mil] *adj./n.m.* thousand **Ça fait, il a acheté le chien. Il a payé dix mille piastres pour. Juste pour prouver à Pascal qu'il avait un meilleur chien que lui.* So he bought the dog. He paid ten thousand dollars for it. Just to prove to Pascal that he had a better dog than him. (EV, An94) ◊ **•des milles** thousands <Lv88> <***Loc:*** EV, LA, SL, An94, Da84, Hi02, Lv88>

mille-pattes [milpat] *n.m.* **1** millipede **2** centipede <***Loc:*** Da84>

millet [mijɛ, mije] *n.m.* millet <***Loc:*** Da84>

millième[1] [miljɛ̃m] *adj./n.* thousandth <***Loc:*** Da84>

millième[2] [miljɛ̃m] *n.* mil (tax) *Il faudra qu'on paye deux millièmes de plus pour les écoles.* We will have to pay two more mils for the school tax. (LA) <***Loc:*** LA>

millier [milje] *n.m.* thousand, about a thousand **Y a des centaines de milliers de cocodris en Louisiane, mais les fédérals disont que c'est eine qualité d'animal en danger de disparaît'.* There are hundreds of thousands of alligators in Louisiana, but the feds say that it's an endangered animal. (ThCa: *Mille misères*) <***Loc:*** Da84, Hi02, ThCa>

million [miljɔ̃] *n.* million **Des millions et des millions de piastres.* Millions and millions of dollars. (EV, An94) <***Loc:*** EV, An94, Da84, Hi02>

millionnaire [miljɔ̃nær] *n.* millionaire **Le roi était beaucoup, beaucoup riche. Il était millionnaire un tas de fois.* The King was very, very rich. He was a millionaire many times over. (EV, An94) <***Loc:*** EV, An94, Da84, Hi02>

mimine [mimin, mimɛ̃n] *n.f.* [*baby talk*] dress <***Loc:*** LF, SJ, SL>

mimosa [mimosa] *n.m.* mimosa <***Loc:*** Da84>

mince [mɛ̃s] *adj.* thin, slender, slim, small *Des petits bras minces.* Thin little arms. (EV) <***Loc:*** EV, Da84, Hi02>

minceur [mɛ̃sœr] *n.f.* slenderness, thinness <***Loc:*** Da84>

mine[1] [min] *n.f.* look, appearance, air, aspect ◊ **•avoir bonne mine** to look good, seem well *Nonc Alphé avait pas bonne mine la dernière fois que je l'ai vu.* Uncle Alphé didn't look well the last time I saw him. (EV) <EV, Da84> **•avoir mauvaise mine** to look bad, seem sick <Da84> **•avoir une mine de chien** ***a*** to look sad, seem depressed ***b*** to look badly groomed ***c*** to look ill <La99> **•faire bonne mine** to be on one's good behavior, be nice <Da84> **•faire mauvaise mine** to give a bad impression <Da84> <***Loc:*** EV, SM, VM, Da84, La99, Lv88>

mine[2] [min] *n.f.* **1** mine (excavation) **2** mine, hidden explosive <***Loc:*** Da84>

mine mine (mini mini) [minmin, minimini] *interj.* here kitty! (used to call a cat) <***Loc:*** SL>

miner [mine] **I** *v.tr.* **1** to mine (minerals, ore) *Ça mine du sel à la Saline.* They mine salt at Avery Island. (VM) **2** to mine, lay explosive mines in or under *Ils ont essayé de miner la rivière pendant la guerre.* They tried to mine the river during the war. (LA) **II se miner** *v.pron.* to erode, wash away *La terre s'a minée.* The ground has eroded. (VM) <***Loc:*** JE, LA, VM, Da84>

minéral [mineral] *n.* mineral, ore *Des droits de minérals.* Mineral rights. (LA) <***Loc:*** LA, Da84>

mineur[1]**, -e** [minœr] *n.* minor, one who has not reached full legal age <***Loc:*** Da84>

mineur[2] [minœr] *n.m.* miner, one who mines <***Loc:*** Da84>

mini [mini] *n.m.* minnow <***Loc:*** JE>

mini mini ♦see **mine mine**

ministère [ministær] *n.m.* ministry <***Loc:*** Da84>

ministre [minist(r)] *n.m.* minister, clergyman <***Loc:*** Da84>

minou [minu] *n.m.* **1** cat *Un tout petit minou.* A very small cat. (LF) **2** kitten **3** [*term of endearment*] (for a cat) kitty <***Loc:*** LF, SL, SM, VM, Da84>

minouche [minuʃ] *n.f.* [*baby talk*] caress ◊ **•faire minouche** to caress <Pe37> <***Loc:*** Pe37>

minuit [mɛ̃nɥi, mɛ̃nyi] *n.m.* midnight <***Loc:*** SM, VM, Da84>

minute [minyt, mɛ̃nyt, mynyt] *n.f.* minute ◊ **•à la minute** in a minute, right away <Da84> <***Loc:*** LF, Da84, Hi02>

miracle [mirak(l)] *n.m.* miracle, marvel <***Loc:*** Da84, Fa77>

miraculeux, -euse [mirakylø, -øz] *adj.* [*eccl.*] miraculous <***Loc:*** Da84>

mire [mir] *n.f.* **1** aim, sighting **2** gun sight ◊ **•prendre sa (bonne) mire / prendre une mire** to take aim **Il a pris sa bonne mire avec sa grande carabine.* He took aim with his big rifle. (EV, An94) <EV, An94, Da84, Lv88> <***Loc:*** EV, JE, An94, Da84, Lv88>

mirer [mire] **I** *v.tr.* to aim, sight, take aim **J'ai miré mon fusil et Kapoww! J'ai tué ce vieux grosbec!* I aimed my gun and Pow! I killed that old grosbeak. (ThCa: *Grosbecs*) **II** *v.intr.* to take aim *Pa mire et boum! il tue un canard français.* Pa sights and boom! he kills a mallard. (Lv88) **III se mirer** *v.pron.* to fix a direction for o.s. *Je m'aurais miré la palette, le tas de palette là pour moi m'assir en haut.* I would have oriented the pallet, the pallet pile, for me to sit on. (SL) ◊ **•mirer adroit** to be a crackshot <VM> <***Loc:*** SL, VM, Da84, Lv88, ThCa>

mirlifiche [mirlifiʃ] *n.f.* trinket, bauble <***Loc:*** JE>

mirliton (maliton, merliton) [mirlitɔ̃, malitɔ̃ mærlitɔ̃] *n.m.* vegetable pear, alligator pear <***Loc:*** CL, IB, LA, LF, SM, TB, VM, Da84, Hi02, Lv88>

miroir [mirwar] *n.m.* mirror <***Loc:*** LA, SL, TB, Da84>

miron [mirɔ̃] *n.m.* gawker, onlooker *Y'a tellement des mirons autour, on peut pas travailler.* There are so many onlookers around that we can't work. (SM) <***Loc:*** SM>

MISDEAL [misdil, mɪsdiˈl] *n.m.* misdeal (in cards) <***Loc:*** EV, JE, SJ, SM, TB, VM, Lv88, Ph36>

mise [miz] *n.f.* **1** stake, ante (in a game) **2** raffle ticket, lottery ticket ◊ **•prendre une mise** to buy a lottery or raffle ticket <Da84> <***Loc:*** Da84>

misérable[1] [mizerab(l)] *adj.* miserable, unfortunate, pitiful, destitute *J'aimerais que ça pourrait revenir comme c'était* *dans le vieux temps, mais on serait bien misérables parce que tu pourrais pas faire les enfants travailler.* I wish things could go back to the way they were in the old days, but we'd be miserable because you'd never get the kids to work. (TB) <***Loc:*** TB, Da84>

misérable[2] [mizerab(l)] *n.* miserable person, destitute person, wretch ◊ **•pauvre misérable** poor devil <Da84> <***Loc:*** Da84>

misérablement [mizerabləmɑ̃] *adv.* miserably *Elle a vi misérablement avec ce bougre.* She spent her life miserably with that guy. (VM) <***Loc:*** VM, Da84>

misère [mizær] *n.f.* **1** misery, poverty, destitution **2** trouble, misfortune, difficulty ◊ **•avoir de la misère** to have trouble, difficulty *Dans ce temps-ça, il y a du monde qu'a eu de la misère.* In those days, there were people who had difficulties. (SL) <SL, Da84> **•être de la misère à** to be difficult to *C'est vraiment de la misère à ramasser.* It is really difficult to pick. (VM) <VM> **•être en misère** to be destitute <Da84> **•faire (de) la misère (à qqn)** ***a*** to give trouble, deal misery *Ça m'a fait plus de misère que si j'aurais resté à la maison.* It gave me more trouble than if I had stayed at home. (EV) ***b*** to tease, torment, nag, harass, pick on *Un jour, c'était presque soleil-couché, le vieux s'amenait sur la plaille, et il avait du tracas avec ce petit bougre, ce petit bougre là après lui faire de la misère et crier dessus.* One day, it was almost sunset, the old man was going along the beach, and he was having trouble with the boy, this boy was tormenting him and yelling at him. (LF) *Il est toujours à faire la misère à ses petites sœurs.* He is always teasing his little sisters. (SM) <EV, LF, SM, Da84> **•mille misères** endless troubles *Il avait mille misères à se faire comprendre.* He had endless trouble to make himself understood. (Lv88) <Da84, Lv88, ThCa> **•sacré misère!** what the hell! (expression of desperation or exasperation) <Da84> <***Loc:*** EV, LF, SL, SM, TB, VM, Da84, Hi02, La99, Lv88, ThCa>

misérer [mizere] *v.intr.* **1** to suffer, be miserable *Nos parents ont miséré un tas.* Our parents suffered a great deal. (Lv88) *Faut pleurer, faut prier, misérer et soufferre.* One must cry, pray, endure and suffer. (Lv88) **2** to wither, waste away *Il était après misérer avec un cancer.* He was wasting away with cancer. (Lv88) **3** to work hard *On a miséré pour sauver le riz.* We worked extremely hard to save the rice. (VM) *C'est un homme qu'a miséré dans sa vie.* That's a man who has worked hard in his life. (VM) **4** to have a hard time (doing s.t.) *Il a miséré pour apprendre le français.* He had a hard time learnig French. (LF) <***Loc:*** LF, SL, VM, Da84, Hi02, Lv88>

miséricorde [mizerikɔrd] *n.f.* mercy, compassion, pity <***Loc:*** Da84, Hi02>

miséricordieusement [mizerikɔrdjøzmɑ̃] *adv.* mercifully, compassionately *Miséricordieusement, je peux pas croire qu'il a fait ça.* Mercifully, I can't believe he did that. (VM) <***Loc:*** VM, Da84>

miséricordieux, -ieuse [mizerikɔrdjø, -jøz] *adj.* merciful, compassionate, pitying <***Loc:*** Da84>

mispelusse ♦see **mispilusse**

mispilusse (mispelusse) [mispilys, mispəlys, myspylys] *n.m.* **1** medlar tree **2** Japanese plum, loquat <***Loc:*** JE, LA, LF, VM, Gu00, Lv88>

missel [misɛl] *n.m.* Mass book, missal <***Loc:*** Da84>

mission [misjɔ̃] *n.f.* **1** mission, errand **2** series of sermons by a missionary lasting three to seven days **3** country church <***Loc:*** Da84, Lv88>

missionnaire [misjɔ̃nær] *n.m.* missionary <***Loc:*** Da84>

MISTAKE [mistɛk, mɪsteˈk] *n.m.* mistake, error <***Loc:*** TB, Da84, Lv88>

mistanflute [mistɑ̃flyt] *n.f.* ◊ **•à la mistanflute** ***a*** hastily ***b*** awry <JE> <***Loc:*** JE>

mistchoug [mistʃug] *n.m.* **1** jack of clubs **2** joker (in a deck of cards) <***Loc:*** EV, Lv88, Ph36>

mistifriser [mistifrize] *v.tr.* to dress up for a special occasion <***Loc:*** JE>

mistigri (mistigris) [mistigri] *n.m.* **1** cat **2** jack of clubs, one-eyed jack **3** joker (in a deck of cards) <***Loc:*** IB, VM, Da84, Lv88>

mistigris ♦see **mistigri**

mitaine [mitɛ̃n] *n.f.* **1** mitten **2** long, fingerless glove *Il n-avait qui mettaient des mitaines, ils avaient des bouts coupés pour attraper le coton.* There were those who put on fingerless gloves, they had the ends cut off in order to grab the cotton. (EV) <***Loc:*** EV, Da84>

mitan [mitɑ̃, mɑ̃tɑ̃, mito] *n.m.* middle, center <***Loc:*** JE>

mitasse [mitas] *n.m./f.* **1** type of Indian legging **2** mitten <***Loc:*** EV, LA, SM, VM, Da84, Lv88, Ph36, Re31>

mite [mi, mit] *n.f.* **1** mite **2** weevil **3** moth <***Loc:*** SB, Da84>

mité, -e [mite] *adj.* **1** full of weevils, weevily **2** moth-eaten *Un capot mité.* A moth-eaten coat. (VM) <***Loc:*** VM, Da84>

miteux, -euse [mitø, -øz] *adj.* **1** full of weevils, weevily **2** moth-eaten *Je peux pas mettre mon vieux chapeau. Il est tout miteux.* I can't wear my old hat. It's all moth-eaten. (VM) <***Loc:*** VM, Da84>

mitre [mit(r)] *n.f.* [*eccl.*] miter (of a bishop) <***Loc:*** Da84>

mobilienne [mobiljɛ̃n, moblijɛ̃n] *n.f.* **1** Mobile cooter (turtle) **2** green turtle **3** name given to any of various large turtles <***Loc:*** AS, IV, JD, LA, LF, PQ, SB, SJ, TB, Re54>

moche [mɔʃ] *n.f.* mush <***Loc:*** TB, VM, Di32>

mode [mɔd] *n.f.* fashion, style, fad WELL *là quand la mode des bogheis a arrêté, là ils ont commencé à avoir des chars.* Well then when buggies went out of fashion, they started having cars. (TB) ◊ **•à la mode** ***a*** in style ***b*** served with ice cream <Da84, Fa77> **•à la vieille mode** old-fashioned <Fa77> <***Loc:*** TB, Da84, Fa77>

modèle [mɔdɛl] *n.m./f.* model, pattern, design *Tout chacun* *avait sa modèle pour faire un bateau.* Everyone had his own design for making a boat. (LF) <***Loc:*** LF, Da84>

modérer [mɔdere] **I** *v.tr.* to moderate, restrain *Il a tout le temps eu du mal à modérer sa colère.* He always had trouble moderating his anger. (LA) **II se modérer** *v.pron.* **1** to restrain o.s. or one's actions *Il était tout le temps en tracas. Il pouvait pas se modérer.* He was always in trouble. He couldn't control himself. (LA) **2** to moderate, abate **Le temps se modère.* The [bad] weather is moderating or breaking up. (Da84) <***Loc:*** LA, Da84>

modeste [modɛs(t)] *adj.* modest *Cette robe est pas beaucoup modeste.* That dress is not very modest. (LA) <***Loc:*** LA, Da84>

modestement [modɛstmɑ̃] *adv.* modestly, simply *Faut marcher la vue basse, les yeux modestement.* One must walk looking down, eyes modestly. (PQ) <***Loc:*** PQ, Da84>

modestie [modɛsti] *n.f.* modesty <***Loc:*** Da84>

modifier [modifje] *v.tr.* to change, modify, alter *Ils ont eu pour modifier la machine pour la mettre dans le bateau.* They had to modify the engine to put it into the boat. (LA) <***Loc:*** LA, Da84>

modiste [modis(t)] *n.f.* seamstress, milliner <***Loc:*** VM, Da84, Lv88>

moelle [mwɛl, mwal] *n.f.* **1** marrow (of bones) **2** pith (of plants) <***Loc:*** Da84, Fa77>

moelleux, -euse [mwalø, -øz] *adj.* marrowy, pithy *Pour faire une bonne sauce, ça prend des os qui sont moelleux.* To make a good sauce, it takes bones that are marrowy. (LA) <***Loc:*** LA, Da84>

mœurs [mœrs] *n.f.pl.* contemporary customs, morals, ways, manners <***Loc:*** Da84>

moi (mon) [mwa, mɔ̃, mwɔ̃] *pron.pers.* **1** *(subj.)* I *Ma sœur et moi parle en français un tas.* My sister and I speak French a lot. (SL) *Moi et toi peut aller, mon mari va nous prêter le* TRUCK. You and I can go, my husband will lend us the truck. (LF) *C'était un bon vieux homme, on était bons padnas moi et lui.* He was a good old boy, we were good friends, he and I. (LF) *Un jour moi reviendrai.* One day I will come back. (VM) *Moi crache dans un bois creux.* I spit into a hollow log. (VM) **2** *(dir.obj.)* (with imperative) me *Je vas parler dans la maison de cour, ça va être jeté à côté, crois-mon.* I am going to talk in court, it will be thrown out, believe me. (LF) **3** *(ind.obj.)* (with imperative) me, to me, for me **Arrête-moi ce tappage.* Stop that racket [for me]. (Da84) *Donne-moi une palette de gomme.* Give me a stick of gum. (VM) **Donne-moi du pain.* Give me some bread. (Da84) **4** *(obj. of prep.)* me *Mais je lui dis, "c'est pas après toi il est fâché, c'est après moi il est fâché."* But I told her, "he's not mad at you, he's mad at me." (EV) **Venez avec moi.* Come with me. (Da84) *Ils sont plus jeunes que moi.* They are younger than me. (AV) *Oh je comprends mieux que je comprenais le n-anglais mais ma parole à moi c'est plus français.* Oh, I understand English better than I used to but my speech is mostly in French. (TB) **5** *(tonic)* me *Je veux du pop rouge, moi.* I want strawberry soda. (VM) *C'était moi tout le temps qui avais pour y aider à faire n'importe qui il avait pour faire.* It was always I who had to help him to do anything he had to do. (EV) *Mon j'aime pas ça qu'on va savoir à soir avec Clinton.* I don't like what we're going to hear tonight from Clinton. (TB) *Je pourrais pas faire ça, j'ai pas la patience moi, pas du tout.* I would not be able to do that, I don't have the patience, not at all. (IB) *Eux-autres connaît mieux que moi.* They know better than I do. (TB) **Moi, je vous dis.* I [myself] tell you. (Da84) *Moi, je crois qu'il a perdu la canique. Il fait drôle!* I think he's lost his mind. He's acting weird. (AC) *Elle est plus vieille que moi.* She is older than me. (PQ) *Moi j'ai sauté par un chassis en arrière.* I jumped out through a back window. (AV) <***Loc:*** AC, AS, AV, EV, JD, LA, LF, PQ, SB, SM, TB, VM, An84, An94, Da84, Gu00, Hi02>

moi-même [mwɑ̃mɛ̃m, mɔ̃mɛ̃m] *pron.pers.* **1** *(obj. of prep.)* myself *Asteur moi j'ai ma compagnie à moi-même et je suis un politicien.* Now I own my own company and I'm a politician. (TB) *Moi, je connais, je suis bonrien, mais je suis bonrien pour moi-même. J'ai jamais fait rien à personne.* Me, I know I'm a good-for-nothing, but I'm a good-for-nothing to myself. I've never done anything to anyone. (EV) *Et là quand j'étais plus vieux, j'ai commencé à travailler pour moi-même.* And then when I was older, I began to work for myself. (TB) *Là, j'ai monté mon* BAND *à moi-même.* Then I started my own band. (EV) **2** *(tonic)* myself *Je* HANDLE *mon tracas moi-même.* I handle my problems myself. (LF) *C'est moi-même qu'a dit ça.* It's me (myself) who said that. (SM) *J'arrange tout ça moi-même.* I fix all that myself. (TB) *Et en temps perdu, plein souvent j'ai continué à lire son livre et à étudier moi-même.* And in my free time, quite often I've continued to read his book and to study on my own. (LF) <***Loc:*** EV, LF, SM, TB, Da84, Hi02>

moindre [mwɛ̃n, mwɛ̃d(r)] *adj.* **1** smaller, lesser *Moi, je vas prendre le moindre des deux.* I'll take the lesser of the two. (LA) **2** least *C'est lui qui veut le faire le moindre de tout.* He wants to do it least of all. (LA) <***Loc:*** LA, Da84>

moindrement [mwɛ̃drəmɑ̃, mɔ̃drəmɑ̃] *adv.* slightly, in the least *Le président a pas moindrement honte qu'il a menti au monde.* The president is not ashamed in the least that he lied to the people. (VM) *Moindrement qu'il se trempe les pieds, il attrape un rhume.* If he wets his feet the least bit, he catches a cold. (LF) ◊ **•pas moindrement acceptable** not in the least acceptable <Da84> <***Loc:*** LF, VM, Da84>

moine [mwɑ̃n] *n.f.* top, spinning top <***Loc:*** JE>

moineau [mɔ̃no, mɑ̃no] *n.m.* sparrow ◊ **•petit-moineau** sparrow <SB> <***Loc:*** AV, JE, LF, SB, SJ, VM, Da84>

moins[1] [mwɛ̃, mwɑ̃s, mwɛ̃s] *adv.* **1** less, fewer *Asteur je mets pus de la viande salée ou du bacon dans mes fèves secs, je* *mets du tasso, c'est moins gras et plus sain, pis ça donne autant de goût.* Nowadays I no longer put salt meat or bacon in my dry beans, I put tasso, it's less fatty and more healthy and it gives as much flavor. (Guoo) *À peu près six pouces, peut-être... peut-être plus, peut-être moins. On va dire six pouces.* About six inches, maybe . . . maybe more, maybe less. Let's say six inches. (EV) *Les SOYBEAN demandent un tas moins de trouble que le riz.* Soybeans are a lot less trouble than rice. (Lv88) *Peut-être tu ferais mieux de t'asseoir là. Il y a moins de vent pour déranger tes cheveux.* Maybe you'd do better to sit there. There's less wind to mess up your hairdo. (ThCa: *La table des veuves*) **2** *(superlative; used with art.def.)* the least *C'est peut-être lui le moins bête de la bande.* He is perhaps the least stupid of the bunch. (LA) *Tu connais dans quel mois les femmes méprisent le moins? Dans février, parce qu'il y a moins de jours.* Do you know in which month women gossip the least? February, because there are fewer days. (Lv88) ◊ **•moins que** less than *Il y en a moins que d'habitude.* There are fewer than usual. (VM) **Ils estiont moins qu'un demi-pouce de différence, mais il avait gagné.* They were less than a half inch apart, but he had won. (EV, An94) **J'en ai moins que lui.* I have less than he. (Da84) <EV, VM, An94, Da84> **•à moins (que)** unless *Tu peux pas aller à moins que tu parles avec ton père avant.* You can't go unless you talk to your father first. (LA) <LA, Da84> **•au moins** at least *Il y en a au moins quatorze dans la glacière.* There are at least fourteen in the ice chest. (LA) <LA, Da84> **•du moins** at least, rather, anyhow <Da84> **•moins à moins** less and less <Da84> **•ni plus ni moins** neither more nor less <Da84> **•plus ou moins** more or less *C'est plus ou moins pareil.* It's more or less the same. (TB) <TB, Da84, Hi02> <***Loc:*** EV, LA, LF, VM, An94, Da84, Hi02>

moins[2] [mwɛ̃, mwɑ̃s, mwɛ̃s] *prep.* **1** minus, less **Trois moins deux laisse un.* Three minus two leaves one. (Da84) **2** till, before (in expressions of time) **Une heure moins dix.* Ten minutes to one. (Da84) <***Loc:*** Da84>

mois [mwa] *n.m.* month *La dernière année c'était pas venu froid. À part qu'on a eu un petit peu de la neige au mois de mars.* The last year it didn't get cold. Except that we had a little snow in March. (TB) ◊ **•dans deux mois** in two months <Da84> **•le mois passé** last month <Da84> **•le mois prochain / le mois qui vient** next month <Da84> **•tous les mois** monthly, every month *Moi, j'ai des BILLS qui sont payables tous les mois.* I have bills that are payable every month. (LA) <LA> <***Loc:*** IB, LA, SL, TB, Da84, Hi02, Lv88>

moiselle (**demoiselle**) [mwazɛl, mwɔ̃mzɛl, dəmwazɛl] *n.f.* dragonfly, mosquito hawk <***Loc:*** AV, EV, JD, SM, TB>

moisi[1], **-e** [mwazi, mwezi] *adj.* mildewed, moldy *La maison est tout moisie.* The house is completely mildewed. (LA) *En-dedans la maison, c'était vert. [...] Un pâle vert, et c'était tout moisi, ça voulait pas sortir.* Inside the house it was green. A pale green, and it was all moldy, it didn't want to come off. (TB) <***Loc:*** LA, TB, Da84>

moisi[2] [mwazi, mwezi] *n.m.* **1** mildew, mold **Ça sent le moisi.* It smells moldy. (Da84) **2** mustiness <***Loc:*** TB, VM, Da84, Fa77>

moisir [mwazir, mwezir] **I** *v.tr.* to mildew *C'est tout ces temps humides qu'a moisi la maison.* It's all this humid weather that has mildewed the house. (LA) **II** *v.intr.* to mildew *Si tu sors pas de la pluie, tu vas moisir.* If you don't get out of the rain, you'll mildew. (LA) **III se moisir** *v.pron.* to become mildewed, get moldy *Laisse pas ça dehors. Ça va se moisir.* Don't leave that outside. It will become mildewed. (LA) <***Loc:*** LA, Da84>

moisissure [mwazisyr] *n.f.* **1** mildew, mold *C'est une sacrée peste, tout la moisissure qu'a rendu le monde malade après l'ouragan!* It's a pestilence, all that mold that got people sick after the hurricane. (LA) **2** mustiness <***Loc:*** LA>

moisson [mwasɔ̃] *n.f.* harvest <***Loc:*** Da84>

moissonage [mwasɔ̃naʒ] *n.m.* harvest <***Loc:*** Da84>

moitié[1] [motʃe, mɔtʃe, motje, mwatje] *n.f.* half ◊ **•à moitié fou** half-crazy <Da84> **•moitié-moitié** half and half <Da84> **•moitié prix** half price <Da84> **•à moitié route** halfway <LF> **•à moitié sauvage** half Indian <AC> **•en moitié** in half **Couper en moitié.* To cut in half. (Da84) <Da84> **•faire récolte à la moitié** to farm on half <Da84> **•la moitié du temps** most of the time *Je compte la moitié du temps en français, ouais. N'importe qui-ce que je fais dans mon idée à mon-même, dans ma tête à mon-même c'est tout fait en français.* I count most of the time in French. Whatever I do in my mind, in my head, it's all done in French. (TB) <TB> <***Loc:*** AC, AV, JE, LA, LF, SM, TB, An94, Da84, Hi02>

moitié[2] [motʃe, mɔtʃe, motje, mwatje] *adv.* **1** half, partially **Il est moitié fou.* He is half crazy. (Da84) **2** halfway, poorly *On était bien connus dans ces temps-là. On faisait tout le temps de la bonne ouvrage, tu connais, c'était pas moitié fait.* We were well known in those days. We always did good work, you know, it wasn't half done. (TB) *C'est moitié fait.* It's poorly done. (VM) <***Loc:*** TB, VM, Da84>

molaire [molær] *n.f.* molar tooth *Il a perdu une molaire.* He lost a molar. (VM) <***Loc:*** VM, Da84>

molène[1] [molɛ̃n] *n.f.* common mullein, turkey mullein plant <***Loc:*** Ho90, Lv88>

molène[2] [molɛ̃n] *n.f.* plump, fat girl <***Loc:*** LF>

moline [molin] *n.m./f.* **1** mechanical cultivator **2** two-wheeled rack to which plows and other field implements are attached <***Loc:*** AV, EV, IB, Lv88>

molle ♦see **mou**

mollet[1] [mɔlɛ, mole] *adj.* soft ◊ **•œuf mollet** soft-boiled egg, coddled egg <Da84> <***Loc:*** Da84>

mollet[2] [mɔlɛ, mole] *n.m.* calf (of the leg) <***Loc***: LA>

molleton [mɔltɔ̃, mɔtlɔ̃] *n.m.* flannel, flannelette <***Loc:*** JE, SL, Da84, Fa77>

molletonne [mɔltɔ̃n] *adj.f.* made of flannelette *Une couverte molletonne.* A flannelette blanket. (SL) <***Loc:*** SL>

mollir [molir] *v.tr.* to soften *Quand il a commencé à la frotter, elle a molli.* When he started rubbing her, she softened. (EV) <***Loc:*** EV, Da84>

moment [mɔ̃mɑ̃] *n.m.* moment, instant ◊ **•à tout moment** all the time, frequently, time after time, again and again *À tout moment c'était nécessaire [de savoir parler français], dans ce temps-là y'en avait en masse du monde qui restait icitte qui pouvait pas parler en anglais ou qu'aurait mieux parlé en français.* It was necessary [to know how to speak French] all the time, in those days, there were a lot of people who lived here and who could not speak English or would speak French better. (AV) *Et à tout moment tu vas voir dans le canal là. C'est un gros business entour icitte. Ils élevont des caïmans.* Time after time you'll see one in the ditch there. That's a big business around here. They raise alligators. (LF) <AV, LF, Da84> **•au moment de** about to **Il a mangé jusqu'à son ventre était au moment de casser.* He ate until his stomach was about to burst. (EV, An94) <EV, An94, Da84> **•c'est le moment** it is the (right) time <Da84> **•dans un moment** in a moment *On va se parler dans un moment.* We'll speak in a moment. (LA) <LA, Da84> **•du moment que** since the time that **Enfin pour dire, du moment que j'ai été assez fort pour travailler, je suis après travailler.* Anyway, from the time that I was fit enough to work, I have been working. (EV, An84) <EV, An84> **•pour le moment** right this moment, at the moment, right now *Pour le moment, il y en a pas qu'est facile à pêcher.* Right this moment, there are none [no fish] that are easy to fish. (SL) <SL> **•sur le moment** at the moment *De petits enfants, oh. Je vas voir. Oh, je pourrais pas te dire sur le moment. À peu près vingt. Dans les vingtaines.* Grandkids, oh. Let me see. I couldn't tell you right now. Around twenty. In the twenties. (TB) <TB> <***Loc:*** AV, EV, LA, LF, SL, TB, An84, An94, Da84>

mommuscade ♦see **muscade**

mon[1] **(ma, mes)** *adj.poss.* (*m.sing.* **mon** [mɔ̃], *f.sing.* **ma** [ma], *m./f.pl.* **mes** [me], *m./f.pl. before a vowel* **mes** [mez]) my *J'ai acheté mon char avec Léon.* I bought my car from Leon. (Lv88) *J'ai besoin de faire arranger mon chat avant il vient trop grand.* I need to have my cat spayed before he gets too big. (LA) *Mon frère et mon.* My brother and me. (AV) *Ayayaie! mon coeur fait mal!* Ouch! my chest hurts! (SM) *Mon opinion de lui a été abaissée.* My opinion of him has been lowered. (EV) *Mon amise qu'est canadien, elle montre le français à les enfants au Bayou Boeuf.* My friend who is Canadian, she teaches French to children in Bayou Boeuf. (LF) **C'est toi qu'après voler ma crème aussi longtemps.* You're the one who's been stealing my cream for so long. (EV, An94) *Moi j'ai jamais de ma vie vu autant d'eau.* I've never in my life seen so much water. (TB) *Il est parent avec ma femme.* He is related to my wife. (VM) *Je trouve que t'as des faux airs avec ma soeur.* I find that you resemble my sister. (SM) *Je vas aux Opelousas pour ajuster mes lunettes.* I go to Opelousas to adjust my glasses. (SL) *Tout cet ouvrage à la pelle a ampoulé mes mains.* All that work with a shovel has blistered my hands. (LA) *Je faisais mes appeleurs moi-même.* I used to make my own duck calls. (TB) <***Loc:*** AS, EV, IB, JE, LA, LF, SL, SM, TB, VM, An94, Da84, Gu00, Lv88>

mon[2] ♦see **moi**

monastère [mɔ̃nastær] *n.m.* monastery <***Loc:*** Da84>

monde[1] [mɔ̃d, mɔ̃n] *n.m.* **1** person, individual *T'as jamais vu un monde faire ça?* Have you ever seen a person do that? (VM) **2** people *Le monde qu'avait de l'argent engageait du monde comme ma grand-mère pour aller frotter le linge.* People who had money would hire people like my grandmother to go scrub the linens. (IB) **3** relatives, kin, kinfolk *C'est son monde qui vient.* Those are his relatives who are coming. (IB) **4** race **5** mankind **6** world ◊ **•bas monde** low-class people <Da84> **•comment dans le monde!** how in the world! <Da84> **•le grand monde** grownups, adults *Quand le grand monde parlait, les petits enfants allaient dehors.* When the grownups would speak, the children would go outside. (Lv88) <Lv88> **•le jeune monde** the young, the young generation *Le jeune monde va pas parler français asteur.* The young generation is not going to speak French now. (Lv88) <Lv88> **•le monde blanc** the white race, white people <Da84> **•le monde de couleur** colored people <Da84> **•le vieux monde** adults, the old generation *Y'a plein de vieux monde qui connaît parler français.* There were a lot of old people who knew how to speak French. (Lv88) <Lv88> **•tout le monde entier** the whole world <Da84> <***Loc:*** IB, PQ, SL, VM, Da84, Hi02, Lv88>

monde[2] [mɔ̃n] *interj.* goodness, gracious *Monde, ça fait chaud!* Goodness, it's hot! (VM) <***Loc:*** VM>

MONKEY BLOOD [mɔ̃kəblʌd, mʌŋkiblʌd] *n.m.* mercurochrome <***Loc:*** VM>

monnaie [mɔ̃nɛ, mɔ̃ne] *n.f.* coin, money <***Loc:*** Da84>

monouque [mɔ̃nuk] *n.f.* [*vulg.*] female genitals <***Loc:*** Lv88>

monseigneur [mɔ̃sɛɲœr] *n.m.* [*eccl.*] Monsignor (title of address for bishops and monsignors) <***Loc:*** Da84>

monsieur [məsjø] *n.m.* mister, sir, gentleman <***Loc:*** Da84, Hi02>

monstre[1] [mɔ̃s, mɔ̃rs, mɔ̃st(r)] *adj.* huge *Il s'a bâti une maison monstre.* He built himself a huge house. (VM) <***Loc:*** VM, Da84>

monstre[2] [mɔ̃s, mɔ̃rs, mɔ̃st(r)] *n.m./f.* **1** monster **2** good-for-nothing, scoundrel, rascal *Les petits monstres ont tout carnagé.* The little good-for-nothings tore up everything. (Lv88) <***Loc:*** IB, TB, Da84, La99, Lv88>

montage [mɔ̃taʒ] *n.m.* rising (of prices, of water, etc.) **Le gros* *tracas à Ma Tchou Flang c'est le montage de* UNEMPLOYMENT *par icite.* Ma Tchou Flang's big worry is the rise in unemployment around here. (Wh83) ◊ **•montage d'eau** high water, flood <Da84> <***Loc:*** Da84, Wh83>

montagne [mɔ̃tɑ̃j, mɔtɑ̃j] *n.f.* mountain <***Loc:*** JE, TB, Da84>

montailler [mɔ̃taje] *v.intr.* to climb around, climb repeatedly <***Loc:*** IB>

montant [mɔ̃tɑ̃] *n.m.* **1** amount, total, sum *Il avait le montant précis dans sa main.* He had the exact amount in his hand. (LA) **2** window mullion ◊ **•montant de porte** doorjamb <Da84> <***Loc:*** LA, LF, TB, VM, Da84>

monter [mɔ̃te] **I** *v.tr.* **1** to go up, climb *Monter une échelle.* To climb a ladder. (VM) *La petite manche penchait assez que c'était malaisé de la monter à bicycle.* The little lane sloped enough that it was difficult to go up on a bicycle. (LA) *Si je boirais deux bières, je monterais le* TELEPHONE POLE *là-bas.* If I drank two beers, I'd be climbing the telephone pole over there. (TB) **2** to mount *Monter un cheval.* To mount a horse. (EV) **3** to take up, bring up, carry up *En premier c'était tout des derricks boulonnés. Eux-autres montait ça* PIECE BY PIECE ALL THE WAY TO THE TOP. At first it was all derricks that were bolted together. They took it up piece by piece all the way to the top. (LF) **4** to start, set up, establish (e.g. a business) *J'avais monté un magasin de linge.* I had started a clothing store. (LF) *Si le marchand gagnait assez d'argent, il montait une deuxième charrette, puis une troisième, et il était classé selon la quantité de ses charrettes.* If the merchant earned enough money, he set up a second wagon, then a third, and he was classed according to the quality of his wagons. (VM) *Là, j'ai monté mon* BAND *à moi-même.* Then I started my own band. (EV) **5** to build **Monter une maison.* To build a house. (Da84) **Monter un magasin.* To build a store. (Da84) **6** to mount, affix, attach *Le* SEAT *était monté sur le chartil.* The seat was mounted on the bed. (LA) *Monter un trawl.* To hang a trawl net (on a frame). (TB) **7** to wind *Monter une montre.* To wind a watch. (VM) **Monter une pendule.* To wind a clock. (Da84) **II** *v.intr.* **1** to rise *Tu vois, l'eau montait, ça venait de la rivière.* You see, the water was rising, it was coming from the river. (SL) *Ça l'a pétrifié de voir l'eau monter si vite.* It petrified him to see the water rise so quickly. (VM) *En printemps l'alcool de bois monte.* In spring the sap rises. (JE) **2** to increase *J'ai arrêté de faire du coton à cause du coût de la graine qui montait.* I stopped raising cotton because the cost of seed was rising. (VM) **3** to ascend, climb *Mais les ratons laveurs et les serpents ont monté pour prendre les oeufs et tuer les petits oiseaux.* But the raccoons and the snakes climbed up to snatch the eggs and kill the baby birds. (TB) **4** to mount, get on (e.g. a horse) *J'ai vu les* REVENUES *à passer, j'ai monté sur un petit cheval rouge, il y avait. Les* REVENUES *passaient dans le chemin.* I saw the revenuers coming by, so I got on a little red horse that was there. The revenuers were passing by on the road. (SL) **5** to get on, get in (e.g. a vehicle) *Quand on était monté dessus le transfert c'était pareil comme on était* GONE *là-bas.* When we were on the bus it was just as if we were already there. (SL) **Ça fait, on monte sur le gros char ici un matin, et puis on a été en Ville.* So we got on the train here one morning, and then we went to New Orleans. (An84) *On a monté dans le char moi et lui et Tante Wavely et puis on avait passé pour prendre ses deux soeurs à lui.* We got in the car, he and I and Aunt Wavely and then we stopped to get his two sisters. (EV) **III se monter** *v.pron.* to amount to *Le compte se monte à au-dessus de cinquante piastres.* The account amounts to more than fifty dollars. (VM) ◊ **•monter à cheval *a*** to get on a horse ***b*** to travel on horseback <Da84> **•monter à la tête** to go to one's head <Da84> **•monter à poil** to ride bare-back <SM, Da84> **•monter dans un char** to get into a car or train <Da84> **•monter de la barrière** to enclose <Lv88> **•monter dessus à pieds joints** to jump on s.o. with both feet <Da84> **•monter en fleurs** to bloom <Da84> **•monter en fruit** to bear fruit <Da84> **•monter en grade** to succeed in business, do a good business *Le magasinier monte en grade.* The storekeeper is doing a good business. (VM) <VM> **•monter en grain(e) *a*** to go to seed ***b*** to never marry, remain an old maid *Je dis, je vas pas rester vieille fille comme ça [...] je dis, un jour à venir faudra je me marie. Je vas pas rester, juste monter en graine, comme on dit, toujours comme un pied de fleurs.* I said, I'm not going to stay an old maid like that, I said one day in the future I'll have to get married. I'm not going to stay, to just "go to seed," like they say, like a flowering plant. (EV) <EV, Da84> **•monter en pomme {tête}** to form a head (of cabbage) <Da84> **•monter sa manivelle** to get wound up as one begins talking <SB, La99> **•monter sur la radio** to appear, speak on the radio *Il monte sur la radio tous les dimanches.* He's on the radio every Sunday. (VM) <VM> **•monter sur le RELIEF** to receive assistance from department of public welfare <VM> **•monter sur ses grands chevaux** to behave arrogantly or self-righteously, get on one's high horse <EV, La99> <***Loc:*** EV, IV, LF, SB, SL, SM, TB, VM, Da84, La99, Lv88>

monteur [mɔ̃tœr] *n.m.* ◊ **•monteur de maisons** house builder <Da84> <***Loc:*** Da84>

montrance [mɔ̃trɑ̃s] *n.f.* appearance, exhibition, display <***Loc:*** JE>

montre [mɔ̃t(r)] *n.f.* **1** watch **2** clock <***Loc:*** SL, Da84>

montrer [mɔ̃tre] **I** *v.tr.* **1** to show, indicate *J'ai planté des pacaniers en arrière. Je vas te montrer ça, j'ai deux rangs de pacaniers en arrière là.* I planted pecan trees out back. I'll show them to you, I have two rows of pecan trees back there. (TB) *Dessus le télévision quand eusse commence à montrer une serpent, je vas changer de station. Carrément.* On TV when they start to show a snake I'll change the channel.

Just like that. (TB) **Bin la veille d'ce jour-là, Monsieur, moi et défunt Sosthène, on a prié l'Bon Dieu qu'i' la soigne pis qu'i' 'i montr' le bon ch'min.* Well, the night before that day, Sir, poor old Sosthène and I prayed to the Good Lord that he would take care of her and show her the right way. (VM, Gu82) **2** to show, exhibit, *Il y a des femmes qu'est comme ça. Ça aime montrer leur lumière.* There are women like that. They love to show their light. (AC, ch: *La lumière dans le chassis*) **3** to teach, show how to do s.t. *C'est nous-autres qui a montré à notre papa et notre maman de parler en anglais.* We are the ones who taught our mom and our dad to speak English. (SL) **II** *v.intr.* to appear *Les petites pattes étaient après montrer.* The little feet were appearing (at the birth of a calf). (Lv88) **III se montrer** *v.pron.* **1** to show o.s., make an appearance *Ils s'ont jamais montré aux noces.* They never showed up at the wedding. (VM) **2** to show off *Il aime se montrer. C'est pour ça qu'il s'habille comme ça.* He likes to show off That's why he dresses like that. (VM) ◊ **•montrer le catéchisse** to teach catechism *Il y avait des vieilles veuves, une qui nous montrait notre catéchisme en français.* There were some old widows, one who taught us our catechism in French. (SL) <SL, Da84> **•montrer l'école** to teach school *Ça demande un tas de patience, montrer l'école.* Teaching school requires much patience. (VM) *J'ai changé mon idée, quand je suis revenu je voulais d'être un maître d'école, j'ai fini l'école pour d'être un maître, j'ai montré l'école dans Lake Charles, à Baton Rouge et dans Ibérie.* I changed my mind, when I came back I wanted to be a school teacher, I finished school to be a teacher, and then I taught school in Lake Charles, Baton Rouge and in Iberia parish. (IB) <IB, VM, Da84> **•montrer le doigt** to give the finger, flip the bird *Ça icitte, montrer le doigt, c'était pas rien du tout quand mon j'ai été BROUGHT UP. Moi j'aurais fait ça à un autre DRIVER sur le chemin, comme ça ici j'aurais fait signe qu'y avait un STATE TROOPER en quelque place.* This here, flipping the bird, that wasn't anything when I was brought up. I would have done that to another driver on the road, that's how I would have made a sign that there was a state trooper somewhere. (LF) <LF> **•se montrer le nez {la figure}** to show one's face <VM> **•se montrer le tchul {derrière}** to make an ass of oneself, act like a fool *Il s'a montré le derrière encore et ça a fini en bataille.* He acted like a fool and it ended up in a fight. (LA) <LA> <***Loc:*** AC, IB, JE, LA, LF, SL, TB, VM, Da84, Lv88>

montreur, -euse [mɔ̃trœr, -øz] *n.* teacher ◊ **•montreuse de catéchisme** woman who teaches children their catechism in French <Lv88> <***Loc:*** Da84, Lv88>

monument [mɔ̃nymɑ̃] *n.m.* monument <***Loc:*** Da84>

MOP[1] [mɔp, mɑp] **I** *v.tr.invar.* to mop *Elle a MOP la galerie pour sa maman.* She mopped the porch for her mom. (SM) **II** *v.intr.invar.* to mop *J'ai MOP juste avant dîner.* I mopped just before dinner. (Lv88) <***Loc:*** EV, SM, VM, Lv88, Ph36>

MOP[2] [mɔp, mɑp] *n.m.* mop <***Loc:*** EV, LA, SM, TB, VM, Da84, Lv88, Ph36>

moquard ♦see **moqueur**

moque[1] [mɔk] *n.m./f.* **1** mug, cup, drinking glass **2** handled drinking cup (used with a bucket) **3** dipper, ladle **4** gravy boat **5** barnacle <***Loc:*** AV, EV, IB, JD, JE, SL, SM, TB, VM, Da84, Gu00, Lv88, Ph36>

moque[2] [mɔk] *n.m.* duck call, birdcall ◊ **•moque à canards / moque-canard** duck call <VM, Lv88> <***Loc:*** VM, Gu00, Lv88>

moquer [moke] **I** *v.tr.* **1** to mimic, mock, imitate *Il moque sa maîtresse.* He mimicks his teacher. (LA) **2** to call (birds) *Avant que ma voix a changé, je pouvais moquer les oies avec ma bouche.* Before my voice changed, I could call geese with my mouth. (VM) **II** *v.intr.* to make fun, joke *Le monde de la Louisiane aime moquer.* People from Louisiana like to joke. (Lv88) **III se moquer** *v.pron.* to jeer at, scoff, laugh at, mock, poke fun at **Moque-toi pas de moi.* Don't make fun of me. (ThCa: *Mille misères*) ◊ **•moquer un canard / moquer des canards** to call ducks **T'aimerais m'oir moquer un canard mieux que ça?* Would you like to see me calling a duck better than that? (Co80) <VM, Co80> <***Loc:*** VM, Co80, Da84, Gu00, Lv88, ThCa>

moquerie [mokri] *n.f.* mockery, scoffing <***Loc:*** Da84>

moqueur[1], **-euse** (**moquard**) [mokœr, mokør, -øz, mokar] *adj.* mocking, fond of making fun of others *Tu parles de moqueuse! Elle allait au bal et trouvait de quoi à dire dessus tout le monde!* Talk about mocking! She would go to the dance and find something to say about everyone. (VM) <***Loc:*** JE, VM, Da84>

moqueur[2] [mokœr, mokør] *n.m.* mockingbird ◊ **•moqueur de canne {bois}** [bird] brown thrasher <SB, Lv88, Re63> **•moqueur français {muet / sauvage / d'hiver}** shrike, French mockingbird, butcher bird <Da84, Re63> <***Loc:*** SB, SL, VM, Da84, Hi02, Lv88, Re63>

moral, -e [moral] *adj.* moral, ethical <***Loc:*** Da84>

morceau [mɔrso] *n.m.* **1** piece, bit, chunk, fragment *Tu mets une chevrette, tu mets un morceau de meuille, tu mets toute qualité d'affaires dessus [le hameçon].* You put a shrimp, you put a piece of mullet, you put all kinds of things on it [the hook]. (JE) *La vitre a brisé en morceaux.* The window shattered into pieces. (LA) **2** part, piece *Des morceaux de remplacement.* Replacement parts. (EV) *Ça c'est le méchant morceau pour l'automobile.* This is the wrong part for the car. (AV) ◊ **•morceau de linge** piece of clothing <Lv88> **•morceau de ménage {butin}** piece of furniture <VM, Lv88> **•morceau de terre** piece of land, piece of property <TB> **•morceau de viande** steak <Hi02> <***Loc:*** AV, EV, JE, LA, LF, TB, VM, Da84, Hi02, Lv88>

mordant, -e [mɔrdɑ̃, -ɑ̃t] *adj.* sarcastic, cutting (of speech) *Un* *discours mordant.* A cutting commentary. (LA) <***Loc:*** LA, Da84>

mordre [mɔrd(r), mɔr, mɔd] *v.tr.* to bite *Alle avait un gros chat, gros comme ça. Et le chat aimait pas l'homme. Il voulait le mordre.* She had a big cat, as big as that. And the cat didn't like the man. It wanted to bite him. (LF) <***Loc:*** LA, LF, SL, Da84>

mordure [mɔrdyr] *n.f.* bite, biting <***Loc:*** EV, LF, SL, TB, VM, Lv88, Ph36>

morelle [morɛl] *n.f.* plant of the nightshade family <***Loc:*** VM, Da84>

mors [mɔr] *n.m.* bit (of a bridle) ◊ **•prendre le mors aux dents** to run away, be uncontrollable, bite the bit, act without restraint <Da84> <***Loc:*** Da84>

mort[1]**, -e** [mɔr, mɔrt] *adj.* **1** dead **Le hibou était par terre; il était mort.* The owl was on the ground; it was dead. (EV, An94) **2** stagnant **Eau morte.* Stagnant water. (Da84) **3** spent, exhausted, worn out *Mort de fatigue.* Dead tired. (VM) <***Loc:*** EV, VM, An94, Da84, Hi02>

mort[2] [mɔr] *n.m.* **1** dead person **2** dummy hand (in card games) ◊ **•faire le mort** to play dead, play possum <Da84> **•né-mort** stillborn <Da84> <***Loc:*** Da84, Hi02>

mort[3] [mɔr] *n.f.* death ◊ **•à la mort** to be dying *Il était déjà à la mort quand j'ai été le voir.* He was already at death's door when I went to see him. (EV) <EV, Da84> **•en mort fausse** drowsy, indolent *Être en mort fausse.* To be drowsy. (LF) <LF> **•la mort n'a pas de fin** [*proverb*] 'you're never too old' (e.g. to get married) <La99> **•à mort** very much, extremely *Les chevrettes, j'aime ça à mort.* I love shrimp to death. (LA) <LA, VM> <***Loc:*** EV, LA, VM, Da84, Hi02, La99>

mortaisage [mɔrtezaʒ] *n.m.* mortising <***Loc:*** Da84>

mortaise [mɔrtɛz, mɔrtwaz] *n.f.* mortise <***Loc:*** JE, Da84>

mortaiser [mɔrteze] *v.tr.* to mortise *Dans le vieux temps, le monde avait l'habitude de mortaiser les chevrons.* In the old days, people used to mortise rafters. (LA) <***Loc:*** LA, Da84>

mortalité [mɔrtalite] *n.f.* **1** death *Le deuxième anniversaire de la mortalité d'Elvis Presley.* The second anniversary of the death of Elvis Presley. (SL) **2** mortality <***Loc:*** SL, VM, Da84, Lv88>

mortel[1]**, -elle** [mɔrtɛl] *adj.* mortal, deadly *Un péché mortel.* A mortal sin. (EV) <***Loc:*** EV, Da84>

mortel[2] [mɔrtɛl] *n.m.* trouble, misery *Il m'a fait des mortels, des misères.* He made trouble and misery for me. (VM) <***Loc:*** VM>

mortel[3] [mɔrtɛl] *adv.* extremely *Ça me démange mortel.* It is making me extremely itchy. (VM) <***Loc:*** VM>

mortellement [mɔrtɛlmɑ̃] *adv.* mortally **Être blessé mortellement.* To be mortally wounded. (Da84) <***Loc:*** Da84>

mortier [mɔrtje] *n.m.* mortar, mortar-mix <***Loc:*** LF, SL, Da84>

mortifiant, -e [mɔrtifjɑ̃, -ɑ̃t] *adj.* mortifying, aggravating, exhibiting bad behavior *Les petites filles sont si jolies et les femmes sont mortifiantes.* Young girls are so pretty and grown women are so aggravating. (VM, ch: *La vie d'un musicien*) <***Loc:*** VM, Da84>

mortifier [mɔrtifje] **I** *v.tr.* **1** to mortify, humiliate *J'étais mortifié quand j'ai vu mon gendre avec cette femme.* I was mortified when I saw my son-in-law with that woman. (LA) **2** to aggravate *Arrête donc de me mortifier comme ça!* Just stop aggravating me like that! (VM) **3** to offend, make angry *C'est comme si son boss l'a mortifiée, ça fait alle a arrêté là-bas.* It is as if her boss offended her, therefore she stopped there. (VM) **II se mortifier** *v.pron.* [*eccl.*] to mortify o.s., practice self-denial (as a religious act) *C'était pus une pénitence. Elle était après se mortifier.* It was no longer a penance. She was punishing herself. (LA) <***Loc:*** EV, LA, VM, Da84>

mort-ivre [moriv(r)] *adj.* dead drunk *Il était soûl mort-ivre; il gringolait tout partout dans le chemin.* He was dead drunk; he was staggering all over the road. (LA) <***Loc:*** JE, LA>

morue [mory] *n.f.* cod <***Loc:*** Da84>

morvant ♦see **morveux**

morve [mɔrv, mɔv] *n.f.* snot, mucus <***Loc:*** SJ, Da84>

morveux[1]**, -euse** (**morvant, -e**) [mɔrvø, -øz, mɔrvɑ̃, -ɑ̃t] *adj.* sniveling, running at the nose, snotty *Des enfants morveux.* Runny-nosed children. (VM) <***Loc:*** SM, VM, Da84>

morveux[2]**, -euse** [mɔrvø, -øz] *n.* **1** brat, unruly child **2** sniveling person <***Loc:*** Da84>

morviat [mɔrvja] *n.m.* phlegm, mucus, snot <***Loc:*** IB, Da84>

mot [mo] *n.m.* **1** word **2** note **3** news ◊ **•mot pour mot** word for word, verbatim <Da84> **•avoir des mots (avec qqn)** to quarrel *Ils ont eu des mots.* They had words. (LA) <LA, SM, VM, La99, Lv88> **•en autres mots** in other words *Mais son popa à elle est mort jeune. En autres mots eux-autres était à neuf. Et il y en a quatre qu'est morts.* But her father died young. In other words there were nine of them. And four of them are dead. (LF) <LF> **•un mot d'écrit** note <Da84> <***Loc:*** LA, LF, SM, VM, Da84, Hi02, La99, Lv88>

motel [motɛl] *n.m.* motel <***Loc:*** Da84>

motelon [mɔtlɔ̃, mɔklɔ̃] *n.m.* **1** clot, lump **2** uneven thread in woven material <***Loc:*** JE, VM, Di32>

motion [mosjɔ̃] *n.f.* motion <***Loc:*** Da84>

motte [mɔt] *n.f.* clod, chunk ◊ **•motte de terre** clod of dirt <Da84> <***Loc:*** Da84, Fa77>

motter [mote] **I** *v.intr.* to clod, form clods *La terre est assez trempe, là, quand tu vas la rabourer, elle va motter.* The ground is so wet, when you go to plow it, it's going to clump up. (VM) **II se motter** *v.pron.* to clod, form into clods <***Loc:*** VM, Da84>

mou[1]**, molle** [mu, mɔl] (*occ. f.* **moute** [mut]) *adj.* **1** soft *Tu bouilles ça jusqu'à ça vient manière mou.* You boil it until it becomes kind of soft. (AV) *Ça la faisait molle (la peau).* It would make it soft (the skin). (AC) **2** flabby *Un ventre mou.* A flabby stomach. (VM) <***Loc:*** AC, AV, VM, Da84>

mou[2] [mu] *n.m.* soft part (of anything) <***Loc:*** Da84>

mouchage [muʃaʒ] *n.f.* blowing of the nose <***Loc:*** Da84>

mouche[1] [muʃ] *n.f.* **1** fly, housefly **2** fishing fly ◊ **•mouche à feu** firefly <IB, JE, LA, VM, Da84, Guoo, Hi02, Lv88> **•mouche à miel** honeybee *C'est comme ça qu'elle allait pour s'occuper des mouches à miel.* This is how she used to go to take care of the bees. (IB) <AL, AV, EV, IB, JE, LA, LF, SB, SM, VM, Da84, Guoo, Hi02, Lv88> **•mouche à ver** ***a*** blowfly ***b*** green fly, maggot fly <VM, Da84> **•mouche catalique** Spanish fly <Da84> <***Loc:*** AL, AV, EV, IB, JE, LA, LF, SB, SL, SM, VM, Da84, Guoo, Hi02, Lv88>

mouche[2] [muʃ] *n.f.* **1** joker (in a deck of cards) **2** wild card with a value between the 10 and the jack (in card games) <***Loc:*** LA>

mouche-nez [muʃne] *n.m.* handkerchief <***Loc:*** JE, TB, VM, Di32, Gr86, Lv88>

moucher [muʃe] **I** *v.tr.* to wipe or blow the nose **Mouche ton nez.* Blow your nose. (Da84) **II se moucher** *v.pron.* to blow one's nose **Mouche-toi.* Blow your nose. (Da84) *Arrête de renifler comme ça et va te moucher plutôt.* Stop sniffling like that and go blow your nose instead. (LA) <***Loc:*** LA, Da84, Lv88>

mouchoir [muʃwar] *n.m.* **1** handkerchief **2** small rectangular parcel of land <***Loc:*** AL, SL, Da84>

moudage [mudaʒ] *n.m.* action of grinding or milling <***Loc:*** VM, Lv88>

mouder ♦see **moudre**

moudeur [mudœr] *n.m.* miller <***Loc:*** JE>

moudre (**mouder**) [mud(r)] (*p.p.* **moulu** [muly], **moudu** [mudy]) *v.tr.* **1** to grind, mill *Ça moudait le maïs pour le gru.* They would grind corn for grits. (Lv88) *Quand tu avais besoin de café, tu le moudais.* When you needed coffee, you would grind it. (JD) **2** to grind, chop up, mince (e.g. meat) *De la viande moudue.* Ground meat. (AC) *Tu peux moudre les bajoues, mettre avec la viande moudue.* You can grind the jowls, put them with the ground meat. (VM) ◊ **•moudre le café** to grind coffee <AC> <***Loc:*** AC, JD, VM, Da84, Lv88>

moudurage [mudyraʒ] *n.* **1** grinding (e.g. of grain) **2** miller's fee, miller payment <***Loc:*** JE>

mouillassant [mujasɑ̃] *adj.* drizzly *Un temps mouillassant.* Drizzly weather. (ch: *La pistache à Tante Nana*) <***Loc:*** Da84>

mouillasse [mujas] *n.f.* rain, drizzle <***Loc:*** EV, Lv88, Ph36>

mouillasser [mujase] *v.intr.* to rain on and off, drizzle, sprinkle *On espérait une grosse pluie, mais ç'a juste mouillassé un petit brin.* We were hoping for a big rain, but it just drizzled a little bit. (Guoo) <***Loc:*** EV, IB, LF, TB, VM, Da84, Guoo, Hi02, Lv88, Ph36>

mouillasserie [mujasri] *n.f.* drizzle <***Loc:*** JE, VM>

mouillasseux, -euse [mujasø, -øz] *adj.* drizzly, rainy *Le temps était trop mouillasseux pour couper du riz hier.* The weather was too rainy for cutting the rice yesterday. (Guoo) <***Loc:*** JE, VM, Da84, Guoo, Lv88>

mouiller [muje] **I** *v.tr.* **1** to wet, dampen *Mouiller une lavette.* To dampen a washcloth. (LA) *Alle ressemblait une poule mouillée.* She looked like a wet chicken. (LA) **2** to spank *Il a mouillé son petit garçon.* He spanked his little boy. (SM) **II** *v.intr.* to rain *Ça va mouiller fort à soir.* It's going to rain hard tonight. (Lv88) *Il avait mouillé une avalasse.* There was a downpour. (Lv88) ◊ **•mouiller averse / mouiller à verse** to rain in torrents <Da84> **•mouiller des chiens et des chats** to rain cats and dogs, rain heavily <Guoo, La99, Lv88> **•mouiller des petits nègres en or / mouiller comme si le Bon Dieu est content** to rain heavily <La99, Lv88> **•mouiller fort / mouiller par barils {baquets / bailles}** to rain heavily *C'était après mouiller fort le jour qu'on a enterré Pawpaw.* It was raining hard the day we buried Pawpaw. (EV) <AC, EV, La99> **•mouiller jusqu'à les chiens {vaches} buvaient debout / mouiller jusqu'à les vaches beuglent** to rain a lot, rain very much <EV, La99> <***Loc:*** AC, AL, AV, EV, IB, LA, LF, SB, SL, SM, TB, VM, Da84, Hi02, Guoo, La99, Lv88, Ph36>

moulage [mulaʒ] *n.m.* **1** act of grinding or milling **2** molding, casting ◊ **•moulage de maïs** corn grinding or milling <Da84> <***Loc:*** SM, Da84, Lv88>

moule[1] [mul] *n.f.* molding, trim, mold <***Loc:*** Da84>

moule[2] [mul] *n.m.* **1** pattern, form, mold (for casting) **2** frame, rack (for stretching out the skin of an animal) <***Loc:*** LF, TB, Da84>

moulé ♦see **moulée**

moulée (moulé) [mule] *n.m./f.* **1** sawdust **2** bran and water mixture used as cattle feed ◊ **•moulée de scie** sawdust <VM> <***Loc:*** JE, TB, VM, Di32>

mouler[1] [mule] (*p.p.* **moulé** [mule], **moulu** [muly]) *v.tr.* to mold, cast (in a mold), shape *Mouler une brique.* To mold a brick. (VM) <***Loc:*** VM, Da84>

mouler[2] [mule] (*p.p.* **moulé** [mule], **moulu** [muly]) *v.tr.* **1** to grind, mill (grains, coffee, etc.) *Dans ces temps il n-avait de la farine maïs que on aurait fait mouler nous-autres même.* In those days, there was cornmeal that we would have ground ourselves. (SL) **2** to grind, chop up, mince (e.g. meat) *Tu moules la viande de cochon et tu la mets dans cette gogue-là.* You mince the pork and you put it in that pig stomach. (AV) *Premièrement, j'étouffe la viande moulue.* First I steam the ground meat. (Lv88) *De la viande moulée.* Ground beef. (Lv88) ◊ **•mouler le café** to grind coffee *Hier au soir j'ai moulé du café.* Last night I ground some coffee. (LF) <AC, LF, VM> <***Loc:*** AC, AV, EV, JE, LF, SB, SL, SM, TB, VM, Da84, Lv88, Ph36>

moulin [mulɛ̃] *n.m.* **1** mill (building, factory, or mechanical device) **2** grinder, churn, mill (for domestic use) ◊ **•moulin à battre** ***a*** churn ***b*** thrashing machine <JE, VM> **•moulin à beurre** butter churn <Lv88> **•moulin à café** coffee mill, coffee grinder <JD, LF, SL, Da84> **•moulin à canne** sugar cane mill <Lv88> **•moulin à coton** cotton mill, gin <SL, Da84> **•moulin à gru** grist mill <Da84> **•moulin à maïs** corn mill <LF, Da84> **•moulin à piles** horse-operated mill of five pestles, hulling mill <JE, VM> **•moulin à riz** rice mill <Da84, Lv88> **•moulin à scie** sawmill <AC, LF, SL, SM, VM> **•moulin à sucre** sugar mill <Da84> **•moulin à vent** windmill <Lv88> **•moulin à viande** meat grinder <EV, Da84, Lv88> <***Loc:*** AC, EV, JD, JE, LA, LF, SL, SM, VM, Da84, Hi02, Lv88>

moulinage [mulinaʒ] *n.m.* **1** milling around, moving around, walking around **2** miller's fee, miller payment **3** ginning (of cotton) <***Loc:*** JE, Da84, Di32>

mouliner [muline] **I** *v.tr.* to gin, pass (cotton) through a gin in order to remove the seeds *Il a pas fini de faire mouliner son coton cette année.* He has not finished ginning his cotton this year. (LA) **II** *v.intr.* to mill around, move around, fly around, walk around *Les oiseaux moulinent dans le ciel.* The birds fly around in the sky. (Lv88) *La mouche est après mouliner pour entrer.* The fly is flying around in order to get in. (Lv88) *Il y a un tas de monde après mouliner.* There are a lot of people milling around. (Lv88) *Les bêtes ont mouliné tout la nuit.* The cattle milled around all night. (VM) **2** to procrastinate *Mouliner en faisant son ouvrage.* To delay in doing one's work. (SJ) ◊ **•mouliner la queue du chien** to procrastinate <La99> <***Loc:*** LA, SJ, VM, Da84, La99, Lv88>

moulinier [mulĩje] *n.m.* miller <***Loc:*** JE, VM, Da84>

moulure [mulyr] *n.f.* molding, trim <***Loc:*** AC, Da84, Fa77>

mouman ♦see **maman**

mouque [muk] *n.f.* clam <***Loc:*** JE>

mourant -e [murɑ̃, -ɑ̃t] *adj.* dying, at the point of death *Son vieux n-oncle est mourant.* His poor old uncle is dying. (LA) <***Loc:*** LA, Da84>

mourir [murir] *v.intr.* to die *On était onze mais il n-a trois qu'a mouri.* We were eleven but three died. (SM) *Ma mouman avait quatre-vingt-seize quand elle a mouri.* My mother was ninety-six when she died. (SM) *Eux-autres a mouri trois semaines de distance.* They died three weeks apart. (AV) ◊ **•faire mourir** to cause to die, put to death <Da84> <***Loc:*** AV, SM, VM, Da84, Hi02, Lv88>

mouroir [murwar] *n.m.* deathbed, death place ◊ **•être sus le mouroir** to be on the point of death <TB, La99> <***Loc:*** TB, La99>

mousquite [muskit] *n.f.* mesquite <***Loc:*** Gu00>

mousse [mus] *n.f.* **1** moss **2** Spanish moss ◊ **•mousse espagnole** Spanish moss <Gu00, Hi02, Lv88> **•mousse-fleur** portulaca, moss rose <EV> <***Loc:*** EV, VM, Da84, Di32, Gu00, Hi02, Lv88>

mousser [muse] *v.tr.* **1** to hurry, urge on *Mousser l'ouvrier.* To urge on the worker. (SJ) **2** to card, comb, brush (wool) with a card <***Loc:*** JE, SJ>

moustache [mustaʃ] *n.f.* **1** mustache **2** whiskers <***Loc:*** TB, Da84>

moustiquaire [mustikær] *n.m.* mosquito net, mosquito bar <***Loc:*** LA, Da84>

moustique [mustik, mustɪk] *n.m.* **1** mosquito **2** gnat or small fly <***Loc:*** AV, IB, IV, JE, LF, SB, SL, SM, TB, VM, Da84, Hi02, Lv88>

moutarde [mutard] *n.f.* **1** mustard **2** mustard greens <***Loc:*** CL, LA, SL, Da84>

moutchon [mutʃɔ̃] *n.m.* stump (e.g. of an amputated limb) <***Loc:*** LF>

mouton [mutɔ̃] *n.m.* **1** lamb **Doux comme un mouton.* Gentle as a lamb. (Da84) **2** sheep **3** mutton <***Loc:*** AV, SL, SM, Da84, Hi02>

mouvant, -e [muvɑ̃, -ɑ̃t] *adj.* **1** moving, shifting *Du sable mouvant.* Shifting sands. (VM) **2** loose (of the ground) *Terre mouvante.* Spongy land. (VM) <***Loc:*** VM, Da84, Lv88>

mouvement [muvmɑ̃] *n.m.* movement, motion ◊ **•se mettre en mouvement** to get going <Da84> <***Loc:*** Da84>

mouver (**MOVE**) [muve, muv] **I** *v.tr.* to move *Ils ont mouvé leur maison de Golden Meadow à Larose.* They moved their house from Golden Meadow to Larose. (VM) **II** *v.intr.* **1** to move, change residence *On a tout* LOAD *l'affaire. On a* MOVE *à la Prairie Ronde.* We loaded everything. We moved to Prairie Ronde (SL) *Il y a juste nous-autres qu'à* MOVE. We were the only ones who moved. (SM) **2** to move, move about *Moi je me rappelle j'avais un Français, il avait pas de machine, il avait une voile pour son bateau, ou quand le courant allait il mouvait.* I remember I had a Frenchman, he had no motor, he had a sail for his boat, or when the current went he moved. (LF) <***Loc:*** LF, SL, SM, VM, Lv88>

MOVE ♦see **mouver**

moyen[1], **-enne** [mojɛ̃, mɔ̃jɛ̃, -ɛ̃n] *adj.* medium, middle-sized **Un moyen garçon.* A medium-sized boy. (Da84) **Moyenne fille.* Middle-sized girl. (Da84) <***Loc:*** Da84>

moyen[2] [mojɛ̃, mɔ̃jɛ̃] *n.m.* **1** means, way **Il voulait s'en revenir, mais il pouvait pas, parce qu'il avait pas moyen de sortir.* He wanted to come home, but he couldn't, because he had no way to get out. (AC, An94) **2** conveyance, vehicle, mode of transportation *T'as laissé ton moyen? J'ai pas de moyen pour aller.* Did you leave your car? I don't have any vehicle to get there. (VM) *Quoi c'est t'as comme moyen?* What do you drive? (VM) *Le monde avait pas des moyens pour aller dans des parties comme ça.* People did not have transportation to go to places like that. (EV) **3** ability ◊ **•avoir les {des} moyens** to have means (i.e. money) *Il a pas les moyens pour s'acheter un char.* He doesn't have the means to buy himself a car. (LA) <LA, Da84> **•être en moyen** to have means **Oh, c'était un homme bien en moyen.* Oh, he was a man of considerable means. (LA, An94) <LA, An94, Da84> **•il y a moyen** it can be, it is possible **Il y a moyen de faire des récoltes, ça fait drôle.* It's possible to really make crops there, it's amazing. (SL, An94) <SL, An94, Da84> **•il y a pas (de) moyen de {pour}** there's no way to, it's impossible to *Tu étais élevé d'une boutique de campagne éyoù on avait tout ce que les gens avaient besoin parce que il y avait pas de moyen pour aller en ville.* You were raised out of a country store where there was everything that people needed because there was no means for going into town. (SL) <SL> **•s'il y a moyen** if there's a way, if it is possible *Je veux mourir dans ma maison, s'il y a moyen.* I want to die at home, if it is possible. (EV) <EV> <***Loc:*** AC, EV, LA, LF, SL, VM, An94, Da84>

moyen[3] [mojɛ̃, mɔ̃jɛ̃] *adv.* rather, somewhat *Il y a plein qu'est morts et il y a plein je veux dire que ils ont* FIGHT *mais la fièvre était tellement fort que il y a plein je veux dire que ça les a brûlé la cervelle. Ça fait après ça ils pouvaient pas apprendre bien, ils étaient moyen en retard.* There are a lot who died and there are a lot, I mean they fought but the fever was so strong that there arre a lot, I mean, whose brains were damaged by the fever. So afterwards they couldn't learn well, they were somewhat retarded. (SJ) <***Loc:*** SJ>

moyennant [mojɛ̃nɑ̃] *adv.* about, approximately *Il a payé moyennant mille piastres pour le vieux char.* He paid approximately a thousand dollars for the old car. (EV) <***Loc:*** EV>

moyenne [mojɛ̃n] *n.f.* average <***Loc:*** Da84>

moyère ♦see **manière**

moyeu [mojø] *n.m.* **1** hub, center **2** hub of a wheel **3** stump (e.g. of an amputated limb) <***Loc:*** EV, VM, Da84, Hi02>

MUCH [mɔtʃ, mʌtʃ] *adv.* much ◊ **•pas MUCH** not much, very little *Ça j'ai c'est pas* MUCH. What I've got is not much. (VM) <VM, Lv88> <***Loc:*** VM, Lv88>

muet, -ette [mɥɛ, mɥe, -ɛt] *adj.* mute *Il était rendu positivement muet.* He had become positively mute. (LA) ◊ **•sourd (et) muet** deaf-mute <Da84> <***Loc:*** LA, Da84>

mulâtre, -esse [mylat(r), -rɛs] *n.* mulatto, person of mixed white and black ancestry <***Loc:*** Da84>

mule [myl] *n.* mule <***Loc:*** Da84, Fa77>

muleron [mylrɔ̃, mylerɔ̃] *n.m.* haystack <***Loc:*** IB, VM, Di32>

mulet [mylɛ, myle] *n.m.* **1** mule (of either sex) **2** he-mule ◊ **•faire son mulet** to yawn <SC, La99> <***Loc:*** IB, JE, SC, VM, Da84, Hi02, La99>

muloche [mylɔʃ] *n.f.* small mule <***Loc:*** JE>

mulon[1] [mylɔ̃, milɔ̃, mulɔ̃] *n.m.* large grindstone <***Loc:*** Lv88>

mulon[2] [mylɔ̃, milɔ̃] *n.m.* haystack *Mulon de foin.* Haystack. (SM) <***Loc:*** AV, IB, SM, VM, Di32, Gr86>

mulonner [mylɔ̃ne, milɔ̃ne, mulɔ̃ne] *v.tr.* to stack (hay) *Mulonner du foin.* To stack hay. (SM) <***Loc:*** JE, SM, Di32, Lv88>

municipal, -e [mynisipal] *adj.* municipal *Il a paru devant le gouvernement municipal.* He appeared before the municipal government. (LA) <***Loc:*** LA, Da84>

munition (**ammunition**) [amynisjɔ̃, mynisjɔ̃] *n.f.* ammunition, munition <***Loc:*** SM, Da84>

mur [myr] *n.m.* **1** wall **2** partition <***Loc:*** SL, Da84, Hi02>

mûr, -e [myr, myrt] *adj.* ripe *Les figues sont mûres.* The figs are ripe. (LA) <***Loc:*** LA, LF, SL, Da84, Hi02>

muraille [myraj] *n.f.* wall <***Loc:*** Da84, Gu00, Hi02, Lv88>

mûre [myr] *n.f.* **1** berry **2** blackberry *Elle allait ramasser les mûres, et puis là elle faisait jusqu'à cinquante* QUARTS *de* BLACKBERRY JAM. She would go and pick blackberries, then she would make up to fifty quarts of blackberry jam. (SL) ◊ **•mûre d'arbre** mulberry <SM, Da84> **•mûre d'éronce / mûre de ronces hautes / mûre douce {haute}** blackberry <TB, Da84, Gu00, Lv88> **•mûre traînante** dewberry, dewberry vine <SM, VM, Da84, Gu00, Lv88> <***Loc:*** AV, CL, SL, SM, TB, VM, Da84, Gu00, Hi02, Lv88>

mûrier [myrje] *n.m.* **1** mulberry tree **2** cedar tree **3** cedarbird, cedar waxwing <***Loc:*** Da84, Gu00, Hi02, Lv88, Re31>

mûrir [myrir] *v.intr.* to ripen, mature *Les tomates sont après mûrir.* The tomatoes are ripening. (LA) ◊ **•faire mûrir** to force-ripen *Tu peux faire mûrir tes poires dans un sac.* You can force-ripen your pears in a paper bag. (LA) <LA, Da84> <***Loc:*** LA, Da84, Fa77>

muscade (**mommuscade**) [myskad, mɔ̃myskad] *n.f.* nutmeg <***Loc:*** SL, VM, Da84>

muscadier [myskadje] *n.m.* nutmeg tree <***Loc:*** Da84>

muscat [myska] *n.m.* **1** muscat wine **2** muscat grape **3** muscadine <***Loc:*** Da84>

muscatel [myskatɛl] *n.m.* muscatel <***Loc:*** Da84, Wh83>

muscle [mysk(l)] *n.m.* muscle <***Loc:*** Da84>

museau [myzo, myzjo] *n.m.* **1** snout, nose **2** face **3** muzzle, calf weaner <***Loc:*** SJ, TB, VM, Da84>

musée [myze] *n.m.* museum <***Loc:*** LF>

musicien [myzisjɛ̃] *n.m.* musician *Il commence à avoir plusieurs jeunes musiciens comme moi qui s'intéressont à notre vieille musique.* There are beginning to be several young musicians like me who are taking an interest in our music. (VM) <***Loc:*** VM, Da84, Fa77, Hi02>

musique [myzik, mizik] *n.m/f.* **1** music **2** musical instrument *Ça c'est une vieille musique.* That's an old hand-cranked organ. (JE) **3** reed (on a musical instrument) *J'ai besoin de changer les musiques dans mon accordéon.* I need to change the reeds in my accordeon. (EV) ◊ **•musique à babines {bouche / gueule}** harmonica <EV, JE, LA, SL, SM, VM, Da84, Lv88, Ph36> **•musique française** traditional Acadian Cajun/Creole music <Lv88> <***Loc:*** EV, JE, LA, SL, SM, VM, Da84, Hi02, Lv88>

musqué, -e [myske] *adj.* musked, musky **Rat musqué.* Muskrat. (VM) <***Loc:*** VM, Da84>

musqette [myskɛt] *n.f.* musket *Quand il voulait bourrer son* *fusil pour tirer la z-oie, il a pris un chiffon de mousse, il l'a bien tapée, la musquette.* When he wanted to stuff his shotgun to shoot the goose, he took a wad of moss, he tapped it well, the musket. (VM) <***Loc:*** VM>

musse [mys] *n.* calf <***Loc:*** LF>

myope [mjɔp, maɔp] *adj.* nearsighted, myopic *Je commence à devenir un peu myope.* I'm starting to become a bit nearsighted. (LA) <***Loc:*** LA, VM, Da84>

myrte rose (**myrtille rose**) [mirtroz] *n.f.* crape myrtle <***Loc:*** JE, TB, Da84>

myrtille [mirtij] *n.f.* **1** crape myrtle **2** blueberry **3** bilberry <***Loc:*** CL, Da84>

myrtille rose ♦see **myrte rose**

mystère [mistær] *n.m.* mystery <***Loc:*** Da84>

mystérieux, -ieuse [misterjø, -jøz] *adj.* mysterious *C'était une place mystérieuse.* That was a mysterious place. (LA) <***Loc:*** LA, Da84>

mystifailler [mistifaje] *v.tr.* to mystify *Ces lumières m'avaient tout mystifaillé.* Those lights had completely mystified me. (LA) <***Loc:*** LA, Da84>

mystifier [mistifje] *v.tr.* to mystify *Il était mystifié quand il a vu qu'elle était pus là.* He was mystified when he saw that she was no longer there. (LA) <***Loc:*** LA, Da84>

nacre [nak(r)] *n.m./f.* mother-of-pearl, nacre <***Loc:*** Da84, Fa77>

nage [naʒ] *n.f.* swim ◊ **•à la nage** swimming **Son chien s'est vite tiré à la nage.* His dog quickly began swimming. (EV, An94) <EV, An94, Da84> **•à la nage de sueur** soaking wet with perspiration <Da84> <***Loc:*** EV, An94, Da84>

nageoire [naʒwar] *n.m.* **1** fin (on a fish) **2** swimming flipper, webbed foot (on a bird) <***Loc:*** VM>

nager [naʒe] *v.intr.* to swim **Tout ça je peux dire, il connaît pas seulement nager.* All I can say is, he doesn't even know how to swim. (EV, An94) <***Loc:*** EV, IV, SL, TB, An94, Da84>

nageur, -euse [naʒœr, -øz] *n.* swimmer *J'ai jamais été bon nageur.* I have never been a strong swimmer. (LA) <***Loc:*** EV, LA, VM, Da84, Fa77>

nain[1]**, -e (nine)** [nɛ̃, nɛ̃n, nin] *adj.* **1** dwarf *Il avait acheté un petit cheval nain pour son garçon.* He had bought a little dwarf horse for his son. (LA) **2** small, undersize <***Loc:*** LA, VM, Da84, Fa77, Lv88>

nain[2]**, -e (nine)** [nɛ̃, nɛ̃n, nin] *n.* dwarf <***Loc:*** LA, VM, Da84, Fa77, Lv88>

naine ♦see **nénaine**

naissance [nesɑ̃s] *n.f.* **1** birth **2** beginning <***Loc:*** AV, Da84>

naissant [nesɑ̃] *adj.* newborn *Le bébé est naissant.* The baby is newborn. (LF) *C'est un naissant.* It's a newborn. (LF) <***Loc:*** LF, Da84>

naître [nɛt(r)] (*p.p.* **éné** [ẽne]**, né** [ne]) *v.intr.* to be born **Il a été né et élevé dans le petit village de Mire.* He was born and raised in the little town of Mire. (LA, An94) *Il y a des petits bébés qui naît qui a pas de bras et qui a pas de mains.* There are some babies who are born who don't have any arms and who don't have any hands. (EV) ◊ **•premier né** firstborn, eldest <Da84> <***Loc:*** AC, AV, EV, LA, TB, An94, Da84>

naïve [naiv] *adj.* naive, simple, guileless *Le vieux dit: "Puisqu'il est si naïve de dire la vérité que ça," il dit, "c'est lui qu'aura ma fille."* The old man says, "Since he is so naïve as to tell the truth in this way," he says, "it is he who will have my daughter." (IB) <***Loc:*** IB, Da84>

naïveté [naivte] *n.f.* naïveté, guilelessness <***Loc:*** Da84>

nambouri ♦see **nombril**

name-name ♦see **niame-niame**

nanan ♦see **nanane**

nanane[1] **(nanan)** [nɑ̃nɑ̃n, nɑ̃nɑ̃] [*baby talk*] **I** *v.tr.invar.* to eat **II** *v.intr.invar.* to eat *J'ai faim, je vas nanane à cette heure.* I'm hungry, I'm going to eat now. (VM) <***Loc:*** IB, LF, SM, TB, VM>

nanane[2] **(nanan)** [nɑ̃nɑ̃n, nɑ̃nɑ̃] *n.m. (occ. f.)* [*baby talk*] **1** food **2** tidbit, tasty morsel **3** meat (of a nut) **4** pulp, edible portion of citrus fruit <***Loc:*** AV, IB, JE, LF, SB, SJ, SL, SM, TB, VM, La99, Lv88>

n-anglais ♦see **anglais**

nap [næp, nap] *n.m.* nap, siesta ◊ **•prendre un nap** to take a nap *Prendre un petit nap.* Take a little nap. (Lv88) <Da84, Lv88> <***Loc:*** Da84, Lv88>

nappille [napij] *n.f.* tablecloth <***Loc:*** JE, Di32>

nappillon [napijɔ̃] *n.m.* small tablecloth <***Loc:*** JE, Di32>

nappe [nap] *n.f.* tablecloth ◊ **•nappe d'autel** altar cloth <Da84> **•nappe de table** tablecloth <SL, Fa77> <***Loc:*** SL, Da84, Fa77>

narcisse [narsis] *n.f.* carnation <***Loc:*** Fa77>

naré, -e [nare] *adj.* sly, cunning <***Loc:*** JE, Di32>

narguer [narge] *v.tr.* to taunt, tease, pick on *Je pense si tu vas les attiner ou de quoi, les narguer, ils vont peut-être te faire de quoi.* I think if you go and tease them [alligators], pick on them, they'll do something to you. (TB) <***Loc:*** LF, SB, TB, Da84, Lv88>

narine [narin] *n.f.* nostril ◊ **•avoir les narines effleurées {ouvertes}** to be angry <La99> <***Loc:*** AC, Da84, Fa77, La99>

nasiller [nazije] *v.intr.* to chatter, gossip <***Loc:*** JE, Di32>

nasonner [nazɔ̃ne] *v.intr.* to grumble **A nasonne, alle est pas cantent.* She's grumbling, she's not happy. (EV, Ph36) <***Loc:*** EV, Ph36>

nation [nasjɔ̃] *n.f.* **1** nation, country *J'étais dans le service et je rencontrais du monde [...] de toutes nations, ça parlait pas l'anglais, n'avait, mais ça parlait plein le français.* I was in the service and I met people from all nations, they didn't speak English, well, some did, but often they spoke French. (LF) **2** ethnic group (e.g. Native Americans or Creoles of color) ◊ **•les Nations Unies** the United Nations <Fa77> <***Loc:*** LF, Da84, Fa77>

national[1]**, -e** [nasjɔ̃nal] *adj.* national **Evidement plaît qu'on la regarde comme eine de les plus grandes économistes national et adviseur de finances, Tchou Flette nous a bien poliement envoyé d'autres suggestions.* Obviously pleased that we regarded her as a leading national economist and financial adviser, Tchou Flette graciously forwarded us further proven suggestions. (Wh83) <***Loc:*** EV, Da84, Wh83>

national[2] [nasjɔ̃nal] *n.* national, citizen <***Loc:*** Da84>

nationale [nasjɔ̃nal] *n.f.* nationality *Oui, la Louisiane c'est un vrai gombo. Il y a des Italiens, des Français, des Espagnes, des Allemands, c'est tout du monde qui vient de différents de nationales, mais ils parlont tout le même français.* Yes, Louisiana is a real gumbo. There are Italians, French, Spanish, Germans, they're all people who come from different nationalities, but they all speak the same French. (LF) <*Loc:* LF>

nationalité [nasjɔ̃nalite] *n.f.* nationality <*Loc:* Da84>

native[1] [nativ] *adj.* native <*Loc:* LF, Da84>

native[2] [nativ] *n.* native *C'est un native de Bayou Lafourche* He's a native of Bayou Lafourche (LF) <*Loc:* LF, Da84>

nativité [nativite] *n.f.* [*eccl.*] nativity <*Loc:* Da84>

nature [natyr] *n.f.* **1** nature **On peut entendre la voix de Dieu dans les cris des oies sauvages et voir sa présence dans la nature.* We can hear the voice of God in the cry of wild geese and see His presence in nature. (ThCa: *Mille misères*) **Jean Sot était fier et bien associé avec la nature.* Jean Sot was proud and well connected with nature. (EV, An94) **2** disposition, character <*Loc:* EV, An94, Da84, Fa77, ThCa>

naturel[1], **-lle** [natyrɛl] *adj.* **1** natural (occurring in nature), not synthetic *Et le petit bayou de la Pointe était un de ces petits bayous naturels. Ça drainait à la mer.* And the little bayou in Pointe aux Chênes was one of those natural little bayous, it drained into the sea. (TB) *Icitte-dedans t'as une huile, une huile espéciale, une huile naturelle qu'empêche l'eau de passer en travers du bois.* In here you've got an oil, a special oil, a natural oil that prevents water from going through the wood. (LF) **2** natural, unprocessed (of food) *On avait tout le manger naturel, on avait notre poulet à nous-autres-mêmes, on avait notre cochon à nous-autres-mêmes, on avait notre lait à nous-autres-mêmes.* We had all the natural food, we had our own chicken, we had our own pig, we had our own milk. (LF) **3** of a normal mental state *Après sa maladie, on dirait qu'elle était pas naturelle.* After her illness, it was as if she was not mentally normal. (SL) **4** natural, normal, usual **Mais c'est pleusement des termes introduit par le développement naturel de usage plutôt que par des gros chiens d'école.* But it's mostly terms introduced through natural development rather than by academic bigwigs. (Wh83) <*Loc:* AC, EV, LA, LF, SL, TB, Da84, Wh83>

naturel[2] [natyrɛl] *adv.* naturally *Et naturel, quand la fille se mariait alle allait avec son mari de place en place.* And naturally, when the girl got married she went with her husband from place to place. (TB) *C'est mieux pour toi d'être naturel plutôt que faire accroire tu peux faire quelque chose.* It's better for you to act naturally than to convince yourself that you can do anything. (Lv88) <*Loc:* LA, TB, Lv88>

naturellement [natyrɛlmɑ̃] *adv.* naturally, of course, obviously **Ça fait, lui, naturellement, il était pas comme ces jeunes petits bougres-là qui allaient au bal sur un* RIDE *ou quelque chose comme ça.* So, naturally, he wasn't like those young guys who hitchhiked to the dance or something like that. (SL, An94) <*Loc:* EV, LA, SL, TB, An94, Da84, Wh83>

naufrage [nofraʒ] *n.m.* havoc, disorder, mess *Garde-moi ce naufrage!* Would you look at this mess! (Lv88) <*Loc:* TB, Lv88>

navet [navɛ, nave] *n.m.* turnip **Ça aimait les navets, ce monde-là, et particulièrement quand ils étiont en cornichons avec du vinaigre.* They liked turnips, those people, and particularly when they were pickled in vinegar. (EV, An94) ◊ •**navet chauvage** Indian turnip <TB> <*Loc:* CL, EV, JE, LA, SM, TB, An94, Da84>

navette [navɛt] *n.f.* bobbin (of a sewing machine) <*Loc:* AC, SL, Da84, Fa77>

navigable [navigab(l)] *adj.* navigable, passable *Ce chemin est pas navigable quand il mouille.* That road is not passable when it rains. (VM) <*Loc:* VM, Da84, Fa77>

navigateur [navigatœr] *n.m.* navigator <*Loc:* Da84>

navigation [navigasjɔ̃] *n.f.* **1** navigation, voyage, travel **2** circulation, traffic *Il y a une grosse navigation à cinq heures.* There's a lot of traffic at five o'clock. (Lv88) <*Loc:* Da84, Lv88>

naviguer [navige] **I** *v.tr.* to transport *Une troupe d'hélicoptères les naviguent aux* RIGS. A bunch of helicopters transport them to the rigs. (Lv88) *Il a mis une grande corde au téléphone pour le naviguer.* He put a long cord on the telephone to carry it around. (Lv88) **II** *v.intr.* **1** to navigate *C'était comme ça qu'on appelle une quille dessus un bateau de voiles, il follait qu'il aye un gros morceau en dedans pour pouvoir le faire naviguer.* That's like what we call a keel on a sailboat, it had to have a big piece inside to make it navigate. (LF) **2** to travel, get around, go (for a ride) *Ils naviguent chaque jour cent milles.* They travel one hundred miles each day. (Lv88) *Tu navigues en bus?* Are you going by bus? (Lv88) *Quand j'étais petit garçon, on naviguait à cheval.* When I was a little boy, we traveled on horseback. (Gu00) *Mon mari naviguait beaucoup pour la compagnie.* My husband used to travel a lot for his business. (IB) **3** to amble about, come and go *Tout ce qu'il fait c'est naviguer toute la journée.* All he does is come and go all day. (SM) <*Loc:* AC, IB, LF, SM, VM, Da84, Gu00, Lv88>

navigueur [navigœr] *n.m.* **1** navigator **2** traveler, one who moves around a lot <*Loc:* JE, SB, SM, VM, Da84, Lv88>

navire [navir] *n.m.* boat, ship, vessel <*Loc:* LF, TB, Da84, Fa77>

nayer ♦see **noyer**

ne [n(ə)] *adv.* (*occ. used with negation*) no, not *La mèche n'a pas d'arbres. C'est juste de l'eau.* The marsh doesn't have any trees. It's just water. (VM) *Ne pleurez pas autant la belle, ne versez pas autant de larmes.* Don't cry so much, girl, don't shed so many tears. (ch: *La veuve de sept ans*) **Ce n'est pas au vingtième siècle que les Acadiens quitteront le dix-septième.* It won't be in the twentieth century that Cajuns leave the seventeenth. (ThCa: *Mille misères*) *Ils n'ont pas pris part dans le dérangement.* They didn't take part in the exodus [from Acadia]. (SL) *N'anvale pas si vite.* Do not swallow so quickly. (JE) **Il n'y a rien qu'est plus malin qu'une froumi.* There is nothing meaner than an ant. (SM, An94) **Il n'y a plus rien.* There is nothing more. (An94) <***Loc:*** JE, SL, SM, VM, An94, ThCa>

nécessaire [nesesær] *adj.* necessary, required *Il faisait juste ça qu'était nécessaire et pas plus.* He would do just what was necessary and no more. (LA) *C'est nécessaire qu'il va au docteur.* He must go to the doctor. (LF) <***Loc:*** AV, LA, LF, Da84>

nécessairement [nesesærmɑ̃] *adv.* necessarily, of necessity *Il y a du monde qui disait que créole, c'est le noir. Pas nécessairement, parce que comme asteur-là, on a des tomates créoles. Dans le vieux temps il y avait des mulets créoles.* There are people who say that Creole refers to blacks. Not necessarily, because like these days, we have Creole tomatoes. In the old days there were Creole mules. (LF) <***Loc:*** EV, LF, Da84, Fa77>

nécessité [nesesite] *n.f.* necessity, need, want <***Loc:*** Da84>

nèche [nɛʃ] *n.f.* window sill <***Loc:*** JE, Di32>

née [ne] *adj.f.* having the maiden name of *Madame Louise Guidry née Trahan.* Mrs. Louise Guidry, maiden name Trahan. (VM) <***Loc:*** EV, VM, Da84>

nèfle [nɛf(l), nærf] *n.f.* Japanese plum <***Loc:*** TB>

néfrier (éflier) [nefryje, nefrije, eflije] *n.m.* medlar tree, Japanese plum tree <***Loc:*** IB, SJ, SM, TB, VM, Lv88>

négative[1] [negativ] *n.m.* film, negative <***Loc:*** Da84>

négative[2] [negativ] *adv.* negatively *Il pense négative.* He thinks negatively. (LF) <***Loc:*** LF>

négligeable [neglizab(l] *adj.* negligible, trifling, unimportant *C'est pas négligeable, tout ça il a fait pour nous-autres.* It's not negligible, everything that he did for us. (VM) <***Loc:*** VM, Da84>

négligeation [neglizasjɔ̃] *n.f.* neglect, negligence <***Loc:*** VM>

négligence [neglizɑ̃s] *n.f.* negligence, carelessness, neglect, thoughtlessness <***Loc:*** Da84>

négligent, -e [neglizɑ̃, -ɑ̃t] *adj.* negligent, neglectful, careless, thoughtless *C'est pas qu'il est mauvais, c'est juste qu'il est négligent.* It's not that he's bad, it's just that he's careless. (LA) <***Loc:*** LA, Da84>

négliger [neglize] **I** *v.tr.* **1** to neglect, be careless about *Il négligeait sa femme et ses enfants.* He neglected his wife and his children. (LA) *Les vaches, la basse-cour, tout quelque chose était joliment négligé depuis qu'alle a quitté.* The cows, the chicken yard, everything was pretty much neglected after she left. (LA) *Il a négligé sa santé.* He neglected his health. (LF) **2** to neglect, forget (to do s.t.) *Il a négligé de se baigner.* He neglected to take a bath. (LF) **II se négliger** *v.pron.* to neglect o.s., be slovenly *Faudrait pas que tu te négliges comme ça.* You shouldn't neglect yourself like that. (LA) <***Loc:*** LA, LF, Da84, Fa77>

négraille[1] [negraj, nigraj] *n.* [*extremely offensive*] black person <***Loc:*** EV, SB, SM>

négraille[2] [negraj, nigraj] *n.f.* [*extremely offensive*] term used to refer to black people collectively <***Loc:*** TB, Da84, Lv88>

nègre[1] [nɛg(r)] *n.m./f.* **1** black person, negro **On ira tout au paradis. Les pécheurs, les bonnes sœurs, les blancs et les nèg's.* We're all going to heaven. Sinners, nuns, whites and blacks. (ThCa: *Mille misères*) **2** Creole language *Parler nègre.* To speak Creole. (Lv88) ◊ **•nègre américain** black person who does not speak Creole or Cajun <Guoo, Lv88> **•nègre créole {français}** black person who speaks Cajun or Creole <Guoo, Lv88> **•cher ti nègre** dear little boy <Da84> **•mon nègre** [*term of endearment*] my man *Mon nègre était malade.* My man was sick. (LA) *Ça va bien à ce matin, mon nègre?* Things are going well this morning, honey? (Guoo) *Toi, bébé, si tu voudrais t'en revenir avec ton nègre, tu connais je te pardonnerais pour tout les choses que tu m'as fait.* You, baby, if you would only come home with your man, you know that I would forgive you for all that you did to me. (EV, ch: *Petit Mamou*) <EV, LA, Guoo, Lv88> **•vieux nègre** ***a*** old friend, my friend ***b*** [*term of endearment*] "old man" *T'as promis de rester avec ton vieux nègre.* You promised to stay with your old man. (Lv88) <Da84, Lv88> <***Loc:*** EV, LA, LF, SL, SM, TB, Da84, Guoo, Lv88, ThCa>

nègre[2] [nɛg(r)] *adv.* [*offensive*] in the manner of black people *Il danse nègre.* He dances like a black person. (SM) <***Loc:*** SM, Da84>

négresse [negrɛs] *n.f.* **1** black woman **2** girlfriend **3** [*term of endearment*] woman ◊ **•ma négresse** [*term of endearment*] my girl, my dear (used for a female of any race) <Gu82> <***Loc:*** EV, LA, Da84, Fa77, Guoo, Lv88>

négrier [negrije, nigrije] *n.* [*extremely offensive*] term formerly used by some to refer to a white person who fraternized with black people <***Loc:*** SJ, TB, Da84, Lv88>

négrillon (nigriot) [negrijɔ̃, nigrijɔ̃, nigrijo] *n.m.* **1** black person **2** black child <***Loc:*** IB, SB, SJ>

Négrite [negrit] *n.f.* name given to a black cow <***Loc:*** JE, Di32>

neige [nɛʒ] *n.f.* snow *La neige tombe.* It's snowing. (LF) <***Loc:*** EV, IV, LF, SM, VM, An94, Da84>

neiger [neʒe] *v.intr.* to snow **Ça neige.* It's snowing. (Fa77) **Il neige.* It is snowing. (Da84) **Il va neiger.* It will snow. (Da84) <***Loc:*** Da84, Fa77>

nénaine (nenaine, naine) [nɛ̃nɛ̃n, nɛ̃n] *n.f.* **1** godmother **2** grandmother, grandma *Naine va venir me voir demain.* Grandma is coming to see me tomorrow. (TB) **3** talkative nuisance, chatterbox *Ça c'est une vieille nénaine. Elle parle tout le temps.* That's an old chatterbox. She talks all the time. (SM) ◊ **•ça, c'est ta nénaine** that's what you say, that's your problem <Lv88> **•être la nenaine (à qqn)** to be bad luck (for s.o.) <TB, La99> **•ta nenaine est caille!** that's what you think! you're fooling yourself! <SM, La99> <***Loc:*** IB, SL, SM, TB, VM, Da84, Fa77, La99, Lv88>

nerf [nær, nærf] *n.m.* **1** sinew, muscle **2** strength, courage, nerve ◊ **•nerf halé** pulled muscle *Je traite pour le mal dans le dos,* A PULLED MUSCLE, *un nerf halé ça.* I treat for backache, a pulled muscle, that's called a "nerf halé." (TB) <TB> **•fait du nerf et de la babiche** (of a person) resilient, able to withstand adversity <La99> <***Loc:*** TB, Da84, Fa77, La99>

nerfé, -e [nærfe] *adj.* extremely nervous or agitated *Il est bien nerfé.* He's extremely agitated. (LF) <***Loc:*** LF, VM>

nerfer [nærfe] *v.tr.* **1** to sever the spinal cord (of an animal) at the first vertebra behind the head (for butchering) *Nerfer un cochon.* To sever a pig's spinal cord. (LA) **2** to cut the tendon of the hind leg (of an animal) **3** to stab *Ils ont nerfé Apollinaire hier soir.* They stabbed Apollinaire last night. (SL) <***Loc:*** JE, LA, LF, SB, SL, VM, Di32>

nerveux, -euse [nærvø, -øz] *adj.* nervous, jittery *Il est assez nerveux, il peut pas rester tranquille.* He's pretty nervous, he can't sit still. (LF) **Et le jeune homme aussi, l'autre bord, là-bas, il pouvait pas dormir. Il était nerveux.* And the young man, too, on the other side, he couldn't sleep. He was nervous. (EV, An94) *Arrête de tapocher sus la table. Ça me rend nerveuse.* Stop tapping on the table. It makes me nervous. (VM) <***Loc:*** EV, LF, An94, Da84>

net[1] **(nette)** [nɛt] *adj.* **1** clean, cleaned-out, tidy, neat *Quand alle a arrivé, la maison était déjà nette.* When she arrived, the house was already clean. (LA) **2** free of expense, net, clear **Un profit nette.* Clear (or net) profit. (Da84) *Le prix net.* The net price. (LF) <***Loc:*** LA, LF, Da84>

NET[2] [nɛt] *n.m.* fishing net <***Loc:*** SM, Gu00>

net[3] [nɛt] *adv.* ◊ **•tout net** completely *Il a oublié tout net.* He completely forgot. (Lv88) **En dernier de sa vie, il avait arrêté de boire tout net, il buvait plus,* NO. At the end of his life, he had completely stopped drinking, he didn't drink anymore. (EV) **L'église catholique m'a abandonné, mon et tous les aut' Cadiens ya bien longtemps. Y se foutont de nous-aut' tout net.* The Catholic Church has abandoned me, me and the other Cajuns long ago. They are completely indifferent to us. (Wh83) <EV, Lv88, Wh83> <***Loc:*** EV, Lv88, Wh83>

nette ♦see **net**[1]

nettement [nɛtmɑ̃] *adj.* finished, over *On peut tous s'en aller, c'est nettement.* We can all leave, it [the party] is over. (LF) *Le bal est nettement.* The dance is over. (LF) <***Loc:*** LF>

netteté [nɛt(ɔ)te] *n.f.* cleanliness, neatness <***Loc:*** Da84>

nettéyer ♦see **nettoyer**

nettéyeurs (netteyures) [netejœr] *n.m.pl.* sweepings, dust <***Loc:*** JE, Di32>

netteyures ♦see **nettéyeurs**

nettoyage [nɛtwajaʒ, netejaʒ] *n.m.* cleaning, cleansing, cleanup <***Loc:*** JE, TB, Da84>

nettoyer (nettéyer) [netwaje, netweje, neteje] *v.tr.* **1** to clean, cleanse *Pour la boucherie de cochon, on nettoyait les tripes, et avec les tripes, on faisait soit des andouilles soit des saucisses.* For the "boucherie," we would clean the tripe, and with the tripe, we made andouilles or sausages. (AC) **2** to dress (food) *Nettoyer une poule, des crabes.* To dress a chicken, crabs. (VM) ◊ **•nettoyer la maison** to clean house *Nettoyer la maison. C'est ça que la femme me fait faire tout le temps.* Clean the house. That's what the wife makes me do all the time. (LF) <EV, LF> <***Loc:*** AC, AV, EV, IB, IV, JE, LA, LF, SB, SM, TB, VM, An94, Da84>

nettoyeur [netwajœr] *n.m.* cleaner <***Loc:*** Da84>

neuf[1]**, neuve** [nœf, nø, nœv] *adj.* new *Un char neuf.* A new car. (LA) ◊ **•tout neuf** brand new <Da84> <***Loc:*** EV, LA, TB, VM, Da84, Lv88, Wh83>

neuf[2] [nœf] *adj./n.m.* nine **J'avais à peu près neuf ans.* I was about nine years old. (LA, An94) ◊ **•des neufs** nines (hand of cards) <JE> <***Loc:*** AC, EV, JE, LA, TB, An94, Da84>

neutre [nœt(r)] *adj.* neutral **Si cette affaire ça arrive et Fontenot, Bertrand et Doucet se met ensemble pour battre Aucoin, le Police Jurie de la paroisse va peut-être rentrer dedans, et si des positions passés veut dire quec'chose, la bande du gouvernement va aller au bord à Aucoin ou rester neutre.* If this situation comes up and Fontenot, Bertrand and Doucet get together to fight Aucoin, the Police Jury of the parish might get involved, and if past positions mean anything, the government gang will either side with Aucoin or remain neutral. (Wh83) <***Loc:*** Wh83>

neuvaine [nøvɛ̃n] *n.f.* [*eccl.*] novena <***Loc:*** Da84>

neuvième [nøvjɛ̃m] *adj./n.* ninth *Il est dans le neuvième livre dans l'école.* He is in the ninth grade at school. (AC) <***Loc:*** AC, Da84>

neveu [n(ə)vø] *n.m.* nephew ◊ **•petit neveu** great-nephew <Da84> <***Loc:*** TB, Da84, Fa77>

névralgie [nevralʒi] *n.f.* neuralgia <***Loc:*** Da84>

neyable ♦see **noyable**

néyer ♦see **noyer**

nez [ne] *n.m.* **1** nose **2** snout **3** end of a loaf of (French) bread ◊ **•nez du prêtre {de l'évêque}** tailbone, rump, bony bottom of a chicken <VM> **•avoir le nez fin *a*** to have a sharp sense of smell *Alle a le nez assez fin, alle peut tout sentir* She's got a sharp sense of smell, she can smell everything (LF) ***b*** to be picky *Il a le nez trop fin pour manger ça que je cuis.* He's too picky to eat what I cook. (AC) ***c*** to be snooty, put on airs *Il a le nez trop fin pour aller dans le vieux char.* He's too good to ride in the old car. (AC) <AC, LF, Da84> **•avoir le nez long** to be wise, informed, know everything *Il a le nez long, il connaît tout.* He knows everything. (LF) <LF, TB, La99> **•avoir le nez rapiqué** to be stuck up <AC, VM> **•avoir un nez comme un bec (à lancette / blanc)** to have a long, pointed nose <La99> **•avoir un nez de manche de pompe** to have a long, pointed nose <La99> **•mettre son nez dans le bol** to interfere, meddle <TB> <***Loc:*** AC, LF, SM, TB, VM, Da84, La99>

ni [ni] *conj.* neither, nor, not **Hormis qu'j'sus bien malade, je r'fuse jâmais d'aller 'oir mes p'tits ni qui'i' v'nont m'oir moi.* Unless I'm very sick, I never refuse to go see my children nor to have them come to see me. (Gu82) ◊ **•ni…ni** neither… nor **Orphelin de père et de mère, ni parents, ni frères et sœurs.* Orphan of father and mother, neither parents, nor brothers and sisters. (Wh83, ch: *J'ai passé devant ta porte)* <EV, Wh83> **•ni (l')un (et) ni l'autre** neither, neither one *Je crois pas que c'est bon ni un et ni l'autre!* I don't think it's good either way! (TB) **Si ni ein et ni l'autre travaillait, là, Nagok faisait le cheval boire à peu près ein demi gallon d'huile à purger pour le délacher et soulager.* If neither worked, then Nagok made the horse drink about a half gallon of castor oil to regulate and relieve him. (Wh83) <TB, Da84, Fa77, Wh83> ***<Loc:*** AC, EV, TB, Da84, Fa77, Gu82, Wh83>

niame-niame[1] **(name-name)** [njãmnjãm, nãmnãm] [*baby talk*] **I** *v.tr.invar.* to eat *Il faut niame-niame ton souper.* You must eat your supper. (IB) **II** *v.intr.invar.* to eat *Tu vas niame-niame pour Mame?* Are you going to eat for Mama? (IB) ***<Loc:*** EV, IB, Re31>

niame-niame[2] **(name-name)** [njãmnjãm, nãmnãm] *n.m.* [*baby talk*] food *Mange ça, cher, c'est du bon niame-niame.* Eat this, dear, it's some good food. (IB) ***<Loc:*** EV, IB, Re31>

nice [nis] *adj.* easily deceived ***<Loc:*** JE, Di32>

NICE [naɪs] *adj.* nice, sweet, gentle *Il est bien NICE.* He's very nice. (LF) ***<Loc:*** AC, JE, LF, Da84>

niche[1] [niʃ, niʒ] *n.f.* **1** nook, alcove **2** dog kennel ***<Loc:*** LA, SL, TB, VM, Da84, Lv88>

niche[2] [niʃ, niʒ] *n.f.* trick, prank, joke, practical joke *Il est tout le temps après jouer des niches.* He's always playing jokes. (VM) *Le monde avait toute sorte de macaqueries, des niches pour faire.* People had all kinds of foolishness, jokes to play. (SL) ***<Loc:*** LA, SL, VM, Da84, Lv88>

nicher [niʃe] **I** *v.intr.* to nest, build a nest *Il y a un moqueur qu'est après nicher dans mon camélia.* There is a mockingbird nesting in my camelia bush. (VM) **II se nicher** *v.pron.* to nestle, cuddle, snuggle up, make o.s. comfortable *Je sortais de me nicher quand le téléphone a sonné.* I had just gotten comfortable in bed when the telephone rang. (VM) ***<Loc:*** VM, Da84>

nichoir [niʃwar] *n.m.* chicken nesting place, laying rack or nest, roost ***<Loc:*** SB, SM, TB, Da84>

nichoix [niʃwa, niʃwar, niʃo] *n.m.* **1** nest egg **2** last-born child in a family ***<Loc:*** EV, IB, JE, LF, TB, VM, Lv88>

nickel [nikɛl, nikel] *n.m.* **1** nickel, five cent coin **2** [metal] nickel ***<Loc:*** IB, JE, SM, Da84, Lv88>

nicotine [nikotin] *n.f.* nicotine ***<Loc:*** Da84>

nid [ni] *n.m.* nest, den ***<Loc:*** LA, An94, Da84>

nièce [njɛs] *n.f.* niece ◊ **•petite-nièce** great-niece <Da84> ***<Loc:*** Da84, Fa77>

nier [nije] *v.tr.* to deny, renounce, repudiate *Tu peux pas nier ton garçon, il te ressemble de trop.* You can't deny your son, he looks too much like you. (VM) ***<Loc:*** VM, Da84>

nifler ♦see **renifler**

nigeant [niʒã] *adj.* **1** mischievous, full of pranks *Il est trop nigeant pour se marier.* He's too mischievous to get married. (VM) **2** painstaking, overly careful of details ***<Loc:*** JE, TB, VM>

nigeau, -euse [niʒo, nigo, -øz] *adj.* slow-moving *Il est nigeau pour laver la vaisselle.* He is slow to wash the dishes. (VM) ***<Loc:*** JE, TB, VM>

nigée [niʒe] *n.f.* brood, nestful ***<Loc:*** JE, Di32, Lv88>

niger ♦see **niquer**

NIGGER-SHOOT [nigaʃut, nɪgəʃut] *n.m.* [*offensive*] slingshot ***<Loc:*** TB, VM, Lv88>

nigriot ♦see **négrillon**

nine ♦see **nain**

ninorant ♦see **ignorant**

nioque [njɔk] *n.m.* **1** nest egg *Un nioque c'est un œuf qu'on met dans le nique. C'est un œuf qu'est pas bon.* A nest egg is an egg that one puts in the nest. It's an egg that's no good. (TB) **2** last-born child in a family **3** bump, bruise, black eye *Et le lendemain j'avais un gros nioque en arrière de ma tête.* And the next day I had a big bump on the back of my head. (EV) **4** dent, bump (as in a car fender) ***<Loc:*** AC, EV, IB, SM, TB, VM, Da84, Lv88>

nioquecer ♦see **noquecer**

nioquer [njoke] *v.tr.* **1** to hit, strike *Il lui en a nioqué un sur le front.* He knocked him on the forehead. (LA) **2** to hit together, particularly in the custom of smacking together hard-boiled eggs (often dyed) on Easter *Ils ont nioqué les œufs après la messe.* They knocked eggs after Mass. (LA) ***<Loc:*** LA, SM, Lv88>

nique [nik, nig] *n.m./f.* **1** nest **2** den ◊ **•nique à chien** dirty room, dirty house <Da84> **•nique à rats** nest of rats <Wh83> **•nique de guêpe** ***a*** wasp nest ***b*** carbuncle <VM> **•nique de Pâques** Easter basket <TB> ***<Loc:*** AL, EV, JE, SL, SM, TB, VM, Da84, Lv88, Wh83>

niquer (niger) [nike, niʒe] **I** *v.intr.* **1** to nest *La poule est niquée sur les œufs.* The hen is nesting on the eggs. (AC) **2** to lie down, snuggle up, make o.s. comfortable *T'as niqué dans le lit tout sale comme ça.* You got comfortable in the bed all dirty like that. (VM) *Mame dort tout le temps. Je suis arrivée hier après l'école. Alle était niquée.* Mom sleeps all the time. I arrived yesterday after school. She was in bed all snuggled up. (EV) **3** to huddle, cower, crouch *Ils sont niqués ensemble devant le feu.* They are huddled together in front of the fire. (VM) **II se niquer** *v.pron.* **1** to nest *Les poules se niquont de bonne heure.* The chickens nest early. (TB) **2** to nestle, cuddle, snuggle up, make o.s. comfortable *Il s'a niqué au lit.* He snuggled up in bed. (EV) *Cette paire a été se niquer en-dessous de les couverts.* That couple went to cuddle underneath the quilt. (LF) *Il est bien niqué, il veut pas s'en aller.* He's really made himself comfortable, he doesn't want to leave. (LF) **3** to go to bed *J'ai été me niquer à bonne heure.* I went to bed early. (SL) ***<Loc:*** AC, EV, LF, SL, TB, VM, Lv88>

nitouche ♦see **sainte nitouche**

niveau [nivo] *n.m.* [tool] level ◊ **•au niveau** level *La table est au niveau.* The table is level. (LF) *Fais le plancher au niveau.* Make the floor level. (LF) <LF> **•de niveau** level *Il* *fallait que tout ça soit de niveau.* All of that had to be level. (SL) <SL, Da84> <***Loc:*** EV, LF, SL, TB, Da84>

niveler [nivle] *v.tr.* 1 to level *Attrape le niveau. On va niveler la fenêtre.* Get the level. We'll level the window. (AC) 2 to flatten, level (land) *Niveler un terrain.* To level a lot. (VM) <***Loc:*** AC, VM, Da84, Fa77>

niveleur [nivlœr] *n.m.* surveyor's level <***Loc:*** Fa77>

noble [nɔb(l)] *adj.* 1 noble, exalted, great *Adieu, la fleur de la jeunesse, la noble qualité de fille.* Goodbye, flower of youth, noble status of maiden. (ch: *Adieu, la fleur de la jeunesse*) 2 vain, haughty, snobbish *C'est ça une personne noble.* That's a haughty person. (VM) <***Loc:*** SM, VM, Da84>

noce [nɔs] *n.f. (often pl.)* wedding, marriage ◊ **•être pas aux noces *a*** to be in an uncomfortable or disagreeable situation ***b*** to not know what one is talking about <La99> <***Loc:*** AC, EV, Da84, Fa77, La99, Ph36>

nocoyau (**nocoillot**) [nokojo] *n.m.* 1 joint, knuckle *J'ai un bobo sur le nocoillot.* I have a sore on my knuckle. (SL) 2 bump, swollenness, knot (as the result of a blow) *Quand il s'a cogné, il s'a fait un beau nocoillot.* When he struck himself he made himself quite a bump. (IB) <***Loc:*** AV, IB, LF, SB, SJ, SL, Lv88>

Noël (**Nouel**) [noɛl] *n.m.* Christmas ◊ **•Papa Noël** Santa Claus, Father Christmas <LF> <***Loc:*** AC, IB, LF, Da84, Gu82>

nœud [nø] *n.m.* 1 knot 2 node, joint (of grasses, cane, etc.) 3 vertebra ◊ **•nœud de rein** any of the individual vertebra making up the backbone <TB> <***Loc:*** AV, SL, TB, VM, Da84, La99, Lv88>

nogalier [nogalje] *n.m.* walnut tree <***Loc:*** Lv88>

noir[1]**, -e** [nwar] *adj.* dark, dismal, tragic *Quand les frères Blanc ont tué M. Begnaud, c'était une affaire noire.* When the Blanc brothers killed Mr. Begnaud, it was a tragic affair. (VM) <***Loc:*** VM, Da84, ThCa>

noir[2]**, -e** [nwar] *adj./n.* black (color) **Ces serpents peut-être grosses et noires et elles voliont doucement.* Those snakes can be big and black and they flew slowly. (ThCa: *Grosbecs*) **Je me rappelle qu'alle avait les yeux noirs, noirs, noirs.* I remember she had eyes that were black as could be. (Gu82) ◊ **•noir à soulier** shoe polish <IB, LF, SL, Lv88> **•noir comme du charbon {de la suie / l'as de pique / un fond de chaudière}** very black <AC, LA, VM, La99> **•noir de lampe** lamp black <Da84> <***Loc:*** AC, AV, EV, LA, VM, Da84, Gu82, La99, Lv88, ThCa>

noir[3] [nwar] *n.m.* 1 black person *Ils ont engagé une femme, ils ont engagé un noir et deux blancs.* They hired a woman, a black man and two whites. (LF) 2 dark, darkness *Mon je peux pas coucher dans le noir. Il faut que j'aye une lumière.* I can't sleep in the dark. I have to have a light. (TB) ◊ **•être dans le noir** to be in trouble *Pour si eusse t'attrape après pêcher, faut que tu les montres ça, t'es dans le clair. Si t'as pas ça, t'es dans le noir.* Because if they catch you fishing, you have to show them that, you're in the clear. If you don't have that, you're in trouble. (TB) <TB> **•faire noir** to be dark, be night *Il va faire noir avant que tu reviens. Fais attention!* It'll be dark before you get back. Be careful! (AC) <AC, Da84> <***Loc:*** AC, EV, IB, LF, SL, TB, Da84, Lv88>

noirâtre [nwarat(r)] *adj.* blackish, dark *Il a acheté un char noirâtre.* He bought a blackish-colored car. (VM) <***Loc:*** VM, Da84>

noircir [nwarsir, nwɔzir] **I** *v.tr.* to blacken, darken *La gazette a noirci mes mains et ma chemise.* The newspaper blackened my hands and my shirt. (AC) **II** *v.intr.* to turn black, darken *Les bananes ont noirci après quelques jours.* The bananas turned black after several days. (AC) *Sa peau a noirci à force qu'il était au soleil.* His skin darkened from being in the sun. (AC) **III se noircir** *v.pron.* to turn black, become dark *Le ciel s'a noirci.* The sky became black. (LA) <***Loc:*** AC, LA, VM, Da84>

noircirer [nwarsire] *v.tr.* to shine (shoes) *Il faut noircirer ses souliers.* One's shoes must be shined. (IB) <***Loc:*** IB>

noiret (**noirot**) [nware, nwaro] *adj.* blackish, darkish hue *Un taureau noiret.* A black bullock. (LA) <***Loc:*** LA, VM>

noirette [nwarɛt] *n.f.* black woman <***Loc:*** SB, SJ, Lv88>

noiron[1]**, -onne** [nwarɔ̃, -ɔ̃n] *adj.* black (esp. of a cow; by extension, a name given to a black cow) *Une vache noironne.* A black cow. (LA) <***Loc:*** EV, LA, SM, VM, Lv88>

noiron[2] [nwarɔ̃] *n.m.* black man <***Loc:*** AV, SB, SJ>

noirot ♦see **noiret**

noix [nwa] *n.f.* 1 nut 2 nut, wing nut ◊ **•noix avec des ailes / noix-z-oreilles** wing nut <AC, JE> <***Loc:*** AC, JE, SL, SM, TB, Da84>

noix de muscade ♦see **noix-muscade**

noix-muscade (**noix de muscade**) [nwamyskad, nwadəmyskad] *n.f.* nutmeg <***Loc:*** VM>

nom [nɔ̃] *n.m.* name **Y faut qu'ein petit porte ein nom Amaricain pour êt' accepté—ein nom comme Rod, Bill, Tom, Brad.* A child must have an English name to be accepted—a name like Rod, Bill, Tom, Brad. (ThCa: *Mille misères*) ◊ **•nom de famille / dernier nom** last name, surname <EV, LF, TB> **•nom donné *a*** given name ***b*** nickname <EV, VM, Lv88> **•nom doux** term of endearment *Négresse, c'est un nom doux que tu vas donner à ta femme. 'Négresse, attrape-moi du café.'* Négresse is a term of endearment you give your wife. 'Négresse, get me some coffee.' (VM) <VM> **•petit nom** nickname *Nous-autres on avait tout le temps connu la vieille femme pour un petit nom, eusse l'appelait Caouenne.* We had always known the old woman by a nickname, they called her Caouenne. (TB) <TB, Da84, Lv88> **•premier nom** first name <AC> <***Loc:*** AC, AV, EV, LA, LF, PQ, SL, SM, TB, VE, VM, An94, Da84, Lv88, ThCa>

nombouril ♦see **nombril**

nombre [nɔ̃m, nɔ̃b(r)] *n.m.* number, quantity <***Loc:*** Da84>

nombril (**nambouri, nombouril, ombril, ombouril**) [nɔ̃bri, nɑ̃buri, nɔ̃buri, ɔ̃bri, ɔ̃bori] *n.m.* navel, belly button ◊ **•c'est là où mon nombril est enterré** that's where I was born <La99> <***Loc:*** AV, EV, IB, JE, SJ, VM, Da84, Fa77, La99, Lv88>

nomination [nɔ̃minasjɔ̃] *n.f.* nomination, appointment <***Loc:*** Da84>

nommé, -e [nɔ̃me] *adj.* one, one certain, one named *Dans le temps que le* FLU *allait, il y avait un nommé Placide Thibodeaux, et il avait une de ses sœurs qui était mort dans le mois d'août avant ça.* In the time that the flu was going on, there was a certain Placide Thibodeaux, and he had one of his sisters who had died in the month of August before that. (AC) <***Loc:*** AC, LA, SM, TB, Da84>

nommer [nɔ̃me] **I** *v.tr.* **1** to name *Les jeunes il y en a plein que je connais pas, mais tout le monde, je peux te les nommer d'un boute à l'autre de la Pointe.* Young people, there are a lot of them that I don't know, but everyone (else), I can name them for you from one end of Pointe aux Chênes to the other. (TB) *Les Français ont nommé ça 'sac-à-lait,' la chair est très blanche.* The French named that 'sack-of-milk,' the flesh is very white. (SL) **2** to nominate, mention *Ils ont nommé B.G. au* SCHOOL BOARD. They nominated B.G. to the school board. (EV) **II se nommer** *v.pron.* to be called *Mais ça faisait ça, ça usait de la graisse, ou du gras, ou quelque chose, et ça mettait de quoi, du* LYE, *quelque chose qui se nommait comme ça, il fallait que ça bouille ça.* But they used to do the following: they used grease or fat or something, and they put in some things, lye, something that was called like that, and that had to boil. (TB) <***Loc:*** EV, IV, SL, TB, VM, Da84>

non[1] [nɔ̃] *n.m.* no, nay <***Loc:*** Da84>

non[2] [nɔ̃] *adv.* no, not ◊ **•non-non** no-no <Da84> **•non plus** neither, either **Il est pas ici non plus.* He is not here either. (Da84) <Da84, Fa77> **•non seulement** not only *Il est non seulement vieux, mais il est aussi malade.* Not only is he old, but he's ill. (AC) <AC, Da84> <***Loc:*** AC, LA, Da84, Fa77>

nonc, n-oncle, noncle ♦see **oncle**

nonote [nɔ̃nɔt] *n.m.* whatnot, set of shelves *Il s'est fait un nonote dans la cuisine.* He set up a whatnot in the kitchen. (SB) <***Loc:*** SB>

noquecer (**nioquecer**) [nɔkse, njokse] *v.tr.* to hit (usu. on the head) *Il était si fâché qu'il l'a nioquecé sus la tête.* He was so mad that he hit him on the head. (AC) <***Loc:*** AC, EV, Lv88>

nord [nɔr] *adj.invar./n.m.* north <***Loc:*** AV, JE, LA, TB, Da84>

nord-est [nɔrdɛs(t), nɔrdɛ] *adj.invar./n.m.* northeast <***Loc:*** VM, Da84, Guoo>

nord-ouest ♦see **noroît**

normal[1]**, -e** [nɔrmal] *adj.* normal *Dans une saison normale je prends beaucoup de poissons.* In a normal season, I catch a lot of fish. (SL) <***Loc:*** LA, SJ, SL, Da84>

normal[2] [nɔrmal] *adv.* normally, naturally, effortlessly *C'est pour ça que je parle le français bien [...], je peux lire normal mais, pour dire, écrire des lettres ou quelque chose comme ça, non.* That's why I speak French well, I can read it normally but, let's say, to write letters or something like that, no. (LF) <***Loc:*** LF>

normand, -e [nɔrmɑ̃, -ɑ̃d] *adj.* Norman *Mon grand-père était normand.* My grandfather was Norman. (SM) <***Loc:*** SM, Da84>

noroît (**nord-ouest**) [nɔrwa, nɔrwɛs(t)] *adj.invar./n.m.* northwest *Le vent est noroît.* The wind is north-west. (Lv88) *Après que l'œil de l'ouragan avait passé, le vent a viré au noroît.* After the eye of the hurricane had passed, the wind quickly turned to the north-west. (VM, Guoo) <***Loc:*** VM, Da84, Guoo, Lv88>

nos ♦see **notre**

notable [notab(l)] *adj.* **1** notable, important *Une personne notable.* An important person. (VM) **2** decent, of good reputation *Tu peux être sûr que ces filles-là sont notables.* You can be sure that those girls are of good reputation. (VM) <***Loc:*** VM, Da84>

notaire [notær] *n.m.* notary ◊ **•notaire publique** notary public <LF, Da84, Fa77> <***Loc:*** LF, Da84, Fa77>

note [not, nɔt] *n.f.* note, notice, written message <***Loc:*** Da84>

noter [note] *v.tr.* to take note, notice, observe **Notez bien.* Note well. (Da84) <***Loc:*** Da84>

notice [notis] *n.f.* **1** notice, notification, advertisement, ad *J'ai perdu mon chien, je vas mettre une notice dans la gazette.* I lost my dog, I'll put an ad in the paper. (Lv88) **2** notice, summons, court summons *Le député shériff a venu avec la notice.* The deputy sherrif came with the summons. (VM) <***Loc:*** TB, VM, Da84, Lv88>

noticer [notise] *v.tr.* to notify, announce *Il s'a fait noticer d'être sûr de se trouver là demain.* He was notified to be sure to be there tomorrow. (TB) <***Loc:*** TB, Lv88>

notifier [notifje] *v.tr.* to notify, give notice *Ils ont notifié le monde de sortir.* The gave the people notice to leave. (Lv88) <***Loc:*** Da84, Fa77, Lv88>

notre (**nos**) (*m./f.sing.* **notre** [nɔt(r)], *m./f.pl.* **nos** [no], **notres** [nɔt(r)], *m./f.pl.* before a vowel **nos** [noz], **notres** [notz]) *adj.poss.* our **Notre voisin.* Our neighbor. (IB, An94) *Nos dents.* Our teeth. (JD) *Eusse nous mettait dessus notres genoux si on parlait en français.* They made us kneel if we spoke French [in school]. (TB) *Elle tenait la maison et cuisait à dîner pour nous-autres, elle lavait notre linge.* She kept the house and cooked dinner for us, she washed our clothes. (IB) *C'est ça notre tracas asteur.* This is precisely our problem right now. (SM) *Ça fait, moi et Henry, on a* RIDE *nos bicycles dans les bois avec nos fusils.* So me and Henry, we rode our bicycles into the woods with our rifles. (JD) *Sur nos bateaux, les trawleurs on parle tout français.* On our boats, all of us trawlers speak French. (Lv88) *Les* *seuls à parler français avec, c'est le vieux monde, les jeunes comme notre âge à nous-autres, proche que jamais.* The only ones to speak French are the old folks, people younger like our age almost never do it. (SM) *Ça a été les meilleures chanteuses a été notre famille à nous-autres icitte.* They were the best singers, our family here. (PQ) *J'aimerais voir notre langue française préservée.* I'd like to see our French language preserved. (LF) *Équand on était petits, nos parents nous amenait au cirque.* When we were little, our parents used to take us to the circus. (LF) ◊ **•le Notre Père** the Our Father <EV, Da84> <***Loc:*** AC, AV, EV, IB, JD, LA, LF, PQ, SL, SM, TB, VM, An94, Da84, Guoo>

nôtre [nɔt(r)] *pron.poss.* ours **C'est les nôtres.* They are ours. (Da84) **C'est le nôtre.* It's ours. (Da84) *Le son de leur voix est différent que le nôtre. Leur voix est plus plate que notre voix à nous-autres.* The sound of their voice is different from ours. Their voice is flatter than ours. (TB) <***Loc:*** TB, Da84>

Nouel ♦see **Noël**

nouer [nwe] **I** *v.tr.* to knot, tangle *Le bougre avait tout noué les cables pour les empêcher de partir.* The guy had tangled the ropes to prevent them from leaving. (LA) **II se nouer** *v.pron.* to get knotted up, get tangled *Ses cheveux s'ont noué dans le vent.* His hair got tangled in the wind. (LA) <***Loc:*** LA, Da84, Fa77>

nourrir [nurir] **I** *v.tr.* **1** to nourish, feed, nurture *Estropier cet homme et là il faut que tu nourris sa famille?* Cripple that man and then you have to feed his family? (IB) **2** to nurse, suckle (a baby) *Ma femme a nourri tous nos enfants au sein.* My wife nursed all of our children. (LA) **II se nourrir** *v.pron.* to nourish o.s., eat *Il était rendu tellement malade qu'il pouvait pus se nourrir.* He had gotten so sick that he could no longer nourish himself. (LA) <***Loc:*** AC, EV, IB, LA, VM, Da84, Fa77>

nourrissant, -e [nurisɑ̃, -ɑ̃t] *adj.* nourishing, nutritious *Elle faisait une soupe qu'était beaucoup nourrissante.* She made a soup that was very nourishing. (LA) <***Loc:*** LA, Da84>

nourrissement [nurismɑ̃] *n.m.* food, feeding <***Loc:*** TB, VM, Lv88>

nourriture [nurityr] *n.f.* **1** food, nourishment **Un jour, ses parents ont parti aussi à la ville pour acheter des nourritures, grosseries.* One day his parents also went to town to buy food, groceries. (EV, An94) **2** feed (for animals) <***Loc:*** EV, An94, Da84, Fa77>

nous [nu] *pron.pers.* **1** *(subj.)* we *Nous irons et nous boirons et nous tarirons les verres et nous les remplirons.* We'll go and we'll drink and we'll drain the glasses and we'll refill them. (VM, ch: *L'oranger*) *Quand l'eau vient trop platte pour les machines, nous hâle les pirogues, nous pagaille.* When the water level is too low for the engines, we take the pirogues, we paddle. (SM) **2** *(dir.obj.)* us *Il nous a pas vus.* He didn't see us. (PQ) *Eusse voulait pas on parle français, eusse nous punissait si on nous attrapait après parler francais avec un autre.* They did not want us to speak French, they would punish us if they caught us speaking French with someone else. (IB) *Ma grand-mère nous lavait avec ça pour pas avoir des puces.* My grandmother washed us with it so that we would not have lice. (IB) *Si ils nous auront découvert! Là, chère, ils nous auront tapé!* If they had discovered us! They would have slapped us! (EV) *On va chez Lorita pour souper. Alle est très avenante, alle nous invite tout le temps.* We're going to Lorita's for supper. She's very nice, she invites us all the time. (LF) *Ils ont bégué pour quelqu'un dans la famille que telle et telle venait nous traiter.* They begged for someone in the family, that one or another would come and treat us. (EV) *La faim nous prenait.* Hunger overwhelmed us. (SL) *Quand on arrivait de l'école, Grand-maman Claire nous espérait à la porte avec des patates chaudes dans sa poche de tablier. C'était notre goûter.* When we arrived home from school, Grandma Claire was waiting for us at the door with hot sweet potatoes in her apron pocket. That was our snack. (VM) **3** *(ind. obj.)* us, to us, for us *Il peut rester trois ou quatre mois sans nous parler.* He can go three or four months without talking to us. (TB) *Après l'ouragan, le gouvernement nous a donné du sucre et de la farine gratis.* After the hurricane, the government gave us sugar and flour for free. (VM) *Moi et toi peut aller, mon mari va nous prêter le* TRUCK. You and I can go, my husband will lend us the truck. (LF) *Grâce à la terre que ma grand-mère nous a laissé, on a de l'argent d'huile qui rentre tous les mois.* Thanks to the land that my grandmother left us, we have oil money coming in monthly. (VM) *Il devrait nous donner de temps en temps une prêche en français,* SUNDAY SCHOOL *ou quelque chose.* He should give us a little sermon now and then in French, Sunday school or something. (TB) **On nous contait des petits contes de ces trois bonriens.* He told us some short stories about the three good-for-nothings. (Gr82) *Hey monsieur D., viens voir ici, viens nous jouer un* TUNE *de ta musique de bouche!* Hey, Mr. D., come over here, come play us a tune on your harmonica! (EV) *Quand j'étais tout petit ma mère nous faisait peur le soir pour qu'on reste autour de la maison. Alle nous disait que y avait un homme qui tournait rougarou.* When I was young my mother would scare us so we would stay around the house. She told us that there was a man who changed into a werewolf. (LF) *Il nous a parlé bien poli.* He spoke to us very politely. (LA) **4** *(obj. of prep.)* us *Sainte Marie, Mère de Dieu, priez pour nous pauvres pécheurs asteur et à l'heure de notre mort.* Holy Mary, Mother of God, pray for us poor sinners now and at the hour of our death. (TB) *Avec nous, elle dit, "Quand vous jetez un mot anglais dans une phrase, ça me gêne."* [When she's] with us, she says, "When you throw an English word into a French sentence, that bothers me." (SL) ◊ **•nous-mêmes** ourselves, us **C'est pour nous-mêmes.* It's for us. (Da84) <Da84> <***Loc:*** AC, EV, LF, PQ, SL, TB, VM, Da84, Gr82>

nous-autres [nuzɔt(r)] *pron.pers.* **1** *(subj.)* we *Nous-autres était jamais comment tu dis ça,* CROWDED. *Nous-autres avait tout le temps de la place.* We were never, what do you call it, crowded. We always had room. (TB) *Nous-autres est après pomper le riz.* We are irrigating the rice. (VM) *Nous-autres va abouter une 'tite cuisine en arrière de la maison.* We're going to add on a little kitchen in the back of the house. (Lv88) **2** *(obj. of prep.)* us *Ça semble comme si eusse sont contre nous-autres.* It seems as if they're against us. (LF) *Dans le vieux temps, quand on allait visiter une fille, souvent on se balançait sur la galerie avec le père et la mère droit là avec nous-autres.* In the old days, when we would go to visit a girl, often we would swing on the porch with the father and mother right there with us. (LA) *Ouais, on avait des bêtes pour nous-autres, et on avait des bonnes vaches à lait.* Yeah, we had cattle, and we had good milking cows. (EV) *Reste avec nous-autres, je peux t'acmoder à soir et on va parler.* Stay with us, I can put you up for the night and we'll talk. (Lv88) *Si quelqu'un aurait voulu prendre avantage de nous-autres, eux-autres aurait pu aisément faire ça.* If someone had wanted to take advantage of us, they could easily have done that. (TB) *Ils ont élargi le chemin en avant de chez nous-autres.* They widened the road in front of our house. (LA) *Des fois ça dit nous-autres même quoi vous-autres a dit sur nous-autres.* Sometimes they tell us what you said about us. (SL) **3** *(obj. of inf.)* us *Ça a donné la main à les enfants de nous attendre nous-autres parler français tu connais.* It helped the children to hear us speak French, you know. (LF) **4** *(tonic)* us *Nous-autres, on use des saucisses boucanées dans notre gombo.* We use smoked sausages in our gumbo. (EV) *Nous-autres on les bûchait pas.* We did not interrogate them. (IB) *Et là tu vas prendre au Petit Caillou ou à Chauvin, il y a plein des mots qu'eusse dit qui est pas pareil que nous-autres. Nous-autres on dit un "*CAP*" eusse eusse dit un "casque."* You take Petit Caillou or Chauvin, there are a lot of words they say that aren't the same as us. We say a "cap," they say a "casque." (LF) *Je trouve que les Indiens a pas autant de mots que nous-autres.* I find that the Indians don't have as many words as we do. (TB) ◊ **•nous-autres-mêmes** ourselves *Dans ces temps il n-avait de la farine maïs que on aurait fait mouler nous-autres-mêmes.* In those days, there was cornmeal that we would have ground ourselves. (SL) *On tirait notres vaches nous-autres-mêmes.* We milked our cows ourselves. (TB) *Et là j'ai commencé à travailler pour nous-autres-mêmes quand défunt pape a venu qu'il pouvait plus travailler par la maladie.* Then I started working for ourselves, when (our) deceased father got to the point where he couldn't work anymore because of illness. (TB) *Quand-ce qu'on a eu un* CAMP *pour nous-autres-mêmes on a amené notre ménage.* When we got a camp of our own, we brought our furniture. (TB) <SL, TB> **•à nous-autres-mêmes** our own *On avait tout la richesse de manger qu'on voulait. On avait tout le manger naturel, on avait notre poulet à nous-autres-mêmes, on avait notre cochon à nous-autres-mêmes, on avait notre lait à nous-autres-mêmes.* We had all the abundance of food that we wanted. We had all the natural food, we had our own chicken, we had our own pig, we had our own milk. (LF) <LF, TB> ***Loc:*** AC, AS, AV, EV, IB, LA, LF, PQ, SL, TB, VM, An94, Lv88>

nouvage ♦see **nuage**

nouveau, -elle [nuvo, -ɛl] *adj.* new *Je suis après faire un grand tour dans tous les villages dans l'état de la Louisiane afficher ma nouvelle médecine que j'ai patenté moi-même et qu'a juste sorti sus le marché.* I am taking a grand tour of all the towns in the state of Louisiana to advertise my new medicine that I invented myself and that just came out on the market. (LF) ◊ **•nouveau arrivé** newcomer <Da84> **•nouveau-né** new-born <Da84> **•à nouveau** again, all over again **Prosper, je suis après me refâcher tout à nouveau encore.* Prosper, I'm getting mad all over again. (EV, An94) <EV, An94> **•de nouveau** once again, once more *Eux-autres triait les chevrettes jusqu'à onze heures, minuit du soir et là et on se réveillait le lendemain matin [...] il faulait que tu recommences tout de nouveau.* They sorted shrimp until eleven or midnight and got up the next day, you had to start all over again. (TB) <TB, Da84> **•quoi il y a de nouveau?** what's new? <Da84> **•tout nouveau, tout beau** a new broom sweeps clean <Da84> <***Loc:*** AC, AV, EV, LF, TB, VM, An94, Da84, Fa77>

nouveau de lune (**renouveau de la lune**) [nuvodlyn, r(ə) nuvodlyn] *n.m.* new moon *Le nouveau de lune est le cinq de mars.* The new moon is March 5. (TB) <***Loc:*** TB, Di32>

nouveauler [nuvole] *v.tr.* to renew **On a invité à Ma Tchou Flette de nouveauler ses recommendations.* Ma Tchou Flette was invited to renew her recommendations. (Wh83) <***Loc:*** Wh83>

nouveauté [nuvote] *n.f.* newness, novelty <***Loc:*** Da84>

nouvelle [nuvɛl] *n.f.* **1** new information, piece of news *La nouvelle m'a mis en bouleverse.* The news bowled me over. (Lv88) **2** *(pl.)* news *Mais dans le temps de la guerre, tous les nouvelles qu'il attendait sus le* RADIO, *il avait un cahier, et il écrisait tout ça.* But during the war, all the news he heard on the radio, he had a notebook, and he wrote it all down. (LF) ◊ **•quelle nouvelle?** what's the news? <Da84> <***Loc:*** LF, TB, Da84, Lv88>

nouvellement [nuvɛlmɑ̃] *adv.* newly, lately *Une maison nouvellement bâtie.* A newly built house. (VM) <***Loc:*** VM, Da84>

novembre [novɑ̃m, novɑ̃b(r)] *n.m.* November <***Loc:*** EV, Da84>

novène [novɛ̃n] *n.m.* [*eccl.*] novena, nine-day devotion in the Catholic Church <***Loc:*** VM, Fa77>

novice [novis] *n.* [*eccl.*] novice, beginner <***Loc:*** Da84>

noviciat [novisja] *n.m.* [*eccl.*] novitiate <***Loc:*** Da84>

noyable (**neyable**) [nwajab(l), nejab(l), nojab(l)] *adj.* floodable, that can be easily flooded *C'est pas de la terre noyable. Elle* *tient pas l'eau.* That isn't floodable land. It doesn't hold water. (VM) <***Loc:*** VM, Da84, Lv88>

noyau [nwajo] *n.m.* **1** seed, pit (of certain fruits) **2** kernel <***Loc:*** AV, SL, Da84, Fa77>

noyer[1] (**nayer, néyer**) [noje, nwaje, neje, naje] **I** *v.tr.* **1** to flood *Noyer un clos de riz.* To flood a rice field. (Lv88) *Le chemin était tout néyé après il a mouillé.* The road was all flooded after it rained. (VM) **2** to drown (a person or animal) *La fille a pas laissé son père noyer les petits chats.* The girl didn't let her father drown the kittens. (LA) **II** *v.intr.* **1** to flood *Ç'a tout noyé à la Nouvelle-Ibérie la semaine passée.* It was all flooded in New Iberia last week. (Lv88) *Le bord icitte ça noye pas tu vois.* This side here doesn't flood, you see. (SM) *On a noyé en 1927.* We flooded in 1927. (Lv88) **2** to drown *Il y avait un petit garçon qu'avait noyé dans le bayou.* There was a little boy who had drowned in the bayou. (SL) **III se noyer** *v.pron.* to drown o.s., be drowned *Il a tombé de dessus un bateau et il s'a noyé.* He fell off a boat and he drowned. (TB) ◊ **•se faire noyer** to drown o.s., be drowned *Trois dans la famille s'a fait noyer.* Three in the family were drowned. (LF) <LF> **•(se) noyer dans son (propre) crachat** ***a*** to talk on without getting to the point ***b*** to talk too much ***c*** to be unable to speak because one has forgotten what one wanted to say <Da84, La99> <***Loc:*** AC, EV, JE, LA, LF, SB, SL, SM, TB, VM, Da84, La99, Lv88>

noyer[2] [nwaje] *n.m.* **1** black walnut tree **2** hickory tree <***Loc:*** AL, CL, LA, SB, SL, VM, Ho90>

nu, -e [ny] *adj.* naked, nude, bare *Il y a une chose j'aurais tout le temps voulu voir, c'était un homme tout nu.* There is one thing that I would have always wanted to see, that is a completely naked man. (IB) ◊ **•nu comme un ver / tout nu** completely naked, stark naked *C'est là je l'ai vu courir devant le monde, tout nu comme un ver.* That's when I saw him running in front of the people, completely naked. (EV) *Baigner tout nu.* To swim naked, skinny dip. (JE) <EV, IB, JE, LA, Da84, La99> **•nu-pieds / pieds-nus** barefoot *Je pouvais pas en acheter, pas d'argent pour acheter des souliers. C'est pour ça que mes pieds sont si larges et si plattes. J'ai marché trop longtemps nu-pieds.* I couldn't buy any, no money to buy shoes. That's why my feet are so wide and so flat. I walked barefoot too long. (TB) <EV, TB, Da84> **•nu-tête / tête-nue** bare-headed *Il était après travailler nu-tête dans le soleil.* He was working bareheaded in the sun. (LA) <LA, Da84> **•se mettre (tout) nu** to get naked *Il s'a mis tout nu et il a sauté dans le vivier.* He got completely naked and jumped into the pond. (LA) <LA, Da84> <***Loc:*** EV, IB, JE, LA, TB, Da84, La99>

nuage (**nouvage**) [nyaʒ, nɥaʒ, nyjaʒ, nwaʒ, niaʒ, njaʒ, ynaʒ, nuvaʒ] *n.m.* **1** cloud **2** mist **3** rain cloud, black cloud ◊ **•nuage de neige** snow cloud <LF> **•nuage de pluie** rain cloud <LF> **•dans les nuages** ***a*** up in the sky, in the clouds *Il a monté, monté jusqu'à qu'il était rendu dans les nuages.* He went up and up until he was up into the clouds. (LA) ***b*** in a dream world, not paying attention to reality <LA, Da84, La99> <***Loc:*** AC, EV, IB, IV, JE, LA, LF, SM, TB, VM, Da84, La99>

nuageux, -euse [nɥaʒø, -øz] *adj.* cloudy, overcast *Et le temps va d'être nuageux pour à soir et demain.* And the weather will be overcast for tonight and tomorrow. (LA) <***Loc:*** LA, Da84>

nudité [nydite] *n.f.* nudity, nakedness <***Loc:*** Da84>

nué (**nuée**) [nɥe, nye, nwe] *n.m./f.* cloud ◊ **•être dans les nués** to be in the clouds, be in a dream world **Là, t-à l'heure, quand j'ai ouvert la porte à peu près dix minutes juste après, j'étais dans les nués.* Then after a while, when I opened the door about ten minutes just after that, I was up in the clouds. (EV, An94) <EV, An94, La99> <***Loc:*** AV, EV, JD, SJ, TB, An94, Da84, La99, Lv88>

nuire [nɥir] *v.intr.* to obstruct, stand in the way, be a nuisance *Ça peut juste nuire à tes affaires.* That can only be a nuissance to your plans. (LA) <***Loc:*** LA, Da84>

nuisable ♦see **nuisible**

nuisance [nɥizɑ̃s] *n.f.* nuisance <***Loc:*** Da84>

nuisible (**nuisable**) [nɥizib(l), nɥizab(l)] *adj.* **1** obnoxious, annoying, bothersome *Ces mouches sont nuisibles.* These flies are annoying. (VM) **2** in the way *Un petit chien nuisible.* A little dog that's in the way. (VM) <***Loc:*** VM, Da84>

nuit [nɥi] *n.f.* night, darkness **La nuit m'a pris.* Darkness overtook me. (Da84) ◊ **•nuit et jour** night and day <Da84> **•à la nuit** at nightfall <SB> <***Loc:*** AC, EV, LA, SB, TB, Da84>

nulle [nyl] ◊ **•(en) nulle part** [nylpar, nynpar] nowhere *On a pas été en nulle part pour notre vacance.* We didn't go anywhere for our vacation. (LA) <LA, VM, Da84> **•nulle place** [nylplas] nowhere *Ça va pas nulle place, à quatre ans c'est des vieux mariés.* They're not going anywhere, after four years they're an old married couple. (TB) <IV, LF, TB, VM> <***Loc:*** IV, LA, LF, TB, VM, Da84>

nullement [nylmɑ̃] *adv.* in no way, by no means, nothing doing *T'es nullement capable de faire ça.* You are in no way able to do that. (VM) <***Loc:*** VM, Da84>

numéro (**luméro**) [nymero, lymero, lymərо, limərо] *n.m.* **1** number **Le numéro de personnes capable de parler Français dedans la paroisse est aussi gros par pourcentage que n'importe quelle place dans la Louisiane.* The number of people able to speak French in the parish is as high as anywhere in Louisiana. (Wh83) **2** size *Après il a eu la fièvre à vingt-quatre heures, ein de ses pieds est deux luméros pus gros que l'autre.* After he had fever for twenty-four hours, one of his feet is two numbers (sizes) bigger than the other. (VM) ◊ **•numéro de licence** license number <TB> **•numéro de téléphone** phone number <LF> **•numéro sept** seven steak <VM> <***Loc:*** AV, EV, LF, SL, SM, TB, VM, Da84, Lv88, Wh83>

numérotage [nymerotaʒ] *n.m.* numbering <***Loc:*** Da84>

numéroter [nymerote] *v.tr.* to number *Il les avait bien numérotés et mis dans des boîtes.* He had them well numbered and placed in boxes. (LA) <***Loc:*** LA, Da84>

numonie ♦see **pneumonie**

nuptial, -e [nypsjal] *adj.* nuptial, wedding **Messe nuptiale.* Wedding mass. (Da84) <***Loc:*** Da84>

nutria [njutria, nutra] *n.m./f.* nutria, coypu <***Loc:*** TB, Da84, Gu00, Lv88>

o ♦see **oh**

obéir [obeir] **I** *v.tr.* to obey *Elle a obéi son père.* She obeyed her father. (LA) **II** *v.intr.* **1** to obey *Il voulait que sa fille espère pour se marier, mais elle a pas obéi.* He wanted his daughter to wait to marry, but she did not obey. (LA) **2** to yield *La planche a obéi à force ils sautaient.* They jumped so much that the board yielded. (Lv88) <*Loc:* LA, Da84, Hi02, Lv88>

obéissance [obeisɑ̃s] *n.f.* obedience, compliance <*Loc:* Da84>

obéissant, -e [obeisɑ̃, -ɑ̃t] *adj.* obedient, submissive **Et Jean Sot était tout le temps très obéissant.* And Jean Sot was always very obedient. (EV, An94) <*Loc:* EV, An94, Da84>

objecter [obʒɛkte, ɔbʒɛkte, obʒekte] *v.intr.* to object, take exception, be opposed *J'objecte à ça.* I object to that. (VM) *Son père objecte de la quitter aller.* Her father is against letting her go. (Lv88) *Ils ont objecté à la nouvelle loi.* They objected to the new law. (LA) *Mon père a objecté que je m'achète des souliers pour jouer à la pelote.* My father objected to my buying shoes to play baseball. (TB) <*Loc:* SM, TB, VM, Da84, Lv88>

objection [ɔbʒɛksjɔ̃] *n.f.* objection, protest <*Loc:* Da84>

objet [ɔbʒɛ, ɔbʒe] *n.m.* **1** object, thing **2** purpose, aim <*Loc:* Da84>

obli ♦see **oubli**

obliance ♦see **oubliance**

obliard ♦see **oubliard**

oblier ♦see **oublier**

oblieur ♦see **oublieur**

obligation [obligasjɔ̃] *n.f.* **1** obligation, duty **2** debt <*Loc:* VM, An94, Da84>

obligé [obliʒe] *adv.* certainly, absolutely, necessarily *Mais obligé, c'est ça.* Well it's got to be that. (VM) *Mais c'est obligé c'est ça il est.* Well, necessarily that's what he is. (VM) *C'est obligé il l'a reçu.* He certainly must have received it. (VM) <*Loc:* VM>

obligeance [obliʒɑ̃s] *n.f.* **1** necessity **2** duty <*Loc:* Da84>

obligeant, -e [obliʒɑ̃, ubliʒɑ̃, -ɑ̃t] *adj.* **1** obliging, accommodating *Elle est obligeante avec sa belle-famille.* She is accommodating to her in-laws. (LA) **2** demanding *Je voudrais pas être marié avec ça. Elle est trop obligeante.* I wouldn't want to be married to her. She is too demanding. (EV) <*Loc:* EV, LA, SB, Da84>

obligément [obliʒemɑ̃] *adv.* certainly, absolutely, necessarily *Mais obligément, ça doit être.* Well, necessarily, it must be so. (VM) <*Loc:* VM>

obliger [obliʒe, ubliʒe] **I** *v.tr.* **1** to oblige, require *Il l'a pas obligé de payer la dette.* He didn't require him to pay the debt. (LA) **2** to compel, force *Il les a obligés de partir.* He forced them to leave. (LA) **II s'obliger** *v.pron.* to force o.s. *Il faut je m'oblige d'aller à la messe.* I have to force myself to go to mass. (LA) ◊ •**être obligé** ***a*** to be obliged **On a été envoyé par le roi pour te tuer, toi et ton petit, et on est obligé de le faire parce que, si nous-autres, on le fait pas, on va être tué.* We were sent by the king to kill you, you and your child, and we are obliged to do it because, if we don't do it, we will be killed. (IB, An94) *Il est obligé de faire cela.* He has to do that. (JE) ***b*** *(hypothesis, speculation)* must *Je dis c'est obligé d'être un avertissement.* I said that it must be a premonition. (TB) *Et j'ai pensé entre mon-même c'est obligé d'être Boyd qu'est là pour venir mettre le* SHOT *à mame.* And I thought to myself that it must be Boyd who was there to give mom her shot. (TB) <EV, IB, IV, JE, SL, TB, VM, An94, Wh83> <*Loc:* EV, IB, IV, JE, LA, SL, TB, VM, An94, Da84, Hi02, Wh83>

obscurité [ɔpskyrite] *n.f.* **1** obscurity **2** darkness, dimness ◊ •**dans l'obscurité** in the dark <EV, LA, VM> <*Loc:* EV, LA, VM, Da84>

observable [ɔpsærvab(l), ɔbzærvab(l), ɔksærvab(l)] *adj.* observable, noticeable <*Loc:* LA, Da84>

observance [ɔpsærvɑ̃s, ɔbzærvɑ̃s, ɔkzærvɑ̃s] *n.f.* observance <*Loc:* LA, Da84>

observant, -e [ɔpsærvɑ̃, ɔbzærvɑ̃, ɔkzærvɑ̃, -ɑ̃t] *adj.* petty, overly concerned with fairness and detail *La femme à Howard est assez observante. Si je fais pour un et pas pour l'autre, ça fait pas.* Howard's wife is so overly concerned with fairness. If I do something for one and not the other, it won't do. (LA) <*Loc:* LA>

observation [ɔpsærvasjɔ̃, ɔbzærvasjɔ̃, ɔksærvasjɔ̃] *n.f.* observation <*Loc:* LA, Da84>

observer [ɔpsærve, ɔbzærve, ɔksærve] **I** *v.tr.* **1** to observe, notice *Je sais pas si t'as observé quand-ce que nous-autres on était après parler et il y avait du monde ici-dedans, c'était après nous regarder comme si qu'on était, uh, qui-ce qu'eux-autres après dire?* I don't know if you observed when we talking and there were people in here, they were looking at us as if we were, oh, what are they saying? (LF) *Petit Poucet était un enfant beaucoup* SMART *et il observait tout et il pouvait se défendre avec les plus vieux.* Petit Poucet was a very smart child and he observed everything and he could hold his own with the older ones. (LA) **2** to observe, obey (e.g. a law) *Mais dedans le Carême ça mangeait pas de viande le mercredi et le vendredi. Aujourd'hui le monde observe plus autant comme eux-autres faisait.* But in Lent they didn't eat meat on Wednesdays or Fridays. Today people don't observe any more like they used to do. (LF) **II s'observer** *v.pron.* **1** to observe each other, watch each other *Les voisins s'observaient passer dans la petite manche.* The neighbors observed each other passing in the little lane. (LA) **2** to be on one's guard *Observe-toi.* Be careful. Behave yourself. (VM) <***Loc:*** EV, LA, LF, VM, Da84, Hi02>

observeur, -euse [ɔpsærvœr, ɔbzærvœr, ɔksærvœr, -øz] *adj.* observant, perspicacious *J'ai jamais vu une fille observeuse comme ça.* I've never seen such an observant girl. (VM) <***Loc:*** VM>

obstacle [ɔpstak(l)] *n.m.* obstacle, hindrance <***Loc:*** Da84>

obstination (**ostination**) [ostinasjɔ̃] *n.f.* **1** stubbornness, obstinacy, bullheadedness *C'est son obstination qui l'a empêché d'être électé.* It's his stubborness that kept him from being elected. (VM) *Sa femme l'a quitté parce qu'il pouvait pas se défaire de son obstination.* His wife left him because he couldn't get over his bullheadedness. (LA) **2** quarrel, fracas, row, loud argument *Tu parles d'une ostination quand il arrive après minuit avec l'odeur de l'essence dessus son col!* Talk about a fracas when he arrives after midnight with the scent of perfume on his collar! (LA) *Mon et mon frère, on a eu une telle ostination qu'on se parle jamais.* My brother and I had such a quarrel that we never speak to each other. (VM) <***Loc:*** IB, LA, TB, VM, Da84, Gr86>

obstiné, -e (**ostiné, -e**) [ostine] *adj.* obstinate, hardheaded, stubborn *Il est obstiné dans son opinion.* He is stubborn about his opinion. (IB) <***Loc:*** IB, Da84>

obstiner (**ostiner**) [ostine] **I** *v.tr.* **1** to nag, fuss at, quarrel with *Ce bougre est tout le temps après ostiner sa femme devant le monde.* That fellow is always fussing at his wife in front of everyone. (LA) *Tu devrais bien arrêter de m'ostiner.* You should really stop fussing at me. (LA) **2** to insist on firmly *Il a obstiné qu'il avait payé la selle.* He insisted that he had paid for the saddle. (LA) *Il m'a ostiné c'était pas lui.* He insisted that it was not him. (Lv88) **II** *v.intr.* to insist, persist, be obstinate *Il voulait pas, il a ostiné.* He didn't want to do it. He was obstinate. (Lv88) **III s'obstiner** *v.pron.* to argue, quarrel with each other *Ça s'ostine tout le temps.* They're always quarreling with each other. (LA) *Ils ont séparé; ils étaient tout le temps après s'ostiner.* They separated; they were always quarreling. (LA) <***Loc:*** EV, IB, LA, LF, SL, VM, Da84, Lv88, Ph36>

obstineur, -euse (**ostineur, -euse**) [ostinœr, -øz] *adj.* **1** stubborn, hard-headed *J'ai jamais vu une femme ostineuse comme ça.* I've never seen such a stubborn woman. (VM) **2** argumentative <***Loc:*** SM, VM, Lv88>

obstruction [ɔpstryksjɔ̃] *n.f.* obstruction, stoppage <***Loc:*** Da84>

obtenable [ɔptənab(l)] *adj.* available **Plus de détails va être lâchés aussi vite qu'ils sont obtenable.* More details will be released as soon as they are available. (Wh83) <***Loc:*** Wh83>

obtenir [ɔbtənir] **I** *v.tr.* to obtain, get *Tu peux obtenir ça à la pharmacie.* You can get that at the pharmacy. (VM) **II s'obtenir** *v.pron.* to get, obtain for o.s. *Il s'a obtenu du gravail pour son chemin de la paroisse.* He obtained some gravel for his road from the parish. (VM) <***Loc:*** VM, Da84>

occasion [okazjɔ̃] *n.f.* **1** occasion, opportunity **2** cause <***Loc:*** LA, Da84, Hi02>

occasionnel, -elle [okazjɔ̃nɛl] *adj.* occasional *C'est juste une affaire occasionnelle.* It's just an occasional thing. (LA) <***Loc:*** LA, Da84>

occasionner [okazjɔ̃ne] *v.tr.* to bring about, cause **Après ça, le groupe s'est dissolu à cause des problèmes personnels occasionnés par le manque de travail pour le groupe.* After that, the group broke up because of personal problems caused by the lack of work for the group. (LA, An84) <***Loc:*** AC, LA, SL, An84, Da84, Gr86, Lv88>

occupant [okypɑ̃] *n.m.* occupant <***Loc:*** Da84>

occupation [okypasjɔ̃] *n.f.* occupation, work, business <***Loc:*** Da84>

occupé, -e [okype, ekype, økupe] *adj.* busy, occupied, engaged *C'est de quoi j'ai assayé d'yeux montrer mais j'ai été assez occupé quand j'étais plus jeune que j'ai pas pu yeux montrer le français comme j'aurais aimé yeux montrer.* That's something I tried to teach them but I was so busy when I was younger that I wasn't able to teach them French like I wanted to. (TB) <***Loc:*** AC, AV, EV, JE, LA, LF, SB, TB, Da84, Hi02>

occuper [okype] **I** *v.tr.* **1** to occupy, dwell in *C'est lui qu'occupe la chambre de mon garçon.* He's the one who occupies my son's room. (LA) **2** to occupy, take up the time of *Ça m'occupe un tas cette affaire d'école.* This matter of school takes up a lot of my time. (Lv88) **3** to worry, cause to worry *Ça l'occupe un tas.* It worries her a lot. (VM) *Je peux pas m'endormir, ça m'occupe tant.* I can't sleep, that worries me so much. (TB) **II s'occuper** *v.pron.* **1** to occupy o.s., busy o.s. *Je m'occupe tous les jours à cuire et propter la maison.* I stay busy every day cooking and cleaning the house. (LA) **2** to look after, take care of (children, etc.) *Quand lui, il est mort, il fallait qu'elle s'occupe de nous-autres et dans ces années-là, le monde avait pas d'argent.* When he died, she had to look after us and in those years, people didn't have any money. (EV, An84) **Pis pas just' ça, a' s'a tout le temps occupé de not' 'tite habitation le temps qu' j' étais à l' ouvrage.* Not only that, she always took care of our little homestead while I was at work. (Gu82) ◊ **•s'occuper avec** to get involved with *La seule manière t'aurais pu te mettre en tracas c'est si t'aurais tombé là et assayer de t'occuper avec la femme d'un autre bougre ou quelque chose, là t'aurais proche sûr eu une bataille.* The only way you could have gotten into trouble is if you would end up there and tried to get involved with the wife of another guy or something, then you would almost certainly have had a fight. (TB) <TB> **•s'occuper de sa tambouille à soi-même** to mind one's own business <SJ> **•s'occuper de ses affaires {oignons}** to mind one's own business *Tu devrais bien t'occuper de tes affaires, toi!* You should mind your own business, you! (LA) *Tu devrais bien t'occuper de tes oignons.* You ought to take care of your own business. (LA) <LA, Da84> <*Loc:* EV, LA, SJ, TB, VM, An84, Da84, Gu82, Lv88>

océan [oseɑ̃, oseɑ̃s] *n.m.* ocean, sea *L'océan a pas de fond.* The ocean has no bottom. (VM) <*Loc:* SM, VM, Da84, Hi02>

octagon [ɔktagɔ̃] *n.m.* octagon <*Loc:* Da84>

octobre [ɔktɔb(r), oktɔb(r)] *n.m.* October <*Loc:* AC, EV, JE, Da84, Hi02>

odeur [odœr] *n.f.* odor, smell, scent *Et ils vont laisser ce pot de chambre en dedans jusqu'à c'est plein et il faudra que tu vives avec cette odeur et te brosses les dents avec cette odeur!* And they're going to leave this chamberpot inside until it's full and you will have to live with that odor and brush your teeth with that odor! (ThCa: *Grosbecs*) <*Loc:* SM, Da84, Hi02, ThCa>

œil [œj] (*pl.* **yeux** [jø], **z-yeux** [zjø]) *n.m.* eye ◊ **•œil de patate** eye of a potato, germ of a potato <Da84> **•yeux creux** sunken eyes <Da84> **•yeux croches** cross-eyed <VM, Lv88> **•yeux barrés (comme un cabri)** evil person, bad person, scoundrel *Tant qu'à toi, z-yeux barrés!* As for you, scoundrel! (EV) *Lui, c'est un z-yeux barrés.* He's a wicked one, a devil. (EV) <AC, EV, La99> **•avoir des yeux noirs comme des socos** to have very dark eyes <La99> **•avoir les yeux dolents** to appear sleepy <La99> **•avoir les yeux égarés** ***a*** to appear tired **Il a les yeux égarés.* He looks tired. (EV, Ph36) ***b*** to be lost or disoriented <EV, La99, Ph36> **•avoir les yeux gouaires** to have a blank look <La99> **•avoir les yeux plus grands que le ventre** to have eyes bigger than one's stomach, be greedy <Da84> **•avoir l'œil sec** ***a*** to be on the lookout ***b*** to be unable to sleep <EV, La99> **•avoir un œil au bois / avoir un œil qui dit merde à l'autre** to be cockeyed <VM, La99> **•avoir un œil qui gagne chez Nonc Pierre** to be cross-eyed <La99> **•faire des gros yeux** to express disapproval <Da84> **•gros yeux / gros-yeux** greedy, gluttonous *T'es gros-yeux. Tu peux pas manger tout ça.* You're being greedy. You can't eat all that. (SM) <SM, La99> <*Loc:* AC, AV, EV, JE, SM, VM, Da84, Hi02, La99, Lv88>

œillet [ejɛ, eje, øjɛ, øje] *n.m.* **1** eyelet (of shoes, etc.) **2** eye of a hook and eye *Accroche et œillet.* Hook and eye. (VM) ◊ **•œillet d'Inde / œillet de dinde / œillet français** marigold *Mon père aimait planter des œillets de dinde dans son jardin pour évader la vermine de son jardinage.* My father liked planting marigolds in his garden to keep away the vermin from his vegetables. (Gu00) <EV, VM, Gu00> <*Loc:* EV, VM, Da84, Gu00>

œuf [œf, zœf] (*pl.* **œufs** [œf, ø], **z-œufs** [zœf, zø]) *n.m.* egg *Des œufs frits.* Fried eggs. (IB) *Les carpes va aller dans le bassin pour pondre leurs œufs.* The carp are going to the bassin to lay their eggs. (SM) ◊ **•œuf cam-cam** hard-boiled egg <SL> **•œuf de caïman {carencro}** illegitimate child <SC, TB, La99> **•œuf de lapin** Easter egg *Les œufs de lapin est tout pigarlés.* The Easter eggs are all speckled. (TB) <TB> **•œuf hardé** soft-shelled egg <TB, Di32> **•œuf mollet** coddled egg <Da84> **•œufs à la neige** ***a*** eggnog ***b*** meringue custard dessert <SL, SM, Lv88> **•blanc d'œuf** egg white <Da84> **•jaune d'œuf** egg yolk <Da84> <*Loc:* AC, AV, EV, IB, IV, SC, SL, SM, TB, VM, An94, Da84, Di32, Hi02, La99>

œuvre [œv(r)] *n.f.* **1** work, labor **2** work of art ◊ **•bonne œuvre** good work <Da84> <*Loc:* Da84, Hi02>

OFF [ɔf] *adv.* off (from work, school) *J'ai pris* OFF. I took off [from work]. (Lv88) *Il après travailler* OFFSHORE, *et quand il va revenir il a six jours* OFF. He works offshore, and when he comes back he'll have six days off. (TB) <*Loc:* TB, Lv88>

offense [ofɑ̃s] *n.f.* offense, wrong <*Loc:* Da84, Lv88>

offenser [ofɑ̃se] **I** *v.tr.* to offend **Je peux pas risquer d'offenser ce bon monde.* I can't risk offending these good people. (LA, An94) **II s'offenser** *v.pron.* **1** to take offense *Il s'a offensé pour rien.* He took offense for nothing. (LA) **2** to offend each other *Chaque fois que ça ouvre la bouche, ça s'offense un à l'autre.* Every time they open their mouths, they offend each other. (VM) <*Loc:* LA, VM, An94, Da84>

offensive [ofɑ̃siv] *adj.* **1** offensive, hurtful, insulting **2** displeasing, offensive *Un renard a une odeur offensive.* A fox has an offensive odor. (VM) <*Loc:* VM, Da84>

offère (offert, offrir) [ofær, ofrir] (*p.p.* **offri** [ofri], **offert** [ofær]) **I** *v.tr.* to offer *Chère, il est venu, puis c'est ça il était venu nous offert, pense donc, d'acheter cette maison, si pauvre qu'on était.* Dear, he came and that's what he had come to offer us, think of it, to buy that house, as poor as we were. (EV) **Il lui offrait toute espèce de bon manger.* He offered her all sorts of good things to eat. (IB, An94) *J'ai offri mon secours.* I offered my help. (VM) **II s'offrir** *v.pron.* **1** to offer to o.s., treat o.s. to *Ils s'ont offert un dîner pour la graduation de leur garçon.* They treated themselves to a dinner for their son's graduation. (VM) **2** to offer one's help <*Loc:* EV, IB, LF, SB, VM, An94, Da84, Gr86, Hi02, Lv88>

offert ♦see **offère**

offertoire [ofærtwar] *n.m.* [*eccl.*] offertory (of the mass) <*Loc:* Da84>

office [ofis] *n.m./f.* **1** office *L'office du docteur est plein le lundi matin.* The doctor's office is full on Monday morning. (Lv88) *L'avocat est dans son office.* The lawyer is in his office. (SL) **2** office, position, function (of president, etc.) **L'maire de Delcambre, c'est un vaillant p'tit jeune homme, il a conduit son office joliment bien.* The mayor of

Delcambre was a fine young man, he performed his duties quite well. (Gr86) **3** post office **4** church service <***Loc:*** EV, IB, SL, SM, TB, VM, An94, Da84, Gr86, Hi02, Lv88, Ph36>

officiant [ofisjɑ̃] *n.m.* [*eccl.*] officiant, officiating priest <***Loc:*** Da84>

officiel[1]**, -lle** [ofisjɛl] *adj.* official *Quand il a dit ça devant tout le monde, ça l'a fait joliment officiel.* When he said that in front of everyone, it made it pretty official. (LA) <***Loc:*** LA, Da84>

officiel[2] [ofisjɛl] *n.m.* official <***Loc:*** TB>

officiellement [ofisjɛlmɑ̃] *adv.* officially *La gouverneuse a déclaré officiellement qu'on avait été nommé à la commission.* The governor declared officially that we had been named to the commission. (VM) <***Loc:*** VM, Da84>

officier[1] [ofisje] *v.tr.* [*eccl.*] to officiate, preside over (ceremonies, etc.) <***Loc:*** Da84>

officier[2] [ofisje] *n.m.* **1** officer, military officer *On avait des prisonniers de Japon. On les prendait à eux-autres, follait qu'eux-autres fait l'ouvrage, rebâtir les maisons et tout pour les officiers.* We had prisoners from Japan. We took them, they had to do the work, rebuild the officers' houses and all. (LF) **2** police officer, sheriff **3** person in charge (within a company, public service) ◊ **•officier de police** police officer <SM> <***Loc:*** LA, SM, TB, Da84, Hi02, Lv88>

offrande [ofrɑ̃d] *n.f.* [*eccl.*] offering, gift <***Loc:*** Da84>

offre [ɔf(r)] *n.m./f.* offer, bid ◊ **•faire un(e) offre** to make an offer or proposal *On va faire un offre dessus la maison aujourd'hui.* We're going to make an offer on the house today. (LA) <LA> <***Loc:*** LA, Da84, Lv88>

offrir ♦see **offère**

oh (**o**) [o] *interj.* oh *"Oh," le vieux dit, "Moi, je vas aller voir."* "Oh," the old fellow said, "I'll go to see." (AS) <***Loc:*** AC, AS, EV, JE, LA, PQ, SL, SM, TB, VM, An94, Da84>

oie (**z-oie, zoie**) [zwa] *n.m./f.* **1** goose (of either sex) *Quand il voulait bourrer son fusil pour tirer la z-oie, il a pris un chiffon de mousse, il l'a bien tapée, la musquette.* When he wanted to stuff his shotgun to shoot the goose, he took a wad of moss, he tapped it well, the musket. (VM) "*The White Goose" ça appelait ça—un petit sac en linge. Il y avait un gros z-oie blanc dessus.* "The White Goose," they called it—a little cloth sack. It had a big white goose on it. (SL) **Être bête come une (z)oie.* To be crazy as a goose. (Da84) **2** snow goose ◊ **•oie aigle** eagle goose, blue goose <Re31> **•oie canadienne / z-oie canadien** Canadian goose, Canada goose <IV, Re31> **•oie couvasse** laying goose <Gr86> **•oie nonnette** white-fronted goose, specklebelly <Re31> **•z-oie blanc {blanche}** snow goose *La z-oie blanche a la peau noire.* The snow goose has black skin. (VM) <IV, LF, VM, Gu00> **•z-oie bleu(e)** blue goose *La jeune z-oie bleue a pas la tête blanche.* The young blue goose doesn't have a white head. (VM) <IV, LF, VM, Gu00> **•z-oie câille** ***a*** white-fronted goose, specklebelly *La zoie câille a les pattes jaunes.* The specklebelly has yellow feet. (VM) ***b*** domestic goose <VM, Gu00, Re31> **•z-oie de cour** domestic goose *J'ai cuit une grosse z-oie de cour pour Noël.* I cooked a big domestic goose for Christmas. (VM) <VM> **•z-oie marron** wild goose <Lv88> **•z-oie pigeon** cormorant <IB> **•être dans le Paris des oies** to be in deep sleep <TB, La99> <***Loc:*** AV, EV, IB, IV, JE, LF, SL, SM, TB, VM, An94, Da84, Gr86, Gu00, Hi02, La99, Lv88, Ph36, Re31>

oignon (**z-oignon**) [ɔ̃jɔ̃, wɑ̃jɔ̃, zɔ̃jɔ̃] *n.m.* onion ◊ **•oignon chauvage** Indian onion <TB> **•oignon d'ali {d'alié}** Indian turnip <IB> **•oignon vert** green onion, scallion <EV, IV, JD, TB> <***Loc:*** CL, EV, IB, IV, JD, JE, LA, SL, SM, TB, Da84, Hi02>

oir ♦see **voir**

oiseau (**z-oiseau, zozo**) [wazo, zwazo, zozo] *n.m.* bird *Mais les ratons laveurs et les serpents ont monté pour prendre les œufs et tuer les petits oiseaux.* But the raccoons and snakes climbed up to get the eggs and kill the young birds. (TB) *L'oiseau se becquait sur la branche.* The bird was preening itself on the branch. (LA) *C'est le mâle qui est le plus beau dans les oiseaux.* It is the male who is the most beautiful among birds. (EV) *Il fait tous ses cabins à zozos.* He makes all his birdhouses. (SL) ◊ **•oiseau bleu** bluebird <Re31> **•oiseau (de) cheminée** chimney swift <AC, Lv88> **•oiseau de cannes** brown thrasher <Re31> **•oiseau de fleurs / z-oiseau-fleur / zozo-fleur** ***a*** hummingbird ***b*** ruby-throated hummingbird <AV, SM, TB, Re31, Lv88> **•oiseau de grapigne {grapine}** bird of prey <Lv88> **•oiseau de maison** house swift <Lv88> **•oiseau de malheur** ***a*** doctor ***b*** priest <Da84> **•oiseau de pluie** ***a*** purple martin, rain bird ***b*** barn swallow <JD, SM, Re31> **•oiseau-mouche / oiseau-à-mouche** hummingbird <IB, Re31> **•oiseau papillon** scissor-tailed flycatcher <Re31, Lv88> **•un oiseau dans la main en vaut deux dans une talle** a bird in the hand is worth two in the bush <Lv88> <***Loc:*** AC, EV, IB, JD, LA, PQ, SL, SM, TB, VM, An94, Da84, Hi02, Lv88, Re31>

olive [oliv] *n.f.* olive <***Loc:*** Da84>

olivier [olivje] *n.m.* **1** any of a variety of laurel trees **2** tupelo, tupelo gum tree **3** sweet-scented olive **4** olive tree **5** Chinese tallow tree ◊ **•olivier de la Chine** sweet-scented olive (ornamental shrub with small white flowers imported from China or Japan) <IB, Re31> <***Loc:*** AS, IB, JD, JE, SB, TB, Da84, Gu00, Lv88, Re31>

ombouril ♦see **nombril**

ombrage [ɔ̃braʒ, ɔ̃broʒ] *n.m./f.* **1** shade *Cet arbre fait de l'ombrage.* This tree gives good shade. (LA) **2** shadow **Faire un ombrage.* To cast a shadow. (La99) ◊ **•à l'ombrage** in the shade *Quand on voulait aller à l'ombrage, on allait en bas le copal.* When we wanted to go in the shade, we went under the sweetgum tree. (SL) *Mets le char à l'ombrage.*

Put the car in the shade. (Lv88) <SL, Lv88> <***Loc:*** AV, LA, SL, SM, VM, Da84, Fa77, La99, Lv88>

ombrager [ɔ̃braʒe] **I** *v.tr.* to shade *Il a planté des chênes pour ombrager son terrain.* He planted oak trees to shade his lot. (VM) **II s'ombrager** *v.pron.* to shade o.s. (e.g. one's eyes) *Il s'a ombragé les yeux pour mieux voir son garçon descendre de l'aéroplane.* He shaded his eyes to better see his son get off the airplane. (LA) <***Loc:*** LA, VM, Da84>

ombre (**lombre, alombre**) [ɔ̃m, ɔ̃b(r), lɔ̃m, lɔ̃b(r), alɔ̃m] *n.m./f.* **1** shade *Dans la lombre de l'arbre.* In the shade of the tree. (Lv88) *Y a pas d'alombre dessus ce bord-là de la maison avant proche six heures et demie.* There's no shade on that side of the house before almost six-thirty. (VM) **2** shadow ◊ **•à l'ombre / à la lombre / à l'alombre** in the shade *Va t'assir à l'ombre.* Go sit in the shade. (VM) *Va t'assir à l'alombre.* Go sit in the shade. (VM) *On va pas bouillir les écrévisses ce bord-là de la maison. Y a pas de l'ombre. On va aller l'autre bord à l'ombre.* We are not going to boil the crawfish on this side of the house. There is no shade. We are going to go to the other side in the shade. (VM) <VM, Da84> <***Loc:*** AL, VM, An94, Da84, Guoo, Lv88>

ombrelle [ɔ̃brɛl] *n.m./f.* **1** umbrella **2** parasol ◊ **•ombrelle de Japon** umbrella plant <VM> <***Loc:*** LA, SM, VM, Da84, Fa77, Guoo, Hi02, Lv88>

ombril ♦see **nombril**

omelette [ɔ̃mlɛt, ɔ̃blɛt, ɔ̃mnɛt] *n.f.* omelet ◊ **•omelette d'œufs** omelet <Da84> <***Loc:*** IB, JE, LF, SB, SJ, Da84>

omission [ɔ̃misjɔ̃] *n.f.* [*eccl.*] omission, oversight *C'était une omission, mais c'était toujours un péché.* It was an omission, but it was still a sin. (VM) <***Loc:*** EV, LA, VM, Da84>

omnipotence [ɔ̃mnipotɑ̃s] *n.f.* [*eccl.*] omnipotence (of God) <***Loc:*** Da84>

omnipotent, -e [ɔ̃mnipotɑ̃, -ɑ̃t] *adj.* [*eccl.*] omnipotent, all powerful <***Loc:*** Da84>

on [ɔ̃, ɛ̃] *(before a vowel* [ɔ̃n, ɔ̃l]*) pron.pers. (subj.)* **1** we *Quand nous-autres ont été enlevé on parlait bien français.* When we were raised, we spoke French well. (SL) *Dès qu'on s'a marié j'ai été rester à Canal Yankee pour sept ans.* When we got married I went to live at Canal Yankee for seven years. (LF) *On était à dix dans la famille.* There were ten of us in the family. (LF) *Moi et ma femme, on a tout le temps parlé français.* My wife and I, we have always spoken French. (LF) *On est après battre le riz, nous-autres.* We're thrashing rice. (VM) *On a été au* SHOW, *nous-autres.* We went to the show. (SM) **2** one, people, they **On dirait, c'est manière drôle de dire ça,* BUT *supposé ça a arrivé.* One would say that it is kind of strange, but supposedly it happened. (SL, An94) *J'avais ça qu'on appelle la ceinture. So j'ai été au docteur.* I had what they call shingles. So I went to the doctor. (TB) *Il a une bonne direction, on croirait jamais qu'il est le fils à ce bon-à-rien.* He has good behavior, one would never believe that he's the son of that good-for-nothing. (VM) *On battait le linge au bayou pour le laver.* They would beat the laundry at the bayou to wash it. (LA) **Petit Jean s'avait engagé avec un géant. Le vieux diable, on l'appelait.* Petit Jean had gotten himself a job with a giant. The old devil, they called him. (An94) <***Loc:*** AC, AV, IB, EV, JE, LA, LF, SL, SM, TB, VM, An84, An94, Da84, Gr82, Guoo, Lv88, Wh83, ThCa>

once [ɔ̃s] *n.f.* **1** ounce *La mesure est peut-être pas à l'once, mais la mesure pourrait remplir un sac de 50 livres.* The measure may not be correct to the ounce, but the measure could fill a 50 pound bag. (LF) *C'est des petits* TWINS. *Des petits bessons. Ça pesait sept livres et cinq -z- onces chaque quand ils sont énés.* They are little twins. They weighed seven pounds five ounces apiece when they were born. (LF) **2** bit, small amount **Il a pas une once d'esprit.* He hasn't a bit of sense. (Da84) <***Loc:*** LF, Da84, Hi02, Lv88>

oncle (**n-oncle, noncle, nonc**) [ɔ̃k(l), nɔ̃k(l)] *n.m.* **1** uncle *Mon mari achetait ça avec son vieux oncle.* My husband used to buy that from his old uncle. (SL) *Je devais parler pour mes tantes et mes noncles.* I had to speak for my aunts and uncles. (SM) **Noncle Paul.* Uncle Paul. (Da84) **Noncle Pierre.* Uncle Peter. (Da84) **2** [*term of endearment or respect for an older man, such as a friend of the family*] 'uncle' <***Loc:*** AC, AV, EV, IB, IV, LA, SJ, SL, SM, TB, VM, An94, Da84, Lv88>

onction [ɔ̃ksjɔ̃] *n.f.* [*eccl.*] unction, anointing ◊ **•Extrême Onction** Extreme Unction, last rites, anointing of the sick <Da84> <***Loc:*** Da84>

ondain ♦see **andain**

onde [ɔ̃d] *n.f.* wave <***Loc:*** Da84>

ondoiement [ɔ̃dwɔjmɑ̃] *n.m.* emergency baptism (Catholic rite) <***Loc:*** LA>

ondoyer [ɔ̃dwɔje] *v.tr.* to baptize without the usual rites and prayers of a church baptism (esp. for a newborn baby at risk of imminent death) *Kurt a été ondoyé. Quand Kurt a été éné, l'évêque était après visiter dans l'hôpital. C'est l'évêque qui l'a ondoyé dans l'hôpital.* Kurt received an emergency baptism. When Kurt was born, the bishop was visiting in the hospital. It was the bishop who baptized him in the hospital. (LA) <***Loc:*** LA, Da84>

ondure [ɔ̃dyr] *n.f.* sty, inflamed swelling on the edge of an eyelid <***Loc:*** VM>

ongle [ɔ̃g(l)] *n.m./f.* **1** nail, fingernail, toenail **2** claw <***Loc:*** SB, SM, VM, Da84, Fa77>

onguent (**longuent**) [ɔ̃gɑ̃, lɔ̃gɑ̃] *n.m.* ointment, salve ◊ **•longuent-graisse** gray liniment <VM> **•onguent à ver** carbolic acid ointment <Da84> <***Loc:*** VM, Da84>

onze [ɔ̃z] *adj./n.m.* eleven **À onze heures le soir.* At eleven o'clock at night. (IV, An94) **Tu connais, quand tu mets onze gallons d'eau dans ton chapeau, puis tu le mets sur ta tête, mais ça tient la tête froide, tu connais, mais l'eau coule *des fois, s'il est pas bien serré.* You know, when you put eleven gallons of water in your hat, and then you put it on your head, well, it keeps your head cold, you know, but the water drips sometimes, if it's not really tight. (EV, An94) <***Loc:*** AV, EV, IV, SM, TB, An94, Da84, Hi02>

onzième [ɔ̃zjɛ̃m] *adj./n.* eleventh *Mon plus vieux garçon a passé en grade au onzième livre.* My oldest son passed into the eleventh grade. (VM) <***Loc:*** VM, Da84>

Opelousas [oplusa(s)] *n.pl.* Opelousas *C'était pour moi et mon vieux frère qui reste aux Opelousas.* It was for me and my old brother who lives in Opelousas. (EV) <***Loc:*** EV, SL>

operater [opərate] *v.tr.* to operate *C'était couru par un* STEAM MOTOR *[...] c'était du* STEAM *qui sortait. C'est un cylindre, ça prendait deux hommes pour l'operater.* It was run by a steam motor, it was steam that came out. It's one cylinder, it took two men to operate it. (AS) <***Loc:*** AS>

opérateur [operatœr] *n.m.* operator <***Loc:*** Da84>

opération [operasjɔ̃] *n.f.* **1** operation *Ils ont appelé le docteur, il était venu, et c'était l'appendicite. Et le docteur a essayé avoir l'opération dans la maison dessus une table.* They called the doctor, he came, and it was appendicitis. And the doctor tried to have the operation in the house on a table. (SB) **2** working, functioning (of a machine, etc.) <***Loc:*** AV, LA, LF, SB, SM, VM, Da84, Gu00, Hi02>

opérer [opere] *v.tr.* **1** to operate on, perform a medical operation on *Depuis qu'il a été opéré pour son cœur.* Since he was operated on for his heart. (TB) **2** to work, operate (a machine) *Il est après opérer le bouledou.* He's operating the bulldozer. (VM) **3** to run, manage **On conte l'histoire d'un pauvre malheureux qui opérait un café.* They tell the story of a poor wretch who ran a café. (Gr86) **4** to castrate *Opérer un verrat.* To castrate a hog. (JE) *Un cheval opéré.* A gelding. (SJ) <***Loc:*** JE, SJ, TB, VM, Da84, Gr86>

opinion [opĩjɔ̃] *n.f.* opinion, idea, view ◊ **•à mon opinion** in my opinion <Da84> **•être d'opinion** to be of the opinion *Je suis de même opinion que vous.* I am of the same opinion as you. (SM) <SB, SM> <***Loc:*** IB, SB, SM, Da84>

opponent [opɔ̃nɑ̃] *n.m.* opponent, adversary **Son opponent a présenté son cas avec plein de vigueur.* His opponent presented his case with much vigor. (Gr82) <***Loc:*** Gr82, Lv88>

opportunité [opɔrtynite] *n.f.* opportunity, chance <***Loc:*** Da84>

opposé[1] [opoze] *n.m.* opposite, contrary ◊ **•à l'opposé** on the contrary, to the contrary *La mère voulait que sa fille se marie avec ce petit bougre, mais à l'opposé son père voulait pas.* The mother wanted her daughter to marry that little fellow, but on the contrary, the father did not. (VM) <VM, Da84> <***Loc:*** VM, Da84, Hi02>

opposé[2] [opoze] ◊ **•opposé de** facing, across from, opposite *L'église est opposée de la grocerie.* The church is across from the grocery. (VM) <VM, Da84, Hi02> <***Loc:*** VM, Da84, Hi02>

opposer [opoze] *v.tr.* **1** to oppose, object to *Elle a opposé mes volontés.* She objected to my wishes. (Lv88) *Je vas pas voter comme toi, je vas t'opposer.* I am not going to vote like you, I am going to oppose you. (Lv88) **2** to prevent *Il l'a opposé de partir.* He prevented him from leaving. (Lv88) *J'en ai de ces gros navires qui naviguent dessus l'eau et soi-disant pour t'opposer de travailler.* I have large ships that sailed the seas and allegedly to prevent you from having to work. (VM, ch: *J'ai marié un ouvrier*) **II s'opposer** *v.pron.* to be opposed <***Loc:*** JD, LF, TB, Da84, Lv88>

opposition [opozisjɔ̃] *n.f.* **1** opposition, resistance **2** those opposed (collectively) ◊ **•mettre opposition à** to oppose *Il a mis opposition au contrat.* He opposed the contract. (LA) <LA, Da84> <***Loc:*** LA, Da84>

oppressé, -e [oprese] *adj.* **1** asthmatic, afflicted with asthma *Il est oppressé un tas.* He often has asthma. (VM) *T'es oppressé, t'es après siller.* You have asthma, you are wheezing. (VM) **2** congested, having respiratory congestion *Elle est oppressée.* She's congested. (LA) **3** hoarse *La dame s'a réveillée à ce matin bien oppressée.* The woman woke up very hoarse this morning. (VM) <***Loc:*** LA, SM, VM, Da84>

oppressement [oprɛsmɑ̃] *n.m./f.* **1** asthma **2** respiratory congestion, stuffiness **3** hoarseness <***Loc:*** SM, VM, Da84, Lv88>

oppresser [oprese] *v.tr.* to congest, cause respiratory congestion *J'ai passé la nuit dehors et ça m'a oppressé.* I spent the night outside and it congested me. (LA) <***Loc:*** LA, Da84>

oppressif, -ive [opresif, -iv] *adj.* asthmatic *Mon grand-père était oppressif.* My grandfather was asthmatic. (VM) <***Loc:*** VM, Da84>

oppression [opresjɔ̃] *n.f.* **1** *(usu. pl.)* asthma, asthma attack *J'ai eu des oppressions quand j'étais petite.* I had asthma (attacks) when I was little. (EV) *La poussière à riz me donnait des oppressions.* Rice dust used to give me asthma attacks. (EV) *Quand ça avait les oppressions [...], ça allait à un arbre et ça te coupait une mèche de cheveux et ça mettait ça dans l'arbre.* When they had asthma, they would go to a tree and they would cut a lock of your hair and they would put it in the tree. (EV) **2** respiratory congestion, stuffiness **3** hoarseness *Des cataplâmes c'est bon pour l'oppression.* Poultices are good for hoarseness. (TB) *Il a l'oppression.* He is hoarse. (TB) **4** oppression, tyranny <***Loc:*** EV, SM, TB, Da84>

option [ɔpsjɔ̃] *n.f.* option, choice <***Loc:*** Da84>

or [ɔr] *n.m./f.* gold ◊ **•d'or / en or** golden, of gold *La montre d'or.* The gold watch. (LA) *Il a acheté une montre en or.* He bought a gold watch. (VM) **Un bracelet en or.* A gold bracelet. (EV, An94) <EV, LA, VM, An94, Da84> <***Loc:*** EV, IV, LA, TB, VM, An94, Da84, Hi02>

oragan ♦see **ouragan**

orage [oraʒ] *n.m./f.* **1** rainshower *Il monte une petite orage dans le sud.* There's a little rainshower coming up from the south. (VM) **2** *(pl.)* storm clouds **3** thunder ◊ **•grosse orage** thundershower with a large amount of rain <VM> **•mauvaise orage** rainstorm with wind and lightning <VM> <***Loc:*** AS, LA, LF, SM, VM, Da84, Guoo, Hi02, Lv88>

orageux, -euse [oraʒø, -øz] *adj.* cloudy, rainy *Il y a du temps orageux qui vient.* There's some rainy weather coming. (LA) <***Loc:*** LA, Da84>

oraison [orezɔ̃] *n.f.* [*eccl.*] prayer ◊ **•oraison dominicale** Lord's prayer <Da84> <***Loc:*** Da84>

orange[1] [orɑ̃ʒ] *adj./n.* orange *La jeune dame avait une belle robe orange.* The young lady was wearing a beautiful orange dress. (VM) <***Loc:*** VM, Hi02>

orange[2] [orɑ̃ʒ] *n.f.* orange ◊ **•petite orange douce** sweet kumquat <LA> **•petite orange haigre** sour kumquat <LA> <***Loc:*** CL, LA, SL, TB, Da84, Hi02>

oranger [orɑ̃ʒe] *n.m.* orange tree <***Loc:*** LA, SL, Da84>

orateur [oratœr] *n.m.* orator, speaker <***Loc:*** Da84>

oratoire [oratwar] *n.m.* oratory, place of prayer, chapel <***Loc:*** Da84>

orchestre [ɔrkɛs(tr)] *n.m.* orchestra <***Loc:*** Da84>

ordinaire[1] [ɔrdinær] *adj.* ordinary, usual, common, average *C'était une jolie étoffe mais c'était bon marché. Ça durait pas et ça convenait pas pour des bals ordinaires.* It was a pretty fabric but it was cheap. It didn't last and it wasn't appropriate for regular dances. (EV) <***Loc:*** EV, Da84>

ordinaire[2] [ɔrdinær] *adv.* usually, ordinarily *Ordinaire, je vas à l'ouvrage à sept heures.* I usually go to work at seven o'clock. (Lv88) *Ordinaire on aime pas ça, nous-autres.* We don't usually like that. (VM) <***Loc:*** VM, Hi02, Lv88>

ordinairement [ɔrdinærmɑ̃] *adv.* ordinarily, usually *Ordinairement, on fait la salade de pomme de terre avec des pommes de terre et des œufs, mais aujourd'hui on a mis des petits morceaux de pomme aussi.* Ordinarily, we make potato salad with potatoes and eggs, but today we added some little pieces of apple too. (LA) <***Loc:*** LA, Da84>

ordination [ɔrdinasjɔ̃] *n.f.* ordination (of priests, ministers, etc.) <***Loc:*** Da84>

ordonnance [ɔrdɔ̃nɑ̃s] *n.f.* ordinance, rule, law, regulation <***Loc:*** Da84>

ordonner [ɔrdɔ̃ne] *v.tr.* **1** to order *Il a ordonné une grande bière.* He ordered a large beer. (Lv88) *Elle a ordonné une volaille rôtie et une demi-douzaine des huîtres.* She ordered a roasted chicken and a half dozen oysters. (ch: *La chanson de cinquante sous*) **2** to order, command (s.o. to do s.t.) *J'ai ordonné mon fils de nettoyer l'écurie.* I ordered my son to clean the stable. (LA) **3** to ordain (to the ministry) *Ils ont ordonné trois jeunes prêtres de la paroisse.* They ordained three young priests from the parish. (EV) <***Loc:*** EV, IB, LA, SM, VM, Da84, Gr86, Lv88>

ordre [ɔrd(r)] *n.m.* **1** order, purchase (of goods) *Voici votre ordre, Madame.* Here is your order, ma'am. (IB) **2** order, command **3** holy orders, ordination **4** orderly condition ◊ **•mettre en ordre** to put in order *Et les bateaux, une fois par an il faut que ça soye inspecté par la Garde de Côte. Et il faut que ça soye tout mis en ordre.* And the boats, once a year they have to be inspected by the Coast Guard. And everything has to be put in order. (LF) <LF> <***Loc:*** IB, LA, LF, SM, VM, Da84>

oreille (**z-oreille**) [orɛj, zorɛj] *n.f.* **1** ear *Ça marquait [les cochons] sur les oreilles.* They marked the pigs on their ears. (SL) **2** moldboard of a plow *Il y avait deux oreilles après. Tu passais ça puis ça ouvrait chaque bord.* There were two moldboards on it. You went through with it and it spread the dirt on each side. (EV) ◊ **•oreille de charrue** plow blade <Da84> **•oreille de chien** 'dogear,' triangular part of a trawl net sewn in to let the net turn and form a corner <TB> **•oreille de cochon** type of fritter, fried pastry dough sometimes dipped in syrup <VM, Lv88> **•oreille de coton** fibrous separation between pods in a cotton boll <JE> **•oreille d'éléphant** elephant ear plant <VM, Lv88> **•à l'oreille** by ear **On figurait que c'était pour leur montrer à eux que quand même si on avait pas d'éducation comme eux ils aviont on pouvait apprendre à jouer de la musique aussi bien que n'importe qui d'autre à l'oreille.* We figured that it was to teach them that even though we didn't have an education like they had we could learn to play music as well as anyone else by ear. (LA, An84) <LA, An84> **•avoir des oreilles d'éléphant {de tayaut} / avoir des oreilles comme un pot de chambre / avoir des oreilles comme un taxi avec les deux portes ouvertes** to have big ears <AV, La99> **•avoir les oreilles claires** to have a keen ear <VM> <***Loc:*** AC, AV, EV, JE, LA, SL, TB, VM, An84, Da84, Hi02, La99, Lv88>

oreillée [oreje] *n.f.* strip of dirt thrown over by a plow <***Loc:*** IB, VM>

oreiller (**oriller**) [orje, orije, oreje] *n.m.* pillow *J'ai dormi dans mon lit. Et moi, faut que moi je me couche sur deux oreillers, cher.* I slept in my bed. And me, I have to sleep with two pillows, dear. (TB) *Mais les mames allait aux bals avec leurs enfants, ça amenait leurs enfants, ça s'amenait des couvertes et des oreillers.* But the mothers went to the dances with their children, they brought their children, they brought blankets and pillows. (LF) <***Loc:*** AL, EV, IB, LA, LF, SL, TB, VM, Da84, Gr86, Hi02, Lv88>

oreillon [orejɔ̃] *n.* pillowcase *La vieille passait son temps à broder des oreillons pour ses petits-enfants.* The old woman spent her time embroidering pillowcases for her grandchildren. (LA) <***Loc:*** LA>

organe[1] [ɔrgɑ̃n] *n.m.* **1** organ **2** penis <***Loc:*** Da84>

organe[2] [ɔrgɑ̃n] *n.f.* effrontery, impudence, boldness <***Loc:*** LF>

organisation [ɔrgɑ̃nizasjɔ̃] *n.f.* organization *Y a deux ans qu'on a formé une organisation des Amis du Français de Lafourche.* Two years ago we formed an organization called the Friends of French in Lafourche. (LF) <*Loc:* LF, Da84>

organiser [ɔrgɑ̃nize] **I** *v.tr.* **1** to organize (e.g. an event) *On a organisé la boucherie.* We organized the hog butchering. (LA) **2** to organize, put in order *Les couteaux et les fourchettes a été organisés.* The knives and forks were put in order. (VM) **II s'organiser** *v.pron.* **1** to organize into a group *On va s'organiser demain pour le ramassage de coton.* We're going to organize ourselves tomorrow for the cotton picking. (LA) **2** to organize o.s., get organized <*Loc:* LA, VM, Da84>

organiste [ɔrgɑ̃nis(t)] *n.m.* organist <*Loc:* Da84, Hi02>

organeau (**argoneau, erganeau**) [ɔrgɑ̃no, argɔ̃no, ærgɑ̃no] *n.m./f.* **1** ring (esp. a large one, as for hanging curtains) *C'est un argoneau en cuivre et tu mets ça sus un baire, vingt-quatre sus le baire, et en avant c'est un galand.* It's a copper ring to put on a mosquito bar, twenty-four on the bar, and in front there is a flounce. (TB) **2** iron ring attached to a rope for tying a horse **3** ring on a net through which a rope is threaded, any of the rings on a skimmer net through which a rope is passed <*Loc:* IB, LF, TB, VM, Lv88>

orge ♦see **auge**

orgue [ɔrg] *n.m.* organ, pipe organ <*Loc:* Da84, Hi02>

orgueil [ɔrgœj] *n.m.* pride, arrogance, vanity <*Loc:* Da84>

orgueilleux, -euse [ɔrgøjø, -øz] *adj.* proud, arrogant, vain *Ils ont tout le temps été du monde orgueilleux dans cette famille.* They have always been proud people in that family. (LA) <*Loc:* LA, Da84, Hi02>

originaire [oriʒinær] *adj.* native **Être originaire de la France.* To be a native of France. (Da84) <*Loc:* Da84>

original, -e [oriʒinal, oreʒinal] *adj.* **1** original *La tache originale.* Original sin. (LA) **2** new *Le char original.* The new car. (LA) **3** strange, odd *Oh, mais elle, elle est originale quand-même.* Oh, she's really strange. (LA) <*Loc:* LA, LF, SL, Da84>

originalement [oriʒinalmɑ̃] *adv.* originally *La maison originalement avait deux chambres.* The house originally had two rooms. (LA) <*Loc:* LA, Da84, Gr86>

origine [oriʒin, oreʒin] *n.f.* origin, source <*Loc:* LF, Da84, Hi02>

originel[1]**, -elle** [oriʒinɛl] *adj.* original **Pêché originel.* Original sin. (Da84) <*Loc:* Da84>

originel[2]**, -elle** [oriʒinɛl] *n.* rascal, scoundrel *Ah! Ma petite originelle.* Oh! You little rascal. (IB) <*Loc:* AV, IB, SJ, La99, Lv88>

originellement [oriʒinɛlmɑ̃] *adv.* originally *La maison originellement avait deux chambres.* The house originally had two rooms. (LA) <*Loc:* LA, Da84>

originer [oriʒine] **I** *v.tr.* to begin, start *Originer quelque chose.* To start something. (Lv88) **II** *v.intr.* to originate *Je sais pas comment le mot a originé mais c'est ça qu'on les appelait, des cap-caps.* I don't know how the word originated but that's what we called them, cap-caps. (LF) <*Loc:* LF, SB, VM, Da84, Gr86, Lv88>

oriller ♦see **oreiller**

orme [ɔrm] *n.m.* elm ◊ **•orme gras** slippery elm <Re31> <*Loc:* CL, SL, Re31>

ornement [ɔrnəmɑ̃] *n.m.* ornament, trim <*Loc:* Da84>

orner [ɔrne] **I** *v.tr.* to ornament, decorate, adorn *On va orner l'arbre dehors avec des lumières.* We're going to decorate the tree outside with lights. (VM) *On va orner la flotte pour la parade.* We're going to decorate the float for the parade. (VM) **II s'orner** *v.pron.* to adorn o.s. *Il s'a orné pour le bal de Mardi Gras.* He got dressed up for the Mardi Gras ball. (VM) <*Loc:* VM, Da84>

orogan ♦see **ouragan**

orphelin, -e [ɔrfəlɛ̃, -in] *n.* orphan *Il lui a demandé si il aurait voulu prendre un orphelin.* He asked him if he would want to take an orphan. (AV) **Ils étaient orphelins. Ça fait, ils étaient misérables.* They were orphans. So, they were poor. (SM, An94) ◊ **•orphelin de mère** motherless <EV, LA, VM> **•orphelin de père** fatherless <EV, LA, VM> **•orphelin de père et de mère** parentless <EV, LA, VM> <*Loc:* AV, EV, LA, SM, VM, An94, Da84, Hi02>

orphelinage [ɔrfəlinaʒ] *n.m.* state of orphanhood <*Loc:* Da84>

orphelinat [ɔrfəlina, ɔrflina, œrfilina] *n.m.* orphanage *L'orphelinat était catholique.* The orphanage was Catholic. (AV) <*Loc:* AV, VM, Da84>

ortalon ♦see **ortolan**

orteil (**z-orteil**) [ɔrte, zɔrtɛj, ɔrtiʒ] *n.m./f.* toe *Moi je boitais avec un orteil qui venait malade à marcher sur les cailloux.* I used to limp with a toe that became sore from walking on pebbles. (LF) ◊ **•orteil de nègre** ***a*** black walnut ***b*** brazil nut <SB, LF, SB, VM, La99> **•le grand {gros} orteil / la grosse orteil** the big toe <LF, Da84> <*Loc:* AV, IB, LA, LF, SB, SM, TB, VM, Da84, Hi02, La99>

ortelon ♦see **ortolan**

ortie [ɔrti] *n.* stinging nettle <*Loc:* IV>

ortolan (**ortelon, ortalon**) [ɔrtolɑ̃, ɔrtəlɔ̃, ɔrtalɔ̃, artolɑ̃] *n.m.* **1** bobolink **2** cedar waxwing **3** black-throated bunting <*Loc:* TB, VM, Da84, Lv88, Re31>

os [ɔs, zo] (*pl.* **os** [os, ɔs, o]) *n.m.* bone *Il a avalé un os de poisson.* He swallowed a fish bone. (AV) *Tu pouvais entendre ses os après crâler.* You could hear his bones cracking. (LA) <*Loc:* LA, SM, TB, VM, Da84, Hi02, Lv88>

oser [oze] *v.intr.* to dare, venture **J'oserais dire.* I dare say. (Da84) *Je connais pas si il va oser dire quelque chose à soir.* I don't know if he will dare to say something tonight. (LA) <*Loc:* LA, Da84, Hi02>

ossaille [osaj] *n.m./f.* **1** bones (collectively) **2** bone *Y'a trop de petites ossailles dans la carpe jaune.* There are too many little bones in a yellow carp. (Lv88) *Un échelon, c'était une ossaille qu'avait de la viande après.* An "échelon" was a bone that had meat on it. (EV) <***Loc:*** EV, SM, TB, Da84, Gr86, Lv88, Ph36>

osseux, -euse [osø, -øz] *adj.* bony, with bones *Ça prend une viande osseuse pour faire une bonne sauce.* It takes a meat with bones to make a good sauce. (VM) <***Loc:*** VM, Da84>

ostination ♦see **obstination**

ostiné ♦see **obstiné**

ostiner ♦see **obstiner**

ostineur ♦see **obstineur**

ôter (**outer**) [ote, ute] **I** *v.tr.* **1** to remove, take off *Tu ôtes l'écale.* You remove the scales. (Lv88) *Il a outé son capot.* He took off his coat. (SM) *Quand tu fais un gombo, et ta viande part à bouillir, ça monte une écume en haut. Il faut tu ôtes ça.* When you make a gumbo, and your meat starts to boil, it makes a froth on the top. You have to take that off. (EV) **2** to remove, take out *La canne est écrasée pour ôter le jus.* The sugarcane is crushed in order to extract the juice. (IB) *À la raffinerie, ça oute le jus des cannes.* At the refinery, they take the juice out of the cane. (LA) **Faire ôter les amygdales.* To have one's tonsils removed. (Da84) **Il lui a ôté les deux yeux.* He plucked both his eyes out. (SL, An94) *Maman m'avait ôtée de l'école.* Mom had taken me out of school. (LA) **3** to take away *La police lui a ôté sa licence.* The police officer took away his license. (Lv88) **4** to turn off *Si tu ôtes le chauffage, t'as frais.* If you turn off the heat, you're cold. (Lv88) **5** to deduct *Ça ôte les taxes dessus mon chèque tous les mois.* They deduct my taxes from my check every month. (VM) **6** to relieve (pain) *Ces petites pilules lui ont ôté son mal de tête.* Those little pills relieved his headache. (LA) **7** to abolish *Il a promis d'outer les taxes et il a fait arien.* He promised to abolish taxes but he didn't do anything. (VM) **II s'ôter** *v.pron.* to remove o.s. **Ôte-toi de là!* Move from here! (Da84) ◊ **•ôter dessus la bouteille** to wean <SB> <***Loc:*** AC, EV, IB, JE, LA, LF, SB, SL, SM, TB, VM, An94, Da84, Hi02, Lv88>

ou [u] *conj.* or **Il y a tout le temps un rat-de-bois ou un chaoui ou un cocodril qui en mangeait trois ou quatre dans ma bande de canards.* There was always a possum or a raccoon or an alligator that would eat three or four of my flock of ducks. (EV, An94) **Il y a des maringouins ou quelque chose qui s'a posé sur moi dans la nuit.* There are mosquitos or something that landed on me during the night. (AC, An94) **Il y avait une vieille femme et un vieux bougre qu'étaient assis sur en avant le foyer un soir, et il y a une souris ou un rat qu'a passé.* There was an old woman and an old man who were sitting on it in front of the fireplace one night, and there's a mouse or a rat that passed by. (SM, An94) **Bien mais, ça se ressemble ou ça se ressemble pas?* Well then, do they resemble each other or not? (EV, An94) ◊ **•ou bien** or, or else *Vous-autres va m'écouter ou bien je vas dire à votre Popa!* You all will listen to me or else I'll tell your Papa! (EV) *Soit que tu viens asteur ou bien tu peux rester jusqu'à demain.* Either you come now, or else you can stay until tomorrow. (LA) <EV, LA, Da84> **•ou qui ou quoi** what *Je sais pas ou qui ou quoi il dit.* I don't know what he is saying. (IB) <IB> **•soit... ou** either . . . or *Et là il y a soit peut-être du* TREASURE *qu'est enterré, ou c'est peut-être quelqu'un qu'est mort.* And there's either maybe treasure buried there, or maybe someone who's dead. (TB) <TB, Wh83> <***Loc:*** AC, AV, EV, IB, IV, LA, LF, SL, SM, TB, VM, An94, Da84, Hi02, Wh83>

où ♦see **ayoù**

ouaché, -e [waʃe] *adj.* settled in comfortably (esp. in a reclining position) *Il était ouaché dans sa chaise.* He was settled comfortably in his chair. (EV) <***Loc:*** EV>

ouacher (s') [waʃe] *v.pron.* **1** to settle o.s. comfortably **Il s'est ouaché dans la chaise et i grouillait pas.* He settled into the chair and didn't move. (EV, Ph36) **2** to go to bed **I s'est ouaché d'bonne heure et il est pas levé encore.* He went to bed early and hasn't gotten up yet. (EV, Ph36) **3** to hide **I s'est ouaché passe qué [=parce que] il avait peur di constabe.* He hid because he was afraid of the policeman. (EV, Ph36) <***Loc:*** EV, Ph36>

ouais ♦see **oui**

ouaise ♦see WAYS

ouanga (**wanga**) [wɑ̃ga] *n.m.* **1** spell, magic spell **La vieille négresse m'a passé in ouanga.* The old black woman put a spell on me. (EV, Ph36) **2** magical charm <***Loc:*** EV, Gr86, Lv88, Ph36, Re31>

ouangateur [wɑ̃gatœr] *n.m.* conjurer, voodoo doctor, one who casts spells <***Loc:*** Re31>

ouaouaron (**wawaron**) [wawarɔ̃, warwarɔ̃, wararɔ̃] *n.m.* **1** bullfrog **2** frog <***Loc:*** AV, EV, SM, VM, Da84, Gu00, Hi02, Lv88, Ph36, Re31>

ouarjoujoum [wardʒudʒum] *onom.* splash **L'homme a sauté dans le bayou avec un "ouarjoujoum."* The man jumped in the bayou with a splash. (Gr86) <***Loc:*** Gr86>

ouapi ♦see **wapi**

oubli (**obli**) [ubli, obli] *n.m.* forgetfulness, oversight ◊ **•par oubli** through forgetfulness <Da84> <***Loc:*** LF, Da84, Lv88>

oubliance (**obliance**) [ublijɑ̃s, oblijɑ̃s] *n.f.* forgetfulness, oversight ◊ **•par obliance** by oversight <Da84> <***Loc:*** SB, Da84, Gr86, Hi02, Lv88>

oubliard, -e (**obliard, -e**) [ubliar, obliar, -ard] *adj.* forgetful *Il est tellement oubliard, il va manquer son enterrement.* He is so forgetful, he'll miss his own funeral. (LA) <***Loc:*** LA, Da84, Gr86>

oublier (**oblier**) [ublije, oblije] **I** *v.tr.* to forget *J'ai oublié.* I forgot. (AV) *Mets-lé là pour pas que je l'oblie.* Put it there so I don't forget it. (TB) **II s'oublier** *v.pron.* to forget (e.g. what one is doing) *Des fois, tu t'oublies et tu retournes dans les mêmes places.* Sometimes you forget yourself and you return to the same places. (LA) <***Loc:*** AC, AS, AV, EV, IB, JE, LA, LF, SB, SL, SM, TB, VM, An94, Da84, Gr86, Hi02, Lv88, Wh83>

oublieur, -euse (**oblieur, -euse, oublieux, -euse**) [ublijœr, oblijœr, ublijø, -øz] *adj.* forgetful *T'es trop jeune pour être tellement oublieur.* You are too young to be so forgetful. (LA) <***Loc:*** LA, Da84, Hi02>

oublieux ♦see **oublieur**

ouest [wɛst] *n.m.* west *Il y a un tas du monde dans l'ouest là qui connaît bien le français.* There are a lot of people in the west who know French well. (TB) <***Loc:*** EV, LA, LF, TB, An94, Da84, Hi02, Wh83>

oui (**ouais**) [wi, wɛ, we, wæ] *adv.* yes, yeah **"O, oui, monsieur," il dit, "ça, c'est correct."* "Oh, yes sir," he says, "that's right." (IV, An94) *Mais ouais, je vas.* But yes, I'm going. (VM) *Quand je parle en français, ça me demande, "Oh, mais vous parlez très bien français." Mais je dis, "Oui, mais j'ai parlé français toute ma vie."* When I speak French, they ask me, "Oh, you really speak French well." But I answer, "Yeah, but I've spoken French all my life." (SL) *Ouais. Je vais au* SHOW *ce soir.* Yes. I'm going to the show tonight. (SM) *Oui, la Louisiane c'est un vrai gombo.* Yes, Louisiana is a real gumbo. (LF) *Oh oui il avait un tremblement.* Oh yes, he had a shake. (TB) **Ah bien oui!* That's for sure! (Da84) **Ah foutre oui!* That's for sure! (Da84) <***Loc:*** AC, AS, AV, EV, IB, IV, JD, JE, LA, LF, SL, SM, TB, VM, An94, Da84, Gu82, Hi02, Lv88, St95>

ouichou [wiʃu] *interj.* cry for chasing away chickens <***Loc:*** EV, Ph36>

ouïe (**z-ouïe**) [wi, zɥi, zwi] *n.f.* gill *Les* GILLNETS, *c'est ça qui prend le poisson dans les ouïes.* The gill-nets, those are the ones that catch the fish by the gills. (IV) <***Loc:*** IV, VM, Da84, Lv88>

ouinque [wɛ̃k] *n.* nothing, not a word **Il a pas dit ouinque.* He did not say a word. (Da84) <***Loc:*** Da84>

ouioui[1] [wiwi] *n.m.* cicada <***Loc:*** SM, Guoo>

ouioui[2] [wiwi] *n.m.* [*baby talk*] urine, pee <***Loc:*** SM>

ouiskie ♦see **whisky**

ouragan (**oragan, orogan**) [uragɑ̃, uragɔ̃, oragɑ̃, urogɑ̃, orogɑ̃, arogɑ̃] *n.m./f.* **1** hurricane *Dans 1957, y a venu une grosse oragan. Alle s'appelait Audrey. Alle a tué au ras de cinq cents personnes.* In 1957, a big hurricane came. It was called Audrey. It killed as many as 500 people. (Guoo) **2** thunderstorm, heavy storm **3** tornado ◊ **•oragan de tonnerre** thunderstorm <LA, Lv88> **•il y a un ouragan dans la Chine** said to point out that something is upside down <VM, La99> <***Loc:*** AV, IB, IV, JE, LA, LF, SB, SJ, TB, VM, Da84, Guoo, Hi02, La99, Lv88>

ourler [urle] *v.tr.* to hem *Je te donnerai une robe de noce toute ourlée-z-en fils d'argent.* I'll give you a wedding dress all hemmed in silver thread. (VM, ch: *Le papier d'épingles*) <***Loc:*** VM, Da84>

ourlet [urlɛ, urle] *n.m.* **1** hem **2** hemline <***Loc:*** SL, Da84>

ours, -e [urs] *n.* **1** (*m.*) bear **2** (*f.*) she-bear, female bear ◊ **•ours noir** black bear <IV, Guoo> <***Loc:*** AC, IV, LF, SL, SM, TB, An94, Da84, Guoo, Hi02>

ousque, oùsque ♦see **ayoù**

outarde [utard] *n.f.* Canada goose <***Loc:*** IB, VM, Da84, Guoo>

outer ♦see **ôter**

outi ♦see **outil**

outil (**outi, z-outil**) [uti, util, zuti] *n.m.* tool, implement *Mon mari est après mener aujourd'hui parce que notre gendre a pas ramassé ses outils.* My husband is carrying on today because our son-in-law didn't bring back his tools. (LA) ◊ **•outils de table** silverware, flatware <VM> <***Loc:*** IB, LA, LF, PQ, SL, TB, VM, An94, Da84, Hi02, Re31>

outrage [utraʒ] *n.m.* insult, outrage <***Loc:*** Da84>

outrager [utraʒe] *v.tr.* to insult, outrage *Quand elle a parti du bal avec ce bougre, ça m'a outragé.* When she left the dance with that fellow, it outraged me. (LA) <***Loc:*** LA, Da84>

outrageux, -euse [utraʒø, -øz] *adj.* insulting, outrageous *C'est outrageux, ça qu'ils sont après dire.* It's outrageous, what they are saying. (LA) <***Loc:*** LA, Da84>

ouvère ♦see **ouverre**

ouverre (**ouvère, ouvrir, rouverre, rouvrir**) [uvær, ovær, ruvær, ruvrir] **I** *v.tr.* **1** to open *Oublie pas d'ouverre la porte pour moi quand j'arrive.* Don't forget to open the door for me when I arrive. (Guoo) *Le marchand va ouvrir la boutique.* The merchant is going to open the shop. (EV) *Ils sont jamais là pour me rouverre la porte.* They are never there to open the door for me. (Guoo) *Va donc rouverre donc mes fosses et la porte du cimetière pour m'en aller dans les flammes de l'enfer brûler.* So, go open up my gravesite and the cemetery gate so that I can go away to burn in the flames of Hell. (ch: *Viens donc t'assir sur la croix de ma tombe*) *Ça c'est le premier magasin qu'on a rouvert.* That's the first store that we opened. (TB) *C'est pour ouvert un* CAN. It is to open a can. (SM) *Il a pas un tas de force pour ouverre sa gueule.* He does not have a lot of strength to open his mouth. (AC) **2** to dredge *On était après ouverre une vieille coulée pour faire un meilleur égout.* We were dredging an old gully to improve the drainage. (EV) **II** *v.intr.* **1** to open *Ça rouvre et ça frème là.* It opens and closes there. (AC) **2** to open (of a flower) *Une rose peut prendre longtemps pour ouvrir.* A rose can take long to open. (LA) **3** to start, open *La chasse ouvre le premier samedi en octobre tous les ans, et là ça ferme la fin de février.* The hunting season starts the first Saturday of October each year, and it closes at the end of February. (SM) **III s'ouverre** *v.pron.* **1** to open *La porte était après s'ouverre doucement.* The door was opening slowly. (Lv88) *La porte s'ouvre à la droite.* The door opens to the right. (LA) **2** to open for o.s. *Comment-ce tu veux que je* DRIVE *là-bas, je peux pas m'ouverre les yeux.* How do you expect me to drive there, I can't open my eyes. (LF) *J'ai fait assez de l'argent pour m'ouverre une petite grosserie.* I made enough money to open myself a little grocery store. (EV) ◊ **•ouvrir son cœur** to open one's heart <Da84> **•ouvrir la lumière** to turn on the light <SM> <***Loc:*** AC, EV, LA, LF, SM, TB, VM, An77, An94, Da84, Gr86, Gu00, Hi02, Lv88>

ouvert, -e [uvær, -ært] *adj.* **1** open *Enfin le vieux PLANTATION STORE est toujours là. Il est pas ouvert.* Well, the old plantation store is still there. It's not open. (IB) **2** exposed **Tout à l'heure, il s'en vient un bougre en travers de la salle qui avait la chemise déboutonnée avec le jabot grand ouvert, avec les culottes qui étaient après pendre un peu bas et il avait le mouchoir juste manière enfoncé dans sa poche.* After a while, there came a guy across the hall who had an unbuttoned shirt with his chest exposed, with pants hanging a bit low and with a handkerchief sort of stuck in his pocket. (SL, An94) <***Loc:*** IB, SL, An94, Da84, Hi02>

ouvertation [uværtasjɔ̃] *n.f.* opening *Une fenêtre c'est une ouvertation, et un chassis c'est avec des vitres dessus.* A "fenêtre" is an opening, and a "chassis" has panes of glass in it. (AS) <***Loc:*** AS>

ouvertement [uværtmɑ̃] *adv.* openly, outwardly *Là je m'ai mis ouvertement pour soigner des petits.* Then I openly started taking care of children. (EV) *Il a fait ça ouvertement devant le diable et tout le monde.* He did that openly in front of the devil and everyone. (LA) <***Loc:*** EV, LA, Da84>

ouverture [uværtyr] *n.f.* **1** opening, gap, hole **2** any opening in a building (e.g. door, window) <***Loc:*** Da84>

ouvrage [uvraʒ] *n.m./f.* **1** task, chore, job *Je faisais toutes sortes d'ouvrages.* I did all kinds of jobs. (AC) *Un ouvrage tue-corps.* A back-breaking job. (VM) **2** labor, work *On était bien connus dans ces temps-là. On faisait tout le temps de la bonne ouvrage, tu connais, c'était pas moitié fait.* We were well known in those days. We always did good work, you know, it wasn't half done. (TB) *Tous les morceaux et l'ouvrage aussi pour vingt piasses.* All the parts and the labor as well for twenty dollars. (EV) *C'est trop d'ouvrage.* It's too much work. (JE) **3** job, work *Il est charpentier, il a pour se baigner après l'ouvrage.* He is a carpenter, he has to take a shower after work. (Lv88) *J'ai arrivé tard à l'ouvrage.* I got to work late. (AV) *On a déjeuné, puis on est parti à l'ouvrage.* We ate breakfast, then we left for work. (EV) **4** occupation, line of work *Quoi c'est ton ouvrage?* What is your occupation? (Lv88) ◊ **•ouvrage de cour** yard work, gardening <Lv88> **•faire ses ouvrages** to do one's chores <Da84> **•prendre l'ouvrage** to go to work <Da84> <***Loc:*** AC, EV, IV, JD, JE, LA, PQ, SJ, SL, SM, TB, VM, An94, Da84, Gr86, Hi02, Lv88, Ph36>

ouvré [uvre] *n.m.* bird's eye cloth (used for making diapers) <***Loc:*** SJ>

ouvreur [uvrœr] *n.m.* opener ◊ **•ouvreur de canne** can opener <LA> <***Loc:*** LA, Da84>

ouvrier [uvrije] *n.m.* carpenter *Mon père c'était un ouvrier, un charpentier.* My father was a carpenter. (SM) *Ma maison ici, c'est moi et mon garçon qu'a tout bâti ça. On avait un ouvrier pour nous aider, et tout le dedans c'est nous-autres, moi et mon garçon qu'a tout fini ça.* My house here, it's my son and I that built it. We had a carpenter to help us, and the inside, it's my son and I that finished all of it. (TB) <***Loc:*** LA, LF, SJ, SL, SM, TB, VM, Da84, Hi02, Lv88>

ouverre ♦see **ouvrir**

ovaire [ovær] *n.m.* ovary <***Loc:*** TB, Da84>

OVEN [ɔv, ʌvən] *n.m.* oven *Un casserole, tu peux mettre ça dans l'OVEN et tu cuis ton manger dedans.* A casserole, you can put that in the oven and you cook your food in it. (JD) <***Loc:*** JD, LF, SM, TB,VM>

OVERCOAT [ovkot, ovokot, o^{u}vəɹko^{u}t] *n.m.* overcoat <***Loc:*** EV, SB, SM, VM, Ph36>

OWN [o^{u}n] *v.tr.invar.* to own *Faut que tu OWN ta terre à toi-même.* You have to own your own land. (TB) *Si j'ownais cette terre là en arrière je pourrais les pêcher dans l'hiver.* If I owned that land back there I could fish for them in the winter. (TB) *Il ownait le bloc entier.* He owned the entire block. (TB) <***Loc:*** AS, TB>

P

p'tit ♦see **petit**

p'us ♦see **pus**

pacane [pakɑ̃n] *n.f.* **1** pecan *J'ai planté des pacaniers en arrière. [...] je plante ça pour quand on va être vieux, on va avoir des pacanes à ramasser.* I planted pecan trees out back. I plant them so that when we're old, we'll have pecans to gather. (TB) **2** least sandpiper **3** female genitals ◊ **•pacane à cochon** wild pecan <Da84> **•pacane amère** pignut, water hickory <SM, VM, Lv88, Re31> **•pas... pacane** nothing *J'ai pas vu pacane.* I didn't see a thing. (La99) *Il m'a vu, mais il m'a pas dit pacane.* He saw me, but he didn't say anything to me. (SM) <SM, La99> <***Loc:*** LA, SL, SM, TB, VM, Da84, Guoo, Hio2, La99, Lv88, Re31>

pacanier [pakɑ̃je] *n.m.* **1** pecan tree *Et on était assis sus la galerie, et on était allongé à côté des pacaniers dessus la galerie.* And we were sitting on the porch, we were stretched out next to the pecan trees on the porch. (TB) **2** pecan wood ◊ **•pacanier amer** bitter pecan, water hickory tree <Re31> **•pacanier greffé** cultivated pecan tree <Re31> **•pacanier sauvage {d'aventure}** wild pecan tree <Re31> <***Loc:*** CL, IV, LA, LF, TB, VM, Da84, Guoo, Hio2, Lv88, Re31>

pacanière [pakɑ̃jær] *n.f.* pecan grove, pecan orchard <***Loc:*** SM, VM, Da84, Guoo, Lv88, Re31>

pacotille [pakotij] *n.f.* **1** cheap stuff, shoddy goods, junk **2** insignificant person or thing **3** nonsense, humbug, foolishness <***Loc:*** SJ, Da84>

padegau ♦see **pategau**

padna (padnat, partner) [padna, pana] *n.m./f.* **1** friend, buddy, chum, pal *C'était un bon vieux homme, on était bons padnas moi et lui.* He was a good old boy, we were good friends, me and him. (LF) **2** partner (in business, a card game, etc.) *Mais A. est un padna dedans le STOCK, tu connais ça qu'est dans le magasin. Il est padna là-dedans.* But A. is a business partner in the stock, you know, the stuff that's inside the store. He's a partner in that. (TB) <***Loc:*** EV, JE, TB, Da84, Guoo, Hio2, Lv88>

padnat ♦see **padna**

padriole ♦see **perdriole**

pagaille [pagaj] *n.f.* **1** paddle, oar *Il s'a trouvé à l'autre bout du lac sans pagaille pour son bateau.* He found himself at the other end of the lake without a paddle for his boat. (Guoo) **2** paddle, type of large flat wooden spoon *Et là les hommes ça prendait ces grosses chaudières noires-là, et ça prend ces petits carreaux de gras, et ça mettait ça dans la chaudière, et ça prendait des pagailles pour brasser ça, tu vois.* And then the men took those big black kettles, and they take these little pieces of fat, and they put them in the kettle, and they took paddles to stir it, you see. (LF) **3** pedal (e.g. of a sewing machine) **4** foot *Ôte tes grosses pagailles.* Move your big feet. (VM) **5** disorder, mess ◊ **•à la pagaille** by means of paddling *On part à la pagaille.* We paddle off. (LF) <LF> <***Loc:*** IV, JE, LA, LF, SM, VM, Da84, Guoo, Hio2, Lv88, Re31>

pagailler (pagayer) [pagaje] **I** *v.tr.* **1** to paddle (a boat) *Tu connais pagailler une pirogue?* Do you know how to paddle a pirogue? (SM) **2** to pedal (the foot pedal of a sewing machine) *J'avais pagaillé cette machine, pis j'étais en famille. Mes pieds étaient enflés.* I had pedaled that machine, and I was pregnant. My feet were swollen. (SL) **II** *v.intr.* to paddle *C'est ça, de temps en temps je vas pagailler ici, pogner des poissons rouges en arrière.* That's it, from time to time I'll paddle around here, catch redfish out back. (TB) <***Loc:*** IV, JE, LA, LF, SL, SM, TB, Da84, Guoo, Hio2, Lv88, Re31>

pagailleur (pagayeur) [pagajœr] *n.m.* paddler, one who paddles (a canoe, pirogue, etc.) <***Loc:*** SM, Re31>

pagayer ♦see **pagailler**

pagayeur ♦see **pagailleur**

page [paʒ] *n.f.* page, sheet (of paper) <***Loc:*** Da84, Hio2>

pagée (paget) [paʒe, paʒɛ] *n.m./f.* section of fence between two posts, panel ◊ **•pagée de barrière** section of fence between two posts <Da84, Lv88> **•pagée de dents** several teeth in a row <LF> <***Loc:*** EV, LF, VM, Da84, Lv88, Ph36>

paget ♦see **pagée**

païen[1], -nne [pajɛ̃, -ɛ̃n] *adj.* pagan, heathen *C'est du monde païen. Eusse va pas à l'église.* They are heathens. They don't go to church. (LF) <***Loc:*** LF, Da84>

païen[2], -nne [pajɛ̃, -ɛ̃n] *n.* pagan, heathen <***Loc:*** Da84>

paillasse[1] [pajas] *n.f.* straw mattress (usu. made of teased corn shucks), corn shuck mattress *Là ça faisait un matelas avec la paille. Ça aurait ôté les morceaux durs d'endans-là. Ça, t'appelais ça une paillasse.* They made mattresses with straw. They would take out the hard pieces. You called it a "paillasse." (SL) <***Loc:*** SL, Da84, Hio2>

paillasse[2] [pajas] *n.m.* **1** clown, buffoon **2** obese or overweight person <***Loc:*** IB, TB, Da84>

paillassée [pajase] *n.f.* contents of a straw mattress <***Loc:*** JE>

paillasson [pajasɔ̃] *n.m.* collar pad made of shucks or moss, put under a horse's wooden collar <***Loc:*** IB, Ph36>

paille [paj] *n.f.* **1** straw **Quand il a revenu, il pouvait pas trouver l'aiguille. Et quand la mère est venue investiguer, il dit, "Je l'ai tirée dans le wagon de paille ici, Mam."* When he came back, he couldn't find the needle. And when his mother came to investigate, he says, "I threw it into the wagon full of straw there, Mom." (EV, An94) **2** shuck, husk, outer leaves (of a stalk of sugarcane, an ear of corn, etc.) *Tu outais les pailles, tu coupais le faît avec un couteau de cannes.* You cut off the outer leaves, you cut off the top [of the cane plant] with a cane knife. (LA) *Là ça faisait des matelas avec la paille.* They used to make mattresses with corn shucks. (SL) ◊ **•paille à {de} maïs** corn shuck, husk <LF, SL, SM, TB, VM, Da84> **•paille chat-tigre** ***a*** needle grass ***b*** Roemer's rush <VM, Lv88, Re31> **•paille de riz** haystack <VM, Fa77> **•paille fine** marsh grass <VM> **•paille jaune** ***a*** switch grass ***b*** broom sage ***c*** bushy beardgrass, bushy bluestem ***d*** feather grass <LA, VM, Da84, Re31> **•à la paille** to bed, in bed <AS, La99> <***Loc:*** AS, EV, IV, JE, LA, LF, SJ, SL, SM, TB, VM, An94, Da84, Fa77, Hi02, La99, Lv88, Re31>

paille-en-queue [pajɑ̃kø] *n.* pintail duck, northern pintail <***Loc:*** IV, JE, LF, SL, TB, VM, Re31>

pailler ♦see **épailler**

paillette [pajɛt] *n.f.* salt water marsh grass <***Loc:*** VM>

paillon [pajɔ̃] *n.m.* pintail duck <***Loc:*** Da84>

pain [pɛ̃] *n.m.* **1** bread *Ma mame cuisait du pain dans la cheminée.* My mother used to bake bread in the fireplace. (TB) **2** one's living, sustenance *Eusse va tout le temps avoir quelqu'un de plus mieux, et c'est pas ça qui me tracasse, mais c'est pour mon gagner mon pain, tu connais?* There's always going to be someone better, and that's not what worries me, but I have to earn my living too, you know? (TB) ◊ **•pain de femme {famille / ménage}** homemade bread <LF, SM, TB> **•pain de froment** wheat bread <Da84> **•pain (de) maïs** cornbread <TB, Da84, Hi02> **•pain (de) poudine** bread pudding <JE> **•pain de sucre** ***a*** hypocrite who appears very virtuous to others ***b*** person with stiff manners <JE, La99> **•pain français** ***a*** French bread, long crusty loaf of white bread ***b*** French toast <IB, JE, SL, Lv88> **•pain grillé** toast, toasted bread <Da84, Lv88> **•pain langui** bread that has not risen enough or has cooked too slowly <Da84> **•pain levé** ***a*** baked cornbread ***b*** homemade bread <VM, Fa77> **•pain moulé** bread crumbs *Mais y a plein du monde qui prendait la cervelle [...] Eux-autres passe ça dans du pain moulé. Et là ça frit ça.* But there are a lot of people who would take the brain. They dip it in bread crumbs. And then they fry it. (LF) <LF> **•pain perdu** French toast *Le matin tu manges du pain perdu, je prends des œufs, je les casse et je les bats bien, je chauffe ma graisse pas trop chaud, mon pain je le jette dedans, je le mets dans ma chaudière et je le fais frire bien, ça c'est bien bon, là tu prends du sirop et tu le vides sur ton pain perdu.* In the morning, you eat French toast, I take some eggs, I break them and beat them well, I cook my fat not too hot, I throw my bread in it, I put it in my skillet and fry it well, it's really good, then you take some syrup and pour it on your French toast. (AV) <AV, LA, LF, SM, TB, VM, Da84, Re31> **•pain tressé** twist-loaf <Re31> <***Loc:*** AC, AV, EV, JE, LA, LF, SL, SM, TB, VM, Da84, Fa77, Hi02, La99, Re31>

pair [pær] *n.m.* udder <***Loc:*** JE>

paire [pær] *n.f.* **1** pair *La première paire de souliers que mon j'ai mis mes pieds dedans là, eh ben, j'ai payé pour mon-même.* The first pair of shoes I ever put my feet in, I paid for myself. (LF) **2** couple *Faudra que tu me donnes une paire de jours.* You'll have to give me a couple of days. (TB) **3** pair (in cards) <***Loc:*** EV, JE, LA, LF, TB, Da84, Hi02>

paisé, -e [peze] *adj.* quiet, silent, reticent, morose *Quoi y a? T'es assez paisé à ce soir.* What's wrong? You are rather quiet tonight. (VM) <***Loc:*** VM>

paix [pɛ, pe] *n.f.* peace, calm **Donne-moi la paix.* Leave me alone. (Da84) **Fous-moi la paix.* Leave me alone. (Da84) ◊ **•paix, toi! / pais-toi!** be quiet! <IB, LF, TB, Lv88> <***Loc:*** IB, LF, TB, Da84, Hi02, Lv88>

pajamas ♦see **pyjamas**

palais [palɛ, pale] *n.m.* **1** palace **2** palate (of the mouth) ◊ **•palais bleu** very mean person <La99> **•palais fendu** cleft palate <EV> <***Loc:*** EV, Da84, La99>

palangre (palanque) [palɑ̃g, palɑ̃k, palɑ̃n] *n.f.* trotline *Une palangre eusse appelait ça, une grande ligne, et eusse amarrait des appâts dessus.* They called that a trotline, a big fishing line, and they tied bait to it. (TB) <***Loc:*** AS, LF, PQ, TB, VM, Da84, Gu00, Re31>

palanque ♦see **palangre**

palao [palao] *n.m.* black bullhead catfish <***Loc:*** SM>

pâle [pal] *adj.* **1** pale *Et un soir eusse avait assayé de nettoyer la maison, en-dedans la maison, c'était vert. [...] Un pâle vert, et c'était tout moisi, ça voulait pas sortir.* And one evening they had tried to clean the house, inside the house it was green. A pale green, and it was all moldy, it didn't want to come off. (TB) **2** colorless *Le whisky que ça faisait dans le temps était pâle.* The whiskey they made in those days was colorless. (LA) <***Loc:*** LA, TB, Da84, Hi02>

paleron [palrɔ̃] *n.m.* post, stump <***Loc:*** IB>

paletot [palto] *n.m.* coat <***Loc:*** IB>

palette [palɛt] *n.f.* **1** paddle *Eux-autres m'a baleiné à moi, moi je m'ai fait baleiner. À la palette. Oh ouais, t'avais le droit de faire ça. Les maîtresses d'école et les maîtres d'école te flaillait. J'ai fait la palette, ils m'ont fait faire la palette!* They whipped me, I got myself whipped. With a paddle. Oh yes, you used to have the right to do that. School teachers would whip you. I made the paddle, they made me make the paddle! (TB) **2** pedal (e.g. gas pedal in a car) *Les enfants, ça se faisait des chars. Ça prendait un gros couvert, et ça enfonçait un morceau de bois dans la terre comme ça-là. Et là eux-autres attachait le couvert comme ça-là. Et là eux-autres mettait un autre morceau de bois pour faire la palette. Et là ça c'était leur char.* Children made themselves cars. They took a big blanket, and they stuck a piece of wood in the earth like that. And they attached the blanket like that. And they put down another piece of wood for the gas pedal. And that was their car. (TB) **3** paddle, type of large flat wooden spoon *Ça brassait les gratons avec une palette.* They would stir cracklins with a big flat wooden spoon. (LA) **4** spatula, pancake turner **5** stick of gum *Tu veux de la gomme? Tiens, je vas te donner une palette pour toi et une pour ton frère.* Do you want some gum? Here, I'll give you a stick for you and one for your brother. (EV) **6** pallet *Les sacs de* FEED *étaient dessus une palette dans le coin.* The sacks of feed were on a pallet in the corner. (LA) **7** wooden flap on a diatonic accordion *J'ai une palette de cassée sur mon accordéon.* I have a broken flap on my accordion. (LA) **8** propeller *Et là ça mettait ça à l'eau et ça quittait ça tout partout épaillé dans les lacs. Les bateaux enroulaient sa palette. Et là les poissons pourrissait dans ça. Et c'est un gaspille.* They would put them [gill nets] in the water and they left them everywhere, scattered throughout the lakes. Boats would get their propellers tangled up. And fish would rot in them. And it's a waste. (TB) **9** pod (of peas, beans, etc.) ◊ **•palette à mouche(s)** flyswatter <LA, VM, Fa77, Lv88> **•palette à z-œufs** egg beater <VM, Fa77, Lv88> **•palette de gomme** stick of gum *Donne-moi une palette de gomme.* Give me a stick of gum. (VM) <EV, VM> **•palette de l'épaule** shoulder blade, scapula <IB, Lv88> **•palette du foyer** small shovel for removing ashes from a fireplace <JE> <***Loc:*** EV, IB, JE, LA, TB, VM, Da84, Fa77, Lv88>

pâlezir ♦see **pâlir**

pâlir (**pâlezir**) [palir, palzir] *v.intr.* to become pale, grow pale, fade *Il a pâli quand il a entendu ça.* He paled when he heard that. (AC) *T'aurais dû voir comment elle avait pâlezi.* You should have seen how she had paled. (LA) <***Loc:*** AC, LA, SM, VM, Da84>

palma Christi (**pauma Christi**) [palmakristi, pɔmakristi] *n.m.* castor bean plant <***Loc:*** IB, VM>

palme [palm] *n.f.* palm, palm branch <***Loc:*** Da84>

palmée [palme] *n.f.* ◊ **•se donner la palmée** to shake hands upon concluding a bargain <JE> <***Loc:*** JE>

palmier [palmje] *n.m.* **1** palm tree **2** palmetto <***Loc:*** VM, Da84>

palon [palɔ̃] *n.m.* dasher, wooden handle of a butter churn *Tu mets le crème dans une grosse jarre et il y avait un palon dedans, on allait en haut et en bas avec le palon.* You put the cream in a large jar and there was a churning stick inside that you moved up and down. (AC) <***Loc:*** AC>

palonnier [palɔ̃je, palɑ̃je] *n.m.* swingtree, swingletree, singletree, swingle-bar, swing bar (wooden bar by means of which a harness is attached to a plow, wagon, or buggy) ◊ **•palonnier double** doubletree <Da84> **•palonnier simple** singletree <Da84> <***Loc:*** AC, EV, SJ, SL, Da84>

pâlot, -otte [palo, palɔt] *adj.* **1** pale *Elle sort jamais. Elle est tout pâlotte.* She never goes outside. She's all pale. (VM) **2** heavy, clumsy, awkward and dull-witted *Pauvre pâlot!* Poor fool! (VM) <***Loc:*** VM>

palotte [palɔt] *adv.* clumsily, awkwardly, with difficulty *Et on faisait peur à les râles, et p'is ça vole palotte. C'est pas comme un canard ou une tourte ou une perdrix, ça. Ça vole mal.* And we scared the rails, and then they fly awkwardly. It's not like a duck or a dove or a quail. They fly poorly. (VM) <***Loc:*** VM>

palourde [palurd] *n.f.* **1** clam **2** freshwater clam, mussel <***Loc:*** LF, TB, Da84, Gu00, Hi02>

pâmer [pɑ̃me] **I** *v.intr.* **1** to choke, stifle, lose one's breath (due to anger, fever, etc.) *Le 'tit bébé a pâmé.* The little baby choked. (Lv88) **2** to hold one's breath until blue in the face (usu. of children) *L'enfant est après pâmer.* The child is holding its breath. (VM) **II se pâmer** *v.pron.* **1** to lose one's breath (from laughing, crying, exertion, rage, etc.) *Il s'a pâmé de rire.* He lost his breath laughing. (LA) **2** to hold one's breath until blue in the face (usu. of children) *Ma 'tite fille s'a pâmée.* My little daughter held her breath until she was blue in the face. (SM) <***Loc:*** LA, SM, TB, VM, Da84, Lv88>

pamphlet [pɑ̃flɛ, pɑ̃fle] *n.m.* pamphlet <***Loc:*** Lv88>

pamplemousse [pɑ̃pləmus] *n.m.* grapefruit <***Loc:*** EV, CL>

panage [pɑ̃naʒ] *n.m.* set of horns, antlers <***Loc:*** JE>

panama [pɑ̃nɑ̃ma] *n.m.* panama hat <***Loc:*** Da84>

panaris [pɑ̃nari] *n.m.* whitlow, infection of the finger or toe around the nail <***Loc:*** Da84>

paner [pɑ̃ne] *v.tr.* to coat with breading for cooking *Ma mère avait jamais vu ça, paner de la volaille pour le cuire dans le four.* My mother had never seen that, breading chicken to cook it in the oven. (LA) ◊ **•paner la botte** to die <La99> <***Loc:*** LA, La99>

panier [pɑ̃je, pɑ̃jɛ̃] *n.m.* **1** basket *Il partait sur son bicycle avec l'accordéon dans le panier.* He left on his bicycle with the accordion in the basket. (LA) **2** hamper *Mets ton linge sale dans le panier.* Put your dirty clothes in the hamper. (LA) **3** muzzle *Il a fallu je mets un panier dessus mon chien. Il voulait mordre le postillon.* I had to put a muzzle on my dog. He wanted to bite the postman. (VM) **4** basket or container with a capacity of 1/4 barrel or 52.5 lbs., used in the seafood fishing industry ◊ **•panier champagne** basket or container with a capacity of 1/3 barrel or 70 lbs., used in the seafood fishing industry <LF, Lv88> **•panier chinois** basket or container with a capacity of 1/2 barrel or 110 lbs., used in the seafood fishing industry <LF, Lv88> **•panier de grosseries** grocery basket <LA> <***Loc:*** AC, AV, JE, LA, LF, PQ, SB, TB, VM, Da84, Hi02, Lv88>

panique [pɑ̃nik] *n.f.* **1** panic **2** scare, fright <***Loc:*** Da84>

paniquer [pɑ̃nike] *v.intr.* to panic *Il a paniqué quand le bougre a sorti son couteau.* He panicked when the guy took out his knife. (LA) <***Loc:*** LA, Lv88>

panne [pɑ̃n] *n.f.* dewlap, loose skin that hangs from the neck of cattle <***Loc:*** JE>

panneau [pɑ̃no] *n.m.* **1** small lead weight formerly used to weigh down the hem of a skirt **2** space under the back seat of a skiff ◊ **•être dans le panneau à qqn** to be wise to s.o.'s tricks <SB, La99> <***Loc:*** JE, SB, La99>

panquet [pɑ̃kɛ, pɑ̃ke] *n.m.* goad, instrument used to prod animals <***Loc:*** JE>

panse [pɑ̃s] *n.f.* **1** stomach (usu. of a cow or pig) prepared as food, tripe *Habitudement c'était la panse de bête, d'animau. Asteur la panse c'est bien lavée avec de l'eau chaud et du soda et c'est cuit avec de la sauce de tomate.* Usually it was the stomach of a cow, a bovine. Nowadays the stomach is washed out well with hot water and baking soda and it's cooked with tomato sauce. (LF) **2** potbelly, paunch *Sa panse lui dépassait la ceinture.* His paunch lapped over his belt. (LA) ◊ **•panse bourrée** pig stomach, stuffed and prepared for eating <EV, JD, SL> **•panse de bête** ***a*** cow stomach ***b*** first cow stomach ***c*** tripe <EV, LA, SM> <***Loc:*** AV, EV, IB, JD, LA, LF, SJ, SL, SM, TB, VM, Da84, Lv88>

pantalon [pɑ̃talɔ̃, patalɔ̃] *n.m.* pants, trousers ◊ **•pantalons courts** short pants, shorts <LF> <***Loc:*** AC, EV, JD, JE, LF, SM, TB, Da84, Hi02>

pantelettes [pɑ̃tlɛt] *n.f.pl.* women's underwear, panties <***Loc:*** Lv88>

panthère [pɑ̃tær] *n.f.* panther <***Loc:*** Da84>

paon [pɑ̃] *n.m.* peacock **Faraud comme un paon.* Dressed up like a peacock. (Da84) <***Loc:*** VM, Da84, Fa77>

papa (**pape, pop, popa, poupa**) [papa, pap, pɔp, popa, pupa, pɔpɔ] *n.m.* father, dad, daddy, papa *Mon popa a* RETIRE *à peu près cinq ans de ça.* My dad retired about five years ago. (LF) *Le vieux monde, ma mame et mon pape, eux parlaient bien peu d'anglais.* The old folks, my mom and my pop, they spoke very little English. (PQ) ◊ **•Papa Noël** Santa Claus <LF> **•popa d'élève** stepfather <TB> **•vieux-pape** [*term of endearment*] grandfather <SM> <***Loc:*** AC, EV, LA, JE, LF, PQ, TB, Da84, Lv88>

papabotte (**pape-à-botte**) [papabɔt] *n.m./f.* upland plover, sandpiper <***Loc:*** JE, Da84, Lv88, Re31>

papaille [papaj] *n.f.* party, social gathering *On a fait fleuri du tactac pour amener à la papaille.* We popped popcorn to take to the party. (TB) <***Loc:*** TB>

papano ♦see **pompano**

pape[1] [pap] *n.m.* pope <***Loc:*** VM, Da84, Fa77>

pape[2] [pap] *n.m.* **1** sparrow **2** painted bunting **3** any of a variety of small, colorful finches, including the canary **4** generic term for a small bird ◊ **•pape choc** blackbird <Re31> **•pape de bois** Baltimore oriole <Re31> **•pape Natchitoches** scarlet tanager <JE> **•pape rouge {vert / doré}** painted bunting <IB> **•petit pape** ***a*** oriole ***b*** sparrow ***c*** bunting ***d*** Baltimore oriole <JE, SB, Lv88> <***Loc:*** IB, JE, PQ, SB, SM, VM, Da84, Hi02, Lv88, Re31>

pape[3] ♦see **papa**

pape-à-botte ♦see **papabotte**

papegai, papegau ♦see **pategau**

papier[1] [papje] *v.tr.* to wallpaper *On a papié ça, on a nettoyé ça, on a resté en dedans* UNTIL *on a bâti une 'tite maison là où Mavis est.* We wallpapered it, we cleaned it, we lived inside until we built a little house where Mavis is. (SL) <***Loc:*** SL>

papier[2] [papje] *n.m.* **1** paper *Tu veux un crayon et un papier?* Do you want a piece of paper and a pencil? (LF) **2** newspaper **3** wallpaper ◊ **•papier-mâché** papier-mâché <Da84> **•papier-nouvelles** newspaper <JE> **•papier sablé {sableux}** sandpaper <VM, Lv88> <***Loc:*** AC, EV, JE, LA, LF, SL, VM, An94, Da84, Hi02, Lv88>

papiéter [papjete] *v.tr.* to wallpaper *On est après papiéter sa chambre.* We're papering his room. (IB) <***Loc:*** AV, IB, SJ>

papillon [papijɔ̃] *n.m.* butterfly <***Loc:*** AV, JE, SM, TB, Da84, Hi02>

papillote [papijɔt] *n.f.* hair curler ◊ **•en papillottes** ***a*** in curlers ***b*** in curls <Da84> **•faire des papillotes** to do fancy acrobatic tricks <SB, La99> <***Loc:*** SB, TB, Da84, La99>

pâquage [pakaʒ] *n.m.* knocking eggs (game in which Easter eggs are broken against each other) **Et la paroisse des Avoyelles a son coutume de Jour de Pâques, le "Pâquage des Œufs."* And Avoyelles Parish has its Easter Sunday custom, the game of "pâquage." (Wh83) <***Loc:*** Wh83>

pâquer [pake] *v.intr.* to knock eggs, play the game of breaking Easter eggs against each other **Alors les Cadiens [...] se délaissaient le dimanche de Pâques en jouant à pâquer.* So on Easter Sunday Cajuns entertained themselves by breaking Easter eggs against each other. (SM) <***Loc:*** SM, Da84, Hi02, Lv88>

Pâques [pak] *n.m.* **1** Easter **2** Easter duties **3** Jewish Passover ◊ **•faire Pâques avant Carême** to become pregnant before getting married <La99> **•faire ses Pâques** to do one's Easter duties, receive communion during the Easter season <Da84> **•petites Pâques** *(n.f.pl.)* Palm Sunday <Re31> <***Loc:*** LF, Da84, Hi02, La99, Re31>

paquet [pakɛ, pake] *n.m.* **1** package, parcel *Il avait de la viande qu'était tout arrangée, et il vendait ça, le monde achetait ça là par petits paquets.* He had meat that was all prepared, and he sold it, people bought it in small packages. (TB) **2** pack, bundle *Un gros paquet de linge, il emmenait sur le dos.* A big pack of clothing that he carried on his back. (TB) **3** paper bag **4** cluster of eggs that a female crab carries under her abdominal apron *Une crabe avec le paquet, tu peux pas ramasser ça. Là avant qu'il a le paquet tu peux les ramasser et les manger. Quand les œufs est en-dedans, en-dedans la coquille, y a plein plein d'œufs.* A crab with the cluster of eggs, you can't gather them. Before they have the eggs you can gather them and eat them. When the eggs are inside, in the shell, there are many, many eggs. (TB) ◊ **•paquet de raisins** bunch of grapes <JE> **•faire son paquet** to pack up and leave <Da84> <***Loc:*** EV, JE, TB, Da84, Lv88>

paqueter [pakte] *v.tr.* to pack, pack up, package *Il a paqueté son linge; il a parti.* He packed his clothes; he left. (VM) <*Loc:* VM, Da84>

par [par] *prep.* **1** by, through the agency or action of *Le petit bougre là s'a fait mordre par une serpent deux ans de ça.* The little guy got bit by a snake two years ago. (LF) *C'est par un musicien, son nom est Happy Fats.* It's by a musician, his name is Happy Fats. (TB) **2** by, by means of *La seule manière tu peux arriver là c'est par bateau.* The only way you can get there is by boat. (TB) *Ça les a reconnus par leurs souliers et leur linge.* They recognized them by their shoes and their clothes. (AC) *Alle a pris Myrtle par les cheveux.* She grabbed Myrtle by the hair. (TB) **3** by way of, through *Moi j'ai sauté par un chassis en arrière.* I jumped out through a back window. (AV) *Alle avait les vers, ça lui sortait par le nez, et les oreilles, la bouche et tout.* She had worms, they were coming out her nose, her ears, her mouth and all. (TB) **4** by, in units of *Y avait un* ICE PICK *et eux-autres cassait ça par petits blocs. Eusse vendait ça cinq sous.* There was an icepick and they broke it into little blocks. They sold them for five cents. (TB) **5** by (used in measurements) *C'était tout vendu un arpent par quarante arpents.* It was all sold [in lots that were] one arpent by 40 arpents. (LF) **6** by, per *La limite des truites grises, c'est vingt-cinq par jour par personne.* The limit on speckled trout is 25 per day per person. (TB) *Vingt-quatre heures par jour.* 24 hours a day. (EV) ◊ **•par ainsi** thus, consequently <JE> **•par après** afterward, after the fact **J'ai su par après que Henri avait été renvoyé en France, à une place nommée Belle Ile.* I found out afterward that Henri had been sent to France, to a place called Belle Ile. (An98) <An98> **•par derrière** from behind <Da84> **•par devant / par en avant** from in front *Les cannes rentrent par en avant.* The sugarcane enters [the machine] from in front. (AS) <AS, Da84> **•par en arrière** in the back *Pour aller au magasin on passait par en arrière.* To go to the store we went the back way. (TB) <TB> **•par en-dessous** underhanded, dishonest <JE> **•par exemple** for example <Da84> **•par exprès** on purpose <Da84> **•par hasard** by chance <Da84> **•par ici** ***a*** this way ***b*** around here *Et là t'es par icitte y a longtemps?* Have you been around here a long time? (TB) <TB, Da84> **•par là** that way, over there **S'en aller par là.* To go that way. (LA, An94) <LA, An94, Da84> **•par rapport à** because of *Je parle plus en anglais asteur par rapport à l'autre monde.* I speak more English now because of other people. (TB) <TB, Hi02> **•par rapport que** because **Par exemple, on peut pas fouiller dans la terre le Vendredi Saint par rapport qu'on va 'oir le sang de Jésus et c'est ein péché mortel.* For example, we can't dig in the earth on Good Friday because we'll see the blood of Jesus and it's a mortal sin. (ThCa: *Mille misères*) <Hi02, ThCa> **•par terre** down, to the ground **Bon, mais, en égrandissant le trou, il a échappé la hache par terre.* Good, but while enlarging the hole, he dropped the ax on the ground. (EV, An94) *On commence à couper les cannes grandes avec ces nouvelles autres machines qu'on a là, un* TWO-ROW *machine alle coupe deux rangs à la fois, alle couche les cannes par terre.* We're starting to cut the tall sugarcane with these other new machines, a two-row machine cuts two rows at once, it flattens the cane. (AS) <AS, EV, An94, Da84> **•par tours** by turns <Da84> **•ça par exemple!** what?! <Da84> <*Loc:* AC, AS, AV, EV, JE, LF, TB, An94, An98, Da84, Hi02, ThCa>

paraboles [parabɔl] *n.* ◊ **•donner des paraboles** to scold, reprimand <JE> <*Loc:* JE>

parachute [paraʃyt] *n.m.* parachute <*Loc:* Da84>

parade [parad] *n.f.* **1** parade *C'est là où tous les petits villages a des parades pour amener le monde d'en dehors.* That's when all the little towns have parades to bring in people from outside. (TB) **2** show ◊ **•pour parade** to show off <Da84> <*Loc:* LF, TB, Da84>

parader [parade] **I** *v.intr.* to parade, show off *Après que sa femme est morte, il a paradé sa misère pour de l'attention.* After his wife died, he paraded his misery to get attention. (LA) **II se parader** *v.pron.* to parade o.s., show off *Ferme le rideau! T'es après te parader tout nu devant le monde!* Close the curtain! You're parading around naked in front of everyone! (LA) <*Loc:* LA, Da84>

paradis [paradi] *n.m.* paradise, heaven <*Loc:* Da84, Hi02>

paraffine [parafin] *n.f.* paraffin <*Loc:* Da84>

parage [paraʒ] *n.m.* planing (of wood) <*Loc:* VM, Da84>

parages (**apparages**) [paraʒ, aparaʒ] *n.m./f.pl.* ◊ **•dans les parages** in the neighborhood, nearby *Il reste dans les apparages.* He lives in the neighborhood. (SM) *Je cherche dans ces parages pour mon chien.* I'm looking in this neighborhood for my dog. (IB) *Si tu viens dans nos apparages, prends garde!* If you come into our neighborhood, beware! (JE) <IB, JE, SM, Da84> <*Loc:* IB, JE, LF, SL, SM, Da84, Lv88>

paragraphe [paragraf] *n.m.* paragraph <*Loc:* Da84>

paraître [parɛt(r)] *v.intr.* **1** to appear, seem **Ça me paraît...* It seems to me . . . (Da84) **Il paraît que...* It seems that . . . (Da84) **2** to make an appearance, show up **Quand Marc Roy a paru dans la porte, Alex Dufour lui a foutu une bonne râclée.* When Marc Roy appeared in the doorway, Alex Dufour socked him hard. (Hi02) <*Loc:* Da84, Hi02>

paralyser [paralize] *v.tr.* to paralyze *Alle est morte en connaissance. Mais alle était paralysée. Alle avait eu un* STROKE. *Alle a duré deux semaines.* She died conscious. But she was paralyzed. She had had a stroke. She lasted two weeks. (TB) <*Loc:* TB, Da84>

paralysie [paralizi, parelizi] *n.f.* paralysis <*Loc:* VM, Da84>

parapel ♦see **parapet**

parapet (**parapel**) [parape, parapɛl] *n.m.* parapet <*Loc:* JE, LA>

parapluie [paraplɥi] *n.m.* **1** umbrella **2** parasol **Taille ta robe de mode à parasol.* Tailor your dress in the parasol style. (ch: *La robe à parasol*) <***Loc:*** Da84>

parasite [parasit] *n.m.* parasite <***Loc:*** VM, Fa77>

parasol [parasɔl] *n.m.* **1** parasol **2** umbrella <***Loc:*** IB, Da84, Lv88>

paratonnerre [paratɔ̃nær] *n.m.* lightning rod <***Loc:*** EV, VM, Da84, Fa77>

paravant ♦see **auparavant**

parc (parque) [park] *n.m.* **1** pen, corral, enclosure (for animals) *Il dit cèze-là que t'attrapes est beaucoup meilleurs que cèze-là qu'est faits dans un parc, qu'est faits dans une cage.* He says that those that you catch are a lot better than those that come from a breeding tank, that are made in a cage. (TB) **2** park *Sa fête qu'eusse avait fêté là-bas c'est au parc l'autre bord.* His birthday that they celebrated, it's in the park on the other side [of the bayou]. (TB) ◊ **•parc à cochon(s)** ***a*** pig sty, hog pen, pigpen ***b*** any dirty place <VM, Da84> **•parc à fumier** dung heap, fertilizer keep <LA> **•parc aux petits** nursery, room where children sleep during a traditional dance <VM> **•parc à veaux {vaches}** calf pen / cow pen <LA, TB> **•mettre au parc** to pen up (usu. to fatten) <Da84> <***Loc:*** LA, TB, VM, Da84, Hi02>

parcage [parkaʒ] *n.m.* penning up, corralling (of animals) <***Loc:*** Da84>

parce que [parskə, paskə] *conj.* because *On les amenait tout partout parce qu'eusse avait pas de char.* We took them everywhere because they didn't have a car. (TB) *Je vais parce que je veux.* I'm going because I want to. (SM) <***Loc:*** AC, AV, EV, IV, JE, LA, LF, SL, SM, TB, An94, Da84, Hi02>

parcelle [parsɛl] *n.f.* parcel, piece, portion <***Loc:*** Da84>

parchemin [parʃəmɛ̃] *n.m.* hull of the coffee bean <***Loc:*** JE>

parchouesse [parʃwɛs] *n.f.* tobacco pouch <***Loc:*** JE>

parcourir [parkurir] *v.tr.* to travel, traverse *Il a parcouri tous les chemins de la paroisse.* He ran all the roads in the parish. (VM) <***Loc:*** VM, Da84>

par-dessous[1] **(par en dessous)** [pardəsu, parɑ̃dəsu, parɑ̃tsu] *adv.* under, underneath, below *Il a été payé par en dessous de la table.* He was paid under the table. (LA) <***Loc:*** LA, Da84, Hi02>

par-dessous[2] [pardəsu] *prep.* under, underneath, below *Le petit a sorti de par-dessous la table.* The child came out from under the table. (EV) <***Loc:*** EV, Da84>

pardessus [pardəsy] *n.m.* **1** overcoat **2** top, top layer *Et là le lendemain quand il faisait froid tu passais, tu ramassais tout le pardessus, c'était comme une crème qui se formait par-dessus. Et tu mettais ça dans une jarre.* And then the next day when it was cold you went by, you collected the top, there was like a cream that had formed on it. And you would put it in a jar. (TB) <***Loc:*** TB, Da84>

par-dessus[1] [pardəsy] *adv.* **1** on top *Et là le lendemain quand il faisait froid tu passais, tu ramassais tout le pardessus, c'était comme une crème qui se formait par-dessus. Et tu mettais ça dans une jarre.* And then the next day when it was cold you went by, you collected the top, there was like a cream that had formed on it. And you would put it in a jar. (TB) **2** over the top *Ça va passer par-dessus.* It will flow over the top. (TB) **3** above, overhead <***Loc:*** LF, TB, Da84, Hi02>

par-dessus[2] [pardəsy] *prep.* **1** above *Tu mets ton hameçon à peu près ça par-dessus l'eau.* You put your hook about that far above the water. (TB) **2** over *Je regardais par-dessus son épaule.* I was looking over his shoulder. (TB) **3** on top of *Une fois un de les boulangers a capoté le TRUCK. Et il avait plein des œufs par-dessus le pain et gâteaux et tout.* One time one of the bakers turned the truck over. And there were a lot of eggs on top of the bread and cakes and all. (LF) <***Loc:*** LF, TB>

pardon[1] [pardɔ̃] *n.m.* pardon, forgiveness <***Loc:*** EV, SL, Da84>

pardon[2] [pardɔ̃] *interj.* forgive me, I'm sorry <***Loc:*** Da84, Hi02>

pardonnable [pardɔ̃nab(l)] *adj.* pardonable, excusable, forgivable *Ça qu'il t'a fait est pas pardonnable.* What he did to you is inexcusable. (EV) <***Loc:*** EV, Da84>

pardonner [pardɔ̃ne] *v.tr.* to pardon, forgive, excuse *Quand même tu fais mal, le Bon Dieu te pardonne.* Even if you do bad, God forgives you. (EV) *Jamais, je vas jamais te pardonner pour avoir fait ça.* I will never, ever forgive you for doing that. (TB) <***Loc:*** EV, TB, Da84>

paré, -e [pare] *adj.* ready, prepared **La fricassée est proche parée.* The fricassee is almost ready. (Hi02) *Ils sont parés pour t'aider.* They are ready to help you. (Lv88) **Le dîner est paré.* Dinner is ready. (Da84) *On a regardé pour deux mois différentes places, on était paré pour prendre quelque chose sur Charles Street.* We looked for a new place for two months, we were ready to take something on Charles street. (IB) ◊ **•tout paré** all ready <Da84> <***Loc:*** AC, EV, IB, LA, LF, SL, TB, VM, An94, Da84, Gu00, Hi02, Lv88, Re31>

parégorique (périgorie) [paregorik, perigori] *n.m./f.* paregoric <***Loc:*** LF, VM, Da84>

pareil, -eille [parej, parɛj] *adj.* **1** identical, the same *C'est peut-être toujours pareil.* Maybe it is still the same. (SL) **2** like, alike, similar, *Souvent des fois il n-a des prononciations qu'est un peu pareilles.* Very often there are pronunciations that are a little bit similar. (SL) **3** like that, such as that, the likes of that **J'ai jamais vu la pareille affaire.* I have never seen such a thing. (Da84) ◊ **•pareil comme** the same as, identical to, just like *Il est pareil comme son père.* He is just like his father. (VM) *Les femmes travaillent dur pareil comme les hommes.* Women work just as hard as men. (Lv88) *Elle a resté avec nous-autres des années et des années, c'était pareil comme un membre de la famille.* She lived with us for years and years, she was like a member of the family. (IB) **Pareil comme deux gouttes d'eau.* Alike as two drops of water. (Da84) <IB, LA, VM, Da84, Lv88, Re31> <***Loc:*** AC, AV, EV, IB, IV, LA, SL, TB, VM, An94, Da84, Lv88, Re31>

pareillement [parejmɑ̃] *adv.* likewise, in the same way *Content de te rencontrer.—Moi, pareillement.* Happy to meet you. —Likewise. (EV) <***Loc:*** EV, Da84>

parent[1] [parɑ̃] *adj.* related, kin *On est parents moi et lui.* He and I are related. (LF) ◊ **•parent par alliance** related by marriage <Da84> **•parent de la fesse gauche** [*ironic or humorous*] related <La99> <***Loc:*** AC, LF, SL, Da84, La99>

parent[2] [parɑ̃] *n.m.* **1** parent *Ça coûte si tellement de l'argent pour élever des enfants aujourd'hui. Et asteur les parents, les deux travaillent.* It costs so much money to raise children today. And these days both of the parents work. (LF) **2** relative, kin ◊ **•grands-parents** grandparents <Da84> **•grands-grands-parents** great-grandparents *Mes grands-grands-parents a revenu de la Chênière, la Chênière dessus la Grande Ile.* My great-grandparents came from Cheniere Caminada, the Cheniere on Grand Isle. (LF) <LF> **•près-parent** near relative <Da84> <***Loc:*** AC, AV, EV, LA, LF, SM, TB, Da84, Hi02>

parentage [parɑ̃taʒ] *n.m./f.* family, relatives, relations *On a été avec des amis qu'avaient du parentage là-bas.* We went with friends who had relatives there. (TB) <***Loc:*** LF, TB, VM, Lv88>

parenté [parɑ̃te] *n.f.* **1** relationship, kinship *Ça vient de la France et on se comprend, [...] tu peux dire que y a de la parenté qu'est là parce que eux-autres aime les mêmes affaires que nous-autres on aime.* They come from France and we understand each other, you can tell that there's a relationship [between us] because they like the same things we like. (TB) **2** kin, relatives **J'ai toujours respecté les fêtes de l'église. J'vas aux baptêmes et aux enterrements de la parenté.* I've always respected Church holidays. I go to my relatives' baptisms and funerals. (ThCa: *Mille misères*) <***Loc:*** AC, AV, SL, TB, Da84, ThCa>

parer[1] [pare] *v.tr.* to ward off, elude, evade, parry *Parer un coup.* To ward off a blow. (EV) <***Loc:*** EV, Da84>

parer[2] [pare] *v.tr.* to prepare, get ready, outfit *Il a pas pu parer son bâteau à temps pour partir.* He couldn't get his boat ready in time to leave. (LA) <***Loc:*** EV, IV, LA, VM>

parer[3] [pare] *v.tr.* to trim, cut down in size, pare *Hache à parer.* Ax used for trimming shingles. (TB) <***Loc:*** TB>

paresse [parɛs] *n.f.* laziness, sloth ◊ **•faire une paresse** to go back to sleep for a short period after being awakened *Tu veux faire une petite paresse ce matin?* Do you want to sleep in for a few extra minutes this morning? (EV) <EV> <***Loc:*** EV, Da84>

paresser [parese] *v.intr.* **1** to idle, be lazy, loaf, take it easy *On a paressé dimanche matin. On a même pas été à la messe.* We took it easy Sunday morning. We didn't even go to Mass. (LA) **2** to sleep in for a short period of time *Quand Daddy travaillait pas le dimanche, tout la famille paressait ensemble dans le lit. On se parlait, on visitait.* When Daddy didn't work on Sundays, the whole family would lounge around in bed together. We'd talk and visit. (VM) <***Loc:*** LA, VM, Da84>

paresseux, -euse [paresø, -øz] *adj.* lazy, slothful *Le monde a tout aujourd'hui. C'est ça qui nous met paresseux!* People have everything today. That's what makes us lazy! (TB) ◊ **•faire le paresseux** to act lazy <Da84> <***Loc:*** AC, AL, JE, TB, Da84, Hi02>

parfait, -e [parfɛ, parfe, -fɛt] *adj.* perfect **Il était si parfait que mon et ma vieille, on l'a appelé comme ça: Parfait. C'était ein bon bébé et pis ein bon 'tit garçon.* He was so perfect that my wife and I named him that: Parfait. He was a good baby and a good little boy. (ThCa: *Mille misères*) <***Loc:*** Da84, ThCa>

parfine [parfin] *n.f.* perfume, fragrance *Ça sent la parfine de la violette.* It smells like violet perfume. (VM) <***Loc:*** VM>

parfum [parfœ̃] *n.m.* **1** perfume, scent **2** extract <***Loc:*** Da84>

pari [pari] *n.m.* bet, wager <***Loc:*** VM, Da84, Fa77>

parier [parje, parije] **I** *v.tr.* to bet, wager *Je parie que tu regardes à ça et tu vas le comprendre bien, huh?* I bet you look at that and you'll understand it well, huh? (TB) **II** *v.intr.* to bet, wager *Parier aux courses.* To bet on the races. (Hi02) **III se parier** *v.pron.* to bet each other *Ils s'ont parié que les enfants s'auraient battu avant la fin de la journée.* They bet on whether or not the children would fight before the end of the day. (VM) <***Loc:*** TB, VM, Da84, Hi02>

parieur [parjœr] *n.m.* bettor, gambler, wagerer <***Loc:*** Da84>

parieux [parjø] *n.m.* heap of branches placed across a stream to form a makeshift bridge <***Loc:*** JE>

parisien[1], **-ienne** [parizjɛ̃, -jɛ̃n] *adj.* Parisian *C'est dur pour nous-autres comprendre le français parisien, parce que eusse parle trop vite pour nous-autres.* It's hard for us to understand Parisian French, because they talk too fast for us. (LF) <***Loc:*** LF, Da84>

parisien[2], **-ienne** [parizjɛ̃, -jɛ̃n] *n.* Parisian <***Loc:*** Da84>

PARK [pɑɹk] *v.tr.invar.* to park (a car) *J'ai pas rien dit de ta manière de* PARK *un char.* I didn't say anything about your way of parking a car. (Lv88) <***Loc:*** TB, Da84, Lv88>

parlage [parlaʒ] *n.m.* **1** saying, expression *"T'as pas assez d'eau à bouillir dans la bombe déjà?" Ça c'est un vieux parlage qu'on fait dès que quelqu'un a de trop à faire.* "Don't you have enough water to boil in the kettle already?" That's an old saying we use when someone has too much to do. (LF) **2** speech, way of speaking *C'est leur patois, leur parlage est différent.* It's their dialect, their speech is different. (TB) *Eux-autres avait bien de la misère à comprendre, c'était par rapport à son parlage.* They had some trouble understanding, it was because of his way of speaking. (TB) <***Loc:*** LF, TB>

parlailler [parlaje] *v.intr.* to chatter, gossip, gab *Arrête de faire ça. Le monde du village est après parlailler.* Stop doing that. People in town are talking. (VM) <***Loc:*** IB, VM, Da84>

parlement [parləmɑ̃] *n.m.* **1** talk, gossip, rumor *Je connais pas si c'est vrai, mais c'est ça le parlement.* I don't know if it's true, but that's the rumor. (VM) **2** conversation, talk, discussion **Le temps [...] avait habitué d'être ein sujet de gros parlement.* Weather used to be a great subject of conversation. (Wh83) **3** speech, way of speaking *Je peux dire la différence éyoù eux-autres reste, par leur parlement, ouais.* I can tell the difference, the places they live, by the way they talk. (TB) ◊ **•avoir beau parlement** to have a fine style of speaking <JE> **•en parlement *a*** in negotiations *Ils sont en parlement de changer le shériff.* They are in negotiations to replace the sheriff. (Lv88) ***b*** having a conversation *Il est en parlement.* He is having a conversation. (VM) <VM, Lv88> **•faire des parlements** to gossip <Da84> **•vilain parlement** nasty, vicious gossip <Da84> <***Loc:*** IB, JE, SL, TB, VM, Da84, Lv88, Wh83>

parlementages [parləmɑ̃taʒ] *n.pl.* gossip, chatter, idle talk <***Loc:*** JE, TB>

parler[1] [parle] **I** *v.tr.* to speak *Quand je parle en français, ça me demande, "Oh, mais vous parlez très bien français." Mais je dis, "Oui, mais j'ai parlé français toute ma vie."* When I speak French, they ask me, "Oh, you really speak French well." But I answer, "Yeah, but I've spoken French all my life." (SL) **II** *v.intr.* **1** to speak, talk *Le monde parle.* People talk. (JE) *Ils pouvaient parler en français mais ils parliont pas avec nous-autres en français.* They were able to speak French but they did not speak French with us. (AV) **2** to gossip *J'ai peur que le monde va parler.* I'm afraid that people will gossip. (LA) **III se parler** *v.pron.* **1** to converse, talk to each other *Ça pourrait s'assir là, tous nous-autres, s'assir là et se parler.* They could sit there, all of us could sit there and talk to each other. (LF) *On va se parler proche tous les jours.* We will talk to each other almost every day. (TB) *Mon et mon frère, on a eu une telle ostination qu'on se parle jamais.* My brother and I had such a quarrel that we never speak to each other. (VM) **2** to talk to oneself *Il se parlait tout le temps à lui-même.* He always talked to himself. (LF) ◊ **•parler à la berloque** to be delirious, rave *Alle parle à la berloque.* She's raving. (TB) <TB> **•parler à l'en plus finir** to talk endlessly <Da84> **•parler à tue-tête / parler à pleine tête** to scream, talk at the top of one's voice <LA, Da84> **•parler comme du tac-tac** to talk in a rapid, staccato fashion <La99> **•parler croche** to speak incorrectly <IB, LA> **•parler de {dessus / après / pour}** to talk about *Après je lui ai parlé dessus ça manière faché.* After I talked to him about it rather angrily. (AC) <AC> **•parler en dessous** to talk behind s.o.'s back <SM, VM> **•parler en grosses lettres** to speak coarsely, speak rudely <Lv88> **•parler en termes *a*** to speak in a careful or affected manner ***b*** to speak frankly <JE, Lv88> **•parler fort** to speak loudly *Baisse ta voix! Tu parles trop fort!* Lower your voice! You talk too loud! (EV) <EV> **•parler français** to say what one thinks, speak one's mind <Lv88> **•parler français comme un Chinois** to speak French badly *Y en a un qui parle français comme un Chinois à peu près.* One of them speaks French badly. (LF) <LF> **•parler gras** to speak 'thick' (with the particular accent of Grand Ile) *Le monde de la Grande Ile, eusse parle gras. [...] J'aime les attendre parler.* People of Grand Isle talk 'thick.' I like to hear them talk. (LF) <LF> **•parler gros nègre** to speak true Creole and not a more-or-less creolized French <Lv88> **•parler lambin** to drawl, speak with a drawl <Da84> **•parler mal de** to speak ill of, criticize *Le monde va parler mal de toi si tu découches tous les soirs.* People will criticize you if you sleep away from home every night. (LA) <LA, Da84> **•parler un tas** to talk a lot <Da84> **•en parlant de la bête, on lui voit la tête** speak of the devil, see his face <Da84> **•en parlant des anges, on voit leurs ailes** speak of angels, see their wings <La99> <***Loc:*** AC, AV, EV, IV, JE, LA, LF, SL, SM, TB, VM, Da84, Hi02, La99, Lv88>

parler[2] [parle] *n.m.* speech *On dirait qu'eux-autres, leur parler est un petit différent, mais pas plein.* You might say that their speech is a little different, but not a lot. (TB) <***Loc:*** TB>

parleur, -euse [parlœr, -øz] *n.* speaker, talker *C'est un parleur courant du français cadien.* He is a fluent speaker of Cajun French. (Lv88) *Il est un vrai parleur.* He's a real talker. (LF) ◊ **•grand parleur et petit faiseur** one who talks much but does little, braggart <Da84> <***Loc:*** LF, Da84, Lv88>

parline ♦see **braline**

parloir [parlwar] *n.m.* parlor, living room <***Loc:*** Da84>

parlure [parlyr] *n.f.* talk, language *Je connais des noirs dont la parlure a gardé beaucoup de ressemblance avec le créole d'Haïti.* I know some blacks whose speech has kept a lot of resemblance with Haitian Creole. (SM) *Le nouveau prêtre a une belle parlure.* The new priest has a beautiful way of expressing himself. (VM) <***Loc:*** JE, SM, VM, Lv88>

parmi [parmi] *prep.* among, amid *Le samedi d'après, un autre aurait tué son veau et il aurait séparé la viande parmi les autres, c'étiont comme un groupe.* The following Saturday, another one would have killed his calf and he would have divided the meat among the other ones, they were like a group. (AC) **Il courait tout parmi tout le monde.* He was running all around among all the people. (EV, An94) <***Loc:*** AC, AV, EV, LA, SL, SM, VM, An94, Da84, Hi02>

paroisse [parwas] *n.f.* **1** county, civil parish **2** church parish ◊ **•paroisses du fleuve** parishes along the Mississippi <Lv88> **•paroisses floridiennes** Florida Parishes <Lv88> **•dans les quatre paroisses** everywhere <La99> <***Loc:*** AC, AV, EV, Da84, Hi02, La99, Lv88>

paroissial, -e [parwasjal] *adj.* parochial, parish *Ils ont eu leur* *réception dans la salle paroissiale.* They held their reception in the parish hall. (LA) <***Loc:*** LA, Da84>

paroissien, -ienne [parwasjɛ̃, -jɛ̃n] *n.m.* **1** parishioner, resident of a civil parish **2** individual, person <***Loc:*** JE, Da84, Lv88>

parole [parɔl] *n.f.* **1** word **Alle a appris ses premières paroles en anglais.* She learned her first words in English. (Gu82) *Et quand ça dit "piastre," eusse connaît qui on après dire, mais eusse dit "Ça c'est une vieille parole!"* And when people say "piastre," they know what we're saying, but they say, "That's an old word!" (TB) **2** speech, speaking *Oh je comprends mieux que je comprenais le n-anglais mais ma parole à moi c'est plus français.* Oh, I understand English better than I used to but my speech is mostly in French. (TB) **3** promise **Donner sa parole.* To give one's word (promise). (Da84) **4** the Word (of God), the Bible *Y avait pas un tas de Protestants. Le monde avait jamais attendu la Parole en anglais, en français, la Bible, avant les Protestants venait.* There weren't many Protestants. People had never heard the Word in English, in French, the Bible, before the Protestants came. (LF) ◊ **•parole d'honneur** word of honor <Da84> **•paroles blessantes** harsh words <Da84> **•avoir des paroles avec qqn** to have a quarrel with s.o. <EV, La99> **•être de bonne parole** to be reliable <Da84> **•prendre la parole** to cut into a conversation, take the floor <Da84> <***Loc:*** EV, LF, TB, Da84, La99, Lv88>

parque ♦see **parc**

parquer[1] [parke] *v.tr.* **1** to corral, pen up *Mon j'ai travaillé dans l'affaire de nutria avec l'homme qui piégeait à Lafitte là-bas. Il en avait acheté 500, acheté des petits, et c'est nous-autres qui les soignait, moi et ma femme. On avait parqué ça, mettre dans un parc.* I worked in the nutria business with the man who fished in Lafitte. He had bought 500 of them, bought little ones, and we're the ones who took care of them, my wife and I. We had fenced them in, put them in a pen. (TB) **2** to herd (e.g. cattle) **Parquer les vaches.* To herd the cattle. (Da84) <***Loc:*** LF, SL, TB, Da84>

parquer[2] [parke] **I** *v.tr.* to park *Et là je vas parquer mon bicycle et là partais là-bas là.* And then I go park my bicycle and I took off that way. (LF) **II se parquer** *v.pron.* to park (one's vehicle) *Je t'as vu passer. T'étais pas sûr de te parquer là-bas, hein?* I saw you drive by. You weren't sure you could park down there, huh? (TB) <***Loc:*** LF, TB>

parquoi ♦see **pourquoi**

parrain [parɛ̃] *n.m.* godfather, sponsor <***Loc:*** VM, Da84, Hi02>

parsonnel ♦see **personnel**

parsonniers ♦see **personniers**

part [par] *n.f.* share, part, portion **Donne-lui sa part.* Give him his share. (Da84) **Part et part égale.* Share and share alike. (Da84) *On pensait pas que le langage allait s'en aller. C'était une grosse erreur dessus notre part à nous-autres.* We didn't think that the language would disappear. That was a big mistake on our part. (TB) ◊ **•à la part** for a share of the profits *Naviguer à la part.* To work on a ship crew for a specified share of the profits. (Lv88) <Lv88> **•à part de** apart from, besides, aside from *J'a tout le temps travaillé à la maison à part d'école ici.* I've always worked at home, besides going to school. (TB) <TB, Da84> **•à part de ça** aside from that, otherwise *Et ça fait que eux-autres réchauffait une jarre de ces viandes rôties là, et à part de ça t'avais de la poule, de la volaille, pleine de la volaille, les œufs.* And so they warmed up a jar of that roasted meat, and besides that you had chicken, a lot of poultry and eggs. (TB) <TB, Da84> **•à part que** except that, apart from, except for *La dernière année c'était pas venu froid. À part qu'on a eu un petit peu de la neige au mois de mars.* The last year it didn't get cold. Except that we had a little snow in the month of March. (TB) <PQ, TB> **•(en) nulle part** nowhere *Tu peux pus trouver des grillades à la chique en nulle part.* You can't find marzigut anywhere anymore. (VM) <LA, VM, Da84> **•en quelque part** somewhere *On jouait pour une danse en quelque part.* We played for a dance somewhere. (SL) <SL, Da84> **•faire part** to take part, be party to, be a part of <Da84> **•prendre part** to take part (in) *Ils n'ont pas pris part dans le dérangement.* They didn't take part in the exodus [from Acadia]. (SL) <SL, Da84> <***Loc:*** AC, EV, LA, PQ, SL, TB, Da84, Lv88>

partage [partaʒ] *n.m.* **1** apportionment, division, distribution (of shares) *Il était pas d'accord avec le partage de la terre de son défunt père.* He didn't agree with the apportionment of his deceased father's land. (VM) **2** part, line where hair is parted *Faire le partage des cheveux.* To make a part in one's hair. (Lv88) <***Loc:*** VM, Da84, Lv88>

partager [partaʒe] **I** *v.tr.* **1** to share *C'est un gros chiche qui veut jamais partager ça qu'il a.* He's a big tightwad who never wants to share what he's got. (EV) **2** to divide up, parcel out, portion out *Elle a partagé sa pomme en quatre morceaux pour donner à ses amies.* She divided up her apple in four pieces to give to her friends. (VM) *Ils ont partagé la terre à mon grand-père en cinq terrains égals.* They divided up my grandfather's land into five equal lots. (VM) **II se partager** *v.pron.* to share with one another, divide with each other *Ils auront besoin de se partager ça qui reste.* They will have to share amongst themselves what is left. (LA) <***Loc:*** EV, LA, Da84, Hi02>

partance [partɑ̃s] *n.f.* **1** departure *Je l'ai vu avant sa partance.* I saw her before her departure. (SM) *Je veux pas être là pour la partance, c'est si triste.* I don't want to be there for the departure, it's so sad. (VM) **2** beginning, start *J'avais fait de la charpente avant d'aller au* TRADE SCHOOL. *C'est ça qui m'a donné ma partance.* I had done carpentry before I went to trade school. That's what gave me my start. (EV) **3** head start ◊ **•en partance / sur sa partance** about to leave

Il est en partance pour la ville. He is about to leave for the city. (LF) *Elle est en partance pour Lafayette.* She is about to leave for Lafayette. (Lv88) <LF, SL, Lv88> **•faire une nouvelle partance** to make a new start <Lv88> **•mauvaise partance, bonne arrivée** a bad beginning, a good ending <Da84, Lv88> **•sur une partance** departing **Il était sur une partance à Brownsville.* He was departing for Brownsville. (Wh83) <Wh83> <***Loc:*** EV, LF, SL, SM, VM,Da84, Lv88, Wh83>

partant[1] [partɑ̃] *n.m.* departing guest *Le prêtre se met à la porte de l'église pour rencontrer les partants.* The priest goes to the door of the church to meet the departing worshippers. (VM) <***Loc:*** VM, Da84>

partant[2] [partɑ̃] *conj.* ◊ **•partant que** as long as **"Ah," elle dit, "Grand Dieu! Partant que c'est un homme," elle dit, "envoyez-moi le tout de suite!"* "Ah," she says, "Good God! As long as it's a man," she says, "send him to me right away!" (LA, An94) <LA, An94> <***Loc:*** LA, An94>

parterre [partær] *n.m.* flower garden, flower bed *Toute la cour en avant chez Grand-maman Tima était en parterres de fleurs.* The whole front yard at Grandma Tima's was flower beds. (Gu00) <***Loc:*** Da84, Gu00>

parti [parti] *n.m.* political party *Le parti des démocrates.* The Democratic Party. (VM) <***Loc:*** LF, VM, Da84>

participation [partisipasjɔ̃] *n.f.* participation <***Loc:*** Da84>

participer [partisipe] *v.intr.* to participate, take part *Je crois pas que ça va participer dans le* POOL *pour le puits d'huile.* I don't think they're going to participate in the pool for the oil well. (LA) <***Loc:*** LA, Da84>

particulier, -ière [partikylje, -jær] *adj.* **1** particular, specific **2** peculiar, particular *Il a toujours été un bougre particulier.* He has always been a peculiar fellow. (LA) **3** difficult, demanding *Il est marié avec une femme qu'est beaucoup particulière.* He is married to a very demanding woman. (LA) <***Loc:*** LA, Da84, Hi02, Lv88>

particulièrement [partikyljærmɑ̃] *adv.* particularly, especially **Ça aimait les navets, ce monde-là, et particulièrement quand ils étiont en cornichons avec du vinaigre.* They liked turnips, those people, and particularly when they were pickled in vinegar. (EV, An94) <***Loc:*** EV, An94, Da84>

partie [parti] *n.f.* **1** part, section *Là-bas dans Canada y a des gazettes, c'est tout français à part que une petite partie qu'est en anglais sur la dernière page.* Up there in Canada there are newspapers that are all in French except a small part that's in English on the last page. (TB) **2** game **Partie de pelote.* Ball game. (Da84) **3** party, social gathering *Aujourd'hui dessus le vendredi tout le monde a tout qualité de parties.* Today on [Good] Friday everyone has all kinds of parties. (LF) ◊ **•partie de noce** wedding party <Da84> **•la majeure partie** majority *La majeure partie des* BOSS *c'était du monde en dehors de la Louisiane.* The majority of the bosses were people from outside Louisiana. (TB) *On parle français aussi mais c'est la majeure partie en anglais.* We speak French too, but the majority is in English. (TB) <TB> **•pour la plus grande partie** for the most part <Da84> <***Loc:*** AC, LA, LF, TB, Da84, Hi02>

partiel, -lle [parsjɛl] *adj.* partial *Un paiement partiel.* A partial payment. (LA) <***Loc:*** LA, Da84>

partiellement [parsjɛlmɑ̃] *adv.* partly, in part *Un temps partiellement couvert avec les hauts dans les soixante-dix.* Partly cloudy weather with highs in the 70s. (LA) <***Loc:*** LA, Da84>

partir [partir] **I** *v.tr.* to start, start up (a machine, a discussion, etc.) *Il peut pas partir la machine.* He cannot start up the machine. (Lv88) *Il a parti la discussion sur la chasse.* He started the discussion about hunting. (Lv88) **II** *v.intr.* **1** to leave, depart, set out *Oh elle a manqué de mourir, moi j'a pris la course, mon. J'ai eu assez peur, mon j'ai parti.* Oh, she nearly died, I took off running. I was so scared, I got out of there. (TB) *Ça me chagrine de te voir partir.* It saddens me to see you leave. (LA) *Je croyais qu'il allait jamais partir.* I thought he would never leave. (EV) *T'as envie partir? Mais certainement!* Do you feel like leaving? Well, certainly! (LA) **Partir de là.* To leave from there. (Da84) **Partir pour la ville.* To head for the city. (Da84) **2** to start, start up (e.g. of a machine) *Y avait un homme eh ben il était arrêté avec sa machine qui voulait pas prendre et partir.* There was a man and he was stuck with his motor that didn't want to start. (TB) *Une fois il était chaud, il aurait parti avec le whisky aussi.* Once he was mad, he would start in with the whisky too. (SL) ◊ **•partir à** to start **Les bêtes ont parti à s'sauver en travers la savanne.* The animals started running away across the meadow. (Gu82) **Partir à se battre.* To begin to fight. (Da84) <Da84, Gu82, Lv88> **•partir à la course** to take off running, run away *Il a venu, il l'a vu, et il a parti à la course, et il a été appeler la loi lui dire que c'était* FOUL PLAY. He came, and he saw him, and he took off running, and he went to call the law to tell them that it was foul play. (TB) <TB> **•partir à la pagaille** to paddle off, paddle away *On part à la pagaille, vous montrer comment le monde de le vieux temps faisiont. Aujourd'hui ça va dans les* OUTBOARD MOTOR. We'll paddle off, to show you how folks in the old days used to do it. Today they go out with outboard motors. (LF) <LF> **•partir à la vole** to fly off, take flight *Il a parti à la vole.* He took flight. (TB) <TB> **•partir après** to go after **Il a regardé Lapin, il dit, "Tu connais une affaire? C'est lui qui a volé mon chèque!" Et il a parti après.* He looked at Lapin, he said, "You know something? He's the one who stole my check!" And he went after [him]. (LA, An94) <LA, An94, Da84> **•partir de la misère** to start trouble *Moi je suis le seul enfant. Et je pars de la misère toujours pour ça. Ils faisont toujours de la misère, les seuls enfants fait toujours de la misère pour ça.* I'm an only child. And I always start trouble because of that. They always make trouble, only children always make trouble because of that. (LF) <LF> **•partir (en) marron** ***a*** to run away, escape, flee (esp. back to the wild) *La bétaille a parti marron.* The animal went back to the wild. (Lv88) *Elle est partie maronne avec un voisin.* She ran away with a neighbor. (Lv88) ***b*** to leave without informing anyone, take 'French leave' *Mon beau-frère Cliff et mon beau-frère Joe avaient parti marron. Ils avaient échappé mes sœurs. Ils avaient été au bal.* My brother-in-law Cliff and my brother-in-law Joe left without notice. They escaped from my sisters and went to the dance. (AC) <AC, AV, VM, Da84, La99, Lv88> **•partir mors aux dents** to bolt suddenly <SM, La99> **•partir son feu** to infuriate *Ça, c'a parti son feu.* That made him fly into a rage. (Lv88) <VM, Lv88> **•partir sous une superstition** to leave hurriedly, without explanation <VM> **•en partant** at the beginning <Da84> **•être parti** to be going, be leaving *Ayoù-ce que t'es parti oui mon bon vieux mari?—Je suis parti au café.* Where are you going, my good old husband?—I'm going to the café. (TB) <TB> ***<Loc:*** AC, AV, JE, LF, SM, TB, VM, An94, Da84, Gu82, Hi02, La99, Lv88>

partisanerie [partizɑ̃nri] *n.f.* party spirit, loyalty to a party or group ***<Loc:*** JE>

partition [partisjɔ̃] *n.f.* partition, division **Les deux frères ont brouillé à cause de la partition de la vieille place.* The two brothers had a falling out because of the partition of the old homestead. (EV, An94) ***<Loc:*** EV, An94, Da84>

partner ♦see **padna**

partout [partu] *adv.* **1** everywhere *C'est français partout, il y a peut-être un peu de différent de mots et de manières mais il y a des différents de manières à parler français en France même.* It's French everywhere, maybe there are a few different words and ways but there are different ways of speaking French in France too. (SL) *Elle faisait des pirouettes partout dans la cour.* She was turning somersaults all over the yard. (LA) **2** wherever *Oh oui partout ayoù je vas, oh ça me convient pas.* Oh wherever I go, oh I am not happy. (EV, ch: *Si j'avais des ailes*) ◊ **•tout partout** everywhere *J'ai cherché tout partout. J'ai pas pu le trouver.* I looked everywhere. I couldn't find it. (SM) *Des filles qui viennent du tout partout.* Girls who come from everywhere. (SL) *Il n-a des bayous qui va tout partout.* There are bayous that go everywhere. (SM) *Ça venait du monde de tout partout dans le pays de l'Amérique.* People would come from everywhere around America. (AC) <AC, EV, IB, LA, SB, SL, SM, TB, VM, An84, Da84, Hi02, Lv88> ***<Loc:*** AC, EV, IB, IV, JE, LA, SB, SL, SM, TB, VM, An84, Da84, Hi02, La99, Lv88>

PARTY [paɹti] *n.m.* party *Un PARTY à soir telle et telle place.* A party tonight at such and such a place. (EV) ***<Loc:*** EV>

parvenir [parvənir] *v.intr.* to come (from), hail (from) **Il parvient de Lafayette.* He comes from Lafayette. (Da84) ***<Loc:*** Da84>

parvenu [parvəny] *n.m.* upstart, nouveau riche ***<Loc:*** Da84>

pas[1] [pa] *n.m.* step, pace, gait ◊ **•pas avançant** step forward, progress *Il reste toujours là. Pour chaque pas avançant il fait un pas reculant.* He always stays there. For every step forward, he takes a step back. (VM) <VM> **•pas de la porte** doorstep *Une fois j'ai eu de l'eau dans ma maison, pas un tas, THOUGH, juste à peu près comme ça-là au pas de ma porte.* One time I had water in the house, not a lot, though, just about that much at my doorstep. (TB) <TB> **•pas de un {deux, etc.}** [dance] one-step, two-step, etc. <Hi02> **•faire un pas en avant et deux en arrière** to take one step forward and two steps back (i.e. not advance well, be unable to get ahead despite some progress) <VM, La99> **•mettre au pas** to put s.o. in his or her place, tell s.o. what you think of him or her <TB> ***<Loc:*** TB, VM, Da84, Hi02, La99>

pas[2] [pa] *adv.* not, no, not any, none **C'est pas de tes affaires.* It's none of your business. (Da84) **C'est pas faisable.* It can't be done, it's not possible. (Da84) **Il y a pas de quoi.* You are welcome. (Da84) **Tu as pas d'affaire ici.* You have no business here. (Da84) **Tu vas pas me dire!* You don't say! (Da84) ◊ **•pas d'affaire!** no way! nothing doing! no deal! <Da84> **•pas d'apparence** not likely, not possible <Da84> **•pas de chance** not a chance, nothing doing <Da84> **•pas de trop** not too much *Ça, je me rappelle pas de trop, c'est plein des années passées, ça.* I don't remember that too well, it was many years ago. (TB) *(Je parle) pas de trop en anglais.* I don't speak English too much. (LF) <JE, LF, TB, Da84> **•pas du tout** not at all *Douze ans de ça il parlait proche que pas du tout en français, il voulait pas parler le français. Mais il a tombé en amour avec la musique cadien.* Twelve years ago he spoke almost no French, he didn't want to speak French. But he fell in love with Cajun music. (LF) <LA, LF, Da84> **•pas encore** not yet *Son idée est pas encore développée là-dessus.* His opinion is not yet developed on that issue. (LA) *Il était pas mort encore.* He was not dead yet. (LA) <EV, LA, VM, Da84> **•pas grand** ***a*** not much *Il avait pas grand éducation.* He didn't have much education. (SL) *Je faisais pas grand argent.* I didn't make much money. (SL) ***b*** not many *C'est rare tu voyais un char passer. Dans ce temps-là y avait pas grands chars.* It was rare that you'd see a car go by. In those days there weren't many cars. (TB) <SL, TB> **•pas jamais** never, not ever *Eusse a savonné sa langue! Et il a pas jamais rejuré après ça.* They soaped his tongue! And he never swore again after that. (TB) <TB, Da84> **•pas rien** nothing, not anything *J'ai pas fait rien.* I did nothing. (SM) *Dis pas rien.* Say nothing. (VM) <IB, SL, SM, VM, Da84> **•pas tout à fait** not quite <LF, Da84> **•pas un foutre** ***a*** not at all, not one bit *Je l'aime pas un foutre.* I don't like him one bit. (VM) ***b*** nothing at all *Il n-a pas un foutre pour faire ici.* There's nothing at all to do here. (SM) <SM, VM, Lv88> ***<Loc:*** AC, AV, EV, IB, IV, JE, LA, LF, SL, SM, TB, VM, Da84, Hi02, Lv88>

pas-bonne [pabɔ̃n] *n.f.* woman of ill repute *Drès que je l'ai vue, je savais que ça c'est une pas-bonne.* As soon as I saw her, I knew she was a woman of ill repute. (VM) <***Loc:*** VM>

passable [pasab(l)] *adj.* fair, passable, tolerable *Comment tu te sens?—Oh, c'est passable.* How do you feel?—Oh, fair. (LA) <***Loc:*** LA, Da84>

passablement [pasabləmɑ̃] *adv.* fairly, passably *Il est passablement bel homme mais sa femme est doublement laide!* He's a fairly handsome man, but his wife is doubly ugly! (VM) <***Loc:*** VM, Da84>

passage [pasaʒ] *n.m./f.* **1** passageway, corridor **2** passage, passing *Mais le chemin était pas large, y avait juste pour un passage d'un char, mais y avait pas grand'monde qu'allait en bas.* But the road was not wide, there was just room for the passage of one car, but there weren't many people who went down it. (TB) **3** ticket, passage on public transportation *J'ai déjà acheté mon passage dessus le char à passagers.* I already bought my train ticket. (VM) *Un passage de bus.* Bus ticket. (Lv88) <***Loc:*** JE, TB, VM, Da84, Lv88>

passager (**passageur**) [pasaʒe, pasaʒœr] *n.m.* passenger *Ç'a commencé là en premier c'était juste pour des passagers. Là ç'a tout* WELL *quand moi j'ai commencé c'était du monde et des automobiles aussi.* It started, at first it was only for passengers. Then it all, well, when I started [riding the ferry] it was people and automobiles also. (SJ) <***Loc:*** JE, SJ, Da84, Lv88>

passageur ♦see **passager**

passant [pasɑ̃] *n.* passer-by, traveler <***Loc:*** Da84>

passe [pas] *n.f.* **1** pass (i.e. channel, route for boats) *Tu vois ayoù la grande passe est?* Do you know where the big pass is? (TB) **2** path, small path *Une passe dans le bois.* A path in the woods. (LA) **3** passage through a barrier, pathway through a field, etc. *Garde! Il y a une passe là. Tu peux rentrer dans la baie en prenant la passe.* Look! There's a pass there. You can get to the bay by taking the pass. (VM) ◊ **•aller {partir} à la passe** to lie in wait for ducks as they come in to roost at night <VM> <***Loc:*** LA, TB, VM, Da84, Lv88>

passé[1], **-e** [pase] *adj.* **1** past, previous *L'année passée on a eu une canne qu'a fait des fleurs.* Last year we had a kind of sugarcane that produced flowers. (AS) *L'année passée, il n-a eu une terrible récolte d'écrivisses.* Last year there was an abundant crawfish harvest. (Lv88) **Si des positions passés veut dire quec'chose, la bande du gouvernement va aller au bord à Aucoin ou rester neutre.* If their past positions are any indication, the government gang will side with Aucoin or remain neutral. (Wh83) **2** ago *J'étais icitte vingt ans passés.* I was here twenty years ago. (Lv88) *Des années passées le moulin était couri juste avec* STEAM *maintenant il y a un tas de l'ectricité.* Some years ago the mill was run just with steam, now there is plenty of electricity. (IB) *J'avais serré le violon longtemps passé, j'avais plus de pratique.* I had put the violin away long ago, I never had any more practice. (Lv88) <***Loc:*** AS, EV, IB, SL, SM, TB, VM, Da84, Lv88>

passé[2] [pase] *n.m.* past *Dans le passé je travaillais au magasin là,* BUT *asteur-là y a douze ans que j'ai pas retourné* BACK *à l'ouvrage.* In the past I worked at the store but now it's been twelve years that I haven't gone back to work. (TB) <***Loc:*** TB, Da84, Hi02>

passé-blanc [paseblɑ̃] *n.* very light-colored mulatto who can pass as white <***Loc:*** Lv88>

passe-droit [pasdrwa] *n.m.* free rein, unlimited right *T'as pas le passe-droit de traiter le monde comme ça!* You don't have free rein to treat people like that! (VM) ◊ **•faire un passe-droit** to wrong by abusing one's rights *Parrain Ové a fait un passe-droit à ma mère. Il avait le droit de vendre sa terre, mais il aurait pas dû parce qu'elle était toujours mineure.* Parrain Ové took advantage of my mother. He had the legal right to sell her land, but he shouldn't have because she was still a minor. (VM) <VM, Da84> <***Loc:*** VM, Da84>

passée [pase] *n.f.* **1** brief appearance *Le soleil a fait qu'une passée.* The sun made only a brief appearance. (Lv88) *Les gâteaux a fait qu'une passée.* The cakes made only one round. (LF) **2** gathering, picking (e.g. of crops) **Faire une passée dans le coton.* To gather the cotton that is ready for harvest. (Da84) *Faire une passée dans un jardin.* To pick vegetables from a garden. (JE) **3** late evening hunt, night hunt **4** scolding, beating ◊ **•aller à la passée** to lie in wait for ducks as they come in to roost at night <SM, Lv88> **•faire une passée *a*** to make a brief appearance, pay a short visit *J'ai fait une petite passée à l'église.* I made a short visit to church. (SM) ***b*** to steal, make a raid, help o.s. to *J'ai fait une passée dans l'argent.* I stole some money. (SM) *J'ai fait une passée dans le gâteau.* I made a raid on the cake. (VM) ***c*** to go through (a field, etc.) harvesting a crop *Faire une passée dans un jardin.* To pick vegetables from a garden. (JE) ***d*** to extend an afternoon hunt into the early evening <JE, SM, VM, Lv88> **•foutre une passée** to give a scolding, beating *J'ai foutu une passée à Pierre.* I gave Pierre a scolding. (SM) <SM> <***Loc:*** JE, SM, VM, Da84, Da92, Lv88>

passe-galon [pasgalɔ̃] *n.m.* bodkin <***Loc:*** IB>

passe-lait [paslɛ, pasle] *n.m.* milk strainer <***Loc:*** AV, SJ>

passe-partout [paspartu] *n.m.* two-handled (logging or tree) saw *Ça c'est ça qu'on appelait un passe-partout pour couper des arbres, pour couper le bois pour la cheminée ou le* STOVE. This is what was called a two-handled saw, to cut trees to be used as firewood in the chimney or the stove. (AC) <***Loc:*** AC, EV, IV, SL, Da84, Hi02>

passe-pieu [paspjø] *n.m.* opening in a fence due to a missing or movable picket, used as a means of passage between adjoining properties <***Loc:*** IB, Lv88>

passeport [paspɔr] *n.m.* passport <***Loc:*** Da84>

passe-porte [paspɔrt] *n.m.* threshold <*Loc:* SL, Lv88>

passer [pase] *v.tr.* **1** to pass, hand *Passe-mon une patate chaude.* Pass me a hot potato. (TB) **2** to pass (from the body), get rid of, excrete *Et là le docteur lui donnait de la médecine, et alle passait les vers.* And then the doctor gave her some medicine, and she passed the worms. (TB) **3** to dip (in), pass (through) *Eux-autres passe ça dans du pain moulé. Et là ça frit ça.* They dipped that in bread crumbs. And then they fried it. (LF) *Tu ôtes le fumier de dans ton chaudin, tu le laves bien bien et tu le passes dans de l'eau manière quède, parce que c'est filant en dedans du chaudin.* You take the fecal matter out of your tripe, you wash it really well and you dip it in warm water, because the inside of tripe is slimy. (EV) **4** to apply, use (a tool, etc.) *Quand ça vient pour retirer ça il faut passer la galère là-dessus.* When it comes time to remove all of that [rough wood] you have to use a plane on it. (LF) **5** to lay, build (a road, a pipeline) *Il s'a amassé une fortune en vendant sa terre pour passer le nouveau chemin.* He amassed a fortune by selling his land to make the new road. (VM) *Je veux te parler concernant le* PIPELINE *que ça veut passer sus notre terre.* I want to talk to you about the pipeline they want to run on our land. (VM) **6** to pass, complete successfully (an exam, a course, a grade) *J'ai étudié, mais j'ai pas passé.* I studied, but I didn't pass. (TB) **7** to pass (a law) *La législature a passé une loi.* The legislature passed a law. (SM) **8** to cure, cause to pass, make (a pain, an illness) go away *Si t'aurais eu de quoi de mauvais mauvais, là t'aurais été voir un docteur. Mais c'était plus te faire traiter, et prendre des tisanes et des petites affaires qu'il connaissait tu vois, il pourrait passer le mal que t'avais.* If you had something really seriously wrong, you would go see a doctor. But more often you went to a folk healer and took herbal teas and little things he knew, you see, he could make the pain you had go away. (TB) **9** to pass on, hand down *Il voulait me passer ses traitements et tout parce que il avait personne d'autre qui voulait, et il voulait le passer à quelqu'un.* He wanted to pass his treatments on to me and all because there was no one else who wanted them, and he wanted to hand them on to somebody. (SJ) **10** to pass, spend (a period of time) *J'ai été passer une semaine à leur maison.* I went to spend a week at their home. (TB) **11** to survive (e.g. a harsh winter, a difficult period) *Tu te couches et tu peux passer un gros froid avec ça-ici dessus le dos.* You get in bed and you can make it through very cold weather with that [quilt] on your back. (TB) **12** to wipe down, mop *Elle aurait passé les* SIDEWALK *au gros rouge.* She would have mopped the sidewalks with crushed red brick. (SL) **13** to check *Mais il faut que mon je soye là avec ma licence là pour être sûr que ces lignes, il faut qu'eusse soit passé tous les jours.* But I have to be there with my license to be sure that these [alligator] lines, they have to be checked every day. (TB) **II** *v.intr.* **1** to pass, go, go by *Je t'as vu passer. T'étais pas sûr de te parquer là-bas, hein?* I saw you drive by. You weren't sure you could park down there, huh? (TB) **Le Bayou Têche passe au ras du Pont-Breaux.* Bayou Teche runs next to Breaux Bridge. (Hi02) *Quand t'es jeune t'as tout le temps tu veux. Ça passe trop vite quand t'es vieux.* When you're young you have all the time you want. It goes by too fast when you're old. (ch: *Le temps est après marcher*) **2** to stop by (usu. for a visit) *Tu pourrais passer voir ta Tante Vivian et ta cousine Marie à Washington en ervenant.* You could stop by to see your Aunt Vivian and your cousin Marie in Washington on your way back. (ThCa: *La douce réunion*) **3** to die, pass away *Le cinquième, c'était un garçon… Il a passé, il est pus dans cette vie.* The fifth one was a boy. He died, he's no longer in this life. (EV) **4** to elapse (of time) *Y avait deux jours qu'avait passé.* Two days had gone by. (TB) **III se passer** *v.pron.* **1** to happen, occur *Une femme qui va s'assir dans un* BEAUTY SHOP *trois ou quatre heures de temps alle connaît tous les nouvelles! Mon je suis pas une de eusse. Mon je connais jamais qui-ce qui se passe.* A woman who goes to sit in a beauty shop for three or four hours knows all the news. I'm not one of them. I never know what's going on. (LF) **2** to forego, do without **Se passer de manger.* To go without food. (Da84) **3** to elapse, go by (of time) *Et des années se passaient.* And years went by. (LF) **4** to spend (time) *Oh je dis je peux pas me passer une autre nuit comme ça je dis avec le mal de tête.* Oh, I said I can't spend another night like that with the headache. (LF) ◊ **•passer à coup de pied** to kick <Da84> **•passer à coups de bâton** to beat with a stick <Da84> **•passer à coups de poing** to beat up <Da84> **•passer à coups de tapes / passer aux tapes** to slap <Da84> **•passer à la baleine** to beat, whisk, whip s.o. <EV, La99, Lv88> **•passer à la bascule** game in which two boys each take one leg and one arm of another and swing him back and forth so that his buttocks strike the buttocks of another who is leaning over <SM> **•passer à la bastringue** to beat up <SL, La99> **•passer à l'examen** to examine <VM> **•passer au bleu** to vanish, disappear quickly *Mon argent a passé au bleu.* My money has gone with the wind. (IB) <IB> **•passer comme une balle** to happen quickly <La99> **•passer de la misère** to live through hardships, have a lot of trouble and hardships in one's life *On a passé plein de la misère pour faire une vie. Tout qualité de choses.* We lived through a lot of hardships to make a living. All kinds of things. (TB) <TB, LF, La99> **•passer des crêpes à qqn** to trick, pull a fast one on s.o. <AC, TB, La99> **•passer des remarques** to make remarks, criticize, critique *T'es tout le temps après passer des remarques ayoù ce ça te regarde pas.* You're always making remarks where it's none of your business. (TB) <TB, Lv88> **•passer du bleu de ciel avec qqn** to suffer misery, a hard time with s.o. <AC, La99> **•passer en avant** to cut ahead or to pass in front <Da84>

•passer en grade to pass, be promoted to the next grade in school *Mon plus vieux garçon a passé en grade au onzième livre.* My oldest son passed into the eleventh grade. (VM) <VM> **•passer la blâme sur** to lay the blame on *Ils avaient essayé de passer la blâme sur Espéra Dugas pour le feu.* They tried to lay the blame for the fire on Espera Dugas. (LA) <LA> **•passer la cheville à qqn** to dupe, deceive, trick s.o. *Il m'a passé la cheville.* He tricked me. (Lv88) <EV, SM, Lv88, Ph36> **•passer la nuit blanche** to spend a sleepless night, not get a wink of sleep <Da84, La99> **•passer la quête** to pass a collection plate, take up a collection <Da84> **•passer le baquet** to slight s.o. *On l'a bien passé le baquet.* We really slighted him. (SL) <SL> **•passer le coton** to gin cotton <VM> **•passer par la porte (d')en arrière** to achieve s.t. by nontraditional or unofficial means <La99> **•passer sur** to run over *Le char a passé sur une vache.* The train ran over a cow. (AV) <AV> **•passer un bloff** to dupe, trick, fool <LF, SM, Lv88> **•passer un cataplâme à qqn** to scold, tell s.o. off <EV, La99> **•passer un coundja (à qqn)** to cast a spell (on s.o.) *Alle m'a passé un coundja.* She put a spell on me. (Lv88) <Lv88> **•passer une bleue (à qqn)** to tell a fib (to s.o.) <La99> **•passer une chique (à qqn)** to say s.t. mean, make a caustic remark (to s.o.) <La99> **•passer une menterie** to tell a lie <Lv88> **•passer une nuit à la plaille** to spend a sleepless night <LF, La99> **•passer un examen** to pass a test, succeed in an examination <SM, VM> **•passez!** shoo! get away! *Passez! veux-tu passer!* Shoo! Get away! Go on! (SM) <IB, SM, Da84> **•se passer le temps** to spend one's time <Da84> **•en passer une à qqn** to put one over on s.o. *[Si] j'aurais assayé de t'en passer une, et puis commencé à parler français, tu comprenais le français mieux que moi!* If I had tried to put one over on you, and started to speak French, you understood French better than me! (TB) **•faire passer qqch à qqn** to cure s.o. of s.t. *"Oh, mais," elle dit, "moi, je vas lui faire passer ça," elle dit, "cette habitude de parier."* "Oh, well," she says, "I am going to cure him of that," she says, "that habit of betting." (AS) <AS> **•s'en passer au bout du bec** to not get or not have any of s.t. <La99> **•son âge l'a passé** she has reached menopause <VM> <***Loc:*** AS, AV, EV, IB, LA, LF, SJ, SL, SM, TB, VM, Da84, Hi02, La99, Lv88, ThCa>

passe-temps [pastɑ̃] *n.m.* pastime, hobby *Ça coûte joliment mais c'est un bon passe-temps.* It costs a lot, but it's a good hobby. (SM) <***Loc:*** SM, Da84>

passette [paset] *n.f.* **1** strainer **2** hallway, corridor <***Loc:*** JE, TB, Lv88>

passeur [pasœr] *n.m.* ◊ **•passeur de chiques** one who makes caustic remarks <La99> <***Loc:*** La99>

pasteur [pastœr] *n.m.* pastor <***Loc:*** Da84>

pastille [pastij] *n.f.* **1** pill, capsule **2** lozenge ◊ **•pastille de mal de tête** aspirin <VM> <***Loc:*** VM, Da84>

pastru [pastry] *n.m.* pastry <***Loc:*** JE>

pataraphe (patcharaque) [pataraf, patʃarak] *n.f.* **1** a lot, a great deal *T'as une pataraphe de papiers.* You have a great deal of papers. (VM) **2** long drawn-out letter or book *Une pataraphe de lettre.* A long drawn-out letter. (LF) **3** flourish (in handwriting) **4** scrawl, illegible handwriting *C'est pas de l'écriture, c'est de la patcharaque.* That's not writing, it's scribbling. (IB) **5** noise <***Loc:*** IB, JE, LF, TB, VM>

patassa [patasa] *n.m.* **1** any of various freshwater fish of the sunfish family (e.g. bluegill, warmouth, crappie, bream) often locally called "perch" or "sun perch" (although not technically true perch) *J'ai attrapé un hourra de patassas avec erien d'autre que des laiches.* I caught a bunch of bream with nothing but earthworms. (VM) **2** dolt, stupid fellow **3** heavy, stout man *Jean est un gros patassa.* John is a fat man. (IB) ◊ **•patassa à grande gueule** goggle-eye, rock bass <VM, Fa77> **•patassa blanc** white perch <Da84> <***Loc:*** AL, EV, IB, IV, JE, LF, SL, SM, TB, VM, Da84, Fa77, Gu00, Hi02, La99, Lv88, Re31>

patasserie [patasri] *n.m.* mess <***Loc:*** TB>

patate [patat] *n.f.* **1** potato *Il faulait qu'on va dans le champ, fouiller des patates, aller fouiller des* EASTER LILY, *haler du bois pour la cheminée.* We had to go into the field, dig up potatoes, go dig up Easter lilies, haul wood for the fireplace. (TB) *Ça va remplir un sac de cinquante livres de patates.* That will fill a bag with 50 pounds of potatoes. (LF) **2** sweet potato **3** any tuber *Les belles-de-nuit, ça fait une patate que tu peux transplanter.* Four o'clocks make a tuber that you can transplant. (VM) **4** chubby or fat person *André était une patate quand il était un bébé.* André was chubby when he was a baby. (EV) *C'est une grosse patate.* He's chubby. (LA) ◊ **•patate anglaise *a*** Irish potato *Les patates anglais, c'était pour manger. On vendait pas les patates anglaises.* The Irish potatoes were for eating. We didn't sell Irish potatoes. (SL) ***b*** potato <AC, CL, EV, IV, JE, LF, SB, SL, VM, Da84, Hi02, Lv88> **•patate douce** sweet potato, yam *Quand j'ai revenu, j'ai commencé acheter des patates douces. Il n-avait beaucoup de patates douces produit ici.* When I came back, I started buying sweet potatoes. A lot of sweet potatoes were produced here. (SL) *Ça dansait ça chantait ça faisait des bêtises, et là la maîtresse bien souvent avait des grands plateaux de patates douces qu'elle avait cuit d'avance.* [The Mardi Gras runners] would dance and sing and act crazy, and then the mistress of the house would quite often have big platters of sweet potatoes that she would have cooked ahead of time. (EV) <AV, CL, EV, IV, JE, LA, LF, SB, SL, SM, VM, Da84, Hi02, Re31> **•patate giraumont** yellow yam <VM> **•patate jambillot {zabillot}** type of native ground artichoke <JE> **•patate jaune** yellow sweet potato <Re31> **•patate ronde** Irish potato <Re31> **•patate yamme** any soft-fleshed variety of reddish-yellow sweet potato <Re31> **•patates frites**

French fried potatoes <Da92> **•en patate** in excess, excessively **Fou en patate.* Very crazy. (La99) **Soûl en patate.* Very drunk (La99) <La99> **•lâche pas la patate** don't give up, stay with it, hang in there <Da84, Lv88> <***Loc:*** AC, AV, CL, EV, IB, IV, JD, JE, LA, LF, SB, SL, SM, TB, VM, Da84, Da92, Hi02, La99, Lv88, Re31>

pataterie [patatri] *n.f.* **1** potato house, potato bin *Il manquait de la place dans la pataterie, ca fait il a embutté ses patates dans le clos et il les a couvert avec de la paille.* There was no more room in the potato shed, so he piled his potatoes in the field and covered them with straw. (VM) **2** mound of potatoes covered with dirt for storage <***Loc:*** IB, SM, VM, Da84, Lv88>

patatras [patatra] *n.m.* bundle *Tout le patatras de papier a tombé sur le plancher.* The whole bundle of paper fell on the floor. (SL) <***Loc:*** SL>

pataucher ♦see **patauger**

pataugeage [patoʒaʒ] *n.m.* wading, walking in mud or shallow water <***Loc:*** Da84>

patauger (**pataucher**) [patoʒe, patoʃe] *v.intr.* to splash around in shallow water, wade or walk around in water or mud (usu. for fun) *Après l'avalasse, les enfants pataugeaient dans le fossé.* After the downpour, the children were splashing around in the ditch. (VM) <***Loc:*** VM, Da84>

patcharaque ♦see **pataraphe**

pâte [pat] *n.f.* dough, batter *Elle aurait ramassé des petits morceaux de pâte comme une petite pelote et pis elle aurait épaillé la pelote bien mince.* She would take little pieces of dough like a little ball, then she would stretch the ball out very thin. (SL) *Des beignets, c'est la même farine, la même pâte que tu démêles pour faire le pain.* Beignets, it's the same flour, the same dough you mix up to make bread. (TB) <***Loc:*** SL, TB, VM, Da84>

pâté [pate] *n.m.* **1** meat pie *Grand-maman d'Érath faisait des pâtés avec des gigiers de z-oie et de canards et alle les assaisonnait avec du thym qu'alle plantait dans son jardin.* Grandma from Erath made meat pies with goose and duck gizzards that she seasoned with thyme that she planted in her garden. (VM) **2** one who overstays his or her welcome ◊ **•pâté de (merde de) vache** cow pie, cow patty, cow dung *Y a rien de plus décourageant que quand tu marches dans une savane et tu rebuttes dessus un pâté de merde de vache.* There's nothing more discouraging than when you're walking in a meadow and you stumble over a cow patty. (Gu00) <Gu00> <***Loc:*** EV, VM, Da84, Gu00, Lv88>

pategau (**padegau, papegau, papégau, papegai**) [patgo, padgo, papgo, papego, papge] *n.m.* **1** turkey shoot, marksmanship contest typically with a stationary target in the form of an animal **2** target in the shape of an animal **3** clay pigeon, skeet **5** trap shoot, skeet shoot, marksmanship contest with clay targets **4** sport of skeet shooting <***Loc:*** IB, Lv88, Re31>

patente [patɑ̃t] *n.f.* patent <***Loc:*** LF, VM, Da84, Fa77>

patenter [patɑ̃te] *v.tr.* **1** to invent *Le bougre qu'a patenté cette affaire, lui, il avait une bonne tête.* The fellow who invented that thing, he sure was smart. (VM) *Je suis après faire un grand tour dans tous les villages dans l'état de la Louisiane afficher ma nouvelle médecine que j'ai patentée moi-même et qu'a juste sorti sur le marché.* I'm doing a big tour in all the towns of the state of Louisiana to advertise my new medecine that I invented myself and that has just come out on the market. (AV) **2** to patent <***Loc:*** AV, VM, Da84>

patience [pasjɑ̃s] *n.f.* patience, forbearance *Je pourrais pas faire ça, j'ai pas la patience moi, pas du tout.* I would not be able to do that, I don't have the patience, not at all. (IB) <***Loc:*** EV, IB, Da84>

patient[1], -e [pasjɑ̃, -ɑ̃t] *adj.* patient *Je suis après l'aider pour d'être patient.* I am trying to help him to be patient. (IB) <***Loc:*** IB, VM, Da84>

patient[2], -e [pasjɑ̃, -ɑ̃t] *n.* patient, one who is under medical care or treatment <***Loc:*** TB>

patienter [pasjɑ̃te] **I** *v.tr.* to make impatient **Ça a venu et ça patientait mon cousin.* That happened and it made my cousin impatient. (LA, An84) **II** *v.intr.* to be patient, have patience *Si vous-autres peut patienter quelques mois, on va vous envoyer votre chèque de FEMA.* If you all can be patient for a few months, we'll send you your FEMA check. (LA) <***Loc:*** LA, An84, Da84>

pâtir [patir] *v.intr.* **1** to suffer *Ma mère était un peu affligée, elle avait une hanche, de petite fille alle a pâti plein avec ça.* My mother was a bit handicapped, she had a [bad] hip, from a young age she has suffered a lot with that. (TB) *Le piquant qu'il a sur le dos. Oh ils vont te faire pâtir, ça te fait mal. Ça va pas te tuer je pense, peut-être y a des places ça te tuerait. Mais ça fait du mal.* The spine that it has on its back, oh, that will make you suffer, it hurts. It won't kill you, I think, maybe there are places where it would kill you. But it hurts. (TB) **2** to want, go hungry, be deprived (of food) *On a pas pâti de rien durant la Dépression, on avait rien, mais on avait de quoi manger.* We weren't deprived of anything during the Depression. We didn't have anything, but we had enough to eat. (Lv88) <***Loc:*** TB, Da84, Lv88>

pâtira [patira] *n.m.* one who suffers in health *Il est un pauvre pâtira.* He's a poor suffering soul. (SM) <***Loc:*** SM>

patocaille [patokaj] *n.m.* hard times, period of difficulty *Dix ans passés on a eu un patocaille.* Ten years ago we had a period of hard times. (EV) <***Loc:*** AV, EV>

patois [patwa] *n.m.* **1** dialect, patois *On a des amis qui parlent très bien français, mais entre eux, dans la famille, ils parlent ce patois-là, toujours entre eux.* We have some friends who speak French very well, but among themselves, within the family, they speak that patois, always among themselves. (SL) *Chaque paroisse a un différent patois.* Each parish has a different patois. (TB) **2** creole (esp. Louisiana Creole) *Les* *jeunes, là ils aiment plus parler français. Les vieux noirs parlaient presque tous le patois, le créole.* The young ones, they don't like to speak French anymore. The old blacks almost all used to speak patois, creole. (SL) <***Loc:*** IB, SL, TB, Da84>

patouiller ♦see **patrouiller**

patrique [patrik] *n.f.* **1** scaly leg (type of illness in poultry) *La patrique est pris dans les poules.* The chickens have been infected with scaly leg. (LA) **2** wasting away <***Loc:*** LA>

patron[1] [patrɔ̃] *n.m.* pattern, model *Tu te coupais un patron. Tu coupais ton patron, là tu coupais tous les chevrons avec ce patron-là.* You cut yourself a model. You cut your pattern, then you cut all your rafter beams with that model. (SL) *Elle pouvait prendre un patron et me faire une chemise dans un petit moment.* She was able to use a pattern and make a shirt for me in a short time. (IB) *Et ça c'est les patrons pour les bateaux qu'on a vus là-bas. Ça c'est les patrons drette-là. Il a été fait drette ici en-dessour là, sur ce ciment ici là.* Those are the patterns for the boats we saw over there. Those are the patterns right there. They were made right here under there, on this cement. (LF) <***Loc:*** AC, EV, IB, JE, LF, SL, Da84>

patron[2]**, -onne** [patrɔ̃, -ɔ̃n] *n.* patron, patron saint *La Sainte Thérèse c'est la patronne de l'église d'Arnaudville.* Saint Theresa is the patron saint of the Arnaudville church. (VM) <***Loc:*** VM, Da84>

patronage [patrɔ̃naʒ] *n.m.* patronage, clientele, customers <***Loc:*** JE, Da84, Lv88>

patroniser [patrɔ̃nize] *v.tr.* to patronize, do business with *Je patronise son magasin.* I patronize his store. (SM) <***Loc:*** IB, JE, SM, Da84, Lv88>

patrouiller (patouiller) [patruje, patuje] *v.intr.* to walk around in the mud <***Loc:*** JE, TB>

patte [pat] *n.f.* **1** paw, foot (of an animal) *Un caïman, il a des pattes assez grandes, il va partir de là et venir là dans deux trois heures, lui il est en dehors de l'eau, l'eau le tracasse plus.* An alligator has rather big feet, he'll come out of there and come here in two or three hours, he's out of the water, the water doesn't trouble him anymore. (TB) **2** leg, foot (of furniture, cooking pot, oil rig, etc.) *On avait ces grosses chaudières en fer, avec des petites pattes en-dessous.* We used to have these big cast iron pots, with little legs under them. (TB) *Et ça c'est un* SPADEFISH. *Ça se tient au ras des* RIG, *au ras des pattes des* RIG *à la mer.* And that's a spadefish. They linger around rigs, around the legs of the oilrigs in the sea. (LF) ◊ **•patte d'alouette** larkspur <IB, VM> **•patte de chat** cat's foot, wild vine that bears small black berries <IB, SM, Lv88> **•patte de cheval** dichondra <TB> **•patte de cochon** pig's foot *On arrangeait tout la tête propre, les oreilles, les pattes de cochon, mettre ça à bouillir ensemble.* We cleaned the head all up, the ears, the pig's feet, and put all of it to boil together. (TB) <TB> **•patte de poule** ***a*** chickpea ***b*** cat's cradle ***c*** lady-finger pea <VM, Da84, Lv88> **•patte jaune** [bird] yellow-legs <JE, Re31> **•patte-plate** flat-footed person *L'armée prend les pattes-plates pour cette guerre.* The army is taking flat-footed people for this war. (VM) <VM> **•à quatre pattes** on all fours *Tu te mettais sus les genoux à quatre pattes pour couper les herbes avec ça.* You got down on all fours to cut the grass with that. (TB) <TB> **•la patte douce** Social Security *Il est pas assez vieux pour toucher la patte douce.* He is not old enough to collect social security. (SL) <EV, SL> <***Loc:*** EV, IB, JE, LF, SL, SM, TB, VM, Da84, Hi02, Lv88, Re31>

patté, -e [pate] *adj.* **1** having large feet *Les garçons entre douze et dix-sept ans sont souvent pattés.* Boys in the 12- to 17-year-old range often have very big feet. (VM) **2** having a rough gait (of a horse) *Il a un cheval patté. C'est pour ça qu'il a eu du mal au dos.* He has a rough-gaited horse. That's why he had a backache. (LA) <***Loc:*** JE, LA, VM>

patteux [patø] *adj.* having a rough gait (of a horse) <***Loc:*** JE>

pâturage [patyraʒ] *n.m.* **1** pasturage, pasture, grazing land *Y avait plein de pâturage, ils les engraissaient encore pour finir la route avant qu'ils arrivaient pour les vendre au marché.* There was a lot of pastureland, they would fatten them [the cows] up again to finish out the journey before they arrived at the market to sell them. (SJ) **2** grass or other plants for feeding livestock **3** pasturing, putting out to pasture *Souvent on changeait les récoltes de riz avec le pâturage de bêtes, et les récoltes de coton avec le maïs pour enrichir la terre.* Often they would alternate the rice crop and the pasturing of cows, and the cotton crop and the corn crop to enrich the land. (VM) <***Loc:*** SJ, VM, Da84>

pauma Christi ♦see **palma Christi**

paume [pɔ̃m] *n.f.* palm of the hand <***Loc:*** Da84>

paupière [popjær, popij] *n.f.* **1** eyelid **2** eyelash **3** butterfly net (used in shrimp fishing) *Des grandes paupières à 22 pieds. Tu peux pas avoir plus grand que 22 pieds.* Big butterfly nets 22 feet long. You can't have bigger than 22 feet. (TB) <***Loc:*** EV, JE, PQ, TB, Da84>

paupiérer [popjere] *v.tr.* to fish (esp. for shrimp) with a butterfly net *Tu peux paupiérer le bayou, et tu peux aller dans les lacs.* You can fish the bayou with a butterfly net, and you can go into the lakes. (TB) <***Loc:*** TB>

paupiéreur [popjerœr] *n.m.* wing net boat, butterfly net boat (used in shrimp fishing) <***Loc:*** Lv88>

paupiller [popije] *v.intr.* to blink <***Loc:*** JE>

pautre ♦see **potre**

pautresse ♦see **potresse**

pautrin ♦see **potre**

pauvre[1] [pɔv(r)] *adj.* **1** poor, impoverished *C'est du monde pauvre mais c'est du monde bien fier et eux-autres a une grosse croyance dans le Bon Dieu.* They're poor people but they're very proud people and they have a strong belief in God. (TB) *Les récolteurs étaient du monde pauvre, eusse* *pouvait pas avoir des esclaves.* Farmers were poor people, they couldn't afford slaves. (LF) *Ils se considéraient pas pauvres.* They didn't consider themselves poor. (SJ) *Il était tellement pauvre, il avait pas des chaussures.* He was so poor, he didn't have shoes. (LA) *Parce que j'ai été assez pauvre je suis dans une position pour aider un tas du pauvre monde et puis je comprends leurs tracas.* Because I was rather poor myself, I am in a position to help many poor people and also I understand their problems. (IB) **2** poor, pitiable, pitiful *Il avait habitude de chamailler ce pauvre homme tous les samedis soirs.* He used to pick on that poor man every Saturday night. (SL) *Ce pauvre monde ont eu pour charroyer tout leur butin pour des mois après que leur vieille grandmère a manqué.* Those poor people had to carry all of their belongings from place to place for months after their old grandmother died. (LA) *Pauvre espèce de crévasse.* Poor, sickly thing. (VM) **Pauvre toi, y'en a pus.* Poor you, there's none left. (Da84) **Pauvre malheureux.* Poor fellow. (Da84) *Pauvre bête, il a caillé la botte.* Poor fellow, he died. (SB) **Et qui c'est qui a tué la pauvre vieille femme?* And who killed the poor old lady? (EV, An94) **3** poor, bad *Mon je suis un pauvre exemple pour dire ca,* BUT *ça aurait dû être fait, on aurait dû le faire nous-autres-mêmes.* I'm a poor example to be saying that, but it should have been done, we should have done it ourselves. (TB) **4** late, deceased *Mais, tu connais, pauvre Léonce était comme ça.* But you know, the late Leonce was like that. (SL) ◊ **•pauvre comme Job** very poor <La99> **•pauvre comme un rat (d'église)** poor as a church mouse <Da84, La99> **•un pauvre petit peu** a very small amount <LF> <***Loc:*** EV, IB, JD, LA, LF, SB, SJ, SL, TB, VM, An94, Da84, Hi02, La99>

pauvre[2] [pɔv(r)] *n.* poor person, one who is impoverished ◊ **•les pauvres** the poor <Da84> <***Loc:*** An94, Da84>

pauvrement [povrəmɑ̃] *adv.* poorly, in poverty *J'ai vi pauvrement dans ma jeunesse.* I lived in poverty in my youth. (VM) <***Loc:*** VM, Da84, Fa77>

pauvreté [povrəte, poværte] *n.f.* poverty, indigence <***Loc:*** JE, Da84>

pauvrie [povri] *n.f.* poverty, indigence <***Loc:*** JE>

pavage [pavaʒ] *n.m.* **1** paving *Le pavage du chemin a arrêté avec l'ouragan.* The paving of the road stopped with the hurricane. (LA) **2** pavement, paved road *Dans l'été, le pavage te brûle les pieds.* In the summer, the pavement burns your feet. (VM) <***Loc:*** LA, VM, Da84>

PAVE [pɛv, peᶦv] *n.m.* pavement, paved road *Y avait pas de* PAVE, *c'était tout des chemins de gravois.* There wasn't any paved road, it was all gravel roads. (Lv88) *J'aime* RIDE *dessus le* PAVE. I like riding on the pavement. (SM) <***Loc:*** SM, VM, Da84, Lv88>

pavé[1], **-e** [pave] *adj.* paved, hard-surfaced *Ça fait juste quelques années que le chemin est pavé.* The road has only been paved for a few years. (LA) <***Loc:*** LA, Da84>

pavé[2] [pave] *n.m.* paved road <***Loc:*** Da84>

pavure [pavyr] *n.f.* planks or branches arranged to permit one to cross running water or a swampy area <***Loc:*** JE, SM, VM, Lv88>

payable [pejab(l)] *adj.* payable, due *Moi, j'ai des* BILLS *qui sont payables tous les mois.* I have bills that are due every month. (LA) <***Loc:*** LA, Da84>

payant[1], **-e** [pejɑ̃, -ɑ̃t] *adj.* paying, high-paying, profitable *Il a un job qu'est pas payant.* He has a job that does not pay well. (LA) <***Loc:*** LA, Da84>

payant[2] [pejɑ̃] *n.m.* payer, one who pays *Le droit est avec le payant.* The rights are with the one who pays. (LA) <***Loc:*** LA, Da84>

paye [pɛj] *n.f.* pay, wages ◊ **•être de bonne paye** to pay one's debts faithfully <Da84> <***Loc:*** Da84>

payement ♦see **paiement**

payer [peje] **I** *v.tr.* **1** to pay (an amount) **Il a acheté le chien. Il a payé dix mille piastres pour.* He bought the dog. He paid ten thousand dollars for [it]. (EV, An94) **2** to pay for *C'est toi qu'a payé la boisson?* Are you the one who paid for the drinks? (TB) **Qui c'est qui va payer les dommages, moi ou toi?* Who will pay for the damages, me or you? (LA, An94) **3** to benefit, be beneficial to **Ça paye d'écouter.* It pays to listen. (Da84) **Ça te payerait de venir.* It would be beneficial for you to come. (Da84) **II** *v.intr.* to pay *Ç'a payé pour la glacière, et les éventails, et l'estricité, ç'a payé pour tout.* They paid for the refrigerator, and the fans, and the electricity, they paid for everything. (TB) *La première paire de souliers que mon j'ai mis mes pieds dedans là, eh ben, j'ai payé pour mon-même.* The first pair of shoes I ever put my feet in, I paid for myself. (LF) *Jésus avait payé pour tous leurs péchés.* Jesus had paid for all their sins. (TB) **III se payer** *v.pron.* **1** to pay o.s., reimburse o.s. *D'après moi, il va se payer pour les dépenses quand ça sera fini.* I guess he'll pay himself back for the expenses after it's all over. (LA) **2** to pay for, pay off (for o.s.) *Tu pourras te bâtir une maison. Et il dit tu pourras travailler et il dit finir de te la payer.* You can build yourself a house. And, he says, you can work and finish paying it off. (TB) ◊ **•payer la traite** to pay for a drink, buy a round of drinks <Lv88> **•payer les frais** to pay the cost, pay expenses <Da84> **•payer par {au} mois** to pay by the month <Da84> **•payer ses comptes** to pay or settle one's accounts <Da84> **•payer un compliment** to pay a compliment <EV, SM, VM, Da84, Lv88> **•payer une visite** to visit, pay a visit *J'ai payé une visite à Robert hier soir.* I visited Robert last night. (SM) *Madame Charles m'a payé une visite aujourd'hui.* Mrs. Charles paid me a visit today. (SJ) <EV, SJ, SM, VM, Da84, Lv88> <***Loc:*** AC, EV, LA, LF, SL, SM, TB, VM, An94, Da84, Hi02, Lv88>

payeur de taxes [pejœrdətaks] *n.m.* taxpayer <***Loc:*** SM, VM, Lv88>

pays[1] [pei, peji] *n.m.* **1** country *Ça qu'on appelle un* SPECKLED

TROUT, nous-autres, c'est un WEAKFISH dans le nord du pays. What we call a speckled trout is called a weakfish in the north of the country. (TB) **2** region, area ◊ **•pays bas** ***a*** low country ***b*** swamp <AV, EV, JD, Da84> **•pays de naissance** birth place, fatherland <Da84> **•pays d'origine** country of origin or birth <Da84> **•pays natal** land or country of birth, native land <Da84> **•pays perdu** ***a*** wilderness ***b*** godforsaken place <Da84> **•de {du} pays** homemade *Savon de pays. Savon du pays.* Homemade soap. (SM, VM) <SM, VM, Da84> **•le vieux pays** Louisiana, for a Texas Cajun <Da84> <***Loc:*** AC, AV, EV, JD, LA, SL, SM, VM, An94, Da84>

pays[2] [pei, peji] *interj.* land sakes *Pays! C'est-il possible?* Land sakes! Is it possible? (EV) <***Loc:*** EV, LA, VM>

peanut-beurre [pinøtbœr] *n.m.* peanut butter <***Loc:*** TB>

peau [po] *n.f.* **1** skin (of a person, an onion, etc.) *Tous les feuilles sortaient dessus, tous les peaux sortaient dessus les BEANS.* All the leaves were coming off, the skins were coming off the beans. (TB) **2** hide, pelt *Il y a plus aucun qualité de peau qui se vend à part que les loutres. Le monde les attrape et ça les vend vivants.* There is no longer any kind of pelt that is sold except otters. People catch them and sell them alive. (TB) **3** leather, uncured leather *Des lisières de peau.* Strips of leather. (Lv88) *Eusse fait des bottes, les grosses bottes, les COWBOY BOOTS avec de la peau.* They make boots, the big boots, cowboy boots out of leather. (TB) ◊ **•peau de canard** goose bumps, gooseflesh <VM, Da84, Fa77, Lv88> **•peau morte** dandruff *Mes cheveux sont pleins de peau morte.* My hair is full of dandruff. (SM) <AL, IB, SM, VM, Da84, Lv88> **•à peau nue** on the bare skin (of clothing) *Elle porte cette robe à peau nue.* She has nothing on but a dress. (LF) <LF> **•avoir la peau dure comme un cocodrie** to be a tough person <EV, La99> <***Loc:*** AL, AV, EV, IB, IV, LF, SM, TB, VM, An94, Da84, Fa77, Hi02, La99, Lv88>

pêchage [peʃaʒ] *n.m.* fishing *Là quand-ce qu'il avait tous les chambres de remplies, ben il arrêtait de faire le pêchage et puis il allait au marché pour vendre sa chevrette.* Then, when he had all the rooms [of the hold] filled, well, he would stop fishing and then he'd go to market to sell his shrimp. (LF) <***Loc:*** LF>

pêchailler [peʃaje] *v.intr.* to fish here and there *On a pêchaillé un peu, mais on a pas attrapé grand chose.* We fished a bit here and there, but we didn't catch much. (LA) <***Loc:*** LA, SM>

péché [peʃe] *n.m.* sin, transgression **Ça c'est un péché.* That's a sin. (Da84) **Laid comme les sept péchés capitaux.* As ugly as the seven capital sins. (Da84) *Jésus avait payé pour tous leurs péchés.* Jesus had paid for all their sins. (TB) ◊ **•péché capital** capital sin <Da84> **•péché d'omission** sin of omission <VM, Da84> **•péché mortel** mortal sin <Da84> **•péché originel** original sin <Da84> **•péché véniel** venial sin <Da84> **•faire un péché** to commit a sin <Da84> <***Loc:*** EV, TB, VM, Da84, Hi02>

pêche[1] [pɛʃ] *n.f.* **1** fishing, angling *J'étais à la pêche hier et puis je n'ai pas pris une, pas un seul.* I was fishing yesterday and didn't catch any, not a single one. (SL) **Moi, je suis parti à la pêche!* I'm going fishing! (LA, An94) **2** fishing, the fishing business *Un bon cinquante du cent du monde jusqu'à oh peut-être 1960, eusse travaillait tout sur l'eau. Soit la pêche aux chevrettes ou la pêche aux huîtres ou la pêche aux poissons. T'avais toute sorte de pêche à faire.* A good fifty percent of people until about 1960 all worked on the water. Either shrimp fishing or oyster fishing or fishing for fish. You had all kinds of fishing to do. (LF) *Fallait bien travailler, il faut travailler dans la pêche depuis l'âge de douze ans.* I needed to work, you have to start work in fishing at twelve years old. (PQ) ◊ **•faire la pêche** to fish *Ayoù tu fais la pêche?* Where do you fish? (VM) **•faire une bonne pêche** to make a good catch, have a good fishing trip <Da84> <***Loc:*** EV, LA, LF, PQ, SL, TB, VM, An94, Da84, Hi02>

pêche[2] [pɛʃ] *n.f.* peach ◊ **•pêche à jus** clingstone peach <Da84> **•pêche à quitte noyau** freestone peach <Da84, Lv88> **•la pêche de la bande** ***a*** the prettiest daughter of the family ***b*** the prettiest girl of a group <La99> <***Loc:*** AV, SL, VM, Da84, Hi02, La99, Lv88>

pécher [peʃe] *v.intr.* to sin, transgress *Elle était après pécher et elle le savait.* She was sinning and she knew it. (LA) <***Loc:*** LA, Da84>

pêcher[1] [peʃe] **I** *v.tr.* to fish, fish for *Il n-a du monde qui pêche des goujons, mais ça c'est un différent de qualité de pêche, parce qu'il faut ça ils les pêchent à la terre.* There are people who fish flathead catfish, but that's a different kind of fishing, because they have to fish for them from the shore. (SL) **II** *v.intr.* **1** to fish *Je pourrais pêcher tous les jours.* I could fish every day. (LA) **Ils estiont après pêcher dessus l'écore du bayou.* They were fishing on the bank of the bayou. (EV, An94) *Le monde c'était tout des planteurs de canne et mon père était un chasseur, il pêchait pour une vie et il élevait des tortues.* People were all sugar cane planters and my father was a hunter, he fished for a living and he raised turtles. (LF) **2** to nod off, doze off *Chaque fois je le regardais, il était après pêcher.* Every time I looked at him, he was nodding off. (LA) ◊ **•pêcher à la ligneguette {ligne}** to fish using a set line or cane pole <EV> **•pêcher des lignes** to fish with trotlines *Je pêche juste des cages à écrevisses et de temps en temps je vas pêcher des lignes, des TROTLINE.* I only use crawfish traps for fishing and from time to time I use trotlines. (SM) <SM> <***Loc:*** AC, EV, JD, LA, SL, SM, TB, An94, Da84, La99>

pêcher[2] [peʃe] *n.m.* peach tree *Et pour quelqu'un qui a le tranchement d'urine, tu connais, je y'eux fais bouillir des feuilles de pêcher.* And for someone who has urine retention, you know, I make them boil peach leaves. (TB) *Ils ont coupé une petite branche de pêcher et ça taillait les enfants.*

They used to cut a little branch from a peach tree and whip the children. (LF) <***Loc:*** LF, SL, TB, Da84>

pêcheur [peʃœr] *n.m.* **1** fisherman *Là tu vois y a des mondes qui travaillent sur des gros bateaux qui va dans l'eau salée, eux-autres a parlé avec des vieux pêcheurs, eh ben eux-autres connaît mieux que moi.* Then you see there are people who work on big boats that go out in saltwater, they talked with old fishermen, well they know better than I do. (TB) *Presque tous les pêcheurs parlent français.* Almost all fishermen speak French. (SM) **2** angler ◊ **•pêcheur à la ligne** angler *Lui il a jamais été d'autre chose qu'un pêcheur à la ligne.* He was never anything but an angler. (TB) <TB> **•pêcheur de {à} crabes {huîtres / chevrettes, etc.}** crab, oyster, shrimp, etc. fisherman *Le monde de Des Allemands là-bas, eusse pêche les barbues, et là eusse ramasse la viande et eusse vend les têtes à les pêcheurs à crabes.* The people from Des Allemands, they fish for catfish, and they collect the meat and they sell the heads to crab fishermen. (TB) <TB> <***Loc:*** SM, TB, Da84, Hi02>

pécheur [peʃœr] *n.m.* sinner *Sainte Marie, Mère de Dieu, priez pour nous pauvres pécheurs asteur et à l'heure de notre mort.* Holy Mary, Mother of God, pray for us poor sinners now and at the hour of our death. (TB) <***Loc:*** TB, Da84, Hi02>

pédale [pedal] *n.f.* pedal, treadle <***Loc:*** Da84>

pedler [pedle] *v.tr.* to peddle *Il passait tous les jours après pedler son pain.* He passed by every day peddling his bread. (LA) <***Loc:*** LA, JE, TB>

pedleur [pedlœr] *n.m.* peddler <***Loc:*** AV, JE, TB>

peigne [pẽj] *n.m.* **1** comb *Quoi il y a eu avec tes cheveux? T'as perdu ton peigne?* What happened to your hair? Did you lose your comb? (LA) **2** sharp row of teeth of certain fish *C'est un poisson fait comme ça mais il a un peigne. Il a des dents comme des piquants chaque bord de ce peigne.* It's a fish that looks like that but it has a sharp row of teeth. It has teeth like thorns on either side. (TB) ◊ **•passer au peigne fin** to investigate carefully <TB> <***Loc:*** LA, SL, TB, Da84>

peigner [pẽje] **I** *v.tr.* **1** to comb (hair) **2** to comb (fiber, e.g. wool or cotton) *Peigner le coton, c'est ôter les grémilles et les saletés, mais carder c'est mettre tous les fils en ligne.* To comb cotton is to take out the impurities, but carding is putting all the fibers in line. (LA) **II se peigner** *v.pron.* to comb one's hair *Va te peigner, paillasse!* Go comb your hair, clown! (VM) ◊ **•se peigner les cheveux** to comb one's hair <Hi02> <***Loc:*** LA, VM, Da84, Hi02>

peignure [pẽjyr] *n.f.* hairdo, coiffure, manner of styling the hair <***Loc:*** LF>

peindre [pẽn, pẽd(r)] **I** *v.tr.* to paint **Il dit que quelqu'un a venu peindre sa bêtaille vert.* He said that someone came and painted his horse green. (AC, An94) **II** *v.intr.* to paint *C'est pas quelqu'un qui connaît bien peindre.* He's not someone who knows how to paint well. (LA) <***Loc:*** AC, LA, An94, Da84, Hi02>

peine [pẽn] *n.f.* **1** penalty, punishment **2** trouble, sorrow, pain ◊ **•à peine** hardly, scarcely, just barely <Da84> **•avoir de la peine à** to have trouble (doing s.t.) *J'ai eu de la peine à dénicher la poule pour avoir les œufs.* I had trouble removing the hen from the nest to get the eggs. (VM) <VM> **•pas avoir la peine** to not need to, not have to *Un bateau plate, carré en avant, ça c'est pour pêcher comme des* HOOPNET, *dans les rivières, là où t'as pas la peine aller dans le bois.* A flat boat, square ahead, this is to fish with hoopnet, in rivers where you don't need to go far into the woods. (SM) *Les* PUT-PUT *c'est une qualité de bateaux on utilisait dans le temps. C'est le train ça faisait. T'avais pas la peine pagayer.* Put-puts were a kind of boat used at one time. It was the noise it made. You did not need to paddle. (SM) <SM> **•ça me fait de la peine** it grieves me, I'm sorry *Alle dit si n-a une d'égaré, alle dit, ça me fait de la peine de dire, mais c'est toi qui l'as égaré.* She said if one of them is missing, I'm sorry to say it, but it's you who lost it. (TB) <EV, TB, Da84> **•c'est pas la peine / ça vaut pas la peine** there's no use, it's not worth it **C'est pas la peine je te conte ça qu'a arrivé, tu vas pas croire.* It's no use for me to tell you what happened, you won't believe it. (EV, An94) *Ça vaut pas la peine bougonner.* It's not worth it to complain. (JE) *C'est pas la peine de faire une babine; tu vas pas aller quand même.* It's no use to pout. You're not going anyway. (LA) *L'affaire est* GONE, *c'est pas la peine brailler.* It's over, there's no use crying. (AC) <AC, EV, JE, LA, SM, TB, An94, Da84> **•en peine** grieving, sorrowful **Je vois vous êtes en peine. Vous avez perdu quelqu'un de votre famille?* I see that you are grieving. Did you lose someone from your family? (LA, An94) <EV, LA, An94> **•faire de la peine** to grieve, make sad or sorry *Et il me faisait de la peine de voir qu'il connaissait pas mieux parler français.* And he made me sad to see that he didn't know any more French than that. (TB) <EV, TB, Da84> **•prendre la peine** to take the trouble *Si je prends la peine d'aller tout le long là-bas-là, il ferait mieux d'être là.* If I take the trouble to go all the way out there, he had better be there. (LA) <LA, Da84> **•sous peine** under penalty *Sous peine de mort.* On pain of death. (VM) <VM, Da84> <***Loc:*** AC, EV, JE, LA, SM, TB, VM, An94, Da84, Hi02>

peineux [pẽnø] *adj.* grieving, sorrowful **Il dit, "D'ayoù tu viens?" Il dit, "Tu sembles peineux."* He says, "Where are you coming from?" He says, "You seem sorrowful." (IV, An94) <***Loc:*** IV, An94>

peintre [pẽt(r)] *n.m.* painter (of pictures), artist <***Loc:*** Da84>

peinturage [pẽtyraʒ] *n.m.* painting, act of painting <***Loc:*** Da84>

peinture [pẽtyr] *n.f.* paint *Ç'a peinturé le devant de leurs maisons* WHITEWASH, *blanc, ça pouvait pas* AFFORD *la peinture.*

They whitewashed the front of their houses, they couldn't afford paint. (LF) <*Loc:* LF, SL, VM, An94, Da84, Lv88>

peinturer [pẽtyre] *v.tr.* **1** to paint (a house, a picture, etc.) *Et après l'ouragan de la Chênière le monde a tout déménagé ici et ç'a peinturé le devant de leurs maisons* WHITEWASH, *blanc, ça pouvait pas* AFFORD *la peinture.* After the Chênière hurricane people all moved here and they whitewashed the front of their houses, they couldn't afford paint. (LF) *Je peux peinturer mes portraits mais je n'ai pas le temps.* I can paint pictures but I don't have the time. (VM) **2** to glaze *C'est pour peinturer un gâteau.* It is to glaze a cake. (SM) <*Loc:* EV, IB, LF, SM, TB, VM, An94, Da84, Lv88>

peintureur, -euse [pẽtyrœr, -øz] *n.* **1** painter, housepainter *Le peintureur a venu pour faire la galerie.* The painter came to do the porch. (Lv88) **2** painter, artist *S'ils ont besoin d'être peinturés, il faut je les amène à une peintureuse à Lafayette. Peinture, c'est une huile on met sur les portraits qui durent pour la vie.* If they need to be painted, I have to take them to a painter in Lafayette. Paint, that's an oil you put on pictures that lasts for life. (VM) <*Loc:* LA, VM, Da84, Lv88>

pêle-mêle [pɛlmɛl] *adv.* pell-mell, in a disorderly fashion *Ils ont tout tombé pêle-mêle par terre.* They all fell pell-mell on the floor. (LA) <*Loc:* LA, Da84, Hi02>

pélerinage [pel(ə)rinaʒ] *n.m.* [*eccl.*] pilgrimage <*Loc:* Hi02>

pélican [pelikɑ̃] *n.m.* **1** pelican **2** brown pelican <*Loc:* JE, SM, Da84, Hi02>

péline (**piline**) [pelin, pilin] *n.f.* **1** palisade, high wooden fence **2** stake, pile, post <*Loc:* JE, Lv88>

pelle [pɛl] *n.f.* **1** shovel *Asteur ils ont une machine pour faire ça, mais dans le temps ça faisait ça à la pelle.* Now they have a machine to do that, but in the past they did that with shovels. (IV) **2** spade, flat shovel ◊ **•pelle-cheuve** shovel <JE, Di32> **•pelle croche** shovel <Da84> **•pelle droite** shovel <AC, Da84> **•pelle plate** spade, flat shovel <AC> <*Loc:* AC, EV, IV, JE, LA, LF, SL, SM, VM, An94, Da84, Di32>

pelletage [pɛltaʒ] *n.m.* shoveling, spading <*Loc:* Da84>

pelletée [pɛlte] *n.m.* shovelful <*Loc:* Da84>

pelleter [pɛlte] *v.tr.* to shovel, spade, dig *Oh, il abattait des bois, et pour faire du bois, tous des jobs comme ça, pelleter des canals.* Oh, he chopped down trees, to get wood, all jobs like that, digging ditches. (TB) <*Loc:* JE, TB, Da84>

pelleteur [pɛltœr] *n.m.* digger, one who shovels or spades <*Loc:* Da84>

pelote (**pelotte, plotte**) [plɔt] *n.f.* **1** ball *Jette la pelote!* Throw the ball! (JE) *Ils ont chiqué de la gomme jusqu'à ils ont fait une grosse pelote.* They chewed gum until they made a big ball. (EV) **2** clot, small lump *La farine a fait des pelotes dans mon roux.* The flour made lumps in my roux. (Lv88) **3** baseball, game of baseball *On jouait à la pelote en arrière de l'école à Cankville.* We played baseball behind the school in Cankville. (LA) *Mes enfants aiment jouer à la pelote.* My children like to play ball. (Gu00) **4** testicle ◊ **•pelote à la main** handball <Lv88> **•pelote au panier** basketball <Lv88> **•pelote au pied** soccer <Lv88> **•pelote en élastique** rubber ball <Da84> <*Loc:* EV, JE, LA, SL, SM, VM, Da84, Gu00, Hi02, La99, Lv88>

pelotte ♦see **pelote**

peluche [plyʃ] *n.f.* material that is plush, velvety, or furry <*Loc:* Da84>

pelure [plyr] *n.f.* peel, skin (of fruits) <*Loc:* Da84>

pénalité [pẽnalite] *n.f.* penalty <*Loc:* JE>

penchant [pɑ̃ʃɑ̃] *n.m.* inclination, leaning, taste <*Loc:* Da84>

pencher [pɑ̃ʃe] **I** *v.tr.* to lean, bend *Elle a penché sa tête d'un côté et de l'autre.* She leaned her head one way and the other. (LA) **II** *v.intr.* **1** to lean, bend *Ça fait j'sutais penchée comme ça-là-là au* LAVATORY *après brosser mes dents.* So I was leaned over like this in the lavatory, brushing my teeth. (TB) **2** to slope, incline *La petite manche penchait assez que c'était malaisé de la monter à bicycle.* The little lane sloped enough that it was difficult to go up on a bicycle. (LA) **III se pencher** *v.pron.* **1** to lean, lean over **Quand Nathan s'est penché pour l'embrasser encore, il a mit [=mis] sa main dessus son genou par accident.* When Nathan leaned over to kiss her again, he put his hand on her knee by accident. (Wh83) **2** to bend over, stoop *C'est à peu près long comme ça là, et ç'a une lame un peu large, pour tu coupes la canne, plutôt que de te pencher et ramasser avec la main, tu vois.* It's about this long, and it has a blade that's fairly wide, so you [can] cut the sugarcane rather than having to stoop to gather it up by hand, you see. (TB) <*Loc:* LA, TB, Da84, Wh83>

pendant [pɑ̃dɑ̃] *prep.* **1** during **Pendant la nuit.* During the night. (Da84) **Les habitants font la récolte de la canne à sucre pendant la roulaison.* Farmers harvest sugar cane during the harvesting season. (Hi02) *Pendant la guerre.* During the war. (SL) **2** for (a period of time) *Je joins toujours de ce monde-là que j'avais affaire avec pendant des années.* I still meet with some of the people that I dealt with for many years. (SL) *Elle a beuglé pendant deux heures.* She wept for two hours. (SB) *Pendant longtemps je faisais du roux mais maintenant c'est un tas plus facile aller au magasin.* For a long time I used to make roux, but now it's a whole lot easier to go to the store [to get it]. (SL) ◊ **•pendant (que)** while *Fait ils se sont couchés, mais pendant que tout ça était après aller, Petit Poucet a pris le bonnet de un des enfants du vieux diable qu'était à peu près sa grosseur à lui et il l'a mis sus sa tête à lui.* So, they went to bed, but while all that was going on, Petit Poucet took the nightcap of one of the old devil's children who was about his size and he put it on his own head. (LA) *Il a venu pendant j'étais dans le clos après ramasser mon gombo.* He came over while I was in the field picking my okra. (Lv88) **Ça fait c'est proche juste les femmes et les petits qui s'assis dans l'église pour* *la messe pendant les hommes se plantent endéhors pour charrer.* So it's mostly just women and children who sit in church for mass, while the men take up positions outside to talk. (Wh83) <LA, SL, SM, Lv88, Wh83> <***Loc:*** AC, EV, LA, SB, SL, SM, An94, Da84, Hi02, Lv88, Wh83>

pendille (**pendriole**) *n.f.* [pɑ̃dij, pɑ̃drijɔl] ◊ **•à la pendille {pendriole}** hanging, suspended <JE, LF, SL, VM> <***Loc:*** JE, LF, SL, VM>

pendilloche ♦see **pendrioche**

pendre [pɑ̃n, pɑ̃d(r)] **I** *v.tr.* **1** to hang, hang up *Alle va aller pendre sa robe là dans le coin là dans sa chambre.* She'll go hang up her dress there in the corner of her room. (TB) *Là j'ai lavé mon linge que j'avais à ce matin sur le dos, il est tout propre, là il est pendu après sécher.* I washed the clothes that I had on this morning, it's all clean, it's hung up drying. (TB) *Il fallait que ça pend la viande en dehors.* They had to hang the meat outside. (TB) **2** to hang, put to death by hanging **Ils les ont attrapés et ils les ont pendus.* They caught them and they hanged them. (SL, An94) *Cet homme vaut pas le câble pour le pendre.* This man is not worth the rope to hang him. (LA) **3** to hang (a door) on hinges *J'ai pendu tout les portes dans la batisse.* I hung all the doors in the building. (SL) **II** *v.intr.* **1** to hang **Tout à l'heure, il s'en vient un bougre en travers de la salle qui avait la chemise déboutonnée avec le jabot grand ouvert, avec les culottes qui étaient après pendre un peu bas et il avait le mouchoir juste manière enfoncé dans sa poche.* Then a guy came across the room with his shirt unbuttoned . . . (SL, An94) *Sa jupe pend dessus un bord.* Her skirt hangs on one side. (AC) **2** to dangle **III se pendre** *v.pron.* to hang o.s. **Il s'a pendu après un arbre.* He hanged himself from a tree. (SL, An94) ◊ **•pendre du babinot** to pout <EV> **•pendre la babine *a*** to show disapproval, pout *Alle pend toujours la babine.* She is always pouting. (LA) ***b*** to be sad or depressed <EV, LA, VM, Da84, La99, Lv88> <***Loc:*** AC, EV, LA, SL, TB, VM, Da84, Hi02, La99, Lv88>

pendrilloche ♦see **pendrioche**

pendrioche (**pendrilloche, pendilloche**) [pɑ̃drijɔʃ, pɑ̃dijɔʃ] *n.f.* **1** anything (usu. gaudy or unsightly) that hangs or dangles *Pendrilloche d'une robe.* Useless hanging piece, ribbon, etc. on a dress (LF) **2** earring (esp. with a pendant ornament) *Ces pendrilloches sont trop longues pour sa petite tête!* Those earrings are too long for her little head! (EV) **3** pendant **4** hook <***Loc:*** JE, LF, SL, SM, VM, Da84, Lv88, Re31>

pendriole ♦see **pendille**

pendule [pɑ̃dyl] *n.f.* **1** clock *J'ai une petite pendule au ras de mon lit.* I have a little clock by my bed. (VM) **2** timer *Je mets la pendule, le temps sur la pendule. Et puis, à quand je le mets dans le développement, je hale les manches. Quand la pendule arrive, elle va sonner.* I set the timer. Then when I put it [the film] in the developer, I pull the handles of the timer. When the timer is finished, it rings. (VM) <***Loc:*** LA, SL, VM, An94, Da84, Gu00, Hi02>

pénésie ♦see **appendésie**

pénétration [pɛ̃netrasjɔ̃] *n.f.* **1** penetration, piercing **2** mental keenness <***Loc:*** Da84>

pénétrer [pɛ̃netre] *v.tr.* to penetrate, pierce, go through, enter **Après mille fois ça commence à pénétrer dans n'importe quel esprit.* After a thousand times, it starts to penetrate into anyone's mind. (*Cris sur le bayou*) <***Loc:*** Da84>

pénible [pɛ̃nib(l)] *adj.* **1** trying, insufferable *Il est pénible avec ses histoires de politique!* He's insufferable with his political stories. (VM) **2** heart-rending *C'était pénible de voir tout ce monde qu'avait perdu tout leur bien dans Rita.* It was heart-rending to see all those people who had lost everything in [Hurricane] Rita. (LA) <***Loc:*** LA, VM, Da84>

péniche [pɛ̃niʃ, piniʃ] *n.f.* small flat-bottom boat *Mais le Bon Dieu a voulu qu'eusse a couru à la péniche et ça c'est ça qu'eusse s'a escapé dedans.* But the Good Lord wanted them to run to the boat and that's what they escaped in. (LF) <***Loc:*** LF, TB, Re31>

pénille [pɛ̃nij] *n.f.* strip of material used in making the homemade rug locally called a 'catalogne' <***Loc:*** JE, Di32>

pénitence [pɛ̃nitɑ̃s] *n.f.* penitence, penance *On faisait des pénitences des fois qu'on allait pas manger du doux du Carème, ou on allait pas,* WELL *j'allais jamais à des bals et des affaires comme ça ou un* SHOW*.* We would do penance sometimes by not eating sweets during Lent, or we didn't go, well, I never went to dances or things like that or to a show. (TB) ◊ **•faire pénitence** to do penance <Da84> <***Loc:*** LF, TB, Da84>

pénitencier (**pénitentier**) [pɛ̃nitɑ̃sje] *n.m.* **1** penitentiary **2** prisoner <***Loc:*** Da84, Lv88>

pénitentiaire [pɛ̃nitɑ̃sjær] *n.m./f.* prison, state penitentiary <***Loc:*** TB, VM, Da84, Lv88>

pénitentier ♦see **pénitencier**

pensée[1] [pɑ̃se] *n.f.* **1** thought, idea **2** opinion <***Loc:*** EV, Da84>

pensée[2] [pɑ̃se] *n.f.* pansy <***Loc:*** Da84>

penser [pɑ̃se] **I** *v.tr.* to think, believe *Je pensais c'était un ours, tu vois.* I thought it was a bear, you see. (LF) *Je pense c'est côté de* CHURCH POINT*.* I think it's near Church Point. (AC) *Je pense qu'elle est folle.* I think she's crazy. (EV) *On pensait pas que le langage allait s'en aller. C'était une grosse erreur dessus notre part à nous-autres.* We didn't think that the language would disappear. That was a big mistake on our part. (TB) *Tu penses que ça va venir? Ouais, je crois ça.* Do you think they're going to come? Yes, I believe so. (EV) **II** *v.intr.* **1** to think *Je vas penser à quelque chose.* I will think of something. (SM) *Qui t'après penser?* What are you thinking about? (AV) *Quand je pense à ça, des fois, je ris, bonne sœur! J'aurais jamais cru que j'aurais été aussi bête que ça!* When I think of that, sometimes I laugh, my goodness! I would never have thought I could be that stupid.

(TB) **2** to think so, be of an opinion *Je pense.* I suppose so. (EV) **Je pense bien.* I think so. (Da84) ◊ **•penser entre moi-même {toi-même, etc.}** to think to myself, yourself, etc. *Alle dit, je peux pas parler longtemps, je vas te rappeler. Alle a jamais rappelé. Alle m'a fait ça une fois à moi. J'ai pensé entre mon-même, je vas te rappeler à toi.* She said, I can't talk long, I'll call you back. She never called back. She did that to me once. I thought to myself, I'll call you back. (TB) <TB> **•pense donc!** expression of astonishment, sometimes disapproval <La99> **•faire penser** to remind *Ça me fait penser à équand j'étais jeune et ça a glacé si dur que la vache à lait avait resté pris par la gueule dans l'eau de la digue.* That reminds me of when I was young and it froze so hard that the milk cow had its muzzle frozen into the watering hole. (ThCa: *La fête à Clomaire*) <ThCa> **•se faire penser** to remind o.s., be reminded <Da84> <***Loc:*** AC, AV, EV, IB, IV, JE, LA, LF, SL, SM, TB, VM, Da84, Hi02, ThCa>

penseur [pɑ̃sœr] *n.m.* thinker <***Loc:*** Da84>

pension [pɑ̃sjɔ̃] *n.f.* **1** pension, lodging **2** cost of lodging **3** pension *Alle est sus ma pension, sus mon* SOCIAL SECURITY. She is on my pension, on my social security. (TB) <***Loc:*** TB, Da84>

pensionnaire [pɑ̃nsjɔ̃nær] *n.m./f.* **1** boarder **2** pensioner *Ça fait trois ans que je suis pensionnaire.* I've been drawing a pension for three years. (Lv88) <***Loc:*** Da84, Lv88>

pensionnat [pɑ̃sjɔ̃na] *n.m.* **1** boarding house **2** boarding school <***Loc:*** Da84>

pensionné, -e [pɑ̃sjɔ̃ne] *n.* boarder, lodger *Il était pensionné au Collège St. Charles là-bas au Grand Côteau.* He was a boarder at St. Charles College over in Grand Coteau. (VM) <***Loc:*** VM, Da84>

pensionner [pɑ̃sjɔ̃ne] **I** *v.tr.* to board, pension *Tu pensionnes ta fille au Sacré Cœur?* Do your board your daughter at Sacred Heart Academy? (LA) **II** *v.intr.* to board, be pensioned *Il pensionne chez Madame Garog.* He has room and board at Mrs.Garog's. (VM) *Tu pensionnes à Lafayette?* You board in Lafayette? (Lv88) <***Loc:*** LA, VM, Da84, Lv88>

pente [pɑ̃t] *n.f.* **1** incline, slope, pitch (of a roof) **2** rut, wheel track **3** spree ◊ **•en pente** sloping, inclined *Un chemin en pente dessus la levée.* An inclined road on the levee. (VM) <VM, Da84> <***Loc:*** JE, VM, Da84>

Pentecôte [pɑ̃tkɔt] *n.f.* Pentecost <***Loc:*** Da84>

penture [pɑ̃tyr] *n.f.* hinge *Ce gros vent l'autre jour a manqué d'arracher la porte de dessus les pentures.* That strong wind the other day nearly tore the door off its hinges. (VM) <***Loc:*** EV, LF, SL, TB, VM, Da84, Gu00>

pépère [pepær] *n.m.* grandfather <***Loc:*** EV, VM, An94, Da84, Lv88>

pépie (**pipi, pipie, pupie**) [pepi, pipi, pypi] *n.f.* pip, mouth disease of chickens **Les poulets ont la pipi.* The chickens have the pips. (Da84) ◊ **•avoir la pépie** (of humans) ***a*** to be thirsty ***b*** to be hoarse <JE, VM> <***Loc:*** JE, LF, SL, VM, Da84>

pepmenthe ♦see **peppermint**

peppermint (**pepmenthe**) [pɛpmɑ̃t, pɛpmɛ̃t, pɑ̃pærmɛ̃t, paprɛ̃mɛ̃n, paparmɑ̃n] *n.m.* peppermint <***Loc:*** JE, TB, Da84, Da92>

péquin [pekɛ̃] *n.m.* [*pej.*] runt, small person <***Loc:*** SL>

percale [pærkal] *n.m.* percale <***Loc:*** Da84>

perçant, -e [pærsɑ̃, -ɑ̃t] *adj.* piercing, shrill, sharp *Un cri perçant.* A piercing cry. (LA) <***Loc:*** LA, Da84>

percé, -e [pærse] *adj.* crazy, nuts *T'es percé, tu peux pas faire ça.* You're crazy, you can't do that. (LF) <***Loc:*** LF>

perce-cuir [pærskɥir] *n.m.* leather punch <***Loc:*** VM>

percentage [pærsɑ̃taʒ] *n.m.* percentage <***Loc:*** JE>

percer [pærse, pœrse] **I** *v.tr.* **1** to bore, drill (a hole) *Ça qu'on appelle des vers de bois, c'était un ver qui perce des trous dans le bois.* What you call woodeating worms, they were worms that bore holes in the wood. (LF) **2** to make (a hole) *On perce un trou là.* We make a hole there. (EV) **3** to pierce **Les oreilles percées.* Pierced ears. (Da84) *Je veux pas que Mame perce le clou.* I don't want Mama to pierce the boil. (VM) **II** *v.intr.* to get a hole, develop a hole *Ça si la culotte aurait percé, elle lui aurait refait lui une autre pièce par dessus ça de là.* If the pants got a hole [in them], she would have put another piece on top of that for him. (EV) **III se percer** *v.pron.* to get holes, become perforated *Le bassin s'a percé avec l'eau salée.* The bucket was perforated by the salt water. (VM) ◊ **•percer ses dents** to teethe, cut teeth (of a baby) *Quand-ce qu'eux-autres était après percer leurs dents.* When they were cutting teeth. (TB) <TB> <***Loc:*** EV, LF, TB, VM, Da84>

perche[1] [pærʃ] *n.f.* **1** trout **2** bass, large-mouthed bass ◊ **•perche rouge** red snapper <Gu00> <***Loc:***SL, VM, Da84, Gu00>

perche[2] [pærʃ] *n.f.* **1** pole, stake *Je vas aller couper mes perches pour mes haricots de rame.* I'm going to go cut my poles for my pole beans. (TB) **2** fishing pole ◊ **•perche-à-ligne** fishing pole *J'ai coupé une branche de sureau pour me faire une perche-à-ligne.* I cut an elder branch to make myself a fishing pole. (VM) <VM> <***Loc:*** LF, TB, VM, Da84>

percher (se) [pærʃe] *v.pron.* to perch, roost *Le z-oiseau s'a perché au faît de l'arbre.* The bird perched itself at the top of the tree. (LA) <***Loc:*** LA, Da84>

perchette [pærʃɛt] *n.f.* perch (for chickens) <***Loc:*** JE>

perchoir [pærʃwar] *n.m.* chicken roost <***Loc:*** Da84>

perdant[1], **-e** [pærdɑ̃, -ɑ̃t] *adj.* **1** losing, suffering defeat *C'est elle qui sera perdante dans ce mariage.* She's the one who will lose in that marriage. (VM) **2** losing, at a loss *Travaille ça-là, tu seras pas perdant.* Work on that, you won't lose. (EV) <***Loc:*** EV, VM, Da84>

perdant[2] [pærdɑ̃] *n.* loser **Être le perdant.* To be the loser. (Da84) <***Loc:*** EV, Da84>

perdition [pærdisjɔ̃] *n.f.* perdition, ruin, waste ◊ **•s'en aller à**

la perdition to go to ruin, go to waste **La maison s'en va à la perdition.* The house is going to ruin. (Da84) **Le maïs s'en va à la perdition.* The corn is going to waste. (Da84) <Da84> <***Loc:*** Da84>

perdre [pærd(r)] **I** *v.tr.* **1** to lose *Quoi il y a eu avec tes cheveux? T'as perdu ton peigne?* What happened to your hair? Did you lose your comb? (LA) *On avait jamais pensé qu'on aurait perdu la langue.* We never thought we would lose the language. (LF) *Après il a fini l'école, il s'a mis à fouiner et il a perdu proche tous ses amis.* After he finished school, he started leading a dissolute life and lost almost all his friends. (LA) *Il a perdu plein d'argent.* He lost a lot of money. (LF) *On a tout perdu.* We lost everything. (VM) **2** to lose (s.o. to death) *Alle a perdu une sœur, pas trop longtemps après alle a perdu une belle-sœur [...]. Je crois qu'eusse sont morts deux semaines de distance.* She lost a sister, then she lost a sister-in-law. I think they died two weeks apart. (TB) **3** to miscarry, lose by miscarriage *Deux fois j'ai perdu mes bébés parce que j'ai fait des affaires que j'aurais pas dû faire.* Twice I miscarried my babies because I did things that I shouldn't have done. (EV) **II** *v.intr.* to have a miscarriage **La femme a perdu.* The woman had a miscarriage. (Da84) **III se perdre** *v.pron.* **1** to get lost, go astray, lose one's way or direction *Il s'a perdu dans le finfifond du bois.* He got lost in the deepest depths of the woods. (VM) **2** to get confused *Des fois quand Nick se perd avec sa mame, il dit, "Mame," il dit, "qui c'est que ça tu uses?"* Sometimes when Nick gets confused [while talking] with his mother, he says, "Mom, what is that [word] you're using?" (LF) ◊ **•perdre connaissance** to lose consciousness *La médecine l'a fait perdre connaissance.* The medicine put him under [i.e. made him lose consciousness]. (AC) <AC, Da84> **•perdre de vue** to lose sight of <Da84> **•perdre du poids** to lose weight *Et mon pape avait perdu du poids depuis que mame avait fait le* SUIT. And my dad had lost weight since my mother had made the suit. (TB) *Elle avait venu chétif, maigre. Elle était blême, sa figure, et puis elle avait perdu un tas de poids.* She had become worn-looking, thin. Her face was pale and she had lost a lot of weight. (SL) <SL, TB> **•perdre la canique / perdre ses {les} caniques** to go crazy, lose one's marbles *Moi, je crois qu'il a perdu la canique. Il fait drôle!* I think he's lost his mind. He's acting weird! (AC) <AC, Da84, La99> **•perdre la carte** to lose one's mind, go crazy, become insane *Quelle idée! Je crois qu'il a perdu la carte!* What an idea! I think he's lost his mind! (SM) <SM, TB, La99> **•perdre la raison** to lose one's mind *Son procès fut jugé d'une voix si-z-horrible, car le jeu et la boisson te fait perdre la raison.* The verdict was announced in such a horrible voice because gambling and drinking make you lose your mind. (PQ, ch: *Le jour de l'Ascension*) <PQ> **•perdre la tête** to go crazy <Da84> **•perdre la vue** to lose one's eyesight <Da84> **•perdre son balan** to lose one's balance or equilibrium *J'ai arrêté de faire des chansons parce que j'ai plus un tas de temps, les moustiques me tracassent et je suis manière malade, tu vois? Tu connais quand-ce c'est que tu perds ton balan, ton équilibre, c'est ça j'empoigne des fois.* I stopped composing songs because I don't have a lot of time anymore, the mosquitoes pester me and I'm somewhat sick, you see? You know when you lose your balance, that's what I get sometimes. (TB) <TB> **•perdre son idée** to lose one's mind *J'ai eu assez de tracas dedans ma vie à me faire perdre mon idée.* I've had enough trouble in my life to make me lose my mind. (VM) *Le jour où tu m'as quitté, j'ai perdu mon idée.* The day you left me, I lost my mind. (Lv88, ch: *Chanson de Vin Bruce*) <VM, Lv88> **•perdre son {l'} équilibre** ***a*** to lose one's balance *Je suis manière malade, tu vois? Tu connais quand-ce c'est que tu perds ton balan, ton équilibre, c'est ça j'empoigne des fois.* I'm somewhat sick, you see? You know when you lose your balance, that's what I get sometimes. (TB) ***b*** to do s.t. strange, do s.t. out of the ordinary ***c*** to go crazy <SM, TB, La99> **•en perdre** to lose ground, lose strength, fade *Quand ça venait pour courir les plus grandes distances, il en perdait.* When it came to running the longest distances, he would lose ground. (EV) <EV> **•je n'ai rien perdu à Chicago** I don't want to go to Chicago <La99> <***Loc:*** AC, AV, EV, JE, LA, LF, SL, SM, TB, VM, Da84, Hi02, La99>

perdreau [pærdro] *n.m.* young quail, young partridge <***Loc:*** Re31>

perdriole (padriole) [pærdrijɔl, padrijɔl] *n.f.* young partridge <***Loc:*** VM>

perdrix [pærdri] *n.m./f.* quail, partridge, bobwhite <***Loc:*** EV, IV, SL, VM, Da84, Lv88>

père [pær] *n.m.* **1** father **Il a revenu* BACK *pour visiter son père et sa mère.* He came back to visit his father and his mother. (LA, An94) **2** father (title for a priest) **Un homme va confesser au prêtre. Il dit, "Père, je veux confesser mes péchés."* A man goes to confess to the priest. He says, "Father, I want to confess my sins." (EV, An94) ◊ **•père levier** stepfather <Da84> <***Loc:*** AC, EV, IV, LA, SL, TB, VM, An94, Da84, Hi02>

perfection [pærfɛksjɔ̃] *n.f.* perfection <***Loc:*** VM, Da84>

perfectionner [pærfɛksjɔ̃ne] **I** *v.tr.* to improve, perfect *Ça m'a pris trois ans d'expérimenter avec un vieux sauvage dans la criée des cannes avant on a pu trouver les ingrédients pour perfectionner ce tonique du Hasitall.* It took me three years of experimentation with an old Indian in the backwoods before we were able to find the ingredients to perfect this Hasitall tonic. (AV) **II se perfectionner** *v.pron.* to improve o.s. *Il commence à se perfectionner dans la routine de faire du riz.* He's starting to improve his rice-producing abilities. (VM) <***Loc:*** AV, VM, Da84>

perfidie [pærfidi] *n.f.* perfidy, treachery, deceit <***Loc:*** Da84>

périgorie ♦see **parégorique**

péril [peri(l)] *n.m.* peril, danger <*Loc:* Da84>

période [perjɔd] *n.f.* period (of time), epoch, era <*Loc:* Da84>

périque (**perique**) [perik] *n.m.* aromatic black tobacco cultivated in St. James parish *Dans le vieux temps, ça torquait le périque pour faire des torquettes.* In the old days, they would twist the perique tobacco into rolls. (LA) <*Loc:* JE, LA, Da84, Lv88, Re31>

périr [perir] *v.intr.* to perish, die *On va tout périr ici, si quelqu'un arrive pas avec du manger.* We'll all die here, if someone doesn't arrive with food. (LA) <*Loc:* LA, VM, Da84, Fa77>

perle [pærl] *n.f.* **1** pearl **2** bead **3** eyeball ◊ **•perles blanches** leucorrhoea <VM> <*Loc:* VM, Da84>

perline [pærlin] *n.m.* washing powder, powdered detergent <*Loc:* VM>

permanence [pærmɑ̃nɑ̃s] *n.f.* permanence <*Loc:* Da84>

permettable [pærmetab(l)] *adj.* permissible *C'est pas permettable dans ce pays.* That's not permissible in this country. (LA) <*Loc:* LA, Da84>

permettre [pærmɛt(r)] **I** *v.intr.* to permit, allow, let *Je te permets pas de me répondre comme ça!* I will not allow you to answer me that way! (AC) *Il était pas permis d'aller au village lui tout seul.* He was not allowed to go to town by himself. (AC) **II se permettre** *v.pron.* to permit o.s., allow o.s. *Je me permets pas de dépenser autant d'argent que ça sus des bagatelles.* I don't allow myself to spend that much money on useless things. (AC) <*Loc:* AC, Da84>

permis [pærmi] *n.m.* permit, license *Pour avoir ton permis et ton estrécité et pour bâtir ta maison, ça qu'il faut faire.* To get your building permit and your electricity and to build your house, that's what you had to do. (LF) <*Loc:* LF, Da84>

permission [pærmisjɔ̃] *n.f.* permission *Et les Cadiens a commencé à faire des records, on a fait des albums, on faisait ça plus à la Nouvelle Orléans, et là lui il donnait sa permission et on a envoyé ça à lui.* And Cajuns began making records, and we made albums, we did that mostly in New Orleans, and then he gave his permission and we sent it to him. (LF) <*Loc:* LF, Da84>

perpétuel, -lle [pærpetɥɛl] *adj.* [*eccl.*] perpetual, continuous *Une dévotion perpétuelle.* A perpetual devotion. (LA) <*Loc:* LA, Da84>

perroquet [pærokɛ, pæroke] *n.m.* parrot <*Loc:* VM, Da84>

perruque [peryk] *n.f.* wig <*Loc:* IB, Da84>

persécuter [pærsekyte] *v.tr.* to persecute, annoy or trouble persistently *Cet homme ça-là a persécuté sa pauvre famille à cause de la boisson.* That man persecuted his poor family because of alcohol. (VM) <*Loc:* VM, Da84>

persécution [pærsekysjɔ̃] *n.f.* persecution <*Loc:* Da84>

persienne [pærsjɛ̃n] *n.f.* shutter, Venetian blind <*Loc:* Da84>

persil [pærsi] *n.m.* parsley <*Loc:* CL, EV, LF, SL, VM, An94, Da84, Hi02>

personnage [pærsɔ̃naʒ] *n.m.* personage, person of importance or renown <*Loc:* Da84>

personnalité [pærsɔ̃nalite] *n.f.* personality, character <*Loc:* Da84>

personne[1] [pærsɔ̃n] *n.f.* person, individual *Mais alle a jamais été bien comme une personne était supposée. Et c'est elle qu'a eu le gris-gris.* But she was never well like a person was supposed to be. And she's the one who had the gris-gris. (TB) ◊ **•personne de parole** person of his or her word <Da84> <*Loc:* AV, EV, SL, SM, TB, Da84, Hi02>

personne[2] [pærsɔ̃n] *pron.indef.* **1** no one, nobody, not anyone, not anybody **Il y a personne ici.* There is no one here. (Da84) *Personne était intéressé là-dedans, tu vois.* Nobody was interested in it, you see. (TB) *Personne te ferait rien de mal.* No one would do you any harm. (SL) *Il y avait pas eu personne de tué.* No one was killed. (AC) *Quand j'étais jeune enfant toujours ici dans la campagne on avait pas beaucoup d'amusement pour les enfants et même personne avait des radio et les TV dans ces temps là.* When I was a young child here in the country we didn't have much fun stuff for kids and nobody even had radio or TV in those days. (LA) **Dis pas à personne.* Don't tell anyone. (LA, An94) *No, j'ai jamais dit à personne jusqu'à j'ai venu grand.* No, I never told anybody until I grew up. (EV) **2** anyone, anybody **Faire mieux que personne.* To do better than anyone [else]. (Da84) ◊ **•personne d'autre** no one else **Personne d'autre que lui.* No one else but him. (Da84) *Personne d'autre était avec lui?* Nobody else was with him? (VM) <VM, Da84> **•pas... personne** no one, nobody *Moi, j'ai pas vu personne.* I saw no one. (AC) <AC, EV, SL, Hi02> <*Loc:* AC, EV, IV, LA, SL, SM, TB, VM, An94, Da84, Hi02>

personnel[1], **-lle** [pærsɔ̃nɛl] *adj.* personal, individual, private *C'est pas mon désir personnel, c'est pour vous-autres que je fais ça.* It is not my personal desire, I'm doing it for you all. (VM) <*Loc:* EV, VM, Da84>

personnel[2] [pærsɔ̃nɛl] *n.m.* personnel, employees, staff <*Loc:* Da84>

personnel[3] [pærsɔ̃nɛl] *adv.* personally *Il a dit ça à moi, personnel.* He told me that, personally. (SM) <*Loc:* SM>

personniers (**parsonniers**) [pærsɔ̃je, parsɔ̃je] *n.m.pl.* group of people who do certain work together without pay (e.g. helping each other plow, build fences, etc.) <*Loc:* JE, Gr86>

perte [pært] *n.f.* **1** loss *Une section de levée pour assayer de protecter le monde pour une ouragan […] Mon je vois si tellement de perte que deux générations d'ici mon je sais pas qui-ce qui va arriver.* A section of levee to try to protect people from a hurricane. I see so much loss [of land] that in two generations I don't know what will happen. (TB) **2** loss, waste *Mais avec 210 livres de chevrettes vertes, de chevrettes fraîches, eux-autres sort avec entre 30 et 33 livres de chevrettes secs. C'est une grosse perte.* But with 210 pounds of fresh shrimp, they end up with between 30 and 33 pounds of dried shrimp. That's a big loss. (TB)

3 miscarriage (loss of fetus) ◊ **•perte de sang** loss of blood, hemorrhage <Da84> **•quelle perte** what a waste, what a loss <Da84> <***Loc:*** TB, Da84>

pesage [pəzaʒ] *n.m.* weighing <***Loc:*** Da84>

pesant [pəzɑ̃, pɛzɑ̃] *n.m.* **1** nightmare **2** delerium <***Loc:*** JE, VM>

pesanteur [pəzɑ̃tœr] *n.f.* weight <***Loc:*** Da84>

pèse [pɛz] *n.m.* scale <***Loc:*** LA>

peser [peze] **I** *v.tr.* to weigh *Le beurre venait en petits barils. Ça fait ils pesaient l'affaire.* Butter used to come in small barrels. So they would weigh the thing. (SJ) *Là les femmes passent en travers encore pour voir s'il y a peut-être des drigailles, ou les épluches, et après ça ils sont pesés sur la balance.* Then the women go through them again to see if there may be some refuse, or peelings, and after that they're weighed on a scale. (LF) **Amène les romaines et pèse son argent.* Bring the scales and weigh his money. (SL, An94) **II** *v.intr.* **1** to be heavy **2** to weigh (an amount) **Peser dix livres.* To weigh ten pounds. (Da84) **Il y a pas de bêtailles qui pèsent seize mille livres.* There are no animals that weigh sixteen thousand pounds. (EV, An94) *Le petit cheval pesait à peu près huit cents livres.* The little horse weighed about 800 pounds. (SL) **3** to bear down **Pèse pas trop fort.* Don't bear down too hard. (Da84) **III se peser** *v.pron.* to weigh o.s. *J'ai mangé assez, j'ai peur de me peser.* I ate so much I'm afraid to weigh myself. (LA) ◊ **•peser (sur) un bouton** to press a button *Y a une petite lumière, il faut que tu pèses le bouton.* There's a little light, you have to press the button. (TB) *Elle pèse sur le bouton, ça sonne chez ma fille.* She presses the button, it rings at my daughter's house. (Lv88) *C'est ça la loi ça nous dit, mais ça peut changer ça si ça veut, c'est juste peser un bouton et puis là l'eau va venir, c'est tout ça prend.* This is the law they tell us, but they can change the law if they want to, they just need to press on a button and then the water will come, that's all it takes. (SM) <SM, TB, Lv88> **•pèse bouton, paie couillon** fancy gadgets are not worth the money one pays for them **Ouais, j'te dis, asteur, c'est 'pèse bouton et paye couillon.'* Yeah, I'll tell you, now, it's fancy gadgets that are not worth the money you pay for them. (Gu82) <Gu82, La99> <***Loc:*** EV, IV, LA, LF, SJ, SL, SM, TB, An94, Da84, Gu82, Hi02, La99, Lv88>

peste [pɛs(t)] *n.f.* **1** pestilence, plague *C'est une sacrée peste, tout la moisissure qu'a rendu le monde malade après l'ouragan!* It's a pestilence, all that mold that got people sick after the hurricane. (LA) **2** nuisance *Tu parles d'une peste, cet homme-là. Il est tout le temps à la maison après essayer de me vendre de l'assurance.* What a nuisance, that guy! He's always at the house trying to sell me insurance. (LA) <***Loc:*** LA, Da84>

pestilence [pɛstilɑ̃s] *n.f.* pestilence, pest, plague, contagion <***Loc:*** Da84>

pet (**pète**) [pɛt] *n.m.* fart ◊ **•avoir un pet accroché *a*** to be bothered by s.t. ***b*** to be in a bad mood ***c*** to not feel well <La99> **•avoir un pet en long *a*** to be contrary, hard to get along with ***b*** to be in a cranky mood <AC, La99> **•(ça compte pas plus qu') un pet dans un ouragan** of little consequence or importance <La99> **•pet de nonne** cream puff <EV, La99> **•pet sec** insignificant thing <LA> <***Loc:*** AC, EV, LA, TB, Da84, La99>

pétarade (**pétarde**) [petarad, petard] *n.f.* proud person <***Loc:*** JD, SC, La99>

pétard [petar] *n.m.* **1** firecracker **2** cap pistol, pop-gun **3** device formerly used to explode a charge by striking it on the ground **4** person with a dynamic or eccentric personality, a 'character' <***Loc:*** VM, Da84, Lv88>

pétarde ♦see **pétarade**

pétchotte [petʃɔt] *n.f.* [*vulg.*] female genitals <***Loc:*** TB>

pète ♦see **pet**

péter [pete] **I** *v.tr.* **1** to deal (a blow) *Péter une tape, un coup.* To deal a blow. (Lv88) *Il m'a pété un coup de poing.* He punched me. (LA) **2** to thrust at, push at, deal to *Pour elle, elle est après me péter les affaires comme ça là.* As for her, she's dealing those situations to me like that. (EV) **II** *v.intr.* to fart *Quand je mange des fèves ou des choux, ça me fait péter.* When I eat beans or cabbage, it makes me fart. (LA) **III se péter** *v.pron.* to throw o.s. *Il s'est pété par terre. Il est tombé par terre.* He threw himself to the ground. He fell on the ground. (AC) ◊ **•péter à cul cassé** to exaggerate, brag <LF, La99> **•péter son camp** to get out, beat it, go away *Allons péter notre camp d'icitte.* Let's get out of here. (JD) <JD> **•péter plus haut que son nez {cul}** to try to do things that are beyond one's social or financial means <La99> **•se péter une ribote** to get drunk <EV, La99> **•va péter à Lacassine** go away, get out of here <La99> <***Loc:*** AC, EV, LA, LF, Da84, Hi02, La99, Lv88>

péteur, -euse (**péteux, -euse, pêteux, -esse**) [petœr, -øz, petø, -øz] *n.* **1** insignificant person, nobody **2** arrogant person, smart-aleck, one who puts on airs **3** child who tries to act grown up **4** punk, tough guy, showoff **5** shiftless person <***Loc:*** EV, VM, Da84, La99>

péteux, pêteux ♦see **péteur**

petiller [pətije] *v.intr.* to sparkle, light up *Mon travail c'était faire des prix à les fermiers [...]. On aurait commencé une conversation en anglais, mais là changer ça en français et je voyais leurs yeux petiller parce que ils aimaient beaucoup mieux faire leur business en français qu'en anglais.* My job was to quote prices to the farmers. We would start a conversation in English but then, changing it to French I would see their eyes light up because they liked much better doing their business in French rather than English. (SL) <***Loc:*** SL>

petit[1], **-e** (**pitit, p'tit, 'tit**) [p(ə)ti, piti, ti, -it] *adj.* **1** small, little *Eux-autres avait une petite cabane, un petit* CAMP *que ça restait dedans.* They had a little cabin, a little camp that they lived in. (TB) *André est venu avec son petit cheval.*

André came with his little horse. (SL) *Oui, le petit prêtre, c'était un jeune prêtre, lui il venait à l'école.* Yes, the little priest, he was a young priest, he would come to the school. (EV) *C'était beaucoup une petite école.* It was a very small school. (AC) *C'est une petite histoire vraie qu'a arrivé à moi quand j'étais un jeune petit garçon.* It's a true little story that happened to me when I was a young little boy. (JD) *Elle était petite hein... elle était plus petite que moi, elle.* She was little, huh . . . she was even smaller than me. (EV) *Ces pendrilloches sont trop longues pour sa petite tête!* Those earrings are too long for her little head! (EV) **2** short (in duration, stature, etc.) *Une petite histoire.* A short story. (EV) **3** young **Les petits enfants.* The children. (Da84) *J'aime les 'tites filles, mais j'aime mieux les 'tits garçons.* I like little girls but I like little boys better. (SM) *Équand on était petits, nos parents nous amenaient au cirque.* When we were little, our parents used to take us to the circus. (LF) **4** younger (of siblings) *Mon petit frère, ma petite sœur.* My younger brother, my younger sister. (SL) ◊ **•petite à petite** little by little, slowly, gradually <Da84> **•tout petit** very little, very small *Les loches qu'on appelle, c'est un tout petit poisson.* Minnows as we call them, they're a very small fish. (TB) <TB, Da84> <***Loc:*** AC, EV, LA, LF, SL, SM, TB, VM, An94, Da84, Lv88>

petit[2], -e (pitit, p'tit, 'tit) [p(ə)ti, piti, -it] *n.m./f.* **1** child, young child **Les pitits.* The children. (Da84) *Est-ce que c'est tes pitits, ça?* Are those your children? (SM) *Qué belle portée de pitits!* What a beautiful bunch of children! (VM) *Les pêcheurs fait pas d'argent avec ça, eusse aime mieux un gros. Eusse met leur appât haut, le petit peut pas attraper.* The fishermen don't make any money with that, they prefer an adult [alligator]. They put their bait high, the little ones can't catch it. (TB) *Ça halait les petits à l'école en wagonnettes, ça appelait,* COVERED WAGONS, *avec deux chevaux.* They transported the kids to school in wagonettes, they called it, covered wagons, with two horses. (EV) **2** offspring, child *Les petits des mes petits à moi pourraient me montrer.* The children of my children could show me. (EV) **3** baby *La petite nièce à ma femme là là a eu un petit avant qu'alle se marie.* My wife's little niece had a baby before she got married. (LF) <***Loc:*** AV, EV, IV, LF, SL, SM, TB, VM, An94, Da84, Hi02>

petite-fille [p(ə)titfij] *n.m.* granddaughter <***Loc:*** Da84>

petitement [p(ə)titmɑ̃] *adv.* poorly, in a small way **Petitement logé.* Poorly housed. (Da84) <***Loc:*** Da84>

petit-enfant [p(ə)titɑ̃fɑ̃] *n.m.* grandchild <***Loc:*** LA, LF, TB, VM, Gu00, Fa77>

petite-nièce [p(ə)titnjɛs] *n.m.* grandniece, great-niece <***Loc:*** Da84>

petitesse [p(ə)titɛs] *n.f.* smallness, scantiness <***Loc:*** Da84>

petit-fils [p(ə)tifis] *n.m.* grandson <***Loc:*** Da84>

pétition [petisjɔ̃] *n.f.* petition, request **Passer une pétition.* To pass a petition. (Da84) <***Loc:*** Da84>

pétitionner [petisjɔ̃ne] *v.tr.* to petition *Pétitionner le juge.* To petition the judge. (EV) <***Loc:*** EV, Da84>

petit-lait [p(ə)tilɛ, p(ə)tile] *n.m.* **1** whey **2** thick milky sap of certain plants <***Loc:*** Da84>

petit-neveu [pətinvø] *n.m.* grandnephew, great-nephew <***Loc:*** Da84>

pétrifiant, -e [petrifjɑ̃, -ɑ̃t] *adj.* petrifying *L'ouragan était pétrifiant.* The hurricane was petrifying. (VM) <***Loc:*** VM, Da84>

pétrifier [petrifje] *v.tr.* to petrify *Ça l'a pétrifié de voir l'eau monter si vite.* It petrified him to see the water rise so quickly. (VM) <***Loc:*** VM, Da84>

pétriller ♦see **pétriner**

pétrin [petrɛ̃] *n.m.* **1** mudhole, boggy area **2** mess, tight spot **3** trough (for mixing dough, breaking ice to be used in shrimp packing, etc.) <***Loc:*** LF, Da84>

pétriner (pétriller) [petrine, petrije] **I** *v.tr.* **1** to knead, mold **2** to stamp, trample **II** *v.intr.* to stamp, trample (in the mud) <***Loc:*** LF, Lv88>

pétrir [petrir] *v.tr.* to knead *Mam Rheul pouvait passer le matin à pétrir son pain.* Mom Rheul could spend an entire morning kneading her bread dough. (LA) <***Loc:*** LA, Da84>

pétrissage [petrisaʒ] *n.m.* kneading (of dough) <***Loc:*** Da84>

pétrole [petrɔl] *n.m.* oil *J'ai fait ça-là à peu près quand je faisais le pétrole. Quand j'amenais les travaillants du Mississippi au Texas, tout la côte de la Louisiane, à peu près 30 ans.* I did that around the time I was working in the oil business. When I took workers from Mississippi to Texas, the whole coastline of Louisiana, for about 30 years. (TB) <***Loc:*** TB>

peu[1] [pø] *n.m.* bit, little bit, small amount **Manger un peu.* To eat a little. (Da84) **Gagner de peu.* To beat by a little. (Da84) **Le peu que j'ai mangé m'a barbouillé le cœur.* The little I ate upset my stomach. (Di32) *J'avais bu un peu et ça m'avait manière brouillé l'idée.* I had drunk a bit and it had sort of blurred my senses. (LA) **Un petit peu à la fois.* A little bit at a time. (Da84) ◊ **•un (petit) peu** slightly, a little **C'était un peu étroit.* It was a bit tight. (LA, An94) *Là si le bateau coulait un petit peu, que la craque s'avait pas bouché, ils prendont du coton exprès, du coton avec du godron dedans.* Then if the boat was leaking a little, if the crack wasn't plugged, they took some cotton brought just for that, cotton with tar in it. (LF) *Il commence à faire un peu trop chaud pour travailler sur ça.* It's starting to be a little too hot to work on that. (LF) *Il a tout le temps été un peu stupide.* He was always a bit stupid. (LA) <JE, LA, LF, VM, An94, Da84> **•un (petit) peu de** a little bit of, a small amount of **Il vendait un petit peu de whiskey à Lafayette.* He sold a little bit of whiskey in Lafayette. (LA, An94) *La dernière année c'était pas venu froid. À part qu'on a eu un petit peu de la neige au mois de mars.* The last year it didn't get cold. Except that we had a little snow in the month of March. (TB) *Il y a peut-être un peu de différent de mots et* *de manières mais il y a des différents de manières à parler français en France même.* Maybe there are a few different words and manners but there are different ways of speaking French in France, too. (SL) <LA, SL, TB, An94> **•un tout petit peu** a tiny bit <Da84> <***Loc:*** AC, AV, EV, IB, IV, JE, LA, LF, SB, SM, TB, VM, An84, An94, Da84, Di32, Guoo, Hio2, La99, Wh83>

peu[2] [pø] *adv.* little, not much, not many, few **Faire aussi peu qu'il peut.* To do as little as he can. (Da84) *Ça mangeait bien peu du bœuf dans ce temps-là. C'était tout le temps de la viande de cochon.* They ate very little beef in those days. It was always pork. (TB) ◊ **•à peu près** about, approximately *Il faut que tu bouilles ça pour à peu près une heure pour cuire les tripes, tu vois.* You have to boil it for about an hour to cook the intestines, you see. (LF) *Et là y a un Rousseau qui reste à peu près deux blocs là-bas.* And there's a Rousseau who lives about two blocks down there. (LF) <EV, IB, LA, LF, SB, SL, TB, VM, An94, Da84, Guoo, Wh83> **•être peu intelligent** to be not very intelligent <Da84> <***Loc:*** Da84, Hio2>

peuple [pœp(l)] *n.m.* people, folks <***Loc:*** Da84>

peur [pœr] *n.f.* fear, terror, fright *Alle a manqué de me faire mourir de peur.* She nearly frightened me to death. (TB) ◊ **•avoir peur à mort** to be very frightened <La99> **•avoir peur (de / que)** to be afraid (of/that) **Ils ont peur de venir par ici.* They are afraid to come around here. (EV, An94) **Le monde avait peur de moi.* People were afraid of me. (EV, An94) *Et il dit que sa mame avait la fièvre typhoïde. [...] Et elle alle nourissait le bébé, tu vois. Et Philippe avait peur qu'alle donne ça à le petit.* And he said that his mother had typhoid fever. And she would feed the baby, you see. And Philippe was afraid that she would give it to the baby. (TB) <TB, Da84, Hio2> **•de peur que** for fear of, for fear that *Ils ont pas dit à rien de peur que leur père aurait compris qu'ils étaient après mentir.* They said nothing for fear that their father would understand that they were lying. (LA) <LA, Da84> **•faire peur (à)** to frighten *Elle a jeté un cri en l'air, alle m'a fait assez peur.* She cried out, she gave me quite a scare. (TB) *C'est ça qui me fait peur.* That's what frightens me. (LA, ch: *Un autre soir ennuyant*) <LA, TB, Da84> **•par la peur** out of fear, on account of fear <Da84> <***Loc:*** AC, EV, JE, LA, SL, SM, TB, VM, An94, Da84, Hio2, La99>

peureux, -euse [pørø, -øz] *adj.* fearful, cowardly, timid *Pauvre garçon, il est tellement peureux que il peut proche pas sortir la nuit.* Poor boy, he's so cowardly that he can hardly go out at night. (LA) <***Loc:*** LA, Da84>

peut-être [pøtɛt(r)] *adv.* maybe, perhaps **Tu connais, garçon, c'est peut-être pas une mauvaise idée, ça.* You know, boy, maybe that's not a bad idea. (IV, An94) **Il est peut-être après dormir.* Maybe he's sleeping. (EV, An94) *À peu près six pouces, peut-être.... peut-être plus, peut-être moins. On va dire six pouces.* About six inches, maybe . . . maybe more, maybe less. Let's say six inches. (EV) *Asteur tu peux aller en Bayou des Allemands dans une heure et demie peut-être, une heure. Mais dans ce temps là, ça peut-être prendait trois heures pour venir à la Pointe.* Now you can go to the Bayou des Allemands in an hour and a half, perhaps, [or] an hour. But in those days it took maybe three hours to come to the Pointe. (TB) **Si c'est bon, plus tard, je vas peut-être aller.* If it's good, later, maybe I'll go. (SL, An94) ◊ **•peut-être que** perhaps, maybe *Peut-être que mon je vas les chercher si vous-autres veut rester ici.* Maybe I'll go get them if you all want to stay here. (TB) <TB> <***Loc:*** AC, AV, EV, IV, LA, SL, TB, VM, An94, Da84>

pharmacie [farmasi, fɔrmasi] *n.f.* pharmacy, drugstore <***Loc:*** EV, LA, VM, Da84>

pharmacien [farmasjɛ̃, fɔrmasjɛ̃] *n.m.* pharmacist, druggist <***Loc:*** EV, Da84>

phonographe [fɔ̃nograf] *n.f.* phonograph <***Loc:*** Da84>

photo [foto] *n.f.* photo, photograph <***Loc:*** TB, Da84>

phrase [fraz] *n.f.* phrase, sentence **Chaque fois il dit ein mot ou eine phrase Cajin, il soutient l'éxistence d'ein deuxième-culture qui est vraiment différent de les manières réglés Américaines.* Every time he says a Cajun word or sentence, he supports the existence of a second culture which is really different from the regular American ways. (Wh83) <***Loc:*** Da84, Wh83>

piaillard [pjajar] *n.m.* killdeer <***Loc:*** Re31>

pialler [pjale] *v.intr.* **1** to whine, complain *Là je suis sûr qu'il va aller pialler à sa mère.* Now I'm sure he will go whine to his mother. (LA) *Arrête donc de pialler comme ça.* Stop whining like that. (LA) **2** to cry, howl *Si j'aurais jonglé lui attraper une gobe là, je peux te dire, il aurait piallé.* If I could have thought to grab a chunk of him, I can tell you, he would have howled. (EV) **3** to peep (of chicks, birds) *Les petits poulets ont piallé tout la nuit.* The chicks peeped all night long. (LA) <***Loc:*** EV, JE, LA, SM, VM, Da84>

piallerie [pjalri] *n.f.* whining, complaining <***Loc:*** Da84>

pialleur, -euse [pjalœr, -øz] *n.* whiner, complainer <***Loc:*** Da84>

piano [pjɑ̃no] *n.m.* **1** piano **2** nickelodeon, jukebox <***Loc:*** VM, Da84, Hio2>

piaquer (**piasser**) [pjake, pjase] *v.intr.* to cheep, peep (of chickens) *Les 'tits poulets piaquent sans fin.* The little chickens peeped endlessly. (Lv88) <***Loc:*** VM, Lv88>

piasse ♦see **piastre**

piasser ♦see **piaquer**

piastre (**piasse**) [pjas(tr)] *n.f.* **1** dollar *La peau de cocodrie vaut vingt piastres le pied.* Alligator skin is worth twenty dollars a foot. (Lv88) *J'ai payé ça trois piasses.* I paid three dollars for that. (VM) **2** silver dollar fish <***Loc:*** AV, EV, LF, SL, SM, TB, VM, Da84, Guoo, Hio2, Lv88>

pic [pik] *n.m.* pick, pick-axe ◊ **•à pic *a*** straight up, straight ahead **Il est assis à pic dans sa chaise.* He is seated straight in his chair. (EV, Ph36) ***b*** steep, at a sharp angle, at a steep slope, inclined **Une couverture à pic.* A steep roof. (Da84) <EV, SL, Da84, Lv88, Ph36> <***Loc:*** EV, LA, SL, Da84, Lv88, Ph36>

pic à poc ♦see **poc à poc**

picailler ♦see **piquailler**

picaillon [pikajɔ̃] *n.m.* **1** old coin **2** small piece, bit, fragment **3** picayune, trifle <***Loc:*** JE, Lv88>

picaillonner [pikajɔ̃ne] *v.intr.* to pinch pennies, be very economical <***Loc:*** JE, Gr86>

picaillonneur [pikajɔ̃nœr] *n.m.* penny-pincher <***Loc:*** JE, Gr86>

picassé, -e [pikase] *adj.* **1** freckled *La petite fille est assez mignonne, toute picassée comme ça.* The little girl is so cute, all freckled like that. (LA) **2** bearing scars, pockmarked *Sa figure est toute picassée.* His face is all scarred. (SL) <***Loc:*** EV, JE, LA, SL, VM, Lv88, Ph36>

picasser [pikase] *v.tr.* to tease, pick on *Il est pas content s'il ne le picasse pas.* He is not happy unless he is teasing him. (IB) <***Loc:*** IB>

pic-bois ♦see **pique-bois**

pichenet (**pichnet, puchné**) [piʃnɛ, piʃne, pyʃnɛ, pyʃne] *n.m.* flick, snap, fillip (e.g. of the fingers, hand), thump *Je vas te foutre un pichenet sur l'oreille.* I'm going to give you a flick on the ear. (LF) **Ça, ça vaut pas un pichnet.* That's not worth a flick of the finger. (Da84) <***Loc:*** LF, VM, Da84, Lv88, Wh83>

pichette ♦see **piquette**

pichnet ♦see **pichenet**

pichou[1] [piʃu] *adj.* mean *Une femme pichou.* A mean woman. (VM) <***Loc:*** AS, VM, La99>

pichou[2] [piʃu] *n.m./f.* **1** bobcat, lynx **2** mean, disagreeable person <***Loc:*** EV, LF, SM, TB, VM, Da84, La99, Lv88, Ph36, Re31>

pichouette [piʃwɛt] *n.f.* **1** naughty, mischievous female (esp. a little girl) **C'est une petite pichouette.* She's a bad little rascal. (Re31) **Quand a ç'té pichouette de Marie, i fau'ra j'la fouette.* As for Mary, that mischievous girl, I need to give her a whipping. (EV, Ph36) **2** short person, runt *Il est un petit pichouette. Il pèse à peu près quatre-vingt livres tout trempe avec pas de linge!* He's a little runt, he weighs about 80 pounds all wet with no clothes on! (TB) <***Loc:*** SB, SM, TB, VM, La99, Lv88, Ph36, Re31>

PICKUP [pikœp] *n.m.* pick-up truck <***Loc:*** Da84, Lv88>

picocher [pikoʃe, pigoʃe] **I** *v.tr.* **1** to peck *Les zozos picochont les fruits.* The birds peck the fruit. (VM) **2** to nag, tease, pick at *Ne va pas le picocher maintenant.* Don't go tease him now. (IB) **II** *v.intr.* **1** to pick at one's food, eat lightly *Arrête donc de picocher comme ça dans ton plat.* Stop picking at your food like that. (LA) *Elle a pas faim. Elle a picoché dans le manger tout l'avant midi.* She's not hungry. She was picking at the food all morning. (SM) *Elle a pas mangé, elle a juste picoché.* She didn't eat, she just picked at her food. (SM) **2** to putter, work lightly *Et là y a huit ans que je suis* RETIRE *de ça. Et là asteur là juste je picoche dans l'un et l'autre.* And it's eight years since I retired from that. And now I just putter in this and that. (TB) **3** to pick a fight *Il a commencé à picocher.* He started to pick a fight. (VM) **4** to nag (at), pick (at) *Elle picoche tout le temps sur lui.* She nags at him all the time. (LF) **Et défunt Monsieur Blanco a pris à picocher après le vieux bougre.* And the late Mr. Blanco began to pick at the old fellow. (SL, An94) <***Loc:*** IB, LA, LF, SL, SM, TB, VM, An94, Da84, Lv88>

picocheur [pikoʃœr] *n.m.* **1** chicken that pecks **2** one who picks at food or eats lightly **3** nag, one who picks at or nags *Je l'aime pas, il est un vrai picocheur.* I don't like him, he's a real nag. (SL) <***Loc:*** SL, SM, Da84, Lv88>

picodinde (**pique aux dindes**) [pikodɛ̃n, pikodɛ̃d] *n.m.* freckle <***Loc:*** AV, SL, Lv88>

picot [piko] *n.m.* **1** stitch, hemstitching *Il faut faire un autre picot droite là.* You have to make another stitch right there. (TB) **2** notch *Il a fait un picot en haut ma toupie.* He made a notch on the upper part of my toy top. (SL) **3** dot, polka-dot *L'étoffe de sa robe est tout pleine de petits picots.* The cloth of her dress is full of little polka-dots. (TB) <***Loc:*** SL, TB, VM>

picote [pikɔt, bikɔt] *n.f.* **1** smallpox *La picote, c'est une maladie défigurante, mais pas autant que la lèpre.* Smallpox is a disfiguring disease, but not as much as leprosy. (VM) **2** chicken pox, varicella *J'ai eu la picote mais j'ai pas été trop malade.* I had chicken pox, but I wasn't too sick. (IB) ◊ **•picote volante / picote de poule / petite picote** chicken pox <EV, LF, SL, SM, TB, VM, Lv88, Ph36> **•grosse {mauvaise} picote** smallpox <EV, JE, Ph36> <***Loc:*** AV, EV, IB, JE, LA, LF, SL, SM, TB, VM, Da84, Lv88, Ph36, Re31>

picoté, -e [pikote] *adj.* pockmarked (as from smallpox) *Sa figure est toute picotée.* His face is all pockmarked. (SM) <***Loc:*** SM, TB, Da84>

picouer [pikwe] *v.tr.* to hemstitch <***Loc:*** VM>

picouette [pikwɛt] *n.f.* ill-tempered girl <***Loc:*** Re31>

PIE [paj] *n.m.* pie <***Loc:*** JE, LF, Lv88, Re31>

pièce[1] [pjɛs] *n.f.* **1** piece, fragment *Mon vase a tout tombé en morceaux, mais j'ai réussi à recoller les pièces ensemble.* My vase fell to pieces, but I succeeded in gluing the pieces back together. (VM) **2** patch (on clothing) *Mettre des pièces sur les genoux des culottes.* To put patches on the knees of pants. (VM) **3** patch (of crop, plants) *Pièce de coton.* Cotton patch. (SM, VM) **Pièce de maïs.* Corn patch. (Da84) **4** room *Cette pièce est un pillage.* This room is a mess. (VM) ◊ **•pièce de musique** piece of music <Da84> **•à la pièce** by the piece <Da84> <***Loc:*** EV, LA, SM, VM, An94, Da84, Hi02>

pièce[2] [pjɛs] *adv.* apiece *C'est à peu près cinq cents piasses* *pièce.* They're about $500 apiece. (TB) *L'homme a payé cent piasses pièce pour ça.* The man paid $100 apiece for them. (TB) <***Loc:*** TB>

piécetager ♦see **piéceter**

piéceter (**piécetager**) [pjɛste, pjɛstaʒe] *v.tr.* to patch, repair, mend **Elle dit, "J'arrange les* NETS *et je piécetage son linge et je fais tout ça."* She says, "I repair the nets and I mend his clothes and I do all that." (EV, An94) <***Loc:*** AL, EV, An94, Da84, Lv88>

pied [pje] *n.m.* **1** foot *Il a coupé son pied creux.* He cut his foot deeply. (SM) **Ses pieds touchaient ses fesses.* She was running very fast. (La99) **2** paw (of an animal) **3** leg (of a table, chair, etc.) *Il faudra que je tourne les pieds de table cet après-midi.* I'm going to have to turn the table legs this afternoon. (VM) **4** foot, base (of a tree, mountain, etc.) *Les patassas sont concentrés au pied des cipres.* The bream are concentrated at the foot of the cypress trees. (LA) **Au pied d'un arbre.* At the base of a tree. (Da84) **5** stalk (of a plant), plant *Des fois, on plantait ça entre les pieds de maïs.* Sometimes we planted it between the cornstalks. (SL) *Comment gros le pied devient?* How big does the plant get? (EV) **6** foot, twelve inches (measure) *Mon garçon est grand, il a six pieds de haut et il pèse presque trois cents livres. Il est grand et gros.* My son is big. He is six feet tall and he weighs almost three hundred pounds. He is tall and big. (TB) *La peau de cocodrie vaut vingt piastres le pied.* Alligator skin is worth twenty dollars a foot. (Lv88) **7** presser foot (of a sewing machine) ◊ **•pied de bêtes** herd *Ils sont après* DIP *le pied de bêtes.* They are dipping the herd. (VM) <VM, Lv88> **•pied de fleur** flower plant <LA> **•pied de lit** foot of the bed <SL, Da84> **•pied de mirliton** chayote, mirliton plant <Re31> **•pied-de-roi / pied-du-roi** ***a*** twelve-inch rule or measuring stick ***b*** carpenter's square ***c*** carpenter's folding ruler *Là, il y avait un pied-de-roi, tu usais ça pour mesurer et ça se ployait pour se mettre dedans ta poche.* Then, there was the folding ruler. You would use it to measure and it folded up so you could put it in your pocket. (LA) <LA, VM, Da84, Lv88> **•pied de sureau** elderberry plant <VM> **•pied d'herbe** stalk of grass <Da84> **•pieds plats** flat feet <AL> **•à pieds joints** knee-deep, all out <Da84> **•donner un pied (à qqn)** to give s.o. an advantage, a 'leg up' <AV, La99> **•être à pied** ***a*** to be on foot ***b*** to have no transportation <Da84> **•faire de ses pieds et ses mains pour arriver** to make great efforts to do s.t. <AV, La99> **•mettre le pied** to set foot <Da84> **•mettre le pied dans la boue** to do s.t. which could have bad consequences <SL, La99> **•pas être à pied** to be very wealthy <La99> **•sus-pied** on foot, standing **Passer la nuit sus-pied.* To stay up all night. (Da84) <Da84> <***Loc:*** AL, AV, EV, LA, LF, SL, TB, VM, Da84, Hi02, La99, Lv88, Re31>

piège [pjɛʒ] *n.m./f.* **1** trap, snare *J'arrive à ce piège là, y a un loutre vivant dedans, ça me vaut 50 piasses.* I arrive at that trap, there's a live otter in it, it's worth 50 dollars to me. (TB) **2** trapping *Il a fait toute sa vie, oui. La pêche, et le piège.* He did that his whole life, fishing and trapping. (TB) ◊ **•aller au piège** to go trapping *Et là on trawlait jusqu'à Christmas. Là ça fermait encore, et tout l'hiver on allait au piège.* And we trawled until Christmas. Then [the season] closed again, and the whole winter we went trapping. (TB) <TB> <***Loc:*** IV, TB, An94, Da84, Hi02>

piégeage [pjeʒaʒ] *n.m.* trapping *Notre job, c'est le piégeage.* Our job, it's trapping. (Lv88) <***Loc:*** VM, Da84, Lv88>

piéger [pjeʒe] *v.tr.* to trap, snare *Et mon père, lui, il piégeait tous les hivers, il allait au piège, il piégeait des rats musqués, des belettes, des chaouis.* And my father, he went trapping every winter, he went trapping for muskrat, mink, raccoons. (TB) <***Loc:*** LF, TB, Da84>

piégeur (**pièegeur**) [pjeʒœr] *n.m.* trapper <***Loc:*** LF, Da84, Hi02, Lv88, Re31>

piejègue [piʒɛg] *n.m.* goatsucker, bullbat, nighthawk <***Loc:*** EV>

pienque[1] [pjɛ̃k] *n.m.* **1** jaybird **2** whiny or difficult child **3** insignificant person <***Loc:*** AV, SM, VM>

pienque[2] [pjɛ̃k] *interj.* nothing doing, no go *Tu veux que je fais ça, mais pienque!* You want me to do it, but no way! (SM) <***Loc:*** SM>

pier (se) [pje] *v.pron.* to get into position to be milked (of a cow) *La vache va se pier et on la tire.* The cow will get into position and we milk her. (Lv88) <***Loc:*** EV, Lv88, Ph36>

pierre [pjær] *n.f.* **1** stone, rock *Il s'a fait un* BARBECUE PIT *en pierre.* He built himself a stone barbecue pit. (LA) **2** calculus, gallstone, kidney stone *Il avait des pierres dans les pigueroins.* He had kidney stones. (Lv88) *Il a des pierres dans le fiel.* He has gallstones. (Lv88) **3** kidney ◊ **•pierre à affiler** sharpening stone <VM> **•pierre à feu** magnifying glass <VM> **•pierre angulaire** cornerstone <Da84> **•pierre à tonnerre** meteorite <AC> **•pierre de sauvage** arrow head <SL> **•les pierres sont après brûler** there is a mist or vapor rising from the ground <La99> <***Loc:*** AC, EV, LA, SJ, SL, VM, An94, Da84, Hi02, La99, Lv88>

piété [pjete] *n.f.* [*eccl.*] piety, godliness <***Loc:*** Da84>

piétinage [pjetinaʒ] *n.m.* trampling <***Loc:*** Da84>

piétinement [pjetinmɑ̃] *n.m.* trampling <***Loc:*** Da84>

piétiner (**piétonner**) [pjetine, pjetɔ̃ne] **I** *v.tr.* to trample, stamp on *Les enfants ont tout piétonné mes fleurs.* The children trampled all over my flowers. (EV) *Les vaches ont assez piétiné la cour de magasin que la terre est assapée.* The cows trampled the barnyard so much that the dirt is compacted. (VM) **II** *v.intr.* to stamp (one's feet) *Ça piétonne juste pour faire du train.* They stamp their feet just to make noise. (EV) <***Loc:*** EV, VM, Da84>

piétonner ♦see **piétiner**

pieu [pjø] *n.m.* **1** board, picket (usu. of split cypress) *C'est ça qu'eux-autres faisait avec ces pieux, t'avais des barrières* *avec ça.* That's what they did with those boards, you had fences made with them. (LF) **2** post ◊ **•pieu deboute** upright board (used for fences) *Là tout ce qu'eux-autres faisait avec les gros cypres, c'était faire ça qu'eux-autres appelait des pieux deboute.* All they did with the big cypresses was to make what they called upright boards. (LF) **Barrière à pieu deboute.* Fence with upright boards. (Da84) <LF, Da84> <***Loc:*** LF, Da84, Lv88>

pieusement [pjøzmɑ̃] *adv.* [*eccl.*] piously <***Loc:*** Da84>

pieux, -euse [pjø, -øz] *adj.* [*eccl.*] pious, devout *Un homme pieux.* A pious man. (LA) <***Loc:*** LA, Da84>

pigarlé, -e [pigarle] *adj.* speckled *Les œufs de lapin est tout pigarlés.* The Easter eggs are all speckled. (TB) <***Loc:*** TB>

pigeon [piʒɔ̃] *n.m.* pigeon ◊ **•pigeon de mer** ***a*** seagull ***b*** Cabot's tern ***c*** Forster's tern ***d*** sea swallow <JE, VM, Da84, Re31> **•pigeon maringouin** goatsucker, bullbat, nighthawk <Da84> **•pigeon ramier** passenger pigeon <Re31> <***Loc:*** JE, VM, Da84, Re31>

pigeon-vole [piʒɔ̃vɔl] *n.* traditional children's game in which players raise an index finger if an animal or object named in the game can fly <***Loc:*** EV, Wh83>

piger [piʒe] *v.tr.* **1** to stare at **2** to dupe, deceive <***Loc:*** JE, LF, Di32>

pignocher (**piguenocher**) [pĩjoʃe, pignoʃe] **I** *v.tr.* **1** to give a beating to **2** to interfere, meddle, tease *Il pignoche, il pignoche jusqu'à ce qu'il fait le train.* He teases, he teases until he starts trouble. (TB) **II se piguenocher** *v.pron.* to fight with each other <***Loc:*** EV, JE, TB, Ph36>

pignon [pĩjɔ̃] *n.m.* **1** the highest point of a pitched roof *Dans la paroisse St. Bernard, le ras de marais a passé par dessus les pignons des maisons.* In St. Bernard Parish, the tidal wave passed over the roof peaks of the houses. (VM) **2** the point of an outside wall created by the roof line, gable *C'était une galerie en avant, et eux-autres avait un pignon. Et là t'avais un autre pignon en arrière et t'avais une galerie sur le bord-là et une galerie bord-là, t'avais trois galeries.* There was a front porch, and they had a gable. And then you had another gable in back and you had a porch on that side and a porch on this side, you had three porches. (LF) *Et mon pape disait s'il a pas de pignon, c'est pas une maison. C'est un* CAMP. And my father used to say if there isn't a gable, it isn't a house. It's a camp. (TB) <***Loc:*** LA, LF, SM, TB, VM, Da84>

pignouf [pĩjuf] *n.m.* uncouth man, rough man <***Loc:*** SM>

pigroin ♦see **pigueroin**

piguenocher ♦see **pignocher**

piguerie [pigri] *n.f.* pigsty, pigpen <***Loc:*** Di32, Re38>

pigueroin (**pigroin**) [pigərwɛ̃] *n.m.* **1** kidney *Il avait des pierres dans les pigueroins.* He had kidney stones. (Lv88) **Maladie de pigroin.* Kidney trouble. (Da84) **2** kidney (as food) *Il faulait il tuait un cochon et là il prendait les débris du cochon, le foie, le cœur, les pigueroins, cuire ça tout ensemble.* He had to kill a pig and then he took the innards, liver, heart, kidneys, and cooked it all together. (IB) <***Loc:*** AV, EV, IB, IV, LA, LF, SL, SM, VM, Da84, Lv88>

pilage [pilaʒ] *n.m.* **1** pounding **2** milling (of grain, etc.) <***Loc:*** Da84>

pile[1] [pil] *n.m./f.* **1** pile, heap, stack *Il fait des grosses piles et il tombe du* SNOW *et là ça tourne tout aux glaces, c'est dur dur.* It makes big piles and the snow falls and then it turns icy and it's very hard. (TB) **2** compost heap *Va mettre ça sus la pile.* Go put that on the compost pile. (VM) ◊ **•en masse et en pile** lots, heaps <Da84> <***Loc:*** TB, VM, Da84>

pile[2] [pil] *n.f.* **1** mortar (in which rice, corn, etc. is hulled or crushed) *Pilez les pacanes dans la pile à Mame.* Crush the pecans in Mom's mortar. (SL) **2** beating, whipping, spanking *Donner une pile.* To give a spanking. (SL) ◊ **•pile et pilon** mortar and pestle <Da84> <***Loc:*** AV, SJ, SL, VM, Da84, La99, Lv88, Re31>

pilée [pile] *n.f.* mortarful, amount equal to the capacity of a mortar *Une pilée de riz.* A mortarful of rice. (VM) <***Loc:*** VM>

piler [pile] **I** *v.tr.* **1** to pound, crush *Pilez les pacanes dans la pile à Mame.* Crush the pecans in Mom's mortar. (SL) **2** to mill, hull in a mortar **Piler du riz.* To mill rice. (Da84) **3** to trample *Piler la terre, piler sous les pieds.* Trample the earth, trample underfoot. (VM) *On a fait un plancher en terre. Mettre ça là, piler ça. C'était tout fait à la main. Ils venaient là et mettre de la chaux.* We made a dirt floor. We put it down, trampled it down. It was all made by hand. They came along and put down lime. (LF) **4** to beat, beat up *Ils l'ont bien pilé dans le* PARKING LOT. They beat him up good in the parking lot. (EV) **II** *v.intr.* to step (in, on, etc.) *Il a pilé dans la boue.* He stepped into the mud. (LF) *Piler sur le pied de quelqu'un.* To step on someone's foot. (LF) <***Loc:*** EV, LF, SB, SL, VM, Da84, La99>

pilier [pilje] *n.m.* **1** footing, piling, support block (of a building) *Il s'avait fait une maison, il a mis ça sur des piliers en briques.* He had made himself a house, he put it up on brick pilings. (EV) **2** pier, post *Un* CAMP *sur des piliers.* A camp on piers. (VM) **3** leg, pedestal (of furniture) *Un pilier de table.* A table pedestal. (VM) ◊ **•pilier de maison** block, footing of a house <Da84> <***Loc:*** EV, VM, Da84>

piline ♦see **péline**

pillage [pijaʒ] *n.m.* **1** plundering, looting, robbing **2** mess *Cette pièce est un pillage.* This room is a mess. (VM) <***Loc:*** VM, Da84>

pillard (**pilleur**) [pijar, pijœr] *n.m.* looter, robber, thief, crook <***Loc:*** Da84>

piller [pije] *v.tr.* to plunder, loot, rob **Piller comme dans la forêt des bandits.* To rob blind, pillage, commit highway robbery. (Da84) <***Loc:*** Da84>

pillerie [pij(ə)ri] *n.f.* pillage, plunder, robbery, looting <***Loc:*** Da84>

pilleur ♦see **pillard**

pilluler ♦see **pulluler**

pilon [pilɔ̃] *n.m.* **1** tamper **2** pile driver **3** pestle <***Loc:*** EV, Da84>

pilonnage [pilɔ̃naʒ] *n.m.* pounding, tamping <***Loc:*** Da84>

pilonner [pilɔ̃ne] *v.tr.* to tamp, pound, pack *Pilonner la terre autour d'un poteau.* To tamp down the earth around a post. (VM) <***Loc:*** VM, Da84>

pilot [pilo] *n.m.* heap, pile, stack *Un pilot de linge sale.* A pile of dirty laundry. (Lv88) <***Loc:*** EV, LF, SL, SM, VM, Da84, Fa77, Ph36, Lv88>

pilotage [pilotaʒ] *n.m.* trampling, stamping <***Loc:*** LF, Lv88>

pilote [pilɔt] *n.m./f.* **1** pilot *Mais je courais un bateau là, j'étais pilote d'un bateau. Oui. J'étais pas instruit mais je pouvais* HANDLE A, *tu connais, une barque.* I ran a boat, I was the pilot of a boat. Yes. I wasn't taught but I could handle a, you know, a small boat. (TB) **2** guide *Il a été ma pilote.* He was my guide. (VM) *Laisse-lé aller le premier, c'est lui le pilote.* Let him go first, he's the guide. (TB) <***Loc:*** JE, TB, VM>

piloter[1] [pilote] *v.tr.* to pilot, guide *Ils pilotent des navires dans le chenal à Port Arthur.* They guide ships in the Port Arthur ship channel. (VM) <***Loc:*** VM, Da84>

piloter[2] [pilote] **I** *v.tr.* **1** to trample, pack down with the feet *Piloter les branches.* To trample the branches. (EV) **2** to pile up *Allons piloter les branches qu'a tombé.* Let's pile up the branches that fell. (VM) **II** *v.intr.* **1** to step randomly and carelessly **2** to stomp, trample **J'ai piloté su les fleurs à Mame.* I trampled on Mom's flowers. (EV, Ph36) **3** to stomp the feet *Le petit a piloté pour pas prendre sa médecine.* The child stomped his feet so as not to take his medicine. (Lv88) <***Loc:*** EV, JE, LF, SB, SJ, VM, Da84, Ph36, La99, Lv88>

pilule [pilyl, pinyl, pynyl, pilyd] *n.f.* pill, capsule *Ma femme des fois prend des pilules de mal à la tête.* My wife sometimes takes headache pills. (LF) <***Loc:*** EV, LF, TB, VM, Da84, Fa77>

pimbêche [pɛ̃bɛʃ] *adj.* lazy, good-for-nothing *Son mari est pimbèche.* Her husband is good-for-nothing. (SM) <***Loc:*** JE, SM, Lv88>

piment [pimɑ̃] *n.m.* pepper *Je fais jaunir [...] la viande et je mets des oignons, des piments, des assaisonnements, et là je remets le riz cru, avec l'eau dedans, et, cuis tout ensemble.* I brown the meat, and I put in onions, peppers, seasonings, and I add in the uncooked rice, with water in it, and cook everything together. (SL) ◊ **•piment banane** banana pepper <VM> **•piment chaud** hot pepper <JE> **•piment doux** sweet pepper, bell pepper <AC, AL, CL, EV, JE, LA, LF, PQ, SL, SM, TB, VM, Da84, Guoo, Hio2, Re31> **•piment enragé** very hot red or cayenne pepper <Da84, Hio2, Lv88, Re31> **•piment fort *a*** hot pepper ***b*** red pepper <EV, PQ, SL, Da84, Guoo, Hio2, Re31> **•piment rouge** red pepper <AC, Re31> **•avoir un piment contre** to have a grudge against, be prejudiced against *J'ai un piment contre lui.* I have a grudge against him. (VM) <VM> **•être piment contre qqn** to be angry with s.o. <VM, La99> <***Loc:*** AC, AL, CL, EV, JE, LA, LF, PQ, SL, SM, TB, VM, Da84, Guoo, Hio2, La99, Lv88, Re31>

pimenté, -e [pimɑ̃te] *adj.* highly peppered or seasoned *C'est une tomate pimentée.* It's a peppered tomato. (TB) <***Loc:*** TB, Da84, Hio2>

pimenter [pimɑ̃te] *v.tr.* to pepper, flavor with pepper *Il a trop pimenté sa viande.* He put too much pepper on his meat. (EV) <***Loc:*** EV, LF, Da84>

pimenterie [pimɑ̃tri] *n.f.* burning of the stomach caused by highly seasoned food *Je m'ai donné une bonne pimenterie.* My stomach is burning from all the spicy food I ate. (VM) <***Loc:*** VM>

pimper[1] [pɛ̃pe] *v.intr.* to drink alcohol *Il peut pimper, lui.* He certainly can drink a lot. (LF) <***Loc:*** LF>

pimper[2] **(se)** [pɛ̃pe] *v.pron.* to primp *Alle est dans sa chambre. Je pense qu'alle est après se pimper là.* She's in her room. I think she's primping in there. (TB) <***Loc:*** TB, VM, Lv88>

pimpette [pɛ̃pɛt] *n.f.* drubbing, severe beating *Il a foutu une pimpette à son beau-frère.* He gave his brother-in-law a severe beating. (LF) <***Loc:*** LF>

pimponner (se) (**pomponner, pouponner**) [pɛ̃pɔ̃ne, pɔ̃pɔ̃ne, pupɔ̃ne] *v.pron.* to primp, dress up with care *Elle met deux heures à se pimponner avant d'aller au bal.* She spends two hours primping before going to the dance. (VM) <***Loc:*** EV, LF, SL, SM, TB, VM, Da84>

pin [pɛ̃] *n.m.* pine, pine tree ◊ **•pin rouge** long leaf pine <SL> **•coco de pin** pine cone <VM> **•île de pins** grove of pine trees in the open prairie <Da84> <***Loc:*** SL, VM, Da84, Hio2>

pince [pɛ̃s] *n.f.* **1** claw, pincer (of crustaceans, etc.) **Les Européens les mangent par glaner toute la viande endéhors de chaque écrévisse et chaque pince.* Europeans eat them by gleaning all of the meat out of each crawfish and each claw. (Wh83) **2** wirecutter *Une pince pour couper ton fil.* A wirecutter for cutting your wire. (LF) **3** clippers, garden shears *J'ai taillé mon gastronia avec une pince.* I trimmed my crape myrtle with shears. (VM) **4** *(pl.)* pliers *Ça va me prendre une paire de pinces pour défaire le robinet.* I'll need a pair of pliers to undo the faucet. (VM) **5** *(pl.)* tongs *Je tourne mon poulet avec des pinces.* I turn my chicken with tongs. (VM) **6** tuck, dart (in a garment) *J'ai mis deux pinces dans ma jupe pour la rapetisser.* I put two darts in my skirt to take it in. (VM) **7** pinch *Pince de sel.* Pinch of salt. (VM, Fa77) ◊ **•pinces à glace** ice tongs <LA> **•pince à linge** clothespin <LA> **•pince de cheveux** lock of hair *C'est pour guérir le croupe qu'on met une pince de cheveux dans le trou d'un bois.* It's to cure croup that we put a lock of hair in the hollow of a tree. (TB) <TB> <***Loc:*** EV, JE, LA, LF, SL, SM, TB, VM, Da84, Fa77, Wh83>

pinceau [pɛ̃so] *n.m.* **1** paintbrush *Je peinture à quatre couleurs avec un pinceau.* I paint [my floats] four different colors with a paintbrush. (TB) **2** shaving brush <***Loc:*** EV, TB, VM, Da84, Lv88>

pincée [pɛ̃se] *n.f.* pinch, small amount **Une pincée de sel.* A pinch of salt. (Da92) <***Loc:*** Da84, Da92>

pince-minette [pɛ̃sminɛt] *n.f.* **1** vain person, pretentious person, fop **2** sanctimonious person <***Loc:*** LF, Lv88>

pince-nez [pɛ̃sne] *n.m.* pince-nez <***Loc:*** VM, Da84>

pincer [pɛ̃se] *v.tr.* **1** to pinch *Les uns là là peut pas pincer parce qu'ils sont trop parés pour changer, ils sont failles. Eusse après assayer mais eusse peux pas faire des durs.* These [crabs] can't pinch because they are too ready to molt, they are weak. They're trying, but they can't make hard ones [claws]. (TB) **2** to grip, squeeze *Il faudra tu pinces le tuyau plus fort si tu veux le défaire.* You'll have to grip the pipe more firmly if you want to take it apart. (VM) <***Loc:*** TB, VM, Da84>

pincette [pɛ̃sɛt] *n.f.* **1** small pinch **2** tweezers ◊ **•à la pincette** between thumb and forefinger *Alle l'attrape à la pincette, alle le tire par la fenêtre.* She grabs him between thumb and forefinger, she pulls him out the window. (TB) <TB> <***Loc:*** TB, Da84>

pinceuse [pɛ̃søz] *n.f.* spring clothespin <***Loc:*** VM>

pine [pin, pɛ̃n] *n.m./f.* penis <***Loc:*** AC, EV, LA, TB, VM, Da84, Hi02>

pinière [pĩjær] *n.f.* **1** pine grove, pine forest **2** piney woods of north and west Louisiana <***Loc:*** SL, Da84, Gu00, Hi02, La99, Re31>

pinouche [pinuʃ] *n.f.* [*baby talk*] penis <***Loc:*** VM>

pintale [pɛ̃tal, pɛ̃tard, pɛ̃taj] *n.m./f.* guinea fowl, guinea hen <***Loc:*** LF, SL, TB, VM, Da84, Lv88, Wh83>

pinte [pɛ̃t] *n.f.* **1** metal drinking cup (usu. with a handle) *Ma vieille tante avait sa pinte d'accrochée dessus sa pompe déhors.* My old aunt had her drinking cup hanging on the pump outside. (Gu00) **2** scoop, dipper, ladle **3** can, tin can **4** aluminum can *Ma voisine marche autour du voisinage pour ramasser des pintes pour vendre.* My neighbor walks around the neighborhood to collect aluminum cans to sell. (Gu00) ◊ **•pinte à café** tin coffee cup <TB> **•pinte d'eau** cup of water <Da84> **•pinte de mesure** measuring cup <LA> <***Loc:*** EV, IB, JD, JE, LA, LF, TB, VM, Da84, Gu00, Lv88>

pinteur [pɛ̃tœr] *n.m.* heavy drinker <***Loc:*** JE, SC, La99>

pintocher [pɛ̃toʃe] *v.intr.* to carouse <***Loc:*** JE>

pintocheur [pɛ̃toʃœr] *n.m.* drunkard, carouser <***Loc:*** JE, VM>

piochage [pjoʃaʒ] *n.m.* hoeing, work done with a hoe <***Loc:*** Da84>

pioche [pjɔʃ, pijɔʃ] *n.f.* **1** hoe *On piochait tout nos cannes à la main, on avait jusqu'à vingt et quelques piocheurs avec des pioches.* We used to hoe all our sugarcane by hand, we had twenty-some hoers with hoes. (AS) **2** square-bladed shovel **3** spades (card game) **4** safety razor ◊ **•pioche à coton** hoe with a flat blade <EV> **•pioche pour rayer** furrowing hoe <EV> <***Loc:*** AS, EV, JE, LA, LF, PQ, SL, SM, VM, Da84>

piocher [pjoʃe] **I** *v.tr.* to hoe *On ramassait du coton, piochait du coton.* We picked cotton, hoed cotton. (AC) **II** *v.intr.* **1** to hoe *J'ai pioché, j'ai travaillé à* SHOCK *du riz.* I hoed, I worked at bundling rice. (EV) **2** to paw the ground (of a bull) *On s'a halé de là quand le taureau a pris à piocher.* We got out of there when the bull started pawing the ground. (VM) **3** to draw cards from a deck *C'est ton tour. Pioche.* It's your turn. Draw. (EV) <***Loc:*** AC, EV, SL, VM, Da84>

piocheur [pjoʃœr] *n.m.* hoer, one who hoes *Le piocheur est endormi dans l'ombre.* The hoer is asleep in the shade. (SL) <***Loc:*** AS, LF, SL>

pipe [pip] *n.f.* **1** pipe (for smoking) **2** pipe, pipeline *Il faulait que tu* GAUGE *tous les* TANK BATTERY, *là éiou tout l'huile rentrait dans ces places là. [...] Faulait que tu* CHECK *à chaque pipe pour voir combien d'huile qu'il était après faire.* You had to gauge all the tank batteries, where the oil was coming in. You had to check each pipe to see how much oil it was producing. (TB) **3** piping, thin strip of covered cord used to trim seams and edges (on a garment or other fabric item) ◊ **•pipe en coton de maïs** corncob pipe <Da84> <***Loc:*** SL, TB, VM, Da84, Hi02>

pipée [pipe] *n.f.* pipeful (of tobacco) <***Loc:*** LF, SL, Da84>

pipeur [pipœr] *n.m.* inveterate pipe smoker <***Loc:*** VM, Da84>

pipi[1] [pipi] *n.m.* urine ◊ **•faire pipi** [*baby talk*] to urinate <Da84> <***Loc:*** Da84>

pipi[2] [pipi] *n.m.* [*baby talk*] chicken <***Loc:*** LF>

pipi[3] ♦see **pépie**

pipie ♦see **pépie**

pipine [pipin] *n.f.* ◊ **•pipine d'eau douce** stroke of bad luck *C'en est une, une pipine d'eau douce que je me tiens.* That's a stroke of bad luck for me. (LF) <LF> **•prendre {avoir} une pipine / se tenir une pipine** to get drunk <La99> <***Loc:*** LF, La99>

piquailler (**picailler**) [pikaje] *v.tr.* **1** to sting repeatedly **Les maringouins m'ont tout picaillé.* The mosquitoes stung me all over. (Da84) **2** to stick or prick repeatedly *Je m'ai fait joliment piquailler en ramassant des mûres.* I got pretty well pricked while picking blackberries. (SL) **II** *v.intr.* [*vulg.*] to have sex indiscriminately *Quand sa femme est pas là, il piquaille.* When his wife is not there, he screws around. (VM) <***Loc:*** LA, SL, VM, Da84>

piquanier [pikɑ̃je] *n.m.* gooseberry <***Loc:*** VM, Fa77>

piquant[1]**, -e** [pikɑ̃, -ɑ̃t] *adj.* **1** thorny *Une liane piquante.* A thorny vine. (LA) **2** pungent, stinging, sharp *J'aime pas mettre cette médecine sus mes bobos parce qu'elle est piquante.* I don't like to put that medicine on my sores because it stings. (LA) **3** spicy, hot and spicy <***Loc:*** LA, Da84>

piquant[2] [pikɑ̃] *n.m.* **1** thorn, sticker *Se planter un piquant.* To get stuck with a thorn. (Lv88) **2** barb (of barbed wire) **3** spine (on the dorsal fin of certain catfish) *Un mâchoiron là, il vient pas gros. Il est un poisson qu'a trois piquants mais ils sont mauvais mauvais, il pique avec.* A gafftopsail catfish doesn't get too big. It's a fish that has three spines that are quite bad, he sticks with them. (TB) **4** stinger *Des aspics, ça c'est eusse-là qu'a les piquants au bout de la tcheue.* Asps, those are the ones that have stingers on the end of their tail. (LF) **5** one who provokes or is easily provoked into a fight *Et d'autres c'était des batailles. J'ai jamais fait une bataille avec un homme, moi. J'avais deux frères qu'était joliment des piquants.* With other people, it was fistfights. I've never fought a man [but] I had two brothers who were quick to fight. (LF) **6** [*vulg.*] penis ◊ **•piquant mourette / piquant (d')amourette / piquant mort raide** ***a*** honey locust (also called sweet locust, black locust, thorn locust, three-thorned acacia, or false acacia) ***b*** prickly ash <JE, Di32, Lv88, Re31> <***Loc:*** EV, JE, LF, SM, TB, VM, Da84, Di32, Hi02, Lv88, Re31>

pique[1] [pik] *n.m./f.* **1** pick (any heavy, sharp, pointed tool) *Un pique. Ça c'est pour commencer ton trou. Tu commences le trou avec un pique, parce que la première terre est dure dure.* A pick. That's for starting your hole. You start your hole with a pick, because the first layer of ground is very hard. (LF) **2** ice pick *Donne-moi la pique pour casser la glace.* Give me the ice pick to break up the ice. (VM) **3** sharp, pointed stick, stake *Et là y a des petits* SLICE *de viande. Et tu peux soit griller sur une pique ou, le vieux temps eusse mettait ça sus, le vieux temps, je me rappelle ça, j'étais jeune, eusse mettait ça sus des moules à rat musqué.* And there are little slices of meat. And you can either grill it on a stake or, in the old days they would put it on, in the old days, I remember, I was young, they put it on muskrat racks. (LF) **4** depth in the ground corresponding to the length of a spade blade *On a planté les graines de fleur dans de la terre pelletée une pique de profondeur.* We planted the flower seeds in the earth dug one spade deep. (TB) **5** spade (in cards) *L'as de pique.* The ace of spades. (EV) <***Loc:*** EV, JE, LF, TB, VM, Da84, Lv88>

pique[2] [pik] *n.m.* yucca <***Loc:*** IB, SJ, Lv88>

pique aux dindes ♦see **picodinde**

piqué[1], **-e** [pike] *adj.* **1** pitted, pockmarked *Sa peau était tout piquée par sa maladie.* His skin was pitted from his illness. (LA) **2** quilted *Ma mère m'a donné une couverture piquée à la main.* My mother gave me a hand-quilted blanket. (LA) **3** moth-eaten, worm-eaten, destroyed or damaged by worms or insects **Bois piqué.* Wormwood. (Da84) **Maïs piqué.* Mite-eaten corn. (Da84) **4** pecky, marked by pocket rot (of cypress) *J'ai usé des planches de cipre piqué pour mon plafonnage.* I used pecky cypress to cover my walls. (VM) **5** decayed, having a cavity (of teeth) *Des fois quand ton eau est pas bonne, t'as les dents piquées.* Sometimes when your water is not good, you have tooth decay. (AS) ◊ **•piqué à l'ail** stuffed with garlic <Da84> <***Loc:*** AS, LA, SL, SM, VM, Da84, La99, Lv88>

piqué[2], **-e** [pike] *adj.* intoxicated, drunk, tipsy *Ils étaient joliment bien piqués quand ils ont arrivé.* They were pretty tipsy when they arrived. (LA) <***Loc:*** LA, SM, La99, Lv88>

pique-bois (**pic-bois**) [pikbwa] *n.m.* woodpecker ◊ **•pique-bois doré {jaune}** golden woodpecker <Re31> **•pique-bois tête rouge** red-headed woodpecker <Re31> **•grande pique-bois** large ivory-billed woodpecker <Re31> <***Loc:*** JE, SB, SM, VM, Da84, Lv88, Re31>

piquée [pike] *n.f.* depth in the ground corresponding to the length of a spade blade <***Loc:*** VM>

pique-nique [piknik] *n.m.* picnic <***Loc:*** LF, Da84>

pique-partout [pikpartu] *n.m.* **1** meddlesome person *Ce petit pique-partout a fouillé tout partout dans mon tiroir.* That little meddlesome person dug all through my drawer. (TB) **2** game in which the player who gets the ball tries to hit any of the other players with it, locally called roly-poly **3** confusion, fight, free-for-all, brawl *Il y a eu un pique-partout hier soir.* There was a melee last night. (SL) **4** orgy *Il y avait assez une grosse bacchanale qui venait de cette maison, je suis sûr qu'ils étiont après avoir un pique-partout là-bas.* There was such a big commotion coming from that house I'm sure they were having an orgy over there. (VM) <***Loc:*** IB, LF, SJ, SL, TB, VM, Lv88>

piquer [pike] **I** *v.tr.* **1** to sting *La guêpe l'a piqué.* The wasp stung him. (LA) *J'ai été ramasser des socos et je m'ai fait piquer par des guêpes.* I was picking muscadines and I got stung by wasps. (Guoo) **2** to stick, prick (with a knife or any sharp point) *C'est pareil comme si tu prends un morceau de viande et puis tu prends une fourchette et piquer ça, et ben c'est comme ça que ça fait, là, la ceinture en-dedans de toi.* It's like if you take a piece of meat and then you take a fork and stab it, well that's what shingles does inside of you. (TB) **3** to stick (one thing into another) *Là j'ai piqué les fleurs là-dedans.* Then I stuck the flowers into it. (TB) **4** to sew, stitch *Ma mère se mettait ensemble avec les femmes du voisinage pour piquer des couiltes.* My mother got together with the women of the neighborhood to sew quilts. (Guoo) **5** to administer a shot to *Alle dit je vas attraper le* FLU. *Non, je dis j'ai été au docteur, eusse m'a piqué dessus chaque bras avec des aiguilles.* She says I'll catch the flu. No, I said I've been to the doctor, they gave me a shot in each arm with needles. (TB) **6** to peck *Les poules piquont quelque chose là.* The hens are pecking something over there. (TB) **7** [*vulg.*] to have intercourse with, have sex with *Je t'ai dit que Tom aurait piqué Youne!* I told you Tom would screw Youne! (Guoo) **II** *v.intr.* [*vulg.*] to have sex, fornicate, copulate *On les a découvert après piquer dans le charretil du* PICKUP. They were caught having sex in the bed of the pickup truck. (VM) **III se piquer** *v.pron.* to stick o.s. (with a splinter or thorn) *Il s'a tout piqué dans les éronces.* He got stuck all over [with thorns] in the briars. (LA) ◊ **•piquer à l'ail** to stuff (a roast, a potato, etc.) with garlic <Da84> **•piquer aux éperons** to spur (a horse) *"Tu vas le lâcher et puis," il dit, "pique-le aux éperons." Il dit, "On va voir comment il va faire."* "You're going to let loose [on the reins] and then," he said, "spur him." He said, "We'll see how he does." (EV) <EV> **•piquer le moulin** to give a whipping or spanking <SM> **•piquer une couverture {un toit}** to reshingle a roof, repair a shingled roof <JE, Da84, Di32> **•piquer une tape (à qqn)** to slap (s.o.) <SM> **•piquer un fossé** to dig a hole <SJ> **•se piquer une bosse** to eat very much <SM> **•se piquer une cuite {brosse}** to get drunk <LA> <***Loc:*** EV, JE, LA, LF, SJ, SM, TB, VM, Da84, Di32, Guoo, Hio2, Lv88>

piquerie [pikri] *n.f.* **1** quilting bee, quilting party *Je vas à la piquerie de quilt après-midi.* I'm going to the quilting bee this afternoon. (VM) **2** shingling party, roofing party <***Loc:*** VM, Da84, Lv88>

piquet [pikɛ, pike] *n.m.* **1** stake *Là ils ont changé la ligne deux ou trois fois depuis ça. Moi j'ai mes piquets chaque boutte.* Then they've changed the [property] line two or three times since then. But I have my stakes at each end. (TB) **2** group of hunters *On se met par piquets épaillés dans le bois pour chasser.* We spread out by groups in the woods for hunting. (Lv88) <***Loc:*** SM, TB, VM, Da84, Lv88>

piquette[1] **(pissette, pisquette, pichette)** [pikɛt, pisɛt, piskɛt, piskwɛt, piʃɛt, pitʃɛt] *n.f.* weak coffee, watered-down coffee *Le café est trop fort pour l'enfant. Donne-lui la piquette.* The coffee is too strong for the child. Give him watered-down coffee. (SM) <***Loc:*** IB, JE, SM, La99, Lv88>

piquette[2] [pikɛt, piket] *n.f.* ◊ **•piquette du jour** daybreak <JE, SM> <***Loc:*** JE, SM>

piquion [pikjɔ̃] *n.m.* goad <***Loc:*** JE, Di32>

piqûre [pikyr] *n.f.* **1** sting *Il a sorti du bois couvert de piqûres.* He came out of the woods covered with stings. (LA) **2** puncture *Son* TIRE *avait juste une petite piqûre mais il était* FLAT *quand même.* His tire had only a little puncture, but it was flat all the same. (LA) **3** wormhole *Les morceaux de bois étaient couverts de piqûres.* The pieces of wood were covered with wormholes. (LA) **4** pit, pockmark *Une figure pleine de piqûres.* A pockmarked face. (VM) <***Loc:*** LA, VM, Da84>

piraque [pirak] *n.m.* penis <***Loc:*** VM>

pirate[1] [pirat] *adj.* intractable, bad, difficult, incorrigible *J'aime pas ça quand ma belle-fille vient visiter. Ses enfants sont assez pirates!* I don't like it when my daughter-in-law comes to visit. Her children are pretty bad! (Guoo) <***Loc:*** Da84, Guoo, Lv88>

pirate[2] [pirat] *n.m.* **1** pirate, robber **2** mean person, unkind person, cruel person **3** badly raised child, insufferable child *Ces petits garçons là sont des vrais pirates.* Those little boys are real scoundrels. (TB) **4** butcher bird, loggerhead shrike <***Loc:*** LF, TB, VM, Da84, La99, Lv88>

pirater [pirate] *v.tr.* **1** to steal *Elle a piraté tout son argent.* She stole all his money. (LA) **2** to disarrange, mess up, upset *Il pirate les choses dans la chambre.* He messes up the things in the room. (IB) <***Loc:*** EV, IB, La99>

pire [pir] *adj.* **1** worse **Aller de mal en pire.* To go from bad to worse. (Da84) **Tant pire pour lui.* That's his hard luck. (Da84) **2** *(superlative; used with art.def.)* the worst ◊ **•(de) pire en pire** worse and worse *Et ça va pire en pire.* And it's getting worse and worse. (TB) <TB> **•faire pire** to do worse <Da84> **•tant pire** so much the worse, too bad <SM, Da84, Lv88, Re31> <***Loc:*** EV, SM, TB, Da84, Hio2, Lv88, Re31>

pirogue [pirɔg] *n.f.* **1** pirogue (a long, narrow type of canoe propelled by paddling) *Pour faire une pirogue, ça c'est le moule qu'ils usont. Ça fait la bonne tenture sur les deux bords.* To make a pirogue, that's the mold they use. That gives you a good flare on both sides. (LF) *Quand l'eau vient trop platte pour les machines, nous hâle les pirogues, nous pagaille.* When the water level is too low for the engines, we take the pirogues, we paddle. (SM) *Pirogue [...] les deux boutes est pointu.* Pirogue . . . both ends are pointed. (JE) **2** dugout canoe <***Loc:*** IV, JE, LA, LF, SM, TB, Da84, Hio2, Re31>

piroguée [piroge] *n.f.* contents of a pirogue, pirogueful *Il a une piroguée de poissons.* He has a pirogueful of fish. (TB) <***Loc:*** JE, TB, Di32>

piroguer [piroge] **I** *v.tr.* to transport in a pirogue *Ça piroguait les canards au Lac Arthur pour les vendre.* They used to transport the ducks to Lake Arthur to sell them. (VM) **II se piroguer** *v.pron.* to ride in a pirogue *Il s'a pirogué dans le bayou.* He rode a pirogue in the bayou. (TB) <***Loc:*** JD, JE, TB, VM, Gr86>

pirogueur, -euse [pirogœr, -øz] *n.* one who travels by pirogue <***Loc:*** Gr86>

piron ♦see **suppuron**

pirouette [pirwɛt] *n.f.* **1** pirouette **2** somersault *Elle faisait des pirouettes partout dans la cour.* She was turning somersaults all over the yard. (LA) **3** whirligig *Il avait mis une de ces petites pirouettes sur sa boîte à poste.* He had put one of those little whirligigs on his mailbox. (LA) <***Loc:*** IB, LA, LF, SJ, TB, Da84>

pirouetter [pirwɛte] *v.intr.* to pirouette, spin on one's toes, turn quickly *Tu devrais bien arrêter de pirouetter tout partout pour un élan et m'écouter.* You ought to stop pirouetting around for a while and listen to me. (LA) <***Loc:*** LA, Da84>

pis[1] [pi, pɥi] *n.m./f.* udder ◊ **•pis enflammé** mastitis, infection of the udder <Wh83> <***Loc:*** JE, VM, Da84, Wh83>

pis[2] ♦see **puis**

piscine [pisin] *n.f.* *[recent]* pool <***Loc:*** TB>

pisé, -e [pize] *adj.* constructed of packed clay ◊ •**pisé de terre** type of construction with clay <Da84> <***Loc:*** Da84>

pisquette ♦see **piquette**

pissat [pisa] *n.m.* urine, piss (usu. of animals) *Du pissat de chien.* Dog urine. (LA) ◊ •**pissat de chat** bad coffee <La99> <***Loc:*** LA, Da84, La99>

pisse-au-lit ♦see **pissenlit**

pissenlit[1] (**pisse-au-lit**) [pisɑ̃li, pisoli] *n.m.* **1** dandelion **2** any of a variety of wildflowers with a showy yellow flower, esp. butterweed, goldenrod, or buttercup *Et plus tard quand le monde a commencé à venir, eusse a découvert qu'il y avait de l'huile, y avait plein des petites fleurs jaunes là, qu'on appelle des pissenlits, eh ben le monde dit "OH, LOOK AT THE BEAUTIFUL GOLDEN MEADOW." Et c'est comme ça que le nom de Golden Meadow a venu.* And later on when people started coming, they discovered that there was oil, there were a lot of little yellow flowers there that they call "pissenlits," and well, people said, "Oh, look at the beautiful golden meadow." And that's how the name Golden Meadow came about. (LF) <***Loc:*** LF, TB, VM, Da92, Ho90>

pissenlit[2] [pisɑ̃li] *n.m.* pad to put on a bed to protect it against bedwetting <***Loc:*** LA>

pisser [pise] **I** *v.tr.* to spurt, gush *Quand le tank a cassé, ça pissait de l'eau tout partout.* When the tank broke, it was spurting water everywhere. (LA) **II** *v.intr.* **1** to piss, urinate *Alle était après nettoyer un NUTRIA et ça lui a pissé dessus.* She was cleaning a nutria and it peed on her. (TB) **2** to spurt forth, gush *Quand j'ai coupé ma main, le sang a pissé.* When I cut my hand, the blood gushed. (SM) ◊ •**pisser sa colère** to vent one's anger <VM> <***Loc:*** EV, LA, SM, VM, Da84, Hi02, Ph36>

pissette ♦see **piquette**

pisseur [pisœr] *n.m.* pisser ◊ •**pisseur en l'air** one who promises much but accomplishes little <Da84> <***Loc:*** Da84>

pissoir [piswar] *n.m.* urinal <***Loc:*** Da84>

pissou [pisu] *n.m.* pad to put on a bed to protect it against bedwetting <***Loc:*** TB>

pistache [pistaʃ, piʃtaʃ] *n.f.* **1** peanut *Tu plantes ça et là après t'arraches ça, et puis tu mets ça à chesser en dehors. Des pistaches.* You plant them and then you dig them up, and then you set them outside to dry. Peanuts. (TB) *Mon grand-père plantait tout le temps des pistaches. On en mangeait quand il faisait froid l'hiver.* My grandfather always planted peanuts. We ate them when it was cold in winter. (Gu00) **2** pistachio *Une année on a planté des pistaches mais tous les froumis l'a mangé.* One year, we planted pistachios but all the ants ate them. (AV) **3** female genitals ◊ •**pistache de terre** peanut <Gu00> •**pistache grillée** roasted peanut <TB, Lv88> •**pistaches à la crème** cream peanuts <Re31> •**pistaches pralinées** sugared peanuts <Re31> •**pistaches salées** salted peanuts <Re31> <***Loc:*** AV, EV, SL, SM, TB, VM, Da84, Gu00, Hi02, Lv88, Re31>

piste (**pistre**) [pis(t), pist(r)] *n.f.* track, trace, mark, footprint *Une piste de poule.* Chicken tracks. (Lv88) **Il a vu des pistes de crème par terre.* He saw cream tracks on the ground. (An94) ◊ •**la piste est sèque** no one is here, the place is empty <La99> <***Loc:*** SM, VM, An94, Da84, Lv88>

pistolet [pistolɛ, pistole] *n.m.* **1** pistol *Tu l'as envoyé un POLICEMAN, alle dit, et mettre le pistolet dans la figure.* You sent her a policeman, she said, who stuck his pistol in her face. (TB) **2** sharp, wily person *Nonc Horace était un pistolet comme son père.* Uncle Horace was a wily character like his father. (EV) **3** unusual and interesting character, often with a dynamic personality *Tant qu'à lui, tu parles d'un pistolet.* As for him, talk about an interesting character. (LA) ◊ •**pistolet à deux manches** unusual and interesting character, often with a dynamic personality <SB, La99> •**pistolet à six coups** six-shooter, pistol <Da84> •**pistolet braqué** cocked gun <Da84> •**pistolet de jambon** bone of a ham <LF> <***Loc:*** EV, JE, LA, LF, SB, TB, Da84, Hi02, La99, Wh83>

piston [pistɔ̃] *n.m.* piston <***Loc:*** Da84>

pistrailler (**pistrer**) [pistraje, pistre] *v.tr.* to leave tracks on, track up by walking on, dirty (a floor) *T'es après pistrailler ma cuisine avec tes pieds trempes.* You're dirtying up my kitchen with your wet feet. (Lv88) *Ga, t'a pistré mon plancher avec tes pagailles sales.* Look, you tracked up my floor with your dirty feet. (VM) <***Loc:*** SM, VM, Lv88>

pistre ♦see **piste**

pistrer ♦see **pistrailler**

pita [pita] *adj.* ◊ •**poule pita** bantam hen <Lv88> <***Loc:*** Lv88>

PITCH[1] [pɪtʃ] *n.m.* pitcher *Il a du monde qui dit un PITCH, ça c'est la chose que tu mets de l'eau dedans, dans la glacière, un PITCH.* There are people who say a "pitch." That's the thing you put water in, in the refrigerator, a pitcher. (LF) <***Loc:*** LF>

PITCH[2] [pɪtʃ] *n.m.* name of a domino game <***Loc:*** VM>

pite (**pitte, pitre**) [pit(r)] *n.m./f.* **1** any of various species of agave **2** Spanish bayonet, Spanish dagger plant *Sus le pied de pite y avait une grosse grappe de fleurs blanches.* On the Spanish dagger plant there was a big cluster of white flowers. (TB) **3** burlap, gunny, coarse fabric made from the fiber of any of various plants (e.g. jute, hemp, sisal) *Un sac de pite.* A burlap bag. (Lv88) *Si t'as pas de coton, tu peux mettre un sac de pite dans ta couilte.* If you don't have any cotton, you can put a burlap sack in your quilt. (Lv88) **4** small rope made by twisting strips of coarse fabric (often used to make chair bottoms) *J'ai arrangé le fond de cette chaise avec la pite.* I repaired the bottom of this chair with burlap rope. (IB) <***Loc:*** IB, TB, VM, Da84, Gu00, Lv88, Re31>

pitié[1] [pitʃe] *n.f.* pity ◊ •**pitié d'affaire** ***a*** sorrowful thing ***b*** slovenly work <VM> •**avoir pitié** to have pity, take pity *Il* *est mort asteur, que le Bon Dieu ait pitié de son âme.* He's dead now, may the Good Lord have pity on his soul. (TB) <TB, Da84> **•faire pitié** ***a*** to be pitiful, be pathetic *Ça fait pitié de voir comme il est après s'abîmer.* It's a pity to see how he is wasting away. (VM) *Alle était si désespoirée ça faisait pitié de la voir.* She was so despairing that it was pitiful to see her. (VM) **Mon cousin peut valser, mais quand il danse le* TWO-STEP, *ça fait pitié!* My cousin can waltz, but when he dances the two-step, it's pathetic! (Hi02) ***b*** to cause to be sad **Si loin que moi je suis de toi, mais ça, ça me fait pitié.* So far away that I am from you, well that makes me sad. (LA, Wh83) <LA, VM, Da84, Hi02, Wh83> **•prendre en pitié** to feel sorry for, have pity on <Da84> **•se prendre en pitié** to feel sorry for o.s. *Il se prend en pitié depuis sa femme a quitté.* He's feeling sorry for himself since his wife left. (LA) <LA, Da84> <***Loc:*** LA, SM, TB, VM, Da84, Hi02, Wh83>

pitié[2] [pitʃe] *interj.* expression of astonishment, pity, or disapproval ◊ **•pitié d'amour** for the love of Pete, for pity's sake <Da84> <***Loc:*** Da84>

pitit ♦see **petit**

piton [pitɔ̃] *n.m.* staple, fence staple <***Loc:*** SM>

pitoyable [pitwajab(l)] *adj.* pitiful, pitiable *C'était beaucoup pitoyable. Là la mère a resté avec cinq z-enfants pour elle et quatre z-enfants pour sa belle-sœur, et là, ça a mouri jusqu'à au grand printemps.* It was very pitiful. The mother was left with five of her own children and four of her sister in law's children, and then they died [one after another] into the springtime. (AC) <***Loc:*** AC, Da84>

pitre, pitte ♦see **pite**

pivardé ♦see **épivardé**

pivarder ♦see **épivarder**

pivelé, -e [pivle] *adj.* **1** spotted, speckled (of the skin or hide) **Un mulet pivelé.* Spotted mule. (Re31) **Une caille pivelée.* Wood thrush. (Re31) **Peau pivelée.* Skin spotted with measles. (Re31) **2** grayish, mottled (usu. with mildew) *Avec l'eau haute, le plafonnage de ma maison était tout pivelé.* With the flood, the walls of my house were mottled with mildew. (VM) **3** *(m.)* mottled, grayish-blue with red spots (of a bull; by extension, name for such a bull) <***Loc:*** EV, SM, VM, Lv88, Ph36, Re31>

pivier (pluvier) [pivje, pivjɛ, pivijɛ, plyvje] *n.m.* any of several species of shorebird (e.g. sandpiper, plover, killdeer) ◊ **•pluvier doré** ***a*** golden plover ***b*** killdeer <IB, Re31> <***Loc:*** EV, IB, JE, SB, TB, Ph36, Re31>

pivot [pivo] *n.m.* pivot, hinge, fulcrum <***Loc:*** VM, Da84, Fa77>

pivoter [pivote] **I** *v.tr.* to pivot, turn on a pivot *Quand le bougre a délivré ma petite bâtisse, il l'a pivotée pour la placer en ligne avec l'autre bâtisse.* When the guy delivered my little building, he pivoted it to place it in line with the other building. (VM) **II** *v.intr.* to pivot, turn on a pivot <***Loc:*** VM, Da84>

placard [plakar] *n.m.* **1** placard, poster *Les candidats avaient mis des placards partout dans le village.* The candidates had placed posters all over town. (LA) **2** spot, stain *Un placard de graisse.* A spot of grease. (Lv88) **3** bruise or spot on skin *Le mal anglais m'a laissé un placard sus le côté.* The shingles left me with a big spot on my side. (VM) **4** small pool, puddle (of liquid) *Un placard de sang par terre.* A puddle of blood on the ground. (VM) **5** task, assignment, quota *Il fallait couper dix rangs pour le placard aujourd'hui.* It was necessary to cut ten rows for today's quota. (IB) <***Loc:*** IB, LA, SM, VM, Da84, Lv88>

place [plas] *n.f.* **1** place, location *Ils sont rentrés dans quatre différentes places.* They went into four different places. (Lv88) *Y a pas de places dedans le pays comme les campagnes de la Louisiane.* There's nowhere in the country like Louisiana's countrysides. (Lv88) **Il a donné la messe dans une place, mais là, il était parti pour l'autre chapelle.* He performed the mass in one place, then he left for the other chapel. (IV, An94) **Ils ont jamais pu trouver la place.* They never could find the place. (VM, An94) **2** spot, place *Chien qui va à la chasse perd sa place.* The dog that goes hunting loses its spot. (Proverb) **Il a retourné le mettre à la même place.* He came back to put it in the same place. (AC, An94) **3** place, position **Moi, à ta place, j'irai retirer cette lettre.* In your place, I would go take back that letter. (IV, An94) **4** room, space *Nous-autres était jamais comment tu dis ça,* CROWDED. *Nous-autres avait tout le temps de la place.* We were never, what do you call it, crowded. We always had room. (TB) *Il manquait de la place dans la pataterie, ca fait il a embutté ses patates dans le clos et il les a couvert avec de la paille.* There was no more room in the potato shed, so he piled his potatoes in the field and covered them with straw. (VM) **5** room, living quarters *J'ai trois bonnes places à louer.* I have three nice rooms for rent. (VM) **6** farm, homestead, plantation *Paul a acheté une place au ras Pont-Breaux.* Paul bought a small farm near Breaux Bridge. (SM) *Cette terre qu'on est dessus là, c'est une partie de la vieille place des Babin.* This land that we're on is part of the old Babin plantation. (TB) ◊ **•place de** instead of *N-a quelqu'uns qu'a parti dès qu'eusse a vu ça, place de rester là, parce que ça c'était la batisse qu'était la plus solide qu'il y avait.* There are some who left when they saw that, instead of staying there, because that was the most solid building there was. (LF) <LF> **•à la place de** instead of <Da84> **•avoir pas de place** to be improper, out of the way, uncalled for *Ça t'étais après parler pour hier, ça avait pas de place.* What you were speaking about yesterday was uncalled for. (VM) <VM> **•(de) place en place** from place to place *Et naturel, quand la fille se mariait alle allait avec son mari de place en place.* And naturally, when the girl got married she went with her husband from place to place. (TB) **Il a voyagé de place en place, de ville en* *ville, et toujours, il avait intérêt de visiter les cimetières.* He traveled from place to place, from town to town, and he was always interested in visiting the cemeteries. (LA, An94) **Ça mettait un jeune bougre sur un cheval et puis le bougre-là passait place en place à ces camps.* They put a young guy on a horse and the guy went from place to place at those camps. (LA, An94) <LA, TB, An94> **•en place de** in place of **Pour z'en, du thé de laurier avec ein cuillier à table de whiskey dans chaque tasse était bu en place du café l'après midi.* For some, bayleaf tea with a tablespoonful of whisky in each cup was drunk in place of coffee in the afternoon. (Wh83) <VM, Fa77, Wh83> **•faire de la place** to make room <Da84> **•mettre en place** to put in place *Il a coupé tous ces morceaux de bois là, et c'était tout mis en place, et ça coulait pas seulement, c'était bien* SEAL *ensemble.* He cut all those pieces of wood, and it was all put in place, and it didn't even leak, it was well sealed together. (TB) <TB> **•mettre qqn à sa place** to set s.o. straight, put s.o. in his or her place <Da84> **•nulle place** nowhere *Ça va pas nulle place, à quatre ans c'est des vieux mariés.* They're not going anywhere, after four years they're an old married couple. (TB) <IV, LF, TB, VM> **•par les places** in great disorder, scattered *Toutes mes lettres sont par les places depuis que je suis ici.* All my letters are in disorder since I arrived here. (IB) <IB> **•prendre la place (de)** to take the place (of) <Da84> **•prendre place** to take place, happen *Il pouvait* VISUALIZE *un portrait de quelque chose qu'allait prendre place.* He could visualize a picture of something that was going to happen. (LF) <LF, Da84> **•sur la place (de)** at the house (of) **Vieux Albert qui restait sur la vieille place à défunt Joseph Hébert.* Old Albert who lived at the deceased Joseph Hébert place. (Co80) <Co80, Lv88> ***<Loc:*** AC, EV, IB, IV, LA, LF, SM, TB, VM, An94, Co80, Da84, Hi02, Lv88, Wh83>

placé, -e [plase] *adj.* **1** living together (without benefit of marriage), shacked up *Sa femme est placée avec un Sabine de en bas du Petit Caillou.* His wife is shacked up with a Sabine from down in Little Caillou. (TB) *L'homme et la femme là sont juste placés.* The man and woman are just living together. (Lv88) **2** adopted or placed in foster care *C'est un enfant placé, mais alle l'aime comme ses enfants à elle.* He's an adopted child, but she loves him like her own children. (TB) ***<Loc:*** AV, TB, Da84, Lv88>

placement [plasmɑ̃] *n.m.* placement, placing ***<Loc:*** Da84>

placer [plase] **I** *v.tr.* **1** to put, place *Il a placé une enveloppe dans ma main.* He placed an envelope in my hand. (ThCa: *Messieurs, mesdames*) *La population dans l'orphelinat était épaisse et ils ont décidé de venir dans le sud voir si ils auriont pas pu placer ces enfants là.* The population in the orphanage was dense, and they decided to come to the south to see if they could place those children there. (AV) **2** to recall, identify *Je l'ai vu avant, mais je peux juste pas le placer.* I've seen him before, but I just can't place him. (VM) **II se placer** *v.pron.* **1** to take one's position, place o.s. *Puis il a continué dans une manière d'une serpent qu'est après se placer pour frapper.* Then he continued in the manner of a serpent that is setting itself up to strike. (ThCa: *Messieurs, mesdames*) **2** to live together (without benefit of marriage) *Asteur il y a un tas de jeunes qui se placent sans se marier.* Today there are a lot of young people who live together without being married. (EV) ◊ **•placer bien ses mots** to speak well, choose one's words carefully <VM> ***<Loc:*** EV, LF, VM, Da84, Lv88, ThCa>

placôté ♦see **plat-côté**

plafond [plafɔ̃] *n.m.* ceiling **Arriver au plafond.* To reach the ceiling. (Da84) ***<Loc:*** JE, SB, VM, Da84, Lv88>

plafonnage [plafɔ̃naʒ] *n.m.* **1** wall *Tu vas pas tapisser le plafonnage?* Aren't you going to paper the wall? (VM) **2** sealing material for walls *J'ai usé des planches de cipre piqué pour mon plafonnage.* I used pecky cypress to cover my walls. (VM) **3** paneling, wainscoting ***<Loc:*** JE, SL, VM, Da84, Di32, Gu00, Lv88>

plafonner [plafɔ̃ne] *v.tr.* to cover, finish the walls or ceiling of *Plafonner une chambre.* To finish the walls of a room. (VM) ***<Loc:*** JE, Da84, Di32, Lv88>

plaider [plede] **I** *v.tr.* to plead (a legal case), defend (a case) in court *C'est le petit Edwards de Crowley qu'a plaidé le cas du monde qu'avait vendu des canards.* It was the little Edwards fellow from Crowley who defended the people who had sold ducks. (EV) **II** *v.intr.* **1** to plead, beg *Sur ses genoux elle a plaidé.* On her knees she pleaded. (Lv88) **2** to enter a plea **III se plaider** *v.pron.* to plead **Se plaider coupable.* To plead guilty. (Da84) ***<Loc:*** EV, Da84, Lv88>

plaiderie [pledri] *n.f.* plea, pleading (in court) ***<Loc:*** JE>

plaie [plɛ, ple] *n.f.* sore, wound ***<Loc:*** Da84>

plaïe ♦see **playe**

plaignant [plɛ̃jɑ̃] *n.* plaintiff ***<Loc:*** Da84>

plaignard, -e [plɛ̃jar, -ard] *n.* griper, complainer, whiner, cry-baby **Il est trop plaignard.* He's too much of a complainer. (EV, Ph36) ***<Loc:*** EV, JE, LF, Da84, Lv88, Ph36>

plaignoux, -euse [plɛ̃ju -øz] *n.* griper, complainer, whiner, cry-baby *Çu-là qui se plaint malade souvent, on l'appelle un plaignoux.* The one who complains of being sick all the time, we call him a whiner. (TB) ***<Loc:*** JE, TB, Di32>

plaille ♦see **playe**

plaindre [plɛ̃n, plɛ̃d(r)] (*p.p.* **plaint** [plɛ̃], **plaindu** [plɛ̃dy]) **I** *v.tr.* to pity, feel sorry for *Je le plaignais jusqu'à j'ai vu qu'il avait menti.* I felt sorry for him until I saw that he had lied. (VM) **II se plaindre** *v.pron.* to gripe, complain, grumble **Il faut pas se plaindre avec le ventre plein.* One should not bellyache with a full belly. (Da84) ***<Loc:*** VM, Da84, Hi02>

plaine (plane) [plɛ̃n] *n.m./f.* **1** maple tree (esp. swamp maple, red maple) **2** maple wood ***<Loc:*** IV, JE, TB, VM, Lv88>

plainte [plɛ̃t] *n.f.* complaint <*Loc:* Da84>

plaintif[1]**, -ive** [plɛ̃tif, -iv] *adj.* plaintive <*Loc:* Da84>

plaintif[2] [plɛ̃tif] *n.m.* plaintiff <*Loc:* JE, Di32>

plaire [plær] (*p.p.* **plu** [ply], **plaît** [plɛ, ple]) **I** *v.tr.* to please, give pleasure *Bébé connaît qui Pop va faire: n'importe quoi pour le plaire.* Baby knows what Papa will do: anything to please him. (AV, ch: *Bébé (de la famille)*) *J'ai arrêté, j'étais pas plaît.* I stopped, I wasn't satisfied. (VM) **II se plaire** *v.pron.* to enjoy o.s. *Je m'ai bien plaît là-bas.* I liked it over there. (VM) <*Loc:* AV, VM, Da84>

plairie ♦see **prairie**

plaisant [plezɑ̃] *adj.* pleasant, nice, agreeable (of a thing or event) *C'était plaisant de passer l'après-midi avec Monsieur Dupuy.* It was nice to spend the afternoon with Mr. Dupuy. (VM) *Eux-autres avaient un MEETING, eusse appelle ça MONDAY NIGHT DISCIPLE. Et ça prie, ça chante, et c'est plaisant.* They have a meeting, they call it Monday Night Disciple. And they pray, they sing, and it's pleasant. (TB) <*Loc:* TB, VM, Da84>

plaisir [plezir] *n.m.* pleasure, fun *Mais c'est sûr un plaisir de parler avec toi.* But it sure is a pleasure to talk to you. (LF) **Mon grand plaisir à moi, c'est... d'observer comment bien corporés les jeunes filles sont!* A great pleasure of mine is . . . to see how well-made the young girls are! (Gr82) ◊ **•avoir du plaisir** to have fun *On a donc eu du plaisir quand mes cousins de Port Arthur a venu.* We sure had fun when my cousins from Port Arthur came over. (VM) *Dans un temps j'élevais des canards pour avoir du plaisir.* At one time I raised ducks for fun. (TB) <VM, Da84, Hi02> **•prendre plaisir** to take pleasure *Il prend trop de plaisir à me faire des misères.* He takes too much pleasure in teasing me. (VM) <VM, Da84> <*Loc:* AV, EV, LF, TB, VM, Da84, Gr82, Hi02>

plaisse [plɛs] *n.m.* adhesive tape <*Loc:* VM>

PLAN [plæn] *v.tr.invar.* to plan to, have the intention to *Il était après PLAN revenir chez moi le lendemain.* He had the intention of coming back to my house the next day. (Lv88) <*Loc:* Lv88>

plan[1] [plɑ̃] *n.m.* **1** plan, intention **Son plan c'est de les mettre dessus la terre juste avant Tchou Flang coupe les herbes pour que le papier peut être déchiraillé par la fourcheuse [=faucheuse].* His plan is to put them on the ground just before Tchou Flang cuts the grass so the paper will be cut up by the lawnmower. (Wh83) **2** plan, drawing, design, blueprint, sketch *Et tous les bateaux en bois qu'a été fait, ils avaient pas de plan pour. Il a jamais eu un plan de fait pour un bateau. Le vieux monde avait tout ça dans leur tête.* And all the wooden boats that were made, they had no blueprints for them. There's never been a blueprint for a boat. The old folks had all of that in their head. (LF) ◊ **•plan de maison** house plan, layout of a house <Da84> **•être dans son plan** to be doing what one likes to do *Alle est dans son plan, asteur, là.* She's enjoying herself very much now. (TB) <EV, TB, La99> <*Loc:* AC, EV, LF, TB, Da84, La99, Wh83>

plan[2] [plɑ̃] ◊ **•en plan avec** even with, flush with, level with *On enlignait les machines dans les bateaux. Enligner, ça veut dire qu'on mettait les machines en plan avec le SHAFT et les PROPELLER, faulait que tout ça soye en ligne pour bien que ça travaille.* We lined up the motors in the boats. Lining up means we put the motors even with the shaft and the propeller, it all had to be lined up so that it would work well. (LF) <LF> <*Loc:* LF>

planchage [plɑ̃ʃaʒ] *n.m.* flooring *Tous les planchages, il faut que ça soye mis, faut que ça soye coupé en dedans.* All of the planking, it has to be put on, it has to be cut inside. (LF) <*Loc:* LF>

planche[1] [plɑ̃ʃ] *n.f.* **1** plank, board **2** heavy, thick plank dragged by a horse to prepare a field for planting ◊ **•planche à repasser** ironing board <VM, Da84, Fa77> **•planche deboute** upright board (type of construction, board and batten) <Da84> <*Loc:* EV, LA, LF, SB, SL, VM, An94, Da84, Fa77>

planche[2] ♦see **plange**

plancher[1] (**planchonner**) [plɑ̃ʃe, plɑ̃ʃɔ̃ne] *v.tr.* to floor, lay a floor in, apply flooring to *Il a planché toute la maison lui-même.* He floored the whole house himself. (Lv88) <*Loc:* SM, VM, Da84, Lv88>

plancher[2] [plɑ̃ʃe] *n.m.* **1** floor, flooring *Ça pendait jusqu'au plancher.* It hung all the way to to the floor. (IB) **Faudra tu frobis le plancher.* You will have to scrub the floor. (EV, An94) **2** deck of a boat *Et après ça, que tout ça c'était fini, ben là ils mettont le plancher ou le DECK sur le bateau.* And after that, when it was all done, they put the deck on the boat. (LF) **3** story, floor *Ils travaillont dans le même collège, le troisième plancher les deux.* They work in the same college, the third floor both of them. (TB) *Alle reste sur le dixième plancher.* She lives on the tenth floor. (TB) ◊ **•plancher de danse** dance floor <VM> <*Loc:* EV, IB, JE, LA, LF, SL, TB, VM, An94, Da84, Hi02, Lv88>

planchonner ♦see **plancher**

plançon [plɑ̃sɔ̃] *n.m.* squared log <*Loc:* JE, Di32>

plane ♦see **plaine**

planer [plɑ̃ne] *v.intr.* to glide, hover, soar, plane **Le carencro plane facilement.* The buzzard glides easily. (Da84) <*Loc:* Da84>

plange[1] (**plonge, planche**) [plɑ̃ʒ, plɔ̃ʒ, plɑ̃ʃ] *adj.* level, flat, even *Le terrain est tout plange icite dans le sud de la Louisiane.* The land is all flat here in the south of Louisiana. (Lv88) **Labourer en planche.* To plow flat, plow level. (Da84) <*Loc:* JE, TB, VM, Da84, Di32, Lv88>

plange[2] (**plonge, planche**) [plɑ̃ʒ, plɔ̃ʒ, plɑ̃ʃ] *adv.* smoothly *Il danse plange.* He dances smoothly. (SM) <*Loc:* SM>

plangir [plɑ̃ʒir] *v.tr.* to level, make even **On plangit la terre* *avec une herse.* The land is leveled with a harrow. (Da84) <***Loc:*** JE, TB, Da84, Di32>

planner [plɑ̃ne] **I** *v.tr.* to plan *Tu ferais mieux de bien planner ton affaire ou ça va te coûter une fortune.* You'd better plan your thing well or it'll cost you a fortune. (LA) **II** *v.intr.* to plan, make plans *Tous les Cajuns se rassemblent pour planner pour l'avenir.* All the Cajuns get together to plan for the future. (Lv88) <***Loc:*** LA, Lv88>

plant [plɑ̃] *n.m.* seed, seedling **Du plant.* Seedlings. (Da92) ◊ **•plant de canne** plant cane, seed cane <SJ> **•plant de chou** ***a*** cabbage seedling ***b*** cabbage plant <Da84> <***Loc:*** SJ, Da84, Da92>

plantage [plɑ̃taʒ] *n.m.* planting (of crops, etc.) <***Loc:*** EV, VM, Da84, Lv88, Ph36>

plantard [plɑ̃tar] *n.m.* cutting (from a plant) <***Loc:*** JE, Di32>

plante[1] [plɑ̃t] *n.f.* **1** plant **2** planting, crop *Le récolteur forçait sa plante de patates douces d'année en année.* The farmer increased his sweet potato crop from year to year. (TB) ◊ **•plante de bonne aventure** plant that comes up spontaneously, volunteer plant <Da84> <***Loc:*** LA, SJ, TB, Da84, Hi02>

plante[2] [plɑ̃t] *n.f.* industrial plant, factory <***Loc:*** Da84>

planter [plɑ̃te] **I** *v.tr.* **1** to plant, sow **Planter du jardinage.* To plant vegetables. (Da84) *Eux-autres plantaient des BEANS blancs, et eux-autres séchait ça.* They planted white beans, and they dried them. (TB) **2** to drive, stick, set **I m'a planté l'aiguille dans l'bras.* He stuck the needle in my arm. (EV, Ph36) *Ça fait, le bougre en arrière de la pirogue là, il plante le devant de la pirogue dans la terre grasse.* So, the guy in back of the pirogue drove the front of the pirogue into wet clay. (JD) **II** *v.intr.* to sink *Pour pas ça plante dans la boue.* So that it doesn't sink in the mud. (Lv88) **III se planter** *v.pron.* **1** to stand o.s. up *Je guettais Mame, je me plantais debout sur une chaise.* I was watching Mom, I stood up on a chair. (AL) **2** to take up a position, settle in **Ça fait c'est proche juste les femmes et les petits qui s'assis dans l'église pour la messe pendant les hommes se plantent endéhors pour charrer.* So, it's mostly just women and children who sit in church for mass, while the men take up positions outside to talk. (Wh83) **Elle s'est plantée là.* She took her position there. (EV, An94) **3** to stick o.s. with *Se planter un piquant.* To get stuck with a thorn. (Lv88) ◊ **•planter (le) chêne** ***a*** to stay, stop, stop suddenly *Il a planté chêne.* He stopped suddenly. (IB) ***b*** to stand on one's head ***c*** to fall forward on one's head, fall head first ***d*** to have a wreck ***e*** to walk on one's hands ***f*** to do a flip and land head first <AC, AV, IB, LF, SM, VM, Da84, La99> **•planter un piquant** ***a*** to cheat, play a dirty trick *Elle m'a planté un piquant.* She played a dirty trick on me. (Lv88) ***b*** to say s.t. bad <Lv88> **•planter un piquet {poteau}** to drive a stake *Il plantait des poteaux à peu près loin comme ça de la levée.* He drove in stakes about so far from the levee. (EV) <EV, Da84> **•se faire planter un piquant** to get cheated in a deal <Da84> <***Loc:*** AC, AL, AV, EV, IB, JD, LA, LF, SL, SM, TB, VM, An94, Da84, Hi02, La99, Lv88, Ph36, Wh83>

planteur, -euse [plɑ̃tœr, -øz] *n.* **1** planter *Le monde c'était tout des planteurs de canne et mon père était un chasseur, il pêchait pour une vie et il élevait des tortues.* People were all sugar cane planters and my father was a hunter, he fished for a living and he raised turtles. (LF) **2** plantation owner **3** *(f.)* planting machine <***Loc:*** EV, LF, SM, VM, An94, Da84, Di32, Lv88>

plaque [plak, plɛk] *n.m./f.* **1** commemorative plaque *Éiou cette plaque là, mame?* Where is that plaque, mom? (TB) **2** metal plate used to cover a hole (e.g. for a burner hole in a wood stove) **3** record *Vin Bruce a frappé une plaque de musique.* Vin Bruce recorded a record. (Lv88) **4** slab *Une plaque de ciment.* A cement slab. (VM) **5** griddle *J'ai une plaque à quatre crêpes.* I have a four pancake griddle. (LA) **6** type of horseshoe that covers the bottom of the hoof (specialized for racing) ◊ **•plaque à gateau** cake pan <VM> **•plaque à PHONOGRAPH** record *Le caouitchouc c'était, que je me rappelle, c'est un plastique noir, ça qu'ils faisont les plaques à PHONOGRAPH avec.* Celluloid was, as I remember, it's a black plastic, what they made phonograph records with. (LF) <LF> <***Loc:*** EV, LA, LF, TB, VM, An94, Da84, Lv88>

plaquemine [plakmin] *n.f.* persimmon ◊ **•plaquemine farouche** wild persimmon <VM> <***Loc:*** AV, EV, TB, VM, Da84, Hi02, Lv88, Ph36, Re31>

plaqueminier [plakmĩje, plakmije, plakmijɛ̃] *n.m.* persimmon tree <***Loc:*** JE, LA, TB, VM, Da84, Hi02, Re31>

plaquer [plake] **I** *v.tr.* **1** to plunk down, place awkwardly or roughly *Il m'a plaqué dans la chaise dans le coin.* He stuck me in the chair in the corner. (SL) **Il est venu plaquer ça drwète dans mon chemin.* He came and plunked that down right in my way. (EV, Ph36) **2** to pack down *La terre est plaquée après ç'a mouillé dur.* The dirt is packed down after it rained hard. (Lv88) **3** to snap, crack, pop, slam *Il plaque le fouet.* He cracks the whip. (VM) *Arrête-moi de plaquer cette gomme.* Quit popping your gum. (VM) **4** to soil, get dirty **Il a plaqué sa culotte dans la boue.* He soiled his pants in the mud. (EV, Ph36) **II se plaquer** *v.pron.* **1** to plunk o.s. down, flop down **2** to fix o.s. in a place, stay <***Loc:*** EV, SL, VM, Da84, Lv88, Ph36>

plarine ♦see **praline**

PLASTIC ♦see **plastique**

plastique (**PLASTIC**) [plastik, plæstik] *n.m.* plastic *Ils ont commencé à faire ça avec du fer. Le fer a commencé à rouiller, c'était pas bon, asteur, ils faisont ça avec du plastique.* They started making it with iron. The iron started to rust, it wasn't good, and now they make it with plastic. (LF) *Le caouitchouc c'était, que je me rappelle, c'est un plastique noir, ça qu'ils faisont les plaques à PHONOGRAPH avec.* Celluloid was, as I remember, it's a black plastic, what they made phonograph records with. (LF) ◊ •**en plastique** plastic, made of plastic <EV> <***Loc:*** LF, SM, Da84, Hi02>

plat[1] [pla] *n.m.* **1** dish, platter, tray **Un plat de viande.* A platter of meat. (Da84) **2** plate, dinner plate *Je lavais les plats toujours et je mets mes souliers moi-même.* I still had to wash the plates and put on my shoes myself. (VM) *J'ai ramassé deux plats d'haricots pour donner à mes deux belles-soeurs.* I gathered two plates of beans to give to my two sisters-in-law. (LF) **3** dish, prepared food *Eux-autres nous avait donné leur adresse et tout, et eux-autres a bien apprécié qu'on pouvait parler avec eux-autres, et demander des bons plats à manger, et voir qui voir alentour.* They gave us their address and all, and they appreciated that we were able to talk to them, and they could ask what was good to eat, and what there was to see in the area. (TB) ◊ •**plat à riz** platter <VM> •**plat (à) vaisselle** dishpan *Ça ici c'est un plat à vaisselle, et ça ici a cent ans. Le plat à vaisselle de défunte mémère.* This here is a dishpan, and this one is a hundred years old. My late grandma's dishpan. (TB) <TB> •**plat creux** soup bowl <SL> •**être dans son plat** to be doing what one likes to do <EV, La99> •**mettre les petits plats dans les gros** ***a*** to cook a lot of food ***b*** to stretch a limited amount of food for unexpected company <SL, La99> <***Loc:*** EV, JE, LA, SL, TB, VM, Da84, Hi02, La99>

plat[2] ♦see **plate**

plat-côté (placôté) [plakote] *n.m.* **1** side of the body (esp. of an animal) **La vache est tombée sur le placôté.* The cow has fallen on its side. (Da84) *Il l'a donné un tape dans le plat-côté.* He hit her in the side. (SL) **2** side of meat, flank *Pour faire du bacon on use les plat-côtés du porc.* To make bacon we use pork flanks. (TB) ◊ •**placôté de porc** side of pork <JE> <***Loc:*** JE, SL, SM, TB, VM, Da84>

plate[1] **(plat)** [pla(t)] *adj.* **1** flat *Un bateau plate, carré en avant, ça c'est pour pêcher comme des HOOPNET, dans les rivières, là où t'as pas la peine aller dans le bois.* A flat boat, square in front, this is to fish with hoopnets, in rivers where you don't need to go far into the woods. (SM) *Si le fond est plat, c'est un skiff.* If the bottom is flat, it's a skiff. (JE) **2** flat, level *Le pays plate de la Louisiane.* The flat country of Louisiana. (Lv88) **3** shallow *C'était mis comme une penture de porte. Et quand il allait dans l'eau creuse, le morceau de bois tombait, et quand il allait dans l'eau plate, le morceau levait, se levait.* It was put on like a door hinge. And when in went into deep water, the piece of wood would fall, and when it went into shallow water, the piece would raise, would rise. (LF) **4** thin *Des crêpes plates.* Thin pancakes. (EV) ◊ •**plat comme une merde {planche / punaise}** very flat <AV, EV, La99> •**à plate** ***a*** flat ***b*** financially broke, impoverished <TB, Da84, La99> •**être à plate** to be lying flat <Da84> <***Loc:*** AV, EV, JE, LF, SM, TB, VM, Da84, Hi02, La99, Lv88>

plate[2] [plat] *n.m.* **1** flat side **2** plate (on a horse's hoof) <***Loc:*** VM, Da84>

plateau [plato] *n.m.* **1** tray, platter *La maîtresse bien souvent avait des grands plateaux de patates douces qu'elle avait cuit d'avance, et des fois des grands plateaux de croquesignoles.* The mistress of the house very often had big platters of sweet potatoes that she had cooked ahead of time, and sometimes big trays of cake doughnuts. (EV) **2** baking pan, roasting pan *Le gâteau est toujours dans le plateau.* The cake is still in the baking pan. (VM) **3** tobacco prepared in strips *Je m'ai mis un plateau.* I took a strip of tobacco. (VM) **4** fiber carded in strips *Des plateaux de coton.* Strips of carded cotton. (LA) <***Loc:*** AC, AL, EV, JE, LA, VM, Da84>

plate-forme [platfɔrm, plætəfɔ̃m] *n.m.* platform (e.g. for drying shrimp, for offshore oil drilling) *Dans ma vie à moi, j'ai commencé à travailler sur les plate-formes à chesser les chevrettes.* In my lifetime, I started working on the shrimp-drying platforms. (TB) <***Loc:*** JE, LF, TB, Da84>

platin [platɛ̃] *n.m.* **1** low, marshy land where water stands most of the year, bottom land, marsh, swamp *On entend les ouaouarons dans les platins.* You can hear bullfrogs in the marshes. (Lv88) **2** pond ◊ •**platin d'eau** lowland <VM> <***Loc:*** CL, EV, JE, LA, SL, SM, VM, An94, Da84, Hi02, Lv88, Ph36>

platine [platin] *n.f.* **1** flattened sausage made of ground pork encased in the intestinal membrane of a pig **2** *(pl.)* side whiskers <***Loc:*** LF, VM>

plâtre [plat(r)] *n.m.* plaster ◊ •**plâtre de Paris** plaster of Paris <Da84> <***Loc:*** Da84>

playe (plaïe, plaille) [plaj] *n.f.* beach *Et tous les jours ce vieux allait marcher sur le BEACH, sur la playe jusqu'à midi, ça revenait BACK bien doucement.* And every day this old man went to walk on the beach until noon, and he came back very slowly. (LF) ◊ •**mettre du linge à la plaille** to lay out clothes on the ground to dry (LF) <LF> <***Loc:*** JE, LF, TB, VM, Gu00, Hi02>

plein[1]**, -e** [plɛ̃, -ɛ̃n] *adj.* **1** full, filled *Et là ça LOAD les cannes dans cette charrette là, et quand le bougre dit que le LOAD est plein, il arrête la machine.* And then they load the cane in this wagon, and when the guy says that the load is full, he stops the machine. (AS) *La dame-jeanne est pleine de whisky.* The demijohn is full of whisky. (AV) *La maison des voisins était plein de punaises.* The neighbor's house was full of bedbugs. (VM) **En pleine connaissance.* Fully conscious. (Da84) *Et le cabinet est plein de tasses craquées.* And the cabinet is full of cracked cups. (LF) *Les enfants sont pleins de canailleries.* Kids are full of mischievous tricks. (SM) *Il lui a envoyé un carton plein de bonbons.* He sent her a cardboard box full of candy. (LA) **2** full (after eating) *Je suis pleine.* I'm full. (LF) **3** *(f.)* pregnant **La femme est pleine.* The woman is pregnant. (Da84) **4** covered **Tu partais propre, et t'arrivais là-bas plein de poussière.* You left clean, and you got there covered in dust. (LA, An94) *Dégrée-toi dehors. Tu vas pas rentrer dans la maison plein* *de boue comme ça.* Undress outside. You're not going to come in the house covered in mud like that. (LA) ◊ **•pleine lune** full moon *T'as jamais vu comment la pleine lune agite les enfants?* Have you ever seen how the full moon excites children? (VM) <IV, VM, An94> **•plein à déborder** brimming, full to the brim <Da84> **•à pleine bouche {gueule}** greedily (of eating) **Manger à pleine bouche.* To devour, eat greedily. (Da84) **Et il mangeait à pleine gueule. Ça lui tombait à chaque bord de la bouche.* And he was eating greedily. It was falling out of each side of his mouth. (EV, An94) <EV, An94, Da84> **•à la pleine course** at full speed, at a dead run **Elle a revenu à la pleine course à la maison, chez mon papa.* She came back at a dead run to the house, to my dad's house. (SL, An94) <EV, SL, An94> **•à pleine tête** loud, very loud **On avait jamais vu des affaires comme ça, des mille et des mille de personnes à la fois qui tapaient des mains et qui criaient à pleine tête, à force qu'ils aimaient la musique qu'on faisait.* We had never seen things like that, thousands and thousands of people all clapping their hands and yelling as loud as they could all at the same time because they liked the music we were playing. (EV, An84) <EV, VM, An84> **•en plein jour** in broad daylight *Ça vient en plein jour icitte les ramasser.* They come here and pick them up in broad daylight. (TB) <TB, Da84> **•tout plein** completely full *Ce bois est tout plein de pourrillons.* This wood is all full of wormholes. (TB) <TB, Da84> ***<Loc:*** AS, AV, EV, JE, LA, LF, PQ, SL, SM, TB, VM, An84, An94, Da84, Hi02>

plein[2] [plɛ̃] *n.m.* ◊ **•plein de (la) lune** full moon *Il aime pêcher au plein de lune.* He likes to fish by the full moon. (LA) **Des fleurs devrait être planté dans le premier quartier de la lune pour avoir les plus jolies fleurs et dans le deuxième quartier ou le plein de la lune pour les meilleur grains.* Flowers should be planted in the first phase of the moon to get the prettiest flowers and in the second phase or full moon for the best seeds. (Wh83) <LA, Da84, Wh83> ***<Loc:*** LA, Da84, Wh83>

plein[3] [plɛ̃] *adv.* **1** much, many, a lot, plenty *J'en connais plein qui vont pas venir.* I know many of them who will not come. (SL) *Prends-toi plein. Y a assez pour une armée.* Help yourself to a lot. There's enough for an army. (TB) *Si eux-autres à du bon temps, du temps sec, ça va plein plus vite que si eux-autres espère en décembre et janvier.* If they have good weather, dry weather, it goes much faster than if they wait for December or January. (TB) *Ça qu'a changé ça plein, c'est après la guerre luméro deux quand les hommes a revenu de l'autre bord.* What changed that a lot, is after WWII when men came back from Europe (lit. the other side). (TB) **2** very *On est une grande paroisse. Une paroisse qu'est long mais pas plein large.* We're a large parish. A parish that's long but not very wide. (LF) ◊ **•plein de** much, many, a lot of, plenty of *Il a plein d'argent.* He has lots of money. (VM) **Avoir plein de temps.* To have a lot of time. (Da84) *Ç'a venu qu'après la guerre t'as eu plein du différent de monde, différent de religions. Pas dire que c'est mauvais, ça a des différentes croyances.* It happened that after the war you had a lot of different people, different religions. That's not to say that it's bad, they have different beliefs. (LF) *Canotte, ça c'est un vieux bateau des vieux temps. Il y en a plus plein de ça. Un canotte, un vieux bateau avec le fond rond.* Lugger, that's an old boat from the old days. There aren't many of those left. A lugger, it's an old boat with a round bottom. (TB) <LF, TB, Da84, VM> **•en plein** fully, entirely, completely *Une fois que j'ai déjeuné je vas marcher le* HALL. *Tout le* HALL *en plein, et revenir, tu vois.* Once I've had breakfast I go walk the halls. The entire length of the hall and back, you see. (TB) <TB> **•on a plein d'huile dans la lampe** you don't have to go yet, it's still early <La99> **•tout en plein** plainly, clearly *Il l'a dit tout en plein.* He stated it clearly. (VM) <VM> ***<Loc:*** EV, LF, SL, TB, VM, An94, Da84, La99>

pléiure (**pleyure**) [plejyr] *n.f.* crease made by a fold ***<Loc:*** JE, TB>

plénière [plɛ̃jær] *adj.* [*eccl.*] plenary, full, complete **Indulgence plénière.* Plenary indulgence. (Da84) <Da84> ***<Loc:*** Da84>

plérion [plerjɔ̃] *n.f.* marsh ***<Loc:*** JE>

pleure [plœr] *n.f.* crying, weeping **Avoir une bonne pleure.* To have a good cry. (Da84) ***<Loc:*** Da84>

pleurer [pløre] *v.intr.* to cry, weep *Ça m'a crevé le cœur assez que j'ai pleuré.* That broke my heart so much that I cried. (TB) **Elle est venue en pleurant.* She came crying. (Da84) *Alle a pris ça assez dur, la fille alle pleurait.* She took it pretty hard, the girl, she was crying. (TB) *Ne pleurez pas autant la belle, ne versez pas autant de larmes.* Don't cry so much, girl, don't shed so many tears. (ch: *La veuve de sept ans*) ***<Loc:*** EV, TB, An94, Da84, Hi02, Lv88>

pleurésie (**purisie**) [plyrezi, pyrizi] *n.f.* pleurisy ***<Loc:*** LF, SM, VM, Da84>

pleureur, -euse [plørœr, -øz] *n.* weeper, crier, mourner ***<Loc:*** Da84>

pleusement ♦see **plussement**

pleuvasser [pløvase] *v.intr.* to drizzle *Il pleuvassait manière quand il a sorti de son* BLIND. It was drizzling when he came out of his blind. (LA) ***<Loc:*** LA, Da84>

pleuvoir [pløvwar] *v.intr.* to rain **Il pleut à verse.* It's pouring down rain, it's raining torrents. (Da84) ***<Loc:*** Da84>

pléyer ♦see **ployer**

pleyure ♦see **pléiure**

pli [pli] *n.m.* **1** fold, crease, pleat *Faire un pli dans une paire de culottes.* To make a pleat in a pair of pants. (LA) **2** wrinkle *Sa figure est plein de plis.* His face is full of wrinkles. (LA) **3** trick (in card playing) *Il croyait qu'il aurait gagné. Il a bourré; il a pas fait un pli.* He thought he would win. He bourréd; he didn't even take a trick. (LA) ***<Loc:*** JE, LA, VM, Da84, Fa77>

plie [pli] *n.m./f.* southern flounder *Mais y a un monsieur qui quitte des appâts vivants dans ses cages pour empoigner des truites et les poissons rouges et les plies.* There's a gentleman who leaves live bait in his box traps for catching trout and redfish and flounder. (TB) <***Loc:*** IB, JE, LF, TB, VM, Da84, Re31>

plier [plije, pleje] **I** *v.tr.* **1** to bend **Moi, j'ai fermé la porte, mais les dards allaient en travers. Mais je les pliais les becs avec mon WRENCH.* I closed the door, but the snouts went through. But I bent their [the giant mosquitoes'] beaks with my wrench. (EV, An94) *Je pouvais plus plier mes jambes du tout, tu connais?* I couldn't bend my legs at all any more, you know? (EV) **2** to fold *On appelait ça des mitaines [...] c'est comme un carreau tu plies comme ça là [...] jusque tu peux mettre bien ta main dedans.* We called them mittens, it's like a square that you fold like that, until you can put your hand inside. (EV) **II** *v.intr.* **1** to bend *Ma jambe est devenue raide. Elle plie pus du tout.* My leg has become stiff. It doesn't bend anymore at all. (LA) **2** to yield, acquiesce, give in *Mais j'ai jamais plié non plus. O non, j'ai dit, je suis pas GUILTY, je dis, j'ai pas fait rien, je dis, je connais pas rien pour ça.* But I never gave in either. Oh no, I said, I am not guilty, I say, I didn't do anything, I say, I don't know anything about it. (EV) **III se plier** *v.pron.* **1** to bend *Essaye de te plier en deux.* Try to bend over double. (LA) **2** to bow (to authority) *Il a eu pour se plier devant le juge.* He had to bow in front of the judge. (LA) **3** to give in *Il faudra tu te plies avant c'est fini.* You'll have to give in before it's all over. (LA) <***Loc:*** EV, JE, LA, An94, Da84>

plissage [plisaʒ] *n.m.* **1** pleating, creasing **2** wrinkling <***Loc:*** Da84>

plissé, -e [plise] *adj.* **1** creased, pleated **2** wrinkled (of cloth) **Bien plissé.* Very wrinkled. (Da84) *Une chemise plissée.* A wrinkled shirt. (SM) **3** wrinkled (of the skin) *La vieille est tout plissée.* The old lady is all wrinkled. (VM) <***Loc:*** SM, VM, Da84>

plisser [plise] *v.tr.* **1** to crease, pleat *Ma mère connaît comment plisser mes culottes.* My mother knows how to pleat my pants. (LA) **2** to wrinkle *C'est pas la peine tu plisses ton front. Il faut le faire.* It's no use you wrinkle your brow. You've got to do it. (LA) <***Loc:*** LA, Da84>

plissure [plisyr] *n.f.* **1** crease, pleat *J'aime pas une plissure dans mes culottes.* I don't like a crease in my pants. (LA) **2** wrinkle *Sa vieille figure était plein de plissures.* Her old face was full of wrinkles. (LA) <***Loc:*** LA, Da84>

plomb[1] [plɑ̃, plɔ̃] *n.m.* **1** lead (metal) *J'ai travaillé un tas quand j'étais jeune avec du plomb et puis j'ai INHALE un tas de ça et je savais pas ça mais le plomb m'a fait STERILE.* I worked a lot with lead when I was young and I inhaled a lot of it and I didn't know it but the lead made me sterile. (IB) **2** lead weight, sinker *Mets-toi un petit plomb sur ta ligne. Tu vas attraper des poissons plus vite.* Put a little sinker on your line. You'll catch fish faster. (LA) *Et le bas du filet a du plomb dessus. Des morceaux lourds pour le tiendre dans le fond.* And the bottom of the net has lead on it. Heavy pieces to keep it at the bottom. (LF) **3** shot (lead pellet), BB shot *J'avais peut-être 50 plombs dans mon petit BB GUN.* I had maybe fifty pellets in my little BB gun. (LF) **4** nickel, five-cent coin <***Loc:*** EV, IB, JE, LA, LF, TB, Da84, Ph36>

plomb[2] ♦see **aplomb**

plombant [plɔ̃bɑ̃] *n.m.* plumb line <***Loc:*** Lv88>

plombé, -e [plɔ̃be] *adj.* leaded, weighted **Un bâton plombé.* A weighted stick, a blackjack. (Da84) ◊ **•pas bien plombé** crazy, not with it, not mentally stable *Le père à lui, il est pas bien plombé.* His father, he's not mentally stable. (VM) <SM, VM, La99, Lv88> <***Loc:*** SM, VM, Da84, La99, Lv88>

plombeau [plɔ̃bo, plɑ̃bo, pɔ̃bo] *n.m.* pommel (of a saddle) <***Loc:*** EV, JE, LA, SL, TB, VM, Da84, Lv88, Ph36>

plomber [plɔ̃be] *v.tr.* **1** to plumb (e.g. a wall) *Ils ont pas bien plombé la maison. Il y a pas une chambre qu'est carrée.* They didn't plumb the house correctly. There's not a room that's square. (LA) **2** to weight with lead *Ils ont plombé la seine pour qu'elle traîne le bas.* They weighted the seine with lead so that it would drag the bottom. (LA) **3** to kill by shooting, fell with a firearm *Plomber un canard.* To shoot a duck. (SJ) <***Loc:*** AV, LA, SJ, Da84, Lv88>

plombter [plɔ̃te] *v.tr.* to shoot, fell with a firearm *Je t'ai dit que je suis adroit, j'ai plombté le z-oiseau.* I'm telling you I'm adroit, I felled the bird. (VM) <***Loc:*** VM>

plonge[1] [plɔ̃ʒ] *n.f* dive, plunge, fall (e.g. into water) *Il a pris une plonge.* He took a plunge. (VM) <***Loc:*** JE, VM, Lv88>

plonge[2] ♦see **plange**

plongée [plɔ̃ʒe] *n.f* dive, plunge, fall (e.g. into water) <***Loc:*** VM, An84>

plongeon [plɔ̃ʒɔ̃] *n.m.* didapper, pied-billed grebe *Les plongeons, ça plonge et c'est dur à tuer ça.* Didappers dive, and they're hard to kill. (TB) ◊ **•grand plongeon** loon <JE> <***Loc:*** JE, TB>

plonger [plɔ̃ʒe] **I** *v.tr.* to plunge, dip, immerse *Il a plongé sa main dans la coulée pour essayer de trouver sa montre.* He plunged his hand into the stream to try to find his watch. (LA) **2** to dive for s.t. *Je pleure mon anneau d'or, dans l'eau il est tombé.—Ne pleurez point, la belle, je vous le plongerai.* I weep for my golden ring, into the water it fell.—Do not weep, fair maiden, I will dive for it for you. (VM, ch: *Isabeau*) **II** *v.intr.* to plunge, take a dip, dive *Dans l'eau haute de 1940, Madame Marceaux a dû plonger dans sa maison pour attraper des bouteilles pour son bébé.* In the 1940 flood, Mrs. Marceaux had to dive into her house to get bottles for her baby. (VM) ◊ **•plonger à casser la vaisselle** to do a cannonball dive <JE> <***Loc:*** JE, LA, TB, VM, Da84>

plongeur[1] [plɔ̃ʒœr] *adj.* diving *C'est un de ces canards* *plongeurs qu'est pas bon à manger.* It's one of those diving ducks that is not good to eat. (LA) <***Loc:*** LA, Da84>

plongeur[2] [plɔ̃ʒœr] *n.m.* **1** diver **2** any of several species of diving birds (e.g. horned grebe, pied-billed grebe, American golden-eye duck) <***Loc:*** JE, Da84, Re31>

plotte ♦see **pelote**

ployable [plwajab(l)] *adj.* flexible, pliable, bendable *Le câble a resté si longtemps dehors qu'il était pus ployable.* The rope stayed outside so long that it was no longer flexible. (LA) <***Loc:*** LA, Da84>

ployage [plwajaʒ, plejaʒ] *n.m.* bending, folding ◊ **•ployage du maïs** bending over of cornstalks above the ears when they begin to ripen <VM> <***Loc:*** JE, VM>

ployant [plwajɑ̃] *adj.* flexible, pliable, bendable *Il s'a acheté de ces bordures ployants pour mettre autour de son jardin.* He bought himself some of those flexible borders to put around his garden. (LA) <***Loc:*** LA, Da84>

ployer (**pléyer**) [plwaje, pleje, ploje, plaje] **I** *v.tr.* **1** to bend **2** to fold **Alle avait ployé le drap et s'avait assis dessus.* She had folded the sheet and had sat down on it. (Gu82) **II** *v.intr.* to bend *J'ai du rhumatisse et mon genou veut pas ployer.* I have rheumatism and my knee doesn't want to bend. (Lv88) **III se ployer** *v.pron.* to bend o.s., bow, bend over *Elle l'a frappé tellement fort qu'il s'a ployé en deux.* She hit him so hard that he bent over double. (LA) <***Loc:*** SL, TB, VM, Da84, Gu82, Lv88>

plucher ♦see **éplucher**

plucheuse [plyʃøz] *n.f.* peeler <***Loc:*** AL>

plue ♦see **pluie**

PLUG[1] [plʌg, plɔg] *v.tr.invar.* **1** to plug, stop up *Et ça travaillait bien oui avec de l'air. Connecter ça comme si que t'aurais voulu mettre de l'air dedans ta* TIRE. *Faulait que tu venais, tu plugais ça-là.* And it ran well on air. [You'd] connect it as if you wanted to put air in your tire. You had to come along and plug the hole. (LF) **2** to plug in **Maw Maw s'est levée et elle a tourné le bouton dessus et l'évantail a parti dans tous les gouts. Bill l'avait* PLUG *mais il l'avait pas mis dessus.* Maw Maw got up and turned the button on and the fan went off full speed. Bill had plugged it in but he had not turned it on. (Wh83) <***Loc:*** LF, TB, Da84, Lv88, Wh83>

PLUG[2] (**plogue**) [plʌg, plɔg] *n.m./f.* **1** electrical outlet *Il y a pas assez de* PLUGS *dans la cuisine.* There are not enough outlets in the kitchen. (LA) **2** stopper *Hale le* PLUG *dans la baignoire avant de sortir.* Pull the stopper in the bathtub before getting out. (LA) **3** plug of tobacco *Il a arrêté pour s'acheter un* PLUG *pour l'après-midi.* He stopped to buy himself a plug of tobacco for the afternoon. (LA) **4** spark plug *Ça fait sûr cinq ans que j'ai pas changé les* PLUGS *dessus mon char.* It's been at least five years since I changed the spark plugs on my car. (LA) **5** wool carded in strips **6** fishing-line bobber *Les poissons pouvont pas caler la plogue.* The fish can't sink the bobber. (VM) <***Loc:*** LA, VM, Da84, Di32, Lv88>

pluie (**plue, pouie, puie**) [plɥi, ply, pɥi, plu] *n.f.* rain ◊ **•la pluie tombe** it's raining <Da84> **•petite pluie fine** fine mist <Da84> <***Loc:*** EV, JE, LA, LF, SL, SM, TB, VM, Da84, Lv88>

plumage [plymaʒ] *n.m.* plumage, feathers <***Loc:*** Da84>

plumas [plyma] *n.m.* feather duster <***Loc:*** EV, IB, JE, SM, TB, VM, Lv88, Ph36>

plume [plym] *n.f.* **1** feather, plume *C'est un z-oiseau qu'est tout noir. Tous les plumes est noirs.* It's a bird that is all black. All of its feathers are black. (LF) **2** pen *Ça je l'ai fait avec une plume et là je prends des crayons et je fais les couleurs.* I did that with a pen, and then I take crayons and I do the colors. (LF) <***Loc:*** AV, IV, LA, LF, SL, SM, TB, Da84, Hi02>

plumeau [plymo] *n.m.* feather duster <***Loc:*** Da84>

plumer [plyme] *v.tr.* **1** to feather, pluck feathers from *Il a plumé la poule.* He plucked the chicken. (SM) **2** to skin, butcher *On va plumer le bœuf quand ça fait froid.* We will skin the ox when it gets cold. (VM) **3** to rob, fleece **Il m'a plumé.* He fleeced me. (Da84) ◊ **•plumer le dinde** to give a whipping <SM> **•comment ça se plume?** how are you? how are things? <La99> <***Loc:*** SM, VM, Da84, Hi02, La99>

plumet [plymɛ, plyme] *n.m.* feather duster <***Loc:*** JE, SJ, Di32, Lv88>

plupart [plypar] *n.f.* most, majority, greatest part **Plus que la plupart de les paroisses dans le Sud de la Louisiane, les Avoyelles à ein identité à eux-autres-mêmes.* More than the majority of parishes in South Louisiana, Avoyelles has an identity of its own. (Wh83) ◊ **•la plupart du temps** most of the time <Da84> **•pour la plupart** for the most part <Da84> <***Loc:*** Da84, Wh83>

plus[1] (**plusse, pus, pu**) [ply, plys, pys, py] *adv.* **1** more **J'en ai plus que lui.* I have more than he has. (Da84) *Mais un cochon est plus aisé à tuer qu'un bœuf.* But a pig is easier to kill than a steer. (TB) *Elle dansait plus que moi.* She danced more than me. (EV) **Je suis pas plus chien que boule.* I am no less than anyone else. (Da84) **Va donc plus vite.* Please go faster. (Da84) *Il fait plus que cinq piastres par jour.* He makes more than five dollars a day. (SM) *J'ai fait à peu près sûr vingt gallons de limonade ou peut-être plus.* I made about 20 gallons of lemonade or maybe more. (EV) *J'ai pus d'argent.* I have more money. (VM) **Pu de vingt ans.* More than twenty years. (Re31) **Pu tôt.* Sooner. (Re31) **2** *(superlative; used with art.def.)* the most *C'est celui-là j'adorais le plus.* He's the one I loved the most. (EV) *Elle m'avait fait la plus jolie robe rose.* She had made the most beautiful pink dress for me. (EV) *Moi je suis la plus vieille.* I'm the oldest. (AC) *La plus jeune est plus vieille que moi un peu.* The youngest one is a little bit older than me. (TB) *Ça c'est à peu près le plus épais que tu vas trouver ça.* This is about the thickest you'll find it. (LF) *C'était le père de ma mère, il avait le plus beau jardin, vous pouviez nourrir la famille* *avec ça.* It was the father of my mother, he had the most beautiful vegetable garden, you could feed the whole family with it. (IB) ◊ **•plus ou moins** more or less *Parce que un Monsieur Hébert de Bourg avait acheté ça pour un magasin là qui était ouvert, je connais pas, 10, 15, 20 ans plus ou moins.* Because a Mr. Hébert from Bourg had bought it as a store that was open, I don't know, 10, 15, 20 years more or less. (TB) *C'est plus ou moins pareil.* It's more or less the same. (TB) <TB, Da84, Hi02> **•au plus loin** at the farthest <Da84> **•bien plus** much more <Da84> **•de plus en plus** more and more <Da84> **•le plus ça va, le pire c'est** the more it goes, the worse it gets <Da84> **•ni plus, ni moins** neither more nor less <Da84> **•non plus** neither, either **Moi non plus.* Me neither. (Da84) **Pas ça non plus.* Not that either. (Da84) *Mais moi non plus, j'ai jamais vu ça.* Well, me neither, I've never seen that. (EV) *N-oncle E lui connaissait pas parler n-anglais non plus.* Uncle E didn't know how to speak English either. (TB) <EV, SL, TB, Da84> **•pas plus que ça** no more than that <Da84> **•tout au plus** at most, at the most <Da84> <*Loc:* AC, EV, IB, JE, LA, LF, PQ, SL, SM, TB, VM, An94, Da84, Hi02, La99, Lv88, Re31, ThCa, Wh83>

plus[2] ♦see **pus**

plusieurs [plyzjœr] *adj.* several, some *Ah, dessus ma place à mon il y a quarante-cinq acres, mais dessus la place de mon grand-grand-père il y avait plusieurs cents acres.* On my farm there are forty-five acres, but on my great-grandfather's farm there were several hundred acres. (TB) *Ouais, j'ai rencontré plusieurs bougres.* Yeah, I met several guys. (EV) **Plusieurs fois.* Several times. (Da84) **Plusieurs jours.* Several days. (Da84) <*Loc:* AC, AV, EV, JE, LA, LF, SM, TB, An94, Da84, Hi02>

plusque ♦see **puisque**

plussement (**pleusement**) [pløsmɑ̃, plœzmɑ̃] *adv.* usually, mostly *Il usait plussement ce chemin-ça pour se rentourner chez lui.* He mostly used that road to go back to his house. (AV) **In vétiver était pleusement trouvé dans le poulailler parce que les poules et pintales aimaient se jouquer dans cette herbe qui profitait des fois 5 pied de haut.* Vetiver was usually found in the henhouse because the chickens and guinea fowl liked to roost in this grass which sometimes grew 5 feet tall. (Wh83) <*Loc:* AV, Wh83>

plutôt [plyto, pyto, pito] *adv.* **1** more *Le vieux vieux bois de cypre il est plutôt rouge que blanc.* The old old cypress wood is more red than white. (LF) **2** rather, fairly **Être plutôt maigre.* To be rather thin. (Da84) **3** if only, would that **Plutôt qu'il aurait fait ça.* If only he had done that / would that he had done that. (Da84) ◊ **•plutôt que (de) / plutôt de** rather than, instead of, in preference to **J'aime celui plutôt que l'autre.* I like this one rather than the other. (Da84) *C'est à peu près long comme ça là, et ç'a une lame un peu large, pour tu coupes la canne, plutôt que de te pencher et ramasser avec la main, tu vois.* It's about this long, and it has a blade that's fairly wide with a hook on it, so you don't have to stoop to gather up the sugarcane, you see. (TB) *Il va venir avec moi plutôt de rester avec sa maman.* He's going to come with me instead of staying with his mother. (SM) *Je vas aller au* SHOW *plutôt de rester à la maison.* I'm going to the movies rather than staying at the house. (VM) <SM, TB, VM, An94, Da84> <*Loc:* EV, LF, SM, TB, VM, An94, Da84, Hi02>

pluvier ♦see **pivier**

pneumonie (**numonie**) [nymɔ̃ni, nimɔ̃ni] *n.f.* pneumonia <*Loc:* IB, SM, Da84, Lv88>

pobon [pobɔ̃, pobɑ̃] *n.m.* preserving jar, fruit jar, canning jar, earthen jar *J'ai fait quelques pobons de confitures.* I made several jars of jam. (SM) *Un pobon de pêches.* A jar of peaches. (IB) <*Loc:* IB, LF, SM, VM, Da84, Lv88, Re31>

poc à poc (**pic à poc**) [pokapɔk, pikapɔk] *adv.* **1** little by little, slowly *Il est après aller pic à poc.* He's going slowly. (LA) **2** so-so, fair, not so well *Comment ça va? Toujours poc à poc.* How's it going? Still so-so. (TB) <*Loc:* JE, LA, SM, TB, VM, Da84, Lv88>

poche [pɔʃ] *n.f.* pocket, pouch ◊ **•avoir la poche pleine** to be wealthy <La99> <*Loc:* LA, Da84, La99, Wh83>

pochée [poʃe] *n.f.* **1** pocketful **2** small sackful (usu. the quantity of corn taken to the mill to be ground) *Mémère moulait une et quelquefois deux pochées de maïs pour faire un pain de maïs doux.* Grandma ground one and sometimes two sackfuls of corn to make a sweet corncake. (TB) <*Loc:* JE, TB, Da84>

pochetée [pɔʃte] *n.f.* pocketful <*Loc:* JE>

pochon [poʃɔ̃] *n.m.* basket <*Loc:* JE>

poêle [pwal, pwɛl, poɛl] *n.f.* **1** frying pan *Une poêle c'est ça que tu fris des patates dedans. Des patates ou des œufs, ou des affaires comme ça.* A frying pan is what you fry potatoes in. Potatoes or eggs, or things like that. (TB) *Et là, tu vas bien beurrer ta poêle avant de mettre ton pain.* And then, you will butter your frying pan well before putting in your bread. (LA) **2** dipper, ladle ◊ **•poêle en fer** iron frying pan <LF> **•poêle luminum** aluminum frying pan <LF> <*Loc:* IB, JE, LA, LF, TB>

poêlée [pwale] *n.f.* panful *Et dans l'après-midi mame grillait une poêlée de café.* And in the afternoon mom would roast a panful of coffee [beans]. (TB) <*Loc:* TB>

poêlon (**poëlon, poilon, pouelon**) [pwalɔ̃, pwelɔ̃] *n.m.* frying pan, skillet <*Loc:* AL, AV, EV, IB, JD, LA, LF, VM, Da84, Lv88>

poème [poɛ̃m] *n.m.* poem <*Loc:* Da84, Hi02>

poète [poɛt] *n.m.* poet <*Loc:* Da84>

pogner ♦see **poigner**

poids [pwa] *n.m.* **1** weight *Tu mettais un petit caillou dans le milieu pour faire du poids.* You would put in a little stone to give it some weight. (LF) *Et mon pape avait perdu du* *poids depuis que mame avait fait le SUIT.* And my dad had lost weight since my mother had made the suit. (TB) **2** load, burden <***Loc:*** LF, SL, TB, Da84>

poignard [pɔ̃jar] *n.m.* **1** dagger **2** butcher knife *Je m'ai coupé au vif avec ce poignard.* I cut myself to the quick with that butcher knife. (VM) <***Loc:*** AL, LF, SM, VM, Da84>

poignarder [pɔ̃jarde] *v.tr.* to stab *Il a passé en arrière de lui et il l'a poignardé dans le dos.* He went behind him and he stabbed him in the back. (LA) <***Loc:*** LA, Da84>

poigne [pwɑ̃j, pɔ̃j] *n.f.* **1** grip, grasp, ability to hold *Il a une bonne poigne.* He has a firm grip. (SM) **2** handful *Une poigne de pacanes.* A handful of pecans. (Lv88) **3** doorknob, knob ◊ **•poigne de (la) porte** doorknob <TB, VM, Fa77> <***Loc:*** EV, JE, LA, SL, SM, TB, VM, Da84, Fa77, Lv88>

poigné ♦see **poignet**

poignée [pwaɲe, pɔ̃je] *n.f.* handful, small quantity *La chevrette sec est bien bon. IN FACT, je vas aller te hacher une poignée d'un petit élan. J'en ai dans mon FREEZER.* Dried shrimp is quite good. In fact, I'll go get you a handful in a moment. I've got some in my freezer. (TB) <***Loc:*** TB, VM, Da84, Fa77>

poigner (**pogner**) [pwɑ̃je, pɔ̃je] *v.tr.* **1** to take, seize, grasp, grab *Les cannes c'était chargé à la main ça. Charger dans un wagon là, on pognait ça par brassées comme ça-là, et jetait ça par-dessus la tête.* The cane was loaded by hand. Loaded in a wagon, we took it by armfuls like that, and threw it up over our heads. (TB) **2** to get, fetch *Pogne-moi un verre.* Grab me a glass. (TB) **3** to catch *Tu peux toujours pogner des chevrettes BROWN.* You can still catch brown shrimp. (TB) *Et là en été dans le temps de les saisons de chevrette il faisait sa vie à pogner les chevrettes avec un épervier.* And then in the summer, during shrimp season, he made a living catching shrimp with a cast net. (TB) **4** to catch by surprise, surprise *Je l'ai pogné quand il a passé.* I caught him by surprise as he went by. (SM) **5** to fool *Je le croyais, mais il m'a bien poigné.* I believed him, but he fooled me good. (SM) <***Loc:*** JE, SM, TB, Lv88>

poignet[1] [pwɑ̃jɛ, pwɑ̃je, pɔ̃je, pɔ̃jɛ̃] *n.m.* **1** wrist **2** cuff, shirt cuff ◊ **•poignet ouvert** dislocated wrist, sprained wrist <SM, VM, Lv88> <***Loc:*** IB, JE, LF, SM, VM, Da84, Lv88>

poignet[2] (**poigné**) [pwɑ̃jɛ, pwɑ̃je, pɔ̃je, pɔ̃jɛ̃] *n.m.* knob, handle <***Loc:*** Da84>

poignette [pwɑ̃jɛt, pɔ̃jɛt, pujɛt] *n.f.* masturbation <***Loc:*** LF, Da84, La99>

poil [pwal, pwɛl] *n.m.* body hair (of human or animal) *Mais c'est pas poilu comme un BEAR. Ça a pas de gros poils comme un BEAR.* It's not hairy like a bear. It doesn't have long hair like a bear. (TB) <***Loc:*** SL, TB, Da84>

poileux, -euse [pwalø, -øz] *adj.* hairy, shaggy *Un chien poileux.* A shaggy dog. (LA) *Un bougre poileux.* A hairy fellow. (LA) <***Loc:*** JE, LA, SM, VM, Da84, Lv88>

poilon ♦see **poêlon**

poilu, -e [pwaly] *adj.* hairy, shaggy *Mais c'est pas poilu comme un BEAR. Ça a pas de gros poils comme un BEAR.* It's not hairy like a bear. It doesn't have long hair like a bear. (TB) <***Loc:*** TB>

poing [pwɛ̃] *n.m.* fist **Bataille à coups de poing.* Fistfight. (Da84) <***Loc:*** Da84>

point[1] [pwɛ̃] *n.m.* **1** dot, period, point *Il a oublié de mettre un point dessus le bout.* He forgot to put a dot on the end. (LA) **2** point (unit for scoring schoolwork, games, sporting events, etc.) *Le marché est pas bon du tout du tout. DOWN cinquante-deux points.* The stock market is not good at all. It's down fifty-two points. (TB) **3** stitch (in sewing) *Fais attention de pas perdre un point.* Be careful not to drop a stitch. (LA) **4** stitch, sharp pain *J'ai un point dans mon côté.* I have a stitch in my side. (SM) **5** point, moment (in time) *Et asteur les affaires est rendu dans un point comme les habitants est pas en bon SHAPE, et je sais pas quoi-ce qui va nous arriver.* And now things have reached a point that farmers are not in good shape, and I don't know what's going to happen to us. (AS) ◊ **•point dans le cœur** heartache, sorrow <VM> **•point de côté** twinge of pain in one's back *Voilà un point de côté qui me prend dans le dos.* I get a twinge in my back. (LA) <LA> **•point de pneumonie** sharp pain of pneumonia <Da84> **•point de vue** point of view <Da84> **•à ce point là** at this point <Da84> **•au point de** at the point of, on the verge of **Au point de la mort.* At the point of death (Da84) **Être au point de se fâcher.* To be at the point of anger (Da84) <Da84> **•avoir un bon point** to be right, have a point <Lv88> **•le point est ceci / le point est ça icite** the point (or reason) is this <LA, Da84> **•mettre les points sur les i** to dot one's i's, be precise, exacting, or meticulous <Da84> <***Loc:*** AS, EV, LA, SM, TB, VM, Da84, Lv88>

point[2] [pwɛ̃] *adv.* not at all, not *Monsieur de la justice, vous n'avez point raison de punir une fille pour l'habit d'un garçon.* Your honor, you are not at all justified in punishing a girl for dressing as a man. (PQ, ch: *Quand la belle entendit dire*) <***Loc:*** PQ, VM, Da84>

pointe [pwɛ̃t] *n.f.* **1** point (of a sharp object) **2** tip *Instruit à la pointe des ongles.* Educated to the fingertips (i.e. well educated). (LF) **3** point of woods projecting into a prairie **4** point of land projecting into a marsh or a body of water *La Pointe au Chênes.* Pointe aux Chênes. (TB) **5** bend in a river, place where two bodies of running water come together ◊ **•pointe de bois** point of woods jutting out into the prairie <Da84> **•pointe de terre** cape, peninsula <Da84> <***Loc:*** AC, EV, LA, LF, SL, An94, Da84, Gu00, Hi02, Lv88>

pointer [pwɛ̃te] **I** *v.tr.* to point, direct *Il a pointé le fusil droit à sa tête.* He pointed the gun right at his head. (LA) **II** *v.intr.* to point (as with the finger) *Elle a demandé ayoù sa bouteille était cachée. Il a juste pointé dans le coin.* She asked where his bottle was hidden. He just pointed to the corner. (LA) **Ça pointait pour ordonner.* They would point when they would command. (Wh83) ◊ **•pointer à** to point to *Quand ils lui ont demandé qui il voulait amener avec lui, il a pointé à sa femme.* When they asked him whom he wanted to take with him, he pointed to his wife. (LA) <LA, Da84> **•pointer (qqn) au doigt** to point out (with the finger), point at, finger (s.o.) *Ça me pointe au doigt en disant, "Garde-lé là, le rouleur et le bambocheur!"* They point at me saying, "Look at him there, the rambler and drunkard!" (ch: *La valse du bambocheur*) **Et c'était trop loin pour eux-autres entendre quoi c'est il disait. Et puis, il les a pointés au doigt.* And it was too far for them to hear what he was saying. And then, he pointed them out. (EV, An94) <EV, An94, Da84> **•pointer la course par derrière (qqn)** to start running after (s.o.) <LF> **•pointer le doigt** to point the finger *La même fille qu'a pointé le doigt à çulà-là, a pointé le doigt à çulà qu'a ce magasin.* The same girl who pointed the finger at him pointed the finger at the one who runs the store. (TB) <TB> <***Loc:*** EV, LA, LF, TB, An94, Da84, Hi02, Lv88>

pointiller [pwɛ̃tije] *v.tr.* to sharpen to a point *Il a passé l'après-midi à pointiller ses hameçons.* He spent the afternoon sharpening his hooks to a point. (LA) <***Loc:*** LA, SL>

pointir [pwɛ̃tir] *v.tr.* to sharpen to a point *On prendait des morceaux de bois, et là tu pointissais le bois, tu connais,... on appelait ça des piques.* We used to take pieces of wood, and then you'd sharpen the wood to a point, you know, . . . we called those stakes. (TB) <***Loc:*** TB>

pointu, -e [pwɛ̃ty] *adj.* **1** pointed *Une serpent poison a la tête pointue.* A venomous snake has a pointed head. (VM) *Pirogue [...] les deux boutes est pointu.* Pirogue [. . .] both ends are pointed. (JE) **2** sharp *Une aiguille pointue.* A sharp needle. (VM) **3** smart, intellectually astute *Un avocat pointu.* An astute lawyer. (EV) <***Loc:*** EV, JE, LF, Da84, La99>

pointure [pwɛ̃tyr] *n.f.* shoe size *Quelle pointure de soulier tu mets?* What size shoe do you wear? (VM) <***Loc:*** JD, SC, VM>

poire [pwar] *n.f.* pear <***Loc:*** CL, Da84, Hi02>

poireau [pwaro, porjo] *n.m.* leek <***Loc:*** EV, JE, Da84>

poirier [pwarje, pwarije] *n.m.* pear tree <***Loc:*** LA, SL, Da84>

pois [pwa] *n.m.* **1** green pea, sweet pea **2** general term used to designate any kind of bean ◊ **•pois à fleur** sweet pea flower <VM> **•pois blanc** white bean <JE> **•pois doux {rond}** green pea, sweet pea <TB> **•pois rouge** red bean <JE> **•petit pois** green pea, sweet pea <Da84> <***Loc:*** TB, VM, Da84, Hi02, Lv88>

poison[1] [pwazɔ̃, pwezɔ̃] *adj.* **1** poisonous *Ce piquant-là est aussi poison que le jour que tu le lèves dedans l'eau.* That spine [on the catfish] is as poisonous as the day you lift him from the water. (TB) **2** venomous *Une serpent poison a la tête pointue.* A venomous snake has a pointed head. (VM) <***Loc:*** JE, TB, VM, Da84>

poison[2] [pwazɔ̃, pwezɔ̃] *n.f. (occ. n.m.)* **1** poison *Il a anvalé la poison.* He swallowed the poison. (SM) **2** herbicide, insecticide *Ça* SPRAY *de la poison pour les herbes.* They spray herbicide for the weeds. (Lv88) <***Loc:*** EV, SL, SM, TB, VM, Da84, Hi02, Lv88, Re31>

poisonné, -e [pwazɔ̃ne] *adj.* venomous *Un serpent poisonné.* A venomous snake. (SM) <***Loc:*** SM>

poisson [pwasɔ̃, pwasɑ̃, pwesɔ̃] *n.m.* **1** fish *Ça se faisait une bonne vie parce que ç'avait tous les fruits de la mer, des poissons, des crabes et de la chevrette, ç'avait tout ça que ça voulait.* They made a good living because they had all the seafood, fish, crabs and shrimp, they had all that they wanted. (LF) **Le poisson, sans boisson, est poison.* Fish without drink is poisonous. (Da84) **2** seafood ◊ **•poisson à femme** ladyfish <TB> **•poisson à peigne** sawfish <TB> **•poisson armé *a*** garfish, armored fish ***b*** alligator garfish, alligator gar ***c*** spotted gar <AL, EV, IB, IV, JE, LF, SL, SM, TB, VM, Da84, Gu00, Hi02, Lv88, Re31> **•poisson à terre sèque *a*** one who has no luck ***b*** one who is lost <La99> **•poisson à voile** sailfish <TB> **•poisson dardeur** stingray <Da84> **•poisson d'avril** April Fool <Da84> **•poisson d'eau douce** freshwater fish <SL> **•poisson d'eau salée** saltwater fish <SL> **•poisson de mer** sea fish, saltwater fish <Da84> **•poisson limon** lemonfish <VM, Fa77> **•poisson qui vole** flying fish <VM, Fa77> **•poisson rouge *a*** redfish *C'est ça, de temps en temps je vas pagailler ici, pogner des poissons rouges en arrière.* That's it, from time to time I'll paddle around here, catch redfish out back. (TB) ***b*** red snapper ***c*** red drum <JE, LF, TB, Da84, Gu00, Lv88, Re31> <***Loc:*** AC, AL, AV, EV, IB, IV, JE, LF, SB, SL, SM, PQ, TB, VM, Da84, Fa77, Gu00, Hi02, La99, Lv88, Re31>

poitrail (potrail) [potraj] *n.m.* **1** breast of a horse **2** breast, chest of a person (esp. an extra large bosom) <***Loc:*** Da84, SM, Da84>

poitresse ♦see **potresse**

poitrinaire[1] **(potrinaire)** [pwatrinær, potrinær] *adj.* consumptive, tubercular, afflicted with tuberculosis *Elle est potrinaire.* She has tuberculosis. (SM) <***Loc:*** SM, VM, Da84>

poitrinaire[2] **(potrinaire)** [pwatrinær, potrinær] *n.m./f.* one who is afflicted with tuberculosis *Dans ce temps-là, ça envoyait les potrinaires au sanitarium.* In those days, they would send people with tuberculosis to the sanitarium. (VM) <***Loc:*** SM, VM, Da84>

poitrine (potrine) [potrin] *n.f.* breast, chest, bosom <***Loc:*** SM, VM, Da84>

poivier ♦see **poivrier**

poivière [pwavjær] *n.f.* pepper shaker <***Loc:*** VM>

poivre [pwav(r)] *n.m.* black pepper <***Loc:*** AC, CL, JE, SL, Da84, Hi02>

poivrer [pwavre] *v.tr.* to pepper *Il a poivré ses œufs assez je pouvais pas les manger.* He put so much pepper on his eggs that I couldn't eat them. (VM) <***Loc:*** VM, Da84>

poivrier (poivier) [pwavrije, pwavje] *n.m.* **1** pepper shaker **2** black pepper plant <***Loc:*** VM, Da84>

poivron [pwavrɔ̃] *n.m.* bell pepper <***Loc:*** CL>

POKENO [pokino] *n.m.* card game <*Loc:* VM, Fa77, Lv88>

poker (**pokeur, poqueur**) [pokœr] *n.m.* poker *Jouer (le) poker.* To play poker. (SJ) <*Loc:* EV, SJ, Da84, Lv88, Ph36>

pokeur ♦see **poker**

pole [pol] *n.m.* shaft, pole (of a carriage) <*Loc:* JE, Di32, Lv88>

poli[1], **-e** [poli] *adj.* **1** polished, glossy, shiny *Un plancher poli.* A polished floor. (VM) **2** polite, refined *Un enfant bien poli.* A polite child. (LA) <*Loc:* LA, VM, Da84>

poli[2] [poli] *adv.* politely *Il nous a parlé bien poli.* He spoke to us very politely. (LA) <*Loc:* LA>

police[1] [polis] *n.f.* **1** police *Y avait quelqu'uns de les police qui travaillaient avec mon qui parlaient français. Et on parlait français parmi nous-autres.* There were a few policemen who worked with me and who spoke French. And we spoke French among ourselves. (LF) **2** police officer *La police lui a ôté sa licence.* The police officer took away his license. (Lv88) <*Loc:* LF, Da84, Hi02, Lv88>

police[2] [pɔlis] *n.f.* policy, insurance policy **Police d'assurance.* Insurance policy. (Da84) <*Loc:* Da84>

POLICEMAN [polismɛ̃n] *n.m.* policeman *Tu l'as envoyé un* POLICEMAN, *alle dit, et mettre le pistolet dans la figure.* You sent her a policeman, she said, who stuck his pistol in her face. (TB) <*Loc:* SM, TB, Da84, Lv88>

poliment [polimɑ̃] *adv.* politely, gently **Ça fait, défunt Martin a été, puis il a dit, bien poliment, "Jeune homme, ici, on marche pas avec des chapeaux sur la tête. Tu vas aller les faire* CHECK." So the late Martin went and he said very politely, "Young man, in here we don't walk around with hats on our heads. You're going to go check them." (LA, An94) <*Loc:* LA, An94, Da84>

polipot [polipɔt] *n.m.* lichen *Il y a beaucoup de polipots sur le tronc de l'arbre.* There are a lot of lichens on the tree trunk. (SL) <*Loc:* SL>

polir [polir] *v.tr.* to polish, shine *Polir les souliers.* To polish shoes. (IB) <*Loc:* IB, Da84>

politesse [politɛs] *n.f.* **1** politeness *Mais une personne dit jamais "toi" à une plus vieille personne, tu dis "vous," c'est comme une politesse.* But a person never says "toi" to an older person, you say "vous," it's a matter of politeness. (TB) **2** good breeding <*Loc:* TB, Da84>

politicien [politisjɛ̃] *n.m.* politician <*Loc:* EV, TB, Da84>

politique [politik] *n.f.* politics ◊ •**faire de la politique** to politic, engage in political activity <Da84> <*Loc:* VM, Da84, Fa77>

politiquer [politike] *v.intr.* to talk politics **"'Tit Maurice" était eine salle de danse, bar, track de chevaux, pit de gaim et grande place pour politiquer.* 'Tit Maurice was a dance hall, bar, horse track, cock-pit, and a great place for talking politics. (Wh83) <*Loc:* Wh83>

POLL [pol] *n.m.* poll, polling place <*Loc:* JE, VM, Lv88>

pollier [polje] *n.m.* poll supervisor <*Loc:* JE>

pollution [polysjɔ̃] *n.f.* pollution <*Loc:* Da84>

polonais[1], **-e** [polɔ̃nɛ, polɔ̃ne, -ɛz] *adj.* Polish *Un prêtre polonais.* A Polish priest. (VM) <*Loc:* VM, Da84>

polonais[2] [polɔ̃nɛ, polɔ̃ne] *n.m.* Polish, the Polish language <*Loc:* Da84>

poltron, -onne [pɔltrɔ̃, -ɔ̃n] *adj.* skittish, jumpy, nervous *Un enfant poltron.* A jumpy child. (LA) <*Loc:* LA, Da84>

pommade [pɔ̃mad] *n.f.* hair gel <*Loc:* LA>

pomme [pɔ̃m] *n.f.* **1** apple **2** head (of lettuce, cabbage, etc.) ◊ •**pomme d'Adam** Adam's apple <Da84> •**pomme de chou** head of cabbage <Da84> •**pomme de mai** mayhaw <CL> •**pomme de pin** pine cone (VM) <VM> •**pomme de terre** potato, Irish potato <AC, AV, EV, IB, LA, LF, SL, SM, VM, Da84, Hi02> •**pomme haigre** crabapple <SJ> •**pomme sauvage** crabapple <VM, Fa77> <*Loc:* AC, AV, EV, IB, LA, LF, SL, SM, TB, VM, Da84, Fa77, Hi02>

pommé, -e [pɔ̃me] *adj.* headed **Chou pommé.* Cabbage that has formed a head, head of cabbage. (Da84) <*Loc:* Da84>

pommeau [pɔ̃mo] *n.m.* pommel (of a saddle) <*Loc:* Da84>

pommer [pɔ̃me] **I** *v.intr.* to head, form a head (of cabbage, etc.) *Il faisait sec cette année, mes choux ont pas pommé.* It was dry this year, my cabbages didn't form heads. (VM) **II se pommer** *v.pron.* to head, form a head (of cabbage, etc.) *Les choux sont après se pommer.* The cabbage plants are forming heads. (VM) <*Loc:* VM, Da84>

pommetier [pɔ̃metje] *n.m.* mayhaw tree <*Loc:* VM, Fa77>

pommette [pɔ̃mɛt] *n.f.* **1** mayhaw **2** mayhaw tree **3** crabapple ◊ •**pommette bleue** species of haw with large, bluish fruit <Re31> <*Loc:* CL, EV, Da84, Lv88, Ph36, Re31>

pommier [pɔ̃mje] *n.m.* **1** apple tree **2** mayhaw tree **3** hawthorn <*Loc:* IB, Da84, Lv88, Re31>

pomon ♦see **poumon**

pomonique ♦see **poumonique**

pompadour [pɔ̃padur] *n.f.* ◊ •**à la pompadour** having the hair combed straight back *Jean se peigne à la pompadour.* John combs his hair straight back. (IB) <*Loc:* IB>

pompano (**papano, pompono**) [pɔ̃pɑ̃no, papɑ̃no, pɔ̃pɔ̃no] *n.m.* any of various fishes from the Gulf of Mexico including the common pompano and the Florida pompano <*Loc:* JE, LF, Da84, Lv88, Re31>

pompe [pɔ̃p] *n.f.* **1** pump, hand pump *Tout l'eau va se rassembler en arrière, et là y a une pompe pour pomper l'eau.* All the water goes into the back [of the boat], and there, there's a pump to pump the water [out]. (LF) **2** air pump **3** water hose *Va chercher la pompe pour laver le bateau.* Go get the hose to wash the boat. (VM) **4** pressurized sprayer *Je m'ai acheté une pompe pour empoisonner les herbes de coco.* I bought a sprayer to poison the nut sedge. (EV) ◊ •**pompe à gaz** gas pump *Quand tu vas aller en l'île tu vas voir deux pompes à gaz pour le char et un tout petit bâtisse, un petit magasin presque au boute.* When you go onto the Island you'll see two gas pumps for cars and a tiny building, a little store almost at the end. (TB) <EV, TB> •**pompe à la main** hand pump *On avait des puits à eau, on pompait de l'eau* *avec des pompes à la main.* We had water wells, we pumped water out with hand pumps. (AS) <AS> <***Loc:*** AS, EV, JE, LA, LF, TB, VM, Da84>

pomper [pɔ̃pe] **I** *v.tr.* **1** to pump *Tu pouvais quitter le bateau, après que t'as bâti le bateau, tu pouvais le mettre à l'eau, le quitter caler pour à peu près trois jours. Tu pompais l'eau dedans.* You could leave the boat, after you've built the boat, you could put it in the water, let it settle for about three days. You pumped water into it. (TB) *Il fallait je pompe du gaz.* I had to pump gas. (Lv88) *Leurs attendants vont venir et pomper le gazoline pour vous. T'as pas besoin de sortir de ton automobile.* Their attendants will come and pump the gas for you. You don't need to get out of your car. (EV) **2** to water, irrigate (with a pump) *Il pompe son riz.* He is irrigating his rice. (SM) *Nous-autres est après pomper le riz.* We are irrigating the rice. (VM) **3** to pump up, inflate by means of a pump *Il a pompé son* TIRE. He inflated his tire. (SM) **4** to introduce, bring in, spread **Cette cochonnerie qu'est pompée dans notre tête.* That trash that is pumped into our heads. (Wh83) **5** to question persistently, pump for information *Il lui a pompé pour savoir quoi ce qu'avait arrivé au bal.* He pumped him to find out what had happened at the dance. (LA) **II se pomper** *v.pron.* to mount one's courage, fortitude, determination or resistance *Il s'a pompé de courage avant de demander à son père pour la marier.* He mounted his courage before asking her father if he could marry her. (VM) <***Loc:*** EV, LA, LF, SM, TB, VM, Da84, Lv88, Wh83>

pompeur [pɔ̃pœr] *n.m.* gager (in the oil industry) *Et là après ça j'ai un job pompeur. C'est moi qui tchéquait les tanks tous les jours.* And after that I got a job as a gager. I was the one who checked the tanks every day. (LF) <***Loc:*** LF, TB>

pompier [pɔ̃pje] *n.m.* **1** blotting paper **2** [*recent*] fireman <***Loc:*** JE, Da84>

pompon [pɔ̃pɔ̃] *n.m.* **1** pom-pom, tuft **2** powder puff **3** [*baby talk*] behind, bottom, buttocks <***Loc:*** JE, SM, Da84>

pomponner ♦see **pimponner**

pompono ♦see **pompano**

pondeuse [pɔ̃døz] *n.f.* laying hen, layer <***Loc:*** Da84>

pondiaire [pɔ̃djær] *n.f.* tube through which an egg passes before it is laid <***Loc:*** SM>

pondoire [pɔ̃dwar] *n.f.* **1** laying house, henhouse, hen cage **2** soft distended belly of a laying hen <***Loc:*** Da84>

pondre [pɔ̃n, pɔ̃nd(r)] (*p.p.* **pond** [pɔ̃], **pondu** [pɔ̃dy]) **I** *v.tr.* to lay (eggs) *Comme asteur-là, tu peux pas les piéger, les attraper, parce qu'eusse après pondre les œufs. Eusse après avoir les petits caïmans asteur-là.* Like right now, you can't trap them, catch them, because they're laying eggs. They're having baby alligators right now. (TB) **II** *v.intr.* to lay eggs *Il pond ici, il lève sa famille. Çu-là-là s'en retourne dans le Canada. Et çu-là icitte, il habite ici.* It lays eggs here, it raises its family. That one goes back to Canada. And this one, it lives here. (TB) **La poule qui chante premier, c'est elle qui a pondu.* The hen that cackles first is the one that laid the egg. (Da84) *La poule a pond.* The chicken laid an egg. (SM) ◊ **•pondre un œuf *a*** to mess up ***b*** to say s.t. unbelievable <EV, La99> <***Loc:*** EV, IV, JE, LF, SM, TB, Da84, Hi02, La99>

pongeux, -euse [pɔ̃ʒø, -øz] *adj.* soft, spongy, fluffy *T'appelais ça une omelette. C'était pongeux, ça gonfle, ça levait.* You called it an omelet. It was fluffy, it puffed up, it rose. (EV) *Alle fait du bon pain pongeux.* She makes good soft bread. (VM) *La terre est pongeuse.* The ground is spongy. (VM) <***Loc:*** EV, VM, Da84, Lv88>

ponkine ♦see **PUMPKIN**

pont [pɔ̃] *n.m.* **1** bridge *Y avait pas de pont. Faulait que t'espères pour le ferry. Je crois qu'il faisait un voyage par heure.* There was no bridge. You had to wait for the ferry. I think they made one trip per hour. (TB) **2** deck of a boat *Chaque côté en-dessour du pont eh ben c'était tout des petites chambres.* Each side under the deck, well, it was all divided into little rooms. (LF) ◊ **•pont à bascule** drawbridge <Da92> **•pont à craques** cattle guard <VM> **•pont à pied** footbridge **Dans ce temps-là, il avait ein 'tit pont à pied qui traversait le bayou et c'était usé par les petits qui venaient à l'école de l'autre bord du bayou.* In those days, there was a little footbridge that crossed the bayou and that was used by children who were coming to school from the other side of the bayou. (Wh83) <Wh83> **•Pont Breaux** Breaux Bridge <SL, Hi02> **•pont de glace** thick layer of ice over a body of water <VM> <***Loc:*** AC, EV, LA, LF, SL, TB, VM, An94, Da84, Da94, Hi02>

ponton [pɔ̃tɔ̃] *n.m.* pontoon *Un pont à pontons.* A pontoon bridge. (VM) <***Loc:*** VM, Da84>

pony [pɔ̃ni] *n.m.* pony <***Loc:*** SM, Da84>

pop[1] [pɔp] *n.m.* soda, pop, soft drink *Vous-autres veut boire du pop ou quelque chose? Tu veux des* POTATO CHIP, *ou?* Do you all want to drink some pop or something? You want potato chips, or? (TB) ◊ **•pop rouge** strawberry soda *Je veux du pop rouge, moi.* I want strawberry soda. (VM) <VM, La99> <***Loc:*** TB, VM, Fa77, La99, Lv88>

pop[2] ♦see **papa**

popa ♦see **papa**

popotte [popɔt] *n.f.* harlot <***Loc:*** SC, La99>

poppé [pope] *n.f.* poppy <***Loc:*** EV, Ph36>

popper [pope] *v.tr.* to pop *Ça poppait le tactac premier. Tu mettais ça dans une bombe et tu poppais ton tactac avec de la graisse.* They popped the popcorn first. You would put that in a cooking pot and you popped your popcorn with some grease. (TB) <***Loc:*** TB>

populaire [popylær] *adj.* **1** popular *Ces grandes barres de candis au peppermint, ça c'était populaire dans ce temps-là.* Those big sticks of peppermint candy, they were popular in those days. (TB) **2** populous, heavily populated *La Louisiane* *était pas populaire. Il n'y est pas grand monde dans la Louisiane. C'était un grand territoire de terre avec peu de monde.* Louisiana was not heavily populated. There were not many people in Louisiana. It was a big territory of land with few people. (AV) <***Loc:*** AC, AV, TB, Da84, Lv88>

popularité [popylarite] *n.f.* popularity **Par rapport à la popularité, ils ont choisi d'être comme tout les autres pour avancer.* Because of popularity, they chose to be like everyone else in order to get ahead. (Wh83) <***Loc:*** Da84, Wh83>

population [popylasjɔ̃] *n.f.* population <***Loc:*** AV, VM, Da84, Fa77>

poque[1] [pɔk] *n.m./f.* **1** punch, fist blow **2** mark left by fist blow or punch <***Loc:*** JE, VM>

poque[2] [pɔk] *n.f.* top, spinning top *Jouer à la poque.* To spin a top. (JE) <***Loc:*** JE>

poquecer ♦see **poquer**

poquer (**poquecer**) [poke, pokse] **I** *v.tr.* to deal (a blow) *Je l'ai poqué un coup de poing.* I dealt him a punch. (SM) **II** *v.intr.* to exchange punches, engage in a brawl, have a fistfight *Charles et Lloyd ont poquecé à l'école hier.* Charles and Lloyd had a fistfight at school yesterday. (SL) <***Loc:*** JE, SL, SM, VM, Lv88>

poqueur ♦see **poker**

porc [pɔr] *n.m.* **1** pig, hog **2** pork <***Loc:*** TB, Da84, Hi02>

porcelain [pɔrslɛ̃] *n.m.* porcelain <***Loc:*** VM, Fa77>

porcelaine (**porcéline**) [pɔrsəlin, pɔrselin] *n.f.* porcelain, china *Les vaisselles étaient fait en porceline blanche.* The dishes were made of white porcelain. (TB) <***Loc:*** TB, VM, Da84>

porcéline ♦see **porcelaine**

pore [pɔr] *n.m.* pore (e.g. in the skin) <***Loc:*** Da84>

poreau [poro] *n.m.* **1** plant gall, tumorous growth on a tree **2** wart <***Loc:*** EV, LF, SB, SM, TB, VM, Da84, Lv88>

poreux, -euse [porø, -øz] *adj.* porous, loosely woven *Mon gilet est trop poreux. Ça tient pas la chaleur.* My sweater is too loosely woven. It's doesn't hold heat. (VM) <***Loc:*** VM, Da84>

port [pɔr] *n.m.* **1** port, harbor *Le port de la Nouvelle Orléans.* The port of New Orleans. (LF) **2** wharf ◊ **•Port Barré** Port Barre (land-locked port) *Il y avait pas de chemin de fer autour ici. Il halait son riz au Port Barré. Il y avait des bateaux qui venaient là en le bayou Courtableau.* There was no railway around here. He would transport his rice to Port Barre. There were boats that came there to Bayou Courtableau. (EV) <EV, Da84> <***Loc:*** EV, LF, Da84>

portable [pɔrtab(l)] *adj.* **1** wearable *Ce pantalon est pus portable. Il y a trop de trous dedans.* This pair of pants is no longer wearable. There are too many holes in it. (VM) **2** portable *Un téléphone portable.* A portable telephone. (VM) <***Loc:*** VM, Da84>

portage[1] [pɔrtaʒ] *n.m.* **1** portage (transportation of a boat by land) **2** transport **3** swampy, woody area that is not easily accessible *Le monde l'autre bord du portage parle pas pareil comme nous-autres.* The people on the other side of the swampy woods don't talk the same way we do. (SM) <***Loc:*** SL, SM, Da84>

portage[2] [pɔrtaʒ] *n.m.* front door, main entrance <***Loc:*** JE>

portager [pɔrtaʒe] *v.intr.* to portage *On a eu pour portager un bon bout pour arriver au Lac Perdu.* We had to portage a good way to reach Lost Lake. (LA) <***Loc:*** LA, Da84, Hi02>

portailler [pɔrtaje] *v.tr.* to carry, carry repeatedly *On était après portailler nos valises tout partout dans l'*AIRPORT. We were carrying our luggage all over the airport. (LA) <***Loc:*** IB, LA>

portale [pɔrtal] *n.m.* front door, main entrance (of a house) <***Loc:*** JE>

portant [pɔrtɑ̃] *adj.* ◊ **•bien portant** healthy, well, in good health <Da84> <***Loc:*** Da84>

porte [pɔrt] *n.f.* **1** door *Frème la porte!* Close the door! (JE) *Barre la porte!* Lock the door! (JE) *On a cogné à la porte.* We knocked at the door. (VM) *Une armoire avec deux portes et des tablettes.* An armoire with two doors and shelves. (AC) **2** doorway **Quand Marc Roy a paru dans la porte, Alex Dufour lui a foutu une bonne râclée.* When Marc Roy appeared in the doorway, Alex Dufour socked him hard. (Hi02) **3** gate *La grande porte est cassée.* The big gate is broken. (IB) *Quand ils arrivaient à la porte du cimitière il faulait qu'ils arrêtent et le prêtre [...] finissait l'enterrement.* When they arrived at the gate of the cemetery they had to stop and the priest would finish the funeral. (LF) **4** entrance **5** paid admission *Et j'ai vu souvent là des... des portes de sept cents tickets.* I often saw 700 paid admissions there. (SL) ◊ **•porte à porte** door to door <EV> **•porte cochère** carport <Da84> **•porte de clos** field gate <Da84> **•porte de communication** communicating door <SB> **•porte de cour** yard gate <Da84, Hi02> **•porte (d') en avant / porte de devant** front door *Il a sorti par la porte de devant.* He went out through the front door. (AC) <AC, TB> **•porte (d')en arrière** back door <TB, Lv88> **•porte en grille** screen door *Là j'ai ouvert la porte en grille, le vent soufflait du nord.* Then I opened the screen door, the wind was blowing from the north. (TB) <TB, Da84> **•porte vitrée** glass door <Da84> **•aller aux portes** to beg, go begging *Ça c'est l'homme qui va aux portes.* That's the man who goes begging. (TB) <TB> **•mettre à la porte** to expel, kick out *Si ça se conformait pas, le constable les mettait à la porte.* If they didn't behave, the constable would kick them out. (LA) <LA, Da84> **•petite porte de jardin** yard gate *Mon papa m'a rejoint à la petite porte de cour en braillant.* My daddy met me at the little yard gate crying. (EV) <EV> <***Loc:*** AC, EV, IB, JE, LA, LF, SJ, SL, SM, TB, VM, An94, Da84, Hi02, Lv88>

portée [pɔrte] *n.f.* **1** range (of the voice, a gun, etc.) **À portée de fusil.* Within gunshot range. (Da84) **2** litter (of offspring) **Une portée de chats.* A litter of cats. (Da84) **Garde voir Wilda et sa portée après sortir de la boutique!* Look at Wilda and her litter of kids coming out of the store! (La99) ◊ **•à portée** nearby, handy, at hand <Da84> <***Loc:*** Da84, La99>

portefeuille [pɔrtfœj] *n.m.* **1** portfolio **2** briefcase **3** wallet, billfold <***Loc:*** EV, Da84>

porte-fouet [pɔrtəfwɛt] *n.m.* whip socket (in a carriage) <Da84>

portemanteau (**porte-manteau**) [pɔrtmɑ̃to] *n.m.* **1** coat rack, clothes rack **2** section in an armoire or chifferobe for hanging clothing <***Loc:*** IB, SM, Da84, Lv88>

portement [pɔrtmɑ̃] *n.m.* health *Il est sûr en bon portement cette année.* He sure is in good health this year. (VM) <***Loc:*** JE, VM>

porte-monnaie [pɔrtmɔ̃nɛ, pɔrtmɔ̃ne] *n.m.* **1** handbag, purse, pocketbook *À la Nouvelle-Orléans, vous savez, les gens sont toujours bien mis, toujours avec leur chapeau, leur porte-monnaie, leurs gants.* In New Orleans, you know, people are always well dressed with their hat, their handbag, their gloves. (Lv88) **2** wallet, billfold *Dans ce temps-là t'aurais pu prendre ton porte-monnaie et t'aurais pu te coucher sur la banquette et mettre ton porte-monnaie sur toi et dormir, et personne aurait touché ton porte-monnaie.* In those days you could have taken your wallet and you could have slept on the sidewalk and put your wallet on top of yourself and slept, and no one would have touched your wallet. (TB) <***Loc:*** EV, LF, SM, TB, Da84, Hi02, Lv88>

porte-paquet [pɔrtpakɛ, pɔrtpake] *n.m.* tattletale, tale-bearer, snitch *Ce porte-paquet va rapporter tout ça alle a attendu.* That tattle-tale will repeat everything she heard. (VM) <***Loc:*** EV, SM, VM, Da84, Lv88, Ph36>

porte-plume [pɔrtplym] *n.m.* penholder <***Loc:*** Da84>

porter [pɔrte] *v.tr.* **1** to carry, bear **Des fois, c'est un sac de bois qu'il porte sur son dos.* Sometimes, it's a sack of wood that he carries on his back. (SL, An94) *C'était un fanal eux-autres appelait ça, c'était une lanterne. Il faulait que tu marches dans le chemin avec ça pour voir ayoù t'allais. Ça fait l'homme portait la lanterne et la femme s'en allait, les enfants en arrière.* It was a lantern as they called it. You had to walk in the road with that to see where you were going. So, the man carried the lantern and the woman went with the children behind her. (TB) *Mais la manière que c'est, D. a jamais été adopté. Il a juste porté le nom d'Esteve.* But the way it went, D. was never adopted. He just bore the name of Esteve. (TB) **2** to wear *Icitte équand le monde est mort, ça porte tout le noir.* Here when somebody dies, they all wear black. (TB) *Elle porte une robe barreautée rouge et blanc.* She is wearing a red and white striped dress. (SB) *On avait des souliers mais les souliers c'était pour le dimanche. C'était pas pour porter toute la semaine.* We had shoes but the shoes were for Sundays. They weren't to be worn every day. (LF) **3** to bring **Elle avait venu lui porter une triste nouvelle.* She had come to bring him sad news. (IV, An94) **Mais elle dit, "Tuez ce chien qui vous suit, et puis ôtez-lui les yeux pour porter au roi."* But she said, "Kill that dog that's following you, and then take out his eyes to bring to the king. (IV, An94) ◊ **•porter attention (à)** to pay attention (to) *J'ai jamais porté attention à qui eusse après dire.* I've never paid attention to what they were saying. (TB) *Je porte pas grand attention, mais je peux dire quand eux-autres vient d'en bas, et si c'est que ça vient d'en haut, parce que le monde d'en haut parle pas pareil comme eusse d'en bas.* I don't pay much attention, but I can tell when they come up from down the bayou or if they come from up the bayou, because people up the bayou don't talk the same as those from down the bayou. (TB) <TB, Da84> **•porter cas (de)** to pay attention (to) *Tu portais pas cas de ça, ils te quittaient tranquille.* You didn't pay any attention to that, they left you alone. (EV) *Porte pas cas de lui. C'est un pur hypocrite.* Don't pay attention to him. He's a pure hypocrite. (LA) <EV, LA, VM> **•porter des nouvelles** to bring news *J'ai peur qu'ils portent des mauvaises nouvelles.* I'm afraid that they are bringing bad news. (LA) <LA, Da84> **•porter des paquets** to gossip, carry tales <Da84> **•porter du bon linge** to wear good clothes *Il a pas la chance de porter du bon linge souvent.* He doesn't often have the opportunity to wear good clothes. (LA) <LA, Da84> **•porter le deuil** to wear mourning *Elle a porté le deuil pour dix ans après que son mari a manqué.* She wore mourning for ten years after her husband died. (LA) <LA, Da84> **•porter plainte** to complain, lodge a complaint *Ils ont décidé de pas porter plainte. Ils allaient régler ça eux-mêmes derrière la petite grosserie.* They decided not to file a complaint. They would take care of the situation themselves behind the little grocery store. (LA) <LA, Da84> **•porter (qqch) comme la peau** to wear every day (e.g. a garment) <SB, La99> **•porter sa croix** to carry one's cross, bear the burden of one's problems *Il faut pas tu te plains, cher. Il faut tu portes ta croix.* You mustn't complain, dear. You must bear your cross. (LA) <LA, Da84> **•porter sur** to affect, influence, damage *Cette maladie porte sur les yeux.* That sickness affects the eyes. (VM) <VM> **•porter un enfant** to carry a child, be pregnant *Je l'ai porté jusqu'au huitième et là je l'ai perdu.* I carried him until the eighth month, then I lost him [because of a miscarriage]. (VM) <VM> **•porter une rancune** to bear a grudge *Ce monde-ça pouvait porter une rancune pour des années.* Those people could carry a grudge for years. (LA) <LA, Da84> **•se porter à / être porté à** to be prone to, be disposed to, have a tendency to **Être porté à la colère.* To be prone to anger. (Da84) <Da84> **•se porter bien** to be well, be in good health <Da84> **•ça porte**

les mêmes caleçons they are always together <La99> **•elle porte les culottes** she 'wears the pants' <La99> <***Loc:*** EV, IV, LA, LF, SB, TB, VM, Da84, Hi02, La99>

porteur [pɔrtœr] *n.m.* **1** bearer, carrier, porter **2** pall bearer <***Loc:*** IB, SJ, Da84>

porteuse [pɔrtøz] *n.f.* sugarcane-carrier, conveyor belt by means of which sugarcane is taken from the cane-shed to the crusher <***Loc:*** IB, SJ>

portier [pɔrtje] *n.m.* doorkeeper <***Loc:*** Da84>

portion [pɔrsjɔ̃] *n.f.* portion, part, share, piece <***Loc:*** Da84>

portrait [pɔrtrɛ, pɔrtre] *n.m.* **1** painting, portrait *Il a* DRAW *le portrait à mon défunt grand-père.* He drew the portrait of my late grandfather. (EV) **2** image, picture *J'avais pas vu un portrait de violon seulement.* I hadn't even seen a picture of a violin. (Lv88) *Il pouvait* VISUALIZE *un portrait de quelque chose qu'allait prendre place.* He could visualize a picture of something that was going to happen. (LF) **3** photograph, picture *Tout quelque chose était beau beau. Là on a été prendre notre portrait.* Everything was beautiful. Then we went to have our picture taken. (EV) *Les portraits de ta famille, c'est pas remplaçable.* Family pictures, those are not replaceable. (EV) **4** *(usu. pl.)* movie, movies *Ils vont voir les portraits à soir.* They are going to the movies tonight. (IB) *Aller aux portraits.* To go to the movies. (SJ) ◊ **•portrait saint** holy picture <Da84> **•portraits grouillants** film, movie <Lv88> **•il est le portrait de son père** he is the image of his father <Da84> **•prendre qqn en portrait / prendre le portrait de qqn** to take s.o.'s picture <Da84, Lv88> **•se faire prendre en portrait** to have one's picture taken <Da84> <***Loc:*** AC, EV, IB, JE, SJ, SL, SM, TB, VM, Da84, Hi02, Lv88>

posé, -e [poze] *adj.* poised, at ease *Ma fille est bien posée avec la compagnie.* My daughter is very at ease with company. (VM) <***Loc:*** VM, Da84>

poser [poze] **I** *v.tr.* to place, set down, put down *Pose la lampe en arrière de la chaise.* Put the lamp down behind the chair. (VM) **Et c'était un marais rond et les canards étaient posés tout le tour au ras de l'écore.* And it was a round marsh and the ducks were sitting all around the edge. (AC, An94) **II se poser** *v.pron.* to alight, perch (of a bird, insect) *C'est un maringouin. Il était après* CHECK *é-où il s'aurait posé.* It's a mosquito. He was checking to see where he would land. (EV) *Et il va venir contre le vent là, ils vont se poser avec les appôts près de toi.* And it [the duck] will come against the wind, they'll alight among the decoys near you. (TB) ◊ **•poser une question** to ask a question **En réponse d'ein question posé dans ein column "Du Chicot" en regarde de Alcide "Bos" Gaspard.* In answer to a question asked in a column of "Du Chicot" concerning Alcide "Bos" Gaspard. (Wh83) <Da84, Da92, Wh83> <***Loc:*** AC, EV, TB, VM, An94, Da84, Da92, Hi02, Wh83>

positif, -ive [pozitif, -iv] *adj.* **1** positive, certain, sure *Je suis sûr et positif qu'il va arriver.* I'm sure and certain that he will arrive. (LA) **2** absolute, honest-to-god **Il s'a fait un positif bonhomme!* He made himself an honest-to-god mannequin! (SL, An94) <***Loc:*** LA, SL, An94, Da84>

position [pozisjɔ̃] *n.f.* **1** situation, position (in space or time) *Tu parles j'étais dans une mauvaise position en bas de la table.* I tell you, I was in a bad position under the table. (LA) **2** job, position *Mon garçon a une bonne position à Lafayette.* My son has a good job in Lafayette. (Lv88) **3** position, attitude, stance (on an issue) **Le Police Jurie de la paroisse va peut-être rentrer dedans, et si des positions passés veut dire quec'chose, la bande du gouvernement va aller au bord à Aucoin ou rester neutre.* The Parish Police Jury may get involved, and if their past positions are any indication, the government gang will side with Aucoin or remain neutral. (Wh83) <***Loc:*** LA, Da84, Hi02, Lv88, Wh83>

positivement [pozitivmɑ̃] *adv.* positively, certainly, surely *Il m'a dit positivement que c'était correct.* He told me absolutely that it was true. (VM) *Il était rendu positivement muet.* He had become positively mute. (LA) <***Loc:*** LA, VM, Da84>

possédé, -e [posede] *n.* **1** possessed person **2** mischievous, disobedient child ◊ **•possédé du diable** possessed person, one who is possessed (by the devil) <Da84> <***Loc:*** LF, Da84>

possession [posesjɔ̃] *n.f.* property, possession ◊ **•prendre possession** to take possession *Les nouveaux voisins ont pas pris possession de la maison encore.* The new neighbors have not yet taken possession of the house. (VM) <VM, Da84> <***Loc:*** VM, Da84>

possibilité [posibilite] *n.f.* possibility <***Loc:*** Da84>

possible[1] [posib(l)] *adj.* possible **C'était possible d'avoir plus que trois ou quatre batailles par soir.* It was possible to have more than three or four fights a night. (LA, An94) <***Loc:*** IV, LA, TB, An94, Da84, Hi02>

possible[2] [posib(l)] *n.m.* **•faire son possible** to do one's best <Da84> <***Loc:*** Da84>

possiblement [posibləmɑ̃] *adv.* possibly, maybe *Ça va t'i bien glacer à soir?—Possiblement.* Is it going to freeze tonight? —Maybe. (VM) <***Loc:*** VM, Da84, Fa77>

postage [postaʒ, pɔsta, pozaʒ, pɔstjab] *n.m.* postage <***Loc:*** IB, JE, VM, Da84, Lv88>

postal, -e [postal] *adj.* postal **Carte postale.* Postcard. (Da84) <***Loc:*** VM, Da84, Fa77>

posté, -e [poste] *adj.* well informed *Il est bien posté sur la guerre.* He is well informed about the war. (VM) *Il est bien posté dans la politique.* He is well informed in politics. (Lv88) <***Loc:*** EV, JE, SL, SM, TB, VM, Da84, La99, Lv88, Ph36>

poste[1] [pɔs(t)] *n.f.* **1** post office **Aller à la poste.* To go to the post office. (Da84) **2** mail **Aller après la poste.* To go after the mail. (Da84) <***Loc:*** SM, Da84, Hi02>

poste[2] [pɔs(t)] *n.m.* post, place, station <***Loc:*** SM, Da84>

poster [poste] **I** *v.tr.* **1** to station *On a été posté dans le sud de la France.* We were stationed in the south of France. (LA) **2** to post, mail **Poster une lettre.* To mail a letter. (Da92) **II se poster** *v.pron.* **1** to station o.s. *Il s'avait posté là en avant de la porte pour pas me manquer.* He had stationed himself in front of the door in order not to miss me. (VM) **2** to learn about, find out about, research *Il s'a bien posté sur l'histoire de sa famille.* He did a lot of research on the history of his family. (LA) **3** to assume an unusual posture while standing *Ga-woir comme il s'a posté.* Look at how he's standing. (VM) <***Loc:*** LA, VM, Da84, Da92>

postes [pɔs(t)] *n.m.pl.* buckshot *Il s'est tourné, parce qu'il l'a tiré dans le dos là-là. Pété un coup de postes et il l'a défoncé un* WHOPPER *de trou.* He turned around because he shot him in the back. Shot him with a round of buckshot and he blew open a whopper of a hole. (EV) **Là, les autres ont été tout moitié blessés, tu connais, avec ces postes-là. Il y a pas rien pour arrêter ça.* Then, the others were all half-wounded, you know, with those buckshot. There's nothing that will stop that. (LA, An94) <***Loc:*** EV, LA, An94, Da84, Da92>

postiche [postiʃ] *adj.* **1** artificial, false **Dents postiches.* False teeth. (Da84, Lv88) **2** annexed, added on (e.g. part of a building) *Galerie postiche.* Added-on porch. (SJ) <***Loc:*** SJ, Da84, Hi02, Lv88>

postillon [postijɔ̃] *n.m.* **1** mailman, mail carrier *Le postillon est arrivé à la maison avec une grosse boîte en carton.* The mailman arrived at the house with a big cardboard box. (Lv88) **2** postmaster **3** letter *Et là quand vous va partir, si vous veut* KEEP IN TOUCH *avec nous-autres, vous prend l'adresse et écrire des postillons.* And then when you leave, if you want to keep in touch with us, take the address and write letters. (LF) <***Loc:*** EV, IB, LF, SL, VM, Da84, Hi02, Lv88, Ph36>

POST-OFFICE [postofis] *n.m.* post office <***Loc:*** TB, Lv88>

postume (**apostume**) [postym, apostym] *n.f.* *(occ. n.m.)* **1** pus *La postume coulait du bobo.* Pus flowed from the wound. (SM) *Il a pincé le bobo et le postume a volé.* He pinched the sore and the pus flew out. (LA) **2** abscess <***Loc:*** EV, IB, JE, LA, SM, VM, Da84, Lv88, Ph36>

pot [po, pɔt] *n.m.* **1** vase *Un pot de fleurs.* A vase of flowers. (LA) **2** pitcher *Sister Theo venait avec un pot de limonade.* Sister Theo would come with a pitcher of lemonade. (SL) **3** pot, jackpot, kitty (e.g. in a card game) **Après chaque joueur mettait sa gage dans le pot, les petits prendaient chaqu'un son tour à rouler le bloc pour avoir ein numéro qui les disait qui faire.* After each player put his bet in the pot, the children each took turns rolling the block that told them what to do. (Wh83) ◊ **•pot à fleur** flower pot <Da84> **•pot d'eau** pitcher (of water) *Il a du monde qui dit un* PITCH, *ça c'est la chose que tu mets de l'eau dedans, dans la glacière, un* PITCH. *Et qui c'est l'autre j'avais nommé? Un pot, un pot d'eau?* There are people who say a pitcher, that's the thing you put water in, in the refrigerator, a pitcher. And what's the other one I mentioned, a "pot d'eau"? (LF) <LF> **•pot de chambre** chamber pot <EV, IB, Da84> **•pot de grès** earthenware crock *Le cochon a donné deux pots de grès de graisse.* The pig yielded two crocks of fat. (VM) <SM, VM> **•pot de lait** pitcher of milk <Da84> **•pot de noce** chamber pot <EV, IB, Da84> **•pot fêlé** one who frequently complains about his health <SM, La99> **•le pot de chambre à Virgile** place where it rains a lot <SL, La99> <***Loc:*** EV, IB, JE, LA, LF, SL, SM, VM, Da84, Hi02, La99, Wh83>

potage [potaʒ] *n.m.* soup <***Loc:*** Da84>

potasse [potas] *n.f.* potash <***Loc:*** EV>

pote ♦see **potre**

poteau [poto] *n.m.* **1** stake, post **2** post, structural support post **Le "Fais Do-Do" était eine grosse batisse blanche avec eine fête [=faît] à pic supporté par ein gros poteau en milieu.* The "*Fais Do-Do*" was a big white building with a pointed roof held up by a large post in the middle. (Wh83) ◊ **•poteau à lumière** telephone pole *Si je boirais deux bières, je monterais le* TELEPHONE POLE *là-bas. Poteau à lumière.* If I drank two beers, I'd be climbing the telephone pole over there. Telephone pole. (TB) <TB> **•poteau de barrière** fencepost *C'était un fifollet eux-autres appelait ça. C'était une boule de feu, et ça dansait sur les barrières, les poteaux de barrière.* They called that a will-o'the-wisp. It was a ball of fire, and it danced on fences, on fenceposts. (TB) <TB> **•poteau de galerie** porch column <TB, VM> **•poteau du coin** ***a*** corner post ***b*** stalwart person, mainstay of a family <Da84> **•faire poteau** to hush, be still <IB> **•poteau, Caillette** see **Caillette** <***Loc:*** AV, EV, IB, LA, SM, TB, VM, Da84, Hi02, La99, Lv88, Wh83>

potiche [potiʃ] *n.f.* **1** pottery **2** hornet's nest <***Loc:*** JE>

potin [potɛ̃] *n.m.* **1** trouble *Plutôt que le potin commence entre eux qu'est pas bien.* Rather than having trouble start between them, which isn't good. (LF) **2** noise *Des rats de maïs là-dedans qui étaient après faire du potin!* [It was] corn rats in there that were making noise. (TB) **3** large iron pot used to boil clothes ◊ **•faire du potin** to make noise *Et les enfants faisaient pas de potin parce que eusse connaît mieux que ça.* And the children made no noise, because they know better than that. (LF) <LF> <***Loc:*** IB, LF, TB>

potrail ♦see **poitrail**

potre[1] (**pautre**) [pɔt(r)] *adj.* untamed (of a horse), not yet broken to the saddle or harness *Un cheval potre.* An untamed horse. (LA) <***Loc:*** LA, Da84>

potre[2] (**pote, pautre, pautrin**) [pɔt(r), potrɛ̃] *n.m.* **1** wild, untamed or unbroken horse, bronco *Ces enfants sont brus commes des potres dans la plaine.* Those children are wild like broncos in the plains. (VM) *Le 'tit garçon a corcobié comme un potre.* The little boy bucked like a bronco. (SM) **2** foal, colt **3** stallion **4** playboy, woman chaser <***Loc:*** JE, SM, VM, Da84, La99, Lv88>

potresse (**pautresse, poitresse**) [potrɛs, pwatrɛs] *n.f.* **1** wild, unbroken mare **2** mare <***Loc:*** JE, VM>

potrinaire ♦see **poitrinaire**

potrine ♦see **poitrine**

pou [pu] *n.m.* **1** louse **2** tick ◊ •**pou de bête** cattle tick <VM> •**pou (de) bois** ***a*** wood tick ***b*** cattle tick <EV, JE, TB, VM, Da84, Fa77, Lv88, Ph36, Re31> •**pou de poule** chicken louse <VM, Da84, Fa77> •**pou de tête** head louse <Da84, Re31> •**être dans les poux de bois** to be overwhelmed with debts <JE> <***Loc:*** EV, JE, TB, VM, Da84, Fa77, Lv88, Ph36, Re31>

pouce [pus] *n.m.* **1** thumb **2** inch *Et chaque bateau avait un espace à peu près je dirais un huitième d'un pouce entre chaque planche qu'était mis sur le bateau.* And every boat had a space about, I would say, an eighth of an inch between each board that was put on the boat. (LF) ◊ •**deux pouces de jambe et le cul tout de suite** [*humorous*] used to describe a very short person <La99> <***Loc:*** AV, EV, IV, LA, LF, SM, Da84, Hi02, La99>

poudine, pouding ♦see **poutine**

poudrage [pudraʒ] *n.m.* powdering <***Loc:*** Da84>

poudre [pud(r), purd] *n.f.* **1** powder *Ma grand-mère, alle aimait du tabac en poudre, du* SNUFF. *Alle mettait ça en dessour de sa lèvre.* My grandmother liked powdered tobacco, snuff. She put it under her lip. (LF) **2** gunpowder **C'est pas toi qu'as inventé la poudre!* You aren't the one who invented gunpowder! (AV, La99) ◊ •**poudre à fusil** gunpowder <Da84> •**poudre à laver** washing powder <VM, Fa77> •**poudre de lait** powdered creamer <LF> <***Loc:*** AV, LF, SM, VM, Da84, Fa77, La99>

poudré [pudre] *n.m.* ◊ •**poudré de neige** light snowfall <JE> <***Loc:*** JE>

poudrer [pudre] **I** *v.tr.* to powder, sprinkle with any powdery substance *Après ça tu poudres ça avec du* CORN STARCH *et tu fais ça deux fois par jour.* After that you sprinkle it with corn starch and you do that twice a day. (TB) **II se poudrer** *v.pron.* to powder o.s. *Se poudrer le nez.* To powder one's nose. (EV) *Laisse-moi me poudrer avant de partir.* Let me powder my face before we leave. (LA) <***Loc:*** EV, JE, LA, TB, VM, Da84, Fa77>

poudrerie [pudrəri] *n.f.* fine sprinkling (of powder, snow etc.) <***Loc:*** JE>

poudriaille [pudrijaj] *n.f.* light snowfall <***Loc:*** JE>

poudrière [pudrijær] *n.f.* powder box <***Loc:*** IB, SM, Da84, Lv88>

poudriller (se) [pudrije] *v.pron.* to dust o.s., cover o.s. in dust, take a dustbath (as chickens) <***Loc:*** JE, TB>

poudrillon (**poudron, poudroir**) [pudrijɔ̃, pudrɔ̃, pudwar] *n.m.* powder puff <***Loc:*** JE, SL, SM, VM, Fa77, Lv88>

poudrin [pudrɛ̃] *n.m.* fine rain or snow <***Loc:*** JE>

poudron ♦see **poudrillon**

poudron ♦see **poudroir**

pouelon ♦see **poêlon**

pouf [puf] *interj.* poof ◊ •**faire pouf** ***a*** to go poof ***b*** to make s.o. lose his temper *Ça y fait pouf.* It makes him lose his temper. (LF) <LF, Da84> <***Loc:*** LF, Da84>

pouie ♦see **pluie**

pouillasse [pujas] *adj.* wretched, miserable <***Loc:*** JE, Di32>

pouillasserie [pujasri] *n.f.* wretchedness, misery <***Loc:*** JE, Di32>

pouille [puj] *n.f.* trouble *Il s'a lancé derrière la barre quand la pouille a pris.* He leapt behind the bar when the trouble started. (LA) <***Loc:*** LA>

pouilleux[1]**, -euse** [pujø, -øz] *adj.* **1** infested with lice *Une z-oie pouilleuse.* A lice-infested goose. (VM) **2** lowly, inconsequential (of a person) <***Loc:*** LA, VM, Da84>

pouilleux[2]**, -euse** [pujø, -øz] *n.* lowlife, bum *Je voudrais pas qu'elle sort avec ce pouilleux.* I wouldn't want her to go out with that bum. (LA) <***Loc:*** LA, VM>

poulailler [pulaje] *n.m.* **1** hen house **J'attend quec'chose dans le poulailler. C'est ein rat de bois qu'est derrière les poules.* I hear something in the chicken house. It's a possum after the chickens. (Wh83) **2** laying coop <***Loc:*** LA, Da84, Wh83>

poulain [pulɛ̃] *n.m.* colt, foal ◊ •**faire le poulain** to be angry <VM, La99> <***Loc:*** VM, Da84, La99>

poularde [pulard] *n.f.* large, fat hen or pullet <***Loc:*** Da84>

poule [pul] *n.f.* **1** chicken *On vadait tuer des poules en dehors, et là alle cuisait les poules fraîches.* We used to go kill chickens outside, and then she would cook up the fresh chickens. (TB) **Quand les poules auront des dents.* When chicken have teeth [i.e. never]. (Da84, La99) **2** hen, roaster **La poule qui chante premier, c'est elle qu'a pondu.* The hen that cackles first is the one that laid the egg. (Da84) ◊ •**poule bénée** Cornish hen <Lv88> •**poule d'eau** coot *Les poules d'eau a pas les nageoires comme un canard.* Coots don't have webbed feet like a duck. (VM) <IB, IV, VM, Da84, Gu00, Hi02, Lv88, Re31> •**poule d'eau de marais** Florida gallinule <Re31> •**poule de bois** large ivory-billed woodpecker <JE, Re31> •**poule frit {frite}** fried chicken *Les* RATTLESNAKE. *Je crois que ça c'est la seule qualité qui est bon à manger. Mon je l'ai jamais mangé, eusse clame que ça a un goût comme la poule frit.* Rattlesnakes. I think that's the only kind that's good to eat. I've never eaten it, they claim it tastes like fried chicken. (TB) <TB> •**poule gingas** speckled hen <Lv88> •**poule grillée** roast chicken <LF> •**poule guinée** guinea hen <Lv88> •**poule lavanée {lavane}** type of dwarf chicken <Lv88> •**poule mouillée** ***a*** wet hen ***b*** spineless, weak, wishy-washy person <Da84> •**poule pita** bantam hen <Lv88> •**poule rôtie** roast chicken <JE, LF, Lv88> <***Loc:*** AV, EV, IB, IV, JE, LA, LF, SL, SM, TB, VM, Da84, Gu00, Hi02, La99, Lv88, Re31>

poulet [pulɛ, pule] *n.m.* **1** young chicken, fryer *On avait tout la richesse de manger qu'on voulait. On avait tout le manger* *naturel, on avait notre poulet à nous-autres-mêmes, on avait notre cochon à nous-autres-mêmes, on avait notre lait à nous-autres-mêmes.* We had all the abundance of food that we wanted. We had all the natural food, we had our own chicken, we had our own pig, we had our own milk. (LF) **2** chick **3** chicken meat ◊ **•poulet d'herbe *a*** hen that sometimes lays its eggs in the field instead of in the henhouse ***b*** illegitimate child <La99> **•poulet frit / poulet rôti** fried chicken <LA, VM, Fa77> **•petit poulet** chick <LA> <***Loc:*** AV, EV, IB, LA, LF, SM, VM, Da84, Fa77, Hi02, La99>

poulette [pulɛt] *n.f.* pullet, young hen <***Loc:*** VM, Da84>

pouliche [puliʃ, poliʃ] *n.f.* **1** filly, young mare **2** very bad girl or woman *Espèce de pouliche, ç'a pas plus de respect qu'arien du tout!* Bad girl, no more respect than I don't know what. (TB) <***Loc:*** TB, VM, Da84, Fa77>

poulie [puli] *n.m./f.* pulley, block and tackle, hoist <***Loc:*** Da84, Lv88>

poulpe [pup] *n.m.* octopus <***Loc:*** VM, Fa77>

pouls [pu] *n.m.* pulse <***Loc:*** VM, Da84, Fa77>

poumon (**pomon, paumon**) [pumɔ̃, pɔ̃mɔ̃, pɔ̃mo] *n.m.* lung <***Loc:*** AC, AL, IB, JE, LA, LF, SB, SM, TB, VM, Da84, Hi02>

poumonique (**pomonique**) [pɔ̃mɔ̃nik] *adj.* pulmonary *Une maladie pomonique.* A pulmonary illness. (VM) <***Loc:*** JE, VM>

pountingue [puntɛ̃ŋ] *n.m.* posterior, bottom *Elle est tombée sur son pountingue.* She fell on her behind. (SM) <***Loc:*** SM>

poupa ♦see **papa**

poupée [pupe] *n.f.* **1** doll *Les filles, on aimait jouer avec des poupées, ça c'était notre meilleur passe-temps.* Girls liked to play with dolls, that was our favorite pastime. (SM) **2** puppet <***Loc:*** LF, SL, SM, Da84>

poupon [pupɔ̃] *n.m.* baby, infant **Cher 'tit poupon.* Dear little baby. (Da84) <***Loc:*** VM, Da84>

pouponner ♦see **pimponner**

poupoune [pupun] *n.f.* **1** woman of questionable morals **2** mistress *Il a humilié sa femme en sortant avec sa poupoune en public.* He humiliated his wife by going out in public with his mistress. (LA) <***Loc:*** EV, LA>

pour [pur] *prep.* **1** for *J'avais acheté du manger pour mes chats.* I had bought food for my cats. (TB) *Crier pour l'aide.* To call for help. (Lv88) *Pour qui tu cherches?* Whom are you looking for? (Lv88) *On va faire un* CHOIR, *il dit, juste pour tes filles, parce que cher Bon Dieu, ça c'est des filles qui peut chanter!* We'll put together a choir, he said, just for your girls, because dear God, those are girls that can sing! (TB) *J'ai pas rien pour faire.* I have nothing to do. (Lv88) **2** for (a period of time) *On a pas eu l'eau haute pour plusieurs années.* We hadn't had flooding for several years. (TB) *J'ai été un barbier pour quelques années.* I was a barber for a few years. (SM) **3** until, till, to (with expressions of time) **Dix minutes pour midi.* Ten minutes to noon. (Da84) **4** toward, to, in the direction of **Partir pour la ville.* To head for the city. (Da84) *Elle est en partance pour Lafayette.* She is about to leave for Lafayette. (Lv88) **5** for, in order to, for the purpose of *On avait juste un éventail comme ça pour t'éventer avec ta main, et il faisait chaud pareil comme il fait ici asteur.* We just had a little fan for fanning yourself by hand like that, and it was hot just like it is here now. (LF) *Ça c'était usé pour fendre le bois. Y avait une grosse lame dessus.* That was used for splitting wood. There's a big blade on it. (LF) **6** about, concerning *Madame Arile, cette-là qui m'a* TEACH *mon catéchisme en français, elle, é contait des contes pour Compère Bouki et Compère Lapin.* Mrs. Arile, the one who taught me my catechism in French, she would tell stories about Brer Bouki and Brer Rabbit. (SL) *Ça pouvait pas la calmer après qu'elle avait eu la nouvelle pour son mari.* They couldn't calm her down after she received the news about her husband. (LA) **7** belonging to *Quand-ce qu'on a eu un* CAMP *pour nous-autres-mêmes on a amené notre ménage.* When we got a camp of our own we brought our furniture. (TB) ◊ **•pour ainsi dire** so to speak <Da84> **•pour (de) même *a*** really, truly *J'ai travaillé pour même dans le clos.* I really worked hard in the field. (Lv88) *Tu dois croire que je suis couillon pour de même!* You must think I'm really stupid! (TB) *Être en amour pour même.* To be truly in love. (SJ) ***b*** however, nevertheless *Pour même, je vais le faire.* Nevertheless, I'm going to do it. (VM) <EV, IB, SJ, TB, VM, An84, Lv88> **•pour moi** according to me, in my opinion *Pour moi, c'est ça. Ça c'est ça on était après charcher pour.* In my opinion, that's what it was. That's what we were looking for. (VM) <VM> **•pour que** so, so that, in order that *J'ai faim, il dit. Chauffe les crabes pour que je mange.* I'm hungry, he says. Heat up the crabs so I can eat. (TB) <LF, TB, Wh83> **•pour toujours** forever <Da84> **•avoir pour *a*** to have to, be obligated *J'ai pour laver le linge demain.* I have to do laundry tomorrow. (SM) ***b*** to want to *J'ai pour aller au show ce soir.* I want to go to the movie tonight. (SM) <SM, VM, Da84, Hi02> **•c'est pour ça** that's why *Il arrêtait pas de traînasser toute la nuit. C'est pour ça que sa femme l'a quitté.* He wouldn't stop gallivanting all night long. That's why his wife left him. (LA) <LA> <***Loc:*** AC, AV, EV, IB, IV, JE, LA, LF, PQ, SJ, SL, SM, TB, VM, An94, Da84, Gu00, Hi02, La99, Lv88, Wh83>

pourcent [pursɑ̃] *n.m.* percent **À 6 pourcent.* At 6 percent. (Da84) <***Loc:*** Da84>

pourcentage [pursɑ̃taʒ] *n.m.* percentage <***Loc:*** Da84>

pourgale [purgal, burgal] *n.f.* reprimand, scolding *Gar, c'était une pourgale sus l'autre côté, t'attends.* Look, there was quite a scolding across the street, you hear. (TB) *Donner une pourgale.* To give a scolding. (LA) <***Loc:*** LA, LF, TB, Da84, Lv88>

pourgaler [purgale, burgale] *v.tr.* **1** to scold, reprimand *Il a* *fait des canailleries et son père l'a pourgalé.* He got into some mischief and his father scolded him. (Lv88) **2** to nag *Ma femme est tout le temps après me pourgaler pour que je peinture la maison.* My wife is always nagging me to paint the house. (VM) <***Loc:*** TB, VM, Da84, Lv88>

pourpier [purpje] *n.m.* portulaca, rose moss ◊ **•petit pourpier** ***a*** milk purslane ***b*** spotted or blotched spurge ***c*** milkweed <VM, Re31> <***Loc:*** VM, Re31>

pourqui [purki] *adv.* why *Pourqui tu vas?* Why are you going? (IB) <***Loc:*** EV, IB>

pourquoi (**parquoi**) [purkwa, parkwa] *adv.* why *Pourquoi les mâles brillent et les femelles est toujours cachées? C'est pour quand il y a des œufs, tu peux pas les voir si aisé.* Why are the males brilliantly colored and the females are camouflaged? It's for when there are eggs, you can't see them as easily. (TB) **Je savais pas pourquoi.* I didn't know why. (IV, An94) *Les autres écoles, je sais pas pourquoi, ils laissont le langage, le français, s'en aller.* The other schools, I don't know why, they're letting the French language disappear. (AS) ◊ **•pourquoi que** why *Je veux croire c'est pourquoi que c'est pas aussi bon que quand Mame en faisait.* I suspect that's why it's not as good as when Mom used to make it. (SL) *C'est pourquoi qu'on faisait ça le soir.* That's why we made it in the evening. (SL) <***Loc:*** AS, EV, IV, JE, LA, SL, SM, TB, An94, Da84, Hi02>

pourri, -e, -ite [puri, -it] *adj.* rotten, spoiled, bad *Une pomme pourrite.* A rotten apple. (LF) *Le bébé de la famille, elle est si canaille et si jolie, si gâtée, elle est pourrie. C'est le bébé de la famille.* The baby of the family, she's so mischievous and so pretty, So spoiled she's rotten. She's the baby of the family. (AV, ch: *Bébé (de la famille)*) <***Loc:*** AV, LF, VM, Da84, Fa77, Lv88>

pourrillon [purijɔ̃] *n.m.* **1** wormhole *Ce bois est tout plein de pourrillons.* This wood is all full of wormholes. (TB) **2** anything old *Jette-ça dehors, ce pourrillon-là.* Throw that outside, that old thing. (VM) ◊ **•en pourrillon** in rotten condition <JE> <***Loc:*** JE, TB, VM>

pourrir [purir] **I** *v.tr.* to cause to rot, cause to spoil *Une mauvaise patate dans le sac aurait pourri tous les autres.* One bad potato in the bag would cause all the others to rot. (EV) **II** *v.intr.* **1** to rot, spoil *À chaque fois qu'eusse mettait un bateau sur le ouaise, un bateau en bois, y avait des places où-ce que le coton venait que ça ça pourrissait. Il faulait mettre du coton frais.* Each time they would put a boat on the dry dock, a wooden boat, there were places where the cotton was rotting. You had to put in fresh cotton. (LF) **2** to stagnate *Dans un tas des places l'eau pourrit.* In many places water stagnates. (SM) <***Loc:*** EV, LF, SM, Da84>

pourrissant, -e [purisɑ̃, -ɑ̃t] *adj.* rotting *La maison sentait le manger pourrissant après l'ouragan.* The house smelled like rotting food after the hurricane. (LA) <***Loc:*** LA, Da84>

pourriture [purityr] *n.f.* **1** rot, rottenness, spoilage *Tu peux pas t'imaginer la pourriture dans la glacière après l'ouragan!* You can't imagine the spoilage in the freezer after the hurricane! (EV) **2** pus *T'aurais dû voir la pourriture qu'a sorti de ce clou quand ils l'ont lancé!* You should've seen the pus that came out of that boil when they lanced it! (VM) **3** infection that develops in a wound *Il a une pourriture sur sa main.* He has an infected sore on his hand. (SM) <***Loc:*** JE, SM, TB, VM, Da84>

poursuire ♦see **poursuivre**

poursuite [pursɥit] *n.f.* **1** pursuit **2** lawsuit, prosecution <***Loc:*** Da84>

poursuivre (**poursuire**) [pursɥiv(r), pursɥir, pursyir] (*p.p.* **poursui** [pursɥi]) **I** *v.tr.* **1** to follow, pursue, chase *Le chien a poursui l'homme.* The dog chased the man. (Lv88) **2** to sue, prosecute *Il va poursuire son voisin.* He is going to sue his neighbor. (SM) **II se poursuivre** *v.pron.* to sue each other *Ça se poursuit pour n'importe qui asteur.* They sue each other for no reason these days. (EV) <***Loc:*** EV, SM, TB, VM, Da84, Lv88>

pourtant [purtɑ̃] *adv.* yet, still, nevertheless, even so, however *Quand même si je dis, il va me dire que je suis fou. Et pourtant je m'ai bien regardé à moi, je me sentais pas de mal.* Even if I say anything [about what I had felt] he'll tell me I'm crazy. And yet I looked at myself, I didn't feel anything wrong with me. (TB) <***Loc:*** TB, An94, Da84>

pourvoir (se) [purvwar] *v.pron.* to provide for o.s. **Se pourvoir à manger.* To provide food for oneself. (Da84) <***Loc:*** Da84>

pourvu [purvy] ◊ **•pourvu que** *conj.* on condition, provided that, provided **Pourvu qu'il reste chez lui.* Provided he stays at home. (Da84) <Da84> <***Loc:*** Da84>

pouscaille [puskaj] *n.f.* hopscotch <***Loc:*** LF>

poussade [pusad] *n.f.* push, shove, jostling *Il m'a donné une poussade.* He gave me a shove. (SM) <***Loc:*** SM, Lv88>

poussailler [pusaje] **I** *v.tr.* to crowd, push, shove (repeatedly and in an annoying way) *Ils ont tellement poussaillé ils ont fini par se faire du mal.* They pushed and shoved so much that they ended up hurting themselves. (SM) **II se poussailler** *v.pron.* to push, shove each other **Dans einne foule l'monne [=monde] s'poussaille.* In a crowd, people push each other. (EV, Ph36) <***Loc:*** EV, IB, SL, SM, TB, Da84, Lv88, Ph36, Re31>

poussant (**pousson**) [pusɔ̃] *n.m.* **1** pinfeather *La poule-là-là a un tas de poussants.* That chicken has lots of pin feathers. (SM) **2** down (of a bird) **3** germ, embryo, sprout *Quand tu mets ton riz de plant dans le canal pour le faire germer, il a déjà des poussants quand tu le plantes.* When you put your seed rice in the canal to germinate it, it already has sprouts when you plant it. (VM) **4** swelling around a fingernail or toenail <***Loc:*** EV, IB, JE, SM, VM, Lv88, Ph36>

pousse [pus] *n.f.* **1** growth, sprout, shoot *Faut tu mets des* CANS *autour de tes pousses de cocombres.* You have to put cans around your cucumber sprouts. (VM) **2** shove, push *Ses amis lui ont donné une pousse pour qu'il demande à la fille de danser.* His friends gave him a push to ask the girl to dance. (VM) <***Loc:*** VM, Da84>

pousse-café [puskafe] *n.m.* coffee spiked with whiskey <***Loc:*** SM, Da84>

poussée [puse] *n.f.* push, drive **Le retournage de le Cajin marron aussi marque l'éxistence d'ein deuxième-culture Américane qu'a pour au dessous 200 ans, temps après temps, résisté la grande poussée de les affaires modernes.* The return of the wild Cajun also marks the existence of a second American culture which has for about 200 years resisted the great push of modernity time after time. (Wh83) <***Loc:*** Wh83>

pousse-pousse [puspus] *n.m.* money, means, wherewithal <***Loc:*** Da84>

pousse-poussière [puspusjær] *n.m./f.* short person <***Loc:*** SM>

pousser [puse] **I** *v.tr.* **1** to push *Asteur tu pousses un bouton et la drague s'en vient en l'air.* Now you push a button and the net goes up in the air. (JE) *Elle a poussé la chaise contre le mur pour masquer le trou.* She pushed the chair against the wall to conceal the hole. (VM) **Le vent me pousse.* The wind is pushing me. (VM, An94) *Avec une voile, s'il était pas tout à fait à le centre du vent ça pourrait te pousser soit d'un bord ou de l'autre.* With a sail, if it wasn't lined up with the wind it could push you to one side or the other. (LF) **Pousse pas la balance trop fort.* Don't push the swing too hard. (EV, Ph36) **2** to push aside, move out of the way *On a acheté un PHONOGRAPH à les enfants, et ça poussait tout le ménage de l'entourage, et ça dansait.* We bought a phonograph for the children, and they pushed all the furniture aside to the walls, and they danced. (TB) **3** to promote, push *Y a du monde qu'après pousser ça icitte plein, pour assayer de ramener le langage.* There are a lot of people promoting it plenty here, to try to bring the language back. (TB) *L'anglais a été poussé si tellement dur que le français a été oublié.* English was pushed so hard that French was almost forgotten. (TB) **4** to push, force (s.t. on s.o.) *Je crois pas que sa mère et son père a poussé le français sus lui avant qu'il commence à faire la musique.* I don't think his mom and dad pushed French on him until he started getting into music. (TB) **5** to herd, drive (animals) *Je pousse mes bêtes à la savanne.* I drive my cattle into the pasture. (SM) **Pousser des bêtes.* To drive cattle. (Da84) **II** *v.intr.* **1** to grow **Le jardinage pousse bien.* The vegetables are growing nicely. (Da84) **2** to drive *On va aller pousser dans l'autre bayou, en arrière.* We'll drive into the other bayou in back. (TB) *Y a plein des mondes qu'a des paupières, [...] et eusse peut pas pousser dans les lacs.* There are a lot of people with butterfly nets, and they can't drive into the lakes. (TB) **3** to provide an animal for community slaughter (when it is one's turn) *Et là t'avais pour notifier, cil-là qu'avait pour pousser chaque fois, parce que t'oubliais quand c'était.* And then you had to notify the one whose turn it was to furnish an animal each time, because you'd forget when it was. (SL) **III se pousser** *v.pron.* to move out of the way, get out of the way *Pousse-toi, t'es dans le chemin!* Move it, you're in the way! (EV) ◊ **•pousser au creux** to corner (an animal) *J'avais un chien vite. Il le trappait, ou bien il le poussait au creux.* I had a fast dog. He would trap it, or he'd corner it. (SL) <SL> **•pousser à vue d'œil** to grow very fast <Da84> **•pousser dessus** to push on (a door, etc.) <Da84> **•pousser en parcage** to take a cow to the bull for mating <SB, La99> **•pousser (qqn) dans les rangs courts** to force s.o. through argument to say or admit s.t. <LA, La99> **•pousser route *a*** to proceed, go on, travel on *Il pousse route pour le bayou.* He travels on toward the bayou. (Lv88) ***b*** to head for, set off for *Y en a plusieurs encore qu'a poussé route plus dans l'EAST.* There are several others who headed east. (LF) ***c*** to leave, depart *Je vais pousser route. C'est tard.* I'm going to leave. It's late. (SM) <LF, SM, Da84, Lv88> **•pousser un cri** to yell <Da84> **•pousser une menterie** to tell a lie <JE> **•pousser un soupir** to heave a sigh <Da84> **•trop pousser** to overcook *Le COOK a trop poussé la viande. Elle est pas mangeable.* The cook overcooked the meat. It's not edible. (SM) <SM> <***Loc:*** EV, IV, JE, LA, LF, SB, SL, SM, VM, An94, Da84, Gu00, La99, Lv88, Ph36>

pousseur [pusœr] *n.m.* drover, one who herds animals ◊ **•pousseur de bêtes** drover, cattle driver, herder, cowboy <SM, VM> <***Loc:*** SM, VM, Lv88>

poussière [pusjɛr] *n.f.* dust <***Loc:*** EV, LA, SL, SM, An94, Da84, Hi02>

poussiéré ♦see **poussiéreux**

poussiérer [pusjere] **I** *v.tr.* to cover with dust, make dusty *T'as rouvert le chassis et ça a tout poussiéré la table.* You opened the window and that got the table all dusty. (VM) **II se poussiérer** *v.pron.* **1** to dust o.s., cover o.s. in dust, take a dustbath (as chickens) **2** to become dusty, get covered with dust *Il faisait assez sec, on s'a tout poussiéré dans le boghei en allant à la messe.* It was so dusty that we got covered in dust in the buggy on the way to Mass. (VM) <***Loc:*** VM, Da84>

poussiéreux, -euse (**poussiéré, -e**) [pusjerø, -øz, pusjere] *adj.* dusty *Tous ses livres étaient poussiéreux.* All her books were dusty. (LA) <***Loc:*** LA, VM, Da84, Fa77, Lv88>

poussinière [pusinjær] *n.f.* the Milky Way <***Loc:*** Da84>

pousson ♦see **poussant**

poustron [pustrɔ̃] *n.m.* feather duster <***Loc:*** Da84>

poutchoume [putʃum] *onom.* splash **•faire poutchoume** to fall into the water with a splash <LF> <***Loc:*** LF, SL>

poutine (**poudine, pouding**) [putin, pudin] *n.f. (occ. n.m.)* **1** pudding *Rose a fait de la poutine à midi.* Rose made pudding at noon. (SL) **2** bread pudding *Vous voyez, à NEW BRUNSWICK la poutine c'est fait avec des pommes de terre.*

Et nous-autres ici on fait ça avec du vieux pain et des œufs, des œufs de poulet. You see, in New Brunswick "poutine" is made with potatoes. And here we make it with old bread, and eggs, chicken eggs. (LF) **3** dumpling *On faisait une fricassée de volaille et puis là on mettait des poutines en dans-là.* We would make a chicken fricassee and put dumplings in it. (LA) **4** heavy clay **5** bait made of cotton and often flavored with blood (used to catch mullet, sheephead, and catfish) ◊ **•poutine de {aux} mûres** blackberry dumpling *Ma mère fait les meilleures poutines aux mûres t'as jamais mangées.* My mother makes the best blackberry dumplings you've ever eaten. (VM) <TB, VM, Guoo> **•poutine de pain** bread pudding <LF> <***Loc:*** AC, AV, EV, IB, JE, LA, LF, SB, SL, SM, TB, VM, An94, Da84, Guoo, Lv88>

pouvoir[1] [puvwar, puwar] *v.intr.* **1** to be able to, can **Je peux pas l'entendre. Il y a trop de train.* I can't hear him. There's too much noise. (EV, An94) *Je peux pas me passer une autre nuit comme ça, je dis, avec le mal de tête.* I can't spend another night like that, I said, with the headache. (LF) *Je ne peux plus durer ça il dit.* I can no longer put up with what he is saying. (Lv88) **Ma bébé a faim et je peux pas trouver ma vache.* My baby is hungry and I can't find my cow. (IV, An94) **Ça peut bien arriver.* It could well happen. (Da84) **2** to be allowed to, may, can **Tu peux pas marier ma fille.* You can't marry my daughter. (EV, An94) **Tu peux pas venir. Toi, t'es trop petit.* You can't come. You're too little. (SL, An94) *Eusse vient cogner à la porte ou eusse sonne la cloche. "Ti-tante? On peut avoir de quoi à boire?"* They come knock on the door or they ring the doorbell. "Auntie, can we have something to drink?" (TB) ◊ **•ça se peut** it is possible **Ça se peut bien.* It could well be, it may well be. (Da84) **Ça se peut pas.* It can't be, that's impossible. (Da84) <Da84> <***Loc:*** AC, AS, AV, EV, IB, IV, JE, LA, LF, SJ, SL, SM, TB, VM, An84, An94, Da84, Gu82, Hi02, Lv88, Ph36, Re31, Wh83>

pouvoir[2] [puvwar, puwar] *n.m.* **1** power, might *Il pouvait traiter pour le mal de tête [...] avec des prières. Il avait comme un pouvoir du Bon Dieu avec ça.* He could treat people for headaches. He had a kind of power from God with that. (TB) *Tu connais que c'est le pouvoir du Bon Dieu.* You know that it's the power of God. (TB) **2** ability, capacity <***Loc:*** TB, Da84, Hi02>

pou-yaille [pujaj] *interj.* exclamation of surprise, pleasure or disgust <***Loc:*** Lv88, Da92>

practiquer ♦see **pratiquer**

prairie (**plairie**) [preri, pleri] *n.f.* **1** prairie, meadow, grassland (esp. those of southwest Louisiana) *Il a eu pour chercher ses vaches à travers la grande prairie.* He had to search for his cows across the expansive prairie. (LA) **2** freshwater marsh (sometimes erroneously called a "swamp") *Nous-autres on faisait des petits bateaux pour faire la pêche dans les mêches, dans les prairies, ou faire la chasse.* We used to make small boats for going fishing in the marshes, or for hunting. (LF) ◊ **•prairie basse** low coastal plain between marsh and prairie <Guoo> **•prairie marron** natural prairie, wild prairie <SM, Lv88> **•prairie molle** alluvial marshland, wetlands, trembling prairie <JE, TB, VM> **•prairie tremblante** alluvial marshland, wetlands, trembling prairie <TB, VM, Guoo, Lv88> <***Loc:*** AC, JE, LA, LF, TB, VM, Da84, Guoo, Hi02, Lv88>

praline (**plarine**) [pralin, plarin] *n.f.* praline, candy made with nuts or seeds and carmelized sugar or syrup *Tu connais qui des pralines est? Ça c'est du candi à la pacane ou du candi à la pistache.* Do you know what pralines are? That's a kind of candy made with pecans or peanuts. (TB) ◊ **•praline au {de} béné** sesame seed praline <SM, Da84, Lv88, Re31> **•praline au lait** milk praline <VM, Fa77> **•praline au tac-tac** popcorn praline <Da84, VM> **•praline aux {à} pistaches** peanut praline <SM, TB> <***Loc:*** AC, JE, LF, SB, SM, TB, VM, Da84, Fa77, Hi02, Lv88, Re31>

praliné [praline] ◊ **•pistaches pralinées** sugared peanuts <Re31> <***Loc:*** Re31>

pratique [pratik] *n.f.* **1** practice, repetition, rehearsal *J'avais serré le violon longtemps passé, j'avais plus de pratique.* I had put the violin away long ago, I never had any more practice. (Lv88) **2** method, usage, custom **Tchou Flette dit qu'ils sont après le faire juste parce que de leurs pratique de conserver.* Tchou Flette said that they are doing it just because of their custom of conserving. (Wh83) **3** client, patient, customer *Je vas te dire ça qu'un avocat m'a dit à moi. Un docteur aussi. Il donnerait une main s'il pourrait parler français. Parce que t'as plus que la moitié peut-être de ses pratiques qu'est français.* I'll tell you what a lawyer told me. A doctor too. He would give a hand if he could speak French. Because you've got more than perhaps half his clients who are French-speaking. (TB) **4** clientele ◊ **•pratique à chagrin** ***a*** person who constantly whines and complains ***b*** 'misery case,' any difficult project or undertaking that is unlikely to be successful *Jouer de la musique, c'est une pratique à chagrin.* Playing music is an undertaking that can come to no good. (VM) *Tu parles d'une pratique à chagrin, c'est arranger les papiers de* INCOME TAX. Talk about a painful task, it's doing one's income tax. (VM) <AC, SM, VM, La99> <***Loc:*** AC, SM, TB, VM, Da84, Hi02, La99, Lv88>

pratiquer (**practiquer**) [pratike, praktike] **I** *v.tr.* **1** to practice (medicine, law, etc.) *Il pratique la loi.* He practices law. (LA) **2** to practice, rehearse *Non, j'ai presque perdu ça. J'ai pas pratiqué ça assez.* No, I've almost lost that ability. I haven't practiced it enough. (TB) **3** to train, make s.o. practice *Il pratique les enfants au baseball.* He trains children to play baseball. (Lv88) **II** *v.intr.* **1** to practice, rehearse *Il y a un* ARENA *drette à peu près à quatre, cinq cents pieds de sa maison. Et ils lassont dedans et ils pratiquont.* There is an arena right about four, five hundred feet from his house. And they lasso in it and they practice. (LF) *On va pratiquer pour le* PLAY *ce soir.* We are going to rehearse for the play tonight. (SM) *Ils sont après practiquer pour le jeu à ce soir.* They are practicing for the game tonight. (VM) **2** to practice, work (at s.t.) *Mais la question est si tu parles français et si tu pratiques un peu, tu peux être capable le lire.* But the thing is if you speak French and you practice a little, you can acquire the ability to read it. (SL) **III se pratiquer** *v.pron.* to practice, rehearse *Il fait des affaires un petit brin plus mieux que mon parce qu'il se pratique plus que mon asteur-là, tu connais?* He does things a little better than I do because he practices more than I do, you know? (TB) <***Loc:*** AC, AV, LF, SL, SM, TB, VM, Da84, Hi02, Lv88>

pratiqueur, -euse [pratikœr, øz] *n.* devout person, one who practices his or her religion <***Loc:*** JE>

précaution [prekosjɔ̃] *n.f.* precaution, care, prudence **Et on peut pas oublier les précautions le monde prendait pour pas être malade.* And we can't forget the precautions people took to not get sick. (Wh83) ◊ **•prendre précaution** to be careful, be cautious <Da84> <***Loc:*** Da84, Wh83>

précautionneux [prekosjɔ̃nø] *adj.* careful *Il avait un garçon mais le garçon il, il était précautionneux, lui, il avait tour avec Pop pour pas travailler dans le clos. Il a aidé un peu, ouais, c'est pas qu'il a pas aidé du tout, mais ça il a aidé, c'est pas un tas.* There was a boy but the boy, he was careful, he toured with Pop in order to not work in the field. He helped a little, yeah, it's not that he didn't help at all, but what he did help [with], it wasn't much. (EV) <***Loc:*** EV>

précautionner [prekosjɔ̃ne] **I** *v.tr.* to caution, warn *Mame m'a précautionné de pas aller au bal avec ce bougre, mais j'ai pas écouté.* Mom warned me not to go to the dance with that guy, but I didn't listen. (VM) **II se précautionner** *v.pron.* to take precautions, be cautious *Précautionne-toi quand tu marches dans la rue d'en Ville.* Be cautious when you walk the streets of New Orleans. (VM) <***Loc:*** VM, Da84>

précédent [presedɑ̃] *n.m.* precedent <***Loc:*** Da84>

précéder [presede] *v.tr.* to precede, go before *Le procès à mon oncle a précédé çulà du gouverneur.* My uncle's trial preceded the governor's. (EV) <***Loc:*** EV, Da84>

prêche [prɛʃ] *n.f.* **1** religious gathering (e.g. church service, prayer meeting) *Le soir qu'on l-a été là-bas pour la petite prêche en français.* The evening that we went down there for the little prayer meeting in French. (TB) **2** sermon *Il devrait nous donner de temps en temps une prêche en français,* SUNDAY SCHOOL *ou quelque chose.* He should give us a little sermon now and then in French, Sunday school or something. (TB) ◊ **•faire la prêche** to preach, deliver a sermon *Le prêtre allait parler, tu connais quand il fait la prêche?* The priest was going to speak, you know when he delivers his sermon? (TB) <TB> <***Loc:*** TB, Da84>

prêchement [prɛʃmɑ̃] *n.m.* preaching, sermon *Il était toujours après son prêchement quand j'ai sorti de l'église.* He was still preaching when I left the church. (LA) <***Loc:*** JD, LA, SC, SJ, Da84, Gr86>

prêcher [preʃe] **I** *v.tr.* **1** to beg, implore, plead with *Et la nègresse ça a prêché sa maîtresse pour ouvère la porte.* And the black woman begged her mistress to open the door. (VM) **2** to hound, nag (to get one's way) *Mon 'tit garçon m'a tant prêché qu'il a fallu que je l'amène chez McDonald's.* My little boy hounded me so much I had to take him to McDonald's. (VM) *Ma femme arrête pas de me prêcher pour que je lui faise une petite maison pour les oiseaux.* My wife won't stop nagging me to make her a little birdhouse. (VM) **II** *v.intr.* to preach *Le Père était après prêcher et puis il était après critiquer les soldats américains.* The Father was preaching and he was criticizing American soldiers. (IB) <***Loc:*** IB, SL, TB, VM, Da84, Lv88>

prêcheur (**pricheur**) [preʃœr, priʃœr] *n.m.* preacher, minister *Y a un prêcheur qui vient de l'Ile, je suis bien padnas avec lui, bon, bon ami.* There's a preacher who comes from the Island, I am good friends with him. (LF) <***Loc:*** JE, LF, SM, VM, Da84, Lv88>

précieusement [presjøzmɑ̃] *adv.* preciously, carefully *Elle garde la robe de baptême précieusement pour la redonner à ses enfants.* She keeps the baptismal dress preciously to give to her children. (VM) <***Loc:*** VM, Da84>

précieux, -ieuse [presjø, -jøz] *adj.* precious, valuable *Ils ont perdu tout ça qu'ils avaient de précieux.* They lost everything they had of value. (LA) <***Loc:*** LA, Da84>

précis, -e [presi, -iz] *adj.* exact, precise *Il avait le montant précis dans sa main.* He had the exact amount in his hand. (LA) <***Loc:*** LA, Da84, Hi02>

prédicateur [predikatœr] *n.m.* **1** fortune teller, one who predicts the future *Les prêcheurs asteur sont des prédicateurs de la fin du monde.* Preachers today are predictors of the end of the world. (VM) **2** predictive sign, predictor *Le temps est prédicateur d'un colonne.* The weather [a yellow glow] is a sign of a tornado. (VM) ◊ **•prédicateur du temps** weatherman, weather forecaster <Gr86> <***Loc:*** VM, Da84, Gr86>

prédiction [prediksjɔ̃] *n.f.* prediction <***Loc:*** Da84>

prédire [predir] *v.tr.* to predict, foretell *Le monde croyait qu'eusse pouvait prédire le mauvais temps.* People believed they could predict bad weather. (LF) <***Loc:*** LF, Da84>

préférable [preferab(l)] *adj.* preferable *Une était pas préférable à l'autre.* One was not preferable to the other. (LA) <***Loc:*** LA, Da84>

préféré, -e [prefere] *adj.* favorite, preferred *Elle a laissé sa terre à son neveu préféré.* She left her land to her favorite nephew. (LA) <***Loc:*** LA, Da84>

préférence [preferɑ̃s] *n.f.* preference <***Loc:*** EV, Da84>

préférencié[1] [preferɑ̃sje] *n.m.* privileged creditor <***Loc:*** JE>

préférencié[2]**, -e** [preferɑ̃sje] *adj.* privileged (of debts) <***Loc:*** JE>

préférer [prefere] *v.tr.* to prefer *En recevant la berouette, c'est le fouette dessus mon dos. Mais, je préfère que la mort.* In receiving the wheelbarrow, it means [also] the whip on my back. Well, I prefer only death. (VM, ch: *La chanson des Savoy*) <***Loc:*** VM, Da84>

préjugé, -e [preʒyʒe] *adj.* prejudiced, biased *Il faulait que leur témoin soye préjugé.* Their witness had to be biased. (LA) <***Loc:*** JE, LA, Da84>

préjuger [preʒyʒe] *v.tr.* **1** to prejudge *Le juge a dit qu'il fallait pas préjuger le cas.* The judge said that we must not prejudge the case. (LA) **2** to prejudice <***Loc:*** LA, Da84>

prélat [prela, prəla] *n.m.* tarpaulin <***Loc:*** JE, LF, VM>

prêle [prɛl] *n.f.* horsetail, equisetum, tall scouring-rush *Oh avec de la prêle aussi. C'est des bâtons, tu cassais ça tout par nœuds ça. Tu casses ça et là tu bouilles ça et ça c'est bon pour ton corps aussi.* Oh, with horsetail too. It's sticks, you would break it by sections. You break it and boil it and it's good for your body too. (TB) <***Loc:*** TB, Ho90>

prélèvement [prelɛvmɑ̃] *n.m.* ◊ **•prélèvement d'un impôt** collection of a tax <JE> <***Loc:*** JE>

prème ♦see **prime**

premesse ♦see **promesse**

premier[1], **-ière** [prəmje, prɛ̃mje, prɔ̃mje, -jær, -jært] *adj.* **1** first *Le premier notaire public qu'on a eu ici était mon grand-père.* The first notary we had here was my grandfather. (LF) **Pascal a tiré le premier coup.* Pascal took the first shot. (EV, An94) *La première paire de souliers que mon j'ai mis mes pieds dedans là, eh ben, j'ai payé pour mon-même.* The first pair of shoes I ever put my feet in, I paid for myself. (LF) **2** chief, primary, main *La première raison de pas fumer, c'est que c'est pas sain.* The main reason for not smoking is that it's unhealthy. (VM) ◊ **•premier cousin** first cousin <VM> **•premier doigt** index finger **Quand il était ein jeune homme, il s'est coupé le premier doigt de la main droite en ouvrant ein can.* When he was a young man, he cut the index finger of his right hand while opening a can. (Wh83) <Wh83> **•premier nom** first name, given name, Christian name <LA, TB> <***Loc:*** AC, EV, IV, LA, LF, SL, SM, TB, VM, An94, Da84, Hi02, Lv88, Wh83>

premier[2] [prəmje, prɛ̃mje, prɔ̃mje] *n.m.* leader, head, premier ◊ **•le premier de** the first of (a month) *J'auras* EIGHTY-FIVE *le premier d'août.* I'll be eighty-five on August first. (SL) <SL> <***Loc:*** SL, Da84, Hi02>

premier[3] [prəmje, prɛ̃mje, prɔ̃mje] *adv.* **1** first *Et là c'est pus comme c'était quand-ce que ç'a premier commencé.* And now it's no longer like it was when that first started. (LF) **Premier arrivé, premier servi.* First come, first served. (VM, An94) **On était là premier.* We were there first. (LA, An94) **2** beforehand *Appelle premier.* Call first. (Lv88) ◊ **•en premier** at first *En premier les dossières c'était deux morceaux de bois.* At first, the backbands were made of two pieces of wood. (LA) *En premier c'était juste pour des passagers. Là quand mon j'ai commencé c'était du monde et des automobiles aussi.* At first it was just for passengers. Then when I started [riding the ferry] it was for people and cars too. (SJ) <EV, LF, LA, SJ, An94> <***Loc:*** EV, LA, LF, VM, An94, Da84, Lv88>

premièrement [prəmjærmɑ̃, prɔ̃mjærmɑ̃, prɛ̃mjærmɑ̃] *adv.* first, in the first place **La belle chanson nommée " 'Tit Maurice" qu'a été premièrement fait par Happy Fats LeBlanc et Doc Guidry.* The beautiful song called " 'Tit Maurice" that was first done by Happy Fats LeBlanc and Doc Guidry. (Wh83) ◊ **•premièrement que** before *C'est moi qu'avais fait premièrement que lui.* I was the one who did that before him. (LA) <JE, LA> <***Loc:*** JE, LA, VM, Da84, Wh83>

prendre [prɑ̃n, prɑ̃d(r)] **I** *v.tr.* **1** to take **Prends-le.* Take it. (Da84) *Mon j'appelle ça voler, parce que quand tu prends quelque chose et pas demander, c'est pas voler ça?* I call that stealing, because when you take something without asking, isn't that stealing? (TB) **2** to take, ingest *Ça prend le* DOPE, *ça prend le* DRINK *de whiskey, et ça rôdaille tout la nuit.* They take drugs, they drink whiskey, they run around all night. (EV) *Je peux pas prendre cette médecine. Ça me soûle.* I cannot take that medicine. It makes me dizzy. (EV) **3** to get, obtain, acquire *Ayoù t'as pris ce siau-là?* Where did you get that bucket? (TB) **4** to grab, seize, snatch *Mais les ratons laveurs et les serpents ont monté pour prendre les œufs et tuer les petits oiseaux.* But the raccoons and the snakes climbed up to snatch the eggs and kill the baby birds. (TB) *Il m'a pris par les bras.* He took me by the arms. (TB) **5** to catch, trap *Tu mettais ça où-ce que, si tu trouvais une place où que le rat musqué entrait en-dessour de son* BURROW, *sa maison, là il prendait sa patte, ou les deux pattes.* You would put that where, if you found a place where the muskrat entered his burrow, his house, he'd catch his paw, or his two paws. (LF) *Alle se halait à côté de sa tour éyou on prendait notre chevrette.* She hurried over to the side of her tower where we used to catch our shrimp. (LF) **6** to pick up, get, fetch *On a monté dans le char moi et lui et Tante Wavely et puis on avait passé pour prendre ses deux sœurs à lui.* We got in the car, he and I and Aunt Wavely and then we stopped to get his two sisters. (EV) **7** to set out upon *On prendait sa* NET, *sa tremaille, on prendait le lac* AND *on l'étendait.* We would take his net, his trammel, and set out on the lake and spread it out. (EV) *Ça prendait le chemin.* They took to the roads. (LF) *Tu prends* HIGHWAY NINETY. You take highway ninety. (TB) **8** to accept, take on (a job, a responsibility) *J'ai eu plein de la chance parce que j'ai appris vite, tous les jobs que je prendais j'apprendais ça vite.* I was lucky because I learned fast, all the jobs that I took I learned quickly. (TB) **9** to receive, get, take *C'est lui qu'a pris le dernier,* POW, *droite dans le dos.* He's the one who took the last one, pow, right in the back. (LA) **10** to take over, overwhelm *La faim nous prenait.* Hunger overwhelmed us. (SL) **11** to take, require *Ça prend une livre de beurre.* It takes a pound of butter. (Lv88) **La* REEL *était une danse qui était malaisée à danser, puis là, ça prenait des bonnes jambes.* The reel was a dance that was hard to do, and then it took good legs. (EV, An84) *Oh, ça prendait des temps infinis pour faire un bateau.* Oh, it took forever to make a boat. (LF) **12** to use *Je me rappelle de ma grand-mère, elle prendait des gazettes pour mettre sur le mur pour* WALLPAPER, *elle faisait ça.* I remember my grand-mother, she took newspapers to put up on the wall for wallpaper, she did that. (IB) *Avant que je mets 200 ou 250 dollars pour tiendre mes culottes en l'air je vas prendre une corde. Je vas prendre une ceinture.* Before I spend 200 or 250 dollars to hold my pants up, I'll use a rope. I'll get a belt. (TB) **II** *v.intr.* **1** to begin, start *La pluie a pris avant j'arrive.* The rain started before my arrival. (Lv88) *Équand l'école va prendre?* When will school start? (SM) **La pluie est prise.* The rain has started. (Da84) *J'ai pris à rire quand il m'a dit ça.* I started to laugh when he told me that. (SM) *Et ça a pris à me faire mal.* And it began to hurt me. (SL) **2** to set in, take root *Défunte 'Tit-tante disait que c'était dur de piocher le coton quand les liserines prenaient dedans parce que ça file partout.* My late aunt used to say that it was hard to hoe the cotton when the morning glories got into them because they spread everywhere. (Gu00) **III se prendre** *v.pron.* **1** to take o.s. *Je connais pas pour qui il se prend, mais il est pas meilleur que nous-autres.* I don't know for whom he takes himself, but he's no better than us. (LA) **2** to take for o.s., help o.s. to, get for o.s. *Prenez-vous un morceau.* Help yourself to another piece [of pie]. (VM) *Et lui s'a pris une autre femme, s'a remarié.* And he got himself another wife, he got remarried. (TB) **3** to live together (without benefit of marriage) *Ils se sont seulement pris.* They are only living together. (SL) **4** to get caught, get taken in a trap (of an animal) *Quand j'étais jeune, il faisait l'affaire de piège, il piégeait. Pour des rats musqués, et des chaouis et des belettes, et n'importé qui-ce qui se prendait dans le piège en hiver.* When I was young he went trapping. For muskrats, raccoons, weasels, and whatever would get caught in the trap in the winter. (TB) ◊ **•à prendre de** starting in, from (a given time) *C'était pas plein des gros bateaux. Mais comme je vous ai dit, à prendre de 1955 jusqu'asteur, c'est des gros bateaux, oh ils mettont des milles et des milles livres de chevrettes.* There weren't a lot of big boats. But like I told you, from 1955 until now, they've had big boats, oh they can take thousands and thousands of pounds of shrimp. (LF) <LF> **•prendre après {sur}** to take after, resemble *Il prend après son père.* He takes after his father. (LA) *Ils ont tous pris sur le père.* They all resemble the father. (VM) <LA, VM, Da84> **•prendre pour** to head for, set out for *Avant qu'on arrive là en* CAMP, *cher, il a pris pour le canal.* Before we arrived at the camp, hon, he headed for the canal. (TB) <TB> **•prendre pour qqn** to take up for s.o., side with or defend s.o. *Si Toute m'aurait traitée pas bien, ça aurait pas fait. Eux aurait pris pour moi.* If Toute had treated me badly, it wouldn't have worked. They would have taken up for me. (LA) <IB, LA, LF, SM, VM, Lv88> **•prendre qqn pour qqch** to take s.o. for s.t. *Je vas vous dire de quoi, je sais pas si vous va me croire ou me prendre pour un couillon.* I'm going to tell you something, I don't know if you'll believe me or take me for an imbecile. (LF) <LF> **•prendre qqn/qqch pour qqn/qqch** to mistake s.o./s.t. for s.o./s.t. else **Prendre Jean pour Pierre.* To mistake John for Peter. (Da84) <Da84> **•se faire prendre** to be caught, get cheated **Le marchand va ouvert la boutique. On va se faire prendre.* The storekeep will open his store. We're going to get caught. (EV, An94) <EV, An94, Da84> **•se prendre la vie** to take one's own life, commit suicide <Da84> **•s'en prendre après (qqn)** to have it in for (s.o.) *J'ai peur qu'il va s'en prendre après moi pour ça.* I'm afraid he's going to have it in for me over that. (LA) <LA, Da84> ***<Loc:*** AC, EV, IB, IV, LA, LF, SJ, SL, SM, TB, VM, An94, Da84, Hi02, La99, Lv88>

preneur [prənœr] *n.m.* ◊ **•preneur de portraits** photographer <LA> ***<Loc:*** LA>

prénoncer ♦see **prononcer**

préoccupation [preokypasjɔ̃] *n.f.* preoccupation ***<Loc:*** Da84>

préoccuper [preokype] *v.tr.* to preoccupy, engross *La bosse dans son sein la préoccupe.* The lump in her breast worries her. (VM) ***<Loc:*** VM, Da84>

préparation [preparasjɔ̃] *n.f.* **1** preparation *On fait des préparations pour un voyage.* We're preparing for a trip. (IB) **2** object destined to serve a particular purpose *Le* SIDEBOARD *c'est une préparation de salle à manger.* The sideboard is intended to be used in the dining room. (VM) *Alle a acheté sa préparation de noce toute faite.* She bought her wedding gown ready-made. (VM) ***<Loc:*** EV, IB, VM, Da84>

préparer [prepare] **I** *v.tr.* to prepare, ready *Il est mort comme à minuit à soir; ils ont pas pu le préparer avant une heure le lendemain après-midi.* He died like around midnight; they couldn't get the body ready before one o'clock the next afternoon. (AC) **II se préparer** *v.pron.* **1** to get ready, prepare o.s. *Et là je la dis "*WELL, *prépare-toi, Tony va appeler, et mon frère va appeler, mon frère est au tracas."* And then I tell her, "Well, get ready, Tony is going to call, and my brother is going to call, my brother is in trouble." (LF) **Quand on se préparait pour faire une boucherie, nous-autres, ça c'était une grosse affaire.* When we would get ready for a "boucherie," that was a big deal. (AC) **2** to dress, dress up *Rose est toujours bien préparée.* Rose is always well dressed. (SL) ***<Loc:*** AC, EV, LA, LF, SL, TB, An94, Da84, Hi02>

près [prɛ, pre] *adv.* **1** near, close, nearby, close by *Ça reste tout près.* They live nearby. (LF) **Le jour est près.* The day is near. (Da84) **2** close (of a relationship) *Ils étaient près lui et puis elle.* They were close, him and her. (IB) *On est onze,* *j'ai trois frères et huit sœurs, on a beaucoup une magnifique famille, on est près.* We are eleven, three brothers and eight sisters, we have a wonderful family, we are close. (SM) **3** close (of kinship) *Tous parents. Il y a que c'est pas près parents. Mais si tu fais un* FAMILY TREE, WAY BACK, *ça va être les mêmes.* All related. There are some who are not close relatives, but if you make a family tree, way back in the past, it's all the same family. (LF) **4** similar *Eux-autres avait plein de leurs mots à eux-autres-mêmes pour des certaines affaires, tu sais, mais c'était assez près que tu pouvais les comprendre bien.* They had a lot of their own words for certain things, you know, but it was close enough that you could understand it well. (TB) ◊ **•près à près** [preapre, prɛaprɛ, prezapre] side by side, close together *Leurs deux maisons sont près à près.* Their two houses are side by side. (Lv88) <EV, IB, SL, SM, TB, VM, Lv88, Ph36> **•près de** ***a*** near, close to *Penche-toi pas trop près de cette tortue cocodril, tu vas te faire chaponner.* Don't bend over too close to that alligator snapping turtle, you will get yourself castrated. (VM) **Venir près de l'eau.* To come near the water. (Da84) **Être près de la ville.* To be near the city. (Da84) ***b*** almost, nearly *Une petite bouteille, c'est quinze, près de seize piastres.* A little bottle is fifteen, almost sixteen dollars. (TB) <JE, TB, VM, Da84> **•à peu près** about, approximately *Mon père a venu acheter un terrain à peu près à dix miles en haut d'ici.* My father came to buy a piece of property about ten miles up the bayou from here. (LF) *Le petit cheval pesait à peu près huit cents livres.* The little horse weighed about 800 pounds. (SL) <EV, IB, LA, LF, SB, SL, TB, VM, An94, Da84, Gu00, Wh83> **•au plus près** at the closest <Da84> **•tout près** nearby, close by *Ça reste tout près.* They live nearby. (LF) <LF, Da84> <***Loc:*** EV, IB, JE, LA, LF, SB, SL, SM, TB, VM, An94, Da84, Gu00, Hi02, Wh83>

prés humides [prezymid] *n.m.pl.* marsh <***Loc:*** JE, Di32>

presbytère [prɛzbitær] *n.m.* presbytery, rectory <***Loc:*** VM, Da84, Fa77>

presbytérien[1]**, -ienne** [prɛzbiterjɛ̃, -jɛ̃n] *adj.* Presbyterian *Une famille presbytérienne.* A Presbyterian family. (LA) <***Loc:*** LA, VM, Da84, Fa77>

Presbytérien[2]**, -ienne** [prɛzbiterjɛ̃, -jɛ̃n] *n.* Presbyterian <***Loc:*** LA, VM, Da84, Fa77>

prescription [preskripsjɔ̃] *n.f.* prescription <***Loc:*** VM, Da84, Fa77>

prescrire [preskrir] *v.tr.* to prescribe *Le docteur m'a prescrit un médecine qui m'endort.* The doctor prescribed a medicine that makes me go to sleep. (VM) <***Loc:*** VM, Da84>

présence [prezɑ̃s] *n.f.* presence ◊ **•présence d'esprit** presence of mind <Da84> <***Loc:*** Da84>

présent[1]**, -e** [prezɑ̃, -ɑ̃t] *adj.* present *Tout le monde présent ici aujourd'hui va témoigner de ça que je dis.* Everybody here today is going to be witness to what I'm saying. (EV) <***Loc:*** EV, Da84>

présent[2] [prezɑ̃] *n.m.* present time ◊ **•à present** now, nowadays *C'est appelé Vacherie Sud à présent.* It's called South Vacherie nowadays. (SJ) **Elle est dans l'hôpital à présent.* She is in the hospital now. (LA, An94) <LA, SJ, An94, Da84, Hi02> <***Loc:*** AV, LA, SJ, Da84, Hi02>

présent[3] [prezɑ̃] *n.m.* gift, present *Mais ça c'est comme ça que moi je donne mes présents, dans des* PAPER BAG. But that's how I give my presents, in paper bags. (TB) <***Loc:*** EV, IB, LF, TB, An94, Da84, Gu00, Wh83>

présentable [prezɑ̃tab(l)] *adj.* presentable *Va te laver! T'es pas présentable comme ça.* Go wash up! You are not presentable like that. (EV) <***Loc:*** EV, Da84>

présentation [prezɑ̃tasjɔ̃] *n.f.* presentation, introduction <***Loc:*** Da84>

présenter [prezɑ̃te] **I** *v.tr.* to present, offer, introduce *Ça peut pas tout mettre dans un* MUSEUM. *Comment ça va présenter une guerre dans un* MUSEUM? They can't put everything in a museum. How are they going to present a war in a museum? (LF) **II se présenter** *v.pron.* **1** to introduce o.s., present o.s. *Il s'a présenté aux parents de sa belle.* He introduced himself to his girlfriend's parents. (VM) **2** to arise, present itself **Des difficultés se présentent.* There are difficulties. (Da84) *Une fois il y avait du mauvais temps qui s'a présenté.* Once there was a storm that arose. (LF) *Si l'occasion se présente, je vas retourner demain au soir.* If I get a chance, I'll go back again tomorrow night. (AC, ch: *J'ai été z-au bal*) **3** to present o.s. correctly, make a certain impression *Mom nous disait mais je connaissais comment faire, comment me présenter, comment faire pour faire une bonne fille.* Mom used to say, but I knew how to behave, how to present myself, to show that I was a good girl. (EV) **La dame se présente bien.* The lady makes a good impression, has a good appearance. (Da84) <***Loc:*** AC, EV, LF, VM, Da84, Hi02>

préservation [prezærvasjɔ̃] *n.f.* preservation <***Loc:*** Da84>

préservative [prezærvativ] *n.f.* **1** preservative *Ils mettont des préservatives dans le lait asteur pour l'empêcher de cailler.* They put preservatives in milk now to keep it from curdling. (VM) **2** condom <***Loc:*** LA, VM>

préserver [prezærve, pærzeve] **I** *v.tr.* **1** to preserve, maintain, safeguard, keep *Ça m'a bien servi de connaître le français. J'aimerais voir notre langue française préservée.* It has served me well to know French. I'd like to see our French language preserved. (LF) **2** to preserve, conserve, keep from perishing (e.g. food) *Ça préservait la viande comme ça.* It preserved the meat that way. (AC) **II se préserver** *v.pron.* to avoid, guard against *Je me préserve d'aller au soleil.* I avoid going in the sun. (VM) <***Loc:*** AC, LF, VM, Da84>

président [prezidɑ̃] *n.m.* president, presiding officer, chairman *J'ai servi comme président pour trois ans.* I served as president for three years. (EV) <***Loc:*** LF, TB, Da84>

présider [prezide] *v.tr.* to preside over *Présider un meeting.* To preside over a meeting. (VM) <***Loc:*** VM, Da84>

presque [presk(ə), prɛʃk(ə), prɛs] *adv.* almost, nearly *J'ai* *presque fini.* I'm almost finished. (SM) *Et là, j'ai été dans le service militaire, et j'ai resté presque trois ans.* And then I was in the armed forces, and I stayed in for about three years. (SL) *Et le monde s'accordait presque aussi bien ou mieux qu'asteur.* And people got along almost as well or better than now. (TB) **Il y en reste presque pus.* There's hardly any left. (Da84) **La journée est presque finie.* The day is almost over. (Da84) <***Loc:*** AC, LF, SL, SM, TB, Da84>

pressant, -e [presɑ̃, -ɑ̃t] *adj.* pressing, urgent *Une affaire pressante.* An urgent affair. (VM) <***Loc:*** VM, Da84>

presse [prɛs] *n.f.* **1** press (for printing, fruit, etc.) *Une presse de coton.* A cotton press. (VM) **2** urgency, haste, hurry **Grâce à leur presse de se faire plus américains que les Américains.* Due to their haste to make themselves more American than the Americans. (De85) ◊ **•à la presse** in a hurry *Être à la presse.* To be in a hurry. (Lv88) *Faire quelque chose à la presse.* To do something in a hurry. (Lv88) <Da84, Lv88> <***Loc:*** VM, Da84, De85, Lv88>

pressé, -e [prese] *adj.* **1** hurried, in a hurry *Moi, je suis pressé. J'ai des affaires à faire.* I'm in a hurry. I've got things to do. (EV, An94) **2** pressing, urgent *Il y avait pas rien de pressé comme y a aujourd'hui.* There wasn't anything pressing like there is today. (SJ) <***Loc:*** EV, SJ, An94, Da84>

pressentiment [presɑ̃timɑ̃] *n.m.* presentiment, foreboding <***Loc:*** Da84>

presser [prese] **I** *v.tr.* **1** to press, squeeze *Presser un limon.* To squeeze a lemon. (VM) **2** to be urgent for *J'ai pas arien qui me presse.* I don't have anything urgent. (TB) **II** *v.intr.* to be urgent **Ça presse.* It is urgent. (Da84) **III se presser** *v.pron.* to hurry, hurry up, make haste <***Loc:*** EV, TB, VM, Da84>

pression [presjɔ̃, preʃjɔ̃] *n.f.* pressure *Y avait de l'eau, mais y avait pas plein de la pression.* There was water, but there wasn't much pressure. (TB) ◊ **•pression de sang** blood pressure <Da84> <***Loc:*** TB, Da84>

prestance [prestɑ̃s] *n.f* appearance *Avoir une belle prestance.* To have a good appearance. (VM) <***Loc:*** VM>

présumer [prezyme] *v.tr.* to presume, assume *Va pas présumer que c'est vrai tant que tu y as pas demandé.* Don't go presuming that it's true until you've asked her. (VM) ◊ **•présume pas tes œufs** [proverb] don't count your chickens before they hatch <VM> <***Loc:*** VM, Da84>

prêt[1] [prɛ, pre, -ɛt] *adj.* ready *Il était tout prêt à faire leur jardin.* He was all ready to start their garden. (TB) *Nous-autres on a été se marier et quand on est revenu tout l'affaire était prêt.* We went to get married and when we came back everything was ready. (EV) *Moi je suis pas prêt lui dire pour il arrête parce que c'est un job il peut faire et il fait de l'argent avec ça.* I'm not ready to tell him to stop because it's a job that he can do and he makes money with that. (EV) <***Loc:*** EV, TB, Da84>

prêt[2] [prɛ, pre] *n.m.* loan *Et là, dans quarante-huit j'ai commencé travailler pour un coopératif qui fait des prêts agricoles.* And then in '48, I started working for a cooperative that makes farm loans. (SL) <***Loc:*** SL>

prêtable [pretab(l)] *adj.* lendable *Mon wagon est pas prêtable. Il est tout sale.* My wagon is not in a lendable state. It's all dirty. (VM) <***Loc:*** VM, Da84>

prête [prɛt] *n.f.* loan *J'ai une prête de cinq piastres à payer.* I have a five dollar loan to pay. (VM) <***Loc:*** VM>

prétendant [pretɑ̃dɑ̃] *n.m.* suitor, wooer <***Loc:*** Da84>

prétende-femme [pretɑ̃dfɑ̃m] *n.f.* fiancée, future wife, bride-to-be <VM>

prétend-mari [pretɑ̃mari] *n.m.* fiancé, future husband <***Loc:*** VM>

prétendre [pretɑ̃n, pretɑ̃d(r)] **I** *v.tr.* **1** to pretend, make believe *Il prétend qu'il me voit pas.* He's pretending not to see me. (VM) *J'ai prétendu que je le connaissais pas.* I pretended that I didn't know him. (SM) **2** to claim *Il prétend que la vache noire est sortie du parc.* He claims that the black cow got out of the corral. (LA) **Ya eine grande différence entr' ein Amaricain qui prétend de parler français comme ein Parisien et ein Cadien qui est français et qui parle son langage comme le Bon Djeu l'a ordonné.* There's a big difference between an American who claims to speak French like a Parisian and a Cajun who speaks his language like the Good Lord ordained. (ThCa: *Mille misères*) **II** *v.intr.* to pretend *Il prétend de t'aimer.* He pretends he loves you. (SM) **III se prétendre** *v.pron.* to pretend to be **Se prétendre riche.* To pretend to be rich. (Da84) <***Loc:*** EV, LA, SL, SM, VM, Da84, Lv88, ThCa>

prétendu, -e [pretɑ̃dy] *n.* **1** *(m.)* fiancé, future husband *Les autres fois, les prétendus donnaient un éventail à leurs prétendues.* In the old days, fiancés gave their betrothed a fan. (VM) **2** *(f.)* fiancée, future wife **"O, mais" il dit, "ça, c'est pas un péché, jouer avec les mains de ta prétendue. Pas de péché là. C'est tout ça t'as fait?"* "Oh, well," he said, "that's not a sin, playing with the hands of your fiancée. No sin there. Is that all you did?" (EV, An94) **3** *(m.)* boyfriend *Ça c'est mon* GRAND-DAUGHTER *et son prétendu.* This is my grand-daughter and her boyfriend. (TB) **4** *(f.)* girlfriend *Je crois qu'il avait une prétendue là-bas.* I think he had a girlfriend over there. (LF) <***Loc:*** EV, LF, SL, TB, VM, An94, Da84>

prétentieux, -ieuse [pretɑ̃sjø, -jøz] *adj.* pretentious *Il est assez prétentieux! Je peux pas le* STAND*!* He's so pretentious! I can't stand him! (VM) <***Loc:*** VM, Da84>

prétention [pretɑ̃sjɔ̃] *n.f.* pretense, pretension <***Loc:*** Da84>

prêter [prete] *v.tr.* to lend, loan *Moi et toi peut aller, mon mari va nous prêter le* TRUCK*.* You and I can go, my husband will lend us the truck. (LF) <***Loc:*** LF, Da84, Lv88>

prêteur [pretœr] *n.m.* lender <***Loc:*** Da84>

prêtre [prɛt(r)] *n.m.* priest ◊ **•prêtre manqué** man who studied to be a priest but failed to be ordained <Da84> **•le prêtre dit pas sa messe deux fois** said when one refuses to repeat o.s. <La99> <***Loc:*** AC, EV, IV, LF, SL, SM, TB, VM, An94, Da84, Hi02, La99, Lv88>

preuve [prœv] *n.f.* proof, evidence <***Loc:*** Da84>

prévenir[1] [prev(ə)nir] *v.tr.* to warn, caution, forewarn *"*Mais, ça c'est ein autre quart de ta vie perdu," le principal a prévenu.* "But that's another quarter of your life wasted," the principal warned. (Wh83) <***Loc:*** Da84, Hi02, Wh83>

prévenir[2] [prev(ə)nir] *n.m.* warning **Et si les ouaouarons grognaient fort juste qu'à [=jusqu'à] tard dans la matinée, c'était ein prévenir de la pluie avant soleil couché.* And if the bullfrogs croaked loud until late in the morning, it was a warning that it would rain before sunset. (Wh83) <***Loc:*** Wh83>

prévention [prevɑ̃sjɔ̃] *n.f.* prevention <***Loc:*** Da84>

prévoir [prevwar] *v.intr.* to foresee, make provisions, plan *Il faut que tu prévoies pour ça.* You have to plan for that. (VM) <***Loc:*** VM, Da84>

prévoyance [prevwajɑ̃s] *n.f.* foresight, precaution <***Loc:*** Da84>

prévoyant, -e [prevwajɑ̃, -ɑ̃t] *adj.* provident, thoughtful, careful *C'est une personne bien prévoyante. Elle a tout le temps de quoi à servir si du monde vient visiter.* She is a very thoughtful person. She always has something to serve if people come to visit. (VM) <***Loc:*** VM, Da84>

pricheur ♦see **prêcheur**

prie-Dieu [pridʒø] *n.m.* **1** prie-dieu, kneeler **2** Carolina wren <***Loc:*** Da84, Hi02, Lv88, Re31>

prier [prije] **I** *v.tr.* to pray to, implore, beg **Bin la veille d'ce jour-là, Monsieur, moi et défunt Sosthène, on a prié l'Bon Dieu qu'i' la soigne pis qu'i' 'i montr' le bon ch'min.* Well, the night before that day, Sir, poor old Sosthène and I prayed to the Good Lord that he would take care of her and show her the right way. (VM, Gu82) **II** *v.intr.* to pray *Je vous souhaite plein de la bonne chance, et je vas prier pour vous.* I wish you much good luck, and I'm going to pray for you. (LF) *J'ai prié pour lui.* I prayed for him. (EV) ◊ **•je vous en prie** please <Da84> <***Loc:*** EV, LF, TB, Da84, Hi02>

prière [prijær] *n.f.* prayer <***Loc:*** AC, EV, IB, LA, LF, TB, VM, An94, Da84, Hi02>

prime[1] [prim] *adj.* **1** prime, excellent *De la viande prime.* Prime cuts of meat. (Lv88) **2** impulsive, quick to react, quick to anger *Un homme prime.* An impulsive man. (VM) *Avoir une colère prime.* To have a quick temper. (VM) **3** alert, lively *Quand j'étais jeune, j'étais prime.* When I was young, I was agile and alert. (LA) **4** early, precocious, early-maturing *Du riz prime.* Early rice. (VM) **5** flammable *La gasoline est prime.* Gasoline is flammable. (SM) <***Loc:*** JE, SM, VM, Da84, Lv88>

prime[2] **(prème)** [prim, prɛ̃m] *n.m./f.* salted beef <***Loc:*** JE, VM, Di32, Lv88>

prince, -esse [prɛ̃s, -ɛs] *n.* **1** *(m.)* prince **2** *(f.)* princess <***Loc:*** VM, Da84, Fa77>

principal[1]**, -e** [prɛ̃sipal] *adj.* principal, primary, main, most important *La raison principale.* The main reason. (EV) <***Loc:*** EV, Da84, Hi02>

principal[2] [prɛ̃sipal] *n.m.* **1** main, essential, or basic thing *Il avait un petit magasin qui vendait des* BEANS *ou des patates, ou le principal.* He had a small store that sold beans or potatoes, the main things. (TB) **2** principal (of a school) *Et on a plusieurs principals qui le veut, mais ils sont pas près de dire arien pas avant qu'ils connaît comment-ce que le* SUPERINTENDENT *veut.* And there are several principals who want it, but they aren't going to say anything until they know what the superintendent wants. (LF) <***Loc:*** LF, TB, Da84, Hi02>

principalement [prɛ̃sipalmɑ̃] *adv.* principally, mainly *C'est ça je pêche là-là, mais on l'appelle localement sacalait. Principalement les noirs sont meilleurs parce que ils sont plus épais.* That [crappie] there is what I fish, but we call it locally "sacalait." Mainly the black ones are best because they're thicker. (SL) *Les Mardi Gras viennent de tout partout, mais principalement Grand Mamou.* (EV, ch: *Chanson des Mardi Gras*) <***Loc:*** EV, SL, TB, Da84, Wh83>

principe [prɛ̃sip] *n.m.* principle, rule, basic law or fact of nature <***Loc:*** Da84>

printanière [prɛ̃tɑ̃jær] *n.f.* blue-winged teal <***Loc:*** TB>

printemps [prɛ̃tɑ̃] *n.m.* spring *Grand-maman Ti-ma avait un gros arkansia dans sa cour qui fleurissait tous les printemps avec des belles grosses grappes de fleurs blanches.* Grandma Ti-ma had a big black locust tree in her yard that blossomed every spring with big beautiful clusters of white flowers. (VM) ◊ **•au {en} printemps / dans le printemps** in the spring *Au printemps ça a été assez bien.* In the spring, it [fishing] was pretty good. (SL) *En printemps l'alcool de bois monte.* In spring the sap rises. (JE) **Ein samedi après midi dans le printemps.* One Saturday afternoon in the spring. (Wh83) <AC, EV, JE, SL, Wh83> <***Loc:*** AC, EV, JE, LA, SL, VM, Da84, Hi02, Lv88, Wh83>

priorité [prijorite] *n.m.* priority **La première priorité est le mâtrissage de la langue Cajine.* The first priority is mastery of the Cajun language. (Wh83) <***Loc:*** Wh83>

pris, -e [pri, -iz] *adj.* **1** taken, occupied (e.g. a place, a seat) *Tu peux pas t'assir ici. C'est déjà pris.* You can't sit here. It's already taken. (EV) **2** started, set in, underway **La querelle est prise.* The quarrel has started. (Da84) **Le feu est pris.* The fire has started. (Da84) *Le beau temps est pris.* The good weather has set in (SM) **L'hiver est prise.* Winter has begun. (Da84) **3** stuck, caught (e.g. in a trap) **Je suis pris.* I am caught. (Da84) **Être pris dans la boue.* To be stuck in the mud. (Da84) **Le trou était pas assez gros pour lui passer. Il était pris.* The hole was not big enough for him to pass through. He was stuck. (EV, An94) **4** caught off guard or unprepared, taken by surprise *J'ai deux milles SHARE dans EQUITY OIL. [...] Et l'affaire d'huile avait retombé vilain, ça fait j'étais pris avec deux mille SHARE.* I have two thousand shares in Equity Oil. And the oil business took a nasty plunge, so I was caught with two thousand shares. (TB) ◊ •**mal pris / malpris** ***a*** not feeling well, not in good shape *Il faut que t'aies besoin, que t'es un peu mal pris.* You must need something since you are not feeling very well. (Lv88) *Quand il est mal pris avec la maladie.* When he is not feeling well due to illness. (Lv88) *Il faut que je suis mal pris pour pas aller à la messe.* I have to not feel well to not go to mass. (Lv88) ***b*** in a difficult situation *On est mal pris avec cet ouragan qui s'en vient.* We're in a bad situation with that hurricane coming. (EV) <EV, Lv88> <***Loc:*** EV, SM, TB, An94, Da84, La99>

prise [priz] *n.f.* **1** grasp, hold, grip, handle *J'ai lâché ma prise dessus mon bébé et il s'a noyé.* I lost my grip on my baby and he drowned. (VM) **2** catch, take (of fish, etc.) *Une prise maigre.* A paltry catch. (VM) **3** snuff *La prise fait éternuer.* Snuff makes you sneeze. (TB) ◊ •**prise de poisson** catch of fish <Da84> •**prise de tabac** pinch of tobacco <Da84> •**prendre une bonne prise** to get a good grasp or grip <Da84> <***Loc:*** JE, TB, VM, Da84>

priser [prize] *v.intr.* to take snuff *Elle l'a quitté parce qu'il prisait et elle trouvait ça dégoûtant.* She left him because he took snuff and it disgusted her. (LA) <***Loc:*** LA>

prison [prizɔ̃] *n.f.* jail, prison ◊ •**mettre en prison** to put in jail *Ils l'ont mis en prison.* They put him in prison. (IV) <IV, An94, Da84> <***Loc:*** EV, IV, VM, An94, Da84>

prisonnier [prizɔ̃je] *n.m.* prisoner, convict <***Loc:*** TB, VM, Da84>

privé, -e [prive] *adj.* private *Une affaire privée.* A private affaire. (EV) <***Loc:*** EV, Da84, Lv88>

priver [prive] **I** *v.tr.* to deprive **Privé de sa mère.* Deprived of his mother. (Da84) **II se priver** *v.pron.* to do without, abstain from, deny o.s. (food, etc.) *Il se privait de pain pour que ses enfants en aient.* He deprived himself of bread so that his children could have some. (LA) <***Loc:*** LA, VM, Da84, Fa77>

privilège [privilɛʒ] *n.m.* privilege, favor <***Loc:*** EV, VM, Da84, Fa77>

prix [pri] *n.m.* **1** prize **2** cost, price *C'était comme on dit un char seconde main. Je me rappelle le prix était douze cents piastres.* It was a second hand car, as they call it. I remember the price was twelve hundred dollars. (TB) ◊ •**à moitié prix** at half price <TB> •**au prix coûtant** at cost <Da84> <***Loc:*** SM, Da84, Hi02>

probabilité [probabilite] *n.f.* probability, likelihood <***Loc:*** Da84>

probable[1] [probab(l)] *adj.* probable, likely *Je connais pas si c'est probable qu'il aurait venu si de bonne heure.* I don't know if it is likely that he would have come so early. (LA) ◊ •**plus que probable** more than likely *Plus que probable, c'est ça qu'a arrivé.* More than likely, that's what happened. (LA) <LA, Da84> <***Loc:*** LA, Da84>

probable[2] [probab(l)] *adv.* probably *Probable, mais moi je pourrais pas vous dire.* Probably, but I couldn't tell you for sure. (TB) <***Loc:*** TB, Da84>

probablement [probabləmɑ̃, prabləmɑ̃] *adv.* probably, likely *Je dirais presque tous les familles ici en bas c'est probablement comme ça que vous allez trouver.* I would say almost all the families down here, that's probably what you'll find. (TB) <***Loc:*** AV, TB, Da84, Wh83>

problème [problɛ̃m] *n.m.* problem, difficulty <***Loc:*** LF, Da84, Wh83>

procès [prosɛ, prose] *n.m.* **1** lawsuit, trial, court action *Le jury a délibéré longtemps après le procès.* The jury deliberated a long time after the trial. (LA) *Le procès à mon oncle a précédé çulà du gouverneur.* My uncle's trial preceded the governor's. (EV) **2** process, method <***Loc:*** EV, LA, VM, Da84, Fa77>

procession [prosesjɔ̃] *n.m.* procession, parade <***Loc:*** Da84>

prochain[1], **-e** [prɔʃɛ̃, -ɛ̃n] *adj.* next, upcoming *Mon frère a donné notice qu'il va courir pour maire dans la prochaine élection.* My brother gave notice that he is going to run for mayor in the next election. (VM) *Ils vont SHIP cent cinquante mille tonnes de cannes ici et l'année prochaine ils vont être dessus un NO-QUOTA.* They're going to ship a hundred and fifty thousand tons of cane [from] here and next year they'll be on a no-quota. (AS) ◊ •**la prochaine fois** next time *"Et tant qu'à toi, mon fils de putain," il dit, "si tu me paies pas cet argent ça tu me dois," et il dit, "si t'arrêtes pas de courir après ma femme," il dit, "la prochaine fois je vas te tuer, ouais!"* "And as for you, you son-of-a-bitch," he says, "if you don't pay me the money you owe me," and he says, "if you don't stop chasing after my wife," he says, "next time I will kill you!" (JD) <JD, LA, Da84> <***Loc:*** AS, JD, LA, Da84>

prochain[2], **-e** [prɔʃɛ̃, -ɛ̃n] *n.* **1** neighbor, fellow man *Aider ses prochains.* To help one's fellow man. (LA) **2** next, next one *J'ai eu quatre garçons, le plus vieux quarante-quatre, le prochain quarante-deux, le prochain quarante, et le prochain trente-huit.* I had four sons, the oldest one is 44, the next one 42, the next one 40 et the next one 38. (IB) <***Loc:*** IB, LA, Da84>

proche [prɔʃ] *adv.* nearly, almost *Il pouvait proche pas marcher du tout.* He almost couldn't walk at all. (SL) *J'ai proche fini.* I'm almost finished. (SM) *On a pas proche fait ça nous-autres on aurait voulu faire.* We didn't nearly do what we would've wanted to do. (EV) *Asteur je vas proche tous les jours.* Now I go almost every day. (TB) ◊ •**proche de** close to, near *Ils ont grouillé dans les Avoyelles proche de Bunkie.* They moved to the Avoyelles, close to Bunkie. (AV) **Ceux-là qui jete la pacane plus proche de la ligne commencent le jeu.* Those who throw the pecan closest to the line begin the game. (Wh83) <AV, Wh83> •**proche**

que almost, nearly *Les seuls à parler français avec, c'est le vieux monde, les jeunes comme notre âge à nous-autres, proche que jamais.* The only ones to speak French are the old folks, people younger like our age almost never do it. (SM) <IV, LF, TB, SM, An94> •**bien proche** almost, nearly <Da84> <***Loc:*** AC, EV, IB, LA, LF, SL, SM, TB, VM, An94, Da84, Hi02>

proclamation [proklɑ̃masjɔ̃] *n.f.* proclamation <***Loc:*** Da84>

proclamer [proklɑ̃me] **I** *v.tr.* to proclaim, declare *Le gouverneur Edwards a proclamé une fête pour le lendemain de Thanksgiving.* Governor Edwards declared a holiday for the day after Thanksgiving. (VM) **II se proclamer** *v.pron.* to proclaim o.s. (e.g. king) *Il s'a proclamé le roi du boudin.* He proclaimed himself Boudin King. (EV) <***Loc:*** EV, VM, Da84>

procure [prokyr] *n.f.* deed <***Loc:*** JE>

production [prodyksjɔ̃] *n.f.* production, output, product <***Loc:*** Da84>

produire [prodɥir] *v.tr.* **1** to produce (goods) *Le* ENVIRONMENTALIST GROUP *a rentré là-dedans qu'a fait ça bien dur pour eux-autres produire un baril d'huile.* The environmentalist group got involved which made it very difficult for them to produce a barrel of oil. (TB) **2** to yield, bear (fruits, seed, etc.) *On a des bananiers ici, ils poussent mais ils produit pas de fruit, rarement, parce que ça prend trop longtemps et avant il y a toujours une gelée.* We have banana trees here, they grow but they don't produce any fruit, [or] rarely, because it takes too long [to ripen] and beforehand there is always a freeze. (SL) **3** to produce, present, bring forth **Produire son batistaire.* To produce his registry of baptism. (Re31) <***Loc:*** SL, TB, Da84, Re31>

produit [prodɥi, prody] *n.m.* **1** product *Les bateaux qu'étaient faits pour les huîtres, ben eux ils avaient pas de trou pour mettre les produits dedans. Le plancher était massif, il avait pas de trou dedans.* The boats that were made for oyster fishing, well, they didn't have a hole to put the products in. The deck was rough cut, there was no hole in it. (LF) **2** *(pl.)* produce, fruits and vegetables *Quand j'ai revenu, j'ai commencé acheter des patates douces. Il n-avait beaucoup de patates douces produit ici. Et j'ai acheté des patates douces pour une ferme de produits à Pont Breaux.* When I came back, I started buying sweet potatoes. A lot of sweet potatoes were produced here. And I bought sweet potatoes for a produce farm at Breaux Bridge. (SL) **3** *(pl.)* proceeds, profit *Il a donné tous les produits du bazar à l'église.* He gave all the proceeds of the bazaar to the church. (VM) <***Loc:*** LF, SL, SM, VM, Da84>

profaner [profɑ̃ne] *v.tr.* [*eccl.*] to profane, desecrate, defile *Ces enfants ont profané les tombes dans le cimetière.* Those children defiled the tombs in the cemetery. (VM) <***Loc:*** VM, Da84>

professer [profese] *v.tr.* [*eccl.*] **1** to profess, proclaim *Il a été obligé de professer la foi catholique avant de marier ma fille.* He had to profess Catholic faith before marrying my daughter. (LA) **2** to practice (a religion) <***Loc:*** LA, VM, Da84>

professeur [profesœr] *n.m.* **1** teacher *Il était premier professeur d'école en bas du bayou. Il a montré les enfants français et anglais ensemble à l'école.* He was the first school teacher down the bayou. He taught the children French and English together at school. (LF) **2** professor *Alle a rencontré un de mes amis là-bas qui vient ici, un professeur de collège.* She met one of my friends there who comes here, a college professor. (TB) <***Loc:*** EV, LF, TB, An94, Da84>

profession [profesjɔ̃] *n.f.* **1** profession, vocation, calling **2** taking of vows <***Loc:*** Da84>

professional ♦see **professionnel**

professionnel[1], **-elle** (**professional**) [profesjɔ̃nɛl, profesjɔ̃nal] *adj.* **1** professional *Je suis pas un musicien professional mais je vais te jouer quelque chose.* I'm not a professional musician, but I'll play you something. (VM) **2** accomplished, excellent <***Loc:*** SM, VM, Da84>

professionnel[2], **-elle** (**professional**) [profesjɔ̃nɛl, profesjɔ̃nal] *n.* professional *C'est un professional. Il joue avec les* BIG LEAGUES. He's a professional. He plays in the Big Leagues. (SM) <***Loc:*** EV, SM, VM, Da84>

profit [profi] *n.m.* **1** profit, gain **2** growth, development *Ga le profit mes haricots avont fait.* Look at the growth of my beans. (VM) <***Loc:*** VM, Da84>

profitable [profitab(l)] *adj.* profitable *Son business était pas profitable. Il a eu pour le fermer.* His business was not profitable. He had to close it. (LA) <***Loc:*** LA, Da84>

profitant [profitɑ̃] *n.m.* waxing (of the moon) *Le déclin de la lune, c'est le contraire du profitant de la lune.* The waning moon is the opposite of the waxing moon. (VM) <***Loc:*** VM>

profiter [profite] *v.intr.* **1** to profit, gain, benefit **Avec ces Cajins "adoptés" la culture profite et réussi.* With these adopted Cajuns the culture benefits and profits. (Wh83) **Venez profiter avec nous-aut'.* Come profit with us. [advertisement] (LGA) **2** to grow **L'herbe profite.* The grass grows. (Da84) *Les patates profitent bien icitte.* Potatoes grow well here. (Lv88) *Une canne a besoin d'humidité pour profiter.* [Sugar] cane needs humidity in order to grow. (IB) *Un enfant qui est à profiter.* A fast-growing child. (SB) *La bonne eau [...] va te faire profiter l'huître pareil comme l'herbe va te faire profiter une vache.* Good water will make your oyster grow just like grass will make your cow grow. (TB) **3** to wax, become full (of the moon) *La lune profite cette semaine.* The moon is becoming full this week. (VM) ◊ •**profiter de l'occasion** to take advantage of the occasion <Da84> <***Loc:*** EV, IB, SJ, TB, VM, Da84, Hi02, Lv88, Wh83>

profond, -e [profɔ̃, -ɔ̃d] *adj.* deep *Dans ce temps-là les champs de cannes allaient dans des 40 et 60 arpents de profond du chemin.* In those days cane fields went 40 to 60 arpents deep from the road. (TB) <***Loc:*** TB, Da84>

programme [progrɑ̃m] *n.m.* **1** program, plan *Ils ont presque venu* EXTINCT *ici en bas. Mais asteur il y en a tout partout, […] mon je sais pas combien, peut-être vingt ans de programme qu'eux-autres a, qu'eux-autres avait fermé la saison.* They almost became extinct down here. But now they are everywhere. I don't know how many years ago maybe twenty years ago they, they started a program to close the hunting season. (TB) **2** program, broadcast (on TV or radio) *J'ai assayé d'écouter ce programme qu'ils ont là en français.* I've tried to listen to that program that they have in French. (TB) **<*Loc:*** AV, EV, TB, Da84>

progrès [progrɛ, progre] *n.m.* progress, improvement, development **<*Loc:*** Da84>

progressif, -ive [progresif, -iv] *adj.* progressive **Cette qualité de musique prouve que la culture Cajine est eine culture vivant, progressif qu'est tout le temps après changer.* This kind of music proves that Cajun culture is a living, progressive culture which is always changing. (Wh83) **<*Loc:*** Da84, Wh83>

prohibition [proibisjɔ̃] *n.f.* prohibition **<*Loc:*** Da84>

projet [proʒɛ, proʒe] *n.m.* **1** project, plan **2** tale **I nous raconte des projets.* He tells us tales. (EV, Ph36) **<*Loc:*** EV, Da84, Ph36>

prolongation [prolɔ̃gasjɔ̃] *n.f.* prolongation, protraction, continuation **<*Loc:*** Da84>

prolongement [prolɔ̃ʒmɑ̃] *n.m.* prolongation, extension **<*Loc:*** Da84>

prolonger [prolɔ̃ʒe] *v.tr.* to prolong, extend, lengthen *J'ai peur que ça va prolonger leur misère.* I'm afraid that this will prolong their misery. (LA) **<*Loc:*** LA, Da84>

promenade [prɔ̃mnad] *n.f.* visit, trip, outing **<*Loc:*** LA, VM, Da84>

promener [prɔ̃mne, purmәne] **I** *v.tr.* to drive, take (a vehicle) out for a ride *Il a été promener une de ces voitures de plairie là, un boghei, boghei de boue.* He went out to drive one of those marsh buggies, mud buggies. (TB) **II se promener** *v.pron.* **1** to go for a stroll, go for a walk *Dessous le laurier blanc, la belle, elle se promène, blanche comme la neige, jolie comme le jour.* Underneath the white laurel, the maiden goes for a stroll, as white as the snow, as beautiful as the day. (PQ, ch: *La belle et le capitaine*) **Va te promener!* Go to hell, take a walk, beat it! (Da84) **2** to ride, go for a ride *On se promenait sur le* BUS. We rode on the bus. (TB) *Et eux-autres avait un vieux* TRUCK. *Et eux-autres venait se promener de temps en temps.* And they had an old truck. And they came to ride around once in awhile. (TB) **Je crois pas Bill a jamais eu ein char parceque mon je l'ai tout le temps connu de ride ein "*BIKE*" dans le voisinage pour aller faire ses commissions ou pour aller se promener.* I don't think Bill ever had a car because I always knew him to ride a bike to run his errands or go for a ride. (Wh83) **3** to go for a visit, take a trip *Alle a été se promener dans le Canada, alle a été se promener à Québec.* She went for a trip around Canada, she went for a trip to Quebec. (TB) ◊ **•se promener à cheval {en boghei} / se promener à la pagaille (etc.)** to go for a ride on a horse / in a buggy / in a paddled boat such as a pirogue, etc. *On pourrait peut-être aller se promener à la pagaille.* Maybe we could go for a ride paddling [in a pirogue]. (LF) <LF> **•se promener à pied** to go for a walk <LF> **<*Loc:*** EV, JE, LF, PQ, TB, Da84, Wh83>

promesse (premesse) [prɔ̃mɛs, prәmɛs] *n.f.* promise, pledge *Rappelle-toi, 'tite fille, les promesses que tu m'as fait.* Remember, little girl, the promises you made to me. (LA, ch: *La valse de samedi soir*) **<*Loc:*** EV, LA, LF, VM, Da84, Hi02>

prometteur [prɔ̃metœr] *n.m.* maker of a promissory note **<*Loc:*** JE>

promettre [prɔ̃mɛt(r)] *v.tr.* to promise, pledge **C'est tout. Je te promets.* That's all. I promise you. (EV, An94) *Et il dit à mon pape il dit, "Je te promets qu'il a un trésor là d'enterré."* And he told my father, "I promise you that there is a treasure buried there." (LF) *Et j'ai* GIVE UP *la musique, j'ai promis à ma femme que c'était pas une vie, mon être dans les* BARROOM *après chanter, pratiquer.* And I gave up music, I promised my wife that it wasn't a life, my being in barrooms singing, practicing. (LF) **<*Loc:*** EV, IV, LF, An94, Da84>

promis [prɔ̃mi] *adj.* promised, pledged, engaged (to be married) *J'étais déjà promis à quelqu'un d'autre quand j'ai rencontré ton père.* I was already promised to someone else when I met your father. (VM) **<*Loc:*** VM, Da84>

PROMOTE [pɹәmoᵘt] *v.tr.invar.* to promote *Ils l'ont* PROMOTE *au troisième livre.* They promoted him to the third grade. (LA) *Ça c'est les trois qu'a fini l'école et qu'a été au collège […]. Mon je sais pas quo'faire eux-autres les promotait pas d'aller, les encourager d'aller à l'école.* Those are the three who finished school and who went on to college. I don't know why they didn't promote going, encourage them to go to school. (LF) **Il y avait un vieux bougre dans le voisinage qui était tout le temps après* PROMOTE *différentes affaires.* There was an old fellow in the neighborhood who was always promoting different things. (SL, An84) **<*Loc:*** LA, LF, SL, An84>

promotion [prɔ̃mosjɔ̃] *n.f.* promotion **<*Loc:*** Da84>

prompt, -e [prɔ̃] *adj.* **1** quick-witted *Il est prompt avec ses réponses, lui.* He's quick-witted with his answers. (VM) **2** quick-tempered, curt *Ton parrain est prompt, mais il est pas méchant.* Your godfather is curt, but he's not mean. (VM) **<*Loc:*** VM, Da84>

prône [prɔ̃n] *n.m.* sermon *À l'église c'était toujours en français les prônes.* At church, the sermons were always in French. (VM) *Durant le prône du prêtre, il dormaillait.* During the priest's sermon, he was dozing off. (VM) **<*Loc:*** TB, VM, Da84>

prononcé, -e [prɔ̃nɔ̃se] *adj.* pronounced, prominent *Un nez prononcé.* A prominent nose. (VM) <***Loc:*** Da84>

prononcer (prenoncer) [prɔ̃nɔ̃se, prənɔ̃se] *v.tr.* **1** to pronounce *Quand même que c'est prononcé un petit peu différent, le monde se comprend, on connait qui-ce qu'eusse veut dire, parce qu'il a tellement des années qu'on se rencontre.* Even if it's pronounced a little bit differently, people understand each other, we know what they're saying, because it's been so many years that we've been meeting. (LF) **2** to recite, say out loud *Allons prononcer le chapelet ensemble.* Let's say the rosary together. (VM) **3** to pronounce, pass a sentence on (in court) *Le juge l'a prononcé coupable.* The judge pronounced him guilty. (VM) <***Loc:*** IB, LF, VM, Da84>

prononciation [prɔ̃nɔ̃sjasjɔ̃, prɔ̃nɔ̃siasijɔ̃] *n.f.* pronunciation *Souvent des fois il n-a des prononciations qu'est un peu pareilles.* Very often there are pronunciations that are a little bit similar. (SL) <***Loc:*** SL, Da84>

PROPEL [propɛl] *n.* propeller <***Loc:*** JE>

prophète [profɛt] *n.m.* [*eccl.*] prophet <***Loc:*** Da84>

prophétie [profesi] *n.f.* [*eccl.*] prophecy <***Loc:*** Da84>

propir [propir] *v.tr.* to clean, clean up, tidy up <***Loc:*** JD, Da84>

proportion [propɔrsjɔ̃] *n.f.* proportion ◊ **•prendre des proportions** to plan carefully (in doing s.t.) <JE> <***Loc:*** JE, Da84>

propos [propo] *n.m.* **1** purpose, design **2** proposal, proposition *Dessus ce propos-là, la belle, elle se promène.* Upon this proposal, the maiden took a stroll. (PQ, ch: *La belle et le capitaine*) ◊ **•à propos de** relative to, concerning, about *Il parlait à propos de son frère.* He was talking about his brother. (LA) <LA, Da84> **•mal à propos** improper, inappropriate *Son idée était joliment mal à propos.* His idea was pretty inappropriate. (LA) <LA, VM, Da84> <***Loc:*** LA, PQ, VM, Da84>

proposer [propoze] *v.tr.* to propose, offer, suggest *Il a proposé un barguine.* He proposed a trade. (LA) *L'homme propose et Dieu dispose.* Man proposes and God disposes. (LA) <***Loc:*** LA, VM, Da84, Fa77>

proposeur [propozœr] *n.m.* proposer, one who proposes s.t. *C'est lui le proposeur de cette loi.* He's the one who proposed this law. (SM) <***Loc:*** SM>

proposition [propozisjɔ̃] *n.f.* proposition, proposal <***Loc:*** Da84>

propre[1] [prɔp(r)] *adj.* **1** clean, neat, spotless *Là j'ai lavé mon linge que j'avais à ce matin sur le dos, il est tout propre, là il est pendu après sécher.* I washed the clothes that I had on this morning, it's all clean, it's hung up drying. (TB) **Tu partais propre, et t'arrivais là-bas plein de poussière.* You would leave clean, and you would arrive over there covered in dust. (LA, An94) **2** decent (of people) *C'est du monde propre.* They are decent people. (LA) **3** own **C'est ses propres souliers.* It's his own shoes. (Da84) **4** full, rightful, true (of a relative) *Mon frère propre.* My full brother (as opposed to half brother). (VM) ◊ **•propre à rien** good-for-nothing <Da84> **•pour propre** dress, dressy *Du linge pour propre.* Dress clothes, Sunday clothes. (LF) <LF> <***Loc:*** EV, LA, LF, TB, An94, Da84, Hi02>

propre[2] [prɔp(r)] *adv.* **1** completely *Ça l'a bouchée propre.* It plugged it up completely. (LA) **2** definitively and quickly *Je l'ai arrêté propre.* I stopped it right there. (VM) <***Loc:*** EV, LA, VM>

proprement [proprəmɑ̃] *adv.* decently, correctly, properly *Quand ils s'ont divorcés, ils ont fait ça proprement. Pas de chicane, pas rien.* When they divorced, they did it right. No fighting, no nothing. (VM) <***Loc:*** VM, Da84>

propreté [proprəte] *n.f.* **1** cleanliness, neatness **2** honesty, decency <***Loc:*** Da84>

propreter ♦see **propter**

propriétaire [proprijetær, proprœritær] *n.m.* proprietor, owner, landlord <***Loc:*** EV, VM, Da84>

propriété [proprijete, propœrte, proprœrite] *n.f.* property, real estate, possession *N-oncle avait un marais à côté de sa propriété.* Uncle had a swamp next to his property. (SJ) <***Loc:*** LF, SJ, TB, VM, Da84>

proptage [prɔptaʒ] *n.m.* cleaning, clean-up <***Loc:*** VM, Da84>

propter (propreter) [prɔpte] **I** *v.tr.* to clean, clean up **Propter la maison.* To clean up the house. (Da84) **Et il dit il y avait un tas des feuilles sur la tombe. Et il avait proprеté la tombe et il avait dansé dessus.* There was a pile of leaves on the grave. And he had cleaned the grave and had danced on top of it. (VM, An94) *J'ai propté ma maison hier. Alle était assez sale que ça m'a pris toute la cernie journée.* I cleaned the house yesterday. It was so dirty that it took me the entire darn day. (Gu00) *J'ai proprеté la poule.* I cleaned the chicken. (VM) **II se propter** *v.pron.* to clean o.s. up, get ready *Il a parti se propreter.* He's gone to get ready. (VM) **2** to clean for o.s. **Se propter une place.* To clean a place for oneself. (Da84) <***Loc:*** IV, LA, SL, VM, An77, An84, Da84, Gu00, Hi02, Lv88>

prospère [prospær] *adj.* prosperous *C'était une famille beaucoup prospère.* That was a very prosperous family. (LA) <***Loc:*** LA, Da84>

prospérer [prospere] *v.intr.* to prosper, be prosperous *Si tu travailles dur, tu vas prospérer.* If you work hard, you will prosper. (LA) <***Loc:*** LA, Da84>

prospérité [prosperite] *n.f.* prosperity, success <***Loc:*** Da84>

prostituée [prostitɥe] *n.f.* prostitute, harlot, whore <***Loc:*** Da84>

prostitution [prostitysjɔ̃] *n.f.* prostitution <***Loc:*** Da84>

protecter [protɛkte] *v.tr.* to protect, guard, care for *Tu vas protecter la maison quand nous-autres sont partis, hein?* You're going to take care of the house when we are gone, right? (VM) *Ça poussait le monde de grouiller plus endedans pour assayer de protecter en tout cas que ç'a eu un* *autre ouragan.* That pushed people to move further inland to try to protect [themselves] in case there would be another hurricane. (LF) <*Loc:* LF, TB, VM, Da84, Fa77, Lv88>

protecteur[1] [protɛktœr] *adj.* protective *Un père protecteur.* A protective father. (VM) <*Loc:* VM, Da84>

protecteur[2] [protɛktœr] *n.m.* protector, defender, guardian <*Loc:* Da84>

protection [protɛksjɔ̃] *n.f.* protection <*Loc:* Da84>

protéger [proteʒe] *v.tr.* to protect, guard *Il va avoir du vent et va avoir des éclairs pour vous faire peur, pour pas que vous-autres me délivre. Mais je vas vous protéger.* There will be wind and there will be lightning to scare you, so you don't deliver me. But I will protect you. (LF) <*Loc:* LF, VM, Da84, Fa77>

protestant[1]**, -e** [protestɑ̃, -ɑ̃t] *adj.* Protestant <*Loc:* LF, Da84, Hi02>

Protestant[2]**, -e** [protestɑ̃, -ɑ̃t] *n.* Protestant *Y avait pas un tas de Protestants. Le monde avait jamais attendu la Parole en anglais, en français, la Bible, avant les Protestants venaient.* There weren't many Protestants. People had never heard the Word in English, in French, the Bible, before Protestants came. (LF) <*Loc:* LF, An94, Da84, Hi02>

prouvable[1] [pruvab(l)] *adj.* provable, subject to proof *Peut-être que le Bon Dieu existe, mais c'est pas prouvable.* Maybe God exists, but it's not provable. (EV) <*Loc:* EV, Da84, Lv88>

prouvable[2] [pruvab(l)] *adj.* probable ◊ **•plus de prouvable** [plydpruvab] more than likely *C'est plus de prouvable lui qu'a lâché mes moutons.* More than likely he's the one who let my sheep loose. (VM) <VM> <*Loc:* VM, Da84, Lv88>

prouvable[3] [pruvab(l)] *adv.* probably, likely *Il va prouvable faire ça.* He's probably going to do it. (VM) **I va venir, prouvabe.* He will probably come. (EV, Ph36) <*Loc:* EV, VM, Lv88, Ph36>

prouvablement [pruvabləmɑ̃] *adv.* probably *C'est prouvablement vrai.* That's probably true. (VM) <*Loc:* VM, Fa77>

prouver [pruve] *v.tr.* to prove *Ça peut vous prouver mes amis, que mon Hasitall et mon sirop de toux, c'est bon pour tous les maladies et tous les caprices quelqu'un peut avoir dans la vie.* That can prove to you, my friends, that my Hasitall and cough syrup, are good for all the illnesses and caprices that someone can have in life. (AV) **Cette qualité de musique prouve que la culture Cajine est eine culture vivant, progressif qu'est tout le temps après changer.* This kind of music proves that Cajun culture is a living, progressive culture which is always changing. (Wh83) <*Loc:* AV, EV, An94, Da84, Wh83>

provenance [prɔvnɑ̃s] *n.f.* source, origin <*Loc:* Da84>

provenir [prɔvnir] *v.intr.* to originate (with), come (from) *Ça provient de mon arrière grand-mère, ça.* That comes from my great grandmother. (VM) <*Loc:* VM, Da84>

proverbe [proværb] *n.m.* proverb <*Loc:* Da84>

providence [providɑ̃s] *n.f.* [*eccl.*] providence (of God) <*Loc:* Da84>

provision [provizjɔ̃] *n.f.* provision, supply, stock *Et là quand le bateau venait en dedans pour ramasser des provisions il amenait un voyage et là c'était vendu.* And then when the boat came in to get supplies it would take a load and sell it. (TB) <*Loc:* TB, Da84>

provisionner [provizjɔ̃ne] **I** *v.tr.* to supply with provisions, stock *Provisionner les bateaux pour la pêche.* To stock boats for fishing. (VM) **II se provisionner** *v.pron.* to provide for o.s., stock up *Se provisionner pour l'hiver.* To stock up for winter. (VM) <*Loc:* VM, Da84>

provoquer [provoke] *v.tr.* **1** to provoke, instigate *T'es après provoquer une bataille avec ça.* You're provoking a fight with that. (VM) **2** to incite, agitate <*Loc:* VM, Da84>

prudence [prydɑ̃s] *n.f.* prudence, discretion <*Loc:* Da84>

prudent, -e [prydɑ̃, -ɑ̃t] *adj.* prudent, careful, cautious *C'est pas prudent de mettre les manches courtes quand il fait froid comme ça.* It's not prudent to wear short sleeves when it's cold like that. (VM) <*Loc:* Da84, Hi02>

prune [pryn] *n.f.* **1** plum **2** prune ◊ **•prune sec** prune, dried plum <TB> <*Loc:* TB, Da84>

prunier [prỹje, pryjɛ̃] *n.m.* plum tree ◊ **•prunier sauvage** wild plum tree <Gu00> <*Loc:* JE, LA, SL, Da84, Gu00>

prussienne [prysjɛ̃n] *n.f.* (*usu. pl.*) sideburn, side-whiskers ◊ **•se raser à la prussienne** to wear sideburns *Il se rase à la prussienne.* He wears sideburns. (IB) <IB> <*Loc:* IB, SM, VM, Lv88>

psiter [psite] *v.intr.* to make a sibilant sound in order to attract s.o.'s attention <*Loc:* JE>

pu ♦see **plus, pus**

puant, -e [pyɑ̃, -ɑ̃t] *adj.* stinky, stinking, foul-smelling *Amène pas ça dans la maison; c'est trop puant!* Don't bring that in the house; it's too stinky. (VM) <*Loc:* VM, Da84, Hi02>

puanteur [pyɑ̃tœr] *n.f.* stench, stink, bad odor <*Loc:* VM, Da84, Fa77>

puantise [pyɑ̃tiz] *n.f.* stench, stink, bad odor <*Loc:* JE>

public[1]**, -ique** [pyblik, plybik] *adj.* public **Chemin public.* Public road (outside the limits of a town corporation). (VM, Da84) **École publique.* Public school (Da84) *Le premier notaire public qu'on a eu ici était mon grand-père.* The first notary we had here was my grandfather. (LF) <*Loc:* LF, VM, Da84>

public[2] [pyblik, plybik] *n.m.* public *Ça travaille dans le public.* They work for the public. (SL) ◊ **•en public** in public *Il a humilié sa femme en sortant avec sa poupoune en public.* He humiliated his wife by going out in public with his mistress. (LA) <LA, Wh83> <*Loc:* EV, LA, SL, VM, Da84, Wh83>

publication [pyblikasjɔ̃] *n.f.* publication *Il y avait pas de publication, il y avait pas de journal, il y avait pas de livres, rien qui était écrit en français avant une vingtaine d'années passées, je pense.* There were no publications, no newspapers, no books, nothing written in French before about twenty years ago, I think. (SL) <*Loc:* SL, Da84>

publicité [pyblisite] *n.f.* ad, advertisement *Je faisais une émission en français le samedi matin pour deux heures de temps en direct, avec de la musique et de la publicité.* I used to do a live two-hour broadcast in French on Saturday morning, with music and advertising. (SL) <***Loc:*** SL>

publier [pyblije] *v.tr.* to publish, publicize, broadcast, print **Et le monde qui passe s'arrête souvent pour un bout de temps parce que, pour ceux qui veut pas le croire, ils ont publié, ils ont mis une grosse plaque et l'histoire du premier pont du Nez Piqué est là pour eux-autres lire.* And people who pass often stop for a while because, for those who don't want to believe it, they published, they put a big plaque and the story of the first Nez Piqué Bridge is there for them to read. (EV, An94) ◊ **•publier les bans** to publish the banns, announce an intended marriage <Da84> <***Loc:*** EV, VM, An94, Da84, Fa77>

publieur [pyblijœr] *n.m.* publisher <***Loc:*** VM, Fa77>

puce [pys] *n.f.* **1** flea **2** louse *Ma grand-mère nous lavait avec ça pour pas avoir des puces.* My grandmother washed us with it so that we would not have lice. (IB) ◊ **•mettre la puce à l'oreille (à qqn)** ***a*** to hint or suggest (to s.o.) ***b*** to warn (s.o.) subtly about a danger ***c*** to make (s.o.) suspicious by one's words <La99> <***Loc:*** IB, Da84, La99>

puchné ♦see **pichenet**

puer [pɥe] **I** *v.tr.* to smell of **Ça pue le chien.* It smells of dogs. (Da84) **II** *v.intr.* to stink, smell bad *Un capot de rat de bois? Ça pue, ça!* A oppossum skin coat? That stinks! (ThCa: *La table des veuves*) ◊ **•puer le tigre {chien}** to stink, smell very bad <SM, Da84> <***Loc:*** SM, Da84, Hi02, ThCa>

puie ♦see **pluie**

puis[1] **(pis, épis, épuis, et puis)** [pɥi, pi, epi, epɥi] *adv.* **1** then, after that, next, later *On parle toujours français et anglais. On commence une conversation en français et puis on finit en anglais des fois.* We always speak French and English. We start a conversation in French and we then finish it in English sometimes. (SL) **Et puis là, il est arrivé.* And then he arrived. (Da84) **Et pis là il a quitté.* After that he left. (Da84) **2** furthermore, besides *Un jour, j'ai décidé j'aurais vendu tous les bêtes. J'étais lasse et puis c'était dur pour nous-autres.* One day, I decided I would sell all the cows. I was tired and besides it was hard for us. (SL) <***Loc:*** AC, EV, IV, LA, SL, SM, VM, Da84, Hi02, Lv88, Re31>

puis[2] **(pis, épis, épuis, et puis)** [pɥi, pi, epi, epɥi] *conj.* and *Ta mère puis ton père.* Your mother and your father. (ch: *Là-bas chez Moreau*) *Mais là avec ça elle avait du riz,* OF COURSE, *puis des fèves plates, des patates douces et de la salade de pommes de terre.* So, with that she had rice, of course, and butter beans, sweet potatos and potato salad. (ThCa: *Le charivari*) *Puis, à penser qu'on l'avait juste invitée à venir avec nous-autres parce que ça faisait pitié de la voir brailler et puis rester regarder les quatre coins de la maison.* Then to think that we had just invited her to come with us because it was so pitiful to see her crying and staying at home staring at the four walls. (ThCa: *La table des veuves*) <***Loc:*** LA, ThCa>

puisque (plusque) [pɥisk, plysk] *conj.* because, since, as, inasmuch as *Plusque Pape veut pas, je peux pas aller.* Because Dad doesn't want it, I can't go. (VM) <***Loc:*** VM, Da84>

puissance [pɥisɑ̃s] *n.f.* power, force, strength <***Loc:*** Da84>

puissant, -e [pɥisɑ̃, -ɑ̃t] *adj.* [*eccl.*] powerful, strong, mighty ◊ **•le Père tout-puissant** the almighty Father <Da84> <***Loc:*** Da84>

puiter [pɥite] *v.intr.* to rain <***Loc:*** JE>

puits [pɥi] *n.m.* **1** well *Tu sais qui il faulait qu'on fait? Mettre une cruche d'eau dedans un puits. Y avait un puits pour avoir de l'eau. [...] Et mettre une corde et quitter ça aller dans le puits pour avoir de l'eau fraîche.* You know what we had to do? Put a water jug in a well. There was a well for getting water. And put a rope on, and let it go down into the well to get cool water. (TB) **2** oil well *Et là après ça ils drillont ça qu'ils voulont, mais ils allont jusqu'à quinze milles pieds. Y a des puits qu'a été plus creux que ça. Et ça dépend qui-ce qu'ils tapont.* And after that they drill what they want to, but they go down as far as fifteen thousand feet. There are wells that that have gone deeper than that. It depends what they hit. (LF) **3** pit *Ils ont fouillé un puits de terre grasse.* They dug a clay pit. (LA) ◊ **•puits à {d'} eau** water well *On avait des puits à eau, on pompait de l'eau avec des pompes à la main.* We had water wells, we pumped water out with hand pumps. (AS) <AS, VM, Fa77> **•puits d'huile** ***a*** oil rig ***b*** oil well *Pour fouiller des puits d'huile dessus la terre.* To dig oil wells on the ground. (SL) <SL, SM, VM, Da84, Gr86, Hi02> <***Loc:*** AS, LA, LF, SL, TB, VM, Da84, Fa77, Hi02>

pulluler (pilluler) [pylyle, pilyle] *v.intr.* **1** to swarm, teem *Les fourmis ont pullulé sur sa jambe quand elle a marché sur le nique.* The ants swarmed on her leg when she stepped on the nest. (VM) **2** to be crawling with, be overrun with (ants, etc.) <***Loc:*** JD, Da84>

PUMPKIN (ponkine) [pɔ̃kin] *n.f.* pumpkin *J'ai mangé de la ponkine pour dîner.* I ate some pumpkin for dinner. (TB) <***Loc:*** TB>

punaise [pynɛz] *n.f.* **1** stink bug *Là il y a les punaises. J'ai des tomates dans mon jardin et ça me les a massacrées et je les ai abandonnées je sais pas combien de fois.* Then there are stink bugs. I've got tomatoes in my garden, and they've massacred them and I've had to abandon them I don't how many times. (SL) **2** bedbug *La maison des voisins était plein de punaises.* The neighbors' house was full of bedbugs. (VM) ◊ **•punaise de bois** wood tick <IB> **•punaise de champ {clos}** corn bug, chinch bug <IB> **•punaise de maison {lit}** bedbug <EV, IB> <***Loc:*** EV, IB, SL, Da84>

PUNCH[1] [pɔ̃ʃ] *n.m. (occ. f.)* punch (beverage of fruit juice, sugar, and water, and sometimes alcohol) <***Loc:*** VM, Da84, Fa77>

PUNCH[2] [pʌntʃ] *n.m.* punch, pointed tool to mark or punch holes <***Loc:*** Da84>

punir [pynir] *v.tr.* **1** to punish **Le Bon Dieu l'a puni pour quelque chose.* God punished him for something. (SL, An94) *Eusse voulait pas on parle français, eusse nous punissait si on nous attrapait après parler francais avec un autre.* They did not want us to speak French, they would punish us if we were caught speaking French with someone else. (IB) **2** to disturb *Ça me punit pas du tout que vous venez icite.* It doesn't disturb me at all that you come here. (VM) <***Loc:*** AC, IB, SL, VM, An94, Da84>

punition [pynisjɔ̃] *n.f.* punishment *Ils avaient pas de punition, non, mais on savait qu'eux-autres aimait pas ça.* There was no punishment, but we knew they didn't like it. (TB) <***Loc:*** SL, TB, An94, Da84>

pupie ♦see **pépie**

pur, -e [pyr] *adj.* **1** pure, unadulterated, unmixed *Moi j'appelle mon langage le cadien, et elle c'était le pur français.* I call my language Cajun, and hers is pure French. (AS) *Lui je crois pas qu'il est un pur Cadien, il a ramassé le patois, tu sais.* I don't think he's a pure Cajun, he picked up the dialect you know. (TB) **Pur nègre.* Pure negro. (Da84) *Il s'a blessé loin dans le fond des bois. C'est par pure chance que son frère l'a trouvé.* He got hurt deep in the woods. It was pure luck that his brother found him. (LA) *Ça qui est assez bon pour mon père est assez bon pour mon. Je vas rester Cadien pur.* What's good enough for my father is good enough for me. I'll remain pure Cajun. (ThCa: *Mille misères*) **2** sexually chaste, virginal *Pour trouver une fille pure, il faut chercher jeune.* To find a chaste girl, it is necessary to search [among the] young. (VM) **3** innocent, good, guiltless <***Loc:*** AS, TB, VM, Da84, ThCa>

pure [pyr] *n.m./f.* **1** billiard ball **2** clear glass playing marble <***Loc:*** SM, VM, Lv88>

purée [pyre] *n.f.* mash, puree <***Loc:*** Da84>

purement [pyrmɑ̃] *adv.* purely *Il était purement couillon.* He was purely foolish. (VM) <***Loc:*** VM, Da84>

pureté [pyrte] *n.f.* purity, innocence, chastity <***Loc:*** Da84>

purgatif, -ive [pyrgatif, -iv] *adj.* purgative *Mange pas trop de prunes. C'est purgatif.* Don't eat too many prunes. They have a purgative effect. (VM) <***Loc:*** VM, Da84>

purgative [pyrgativ] *n.f.* purgative <***Loc:*** Da84>

purgatoire [pyrgatwar] *n.m.* Purgatory <***Loc:*** VM, Fa77>

purge [pyrʒ] *n.f.* **1** purge **2** purgative, laxative *Il faulait que je prends une purge.* I had to take a laxative. (TB) *Une autre chose, quand j'ai fait les ingrédients pour Happy Day Powder, j'ai mis une purge dans la poudre. Tu connais que le mal de tête est souvent occasionné par la constipation.* Another thing, when I put together the ingredients for Happy Day Powder, I put a purgative in the powder. You know that headaches are often caused by constipation. (ThCa: *Messieurs, mesdames*) <***Loc:*** LF, TB, VM, Da84, ThCa>

purger [pyrʒe, pyrʒete] **I** *v.tr.* to purge, clean out *Tous les printemps, ça nous purgeait avec de l'huile de castor.* Every spring, they would purge us with castor oil. (VM) **II se purger** *v.pron.* to purge o.s., take a laxative *Il se purge avec du* COAL OIL *et du sucre.* He purges himself with coal oil and sugar. (LA) <***Loc:*** JE, LA, VM, Da84>

purification [pyrifikasjɔ̃] *n.f.* **1** purification, cleansing, disinfecting **2** [*eccl.*] Purification <***Loc:*** Da84>

purifier [pyrifje, pyryfje] **I** *v.tr.* to purify, refine, cleanse *C'est à la grande sucrerie qu'ils purifiont le sucre.* It's at the big sugar mill that they refine the sugar. (VM) **II se purifier** *v.pron.* to purify o.s., cleanse o.s. *Tu te confesses pour te purifier avant d'aller à la communion.* You confess to purify yourself before going to communion. (VM) <***Loc:*** VM, Da84>

purisie ♦see **pleurésie**

puron ♦see **suppuron**

pus[1] (**pu, p'us, plus**) [py] *adv.* no more, no longer **J'en ai pu.* I have no more. I don't have any more. (Da84) **Il vient pu ici.* He no longer comes here. (Da84) **Il y en a pu.* There is no more. (Da84) *J'avais faim, mais j'ai p'us faim depus j'ai mangé.* I was hungry, but I'm no longer hungry since I ate. (SM) **Il a pus de dépense.* He has no more expenses. (Da84) **Il peut pus rien faire.* He can no longer do anything. (Da84) **Il peut pus manger.* He cannot eat any more. (Da84) **Je peux pu attendre.* I cannot wait any longer. (Re31) <***Loc:*** AC, AV, EV, IB, JE, LA, LF, SM, TB, VM, An94, Da84, Hi02, Re31, Wh83>

pus[2] ♦see **plus**

pustule [pystyl] *n.f.* pustule, pimple <***Loc:*** Da84>

putain (**putaine**) [pytɛ̃, pytɛ̃n] *n.f.* whore, prostitute, hooker **Fils de putain!* Son of a bitch! (Da84) <***Loc:*** IB, LA, SM, VM, Da84, Hi02>

putaine ♦see **putain**

putainer [pytɛ̃ne] *v.intr.* **1** to frequent prostitutes *Elle pouvait pas l'empêcher de putainer d'un bord et de l'autre.* She couldn't prevent him from frequenting prostitutes everywhere. (LA) **2** to be promiscuous, whore around *Elle devrait bien arrêter de putainer comme ça, à cause de sa petite fille.* She ought to stop carrying on like a prostitute like that because of her daughter. (LA) <***Loc:*** LA, Da84>

putainerie [pytɛ̃nri] *n.f.* prostitution <***Loc:*** Da84>

PUTTPUTT (**PUT-PUT**) [pœtpœt, pɔtpɔt] *n.m.* **1** inboard motor (on a boat) **2** very slow boat (2-3 hp) *Les* PUT-PUT *c'est une qualité de bateaux on utilisait dans le temps. C'est le train ça faisait. T'avais pas la peine pagayer.* Put-puts were a kind of boat used at one time. It was the noise it made. You did not need to paddle. (SM) <***Loc:*** LF, SM>

pyjamas (**pajamas**) [piʒɑ̃ma, paʒɑ̃ma] *n.m.pl.* pyjamas, night clothes <***Loc:*** AL, Da84>

Q

qu' ♦see **que**

quadrille [kadrij] *n.f.* quadrille, square dance <***Loc:*** Da84>

qual ♦see **quel**

qualification [kalifikasjɔ̃] *n.f. (usu. pl.)* qualification <***Loc:*** SM, Di32, Lv88>

qualifié, -e [kalifje] *adj.* qualified, having the necessary qualifications <***Loc:*** SM, Da84, Di32>

qualifier [kalifje] *v.tr.* to qualify *Son école le qualifie pas pour faire ça.* His education doesn't qualify him to do that. (LA) <***Loc:*** LA, Da84, Di32>

qualité [kalite] *n.f.* **1** quality **On avait du monde ici qui jonglait qu'un musicien, c'était quelqu'un qu'avait pas trop des bonnes qualités, pas trop responsable, mais moi, je me considère pas comme ça.* There were people here who thought that a musician was someone who didn't have too many good qualities, not responsible, but I don't consider myself like that. (VM, An84) **2** sort, kind, type, variety *Toutes qualités de poissons.* All sorts of fish. (Lv88) *On a perdu toutes qualités d'affaires.* We lost all kinds of things [in the hurricane]. (JE) *Il n-a toutes qualités de monde.* There are all kinds of people. (Lv88) *C'est les seules qualités de fleurs que je connais, moi.* Those are the only varieties of flowers I'm familiar with. (VM) ◊ **•différentes qualités de / différent de qualités de** different kinds of *Différentes qualités de musique.* Different types of music. (Lv88) *Il n-a beaucoup de différent de qualités de serpents.* There are a lot of different kinds of snakes. (SL) *Dans le maïs, il y a des chenilles, différent de qualités de chenilles.* In the corn, there are caterpillars, different kinds of caterpillars. (SL) <SL, Lv88> <***Loc:*** JE, SL, SM, VM, An84, Da84, Gu00, Hi02, Lv88>

quand[1] (**équand, et quand**) [kɑ̃, kɑ̃t, ekɑ̃] *conj.* **1** when **Je me rappelle équand on était pitites.* I remember when we were young. (Gu82) *Je vas venir quand que je pourra.* I'll come when I can. (TB) **Il va venir quand il sera paré.* He will come when he is ready. (Da84) **2** whenever *Lui mettait son pied par terre, équand il voulait que nous-autres on fait quelque chose.* He would put his foot down, whenever he wanted us to do something. (TB) ◊ **•quand même** [kɑ̃mɛ̃m, kamɛ̃m] ***a*** even so, anyway *Ils ont dansé quand même.* They danced anyway. (AV) *Il le faisait quand même.* He did it anyway. (AC) *Ouais, une sage-femme. [...] Mais quand même elle était bonne bonne.* Yes, a midwife. But even so, she was very good. (EV) ***b*** *(intensifier)* really **Ça c'est fort quand-même.* That's really strong. (Da84) **Ça, quand même!* Now really! (expression of disapproval or reproach) (La99) <AC, AV, EV, LA, Da84, La99> **•quand même (que)** even when, even if, even though *Quand même eusse comprend, eusse veut pas parler.* Even when they understand, they don't want to speak it. (TB) *L'hiver c'était plein froid. Quand même que t'étais en-dedans, c'était plein froid.* In the winter it was quite cold. Even if you were indoors, it was quite cold. (LF) *Tu connais, quand même tu fais mal, le Bon Dieu te pardonne.* You know, even if you do [something] bad, the Good Lord will forgive you. (EV) *Quand même tu me dis ça, je peux pas le croire.* Even if you tell me that, I can't believe it. (Lv88) *Eux-autres te paye quand même tu peux plus travailler.* They pay you even though you can't work any more. (TB) *Quand même que c'est prononcé un petit peu différent, le monde se comprend.* Even if it's pronounced a little bit differently, people understand each other. (LF) <AV, EV, LF, TB, Da84, La99, Lv88> **•quand même que... ou non** whether . . . or not *J'aime parler. Et je dis, quand même qu'eusse me comprend ou non, que c'est en anglais ou en français, j'ai dit je vas parler.* I like to talk. And I say, whether they understand me or not, whether it's in English or in French, I said I'm going to talk. (TB) <TB> <***Loc:*** AV, EV, LF, TB, Da84, Gu82, Hi02, La99, Lv88>

quand[2] (**équand, et quand**) [kɑ̃, kɑ̃t, ekɑ̃] *adv.interrog.* when *Quand-ce tu comptes arriver là-bas?* When do you expect to get there? (TB) **Équand ce que tu reviens, mon bon vieux mari?* When will you come back, my good old husband? (ch: *Mon bon vieux mari*) **Et quand tu vas venir?* When are you coming? (Da84) <***Loc:*** AC, AV, EV, LF, SM, TB, VM, Da84, Gu00, Hi02, La99, Lv88>

quant [kɑ̃t] ◊ **•quant à** as for, in regard to *Quant à toi, tu vas jamais comprendre!* As for you, you'll never understand! (VM) <***Loc:*** VM, Da84, Hi02>

quantième (**comptième, quantier**) [kɑ̃tjɛ̃m, kɑ̃tʃe] *n.m.* date (of the month, year, etc.) *Équel quantième du mois on est aujourd'hui?* What's the date today? (TB) **Quel comptième on est aujourd'hui?* What is today's date? (Da84) <***Loc:*** TB, Da84, Hi02>

quantier[1] (**cantier**) [kɑ̃tje, kɑ̃tʃe] *n.m.* **1** moccasin or shoe of rawhide or deerskin **Défunt Sosthène faisait des cantiers pour travailler à l'entour de l'habitation... I' faisait ça avec d'la peau, côme d'la peau de vache ou d'la peau de rat musqué. I' coupait des lisières de peau pour faire côme des cordes... pis i'cousait ça avec ces babiches-là.* Late Sosthène would make mocassins to work around the farm . . . He would make them with skins, like cow hide or muskrat skins. He would cut thin lengths of skin, to make like cords . . . then he would sew them with those lashes.

(Gu82) **2** old shoe *Mets tes quantiers et va dans la cour.* Put on your old shoes and go out in the yard. (SM) *Ote tes cantiers avant de rentrer dans la maison.* Take off your old shoes before you come into the house. (Lv88) <*Loc:* EV, LA, LF, SJ, SL, SM, TB, Gu82, Lv88, Ph36, Re31>

quantier[2] ♦see **quantième**

quantité [kɑ̃tite] *n.f.* **1** quantity, amount *Tu peux mettre la quantité que tu veux, t'as pas de limites pour les lignes.* You can put out the quantity you want, there's no limit on alligator lines. (TB) *Des chevreuils, il y en avait en haut d'ici, mais pas des grosses quantités, il y en avait un peu de ça, THOUGH.* Deer, there used to be some up the bayou from here, but not in large numbers; there were some though. (TB) **2** considerable quantity, large number **Il y en a une quantité.* There are a lot [of them]. (Da84) <*Loc:* EV, TB, Da84>

quarantaine [karɑ̃tɛ̃n] *n.f.* about forty **Il a une quarantaine d'années.* He is about forty years old. (Da84) ◊ **•faire une quarantaine** to make a scene, create an uproar <AV, SJ> <*Loc:* AV, SJ, Da84>

quarante [karɑ̃t] *adj./n.m.* forty **Ils avaient quarante sous dans leurs poches entre eux-autres deux.* They had forty cents in their pockets between the two of them. (SL, An94) <*Loc:* AC, AV, EV, SC, SL, TB, An94, Da84, Hi02, La99>

quarante-quatre [karɑ̃tkat(r)] *n. (usu. pl.)* red bean **J'ai mangé des quarante-quatre pour dîner.* I ate red beans for dinner. (SC, La99) <*Loc:* SC, La99>

quarantième [karɑ̃tjɛ̃m] *adj./n.* fortieth *Ils sont après célébrer leur quarantième anniversaire de mariage.* They are celebrating their fortieth wedding anniversary. (LA) <*Loc:* LA, Da84>

quarantine [karɑ̃tin] *n.f.* quarantine <*Loc:* Da84>

quarantiner [karɑ̃tine] **I** *v.tr.* to quarantine, isolate, segregate *Ils ont jamais réussi à quarantiner les Cadiens en bas du bayou.* They were never able to quarantine the Cajuns on the lower part of the bayou. (LA) **II se quarantiner** *v.pron.* to quarantine o.s. *Le monde a eu pour se quarantiner pour pas attraper la grande fièvre.* People had to quarantine themselves to avoid catching yellow fever. (LA) <*Loc:* LA, Da84, Lv88>

quart [kar] *n.m.* **1** quarter, one fourth *À peu près un quart de mile d'ici.* Approximately a quarter mile from here. (TB) **2** quart **Un quart de vin.* A quart of wine. (Da84) ◊ **•quart de gallon** quart <Da84> **•quart d'heure** quarter of an hour *J'ai fait de la radio pendant vingt-cinq ans. Une émission concernant l'agriculture, pendant un quart d'heure tous les matins.* I did radio [broadcasts] for twenty-five years. A program about agriculture, for a quarter of an hour every morning. (SL) <SL> <*Loc:* LA, SL, TB, Da84, Hi02, Lv88>

quarteron, -onne [kartrɔ̃, kaltrɔ̃, -ɔ̃n] *n.* **1** person who has one black and three white grandparents **2** light-skinned mulatto, usu. with predominantly Caucasian features **3** person of mixed white and African-American blood (regardless of the proportion of each race) *Ah oui, il y en a de ces quarterons en bas du bayou.* Oh yes, there are mixed bloods down the bayou. (TB) <*Loc:* SJ, TB, Lv88>

quarti [kwarti, karti] *n.m.* **1** two and a half cents **2** amount or quantity of goods that could be bought for two and a half cents (esp. on plantations) *Un quarti de sel et un quarti de sucre.* Half a nickel's worth of salt and half a nickel's worth of sugar. (SJ) <*Loc:* IB, SJ, SM, Lv88, Re31>

quartier [kartje] *n.m.* **1** fourth part, quarter (of meat, land, etc.) *On les mettait par quartier, quatre quartiers par bête: deux quartiers d'en avant et deux quartiers d'en arrière. [...] là où les côtes commencent, ça c'est le quartier d'en avant.* They [carcasses of butchered animals] were divided up into quarters, four quarters per animal: two forequarters and two hindquarters. Where the ribs begin, that's the front quarter. (VM) *Il a eu pour vendre un quartier pour payer ses taxes.* He had to sell a quarter [of his section] to pay his taxes. (LA) **2** quarter, phase of the moon **3** area or district of a city **Le Quartier Français.* The French Quarter (in New Orleans). (Da84) **4** *(pl.)* living quarters *J'ai une amie qu'a transformé ses quartiers d'esclaves en BED AND BREAKFAST.* I have a friend who turned her [former] slave quarters into a Bed & Breakfast. (VM) <*Loc:* LA, SL, VM, Da84, Hi02>

quasiment [kazimɑ̃] *adv.* almost, nearly <*Loc:* JD, Di32>

quatorze [katɔrz] *adj./n.m.* fourteen **Depuis l'âge de quatorze ans, je suis après rouler manche à manche.* Since I was fourteen years old, I've been rambling from one back road to another. (ch: *La valse du bambocheur*) <*Loc:* AC, EV, TB, An94, Da84, Hi02>

quatorzième [katɔrzjɛ̃m] *adj./n.* fourteenth *C'est le quatorzième veau qu'on perd cette année.* That's the fourteenth calf we're losing this year. (LA) <*Loc:* LA, Da84>

quatre [kat(r)] *(before a consonant* [kat], *before a vowel* [katr, katz]) *adj./n.m.* four **Le quatre de juillet.* The fourth of July. (Da84) ◊ **•quatre-par-quatre** four-by-four (piece of lumber) *Je crois que c'était une trente-et-un MODEL T FORD. Il pagaillait à Houma avec ça dans la boue. Et il follait qu'eusse se met des chaînes et ç'apportait un quatre-par-quatre ou une grosse branche de bois là.* I think it was a 1931 Model T Ford. He used to paddle to Houma in that in the mud. And they would have to put on chains and they would bring along a four-by-four or a big branch [just in case]. (TB) <TB, Lv88> **•quatre-par-six** four-by-six (piece of lumber) <Lv88> **•quatre-z-as** four aces (hand of cards) <JE> **•deux-par-quatre** two-by-four (piece of lumber) *C'était fait avec un deux-par-quatre, deux pouces d'épais et quatre pouces de large.* That was made with a two-by-four, two inches thick and four inches wide. (LF) <LF> **•faire les quatre-cents coups** to raise all kinds of hell <Da84> **•un de ces quatre matins** one of these days <AV, La99> <*Loc:*

AC, AV, EV, IV, JE, LF, SM, TB, VM, An94, Da84, Hi02, La99, Lv88>

quatre heures [katrœr] *n.* four o'clock (flowering plant) <***Loc:*** VM>

quatre-chemins [katʃmɛ̃] *n.f.pl.* crossroads, intersection *Fais attention quand tu arrives aux quatre-chemins.* Be careful when you get to the intersection. (VM) <***Loc:*** VM>

Quatre-Temps [kat:ɑ̃] *n.m.* [*eccl.*] Ember Days (days of fasting and abstinence at the beginning of each season in the ecclesiastical calendar) *Les autres fois, le monde faisait maigre les mercredis, jeudis et samedis des Quatre-Temps.* In the old days, people would fast on the Wednesday, Thursday, and Saturday of Ember Days. (VM) <***Loc:*** VM, Da84>

quatre-vingts [katrəvɛ̃] *adj./n.m.* eighty *Il m'a payé quatre-vingts piastres pour le veau.* He paid me eighty dollars for the calf. (LA) <***Loc:*** LA, Da84, Hi02>

quatre-vingt-dix [katrəvɛ̃dis] *adj./n.m.* ninety **Jake pesait à peu près quatre-vingt-dix livres, tu sais.* Jake weighed about ninety pounds, you know. (IB, An94) **O moi, je m'en va's condamné pour quatre-vingt-dix-neuf ans.* Oh me, I'm going away, condemned for ninety-nine years. (ch: *La valse de quatre-vingt-dix-neuf ans*) <***Loc:*** EV, IB, An94, Da84, Hi02>

quatre-vingt-dixième [katrəvɛ̃dizjɛ̃m] *adj./n.* ninetieth <***Loc:*** EV, LA>

quatre-vingtième [katrəvɛ̃tjɛ̃m] *adj./n.* eightieth <***Loc:*** EV, LA>

quatre-z-yeux [katzjø] *n.* type of jellyfish <***Loc:*** JE>

quatrième [katrijɛ̃m] *adj./n.* fourth *Et puis là d'autres enfants à Monsieur Amédé Miller, aussi, eux restait la quatrième terre de la terre à nous-autres.* And then other children of Mr. Amédé Miller also lived on the fourth estate over from us. (IB) <***Loc:*** IB, An94, Da84>

quatrièmement [katrijɛ̃m:ɑ̃] *adv.* fourthly, in the fourth place *Et quatrièmement, t'as pas assez d'argent pour commencer.* And fourthly, you don't have enough money to get started. (LA) <***Loc:*** LA, Da84>

que[1] [kə] (*before a vowel* **qu'** [k]) *adv. (excl.)* how **Que c'est beau.* How beautiful. (Da84) <***Loc:*** Da84>

que[2] [kə] (*before a vowel* **qu'** [k]) *conj.* **1** that *C'est foutant que je peux pas faire ce que je veux.* It's annoying that I can't do what I want. (LF) **Je m'étais aperçu qu'il y avait quelque chose qui était* WRONG. I had realized that there was something wrong. (SL, An94) *Il faudra que je fais mon idée.* I'll have to make up my mind. (ch: *La valse d'ennui*) **Je crois que tu es riche.* I think that you are rich. (Da84) **2** until, till **Espère que j'arrive.* Wait till I arrive. (Da84) **3** whether **Qu'il soit riche ou pauvre, ça fait aucune différence.* Whether he is rich or poor makes no difference. (Da84) **4** only **Il a que se taire.* He has only to shut up. (Da84) **Tu as juste qu'à me dire.* You have only to tell me. (Da84) *Et mon j'avais pas d'enfants, et elle alle avait qu'une petite fille.* And I had no children, and she had only a little girl. (TB) **5** *(second element in comparative constructions)* as, than **Aussi grand que lui.* As tall as he is. (Da84) *Aussi bien que je peux voir* As far as I can see. (Da84) **J'en ai moins que lui.* I have less than he has. (Da84) **J'aime un tas, ça c'est plus que toi tu peux dire pour moi.* I love [you] so much; that's more than you can say for me. (ch: *I don't want you anymore*) **Ça que j'trouve encore plus trist' que ça, c'est que […] j'ai des enfants qui croyont […] qu'i' sont des Amaricains.* What I find even sadder than that is that I have children who think they are [Anglo-]Americans. (Gu82) **Alle avait jâmais a'tendu arien d'aut' que l'français cadjin.* She had never heard anything other than Cajun French. (Gu82) **Il a pas de support que le mien.* He has no other support than mine. (Da84) **Personne d'autre que vous.* No one else besides you. (Da84) <***Loc:*** AC, AV, EV, IB, IV, LA, LF, SB, SL, TB, VM, An84, An94, Da84, Di32, Gu82, La99, Lv88, Ph36, Wh83>

que[3] [kə] (*before a vowel* **qu'** [k]) *pron.rel.* **1** which, that *Ça c'est eine allure que t'as avec cette robe.* That's quite a look that you've get with that dress. (TB) *La première paire de souliers que mon j'ai mis mes pieds dedans là, eh ben, j'ai payé pour moi-même.* The first pair of shoes that I ever put my feet in, well, I paid for myself. (TB) **2** whom **J'ai marié une chère tite fille, une petite fille que moi j'aimais.* I married a dear li'l girl, a little girl whom I loved. (ch: *Cajun crawl*) **3** about which, about whom *Le garçon que je te parle.* The boy whom I'm talking to you about. (Lv88) **4** of which *Dans ce temps-là que je parle.* In the time I'm talking about. (Lv88) **Il y a bien des choses que j'ai besoin.* There are many things that I need. (Re31) **5** whose *L'homme que son garçon est mort.* The man whose son is dead. (Gu50) **6** where **Oui, la place que moi, je voudrais mourir, c'est dans les bras de mon 'tit bébé.* Yes, the place where I would like to die is in the arms of my little darling. (ch: *Reno waltz*) **7** when **C'est ça la valse qui jouait au temps, dans le temps que je courtisais.* That's the waltz that was playing then, at the time when I was courting [her]. (ch: *La valse du malchanceux*) <***Loc:*** JE, VM, Da84, Hi02, Lv88, Re31>

que[4] [kə] (*before a vowel* **qu'** [k]) *pron.interrog. (usu. in compound expr.)* ◊ **•qu'est-ce que** what *Qu'est-ce que c'est ça?* What's that? (VM) <VM> <***Loc:*** JE, VM, Da84, Hi02, Lv88, Re31>

que[5] [kə] (*before a vowel* **qu'** [k]) *(interrog. marker used after question words) D'où que tu viens?* Where are you from? (Lv88) *Mais je dis comment que tu vas aller parler avec ce monde-là?* But I said, how are you going to go and talk to those people? (LF) *La raison pourquoi que mon je parle toujours français c'est que mes grands-parents tout le temps parlaient français.* The reason I still speak French is that my grandparents always spoke French. (LF) *Ça lui mande quo'faire que tu viens jamais nous visiter.* They ask him, why don't you ever come visit us? (LF) <*Loc:* LF, Lv88>

qué[1] [ke] *pron.interrog.* what (used to ask for repetition of something not heard clearly) *Un qué?* A what? (PQ) <*Loc:* PQ>

qué[2] ♦see **quel**

quède (**quiède, tiède**) [kɛd, kjɛd, tjɛd, tʃɛd] *adj.* **1** lukewarm, tepid *L'eau est quède.* The water is lukewarm. (LF) *L'eau quède, ni chaud ni glacé.* Lukewarm water, neither hot nor cold. (JE) *Un tas des fois, on mettait ça au soleil quand on ramassait du coton, puis là le soir c'était quède là, tu connais.* Many times, it would be placed in the sun when the cotton was collected, then in the evening it would be tepid, you know. (LA) **2** ordinary, middling, mediocre *Je connais pas quoi faire, mais mes tomates sont manière tièdes cette année.* I don't know why, but my tomatoes are very mediocre this year. (SM) <*Loc:* AC, AV, IB, JE, LA, LF, SB, SJ, SM, TB, Da84, Lv88>

quédir [kedir, kjedir, kɛdzir] **I** *v.tr.* to make lukewarm (by heating or cooling) *Si tu mets ton gombo devant l'éventail, ça va le quédir plus vite.* If you put your gumbo in front of the fan, it will cool it faster. (LA) **II** *v.intr.* to grow lukewarm, become tepid *Bois ton café avant ça quédit.* Drink your coffee before it becomes lukewarm. (LA) <*Loc:* LA, VM, Lv88>

quel[1], **-lle** (**qual, -e, queul, -e, équel, -lle, aquel, -lle**) [kɛl, kal, kœl, ekɛl, akɛl] (*before a consonant often* **qué, queu, équé, aqué** [ke, kø, eke, ake]) *adj.* **1** *(interrog.)* what, which **Quelle étoile dans le ciel qui est toi aujourd'hui?* Which star in the sky are you today? (ch: *Quelle étoile*) *Équelle fille tu parlais pour?* Which girl were you talking about? (VM) **Qué jour qu'on est aujourd'hui?* What day is it today? (La99) **Quelle heure qu'il est?* What time is it? (La99) **Dans quelle année que t'es né?* In what year were you born? (La99) **Quel âge que tu as?* How old are you? (La99) *Qué cheval est pour vous?* Which horse is yours? (SB) **Qué jour que tu viendras me voir?* What day will you come to see me? (Di32) **Queu mal je te fais?* What harm am I doing you? (Di32) *Il va faire 29 dans janvier pour sûr, je me rappelle pas juste équé date c'était.* He'll be 29 in January, for sure, I don't remember just what date it was. (TB) *Equel âge que Tante L. a?* How old is Aunt L.? (TB) **2** *(excl.)* what, what a **Quelle beauté!* What beauty! (Da84) <*Loc:* JE, TB, VM, Da84, Di32, Gu82, La99>

quel[2], **-lle** (**qual, -e, queul, -e, équel, -lle, aquel, -lle, lequel, laquelle**) [kɛl, kal, kœl, ekɛl, akɛl, akœl, ekøl, løkɛl, løkøl] *pron.interrog.* **1** which, which one **Quel tu choisis?* Which one do you choose? (Da84) *C'est quel des deux qu'est l'aîné?* Which of the two is the oldest? (LA) *Équel c'est que tu parlais pour?* Which one were you talking about? (VM) **D'équel que tu parles?* Which one are you talking about? (La99) *Aquelle de mes soeurs?* Which one of my sisters? (TB) **Ça c'est mes chevals. Équel que tu veux acheter?* These are my horses. Which one do you want to buy? (La89) **A équelles de tes soeurs que cet enfant appartient?* To which one of your sisters does this child belong? (La99) **2** who, whom **Quel qui est le plus fort?* Who is the strongest? (Da84) *Équel tu as fait ça pour?* Whom did you do that for? (LF) *Je sais pas équel c'est qu'a tiré le premier coup.* I don't who it is who fired the first shot. (VM) <*Loc:* EV, LA, LF, VM, Hi02, La99>

quéloëtement [kelwɛtmɑ̃] *n.m.* **1** winking **2** blinking <*Loc:* JE, VM, Di32>

quéloëter [kelwete, kalwete] *v.intr.* **1** to wink **2** to blink <*Loc:* JE, LA, TB, VM, Di32>

quelqu'un, -e (**quèqu'un, -e**) [kekɛ̃, kekœ̃, køkɛ̃, tʃekɛ̃, -ɛ̃n] *pron.indef.* someone **Je vois vous êtes en peine. Vous avez perdu quelqu'un de votre famille?* I see that you are grieving. Did you lose someone from your family? (LA, An94) *On va tout périr ici, si quelqu'un arrive pas avec du manger.* We'll all die here, if someone doesn't arrive with food. (LA) **Quelqu'un m'appelle.* Someone is calling me. (SM, An94) **Il y a quelqu'un là?* Is someone there? (Da84) ◊ **•quelqu'un d'autre** someone else *J'étais déjà promis à quelqu'un d'autre quand j'ai rencontré ton père.* I was already promised to someone else when I met your father. (VM) <LA, SL, SM, VM, An94> **•quelqu'uns** a few, some *Y avait quelqu'uns de les police qui travaillait avec mon qui parlait français. Et on parlait français parmi nous-autres. Mais on conduisait tout notre ouvrage en anglais.* There were some of the police who spoke French. We would speak French together. But we carried out all our work in English. (LF) <LF, TB> **•quelques-uns / quelques-unes** a few, some **Quelques unes des femmes sont malades.* Some of the women are sick. (Da84) <Da84> **•tout quelqu'un** everyone **Et tout quelqu'un avait des bons couteaux.* And everyone had good knives. (SL, An94) **Il jouait des niches, et tout quelqu'un l'aimait parce qu'il les faisait rire.* He played jokes, and everyone liked him because he made them laugh. (LA, An94) <AC, LA, LF, SL, SM, An94, Hi02> <*Loc:* AC, AV, EV, JE, LA, LF, SM, TB, VM, An94, Da84, Hi02, Re31>

quelque (**quèque**) [kɛlk(ə), kɛk] *adj.indef.* **1** some *J'ai essayé de penser à quelque manière de m'esquiver.* I tried to think of some way to avoid it. (ThCa: *Grosbecs*) *Tu devrais aller autour de Lafayette pour quelque temps.* You should go spend some time around Lafayette. (TB) *Ça fait là alle a rencontré Tommy, là, quelque temps après ça s'a marié.* So she met Tommy, and some time later they got married. (TB) **2** *(pl.)* some, a few **J'ai quelques piastres.* I have a few dollars. (Da84) **Quelques jours passés.* A few days ago. (Da84) **Il vendait un petit peu de whiskey à Lafayette. [...] Et bien là il amenait quelques galons pour vendre.* He sold a little bit of whiskey in Lafayette. So he would bring a few gallons to sell. (LA, An94) **Y avait quèques années qu'il avait arrêté de faire récolte.* He had stopped farming several years before. (VM, Gu82) *On piochait tout nos cannes à la main, on avait jusqu'à vingt et quelques piocheurs avec des pioches.* We used to hoe all our sugarcane by hand, we had twenty-some hoers with hoes. (AS) **Il avait un tas de la terre. Il avait deux cent et quelques arpents de terre.* He had a lot of land. He had two hundred and some arpents of land. (LA, An94) <***Loc:*** AC, AS, AV, IV, LA, SL, TB, VM, An94, Da84, Gu82, ThCa>

quelque chose (**quèque chose, quichose**) [kɛkʃoz, kɛkʃɔʒ, kɛtʃɔz, kiʃoz] *adv.indef.* something *Tiendre quelque chose en ta main.* To hold something in your hand. (JE) **Je veux te dire quelque chose.* I want to tell you something. (CL, An94) **Si eux-autres ont rêvé que tu leur as donné quelque chose, il faut tu leur donnes.* If they dreamed that you gave them something, you have to give it to them. (SL, An94) **Ils ont compris qu'il y avait quelque chose de drôle.* They understood that there was something funny. (EV, An94) *Il a trouvé quichose bien joli dans la malle.* He found something quite nice in the mail. (SB) ◊ **•tout quelque chose** everything **Faut que tout quèque chose souaye vite.* Everything must be quick. (Gu82) *Tout quelque chose était beau beau.* Everything was beautiful. (EV) <EV, LA, SM, An94, Gu82, Hi02> <***Loc:*** AC, EV, IV, JE, LA, SB, SL, SM, TB, VM, An94, Da84, Hi02, Gu82>

quelque part (**en quelque part**) [kɛkpar, ɑ̃kɛkpar] *adv.indef.* somewhere **Ça fait, Petit Jean a entendu ça. Il a sorti. Il s'a attrapé un* LOG *et il l'a mis dans son lit, et puis il s'a fourré quelque part.* So, Little John heard that. He went out. He got himself a log and he put it in his bed, and then he hid somewhere. (AC, An94) **Il a été en quelque part.* He went somewhere. (Da84) <***Loc:*** AC, SL, An84, An94, Da84>

quelque place (**en quelque place**) [kɛkplas, ɑ̃kɛkplas] *adv. indef.* somewhere *Eusse venait de quelque place dans la Louisiane.* They came from somewhere in Louisiana. (TB) *Vous allez quelque place d'autre avec votre message?* Are you going anywhere else with your message? (ThCa: *Messieurs, mesdames*) *Il a follu qu'il grouille en quelque place d'autre pour trouver une femme.* He had to move somewhere else to find a wife. (TB) <***Loc:*** LF, SL, TB, Hi02, ThCa>

quelque temps [kɛktɑ̃] *adv.indef.* sometime *Je vas passer par là quelque temps après midi.* I'll stop by there sometime after noon. (VM) <***Loc:*** VM>

quelquefois (**quèquefois**) [kɛlkəfwa, kɛkfwa] *adv.indef.* sometimes, occasionally *Quelquefois je me demande pourquoi* EVEN *je suis toujours là.* Sometimes I ask myself why I'm even still here. (SL) *Mais quèquefois les règlements étiont difficiles à suire.* But sometimes the rules were hard to follow. (ThCa: *Mille misères*) *Mémère moulait une et quelquefois deux pochées de maïs pour faire un pain de maïs doux.* Grandma ground one and sometimes two sackfuls of corn to make a sweet corncake. (TB) <***Loc:*** JD, SL, TB, Da84, Re31, ThCa>

quémander ♦see **tchamander**

quémandeur ♦see **tchamandeur**

quèqu'un ♦see **quelqu'un**

quèque chose ♦see **quelque chose**

quèque[1] [kɛk] *pron.interrog.* what *Quèque ça veut dire?* What does that mean? (VM) <***Loc:*** VM, Di32>

quèque[2] ♦see **quelque**

quèquefois ♦see **quelquefois**

querçon ♦see **tiercent**

querellailler [krɛlaje] **I** *v.tr.* to nag *Ma femme est tout le temps après me querellailler.* My wife is always nagging me. (LA) **II** *v.intr.* to quarrel, fuss, argue continuously or repeatedly *Ils estiont après querellailler entre eux-autres quand Mame a mis son pied par terre.* They were kind of quarreling among themselves when Mom put her foot down. (LA) <***Loc:*** LA, Da84>

querelle [kərɛl] *n.f.* quarrel, fuss, dispute ◊ **•en querelle** on the outs, not on speaking terms **Adam et le Bon Djeu était tout l'temps encrèles [=en querelle].* Adam and God were always on the outs. (Gr86) <EV, An94, Gr86> <***Loc:*** EV, An94, Da84, Gr86, Hi02>

quereller [krele] **I** *v.tr.* to scold **Clifton, je crois je vas foutre ça par terre. Je vas et je bois. Je me saoule. Là, le lendemain, ma femme me querelle.* Clifton, I think I'm going to throw that down. I go and I drink. I get drunk. Then the next day, my wife scolds me. (EV, JD, An84) **II** *v.intr.* to quarrel, fuss, argue *Ils ont querellé pour quelque chose.* They argued about something. (EV) **III se quereller** *v.pron.* to quarrel, bicker, make a fuss *Ils sont tout le temps après se quereller.* They are always quarreling. (LA) *Ils sont après se quereller avec leur cousins, les Babineaux.* They are quarreling with their Babineaux cousins. (LA) <***Loc:*** AC, EV, JD, LA, SM, An84, Da84, Hi02>

querelleur, -euse [krelœr, -øz] *adj.* quarrelsome *Merci bon Dieu, ma femme est pas querelleuse.* Thank God my wife is not quarrelsome. (LA) <***Loc:*** LA, Da84>

question [kɛstjɔ̃] *n.f.* **1** question **Je veux demander une question avant que je parte.* I want to ask a question before I leave. (EV, An94) **2** question, matter, issue *Mais la question est si tu parles français et si tu pratiques un peu, tu peux être capable le lire.* But the thing is if you speak French and you practice a little, you can acquire the ability to read it. (SL) **La question est ceci.* The question is this. (Da84) <***Loc:*** AC, AV, EV, SL, SM, An94, Da84, Hi02>

questionnement [kɛstjɔ̃nmɑ̃] *n.m.* questioning <***Loc:*** Da84>

questionner [kɛstjɔ̃ne] **I** *v.tr.* to question, ask *Je peux pas croire qu'il va me questionner pour ça.* I can't believe that he is going to question me about that. (LA) **II** *v.intr.* to inquire, ask *Je crois que tu devrais questionner pour savoir ayoù il reste.* I think you should ask to find out where he lives. (LA) <***Loc:*** LA, Da84>

questionneur, -euse [kɛstjɔ̃nœr, -øz] *n.* questioner, inquirer <***Loc:*** Da84>

quête [kɛt] *n.f.* **1** collection of funds (generally for religion or charity) **2** collection basket ◊ **•faire {passer} la quête *a*** to take up an offering, pass the basket or collection plate (at church) *Passer la quête à la messe.* To take up the offering during mass. (VM) *Ils ont passé la quête après la communion.* They took up the collection after communion. (EV) ***b*** to take up a collection *On va faire la quête. On va passer le chapeau.* We're going to take up a collection. We're going to pass the hat. (VM) ***c*** to ask for charity, ask for alms *Elle était rendu à faire la quête pour manger.* She was reduced to asking for charity in order to eat. (LA) <EV, LA, VM, Da84> <***Loc:*** EV, LA, VM, Da84, Fa77>

quêter (**tchêter**) [tʃete] **I** *v.tr.* to beg *Les petits de cette école sont tout le temps après me tchêter pour quelque chose.* The kids from that school are always begging me for something. (EV) **II** *v.intr.* to beg *Hier elle m'a demandé d'y donner cette vieille chaudière. Elle est tout le temps après tchêter.* Yesterday she asked me to give her that old pot. She's always begging for something. (EV) <***Loc:*** EV>

quêteur, -euse (**tchêteur, -euse, quêteux, -euse**) [tʃetœr, ketø, -øz] *n.* one who is always begging, beggar <***Loc:*** EV, VM>

quêteux see **quêteur**

queu ♦see **quel**

queue (**cheue, tcheue**) [kø, tʃø, tʃjø] *n.f.* **1** tail *La viande qu'est plus délicat c'est celle-là qu'est alentour le cou [...]. La partie qu'est sur la queue, la grande queue, c'est dur, c'est pas aussi tendre. Oh ouais, le cocodrie est bon à manger.* The most delicate meat is around the neck. The part on the tail, the big tail, it's hard, it's not as tender. Oh yes, alligator is good to eat. (IB) *Là le* RED SNAPPER *est proche pareil, mais il a pas les taches dessus la queue du tout.* The red snapper is almost the same, but he doesn't have the spots on his tail at all. (TB) **2** end (of a line, etc.) *Il a eu pour aller à la queue de la ligne.* He had to go to the end of the line. (LA) ◊ **•queue à ciseaux** Forster's tern <Re31> **•queue creuse** 'hollow tail' (malady believed by farmers to afflict livestock) <VM> **•queue de billard** pool cue *J'étais après venir avec ma queue de billard.* I was on my way with my pool cue. (LA) <LA> **•queue de capot** coattail **Quand il mentissait, il fallait tout le temps lui haler sur sa queue de capot.* When he would lie, one always had to pull on his coattail. (LA, An94) <LA, An94> **•queue de chaqui** barnyard grass <SB> **•queue de chat *a*** cattail plant ***b*** broom sedge <SB, Gu00, Hi02, Ho90, Lv88> **•queue de la comète *a*** one who is late for every and any occasion ***b*** rather insignificant person <SM> **•queue de loup** wild rice <Ho90> **•queue de rat *a*** rat-tail file *Tu peux pas faire un trou rond sans user une queue de rat.* You can't make a round hole without using a rat-tail file. (TB) ***b*** cattail plant <TB, Da84, Ho90, Hi02, Lv88, Re31> **•queues d'ail** garlic greens *Quand tu prépares une daube de poisson armé, tu la piques avec du persil, des queues d'oignon, des queues d'ail, du sel et du poivre.* To prepare a garfish roast, you cut slits in it and fill them with a mixture of parsley, onion tops, garlic greens, salt, and pepper. (VM) <VM> **•queues de betteraves** beet leaves, beet greens <LA> **•queues de navet** turnip greens <LA> **•queues d'oignon *a*** onion tops, shallot leaves *Je mets des saucisses et une poule et du persil, de la célérie, et des queues d'oignon, et du filé. Et faut pas oublier les oignons aussite.* I put in sausage and a chicken, and parsley, and onion tops, and filé powder. And you can't forget the onions too. (TB) ***b*** green onions *Et là quand il est presque cuit, je mets des queues d'oignon en dedans.* And then, when it is almost cooked, I put the green onions in. (SM) <AV, EV, IB, IV, JD, JE, LA, LF, SB, SM, TB, VM> **•avoir la queue sur le dos** to be on the go <La99> **•en queue de chemise** pantless, wearing only a shirt *Tu peux croire, il a sorti en queue de chemise. J'avais assez honte, je te dis.* Can you believe it, he came out wearing only his shirt. I was quite embarrassed, let me tell you. (TB) <SM, TB, Lv88> **•fausse queue** switch, hairpiece consisting of a tress of false hair <VM> **•la queue raide** at top speed **Mais ça qu'était plus drôle c'est qu'les bêtes ont parti à s'sauver en travers la savanne la tcheue raide.* But the funniest thing was that the animals took off across the prairie at top speed. (Gu82) <Gu82> **•longue queue** cuckoo bird <Lv88> <***Loc:*** AC, AV, EV, IB, IV, JD, JE, LA, LF, SB, SM, TB, VM, An94, Da84, Gu00, Gu82, Hi02, Ho90, La99, Lv88, Re31>

queul ♦see **quel**

qui[1] [ki] *conj.* if *Qui elle en a, ça va faire.* If she has any, that will do. (AV) <***Loc:*** AV, TB>

qui[2] (**ti**) [ki, ti] (*before a vowel, usually* **qu'** [k], **t'** [t]) *pron. rel.* **1** who *C'est mémère qu'avait une vache qui s'appelait Caillette.* It's grandma who had a cow who was named Caillette. (TB) **Y avait du monde qu'achetait du charbon.* There were some people who used to buy coal. (Gu82) *C'est quelqu'un qui donne des candjas.* That's someone who casts spells. (TB) **Tous les deux pour la même, ni moi ni toi qui l'aura.* Both of us [are longing] for the same girl, [it's] neither you nor I who will have her. (ch: *Tous les deux pour la même*) *C'est lui t'a fait ça.* He's the one who did that. (LA) **2** that, which *Une guêpe anglaise c'est eusse qui fait des niques en papier. Et là les guêpes noires est eusse qui fait leur nique en boue.* An 'English' wasp, they're the ones that make nests out of paper. And black wasps are the ones that make their nest out of mud. (LF) *Y avait un homme eh ben il était arrêté avec sa machine qui voulait pas prendre et partir.* There was a man and he was stuck with his motor that didn't want to start. (TB) *Un grognard, il y a quequechose ti fait du train, tu vois.* A croaker, there's something [about it] that makes noise, you see. (JE) **3** *(obj. of prep.)* who, whom *Je sais pas, comme je vous dis, c'est selon avec qui j'après parler.* I don't know, it's like I told you, it depends on whom I'm talking to. (TB) <*Loc:* AV, EV, IB, IV, JE, LA, LF, TB, Da84, Gu82, Hi02>

qui[3] [ki] *pron.interrog.* **1** who, whom **Qui c'est ça?* Who is that? (Da84, LA) *Qui c'est que ça?* Who's that? (JE) **Qui elle travaille pour?* Whom does she work for? (Hi02) *Avec qui tu as été au village?* With whom did you go to town? *(VM) Tu as vu qui?* Whom did you see? (VM) **Qui il veut?* Whom does he want? (La89) **Pour qui c'est que ces souliers?* Whose shoes are these? (La89) *À ce matin je savais pas qui-ce qu'était après appeler de bon matin comme ça.* This morning I didn't know who was calling early like that. (TB) *Je connais pas si je vas aller, c'est dépendant qui sera là avec nous-autres.* I don't know if I'm going, it depends on who will be there with us. (LA) **2** what *Qui tu veux dire?* What do you mean? (LF) **Qui vous aut' fait-là?* What are you doing there? (An77) *Qui tu veux je te cuis?* What do you want me to cook for you? (Lv88, ch: *Yousqu't'es parti*) *Qui t'appelles ça?* What do you call that? (JE) *Je sus pas tracassée. Tracassée pour qui?* I'm not worried. Worried about what? (VM) *Depuis '36 j'habite ici. Ça donne qui, 64 ans?* I've lived here since 1936. That makes what, 64 years? (TB) *Mon grand-père a tapé des chousses, tu connais qui un chousse est?* My grandfather struck tree stumps, you know what a stump is? (LF) *Quand l'eau est après monter qui faut tu fais?* When water is rising, what should you do? (SM) *Qui tu crois?* What do you think? (Lv88) *Tout ce qu'il fait c'est leur montrer qui faire.* All that he does is show them what to do. (LF) *Quand tu vas te déranger tu connais plus qui t'après faire, tu connais plus qui tu dis.* When you take leave of your senses you don't know what you're doing anymore, you don't know what you're saying anymore. (TB) **3** *(excl.)* *Qui, tu rôdailles toute la journée icitte?* What, you hang out all day long here? (TB) ◊ **•qui ce qui / qui c'est qui** *(subj.)* ***a*** who *Qui-ce qui le chantait?* Who sang it? (TB) *Mais qui-ce qui va les* CHECK *là-bas s'ils ont tout pris ou pas?* But who is going to go down there to check to see if they took all of them or not? (LF) ***b*** what *Il dit, "Qui-ce qu'après vivre icitte avec vous-autres dans les forêts?" Je dis, "Il y a des lapins, y a des écureuils, y a des nutrias qu'on appelle, et y en a des rats de bois, et y en a des chaouis."* He said, "What is living here in the forest with you all?" I said, "There are rabbits, there are squirrels, there are nutrias as we call them, and there are oppossums and there are raccoons." (TB) **•qui ce que / qui c'est que** *(obj.)* ***a*** whom, who *J'ai dit qui-ce que j'étais.* I said who I was. (LF) ***b*** what *Qui-ce qu'on peut parler après?* What can we talk about? (TB) *Et là qui-ce t'après faire, un livre?* So, what are you doing, making a book? (LF) *Il disait qui-ce qu'il faisait le bougre, mais ça nommait pas sa batisse.* The guy would say what he did [for a living], but he wouldn't name the building. (LF) **Ça dépend de qui-ce que je parle.* It depends on what I am talking about. (LF) ***c*** who is, who are *Qui-ce que c'est le pape à L.?* Who is L's father? (TB) ***d*** what is, what are *Tu connais qui c'est une bouillabaisse?* Do you know what a bouillabaisse is? (LF) *Qui c'est ça?* What's that? (SM) *Qui c'est que ça?* What's that? (AC, AV JE, LF, SJ, SM, TB) *Qui c'est ton tracas?* What's the matter with you? (LF) *Tony uh oh qui c'est son nom encore?* Tony uhm, oh, what is his name again? (LF) *Qui-ce que c'est?* What's that? (LF, TB) *Qui-ce que ça c'est?* What's that? (TB) *Qui-ce que c'est que ça?* What is that? (TB) *Moi je me rappelle jusqu'à que j'étais à l'école je savais pas qui c'était qu'un* BUSHEL. I remember, until I went to school I didn't know what a bushel was. (LF) **•qui ça dit?** how's it going? what's up? what's new? what's happening? <LF, TB> **•qui d'autre *a*** who else ***b*** what else *Je sais pas qui d'autre je pourrais vous dire, vous expliquer.* I don't know what else I could tell you, explain to you. (TB) <TB> **•qui il y a / qui y a / qui i-n-a / qui il a** what's the matter, what's wrong, what is it *Qui y a?* What's the matter? (Gu00) *Qui y a avec toi?* What's the matter with you? (LF) *Qui il a?* What's wrong?' (TB) *Qui il y a?* What's the matter? (EV) *Qui i-n-a?* What's the matter? (Lv88) *Je sais pas qui y a, c'est trop tranquille.* I don't know what's wrong, it's too quiet. (TB) <AV, EV, JE, LF, SM, VM, Gu00, Lv88> **•pour qui** for what, for what reason, why *Pour qui t'as fait ça?* Why did you do that? (LF) <*Loc:* AC, AV, EV, JE, LA, LF, SJ, SM, TB, VM, Da84, Gu00, Hi02, La89, Lv88>

qui[4] [ki] *onom.* kee (cry imitating a bird) *Quand-ce que l'hiver est après arriver, tu les attends passer. Avant que le froid arrive tu les attends, qui! qui! qui!* When the winter is about to come, you hear them flying over. Before the cold comes you hear them, kee! kee! kee! (TB) <*Loc:* TB>

quiaque-quiaque [kjak:jak] *onom.* haha (sound imitating laughter) <*Loc:* LA, SM>

quiaquer [kjake] *v.intr.* **1** to laugh heartily **2** to talk much <*Loc:* JD>

quichose ♦see **quelque chose**

quiède ♦see **quède**

quiédeur (**tiédeur**) [kjedœr, tjedœr] *n.f.* tepidity, lukewarmness <*Loc:* Da84>

quille [kij] *n.f.* **1** border (e.g. of wallpaper) **2** strip, jamb, molding **3** keel *Après que ç'avait fait la quille ça mettait l'étrave. L'étrave c'était le devant du bateau.* After they had made the keel, they put on the bow. The bow is the front of the boat. (LF) **4** leg ◊ **•avoir une quille** to have a big nose <La99> <*Loc:* JD, JE, TB, Da84, La99>

quilt (**quilte, couilte**) [kwil(t), kil(t)] *n.f.* *(occ. m.)* quilt **Alle arrêtait pas de carder son coton ou de piquer eine couilte* *qu'alle avait faite avec des r'tailles.* She never stopped carding her cotton or stitching a quilt that she made from scraps. (Gu82) ◊ **•quilte d'alliance** wedding quilt (made for a daughter given away in marriage) **Et tu connais que c'est pas la première fois que Mom fait une quilte d'alliance.* You know this isn't the first time that Mom has made a wedding quilt. (ThCa: *La dernière quilte*) <***Loc:*** AV, SB, SJ, VM, Gu82, Gu00, Lv88, ThCa>

quilte ♦see **quilt**

quilter (**couilter**) [kwilte] **I** *v.tr.* to quilt *Cette couilte a été couiltée par ma grand-mère.* This quilt was made by my grandmother. (VM) **II** *v.intr.* to quilt, make quilts *On avait habitude de couilter dans l'hiver.* We used to make quilts in the winter. (SL) <***Loc:*** SL, SM, VM>

quilteuse [kwiltøz] *n.f.* female quilter, quilt maker **Mayo, un des enfants est sous la quilte, dérangeant les quilteuses.* Mayo, one of the children is under the quilt, bothering the quilters. (ThCa: *La dernière quilte)* <***Loc:*** ThCa>

quinapan [kinapɑ̃] *n.f.* clique *Être dans la quinapan.* To be in the clique. (SL) <***Loc:*** SL>

quincailler ♦see **tchincailler**

quincaillerie ♦see **tchincaillerie**

quinine [kinin, kini] *n.m./f.* quinine <***Loc:*** TB, Da84>

quinqué, -e [kɛ̃ke] *adj.* well dressed, dressed with taste *Elle est toujours bien quinquée.* She is always well dressed. (IB) <***Loc:*** IB, SJ>

quinte (**quinteau**) [kɛ̃t, kɛ̃to] *n.m.* small pile or stack (as of hay stacked for drying) *Rentrez les quintes de foin avant la pluie.* Bring in the piles of hay before the rain. (IB) *Le quinteau de riz est fait il y a une semaine.* The stack of rice was made a week ago. (SB) <***Loc:*** IB, SJ>

quinteau ♦see **quinte**

quinzaine [kɛ̃zɛ̃n] *n.f.* about fifteen *J'ai acheté la compagnie y a une quinzaine d'années.* I bought the company some fifteen years ago. (TB) *T'es pris ici avec une douzaine, une quinzaine de caïmans avec pas d'écorcheurs. Et là tu vas perdre tout.* You're stuck here with a dozen or about fifteen alligators and no skinners. And then you'll lose everything. (TB) <***Loc:*** TB, Da84>

quinze [kɛ̃z] *adj./n.m.* fifteen **J'ai vendu mon 'tit mulet, pour quinze sous.* I sold my little mule for fifteen cents. (ch: *'Tit galop pour Mamou)* <***Loc:*** AC, AV, EV, TB, An94, Da84, Hi02>

quinze-côtes (**tchaise-côtes**) [kɛ̃zkɔt, tʃɛzkɔt] *n.m.* thin, long-legged man *Je vas arrêter woir si tchaise-côte va venir avec mon.* I'm going to stop and see if beanpole wants to come with me. (TB) <***Loc:*** JE, TB>

quinzième [kɛ̃zjɛ̃m] *adj./n.* fifteenth *C'est la quinzième fois je lui dis de pas faire ça.* That's the fifteenth time I've told him not to do that. (LA) <***Loc:*** LA, Da84>

quiqui [kiki] *n.m.* throat ◊ **•prendre au quiqui** to take someone by the throat, choke <LF> <***Loc:*** LF>

quiquiner [kikine] *v.tr.* to bother, annoy *Tout ce bruit me quiquine.* All that noise bothers me. (IB) <***Loc:*** IB, SB>

quiquisse ♦see **titisse**

quiquitte[1] [kikit] *n.m./f.* [*baby talk*] chicken <***Loc:*** EV, IB, SM, Gr86, Ph36>

quiquitte[2] [kikit, kitkit] *interj.* call for chickens <***Loc:*** IB, SB>

QUIT [kwɪt] *v.tr.invar.* to quit, abandon, leave *Je vas* QUIT *mon job.* I'm going to quit my job. (Lv88) <***Loc:*** Lv88>

quittable [kitab(l)] *adj.* ready to leave, on the point of departure *On est quittables, nous-autres.* We're ready to leave. (VM) <***Loc:*** VM>

quittage [kitaʒ] *n.m.* sacrifice, s.t. left behind or abandoned *Il y aurait un quittage de quelque chose.* There would be something left behind. (EV) <***Loc:*** EV>

quittance [kitɑ̃s] *n.f.* **1** receipt **2** performance of a duty, payment of a debt *Moi, j'y ai aidé à sauver sa récolte. Il m'a aidé à remettre ma couverture. Ça c'était sa quittance.* I helped him bring in his crop. He helped me put my roof back on. That was his way of paying me back. (LA) <***Loc:*** LA, Da84>

quitte [kit] *adj.* **1** even, paid up, in the clear *Là asteur on est quitte.* Now we're even. (LA) **2** free (from an obligation) **Il est quitte à ç't heure, il a fini ses études.* He's free now, he has finished his studies. (EV, Ph36) ◊ **•autant {tant} quitte** might as well, just as well *T'as tant quitte venir asteur. Il faudra tu te décides un jour ou l'autre.* You might as well come now. You'll have to make up your mind one day or another. (LA) <LA, Da84> ◊ **•avoir plus quitte** to have better (do s.t.) *T'as plus quitte pas dire ça.* You'd better not say that. (Lv88) **Tu as plus quitte t'en aller.* You had better leave. (Da84) **Tu as plus quitte te taire.* You had better shut up. (Da84) **On a plus quitte s'en aller.* We had better leave. (Da84) <Da84, Lv88> <***Loc:*** EV, LA, Da84, Lv88, Ph36>

quitté, -e [kite] *adj.* separated, divorced *S'il a été marié ils sont quittés lui et sa femme.* If he was married, they are separated, he and his wife. (LA) **Pas bien longtemps après qu'ils ont été quittés...* Not too long after they were divorced . . . (ThCa: *Le charivari*) ◊ **•être quitté de qqn** to be separated or divorced from s.o. <Lv88> <***Loc:*** LA, Lv88, ThCa>

quitter [kite] **I** *v.tr.* **1** to let, allow, permit **Quitte-les venir.* Let them come. (Da84) **Quitte-moi t'aider.* Let me help you. (Da84) *Quitte-moi te donner la main.* Let me help you. (LF, TB) *Ça nous quittait pas jouer avec la machine.* They didn't let us play with the machine. (Lv88) **I' quittait pas personne parler avec sa fille.* He didn't allow anyone to talk to his daughter. (An77) *Il m'a quitté avoir son char à soir.* He let me have his car tonight. (Lv88) *Vivre et quitte vivre.* Live and let live. (Lv88) *Eux-autres quittait pas les Sauvages aller à l'école du monde blanc.* They didn't let Indians go to white people's schools. (TB) **Quitte-moi te raconter quelque chose pour ton père et moi.* Let me tell you something about your father and me. (LA, An94) **2** to keep, maintain (in a condition or state) *Tu les quittes réveillés jusqu'à onze heures douze heures du soir.* You keep them awake until eleven o'clock, twelve o'clock at night. (AV) *Et tu mets ta graisse, et là tu quittes ça un peu chaud.* And you put in the fat, and you keep it kind of hot. (EV) **3** to leave *Tu peux quitter ça dehors.* You can leave that outside. (EV) *Y a une femme qu'a appelé deux fois et qu'a quitté un message sur ma machine et je connais pas qui-ce qu'alle dit.* There's a woman who's called twice and who left a message on my machine and I don't know what she's saying. (LF) *Ça les quitte deux ou trois mois dans la bonne eau là.* They leave them [the oysters] in the good water for two or three months. (TB) *Quitte le PHONE là où il est!* Leave the phone right where it is! (EV) *Il dit, "Je t'adviserais," il dit, "lui quitter son nom il est venu avec." Et Pape lui dit, "Je vas pas changer son nom."* He said, "I'd advise you," he said, "to leave him with the name he came with." And Pop said to him, "I won't change his name." (AV) **4** to leave, abandon *Vivienne, ma femme, m'a quitté pour s'en aller à New York.* Vivienne, my wife, left me to go to New York. (ThCa: *La douce réunion*) **J'ai quitté ma vieille mère.* I left my old mother. (ch: *Quitter la maison*) *Elle a été quittée.* She was abandoned [by her husband]. (Lv88) *Sa femme l'a quitté. Elle l'a attrapé après chiennailler.* His wife left him. She caught him sleeping around. (LA) **5** to leave (a location) *Et on quittait l'école et on allait au CAMP pour trois mois.* And we left school and we went to our camp for three months. (TB) **II** *v.intr.* **1** to stop, cease, quit *Il a quitté de boire.* He quit drinking. (Lv88) **2** to leave, depart *Il a quitté pour l'église.* He left for church. (IB) **J'ai quitté de la maison.* I left home. (ch: *Quitter la maison*) **III se quitter** *v.pron.* to break up, separate, divorce *Ils se sont quittés.* They split up. (Lv88) ◊ **•quitter tomber** to drop *Oui, mangeur d'oeuf. Ces grosses serpents va manger un oeuf et là s'il peut pas la casser à la quitter tomber, il va tourner au ras d'un arbre ou d'un poteau. Il va casser l'oeuf après qu'il l'a envalé.* Yes, a yellow chicken snake. Those big snakes will eat an egg and then if they can't break it by dropping it, they'll turn around a tree or a post. He'll break the egg after he's swallowed it. (TB) <TB> **•quitter tranquille** to leave alone, leave in peace *Je croyais peut-être, tu connais, il m'aurait quittée tranquille et il aurait rafraîchi là-dessus.* I though perhaps, you know, he would leave me alone and that he would have cooled to the idea. (EV) <AV, EV, JE, EV, IB, IV, Ph36> <***Loc:*** AC, AV, EV, IB, IV, JE, LA, LF, PQ, SL, SM, TB, VM, An77, An94, Da84, Hi02, Lv88, ThCa>

quo' faire ♦see **quoi faire**

quoi[1] [kwa, ko] *pron.indef.* ◊ **•de quoi *a*** something *C'est peut-être de quoi que je connais pas.* It might be something that I'm not familiar with. (TB) *Oh j'ai mangé de quoi de bon.* Oh, I ate something good. (LF) *Dis à Ti-Jean de venir me voir, j'ai de quoi à lui dire.* Tell Li'l John to come see me, I have something to tell him. (VM) ***b*** something of value, substance, wealth *J'ai travaillé dur tout ma vie, mais asteur j'ai de quoi.* I have worked hard all my life, but now I have some means. (VM) *J'ai un tit brin de quoi asteur qu'ils ont trouvé de l'huile dessus ma terre.* I have a little bit of money now that they have found oil on my land. (VM) **T'as pour avoir de quoi pour avoir une femme.* You have to have wealth to have a wife. (SL, An94) <IV, LF, SL, TB, VM, An94> **•il y a pas de quoi** you're welcome, don't mention it <Da84> <***Loc:*** IV, LF, SL, TB, VM, An94, Da84>

quoi[2] [kwa, ko] *pron.rel.* what, which *Tu peux jamais dire quoi elle va faire. Elle est manière fêlée.* You can never tell what she's going to do. She's a little nutty. (LA) *Tu vas pas mettre quoi je dis sur le TAPE?* You're not going to put what I say on tape, are you? (Lv88) *C'était selon quoi tu pêchais.* It depended on what you were fishing for. (IV) **'Garde donc quoi t'après faire avec moi.* Look what you're doing to me. (ch: *Chère Alice*) *Tu sais pas quoi tu dis.* You don't know what you're saying. (LA) **Je sais pas quoi faire.* I don't know what to do. (Da84) *Je m'en fous pas mal quoi tu dis.* I don't care what you say. (LA) <***Loc:*** IV, LA, LF, SL, TB, An94, Da84, Hi02>

quoi[3] [kwa, ko] *pron.interrog.* what **Quoi il a dit?* What did he say? (Da84) *Quoi ça veut dire?* What does that mean? (Lv88) *Quoi tu crois?* What do you think? (Lv88) *Mais je dis: "quoi je vas faire?"* But I said: "what I am going to do"? (AC) *Quoi tu mets sur le hameçon?* What do you put on the hook? (JE) **Quoi ils vouliont foutre avec une pareille grosse chaudière?* What did they want to do with such a big pot? (SL, An94) ◊ **•quoi ce qui / quoi c'est qui** *(subj.)* what **Quoi-ce qui bouche le trou?* What's stopping the hole? (AC, An94) *Et asteur les affaires est rendu dans un point comme les habitants est pas en bon SHAPE, et je sais pas quoi-ce qui va nous arriver.* And now things have reached a point that farmers are not in good shape, and I don't know what's going to happen to us. (AS) <EV, IB, JD, LA, LF, SM, VM, Da84, Hi02, Lv88> **•quoi ce (que) / quoi c'est (que)** *(obj.)* ***a*** what *Quoi c'est tu brasses là?* What are you doing over there? (VM) *Quoi c'est tu veux?* What do you want? (Lv88) **Et c'était trop loin pour eux-autres entendre quoi c'est il disait. Et puis, il les a pointés au doigt.* And it was too far for them to hear what he was saying. And then, he pointed them out. (EV, An94) ***b*** what is, what are **Quoi c'est?* What is it? (Da84) *Quoi c'est ça?* What's that? (SM) *Quoi c'est ton nom?* What is your name? (Lv88) *Quoi c'est le tracas, quoi i-n-a?* What's the problem, what's the matter? (LA) *Quoi c'est avec vous?* What's the matter with you? (IB) **Quoi c'est vous-autres espère?* What is it you're waiting for? (Hi02) *Quoi ce que c'est?* What's that? (IV) *Quoi-ce que y a?* What's wrong? *Quoi ce que t'as?* What's the matter with you? (IV) **Il dit, "Quoi-ce qu'il y a,* *maman? On dirait que t'es jongleuse."* He said, "What's the matter, Mama? It seems that you are pensive." (IB, An94) <EV, IB, JD, LA, LF, SM, VM, Da84, Hi02, Lv88> **•quoi ça dit?** how's it going? what's up? what's new? what's happening? <Gu00, La99, Lv88> **•quoi (il) y a? / quoi i-n-a?** what's the matter? <AC, EV, JD, LA, LF, VM, An94, Da84, Gu00> <***Loc:*** AC, EV, IB, IV, JD, JE, LA, LF, SL, SM, TB, VM, An94, Da84, Hi02, La99, Lv88>

quoi[4] [kwa, ko] *interj.* what <***Loc:*** Da84>

quoi faire (**quo' faire, cofaire**) [kofær] *adv.interrog.* why *Cofaire tu vas pas travailler?* Why aren't you going to work? (Lv88) **Quoi faire Monsieur Latiolais a fait tout ça?* Why did Mr. Latiolais do all that? (Hi02) **Mon, je vois pas qui je t'ai fait. Quo'faire donc tu veux pas t'en revenir au Port Arthur.* I don't know what I did to you. Why don't you want to come back to Port Arthur? (ch: *Port Arthur*) *Quoi-faire tu veux savoir?* Why do you want to know? (JE) **I' travaillont tout l'temps et quo' faire?* They worked all the time, and what for? (Gu82) <***Loc:*** IB, JE, SB, SM, TB, VM, Da84, Gu00, Gu82, Hi02, Lv88>

quoique [kwak] *conj.* although, even though **Quoiqu'il est jeune, il est sage.* Even though he is young, he is wise. (Da84) <***Loc:*** Da84>

R

rabâcher [rabaʃe] *v.tr.* to mumble *Il a rabâché quelque chose avant de partir mais j'ai rien compris.* He mumbled something before he left but I didn't understand a single word. (SL) <***Loc:*** SL>

rabaissement [rabesmɑ̃] *n.m.* lowering (of prices) <***Loc:*** Da84>

rabaisser [rabese] *v.tr.* to lower (a price) again *Ils ont rabaissé les prix chez Abdalla depuis qu'ils ont décidé de fermer.* They lowered the prices at Abdalla's again since they decided to close. (VM) <***Loc:*** VM, Da84>

rabasilière [rabaziljær] *n.f.* swamp <***Loc:*** AV, Gr86>

rabasseau [rabaso] *n.m.* rake *Alle a ramassé les herbes avec le rabasseau.* She raked up the grass with the rake. (TB) <***Loc:*** TB>

rabat [raba] *n.m.* **1** rolled hem *J'ai fait un rabat dans sa chemise.* I put a rolled hem in his shirt. (VM) **2** roof built over a doorway for protection from the elements *Il faut ramancher le rabat.* We need to fix the roof over the door. (TB) <***Loc:*** JE, TB, VM>

rabatter ♦see **rabattre**[2]

rabattre[1] [rabat(r)] *v.tr.* **1** to flatten, press down *Le vent avait rabattu les cannes.* The wind had put down the cane. (LA) **2** to make a rolled hem *J'ai bien rabattu ça comme il faut.* I made sure to put in a good hem. (VM) <***Loc:*** LA, VM, Da84>

rabattre[2] (**rabatter**) [rabat(r), rabate] *v.tr.* to repeat (the same thing) over and over again *Il rabatte toujours la même affaire.* He always repeats the same thing. (TB) *Il rabatte toujours la même chose.* He always repeats the same thing. (IB) *Il rabattait la même vieille histoire.* He repeated the same old story over and over. (VM) <***Loc:*** IB, JE, TB, VM, Di32, Lv88>

rabiot [rabjo] ◊ **•en rabiot** separated, divorced (of a married couple) <JE> <***Loc:*** JE>

rabiotte [rabjɔt] *n.* **1** *(m.)* divorced man **2** *(f.)* divorced woman *Il a marié une rabiotte.* He married a divorcée. (SM) <***Loc:*** IB, SM, VM, La99, Lv88>

raboron [rabɔrɔ̃] *n.* person of short stature, runt *Il est raboron, lui. Il a pas grandi du tout.* He's a runt. He hasn't grown at all. (LF) <***Loc:*** LF>

rabot[1] [rabo] *n.m.* **1** large clod of dirt **2** unevenness (of a road) <***Loc:*** JD, JE, LF, TB, Da84>

rabot[2] [rabo] *n.m.* plane, wood plane *C'est tout des outils fait avec du bois. Ça c'était ça qu'on appelait un rabot ou un* WOOD PLANER. *Et il a deux grosseurs.* Those are all wooden tools. That's what they called a wood planer. And it comes in two sizes. (LF) ◊ **•passer (qqch) au rabot** to plane (s.t.) <LF> <***Loc:*** JE, LF>

raboter [rabote] *v.intr.* to be bumpy *Le chemin à L'Anse Bourbeuse rabotait.* The road to L'Anse Bourbeuse was bumpy. (LA) <***Loc:*** LA>

raboteux, -euse [rabotø, -øz] *adj.* rough, uneven, bumpy (esp. of a road) *La petite manche qui va à la vieille maison devient raboteux après quelques années, et tous les temps en temps, il faut l'égaliser.* The lane that goes to the old house gets rough after a few years and every now and then, it must be graded. (LA) <***Loc:*** LA, Da84>

rabougri [rabugri] *n.m.* clumsy, ungainly person ◊ **•vieux rabougri** old man who likes to flirt <SM> <***Loc:*** AS, SJ, SM, VM, La99>

rabourage (**labourage**) [raburaʒ, laburaʒ] *n.m.* plowing, tillage <***Loc:*** SL, Da84>

rabourer (**labourer**) [rabure, rabule, labure] **I** *v.tr.* to plow, till *Rabourer la terre.* To plow the land. (JE) **II** *v.intr.* to plow, till *Je rabourais avec une paire de mulets, deux mulets et une charrue.* I used to plow with a pair of mules, two mules and a cart. (IB) *On raboure pour planter à l'automne.* We are plowing in order to plant in autumn. (Lv88) *Une charrue qui rabourait trois pieds de creux.* A plow that tills three feet deep. (VM) ◊ **•labourer en planche** to plow flat, plow level <Da84> **•labourer en rang** to plow in rows <Da84> **•rabourer à travers les rangs** to do things the hard way, make things hard for o.s. <LA, La99> <***Loc:*** AC, AV, IB, JD, JE, LA, LF, SB, SL, SM, TB, VM, Da84, Di32, Gr86, La99, Lv88>

raboureur (**laboureur**) [raburœr, rabulœr, laburœr] *n.m.* **1** plowman **2** farmer <***Loc:*** JE, SB, SL, SM, TB, VM, Da84, Di32, Gr86, Hi02, Lv88>

raboustin [rabustɛ̃] *n.m.* man of short stature, runt <***Loc:*** JD>

raboutage [rabutaʒ] *n.m.* piecing, patching <***Loc:*** Da84>

rabouter (**raboutiner**) [rabute, rabutine] *v.tr.* **1** to join end to end *J'ai libouté les planches.* I placed the planks end to end. (SM) **2** to lengthen, extend *J'ai raboutiné la corde à linge.* I lengthened the clothesline. (VM) *Elle a rabouté sa robe.* She lengthened her dress. (SB) **3** to add on to, enlarge by addition *On a rabouté, rabouté des boutes dessus, mais j'ai tout élevé mes trois enfants dans une petite maison.* We added, added parts onto it, but I raised my three kids in a small house. (TB) *Ils ont fait ça quand ils ont rabouté leur maison.* They did that when they added on to their house. (LA) **4** to patch, patch up, piece together *C'est une maison tout raboutée.* It's a house that's all patched together. (SM) *Rabouter des morceaux de ficelle.* To piece together bits of string. (SJ) *J'ai pas fini de rabouter les planches dessus* *la galerie.* I have not finished patching the planks on the porch. (LA) <***Loc:*** AV, EV, JD, JE, LA, SB, SJ, SM, TB, VM, Da84, Ph36, Re31>

raboutiner ♦see **rabouter**

racacha ♦see **racatcha**[2]

racage ♦see **racaille**

racaille (**racage**) [rakaj, rakaʒ] *n.f.* ◊ •**tomber en racaille** ***a*** to fall apart, fall to pieces *Ça tombe en racaille.* It's falling apart. (TB) ***b*** to fall in a heap *Il a tombé en racage.* He fell in a heap. (LF) <LF, TB> <***Loc:*** LF, TB>

racatcha[1] [rakatʃa] *adj.* **1** old, worn, worn out *Alle a une robe toute racatcha.* She has a worn-out old dress. (AV) *Une vieille voiture racatcha.* An old rattletrap carriage. (SJ) **2** vulgar, coarse, unrefined <***Loc:*** AV, SJ, SM>

racatcha[2] (**racacha**) [rakatʃa] *n.m.* **1** bur (esp. hedgehog grass or sandbur) **2** spur (of a rooster, of a horseman) **3** bunion **4** anything old and in bad condition (esp. a car, a horse, or a person) *Il vient dans son racatcha.* He's coming in his old jalopy. (AV) **5** worthless fellow, bum *Il fait jamais rien, le vieux racatcha.* He never does anything, the old bum. (TB) **6** rabble, riffraff **Ti peux tirer tout ç'té racatcha déhors, ça vaut pas rien.* You can't throw all that rabble out, they're worthless. (EV, Ph36) <***Loc:*** AV, EV, IB, JE, LF, SM, TB, VM, Da84, Di32, Hi02, Ho90, Lv88, Ph36>

racca [raka] *n.m.* horse that paces or racks ◊ •**aller le racca** {**rack**} to pace, rack <VM, Da84> <***Loc:*** VM, Da84>

raccommodable [rakmodab(l)] *adj.* repairable, mendable *Je veux pas ce capot. Il est pas raccommodable.* I don't want that coat. It's not mendable. (EV) <***Loc:*** EV, Da84>

raccommodage (**racmodage**) [rakmodaʒ, rɑ̃kmodaʒ] *n.m.* repair, mending, darning, patching *J'ai un tas de racmodage à faire.* I have tons of mending to do. (TB) *Alle a fait un racmodage sus ses bas.* She mended her stockings. (SB) <***Loc:*** AV, IB, JD, LF, SB, SL, SM, TB, VM, Da84, Lv88, Re31>

raccommoder (**racmoder**) [rakmode] *v.tr.* to repair, mend, patch, patch up *Ma mère a eu pour raccommoder mes vieilles chemises parce qu'on pouvait pas en acheter d'autres.* My mother had to patch my old shirts because we couldn't buy more. (LA) <***Loc:*** AV, IB, JD, LA, LF, SB, SL, SM, TB, VM, Da84, Lv88, Re31>

raccoquillé, -e [rakokije, rakotʃije] *adj.* **1** shrunken, contracted, curled up *Le nerf est tout raccoquillé.* The muscle is all contracted. (SM) **2** hunched over, bunched up *Il l'a trouvé tout raccoquillé avec des crampes.* He found him all hunched over with cramps. (VM) <***Loc:*** JD, SM, VM, Da84>

raccoquiller [rakokije, rakotʃije, rɑ̃kokije] **I** *v.intr.* to contract (with cold, etc.) *Il pouvait pas la trouver. Elle avait raccoquillé dans le froid.* He couldn't find it. It had contracted in the cold. (LA) **II se raccoquiller** *v.pron.* **1** to curl up *L'enfant s'est raccoquillé en bas des couvertes.* The child curled up under the covers. (VM) *Il s'a racoquillé à force qu'il avait froid.* He curled up because he was so cold. (LF) **2** to huddle, huddle up *Les chiens s'avaient raccoquillé dans le coin de la galerie à l'abri du vent de nord.* The dogs had huddled up in the corner of the porch away from the north wind. (LA) <***Loc:*** LA, LF, SM, VM, Da84, Lv88>

raccordement [rakɔrdəmɑ̃] *n.m.* refitting, fitting together again <***Loc:*** Da84>

raccorder [rakɔrde] *v.tr.* **1** to refit *Et Mom aurait raccordé une culotte, ben elle aurait raccordé les culottes à Pop là jusqu'à quatre fois par dessus la même pièce.* And Mom would refit pants, she would refit Pop's pants up to four times on the same material. (EV) **2** to restring (an instrument) **Je l'ai raccordé. J'ai mis des cordes dessus.* I restrung it. I put strings on it. (VM, An84) **3** to tune, retune (an instrument) *J'ai eu pour raccorder mon violon à cause de la chaleur.* I had to retune my violin because of the heat. (LA) <***Loc:*** EV, LA, VM, An84, Da84>

raccourci [rakursi] *n.m.* shortcut *Le raccourci est bourbeux.* The shortcut is muddy. (SM) ◊ •**raccourci à défunt Pétain / raccourci à Philémon** ***a*** supposed shortcut that actually takes longer than the normal route ***b*** effort that is not worth the trouble <La99> <***Loc:*** JD, LF, SM, Da84, La99, Re31>

raccourcir [rakursir] **I** *v.tr.* to shorten *Ils ont raccourci le chemin à Delcambre avec le BYPASS.* They shortened the road to Delcambre with the bypass. (LA) **II** *v.intr.* to shorten, shrink *Ma mère a chessé ma chemise et les manches ont raccourci.* My mother dried my shirt and the sleeves shortened. (LA) **III se raccourcir** *v.pron.* to become shorter, shrink **Les jours se raccourcissent.* The days are getting shorter. (Da84) <***Loc:*** JD, LA, Da84>

raccourcissement [rakursismɑ̃] *n.m.* shortening, shrinking <***Loc:*** Da84>

raccoutumer (**réaccoutumer**) [rakutyme, reakutyme] **I** *v.tr.* to reaccustom, retrain (an animal) *Il faut je raccoutume mon chien de rester dehors.* I have to retrain my dog to stay outside. (EV) **II se raccoutumer** *v.pron.* to reaccustom o.s., get accustomed again *J'ai eu pour me raccoutumer à la chaleur après mes vacances au Canada.* I had to reaccustom myself to the heat after my vacation to Canada. (LA) *Il a pas pu se réaccoutumer à la vie de campagne.* He wasn't able to get reaccustomed to country life. (LA) <***Loc:*** EV, LA, Da84, Ph36>

raccroc [rakro] *n.m.* **1** inlet, small bay extending from a stream *Il a mis le bateau dans le raccroc.* He put the boat in the inlet. (LF) **2** rip, tear (e.g. in cloth) *Elle a un raccroc dans sa robe.* She has a tear in her dress. (SB) <***Loc:*** LF, SB>

raccrochage [rakroʃaʒ] *n.m.* rehooking, rehanging, reconnecting <***Loc:*** Da84>

raccrocher [rakroʃe] **I** *v.tr.* to rehook, rehang, reconnect *Raccroche le PHONE!* Hang up the phone! (EV) **II se raccrocher** *v.pron.* **1** to hook on again, become rehooked *Je savais* *qu'il s'aurait raccroché dessus ce dope-là.* I knew he'd get hooked on that dope stuff again. (LA) **2** to cling, hang *J'aime pas mettre ce* SWEATER *parce qu'il y a toujours des petits bouts de fils qui se raccrochent après.* I don't like to wear that sweater because there are always little pieces of thread clinging to it. (LA) ◊ •**raccrocher sus qqn** to hang up on s.o. *Il ferait mieux de pas raccrocher sus moi.* He'd better not hang up on me. (LA) <LA> <***Loc:*** EV, LA, Da84>

raccroupi [rakrupi] *n.m.* one who likes to sit in place (e.g. by the fire) and do nothing *C'est rien qu'un vieux raccroupi.* He's just an old guy who likes to sit by the fire. (TB) <***Loc:*** JE, TB>

race [ras] *n.f.* **1** race (of humans) **Il faut que je me range avec mes frères et sœurs de ma race noire, qu'importe leur langue.* I have to take my place next to my brothers and sisters of the black race, whatever their language. (ThCa: *Mille misères*) **2** breed, stock, subspecies (of animals) **3** ethnicity **Comment ça se fait que les 'tits enfants de mon sang sont pas de ma race, la race acadienne?* How can it be that the grandchildren of my own blood are not of my race, the Acadian race? (ThCa: *Mille misères*) **4** relatives *Ils étont, tous, ma race.* They were all my relatives. (VM) *Jean a une grande race.* John has a big family (with lots of offspring). (JE) <***Loc:*** JE, VM, Da84, ThCa>

rachanter [raʃɑ̃te] *v.intr.* to prattle, talk meaninglessly *Ne l'écoutez pas, il rachante.* Don't listen to him, he prattles on. (SB) <***Loc:*** SB>

raché ♦see **ratché**

racheter [raʃte] **I** *v.tr.* **1** to buy again, buy back *Et quand ils ont parti j'ai tout racheté l'affaire mais pas la terre.* And when they left I bought the whole thing back but not the land. (LF) **2** to redeem *Il voulait racheter son honneur après qu'il a sorti de la prison.* He wanted to redeem his honor after he got out of prison. (VM) **II se racheter** *v.pron.* to repurchase for o.s., purchase more (of s.t.) for o.s. **Se racheter du linge.* To buy oneself some more clothes. (Da84) <***Loc:*** AC, EV, LF, VM, Da84>

racheux, -euse (arracheux, -euse) [raʃø, araʃø, -øz] *adj.* rough, coarse *Alle a une peau racheuse.* She has rough skin. (VM) *Une langue de bête est racheuse avant que tu la nettoies.* A beef tongue is rough before you clean it. (LA) *Cette chemise est trop arracheuse.* This shirt is too coarse. (JE) <***Loc:*** JD, JE, LA, LF, SM, TB, VM, Da84, Lv88>

racinage [rasinaʒ] *n.m.* **1** root crop **2** rooting <***Loc:*** Da84>

racine [rasin] *n.f.* **1** root *Les racines du bois.* The roots of the tree. (AV) **2** origin **3** penis **Pierre voulait montrer il était plus homme que l'autre et sa racine était encore plus longue.* Pierre wanted to show that he was even more of a man than the other and that his penis was longer. (EV, Gr86) <***Loc:*** AV, EV, LA, SM, Da84, Gr86, Hi02>

raciner ♦see **enraciner**

racineux, -euse [rasinø, -øz] *adj.* having many roots *Un frêne, c'est un arbre racineux.* A green ash is a tree with many roots. (LA) <***Loc:*** JD, LA, Lv88>

raciste [rasis(t)] *n.* racist <***Loc:*** Da84>

rack ♦see **racca**

raclage [raklaʒ] *n.m.* **1** cutting, cropping (of grass, etc.) **2** clean sweep, big win in which one takes the entire pot (usu. at cards) *J'ai eu pour partir après le raclage à Bobby. Il me restait pus un sou pour jouer.* I had to leave after Bobby's clean sweep. I didn't have a penny left to play with. (LA) ◊ •**raclage d'herbe** close mowing or cutting of grass <Da84> <***Loc:*** LA, Da84>

raclée (râclée) [rakle] *n.f.* **1** whipping, beating **Donner une raclée.* To give a whipping. (Da84) *Il nous a foutu chacune une raclée.* He gave each of us a whipping. (EV) **2** rake ◊ •**raclée des herbes** rake <PQ> <***Loc:*** EV, JD, PQ, Da84, Hi02, La99>

racler [rakle] *v.tr.* **1** to crop, cut short *L'ouragan a raclé tous les arbres dans la cour à ma belle-mère.* The hurricane clipped all the trees in my mother-in-law's yard. (LA) **2** to scrape, shave (a cultivated row) *Une fois, moi et André, on était après racler les bâtons de coton.* Once, me and André, we were scraping the cotton stalks. (SL) **3** to take everything, make a clean sweep *J'ai raclé mon dîner.* I cleaned my plate. (SM) **Ces gens ont raclé la table.* These people cleaned out the table (i.e. ate all the food). (Da84) **4** to whip, beat *Je vas bien te racler si t'es pas sage, petit.* I'll whip you good if you don't behave, child. (VM) **5** to beat down, devastate, destroy *Les cochons ont raclé mon jardin.* The pigs destroyed my garden. (SM) *Ces enfants ont raclé toutes mes fleurs là où ils jouont.* Those kids trampled all of my flowers where they play. (VM) <***Loc:*** EV, IB, JD, LA, SL, SM, VM, Da84, La99, Lv88, Ph36>

raclin [raklɛ̃] *n.m.* **1** scrawny, underfed horse *Ce raclin va tomber en route.* That scrawny horse will fall down along the way. (SB) **2** good-for-nothing person *Tu parles d'un raclin, c'est ça.* Talk about a lowlife, there's one. (SB) <***Loc:*** SB>

raclure [raklyr] *n.f.* **1** beating, whipping **2** lining of the intestine, which is scraped off and discarded before sausage is made <***Loc:*** EV, SM, La99>

racmodage ♦see **raccommodage**

racmoder ♦see **raccommoder**

racoin [rakwɛ̃] *n.m.* corner, nook *J'ai cherché pour lui dans tous les racoins.* I looked for him in every nook and cranny. (SM) <***Loc:*** AV, EV, IB, JD, SM, VM, Da84, Lv88, Ph36, Re31>

racointer [rakwɛ̃te] *v.tr.* to put into a corner **J'ai racointé ça, c'était dans mon chemin icite.* I put that in a corner, it was in my way here. (EV, Ph36) <***Loc:*** EV, Ph36>

racontage [rakɔ̃taʒ] *n.m.* storytelling <***Loc:*** Da84>

raconte [rakɔ̃t] *n.f.* story, narration *Fais-moi la raconte de* *comment t'as appris à jouer.* Tell me the story of how you learned to play. (EV) <*Loc:* EV, Hio2>

raconter (**aconter**) [rakɔ̃te, akɔ̃te] *v.tr.* **1** to relate, tell, narrate **Ça, c'est une belle histoire, mais je peux pas la raconter, moi.* That's a beautiful story, but I can't tell it. (IV, An94) **Guillory m'a raconté l'autre jour comment il avait joué eine niche dessus Hebert ein Halloween des années passées.* Guillory told me the other day how he had played a trick on Hebert one Halloween years ago. (Wh83) *Et l'histoire j'aimerais vous raconter aujourd'hui, c'est ça qu'a arrivé à moi et mon petit padna quand on avait alentour de, je pense, treize ans chacun.* And the story I'd like to tell you today is about what happened to me and my friend when we were each around, I think, thirteen years old. (JD) **2** to declare, confess **J'irais me reposer, auprès de toi ma belle, te raconter mes peines [...] et ensuite mes amitiés.* I would go lie near you, my beauty, to tell you my troubles and then my affections. (ch: *Si j'aurais des ailes*) <*Loc:* IV, JD, LA, LF, SB, An94, Da84, Hio2, Wh83>

raconteur [rakɔ̃tœr] *n.m.* storyteller **Mon père était un chanteur et raconteur de contes.* My father was a singer and a storyteller. (Gr86) <*Loc:* LF, Da84, Gr86, Hio2>

radio [ɹeˈdijo radijo, regjo] *n.m./f.* radio <*Loc:* AV, IB, LA, SL, TB, Da84, Hio2, Lv88>

radis [radi] *n.m.* radish <*Loc:* AV, JE, SM>

radmettre ♦see **réadmettre**

radotage [radotaʒ] *n.m.* gossip, idle talk, gabbing *Tu vas me rendre folle avec ton radotage!* You're going to drive me crazy with your chatter! (EV) <*Loc:* EV, Da84>

radote [radɔt] *n.f.* babbling, gabbing, idle talk, foolish talk *Et tu connais quand-ce que quelqu'un est juste après te parler et que tu trouves il est pas après faire de la raison, juste après parler, parler pour arien, tu connais? Ma grand-mère disait "Arrête cette radote-là."* And you know when someone is just talking to you and you find that he isn't making any sense, he's just talking, talking for no reason, you know? My grandmother used to say, "Stop that babbling." (TB) <*Loc:* LF, TB>

radotement [radɔtmɑ̃] *n.m.* **1** gossip, idle talk **2** rumor <*Loc:* Da84>

radoter (**ragoter**) [radote, ragote] *v.intr.* **1** to gab, gossip, make idle talk *Ça, c'en est une qui peut radoter. Tu devrais attendre ça qu'elle a dit pour sa belle-fille.* She is one who can gossip. You should hear what she said about her daughter-in-law. (EV) **2** to ramble on, talk endlessly *Arrêtez donc de radoter. On veut notre argent.* Stop rambling on. We want our money. (ThCa: *Martin Weber*) <*Loc:* EV, JD, LF, TB, Da84, ThCa>

radoteur, -euse [radotœr, -øz] *n.* **1** gossiper, gossipmonger, gabber **2** chatterbox, one who talks too much <*Loc:* LF, Da84>

radoucir [radusir] *v.tr.* **1** to sweeten again *Mon père avait l'habitude de radoucir son thé.* My father always put more sugar in his tea. (EV) **2** to retame (an animal) *On a retrouvé le chat après quelques mois, mais on a jamais pu le radoucir.* We found the cat after several months, but we never were able to retame it. (LA) **3** to retrain (an animal) *On a eu pour radoucir le cheval quand ma fille a revenu du collège.* We had to retrain the horse when my daughter returned from college. (LA) <*Loc:* EV, LA, Da84>

rafale [rafal] *n.f.* gust of wind *Ça passait des rafales hier au soir quand ça mouillait.* It was gusting last night during the rain. (LA) <*Loc:* LA>

rafalé[1], **-e** [rafale] *adj.* sated, filled up **Il est rafalé su ç'dessert.* He got filled up on this dessert. (EV, Ph36) <*Loc:* EV, Ph36>

rafalé[2], **-e** [rafale] *n.* greedy person *C'est trop un rafalé pour inviter à dîner.* He's too much a glutton to invite for dinner. (VM) <*Loc:* VM>

rafalement [rafalmɑ̃] *n.m.* downdraft, backdraft <*Loc:* Da84>

rafaler [rafale] *v.intr.* **1** to gust (of the wind) *Le vent était après rafaler.* The wind was gusting. (LA) **2** to change direction (of the wind) **Le vent rafale.* The wind changes direction (i.e. is variable). (Da84) **3** to backdraft **La cheminée rafale.* The chimney backdrafts. (Da84) *Le vent rafalait derrière le magasin.* There was a backdraft behind the barn. (LA) <*Loc:* LA, SM, Da84, Lv88>

raferdir ♦see **refroidir**

rafficher [rafiʃe] *v.tr.* **1** to repost, post again **2** to arrange, settle *Il va rafficher cette affaire pour moi.* He's going to take care of that matter for me. (IB) <*Loc:* EV, IB, Ph36>

raffiler (**réaffiler**) [rafile, reafile] *v.tr.* to resharpen *Raffiler un couteau.* To resharpen a knife. (LA) <*Loc:* LA, Da84>

raffinage [rafinaʒ] *n.m.* refining <*Loc:* Da84>

raffinement [rafinmɑ̃] *n.m.* **1** refining **2** refinement, nicety, culture <*Loc:* Da84>

raffiner [rafine] **I** *v.tr.* to refine *Raffiner du sucre.* To refine sugar. (VM) **II se raffiner** *v.pron.* to become refined *Tant qu'à lui, c'est un Cadien qui s'a raffiné depuis qu'il a été au Texas.* As for him, he's a Cajun who became refined after he went to Texas. (VM) <*Loc:* VM, Da84>

raffinerie [rafinri] *n.f.* refinery ◊ •**raffinerie de sucre** sugar refinery <Da84> •**raffinerie d'huile** oil refinery <Da84> <*Loc:* SM, Da84>

raffle [raf(l)] *n.f.* raffle, lottery <*Loc:* JE, VM, Da84, Lv88>

raffler [rafle] *v.tr.* to raffle, raffle off *Raffler une couverte.* To raffle off a blanket. (EV) <*Loc:* EV, IB, JE, SL, VM, Da84, Lv88>

rafistolage [rafistolaʒ] *n.m.* mending, patching, repairing <*Loc:* Da84>

rafistolé, -e [rafistole] *adj.* **1** mended, patched up, repaired *Une chemise rafistolée.* A mended shirt. (EV) **2** dressed up, elegantly dressed *L'homme dans l'hôtel était tout rafistolé.* The man in the hotel was all dressed up. (SM) <*Loc:* EV, SM, Da84>

rafistoler (**afistoler, rapistoler**) [rafistole, afistole, rapistole]

I *v.tr.* **1** to mend, patch up, repair *Ils ont rafistolé la maison.* They fixed up the house. (SM) *Jean et Marie ont rafistolé leur dispute.* John and Mary have patched up their quarrel. (IB) *Je rapistole ses chaussons.* I'm darning his socks. (IB) **2** to effectively put in order *J'ai bien afistolé l'affaire.* I carefully arranged the affair. (Lv88) **II se rafistoler** *v.pron.* to dress extravagantly *Elle s'est afistolée.* She got dressed up extravagantly. (Lv88) <***Loc:*** EV, IB, JE, SB, SM, TB, VM, Da84, Lv88, Ph36>

raforcir ♦see **renforcir**

rafraîchir [rafreʃir] **I** *v.tr.* to refresh, cool off *De la mauve. J'en ai bu plein de ça avec défunte mémère. C'était pour te rafraîchir. Tu pouvais boire ça n'importe qui temps.* Mallow. I drank a lot of that with my late grandmother. It was to refresh you. You could drink that whenever. (TB) **II se rafraîchir** *v.pron.* to cool off, be refreshed **Le temps se rafraîchit.* The weather is cooling off. (Da84) <***Loc:*** EV, TB, SJ, Da84>

rafraîchissant, -e [rafreʃisɑ̃, -ɑ̃t] *adj.* cooling, refreshing *Un bon gobelet de limonade, ça serait rafraîchissant droite asteur.* A good glass of lemonade would be refreshing right now. (EV) <***Loc:*** EV, TB, Da84>

rafraîchissement [rafreʃismɑ̃] *n.m.* refreshing, cooling <***Loc:*** LA, Da84>

rafroidir ♦see **refroidir**

ragaillardir [ragajardir] *v.intr.* to get well, recover, recuperate <***Loc:*** JD>

rage [raʒ] *n.f.* **1** rabies, hydrophobia **2** rage, uncontrolled anger <***Loc:*** Da84, Hi02>

ragé ♦see **enragé**

ragir ♦see **réagir**

ragoter ♦see **radoter**

ragoton [ragotɔ̃] *n.m.* man of short stature, runt *Il va rester un ragoton toute sa vie.* He'll remain a short, stubby guy all his life. (TB) <***Loc:*** TB>

ragouillage [ragujaʒ] *n.m.* bad cooking, badly prepared dish *J'ai fait juste un ragouillage.* I just threw something together. (VM) <***Loc:*** JE, VM, Di32, Lv88>

ragouiller [raguje] *v.tr.* to make a stew or hash with (leftovers, esp. of meat) *Je vas ragouiller ça qui reste.* I'm going to make a stew out of what's left. (VM) <***Loc:*** JE, VM, Di32, Lv88>

ragoût [ragu] *n.m.* stew, ragout ◊ •**ragoût de patates** potato stew <LF> <***Loc:*** LF, Da84>

rai ♦see **rais**

raide[1] [rɛd, red] *adj.* **1** stiff, rigid, unbending *T'es raide comme un jarret de bœuf.* You are as stiff as a bull's hock. (LA) *Raide comme un clou.* As stiff as a nail. (LA) **2** firm *Le candi était pas encore raide assez pour le couper.* The fudge was not yet firm enough to cut. (EV) **3** tight (of a rope) *Hale le câble aussi raide que tu peux.* Pull the rope as tight as you can. (LA) <***Loc:*** EV, LA, Da84>

raide[2] [rɛd, red] *adv.* **1** heavily, hard *La pluie tombe raide.* It is raining hard. (SM) **2** instantly, immediately *Tuer raide.* To kill instantly. (SM) <***Loc:*** SM>

raidement [rɛdmɑ̃] *adv.* at a good clip or pace **Ça marche raidement.* Things are moving at a good clip. (Da84) <***Loc:*** Da84>

raidir (**raidzir**) [redir, rɛdzir] **I** *v.tr.* **1** to stiffen, make rigid **2** to tighten *Raidir un câble.* To tighten a rope. (LA) **3** to straighten *Raidir une planche.* To straighten a plank. (LA) **II** *v.intr.* **1** to stiffen **2** to straighten, straighten up *Quand il a attendu la nouvelle, il a raidi du coup.* When he heard the news, he straightened up on the spot. (LA) <***Loc:*** JE, LA, VM, Da84>

raidissoir [rediswar] *n.m.* wire stretcher <***Loc:*** VM>

raie [rɛ, re] *n.f.* furrow (between rows in a field) *Il faut tu mets tes cannes coupées en travers des rangs. Dans la raie tu pouvais passer ta main, tu pouvais attraper une brassée de cannes.* You have to put your cut cane across the rows. In the furrow you could run your hand along and you could grab an armful of cane. (LA) <***Loc:*** AC, IV, LA, Da84>

raignure ♦see **rainure**

rail [rɛl] *n.m.* rail (of a railroad track) *Marche pas sur les rails, le char va passer bétôt.* Don't walk on the rails, the train will come by soon. (VM) <***Loc:*** VM, Da84>

raine [rɛ̃n] *n.f.* frog *La raine chante beaucoup.* The frog sings a lot. (AV) <***Loc:*** AV>

rainette (**grainette, ranette, renette**) [rɛ̃nɛt, grɛ̃nɛt, rɑ̃nɛt, rønɛt] *n.f.* any small green frog, such as a tree frog or rain frog <***Loc:*** AC, AV, EV, JE, SL, VM, Da84, Gu00, Hi02, Ph36>

rainure (**raignure**) [rɛ̃nyr, rɛ̃jyr] *n.f.* **1** rut (in a road) *Il y avait des rainures dans le chemin.* There were ruts in the road. (SL) *La raignure où le char passait était plein d'eau.* The rut where the car passed was full of water. (TB) **2** groove of a tongue-and-groove coupling <***Loc:*** LF, SL, TB, Gr86>

rais (**rai**) [rɛ, re] *n.f.* spoke (of a wheel) *Il y avait des rais de wagon en bois tout le tour.* There were wooden wheel spokes all the way around. (EV) <***Loc:*** EV, VM, Da84>

raisé, -e [reze] *adj.* streaked *J'ai lavé la robe mais c'est toujours raisée.* I washed the dress but it's still streaked. (VM) <***Loc:*** VM>

raiser [reze] *v.tr.* **1** to make furrows for sowing *La semaine passée, on a raisé la terre pour planter le maïs.* Last week, we made furrows to plant the corn. (Lv88) *Il a raisé le rang pour planter les cannes.* He plowed the row to plant sugar cane. (SM) **2** to bring up dirt to the roots of *Raiser ses pieds de tomate.* To build up dirt around the base of one's tomato plants. (VM) **3** to turn over (eggs) in an incubator *Ils ont oublié de raiser les œufs et ils les ont tout perdus.* They forgot to turn over the eggs and they lost them all. (VM) <***Loc:*** JE, SL, SM, VM, Da84, Lv88>

raisin [rezɛ̃, resɛ̃] *n.m.* **1** grape **2** raisin ◊ •**du raisin** seaweed <JE> <***Loc:*** JE, SM, VM, Da84, Hi02>

raison [rezɔ̃] *n.f.* **1** reason *Enfin j'ai commencé mon à travailler et je faisais plus dans un mois que mon pauvre vieux papa faisait dans toute l'année. Ça fait, je voyais pas de raison d'aller finir l'école.* Finally I started to work and I made more in a month than my poor old dad made in a whole year. So I saw no reason to go finish school. (TB) **Pour cette raison.* For this reason. (Da84) **2** sense, reason, good sense *Son procès fut jugé d'une voix si-z-horrible, car le jeu et la boisson te fait perdre la raison.* The verdict was announced in such a horrible voice because gambling and drinking make you lose your mind. (PQ, ch: *Le jour de l'Ascension*) *Ce malheureux garçon, tout rempli de boisson, parle à son père sans entendre raison.* That miserable boy, all full of liquor, speaks to his father without listening to reason. (PQ, ch: *Le jour de l'Ascension*) **3** speech, manner of speech *T'as sûr une bonne raison en français pour un Américain.* You sure have a good manner of speaking French for an Anglophone. (VM) ◊ **•avoir raison** to be right *Ils avaient raison pour ça.* They were right about that. (PQ) <PQ, Da84> **•en raison que** because, since *Et asteur, en raison que le cipre est tellement rare, ils usont du bois qui vient de Honduras, ça qu'on appelle du SPANISH CEDAR.* And today, since cypress is so rare, they use wood that comes from Honduras, what they call Spanish cedar. (LF) <LF> **•faire de la raison** to make sense *Et tu connais quand-ce que quelqu'un est juste après te parler et que tu trouves il est pas après faire de la raison, juste après parler, parler pour arien, tu connais? Ma grand-mère disait "Arrête cette radote-là."* And you know when someone is just talking to you and you find that he isn't making any sense, he's just talking, talking for no reason, you know? My grandmother used to say, "Stop that babbling." (TB) <TB> **•la raison qui fait** the reason why *Ça c'est la raison qui fait on part.* That's the reason why we are leaving. (AV) <AV> **•se faire des raisons** to make excuses <Da84> <***Loc:*** AV, EV, PQ, TB, VM, Da84>

raisonnable [rezɔ̃nab(l)] *adj.* right, reasonable, sensible, fair, just *Ça sera pas raisonnable que je fais ça.* It wouldn't be right for me to do that. (VM) <***Loc:*** EV, VM, Da84>

raisonnablement [rezɔ̃nabləmɑ̃] *adv.* reasonably, sensibly *Il manie son argent raisonnablement.* He handles his money reasonably. (AC) <***Loc:*** AC, Da84>

raisonnement [rezɔ̃nmɑ̃] *n.m.* reasoning, reason <***Loc:*** Da84>

raisonner [rezɔ̃ne] *v.intr.* to reason *Moi, je trouve pas qu'il raisonne trop bien dans cette affaire.* I don't find that he is reasoning very well in this matter. (LA) <***Loc:*** LA, Da84>

raiton [retɔ̃] *n.m.* little stingray <***Loc:*** Re31>

rajeunezir ♦see **rajeunir**

rajeunir (rajeunezir) [raʒœnir, raʒœnzir, raʒœʒir] *v.intr.* to get younger, rejuvenate *Ça vous fait du bon, il me semble que vous rajeunezissez.* It does you good, it seems to me that you are getting younger. (VM) <***Loc:*** IB, JE, SL, VM, Da84>

rajouter (réajouter) [raʒute, reaʒute] *v.tr.* **1** to add to again *On a eu pour rajouter au gombo quand les enfants ont arrivé.* We had to add to the gumbo again when the kids arrived. (LA) **2** to piece together *Il a rajouté sa porte.* He put his door together with several pieces. (AC) <***Loc:*** AC, LA, Da84>

rajustement (réajustement) [raʒystmɑ̃, reaʒystmɑ̃] *n.m.* readjustment <***Loc:*** Da84>

rajuster (réajuster) [raʒyste, reaʒyste] *v.tr.* to readjust *Il a rajusté sa cravate avant de rentrer dans la salle.* He readjusted his tie before going into the dancehall. (LA) **II se rajuster** *v.pron.* to readjust o.s., readjust one's clothes *Il s'a rajusté avant de sortir.* He readjusted himself before going out. (LA) <***Loc:*** LA, Da84>

râle[1] [ral] *n.m./f.* **1** rail, any of various marsh birds **Maigre comme une râle.* Skinny as a rail. (Da84) **2** quail *Il a tiré deux râles.* He shot two quail. (SL) **3** marsh hen ◊ **•râle bleu(e) / râle d'eau** marsh guinea, marsh hen, purple gallinule <VM, Re31> **•râle poule d'eau** marsh water hen <Re31> **•râle grise** clapper rail <VM> **•râle masqué** sora rail (with a black face and throat) <TB, Re31> **•grande râle de prairie** king rail <Re31> <***Loc:*** IB, SB, SL, SM, TB, VM, Da84, Guoo, Re31>

râle[2] [ral] *n.m./f.* rattle (in the throat) *Il avait la râle et son souffle était bien bien court.* He had a rattle in the throat and his breath was very very short. (EV, Gr86) ◊ **•râle de la mort** death rattle <Da84> <***Loc:*** EV, JE, Da84, Gr86>

râlement [ralmɑ̃] *n.m.* rattle (in the throat) <***Loc:*** Da84>

râler [rale] *v.intr.* **1** to rattle in the throat or bronchial tubes *Le pauvre bougre était couché dans son lit. Je l'entendais après râler de l'autre chambre.* The poor fellow was lying in his bed. I could hear him rattling from the next room. (LA) **2** to make noise, growl *Ton estomac râle.* Your stomach is growling. (VM) <***Loc:*** LA, TB, VM, Da84>

ralingue [ralɛ̃, relɛ̃ŋ] *n.f.* weighted rope *T'amarres la trawl, une ralingue de chaque bord. Il a une qui va dessus la gauche et une qui va sur la droite.* You attach the trawl with a weighted rope on each side. It has one that goes on the left and one that goes on the right. (TB) <***Loc:*** LF, TB>

rallongement [ralɔ̃ʒmɑ̃] *n.m.* **1** lengthening **2** extension, addition <***Loc:*** Da84>

rallonger [ralɔ̃ʒe] *v.tr.* to lengthen, extend *Il faudra qu'on rallonge le hangar pour mettre les nouveaux veaux à l'abri.* We'll have to extend the barn to shelter the new calves. (LA) <***Loc:*** LA, Da84>

rallumer [ralyme] **I** *v.tr.* to relight, rekindle *Laisse faire. On va rallumer le feu demain matin.* Let it be. We'll relight the fire tomorrow morning. (LA) **II se rallumer** *v.pron.* to be rekindled, be relighted *Le feu s'a rallumé dans le vent.* The fire rekindled itself in the wind. (LA) <***Loc:*** EV, LA, Da84>

ramancher[1] **(remmancher)** [rɑ̃mɑ̃ʃe] *v.tr.* **1** to refit a handle (to a tool) *Ramancher une pioche.* To refit the handle of a hoe. (VM) *Il faudra remmancher la pelle avant de faire le fossé.* It will be necessary to refit a handle on the shovel before digging the ditch. (LA) **2** to set (a broken bone) *Il a crié fort quand le docteur a eu pour ramancher sa jambe.* He yelled out when the doctor had to set his leg. (VM) **3** to fix, repair *Il a ramanché l'automobile.* He repaired the car. (SM) *Sa machine à coudre était cassée, il l'a ramanchée avec du fil.* Her sewing machine was broken, he fixed it with some wire. (AC) **4** to put back together *J'ai eu des affaires d'amenées icitte-là avant qu'était tout défait dans morceaux, et j'ai ramanché ça* BACK *et partais ça.* I've had things brought here before that were all taken apart into pieces, and I put it back together and started it up. (TB) **5** to assemble, put together, make *Il a ramanché une barouette avec des boutes de planches et quelques clous.* He put together a wheelbarrow with some bits of board and some nails. (TB) **6** to improvise (a solution) *Il va remmancher quelque chose plutôt que dire il a perdu.* He'll improvise something before admitting that he lost. (LA) <***Loc:*** AC, JE, LA, SM, TB, VM, Da84>

ramancher[2] **(ramâcher)** [rɑ̃mɑ̃ʃe, rɑ̃maʃe] **I** *v.tr.* **1** to mutter, mumble *Il était planté là après ramancher toute sorte de couillonade.* He was there muttering all sorts of silliness. (LA) **2** to garble, mix up (e.g. a story) *Il a ramanché une histoire.* He got the story all mixed up. (SM) **3** to make up, invent, fabricate *Il a ramanché toutes espèces de choses sur toi.* He made up all sorts of things about you. (VM) **4** to narrate, tell **I nous a ramanché einne histoire.* He told us a story. (EV, Ph36) **II** *v.intr.* to talk idly, talk unintelligible drivel *Arrête donc de ramancher comme ça.* Stop talking idly like that. (LA) <***Loc:*** AV, EV, IB, LA, SB, SJ, SM, TB, VM, Lv88, Ph36>

ramarrer [rɑ̃mare] *v.tr.* to retie *Il faudra tu ramarres tes souliers. Ils sont tout démarrés.* You'll have to retie your shoes. They are untied. (LA) <***Loc:*** JD, LA, SM, Da84, Lv88>

ramassage [rɑ̃masaʒ] *n.m.* **1** gathering, picking, collection *Le ramassage de coton commence demain.* The cotton picking begins tomorrow. (SM) *On a fait un ramassage d'œufs pour la crème.* We collected eggs for the ice cream. (SL) **2** communal harvest *Ils ont fait un ramassage.* They made a communal harvest. (VM) <***Loc:*** SL, SM, VM, Da84, Lv88>

ramasse [rɑ̃mas] *n.f.* **1** harvest, harvesting, collection *C'était le temps de la ramasse de coton. Ça fait, lui fallait il prend son sac de coton puis il va aller le ramasser tout seul.* It was cotton harvest time. So, he had to take his cotton sack and he went to pick it by himself. (EV) **2** lot, heap, pile **Il a attrapé une ramasse de poisson.* He caught a lot of fish. (Da84) **3** beating, whipping, thrashing, shower of blows ◊ **•foutre une ramasse (à qqn)** ***a*** to slap (s.o.) *Et ma mame me disait "Frème la porte, les moustiques va rentrer." Et alle retournait, et je retournais, je rouvais la porte encore jusqu'à je m'ai fait foutre une ramasse.* And my mother told me, "Shut the door, the mosquitos will come in." And she would turn her back, and I would go back, I would open the door again, until I got myself slapped. (LF) ***b*** to give a sound drubbing (to s.o.) *Donner une ramasse de coups de bâton.* To beat with a stick. (JD) <JD, LF> <***Loc:*** EV, JD, LF, Da84, Lv88>

ramassé ♦see **ramassis**

ramasse-coton [rɑ̃maskotɔ̃] *n.f.* cotton picking, gathering of cotton **La ramasse-côton est proche finie.* The cotton picking is almost over. (EV, Ph36) <***Loc :*** EV, SM, Ph36>

ramasser[1] [rɑ̃mase] **I** *v.tr.* **1** to pick up *Je vas pas te redemander de ramasser ton linge.* I'm not going to ask you again to pick up your clothes. (EV) *L'avalasse a ramassé tout ça.* The flood picked up all that. (VM) **2** to pick, gather, harvest *Il a ramassé du coton.* He picked some cotton. (SL) *J'ai ramassé des figues.* I picked some figs. (SM) *Ramasser les roses du jardin.* To pick roses from the garden. (JD) **3** to collect, gather up *On ramassait l'eau de la couverture.* We were collecting water from the roof. (Lv88) *Maintenant, on va ramasser la musique acadienne.* Now we will collect Acadian music. (Lv88) **4** to pick up, collect for transport (e.g. in a vehicle) *Ils vont ramasser votre prescription chez vous.* They will stop by your house to pick up your prescription. (AC) *Il envoie un* TRUCK *pour ramasser les bêtes.* He sends a truck to pick up the cattle. (Lv88) **5** to give (s.o.) a lift, take (s.o.) along (in a vehicle) *C'est peut-être les hommes qu'a venu te ramasser pour aller à l'ouvrage.* Maybe it's the men who've come to get you to go to work. (LF) *Je venais de Lafayette une fois et j'ai ramassé un soldat français. Ça c'était dans les années quarante.* Once I was coming from Lafayette and I gave a French soldier a lift. That was in the forties. (SL) **6** to apprehend, arrest, take into custody **Moi je m'ai mis dans le tracas, la loi m'as ramassé, moi je suis parti dans la prison.* I got into trouble, the law apprehended me, and I went to prison. (ch: *La porte d'en arrière*) **7** to tidy up, straighten up, put in order **J'ai manière honte que j'ai pas eu le temps ramasser la maison.* I'm a bit embarrassed that I didn't have time to straighten up the house. (ThCa: *Le charivari*) **8** to pick up, learn (e.g. a language) without formal instruction *Lui je crois pas qu'il est un pur Cadien, il a ramassé le patois, tu sais.* I don't think he's a pure Cajun, he picked up the dialect, you know. (TB) **II se ramasser** *v.pron.* to be deposited or piled up *Pendant l'ouragan* AUDREY *toutes qualités d'affaires s'ont ramassé contre la levée du* INTERCOSTAL. During hurricane Audrey, all kinds of things got piled up against the Intercostal levee. (VM) *Un corps s'a ramassé au Lac Arthur.* A corpse ended up deposited at Lake Arthur. (VM) ◊ **•ramasser dans les rangs hauts** to have it easy <LA, La99> <***Loc:*** AC, AV, EV, IB, JD, LA, LF, SB, SL, SM, TB, VM, Da84, Hi02, La99, Lv88, Ph36, ThCa>

ramasser[2] [rɑ̃mase] *v.tr.* to correct in a brusque way, dress down *Son frère croyait il était malin, mais il l'a ramassé devant tout le monde.* His brother thought he was clever, but he dressed him down in front of everyone. (LA) <***Loc:*** LA>

ramasserie [rɑ̃masri] *n.f.* **1** harvest (often done as a cooperative community event) *Une ramasserie de pacanes, de coton.* A (communal) harvest of pecans, of cotton. (Lv88) **2** cotton picking (often done as a cooperative community event) *Si quelqu'un tombait malade et pouvait pas ramasser leur coton, eux faisait une ramasserie.* If someone got sick and could not harvest their cotton, they did a cooperative community cotton picking [for that person]. (LA) **3** *(pl.)* leftovers, scraps (of a meal) *Ramasseries du dîner.* Scraps from the dinner table. (SJ) <***Loc:*** AV, IB, JD, JE, LA, SJ, SL, VM, Lv88>

ramasseur [rɑ̃masœr] *n.m.* picker, gatherer, harvester *Les ramasseurs sont là pour ramasser le coton.* The pickers are there to harvest the cotton. (SM) *J'ai ramassé mon coton avec vingt ramasseurs.* I harvested my cotton with twenty pickers. (VM) ◊ **•ramasseur de coton** cotton picker *Il y avait pas de manger pour les ramasseurs de coton.* There wasn't any food for the cotton pickers. (SL) <SL, Da84> <***Loc:*** SL, SM, VM, Da84>

ramasseuse [rɑ̃masøz] *n.f.* reaping machine, harvester ◊ **•ramasseuse à coton** cotton harvesting machine <EV> <***Loc:*** EV, SM, Lv88>

ramassis (ramassé) [rɑ̃masi, rɑ̃mase] *n.m.* **1** *(pl.)* food scraps, feed slop, swill *Donner des ramassis aux cochons.* To feed the pigs. (EV) **2** pile of trash, driftwood or flotsam deposited by floods or waves (esp. hurricane or storm-related) *Un ramassis, c'est un amas de drigailles.* A 'ramassis' is a pile of worthless trash. (LF) <***Loc:*** EV, LF, VM>

rame[1] [rɑ̃m] *n.f.* stake (for staking plants) *T'aurais amarré tes pieds de tomates après des rames.* You would have tied your tomato stalks to stakes. (EV) ◊ **•haricot (de) rame** vining string bean, pole bean <AV, IB, JD, LA, LF, SB, SM, TB, Da84> <***Loc:*** AV, EV, IB, IV, LA, LF, SB, SM, TB, Da84>

rame[2] [rɑ̃m] *n.f.* oar <***Loc:*** SB>

rameau [rɑ̃mo] *n.m.* **1** branch of a magnolia (or other tree) blessed by a priest on Palm Sunday **2** magnolia tree *Les rameaux font des larges fleurs blanches.* Magnolias produce large white flowers. (AV) <***Loc:*** AV, EV, IB, JD, JE, SM, TB, Da84, Ho90, Lv88, Ph36, Re31>

ramener (remener, remmener) [rɑ̃mne, rəmne] *v.tr.* **1** to bring back, take back, lead back **Ramène-le chez lui.* Take him back home. (Da84) *Et je m'ai saoulé que je pouvais plus marcher, ils m'ont ramené* BACK *à la maison.* And I drank until I couldn't walk, they brought me back to the house. (ch: *La porte d'en arrière*) **2** to restore *Là ils ont ramené la langue de français, mais pas des Cadiens.* They restored the French language, but not the Cajuns'. (SL) <***Loc:*** AC, EV, LA, SL, TB, Da84>

ramequin [rɑ̃mkɛ̃] *n.m.* feast, banquet <***Loc:*** JE, Di32, Gr86>

ramer[1] [rɑ̃me] *v.tr.* to stake, support (plants) with a stake **Ramer des fèves plattes.* To stake butter beans. (Da84) *Quand tes tomates venaient assez haut, tu les ramais.* When the tomatoes got tall enough, you would stake them. (EV) <***Loc:*** EV, IV, Da84>

ramer[2] [rɑ̃me] *v.tr.* to row (using oars) *Ramer les skiffs pour aller travailler et revenir. Hiver comme été.* Rowing skiffs to go to work and back. Winter and summer alike. (SB) <***Loc:*** SB>

rametien [rɑ̃mtʃɛ̃] *n.m.* **1** chatting **2** gossip **3** patois, dialect, brogue <***Loc:*** AV, EV, Ph36>

rameur [rɑ̃mœr] *n.f.* plant that creeps or climbs <***Loc:*** VM>

ramollir [rɑ̃molir] **I** *v.tr.* to soften, resoften *Là il faullait ramollir le beurre.* Then you had to soften the butter. (LA) **II se ramollir** *v.pron.* to become soft, grow soft *Il est juste après se ramollir assis à la maison à rien faire.* He's just growing soft sitting at home doing nothing. (LA) <***Loc:*** LA, Da84>

ramoner [rɑ̃mɔ̃ne] *v.tr.* **1** to reprimand, rebuke, reprove *Elle l'a bien ramoné devant tout le monde.* She reprimanded him severely in front of everyone. (LA) **2** to beat up *Il l'a ramoné à coups de poing.* He beat him up with punches. (SM) <***Loc:*** LA, SL, SM, Lv88>

rance[1] [rɑ̃s] *adj.* rancid *Le beurre est rance. Je peux le sentir d'ici.* The butter is rancid. I can smell it from here. (LA) <***Loc:*** EV, JE, LA, SM, Da84>

rance[2] [rɑ̃s] *n.f.* **1** rafter, post, stake **2** long piece of wood or other material used as a lever to lift heavy objects *Il a usé une rance pour lever l'arbre.* He used a lever to lift the tree. (SM) **3** wooden roller used for moving buildings *On a halé la maison sur des rances.* They towed the house along on rollers. (VM) <***Loc:*** SL, SM, TB, VM, Lv88>

rancée ♦see **rincée**

rancer ♦see **rincer**

ranche [rɑ̃ʃ] *n.f.* **1** spoke (of a wheel) **2** light rail (along the side of a cart) <***Loc:*** IB, JE, Di32, Lv88>

rancir [rɑ̃sir] *v.intr.* to become rancid *Si tu laisses le beurre trop longtemps sur le comptoir, ça va rancir.* If you leave the butter on the counter too long, it will become rancid. (LA) <***Loc:*** LA, Da84>

rancœur [rɑ̃kœr] *n.f.* rancor, bitterness <***Loc:*** Da84>

rancœurer ♦see **acœurer**

rancune [rɑ̃kyn] *n.f.* rancor, malice, extreme ill will ◊ **•par rancune** out of spite, out of malice *Il a tourné son dos sur son garçon par rancune.* He turned his back on his son out of spite. (LA) <LA, Da84> <***Loc:*** LA, Da84>

rancuneux, -euse [rɑ̃kynø, -øz] *adj.* spiteful, rancorous *Contrarie-le pas. C'est un bougre qu'est beaucoup rancuneux.* Don't cross him. That's a fellow who is very spiteful. (LA) <***Loc:*** JD, LA, Da84, Lv88>

rançure ♦see **rinçure**

ranette ♦see **rainette**

rang [rɑ̃] *n.m.* **1** row **Rang de chaises.* Row of chairs. (Da84) **Rang de maïs.* Row of corn. (Da84) *Rangs de canne.* Rows of sugar cane. (TB) **2** ring (on a turtle's back) *Les rangs venaient manière en arrière. Fallait pas tu la touches ici, elle t'aurait mordu.* The rings come around in the back. Better not touch her here, she [the snapping turtle] would have bitten you. (EV) ◊ **•être à rang d'oignons** to be assembled in a large crowd <TB, La99> **•trois-rangs** snapping turtle <EV> <***Loc:*** AC, EV, LA, SM, TB, VM, Da84, La99>

rangé, -e [rɑ̃ʒe] *adj.* arranged, tidy, in order *Son garage est tout le temps bien rangé.* His garage is always in order. (LA) <***Loc:*** LA, Da84>

rangée [rɑ̃ʒe] *n.f.* row, line, file *Il y avait deux rangées de bancs là.* There were two rows of benches there. (EV) **Rangée d'arbres.* Row of trees. (Da84) <***Loc:*** EV, Da84>

ranger (se) [rɑ̃ʒe] *v.pron.* **1** to seek refuge, take refuge *Si l'ouragan vient, range-toi chez nous-autres.* If the hurricane comes, come take refuge at our house. (VM) **Pendant la Révolution d'France, i' (les nobles) s'sont rangés ici.* During the Revolution in France, they (the nobility) sought refuge here. (Gr82) **2** to settle, make one's home in a new place *Et ils se sont tous rangés ici à St. Martin, près de la Nouvelle-Orléans.* And they all established themselves here in St. Martin, near New Orleans. (SM) **3** to return home *Il y avait deux ans qu'on l'avait pas vu. Là il s'a rangé.* We hadn't seen him in two years. Then he returned home. (AC) **4** to come, arrive *Je m'ai rangé à huit heures.* I arrived at eight o'clock. (VM) <***Loc:*** AC, JE, SM, TB, VM, Da84, Gr82, Lv88>

rangeux, -euse [rɑ̃ʒø, -øz] *adj.* careful, orderly, meticulous *Il a marié une femme beaucoup plus rangeuse que lui.* He married a woman who is much more meticulous than he. (LA) <***Loc:*** JE, LA, VM>

rantion ♦see **ration**

rantionner ♦see **rationner**

râpage [rapaʒ] *n.f.* grating, rasping <***Loc:*** Da84>

rapapiote [rapapjɔt] *n.m.* thin, shriveled, emaciated person (esp. a child) *Ces espèces de petits rapapiotes sont toujours flanqués ici.* Those miserable little children are always stuck here. (IB) <***Loc:*** IB>

raparaître ♦see **reparaître**

râpe [rap] *n.f.* **1** rasp, coarse file **2** scraper *Et là ça grattait le cochon avec des râpes. Me rappelle qu'eux-autres faisait ça comme ça. Eux-autres pendait le cochon et eux-autres faisait des râpes comme ça.* And they scraped the pig with scrapers. I remember that they did it like this. They hung the pig up and they scraped it like this. (LF) **3** grater **4** plane, wood plane <***Loc:*** AC, JE, LA, LF, SL, SM, VM, Da84>

râper [rape] *v.tr.* **1** to rasp, file (wood or other materials) *On a eu besoin de râper les bords un peu pour pouvoir les mettre.* We had to rasp the ends a bit in order to fit them. (LA) **2** to scrape *Et là ça grattait le cochon avec des râpes. […] Eux-autres pendait le cochon et eux-autres faisait des râpes comme ça. Ça râpait le cochon.* And they scraped the pig with scrapers. They hung the pig up and they scraped it like this. They scraped the pig. (LF) **3** to grate (cheese, etc.) *Râper du fromage pour mettre dans la salade.* Grating cheese to put on salad. (LA) <***Loc:*** EV, LA, LF, TB, Da84>

rapetissant, -e [raptisɑ̃, -ɑ̃t] *adj.* shrinking *La laine, c'est une étoffe qu'est rapetissante.* Wool is a material that shrinks. (LA) <***Loc:*** LA, Da84>

rapetisser [raptise] **I** *v.tr.* **1** to reduce in size, make smaller, take in (a garment) *T'auras besoin de rapetisser ton capot avant de le mettre.* You'll have to take in your coat before wearing it. (LA) **2** to shrink *L'eau chaude peut rapetisser ton linge.* Hot water can shrink your clothes. (LA) **II** *v.intr.* to shrink, get smaller **Il y a tout le temps un rat-de-bois ou un chaoui ou un cocodril qui en mangeait trois ou quatre dans ma bande de canards. Et tous les jours, ça revenait, ça rentrait dans le parc, la bande rapetissait.* There was always a possum or a raccoon or an alligator that would eat three or four ducks among my flock. And everyday, they would come back, they would go into the pen, the flock would get smaller. (EV, An94) <***Loc:*** EV, LA, TB, An94, Da84>

râpeuse [rapøz] *n.f.* grater <***Loc:*** EV>

rapiat [rapja] *adj.* selfish, greedy, rapacious *J'aimerais acheter dans son magasin, mais il est trop rapiat.* I would like to shop in his store, but he is too greedy. (SM) <***Loc:*** JE, SM, VM, Di32>

rapides [rapid] *n.pl.* rapids ◊ **•sauter les rapides** to decend or leap the rapids <Re31> <***Loc:*** Re31>

rapiéçage (**rapiécetage**) [rapjesaʒ, rapjestaʒ] *n.m.* patching, patching up, mending <***Loc:*** Da84>

rapiécement [rapjesmɑ̃] *n.m.* patching, patching up, mending <***Loc:*** LA, VM>

rapiécer (**rapiéceter**) [rapjese, rapjeste] *v.tr.* to patch, patch up, piece together, mend **Mes culottes rapiécetées.* My patched-up pants. (Wh69) <***Loc:*** Da84, Lv88, Wh69>

rapiécetage ♦see **rapiéçage**

rapiéceter ♦see **rapiécer**

rapigner [rapĩje] *v.intr.* to haggle, bargain (in order to get a lower price) *Il dit que je rapigne de trop.* He says I haggle too much. (TB) <***Loc:*** TB>

rapiqué, -e [rapike, raplike] *adj.* **1** in an upright position *Ti-Jean est assis rapiqué dans sa chaise.* Little John is seated upright in his chair. (IB) **2** cheerful, in a good humor *Il était bien rapiqué la dernière fois je l'ai vu.* He was quite cheerful the last time I saw him. (AC) **3** trying to act like a younger person *A l'âge de cinquante ans ce vieux homme était très rapiqué.* At the age of fifty that old man was constantly trying to act younger. (TB) <***Loc:*** AC, IB, TB, VM, Da84>

rapiquer [rapike] *v.intr.* to begin to feel better (after an illness) *Hier elle était bien malade, mais on dirait qu'elle a rapiqué aujourd'hui.* Yesterday she was really sick, but it seems as though she's doing better today. (VM) <***Loc:*** VM, Da84>

rapistoler ♦see **rafistoler**

raponneau [rapɔ̃no] *adj.* wretched-looking, of poor appearance <***Loc:*** JD>

rappareiller [rapareje] *v.tr.* **1** to pair off, match up *Elle est après rappareiller des vieux souliers.* She is matching up some old shoes. (SM) *Je suis après rappareiller tous ces vieux bas.* I'm pairing up all of these old stockings. (VM) **2** to match, find or provide an equal for *Prends ce morceau d'étoffe pour voir si tu peux me le rappareiller.* Take this piece of fabric to see if you can match it exactly for me. (SB) <***Loc:*** SB, SM, VM, Di32>

rappeler[1] [raple] **I** *v.tr.* to remember, recall *Je rappelle pas qu'est-ce que c'est ça.* I don't remember what it is. (JE) **II se rappeler** *v.pron.* to remember, recall *Je me rappelle pas.* I don't remember. (EV) *Je peux pas me rappeler.* I can't remember. (TB) *C'est pas comme ça là ça se nommait mais je peux plus me rappeler.* That's not what it was called but I can't remember anymore. (VM) ◊ **•se rappeler BACK** to remember *Tu parles de se rappeler BACK ces noms-là.* You're talking about summoning to mind those names. (VM) <VM> <***Loc:*** AC, AV, EV, IV, JE, LA, SL, TB, VM, Da84, Hi02>

rappeler[2] [raple] *v.tr.* to call again, call back *Rappelle-moi quand t'auras une chance.* Call me back when you get a chance. (VM) <***Loc:*** VM>

rappliquer [raplike] *v.tr.* to reapply *J'ai eu pour rappliquer trois fois pour mon argent de FEMA avant de recevoir mon chèque.* I had to reapply three times for my money from FEMA before receiving my check. (LA) <***Loc:*** LA, Da84>

rappointer [rapwɛ̃te] *v.tr.* to reappoint *Je peux pas croire qu'ils ont rappointé ce bougre après tout l'argent qu'il a volé.* I can't believe they reappointed that fellow after all the money he stole. (VM) <***Loc:*** TB, VM, Da84>

rappointir [rapwɛ̃tir] *v.tr.* to resharpen (to a point) *Rappointir un crayon.* To resharpen a pencil. (LA) <***Loc:*** LA, Da84>

rapport[1] [rapɔr] *n.m.* profit, gain *Avec l'ouragan, on a pas eu un tas de rapport dessus les cannes.* With the hurricane, we didn't have much gain with the cane. (VM) <***Loc:*** VM>

rapport[2] [rapɔr] *n.m.* report, account, tale *Il follait que tu TURN IN un rapport tous les matins. Si tu travaillais le soir, follait que tu TURN IN un rapport. Dire qui les puits faisaient.* You had to turn in a report every morning. If you worked in the evening you had to turn in a report to tell how the oil wells were doing. (TB) *Carculer combien de gaz qu'eux-autres faisait, et je faisais des rapports sur ça.* Calculating how much gas they were producing, and I filled out reports on that. (LF) <***Loc:*** LF, TB>

rapport[3] [rapɔr] *n.m.* relationship, connection *J'ai tout le temps eu un bon rapport avec ma belle-mère.* I have always had a good relationship with my mother-in-law. (EV) ◊ **•(par) rapport à *a*** because of *Condamné pour quatre-vingt-dix-neuf ans, c'est juste rapport aux paroles toi, t'as dit, qui m'a fait souffert aussi longtemps pour ça.* Condemned for ninety-nine years, it's all because of the words you said that made me suffer for so long over that. (ch: *La valse de quatre-vingt-dix-neuf ans*) *Alle comprend plus, par rapport à sa belle-mère, elle soignait sa belle-mère.* She understands more because of her mother-in-law, she used to take care of her mother-in-law. (TB) ***b*** on account of *Il l'a fait rapport à vous.* He did it on account of you. (VM) <AC, EV, LF, TB, VM, Da84, Hi02, Lv88> **•(par) rapport que** because **On est fier, nous-aut', que l'écrivisse est le symbole des Cadjins par rapport que c'est l'animal le plus courageux dedans le monde.* We're proud that the crawfish is the symbol of the Cajuns because it's the bravest animal in the world. (ThCa: *Mille misères*) <ThCa> <***Loc:*** AC, EV, LF, TB, VM, Da84, Hi02, Lv88, ThCa>

rapporter[1] [rapɔrte] **I** *v.tr.* to yield, produce (payment, profit, interest) **J'ai espoir que je pourrai RETIRE avec l'argent que les BEAN vont rapporter.* I hope I will be able to retire with the money that the beans will bring in. (Gu82) **II** *v.intr.* **1** to bear fruit, produce fruit **Les pruniers rapportent bien.* The plum trees are bearing well. (Da84) **2** to bear interest, yield interest *Mon compte rapporte pas beaucoup depuis quelques années.* My savings account doesn't bear much interest since the last few years. (LA) <***Loc:*** LA, VM, Da84, Gu82>

rapporter[2] [rapɔrte] **I** *v.tr.* to report, relate (e.g. news) *C'est ça qu'ils ont rapporté aux nouvelles hier au soir.* That's what they reported on the news last night. (VM) **II** *v.intr.* to bear tales, tattle *Arrêtez de rapporter comme ça, z-enfants!* Stop tattling like that, children! (LA) <***Loc:*** LA, VM>

rapporter[3] [rapɔrte] **I** *v.tr.* to bring back *Tu peux emprunter ma chaudière, mais sois sûr de la rapporter.* You can borrow my pot, but be sure to bring it back. (VM) **II** *v.intr.* to follow through **Et quand il a arrivé à la place ayoù eux devaient se battre-là, il a demandé si son camarade était là, mais eux lui a dit non. Il avait pas venu, il avait pas rapporté.* And when he arrived at the place where they were supposed to fight, he asked if his friend was there, but they told him no. He had not come, he had not followed through [with his promise]. (LA, An94) <***Loc:*** EV, IB, LA, VM, An94, Da84, Gu82>

rapporter[4] [rapɔrte] *v.tr.* to add on *Pape avait rapporté un bout dessus sa chambre et là il a mis un lit en dedans pour mon frère.* Pop had added a bit to the room and then he put a bed in there for my brother. (EV) <***Loc:*** EV>

rapporteur [rapɔrtœr] *n.m.* **1** news reporter **2** tale bearer, snitch, tattle-tale, gossip <***Loc:*** SB, Da84>

rapprendre (**réapprendre**) [raprɑ̃n, raprɑ̃d(r), reaprɑ̃n, reaprɑ̃d(r)] *v.tr.* to relearn *Ça faisait si longtemps que j'étais marié avec ce maudit Texien que j'ai eu pour rapprendre à faire un roux après que je l'ai quitté.* I had been married for so long to that damned Texan that I had to relearn to make a roux after I left him. (VM) <*Loc:* EV, IB, VM, Da84, Ph36>

rapproché, -e [raproʃe] *adj.* near, close *Le bois ressemble rapproché dans le brouillard. C'est signe de pluie.* The woods seem near in the fog. That's a sign of rain. (VM) <*Loc:* VM, Da84>

rapprochement [raprɔʃmɑ̃] *n.m.* **1** drawing closer **2** reconciliation (of persons) <*Loc:* Da84>

rapprocher [raproʃe] **I** *v.tr.* **1** to bring closer *J'ai rapproché mon char de la maison avant l'ouragan pour le protéger du vent.* I put my car closer to the house before the hurricane to protect it from the wind. (LA) **2** to bring closer together **II se rapprocher** *v.pron.* **1** to draw near or nearer, come closer, approach **Rapprochez-vous.* Come closer. (Da84) **2** to become reconciled ◊ **•rapprocher les deux bouts** to make ends meet *Avec tous ces petits, il a de la misère à rapprocher les deux bouts.* With all those kids, he has a hard time making ends meet. (EV) <EV> <*Loc:* EV, LA, Da84>

raquette [raket] *n.f.* **1** racket (for tennis, badminton, etc.) **2** cactus **3** prickly pear cactus <*Loc:* AV, SM, Da84, Guoo, Ho90>

rare [rar] *adj.* rare, scarce, uncommon *Les prêcheurs en français est rares asteur.* Preachers in French are rare now. (TB) *Équand-ce que les cipres a commencé à venir rares, qu'il y avait plus de cipres, eh ben ils ont commencé à faire des pirogues en planches.* When the cypress started getting rare, when there was no more cypress, well, they started making pirogues with boards. (LF) <*Loc:* EV, LF, SM, TB, Da84, Hi02>

rarement [rarmɑ̃] *adv.* **1** rarely, seldom *Il vient ici? —Rarement.* Does he come here? —Rarely. (VM) *On a des bananiers ici, ils poussent mais ils produit pas de fruit, rarement, parce que ça prend trop longtemps et avant il y a toujours une gelée.* We have banana trees here, they grow but they don't produce any fruit because it takes too long [to ripen] and beforehand there is always a freeze. (SL) **2** ever *La plus belle eau que j'ai rarement vue.* The prettiest water I've ever seen. (SM) <*Loc:* SL, SM, VM, Da84>

rareté [rarte] *n.f.* rarity, scarceness <*Loc:* Da84>

rarranger [rarɑ̃ʒe] **I** *v.tr.* **1** to rearrange **2** to tidy up again, straighten up again *J'ai eu pour rarranger tous les lits que les enfants avaient défaits.* I had to remake all the beds that the children had undone. (VM) **3** to mend, repair *Je vas le rarranger t'à l'heure.* I'll mend it shortly. (TB) **4** to resolve *On aurait rarrangé les affaires là, chère.* We would have resolved our issues right there, honey. (EV) **II se rarranger** *v.pron.* **1** to adjust o.s., adjust one's clothing **2** to reconcile, become reconciled *Ils s'ont rarrangés.* They reconciled. (VM) <*Loc:* EV, TB, VM>

ras[1] [ra] *adj.* ◊ **•jour ras** slack day (in fishing) <JE> <*Loc:* JE>

ras[2] [ra] *n.m.* ◊ **•à ras** full to the brim *Une grosse pluie qu'avait tombé. On arrive au canal. C'était à ras.* A heavy rain had fallen. We arrived at the canal. It was full to the brim. (SL) <SL> **•au ras** nearby, close by *Il reste au ras.* He lives nearby. (SM) *T'as mis ça au ras.* You put that close by. (VM) **Droite au-ras.* Right nearby. (Da84) <SM, VM, Da84> **•au ras (de)** ***a*** near, close to, next to *Au ras de chez moi.* Near my house. (Lv88) *Il avait une petite maison au ras de la maison à Mame et Pape.* He had a little house next to Mom and Pop's house. (EV) *Elle me mettait couché au ras d'elle pour me tiendre chaud, pour pas j'attrape du mal.* She put me to bed right next to her, to keep me warm so that I wouldn't get sick. (SL) *J'ai planté mon rosier droite au ras de ma porte de devant.* I planted my rose bush right next to my front door. (VM) *Elle reste au ras la poste.* She lives near the post office. (SM) ***b*** approximately, about, around *L'oragan Audrey a tué au ras de cinq cents personnes.* Hurricane Audrey killed nearly five hundred people. (Lv88) **Pas loin d'icitte, au ras de trente mille piastres.* Not far from here, around thirty thousand dollars. (ThCa: *La table des veuves*) *Au ras de Christmas.* Around Christmas. (EV) <EV, SL, SM, TB, VM, Da84, Guoo, Lv88> <*Loc:* AC, EV, LA, LF, SL, SM, TB, VM, Da84, Guoo, Lv88, ThCa>

rasage [razaʒ] *n.m.* shaving <*Loc:* Da84>

rasant, -e [razɑ̃, -ɑ̃t] *adj.* extremely sharp *Mon couteau est assez affilé il est rasant.* My knife is so well sharpened that it's razor sharp. (LA) <*Loc:* LA, Da84>

rase[1] [raz] *adj.* flush, even *Le clos de riz était rase.* The rice field was cut flush to the ground. (LA) <*Loc:* LA, Da84>

rase[2] [raz] *n.f.* ◊ **•à (la) rase** ***a*** to the brim *Il a rempli sa tasse à rase de café. Ça m'étonne donc pas que ç'a débordé.* He filled his cup to the brim with coffee. It doesn't surprise me then that it overflowed. (VM) *Plein à la rase.* Full to the brim. (Lv88) ***b*** flush *Et une grosse pluie qu'avait tombé. On arrive au canal là, c'était à rase.* There had been a big rain. We get to the canal there, it [the water] was flush with the bank. (SL) **Couper à la rase.* To cut flush with the surface. (Da84) <SL, SM, VM, Da84, Guoo, Lv88> <*Loc:* SL, SM, VM, Da84, Guoo, Lv88>

rasé, -e [raze] *adj.* **1** shaven *Je veux me faire enterrer bien rasé.* I want to be buried well-shaven. (EV) **2** worn (of the teeth of animals) *Un vieux cheval avec les dents rasées.* An old horse with worn teeth. (LA) **3** done for, finished *Il est rasé pour toujours en politique.* His political career is done for. (SB) <*Loc:* EV, LA, SB, VM, Da84>

rasée (rasure) [raze, razyr] *n.f.* ◊ **•à la rasée {rasure}** ***a*** to the brim ***b*** flush <VM, Da84, Guoo, Lv88> <*Loc:* SL, SM, VM, Da84, Guoo, Lv88>

raser[1] [raze] **I** *v.tr.* **1** to shave *Mon père était barbier. Il allait raser les morts au* FUNERAL HOME. My father was a barber. He used to go shave the dead at the funeral home. (LA) **2** to rasp (e.g. wood) *C'est pour raser le bois.* It is used to rasp wood. (SM) **II se raser** *v.pron.* to shave o.s. **Tous les matins je me rase avant je bois mon café.* Every morning I shave before I drink my coffee. (Hi02) ◊ **•raser les cannes** to cut the cane at the end of summer so that it will resprout <SM, Lv88> <***Loc:*** LA, SM, Da84, Hi02, Lv88>

raser[2] [raze] *v.intr.* to be blissful, be very happy *Il s'est choqué après moi, mais je lui ai donné un gros morceau de tarte et après ça il rasait.* He got mad at me, but I gave him a big piece of pie and after that he was really happy. (EV) <***Loc:*** EV>

raseur [razœr] *n.m.* barber *Je vais passer chez le raseur à ce soir.* I'm going to the barber this evening. (VM) <***Loc:*** JE, TB, VM, Lv88>

raseuse [razøz] *n.f.* **1** sickle bar mower **2** cane shaver, machine that cuts sugar cane shoots after the first freeze <***Loc:*** EV, SM, VM, Lv88>

rasoir[1] [razwar] *adj.* rapacious, greedy *J'aime pas* DEAL *avec lui. Il est trop rasoir.* I don't like to deal with him. He's too rapacious. (SM) <***Loc:*** SM>

rasoir[2] [razwar] *n.m.* razor <***Loc:*** SM, Da84>

rasoir[3] [razwar] *n.m.* shin <***Loc:*** EV>

raspaille [raspaj] *n.f.* children's game of hide-and-seek or 'I spy' <***Loc:*** SJ>

rassasiant, -e [rasazjɑ̃, -ɑ̃t] *adj.* **1** satisfying *Boire une bière fraîche après une journée de travail au soleil, c'est rassasiant.* Drinking a cold beer after a day of work in the sun is very satisfying. (VM) **2** filling <***Loc:*** VM, Da84>

rassasier (**rassasir**) [rasazje, rasazir] **I** *v.tr.* to satisfy, sate, satiate *J'ai bu un gros verre d'eau et ça m'a toujours pas rassasié.* I drank a big glass of water and it still didn't sate me. (VM) **II se rassasier** *v.pron.* to satisfy o.s., get one's fill, appease one's hunger *Il peut pas se rassasir à manger.* He can't get his fill of eating. (VM) *Je peux pas me rassasir.* I can't get enough. (SM) <***Loc:*** SM, VM, Da84>

rassasir ♦see **rassasier**

rassemblée [rasɑ̃ble] *n.f.* assembly, gathering ◊ **•rassemblée de famille** family reunion <EV> <***Loc:*** EV, IB, Da84, Lv88, Ph36>

rassembler [rasɑ̃ble] **I** *v.tr.* to assemble, gather together *On va rassembler tous les enfants et on va prendre un portrait pour Mame.* We're going to get all the children together and we'll take a picture for Mom. (VM) **II** *v.intr.* to assemble, gather, come together *On a rassemblé hier au soir.* We got together last night. (VM) **III se rassembler** *v.pron.* to assemble, come together **Ein matin éoù-ce qu'i'faisait bien froid les parents et les voésins se rassembliont avant le jour pour aider avec la boucherie.* One morning when it was really cold out my parents and neighbors got together before daybreak to help with the pig roast. (Gu82) *On se rassemblait comme ça là. Là des fois on avait des bals le dimanche après-midi.* We would get together like that. Sometimes we would have balls on Sunday afternoons. (EV) *Tous les Cadiens se rassemblent pour planner pour l'avenir.* All the Cajuns get together to plan for the future. (Lv88) <***Loc:*** EV, VM, Da84, Gu82, Hi02, Lv88>

rasseoir (**rassir**) [raswar, rasir] **I** *v.tr.* to reseat *Rasseoir un enfant.* To reseat a child. (EV) *Les enfants qui étaient rassis ont eu chacun une dragée.* The children who were reseated each got a hard candy. (LA) **II se rasseoir** *v.pron.* to sit down again *Rassisez-vous!* Sit back down! (VM) *T'as le temps, rassis-toi.* You've got time, sit back down. (TB) <***Loc:*** EV, JD, JE, LA, TB, VM, Da84, Lv88>

rassir ♦see **rasseoir**

rassis, -e [rasi, -iz] *adj.* stale *Tout ce qu'on a, c'est du pain rassis.* All we have is stale bread. (LA) <***Loc:*** LA, Da84>

rassurer (**réassurer**) [rasyre, reasyre] **I** *v.tr.* **1** to reassure *Ça me rassure pas d'attendre parler tous ces politiciens.* It does not reassure me to hear all those politicians talking. (LA) **2** to reinsure *Les compagnies d'assurance vont jamais rassurer les maisons en Ville.* The insurance companies will never reinsure the houses in New Orleans. (VM) **II se rassurer** *v.pron.* **1** to be reassured, reassure o.s. *Ma mère s'a rassuré quand elle m'a vu tourner dans la manche.* My mother was reassured when she saw me turn into the lane. (LA) **2** to make sure **3** to get reinsured *Il y a un tas de monde qui va pas pouvoir se rassurer.* There are a lot of people who will not be able to get reinsured. (LA) <***Loc:*** EV, LA, VM, Da84, Ph36>

rasure ♦see **rasée**

rat [ra] *n.m.* **1** rat **2** muskrat *T'allais au piège, tu prenais des bétailles, comme des* NUTRAS, *des rats, des gros rats eusse disait, des belettes, des loutres.* You would go trapping, you'd catch animals, like nutrias, muskrats, big rats as they would say, minks, otters. (LF) ◊ **•rat de bois** opossum, possum <AV, EV, IB, LF, SB, SL, SM, TB, Da84, Gu00, Hi02, Lv88, Ph36> **•rat musqué** muskrat *Mais ça partait d'ici, ça allait dans l'ouest, piéger les rats musqués.* But they used to go out from here, they went west to trap muskrats. (TB) *On a piégé 17 ans la même place. Et un hiver on a empoigné 8,500 rats musqués.* We trapped for 17 years in the same place. And one winter we caught 8,500 muskrats. (TB) <IB, LF, PQ, TB, Da84, Gu00, Hi02> **•faire le rat de bois** to play possum <Da84> <***Loc:*** AV, EV, IB, LF, PQ, SB, SL, SM, TB, Da84, Gu00, Hi02, Ph36, Re31>

ratanier ♦see **latanier**

ratapieux ♦see **ratapiot**[1]

ratapiot[1] (**ratapieux**) [ratapjo, ratapjø] *adj.* stingy <***Loc:*** JE, Di32>

ratapiot[2] [ratapjo] *n.m.* stingy man <***Loc:*** SM>

ratata [ratata] *n.m.* ◊ **•être sur un ratata** to be all dressed up <LF> <***Loc:*** LF>

ratatille ♦see **ratatin**

ratatin (**ratatille**) [ratatɛ̃, ratatij] *n.m.* mess *Marie va faire un ratatin de ça.* Mary will make a mess of that. (IB) <***Loc:*** IB>

ratatiner [ratatine] **I** *v.tr.* to shrivel, cause to shrivel up *La chesseresse a ratatiné mes cocombres.* The drought shriveled up my cucumbers. (VM) **II** *v.intr.* to shrivel up *Et quand-ce que ça continuait à cuire, et cuire et cuire, ça ratatinait, ça vient comme les gratons.* And when it would keep on cooking and cooking and cooking, it would shrink up, it becomes like cracklings. (LF) **III se ratatiner** *v.pron.* to shrivel up, shrink *Son pis s'a ratatiné depuis qu'elle a perdu son veau.* Her udder shrank after she lost the calf. (LA) <***Loc:*** EV, LA, LF, VM, Da84>

ratatouille [ratatuj] *n.f.* **1** thick stew **2** bad, unappetizing cooking **3** heavy rain, downpour **On a attrapé une ratatouille.* We caught a downpour. (Da84) **4** beating, spanking, whipping *Il a attrapé une bonne ratatouille.* He got a good beating. (SM) *Je l'ai donné une bonne ratatouille.* I gave him a good whipping. (VM) **5** reprimand, bawling out, scolding *Je lui donnerai une bonne ratatouille.* I'll give him a good scolding. (SB) **6** get-together where people sing, usu. at Christmas time <***Loc:*** AV, EV, IB, SB, SC, SJ, SL, SM, TB, VM, Da84, Gr86, La99, Ph36>

ratché, -e (**raché, -é**) [ratʃe] *adj.* **1** stingy, avaricious *C'était l'homme le plus ratché du monde.* He was the stingiest man on Earth. (VM) **2** wretched, miserable, pitiful <***Loc:*** JD, VM, Da84, La99>

rate[1] [rat] *n.f.* spleen *Ça use la rate du cochon pour attraper des écrevisses.* They use the spleen of the pig to catch crawfish. (EV) ◊ **•avoir pas de rate** to have a lot of stamina <Da84> <***Loc:*** EV, SM, Da84, La99>

rate[2] [rat] *n.f.* female rat <***Loc:*** SL, Da84>

rate[3] [rat] *n.f.* grater <***Loc:*** Da84>

râteau [rato] *n.m.* rake <***Loc:*** EV, JE, LA, LF, TB, VM, Da84, Hi02>

râtelier [ratelje] *n.m.* **1** hay rack *Nous-autres, on mettait un râtelier. Tu mettais le foin dans un râtelier, et ça mangeait ça.* We put up a hay rack. You would put the hay in a hay rack, and they [the animals] would eat it. (EV) **2** hitching-rack **3** set of false teeth, dentures *Alle a perdu son râtelier en haut.* She lost her dentures upstairs. (VM) <***Loc:*** EV, LF, SM, VM, Da84, Guoo, Hi02>

rater [rate] **I** *v.intr.* **1** to fail **Son plan a raté.* His plan failed. (Da84) **2** to misfire, fail to fire **Le fusil a raté.* The gun misfired. (Da84) **II se rater** *v.pron.* to miss by a narrow margin, come very near *Il s'a raté de se le faire mettre.* He nearly got taken. (TB) <***Loc:*** TB, Da84>

ration (**rantion**) [rasjɔ̃, rɑ̃sjɔ̃] *n.f.* ration, share, portion, allowance <***Loc:*** Da84>

rationnement [rasjɔnmɑ̃] *n.m.* **1** ration, share, portion, allowance **2** rationing <***Loc:*** Da84>

rationner (**rantionner**) [rasjɔne, rɑ̃sjɔne] *v.tr.* to ration, portion out, parcel out *Certaines choses étaient rationnées je me rappelle pendant la guerre, c'était un peu plus cher, le sucre était rationné, n-avait quelques autres choses qu'étaient rationnées, des pneus pour les autotomobiles, ça c'était rationné.* I remember, a few things were rationed during the war, it was a little bit more expensive, sugar was rationed, some other things were rationed, tires for cars, that was rationed too. (IB) <***Loc:*** IB, Da84>

râtoler, ratôler ♦see **râtonner**

râtonner (**râtoler, ratôler**) [ratɔ̃ne, ratole, rakɔ̃ne] *v.tr.* **1** to rake, rake up *Si tu râtonnes les feuilles, je vas te donner six escalins.* If you rake the leaves, I will give you seventy-five cents. (EV) *Il faut ratôler ces feuilles.* You need to rake up those leaves. (IB) **2** to scrape, scrape off <***Loc:*** EV, IB, JD, LF, SB, SL, SM, TB, VM, Da84, Lv88, Ph36>

rattacher [rataʃe] *v.tr.* to reattach, refasten, renail *J'ai été obligé de rattacher le zinc dessus la couverture.* I had to reattach the tin on the roof. (VM) <***Loc:*** VM, Da84>

rattraper [ratrape] **I** *v.tr.* **1** to retake, recoup, recover (losses) *Je vas jamais rattraper mon argent. Il faudra que je ferme mon business.* I'll never recoup my money. I'll have to close my business. (LA) **2** to recall, retrieve (a memory) *Allons voir qui je voulais te dire asteur, je peux pas le rattraper là qui on était après parler pour.* Let's see what I wanted to tell you now, I can't recall what we were talking about. (EV) **3** to recatch (an animal) *Il s'a sauvé dedans tout le bois, et les hommes a couru après, mais ils l'ont rattrapé.* He [the horse] escaped in all the trees and the men ran after him, but they caught him. (EV) **4** to overtake (in a race or contest) *Ils les ont rattrapés dans la dernière manche.* They caught up with them in the last inning. (VM) **II se rattraper** *v.pron.* **1** to recover one's losses **2** to catch up, get caught up (e.g. on work) *J'ai assez d'ouvrage, je vas jamais me rattraper.* I have so much work that I'll never get caught up. (VM) <***Loc:*** EV, LA, VM, Da84>

raugmenter [rogmɑ̃te, ragmɑ̃te] **I** *v.tr.* to increase, raise (a price) *Il raugmente le prix.* He raises the price. (IB) **II** *v.intr.* to increase, improve (of business) *Les affaires raugmentont asteur.* Business is improving now. (VM) <***Loc:*** IB, JD, VM, Di32>

ravage [ravaʒ] *n.m.* ravage, havoc <***Loc:*** Da84>

ravager [ravaʒe] *v.tr.* to ravage, cause havoc, devastate *L'ouragan a ravagé notre paroisse.* The hurricane ravaged our parish. (VM) <***Loc:*** VM, Da84>

ravaler ♦see **renvaler**

ravaud [ravo] *n.m.* trouble, disturbance ◊ **•faire le ravaud** to stir up trouble, pick a quarrel *Il est toujours après faire le ravaud au bal.* He's always stirring up trouble at the dances. (VM) <JE, VM> <***Loc:*** JE, VM>

ravert ♦see **ravet**

ravet (**ravert**) [ravɛ, rave, ravær] *n.m.* cockroach, roach *C'est plein de zireté de raverts.* It's full of cockroach filth. (TB) ◊ •**ravert de bois** wood roach *Si tu coupes du bois pour se chauffer, tu vas le mettre soit dans une pile sur le dehors de la maison, et les raverts va se mettre là-dedans, on appelle ça des raverts de bois.* If you cut wood for heating, you put it in a pile outside the house, the cockroaches will get in there, we call those wood roaches. (LF) <LF> •**avoir un ravet dans la poche** (said of a white person) to have some black ancestry <La99> <***Loc:*** AC, AL, AV, EV, IB, JD, JE, LA, LF, SB, SJ, SL, SM, TB, VM, Da84, Gu00, Hi02, La99, Lv88, Ph36, Re31>

ravigaud [ravigo] *n.m.* whim, caprice, fancy, notion *Le ravigaud m'a pris de le faire.* I did it on a whim. (VM) *Elle a eu un ravigaud de venir nous voir avec le bébé.* She had a notion to come and see us with the baby. (Lv88) *Il a un ravigaud d'aller avec toi.* He's got a notion to go with you. (SM) <***Loc:*** IB, JE, SM, VM, Di32, Lv88>

ravigorer [ravigore] *v.intr.* to take on new strength or new life <***Loc:*** JD>

ravioter [ravjote] *v.tr.* to revive, pick up, give new strength or life to *Ce coup de whisky va le ravioter.* This drink of whiskey will revive him. (LF) <***Loc:*** LF>

raviser [ravize] *v.tr.* to stare at *Jean est toujours à raviser Pierre.* John is always staring at Pierre. (IB) <***Loc:*** IB, JE, Di32>

ravoir (**réavoir**) [ravwar, rawar, reavwar, reawar] (*p.p.* **réeu, réu** [rejy]) *v.tr.* **1** to have again, get again **Réavoir la fièvre.* To have a fever again. (Da84) *Alle avait revenu pour que je la traite encore, à force que j'i avais fait du bien. Et pauvre bête, elle a jamais réeu ça* BACK. She had come back so I could treat her again, I had done her so much good. And poor thing, she never got it back again. (TB) **2** to get back, recover (a possession) *Il a jamais pu ravoir sa jument.* He was never able to recover his mare. (LA) <***Loc:*** JD, LA, TB, Da84>

rayer [reje] *v.tr.* **1** to candle (eggs) *Il a rayé des œufs pour voir s'ils étaient bons.* He candled some eggs to see if they were good. (SM) **2** to dig (e.g. a furrow) *Il me reste juste pour rayer un fossé à ce matin.* All I have left to do is dig a furrow this morning. (LA) <***Loc:*** EV, JD, LA, SM>

rayon [rejɔ̃] *n.m.* ray, beam <***Loc:*** Da84>

raz [ra] *n.m.* ◊ •**raz de marée** tidal wave *Ils disont que c'est un raz de marée qu'a tué tout ce monde à Camaron en 1957.* They say it's a tidal wave that killed all those people in Cameron in 1957. (VM) <VM, Gu00> <***Loc:*** VM, Gu00>

re- (**er-, eur-, ar-, r'-**) [r(ə), ər, ar-, ær, r] *verb prefix* re-, again, back, more [*Note:* The pronunciation and spelling of this prefix are regionally variable. In the interest of space, we have noted the variant pronunciations but not the variant spellings in the relevant articles. The reader can expect to encounter variant spellings in the contextual examples provided in the entries as well as in texts written in Louisiana French.]

réaccoutumer ♦see **raccoutumer**

réaction [reaksjɔ̃] *n.f.* reaction <***Loc:*** Da84>

réadmettre (**radmettre**) [readmɛt(r) radmɛt(r)] *v.tr.* to readmit <***Loc:*** EV, Da84, Ph36>

réaffiler ♦see **raffiler**

réagir (**ragir**) [reaʒir, raʒir] *v.intr.* to react *Il l'a cogné tellement fort, le bougre a jamais seulement réagi.* He hit him so hard, the fellow never even reacted. (LA) <***Loc:*** EV, IB, LA, Da84, Hi02, Ph36>

réajouter ♦see **rajouter**

réajustement ♦see **rajustement**

réajuster ♦see **rajuster**

réaliser [realize] *v.tr.* to realize, be aware of *Il réalisait pas quoi il faisait.* He didn't realize what he was doing. (LA) <***Loc:*** LA, Da84>

réalité [realite] *n.f.* reality, fact <***Loc:*** Da84>

réapparaître [reaparɛt(r)] *v.intr.* to reappear, show up again *Ils ont réapparu dans le chassis.* They reappeared in the window. (LA) <***Loc:*** LA, Da84>

réapprendre ♦see **rapprendre**

réarmer (se) [rearme] *v.pron.* to rearm o.s. *Après que ses enfants ont quitté la maison, il s'a réarmé.* After his children left home, he started to keep guns again. (LA) <***Loc:*** LA, Da84>

réassurer ♦see **rassurer**

réavoir ♦see **ravoir**

rebaisser [r(ə)bese, ərbese, ærbese] *v.tr.* **1** to lower again **Et elle a élevé son* BUN. *Quand elle l'a élevé, elle l'a vite rebaissé.* And she raised [the top of] her [hot dog] bun. When she raised it, she quickly lowered it again. (EV, An94) **2** to reduce (a price) *J'imagine qu'ils vont rebaisser les prix après les fêtes.* I imagine that they will reduce the prices after the holidays. (LA) <***Loc:*** EV, LA, An94, Da84>

rebaptiser [r(ə)batize, rebatize, r(ə)baptize, ərbatize, ærbatize] *v.tr.* to rebaptize *Ils ont eu pour rebaptiser le petit pour sa belle-famille.* They had to rebaptize the child for the benefit of her in-laws. (LA) <***Loc:*** LA, Da84>

rebâtir [r(ə)batir, ərbatir, ærbatir] **I** *v.tr.* to rebuild **Y a eu des voésins qu'ont eu pour tout r'bâtir leurs maisons.* There were some neighbors who had to completely rebuild their houses. (Gu82) *Mais la maison est cassée, et rebâtie.* But the house has been demolished and rebuilt. (TB) **II se rebâtir** *v.pron.* to rebuild one's home *Si l'ouragan prend ta maison, t'as de l'ensurance pour te rebâtir encore.* If the hurricane takes your house, you've got insurance to rebuild again. (TB) <***Loc:*** TB, Da84, Gu82>

rebattre [r(ə)bat(r), ərbat(r), ærbat(r)] *v.tr.* **1** to beat again *Quand le bougre a revenu, il l'a rebattu encore.* When the fellow came back, he beat him again. (LA) **2** to rethresh

Rebattre le riz.* To rethresh the rice. (Da84) **3 to reforge **Rebattre la charrue.* To reforge the plow. (Da84) <***Loc:*** LA, Da84>

rebiffé, -e [r(ə)bife, ərbife, ærbife] *adj.* angry *Les petis garçons ont dévasté les cannes de l'homme qu'était bien rebiffé.* The little boys destroyed the sugar cane of the man who was quite angry. (TB) <***Loc:*** TB>

rebiffer [r(ə)bife, ərbife, ærbife] **I** *v.intr.* to be impudent **II se rebiffer** *v.pron.* to get angry *Il se rebiffe pour arien.* He gets angry for nothing. (TB) <***Loc:*** JE, TB, VM>

reblanchir [r(ə)blɑ̃ʃir, ərblɑ̃ʃir, ærblɑ̃ʃir] *v.tr.* **1** to rewhiten, whiten again **2** to rebleach, bleach again **3** to rewhitewash, whitewash again *Il faudra reblanchir la maison au printemps.* We'll have to rewhitewash the house this spring. (LA) <***Loc:*** LA, Da84>

reboire [r(ə)bwar, ərbwar, ærbwar] *v.intr.* to drink alcohol again *Il a promis de rester à jeun mais il avait rebu avant la fin de semaine.* He promised to stay sober, but he had drunk again before the weekend. (LA) <***Loc:*** EV, LA, Da84>

rebond [r(ə)bɔ̃, ərbɔ̃, ærbɔ̃] *n.m.* rebound *Ça a fait un erbond, ça fait qu'il s'a coupé.* It rebounded back, so he cut himself. (VM) <***Loc:*** VM, Da84>

rebondir [r(ə)bɔ̃dir, ərbɔ̃dir, ærbɔ̃dir] *v.intr.* **1** to rebound, spring back, bounce back *Ça l'a bien secoué quand ça a erbondi.* It really shook him when it sprang back. (VM) **2** to bounce, bounce around *Ils étaient après galoper leurs chevaux avec Roy rebondissant dans le chartil du wagon.* They were galloping their horses with Roy bouncing around in the bed of the wagon. (VM) <***Loc:*** VM, Da84>

rebondissant [r(ə)bɔ̃disɑ̃, ərbɔ̃disɑ̃, ærbɔ̃disɑ̃] *adj.* bouncy, springy, elastic <***Loc:*** Da84>

rebondissement [r(ə)bɔ̃dismɑ̃, ərbɔ̃dismɑ̃, ærbɔ̃dismɑ̃] *n.m.* rebound, act of rebounding <***Loc:*** Da84>

reboucher [r(ə)buʃe, ərbuʃe, ærbuʃe] **I** *v.tr.* **1** to restop, recork (a bottle) *Rebouche pas la bouteille, j'ai toujours soif.* Don't restop the bottle, I'm still thirsty. (LA) **2** to reblock, replug (a pipe) **3** to redam (a ditch) **II se reboucher** to close up, reclose (of a hole) *Elle s'a fait repercer les oreilles parce que les trous s'avait rebouché.* She had her ears repierced because the holes had reclosed. (LA) <***Loc:*** LA, Da84>

rebouillir [r(ə)bujir, ərbujir, ærbujir] **I** *v.tr.* to reboil, boil again *C'est pas bon de rebouillir un gombo.* It's not good to reboil a gumbo. (LA) **II** *v.intr.* to reboil, boil again *Quand ça commence à rebouillir, c'est là que tu mets le sucre.* When it starts to boil again, that's when you add the sugar. (EV) <***Loc:*** AC, EV, LA, Da84>

rebouquer[1] [r(ə)buke, ərbuke, ærbuke] *v.intr.* **1** to back down *Il a rebouqué quand je lui ai dit ça que je pensais de ses caprices.* He backed down when I told him what I thought of his fancies. (VM) **2** to be repulsed, be taken aback *Il a rebouqué sur l'idée qu'elle aurait pu faire quelque chose comme ça.* He was taken aback by the idea that she could have done something like that. (VM) <***Loc:*** JE, VM, Lv88>

rebouquer[2] **(se)** [r(ə)buke, ərbuke, ærbuke] *v.pron.* to become angry again, get mad again *Elle va se rebouquer si on lui dit ça.* She'll get mad again if we tell her that. (IB) <***Loc:*** IB>

rebours [r(ə)bur, ərbur, ærbur] *n.m./f.* reverse, opposite *Il a fait la rebours de qu'il a dit.* He did the opposite of what he said. (JE) ◊ **•à (la) rebours *a*** in reverse **Mettre à la rebours.* To put in reverse. (Da84) ***b*** awkwardly *Ils faisont tout le temps les affaires à la rebours, eusse.* They always did things awkwardly. (VM) <VM, Da84, Guoo, Lv88> **•à la rebours du bon sens** contrary to good sense *Il est tout à la rebours du bons sens.* He is in complete contradiction of good sense. (Lv88) <SM, Lv88> <***Loc:*** JE, LF, SM, VM, Da84, Guoo, Lv88>

reboutonner [r(ə)butɔ̃ne, ərbutɔ̃ne, ærbutɔ̃ne] *v.tr.* to button again *Arboutonne ton capot.* Button your coat again. (JE) <***Loc:*** JE>

rebrasser [r(ə)brase] *v.tr.* **1** to stir again **2** to shuffle (cards) <***Loc:*** JE, TB>

rebut [r(ə)by, ərby, ærby] *n.* reject, misfit, outcast **Jean c'est in vrai rebut, ça l'invite pas jamais.* John is a real outcast, they never invite him. (EV, Ph36) <***Loc:*** EV, SM, Ph36>

rebuté, -e [r(ə)byte, ərbute, ærbute] *adj.* balky, rebellious *Un enfant rebuté.* A rebellious child. (VM) <***Loc:*** VM, Da84>

rebuter [r(ə)byte, ərbute, ærbute] **I** *v.intr.* **1** to trip *Il m'a foutu une jambette; il m'a fait rebuter.* He stuck his leg out; he made me trip. (VM) **2** to balk, draw back *Il erbute au travail.* He balks at work. (VM) **II se rebuter** *v.pron.* to rebel, balk *On était après dételer les mulets pour aller dîner. Tout d'un coup, July s'a rebuté. Il a commencé à corcobier assez fort que je pouvais pas le tenir.* We were unharnessing the mules to go eat supper. All of a sudden July balked. He started to buck so hard that I couldn't hold him. (ThCa: *La dernière quilte*) <***Loc:*** TB, VM, Da84, ThCa>

recacheter [r(ə)kaʃte, ərkaʃte, ærkaʃte] *v.tr.* to reseal (an envelope, etc.) *J'ai décacheté sa lettre par accident; je l'ai recachetée et il s'en a jamais aperçu.* I unsealed his letter by accident; I resealed it and he never noticed. (VM) <***Loc:*** VM, Da84>

recarguer [r(ə)karge, ərkarge, ærkarge] **I** *v.tr.* to lean back, prop *Il a recargué la chaise contre la porte.* He propped the chair against the door. (LA) **II** *v.intr.* to lean back **III se recarguer** *v.pron.* to lean back *Il s'a recargué contre un arbre pour quelques minutes.* He leaned up against a tree for a few minutes. (LA) <***Loc:*** JE, LA, SM, VM, Da84, Lv88>

réception [resɛpsjɔ̃] *n.f.* reception <***Loc:*** AV, Da84>

recette (arcette) [r(ə)sɛt, ərsɛt, ærsɛt] *n.f.* recipe *Je fais pas des recettes, je cuis comme mère cuisait, juste comme ça.* I don't use recipes, I cook like mother cooked, that's all there is to it. (SL) <***Loc:*** EV, LA, SL, Da84, Lv88>

recevoir (**reçoir**) [r(ə)səvwar, ərsəvwar, ærsəvwar, ərsevwar, r(ə)s(ə)war, ərs(ə)war, ærs(ə)war, ærsewar, s(ə)war] *v.tr.* **1** to receive, get *Tu vas recevoir quelque chose.* You're going to receive something. (JE) *Tu vas reçoir une lettre.* You're going to receive a letter. (LF) **Recevoir une saucée.* To get a heavy rain. (JD, La99) **2** to receive, welcome, show hospitality to *La prochaine fois, je vas te reçoir, toi et ta famille.* The next time, I will receive you, you and your family. (Lv88) **Voulez-vous reçoir cette bande de Mardi gras?* Will you accept these Mardi Gras revelers? (Hi02) <***Loc:*** AC, EV, JD, JE, LA, LF, SB, TB, Da84, Hi02, La99, Lv88>

rechaner [r(ə)ʃɑ̃ne, ərʃɑ̃ne, ærʃɑ̃ne] *v.intr.* **1** to curl the upper lip and show the teeth (of a horse, a donkey) *Ga le cheval, il est après rechaner.* Look at the horse, he is showing his teeth. (VM) **2** to snarl <***Loc:*** JE, VM>

rechange [r(ə)ʃɑ̃ʒ, ərʃɑ̃ʒ, ærʃɑ̃ʒ] *n.m.* **1** replacement, exchange **2** change of clothing *Préparez vous-autres chacun un rechange.* Each of you prepare a change of clothes. (LF) ◊ **•rechange de bain** bathing suit <JE> <***Loc:*** JE, LF, Da84, Lv88>

rechanger [r(ə)ʃɑ̃ʒe, ərʃɑ̃ʒe, ærʃɑ̃ʒe] **I** *v.intr.* to change again *Entrement que ça, je sais pas comment le monde aurait vi. Mais là, ça a rechangé, par exemple.* Other than that, I don't know how people would have survived. But then, things changed again, however. (AC) **II se rechanger** *v.pron.* to change one's clothes *Espère, j'ai pour me rechanger.* Hang on, I need to change my clothes. (VM) <***Loc:*** AC, TB, VM, Da84>

réchappe [reʃap] *n.f.* ◊ **•il y a pas de réchappe** ***a*** there's no escape, there's no way out *Il y a pas de réchappe, il faudra il paye.* There's no way around it, he has to pay. (Lv88) ***b*** there's no hope of recovery or recuperation *Mais je te dis qu'il est bien malade, j'ai peur qu'il n'y a pas de réchappe.* But I'm telling you that he is really sick, I'm afraid there's no [means of] recovery. (VM) *Y'a pas de réchappe possible, il est si bas.* There is no hope of recovery, he is so weak. (Lv88) <EV, SM, TB, VM, Da84, Lv88, Ph36> <***Loc:*** EV, SM, TB, VM, Da84, Lv88, Ph36>

réchapper [reʃape] *v.tr.* **1** to save, rescue *Il est mort, ils ont pas pu le réchapper.* He died, they weren't able to save him. (Lv88) *Ils ont réchappé cent poulets quand même de la maladie.* They saved a hundred chickens from the sickness anyway. (SM) **2** to recover, end up with *Il avait cinq enfants. Ma maman en a eu dix et elle en a réchappé cinq. Ils sont tous morts petits à naissance.* He had five children. My mother had ten and she ended up with five. They [the others] all died at birth. (AV) **3** to drop again, drop back **Il a fallu qu'il se coupe un morceau après sa jambe à lui pour le dernier morceau. Autrement il l'aurait réchappé.* He had to cut a piece from his own leg for the last piece [to feed to the bird]. Otherwise [the bird] would have dropped him. (AC, An94) **II** *v.intr.* **1** to escape *Il pourra pas réchapper de là.* He won't be able to escape from there. (LA) **2** to recover (from sickness) **Il va réchapper.* He will recover. (Da84) *S'il est pas trop massacré, tu lui donnes un* SHOT *pour il réchappe.* If [the rooster] is not too mangled, give him a shot so that he'll recover. (Lv88) <***Loc:*** AC, AV, EV, LA, SB, SM, An94, Da84, Lv88>

recharger [r(ə)ʃarʒe, ərʃarʒe, ærʃarʒe] *v.tr.* **1** to recharge, reload (a gun) *Il a pas pu recharger son fusil assez vite pour le tirer encore.* He wasn't able to reload his shotgun fast enough to shoot it again. (LA) **2** to load again (e.g. a truck) <***Loc:*** LA, Da84>

réchaud [reʃo] *n.m.* **1** heater **On s'assisait autour du réchaud, les dos glaciont et les genoux brûliont.* We would sit around the heater, our backs were freezing and our knees were burning. (Gu82) **2** stove, portable stove *Son réchaud était sale, il pouvait pas allumer son réchaud.* His stove was dirty, he was unable to light his stove. (SM) ◊ **•réchaud à {en} bois** wood stove, wood heater *Y avait pas d'électricité, et eusse se chauffait avec des gros réchauds à bois ou avec du charbon.* There was no electricity, and they heated themselves with big wood heaters or with coal. (TB) <TB> **•réchaud à coloïe** kerosene heater *Y avait des réchauds à coloïe, et des* STOVES *à coloïe, et des lampes pour le soir pour que le monde peuve voir éiou c'est.* There were kerosene heaters, and kerosene stoves, and lamps for the evening so people could see where they were. (TB) <TB> <***Loc:*** SM, TB, Da84, Gu00, Gu82, Hi02, Lv88>

réchauffage [reʃofaʒ] *n.m.* **1** rewarming, reheating **2** warming <***Loc:*** Da84>

réchauffement [reʃofmɑ̃] *n.m.* **1** rewarming, reheating **2** heat development (in hot beds, manure, etc.) <***Loc:*** Da84>

réchauffer (**rechauffer**) [reʃofe, ərʃofe] **I** *v.tr.* **1** to reheat, heat up again, warm up again *Si tu réchauffes la soupe, c'est ça que je vas manger.* If you reheat the soup, that's what I'll eat. (LA) *J'ai pas envie de manger du gombo réchauffé.* I don't feel like eating reheated gumbo. (LA) **2** to heat up, warm up *Et elle avait l'habitude de chauffer un fer à repasser et le mettre dans son lit, pour réchauffer ses pieds le soir.* And she had a habit of heating an iron and putting it into the bed to warm up her feet at night. (LA, An94) **II se réchauffer** *v.pron.* **1** to warm o.s. *Et ça usait le bois pour se réchauffer dans l'hiver et pour brûler dans le* STOVE *pour cuire.* And they used the wood to warm themselves in the winter and to burn in the stove for cooking. (LF) **2** to warm up, get warm, get warmer **Le temps se réchauffe.* The weather is warming up. (Da84) <***Loc:*** LA, LF, An94, Da84>

rechausser[1] [r(ə)ʃose, ərʃose, ærʃose] *v.tr.* to replace shoes or stockings for *Il a pas assez d'argent pour rechausser ses enfants.* He doesn't have enough money to replace his children's shoes. (LA) <***Loc:*** LA, Da84>

rechausser[2] ♦see **renchausser**

recherche (**reserche**) [r(ə)ʃærʃ, ərʃærʃ, ærʃærʃ, r(ə)særʃ] *n.f.* **1** search, quest *Il a fait une recherche pour son cheval.* He conducted a search for his horse. (SM) **2** research, investigation <***Loc:*** SM, VM, Da84, Gr86, Lv88>

recherché, -e [r(ə)ʃærʃe, ərʃærʃe, ærʃærʃe] *adj.* rare, choice, sought after, in great demand **Elle était facilement la fille la plus recherchée dans toute la cyprière.* She was easily the most sought-after girl in the swamp. (So97) <***Loc:*** VM, Da84, So97>

rechercher [r(ə)ʃærʃe, ərʃærʃe, ærʃærʃe] *v.tr.* to search for again, look for again *Il était dans la salle après rechercher le même chapeau qu'il avait perdu la semaine d'avant.* He was in the dance hall looking for the same hat that he had lost the week before. (LA) <***Loc:*** LA, Da84>

rechigner [r(ə)ʃĩje, ərʃĩje, ærʃĩje] *v.intr.* **1** to bray, neigh *Ces bêtes rechignent tout le temps.* Those animals neigh all the time. (IB) **2** to curl the upper lip and show the teeth (of a horse, a donkey) <***Loc:*** IB, JE, Di32>

rechute [r(ə)ʃyt, ərʃyt, ærʃyt] *n.f.* relapse, setback ◊ **•avoir une rechute** to have a relapse (of sickness, etc.) <Da84> <***Loc:*** Da84>

rechuter [r(ə)ʃyte, ərʃyte, ærʃyte, ʃyte] *v.intr.* **1** to relapse, have a relapse, fall sick again *C'est juste un petit rhume, mais il faut je reste égale ou je vas rechuter.* It's just a little cold, but I have to avoid temperature changes or I'll relapse. (AC) *Mame a rechuté après sa fluxion et elle a jamais repris sa force.* Mom relapsed after her pneumonia and she never regained her strength. (AC) **2** to fall back into sin *Elle a rechuté dès que Carême a fini.* She fell back into sin as soon as Lent was over. (LA) **3** to have a setback *Si on fait pas attention avec notre argent, on va rechuter.* If we are not careful with our money, we'll have a setback. (LA) <***Loc:*** AC, EV, JE, LA, TB, VM, Da84, Ph36>

récit [resi] *n.m.* eulogy <***Loc:*** JD>

récitation [resitasjɔ̃] *n.f.* recitation <***Loc:*** Da84>

réciter [resite] *v.tr.* to recite, recount *Mon oncle pouvait réciter tout l'histoire de la famille.* My uncle could recite the whole history of the family. (LA) <***Loc:*** LA, Da84>

réclame [reklɑ̃m] *n.f.* claim <***Loc:*** Da84>

reclamer (**réclamer**) [r(ə)klɑ̃me, ərklɑ̃me, ærklɑ̃me, reklɑ̃me] *v.tr.* **1** to claim, lay claim to *Les petits enfants ont reclamé tous les biens de leur grand-mère qui était morte.* The grandchildren claimed all the possessions of their grandmother who had died. (TB) **2** to claim, maintain, state **I' réclamait qu'i pouvont pas trouver persônne d'aut' qui peut faire le job aussi bien que moi.* They maintained that they could not find anyone else who could do the job as well as me. (Gu82) *Moi je dis c'est troisième cousin* BUT *eux-autres reclame c'est deuxième cousin, moi je sais pas.* I said we're third cousins but they claim it's second cousins, I don't know. (TB) *Il reclame qu'il va revenir, mais je crois qu'il est* GONE *pour de bon.* He claims that he's coming back, but I believe he's gone for good. (LA) <***Loc:*** LA, TB, VM, Da84, Gu82, Hi02, Lv88>

reçoir ♦see **recevoir**

recoller [r(ə)kole, ərkole, ærkole] *v.tr.* to reglue *Je vas essayer de recoller le haut de ton violon avant que t'arrives.* I'll try to reglue the top of your violin before you arrive. (VM) <***Loc:*** VM, Da84>

récolte [rekɔlt, rekolt] *n.f.* crop, harvest *Alors, j'ai été visiter parmi les fermiers et mesurer la quantité de récolte ils avient.* So, I would go out to visit the farmers and measure the amount of crop they had. (SL) *Les* SOYBEAN *[...] c'est une récolte qui existait pas ici ça, trente ans passé.* Soybeans, that's a crop that didn't exist here thirty years ago. (SL) ◊ **•faire récolte** ***a*** to farm, raise crops *Quand j'étais jeune, j'ai pas été à l'école, parce qu'il faulait que j'aide mon pape, faire récolte, travailler.* When I was young, I didn't go to school, because I had to help my dad, do the farming and work. (TB) **Y avait quèques années qu'il avait arrêté de faire récolte.* It's been a few years since he stopped farming. (VM, Gu82) ***b*** to harvest *Je faisais récolte pour Monsieur Daigle.* I harvested for Mr. Daigle. (AC) <AC, LF, TB, VM, Gu82, Lv88> <***Loc:*** AC, EV, LF, SL, SM, TB, VM, Da84, Gu82, Hi02, Lv88>

récolter [rekɔlte] *v.tr.* to reap, harvest *Il a récolté sa misère.* He reaped his own misery. (LA) <***Loc:*** LA, Da84>

récolteur [rekɔltœr, rekoltœr] *n.m.* farmer, planter *Les récolteurs de patates douces ont eu de la misère cette année par rapport à la chesseresse.* The sweet potato farmers had trouble this year because of the drought. (Gu00) *Elle fait un tas du* BUSINESS *avec des récolteurs.* She does a lot of business with farmers. (SL) <***Loc:*** SL, SM, TB, Gu00, Lv88>

récoltier [rekɔltje] *n.m.* farmer, planter *La canne était un produit joliment important pour les récoltiers dans la Louisiane.* Sugar cane was a pretty important product for the farmers of Louisiana. (Lv88) *Les récoltiers avaient beaucoup besoin de pluie.* The farmers really needed rain. (VM) *Quoi les récoltiers allont faire avé les hommes tous partis à l'armée?* What will the farmers do, with all the men gone in the army? (VM) <***Loc:*** AC, JE, LA, SL, SM, VM, Da84, Gu00, Hi02, Lv88>

recommandable [r(ə)kɔ̃mɑ̃dab(l), ərkɔ̃mɑ̃dab(l), ærkɔ̃mɑ̃dab(l)] *adj.* recommendable, advisable *Fais pas ça. C'est pas recommandable.* Don't do that. It's not advisable. (VM) <***Loc:*** VM, Da84>

recommandation [r(ə)kɔ̃mɑ̃dasjɔ̃, ərkɔ̃mɑ̃dasjɔ̃, ærkɔ̃mɑ̃dasjɔ̃] *n.f.* recommendation, reference <***Loc:*** Da84>

recommander[1] [r(ə)kɔ̃mɑ̃de, ərkɔ̃mɑ̃de, ærkɔ̃mɑ̃de] *v.tr.* to order (goods or services) *Il a recommandé de l'étoffe pour sa femme.* He ordered cloth for his wife. (LA) ◊ **•recommander une messe** to have a mass said <Da84> <***Loc:*** EV, LA, Da84, Ph36>

recommander[2] [r(ə)kɔ̃mɑ̃de, ərkɔ̃mɑ̃de, ærkɔ̃mɑ̃de] *v.tr.* to recommend *Il a recommandé son employé pour un meilleur job.* He recommended his worker for a better job. (LA) <***Loc:*** LA>

recommencement [r(ə)kɔ̃mɑ̃smɑ̃, ərkɔ̃mɑ̃smɑ̃, ærkɔ̃mɑ̃smɑ̃] *n.m.* new beginning, new start <***Loc:*** Da84>

recommencer [r(ə)kɔ̃mɑ̃se, ərkɔ̃mɑ̃se, ærkɔ̃mɑ̃se] **I** *v.tr.* to begin again, start again *Les bougres de la pointe ont pas recommencé leurs niches?* The fellows from the point haven't started their tricks again? (VM) **II** *v.intr.* to begin again, get a new start **Mais j'avais arrêté pour vingt ans quand j'ai recommencé encore avec Sady et Amédé et Angelas.* But I had stopped for twenty years when I started again with Sady and Amédé and Angelas. (SL, An84) <***Loc:*** SL, VM, An84, Da84>

récompense [rekɔ̃pɑ̃s] *n.f.* recompense, reward, compensation <***Loc:*** Da84>

récompenser [rekɔ̃pɑ̃se] *v.tr.* to reward, repay, compensate **La vérité va peut-être te faire du mal, mais quelqu'un va toujours te récompenser.* The truth might hurt you, but someone will always pay you back. (ch: *La valse de quatre-vingt-dix-neuf ans*) <***Loc:*** Da84>

recompter [r(ə)kɔ̃te, ərkɔ̃te, ærkɔ̃te] *v.tr.* to recount, count again *Il faudra on recompte encore. Ça sort jamais pareil.* We'll have to count again. It never comes out the same. (LA) <***Loc:*** LA, Da84, Lv88>

réconcilier [rekɔ̃silje] **I** *v.tr.* to reconcile *Le prêtre a jamais pu réconcilier l'homme et la femme.* The priest was never able to reconcile the man and the woman. (LA) **II se réconcilier** *v.pron.* to be reconciled, make up *Tout le monde dans le voisinage est après souhaiter que ça va se réconcilier.* Everyone in the neighborhood is hoping that they will be reconciled. (LA) <***Loc:*** LA, Da84>

reconduire [r(ə)kɔ̃dɥir, ərkɔ̃dɥir, ærkɔ̃dɥir] *v.tr.* **1** to lead back *Son cheval l'a reconduit à sa maison.* His horse led him back to his house. (LA) **2** to drive back <***Loc:*** LA, Da84>

reconnaissable [r(ə)kɔ̃nesab(l), ərkɔ̃nesab(l), ærkɔ̃nesab(l)] *adj.* recognizable *Ils l'ont massacré jusqu'à qu'il était pus reconnaissable.* They beat him up until he was no longer recognizable. (LA) <***Loc:*** LA, Da84>

reconnaissance [r(ə)kɔ̃nesɑ̃s, ərkɔ̃nesɑ̃s, ærkɔ̃nesɑ̃s] *n.f.* **1** recognition **2** gratitude **3** reward *Il donne des reconnaissances à ceux qui l'ont électé.* He gives rewards to those who elected him. (VM) <***Loc:*** VM, Da84>

reconnaissant, -e [r(ə)kɔ̃nesɑ̃, ərkɔ̃nesɑ̃, ærkɔ̃nesɑ̃, -ɑ̃t] *adj.* grateful, appreciative *Il était beaucoup reconnaissant pour tout l'aide qu'ils lui ont donné.* He was very grateful for all the help they gave him. (LA) <***Loc:*** LA, Da84>

reconnaître [r(ə)kɔ̃nɛt(r), ərkɔ̃nɛt(r), ærkɔ̃nɛt(r)] **I** *v.tr.* **1** to recognize *Il va t'arconnaître.* He is going to recognize you. (JE) *De loin, loin je reconnaissais son sifflet.* From far, far away, I recognized his whistling. (AC) *Et ils m'ont reconnu quand j'ai passé.* And they recognized me when I passed by. (TB) **2** to be grateful for *Je reconnais l'aide ils m'ont donné.* I am grateful for the help they gave me. (LA) **II se reconnaître** *v.pron.* to recognize each other *On se reconnaît pus. On se voit pus assez souvent.* We don't recognize each other anymore. We no longer see each other often enough. (LA) <***Loc:*** AC, EV, JE, LA, TB, Da84, Hi02, Lv88>

reconsidérer [r(ə)kɔ̃sidere, ərkɔ̃sidere, ærkɔ̃sidere] *v.tr.* to reconsider *Ils aimeraient que je reconsidère ma position.* They would like me to reconsider my position. (LA) <***Loc:*** LA, Da84>

reconsolable [r(ə)kɔ̃solab(l), ərkɔ̃solab(l), ærkɔ̃solab(l)] *adj.* consolable *Son chagrin pour son père n'est pas reconsolable.* Her grief for her father is not consolable. (IB) <***Loc:*** EV, IB, Ph36>

reconsolation [r(ə)kɔ̃solasjɔ̃, ərkɔ̃solasjɔ̃, ærkɔ̃solasjɔ̃] *n.f.* consolation <***Loc:*** EV, Ph36>

reconsoler [r(ə)kɔ̃sole, ərkɔ̃sole, ærkɔ̃sole] **I** *v.tr.* to console, comfort *Il a reconsolé l'enfant qui pleurait.* He consoled the crying child. (SM) *Je pouvais arien faire pour l'erconsoler.* I could do nothing to console her. (VM) **II se reconsoler** *v.pron.* to console o.s. *Ma chère sœur, reconsole-toi. Papa te mettra au couvent.* My dear sister, console yourself. Papa will place you in a convent. (IB, ch: *Une fille de quatorze ans*) <***Loc:*** EV, IB, JE, SB, SL, SM, TB, VM, Da84, Hi02, Lv88, Ph36>

reconstituer [r(ə)kɔ̃stitɥe, ərkɔ̃stitɥe, ærkɔ̃stitɥe] *v.tr.* to reconstitute *Ils ont jamais pu reconstituer la recette à défunt Arthur pour faire du whisky.* They were never able to reconstitute the late Arthur's recipe for making whiskey. (LA) <***Loc:*** LA, Da84>

reconstruction [r(ə)kɔ̃stryksjɔ̃, ərkɔ̃stryksjɔ̃, ærkɔ̃stryksjɔ̃] *n.f.* reconstruction, rebuilding *Durant le temps de la Reconstruction, le monde a déménagé dans les prairies.* During Reconstruction, people moved to the prairies. (VM) <***Loc:*** VM, Da84>

reconstruire [r(ə)kɔ̃strɥir, ərkɔ̃strɥir, ærkɔ̃strɥir] *v.tr.* to reconstruct, rebuild *Il y a un tas du monde qui va pas reconstruire leurs maisons après l'ouragan.* There are many people who will not rebuild their houses after the hurricane. (VM) <***Loc:*** VM, Da84>

recopié, -e [r(ə)kopje, ərkopje, ærkopje] *adj.* resembling trait for trait *C'était mon père recopié.* He was the spitting image of my father. (SB) <***Loc:*** JE, SB, Di32>

recopier [r(ə)kopje, ərkopje, ærkopje] *v.tr.* to recopy *Il faudra que je faise recopier mes documents.* I'll have to have my documents recopied. (LA) <***Loc:*** LA, Da84>

record (récord, RECORD) [rekɔr(d), r(ə)kɔr(d) ɹɛkə(ɹ)d] *n.m.* record (music recording) **On a été en ville... et puis on a fait ces records.* We went to town . . . and we made these records. (An84) *Il était le premier personne qu'a jamais fait* *un record cadien dans* NASHVILLE. *Des records cadiens avait été faits depuis 1928, mais ç'avait jamais été fait à* NASHVILLE. He was the first person who ever cut a Cajun record in Nashville. Cajun records were being produced since 1928, but it hadn't been done at Nashville. (LF) <***Loc:*** AC, EV, LF, An84, Da84, Lv88>

récorder (**recorder**) [rekɔrde, r(ə)kɔrde, rakɔrde] *v.tr.* to record *J'ai récordé tout ce qui s'a passé jusqu'à la fin.* I recorded everything that happened until the end. (Lv88) *Il est après prendre tout ça recordé en français.* He's recording all of that in French. (TB) *Tout ça a été récordé icite, chez moi.* All of that was recorded here, at my house. (Lv88) *Papa Cairo, il a récordé un deuxième disque.* Papa Cairo, he cut a second record. (SL) **La musique Française Cajine était première raccordée [=récordée] dans 1928 par Joe Falcon.* Cajun French music was first recorded in 1928 by Joe Falcon. (Wh83) <***Loc:*** AC, SL, TB, Da84, Gr86, Lv88, Wh83>

recorder[1] [r(ə)kɔrde, ərkɔrde, ærkɔrde] *v.tr.* to restack (firewood, bricks, etc.) **Recorder le bois.* To restack a cord of wood. (Da84) <***Loc:*** Da84>

recorder[2] ♦see **récorder**

récordeur [rekɔrdœr] *n.m.* tape recorder *Alle prendait les témoignages avec son petit récordeur.* She was taking testimonies with her little tape recorder. (Lv88) <***Loc:*** Gr86, Lv88>

recoucher [r(ə)kuʃe, ərkuʃe, ærkuʃe] **I** *v.tr.* to put back to bed, put to bed again *Arrête de faire ton train. Je veux pas avoir besoin de recoucher les enfants.* Stop making noise. I don't want to have to put the children to bed again. (LA) **II se recoucher** *v.pron.* to lie down again, go back to bed *Je m'ai levé, j'ai sorti sur le* DECK. *Pas de vent. Bien bien calme. J'ai pas rien dit, j'ai pas réveillé mon cousin et l'autre. J'ai retourné me recoucher.* I got up. I went out on the deck. No wind. Very calm. I didn't say anything, I didn't wake up my cousin or the other guy. I returned and went back to bed. (TB) <***Loc:*** LA, TB, Da84>

recoudre [r(ə)kud(r)] (*p.p.* **recoudu** [r(ə)kudy, ərkudy, ærkudy], **recousu** [r(ə)kuzy, r(ə)kuzy, ərkuzy]) *v.tr.* to resew, restitch *Mame a recousu ma chemise.* Mom resewed my shirt. (LA) <***Loc:*** LA, Da84>

recouper [r(ə)kupe, ərkupe, ærkupe] *v.tr.* to recut, cut again *J'ai pas coupé ça bien. Il faudra je le recoupe encore.* I didn't cut that well. I'll have to cut it again. (LA) <***Loc:*** LA, Da84>

recourir [r(ə)kurir, ərkurir, ærkurir] *v.tr.* **1** to rerun, run again *Edwin Edwards pourra jamais recourir pour gouverneur, mais il devrait.* Edwin Edwards will never be able to run for governor again, but he should. (LA) **2** to redo, go back over ◊ **•recourir les manques** to replant the empty spaces in a row of crop, trees, etc. *J'ai eu pour recourir les manques dans ma pièce de coton pour replanter.* I had to go back over the empty spaces in my cotton patch to replant. (LA) <LA, Da84> <***Loc:*** JD, LA, Da84>

recours [r(ə)kur, ərkur, ærkur] *n.m.* recourse, resort ◊ **•avoir recours (à)** to have recourse (to), resort (to) *On a essayé de l'empêcher, mais il y avait pas de recours.* We tried to prevent it, but there was no recourse. (VM) <VM, Da84> <***Loc:*** VM, Da84>

recouverre (**recouvrir**) [r(ə)kuvær, ərkuvær, ærkuvær, r(ə)kuvrir, ərkuvrir, ærkuvrir] **I** *v.tr.* to reroof, recover (a roof) *On aurait pour recouverre la couverture, mais tous les ouvriers sont beaucoup occupés.* We would have to recover our roof, but the carpenters are all very busy. (LA) **II** *v.intr.* to recover, recuperate *Il est à recouvrir de sa maladie.* He is recuperating from his illness. (SM) **III se recouverre** *v.pron.* **1** to cover o.s. again *Il s'a recouvert au milieu de la nuit.* He covered himself back up in the middle of the night. (VM) **2** to become cloudy or overcast again **Le temps se recouvre.* The weather is getting overcast again. (Da84) <***Loc:*** LA, SM, VM, Da84>

recouvrir ♦see **recouverre**

recracher [r(ə)kraʃe, ərkraʃe, ærkraʃe] *v.intr.* **1** to spit again *Je lui a dit de pas cracher encore, mais il a recraché sur son frère.* I told him not to spit again, but he spit again on his brother. (VM) **2** to spit up <***Loc:*** VM, Da84>

recreuser ♦see **recreusir**

recreusir (**recreuser**) [r(ə)krøzir, ərkrøzir, ærkrøzir, r(ə)krøze, ərkrøze, ærkrøze] *v.tr.* **1** to hollow out again **2** to deepen (a hole) *Ton fossé est pas assez creux. Il faudra tu le recreusis.* Your ditch is not deep enough. You'll have to dig it deeper. (VM) <***Loc:*** VM, Da84>

recrier [r(ə)krije, ərkrije, ærkrije] *v.intr.* to yell out again *Il a pas attendu. Il faudra tu recries après.* He didn't hear. You'll have to yell for him again. (VM) <***Loc:*** VM, Da84>

récrire [rekrir] *v.tr.* **I** *v.tr.* to rewrite, write again *Il faudra que tu récris la recette. Je l'ai perdue.* You'll have to rewrite the recipe. I lost it. (LA) **II** *v.intr.* to write in response, write back *Il a écrit une lettre à sa sœur dans la Californie et elle lui a récrit.* He wrote a letter to his sister in California and she wrote back to him. (VM) <***Loc:*** LA, VM, Da84>

recrochir [r(ə)kroʃir, ərkroʃir, ærkroʃir] *v.tr.* to rebend *Je venais juste de dressir mon poteau d'antenna après Katrina, quand le vent de Rita l'a recrochi encore.* I had just straightened my antenna pole after Katrina when Rita's winds rebent it. (VM) <***Loc:*** VM, Da84>

recroiser [r(ə)krwaze, ərkrwaze, ærkrwaze] *v.tr.* **1** to recross, cross again *J'ai eu pour recroiser le bayou trois fois aujourd'hui.* I had to recross the bayou three times today. (VM) **2** to cross (s.o.) again, vex again *Je vas jamais la recroiser encore.* I'll never cross her again. (VM) <***Loc:*** VM, Da84>

reçu [r(ə)sy, ərsy, ærsy] *n.m.* receipt <***Loc:*** Da84>

recuire [r(ə)kɥir, ərkɥir, ærkɥir] *v.tr.* to recook, cook again *J'ai recuit mes confitures parce que je les avais gardées trop longtemps.* I recooked my preserves because I had kept them too long. (VM) <*Loc:* VM, Da84>

reculer (**culer**) [r(ə)kyle, ərkyle, ærkyle, kyle] **I** *v.tr.* to back up, move back *Reculez la ligne un peu, il y a pus de place en avant.* Back up the line a bit, there's no more room up front. (LA) **II** *v.intr.* **1** to back up, move back **Il a pas bien regardé en reculant et y a ein* TRUCK *qui l'a abordé par en arrière.* He didn't look carefully while backing up [in his car] and a truck hit him in the rear end. (VM, Gu82) **Cule!* Move back! (Da84) **2** to draw back *Il a arculé.* He drew back. (JE) **3** to fall back *Que le tonnerre grogne et que la muraille recule.* May the thunder roar and may the wall fall back. (IB, ch: *Trinquons*) **III se reculer** *v.pron.* to back up, move back, get out of the way **Cule-toi.* Get out of the way. (Da84) <*Loc:* IB, JE, LA, SM, TB, VM, Da84, Gu82, Lv88>

reculoir ♦see **reculoire**

reculoire (**reculoir**) [r(ə)kylwar, ərkylwar, ærkylwar] *n.m./f.* **1** breeching (part of a harness) **2** saddle-tie, crupper **3** stern cable <*Loc:* VM, Da84, Lv88>

reculons [r(ə)kylõ, ərkylõ, ærkylõ] ◊ •**à reculons** backwards *Une écrevisse nage à reculons.* A crawfish swims backwards. (VM) <VM> •**aller en reculons** to go backwards <Da84> <*Loc:* VM, Da84>

redéfaire [r(ə)defær, ərdefær, ærdefær] *v.tr.* to undo again, take apart again *J'avais arrangé la barrière et ils ont eu pour la redéfaire pour passer la maison.* I had fixed the fence and they had to take it apart again to pass the house. (VM) <*Loc:* VM, Da84>

redemander [r(ə)d(ə)mɑ̃de, ərd(ə)mɑ̃de, ærd(ə)mɑ̃de] *v.tr.* to ask again *Je vas pas te redemander de ramasser ton linge.* I'm not going to ask you again to pick up your clothes. (EV) <*Loc:* EV, Da84>

rédempteur [redɑ̃ptœr] *n.m.* [*eccl.*] redeemer, savior <*Loc:* Da84>

rédemption [redɑ̃psjõ] *n.f.* [*eccl.*] redemption <*Loc:* Da84>

redescendre [r(ə)desɑ̃n, r(ə)desɑ̃d(r), ərdesɑ̃n, ərdesɑ̃d(r), ærdesɑ̃n, ærdesɑ̃d(r)] **I** *v.tr.* **1** to go down again (e.g. stairs, a ladder, etc.) **2** to take down again *Redescends la chaudière. C'est l'heure pour faire un gombo.* Take the pot back down. It's time to make a gumbo. (LA) **II** *v.intr.* to come down again, go down again *C'est pas monter qu'est le tracas, c'est redescendre.* It's not going up that's the problem, it's going down again. (VM) <*Loc:* LA, VM, Da84>

redevoir [r(ə)dəvwar, ərdəvwar, ærdəvwar] *v.tr.* to still owe, owe (a certain amount) more *Il reclame que je lui redois cinq piastres, et pourtant je l'ai déjà payé.* He claims that I still owe him five dollars, and yet I already paid him. (VM) <*Loc:* VM, Da84>

redire [r(ə)dir, ərdir, ærdir] *v.tr.* **1** to repeat, say again **2** to retell, tell again *Tu veux nous redire l'histoire? On va te laisser parler.* Do you want to tell us the story again? We will let you talk. (VM) <*Loc:* VM, Da84>

rediviser [r(ə)divize, ərdivize, ærdivize] *v.tr.* to subdivide *Ils ont redivisé le terrain qu'ils avaient hérité pour faire un* SUBDIVISION. They subdivided the land they had inherited to make a subdivision. (EV) <*Loc:* EV, Da84>

redonner [r(ə)dõne, ərdõne, ærdõne] *v.tr.* to give back, restore *Une chance manquée est pas redonnée.* A missed opportunity is not given back. (ch: *Le temps est après marcher*) <*Loc:* TB, Da84>

redoublage [r(ə)dublaʒ, ərdublaʒ, ærdublaʒ] *n.m.* lining (of clothing, etc.) <*Loc:* Da84>

redoubler [r(ə)duble, ərduble, ærduble] *v.tr.* to line, add lining to (e.g. a garment) *Les jeunes filles d'aujourd'hui connaît pas qui c'est piquer ou redoubler une couverte.* Girls today don't know what it is like to stitch or line a quilt. (TB) <*Loc:* TB, Da84>

redoutable [r(ə)dutab(l), ərdutab(l), ærdutab(l)] *adj.* frightening, imposing *Fais attention avec lui. Il a une colère redoutable.* Be careful with him. He has a frightening temper. (LA) *C'était un mauvais petit homme. Il avait une réputation redoutable.* He was a bad little man. He had a frightening reputation. (SL) <*Loc:* LA, SL>

redouter [r(ə)dute, ərdute, ærdute] *v.tr.* to fear, be afraid of, be apprehensive of *C'est une personne à redouter.* That's someone to be afraid of. (LA) <*Loc:* LA, Da84>

redresser[1] [r(ə)drese, ərdrese, ærdrese] *v.tr.* to retrain *Redresser un chien.* To retrain a dog. (VM) <*Loc:* VM>

redresser[2] [r(ə)drese, ərdrese, ærdrese] *v.tr.* to straighten up, raise up (a post, a tree, etc.) *Il a eu pour redresser son jeune copal après l'ouragan.* He had to straighten up his young sweet gum tree after the hurricane. (LA) <*Loc:* LA, Da84>

redressir (**redroitsir**) [r(ə)dresir, ərdresir, ærdresir, r(ə)drwatsir, ərdrwatsir, ærdrwatsir] **I** *v.tr.* **1** to straighten, stand up straight, put or put back in an upright position *J'ai redressi mon gastronia qu'avait tombé dans le gros vent.* I straightened out my crape myrtle that had fallen in the high wind. (VM) **2** to straighten, put back in the correct or expected position *Il a redroitsi ma bague.* He straightened my ring. (SL) **II se redressir** to stand up straight *Redressis-toi bien.* Stand up straight (LA) <*Loc:* LA, SL, VM, Lv88>

réduction [redyksjõ] *n.f.* **1** reduction, decrease **2** discount <*Loc:* Da84>

réduire [redɥir] **I** *v.tr.* to reduce (in quantity) *Réduire un salaire.* To reduce a salary. (LA) *Réduire une sauce.* To reduce [the quantity of water in] a sauce. (VM) *À des prix réduits.* At reduced prices. (VM) **II** *v.intr.* to diminish, decline *On dirait que mon bois de feu est après réduire plus vite que ça devrait.* It seems as if my firewood supply is diminishing faster than it ought to. (IV) **III se réduire** *v.pron.* to diminish, be reduced *Quand tu cuis tes pralines, tu les tires pas* *avant que ta sauce se réduit.* When you cook pralines, you don't take them off the heat until your liquid has reduced. (VM) <***Loc:*** IV, LA, VM, Da84>

réélecter [reelɛkte] *v.tr.* to reelect *Il y a pas de chance que ce couillon soit réélecté!* There's no chance that that fool will be reelected! (VM) <***Loc:*** VM, Da84, Gr86>

réélection [reelɛksjɔ̃] *n.f.* reelection <***Loc:*** Da84>

réélire (**réélure**) [reelir, reelyr] (*p.p.* **réélu**) *v.tr.* to reelect *Réélire un sénateur.* To reelect a senator. (VM) <***Loc:*** VM, Da84>

réellement [reɛlmɑ̃] *adv.* really, truly, in fact **Je crois réellement que j'l'ai taillé assez fort qu'il a pas pu s'assire pour trois jours.* I think I really gave him such a whipping that he couldn't sit down for three days. (Gu82) *C'était réellement un grand bois.* It was a really big woods. (SM) <***Loc:*** AC, SM, Da84, Gu82>

réélure ♦see **réélire**

réengager ♦see **rengager**

réenterrer ♦see **renterrer**

refaçonner [r(ə)fasɔ̃ne, ərfasɔ̃ne, ærfasɔ̃ne] *v.tr.* to refashion, redesign, remake *Il faudra que je refaçonne ce morceau pour ma charrue parce qu'il y a pus personne qui travaille là-dessus.* I'll have to remake that piece for my plow myself from scratch because nobody does that kind of work anymore. (LA) <***Loc:*** LA, Da84>

refaire [r(ə)fær, ərfær, ærfær] **I** *v.tr.* to remake, redo, do again *Une erreur se fait une fois dans ta vie. La deuxième là si tu peux charrer bien à un enfant là il va comprendre, peut-être il va jamais refaire la même erreur!* A mistake is made once in your life. The second time if you can speak well to a child, he'll understand, maybe he'll never make the same mistake again! (EV) *Enfin il m'a donné la maison, et ils l'ont tout défait et pis ils ont halé ça au village et ils me l'ont refait.* Finally, he gave me the house, and they had it taken apart, and then they hauled it to town and they reconstructed it for me. (VM) **Le lit est refait.* The bed is remade. (Da84) **II** *v.intr.* to reconcile, become reconciled *Ils ont eu une dispute, mais ils ont refait encore.* They had a fight, but they reconciled again. (SM) **III se refaire** *v.pron.* **1** to improve in health, get better, convalesce after an illness *Il a été malade, mais il est après se refaire.* He was sick, but he's getting better. (SM) **2** to recover (e.g. from a shock), pull o.s. together *Je pouvais juste pas me refaire après la mort de mon mari.* I just couldn't get back on my feet after my husband's death. (VM) **3** to clear up, improve (of the weather) *Le temps va se refaire après la pluie.* The weather will clear up after the rain. (SM) **Le temps est après se refaire.* The weather is improving. (Da84) **4** to increase, wax (of the moon) *La lune est après se refaire.* The moon is waxing. (VM) **5** to become better looking, recover one's former good looks **La fille s' refait.* The girl is getting better looking. (EV, Ph36) ◊ •**se refaire à** ***a*** to accept, reconcile o.s. to, get over *Il pouvait pas se refaire à l'idée que la femme l'avait quitté.* He couldn't get over the idea that his wife had left him. (LA) ***b*** to reconcile with, become reconciled with, make up with (s.o.) *Marie s'est refait à Louise.* Marie made up with Louise. (SM) <LA, SM, VM, Da84> <***Loc:*** EV, IB, JE, LA, SM, TB, VM, Da84, La99, Lv88, Ph36>

refendre [r(ə)fɑ̃n, r(ə)fɑ̃d(r), ərfɑ̃n, ərfɑ̃d(r), ærfɑ̃n, ærfɑ̃d(r)] **I** *v.tr.* to resplit, resaw (lengthwise) **II** *v.intr.* to split again *J'avais arrangé la patte de la chaise le mieux je pouvais mais elle a refendu.* I had fixed the chair leg the best I could, but it split again. (LA) <***Loc:*** LA, Da84>

référence [referɑ̃s] *n.f.* **1** reference **2** character reference <***Loc:*** Da84>

refermer [r(ə)færme, ərfærme, ærfærme] **I** *v.tr.* to reclose, shut again *J'ai eu pour refermer tous les chassis quand la pluie a recommencé.* I had to close all the windows again when the rain restarted. (EV) **II se refermer** *v.pron.* to shut itself again **La porte s'a refermée.* The door closed itself again. (Da84) <***Loc:*** EV, Da84>

referrer [r(ə)fere, ərfere, ærfere] *v.tr.* **1** to reshoe (a horse) *J'ai pas assez d'argent pour referrer mon cheval.* I don't have enough money to reshoe my horse. (LA) **2** to reclad (with iron) *Referrer un* BARBECUE PIT. To reclad a barbecue pit. (LA) <***Loc:*** LA, Da84>

réfléchir [refleʃir] *v.intr.* to think, reflect, ponder **Ça va réfléchir. Vous-autres vas se comprendre plus tard.* They'll think it over. Y'all will come to an understanding later. (SL, An94) <***Loc:*** SB, SL, An94, Da84>

réflecter [reflɛkte] *v.intr.* **1** to reflect *Je pouvais pas voir parce que les lumières du char étaient après réflecter dans les vitres.* I couldn't see because the car's headlights were reflecting in the window. (LA) **2** to be reflected or mirrored *Le prix de cette boutique a réflecté sur l'autre.* The price at this store reflects on the other. (Lv88) <***Loc:*** LA, Da84, Lv88>

refleurir [r(ə)flørir, ərflørir, ærflørir] *v.intr.* to rebloom, reblossom, bloom again *Je vas te dire quoi. Mes poiriers ont refleuri après l'ouragan. Si on a pas de glace, je vas faire des poires pour le Jour de l'An!* I tell you what. My pear trees reflowered after the hurricane! If we don't get a freeze, I'm going to have pears for New Year's! (LA) <***Loc:*** LA, Da84>

réflexion [reflɛksjɔ̃] *n.f.* thought, reflection, consideration <***Loc:*** Da84>

re-FLOOD [r(ə)flød] *v.intr.invar.* to flood again, reflood *La terre peut baisser y a des places peut-être trois ou quatre pieds, du moment que tu chesses. Et là dès que ça re-*FLOOD *là, eh ben là tu vois plus de terre du tout, tu vois plus d'herbe, pas rien du tout. C'est juste de l'eau.* The ground can sink maybe three or four feet in places, when you drain it. And then when it floods again, you don't see any land at all, you see no grass, nothing at all. It's just water. (LF) <***Loc:*** LF>

refondre [r(ə)fɔ̃n, r(ə)fɔ̃d(r), ərfɔ̃n, ərfɔ̃d(r), ærfɔ̃n, ærfɔ̃d(r)] *v.tr.* to remelt *Si tes pralines viennent dures, tu peux les refondre.* If your pralines get too hard, you can remelt them. (LA) <***Loc:*** LA, Da84>

reforger [r(ə)fɔrʒe, ərfɔrʒe, ærfɔrʒe] *v.tr.* to reforge *Reforger une lame de charrue.* To reforge a plowshare. (LA) <***Loc:*** LA, Da84>

réformation [refɔrmasjɔ̃] *n.f.* reformation <***Loc:*** Da84>

réforme [refɔrm] *n.f.* reform, amendment <***Loc:*** Da84>

reformer [r(ə)fɔrme, ərfɔrme, ærfɔrme] *v.tr.* to re-form, form again *Reformer des rangs dans un clos.* To reform rows in a field. (LA) <***Loc:*** LA, Da84>

réformer [refɔrme] **I** *v.tr.* to reform, improve *Elle l'a marié en croyant qu'elle pourrait le réformer.* She married him thinking that she would be able to reform him. (LA) **II se réformer** *v.pron.* to mend one's ways, reform o.s. *Il va jamais se réformer, ça fait pas rien quoi c'est son père fait.* He'll never reform himself, no matter what his father does. (LA) <***Loc:*** LA, Da84>

refouiller [r(ə)fuje, ərfuje, ærfuje] *v.tr.* to redig, dig deeper *Le puits a tari. Il faudra le refouiller.* The well went dry. We'll have to redig it. (LA) <***Loc:*** LA, Da84>

refoule [r(ə)ful, ərful, ærful] *n.f.* reflux, flowing back, ebb *Quand il y a une chesseresse, il y a une refoule d'eau salée dans le maîche.* When there's a drought, there's a backflow of salt water into the marsh. (VM) <***Loc:*** JE, VM, Lv88>

refouler[1] [r(ə)fule, ərfule, ærfule] *v.tr.* to repack, retamp *Il a eu pour refouler son insulation dans le mur. Ça avait commencé à tomber.* He had to stuff his insulation back into the wall. It had started falling out. (LA) <***Loc:*** LA, LF, TB, Da84>

refouler[2] **(se)** [r(ə)fule, ərfule, ærfule] *v.pron.* to sprain, twist (e.g. one's ankle) *Si tu te refoulais un pied, eh ben eux-autres te traitait pour ça.* If you sprained a foot, well they treated you for that. (TB) *Et j'étais après dompter un cheval un jour et quelque manière je m'ai refoulé la main comme ça. Et ç'a enflé.* I was taming a horse one day and somehow I sprained my hand like that. And it swelled up. (LF) <***Loc:*** LA, LF, TB, Da84>

refouloir [r(ə)fulwar, ərfulwar, ærfulwar] *n.m.* tamp, tamper, ram <***Loc:*** Da84>

refrain [r(ə)frɛ̃, ərfrɛ̃, ærfrɛ̃] *n.m.* refrain <***Loc:*** Da84>

refrapper [r(ə)frape, ərfrape, ærfrape] *v.tr.* to strike again, knock again *Quand il s'a levé, le constable l'a refrappé encore.* When he got up, the bouncer hit him again. (LA) <***Loc:*** LA, Da84>

refrédir ♦see **refroidir**

réfrigérateur [refriʒəratœr, ərfriʒəratœr, ærfriʒəratœr] *n.m.* refrigerator *Anciennement, il y avait pas de réfrigérateurs.* In the past, there were no refrigerators. (SL) <***Loc:*** SL>

refroidir (**rafroidir, raferdir, refrédir**) [r(ə)frwadir, ərfrwadir, ærfrwadir, rafrwadir, rafærdir, rafrədir, rafredir, r(ə)fredir, refredir] **I** *v.tr.* to cool off, chill, make cooler or colder *Rafroidis la soupe.* Cool off the soup. (SM) **II** *v.intr.* **1** to chill, cool, keep cold *Pour refroidir y avait des marchands de glace qui passaient, un* TRUCK *y avait des gros blocs de glace.* For keeping cool there were ice merchants who came by, a truck that had big blocks of ice. (TB) *Et là dans l'été y avait pas de glacières, et tu faisais pas boucherie dans l'été parce que tu peux pas refroidir assez pour la sauver.* In summer there were no refrigerators, and you didn't butcher hogs in summer because you couldn't cool enough to save. (TB) **2** to cool off, become cold *Ça a rafroidi un tas, hein?* It cooled off a lot, eh? (VM) *Ça rafroidit dehors.* It is getting cold outside. (SM) *Il a refrédi sous les arbres.* He cooled off under the trees. (SB) **III se refroidir** *v.pron.* to cool off, become cold or colder **Le temps se refroidit.* It's getting colder. (Da84) *Le temps s'a rafroidi.* The weather has gotten colder. (SM) <***Loc:*** EV, JE, SB, SM, TB, VM, Da84, Lv88, Ph36>

réfugié, -e [refyʒje] *n.* refugee <***Loc:*** Da84>

réfugier (se) [refyʒje] *v.pron.* to take refuge, take shelter *Ils ont eu pour se réfugier dans le camp.* They had to take refuge in the camp. (LA) <***Loc:*** LA, Da84>

refusailler [r(ə)fyzaje, ərfyzaje, ærfyzaje] *v.tr.* to refuse repeatedly <***Loc:*** IB>

refuser [r(ə)fyze, ərfyze, ærfyze] *v.tr.* to refuse, reject, turn down **Hormis qu'j'sus bien malade, je r'fuse jâmais d'aller 'oir mes p'tits.* Unless I'm really sick, I never refuse to go visit my kids. (VM, Gu82) *"Si quelqu'un vient vous inviter, refusez pas personne!" Pop nous a dit.* "If someone comes to invite you [to dance], don't turn down anyone!" Pop told us. (EV) <***Loc:*** EV, TB, VM, Da84, Gu82, Hi02>

regagner [r(ə)gɑ̃je, ərgɑ̃je, ærgɑ̃je] *v.tr.* **1** to win back, win again **2** to regain, recover *Je crois pas qu'on pourra regagner notre terre.* I don't think we'll be able to regain our land. (LA) ◊ **•regagner son chemin** to get back on track <LA> <***Loc:*** LA, Da84>

regaincher [r(ə)gɛ̃ʃe, ərgɛ̃ʃe, ærgɛ̃ʃe] *v.tr.* **1** to patch up (e.g. clothes) **2** to freshen (one's appearance) <***Loc:*** SM>

regard [r(ə)gar, ərgar, ærgar] *n.m.* **1** glance, look **2** appearance <***Loc:*** Da84>

regardable [r(ə)gardab(l), ərgardab(l), ærgardab(l)] *adj.* presentable, sightly, fine-looking *C'est mieux pas prendre mon portrait aujourd'hui. Je suis pas regardable.* It's better not to take my picture today. I'm not presentable. (EV) *Ça c'est pas regardable.* That's not worth looking at. (SM) <***Loc:*** EV, JE, LF, SB, SM, TB, VM, Lv88>

regardailler [r(ə)gardaje, ərgardaje, ærgardaje] *v.tr.* to look at repeatedly <***Loc:*** IB>

regardant, -e [r(ə)gardɑ̃, ərgardɑ̃, ærgardɑ̃, -ɑt] *adj.* **1** exacting, particular, easily offended *Fais attention quoi tu dis en avant d'elle. Elle est assez regardante. Elle manque pas rien.* Be careful what you say in front of her. She is so easily offended. She doesn't miss anything. (LA) **2** greedy, stingy *Il est aregardant comme tout.* He is stingy as anything. (JE) **3** exacting in the expectation of payment *Il est trop regardant. Il devrait l'aider juste parce que c'est son frère.* He only works for pay. He ought to help him just because that's his brother. (LA) <***Loc:*** JE, LA, LF, SM, Da84, Lv88>

regarder (garder) [r(ə)garde, ərgarde, ærgarde garde] **I** *v.tr.* **1** to look at, view, watch *Tu me fais du mal chaque fois je te regarde, ma vilaine.* You hurt me every time I look at you, you rascal. (ch: *Madame Atchen*) *Je regardais le chat comme ça et Mom dit, "Non, non!" elle dit, "regarde pas le chat, ça va te marquer ton enfant."* I was looking at the cat like that and Mom said, "No, no!" she said, "don't look at the cat, it will mark your child." (EV) **2** to observe (a holiday) *Dans ce temps-là, le monde regardait le Carème, asteur c'est pus comme ça. Et y avait pas de danses, dans le Carème.* In those days people observed Lent, today it's not like that. And there were no dances, during Lent. (TB) **3** to hold in regard, have regard for *Maman, alle dit,* THANK YOU *pour avoir venu avec tes filles. Y a juste vous-autres qui nous regarde.* Mom, she said, thank you for coming with your daughters. You're the only ones who have any regard for us. (TB) *Elle regardait Geneviève pareil comme sa mère.* She held Genevieve in the same regard as her own mother. (IV) **4** to concern, be the business of **Ça me regarde pas.* It's none of my business. (Da84) **II** *v.intr.* **1** to look **Garde donc!* Will you look! (Da84) **Garde voir!* Please look! (Da84) *Ils sont après regarder, pour acheter une maison, une place, et ils sont après calculer pas trop loin de l'école.* They are looking around, to buy a house, a place, and are thinking of something not too far from school. (IB) **Regardez, donc, malheureuse, tu m'abandonnes pour toujours.* So look, unhappy one, you're leaving me forever. (ch: *Mon chère bébé créole*) **2** to look, seem, appear *Vous regardez bien, on croirait pas vous-autres avez soixante-dix ans.* You look good, one wouldn't believe you are seventy years old. (Lv88) *J'ai coupé les herbes, ça regarde un tas mieux asteur.* I cut the grass, it looks a lot better now. (Lv88) *Ça regarde pas mauvais.* It doesn't look bad. (Lv88) **III se regarder** *v.pron.* to look at o.s., look at each other *Quand même si je dis, il va me dire que je suis fou. Et pourtant je m'ai bien regardé à moi, je me sentais pas de mal.* Even if I say it, he'll say that I am crazy. And yet I looked myself over well and I didn't feel bad. (TB) ◊ **•regarder croche** to be cross-eyed, look cross-eyed <VM> **•regarder pour** to look for *Si tu le mets à l'envers, il va voir l'appât, mais une crabe va pas aller nager en l'air pour aller en dedans. Il marche sur le fond et il va regarder pour un trou pour rentrer en dedans.* If you put it [the trap] upside down, a crab will see the bait, but it won't swim up to go inside. It walks on the bottom and it will look for a hole to get in. (TB) **J'ai regardé dans tous les coins du pays pour un autre avec des chers yeux bleus comme toi.* I've looked all over the country for another with dear blue eyes like yours. (ch: *Une autre chance*) **Oui, tous les soirs, moi j'suis là 'près regarder pour toi.* Yes, every night, I'm looking for you. (ch: *Quelle étoile*) <EV, IB, TB> <***Loc:*** AC, EV, IB, IV, LA, TB, VM, Da84, Hi02, Lv88>

regimber (reginguer) [r(ə)ʒɛ̃be, ərʒɛ̃be, ærʒɛ̃be, r(ə)ʒɛ̃ge, ərʒɛ̃ge, ærʒɛ̃ge] **I** *v.intr.* **1** to kick, jump, rear *Le cheval a regimbé quand je lui a passé les éperons.* The horse reared when I spurred it. (VM) **2** to revolt, balk, rebel *L'enfant a regimbé quand je lui ai dit qu'elle pouvait pas aller au bal.* The child revolted when I told her she couldn't go to the dance. (VM) **3** to caper, dance about **II se regimber** *v.pron.* to balk, rebel *C'est pas la peine que tu te regimbes. Il faudra toujours que tu m'aimes.* There's no use for you to balk. You'll have to love me in the end. (VM) <***Loc:*** JE, VM, Da84>

régime[1] [reʒim] *n.m.* regime, form of government ***Loc:*** <Da84>

régime[2] [reʒim] *n.m.* cluster, bunch **Régime de bananes.* Bunch of bananas. (Da84) <***Loc:*** Da84>

régiment [reʒimɑ̃] *n.m.* military regiment <***Loc:*** SL, SM>

reginguer ♦see **regimber**

région [reʒjɔ̃] *n.f.* region, area <***Loc:*** LF, Hi02>

registre[1] [r(ə)ʒist(r), ərʒist(r), ærʒist(r)] *n.m.* **1** register, record book **2** baptismal registry *Et quand il a mis mon nom sur mon registre quand j'ai été iné, il a esplé ça en français.* And when he put my name on my register when I was born, he spelled it in French. (TB) <***Loc:*** TB, Da84>

registre[2] [r(ə)ʒist(r), ərʒist(r), ærʒist(r)] *n.m.* damper, vent, air vent <***Loc:*** Da84>

régistre[3] [reʒis(tr)] *n.m.* cash register *Attrape-moi six escalins en dedans le régistre.* Get me seventy-five cents from the cash register. (VM) <***Loc:*** VM>

registrer [r(ə)ʒistre, ərʒistre, ærʒistre] *v.intr.* to register to vote **Les vieilles femmes et les vieux hommes devraient aller registrer.* Old women and old men should go register to vote. (VM, Gr86) <***Loc:*** VM, Gr86>

règle [rɛg(l)] *n.f.* **1** rule, order, law **2** ruler (for measuring) *On se faisait punir et taper, mettre à genoux sur des grains de maïs, ou prendre une règle et te taper le bout des doigts si tu parlais français à l'école.* We got ourselves punished and hit, put on our knees on kernels of corn, or [they'd] take a ruler and hit the ends of your fingers if you spoke French in school. (LF) **3** *(pl.)* menses, menstrual period <***Loc:*** IB, LA, LF, SJ, Da84>

réglé [regle] *adv.* regularly, on a regular basis *Asteur je vas plus à la messe réglé.* These days I don't go to Mass regularly anymore. (Lv88) *C'était pas un homme qui travaillait réglé. Il vagabondait d'un bord et de l'autre.* He wasn't a man who worked regularly. He used to wander around from place to place. (LA) *Mais j'ai jamais retenu un autre job* *réglé.* But I've never held another steady job. (TB) *J'ai un garçon qui* RIDE *réglé.* I have a son who rides regularly. (LF) <***Loc:*** EV, LA, LF, PQ, TB, Lv88>

règlement [rɛgləmɑ̃] *n.m.* **1** setting (of time pieces) **2** rule **Habitude je suivais les règlements.* Usually I followed the rules. (ThCa: *Mille misères*) **3** settlement (of an account, a difficulty, etc.) ◊ **•réglement de comptes** getting even, settling the score *C'était pas juste une bataille. C'était un règlement de comptes.* It wasn't just a fight. It was a settling of the score. (LA) <LA> <***Loc:*** LA, Da84, ThCa>

régler [regle] **I** *v.tr.* **1** to regulate, order *Quand j'ai fini l'école en 1938, j'ai commencé travailler pour, ça s'appelait l'*AGRICULTURE ADJUSTMENT ADMINISTRATION. *C'était une agence du gouvernement qu'a commencé à régler la quantité de récolte, principalement du coton, que les fermiers pouvaient planter.* When I finished school in 1938, I began working for, it was called the Agriculture Adjustment Administration. It was a government agency that began to regulate the amount of crops, principally cotton, that the farmers could plant. (SL) **2** to set (a time piece) **Régler la montre, la pendule.* To set the watch, the clock. (Da84) **3** to settle (e.g. a dispute), often by fighting *Chez nous ça pouvait pas régler leurs affaires au bal parce que le constable était trop brut, ça fait ça espérait le lendemain après la messe.* Where I lived, they couldn't settle their disputes at the dance because the bouncer was too strict, so they waited until the next day after Mass. (LA) **II** *v.intr.* to menstruate **III se régler** *v.pron.* to regulate one's digestion, keep o.s. regular *Il prend de la médecine pour se régler.* He takes medicine to keep himself regular. (LA) ◊ **•régler ses affaires** to put one's affairs in order <Da84> **•régler ses comptes** to pay or settle one's accounts <Da84> <***Loc:*** AL, IB, LA, SJ, SL, VM, Da84>

régner [rẽje] *v.intr.* to reign, rule, prevail *C'est elle qui régnait sus sa famille.* She's the one who reigned over her family. (LA) <***Loc:*** LA, Da84>

regonfler [r(ə)gɔ̃fle, ərgɔ̃fle, ærgɔ̃fle] **I** *v.tr.* to reinflate *Ils ont eu pour regonfler le* TIRE *après juste quelques jours.* They had to reinflate the tire after just a few days. (LA) **II** *v.intr.* to swell again, swell up again *Son bras a regonflé durant la nuit.* His arm swelled up again during the night. (LA) **III se regonfler** *v.pron.* to swell again, swell up again *Le ouaouaron s'a regonflé.* The bullfrog swelled up again. (LA) <***Loc:*** LA, Da84>

regouler (se) [r(ə)gule, ərgule, ærgule] *v.pron.* to eat one thing to the point of disgust *Il a mangé tellement des poires il s'est regoulé.* He ate so many pears that he got digusted by them. (SL) ◊ **•être regoulé** to be fed up, be disgusted *Il est regoulé sus ça.* He is fed up with that. (TB) <TB> <***Loc:*** SL, TB, Di32>

regratter [r(ə)grate, ərgrate, ærgrate] **I** *v.tr.* to rescrape, rescratch, scrape or scratch again *Elle a regratté une autre allumette.* She struck another match. (SL) **II se regratter** *v.pron.* to scratch o.s. again or repeatedly *Il pouvait pas s'empêcher de se regratter.* He couldn't keep from scratching himself repeatedly. (LA) <***Loc:*** LA, SL, Da84>

regreffer [r(ə)grefe, ərgrefe, ærgrefe] *v.tr.* to regraft *On va essayer de regreffer la branche sur le plaqueminier.* We will try to regraft the branch on the persimmon tree. (LA) <***Loc:*** LA, Da84>

regret [r(ə)grɛ, ərgrɛ, ærgrɛ, r(ə)gre, ərgre, ærgre] *n.m.* regret, sorrow *J'ai pas de regrets, on a fait une bonne vie.* I have no regrets, we've had a good life. (TB) ◊ **•avoir du regret** to be regretful, be sorry *J'ai eu du regret après que j'ai pas accepté.* I was sorry afterwards that I didn't accept. (SJ) <SJ> <***Loc:*** EV, SJ, TB, Da84, Hi02>

regrettable [r(ə)gretab(l), əgretab(l), ærgretab(l)] *adj.* regrettable, deplorable, unfortunate *C'est beaucoup regrettable, la manière qu'il traitait ses enfants.* It's really deplorable the way he treated his children. (LA) <***Loc:*** LA, Da84>

regretter [r(ə)grete, ərgrete, ærgrete] *v.tr.* **1** to regret, be sorry for *J'ai regretté bien ça.* I really regretted that. (SL) *Je regrette ça j'ai fait.* I am sorry for what I did. (LA) **J'crois qu'Sosthène er'grettait qu'il avait pas écouté son vieux grand-père.* I think Sosthène regretted that he hadn't listened to his old grandfather. (Gu82) **2** to miss *T'eurgrettes les* GOOD TIMES *on avait?* You miss the good times we used to have? (SM) *T'eurgrettes ton argent?* You miss your money? (VM) <***Loc:*** AC, AV, EV, LA, SL, SM, TB, VM, Da84, Gu82, Hi02>

regricher (égricher, gricher) [r(ə)griʃe, ərgriʃe, ærgriʃe, egriʃe, griʃe] **I** *v.tr.* **1** to go against (e.g. a current, the wind) **Regricher le courant.* To go against the current. (Da84) **Regricher le vent.* To go against the wind. (Da84) **2** to rise up against, stand up to, go against **Il y en a qui ont regriché le cour [=cours], pour retrouver l'Acadie devenue Nova Scotia* There were some who went against the current to get back to Acadia, which had become Nova Scotia. (Ar82) **3** to bristle, raise up **Quand il était fâché, i' grichait les cornes-là.* When he was angry, he raised up those horns. (An77) **II** *v.intr.* **1** to become ruffled, stand on end (of hair) *Ses cheveux ont argriché.* His hair stood on end. (Lv88) *Ses cheveux est regriché.* His hair stood back up [after being combed down]. (SM) **Ses cris fait égricher ses ch'feux.* His cries make your hand stand on end. (EV, Ph36) **2** to get riled up, get emotionally shaken up, lose one's temper *Il a regriché quand il a entendu la nouvelle.* He got riled up when he heard the news. (LA) **3** to bristle up *Le chat est griché.* The cat is bristled up. (Lv88) **4** to be in a bad mood, be grouchy *Il était argriché, je sais pas ça il avait.* He was grouchy, I don't know what was wrong with him. (Lv88) *Il regriche comme un chat en colère.* He is as grouchy as an angry cat. (Lv88) **III se regricher** *v.pron.* **1** to stand up, rise up **2** to get riled up, get on the defensive *Egriche-toi pas!* Don't get in a huff! (EV) **3** to bristle up **Le chien s'a regriché.* The dog bristled up. (Da84) ◊ **•regricher les cheveux** to bristle up <Da84> **•se regricher contre** to go against, oppose *Il s'a regriché contre la famille de sa femme.* He went against his wife's family. (LA) *Tu t'as griché contre moi.* You sided against me. (VM) <LA, VM> <***Loc:*** EV, JD, LA, LF, SM, VM, Da84, An77, Ar82, Lv88>

regrouiller [r(ə)gruje, ərgruje, ærgruje] *v.intr.* to move again, budge again *Le petit va regrouiller de son coin si tu tournes le dos.* The little child will move back out of his corner if you turn your back. (IB) <***Loc:*** IB>

régulateur[1] [regylatœr] *n.m.* digestion aid, laxative *Je peux pas me passer de mon régulateur.* I can't do without my laxative. (VM) <***Loc:*** VM>

régulateur[2] [regylatœr] *n.m.* member of a group organized in St. Martinsville in the early 1880s to restore white rule <***Loc:*** SM>

régulation [regylasjɔ̃] *n.f.* regulation, rule <***Loc:*** Da84, Gr86>

régulier[1]**, -ière** [regylje, reglije, -jær] *adj.* **1** regular, steady *J'étais parti pour servir le grand roi, servir le grand roi sur l'armée régulière.* I had left to serve the high king, to serve the high king in the regular army. (LA, ch: *Grand Dieu, comme je suis à mon aise*) **2** punctual *C'était un ouvrier qu'était régulier. Il commençait tous les jours à sept heures.* He was a punctual carpenter. He started every day at seven o'clock. (LA) <***Loc:*** LA, Da84>

régulier[2] [regylje] *adv.* regularly, on a regular basis *Ça prend quatre à cinq semaines, on travaille pas régulier.* It takes four to five weeks [to make a violin], we don't work regularly. (Lv88) <***Loc:*** Lv88>

régulièrement [regyljærmɑ̃] *adv.* regularly, on a regular basis *Il jouait pas régulièrement.* He did not play regularly. (EV) <***Loc:*** EV, Da84>

réhabituer (**rhabituer**) [reabitɥe, rabitɥe] **I** *v.tr.* to reaccustom, refamiliarize *Réhabituer ses enfants à l'école après les vacances.* To reaccustom one's children to school after vacation. (LA) **II se réhabituer** *v.pron.* to reaccustom o.s., get used to again *Il faudra se rhabituer à la chaleur.* We'll have to reaccustom ourselves to the heat. (LA) <***Loc:*** LA, Da84>

rehausser [r(ə)hose, ərhose, ærhose] *v.tr.* to raise *Et ça a calé, faulait que eux-autres rehaussait ça souvent des fois depuis ça.* And it sank, they had to raise it up a number of times after that. (TB) **Rehausser le prix.* To raise the price. (Da84) <***Loc:*** TB, Da84>

réimprimer [reɛ̃prime] *v.tr.* to reprint *Ils ont eu pour réimprimer toutes les invitations à la noce.* They had to reprint all the wedding invitations. (LA) <***Loc:*** LA, Da84>

rein [rɛ̃] *n.m.* **1** backbone, back, spine *Le rein c'est le dos mais un piguerouin c'est* KIDNEY. The "rein" is the back but the "piguerouin" is the kidney. (IB) **2** *(pl.)* lower back, lumbar region *T'as mal aux reins?* Does your back hurt? (LF) ◊ **•pas avoir de rein encore** to not yet be strong enough (of young people) <Lv88> <***Loc:*** EV, IB, JE, LF, TB, Da84, Lv88>

reine [rɛ̃n] *n.f.* **1** queen **2** beauty queen, winning contestant in a women's pageant *Et là j'ai un certificat, j'étais la reine dans 1990. Ça ça vient du village de Houma.* And I have a certificate, I was queen in 1990. That comes from the city of Houma. (TB) **3** queen (in a deck of cards) <***Loc:*** SB, TB, Da84, Hi02>

reinquer ♦see **reintier**

réinstaller (**rinstaller**) [reɛ̃stale, rɛ̃stale] **I** *v.tr.* to reinstall *Don a réinstallé mon* RADIO. Don reinstalled my radio. (LA) **II se réinstaller** *v.pron.* to reestablish o.s., settle back in *Ils ont essayé de se réinstaller dans le voisinage, mais personne les voulait.* They tried to reestablish themselves in the neighborhood, but no one wanted them. (LA) <***Loc:*** EV, LA, Da84, Ph36>

reintier (**reinquer**) [rɛ̃tje, rɛ̃tʃe, rɛ̃tʃɛ̃, rɛ̃ke] *n.m.* **1** backbone, back, spine *J'ai mal au reintier.* My back hurts. (SM) *Longtemps passé, on coupait ça chaque bord du reintier.* A long time ago, it would be cut on each side of the backbone. (AC) **2** backstrap loin (of a butchered animal) *Ça coupait là le cochon en deux et là il y avait le reintier. Il y avait un reintier chaque bord.* They would cut the pig there in two and there would be the backstrap loin. There was a backstrap loin on each side. (LA) **3** pork chine, pork backbone with meat *Une fricassée reintier.* Pork chine stew. (Lv88) *Là les femmes dans la cuisine disaient: "Eh amène le reintier, on va faire une sauce!"* Then, women in the kitchen would say: "Hey, bring the backbone we're going to make a sauce!" (IB) <***Loc:*** AC, AV, EV, IB, IV, JD, JE, LA, LF, SB, SL, SM, TB, VM, Da84, Hi02, Lv88, Ph36>

rejeter [r(ə)ʒəte, ərʒəte, ærʒəte, rəʃte] **I** *v.tr.* to vomit, throw up *Elle rejette tout, même l'eau.* She vomits everything, even water. (Lv88) **II** *v.intr.* to vomit, throw up **J'sus assez larguée d'a'tend [=attendre] parler de not' magnière [=manière] de parler à nous-aut', j'pourrais rej'ter.* I am so tired of hearing about our way of speaking, I could vomit. (Gu82) <***Loc:*** LA, SM, TB, VM, Da84, Gu82, Lv88>

rejoindre [r(ə)ʒwɛ̃n, r(ə)ʒwɛ̃d(r), ərʒwɛ̃n, ərʒwɛ̃d(r), ærʒwɛ̃n, ærʒwɛ̃d(r)] **I** *v.tr.* to meet, meet up with, encounter *Venez jamais me rejoindre sans le papier signé.* Don't show up to meet me without the signed paper. (Lv88) *J'ai rejoint quelqu'un sur ma route.* I met someone on my way. (SM) *Je l'ai rejoint au village.* I met him in town. (VM) *Et quand vous avez rejoint Darrell, dimanche?* And when did you meet up with Darrell, on Sunday? (VM) **II se rejoindre** *v.pron.* to meet each other, get together with one another *C'est une occasion pour se rejoindre avec la famille et les amis.* It is an occasion to get together with family and friends. (Lv88) **Et le soir, il nous faisait se rejoindre pour jouer de la musique.* And in the evening he would have us get together to play music. (An84) <*Loc:* AC, EV, LA, SL, SM, TB, VM, An84, Da84, Gr86, Hi02, Lv88, Ph36>

rejouer [r(ə)ʒwe, ərʒwe, ærʒwe] *v.tr.* to replay, play again *On a eu pour rejouer la danse une dizaine de fois.* We had to replay the song about ten times. (VM) <*Loc:* EV, VM, Da84>

rejuger [r(ə)ʒyʒe, ərʒyʒe, ærʒyʒe] *v.tr.* to rejudge, judge again *Ils auront besoin de les rejuger.* They will have to rejudge them. (LA) <*Loc:* LA, Da84>

relâcher [r(ə)laʃe, ərlaʃe, ærlaʃe] **I** *v.tr.* **1** to relax, slacken **2** to release, set free **Relâcher le chaoui.* To set the raccoon free. (Da84) **II se relâcher** *v.pron.* to slacken, relax <*Loc:* Da84>

rélargir [relarʒir] *v.tr.* to broaden, widen, enlarge *On aurait besoin que ça vient rélargir le fossé pour amener l'eau.* We would need them to come and enlarge the ditch to carry the water away. (LA) <*Loc:* LA, Da84>

relation [r(ə)lasjɔ̃, ərlasjɔ̃, ærlasjɔ̃] *n.f.* relation, connection ◊ •**avoir des relations** to have sexual intercourse <VM> <*Loc:* VM, Da84>

relaver [r(ə)lave, ərlave, ærlave] *v.tr.* to rewash, wash again *Il faudra que je relave mon char asteur.* I'll have to rewash my car now. (LA) <*Loc:* LA, Da84>

relevé, -e [r(ə)l(ə)ve, ərləve, ærləve] *adj.* recovered, back on one's feet (after an illness) *J'étais content de voir qu'il était relevé.* I was happy to see that he was back on his feet. (LA) <*Loc:* LA, Da84>

relever [r(ə)l(ə)ve, ərləve, ærləve] **I** *v.tr.* **1** to raise up again, lift up again *Je peux pas relever ça.* I can't lift that back up. (VM) **2** to spruce up, tidy up (a place) **Relever la place.* To tidy up, clean up the place. (Da84) **3** to copy, reproduce *Il faut que je relève ce patron.* I need to copy this pattern. (TB) **II** *v.intr.* to recover (from an illness) *Je connais pas si il va relever après tout ça.* I don't know if he will recover after all that. (LA) **III se relever** *v.pron.* **1** to get up again, right o.s. **Il a tombé par terre, mais en tombant, il s'a relevé et il a parti avec le* GANG. He fell, but on his way down, he got up again and he left with the gang. (LA, An94) **2** to recover (from an illness), get up (from a sickbed) *On s'erleuve pas tout le temps de la tatanos, non!* People don't always recover from lockjaw. (TB) *Il va jamais s'eurlever de son lit.* He will never get up from his sickbed. (SM) **3** to clear up (of the weather) *Le temps va s'eurlever je crois.* The weather is going to clear up, I think. (VM) ◊ •**relever le nom de** to perpetuate the name of (by giving it to a child) <Da84> <*Loc:* EV, JE, LA, SM, TB, VM, An94, Da84>

RELIEF [ɹəlif] *n.m.* department of public welfare <*Loc:* VM>

religieuse[1] ♦see **religieux**

religieuse[2] [r(ə)liʒjøz, ərliʒjøz, ærliʒjøz] *n.f.* black-necked stilt <*Loc:* Lv88, Re31>

religieux[1], **-ieuse** [r(ə)liʒjø, ərliʒjø, ærliʒjø, -øz] *adj.* religious, devout **Toutes les vieilles femmes, elles sont beaucoup religieuses.* All of the old women are very devout. (EV, An94) <*Loc:* EV, An94, Da84, Hi02>

religieux[2], **-ieuse** [r(ə)liʒjø, ərliʒjø, ærliʒjø, r(ə)lyʒjø, ərlyʒjø, ærlyʒjø, -øz] *n.* **1** *(m.)* monk **2** *(f.)* nun **3** devout person *Ça c'est une religieuse. Alle va monter au ciel, sûr.* She's a devout person. She'll go to heaven, for sure. (VM) <*Loc:* LF, SM, VM, Da84, Hi02>

religion [r(ə)liʒjɔ̃, ərliʒjɔ̃, ærliʒjɔ̃, r(ə)lyʒjɔ̃, ərliʒjɔ̃, ærliʒjɔ̃, r(ə)liʒɔ̃, ərliʒɔ̃, ærliʒɔ̃, liʒɔ̃] *n.f.* religion <*Loc:* LF, SL, SM, TB, Da84, Hi02>

relique [r(ə)lik] *n.m.* [*eccl.*] relic <*Loc:* Da84>

relire [r(ə)lir, ərlir, ærlir] *v.tr.* to reread, read again *J'ai pas pris la peine de relire le contrat.* I didn't take the trouble to reread the contract. (LA) <*Loc:* LA, Da84>

reloger [r(ə)loʒe, ərloʒe, ærloʒe] **I** *v.tr.* to relocate, move to new lodgings *On a passé la fin de semaine à reloger mon garçon.* We spent the weekend relocating my son. (VM) **II se reloger** *v.pron.* to relocate, move to new lodgings *La quantité de monde qu'a eu pour se reloger!* The number of people who had to relocate! (LA) <*Loc:* LA, VM, Da84>

relouer [r(ə)lue, ərlue, ærlue] *v.tr.* to rerent, sublet *Ils ont reloué la petite maison à un homme et une femme qu'avaient pas d'enfants.* They sublet the little house to a man and a woman with no children. (LA) <*Loc:* LA, Da84>

reluquer [r(ə)lyke, ərlyke, ærlyke] **I** *v.tr.* to stare at, ogle *Alle était après nous reluquer à en plus finir.* She was staring at us like there was no tomorrow. (TB) **II** *v.intr.* to look, gaze *Elle est toujours après reluquer où elle a pas d'affaire.* She's always looking where she has no business. (SB) <*Loc:* SB, TB>

reluqueuse [r(ə)lykøz, ərlykøz, ærlykøz] *n.f.* **1** woman who stares **2** busybody, prying woman <*Loc:* TB>

remâcher [r(ə)maʃe, ərmaʃe, ærmaʃe] *v.tr.* to rechew, chew again <*Loc:* Da84>

remanger [r(ə)mɑ̃ʒe, ərmɑ̃ʒe, ærmɑ̃ʒe] *v.intr.* to eat again *Je vas jamais remanger là encore.* I'll never eat there again. (LA) <*Loc:* LA, Da84>

remanier [r(ə)mɑ̃je, ərmɑ̃je, ærmɑ̃je] *v.tr.* to rehandle, handle again *J'ai pas envie de remanier ce voyage de bois.* I don't feel like rehandling that load of wood. (LA) <*Loc:* LA, Da84>

remarcher [r(ə)marʃe, ərmarʃe, ærmarʃe] *v.intr.* to walk back *Après dîner on remarchait* BACK *à l'école et là après ça on a remarché* BACK *à la maison.* After lunch we walked back to school and then after that [at the end of the school day] we walked back home. (LF) <*Loc:* LF>

remariage [r(ə)marjaʒ, ərmarjaʒ, ærmarjaʒ] *n.m.* remarriage <*Loc:* Da84>

remarier [r(ə)marje, ərmarje, ærmarje] **I** *v.tr.* to remarry, perform a marriage ceremony for again *Il les a remariés pour leur cinquantième anniversaire.* He remarried them for their fiftieth anniversary. (LA) **II se remarier** *v.pron.* to remarry, marry again, get remarried *Elle s'est remariée sept fois.* She remarried seven times. (EV) *Jusqu'à que mon pape se remarie, c'est eusse qui nous a soigné nous-autres trois.* Until my dad remarried, they're the ones who took care of the three of us. (TB) *Il a déshonoré sa défunte femme quand il s'a remarié deux mois plus tard.* He dishonored his late wife when he remarried two months later. (VM) <***Loc:*** AS, EV, LA, LF, TB, VM, Da84>

remarquable [r(ə)markab(l), ərmarkab(l), ærmarkab(l)] *adj.* **1** remarkable, outstanding *Elle dit, "Ça va être bien remarquable," tu sais. Elle dit, "Ça va être joli," elle dit, "nous-autres se marier aussi, se remarier."* She says, "It will be remarkable," you know. She says, "It will be beautiful," she says, "us getting married, too, getting remarried." (AS) **2** noticeable <***Loc:*** AS, Da84>

remarque [r(ə)mark, ərmark, ærmark] *n.f.* **1** remark, comment *Passer des remarques.* To make remarks. (SM) *Oh des fois on va faire une remarque en français.* Oh, sometimes we'll make a remark in French. (TB) **2** sign, mark **Ça c'est la remarque d'un fou.* This is the mark of a fool. (Da84) ◊ **•remarque de tombe** grave marker <SL> <***Loc:*** SL, SM, TB, Da84>

remarquer[1] [r(ə)marke, ərmarke, ærmarke] *v.tr.* **1** to remark, comment *Il a remarqué qu'il voulait pas faire ça.* He remarked that he didn't want to do that. (LA) **2** to notice *"Ouais, mais," il dit, "si t'as remarqué, le coq change de poule à chaque coup."* "Yes, but," he says, "if you noticed, the rooster changes hens each time." (AS) <***Loc:*** AS, EV, LA, TB, Da84, Hi02>

remarquer[2] [r(ə)marke, ərmarke, ærmarke] *v.tr.* to mark again *Remarquer des bêtes.* To rebrand cattle. (LA) <***Loc:*** LA, Da84>

remâter [r(ə)mate, ərmate, ærmate] **I** *v.tr.* to stand s.t. up again *Il a remâté le bougre contre la barre.* He stood the fellow back up against the bar. (LA) **II se remâter** *v.pron.* **1** to stand up on hind legs again, rear back again (of a horse) *Le cheval a remâté quand il a vu la serpent.* The horse reared again when it saw the snake. (LA) **2** to rise up (against) *Reste tranquille et t'armâte pas sur moi.* Be still and do not rise up against me. (JE) **3** to oppose, resist, rebel *Je m'ai remâté contre.* I rebelled against it. (VM) <***Loc:*** JE, LA, TB, VM, Da84>

remballer [rɑ̃bale] *v.tr.* to rebale, repack *Ils ont eu pour remballer les petites balles en grandes balles.* They had to rebale the little bales into big bales. (LA) <***Loc:*** LA, Da84>

rembarquement [rɑ̃barkmɑ̃] *n.m.* reembarkation <***Loc:*** Da84>

rembarquer [rɑ̃barke] **I** *v.tr.* to reembark, reload *Il a fallu qu'ils rembarquent tous ces sacs d'écrevisses parce qu'ils les avaient déchargés à la mauvaise place.* They had to reload all those sacks of crawfish because they had unloaded them at the wrong place. (VM) **II** *v.intr.* to get back into (a vehicle), get in again *On va rembarquer dans le char dans quelques minutes.* We'll get back in the car in a few minutes. (SM) **III se rembarquer** *v.pron.* to go aboard again *Ils s'ont rembarqués dans le bateau.* They went aboard the boat again. (LA) <***Loc:*** LA, SM, VM, Da84>

rembarrer [rɑ̃bare] *v.tr.* **1** to lock in, lock up *Tous les soirs on a plein de trouble à rembarrer le chien dans l'hangar.* Every evening we have a lot of trouble locking the dog up in the shed. (TB) **2** to contradict, interrupt <***Loc:*** AV, LF, TB>

rembellezir ♦see **rembellir**

rembellir (rembellezir) [rɑ̃belir, rɑ̃bɛlzir] **I** *v.tr.* to restore the beauty of, beautify again *Ils sont après essayer de rembellir la vieille place.* They are trying to beautify the old place again. (LA) **II** *v.intr.* to become more beautiful *Moi, je trouve alle a rembellezi là-bas.* I think she got more beautiful over there. (VM) <***Loc:*** LA, VM, Da84>

remboursable [rɑ̃bursab(l)] *adj.* reimbursable, repayable *C'est remboursable à la fin du mois.* It's reimbursable at the end of the month. (VM) <***Loc:*** VM, Da84>

remboursement [rɑ̃bursmɑ̃] *n.m.* reimbursement, repayment <***Loc:*** Da84>

rembourser [rɑ̃burse] *v.tr.* to reimburse, repay *Je lui ai prêté cent piastres; il m'a jamais remboursé.* I lent him a hundred dollars; he never repaid me. (VM) <***Loc:*** VM, Da84>

remède (eurmède) [r(ə)mɛd, ərmɛd, ærmɛd] *n.m.* remedy, cure, medicine *Ça se faisait des remèdes eux-autres-mêmes.* They would make their own medicine. (AC) *Le docteur m'a donné des eurmèdes, mais je les ai pas pris.* The doctor gave me medecines, but I didn't take them. (SM) <***Loc:*** AC, SM, TB, VM, Da84>

remêler [r(ə)mele, ərmele, ærmele] *v.tr.* to remix, mix again *Là il faut tu remêles tout ça dans une grande chaudière.* Then you have to remix all of that in a big pot. (LA) <***Loc:*** LA, Da84>

remener ♦see **ramener**

remerciement [r(ə)mærsimɑ̃] *n.m.* thanks, thanksgiving ◊ **•le Jour de Remerciement** Thanksgiving Day <Da84> <***Loc:*** Da84>

remercier [r(ə)mærsje, ərmærsje, ærmærsje] *v.tr.* to thank **Les Mardi Gras vous remercient.* The Mardi Gras revelers thank you. (Hi02) <***Loc:*** Da84, Hi02>

remettre [r(ə)mɛt(r), ərmɛt(r), ərmet(r), ærmɛt(r), ærmet(r),] **I** *v.tr.* **1** to put back, return, replace *Et ça le prendait, ça travaillait, tu connais, dessus un violon pour un certain du temps. Là, ça le pendait, ça le mettait de côté. Et là, ça revenait, ça travaillait dessus pour un bout de temps. Là, ça le remettait de côté.* And they'd take it, they'd work on it, you know, on a violin for a certain period of time. Then they'd hang it up, put it aside. And then they'd come back to it, they'd work on it for a while. Then they'd put it back. (SL) *Et le bateau est monté là-dessus, il est nettoyé en-dessour* *et il est peinturé, et là eux-autres le quittont chesser pour un ou deux jours, là le remettont* BACK *à l'eau.* And the boat is raised up on there, it is cleaned underneath and it is painted, and then they let it dry for a day or two, then they put it back in the water. (LF) **2** to put some more in or on, apply some more *Quand il était cuit on remettait un petit brin d'eau.* When it was cooked, we would put in a little more water. (AC) *Moi et ma femme on a décidé d'aller dans la banque et de sortir cet argent-là. On a sorti un gros tas. Et on l'a jamais remis autre jusqu'aujourd'hui* BUT *je regrette arien, j'ai fait une bonne vie.* My wife and I decided to go to the bank and take out that money. We took out a large sum. And we never put in any more until now but I regret nothing, I've had a good life. (AS) **3** to put on again *Tu peux ermettre ton capot parce qu'ils vont prendre ton portrait.* You can put your jacket back on because they're going to take your picture. (EV) **Y a fallu qu'i' perde eine avant-midi d'ouvrage dans l'clos pour aller dire à c't animal-là que si jâmais a' r'mettait la main su' not' 'tite fille i'l'aurait fait faire, elle aussite, quèque chose qu'alle était pas capab' de faire. I' l'aurait fait pagayer eine pirogue pleine de trous.* He had to miss a whole morning of work in the fields in order to go tell that brute that if she ever laid another hand on our little girl he would make her, too, do something that she couldn't possibly do. He would've made her paddle a boat full of holes. (VM, Gu82) **4** to add in *Je fais jaunir [...] la viande et je mets des oignons, des piments, des assaisonnements, et là je remets le riz cru, avec l'eau dedans, et, cuis tout ensemble.* [To make a jambalaya] I brown the meat, and I add onions, peppers, seasonings, and I add in the uncooked rice, with water in it, and cook everything together. (SL) **5** to put back together, reassemble *Je peux défaire une machine et tout soucouer les morceaux d'un* CAN *de cinq gallons et là les remettre à* BACK. I can take a machine apart and shake all the pieces up in a five gallon can and then put them back together. (TB) **6** to turn on again (e.g. an appliance) *Oui, il a remis ça* BACK *dessus.* Yes, he turned it [the tape recorder] back on. (TB) **7** to postpone, put off *Ils ont ermis la game à dimanche.* They postponed the game until Sunday. (SM) *Un travail remis est jamais fini.* A job that is put off is never finished. (LA) **8** to pep s.o. up *Et là j'ai lit les* FUNNY PAPER, *et là après ça ça l'a remis, tu vois.* And then I read the funny papers, and after that it pepped her up, you see. (TB) **II se remettre** *v.pron.* **1** to remember **Je me remets de ça.* I remember that. (Da84) **2** to get back to **Se remettre à l'ouvrage.* To get back to work. (Da84) ◊ **•remettre à demain** to put off until tomorrow <Da84> <***Loc:*** AC, AS, EV, LA, LF, SL, SM, TB, VM, Da84, Gu82>

remeubler [r(ə)møble, ərmøble, ærmøble] *v.tr.* to refurnish *Il y a du monde qu'ont été obligé de rebâtir leurs maisons et d'autres qu'ont juste eu pour les réparer et remeubler.* There are people who had to rebuild their houses and others who just had to repair and refurnish them. (VM) <***Loc:*** VM, Da84>

remise[1] [r(ə)miz, ərmiz, ærmiz] *n.f.* remittance, remission <***Loc:*** Da84>

remise[2] **(armise)** [r(ə)miz, ərmiz, ærmiz] *n.f.* carriage house, garage *La voiture est dans la remise.* The buggy is in the carriage house. (SB) <***Loc:*** SB, Da84>

rémission [remisjɔ̃] *n.f.* [*eccl.*] remission, forgiveness (of sins) <***Loc:*** Da84>

remmancher ♦see **ramancher**

remmener ♦see **ramener**

remontage [r(ə)mɔ̃taʒ, ərmɔ̃taʒ, ærmɔ̃taʒ] *n.m.* rising <***Loc:*** Da84>

remonter [r(ə)mɔ̃te, ərmɔ̃te, ærmɔ̃te] **I** *v.tr.* **1** to ascend, climb (e.g. a mountain) **2** to wind up again *Il a oublié de remonter la pendule.* He forgot to wind the clock. (LA) **II** *v.intr.* **1** to go up again, climb again **Sa fièvre est après remonter.* His fever is rising again. (Da84) **Ça fait qu'elle a descendu en bas de la montagne et elle a trouvé de quoi qui coupait. Elle a remonté, elle lui a ôté la peau et puis là, elle se l'a mise sur le dos, et elle a parti à s'en aller.* So, she descended the mountain and she found something that would cut. She climbed back up, she took off the pelt and then she put it on her back and she went away. (IV, An94) **2** to rise, go up (of prices) *Le prix des haricots a remonté.* The price of beans has gone up. (TB) ◊ **•remonter à cheval** to go on horseback again <Da84> **•remonter le vent {courant}** to go against the wind, go against the current <Da84> **•aller en remontant** to go upwards *Le chemin allait en remontant la levée.* The road went up the levée. (VM) <VM, Da84> <***Loc:*** IV, LA, TB, VM, An94, Da84>

remontrance (armontrance) [r(ə)mɔ̃trɑ̃s, ərmɔ̃trɑ̃s, ærmɔ̃trɑ̃s] *n.m./f.* reprimand, remonstrance *C'est un vieux armontrance eux-autres ont fait.* It's an old remonstrance that they made. (Lv88) ◊ **•faire des remontrances** to reprimand <Da84> <***Loc:*** Da84, Lv88>

remontrer [r(ə)mɔ̃tre, ərmɔ̃tre, ærmɔ̃tre] **I** *v.tr.* **1** to show again, exhibit again **2** to teach *Ça c'est terrible, la maîtresse peut arien le remontrer.* It's terrible, the schoolteacher can't teach him anything. (VM) **3** to reteach *Il faudra lui remontrer comment parler après son* STROKE. It will be necessary to reteach him to speak after his stroke. (LA) **II se remontrer** *v.pron.* to show o.s. again *Je crois pas qu'il va se remontrer ici encore.* I don't think he will show himself around here again. (LA) <***Loc:*** LA, VM, Da84>

remordre [r(ə)mɔrd(r), ərmɔrd(r), ærmɔrd(r)] *v.tr.* to bite again *Il l'a remordu sur l'oreille.* He bit him again on the ear. (LA) <***Loc:*** LA, Da84>

remords [r(ə)mɔr] *n.m.* remorse, sorrow ◊ **•remords de conscience** pang of remorse, pang of conscience <Da84> <***Loc:*** Da84>

remoudre [r(ə)mud(r), ərmud(r), ærmud(r)] *v.tr.* to regrind, remill *Remoudre le café.* To regrind coffee. (VM) <*Loc:* VM, Da84>

remouiller [r(ə)muje, ərmuje, ærmuje] **I** *v.tr.* to rewet, remoisten *Remouille ta chemise avant tu la grilles.* Rewet your shirt before you scorch it. (VM) **II** *v.intr.* **1** to rain again **Il va remouiller aujourd'hui.* It will rain again today. (Da84) **2** to be on the verge of giving birth (of a cow, mare, etc.) <*Loc:* VM, Da84>

rémoulade [remulad] *n.f.* highly seasoned stew <*Loc:* Da84>

remous [r(ə)mu] *n.m.* **1** water eddy (caused by movement under the water) **2** undercurrent <*Loc:* Da84>

rempaqueter [rɑ̃pakte] *v.tr.* to repack, repackage *Rempaqueter un sofa pour le renvoyer.* To repack a sofa to send it back. (VM) <*Loc:* VM, Da84>

remparer (se) [rɑ̃pare] *v.pron.* to take or retake possession *Il s'a remparé du butin de sa famille.* He retook possession of his family's goods. (VM) <*Loc:* JE, VM, Da84>

rempirer [rɑ̃pire] **I** *v.tr.* to make worse, worsen *T'es juste après rempirer ton cas quand tu parles comme ça.* You're just making your case worse when you talk like that. (EV) **II** *v.intr.* to worsen, get worse (e.g. in sickness) **Les affaires rempirent.* Things are getting worse. (Da84) *La femme était mieux, mais elle a rempiré.* The woman was better, but she took a turn for the worse. (SM) *Le docteur croyait ça il était guérissable, mais il rempire tous les jours.* The doctor believed it was curable, but he is getting worse every day. (VM) <*Loc:* EV, IB, SB, SL, SM, TB, VM, Da84, Gr86, Lv88, Ph36>

remplaçable [rɑ̃plasab(l)] *adj.* replaceable *Ta fourniture, c'est une chose, mais les portraits de ta famille, c'est pas remplaçable.* Your furniture, that's one thing, but family pictures, those are not replaceable. (EV) <*Loc:* EV, Da84>

remplaçant [rɑ̃plasɑ̃] *n.m.* replacement, substitute *Quand je vas prendre ma retraite, ils vont jamais trouver un remplaçant pour moi.* When I retire, they will never find a replacement for me. (VM) <*Loc:* VM, Da84>

remplacement [rɑ̃plasmɑ̃] *n.m.* **1** replacement, substitution **2** replacement, substitute **Mon remplacement arrive à quatre heures. Y a plus qu'ein mois que j'ai pas vu ma femme et mes enfants.* My replacement arrives at four o'clock. It's been more than a month that I haven't seen my wife and kids. (Gu82) <*Loc:* Da84, Gu82>

remplacer [rɑ̃plase] *v.tr.* to replace, substitute for *Elle était juste après me remplacer là.* She was just replacing me there. (EV) <*Loc:* EV, Da84>

remplie [rɑ̃pli] *adj.f.* pregnant *Elle est remplie.* She is pregnant. (SM) <*Loc:* SM, Da84>

remplier ♦see **replier**

remplir [rɑ̃plir] **I** *v.tr.* **1** to fill, fill up *WELL, il remplissait le TRUCK de ses enfants, eux-autres avait une grosse famille.* Well, he filled up the truck with his kids, they had a big family. (TB) *J'avais pompé de l'eau, j'avais rempli les deux barils.* I had pumped water, I had filled up the two barrels. (VM) *Ce malheureux garçon, tout rempli de boisson, parle à son père sans entendre raison.* That miserable boy, all full of liquor, speaks to his father without listening to reason. (PQ, ch: *Le jour de l'Ascension*) **Ein jour j'm'ai aperçue que le lait que Pierre rentrait était bleu. Ça fait le lend'main matin j'ai guetté par le chassis et j'ai découvert Pierre après remplir son siau à la pompe.* One day I noticed that the milk that Pierre was bringing in was blueish. So, the next morning I watched from the window and I caught Pierre topping off his bucket at the [water] pump. (VM, Gu82) **2** to impregnate, cause to become pregnant *La truie a été remplie depuis la semaine passée.* The sow is pregnant since last week. (SB) **3** to fill out (a form) *T'avais un FORM que tu remplissais tout ce que ça que le puits faisait: l'huile, l'eau, et le gaz. Et là la pression que le puits avait.* You had a form where you filled out what the oil well produced: oil, water, and gas. And the pressure that the well had. (LF) **II se remplir** *v.pron.* **1** to fill up *Ça se remplit, le BAG se remplit. Et là équand il est plein, juste tu hales ça dans le bateau.* The bag fills up. And when it's full, you just haul it into the boat. (TB) **2** to fill o.s. ◊ •**remplir à déborder** to fill to overflowing <Da84> <*Loc:* EV, LF, PQ, SB, SM, TB, VM, Da84, Gu82, Hi02, Ph36>

remployer[1] [rɑ̃plwaje] *v.tr.* **1** to rehire, reemploy **2** to reuse, reemploy (e.g. a tool) <*Loc:* Da84>

remployer[2] ♦see **reployer**

remuage [r(ə)mɥaʒ, ərmɥaʒ, ærmɥaʒ] *n.m.* moving, movement <*Loc:* Da84>

remuement [r(ə)mymɑ̃, ərmymɑ̃, ærmymɑ̃] *n.m.* movement <*Loc:* Da84>

remuer [r(ə)mɥe, ərmɥe, ærmɥe] **I** *v.tr.* to move, stir *Le vent était après remuer les feuilles.* The wind was stirring the leaves. (VM) **II se remuer** *v.pron.* to move, stir *Les jeunes chats avaient juste commencé à se remuer.* The kittens had just started to stir. (LA) <*Loc:* LA, VM, Da84>

rémunérer [remynere] *v.tr.* to remunerate, reward *Je suis pas bien rémunéré pour ça je fais.* I'm not well paid for what I do. (VM) <*Loc:* VM, Da84>

renâcler [rənakle, ərnakle, ærnakle] *v.intr.* to snort *Le cheval a arnaclé.* The horse snorted. (JE) <*Loc:* JE, SL, TB, Da84>

renaissance [r(ə)nesɑ̃s, ərnesɑ̃s, ærnesɑ̃s] *n.f.* **1** rebirth **2** revival, renewal <*Loc:* Da84, Hi02>

renard, -e [r(ə)nar, ərnar, ærnar, -ard] *n.* **1** *(m.)* fox **2** *(f.)* vixen, she-fox <*Loc:* AL, Da84, Hi02>

rencaisser [rɑ̃kese] *v.tr.* to reencase, rebox, repack *Rencaisser son linge.* To repack one's clothes. (VM) <*Loc:* VM, Da84>

rencharger [rɑ̃ʃarʒe] *v.tr.* **1** to charge, entrust, put in charge *J'y ai renchargé de le faire.* I put him in charge of doing it. (VM) **2** to instruct, bring to understand definitely *Je l'ai* *bien renchargé que je voulais pas ça.* I made him understand that I didn't want that. (VM) <***Loc:*** VM, Da84>

renchaussage [rɑ̃ʃosaʒ] *n.m.* 'laying by' of sugar cane crop <***Loc:*** SJ>

renchausser (**rechausser**) [rɑ̃ʃose, raʃose] *v.tr.* to bank up, reinforce, bring dirt up around (plants) *Renchausser un pied de tomate.* To bring up dirt around a tomato plant. (LA) *Il a passé la semaine à rechausser son maïs.* He spent the week rebanking his corn. (LA) <***Loc:*** AV, IB, LA, SJ, SL, SM, TB, VM, Da84, Lv88>

renchérir [rɑ̃ʃerir] **I** *v.tr.* to raise (a price) *Ils ont renchéri le prix du gaz.* They raised the price of gas again. (VM) **II** *v.intr.* to become more expensive *Les écrevisses vont renchérir cette année.* Crawfish is going to be more expensive this year. (LA) <***Loc:*** LA, VM, Da84>

rencontre [rɑ̃kɔ̃t(r)] *n.f.* encounter, meeting <***Loc:*** Da84>

rencontrer [rɑ̃kɔ̃tre, rakɔ̃tre] **I** *v.tr.* to meet, encounter *Le prêtre se met à la porte de l'église pour rencontrer les partants.* The priest goes to the door of the church to meet the departing worshippers. (VM) **2** to make the acquaintance of, meet *Alle a rencontré un de mes amis là-bas qui vient ici, un professeur de collège.* She met one of my friends there who comes here, a college professor. (TB) *J'étais déjà promis à quelqu'un d'autre quand j'ai rencontré ton père.* I was already promised to someone else when I met your father. (VM) **II** *v.intr.* to meet, meet up *Vous peut appeler, peut-être on pourrait rencontrer encore.* You can call, maybe we could meet up again. (IB) **III se rencontrer** *v.pron.* to meet each other *Le monde a commencé à vouloir se rencontrer et puis ça se battait pas.* People started wanting to meet each other and so they didn't fight. (SL) *Et il a fait ça quatre fois qu'on se rencontre.* And he did that the four times that we met up. (TB) <***Loc:*** AC, AV, EV, IB, SL, TB, Da84>

rendez-vous [rɑ̃devu] *n.m.* **1** duel, meeting to settle a score **Ça fait, ils ont fait un rendez-vous pour le dimanche matin [...]. Ils se seraient battus aux armes.* So they scheduled a duel for Sunday morning. They would use firearms. (SL, An94) **2** rendezvous, trysting place, meeting place ◊ **•faire un rendez-vous** to make an appointment <Lv88> <***Loc:*** EV, SL, An94, Da84, Hi02, Lv88>

rendormir [rɑ̃dɔrmir] **I** *v.tr.* to put back to sleep *Je pourras jamais rendormir les petits si tu les réveilles asteur.* I will never be able to get the children back to sleep if you wake them now. (LA) **II se rendormir** *v.pron.* to go back to sleep *Réveille-toi et rendors-toi; tu ronfles!* Wake up and go back to sleep; you're snoring! (LA) <***Loc:*** LA, Da84>

rendre [rɑ̃n, rɑ̃d(r)] **I** *v.tr.* **1** to render, yield (fruit, etc.) **2** to give back, restore *Il lui a rendu mieux qu'il a eu.* He gave him back better than he got. (LA) **3** to cause to be, cause to become, render *Tu vas me rendre folle avec ton radotage!* You're going to drive me crazy with your chatter! (EV) **Mon souper m'a rendu malade.* My dinner made me sick. (An94) **4** to reduce by melting, render (e.g. lard) *Rendre de la graisse de cochon.* To render pork fat. (LA) **II** *v.intr.* **1** to yield fruit **La récolte rend bien.* The crop is yielding well. (Da84) **2** to become **Mais la petite fille, elle était rendue grande.* But the little girl, she had become grown-up. (IV, An94) *Ça fait, il était rendu vieux garçon.* So he had become an old bachelor. (SL, An94) **C'était rendu à midi. L'homme voulait s'en aller dîner.* It had gotten to be noon. The man wanted to leave to eat lunch. (SL, An94) **III se rendre** *v.pron.* **1** to cause o.s. to be, cause o.s. to become *Je m'ai rendu malade avec du maquechou une fois, et ensuite j'ai jamais pu me rengoûter après le maïs tendre.* I got sick from eating maquechou once, and after that I never could recover my taste for corn. (VM) **2** to arrive at, reach (a destination) **Mon père s'a rendu icitte dans la Louisiane ayou il a recommencé avec à rien d'autre que la terre que les Espagnols lui ont donnée.* My father arrived here in Louisiana where he started all over with nothing more than the land the Spanish gave him. (Ar98, *Suite du loup*) ◊ **•rendre au monde** to deliver, give birth to, bring into the world *J'ai eu mille misères pour la rendre au monde.* I had a devil of a time giving birth to her. (EV) <EV> **•rendre compte (de)** to give account (of) <EV, Da84> **•rendre justice** to render justice <Da84> **•rendre malade** to cause to be sick *Mon souper m'a rendu malade.* My dinner made me sick. (An94) <An94, Da84> **•se rendre chez soi** to reach home <Da84> **•se rendre malade** to make o.s. sick <Da84> **•se rendre utile** to make o.s. useful <Da84> **•se rendre compte** to find out (for o.s.), verify *J'ai été là-bas juste pour me rendre compte.* I went over there just to see for myself. (VM) <VM, Da84> <***Loc:*** EV, IV, LA, SL, TB, An94, Da84, Hi02>

rendu [rɑ̃dy] *adj.* **1** arrived *On est pas encore rendu.* We haven't arrived yet. (LA) **Il dit, "Maman," il dit, "j'étais rendu loin! Et j'ai vu une bêtaille qu'était beaucoup grosse!"* He said, "Mom," he said, "I ended up far away! And I saw a beast that was really big!" (LA, An94) **2** at the limit (of what is acceptable or tolerable) **Ça c'est rendu.* That's the limit. (Da84) ◊ **•être rendu** to reach a state **Ça fait, il était rendu vieux garçon.* So he had gotten to the point where he was an old bachelor. (SL, An94) <SL, An94, Da84> <***Loc:*** LA, SL, An94, Da84>

renduire [rɑ̃dɥir] *v.tr.* to coat, paint *Renduire une barrière avec de la chaux.* To whitewash a fence. (VM) <***Loc:*** VM>

renduit [rɑ̃dɥi] *n.m.* coat, layer (of paint) <***Loc:*** VM>

rendurcir [rɑ̃dyrsir] **I** *v.tr.* to harden again *La chesseresse a rendurci la terre dans le platin.* The drought has made the dirt in the lowland hard again. (LA) **II se rendurcir** *v.pron.* to harden *On va passer la herse avant la terre se rendurcit.* We'll pass the harrow before the soil rehardens. (LA) <***Loc:*** LA, Da84>

rêne (**riêne**) [rɛ̃n, rjɛ̃n] *n.f.* rein (of a harness) *Ça passait les guides et les rênes dans les hèmes.* The traces and the reins would go through the hames. (AC) <***Loc:*** AC, EV, VM, Da84, Ph36>

rêner [rɛ̃ne] *v.tr.* to rein, guide with reins, drive (horses) *Rêner des chevaux.* To rein horses. (LA) <***Loc:*** JE, LA, SM, TB, VM, Da84, Lv88>

renette ♦see **rainette**

renfermer [rɑ̃færme] **I** *v.tr.* to enclose, pen up, confine *Tu le renfermes dans une cage avec ces tout petits poulets là.* You enclose it in a cage with those tiny little chicks. (IV) **II se renfermer** *v.pron.* to shut o.s. in, seclude o.s., lock o.s. up *Elle se renferme dans la maison toute la journée.* She shuts herself in the house all day long. (EV) <***Loc:*** EV, IV, Da84>

renfiler [rɑ̃file] *v.tr.* to thread, rethread (a needle) *Renfiler une aiguille.* To thread or rethread a needle. (VM) <***Loc:*** VM, Da84>

renfoncer [rɑ̃fɔ̃se] **I** *v.tr.* to resink, drive in again **Renfoncer un poteau.* To resink a post. (Da84) **II se renfoncer** *v.pron.* to sink deeper *Il s'a renfoncé dans le rouin.* He sank deeper in the rut. (VM) <***Loc:*** VM, Da84>

renforçage [rɑ̃fɔrsaʒ] *n.m.* reinforcing, strengthening <***Loc:*** Da84>

renforcement ♦see **renforcissement**

renforcer ♦see **renforcir**

renforcir (**raforcir, renforcer**) [rɑ̃fɔrsir, rafɔrsir, rɑ̃fɔrse] **I** *v.tr.* to reinforce, strengthen *Ce thé m'a renforci.* This tea strengthened me. (VM) *L'ammonia m'a renforci.* The ammonia strengthened me. (SM) **II** *v.intr.* to grow stronger, become stronger *Le vent renforcissait.* The wind grew stronger. (Lv88) **III se renforcir** *v.pron.* to gain strength, grow stronger *Il a été bien malade cet hiver, mais il est après renforcir asteur.* He was very sick this winter, but he's getting stronger now. (VM) <***Loc:*** SM, TB, VM, Da84, Lv88>

renforcissant [rɑ̃fɔrsisɑ̃] *adj.* strengthening, sustaining *Mange ta viande. C'est renforcissant.* Eat your meat. It makes you strong. (VM) <***Loc:*** VM, Da84>

renforcissement (**renforcement**) [rɑ̃fɔrsismɑ̃, rɑ̃fɔrsmɑ̃] *n.m.* reinforcement, strengthening <***Loc:*** Da84>

renfort [rɑ̃fɔr] *n.m.* reinforcement, strengthening piece (e.g. in a shoe) <***Loc:*** Da84>

renfouillé, -e [rɑ̃fuje] *adj.* isolated, hidden away from civilization *Il est renfouillé là-bas dans le bois.* He lives in the woods hidden from civilization. (LF) <***Loc:*** LF>

rengager (**réengager**) [rɑ̃gaʒe, reɑ̃gaʒe] *v.tr.* to rehire, reemploy *Tant qu'à lui, je vas pas le rengager! Il arrive assis.* As for him, I'm not going to hire him. He arrives sitting down (i.e. he's lazy). (LA) <***Loc:*** LA, Da84>

rengoûter (se) [rɑ̃gute] *v.pron.* to recover one's taste (for) *Je m'ai rendu malade avec du maquechou une fois, et ensuite j'ai jamais pu me rengoûter après le maïs tendre.* I got sick from eating maquechou once, and after that I never could recover my taste for corn. (VM) <***Loc:*** VM, Da84>

rengraisser [rɑ̃grese] **I** *v.tr.* **1** to fatten, fatten up *Cette levure va rengraisser les cochons.* This yeast will fatten up the pigs. (VM) **2** to refatten, fatten up again **II** *v.intr.* **1** to get fat, become stout *Il était maigre, mais il a rengraissé.* He was thin, but he got fat. (SM) **2** to regain weight, get fat again *Il a rengraissé quand il a arrêté de fumer.* He put on weight again after he quit smoking. (VM) **III se rengraisser** *v.pron.* to regain weight, get fat again *Ma tante s'a rengraissé après son opération.* My aunt regained weight after her operation. (VM) <***Loc:*** SM, TB, VM, Da84, Lv88>

renier [r(ə)nje, ərnje, ærnje] *v.tr.* to repudiate, disavow, reject *Il peut pas renier ses enfants. Il les a marqués.* He can't disavow his children. He stamped them with his traits. (VM) <***Loc:*** VM, Da84>

reniflement [r(ə)nifləmɑ̃] *n.m.* sniffle, sniffling <***Loc:*** Da84>

renifler (**nifler**) [r(ə)nifle, ərnifle, ærnifle, nifle] **I** *v.tr.* **1** to smell *J'ai venu parce que j'ai niflé des tartes.* I came because I smelled pies. (VM) **2** to sniff, snort, take (a drug) by inhaling *Sa narine a ulcéré à force elle a reniflé ce dope.* Her nostril ulcerated because she sniffed so much of that dope. (LA) **II** *v.intr.* **1** to sniff, sniffle *Arrête de renifler comme ça et va te moucher plutôt.* Stop sniffling like that and go blow your nose instead. (LA) **2** to sniff around *Je veux pas de ces garçons après renifler autour de la maison!* I don't want those guys sniffing around the house! (LA) <***Loc:*** JE, LA, VM, Da84>

renommée [r(ə)nɔ̃me, ərnɔ̃me, ærnɔ̃me] *n.f.* **1** fame, renown **2** reputation <***Loc:*** SL, Da84>

renommer [r(ə)nɔ̃me, ərnɔ̃me, ærnɔ̃me] *v.tr.* to renominate, rename *Ils l'ont renommé au conseil.* They renamed her to the council. (EV) <***Loc:*** EV, Da84>

renoncer [r(ə)nɔ̃se, ərnɔ̃se, ærnɔ̃se] *v.tr.* to renounce, repudiate, give up *Il a renoncé ses enfants.* He repudiated his own children. (VM) <***Loc:*** VM, Da84>

renouer [r(ə)nue, ərnue, ærnue] *v.tr.* to reknot, retangle *Le nouveau travaillant a tout renoué le câble que j'use pour amarrer le bateau.* The new worker completely tangled the rope that I use to tie the boat. (VM) <***Loc:*** VM, Da84>

renouveau de la lune ♦see **nouveau de lune**

renouvelable [r(ə)nuv(ə)lab(l), ərnuv(ə)lab(l), ærnuv(ə)lab(l)] *adj.* renewable *Mon* LEASE *est renouvelabe à la fin du mois.* My lease is renewable at the end of the month. (VM) <***Loc:*** VM, Da84>

renouveler [r(ə)nuv(ə)le, ərnuv(ə)le, ærnuv(ə)le] **I** *v.tr.* **1** to renew *J'ai pour renouveler ma licence dans juin.* I have to renew my license in June. (LA) **2** to renovate *Renouveler une maison.* To renovate a house. (VM) **II se renouveler** *v.pron.* to be renewed *Le contrat va se renouveler à la fin de l'année.* The contract will be renewed at the end of the year. (VM) ◊ •**renouveler la mémoire** to remind <Da84> •**renouveler les connaissances** to renew acquaintances <Da84> <***Loc:*** LA, TB, VM, Da84>

renouvellement [r(ə)nuvɛlmɑ̃, ərnuvɛlmɑ̃, ærnuvɛlmɑ̃] *n.m.* 1 renewal 2 renovation <*Loc:* Da84>

rénovation [renovasjɔ̃] *n.f.* 1 renovation 2 renewal <*Loc:* Da84>

renseignement [rɑ̃sɛ̃jmɑ̃] *n.m.* 1 teaching 2 information 3 news <*Loc:* Da84>

renseigner [rɑ̃sɛ̃je] **I** *v.tr.* to teach, inform *On aura pour renseigner les vieux dessus les nouvelles lois de SOCIAL SECURITY.* We're going to have to inform the old people about the new Social Security laws. (VM) **II se renseigner** *v.pron.* to inform o.s., inquire *J'ai eu besoin de me renseigner sur les deux candidats.* I had to inquire about the two candidates. (LA) <*Loc:* LA, VM, Da84>

rente [rɑ̃t] *n.f.* income, profit, revenue ◊ **•rente des vieux** old age pension <Gr86> <*Loc:* Da84, Gr86>

renterrer (**réenterrer**) [rɑ̃tere, reɑ̃tere] *v.tr.* to rebury, reinter *Il faudra renterrer tout ce monde qu'a été déterré par l'ouragan.* They will have to rebury all those people who were disinterred by the storm. (VM) <*Loc:* VM, Da84>

rentourner [rɑ̃turne] **I** *v.tr.* to return, give back *Rentourne tout ça avant que ça s'aperçoit.* Return all of that stuff before they notice. (LA) **II** *v.intr.* to return, come back *Le même matin, j'étais après rentourner là, N-oncle K. est venu [...] chez Pop.* The same morning, I was coming back and Uncle K. came to Pop's house. (EV) **III se rentourner** *v.pron.* to come back, go back, return *Tous les fins de semaine il se rentournait à Eunice.* Every weekend he returned to Eunice. (EV) *Il fallait il se rentourne avec sa moman et son popa.* He had to go back with his mom and dad. (EV) <*Loc:* EV, LA, SL, VM, Da84>

rentrer [rɑ̃tre] **I** *v.tr.* to bring in, bring back **Ein jour j'm'ai aperçue que le lait que Pierre rentrait était bleu.* One day I noticed that the milk that Pierre was bringing in was blueish. (Gu82) **Après que la récolte était rentrée, Sosthène vendait au village ça qu'on avait d'extra, ça qu'on pouvait pas user.* After the harvest was brought in, Sosthène would sell in town what was extra, what we couldn't use. (Gu82) **II** *v.intr.* 1 to enter, go in, come in *Rentre vite, laisse pas les moustiques passer.* Enter quickly, don't let the mosquitos get inside. (VM) *Rentre dans la maison une minute.* Come into the house for a minute. (SM) **On a rentré par la porte d'en arrière. Grandm'man, elle, avait rentré par la porte d'en avant.* We came in by the back door. Grandma, she had come in by the front door. (Gu82) 2 to get in, get into *Rentre dans le char.* Get in the car. (LF) ◊ **rentrer dans le tracas** to get into trouble *Il s'a faufilé parmi des bons-à-rien et il a rentré dans le tracas.* He was hanging around with some ne'er-do-wells and he got into trouble. (LA) <LA> **•rentrer derrière** to get after, scold *Il a rentré derrière Charles pour ça.* He got after Charles about that. (EV) <EV> <*Loc:* AC, AV, EV, JE, LA, LF, SB, SL, SM, TB, VM, Da84, Gu82, Hi02>

renvaler (**ravaler**) [rɑ̃vale, ravale] *v.tr.* to reswallow *Renvaler son crachat.* To reswallow one's spit. (VM) ◊ **•renvaler ses paroles** to eat one's words *Je vas te faire renvaler tes paroles, toi!* I'll make you eat your words! (LA) <LA> <*Loc:* LA, VM, Da84>

renvenir [rɑ̃vnir] *v.intr.* to return, come back **Il est renvenu.* He came back. (Da84) <*Loc:* Da84>

renvers ♦see **envers**

renverse [rɑ̃værs] *n.f.* reverse ◊ **•à la renverse** in reverse, backwards *Le boghei a tombé à la renverse dans le fossé.* The buggy fell backwards into the ditch. (VM) <VM, Da84> <*Loc:* VM, Da84>

renverser (**reverser**) [rɑ̃værse, r(ə)værse, ərværse, ærværse] **I** *v.tr.* to overturn, turn upside down *Là tout d'un coup je l'ai empoignée et je l'ai renversée sus la berce.* Then all of a sudden I grabbed her and I turned her upside down on the rocker. (AV) **II se renverser** *v.pron.* to turn over, flip *Le tracteur s'a renversé dessus mon oncle.* The tractor turned over on my uncle. (VM) <*Loc:* AV, VM, Da84>

renvoyer [rɑ̃vwaje, rɑ̃waje] **I** *v.tr.* to send back *Des portraits, il a pris je sais pas combien. Et là il a été à GERMANY, il a retourné et là il a renvoyé un STACK de portraits, t'aurais dû voir.* Pictures, he took I don't know how many. And then he went to Germany, he went back, and he sent back a stack of pictures, you should have seen it. (LF) *Quand on va renvoyer BACK les soldats?* When are they going to send the soldiers back? (VM) 2 to send off, send away *Ils ont renvoyé leur fille quand ils ont trouvé qu'elle était en famille.* They sent their daughter away when they found out she was pregnant. (EV) **II se renvoyer** *v.pron.* to go back home *C'est l'heure que je me renvoie.* It's time I go back home. (VM) <*Loc:* EV, LF, TB, VM, Da84>

renvoyure [rɑ̃vwajyr] *n.f.* milk left in a cow's udder for the calf after milking <*Loc:* VM>

réoccuper (**roccuper**) [reokype, rokype] **I** *v.tr.* to reoccupy, occupy again *Essaie de réoccuper les enfants à faire leur ouvrage.* Try to reoccupy the children with doing their work. (LA) **II se réoccuper** *v.pron.* to reoccupy o.s., get back to (doing s.t.) *J'ai crié quand ma mère m'a dit que la guerre avait fini. Là je m'ai réoccupé à cirer mes souliers.* I yelled when my mother told me that the war had ended. Then I went back to shining my shoes. (VM) <*Loc:* LA, VM, Da84>

réordonner (**rordonner**) [reɔrdɔ̃ne, rɔrdɔ̃ne] *v.tr.* to reorder *J'ai eu pour réordonner la robe, parce qu'elle avait jamais arrivé.* I had to reorder the dress because it had never arrived. (LA) <*Loc:* LA, Da84>

réorganisation [reɔrgɑ̃nizasjɔ̃] *n.f.* reorganization <*Loc:* Da84>

réorganiser [reɔrgɑ̃nize] **I** *v.tr.* to reorganize *On aura du mal à réorganiser le conseil du village après les élections.* We're going to have trouble reorganizing the town council after the elections. (VM) **II se réorganiser** *v.pron.* to reorganize o.s. *Ils s'ont réorganisé pour chasser dans les clos de riz après qu'ils ont perdu leur camp à la Chênière.* They reorganized themselves to hunt in the rice fields after they lost their camp at Chênière. (LA) <*Loc:* LA, VM, Da84>

réparable [reparab(l)] *adj.* repairable, mendable *Ta chaise est par réparable. Tu peux la jeter.* Your chair is not repairable. You can throw it away. (VM) <*Loc:* VM, Da84>

réparage [reparaʒ] *n.m.* **1** repair *Mais j'ai vendu la petite maison. Elle avait besoin un tas de réparages.* But I sold the little house. It needed a lot of repairs. (SL) **2** repairing, mending *Le réparage de ma barrière m'a coûté cinquante piastres.* Repairing my fence cost me fifty dollars. (SM) <*Loc:* EV, JE, SB, SL, SM, TB, Da84, Lv88, Ph36>

reparaître (**raparaître**) [r(ə)parɛt(r), ərparɛt(r), ærparɛt(r), raparɛt(r)] *v.intr.* to reappear, show up again *Elle va pas reparaître avant la fin du mois pour collecter son argent.* She won't show up again before the end of the month to collect her check. (VM) <*Loc:* VM, Da84>

réparation [reparasjɔ̃] *n.f.* **1** repair *Tous mes réparations, je faisais tout ça moi-même. Je soude du* ALUMINUM *et du fer, et du* STAINLESS STEEL. All of my repairs, I did them all myself. I solder aluminum and iron, and stainless steel. (TB) **2** amends, redress, reparation *Le juge lui a obligé de faire des réparations pour la barrière que son taureau avait cassé.* The judge obliged him to make reparations for the fence that his bull had broken. (VM) <*Loc:* TB, VM, Da84, Hi02>

réparement [reparmɑ̃] *n.m.* **1** repair **2** reparation <*Loc:* EV, SM, Ph36>

réparer (**reparer, remparer**) [repare, r(ə)pare, ərpare, ærpare, rɑ̃pare] **I** *v.tr.* **1** to repair, fix, mend *On faisait des lignes que l'huile flotte dedans. Et on réparait les* SEPARATORS *que l'huile flowait dedans.* We laid pipeline that oil floats in. And we repared the separators that oil flows through. (LF) **C'est côme [=comme] ça si je peux toujours 'oir Pepère Gustav [...] en réparant ein fil de carrelet.* That's how I still remember Grandpa Gustave, mending the twine of a cast net. (VM, Gu82) **2** to redo *J'avais pas bien fait l'ouvrage, j'avais pour le remparer.* I hadn't done the work well, I had to do it over again. (VM) **3** to make good (i.e. repair wrongs) *Il faudra je répare le dédommage que je lui ai fait.* I will have to make reparation for the damage I caused him. (LA) **II se réparer** *v.pron.* **1** to clear up (of the weather) *La pluie est finie, le temps va se réparer.* The rain is over, the weather will clear up. (VM) **2** to put o.s. to rights <*Loc:* AC, JE, LA, LF, TB, VM, Da84, Gu82, Hi02, Lv88>

répareur [r(ə)parœr, ərparœr, ærparœr] *n.m.* repairman <*Loc:* SB>

reparler [r(ə)parle, ərparle, ærparle] *v.intr.* to speak again **Je m'en vais lui reparler.* I'm going to talk to him again. (Da84) <*Loc:* Da84>

repartager [r(ə)partaʒe, ərpartaʒe, ærpartaʒe] *v.tr.* to reapportion, redivide *Ils auront pour repartager la terre. Deux des enfants sont pas d'accord avec les autres.* They will have to redivide the land. Two of the children don't agree with the others. (LA) <*Loc:* LA, Da84>

repartir [r(ə)partir, ərpartir, ærpartir] **I** *v.tr.* to restart *J'ai pas pu repartir le tracteur, ça fait j'ai laché.* I couldn't restart the tractor, so I knocked off. (LA) **II** *v.intr.* **1** to go away again, leave again *On a reparti après qu'on a fini d'arranger le* FLAT. We left again after we finished fixing the flat. (LA) **2** to start up again, start out again *Mais là, ça a rechangé, par exemple. Ça avait reparti beaucoup bien.* Then, things changed again though. Things had gotten restarted pretty well. (AC) <*Loc:* AC, LA, Da84>

repas [r(ə)pa, ərpa, ærpa] *n.m.* meal <*Loc:* EV, TB, Da84, Hi02>

repassage [r(ə)pasaʒ, ərpasaʒ, ærpasaʒ] *n.m.* **1** ironing (of clothes) *J'ai lavé aujourd'hui et j'ai un gros repassage pour demain.* I washed today and I have a lot of ironing for tomorrow. (TB) **2** revision, going over s.t. again (e.g. a lesson) **3** passing again, recrossing <*Loc:* EV, TB, Da84>

repasser (**erpasser**) [r(ə)pase, ərpase, ærpase] **I** *v.tr.* **1** to iron (clothes, etc.) *On erpassait un tas parce que dans ce temps-là le monde erpassait un tas leur linge.* We used to iron a lot because in those days people used to iron their clothes a lot. (AC) **2** to go over again (a lesson, figures, etc.) *J'ai tout repassé les numéros pour voir ayoù l'erreur était.* I went over the numbers again closely to find where the error was. (VM) **II** *v.intr.* to pass by again *Deux semaines après, le bougre repasse encore.* Two weeks later, the guy passes by again. (SL) <*Loc:* AC, EV, SL, TB, VM, Da84, Lv88>

repayer [r(ə)peje, ərpeje, ærpeje] *v.tr.* **1** to pay again **2** to repay, pay back *Tu pourrais me repayer dans quelques semaines.* You can repay me in a few weeks. (LA) <*Loc:* LA, Da84>

repécher [r(ə)peʃe, ərpeʃe, ærpeʃe] *v.intr.* [*eccl.*] to sin again <*Loc:* Da84>

repêcher [r(ə)peʃe, ərpeʃe, ærpeʃe] *v.tr.* to refish (a certain place) *J'ai jamais repêché cette place depuis que mon ami est mort.* I never refished that place after my friend died. (VM) <*Loc:* VM, Da84>

repeindre [r(ə)pɛ̃n, r(ə)pɛ̃d(r), ərpɛ̃n, ærpɛ̃d(r), ærpɛ̃n, ærpɛ̃d(r)] *v.tr.* to repaint *Il faudra je faise repeindre mon char.* I'll have to have my car repainted. (LA) <*Loc:* LA, Da84>

repeinturer [r(ə)pɛ̃tyre, ərpɛ̃tyre, ærpɛ̃tyre] *v.tr.* to repaint *Johnny est après essayer de repeinturer sa maison avant sa femme retourne de ses vacances.* Johnny is trying to repaint his house before his wife returns from her vacation. (VM) <*Loc:* VM, Da84>

rependre [r(ə)pɑ̃n, r(ə)pɑ̃d(r), ərpɑ̃n, ərpɑ̃d(r), ærpɑ̃n, ærpɑ̃d(r)] *v.tr.* to rehang *On a rependu tous les portraits après qu'ils* *ont peinturé les chambres.* We rehung all the pictures after they painted the rooms. (LA) <***Loc:*** LA, Da84>

repenser [r(ə)pɑ̃se, ərpɑ̃se, ærpɑ̃se] **I** *v.tr.* to rethink, reconsider, think over again *Tu peux repenser ton affaire, mon garçon.* You can rethink your situation, son. (LA) **II** *v.intr.* to think again *Depuis qu'elle a quitté, elle a jamais repensé à nous-autres.* Since she left, she never thought about us again. (VM) <***Loc:*** LA, VM, Da84>

repentant, -e [r(ə)pɑ̃tɑ̃, ərpɑ̃tɑ, ærpɑ̃tɑ̃, -ɑ̃t] *adj.* [*eccl.*] repentant <***Loc:*** Da84>

repenti, -e [r(ə)pɑ̃ti, ərpɑ̃ti, ærpɑ̃ti] *n.* [*eccl.*] repentant, penitent *C'était un soûlard, mais il est repenti asteur.* He was a drunkard, but he is repentant now. (VM) <***Loc:*** VM, Da84>

repentir (se) [r(ə)pɑ̃tir, ərpɑ̃tir, ærpɑ̃tir] *v.pron.* to repent *Sa femme le reprendrait s'il voudrait se repentir.* His wife would take him back if only he would repent. (LA) <***Loc:*** LA, Da84>

repercer [r(ə)pærse, ərpærse, ærpærse] *v.tr.* to rebore, repierce *Elle s'a fait repercer les oreilles parce que les trous s'avaient rebouché.* She had her ears repierced because the holes had reclosed. (LA) <***Loc:*** LA, Da84>

reperdre [r(ə)pærd(r), ərpærd(r), ærpærd(r)] *v.tr.* to lose again *Il aura de la misère à reperdre son poids.* He'll have trouble losing his weight again. (LA) <***Loc:*** LA, Da84>

repeser [r(ə)pəze, ərpəze, ærpəze] *v.tr.* to reweigh *Repèse ces chevrettes-là. Je crois pas qu'il y a dix livres.* Reweigh those shrimp. I don't believe that there are ten pounds. (LA) <***Loc:*** LA, Da84>

répétailler [repetaje] *v.tr.* to repeat over and over *T'es tout le temps après répétailler tes mêmes vieilles histoires!* You're always repeating your same old stories over and over again! (VM) <***Loc:*** VM, Da84>

répéter [repete] **I** *v.tr.* to repeat *WELL, répète pas ça, c'est peut-être pas vrai, pas sûr. Mais il me semble que quelqu'un m'a dit, c'était quelque chose comme vingt-cinq mille piastres.* Well, don't repeat that, maybe it's not true, not sure. But it seems to me that someone told me that it was something like twenty-five thousand dollars. (ThCa: *La table des veuves*) **II se répéter** *v.pron.* to repeat o.s. *Il se répète souvent.* He repeats himself often. (EV) <***Loc:*** EV, Da84, Hi02, ThCa>

répétition [repetisjɔ̃] *n.f.* repetition, recurrence <***Loc:*** Da84>

repétrir [r(ə)petrir, ərpetrir, ærpetrir] *v.tr.* to reknead *Là, quand ta pâte a levé, tu la repétris.* Then, when your bread dough has risen, you reknead it. (LA) <***Loc:*** LA, Da84>

repimper (se) [r(ə)pɛ̃pe, ərpɛ̃pe, ærpɛ̃pe] *v.pron.* to dress carefully, doll o.s. up, primp *Il s'a repimpé encore pour sortir.* He got all dressed up again to go out. (VM) <***Loc:*** JE, VM>

replacement [r(ə)plasmɑ̃, ərplasmɑ̃, ærplasmɑ̃] *n.m.* replacing, replacement *Elle a eu un replacement, un HIP REPLACEMENT, longtemps passé.* She had a replacement, a hip replacement, a long time ago. (TB) <***Loc:*** TB, Da84>

replacer [r(ə)plase, ərplase, ærplase] **I** *v.tr.* to replace, put back *Replacer une épaule démanchée.* To put back a dislocated shoulder. (VM) **II se replacer** *v.pron.* to get back into place *Replace-toi! On a pas fini de prendre les portraits!* Get back into place! We haven't finished taking pictures! (VM) <***Loc:*** VM, Da84>

replanter [r(ə)plɑ̃te, ərplɑ̃te, ærplɑ̃te] *v.tr.* to replant *Replanter les manques.* To replant the void spots [in a field or row]. (LA) <***Loc:*** LA, Da84>

replier (**remplier**) [r(ə)plije, ərplije, ærplije, rɑ̃plije] *v.tr.* **1** to refold *Replie ton linge avant de le mettre dans le tiroir.* Refold your clothes before putting them in the drawer. (EV) **2** to bend back, fold back **3** to tuck in <***Loc:*** EV, Da84>

replisser [r(ə)plise, ərplise, ærplise] *v.tr.* **1** to repleat *Il faudra que je repasse ce pantalon encore pour le replisser.* I'll have to iron these pants again to repleat them. (VM) **2** to rewrinkle *Les petites filles s'assisaient pas avant d'aller à la messe pour pas replisser leur robe.* Little girls wouldn't sit down before going to Mass so that they didn't rewrinkle their dresses. (VM) <***Loc:*** VM, Da84>

reployer (**remployer**) [r(ə)plwaje, ərplwaje, ærplwaje, rɑ̃plwaje, rɑ̃pleje] *v.tr.* **1** to refold *Reployer ses draps.* To refold one's sheets. (VM) **2** to bend back *Le vent a reployé un morceau de zinc dessus ma couverture.* The wind bent back a sheet of galvanized iron on my roof. (VM) <***Loc:*** IB, TB, VM, Da84>

repomper [r(ə)pɔ̃pe, ərpɔ̃pe, ærpɔ̃pe] *v.tr.* to pump back *Dès que ce gaz là revient d'OFFSHORE là ils le séparont à ce PLANT là. [...] Souvent des places après qu'il est tout séparé, ils le repompont dans la même ligne.* As soon as the gas comes in from offshore they separate it at that plant. A lot of places after it's all separated, they pump it back through the same pipeline. (LF) <***Loc:*** LF>

répondre [repɔ̃n, repɔ̃d(r)] (*p.p.* **répond** [repɔ̃], **répondu** [repɔ̃dy]) **I** *v.tr.* to respond to, answer *J'ai répondu mes questions moi-même.* I answered my own questions. (VM) **II** *v.intr.* to respond, reply, answer *Elle a appris avec les enfants qui a été à l'école à répondre en anglais.* She learned with the children who went to school how to answer in English. (EV) *Ça fait, on répond, on dit, "SURE, COME ON."* So we reply, we say, "sure, come on." (JD) *J'ai pas répond quand il m'a parlé.* I didn't answer when he talked to me. (SM) ◊ **•répondre au téléphone** to answer the telephone **Excusez-moi, Monsieur, faut qu'j'réponde au téléphone.* Pardon me, sir, I have to answer the phone. (Gu82) <Gu82> <***Loc:*** EV, JD, LA, SM, VM, Da84, Gu82, Lv88>

réponse [repɔ̃s] *n.f.* response, reply, answer **Donner réponse.* To give a reply. (Da84) <***Loc:*** Da84>

reporter [r(ə)pɔrte, ərpɔrte, ærpɔrte] *v.tr.* to carry back, bring back, take back *Reporte-moi ce bassin quand t'auras fini avec.* Carry this tub back to me when you've finished with it. (VM) <***Loc:*** VM, Da84>

repos [r(ə)po, ərpo, ærpo] *n.m.* repose, rest ◊ **•prendre un repos** to take a rest <Da84> <*Loc:* SM, TB, Da84, Hi02>

reposant, -e [r(ə)pozɑ̃, ərpozɑ̃, ærpozɑ̃, -ɑ̃t] *adj.* restful, relaxing *C'est bien reposant de s'assir dessus la galerie.* It is very restful to sit on the porch. (LA) <*Loc:* LA, Da84>

reposé, -e [r(ə)poze, ərpoze, ærpoze] *adj.* rested, reposed *Les enfants étaient pas bien reposés. C'est pour ça que ça braillait.* The children were not well rested. That's why they were crying. (LA) <*Loc:* LA, Da84>

reposer [r(ə)poze, ərpoze, ærpoze] **I** *v.tr.* **1** to rest *Je repose mes jambes.* I rest my legs. (SL) **2** to relax s.o. *Ça me repose à parler. J'aime parler.* It relaxes me to talk. I like to talk. (TB) **II** *v.intr.* to stay, remain *Ça a commencé faire des battures, des* SANDBAR, *ça empêchait l'eau passer. Le sable a tout reposé et ça a fait une petite levée tout au long de ces bayous là.* Sandbars started building up, it prevented the water from going through. The sand would stay there and a levee would appear all along the bayou there. (SM) **III se reposer** *v.pron.* **1** to rest *Et quand je suis seule j'aime mieux rester sur ma chaise. Comme ça je peux me reposer mieux, sur ma chaise que dans le lit.* And when I'm alone I prefer to stay in my chair. That way I can rest better, in my chair than in bed. (TB) **2** to relax *Mais j'ai plein du monde qui vient ici [...] et y a plein de mes enfants qui me dit tu devrais arrêter ça, tu devrais te reposer.* But I have a lot of people who come here, and a lot of my children tell me you should stop that, you should relax. (TB) <*Loc:* AC, SL, SM, TB, Da84>

repousse [r(ə)pus, ərpus, ærpus] *n.f.* regrowth, new growth <*Loc:* Da84>

repousser [r(ə)puse, ərpuse, ærpuse] **I** *v.tr.* **1** to push back *Il a repoussé le bateau à l'eau.* He pushed the boat back into the water. (LF) **2** to drive back, repel, repulse *Il était après essayer de repousser les vaches, mais il pouvait pas.* He was trying to drive the cows back, but he was not able. (LA) **II** *v.intr.* to grow again, grow back *Saute crapeau, ta queue va brûler, prends courage alle va repousser.* Jump, toad, your tail will burn, take heart, it will grow back. (TB, ch: *Saute crapaud*) <*Loc:* JE, LA, LF, TB, Da84>

reprendre [r(ə)prɑ̃n, r(ə)prɑ̃d(r), ərprɑ̃n, ərprɑ̃d(r), ærprɑ̃n, ærprɑ̃d(r)] **I** *v.tr.* **1** to take back, retake *Il voulait pas reprendre l'argent.* He didn't want to take back the money. (LA) *Sa femme le reprendrait s'il voudrait se repentir.* His wife would take him back if only he would repent. (LA) **2** to take up again, begin again **Là, j'ai décidé j'aurais arrêté ça, j'aurais repris à jouer du violon.* Then I decided that I would stop that, that I would take up the fiddle again. (EV, An84) **3** to interrupt or correct (s.o.) in conversation *Son père aime pas quand elle le reprend comme ça.* His father doesn't like it when she corrects him like that. (LA) **II** *v.intr.* **1** to start again **La chicane a repris. Ils se sont quittés encore.* The argument started again. They separated again. (SM, An94) **2** to grow back, revive (of a plant) *Je connais pas si le plaqueminier que j'ai transplanté va reprendre.* I don't know if the persimmon tree I transplanted will revive. (LA) **III se reprendre** *v.pron.* **1** to correct o.s. **2** to pull o.s. together, stop o.s. *Il avait envie de lui tirer une chique, mais il s'a repris.* He felt like criticizing him, but he restrained himself. (LA) **3** to get back together, reunite (of separated spouses or partners) **Ça fait, ils ont décidé ils se seraient repris.* So they decided they would reunite. (SM, An94) ◊ **•reprendre courage** to take courage again <Da84> **•reprendre du poids** to regain weight *Alle a encore des mals dans l'estomac, mais alle a repris du poids, alle a* PICK UP. She still has stomachaches but she has regained some weight, she has picked up. (TB) <TB> **•en reprendre** to get better **Il en reprend.* He is getting better. (Da84) <Da84> <*Loc:* EV, LA, SM, TB, An84, An94, Da84>

représentant, -e [r(ə)prezɑ̃tɑ̃, ərprezɑ̃tɑ̃, ærprezɑ̃tɑ̃, -ɑ̃t] *n.* representative (esp. in a legislative body) *Il a décidé de courir pour représentant.* He decided to run for representative. (LA) <*Loc:* LA, Da84>

représenter [r(ə)prezɑ̃te, ərprezɑ̃te, ærprezɑ̃te] **I** *v.tr.* to represent, depict *Et là depuis les dernières années, quinze, vingt ans, ils ont commencé à faire des masques qui représentent toute espèce de chose, le président, ou des macaques, et toute espèce de chose.* And then in the last 15 or 20 years, they've started making masks that represent all kinds of things, the president, or monkeys, and all kinds of things. (LF) **II se représenter** *v.pron.* to represent o.s. *La manière qu'il se représentait, c'est pas drôle que le monde l'aimait pas.* Given the way he represented himself, it's no wonder that people didn't like him. (LA) <*Loc:* LA, LF, Da84, Hi02>

réprésenteur (**représenteur**) [reprezɑ̃tœr, r(ə)prezɑ̃tœr, ərprezɑ̃tœr, ærprezɑ̃tœr] *n.m.* representative *Je suis emmêlé dans la politique, je suis un réprésenteur et quand moi je parle à mon monde sus le* RADIO *ou sus le* TELEVISION *la moitié du temps je yeux parle en français.* I'm involved in politics, I'm a representative, and when I talk to my people on the radio or the television, most of the time I talk to them in French. (TB) ◊ **•représenteur de l'état** state representative *Il était un représenteur de l'état des années de ça.* He was a state representative many years ago. (LF) <LF> <*Loc:* LF, TB>

repris, -e [r(ə)pri, ərpri, ærpri, -iz] *adj.* **1** recaptured, retaken *Le pays est repris.* The country has been retaken. (LA) **2** started again **La pluie est reprise.* The rain has started again. (Da84) <*Loc:* LA, Da84>

reprochable [r(ə)proʃab(l), ərproʃab(l), ærproʃab(l)] *adj.* reproachable *C'est un bougre qu'est pas reprochable.* He is a fellow who is irreproachable. (LA) <*Loc:* LA, Da84>

reproche [r(ə)prɔʃ, ərprɔʃ, ærprɔʃ] *n.m.* reproach ◊ **•faire des reproches** to reproach <Da84> <*Loc:* Da84>

reprocher [r(ə)proʃe, ərproʃe, ærproʃe] **I** *v.tr.* to reproach, find fault with, blame *Il peut pas reprocher son frère pour la manière il a traité sa mère.* He can't reproach his brother for the way he treated his mother. (LA) **II se reprocher** *v.pron.* to reproach or blame o.s. *Reproche-toi pas. C'est pas ta faute.* Don't blame yourself. It's not your fault. (LA) <***Loc:*** LA, Da84>

reproduire [r(ə)prodɥir, ərprodɥir, ærprodɥir] *v.tr.* to reproduce, duplicate, copy *Il a reproduit la lettre telle qu'elle était.* He reproduced the letter exactly as it was. (LA) <***Loc:*** LA, Da84>

républicain [repyblikɛ̃] *n.* Republican, member of the Republican party *Ça c'est à peu près une affaire des républicains.* That's likely a Republican issue. (LA) <***Loc:*** LA, Da84, Gr86, Hi02>

republier [r(ə)pyblije, ərpyblije, ærpyblije] *v.tr.* to republish *Ils ont eu pour republier leurs bans de mariage à cause de l'erreur du prêtre.* They had to republish their marriage bans because of the priest's error. (LA) <***Loc:*** LA, Da84>

république [repyblik] *n.f.* republic <***Loc:*** Da84>

répudier [repydje] *v.tr.* [*eccl.*] to repudiate, disown <***Loc:*** Da84>

répugnance [repỹjɑ̃s] *n.f.* repugnance, loathing, disgust <***Loc:*** Da84>

répugnant, -e [repỹjɑ̃, -ɑ̃t] *adj.* repugnant, loathsome, disgusting *Il trouvait l'odeur de la viande répugnante.* He found the odor of meat repugnant. (VM) <***Loc:*** VM, Da84>

répugné, -e [repỹje, repĩje] *adj.* disgusted, fed up **Je suis répugné.* I am disgusted. (Da84) *Il est répugné sus ça.* He is fed up with that. (TB) <***Loc:*** TB, Da84>

réputation [repytasjɔ̃] *n.f.* reputation <***Loc:*** EV, Da84>

requin (**réquin**) [r(ə)kɛ̃, rekɛ̃, ərkɛ̃, ærkɛ̃] *n.m.* shark *Il mange comme un requin.* He eats like a shark. (JE) <***Loc:*** IB, JE, LF, TB, VM, Gu00>

requinquiné, -e [r(ə)kɛ̃kine, ərkɛ̃kine, ærkɛ̃kine] *adj.* **1** spruced up, smartened up **2** spry, lively, alert <***Loc:*** SM>

rerentrer [r(ə)rɑ̃tre, ərrɑ̃tre, ærrɑ̃tre] *v.intr.* to reenter, come back in *Il a rerentré dans la maison.* He came back into the house. (LA) <***Loc:*** LA, Da84>

reserche ♦see **recherche**

réservation [rezærvasjɔ̃] *n.f.* reservation <***Loc:*** Da84>

réserve [rezærv] *n.f.* reserve, reservation *Depuis qu'ils ont fait une réserve, le monde vient comme ça dedans. Et pour ce monde là, y en a plein d'eux-autres, pas plein mais assez, qui connaît pas qui c'est qu'un fusil.* Since they've made a reserve, people come just like that. And of those people there are a lot, not a lot maybe but enough, who don't know what a gun is. (TB) ◊ **•avec réserve** with reserve *Il s'en allait doucement, avec réserve.* He went slowly, with reserve. (VM) <VM, Da84> **•en réserve** in reserve *Il avait du gaz en réserve dans la cabane.* He had gas in reserve in the cabin. (LA) <LA, Da84> **•sans réserve** without reserve, without restraint *Il a donné tout ça il pouvait, sans réserve.* He gave all he could, without reserve. (LA) **Il est sans réserve.* He shows no restraint. (EV, Ph36) <EV, LA, Da84, Ph36> <***Loc:*** EV, LA, TB, VM, Da84, Ph36>

réservé, -e [rezærve] *adj.* **1** reserved (of a place) *Excuse-moi. C'est une place réservée.* Excuse me. This place is reserved. (LA) **2** shy, reserved *Il est manière un peu réservé, c'est pas qu'il voudrait pas.* He's a bit reserved, it's not that he'd be unwilling. (LF) ◊ **•réservé que** except that <Da84> <***Loc:*** LA, LF, Da84>

réserver [rezærve] *v.tr.* to reserve, keep back, set aside *Ils ont réservé un peu d'argent pour le voyage.* They reserved a little money for the trip. (LA) ◊ **•réserver une place** to reserve a place <Da84> <***Loc:*** LA, Da84>

réservoir [rezærvwar] *n.m.* reservoir, container <***Loc:*** Da84>

résidence [rezidɑ̃s] *n.f.* residence, abode, dwelling, home <***Loc:*** EV, LF, Da84>

résident [rezidɑ̃] *n.m.* resident <***Loc:*** Da84, Gr86>

résigné, -e [rezĩje] *adj.* resigned *Il est résigné à l'idée qu'il va mourir là ayoù il reste asteur.* He is resigned to the idea that he will die where he now lives. (LA) <***Loc:*** LA, Da84>

résigner [rezĩje] *v.tr.* **1** to resign (from a job) *Il a résigné son job d'un coup de colère.* He resigned his job in a fit of pique. (LA) **2** to give up, resign *J'ai résigné mon idée de rester bien tranquille ici.* I gave up my idea of remaining here undisturbed. (EV) <***Loc:*** EV, LA, Da84>

résipére, résipère ♦see **érésipèle**

résistance [rezistɑ̃s] *n.f.* resistance <***Loc:*** Da84>

résistant, -e [rezistɑ̃, -ɑ̃t] *adj.* resistant, tough *C'est du bois qu'est joliment résistant.* That is wood that is pretty tough. (LA) <***Loc:*** LA, Da84>

résister [reziste] **I** *v.tr.* to resist, oppose, hold out against *Il a résisté sa famille aussi longtemps qu'il pouvait.* He resisted his family as long as he could. (LA) **II** *v.intr.* **1** to resist **2** to live long *Je vas résister longtemps, moi.* I'm going to live a long time. (VM) <***Loc:*** LA, VM, Da84, Wh83>

résolu (**résou**) [rezoly, rezu] *adj.* **1** determined, resolute, resolved *Il a resté résolu de faire ça longtemps après l'enterrement.* He remained resolved to do that long after the burial. (LA) *Il est résou de partir.* He is determined to leave. (SL) **2** robust, sturdy *Un homme bien résolu.* A sturdy, well-defined man. (VM) <***Loc:*** JE, LA, SL, VM, Da84, Lv88>

résolution [rezolysjɔ̃] *n.f.* resolution, determination <***Loc:*** Da84>

résonance [rezɔ̃nɑ̃s] *n.f.* resonance <***Loc:*** Da84>

résonnant, -e [rezɔ̃nɑ̃, -ɑ̃t] *adj.* resonant, resounding *Ça fait un train résonnant.* It makes a resounding noise. (LA) <***Loc:*** LA, Da84>

résonnement [rezɔ̃nmɑ̃] *n.m.* resonance, reverberation <***Loc:*** Da84>

résonner [rezɔ̃ne] *v.intr.* to reverberate, resound **Il a une cloche d'église pendue dans le cou. "Badingue, badangue!" Nous-*

autres, on connaît ayoù il est. Mais ça résonne dans les quatre coins. He has a church bell hanging from his neck. "Bading, badang!" We know where he is. But it resounds in the four corners of the land. (EV, An94) <***Loc:*** EV, An94, Da84>

re-sonner ♦see **ressonner**

résou ♦see **résolu**

respect [respɛ, respe] *n.m.* respect **Au respect que je vous dois.* According to the respect I owe you. (Da84) <***Loc:*** Da84, Hi02>

respectable [respɛktab(l)] *adj.* respectable *C'est plus respectable tu dis 'vous' à une vieille personne.* It's more respectable to say 'vous' to an older person. (TB) <***Loc:*** TB, Da84, Hi02>

respecter [respɛkte] **I** *v.tr.* to respect, have regard for *Il respecte son père et sa mère.* He respects his father and his mother. (LA) **II se respecter** *v.pron.* to respect o.s. or one another *Il se respecte pas du tout. C'est pour ça qu'il boit autant.* He has no respect for himself. That's why he drinks so much. (LA) <***Loc:*** EV, LA, Da84, Hi02>

respectueux, -euse [respɛktɥø, -øz] *adj.* respectful, polite *C'est des enfants beaucoup respectueux.* They are very polite children. (LA) <***Loc:*** LA, Da84>

respiration [respirasjɔ̃] *n.f.* respiration, breathing <***Loc:*** Da84>

respire [respir] *n.m. (occ. f.)* breath *Elle a un respire bien court.* She is very short of breath. (SB) ◊ **•prendre son respire** ***a*** to draw breath *Il a pris son dernier respire à minuit.* He drew his last breath at midnight. (SL) ***b*** to catch one's breath *Il était étouffé. Il pouvait pas prendre son respire.* He was winded. He couldn't catch his breath. (SM) <SL, SM> <***Loc:*** IB, JE, SB, SL, SM>

respirer [respire, rɑ̃spire] *v.intr.* to breathe, respire, inhale and exhale *Il respirait fort. "Ouh," il dit, "je sens la viande fraîche."* He breathed deeply. "Ooh," he said, "I smell fresh meat." (LA) <***Loc:*** LA, TB, VM, Da84, Hi02>

responsabilité [respɔ̃sabilite] *n.f.* responsibility, accountability <***Loc:*** EV, Da84>

responsable[1] [respɔ̃sab(l)] *adj.* responsible, accountable *Faulait tu soyes responsable de toi-même.* You had to be responsible for yourself. (IB) <***Loc:*** IB, TB, Da84>

responsable[2] [respɔ̃sab(l)] *n.* responsibility *Mais je lui ai montré comment signer son nom. Parce que je voulais pas tout le temps aller, moi, à la banque, c'était ses responsables à lui aussi, tu vois. Et il a appris comment signer son nom mais c'est tout.* But I taught him how to write his name. Because I didn't want to always go to the bank, they were his responsibilities too, you see. And he learned how to sign his name but that's all. (TB) <***Loc:*** TB>

ressaisir [r(ə)sezir, ərsezir, ærsezir] *v.tr.* to recapture, seize again, grab again, catch again *Il a ressaisi le lapin.* He grabbed the rabbit again. (LA) <***Loc:*** LA, Da84>

ressauter [r(ə)sote, ərsoste, ærsote] **I** *v.tr.* to jump over again *Le bœuf a ressauté la barrière.* The bull jumped the fence again. (LA) **II** *v.intr.* **1** to jump again *Il a eu pour ressauter encore.* He had to jump again. (LA) **2** to give a start, jump out of surprise <***Loc:*** LA, Lv88>

ressemblance [r(ə)sɑ̃blɑ̃s, ərsɑ̃blɑ̃s, ærsɑ̃blɑ̃s] *n.f.* resemblance, likeness <***Loc:*** Da84>

ressemblant [r(ə)sɑ̃blɑ̃, ərsɑ̃blɑ̃, ærsɑ̃blɑ̃] *n.m.* ◊ **•dans mon ressemblant** it seems to me *Dans mon ressemblant, on dirait que c'est pas bien.* It seems to me that it doesn't look good. (TB) <TB> <***Loc:*** TB>

ressembler [r(ə)sɑ̃ble, ərsɑ̃ble, ærsɑ̃ble] **I** *v.tr.* to resemble, look like *Tu peux pas nier ton garçon, il te ressemble de trop.* You can't deny your son, he looks too much like you. (VM) **A' r'semblait eine orpheline.* She looked like an orphan. (Gu82) **II** *v.intr.* to appear, seem **Il s'a fait du mal asoir, et ça ressemb' pas trop bon.* He hurt himself tonight, and it doesn't look too good. (ThCa: *La table des veuves*) *Il ressemble vaillant.* He seems nice. (Lv88) **Toi, tu me ressembles pas jamais être contente.* It seems to me you're never happy. (ch: *Calcasieu Waltz*) *Comment ça te ressemble?* How does that look to you? (TB) *Tu vois je suis manière* COLORBLIND. *Vert et bleu ça me ressemble les mêmes.* You see I'm somewhat colorblind. Green and blue look the same to me. (TB) **III se ressembler** *v.pron.* to resemble each other, look like one another *"Mais," il dit, "c'est des jumelles." Et il dit, "Ça se ressemble autant que deux petits peut se ressembler."* "Well," he said "they are twins." And he said, "They look as much like each other as two children can." (EV, An94) ◊ **•ressembler le diable avant jour** to look terrible (said of one who has spent the night out drinking) <SL, La99> **•ressembler (pareil) comme {à}** to look like, resemble *Les yeux bleus, les cheveux blonds. Elle ressemble pareille comme Mémère.* Blue eyes, blond hair. She looks just like Granny. (AC, ch: *Two-step à Tina*) *Ça ressemble pas pareil comme ça sonne.* That [written French] doesn't look like it sounds. (VM) **Mon vieux* HOME *est plus le même depuis que t'es* GONE, *ça ressemble juste comme une place abandonnée.* My old home is no longer the same since you've been gone, it just seems like an abandonned place. (ch: *Old Home Waltz*) *Ça ressemble à un marteau.* It looks like a hammer. (TB) *Il ressemblait pareil à un* COWBOY. He looked like a cowboy. (TB) <AC, TB, VM> **•se ressembler comme deux gouttes d'eau** to resemble each other very closely, be alike as two peas in a pod <Da84, La99> <***Loc:*** AC, EV, LA, SL, TB, VM, An94, Da84, Gu82, Hi02, La99, Lv88, ThCa>

ressemelage [r(ə)səmlaʒ] *n.m.* resoling (of shoes) <***Loc:*** Da84>

ressemeler [r(ə)səmle, ərsəmle, ærsəmle] *v.tr.* to resole *J'ai pas assez d'argent pour faire ressemeler mes souliers.* I don't have enough money to have my shoes resoled. (LA) <***Loc:*** LA, Da84>

ressentir [r(ə)sɑ̃tir, ərsɑ̃tir, ærsɑ̃tir] *v.intr.* 1 to feel, feel again *Elle a commencé à pouvoir ressentir le coton après son bébé est né.* She started being able to feel cotton again after her baby was born. (LA) 2 to smell again *Je commence à ressentir du gaz dans la maison.* I am starting to smell gas in the house again. (LA) <***Loc:*** LA, Da84>

resserrer[1] [r(ə)sere, ərsere, ærsere] *v.tr.* to retighten, tighten again *Il a resserré les boulons.* He retightened the nuts. (LA) <***Loc:*** LA, Da84>

resserrer[2] [r(ə)sere, ərsere, ærsere] *v.tr.* to put away, store *Resserre les groceries pour moi.* Put away the groceries for me. (LA) <***Loc:*** LA, Da84>

reservir [r(ə)særvir, ərsærvir, ærsærvir] **I** *v.tr.* to serve again *Tu veux que je te ressers du gombo?* Do you want me to serve you some more gombo? (LA) **II** *v.intr.* to be used again, be useful again *Sauve ça. Ça peut resservir.* Save that. It can be useful again. (LA) **III se resservir** *v.pron.* to serve o.s. again (e.g. at a meal) *Resservez vous-autres. Il y en reste.* Serve yourselves seconds. There's more. (LA) <***Loc:*** LA, Da84>

ressonner (re-sonner) [r(ə)sɔ̃ne, ərsɔ̃ne, ærsɔ̃ne] **I** *v.tr.* to ring again *Le prêtre a ressonné la cloche.* The priest rang the bell again. (LA) **II** *v.intr.* to ring again **La cloche re-sonne.* The bell is ringing again. (Da84) <***Loc:*** LA, Da84>

ressorer [resore] *v.intr.* to air dry, drip dry *Je vas mettre mon linge dessus le fil à linge et dans rien de temps ça sera bien ressoré.* I'm going to put my clothes on the line and in no time, they will be well dried. (EV) <***Loc:*** EV>

ressort [r(ə)sɔr, ərsɔr, ærsɔr] *n.m.* spring, coil ◊ **•ressort de lit** bedspring <Da84> <***Loc:*** Da84>

ressortir [r(ə)sɔrtir, ərsɔrtir, ærsɔrtir] **I** *v.tr.* to bring out *Elle a ressorti son vieux matelas pour son garçon qu'avait quitté sa femme.* She brought her old matress back out for her son who had left his wife. (LA) **II** *v.intr.* to come out again, go out again *Les crabes dedans ces* AUTOMATIC TRAPS *là [...], quand alle rentre alle peut pas ressortir.* The crabs in those automatic traps, when she goes in there she can't get back out. (TB) *L'alligateur fait plus qu'un langage comme ça, mais ça c'est lui qu'on usait pour les faire ressortir pour les tuer, ceux qui était dans un trou.* The alligator makes more sounds than just that one, but that's the one we used [imitated] to get them to come back out in order to kill them, the ones that were in a hole. (TB) ◊ **•faire ressortir** to bring out, accentuate <Da84> <***Loc:*** EV, TB, VM, Da84>

ressoubler [r(ə)suble, ərsuble, ærsuble] *v.tr.* 1 to ransack, rummage through (while searching for s.t.) 2 to unearth, come across *J'ai ressoublé ça dedans le fond de l'armoire.* I unearthed that in the bottom of the armoire. (TB) <***Loc:*** TB>

ressoudre ♦see **ressourdre**

ressoûler (se) [r(ə)sule, ərsule, ærsule] *v.pron.* to get drunk again *Et je m'ai jamais ressoûlé* BACK. And I've never gotten drunk again. (LF) <***Loc:*** LF>

ressource [r(ə)surs, ərsurs, ærsurs] *n.f.* 1 resource 2 resourcefulness 3 funds, means (money) <***Loc:*** Da84>

ressourdir ♦see **ressourdre**

ressourdre (ressoudre, ressourdir) [r(ə)sud(r), ərsud(r), ærsud(r), r(ə)surdir, ərsurdir, ærsurdir] (*p.p.* **ressoud, ressoudu** [r(ə)su, ərsu, ærsu, r(ə)sudy, ərsudy, ærsudy]) **I** *v.tr.* to recover from the water *Il a arsoud le chapeau.* He recovered the hat from below the surface of the water. (LF) **II** *v.intr.* 1 to show up, appear, reappear *Tu peux jamais dire quand il va ressourdre.* You can never tell when he will show up. (LA) *Mam' cuit tout le temps de trop le dimanche, parce qu'alle a peur que que'qu'un ressoud.* Mom always cooks too much on Sundays because she's afraid that someone will show up. (Guoo) *Regarde qui c'est qui ressoud.* Look who's back. (LA) 2 to resurface, come up from under the water *Son mari a tombé du bateau dedans le bayou et il a jamais ressoud.* Her husband fell off the boat into the bayou and he never resurfaced. (Guoo) *Tout d'un coup, il a arsoudu.* All at once he came up. (JE) *Je t'ai pas toujours dit, la belle, et quand ce bâtiment câlerait, O, il aurait une carlet à plus jamais ressourdre?* Haven't I always told you, maiden, that when this vessel sinks, oh, it will have a net that will never come up again. (VM, ch: *J'ai marié un ouvrier*) *Je prendais un vingt-deux là équand ça ressoudait, mais j'en ai jamais tué un, je l'ai touché je pense, mais j'ai pas pu en attraper un.* I would take a .22 for when it [the tarpon] would resurface, but I never killed one, I grazed it I think, but I was never able to catch one. (TB) ◊ **•faire ressourdre** to start, jump (a rabbit) *J'ai fait ressourdre le lapin.* I jumped the rabbit. (TB) <TB> <***Loc:*** JE, LA, LF, TB, VM, Da84, Guoo, Lv88>

ressouvenir (se) [r(ə)suvnir, ərsuvnir, ærsuvnir] *v.pron.* to remember, recall *Je peux pas me ressouvenir de son nom.* I can't remember his name. (LA) <***Loc:*** LA, Da84>

ressuscitation [resysitasjɔ̃] *n.f.* [*eccl.*] 1 resuscitation 2 resurrection <***Loc:*** Da84>

ressusciter [resysite] **I** *v.tr.* to resuscitate, revive, bring back to life *Quand il ont lavé sa figure, ça l'a ressuscité.* When they washed his face, it revived him. (LA) **II** *v.intr.* to come back to life *Il a ressuscité assez longtemps pour voir sa famille.* He revived long enough to see his family. (LA) <***Loc:*** LA, Da84>

ressuyer [resɥije] *v.tr.* to wipe off again, dry off again *Il faudra ressuyer le comptoir.* It will be necessary to wipe the counter again. (LA) <***Loc:*** EV, LA, Da84>

restant [restɑ̃] *n.m.* 1 remnant, leaving, leftover part **Les restants de table.* Leftovers from a meal. (Da84) 2 remainder, rest *Et là j'ai une de mes filles qui reste au Mississippi. Et le restant reste ici.* And I have one of my daughters who lives in Mississippi. And the rest live here. (TB) *Il a eu pour* *se médeciner le restant de sa vie après son opération.* He had to take medicine for the rest of his life after his operation. (LA) *Cet homme avait eu un œil d'arraché dans une bataille avec son voisin. Il a fait le restant de sa vie borgne.* That man had an eye pulled out in a fight with his neighbor. He spent the rest of his life one-eyed. (LA) **Hé, chère, aujourd'hui j'suis condamné [...] quatre-vingt-dix-neuf ans [...], ça c'est le restant de ma vie.* Hey, babe, today I'm condemned, ninety-nine years, that's the rest of my life. (ch: *La Valse du bambouchear*) <***Loc:*** AC, TB, Da84, Lv88>

restaurant (**estaurant, estaurat, restaurat**) [restorɑ̃, estorɑ̃, estora, restora] *n.m.* restaurant, café *Je vas dîner à l'estaurant à midi.* I'm going to eat at the restaurant at noon. (VM) <***Loc:*** EV, TB, VM, Da84>

restaurat ♦see **restaurant**

restauration [restorasjɔ̃] *n.f.* restoration <***Loc:*** Da84>

restaurer [restore] *v.tr.* to restore *Ils sont après restaurer la vieille maison des Courville.* They are restoring the old Courville house. (LA) <***Loc:*** LA, Da84>

reste [rɛs(t)] *n.m.* **1** rest, balance, remainder **2** *(pl.)* human remains, funerary remains *C'était du monde de la Ville Platte qu'a venu pour les restes. Et ils les ont enterrés dedans le cimetière à la Ville Platte.* It was people from Ville Platte who came for the remains. And they buried them in the cemetery in Ville Platte. (SL) ◊ **•de reste** left over, more than enough **Il y en a de reste.* There is more than enough. (Da84) <Da84> <***Loc:*** LA, SL, Da84>

rester [reste] *v.intr.* **1** to remain, be left **Il reste deux piastres.* There are two dollars left. (Da84) **Il y en reste trois.* There are three left. (Da84) **Mes parents ils sont presque tous morts, ceux-là qui restent, il y en a plus un qui veut me voir.* My relatives are almost all dead, [among] those who remain, not a single one wants to see me. (ch: *Je suis orphelin*) **2** to stay, remain *Dedans les parlements de mon pape et ma mame et le monde qui venait parler avec eusse, eh ben nous-autres on pouvait pas rester et écouter.* In the discussions of my dad and mom and the people who came to see them, well, we weren't allowed to stay and listen. (TB) **Tes menteries vont rester sur ta conscience.* Your lies will remain on your conscience. (ch: *La valse de quatre-vingt-dix-neuf ans*) **Je va's rester ayoù j'suis parce que je connais tu me veux plus.* I'm going to stay where I am because I know you don't want me anymore. (ch: *Quitter la maison*) **Si tu resterais si loin, 'tit monde, toi, jolie ça m'a fait du mal.* If you would stay so far away, darling, you, pretty one, that hurt me. (ch: *Eunice Two Step*) **3** to reside, dwell, live (in a place) *Mon garçon reste à Lafayette.* My son lives in Lafayette. (Lv88) *Éou tu restes?* Where do you live? (SM) *Il reste à l'autre bord du village.* He lives on the other side of town. (VM) **Les vieux restiont à la maison avec nous aut'. Y avait pas ces maisons éoù i mettont les vieux pour mourir.* Our old folks used to live at home with us. There weren't places where they put the old people to die. (Gu82) *Les Rivette restaient à peu près un demi-mile de nous-autres.* The Rivettes lived about a half-mile from us. (SL) *J'ai resté tout ma vie ici.* I have lived here all my life. (SM) ◊ **•rester à côté** to keep away *Il a resté à côté de Lafayette pour une dizaine d'années.* He stayed away from Lafayette for about ten years. (LA) <LA, Da84> **•rester à part** to remain aloof or apart <Da84> **•rester avec** to stay with it, hold on **Reste avec!* Stay with it, don't give up. (Da84) <Da84> **•rester avec la chuille** to be duped, be fooled, be had **J'ai resté avec la chuille.* I was duped. (EV, Ph36) *J'ai resté avec la chuille.* I've been had. (Lv88) <EV, SM, Lv88, Ph36> **•rester bête** to remain silent <SM> **•rester chez soi** to stay at home <Da84> **•rester de l'arrière** to be in arrears *Il a resté six mois de l'arrière.* He was six months in arrears. (TB) <TB> **•rester en arrière** to stay behind, lag behind, stay back <Da84> **•rester en vie** to stay alive, remain alive <Da84> **•rester en ville** to stay in the city, live in the city <Da84> **•rester pour graine** to remain an old maid, not marry in one's lifetime <La99> **•rester pour (qqn)** ***a*** to live on (s.o.'s land) *Avant on se marie, ça restait pour Dr. Jenkins.* Before we were married, they were living on Dr. Jenkin's land. (EV) ***b*** to sharecrop (for s.o.), tenant farm *Il restait pour M. Jean Conques.* He used to sharecrop for Mr. Jean Conques. (LA) <EV, LA> **•rester seul** to live alone <Da84> **•rester tranquille** to keep quiet <Da84, Lv88> **•ça reste à (qqn)** it's up to (s.o.) **Ça, ça reste à vous.* That's up to you. (Da84) <Da84> <***Loc:*** AC, EV, LA, LF, SL, SM, TB, VM, Da84, Gu82, Hi02, La99, Lv88>

restriction [restriksjɔ̃] *n.f.* restriction, limitation <***Loc:*** Da84>

résultat [rezylta] *n.m.* result, effect, consequence, outcome <***Loc:*** Da84>

résurrection [rezyrɛksjɔ̃] *n.f.* [*eccl.*] resurrection <***Loc:*** Da84>

résypère ♦see **érésipèle**

rétablir [retablir] **I** *v.tr.* **1** to reestablish, restore *Rétablir la paix.* To reestablish order. (LA) *Il pourra jamais rétablir son honneur.* He will never be able to restore his honor. (LA) **2** to rebuild *La paroisse a rétabli le pont.* The parish government rebuilt the bridge. (LA) **3** to cure *Les traitements l'ont rétabli.* The treatments cured him. (LA) **II se rétablir** *v.pron.* to recover one's health, get well *Je crois pas qu'il va jamais se rétablir.* I don't think he will ever get well. (LA) <***Loc:*** LA, Da84>

rétablissement [retablismɑ̃] *n.m.* **1** restoration (of order, etc.) **2** recovery (of health) <***Loc:*** Da84>

retaille [r(ə)taj, ərtaj, ærtaj] *n.f.* remnant, scrap (of cloth, wood, etc.) *Elle a fait une quilt avec les plus belles retailles qu'elle gardait dans son vieux bureau.* She made a quilt with the prettiest scraps of cloth that she kept in her old desk. (Lv88) **Alle arrêtait pas de carder son coton ou de piquer eine couilte qu'alle avait faite avec des r'tailles.* She never stopped carding her coton or stitching a quilt that she made from scraps. (Gu82) <*Loc:* SM, TB, VM, Da84, Gu82, Lv88>

retailler [r(ə)taje, ərtaje, ærtaje] *v.tr.* to recut, reprune (trees) *Il faut pas que tu retailles les arbres chaque année.* You mustn't reprune the trees every year. (LA) <*Loc:* LA, Da84>

retard [r(ə)tar, ərtar, ærtar] *n.m.* delay ◊ •**en retard** ***a*** late ***b*** developmentally delayed, retarded *Y a plein qu'est morts et y a plein je veux dire que ils ont* FIGHT *mais la fièvre était tellement fort que il y a plein je veux dire que ça les a brûlés la cervelle. Ça fait après ça ils pouvaient pas apprendre bien, ils étaient moyen en retard.* There are a lot who died and there are a lot, I mean, they fought but the fever was so strong that there were a lot, I mean, whose brains were damaged by the fever. So, afterwards they couldn't learn well, they were somewhat retarded. (SJ) <SJ, Da84, Hi02> <*Loc:* SJ, Da84, Hi02>

retarder [r(ə)tarde, ərtarde, ærtarde] *v.tr.* **1** to delay, postpone *Ils ont eu pour retarder la course.* They had to delay the race. (LA) **2** to set back (a timepiece) **Retarder une pendule.* To set a clock back. (Da84) <*Loc:* LA, Da84>

retendre [r(ə)tɑ̃n, r(ə)tɑ̃d(r), ərtɑ̃n, ərtɑ̃d(r), ærtɑ̃n, ærtɑ̃d(r)] *v.tr.* to stretch again (wire, rope, etc.) *Ils ont retendu le fil après que les vaches avaient passé.* They restretched the wire after the cows had passed through. (LA) <*Loc:* LA, Da84>

retenir (**retiendre**) [rətnir, ərtnir, ærtnir, r(ə)tʃɛ̃n, r(ə)tʃɛ̃d(r), ərtʃɛ̃n, ərtʃɛ̃d(r), ærtʃɛ̃n, ærtʃɛ̃d(r), r(ə)tjɛ̃, ərtjɛ̃, ærtjɛ̃] **I** *v.tr.* to retain, keep back, withhold (money, etc.) *Je crois qu'il est après retiendre de l'argent.* I think he's holding some money back. (LA) **II se retenir** *v.pron.* to restrain o.s., hold o.s. back *Essaie de te retiendre. C'est un bougre dangereux.* Try to hold yourself back. He is a dangerous fellow. (LA) ◊ •**retiendre en mémoire** to bear in mind <Da84> <*Loc:* JE, LA, TB, Da84>

retiendre ♦see **retenir**

rétif, -ive [retif, -iv] *adj.* stubborn, balky *Elle a tout le temps été rétive.* She was always stubborn. (LA) ◊ •**faire rétif** to balk (of a horse, a mule) <Da84> <*Loc:* LA, Da84>

RETIRE [ɹitaɪ, ɹətaɪɹ] *v.intr.invar.* to retire *Il a* RETIRE *cinq ans passés.* He retired five years ago. (Lv88) **J'ai espoir que je pourrai* RETIRE *avec l'argent que les* BEAN *vont rapporter.* I hope I will be able to retire with the money that the beans will bring in. (Gu82) *J'ai travaillé là jusqu'à j'ai* RETIRED *en 1980.* I worked there until I retired in 1980. (IB) *Je croyais t'avais* RETIRED, *toi.* I thought you retired. (EV) <*Loc:* EV, IB, Gu82, Lv88>

retiré, -e [r(ə)tire, ərtire, ærtire] *adj.* **1** retiring, quiet, unpretentious *Une personne retirée.* A retiring person. (VM) **2** retired (from a profession) *Un juge retiré.* A retired judge. (Lv88) <*Loc:* VM, Da84, Lv88>

retirer[1] [r(ə)tire, ərtire, ærtire] **I** *v.tr.* **1** to take out *C'est moi qui tuais pour mon pape. Et il lavait bien la panse de bœuf et il le ramassait et là il faut que tu bouilles ça et il faut que tu retires le dedans et tout, tu connais.* I was the one who did the slaughtering for my father. And he would wash out the cow stomach well and he took it, and you have to boil it and take out the insides and all, you know. (LF) **2** to remove, take off *Une hache à pied. Le monde a usé ça pour faire leurs pirogues, pour retirer le plus gros du bois.* A foot axe. People used that to make their pirogues, to remove the rough areas of the wood. (LF) *Il a rentré dans la petite galerie, il s'assit sur la berceuse, il a retiré ses bottes. Il les avait pas lavées, tu vois.* He came into the little porch, he sat down on the rocking chair, he removed his boots. He hadn't washed them, you see. (TB) **3** to withdraw (support, money, etc.) *J'ai retiré l'argent que j'avais donné à ce candidat.* I withdrew the money that I had contributed to that candidate. (VM) **4** to draw again **Retirer de l'eau.* To draw water again. (Da84) **5** to milk again **Retirer les vaches.* To milk the cows again. (Da84) **6** to serve, dish out *Va chercher la gibote pour que je retire la soupe.* Go get the dipper so I can dish out the soup. (TB) **II se retirer** *v.pron.* **1** to withdraw *O il y aurait bien longtemps, je m'en aurais retiré.* Oh I would have withdrawn long ago. (IB, ch: *Madamoiselle Emélie*) **2** to come off, fall off *Et là dès que c'est cuit là, eh ben la viande se retire sur les os. Là ils jetont les os. Là ça gèle avec cette couenne là en-dedans là. Ça gèle, ça vient dur. C'est ça ils appelont de la gelée.* And when it's cooked, the meat comes off the bones. Then they throw away the bones. Then it gels with that pig skin in it. It gels, it gets hard. That's what they call head cheese. (LF) ◊ •**retirer de l'argent** to withdraw money (from an account) <Da84> •**retirer qqch dans la figure à qqn** to throw s.t. back in s.o.'s face, use s.o.'s words against him or her <EV> <*Loc:* EV, IB, LF, TB, VM, Da84>

retirer[2] [r(ə)tire, ərtire, ærtire] *v.tr.* to shoot again, fire (a gun) again <*Loc:* LA, Da84>

retomber [r(ə)tɔ̃be, ərtɔ̃be, ærtɔ̃be] *v.tr.* to fall again, fall back **Elle a retombé par terre.* She fell back to the ground. (Da84) <*Loc:* EV, Da84>

retordre [r(ə)tɔrd(r), ərtɔrd(r), ærtɔrd(r)] *v.tr.* **1** to retwist, rebend **2** to wring out again *J'ai eu pour retordre le linge qu'était étendu sur la corde après la pluie.* I had to wring out the clothes on the line again after the rain. (VM) <*Loc:* VM, Da84>

retoucher [r(ə)tuʃe, ərtuʃe, ærtuʃe] *v.tr.* **1** to touch again *Il s'a fâché, il a pris le* TABLET *et le* PRIMER BOOK, *il a été, il l'a mis dedans le tiroir du garde-manger. Et il dit "Je veux pas retoucher ça."* He got mad, he took the writing tablet and the primer book, he went, he put them in the larder. And he said "I don't want to touch that again." (TB) **2** to retouch, touch up *Retoucher le mur ayoù on a manqué une place.* To retouch a wall where one missed a spot. (VM) <***Loc:*** TB, VM, Da84>

retour [r(ə)tur, ərtur, ærtur] *n.m.* **1** return *J'ai jamais eu de retour de cet argent que j'avais investi dans son magasin.* I never had a return on the money I had invested in his store. (EV) **2** end result, ultimate outcome *Quoi c'était le retour de ton meeting avec ces bougres?* What was the outcome of your meeting with those fellows? (VM) ◊ **•avoir le retour d'âge** to go through menopause <LF, SJ, SL> **•de {en} retour** back, returned **Il est de retour.* He is back, he has returned. (Da84) <Da84> <***Loc:*** EV, LF, SJ, SL, VM, Da84>

retourner [r(ə)turne, ərturne, ærturne] **I** *v.tr.* to turn over *C'est l'heure pour retourner les crêpes.* It's time to turn the pancakes. (EV) **II** *v.intr.* **1** to go back, return *Il fallait il retourne pour faire son service.* He had to go back to do his military service. (TB) *Là, la dame retournait se mettre ayoù elle était, s'assir ayoù elle était, tu connais.* The woman went back to where she was, sat down where she had been, you know. (VM) *Il voulait pas retourner à l'école.* He didn't want to go back to school. (AC) **2** to come back, return *Johnny est après essayer de repeinturer sa maison avant sa femme retourne de ses vacances.* Johnny is trying to repaint his house before his wife returns from her vacation. (VM) **III se retourner** *v.pron.* to come back, go back, return *Et un soir, ils aviont apporté des contes et puis nous-autres fallait on s'en retourne, chère enfant, en wagon.* And one evening, they had come back with some stories and we had to go back, child, in a wagon. (EV) *Et quelque temps après ça quand il s'est retourné* BACK *eusse s'en allait dans l'ouest.* And some time after that, when he went back, they [the ducks] were heading west. (TB) ◊ **•se retourner de bord** to turn o.s. around *Retourne-toi de bord et regarde-moi dans les yeux.* Turn around and look me in the eyes. (LA) <LA, Da84> <***Loc:*** AC, EV, LA, TB, VM, Da84, Hi02>

retracer [r(ə)trase, ərtrase, ærtrase] *v.tr.* to retrace (a line, tracks, etc.) **Il a pris à le retracer en regrichant la trace, ayoù ce qu'il devenait.* He started to retrace the trail, backtracking, in the direction that it [the deer] had come from. (AC, An94) <***Loc:*** AC, An94, Da84>

rétraction [retraksjɔ̃] *n.f.* retraction <***Loc:*** Da84>

retraite [r(ə)trɛt, ərtrɛt, ærtrɛt] *n.f.* **1** retreat, withdrawal **2** retreat (spiritual or religious exercise) **3** retirement ◊ **•faire une retraite *a*** to make a retreat ***b*** to go on a retreat <Da84> **•prendre sa retraite** to retire *J'étais bien connu avec tous les compagnies, équand j'ai pris ma retraite, eusse voulait pas que je quitte ca.* I was well known with all the companies. When I retired they didn't want me to quit. (TB) *Quand je vas prendre ma retraite, ils vont jamais trouver un remplaçant pour moi.* When I retire, they will never find a replacement for me. (VM) <SL, TB, VM> <***Loc:*** SL, TB, VM, Da84>

retrancher [r(ə)trɑ̃ʃe, ərtrɑ̃ʃe, ærtrɑ̃ʃe] *v.tr.* to reslice, recut *Il faudra je retranche la daube. Il y a plus de monde que je croyais.* I'll have to reslice the roast. There are more people than I thought. (LA) <***Loc:*** LA, Da84>

retravailler [r(ə)travaje, ərtravaje, ærtravaje] **I** *v.tr.* to rework *Je vas retravailler ma manche samedi après-midi avant la messe.* I'll rework my lane Saturday afternoon before Mass. (LA) **II** *v.intr.* to work again *Il a pas retravaillé depuis son* STROKE. He hasn't worked again since his stroke. (EV) <***Loc:*** EV, LA, Da84>

retraverser [r(ə)traværse, ərtraværse, ærtraværse] *v.tr.* to recross, cross over again *Il traversait et retraversait le bayou en cherchant son canard qu'avait tombé loin du* BLIND. He crossed and recrossed the bayou looking for his duck that had fallen far from the blind. (LA) <***Loc:*** LA, Da84>

retremper [r(ə)trɑ̃pe, ərtrɑ̃pe, ærtrɑ̃pe] **I** *v.tr.* to wet again *Retrempe ta chemise avant de la repasser.* Rewet your shirt before ironing it. (LA) **II se retremper** *v.pron.* **1** to get wet again *Il s'a retrempé pour une troisième fois la même nuit.* He got wet for the third time the same night. (LA) **2** to urinate involuntarily, wet o.s. ◊ **•retremper le lit** to wet the bed *Il retrempe le lit proche tous les soirs.* He wets the bed nearly every night. (LA) <LA> <***Loc:*** LA, Da84>

retresser [r(ə)trese, ərtrese, ærtrese] *v.tr.* to rebraid (hair, twine, etc.) *Je lui ai retressé les cheveux comme avant.* I rebraided her hair like before. (VM) <***Loc:*** VM, Da84>

retroussement [r(ə)trusmɑ̃, ərtrusmɑ̃, ærtrusmɑ̃] *n.m.* rolling up (of pants, sleeves, dress) *Je savais la bataille aurait commencé quand j'ai vu le retroussement des manches.* I knew the fight would start when I saw the rolling up of sleeves. (VM) <***Loc:*** VM, Da84>

retrousser (trousser) [r(ə)truse, ərtruse, ærtruse, truse] **I** *v.tr.* to turn up, roll up *Retrousse tes manches de chemise.* Roll up your shirt sleeves. (LA) *J'ai troussé mes manches et j'ai commencé derrière le char.* I rolled up my sleeves and started on the car. (LA) **II se retrousser** *v.pron.* to tuck up, roll up (one's dress, sleeves, pants) *Elle s'a retroussé la robe.* She raised up her dress. (VM) <***Loc:*** LA, VM, Da84>

retrouver [r(ə)truve, ərtruve, ærtruve] **I** *v.tr.* to find again, rediscover **Toi, veux pas, toi, 'tite fille, de me retrouver.* You don't want to come find me again. (ch: *Two step de maman*) *Ils les ont pas retrouvés avant que ça pouvait plus les reconnaître, enfin, ça les a reconnus par leurs souliers et leur linge manière.* They didn't find them until they couldn't recognize them anymore, they recognized them somehow by their shoes and by their clothing. (AC) **II se retrouver** *v.pron.* **1** to regain one's bearings (after being lost) *On se retrouvait au ras d'un clos, on s'est fourré en dessous de la barrière, on est rentré dans le clos, chère.* We found ourselves next to a field, we went under the fence, we went into the field, dear. (EV) **2** to find each other again ◊

•se retrouver à la bonne place to find o.s. at the right place <Da84> <***Loc:*** AC, EV, TB, Da84>

reunette ♦see **rainette**

réunion [reynjɔ̃] *n.f.* reunion, meeting, gathering <***Loc:*** Da84, Hi02>

réunir [reynir, rynir] **I** *v.tr.* to reunite, rejoin, bring back together **II se réunir** *v.pron.* to reunite, reassemble, meet <***Loc:*** EV, Da84, Ph36>

réuser [reyze] *v.tr.* to reuse, use again *Elle avait pour détortiller les vieux fils avant de les réuser.* She had to unravel the old threads before reusing them. (LA) <***Loc:*** LA>

réussir (**érussir**) [reysir, erysir, rysir] *v.intr.* to succeed, be successful *Il érussit jamais à rien.* He never succeeds at anything. (VM) <***Loc:*** EV, LA, TB, VM, Da84, Hi02, Ph36, Wh83>

réussite [reysit] *n.f.* success <***Loc:*** Da84>

revange ♦see **revenge**

revanger ♦see **revenger**

rêve [rɛv] *n.m.* dream **Là je m'ai aperçu ça c'était juste un rêve.* Then I realized it was just a dream. (ch: *Juste un rêve*) *O toi, chérie, si tu veux faire un joli rêve, essaie de sommeiller dans les bras de ton nègre.* Oh dearest, if you want to have a sweet dream, try sleeping in the arms of your loving man. (IB, ch: *J'ai vu Lucille*) ◊ **•rêve de poule** unrealistic idea or plan <La99> <***Loc:*** EV, IB, SL, An94, Da84, Hi02, La99>

réveil [revɛj] *n.m.* **1** waking, awakening **2** alarm clock <***Loc:*** Da84, Lv88>

réveille [revɛj] *n.f.* alarm clock <***Loc:*** AV, SB, SJ, SM, Lv88>

réveillé, -e [reveje] *adj.* **1** awake, awake again *Parce qu'il venait, j'étais réveillée.* Because he was coming, I was awake. (AC) **2** sly, mischievous *Il était réveillé pour même.* He was crafty for sure. (VM) <***Loc:*** AC, VM>

réveiller [reveje] **I** *v.tr.* to awaken, wake up *Vers minuit du soir, ça m'a réveillé à force que le bateau roulait.* Around midnight, it woke me up because the boat was rolling so much. (TB) *Il m'a réveillé doucement, il voulait pas réveiller l'autre.* He woke me up softly, he didn't want to wake up the other guy. (TB) **II** *v.intr.* to awaken, wake up **J'ai reveillé à ce matin avec un cœur aussi cassé.* I woke up this morning with such a broken heart. (ch: *Juste un rêve*) **II se réveiller** *v.pron.* to awaken, wake up *Ce soir là, quand il s'est réveillé lui-même, il a arrêté tout ça.* That night, when he woke up, he stopped all that [drinking]. (EV) *Tout d'un coup, je m'ai réveillé là, chère, en peur.* All of a sudden, I woke up frightened, dear. (EV) *Là, quand je m'ai bien réveillé, j'ai vu c'était pas vrai et j'ai prié pour lui.* Then when I really woke up, I saw that it wasn't true and I prayed for him. (EV) <***Loc:*** AC, EV, IB, SL, TB, Da84>

revenant [r(ə)v(ə)nɑ̃, ərvənɑ̃, ærvənɑ̃] *n.m.* ghost, spook, apparition *On avait fermé nos yeux qu'on avait peur du revenant.* We had closed our eyes [because] we were afraid of the ghost. (EV) <***Loc:*** EV, Da84, Hi02>

revendre [r(ə)vɑ̃n, r(ə)vɑ̃d(r), ərvɑ̃n, ərvɑ̃d(r), ærvɑ̃n, ærvɑ̃d(r)] *v.tr.* to resell, sell again *Là lui qui l'a acheté avec moi, là lui il faut qu'il dit à quel homme qu'il l'a revendu, jusqu'à que ça va éiou-ce qu'il était perdu.* Then the one who bought it from me, he has to tell whatever man he resold it to, until it gets back to where it [the alligator tag] was lost. (TB) <***Loc:*** TB, Da84>

revenge (**revange, arvange**) [r(ə)vɑ̃ʒ, ərvɑ̃ʒ, ærvɑ̃ʒ] *n.f.* revenge *Je vas avoir mon arvange.* I shall get my revenge. (JE) ◊ **•prendre sa revenge** to get one's revenge <Da84> <***Loc:*** JE, LF, SM, TB, Da84, Lv88>

revenger (**revanger, arvanger**) [r(ə)vɑ̃ʒe, ərvɑ̃ʒe, ærvɑ̃ʒe] **I** *v.tr.* to avenge, get revenge for *J'ai revengé la mort de mon frère.* I avenged the death of my brother. (LA) **II se revenger** *v.pron.* to avenge o.s., get revenge **J'ai envie de me revenger.* I want to get my revenge. (An77) *Il va s'arvanger.* He will avenge himself. (JE) *Ça jouait des 'tits tours pour se revenger.* They played little tricks to get their revenge. (Lv88) *Il s'aurait revengé si jamais Martin Weber croisait son chemin encore.* He would have gotten his revenge if Martin Weber ever crossed his path again. (LA) <***Loc:*** JE, LA, LF, SB, An77, Da84, Lv88>

revenir [r(ə)v(ə)nir, ərvənir, ærvənir] **I** *v.intr.* **1** to return, come back *La dame est jamais revenue* BACK. The lady never came back. (IB) **Moi j'vois pas quoi faire si tu reviens pas, bébé.* I don't know what I'll do if you don't come back, baby. (ch: *Ma blonde est partie*) **Ça fait du bien d'êt' ervenue chez moi.* It feels good to be back home. (Gu82) **Pour r'venir à quoi-ce qu'on disait.* To come back to what we were saying. (Gu82) **Ouai, catin, je va's revenir à me refaire tout ça t'as fait.* Yes, babydoll, I'll come back and relive everything you did to me. (ch: *Euncie two step*) **Quand j'ai quitté de la maison [...] j'avais dit que j'aurais jamais rev'nu.* When I left home, I had said that I would never come back. (ch: *J'ai fait une grosse erreur*) **2** to recur *Les bessons, ça revient tous les deux générations.* Twins recur every other generation. (VM) **II s'en revenir** *v.pron.* to return, come back **La première journée d'école, Emma s'en a r'venue à la maison en braillant.* The first day of school, Emma came home crying. (Gu82) **Hé, toi, chère, il faut toi tu t'en reviens.* Hey, you, darling, you have to come back. (ch: *Lacassine special*) ◊ **•revenir au même** to amount to the same thing, boil down to the same thing *Des fois eusse dit des affaires en anglais qu'a pas d'allure non plus, enfin, ça c'est ça, ça revient toujours au même.* Sometimes they say things in English that don't make sense either, well, that's the way it is, it boils down to the same thing. (TB) <TB> **•revenez! / reviens! / reviens BACK!** come back! (an invitation to return, e.g. a merchant's send-off to a customer) <Da84, La99> **•ça lui revient** he has it coming to him (as a reward or retribution) <Da84> <***Loc:*** AC, EV, IB, JE, LA, LF, SL, TB, VM, Da84, Gu82, Hi02>

revenu [rəv(ə)ny, ərvəny, ærvəny] *n.m.* income, profit, revenue <***Loc:*** Da84>

REVENUE [ɹɛvənu¤] *n.m.* revenuer, Treasury Department revenue agent (responsible for the destruction of illegal stills and arrest of bootleggers) *J'ai vu les* REVENUES *à passer, j'ai monté sur un petit cheval rouge, il y avait. Les* REVENUES *passaient dans le chemin.* I saw the revenuers coming by, so I got on a little red horse that was there. The revenuers were passing by on the road. (SL) <***Loc:*** SL>

rêver [reve] **I** *v.tr.* to dream **J'ai rêvé hier au soir que tu m'avais donné ton cheval.* I dreamed last night that you had given me your horse. (SL, An94) **II** *v.intr.* to dream *Bien rare que je vas rêver à quelque chose.* It's quite rare for me to dream of anything. (TB) *Je rêve après des choses que je vas faire.* I dream about things that I'm going to do. (TB) **J'avais rêvé-z-à mes chers 'tits yeux noirs, qui est partie.* I dreamed about my dear little black-eyed girl, who has gone away. (ch: *'Tits yeux noirs*) <***Loc:*** SL, TB, An94, Da84, Hi02>

reverdir [r(ə)værdir, ərværdir, ærværdir] *v.intr.* to become green again *Ça va prendre quelque temps avant que les maîches vont reverdir.* It'll take some time before the marshes become green again. (VM) <***Loc:*** VM, Da84>

révérence [reverɑ̃s] *n.f.* reverence <***Loc:*** Da84>

révérend [reverɑ̃] *adj.* [*eccl.*] reverend <***Loc:*** Da84>

revers [r(ə)vær, ərvær, ærvær] *n.m.* reverse, wrong side (of cloth, clothing, etc.) <***Loc:*** Da84>

reverser[1] [r(ə)værse, ərværse, ærværse] *v.tr.* to repour, pour again *Reverse-moi un verre de vin.* Pour me another glass of wine. (VM) <***Loc:*** VM, Da84>

reverser[2] ♦see **renverser**

rêveur, -euse [revœr, -øz] *n.* dreamer <***Loc:*** Da84>

revider [r(ə)vide, ərvide, ærvide] *v.tr.* to pour out again, empty again *Combien de fois il faudra qu'on revide la glacière cette année?* How many times will we have to empty the refrigerator again this year? (EV) <***Loc:*** EV, Da84>

revirer [r(ə)vire, ərvire, ærvire] *v.intr.* **1** to turn around, turn back **Il a voulu revirer dans son vieux char, il a embourbé.* He wanted to turn back in his old car, he got stuck in the mud. (An77) *Tu pouvais revirer au bout du chemin là à la Pointe là-bas si c'était pour venir ici et parler d'anglais.* You might as well have turned back at the top of the road to Pointe aux Chênes if you were coming down here to speak English. (TB) *Et eusse a erviré et eusse a revenu* BACK *chez eux.* And they turned around and came back home. (LF) **2** to go back *Mais si tu revires vers l'affaire à peu près 20 ou 25 ans passés le Cadien aurait pu jamais avoir une compagnie parce que les bougres qu'avaient les banques et tout, eux-autres voulait pas faire barguine avec les Cadiens.* But if you go back to 20 or 25 years ago the Cajun could never have had a company, because the guys who had the banks and all, they didn't want to bargain with Cajuns. (TB) ◊ **•revirer à l'endroit** to turn right side out *Revire ma robe à l'endroit.* Turn my dress right side out. (TB) <TB> **•(se) revirer de bord** to turn around *Et juste j'ai reviré de bord et mettre le verre sur le cabinette et le* ALKA SELTZER *aussitte,* MAN, *c'est comme un logue qu'a tombé par terre.* And I just turned around to put the glass on the cabinet and the Alka Seltzer too, man, it was like a log that fell to the ground. (TB) *Tu peux te revirer de bord, je veux pus te voir.* You can just turn around, I don't want to see you anymore. (LA) <LA, TB> <***Loc:*** EV, IB, LA, LF, SM, TB, VM, An77, Da84, Lv88, Ph36>

revivre [r(ə)viv(r), ərviv(r), ærviv(r)] *v.intr.* to revive, come back to life *Son deuil est fini. Elle pourra revivre asteur.* Her mourning is over. She will be able to live again. (VM) <***Loc:*** VM, Da84>

revoir [r(ə)vwar, ərvwar, ærvwar] **I** *v.tr.* to see again *Il avait un gros sac d'or et les belles bottes du diable. Fait, tout était magnifique, ils estiont contents de le revoir.* He had a big sack of gold and the devil's beautiful boots. So, everything was wonderful, they were happy to see him again. (LA) *Au revoir, mes amis. Je vas vous revoir sur mon autre grand tour.* Goodbye, my friends. I will see you again on my other big tour. (AV) *Je le revoyais pas avant le lundi matin.* I didn't see him again before Monday morning. (AC) **II se revoir** *v.pron.* to see each other again, meet each other again *On va se revoir la semaine qui vient.* We'll meet again next week. (LA) **On va se revoir plus tard.* We'll see each other again later. (La99) ◊ **•au revoir** [orəvwar, arəwar, ɑ̃rəvwar] goodbye, so long <SB, SM, Da84, Hi02> **•on va se revoir** see you later, good-bye for now <La99, Lv88> <***Loc:*** AC, AV, LA, Da84, Hi02, La99, Lv88>

revoler[1] [r(ə)vole, ərvole, ærvole] *v.intr.* to fly again *Après le 11 de septembre, je crois pus que je vas revoler.* After September 11th, I don't think I'll ever fly again. (VM) <***Loc:*** LA, VM, Da84>

revoler[2] [r(ə)vole, ərvole, ærvole] *v.tr.* to steal again *Ces malfaicteurs ont revolé ma faucheuse.* Those ne'er-do-wells stole my lawnmower again. (LA) <***Loc:*** LA, VM, Da84>

révoltant, -e [revɔltɑ̃, -ɑ̃t] *adj.* revolting, disgusting *Ça me dégoûte. C'est révoltant!* That disgusts me. It's revolting! (ThCa: *Mille misères*) <***Loc:*** Da84, ThCa>

révolte [revɔlt] *n.f.* revolt, revolution, rebellion <***Loc:*** Da84>

révolter [revɔlte] **I** *v.intr.* to revolt, rebel *Les esclaves ont révolté.* The slaves revolted. (VM) **II se révolter** *v.pron.* to revolt, rebel *Il est rendu à l'âge qu'il se révolte contre tout quelque chose et tout quelqu'un.* He's gotten to the age where he rebels against everything and everyone. (VM) <***Loc:*** VM, Da84>

révolution [revolysjɔ̃] *n.f.* revolution **Pendant la Révolution d'France, i' (les nobles) s'sont rangés ici.* During the

Revolution in France, they (the nobility) sought refuge here. (Gr82) <***Loc:*** Da84, Gr82>

révolutionnaire [revolysjɔ̃nær] *adj.* revolutionary **C'était une autre cause révolutionnaire que j'allais embrasser, mais cette fois, c'était beaucoup plus important parce que ça me touchait directement.* It was another revolutionary cause that I would embrace, but this time it was more important because it concerned me directly. (LA, An84) <***Loc:*** LA, An84>

revomir [r(ə)vɔ̃mir, ərvɔ̃mir, ærvɔ̃mir] *v.tr.* to vomit again *Il a revomi trois fois.* He vomited three more times. (VM) <***Loc:*** VM, Da84>

révoquer [revoke] *v.tr.* to revoke, repeal *Révoquer une licence.* To revoke a license. (LA) <***Loc:*** LA, Da84>

revue [r(ə)vy, ərvy, ærvy] *n.f.* review <***Loc:*** Da84>

rézard ♦see **lézard**

rézipère ♦see **érésipèle**

rhabiller [rabije] **I** *v.tr.* to dress again *Rhabille le bébé. Il faudra qu'on l'amène à l'hôpital.* Get the baby dressed again. We'll have to take him to the hospital. (EV) **II se rhabiller** *v.pron.* to get dressed again *J'ai eu pour me rhabiller deux fois dans la même journée à cause de la pluie.* I had to dress twice in the same day because of the rain. (LA) <***Loc:*** EV, LA, Da84>

rhabituer ♦see **réhabituer**

rhinocéros [rinoserɔs] *n.m.* rhinoceros <***Loc:*** Da84>

rhumatise [rymatiz] *n.f.* rheumatism *Etre attaqué de la rhumatise.* To suffer from rheumatism. (AV) <***Loc:*** AV, SJ>

rhumatisme (**rhumatisse**) [rymatis] *n.m.* rheumatism <***Loc:*** EV, IB, LF, SB, SL, SM, TB,VM, Da84>

rhumatisse ♦see **rhumatisme**

rhume [rym, rœ̃m] *n.m.* **1** cold *Le thé de mamou décolle le rhume.* Mamou tea helps to break up a cold. (VM) **2** mucus, nasal discharge *J'ai craché du rhume.* I spit up some mucus. (LA) ◊ •**rhume de cerveau** head cold <Da84> •**avoir le rhume** to have a cold <Da84> •**prendre un rhume** to catch a cold <Da84> <***Loc:*** AC, AV, LA, VM, Da84, Hi02>

ribandelle ♦see **ribondelle**

ribondelle (**ribandelle, rubandelle**) [ribɔ̃dɛl, ribɑ̃dɛl, rybɑ̃dɛl] *n.f.* **1** ribbon, band **2** strip, torn piece, tatter **Son linge est tout en ribondelle.* Her clothes are in tatters. (Da84) *Il a déchiré sa culotte en ribandelles.* He tore his pants to shreds. (SM) <***Loc:*** AV, IB, JE, LF, SB, SJ, SL, SM, VM, Da84, Lv88>

ribote (**ribotte**) [ribɔt, ribot] *n.f.* drunken spree **Il s'a sacré une ribotte.* He got drunk. (Da84) *Ils auront fait une ribote pour Christmas.* They would get drunk at Christmas. (EV) <***Loc:*** EV, Da84, La99>

riboter (**ribotter**) [ribote] *v.intr.* to drink heavily, get drunk *Ils ont riboté toute la fin de semaine.* They drank all weekend. (LA) <***Loc:*** LA, PL, Da84, Lv88>

riboteur, -euse (**ribotteur, -euse**) [ribotœr, -øz] *n.* **1** habitual drunkard **2** reveler, partier <***Loc:*** Da84, Lv88>

riboteux, -euse [ribotø, -øz] *adj.* drunk <***Loc:*** Lv88>

ribotte ♦see **ribote**

ribotter ♦see **riboter**

ribotteur ♦see **riboteur**

ricane [rikɑ̃n] *n.f.* **1** laughing fit **2** ruckus, uproar <***Loc:*** LA, VM, Da84>

ricanement [rikɑ̃nmɑ̃] *n.m.* laughter, loud laughter *Y a trop de ricanement ici.* There's too much laughter here. (SM) <***Loc:*** SM, Lv88>

ricaner [rikɑ̃ne, rigɑ̃ne] *v.intr.* **1** to laugh, laugh loudly *'Coute les enfants ricaner dans l'autre chambre.* Listen to the kids laughing in the other room. (SM) *T'as ricané un tas hier au soir.* You laughed a lot last night. (VM) **2** to laugh in a condescending or mocking way, sneer *S'il arrête pas de ricaner comme ça, je vas lui péter une tape.* If he doesn't stop laughing like that, I'll slap him. (LA) <***Loc:*** LA, SM, TB, VM, Da84, Lv88>

ricaneur, -euse [rikɑ̃nœr, -øz] *adj.* easily given to laughter, always laughing *Il est ricaneur.* He loves to laugh. (SM) *C'est une ricaneuse.* She's someone who laughs a lot. (SM) <***Loc:*** SM>

richard [riʃar] *n.m.* rich man **Moi j'suis pas riche. Ils viendraient m'offrir de vivre comme un gros richard dans une grande ville, pas pour cinq mille piasses j'quitterais mon pays!* I'm not rich. They could come and offer to have me live like a rich man in a big city, not for five thousand dollars would I leave my homeland! (Gr86) <***Loc:*** Gr86>

riche [riʃ] *adj.* rich, wealthy *T'avais le planteur riche qu'était bien éduqué qu'avait beaucoup d'argent. Ah ben, lui, il est venu ici.* You had the rich planter who was well educated, who had a lot of money. Well, he came here. (SM) *Tu vois ça fait de l'argent. C'est pas du monde de riche, mais c'est du monde qui fait de l'argent un peu.* You see, they make money. They're not rich people, but they're people who make a little money. (TB) ◊ •**riche comme Crésus** very wealthy <La99> •**les riches** the wealthy, the rich <Da84> <***Loc:*** LA, LF, SM, TB, Da84, Hi02, La99>

richement [riʃmɑ̃] *adj.* richly *Tu seras après vivre richement.* You will be living richly. (VM) <***Loc:*** VM, Da84>

richesse [riʃɛs] *n.f.* riches, wealth *On avait tout la richesse de manger qu'on voulait. On avait tout le manger naturel, on avait notre poulet à nous-autres-mêmes, on avait notre cochon à nous-autres-mêmes, on avait notre lait à nous-autres-mêmes.* We had all the abundance of food that we wanted. We had all the natural food, we had our own chicken, we had our own pig, we had our own milk. (LF) <***Loc:*** LF, Da84>

ricocher [rikoʃe] *v.intr.* to ricochet, rebound *Les plombs à Duhon ont ricoché tout partout dans sa chambre à coucher.* The lead pellets from Duhon's gun ricocheted all around his bedroom. (LA) <***Loc:*** LA, Da84>

ricochet [rikoʃe] *n.m.* ricochet, rebound <***Loc:*** Da84>

ricrac [rikrak] *n.* rickrack ◊ **•faire des ricracs** to do s.t. in order to make a good impression <SL, La99> <***Loc:*** SL, La99>

ride[1] [rid] *n.f.* wrinkle <***Loc:*** Da84>

RIDE[2] [ɹaɪd] *n.m./f.* ride, transportation, passage *J'ai un* RIDE *pour aller en Ville.* I have a ride to go to New Orleans. (VM) *Une chance dans dix, t'aurais un mille de* RIDE. One chance in ten that you'll get a mile's ride. (Lv88) <***Loc:*** JE, SL, VM, An94, Lv88>

RIDE[3] [ɹaɪd] **I** *v.tr.invar.* to ride *Quitte-moi* RIDE *ta* BICYCLE. Let me ride your bicycle. (VM) **II** *v.intr.invar.* to ride, take a ride *Tu veux* RIDE *avec nous-autres?* Do you want to ride with us? (VM) *Et tu as* RIDE *avec lui?* And you rode with him? (VM) *Il voulait aller* RIDE *dans le nouveau char.* He wanted to go for a ride in the new car. (Lv88) ◊ **•RIDE à cheval** to ride on horseback, ride a horse *Elle a été* RIDE *à cheval ce matin.* She went horseback riding this morning. (Lv88) <Lv88> <***Loc:*** EV, JE, LA, TB, VM, Lv88>

ridé, -e [ride] *adj.* wrinkled *Une personne qui reste au soleil de trop va venir tout ridée.* A person who stays too much in the sun will become all wrinkled. (LA) <***Loc:*** LA, Da84>

rideau [rido] *n.m.* curtain, shade <***Loc:*** AV, Da84>

ridelle (**aridelle**) [ridɛl, aridɛl] *n.f.* **1** railing (used to reinforce the top of a cab, truck, wagon, cart, etc.) **2** light rail (along the side of a cart) <***Loc:*** Da84, Lv88>

rider [ride] **I** *v.tr.* to wrinkle *Mets ton garde-soleil. Le soleil va rider ta figure.* Put on your sunbonnet. The sun will wrinkle your face. (VM) **II se rider** *v.pron.* to become wrinkled, shrivel up <***Loc:*** VM, Da84>

ridicule [ridikyl, redikyl] *adj.* ridiculous *Une idée ridicule.* A ridiculous idea. (VM) <***Loc:*** JD, VM, Da84>

ridiculer [ridikyle] *v.tr.* to ridicule, poke fun at *Si t'arrêtes pas de me ridiculer, je vas partir.* If you don't stop ridiculing me, I'll leave. (VM) <***Loc:*** VM, Da84>

rien[1] (**arien, à-rien**) [rjɛ̃, arjɛ̃] *n.m.* trifle ◊ **•un petit rien tout neuf** nonsensical response used to avoid answering questions (e.g. reply to a nosy child who asks "what's that?") <Da84, La99> <***Loc:*** JE, LA, SM, Da84, La99>

rien[2] (**arien, à-rien, erien**) [arjɛ̃, ərjɛ̃, rjɛ̃] *pron.indef.* nothing *Ça parle de trop mais ça dit pas rien.* They talk too much but they say nothing. (IB) *T'es pas malade. E-n'a pas arien avec toi.* You're not sick. There's nothing wrong with you. (SM) *J'ai pas rien fait.* I didn't do anything. (Lv88) *Et ça vous coûte pas arien.* And that costs you nothing. (EV) *Arien il fait à cet enfant-là.* He does nothing to this child. (Gu00) **Faire à-rien.* To do nothing. (Da84) *Arien, tout nu,* EXCEPT *sa paire de* TENNI'SHOES! Nothing, completely naked, except for his pair of tennis shoes! (Gu00) ◊ **•rien que / yanque / yienque / yinque** [rjɛ̃k, jɛ̃k] only, just **Il y a pas rien que toi pour moi aimer dans le pays icite.* There's only you for me to love in this country. (ch: *La vieille malheureuse*) *Y avait dans les deux, trois cents enfants pour rien qu'un maître d'école.* There were two, three hundred children for just one school teacher. (TB) *Ça c'est rien que B qui peut parler français.* Only B can speak French. (TB) *Il a yienque une piasse.* There's only one dollar. (SM) <EV, IB, LF, SL, SM, TB, Da84, Ph36> **•avoir rien à son épreuve *a*** to have no match, have no equal ***b*** to have nothing one would not do *Il a rien à son épreuve.* There's nothing he wouldn't do. (LF) <LF, Da84> **•ça fait (pas) rien** it's okay, it doesn't matter, it doesn't make any difference *On est comme quatrièmes cousins. Et là* WELL *asteur ça fait pas rien, je suis marié, et je vas pas aller me démarier parce qu'on est parents! Mame et pape est premiers cousins.* We are like fourth cousins. And, well, now it doesn't make any difference, I'm married, and I'm not going to go get unmarried just because we're related! Mom and Dad are first cousins. (LF) **Ça me fait pas rien.* It's okay by me. (Da84) **Ça me fait rien.* It doesn't bother me. (Da84) <LF, Da84> **•c'est (pas) rien** it's nothing (Da84) <Da84> **•de rien** you're welcome (in response to "thank you") <Da84, Hi02> **•être à rien faire** to be idle, do nothing <Da84> **•(pas) rien du tout** nothing at all **C'est rien du tout.* It's nothing at all. (Da84) **C'était eine 'tite accident d'arien du tout.* It was a little accident that was really nothing at all. (VM, Gu82) <VM, Da84, Gu82> **•plus . . . rien** nothing anymore *Il a mangé ça. Je pouvais plus faire rien.* He ate that. I couldn't do anything anymore. (SL) <SL> <***Loc:*** AC, EV, AV, EV, IV, JE, LA, LF, SL, SM, TB, VM, Da84, Gu00, Gu82, Hi02, Lv88>

riêne ♦see **rêne**

rienquetement (**yienquetement**) [rjɛ̃ktəmɑ̃, jɛ̃ktəmɑ̃] *adv.* only, exactly *C'est rienquetement ça!* That's exactly it! (TB) <***Loc:*** EV, TB, Ph36>

rifler [rifle] **I** *v.tr.* **1** to brush, graze, touch lightly *Il m'a riflé en passant.* He brushed me while passing by. (SM) *Oups, je l'ai riflé.* Oops, I brushed up against him. (VM) *Il a riflé mon char.* He grazed my car. (Lv88) **2** to have a close call (with adversity) *Ç'a riflé qu'il se fasse tuer.* He almost got himself killed. (SM) *Il a riflé la mort.* He had a brush with death. (SM) *Ça c'est rifler la mort, hein?* That was a close call with death, wasn't it? (VM) **II** *v.intr.* to almost (do s.t.) *J'ai riflé échapper le verre.* I almost dropped the glass. (Lv88) <***Loc:*** EV, IB, JE, LF, SB, SL, SM, TB, VM, Da84, Lv88, Ph36>

riflette [riflɛt] *n.f.* edge *Il a marché sur la riflette de la fenêtre.* He walked on the edge of the window. (SB) <***Loc:*** SB>

riflure [riflyr] *n.f.* scratch *Il avait deux ou trois riflures sus ses mains.* He had two or three scratches on his hands. (TB) <***Loc:*** JE, TB>

RIG [rig, ɹɪg] *n.m.* **1** oil rig **2** rig <***Loc:*** Lv88>

rigolet [rigolɛ, rigole] *n.m.* **1** drill, small furrow or trench for planting seeds *Le rigolet est plein d'eau.* The drill is full of water. (IB) **2** small trench, channel, drain (to drain an area) **3** rivulet, small stream <***Loc:*** AV, IB, SJ, VM, Da84, Lv88>

rikiki ♦see **riquiqui**

rime [rim] *n.m./f.* rhyme **Ç'a ni rime ni bon sens.* This has neither rhyme nor reason, this doesn't make sense. (Da84) ◊ **•faire pas de rime** to not make sense *Ça fait pas de rime.* That doesn't make any sense. (VM) <TB, VM> <***Loc:*** TB, VM, Da84, Gr86>

rimer [rime] *v.intr.* **1** to rhyme **2** to make sense **Ça rime pas.* It doesn't make sense. (Da84) <***Loc:*** Da84>

rimpinpin [rɛ̃pɛ̃pɛ̃] *n.m.* ◊ **•habillé sur le rimpinpin** dressed up smartly <LF> <***Loc:*** LF>

rinçage [rɛ̃saʒ] *n.m.* rinsing <***Loc:*** Da84>

rincée (**rancée**) [rɛ̃se] *n.f.* **1** beating, thrashing, whipping, spanking *Tu vas attraper une bonne rincée équand tu rentres chez toi.* You're going to get a good thrashing when you get home. (VM) *Je l'ai foutu une rincée.* I gave him a beating. (SM) **2** sudden and short downpour <***Loc:*** AV, JD, SM, VM, Da84, La99, Lv88>

rincer[1] (**rancer, rinser**) [rɛ̃se] **I** *v.tr.* to rinse *Et t'avais une baille pour frotter, l'autre baille pour rincer.* And you had one washtub for scrubbing, the other for rinsing. (TB) **II se rincer** *v.pron.* to rinse o.s. *T'as pas fini de te rinser?* You're not finished rinsing yourself off? (LA) **Se rincer la bouche.* To rinse one's mouth. (Da84) ◊ **•rincer ses yeux** to ogle, stare longingly at *Une jolie fille entrait et les hommes rinçaient leurs yeux et se disaient: "C'est pas une vache, non, ça!"* A pretty girl came in and the men stared at her and said to each other, "She's certainly not ugly!" (Gr86) <Gr86> <***Loc:*** LA, TB, Da84, Gr86>

rincer[2] (**rancer, rinser**) [rɛ̃se] *v.tr.* to beat, thrash, whip *Je l'ai assez rincé pour ça il a fait quand même.* Anyway I gave him a pretty good whipping for what he did. (VM) <***Loc:*** AL, EV, VM, Da84, La99, Lv88>

rinçure (**rançure**) [rɛ̃syr, rɑ̃syr] *n.f.* beating, whipping, thrashing **Mon père il prenait sa ceinture et il m'donnait une bonne rinçure.* My father took his belt and he gave me a good whipping. (Gr86) <***Loc:*** EV, Gr86, La99>

ringe [rɛ̃ʒ] *n.f.* cud (of ruminants) <***Loc:*** VM>

ringer [rɛ̃ʒe] *v.intr.* to chew cud *La vache est après ringer.* The cow is chewing her cud. (VM) <***Loc:*** JE, VM, Di32>

rinser ♦see **rincer**

rinstaller ♦see **réinstaller**

rinviter [rɛ̃vite] *v.tr.* to invite again, reinvite, invite back <***Loc:*** EV, IB, Ph36>

ripage [ripaʒ] *n.m.* wood shavings <***Loc:*** Da84>

ripe [rip] *n.f.* wood shaving *Les enfants font des boucles avec les ripes.* The children make curls with the wood shavings. (SM) <***Loc:*** EV, IB, JE, SB, SL, SM, TB, VM, Da84, Lv88, Ph36>

ripopée [ripope] *n.f.* **1** mob, gang, rabble *Y'a une ripopée d'monde dehors.* There's a gang of people outside. (SM) **2** bunch of noisy or annoying children *Elle s'en vient avec une ripopée d'enfants.* She's coming with a gang of children. (SL) **3** crowd, following *Il était suivi d'une ripopée de chiens.* He was being followed by a large pack of dogs. (IB) **4** rubbish, nonsense *C'est de la ripopée ce qu'il te dit là.* What he told you is a bunch of nonsense. (SB) <***Loc:*** IB, SB, SJ, SL, SM, Da84, Lv88>

ripopette [ripopɛt] *n.f.* **1** large number of children in a single family **2** crowd, following *Je vois cette ripopette qui vient.* I see that large crowd coming. (IB) <***Loc:*** IB, SM>

riquiqui[1] (**rikiki**) [rikiki] *n.m./f.* **1** person of short stature, runt **2** imbecile, nitwit **3** poor, wretched, ill-clad person **Une famille de riquiquis.* A family of poor, ill-clad people. (Re38) <***Loc:*** EV, SM, VM, Da84, Lv88, Re38>

riquiqui[2] (**rikiki**) [rikiki] *n.m.* large group, crowd **...me laissent une riquiqui d'enfants à élever toute seule....* leave me with a bunch of kids to raise alone. (SM, Ca83) *Ce riquiqui est après jouer là dans la rue.* That crowd is playing out there in the street. (VM) <***Loc:*** IB, SM, VM, Ca83>

riquiqui[3] (**rikiki**) [rikiki] *n.m. (usu. pl.)* the giggles *Qui il y a avec toi? T'as les rikikis?* What's wrong with you? Do you have the giggles? (EV) **Mais il a l'riquiquis, lui! Qui c'est qu'il [=qui le] chatouille?* He sure has the giggles! What's tickling him? (EV, Ph36) <***Loc:*** EV, Ph36, Re38>

rire[1] [rir] *v.intr.* **1** to laugh **Allons à la cantine, O boire et bien rire, et bien se divertir, O nous et nos amis.* Let's go to the canteen, oh to drink and laugh hard and have a real good time, oh we and our friends. (ch: *Si j'aurais des ailes*) **2** to smile *Il a manière ri pour se prendre en portrait.* He barely smiled for his picture. (LA) ◊ **•rire après {de}** to laugh at *Je lui ai fait l'école jusqu'à que sa sœur a venu, alle a commencé à rire après lui et à dire que, oh, c'était un déshonneur de ça qu'il était après faire.* I taught him school until his sister came, she began to laugh at him and to say that, oh, what he was doing was a dishonor. (TB) *Et mes deux plus vieux eusse avait peur de parler français, peur que ça disait pas les bonnes paroles et qu'on allait rire après eux.* And my two oldest ones were afraid to speak French, afraid they weren't saying the right words and that we would laugh at them. (LF) <LF, TB> **•rire à se foutre par terre** to laugh very heartily <La99> **•rire comme un fou** to laugh heartily, laugh like crazy **On faisait des farces, on riait côme des fous.* We would tell jokes, we would laugh like crazy. (Gu82) <Gu82, La99> **•rire dans sa barbe** to laugh up one's sleeve, laugh to o.s. <Da84> <***Loc:*** EV, LA, LF, SL, TB, Da84, Hi02, La99>

rire[2] [rir] *n.m.* laugh, laughter <***Loc:*** Da84>

ris [ri] *n.m.pl.* sweetbread *Dehors, ça faisait de la fricassée, là ça cuisait du foie, et de la rate et ça ils appellent les ris étaient beaucoup bon pour manger moi* COWBOY STEW. Outside, they were preparing some stew, they were cooking liver and spleen, and what they call the sweetbreads were really good to eat, goodness me, cowboy stew. (AC) <***Loc:*** AC, VM, Da84>

risable ♦see **risible**

risée [rize] *n.f.* laughingstock ◊ **•faire une risée de soi-même** to make a laughingstock of o.s. <Lv88> <***Loc:*** Lv88>

risible (**risable**) [rizib(l), rizab(l)] *adj.* ridiculous, funny, laughable *C'était risible, la manière qu'il a raconté ça.* It was funny, the way he recounted that. (VM) <***Loc:*** SB, TB, VM, Da84>

risque [ris(k)] *n.m.* risk, chance, hazard <***Loc:*** Da84>

risqué, -e [riske] *adj.* risky, hazardous *Et il voulait pas qu'on travaille avec pas de l'assurance dessus. C'était trop risqué.* And he didn't want us to work with no insurance. It was too risky. (TB) <***Loc:*** TB, Da84>

risquer [riske] **I** *v.tr.* to risk, venture, take a chance **Il dit, "Je peux pas risquer d'offenser ce bon monde. Ils sont trop bons pour moi."* He said, "I can't risk offending those people. They are too good to me." (LA, An94) **II se risquer** *v.pron.* to risk o.s., take one's chances *Je vas me risquer. J'ai rien à perdre.* I'll take my chances. I have nothing to lose. (LA) <***Loc:*** LA, An94, Da84>

risqueux, -euse [riskø, -øz] *adj.* imprudent, rash *C'est trop risqueux, ça.* That's too imprudent. (VM) <***Loc:*** JE, VM>

river [rive] *v.tr.* to rivet, clinch *River une crampe.* To rivet a staple. (LA) <***Loc:*** LA, Da84>

rivet [rivɛ, rive] *n.m.* rivet <***Loc:*** Da84>

riveter [rivte] *v.tr.* to rivet, clinch *Riveter une crampe.* To rivet a staple. (VM) <***Loc:*** VM, Da84>

riveur [rivœr] *n.m.* riveter <***Loc:*** Da84>

rivière [rivjær] *n.f.* **1** river *Avant qu'eux-autres fait des levées pour arrêter l'eau de passer par dessus les bords de la rivière, eh ben y avait une grande différence la manière que la terre était ici.* Before they made levees to stop the water from going over the riverbanks, well there was a big difference in how the land was around here. (TB) **J'étais après marcher au long de la rivière. J'étais après jongler à ça qu'avait arrivé.* I was walking along the river. I was thinking about what had happened. (ch: *Juste un rêve*) **2** large bayou, large stream <***Loc:*** AV, EV, LA, SL, SM, TB, VM, Da84, Gu00, Hi02, Lv88>

riz [ri] *n.m.* rice ◊ **•riz de l'âne {de long}** any of various wild grasses such as barnyard grass, water grass, cockspur grass (locally called wild millet or wild rice, although of the grass family and not true rice) <Ho90, Re31> **•riz farouche {sauvage}** any of various wild grasses such as barnyard grass, water grass, cockspur grass (locally called wild millet or wild rice, although of the grass family and not true rice) <Da84, Ho90, Re31> **•riz de providence** rice raised without benefit of irrigation (i.e. depending on providence for rain) <Da84> <***Loc:*** CL, EV, SL, SM, TB, VM, Da84, Hi02, Ho90, Re31>

robal [robal] *n.m.* whiting (locally called channel mullet or southern kingfish) <***Loc:*** LF>

robe [rɔb] *n.f.* **1** dress, gown *Il fait des côtés de quilts avec les retailles de les vieilles robes qu'ils ont fait longtemps passé.* He makes the sides of quilts with remnants of old dresses that they made a long time ago. (SM) **Taille ta robe de mode à parasol.* Tailor your dress in the parasol style. (ch: *La robe à parasol*) **2** robe **3** corn husk, corn shuck **4** veil surrounding a hornet's nest ◊ **•robe de maïs** corn husk *Jette les robes de maïs aux vaches.* Throw the corn shucks to the cows. (SB) <SB, SL, SM, Da84> **•robe de noces** wedding dress *Ça se mettait comme une robe de noces, ou ça mettait des habillements, ça se masquait avec du linge qu'eux-autres avait pas avant, tu connais pour pas que le monde les reconnaît.* They [Mardi Gras revelers] would put on like a wedding dress, or they would put on garments, they were disguising themselves with clothes they didn't have before, you know, so people wouldn't recognize them. (TB) <TB> **•robe de nuit** nightgown <LF> **•grande robe** long dress *Ça mettait des grandes robes qui traînaient au plancher.* They used to wear long dresses that dragged on the floor. (SL) <SL> **•petite robe** skirt **Oh, Alice, va, donc, mettre ta 'tite robe de grandes barrés, 'garde donc, quoi c'qui vient.* Oh, Alice, so go put on your little skirt with the big stripes, for look who's coming. (ch: *Chère Alice*) <SL> <***Loc:*** AC, EV, JE, LF, SB, SL, SM, TB, VM, Da84, Hi02, Lv88>

robinet [robinɛ, robine, rubinɛ, rubine] *n.m.* faucet, tap <***Loc:*** EV, LA, TB, Da84, Hi02>

robio [robjo] *n.m.* simpleton, nitwit <***Loc:*** LF>

robuste [robys(t)] *adj.* robust, strong, solid *Sa femme est pas grosse, elle est juste robuste. Et tu parles de robuste! Elle pourrait haler une herse.* His wife isn't fat, she's just solid. And talk about solid! She could pull a harrow. (LA) <***Loc:*** AV, LA, Da84>

roccuper ♦see **réoccuper**

rocher [roʃe] *n.m.* large rock <***Loc:*** Da84, Lv88>

rôdailler [rodaje] *v.intr.* **1** to gallivant, run around *Il veut rôdailler tout le temps.* He wants to run around all the time. (VM) *Okay, la femme qui est en famille, c'est ça la raison il y a autant de petits qui naît pas comme il faut, eux-autres ça va, ça prend le* DOPE, *ça prend le* DRINK *de whiskey, et euh... ça ça rôdaille tout la nuit.* Okay, the woman who is pregnant, that's the reason there are so many children who are born with birth defects, they go, they take drugs, they drink whiskey, they run around all night. (EV) **2** to roam, wander, drift *Il rôdaillait d'un bord et de l'autre.* He drifted back and forth. (LA) **3** to travel a great deal *Je peux pus rôdailler comme avant depuis que j'ai eu mes enfants.* I can't run the roads like I used to since I had my children. (EV) <***Loc:*** AV, EV, JE, LA, LF, SB, SL, SM, TB, VM, Da84, Lv88>

rôdailleur, -euse [rodajœr, -øz] *n.* **1** one who gallivants or runs around **2** one who runs around rather than taking care of responsibilities **3** roamer, rover, rambler, wanderer, drifter, vagabond *Le shérif, c'est pour les rôdailleurs, les batailleurs.* The sheriff, he handles the vagrants and the brawlers.

(Lv88) <*Loc:* AV, JE, LF, SB, SL, SM, TB, VM, Da84, Lv88>

rodaire (**rodère**) [rodær] *n.m.* corral, pen for gathering animals (for selling, branding, etc.) <*Loc:* JE, LF, VM, Di32, Lv88>

rode [rɔd] *n.* ◊ **•être en rode** to be on the go *Il est tout le temps en rode.* He's always on the go. (LF) <LF> <*Loc:* LF>

rodéo [rodeo] *n.m.* **1** rodeo **2** fishing rodeo, sportfishing competition *Y a un rodéo l'autre boutte ou qui?* There's a fishing rodeo over there or what? (TB) <*Loc:* TB>

rôder [rode] *v.intr.* **1** to gallivant, run around *Il est après rôder. Il est pas ici.* He's out gallivanting around. He's not here. (SM) **2** to roam about, prowl, be on the prowl **3** to travel a great deal *J'ai pas pris ce job parce qu'il aurait faulu je rôde de trop.* I didn't take that job because I would've had to travel too much. (EV) <*Loc:* EV, SM, Da84>

rodère ♦see **rodaire**

rôdeur, -euse [rodœr, -øz] *n.m.* **1** one who gallivants or runs around **2** one who roams or prowls around **3** one who is always on the move *Elle passe son temps à aller et revenir de la ville. C'est une vraie rôdeuse.* She spends her time going back and forth to New Orleans. She's always on the move. (SM) <*Loc:* SM, Da84>

rodingot [rodɛ̃go] *n.m.* frock coat <*Loc:* AV>

rogation [rogasjɔ̃] *n.f.* [*eccl.*] rogation days <*Loc:* Da84>

rognon [rɔ̃jɔ̃, hɔ̃jɔ̃] *n.m.* **1** flank, side of ribs **2** kidney <*Loc:* IB, JE, LF, TB, Da84>

rogoyo [rogojo] *n.* mischievous person <*Loc:* VM>

roi[1] [rwa] *n.m.* **1** king **2** Mardi Gras king *Çula-là qu'était mon roi, il est mort, pauvre Claude. Il est mort y a deux ans. Il est mort d'un* ANEURYSM. The one who was my king [at Mardi Gras] died, poor Claude. He died two years ago. He died of an aneurysm. (TB) **3** king (in a deck of cards) **4** prairie king snake **5** king mackerel ◊ **•roi Bertaud** wren <Lv88, Re54> <*Loc:* EV, IV, JE, LF, TB, VM, Da84, Hi02, Lv88, Re54>

roi[2] [rwa] *n.m.* spinning wheel <*Loc:* VM>

roitelet (**rotelet, lotret**) [rwatle, rɔtle, rotle, lɔtle, lotre] *n.m.* wren <*Loc:* AV, JE, TB, Re31>

roler [role] *v.tr.* **1** to roll up, roll *Roler un tortignon.* To roll up a bun (hairstyle). (VM) **2** to tuck in (a bedsheet) *Role ce drap bien.* Tuck in that sheet well. (IB) <*Loc:* EV, IB, JE, VM, Da84, Di32>

rolet [role] *n.m.* small roll of wool or cotton thread <*Loc:* JE, Di32, Lv88>

rolle [rɔl] *n.f.* heavy roller used for crushing sugar cane, cane-crusher <*Loc:* IB, SJ>

rolon [rolɔ̃] *n.m.* **1** rounded log *Dans les vieux temps, le monde déménageait des bâtisses. Ça aurait mis des rolons en-dessous et ça l'aurait halé avec des mulets.* In the old days, people used to move buildings. They would put rounded logs underneath and they would pull it with mules. (LA) **2** small tree limb, cut and placed over a bad road *Je vais passer sur la manche à rolons.* I'm going to cross over on the path with the improvised causeway. (SM) <*Loc:* IB, LA, SM, VM, Di32, Lv88>

romaine [rɔ̃mɛ̃n] *n.f.* **1** *(usu. pl.)* scale, balance, counterbalance scale *T'avais une planche sur le wagon, d'attachée, et les romaines, et tu pesais et tu le vidais dans le wagon.* You had a board on the wagon, attached to it, and the scales, and you would weigh [as you were loading] and you filled up the wagon [that way]. (SL) **2** loose dress resembling a priest's cassock ◊ **•romaine à viande** meat scale, deli scale *Une romaine à viande, c'est la romaine est carrée comme ça. Elle a une petite tablette en haut. Tu mets un bassin et tu pèses ce tu veux.* A meat scale, it's a scale that's about this big of a square. It has a little platform on top. You put a pan [on it] and measure how much you want. (AC) <AC> <*Loc:* AC, SL, SM, VM, Da84, Di32, Lv88>

roman [rɔ̃mɑ̃] *n.m.* novel, romance <*Loc:* Da84>

ronce ♦see **éronce**

rond[1]**, -e** [rɔ̃, rɔ̃d] *adj.* **1** round, circular **Et c'était un marais rond et les canards étaient posés tout le tour au ras de l'écore.* And it was a round pond and the ducks were all around next to the bank. (AC, An94) *Des danses rondes.* Round dances. (SM) *Le chien est assez gros, garde, il est rond!* The dog is so fat he's round! (VM) **2** plump **3** drunk **Il est rond, il a eu quat coups.* He's drunk, he's had four shots. (EV, Ph36) ◊ **•en rond** in a circle <SM> **•tout rond** whole *Il a envalé ça tout rond.* He swallowed it whole. (LA) <LA, Da84> **•se coucher tout rond** to go to bed with all one's clothes on *Il faisait assez froid hier au soir, je m'ai couché tout rond.* It was so cold last night that I went to bed with all my clothes on. (VM) <VM, Da84> <*Loc:* AC, EV, IB, LA, LF, SL, SM, TB, VM, An94, Da84, Fa77, Hi02, La99>

rond[2] [rɔ̃] *n.m.* circle, ring *Les deux batailleurs se sont empoignés un et l'autre au milieu du grand rond.* The two fighters grabbed each other in the middle of the ring. (LA) ◊ **•faire grand rond** to form a big ring, clear out an area (to make room for a fight about to take place) <Da84> <*Loc:* LA, TB, Da84, Hi02>

ronde [rɔ̃d, rɔ̃n, rɑ̃d, rɑ̃n] *n.f.* radius **Pour dix miles à la ronde.* For a radius of ten miles. (Da84) <*Loc:* JD, Da84>

rondelle [rɔ̃dɛl] *n.f.* **1** ring, circular object **2** washer (for a screw or bolt) ◊ **•rondelle d'oignon** onion ring <JD> <*Loc:* JD, Da84>

rondeur [rɔ̃dœr] *n.f.* roundness <*Loc:* Da84>

rondin [rɔ̃dɛ̃] *n.m.* **1** round handle **2** small piece of wood *Il a ramassé seulement les rondins.* He only collected the small pieces of wood. (SB) <*Loc:* EV, SB>

rondinage [rɔ̃dinaʒ] *n.m.* scolding, reprimand *Donner un rondinage à quelqu'un.* To give someone a good scolding. (SJ) <*Loc:* SJ>

rondiner [rɔ̃dine] *v.tr.* **1** to make round *Je veux rondiner ce* *morceau de bois.* I want to make that piece of wood round. (IB) **2** to scold <*Loc:* AV, IB, SJ>

ronflement [rɔ̃fləmɑ̃] *n.m.* **1** snoring **2** humming (e.g. of machinery) <*Loc:* Da84>

ronfler [rɔ̃fle] *v.intr.* **1** to snore **Ça se fait, ils se sont couchés, et le vieux-là, ça a pas été cinq minutes avant il a commencé à ronfler.* So, they went to bed, and the old man, it was no more than five minutes before he started snoring. (EV, An94) *Réveille-toi et rendors-toi; tu ronfles!* Wake up and go back to sleep; you're snoring! (LA) **2** to hum, whir (e.g. of a machine) **3** to whiz *La bataille a commencé. Les balles ronflaient dans l'air.* The battle started. Bullets whizzed through the air. (Gr86) <*Loc:* EV, An94, Da84, Gr86>

ronfleur, -euse [rɔ̃flœr, -øz] *n.* snorer <*Loc:* Da84>

ronger [rɔ̃ʒe] *v.tr.* to gnaw *Les rats ont tout rongé mes soliveaux.* The rats chewed my beams all up. (EV) <*Loc:* EV, Da84>

rongeur [rɔ̃ʒœr] *n.m.* rodent <*Loc:* Da84>

ronquouin [rɔ̃kwɛ̃] *n.m.* one-testicled animal *Ça c'est un bon veau, mais celui-là c'est un ronquouin.* That's a good calf, but that one's one-testicled. (SM) <*Loc:* SM>

ronron [rɔ̃rɔ̃] *n.m.* purring <*Loc:* Da84>

ronronnement [rɔ̃rɔ̃nmɑ̃] *n.m.* purring <*Loc:* Da84>

ronronner [rɔ̃rɔ̃ne] *v.intr.* to purr *Un chat qui ronronne.* A cat that purrs. (LA) <*Loc:* LA, Da84>

root-bière [rutbjær] *n.m.* root beer <*Loc:* LF, TB>

rôquelaure [roklɔr] *n.* good-for-nothing **Ces hommes sont des rôquelaures.* Those guys are good for nothing. (EV, Ph36) <*Loc:* EV, Ph36>

roquer [roke] *v.tr.* **1** to hit *Je l'ai roqué sur la tête.* I hit him in the head. (Lv88) **2** to whip, beat **Pape m'a rôqué pass qué [=parce que] j'avais bu.* Dad beat me because I had drunk booze. (EV, Ph36) <*Loc:* EV, IB, SM, Lv88, Ph36>

roqueter [rokte] *v.tr.* to win hands down, take all the winnings in (a game) *Jean a bien roqueté le jeu à soir.* John won everything tonight hands down. (IB) <*Loc:* IB>

roquette [rokɛt] *n.f.* roquette, arugula <*Loc:* Da84>

rordonner ♦see **réordonner**

rosaire [rozær] *n.m.* rosary, rosary beads <*Loc:* Da84>

rose[1] [roz] *adj./n.* pink (color) *Elle m'avait fait la plus jolie robe rose.* She had made me the prettiest pink dress. (EV) *Tu vois dans la dernière patte? Tu regardes, il a une ligne, soit il va être blanc, rose ou rouge. Et quand il est rouge, il est paré, dans pas longtemps, un à trois jours, il change de peau.* You see on its [the crab's] hind leg? You examine it, it has a line, either it will be white, or pink, or red. When it is red, he's ready, in a not very long time, one to three days, he will molt. (TB) <*Loc:* EV, TB, Da84, Hi02>

rose[2] [roz] *n.f.* rose ◊ **•rose de montagne** rosa de montana <VM> <*Loc:* JD, SL, VM, Da84, Hi02>

roseau [rozo] *n.m.* any of various types of reed or cane, such as common reed grass and marsh cane ◊ **•roseau de cochon** smooth cordgrass <Ho90> **•roseau d'Egypte** mariposa lily <VM> <*Loc:* VM, Da84, Gu00, Ho90, Lv88>

rosée [roze] *n.f.* dew <*Loc:* VM, Da84>

roséole [rozeɔl] *n.f.* roseola, German measles <*Loc:* EV, Da84>

rosette [rozɛt] *n.f.* bow, rosette *Des petites rosettes pour mettre dessus chaque côté de le* MANTLE. *Pour le* SHOWER *samedi.* Little rosettes to put on each side of the mantle. For the shower Saturday. (TB) <*Loc:* TB, Da84>

rosier [rozje] *n.m.* rosebush ◊ **•rosier filant** climbing rosebush <VM> <*Loc:* EV, VM, Da84>

rosine [rozin] *n.f.* **1** rosin, resin *Il y avait de la rosine sus le morceau de bois.* There was resin on the piece of wood. (TB) **2** line with metal resonator hung around a house as part of a traditional prank *Des années passées, quand on était manière pour faire peur à quelqu'un, ils allaient, ils prenaient une ligne entour de la maison, ils attachaient ça sur du zinc, ça frottait et ça sonnait comme des petits chats après se battre là, quand une veuve ou un veuf se mariait, ils allaient jouer la rosine, c'était une vieille coutume entour d'ici.* Years ago, when people wanted to sort of scare someone, they would go and set a string around the house, they would tie it up to a piece of metal, it would rub and make noise like small cats fighting, when a widow or a widower got married, people would 'play the rosine,' it was an old custom around here. (IB) <*Loc:* IB, TB, VM>

rot [rɔt] *n.m.* belch <*Loc:* Da84>

rotelet ♦see **roitelet**

roter [rote] *v.intr.* to belch **Nagok traitait ein cheval gonflé par lui donner juste du foin sec à manger ou par emmarer ein petit morceaux de bois en travers de sa geuele [=gueule] pour le tchein [=tiendre] ouvert pour le faire rôter [=roter] et l'aider a dégonfler.* Nagok treated a bloated horse by giving it only dry hay to eat or by tying a small piece of wood through his mouth to keep it open and make him belch and help him deflate. (Wh83) <*Loc:* Da84, Wh83>

rôti (**routi**) [ruti] *n.m.* **1** roast *C'était tout le temps de les volailles. Ou c'était du roûti de cochon.* It was always chickens. Or it was roast pork. (LF) **2** a share of assorted meats from community slaughtering *Un rôti, c'est des gratons et du boudin et […] un assemblage de viande. Chacun avait sa part.* A "rôti," that's cracklings and boudin sausage and an assortment of [other] meats. Each one [of us] had a portion. (SL) **3** community roast *On donnait des rôtis, tu connais. Mais c'était tout le temps des cochons qu'étaient gros comme moi proche.* We organized community roasts, you know. And there were always pigs that were almost as big as me. (LA) **4** portion of meat <*Loc:* AC, AV, JE, LA, LF, SB, SL, SM, TB, VM, Da84, Lv88>

rôtie (**routie**) [ruti] *n.f.* roast chicken *De la routie.* Some roast chicken. (AC) <*Loc:* AC>

rôtir (**routir**) [rotir, rutir, rutje] **I** *v.tr.* **1** to roast, broil *Il a routi* *la poule.* He roasted the chicken. (SM) *J'ai oublié d'amener la poule roûtie.* I forgot to bring the roast chicken. (LF) **2** to fry *Alle m'a rôti un bœuf.* She fried up a beef steak for me. (VM) *Je vas me routir des œufs.* I'm going to fry some eggs for myself. (VM) **3** to deep fry *Du poulet rôti.* Fried chicken. (SL) **4** to brown, cook *Il faut tu rôtis ta viande bien bien jaune pour faire une bonne sauce.* You have to really brown your meat well to make a good gravy. (LA) **II** *v.intr.* to get too hot, 'roast' *On a routi devant le feu.* We roasted in front of the fire. (SM) ◊ **•faire rôtir** to roast <Da84> <***Loc:*** LA, SL, SM, VM, Da84>

rôtisserie [rotisri] *n.f.* roaster, grill <***Loc:*** Da84>

roucheter [ruʃte] *v.tr.* to whip, beat *Le nègre a rouchеté ce bougre.* The negro beat that fellow. (IB) <***Loc:*** IB>

roue [ru] *n.f.* **1** wheel *Il avait une voiture, une bonne voiture. Et il allait peut-être 30, 40 milles à l'heure. Peut-être moins. Là il a une roue qui s'a dévissé avant qu'il peuve arrêter la voiture, et il a usé le* HUB *éiou tu visses là.* He had a car, a good car. And it would go 30 or 40 mph. Perhaps less. Then he had a wheel that came unscrewed before he could stop the car, and he used the hub where you screw it on there [to stop]. (TB) **2** steering wheel ◊ **•la roue tourne** things change, time marches on <AV, La99> <***Loc:*** AV, JE, SM, TB, VM, Da84, Hi02, La99, Lv88>

roué, -e [rwe] *adj.* sharp, cunning, smart *Un enfant roué.* A sharp child. (LA) <***Loc:*** LA, Da84>

rouette [rwɛt, ruwɛt] *n.m./f.* spinning wheel <***Loc:*** LA, VM, Lv88>

roufian, -e [rufjɑ̃, -ɑ̃n] *n.* meddler, busybody <***Loc:*** LF>

roufianer [rufjɑ̃ne] *v.intr.* to butt in, meddle *Il est après roufianer dans tes affaires.* He's meddling in your business. (LF) <***Loc:*** LF>

roufianeur, -euse [rufjɑ̃nœr, -øz] *n.* meddler, busybody <***Loc:*** LF>

rougarou ♦see **loup-garou**

rouge[1] [ruʒ] *adj./n.* red (color) *Les grosses fourmis rouges font des buttes de terre et mordent.* The big red ants make anthills and bite. (Gu00) *Elle porte une robe barreautée rouge et blanc.* She is wearing a red and white striped dress. (SB) ◊ **•rouge comme une bête rouge / rouge comme une betterave {une écrevisse / une tomate / un piment}** very red <AV, SM, La99> **•rouge comme un écarlate** scarlet-colored <AV, SJ> <***Loc:*** AC, AV, EV, IB, IV, LA, LF, SB, SJ, SL, SM, TB, VM, An94, Da84, Gu00, Hi02, La99, Lv88>

rouge[2] [ruʒ] *n.m.* rouge, blusher, make-up applied to the cheeks <***Loc:*** Da84>

rougeâtre [ruʒat(r)] *adj.* reddish *Le plus vieux qu'un cipre est, plus le rougeâtre que le bois va être. Ça c'est du bois qu'est coupé jeune, et il est toujours plein blanc.* The older a cypress is, the more reddish the wood will be. That is wood that was cut young, so it's still quite white. (LF) <***Loc:*** LF, Da84, Gr86>

rougelles [ruʒɛl] *n.f.pl.* measles *Le thé de sassafras est bon pour les rougelles.* Sassafras tea is good for the measles. (TB) <***Loc:*** TB>

rougeole [ruʒɔl] *n.f.* measles *J'ai resté trois mois et trois semaines dans l'hôpital avec la rougeole.* I stayed for three months and three weeks in the hospital with the measles. (TB) <***Loc:*** AV, IB, LA, SM, TB, Da84>

rougette [ruʒɛt] *adj.* having a reddish coat (of a cow; by extension, name for a reddish-colored cow) *Une taure rougette.* A reddish colored heifer. (VM) <***Loc:*** SM, VM, Da84>

rougeur [ruʒœr] *n.f.* redness <***Loc:*** Da84>

ROUGH [ɹʌf, rɔf] *adj.* **1** rough, coarse *Un couteau à deux manches. Ça c'était usé habitudement sur le dehors d'un bateau, d'un petit bateau pour faire de l'ouvrage* ROUGH. *C'était pas de l'ouvrage finie, c'était de l'ouvrage* ROUGH *que tu usais ça.* A two-handled draw knife. That was usually used on the outside of a boat, of a little boat for rough work. It wasn't delicate work, it was rough work that you used that for. (LF) **2** rude, surly *C'est un homme* ROUGH. He's a rough man. (VM) **3** difficult, challenging *Quand c'est* ROUGH, *il faut marcher.* When times are tough, you have to keep moving ahead. (VM) <***Loc:*** JE, LF, TB, VM, Di32, Lv88>

rougir [ruʒir] **I** *v.tr.* to redden *Mon père m'a rougi le derrière.* My father reddened my behind. (LA) **II** *v.intr.* to blush *Awhh, M. LeBlanc, tu vas me faire rougir.* Aw, Mr. LeBlanc, you're going to make me blush. (ThCa: *Messieurs, mesdames…*) <***Loc:*** LA, Da84, ThCa>

rouille [ruj] *n.f.* rust <***Loc:*** Da84>

rouiller [ruje] **I** *v.tr.* to rust, cause to rust *L'eau salée a tout rouillé la serrure de ma porte.* The salt water rusted my door lock. (VM) **II** *v.intr.* to rust, become rusty *Ils ont commencé à faire ça avec du fer. Le fer a commencé à rouiller, c'était pas bon, asteur, ils faisont ça avec du plastique.* They started making it with iron. The iron started to rust, it wasn't good, and now they make it with plastic. (LF) **III se rouiller** *v.pron.* to rust, become rusty *Si c'est pas* GALVANIZE, *ça se rouille aisé.* If it's not galvanized, it rusts easily. (LA) <***Loc:*** LA, LF, VM, Da84>

rouillure [rujyr] *n.f.* rustiness, rusty spot <***Loc:*** Da84>

rouin [rwɛ̃] *n.m.* track, rut (made by wheels) *Ils ont sui les rouins de mon boguet.* They followed the tracks of my carriage. (Lv88) *Les roues de wagons et de bogheis faisaient des rouins dedans la boue quand il mouillait.* The wheels of wagons and carriages made ruts in the mud when it rained. (Gu00) *Les rouins sont assez creux par icite.* The ruts in the road are pretty deep here. (VM) <***Loc:*** VM, Da84, Gu00, Lv88>

roulage [rulaʒ] *n.m.* **1** act of rolling **2** transporting of wood, cane, etc. **3** grinding of sugar cane *Le roulage de cannes a occupé plein de monde.* The cane grinding occupied a lot of people. (TB) <***Loc:*** JE, TB, VM, Da84, Di32, Lv88>

roulailler [rulaje] *v.intr.* **1** to roll, roll around *Il s'a tout roulaillé* *dans l'herbe.* He rolled all around in the grass. (TB) **2** to run around, gallivant, gad about *Roulailler d'un bord et de l'autre, je connais p'us comment je vas faire.* Running around here and there, I don't know any longer how I'm going to make it (ch: *Je peux pas t'oublier*) *Il aura jamais rien parce qu'il roulaille tout le temps.* He'll never have anything because he gads about too much. (SL) <***Loc:*** SB, SL, TB, Da84, Hi02, Lv88>

roulailleur, -euse [rulajœr, -øz] *n.* wanderer <***Loc:*** Da84>

roulaison [rulezɔ̃] *n.f.* **1** sugar cane harvest *Je vais faire la roulaison à* ST. JOHN. I'll work the sugar cane harvest in St. John Parish. (SM) **2** sugar harvesting and grinding season *Eh ben eusse allait alentour de Opelousas et Lafayette et tout chercher des hommes. Et eusse avait des petites maisons, des petites cabanes manière que eusse restait là dans le temps de la roulaison.* And, well, they went around Opelousas and Lafayette and all looking for men. And they would have little houses, little cabins, like what they lived in during the time of the cane harvesting season. (LF) <***Loc:*** AV, IB, JE, LF, SB, SJ, SL, SM, TB, VM, Da84, Gr86, Hi02, Lv88>

rouleau [rulo] *n.m.* **1** roll, coil, spool *Oublie pas d'acheter un rouleau de fil pour faire ta robe.* Don't forget to buy a spool of thread to make your dress. (TB) **2** roller *Ils prendaient des planches et tout avec des rouleaux. Et ils mettaient la maison dessus et la roulaient* BACK. They took boards and all, with rollers. And they would put the house on it and roll it back. (SJ) **3** rolling pin **4** rolled or wrapped bundle, bale *Il y a un* DRUMMER *qu'a perdu un rouleau de fouets à boghei dans le chemin.* There's a drummer who lost a bundle of draft horse whips on the way. (EV) **5** cutworm **6** pill bug, roly poly <***Loc:*** AV, EV, IB, SJ, SM, Da84>

roulement [rulmɑ̃] *n.m.* rolling, rumble ◊ **•roulement de tonnerre** roll of thunder <Da84> <***Loc:*** Da84>

rouler [rule] **I** *v.tr.* **1** to roll *Aujourd'hui, je suis condamné, condamné à rouler ma bourouette sur ma planche de six pouces.* Today I'm condemned, condemned to roll my wheelbarrow on my six inch plank. (ch: *La valse du bambocheur*) **2** to move (a house) by means of rollers *Ils prendaient des planches et tout avec des rouleaux. Et ils mettaient la maison dessus et la roulaient* BACK. They took boards and all, with rollers. And they put the house on it and they'd roll it back. (SJ) **3** to wind, roll up, coil *Rouler un câble.* To roll up a rope. (LA) **II** *v.intr.* **1** to roll, pitch from side to side (of a boat) *Vers minuit du soir, ça m'a réveillé à force que le bateau roulait.* Around midnight, it woke me up because the boat was rolling so much. (TB) **2** to rumble, roll, roar *Quand la tonnerre roule les tortues sortent.* When thunder rolls the turtles come out. (proverb, Lv88) **3** to roam, run around, gallivant *Moi, j'ai roulé, je m'ai mis à malfaire. J'avais la tête dure, j'ai rentré dans le tracas.* I ran around, I started getting into trouble. I had a hard head, I got in trouble. (ch: *Les barres de la prison*) **4** to work in the sugar cane harvest *Tu vas rouler cette année?* Are you going to work in the cane harvest this year? (TB) **5** to fare, get along **Comment ça roule?* How are you? How are you getting along? (Da84) *Laissez les bons temps rouler.* Let the good times roll. (proverb) **III se rouler** *v.pron.* to roll o.s. over, turn o.s. over, roll around *Les cochons se roulent dans la boue quand il fait chaud.* Pigs roll in the mud when it's hot. (VM) ◊ **•rouler les cannes** to crush and grind sugar cane *J'ai travaillé à une sucrerie là-bas éiou eux-autres roulait les cannes.* I worked in a sugar mill where they ground the cane. (TB) <TB> **•rouler les (grands) chemins** to run the roads <VM, Gr86> <***Loc:*** LA, SJ, TB, VM, Da84, Gr86, Hi02, Lv88>

roulette [rulet, rulɛt] *n.f.* **1** roller, caster **2** washer **3** ring, circular object **4** round, round slice or section *Tu coupes le coucha en roulettes.* You cut the squash into rounds. (Lv88) **5** wooden or iron hoop that children roll with a stick **6** game of roulette **7** rocker, blade, runner (curved wooden bottom) of a rocking chair **8** trundle bed ◊ **•ça va sur des roulettes** it's going very well <La99> <***Loc:*** SM, TB, VM, Da84, La99, Lv88>

rouleur, -euse [rulœr, -øz] *n.* wanderer <***Loc:*** Da84>

roulon [rulɔ̃] *n.m.* roll, bun (of hair) *On se tisait les cheveux pour faire des roulons.* We teased our hair to put it up in rolls. (TB) <***Loc:*** TB>

roumarin [rumarɛ̃] *n.m.* rosemary <***Loc:*** SJ>

roupe [rup] *n.f.* baby's cloak, child's coat <***Loc:*** LF, SL, Lv88>

roupette [rupɛt] *n.m.* testicle <***Loc:*** SB, SM>

roupie [rupi] *n.f.* snood, dewbill (pendulous skin over the beak of a turkey) <***Loc:*** VM>

roupille [rupij] *n.f.* snot, mucus (hanging from the nose) <***Loc:*** Da84>

roupiller [rupije] *v.intr.* to doze <***Loc:*** Re31>

rouscailler [ruskaje] *v.intr.* to philander, chase women *Il fait que rouscailler depuis quelques années.* All he does is chase women, since a few years ago. (SM) <***Loc:*** JE, SM>

rouscailleur [ruskajœr] *n.m.* philanderer, woman-chaser *C'est un vrai rouscailleur. Il passe son temps à rouscailler.* He's a real philanderer. He spends his time chasing women. (SM) <***Loc:*** JE, SM>

roussequette [rusket] *n.f.* spanking, whipping, beating <***Loc:*** VM, La99>

roussetée [ruste] *n.f.* whipping, beating *Je l'ai donné une roussetée de coups de bâton.* I showered him with blows with my stick. (SL) <***Loc:*** EV, SL, La99, Ph36>

rousseture [rustyr] *n.f.* whipping, beating *J'ai pour te flanquer la meilleure rousseture que tu as jamais attrapée.* I'm going to give you the best whipping you ever had. (SB) <***Loc:*** SB, La99>

rousta [rusta, rusa] *n.m.* rooster *Une vieille poule ça fait mieux dans un gombo qu'un jeune poulet parce que quand* *tu bouilles le gombo pour longtemps, un jeune poulet va casser et un rousta ou une vieille poule dans un gombo ça reste ensemble.* An old hen is better in a gumbo than a young chicken because when you boil the gumbo for a long time, a young chicken is going to break into pieces whereas a rooster or an old hen, it will stay together. (AV) <***Loc:*** AV, VM>

roustailler [rustaje] *v.tr.* to beat, whip *Je sais qu'on va le roustailler pour ça.* I know they'll beat him for that. (IB) <***Loc:*** IB>

routabaga ♦see **rutabaga**

route [rut] *n.f.* **1** route, road, way *La route marche mal.* The road is not good. (VM) **2** journey *Y avait plein de pâturage, ils les engraissaient encore pour finir la route avant qu'ils arrivaient pour les vendre au marché.* There was a lot of pasture land, they would fatten them [the cows] up to finish out the journey before they arrived at the market to be sold. (SJ) ◊ **•en route** on the road *Et des fois on est en route, je dis à ma femme, "Oh Lord, le char va casser." Et on va pas aller plus qu'un mille d'ici. And I'll be damned, le char est cassé.* And sometimes we're on the road, I'll say to my wife, "Oh Lord, the car is going to break down." And we go no further than a mile from here and I'll be damned, the car breaks down. (LF) <LF> **•faire route** to travel *Dans ce temps que mon je sus après parler asteur-là, ça prendait oh peut-être 45 minutes, pour sûr, parce que ces vieilles carrioles, ça faisait pas route trop vite.* In the days that I'm talking about now, it took about 45 minutes, for sure, because those old two-wheeled wagons, they didn't travel very fast. (TB) *Et puis là ça c'est épaillé tout partout, tu vois? Ça fait route, ça reste pas tout le temps dans la même place.* And then they [nutrias] spread out everywhere, you see? They move around, they don't always stay in the same place. (TB) <TB> **•faire une grande route** to go a long way, take a long journey <Da84> <***Loc:*** EV, LF, TB, VM, Da84, Lv88>

routi ♦see **rôti**

routie ♦see **rôtie**

routine [rutin] *n.f.* **1** routine **2** trick, attempt at deception *T'as fait une routine avec alle.* You played a trick on her. (VM) **3** small path, cowpath *Il a tombé dessus une petite routine qui serpentait dans le bois.* He came upon a little cowpath that wound around in the woods. (LA) *Tous les jours ce vieux homme prend la même routine pour aller à son champ.* Every day that man takes the same path to go to his field. (TB) ◊ **•routine à la volonté** turnrow, headland (strip of uncultivated land at the end or side of a field where a plow can turn) <SM> **•routine à volonté** highway, road *Regarde le char qui vient dans la routine à volonté.* See the car coming down the highway. (IB) <IB> <***Loc:*** IB, LA, SM, TB, VM, Da84>

routir ♦see **rôtir**

rouverre, rouvrir ♦see **ouverre**

roux [ru] *n.m.* roux (flour browned in fat and used for thickening gravies, gumbo, courtbouillon, and many other Cajun dishes) *Pendant longtemps je faisais du roux mais maintenant c'est un tas plus facile aller au magasin.* For a long time I used to make roux, but now it's a whole lot easier to go to the store (to get it). (SL) *C'est pas un gumbo si vous avez pas un roux.* It is not a gumbo if you do not have a roux. (IB) *Ma grand-mère mettait pas de roux dans son gombo. Elle l'épaississait avec du filé.* My grandmother didn't make her gumbo with a roux. She thickened it with filé. (VM) *Le roux c'est fait avec de la farine et de la graisse, tu mets de la farine et de la graisse dans un chaudron et tu cuis ça jusqu'à ça devient brun et c'est ça tu mets dans le gombo pour donner le gombo le goût et pour donner le gombo une jolie couleur.* Roux is made from flour and lard; you put the flour in the lard in a caldron and you cook it until it browns, and that's what you put in a gumbo to give the gumbo its taste and to give the gumbo a nice color. (AV) <***Loc:*** AV, IB, SB, SL, VM, Da84, Gu00, Hi02>

ruban [rybɑ̃] *n.m.* **1** ribbon **2** magnetic tape for recording sound, audio tape *Il prendait ses témoignages sur le ruban.* His testimony was recorded on tape. (Lv88) <***Loc:*** SL, Da84, Gr86, Hi02, Lv88>

rubandelle ♦see **ribondelle**

rubis [rybi] *n.m.* ruby <***Loc:*** Da84>

ruche [ryʃ] *n.f.* hive, beehive <***Loc:*** SM, Da84>

rude [ryd] *adj.* crude, rude, rough <***Loc:*** Da84>

rudement [rydmɑ̃] *adv.* roughly, hard, harshly <***Loc:*** Da84>

rue [ry] *n.f.* street *Eusse passait dans les rues pour faire de la boucane pour les moustiques.* They would pass in the streets to make smoke because of the mosquitoes. (LF) ◊ **•grande rue / grand'rue** main street **Notre band était après jouer sur la grand'rue à Jack's Place.* Our band was playing on Main street at Jack's Place. (LA, An84) <LA, An84, Da84> <***Loc:*** AV, EV, LA, LF, SM, TB, An84, An94, Da84, Hi02, Wh83>

ruette [rwɛt] *n.f.* space between a bed and the wall <***Loc:*** AV, JD>

ruine [rɥin] *n.f.* ruin, destruction, decay ◊ **•aller en ruine** to go to ruin <Da84> <***Loc:*** Da84>

ruiner (**aruiner**) [rɥine, arɥine] **I** *v.tr.* to ruin, spoil, destroy *Tu vas m'aruiner.* You are going to ruin me. (JE) **II se ruiner** *v.pron.* to ruin o.s., go to ruin *Il avait racheté la boutique pour venir ici à Eunice puis il s'est ruiné.* He had bought back the store to come to Eunice, then he went broke. (EV) <***Loc:*** EV, JE, LF, Da84>

rumeur [rymœr] *n.f.* rumor <***Loc:*** Da84>

ruse [ryz] *n.f.* wile, ruse, cunning <***Loc:*** Da84>

rusé, -e [ryze] *adj.* wily, crafty, cunning, shrewd *Guette-lé. Il est rusé.* Keep an eye on him. He's crafty. (VM) <***Loc:*** VM, Da84>

Russe ♦see **Russie**

Russie (**Russe**) [rysi, rys] *n.f.* Russia <***Loc:*** Da84, Lv88>

russien[1]**, -ienne** [rysjɛ̃, -jɛ̃n] *adj.* Russian <***Loc:*** EV, LA, LF, VM, Lv88>

russien[2] [rysjɛ̃] *n.m.* Russian language *Pushkin, lui, il écrisait mieux en français qu'en russien.* Pushkin wrote better in French than in Russian. (EV) <***Loc:*** EV>

rutabaga (**routabaga**) [rutabaga] *n.m.* rutabaga <***Loc:*** EV, Da84>

RYE [ɹaɪ] *n.m.* rye whiskey <***Loc:*** Lv88>

RYE GRASS [ɹaɪgɹæs] *n.f.* rye grass <***Loc:*** Da84>

S

sa ♦see **son**

sabbat [saba] *n.m.* **1** Sabbath, Sunday **2** noise, uproar, din *Qué sabbat tu mènes là!* You are causing such an uproar! (VM) <***Loc:*** VM, Da84, Di32>

Sabine [sabin] *n.* [*offensive*] person of mixed white, Native American, and/or African American blood, esp. a member of one of the Native communities of Terrebonne and Lafourche Parishes traditionally known as the Houma Indians *Sa femme est placée avec un Sabine de en bas du Petit Caillou. Moi j'ai pris ça dur. Y avait juste trois mois qu'il était mort.* His wife is shacked up with a Sabine from down in Little Caillou. I took that hard. It had only been three months since he died. (TB) <***Loc:*** LF, TB, Lv88>

sable[1] [sab(l)] *n.m.* sand <***Loc:*** IB, JE, SB, SM, Da84, Di32, Hi02, Lv88>

sable[2] [sab(l)] *n.m.* [sugar cane industry] large paddle used to push aside or remove foam from boiling cane juice <***Loc:*** IB, JE, SB, SM, Da84, Di32, Hi02, Lv88>

sablé, -e [sable] *adj.* sandy, sanded **Papier sablé.* Sandpaper. (Da84) <***Loc:*** SM, Da84, Lv88>

sabler [sable] *v.tr.* [sugar cane industry] to push aside or remove foam from boiling cane juice with a paddle (called a "sable") when transferring the juice from one kettle to another <***Loc:*** IB, JE, Di32, Lv88>

sableux, -euse [sablø, -øz] *adj.* sandy, sanded **Terre sableuse.* Sandy soil. (Da84) **Papier sableux.* Sandpaper. (Da84) <***Loc:*** JE, LA, VM, Da84, Di32>

sablière [sablijær] *n.f.* sill <***Loc:*** EV, Da84>

sabot [sabo] *n.m.* **1** any heavy, clumsy shoe, clodhopper **2** hoof *Il y en a qui mettait des fers pour aider aux sabots.* Some people put on irons to help the hoofs. (EV) **3** horseshoe ◊ **•sabot de cheval *a*** hoof of a horse ***b*** ponyfoot, dichondra (a small creeping grass) <TB, VM, Ho90, Re31> <***Loc:*** EV, SB, SM, TB, VM, Da84, Ho90, Re31>

sabotage [sabotaʒ] *n.m.* sabotage, vandalism, wanton destruction (of property) <***Loc:*** Da84>

saboteur [sabotœr] *n.m.* saboteur, person engaged in sabotage <***Loc:*** Da84>

sabotière (sorbetière) [sabotjær, sɔrbətjær, sarbotjær] *n.f.* ice cream churn, machine, or freezer <***Loc:*** AC, AV, EV, IB, LA, SL, SM, VM, Da84, Lv88, Ph36>

saboulée [sabule] *n.f.* **1** shower of blows, series of blows **2** reprimand <***Loc:*** EV, SM, La99, Lv88, Ph36>

sabouler [sabule] **I** *v.tr.* **1** to beat *Il l'a saboulé à coups de pieds.* He beat him with his feet. (Lv88) **2** to reprimand, scold *Sa mère l'a bien saboulé le lendemain matin.* His mother scolded him well the next morning. (LA) **II se sabouler** *v.pron.* **1** to have a fistfight **2** to fight with mudballs <***Loc:*** LA, SB, SM, La99, Lv88>

sabre [sab(r)] *n.m./f.* **1** sword, saber **2** scythe, cane knife *Couper la canne au sabre.* To cut the cane with a cane knife. (LF) *Et eusse mettait les cabris là-dedans, les cabris mangeaient les herbes, tu vois, on avait pas besoin de les couper au sabre après.* And they put the goats in there, the goats ate the grass, you see, we didn't need to cut it with a scythe then. (TB) **3** sawfish *C'était un poisson avec un grand bec, il a des dents chaque bord comme une scie, on appelle ça un sabre.* It was a fish with a big snout, it has teeth on both sides like a saw, we call that a sawfish. (LF) **4** ribbonfish *Là y'a un autre poisson qu'eusse appelle un sabre, ils appellent ça en anglais A RIBBONFISH.* Then there's another fish that they call a "sabre," in English they call that a ribbonfish. (LF) ◊ **•sabre à canne** cane knife, scythe used for cutting sugarcane *Parce qu'y avait pas des RIDING LAWN MOWER là, il y avait pas de ça dans ce temps-là non. Et faulait que tu prends ça à la pioche ou avec une sabre à canne.* Because there were no riding lawn mowers then, there was none of that in those days. You had to do it by hoe or with a scythe. (TB) <TB> <***Loc:*** JE, LF, SB, SM, TB, Da84, Lv88>

sabrer [sabre] *v.tr.* to cut with a scythe *Il a eu pour sabrer les herbes.* He had to cut the grass with a scythe. (VM) <***Loc:*** LF, VM, Lv88>

sabreur [sabrœr] *n.m.* cane cutter <***Loc:*** LF, Lv88>

sac [sak] *n.m.* **1** sack, bag, pouch **2** [*vulg.*] scrotum ◊ **•sac à boisson** drunkard <EV, La99, Lv88, Ph36> **•sac à {en} papier *a*** paper bag ***b*** expression of disapproval or reproach <IB, SB, Da84, La99> **•sac à tous grains** temperamental person <SB, La99> **•sac de pitre** peat sack, gunny sack, burlap sack, sack made of rough cloth (used for cotton, grain, etc.) *Les autres fois, le riz était moudu et mis dans des sacs de pitre.* In the past, the rice was ground up and put in burlap bags. (Gu00) <SM, Da84, Gu00, Lv88> **•sac de trôle** bag of a trawl net <TB> <***Loc:*** EV, IB, LF, SB, SL, TB, Da84, Gu00, Hi02, La99, Lv88, Ph36>

sacacoua ♦see **sassaquoi**

sacage [sakaʒ] *n.m.* large amount *On a fait un sacage de maïs cette année.* We produced a huge amount of corn this year. (TB) <***Loc:*** JE, TB, Di32>

sacalait ♦see **sac-à-lait**

sac-à-lait (sacalait) [sakalɛ, sakale] *n.m.* **1** white perch *Quand l'eau est claire dans le bayou, la pêche est bonne pour les sacalaits.* When the water is clear in the bayou, it is good for fishing white perch. (VM, Gu00) **2** crappie (white or black) *C'est ça je pêche là-là, mais on l'appelle localement sacalait. Principalement les noirs sont meilleurs parce que ils sont plus épais.* That there [crappie] is what I fish, but we call it locally "sacalait." Mainly the black ones are best because they're thicker. (SL) <*Loc:* AL, AV, EV, IB, JE, LF, SB, SL, SM, TB, VM, Da84, Gu00, Hi02, Lv88, Ph36, Re31>

sacamité ♦see **sagamité**

sac-à-plomb [sakaplɔ̃] *n.m.* pied-billed grebe <*Loc:* JE, Lv88, Re31>

sacré (**cré**) [sakre, kre] *adj.* **1** [*eccl.*] sacred, holy, consecrated, blessed *Malgré qu'il s'a détruit, il a été enterré dans de la terre sacrée.* Even though he committed suicide, he was buried in sacred ground. (LA) **2** damned, darned *Sors ton sacré nez de mes affaires!* Get your damned nose out of my business! (LA) ◊ •**sacré bleu** [*mild oath*] good heavens <La99> •**sacrée boucane {misère}** [*mild oath*] holy smoke <Da84> •**sacré couillon** [*vulg.*] damn nut <Da84> •**sacré diable** curses <Lv88> •**sacré fils de garce {putain}** [*vulg.*] damn son-of-a-bitch <Da84> •**sacré tonnerre** [*mild oath*] holy thunder <Da84> <*Loc:* EV, LA, SL, An94, Da84, Hi02, La99, Lv88>

sacrement[1] [sakrəmɑ̃] *n.m.* sacrament <*Loc:* TB, Da84>

sacrement[2] ♦see **sacrément**

sacrément (**sacrement**) [sakremɑ̃, sakrəmɑ̃] *adv.* **1** darn well **T'as sacrément menti.* You darn well lied. (Da84) **2** very, extremely *Les chat-tigres, c'est sacrement mauvais pour les volailles et les petits lapins.* Lynxes are very bad news for chickens and small rabbits. (TB) <*Loc:* TB, Da84>

sacrer [sakre] **I** *v.tr.* **1** to deal, deliver (a blow) *Il m'a sacré donc un coup de poing et ils m'ont tiré dans la fenêtre.* He punched me and they tossed me in the window. (Lv88) **2** to hit *Il lui a sacré sur la tête.* He hit him on the head. (SB) **3** to throw, fling **Ils l'ont sacré à travers de la fenêtre.* They threw him out the window. (IV, An94) **Il a sacré cent piastres dans le cercueil.* He threw a hundred dollars into the coffin. (An94) **Sacrer par terre.* To throw down. (EV, Ph36) **II** *v.intr.* to swear, curse *Sacrer en français est un art chez les Cadiens.* To swear in French is an art for Cajuns. (Lv88) **III se sacrer** *v.pron.* to not care, not give a damn *Je m'en sacre de ça que tu crois.* I don't care what you think. (LA) ◊ •**sacrer le camp** to leave, clear out, take off <EV, Lv88, Ph36> •**sacrer un coup de fusil** to shoot, fire a gunshot <SM, VM, Lv88> •**sacrer un coup de main** to strike with the side of the hand <Lv88> •**sacrer un coup de pied** to kick <SM, VM, Da84> •**sacrer un coup de poing** to punch <SM, VM> •**sacrer une gratte {volée} à qqn** to beat s.o. <AC, JE, SM, La99> •**sacrer une raclée** to give a whipping <Da84> •**sacrer une tape** to slap <Da84> <*Loc:* AC, EV, IV, JE, LA, SB, SM, TB, VM, An94, Da84, La99, Lv88, Ph36>

sacrifice [sakrifis, sakrefis] *n.m.* sacrifice <*Loc:* LF, Da84>

sacrifier [sakrifje] **I** *v.tr.* to sacrifice, give up *Il a pas envie de sacrifier son job.* He doesn't want to give up his job. (LA) **II se sacrifier** *v.pron.* to sacrifice o.s., one's time, etc. *Elle se sacrifie pour son mari et ses enfants.* She sacrifices herself for her husband and children. (VM) <*Loc:* LA, VM, Da84>

sacrilège [sakrilɛʒ] *n.m.* [*eccl.*] sacrilege <*Loc:* Da84>

sacristain [sakristɛ̃] *n.m.* [*eccl.*] sacristan, sexton <*Loc:* Da84>

sacristie [sakristi] *n.f.* [*eccl.*] sacristy <*Loc:* Da84>

sacristine [sakristin] *n.f.* [*eccl.*] sacristan <*Loc:* Da84>

safétida ♦see **assafœtida**

safre [saf(r)] *adj.* gluttonous, greedy *Ce safre a mangé tout mon gâteau.* That glutton ate my whole cake. (SL) <*Loc:* SL, VM, Di32, Lv88>

safrement [safrəmɑ̃] *adv.* greedily, gluttonously <*Loc:* VM, Di32>

safreté [safrəte] *n.f.* gluttony <*Loc:* JE, SL, Di32, Lv88>

sagamité (**sacamité**) [sagɑ̃mite, sakɑ̃mite, sokɑ̃mite] *n.f.* hominy <*Loc:* IB, LF, SL, SM, VM, Da84, Di32, Hi02, Lv88, Re31>

saganer [sagɑ̃ne] *v.tr.* **1** to beat, shake (e.g. as punishment) *Je l'ai bien sagané, cet enfant.* I have punished him well, this child. (VM) **2** to muddy, sully *T'as tout sagané ta robe.* You got your dress all dirty. (TB) **3** to pelt (with rocks, dirt, etc.) **4** to shoot repeatedly (as into a flock of birds) **5** to waste, squander *Saganer sa vie.* To waste one's life. (IB) **6** to bungle, botch, do (one's work) in a slipshod manner <*Loc:* IB, LA, TB, VM, Di32>

sage[1] [saʒ] *adj.* calm, mellow <*Loc:* JE, Da84, Di32>

sage[2] [saʒ] *n.* wise person, sage *La terre nourrit tout, les fous, les saouls, les sages.* The earth nourishes all, the fools, the drunks, the sages. (VM, ch: *La terre nourrit tout*) <*Loc:* VM, Da84>

sagesse [saʒɛs] *n.f.* wisdom <*Loc:* Da84>

sagoter [sagote] *v.tr.* to agitate clothing in a tub of water *Je vas sagoter cette guenille dans l'eau.* I'm going to shake this rag in water. (TB) <*Loc:* TB>

sagouiller [saguje] *v.tr.* **1** to dirty, sully *Alle a sagouillé le linge.* She got the clothes all dirty. (TB) **2** to bungle, botch, do in a slipshod manner <*Loc:* TB>

saïbote ♦see SIDEBOARD

saignant, -e [sɛ̃jɑ̃, -ɑ̃t] *adj.* bloody, bleeding *Il a sorti de la bataille tout saignant.* He came out of the fight all bloody. (LA) <*Loc:* LA, Da84>

saigner [sɛ̃je] **I** *v.tr.* to bleed (an animal), kill by bleeding **Saigner un cochon.* To bleed a pig. (Da84) **II** *v.intr.* to bleed *Faut que tu y coupes et y quitter saigner pour ôter le sang de dans la viande.* You have to cut it and let it bleed to get the blood out of the meat. (TB) **Il avait saigné jusqu'à il avait plus de sang.* He had bled until he had no more blood.

(EV, An94) ◊ **•saigner à mort** to bleed to death <Da84> **•faire saigner** to cause to bleed **Eux a attrapé le cochon, eux avaient commencé pour le faire saigner.* They caught the pig, they had started to bleed it. (LA, An94) <LA, An94, Da84> <***Loc:*** EV, LA, TB, An94, Da84, Hi02>

saigneux, -euse [sɛ̃jø, -øz] *adj.* bloody, bleeding <***Loc:*** Da84>

sain [sɛ̃] *adj.* healthy, sound, hale *Il n'y a ni médecin ni chirurgien qui peut remettre mon corps en sain.* There is no doctor or surgeon to make my body healthy once again. (PQ, ch: *Sainte Catherine*) ◊ **•sain et sauve** safe and sound <Da84> <***Loc:*** PQ, Da84>

saint[1], -e [sɛ̃, sɛ̃t] *adj.* **1** holy, saintly *C'était une petite fille sainte.* She was a holy little girl. (AC) **2** [*ironic*] blessed *Ça c'est la meilleure idée t'as eu toute la sainte journée, mon garçon!* That's the best idea you've had the whole blessed day, my boy! (JD) <***Loc:*** AC, JD, Da84, Hi02>

saint[2], -e [sɛ̃, sɛ̃t] *n.* saint <***Loc:*** LA, PQ, Da84, Hi02>

sainte-hale-ça [sɛ̃thalsa] *n.f.* long, hard, steady work <***Loc:*** LA>

sainte nitouche (sainte mitouche) [sɛ̃tnituʃ, sɛ̃tmituʃ] *n.* **1** untouchable or touchy person, touch-me-not **2** holier-than-thou person, hypocrite, sanctimonious person, one who pretends to be innocent **3** person who is aloof <***Loc:*** AS, AV, IB, LF, SJ, SL, SM, Da84, La99>

Saint-Esprit [sɛ̃tɛspri] *n.m.* Holy Spirit <***Loc:*** Da84>

saint-frusquin [sɛ̃fryskɛ̃] *n.m.* rump, derriere, behind *Il a attrapé un coup sur le saint-frusquin.* He caught a blow on the behind. (SB) <***Loc:*** SB>

saint-jean [sɛ̃ʒɑ̃] *n.m.* goldenrod *Les saint-jeans fleurit plein autour la fête de Saint-Jean. C'est pour ça qu'on les appelle par ce nom-là.* Goldenrods bloom a lot around the time of St. John's feast. That's why they're called by that name. (TB) <***Loc:*** TB>

Saint-Médard [sɛ̃medar] *n.f.* period of rain or drought beginning June 8 and lasting forty days <***Loc:*** LA>

saisir [sezir] *v.tr.* **1** to grasp, grab, seize **Il a saisi son argent et il a parti en courant.* He grabbed his money and he took off running. (LA) *Elle m'a saisi la main comme une cossarde saisit une souris.* She seized my hand like a hawk grabs a mouse. (VM) **2** to seize (assets) by law *Saisir les affaires de quelqu'un qui fait banqueroute.* To seize the belongings of someone who has gone bankrupt. (VM) **3** to surprise *Ça m'a saisi quand j'ai entendu la nouvelle.* That surprised me when I heard the news. (VM) <***Loc:*** LA, VM, Da84>

saison [sezɔ̃] *n.f.* **1** season **2** season (period of time for a particular activity) *Il est à la trawl dans Mississippi asteur. La saison rouvre aujourd'hui là-bas.* He is trawling in Mississippi now. The season opens today over there. (TB) ◊ **•saison de mai** spring shrimping season <TB> **•saison haute** high season (for shrimp fishing) <JE> **•en saison *a*** in season (fruit, vegetable, game, etc.) ***b*** in heat (of a female animal) *Joue pas avec la chienne. Elle va te mordre. Elle est en saison.* Don't play with the dog. She'll bite you. She's in heat. (SM) <SM, VM, Da84> <***Loc:*** JE, SL, SM, TB, VM, Da84>

saisonnage [sezɔ̃naʒ, sasɔ̃naʒ] *n.m.* seasoning *On bouillait notre viande, et on met tout des saisonnages, du persil, des queues d'oignons, des oignons.* We boiled our meat, and we put in all the seasonings, parsley, onion tops, onions. (TB) <***Loc:*** TB>

saisonner ♦see **assaisoner**

salade [salad] *n.f.* **1** salad **2** lettuce *J'ai sûr des beaux rangs de salade dans mon jardin.* I sure have nice rows of lettuce in my garden. (TB) **3** duckweed **4** beating *Il lui a passé une salade.* He gave him a beating. (LA) *Flanquer une salade sur la gueule.* To punch someone in the face. (LF) <***Loc:*** AV, JE, LA, LF, SB, TB, Da84, Di32, Hi02, La99, Lv88>

salaire [salær] *n.m.* salary, wages <***Loc:*** Da84>

salaud[1] (salop) [salo] *adj.m.* **1** dirty (physically and morally) **Il était sale et barbeux, maudit et salop.* He was dirty and unshaven, mean and indecent. (EV, Gr86) **2** untrustworthy, deceitful *Il est salaud.* He is untrustworthy. (SM) <***Loc:*** EV, SM, Da84, Gr86>

salaud[2] (salop) [salo] *n.m.* **1** dirty person (physically and morally) **2** one who is untrustworthy or deceitful, double-crosser *Il m'a promis un job, mais il l'a donné à quelqu'un d'autre. C'est un foutu salaud.* He promised me a job but he gave it to someone else. He's a damned double-crosser. (SM) **3** rascal **Ah mon petit salop!* You dirty little rascal! (Da84) <***Loc:*** EV, SM, Da84, Gr86>

sale [sal] *adj.* **1** dirty, filthy *Excuse ma maison, elle est sale.* Excuse my house, it is filthy. (LA) **2** indecent, immoral *C'est un homme sale.* He is an indecent man. (LA) <***Loc:*** LA, Da84>

saler [sale] *v.tr.* to salt (e.g. food) *Il faulait qu'on achète du sel, et on salait ça et mettre ça dans des grandes jarres, des grands vaisseaux.* We had to buy salt, and we salted it [meat] and put it in big jars, big containers. (TB) *C'est pas toi qu'as salé la mer!* [insult for someone arrogant or not very intelligent] (La99) **Viande salée.* Salted meat. (Da84) **Eau salée.* Saltwater. (Da84) <***Loc:*** EV, SL, TB, An94, Da84, La99>

saleté [salte] *n.f.* **1** dirt, filth **2** dirty deed ◊ **•faire des saletés** to do dirty deeds, commit immorality <Da84> <***Loc:*** Da84>

salezir ♦see **salir**

salière [saljær] *n.f.* salt shaker <***Loc:*** VM>

salir (salezir) [salir, salzir] **I** *v.tr.* to dirty, soil, defile **T'avais justement un bon change de bon linge. Si tu te battais, t'allais le déchirer, salir, et tout ça.* You had just one good change of clothes. If you fought, you would tear it, dirty it, and all that. (IV, An94) **II** *v.intr.* to defecate **III se salir** *v.pron.* **1** to get dirty *Faisez attention de pas vous salir dehors.* Be careful not to get dirty outside. (LA) **2** to soil o.s. (esp. of babies) <***Loc:*** IB, IV, JE, LA, An94, Da84>

salissant, -e [salisɑ̃, -ɑ̃t] *adj.* **1** dirtying, soiling **Ouvrage salissant.* Dirty work. (Da84) **2** easily dirtied **Du linge salissant.* Clothes that get dirty easily. <Da84> <***Loc:*** Da84>

salive [saliv] *n.f.* saliva, spittle <***Loc:*** Da84>

salivure [salivyr] *n.f.* salivation, an abnormally increased flow of saliva <***Loc:*** JE, SM, Di32>

salle [sal] *n.f.* **1** hall, large room, room **2** dance hall *Chien était dans la salle après danser cochon.* Chien [a nickname] was in the dancehall dancing in a vulgar manner. (LA) ◊ **•salle à manger *a*** dining room *En arrière de la cheminée t'avais la cuisine et là t'avais un foyer, un foyer en avant de la salle à manger, c'est ça qu'eusse se réchauffait avec.* Behind the chimney you had the kitchen and then you had a fireplace, a fireplace in front of the dining room, that's what they used for heating. (LF) ***b*** kitchen <JE, LA, LF, Da84, Guoo> **•salle de danse *a*** dance hall ***b*** nightclub where one dances to Cajun music <LA, An94, Da84, Guoo, Hio2> <***Loc:*** JE, LA, LF, SL, An94, Da84, Guoo, Hio2>

salon [salɔ̃] *n.m.* living room, parlor, salon <***Loc:*** Da84, Guoo>

saloon [sulun] *n.m.* saloon, barroom *Il y avait un* SIGN *dans ce saloon là qui disait '*DON'T LOSE YOU HEAD BECAUSE THAT'S THE BEST PART OF YOUR BODY*'.* There was a sign in that saloon that said 'Don't lose your head because it's the best part of your body.' (TB) <***Loc:*** TB, VM>

salop ♦see **salaud**

salope[1] **(salote)** [salɔp, salɔt] *adj.f.* repulsive, filthy untidy *Elle est salope.* She is repulsive. (SM) <***Loc:*** SM, VM, Lv88>

salope[2] **(salote, salôte)** [salɔp, salɔt] *n.f.* **1** repulsive, filthy untidy woman *Tu veux pas te marier avec cette espèce de salope.* You don't want to marry that sort of dirty woman. (LA) **2** slut, whore **Il y avait une fois une vieille salôte qu'a donné naissance à trois petits bâtards.* There was once an old whore who gave birth to three bastards. (EV, Gr86) <***Loc:*** EV, LA, SM, VM, Gr86, Lv88>

saloper [salope] **I** *v.tr.* to botch, do in a slovenly way, do negligently *Je suis sûr qu'il va saloper le job.* I'm sure that he will botch the job. (LA) *Il est après saloper sa vie.* He is botching his life. (LA) **II** *v.intr.* to lead an indecent life <***Loc:*** JD, LA, Lv88>

saloperie[1] [salopri] *n.* good-for-nothing, rascal, immoral person, indecent person *Le saloperie est parti avec ça.* The rascal made off with that. (SB) *Ce saloperie de Jean a volé mon argent.* That rascal John stole my money. (IB) <***Loc:*** IB, JD, LA, SB, SM, TB, Da84, Lv88>

saloperie[2] [salopri] *n.f.* **1** filth, dirtiness, dirt **2** smut, indecency, immorality **Dire des saloperies.* To tell dirty stories or jokes. (Da84) ◊ **•faire des saloperies *a*** to do indecent things ***b*** to play dirty tricks <Da84> <***Loc:*** SM, Da84, Lv88>

saloperie[3] [salopri] *interj.* son-of-a-gun, dog-gone it, oh shucks <***Loc:*** Da84>

salote, salôte ♦see **salope**

salpêtre [salpɛt(r)] *n.m.* saltpeter, sodium nitrite <***Loc:*** Da84>

saluer [salɥe] *v.tr.* **1** to salute, greet *Il a passé au ras de moi; il m'a pas seulement salué.* He passed right by me; he didn't even greet me. (VM) **2** to bow (in a dance) *Il a salué sa cavalière.* He bowed to his dance partner. (LA) **3** to hail *Saluer un bateau.* To hail a boat. (VM) <***Loc:*** LA, VM, Da84>

salut [saly] *n.m.* **1** salvation, welfare **2** salute, greeting, salutation <***Loc:*** Da84>

samedi [sɑ̃mdi] *n.m.* Saturday ◊ **•Samedi Saint** Holy Saturday <Da84> <***Loc:*** EV, Da84, Hio2>

SAMPLE [sɛ̃p(l)] *n.m.* sample, specimen *Il veut un* SAMPLE *de cette étoffe.* He wants a sample of this cloth. (AV) <***Loc:*** VM, Da84>

sanctifiant, -e [sɑ̃ktifjɑ̃, -ɑ̃t] *adj.* [*eccl.*] sanctifying **Grâce sanctifiante.* Sanctifying grace. <Da84> <***Loc:*** Da84>

sanctifier [sɑ̃ktifje] *v.tr.* [*eccl.*] to sanctify, bless <***Loc:*** Da84>

sanctuaire [sɑ̃ktɥær] *n.m.* **1** sanctuary of a church **2** sanctuary, protected area for birds, wildlife, etc. <***Loc:*** Da84>

sandale [sɑ̃dal] *n.f.* sandal <***Loc:*** Da84>

sandwich [sɑ̃dwitʃ] *n.m.* sandwich <***Loc:*** Da84>

sang [sɑ̃] *n.m.* **1** blood **Ça lui a coupé le nez et il a saigné quelques gouttes de sang.* It cut his nose and he bled a few drops of blood. (VM, An94) **Il avait saigné jusqu'à il avait plus de sang.* He had bled until he had no more blood. (EV, An94) **2** parentage, ancestry ◊ **•sang clair** anemia <SM> **•sang doux** diabetes <Lv88> **•sang hâcre** acid blood condition that causes a rash <VM> **•sang mêlé** mixed blood **J'ai le sang mêlé.* I have mixed blood. (EV, An94) <EV, An94> **•sang (trop) bas** low blood pressure *Il a le sang bas.* He has low blood pressure. (LA) <LA, SM, VM, Lv88> **•sang (trop) haut / sang trop fort** high blood pressure *Il a le sang haut.* He has high blood pressure. (LA) <LA, SM, VM, Lv88> **•mauvais sang *a*** syphilis ***b*** anemia <SM, VM> **•(se) faire du mauvais sang** to make bad blood, get angry <Da84, SM, La99, Lv88> <***Loc:*** EV, IV, JE, SL, SM, VM, An94, Da84, Hio2, La99, Lv88>

sangle [sɑ̃ŋ, sɑ̃g(l)] *n.f.* **1** belly band (of a saddle or harness), girth **2** cinch strap *Il y avait deux sangles après la selle.* There were two cinch straps attached to the saddle. (EV) <***Loc:*** EV, IB, Da84>

sangler [sɑ̃gle] **I** *v.tr.* **1** to fasten, cinch (e.g. a belly band, cinch, harness, or saddle) *T'as pas sanglé la selle assez serré.* You didn't cinch the saddle tightly enough. (EV) **2** to hit, beat with a strap *Cet homme haïssable avait l'habitude de sangler ses enfants.* That hateful man had the habit of beating his children with a strap. (LA) **3** to impose *Tout ça il a fait, c'est de sangler des taxes dessus le dos des pauvres malheureux.* All he did was impose taxes on the backs of the poor people. (VM) **II se sangler** to saddle o.s. (with a debt or burden) **Je m'ai sanglé avec une grosse dette.* I assumed a large debt. (Da84) <***Loc:*** EV, LA, SM, VM, Da84, Di32, Lv88, Ph36>

sang-mêlé [sɑ̃mele] *n.* half-breed, person of mixed blood or impure race *Le monde de ce village c'est des sang-mêlé.* The people of that town are of mixed blood. (LA) <***Loc:*** JE, LA, VM, Da84, Di32>

sangsue [sɑ̃sy] *n.f.* leech <***Loc:*** TB, Da84>

sani ♦see **cerni**

sans [sɑ̃] *prep.* without *C'est bon quand tu peux danser sans musique.* It's good when you can dance without music. (EV) **On peut faire sans travailler le dimanche.* We can do it without working on Sunday. (SL, An94) ◊ **•sans cesse** endless, ceaseless <Da84> **•sans connaissance** unconscious <Da84> **•sans doute** no doubt, without a doubt <Da84> **•sans (que)** ***a*** unless *Et on veillait le mort, bien sûr. On aurait jamais laissé le mort sans que quelqu'un soit là.* And we waked the body, of course. We would've never left the body unless someone was there. (TB) ***b*** without **T'auras pas battu dans la salle sans il te fout dehors.* You wouldn't have fought in the dance hall without him throwing you out. (LA, An94) <LA, TB, An94, Da84> **•ça va sans dire** it goes without saying <Da84> <***Loc:*** AV, EV, IB, IV, LA, LF, SL, TB, VM, An94, Da84, Gu00, Hi02, Wh83>

sans-cœur [sɑ̃kœr] *n.* heartless, cruel, pitiless person *Tu es rien qu'un sans-cœur.* You're nothing but a cruel man. (SB) <***Loc:*** SB, Da84, Di32>

sans-joie [sɑ̃ʒwa] *n.m.* great blue heron <***Loc:*** Lv88, Re31>

Santa Claus [sɑ̃taklɔz, sɛ̃teklɔz] *n.prop.* Santa Claus <***Loc:*** AC, EV, IB, Lv88, Ph36>

santé [sɑ̃te] *n.f.* health *J'ai pas pu m'empêcher de marcher à lui. Je dis, "Il y a une question j'aimerais te demander. Quoi c'est tu fais pour ta santé?" Il dit, "Je vas au bal proche tous les soirs."* I couldn't help but walk over to him. I said, "There's a question I'd like to ask you. What do you do for your health?" He said, "I go to the dance almost every night." (ch: *La neige sur la couverture*) ◊ **•à votre santé** to your health <Da84> **•en bonne santé** in good health <Da84> **•en mauvaise santé** in bad health <Da84> <***Loc:*** AL, LF, Da84, Lv88>

saoul ♦see **soûl**

saper[1] [sape] *v.tr.* to pack earth (esp. around the base of a plant) *Saper la terre autour d'une plante.* To pack the soil around the roots of a plant. (SJ) <***Loc:*** AV, IB, SJ>

saper[2] ♦see **assaper**

sapré [sapre] *adj.* [*euphemism for* **sacré**] darned, doggone *Sapré petit garçon, c'est bon à rien.* Darned little boy, he's good for nothing. (TB) <***Loc:*** TB>

saprement [saprəmɑ̃] *adv.* [*euphemism for* **sacrément**] very, extremely, darned, doggone *C'est saprement sale.* It's very dirty. (TB) <***Loc:*** TB>

sapristi [sapristi] *interj.* expression of surprise, impatience, or hopelessness **Sapristi d'affaire!* That's a hell of a thing! (Da84) <***Loc:*** Da84>

saquée [sake] *n.f.* sackful *On a jeté toute une saquée de riz sur les mariés.* We threw a whole sackful of rice on the newlyweds. (VM) <***Loc:*** TB, VM>

saquer [sake] *v.tr.* to hit, strike *Saque-lé là.* Hit him there. (TB) <***Loc:*** JE, TB, Di32>

sarbacane ♦see **sarboucane**

sarboucane (**sarbacane, serboucane**) [sarbukɑ̃n, sarbakɑ̃n, særbukɑ̃n, særabukɑ̃n] *n.f.* blowgun, blowpipe, peashooter *Les autres fois le monde avait des serboucanes pour tuer les petits oiseaux.* In the past people had blowguns to kills small birds. (TB) <***Loc:*** AV, EV, IB, JD, JE, LF, TB, Da84, Lv88, Ph36>

sarcelle [særsel] *n.f.* **1** blue-winged teal duck, teal **2** green-winged teal duck ◊ **•sarcelle aile bleue** blue-winged teal <Re31> **•sarcelle aile verte** green-winged teal <Re31> **•sarcelle de nord / sarcelle d'hiver** northern teal / winter teal (names for the green-winged teal) <Re31> **•sarcelle d'été / sarcelle automnière / sarcelle printanière** summer / fall / spring teal (seasonal names for the blue-winged teal) <Re31> <***Loc:*** AL, EV, IB, JE, LF, SL, TB, VM, Da84, Gu00, Re31>

sardine [sardin] *n.f.* **1** sardine **2** shad <***Loc:*** IV, SB, SM, VM, Da84>

sassepareille ♦see **chassepareille**

sasacoua ♦see **sassaquoi**

sassafran, sassafrance ♦see **sassafras**

sassafras (**sassafran, sassafrance**) [sasafrɑ̃, sasafrɑ̃s] *n.m.* **1** sassafras tree **2** sassafras (leaves of the sassafras tree, used for tea or dried and crushed to be used as a seasoning and thickening agent) *Le thé de sassafran (filé) est bon pour faire sortir la rougeole.* Sassafras tea is good to cure the measles. (SM) <***Loc:*** AC, CL, EV, IB, LA, SL, SM, TB, VM, Da84>

sassaquoi (**sassacoua, sacacoua**) [sasakwa, sakakwa] *n.m.* **1** noise, uproar, racket, hubbub, disturbance *Ils ont mené un sassaquoi toute la nuit.* They made a lot of noise all night long. (Lv88) **2** imposing and noisy person **C'est un sacacoua.* He's a windbag. (Re31) <***Loc:*** AV, EV, JE, SL, SM, TB, Lv88, Ph36, Re31>

Satan [satɑ̃] *n.prop.* Satan, the devil <***Loc:*** Da84>

satin [satɛ̃] *n.m.* satin <***Loc:*** Da84>

satine [satin] *n.f.* sateen <***Loc:*** Da84>

satisfaction [satisfaksjɔ̃] *n.f.* **1** satisfaction **2** atonement <***Loc:*** Da84>

satisfaire [satisfær] *v.tr.* to satisfy, make amends, gratify, sate *Asteur ils mettont leurs bas pour* Christmas. *Mais nous-autres on prendait notre bas, on essayait de trouver le plus grand bas qu'on pouvait pour le mettre dessus le foyer pour qu'eusse nous amène plein mais eusse remplissait jamais le bas, eusse mettait juste assez pour te satisfaire.* Today they put up their stocking for Christmas. But we would take our stocking, we tried to find the biggest stocking we could to put on the hearth so they would bring us a lot, but they never filled the stocking, they put in just enough to satisfy you. (LF) <*Loc:* LF, Da84>

satisfait, -e [satisfɛ, satisfe, -ɛt] *adj.* **1** satisfied, pleased *Ça fait sois pas trop gourmand, sois satisfait avec ce que tu as.* So don't be too gluttonous, be satisfied with what you've got. (LA) **2** convinced, persuaded *Je suis satisfait qu'il va pas être électé.* I am convinced that he will not be elected. (SM) ◊ **•pas satisfait après** vexed with, annoyed at *Il est pas satisfait après toi.* He is annoyed with you. (VM) <VM> <*Loc:* AC, SB, SL, SM, VM, Da84, Lv88>

sauce [sos, sɔs, søs] *n.f.* sauce *C'est bon pour manger ceux-là là, proche tout quelqu'un fait une sauce avec le poisson ça.* Those are good to eat, almost everyone makes a sauce with that fish. (SM) **2** gravy ◊ **•sauce aux tomates** tomato sauce <Da84> **•sauce blanche** cream gravy <VM, Fa77> **•sauce de débris** organ-meat stew <LA> **•sauce piquante** ***a*** highly seasoned stew ***b*** highly seasoned sauce that accompanies many traditional meat and fish dishes ***c*** hot sauce <Da84, Hi02, Lv88> **•sauce rouillée** brown gravy <LA, Da84> **•être dans sa sauce** to be doing what one likes to do <EV, La99> <*Loc:* AC, EV, JD, LA, SB, SL, SM, VM, Da84, Fa77, Hi02, La99>

saucé, -e [sose] *adj.* **1** drunk, 'sauced' **Il est saucé déjà.* He's already drunk. (EV, Ph36) **2** soaked, drenched *T'es tout saucé là.* You're all soaked. (TB) <*Loc:* EV, SM, TB, La99, Ph36>

saucée [sose] *n.f.* **1** heavy rain **On a attrapé une saucée.* We caught a drenching rain. (Da84) **2** short visit ◊ **•faire une (petite) saucée** to make a short visit *Faire une saucée chez Mom.* To make a short visit at Mama's. (SL) <JD, SL, TB, Da84, La99> <*Loc:* JD, LF, SL, TB, Da84, La99, Lv88>

saucer [sose] *v.tr.* **1** to dip into sauce (or any liquid) **Saucer le pain dans la sauce.* To dip the bread in the gravy. (Da84) *Tu prends ton pain et tu le sauçais dans l'œuf.* You take your bread and you would dip it into the egg. (LF) **2** to soak (e.g. clothes) *J'ai saucé mon linge une heure de temps.* I soaked my clothes for an hour. (TB) **3** to wet (e.g. with rain) <*Loc:* JE, LF, TB, Da84>

saucière [sosjær] *n.f.* gravy boat <*Loc:* Da84>

saucisse [sosis] *n.f.* sausage ◊ **•saucisse boucanée** smoked sausage <VM, Fa77> <*Loc:* AC, EV, LA, SL, VM, Da84, Fa77>

saucisseur [sosisœr] *n.m.* sausage maker <*Loc:* LA>

sauf [sof] *prep.* except, barring *Ils ont tous échappé sauf le petit.* They all got away except the little one. (LA) ◊ **•sauf que** except that, unless, barring *Elle aurait eu du bois de cheminée sauf que son maudit mari était trop paresseux pour venir ici en chercher.* She would've had firewood except that her damned husband was too lazy to come pick some up here. (LA) <LA, Da84> **•sauf que pour** except for *Ma mère a invité tout le monde sauf que pour mon frère.* My mother invited everyone except for my brother. (LA) <LA> <*Loc:* LA, Da84, Hi02>

saule [sol] *n.m.* willow tree ◊ **•saule pleurant** weeping willow tree <VM> <*Loc:* CL, IV, LF, TB, VM, Da84, Gu00, Hi02>

saulier [solje] *n.m.* willow tree <*Loc:* VM>

saulière [soljær] *n.f.* willow grove <*Loc:* IB, JE, SB, TB, VM, Lv88>

saumâtre [sõmat(r)] *adj.* brackish, salty *On avait plein des congos. Mais l'eau salée et saumâtre a venu, ça c'est la seule chose de bien que l'eau saumâtre a fait pour nous, ôter les mauvais serpents.* We had a lot of water moccasins. But salt water and brackish water came in, that's the only good thing that brackish water did for us, to get rid of the bad snakes. (TB) <*Loc:* TB, Da84>

saumon [sõmɔ̃] *n.m.* salmon <*Loc:* Da84>

saumure [sõmyr] *n.f.* brine, pickling solution *Il a fait la saumure pour conserver la viande.* He made brine to preserve the meat. (SB) <*Loc:* AC, SB, Da84>

saut [so] *n.m.* jump, leap, fall **Il a eu un mauvais saut.* He had a bad fall. (Da84) <*Loc:* Da84>

sautaillage [sotijaʒ] *n.m.* jumping around *En principe, les enfants pouvaient jouer dans la cour s'ils étaient bien sages. Il y avait pas de jeux et de cris et de sautaillage.* Generally, children could play in the yard if they behaved themselves. There were no games or yelling or jumping around. (TB) <*Loc:* TB>

sautaillement [sotajmɑ̃] *n.m.* jump, jumping, hopping, skipping, jumping around <*Loc:* Lv88>

sautailler [sotaje] *v.intr.* to jump about, hop, leap, jump up and down *J'aime pas qu'il vient ici parce que ses enfants sautaillent sur mon lit.* I don't like him to come here because his children jump on my bed. (VM) <*Loc:* IB, JE, LA, SM, VM, Lv88>

sauter [sote] *v.tr.* **1** to jump, jump over **Sauter la fosse.* To jump the ditch. (Re31) *Il faut que j'amarre mon chien parce que c'est un sauteur. Il va sauter la barrière.* I have to tie up my dog because he's a jumper. He'll jump the fence. (EV) **2** to skip, pass over, overlook, leave out **3** to flush, force out *Les chiens ont sauté un lapin.* The dogs flushed out a rabbit. (IV) **II** *v.intr.* to jump, leap *Et un soir après gambler, j'ai perdu tout mon argent. Et j'ai été pour sauter dans la Rivière Rouge.* And one night while gambling, I lost all my money. I went to jump into the Red River. (ch: *La valse de la Rivière Rouge*) **J'ai sauté sur ce cheval.* I jumped onto the horse. (SL, An94) **Il est un peu haut. Je vais essayer de sauter et essayer de l'attraper.* It's a bit high. I will try to jump and try to grab it. (LA, An94) ◊ **•sauter (à) la corde** to skip rope, jump rope <SM, Lv88, Re31> **•sauter crapaud (pour qqn)** to be a 'yes man' for s.o., slavishly obey and follow <La99> **•sauter le (manche à) balai** to live together (without benefit of marriage) <IB, LF, SL, TB,

VM, La99, Lv88> **•sauter les rapides** to decend or leap the rapids <Re31> **•sauter sur le casaquin de qqn** to jump on s.o., beat s.o. up <La99> <***Loc:*** AC, AV, EV, IB, IV, LA, LF, SL, SM, TB, VM, An94, Da84, Hi02, La99, Lv88, Re31>

sauterelle [sotrɛl] *n.f.* **1** grasshopper **2** mosquito hawk, dragonfly ◊ **•sauterelle cheval** lubber grasshopper <Lv88, Re31> **•sauterelle de maiche** marsh grasshopper <VM> <***Loc:*** LA, LF, PQ, SL, SM, TB, An94, Da84, Hi02, Lv88, Re31>

sauteur [sotœr] *n.m.* jumper, vaulter *Il faut que j'amarre mon chien parce que c'est un sauteur. Il va sauter la barrière.* I have to tie up my dog because he's a jumper. He'll jump the fence. (EV) <***Loc:*** EV, Da84>

sauvage (**chauvage**) [sovaʒ, ʃovaʒ] *adj.* **1** savage, untamed, wild, uncivilized, undomesticated *Le monde du Marais Bouleur c'est du monde sauvage.* The people of Marais Bouleur are wild. (VM) **2** wild, not cultivated *Riz sauvage.* Wild rice, providence rice. (VM) *Les oignons de mer, c'est des oignons sauvages.* Sea onions are wild onions. (VM) **3** Native American, American Indian **Beaucoup des années passées, depuis les Cadiens est ici, il y a un bayou, et le nom du bayou, c'est le bayou Nez Piqué, et c'est un nom sauvage.* For many years, since the arrival of the Cajuns, there has been a bayou and the name of the bayou is Bayou Nez Piqué, and it's an Indian name. (EV An94) *Ma mère parlait pas bien en français, elle était à moitié sauvage, à moitié indien, Cherokee.* My mother did not speak French well, she was half Indian, Cherokee. (AC) ◊ **•faire sauvage** said of visitors who leave when others arrive <LA> <***Loc:*** AC, EV, SM, VM, An94, Da84, Hi02, Lv88>

sauvage, -esse (**chauvage, -esse**) [sovaʒ, ʃovaʒ, -ɛs] *n.* **1** *(m.)* American Indian, Native American man *Un vieux sauvage.* An old Indian man. (AV) **2** *(f.)* American Indian, Native American woman *La vieille chauvagesse était après cuire son pain.* The old Indian woman was baking her bread. (Lv88) <***Loc:*** AC, AV, EV, IB, JD, LA, LF, SM, TB, VM, Da84, Hi02, Lv88>

sauve [sov, sof] *adj.* **1** safe, unhurt, free of harm, out of danger *Ma mame et mon pape et mes sœurs, ça vient chez moi quand il y a une ouragan parce qu'on est sauve là.* My mom and dad and my sisters, they come to my place when there is a hurricane because we are safe there. (TB) **2** safe, secure, affording protection *Il va aller se mettre dans une place qu'est sauve.* It will go into a place that is safe. (TB) ◊ **•sain et sauve** safe and sound <Da84> <***Loc:*** TB, Da84>

sauver [sove] **I** *v.tr.* **1** to save, keep *On sauvait le sang du cochon pour faire des boudins noirs.* We saved the blood of the pig to make black boudin. (Lv88) **2** to save, rescue *Mon grand-père a sauvé un rougarou.* My grandfather rescued a weredog. (JE) **Ma maman a soigné sa jambe et tout, elle et sa vieille femme. Ils ont pas pu le sauver.* My mom took care of his leg and all, her and his old wife. They weren't able to save him. (SL, An94) **3** to save, prevent from wasting (money or time) *Ça aurait sauvé un tas de temps.* That would have saved a lot of time. (Lv88) *Beaucoup de bons spécials pour vous sauver de l'argent.* Many good specials to save you money. (EV) **4** to put away *Sauver la vaisselle.* To put away the dishes. (VM) **4** to harvest *Sauver le riz.* To harvest rice. (VM) *Il y avait du riz qui restait dans les clos après avoir sauvé la récolte.* There was some rice left in the fields after the harvest was done. (Lv88) **II se sauver** *v.pron.* **1** to save o.s. *Le bateau a calé. Et lui il s'a sauvé sur un baril en bois.* The boat sank. And he saved himself on a wooden barrel. (LF) *Dans la famille c'est moi qui fournis une place pour que la famille se sauve quand y a une ouragan là.* In the family, I'm the one who provides a place for the family to escape to when there's a hurricane. (TB) **2** to run away, escape *Après ça, j'ai été obligé de me sauver et me cacher.* After that, I had to run away and hide. (SL) **Il y avait un homme qui était après voyager à pied dans le bois et il y a un gros, gros chat, terrible gros chat qui a tombé derrière lui. Il a pris à se sauver, sauver, sauver.* There was a man who was walking in the woods and there's a great big cat, a huge cat that came up behind him. He started running away. (AC, An94) <***Loc:*** AC, AV, EV, JD, JE, LA, LF, SJ, SL, SM, TB, VM, An94, Da84, Hi02, Lv88>

sauveur, -euse [sovœr, -øz] *n.m.* savior, rescuer, saver <***Loc:*** Da84>

savane (**savanne**) [savɑ̃n] *n.f.* **1** pasture, prairie, uncultivated land, meadow, grassland *Souvent des fois, on allait là-bas dans la savane, on s'en venait* BACK *avec deux cents lapins.* Many times, we would go there in the meadow and bring back two hundred rabbits. (IB) **2** enclosed pasture (i.e. fenced-in area for grazing) ◊ **•en savane** lying fallow **J'ai mis une partie de mon clos en savane.* I left a piece of the field fallow. (Di32) <Di32> <***Loc:*** AC, AV, EV, IB, LA, LF, SB, SL, SM, TB, VM, An94, Da84, Di32, Gu00, Hi02, Lv88, Ph36, Re31>

savaner[1] [savɑ̃ne] *v.tr.* to separate the hull from the kernel (of beans, peas, rice, etc.) *J'ai savané mes fèves.* I hulled my beans. (IB) <***Loc:*** IB>

savaner[2] [savɑ̃ne] *v.tr.* to squander, waste *Savaner sa jeunesse.* To throw away one's youth. (SJ) <***Loc:*** SJ>

savanne ♦see **savane**

savant[1]**, -e** [savɑ̃, -ɑ̃t] *adj.* **1** educated, literate *Pour écrire des lettres, ça trouvait une personne savante.* To write letters, they would find someone educated. (LA) **2** knowledgeable *Je peux défaire une machine et tout secouer les morceaux d'un* CAN *de cinq gallons et là les remettre à* BACK. *Je suis joliment savant là-dedans.* I can take a machine apart and shake all the pieces up in a five gallon can and then put them back together. I'm quite knowledgeable about that. (TB) <***Loc:*** LA, TB, Da84>

savant[2]**, -e** [savɑ̃, -ɑ̃t] *n.* **1** learned person, wise person **2** one who knows everything that is going on <*Loc:* VM, Da84>

savate [savat] *n.f.* **1** any low top, low quarter, slip-on shoe **2** woman's dress shoe **3** slipper, bedroom slipper ◊ **•savate de chambre {maison}** slipper <LF, VM> <*Loc:* AV, EV, IB, IV, JD, JE, LA, LF, SB, SJ, SL, SM, TB, VM, Da84, Hi02, Lv88, Re31>

savoir[1] [savwar, sawar] *v.tr.* **1** to know, be informed of, understand *Je veux savoir pourquoi ça m'avait sui hier au soir.* I want to know why they followed me last night. (LF) *Quoi-faire tu veux savoir?* Why do you want to know? (JE) *Je suis tout le temps le dernier pour savoir.* I'm always the last one to know. (JE) *Vous sait que c'est vrai.* You know it's true. (TB) *Et là c'était comme un navire allait laisser le port de la Nouvelle Orléans, notre job c'était pour mettre les messages dans les codes et là t'envoyais ça dessus le radio dans différentes places pour les laisser savoir équand le navire allait laisser le port et quand il devrait arriver là-bas et qui-ce qu'il y avait dessus le navire.* And then when a ship was going to leave the port of New Orleans, our job was to put the messages in codes and then you would send that out on the radio to different places to let them know when the ship was going to leave the port and when it should arrive there and what there was on the ship. (LF) *Comment on était pas malade, je ne sais pas.* How we didn't get sick, I don't know. (IB) **2** to know, be acquainted with (a person) *Elle savait tout le monde.* She knew everybody. (Lv88) *Je savais pas mon père, il était mort.* I did not know my father, he was dead. (IB) ◊ **•savoir et où son pain est beurré** to know where one's bread is buttered, know where one's interests lie <Da84> **•savoir mieux** to know better **Il aurait dû savoir mieux que ça.* He should have known better than that. (IV, An94) <IV, An94> **•savoir où cabri porte la queue** to know how far to go in a given situation <SM> <*Loc:* AC, EV, IB, IV, JE, LA, LF, PQ, SB, SL, SM, TB, VM, An94, Da84, Hi02, Lv88>

savoir[2] [savwar, sawar] *n.m.* knowledge, learning *Pourtant, il a assez de savoir pour connaître mieux.* Yet he has enough knowledge to know better. (LA) <*Loc:* LA, Da84>

savoir-faire [savwarfær] *n.m.* know-how, practical knowledge <*Loc:* Da84, Hi02>

savon [savɔ̃] *n.m.* soap ◊ **•savon du pays** homemade lye soap <EV, LA, SL, SM, VM, Da84> <*Loc:* AC, EV, LA, SL, SM, TB, VM, Da84, Hi02>

savonnage [savɔ̃naʒ] *n.m.* reprimand, scolding *Donner un bon savonnage à quelqu'un.* To give someone a good scolding. (SJ) <*Loc:* AV, IB, SJ, Lv88>

savonner [savɔ̃ne] **I** *v.tr.* to soap, wash with soap *Il a bien savonné ses mains.* He soaped his hands well. (LA) *Eusse a savonné sa langue! Et il a pas jamais rejuré après ça.* They soaped his tongue! And he never swore again after that. (TB) **II se savonner** *v.pron.* to soap o.s. *Le bébé s'avait tout savonné avant que sa mère retourne.* The baby had completely soaped himself before his mother returned. (LA) ◊ **•se savonner la figure** to wash one's face with soap *Va te savonner la figure avant de t'assir à la table.* Go and wash your face with soap before sitting at the table. (LA) <LA, Da84> <*Loc:* LA, TB, Da84>

savonnette [savɔ̃nɛt, savɔ̃net] *n.f.* **1** bar of dainty, perfumed soap **2** soapbox **3** soap dish **4** shaving mug **5** shaving brush <*Loc:* AV, IB, LF, SJ, SL, SM, VM, Lv88>

savonnure (savonnière) [savɔ̃nyr, savɔ̃nœr, savɔ̃njær] *n.f.* **1** soapy water, dishwater *J'ai mis le linge dans la savonnure.* I put the laundry in the soapy water. (IB) **2** soap suds *J'ai fait un tas de savonnure dans l'eau.* I made a lot of soap suds in the water. (SL) **3** soaping up, lathering *Je l'ai donné une bonne savonnure.* I gave him a good soaping up. (TB) <*Loc:* EV, IB, JD, LA, LF, SL, SM, TB, VM, Da84, Lv88, Ph36>

SAY-SO (séceau) [seso] *n.m.* ice-cream cone ◊ **•SAY-SO de crème** ice-cream cone <Re31> <*Loc:* EV, LA, SM, VM, Da84, Lv88, Ph36, Re31>

scabreux, -euse [skabrø, -øz] *adj.* rough, difficult *Ils ont passé un temps scabreux.* They went through a difficult period. (LA) *Les affaires sont scabreux avec la guerre.* Business is bad with the war. (VM) <*Loc:* LA, VM, Da84>

scandale (escandale) [skɑ̃dal, ɛskɑ̃dal, eskɑ̃dal] *n.m./f.* **1** scandal **2** noisy argument, quarrel, row **3** uproar, noise, racket *C'était une grande escandale.* There was a great uproar. (LF) ◊ **•faire un scandale** ***a*** to create a big row or fuss ***b*** to raise hell, raise a ruckus <Da84> <*Loc:* LF, SM, VM, Da84, Lv88>

scapulaire (escapulaire, caspulaire) [skapylær, ɛskapylær, kaspylær] *n.m.* scapular <*Loc:* LF, SJ, SM, Da84>

scarf [skarf] *n.m.* scarf <*Loc:* SL, Lv88>

scarlatine [skarlatin] *n.f.* scarlet fever <*Loc:* Da84>

scélérat [selera] *n.m.* rascal, scoundrel, villain <*Loc:* Da84>

scène [sɛ̃n] *n.f.* **1** scene **2** quarrel, row ◊ **•faire une scène** to make a scene *Fais pas une scène devant tout le monde.* Don't make a scene in front of everyone. (LA) <LA, Da84> <*Loc:* LA, Da84>

sciage [sjaʒ] *n.m.* sawing <*Loc:* Da84>

scie [si] *n.f.* saw ◊ **•scie à bois** carpenter's saw <JE> **•scie à électricité** power saw, circular saw <JE> **•scie à fer** hacksaw <JE> **•scie à (la) main** handsaw *On les coupait avec une scie à la main.* We would cut them with a handsaw. (AC) <AC, SL, TB> **•scie de travers** crosscut saw <TB> **•scie électrique** electric saw <LF> **•scie ronde** circular saw <SM, Lv88> <*Loc:* AC, EV, JE, SL, SM, TB, Da84, Hi02>

science [sjɑ̃s] *n.f.* science, learning <*Loc:* Da84>

scientiste [sjɑ̃tist] *n.m.* scientist <*Loc:* Da84>

scier [sje] *v.tr.* to saw, cut with a saw *On va dans le bois, prend à scier des logs.* We go to the woods, start cutting logs. (SL) <*Loc:* EV, SL, Da84>

scierie [siri] *n.f.* sawing <*Loc:* Da84>

scieur [sjœr] *n.m.* sawyer <*Loc:* JE, Da84>

scigailler [sigaje] *v.tr.* to cut, saw *Il a scigaillé la corde.* He cut the rope. (AV) <*Loc:* AV>

scorpion [skɔrpjɔ̃] *n.m.* scorpion <*Loc:* Da84>

SCREEN [skrin] *n.m.* screen (for doors and windows) <*Loc:* EV, Lv88, Ph36>

sculpture [skyltyr, skylptyr] *n.f.* sculpture, carving <*Loc:* LF, Da84>

se [s(ə)] *(before a vowel* **s'** [s]*) pron.pers.* **1** *(refl.)* himself, herself, itself, oneself **Il s'a levé debout et il a laché sa main gauche.* He got up and let go of his left hand. (EV, An84) *Et un homme s'habituait à faire quelque chose comme ça et après ça il était en demande.* And a man would get used to doing something like that, and after that he was in demand. (LF) *Elle avait été au couvent pour se mettre sœur.* She had gone to the convent to become a nun. (SL) **Se faire du pain.* To make oneself some bread. (Da84) **2** *(refl.)* ourselves *On s'est bâti en 1960.* We built ourselves a house in 1960. (Lv88) *On s'a plaint assez. C'est l'heure de se mettre à l'ouvrage.* We've complained enough. It's time to get to work. (LA) *On se met par piquets épaillés dans le bois pour chasser.* We spread out by groups in the woods for hunting. (Lv88) **3** *(refl.)* yourself, yourselves *Comment vous s'appelez?* What is your name? (LF) *Peut-être que vous se rappelez de ça.* Maybe you remember that. (TB) *Si vous se fait prendre, les* FINE *est mauvais.* If you get caught, the fines are stiff. (TB) *M. peut m'appeler si alle meurt avant que vous-autres s'en revient.* M. can call me if she dies before you all come back. (TB) **4** *(refl.)* themselves *Si ça se conformait pas, le constable les mettait à la porte.* If they didn't behave themselves, the bouncer would kick them out. (LA) *Dans le temps, les femmes se voilaient pour aller à confession.* In the old days, women wore a veil to go to confession. (VM) *Les poules étaient après se vanner en bas de la maison ayoù la terre était toujours sec.* The chickens were taking a dust bath under the house where the dirt was still dry. (LA) **5** *(recip.)* each other *Ça s'embrassait à chaque fois que ça se voyait.* They kissed each time they saw each other. (EV) *Moi et toi se regarde vis-à-vis.* You and I are looking at each other face to face. (LF) *Dans le vieux temps, ça pouvait pas se becquer comme asteur.* In the old days, they couldn't kiss each other like now. (LA) *Mon et mon frère, on a eu une telle ostination qu'on se parle jamais.* My brother and I had such a quarrel that we never speak to each other. (VM) **Bien mais, ça se ressemble ou ça se ressemble pas?* Well then, do they resemble each other or not? (EV, An94) *Les deux garçons se halaillaient l'un à l'autre.* The two boys argued with each other. (Lv88) <*Loc:* EV, LA, LF, SL, TB, VM, An84, An94, Da84, Hi02, Lv88>

seau ♦see **siau**

sec[1] **(sèque)** [sɛk] *adj.* *(f.* **sèche** [sɛʃ] *is rare)* **1** dry *Une poussière sec.* Dry dust. (Lv88) **Il sifflait, il chantait, mais tout d'un coup, tandis qu'il traversait un marais sec, il a vu des craques dans la terre, des grosses craques.* He was whistling, he was singing, but all of a sudden, while he was crossing a dry swamp, he saw cracks in the earth, big cracks. (EV, An94) **"Mais," il dit, "j'ai venu pour te dire qu'elle est sèque. Elle est parée pour une seconde couche."* "Well," he says, "I came to tell you that she's dry. She's ready for a second coat." (SL, An94) **2** dried *Des prunes secs.* Dried prunes. (Lv88) **3** sharp, harsh (e.g. words, manner of speaking) *Il m'a parlé dans une manière joliment sec.* He spoke to me in a rather sharp manner. (LA) **4** sharp, crisp (of a sound) *Et il dit le bon son, c'est sec, il faut que ça soye un son sec. C'est ça qu'un canard fait.* And he said that the right sound is crisp, it has to be a crisp sound. That's what a duck makes. (TB) ◊ **•être à sec** to be in a dry area <Da84> **•il fait sec** the weather is dry *Moi je pêche dans les bayous, mais l'eau est tellement basse, tellement il fait sec que l'eau est pas bonne, et alors un poisson mord pas.* I fish in the bayous, but the water is so low, it's so dry that the [condition of the] water isn't right, and so a fish won't bite. (SL) <SL> <*Loc:* AC, EV, LA, LF, SL, TB, VM, An94, Da84, Lv88, Wh83>

sec[2] [sɛk] *adv.* in a dry, sharp manner *Il m'a répondu sec.* He answered me sharply. (LA) <*Loc:* LA>

sécataire [sekatær] *n.m.* pruning scissors <*Loc:* SM>

séceau ♦see **SAY-SO**

séchade [seʃad] *n.f.* drying *J'ai fait une séchade de linge.* I dried a load of clothes. (SB) <*Loc:* SB>

séchage ♦see **chessage**

sèche ♦see **chesse**

sécher ♦see **chesser**

sécheresse ♦see **chesseresse**

sécheuse ♦see **chesseuse**

second[1], **-e** [səgɔ̃, -ɔd] *adj.* second **"Mais," il dit, "j'ai venu pour te dire qu'elle est sèque. Elle est parée pour une seconde couche."* "Well," he says, "I came to tell you that it she is dry. She's ready for a second coat." (SL, An94) *Un jurement tous les seconds mots elle dit.* A curse word every other word that she says. (Lv88) ◊ **•(de) seconde main** secondhand, used **C'était pas un violon neuf. C'était un seconde main.* It wasn't a new violin. It was a used one. (JD, An84) *Un char de seconde main.* A secondhand car. (LA) <JD, LA, TB, An84> <*Loc:* JD, LA, SL, An84, An94, Da84>

second[2] [səgɔ̃] *n.m.* bass key (on an accordion) <*Loc:* EV>

seconde [səgɔ̃d] *n.f.* second (of time) *Si tu fous un baril par terre, cinq secondes de* PENALTY. *Alors tu peux pas gagner, si tu vois quelqu'un qui fout un baril par terre tu sais qu'il a pas gagné.* If you knock a barrel over, five seconds penalty. So you can't win, if you see someone knock a barrel over you know he hasn't won. (LF) <***Loc:*** LF, Da84, Hi02>

seconder (**segonner**) [səgɔ̃de, səgɔ̃ne] *v.intr.* to second, back up, play second (harmony) fiddle *J'avais pas l'habitude de seconder.* I was not used to playing second fiddle. (VM) <***Loc:*** VM, An84, Da84, Gr86, Hi02>

secondeur (**segonneur**) [səgɔ̃dœr, səgɔ̃nœr] *n.m.* accompanying fiddler, second fiddler <***Loc:*** EV, Gr86>

secouage [səkuaʒ] *n.m.* shaking, jolting, jolt <***Loc:*** Da84>

secouée [skwe] *n.f.* blow (physical or moral) <***Loc:*** JD>

secouement [səkumɑ̃] *n.m.* shaking, jolting, jolt <***Loc:*** Da84>

secouer (**escouer**) [səkue, sukwe, sukuje, ɛskue, ɛskwe, eskwe] **I** *v.tr.* **1** to shake *Je peux défaire une machine et tout secouer les morceaux d'un* CAN *de cinq gallons et là les remettre à* BACK. I can take a machine apart and shake all the pieces up in a five gallon can and then put them back together. (TB) *Je vas au bal tous les samedis pour escouer mes vieilles pattes.* I go to the dance every Saturday to shake up my old feet. (Lv88, ch: *Lâche pas la patate*) **2** to shock, jolt *Ça m'a escoué, cette nouvelle.* It shocked me, this news. (SM) **II** *v.intr.* **1** to shake *La maison était après secouer.* The house was shaking. (JE) *Le bateau secoue.* The boat is shaking. (LF) **2** to shake o.s. off *Quand ce petit chien s'a mis à secouer, il a laissé de la boue tout partout.* When that little dog started shaking himself off, he left mud everywhere. (EV) **III se secouer** *v.pron.* to shake o.s. *Le chien s'a secoué en sortant du lac.* The dog shook itself after coming out of the lake. (VM) **À chaque fois on jetait de la terre, il s'escouait.* Each time we threw dirt, he would shake himself. (EV, An94) ◊ **•secouer la main** to shake hands (in greeting) *On était pas gêné pour dire bonjour ou secouer la main.* We were not uncomfortable to say hello or to shake hands. (IB) <IB> <***Loc:*** EV, IB, JE, LF, SB, SL, SM, TB, VM, An94, Da84, Gr86, Hi02, Lv88>

secourir [səkurir, sukurir] (*p.p.* **secouri** [səkuri]) *v.tr.* to aid, help, assist *Pour ça je l'ai secouri, il m'a donné trois piastres.* Because I helped him, he gave me three dollars. (VM) **Tout ce que te demande, c'est de secourir le monde, surtout les vieilles veuves.* All that I ask of you, it's to help the people, especially the old widows. (IV, An94) <***Loc:*** IV, VM, An94, Da84>

secours [səkur, sekur, sukur] *n.m.* help, aid, assistance *Il y avait pas de docteur et c'est le seul secours que le monde avait.* There was no doctor and that was the only help that people had. (TB) *Donne-moi du secours.* Help me. (VM) *J'ai offri mon secours.* I offered my help. (VM) <***Loc:*** EV, TB, VM, An94, Da84, Hi02>

secousse (**escousse**) [səkus, ɛskus, eskus] *n.m./f.* **1** shock, blow, jolt *Il s'a donné un joli escousse équand il a tombé.* He gave himself a good jolt when he fell. (VM) **2** crisis *Il a eu une autre escousse.* He had another crisis. (Lv88) *J'ai eu encore une mauvaise escousse.* I had another nasty shock. (SM) **3** moment, short period of time *Il y a une secousse que je t'espère.* I've been waiting for you for a while (VM) *Je vais venir te ramasser dans une secousse.* I'll come and pick you up in a moment. (Lv88) *Je l'ai attendu une secousse.* I waited a moment for him. (SM) **4** fit, short period of intense activity *J'avais un escousse de travailler à ce matin.* I had a fit of working this morning. (VM) ◊ **•par escousse(s)** from time to time, intermittently *Il travaille par escousse.* He works intermittently. (SM, VM) <SM, VM> **•tout d'un(e) escousse** all at once, all of a sudden **Ça fait, tout d'un escousse, elle dit, "*BOY, BOY*! Ça, c'est un vilain temps pour le monde qu'est pas chez eux!* So, all of a sudden, she said, "Boy, boy! That's terrible weather for people who are not home." (SL, An94) <SL, An94, Lv88> <***Loc:*** SL, SM, VM, An94, Da84, Hi02, Lv88>

secret[1] [səkrɛ, səkre, səgre] *adj.* secret, hidden, private *Un amour secret.* A secret love. (LA) ◊ **•en secret** in secret, secretly *Ils étaient mariés en secret dix mois avant que son père a su.* They were secretly married for ten months before her father found out. (EV) <EV, Da84> <***Loc:*** EV, LA, Da84>

secret[2] [səkrɛ, səkre, səgre, sagre] *n.m.* secret *Tu peux pas 'i dire arien. Alle peut pas garder un secret. C'est plus fort que elle.* You can't tell her anything. She can't keep a secret. It's bigger than she is. (VM, Gu00) **Je vas te dire un petit secret.* I'm going to tell you a little secret. (LA, An94) <***Loc:*** LA, LF, VM, An94, Da84, Gu00, Lv88>

secrétaire [səkretær] *n.* **1** secretary **2** writing desk <***Loc:*** Da84>

section [sɛksjɔ̃] *n.f.* **1** section, division *Une section de levée pour assayer de protecter le monde pour une ouragan [...] Mon je vois si tellement de perte que deux générations d'ici mon je sais pas qui-ce qui va arriver.* A section of levee to try to protect people from a hurricane. I see so much loss [of land] that in two generations I don't know what will happen. (TB) **2** parcel of land measuring 640 acres (one square mile) ◊ **•être en section** to be rough, difficult **Les affaires sont en section.* Things are rough. (Da84) <Da84> <***Loc:*** LF, Da84, Lv88>

séculier [sekylje] *adj.* [*eccl.*] secular, worldly **Prêtre séculier.* Secular priest. (Da84) <***Loc:*** Da84>

sécurité [sekyrite, sykyrite] *n.f.* **1** security, safety **2** collateral guarantee <***Loc:*** SM, VM, Da84>

segonner ♦see **seconder**

segonneur ♦see **secondeur**

seigneur [sẽɲœr, sẽjœr] *n.m.* lord **Mon Dieu Seigneurl* My Lord! Good Lord! (Da84) <***Loc:*** Da84, Hi02, La99>

seillon ♦see **sillon**

seillonner ♦see **sillonner**

sein [sẽ] *n.m.* bosom, breast *La bosse dans son sein la préoccupe.* The lump in her breast worries her. (VM) <***Loc:*** VM, Da84, Hi02>

seine [sẽn] *n.f.* **1** net, seine, seine fishing net *Une seine, il faut tu la hales, tu la hales jusqu'à t'arrives au* BOAT. A fishing net, you have to haul it, you haul it until you get to the boat. (JE) *Et ça empoignait la chevrette avec des filets, les Cadiens appellent ça une seine. Et ça se mettait à l'eau et eusse halait la seine et eusse faisait un cercle pour entasser les chevrettes pour les ramasser.* And they would catch the shrimp with nets, Cajuns call it a "seine." It would be put in the water and they would haul the net and they would make a circle to collect the shrimp, to pick them up. (LF) **2** gillnet ◊ **•seine à poisson** monofilament fishing net, seine <LF> **•seine à trois mailles** type of seine with a pouch <IV> **•aller à la seine** to go seining <Da84> <*Loc:* IV, JE, LF, SL, SM, TB, Da84>

seiner [sẽne] **I** *v.tr.* to seine, catch with a net *Une seine c'est pour seiner les chevrettes ça.* A seine is for catching shrimp. (TB) **II** *v.intr.* to fish with a seine *Les pêcheurs vont pour seiner ou trawler.* Fishermen either go seining or trawling (Lv88) *On seinait pour les écrevisses au long de la levée.* We seined to catch crawfish along the levee. (SM) <*Loc:* EV, IV, LA, SL, SM, TB, VM, Da84, Lv88, Ph36>

seize [sɛz] *adj./n.m.* sixteen **Il est revenu avec une carpe de seize livres.* He came back with a sixteen-pound carp. (EV, An94) <*Loc:* AC, EV, TB, An94, Da84, Hi02>

seizième [sɛzjẽm] *adj./n.* sixteenth *Leur seizième enfant.* Their sixteenth child. (EV) *Ils ont pas eu plus qu'un seizième dans leur* LEASE. They didn't get more than a sixteenth in their lease. (LA) <*Loc:* EV, LA, Da84>

séjour [seʒur] *n.m.* stay, sojourn <*Loc:* Da84>

sel [sɛl] *n.m.* salt **Oublie pas aussi de mettre sel et persil dans le gumbo.* Also don't forget to put salt and parsley in the gumbo. (EV, An94) ◊ **•sel à purger** Epsom salts <IB, SB, SM> **•sel d'epsom** [sɛldapsɔ̃, sɛldapsɔ̃m] Epsom salts <SM, TB, Da84> **•sel de table** table salt <TB> <*Loc:* EV, IB, IV, JE, SB, SL, SM, TB, An94, Da84, Hi02>

sélecter [selɛkte] *v.tr.* to select, choose *Sélecter un nouveau char.* To select a new car. (VM) <*Loc:* VM, Da84>

sélection [selɛksjɔ̃] *n.f.* selection, choice <*Loc:* Da84>

selle [sɛl] *n.f.* **1** saddle *Il y avait un chemin le long du Bayou Lafourche que le monde passait à pied pour haler la cordelle du bateau. Tu vois t'avais une cordelle tu pouvais te la haler[...] J'aurais pu prendre mon cheval et l'amarrer sur la selle et la haler jusqu'à qu'un autre le prend.* There was a road along Bayou Lafourche that people travelled on foot to tow the boat with a cordelle. You see you had a cordelle, you could haul it. I could have taken my horse and tied it to the saddle and hauled it until another took it. (LF) **2** bowel movement, feces ◊ **•aller à la selle / avoir une selle** to have a bowel movement <Da84> <*Loc:* AV, IB, JE, LF, SL, An94, Da84, Hi02>

seller [sele] *v.tr.* to saddle, saddle up *Moi, je prends mon vieux cheval et j'attrape ma vieille selle. Je selle mon vieux cheval pour aller chercher ma belle.* I take my old horse and I get my old saddle. I saddle my old horse to go get my girl. (ch: *Travailler, c'est trop dur*) ◊ **•c'est sellé et bridé** all is complete, nothing is missing (of a situation) <JD, La99> <*Loc:* JD, Da84, Hi02, La99>

selon [səlɔ̃] *prep.* according to *Selon le bougre du temps ça va pas mouiller demain.* According to the weatherman, it's not going to rain tomorrow. (LA) ◊ **•c'est selon** it depends <LF, TB, Da84> <*Loc:* LA, LF, TB, Da84, Hi02>

semage [sẽmaʒ, səmaʒ] *n.m.* **1** sowings, seeds **2** sowing time *Pendant le semage.* At sowing time. (SJ) <*Loc:* AV, IB, SB, SJ, Lv88>

semaine [s(ə)mẽn] *n.f.* week ◊ **•semaine des quatre jeudis** when pigs fly (i.e. never) <LF> **•la semaine passée** last week <TB, Da84> **•la semaine prochaine** next week <Da84> **•la semaine qui vient** next week <Da84> **•la Semaine Sainte** Holy Week <TB, Da84> **•avoir une semaine** to menstruate <VM> **•par semaine** per week, weekly <SL, VM> <*Loc:* AC, EV, LF, SL, TB, VM, An94, Da84>

semblance [sɑ̃blɑ̃s] *n.f.* resemblance, semblance, likeness <*Loc:* JD, SB, Da84>

semblant [sɑ̃blɑ̃] *n.m.* feint, pretense **C'est juste des semblants.* That's just pretense. (Da84) ◊ **•faire semblant (de)** to make believe, pretend, feign **Et ils ont fait semblant d'aller marcher dans le bois. Et quand ils ont été un peu loin, ils ont tous parti et ils sont rentournés au wagon.* And they pretended to go walking in the woods. And when they had gone a little way, they all left and they returned to the wagon. (LA, An94) <LA, An94, Da84> <*Loc:* LA, An94, Da84>

sembler [sɑ̃ble] *v.intr.* **1** to seem, appear *Mais Dud, c'est la cinquième fois qu'on est venu ici au Docteur Latour et tu sembles assez gaillard.* But Dud, it's the fifth time we have come here to Dr. Latour's and you seem to be in good health. (ThCa: *Messieurs, mesdames*) *Il semble d'être beaucoup intéressé après elle.* He seems to be very interested in her. (EV) **2** to resemble *Elle avait des durillons et des cors sur les orteils qui semblaient à des nœuds de bois gras.* She had corns and callouses on her toes that ressembled knots of long-leaf pine. (AV) <*Loc:* AV, EV, LF, SM, Da84, ThCa>

semelle [smel, symɛl] *n.f.* sole (of a shoe) <*Loc:* SM, Da84, Lv88>

semence [səmɑ̃s] *n.f.* **1** seed **2** semen <*Loc:* AC, Da84>

semer [səme] *v.tr.* **1** to sow, plant *Ma grand-mère semait toujours son persil le vendredi saint.* My grandmother always planted her parsley seed on Good Friday. (VM) **2** to spread (gossip, rumors, etc.) *Qui ce qui a semé cette histoire?* Who spread that story? (LA) **3** to abandon, cast off *Comment t'as eu ton chien? Il y a quelqu'un qui a semé ça ici.* How did you get your dog? Somebody abandoned it here. (LA) ◊ **•semer de la merde** to cause trouble (through gossip) <EV> <*Loc:* EV, LA, VM, Da84>

séminaire [sẽminær] *n.m.* seminary <***Loc:*** Da84>

séminarien [sẽminarjẽ] *n.m.* [*eccl.*] seminarian <***Loc:*** Da84>

séminariste [sẽminarist] *n.m.* [*eccl.*] seminarian <***Loc:*** Da84>

sénat [sena] *n.m.* senate <***Loc:*** Da84>

sénateur [senatœr] *n.m.* senator <***Loc:*** Da84>

séné [sẽne] *n.m.* senna <***Loc:*** SM>

senelle [snɛl] *n.f.* cinch ◊ •**être une senelle** to be a cinch, be easy *Mais, ça, c'est une senelle.* But it's a cinch. (VM) <VM> <***Loc:*** EV, VM, Ph36>

sens [sɑ̃s] *n.m.* **1** sense **2** direction **Dans ma famille on a jamais eu besoin de 'garder dans ein liv' pour sa'oir dans quel sens le vent soufflait.* In my family we have never needed to look in a book to know which way the wind was blowing. (ThCa: *Mille misères*) ◊ •**bon sens** good sense, common sense **Ça fait pas de bon sens.* That does not make sense. (Da84) <Da84, Hi02> <***Loc:*** Da84, Hi02, ThCa>

sensation [sɑ̃sasjɔ̃] *n.f.* feeling, sensation <***Loc:*** Da84>

sensible (**sensive**) [sɑ̃sib(l), sɑ̃siv] *adj.* sensitive, tender **Jean Sot avait le cœur, on conte, beaucoup sensible. Il aimait tout le monde.* Jean Sot, they say, had a very tender heart. He loved everyone. (EV, An94) <***Loc:*** EV, An94, Da84>

sensive ♦see **sensible**

sentence [sɑ̃tɑ̃s] *n.f.* sentence, verdict <***Loc:*** Da84>

senteur [sɑ̃tœr] *n.f.* odor, smell, scent <***Loc:*** Da84>

sentiment [sɑ̃timɑ̃] *n.m.* **1** feeling *Là on est après brûler nos cannes [...] Le sentiment du monde alentour ici dans les terres d'agriculture de faire des cannes, c'est manière contre nous-autres parce que ça envoye un tas de drigailles dans l'air.* Now we're burning sugarcane stubble. The feeling of people around here in the sugarcane farming area is somewhat against us because it throws a lot of junk [i.e. chaff and dust] into the air. (AS) **2** sentiment, affection **Il aimait jusqu'à la nature, les arbres, les fleurs, la terre. Il avait un grand sentiment pour tout ce qui existait.* He even loved nature, trees, flowers, the earth. He had great affection for everything that existed. (EV, An94) **3** opinion, idea <***Loc:*** EV, An94, Da84>

sentir [sɑ̃tir] (*p.p.* **senti** [sɑ̃ti], **sentu** [sɑ̃ty]) **I** *v.tr.* **1** to feel **Il a senti le fouette.* He felt the whip. (Da84) **Il connaît le chien était après le toucher, mais il sentait pas à rien. C'est comme si c'était juste du vent.* He knew the dog was touching him, but he didn't feel anything. It was as if it was just the wind. (SM, An94) **2** to smell **Il a senti le dîner.* He smelled the dinner. (Da84) **Je sens de la viande fraîche.* I smell fresh meat. (LA, An94) **3** to smell of, have the smell of *Ça sent le melon ici-dans.* It smells like melon in here. (EV) **II** *v.intr.* to smell, have an odor *L'eau sentait, ça sentait, des mauvaises odeurs dans tout le bayou. Tout le chemin.* The water smelled, it smelled, bad odors throughout the bayou. The whole way. (TB) **Ça sent bon.* That smells good. (Da84) **III se sentir** *v.pron.* to feel **Ça fait, mon papa a dit, "Si tu te sens comme ça,* GO AHEAD." So my dad said, "If that's the way you feel, go ahead." (LA, An94) **Je me sens assez bien que je peux courir en travers d'une barrière à fil de fer sans attraper aucune blessure.* I feel so good that I can run across a barbed wire fence without getting any injury. (ThCa: *Messieurs, mesdames*) ◊ •**se sentir bête** to feel foolish <Da84> •**se sentir bien** to feel well <Da84> •**se sentir chéti** to feel badly <Da84> •**se sentir faille** to have a weak spell, feel faint *Quand j'espère trop longtemps avant de manger, je me sens faille.* If I wait too long before I eat, I feel faint. (Gu00) <SM, Gu00, Lv88> •**se sentir foutaise {malade}** to feel sick <Da84, Lv88> <***Loc:*** EV, LA, SL, SM, TB, An94, Da84, Gu00, Hi02, Lv88, ThCa>

séparable [separab(l)] *adj.* separable *Ces amis sont pas séparables. C'est comme St. Roch et son chien.* Those two friends are inseparable. They're like St. Roc and his dog. (LA) <***Loc:*** LA, Da84>

séparation [separasjɔ̃] *n.f.* **1** separation **2** partition (inside a room) <***Loc:*** SL, TB, Da84>

séparément [separemɑ̃] *adv.* separately *Chacun a fait sa liste séparément.* Each one made his list separately. (EV) <***Loc:*** EV, Da84>

séparer [separe] **I** *v.tr.* **1** to separate, part *C'était juste le bayou qui sépare le monde là-bas et le monde ici.* There was just the bayou that separates the people over there from the people here. (TB) **2** to divide, distribute *Le samedi d'après, un autre aurait tué son veau et il aurait séparé la viande parmi les autres, c'étiont comme un groupe.* The following Saturday, another one would kill his calf and he would divide the meat among the other ones, they were like a group. (AC) **Alors là, ils ont appelé tout le monde et puis ils l'ont séparé. Et il a donné cinquante barils de graisse. Et l'armée a pris la viande, et il y en a eu pour une année, avec cette viande de ce cocodril-là.* So then they called everyone and then they separated it [the alligator carcass]. And it gave fifty barrels of grease. The army took the meat, and there was a year's worth with this meat from this alligator. (EV, An94) **II se séparer** *v.pron.* to separate, part, come apart, split up *Plus tard dans la vie, la chicane a pris. On pouvait plus s'accorder, on s'a séparé.* Later in life the fighting started. We couldn't get along anymore, we split up (ch: *French blues*) *Et puis le beurre prendait à se faire et ça se séparait et c'était le gras du crème.* And then the butter would start to form and the fat of the cream would separate. (AC) ◊ •**être séparé** to be separated (of a couple) *On est séparé mais on est toujours amis, elle vient toujours, à tous moments faire un tour.* We are separated but we are still friends, she always comes, she stops by all the time. (AV) <AV> <***Loc:*** AC, AV, EV, LA, LF, TB, An94, Da84, Hi02>

sept [sɛt] *adj./n.m.* seven *Ma maison a sept chambres.* My house has seven rooms. (Gu00) *Le sept de juillet.* The seventh of July. (LF) <***Loc:*** AC, AV, EV, IV, LA, LF, PQ, SL, SM, TB, An94, Da84, Gu00, Hi02, Lv88>

septembre [septɑ̃m, sɛptɑ̃b(r), sɛktɑ̃m, sɛktɑ̃b(r)] *n.m.* September <*Loc:* AC, EV, LF, SM, TB, Da84, Hi02, Lv88>

septième [sɛtjɛ̃m] *adj./n.* seventh *Ma mère était la septième de huit filles.* My mother was the seventh of eight daughters. (EV) <*Loc:* AC, EV, Da84>

séquelle [sekɛl] *n.f.* gang, bunch ◊ **•toute la sacrée séquelle** the whole damn bunch, the whole shebang <Da84> <*Loc:* Da84>

séquence [sekɑ̃s, sẽkɑ̃s] *n.f.* **1** sequence **2** straight (in poker) <*Loc:* LF, Da84>

séquir [sekir] **I** *v.tr.* to dry, cause to dry **II** *v.intr.* to dry, dry out, become dry <*Loc:* JD>

sérail [seraj, saraj, sœraj] *n.m.* noise, uproar, disturbance *Faire un grand sérail.* To make a loud racket. (SJ) *C'était un grand sérail quand le toit a tombé.* There was a great noise when the roof fell in. (IB) *Et le soir eusse attendait les sérails dedans la cuisine, quelqu'un qui lavait la vaisselle et tout.* And in the evening they heard noises in the kitchen, someone who was washing the dishes and all. (TB) ◊ **•en sérail** on the outs *On est tout le temps en sérail.* We're always on the outs. (TB) <TB> <*Loc:* AV, EV, IB, LA, LF, SB, SJ, SL, SM, TB, Lv88, Ph36>

serboucane ♦see **sarboucane**

serclage [særklaʒ] *n.m./f.* **1** weeding **2** weeding season <*Loc:* IB, SJ>

sercler [særkle] *v.tr.* to weed, cut (weeds) with a sickle or scythe <*Loc:* IB, JE, SJ>

sercleur [særklœr] *n.m.* weeder, one who weeds <*Loc:* IB, SJ>

serein [serɛ̃, sərɛ̃] *n.m.* **1** dew *Quand j'ai pas rentré le linge à l'heure, Mame m'a disputé parce que le serein avait tombé dessus.* When I didn't take the laundry in on time, Mom fussed at me because the night mist had gotten on it. (VM) **2** mist, fog <*Loc:* AV, SL, VM, Da84, La99>

sérénade [serẽnad, serẽnaj] *n.f.* **1** serenade **2** scolding, reprimand *Donner une sérénade à quelqu'un.* To give someone a good scolding. (SJ) <*Loc:* AV, IB, SJ, Da84>

serge [særʒ] *n.f.* serge (twilled woolen fabric) <*Loc:* Da84>

sergent [særʒɑ̃] *n.m.* sergeant <*Loc:* Da84>

série [seri] *n.f.* **1** series, run **2** spell, period ◊ **•série de beau temps** spell of good weather <Da84> **•série de pluie** spell of rain <Da84> <*Loc:* Da84>

sérieusement [serjøzmɑ̃] *adv.* seriously **Les autres fois la Semaine Sainte était beaucoup important à les Cajins et c'était observée sérieusement.* Formerly Holy Week was very important to Cajuns and it was observed seriously. (Wh83) <*Loc:* Da84, Wh83>

sérieux[1], -euse [serjø, sørjø, -øz] *adj.* **1** serious *Asteur, on jeûne proche pus durant Carême, mais dans le temps, c'était sérieux.* Today, we hardly fast anymore during Lent, but in the old days, it was serious. (LA) **2** grave *Sa maladie était rendue bien sérieux.* His illness had become quite grave. (LA) ◊ **•sérieux comme une manne de tripes** very serious <EV, La99> <*Loc:* AV, EV, LA, VM, An94, Da84, La99>

sérieux[2] [serjø, sørjø] *adv.* seriously *Il était pris sérieux dans le trou.* He was seriously caught in the hole. (LA) <*Loc:* LA>

seringue (syringue) [sərɛ̃g, sərɛ̃ʒ, sirɛ̃g] *n.f.* syringe <*Loc:* Da84, Lv88>

serment [særmɑ̃] *n.m.* oath, swearing ◊ **•faire serment** to swear *Je fais serment que je vas jamais quitter encore.* I swear that I'll never leave again. (LA) <AL, LA> **•faux-serment** perjury, false oath <Da84> <*Loc:* AL, LA, Da84, Hi02>

sermenter [særmɑ̃te] *v.intr.* to swear, take an oath **"Lui, il veut tout le temps dire une plus fort que moi, mais guette, je vas lui en dire une à ce matin qui est plus fort." Il dit, "Il faudra que tu sermentes. Et quand je vas lui dire ça, toi, tu dis que t'as vu ça."* "He always wants to tell a taller one than me, but watch, I'll tell him one this morning that is taller." He says, "You will have to swear. And when I will tell this to him, you say that you saw it." (IV, An94) <*Loc:* IV, An94, Da84>

sermon [særmɔ̃] *n.m.* sermon <*Loc:* JD, Da84>

serpent [særpɑ̃] *n.m./f.* snake, serpent *Le petit bougre là, là s'a fait mordre par une serpent deux ans de ça. C'est moi qui l'a sauvé. J'ai coupé ayoù la serpent l'a mordu sur le bout du doigt, j'ai sucé.* The little guy got bit by a snake two years ago. I'm the one that saved him. I cut where the snake bit him on the end of the finger, I sucked on it. (LF) ◊ **•serpent (à) sonnette(s)** rattlesnake <AV, SL, SM, TB, VM, Da84, Lv88, Re31> **•serpent à tête plate** water moccasin <VM> **•serpent barré(e)** garter snake <VM, Gu00, Lv88> **•serpent congo** water moccasin, cottonmouth <TB, VM, Da84, Gu00> **•serpent cotonnade** garter snake <SB> **•serpent d'eau** ***a*** water moccasin ***b*** any of a variety of nonvenomous water snakes <SL, Da84, Gu00> **•serpent de canne** copperhead <SL> **•serpent des herbes** yellow-bellied water snake <JE> **•serpent fouetteuse** ***a*** whip snake ***b*** coachwhip snake ***c*** blue runner snake <LA, Da84, Gu00, Lv88> **•serpent mangeur / mangeuse d'œufs** ***a*** yellow chicken snake ***b*** king snake <EV, IB, LA, Lv88, Ph36, Re31> **•serpent siffleuse** ***a*** spreading adder ***b*** ground adder <Da84> **•comme un(e) serpent à sonnette** untrustworthy <VM, La99> <*Loc:* AV, EV, IB, JE, LA, LF, SB, SL, SM, TB, VM, An94, Da84, Gu00, Hi02, La99, Lv88, Ph36, Re31>

serpenter [særpɑ̃te] *v.intr.* to wind, meander, snake *Il a tombé dessus une petite routine qui serpentait dans le bois.* He came upon a little cowpath that wound around in the woods. (LA) <*Loc:* LA, Da84>

serpentine [særpɑ̃tin] *n.f.* rickrack <*Loc:* VM, Fa77>

serré, -e [sere] *adj.* **1** tight, tightened *Et s'il commence à couler eh ben tout ce que t'as besoin de faire c'est le visser un petit peu plus serré.* And if it starts to leak, well, all you have to do is screw a little bit tighter. (LF) **2** rare, not abundant *L'argent était bien serré dans ce temps-là.* Money was tight in those days. (Lv88) **3** packed in *Mes livres sont trop serrés sus la tablette.* My books are too packed on the shelf. (VM) <***Loc:*** LA, LF, TB, VM, Da84, Lv88>

serre-joint [særʒwɛ̃] *n.m.* clamp <***Loc:*** JE>

serrer [sere] **I** *v.tr.* **1** to tighten *Il faudra serrer la ceinture pour pouvoir le faire jusqu'à l'été.* We'll have to tighten our belts in order to make it till summer. (LA) *En premier c'était tout des* DERRICKS *boulonnés. Eux-autres montait ça* PIECE BY PIECE ALL THE WAY TO THE TOP. *Et eux-autres serrait les boulons et après ils ont venu avec des* JACKKNIFE. At first it was all derricks that were bolted together. They took it up piece by piece all the way to the top. And they tightened the bolts and later they came along with jackknives. (LF) **2** to squeeze, press *Il a attrapé mon bras il l'a serré aussi fort qu'il pouvait.* He grabbed my arm and he squeezed it as hard as he could. (LA) **3** to put away, put back in place **Serrer le fusil.* To put away the gun. (Da84) *Il a serré ça dans le buffet.* He put it back into the sideboard. (Lv88) *Marie serre le linge.* Mary is putting away the clothes. (IB) **4** to put aside, save (money) **Le vieux monde enterrait leur argent [...] C'était le seul moyen ils avaient de serrer leur argent.* Old folks would bury their money. It was the only way for them to keep their money safe. (An77) *On a serré de l'argent pour nous-autres bâtir la maison.* We saved money to build ourselves a house. (EV) **II** *v.intr.* to economize, be thrifty *Elle aime à serrer.* She likes to economize. (AV) ◊ **•serrer les nœuds** to tighten the mesh links of a trawl net <TB> <***Loc:*** AC, AV, EV, IB, JD, LA, LF, SB, SJ, SL, TB, An77, An94, Da84, Lv88>

serrure [seryr] *n.f.* door lock ◊ **•serrure de porte** hardware of a doorknob and lock <EV> <***Loc:*** EV, VM, Da84>

servable [særvab(l)] *adj.* **1** usable, good for use *Tu vas jeter ça, mais c'est encore servable.* You are going to throw it away, but it is still usable. (VM) **2** in use *Ce mot-là est pas servable pour nous-autres.* This word is not in use among us. (VM) <***Loc:*** VM>

servant, -e [særvɑ̃, -ɑ̃t] *n.* **1** servant **2** *(f.)* maid <***Loc:*** Da84>

service [særvis] *n.m.* **1** service *Un char deuxième main qui va te donner des années de service sans avoir de tracas.* A second-hand car that will give you years of service without problems. (EV) **2** military service, armed forces, military *J'ai mis quatre ans dans le service dans la Guerre Luméro Deux.* I spent four years in the military in World War II. (TB) **3** set (of plates, glasses, etc.) *Un service d'assiettes.* A set of plates. (LA) **4** church service *Des chansons en français mais pas des services en français. Pas catholique.* Songs in French but not services in French. Not at Catholic churches. (TB) **5** funeral service *Ces affiches donnaient le nom, l'âge et la résidence du mort et le lieu et l'heure du service, d'habitude vingt-quatre heures après la mort.* Those posters gave the name, age and residence of the deceased and the place and time of the service, usually twenty-four hours after the time of death. (VM) ◊ **•service militaire** armed forces *Et là, j'ai été dans le service militaire, et j'ai resté presque trois ans.* And then I was in the armed forces, and I stayed in for about three years. (SL) <LA, SL> **•en service** in use *T'as vu ce* PLANT *là qu'est pas en service.* You saw that factory that is not in use. (LF) <LF> **•faire son service** to do one's military service *Il faulait qu'il retourne pour faire son service, tu vois. Il avait deux ans de service à faire dans l'armée.* He had to go back [to France] to do his service, you see. He had two years of service to do in the army. (TB) <TB> **•hors de service** beyond repair, useless *La vieille emballeuse est hors de service depuis longtemps.* The old baler has been beyond repair for a long time. (LA) <LA, Da84> <***Loc:*** LA, LF, SL, TB, VM, Da84>

serviette [særvjɛt, sarjɛt] *n.f.* **1** napkin **2** towel *Faulait que tu vas te laver avec une serviette.* You had to go and wash with a towel. (TB) **3** dishrag, dishcloth ◊ **•serviette à bébé** baby bib <SL> <***Loc:*** JD, SL, TB, Da84>

servir [særvir] **I** *v.tr.* **1** to serve (e.g. a meal) *Après qu'elle a servi le poulet, elle s'a assis avec nous-autres.* After she served the chicken, she sat with us. (LA) **2** to serve, wait on, attend to **Et il y a une que, naturellement, il y a une qu'a été servie avant l'autre.* And there was one, naturally, there was one that was served before the other. (EV, An94) *"Mais," il dit, "comment t'as trouvé ma femme?" Il dit, "Elle t'a bien servi?"* "Well," he says, "how did you find my wife?" He says, "Did she wait on you well?" (IV) **3** to serve, be of service to *Le shérif servait la cour de la paroisse. Le constable il servait la cour de le juge de paix.* The sheriff served the parish court. The constable served the justice of the peace. (LF) *Ça m'a bien servi de connaître le français. J'aimerais voir notre langue française préservée.* It has served me well to know French. I'd like to see our French language preserved. (LF) **II** *v.intr.* to act (as), serve (as) *Mon père était dans la Première Guerre Mondiale, il a servi d'interprète en France.* My father was in World War I, he served as an interpreter in France. (SL) **III se servir** *v.pron.* **1** to serve o.s. **Servez-vous!* Help yourself! (Da84) **2** to use *Tu peux barrer quelque chose sans te servir d'un cadenas.* You can lock something without using a padlock. (IB) ◊ **•servir de caution {cautionnement / CO-SIGN}** ***a*** to vouch for *Il avait pas personne pour lui servir de* CO-SIGN. He had no one to vouch for him as a co-signer. (IV) ***b*** to stand bail, go bail (for s.o.) *C'est son oncle qui l'a servi de cautionnement.* It's his uncle who guaranteed his bail. (VM) <IV, VM, Da84> **•être servi** to be used *Ce terme-là est pas beaucoup servi.* That word isn't used much. (VM) *C'était pas servi. On savait pas ça c'était.* It wasn't used. We didn't know what it was. (SL) *C'était servi pour affiler le rasoir.* It was used to sharpen the razor. (Lv88) *Le chemin de fer était* *servi pour haler les cannes.* The railroad was used to haul sugar cane. (Lv88) <SL, VM, Lv88> **•faire servir** to breed *Mon père a fait servir des bêtes, des cochons, et des poules et faire des jardins.* My father bred cattle, pigs and chickens and grew vegetables. (SL) <SL> <***Loc:*** EV, IB, IV, LA, LF, SL, TB, VM, An94, Da84, Lv88>

ses ♦see **son**

sésame [sezãm] *n.m.* sesame seed <***Loc:*** Da84>

session [sesjɔ̃] *n.f.* session, setting <***Loc:*** Da84>

SET[1] [sɛt] *v.tr.invar.* to set *Tu la SET sur zéro.* You set it at zero. (AC) <***Loc:*** AC>

SET[2] [sɛt] *n.m.* set (e.g., of tools) *Il a tout le SET de livres.* He has the whole set of books. (SL) ◊ **•SET de vaisselle** set of dishes <LF> <***Loc:*** JE, LF, SB, SL, TB, Da84, Lv88>

seul, -e [sœl] *adj.* **1** only **Mon seul ami.* My only friend. (Da84) **La seule raison je fais ça je suis après faire-ça, c'est pour me revenger.* The only reason I am doing this is to get revenge. (EV, An94) *Il y avait un seul hôtel à Mamou.* There was only one hotel in Mamou. (EV) **Et c'était le seul temps le monde mangeait des gâteaux, quand il y avait des noces.* And it was the only time people ate cakes, when there was a wedding. (An94) **2** alone **Et toujours, ils ont quitté Petit Poucet dans le bois tout seul.* And anyway, they left Petit Poucet in the woods all alone. (LA, An94) **3** unmarried, single *Il était seul dans ce temps ça, il avait pas encore rencontré sa femme.* He was single in those days, he had not yet met his wife. (LA) **4** complete, utter *C'était un seul déboulis chez Kress.* It was a complete madhouse at Kress'. (AV) ◊ **•seul (d')enfant** only child *Mame était seule d'enfant.* Momma was an only child. (VM) *Mon je suis le seul enfant. Et je pars de la misère toujours pour ça. Ils faisont toujours de la misère, les seuls enfants fait toujours de la misère pour ça.* I'm an only child. And I always start trouble because of that. They always make trouble, only children always make trouble because of that. (LF) <LF, VM> **•tout seul** ***a*** all alone *Et il pouvait pas aller lui tout seul, c'était trop loin pour lui il va à pied.* And he couldn't go all alone, it was too far for him to go on foot. (EV) *Il dit, "J'ai peur de coucher dans le bois moi tout seul."* He said, "I'm afraid to sleep in the woods all alone." (LA) ***b*** by oneself, without assistance *Mon petit garçon peut se déboutonner tout seul.* My little boy can unbutton himself all by himself. (EV) *Il les a tout bouledou, lui tout seul.* He intimidated them all by himself. (LA) <AC, EV, LA, VM, Da84, Hi02> <***Loc:*** AC, EV, JE, LA, LF, SL, SM, TB, VM, An94, Da84, Hi02, Wh83>

seulement [sœlmɑ̃] *adv.* **1** only *Il y a seulement lui qui aurait pu faire ça.* Only he could have done that. (LA) **2** even *Lui il est mort quand-ce que mon grand-père était enfant, il se rappelle pas de son pape seulement.* He died when my grandfather was a child, he doesn't even remember his father. (TB) *Dans ce temps là, là on avait pas seulement de char.* In those days, we didn't even have a car. (EV) *Le monde connaissait pas seulement lire leur nom.* People didn't even know how to read their name. (TB) **3** but, however **Seulement, cil-là qui avait la babine coupée était un tas plus mauvais.* However, the one with the cut lip was much worse off. (SL, An94) ◊ **•non seulement** not only *Non seulement qu'il quittait pas, mais il a mangé tout le dîner. Il y a pas resté à rien pour souper.* Not only would he not leave, but he ate all the food from dinner. There was nothing left for supper. (LA) <AC, LA, Da84> **•si seulement** if only *Si seulement il pourrait arriver à l'heure pour une fois.* If only he could arrive on time for once. (LA) <LA, Da84> <***Loc:*** AC, EV, LA, SL, TB, VM, An94, Da84, Lv88>

sève [sɛv] *n.f.* sap (of plants) ◊ **•prendre une nouvelle sève** to make a new spurt of growth <Da84> <***Loc:*** Da84>

sévère [sevær] *adj.* **1** severe, harsh *Dans ces temps ça, les affaires étaient sévères.* In those days, things were severe. (LA) **2** strict, rigid *Notre papa était beaucoup sévère dessus nous-autres, ça fait on a tout le temps été craintif.* Our Pop was very strict with us, therefore we were always fearful. (EV) <***Loc:*** EV, LA, Da84>

sevrage [səvraʒ] *n.m.* weaning <***Loc:*** Da84>

sevrer [səvre] *v.tr.* to wean *La vache va bientôt sevrer son veau.* The cow will soon wean her calf. (LA) <***Loc:*** AC, LA, LF, SB, TB, Da84>

sexe [sɛks] *n.m.* sex, gender <***Loc:*** Da84>

SHADE [ʃɛd, ʃed] *n.m.* **1** window shade **2** lampshade <***Loc:*** AV, EV, IB, LF, SM, VM, Lv88, Ph36>

SHAMPOO [ʃæmpu] *n.m.* shampoo <***Loc:*** Da84, Lv88>

SHED [ʃɛd, ʃed] *n.m.* **1** shed *Et mon grand-père avait des patates douces. Dedans un SHED, il avait.* And my grandfather had sweet potatoes. He had them in a shed. (LF) **2** barn **3** toolshed *Je connaissais un homme du Grand Caillou qu'avait un SHED en arrière et il avait un vrai tas de différentes affaires là dans son SHED, et il avait été empoigner ses trôles parce que la trôle était pour commencer.* I knew a man from Grand Caillou who had a toolshed out back and he had a whole pile of different things in his shed, and he had gone to get his trawls because the trawling season was about to begin. (TB) <***Loc:*** EV, JE, LF, SL, TB, VM, Da84, Lv88, Ph36>

shérif [ʃerif] *n.m.* sherrif <***Loc:*** LF, SL, TB, Da84, Lv88>

SHINE [ʃaɪn] *n.m.* shoe polish <***Loc:*** VM>

SHOCK[1] [ʃɔk] *v.tr.invar.* to shock, bundle *On est après SHOCK le riz.* We are bundling the rice. (VM) <***Loc:*** EV, VM>

SHOCK[2] [ʃɔk] *n.m.* shock (of rice) <***Loc:*** VM>

SHOP[1] **(shop)** [ʃɔp] *v.intr.invar.* to shop *Peut-être alle est partie SHOP avec tout cet argent-là.* Maybe she went shopping with all that money. (ThCa: *La table des veuves*) <***Loc:*** Lv88, ThCa>

SHOP[2] **(shop, choppe, échoppe)** [ʃɔp, eʃɔp] *n.m./f.* **1** shop, store **Son garçon a toujours une SHOP au Liberty Theater.* His son still has a shop at the Liberty Theater. (An84) *Je louais une petite échoppe de barbier.* I used to rent a little barbershop. (Gr86) **2** shed **3** shop, workshop, workroom *Tu faisais de l'ouvrage dans une* SHOP, *comme ouvert les huîtres. Une shop à z-huîtres. Des shops à poisson, pour nettoyer le poisson.* You did work in a shop, like opening oysters. An oyster shop. Fish shops, for cleaning fish. (LF) <*Loc:* AV, JE, LF, SL, TB, VM, An84, Gr86, Lv88, Wh83>

SHOT [ʃɔt] *n.m.* shot, injection ◊ **•prendre un SHOT** to take a shot *Faut je prends un* SHOT *tous les jours.* I have to take a shot every day. (TB) <TB> <*Loc:* TB>

shou [ʃu] *interj.* cry to make pigs or chickens go away <*Loc:* SM>

shove (**cheuve**) [ʃɔv, ʃov, ʃœv] *n.f.* shovel **Je calcule, je suis autant que l'homme qu'est après travailler à la shove, ou le mécanicien, ou n'importe quel autre métier.* I figure that I'm worth as much as the man who works the shovel, or the engineer, or someone who does any other type of work. (VM, An84) ◊ **•shove à riz** round-edged shovel with holes in the blade <EV> <*Loc:* AC, EV, IB, JE, LA, PQ, SL, VM, An84, Da84, Di32, Fa77, Lv88>

shovel (**chauvelle, chevelle**) [ʃovɛl, ʃəvɛl] *n.f.* shovel *Et après une heure et demie, deux heures, eux-autres va avec des chauvelles et eux-autres les brasse.* And after an hour and a half, two hours, they take shovels and they stir them. (TB) <*Loc:* IB, TB>

shoveler (**chauveler**) [ʃovle] *v.tr.* to shovel *Il a chauvelé les drines avec la chauvelle.* He shoveled out the drains with a shovel. (TB) <*Loc:* TB>

SHOW [ʃo] *n.m.* **1** show, showing, performance (of a film, play, etc.) *Et là le monsieur me dit faut que toi tu viens pour parler il dit. Il dit c'est toi qui vas faire le* SHOW. And then the man tells me, you have to come and talk, he says. He says, you're the one who's going to do the show. (TB) **2** television program, show *T'as vu des* LANDING BOATS *là qu'eusse fait sur le* SHOW *là, et ça avait à peu près douze pieds de large, et à peu près près de quarante pieds de long.* Did you see the landing boats that they had on the TV show, they were about twelve feet long and about nearly forty feet long. (LF) **3** movie, movies, movie theater *On allait au* SHOW *tous les samedis.* We went to the movies every Saturday. (JD) <*Loc:* AV, JD, LF, TB, VM, An94, Lv88, Wh83>

si[1] [si] *adv.* so **Si bon.* So good. (Da84) **Il y a si longtemps de ça.* It was so long ago. (VM, An94) *Ton maïs te fait une bonne viande, et si tu le donnes du slop, ta viande va pas être si bonne.* Corn makes for good meat, and if you give him slop (to eat), your meat won't be so good. (TB) ◊ **•si… que** as… as *"Ouais," il dit, "elle peut l'avoir, si vite qu'elle me donne le vingt piastres."* "Yes," he says, "she can have it, as soon as she gives me the twenty dollars." (IV) <IV, St95> **•si tant** so much *Il a parlé si tant qu'il a un mal de gorge.* He talked so much that he has a sore throat. (SM) <EV, LA, SM> <*Loc:* AC, EV, IB, IV, LA, SL, SM, TB, VM, An94, Da84, Lv88, St95, ThCa>

si[2] [si] *conj.* if *Si mon père aurait été au village, il aurait acheté du pain, il nous aurait fait des sandwichs avec du pain.* If my father had gone to the city, he would have bought bread, and he would have made some sandwiches for us with the bread. (IB) **J'ai faim. J'ai venu voir si t'aurais pas quelque chose pour me donner à manger.* I'm hungry. I came to see if you might not have something to give me to eat. (SL, An94) ◊ **•si c'est que** if *Dans ce temps-là il y avait des traiteuses qui pouvaient dire si c'est que t'avais eu un gris-gris.* In those days there were folk healers who could say if someone had cast a spell on you. (TB) <TB> **•si jamais** if ever *Si jamais il t'arrive quelque chose à toi, Madeleine pourra gagner sa vie.* If anything ever happens to you, Madeleine will be able to earn a living. (ThCa: *Le charivari*) <Da84, ThCa> **•si tu veux** if you wish <Da84> **•comme si** as if *Comme si il va venir asteur.* As if he's going to come now. (LA) *Notre cousin de Béville nous dédaigne comme si il se croit plus que nous-autres.* Our cousin in Abbeville looks down on us as if he thinks he's better than we are. (VM) <EV, IV, LA, LF, SL, SM, TB, VM, An94, Da84, La99> **•faire comme si** to act as if, act like **Il faisait comme si il était après rire.* He acted like he was laughing. (LA, SL, An94) <SL, An94> <*Loc:* AC, AV, EV, IB, IV, JD, JE, LA, LF, SL, SM, TB, VM, An84, An94, Da84, Gr86, Gu00, Hi02, La99, Lv88, ThCa, Wh83>

siau (**seau**) [sjo, sijo, syo, sjø] *n.m.* **1** pail, bucket *Ma grand-mère avait un siau avec des trous dedans, et eusse mettait le lait dedans le siau, et ça le mettait dans le puits pour tiendre le lait frais. Comme ça, la chaleur le faisait pas aigrir.* My grandmother had a bucket with holes in it, and they would put the milk in the bucket, and they put it in the well to keep the milk cool. That way, the heat didn't make it turn sour. (LF) **2** boiler ◊ **•à siau** enough, plenty **J'en ai à siau.* I have plenty. (Da84) <Da84> **•il mouille par siaux** it's raining hard <Gu00, Lv88> <*Loc:* AV, EV, IB, JD, JE, LF, SB, SJ, SL, SM, TB, VM, Da84, Gu00, Hi02, Lv88, Ph36>

siblème ♦see **ciblème**

SIDEBOARD (**saïbote**) [saɪdbɔd, sajbot] *n.m.* sideboard *Je mets tous mes apprêtements dessus le* SIDEBOARD. I put all of my crafts on the sideboard. (VM) <*Loc:* EV, VM, Di32, Lv88, Ph36>

siècle [sjɛk(l)] *n.m.* **1** century **2** era, age ◊ **•dans les siècles des siècles** for endless ages <Da84> <*Loc:* TB, Da84>

siège [sjɛʒ] *n.m.* **1** seat, chair **2** seat, position in a body of officials **3** period during which a court or a legislative body is in session ◊ **•le Saint-Siège** the Holy See <Da84> <*Loc:* SM, Da84, Di32>

siéger [sjeʒe] *v.intr.* **1** to sit, be located *Durant la Guerre des Confédérés, le gouvernement a siégé aux Opelousas.* During the Civil War, the government was located in Opelousas.

(EV) **2** to occupy a seat as a member of a body of officials *Il a siégé comme juge jusqu'à sa mort.* He sat as judge until his death. (LA) <*Loc:* EV, LA, VM, Di32>

sien, sienne [sjɛ̃, -ɛ̃n] *pron.poss.* his, hers *Mon jardin colle au sien.* My garden adjoins his. (SM) *Faulait je mets ma main par-dessus la sienne, c'était glacée comme tout. Je dis "Claude, t'es malade." Il dit "Je me sens pas bien."* I had to put my hand over his, it was cold as ice. I said, "Claude, you're sick." He said, "I don't feel well." (TB) **Et Kossuth était* GONE *à sa boucherie, et Johnny était* GONE *à la sienne. Et ils se sont croisés là-là.* And Kossuth had left to his butchery, and Johnny had gone to his. And they crossed each other right there. (EV, An94) <*Loc:* EV, LA, SM, TB, VM, An94>

sifflage [siflaʒ] *n.m.* whistling <*Loc:* SB, Da84>

sifflant, -e [siflɑ̃, -ɑ̃t] *adj.* whistling **Une casserole sifflante.* A whistling kettle. (Da84) <*Loc:* Da84>

sifflement [sifləmɑ̃] *n.m.* whistling <*Loc:* Da84>

siffler [sifle, syfle] **I** *v.tr.* **1** to whistle *C'est pour ça le monde l'appelle le petit siffleur. Il siffle sa chanson toute la journée.* That's why people call him the little whistler. He whistles his song all day long. (ch: *Le petit siffleur*) **2** to steal *Il a sifflé ça quand je le regardais pas.* He stole that when I wasn't watching him. (VM) **II** *v.intr.* **1** to whistle, hiss *Tu pourrais peut-être siffler quand tu danses.* Maybe you could whistle when you dance. (EV) **2** to ring (of the ears) *Son oreille a commencé à siffler.* His ear started ringing. (SB) ◊ •**siffler après** to whistle at, call by whistling *Siffler après un chien.* To call a dog by whistling. (LA) <LA, Da84> •**siffler dans le vent** ***a*** to do s.t. useless ***b*** to waste time <EV, La99> •**pas siffler** to keep silent, not open one's mouth *Alle a pas sifflé toute l'après-midi.* She didn't open her mouth all afternoon. (VM) <VM> <*Loc:* EV, LF, SB, SL, VM, Da84, Hi02, La99>

sifflet [siflɛ, sifle] *n.m.* whistle ◊ •**sifflet à z-oie** goose whistle (for calling geese during a hunt) <LF> •**sifflet de canard** duck call, duck whistle <TB> <*Loc:* LF, TB, Da84>

siffleur, -euse [siflœr, -øz] *n.* **1** whistler *C'est pour ça le monde l'appelle le petit siffleur. Il siffle sa chanson toute la journée.* That's why people call him the little whistler. He whistles his song all day long. (ch: *Le petit siffleur*) **2** hognose snake, puff adder <*Loc:* Da84, Lv88, Re31>

signal [siɲal] *n.m.* signal <*Loc:* Da84>

signature [siɲatyr] *n.f.* signature <*Loc:* Da84>

signe [sin, siɲ] *n.m.* **1** sign, mark, token, indication **2** beauty mark, mole, birthmark *Ma sœur avait vu un signe sus le dos à Mame.* My sister had seen a mole on Mom's back. (EV) **3** gesture **4** signature ◊ •**signe de beauté** mole, birthmark <Da84> •**signe de maladie** symptom <Da84> •**signe postiche** false mole, beauty mark <Da84> •**faire le signe de (la) croix** to make the sign of the cross *Il a fait son signe de la croix et puis il a fait des prières.* He made his sign of the cross and then he said some prayeres. (EV) <EV, LF> •**faire signe** to signal, indicate *Ça icitte, montrer le doigt, c'était pas rien du tout quand moi j'ai été* BROUGHT UP. *Moi j'aurais fait ça à un autre* DRIVER *sur le chemin, comme ça ici j'aurais fait signe qu'y avait un* STATE TROOPER *en quelque place.* This here, flipping the bird, that wasn't anything when I was brought up. I would have done that to another driver on the road, that's how I would have made a sign that there was a state trooper somewhere. (LF) <EV, LA, LF, SL, An94> <*Loc:* AC, EV, JE, LA, LF, SL, An94, Da84, Lv88>

signer [siɲe] *v.tr.* to sign (e.g. a document) *L'affaire était faite; il y avait pas un qu'a refusé de signer.* The deal was done. Not one of them refused to sign. (ThCa: *Messieurs, mesdames*) <*Loc:* AC, EV, Da84, ThCa>

signification [siɲifikasjɔ̃] *n.f.* significance, meaning <*Loc:* Da84>

silement [silmɑ̃] *n.m.* **1** buzzing, ringing (in the ears) *J'ai un silement dans les oreilles.* I have a buzzing in my ears. (VM) **2** wheezing (in the chest) *Un silement dans le potrail.* A wheezing in the chest. (VM) <*Loc:* JE, SB, VM, Lv88>

silence [silɑ̃s] *n.m.* silence <*Loc:* Da84>

silhouette [silwɛt] *n.f.* silhouette, outline <*Loc:* Da84>

siller (ciller) [sile] **I** *v.tr.* **1** to sic, urge (an animal) to attack *On a sillé le chien après.* We sicced the dog on [him]. (VM) **2** to provoke *L'un est toujours après siller l'autre.* One is always provoking the other. (VM) **II** *v.intr.* **1** to hiss (of a snake, goose, etc.) *La z-oie va siller après toi, si alle est après couver.* The goose will hiss at you if she is brooding. (VM) **2** to buzz, ring (of the ears) *Tes oreilles ont dû siller hier, parce qu'on a parlé de toi toute la journée.* Your ears must have been ringing yesterday, because we talked about you all day. (VM) **3** to wheeze, breathe with whistling or a rattle in the throat *T'es oppressé, t'es après siller.* You have asthma, you are wheezing (VM) **4** to whiz, whistle (e.g. a bullet) *Les balles ont sillé au-dessus de nos têtes.* The bullets whistled over our heads. (LA) ◊ •**siller sur l'estomac** to wheeze *Je l'entends siller sur l'estomac.* I hear him wheezing. (SL) <SL> <*Loc:* IB, LA, SM, VM, Da84, Di32, Lv88>

silliette [siljɛt] *adj.* sickly <*Loc:* SL>

sillon (seillon) [sijɔ̃, sejɔ̃] *n.m.* furrow <*Loc:* AV, IB, SB, SJ, VM, Da84, Lv88>

sillonner (seillonner) [sejɔ̃ne] *v.tr.* **1** to plant in raised rows *Seillonner des patates.* To plant sweet potatoes in rows (by banking the dirt up around them). (SJ) **2** to furrow, plow *Il a seillonné sa terre à trois coups.* He plowed his land three times. (AV) <*Loc:* AV, SJ>

simagrée ♦see **simagris**

simagris (simagrée) [simagri, simagre] *n.f.* **1** contorted facial expression, face, grimace *Arrête de faire des simagris. Le vent va virer au nord et ta figure va rester comme ça!* Stop making faces. The wind will turn north and your face will stay like that! (VM) *Elle faisait beaucoup de simagris.* She was making a lot of faces. (SB) **2** affectation, air *Elle fait toutes ces simagris depuis qu'elle est riche.* She puts on all those airs since she has become rich. (IB) **3** ritual words or gestures used by a folk healer during a treatment *Et c'est manière dur à croire que quelqu'un va te dire une simagris sur quelque chose là et il va te faire du bien pour une coupure ou pour un coup de bâton dans le dos.* And it's somewhat hard to believe that someone is going to pronounce some magic words on something and that he'll do you some good for a cut or a wound from a stick in the back. (TB) *Le traiteur fait des simagrées quand il donne un traitement.* The folk healer makes motions with his hands when giving a treatment. (TB) <***Loc:*** AV, IB, SB, TB, VM, Da84>

simarouba [simaruba] *n.m.* simarouba (Amazon hardwood tree) <***Loc:*** JD, Lv88>

simple [sɛ̃p(l)] *adj.* **1** simple, easy *Ça fait quand-ce que j'ai pris le CODOFIL c'était bien pour moi parce que je pouvais parler en français, la conversation était simple.* So when I took the CODOFIL course it was good for me because I could speak French, conversation was easy. (LF) **2** mere *C'était une simple question.* It was a mere question. (LA) *Un simple malentendu.* A mere misunderstanding. (LA) **3** plain, ordinary *Je peux juste pas croire que dans cette petite bouteille que tu as volée de la* NURSE *à Doc Latour, que c'est seulement du "*VITAMIN B-I*", quelque chose si simple que ça.* I just can't believe that in this little bottle that you stole from Dr. Latour's nurse is only vitamin B-1, something as ordinary as that. (ThCa: *Messieurs, mesdames*) **4** simple-minded *Le bougre, il était manière simple. Il connaissait pas trop quoi c'est qu'allait* ON. The guy, he was sort of simple-minded. He didn't understand too well what was going on. (AS) **5** single *Une charrue simple.* A single plow. (EV) <***Loc:*** AS, EV, LA, LF, VM, Da84, ThCa>

simplement[1] [sɛ̃pləmɑ̃] *adj.* simple *Ça me dérange pas parce que je suis pas intéressé pour la simplement des raisons que j'ai eu tout ça je voulais à ce bout ici.* It doesn't bother me because I'm not interested for the simple reason that I had everything I wanted right here. (AV) <***Loc:*** AV>

simplement[2] [sɛ̃pləmɑ̃] *adv.* simply *Tu peux faire ça plus simplement.* You can do that more simply. (VM) **•tout simplement** simply <Da84> <***Loc:*** EV, VM, Da84>

sinapisse [sinapis] *n.m.* sinapism, mustard plaster <***Loc:*** LF>

sincère [sɛ̃sær] *adj.* sincere, honest *C'est un homme beaucoup sincère. Il a du sentiment pour sa famille.* He's a very sincere man. He has strong feelings for his family. (LA) <***Loc:*** LA, Da84>

sincèrement [sɛ̃særmɑ̃] *adv.* sincerely *Ça c'en est un qui parle sincèrement sans fournir.* He's one who speaks sincerely but doesn't follow through. (LA) <***Loc:*** LA, Da84>

sincérité [sɛ̃serite] *n.f.* sincerity <***Loc:*** Da84>

singo [siŋgo] ◊ **•être après {à} singo** to take a nap *Quand j'ai arrivé chez lui, il était après singo.* When I arrived at his house, he was napping. (LA) <LA, Lv88> **•faire singo** to take a nap <SM, La99, Lv88> <***Loc:*** LA, SB, SM, La99, Lv88>

singoter [sɛ̃gote, sinote] *v.intr.* to doze *Le nègre aime à singoter sur sa chaise.* The black man likes to doze in his chair. (IB) <***Loc:*** IB>

SINK (zinc) [sɛ̃k, siŋk, zɛ̃k] *n.m.* sink, kitchen sink <***Loc:*** VM, Lv88>

sipion ♦see **espion**

sirop [siro, syro] *n.m.* **1** syrup *Le jus était cuit, chauffé jusqu'à qu'il venait en sirop.* The juice was cooked, heated, until it became a syrup. (LA) *Sirop de canne.* Cane syrup. (EV) **2** term used in the making of open-kettle cane syrup to indicate the third kettle in a series of kettles ◊ **•sirop de batterie** cane syrup cooked in an open pot, open-kettle syrup <TB, Da84, Lv88, Re31> **•être dans son sirop** to relish one's own situation <La99> **•le sirop et biscuits cassent pas égal** vengeance never evens out a wrong <La99> <***Loc:*** AC, AV, EV, IB, LA, SB, TB, VM, Da84, Hi02, La99, Lv88, Re31>

siroté, -e [sirote] *adj.* sticky, gluey *T'as pas bien lavé la vaisselle. C'est toujours siroté.* You didn't wash the dishes well. They're still sticky. (LA) *Les mains sirotées de godron.* Hands sticky with tar. (LF) <***Loc:*** LA, LF, Lv88>

siroter[1] [sirote] *v.tr.* **1** to add syrup to, cover with syrup *J'ai siroté mes biscuits.* I put syrup on my biscuits. (LA) **2** to sugarcoat, embellish, make s.t. seem better than it is *Arrête de siroter les affaires. Dis-moi la vérité.* Stop sugarcoating things. Tell me the truth. (VM) <***Loc:*** JD, LA, VM, Lv88>

siroter[2] [sirote] *v.intr.* to sob <***Loc:*** SL, Lv88>

siroteux, -euse [sirotø, -øz] *adj.* syrupy *Les patates douces sont siroteuses.* Sweet potatoes are syrupy. (VM) <***Loc:*** VM>

sirugien, sirurgien ♦see **chirurgien**

sisi [sisi] *n.m.* ◊ **•sisi à dents** ***a*** expression used to avoid answering a question or naming s.t. one does not wish to reveal *Qu'est-ce que tu as dans cette boîte? —Sisi à dents.* What do you have in that box? —Wouldn't you like to know. (SB) ***b*** mythical trap or snare against which children were warned *C'est un sisi à dents pour arracher les dents des demandants.* It's a tooth-puller to pull out the teeth of those who keep asking. (IB) <IB, SB, SJ, La99> <***Loc:*** IB, SB, SJ, La99>

sissite [sisit] *v.intr.invar.* [*baby talk*] to sit, sit down *Sissite sur le plancher, cher.* Sit on the floor, hon. (SL) *J'ai sissite sur le plancher.* I sat on the floor. (SL) *Sissite-toi.* Sit down. (IB) <***Loc:*** IB, SL>

sitôt [sito] ◊ **•sitôt que** as soon as *On va partir sitôt qu'il arrive.* We'll leave as soon as he gets here. (LA) <LA> **•pas de sitôt** not soon, not for a long time <Da84> <***Loc:*** LA, Da84>

situation [sitɥasjɔ̃] *n.f.* **1** situation *C'est selon avec qui je suis après parler, si c'est que le monde après se forcer pour parler anglais, je parle français avec eusse. C'est selon la situation.* It depends who I'm talking to, if the people are forcing themselves to speak English, I speak French with them. It depends on the situation. (TB) **2** position **3** predicament <***Loc:*** TB, Da84>

situer [sitɥe] **I** *v.intr.* to be located *Sa boutique est située juste en dehors du village.* Her store is located right outside of town. (LA) **II se situer** *v.pron.* to situate o.s. *Il s'a situé en arrière de la salle pour le voir.* He situated himself in the back of the room so he could see him coming. (LA) <***Loc:*** LA, Da84>

sive [siv] *n.f.* shallot <***Loc:*** EV, Ph36>

six [sis] (*before a consonant* [si], *before a vowel* [siz]) *adj./n.m.* six *Mon garçon est grand, il a six pieds de haut et il pèse presque trois cent livres. Il est grand et gros.* My boy is big, he is six feet tall and he weighs almost three hundred pounds. He is tall and big. (TB) *Aujourd'hui, je suis condamné, condamné à rouler ma bourouette sur ma planche de six pouces.* Today I'm condemned to roll my wheelbarrow on my six-inch plank. (ch: *La valse du bambocheur*) ◊ **•six par huit** six by eight lumber <Lv88> **•six par six** six by six lumber <Lv88> <***Loc:*** AC, AV, EV, IV, LA, SL, SM, TB, An94, Da84, Hi02, Lv88>

six-barbes [sibarb] *n.m.* sea-bob, small shrimp formerly considered unmarketable but now sold for use as popcorn shrimp <***Loc:*** LF, TB>

sixième [sizjɛ̃m] *adj./n.* sixth *C'est la sixième fois qu'il m'appelle aujourd'hui.* That's the sixth time he's called me today. (EV) *Jusqu'à dans le sixième.* Until the sixth grade. (SM) <***Loc:*** EV, SM, Da84>

SKATE [skɛt, ske^{i}t] *v.intr.invar.* to skate *On pouvait* SKATE *dessus le pont.* We could skate on the bridge. (SM) <***Loc:*** EV, SM, Da84, Lv88, Ph36>

ski[1] [ski] *v.intr.invar.* to ski *Ils ont été ski dans Colorado pour Mardi Gras.* They went skiing in Colorado for Mardi Gras. (VM) <***Loc:*** VM, Da84>

ski[2] [ski] *n.m.* ski <***Loc:*** Da84>

skiff (**esquif**) [skif, ɛskif] *n.m.* skiff, small flat-bottomed rowboat with a pointed bow and square stern ◊ **•skiff à rames** type of rowboat <LF> **•skiff à z-huîtres** oyster skiff, a boat approximately 18-20 ft. long and about 8 ft. wide <LF> <***Loc:*** IV, LF, SB, SM, TB, VM, Da84, Lv88>

SKIMMER [skimə] *n.m.* skimmer, type of trawl used in shrimp fishing <***Loc:*** TB>

slip[1] [slip] *n.m.* slip, act of slipping <***Loc:*** Da84>

slip[2] [slip] *n.m.* slip (woman's undergarment) <***Loc:*** EV, Da84>

slip[3] [slip] *n.m.* slipper, bedroom slipper, house slipper <***Loc:*** Da84>

SMART (**smatte**) [smart, smat] *adj.* smart, sharp, cunning *Il est* SMART, *il a été éduqué au collège.* He is smart, he went to college. (Lv88) *Et Petit Poucet était plus* SMART *que les autres et il était aimé plus par le papa et la maman.* And Tom Thumb was smarter than the others and he was loved more by his father and his mother. (LA, An94) ◊ **•smatte comme la tomate à Firin du Marais Plate** unintelligent <La99> **•smatte comme une fève plate** ***a*** intelligent ***b*** [*used ironically*] not very intelligent <La99> **•smatte comme une tomate** very intelligent <La99> <***Loc:*** EV, LA, LF, SB, SL, SM, TB, VM, An94, Da84, Hi02, La99, Lv88, Ph36>

smatte ♦see **SMART**

SMILE [smaɪl] *n.m.* shot, small quantity of alcohol *Loule, tu veux un petit* SMILE? Lou, you want a little drink? (SL) <***Loc:*** SL>

SNAP [snæp] *n.m.* snap (fastener on clothing) <***Loc:*** VM>

snelle [snɛl, snel] *n.f.* snail <***Loc:*** SM, Da84, Lv88>

sobriquer [subrike] *v.tr.* to nickname, give a nickname to <***Loc:*** IB, SJ>

sobriquet [subrikɛ, subrike] *n.m.* **1** nickname **2** pet name <***Loc:*** AV, SM, VM, Lv88>

socau ♦see **soco**

sociable [sosjab(l)] *adj.* sociable *C'est du monde beaucoup sociable. On les voit tout partout.* They're very sociable people. We see them everywhere. (EV) <***Loc:*** EV, Da84>

société [sosjete] *n.f.* **1** society, community **2** company **3** association, organization, society *Je me demande si les dinosaures ont formé des sociétés pour la préservation des dinosaures.* I wonder if dinosaurs formed societies for the preservation of dinosaurs. (ThCa: *Mille misères*) ◊ **•de société** in partnership **On a acheté ça de société, moi et mon père, ce violon-là.* We bought that in partnership, my father and I, that violin there. (JD, An84) <JD, An84> <***Loc:*** JD, An84, Da84, ThCa>

soco (**socau**) [soko] *n.m.* **1** muscadine vine **2** muscadine, southern fox grape *J'ai été ramasser des socos et je m'ai fait piquer par des guêpes.* I was picking muscadines and I got stung by wasps. (Gu00) ◊ **•soco blanc** white muscadine <Re31> <***Loc:*** AL, AV, EV, IB, LF, SB, SL, SM, TB, VM, Da84, Di32, Gu00, Hi02, Lv88, Ph36, Re31>

soda [soda] *n.m.* soda, baking soda ◊ **•soda à pain** baking powder <VM> <***Loc:*** AV, EV, IB, LF, SB, SJ, SL, TB, VM, Da84, Lv88, Ph36>

sœur [sœr] *n.f.* **1** sister *Cette femme-là est ma sœur et cette femme-là est ma cousine.* That woman is my sister and that woman there is my cousin. (JE) **2** nun *Ils ont tout fini l'école, les miens, parce qu'ils ont tout été à l'école catholique. Et les garçons étaient avec les frères, et les petites filles étaient avec les sœurs.* They all finished school, my kids, because they all went to Catholic school. And the boys went with the monks, and the little girls went with the nuns. (TB) ◊ **•demi-sœur** ***a*** half sister ***b*** step-sister <TB, Da84> <***Loc:*** AC, EV, JE, LA, PQ, SM, TB, Da84, Hi02>

sofa [sofa] *n.m.* sofa, settee, couch, divan <***Loc:*** EV, IB, JE, LA, TB, VM, Da84, Gu00, Hi02, Lv88>

soguer [soge] *v.intr.* **1** to loaf, waste time *J'ai été après soguer dans ma berce tout l'après-midi.* I was loafing in my rocking chair all afternoon. (Lv88) *Passer sa vie à soguer.* To spend one's life loafing. (AV) **2** to doze off, snooze, take a cat nap *J'ai passé toute la journée à soguer.* I spent the whole day snoozing. (VM) ◊ **•être à soguer** to have a hangover <SL> <***Loc:*** AV, SJ, SL, TB, VM, Lv88>

soi [swa] *pron.* ◊ **•chez soi** at one's home <PQ, Da84> <***Loc:*** PQ, Da84>

soi-même [swãmɛ̃m] *pron.* himself, herself, itself, oneself *Il faut qu'un monde s'aide soi-même avant de demander de l'aide aux autres.* A person has to help himself before he asks for help from others. (VM) <***Loc:*** VM, Da84>

soi-disant [swadizɑ̃] *adv.* it is said, so said, supposedly, allegedly **T'as entendu parler de l'homme dans la lune. Mais soi-disant, c'était une punition. Le Bon Dieu l'a puni pour quelque chose... Soi-disant, c'est un homme qui est dans la lune parce qu'il a été après du bois le dimanche.* You've heard about the man in the moon. Supposedly, it was a punishment. The Good Lord punished him for something . . . Supposedly, he's a man who's in the moon because he went to get wood on Sunday. (SL, An94) *C'est soi-disant un péché de blasphémer.* It is supposedly a sin to curse. (LA) <***Loc:*** LA, LF, SL, An94, Da84>

soie [swa] *n.f.* silk ◊ **•soie de coton** cotton silk fiber <Da84> <***Loc:*** Da84>

soif [swaf] *n.f.* thirst ◊ **•avoir soif** to be thirsty **Ils avaient faim et ils avaient soif. Ils étaient après dire comment pauvres ils étaient.* They were hungry and they were thirsty. They were saying how poor they were. (SL, An94) *Rebouche pas la bouteille, j'ai toujours soif.* Don't re-cork the bottle, I'm still thirsty. (LA) <LA, SL, An94, Da84, Hi02> <***Loc:*** LA, SL, An94, Da84, Hi02>

soiffer [swafe] **1** to drink greedily **2** to devour *Soiffer son manger.* To gulp down one's food. (SJ) <***Loc:*** SJ, Lv88>

soiffeur [swafœr] *n.m.* drunkard <***Loc:*** SM, La99>

soigné, -e [swɑ̃je] *adj.* groomed, cared for **Un chien bien soigné.* A well-groomed dog. (Da84) **Puis dans le temps, le bougre avait un beau cheval. Il avait une belle queue et il brossait ce crin et puis c'était soigné comme tu soignes ton char aujourd'hui.* And in those days, the fellow had a beautiful horse. It had a beautiful tail and he brushed that mane and it was cared for like cars are cared for today. (SL, An94) <***Loc:*** EV, SL, An94, Da84>

soigner [swɑ̃je, swɛ̃je, sɔ̃je] **I** *v.tr.* **1** to take care of, tend to, care for *Si le Bon Dieu veut m'aider je veux soigner les malades.* If the Good Lord is willing to help me, I want to care for the ill. (SL) *J'ai travaillé pour le shérif, j'ai soigné l'école pour douze ans.* I worked for the sheriff, I took care of the school for 12 years. (TB) *Je soignais des enfants. J'ai fait ça pour vingt ans de temps.* I took care of children. I did that for twenty years. (EV) **2** to keep (e.g. bees) *Ma mère soignait des abeilles, des mouches à miel, ça fait ils en avaient un tas.* My mother kept bees, honeybees, so they had a lot. (IB) **II se soigner** *v.pron.* to take care of o.s. *Soignez-vous-autres et revenez!* Take care of yourselves and come back! (LA) *Soignez-vous bien!* Take care! (Hi02) ◊ **•soigner un petit chien {veau} (pour qqn)** to hold a grudge and plan or await revenge (against s.o.) <EV, La99> <***Loc:*** AC, EV, IB, LA, SL, SM, TB, Da84, Hi02, La99, Lv88>

soigneur, -euse [swɑ̃jœr, -øz] *n.* nurse ◊ **•soigneuse de malade** practical nurse <Da84> <***Loc:*** Da84>

soin [swɛ̃] *n.m.* care, attention ◊ **•avec soin** carefully, with care <Da84> **•mal soin** neglect, carelessness *C'est le mal soin qu'a fait ça.* It's neglect that caused that. (VM) <VM> **•prendre en soin** to be responsible for, take care of *J'ai pris les enfants en soin quand ils étiont en ville.* I took care of the kids while they were in town. (VM) <EV, VM> <***Loc:*** EV, LA, VM, Da84>

soir [swar] *n.m.* evening, night *Je vas au bal proche tous les soirs.* I go to the dance almost every night. (ch: *La neige sur la couverture*) ◊ **•à soir / (à) ce soir / asoir** tonight, this evening *Il y a un bal à soir.* There's a dance tonight. (SM) *Tu vas pas au* SHOW *à ce soir?* You aren't going to the show tonight? (VM) <IB, IV, LA, LF, SM, TB, VM, Da84, Hi02, Lv88, Wh83> <***Loc:*** AC, AS, EV, IB, IV, LA, LF, SL, SM, TB, VM, An84, An94, Da84, Gu00, Hi02, Lv88, Wh83>

soirée [sware] *n.f.* **1** evening **2** evening visit **3** evening party **Ceux-là qu'avaient des grands chambres invitaient monde d'aller pour une 'tite soirée.* Those who had big rooms invited people to go to a little evening social. (St95) **Jeudi soir on a eu une petite soirée.* Thursday night we had a little party. (LA, An94) ◊ **•faire une soirée *a*** to spend the evening ***b*** to give an evening party **On va faire une petite soirée juste pour nous-autres et on va pas inviter personne.* We'll have a little party just for ourselves and we won't invite anyone. (LA, An94) <LA, An94, Da84> <***Loc:*** LA, SM, VM, An94, Da84, Hi02, St95>

soit [swa] *conj.* ◊ **•soit... soit** either . . . or **Soit lui, soit moi.* Either him or me. (Da84) <Da84> **•soit... ou** either . . . or *Soit une caisse ou une boîte.* Either a carton or a box. (JE) *Eusse travaillait tout sur l'eau. Soit la pêche aux chevrettes ou la pêche aux huîtres ou la pêche aux poissons. T'avais toute sorte de pêche à faire.* They all worked on the water. Either shrimp fishing or oyster fishing or fishing for fish. You had all kinds of fishing to do. (LF) *On avait pas de char dans ce temps là, fallait soit qu'on marche ou* RIDE *des bicycles.* We didn't have a car in those days, we had to either walk or ride bicycles. (TB) <JE, LF, TB> **•soit que... ou que** whether . . . or **Soit qu'il vient ou qu'il vient pas.* Whether he comes or not. (Da84) <Da84> <***Loc:*** AV, EV, JE, LF, SL, SM, TB, Da84>

soixantaine [swasɑ̃tɛ̃n] *n.f.* about sixty <*Loc:* TB, Da84>

soixante [swasɑ̃t, swesɑ̃t, swezɑ̃t] *adj./n.m.* sixty *Il y avait soixante z-œufs dans la caisse.* There were sixty eggs in the case. (LA) <*Loc:* EV, LA, SM, TB, VM, An94, Da84, Hi02>

soixante-dix [swasɑ̃tdis, swesɑ̃tdis] *adj./n.m.* seventy *Cette maison a soixante-dix ans de vieille.* That house is seventy years old. (LA) *Vous regardez bien, on croirait pas vous-autres avez soixante-dix ans.* You look good, one wouldn't believe you are seventy years old. (Lv88) *Un temps partiellement couvert avec les hauts dans les soixante-dix.* Partly cloudy weather with highs in the 70s. (KRVS) <*Loc:* LA, Da84, Hi02, Lv88>

soixante-dixième [swasɑ̃tdizjɛ̃m, swesɑ̃tdizjɛ̃m] *adj./n.* seventieth <*Loc:* Da84>

soixantième [swasɑ̃tjɛ̃m, swesɑ̃tjɛ̃m] *adj./n.* sixtieth *Ils ont fêté leur soixantième anniversaire de mariage.* They celebrated their sixtieth wedding anniversary. (LA) <*Loc:* LA, Da84>

soja [soʒa] *n.m.* soybean <*Loc:* CL>

soldat[1] [sɔlda] *n.m.* soldier <*Loc:* LF, SM, Da84, Hi02>

soldat[2] (**soldat chien**) [sɔlda, sɔldaʃjɛ̃] *n.m.* black-necked stilt <*Loc:* Lv88>

soldat chien ♦see **soldat**[2]

sole [sol] *n.f.* **1** sill, large timber beam (main support of a building) **2** beam *Les enfants ont corcobié assez en haut qu'ils ont cassé la grosse sole du milieu.* The children bucked around so much up there that they broke the big center beam. (LA) <*Loc:* LA, SL, Da84>

soleil [solɛj, solej] *n.m.* **1** sun *Le soleil a fait qu'une passée.* The sun made only a brief appearance. (Lv88) *La gelée le matin, quand le soleil se lève, ça brille.* The frost in the morning sparkles when the sun rises. (VM) **2** sunshine, sunlight *Une personne qui reste au soleil de trop va venir tout ridée.* A person who stays too much in the sun will become all wrinkled. (LA) *Boire une bière fraîche après une journée de travail au soleil, c'est rassasiant.* Drinking a cold beer after a day of work in the sun is very satisfying. (VM) **3** sunflower ◊ •**soleil baissant** setting sun <Da84> •**soleil couché / soleil-coucher** sunset *Il fallait aller à l'ouvrage jusqu'à soleil couché.* We had to work until sunset. (Lv88) *Il était pas chez lui avant le soleil couché.* He was not home before sunset. (Lv88) <LA, LF, An94, Gu82, Lv88, Wh83> •**soleil levant** the rising sun <Da84> •**soleil levé / soleil-lever** ***a*** sunrise, at sunrise ***b*** the risen sun <LA, An94, Da84, Lv88> •**(de) soleil levant (à) soleil couché** from dawn to dusk *On travaillait de soleil levant à soleil couché.* We worked from dawn to dusk. (LA) <LA, Lv88> •**faire beau soleil** to be bright sunlight <Da84> •**mettre au beau soleil** to expose to full sunlight *Quand un bébé était un peu jaune, tu le mettais au beau soleil et ça le guérissait.* When a baby was a bit jaundiced, you would expose it to full sunlight and that would cure it. (LA) <LA, Da84> •**mettre au soleil** to put or hang in the sun *J'aime mettre mon linge au soleil.* I like to hang my clothes in the sun. (LA) <LA, Da84> <*Loc:* LA, LF, SL, VM, An94, Da84, Gu82, Hi02, Lv88, Wh83>

soleiller [soleje] **I** *v.tr.* to sun, expose to sunlight *J'ai soleillé le linge à ce matin.* I hung out the washing in the sun this morning. (VM) *J'ai soleillé les matelas.* I put the mattresses out in the sun. (SM) **II** *v.intr.* to sun, sunbathe *Les hommes soleillaient en arrière du magasin.* Men would sunbathe behind the shop. (Lv88) **III se soleiller** *v.pron.* to sun o.s., sunbathe *Le chat se soleille sur la galerie.* The cat is sunning itself on the porch. (Lv88) *J'ai été me soleiller.* I went sunbathing. (VM) <*Loc:* AV, EV, IB, LA, LF, SB, SJ, SL, SM, TB, VM, Da84, Lv88, Ph36>

solemnité ♦see **solennité**

solennité (**solemnité**) [solɑ̃nite] *n.f.* [*eccl.*] solemnity, festive observance <*Loc:* Da84>

solennel [solɑ̃nɛl] *adj.* [*eccl.*] solemn <*Loc:* Da84>

soliard [sɔljar] *n.* ◊ •**tomber en soliard** to faint, pass out <EV, Lv88, Ph36> <*Loc:* EV, Lv88, Ph36>

solide [solid] *adj.* **1** solid *N-a quelqu'uns qu'a parti dès qu'eusse a vu ça, place de rester là, parce que ça c'était la batisse qu'était la plus solide qui y avait.* There are some who left when they saw that, instead of staying there, because that was the most solid building there was. (LF) **2** firm, sturdy *C'était joliment un bougre solide dans ces temps.* He was a pretty firm fellow in those days. (SL) **3** strong *Le mur est pas trop solide.* The wall is not very strong. (LA) **4** sound, trustworthy *Sa promesse était solide.* His promise was sound. (LA) <*Loc:* LA, LF, SL, SM, Da84>

solider ♦see **assolider**

solitaire[1] [solitær] *adj.* solitary, alone *Un loup solitaire.* A lone wolf. (LA) <*Loc:* LA, Da84>

solitaire[2] [solitær] *n.* solitaire, card game played by one person alone <*Loc:* Da84>

solitude [solityd] *n.f.* solitude, seclusion <*Loc:* Da84>

solive [soliv] *n.f.* joist, support beam <*Loc:* Hi02>

soliveau [solivo] *n.m.* **1** joist, support beam *Ils ont eu besoin d'abouter les derniers soliveaux pour finir.* They had to join the last beams to finish the job. (LA) *Les rats ont tout rongé mes soliveaux.* The rats chewed my beams all up. (EV) **2** threshold, sill <*Loc:* AV, EV, IB, LA, SJ, SL, SM, Da84, Lv88>

solqui ♦**see sulky**

solution [solysjɔ̃] *n.f.* solution (of a problem) <*Loc:* Da84>

sombre [sɔ̃m, sɔ̃b(r)] *adj.* dark, somber, gloomy *Elle mettait tout le temps des couleurs sombres.* She always wore somber colors. (LA) <*Loc:* LA, Da84>

somme[1] [sɔ̃m] *n.f.* sum, total, amount <*Loc:* SM, Da84>

somme[2] [sɔ̃m] *n.m.* **1** nap *Mon petit garçon est grognard quand il se réveille de son somme.* My little boy is grouchy when he wakes from his nap. (VM) **2** sleep ◊ •**faire {prendre}**

un somme to take a nap <AL, Da84> <*Loc:* AL, SM, VM, Da84>

sommeil [sɔ̃mɛj] *n.m.* sleep, slumber <*Loc:* Da84>

sommeiller [sɔ̃meje] *v.intr.* to sleep, doze, take a nap *O toi, chérie, si tu veux faire un joli rêve, essaie de sommeiller dans les bras de ton nègre.* Oh dearest, if you want to have a sweet dream, try sleeping in the arms of your loving man. (IB: ch, *J'ai vu Lucille*) <*Loc:* IB, Da84>

somnambule [sɔ̃mnɑ̃byl, sɔ̃nɑ̃byl] *n.f.* fortune-teller <*Loc:* JE, SJ, La99, Lv88>

son[1] **(sa, ses)** *adj.poss.* (*m.sing.* **son** [sɔ̃], *f.sing.* **sa** [sa], *m./f.pl.* **ses** [se], *m./f.pl. before a vowel* **ses** [sez]) his, her, its **Il y a un jeune bougre qui s'en vient sur son* MOTORCYCLE. There is a young guy who comes on his motorcycle. (IV, An94) *Et naturelle, quand la fille se mariait alle allait avec son mari de place en place.* And naturally, when the girl got married she went with her husband from place to place. (TB) *Il voulait racheter son honneur après qu'il a sorti de la prison.* He wanted to redeem his honor after he got out of prison. (VM) *Son frère croyait il était malin.* His brother thought he was clever. (LA) *Il a fait des macaqueries quand son papa est parti.* He got into mischief when his dad was gone. (SM) **Il a descendu de son char.* He got out of his car. (EV, An94) *Il travaille pour son manger.* He works for his food. (SM) **Il avait son casse-tête dans sa ceinture.* He had his hammer in his belt. (IV, An94) **Il avait cinq sous dans sa poche.* He had five cents in his pocket. (SL, An94) *Il s'a présenté aux parents de sa belle.* He introduced himself to his girlfriend's parents. (VM) *Noncle avait un marais à côté de sa propriété.* Uncle had a swamp next to his property. (SJ) *Après que sa femme est morte, il a paradé sa misère pour de l'attention.* After his wife died, he paraded his misery to get attention. (LA) **Alle a appris ses premières paroles en anglais.* She learned her first words in English. (Gu82) *Après il a fini l'école, il s'a mis à fouiner et il a perdu proche tous ses amis.* After he finished school, he started leading a dissolute life and he lost almost all his friends. (LA) *J'aime pas ça quand ma belle-fille vient visiter. Ses enfants sont assez pirates!* I don't like it when my daughter-in-law comes to visit. Her children are pretty bad. (Gu00) *C'est un enfant placé, mais alle l'aime comme ses enfants à elle.* He's an adopted child, but she loves him like her own children. (TB) **Ses trois filles et sa femme étaient dans la maison.* His three daughters and his wife were in the house. (LA, An94) **Il voulait que ses garçons arrêtent de gambler.* He wanted his sons to stop gambling. (An94) <*Loc:* AC, AV, EV, IB, IV, JE, LA, LF, SB, SJ, SL, SM, TB, VM, An94, Da84, Gu00, Gu82, La99, Lv88, Ph36, Re31,Wh83>

son[2] [sɔ̃] *n.m.* sound <*Loc:* TB, Da84>

son[3] [sɔ̃] *n.m.* **1** sawdust **2** dandruff *Il a du son dans la tête.* He has dandruff in his hair. (AV) ◊ **•son de scie {bois}** sawdust *Ça achetait la glace dans des gros blocs, et eusse mettait ça dans du son de scie.* They bought ice in big blocks, and they put it in sawdust. (LF) <EV, IB, LA, LF, SB, SL, SM, TB, Da84, Lv88, Ph36> <*Loc:* AV, EV, IB, LA, LF, SB, SL, SM, TB, Da84, Lv88, Ph36>

sondage [sɔ̃daʒ] *n.m.* sounding, probing, testing <*Loc:* Da84>

sonder [sɔ̃de] *v.tr.* **1** to sound, test for, explore *Il sonde la hauteur du fleuve.* He's testing the depth of the river. (SB) *J'ai travaillé sur un* CREW *qui sondait pour l'huile.* I worked on a crew that tested for oil. (LA) **2** to auscultate *Le docteur a sondé mon ventre.* The doctor auscultated my stomach. (SM) <*Loc:* LA, SB, SM, VM, Da84, Lv88>

songe [sɔ̃ʒ] *n.m.* dream <*Loc:* Da84>

songer [sɔ̃ʒe] *v.intr.* to ponder, consider *Adieu, Théogène, ayoù tu te sauves? Songez, petit, j'ai perdu mon chapeau.* Adieu, Théogène, where are you running? Consider, little one, I've lost my hat. (VM, ch: *Théogène Dubois*) <*Loc:* VM, Da84>

sonnailler [sɔ̃naje] *v.tr.* to ring repeatedly, ring off and on *Ce maudit téléphone sonnaillait toute la grande journée.* That damn telephone would ring repeatedly all day long. (LA) <*Loc:* LA, Da84>

sonner [sɔ̃ne] **I** *v.tr.* to sound, ring, strike (e.g. a bell, a chord) **Ça fait, on allait ensemble voir comment il accordait ça. Il sonnait une corde. Là, nous-autres, on essayait.* So we would go together to see how he would tune it up. He would sound a string. Then we would try. (EV, An94) **II** *v.intr.* **1** to sound, ring **Là, je vas te jouer une valse t'as jamais entendu. Je connais pas si ça va sonner bien, mais je vas te la jouer quand même.* Now I'll play a waltz that you never heard. I don't know if it will sound good, but I'll play it for you anyway. (JD, An84) **2** to sound, give a particular impression *C'est tout pareil. Tu peux user n'importe équel, selon équel qui sonne mieux équand t'après le dire.* It's all the same. You can use either one, depending on which one sounds better when you're saying it. (TB) *En anglais ça sonne un peu mieux que ça. Mais ça, il le voulait en français.* In English it sounds a little better than that. But he wanted it in French. (TB) <*Loc:* EV, JD, TB, An84, An94, Da84, Hi02>

sonnerie [sɔ̃nri] *n.f.* ringing **La sonnerie de cloches.* The ringing of bells. (Da84) <*Loc:* Da84>

sonnette [sɔ̃nɛt] *n.f.* **1** small bell **2** rattlesnake *La sonnette a manqué me mordre.* The rattlesnake nearly bit me. (SL) <*Loc:* JE, LF, SL, TB, Da84, Lv88>

sonneur [sɔ̃nœr] *n.m.* bell ringer <*Loc:* Da84>

sorbet [sɔrbɛj] *n.m.* sherbet <*Loc:* LF>

sorbetière ♦see **sabotière**

sorcier, -ière [sɔrsje, -jær] *n.* **1** *(m.)* magician, wizard **2** *(f.)* witch, wizard, sorceress <*Loc:* Da84>

sorgho [sɔrgo, solgo] *n.m.* sorghum <*Loc:* VM, Da84>

sorrel [sorɛl] *adj.* sorrel *Vous avez peut-être pas vu par hasard une petite jument sorrel, queue coupée queue ouverte avec* *deux poulains derrière?* Might you have seen by chance a little sorrel mare, with a cut and fanned tail with two colts following her? (LA) <*Loc:* LA, Lv88>

sort [sɔr] *n.m.* lot, fate, destiny, condition <*Loc:* Da84>

sortant [sɔrtɑ̃] *n.m.* the outgoing, those leaving <*Loc:* Da84>

sorte [sɔrt] *n.f.* kind, sort, type **Quelle sorte de monde c'est ça?* What kind of people are these? (Da84) **Ça fait, le bougre a continué à raconter toutes sortes des affaires.* So, the guy continued to recount all kinds of things. (SL, An94) *T'avais toute sorte de pêche à faire.* There were all kinds of fishing to do. (LF) *Il était planté là après ramancher toute sorte de couillonades.* He was there muttering all sorts of silliness. (LA) *Tu vas dans l'Atchafalaya, tu vois pas personne, c'est tranquille, là tu vois toutes sortes de zozos, toutes sortes de bétails.* You go into the Atchafalaya, you don't see anyone, it's quiet, there you see all kinds of birds, all kinds of animals. (SM) <*Loc:* EV, LA, LF, SL, SM, An94, Da84>

sortir [sɔrtir, surtir] **I** *v.tr.* to bring out, take out *Ils ont sorti un nouveau papier. Ça c'est pas de bonnes nouvelles en nulle place.* They brought out a new paper. There is no good news anywhere. (VM)-**Et quand ils ont foncé, il a sorti son pistolet, puis il a crié, "Grand rond!"* And when they rushed forward, he took out his pistol and he yelled, "Big circle!" (LA, An94) *Il a paniqué quand le bougre a sorti son couteau.* He panicked when the fellow took out his knife. (LA) **II** *v.intr.* **1** to come out, emerge *Le petit a sorti de pardessous la table.* The child came out from under the table. (EV) **La maîtresse de la maison a sorti.* The lady of the house came out. (LA, An94) *T'aurais dû voir la pourriture qu'a sorti de ce clou quand ils l'ont lancé!* You should've seen the pus that came out of that boil when they lanced it! (VM) *Alle avait les vers, ça lui sortait par le nez, et les oreilles, la bouche et tout.* She had worms, they were coming out her nose, her ears, her mouth and all. (TB) **2** to go out *Pauvre garçon, il est tellement peureux que il peut proche pas sortir la nuit.* Poor boy, he's so cowardly that he can hardly go out at night. (LA) *Moi, je trouvais que ses culottes étaient trop* TIGHT, *mais sa mère la laissait sortir comme ça.* I thought that her pants were too tight, but her mother would let her go out like that. (LA) **III s'en sortir** *v.pron.* to find a way out, extricate o.s. *Je suis pas sûr que je pourras m'en sortir.* I don't know if I'll be able to find a way out. (LA) ◊ **•sortir à jeu** to tie, come out even *Ils ont sorti à jeu.* They came out even. (VM) <VM> **•sortir avec *a*** to date *Il sort avec la même fille depuis des années.* He has been dating the same girl for years. (LA) *Je voudrais pas qu'elle sort avec ce pouilleux.* I wouldn't want her to date that bum. (LA) ***b*** to go out with **Et pour eux-autres s'amuser bien, ils ont pris à sortir avec nous-autres tout doucement.* And in order to have a good time, they slowly started going out with us. (EV, An84) ***c*** to produce, come out with (s.t. new) **Tu vois, Joe Falcon venait de sortir avec un* RECORD *de musique d'accordéon.* You see, Joe Falcon had just come out with a record of accordion music. (SL, An84) <EV, LA, SL, An84, Da84> **•sortir de *a*** to have just (done s.t.) **Je sors d'arriver.* I just got here. (Da84) *Alle sort de me parler de ça.* She just told me about that. (VM) *Il sort de finir l'ouvrage.* He just finished the task. (Lv88) ***b*** to come from, come out from, leave from **Et le soir, il sortait de là, et il prendait le bayou et il mangeait les bêtes.* And at night, it would come out from there and it would follow the bayou and it would eat the cows. (EV, An94) *Il était toujours après son prêchement quand j'ai sorti de l'église.* He was still preaching when I left the church. (LA) <EV, LA, LF, SL, SM, TB, VM, An94, Da84, Hi02, Lv88> **•sortir du chemin** to get out of the way <Da84> **•sortir en arrière** to lose, not get what one expects **Tu sortais jamais en arrière. Tu recevrais autant de viande que t'avais donnée aux autres.* You never lost out. You got as much meat as you had given to the others. (Gu82) <Gu82, Lv88> **•sortir l'avant / sortir en avant** to make a profit, come out ahead *Il a sorti l'avant dans ce business.* He came out of that deal with a profit. (JE) *Avec tous ces dépenses, j'ai sorti en avant quand même.* With all these expenses, I came out ahead anyway. (Lv88) <JE, TB, Lv88> **•faire sortir** to force out **Faire sortir le monde.* To force the people out. (Da84) <Da84> <*Loc:* EV, JE, LA, LF, SL, SM, TB, VM, An84, An94, Da84, Gu82, Hi02, La99, Lv88>

sot[1]**, sotte** [so, sɔt] *adj.* foolish, silly, stupid ◊ **•sot comme un panier percé** very stupid <AV, La99> <*Loc:* AV, EV, TB, An94, Da84, La99, Lv88>

sot[2]**, sotte** [so, sɔt] *n.* idiot, fool, stupid person **Ça, c'était Jean Sot, le sot, l'imbécile, le fou.* That was Foolish John, the fool, the imbecile, the nut. (EV, An94) <*Loc:* AV, EV, An94, Da84, La99, Lv88>

sottiseux, -euse [sotizø, -øz] *n.* one who says silly, foolish things <*Loc:* JE, TB>

sou [su] *n.m.* cent, penny **J'ai pas le sou.* I am broke. (Da84) **Il vaut pas un sou.* He's not worth a penny. (Da84) *J'ai payé cinq sous.* I paid five cents. (EV) *Et là, tu pouvais t'acheter un* SOUP BONE *pour dix sous, cinq ou dix sous.* And you could buy yourself a soup bone for ten cents, five or ten cents. (SL) ◊ **•cinq-sous** nickel <EV, TB, Lv88> **•cinq sous commencent la piastre** getting started is the hardest part of a project <LA, La99> **•dix-sous** dime <Lv88> **•vingt-cinq-sous** quarter <Lv88> <*Loc:* AV, EV, LA, SL, SM, TB, VM, An94, Da84, Hi02, La99, Lv88>

soubler [suble] *v.intr.* to whistle <*Loc:* Hi02>

souche ♦see **chousse**

souci [susi] *n.m.* ◊ **•sans souci la rose** carefree *Mais vous êtes sans souci la rose.* But you are carefree. (TB) <TB> <*Loc:* TB>

soucille (**sousille, souille**) [susi, susij, sosij, sosi, suzij, suj] *n.f.* pillowcase, pillowslip ◊ **•soucille d'oreiller** pillowcase

<IB, LA, SM, TB, VM, Da84, Guoo> <***Loc:*** IB, LA, SM, TB, VM, Da84, Guoo, Lv88>

soucoupe [sukup, s(ə)kup] *n.f.* saucer <***Loc:*** JE, LA, LF, SB, SL, SM, Da84>

soudable [sudab(l)] *adj.* solderable, weldable *On l'a soudé assez de fois, c'est p'us soudable.* We welded it so many times, it's no longer solderable. (VM) <***Loc:*** VM, Da84>

souder [sude] *v.tr.* to solder, braze, weld *Il est un soudeur asteur. Il soude, il a son business à lui-même.* He's a welder now. He welds, he has his own business. (TB) <***Loc:*** IB, LF, TB, Da84>

soudeur [sudœr] *n.m.* solderer, welder <***Loc:*** LA, TB, Da84>

soudeuse [sudøz] *n.f.* welding machine <***Loc:*** Da84>

soudrillonne [sudrijɔ̃n] *n.f.* dirty woman *Va donc te laver, espèce de soudrillonne.* Go wash up, filthy woman. (TB) <***Loc:*** TB>

soudure [sudyr] *n.f.* **1** solder **2** soldering **3** soldered joint, weld <***Loc:*** IB, Da84>

soué [sue, sui] *interj.* cry to call pigs <***Loc:*** EV, SM, Ph36>

soufferre (**souffert, souffrir**) [sufær, sufrir] **I** *v.tr.* to suffer, endure (e.g. pain, death) *Il y en a qu'a souffert la mort.* There are those who suffered death. (ch: *Acadie à la Louisiane*) **II** *v.intr.* to suffer *Et là eux-autres va hacher les pensions et ça laisse les petits manière à souffert.* And then they go get the support checks, and they leave the little ones to suffer somewhat. (TB) *Il va souffert beaucoup.* He will suffer a lot. (Lv88) *Faut pleurer, faut prier, misérer et souffert.* One must cry, pray, struggle, and suffer (Lv88, ch: *Un saint sur la terre*) ◊ **•soufferre du bleu de ciel avec** to suffer misery or a hard time with <La99> **•soufferre les conséquences** to suffer the consequences <Da84> **•soufferre des martyres** to suffer torments, be tortured <Da84> <***Loc:*** LA, LF, SB, SL, TB, VM, An94, Da84, Hio2, La99, Lv88>

souffert ♦see **soufferre**

souffle [suf(l)] *n.m.* **1** breath *Il y a un monsieur qui me dit c'est bon pour tes poumons, tes* LUNGS, *il dit quand tu fais, quand tu souffles là-dedans, il dit, ça travaille ça-là, ça te donne du souffle.* There's a man that tells me that it's good for your lungs, he says when you do that, when you blow into it [the duck call], it works them, it gives you breath. (TB) **2** wind ◊ **•souffle court** asthma *85 ans, cher. Je crois pas ça. Je le crois quand je commence à venir avec le souffle court, là je le crois, mais à part de ça...* I'm 85. I can't believe that. I believe it when I start to get asthma, then I believe it, but otherwise . . . (TB) <TB> <***Loc:*** TB, Da84>

souffle-poussière [sufpusjær] *n.* short person <***Loc:*** VM>

souffler [sufle] **I** *v.tr.* **1** to blow out **Il a soufflé la lampe. Il a été se coucher.* He blew out the lamp. He went to bed. (SL, An94) **2** to inflate *Souffler des* TIRES. To inflate tires. (LA) **3** to utter **Souffle pas un mot.* Don't breathe a word. (Da84) **II** *v.intr.* **1** to breathe *Si vous allumez une cigarette je vas vous dire* WELL *vous pouvez rester mais la cigarette va en-dehors. J'ai de la misère à souffler quand je suis autour de ça.* If you light a cigarette I'll tell you, well, you can stay but the cigarette goes outside. I have trouble breathing when I'm around that. (TB) *Si ton nez était bouché, ça aidait pour tu pouvais souffler meilleur.* If your nose was blocked, it helped so that you could breathe better. (AC) *Je suis sûre qu'il est mort. Il souffle plus.* I'm sure he's dead. He's not breathing any more. (TB) **2** to blow **Dans ma famille on a jamais eu besoin de 'garder dans ein liv' pour sa'oir dans quel sens le vent soufflait.* In my family, we never had to look in a book to see which way the wind was blowing. (ThCa: *Mille misères*) **III se souffler** *v.pron.* to inflate o.s., puff o.s. up **Il se soufflait jusqu'à t'à l'heure il se soufflait de trop, il a cassé.* He [the frog] inflated himself until soon he had puffed himself up too much and he popped. (LA, An94) ◊ **•souffler une tape** to slap <VM> **•se souffler dans les narines *a*** to get physically close in a conflict or argument ***b*** to be on the verge of fighting <La99> <***Loc:*** AC, EV, LA, SL, TB, VM, An94, Da84, Hio2, La99, ThCa>

soufflet [suflɛ, sufle] *n.m.* bellows (on an accordion) <***Loc:*** EV>

souffrance [sufrɑ̃s] *n.f.* pain, suffering <***Loc:*** Da84>

souffrant, -e [sufrɑ̃, -ɑ̃t] *adj.* suffering, aching *Elle était souffrante la semaine passée.* She was suffering last week. (LA) <***Loc:*** LA, SM, Da84>

souffrir ♦see **soufferre**

soufre [suf(r)] *n.m.* sulphur, brimstone <***Loc:*** Da84>

souhait [swɛ, swe] *n.m.* wish, desire <***Loc:*** Da84>

souhaitable [swatab(l)] *adj.* desirable *Ça serait souhaitable qu'il mouille plus que ça.* It would be desirable that it rain more than this. (VM) <***Loc:*** VM, Da84>

souhaiter [swate] **I** *v.tr.* to want, wish, desire, hope *Ça pourrait taper le Mexique,* BUT *je souhaite ça vient pas.* It could hit Mexico, but I hope it doesn't come. (TB) *Je sais pas qui il va faire avec moi, mais je souhaite qu'il me fait pas de tort.* I don't know what he's going to do with me, but I hope he doesn't do me wrong. (TB) **II se souhaiter** *v.pron.* to wish for, desire for o.s. **Se souhaiter de l'argent.* To wish for money. (Da84) ◊ **•c'est à souhaiter** it is desirable, it is to be hoped for <Da84> <***Loc:*** SB, TB, Da84, Hio2>

souille ♦see **soucille**

souillon, -onne [sujɔ̃, -ɔ̃n] *adj.* dirty, filthy *Ça ça m'a pas amusé parce que je suis pas si souillonne que ça.* I didn't like that because I'm not that dirty. (St95) <***Loc:*** St95>

souillonner [sujɔ̃ne] *v.tr.* to dirty, soil *Alle a tout souillonné le linge.* She got the clothes all dirty. (TB) <***Loc:*** TB>

soûl, -e (**saoul**) [su, sul] *adj.* **1** drunk, tipsy *Les là qu'étaient trop saouls, on les envoyait à leur camp.* Those who were too drunk were sent to their camp. (IB) *Tu dois l'attendre baranquer quand il est soûl.* You should hear him babble when he's drunk. (VM) *Il est tout le temps soûl. C'est un bon-à-rien.* He's always drunk. He's a worthless fellow.

(SM) **2** dizzy *Il est soûl d'avoir trop tourné.* He is dizzy from having spun around too much. (SL) ◊ **•soûl en farine {patate} / soûl comme un cochon {une grive}** very drunk <La99> <***Loc:*** IB, LF, SL, TB, VM, Da84, Hi02, La99>

soulageant, -e [sulaʒɑ̃, -ɑ̃t] *adj.* soothing, healing *Une baume soulageante.* A soothing balm. (LA) <***Loc:*** LA, Da84>

soulagement [sulaʒmɑ̃] *n.m.* relief, soothing, alleviation (of pain) <***Loc:*** Da84>

soulager [sulaʒe] **I** *v.tr.* to ease, relieve, alleviate, soothe *T'as pas quelque chose qui pourrait soulager un mal d'oreille?* Don't you have anything that could relieve an earache? (EV) *Je mets une planche en-dessous de mon matelas, ça soulage mon mal de dos.* I put a board underneath my mattress, it eases my back pain. (VM) **II se soulager** *v.pron.* to console o.s., make o.s. feel better *J'ai juste moi seul pour me reconsoler, juste mes chansons pour me soulager.* I have just myself to console me, just my songs to ease my pain. (ch: *Une dernière chanson*) *Je me soulage à brailler.* I make myself feel better by crying. (VM) ◊ **•soulager (qqn) de sa porte-monnaie** to steal someone's wallet <AV, La99> <***Loc:*** AV, EV, VM, Da84, La99>

soûlant, -e [sulɑ̃, -ɑ̃t] *adj.* intoxicating *Les graines de lilas sont soûlantes pour les grives.* Chinaball berries are intoxicating to robins. (VM) <***Loc:*** VM, Da84>

soûlard[1]**, soûleuse (souleur, -euse)** [sular, suløz, sulœr] *adj.* habitual drinker, drunkard, alcoholic *Il a eu le malheur de marier une femme soûleuse.* He had the misfortune of marrying an alcoholic woman. (VM) <***Loc:*** TB, VM, Da84>

soûlard[2]**, soûleuse** [sular, suløz] *n.* drunkard *Pauvre Marie, la femme à Gros, ça devait être dur d'avoir marié un soûlard comme ça.* Poor Marie, Gros' wife, it must have been hard to have married a drunkard like that. (ThCa: *La fête à Clomaire*) <***Loc:*** Da84, ThCa>

soûler [sule] **I** *v.tr.* **1** to intoxicate, get s.o. drunk *La bière va te soûler aussi bien que le whisky.* Beer will get you as drunk as well as whisky does. (EV) **2** to make dizzy, cause to be dizzy *Je peux pas prendre cette médecine. Ça me soûle.* I cannot take that medicine. It makes me dizzy. (EV) **II se soûler** *v.pron.* **1** to get drunk *J'ai pris son capot et j'ai été me soûler.* I took his coat and went to get drunk. (IB) **2** to get dizzy *Il s'est soûlé à force qu'il a tourné.* He got dizzy from spinning around so much. (SL) <***Loc:*** AL, EV, IB, LF, SL, Da84, Hi02>

soûlerie [sulri] *n.f.* drunken spree, binge <***Loc:*** Da84>

soulèvement [sulɛvmɑ̃] *n.m.* raising, lifting *J'ai eu pour emprunter des* JACKS *pour le soulèvement de la bâtisse.* I had to borrow some jacks for the raising of the building. (LA) <***Loc:*** LA, Da84>

soulever [sul(ə)ve] **I** *v.tr.* **1** to raise, lift *Tu veux bien soulever ton bout?* Would you please lift your end? (LA) **2** to steal, pickpocket *Il m'a soulevé cinq piastres.* He stole five dollars from me. (VM) **3** to reprimand, scold *Je l'ai soulevé pour avoir dit une menterie.* I reprimanded him for lying. (SL) **II se soulever** *v.pron.* to get up, rise, pick o.s. up *J'ai de la misère à me soulever quand je tombe.* I have trouble getting myself up when I fall. (VM) <***Loc:*** JE, LA, SL, VM, Da84>

soulier [sulje, suje, ʃulje] *n.m.* shoe *On allait à l'école nu-pieds, pas de souliers, tu mettais des souliers quand c'était froid mais quand le temps réchauffait, pas de souliers, c'était naturel pour tous les enfants, presque tous les enfants.* We went to school barefoot, no shoes, you put shoes on when it was cold but when it warmed up, no shoes, it was natural for all children, almost all children. (IB) ◊ **•soulier de bain** bath slipper <TB> **•soulier de chambre** slipper <LF> **•soulier de cheval** horseshoe <JE> **•soulier de maison *a*** house slipper, house shoe ***b*** slipper, bedroom slipper <SL, TB, VM> **•souliers amarrés** shoes with laces <Lv88> **•souliers d'ouvrage** work shoes <Lv88> **•souliers en caoutchouc** rubber shoes <Da84> **•soulier en élastique *a*** rubber shoes, overshoes ***b*** tennis shoes <Da84> **•soulier fin** dress shoe <Da84> **•soulier sauvage** moccasin <Re31> **•gros soulier** work shoe <Da84> <***Loc:*** AC, CL, EV, IB, JE, LA, LF, SB, SL, TB, VM, Da84, Hi02, Lv88, Re31>

soumettre (se) [sumɛt(r)] *v.pron.* **1** to submit, comply, yield, give in *Il aimerait mieux mourir que se soumettre.* He would rather die than submit. (LA) **2** to apologize *Il a venu se soumettre à moi pour ça.* He came to apologize to me for that. (VM) <***Loc:*** LA, VM, Da84>

soupape [supap] *n.f.* valve <***Loc:*** Da84>

soupçonneur [supsɔ̃nœr] *n.m.* person of whom one must be suspicious <***Loc:*** VM, Lv88>

soupe [sup] *n.f.* soup, broth, bouillon *La soupe était après bouillir à gros bouillons.* The soup was boiling briskly. (EV) *Si tu réchauffes la soupe, c'est ça que je vas manger.* If you reheat the soup, that's what I'll eat. (LA) *Rafroidis la soupe.* Cool off the soup. (SM) ◊ **•soupe maigre *a*** soup without meat ***b*** broth with roux to which onions, bell pepper, and cornbread croutons are added <EV> <***Loc:*** EV, LA, SM, Da84, Hi02>

souper[1] [supe] **I** *v.tr.* to eat for supper, dine on *On a soupé un canard hier au soir.* We dined on a duck yesterday evening. (Lv88) *J'ai soupé des volailles.* I ate poultry for supper. (VM) **II** *v.intr.* to sup, have dinner, eat supper (the evening meal) **Mais nous, on va souper. Quand lui, il va arriver, il va manger.* We are going to eat supper. When he arrives, he will eat. (SL, An94) *Quand ça vient le temps pour souper, pour dîner, on se met à table.* When it's time to eat supper, we sit down at the table. (AV) *On est tout paré pour aller souper chez Bélizaire asteur?* Are we all ready to go eat supper at Belizaire's now? (ThCa: *La dernière quilte*) <***Loc:*** AV, LA, SL, VM, An94, Da84, Hi02, Lv88, ThCa>

souper[2] [supe] *n.m.* supper, evening meal **Mon souper m'a rendu malade.* My supper made me sick. (An94) **Le* *souper est paré.* Supper is ready. (LA, An94) <***Loc:*** EV, IB, LA, SL, An94, Da84, Hi02, Lv88>

soupière [supjær] *n.f.* soup bowl, soup tureen <***Loc:*** Da84>

soupir [supir] *n.m.* sigh, gasp <***Loc:*** Da84>

soupirer [supire] *v.intr.* to sigh, gasp *Elle soupirait chaque fois qu'elle entendait mon nom.* She gasped each time she heard my name. (VM) <***Loc:*** VM, Da84>

souple [sup(l)] *adj.* **1** quick, supple, agile *Mon frère était bien souple quand il était jeune.* My brother was very agile when he was young. (VM) **2** moist, wet **Ces draps sont trop souples, il faut les étendre au soleil.* These sheets are too wet, they must be hung in the sun. (Di32) <***Loc:*** VM, Da84, Di32>

souquer [suke] *v.tr.* to seize, squeeze tightly *Souquer une corde.* To squeeze a rope tightly. (VM) <***Loc:*** JE, VM, Lv88, Di32>

source [surs] *n.f.* **1** spring (of water) **Là, elle a trouvé de l'eau, une source d'eau qui coulait.* There, she found water. A spring of water that was running. (IV, An94) **2** source, origin ◊ •**eau de source** spring water <Da84> <***Loc:*** IV, SM, An94, Da84>

sourcil [sursi, susi] *n.m.* eyebrow <***Loc:*** LF, SB, SL, SM, VM, Da84>

sourd[1], -e [sur, -d] *adj.* deaf *Il est sourd, lui, il peut pas t'attendre.* He is deaf, he can't hear you. (VM) ◊ •**sourd comme un poteau {pot} / sourd comme un pot de chambre** very deaf <AV, La99> <***Loc:*** AV, VM, Da84, La99>

sourd[2], -e [sur, -d] *n.* deaf person <***Loc:*** AV, VM, Da84, La99>

sourd[3] [sur] *n.m.* salamander <***Loc:*** SM, Di32, Lv88>

sourd-et-muet [suremɥe, suremɥɛt] *n.* deaf-mute, one who is deaf and dumb *Elle a marié un sourd-et-muet.* She married a deaf-mute. (LA) <***Loc:*** JD, LA, Da84>

sourdine [surdin] *n.f.* ◊ •**à la sourdine *a*** in a sneaky or stealthy way ***b*** unexpectedly *Arriver à la sourdine.* To arrive unexpectedly. (LA) <LA, SJ> <***Loc:*** LA, SJ>

sourdre (**sourder**) [surd(r), sɔrd(r), surde] (*p.p.* **sourdu** [surdy], **sourdé** [surde], **sourd** [sur]) **I** *v.tr.* to find, dig up, bring out *Mais où t'as sourdé ce vieux sweater-là?* But where did you dig up that old sweater? (TB) **II** *v.intr.* **1** to appear, come out **2** to show up unexpectedly *Il a sourd en arrière.* He showed up in back unexpectedly. (Lv88) **3** to surface, float to the top *Non, il avait calé, c'était l'hiver, et il a calé, et là quand-ce que l'été a pris, la chaleur a pris, il a sourdu, c'est là qu'eusse l'a trouvé.* No, he had sunk, it was winter and he had sunk, and then when summer started, warm weather began, he came to the surface, and that's when they found him. (TB) ◊ •**faire sourdre *a*** to cause to sprout *L'eau a fait sourdre les* BEANS. The water made the beans sprout. (Lv88) ***b*** to start, flush, jump (a game animal) **Il a fait sourdre un lapin des broussailles.* He jumped a rabbit from the brush. (Di32) <JE, Di32, Lv88> <***Loc:*** JD, JE, TB, VM, Da84, Di32, Lv88>

sourge [surʒ] *adj.* soft, light, fluffy *Le secret de faire des poutines sourges, c'est de les cuire doucement et couverts.* The secret of making fluffy puddings is to cook them slowly, and covered. (VM) **Du pain sourge.* Soft bread. (Di32) *Le gâteau est sourge.* The cake is spongy. (VM) <***Loc:*** VM, Di32, Gu00, Lv88>

sourire[1] [surir] *v.intr.* to smile, grin **"Ho! Mais si le Bon Dieu est aussi bon que tu dis," il dit, "Il va te donner du linge." Elle a été obligée de sourire.* "Ho! But if God is as good as you say," he said, "He's going to give you some clothes." She had to smile. (IV, An94) <***Loc:*** IV, An94, Da84>

sourire[2] [surir] *n.m.* smile, grin <***Loc:*** Da84>

souris [suri] *n.m./f.* mouse <***Loc:*** AV, JE, SM, Da84, Di32, La99, Lv88>

souris-chaude (**souris-chauve**) [suriʃod, suriʃɔd, suriʃov, suriʃof] *n.f.* bat ♦cf **chauve-souris** <***Loc:*** AV, EV, IB, JD, LA, LF, SL, SM, TB, VM, Lv88, Ph36, Re31>

soursoubler [sursuble, sorsuble] *v.tr.* to ransack, turn topsy-turvy, mess up (e.g. while looking for s.t.) *Il a tout soursoublé sa chambre pour le chercher.* He messed up his whole room to look for it. (VM) <***Loc:*** JE, TB, VM, Di32, Lv88>

sous [su, sur] *prep.* under, below, beneath **Un gros mariage, tu connais, des autres fois passées, ça faisait le dessert dehors sous les arbres, l'été.* A big wedding, you know, in the olden days, they would have the reception outside under the trees in the summer. (EV, An94) <***Loc:*** EV, LF, VM, An94, Da84, Di32, Hi02>

sous-marin [sumarɛ̃] *n.m.* submarine <***Loc:*** LF>

sousille ♦see **soucille**

sousouille [susuj] *n.m.* [*baby talk*] shoe <***Loc:*** LF>

sous-jupe [suʒyp] *n.f.* slip, petticoat <***Loc:*** Da84>

sous-queue [sukø] *n.f.* crupper *Mettre la sous-queue au cheval.* To put the crupper on a horse. (SJ) <***Loc:*** AV, SJ>

soutadaire (**soutadère, soutadière, soutardère**) [sutadær, sutadjær, sutardær] *n.f.* **1** saddle pad, saddle blanket **2** very dirty item of clothing <***Loc:*** AV, EV, IB, JD, SB, SJ, SL, SM, VM, Da84, Di32, Lv88, Ph36, Re31>

soutadère ♦see **soutadaire**

soutadière ♦see **soutadaire**

soutane [sutɑ̃n] *n.f.* cassock <***Loc:*** Da84>

soutardère ♦see **soutadaire**

soutenable [sutnab(l)] *adj.* tenable, sustainable, defensible *Ta position est pas soutenable.* Your position is not defensible. (LA) <***Loc:*** LA, Da84>

soutenir (**soutiendre**) [sutnir, sutjɛ̃n, sutjɛ̃d(r)] **I** *v.tr.* **1** to support, hold up *Ils ont passé avec; ça l'apportait. Je pense il y avait trois quatre z-hommes qui le soutenaient.* They passed by with [his body]; they were carrying him. I think there were three or four men holding him up. (EV) **2** to support (financially), give support to, keep up (e.g. a family) *Il soutient pas ses enfants.* He doesn't support his children. (LA)

3 to maintain, claim **4** to take up for *Elle soutient trop son garçon.* She takes her son's side too much of the time. (LA) **II se soutenir** *v.pron.* **1** to support o.s. or each other **2** to hold o.s. up <***Loc:*** EV, LA, SB, SL, Da84, Lv88>

souterrain[1] [suterɛ̃] *adj.* underground, subterranean *Un nique souterrain.* An underground nest. (LA) <***Loc:*** LA, Da84>

souterrain[2] [suterɛ̃] *n.m.* **1** cave, cavern **2** mole tunnel <***Loc:*** EV, Da84>

soutien [sutjɛ̃] *n.m.* sustenance, support, upkeep *Elle a élevé ses cinq enfants sans aucun soutien de sa famille.* She raised her five children without any help from her family. (VM) <***Loc:*** VM, Da84>

soutiendre ♦see **soutenir**

souvenance [suvnɑ̃s] *n.f.* memory **Il a fait une autre lettre pour envoyer au roi, lui dire que—et elle avait un petit—il a dit que, dessus la lettre, qu'il fallait qu'il détruit Geneviève et son petit parce qu'il voulait pas de souvenance si elle était tournée comme ça.* He wrote another letter to send to the king, to tell him that—and she had a child—he said, in the letter, that it would be necessary to kill Genevieve and her child because he didn't want any memory [of her] if she had turned out like that. (IV, An94) <***Loc:*** IV, An94>

souvenir[1] **(se)** [suvnir] *v.pron.* to remember, recall *Je me souviens, chère, aussi bien de les jeux de cartes chez Nonc Willy.* I remember, dear, very well the card games at Uncle Willy's. (AV, ch: *Nonc Willy*) <***Loc:*** AV, Da84, Hi02>

souvenir[2] [suvnir] *n.m.* **1** remembrance, recollection **2** souvenir, keepsake *Il y a plein du monde de la France qui vient ici à ma boutique pour voir les souvenirs qu'on a de la Paroisse, et eux-autres peut pas croire que je parle en français.* There are a lot of people from France who come here to my store to see the souvenirs that we have of the parish, and they can't believe that I speak French. (LF) <***Loc:*** LF, Da84>

souvent [suvɑ̃] *adv.* often, frequently *Les politiciens travaillent souvent en graissant la main.* Politicians often work on things by bribing. (LA) *J'ai habitude aller souvent au NURSING HOME.* I used to go often to the nursing home. (EV) *Ça a pas l'habitude d'être icitte, lui, c'est pas souvent qu'il reste icitte.* He's not used to being here, it's not often that he stays here. (TB) *Ma femme vient avec moi beaucoup souvent.* My wife comes with me very often. (SM) ◊ **•souvent de(s) fois / souventefois** frequently, often *Souvent des fois notre père me disait si vous-autres va dans les différentes places, guettez qui vous-autres dit.* Often our father would tell me, if you all go to different places, watch what you say. (LF) *J'ai fait ça souventefois.* I've done that quite often. (TB) <JD, JE, LA, LF, SL, SM, TB, Da84, Lv88> <***Loc:*** EV, JD, JE, LA, LF, SL, SM, TB, VM, Da84, Lv88>

SOYBEAN [sɔibin] *n.m./f.* soybean *Les SOYBEAN [...] c'est une récolte qui existait pas ici ça, trente ans passés.* Soybeans, that's a crop that didn't exist here thirty years ago. (SL) <***Loc:*** EV, SL, An94, Da84, Lv88, Ph36>

spaghetti [spageti] *n.m.* spaghetti <***Loc:*** Da84>

sparadraffe [sparadraf] *n.m.* adhesive bandage or plaster *Poser un sparadraffe.* To put on an adhesive bandage. (SJ) <***Loc:*** IB, SJ>

spatule [spatyl] *n.f.* **1** any long-legged bird with a spatula-shaped beak **2** roseate spoonbill duck **3** paddlefish, spoonbill catfish <***Loc:*** VM, Lv88, Re31>

spécial, -e [spesjal] *adj.* special, particular *Vous-autres faisait quelque chose spéciale avec l'argent qu'il faisait avec la musique ou vous-autres mettait ça avec l'autre argent pour faire le ménage aller?* Did you all do anything special with the money that he made with the music or did you put that in with the other money to make the household run? (EV) <***Loc:*** EV, Da84, Hi02>

spécialement [spesjalmɑ̃] *adv.* specially, especially *On les voulait pas là pour commencer avec. Spécialement si le père et la mère étaient pas là.* We didn't want them there in the first place. Especially if the father and mother weren't there. (LA) <***Loc:*** LA, Da84>

spécialiser (se) [spesjalize] *v.pron.* to specialize *Son HACK était un tout petit magasin et souvent il se spécialisait dans des articles de cuisine, des groceries, ou des outils.* His hack was a little store and often he would specialize in cooking utensils, groceries, or tools. (VM) <***Loc:*** VM, Da84>

spécialiste [spesjalis(t)] *n.* expert, specialist *Ma femme aura pour voir un spécialiste.* My wife will have to see a specialist. (LA) <***Loc:*** LA, Da84>

spécialité [spesjalite] *n.f.* specialty <***Loc:*** Da84>

SPEED[1] [spid] *v.intr.invar.* to go fast, speed **Ç't homme aime SPEED.* That man likes to drive fast. <EV, Ph36> <***Loc:*** EV, SB, Lv88, Ph36>

SPEED[2] [spid] *n.m.* speed **•tout SPEED** full speed ahead <JE> <***Loc:*** EV, JD, JE, Ph36>

spirituel, -lle [spiritɥɛl] *adj.* [*eccl.*] spiritual <***Loc:*** Da84>

splouque [spluk] *n.m.* **1** guy, fellow **Ç'splouque veut pas partir, i faut l'mette déhors.* That guy doesn't want to leave, we need to throw him out. (EV, Ph36) **2** ladies' man <***Loc:*** EV, SM, Ph36>

SPORT[1] [spɔrt] *v.intr.invar.* to show off, have a big time *Boy, il a SPORT là.* Boy, he was showing off there. (VM) <***Loc:*** VM>

SPORT[2] [spɔrt] *adj.* funny **Ça c'est SPORT comme i fait ces tôrs de forces.* That's funny how he performs those stunts. (EV, Ph36) <***Loc:*** EV, Ph36>

SPORT[3] [spɔrt] *n.m.* **1** recreational hunter **2** athlete **3** fancy dresser **4** nice, easy-going person **Il est un bon SPORT.* He is a good sport. (Da84) <***Loc:*** Da84>

SPRAY [spre] *v.tr.invar.* to spray *Ils vont SPRAY les moustiques avec l'hélicoptère.* They are going to spray the mosquitos with the helicopter. (Lv88) <***Loc:*** Lv88>

SPRING [spriŋ] *n.m.* spring, metal coil <*Loc:* EV, VM, Lv88, Ph36>

squelette (**esquelette**) [ɛskəlɛt] *n.m.* skeleton <*Loc:* IB, Da84>

stable (**estable**) [ɛstab(l)] *adj.* stable, solid, firm *C'est pas estable, je dois l'assolider.* It's not stable, I have to make it solid. (VM) <*Loc:* VM, Da84>

STACK [stæk] *v.tr.invar.* to stack *Dès qu'eux-autres sortait du trou dans le champs là, eux-autres halait trois tuyaux ensemble et eux-autres stackait ça dans le* DERRICK. When they came out of the hole in the oil field, they dragged three pipes together and they stacked them in the derrick. (LF) <*Loc:* LF, TB>

STAMP [stẽp] *n.m.* stamp <*Loc:* EV, SL, Da84, Lv88, Ph36>

STAND[1] [stẽn] *v.tr.invar.* to tolerate, endure, stand *Je peux pas* STAND *quelqu'un comme ça.* I can't stand someone like that. (Lv88) <*Loc:* LF, VM, Da84, Lv88>

STAND[2] [stẽn] *n.m.* **1** stand, position **Faire un* STAND. To make a stand, take a position. (Da84) **2** stand (of crops) **J'ai un bon* STAND *de maïs.* I have a good stand of corn. (Da84) **3** stand, small shop **Un* FRUIT STAND. A fruit stand. (Da84) **4** stand (in court) <*Loc:* EV, SB, TB, Da84, Lv88, Ph36>

STARTER [startər] *n.m.* starter (for a machine) <*Loc:* Da84>

station [stasjɔ̃, estasjɔ̃, ɛstasjɔ̃] *n.m./f.* **1** station (railroad, bus, etc.) *Drète au ras du station.* Right next to the station. (Lv88) **2** television station, channel *Dessus le télévision quand eusse commence à montrer une serpent, je vas changer de station. Carrément.* On TV when they start to show a snake, I'll change the channel. Just like that. (TB) **3** radio broadcasting station ◊ **•station de gaz** gas station *Nous on va dire une estation de gaz, eux ils disont un* GAS STATION. We call it an "estation de gaz," and they call it a "gas station." (IV) <IV, Fa77> **•station d'huile** gas station *C'est proche que vis-à-vis avec la station d'huile.* It's almost right across from the gas station. (LF) <LF> <*Loc:* IV, LF, SB, TB, VM, Da84, Fa77, Lv88>

statue (**estatue**) [staty, ɛstaty, estaty] *n.f.* statue <*Loc:* IB, LF, SB, SM, VM, Da84, Lv88>

stchoune [stʃun] *n.m.* child's playing marble made of crystal <*Loc:* LF>

STEAK [stek] *n.m.* steak ◊ **•ROUND STEAK** round steak <AC> <*Loc:* AC, EV, VM, Da84, Ph36, Re31>

STEAM [stim] *n.m.* steam <*Loc:* AV>

step-in [stɛpɪn] *n.m.* *(sing./pl.)* woman's underpants <*Loc:* JE, LF, TB>

stock [stɔk] *n.m.* stock <*Loc:* Da84>

STOP[1] [stɔp] *n.* stop sign, stoplight <*Loc:* Da84>

STOP[2] [stɔp] *interj.* stop! <*Loc:* Da84>

STOVE [stov, sto^{u}v, stɔv] *n.m.* **1** stove, cookstove *Et une chaudière, tu mets ça sur le* STOVE. And a cooking pot, you put that on the stove. (JD) **2** stove, heater *Quand ça faisait froid, on avait juste un foyer et puis un* STOVE. When it was cold, we just had a fireplace and a stove. (IB) ◊ **•STOVE à {au} bois** wood stove *Et ça qu'eux-autres pouvait pas user, eux-autres faisait du bois pour brûler dedans le foyer et le* STOVE, *on avait un* STOVE *à bois.* And what they couldn't use, they made wood to burn in the fireplace and the stove, we had a wood stove. (LF) <AC, LF, TB> **•STOVE à coloïe** kerosene stove *Les commodes était tout en-dehors, les lumières c'était des lampes, des* STOVES *à bois, des* STOVES *à coloïe qu'eux-autres appelle.* The toilets were all outdoors, lights were lamps, wood stoves, kerosene stoves as they called them. (TB) <TB> **•STOVE à gaz** gas stove *J'ai un bon* STOVE *à gaz.* I have a good gas stove. (Lv88) <Lv88> <*Loc:* AC, AV, EV, IB, JD, JE, LF, SB, SM, TB, VM, Da84, Gu00, Hi02, Lv88, Ph36>

STRAIGHT [strɛt, stre^{i}t, stret] *adj.* straight, pure, undiluted, not mixed *Je vais le boire* STRAIGHT. I'm going to drink it straight. (VM) <*Loc:* TB, VM, Lv88>

STRAP [stræp, strẽp] *n.m.* **1** strap, boot strap **2** razor strap <*Loc:* EV, JD, SB, VM, Da84, Lv88, Ph36>

strict [strik(t)] *adj.* strict, severe *Sa famille a toujours été un peu strict.* His family was always a bit strict. (LA) <*Loc:* LA, Da84>

STRIKE[1] [straɪk] *v.intr.invar.* to strike, to go on strike *Sur les jobs, ça va* STRIKE *asteur.* On jobs now, workers will strike. (Lv88) <*Loc:* EV, Lv88, Ph36>

STRIKE[2] [straɪk] *n.m.* strike *Il a voté d'aller sur* STRIKE. He voted to go on strike. (Lv88) <*Loc:* EV, Lv88, Ph36>

STROKE [strok] *n.m.* stroke <*Loc:* VM>

stupide [stypid] *adj.* stupid, dumb *Il a tout le temps été un peu stupide.* He was always a bit stupid. (LA) <*Loc:* LA, Da84>

suaire [sɥær] *n.m.* [*eccl.*] type of decorative cloth put underneath the head of a corpse for a funeral ◊ **•Saint suaire** the Holy Shroud (of Christ) <Da84> <*Loc:* Da84>

subdiviser [sybdivize] *v.tr.* to subdivide *Ils ont subdivisé leur terre pour la vendre.* They subdivided their land to sell it. (LA) <*Loc:* LA, Da84>

subdivision [sybdivizjɔ̃] *n.f.* subdivision <*Loc:* Da84>

subir [sybir] *v.tr.* to undergo, suffer, sustain (a loss or pain) *Ils ont subi un hourra de maladies dernièrement.* They have suffered many illnesses lately. (LA) ◊ **•subir les conséquences** to suffer the consequences <Da84> <*Loc:* LA, Da84>

subit (**subite**) [sybi, sybit] *adv.* suddenly, quickly *Elle a parti subite.* She left suddenly. (LA) *Ma sœur est mort subit.* My sister died suddenly. (SM) <*Loc:* LA, SM, Da84, Hi02>

subite ♦see **subit**

subitement [sybitmɑ̃] *adv.* suddenly, quickly *Il a quitté son job subitement et il a disparu.* He left his job suddenly and he disappeared. (LA) <*Loc:* LA, Da84>

subsister [sybziste] *v.intr.* to subsist, eke out an existence *Ils étaient à peine après subsister dans le fond des bois.* They were barely surviving deep in the woods. (LA) <*Loc:* LA, Da84>

succéder [syksede] *v.tr.* to follow, succeed (e.g. in office) *C'est Père Matte qu'a succédé Père Garneau.* Father Matte is who succeeded Father Garneau. (VM) <*Loc:* VM, Da84>

succès [syksɛ, sykse] *n.m.* success <*Loc:* EV, Da84>

succession [syksɛsjɔ̃] *n.f.* succession, heritage <*Loc:* Da84>

succomber [sykɔ̃be] *v.intr.* [*eccl.*] to succumb, yield *Succomber à la tentation.* To succumb to temptation. (LA) <*Loc:* LA, Da84>

suce [sys] *n.f.* all-day sucker, candy <*Loc:* VM>

suce-fleur [sysflœr] *n.m.* **1** hummingbird **2** effeminate male <*Loc:* EV, IB, JD, SB, SM, VM, Da84, La99, Lv88, Ph36>

sucer [syse] *v.tr.* to suck, suckle **Sucer des cannes à sucre.* To suck on sugar cane. (Da84) <*Loc:* Da84>

suceron [sysərɔ̃] *n.m.* nipple of a baby bottle *Le suceron du petit est perdu.* The nipple of the baby's bottle is missing. (TB) <*Loc:* TB>

sucette [sysɛt] *n.f.* **1** lollipop, sucker **2** nipple of a bottle **3** pacifier <*Loc:* AV, IB, LF, SM, TB>

suceur [sysœr] *n.m.* homosexual ◊ **•suceur-de-fleurs** ladies' man <SM> <*Loc:* SM, La99>

sucre [syk(r), søk(r)] *n.m.* sugar ◊ **•sucre en poudre** powdered sugar <TB> <*Loc:* AV, EV, IB, JE, SL, TB, VM, Da84, Hi02>

sucrer [sykre] *v.tr.* **1** to sweeten, sugar *Dans le temps, on sucrait le café dans la grègue.* In those days, we sweetened coffee in the pot. (LA) *Thé sucré.* Sweetened tea. (LA) **2** to trick, fool **Tu peux pas me sucrer avec ça.* You can't fool me with that. (AC, La99) <*Loc:* AC, LA, Da84, La99>

sucrerie [syklәri, siklәri] *n.f.* **1** sugar mill, sugar refinery, sugarcane factory **2** syrup mill (distinguished from a "raffinerie," which refines sugar) <*Loc:* AV, IB, LA, LF, SL, SM, TB, VM, Da84, Lv88, Re31>

sucrier [sykrije, sukrije, sykәrje] *n.m.* **1** sugar bowl **2** sugarcane farmer, planter **3** employee of a sugar factory <*Loc:* JD, LA, Da84, Lv88, Re31>

sucrose [sykrɔs] *n.f.* sucrose <*Loc:* TB, VM>

sud [syd] *adj.invar./n.m.* south *Casey Jones c'était un petit homme du nord. Il est venu au sud, en linge de dessous.* Casey Jones was a little man from the North. He came south in his underwear. (ch: *Casey Jones*) <*Loc:* Da84, Hi02>

sud-est [sydɛs(t), sydɛ] *adj.invar./n.m.* southeast *Un nom de famille du sud-est.* A family name from the southeast. (EV) <*Loc:* EV, VM, Da84>

sud-ouest ♦see **suroît**

suée [sɥe] *n.f.* thrashing, whipping, beating *Foutre une suée à quelqu'un.* To give somebody a good thrashing. (LF) <*Loc:* LF>

suer [sɥe] *v.intr.* to sweat, perspire *Mets l'AIR CONDITION. Je suis après suer.* Put the air conditioning on. I'm sweating. (VM) ◊ **•suer comme un bâtard à une réunion de famille / suer comme un nègre à la messe / suer comme les Ponce Pilate** ***a*** to sweat profusely ***b*** to be in a very awkward or uncomfortable situation <La99> **•suer des caravelles** to have a lot of difficulty doing s.t. <AV, La99> <*Loc:* AV, Da84, La99>

sueur [sɥœr] *n.f.* sweat, perspiration **À la sueur de son front.* By the sweat of his brow. (Da84) <*Loc:* Da84>

suffire [syfir] **I** *v.intr.* to suffice, be enough **Suffit qu'il a dit ça.* It suffices that he said this. (Da84) **II se suffire** *v.pron.* [*pej.*] to think highly of o.s. *Tant qu'à lui, il se suffit!* As for him, he thinks a lot of himself (LA) ◊ **•suffit que** it suffices *Suffit que tu lui parles de ça, et puis il va le faire.* All you have to do is talk to him about it and he'll do it. (VM) <VM, Da84> **•ça suffit** it's enough <Da84> <*Loc:* LA, VM, Da84>

suggestion [sygʒɛstjɔ̃] *n.f.* suggestion <*Loc:* Da84>

suicide [sɥisid] *n.m.* **1** suicide **2** one who commits suicide <*Loc:* Da84>

suie [sɥi] *n.f.* soot, lampblack <*Loc:* VM, Da84>

suif [sɥif] *n.m.* tallow, fat (of animals) ◊ **•suif de mouton** sheep tallow <Da84> <*Loc:* VM, Da84>

suifeux, -euse [sɥifø, -øz] *adj.* full of tallow *Le barbedeau n'est pas aussi suifeux qu'un mouton* The Barbados [sheep] is not as full of tallow as a regular sheep. (VM) <*Loc:* VM>

suiffrer [sɥifre] *v.tr.* to tallow, rub with tallow <*Loc:* Da84>

suire ♦see **suivre**

SUIT [sut, sɔt, sot] *n.m.* suit *Il s'a sûr acheté un joli SUIT.* He sure bought himself a fine suit. (TB) ◊ **•SUIT à {de} bain / sot-à-bain** swimming suit <EV, IB, Lv88> <*Loc:* AC, AV, EV, IB, LF, SB, TB, VM, Da84, Lv88, Ph36>

suite [sɥit] *n.f.* continuation, succession, consequence ◊ **•ainsi de suite** and so forth, etcetera *Là il a eu pour retourner à l'hôpital, puis ils ont trouvé un cancer, puis il a eu un autre STROKE et ainsi de suite.* Then he had to go back to the hospital, then they found cancer, then he had another stroke, etc. (VM) <VM, Da84> **•de suite** in succession, in a row *Elle était si maigre, pauvre bête, que le prêtre l'a manquée à la table sainte deux dimanches de suite.* She was so thin, poor thing, that the priest missed her at the holy altar two Sundays in a row. (ThCa: *La fête à Clomaire*) <Da84, ThCa> **•tout de suite** right away, immediately **Il a parti tout de suite.* He left right away. (EV, An94) *Ouais, et là, et j'avais toujours l'habitude de les vendre tout de suite pour l'élevage.* Yes, and then, I usually sold them [horses] right away for breeding. (ThCa: *La table des veuves*) <EV, LA, Da84, An94> <*Loc:* EV, LA, VM, An94, Da84, Hi02, ThCa>

suivant, -e [sɥivɑ̃, -ɑ̃t] *adj.* following, next *La personne suivante qui va appeler va gagner une livre de MELLOW JOY.* The next person who calls will win a pound of Mellow Joy. (VM) <*Loc:* VM, Da84, Hi02>

suivre (suire) [sɥiv(r), sɥir, swir] (*p.p.* **sui,** [sɥi], **suit** [sɥi], **suivi** [sɥivi]) *v.tr.* **1** to follow *J'ai suit quelqu'un.* I followed somebody (AC) *Le petit garçon m'a suit partout.* The little boy followed me everywhere. (SM) *Je vais te suivre à la mer.* I will follow you to the sea. (TB) *C'est des poissons qui* MIGRATE *dedans le golfe, ils partont et puis ils suisont le* SHORE. Those are fish that migrate into the gulf, they leave and they follow the shore. (LF) *Je voulais savoir quo'faire il m'a suit hier au soir.* I wanted to know why he followed me last night. (TB) **2** to keep up with *Je peux toujours, quand je dis un chapelet en français je peux le suivre.* I always can keep up with him when I say the rosary in French (SL) **3** to succeed (in office) **II se suivre** *v.pron.* to succeed, follow each other *Tous les fêtes dans notre famille se suivent.* All the birthdays in our family are one after another. (EV) <***Loc:*** AC, AV, EV, JE, LA, LF, SB, SL, SM, TB, Da84, Hi02, Lv88>

sujet[1] [syʒɛ, syʒe] *adj.* subject, prone, liable, likely (to) **Être sujet au mal de tête.* To be subject to headache. (Da84) **Être sujet de se faire tuer.* To be liable to get killed. (Da84) *Il est sujet à venir.* He is likely to come. (LA) <***Loc:*** LA, VM, Da84>

sujet[2] [syʒɛ, syʒe, ʃyʒe] *n.m.* subject, point or person in question <***Loc:*** Da84>

sujéti, -e [syzeti] *adj.* subject, eligible *Les hommes mariés sont sujétis, eux aussite, à l'armée.* Married men are also eligible for the draft. (VM) <***Loc:*** VM>

sulky (**solqui**) [sɔlki, solki, solke, soki] *n.m.* sulky, small two-wheeled horse-drawn wagon that seats only the driver <***Loc:*** LA, VM, Da84, Lv88>

supérieur, -e [syperjœr] *adj.* superior **Mère Supérieure.* Mother Superior (head nun). (Da84) <***Loc:*** Da84>

superintendant [syperɛ̃tɑ̃dɑ̃] *n.m.* superintendent <***Loc:*** AV, Da84>

supernaturel, -lle [sypærnatyrɛl] *adj.* supernatural <***Loc:*** VM, Lv88>

superstitieux, -euse [sypærstisjø, supærtisjø, -øz] *adj.* superstitious *C'est du monde bien superstitieux. Ça va virer de bord si ça voit un chat noir devant eusse.* Those are superstitious people. They'll turn around if they see a black cat in front of them. (VM) <***Loc:*** VM, Da84>

superstition [sypærstisjɔ̃, sypærtisjɔ̃, sypærdisjɔ̃] *n.f.* superstition <***Loc:*** VM, Da84>

supplice [syplis] *n.m.* torture, suffering *Cher, elle a souffert des supplices avec cet homme-là.* Honey, she suffered tortures with that man. (VM) ◊ **•être au supplice** to be desperate, be in desperation, be helpless <Da84> **•le dernier supplice** the throes of death, last agony, death agony <Da84> <***Loc:*** VM, Da84>

supplier [syplije] *v.tr.* to beg, implore, beseech *Il m'a supplié de pas le quitter.* He begged me not to leave him. (LA) <***Loc:*** LA, Da84>

support [sypɔr] *n.m.* **1** support, prop **2** upkeep, maintenance, support *C'est tout sur le support du gouvernement.* They are all on government support. (Lv88) **3** political support, alliance *Oui, et c'est pour ça que Huey a donné son support à Shelby Taylor qui court contre moi.* Yes, and that's why Huey gave his support to Shelby Taylor who is running against me. (ThCa: *Messieurs, mesdames*) <***Loc:*** VM, Da84, Lv88, ThCa>

supporter [sypɔrte] *v.tr.* **1** to bear, tolerate, endure *Ce vieux tchu, je peux pas le supporter!* That old ass, I can't stand him! (LA) **2** to uphold, support *Supporter une citerne.* To hold up a cistern. (VM) **3** to provide for, support (financially) *Il pouvait pas marier une négresse mais il fallait il supporte l'enfant.* He could not marry a black woman, but he had to support the child. (Lv88) *Et si l'homme qu'était marié s'en allait et qu'il a assayé de pas supporter sa famille, les hommes de la campagne allaient par derrière lui.* And if the man who was married went off and tried to not support his family, the men of the countryside went after him. (TB) **4** to give support to (in an election), be a partisan of *Supporter un candidat.* To support a candidate. (EV) <***Loc:*** EV, IB, LA, LF, SB, SJ, SL, SM, TB, VM, Da84, Lv88, Ph36>

supposant [sypozɑ̃] *adv.* supposing it is the case that, let's suppose that *Supposant il est parti de chez lui à neuf heures, il devrait être rendu asteur.* Supposing that he left at nine, he should be there by now. (LA) <***Loc:*** LA>

supposé[1]**, -e** [sypoze] *adj.* ◊ **•être supposé de** to be supposed to *Pour le Vendredi Saint t'es pas supposé de fouiller dans la terre.* For Good Friday you're not supposed to dig in the earth. (TB) **Il est supposé de venir.* He is supposed to come. (Da84) *Dès que la maîtresse allait me demander de quoi, j'étais supposée de répondre* YES OR NO. When the teacher would ask me something I was supposed to answer yes or no. (LF) <LF, TB, Da84> <***Loc:*** JE, LF, TB, Da84>

supposé[2] [sypoze] *adv.* supposedly *Moi j'étais après prendre des tests la semaine passée, pour supposé j'avais des trous dans mes tripes, le docteur m'avait dit ça.* I was taking tests last week, supposedly I had holes in my intestines, the doctor had told me that. (LF) **On dirait, c'est manière drôle de dire ça,* BUT *supposé ça a arrivé. C'est une histoire vraie.* It seems rather strange to say that, but supposedly it happened. It's a true story. (SL, An94) <***Loc:*** LF, SL, TB, VM, An94>

supposer [sypoze] *v.tr.* to suppose, assume, conjecture *Et là quand le candi était cuit dans la cheminée ça prendait une cuillère, je suppose, ça mettait ça dans chaque de les pailles.* And when the candy was cooked in the fireplace, they took a spoon, I suppose, they put it in each of the cornhusks. (TB) <***Loc:*** TB, Da84, Hi02>

suppurer [sypyre, sypire] *v.intr.* to suppurate, ooze *Une plaie qui suppure.* A wound that oozes. (VM) <***Loc:*** EV, VM, Da84>

suppuron (puron, piron) [sypurɔ̃, pyrɔ̃, pirɔ̃] *n.m.* pimple, blackhead <*Loc:* IB, JE, SJ, TB, VM Lv88>

sur (sus) [syr, sy] *prep.* **1** on **Je compte sur toi.* I am counting on you. (Da84) *Il ferait mieux de pas raccrocher sus moi.* He'd better not hang up on me. (LA) *Il a tourné son dos sur son garçon par rancune.* He turned his back on his son out of spite. (LA) *Les filles étaient sur un bord et les garçons étaient sur l'autre.* Girls were on one side and boys on the other. (TB) **Un bougre du Texas et un bougre de la Louisiane, et ils se sont rencontrés sur le pont, tu sais, sur le même pont.* A guy from Texas and a guy from Louisiana, they met on the bridge, you know, the same bridge. (An94) *J'ai une palette de cassée sur mon accordéon.* I have a broken flap on my accordion. (LA) *On a regardé pour deux mois différentes places, on était paré pour prendre quelque chose sur Charles Street.* We looked for a place for two months, we were ready to take something on Charles street. (IB) *Là-bas dans Canada y a des gazettes, c'est tout français à part que une petite partie qu'est en anglais sur la dernière page.* Up there in Canada there are newspapers that are all in French except a small part that's in English on the last page. (TB) *Je suis emmêlé dans la politique, je suis un réprésenteur et quand moi je parle à mon monde sus le* RADIO *ou sus le* TELEVISION *la moitié du temps je yeux parle en français.* I'm involved in politics, I'm a representative, and when I talk to my people on the radio or the TV, most of the time I talk to them in French. (TB) *Alle reste sur le dixième plancher.* She lives on the tenth floor. (TB) *Et on était assis sus la galerie.* We were sitting on the porch. (TB) **Ça tire sus midi.* Noon is drawing near. (Da84) **2** on, onto *Tout le patatras de papier a tombé sur le plancher.* The whole bundle of paper fell onto the floor. (SL) *Tu prends du sirop et tu le vides sur ton pain perdu, ça c'est bien bon.* You take some syrup and pour it on your French toast, it's good. (AV) *Va mettre ça sus la pile.* Go put that on the compost pile. (VM) *Un jour ils ont attelé le wagon et ils ont parti avec deux chevaux attelés sus le wagon.* One day they hitched the wagon and they left with two horses hitched onto the wagon. (LA) **3** upon, on top of *Marche pas sur les rails, le char va passer bétôt.* Don't walk on the rails, the train will come by soon. (VM) *Un* CAMP *sur des piliers.* A camp on piers. (VM) *Et quand je suis seule j'aime mieux rester sur ma chaise. Comme ça je peux me reposer mieux, sur ma chaise que dans le lit.* And when I'm alone I prefer to stay in my chair. That way I can rest better, in my chair than in bed. (TB) *Si tu laisses le beurre trop longtemps sur le comptoir, ça va rancir.* If you leave the butter on the counter too long, it will become rancid. (LA) **Ça fait, j'étais à cheval et il y avait pas de selle, pas rien sur le cheval.* So I was on the horse and there was no saddle, there was nothing on the horse. (SL, An94) *Piler sur le pied de quelqu'un.* To step on someone's foot. (LF) **4** about, concerning *Il a ramanché toutes espèces de choses sur toi.* He made up all sorts of things about you. (VM) *Il a parti la discussion sur la chasse.* He started the discussion about hunting. (Lv88) *Des fois ça dit nous-autres même quoi vous-autres a dit sur nous-autres.* Sometimes they tell us what you said about us. (SL) **5** on, astride, aboard (a means of transportation) *Assieds-toi sur le bateau, à droite là.* Have a seat on the boat, over on the right. (PQ) *On se promenait sur le* BUS. We rode on the bus. (TB) *Il partait sur son bicycle avec l'accordéon dans le panier.* He left on his bicycle with the accordeon in the basket. (LA) **6** over *C'est elle qui régnait sus sa famille.* She's the one who reigned over her family. (LA) ◊ **•sur le moment** at the moment <SL, Da84> <*Loc:* AV, EV, IB, LA, LF, PQ, SL, TB, VM, An94, Da84, Hi02, Lv88>

sûr[1]**, -e** [syr] *adj.* sure, secure, certain **T'es sûr tout est correct?* Are you sure everything is okay? (EV, An94) **Ça c'est sûr.* That's for sure. (Da84) ◊ **•à coup sûr** with certainty *Tirer à coup sûr.* To shoot with accuracy or certainty. (VM) <VM, Da84> <*Loc:* EV, LA, SB, SL, SM, VM, An94, Da84, Hi02>

sûr[2] [syr, sœr, sir] *adv.* certainly, surely *Il élevait des cannes lui aussi. Il était proche sûr le plus gros fermier des cannes.* He raised cane also. He was almost certainly the biggest cane farmer. (LA) *J'avais sûr quatorze ans.* I was surely fourteen years old. (Lv88) *Je suis sûr content vous avez venu.* I'm certainly glad you came. (Lv88) *Ça c'est sûr bon.* That certainly is good. (SM) *Il va arriver demain sûr.* He will surely arrive tomorrow. (SM) ◊ **•bien sûr** surely, of course, assuredly *T'as envie d'aller avec moi? —Mais, bien sûr!* Do you feel like going with me?—Well, of course! (EV) <EV, Da84> **•pas sûr** not certain **Pas sûr qu'il vont l'enterrer creux comme ça, non, si je vas pas.* It is not certain that they will bury him that deep if I don't go. (SL, An94) <SL, An94> **•pour sûr** for sure *Ça c'est un cheval pour sûr.* That's a horse, for sure. (JE) *Pas de nom français pour sûr.* [There's] no French name [for that] for sure. (SL) <JE, SB, SL, Lv88> <*Loc:* EV, JE, LA, SL, SM, VM, An94, Da84, Lv88, Ph36>

sureau [syro, siro, suro, sirjo] *n.m.* **1** elder tree, elder bush, elder wood *Eusse prend des feuilles du sureau, des bâtons de sureau, et bouillir ça, et laver leur jambe avec ça, des bobos.* They take elder leaves, sticks of elder, and boil it, and wash their leg and sores with that. (TB) **2** elderberry *Je connais pour le manger des chevreuils, il y a des sureaux. Ça fait une grappe manière comme des petits raisins, ça fait une belle grosse fleur blanche.* I know for deer food, there are elderberries. They make a cluster kind of like little grapes. They make a big, white flower. (VM) <*Loc:* IB, JD, TB, VM, Da84>

sûrement [syrmɑ̃] *adv.* surely, certainly, for sure **Je suis sûrement pas un conteur de contes, mais j'ai appris des contes,* *quand j'étais petit avec mon père et ma mère.* I am certainly no storyteller, but I learned some stories when I was little from my father and mother. (EV, An94) <***Loc:*** EV, An94, Da84>

sûreté [syrte] *n.f.* **1** safety, surety, security, assurance **2** certainty *Est-ce que c'est une sûreté qu'il va venir?* Is it a certainty that he will come? (SM) ◊ **•prendre des sûretés** to take precautions *On va prendre des sûretés pour pas que ça arrive encore.* We're going to take precautions so that it doesn't happen again. (LA) <LA, Da84, Lv88> <***Loc:*** LA, SM, VM, Da84, Lv88>

surfaire [syrfær] *v.tr.* to redo, do again *Surfais-lé, tu l'as pas bien fait.* Do it again, you didn't do it right. (TB) <***Loc:*** TB>

suriner ♦see **chouriner**

surjet [syrʒɛ, syrʒe] *n.m.* flat seam, hem *J'ai faufilé le surjet.* I basted the flat seam. (IB) <***Loc:*** IB, JE>

surjeter [syrʒəte] *v.tr.* to sew by hand over an unfinished seam on the inner part of a garment <***Loc:*** IB>

surlendemain [syrlɑ̃dəmɛ̃] *n.m.* day after next, day after tomorrow <***Loc:*** Da84>

surmonter [syrmɔ̃te] **I** *v.tr.* to surmount, surpass, outdo, overcome *Je connais pas si il pourra surmonter sa misère.* I don't know if he will be able to surmount his pain. (LA) **II se surmonter** *v.pron.* to outdo o.s. or each other *Ça essayait de se surmonter un à l'autre.* They were trying to outdo each other. (LA) <***Loc:*** LA, Da84>

suroît (sud-ouest) [syrwa, sydwɛs(t)] *adj.invar./n.m.* southwest *Un vent suroît.* A southwest wind. (VM) **D'autres croient qu'il est toujours en vie, dans une forme ou d'autre de fou qu'on trouve toujours dans tous les villes dans le sud-ouest de la Louisiane.* Others believe that he's still alive, in one form or another of the fools that you find in all the towns in Southwest Louisiana. (EV, An94) <***Loc:*** EV, JE, VM, An94, Da84, Lv88>

surpasser [syrpase] *v.tr.* to surpass, go beyond, outdo **Défunt Pap était mort et on avait une assurance, mais je crois on l'a surpassée à préparer défunt Pap pour l'enterrer.* Grandpa died and we had insurance but I think we went beyond it to prepare late Grandpa for burial. (EV, An84) *Mais ça, ça me surpasse.* Well, that outdoes me. (LA) <***Loc:*** EV, LA, An84, Da84>

surprenant, -e [syrprɛ̃nɑ̃, -ɑ̃t] *adj.* surprising, amazing, astonishing **Il y avaient pas beaucoup de places pour jouer, et il y avait pas beaucoup d'argent. C'est surprenant combien peu.* There were not many places to play, and there wasn't much money. It's surprising how little. (LA, An84) <***Loc:*** LA, An84, Da84>

surprendre [syrprɑ̃n, syrprɑ̃d(r)] **I** *v.tr.* to surprise, astonish *Tu peux pas me surprendre. Si tu me surprends ça c'est* IT. *Je vais* PASS OUT. You can't surprise me. If you surprise me that's it. I'll pass out. (TB) **II se surprendre** *v.pron.* **1** to surprise o.s. *Je m'ai surpris moi-même quand j'ai fini si de bonne heure.* I surprised myself when I finished so early. (LA) **2** to surprise each other *Ils s'ont surpris au bal.* They surprised each other at the dance. (LA) <***Loc:*** LA, TB, Da84, Hi02>

surpris, -e [syrpri, -iz] *adj.* surprised, astonished *Il est surpris de voir combien ils ont avancé avec la maison.* He is surprised to see how much they have advanced with the house. (LA) <***Loc:*** LA, Da84>

surprise [syrpriz] *n.f.* **1** surprise, astonishment **2** surprise lily <***Loc:*** EV, Da84, Hi02>

surtout [syrtu] *adv.* **1** above all, especially **Tout ce que te demande, c'est de secourir le monde, surtout les vieilles veuves.* All I ask of you is to take care of the people, especially the old widows. (IV, An94) **2** mostly *Surtout on fait de l'étouffée.* Mostly we make étouffée. (SL) <***Loc:*** IV, SL, An94, Da84>

surveillance [syrvejɑ̃s] *n.f.* supervision, surveillance <***Loc:*** Da84>

surveillant [syrvejɑ̃] *n.m.* one who supervises or watches <***Loc:*** Da84>

surveiller [syrveje] *v.tr.* to supervise, take care of, watch over, keep an eye on *Les mères et les grand-mères prenaient leurs places autour de la salle pour guetter tout ce qui se passait et pour surveiller leụrs filles.* The mothers and grandmothers would take their places around the hall to watch everything that was going on and to keep an eye on their girls. (VM) <***Loc:*** VM, Da84>

survivre [syrviv(r)] (*p.p.* **survi** [syrvi]) *v.intr.* to survive **Et la question revenait tout le temps: Est-ce que tu crois que cette musique et cette langue et cette culture vont survivre?* And the question would always come back: Do you think that this music and this language and this culture will survive? (EV, An84) *Ils ont essayé de le sauver, mais il a pas survi.* They tried to save him, but he didn't survive. (LA) <***Loc:*** EV, LA, An84, Da84, Hi02, Lv88>

sus ♦see **sur**

susceptible [syseptib(l)] *adj.* susceptible, touchy, sensitive, easily provoked *Tu peux pas lui dire arien. Il est beaucoup susceptible.* You can't tell him anything. He's very touchy. (LA) <***Loc:*** LA, Da84>

suspect, -e [syspɛk(t)] *adj.* **1** suspicious *C'était beaucoup suspect, la manière qu'il faisait alentour d'elle.* It was highly suspicious, the way he acted around her. (LA) **2** sensitive, touchy, easily offended, prudish ***WELL, *les petits contes cochons, tu connais, on racontait pas ça quand il y avait des filles, tu connais, parce que dans ces temps-ça, c'était un tas plus suspect qu'asteur.* Well, the little dirty jokes, you know, we didn't tell them when there were girls, you know, because in those days, people were a lot more easily offended than now. (LA, An94) **3** exacting, hard to please, fastidious, meticulous *J'aime pas travailler pour lui parce qu'il est trop suspect.* I don't like working for him because he's too hard to please. (SL) **4** ill-tempered **5** proud, haughty **6** strange, bizarre <*Loc:* EV, JD, LA, SB, SL, SM, VM, An94, Da84, Lv88, Pe37, Ph36, Re31>

suspecter [syspɛkte] *v.tr.* to suspect, be suspicious of *Je connais pas pour les autres, mais lui, je l'ai toujours suspecté.* I don't know about the others, but him, I always suspected him. (LA) <*Loc:* LA, Da84>

suspendre [syspɑ̃n , syspɑ̃d(r)] *v.tr.* **1** to hang, hang up *Suspends tes canards sous la corniche de la maison.* Hang your ducks under the eave of the house. (VM) **2** to defer, postpone *Son cas a été suspendu jusqu'à dans l'été.* Her case was deferred until summertime. (LA) ◊ **•laisser (qqn) suspendu** to leave s.o. in suspense, leave s.o. hanging *Il a pas fini son histoire, il nous a laissés là suspendus.* He didn't finish his story. He left us hanging. (VM) <VM, Da84> <*Loc:* LA, VM, Da84>

susurrer [sysyre] *v.intr.* to whisper, murmur *Ils étaient dans le coin après susurrer.* They were in the corner whispering. (LA) <*Loc:* LA, Da84>

SWAMP [swɑ̃p] *n.m.* swamp *Les Cadiens, quand ils ont venu ici je pense qu'il y avait arien d'autre que les* SWAMPS, *et là eux-autres a tapé de l'huile.* The Cajuns, when they came here I think there was nothing but swamps, and then they struck oil. (LF) <*Loc:* JE, LF, SB, VM, Lv88>

swampeur [swɑ̃pœr] *n.m.* worker in the swamps, often affiliated with the lumber industry <*Loc:* JE, Lv88>

SWEATER [swɛtœr, swera, sware] *n.m.* sweater <*Loc:* AV, LF, TB, VM, Da84>

SWITCH[1] (**switcher**) [switʃ, switʃe] *v.tr.* to switch *Ils ont* SWITCH *les chars dans la nuit.* They switched [railroad] cars in the night. (LA) <*Loc:* JE, LA, SB, Da84, Lv88>

SWITCH[2] [switʃ] *n.m.* **1** electric switch *Le* SWITCH *était juste un tout petit bouton tu halais.* The switch was just a little button that you pushed. (AC) **2** railroad switch **3** small whip **4** exchange, switch <*Loc:* AC, EV, JE, SB, VM, Da84, Lv88, Ph36>

switchement [switʃmɑ̃] *n.m.* switching *Le switchement prend pas beaucoup de temps.* [Railroad] switching doesn't take long. (SB) <*Loc:* SB>

switcher ♦see **SWITCH**

switcheur [switʃœr] *n.m.* switchman, person who operates railroad switches <*Loc:* JE, SB>

symbole [sɛ̃bɔl] *n.m.* [*eccl.*] symbol, creed ◊ **•le Symbole des Apôtres** the Apostles Creed <Da84> <*Loc:* Da84>

sympathique [sɛ̃patik] *adj.* sympathetic *Il est bien sympathique avec ce mouvement.* He is very sympathetic with this movement. (IB) <*Loc:* IB, Da84>

symptôme [sɛ̃ptɔ̃m] *n.m.* symptom, indication, sign <*Loc:* Da84>

syphoïde ♦see **typhoïde**

syringue ♦see **seringue**

système [sistɛ̃m] *n.m.* system *Mais c'est malheureux que le système d'école est tellement sale, c'est corrupté par le diable. Ça les enseigne que eux-autres vient des bétailles.* But it's awful how the school system is so dirty, it's corrupted by the devil. They teach them that they come from animals. (LF) ◊ **•système nerveux** nervous system <Da84> <*Loc:* LF, Da84>

T

t'[1] ♦see **qui**

t'[2] ♦see **te**, **tu**

T.V. (**tivi**) [tivi] *n.m.* television <*Loc:* Fa77, Lv88>

ta ♦see **ton**

tabac [taba] *n.m.* tobacco ◊ •**tabac à chiquer** chewing tobacco <Da84> •**tabac en poudre** snuff <LF> <*Loc:* AV, EV, LF, SM, An94, Da84, Hi02>

tabaquière ♦see **tabatière**

Tabasco [tabasko] *n.m.* Tabasco (hot pepper sauce) <*Loc:* AV, Lv88>

tabatière (**tabaquière**) [tabatjær, tabatʃær, tabakjær] *n.f.* snuffbox, tobacco pouch, tobacco box <*Loc:* IB, TB, Da84, Lv88>

tabernacle [tabærnak(l)] *n.m.* [*eccl.*] tabernacle <*Loc:* Da84>

tabilier ♦see **tablier**

table [tab(l)] *n.f.* table ◊ •**table à scie** table saw <AV, JE> •**table à travailler** workbench <SL> •**table de POOL** pool table <LF> •**table d'opération** operating table <AV, LF> •**table sainte** communion rail <AV, Da84> •**mettre la table** to set the table *J'ai mis la table, et je lui ai mis son 7-UP, et les CRACKER.* I set the table, and I gave him his 7-Up and the crackers. (TB) <EV, TB, An94, Da84> •**se mettre à (la) table** to sit at the table *Quand ça vient le temps pour souper, pour dîner, on se met à table.* When it's time to eat supper, we sit down at the table. (AV) <AC, AV, EV, SL, An94, Da84> <*Loc:* AC, AV, EV, IV, JE, LA, LF, SL, TB, VM, An94, Da84, Hi02>

tableau [tablo] *n.m.* blackboard <*Loc:* AV, Da84>

tablée [table] *n.f.* tableful (e.g. of food or guests) <*Loc:* Da84>

tablette [tablɛt] *n.f.* **1** shelf *Une armoire avec deux portes et des tablettes.* An armoire with two doors and shelves. (AC) **2** tablet, writing pad **Pour acheter plus des tablettes d'écriture.* To buy more writing tablets. (Wh83) **3** tablet, medicine tablet <*Loc:* AC, AV, LA, TB, VM, Da84, Lv88, Wh83>

tablier (**tabilier**) [tablije, tabilje] *n.m.* apron <*Loc:* AV, IB, LA, SM, TB, VM, Da84, Lv88>

tacalac [takalak] *adj.* crazy, foolish, silly *Ce bougre a tout le temps été tacalac.* That fellow has always been foolish. (LA) <*Loc:* LA>

tachant, -e [taʃɑ̃, -ɑ̃t] *adj.* staining, causing stains *Des mûres et des plaquemines sont beaucoup tachantes.* Blackberries and persimmons stain badly. (LA) <*Loc:* LA, Da84>

tache [taʃ] *n.f.* **1** stain, spot *Il y avait une mauvaise tache sur le devant de sa robe.* There was a bad stain on the front of her dress. (LA) **2** blemish (on the skin, e.g. a birthmark) **3** spot (on the coat or skin of an animal) *Là le RED SNAPPER est proche pareil, mais il a pas les taches dessus la queue du tout.* The red snapper is almost the same, but he doesn't have the spots on his tail at all. (TB) <*Loc:* LA, TB, VM, Da84, Hi02>

tâche[1] [taʃ] *n.f.* task, job *Mon père disait toujours dix rangs de coton à faire aujourd'hui, ça c'est notre tâche.* My father always said ten rows of cotton to do today, that's our task. (AV) <*Loc:* AV, EV, VM, Da84, Lv88>

tâche[2] [taʃ] *n.f.* ditch or hole used to prepare bousillage for the construction of houses <*Loc:* EV, VM, Da84, Lv88>

tacher [taʃe] **I** *v.tr.* to stain, spot, soil *Ma robe est tout tachée.* My dress is all stained. (AV) **II se tacher** *v.pron.* to stain, spot, soil o.s. *Je m'ai tout taché avec la peinture.* I got paint stains all over myself. (AV) <*Loc:* AV, Da84>

tâcheron [taʃrɔ̃] *n.m.* worker who prepares bousillage <*Loc:* Di32, Lv88>

tac-tac (**tactac**) [taktak] *n.m.* **1** popcorn *On a fait des boules de tac-tac. Avec le sirop, on met ça ensemble.* We made popcorn balls. With syrup, you put them together. (AV) **2** noisy chatter **Arrêtez votre tactac!* Stop your chattering! (La99) <*Loc:* AV, EV, IB, LF, SB, SL, SM, TB, VM, Da84, La99, Hi02, Lv88, Ph36, Re31>

tactac ♦see **tac-tac**

tactique [taktik] *n.f.* tactic <*Loc:* Da84>

tafia [tafja] *n.m.* **1** rum made from molasses, sugar cane, and brown sugar **Le tafia dit toujours la vérité.* Tafia always tells the truth. (Re31) **2** weak or bad-tasting coffee <*Loc:* EV, VM, La99, Lv88, Ph36, Re31>

tafiateur [tafjatœr] *n.m.* drunkard <*Loc:* Re31>

TAG [tag] *n.m.* (*occ. f.*) **1** tag, ticket *Chaque bête avait un TAG sur le dos.* Each animal had a tag on its back. (VM) **2** game of tag *Jouer TAG.* To play tag. (Lv88) *Jouer à la TAG.* To play tag. (LF) *Les jeunes a joué TAG. Ça c'était une grosse game.* The young people played tag. That was a popular game. (AV) <*Loc:* AV, LF, VM, Lv88>

taïaut[1] (**tayaut**) [tajo] *n.m.* **1** hound, bloodhound *Ce taïaut est un bon chien à chevreuil.* This hound is a good deer dog. (TB) **2** beagle *On chasse juste le lapin farouche avec un taïaut.* We only chase wild rabbits with beagles. (Lv88) **3** mongrel, mutt *Un taïaut de chasse.* A mongrel hunting dog. (SJ) *Un chien taïaut.* A mongrel. (AV) <*Loc:* AV, EV, IB, LF, SB, SJ, SL, SM, VM, An94, Da84, Lv88, Ph36, Re31>

taïaut[2], **-e** [tajo, -ot] *n.* person of low class **N'appelez jamais une femme "une taïaute." C'est criminel et les chances sont qu'elle va te crimer aussi.* Never call a woman a "taïaute."

It's terrible and chances are she'll beat you, too. (Re76) <*Loc:* Re76>

taïaut[3] [tajo] *interj.* tally ho! <*Loc:* VM>

taillage [tajaʒ] *n.m.* cutting, trimming <*Loc:* Da84>

taillant [tajɑ̃] *n.m.* cutting edge (of a knife, etc.) *Le taillant de la hache.* The blade of the ax. (AV) <*Loc:* AV, EV, VM, Da84>

taille[1] [taj] *n.f.* **1** waist **2** stature, size, shape (of a person) ◊ **•avoir une belle taille** to have a nice figure *Elle a une belle taille, ma femme.* My wife has a nice figure. (AV) <AV, Da84> **•prendre en taille douce** to deal with gently, tactfully *On gagnera l'enfant si on le prend en taille douce au lieu de le gronder.* We'll win the child over if we deal with him gently instead of scolding him. (Pe37) <SM, Pe37> <*Loc:* AV, SL, Da84, Hi02, Lv88>

taille[2] [taj] *n.f.* hill, mound, patch, plot (of a plant in a garden) **Comme même il y'en avait dans le jardin pleusement, ein taille de moutarde était plantée dans la cour et quittée éspécialement pour monter en graine.* Even though there was usually some in the garden, a hill of mustard was planted in the yard and left especially to go to seed. (Wh83) <*Loc:* Wh83>

tailler [taje] *v.tr.* **1** to cut *Je peux tailler l'étoffe pour faire une robe.* I can cut the material to make a dress. (AV) **2** to carve, trim *Il a taillé un morceau de bois pour remplacer la patte de la chaise.* He carved a piece of wood to replace the chair leg. (LA) **3** to clip, trim, prune **4** to whip, give a whipping to **Je l'ai taillé assez fort qu'il a pas pu s'assire pour trois jours.* I whipped him so hard that he couldn't sit down for three days. (Gu82) *Ils ont coupé une petite branche de pêcher et ça taillait les enfants.* They used to cut a little branch from a peach tree and whip the children. (LF) ◊ **•tailler flèche** to cut straight, trim evenly <VM> **•bien taillé** shapely *Elle avait le toupet si bien taillé.* She had such a shapely hairdo. (AC, ch: *La fille de la veuve*) <AC, Da84> <*Loc:* AC, AV, EV, IB, LA, LF, SB, SL, SM, TB, VM, An94, Da84, Gu82, Lv88, Ph36>

tailleur [tajœr] *n.m.* tailor <*Loc:* Da84>

taillon [tajɔ̃] *n.m.* small piece <*Loc:* Lv88>

taïque [taik] *n.f.* **1** [*offensive*] squaw, Indian woman **Elle est méchante comme une taïque.* She's as mean as a squaw. (Re31) **2** ugly woman **3** dark-complexioned woman **4** person with long, disheveled hair <*Loc:* SM, TB, Da84, Lv88, Re31>

tairabi ♦see **tarabi**

taire[1] [tær] **I** *v.tr.* to hush, shut up *Je vas me le taire.* I'll shut him up for myself. (VM) **II se taire** *v.pron.* to shut up, keep silent **Fillette, jeunesse, mais taisez-vous. Vous n'avez pas encore quinze ans.* Little girl, young girl, be quiet. You are not yet fifteen years old. (IB, ch: *Une fille de quatorze ans*) ◊ **•faire taire** to shut s.o. up *Il peut pas les faire taire.* He can't make them shut up. (LA) *Tu peux pas les faire taire, ce monde-ça.* You can't make them shut up, those people. (VM) <LA, VM, Da84> <*Loc:* LA, VM, Da84>

taire[2] ♦see **terre**[2]

tairière ♦see **tarière**

tairir ♦see **tarir**

taiser (se) [teze] *v.pron.* to be silent, become silent *Il veut pas se taiser.* He won't shut up. (SL) <*Loc:* SL, TB, VM, Lv88>

talbot [talbo, tabo] *n.m.* hobble, weight tied to an animal to prevent it from running <*Loc:* IB, JD, VM, Di32>

talboter [talbote] *v.tr.* to hobble, tie a weight to an animal to prevent it from running *Ils ont eu pour talboter le bœuf.* They had to hobble the bull. (JD) <*Loc:* JD, VM, Di32>

t'à l'heure ♦see **talheure**

talheure[1] (**tout à l'heure, t'à l'heure**) [talœr, tutalœr] *adv.* **1** soon, after a while, shortly *On va aller au village talheure.* We're going to go to town shortly. (AV) *Y'a un voisin qui va venir tout à l'heure.* There is a neighbor who is going to come soon. (AC) **Ça fait, le bougre, lui, tout à l'heure, le mal au ventre l'a pris, le marié.* So the fellow, after a while, he got a stomachache, the groom. (EV, An94) **2** a short while ago *J'ai pas pu vous dire tout à l'heure.* I couldn't tell you a little while ago. (LF) *Il est venu t'à l'heure.* He came a little while ago. (SM) **Je suis après chercher le savon. Je m'en avais servi pour me laver les mains tout à l'heure.* I'm looking for the soap. I used it to wash my hands a little while ago. (ThCa: *Le charivari*) <*Loc:* AC, AV, EV, LF, SB, SM, TB, VM, An94, Da84, La99, Lv88, ThCa>

talheure[2] (**tout à l'heure, t'à l'heure**) [talœr, tutalœr] *interj.* see you soon <*Loc:* Da84>

talle (**tallée**) [tal, tale] *n.f.* **1** clump of bushes, briars, or shrubs **2** hunter's blind ◊ **•talle d'éronces** blackberry bush, bramble *Je vas ramasser des mûres dans la talle d'éronces.* I'm going to pick blackberries in the blackberry bushes. (AV) <AV, EV, IB, SM, Da84, Lv88, Ph36> **•talle d'herbe** clump of grass <Da84> <*Loc:* AV, EV, IB, LF, SJ, SL, SM, VM, Da84, Lv88, Ph36>

tallée[1] [tale] *n.f.* **1** lot, bunch **2** trick (in a card game) <*Loc:* AV, SM, Da84, Lv88>

tallée[2] ♦see **talle**

taller [tale] *v.intr.* **1** to stool, grow into a clump *Si tu laisses ton riz à sec quelque temps, il va taller.* If you leave your rice field dry for a while, the rice will stool. (VM) **2** to bush out, take the shape of a bush *Les rosiers est tout tallé. Ils sont bien* SHAPED. *T'as pas des branches dans toutes directions.* The rose bushes are taking shape. They're well shaped. You don't have branches [growing] in all directions. (AV) *Le bois est tout tallé.* The tree is all bushed out. (AV) <*Loc:* AV, EV, VM, Da84, Ph36>

talocher [taloʃe] *v.tr.* to hit, strike *Je l'ai taloché avec le bâton.* I hit him with the stick. (TB) <*Loc:* TB>

talon [talɔ̃] *n.m.* heel ◊ **•avoir les talons jaunes** to be old and unmarried <La99> <*Loc:* Da84, Hi02, La99>

talonner [talɔ̃ne] *v.tr.* **1** to spur with the heel, press one's heels into *Talonner son cheval, ça le fait galoper plus vite.* Spurring one's horse makes it gallop faster. (AV) **2** to stomp, stamp noisily with the feet *Ils ont talonné le plancher.* They stomped the floor. (AV) **3** to trample *Il talonne l'herbe.* He tramples the grass. (SB) <***Loc:*** AV, IB, SB, SJ, Da84>

tambouille (tombouille) [tɑ̃buj, tɔ̃buj] *n.f.* **1** cooking *Une bonne tambouille.* Good cooking. (Lv88) **2** potful, large quantity (of cooked food) *J'ai cuit une tambouille d'haricots blancs.* I cooked a potful of white beans. (SB) **3** anything cooked, esp. meat <***Loc:*** SB, SJ, SM, TB, VM, La99, Lv88>

tambouiller [tɑ̃buje] *v.tr.* to cook *On va parler tranquille, j'ai tambouillé mon dîner à bonne heure.* We can have a nice chat, I cooked dinner early. (Lv88) <***Loc:*** TB, Lv88>

tambour [tɑ̃bur, tɑ̃bor] *n.m.* **1** drum **2** drumfish, black drum, saltwater drum *Il a pas la couleur des tambours, le tambour est manière bleu, vert-bleu.* It doesn't have the color of a drumfish, the drum is somewhat blue, blue-green. (TB) **3** embroidery hoop *Broder au tambour.* To embroider using a hoop. (SJ) ◊ **•tambour battant** in abundance *Avoir de l'argent tambour battant.* To be rolling in money. (SJ) <IB, SJ> <***Loc:*** IB, JE, LF, SJ, TB, VM, Da84, Gu00, Hi02, Re31, Wh83>

tamis [tɑ̃mi] *n.m.* sifter, sieve, strainer *Un tamis, c'est pour tamiser la farine.* A sifter is for sifting flour. (LA) <***Loc:*** AL, AV, LA, TB, Da84>

tamisage [tɑ̃mizaʒ] *n.m.* sifting, screening <***Loc:*** Da84>

tamiser [tɑ̃mize] **I** *v.tr.* **1** to sift, screen *J'ai tamisé ma farine pour faire mon gâteau.* I sifted my flour to make my cake. (AV) *Tamiser le riz.* To screen rice. (VM) **2** to search, scrutinize thoroughly *On a tamisé la cour et on a pas trouvé ta bague.* We scrutinized the yard thoroughly and didn't find your ring. (VM) **3** to beat up, give a beating to *Si t'arrêtes pas de faire ça, je vas te tamiser.* If you don't stop doing that, I'll give you a beating. (VM) **II** *v.intr.* to shake while dancing in such a way that the whole body trembles *Quand ils font le zydeco DANCE, ils s'apé tamiser.* When they do the zydeco dance, they're shaking. (AV) **III se tamiser** *v.pron.* to shake o.s., shake about *Il est après se tamiser.* He's dancing and shaking about. (TB) <***Loc:*** AV, EV, TB, VM, Da84, La99>

tamponne [tɑ̃pɔ̃n] *n.f.* short, stout woman <***Loc:*** EV, IB, Lv88, Ph36, Re31>

tandis [tɑ̃di] *conj.* while *Je vas aller au village tandis tu vas au docteur.* I'm going to go to town while you go to the doctor. (AV) *Tandis tu vas marcher, moi je vas faire ça.* While you go for a walk, I'm going to do this. (AV) ◊ **•tandis que** while **Il sifflait, il chantait, mais tout d'un coup, tandis qu'il traversait un marais sec, il a vu des craques dans la terre, des grosses craques.* He was whistling, he was singing, but all of a sudden, while he was crossing a dry swamp, he saw cracks in the earth, big cracks. (EV, An94) **Je vas te dire quelque chose tandis que j'y pense là.* I'm going to tell you something while I'm thinking of it. (IV, An94) *Il a mangé tous les cornichons de navets qu'il a pu tandis que le vieux était au magasin.* He ate all the pickled turnips he could while the old man was at the store. (EV, An94) <EV, IV, LA, An94, Da84> <***Loc:*** AV, EV, IV, LA, An94, Da84>

TANK [tɛ̃k] *n.m.* **1** tank (liquid container) *Et y a des poissons vivants dans les TANKS.* And there are live fish in the tanks. (TB) **2** military tank ◊ **•TANK à butane** butane tank <LF> **•TANK à gaz** gas tank <TB> <***Loc:*** EV, LF, SL, TB, Da84, Lv88, Ph36>

tannable [tɑ̃nab(l), tɛ̃nab(l)] *adj.* dull, boring *C'est une journée beaucoup tannable.* It's a very dull day. (AV) <***Loc:*** AV>

tannage [tɑ̃naʒ] *n.m.* tanning, dressing (of hides) <***Loc:*** Da84>

tanné, -e [tɑ̃ne] *adj.* **1** tanned *Des peaux tannées.* Tanned hides. (LA) **2** sated, surfeited **J'en suis tanné.* I am fed up with it. (Da84) **3** weary, tired (of) *Je suis tanné de ça.* I'm tired of that. (LA) <***Loc:*** LA, Da84, Hi02>

tanner [tɑ̃ne] **I** *v.tr.* **1** to tan (hides, leather) *Ça tanne des peaux de vaches à côté de la tuerie des Martin.* They tan cow hides next to the Martins' slaughterhouse. (LA) **2** to bore **Ses histoires m'tanent.* His stories bore me. (EV, Ph36) **II** *v.intr.* to tire, grow tired (of) *J'ai tanné des haricots.* I'm tired of beans. (AV) *J'ai tanné de rester dans la ville.* I'm tired of living in New Orleans. (AV) **III se tanner** *v.pron.* **1** to get tired (of), be fed up (with) *Je m'ai tanné de tout le temps aller là-bas pour THANKSGIVING, ça fait je reste ici asteur.* I got tired of always going over there for Thanksgiving, so I stay here now. (LA) **2** to become bored, have enough, grow tired (of doing s.t.) *Quand vieux Émar s'est tanné, lui, il a embarqué et il a GONE.* When old Emar got bored, he left. (EV) <***Loc:*** AV, EV, LA, Da84, Ph36>

tannerie [tɑ̃nri] *n.f.* tannery <***Loc:*** AC, Da84>

tant [tɑ̃] *adv.* **1** so much **Mange pas tant que ça.* Don't eat so much. (Da84) **2** so many *Il y avait tant de familles qui se mettaient ensemble, et tous les samedis, ils tuaient un veau, chacun à son tour.* There were so many families that got together, and every Saturday, they slaughtered a calf, they took turns. (SL) *Asteur eux-autres te ALLOW juste tant de TAGS, ça va par les arpents de terre que t'as.* Now they allow you just so many tags, it goes by the number of acres of land you own. (TB) **3** so long, so often ◊ **•tant de fois** so many times *Tant de fois, je vas au bal.* I go to the dance so many times. (AV) <AV, Da84> **•tant mieux** so much the better *Il dit qu'il veut pas aller. Mais tant mieux. On a pas besoin de lui quand même.* He says he doesn't want to go. Well, so much the better. We don't need him anyway. (LA) <AV, LA, Da84> **•tant pire** so much the worse, too bad **Tant pire pour lui.* Too bad for him, that's his hard luck. (Da84) <SB, TB, Da84> **•tant qu'à** as for, with regard to *Tant qu'à lui, c'est bien fou.* As for him, it's quite crazy.

(SM) *Tant qu'à moi, ça me fait arien.* As for me, that doesn't do anything for me. (VM) *Tant qu'à mon, je suis fière.* As for me, I'm proud. (AV) *Tant qu'à nos traditions...* As for our traditions . . . (Lv88) <AV, EV, IB, LF, SB, SL, SM, TB, VM, Lv88, Ph36> **•tant qu'à faire** in that case *Tant qu'à faire, reste à la maison.* In that case, stay home. (AV) <AV, Da84> **•tant qu'à pour lui** [*implies a negative judgment*] as for him, as far as he's concerned *Tant qu'à pour lui, il vaut rien.* As for him, he's worthless. (AV) <AV, Da84> **•tant que** ***a*** as long as *Et tant qu'il y avait le sucre dans la chose, alle aurait mangé là. Il n'avait pas de tracas. Mais quand il n'avait plus de sucre,* LOOK OUT. As long as there was sugar in the thing, she would eat it. There was no trouble. But when there was no more sugar, look out! (EV) *Je vas jamais oblier ça tant que je vas vivre.* I won't forget that as long as I live. (TB) ***b*** while *Et tant qu'on était là-bas y avait plusieurs familles qui délogeaient, ça venait manière comme un petit village.* And while we were there, there were several families who moved, it became somewhat like a little town. (TB) ***c*** as much as *Il va à l'école tant qu'il faut.* He goes to school as much as he has to. (LA) <LA, LF, TB, Da84, Hi02> **•tant qu'à pour** as for *Mais tant qu'à pour moi, je suis ici, mais pour rester.* But as for me, I'm here to stay. (LA, ch: *La valse de l'héritage*) <LA> **•c'est tant quitte** it's worth as much <Lv88> **•si tant** so, so much, so many *Y'a pas si tant d'années.* Not so many years ago. (Lv88) *Ses planchers brillent si tant.* His floors shine so much. (Lv88) <TB, Lv88> ***<Loc:*** AC, AV, EV, IB, IV, LA, LF, PQ, SB, SL, SM, TB, VM, An94, Da84, Hi02, Lv88, Ph36>

tante [tɑ̃t] *n.f.* aunt *Je devais parler pour mes tantes et mes noncles.* I had to speak for my aunts and uncles. (SM) ◊ **•tante par alliance** aunt by marriage <Da84> **•grande tante** great aunt <Da84> ***<Loc:*** EV, LA, PQ, SM, TB, An94, Da84, Hi02>

tantôt [tɑ̃to] *adv.* soon, presently **Je vas venir tantôt.* I'll come soon. (Da84) *Tantôt, je vas faire mon ouvrage.* I'll do my work soon. (AV) *Je vas cuire mon dîner tantôt.* I'm going to cook my dinner soon. (AV) ◊ **•tantôt-bétôt** sooner or later *Il va arriver tantôt-bétôt.* He will arrive sooner or later. (VM) <VM, Da84> ***<Loc:*** AV, VM, Da84>

taoubas [tauba] *n.m.* noisy gathering ***<Loc:*** AV, Re31>

taon [tɑ̃] *n.m.* **1** horsefly **2** sandfly **3** ox-fly ***<Loc:*** LF, SM, Da84>

tapage (**tapaillage**) [tapaʒ, tapajaʒ] *n.m.* uproar, racket, noise, disturbance ***<Loc:*** SL, Da84>

tapager [tapaʒe] *v.intr.* **1** to make noise, create an uproar, create a disturbance *Ils ont tapagé jusqu'à après minuit.* They created an uproar until after midnight. (LA) **2** to talk loudly and endlessly, to the point of being annoying ***<Loc:*** LA, VM, Lv88>

tapaillage ♦see **tapage**

TAPE [teᶦp, tɛp] *n.m.* **1** measuring tape **2** audio tape **3** adhesive tape ◊ **•mettre sur le TAPE** to tape-record, put on tape *Tu vas pas mettre quoi je dis sur le* TAPE*?* You're not going to put what I say on tape, are you? (Lv88) <Lv88> ***<Loc:*** JE, Lv88>

tape [tap] *n.f.* slap **Elle a réveillé le vieux bougre à coup de tapes.* She woke up the old man by slapping him around. (EV, An94) ◊ **•vire-tape** slap with the back of the hand <VM> ***<Loc:*** EV, VM, An94, Da84>

tapé [tape] *adj.* ◊ **•c'est bien tapé** it serves him/her right, she/he had it coming, it is well deserved <Da84, Lv88> ***<Loc:*** Da84, Lv88>

tapée [tape] *n.f.* heap, a lot, large or excessive amount *Une tapée de piment rouge.* A whole bunch of red pepper. (VM) **J'ai attrapé une tapée de poisson.* I caught a lot of fish. (Da84) *Il a dit une tapée de menteries.* He told a bunch of lies. (SM) *Il y a une tapée de monde.* There's a whole bunch of people. (LA) *J'ai apporté une tapée de viande.* I brought a huge amount of meat. (SB) ***<Loc:*** LA, SB, SM, VM, Da84>

tape-en-gueule [tapɑ̃gøl] *n.m.* clabber, curds and whey ***<Loc:*** SM>

taper [tape] **I** *v.tr.* to slap, strike, hit *Si ils nous auront découvert! Là, chère, ils nous auront tapés!* If they had discovered us! They would have slapped us! (EV) *Eh ben il fallait que tu prends un bâton et taper, taper, taper. Ça ça le faisait* FLUFFY *encore. Là le lit était paré pour le soir.* Well, you had to take a stick and hit it, hit it, hit it. That made it fluffy again. Then the bed was ready for the night. (TB) *On le foutait une balle, ou ça se prenait une hache et le taper dans la tête.* We would shoot a bullet in it or take an axe and hit it in the head. (TB) **II** *v.intr.* **1** to clap *Le monde tapait comme des fous.* The people were clapping like they were crazy. (LA) **2** to knock *Alle a venu taper à la porte.* She came to knock on the door. (LF) **3** to strike, occur (e.g. of a disease) *Quand la fièvre jaune a tapé dessus le bayou et y a plein du monde qu'est mort.* When yellow fever struck on the bayou and a lot of people died. (LF) **III se taper** *v.pron.* to slap each other *Ils se sont tapés.* They slapped each other. (AV) ◊ **•taper ça à qqn / taper sa réponse à qqn** to put s.o. in his place, answer smartly *Il croyait qu'il m'avait bouché, mais je lui ai tapé ça, je te dis.* He thought he had shut me up, but I put him in his place, I'll tell you. (LA) *J'ai vu ma chance quand il m'a dit ça et je lui ai bien tapé ma réponse.* I saw my chance when he said that to me, and I came back with a cutting rejoinder. (SB) <LA, SB, VM> **•taper la savate** to dance *On va aller au bal taper la savate à soir.* We're going to go dancing tonight. (LF) <LF> ***<Loc:*** AV, EV, IV, LA, LF, SB, TB, VM, Da84>

tapis [tapi] *n.m.* **1** carpet **2** rug **3** cover ◊ **•tapis de table** oilcloth <VM> ***<Loc:*** LA, TB, VM, Da84>

tapisser [tapise] *v.tr.* to wallpaper, hang wallpaper or tapestry

Ma femme a tapissé les murs de la cuisine elle-même. My wife wallpapered the kitchen walls herself. (LA) <***Loc:*** LA, Da84>

tapisserie [tapisri] *n.f.* **1** wallpaper **2** tapestry **3** wallpapering, hanging wallpaper or tapestry <***Loc:*** Da84, Pe37>

tapisseur [tapisœr] *n.m.* **1** upholsterer **2** tapestry worker **3** paper hanger <***Loc:*** SM, VM, Lv88>

tapocher [tapoʃe] *v.tr.* **1** to tap, strike, hit *Le professeur a tapoché le petit garçon.* The teacher slapped the little boy. (SB) **2** to slap around, give several light slaps to *Elle est tout le temps après tapocher ses enfants.* She's always slapping her kids around. (VM) **3** to tap or beat repeatedly *Arrête de tapocher sus la table. Ça me rend nerveuse.* Stop tapping on the table. It makes me nervous. (VM) **4** to stomp, stamp with the feet <***Loc:*** AV, IB, SB, SJ, SL, SM, TB, VM, Da84, Lv88, Re31>

tapoir [tapwar] *n.m.* batter (in baseball) <***Loc:*** IB>

tapon [tapɔ̃] *n.m.* bottlecap <***Loc:*** IB>

taqué, -e [take] *adj.* withdrawn, taciturn <***Loc:*** VM>

taquer [take] *v.tr.* to latch, lock *Va taquer la porte pour moi.* Go lock the door for me. (SM) <***Loc:*** LA, LF, SB, SL, SM, Da84, Lv88>

taquet [takɛ, take] *n.m.* **1** latch, catch, hook, cleat (of a door or gate) **2** tongue **Son taquet est trop long.* His tongue is too long. (EV, Ph36) <***Loc:*** EV, LA, LF, SB, SM, TB, VM, Da84, Lv88, Pe37, Ph36>

taqueté, -e [takte] *adj.* spotted, speckled *Une vache taquetée.* A spotted cow. (IB) <***Loc:*** IB, LF>

taquiner [takine] *v.tr.* to tease, antagonize, annoy *Il m'a bien taquiné tout l'après-midi.* He teased me all afternoon. (AV) <***Loc:*** AV, SL, Da84>

taquinerie [takinri] *n.f.* act of teasing, antagonizing, annoying <***Loc:*** Da84>

tarabi (**tarabie, tairabi, tournabie**) [tarabi, tærabi, turnabi] *n.m.* **1** rope jack (rope-making tool) **2** instrument used to make horse reins out of horse hair <***Loc:*** SM, VM, Da84, Gu00, Lv88>

tarabie ♦see **tarabi**

taraud [taro] *n.m.* thread (on bolts, screws) <***Loc:*** AV, JE, LA, Da84>

tarauder (**tarauter**) [tarode, tarote] *v.tr.* to thread, cut threads on, tap (screws, bolts, nuts, etc.) *Il est tarauté à l'envers du bon sens.* It's threaded in the wrong direction. (AV) *Tarauter un tuyau.* To thread the end of a piece of pipe. (SJ) <***Loc:*** AV, IB, SB, SJ, Da84, Lv88>

tarauter ♦see **tarauder**

tard[1] [tar] *n.m.* ◊ •**au tard** late **Arriver au tard.* To arrive late. (Da84) <Da84> •**sur le tard** late in the evening, at nightfall *Tous les soirs, sur le tard, il fallait qu'on moule du café.* Every night, late in the evening, we had to grind coffee. (TB) <LA, SM, TB, Da84> <***Loc:*** LA, SM, TB, Da84>

tard[2] [tar] *adv.* late *On s'est marié tard au printemps.* We got married late in spring. (EV) *J'ai arrivé tard à l'ouvrage.* I got to work late. (AV) ◊ •**au plus tard** at the latest *Fais ça demain au plus tard.* Do that by tomorrow at the latest. (VM) <VM, Da84> •**être tard** to be late <VM> •**plus tard** later *Là, plus tard quand j'ai eu dix-huit ans je m'ai marié.* Later, when I turned eighteen, I got married. (AC) <AC, LA, SL, VM, An94, Da84> •**tôt ou tard** sooner or later *Tôt ou tard, il faudrait il se décide.* Sooner or later, he'll have to make up his mind. (LA) <LA, Da84> •**trop tard** too late **Le médecin après la mort, c'est trop tard.* The doctor after death, it's too late. (Da84) <Da84> <***Loc:*** AC, AV, EV, LA, SL, TB, VM, An94, Da84, Hi02, Lv88>

tarder [tarde, tardze] **I** *v.tr.* to delay, make late *Il m'a tardé pour aller au village.* He made me late for going to town. (AV) **II** *v.intr.* to delay, be late *Car les messieurs de la justice ne tarderont pas longtemps.* For the ministers of justice will not tarry long. (PQ, ch: *Quand la belle entendit dire*) <***Loc:*** AV, PQ, TB, Da84>

target [tarʒɛ, tarʒe] *n.m.* bolt, latch *Mettre le target sur la porte.* To bolt the door. (SJ) <***Loc:*** AV, IB, SJ>

tarière (**tairière**) [tarjær, terjær, tærjær] *n.m.* any of several boring tools such as a hand-drill, bit and brace, wimble, auger, or gimlet <***Loc:*** AV, IB, SB, SJ, VM, Da84, Gu00, Lv88>

tarif [tarif] *n.m.* tariff, charge, tax <***Loc:*** Da84>

tarir (**térir, tairir**) [tarir, terir, tærir] **I** *v.tr.* **1** to exhaust, use up *Le puits est téri, il faulait fouiller un autre.* The well is dry, we had to dig another one. (VM) **2** to drain, drain out *Nous irons et nous boirons et nous tarirons les verres et nous les remplirons* We'll go and we'll drink and we'll drain the glasses and we'll refill them. (VM, ch: *L'oranger*) **3** to reduce (a sauce) *J'ai levé la mèche pour térir ma sauce.* I raised the flame to reduce my sauce. (VM) **II** *v.intr.* **1** to dry up, run dry (e.g. a well, a milk cow, etc.) *Caillette a téri. Son veau a péri.* Caillette [the cow] dried up and her calf perished. (VM) **2** to cook down *On va laisser la sauce tarir. Ça va l'épaissir.* We'll let the sauce cook down. That'll thicken it. (VM) <***Loc:*** AV, SM, TB, VM, Da84, Lv88>

tarpoline [tarpolin] *n.f.* tarpaulin <***Loc:*** AV, IB, SB, SJ, SL, SM>

tarpon [tarpɔ̃] *n.m.* tarpon <***Loc:*** Da84, Gu00>

tarte [tart] *n.f.* pie, tart *Il a grappillé le dernier morceau de tarte.* He seized the last piece of pie. (LA) ◊ •**tarte à la bouillie** custard pie <LA> •**tarte à la patate douce** sweet potato pie <TB> •**tarte couvert** turnover <LA> <***Loc:*** LA, SL, TB, Da84, Hi02>

tartine [tartin] *n.f.* slice *Donne-moi une tartine de fromage.* Give me a slice of cheese. (IB) *Une tartine de pain.* A slice of bread. (SB) <***Loc:*** IB, SB>

tas [ta] *n.m.* heap, pile, bunch, large quantity, a lot *Tu pouvais acheter un vrai tas d'affaires pour vingt piastres.* You could buy a whole lot of stuff for $20. (TB) ◊ •**mettre en tas** to pile up, heap up *Et il les a tout mis en tas jusqu'à le jour que on a commencé la maison.* And he piled them [bricks] up until the day when we started the house. (EV) <EV, Da84> **•un tas** much, a lot **J'en ai un tas.* I've got a lot of it. (Da84) *Ça va un tas plus vite.* It goes much faster. (SM) *Il va mouiller un tas à soir.* It's going to rain a lot tonight. (Lv88) *Ma sœur et moi parle en français un tas.* My sister and I speak French a lot. (SL) *Le monde allait un tas dans des bogheis.* People went in buggies a lot. (SL) *Elle est jolie, mais pas un tas.* She's pretty, but not that pretty. (SM) <AC, EV, IB, JE, LA, LF, SB, SL, SM, VM, An94, Lv88, Ph36> **•un tas de** a lot of, many, much *Ma mère élevait un tas des volailles qui pondaient un tas des œufs.* My mother raised a lot of poultry which laid many eggs. (IB) *Y'avait pas un tas des femmes qui travaillaient à côté de la maison.* There were not many women who worked outside the house. (AC) *Il a élevé un tas d'enfants.* He raised many children. (VM) *Il fait un tas de cancan.* He makes a lot of trouble. (SM) *Il y avait pas un tas de cassage après le bal.* There wasn't much breakage after the dance. (LA) <AC, EV, IB, JE, LA, LF, SB, SL, SM, VM, An94, Lv88, Ph36> **•un tas des fois** many times *Ça voulait pas on parle français, quand j'étais à l'école je me faisais fouetter un tas des fois.* They did not want you to speak French, at school I was whipped many times. (AC) <AC, SL> **•un tas dur** a great deal *On a un tas dur de ça.* We have a great deal of that. (TB) <TB> <***Loc:*** AC, EV, IB, IV, JE, LA, SL, SM, TB, VM, An94, Da84, Hi02, Lv88>

tasse [tas] *n.f.* cup *Une tasse de lait.* A cup of milk. (LF) ◊ **•tasse à café** coffee cup, porcelain cup <AV, JE, LF, TB, Da84> **•tasse de café** cup of coffee **Elle lui a donné une tasse de café.* She gave him a cup of coffee. (EV, An94) <EV, JE, An94, Da84> **•tasse de pissat chaud** cup of weak coffee <EV, La99> **•tasse à mesure** measuring cup <JD> **•demi-tasse** ***a*** half-cup ***b*** demitasse <Da84> <***Loc:*** AC, AV, CL, EV, IB, JD, JE, LA, LF, SB, SM, TB, An94, Da84, Hi02, La99>

tasseau[1] [taso] *n.m.* rectangular bark basket used for berry picking <***Loc:*** SJ>

tasseau[2] ♦see **tasso**

tassée [tase] *n.f.* cup, cupful *Rentre, je vas te faire une tassée de café.* Come in, I'll make you a cup of coffee. (TB) <***Loc:*** TB>

tasso (tasseau) [taso] *n.m.* tasso, sun-dried or smoked meat (esp. pork, beef, or fish) cut into strips resembling jerky *Asteur je mets p'us de la viande salée ou du bacon dans mes fèves secs, je mets du tasso, c'est moins gras et plus sain, pis ça donne autant de goût.* Nowadays I no longer put salted meat or bacon in my dry beans, I put tasso, it's less fatty and more healthy and it gives as much flavor. (Gu00) *Le tasso, c'est la viande séchée à la fumée, qui la conserve.* Tasso is meat that is smoked while it's dried, to preserve it. (SL) *Du tasseau, de la panse bourrée, du béquine, des saucisses...* Tasso, stuffed stomach, bacon, sausages . . . (EV) *Des tasseaux c'est bon à cuire avec des tomates.* Strips of dried and salted fish are good cooked with tomatoes. (TB) **Pour faire le délivrage du petit plus aisé, [...] ça aidait si la femme buvait du thé de farine maïs et chiquait du tasso.* To make the delivery of the baby easier, it helped if the woman drank corn meal tea and chewed jerky. (Wh83) *Jambalaya [...] on fait avec de la volaille et du tasso.* Jambalaya we make with poultry and smoked dried meat. (SL) <***Loc:*** EV, IB, LF, SB, SC, SL, SM, TB, VM, Da84, Gu00, Hi02, La99, Lv88, Ph36, Re31, Wh83>

tata [tata] *interj.* [*baby talk*] thank you *Tata pour le bonbon.* Thank you for the candy. (SM) **Dis tata à l'homme.* Tell the man thank you. (EV, Ph36) <***Loc:*** EV, IB, LF, SB, SL, SM, Da84, Ph36>

tataille [tataj] *n.f.* **1** threatening beast, monster *Va pas dehors. Une tataille va t'attraper.* Don't go outside. A monster will get you. (LA) **Le Ta-Taille ça dit est ein gros bétaille qui ressemble manière comme ein ravert. Il vient après la nuit et coupe les orteils des petits méchants.* The "Ta-Taille" is said to be a giant creature that resembles a cockroach. It comes after dark and cuts off the toes of mean children. (Wh83) **2** frightening bug *Traîne-toi pas en dessous de la maison. Il y a plein de tatailles en bas-là.* Don't go crawling under the house. It's full of scary bugs under there. (VM) <***Loc:*** AV, LA, VM, Lv88, Wh83>

tâtailler [tataje] *v.tr.* to paw, feel up, grope *Il aime beaucoup tâter quelqu'un. Il est après tâtailler, toucher dans les mauvaises places.* He really likes to grope people. He's groping, touching in the wrong places. (AV) <***Loc:*** AV, LA, SB, VM>

tatamage [tatamaʒ] *n.m.* noise, racket, uproar *Ils ont fait un tatamage hier soir chez le voisin.* They made quite a racket last night at the neighbor's. (SB) <***Loc:*** SB>

tatanas ♦see **tétanos**

tâter [tate] *v.tr.* **1** to cull *Tâter les poules.* To cull hens (in order to separate layers from the rest of the flock). (SJ) **2** to paw, feel up, grope *Il aime beaucoup tâter quelqu'un. Il est après tatailler, toucher dans les mauvaises places.* He really likes to grope people. He's groping, touching in the wrong places. (AV) <***Loc:*** AV, SJ, Da84>

tatine [tatin] *n.f.* tatting, type of knotted lace <***Loc:*** SB, Lv88>

tatiner [tatine] *v.intr.* **1** to dabble *Il a tatiné dans l'élevage des lapins.* He dabbled in rabbit breeding. (LA) **2** to tat, do tatting <***Loc:*** EV, LA, SM, Lv88, Ph36>

tâton [tatɔ̃] *n.m.* probe, feeler <***Loc:*** Da84>

tâtonner [tatɔ̃ne] **I** *v.intr.* **1** to feel one's way, feel around *On a eu pour tâtonner dans le noir pour trouver la lampe.* We had to feel around in the dark to find the lamp. (VM) **2** to paw, feel up, grope *Arrête-toi de me tâtonner.* Stop pawing me. (TB) **3** to waste time *T'es après tâtonner, dépêche-toi.*

You're wasting time, hurry up! (AV) **II se tâtonner** *v.pron.* to pet, grope, feel each other up *Le jeune monde a p'us de honte. Ils étaient après se tâtonner grand debout à bic à blanc droite là devant tout le monde dessus le plancher de danse.* Young people have no shame anymore. They were petting standing up right there on the dance floor in public in front of everyone. (LA) ◊ **•tâtonner pour des tortues** to feel underwater for turtles <Da84> <***Loc:*** AV, EV, LA, SM, TB, VM, Da84, La99, Ph36>

tatou [tatu] *n.m.* armadillo <***Loc:*** Da84>

tatouiller [tatuje] *v.tr.* to tickle *Il aime trop à tatouiller.* He's too fond of tickling. (SB) <***Loc:*** SB>

taupe [top, tɔp] *n.f.* mole (small burrowing mammal) <***Loc:*** EV, Da84, Fa77, Guoo>

taupin [topɛ̃] *n.m.* **1** burly, large, strong man **2** heavy, fat person ◊ **•Taupin vaut Maurin** ***a*** one is as bad as the other (of two things or people) ***b*** there is no point in arguing <La99> <***Loc:*** VM, Da84, La99>

taure [tɔr] *n.f.* heifer *Ils ont eu pour corailler les taures.* They had to pen up the heifers. (LA) <***Loc:*** AV, EV, IB, LA, SB, SM, TB, VM, Da84, Fa77, Guoo, Lv88>

taureau [toro] *n.m.* **1** bull *Un taureau l'a coffré.* A bull gored him. (VM) *On s'a halé de là quand le taureau a pris à piocher.* We got out of there when the bull started pawing the ground. (VM) **2** tough guy **3** one who thinks he's better or stronger than others ◊ **•taureau du bois** bully, cock-of-the-walk <VM> **•c'est pas toi qu'es le taureau du côteau** insult used for someone arrogant or not very intelligent. <La99> **•le taureau sur le côteau {la butte}** ***a*** the leader ***b*** the strongest or toughest of a group <AC, La99> <***Loc:*** AC, AV, EV, SM, VM, Da84, Guoo, Hi02, La99>

taurin [torɛ̃] *n.m.* drunken man who makes trouble <***Loc:*** SM>

taxable [taksab(l)] *adj.* taxable *Les médecines sont pas taxables.* Medicines aren't taxable. (EV) <***Loc:*** EV, VM, Da84, Lv88>

taxe [taks] *n.f.* tax <***Loc:*** EV, LF, SM, TB, VM, Da84, Lv88>

taxer [takse] *v.tr.* to tax *Le gouvernement arrête pas de nous taxer.* The government doesn't stop taxing us. (VM) <***Loc:*** VM, Da84, Fa77>

taxi [taksi] *n.m.* taxi, taxicab <***Loc:*** Da84>

tayaut ♦see **taïaut**

tcha [tʃa] *interj.* cry to call cows <***Loc:*** SM>

tchac (**chaque, tchoc, tchaqué, chaqué, -e**) [tʃak, tʃɔk, tʃake] *adj.* **1** intoxicated, drunk *Il était manière tchac, ça fait il voulait danser avec tout quelqu'un.* He was sort of drunk, so he wanted to dance with everyone. (EV) **2** tipsy, slightly inebriated *Quelqu'un qui boit, il est tchoc.* Someone who drinks is tipsy. (AV) <***Loc:*** AV, EV, IB, LF, SM, TB, VM, Da84, La99, Lv88, Ph36>

tchacafané [tʃakafɑ̃ne] *n.m.* insignificant person <***Loc:*** SM>

tchacailler ♦see **tchincailler**

tchacaillerie [tʃakajri] *n.f.* drinking binge, bout of drinking *Il est sur une tchacaillerie.* He is on a drinking binge. (SL) <***Loc:*** SL>

tchacailleur ♦see **tchicailleur**

tchacalata [tʃakalata] *n.m.* chicken hawk <***Loc:*** LF>

tchacara [tʃakara] *n.m.* rattle-trap vehicle, jalopy *Il a halé son bois dans son tchacara.* He hauled his wood in his old wagon. (AV) <***Loc:*** AV, IB>

tchacouelle (**catchouelle**) [tʃakwɛl, katʃwɛl] *n.m.* **1** skillet **2** water dipper, large cup with a long handle *La tchacouelle a tombé dans le puits.* The dipper fell into the well. (AV) <***Loc:*** AL, AV, EV>

tchaffié ♦see **tchifaillé**

tchaise-côtes ♦see **quinze-côtes**

tchamander (**tchémander, tchinmander, chamonder, quémander**) [tʃamɑ̃de, tʃemɑ̃de, tʃamɔ̃de, tʃɛ̃mɑ̃de] **I** *v.tr.* to beg for *Tchamander de l'argent pour son école, pour son église.* To beg for money for one's school, for one's church. (EV) **II** *v.intr.* to beg (objectionably, frequently, or in a whining way) *Viens pas tchamander icitte!* Don't come begging around here. (EV) <***Loc:*** EV, SM, VM, Da84, Hi02, Lv88>

tchamanderie (**chamanderie**) [tʃamɑ̃dri] *n.f.* begging <***Loc:*** Da84>

tchamandeur, -euse (**tchémandeur, -euse, chamandeur, -euse, chomandeur, -euse, quémandeur, -euse**) [tʃɑ̃mɑ̃dœr, -øz, tʃemɑ̃dør, -øz, tʃɔ̃mɔ̃dœr, -øz, tʃamɔ̃dœr, -øz] *n.* **1** beggar, mendicant *La fille dit un vieux tchamandeur est à la porte.* The girl says there's an old beggar at the door. (SM) **2** insistently demanding person <***Loc:*** SL, SM, Da84, Lv88>

tchambo [tʃɑ̃bo] *v.tr.invar.* to hold *Tchambo le sac pour moi.* Hold the bag for me. (SB) <***Loc:*** SB>

tchampourra (**chambouhourra, champoura**) [tʃɑ̃pura, tʃɑ̃bura] *n.m.* **1** commotion, racket, ruckus *J'ai été là-bas, il y avait le plus gros champoura.* I was over there, there was the biggest commotion. (VM) *Les petits font un tchampourra quand ils jouent ensemble.* The kids make a racket when they play together. (SM) *On a fait un chambouhourra chez elle hier soir.* They made a big commotion at her house last night. (IB) **2** mess, disorder *Faire un tchampourra de son ouvrage.* To make a mess of one's task. (SJ) *Elle a fait un tchampourra de ce gâteau.* She made a mess of the cake. (IB) **3** fair, festival, festive occasion **4** riffraff **Tout ç' chambouhourra vaut pas dix sous.* All that riffraff isn't worth a dime. (EV, Ph36) <***Loc:*** AV, EV, IB, SJ, SM, VM, Ph36, Re31>

tchanfré ♦see **camphré**

tchapin [tʃapɛ̃] *n.m.* sag in trousers that are too large for the wearer *Ce patalon y fait un tchapin dans le dos.* These trousers sag in the back. (LF) <***Loc:*** LF>

tchaqué ♦see **tchac**

tchaquer (**chaquer**) [tʃake, tʃɔke] **I** *v.tr.* to intoxicate, get s.o. drunk *On l'a tchaqué la veille de ses noces et il était toujours* *tchaqué quand il a arrivé à l'autel.* We got him drunk the night before his wedding and he was still drunk when he arrived at the altar. (VM) **II se tchaquer** *v.pron.* to get drunk, get tipsy **On commençait à se chaquer en haut là et on jouait aussi fort comme on pouvait.* We would start getting tipsy up there and we would play as loud as we could. (An84) *J'avais été au bal le dimanche au soir et je m'ai manière... Je m'ai tchaqué bien.* I had gone to the dance on Sunday night and I sort of . . . I got good and drunk. (SL) <***Loc:*** SB, SL, SM, VM, An84, Da84, Guoo, Hio2, La99, Lv88>

tcharabo [tʃarabo] *n.* rifle <***Loc:*** AV, JD>

tcharara (charara) [tʃarara] *n.f.* weak coffee <***Loc:*** AV, EV, Ph36, Re31>

tcharatte [tʃarat] *n.f.* mockingbird <***Loc:*** SB>

tchaurisse (chaurice, chourice) [tʃoris, tʃuris, ʃoris] *n.m./f.* thick, spicy sausage made with coarsely-chopped meat <***Loc:*** AV, SM, Guoo, Lv88, Re31>

tcheck [tʃek] *n.m.* biscuit dough cooked in the shape of a large flat cake <***Loc:*** SM>

tchèque ♦see **CHECK**

tchéquer ♦see **CHECK**

tchêter ♦see **quêter**

tchêteur ♦see **quêteur**

tcheue ♦see **queue**

tchie [tʃi] *n.f.* small piece of cotton left in the boll after picking <***Loc:*** AV>

tchicadence [tʃikadɑ̃s] *n.f.* tip of a whip <***Loc:*** Lv88>

tchicailler ♦see **tchincailler**

tchicailleur (tchacailleur) [tʃikajœr, tʃakajœr] *n.m.* **1** troublemaker *Il était tchacailleur.* He was a troublemaker. (EV) **2** loafer, dawdler <***Loc:*** AV, EV>

tchifaillé, -e (tchaffié, -e) [tʃifaje, tʃafje] *adj.* tackily or gaudily dressed *C'est ça qui sortont tchaffiés.* Those are the ones who go out dressed gaudily. (VM) <***Loc:*** VM>

tchincailler (tchacailler, tchicailler, chéquailler, quincailler) [tʃɛ̃kaje, tʃakaje, tʃikaje, tʃekaje] **I** *v.tr.* to tease, annoy, irritate *Il était tout le temps après tchincailler ces bougres-là. Et puis ils s'ont mis ensemble et ils l'ont bûché.* He was always teasing those guys. And they got together and they beat him up. (LA) **Ç't homme me chéquaille.* That man annoys me. (EV, Ph36) **II** *v.intr.* **1** to bother with, fool around with *Moi, j'ai jamais quincaillé avec du bois dur.* I've never bothered with hardwood. (SL) **2** to waste one's time, fool around, loaf **I fait pas rien, i chéquaille.* He doesn't do anything, he wastes his time. (EV, Ph36) <***Loc:*** AV, EV, LA, Da84, Lv88, Ph36>

tchincaillerie (quincaillerie) [tʃɛ̃kajri] *n.f.* **1** cheap bric-a-bric, shoddy goods, junk *Ça va acheter des quincailleries dans les machines pour 25 sous.* They'll buy cheap prizes in the vending machine for a quarter. (Lv88) *Acheter des tchincailleries.* To buy junk. (VM) *J'achète jamais là-bas. C'est rien que des tchincailleries.* I never buy there. It's nothing but cheap junk. (VM) **2** useless or worthless objects, junk, trash *Mon mari a réparé son char dans le garage hier et il a laissé des tchincailleries à la traîne tout partout.* My husband fixed his car in the garage yesterday and he left junk lying around all over the place. (Guoo) *Laisser des tchincailleries dans le garage.* Leave trash in the garage. (VM) <***Loc:*** LA, SM, VM, Da84, Guoo, Lv88>

tchine (chine) [tʃin] *adj.* **1** extremely curly, frizzy, kinky, tightly curled (of hair) *Avant son opération, ma mère avait les cheveux assez frisés, ils étiont proche tchines.* Before her operation, my mother's hair was so tightly curled it was almost kinky. (Guoo) *Cheveux chines.* Kinky hair. (VM) **2** frizzly (of a hen) *Poule chine.* Frizzly hen. (VM) <***Loc:*** JD, VM, Guoo>

tchinque-tchinque [tʃɛ̃ktʃɛ̃k] *adj.* tacky *Elle est jolie, mais un peu tchinque-tchinque.* She is pretty, but a bit tacky. (SM) <***Loc:*** SM>

tchinqui-tchinque (chinc-chinc) [tʃɛ̃nkitʃɛ̃nk, tʃɛ̃nktʃɛ̃nk] *n.m.* **1** [*pej.*] loud, jazzy hillbilly music, chanky-chank **2** musical instrument <***Loc:*** VM, Hio2>

tchiper (chiper) [tʃipe] *v.intr.* to gossip **A chippe su tout l' monne.* She gossips about everyone. (EV, Ph36) <***Loc:*** EV, Ph36>

tchique[1] [tʃik] *n.f.* **1** bun, roll, twist, or knot of hair worn at the back of the head **2** nub of the stem of a gourd plant (e.g. a pumpkin) <***Loc:*** LF, VM>

tchique[2] (**CHEEK**) [tʃik] *n.f.* nerve, brass *Avoir de la tchique.* To have a lot of nerve. (LF) <***Loc:*** LF>

tchique[3] [tʃik] *interj.* cry for calling calves <***Loc:*** EV, SM, Lv88, Ph36>

tchiqué [tʃike] *interj.* cry used to chase away calves <***Loc:*** EV, SM, Ph36>

tchiquette [tʃikɛt] *n.f.* ◊ •**acheter à la tchiquette** to buy very little (of s.t.) at a time <LA, SM, Lv88> <***Loc:*** LA, SM, Lv88>

tchiquine [tʃikin] *adj.* very skinny, sickly looking *Il faudra que tu donnes du* FEED *à ta taure. Alle commence à être joliment tchiquine.* You need to give some feed to your heifer. She is starting to be quite sickly looking. (Guoo) <***Loc:*** VM, Guoo>

tchoc[1] **(choc, choque)** [tʃɔk, tʃak] *n.m.* **1** blackbird **2** any of various birds with dark plumage ◊ •**tchoc à vache** cowbird <Guoo, Lv88> •**tchoc aux ailes rouges / choc aile rouge** redwing blackbird <Guoo, Lv88, Re31> •**beau tchoc** good-for-nothing <Lv88> <***Loc:*** AV, EV, IB, JE, LA, LF, SB, SM, TB, VM, Da84, Guoo, Lv88, Ph36, Re31>

tchoc[2] ♦see **tchac**

tchocouette [tʃokwɛt] *n.f.* lock of hair, braid <***Loc:*** AV>

tchololo [tʃololo] *n.m.* uproar, scandal *Il a tapé sa femme et ç'a fait un tchololo dans la famille.* He hit his wife and that caused an unproar in the family. (LF) <***Loc:*** LF>

tchompète [tʃɔ̃pɛt] *n.f.* sweetened water <*Loc:* SM>

tchonque ♦see CHUNK

tchopine ♦see **chopine**

tchoque-à-bloque (**chock-a-block, choque-à-bloque**) [tʃokablɔk] *adj.* **1** full **2** tightly packed *Le monde était tchoque-à-bloque dans les salles quand Joe et Cléoma jouaient.* The dance halls were packed with people when Joe and Cléoma played. (LA) **3** so-so, fair *Comment ça va? Choque-à-bloque, et toi?* How's it going? So-so, and you? (VM) <*Loc:* LA, VM, Lv88>

tcho-tcho [tʃotʃo] *n.* suckling pig <*Loc:* AV, La99>

tchote [tʃɔt] *n.f.* curler paper <*Loc:* LF>

tchou ♦see **tchouque**

tchouflangue [tʃuflɑ̃ŋ] *n.f.* small cheap business or place of amusement <*Loc:* LF>

tchoune [tʃun] *n.f.* sow <*Loc:* IB, LF, SB>

tchounie [tʃuni] *n.* pet pig <*Loc:* IB>

tchoupe ♦see **tchouque**

tchouque (**tchou, tchoute, tchoupe, tchouque-tchouque**) [tʃuk, tʃu, tʃo, tʃut, tʃup, tʃuktʃuk] *interj.* cry for calling pigs <*Loc:* AV, IB, SB, SJ, SL, SM>

tchourouc [tʃuruk] *n.m.* sandpiper, pectoral sandpiper <*Loc:* IB, JE, Lv88>

tchoute ♦see **tchouque**

tchu[1] (**chu**) [tʃy] *adj.* stupid *Ça c'est chu d'oblier ça.* It's stupid to forget that. (VM) <*Loc:* VM>

tchu[2] (**cul, cu, chu**) [tʃy, ky] *n.m./f.* **1** backside, derriere, rump, butt, ass, bottom *Ta culotte est après pendre si bas que je te vois le tchu.* Your pants are hanging so low that I see your behind. (VM) **2** end **3** idiot *Espèce de tchu.* Idiot! (VM) ◊ •**cul de bonbon** dandy <AC, La99> •**cul de chaoui** [*vulg.*] coonass <Lv88> •**cul-de-sac** dead end, blind alley <Da84> •**cul passe sus la tête** to do a flip <La99> •**cul plat** foolish person <La99> •**avoir le cul rouge** ***a*** to be angry ***b*** to have the blues <SM, VM, La99> •**nu tchu** buck naked <VM> •**ton cul!** [*vulg.*] says you! go to hell! <La99> <*Loc:* AC, AV, JE, SM, VM, Da84, La99>

te (**t'**) [tə, t] *pron.pers.* **1** *(dir.obj.)* you **Lapin, je voulais te brûler, mais je veux te jeter dans les éronces-là!* Rabbit, I wanted to burn you, but I want to throw you in the briars there! (SM, An94) *Ça qui me donne autant chagrin, je vas jamais te voir encore.* What makes me so sad is that I'm never going to see you again. (ch: *La valse d'amitié*) *Je vais venir te ramasser dans une secousse.* I'll come and pick you up in a moment. (Lv88) **2** *(ind.obj.)* to you, for you *Tu jongles pas que il y a quelqu'un qui peut t'emmener une mauvaise nouvelle.* You don't think that someone could bring you bad news. (VM, ch: *La nouvelle d'un étranger*) **Là, je vas te jouer une valse t'as jamais entendu. Je connais pas si ça va sonner bien, mais je vas te la jouer quand même.* Now I'll play a waltz that you never heard. I don't know if it will sound good, but I'll play it for you anyway. (JD, An84) *"O!" elle dit, "je vas pas te dire, parce que tu peux pas le faire."* "Oh," she said, "I'm not going to tell you because you can't do it." (SL, An94) **3** *(refl.)* yourself **Ça fait, mon papa a dit, "Si tu te sens comme ça,* GO AHEAD.*"* So my dad said, "If that's the way you feel, go ahead." (LA, An94) *Faulait que tu vas te laver avec une serviette.* You had to go and wash with a towel. (TB) *Mange pas de trop, tu vas te faire malade.* Don't eat too much, you'll make yourself sick. (LA) *Faut que tu te ménages; tu joues à la pelote demain.* You have to rest up; you're playing ball tomorrow. (LA) *Elle est mielleuse, mais tu peux pas te fier à elle.* She's sweet, but you cannot trust her. (VM) <*Loc:* AC, AL, AV, EV, IB, IV, JD, JE, LA, LF, SB, SL, TB, VM, An84, An94, Da84, Fa77, Lv88>

TEACH [titʃ] **I** *v.tr.invar.* to teach *Madame Arile, cette-là qui m'a* TEACH *mon catéchisme en français, elle, é contait des contes pour Compère Bouki et Compère Lapin.* Mrs. Arile, the one who taught me my catechism in French, she would tell stories about Brer Bouki and Brer Rabbit. (SL) **II** *v.intr. invar.* to teach **Il y a un petit prêtre qui est venu à l'*ADULT SCHOOL *pour nous* TEACH. There's a little priest who came to Adult School to teach us. (EV) <*Loc:* EV, LF, SL, TB, Lv88, Ph36>

TEAKETTLE [tikɛl, tikɛt, tikɛdl] *n.m.* teakettle, kettle for boiling water <*Loc:* LF>

TEAM [tim] *n.m.* **1** team *Moi j'ai joué deux ans mais asteur tu dis au monde que t'as joué dessus un* TEAM *de six hommes eux-autres rit après toi parce que ils ont jamais entendu parler de ça.* I played for two years, but today if you tell people that you played on a team of six men they laugh at you because they've never heard of that. (LF) **2** team, pair, harnessed team *J'avais un* TEAM *de mulets pour rabourer à neuf ans.* I had a team of mules for plowing when I was nine years old. (SL) *Il a un bon* TEAM *pour rabourer.* He has a good team for plowing. (SM) <*Loc:* EV, LF, SB, SL, SM, VM, Da84, Lv88, Ph36>

teigner ♦see **éteigner**

teindeur [tɛ̃dœr] *n.m.* dyer, one who dyes <*Loc:* VM, Lv88>

teindre [tɛ̃n, tɛ̃d(r)] (*p.p.* **teindu** [tɛ̃dy], **teint** [tɛ̃]) **I** *v.tr.* to dye, color, tint *Des œufs teindus pour Pâques.* Eggs dyed for Easter. (Lv88) *Il a teindu la chemise.* He dyed the shirt. (AV) *J'ai teint mes cheveux hier.* I dyed my hair yesterday. (AV) **Et il le mettait dans ce baril là. Ce baril là le teindait rouge.* And he would put it [whiskey] in that barrel. That barrel would give it a red tint. (VM) **II se teindre** *v.pron.* to dye (e.g. one's hair) **Se teindre les cheveux.* To dye one's hair. (Da84) <*Loc:* AV, VM, Da84, Lv88>

teint [tɛ̃] *n.m.* complexion <*Loc:* Da84>

teinter [tɛ̃te] *v.tr.* to dye, color, tint <*Loc:* Da84>

teinture [tɛ̃tyr] *n.f.* **1** dye, color, tint **2** tincture of iodine <*Loc:* Da84>

tel[1] **(telle)** [tel, tɛl] *adj.* **1** a certain **Il dit, "juste dis tu veux de la pluie tel temps, et tu l'auras."* He says, "Just say that you want rain at a certain time and you will have it." (SL, An94) **2** as is, in the same way *Il devait arranger ma maison, mais il l'a laissée telle.* He needed to clean up my house but he left it as is. (SM) ◊ **•tel comme** just like *Et la vieille Indien à peu près cent ans, alle dit, "Garde voir. Tu bois droite ayoù la craque, telle comme moi!"* And the old Indian, about 100 years old, she says, "Look at that! You drink at the crack, just like me!" (LF) **Il est bon tel comme il est.* He is good just the way he is. (Da84) *Les Miguez là, eusse salait les ours, telle comme tu sales la viande de cochon, ou quelque chose comme ça.* Those Miguez, they would salt the bears, just as you salt pork or something like that. (LF) <LF, Da84> **•tel et tel / telle et telle** ***a*** such and such *Un* PARTY *à soir telle et telle place.* A party tonight at such and such a place. (EV) *Telle et telle personne a été au cinéma.* Such and such a person went to the movies. (AV) ***b*** some . . . or another *So, il les a dit que tel et tel temps que il faudra qu'eux-autres déloge parce que une de ses enfants voulait rester dans la maison.* So, he told them that sometime or another they would have to move out because one of his children wanted to live in the house. (TB) <AV, EV, TB> **•comme tel** as such, as is *Je vas prendre ça comme tel.* I'll take that as is. (EV) <EV, Da84> <***Loc:*** AV, EV, SL, SM, An94, Da84>

tel[2] **(telle)** [tel, tɛl] *pron.indef.* one, someone **Un tel m'a dit.* Someone told me. (Da84) ◊ **•tel et tel** so and so *Mom me dit des fois des histoires parce que tel et tel avait vu le défunt grand-père assis dans le bois ou quelque chose.* Mom sometimes tells me stories because so and so had seen the late grandfather sitting in the woods or something. (EV) <AV, EV, Da84> <***Loc:*** AV, EV, TB, Da84>

télégramme [telegrɑ̃m] *n.m.* telegram <***Loc:*** AV, Da84, Fa77>

télégraphe [telegraf] *n.m.* telegraph <***Loc:*** Da84>

télégrapher [telegrafe] **I** *v.tr.* to telegraph, send a telegram *Il a télégraphé à sa fiancée.* He sent a telegram to his fiancée. (AV) **II** *v.intr.* to telegraph, send a telegram to *Ils lui ont télégraphé de venir.* They telegraphed him to come. (AV) <***Loc:*** AV, IB, LF, SJ, SL, TB, Da84>

téléphone [telefɔ̃n, telefɔrn] *n.m.* telephone *Ce maudit téléphone sonnaillait toute la grande journée.* That damn telephone would ring repeatedly all day long. (LA) <***Loc:*** AC, EV, LA, LF, TB, An94, Da84>

téléphoner [telefɔ̃ne, telefɑ̃ne, telefɔrme, telefɔrne, telesfɔrme] *v.intr.* to telephone, call on the phone *J'ai téléphoné à mon mère aujourd'hui.* I called my mother today. (AV) *Télésformez le docteur pour moi.* Phone the doctor for me. (IB) <***Loc:*** AV, IB, SM, Da84>

télévision [televiʒən] *n.m./f.* **1** television *Il n-a la passion du Christ sur le télévision.* The passion of Christ is on the television. (Lv88) *M. D. aime bien la télévision, il guette tous les soirs.* M. D. likes television, he watches [it] every evening. (AV) **2** television set <***Loc:*** AV, SL, Da84, Lv88>

tellement [tɛlmɑ̃] *adv.* **1** so *Pauvre bête, il bégayait tellement mauvais que il pouvait pas user le phone du tout.* Poor thing, he stuttered so badly that he couldn't use the telephone at all. (LA) *Il est tellement gros!* He's so fat! (AV) **Il y en a un des petits ouaouarons qu'a vu un gros bœuf, et le bœuf lui a fait peur, tellement il était gros.* There was one of the little frogs that saw a big bull and the bull scared it, so big was it. (LA, An94) **2** so much *Alle avait tellement maigri, la pauvre bête, jusqu'à alle caracolait.* She had lost so much weight, poor thing, that she was staggering. (AV) **Il y a l'histoire de Fin Voleur, mais c'est proche un embarras, tellement c'est long.* There's the story of Fin Voleur, but it's almost a bother, so long is it. (SL, An94) ◊ **•si tellement** ***a*** so **Le monde vit si tellement vieux.* People live to be so old. (An94) ***b*** such **Mais il y avait si tellement un bon constable là, seulement lui, il a cogné, ouais.* But there was such a good constable there, but he would hit. (SL, An94) ***c*** so much **Comme tu aimes Rover si tellement, je serais content de l'amener.* Since you love Rover so much, I would be happy to take him. (LA, An94) ***d*** so many *Il y avont si tellement de choses à compter.* There were so many things to count. (VM) ***e*** in such a way <LA, SL, VM, An77, An94, Lv88> <***Loc:*** AV, EV, JD, LA, SL, VM, An77, An94, Da84, Hi02>

téméraire [tẽmerær] *adj.* **1** rash, daring **Jugement téméraire.* Rash judgment. (Da84) **2** risk-taking, audacious, daring *J'aime pas laisser mes enfants aller jouer là-bas. Ses enfants sont trop téméraires.* I don't like to let my kids go over there to play. His children are too audacious. (EV) <***Loc:*** EV, Da84>

témérité [tẽmerite] *n.f.* temerity, rashness, audacity, effrontery <***Loc:*** Da84>

témoignage [tẽmwɑ̃jaʒ] *n.m.* testimony *Alle prendait les témoignages avec son petit récordeur.* She was taking testimonies with her little tape recorder. (Lv88) ◊ **•faux témoignage** false witness <Da84> <***Loc:*** AV, Da84, Lv88>

témoigner [tẽmwɑ̃je] **I** *v.tr.* to swear *Il a témoigné qu'il l'avait vu avec la femme à Howard.* He swore that he had seen him with Howard's wife. (LA) **II** *v.intr.* to testify, bear witness *Il a témoigné à la Cour hier.* He testified in court yesterday. (AV) <***Loc:*** AV, LA, Da84>

témoin [tẽmwẽ] *n.m.* **1** witness **2** second (in a duel) *Il y a deux hommes qu'étaient ses témoins. Et Antoine était pareil.* There were two men who were his seconds in the duel. And Antoine was the same. (EV) ◊ **•témoin oculaire** eyewitness <Da84> <***Loc:*** EV, Da84, Fa77>

tempe [tɑ̃p] *n.f.* **1** temple (side of the forehead) **2** sideburn <***Loc:*** AC, Da84, Fa77>

tempérament [tɑ̃peramɑ̃] *n.m.* temperament, character, disposition <***Loc:*** Da84>

température [tɑ̃peratyr] *n.f.* temperature <*Loc:* AV, Da84, Fa77>

tempête [tɑ̃pɛt] *n.f.* **1** tempest, storm **2** sudden storm <*Loc:* TB, Da84, Fa77>

temps[1] [tɑ̃, tɑ̃p] *n.m.* **1** time **Il y a plein de temps.* There's plenty of time. (Da84) **Y a plusieurs temps qu'il est pas venu.* It's been a while since he has come. (EV, Ph36) *La vieille passait son temps à broder des oreillons pour ses petits-enfants.* The old woman spent her time embroidering pillowcases for her grandchildren. (LA) *Une cigale de nuit [...]. C'est une bétaille qui reste dans la terre pour longtemps, des années de temps.* A seven-year locust. It's an insect that lives in the ground for a long time, years at a time. (LF) *Le boudin, ils preniont du riz, le foie, et de la viande, ils moulaient ça tout ensemble et ils cuisaient ça un bout de temps.* [To make] boudin, they would take rice, liver, and meat, they would mince it all together and they would cook it for a while. (AV) *C'est dommage qu'il passe son temps en coursaillerie.* It's too bad that he spends his time at debauchery. (SM) **Les temps sont durs.* Times are hard. (Da84) **2** time, moment **Le temps est arrivé.* The time has come. (Da84) *Il a fait comme si il voulait se battre, mais il a caillé quand c'était temps pour se battre.* He was acting like he wanted to fight, but he backed down when it was time to fight. (SM) *Dans un temps j'élevais des canards pour avoir du plaisir.* At one time I raised ducks for fun. (TB) **3** beat *Valse à deux temps.* Waltz with two variant beats. (LA, SM) ◊ **•temps de guerre** wartime tour of duty *J'ai passé mon temps de guerre en Italie.* I did my wartime tour of duty in Italy. (SL) <SL> **•à temps** on time, in time **Juste à temps.* Just in time. (Da84) <Da84> **•au même temps** at the same time <Da84> **•avoir un {du} bon temps** to have a good time *Je vas avoir un bon temps ce soir avec Albert.* I'm going to have a good time this evening with Albert. (AV) *Il aimait beaucoup bêtiser et rire et avoir du bon temps.* He liked to fool around and laugh and have a good time. (Lv88) <AV, IB, LF, SB, SL, SM, TB, Da84, Lv88> **•avoir un temps dur** to have a hard time <Da84> **•beaucoup de temps** a long time <SM, VM> **•c'est temps** it's time **C'est temps de se lever.* It's time to get up. (Da84) <Da84> **•aucun temps** no time, no time at all **Well, ça pas pris aucun temps.* Well, that didn't take any time at all. (Gu82) *Il va être ici dans aucun temps.* He'll be here in no time. (SM) <SM, Gu82, Lv88> **•dans ce temps-là / dans ce temps ça-là / dans ces temps-ça** in those days, at that time *Oui mais les ouragans était dangereux dans ce temps ça là. Il y a eu des dommages de la levée.* Yes, but hurricanes were dangerous in those days. There was damage to the levee. (SB) *C'est moi qu'étais en charge de bâtir ce bateau-là. Pape était mort dans ces temps-là.* I'm the one who was in charge of building this boat. Dad was dead at that time. (TB) **Si t'avais trente-cinq sous pour aller au bal dans ces temps ça-là, tu dansais brave.* If you had thirty-five cents to go to the dance in those days, you danced confidently. (An94) <EV, IB, LF, SB, TB, VM, An94, Lv88> **•dans l'air du temps** way up high <Da84> **•dans le vieux temps** in the old days *Ils ont chauté le devant de la maison comme dans le vieux temps.* They whitewashed the front of the house with lime like in the old days. (LA) *Et dans le vieux temps eux-autres faisait les draps avec du coton jaune.* And in the old days they made sheets with yellow cotton. (TB) <LA, LF, TB, An94> **•dans rien de temps** in no time at all <SM, Da84> **•(de) temps en temps** once in a while, from time to time, occasionally *Temps en temps, je fais* FUN *de lui.* Occasionally I make fun of him (JE) *Tu mets une* CUP *de farine et une* CUP *de* COOKING OIL *et puis là tu le mets en dedans pour trente minutes et là tu le brasses de temps en temps.* You take a cup of flour and a cup of cooking oil, and then you put it inside for thirty minutes, and then you stir it from time to time. (SM) <JE, SM, Da84> **•du temps que** while, when *Du temps que je travaillais pour Texaco, on travaillait toujours sur les bateaux. Ça fait j'ai jamais arrêté de faire la charpente.* While I was working for Texaco, we still worked on boats. So, I've never stopped doing carpentry work. (TB) <TB> **•en ces temps-là** at that time <AC> **•en temps perdu** in my free time *Et en temps perdu, plein souvent j'ai continué à lire son livre et à étudier moi-même.* And in my free time, quite often I've continued to read his book and to study on my own. (LF) <LF> **•jusqu'à temps** until <Lv88> **•le temps à Pascal est fini** the times of abundance are over <La99> **•le temps me dure (de / que)** I am anxious (to), I can hardly wait (for) *Le temps me dure qu'il arrive.* I can't hardly wait till he arrives. (VM) **Le temps me dure d'arriver.* I am anxious to get there. (Da84) <VM, Da84> **•mettre du temps** to take time, take a while *Il est timide. Il met du temps à se dégêner.* He is timid. It takes him a while to get over his shyness. (VM) <VM, Da84> **•prendre son temps** to take one's time <Da84> **•tous les temps en temps** from time to time *Je passe à travers des Opélousas tous les temps en temps.* I pass through Opelousas from time to time. (Lv88) *Il me donnait une petite chique tous les temps en temps.* He would give me a small chew once in a while. (AC) <AC, Lv88> **•tout le temps** always, all the time *Il est tout le temps soûl. C'est un bon-à-rien.* He's always drunk. He's a worthless fellow. (SM) *Il mange tout le temps.* He's always eating. (JE) <EV, IB, JE, LA, SM, TB, VM, An94, Lv88, Wh83> **•le vieux temps passé** the old days *Ça ressemble à le vieux temps passé.* It's just like the old days. (AV) <AV, Lv88> **•il y a plusieurs temps** it's been a long time <Lv88> **•il y plusieurs temps passés** a long time ago, in the past *Il y a plusieurs temps passés, c'était vaillant.* A long time ago, it was nice. (AV) <AV> <*Loc:* AC, AV, EV, IB, JE, SB, SL, SM, TB, VM, An94, Da84, Gu00, Gu82, Hi02, La99, Lv88, Wh83>

temps[2] [tɑ̃, tɑ̃p] *n.m.* weather *Ça tout dépend dessus le temps dans le Nord de l'Amérique.* It all depends on the weather in North America. (SM) *Le temps était après se baisser.* The weather was getting overcast. (LA) *Il y a un mauvais temps qui se brasse dans l'est.* There's some bad weather stirring up in the east. (LA) ◊ •**temps bleu** thunderstorm *Tu ferais mieux de te dépêcher! Tu vois le temps bleu qui s'en vient?* You've got to hurry. Do you see the thunderstorm that's coming? (Guoo) <Guoo> •**temps boucané** ***a*** gloomy, overcast weather ***b*** hazy weather *Le temps est boucané.* The weather is hazy. (SM) <TB, SM, La99> •**temps couvert** cloudy, overcast weather <Da84> •**temps sec** drought <TB> •**avoir du bon {beau} temps** to have good weather <Da84> •**faire beau temps** to be good weather <Da84> •**faire mauvais temps** to be bad weather <Da84> •**le temps est à la pluie** it's rainy weather <Da84> •**le temps est après se gâter** the weather is spoiling <Da84> •**le temps est couvert** it's cloudy <Da84> <***Loc:*** LA, SM, TB, Da84, Guoo, Wh83>

tenable [tənab(l)] *adj.* tenable <***Loc:*** Da84>

tenant [tənɑ̃] *n.m.* tenant farmer, sharecropper <***Loc:*** VM>

tend-fil [tɑ̃fil] *n.m.* wire stretcher <***Loc:*** Fa77>

tendance [tɑ̃dɑ̃s] *n.f.* tendency, inclination <***Loc:*** Da84>

tendon (**tendron**) [tɑ̃dɔ̃, tɑ̃drɔ̃] *n.m.* tendon, sinew *Mon tendron dans mon pied fait mal.* The tendon in my foot hurts. (AV) <***Loc:*** AV, Da84>

tendre[1] [tɑ̃n, tɑ̃d(r)] **I** *v.tr.* **1** to tighten (a wire) *Tendre un fil.* To tighten a wire. (LA) **2** to set (a trap) *Il a tendu le piège.* He set the trap. (LA) **3** to spread out (clothing to dry) *Elle tend son linge sur l'herbe.* She spreads her clothes on the grass. (SB) **II se tendre** *v.pron.* to get taut, get tight *La peau sus la chaise s'a tendu à mesure que ça chessait.* The skin on the chair tightened as it dried. (VM) <***Loc:*** LA, SB, VM, Da84>

tendre[2] [tɑ̃n, tɑ̃d(r)] *adj.* tender, affectionate *Le monde était beaucoup tendre.* People were very affectionate. (AV) <***Loc:*** AV, SB, Da84>

tendrement [tɑ̃drəmɑ̃] *adv.* tenderly, fondly, affectionately *Si j'avais un amant qui m'aimerait si tendrement.* If I had lover who loved me so tenderly. (IB, ch: *Les amours sont courts*) <***Loc:*** IB, Da84>

tendresse [tɑ̃drɛs] *n.f.* tenderness, kindness, softness <***Loc:*** Da84>

tendron ♦see **tendon**

tendzir ♦see **attendrir**

teneur [tənœr] *n.m.* keeper ◊ •**teneur de magasin** storekeeper <Da84> <***Loc:*** Da84>

tenir (**tiendre**) [t(ə)nir, tjɛ̃n, tjɛ̃d(r), tʃɛ̃n, tʃɛ̃d(r)] **I** *v.tr.* **1** to hold, hold onto *Cette femme va tenir le bébé.* That woman is going to hold the baby. (LF) *Tu pouvais pas être vu marcher dans le chemin à tiendre la main de la fille, non.* You couldn't be seen walking in the road holding the girl's hand, no. (TB) *Tiendre quelque chose en ta main.* To hold something in your hand. (JE) *Cette femme est après tiendre un bébé.* That woman is holding a baby. (LA) *Tiens ça.* Hold this. (AC) **2** to hold, contain **Le bassin tient deux gallons.* The pan holds two gallons. (Da84) **3** to hold, hold back, retain *Dans le bayou y a une bôme pour tiendre les herbes du bayou.* In the bayou there is a boom to hold back the grasses. (TB) **4** to keep, maintain (in a certain place or state) *Elle me mettait couché au ras d'elle pour me tiendre chaud.* She laid me down next to her to keep me warm. (SL) *Ce plancher est du ciment avec les tuyaux pour tiendre à peu près 85 degrés de chaleur dans cette eau tout le temps, tous les 24 heures.* This floor is made of cement with pipes to keep about 85 degrees of heat in this water all the time, 24 hours a day. (TB) *On après te tiendre icitte?* Are we keeping you? (LF) *Sur une roue qui le tient en bas de l'eau contre la terre, comme ça le poisson peut pas sortir.* On a wheel which keeps it at the bottom of the water so that the fish cannot get out. (SM) **5** to run, operate, manage (a store, business, etc.) **Tenir un café.* To manage or run a café. (Da84) *Mon père tenait un magasin de groceries.* My father ran a grocery store. (LF) **6** to have for sale *La seule petite grocerie icitte qui tient des pralines fraîches.* The only little grocery store around here that has fresh pralines. (Lv88) **II** *v.intr.* **1** to hold, hold out, last **Cette colle peut pas tenir.* This glue cannot hold. (Da84) **Son argent va pas tenir.* His money won't hold out. (Da84) **2** to stay, stay away *Ça tient dans les bois dans l'eau douce.* They [wood ducks] stay in the woods in the fresh water. (JE) **III se tenir** *v.pron.* to keep o.s., hold o.s. *Tiens-toi droite.* Sit up straight. (EV) **Se tenir assis.* To remain seated. (Da84) **Se tenir ensemble.* To hold together, keep together. (Da84) **Se tenir paré.* to keep o.s. ready. (Da84) **Se tenir réveillé.* To stay awake. (Da84) **Se tenir tranquille.* To keep quiet. (Da84) ◊ •**tenir à** to like, have a liking for, care for **Je tiens pas à la viande.* I don't care for meat. (Da84) <Da84> •**tenir à sa parole** to keep one's word <Da84> •**tenir bon** to hold fast, hold on **Tiens bon!* Hold tight! <Da84> •**tenir compagnie** to keep (s.o.) company *Moi je veux aller fumer en dehors, tu vas y tiendre compagnie un élan?* I'm going to go smoke outside, are you going to keep him company for a spell? (TB) <TB> •**tenir compte** to keep score, keep track of, keep account of <Da84> •**tenir de** ***a*** to like, have a liking for, care for **Je tiens pas de danser.* I don't care to dance. (Da84) ***b*** to take after **Il tient de sa mère.* He takes after his mother. (Da84) <EV, Da84> •**tenir des livres** to keep the books *Et là j'appelais tout le monde pour que ça vient travailler dans la facterie. Et je tenais des livres, je tenais leurs livres.* And I called all those people to have them come to work in the factory. And I kept the books, I kept their books. (TB) <TB, Da84> •**tenir en l'air** to hold up *Je dis, t'écoutes, Défêné, avant que je mets 200 ou 250* *dollars pour tiendre mes culottes en l'air je vas prendre une corde.* I said, listen, Déféné, before I put out $200 or $250 to hold my pants up [with an alligator skin belt], I'll get a rope. (TB) <TB> **•tenir ensemble** to hold together *Juste de la terre, de la mousse, et de la chaux, et tout travailler ça avec tes pieds et tout l'affaire comme ça. Pareil comme tu prendais une brique et de la mettre, mais c'était en terre. Et de la mousse pour tenir l'affaire ensemble.* Just earth, and moss, and lime, and work that down with your feet and all that. Just as if you took a brick and put it down, but it was made of earth. And moss to hold the whole thing together. (LF) <LF> **•tenir l'école** to teach school <VM> **•tenir (la) maison** to keep house *Elle tenait la maison et cuisait à dîner pour nous-autres, elle lavait notre linge.* She kept the house and cooked dinner for us, she washed our clothes. (IB) <IB, Da84> **•tenir la paix** to keep the peace *Ça fait pour tiendre la paix sur le job on parlait en anglais.* So, to keep the peace on the job we spoke English. (TB) <LF, TB> **•tenir une brique** to be drunk <JE, La99> **•tenir une conversation** to have a conversation, hold a conversation *La seule qui peut parler français et tiendre une conversation c'est ma plus vieille.* The only one who can speak French and hold a conversation is my oldest daughter. (TB) *Ils pouvont pas tiendre une conversation en français.* They can't hold a conversation in French. (TB) <TB, Da84> **•se tenir à côté** to keep away, stay away *Tiens-toi à côté. C'est dangereux.* Keep away. It's dangerous. (LA) <LA, Da84> **•se tenir comme un gris-gris** to hold on very tightly to one another <LF, La99> **•se tenir debout** to remain standing <Da84> **•se tenir en bonne santé** to keep fit <Da84> ***<Loc:*** AC, AV, EV, IB, JE, LA, LF, SB, SL, SM, TB, VM, Da84, Hi02, La99, Lv88, Ph36>

tennis [tẽnis] *n.m.* **1** tennis **2** tennis ball **3** tennis racket **4** tennis court **5** tennis shoe ***<Loc:*** Da84>

tentable [tɑ̃tab(l)] *adj.* tempting, appealing, desirable *Il est beaucoup tentable, ce vaillant homme.* This handsome man is very appealing. (AV) ***<Loc:*** AV, Da84, Hi02>

tentation [tɑ̃tasjɔ̃] *n.f.* temptation ***<Loc:*** Da84>

tente [tɑ̃t] *n.f.* tent ***<Loc:*** AC, Da84>

tenter[1] [tɑ̃te] *v.tr.* **1** to tempt, attract, interest *Peut-être que vous serait intéressé avoir votre* TAPE RECORDER *et tout, c'est juste pour voir si ça vous tente.* Perhaps you'd be interested in having your tape recorder and all, it's just to see if that interests you. (LF) *Ça m'a jamais tenté, il y a trop d'autres choses à manger.* That has never tempted me, there are too many other things to eat. (LF) **2** to try, attempt, undertake *Tenter sa chance.* To try one's luck. (VM) ***<Loc:*** AV, LF, VM, Da84>

tenter[2] [tɑ̃te] *v.intr.* to camp, live in a tent *Ils avont tenté un mois avant ils pouviont bâtir une maison.* They had lived in a tent for a month before they could build a house. (VM) ***<Loc:*** VM>

tenture [tɑ̃tyr] *n.f.* flare, spread (of a boat) *Pour faire une pirogue, ça c'est le moule qu'ils usont. Ça fait la bonne tenture sur les deux bords.* To make a pirogue, that's the mold they use. That gives you a good flare on both sides. (LF) ***<Loc:*** LF, TB>

terboliser (**tribouliser**) [tærbolize, tribulize] *v.tr.* to disturb, upset, perturb *Tribouliser quelqu'un par une mauvaise nouvelle.* To upset someone with bad news. (SJ) *Une nouvelle triboulisante.* Upsetting news. (SJ) ***<Loc:*** IB, SB, SJ>

tère ♦see **terre**[2]

térébenthine [terebɑ̃tin, terabɑ̃tin, tærbɑ̃tin, tyrbɑ̃tin, turmɑ̃tin] *n.f.* turpentine *C'est bon pour traiter ça, la térébenthine; mon j'en garde tout le temps.* Turpentine is good for treating illnesses. I always keep some on hand. (TB) ***<Loc:*** AC, AV, TB, Da84>

térir ♦see **tarir**

terme [tærm] *n.m.* **1** word, term *Les termes de "*BUSHEL*" et tout ça c'était pas quelque chose qu'était commun.* Terms like "bushel" and all that were not common. (LF) *Ce terme-là est pas beaucoup servi.* That word isn't used much. (VM) **2** term, condition (e.g. of a sale) **3** term (of office, of a prison sentence, etc.) *J'ai couru dans 1952, et j'ai gagné et j'ai resté trois termes de quatre ans. Douze ans. Et là j'ai* GIVE UP *ça, et je travaillais dans l'office d'assesseur.* I ran in 1952, and I won, and I stayed for three four-year terms. Twelve years. And then I gave that up and I worked in the assessor's office. (LF) **Hébert et Guillory, mes vieux amis de la Grand Prairie qu'est aseteur "après servir des termes de vie" comme ça dit, dans ein* NURSING HOME *dans les Opélousas.* Hebert and Guillory, my old friends from Grand Prairie who are serving life terms, as they say, in a nursing home in Opelousas. (Wh83) **4** term, quarter (period of time in school) **Un terme d'école.* A school term. (Da84) ◊ **•en termes** plainly, frankly <JE, VM> ***<Loc:*** JE, LF, VM, Da84, Lv88, Wh83>

terminer [tærmine] **I** *v.tr.* to terminate, end, conclude, wind up, finish *L'histoire a été terminée.* The story was ended. (AV) **II** *v.intr.* to come to an end, finish *Ça va terminer mal.* That's going to end badly. (VM) *Ça jouait tout le temps "*HOME SWEET HOME*" pour annoncer que le bal terminait.* They always used to play "Home Sweet Home" to announce that the dance was over. (EV) ***<Loc:*** AV, EV, VM, Da84>

termite [tærmit] *n.f.* termite, white ant ***<Loc:*** Da84>

ternir [tærnir] **I** *v.tr.* to cause to dull, tarnish *Si tu laisses tes affaires en argent dehors, ça va les ternir.* If you leave your silver things out, it will tarnish them. (LA) **II** *v.intr.* to dull, tarnish *Ils ont amené mon bon plat au bois et il a terni.* They took my good platter to the woods and it got tarnished. (VM) **III se ternir** *v.pron.* to tarnish, become tarnished *Si tu soignes pas tes affaires, ça va se ternir.* If you don't take care of your things, they will tarnish.. (LA) ***<Loc:*** LA, VM, Da84>

terrain [terɛ̃] *n.m.* **1** lot, plot of land *Mon père a venu acheter un terrain à peu près à dix miles en haut d'ici.* My father came to buy a piece of property about ten miles up the bayou from here. (LF) **2** ground, terrain ◊ **•terrain d'école** school playground <VM> **•terrain du jeu** sport field (for baseball, football, etc.) *On charge l'entrée du terrain du jeu.* We charge admission to the field [for sports]. (Lv88) <Lv88> <***Loc:*** EV, LF, VM, Da84, Fa77, Lv88>

terrasse [teras] *n.f.* terrace, embankment, bank <***Loc:*** Da84>

terrassé, -e [terase] *adj.* tired **Alle est térrassée à ç'soir, alle a travaillé dur.* She is tired tonight, she worked hard. (EV, Ph36) <***Loc:*** EV, Ph36>

terrasser [terase] *v.tr.* to terrace, bank up *Terrasser un clos de riz avec des levées.* To terrace a rice field with levees. (VM) *Terrasser un terrain pour planter.* To terrace a plot of land to plant. (SL) <***Loc:*** SL, VM, Da84>

terre[1] [tær] *n.f.* **1** earth, world *Qui a créé la terre et le ciel?* Who created the earth and the heavens? (LA) **Mais moi, j'vas vous dire la franche vérité: y a pas parsône dessus la terre qu'est plus bête qu'ein Amaricain.* But I'm going to tell you the honest to goodness truth: there is no one on earth dumber than an American. (Gu82) **2** dirt, soil, earth *On a fait un plancher en terre. Mettre ça là, piler ça. C'était tout fait à la main. Ils venaient là et mettre de la chaux.* We made a dirt floor. We put it down, packed it down. It was all made by hand. They came along and put down lime. (LF) *Les poules étaient après se vanner en bas de la maison ayoù la terre était toujours sec.* The chickens were taking a dust bath under the house where the dirt was still dry. (LA) **3** ground *Il a calé un poteau dans la terre.* He planted a pole into the ground. (SM) *Ils ont cassé la terre pour le nouveau presbytère.* They broke ground for the new rectory. (EV) *Une cigale, ça commence avec un ver dans la terre, une larve.* A cicada begins his life as a worm in the ground, a grub worm. (AV) *Malgré qu'il s'a détruit, il a été enterré dans de la terre sacrée.* Even though he committed suicide, he was buried in sacred ground. (LA) **4** land *Il y avait pas la moitié de la terre qu'était cultivable.* Less than half of the land was arable. (LA) *Ça, c'était du monde qui connaissait comment cultiver la terre.* They were people who knew how to cultivate the land. (LA) *La levée d'un clos de riz suit les contours de la terre.* The rice field levee follows the contour of the land. (LA) **5** land, property *Je veux te parler concernant le* PIPELINE *que ça veut passer sus notre terre.* I want to talk to you about the pipeline they want to run on our land. (VM) *Ils ont continué le chemin jusqu'à la terre des écoles.* They continued the road up to the school board property. (LA) *Et puis là d'autres enfants à Monsieur Amédé Miller, aussi, eux restait la quatrième terre de la terre à nous-autres.* And then other children of Mr. Amédé Miller also lived on the fourth estate over from us. (IB) ◊ **•terre de bois** woodland <Da84> **•terre égale** level land <AC> **•terre forte** fertile soil <AC> **•terre friable** dirt, loose soil <Da84> **•terre grasse *a*** clay, clay soil ***b*** gumbo, type of sticky soil <EV, VM, Da84> **•terre haute** high ground, land that does not flood <Lv88> **•terre meuble** dirt, loose soil <Da84> **•terre mourante** black, porous, rich soil <EV> **•terre neuf** newly cleared land that has not yet been cultivated <EV, Lv88, Ph36> **•terre niveau** level land <AC> **•terre pauvre** poor, unfertile soil <AC> **•terre plange** level land <Da84> **•terre rapportée** silt, alluvium <Da84, Lv88> **•terre riche** fertile soil <AC> **•terre sainte** holy land <Da84> **•terre tremblante {mouvante}** quicksand <VM, Da84, Lv88> **•à terre *a*** on the ground, onto the ground *[La] paille est tout partout à terre.* Straw is all over the place on the ground. (JE) ***b*** on land, onto land *Ç'avait tout poussé les bateaux à terre avec l'eau.* It [the hurricane] had pushed the boats onto land with the water. (JE) <JE> **•à la terre** on the shore *Il n-a du monde qui pêche des goujons, mais ça c'est un différent de qualité de pêche, parce qu'il faut ça ils les pêchent à la terre.* There are people who fish flathead catfish, but that's a different kind of fishing, because they have to fish them from the shore. (SL) <SL> **•mettre par terre** to put down, set down <Da84> **•par terre** on the ground, on the floor *Y'a une craque dans le verre qu'a été capoté par terre.* There's a crack in the glass that was dropped on the floor. (Lv88) *Dans les Philippines, tout le monde se couche par terre.* In the Philippines, everyone sleeps on the ground. (VM) *J'espère un gros vent va venir là et à peu près tout jeter par terre.* I expect a strong wind to come and blow just about everything to the ground. (SL) **Le hibou était par terre; il était mort. Et ils l'ont examiné.* The owl was on the ground; it was dead. And they examined it. (EV, An94) <EV, JD, TB, VM, An84, An94, Da84, Lv88> <***Loc:*** AC, AV, EV, IB, JD, JE, LA, SL, TB, VM, An84, An94, Da84, Gu82, Hi02, Lv88, Ph36>

terre[2] **(taire, tère)** [tær] *n.m./f.* stingray *Les taires a des piquants aussi, ça c'est d'autre chose. C'est mauvais.* Stingrays have spines too, that's another thing. They're bad. (TB) <***Loc:*** IB, LF, TB, VM, Da84, Gu00, Lv88, Re31>

Terrebonnier [tærbɔ̃je] *n.m.* person from Terrebonne parish *Le monde de Lafourche va dire "ces Terrebonniers là."* People in Lafourche Parish will say "those Terrebonniers." (TB) <***Loc:*** TB>

terrestre [terɛs(t)] *adj.* terrestrial, earthly **Paradis terrestre.* Garden of Eden, earthly paradise. (Da84) <***Loc:*** Da84>

terreur [terœr] *n.f.* terror, dread, fear <***Loc:*** Da84>

terrible[1] [terib(l)] *adj.* **1** terrible, dreadful *Il était beaucoup terrible, lui. Il avait la tête dure, dure.* He was really terrible. He was very hard headed. (EV) **Enfant terrible.* Problem child. (Da84) **2** abundant, in great quantity *L'année passée, il n-a eu une terrible récolte d'écrivisses.* Last year there was an abundant crawfish harvest. (Lv88) *Il y avait des écrevisses terribles quand il a laissé l'eau aller sur son riz.*

There were great quantities of crawfish when he flooded his rice. (VM) <***Loc:*** AC, AV, EV, VM, Da84, Lv88>

terrible[2] [terib(l)]] *adv.* very, extremely **Il y avait un homme qui était après voyager à pied dans le bois et il y a un gros, gros chat, terrible gros chat qui a tombé derrière lui.* There was a man who was traveling on foot in the woods and a big cat, extremely big cat came after him. (AC, An94) *J'aimais terrible la musique.* I really loved music. (EV) <***Loc:*** AC, EV, An94>

terriblement [teribləmɑ̃] *adv.* **1** terribly, dreadfully, awfully **Terriblement malade.* Terribly sick. (Da84) **2** really *Ça a été beaucoup bien, terriblement bien.* That went very well, really well. (EV) *J'aimais terrible la musique et j'aimais terriblement danser et j'ai pas pour me vanter, j'étais une bonne danseuse.* I really loved music and I really loved to dance and I don't have to brag about it, I was a good dancer. (EV) <***Loc:*** EV, Da84, Fa77>

terrier [terje] *n.m.* hole digger <***Loc:*** VM>

terrifiant, -e [terifjɑ̃, -ɑ̃t] *adj.* terrifying *Une orage terrifiante.* A terrifying rainstorm. (LA) <***Loc:*** LA, Da84>

terrifier [terifje] *v.tr.* to terrify, frighten *Le jeune m'a terrifié.* The young man frightened me. (AV) <***Loc:*** AV, Da84>

terrine [terin] *n.f.* bowl, serving bowl <***Loc:*** SM>

territoire [teritwar] *n.m.* **1** territory **Il y avait des Indiens droite ici pendant un temps. C'était leur territoire.* There were Indians right here for a time. It was their territory. (SL, An94) **2** region, area, district *Si jamais vous part pour ce territoire là, j'ai une sœur qui reste là-bas à Ibérie.* If you ever head over to that area, I have a sister who lives down there in Iberia. (LF) **3** bailiwick ◊ •**territoire des Indiens** Indian territory <Da84> <***Loc:*** AV, LF, SL, An94, Da84>

tes ♦see **ton**

test [tɛs(t)] *n.m.* test *Le docteur a analysé les résultats de mon test.* The docteur analyzed the results of my test. (VM) *Faut qu'alle soye là-bas de bon matin pour prendre ses tests pour son sang.* She has to be there early to get her blood tests. (TB) <***Loc:*** LA, LF, TB, VM, Da84>

testament [tɛstɑ̃mɑ̃] *n.m.* **1** testament **2** last will and testament <***Loc:*** Da84>

testicule [testikyl] *n.f.* testicle <***Loc:*** Da84>

testifier [tɛstifje] *v.intr.* to testify, bear witness *Il a testifié au juge.* He testified to the judge. (AV) <***Loc:*** AV, Da84>

têt [tɛt] *n.* lodging for farm stock ◊ •**têt à cochons** pigshed <Lv88> •**têt à poules** chicken coop <LA> <***Loc:*** LA, Lv88>

tétanos (tatanas) [tetɑ̃nos, tatɑ̃nas, tatɑ̃na, tatɑ̃nɔs, tẽtɑ̃nɔs] *n.m.* tetanus, lockjaw *On s'erleuve pas tout le temps de la tatanos, non!* People don't always recover from lockjaw. (TB) <***Loc:*** LF, SB, TB, VM, Da84, Fa77>

tête[1] [tet, tɛt] *n.f.* **1** head *Il a une méchant grosse tête.* He has a heck of a big head. (EV) *Je l'ai roqué sur la tête.* I hit him in the head. (Lv88) **Il ont mis la tête en bas à l'abri du vent.* They put their heads down to shelter them from the wind. (Gu82) *Y a deux jeunes garçons qui s'a fait tuer là, couper la tête.* There are two boys who got killed there, they got their heads cut off. (TB) **2** head, mind *Ça éclaircit la tête plus si tu bois du café.* It clears your head more if you drink some coffee. (TB) *Je dis ça dans mon idée, tu connais tes traitements, tu dis des prières dans ta tête.* I say them [the prayers] in my mind, you know the treatments, you say the prayers in your head. (TB) **3** head of hair *Les mouches m'a pris dans les cheveux dessus le chemin! Oh, parle d'une affaire, ma tête était pleine de mouches à miel.* The bees got into my hair on the road! Oh, talk about a dilemma, my hair was full of bees. (TB) **4** head, highest position of leadership or authority *Y en a qu'est des gens de grands accomplissements qui travaillent à la tête des banques ou des bonnes positions, des ingénieurs et tout.* There are some who are people of great accomplishments, who work at the head of banks or good positions, engineers and all. (TB) **5** head, chief, leader *Il était le tête de les Indiens, tous les Indiens, il était le* CHAIRMAN OF THE TRIBAL COUNCIL. He was the head of the Indians, he was the chairman of the tribal council. (TB) **6** certain place on a trawlnet where the mesh comes together ◊ •**tête à raisins** [*offensive*] black person <Lv88> •**tête à tête** private talk, face to face <Da84, Hi02> •**tête baille** towheaded <Da84> •**tête chauve** bald-headed <Da84> •**tête d'ail** bulb or head of garlic <Da84> •**tête de bête / tête d'animaux** head of cattle *Avant la grande eau, il avait 250 têtes de bêtes dans le bois.* Before the flood, he had 250 head of cattle in the woods. (SL) <LF, SL> •**tête de caouène** ***a*** hardhead ***b*** female genitalia <Lv88> •**tête de chat** clevis (as on a plow) <IB> •**tête de chou** head of cabbage <SM, VM, Da84> •**tête de femme** ironweed <SB> •**tête de laitue** head of lettuce <SM, VM> •**tête de lampe** lamp burner <VM> •**tête de lit** head of the bed <SL> •**tête de pluie** large cloud that brings rain *Cette tête de pluie ressemble du tactac.* That raincloud looks like popcorn. (Gu00) <Gu00> •**tête d'oignon** onion <VM> •**tête d'oreiller** pillowcase <SB, SL, SM, VM, Lv88> •**tête-dure** hard-headed, stubborn ***a*** *Il est tête-dure comme tout.* He's as stubborn as can be. (SM) ***b*** hardheaded person, stubborn person *Une de ces têtes-dures.* One of those hardheads. (TB) <EV, IB, SM, TB, VM, Da84, Ph36> •**tête dure comme un bourriquet** very stubborn <La99> •**tête rouge** redhead duck *Et ça ici c'est le tête rouge, le REDHEAD.* This one is the redhead. (TB) <LF, TB> •**tête-vert** mallard duck *Nous on appelle ça le tête-vert. Le Français appelle ça un col-vert.* We call that [the mallard] a 'green-head.' The Frenchman calls it a 'green-collar.' (TB) <AL, TB> •**à haute tête** out loud <VM, La99> •**à pleine tête** ***a*** very loudly, at the top of one's lungs *Un vieux homme a passé et il disait à pleine tête: "Moi, j'veux mourir."* An old man passed by and was saying at the top of his lungs: "I want to die." (VM) *Ils criaient à pleine* *tête à force ils aimaient la musique.* They liked the music so much they were screaming at the top of their lungs. (Lv88) ***b*** out loud <VM, La99, Lv88> **•avoir la tête égrichée** to have disheveled or wild hair <EV> **•avoir tous leur tête dans le même bonnet** to think alike, be in complete agreement (of several people) <La99> **•avoir une bonne tête** to be smart <Da84> **•avoir une tête** to have a good memory <AV> **•avoir une tête de caïman** to be obstinate, be stubborn <SB> **•avoir une tête de poule** to have a poor memory <AV, La99> **•en tête** head, in charge **L'homme en tête.* The man in charge. (Da84) <Da84> **•être à la tête** to be at the head <Da84> **•être dans (qqch) par dessus la tête** to be over one's head (in troubles, etc.) <Da84> **•faire à sa tête** to be headstrong <Da84> **•prendre la tête** to take the lead <Da84> **•se mettre à la tête** to take charge <Da84> ***<Loc:*** AC, AL, AV, EV, IB, JE, LA, LF, SB, SL, SM, TB, VM, An94, Da84, Gu00, Gu82, Hi02, La99, Lv88, Ph36>

tête[2] [tɛt, tet] *n.m.* **1** teat (of an animal) **2** breast (of a human) ***<Loc:*** LF, SB>

tété [tete] *n.m.* **1** nipple (of a human) *Elle a eu du mal à faire son premier prendre le tété.* She had trouble getting her firstborn to take the nipple. (LA) **2** teat (of an animal) **"Well," il dit, "j'ai vu une vache avec cinq veaux." "Oh oh! Mais," il dit, "quoi ce que ça fait? Il y a un veau qui avait pas de tété?"* "Well," he says, "I saw a cow with five calves." "Oh oh!" he says, "what happened? There's a calf without a teat?" (SL, An94) ***<Loc:*** IB, LA, SL, SM, VM, An94, Da84, Lv88>

tétée [tete] *n.f.* nursing, breastfeeding (of an infant) *Son enfant braillait parce qu'il avait pas eu une pleine tétée.* Her child was was crying because he had not had a full nursing. (LA) ***<Loc:*** LA>

téter [tete] **I** *v.tr.* to nurse, suckle *La vache est après téter son veau.* The cow is nursing her calf. (LA) **II** *v.intr.* to nurse, suckle *Je connais pas quoi il y a. Le veau veut p'us téter du tout.* I don't know what's wrong. The calf will no longer nurse at all. (LA) *Ils laissent p'us téter le veau comme il veut dès qu'ils recommencent à tirer la vache.* They don't let the calf nurse at will any longer once they start milking the cow. (VM) ◊ **•faire téter** to nurse <Da84> **•si on peut pas téter maman, il faut téter mémère** you take what you can get, you have to make the best of a bad situation <SL, La99> ***<Loc:*** LA, SL, VM, Da84, Fa77, La99>

tétine [tetin] *n.f.* **1** nipple (of a human) **2** teat (of an animal) ◊ **•tétine de négresse** prairie coneflower <VM> ***<Loc:*** VM, Da84, Fa77>

téton [tetɔ̃] *n.m.* **1** breast (of a human) *Mae West avait des gros tétons.* Mae West had big breasts. (IB) **2** teat (of an animal) **Oublie pas de les dire, aussi, elle a une corne creuse et un téton gâté!* Don't forget to tell them, too, she [a cow] has a hollow horn and a spoiled teat! (EV, An94) ◊ **•téton de négresse** black-eyed susan <LF> ***<Loc:*** EV, IB, LF, An94, Da84, Hi02>

têtu, -e [tety] *adj.* stubborn, obstinate, hard-headed *Mon mari est beaucoup têtu. Il a la tête dure.* My husband is very stubborn. He has a hard head. (AV) ***<Loc:*** AV, Da84, Hi02>

texien [tɛksjɛ̃] *adj.* Texan ***<Loc:*** Hi02>

Texien, -ienne [tɛksjɛ̃, -jɛ̃n] *n.* Texan *Mon frère c'est un Texien. Il a resté 15 ans là-bas.* My brother is a Texan. He lived there for 15 years. (AV) ***<Loc:*** AV, Hi02, Lv88>

thé [te] *n.m.* **1** tea *Mon père avait l'habitude de radoucir son thé.* My father had the habit of adding more sugar to his tea [than was already added]. (EV) *Ce thé m'a renforci.* This tea strengthened me. (VM) **2** herbal tea *Des fois, Mom elle faisait du thé de sassafras ou du thé d'autre chose pour nous-autres boire ça, si on voulait boire quelque chose.* Sometimes Mom would make sassafras tea or some other kind of tea for us to drink if we wanted to drink something. (EV) *Ils bouillissaient la graine du mamou pour faire un thé.* They boiled the seeds of the coral tree to make tea. (Lv88) **3** medicinal tea *Les mangliers poussent tout partout dans les prairies. Si tu fais un thé avec les feuilles, y a rien de meilleur pour casser la fièvre.* Baccharis grow all over the place in the prairies. If you make a tea with the leaves, there's nothing better to break a fever. (Gu00) *Monsieur Trahan m'a amené de la vinéraire quèque temps passé. Il m'a dit que si tu fais un thé avec, c'est bon pour le rhume.* Mr. Trahan brought be some everlasting flowers a while back. He told me that if you use them for tea, it's good for a cold. (Gu00) ◊ **•thé de chardon** thistle tea <Da84> **•thé de laurier** bay leaf tea <Fa77> **•thé de mamou** mamou tea *C'est curatif, du thé de mamou.* Mamou tea is curative. (VM) *Y a rien de mieux que du thé de mamou pour décoller un rhume.* There's nothing better than mamou tea to clear up a cold. (VM) <SL, SM, VM> **•thé de sassafras** sassafras tea <SM> ***<Loc:*** EV, SL, SM, TB, VM, Da84, Fa77, Gu00, Hi02, Lv88>

théâtre [teat(r)] *n.m.* **1** theater **2** play, drama *Une belle salle pour faire des théâtres et des danses.* A lovely room for holding plays and dances. (SM) ***<Loc:*** SM, Da84, Fa77>

thermomètre [tærmɔ̃mɛt(r)] *n.m.* thermometer ***<Loc:*** AV, VM, Da84, Fa77>

thym [tɛ̃] *n.m.* thyme *Grand-maman d'Érath faisait des pâtés avec des gigiers de z-oie et de canards et alle les assaisonnait avec du thym qu'alle plantait dans son jardin.* Grandma from Erath made meat pies with goose and duck gizzards that she seasoned with thyme that she planted in her garden. (VM) ***<Loc:*** AV, VM>

ti[1] [ti] *adv.* particle used for emphasis (esp. in interrogatives) *Vous avez ti soupé?* Have you really eaten? (TB) *Vous avez ti été là-bas?* Have you ever been there? (SL) *Tu vas ti venir ou non?* Are you coming or not? (SM) *Ils en ont ti fait des canailleries quand ils étaient jeunes.* They sure did some bad things when they were young. (LA) ***<Loc:*** EV, LA, SL, SM, TB>

ti[2] ♦see **qui**

tibereuse [tibrøz] *n.f.* tuberose <*Loc:* VM>

tic [tik] *n.m.* tic, twitch ◊ •**tic douloureux / tic St. Honoré** facial neuralgia <Da84> <*Loc:* Da84>

tiche ♦see **tige**

ticket (**tiquette**) [tikɛ, tike, tikɛt, tiket] *n.m.* *(occ. f.)* **1** ticket (of admission, etc.) *Il faut que je foute un* CALL *à quelqu'un pour avoir des tickets.* I have to make a call to someone to get tickets. (LF) **2** ticket (given as a penalty, e.g. a traffic ticket) *Et là faut que t'achètes tes* TAG, *et si t'as pas de* TAG *sus la tcheue, tu vas te faire donner un ticket et te faire frémer en prison.* Then you have to buy tags, and if you don't have a tag on the tail [of the alligator], you'll be given a ticket and get yourself put in prison. (TB) **3** tag, price tag, label **4** coupon, voucher *Moi, j'ai travaillé pendant la guerre. [...] J'ai travaillé au* RATION BOARD, *où ils donnaient des tickets pour acheter de quoi.* I worked during the war. I worked at the ration board, where they were giving out coupons for purchasing something [to eat]. (SL) **5** ballot <*Loc:* AV, EV, IB, LF, SB, SJ, SL, SM, TB, VM, Da84, Fa77, Hi02, Lv88>

tic-tac [tiktak] *n.m.* tick-tock (of a clock) <*Loc:* Da84>

TIE [taɪ] *n.m.* railroad crosstie <*Loc:* VM>

tiède ♦see **quède**

tiédeur ♦see **quiédeur**

tien, tienne [tʃɛ̃, tʃɛ̃n] *pron.poss.* yours, your own **Le tien est plus gros que le mien.* Yours is bigger than mine. (Da84) *Il fume, le tien?* Does yours smoke? (TB) *Tous mes mêmes numéros j'ai sur la mienne là, faut que tu l'aies sur la tienne avec mon nom et mon adresse et tout dessus.* All of my numbers that I have on mine, you have to have on yours with my name and my address and all on it. (TB) ◊ •**ton tien** yours <LF> •**eusse tiennes** yours *Mes paroles de ma bouche sort pas pareil comme eusse tiennes.* The words from my mouth don't come out the same way as yours do. (LF) <LF> •**te le tien** yours *T'as bu te le tien?* Did you drink yours? (LF) <LF> <*Loc:* AV, JE, LF, TB, Da84, Hi02>

tiendre ♦see **tenir**

tienne ♦see **tien**

tiens [tjɛ̃, tʃɛ̃] *interj.* there! here! well, look here **Mais tiens, là il arrive!* There he comes! (Da84) *Tiens! Prends ça.* Here! Take this. (JE) <*Loc:* AV, JE, Da84>

tiercent (**tierçon, cairson, querçon**) [tjærsɑ̃, tjærsɔ̃, kærsɔ̃] *n.m.* small barrel that holds 33 1/3 gallons (i.e. 1/3 of 100) *J'ai vendu deux poules et trois douzaines d'œufs et ça m'a donné assez d'argent pour acheter un cairson de sucre.* I sold two chickens and three dozen eggs and that gave me enough money to buy a barrel of sugar. (Gu00) <*Loc:* AC, JD, VM, Da84, Gu82, Gu00, Lv88>

tierçon ♦see **tiercent**

tierlambèche (**tirelambêche**) [tʃærlɑ̃bɛʃ, tirlɑ̃bɛʃ] *n.f.* small bit ◊ •**en tierlambèches** to shreds, in tatters *Elle a déchiré la lettre en tierlambèches.* She ripped the letter to shreds. (LA) *Elle a déchiré les draps en tierlambèches.* She tore the sheets in tatters. (LA) <LA, Lv88> <*Loc:* LA, VM, Lv88>

tiers [tjær] *n.* third **Un tiers de gallon.* One third of a gallon. (Da84) <*Loc:* Da84, Hi02>

tige (**tiche**) [tiʃ] *n.f.* **1** stem **2** petiole (of a leaf) <*Loc:* LF, VM, Da84>

TIGHT [taɪt] *adj.* **1** tight, close-fitting *Moi, je trouvais que ses culottes étaient trop* TIGHT, *mais sa mère la laissait sortir comme ça.* I thought that her pants were too tight, but her mother would let her go out like that. (LA) **2** financially difficult, austere, tight *Dans ce temps là, tu connais, les affaires étaient* TIGHT. In those days, you know, things were tight. (EV) *Et quand les affaires venaient assez* TIGHT *que il y avait pas de bon sucre, il y en a plein qui usait du sirop dans le café.* When times were so hard that there was no good sugar, many would use syrup in their coffee. (TB) **3** miserly, stingy, tight *C'est le bougre le plus* TIGHT *du village.* He was the stingiest person in town. (VM) **4** intoxicated, drunk *Elle devait être* TIGHT *si alle a parlé comme ça.* She must have been drunk if she spoke like that. (LA) *J'étais manière* TIGHT *quand j'ai quitté le bal.* I was a little drunk when I left the dance. (LA) <*Loc:* EV, LA, TB, VM, Lv88>

tignasse ♦see **crignasse**

tignon (**chignon, tillon, tiyon**) [tijɔ̃, tiɲɔ̃, ʃiɲɔ̃] *n.m.* **1** turban, headscarf, kerchief tied around the head **2** bun, roll, twist, or knot of hair worn at the back of the head <*Loc:* AV, IB, EV, LF, SB, SL, SM, VM, Da84, Gu00, Lv88, Ph36, Re31>

tigre, -resse [tig(r), tigrɛs] *n.* **1** *(m.)* tiger **2** *(f.)* tigress <*Loc:* AV, Da84, Hi02>

ti-gris [tigri] *n.m.* sparrow <*Loc:* AV, VM, Fa77>

tille [tij] *n.f.* hand adze used to gouge wood, as in making pirogues or barrel staves ◊ •**tille ronde** tool used to carve out pirogues <Lv88> <*Loc:* Lv88>

tiller (**étiller**) [tije, etije] *v.tr.* **1** to split, tear, pull apart (esp. lengthwise or along the grain) *Je vas tiller une logue aujourd'hui.* I'm going to split a log today. (TB) *Ça prenait des pailles de maïs, c'était tout étillé.* They would take corn husks, and they were completely torn into strips. (SL) **2** to pull or shake apart (strands of Spanish moss, e.g. in a mattress) in order to fluff and clean them *On étille la mousse.* We pull the Spanish moss apart. (IB) **Tiller de la mousse.* To fluff up moss. (Da84) **3** to shred *Sa robe est tout étillée.* Her dress is all ripped to shreds. (VM) *Des années passées, défunt mom bouillait la viande, là elle cassait la viande avec les mains, on appelait ça "tiller", c'était pas moulé c'était tillé, elle faisait le boudin avec ça.* Years ago, my late mother boiled meat, she split the meat by hand, we called it "tiller", it was not ground, it was shredded, she made boudin with it. (IB) **4** to beat, whip *Il y a tombé dessus, et l'a étillé.* He fell on him and gave him a good beating. (LF) <*Loc:* AV, IB, LF, SL, SM, TB, VM, Da84, Lv88, Re31>

tilleul [tijœl] *n.m.* linden <***Loc:*** AC>

tillon ♦see **tignon**

timbré, -e [tɛ̃bre] *adj.* crazy, foolish <***Loc:*** AC>

timide [timid] *adj.* timid, shy, bashful *Il est timide. Il met du temps à se dégêner.* He is timid. It takes him a while to get over his shyness. (VM) <***Loc:*** AC, VM, Da84>

timidité [timidite] *n.f.* timidity, shyness, bashfulness <***Loc:*** Da84>

tiner ♦see **attiner**

tingue-lingue [tɛ̃gɛ̃lɛ̃] *n.m.* ◊ •**grand tingue-lingue** tall, thin, long-legged lanky person <Lv88> <***Loc:*** Lv88>

TIP [tip] *n.m.* **1** tip, gratuity **2** tip, useful bit of information <***Loc:*** EV, Lv88, Ph36>

tiquette ♦see **ticket**

tirage[1] [tiraʒ] *n.m.* milking (of cows) *Il y a plus eu de trouble pour le tirage de vaches et le faisage de vider le pot.* There's more trouble for the milking of the cows and the emptying of the pots. (EV) <***Loc:*** EV, Fa77, Gr86, Lv88>

tirage[2] [tiraʒ] *n.m.* **1** shot, gunshot, detonation (of a gun) *Y'avait un tirage au bal samedi soir.* There was a gunshot at the dance on Saturday night. (Lv88) **2** shooting *"Tu as vu le tirage?," demande l'avocat.* "Did you see the shooting?" the lawyer asked. (EV) <***Loc:*** EV, Fa77, Gr86, Lv88>

tiraille [tiraj, tʃiraj, toraj] *n.f.* hard, tough, sinewy meat of poor grade *C'est juste de la tiraille qu'il m'a envoyée aujourd'hui.* All he sent me today was tough, sinewy meat. (TB) <***Loc:*** IB, LF, SB, SJ, SL, SM, TB, VM, Da84, Lv88>

tirailler[1] [tiraje] **I** *v.tr.* to pull, pull in all directions *Sa famille la tiraille d'un bord à l'autre.* Her family pulls her from one direction to the other. (VM) **II** *v.intr.* **1** to pull on persistently *Elle est toujours après tirailler sur ma robe.* She's always tugging on my dress. (SM) **2** to move along <***Loc:*** LA, SM, VM, Da84>

tirailler[2] [tiraje] *v.intr.* to shoot, fire (a gun) wildly or aimlessly *Il était après tirailler tout partout comme un fou quand je l'ai vu.* He was shooting wildly like a fool when I saw him. (LA) <***Loc:*** LA, SM, VM, Da84>

tire[1] [tir] *n.f.* **1** damper (in a flue) **2** draft (of a flue, chimney, etc.) <***Loc:*** Da84>

tire[2] [tir] *n.f.* small strap formerly used on boots and shoes (to help pull them on) ◊ •**tire de botte** boot strap <Da84> <***Loc:*** Da84>

tire[3] [tir] *n.* ◊ •**cheval de tire** draft-horse <***Loc:*** Di32, Gu86, Lv88>

TIRE[4] [taj, tajə] *n.m./f.* tire <***Loc:*** AV, LA, LF, SL, TB, VM, Da84, Lv88>

tire-bouchon [tirbuʃɔ̃] *n.m.* corkscrew <***Loc:*** AC, Da84, Fa77>

tire-braises [tirbrɛz] *n.m.* fireplace tongs <***Loc:*** AC>

tirelambêche ♦see **tierlambêche**

tire-larigot [tirlarigo] ◊ •**à tire-larigot** in great quantity, a lot *Ils sont venus à tire-larigot.* They came in very great numbers. (SB) <SB, La99> <***Loc:*** SB, La99>

tire-point [tirpwɛ̃] *n.m.* triangular file *Limer au tire-point.* To sharpen [a knife] with a triangular file. (SJ) <***Loc:*** SJ, VM>

tirer[1] [tire] **I** *v.tr.* **1** to pull, draw, drag *Alle l'attrape à la pincette, alle le tire par la fenêtre en disant qu'il était soûl.* She pinches his ear and pulls him out the window saying that he was drunk. (TB) **2** to milk *Je tire ma vache deux fois par jour.* I milk my cow twice a day. (Gu00) *On tirait les vaches deux fois par jour. C'était pas du lait à la glace mais c'était du lait frais.* We milked the cows twice a day. It wasn't iced milk but it was fresh milk. (LF) *Pape avait une vache à tirer le lait.* Dad had a milking cow. (IB) **3** to draw, select randomly (e.g. a name or number in a raffle or drawing) *Tirer les numéros pour le* RAFFLE. To draw numbers for the raffle. (AV) **4** to tear *Tirer le papier.* To tear the paper. (IB) **5** to remove, take off *J'ai tiré mon capot sur mon siège.* I removed my coat from my seat. (AV) *Quand tu cuis tes pralines, tu les tires pas avant que ta sauce se réduit.* When you cook pralines, you don't take them off the heat until your liquid has reduced. (VM) **6** to serve, dish out *Le dîner est tiré.* Dinner is dished out. (SB) **II** *v.intr.* to draw, puff (on a cigarette, pipe, etc.) *Il a tiré sur sa pipe.* He drew on his pipe. (LA) **III se tirer** *v.pron.* to throw o.s., jump *Le chien s'est tiré à la nage pour chercher le canard.* The dog jumped into the water to get the duck. (Lv88) *Il a ouvert la porte et le chien s'est tiré sur lui.* He opened the door and the dog jumped on him. (Lv88) *Elle s'est tirée dans mes bras.* She thew herself into my arms. (Lv88) ◊ •**tirer (à) la courtepaille** to draw straws, draw lots *On a tiré la courtepaille pour voir lequel qui serait mangé.* We drew straws to see which one would be eaten. (IB, ch: *Sept ans sur mer*) <IB, Da84> •**tirer au sort** to cast lots, draw lots <Da84> •**tirer avec la fine mire** to be precise in one's work or skill <EV, La99> •**tirer de l'eau** to draw water <Da84> •**tirer des cartes** to do card readings, practice cartomancy (fortunetelling with cards) *Je tire pas des cartes, non. C'est pas de quoi que je m'embête de ça. Si je tirais les cartes et que j'aurais appris ça j'aurais appris pour la bonne chose, mais je veux pas apprendre ça.* I don't do card readings, no. That's not something I bother with. If I read cards and if I had learned that, I would use it for good, but I don't want to learn that. (TB) <LF, TB> •**tirer la bonne aventure (à qqn)** to tell (s.o.'s) fortune <VM, Da84, La99> •**tirer la courte paille** to have a hard life <AV, La99> •**tirer la gazette** to subscribe to a newspaper <VM> •**tirer le diable par la queue** ***a*** to make great efforts ***b*** to be in an embarrassing position ***c*** to be in a miserable position, be suffering ***d*** to fight with fury <AV, JD, TB, La99> •**tirer une course** to run an errand <LA> •**tirer un portrait** to take a picture, photograph <Da84, Lv88> •**tirer sur la fin {à sa fin}** to draw near the end, draw to the end <Da84> •**tirer sur midi** to draw near noon <Da84> •**tirer une carotte** to tell a falsehood <JD, La99> **•tirer une chique à qqn** to criticize s.o. *Il avait envie de lui tirer une chique, mais il s'a repris.* He felt like criticizing him, but he restrained himself. (LA) <LA> **•tirer une course** ***a*** to run a race, take part in a race *J'ai tiré une course avec lui.* I ran a race with him. (SM) *J'ai tiré une course avec lui et j'ai perdu.* I ran a race with him and I lost. (Lv88) ***b*** to scram, run away <SM, VM, Da84, Lv88> **•tirer une poignette** to masturbate <La99> **•se tirer dans l'eau** to dive into the water <VM> **•avoir tiré son pétard** to have come to the end of one's high point, be on the decline <EV, La99> **•tiré à quatre épingles** dressed to perfection <Da84> <***Loc:*** AC, AV, EV, IB, JD, LA, LF, SB, SL, SM, TB, VM, Da84, Hi02, Gu00, La99, Lv88>

tirer[2] [tire] **I** *v.tr.* **1** to shoot, fire (a gun) *Il a pas pu recharger son fusil assez vite pour le tirer encore.* He wasn't able to reload his shotgun to shoot it again. (LA) *Il a tiré son fusil.* He shot his gun. (Lv88) **2** to shoot, injure or kill by shooting *Je vas tirer le chevreuil.* I'm going to shoot the deer. (SM) *Tirer quelqu'un avec un fusil.* To shoot someone with a gun. (SM) *Tu le tires par en-dessour.* You shoot it [the duck] from underneath. (TB) *Ils l'ont tiré drète devant moi. Ils l'ont tiré dans la figure.* They shot him right in front of me. The shot him in the face. (EV) *Madame Bosso, tirez-moi pas! C'est pas moi qu'a pris ta fille.* Madame Bosso, don't shoot me! It's not me who took your daughter. (ch, *Madame Bosso*) **3** to throw, cast, toss *J'ai tiré des cailloux dans sa figure.* I threw rocks in his face. (Lv88) *Tire la pelote en l'air, je vas l'attraper.* Throw the ball in the air, I'll catch it. (Gu00) **II se tirer** *v.pron.* to shoot o.s. **Quand j'ai pris mon pistolet un jour, c'est pour aller me tirer.* When I took my pistol one day, it was to go shoot myself. (Wh69) *Il s'a tiré avec le fusil.* He shot himself with the gun. (SM) *Il a désarmé son voisin avant qu'il se tire lui-même.* He disarmed his neighbor before he shot himself. (VM) ◊ **•tirer des chiques {une chique}** to hurl insults, make caustic remarks <Da84, La99> **•tirer des coups de pied** to kick (of animals) <Da84> **•tirer un coup de poing** to punch, throw a punch <AV> **•tirer une patate chaude (à qqn)** ***a*** to pose a difficult problem (to s.o.) ***b*** to put (s.o.) on the spot <EV, La99> **•tirer une tape** to slap <AV> **•tirer un œil** to cast a glance <Lv88> **•tirer un saut** to visit quickly <Lv88> <***Loc:*** AC, AV, EV, IB, JD, LA, LF, SB, SL, SM, TB, VM, Da84, Hi02, Gu00, La99, Lv88, Wh69>

tireur, -euse [tirœr, -øz] *n.* shooter, marksman ◊ **•tireur de bonne aventure** fortune teller <Da84, La99> **•tireur de chiques** one who makes caustic remarks <La99> **•tireur de portraits** photographer *Quand on a descendu du grand char à Crowley un tireur de portraits a fait un* SNAPSHOT *de nous-autres ensemble et il l'a donné à Huey Long.* When we got out of the train in Crowley, a photographer took a snapshot of us together and he gave it to Huey Long. (ThCa: *Messieurs, mesdames*) <EV, LF, SB, TC, VM, Da84, Lv88, Ph36> **•tireuse de cartes** fortune teller <Fa77> <***Loc:*** EV, LF, SB, TC, VM, Da84, Fa77, La99, Lv88, Ph36, ThCa>

tire-vache [tirvaʃ] *n.m.* milking-pail <***Loc:*** IB, SM, VM, Lv88>

tiroir [tirwar] *n.m.* drawer <***Loc:*** SL, Da84, Fa77>

tisane [tizɑ̃n] *n.f.* **1** tea **2** herbal tea **3** medicinal tea *Il aurait pris une racine d'un certain bois. Il te donnait et t'aurais pris ça et faire la tisane avec ça. Et tu buvais ça pour tant de jours, il t'aurait dit combien de jours de boire ça pour.* He would take the root of a certain tree. He gave that to you and you would take that and make an medicinal tea with it. And you drank that for so many days, he would tell you how many days to drink that. (TB) <***Loc:*** TB, Da84, Hi02>

tiser (se) [tize] *v.pron.* ◊ **•se tiser les cheveux** to tease one's hair *On se tisait les cheveux pour faire des roulons.* We teased our hair to make rolls. (TB) <TB> <***Loc:*** TB>

tison [tizɔ̃] *n.m.* **1** burning log or stick **2** poker (used to stir a fire) <***Loc:*** EV, Da84, Lv88, Ph36>

tisonner (**attisonner**) [tizɔ̃ne, atizɔ̃ne] *v.tr.* **1** to poke, stir (a fire) *J'ai tisonné le feu dans la cheminée.* I stirred the fire in the fireplace. (AV) *Arrête d'attisonner le feu comme ça.* Stop poking the fire like that. (TB) **2** to tease *Il m'a tisonné jusqu'à j'étais fâché.* He teased me until I got angry. (AV) <***Loc:*** AC, AV, IB, SJ, TB, Da84, Lv88>

tisonnier [tizɔ̃je] *n.m.* poker (used to stir a fire) <***Loc:*** AC>

'tit-fer [tifær] *n.m.* triangle, steel triangle used as a musical percussion instrument <***Loc:*** Hi02>

'tit ♦see **petit**

titisse (**quiquisse**) [titis, kikis] *n.m.* **1** sparrow **2** generic term for almost any small bird whose specific name is unknown to the speaker **3** small, thin person *Ce pauvre titisse aura froid cet hiver.* That poor thin man will be cold this winter. (IB) **4** [*baby talk*] penis ◊ **•petit quiquisse** sparrow <SM> <***Loc:*** IB, SB, SM, Da84, Lv88>

titite [titit] *n.m./f.* doll, small toy baby <***Loc:*** LF>

tit-nom [tinɔ̃] *n.m.* nickname *C'est pas son vrai nom. C'est son tit-nom.* That's not his real name. It's his nickname. (SM) <***Loc:*** SM, VM>

titre [tit(r)] *n.m.* title, heading, headline <***Loc:*** Da84>

tivi ♦see **T.V.**

tiyon ♦see **tignon**

TOAST [tos(t)] *n.m.* toast (to a person or cause) ◊ **•faire un TOAST** to propose a toast <Da84> <***Loc:*** Da84>

tocail ♦see **tocaille**

tocaille (**tocail**) [tokaj] *n.m.* **1** namesake, person bearing the same given name *Il s'appelle Edward. C'est mon tocaille.* His name is Edward. He's my namesake. (SM) **2** double, person who closely resembles another **3** rascal <***Loc:*** EV, IB, LF, SM, VM, Da84, Lv88, Ph36>

tocate [tokat] *n.f.* **1** infatuation *Il a une tocate pour la petite fille.* He has an infatuation with that little girl. (SM) **2** penchant, predilection *Elle a une tocate pour les suce-fleurs.*

She's got a thing for hummingbirds. (VM) **3** whim, fad <*Loc:* SM, VM>

toddé ♦see **todie**

todie (**toddé**) [todi, tode] *n.m.* **1** hot toddy, a type of grog **2** toddy, shot of liquor (usually mixed with sugar and water) <*Loc:* EV, IB, SM, TB, VM, Da84, Lv88, Ph36>

toffé [tofe] *n.m.* thick syrup <*Loc:* SL>

toi [twa] *pron.pers.* **1** *(subj.)* you *Moi et toi peut aller, mon mari va nous prêter le* TRUCK. You and I can go, my husband will lend us the truck. (LF) **2** *(dir.obj.)* (with imperative) you, yourself *Je dis, "Tracasse-toi pas, je dis, ce monde-là c'est tout du monde qui veut faire du tracas."* I said, "Don't worry, those people are just people who want to cause trouble." (LF) *Penche-toi pas trop près de cette tortue cocodril, tu vas te faire chaponner.* Don't bend over too close to that alligator snapping turtle, you will get yourself castrated. (VM) *Chesse-toi bien après tu sors de la baignoire.* Dry yourself well after you get out of the tub. (LA) *Tiens-toi à côté. C'est dangereux.* Keep away. It's dangerous. (LA) **3** *(ind.obj.)* (with imperative) for you, for yourself *Prends-toi plein. Y a assez pour une armée.* Help yourself to a lot. There's enough for an army. (TB) *Mets-toi un petit plomb sur ta ligne. Tu vas attraper des poissons plus vite.* Put a little sinker on your line. You'll catch fish faster. (LA) **4** *(obj. of prep.)* you **C'est pour toi.* It's for you. (Da84) **Mais je lui dis, "c'est pas après toi il est fâché, c'est après moi il est fâché."* But I told her, "he's not mad at you, he's mad at me." (EV) *Eh ben, aie pas peur on va pas parler après toi en arrière de ton dos, parce qu'on a pas été élevé comme ça.* Well, don't be scared that we will talk about you behind your back, because we weren't raised like that. (TB) *Je m'adresse pas à toi.* I'm not talking to you. (VM) *C'est mieux pour toi d'être naturel plutôt que faire accroire tu peux faire quelque chose.* It's better for you to act naturally than to convince people that you can do anything. (Lv88) **5** *(tonic)* you *Toi tu vas pas rire autant, je pense.* You won't laugh as much, I think. (TB) *Oh! 'tite fille, mais rappelle-toi, bébé, les accroires, chère, toi tu m'as faits.* Oh girl, remember the lies you told me, baby. (Lv88) **C'est toi qu'après voler ma crème aussi longtemps.* You're the one who's been stealing my cream for so long. (EV, An94) *Je vaux autant comme toi.* I'm worth as much as you. (SM) **C'est toi ça?* Is that you? (Da84) <*Loc:* AC, AV, EV, LA, LF, SL, SM, TB, VM, An94, Da84, Hi02, Lv88>

toi-même [twamɛ̃m] *pron.* **1** *(obj. of prep.)* you, yourself *Tes enfants à toi-même.* Your own children. (EV) **2** *(tonic)* you, yourself **Viens donc toi-même.* Please come yourself. (Da84) <*Loc:* AC, EV, Da84>

toie [twa] *n.f.* caul, membrane around a baby in the womb <*Loc:* VM>

toile [twal, twɛl] *n.f.* **1** linen, cloth, canvas **2** raincoat **3** diaphragm (of the body) ◊ **•toile cirée** ***a*** oilcloth ***b*** tarpaulin ***c*** raincoat <IB, Da84, Fa77> <*Loc:* AC, EV, IB, Da84, Fa77, Gu00>

toilette[1] [twalɛt] *n.f.* **1** toilet **2** dresser, dressing table ◊ **•aller à la toilette** to go to the bathroom <TB> <*Loc:* AC, EV, LA, TB, Da84, Gu00, Hi02, Lv88>

toilette[2] [twalɛt] *n.f.* **1** diaphragm (of the body) **2** peritoneum *La toilette c'est ça qui enveloppe tout la panse du cochon.* The peritoneum is what surrounds the pig's abdomen. (TB) <*Loc:* TB, Da84>

toise [twaz] *n.f.* **1** triangular surveying device made of three pieces of wood and measuring six feet at its base, formerly used to survey land in arpents **2** former unit of height equalling approximately six feet <*Loc:* Da84, Lv88, Re31>

toiser [twaze] *v.tr.* to survey with a 'toise' *Ça avait habitude de toiser la terre eux-mêmes pour la diviser en héritage.* They used to survey land in arpents themselves to divide it into inherited lots. (LA) <*Loc:* LA, Da84>

toit [twa] *n.m.* roof <*Loc:* SM, Da84>

tolérance [tolerɑ̃s] *n.f.* toleration, endurance <*Loc:* Da84>

tomate [tomat] *n.f.* tomato <*Loc:* CL, JE, SL, TB, Da84, Hi02, Re31>

tombe [tõm, tõb] *n.f.* tomb, grave <*Loc:* IV, LF, SB, SL, An94, Da84>

tombeau [tõbo] *n.m.* **1** grave, tomb **2** burial vault <*Loc:* Da84, Hi02>

tomber [tõbe] **I** *v.tr.* to drop, reduce (of rate, value, etc.) *Ça va peut-être tomber la valeur du* FRANC. They might drop the value of the franc. (TB) **II** *v.intr.* **1** to fall, drop *La femme a tombé par terre.* The woman fell on the ground. (AV) *Quand je suis venu, venu pour la tirer, alle tombait par terre.* When I came, came to milk her, she would fall down on the ground. (EV) **2** to decline in price *Le gazoline a tombé.* Gas went down in price. (AV) **3** to subside (of water), abate, die down (of wind, noise) *Le vent a tombé.* The wind died down. (AV) ◊ **•tomber à la renverse** to fall backwards <AC> **•tomber à plate sus le ventre / tomber à plein ventre** to fall on one's stomach <AC> **•tomber d'accord** to reach an agreement <VM, Da84> **•tomber dans le panneau** to happen advantageously <SB, La99> **•tomber dans les défaillances** to lose consciousness <Lv88> **•tomber dans les fesses à BLACK** to faint <AV, La99> **•tomber de l'eau** to urinate <VM> **•tomber derrière (qqn)** to plead with, get after (s.o.) *Happy Fats a tombé derrière Tante Maria pour elle lui fait des crêpes.* Happy Fats pleaded with Aunt Maria for her to make him some crepes. (LA) <LA> **•tomber des petits nègres la tête en bas** to rain heavily <SM, La99> **•tomber d'un mal / tomber du haut mal** to have an epileptic seizure <Da84, Lv88> **•tomber en amour (avec)** to fall in love (with) *Douze ans de ça il parlait procheque pas du tout en français, il voulait pas parler le français. Mais il a tombé en amour avec la musique cadien.* Twelve years ago he spoke almost no French, he didn't want to speak French.

But he fell in love with Cajun music. (LF) *Alle tombe en amour avec Jean.* She falls in love with John. (AV) <AC, AV, IB, JE, LF, SM, TB, Da84, Lv88> **•tomber en botte *a*** to go to ruin or disrepair, fall to pieces *La maison est après tomber en botte.* The house is falling to pieces. (SL) ***b*** to fall into a swoon ***c*** to go bankrupt, go to rack and ruin *Les affaires vont tomber en botte.* Business will go to rack and ruin. (SL) *Le magasin va tomber en botte.* The store will go bankrupt. (LF) <AV, LF, SL, La99> **•tomber en confiture** to faint <La99> **•tomber en défaillance** to faint *Les autres fois quand il fallait jeûner avant d'aller communier, y avait du monde qui tombait en défaillance durant la messe.* In the old days when one had to fast before taking communion, some people would faint during mass. (VM) <EV, LF, VM, La99, Lv88, Ph36> **•tomber en doise {douale}** to fall into ruin or disrepair, become dilapidated *Regarde cette cabane. Elle est après tomber en douale.* Look at that shack. It is going to ruin. (VM) <TB, VM, La99> **•tomber en poudre {poussière}** to turn to naught, crumble (into dust) <Da84> **•tomber en racaille {racage} *a*** to fall apart, fall to pieces *Ça tombe en racaille.* It's falling apart. (TB) ***b*** to fall in a heap *Il a tombé en racage.* He fell in a heap. (LF) <LF, TB> **•tomber en ruine** to fall into ruin or disrepair, become dilapidated <TB, La99> **•tomber en soliard** to faint <EV, Ph36> **•tomber en train** to get into a fight <VM> **•tomber en-val-en-zèle / tomber en val et en zèle** to fall apart, become dilapidated *La barrière est tombée en-val-en-zèle.* The fence fell apart. (TB) <TB, La99> **•tomber malade** to get sick *Là, elle a tombé malade et elle est morte.* She fell sick and she died. (EV) <EV, Da84> **•faire tomber** to cause to fall <Da84> <***Loc:*** AC, AV, EV, IV, JE, LA, LF, SB, SL, SM, TB, VM, An94, Da84, Hi02, La99, Lv88, Ph36>

tombouille ♦see **tambouille**

ton (**ta, tes**) (*m.sing.* **ton** [tɔ̃], *f.sing.* **ta** [ta], *m./f.pl.* **tes** [te], *m./f.pl.* before a vowel **tes** [tez]) *adj.poss.* your *Mets ton garde-soleil. Le soleil va rider ta figure.* Put on your sun bonnet. The sun will wrinkle your face. (VM) **Tes mains.* Your hands. (Da84) **J'ai rêvé hier au soir que tu m'avais donné ton cheval.* I dreamed last night that you had given me your horse. (SL, An94) *Je vas pas te redemander de ramasser ton linge.* I'm not going to ask you again to pick up your clothes. (EV) **Ta mère.* Your mother. (Da84) **Tes enfants.* Your children. (Da84) **Ton père.* Your father. (Da84) *Je vas te faire renvaler tes paroles, toi!* I'll make you eat your words! (LA) <***Loc:*** AC, AV, EV, IB, IV, LA, LF, SL, SM, TB, VM, An94, Da84, La99, Lv88, Wh83>

tondeur [tɔ̃dœr] *n.m.* shearer, one who shears (sheep) <***Loc:*** Da84>

tondeuse [tɔ̃døz] *n.f. (usu. pl.)* shears, shearing tool for sheep <***Loc:*** Da84>

tondre[1] [tɔ̃n, tɔ̃d(r)] *v.tr.* to shear, clip *Il est après charcher les fauces pour tondre les moutons.* He is looking for the shears in order to shear the sheep. (VM) <***Loc:*** EV, VM, Da84>

tondre[2] [tɔ̃n, tɔ̃d(r)] *n.m.* fungus collected for kindling <***Loc:*** Re31>

tonibas [tɔ̃niba] *interj.* my goodness! good heavens! *Tonibas! Ça c'est trop bête.* My goodness, that's too stupid. (SB) *Tonibas de sac!* Goodness gracious! (SB) *Cré tonibas!* Goodness! (IB) <***Loc:*** AV, IB, SB>

tonique [tɔ̃nik] *n.* tonic <***Loc:*** AV, Da84>

tonnage[1] [tɔ̃naʒ] *n.m.* sheep-shearing, clipping *Pendant le tonnage de moutons.* While the sheep are being sheared. (SJ) <***Loc:*** AV, SJ, Lv88>

tonnage[2] [tɔ̃naʒ] *n.m.* tonnage *Y a une qualité de canne qui te donne un bon tonnage.* There's a kind of cane that gives you a good tonnage. (SJ) <***Loc:*** SJ>

tonnant ♦see **étonnant**

tonne [tɔ̃n] *n.m./f.* **1** cistern (to catch and store rainwater) **2** ton (2000 pounds) <***Loc:*** EV, IB, SM, Da84, Lv88, Ph36>

tonneau [tɔ̃no] *n.m.* funnel <***Loc:*** Da84>

tonner [tɔ̃ne] *v.intr.* to thunder **Il tonne.* It is thundering. (Da84) *Équand il tonne, il fait un éclair.* When it thunders, there is lightning. (TB) <***Loc:*** AC, TB, Da84>

tonnerre [tɔ̃nær] *n.m.* **1** thunder **Que le tonnerre m'écrase en mille poussières.* May the thunder crush me into a thousand specks of dust! (Da84) *On a besoin du tonnerre pour les fleurs.* We need thunder [rain] for the flowers. (VM) **2** tough guy, troublemaker *Jean est un tonnerre quand il commence.* John is a bear when he gets going. (IB) ◊ **•tonnerre à la voile** noisy, unruly person <SM, La99> **•tonnerre de foutre** Can you imagine it? For heaven's sake! *Il devait arriver à cinq heures et il n'est pas venu avant minuit—tonnerre de foutre!* He was supposed to arrive at five o'clock and he didn't get here until midnight—can you imagine? (SB) <SB> **•tonnerre est-il {c'est-ti} possible?** Is it really possible? Can it really be? <Lv88> **•tonnerre, mes chiens!** expression of anger, pain or surprise <La99> **•coup de tonnerre** thunderclap <Da84> **•petit tonnerre** highly active child <La99> **•(que le) tonnerre m'écrase!** expression of anger, pain or surprise <La99, Lv88> **•sacré tonnerre!** holy thunder! <Da84> <***Loc:*** AC, AV, IB, JD, LF, SM, VM, Da84, Hi02, La99, Lv88>

tonquin (**donquin**) [tɔ̃kɛ̃, dɔ̃kɛ̃] *adj.* ◊ **•petit cochon tonquin** very short, fat pig <SM> <***Loc:*** SM>

top [tɔp] *n.m.* **1** top, surface *Une paupière c'est pour la pluie, quand la chevrette vient sur le top de l'eau.* A butterfly net is for when it rains, when the shrimp come up to the top of the water. (TB) **2** roof *Le top de la maison était couvert avec des bardeaux.* The roof of the house was covered with shingles. (TB) **3** top, roof (of a car or buggy) *Ils ont pris les guides, et ils les ont amarrés sur le top du boghei.* They took the reins, and they tied them to the top of the buggy.

(EV) **4** hood (of a car) <***Loc:*** EV, SB, SM, TB, VM, Da84, Ph36>

topette [topɛt, topet] *n.f.* **1** small flask *Il garde une topette dans sa poche tout le temps.* He keeps a flask in his pocket all the time. (SM) *Manier la topette raide.* To drink to excess. (SJ) **2** drinking spree, drinking bout *On s'est foutu une topette hier soir.* We went on a drinking bout last night. (AV) <***Loc:*** AV, EV, IB, LF, SB, SJ, SL, SM, TB, Da84, Lv88, Ph36>

topinambour [tupinɑ̃bur, tɔ̃pinɔ̃bur] *n.m.* Jerusalem artichoke <***Loc:*** AC, AV, IB, SJ, SM, TB, VM, Da84, Re31>

toqué[1], -e [toke] *adj.* **1** crazy, cracked, batty *Elle est toquée.* She's crazy. (AV) *Mon père était pas toqué sur les écoles non plus.* My father wasn't crazy about schools either. (SM) **2** drunk, tipsy *Elle est toquée, elle est saoule.* She's drunk. (AV) <***Loc:*** AV, EV, SB, SM, VM, Da84, Hi02, La99>

toqué[2], -e [toke] *n.* crazy person <***Loc:*** Hi02>

toquer [toke] **I** *v.tr.* to strike, hit *Il a toqué son coude contre le mur.* He hit his elbow against the wall. (VM) **II** *v.intr.* to beat (of the heart) *Son cœur toquait vite et fort.* His heart was beating fast and hard. (VM) ◊ **•toquer un coup de pied** to kick <Da84> <***Loc:*** VM, Da84, Lv88>

tôr ♦see **tour**

torche [tɔrʃ] *n.f.* **1** amount of bousillage one can hold in two hands **2** rag used to wipe the bottom after a bowel movement <***Loc:*** SB, Lv88>

torcher (**étorcher**) [tɔrʃe, etɔrʃe] **I** *v.tr.* **1** to wipe (the bottom, esp. of a child) *Je suis tanné d'avoir besoin de le torcher.* I am fed up with having to wipe his bottom. (LA) **2** to wipe or sponge (any part of the body) **II se torcher** *v.pron.* to wipe one's bottom *Il est rendu qu'il peut p'us seulement se torcher.* He has reached the point where he can no longer even wipe himself. (LA) <***Loc:*** AC, IB, LA, Da84>

torchon [tɔrʃɔ̃] *n.m.* **1** any wad of material used to clean one's bottom **2** duster, any wad of material used to dust, clean up or scrub **3** loofah, dishcloth gourd <***Loc:*** AC, IB, LA, LF, SJ, VM, Da84, Lv88>

torcou [tɔrku] *n.m.* wryneck woodpecker <***Loc:*** Lv88>

tordre [tɔrd(r)] **I** *v.tr.* **1** to twist, bend **Après ça, il a attrapé une vieille couveuse qui était après couver sur quelques œufs de z oie. Et il lui a tordu le cou.* After that, he caught an old hen who was sitting on several goose eggs. And he wrung its neck. (EV, An94) **2** to wring out (clothing) **II se tordre** *v.pron.* **1** to twist o.s. *J'aime à me tordre avec la musique.* I like to twist with the music. (AV) **2** to wring (one's hands) *Il était assez nerveux, il se tordait les mains.* He was so nervous, he was wringing his hands. (LA) <***Loc:*** AV, EV, LA, An94, Da84, Fa77>

tordu, -e [tɔrdy] *adj.* twisted, crooked, bent, deformed *Le vieux chêne était tout tordu.* The old oak was all twisted. (LA) <***Loc:*** LA, Da84>

tornado (**tournado**) [tɔrnado, turnado] *n.m.* tornado <***Loc:*** EV, JD, SB, SM>

toron [torɔ̃] *n.m.* clod *Ses grands cantiers avaient des gros torons de boue dessus.* His big old shoes had clods of dirt on them. (TB) <***Loc:*** TB>

torquer [tɔrke] *v.tr.* to twist, roll (tobacco) *Dans le vieux temps, ça torquait le périque pour faire des torquettes.* In the old days, they would twist the perique tobacco into rolls. (LA) <***Loc:*** LA, Lv88>

torquette [tɔrkɛt, turkɛt, tɔrgɛt] *n.f.* **1** roll of tobacco *Pépère avait l'habitude de chiquer des torquettes.* Grandpa used to chew rolls of tobacco. (TB) **2** [*pej.*] woman **Garde-donc ç'te torquette, a marche comme einne vache.* Just look at that woman, she walks like a cow. (EV, Ph36) <***Loc:*** EV, IB, SM, TB, VM, Lv88, Ph36>

tort [tɔr] *n.m.* harm, hurt, damage, wrong ◊ **•avoir tort** to be wrong, be in the wrong *Quand on avait l'accident, l'homme avait tort.* When we had the accident, the man was in the wrong. (AV) <AV, Da84> **•en tort / dans le tort** in the wrong *L'homme était en tort.* The man was in the wrong. (AV) <AV, Da84> **•faire (de / du) tort *a*** to harm *Quelqu'un qui veut faire un crime ou faire du mal ou du tort à quelqu'un, il va le faire.* Someone who wants to commit a crime or to hurt or harm someone, he's going to do it. (IB) ***b*** to do wrong *Je sais pas qui il va faire avec moi, mais je souhaite qu'il me fait pas de tort.* I don't know what he's going to do with me, but I hope he doesn't do me wrong. (TB) ***c*** to make sick *Le manger m'a fait du tort.* The food made me sick. (AV) <AV, IB, TB, Da84> <***Loc:*** AV, IB, TB, Da84>

torticolis (**torticoulis**) [tɔrtikoli, tɔrtikuli, turtikuli, tartikuli, tatikuli] *n.m.* stiff neck, crick in the neck <***Loc:*** SM, TB>

torticoulis ♦see **torticolis**

tortignon ♦see **tortillon**

tortiller [tɔrtije] *v.tr.* **1** to twist, wind, wind around, twirl around *Il a tortillé la corde.* He twisted the rope. (AV) *Ça faisait des bonnes saucisses. Ils avaient une jarre de sept galons. Et tu tortillais ça en dedans-là jusqu'à ça venait en haut.* They made good sausages. They had a seven-gallon jar. And you would twist that around in there until it got to the top. (SL) **2** to twist, tie up *Je l'aurais tortillé avec une liane et puis je le halais.* I would tie it up with a vine and then I would pull it. (SL) **3** to wrap *Tortille bien le bebé avant de sortir dans le froid.* Wrap the baby up well before going out in the cold. (VM) **II** *v.intr.* to wriggle, twist around *Arrête donc de tortiller comme ça!* Will you stop twisting around like that! (AV) <***Loc:*** AV, SL, VM, Da84>

tortillon (**tortignon, tourtillon**) [tɔrtijɔ̃, turtijɔ̃] *n.m.* (*occ. f.*) **1** bun, tight roll of hair worn at the back of the head *Sa tortillon est toute défaite.* Her bun has come completely undone. (IB) **2** whirlpool, eddy *Il s'a fait prendre dans le tourtillon.* He got caught in the eddy. (TB) <***Loc:*** IB, LF, SB, SL, SM, TB, VM, Da84>

tortue [tɔrty, tørty] *n.f.* **1** turtle *À l'autre place qu'on avait, j'avais un homme qui venait de Shriever, qu'avait une ferme* *de tortues. Des petites tortues qu'eusse vendait dans des magasins.* At the other business we had, I had a man who came from Shriever, who had a turtle farm. Little turtles that they sold in stores. (LF) **2** any small bug or worm that curls up when touched ◊ **•tortue blanche** Atlantic ridley (sea turtle) <JE> **•tortue câille** slider (kind of turtle) <VM, Guoo> **•tortue caïman** alligator snapping turtle, (freshwater) loggerhead snapping turtle <LF, SB, Lv88> **•tortue cocodril** alligator snapping turtle, (freshwater) loggerhead snapping turtle <TB, VM, Guoo, Lv88> **•tortue caouenne *a*** alligator snapping turtle, (freshwater) loggerhead snapping turtle ***b*** common snapping turtle <EV, LF, SB, TB> **•tortue cou barré** stripe-necked turtle <Lv88> **•tortue de boue** mud turtle <Lv88> **•tortue de canne** three-toed box turtle <SB, Lv88> **•tortue de cyprière *a*** map turtle ***b*** alligator snapping turtle, (freshwater) loggerhead snapping turtle <SB, VM> **•tortue de lac** map turtle <VM> **•tortue de mer** sea turtle <Da84, Guoo> **•tortue de mer ridley** Atlantic ridley (sea turtle) <VM> **•tortue de mer verte** green sea turtle <VM> **•tortue de rosée** three-toed box turtle <VM, Lv88> **•tortue double-porte** common snapping turtle <VM> **•tortue mobilienne *a*** Mobile cooter ***b*** green turtle ***c*** name given to any of various large turtles <AS, JD, LA, LF, PQ, SB, SJ, TB, Lv88> **•tortue molle / tortue écaille molle / tortue caille molle *a*** (freshwater) softshell turtle ***b*** leatherback sea turtle <JE, SB, SL, VM, Da84, Guoo, Lv88> **•tortue musquée** musk turtle, stinkpot <SB> **•tortue noire** diamondback terrapin <SB> **•tortue perroquet** hawksbill sea turtle <TB> **•tortue puante** musk turtle, stinkpot <LA, SL, VM, Da84, Guoo, Lv88> **•tortue ventre jaune** yellow-bellied turtle <Guoo, Lv88> **•tortue verte** green turtle <LF, TB> **•être comme la tortue** to carry one's belongings on one's back <AV, La99> **•vieille tortue** slowpoke <SB> <***Loc:*** AL, AV, EV, IB, IV, JD, JE, LA, LF, SB, SJ, SL, SM, TB, VM, Da84, Guoo, Hio2, La99, Lv88>

tôt [to] *adv.* early *Il faut je me lève tôt le matin dans l'hiver.* I have to get up early in the morning during the wintertime. (LA) ◊ **•tôt ou tard** sooner or later <Da84> <***Loc:*** AV, LA, SM, An94, Da84, Hio2>

totage [totaʒ] *n.m.* totality, entirety <***Loc:*** VM>

toteau (toto) [toto] *n.m.* **1** fried biscuit dough **2** shortening bread **3** [*baby talk*] cake <***Loc:*** LF, SL, VM, La99>

toto[1] **(toutouille)** [toto, tutuj] *n.m.* [*baby talk*] shoe <***Loc:*** LF, SL, SM, La99>

toto[2] ♦see **toteau**

touche [tuʃ] *n.f.* **1** touch, touching **2** helping hand **3** slap *Je vas te donner une bonne touche si tu restes pas tranquille.* I'm going to slap you good if you don't stay quiet. (TB) **4** reprimand, punishment **5** drag, draw (on a cigarette, pipe, etc.) *Il a pris une touche sur ma cigaritte.* He took a drag on my cigarette. (SL) **6** playing (of a musical instrument) *Foutre une touche à une musique à bouche.* To play the harmonica a bit. (LA) <***Loc:*** LA, SB, SL, TB, VM, Da84, La99, Lv88>

touché [tuʃe] *adv.* ◊ **•à touché** touching, very close, near, nearby **Il reste à touché de chez moi.* He lives right near me, next door to me. (Da84) <Da84> <***Loc:*** Da84>

toucher [tuʃe] **I** *v.tr.* **1** to touch, handle, feel **Et quand il a été pour lui ôter son pied, il dit, "Touche pas mon pied, criminel que t'es."* When he went to remove his foot [from the stirrup], he says, "Don't touch my foot, criminal that you are." (IV, An94) **2** to touch (emotionally) **Toucher le cœur.* To touch one's heart. (Da84) *Ça m'a touché quand il a chanté pour l'enterrement de son frère.* I was touched when he sang at his brother's funeral. (LA) *Il a touché mon cœur.* He touched my heart. (AV) **3** to concern **C'était une autre cause révolutionnaire que j'allais embrasser, mais cette fois, c'était beaucoup plus important parce que ça me touchait directement.* It was another revolutionary cause that I would embrace, but this time it was more important because it concerned me directly. (LA, An84) **4** to collect (money) *Il est pas assez vieux pour toucher la patte douce.* He is not old enough to collect social security. (SL) *Toucher de l'argent.* To receive some money. (AC) *Tu vas toucher dans le puits?* Are you going to collect in the well pool? (LA) **5** to ride (a horse) competitively or for money *Moi, j'avais envie de toucher le cheval, parce que si je gagnais, je faisais quelques sous.* I wanted to ride horses competetively because if I won, I would make some money. (EV) **6** to herd, drive (cattle) **7** to drive for hire (a team, a car, etc.) *Il a touché un gros* TRUCK *pour des années.* He drove a semi for years. (EV) **8** to drive *Alle touchait le char à quarante milles à l'heure.* She was driving the car at forty miles an hour. (TB) **II** *v.intr.* **1** to be touching **Il dit, "Comment tu veux moi, je tiens bon, mes quatre pattes, elles touchent pas par terre!"* He says, "How do you want me to hold tight, my four feet are not touching the ground!" (SM, An94) **2** to be contiguous *Les deux terrains touchent pas.* The two lots are not contiguous. (LA) **III se toucher** *v.pron.* **1** to touch o.s. or each other **2** to be contiguous **Les deux maisons se touchent.* The two houses are contiguous. (Da84) ◊ **•toucher à** to be near **Toucher à la fin.* To be near the end. (Da84) <Da84> <***Loc:*** AC, AV, EV, IV, LA, SL, SM, VM, An84, An94, Da84, Hio2>

toucheron [tuʃrɔ̃] *n.m.* big whip used by stock herders <***Loc:*** VM>

toucheur [tuʃœr] *n.m.* **1** jockey **2** stock herder, driver, cowboy **3** car or carriage driver **4** faith healer ◊ **•toucheur de cheval** jockey <EV> **•toucheur de bêtes** drover, cattle driver <Da84> <***Loc:*** EV, VM, Da84, Lv88, Ph36>

touine [twin] *n.m.* twin <***Loc:*** EV, JD, SL>

toujours [tuʒur] *adv.* **1** still *Quand ils l'ont arrêté, il avait tout l'argent toujours dessus lui.* When they arrested him, he still had all the money on him. (LA) **J'ai toujours les* *mêmes sentiments qui me fâchaient en 1975, et ça me fâche d'autant plus aujourd'hui.* I still have the same feelings that angered me in 1975, and they anger me that much more today. (LA, An84) *Je joins toujours de ce monde-là que j'avais affaire avec pendant des années.* I still meet with some of the people that I dealt with for many years. (SL) *Si t'as pas affiché ta terre, le monde va peut-être toujours chasser dessus.* If you haven't posted your land, people still might hunt on it. (VM) **2** always, forever, at all times **Il est toujours malade.* He is always sick. (Da84) **Il est toujours là.* He is always there. (Da84) *C'est toujours une canotte si le fond est rond.* It's always a 'canotte' if the bottom is round. (JE) *Et n-en a toujours un tas de monde qui va à la messe ça parle français.* There are always a lot of people who go to mass that speak French. (SL) *Des fois eusse dit des affaires en anglais qu'a pas d'allure non plus, enfin, ça c'est ça, ça revient toujours au même.* Sometimes they say things in English that don't make sense either, well, that's the way it is, it always boils down to the same thing. (TB) *Le riz de plant et les machineries augmentent toujours et on a presque pas rien pour le riz.* The seed rice and the machinery are always increasing [in price] and we get almost nothing for the rice. (VM) **3** anyway, in any case *J'ai été mordu. Toujours, c'était mauvais.* I got bitten. In any case, it was bad. (EV) **Et toujours, sur sa route, l'après-midi était après s'avancer.* And in any case, on his way, afternoon was approaching. (LA, An94) **Le renard était dans le bois où ils habitent et, toujours, il avait beaucoup faim.* The fox was in the woods where they live and, in any case, he was very hungry. (LA, An94) <***Loc:*** AC, EV, JE, LA, PQ, SL, SM, TB, VM, An84, An94, Da84, Hi02>

touloulou ♦see **tourloulou**

toupet[1] [tupɛ, tupe] *n.m.* **1** forelock (of a horse), bangs (of a person's hair) **2** hairdo *Elle avait le toupet si bien taillé.* She had such a shapely hairdo. (AC, ch: *La fille de la veuve*) **3** false hairpiece <***Loc:*** AC, TB, Da84, Lv88>

toupet[2] [tupɛ, tupe] *n.m.* audacity, nerve, brazenness ◊ **•avoir le {du} toupet** to have the nerve, have a lot of nerve *Et là il allait attaquer un autre nid, ici de l'avant, il a du toupet. Un raton laveur a du toupet oui. Il va faire n'importe qui pour manger.* And then he would go to attack another nest, from here on, he has nerve. A raccoon has nerve, oh yes. He'll do anything to eat. (TB) <AC, TB, Da84> <***Loc:*** AC, TB, Da84>

toupie [tupi] *n.f.* top, spinning top <***Loc:*** AC, Da84>

tour (tôr) [tur] *n.m.* **1** turn, revolution (of a wheel, key, etc.) **2** trip, visit *J'après faire un grand tour dans tous les villages dans l'état de la Louisiane.* I'm taking a big trip around to all the towns in the state of Louisiana. (AV) **3** turn (in a rotation or order) *Il a perdu son tour pour danser avec la belle blonde quand il a été boire une bière à la barre.* He lost his turn to dance with the pretty blonde girl when he went to drink a beer at the bar. (LA) **Ils ont dansé chacun son tour avec la même fille.* They each took a turn dancing with the same girl. (SL, An94) *Il y avait tant de familles qui se mettaient ensemble, et tous les samedis, ils tuaient un veau, chacun à son tour.* There were so many families that got together, and every Saturday, they slaughtered a calf, they took turns. (SL) **4** trick, prank *Il a fait des mauvais tours dans sa vie.* He pulled off some malicious pranks in his life. (LA) ◊ **•tour dans le dos** backache, strain in the back <Lv88> **•tour de force** feat of strength, stunt **Ça c'est* SPORT *comme i fait ces tôrs de forces.* That's funny how he performs those stunts. (EV, Ph36) <AC, EV, Da84, Ph36> **•tour de lune** crazy or bizarre stunt, escapade <Da84> **•tour de reins** wrench in the back, twisting of the back, backache *Il a levé la voiture et il a attrapé un tour de reins.* He picked up the car and wrenched his back. (SM) <SL, SM, Da84> **•tour d'ongle *a*** whitlow, infection of the finger or toe around the nail ***b*** hangnail <AC, EV, IB, VM, Lv88, Ph36> **•avoir {faire} le tour d'âge** to go through menopause *Alle est après avoir son tour d'âge.* She is going through menopause. (VM) <LF, SJ, SL, SM, VM, La99, Lv88> **•avoir un tour de lune** to be in a contrary mood <SB, La99> **•faire le tour *a*** to go around (an object) *Et là tu viens à la course et tu fais le tour de ce baril-là.* And then you come running up and you go all the way around that barrel. (LF) ***b*** to avoid trouble *Il va faire le tour tout ça il y aura moyen.* He will try to avoid trouble as much as he can. (EV) <EV, LF, Da84> **•faire le tour de la maison** to go around the exterior of a house <Da84> **•faire le tour des bêtes** to round up cattle <Da84> **•faire un tour *a*** to make a round, make a circle *Et là chaque fois qu'alle faisait un tour, mettait une ou deux mailles sur le filet de plus, jusqu'à qu'alle faisait un épervier.* And each time she made a circle she put one or two more links of mesh on the net, until she had made a castnet. (LF) ***b*** to make a short visit <Da84> **•prendre son tour** to take one's turn <Da84, Wh83> **•tout le tour** all around **Et c'était un marais rond et les canards étaient posés tout le tour au ras de l'écore.* And it was a round pond and the ducks were all around next to the bank. (AC, An94) **J'ai vu les chandelles allumées tout le tour de son cercueil.* I saw lighted candles all around his coffin. (Wh69) *Il y avait trente z-acres pour couper les chemins tout le tour pour lui passer avec la coupeuse. Il halait ça avec un* TRACTOR*.* There were thirty acres to cut paths all around so that he could get through with the combine. He hauled it with a tractor. (EV) <AC, EV, An94, Wh69> <***Loc:*** AC, AV, EV, LA, LF, SL, SM, TB, VM, An94, Da84, La99, Lv88, Ph36, Wh69, Wh83>

tourbillon [turbijɔ̃, turbyjɔ̃] *n.m.* **1** swirl, eddy **2** any type of whirlwind, such as a dust devil, tornado, or waterspout <***Loc:*** AV, EV, JD, LA, LF, TB, VM, Da84, Gu00>

tourbine [turbin] *n.m.* tornado <***Loc:*** LF>

touriste [turis(t)] *n.m.* tourist <*Loc:* TB, Hi02>

tourloulou (**touloulou, tourlourou, trouloulou**) [turlulu, turluru, trululu] *n.m.* **1** fiddler crab **2** doodlebug, larva of the tiger beetle <*Loc:* IB, LA, LF, TB, Hi02, Re31>

tourlourou ♦see **tourloulou**

tourment [turmɑ̃] *n.m.* torment, torture <*Loc:* Da84>

tourmenter [turmɑ̃te] *v.tr.* **1** to torment, torture *Ce vieux bougre était après tourmenter ces pauvres enfants.* That old fellow was tormenting those kids. (LA) *Les Japons a tourmenté les soldats.* The Japanese tortured the soldiers. (AC) **2** to annoy, plague, vex **3** to worry, cause to worry <*Loc:* AC, LA, Da84>

tournabie ♦see **tarabi**

tournado ♦see **tornado**

tournage [turnaʒ] *n.m.* **1** turnrow, headland (strip of uncultivated land at the end or side of a field where a plow can turn) **2** turnaround (for vehicles) <*Loc:* LF, TB>

tournaille [turnaj] *n.f.* turnrow, headland (strip of uncultivated land at the end or side of a field where a plow can turn) <*Loc:* Da84>

tournailler [turnaje] **I** *v.tr.* to turn *Il va essayer de tournailler sa chance.* He is going to try to turn his luck around. (LA) **II** *v.intr.* to mill around, turn around and around, go back and forth *Il était après tournailler et tournailler de bord, perdu comme une caille.* He was going around and around, as lost as a meadowlark. (LA) **2** to whirl, spin ◊ •**tournailler la queue du chien** to procrastinate <La99> <*Loc:* IB, LA, TB, Da84, La99, Lv88>

tournant [turnɑ̃] *n.m.* turnrow, headland (strip of uncultivated land at the end or side of a field where a plow can turn) <*Loc:* IV>

tourne [turn] *n.f.* **1** trump card **2** turnrow, headland (strip of uncultivated land at the end or side of a field where a plow can turn) <*Loc:* TB, Lv88>

tourné, -e [turne] *adj.* **1** turned, turned around *Un cable tourné en ronds.* A rope turned in rounds. (LA) **2** changed, altered **Il a dit dessus la lettre qu'il fallait qu'il détruit Geneviève et son petit parce qu'il voulait pas de souvenance si elle était tournée comme ça.* He said in the letter that he must kill Geneviève and her child because he wanted no memory of her if she had changed that way. (IV, An94) <*Loc:* IV, LA, An94, Da84>

tourne-avis, tourne-à-visse ♦see **tournevis**

tournée [turne] *n.f.* tour, trip, visit, journey <*Loc:* AV, Da84, Lv88>

tournement [turnəmɑ̃] *n.m.* turning, spinning ◊ •**tournement de tête** dizziness <Da84> <*Loc:* Da84>

tourne-queue [turnkø] *n.m.* mosquito larva <*Loc:* Lv88, Re31>

tourner [turne] **I** *v.tr.* **1** to turn **Il avait un moulin à maïs. Il tournait ça à chevaux.* He had a corn mill. He turned it with horses. (EV, An94) **2** to rotate, turn around **Père, tourne ce col et puis ton capot, vire-le devant derrière.* Father, turn around that collar and your coat, turn it backwards. (IV, An94) **3** to shape or turn on a lathe *Il faudra que je tourne les pieds de table cet après-midi.* I'm going to have to turn the table legs this afternoon. (VM) **4** to wind *Tourner une montre.* To wind a watch. (LA) **5** to turn out *Ça a tourné que Louis a pas pu finir la course avec son frère.* It turned out that Louis could not finish the race with his brother. (LA) **6** to turn, render, cause to become (a certain way) *Tu vides du café dans du lait, ça le tourne marron, mais marron blanc.* You pour coffee into some milk, it turns it brown, light brown. (LA) **II** *v.intr.* **1** to turn, turn into, become *Je crois je tournais sur 13 ou 14 là.* I think I was turning 13 or 14. (TB) *Quand j'étais tout petit ma mère nous faisait peur le soir pour qu'on reste autour de la maison. Alle nous disait que y avait un homme qui tournait rougarou.* When I was young my mother would scare us so we would stay around the house. She told us that there was a man who changed into a werewolf. (LF) *Après qu'il a un certain âge il tourne cette couleur-là, il peut être blanc. Il va venir cette couleur-là.* After it's a certain age it turns that color, it might start out white. It'll turn that color. (TB) *Quand alle s'a marié, alle a tourné Catholique.* When she married, she became Catholic. (LA) **2** to turn, turn a corner, change direction *T'as besoin de tourner drette-là.* You need to turn right there. (TB) *Tourne à la droite.* Turn right. (JE) *T'as besoin de tourner à droite ici-là.* You need to turn right, right here. (TB) **3** to rotate, turn around *Il était planté au milieu du chemin après tourner et tourner.* He was there in the middle of the street, turning around and around. (LA) **III se tourner** *v.pron.* to turn, turn around **Ça se fait, il se tourne à son ami.* So, he turned around to his friend. (EV, An94) ◊ •**tourner bout pour bout** to turn over, turn completely around *Il a tourné bout pour bout.* He turned all the way around. (SL) <SL, Lv88> •**tourner casaque** to flee, run away, take to one's heels <JD> •**tourner de bord** to turn around <TB, Da84> •**tourner en candi** to crystallize (of sugar) <Da84> •**tourner en eau de boudin** ***a*** to become insignificant ***b*** to not come about <AV, SL, La99> •**tourner en merde** to go to hell, fall apart, turn to shit *Tout ces grandes idées, ça va tout tourner en merde.* All those grand ideas, it will all fall apart. (LA) <LA> •**tourner le dos** to turn one's back *Tu m'as dit tu m'aimais, et aujourd'hui, garde donc là, tu me tournes le dos.* You said you loved me and today, look, you are turning your back on me. (LA) <LA> •**être mal tourné** to be on the wrong road <Da84> <*Loc:* AC, AV, EV, IV, JD, JE, LA, LF, SB, SL, TB, VM, An94, Da84, Hi02, La99, Lv88, Wh83>

tournerie [turnri] *n.f.* ◊ •**tournerie de crêpes** get-together on the day of Candlemas, at which crêpes are traditionally made and eaten <Lv88> <*Loc:* Lv88>

tournevis (**tourne-avis, tourne-à-visse**) [turnavis, turnavi, turndavis] *n.m.* screwdriver <***Loc:*** AC, AV, EV, IB, JE, LA, LF, SB, SL, SM, TB, VM, Da84>

tourniole [tɔrɲɔl] *n.f.* whitlow, infection of the finger or toe around the nail <***Loc:*** Lv88>

tourniquet [turnikɛ, turnike] *n.m.* cowlick <***Loc:*** LF, SB>

tournoi [turnwa] *n.m.* tournament, match <***Loc:*** Da84>

tournure [turnyr] *n.f.* **1** turn, curve *Il y avait une mauvaise tournure dans le petit chemin.* There was a bad turn in the little road. (LA) **2** turnrow, headland (strip of uncultivated land at the end or side of a field where a plow can turn) *Il s'a arrêté pour boire de l'eau sur la tournure.* He stopped to drink some water on the turnrow. (IV) **3** trick, ruse, deception **4** inclination, bent ◊ **•avoir une mauvaise tournure** to have a bad bent or inclination <Da84> <***Loc:*** IV, LA, VM, Da84>

tourte [turt, tot] *n.m./f.* dove *Les tourtes roûties étaient bien bonnes.* The roasted doves were really good. (TB) <***Loc:*** AC, EV, IB, JE, LA, LF, SB, SL, SM, TB, VM, Da84, Hi02, Lv88>

tourterelle [turtrɛl, turtɛl] *n.f.* dove <***Loc:*** SL, TB, Da84>

tourtière [turtjær] *n.f.* **1** pâté **2** cake <***Loc:*** Lv88>

tourtillon ♦see **tortillon**

tous[1] [tu] *pron.indef.* all, everyone *La durance de la saison de pluie a été remarquée par tous.* The duration of the rainy season was noticed by everyone. (TB) *On peut tous s'en aller, c'est nettement.* We can all leave, it [the party] is over. (LF) **L'boguet était trop pitit, an [=on] pouvait pas tous embarquer.* The buggy was too small, we couldn't all get in. (EV, Ph36) ◊ **•nous tous** all of us <Da84> <***Loc:*** AV, EV, IV, LA, LF, SL, SM, TB, An94, Da84, Hi02, Ph36>

tous[2] ♦see **tout**

toussailler [tusaje] *v.intr.* to cough, cough often or frequently *Il a toussaillé proche tout la nuit.* He coughed almost all night long. (LA) <***Loc:*** IB, LA, SB, SM, Da84, Lv88>

Toussaint [tusɛ̃, tusɛ̃t] *n.f.* All Saints' Day, the feast of All Saints (November 2) <***Loc:*** AC, EV, IB, Da84, Hi02, Lv88>

tousser [tuse] **I** *v.tr.* to cough up *Il a toussé le rhume.* He coughed up the cold. (AC) **II** *v.intr.* to cough *Et tu voyais que le pauvre bête avait tombé dans le bayou parce qu'il était après tousser et cracher et tout quelque chose.* And you could see that the poor fellow had fallen into the bayou, because he was coughing and spitting and everything. (JD) <***Loc:*** AC, EV, JD, Da84, Hi02>

tousserie [tusri] *n.f.* coughing, coughing spell <***Loc:*** Da84>

tout[1], **-e** (*m.sing.* **tout** [tu], *f.sing.* **toute** [tut] *occ.* **tout** [tu], *m.pl.* **tous** [tu], *f.pl.* **toutes** [tut] *occ.* **tous** [tu]) *adj.* **1** all, whole, entire *J'ai parlé français toute ma vie.* I've spoken French all my life. (SL) *Il beurdasse toute la journée.* He piddles around all day. (SM) *C'est venu que il a été en banqueroute. Ça fait toute l'affaire a été perdue.* It ended up going bankrupt. So, the whole business was lost. (SJ) *Il a barboté toute la nuit.* He was out drinking all night. (Lv88) *T'es brave de travailler toute cette place tout seul.* You're brave to work this whole farm by yourself. (EV) **Tous nous-autres.* All of us. (Da84) **Toute la journée.* All day long. (Da84) *J'ai resté tout ma vie ici.* I have lived here all my life. (SM) **2** each, every *Il les a touchés tout chacun sur la tête pour voir quel qu'avait pas de chapeau.* He touched each one on the head to see which one had no hat. (LA) *Mon grand-père et ma grand-mère allont au bal tous les samedi soirs.* My grandfather and grandmother go to the dance every Saturday night. (Gu00) *La couverture de tous les maisons qu'était bâti c'est des bardeaux.* The roof of all the houses that were built was with shingles. (LF) ◊ **•tout-dans-le-monde** rascal (used in humorous reference to a child) *Cette petite tout-dans-le-monde.* This little rascal. (LF) <LF> **•tout le monde** everyone, everybody **Tout le monde allait à la messe. Il y avait pas d'excuse.* Everyone went to Mass. There was no excuse [not to]. (IV, An94) <EV, IV, SM, VM, An94, Hi02> **•tout le temps** all the time, always *Elle m'achale, elle est tout le temps après babiller.* She gets on my nerves, she's always grumbling. (Lv88) <IB, An94, Da84, Hi02> **•tout quelqu'un** everyone *Ses frères a passé voir tout quelqu'un.* His brothers stopped by to say hello to everyone. (SM) *Tout quelqu'un partait à leur maison à se coucher.* Everyone went to their houses to go to bed. (LF) *Tout quelqu'un parlait français c'était pas comme asteur.* Everybody would speak French it was not like it is now. (AC) <AC, LF, SM, Hi02> **•tout quelque chose** everything <LA, SM, An94, Hi02> **•à toutes heures** at all hours <Da84> **•à tout moment** repeatedly, often, very frequently <Da84> **•de toute part** from everywhere, from all over <Da84> **•du tout** at all *Proche tous mes frères et mes sœurs parlent pas français du tout.* Nearly all of my brothers and sisters do not speak French at all. (SL) <SL> **•pas tout là** slightly mentally deranged <La99> <***Loc:*** AC, EV, IB, JE, LA, LF, SJ, SL, SM, An94, Da84, Gu00, Hi02, Lv8, Wh83>

tout[2] [tu] (*before a vowel or optionally before a feminine adjective beginning with a consonant* [tut]) *adv.* wholly, entirely, all **Tout nouveau, tout beau.* New broom sweeps clean. (Da84) **Habillé tout en rouge.* All dressed up in red. (Da84) *Mon père avait des belles de nuit jaunes dans sa cour. Les miennes sont toutes rouges.* My father had yellow four o'clocks in his yard. Mine are all red. (Gu00) *Il est tout basané.* He is all freckled. (JE) ◊ **•tout à fait** completely **Tout à fait noire.* Completely black. (Da84) <Da84> **•tout au plus** at most, at the most <Da84> **•tout de même** [tudmɛ̃m] nevertheless, all the same *Il m'a dit ça tout de même.* He told me nevertheless. (IB) <IB> **•tout de suite / toutesuite** [tutswit] right away, immediately **"Ah," elle dit, "Grand Dieu! Partant que c'est un homme," elle dit, "envoyez-moi le tout de suite!"* "Ah," she says, "Good God! As long as it's a man," she says, "send him to me right away!" (LA, An94) <EV, LA, Da84, An94> **•tout droite** ***a*** straight ahead ***b*** instantly, immediately, at once *Deux étaient tués tout droite.* Two were killed instantly. (LA) <LA, Da84> **•tout d'un coup** all of a sudden *Là tout d'un coup je l'ai empoignée et je l'ai renversée sus la berce.* Then all of a sudden I grabbed her and I turned her upside down on the rocker. (AV) <AV, EV, JE, LA, TB, An94, Da84> **•tout fait** ready made <Da84> **•tout partout** everywhere *Mes mirlitons sont après filer tout partout dessus la galerie.* My vegetable pears are climbing all over the porch. (LA) <AC, EV, LA, SL, SM, TB, VM, An84, Da84, Hi02, Lv88> **•tout petit** very little, very small *Un tout petit minou.* A very small cat. (LF) <AC, IV, LF, TB, VM, Da84> **•pas tout à fait** not quite *Avec une voile, s'il était pas tout à fait à le centre du vent ça pourrait te pousser soit d'un bord ou de l'autre.* With a sail, if it wasn't lined up with the wind it could push you to one side or the other. (LF) <LF, Da84> <***Loc:*** AC, AV, EV, IB, IV, JE, LA, LF, SL, SM, TB, VM, An84, An94, Da84, Gu00, Hi02, Lv88, La99, Wh83>

tout[3] [tu] *pron.indef.* all, everything *J'ai laissé tout en dedans—les rideaux, et la glacière, il a eu un bon barguine.* I left everything inside—the curtains, the refrigerator, he got a good bargain. (SL) *Il comprend tout et il peut dire quelques affaires, mais il parle pas bien en français.* He understands everything and he can say a few things, but he doesn't speak French well. (LF) **Ça nomme le bougre et tout.* They name the fellow and everything. (EV, An94) ◊ **•après tout** after all <Da84> **•c'est tout** that's all <Da84> **•pas du tout** not at all *Pauvre bête, il bégayait tellement mauvais que il pouvait pas user le* PHONE *du tout.* Poor thing, he stuttered so badly that he couldn't use the telephone at all. (LA) <LA, LF, Da84> <***Loc:*** EV, LA, LF, SL, An94, Da84, Hi02>

tout à l'heure ♦see **talheure**

tout de mains ♦see **tout-mains**

tout-mains (**tout de mains**) [tumɛ̃, tudmɛ̃] *adj.* versatile, dexterous *Elle est tout de mains. Elle peut faire n'importe quoi.* She is versatile. She can do anything. (VM) <***Loc:*** VM>

toutout [tutu] *n.m.* namby-pamby, easily influenced person <***Loc:*** IB>

toutouille ♦see **toto**

tout-puissant [tupɥisɑ̃] *adj.* all-powerful, almighty ◊ **•Dieu tout-puissant** almighty God <Da84> <***Loc:*** Da84>

toux (**tousse**) [tu, tus] *n.f.* cough <***Loc:*** AC, AV, EV, LF, SM, Hi02>

toyasse [tojas] *n.f.* weak coffee *Ça c'est une fois que t'as fait de la toyasse.* That's one time that you made weak coffee. (TB) <***Loc:*** TB>

tracas [traka] *n.m.* **1** trouble, worry, anxiety *N-avait danger mais il y'a pas eu de tracas.* It was dangerous but we didn't have any trouble. (IB) *Si ta canique est restée dans le cercle, là t'avais un tracas.* If your marble stayed in the circle, then you were in trouble. (AC) **2** difficulty, problem *Un char deuxième main qui va te donner des années de service sans avoir de tracas.* A second-hand car that will give you years of service without problems. (EV) **Si ça vous donne trop de tracas de prêcher en français...* If it's too much trouble for you to preach in French . . . (TaCh: *Mille misères*) *Dans à peu près un mois, un mois et demi, tu mets un Français de la France, de Paris, et tu mets un Cadien d'ici ensemble, eh ben eusse pourrait se parler avec pas de tracas du tout.* In about a month or a month and a half, you put a Frenchman from France, from Paris, and you put a Cajun together, they would be able to talk to each other with no trouble at all. (TB) *C'est ça notre tracas asteur.* This is precisely our problem right now. (SM) ◊ **•avoir (du) tracas** to have trouble *J'avais tracas avec une oreille, je pouvais pas attendre.* I had problems with one ear, I could not hear. (SM) *J'arrête au bord du chemin, j'ai du tracas avec mon char.* I stop on the side of the road, I have problems with my car. (IB) <IB, SM, Da84> **•faire du tracas** to cause trouble, make trouble *Je dis, "Tracasse-toi pas, je dis, ce monde-là c'est tout du monde qui veut faire du tracas."* I said, "Don't worry, those people are just people who want to cause trouble." (LF) <LF, Da84> **•prendre le tracas** to take the trouble <Da84> **•se mettre en tracas / se mettre dans le tracas** to get into trouble *Eux-autres aime pas se marier parce qu'eux-autres peut se mettre en tracas. Ça dure pas.* They don't like to get married, because they can get into trouble. It doesn't last. (TB) *La seule manière t'aurais pu te mettre en tracas c'est si t'aurais tombé là et assayer de t'occuper avec la femme d'un autre bougre ou quelque chose, là t'aurais proche sûr eu une bataille.* The only way you could have gotten into trouble is if you would have ended up there and tried to get involved with the wife of another guy or something, then you would almost certainly have had a fight. (TB) <TB, Hi02> <***Loc:*** AC, EV, IB, LF, SM, TB, Da84, Hi02, La99, Lv88, ThCa>

tracassant, -e [trakasɑ̃, -ɑ̃t] *adj.* worrisome, worrying, troublesome, annoying *C'est une affaire tracassante.* This a troublesome thing. (LA) <***Loc:*** LA, Da84>

tracasser [trakase] **I** *v.tr.* **1** to worry, cause to worry *Ils ont fait des farces comme ça là, souvent, mais ça me tracassait pas.* They made jokes like that often, but it didn't worry me. (EV) **2** to pester, bother, annoy *Je me rappelle quand j'étais petite je tracassais Mom pour boucherie. "Mom, je veux aider! Je veux faire quelque chose!"* I remember when I was young, I would pester my mother to be involved with the "boucherie." "Mom, I want to help! I want to do something!" (EV) *J'ai arrêté de faire des chansons parce que j'ai plus un tas de temps, les moustiques me tracassent et je suis manière malade, tu vois?* I stopped composing songs because I don't have a lot of time anymore, the mosquitoes pester me and I'm somewhat sick, you see? (TB) *S'il avait pas d'ouvrage ça le tracasserait un tas.* It would bother him a lot if he had no work. (SM) **II se tracasser** *v.pron.* to worry, fret **Et là, il lui a dit qu'il fallait pas qu'elle se tracasse, qu'il allait parler au roi pour la soigner, pour prendre cas d'elle.* Then, he told her that she shouldn't worry, that he would speak to the king to care for her, to take up her case. (IV, An94) **Tracasse-toi pas!* Don't worry! (Da84) *Tracasse-toi pas de moi.* Don't worry about me. (Lv88) ◊ **•être tracassé** to be worried *Il est tracassé pour son vieux père.* He is worried about his old dad. (Lv88) *Ils étaient beaucoup tracassés parce que j'avais la fièvre beaucoup haut.* They were very anxious because I had a very high fever. (AV) *Je suis tracassé pour mon père.* I am worried for my father. (SM) <AV, SM, Da84, Lv88> <***Loc:*** AV, EV, IV, SM, TB, An77, An94, Da84, Hi02, Lv88>

trace [tras] *n.f.* **1** trail, track, trace, footprint *Y'avait des traces autour du puits.* There were tracks around the ditch. (Lv88) **Il voyait des traces autour de son puits, des traces à Lapin autour de son puits.* He saw footprints around his well, Lapin's footprints around his well. (SM, An94) **2** small passage, path, trail, or canal *Il suit une trace dans le mèche pour aller piéger.* He follows a trail through the marsh to go trapping. (Lv88) <***Loc:*** AC, SM, An94, Da84, Lv88>

tracer [trase] *v.tr.* **1** to trace, draw *Il a tracé le portrait sur un morceau de papier.* He traced the picture on a piece of paper. (LA) **2** to track *Le taïaut a tracé et tué deux lapins.* The hound tracked and killed two rabbits. (Lv88) **3** to trace (back to the beginning) *On a tracé l'histoire de mon grand-père.* We traced the history of my grandfather. (Lv88) *Les vieilles acadiennes traçaient les ancêtres pour découvrir les maladies.* The old Acadians traced their ancestors to find out about illnesses. (Lv88) <***Loc:*** AC, LA, An94, Da84, Lv88>

traceur [trasœr] *n.m.* tracker **Il était beaucoup bon traceur, beaucoup, beaucoup bon. Il traçait n'importe quoi.* He was a very good tracker, very, very good. He would track anything. (AC, An94) <***Loc:*** AC, An94>

TRACK [trak, tɹæk, tɹɛk] *n.m./f.* **1** path, track **2** railroad track *L'auto a arrêté sur le* TRACK. The car stopped on the train track. (AV) **3** race track **4** track team <***Loc:*** AV, EV, LF, SB, SL, SM, VM, Da84, Lv88, Ph36>

tracteur ♦see **TRACTOR**

TRACTOR (tracteur) [trakta, traktœr] *n.m.* tractor *Le tracteur s'a renversé dessus mon oncle.* The tractor turned over on my uncle. (VM) <***Loc:*** SL, VM, Da84, Hi02>

tradition [tradisjɔ̃] *n.f.* tradition <***Loc:*** SM, Da84, Hi02>

traditionnel, -lle [tradisjɔ̃nɛl] *adj.* traditional, customary *La musique traditionnelle.* Traditional music. (LA) <***Loc:*** LA, Da84, Hi02>

traduire [tradɥir] *v.tr.* to translate, interpret *Un tas des soldats cadiens dans la guerre avaient pour traduire pour les officiers.* A lot of Cajun soldiers in the war had to translate for the officers. (LA) <***Loc:*** LA, Da84, Hi02>

traduiseur [tradɥizœr] *n.m.* translator <***Loc:*** Da84>

trafic [trafik] *n.m.* **1** vehicular traffic **2** traffic, trade <***Loc:*** EV, LF, TB, VM, Da84, Lv88>

trafiquer [trafike] **I** *v.tr.* **1** to shuttle, take back and forth *Il trafiquait les enfants tous les jours à l'école.* He would take the children back and forth to school every day. (LA) **2** to traffic, deal, trade *Dans ce temps là, ça trafiquait du whisky.* In those days, they used to traffic whiskey. (SL) **II** *v.intr.* **1** to go back and forth, come and go *Il est tout le temps à trafiquer entre ici et Pont Breaux.* He is always going back and forth between here and Breaux Bridge. (SM) *Ça trafique toute la journée dans la salle à manger; ça fait pas de bien de l'nettoyer.* People come and go all day long through the dining room; it does no good to clean it. (TB) **2** to travel, circulate *Il trafique tous les jours à Cécilia.* He travels to Cecilia every day. (Lv88) *Ça trafique tout partout asteur.* People travel everywhere these days. (Lv88) <***Loc:*** LA, SB, SL, SM, TB, VM, Da84, Lv88>

trafiqueur [trafikœr] *n.m.* dealer, merchant. *Il est un trafiqueur d'œufs.* He is an egg dealer. (SL) <***Loc:*** SL>

tragédie [traʒedi] *n.f.* tragedy, misfortune *C'était une tragédie, ça qu'a arrivé l'autre soir après le bal.* It was a tragedy, what happened the other evening after the dance. (LA) <***Loc:*** LA, Da84, Fa77>

trahir [trair] *v.tr.* to betray, double-cross *Il trahirait son frère.* He would betray his own brother. (VM) <***Loc:*** VM, Da84>

traider [trede] *v.tr.* to trade *Et là avant ça je restais dans des* CAMPBOAT, *on traidait. Quand le monde avait des* CAMPBOAT, *vadait au piège, moi je prendais leur maison.* And then I lived in a campboat, we would trade. When people had campboats and went trapping, I took their house. (TB) <***Loc:*** TB>

traillail [trajaj] *n.m.* noise, commotion *Et mon beau-frère dit qu'il attendait du potin, du traillail dans la nuit, plein du marchage qu'était fait...* And my brother-in-law said he heard some noise, some racket at night, a lot of walking going on . . . (LF) <***Loc:*** LF>

train[1] [trɛ̃] *n.m.* locomotive, train <***Loc:*** SL>

train[2] [trɛ̃] *n.m.* **1** noise, racket **Quand il a parti la machine, ça faisait le même train.* When he started up the engine, it was making the same noise. (Wh83) **Il y en avait un drôle de train.* There was a strange noise. (EV, An94) *Tu vas aller parmi ce poisson-là et tu vas emmener du train pour les faire peur, comme ça ils vont aller nager, ils vont aller se prendre dans ton tramail.* You're going to see the fish and you're going to make noise to scare the fish and then they're going to be caught in your trammel. (SM) **2** trouble, altercation, dispute, quarrel, fuss *Je veux pas de train, je veux pas chicaner.* I don't want any trouble, I don't want to fight. (Lv88) *Il cherche tout le temps du train à son voisin.* He's always looking for a dispute with his neighbor. (Lv88) *Mais j'aime ce bayou icitte, y a pas de train ici.*

But I like this bayou, there's no trouble here. (TB) *Ça se battait. Il y avait des fois que ça allait bien aisé, et d'autres fois, il y avait du train.* They would fight. Sometimes things would go well, and other times there were altercations. (EV) ◊ **•faire du train** to make noise *On faisait du train avec des bâtons et on poussait les râles éyoù la levée, la barrière était haute.* We would make noise with sticks and we'd push the rails to where the levee, the fence was high. (VM) *T'arrêtes pas faire du train jusqu'à les deux t'invitent dans la maison pour manger ou boire quelque chose.* You don't stop making noise until both of them invite you inside the house to eat or drink something. (AV) <AV, VM, Da84> <*Loc:* AV, EV, LA, SB, SL, SM, VM, An94, Da84, Hi02, La99, Lv88>

train[3] [trɛ̃] *n.m.* speed, pace, rate ◊ **•aller au train des vieux** to go slowly and carefully, in the manner of old folks <Da84, La99> **•aller bon train** to go at a good clip <Da84> **•aller (à) petit train** to go slowly **Ils ont vu l'homme était après s'en aller à petit train pour s'en aller chez lui.* They saw that the man was going slowly to go home. (SL, An94) <SL, VM, An94, Da84, Lv88> **•aller le train** ***a*** to pace (of a horse) ***b*** to go slowly <SB, Da84> **•faire le train** to do daily chores (on a farm) <Lv88> **•se mettre en train** to make a beginning, make a start <Da84> **•petit train va loin** slow and steady wins the race <Lv88> <*Loc:* AV, EV, LA, SB, SL, SM, VM, An94, Da84, Hi02, La99, Lv88>

train[4] [trɛ̃] ◊ **•être en train de / être entrain de** to be about to (do s.t.) *Il est en train de dire quelque chose à ce bougre.* He is about to tell that fellow something. (VM) *Je suis en train de laver mon char.* I'm about to wash my car. (Gu00) **Je suis entrain de manger.* I am about to eat. (Da84) **Je suis en train de commencer.* I am about to begin. (Da84) <EV, VM, Da84, Gu00, Hi02> <*Loc:* EV, VM, Da84, Gu00, Hi02>

traînage [trɛ̃naʒ] *n.m.* dragging, hauling ◊ **•traînage de maison** house moving <Da84> <*Loc:* Da84>

traînaille [trɛ̃naj] *n.f.* **1** things that are scattered or lying around **2** riffraff <*Loc:* EV, SB, Da84, Lv88, Ph36>

traînailler [trɛ̃naje] *v.intr.* **1** to run around, dissipate, gallivant *Quand il était jeune, tout ça il faisait, c'était traînailler les rues et bambocher toute la nuit.* When he was young, all he did was run around in the streets and drink all night long. (LA) **2** to linger, loiter about *Lui, il peut traînailler toute la journée après faire rien du tout.* He can loiter about all day long doing nothing. (LA) ◊ **•traînailler les chemins** to wander about as a hobo *Tout ce qu'il fait c'est traînailler les chemins.* All he does is wander around like a hobo. (SM) <SM> <*Loc:* AV, LA, SB, SM, Da84, Hi02, Lv88>

traînailleur [trɛ̃najœr] *n.m.* good-for-nothing, loiterer, loafer <*Loc:* AV, Lv88>

traînant, -e [trɛ̃nɑ̃, -ɑ̃t] *adj.* dragging, trailing, hanging ◊ **•mure traînante** dewberry <VM> <*Loc:* VM, Da84>

traînard [trɛ̃nar] *n.m.* **1** gallivanter **2** bum, hobo <*Loc:* Da84>

traînassant [trɛ̃nasɑ̃] *adj.* sluggish, listless, out of sorts, not well *On est tout manière traînassant aujourd'hui.* We're all a little out of sorts today. (LA) <*Loc:* LA, VM, Da84, Lv88>

traînasse [trɛ̃nas] *n.f.* **1** trail made through marsh grass for the passage of pirogues or small boats *Le petit chaland entre dans une traînasse et s'arrête à une palangre.* The little boat goes into a boat trail and stops at a trot line. (Lv88) **2** trail where logs are dragged out of the swamps **3** portage, place where boats are carried from one body of water to another **4** a following (usu. of children, charges, or dependents) **M. Durel et sa traînasse sont après venir.* M. Durel and his following are coming. (EV, Ph36) *Avoir une traînasse.* To have a large number of dependents. (SJ) **5** things that are scattered or lying about *Ramasse tes traînasses.* Pick up the things you've left lying around. (TB) <*Loc:* AV, EV, IB, LF, SB, SJ, TB, VM, Da84, La99, Lv88, Ph36, Re31>

traînasser [trɛ̀nase] *v.intr.* to gallivant, dissipate, run around *Il arrêtait pas de traînasser toute la nuit. C'est pour ça que sa femme l'a quitté.* He wouldn't stop gallivanting all night long. That's why his wife left him. (LA) <*Loc:* LA, Da84>

traîne[1] [trɛ̃n] *n.f.* sleigh <*Loc:* Da84, Lv88>

traîne[2] [trɛ̃n] *n.f.* ◊ **•à la traîne** ***a*** on the run, on the go *Elle est tout le temps à la traîne dans le village.* She's always on the run in town. (LA) ***b*** in disorder *Il laisse ses affaires à la traîne. C'est pourquoi il peut pas les trouver.* He leaves his things in disorder. That's why he can't find them. (SM) <SM, VM, Re31> <*Loc:* LA, SM, VM, Re31>

traîné, -e [trɛ̃ne] *n.* vagabond <*Loc:* Lv88>

traîneau [trɛ̃no] *n.m.* **1** sled, skid **2** marsh buggy (vehicle used for traveling over marsh land) **3** railway coach, train car <*Loc:* AC, LF, SL, VM, Da84>

traîner [trɛ̃ne] **I** *v.tr.* **1** to drag, draw, haul *Ça me traînait un bout.* It dragged me a ways. (SL) *J'ai juste* WAX *le plancher. Traîne pas ça dessus; tu vas l'écorcher!* I just waxed the floor. Don't drag that on it; you'll scratch it! (LA) *Un* SKIMMERNET *est meilleur, tu peux travailler ça le jour ou le soir. Paupière, juste le soir. C'est un* FRAME *carré, et il va pas traîner le fond.* A skimmernet is better, you can work that during the day or the evening. A butterfly net, only in the evening. It's a square frame, and it won't drag the bottom. (TB) **2** to wear for everyday use (e.g. for work) *Il traîne ses bons souliers.* He's wearing his good shoes for everyday use. (TB) **II** *v.intr.* **1** to loiter, hang around *Arrêtez de traîner à l'entour d'ici.* Stop hanging around here. (LA) **2** to travel around, wander around, gallivant *Quand j'ai eu mon premier char, je traînais un tas.* When I got my first car, I rode around a lot. (SL) **III se traîner** *v.pron.* to drag o.s., crawl *Le bébé est juste après commencer à se traîner.* The baby is just starting to crawl. (LA) ◊ **•traîner les rues** to run the streets, gallivant <Da84> **•traîner les savates** to lag behind in one's work <SB, La99> **•traîner une maison**

to move a house, haul a house <Da84> **•pas (se) traîner les pattes {talons}** ***a*** to go quickly ***b*** to do s.t. quickly without wasting time <AC, La99> <*Loc:* AC, AV, LA, LF, SB, SL, TB, Da84, Hi02, La99>

traîneur, -euse [trẽnœr, -øz] *n.* loafer, bum <*Loc:* SM, VM, Da84, Lv88>

traîneuse [trẽnøz] *n.f.* **1** loose woman **2** prostitute <*Loc:* SM, Da84, Lv88>

traire [trær] *v.tr.* to milk (a cow) *Traire la vache.* To milk the cow. (SM) <*Loc:* SB, SM, Da84>

trait [trɛ, tre] *n.m.* **1** trace (of a harness) *Là, dessus le collier de bois, il y avait des crochets chaque bord. Tu mettais ça ils appellent des traits, des mailles de chaînes, deux chaînes chaque bord.* Then, on the wooden collar, there were hooks on each side. You would put what they called traces, links of chain, two chains on each side. (AC) **2** feature (of a face) ◊ **•trait de chaîne** harness rigging <EV> <*Loc:* AC, EV, Da84>

traitable [tretab(l)] *adj.* treatable, curable *Une bonne chose pour elle, son cancer est traitable.* A good thing for her, her cancer is treatable. (LA) <*Loc:* LA, Da84>

traitement [trɛtmɑ̃] *n.m.* treatment, remedy, folk healing *Il m'a dit comme ça que lui il connaît pas traiter du tout, il connaît pas arien du tout dans les traitements.* He told me like that that he knows nothing about folk healing, he knows nothing at all about folk healing. (TB) <*Loc:* TB, Da84>

traiter [trete] **I** *v.tr.* **1** to treat (an illness or a sick person) by means of prayers, incantations, herbs, or other folk remedies *Moi, je traite pour le coup de soleil.* I treat for sunburns. (Guoo) *Mon père traitait les animaux, et ça venait tous à la maison avec leurs animaux ou lui il allait chez eux pour traiter n'importe qui n-avait avec eux.* My father treated animals, and they all would come to the house with their animals or he would go to their home to treat whatever was wrong with them. (IB) *Ils ont bégué pour quelqu'un dans la famille que telle et telle venait nous traiter.* They begged for someone in the family, that one or another would come and treat us. (EV) **2** to treat or deal with *Il traite ses amis bien.* He treats his friends well. (LA) **II** *v.intr.* **1** to treat medically *Mon docteur traite pas pour les maladies de cœur.* My doctor does not treat heart ailments. (LA) **2** to treat (by folk remedies) *Mme. Ozémé Buquet a traité à Cilé pour la maladie d'os.* Mrs. Ozémé Buquet treated Cilé for rickets. (TB) *Ça traite beaucoup pour le résipère.* They treat a lot for Saint Anthony's fire. (Lv88) **III se traiter** *v.pron.* to treat o.s. or each other in a particular way *Ils se traitont comme des chiens.* They treat each other like dogs. (LA) ◊ **•traiter de fou** to call (s.o.) a fool, treat as a fool *Ils m'ont traité de fou quand j'ai dit que je voulais m'acheter une maison.* They called me a fool when I said I wanted to buy myself a house. (LA) <LA, Da84> **•traiter de père** to treat as a father <Da84> **•traiter de voleur** to call (s.o.) a thief, treat as a thief <Da84> <*Loc:* AC, EV, IB, IV, LA, LF, TB, Da84, Guoo, Hi02, Lv88>

traiteur, -euse [tretœr -øz] *n.* traditional healer, faith healer *Quand j'avais 13 ans, j'ai eu une mauvaise dartre. Ma mère m'a amené chez une vieille traiteuse à la campagne.* When I was thirteen I had a bad mole. My mom took me to an old faith healer in the country. (Guoo) *Plein de mes amis dit, t'aurais dû aller voir un traiteur. Allez voir un traiteur. Je dis non, le docteur m'a donné les médecines, si ça ça fait pas, là je vas aller voir un traiteur.* Many of my friends said, you should have gone to see a healer. Go see a healer. I said, no, the doctor gave me medicine, if that doesn't work, then I'll go see a healer. (TB) <*Loc:* AC, AV, EV, IB, LF, SB, SJ, SL, SM, TB, VM, Da84, Guoo, Hi02, Lv88, Ph36>

traître[1] [trɛt(r)] *adj.* vicious, deceitful, treacherous, perfidious ◊ **•traître comme la mort** terribly deceitful <AV, La99> **•en traître** treacherously, by surprise, sneakily *Il a arrivé au bal en traître.* He came to the dance sneakily. (LA) <LA, Da84> <*Loc:* AV, IB, LA, Da84, La99>

traître[2] [trɛt(r)] *n.m.* traitor, deceitful person *Lui il a été pour d'être un prêtre et moi j'ai été pour d'être un traître.* He became a priest and I became a traitor (IB) <*Loc:* AV, IB, LA, Da84, La99>

trallée [trale, tralale] *n.f.* **1** bunch, large quantity, large number or group *Il a une trallée d'enfants.* He has a bunch of children. (SM) **2** group (e.g. of children) being chaperoned <*Loc:* AV, EV, IB, LF, SB, SJ, SL, SM, TB, Da84, Lv88>

tramail (tramaille, tremaille, trois-mailles) [tramaj, trəmaj, trwamaj] *n.m.* **1** three-panel net *Il a un set de grosses mailles ce bord ici et un set de grosses mailles l'autre bord, ça c'est trois mailles, ça s'appelle ça trois-mailles.* He has a set of wide knit nets on this side and a set of wide knit nets on the other side, that's three paneled nets, they call that three-panel nets. (JE) **2** trammel, gill net, small seine *Un trois-mailles... ils avaient un sac dessus. Et tu mettais deux bâtons, et tu halais les bâtons tout doucement à terre, et tout ça qu'il avait dedans le filet allait dedans le sac. C'était pas grand, c'était à peu près, oh, je dirais peut-être cent livres, cent cinquante livres de poissons.* A trammel . . . they had a bag on them. And you attached two poles, and you pulled the poles slowly toward land, and everything that there was in the net went into the sack. It wasn't big, it was about, oh, I would say a hundred pounds, a hundred and fifty pounds. (LF) <*Loc:* EV, JE, LF, SM, Da84>

tramaille ♦see **tramail**

tramailler (trois-mailler) [tramaje, trwamaje] *v.intr.* to trammel, fish with a trammel *Là ça c'est une seine mais ça appelle ça tramailler.* There that's a "seine," but they call [fishing with] it "trammeling." (SM) <*Loc:* LF, SM>

TRAMP [trɑ̃p, ɹɛ̃p] *n.m.* hobo, tramp, bum, vagabond <*Loc:* Da84, Lv88>

tranchant [trɑ̃ʃɑ̃] *n.m.* edge, cutting edge <*Loc:* Da84>

tranche [trɑ̃ʃ] *n.f.* **1** slice, slab **2** cut ◊ •**tranche de pain** slice of bread <AC, LA, An94, Da84> <***Loc:*** AC, LA, An94, Da84>

tranchée [trɑ̃ʃe] *n.f.* slice, section (of an orange, etc.) *Donne à Jean une tranchée de ton orange.* Give John a slice of your orange. (IB) <***Loc:*** IB>

tranchement [trɑ̃ʃmɑ̃] *n.m.* ◊ •**tranchement d'urine** urinary retention, ischuria *Et pour quelqu'un qui a le tranchement d'urine, tu connais, je yeux fais bouillir des feuilles de pêcher.* And for someone who has urine retention, you know, I make them boil peach leaves. (TB) <TB> <***Loc:*** TB>

trancher [trɑ̃ʃe] **I** *v.tr.* to slice, cut, carve **Mon oncle était par derrière lui, et il était après trancher son derrière avec le fouet.* My uncle was after him, and he was cutting his behind with the whip. (IV, An94) **II** *v.intr.* to cut easily, be sharp *Il avait un couteau qui tranchait.* He had a knife that was sharp. (LA) <***Loc:*** AC, IV, LA, An94, Da84>

trancheuse [trɑ̃ʃøz] *n.f.* **1** slicer **2** disk plow **3** disk harrow <***Loc:*** VM, Da84>

tranquille [trɑ̃kil] *adj.* quiet, still, calm, tranquil *Tu vas dans l'Atchafalaya, tu vois pas personne, c'est tranquille.* You go into the Atchafalaya basin, you don't see anyone, it's quiet. (SM) *Mame nous disait mais je connaissais comment faire, comment me présenter, comment faire pour faire une bonne fille, une fille tranquille et sage.* Mom used to tell us, but I knew how to present myself, how to act to be a quiet and well-behaved girl. (EV) *Restez tranquilles!* Be quiet! (TB) <***Loc:*** AC, AL, EV, SM, TB, Da84, Hi02>

tranquillement [trɑ̃kilmɑ̃] *adv.* peacefully, quietly *Dis pas rien. Il est après dormir bien tranquillement.* Don't say anything. He's sleeping quietly. (LA) <***Loc:*** LA, Da84>

tranquilliser [trɑ̃kilize] **I** *v.tr.* to quiet, calm, tranquilize *Ils avaient bu et il pouvait p'us les tranquilliser.* They had drunk, and he couldn't calm them down anymore. (LA) **II se tranquilliser** *v.pron.* to calm down, quiet down, become quiet *Tu ferais mieux de te tranquilliser avant ton père arrive.* You had better calm down before your father gets here. (LA) <***Loc:*** LA, Da84>

tranquillité [trɑ̃kilite] *n.f.* quietness, tranquility, calm, stillness <***Loc:*** Da84>

transfer ♦see **transfert**

transférer [trɑ̃sfere] **I** *v.tr.* **1** to transfer, move from one place or job to another *Mon oncle a été tranféré à Houston.* My uncle was transferred to Houston. (LA) **2** to transport *Y'a un bus qui va te transférer à la Ville Platte.* There is a bus that will take you to Ville Platte. (Lv88) **II** *v.intr.* to be part of, be included in *Je voulais pas être transféré dans la dispute.* I didn't want to be included in the dispute. (VM) <***Loc:*** LA, TB, VM, Da84, Lv88>

transfert (**transfer**) [trɑ̃sfær] *n.m.* **1** transfer, removal **2** bus (esp. a school bus) *Quand on était monté dessus le transfer c'était pareil comme on était* GONE *là-bas en ville.* When we had gotten on the bus, it was just as if we had gone to New Orleans. (SL) **3** horse-drawn school bus ◊ •**transfert d'école** school bus <SJ, Hi02> <***Loc:*** AV, IB, SJ, SL, SM, VM, Da84, Hi02, Lv88>

transmettre [trɑ̃smɛt(r)] *v.tr.* to transfer from one place to another *Elle a transmis sa viande dans une plus grande chaudière.* She transferred her meat to a bigger pot. (LA) <***Loc:*** LA, Da84>

transmission[1] [trɑ̃smisjɔ̃] *n.f.* transmission, conveying, passing on <***Loc:*** Da84>

transmission[2] [trɑ̃smisjɔ̃] *n.f.* transmission (of a car or truck) <***Loc:*** Da84>

transmission[3] [trɑ̃smisjɔ̃] *n.m.* transom <***Loc:*** Da84>

transom [trɑ̃sɔ̃] *n.m.* transom <***Loc:*** Da84>

transpiration [trɑ̃spirasjɔ̃] *n.f.* **1** sweating, perspiration **2** sweat <***Loc:*** Da84>

transpire [trɑ̃spir] *n.f.* sweat *Le garçon a une transpire qui sent fort.* The boy has strong-smelling sweat. (SB) <***Loc:*** SB>

transpirer [trɑ̃spire] *v.intr.* to sweat, perspire *Il faisait chaud. J'ai jamais transpiré comme ça dans ma vie.* It was hot. I never perspired like that in my life. (LA) <***Loc:*** AC, LA, Da84, Fa77>

transplanter [trɑ̃splɑ̃te] **I** *v.tr.* to transplant *C'est proche l'heure de transplanter mes tomates dans mon jardin.* It's almost time to transplant my tomato plants into my garden. (LA) **II se transplanter** *v.pron.* to move o.s., transplant o.s., be transplanted *Il s'a transplanté ici du Texas.* He moved here from Texas. (LA) <***Loc:*** LA, Da84>

transportable [trɑ̃spɔrtab(l)] *adj.* transportable, movable *La maison en briques était pas transportable.* The brick house was not movable. (LA) <***Loc:*** LA, Da84>

transportation [trɑ̃spɔrtasjɔ̃] *n.f.* transportation <***Loc:*** Da84, Lv88>

transporter [trɑ̃spɔrte] *v.tr.* to transport *Le petit bateau, ça que je suis après faire asteur là, c'était un bateau qui transportait les huîtres.* The little boat, the one I'm making now, that was a boat for transporting oysters. (LF) <***Loc:*** AC, LF, Da84>

transposer [trɑ̃spoze] *v.tr.* to transpose *L'ouvrier a transposé ses marques et il a mal coupé la planche.* The carpenter transposed his marks and cut the plank wrong. (LA) <***Loc:*** LA, Da84>

transvider [trɑ̃svide] *v.tr.* to pour from one container into another, decant *Là tu vas transvider ton jus dans un bocal.* Then you will pour your juice into a jar. (LA) <***Loc:*** AV, IB, LA, SB, SJ, Da84, Lv88>

trapeuze ♦see **trapèze**

trapèze (**trapeuze**) [trapɛz, trapøz] *n.f.* trapeze <***Loc:*** Da84, Lv88>

trapiller ♦see **trapigner**

trappe [trap] *n.f.* trap, snare ◊ •**trappe à souris** mousetrap <Da84, Lv88> <***Loc:*** Da84, Lv88, Re31>

trape-sottes [trapsɔt] *n.m.* con, con game **Son affaire qu'il a, c'est in vrai trape-sott'.* That thing he's got going is a real con game. (EV, Ph36) <***Loc:*** EV, Ph36>

trapper [trape] *v.tr.* to trap, catch *On a habitude de trapper des nutrias pour la peau, mais asteur ça vaut p'us rien.* We used to trap nutria for their fur, but now it's not worth anything. (LA) <***Loc:*** LA, TB, Da84>

trappeur (**attrapeur**) [trapœr, atrapœr] *n.m.* trapper <***Loc:*** Da84, Lv88, Re31>

trapigner (**trapiller, tripiller**) [trapĩje, trapije, tripije] **I** *v.tr.* to trample *Il a tripillé les fleurs dans le jardin.* He trampled on the flowers in the garden. (TB) **II** *v.intr.* to walk back and forth <***Loc:*** LA, TB, Fa77>

trapinailler [trapinaje] *v.intr.* to be constantly on the go *Jean trapinaille un tas.* John is always on the go. (IB) <***Loc:*** IB>

TRASH [tɹæʃ, trɛʃ] *n.f.* **1** *(usu. pl.)* trash, rubbish *Sors les TRASH.* Take out the trash. (LA) **2** worthless person, trash *Vous-autres veut pas sortir avec elle, c'est rien qu'une DAMN TRASH.* You don't want to go out with her, she's nothing but damn trash. (VM) <***Loc:*** LA, VM>

travail [travaj] *n.m.* **1** work, labor, toil **2** job, occupation **3** workmanship <***Loc:*** AC, EV, Da84, Hi02>

travaillant[1], **-e** [travajɑ̃, -ɑ̃t] *adj.* hardworking, industrious <***Loc:*** SJ, TB, Lv88>

travaillant[2], **-e** [travajɑ̃, -ɑ̃t] *n.* worker, working man or woman, laborer ◊ **•travaillant à la part** sharecropper <VM> **•travaillant de champs {clos}** field laborer, farm hand <IB, SJ> **•travaillant de forge** blacksmith <SJ> <***Loc:*** AC, AV, IB, LF, SB, SJ, SL, SM, TB, VM, Da84, Lv88>

travailler [travaje] **I** *v.tr.* **1** to work, work at, shape (e.g. a piece of wood) *Ça pouvait me prendre une semaine pour travailler un morceau de bois jusqu'à qu'il était paré pour user sur le violon.* It could take me a week to work a piece of wood before it was ready to use on the violin. (AC) **2** to work, farm (a piece of land, a garden) *Le monde travaillait tout leurs champs avec des chevals.* People all worked their fields with horses. (TB) **3** to run, operate *Il travaillait la machine qui chargeait les cannes.* He ran the engine that loaded the cane. (LA) **II** *v.intr.* **1** to work, toil, labor **Il avait des bougres qui travaillaient pour lui.* He had fellows who worked for him. (LA, An94) *J'ai commencé à travailler dans l'affaire de pêche.* I started working in the fishing business. (TB) **2** to function, work, operate *Le FERTILIZER, ça travaille vite, mais pas pour longtemps.* Fertilizer works fast, but not for long. (Lv88) *On est après essayer faire partir une petite machine qui travaille plus.* We're trying to start up a little machine that doesn't work anymore. (EV) *Il y a quelque chose de WRONG, cette accordéon, alle travaille pas bien.* There's something wrong, this accordeon, it doesn't work right. (JE) *Ils ont fait un test trois mois après pour voir si ça avait travaillé.* They did a test three months later to see if it had worked. (VM) *C'est un de les premiers STOVE à l'électricité, j'ai trouvé ça au bord du chemin, et puis ça travaille.* This is one of the first electric stoves, I found it on the side of the road, and it works. (IB) ◊ **•travailler à la charpente** to do carpentry <Da84> **•travailler à la journée** to work by the day, work as a day laborer <Da84> **•travailler à la moitié** to sharecrop on halves *Lui, il fallait il donne la moitié. Il travaillait à la moitié.* He had to give half [of his crop to the boss]. He sharecropped on half. (SL) <SL> **•travailler à la part** to work for a share of profits, sharecrop *Il avait pas sa terre à lui-même, ça fait il travaillait à la part.* He didn't have his own land, so he sharecropped. (LA) <LA> **•travailler à la tâche** to work by the job, task, or piece <Da84> **•travailler au troisième** to sharecrop on thirds <EV> **•travailler comme un neuf / travailler comme un papier de musique** to work well, go smoothly, work like a charm <La99, Lv88> **•travailler par jour** to work by the day <Da84> **•travailler par semaine** to work by the week <Da84> <***Loc:*** AC, EV, JE, IB, IV, JE, LA, SL, SM, TB, VM, An94, Da84, Hi02, La99, Lv88>

travailleur, -euse [travajœr, -øz] *n.* worker, laborer ◊ **•bon travailleur** hard-working man, good worker <Da84> <***Loc:*** AC, Da84>

travers[1] [travær] *n.m.* width, breadth ◊ **•à travers / en travers (de)** ***a*** through *Comme ça la graisse passe en travers les petits trous.* That way the grease goes through the little holes. (SL) *Je passe à travers des Opélousas tous les temps en temps.* I pass through Opelousas from time to time. (Lv88) *Il y avait assez de brûlots! Oh, c'est une mauvaise bétaille. Ça passe en travers des SCREEN et tout.* There were so many gnats! Oh, that's a bad bug. They go through the screens and all. (TB) *Icitte-dedans t'as une huile, une huile espéciale, une huile naturelle qu'empêche l'eau de passer en travers du bois.* In here you've got an oil, a special oil, a natural oil that prevents water from going through the wood. (LF) *Tu peux regarder en travers d'un petit châssis.* You can look through a little window. (Lv88) *Une course en travers de la ville.* A race through the city. (SL) ***b*** across *[Les râles] le soir, tu vois, ça court en travers du chemin, comme un ROADRUNNER.* [Rails] at night, you see, they run across the road, like a roadrunner. (VM) *La nouvelle boutique drouète en travers de la rue de la banque.* The new store right across the street from the bank. (EV) **Ils ont commencé à fouiller. Et dès qu'ils ont fouillé un bout, il y avait un gros bœuf qui s'en venait en travers de le bois avec la flamme qui lui sortait du nez.* They started to dig. And as soon as they had dug a bit, a big bull came at them from across the woods with flame coming out of his nostrils. (SM, An94) ***c*** through (an amount of time) *Jeudi en travers du samedi.* From Thursday through Saturday. (SL) *L'endedans des tuyaux avait calciné à travers les années.* The inside of the pipes had calcified through the years. (LA) *La saison d'écrevisses* *court en travers de septembre et d'octobre.* Crawfish season runs through September and October. (Lv88) *Des fois il travaillait en travers de beaucoup de z-heures.* Sometimes he worked many hours. (Lv88) ***d*** through, from *J'ai eu ça en travers d'une grosse compagnie.* I got that through a big company. (Lv88) *J'ai appris tout ça je connais à travers mon papa.* I learned everything I know through my dad. (Lv88) ***e*** crosswise *Il a resté pris en travers du chemin.* He stayed stuck crosswise in the road. (LA) <EV, LA, LF, SB, SL, SM, TB, VM, An94, Da84, Lv88> **•aller à travers** to go wrong *Je peux pas m'avancer; tout va à travers.* I can't get ahead, everything is going wrong. (TB) <TB> **•être de {en} travers** to be cross or ill-humored, grouchy, be in a bad mood *Je suis en travers depuis trois mois.* I've been in a bad mood for three months. (SM) <LF, SL, SM, Da84, La99> <***Loc:*** EV, LA, LF, SB, SL, SM, TB, VM, Da84, La99, Lv88>

travers[2] [travær] *n.m.pl.* small drains that conduct surplus water in a field to ditches between the cuts <***Loc:*** SJ>

traverse [traværs] *n.f.* **1** crossing, sea voyage **2** ferry, watercraft used for crossing a bayou or other body of water <***Loc:*** LF, TB, VM>

traverser [traværse, travœrse] *v.tr.* to cross, cross over, traverse *Droite au ras du* FERRY *de Galveston ayoù tu traverses la baie là, il y avait un* SALOON *là.* Right next to the Galveston ferry where you cross the bay, there was a saloon there. (TB) *J'attends la complétion du pont avant d'essayer de traverser la rivière.* I'm waiting for the completion of the bridge before trying to cross the river. (SM) *Il m'a crié* LOOK OUT *quand j'étais après traverser la grande rue.* He yelled out to me to look out when I was crossing the main street. (VM) <***Loc:*** AC, IB, SL, SM, TB, VM, Da84, Lv88>

traversin [traværsɛ̃, travœrsɛ̃] *n.m.* bolster, long pillow, double pillow <***Loc:*** AC, LA, SL, VM, Da84>

travouil [travuj] *n.m.* spool or reel used to put string in skeins <***Loc:*** Lv88>

travouiller [travuje] *v.tr.* to wind (string) into a hank or skein *Après que tu fais ton fil, il faut que tu le travouilles.* After you make your thread, you have to wind it into a hank. (VM) <***Loc:*** VM, Lv88>

trawl ♦see **trôle**

trawler ♦see **trôler**

trawleur ♦see **trôleur**

trayon [trejɔ̃, trijɔ̃] *n.m.* teat (of a cow, etc.) <***Loc:*** AC, SM>

TREAT [tɹit] *n.m.* **1** treat **2** invitation, offer <***Loc:*** SB, VM, Lv88>

trèfle [trɛf(l)] *n.m.* **1** clover **2** clubs (in cards) ◊ **•trèfle à quatre feuilles** four-leaf clover <Hi02> **•trèfle salé** wood sorrel, oxalis <LF> <***Loc:*** AC, JE, LF, VM, Da84, Hi02>

treize [trɛz] *adj./n.m.* thirteen <***Loc:*** AC, EV, LA, SM, An94, Da84, Hi02>

treizième [trɛzjɛ̃m] *adj./n.* thirteenth <***Loc:*** AC, Da84>

trelle ♦see **trille**

treller [trele] *v.intr.* to low (of a calf) <***Loc:*** SB>

tremaille ♦see **tramail**

tremblade [trɑ̃blad] *n.f.* trembling, shaking *La fille a la tremblade.* The girl is trembling. (SB) <***Loc:*** SB>

tremblant, -e [trɑ̃blɑ̃, -ɑ̃t] *adj.* trembling, shivering, shaking *J'étais tremblant quand on a arrivé pour manger.* I was trembling when we arrived to eat. (VM) *Pour arriver au* BLIND, *il fallait traverser du maîche tremblant.* To get to the blind, you had to cross a trembling marsh. (LA) <***Loc:*** LA, VM, Da84>

tremble [trɑ̃m, trɑ̃b(l)] *n.m.* fever chills ◊ **•avoir le tremble** to have chills (due to fever) <VM> <***Loc:*** VM>

tremblement [trɑ̃bləmɑ̃] *n.m.* **1** trembling, shaking, quivering, shivering *Oh oui il avait un tremblement.* Oh yes, he had a shake. (TB) **2** seizure **Le maître d'école a dit que juste quec semaines après Scotty avait déménagé, le principal a trouvé Bengi endessous ein arbre après recess, après avoir ein mauvais tremblement.* The teacher said that just a few weeks after Scotty moved, the principal found Bengi under a tree at recess having a terrible seizure. (Wh83) ◊ **•tremblement de terre** earthquake, tremor <EV, An94, Da84> **•tous les tremblements de terre** every once in a while <SL, La99> <***Loc:*** EV, PQ, SL, TB, An94, Da84, La99, Wh83>

trembler [trɑ̃ble] *v.intr.* to shake, tremble, shiver, quake *Mais lui il tremblait. Et je dis "Daddy, tu te sens bien?"* But he was shaking. And I said, "Daddy, do you feel all right?" (TB) <***Loc:*** AC, TB, Da84>

trempe[1] [trɑ̃p] *adj.* wet, soaked, damp *Faulait mettre des bons capots pour arriver sans d'être trempe.* We had to put on good coats to arrive without being completely wet. (IB) *De la terre trempe.* Wet ground. (Lv88) *Un automne trempe.* A wet autumn. (Lv88) ◊ **•mettre à la trempe** to soak, set in liquid *J'ai mis mon pain à la trempe dans mon lait.* I put my bread to soak in my milk. (EV) <EV, Da84> <***Loc:*** AC, EV, IB, SM, TB, VM, Da84, Gu00, Hi02, Lv88>

trempe[2] [trɑ̃p] *n.f.* beating, whipping *Son père lui a foutu une trempe quand il est arrivé chez lui.* His father gave him a beating when he got home. (SB) <***Loc:*** SB>

trempée [trɑ̃pe] *n.f.* beating, volley of blows <***Loc:*** VM>

tremper [trɑ̃pe] **I** *v.tr.* **1** to wet, moisten, cause to be wet *Va tremper cette serviette pour moi.* Go wet this towel for me. (LF) **2** to soak *Tu trempais ton pain dans un bol avec du lait et un œuf battu.* You would soak your bread in a bowl of milk and a beaten egg. (LA) **3** to dip, dunk *J'ai trempé mon pain dans le lait.* I dunked my bread in the milk. (EV) **II** *v.intr.* to soak *Là tu laissais ça tremper toute la nuit.* Then you let that soak all night. (LA) **III se tremper** *v.pron.* **1** to get wet, get soaked, be soaked *Il s'a tout trempé dans la pluie.* He got soaked in the rain. (LA) **2** to wet o.s., urinate in one's clothing *Tu t'as trempé?* Did you wet your pants?

(LA) ◊ **•tremper le lit** to wet the bed *T'as trempé ton lit.* You wet your bed. (VM) <VM, Da84> <***Loc:*** AC, AV, EV, IB, IV, JE, LA, LF, SM, TB, VM, Da84>

trentaine [trɑ̃tɛ̃n] *n.f.* about thirty <***Loc:*** Da84>

trente [trɑ̃t] *adj./n.m.* thirty *Ils ont au-dessus trente ans d'expérience.* They have more than thirty years of experience. (EV) ◊ **•se mettre en trente-quatre {trente-six}** to outdo o.s., make a great effort *Mais je peux pas me mettre en trente-quatre!* I can't divide myself into thirty-four [= I can't make that great an effort]. (Lv88) *Il s'a mis en trente-six pour aller voir sa belle.* He outdid himself [dressing up] to see his girlfriend. (SM) <SM, Lv88> <***Loc:*** AC, EV, SM, VM, Da84, Hi02, Lv88>

trentième [trɑ̃tjɛ̃m] *adj./n.* thirtieth <***Loc:*** AC, Da84>

très [tre] *adv.* very, very much, greatly, much *Il était très farce.* He was very comical. (LA) *Les Français ont nommé ça "sac-à-lait": la chair est très blanche.* The French named that "sack-of-milk": the flesh is very white. (SL) *On va chez Lorita pour souper. Alle est très avenante, alle nous invite tout le temps.* We're going to Lorita's for supper. She's very nice, she invites us all the time. (LF) <***Loc:*** LA, LF, SL, Da84, Hi02>

trésor [trezɔr] *n.m.* **1** treasure **2** wealth, riches <***Loc:*** Da84>

trésorier [trezorje] *n.m.* treasurer <***Loc:*** Da84>

tresse [trɛs] *n.f.* tress, braid ◊ **•tresse d'ail** string of garlic *Le marchand avait des tresses d'ail à cinquante sous pièce.* The merchant had strings of garlic for fifty cents apiece. (TB) <TB> <***Loc:*** AC, TB, Da84>

tresser [trese] *v.tr.* to braid, plait (hair, etc.) *Sa mère pouvait passer des heures à lui tresser ses cheveux.* Her mother could spend hours braiding her hair. (LA) <***Loc:*** AC, LA, SL, Da84>

tréteau [treto] *n.m.* **1** sawhorse **2** tripod **3** scaffold **4** stand **5** trestle <***Loc:*** AC, EV, VM, Da84>

triage [triaʒ] *n.m.* choosing, sorting <***Loc:*** Da84>

triangle [triɑ̃g(l)] *n.m.* **1** triangle **2** triangle, steel triangle used as a musical percussion instrument <***Loc:*** AC, Da84>

TRIBE ♦see **tribu**

tribord [tribɔr] *n.* ◊ **•(de) tribord et babord {bâbord}** ***a*** all over the place, helter-skelter, in all directions, on every side *Courir de tribord et babord.* To run in all directions. (LF) ***b*** in disorder *C'est tout de tribord et bâbord icite.* Everything is topsy-turvy here. (Lv88) ***c*** inconsistently, in a wavering fashion <LF, SL, La99, Lv88> <***Loc:*** LF, SL, La99, Lv88>

tribouliser ♦see **terboliser**

tribu (**TRIBE**) [triby, tɹaɪb] *n.f.* tribe <***Loc:*** Da84>

tribuchet [tribyʃe] *n.m.* spring trap (for catching birds), home-made bird trap <***Loc:*** IB, SJ>

tribulation [tribylasjɔ̃] *n.f.* [*eccl.*] trouble, tribulation <***Loc:*** Da84>

tribune (**trubine**) [tribyn, trybin] *n.f.* **1** choir loft **2** gallery in the church where the organ is located <***Loc:*** VM, Da84>

tricher [triʃe] **I** *v.tr.* to cheat, trick, deceive *Il m'a triché sur le riz. Il m'a pas donné un plein sac.* He cheated me on the rice. He didn't give me a full sack. (VM) **II** *v.intr.* to cheat ◊ **•tricher sur la grègue** to take coffee from the pot before it is done brewing <VM> <***Loc:*** VM, Da84>

tricherie [triʃri] *n.f.* cheating <***Loc:*** Da84>

tricheur [triʃœr] *n.m.* cheater, crook <***Loc:*** Da84>

tricoler [trikole] *v.intr.* to stagger, totter, waver *Il tricolait tout partout quand il a arrivé dans la maison saoul.* He was staggering all over when he came home drunk. (LA) <***Loc:*** IB, JE, LA, LF, SJ, TB, VM, La99, Lv88>

tricot [triko] *n.m.* **1** knit, knitted cloth **2** sweater *Mets ton tricot. Il fait frais déhors.* Put on your sweater. It's chilly outside. (LA) <***Loc:*** LA, Da84>

tricoter [trikote] *v.tr.* **1** to knit *Elle a tricoté un beau* CAP *pour son père.* She knitted a beautiful cap for her father. (LA) **2** to weave in and out, stagger, totter, waver (while walking) <***Loc:*** LA, Da84, Fa77>

TRICYCLE [tɹaɪsɪkəl] *n.m.* tricycle <***Loc:*** SL>

trier [trie, trije] *v.tr.* to choose, sort, pick out, select *Ça c'est les machines qu'épluchent des chevrettes. Et là les femmes se met sur la bande pour trier, arracher les épluches et les chevrettes cassées et les petits poissons que peut-être qui va passer.* Those are machines that peel the shrimp. Women stand at the conveyor belts to sort, pull out the peels and broken shrimp and little fish that might come by. (LF) *Dans les huit que j'ai vus, il a fallu que j'en trie un.* Of the eight [doctors] that I saw, I had to choose one. (VM) *Et quand on faisait des prâlines de pistache là moi et ma sœur on allait au magasin et on triait les belles pailles de maïs.* And when we made peanut pralines, my sister and I would go to the barn and pick out the finest corn shucks. (EV) ◊ **•trier les cheveux** to part one's hair *Il avait du mal à trier ses cheveux sans un miroir.* He had a hard time parting his hair without a mirror. (LA) <EV, LA> <***Loc:*** EV, LA, LF, VM, Da84>

trille (**trelle**) [trij, trɛl] *n.f.* trellis <***Loc:*** AC, IB>

trimage [trimaʒ] *n.m.* noise, uproar <***Loc:*** VM>

trinité [trinite] *n.f.* trinity ◊ **•Sainte Trinité** Holy Trinity <Da84> <***Loc:*** Da84>

trinquer [trɛ̃ke] *v.intr.* to make a toast *Trinquons, trinquons, mes chers camarades, mais oublions jamais la raison.* Let's toast, let's toast, dear friends, but let's never forget reason. (IB, ch: *Trinquons*) <***Loc:*** IB, Hi02>

triomphe [triɔ̃f] *n.m.* triumph, victory <***Loc:*** Da84>

tripage [tripaʒ] *n.f.* offal, entrails (collectively) <***Loc:*** Da84>

tripe [trip] *n.f.* **1** *(usu. pl.)* intestines, guts *Moi j'étais après prendre des tests la semaine passée, pour supposé j'avais des trous dans mes tripes, le docteur m'avait dit ça.* I was taking tests last week, supposedly I had holes in my intestines, the doctor had told me that. (LF) **2** intestines used as food, esp. for sausage casing ◊ **•tripe épurée** very skinny person <SM, Lv88> **•tripes à la chique** traditional dish of veal tripe <SM, VM, Lv88> **•avoir des tripes dans les pieds** to be a big eater <La99> **•la tripe du nord** large intestine <VM> <***Loc:*** AV, EV, LA, LF, SM, TB, VM, Da84, La99, Lv88>

tripiller ♦see **trapigner**

tripler [triple] **I** *v.tr.* to triple *Il a triplé sa rente de coton depuis l'année passée.* He tripled his cotton profits since last year. (VM) **II** *v.intr.* to triple *Le prix du gaz a proche triplé.* The price of gas has almost tripled. (LA) <***Loc:*** LA, VM, Da84>

tripoter [tripote] **I** *v.tr.* to fondle, feel up *Le garçon a tripoté la jeune fille.* The boy felt the girl up. (SB) **II** *v.intr.* to tinker, putter around <***Loc:*** SB, Da84, Re31>

triste [tris(t)] *adj.* **1** sad, sorrowful *Alle est triste, alle sort d'enterrer son défint.* She's sad, she's just come from burying her deceased husband. (VM) *Quelle triste nouvelle. C'est chagrinant.* What sad news. It's heartbreaking. (VM) *Une triste vie* BUT *c'était une bonne vie. Aujourd'hui le monde est fou.* A sad life but it was a good life. Today people are crazy. (TB) **C'est triste quand-même.* That's terrible. (Da84) *On allait ensevelir les enfants qui étaient morts jusqu'à trois dans la même maison. [...] C'était beaucoup triste de voir des choses comme ça.* We would go and prepare for burial the babies who had died, up to three in the same house. It was very sad to see things like that. (AC) *Je me fais l'idée c'était une triste affaire pour une femme, elle avait pas de défense.* I imagine that it was a sad affair for a woman, she was vulnerable. (EV) **2** pathetic, pitiful **Ça c'est un triste homme.* That's a poor excuse of a man. (Da84) **Ça c'est une triste chose.* That's a pitiful thing. (Da84) <***Loc:*** AC, AV, EV, TB, VM, Da84, Hi02>

tristement [tristəmɑ̃] *adv.* pitifully, sadly, miserably, sorrowfully *Il s'en allait tout tristement au cimitière des Abshire hier pour faire de la misère à son père. Quoi faire? Quoi faire?* He went sadly to the Abshire's cemetery yesterday to torment his father. What to do? What to do? (VM) <***Loc:*** VM, Da84, Fa77>

tristesse[1] [tristɛs] *n.f.* **1** sadness, sorrow *Et p'is c'est trop de tristesse, mon j'ai le cœur sur mes bras quand je vois tous ces enfants là, tu sais.* And then it's too sad, I have my heart on my sleeve when I see all those children there, you know. (TB) **2** shame, pity *C'est une tristesse je pense, ce que le gouvernment faisait.* It's a shame, I think, what the government was doing. (TB) *C'était une tristesse, ça qu'a arrivé au monde de Camaron durant l'Ouragan Audrey.* That was a horrible thing that happened to the people of Cameron during Hurricane Audrey. (VM) <***Loc:*** AC, TB, VM, Da84, La99>

tristesse[2] [tristɛs] *interj.* mercy! (expression of astonishment or pity) <***Loc:*** LA, LF, VM, La99>

triter [trite] *v.tr.* to treat (to a meal, etc.) *C'est à son tour à triter.* It's his turn to treat. (LF) <***Loc:*** LF, Da84>

triure [trijyr] *n.f.* part (in the hair) <***Loc:*** VM, Fa77>

trois [trwa] *adj./n.m.* three *J'ai mis deux ou trois changes de linge en dedans.* I put two or three changes of clothes in it. (EV) *Mon grand-père a vi jusqu'à l'âge de cent trois ans.* My grandfather lived until the age of a hundred and three. (LF) *Les trois dernières années, on a pas eu d'eau du tout, on a presque pas pêché, tout l'Amérique est dans une sécheresse.* The last three years, we didn't have water at all, we almost didn't fish, all of America is going through a drought. (SM) ◊ **•trois de la même qualité** three of a kind (hand of cards) <JE> <***Loc:*** AC, AV, EV, JE, LA, LF, PQ, SB, SL, SM, TB, VM, An94, Da84, Gr82, Gu00, Hi02, Lv88, Wh83>

troisième [trwazjɛ̃m] *adj./n.* third *Quand j'étais dans le troisième livre, je parlais pas en anglais.* When I was in the third grade, I couldn't speak English. (LA) *Il est au collège, il est dans sa troisième année de collège à Shreveport, Centenary.* He's in college, he's in his third year of college in Shreveport, Centenary. (VM) **La deuxième fois, il a dit, "Quand je vas revenir la troisième fois, ça sera pas joli!"* The second time, he said, "When I come back a third time, it won't be pretty!" (LA, An94) <***Loc:*** EV, LA, LF, VM, An94, Da84>

trois-mailles ♦see **tramail**

trois-mailler ♦see **tramailler**

trois-pieds [trwapje] *n.m.* tripod *Mémère faisait tout le temps son café sus un trois-pieds qu'alle mettait dans le fouyer l'hiver.* Grandma always made her coffee in a tripod that she put in the fireplace in winter. (TB) <***Loc:*** TB>

trois-rangs [trwarɑ̃] *n.f.* loggerhead turtle <***Loc:*** AL>

trôle (trawl) [trɔl] *n.f. (occ. m.)* **1** trawl net, trawl line, trawl *Après avoir traîné le trôle pour deux heures de temps, les hommes ont levé cinq bailles de chevrettes.* After dragging the trawl for two hours, the men pulled up five tubfuls of shrimp. (TB) *Vous-autres est bien à la fraîche, mais c'est l'heure de rentrer la trawl.* You are comfortable in the shade but it's time to pull in the trawl net. (Lv88) **2** trawling *Il y a des bougres qu'on parle joliment français comme je t'ai dit à la trôle.* There are fellows to whom we speak French pretty much, as I told you, while trawling. (JE) *C'est le temps qu'on a parlé français en trawl.* That's the time when we spoke French while trawling. (JE) **3** trawling season *Il avait été empoigner ses trôles parce que la trôle était pour commencer.* He had gone to get his trawls because the trawling season was about to begin. (TB) ◊ **•aller aux trôles** to go trawling, catch shrimp with a trawl *J'ai commencé à aller aux trôles dans 1941. Ça fait qu'il y a longtemps que je suis après jouer avec ce maillage.* I began going trawling in 1941. So, I've been playing with that mesh for a long time. (TB) *L'été ça faisait leur vie à aller aux trôles pour des chevrettes.* In the summer they made their living going trawling for shrimp. (TB) <TB> <***Loc:*** JE, LF, PQ, SM, TB, Gu00, Lv88>

trôler (**trawler**) [trole] **I** *v.tr.* to trawl, catch with a trawl *On avait habitude trôler des chevrettes pour une semaine à la fois.* We used to trawl shrimp for a week at a time. (IB) **II** *v.intr.* to trawl *Elle, alle a trôlé 17 ans avec moi. Sur le bateau.* She went trawling with me for 17 years. On the boat. (TB) *Je m'en rappelle quand mon pape trôlait il a déjà pogné un comme ça, il dit que c'est un espadron.* I remember when my daddy used to trawl, he caught one like that, he said it was a sawfish. (LF) <***Loc:*** IB, IV, LF, TB>

trôleur (**trawleur**) [trolœr] *n.m.* trawler *Mon père, il piégeait et il trôlait. Il était un pêcheur et un trôleur.* My father fished and trawled. He was a fisherman and a trawler. (TB) *Sur nos bateaux, les trawleurs on parle tout français.* On our boats, all of us trawlers speak French. (Lv88) <***Loc:*** TB, Lv88>

trombone [trɔ̃bɔ̃n] *n.m.* trombone <***Loc:*** Da84>

trompe[1] [trɔ̃p] *n.f.* **1** trunk (of an elephant) **2** Jew's harp <***Loc:*** AC, VM, Da84, Lv88>

trompe[2] [trɔ̃p] *n.f.* mistake, error *Il a fait une trompe quand il a compté l'argent.* He made a mistake when he counted the money. (LF) *J'ai fait une trompe pas pour bêtiser.* I made a serious mistake. (TB) <***Loc:*** LF, TB>

tromper [trɔ̃pe] **I** *v.tr.* **1** to deceive, betray the trust of *Son garçon l'a trompé. Il a mis leur terre à son nom, et puis là il l'a perdue dans une partie de cartes.* His son betrayed him. He put their land in his name, and then he lost it in a card game. (VM) **2** to cheat on *Il a trompé sa femme.* He cheated on his wife. (LA) **II se tromper** *v.pron.* to make a mistake, be mistaken, be wrong *Je croyais je voulais partir, mais je me trompais.* I thought I wanted to leave, but I was mistaken. (LA) *Ça c'était en cinquante-deux si je, je crois pas je me trompe.* That was in fifty-two if I, I don't think I'm mistaken. (TB) ◊ **•se faire tromper** to be fooled *Je m'ai fait tromper.* I got myself taken. (VM) <VM> <***Loc:*** LA, TB, VM, Da84, Hi02>

tromperie [trɔ̃pri] *n.f.* fraud, deceit, cheating <***Loc:*** Da84>

trompette [trɔ̃pɛt] *n.f.* trumpet, horn <***Loc:*** Da84>

trompeur, -euse (**trompeux, -euse**) [trɔ̃pœr, trɔ̃pø, -øz] *adj.* deceitful, misleading, cheating *Il est beaucoup trompeur.* He is very deceitful. (LA) <***Loc:*** LA, VM, Da84>

trompeux ♦see **trompeur**

tronc [trɔ̃] *n.m.* trunk (of a tree) <***Loc:*** SL, Da84>

trône [trɔ̃n] *n.m.* throne <***Loc:*** Da84>

trop [tro] *adv.* **1** too, excessively *Il s'a aperçu trop tard que l'eau montait.* He realized too late that the water was rising. (LA) *Il commence à faire un peu trop chaud pour travailler sur ça.* It's starting to be a little too hot to work on that. (LF) *Je sors p'us avec elle parce qu'elle est trop collante.* I don't go out with her any more because she is too clingy. (VM) *Alle peut pas rester trop au* STOVE. *Elle peut pas avoir trop chaud.* She can't stay near the stove too long. She's not supposed to get too hot. (TB) **2** too much *Ça se saoule trop, tu peux pas dépendre dessus eux-autres.* They get drunk too much, you can't depend on them. (Lv88) **Je peux pas l'entendre. Il y a trop de train.* I can't hear him. There's too much noise. (EV, An94) *À la bouilliture de chevrettes il a pas beaucoup mangé. C'est parce qu'il est pas supposé de manger trop de chevrettes.* At the shrimp boil he didn't each much. It's because he's not supposed to eat too much shrimp. (TB) *J'ai pas trop confiance en la Croix Rouge.* I don't have much faith in the Red Cross. (IB) *Toi, tu veux trop barguiner.* You try to bargain too much. (JE) *Ma main est toute ampoulée, j'ai trop pioché.* My hand is all blistered, I dug too much. (Lv88) ◊ **•de trop** too much *Le fait d'*OFFSHORE *je connais pas de trop. J'ai jamais pêché de trop là-bas.* The offshore business I don't know very well. I've never fished too much out there. (TB) *J'aime pas trotter un cheval. Ça te bouscule de trop.* I don't like to trot a horse. It shakes you up too much. (LA) *[Je parle] pas de trop en anglais* I don't speak English too much. (LF) <LA, LF, TB, Da84> <***Loc:*** AV, EV, IB, JE, LA, LF, SB, SL, SM, TB, VM, An94, Da84, Gr82, Hi02, Lv88, Ph36>

trot (**trotte**) [trɔt] *n.m.* **1** trot, run **2** distance ◊ **•aller petit trotte** to go at a slow pace <Da84> **•faire un petit trotte** to make a short run (to go to the store, etc.) <Da84> <***Loc:*** VM, Da84, Lv88>

trotte ♦see **trot**

trotter [trote] **I** *v.tr.* to trot (a horse) *J'aime pas trotter un cheval. Ça te bouscule de trop.* I don't like to trot a horse. It shakes you up too much. (LA) **II** *v.intr.* to trot *Cette jument pouvait trotter toute la journée sans devenir fatiguée.* That mare could trot all day long without getting tired. (LA) <***Loc:*** LA, Da84>

trotteur[1]**, -euse** [trotœr] *adj.* trotting *Une jument trotteuse.* A trotting mare. (LA) <***Loc:*** LA, Da84>

trotteur[2] [trotœr] *n.m.* trotter <***Loc:*** Da84>

trottoir [trotwar] *n.m.* sidewalk <***Loc:*** Da84>

trou [tru] *n.m.* hole, gap, opening *J'ai tombé dans un trou de cocodrie quand j'étais petit, et j'ai manqué de jamais de m'en débourber.* I fell into an alligator hole when I was little, and I almost never got out of there. (VM) *Ils ont détecté un trou dans le tuyau de gaz.* They found a hole in the gas line. (LA) *Il était après s'asphyxier au fond du trou quand ils l'ont trouvé.* He was suffocating at the bottom of the hole when they found him. (LA) ◊ **•trou de la souris** east, when speaking of the direction in or from which the wind blows <JE, La99, Lv88> **•trou de taureau** ***a*** natural pool, pond, hollow in a prairie ***b*** hole in the ground supposedly made by an enraged bull <VM, Lv88> **•bouche-trou** stop-gap <Da84> **•mettre dans le trou** to dupe, deceive <VM> <***Loc:*** EV, JE, LA, LF, VM, Da84, Gu82, Hi02, La99, Lv88>

troublant, -e [trublɑ̃, -ɑ̃t] *adj.* troubling, bothersome, disturbing *C'était une nouvelle beaucoup troublante.* It was very disturbing news. (VM) <***Loc:*** VM, Da84>

trouble[1] [trub(l)] *adj.* **1** murky, muddy (of water) *Tu peux pas attraper du poisson dans l'eau trouble.* You can't catch fish in troubled water. (LA) **2** troubled, unsettled, worried *C'est une affaire trouble, ça.* That's an unsettled affair. (LA) <***Loc:*** LA, Da84>

trouble[2] [trub(l)] *n.m.* **1** bother, hassle, trouble *Les soybean demandent un tas moins de trouble que le riz.* Soybeans are a lot less trouble than rice. (Lv88) **2** trouble, discord, disorder ◊ **•faire du trouble** to cause trouble *Leur garçon leur fait du trouble depuis l'âge de quinze ans.* Their son has been giving them trouble since he was fifteen. (VM) <VM, Da84> **•(se) donner le trouble / (se) prendre le trouble** to take the trouble *Si tu prends le trouble d'aller loin là-bas, tu veux avoir quelque chose pour ramener.* If you take the trouble to go way out there, you want to have something to take back. (LA) <LA, Da84> <***Loc:*** EV, LA, VM, Da84, Hi02, Lv88>

troubler [truble] **I** *v.tr.* **1** to disturb, trouble, bother *La femme que j'ai prise, elle m'a troublé l'esprit.* The woman I married has troubled my mind. (VM, ch: *Je me suis marié*) **2** to cloud up (a liquid) *Si tu fais pas attention, ça va troubler ta bière.* If you're not careful, it will cloud up your beer. (LA) **II se troubler** *v.pron.* to cloud up, become cloudy (of a liquid) *On savait qu'il y avait quelque chose de drôle quand l'eau s'a troublé.* We knew that there was something wrong when the water became cloudy. (LA) <***Loc:*** IB, LA, VM, Da84>

troué, -e [truwe] *adj.* holey, having holes, pierced with holes <***Loc:*** AC>

troufignon [trufijɔ̃] *n.m.* **1** small hole *Je raccommode ce troufignon.* I'm darning this small hole. (IB) **2** butt, ass, derriere, rump *Ton grand troufignon!* Your big ass! (SB) <***Loc:*** IB, SB>

trouloulou ♦see **tourloulou**

troupe [trup] *n.f.* group, troop, bunch *Une troupe de helicopters les naviguent* OFF-SHORE. A group of helicopters transported them offshore. (Lv88) *Ils ont envoyé une troupe de garçons pour arranger les barrières et refaire les magasins après l'ouragan.* They sent a troop of boys to repair the fences and rebuild the barns after the hurricane. (LA) *Grand-m'man nous laissait jamais aller en nulle part sans qu'il y ait une troupe avec nous-autres.* Grandma never let us go out anywhere unless there was a bunch of people with us. (VM) <***Loc:*** LA, Da84, Lv88>

troupeau [trupo] *n.m.* **1** herd (of animals) **2** flock (of sheep) **3** pack (of dogs) ◊ **•troupeau de bêtes** herd <VM> <***Loc:*** VM, Da84, Hi02>

trousseau [truso] *n.m.* trousseau, hope chest ◊ **•trousseau de bébé** layette <VM> <***Loc:*** VM, Da84>

trousser ♦see **retrousser**

trouvaille [truvaj] *n.f.* find, discovery <***Loc:*** Da84>

trouve [truv] *n.f.* windfall, discovery, lucky hit <***Loc:*** SB, Lv88>

trouver [truve] **I** *v.tr.* **1** to find, discover *On a pas trouvé à rien.* We didn't find anything. (JD) *Le cipre est dur à trouver mais les vieilles maisons étaient faites avec ça.* Cypress is hard to find but old houses were made with it. (IB) *Sa dégaine l'empêche de trouver un mari.* Her slovenliness prevents her from finding a husband. (VM) *Il est bien pour vivre depuis on a trouvé l'huile sur sa terre.* He's well off since oil was found on his land. (SM) **2** to find, consider *Mémère avait trouvé ce nom là joli.* Grandma had found that name pretty. (EV) **Tu trouves?* Do you think so? (Da84) **Monsieur Johnson, moi, je peux pas dire autant de vous. Je vous trouve pas beau.* Mr. Johnson, I can't say as much about you. I don't find you handsome. (SM, An94) *Je trouve que t'as des faux airs avec ma sœur.* I find that you resemble my sister. (SM) *Je l'ai pas trouvé amusant du tout.* I didn't find him funny at all. (LA) **3** to find, determine (after judicial inquiry) *Ils l'ont amené en cour, mais le juge l'a trouvé innocent.* They took him to court, but the judge found him innocent. (EV) **II se trouver** *v.pron.* **1** to find o.s. **Je me trouve malpris.* I find myself in trouble. (Da84) *Il a bien mérité de se trouver avec une femme comme ça. Comme dit le bougre, l'un vaut l'autre et l'autre vaut rien.* He deserves to end up with a woman like that. As they say, one is as good as the other and the other is worthless. (EV) **2** to consider o.s. **Je me trouve riche.* I consider myself rich. (Da84) **3** to be located **Le Pont-Breaux se trouve dedans la Paroisse Saint-Martin.* Breaux Bridge is located in St. Martin Parish. (Hi02) **4** to be found *Ça se trouve pas dessus tous les cartes.* It can't be found on all the maps. (SL) ◊ **•trouver à redire** to find fault, object <Da84> **•trouver le temps long** to perceive that time moves slowly (i.e. be bored or lonely) *Je trouvais le temps long de pas le voir.* It was as if time passed slowly because I didn't see him. (AC) <AC> **•trouver son maître** to meet one's match <Da84> **•se trouver bête** to feel foolish <Da84> <***Loc:*** AC, AV, EV, IB, JD, LA, LF, SL, SM, TB, VM, An94, Da84, Hi02, Lv88, St95, Wh83>

trubine ♦see **tribune**

TRUCK [trœk, trɔk] *n.m.* truck, pick-up truck ◊ **•TRUCK d'école** school bus <Lv88> <***Loc:*** AC, EV, LA, LF, SL, TB, VM, Da84, Hi02, Lv88, Ph36>

truelle [tryɛl] *n.f.* trowel <***Loc:*** AC, SL, Da84>

truie [trɥi] *n.f.* **1** sow, female pig **2** sloppy, slovenly or morally loose woman ◊ **•avoir pas plus d'à peu près qu'une truie aux socos** to not have good judgment, not have good sense <EV, La99> **•vieille truie** old sow (game played with sticks and a tin can) <Da84> <***Loc:*** AV, EV, IB, IV, SM, Da84, La99>

truite [tryt, trɥit] *n.f.* **1** trout, speckled trout, sea trout **2** bass, largemouth bass **3** minnow ◊ **•truite barrée** striped bass <AL> **•truite blanche** sand sea trout, white trout <LF, TB> **•truite d'eau douce** black bass *Y a des grosses* *truites d'eau douce au marché de poisson.* There are some big black bass at the fish market. (TB) <TB> **•truite de mer** sea trout <LF> **•truite grise** speckled trout, spotted sea trout <LF, TB> **•truite verte** ***a*** largemouth bass ***b*** spotted bass <LF, JE, TB, Re31> <***Loc:*** AL, IV, JE, LF, TB, VM, Da84, Gu00, Lv88, Re31>

tu (t') [ty, ti] (*before a vowel* **t'** [t]) *pron.pers. (subj.)* you *Je vais casser ton cou si tu me bloffes!* I'll break your neck if you deceive me! (SM) *Bois une petite goutte et tu vas te sentir mieux.* Drink a little sip and you'll feel better (EV) *Quand tu passes en avant de chez Madame Kelly tu vois pas sa maison à force qu'alle est dans une boisure.* When you pass by Mrs. Kelly's you don't see her house for all the thick foliage. (TB) *Chesse-toi bien après tu sors de la baignoire.* Dry yourself well after you get out of the tub. (LA) *Arrête de faire le bouffon, tu me fais honte!* Stop acting like a clown! You're embarrassing me! (VM) *Qui tu mets dessus?* What do you put on it? (JE) *Quoi tu mets sur le hameçon?* What do you put on the hook? (JE) <***Loc:*** AC, AV, EV, IB, IV, JE, LA, LF, SL, SL, SM, TB, VM, An84, An94, Da84, Gu82, Hi02, La99, Lv88>

tuberculose [tybærkyloz] *n.f.* tuberculosis, consumption <***Loc:*** Da84>

tuer [tɥe, tʃɥe] **I** *v.tr.* 1 to kill **Si t'aurais des chiens de chasse, des taïaux comme ça moi j'ai, tu pourrais tuer un chevreuil.* If you had huntings dogs, hounds like I have, you could kill a deer. (EV, An94) *Des punaises [...] j'en ai tué. Le seul moyen je peux les tuer, c'est avec un marteau.* Stink bugs, I've killed a lot of them. The only way I can kill them is with a hammer. (SL) 2 to slaughter (an animal) *C'est là la boucherie était, tu vois, chez un qui tuait tout le temps.* That's where the butchery was, you see, at the home of someone who slaughtered all the time. (SL) **II se tuer** *v.pron.* to kill o.s., commit suicide *Son frère s'a tué avec un fusil.* His brother committed suicide with a shotgun. (LA) ◊ **•tuer du {le} temps** to kill time *On était juste après tuer le temps à jouer aux cartes.* We were just killing time playing cards. (LA) <LA, Da84> **•tuer la chandelle** to snuff out the candle <VM> **•tuer raide** to knock s.o. dead *Ça va te tuer raide. Ici en bas du bayou il y a pas de serpent qu'est pas* POISONOUS. That will knock you dead. Down the bayou here there aren't any snakes that aren't poisonous. (LF) <LF> **•tuer un oiseau au vol** to kill a bird in flight, kill a bird on the wing <Da84> **•tue-corps** back-breaking *Un ouvrage tue-corps.* A back-breaking job. (VM) <VM, Da84> **•se tuer à travailler** to kill o.s. working <Da84> <***Loc:*** AC, AV, EV, IV, LA, LF, SL, TB, VM, An94, Da84, Hi02, Wh83>

tuerie [tyri] *n.f.* 1 slaughterhouse *Ils ont emmené leurs cochons à la tuerie.* They brought their pigs to the slaughterhouse. (Lv88) *Ça c'était dans une tuerie, c'était pas pour vendre de la viande, c'était juste pour les halles.* That was in a slaughterhouse, it wasn't to sell meat, it was just for the slaughterhouse. (VM) 2 slaughter, massacre **Tous les habitants avaient un chien à rats. En juin, quand on rentrait le nouveau maïs dans les magasins à maïs, on faisait une tuerie de rats avec les voisins. Et chacun venait avec son petit chien.* All the farmers had a rat dog. In June, when we brought the new corn into the corncribs, we had a rat killing with the neighbors. Everyone came with their dog. (Gr86) <***Loc:*** TB, VM, Da84, Gr86, Lv88>

tue-tête [tytɛt] *adv.* ◊ **•à tue-tète** at the top of one's voice *Il parlait à tue-tête.* He was speaking at the top of his voice. (LA) <LA, Da84> <***Loc:*** LA, Da84>

tueur [tyœr] *n.m.* 1 killer, slayer, murderer 2 butcher <***Loc:*** Da84>

TUG [tɔg] *n.m.* tug boat *Parce qu'il va plus vite qu'un* TUG, *il va plus vite qu'un* LUGGER, *c'est pour ça que ça appelle ça un bateau de course.* Because it goes faster than a tug boat, it goes faster than a lugger, that's why it's called a racing boat. (TB) <***Loc:*** JE, TB>

tulipier [tylipje] *n.m.* yellow poplar tree <***Loc:*** LA>

tumeur [tymœr, timœr] *n.f.* 1 tumor, lump 2 swelling <***Loc:*** TB, Da84, Fa77>

TUNE [tun, tʃun] *n.m.* tune, melody, musical air *Hey monsieur D., viens voir ici, viens nous jouer un* TUNE *de ta musique de bouche!* Hey, Mister D., come over here, come and play us one of your harmonica tunes! (EV) <***Loc:*** EV, LF, SB, SL>

turine [tyrin] *n.f.* tureen <***Loc:*** IB>

turluter [tyrlyte] **I** *v.tr.* to hum *Les vieux turlutaient des airs de violon pour danser dans Carême.* The old folks used to hum fiddle tunes to dance to during Lent. (LA) **II** *v.intr.* 1 to hum *Il pouvait turluter pour des heures.* He could hum for hours. (LA) 2 to whirl around <***Loc:*** LA, TB, Lv88>

turlutte [tyrlyt] *n.f.* 1 fight 2 loud noise **Qui c'est qui fait ç'té turlutte?* Who's making that racket? (EV, Ph36) <***Loc:*** EV, Ph36>

turlututu [tyrlytyty] *n.m.* odd-looking hat *Ça c'est le beau turlututu que t'as sus la tête.* That sure is a funny-looking hat that you have on your head. (TB) <***Loc:*** TB>

tuteur [tytœr] *n.m.* 1 tutor, guardian 2 stake, support, guide (e.g. for a tree) *On a mis des tuteurs pour dresser le petit chêne qu'on avait planté.* We put up guides to support the young oak tree that we had planted. (LA) <***Loc:*** LA, Da84>

tuyau [tijo] *n.m.* 1 tube, pipe, duct, flue *Ils aviont un tuyau qui venait de là dans la boucanière.* They had a pipe that was running from there to inside the smoke house. (AC) 2 drinking straw ◊ **•tuyau de pipe** pipe stem <Da84> **•tuyau à boire** drinking straw <LF> <***Loc:*** AC, EV, IB, LF, SM, TB, VM, Da84, Lv88>

TWO-STEP [tustɛp] *n.m.* two-step (popular Cajun dance) <***Loc:*** Da84, Gu00, Hi02, Lv88>

TYPEWRITER [taipraitə] *n.m.* typewriter <***Loc:*** EV, Da84, Lv88, Ph36>

typhoïde[1] (**syphoïde**) [tifoid, sifoid, ɛstifoid] *adj.* ◊ •**fièvre typhoïde** typhoid, typhoid fever *Il y avait pas de docteur, [...] le monde traitait pour des maladies comme ça de la fièvre typhoïde.* There weren't doctors, people treated for illnesses like that, typhoid fever. (TB) <TB> <***Loc:*** AC, AV, SL, SM, TB, Da84>

typhoïde[2] (**syphoïde**) [tifoid, sifoid, ɛstifoid] *n.f.* typhoid, typhoid fever *Leurs maris étaient morts il y avait des années de la typhoïde.* Their husbands had died years ago of typhoid fever. (SL) <***Loc:*** AV, LF, SL, SM, TB, Da84>

U

ulcère [ylsær, yksær] *n.m.* ulcer <***Loc:*** SM, VM, Da84>

ulcérer [ylsere] **I** *v.tr.* to ulcerate *Ce mors a ulcéré la langue de mon cheval tellement il l'a usé.* This bit ulcerated my horse's tongue because he had worried it so much. (LA) **II** *v.intr.* to become ulcerated *Sa narine a ulcéré à force elle a reniflé ce* DOPE. Her nostril ulcerated because she sniffed so much of that dope. (LA) **III s'ulcérer** *v.pron.* to become ulcerated *Mes gencives sont après s'ulcérer.* My gums are becoming ulcerated. (VM) <***Loc:*** LA, VM, Da84>

un (ein, eun), une (eine, einne, eunne) (*m.sing.* **un, ein, eun** [ɛ̃], *before a vowel* [ɛ̃n], *f.sing.* **une, eine, einne, eunne** [ɛ̃n, œ̃n]) *adj./n.* one *Je suis né à peu près un mile à l'est d'ici.* I was born about one mile to the east of here. (SL) *Des fois on peut bien aller eine semaine.* Sometimes we can go for one week. (JE) *Au bout d'un an et un jour.* After one year and one day. (JE) **Un jour elle dit à son papa, "Papa je veux me marier."* One day she told her dad, "Papa, I want to get married." (ch: *La fille de quatorze ans*) **Par un beau dimanche mais j'ai mis aller la voir.* One beautiful Sunday I went to see her. (ch: *Aux Natchitoches*) <***Loc:*** EV, JE, SL, SM, VM, An94, Da84>

un (ein, eun), une (eine, einne, eunne) (*m.sing.* **un, ein, eun** [ɛ̃], *before a vowel* [ɛ̃n], *f.sing.* **une, eine, einne, eunne** [ɛ̃n, œ̃n], *m./f.pl.* **des** [de], *before a vowel often* [dez]) *art.indef.* a, an (*pl.* = some) *Un rougarou, ça peut être un homme ou une femme.* A werewolf, it can be a man or a woman. (JE) *Il y avait une grosse bande de petits ouaouarons.* There was a large group of little frogs. (LA, An94) **Il est manière effronté pour un bougre qu'a un business.* He's kind of nervy for a fellow with a business. (ThCa: *La table des veuves*) *Tu veux une allumette? Moi j'en ai une.* Do you want a match? I've got one. (SM) *Là, il s'a trouvé embourbé dans une vilaine affaire.* Then he found himself involved in an ugly affair. (EV) *Ils ont mis un empêchement contre lui.* They put a restraining order on him. (VM) **Alle avait des gingas, des canards d'Inde, des pintales.* She had some barred Plymouth Rock chickens, some Muscovy ducks, and some guinea fowl. (VM, Gu82) *T'as demandé pour un crayon? Moi j'en ai un.* Did you ask for a crayon? I've got one. (SM) <***Loc:*** EV, JE, LA, SM, TB, VM, An94, Da84, Gu82, Gu00, ThCa>

un (ein, eun), une (eine, einne, eunne) (*m.sing.* **un, ein, eun** [ɛ̃, ɛ̃n], *f.sing.* **une, eine, einne, eunne** [ɛ̃n, œ̃n]) *pron.indef.* one *Une était pas préférable à l'autre.* One was not preferable to the other. (LA) *Trois chaises, une au milieu et une chaque bout.* Three chairs, one in the middle and one [on] each end. (EV) *Quand un dansait avec la fille, l'autre dansait avec quelqu'un d'autre. Ça fait, eux s'échangeait ça toute la nuit.* When one would dance with the girl, the other would dance with someone else. So they exchanged them between themselves all night long. (SL) *Tu veux une allumette? Moi j'en ai une.* Do you want a match? I've got one. (SM) *T'as demandé pour un crayon? Moi j'en ai un.* Did you ask for a crayon? I've got one. (SM) *Quand les enfants se sont endormis, il a ôté le bonnet à un et il l'a mis sur sa tête à lui.* When the children went to sleep, he took the bonnet from one and put it on his own head. (LA) ◊ **•un par un** one by one <Da84> **•l'un l'autre / l'un à l'autre** one another, each other *Le monde s'aidait l'un à l'autre.* People helped each other. (SL) *On rit après l'un à l'autre.* We laugh at each other. (LF) <LA, LF, SL, SM, VM, Lv88> **•un et l'autre *a*** one another, each other *Les deux batailleurs se sont empoignés un et l'autre au milieu du grand rond.* The two fighters grabbed each other in the middle of the ring. (LA) ***b*** somebody, someone *Un et l'autre ramassait un jeune cochon pour une piasse ou deux.* Someone would pick up a young pig for a dollar or two. (TB) ***c*** this and that, one thing and the other *Et là y a huit ans que je suis* RETIRE *de ça. Et là asteur là juste je pigoche dans l'un et l'autre.* And it's eight years since I retired from that. And now I just putter in this and that. (TB) <LA, LF, TB> **•pas un seul** not a single one *J'étais à la pêche hier et puis je n'ai pas pris une, pas un seul.* I was fishing yesterday and didn't catch one thing, not a single one. (SL) <SL, Da84> <***Loc:*** AC, EV, LA, LF, PQ, SL, SM, TB, Da84>

uni, -e [yni] *adj.* **1** united **Les États-Unis.* The United States. (Da84) **2** smooth *Il a travaillé sa pièce jusqu'à que la terre était bien unie.* He worked his field until the earth was very smooth. (VM) **3** even, level *Allons dire, vous voulez prendre un comme ça et de le remplir uni, ça va remplir un sac de 50 livres de patates.* Let's say you want to take one like that and fill it level, it will fill a 50-pound sack of potatoes. (LF) **4** solid-colored, of one color *Elle portait une robe toute unie.* She was wearing a solid-colored dress. (Lv88) <***Loc:*** LF, SM, VM, Da84, Lv88>

uniforme [ynifɔrm] *adj.* uniform, alike, same *Il a planté tous ses poteaux uniformes.* He set all of his posts so as to be uniform. (VM) <***Loc:*** VM, Da84>

uniment [ynimɑ̃] *adv.* plainly, simply, unceremoniously *On l'a fait tout uniment.* We did it very simply. (VM) <***Loc:*** VM>

union [ynjɔ̃] *n.f.* **1** union, alliance **2** labor union <***Loc:*** Da84>

unique [ynik] *adj.* **1** only, sole **Un fils unique.* An only son. (Da84) **2** unique *Un caractère unique.* A unique character. (LA) <***Loc:*** LA, Da84, Hi02>

unir [ynir] **I** *v.tr.* **1** to unite, join together *Ils sont après essayer d'unir le monde d'en haut et le monde d'en bas pour supporter le même candidat.* They're trying to unite the people from upstream with those from downstream to support the same candidate. (VM) **2** to smooth, make even, make level *Unir deux planchers.* To smooth the joint between two floors. (VM) **II s'unir** *v.pron.* to unite, combine, join together *On va s'unir derrière Mr. B.* We will unite in support of Mr. B. (VM) <*Loc:* IB, SJ, VM, Da84>

unité [ynite] *n.f.* unity, oneness <*Loc:* Da84>

univers [yniværs] *n.m./f.* **1** universe **2** world <*Loc:* AV, SJ, Da84, Hi02>

université [yniværsite] *n.f.* university <*Loc:* LA, LF, Da84, Hi02>

urine [yrin] *n.f.* urine <*Loc:* Da84>

uriner [yrine] *v.intr.* to urinate *Il a pas pu uriner pour ses tests.* He couldn't urinate for his medical exams. (LA) <*Loc:* LA, Da84>

usable [yzab(l)] *adj.* usable *Il m'a laissé sa vieille machine qu'est même pas usable.* He left me his old tractor that is not even usable. (LA) <*Loc:* LA, Da84>

usage [yzaʒ] *n.m./f.* **1** use, usage *Si t'as pas d'usage de ça, donne-moi le.* If you don't have any use for that, give it to me. (Lv88) *Et çu-là c'était une qu'était usé pour la même chose aussite, des différents d'usages pour.* And that's one that was used for the same thing, different uses for it. (LF) **2** custom, practice *C'était l'usage chez nous-autres de mettre des canards blessés dans la basse-cour pour attirer les canards farouches.* It was the custom here to place wounded ducks in the chicken yard to attract wild ducks. (VM) **3** good manners *Il a pas d'usage, lui.* He doesn't have any manners. (Lv88) ◊ **•faire usage de** to use, make use of *Tu crois il va faire usage du cadeau qu'on lui a donné?* Do you think he will make use of the gift we gave him? (VM) <VM, Da84> <*Loc:* LF, VM, Da84, Lv88>

usance [yzɑ̃s] *n.f.* **1** use *Il m'a donné l'usance de son cheval.* He gave me the use of his horse. (VM) **2** durability *C'est d'une bonne usance.* It's very durable. (VM) <*Loc:* VM>

use [yz] *n.f.* use *C'était des outils pour des faiseurs de baril. Mais les Américains ou les Cadiens de la Louisiane a trouvé une use pour ça, so ils ont usé ça pour le dedans des pirogues.* They were tools for barrelmakers. But Americans or Cajuns of Louisiana found a use for them, so they used them for the insides of pirogues. (LF) <*Loc:* LF>

usé, -e [yze] *adj.* **1** used *Du linge usé.* Hand-me-down clothing. (Lv88) *Des chars usés.* Used cars. (Lv88) *Le mouchoir est pas usé. Il est propre.* The handkerchief is not dirty (i.e. used). It's clean. (SM) **2** used up, worn out *Les dents de la vieille vache sont tout usées. Elle va pas faire l'hiver.* The old cow's teeth are all worn out. She won't make it through the winter. (LA) <*Loc:* SM, VM, Da84, Lv88>

user [yze] **I** *v.tr.* **1** to use *On use des fusils à chasser.* We use guns to hunt. (JE) *C'est ça la cuillère tu uses pour frire ton œuf.* That's the spoon you use to fry your egg. (SL) *On nettoyait les pailles de maïs, les coupait et tu usais ça pour un vaisseau pour mettre la plarine dedans.* We cleaned the corn shucks, cut them off and you used them for a container to put your praline in. (TB) *Nous-autres, on use des saucisses boucanées dans notre gombo.* We use smoked sausages in our gumbo. (EV) *Il usait l'huile pour graisser ses machineries.* He would use oil to lubricate his equipment. (AC) *Le laurier est usé pour faire un thé.* Laurel is used for making tea. (Lv88) *Tu pourrais m'user pour t'aider.* You could use me to help you. (Lv88) *C'est pas des mots on use icitte.* Those are not words that we use here. (Lv88) *J'aime pas user de gros mots, non.* I don't like to use bad words. (LA) **2** to use up, wear out, consume *Et pour pas user les batteries, temps que les nouvelles étaient finies l'affaire était teindue.* And so as not to use up the batteries, when the news was over the thing was shut off. (LF) *Y'avait pas d'ectricité ça fait faulait on tue notre volaille le jour qu'on le usait.* There was no electricity, so we had to kill our poultry the day we ate it. (AC) **3** to worry, toy with *Ce mors a ulcéré la langue de mon cheval tellement il l'a usé.* This bit ulcerated my horse's tongue because he had worried it so much. (LA) **II s'user** *v.pron.* to wear out *Ces nouvelles bandes en élastique, ça s'use tellement vite qu'il faut que tu les changes tous les ans.* Those new rubber belts wear out so fast that you have to change them every year. (VM) ◊ **•user son jugement** to use one's judgment *J'y ai dit de user son* OWN *jugement, elle alle connaît mieux que mon.* I told her to use her own judgment, she knows better than I do. (TB) *Il faut tu uses ton jugement. Il faut tu jongles si c'est une personne blanc ou une personne brun.* You have to use your judgment. You have to think about whether it's a white person or a dark-skinned person. (VM) <TB, VM> <*Loc:* AC, EV, IB, JE, LA, LF, SL, TB, VM, Da84, Hi02, Lv88>

usine [yzin] *n.f.* **1** mill, factory **2** cottonseed oil compress, place where oil is pressed out of seeds (esp. cotton seeds) <*Loc:* SM, Da84>

usiner [yzine] *v.tr.* to stuff and mount (an animal) *On a usiné tous les oiseaux qu'on avait.* We stuffed and mounted every bird that we had. (IB) <*Loc:* IB>

usufruit [yzyfrɥi] *n.m.* usufruct <*Loc:* Da84>

usure [yzyr] *n.f.* usury <*Loc:* EV, Da84>

usurier, -ière [yzyrje, -jær] *adj.* **1** which uses much, which uses up quickly **2** said of one who wears out his clothes quickly <*Loc:* JE, Di32, Lv88>

utile [ytil] *adj.* useful, helpful *L'accointance du monde de l'huile est bien utile.* It is very useful to know people who work in the oil business. (Lv88) *Le petit bougre à n-oncle Bie était beaucoup utile quand il a venu passer quelques semaines.* Uncle Bie's kid was very helpful when he came to spend a few weeks with us. (LA) <***Loc:*** LA, Da84, Hi02, Lv88>

utiliser [ytilize] *v.tr.* to utilize, make use of, employ *Il avait le boghei et un* TRUCK *aussite. Il utilisait les deux.* He had a wagon and a truck, too. He used both. (LA) <***Loc:*** LA, Da84>

utilité [ytilite] *n.f.* **1** utility, usefulness **2** use, usage *J'élève des tomates pour mon utilité.* I raise tomatoes for my own use. (Lv88) *On faisait ça pour l'utilité de la famille.* We made that for the family's use. (SM) *Le coton jaune, c'est seulement pour ton utilité à toi.* Yellow cotton, it's only good for your own use. (Lv88) <***Loc:*** SM, Da84, Lv88>

va-et-vient (**va-t-et-vient, vat-à-vient**) [vaevjɛ̃, vatevjɛ̃, vatavjɛ̃] *n.m.* come and go, goings and comings *Il y a trop de va-t-et-vient ici.* There's too much coming and going here. (SM) <***Loc:*** EV, IB, JD, LA, LF, SJ, SL, SM, Da84, Lv88, Ph36>

vacance [vakɑ̃s] *n.f.* vacation *Il a parti sur une vacance.* He left on vacation. (Lv88) *Prendre mes vacances.* To take my vacation. (SM) *On avait une vacance d'un mois entre le mois de mai et le mois d'août.* We had a one month vacation between the month of May and the month of August. (TB) ◊ **•en vacances** ***a*** on vacation **Il est parti en vacances.* He left on vacation. (EV, An94) ***b*** at large (of livestock) <SM, VM> <***Loc:*** EV, LA, SM, TB, VM, An94, Da84, Lv88, Wh83>

vacant, -e [vakɑ̃, -ɑ̃t] *adj.* empty, vacant *Une terre vacante.* An unoccupied land. (VM) **[Sa femme] le veillait et le guettait avec un œil sec et vacant.* His wife watched him with a dry and vacant eye. (Gr86) <***Loc:*** VM, Da84, Gr86>

vaccin [vaksɛ̃] *n.m.* vaccine <***Loc:*** Da84>

vaccination [vaksinasjɔ̃] *n.f.* vaccination <***Loc:*** Da84>

vaccine [vaksin] *n.f.* vaccine <***Loc:*** Fa77, Lv88>

vacciner [vaksine] *v.tr.* to vaccinate, inoculate *Je vas vacciner mes taures avant de les lâcher dans la savane.* I'm going to vaccinate my heifers before letting them out in the pasture. (LA) <***Loc:*** LA, Da84>

vaccineur [vaksinœr] *n.m.* **1** one who vaccinates **2** veterinarian *Je vas charcher le vaccineur pour la bête.* I'm going to get the veterinarian for the cow. (VM) <***Loc:*** VM>

vache [vaʃ] *n.f.* cow ◊ **•vache à lait** ***a*** milk cow ***b*** coward, weak man <IB, SJ, SL, SM, Da84, Hi02> **•vache de mer** manatee, sea-cow <VM> **•vache figure blanche** Hereford cow <VM> **•vache habillée en zinc** hateful or mean person <SM, La99> <***Loc:*** IB, SJ, SL, SM, VM, Da84, Hi02, La99>

vacher[1] **(se)** [vaʃe] *v.pron.* to fall down *Il s'est vaché par terre.* He fell to the ground. (AV) <***Loc:*** AV>

vacher[2] [vaʃe] *n.m.* cowboy, cow herder, cowpoke *Dans le vieux temps, c'était tout des vachers par icite.* In the old days, it was all cowboys around here. (Lv88) <***Loc:*** Da84, Hi02, Lv88>

vacherie [vaʃri] *n.f.* **1** cattle ranch *Comment ça a commencé la vacherie, c'est quand ils avaient habitude d'amener les vaches, les animaux, ils transféraient les animaux du ouest et tout, et il y avait certaines places qu'ils arrêtaient. C'était une place qu'était à peu près de cinq milles d'ici, ils appelaient la Vacherie. C'est là ils tenaient les animaux.* How they started the cattle ranch, it's when they used to bring the cows, the cattle, they would transfer cattle from the west and all, and there were certain places where they would stop. There was a place that was about five miles from here, they called it Vacherie. That's where they held the cattle. (SJ) **2** breeding, raising, rearing of cattle *Ils ont quitté la vacherie pour faire récolte de coton.* They quit raising cattle to harvest cotton. (Lv88) **3** herd of cattle **4** pasture <***Loc:*** SJ, VM, Da84, Hi02, Lv88>

vadrouille [vadruj] *n.f.* mop <***Loc:*** Lv88>

vagabond [vagabɔ̃, vakabɔ̃] *n.m.* vagrant, rover, vagabond, tramp, hobo <***Loc:*** LF, VM, Da84>

vagabonder [vagabɔ̃de] *v.intr.* to roam, wander around *C'était pas un homme qui travaillait réglé. Il vagabondait d'un bord et de l'autre.* He wasn't a man who worked regularly. He wandered around from place to place. (LA) <***Loc:*** LA, Da84>

vaillant, -e [vajɑ̃, -ɑ̃t] *adj.* **1** good, kind, pleasant, nice, likeable *Une banque avec tous ses vaillants employés qui parlent français ou anglais.* A bank with all its nice employees who speak French or English. (EV) *C'est vaillant quand il n-a de la compagnie ou quelque chose, mais là après ça, quand c'est juste eux-autres, ça se chamaille.* They are nice [with each other] when they have company, but afterwards, when it's just them, they fight. (AV) *Il n-avait une vaillante personne, elle nous a laissé user sa maison.* There was a nice person, she let us use her house. (IB) **Il y en a quelques uns qui ont resté qui étaient vaillants et doux.* There were some who stayed who were good and gentle. (SL, An94) **2** considerate, helpful, friendly **Ça fait, la maman voulait d'être vaillante et bonne pour la fille.* So, the mother wanted to be considerate and good for the daugher. (LA, An94) **3** healthy, vigorous *Il est vaillant depuis qu'il a revenu de son voyage.* He is healthy since he returned from his trip. (SL) **4** valiant, courageous, brave *Son garçon a fait un vaillant soldat.* His son made a valiant soldier. (LA) *Tu vas être vaillante équand ta mère est à l'hôpital.* You will be brave when your mother is at the hospital. (VM) **5** handsome, good-looking *Le petit bougre à Lorita est bien vaillant asteur qu'il a perdu soixante-quinze livres.* Lorita's boy is really handsome now that he's lost seventy-five pounds. (LF) **6** smart *Il est vaillant, j'ai un tas de confiance à lui.* He is smart, I have a lot of confidence in him. (IB) ◊ **•vaillant bougre** good man, nice fellow *C'était aussi vaillant bougre que tu pouvais mettre les yeux dessus.* He's as nice as any guy you'll ever see. (LA) *Il a été bien* NICE *avec moi. C'est un vaillant bougre.* He was very nice with me. He's a good guy. (SM) <LA, SM> **•du vaillant monde** nice people *Du bon* *manger cadien servi par du vaillant monde.* Good Cajun food served by nice people. (EV) *J'ai rencontré l'homme et la femme, les deux du vaillant monde.* I met the man and the woman, both are nice people. (EV) <EV, LA, SM, Da84> <***Loc:*** AV, EV, IB, JD, LA, LF, SB, SJ, SL, SM, TB, VM, An94, Da84, Hi02, Lv88, Ph36>

vaillantise [vajɑ̃tiz] *n.f.* boasting, bragging <***Loc:*** Lv88>

vain, -e [vɛ̃, vɛ̃n] *adj.* vain, conceited ◊ **•en vain** in vain, futile, useless *Prier en vain.* To pray in vain. (LA) <LA, Da84, Fa77> <***Loc:*** LA, Da84, Fa77>

vaisseau [veso] *n.m.* **1** small container (e.g. jar, dish) *Ça c'était dans le temps de la dépression et tout ça-là, y avait pas un cinq sous dans le vaisseau.* That was in the time of the Depression and all, there wasn't a nickel in the jar. (TB) *On nettoyait les pailles de maïs, les coupait et tu usais ça pour un vaisseau pour mettre la plarine dedans.* We cleaned the corn shucks, cut them off, and you used them for a container to put your praline in. (TB) *Va me chercher un vaisseau pour mettre le sang.* Go and find me a container to put the blood in. (VM) **2** boat, ship, vessel *Un vaisseau sur la mer.* A boat on the ocean. (LA) <***Loc:*** IB, LA, TB, VM, Da84, Gu00, Lv88>

vaisselle [vesɛl] *n.f.* dishes, chinaware, tableware *Les enfants aimont sûr pas laver les vaisselles.* The children sure don't like to wash dishes. (TB) <***Loc:*** AC, SL, TB, Da84, Hi02>

valdrague [valdrag] *n.f.* ruin ◊ **•à la valdrague** ***a*** any-which-way, in disorder *C'est tout à la valdrague chez eux.* It's all a mess at their house. (Lv88) *Laisser aller à la valdrague.* Allow to go to pot. (Lv88) ***b*** slovenly *Une femme toute à la valdrague est une femme nu-pieds, sale et alle a du linge déchiré.* A slovenly woman is barefoot, dirty, and she has torn clothing. (TB) ***c*** abandoned *Si la mame laisse l'enfant à la valdrague et qu'alle a un job, ils vont coincer ton* CHECK. *T'appelles ça* GARNISH *ici.* If the mom leaves the child abandoned and she has a job, they'll block your paycheck. They call that a garnish here. (TB) <TB, VM, Lv88> <***Loc:*** JD, TB, VM, Da84, Lv88>

valence [valɑ̃s] *n.f.* valence <***Loc:*** Da84>

VALENTINE (**valentine**) [vælɛ̃ntajn, valɑ̃tin] *n.m./f.* **1** valentine **2** *(f.)* old maid *T'as ti vu cette valentine après assayer d'attirer l'attention des hommes?* Did you see that old maid trying to get the men's attention? (JD) <***Loc:*** JD, SL, Da84, Lv88>

valet [vale] *n.m.* **1** male servant **2** jack (in a deck of cards) <***Loc:*** JE, Da84>

valeur [valœr] *n.f.* **1** value, worth, price *Et quand le prix est bon, un pied vaut de la valeur, oui. Le plus haut que moi j'ai jamais vendu, c'est soixante dollars pour un pied, du bout de la queue au bout du nez.* And when the price is good [on alligator hide], one foot is worth something, yes. The highest I've sold at is sixty dollars a foot, from the end of the tail to the tip of the nose. (TB) **2** merit *Tout le monde a de la valeur.* Everybody has merit. (IB) <***Loc:*** IB, TB, Da84, Hi02>

valide [valid] *adj.* valid, good, correct <***Loc:*** Da84>

validité [validite] *n.f.* validity <***Loc:*** Da84>

valise [valiz] *n.f.* suitcase <***Loc:*** Da84>

valoir (**voloir**) [valwar, volwɑr] *v.intr.* **1** to be worth **Ça vaut trois piastres.* It's worth three dollars. (Da84) *Tu crois que ça va voloir le prix?* Do you think it will be worth the price? (VM) *Il vaut dix mille piasses.* It's worth ten thousand dollars. (SM) **Ça vaut la peine.* It's worth the trouble. (Da84) **Il vaut pas un coup de bâton.* He's not worth a lick (with a stick). (Da84) **Ça vaut pas baisser et ramasser.* That's not worth bending down and picking up. (AC, La99) **Ça vaut rien.* It's worth nothing. (Da84) **Ça vaut pas cinq sous de pistaches.* That's not worth a nickel's worth of peanuts. (EV, La99) **Valoir peu de chose.* To not be worth much. (Da84) **2** to possess assets worth, be worth **I vaut 20,000 dollars.* He is worth $20 grand. (EV, Ph36) ◊ **•valoir mieux** to be better *Vaudrait mieux qu'il reste à la maison.* It would be better for him to stay at home. (LA) **Mieux vaut prendre garde que pardon.* It's better to be safe than sorry. (Da84) <LA, Da84> **•faire valoir** to validate or demonstrate the worth of, raise the value of *Il essayait de faire valoir sa place devant son gendre.* He was trying to demonstrate the value of his farm in front of his son-in-law. (LA) <LA, Da84> **•l'un vaut l'autre et l'autre vaut rien / l'un vaut l'autre et les deux vaut rien** of two things or people, neither is worth very much <AV, La99> <***Loc:*** AC, AV, EV, LA, LF, SC, SM, VM, An94, Da84, Hi02, La99, Ph36, Wh83>

valse [vals] *n.f.* waltz **Ça danse les polkas du vieux temps, les mazurkas, les valses aussi.* They dance the old-time polkas, mazurkas, waltzes too. (ch: *Le sud de la Louisiane*) *C'est ça la valse qui t'après jouer le soir où je l'ai demandée.* That's the waltz that was playing the night that I asked for her hand. (ch: *La valse du malchanceux*) ◊ **•valse à deux-temps** waltz with two variant beats <LA, SM> <***Loc:*** SM, Da84, Gu00, Hi02>

valser [valse] *v.intr.* to waltz **Mon cousin peut valser, mais quand il danse le* TWO-STEP, *ça fait pitié!* My cousin can waltz, but when he dances the two-step, it's pathetic! (Hi02) <***Loc:*** Da84, Hi02>

valsovienne [valsovjɛ̃n] *n.f.* lively dance, jig *Faire quelqu'un danser la valsovienne.* To make someone step lively. (SB) <***Loc:*** IB, SB>

vanille [vɑ̃nij] *n.f.* vanilla *Mets de l'essence à la vanille et puis roule ta pâte dans la farine et forme-toi des croquecignoles comme tu veux.* Put in some vanilla extract and then roll your dough in flour and shape your doughnuts as you like. (TB) <***Loc:*** AV, LF, TB, Da84>

vanité [vɑ̃nite] *n.f.* vanity, conceit <***Loc:*** Da84>

vannage [vɑ̃naʒ] *n.m.* winnowing <***Loc:*** Da84>

vanne [vɑ̃n] *n.f.* winnowing vessel (usu. a basket) <***Loc:*** Da84>

vanner [vɑ̃ne] **I** *v.tr.* to winnow *Dans le temps, ça avait habitude de vanner le riz pour séparer la graine.* In the old days, they used to winnow the rice to separate the grain. (LA) **II se vanner** *v.pron.* to take a dust bath (of birds) *Les poules étaient après se vanner en bas de la maison ayoù la terre était toujours sec.* The chickens were taking a dust bath under the house where the dirt was still dry. (LA) <***Loc:*** LA, VM, Da84, Lv88>

vanter [vɑ̃te] **I** *v.intr.* to boast, brag *Il disait c'est pas pour vanter mais il était un bon mari.* He was saying that he wasn't being boastful but that he was a good husband. (EV) **II se vanter** *v.pron.* to boast, brag *J'aimais terrible la musique et j'aimais terriblement danser et j'ai pas pour me vanter, j'étais une bonne danseuse.* I really liked music and I really liked to dance and I don't have to boast about it [but] I was a good dancer. (EV) *Je vais peut-être me vanter, mais je crois que dans mon jeune temps, j'étais un vrai bon appeleur.* I may be boasting but I think that in my younger days I was quite a good duck caller. (TB) <***Loc:*** EV, TB, Da84>

vanterie [vɑ̃tri] *n.f.* **1** boast **2** boasting, bragging <***Loc:*** Da84>

vanteur[1]**, -euse** (**vanteux, -euse**) [vɑ̃tœr, vɑ̃tø, -øz] *adj.* boastful, proud *Prends ça elle dit avec un peu de sel. Elle est beaucoup vanteuse.* Take what she says with a grain of salt. She is very boastful. (LA) <***Loc:*** AC, JD, LA, LF, SL, SM, VM, Da84, La99, Lv88>

vanteur[2]**, -euse** [vɑ̃tœr, -øz] *n.* braggart, boaster, bragging person <***Loc:*** IB, JD, LA, SJ, SM, VM, Da84, La99, Lv88>

vanteux ♦see **vanteur**

vapeur [vapœr] *n.f.* vapor, steam <***Loc:*** SM, Da84, Hi02>

vaporiser [vaporize] *v.tr.* to vaporize *Vaporiser du Flit.* To vaporize Flit [insecticide]. (VM) <***Loc:*** VM, Da84>

variable [varjab(l)] *adj.* variable, changing, unsteady *Le temps est beaucoup variable au long de la côte.* The weather is quite variable along the coast. (VM) <***Loc:*** VM, Da84>

variation [varjasjɔ̃] *n.f.* variation, change, difference <***Loc:*** Da84>

varié, -e [varje] *adj.* varied, mixed, assorted *Elle avait des poules variées dans sa basse-cour.* She had assorted chickens in her chicken yard. (LA) <***Loc:*** LA, Da84>

varier [varje] *v.intr.* to vary, differ *Ça qu'est à la mode peut varier beaucoup parmi les jeunes.* What's in style can vary quite a bit among young people. (LA) <***Loc:*** LA, Da84>

variété [varjete] *n.f.* **1** variety, type, kind *Les variétés de canards.* The varieties of ducks. (SL) **2** diversity **La variété fait la beauté.* Variety makes for beauty. (Da84) **3** type of dance *Ils ont dansé la variété.* They danced a variety (type of dance). (SM) <***Loc:*** SL, SM, Da84>

varlope (**verlope**) [varlɔp, værlɔp] *n.f.* plane, jack-plane, carpenter's plane <***Loc:*** IB, SB>

varloper (**verloper**) [varlope, værlope] *v.tr.* to plane *Verloper une planche.* To plane a board. (SB) <***Loc:*** AV, IB, SB>

varlopure [varlopyr] *n.f.* wood shavings (from a plane) <***Loc:*** Lv88>

varveau [varvo] *n.m.* **1** fishing net shaped like a funnel **2** weir (type of fishing net) <***Loc:*** VM, Lv88>

vase[1] [vaz] *n.f.* silt, slime, wet mud <***Loc:*** Da84>

vase[2] [vaz] *n.m.* vase, pot <***Loc:*** Da84, Fa77>

vaséline [vazelin] *n.f.* Vaseline *Il a mis de la vaséline dessus.* He put vaseline on it. (VM) <***Loc:*** VM, Da84>

vaséliner [vazeline] *v.tr.* to apply Vaseline to *Il a bien vaséliné ses bobos.* He applied lots of Vaseline to his sores. (LA) <***Loc:*** LA, Da84>

vaseux, -euse [vazø, -øz] *adj.* silty, slimy, muddy *C'était beaucoup vaseux autour du puits.* It was very muddy around the well. (VM) <***Loc:*** VM, Da84>

vasière [vazjær] *n.f.* muddy expanse <***Loc:*** VM>

vaste [vas(t)] *adj.* vast, huge, extensive *Il avait une vaste terre.* He had a vast estate. (VM) <***Loc:*** VM, Da84>

vat-à-vient, va-t-et-vient ♦see **va-et-vient**

Vatican [vatikɑ̃] *n.m.* [*eccl.*] Vatican <***Loc:*** Da84>

vaudou ♦see **voudou**

vaurien [vorjɛ̃] *n.m.* worthless man, rascal, scoundrel, loser, good-for-nothing <***Loc:*** Da84, Gr86, Hi02>

vauriennerie [vorjɛ̃nri] *n.f.* **1** worthless thing or person **2** trash, junk <***Loc:*** Da84, Gr86>

va-vite [vavit] *n.m./f.* diarrhea ◊ **•avoir la va-vite** to have diarrhea <La99> <***Loc:*** EV, JD, SM, Hi02, La99, Lv88, Ph36>

veau [vo] *n.m.* **1** calf *Il faudra qu'on rallonge le hangar pour mettre les nouveaux veaux à l'abri.* We'll have to extend the barn to shelter the new calves. (LA) **2** veal ◊ **•veau engraissé** fatted calf **Durant le temps chaud eune des voésins tuait ein veau engraissé.* During the hot spell, one of the neighbors butchered a fatted calf. (Gu82) <Gu82> <***Loc:*** AC, AV, EV, LA, SL, SM, TB, VM, Da84, Hi02>

végétable (**végétau**) [veʒetab(l), veʒeto] *n.m.* vegetable <***Loc:*** SB, Da84, Lv88>

végétau ♦see **végétable**

végétir [veʒetir] *v.intr.* to remain in one place, take root *Ce bougre va végétir dans ce petit village.* That guy is going to take root in that small town. (IB) <***Loc:*** IB>

veillage [vejaʒ] *n.f.* evening spent socially *Faire une veillage.* To spend an evening socially. (JD) <***Loc:*** JD>

veille (**veuille**) [vɛj, vœj] *n.f.* eve, day before **Le monde était pas beaucoup éclairé et ça croyait dans la superstition que dessus la veille de Halloween, les vaches parlaient.* People weren't very enlightened and they believed in the superstition that on the eve of Halloween, cows would talk. (Wh83) ◊ **•veille de Christmas** Christmas Eve <TB> **•veille de l'an** New Year's Eve <EV, Ph36> **•veille de la Toussaint** Halloween <Gu82> **•veille de Noël** Christmas Eve <Da84> **•à la veille** with the intention of spending the night *Mais*

Ariane, t'es venue à la veille? Well, Ariane, have you come to spend the night? (EV) <EV, An94> **•aller à la veille** to make an evening visit *On aimait aller à la veille en premier qu'on était marié chez les voisins. On travaillait le jour et le soir, on allait visiter.* We liked making evening visits at the neighbors' house when we were first married. We would work during the day and in the evening, we would go visiting. (EV) **Ein soir, on a été à la veille chez lui.* One evening, we made a visit to his place. (Wh83) <EV, Da84, Lv88, Wh83> **•avant-veille** eve of the eve, two days before **Avant-veille de Noël.* The day before Christmas Eve. (Da84) <Da84> <***Loc:*** AC, EV, TB, An94, Da84, Gu82, Gr86, Ph36, Wh83>

veillée [veje] *n.f.* **1** evening **2** evening visit, evening spent with neighbors *Et le monde ça visitait un à l'autre, les voisins allait visiter, ça appelait ça la veillée.* And people visited each other, neighbors went visiting, they called that a "veillée." (LF) *Paul a fait un bout de veillée avec nous-autres.* Paul spent part of the evening with us. (SM) **3** evening party ◊ **•faire la veillée** ***a*** to spend the night, stay overnight ***b*** to make an evening visit *On s'assisait sur les galeries, et y avait pas de traffic qu'il y a aujourd'hui. Et le monde s'assisait avec les voisins, ça parlait, et tant que c'était après faire la veillée ou parler ça faisait le filet.* We would sit on the porches, and there was no traffic like there is today. And people sat with their neighbors, they talked, and while they were having their evening visit or talking they were making the net. (LF) <AC, LF, SL> **•faire une veillée** to make an evening visit **Il faisait des veillées à l'une et l'autre maison.* He would make evening visits at one house and another. (SL, An94) <SL, An94, Da84> <***Loc:*** AC, LF, SL, SM, An94, Da84, Hi02, Re31>

veiller [veje] **I** *v.tr.* **1** to keep watch, stay up and watch over *Parce que il fallait que les hommes veillent la viande le soir. Il fallait que ça prend la viande en dehors, et faut que ça égoutte ça.* Because the men had to watch over the meat at night [because] they had to take the meat outside and bleed it. (TB) **2** to keep a vigil or hold a wake over (the deceased) *Veiller un mort.* Keep a vigil over the dead. (AC) **II** *v.intr.* **1** to stay awake *J'ai veillé tard hier soir en espérant mon garçon.* I stayed awake late last night waiting up for my son. (LA) **2** to pay an evening visit, pass an evening (with) *On allait veiller, soit nous-autres on allait veiller chez eux-autres, ou eux-autres venait veiller à la maison.* We used to go visiting, either we would spend the evening at their place, or they would spend the evening at our house. (TB) *Dans ce temps-là, comment dur que la vie était à faire, t'avais toujours le temps d'aller veiller chez tes amis.* In those days, as hard as life was to live, you always had the time to go for an evening visit with your friends. (TB) *Venez donc à soir veiller avec nous-autres.* Come in the evening for a visit with us. (SM) ◊ **•veiller les malades {un malade}** to sit up with, keep watch over the sick <AC, Da84> **•veille voir** ***a*** be careful, watch out *Veille voir, il va te taper.* Be careful, he'll hit you. (LF) ***b*** wait *Veille woir je veux te montrer ça ici.* Wait, I want to show you this. (TB) <LF, TB> <***Loc:*** AC, LA, LF, SM, TB, VM, Da84, Re31>

veillerie [vejri] *n.f.* **1** evening visit *Il a fait la veillerie jusqu'à minuit chez Rose.* He visited at Rose's until midnight. (SL) **2** staying up at night, staying up late *Il a fait la veillerie avec sa mère hier soir.* He sat up with his mother last night. (SJ) **Ta veillerie hier au soir t'a pas fait d'bien, ti t'endors aujôrd'hui.* Your staying up late last night didn't do you much good; you're falling asleep today. (EV, Ph36) <***Loc:*** EV, SJ, SL, SM, VM, Lv88, Ph36>

veilloche [vejɔʃ] *n.f.* small pile, stack (of straw, rice, wheat, etc.) in a field <***Loc:*** Gr86, Lv88>

veillocher [vejɔʃe] *v.tr.* to stack up, pile up, put in stacks or piles **Y avait du monde à veillocher du riz, à l'mettre en tas, à faire des meules.* There were people to put rice in piles, to make stacks. (Gr86) <***Loc:*** Gr86>

veine[1] [vɛ̃n] *n.f.* **1** vein **2** veining or grain (in wood, marble, etc.) ◊ **•veine de sang** vena cava *Il faut un couteau qui coupe en allant en bas pour qu'il coupe la veine de sang. [...] C'est la meilleur moyère entre les jambes à l'avant, juste à la gorge.* You have to have a knife that cuts from underneath to sever the vena cava. The best way to do it is between the front legs up to the throat. (VM) <VM> <***Loc:*** VM, Da84>

veine[2] [vɛ̃n] *n.f.* vein, humor, mood **Il était dans une bonne veine.* He was in a good mood. (Da84) <***Loc:*** Da84>

velimer ♦see **vénimer**

velimeux ♦see **vénimeux**

velin ♦see **vénin**

vélocipède (vérocypèle) [velosipɛd, verosipɛl] *n.m.* bicycle *Y a un vieux t-homme qu'était fier de me dire que c'était pas un* BICYCLE, *mais un vérocypèle.* There's an old man who was proud to tell me that it [the word] wasn't "bicycle," but "vérocypèle." (Gu00) <***Loc:*** AV, Gu00>

velours [vlur] *n.m.* velvet <***Loc:*** Da84, Fa77>

vendage [vɑ̃daʒ] *n.m.* sale, selling *Elle a le vendage d'une bonne ligne de linge.* She sells a good line of clothing. (Lv88) *C'est demain le vendage de sa propriété.* Tomorrow is the selling of his property. (SM) <***Loc:*** SM, TB, VM, Lv88>

venderdi ♦see **vendredi**

vendeur [vɑ̃dœr] *n.m.* salesman, seller, merchant <***Loc:*** EV, An94, Da84, Hi02, Wh83>

vendre [vɑ̃n, vɑ̃d(r)] **I** *v.tr.* to sell *Ma mère achetait un tas des étoffes pour faire le linge. Dans le temps là ça vendait pas le linge tout fait.* My mother bought a lot of fabric to make clothes. In those days they didn't sell ready-made clothes. (AC) **Et ils ont vendu la peau à des* FACTORIES *qui faisaient des souliers.* And they sold the skin to factories that made shoes. (EV, An94) **Il élevait et vendait des jardinages pour faire sa vie.* He grew and sold vegetables to make a living. (Wh83) **II se vendre** *v.pron.* to be sold *Il y a plus aucun qualité de peau qui se vend à part que les loutres. Le monde les attrape et ça les vend vivants.* There isn't any kind of pelt that sells anymore except for otters. People catch them and sell them alive. (TB) ◊ **•vendre à crédit** to sell on credit <Da84> **•vendre à la côte** to sell in the neighborhood, sell to one's neighbors *Ça fait on pêchait, on vendait ça, eux-autres appelait ça vendre ça à la côte, tu vois. Passer de maison en maison.* So, we would fish, we would sell that, they used to call that selling in the neighborhood, you see. To go from door to door. (TB) <TB> **•vendre à la pièce** to sell by the piece <Da84> **•vendre en détail** to sell retail <Da84> **•vendre en gros** to sell in large lots, sell wholesale *Dans les vieux magasins, ça vendait en gros et ça vendait aussi à la pièce.* In the old stores, they used to sell in large lots and they also sold by the piece. (LA) <LA> <***Loc:*** AC, EV, IV, LA, SL, SM, TB, VM, An94, Da84, Gu82, Hi02, Wh83>

vendredi (venderdi) [vɑ̃drədi, vɑ̃dərdi] *n.m.* Friday ◊ **•Vendredi Saint** Good Friday <EV, LA, VM, Da84> <***Loc:*** EV, LA, VM, Da84, Hi02, Lv88>

vénération [vẽnerasjɔ̃] *n.f.* [*eccl.*] veneration, respect, reverence **La Toussaint est célébrée avec eine vénération et intensité égale avec Chrismise.* All Saints' is celebrated with a veneration and an intensity equal to Christmas. (Wh83) <***Loc:*** Da84, Wh83>

vénérer [vẽnere] *v.tr.* to venerate, revere *C'était rendu à vénérer tous les saints pour essayer d'avoir de l'aide.* They had gotten to the point of venerating all the saints to try to get some help. (LA) <***Loc:*** LA, Da84>

vengeance [vɑ̃ʒɑ̃s] *n.f.* revenge, vengeance <***Loc:*** Da84>

venger [vɑ̃ʒe] **I** *v.tr.* to revenge, avenge *Il était après essayer de venger son père quand il m'a coincé.* He was trying to avenge his father when he cornered me. (LA) **II se venger** *v.pron.* to take revenge, avenge o.s. *C'est jamais une bonne idée de se venger.* It's never a good idea to take revenge. (LA) <***Loc:*** LA, Da84>

véniel, -lle [vẽnjɛl] *adj.* [*eccl.*] venial, minor **Péché véniel.* Venial sin. (Da84) <***Loc:*** Da84>

vénimer (velimer) [vẽnime, vəlime] *v.tr.* to poison <***Loc:*** VM>

vénimeux, -euse (velimeux, -euse) [vẽnimø, vəlimø, -øz] *adj.* poisonous *Une serpent vénimeuse.* A poisonous snake. (LA) <***Loc:*** LA, VM>

vénin (velin) [vẽnẽ, vənẽ, vəlẽ] *n.m.* poison, venom <***Loc:*** VM, Da84>

venir (viendre) [vnir, mnir, vjẽn, vjẽd(r)] **I** *v.intr.* **1** to come **Viens p'us autour d'ici.* Don't come around here anymore. (Da84) **Si tu veux venir me joindre, à soir, je vas te montrer.* If you want to come and join me tonight, I'll show you. (EV, An94) *C'est à cause ces gros bateaux-là qui vient de tous ces pays-là.* It is because of all these boats which come from all these countries there. (SM) *Il a menu à la Louisiane du Texas.* He came to Louisiana from Texas. (JE) **C'était une tortue qu'était après venir en travers du bayou.* It was a turtle that was coming across the bayou. (LA, An94) *La voiture va viendre dans une demi-heure.* The car will come in a half hour. (SJ) *'Garde donc quoi ce qui vient en travers du clos sur grand Henry.* Look what's coming across the field on big Henry [the horse]. (ch: *Chère Alice*) **2** to come from, be from (a place) *Elle a né icitte, sa maman viendait d'icitte, son popa a été né dans le Texas.* She was born here, her mom came from here, her dad was born in Texas. (AV) **Venir de la ville.* To come from the city (i.e. New Orleans). (Da84) **Venir de loin.* To be from far away. (Da84) **3** to become *Le jus était cuit, chauffé jusqu'à qu'il venait en sirop.* The juice was cooked, heated, until it became a syrup. (LA) *Un et l'autre ramassait un jeune cochon pour une piasse ou deux, et là on met ça en dehors, et on feedait ça, jusqu'à que ça vient bon à tuer.* One or the other of them would pick up a young pig for a dollar or two, and then we put it outside, we fed it until it was good to slaughter. (TB) *Après qu'il a un certain âge il tourne cette couleur-là, il peut être blanc. Il va venir cette couleur-là.* After it's a certain age it turns that color, it might start out white. It'll turn that color. (TB) *Venir fou.* To become crazy. (SM) **4** to have just (done s.t.) **Venir d'arriver.* To have just arrived. (Da84) **II s'en venir** *v.pron.* to come *Tu le voyais apé s'en venir en travers de la savane.* You'd see him coming across the pasture [toward our place]. (SL) **Il y a un jeune bougre qui s'en vient sur son MOTORCYCLE.* There's a young guy who's coming on his motorcycle. (IV, An94) *Et là quand le prêtre a arrivé, il s'en venait à la course parce que y a une femme qu'a venu, et je lui ai dit qu'il était mort.* And then when the priest arrived, he came running up because a woman had come, and I told her he was dead. (TB) **Ils ont vu un gros cheval s'en venir à travers du bois avec un homme dessus.* They saw a big horse come through the woods with a man on it. (SM, An94) *Il a quitté la campagne pour s'en venir au village.* He left the country to come to town. (Lv88) ◊ **•venir à bout** to make ends meet *Parce qu'il faisait un jardin, la seule manière qu'on pouvait venir à bout, il faulait se faire un peu du manger pour laisser cette piastre ou deux qu'il faisait acheter ça qu'on pouvait pas faire.* Because he did some gardening, the only way we could make ends meet, we had to produce a little food to leave that dollar or two he earned to buy what we couldn't make. (TB) <TB> **•venir à cheval** to come on horseback <Da84> **•venir à l'idée** to come to mind *Ça me vient pas à l'idée là.* It does not come to my mind now. (AC) <AC> **•venir après** to come after, come get *Tu peux venir après ton char, c'est tout paré.* You can come get your car, it's ready. (Lv88) <Da84,

Hi02, Lv88> **•venir BACK** to come back **Il va là-bas au parc regarder. Il vient BACK dans la maison.* He goes over there to the corral to look. He comes back in the house. (IV, An94) <IV, SM, An94> **•venir en âge** to attain the age of legal adulthood <SJ> **•venir en famille** to get pregnant *Martha est venue en famille.* Martha became pregnant. (EV) *Elle a venu en famille.* She became pregnant. (AC) <AC, EV> **•venir en l'air** to come up (to the surface) *Et la chevrette vient en l'air la nuit, tu vois. Eusse vient en l'air pour la clairté.* And the shrimp come up at night, you see. They come up for the light. (TB) <TB> **•venir en traître** to sneak up (deceitfully) <Da84> **•venir faille** to have a weak spell, faint, swoon *J'ai venu faille à l'église.* I fainted at church. (VM) <VM> **•venir faire une tournée {un tour}** to come over for a visit <Da84> **•venir se poquer** to drop in uninvited <SM> **•venir un fil {un cheveu / deux cheveux} de sa mort** to come very close to dying, almost die <AV, La99> **•qui vient** coming, upcoming, next (in time) **L'année qui vient.* Next year, the coming year. (Da84) <SJ, Da84> ***<Loc:*** AC, AV, EV, IV, JE, LA, LF, SB, SJ, SL, SM, TB, VM, An94, Da84, Hi02, La99, Lv88>

vent [vɑ̃] *n.m.* wind **Il ont mis la tête en bas à l'abri du vent.* They put their heads down to shelter them from the wind. (Gu82) ◊ **•vent à décorner un bœuf** very strong wind <La99> **•vent de grâce** helpful or welcome wind *Là plus tard le soir le vent a commencé à venir et eusse pensait que c'était comme un vent de grâce, so eusse s'a pas tracassé.* Then later the wind started coming and they thought it was like a helpful wind; so, they didn't get worried. (LF) <LF> **•vent de nord** north wind **Dans octobre quand les premiers vents de nord cômenciont, tu 'oyais les oies et les canards arriver.* In October when the first north winds began blowing, you'd see the geese and ducks arrive. (Gu82) <Da84, Gu82> **•vent des Lantier** a cold northeast wind <AC, La99> **•vent du large** southwest wind, wind from the ocean <JE, La99> **•vent fringant** nippy wind coming from several directions <VM> **•vents de Carême** strong spring winds, 'March winds' <LA, VM, Gu00, La99, Lv88> **•gros vent** heavy wind *J'espère un gros vent va venir là et à peu près tout jeter par terre.* I expect a strong wind to come and blow just about everything to the ground. (SL) <SL> ***<Loc:*** AC, JD, JE, LF, SL, TB, VM, Da84, Gu00, Gu82, Hi02, La99>

ventail ♦see **éventail**

vent-debout (**vent debout**) [vɑ̃dəbu, vɑ̃dbut] *adj.* ◊ **•avoir le vent debout *a*** to be in despair ***b*** to be worried <JD, La99> **•être vent-debout *a*** to be in a dither, be in a quandary, be in a difficult situation ***b*** to be extremely worried, be out of one's senses with worry *Elle était vent-debout, son enfant était pas c'ez elle.* She was worried, her child wasn't at home. (LF) *Alle était vent-debout de voir le mauvais temps et son mari pas là.* She was worried sick with the bad weather and her husband not there. (TB) <JD, LF, TB, VM, Da84, La99, Lv88> ***<Loc:*** JD, LF, TB, VM, Da84, La99, Lv88>

vente [vɑ̃t] *n.f.* sale, selling **•vente publique** auction <Da84> ***<Loc:*** Da84>

venter [vɑ̃te] **I** *v.tr.* to fan *Il vente le bébé malade.* He fans the sick baby. (SM) **II** *v.intr.* to be windy **Il vente fort.* The wind is blowing strongly. (Da84) *Et allons dire que c'était pas trop une belle ouragan, ça. Il a venté, et le magasin à maïs là, moi je croyais qu'il allait prendre des ailes et puis s'en aller là-dedans.* Let's say it wasn't a very nice hurricane. It was windy, and the corn crib, I thought it was going to sprout wings and take off in it. (TB) *Bougre, le vent ventait, ventait. Il y avait des ours là. Les chênes se frottaient ensemble comme ça là, là, ça faisait un jargon.* Man, the wind was blowing and blowing. There were bears. The oaks were rubbing against each other like that, it was making noise. (LF) ***<Loc:*** LF, SM, TB, Da84>

venteux, -euse [vɑ̃tø, -øz] *adj.* windy *C'est un temps de l'année qu'est beaucoup venteux.* That's a time of year that is very windy. (LA) ***<Loc:*** LA, Da84>

ventrage [vɑ̃traʒ] *n.m.* abdominal region, belly *Ouvrir le ventrage.* To [cut] open the abdomen. (SB) ***<Loc:*** AV, IB, SB>

ventre [vɑ̃t(r)] *n.m.* belly, stomach, abdomen ◊ **•ventre jaune *a*** yellow-belly, coward *Les bougres ventre jaune sur le job, c'est pas du bon ouvrage.* Lazy workers don't make for good labor. (Lv88) ***b*** yellow-bellied turtle *Les ventre-jaune, c'était pas bon à manger, mais il y en a qui les mangeaient quand même.* Yellow-bellied turtles, they weren't good to eat, but there are some [people] who would eat them anyway. (EV) <EV, Da84, Gu00, Lv88> **•ventre-rouge** radical, free-thinker, non-conformist <VM> **•avoir le ventre plein** to be fed up with something <La99> **•avoir mal au ventre** to have a stomachache <Da84> ***<Loc:*** EV, IV, LA, SM, Da84, Gu00, La99>

ventrée [vɑ̃tre] *n.f.* bellyful, large portion *Mon cheval s'a foutu une ventrée de foin.* My horse ate a bellyful of hay. (SM) ***<Loc:*** SL, SM, VM, Da84>

venure [vənyr] *n.f.* arrival ***<Loc:*** VM>

vénus [vẽnys] *n.f.* **1** Venus **2** woman of mixed Caucasian and American Indian descent ***<Loc:*** JD, Da84, La99>

ver [vær] *n.m.* **1** worm **2** earthworm ◊ **•ver à mille pattes** centipede <EV, Lv88, Ph36> **•ver blanc** grub worm <Da84> **•ver de bois** woodeating worm <LF> **•ver de cœur** heartworm *J'ai peur les vers de cœur va le prendre et tout le tuer.* I'm afraid the heartworms will attack and kill it. (SL) <SL> **•ver de lèche** earthworm <Da84> **•ver de terre *a*** earthworm ***b*** cocoon <VM, Da84> **•ver solitaire** tapeworm <Da84> ***<Loc:*** EV, LF, SL, TB, VM, Da84, Hi02, Lv88, Ph36>

verbouteille ♦see **verre-bouteille**

verdage [værdaʒ] *n.m.* greens, edible greens, green vegetables ***<Loc:*** JD>

verdir (**verdzir**) [værdir, værdzir] **I** *v.tr.* to color green, make green *La mousse a verdi la maison.* The moss turned the house green. (VM) **II** *v.intr.* to become green, turn green *Les herbes sont après verdir.* The grass is turning green. (VM) <***Loc:*** VM, Da84>

verdure [værdyr] *n.f.* **1** greenness **2** greenery **3** greens, edible greens, green vegetables *Le docteur y a dit de manger plus de verdure.* The doctor told him to eat more greens. (LA) <***Loc:*** Da84>

verdzir ♦see **verdir**

véreuse [verøz] *n.f.* short coat *Ma véreuse est su le dos de cette chaise.* My short coat is on the back of that chair. (TB) <***Loc:*** TB>

verge [værʒ] *n.f.* open-ended sewing thimble ◊ •**verge d'or** goldenrod <Ho90> <***Loc:*** VM, Ho90>

verger [værʒe] *n.m.* **1** orchard, fruit orchard **2** flower garden <***Loc:*** IB, LA, Da84>

vergerolle [værʒərɔl] *n.* daisy fleabane (type of wild daisy) <***Loc:*** Ho90>

verglacer [værglase] *v.intr.* to sleet *Il fait frais quand il est après verglacer.* It is cold when it is sleeting. (AL) <***Loc:*** AL, LA, SL, Da84, Lv88>

verglan ♦see **verglas**

verglas (**verglan**) [værgla, værglã] *n.m.* **1** sleet *Le verglan a cassé les vitres.* The sleet broke the windows. (AV) **2** frost **3** slush, melted snow <***Loc:*** AL, AV, LA, SM, TB, Da84, Lv88, Re31>

vergogne [værgɔ̃j] *n.f.* shame <***Loc:*** Da84>

vergue [værg] *n.f.* horse-drawn shaft for operating machinery <***Loc:*** VM>

vérifiable [verifjab(l)] *adj.* verifiable *Je me demande si c'est réellement vérifiable après si longtemps.* I wonder if it is really verifiable after so long. (LA) <***Loc:*** LA, Da84>

vérifier [verifje] *v.tr.* **1** to verify, prove *Je connais pas comment ça croit que ça va vérifier qui a fait quoi si longtemps passé.* I don't know how they think they will verify who did what so long ago. (LA) **2** to compare *Allons les vérifier pour voir qui c'est le meilleur.* Let's compare them to see which one is the best. (VM) <***Loc:*** LA, VM, Da84>

véritable [veritab(l)] *adj.* true, actual, real, veritable **C'est du véritable sirop.* This is real syrup. (Da84) <***Loc:*** Da84>

varlope ♦see **verlope**

varloper ♦see **verloper**

vérité [verite] *n.f.* truth *Mais je vas te dire la vérité.* But I'll tell you the truth. (EV) ◊ •**la franche vérité** the honest truth, the way it really is **Mais moi, j'vas vous dire la franche vérité: y a pas parsône dessus la terre qu'est plus bête qu'ein Amaricain.* But I'm going to tell you the honest to goodness truth: there is no one in the world dumber than an American. (Gu82) <VM, Gu82> <***Loc:*** EV, VM, Da84, Gu82, Hi02>

vermicelle [værmisɛl, værmiʃɛl] *n.m.* **1** vermicelli **2** very thin person <***Loc:*** VM, Da84>

vermifuge [værmifyʒ] *n.m.* vermifuge (deworming medicine) <***Loc:*** Da84>

vermine [værmin] *n.f.* vermin *Mon père aimait planter des œillets d'Inde dans son jardin pour évader la vermine de son jardinage.* My father liked planting marigolds in his garden to keep away the vermin from his vegetables. (Gu00) **Les vermines sont après manger tout ça j'ai dans l'jardin.* The insects are eating everything I have in the garden. (EV, Ph36) <***Loc:*** EV, SM, TB, Da84, Gu00, Ph36>

vernailler [værnaje] *v.intr.* to loaf, wander aimlessly <***Loc:*** VM>

vernir [værnir] *v.tr.* to varnish, glaze *Ça ici, j'ai fait ça, ça c'est du cèdre. Tu vois ça semble qu'il a été verni et qu'il est craqué et tout. Ça semble il a été verni, c'est pas vrai non.* This here, I made that. That's cedar wood. You see it looks like it was varnished and that it's cracked and all. It looks varnished, but it's not, really. (TB) <***Loc:*** TB, Da84>

vernis [værni] *n.m.* **1** varnish **2** surface, outer layer (e.g. of skin) *Oter le vernis de la jambe.* To skin the leg. (AV) <***Loc:*** AV, Da84>

vernissage [værnisaʒ] *n.m.* varnishing <***Loc:*** Da84>

vérocypèle ♦see **vélocipède**

verrat [vera] *n.m.* boar, boar hog, male pig **Lui, il a un verrat là-bas. Je vas emmener la truie là-bas et puis la* BREED. He has a boar hog over there. I'll take the sow over there to breed her. (IV, An94) *Onze verrats et une truie, ça fait douze cochons.* Eleven boars and a sow, that makes twelve pigs. (VM) <***Loc:*** AL, IB, IV, VM, An94, Da84>

verre [vær] *n.m.* **1** glass *Il y a jusqu'à des chaudières en verre asteur.* There are even cooking pots made of glass now. (VM) **2** drinking glass **Un verre d'eau.* A glass of water. (Da84) **3** *(pl.)* glasses, eyeglasses, spectacles *J'ai eu la malchance de casser mes verres ce matin.* I had the misfortune to break my spectacles this morning. (SJ) ◊ •**verre à boire** drinking glass <LF> <***Loc:*** AV, IB, IV, JD, JE, LA, LF, SB, SJ, SL, SM, TB, VM, Da84, Hi02>

verre à bouteille ♦see **verre-bouteille**

verre-bouteille (**verbouteille, verre à bouteille, verre de bouteille**) [værbutɛj, værabutɛj, værdəbutɛj] fragment of broken glass, shard of glass *Je m'avais coupé en bas le pied avec un verre-bouteille et puis ça saignait.* I had cut myself on the bottom of the foot with a shard of broken glass and it was bleeding. (SL) <***Loc:*** LA, LF, SL, SM, Da84, Lv88>

verre de bouteille ♦see **verre-bouteille**

verrée [vere] *n.f.* glassful, the contents of a glass <***Loc:*** TB>

verrue (**verrure, verrule**) [very, veryr veryl] *n.f.* wart <***Loc:*** JD, LA, SM, TB, VM, Da84, Lv88>

verrule, verrure ♦see **verrue**

vers[1] [vær] *n.m.* verse (of the Bible, of poetry, etc.) <***Loc:*** Da84, Hi02>

vers[2] [vær] *prep.* **1** toward, to, in the direction of **Donner la tête vers la ville.* To head for the city. (Da84) **2** about, approximately, around **Il l'a amené à une factrie de bière vers minuit le soir.* He took him to a brewery around midnight. (IV, An94) **Vers trois heures de l'après-midi.* About 3 p.m. (Da84) <***Loc:*** IV, LA, TB, An94, Da84, Hi02>

verser [værse] *v.tr.* **1** to pour, pour out *C'est quand j'allais la voir, elle me versait à boire.* When I went to see her, she poured me a drink. (IB, ch: *Je m'ai fait une maîtresse*) **2** to tip over, spill *Fais attention, tu vas verser ta bière.* Be careful, you'll spill your beer. (LA) **3** to shed (tears) *Ne pleurez pas autant, la belle, ne versez pas autant de larmes.* Weep not so, maiden, shed not so many tears. (IB, ch: *La veuve de sept ans*) <***Loc:*** IB, LA, Da84>

verset [verse, værse] *n.m.* **1** scripture verse, passage **2** stanza *Le second verset.* The second stanza. (SB) <***Loc:*** SB, Da84>

version [værsjɔ̃, værzjɔ̃] *n.f.* version <***Loc:*** Da84>

vert[1], -e [vær, vært] *adj.* **1** unripe (of fruit or vegetables) *Ça peut te rendre malade si tu manges des plaquemines vertes.* It can make you sick if you eat unripe persimmons. (LA) *Café vert.* Unroasted coffee beans. (SM) **2** green, inexperienced, innocent (of a person) **Mom m'a jamais expliqué rien. J'ai été aussi vert qu'un arbre dedans la cour là.* Mom never explained anything to me. I was as green as that tree in the yard. (EV) *Ils étaient verts, verts, le jeune monde dans ce temps-là. Ça connaissait pas rien.* They were so green, young people in those days. They didn't know anything. (EV) ◊ **•vert comme de l'herbe** naïve <LA, La99> <***Loc:*** AC, EV, JE, LA, LF, SL, SM, TB, VM, An94, Da84, Hi02, La99, Re31>

vert[2], -e [vær, vært] *adj./n.* green (color) **Eux avaient peint sa jument verte avec de la peinture.* They had painted his mare green with paint. (SL, An94) ◊ **•vert comme de l'herbe {des herbes}** green as grass, very green in color <LA, La99> **•vert de Paris** Paris green (bright green pigment, also used as an insecticide, containing copper and arsenic) <Da84> <***Loc:*** AC, EV, JE, LA, LF, SL, SM, TB, VM, An94, Da84, Hi02, La99, Re31>

vert[3] [vær] *n.m.* greenery <***Loc:*** Da84>

vert de gris [værdəgri] *n.m.* verdigris <***Loc:*** Da84>

vertical [værtikal] *adj.* vertical <***Loc:*** Da84>

vertu [værty] *n.f.* [*eccl.*] virtue, chastity <***Loc:*** Da84>

vertueux, -euse [værtɥø, -øz] *adj.* virtuous *C'était pas ça que t'appelles une femme vertueuse.* She wasn't what you would call a virtuous woman. (LA) <***Loc:*** LA, Da84>

verveine [værvɛ̃n] *n.f.* verbena <***Loc:*** EV>

veste [vɛst] *n.m.* vest *Je veux un* SUIT *avec un veste.* I want a suit with a vest. (TB) <***Loc:*** TB>

vestibule [vɛstibyl] *n.m.* vestibule, lobby <***Loc:*** Da84>

vestige [vɛstiʒ] *n.m.* vestige, trace, remains *Il y avait une habitation là, mais asteur il reste juste les vestiges.* There was once a farm there, but now there are only the remains. (VM) <***Loc:*** VM, Da84>

vétéran [veterɑ̃] *n.m.* veteran <***Loc:*** Da84>

vétérinaire[1] [veterinær, vetrinær] *adj.* veterinary *Donne pas ça à ton enfant, c'est une médecine vétérinaire.* Don't give that to your child, it's a veterinary medicine. (VM) <***Loc:*** VM, Da84>

vétérinaire[2] [veterinær, vetrinær] *n.m.* veterinarian <***Loc:*** Da84, Hi02>

vêtir [vetir] **I** *v.tr.* to clothe, dress *J'aimerais mieux les vêtir que les nourrir.* I would rather clothe them than feed them. (LA) *Ça vendait les catins vêtues.* They sold clothed dolls. (LA) **II se vêtir** *v.pron.* to dress o.s. *Il était rendu qu'il pouvait pus seulement se vêtir.* He had reached the point where he could no longer even dress himself. (LA) <***Loc:*** LA, Da84>

vétiver (**vetiver, veutivert**) [vetivær, vətivær] *n.* type of tufted perennial grass, pampas grass <***Loc:*** Da84, Ho90>

veuf ♦see **veuve**

veuille ♦see **veille**

veutivert ♦see **vétiver**

veuve[1] [vœv] *adj.* (*m.* **veuf** [vœf] *is rare*) widowed **La vieille maman était veuve et elle voulait sa fille trouve à se marier, mais ça prenait du temps.* The old mother was widowed and she wanted her daughter to find someone to marry, but it was taking some time. (LA, An94) <***Loc:*** LA, An94, Da84, Lv88>

veuve[2] [vœv] *n.* (*m.* **veuf** [vœf] *is rare*) **1** widow, widower *Quand j'ai rencontré Philippe et qu'il m'a dit qu'il était veuve, j'ai commencé à prier pour sa femme.* When I met Philip and he told me he was a widower, I began to pray for his wife. (TB) *Un homme veuve.* A widower. (LF) **Tout ce que je te demande, c'est de secourir le monde, surtout les vieilles veuves.* All I ask you is to help people, especially the old widows. (IV, An94) **C'est les veuves de la coulée qu'est parties au village.* All the widows on the creek have left for town. (ch: *Les veuves de la coulée*) **2** person unaccompanied by his or her partner (e.g. for the evening or an event) *À soir, nous-autres va à la barre avec les veuves.* Tonight we are going to the bar with [just] the guys. (Lv88) ◊ **•veuve délaissée** grass widow (i.e. a woman who is either divorced or separated) <Da84> **•veuve rabiotte** woman whose husband has left her <SM, La99, Lv88> **•faire la veuve** to act like a widow <Da84> <***Loc:*** AC, IB, IV, JD, LA, LF, SM, TB, An94, Da84, La99, Lv88>

vexant, -e [vɛksɑ̃, -ɑ̃t] *adj.* vexing, annoying *Ma belle-sœur est vexante.* My sister-in-law is annoying. (VM) <***Loc:*** VM, Da84>

vexer [vɛkse] *v.tr.* to vex, annoy, bother *Il m'a vexé avec ses histoires.* He vexed me with his stories. (VM) <***Loc:*** VM, Da84>

viande [vjɑ̃n, vjɑ̃(d)] *n.f.* meat **On avait pas de glacières ni de* DEEP FREEZE *mais on manquait jâmais de viande fraîche.* We didn't have refrigerators or freezers but we never lacked fresh meat. (Gu82) ◊ **•viande de bête** beef <EV, SL, SM,

Ph36> •**viande de bœuf** beef <Da84> •**viande de chevreuil** venison <IB> •**viande de cochon** pork <EV, LF, SM, TB, VM, Da84, Ph36> •**viande de mouton** mutton, lamb <Da84> •**viande de veau** veal <Da84> •**viande farouche** game (meat) *On mange proche jamais de la viande farouche.* We almost never eat game. (AC) **Les jeunes d'asteur [...], tu peux proche pas les blâmer de pas vouloir manger d'la viande farouche.* Young people today, you can hardly blame them for not wanting to eat game meat. (Gu82) <AC, Gu82> •**viande fumée** smoked meat <SL> •**viande hachée** ground meat <EV, Da84> •**viande moulue** ground meat <EV, Da84> •**viandes d'en-dedans** organ meat <LF> •**viande salée** salted meat, meat preserved by salting process <SL> <***Loc:*** AC, EV, JE, LA, LF, SL, SM, TB, VM, Da84, Gu82, Hi02, Ph36>

vibration [vibrasjɔ̃] *n.f.* vibration <***Loc:*** Da84>

vicaire [vikær] *n.m.* vicar, assistant pastor ◊ •**vicaire général** vicar general <Da84> <***Loc:*** Da84>

vice [vis] *n.m.* vice <***Loc:*** Da84>

vice-président [visprezidɑ̃] *n.m.* vice-president <***Loc:*** Da84>

vicieux, -euse [visjø, -øz] *adj.* vicious, cruel, heartless *C'était un petit homme vicieux.* He was a cruel little man. (SL) <***Loc:*** SL, Da84>

victime [viktim] *n.f.* victim <***Loc:*** Da84>

victoire [viktwar] *n.f.* victory <***Loc:*** Da84>

vidage [vidaʒ] *n.m.* emptying <***Loc:*** Da84>

vide[1] [vid] *adj.* empty, void, vacant **Ça fait, tu peux pas aller te marier avec les poches vides.* So, you can't get married with empty pockets. (SL, An94) <***Loc:*** SL, An94, Da84, Hi02>

vide[2] [vid] *n.m.* blank space, void <***Loc:*** Da84>

vider [vide] **I** *v.tr.* **1** to empty, drain **Ça fait un matin je rentre là Mom dit, "Il faut tu vas vider ton pot de chambre."* So, one morning I come home and Mom says, "You need to go and empty your chamber pot." (EV) **Être trop bête pour vider un pot de chambre.* To be hopelessly stupid. (Da84) **2** to pour *Et puis après ça il vidait du whisky dessus chaque feuille.* And then after that he would pour some whiskey on each [tobacco] leaf. (AC) *Vide l'eau dans le verre.* Pour the water into the glass. (SM) *Il a vidé un peu d'eau dans son vin.* He poured a little bit of water in his wine. (Lv88) **II se vider** *v.pron.* to become empty *La citerne avait un trou dedans et elle s'a vidé.* The cistern had a hole in it and it became empty. (VM) ◊ •**vider la mer avec un baril défoncé** to empty the sea with a leaky barrel, do a task that requires great effort but accomplishes nothing <SL, La99> <***Loc:*** AC, AV, EV, SL, SM, TB, VM, Da84, Hi02, La99, Lv88>

vie [vi] *n.f.* **1** life *Tu vas faire une meilleure vie avec un homme qu'est brave.* You will have a happier life with a brave man. (AS) **2** lifestyle *Il mène une vie de chien.* He has the lifestyle of a dog. (LA) **3** lifetime *Il a dépensé l'argent de sa vie d'ouvrage pour acheter cette maison.* He spent the money of a lifetime of work to buy that house. (VM) **4** life story *Il a raconté sa vie à ses petits enfants.* He told his life story to his grandchildren. (LA) **5** livelihood, living, means of support **Non, moi, je fais ma vie ici. Moi, je veux pas aller là-bas.* No, I make my living here. I don't want to go there. (SL, An94) ◊ •**vie de garçon** ***a*** bachelor life *Et on a fait notre vie de garçon ensemble.* And we spent our bachelor days together. (TB) ***b*** boyhood, bachelorhood *C'est plusieurs années qu'on a resté au Cutoff. Tout ma vie de garçon était là et une dizaine d'années que j'étais marié.* We lived in Cutoff for several years. My whole bachelorhood was spent there and about ten years that I was married. (LF) <LF, TB> •**avoir la vie dans sa main** to almost die <VM, La99> •**bon comme la vie** exceedingly good *Il ferait n'importe quoi pour moi. C'est bon comme la vie.* He would do anything for me. He's as good as life. (SM) <SM> •**en vie** alive, living *Les deux plus jeunes filles est toujours en vie.* The two youngest girls are still alive. (TB) <EV, JE, TB, An94, Da84> •**faire une {sa} vie** to work for one's living, make or earn a living *Je pouvais pas faire une vie avec ça.* I could not make a living with that. (SM) *L'été ça faisait leur vie à aller au trawl pour des chevrettes.* In the summer they made their living going trawling for shrimp. (TB) <AC, SL, SM, TB, An94, Lv88> •**la vie durante** for one's lifetime, during one's lifetime <Da84> •**pour une vie** for a living *Qu'est-ce que tu fais pour une vie?* What do you do for a living? (Lv88) *On pêche pour notre vie.* We fish for a living. (Lv88) *J'ai essayé pêcher des écrevisses pour une vie.* I tried to catch crawfish for a living. (SM) <SM, VM, An94, Lv88> •**tout(e) sa vie** one's entire life **Il'avont couri tout leur vie pis il'avont pas pris le temps d'rire.* They ran ragged their whole lives and they haven't taken the time to laugh. (Gu82) *Il a fait ça toute sa vie.* He did that for his entire life. (AC) *Alle restait malade toute sa vie.* She stayed sick for her entire life. (TB) <AC, EV, TB, An94, Gu82> <***Loc:*** AC, AS, EV, JE, LA, LF, SL, SM, TB, VM, An94, Da84, Gu82, Hi02, La99, Lv88>

vieillard [vjejar] *n.m.* old man <***Loc:*** Da84>

vieille ♦see **vieux**

vieillerie [vjejri] *n.f.* **1** old junk, old things **2** old age *Je peux pus voir. C'est pas bon. C'est la viellerie qui fait ça.* I can't see anymore. It's not good. It's old age that does that. (EV) <***Loc:*** EV, Da84>

vieillesse [vjejes] *n.f.* old age <***Loc:*** LF, Da84, Hi02>

vieillezir ♦see **vieillir**

vieillir (**vieillezir**) [vjejir, vjejzir] **I** *v.tr.* to age *La boisson vieillezit un monde.* Liquor ages a person. (VM) **II** *v.intr.* to age, grow old *C'est mieux de vieillezir que pas vieillezir.* It's better to grow old than not to [and die]. (SL) <***Loc:*** SL, VM, Da84, Lv88>

viendre ♦see **venir**

vierge [vjærʒ] *n.f.* virgin *Ça me fait de la peine de le dire, mais elle était pas vierge quand elle s'a marié.* It hurts me to say it, but she was not a virgin when she married. (VM) **Sainte Vierge Marie!* Holy Virgin Mary! (used to express surprise) (La99) ◊ **•la Sainte Vierge** the Blessed Virgin **Que la Sainte Vierge doit honnir.* The Holy Virgin must be ashamed (used to express disapproval). (La99) <LA, VM, Da84, La99, Lv88> <***Loc:*** LA, VM, Da84, La99, Lv88>

vieux, vieille[1] [vjø, vjɛj] *adj.* old **C'est pas ein deshôneur d'êt' vieux, mais c'est sûr pas aisé.* It's not a dishonor to be old, but it sure isn't easy. (Gu82) *Mes autres frères sont morts, le plus jeune est mort et le plus vieux est mort.* My other brothers are all dead, the youngest is dead and the oldest is dead. (SM) **I' voulont défaire ma vieille maison et m'en r'bâtir eine neuve.* They want to tear down my old house and build me a new one. (Gu82) ◊ **•vieille fille** old maid, spinster <Da84> **•vieux garçon** old bachelor <SM, Da84> **•vieux monde** old folks, elderly people *Le vieux monde, ma mame et mon pape, eux parlait bien peu d'anglais.* The old folks, my mom and my pop, used to speak very little English. (PQ) <PQ> **•vieux nègre** ***a*** *[term of endearment]* (usu. unrelated to race) old boy, friend ***b*** suitor (used in self-endearing appeal, esp. in songs) **Tu devrais bien écouter ton vieux nèg' une fois.* You should really listen for once to your old beau. (ch: *Jolie catin*) <Da84, Lv88> **•le vieux temps / les (bons) vieux temps** the (good) old days **Ça danse les polkas du vieux temps.* They dance the polkas from the old days. (ch : *Le sud de la Louisiane*) **Ouais, ça c'était les bons vieux temps.* Yep, them were the good old days. (Gu82) <EV, LA, TB, An94, Gu82> <***Loc:*** AC, AV, EV, IV, LA, LF, PQ, SL, SM, TB, VM, An94, Da84, Gu82, Hi02>

vieux, vieille[2] [vjø, vjɛj] *n.* **1** *(m.)* old man **Le vieux a essayé d'étrangler son fils.* The old man tried to strangle his son. (EV, An94) **Le vieux a retourné chez lui et il lui avait amené son fusil.* The old man went home and he had brought his gun. (SL, An94) **2** *(m.)* husband **Ça fait qu'ils se sont remariés. Et la vieille lui a demandé un* HONEYMOON *aussi, tu sais, le vieux et la vieille.* So, they got remarried. And the wife asked him for a honeymoon, too, you know, the husband and wife. (An94) **3** *(f.)* old woman *Et j'ai eu un docteur pour tous mes petits, excepté un, il a fallu que je prende une vieille femme, mais la vieille elle a travaillé aussi bien qu'un docteur.* And I had a doctor for [delivering] all of my children, except one, I had to get an old lady, but the old woman worked as well as a doctor. (EV) **4** *(f.)* wife **Ma femme m'a acheté ein habit neuf pour porter demain au soir. J'avais pas trop envie de porter un* SUIT, *mais la vieille m'a dit que Raymond l'avait demandé.* My wife bought me a brand new suit to wear tomorrow evening. I don't feel much like wearing a suit, but the wife told me that Raymond asked me to. (Gu82) **5** *(pl.)* old people, old folks **Les jeunes d'asteur voulont p'us écouter les vieux côme avant.* Young people today don't want to listen anymore to old folk like before. (Gu82) ◊ **•ma vieille** ***a*** my wife *Ma vieille veut pas aller. Et ta vieille?* My wife doesn't want to go. And your wife? (SM) ***b*** my mother ***c*** my friend <EV, SL, SM, Da84, Lv88, Ph36> **•mon vieux** ***a*** my husband *Moi, je veux aller, mais mon vieux veut pas.* I want to go, but my husband doesn't want to. (SM) ***b*** my father ***c*** my friend <EV, SL, SM, Da84, Lv88, Ph36> <***Loc:*** EV, LA, SL, SM, An94, Da84, Gu82, Hi02, Lv88, Ph36>

vieux garçon [vjøgarsɔ̃] *n.m.* zinnia <***Loc:*** AV, EV, IB, JD, LF, SJ, SL, SM, Ph36>

vieux-mame [vjømɑ̃m] *n.f.* *[term of endearment]* grandma, grandmother *Vieux-mame, tu veux je fais ça?* Grandma dear, do you want me to do that? (SL) <***Loc:*** SL, SM>

vieux-pape [vjøpap] *n.m.* *[term of endearment]* grandpa, grandfather <***Loc:*** SM>

vif[1]**, vive** [vif, viv] *adj.* lively, spry, quick, alert *Elle est vif avec ses ouvrages.* She is quick with her work. (Lv88) *C'est une petite fille qu'est vive.* She is a lively little girl. (VM) <***Loc:*** VM, Da84, Lv88>

vif[2] [vif] *n.m.* quick, flesh beneath the skin *Je m'ai coupé au vif avec ce poignard.* I cut myself to the quick with that butcher knife. (VM) <***Loc:*** VM>

vif-argent [vifarʒɑ̃] *n.m.* mercury, quicksilver <***Loc:*** Da84>

vigilance [viʒilɑ̃s] *n.f.* **1** vigilance, watchfulness **2** vigilante movement **Oh, mais cher, il y en avait amené un tas ici pour le temps de la vigilance.* Oh, well dear, a lot went on around here during the vigilante movement. (VM, An94) **3** vigilante committee *Ils m'ont dit que c'était la vigilance qu'avait pendu le petit Légé.* They told me it was the vigilantes who had hanged the little Légé boy. (VM) <***Loc:*** AC, VM, An94, Da84>

vigilant[1]**, -e** [viʒilɑ̃, -ɑ̃t] *adj.* vigilant, watchful *Tu pourras pas arriver près de chez eux-autres. Ils ont un chien vigilant.* You won't be able to approach their house. They have a vigilant dog. (VM) <***Loc:*** VM, Da84>

vigilant[2] [viʒilɑ̃] *n.m.* vigilante, member of a vigilance committee <***Loc:*** VM, Da84>

vigile [viʒil] *n.f.* **1** vigil **2** vigil of feast days <***Loc:*** Da84>

vigne [viŋ, vin, viɲ] *n.f.* vine ◊ **•vigne de raisin** grapevine <Fa77> <***Loc:*** LF, Fa77>

vigoureux, -euse [vigurø, -øz] *adj.* vigorous, lively, strong, robust *Elle est beaucoup vigoureuse.* She is full of life. (IB) <***Loc:*** IB, Da84>

vigueur [vigœr] *n.f.* vigor, force, strength <***Loc:*** Da84>

vilain[1]**, -e** [vilɛ̃, -ɛ̃n] *adj.* **1** ugly *Ça c'est vilain.* That's ugly. (SM) *Elle est vilain.* She is ugly. (SM) **2** evil, nasty, dirty **Là, après ça, on avait deux jeunes bougres qui ont pris à jouer, et ils estiont bons joueurs. Mais il avions des vilaines manières.* Then, after that, there were two young fellows who started to play, and they were good musicians. But they had evil ways. (EV, An84) **3** rude *Fais pas ça. C'est vilain.*

Don't do that. It's rude. (VM) **4** ugly, bad, nasty (of the weather) *Et hier au soir le temps était assez vilain.* And last night the weather was quite nasty. (TB) ◊ **•vilain comme un coin de banquette / vilain comme un péché {un macaque / le diable}** very ugly <AV, SL, VM, La99> **•vilain mot** bad word, dirty word *Y a des mots que nous-autres on dit là, eh ben pour eusse c'est un vilain mot.* There are words that we say here, for them they are bad words. (LF) *Et "nègre" veut pas dire "NIGGER," c'est pas un mot vilain. C'est juste dire que c'est un homme de couleur. Un noir. Tu vas dire "un nègre," ou "une négresse," et c'est pas une insulte.* And "nègre" doesn't mean "nigger," it's not an ugly word. It's just to say that someone is a man of color. A black man. You'll say a "nègre," or a "négresse," and it's not an insult. (LF) <LF> **•faire des vilaines choses** to do nasty things or immodest acts <Da84> ***<Loc:*** AV, EV, IB, IV, JD, JE, LA, LF, SB, SL, SM, TB, VM, An84, An94, Da84, Hi02, La99, Lv88>

vilain[2], -e [vilɛ̃, -ɛ̃n] *n.* ugly person ◊ **•mon vilain** you rascal *Tu me fais du mal chaque fois je te regarde, ma vilaine.* You hurt me every time I look at you, you rascal. (ch: *Madame Atchen*) <Da84> ***<Loc:*** Da84>

vilain[3] [vilɛ̃] *adv.* badly, in an ugly or nasty way *Et l'affaire d'huile avait retombé vilain, ça fait j'étais pris avec deux mille SHARE, j'avais payé treize milles.* And the oil business had fallen badly, so I was stuck with two thousand shares, I had paid thirteen thousand. (TB) ***<Loc:*** TB>

vilainement [vilɛ̃nmɑ̃] *adv.* in an ugly or unkind way *Il a fait ça vilainement.* He did that in an unkind way. (EV) ***<Loc:*** EV, Da84>

vilebrequin ♦see **virebrequin**

village [vilaʒ] *n.m.* **1** town *Il a quitté la campagne pour s'en venir au village.* He left the country to come to town. (Lv88) **2** city *Lafayette est un gros village.* Lafayette is a big city [about 100,000 inhabitants]. (Lv88) *On avait des chiens et des chats mais pas d'autres animaux parce qu'on restait dans le village.* We had dogs and cats but no other animals because we used to live within the city limits. (IB) ***<Loc:*** AC, AV, EV, IB, LA, SL, TB, VM, An94, Da84, Hi02, Lv88>

ville (Ville) [vil] *n.f.* city (used almost exclusively to refer to New Orleans) *Les sœurs de la Ville m'a envoyé le programme de son enterrement.* The nuns from New Orleans sent me the program from her funeral service. (SL) ◊ **•en ville** in town, specifically New Orleans *J'aviserais pas quelqu'un d'assayer de coucher sur la rue en ville asteur.* I would not advise someone to try to sleep on the street in New Orleans nowadays. (TB) *Ils ont été en ville pour leur vingtième anniversaire.* They went to New Orleans for their twentieth anniversary. (LA) <LA, TB, Da84> ***<Loc:*** EV, LA, SL, SM, TB, VM, Da84, Hi02, Lv88, Ph36>

vin [vɛ̃] *n.m.* **1** wine *Ça boit beaucoup du vin.* They drink a lot of wine. (AV) **2** homemade wine (made from cherries, peaches, or other fruits) *Il faisait du vin avec des fruits. Avec des merises, avec des figues et avec des pêches. [...] Tu mettais ça à haigrir avec du sucre.* He used to make wine with fruit, with wild cherries, with figs, and with peaches. You would let it ferment with sugar. (VM) **3** juice ◊ **•vin à vingt batailles au gallon** very strong wine <SM, La99> **•vin de canne** sugar cane juice <IB, SJ, SL, SM, VM, Da84> **•vin de mûre** berry juice <Da84> **•vin hâcre *a*** bitter wine (esp. wine that has gone bad) ***b*** dry wine <LA, VM> ***<Loc:*** AV, CL, EV, LA, SJ, SL, SM, VM, An94, Da84, Hi02, La99, Lv88>

vinaigre [vinɛg(r)] *n.m.* vinegar ◊ **•être dans son vinaigre** to be inebriated <EV, La99, Lv88, Ph36> ***<Loc:*** AV, EV, TB, An94, Da84, Hi02, La99, Lv88, Ph36>

vinaigrer [vinegre] *v.tr.* to season with vinegar *Il a vinaigré sa viande.* He seasoned his meat with vinegar. (LA) ***<Loc:*** LA, Da84>

vindication [vɛ̃dikasjɔ̃] *n.f.* vengeance, revenge *Je vas prendre une vindication contre lui.* I will take revenge on him. (VM) ***<Loc:*** VM>

vinéraire ♦see **vulnéraire**

vingt [vɛ̃] *adj./n.m.* twenty *Elle peut l'avoir, si vite qu'elle me donne le vingt piastres.* She can have it, as soon as she gives me the twenty dollars. (IV) ***<Loc:*** AC, AV, CL, EV, IV, LA, SL, TB, VM, An94, Da84, Hi02>

vingtaine [vɛ̃tɛ̃n] *n.f.* about twenty, a score *Il y avait pas de publication, il y avait pas de, de journal, il y avait pas de livre, rien qui était écrit en français avant une vingtaine d'années passé, je pense.* There were no publications, no newspapers, no books, nothing that was written in French before about twenty years ago, I think. (SL) ***<Loc:*** SL, TB, An94, Da84>

vingt-cinq sous [vɛ̃tsɛ̃su] *n.m.* quarter, 25-cent coin ***<Loc:*** CL, IV, LA, An94, Hi02>

vingt-deux [vɛ̃tdø] *n.m.* .22-caliber rifle *Je prendais un vingt-deux là équand ça ressoudait, mais j'en ai jamais tué un, je l'ai touché je pense, mais j'ai pas pu en attraper un.* I would take a .22 for when it [the tarpon] would resurface, but I never killed one, I grazed it I think, but I was never able to catch one. (TB) ***<Loc:*** TB>

vingtième [vɛ̃tjɛ̃m] *adj./n.* twentieth *Ils ont été en ville pour leur vingtième anniversaire.* They went to New Orleans for their twentieth anniversary. (LA) ***<Loc:*** LA, An94, Da84>

violence [vjolɑ̃s] *n.f.* violence ***<Loc:*** Da84>

violent, -e [vjolɑ̃, -ɑ̃t] *adj.* violent, fierce, brutal *Si ma mie-z-elle est morte, j'aurai le cœur violent.* If my love is dead, I will have a violent heart. (PQ, ch: *La belle et les capitaines*) ***<Loc:*** PQ, Da84>

violer [vjole] *v.tr.* **1** to violate, transgress (a law) *Les représentants ont pas plus le droit de violer la loi que n'importe qui d'autre.* Representatives have no more right to violate the law than anyone else. (LA) **2** to profane (a holy place) *Violer un cimetière.* To profane a cemetery. (LA) **3** to rape *Il en a violé Dieu sait combien avant qu'il l'ont attrapé.* He raped God knows how many before they caught him. (LA) <***Loc:*** LA, Da84>

violet (**violette**) [vjolɛ, vjole, vjolɛt] *adj./n.* violet, purple (color) *Une belle petite robe violette.* A pretty little purple dress. (LA) <***Loc:*** LA, TB, Da84, Hi02>

violette[1] [vjolɛt] *n.f.* violet, flower of the violet family ◊ **•violette marronne {farouche / sauvage}** wild violet <EV, VM, Ho90> <***Loc:*** EV, Da84, Ho90>

violette[2] ♦see **violet**

violon [vjolɔ̃, vjølɔ̃] *n.m.* **1** violin **2** red head duck <***Loc:*** AC, AV, EV, JD, JE, LF, SL, Da84, Hi02, Lv88, Re31>

violoneux [vjolɔ̃nø] *n.m.* violinist, fiddler <***Loc:*** Di32, Hi02>

vipère [vipær] *n.f.* viper, adder <***Loc:*** Da84>

virage [viraʒ] *n.m.* **1** turning, curve (e.g. in a road) **2** action of turning **3** swerve, swerving, careening *C'était un virage que cette auto a fait.* That's quite a swerve that car made. (SJ) <***Loc:*** SJ, VM, Da84>

virebrequin (**vilebrequin, birebiquin, vilevaquin**) [virbrəkɛ̃, vilbrəkɛ̃, vivrəkɛ̃, birbikɛ̃, vilvakɛ̃] *n.m.* any of several boring tools such as a hand-drill, bit and brace, wimble, auger, or gimlet ◊ **•avoir une gueule comme un vilevaquin** to always say the wrong thing <TB, La99> <***Loc:*** AV, EV, IB, JD, LA, LF, SB, SJ, SL, SM, TB, VM, Da84, La99, Lv88, Ph36>

vire-cul [virky] *n.m.* mosquito larva, wiggle-tail <***Loc:*** LA, SM>

vire-de-bord [virdəbɔr] *n.m.* mosquito larva, wiggle-tail <***Loc:*** Lv88, Re31>

virée [vire] *n.f.* turnrow, headland (strip of uncultivated land at the end or side of a field where a plow can turn) <***Loc:*** VM, Br55, Di32, Gr86, Lv88>

virement [virmɑ̃] *n.m.* turn, turning <***Loc:*** Da84>

virer [vire] **I** *v.tr.* **1** to turn *Vire ton cheval de bord et va-t-en.* Turn your horse around and go away. (VM) *Le portrait était par terre, viré en l'air, avec la figure en l'air, et la vitre était tout cassée.* The picture was on the ground, turned upwards, face up, and the glass was all broken. (TB) **2** to dissuade, persuade not to, turn s.o. away from *Je l'ai viré de le faire.* I persuaded him not to do it. (VM) **II** *v.intr.* **1** to turn *Au bout du chemin, vous virez en-bas.* At the end of the road, you turn down there. (Lv88) *Vire à la droite.* Turn right. (JE) **2** to turn, turn into, become *Il a viré baptiste après qu'il s'a marié.* He turned Baptist after he married. (LA) **III se virer** *v.pron.* to turn, turn around *Il s'a viré pour la regarder dans les yeux.* He turned around to look her in the eyes. (LA) ◊ **•virer à l'envers** to turn inside out *Les tripes. Et là faulait qu'alle les vire à l'envers et gratter de ce bord-là aussitte.* The intestines. Then she had to turn them inside out and scrape that side too. (TB) <TB> **•virer de bord** ***a*** to turn around *Il a viré de bord au milieu du chemin.* He turned around in the middle of the road. (LA) ***b*** to change one's opinion *Il a viré de bord et voté contre le président le deuxième coup.* He changed his opinion and voted against the president the second time. (VM) <LA, SJ, SM, VM, Da84, Lv88> **•se virer de bord** to turn around *Et la femme s'a viré de bord et l'a flaillé une tape dans la figure.* And the woman turned around and gave him a slap in the face. (TB) *Vire-toi de bord.* Turn around. (LA) <LA, TB> <***Loc:*** JE, LA, LF, SJ, SM, TB, VM, Da84, Hi02, Lv88>

vireveau [virvo] *n.m.* windlass, hand-winch <***Loc:*** VM, Lv88>

vire-vire[1] [virvir] *n.m.* **1** mosquito larva, wiggle-tail **2** western willet <***Loc:*** IB, LF, SL, SM, VM, Da84, Lv88, Re31>

vire-vire[2] [virvir] *n.m.* whirlpool <***Loc:*** VM>

virginité [virʒinite, værʒinite] *n.f.* virginity <***Loc:*** Da84>

virole [virol] *n.f.* [hardware] nut <***Loc:*** TB, VM, Fa77>

viron [virɔ̃] *n.m.* walk, round *Tous les jours il fait son viron par la poste.* Every day he takes his walk to the post office. (VM) <***Loc:*** VM, Lv88>

vironer [virɔ̃ne] *v.intr.* to change course often, veer *Elle virone trop pour finir son ouvrage.* She changes course too often to get her job done. (IB) *Vironer d'un côté à l'autre.* To veer from one side to the other. (AV) <***Loc:*** AV, IB>

vis (**avis, avisse**) [vis, avis] *n.m./f.* **1** screw *J'ai de besoin de des avis pour mettre cette plaque-là.* I need some screws to install that plate. (VM) **2** wood screw ◊ **•avisse à quatre coins** Phillips head screw <JE> **•avisse à tête platte** flat-head screw <JE> <***Loc:*** EV, JE, LF, SB, SL, SM, VM, Da84, Lv88>

vis-à-vis (**vis à vis**) [vizavi] *adv.* face to face *Moi et toi se regarde vis-à-vis.* You and I are looking at each other face to face. (LF) ◊ **•vis-à-vis (de)** ***a*** facing, across from *Ils ont* DREDGE *quelques années passées, ils ont arrêté vis-à-vis le cimetière.* They dredged several years ago, they stopped right across from the cemetery. (TB) *J'ai été énée à la Pointe aux Chiens. Drette au long du bord sur le Bayou Lafourche, proche vis-à-vis de là où ce que mon mari était éné, lui il était éné sur Terrebonne.* I was born in Pointe aux Chênes. Right on the Lafourche side, almost right across from where my husband was born, he was born in Terrebonne. (TB) *C'est proche que vis-à-vis avec la station d'huile.* It's almost right across from the gas station. (LF) ***b*** in line with, even with *Ils restiont vis-à-vis ma maison.* They lived in line with my house. (VM) *Il est vis-à-vis de moi.* He is even with me, lined up with me. (LF) ***c*** side by side *Je reste vis-à-vis de ma fille.* I live next door to my daughter. (AV) <***Loc:*** AV, EV, LF, SB, SM, TB, VM, Da84, Hi02>

visage [vizaʒ] *n.m.* face, visage <***Loc:*** Da84>

visible [vizib(l)] *adj.* visible, in sight <***Loc:*** Da84>

vision [vizjɔ̃, vyzjɔ̃] *n.f.* apparition, ghost *Avoir une vision.* To see an apparition. (AV) <*Loc:* AV, SB, Da84>

visitation [vizitasjɔ̃] *n.f.* visitation, official visitation or inspection <*Loc:* Da84>

visite [vizit] *n.f.* visit, call *Bien merci d'avoir eu venu. Votre visite m'a bien désennuyé.* Thanks for coming. Your visit has really cheered me up. (LA) <*Loc:* LA, SM, VM, Da84>

visiter [vizite] **I** *v.tr.* to visit, call on *Et son mari il était mort. Et un bougre venait la visiter.* And her husband was dead. And a guy would come to visit her. (LF) *Il a revenu pour visiter son père.* He came back to visit his father. (Lv88) **II** *v.intr.* to visit, go visiting *J'aime pas ça quand ma belle-fille vient visiter. Ses enfants sont assez pirates!* I don't like it when my daughter-in-law comes to visit. Her children are pretty bad. (Gu00) *On visite un tas le dimanche.* We do a lot of visiting on Sundays. (Lv88) **III se visiter** *v.pron.* **1** to visit each other *Ça a commençé à se visiter.* They started to visit each other. (AC) *Et asteur le monde se visite pas. C'est pas comme c'était. Parce que y a plus d'affaires à faire, et y a plein du monde qui connait pas leurs voisins.* And today people don't visit. It's not like it used to be. Because there are more things to do, and there are a lot of people who don't know their neighbors. (LF) **2** to date *Ça se visitait pas comme aujourd'hui.* They didn't date like today. (LA) <*Loc:* AC, AV, EV, LA, LF, Da84, Gu00, Lv88>

visiteur [vizitœr] *n.m.* visitor, caller <*Loc:* Da84>

vissage [visaʒ] *n.m.* screwing (of screws or bolts) <*Loc:* Da84>

visser (avisser) [vise, avise] **I** *v.tr.* **1** to screw *J'ai jamais pu avisser l'étau assez serré pour tiendre la lame.* I never was able to screw the vice tight enough to hold the blade. (VM) *Et s'il commence à couler eh ben tout ce que t'as besoin de faire c'est le visser un petit peu plus serré.* And if it starts to leak, well, all you have to do is screw it a little bit tighter. (LF) *Ça c'est tous des vis pour avisser dans du bois.* All these are screws to screw into wood. (AC) **2** to fix with a screw **II se visser** *v.pron.* to be screwed *Ça se visse mal.* It is difficult to screw in. (LA) <*Loc:* AC, LA, LF, TB, VM, Da84, Lv88>

vitamine [vitamin] *n.f.* vitamin <*Loc:* Da84>

vite[1] [vit] *adj.* fast, quick *C'était pas des bateaux vites.* These were not fast boats. (SM) *Le service est vite.* The service is fast. (AC) **Il avait le plus beau coureur, le plus vite il y avait.* He had the most beautiful race horse, the fastest there ever was. (EV, An94) <*Loc:* AC, EV, IV, LA, LF, SM, TB, An94, Da84, Lv88>

vite[2] [vit] *adv.* **1** fast, quickly **Viens vite!* Come quickly (Da84) **Le chat a couri plus vite que le gros tchoque, et il l'a attrappé.* The cat ran faster than the blackbird, and he caught it. (Hi02) *Un pivier c'est des petits oiseaux qui marche vite, vite, vite là.* A sandpiper, that's those little birds that walk really, really fast. (JE) *Je m'ai vite dessoûlé quand mon char a rentré dans le fossé.* I sobered up quickly when my car went into the ditch. (VM) **2** soon *Il sera ici bien vite.* He will be here very soon. (VM) ◊ **•à la va vite** quickly and not very well *Il travaille à la va vite.* He works too quickly and not very well. (LA) *Paul fait tout à la va-vite.* Paul does everything fast. (SM) *Il peut pas garder un job parce que ça travaille tout le temps à la va vite.* He can't keep a job because he always rushes and does shoddy work. (EV) <EV, LA, SL, SM, La99> <*Loc:* AC, AV, EV, IV, JE, LA, LF, SL, SM, VM, Da84, Gu82, Hi02, La99>

vitement [vitmɑ̃] *adv.* quickly *Il court si vitement.* He runs so fast. (Lv88) **Le seau d'écrevisses a été vitement donné.* The bucketful of crawfish was quickly distributed. (Wh83) <*Loc:* Da84, Lv88, Wh83>

vitesse [vitɛs] *n.f.* speed, quickness, velocity <*Loc:* Da84>

vitrage [vitraʒ] *n.m.* **1** pane of glass *Tu vas casser tous les vitrages si tu arrêtes pas de jeter ces cailloux là.* You're going to break all the window panes if you don't stop throwing those rocks. (IB) **2** window *Quand l'ouragon a passé, tout ses vitrages ont cassé.* When the hurricane passed, all of his windows broke. (VM) **3** stained glass window <*Loc:* AV, IB, IV, SB, VM, Lv88>

vitre [vit(r), virt] *n.f.* **1** glass *Il avait une porte qu'était proche tout fait en vitre.* He had a door that was almost all glass. (VM) **2** pane of glass, windowpane **Tout ce que nous autres on a eu pour faire c'est remettre les bardeaux et les vitres et chesser les matelas.* All that we had to do was replace the shingles and the windowpanes and dry out the mattresses. (Gu82) **3** window *La pluie vient. Baisse les vitres.* The rain is coming. Close the windows. (SM) **4** plate glass window *La vitre était tout ensemble comme dans une porte. Comme devant un magasin.* The plate glass window was a solid piece like a door. Like in front of a store. (LF) **5** lens (of eyeglasses) *J'ai changé les vitres de mes lunettes.* I changed the lenses of my glasses. (SM) ◊ **•vitre de châssis** windowpane **Ç'a cassé toutes les vitres dans les châssis.* That broke all the glass in the windows. (Gu82) <EV,Gu82> **•vitres de lunettes** eyeglass lenses <Lv88> <*Loc:* EV, LF, SM, TB, VM, Da84, Gu82, Lv88>

vitré, -e [vitre] *adj.* **1** made with fitted glass **Porte vitrée.* Glass door. (Da84) *Salon vitré.* Glass porch, solarium. (VM) **2** calm, like glass *L'eau du lac était vitrée.* The water on the lake was like glass. (VM) **3** glassy, glazed (of the eyes) **Avoir les yeux vitrés.* To have glassy eyes. (Da84) **4** glazed (of ceramic, pottery) *Un pot de fleur vitré.* A glazed flower vase. (LA) <*Loc:* LA, VM, Da84, Fa77, Gr86, La99>

vitreau [vitro] *n.m.* **1** stained-glass window **2** showcase, window display <*Loc:* VM, Lv88>

vitrer [vitre] *v.tr.* to fit glass into, glaze *Vitrer des chassis.* To glaze windows. (LA) <*Loc:* LA, Da84>

vitrière [vitrijær] *n.f.* **1** showcase, glass case **2** store window <*Loc:* LA, LF, Da84, Lv88>

vivable [vivab(l)] *adj.* livable, habitable, inhabitable *C'est pas vivable ici, à force il fait chaud.* It's not livable here, it's so hot. (VM) <***Loc:*** JD, SJ, TB, VM, Da84>

vivant[1]**, -e** [vivɑ̃, -ɑ̃t] *adj.* **1** living, alive *Et y a des poissons vivants dans les* TANKS. And there are live fish in the tanks. (TB) **2** lively <***Loc:*** LA, TB, Da84, Hi02>

vivant[2] [vivɑ̃] *n.m.* **1** lifetime *Il avait jamais vu ça de son vivant.* He had never seen that in his life. (VM) **2** living being *Il est retourné parmi les vivants.* He has returned among the living. (VM) *Mon oncle a fait un testament qui laissait sa terre au dernier vivant, sous condition qu'il ait pas d'enfants.* My uncle made a will that left his land to the last remaining survivor on condition that he have no children. (LA) <***Loc:*** LA, VM, Da84>

vivement [vivmɑ̃, vifmɑ̃] *adv.* quickly, spryly <***Loc:*** VM, Da84>

vivier [vivje] *n.m.* **1** fish pond, pond **2** pool, pond, water-hole **3** box or cage submerged in water to store and keep caught fish or crabs alive <***Loc:*** AC, EV, LF, SM, Da84, Lv88, Ph36>

vivocher [vivoʃe] *v.intr.* to live poorly, live sparsely *On était assez pauvre, c'était juste vivocher qu'on faisait.* We were so poor, it was just scraping by that we did. (VM) <***Loc:*** SM, VM, Lv88>

vivre [viv(r)] (*p.p.* **vi** [vi]) *v.intr.* **1** to live **I' viviont bien. Tu pouvais pas trouver eine paire de monde plus contents que ces deux-là.* They led a good life. You couldn't find a happier pair than those two. (Gu82) *On était huit qu'a vi.* Eight of us lived. (SM) *Tant que mon mari a vi.* While my husband was alive. (Lv88) *Y a plein plein du monde qu'est noyé dans le fleuve là, durant le temps que moi j'ai vi.* There are lots and lots of people who drowned in the river, during the time that I've lived. (SB) **Si on aurait jamais retourné au bal, il aurait peut-être vi un 'tit brin plus longtemps.* If we had never returned to the dance, he might have lived a little bit longer. (ThCa : *La table des veuves*) **Ouais, ça c'était eine grand-mère. [...] Alle avait la joie de viv'.* Yeah, that was a real grand-mother. For her, it was a delight to live. (Gu82) **2** to subsist *On vivait mais on venait pas riche.* We were subsisting but we weren't getting rich. (VM) **3** to reside *C'est pour ça je l'aime ça alentour icitte, je crois pas je pourrais vivre dans un village.* It's for that reason I like living around here, I don't think I could live in a town. (SM) ◊ **•vivre en désordre** to live together out of wedlock *La fille à son oncle vit en désordre.* His uncle's daughter is living out of wedlock. (SL) <SL> **•vivre en espoir et mourir comme un vieux chien** to have a miserable life, live [for nothing but] hope and die like an old dog <TB, La99> **•vivre sa vie** to live one's life *Mon père a vi son vie à essayer de les faire* RECOGNIZE *mon grand-père.* My father tried all his life to make them acknowledge [the contribution of] my grandfather. (AC) <AC> **•être bien pour vivre** to be well off financially *Il est bien pour vivre depuis on a trouvé l'huile sur sa terre.* He's well off since oil was found on his land. (SM) <SM> <***Loc:*** AC, EV, IV, LA, SB, SL, SM, TB, VM, An94, Da84, Gu82, Hi02, La99, Lv88, ThCa>

vlimon ♦see **limon**[4]

vocation [vokasjɔ̃] *n.f.* [*eccl.*] vocation, calling <***Loc:*** Da84>

voésin ♦see **voisin**

vœu [vø] *n.m.* vow, promise <***Loc:*** Da84>

voici [vwasi] *prep.* here is, here are <***Loc:*** Da84, Hi02>

voilà (**en v'là**) [vwala, wala, ɑ̃vla] *prep.* there is, there are *Voilà la raison pourquoi que ça mettait deux planches là, deux planches là, deux planches là jusqu'à que ça venait jusqu'à en haut.* There's the reason why they put two boards here, two boards there, two boards here until they got to the top. (LF) **Peut-êt' j' sus arien qu'ein couillon de* COONASS *mais en v'là qu'que choge que mon je connais et que les maît's d'école ont jamais voulu comprend'.* Maybe I'm nothing but an old coonass, but there's something that I know and that schoolteachers have never wanted to understand. (*Mille misères*) <***Loc:*** IV, LA, LF, SM, An94, Da84, Hi02>

voile[1] [vwal, wal] *n.f.* **1** sail *Le gouvernail. Ce morceau dans le milieu, c'était plutôt pour le tiendre aussi droite que peut. Ça c'était pour le gouverner, pour le tiendre, pour qu'il va droite parce que avec une voile, s'il était pas tout à fait à le centre du vent ça pourrait te pousser soit d'un bord ou de l'autre.* The rudder. The piece in the middle, it was more to keep you as straight as possible. It was to steer you, to hold it so it would go straight, because with a sail, if it wasn't lined up with the wind it could push you to one side or the other. (LF) **2** sailfish *Comme un* SAILFISH, *on appelle ça comme une voile.* Like a sailfish, we call that like a sail. (LF) ◊ **•autant à l'ancre qu'à la voile** either way is fine, it doesn't matter to me <VM> <***Loc:*** LF, VM>

voile[2] [vwal, wal] *n.m.* **1** veil **2** window curtain **3** screen **4** veil, caul ◊ **•voile de lampe** lampshade <Lv88> <***Loc:*** LF, Da84, Lv88>

voiler[1] [vwale] **I** *v.tr.* **1** to veil *Les nuages voilent la lune.* The clouds veil the moon. (VM) **2** to screen **II se voiler** *v.pron.* to wear a veil *Dans le temps, les femmes se voilaient pour aller à confession.* In the old days, women wore a veil to go to confession. (VM) <***Loc:*** VM, Da84>

voiler[2] [vwale] *v.intr.* to wobble *La roue voile.* The wheel is wobbling. (AV) <***Loc:*** AV>

voilette [vwalɛt] *n.f.* veil, caul <***Loc:*** VM, Br55>

voir[1] (**oir**) [vwar, war] **I** *v.tr.* **1** to see *Il a été voir.* He went to see. (AC) *Si tu voirais la robe à Myrtle!* If you saw Myrtle's dress! (SL) *Allons les vérifier pour voir qui c'est le meilleur.* Let's compare them to see which one is best. (VM) **J'crois des fois qu'i' sont plus contents de me 'oir partir qu'i' sont de me 'oir arriver.* Sometimes I think they are happier to see me leave than to see me come home. (Gu82) **2** to visit *Je vas venir voir vous-autres.* I'm going to come and see/visit you.

(VM) *Il est venu nous voir.* He came to see us. (SM) **Je va's faire jamais vous-autres vas me voir encore.* I'm going to make sure that y'all will never see me gain. (lyrics: *La valse à Abe*) **Elle veut plus me voir après aujourd'hui.* She doesn't want to see me anymore after today. (ch: *Bunk's Blues*) **3** to stand, endure, put up with *Moi j'aime pas ça qu'on va savoir à soir avec Clinton. Je voudrais bien qu'eux-autres le fourrait endessous de la prison. Maudit Clinton, je peux pas le voir.* I don't like what we're going to hear tonight from Clinton. I'd like it if they threw him in prison. Damned Clinton, I can't stand him. (TB) **4** to understand **Tu vas voir mais pour toi-même que moi, mais je mérite pas tout ça mais t'apès faire.* You'll see for yourself that I don't deserve what you're doing to me. (ch: *Allons à Lafayette*) **II se voir** *v.pron.* **1** to see o.s. or each other *Ça s'embrassait à chaque fois que ça se voyait.* They kissed each time they saw each other. (EV) **2** to imagine o.s. in a certain way *Il se voit docteur déjà.* He imagines himself to be a doctor already. (VM) ◊ **•voir à** to check on, tend to *Une fois défunt pépère était assis sur sa vieille berceuse, il regardait et il se lève, il va pour aller voir à ses chevals.* Once my late grandpa was sitting on his old rocker, he was looking and he gets up, he goes to check on his horses. (TB) <LA, TB> **•voir bleu** ***a*** to be subject to attacks of dizziness ***b*** to be stunned after a blow, see stars <VM> **•voir (du) bleu** to experience suffering, endure intense suffering *T'as vu bleu dans ta misère.* You really had it hard in your misfortune. (VM) *J'ai vu du bleu au dentiste.* I suffered at the dentist's. (SM) <SM, VM> <***Loc:*** AC, AV, EV, IV, LA, LF, SL, SM, TB, VM, An94, Da84, Gu82, Hi02, La99, Lv88>

voir[2] [vwar] *v.intr.* to menstruate, have one's menstrual period <***Loc:*** IB, LF>

voir[3] (**oir, oire, woir**) [vwar, war] *adv.* (used to mark the imperative) **1** please **Dis-moi voir.* Please tell me. (Da84) **Essaye oire.* Please try. (Da84) **Garde voir ça.* Please look at that. (Da84) **Garde oire ici.* Please look here. (Da84) **Viens voir ici.* Please come here. (Da84) **Donne-moi oire du pain.* Please give me some bread. (Da84) **2** then, so, indeed *Je sais pas éiou c'est. Ouvre voir ce cabinet-là.* I don't know where it is. So open that cupboard. (TB) *'Garde oir.* Then look. (Lv88) *Goûte-voir.* Have a taste then. (SM) *Arrête-voir.* So stop. (SM) *Veille voir, il va te taper.* Be careful, he'll hit you. (LF) <***Loc:*** LF, SM, TB, VM, Da84, Lv88>

voisin[1], **-e** [vwazɛ̃, wazɛ̃, -in] *adj.* neighboring, next, adjacent, bordering ◊ **•voisin (de)** next to, next door to *Elle qui reste l'autre côté du chemin voisin de L.* The one who lives on the other side of the road next door to L. (TB) *On a délogé ici, j'ai bâti une petite maison voisin icitte là.* We moved here, I built a small house next door to this one. (TB) <TB> <***Loc:*** TB, Da84>

voisin[2], **-e** (**voésin, -e**) [vwazɛ̃, wazɛ̃, vwezɛ̃, -in] *n.* neighbor *Ma voisine marche autour du voisinage pour ramasser des pintes pour vendre.* My neighbor walks around the neighborhood to collect aluminum cans to sell. (Gu00) *Mes enfants a fait ça déjà, s'habiller au Mardi Gras et passer, aller c'ez les voisins.* My children have done that, get dressed up for Mardi Gras and pass by the neighbors. (TB) *La maison des voisins était plein de punaises.* The neighbors' house was full of bedbugs. (VM) **Durant le temps chaud eune des voésins tuait ein veau engraissé puis chacœune des aut's voésins allait charcher son roûti de viande.* During the hot spell, one of the neighbors butchered a fatted calf, then each of the other neighbors would fetch his/her roast. (Gu82) <***Loc:*** EV, IV, LF, SM, TB, VM, An94, Da84, Gu82, Gu00, Hi02, Lv88>

voisinage [vwazinaʒ, wazinaʒ] *n.m.* **1** neighborhood, vicinity, surrounding **Ils ont quitté le voisinage et Jean Sot a jamais pu trouver ses parents.* They left the neighborhood and Jean Sot was never able to find his parents. (EV, An94) **2** community *Sur l'autre bord, il n-a des voisinages qui parlent pas français du tout.* On the other side, there are communities that don't speak French at all. (Lv88) **3** the neighbors, people living in the surrounding area *Dans ces temps ça si quelqu'un voulait bâtir une maison ou arranger une maison tout le voisinage ça se mettait tous ensemble et ça les y aidait.* In those days, when someone wanted to build a house or to renovate a house all the neigborhood would get together to help this person. (AC) ◊ **•faire le voisinage** to share food (e.g. a catch of fish or seafood) with the neighbors <LF> <***Loc:*** AC, AL, AV, EV, LA, LF, SM, TB, An94, Da84, Hi02, Lv88>

voisiner [vwazine] **I** *v.intr.* **1** to be neighborly *Le monde voisinait plus dans le temps.* People were more neighborly in the old days. (VM) **2** to share food (e.g. a catch of fish or seafood) with the neighbors *Voisiner, quand mon père arrivait de la mer, il amenait quelques siaux d'huîtres. Et il faisait le voisinage,* HE WOULD BRING *tout le monde dans la côte* A BUCKETFUL. Sharing food with the neighbors, when my father came back from sea he brought several buckets of oysters. And he would share with the neighbors, he would bring everyone in the neighborhood a bucketful. (LF) **II se voisiner** *v.pron.* to visit one's neighbors *On a resté voisin pour des années, mais on se voisinait pas.* We lived as neighbors for years, but we didn't visit each other. (VM) <***Loc:*** LF, VM, Da84>

voiture [vwatyr] *n.f.* **1** carriage, conveyance, vehicle (generic for buggy, surrey, coach, cariole, etc.) **2** [*recent*] car, automobile *Y avait un chemin de gravois entre ici et le Bayou des Allemands. Mais les gravois était gros comme ça. Il avait une voiture, une bonne voiture. Et il allait peut-être 30, 40 milles à l'heure.* There was a gravel road between here and Bayou des Allemands. But the gravel was this big. He had a car, a good car. And it would go 30 or 40 mph. (TB) <***Loc:*** EV, LA, SM, TB, An94, Da84, Lv88>

voix [vwa] *n.f.* **1** voice **2** speech **3** vote <*Loc:* LA, SM, PQ, An94, Da84, Hi02>

vol[1] [vɔl] *n.f.* flight, flying ◊ **•à la vol {vole}** flying, in flight *Il a tiré le canard à la vol.* He shot the bird in flight. (LA) **Le maudit poisson s'est envolé jusque dans un arbre. Il s'en allait à la vole et je l'ai jamais vu encore.* The damned fish flew all the way to a tree. He took flight and I never saw him again. (Gr86) <LA, Gr86> <*Loc:* EV, LA, An94 Da84, Gr86>

vol[2] [vɔl] *n.m.* theft, stealing, robbery, burglary **Ils l'ont emmené avec eux-autres. Ils ont fait leurs vols.* They took him with them. They did their robberies. (SL, An94) <*Loc:* Da84>

volaille [volaj] *n.f.* **1** poultry *Jambalaya [...] on fait avec de la volaille et du tasso.* Jambalaya we make with poultry and smoked dried meat. (SL) *Et ça fait que eux-autres réchauffait une jarre de ces viandes rôties là, et à part de ça t'avais de la poule, de la volaille, pleine de la volaille, les œufs.* And so they warmed up a jar of that roasted meat, and besides that you had chicken, poultry, a lot of poultry and eggs. (TB) **2** chicken *C'est pas du rouge rouge comme un animau, et c'est pas une chair qu'est blanche comme une volaille non plus.* It's not a deep red meat like a cow, and it's not a flesh that's white like a chicken either. (LF) *Ah ben si ça voulait se faire un gombo eh ben là alle vadait dedans sa cour alle tuait sa volaille.* Well, if they wanted to make themselves a gumbo, well, she went into her yard and she killed her chicken. (TB) <*Loc:* AC, EV, IB, IV, LA, LF, SL, SM, TB, VM, An94, Da84>

volant[1]**, -e** [volɑ̃, -ɑ̃t] *adj.* flying *Un écureuil volant.* A flying squirrel. (VM) <*Loc:* VM, Da84>

volant[2] [volɑ̃] *n.m.* **1** scythe **2** ditch-bank blade **3** ruffle *La robe a un gros volant en bas.* The dress has a big ruffle on the bottom. (AV) <*Loc:* AV, LA, SM, VM, Da84, Lv88>

volée[1] [vole] *n.f.* **1** flight of birds, flock of birds in flight **2** whipping, thrashing *Il y a sacré une volée.* He gave him a thrashing. (VM) ◊ **•aller à la volée** to go on a late evening hunt <Da84> <*Loc:* VM, Da84>

volée[2] [vole] *n.m./f.* American lotus, American nelumbo, yellow lotus, water chinquapin <*Loc:* Da84, Ho90, Lv88, Re31>

voler[1] [vole] *v.intr.* **1** to fly **Ça prend quinze minutes, un petit yinquis, pour voler dessus le bout pour arriver à l'autre bout.* It takes fifteen minutes for a little field sparrow to fly from one end to the other. (EV, An94) **2** to fly, fly off (as a result of being hit, thrown, or blown) **Ça fait, la troisième fois, il a venu avec un bâton, puis il a pris à cogner et puis les chapeaux a pris à voler.* So, the third time he came with a stick, and he started hitting and then the hats started flying. (LA, An94) *Les feuilles volaient dans le vent.* The leaves were flying in the wind. (VM) **3** to fly, take a plane *C'est pas que j'ai peur des automobiles asteur. Moi je vas aller en l'air. Moins de danger. Moi j'aime voler.* It's not that I'm afraid of automobiles now. I'll go by air. Less danger. I like to fly. (TB) **4** to spurt forth, gush *Le sang a volé quand il s'a coupé.* The blood gushed out when he cut himself. (SM) ◊ **•voler en pointe** to fly in a triangular formation **Les oies et les canards [...] i' voliont en pointe devant le soleil-couché.* The geese and the ducks, they would fly in formation in front of the setting sun. (Gu82) <Gu82> <*Loc:* EV, LA, SM, TB, VM, An94, Da84, Gu82, Hi02>

voler[2] [vole] **I** *v.tr.* **1** to steal **Lapin a venu le soir pour voler de l'eau.* Lapin came at night to steal water. (SM, An94) **2** to kidnap **Voler une fille.* To kidnap a girl. (Da84) **II** *v.intr.* to steal, rob **Quand il est devenu assez fort, ils l'ont envoyé voler comme eux-autres.* When he was old enough, they sent him to steal like them. (SL, An94) ◊ **•voler comme dans la forêt des bandits** to commit highway robbery <Da84> <*Loc:* AC, IV, LA, SL, SM, An94, Da84, Hi02>

voleur[1] [volœr] *adj.* thieving, stealing *Il est juste assez voleur pour gagner l'élection.* He's just thieving enough to win the election. (VM) <*Loc:* VM, Da84>

voleur[2] [volœr] *n.m.* thief, robber <*Loc:* Da84>

voliche [voliʃ] *n.f.* weatherboard, siding, clapboard siding *Ils vont mettre des voliches sur le pignon de la maison.* They're going to put weatherboard on the gable of the house. (SM) <*Loc:* AV, EV, IB, JD, LA, LF, SB, SJ, SL, SM, TB, VM, Da84, Lv88>

volichage [voliʃaʒ] *n.m.* **1** weatherboarding (material) **2** process of weatherboarding a house <*Loc:* SM, VM, Da84>

volicher [voliʃe] *v.tr.* to weatherboard, apply weatherboard to *Ils ont voliché la maison.* They applied weatherboard to the house. (VM) <*Loc:* LA, LF, SJ, SL, SM, VM, Da84, Lv88>

volier [volje] *n.m./f.* flight of birds, flock of birds in flight *Il y une volier de z-oies qu'a passé par dessus de la maison.* A flight of geese passed over the house. (VM) *Ça donc qué grande volier de canards.* Well, what a big flock of ducks. (VM) <*Loc:* AV, IB, LF, VM, Re31>

volière [voljær] *n.f.* flock, covey of birds *Une volière de perdrix.* A covey of quail. (LA) <*Loc:* LA, SM, Da84>

voloir ♦see **valoir**

volontaire[1] [volɔ̃tær] *adj.* **1** volunteer *Ça usait des hommes volontaires pour battre les feux.* They used volunteer men to fight fires. (VM) **2** willing *Il était pas ça que tu pourrais appeler volontaire.* He wasn't exactly what you would call willing. (LA) <*Loc:* LA, VM, Da84, Lv88>

volontaire[2] [volɔ̃tær] *n.m.* volunteer *Nous-autres on a été volontaires, vous voyez. On a pas été* DRAFT. We were volunteers, you see. We weren't drafted. (TB) <*Loc:* TB, Da84>

volonté [volɔ̃te] *n.f.* **1** will *Les Mardi Gras vous remercient bien de votre bonne volonté.* The Mardi Gras participants thank you very much for your good will. (EV, ch: *Chanson de Mardi Gras*) **2** wish *Elle a opposé mes volontés.* She objected to my wishes. (Lv88) <*Loc:* EV, Da84, Lv88>

voltigement [voltiʒmɑ̃] *n.m.* fluttering <*Loc:* Da84>

voltiger [voltiʒe] *v.intr.* **1** to fly about, hover, flutter *Je vois la terre sur toutes côtés, trois pigeons blancs qui sont à voltiger.* I see land on all sides, three white pigeons fluttering about. (IB, ch: *Sept ans sur mer*) **2** to fly, take a plane *T'as voltigé jusqu'à Houston?* You flew to Houston? (Lv88) **3** to fly, fly off (as a result of being hit, thrown, or blown) **L'anneau a voltigé.* The ring flew off. (VM, An84) <*Loc:* IB, VM, An84, Da84, Hi02, Lv88>

volume[1] [volym] *n.f.* lint *Balie propre, laisse pas la volume dessous le lit.* Sweep clean, don't leave lint under the bed. (VM) <*Loc:* LA, VM>

volume[2] [volym] *n.m.* volume, size, mass *Le volume de sirop dans le baril.* The volume of syrup in the barrel. (VM) <*Loc:* VM, Da84>

volume[3] [volym] *n.m.* volume (of a book) <*Loc:* Da84>

volumé, -e [volyme] *adj.* fluffy *Batte-lé jusqu'à ça vient volumé.* Beat it until it becomes fluffy. (VM) <*Loc:* VM>

volumer [volyme] *v.tr.* to make fluffy and soft by shaking or beating *Volume bien les matelas.* Fluff up the mattresses well. (VM) *On a passé l'après-midi à volumer la mousse.* We spent the afternoon fluffing up the Spanish moss. (VM) *Il faut j'use un bâton pour volumer mon traversin.* I have to use a stick to fluff my bolster. (LA) <*Loc:* LA, VM>

vomi ♦see **vomit**

vomir [vomir] *v.intr.* to vomit *La fièvre jaune te fait vomir noir.* Yellow fever makes you vomit black. (VM) <*Loc:* EV, VM, Da84>

vomis ♦see **vomit**

vomissage [vɔ̃misaʒ] *n.m.* **1** vomiting *Le vomissage a duré une demi-heure.* The vomiting lasted a half hour. (SJ) **2** vomit, vomited substance *Il a marché dans le vomissage.* He walked in the vomit. (SM) <*Loc:* JD, SJ, SL, SM, VM, Da84, Lv88>

vomissement [vɔ̃mismɑ̃] *n.m.* **1** vomiting **2** vomit **3** upset stomach, nausea <*Loc:* SM, Da84>

vomit (**vomi, vomis**) [vɔ̃mi] *n.m.* vomit, vomited substance *Le chat a marché dans le vomit.* The cat walked in the vomit. (SL) <*Loc:* AV, EV, IB, LF, SB, SL, SM, VM, Da84, Ph36>

vorace [voras] *adj.* voracious *Un chien vorace.* A voracious dog. (VM) <*Loc:* VM, Da84>

vos ♦see **votre**

votant [votɑ̃] *n.* voter <*Loc:* Da84>

vote [vɔt] *n.m.* vote <*Loc:* LF, Da84>

voter [vote] *v.intr.* to vote *Je peux pas croire qu'ils ont voté pour les républicains.* I can't believe they voted for the Republicans. (LA) <*Loc:* LA, Da84, Hi02>

voteur [votœr] *n.* voter **Mon "bill" a affecté cent mille voteurs et peut-être plus.* My bill affected 100,000 voters and perhaps more. (ThCa: *Messieurs, mesdames*) <*Loc:* ThCa>

votre (**vos**) (*m./f.sing.* **votre** [vɔt(r)], *m./f.pl.* **vos** [vo], *m./f.pl.* before a vowel **vos** [voz]) *adj.poss.* your **Votre chambre.* Your room. (Da84) **Votre maison.* Your house. (Da84) **Vos chambres.* Your rooms. (Da84) **Arrêtez votre tactac!* Stop all your talking! (La99) *Qui c'est votre nom?* What is your name? (LF) <*Loc:* AC, LF, Da84, La99>

vôtre [vot] *pron.poss.* yours **La vôtre.* Yours. (Da84) <*Loc:* Da84>

voudou[1] (**houdou**) [vudu, hudu] *adj.* of or pertaining to voodooism or a voodoo **Une danse voudou.* A voodoo dance. (Re31) **La religion voudou.* The voodoo religion. (Re31) <*Loc:* Gr86, Re31>

voudou[2] (**houdou**) [vudu, hudu] *n.m./f.* practicer of voodoo rites **Il est un voudou.* He is a voodoo. (Re31) **Elle est une voudou.* She is a voodoo. (Re31) **La danse des voudoux.* The dance of the voodoos. (Re31) <*Loc:* Gr86, Re31>

voudou[3] (**vaudou, houdou**) [vudu, vodu, hudu] *n.m.* **1** voodoo **2** spell, charm **3** evil spell, curse <*Loc:* IB, LF, SB, SJ, SM, Da84, Hi02, Lv88>

vouer [vwe] **I** *v.tr.* to dedicate, vow, pledge **Voué à la Sainte Vierge.* Vowed or dedicated to the Blessed Virgin. (Da84) **II se vouer** *v.pron.* to pledge o.s., vow o.s. (e.g. in marriage) *Elle s'a voué à ce bougre malgré son père.* She pledged herself to that guy in spite of her father. (LA) <*Loc:* LA, Da84>

vouiche [vwiʃ] *interj.* yes *Ah! Ben vouiche.* Well, of course. (JD) <*Loc:* JD>

vouloir[1] [vulwar] **I** *v.tr.* **1** to want **Je veux toi, tu soyais content de ça j'après faire.* I want you to be happy with what I'm doing. (ch: *Valse de Cajun*) *Je voulais te dire mais je pouvais pas.* I wanted to tell you but I couldn't. (JE) *Je voudrais pas qu'elle sort avec ce pouilleux.* I wouldn't want her to go out with that bum. (LA) **Je connais tu me veux plus.* I know you don't want me anymore. (ch: *Quitter la maison*) *Tu veux de la gomme?* Do you want some gum? (EV) *Y avait un homme eh ben il était arrêté avec sa machine qui voulait pas prendre et partir.* There was a man and he was stuck with his motor that didn't want to start. (TB) *Quand il parle de ça qu'il veut faire avec sa vie il a pas beaucoup d'à-peu-près.* When he talks about what he wants to do with his life, he doesn't have much common sense. (AC) *Douze ans de ça il parlait procheque pas du tout en français, il voulait pas parler le français. Mais il a tombé en amour avec la musique cadien.* Twelve years ago he spoke almost no French, he didn't want to speak French. But he fell in love with Cajun music. (LF) *Il voulait pas on se marie.* He didn't want us to marry. (EV) *Peut-être que mon je vas les chercher si vous-autres veut rester ici.* Maybe I'll go get them if you all want to stay here. (TB) **J'sais pas si c'est vrai qu'y a pas ein tas d'hômes qui pouvont faire le job que moi je fais, mais c'est sûr qu'y en a pas ein tas qui vouderiont le faire.* I don't know if it's true that there aren't many men who can do the work that I do, but it's certain that there aren't many who would want to do it. (Gu82) **2** to intend **Il* *a voulu quitter la banque, il a pas bien regardé en reculant et y a ein* TRUCK *qui l'a abôrder par en arrière.* He intended to leave the bank, [but] he didn't look carefully when he was backing up and a truck hit him from behind. (Gu82) **3** to require, demand *Mame veut absolument qu'on va à la messe.* Mama demands that we go to church. (VM) **II** *v.intr.* **1** to want to, wish to *Je vais parce que je veux.* I'm going because I want to. (SM) *C'est ça la loi ça nous dit, mais ça peut changer ça si ça veut, c'est juste peser un bouton et puis là l'eau va venir, c'est tout ça prend.* This is the law they tell us, but they can change the law if they want to, they just need to press on a button and then the water will come, that's all it takes. (SM) **I' pourra aller là où i' voudra avec sa chère 'tite femme.* He can go wherever he wants with his dear little wife. (Gu82) **Mais il' ont jâmais voulu.* But they never had the desire. (Gu82) **2** to will **Si le Bon Dieu veut, dans quèques années i' sera peut-êt' le "boss" à son vieux père.* If the Good Lord wills, in a few years he might be his old man's boss. (Gu82) **Vouloir c'est pouvoir.* Where there's a will, there's a way. (Da84) **3** to agree *Je crois il va arriver. —Moi, je veux.* I think he'll arrive. —I agree. (VM) **4** to almost, nearly (do s.t.) *Ça a volu être vert.* That was near (to being) green. (VM) *Il a volu tomber.* He almost fell. (VM) *Tu ramassais un voyage qu'était un peu plus lourd sur un bord ou l'autre, la fourche voulait tourner dans tes mains.* If you picked up a forkload that was heavier on one side or the other, the pitchfork would almost turn in your hands. (EV) **III se vouloir** *v.pron.* to wish to be, wish for o.s. **Se vouloir riche.* To wish to be rich. (Da84) ◊ **•vouloir dire** to mean, signify **Je comprends exactement qui tu veux dire.* I understand exactly what you mean. (EV, An94) <EV, LA, LF, SJ, TB, VM, An94, Da84, Lv88, Wh83> **•vouloir pas de** to not want s.t. (with emphasis) **Je connais tu veux pas de moi.* I know you don't want me. (ch: *Quitter la maison*) **Joli cœur, pourquoi donc tu veux pas de me voir, jolie?* Dear heart, why don't you want to see me, darling? (ch: *La valse de la Rosa*) <ch> **•en vouloir à** to have it in for, hold a grudge against *C'est comme si j'y en veux toujours quand-même il est mort.* It's as if I hold it against him still, even though he's dead. (EV) <EV> **<*Loc:*** AC, EV, IB, JE, LA, LF, SJ, SL, SM, TB, VM, An94, Da84, Gu00, Gu82, Hi02, Lv88, Ph36, Wh83>

vouloir[2] [vulwar] *n.m.* will, willpower *Il a le vouloir, mais pas le pouvoir.* He has the will, but not the means. (VM) **<*Loc:*** VM, Da84>

vous [vu] (*before a vowel* [vuz]) *pron.pers. (sing. polite or pl.)* **1** *(subj.)* you *On veut pas l'argent vous va gagner.* We don't want the money that you will earn. (AC, ch: *Restez, Mom et Pop*) *Vous venez nous rejoindre [...] au gumbo ce soir.* Y'all come join us at the gumbo [feast] tonight. (ch: *La danse de Mardi Gras*) *Peut-être que vous serait intéressé avoir votre* TAPE-RECORDER *et tout.* Perhaps you'd be interested in having your tape recorder and all. (LF) *Si vous se fait prendre, les* FINE *est mauvais.* If you get caught the fines are stiff. (TB) **Faut vous soit pas canaille, faut pas vous-autres va trop loin.* You must not be mischievous, you must not go too far. (LA, An94) **2** *(dir.obj.)* you *C'est juste pour voir si ça vous tente.* It's just to see if that interests you. (LF) *Au revoir, mes amis. Je vas vous revoir sur mon autre grand tour.* Good-bye, my friends. I will see you again on my other big tour. (AV) *"Si quelqu'un vient vous inviter, refusez pas personne!" Pop nous a dit.* "If someone comes to invite you (to dance), don't turn down anyone!" Pop told us. (EV) **3** *(ind.obj.)* you, to you, for you **Mais moi, j'vas vous dire la franche vérité: y a pas parsône dessus la terre qu'est plus bête qu'ein Amaricain.* But I'm going to tell you the honest to goodness truth: there is no one in the world dumber than an American. (Gu82) *Et l'histoire j'aimerais vous raconter aujourd'hui, c'est ça qu'a arrivé à moi et mon petit padna.* And the story I'd like to to tell you today is about what happened to me and my friend. (JD) *Prenez-vous un morceau.* Help yourself to a piece [of pie]. (VM) *On part à la pagaille, vous montrer comment le monde de le vieux temps faisiont.* We'll paddle off, to show you how folks in the old days used to do it. (LF) *Ça peut vous prouver mes amis, que mon Hasitall et mon sirop de toux, c'est bon pour tous les maladies et tous les caprices quelqu'un peut avoir dans la vie.* That can prove to you, my friends, that my Hasitall and my cough syrup, are good for all the illnesses and caprices that someone can have in life. (AV) **4** *(obj. of prep.)* you *Je vas prier pour vous.* I'm going to pray for you. (LF) **5** *(refl.)* yourself, yourselves *Prenez-vous un morceau.* Help yourself to another piece [of pie]. (VM) *Faisez attention de pas vous salir dehors.* Be careful not to get dirty outside. (LA) **Servez-vous!* Help yourself [to food]. (Da84) ◊ **•vous-même** you, yourself <Da84> **<*Loc:*** AC, AV, EV, IB, IV, JD, LA, LF, PQ, SL, SM, TB, VM, An94, Da84, Gu82, Hi02, Lv88, ThCa, Wh83>

vous-autres [vuzɔt] *pron.pers.pl.* **1** *(subj.)* you, you all *Vous-autres est bien à la fraîche, mais c'est l'heure de rentrer la trawl.* You are comfortable in the shade but it's time to pull in the trawl net. (Lv88) *Vous-autres faisait quelque chose spéciale avec l'argent qu'il faisait avec la musique ou vous-autres mettait ça avec l'autre argent pour faire le ménage aller?* Did you all do anything special with the money that he made with the music or did you put that in with the other money to make the household run? (EV) *Si vous-autres peut patienter quelques mois, on va vous envoyer votre chèque de FEMA.* If y'all can wait a few months, we'll send you your FEMA check. (LA) *Vous-autres veut boire du pop ou quelque chose? Tu veux des* POTATO CHIP, *ou?* Do you all want to drink some pop or something? You want potato chips, or? (TB) **2** *(obj. of prep.)* you, you all *C'est pas mon désir personnel, c'est pour vous-autres que je fais ça.* It is not my personal desire, I'm doing it for you all. (VM) **3** *(obj. of inf.)* you, you all *Je vas venir voir vous-autres.* I'm going to come and see you. (VM) **4** *(refl.)* yourselves *Effrayez-vous-autres pas.* Don't be frightened. (LA) ◊ **•vous-autres même** you yourselves <Da84> <***Loc:*** AC, EV, LA, LF, SL, TB, VM, An77, An94, Da84, Hi02, Lv88, Wh83>

voyage [vwajaʒ, wajaʒ, vojaʒ] *n.m.* **1** journey, trip, voyage *Follait que t'espères pour le ferry. Je crois qu'il faisait un voyage par heure.* You had to wait for the ferry. I think it made one trip per hour. (TB) *Il est vaillant depuis qu'il a revenu de son voyage.* He is healthy since he returned from his trip. (SL) **Les Mardi Gras sont dessus un grand voyage.* The Mardi Gras riders are on a great journey. (ch: *La danse de Mardi Gras*) **2** load, wagonload, truckload *Quand tu partais avec un voyage d'hommes là tu pouvais mettre une cinquantaine d'hommes dans le bateau.* When you set off with a load of men, you could put about 50 men in the boat. (LF) *Tu ramassais un voyage qu'était un peu plus lourd sur un bord ou l'autre, la fourche voulait tourner dans tes mains.* If you picked up a forkload that was heavier on one side or the other, the pitchfork would almost turn in your hands. (EV) **Un voyage de bois.* A load of wood. (Re31) *J'ai halé trois voyages de foin dans mon magasin.* I hauled three loads of hay into my barn. (VM) ◊ **•bon voyage** 'have a nice trip' <Da84> **•faire un voyage *a*** to carry a load ***b*** to take a trip *Y avait pas de pont. Faulait que t'espères pour le ferry. Je crois qu'il faisait un voyage par heure.* There was no bridge. You had to wait for the ferry. I think they made one trip per hour. (TB) <Da84> <***Loc:*** AV, EV, IB, LF, SJ, SL, SM, TB, VM, Da84, Lv88, Re31>

voyager [vwajaʒe, wajaʒe, vojaʒe] **I** *v.tr.* **1** to travel (a route, a road, etc.) *Il voyageait un chemin de campagne.* He traveled a country road. (Lv88) **2** to transport, carry *J'ai voyagé mes valises moi toute seule.* I carried my suitcases all by myself. (Lv88) **3** to wave *Capitaine, Capitaine, voyage ton flag.* Captain, Captain, wave your flag. (ch: *La danse de Mardi Gras*) **II** *v.intr.* to travel, journey, take a trip *Ils ont voyagé dans le bois.* They traveled in the woods. (LA) <***Loc:*** LA, LF, TB, An94, Da84, Hi02, Lv88>

voyageur[1] [vwajaʒœr, wajaʒœr, vojaʒœr] *adj.* traveling, migratory **Comis voyageur.* Traveling salesman. (Da84) <***Loc:*** Da84>

voyageur,[2] **-euse** [vwajaʒœr, wajaʒœr, vojaʒœr, -øz] *n.* traveler <***Loc:*** LF, Da84, Hi02>

voyant, -e [vwajɑ̃, wajɑ̃, vojɑ̃, -ɑ̃t] *adj.* highly visible, bright *Il y a du monde qui peinture leurs maisons des couleurs voyantes.* There are people who paint their houses highly visible colors. (VM) <***Loc:*** VM, Da84>

voyer [voje] *v.tr.* **1** to throw *Beau Geste a voyé le melon-là parterre, puis il a parti.* Beau Geste threw the melon to the ground, then he left. (SL) *Il a voyé la balle à Jean.* He threw the ball to John. (SJ) **2** to send *Il a voyé ça à sa fille.* He sent that to his daughter. (SL) ◊ **•voyer pour** to send for *Elle a voyé pour son mari.* She sent for her husband. (SL) <SL> <***Loc:*** SJ, SL, SM>

voyeur [vwajœr, wajœr, vojœr] *n.m.* voyeur, peeping Tom <***Loc:*** Da84>

vrai[1], **-e** [vre, vrɛ] *adj.* **1** true **Chère bassette tu m'as dit tu m'aimais, aujourd'hui moi j'peux voir c'est pas vrai, c'était tous des accroires tu m'faisais.* Dear little woman, you told me that you loved me, [but] today I can see it's not true, it was all an act that you made me believe in. (ch: *Ma chère bassette*) *C'est une petite histoire vraie qu'a arrivé à moi quand j'étais un jeune petit garçon.* It's a true little story that happened to me when I was a young little boy. (JD) **2** real, genuine **C'est du vrai sirop.* This is real syrup. (Da84) **Eine vraie richesse.* A real treasure. (Gu82) **J'ai eune de me garçons qu'est après étudier pour êt' ein vrai ingénieur.* One of my boys is studying to become a real engineer. (Gu82) **3** real, veritable *C'est des vrais petits diables, ces enfants là. Si c'est brigand!* Those kids are real devils. Are they rowdy! (TB) *Il est un vrai brise-fer.* He's a regular bull in a china shop. (JE) <***Loc:*** EV, IB, IV, JD, JE, LA, LF, SL, SM, TB, VM, An94, Da84, Gu82, Hi02, Lv88, Ph36>

vrai[2] [vre, vrɛ] *n.m.* truth ◊ **•pour vrai dire** to tell the truth <Da84> <***Loc:*** Da84>

vrai[3] [vre, vrɛ] *adv.* truly, really *Il est mort? Vrai?* He's dead? Really? (SM) <***Loc:*** SM>

vraiment [vremɑ̃] *adv.* truly, really **Je crois dans tout le monde, c'est juste quelques-uns qui connaissaient vraiment la musique cadienne.* I think that in all the world there are just a few who really knew Cajun music. (AV) **Vraiment?* Is that so? (Da84) *Je crois pas qu'il y a personne de la Louisiane qu'est là-bas autrement que c'est quelqu'un qui veut vraiment être.* I think that there is nobody from Louisiana there unless it is someone who really wants to be. (TB) **Chaque fois il dit ein mot ou eine phrase Cajin, il soutient l'éxistence d'ein deuxième-culture qui est vraiment différent de les manières réglés Américaines.* Every time he says a Cajun word or sentence, he supports the existence of a second culture which is really different from the regular American ways. (Wh83) <***Loc:*** AC, AV, EV, TB, VM, Da84, Hi02, Wh83>

vrille [vrij] *n.f.* **1** drill, bit, gimlet **2** corkscrew **3** tendril <***Loc:*** Da84>

vue [vy] *n.f.* **1** view **2** sight, eyesight, vision *Avoir la vue embrouillée.* To have blurry vision. (LA) ◊ **•à vue d'œil** visibly <Da84> **•en vue de** in view of, with an eye to *Il a égalisé son terrain en vue de se faire une maison.* He leveled his lot in view of building a house. (VM) <VM, Da84> <***Loc:*** LA, PQ, VM, Da84, Lv88>

vulgaire [vylgær] *adj.* vulgar, coarse, rude *Fais pas ça, c'est vulgaire.* Don't do that, it's vulgar. (LA) <***Loc:*** LA, Da84>

vulière [vyljær] *adj.* clear, evident, apparent, obvious *Tes enfants mangent bien? —Mais c'est vulière. Tu vois pas* *comment ils sont gros et gras?* Do your children eat well? —Well, it's evident. Don't you see how portly they are? (VM) <***Loc:*** LA, VM, Fa77>

vulnéraire (**vinéraire**) [vyneræɾ, vineræɾ] *n.f.* **1** everlasting, pearly everlasting (type of wildflower) *Monsieur Trahan m'a amené de la vinéraire quèque temps passé. Il m'a dit que si tu fais un thé avec, c'est bon pour le rhume.* Mr. Trahan brought be some everlasting flowers a while back. He told me that if you use them for tea, it's good for a cold. (Guoo) **2** saltmarsh aster (medicinal plant) <***Loc:*** IB, TB, VM, Guoo>

wagon (**waguine**) [wagɔ̃, wogɔ̃, wagin, wogin] *n.m.* **1** four-wheeled wagon *Un wagon a quatre roues. Il était plus grand qu'une charrette. Une charrette avait juste deux roues.* A wagon has four wheels. It was bigger than a cart. A cart had just two wheels. (EV) **2** wooden wagon pulled by draft animals *Si tu voulais aller en quelque part il faut que tu marches ou tu vas dans un wagon avec des mulets.* If you wanted to go someplace you had to walk or you went in a mule-drawn wagon. (SL) **3** litter, stretcher <***Loc:*** AC, EV, IB, JE, LA, LF, SB, SJ, SL, SM, TB, An94, Da84, Di32, Gu00, Hi02, Lv88, Ph36>

wagonner [wagɔ̃ne] *v.intr.* to drive a wagon <***Loc:*** JE>

wagonneur ♦see **wagonnier**

wagonnette [wagɔ̃nɛt, wæginɛt] *n.f.* **1** small wagon, small cart **2** covered wagon *Ça halait les petits à l'école en wagonnettes, ça appelait,* COVERED WAGONS, *avec deux chevaux.* They transported the kids to school in wagonettes, they called it, covered wagons, with two horses. (EV) <***Loc:*** EV, Da84>

wagonnier (**wagonneur**) [wagɔ̃je, wagɔ̃nœr] *n.m.* wagoner, wagon driver <***Loc:*** JE, Di32, Gr86>

waguine[1] [wagin] *n.f.* **1** spring wagon **2** two-wheeled cart <***Loc:*** LF, SM, TB, Di32>

waguine[2] ♦see **wagon**

wanga ♦see **ouanga**

wapi (**ouapi**) [wapi] *n.m.* small rug woven from scraps of cloth <***Loc:*** VM>

warou ♦see **loup-garou**

warrant [warɑ̃] *n.m.* warrant, arrest warrant, search warrant *Follait que le juge de paix décide s'il va faire une charge, si c'était sérieux, et les laisser signer l'*AFFIDAVIT *et là follait que j'ai fait un warrant.* The justice of the peace had to decide if he was going to bring charges, if it was serious, and let them sign the affidavit, and then I had to issue a warrant. (LF) <***Loc:*** EV, JE, LF, SL, VM, Da84, Di32, Lv88, Ph36>

WASHBOARD [wɑʃbod, waʃbo] *n.m.* washboard (used for music) <***Loc:*** LF, Lv88>

WASHER [wɑʃə] *n.f.* washer <***Loc:*** EV, Da84, Lv88, Ph36>

WATCHMAN [wɑtʃmən, watʃmɛ̃, watʃmɛ̃n, watʃmɑ̃n] *n.m.* watchman, guard <***Loc:*** EV, JE, SB, TB, VM, Da84, Di32, Gr86, Lv88, Ph36>

WAVE[1] [wev, wɛv] *v.tr.invar.* to wave, set waves in (the hair) <***Loc:*** EV, Lv88, Ph36>

WAVE[2] [wev, wɛv] *n.m.* permanent wave (for hair) <***Loc:*** EV, Lv88, Ph36>

WAYS (**ouaise**) [wez, wɛz] *n.m./f.* **1** ways, ground ways (shipbuilding term for a track used in the launching of boats) *Mon pape s'avait fait une ouaise pour haler les petits bateaux, il avait le bois pour le faire, il l'a fait.* My dad had made a ways for hauling little boats, he had the wood to do it and he did it. (LF) **2** dry dock *Et quand-ce que les bateaux, une fois par an il faut que ça soye inspecté par la Garde de Côte. Et il faut que ça soye tout mis en ordre. Et là c'est là où ce qu'ils montont leur bateau sur des* WAYS. And when the boats, once a year they had to be inspected by the Coast Guard. And everything had to be put in order. And that's when they put their boat up on a dry dock. (LF) <***Loc:*** LF, TB>

wawaron ♦see **ouaouaron**

WEEKEND (**WEEK-END**) [wikɛ̃n(d)] *n.m.* weekend <***Loc:*** AC, EV, Da84, Hi02>

weev [wiv] *n.* boll weevil <***Loc:*** SL>

WELFARE [wɛlfɛɹ] *n.m.* welfare *On avait ses chèques de* WELFARE, *ça aidait aussi.* We had his welfare checks, that helped, too. (AC) <***Loc:*** AC, Lv88>

WELL (**well**) [wɛl, wæl] *interj.* well, so *Il m'a mandé comment-ce que tu disais* HOWDY *en français. Je dis, well, ça c'est "bonjour."* He asked me how how say howdy in French. I said, well, that's "bonjour." (TB) <***Loc:*** AC, AV, EV, LA, SL, TB, VM>

whiskey, whiskie ♦see **whisky**

whisky (**whiskey, whiskie, ouiskie**) [wiski] *n.m.* whiskey *Le whisky que ça faisait dans le temps était pâle.* The whiskey they made in those days was colorless. (LA) ◊ •**whisky camphré** camphorated whiskey (home remedy for various ills) <VM> <***Loc:*** EV, JD, LA, SL, VM, An94, Da84, Di32, Hi02, Ph36>

windrow [winro] *v.tr.invar.* to windrow (sugarcane) <***Loc:*** JD, SB, Lv88>

woir ♦see **voir**

WRENCH [ɹɛ̃ntʃ] *n.m.* wrench <***Loc:*** Di32, Lv88>

WRONG [ɹɔ̃ŋ] *adj.* wrong *T'es pas* WRONG. You're not wrong. (Lv88) **T'es jamais* WRONG. You are never wrong. (EV, An94) ◊ **Je m'étais aperçu qu'il y avait quelque chose qui était* WRONG. I had noticed that there was something that was wrong. (SL, An94) ◊ •**aller** WRONG to go wrong *On va jamais aller* WRONG. We will never go wrong. (SL) <SL> •**y avoir qqch de** WRONG to have s.t. wrong *Il y a quelque chose de* WRONG, *cette accordéon, alle travaille pas bien.* There's something wrong, this accordeon, it doesn't work right. (JE) **Moi, je connais pas quoi ça il y a de* WRONG. I don't know what's wrong. (IV, An94) *Il y a quèque chose de* WRONG *dedans.* There's something wrong about that. (VM) <IV, JE, VM, An94> <***Loc:*** EV, IV, JE, SL, TB, VM, An94, Lv88>

y[1] [i] *adv.* there **Allons-y.* Let's go there. (Da84) ◊ **•il y a / il n-a** [ija, ja, ina, ena] there is, there are **Il y a personne ici.* There is no one here. (Da84) **Je peux pas l'entendre. Il y a trop de train.* I can't hear him. There's too much noise. (EV, An94) **Il y en a pas.* There is none. (Da84) *Quoi il n-a?* What's the matter? (Guoo) *Qui il n-a?* What's the matter? (Guoo) *Souvent des fois il n-a des prononciations qu'est un peu pareilles.* Very often there are pronunciations that are a little bit similar. (SL) *Peut-être il va y avoir un là-bas.* There might be one in there. (LF) *L'année passée, il n-a eu une terrible récolte d'écrivisses.* Last year there was an abundant crawfish harvest. (Lv88) *Il y avait pas de publication, il y avait pas de journal, il y avait pas de livres, rien qui était écrit en français avant une vingtaine d'années passées, je pense.* There were no publications, no newspaper, no books written in French before about twenty years ago, I think. (SL) <AC, AV, EV, IV, JE, LA, LF, PQ, SJ, SL, SM, TB, VM, An94, Da84, Gr82, Guoo, Lv88, Ph36, Wh83> **•il y a** ago *Je suis fier d'avoir entamé chez nous, il y a trois ans, la Fête Internationale Acadienne.* I am proud to have launched here, three years ago, the International Acadian Festival. (Lv88) <Lv88> ***<Loc:*** AC, AV, EV, IV, JE, LA, LF, SL, SM, TB, An94, Da84, Hi02>

y[2] ♦see **lui**

yaïe (yaille, aïe) [jaj, aj] *interj.* boy, man, wow ◊ **•oh (y) yaïe / oh yé yaïe** oh boy, man, wow *Cher, tu sais pas. Oh yaïe.* Dear, you don't know the half of it. Man! (TB) *Mais papa aimait pas L., cher. Je crois pas que L. save, mais oh yé yaïe.* But daddy didn't like L, dear. I don't think L knew that, but oh boy. (TB) **Oh, y yaïe, toi 'tite fille, je serai curieux de te rejoindre quand même un autre fois.* Oh boy, you little girl, I wonder what it would be like to get together again. (ch: *La valse à Austin Ardoin*) **Y aïe, tu dis que moi, je connais pas, tu m'abandonnes.* Oh boy, you say that me, I don't know, you're abandoning me. (ch: *Madam Atchen*) <TB, VM> ***<Loc:*** AC, TB, VM>

yaille ♦see **yaïe**

yam (yamme) [jɑ̃m, jæm] *n.m.* yam, sweet potato ***<Loc:*** EV, Da84, Hi02, Lv88, Ph36, Re31>

yamme ♦see **yam**

yankee[1] **(yinquis)** [jẽki] *n.m.* sparrow **Ça prend quinze minutes, un petit yinquis, pour voler dessus le bout pour arriver à l'autre bout.* It takes fifteen minutes for a little sparrow to fly from one side and arrive on the other side. (EV, An94) ***<Loc:*** EV, An94, Ph36>

Yankee[2] **(Yinqui, Yankie)** [jẽki] *n.m.* **1** American from the North, Yankee, Northerner *Et dans ce temps-là on l'appelait pas* GOLDEN MEADOW, *on l'appelait ça Canal Yankee. Peut-être que t'es familier avec ça. Y avait un canal et c'était des Yankees qui restait là. On disait Canal Yankee.* And in those days we didn't call it Golden Meadow, we called it Canal Yankee. Maybe you're familiar with that. There was a canal and it was Yankees who lived there. We called it Canal Yankee. (LF) **2** Union soldier (during the Civil War) ◊ **•ça aurait pas pris un Yinqui** ***a*** that's easy to do ***b*** that's easy to understand <EV, La99> ***<Loc:*** EV, IB, JD, LF, SL, SM, Da84, Di32, La99, Lv88, Ph36>

Yankie ♦see **Yankee**

yanque ♦see **rien que**

yard (yarde) [jard] *n.m./f.* yard (3 feet) *Le coton est quinze sous la yarde.* Cotton is fifteen cents a yard. (IB) ***<Loc:*** EV, IB, LA, TB, VM, Da84, Lv88>

yarde ♦see **yard**

YEAST (isse) [jis(t), is] *n.m./f.* **1** yeast **2** baking powder ◊ **•YEAST macaque** Parrot and Monkey brand baking powder <SL, La99> ***<Loc:*** IB, SL, SM, TB, VM, La99, Lv88>

YEASTCAKE (issequèque) [jiskeⁱk, iskɛk] *n.* yeast cake ***<Loc:*** TB>

yeille ♦see **yelle**

yelle (yeille) [jɛl, jɛj] *n.f.* youngest daughter of a family ***<Loc:*** JE, Di32>

yenne [jẽn] *n.f.* disorderly woman ***<Loc:*** JD>

yeur ♦see **yeux**

yeux[1] **(y'eux, yeur)** [jø, jœr] (*before a vowel* [jøz]) *pron. (ind.obj.)* them *Çulà qui pouvait trouver le fouet, il pouvait courser les autres et y'eux faire peur.* The one who found the whip, he could chase the others and scare them. (VM) *Ma mame yeux parlait français, alle a assayé de yeux montrer à parler français.* My mother spoke to them in French, she tried to teach them to speak French. (LF) *Je vas y'eux donner des serviettes de bain.* I will give them towels. (La03) *Il fallait les habiller dans le linge que les voisins nous donnaient pour yeux mettre.* We had to dress them in the clothing that the neighbors gave us for them to wear. (EV) ***<Loc:*** EV, LF, TB, VM, Da84, Hi02>

yeux[2] ♦see **eux**

yeux[3] ♦see **œil**

yéya [jeja] *n.m.* [*baby talk*] horse ***<Loc:*** JE, Di32>

yienque ♦see **rien que**

yienquetement ♦see **rienquetement**

Yinqui ♦see **Yankee**

yinquis ♦see **yankee**

yinque ♦see **rien que**

yinyin ♦see **gningnin**

y'où ♦see **ayoù**

yoyo [jojo] *n.m.* yoyo <***Loc:*** AV, Da84>

youk [juk] *n.m.* euchre <***Loc:*** VM, Di32>

youque (**yuque**) [juk, jyk] *n.m.* yoke (of a shirt or dress) <***Loc:*** LF, TB, VM>

youquer [yuke] *v.tr.* **1** to yoke **2** to fool, trick, get the best of <***Loc:*** JD, SB>

yoyotte ♦see **gnognotte**

yuque ♦see **youque**

Z

z-acre ♦see **acre**
z-agrafe ♦see **agrafe**
z-aignée ♦see **araignée**
z-ail ♦see **ail**
z-aile ♦see **aile**
z-ampoule ♦see **ampoule**
z-ananas ♦see **ananas**
z-araignée ♦see **araignée**
z-arbre ♦see **arbre**
zarico ♦see **haricot**
zaricot (**ZYDECO**) [zariko, zaɪdəko] *n.m.* zydeco music <***Loc:*** EV, LA, VM>
z-automobile ♦see **automobile**
ZEBRA [zibɹə] *n.m.* zebra <***Loc:*** AV, Da84>
zèle [zɛl] *n.m.* zeal, enthusiasm <***Loc:*** Da84>
z-enfants [zɑ̃fɑ̃] *interj.* goodness! *Zenfants! Quoi je vas faire?* Goodness! What will I do? (VM) <***Loc:*** SM, VM>
zéro [zero] *n.m.* **1** zero, naught **2** incapable or incompetent person <***Loc:*** EV, JD, Da84, Hi02>
z-habitant ♦see **habitant**
z-hameçon ♦see **hameçon**
z-haricot ♦see **haricot**
z-herbe ♦see **herbe**
z-hibou ♦see **hibou**
z-huître ♦see **huître**
z-huîtreur ♦see **huîtreur**
zibré [zibre] *n.m.* zebra <***Loc:*** Fa77>
zieu ♦see **zyeu**
zieuter [zjøte] *v.tr.* **1** to look at, look over *Il y avait des chemises à vendre puis j'étais apres les zieuter.* There were shirts for sale and I was looking them over. (LA) **2** to stare at, glare at *Quand j'ai rentré dans la barre, il m'a zieuté comme si il voulait me tuer.* When I entered the bar, he glared at me like as if he wanted to kill me. (LA) <***Loc:*** LA>
zigonner [zigɔ̃ne] *v.tr.* to pull (a horse) from side to side by pulling on one rein then the other **Ce cheval est bien amain, pourquoi le zigonner?* This horse is quite handy, why pull him from one side to the other like that? (Di32) *Il est après zigonner le cheval.* He is pulling the horse from side to side. (VM) <***Loc:*** JE, VM, Di32, Lv88>
zigzag (**zigzaque**) [zigzag, zigzak] *n.m.* zigzag *Le petit garçon est après faire des zigzaques.* The little boy is zigzagging. (VM) <***Loc:*** VM, Da84>
zigzaguer (**zigzaquer**) [zigzage, zigzake] *v.intr.* to zigzag *Son char zigzaguait assez, je croyais qu'il était soûl.* His car was zigzagging so much, I thought he was drunk. (VM) <***Loc:*** VM, Da84>
zigzaque ♦see **zigzag**
zigzaquer ♦see **zigzaguer**
zinc[1] [zɛ̃, zɛ̃k] *n.m.* **1** galvanized or corrugated iron *Couverture en zinc.* Roof of tin or corrugated iron. (TB) **2** any of a variety of metals (esp. zinc, iron, and tin) *Un bassin en zinc.* A tinplate basin. (Lv88) *Une couverture en zinc.* A tin roof. (LA) <***Loc:*** JE, LA, SJ, SL, TB, VM, Da84, Di32, Lv88>
zinc[2] ♦see **SINK**
z-indien ♦see **indien**
z-Indien ♦see **Indien**
z-intestin ♦see **intestin**
zinzin [zɛ̃zɛ̃] *n.m.* **1** American widgeon, baldpate duck **2** light-colored or light-weight summer suit (usu. worn in fall or winter in Louisiana) **3** stupid or foolish person *Espèce de grand zinzin.* You big nitwit. (TB) ◊ **•avoir les zinzins** to have the blues <JD, SC, La99> **•c'est ton zinzin** it's your butt on the line *C'est ton zinzin si tu crois tu vas t'esquiver avec ça.* It's your behind if you think you're going to get away with that. (VM) <***Loc:*** JD, JE, LF, SC, SM, TB, VM, La99, Re31>
zip [zip, zɪp] *n.m.* zipper <***Loc:*** JE, SM, VM, Lv88>
zirable [zirab(l)] *adj.* nasty, disgusting, revolting, repulsive *Tu parles la table était zirable quand on a eu fini de faire boucherie.* Are you kidding? The table was disgusting when we finished up with the butchering. (Guoo) *C'est sale. Tu peux être sale et pas zirable. Je crois pas que tu peux être zirable et pas être sale.* It's dirty. You can be dirty and not revolting. I don't think you can be revolting and not be dirty. (LF) *La fille ça tu sors avec là est zirable.* The girl you are going out with is repulsive. (SM) <***Loc:*** JD, LA, LF, SL, SM, TB, VM, Da84, Di32, Guoo, Hi02, Lv88>
zirablement [zirabləmɑ̃] *adv.* disgustingly, repulsively *Ça s'embrassait zirablement devant le public.* They kissed disgustingly in public. (VM) <***Loc:*** VM, Da84>
zire [zir] *n.m.* disgust ◊ **•avoir zire (de)** to be disgusted, be repelled, be revolted (by) *Et la tasse était pas propre. Alle était* SMUDGE. *Et lui il se sert pas, il voulait pas boire le café, il avait honte, il avait zire de la tasse.* And the cup wasn't clean, it was smudged. And he doesn't use it, he didn't want to drink the coffee, he was embarrassed, he was disgusted by the cup. (LF) *Y a du monde qu'a zire de toucher des 'tites rainettes.* Some people are revolted by touching little frogs. (Guoo) **J'ai zire de cette viande.* I am disgusted with this meat. (Da84) <LF, SM, VM, Da84, Guoo, Lv88> **•faire {donner} zire** to be repulsive, cause repugnance *Le crapaud me fait zire.* The toad is repugnant to me. (Lv88) <LF,

Lv88> <***Loc:*** IB, JD, LA, LF, SJ, SL, SM, TB, VM, Da84, Di32, Guoo, Lv88>

zireté [zirte] *n.f.* **1** repulsiveness **2** repulsive thing *Ma tante a dit que c'était une zireté de voir toutes ces serpents dans ce portrait.* My aunt said it was revolting to see all the snakes in the picture. (Guoo) **3** filth *C'est plein de zireté de raverts.* It's full of cockroach filth. (TB) <***Loc:*** JE, LF, SL, TB, VM, Da84, Guoo>

zirou [ziru] *adj.* easily revolted, squeamish <***Loc:*** JE, Di32>

z-œufs ♦see **œuf**

zoie, z-oie ♦see **oie**

z-oignon ♦see **oignon**

z-oiseau ♦see **oiseau**

zombi [zɔ̃bi, ʒɔ̃bi] *n.m.* **1** phantom, ghost, apparition **2** anything big or grotesquely out of proportion **3** tooth fairy ◊ •**faire zombi** to play possum <Re31> <***Loc:*** IB, SB, TB, Lv88, Re31>

zoo [zu] *n.m.* zoo <***Loc:*** SM>

z-oreille ♦see **oreille**

z-orteil ♦see **orteil**

z-ouïe ♦see **ouïe**

z-outil ♦see **outil**

zozo[1] [zozo] *n.* small-minded, foolish person <***Loc:*** JE, Di32>

zozo[2] *n.m.* [*baby talk*] bird <***Loc:*** IB, SL>

zozo[3] ♦see **oiseau**

ZYDECO ♦see **zaricot**

zyeu (**zieu**) [zjø] *n.m.* **1** *(sing.)* eye *Il a un zyeu en vitre.* He has a glass eye. (SM) **2** *(pl.)* eyes <***Loc:*** JD, SB, SM, Di32, Lv88>

z-yeux ♦see **œil**

English-Louisiana French Index

A

a *art.* le, un
aback *adv.* **be taken aback** rebouquer
abandon *v.* abandonner, dégrader, délaisser, déserter, lâcher, QUIT, quitter, semer, laisser (qqn) en plan **abandon o.s.** se livrer à
abandoned *adj.* à la valdrague **something left behind or abandoned** quittage **one who has been abandoned by a partner or loved one** délaissé
abandonment *n.* abandon
abate *v.* se modérer, tomber
abbess *n.* abbesse
abbot *n.* abbé
abdomen *n.* ventre
abdominal *adj.* **abdominal region** ventrage
abduct *v.* enlever
ability *n.* capacité, faculté, habilité, moyen, pouvoir
able *adj.* capable, compétent, habile, HOP **be able** pouvoir
abnormal *adj.* abnormal
aboard *adv.* sur **go aboard again** se rembarquer
abode *n.* demeure, résidence
abolish *v.* ôter, abolir
abominable *adj.* abominable
abominate *v.* abominer
abomination *n.* abomination
abort *v.* avorter
abortion *n.* avortement, fausse-couche
about *adv.* (à) côté de, approchant, au ras (de), autour, dans un approchant, environ, moyennant, à peu près **about to** au moment de **be about to** en train de / entrain de, être après pour, être pour
about *prep.* après, dans l'alentour de / dans les alentours de, de, dessus, pour, sur, vers, à propos de **rattle on and on about s.t.** en faire tout un chapitre
above *adv.* par-dessus **over and above** par-dessus le marché
above *prep.* en dessus, en haut (de), par-dessus
abridge *v.* abréger
abroad *n.* l'autre bord
abrogation *n.* abrogation
abscess *n.* abcès, dépôt, humeur, postume **core of an abscess or boil** mèche
absence *n.* absence **in my absence** dans mon absence
absent *adj.* GONE
absinthe *n.* absinthe, herbe sainte **absinthe liqueur** absinthe
absolute *adj.* absolu, positif
absolutely *adv.* absolument, obligé, obligément
absolution *n.* absolution
absolve *v.* absoudre
absorber *n.* **shock absorber** chacaça
abstain *v.* faire abstinence de, s'abstenir, se priver **abstain from eating meat** faire maigre
abstaining *adj.* abstinent
abstinence *n.* abstinence
abstinent *adj.* abstinent
abundance *n.* abondance **in abundance** tambour battant **have an abundance** écraser la mûre (pour) **the times of abundance are over** le temps à Pascal est fini
abundant *adj.* abondant, terrible **be abundant** forcer **not abundant** serré
abuse *n.* abus, bourlingue, injure **utter violent abuse** bagueuler
abuse *v.* abuser, abîmer, ambitionner dessus qqn, bourlinguer, bourrasser, maganer, maltraiter **verbally abuse** agoniser
abusive *adj.* abusif
acacia *n.* acacia **false acacia** févier
academy *n.* académie
Acadia *n.* Acadie
Acadian *adj.* acadien **Acadian French** acadien
Acadian *n.* Acadien **Louisiana Acadian** acadien, Cadien *pl.* **language of the Acadians** acadien
Acadiana *n.* Acadiana
accelerator *n.* **accelerator pedal** marchette
accent *n.* accent
accentuate *v.* faire ressortir
accept *v.* accepter, prendre, se refaire à
acceptable *adj.* acceptable **not in the least acceptable** pas moindrement acceptable
acceptance *n.* acceptance, acceptation
access *n.* accès
accessible *adj.* approchable
accessory *npl.* **wedding garments and accessories** agrès de noces **fancy or dressy clothes and accessories** farauderie
accident *n.* accident **by accident** par accident
accidentally *adv.* par accident
accommodate *v.* accommoder **accommodate o.s.** s'accommoder **a woman who marries must accommodate herself to her husband's habits, family, etc.** qui prend mari, prend pays
accommodating *adj.* accordant, arrangeant, complaisant, obligeant
accommodation *n.* accommodation, logement
accompany *v.* accompagner
accomplish *v.* accomplir, achever
accomplished *adj.* professionnel
accomplishment *n.* accomplet, accomplissement
accord *n.* accord, accordement **be in accord** convenir
according *prep.* **according to** accordant, d'après, selon
accordion *n.* accordéon **diatonic accordion** accordéon français **accordion player** accordioniste
accost *v.* aborder
account *n.* compte, dicton, exposé, rapport **bank account**

acompte **charge account** acompte **give account** rendre compte (de) **keep account of** tenir compte **on account of** (par) rapport à, à cause de **written account of one's life** mémoire *pl.* **pay or settle one's accounts** payer ses comptes, régler ses comptes

accountability *n.* responsabilité

accountable *adj.* responsable

accoutrement *npl.* **accoutrements** gréement

accumulate *v.* cumuler, s'amasser

accuracy *n.* exactitude

accurate *adj.* exact

accusation *n.* accusation, charge

accuse *v.* accuser, charger **accuse o.s.** s'accuser

accused *n.* accusé

accuser *n.* accuseur

accustom *v.* accoutumer

accustomed *adj.* habitué **be accustomed** avoir habitude (de) **become accustomed** s'accoutumer, s'habituer **get accustomed again** se raccoutumer **be accustomed to the ways** être habitué avec **one who is accustomed** habitué

ace *n.* as, boulette **ace of spades** as de pic *pl.* **four aces** quatre-z-as

ache *n.* avoir du mal, douleur, mal

ache *v.* faire (du) mal

achieve *v.* compléter **achieve s.t. by nontraditional or unofficial means** passer par la porte (d')en arrière

aching *adj.* souffrant

acid *n.* acide **acid blood condition** sang hâcre **battery acid** acide de batterie **carbolic acid** (acide) carbolique, acide carbolique **citric acid** acide de citron **carbolic acid ointment** onguent à ver

acidic *adj.* acide, hâcre

acidity *n.* acidité

acknowledge *v.* admettre

acolyte *n.* acolyte

acorn *n.* gland

acquaintance *n.* accointance, connaissance **make the acquaintance** faire la connaissance (de), rencontrer *pl.* **renew acquaintances** renouveler les connaissances

acquainted *adj.* **be acquainted** savoir, se connaître **get acquainted** faire la connaissance (de), s'accointer

acquiesce *v.* plier

acquire *v.* prendre, contracter **acquire property or anything of value** se gagner de quoi

acquit *v.* **acquit o.s.** s'acquitter

acquittal *n.* acquittance, acquittement

acre *n.* acre

acrid *adj.* hâcre

across *adv.* en biais **across from** en face de, opposé de

across *prep.* à travers / en travers (de)

act *n.* acte, fait **be in the act of** être après

Act *n.* **Act of Contrition** le confesse à Dieu

act *v.* ACT, agir, agiter **act as** servir **act like** faire comme si **act as if** faire comme si **one who acts** faiseur

action *n.* acte, action **court action** procès **take action** agir **through the agency or action of** par

active *adj.* actif **highly active child** petit tonnerre

activity *n.* action, activité **stop activity** lâcher **exhibit great activity or energy** grouiller **be full of activity** boulotter **line of work or activity** ligne **short period of intense activity** secousse **period of time for a particular activity** saison *pl.* **assortment of activities** bal et bazar et course et bataille

actor *n.* acteur

actress *n.* acteur, actrice

actual *adj.* véritable

actually *adv.* pour même

ad *n.* notice, publicité

Adam *n.* **Adam's apple** gargand, gargoton, pomme d'Adam

adapt *v.* adapter **adapt o.s.** s'accommoder, s'adapter

adaptable *adj.* adaptable

add *v.* abouter, additionner, ajouter, figurer, mettre, rabouter, rapporter, remettre, abouter, additionner, allonger, égrandir **add to again** rajouter **add on to one's house** s'égrandir

added *adj.* postiche

adder *n.* vipère **ground adder** serpent siffleuse **puff adder** siffleur **spreading adder** serpent siffleuse

adder's-tongue *n.* langue de serpent

addicted *adj.* **get addicted** s'addicter

adding *n.* addition, égrandissement

addition *n.* aboutage, addition, allonge, allongement, rallongement, ajoutement **addition to the back of house** cabousse

additional *adj.* d'autre, extra

address *n.* adresse **make an address or speech** adresser

address *v.* adresser la parole à qqn, adresser, s'adresser, adresser **address in a desultory or insolent manner** apostropher

adelia *n.* bois blanc

adept *adj.* bon à marier, habile **adept at** fort pour **be expert at, adept at** avoir la main pour

adjacent *adj.* voisin, à collé de **be adjacent** abouter, border, se joindre

adjoin *v.* attenir, coller à {après}, se joindre

adjoining *adj.* joignant **be adjoining** coller à {après}

adjust *v.* adapter, ajuster, arranger **adjust o.s.** s'ajuster, se rarranger **adjust one's clothes** s'ajuster

adjustable *adj.* adaptable

adjusted *adj.* **poorly adjusted** malajusté

adjuster *n.* ajusteur

adjusting *n.* ajustage

adjustment *n.* ajustage, ajustement

administer *v.* courir, foutre

administering *n.* **act of administering** administration

administration *n.* administration

admirable *adj.* admirable

admire *v.* admirer **admire o.s. or each other** s'admirer

admissible *adj.* admettable, admissible
admission *n.* admission **admission fee** admission **admission of guilt** admission **paid admission** porte
admit *v.* admettre, avouer, déclarer
admittable *adj.* admettable
admittance *n.* accès, entrée, entrance
ado *n.* **much ado** estampique **much ado about nothing** une grande estampique pour rien
adopt *v.* adopter, adopter
adopted *adj.* **adopted or placed in foster care** placé
adoption *n.* adoption
adorable *adj.* adorable
adoration *n.* adoration
adore *v.* adorer
adorer *n.* adorateur
adorn *v.* adorner, garnir, orner **adorn o.s.** s'orner, se garnir
adornment *n.* embellissement
adroit *adj.* aplomb
adroitness *n.* aplomb
adult *n.* grand, majeur **you think you are behaving like an adult, but you are being foolish or impudent** tu crois (que) t'es maître et majeur *pl.* **adults** le grand monde, le vieux monde
adultery *n.* adultère **commit adultery** découcher
adulthood *n.* majorité, maturité **attain the age of legal adulthood** venir en âge
advance *n.* avance **in advance of** avant *pl.* **make advances** faire des avances
advance *v.* avancer, marcher, faire des avances (d'argent)
advanced *adj.* avancé
advancement *n.* avancement
advancing *n.* avancement
advantage *n.* avantage **take advantage** abuser **take advantage of** prendre avantage de **take advantage of s.o.** ambitionner dessus qqn **take advantage of the occasion** profiter de l'occasion **take advantage of a cool breeze** attraper la fraîche **take the advantage** prendre (l')avantage **gain the advantage over** engagner **have the advantage over** emmancher **give s.o. an advantage, a leg up** donner un pied (à qqn)
advantageous *adj.* avantageux
Advent *n.* avent
adventure *n.* aventure
adversary *n.* opponent
adversity *n.* **able to withstand adversity** fait du nerf et de la babiche
advertise *v.* afficher
advertisement *n.* affiche, avertissement, notice, publicité
advertiser *n.* afficheur
advertising *n.* affichage
advice *n.* avis, conseil **give advice** aviser **take advice** prendre l'avis
advisable *adj.* recommandable
advise *v.* aviser, conseiller **advise against** déconseiller
advisor *n.* aviseur, conseilleur, consultant
adze *n.* herminette **cooper's adze** herminette **hand adze** tille
afar *adv.* **from afar** de loin
affable *adj.* charrant
affair *n.* affaire **complicated affair** emmanchure **have an affair** bêtiser, s'amouracher *pl.* **affairs** business
affect *v.* affecter, porter sur
affectation *n.* simagris
affected *adj.* fionneur, gesteux **person with affected manners** fionneur **act in a pretentious, haughty or affected way** fionner
affection *n.* affection, amitié, amour, attachement, sentiment **physical affection** licherie **lavish inordinate affection on** gâter **saying that describes a couple who make a show of affection in public, but who fight frequently in private** c'est un 'cher' ici, 'cher' la-bàs
affectionate *adj.* tendre **ironic or affectionate term for a person** coco
affectionately *adv.* tendrement
affidavit *n.* affidavit
affiliation *n.* bord
affirm *v.* affirmer
affirmative *adj.* affirmative
affix *v.* monter
afflict *v.* affliger
afflicted *adj.* abattu, afflictionné
affliction *n.* affliction, désolation
afford *v.* AFFORD
affront *n.* affront
affront *v.* affronter
afloat *adj.* à la flotte
aforementioned *adj.* **aforementioned one** dit
aforesaid *n.* dit
afraid *adj.* craignant, craintif **be afraid** avoir froid aux yeux, avoir la {une} cache, avoir peur (de / que), craindre, frémir, redouter
Africa *n.* Afrique
African *adj.* africain
African-American *n.* **insulting name for an African-American, a mulatto, or a Cajun** bougali *pl.* **term used to refer to African-Americans collectively** négraille
after *adj.* dépassé
after *adv.* après, par après **right after** droite après
after *conj.* après (que)
after *prep.* après, dedans, au bout de
afternoon *n.* après-midi **afternoon show** matinée **good afternoon** bonjour **this afternoon** après-midi, cet après-midi
afterward *adv.* après, par après
afterwards *adv.* par après
again *adv.* BACK, encore, re-, à nouveau **again and again** à tout

moment **never again** jamais encore **once again** de nouveau **all over again** à nouveau

against *prep.* contre **up against** contre **hold s.t. against** avoir une dent contre qqn

agave *n.* pite

age *n.* siècle, âge **of age** fort **old age** vieillerie, vieillesse **advanced in age** hors d'âge **difference in age** différence **of legal age** en âge, majeur **at the age of reason** fort **of the age of majority** grand, maître et majeur **be of ripe age** avoir un bon âge **good or ripe age** bel {belle} âge *pl.* **for endless ages** dans les siècles des siècles

age *v.* vieillir

aged *adj.* d'âge, âgé

agency *n.* agence **through the agency or action of** par

agent *n.* agent, commissionnaire **county agent** agent de la paroisse **drying agent** déchessant **FBI agent** fédéral **station agent** agent de tickettes {gare}

aggravate *v.* affoler, agoniser, engraver, mortifier

aggravated *adj.* **become aggravated** s'affoler

aggravating *adj.* enquiquinant, mortifiant

aggressive *adj.* **bred to be aggressive for cockfighting** gaïme

agile *adj.* agile, souple

agility *n.* agilité

agitate *v.* mettre en bouleverse, provoquer **agitate clothing in a tub of water** sagoter

agitated *adj.* agité, effardé **be agitated** s'agiter **restless or agitated person or animal** loup-garou **extremely nervous or agitated** nerfé

agitation *n.* agitation **great agitation** estampique **experience a strange agitation** faire drôle

agitator *n.* batteur

agnail *n.* belle-mère

ago *adv.* de ça, il y a, passé **a long time ago** longtemps passé **that was a long time ago** ça date du temps d'Artaguette **a week, a month, two days ago** ça donne une semaine {un mois / deux jours} que

agony *n.* agonie **death agony** agonie de la mort, le dernier supplice **be in agony** agoniser

agree *v.* approuver, cager, concourir, consentir, convenir, vouloir, être d'accord **agree with one another** s'accorder

agreeable *adj.* agréable, charmant, complaisant, conscencieux, consentieux, plaisant

agreeableness *n.* complaisance

agreed *adj.* attendu, convenu

agreement *n.* accord, accordement, adonnance, arrangement, assent, consentement, contrat, convenance **reach an agreement** se comprendre, tomber d'accord **be in complete agreement** avoir tous leur tête dans le même bonnet

agricultural *adj.* agricole

agriculture *n.* agriculture

ah *interj.* ah

ahead *adj.* avancé

ahead *adv.* en avance, en avant **ahead of** avant, en avant de **ahead of time** d'avance **be ahead** être de l'avant **straight ahead** droite, tout droite

aid *n.* aide, aideur, assistance, assistant, secours **digestion aid** régulateur

aid *v.* aider, assister, secourir

aiding *adj.* auxiliaire

aim *n.* but, mire, objet **take aim** mirer, prendre sa (bonne) mire / prendre une mire

aim *v.* braquer, mirer

air *n.* air, mine, simagris **air conditioning** air froide **air pump** pompe **air vent** registre **cool air** fraîcheur **musical air** TUNE **let air out of** dégonfler **on the air** sur {dessus} l'air **in the air, the sky** l'air du temps **in the open air** en pleine air **up in the air** en l'air **be full of hot air** flafla *pl.* **put on airs** avoir le nez fin, faire {prendre} des fions, se donner des airs, se flanquer des fions **one who puts on airs** fionneur, péteur

air *v.* **air out** airer

air-dry *v.* ressorer

airhead *n.* biorque

airplane *n.* aéroplane, avion **ultralight airplane** cigale

airship *n.* BALLOON

aisle *n.* allée

alarm *n.* alarme **alarm clock** réveil, réveille **state of alarm** alarme

alarming *adj.* inquiétant

alburnum *n.* aubelle

alcohol *n.* alcool, liqueur **drink alcohol** boire, pimper **drink alcohol again** reboire **one who does not drink alcohol** buveur de lait

alcoholic *adj.* **alcoholic beverage** boisson **alcoholic drink** DRINK **give s.o. alcoholic beverages** biter

alcoholic *n.* soûlard

alcove *n.* niche

alderman *n.* membre de conseil (du village)

alert *adj.* prime, requinquiné, vif

alewife *n.* gaspareau

alfalfa *n.* alfalfa

algae *n.* **blue-green algae** limon

alibi *n.* excuse

alight *v.* se poser

align *v.* aligner

aligning *n.* alignement

alignment *n.* alignement

alike *adj.* pareil, uniforme **be alike as two peas in a pod** se ressembler comme deux gouttes d'eau

alive *adj.* en vie, vivant **be alive** exister **stay alive** rester en vie

all *adj.* tout

all *adv.* tout

all *pron.* tous, tout, toute chose **above all** avant tout, surtout **after all** après tout, au bout du compte, enfin, à la fin du compte **at all** du tout **that's all** c'est tout **not at all** pas du tout, pas un foutre, pas une miette, point

allegedly *adv.* soi-disant

alleluia *interj.* alléluia

allergy *npl.* **allergies** fièvre d'automne

alleviate *v.* alléger, soulager, apaiser

alleviation *n.* soulagement

alley *n.* allée **blind alley** cul-de-sac

alliance *n.* alliance, fédération, support, union

alligator *n.* alligator, caïman, cocodrie **go alligator hunting** aller aux caïmans *pl.* **one who skins alligators** écorcheur

allocate *v.* alloquer, apportionner

allot *v.* assigner

allotment *n.* concession

allow *v.* laisser, permettre, quitter **allow o.s.** se laisser, se permettre **allow to enter** admettre **allow o.s. to be cheated** se laisser mettre dedans

allowance *n.* ration, rationnement

allowed *adj.* **be allowed** pouvoir

alluvium *n.* terre rapportée

almanac *n.* almanach, calendrier

almighty *adj.* tout-puissant **almighty God** Dieu tout-puissant **the almighty Father** le Père tout-puissant

almond *n.* amande **earth almond** cache-cache

almost *adv.* approchant, bien proche, en approchant, presque, proche que, proche, près de, quasiment, vouloir, manquer de, rifler **be almost** donner sur

alms *npl.* aumône, charité **give alms** faire la charité **ask for alms** faire {passer} la quête

aloe *n.* alouase

alone *adj.* seul, solitaire **all alone** tout seul **leave alone** quitter tranquille **let alone** laisser tranquille **go away and leave me alone** va te coucher

along *adv.* **get along** s'emmancher

along *prep.* à {au / en / le} long de

aloof *adj.* **person who is aloof** sainte nitouche

aloud *adv.* fort

alphabet *n.* alphabet, béaba

already *adv.* déjà

also *adv.* aussi, itou

altar *n.* autel **altar boy** acolyte, enfant de chœur **altar cloth** nappe d'autel

alter *v.* berdasser, changer, modifier

altercation *n.* accrochage, train

altered *adj.* tourné

alternation *n.* contrepoint

althea *n.* althéa

although *conj.* malgré que, quoique

altitude *n.* altitude, hauteur

alum *n.* alun

aluminum *n.* aluminium, étain **made of stainless metal or aluminum** brillant

always *adv.* toujours, tout le temps, à demeure

amaryllis *n.* lys de Saint-Joseph **red amaryllis** chapeau de St. Jacques

amass *v.* amasser, s'amasser

amaze *v.* étonner

amazement *n.* étonnement

amazing *adj.* surprenant

ambassador *n.* ambassadeur

ambition *n.* ambition, aspiration

ambitious *adj.* ambitieux, ambitionneux **be ambitious** ambitionner

amble *v.* **amble about** naviguer

ambulance *n.* ambulance

ambush *n.* embuscade **lie in ambush** faire l'embuscade

ameliorate *v.* bonifier

amen *interj.* ainsi soit-il, amen

amend *v.* amender

amendable *adj.* amendable

amendment *n.* amendement, réforme

amends *npl.* réparation **make amends** donner satisfaction, satisfaire

America *n.* Amérique

American *adj.* américain

American *n.* Américain **American from the North** Yankee **American of Italian origin** dégo **Native American** Indien, indien, sauvage

Americanize *v.* américaniser

Americanized *adj.* **become Americanized** s'américaniser

amiable *adj.* accordant, aimable, amiable

amicable *adj.* amicable

amicably *adv.* amicablement

amid *prep.* parmi

amidst *prep.* entremis

ammonia *n.* ammonia

ammunition *n.* ammunition, munition

among *prep.* dans, entre, entremis, parmi

amortize *v.* amortir

amount *n.* montant, quantité, somme **large amount** chouinque, sacage **small amount** bout, fraction, goutte, once, peu, pincée, un pauvre petit peu, un peu de **greatest number or amount** majorité **large or excessive amount** tapée

amount *v.* **amount to** se monter **no longer amount to anything** compter plus z-herbes

amphiuma *n.* congo, congre

amplifying *adj.* **amplifying device** cornet

amply *adv.* largement

amputate *v.* amputer

amputation *n.* amputation

amulet *n.* gris-gris

amuse *v.* amuser, divertir, désennuyer **amuse o.s.** se divertir **enjoy or amuse o.s. or each other** s'amuser

amusement *n.* amusement, amusette, divertissement

an *art.* un
analyze *v.* analyser
anatomy *n.* anatomie
ancestor *n.* ancêtre
ancestry *n.* chicot, chousse, sang
ancient *adj.* ancien
and *conj.* et, puis **and then** et là **and so forth** ainsi de suite
andiron *n.* chenet, chevalet
andouille *n.* andouille
anemia *n.* mauvais sang, sang clair
angel *n.* ange **guardian angel** ange gardien *pl.* **speak of angels, see their wings** en parlant des anges, on voit leurs ailes
angelus *n.* angélus
anger *n.* colère, fureur **uncontrolled anger** rage **fit of anger** coup de colère **prone to anger** coléreux **provoking to anger** choquant **quick to anger** chocatif, prime **vent one's anger** pisser sa colère **expression of anger, pain, or surprise** (que le) tonnerre m'écrase!, tonnerre, mes chiens **get over one's anger** se défâcher **expression used to show surprise, irritation or anger** fils de chien {garce / putain} / fils de putain de bordel {garce}, fils de monstre {pistache / poteau} / fils de poteau de barrière
anger *v.* achaler, choquer, enrager, foutre en feu, fâcher
angering *adj.* choquant
angina *n.* angine
angle *n.* angle, biais, encoignure **right angle** équerre **at a sharp angle** à pic
angler *n.* pêcheur à la ligne, pêcheur
angling *n.* pêche
Anglo *n.* Américain
Anglophone *adj.* américain
Anglophone *n.* Anglais **Anglophone not of Cajun ethnicity** cou-rouge
angry *adj.* achalé, bouqué, chaud, choqué au fiel, en fantaisie, enragé, farouche, fâché après {avec}, fâché comme un chien enragé / fâché comme une dinde {une garce / une guêpe / une hornette / un taureau / un tigre}, fâché, rebiffé **be angry** avoir le crin raide, avoir le cul rouge, avoir les narines effleurées {ouvertes}, bouillonner de rage, faire le poulain, prendre ça à coups de bâton, se fâcher, se manger de rage, être choqué après {avec} qqn, être piment contre qqn **become angry** bourdonner, s'embrouiller, se chagriner, se chauffer **get angry** bagueuler, prendre une colère, se faire du mauvais sang, se fâcher après, se fâcher, se mettre en colère, se rebiffer **make angry** mortifier **become angry again** rebouquer **get angry, mad, upset** se choquer **make s.o. angry** faire fâcher, faire manger du chien enragé **I'm so angry about that** bûche ça à coups de bâton! / bûche ça avec une chaîne! **that makes him or her angry** ça fait bouillir sa chaudière
anguish *n.* agonie
angular *adj.* angulaire
anhinga *n.* bec-à-lancette
animal *n.* bétaille, bête, bébête **domestic animal** animal **wild animal** bête farouche **any horned animal** bête à corne **provide an animal for community slaughter** pousser **runted or undersized animal** chacta **huge and strong man or animal** colosse *pl.* **barnyard animals** basse-cour **farm animals** animal **water the animals** faire boire
animate *v.* animer
animated *adj.* animé, dégagé
animation *n.* feu
anise *n.* anis
anisette *n.* absinthe, anisette
ankle *n.* cheville de {du} pied, cheville, jointure du pied **ankle of a horse** joint
ankle-boot *n.* broquin
annex *n.* aboutage, addition, allonge, briset
annex *v.* annexer
annexed *adj.* postiche
anniversary *n.* anniversaire
announce *v.* annoncer, faire dire, noticer **announce an intended marriage** publier les bans
announced *adj.* **be announced** se déclarer
announcement *n.* annonce, annoncement
announcer *n.* annonceur
annoy *v.* abominer, achaler, agacer, brûler, bâdrer, chamailler, chicoter, choquer, déranger, embêter, emmerder, emmicher, foutumasser, gêner, harasser, irriter, quiquiner, taquiner, tchincailler, tourmenter, tracasser, vexer **annoy or trouble persistently** persécuter **one who annoys, pesters or makes trouble** embarrateur
annoyance *n.* agacerie, damnation, dérangement, embêtation, embêtement
annoyed *adj.* achalé **annoyed at** pas satisfait après **be annoyed** s'embêter
annoying *adj.* achalant, agaçant, choquant, embarrateur, embêtant, emmerdant, gênant, maudit, nuisible, tracassant, vexant **annoying person** drigaille, emmicheteur **bunch of noisy or annoying children** ripopée
annoying *n.* taquinerie
annual *adj.* annuel
annul *v.* annuler
annulment *n.* annulement
anointing *n.* onction **anointing of the sick** extrême-onction, Extrême Onction
another *adj.* **some . . . or another** tel et tel / telle et telle
answer *n.* réponse **give an answer** donner réponse
answer *v.* répondre, exaucer **answer smartly** taper ça à qqn / taper sa réponse à qqn **answer the telephone** répondre au téléphone
ant *n.* fourmi **white ant** termite
antagonize *v.* taquiner
antagonizing *n.* taquinerie

ante *n.* mise
antenna *n.* baleine
Anthony *n.* **Saint Anthony's fire** érésipèle
anthrax *n.* anthrax, charbon
antic *n.* macaquerie
anticipate *v.* anticiper
anticipation *n.* anticipation
antidote *n.* contrepoison
antiseptic *adj.* antiseptique
antiseptic *n.* antiseptique
antler *npl.* **set of horns, antlers** panage
anvil *n.* enclume
anxiety *n.* anxiété, tracas **expect with anxiety** appréhenter
anxious *adj.* anxieux, inquiet **I am anxious** le temps me dure (de / que) **one is impatient, anxious, in a hurry** le temps dure (à qqn de faire qqch)
any *adj.* de **any one, any** n'importe quel **not any** aucun
any *pron.* **not any** aucun, pas
any-which-way *adv.* à la valdrague
anybody *pron.* **not anybody** personne
anyhow *adv.* du moins, n'importe comment, n'importe
anyone *pron.* n'importe qui **not anyone** personne
anything *pron.* n'importe qui, n'importe quoi **not anything** pas rien
anytime *adv.* n'importe quand
anyway *adv.* n'importe comment, n'importe, quand même, toujours
anywhere *adv.* n'importe ayoù
apart *adj.* différent
apart *adv.* à côté **apart from** à part de, à part que **apart from that** autrement de {que} ça **coming apart** démoyé **falling apart** démoyé **far apart** loin à loin
apartment *n.* appartement
ape *v.* faire des macaqueries dessus qqn
apiece *adv.* pièce
apocalypse *n.* apocalypse
apologize *v.* demander pardon, s'excuser, se soumettre
apoplexy *n.* apoplexie
apostasy *n.* apostasie
apostate *n.* apostat
apostle *n.* apôtre *pl.* **one of the twelve apostles** disciple
Apostles' *n.* **the Apostles' Creed** le crois en Dieu, le Symbole des Apôtres
apostolate *n.* apostolat
apostolic *adj.* apostolique
appalling *adj.* effrayant
apparent *adj.* vulière
apparently *adv.* apparemment
apparition *n.* loup-garou, revenant, vision, zombi
appeal *n.* appel **court of appeal** cour d'appel
appeal *v.* appeler sur {dessus}, invoquer
appealing *adj.* frayant, invitant, tentable
appear *v.* apparaître, débouquer, monter sur la radio, montrer, paraître, regarder, ressembler, ressourdre, sembler, sourdre **make appear thinner** amincir
appearance *n.* air, allure, apparence, mine, montrance, prestance, regard **bad appearance** mauvaise mine **brief appearance** passée **first appearance** début **make an appearance** paraître, se montrer **make one's appearance** faire son apercevance **of neglected appearance** dégainé **of poor appearance** raponneau **mar the appearance of** défigurer **make a brief appearance** faire une passée **slovenly or unkempt appearance** dévaldrague
appease *v.* apaiser
appeasement *n.* apaisement
appendage *n.* appendice
appendicitis *n.* appendicite
appendix *n.* appendice
appetite *n.* appétit **have a large appetite** manger comme quatre / manger comme un cochon {ours / requin}
appetizing *adj.* appétissant
applaud *v.* applaudir
applause *n.* applaudissement
apple *n.* pomme **apple tree** pommier **Adam's apple** gargand, gargoton, pomme d'Adam **balsam apple** mexicain
appliance *n.* machine
applicable *adj.* applicable
applicant *n.* applicant
application *n.* application, applicage **make an application** faire (une) application **submit an application** mettre une application
apply *v.* appliquer, faire (une) application, passer, appliquer **apply o.s.** s'appliquer **apply some more** remettre
applying *n.* applicage
appoint *v.* appointer **appoint o.s.** s'appointer
appointment *n.* appointement, nomination **make an appointment** citer, faire un rendez-vous
apportion *v.* alloquer, apportionner
apportionment *n.* partage
appraisal *n.* estimation
appraise *v.* estimer
appreciate *v.* apprécier
appreciation *n.* appréciation
appreciative *adj.* reconnaissant
apprehend *v.* ramasser
apprehension *n.* **feel fear or apprehension** frémir
apprehensive *adj.* **be apprehensive of** redouter
apprentice *n.* apprenti
apprenticeship *n.* apprentissage
approach *v.* aborder, approcher, s'amener, s'approcher, s'avancer, se rapprocher
approchable *adj.* approchable
appropriate *adj.* bon, commode
appropriate *v.* approprier

appropriateness *n.* **sense of appropriateness** à-propos
appropriation *n.* appropriation
approve *v.* applaudir, approuver
approximately *adv.* (à) côté de, au ras (de), autour (de), dans l'alentour de / dans les alentours de, manière, moyennant, vers, à peu près
approximation *n.* à-peu-près
apricot *n.* abricot **apricot tree** abricotier
April *n.* avril **April Fool** poisson d'avril **be tricked on April Fool's Day** manger le poisson d'avril
apron *n.* tablier
aptitude *n.* **having no aptitude** malpris à
Arab *n.* Arabe
Arabian *adj.* arabe
arabic *adj.* **gum arabic** gomme arabique
Arabic *adj.* arabe **Arabic language** Arabique
Arabic *n.* Arabique
arable *adj.* arable, cultivable
arbitrary *adj.* arbitraire
arbor *n.* berceau
arch *n.* arc, arche
archangel *n.* archange
archbishop *n.* archevêque
architect *n.* architecte
architecture *n.* architecture
ardent *adj.* ardent
ardor *n.* ardeur
area *n.* entourage, pays, région, territoire
argue *v.* argumenter, bagueuler, chicaner, chicoter, quereller, s'ostiner, se contrarier **argue continuously or repeatedly** querellailler **argue with each other** se disputer, se halailler
arguing *n.* **there is no point in arguing** Taupin vaut Maurin
argument *n.* argument, chicane, dispute, halaillage, halaillement **loud argument** obstination **noisy argument** scandale
argumentative *adj.* obstineur
arise *v.* se présenter
arithmetic *n.* arithmétique, calcul, mathématique
ark *n.* arche **Noah's ark** arche
Arkansas *n.* Arkansas
arm *n.* arme, bras **arm wrestle** coucher au poignet **arm in arm** bras dessus bras dessous *pl.* **arms** armement **span of both arms fully extended** brasse
arm *v.* armer **arm o.s.** s'armer
armadillo *n.* armadillo, madrille, tatou
armament *n.* armement
armchair *n.* chaise bourrée, fauteuil
armful *n.* brassée
armhole *n.* mancheur
armistice *n.* armistice
armoire *n.* armoire, boutique **section in an armoire or chifferobe for hanging clothing** portemanteau
armpit *n.* endessous du bras
army *n.* armée, militaire
aromatic *adj.* aromatique
around *adv.* alentour (de) / à l'entour (de), alentour, au ras (de), autour (de), autour **all around** tout le tour
around *prep.* autour (de), dans l'alentour de / dans les alentours de, vers
arouse *v.* animer
arpent *n.* arpent
arrange *v.* amarrer, arranger, arrimer, disposer, rafficher, emmancher **arrange in order** classer **arrange in a somewhat illicit way** maquemousser
arranged *adj.* rangé
arrangement *n.* aises, ajustement, arrangement, disposition
arrear *npl.* **be in arrears** rester de l'arrière
arrest *n.* arrêt **arrest warrant** warrant
arrest *v.* arrêter, ramasser
arrival *n.* arrivée, venure
arrive *v.* arriver, s'amener, se ranger **arrive at** atteindre, se rendre
arrived *adj.* rendu
arrogance *n.* arrogance, fierté, glorieuseté, orgueil
arrogant *adj.* arrogant, orgueilleux, trop grand pour ses culottes **arrogant person** péteur **insult used for s.o. arrogant or not intelligent** c'est pas toi qu'es le taureau du côteau
arrow *n.* flèche **arrow head** pierre de sauvage
arrowhead *n.* **arrowhead plant** langue de {du} bœuf
art *n.* art **work of art** œuvre
artery *n.* altère
artesian *adj.* artésien
artful *adj.* **artful, crafty, sly man** homme d'affût
arthritis *n.* ARTHRITIS
Arthur *n.* **Lake Arthur** Lac Arthur
artichoke *n.* artichaut **globe artichoke** artichaut **Jerusalem artichoke** topinambour **native ground artichoke** patate jambillot {zabillot}
article *n.* article
articulate *v.* s'expliquer
artificial *adj.* faux, postiche
artillery *n.* artillerie
artisan *n.* artisan
artist *n.* artiste, peintre, peintureur **con artist** fraudeur **touch-up artist** brosseur du portrait
arugula *n.* roquette
as *conj.* puisque, que, à mesure que **as for** autant que pour, quant à, tant qu'à pour, tant qu'à **as if** comme si **as is** comme tel, tel **as... as** aussi... que / aussi... comme, si... que **as... as** aussi... comme **as for him** tant qu'à pour lui **as long as** aussi longtemps que, dès que / desque / drès que **as much as** autant que {comme} **as soon as** aussitôt que **as they say** comme dit l'autre {le bougre} **as well as** ainsi que, aussi

bien que **as it should be** comme de juste **as the saying goes** comme dit l'autre {le bougre} **as much as one wishes** à son contentement **just as** pareil comme

as *prep.* comme

asafoetida *n.* assafœtida

asbestos *n.* asbeste

ascend *v.* engrucher, monter, remonter

ascension *n.* ascension

ascent *n.* ascension

ash *n.* cendre, frêne **ash receptacle** cendrier **prickly ash** bois d'amourette, frêne piquant, piquant mourette / piquant (d') amourette / piquant mort raide *pl.* **ashes** cendre

Ash *n.* **Ash Wednesday** Mercredi des Cendres

ashamed *adj.* **be ashamed** avoir honte **you should be ashamed of yourself** va te cacher / va te faire cacher à Lafayette, va te coucher

ashtray *n.* cendrier

aside *adv.* à côté **aside from** à part de **aside from that** à part de ça

ask *v.* demander pour, demander, questionner **ask again** redemander **ask around** s'informer **ask o.s.** se demander **ask a question** poser une question **ask for alms** faire {passer} la quête **ask for charity** demander la charité, faire {passer} la quête **one who asks or solicits** demandant

askew *adj.* bisquencoin

asleep *adj.* endormi **while asleep** en dormant **fall asleep at the switch** dormir sur un rôti **be tired, asleep on one's feet** dormir debout

asp *n.* aspic

aspect *n.* mine **of mournful aspect** défiguré

asphalt *n.* **asphalt road** chemin de godron

asphyxiate *v.* asphyxier

aspic *n.* **aspic salad** aspic

aspiration *n.* aspiration

aspirin *n.* aspirine, calmant, calme, pastille de mal de tête

ass *n.* cocodrie, tchu, troufignon, âne **make an ass of o.s.** se montrer le tchul {derrière}

assail *v.* bombarder

assassin *n.* assassin, assassineur

assassinate *v.* assassiner

assassination *n.* assassin, assassinat, assassination

assault *n.* assaut, attaque

assault *v.* attaquer

assemblage *n.* assemblage

assemble *v.* assembler, emmancher, ramancher, rassembler, s'assembler, se joindre, se rassembler **assemble hastily** garrocher ensemble

assembling *n.* assemblage

assembly *n.* assemblage, assemblée, audience, congrégation, meeting, rassemblée

assent *n.* assent

assert *v.* affirmer

assess *v.* acertainer, assesser

assessment *n.* assessement

assessor *n.* assesseur

asset *npl.* **assets** fonds **possess assets, worth** valoir

asshole *n.* champignon

assign *v.* assigner

assignment *n.* placard, assignement

assist *v.* aider, assister, secourir

assistance *n.* aide, assistance, coup de main, secours **provide assistance** donner un coup de main **without assistance** tout seul **receive assistance from department of public welfare** monter sur le RELIEF **insurance or public assistance** bénéfice

assistant *n.* aide, aideur, assistant

associate *n.* associé, compagnon

associate *v.* associer, se coller sur, se mettre ensemble, fraterniser **associate o.s.** s'associer

associated *adj.* connecté avec

association *n.* association, CLUB, société

assorted *adj.* assorti, varié

assortment *n.* assortiment

assume *v.* assumer, espérer, présumer, supposer **assume an unusual posture** se poster

Assumption *n.* assomption **Feast of the Assumption** assomption

assurance *n.* assurance, sûreté

assure *v.* acertainer, assurer, garantir

assured *adj.* **be assured** s'assurer

assuredly *adv.* assurément, bien sûr

aster *n.* **saltmarsh aster** vulnéraire

asthma *n.* asthme, oppressement, oppression, souffle court **asthma attack** oppression **afflicted with asthma** oppressé

asthmatic *adj.* oppressif, oppressé

astonish *v.* surprendre, étonner

astonished *adj.* surpris **be astonished** s'étonner

astonishing *adj.* surprenant, étonnant

astonishment *n.* surprise, étonnement **expression of astonishment, sometimes disapproval** pense donc! **expression of astonishment, pity, or disapproval** pitié

astound *v.* abasourdir

astraddle *adv.* acadiac, à calibarda, à califourchon

astride *adv.* acadiac, sur, à calibarda, à califourchon

astronomer *n.* astronome

astute *adj.* **intellectually astute** pointu

at *prep.* après, chez, dessus, à

Atchafalaya *n.* **the Atchafalaya Basin** le bassin de l'Atchafalaya

athlete *n.* SPORT

Atlantic *adj.* **Atlantic ocean** atlantique

atomic *adj.* **atomic bomb** bombe atomique

atonement *n.* satisfaction

atrophy *v.* déchesser

attach *v.* amarrer, attacher, macorner, monter, accrocher **attach with a pin** attacher

attached *adj.* accroché après, après **become attached** attacher, s'attacher, s'enticher **emotionally attached** gâté après (qqn)

attaching *n.* attachage

attachment *n.* attache, attachement

attack *n.* assaut, attaque de maladie, attaque **asthma attack** oppression **heart attack** attaque de cœur

attack *v.* attaquer **attack each other** s'attaquer **urge to attack** siller

attacker *n.* attaqueur

attain *v.* atteindre, frapper **attain in competition** gagner **attain the age of legal adulthood** venir en âge

attempt *n.* essai

attempt *v.* entreprendre, essayer, tenter **attempt to influence** cabaler

attend *v.* assister, servir, fréquenter

attendance *n.* assistance, compagnie

attendant *n.* attendant

attention *n.* attention, soin **pay attention** faire attention, hourra, LOOK OUT, porter attention (à), porter cas (de), se guetter **pay attention to** guetter **draw attention to o.s.** s'afficher **give amourous attention** courtiser **lack of attention** manque d'attention **not paying attention to reality** dans les nuages **used to call attention** hem, hé **make a sibilant sound in order to attract s.o.'s attention** psiter

attentive *adj.* attentionné

attest *v.* certifier

attic *n.* grénit

attire *n.* **bizarre attire** attriquage, attriquement **flashy, gaudy attire** harnachement

attitude *n.* attitude, position

attorney *n.* avocat **attorney general** avocat général **district attorney** avocat (de) district

attract *v.* attirailler, attirer, tenter

attraction *n.* attraction

attractive *adj.* attirant

attractiveness *n.* attraction

auburn *adj.* châtain

auction *n.* encan, vente publique **auction barn** encan **auction house** encan **sell at auction** encanter **put up for auction** mettre à l'encan

auction *v.* **auction off** encanter

auctioneer *n.* crieur, encanteur

audacious *adj.* audacieux, téméraire

audaciously *adv.* avec audace

audacity *n.* audace, fiel, toupet, témérité

audience *n.* audience

audio *n.* **audio tape** ruban, TAPE

audition *n.* audition

auditor *n.* auditeur

auger *n.* **ground auger** mèche-terrière

augment *v.* augmenter

augmentation *n.* augmentation

August *n.* août

aunt *n.* tante **aunt by marriage** tante par alliance **great aunt** grande tante

auricular *adj.* auriculaire

auscultate *v.* sonder

austere *adj.* TIGHT

author *n.* auteur, écrivain

authority *n.* autorité, commission, jurisdiction **submit to authority** fléchir **highest point of leadership or authority** tête *pl.* **the authorities** les autorités

authorization *n.* autorisation

authorize *v.* approuver, autoriser, commissionner, donner le pouvoir, déléguer

autograph *n.* autographe

automatic *adj.* automatique

automatically *adv.* automatique

automobile *n.* automobile, char, voiture

autumn *n.* automne

auxiliary *adj.* auxiliaire

available *adj.* obtenable

avalanche *n.* avalasse

avarice *n.* avarice, chicheresse, chichetesse, chicheté

avaricious *adj.* avare, chiche, intéressé, ratché

avenge *v.* revenger, venger **avenge o.s.** se revenger, se venger

avenue *n.* avenue

average *adj.* ordinaire

average *n.* moyenne

aversion *n.* **cause aversion** dégoûter **have an aversion** avoir dédain de

avert *v.* détourner

avid *adj.* avide

avidity *n.* avidité

avocado *n.* avocat

avoid *v.* aider, esquiver, se préserver, éviter **expression used to avoid answering a question or naming s.t. one does not wish to reveal** sisi à dents

avow *v.* avouer

avowal *n.* déclaration

Avoyelles *n.* **Avoyelles Parish** Avoyelles

await *v.* attendre, espérer

awake *adj.* réveillé **awake again** réveillé **stay awake** veiller **up and awake** debout

awaken *v.* réveiller, se réveiller, éveiller

awakening *n.* réveil

aware *adj.* **become aware** s'apercevoir **be aware of** réaliser

away *adv.* au large, GONE **away from** (à) côté de **away from the road or bayou** large **far away** au large **right away** carrément, immédiatement, tout de suite / toutesuite, tout de suite, à la minute

awful *adj.* bétaille, cruel, horrible

awfully *adv.* diablement, terriblement

awkward *adj.* emplâtre comme du goudron, gauche, gommeux, maladroit, malpris à **awkward and dull-witted** pâlot **awkward and slow** emplâtre **awkward and slow-moving person** cataplasme **clumsy, awkward person** bidet **any awkward or clumsy act or utterance** gaucherie **be in a awkward or uncomfortable situation** suer comme un bâtard à une réunion de famille / suer comme un nègre à la messe / suer comme les Ponce

awkwardly *adv.* palotte, à (la) rebours

awkwardness *n.* dégaine, gaucherie

awl *n.* alêne

awning *n.* auvent

awry *adv.* à la mistanflute

ax *n.* casse-tête, hache **ax used for trimming of shingles** hache à parer **double-edged ax** hache à deux taillants **foot ax** hache à pied **single-edged ax** hache à un taillant

axle *n.* essieu **axle grease** graisse à charette

azalea *n.* azélia

B

babble *n.* bavardage

babble *v.* bagueuler, bavarder

babbler *n.* bavard, bavardeur

babbling *n.* radote

babe *n.* bèbe

baby *n.* bébé, bèbe, enfant, petit, poupon, bébé **baby bed** lit à bébé **baby bib** bavette, serviette à bébé **baby bottle** biberon, bouteille de bébé / bouteille à {de} lait, bouteille, fiole **baby carriage** boghei **baby doll** catin à viser **baby tooth** caquisse **toy baby** titite

baccharis *n.* manglier

bachelor *n.* bachelier, vieux garçon **bachelor life** vie de garçon **bachelor quarters** garçonnière **bachelor's button** vieux garçon **old bachelor** vieux garçon

bachelorhood *n.* vie de garçon

back *adv.* BACK, de {en} retour, re-, à BACK **take one step forward and two steps back** faire un pas en avant et deux en arrière

back *n.* (d')en arrière, dos, rein, reintier, dossier **back of a boat** derrière du bateau **in back** en arrière **lower back** rein **strained back** détour de reins **in back of** derrière **lower back pain** mal aux reins **behind one's back** dans le dos **behind s.o.'s back** en arrière (de) **in the back** en arrière (de), en arrière, par en arrière **turn one's back** tourner le dos **break the back of** éreinter **sprain in the back** forçure **strain in the back** tour dans le dos **talk behind s.o.'s back** parler en dessous **twisting of the back** tour de reins **wrench in the back** tour de reins **space under the back seat of a skiff** panneau **hurt or break one's back** s'éreinter **carry one's belongings on one's back** être comme la tortue **the width of a person's back** écarrure **twinge of pain in one's back** point de côté

back *v.* BACK **back down** bouquer, cailler, caler, caponner, rebouquer **back out** caler le bouchon **back up** BACK, faire BACK, reculer, se reculer, seconder

back-biting *n.* mépris

back-breaking *adj.* tue-corps

backache *n.* mal aux reins, tour dans le dos, tour de reins

backbone *n.* rein, reintier, épine

backdraft *n.* rafalement

backdraft *v.* rafaler

background *n.* **person's background** dossier

backhand *n.* dossière

backside *n.* tchu

backstrap *n.* **backstrap loin** reintier

backwards *adv.* devant derrière, à la renverse, à l'envers / à renvers, à reculons

backwoods *n.* criée des cannes

bacon *n.* béquine, jambon, lard entrelardé

bad *adj.* chéti, croche, espiègle, indigne, malva, maudit, mauvais comme une puce {la gale} / mauvais comme un {une} serpent à sonnette, mauvais, méchant, pauvre, pirate, pourri, vilain **bad condition** dépit **bad luck** malheur **bad mood** humeur furvoyante **bad people** du chéti monde **bad person** calypson, yeux barrés (comme un cabri) **bad taste** mauvais goût **bad things** mauvaises affaires **bad girl or woman** pouliche **be bad** avoir un cœur noir **feel bad** se sentir chéti **go bad** se gâter **half bad** à demi mal **look bad** avoir mauvaise mine **morally bad** chéti **smell bad** puer le tigre {chien} **too bad** foutant, tant pire **be bad luck** être la nenaine (à qqn) **exhibiting bad behavior** mortifiant **in bad condition** mal harnaché **in bad shape** mal harnaché, malfoutu **in bad taste** mardi gras **from bad to worse** de mal en pire **as bad as the mange** maudit comme une gale **it's too bad** c'est bernique, c'est dommage **say s.t. bad** planter un piquant **be in bad condition** être au dépit **in a bad mood** de {en} mauvaise humeur, enflé, mal en train **go from bad to worse** dégrouler **in a bad, mean way** mauvais **wicked, evil, bad, malicious person or thing** maudit, méchant **they are equally bad** ça chie dans le même sac **be in a bad mood** avoir un pet accroché, avoir une croche (d') accrochée, babiller, être dans les brindezingues, être dans ses feurdaines, être en chimère **be in a bad way** filer un mauvais coton **anything old, in bad shape or disrepair** baraque **one is as bad as the other** caca pour merde, c'est la faim et la soif, Taupin vaut Maurin **anything old and in bad condition** racatcha **do s.t. which could have bad**

consequences mettre le pied dans la boue **person who is in a bad humor** bâton merdeux

bad *n.* mal **take the good with the bad** manger les grillots avec le tactac

bad-tempered *adj.* babillard

badge *n.* emblème

badly *adv.* mal, chétiment, vilain

badness *n.* maudiceté, mauditerie, méchanceté

baffle *v.* bafouer, interboler

bag *n.* sac **game bag** carnassière, carrelet, havresac **hunting bag** carnassière, carrelet **paper bag** paquet, sac à {en} papier **travel bag** cabas **put into a bag** ensaquer *pl.* **have bags under one's eyes** avoir les yeux cernés

bag *v.* ensaquer

bagasse *n.* bagasse

baggage *n.* bagage **baggage car** char à bagages

bagging *n.* ensachage

baguette *n.* flûte de pain

bail *n.* anse, caution **put up bail** cautionner **stand or go bail** servir de caution {cautionnement / CO-SIGN}

bail *v.* **bail out** cautionner

bailiff *n.* crieur de cour, crieur

bailing *n.* cautionnement

bailiwick *n.* territoire

bait *n.* aboëtte, appât, poutine

bait *v.* aboëtter, appâter, empatter

bake *v.* farcir

baked *adj.* farci

baker *n.* boulanger

bakery *n.* bakerie, boulangerie

baking *n.* **baking pan** casse, plateau **baking powder** BAKING, soda à pain, YEAST **baking soda** soda **Parrot and Monkey brand baking powder** YEAST macaque

balance *n.* balan, balance, reste, romaine, équilibre, balance **lose one's balance** perdre son {l'} équilibre **lose one's balance or equilibrium** perdre son balan

balance *v.* balancer **balance o.s.** se balancer

balanced *adj.* **be balanced** être dessus un balan

balancing *n.* balan

bald *adj.* BALD HEAD, chauve **be bald** avoir la batture

bald-headed *adj.* tête chauve

bale *n.* botte, rouleau, balle **bale of hay** botte de foin *pl.* **put into bales** baller

bale *v.* baller, botteler, emballer

baled *adj.* **be baled** s'emballer

baler *n.* emballeuse

baling *n.* emballage **baling machine** emballeuse

balk *v.* rebuter, regimber, se rebuter, se regimber, faire rétif

balky *adj.* buté, rebuté, rétif

ball *n.* bal, BALL, balle, boule, boulotte, pelote **ball game** game de pelote **ball player** joueur de pelote **ball of gum** boule de gomme **billiard ball** pure **dust ball** duvet **masked ball** bal masqué **popcorn ball** boule de tactac **rubber ball** pelote en élastique **tennis ball** tennis **wedding ball or dance** bal de noce

ballad *n.* **sad or tragic ballad** complainte

ballet *n.* ballet

balloon *n.* BALLOON, bouloune

ballot *n.* ticket

ballroom *n.* HALL

balsam *n.* liège

balsamine *n.* belsamine, herbe honteuse

Baltimore *n.* **Baltimore oriole** pape de bois

balustrade *n.* ballustrade

bamboo *n.* bambou, canne farouche, canne marronne, canne sauvage, canne terre haute, canne à fuseau, canne à pêche {pêcher}, canuche

banana *n.* banane **banana tree** bananier

band *n.* BAND, bande, bastringue, batelée, lichefrippe, ribondelle, bague, bande, cavaillade, gang **band of cloth** bande **band or girdle of elastic material** corselette **belly band** sangle **jazz band** JAZZ BAND **rubber band** élastique

bandage *n.* bandage **finger bandage** doignon, fourreau **adhesive bandage or plaster** sparadraffe

bandage *v.* bander

bandit *n.* bandit

bang *npl.* **bangs** toupet

banish *v.* bannir, déporter, exiler

banishment *n.* bannissement, exil

banister *n.* ballustrade

banjo *n.* banjo

bank *n.* banc, banque, levée, terrasse, écore **bank account** acompte **bank of a stream that has no levee** bordure **cloud bank** château **be on the bank** être en bas l'écore *pl.* **not trust banks** cacher son argent dans des cornes à bœuf

bank *v.* endosser, entourer **bank up** butter, chausser, rechausser, renchausser, terrasser

banker *n.* banquier

banking *n.* entourage

bankrupt *adj.* **go bankrupt** faire banqueroute, tomber en botte **one who is bankrupt** banqueroutier

bankruptcy *n.* banqueroute

banns *npl.* bans **publish the banns** publier les bans

banquet *n.* banco, banquet, festin, ramequin

bantam *n.* **bantam chicken** bendé

banter *v.* bêtiser

bantering *n.* **silly bantering** folerie

baptism *n.* baptême **baptism record or certificate** baptistaire **emergency baptism** ondoiement

baptismal *adj.* **baptismal registry** registre

Baptist *adj.* baptiste

Baptist *n.* Baptiste **Saint John the Baptist** St. Jean Baptiste

baptistery *n.* baptistaire

baptize *v.* baptiser **baptize without a church ceremony**

endoyer **baptize without the usual rites and prayers of a church baptism** ondoyer

baptizer *n.* baptiseur

bar *n.* bar, BARROOM, cabaret, café, comptoir, barre **bar or beam used for leverage** levier **candy bar** barre de candi **mosquito bar** bère, drap à maringoins, moustiquaire **rein bar** croix **swing bar** palonnier **transversal bar in row-boats** barre **lock with a bar** barrer **thin, straight cylindrical piece or bar of metal or wood** barreau *pl.* **enclose with bars** barreauter **made of bars** barreauté **put upright bars in a banister** bâtonner

bar *v.* barreauter **bar off** décacher

barb *n.* croc, dardon, piquant

barbecue *n.* barbecue **barbecue pit** barbecue

barbecue *v.* barbecue

barbel *n.* barbe, barbillon

barber *n.* barbier, raseur

barbershop *n.* BARBER-SHOP

barbwire *n.* **barbwire fence** barrière à (fil de fer à) piquants

bare *adj.* nu, à l'air **bare or barren spot** manque

bare *v.* grincher **bare o.s.** se découvrir **bare the chest of** dépoitrailler **bare the roots of** décoller **bare one's neck and shoulders** se décolleter

bare-back *adv.* **ride bare-back** monter à poil

bare-headed *adj.* nu-tête / tête-nue

barefoot *adj.* nu-pieds / pieds-nus

barely *adv.* à gros grain, à peine

bargain *n.* barguine, DEAL **at a bargain** au marché **strike a bargain** faire marché

bargain *v.* barguiner, rapigner **one who bargains or haggles** barguineur

barge *n.* berge, chaland **flat barge** cageux

baring *n.* **baring of the neck, shoulders, etc.** décolletage

bark *n.* barque, écorce

bark *v.* jappailler, japper

barking *n.* jappement

barn *n.* hangar, magasin de {à} foin, magasin de {à} maïs, magasin, SHED **auction barn** encan **hay barn** magasin de {à} foin **build o.s. a barn, a store** se bâtir un magasin

barnacle *n.* grabon, moque

barnyard *n.* cour de magasin **barnyard animals** basse-cour

barometer *n.* baromètre

baron *n.* baron

baroness *n.* baron

Barre *n.* **Port Barre** Port Barré

barrel *n.* baril, barrique, boucaut **barrel bung** bombe **barrel hoop** frette **barrel maker** faiseur de baril **barrel stave** douelle **barrel of a double-barreled shotgun** fourche **barrel that holds 33 1/3 gallons** tiercent **gun barrel** canon de fusil **rinse water barrel** baril de lavure **forty gallon oil barrel** baril **one half of a barrel used as a washtub, water trough, etc.** barrique *pl.* **put into casks or barrels** enformer

barren *adj.* **bare or barren spot** manque

barrier *n.* barrière **barrier made of boards** barrière en pieux debout **barrier made of floating logs** bôme **erect a fence or barrier around** entourer

barring *conj.* sauf que

barring *prep.* sauf

barroom *n.* BARROOM, cabaret, café, saloon

barter *v.* barguiner, brocanter, changeoter, faire (un/une) barguine (avec), s'échanger, se barguiner, échanger

barterer *n.* brocanteur

bartering *n.* brocantage

base *adj.* **base person** cœur noir

base *n.* bas, base, but, pied

base *v.* **base o.s.** se fonder **base on** baser sur **base o.s., one's ideas or actions on** se baser sur

baseball *n.* BALL, pelote **baseball cap** CAP, casque à bec, casque, casquette **game of baseball** pelote

bashful *adj.* gêné, honteux, timide **be bashful** se gêner **be timid, shy, bashful** avoir honte

bashfulness *n.* gêne, honte, timidité

basic *adj.* **main, essential, or basic thing** principal

basil *n.* basilique

basilica *n.* basilique

basin *n.* baille, bassin

basis *n.* base **on a regular basis** réglé, régulier, régulièrement

basket *n.* cabas, corbeille, manne, panier, pochon **basket or container** champagne, panier champagne, panier chinois, panier **bushel basket** boisseau, manne **collection basket** quête **Easter basket** nique de Pâques **grocery basket** panier de grosseries **rectangular bark basket used for berry picking** tasseau

basketball *n.* pelote au panier

bass *n.* perche, truite **bass drum** basse **bass key** second **black bass** truite d'eau douce **double bass** basse **large-mouthed bass** perche **largemouth bass** grande gueule, truite verte, truite **rock bass** patassa à grande gueule **spotted bass** truite verte **string bass** basse **striped bass** barre, truite barrée

bassinet *n.* bassinet

bastard *n.* bâtard, champignon **bastard file** briqué, lime-rapé {-râpe}

bastardization *n.* abâtardissage, abâtardissement

bastardize *v.* abâtardir

bastardized *adj.* abâtardi, abâtardi **be bastardized** s'abâtardir

bastardizing *n.* abâtardissage, abâtardissement

baste *v.* faufiler

bat *n.* chauve-souris, couvre-joint, souris-chaude **bat of carded wool or cotton ready for spinning** écardon

bat *v.* **bat one's eyelids** battre les yeux

bath *n.* bain **bath slipper** soulier de bain **public bath** baignoire **take a bath** prendre un bain, se baigner **take a dust bath** se vanner

bathe *v.* baigner, se baigner

bather *n.* baigneur
bathhouse *n.* baignoire
bathing *n.* baignage **bathing suit** rechange de bain
bathroom *n.* cabine, cabinet, cacatoir, chambre à bain(s), commode **go to the bathroom** aller à la cabine, aller à la commode, aller à la toilette
bathtub *n.* bac à bain, bac, baignoire, baille à bain {baigner}, baille à laver, baille, bain, bassin
batiste *n.* batiste
battalion *n.* bataillon
batten *n.* couvre-joint, latte
batter *n.* pâte, tapoir
batter *v.* bosser
battery *n.* batterie **battery acid** acide de batterie
battle *n.* bataille
battlefield *n.* champ de bataille
batty *adj.* toqué
bauble *n.* bébelle, fanfreluche, mirlifiche *pl.* **baubles** affûtiaux
bawl *v.* brailler, gueuler **bawl out** agoniser, foutre HELL, foutre une chauffe, foutre une pourgale (à)
bawling *adj.* gueulard
bawling *n.* braille, braillerie **bawling out** ratatouille
bay *n.* anse, baie **bay leaf** laurier **bay tree** laurier **bay extending from a stream** raccroc **red bay tree** petit laurier **sweet bay tree** laurier doux
bayberry *n.* cirier
bayonet *n.* baïonnette **bayonet tree** baïonnette **Spanish bayonet** pite
bayou *n.* bayou, rivière **down the bayou** en bas **up the bayou** en haut du bayou, en haut **head waters of a bayou** marais **low area near a bayou** marais **mouth of a river or bayou** engueulement
bazaar *n.* bazar
BB *n.* **BB shot** plomb
be *v.* se faire, être, aller, avoir, faire **be from** venir **leave be** laisser tranquille **let be** laisser faire **cause to be** mettre, rendre **it can be** il y a moyen **pretend to be** se prétendre **wish to be** se vouloir **as it should be** comme de juste **can it really be?** tonnerre est-il {c'est-ti} possible? **cause o.s. to be** se rendre
beach *n.* playe
bead *n.* perle *pl.* **prayer beads** chapelet **rosary beads** rosaire **blessed rosary beads** chapelet bénit **say the beads** égrainer le chapelet
beadle *n.* bedeau
beagle *n.* chien à lapins, taïaut
beak *n.* bec
beakfull *n.* becquetée
beam *n.* flèche, lambourde, madrier, rayon, sole **floor beam** lambourde **support beam** solive, soliveau **timber beam** sole **bar or beam used for leverage** levier
bean *n.* BEAN, fève gourgane, fève, graine, haricot, pois **bean trellis** berceau de fèves **bunch bean** fève foulée **bush bean** haricot de chaland, haricot nain **butter bean** fève platte {plate}, haricot cire **Christmas bean** fève platte {plate} **coffee bean** graine de café **dwarf bean** fève foulée, fève nain {nine} **green bean** BEAN vert, haricot **jelly bean** crotte de poule **kidney bean** fève de foie **lima bean** fève platte {plate} **navy bean** fève blanche **pole bean** haricot (de) rame **red bean** fève rouge, pois rouge, quarante-quatre **snap bean** haricot **string bean** fève à la brasse, haricot (de) rame, haricot **stringless bean** haricot de factrie **wax bean** haricot cire **white bean** BEAN blanc, fayot, fève marronne, pois blanc **yard-long bean** haricot à brasse **castor bean plant** palma **coral bean tree** mamou **bush butter bean** fève platte naine **long green bean** fève de yard **vining string bean** haricot (de) rame **butter pea lima bean** marionnette **hull of the coffee bean** parchemin *pl.* **red beans and rice** bécassine créole
beanie *n.* caloquinte, calotte
bear *n.* ours **black bear** ours noir **female bear** ours **stuffed bear** catin de l'ours **teddy bear** catin de l'ours
bear *v.* endurer, porter, supporter, produire **bear down** peser **bear tales** rapporter **bear a grudge** porter une rancune **bear in mind** retiendre en mémoire **bear the burden of one's problems** porter sa croix
bearable *adj.* endurable
beard *n.* barbe **beard stubble** chicot
bearded *adj.* barbeux
beardgrass *n.* **bushy beardgrass** paille jaune
bearer *n.* porteur **pall bearer** apporteur, porteur **tale bearer** rapporteur
bearing *npl.* **regain one's bearings** se retrouver
beast *n.* bétaille **threatening beast** tataille **wild beast** bête farouche **you beast!** espèce de bétaille!
beat *adj.* **anything old or beat up** hariat
beat *n.* temps
beat *v.* abominer, abîmer, assaper, bûchailler, bûcher, baleiner, battre, BEAT, bâcler, canonner, carder, crimer, flauber, hacher, herser, louper, massacrer, passer à la baleine, piler, racler, rincer, roquer, roucheter, roustailler, sabouler, saganer, tiller, écouenner, élinguer, épiauler, étriper, battre, brasser, toquer **beat again** rebattre **beat down** abattre, racler **beat it** filer, flanquer son camp, foutre le camp, foutre le champ, haler ses caniques, péter son camp, se haler, va te cacher / va te faire cacher à Lafayette **beat mercilessly** assommer **beat s.o.** sacrer une gratte {volée} à qqn **beat unmercifully** extravaguer **beat up** abîmer, bûcher, battre, crimer, donner des coups, doubler, esquinter, foutre des coups (à qqn), hacher, massacrer, passer à coups de poing, passer à la bastringue, piler, ramoner, tamiser, émecter **beat violently** épurer **beat each other** se bûcher **beat s.o. up** en foutre à qqn, foutre ça à qqn, sauter sur le casaquin de qqn **beat up severely** assommer **beat s.o. in competition** faire

chiquer poteaux à qqn **beat with a stick** bâtonner, passer à coups de bâton **beat with a strap** sangler **not beat around the bush** pas aller les quatre chemins **beats me** ça me BEAT **that beats everything** ça par exemple! **that beats me** ça me gagne! **one who beats others** bûcheur

beaten *adj.* **he/she should be beaten!** prends ça à coups de bâton!

beater *n.* brasseur, char-à-banc, batteur **egg beater** palette à z-œufs

beating *n.* bûchée, battage, dandine, douille, décoction, dégelée, passée, pile, raclure, raclée, ramasse, ratatouille, rincée, rinçure, roussequette, rousseture, roussetée, salade, suée, trempe, trempée **beating of plowshare to sharpen it** battage (de) charrue **severe beating** pimpette **give a beating** flanquer une décoction, massacrer la couenne, pignocher, tamiser **give a scolding, beating** foutre une passée

beau *n.* cavalier

beautification *n.* embellissement

beautiful *adj.* beau **become more beautiful** rembellir **become more beautiful or more handsome** se bellesir

beautify *v.* embellir **beautify again** rembellir

beauty *n.* beauté **beauty mark** signe postiche, signe **beauty queen** reine **restore the beauty of** rembellir

beaver *n.* castor

because *conj.* (par) rapport que, car, d'abord que, depuis (que), en raison que, par rapport que, parce que, puisque, à cause que **because of** (par) rapport à, par rapport à, à cause de

become *v.* aboutir, devenir, rendre, tourner, venir, virer, faire, se mettre **become of** devenir **cause to become** mettre, rendre, tourner **cause o.s. to become** se rendre

becoming *adj.* décent

bed *n.* lit, chartil **bed canopy** ciel de lit **bed cover** couverte **bed frame** carré de lit **bed linens** linge **bed post** colonne **bed staff** bâton à {de} lit **bed in bed** à la paille **baby bed** lit à bébé **camp bed** couchette **canopy bed** lit à ciel **double bed** lit double, lit qui couche un {deux} **flower bed** banquette, parterre **folding bed** baudette **iron bed** bois de lit en fer **made-up bed** lit gréyé **oyster bed** banc d'huîtres **roll-away bed** lit à roulettes **single bed** lit qui couche un {deux}, lit étroit {simple} **trundle bed** lit à roulettes, roulette **twin bed** lit étroit {simple} **go to bed** s'ouacher, se coucher, se niquer **make a bed** arranger un lit **out of bed** debout **put to bed** coucher, mettre (à) coucher / mettre au lit, mettre au lit **wet the bed** retremper le lit, tremper le lit **go to bed early** se coucher avec les poules **put to bed again** recoucher **go to bed with all one's clothes on** se coucher tout rond **foot of the bed** pied de lit **go back to bed** se recoucher **head of the bed** tête de lit **headboard of a bed** barre du lit **put back to bed** recoucher **space between a bed and the wall** arouelle **get up out of bed** se lever **said of one who goes to bed early** calibossé **get up on the wrong side of the bed** se lever sur le mauvais pied

bedbug *n.* punaise de maison {lit}, punaise

bedding *n.* linge, litage

bedraggled *adj.* **any bedraggled, forlorn-looking man or boy** juif-errant

bedroom *n.* chambre à coucher, chambre à lit **bedroom slipper** savate, slip, soulier de maison

bedsheet *n.* drap

bedspread *n.* courtepointe **quilted bedspread** édradon

bedspring *n.* ressort de lit

bee *n.* bourdon **bee hive** caisse à mouches, chouce de miel, cloche, ruche **carpenter bee** bourdon de bois / bourdon de la maison **quilting bee** piquerie

beech *n.* **beech tree** hêtre

beef *n.* bœuf, viande de bœuf, viande de bête **beef stew** fricassée de viande **salted beef** prime

beer *n.* bière **homemade beer** bière créole **root beer** rootbière

beet *n.* betterave **beet greens** queues de betteraves **beet leaves** queues de betteraves

beetle *n.* barbot, bête à Bon Dieu, petite bétaille **blister beetle** catalique **dung beetle** fouille-merde **green beetle** bourdon de terre **Japanese beetle** hanneton **May beetle** bête à chandelle **whirligig beetle** café, castor **big black beetle** capecape **larva of a tiger beetle** charlotte, tourloulou **larva of the tiger beetle or pill bug** loulou

before *adv.* auparavant

before *conj.* avant (que), premièrement que

before *prep.* auparavant de, avant de, avant, devant, moins

beforehand *adv.* auparavant, d'avance, premier

beg *v.* béguer, aller aux portes, bourlinguer, mendianer, plaider, prier, prêcher, quêter, supplier, tchamander, demander la charité, tchamander **sit on its haunches and beg** faire (sa) belle **one who is always begging** quêteur

beggar *n.* bégueur, quêteur, tchamandeur

beggary *n.* mendianité

begging *adj.* demandant

begging *n.* mendianité **go begging** aller aux portes

begin *v.* commencer, entamer, originer, prendre, se mettre à **begin again** recommencer, reprendre

beginner *n.* débutant, novice

beginning *n.* commencement, début, entrain, naissance, partance **new beginning** recommencement **from beginning to end** de fond en comble **at the beginning** en partant **make a beginning** faire un entrain, se mettre en train **a bad beginning, a good ending** mauvaise partance, bonne arrivée

begonia bogonia

begrudge *v.* envier

behave *v.* agir, se comporter, se conduire **behave arrogantly** faire le grand pour ses culottes **behave defiantly** faire le détestable **behave impolitely** faire l'effronté **behave arrogantly or self-righteously** monter sur ses grands chevaux **you think you are behaving like an adult, but you are**

being foolish or impudent tu crois (que) t'es maître et majeur

behaved *adj.* emmené

behavior *n.* comporte, conduite, direction **exhibiting bad behavior** mortifiant **be on one's good behavior** faire bonne mine

behind *adv.* en arrière **be behind** être en arrière **from behind** par derrière, par en arrière de **right behind** droite en arrière

behind *n.* derrière, saint-frusquin, pompon **it's your behind if you think you're going to get away with that** c'est ton zinzin **have a skinny behind** avoir des fesses de moiselle

behind *prep.* derrière, en arrière (de)

being *n.* être **living being** vivant **imaginary being used to frighten children** badjo, croquemitaine

belch *n.* rot

belch *v.* roter

belfry *n.* clocher

Belgium *n.* Belgique

belie *v.* démentir

belief *n.* croyance

believable *adj.* croyable

believe *v.* croire, figurer, penser **make believe** faire accroire, faire semblant (de), prétendre **I don't believe you** belle affaire!, cache-toi, va te cacher / va te faire cacher à Lafayette, va te coucher **know what to believe** connaître où cabri porte la queue **that's hard to believe** ça c'est fort (quand même)

believer *n.* croyant

bell *n.* cloche, sonnette, cloche **bell ringer** sonneur **jingle bell** cloche

bellow *npl.* **bellows** soufflet

bellow *v.* beugler, hurler

bellowing *n.* beuglage, beuglement

belly *n.* ventrage, ventre **belly band** sangle **belly button** bourrique, cabri, nombril **big belly** bedaine **soft distended belly of a laying hen** pondoire

bellyache *n.* mal au {de} ventre, mal d'estomac

bellyful *n.* ventrée

belong *v.* appartenir **belong to** être pour

belonging *npl.* **household belongings** butin **carry one's belongings on one's back** être comme la tortue

belonging *prep.* **belonging to** pour, de, à

beloved *adj.* cher, chéri

beloved *n.* bien-aimé

below *adv.* bas, en bas, en dessous, par-dessous

below *prep.* dessous, par-dessous, sous

belt *n.* ceinture **mechanical belt** bande **buckle o.s., one's belt** se boucler

bench *n.* banc **bench mark** borne **work bench** table à travailler, établi

bend *n.* cobissure, croche, coude **bend in a river** pointe

bend *v.* cabosser, cobir, crochir, fléchir, pencher, plier, ployer, se plier, tordre **bend back** replier, reployer **bend o.s.** se ployer **bend over** se baisser, se pencher, se ployer **bend in or out with a hat** cabaner

bendable *adj.* ployable, ployant

bender *n.* **go on a bender** se foutre une cuite, se prendre une cuite

bending *n.* ployage **bending over of cornstalks** ployage du maïs

beneath *adv.* bas, en bas, en dessous

beneath *prep.* dessous, sous

benediction *n.* bénédiction

benefactor *n.* bienfaiteur

beneficial *adj.* **be beneficial** payer

beneficiary *n.* bénéficié

benefit *n.* avantage, bénéfice *pl.* **benefits** bénéfice

benefit *v.* bénéficier, jouir, payer, profiter

bent *adj.* assodié, chirvauché, cobi, courbé, croche, crochu, tordu **bent over** en deux **bent in two** en deux **become bent or warped** se crochir

bent *n.* tournure **have a bad bent or inclination** avoir une mauvaise tournure

bequeath *v.* laisser

beret *n.* béret

berry *n.* mûre **berry juice** vin de mûre **berry preserves** confiture aux mûres

beseech *v.* supplier

beside *prep.* (à) côté de, côté, en dehors de, sur le côté de

besides *adv.* aussi bien, puis, à part de

besides *conj.* bien que

besides *prep.* autre que, dehors

besmear *v.* beurriner, emberner, embeurriner **besmear o.s.** s'emberner **besmear with excrement** emmerder **besmear o.s. with excrement** s'emmerder **besmear with mud or dirt** embarbouiller **besmear with excrement or some unpleasant substance** emmicheter **besmear o.s. with excrement or some unpleasant substance** s'emmicheter

best *adj.* meilleur

best *adv.* mieux

best *n.* fleur **do one's best** faire son mieux, faire son possible **get the best of** engagner, youquer **make the best of a situation** manger les grillots avec le tactac **take the best of s.t. first without consideration for others** manger le pain blanc en premier **put on one's Sunday best** se farauder **you have to make the best of a bad situation** si on peut pas téter maman, il faut téter mémère

best *v.* faire manger de l'avoine (à qqn)

bet *n.* gage, gageure, pari

bet *v.* gager, gambler, parier **bet each other** se parier

betray *v.* beurrer, foutre dedans, trahir **betray the trust of** tromper

betroth *v.* fiancer

betrothal *n.* accordement

better *adj.* meilleur **be better** aller {être} mieux, valoir mieux **get better** en reprendre, improuver, s'amollir, se refaire **make better** abonnir, improuver **be getting better** aller {être} mieux **begin to feel better** rapiquer **make o.s. feel better** se soulager **so much the better** tant mieux **make s.t. seem better than it is** siroter **make something seem better than it is by exaggeration** faire des fleurs **become or be made better** s'abonnir **one who thinks he's better or stronger than others** taureau

better *adv.* mieux **much better** beaucoup mieux / un tas mieux **I had better, you had better, he had better, etc.** je ferais mieux / tu ferais mieux / il ferait mieux, etc.

better *n.* **so much the better** tant mieux

better *v.* bonifier **better o.s.** se bonifier

betting *n.* gamblage

bettor *n.* gageur, parieur

between *prep.* entre

bewildered *adj.* extravagué

bewitch *v.* charmer

bias *n.* biais **bias tape** biais

biased *adj.* préjugé

bib *n.* **baby bib** bavette, serviette à bébé

Bible *n.* bible **the Bible** parole

biblical *adj.* biblique

bicker *v.* chamailler, chicaner, se chamailler, se chicaner, se chipoter, se quereller **bicker with one another** se disputailler

bickering *n.* bisbille, halaillement

bicycle *n.* bicycle, vélocipède **by bicycle** à bicycle

bid *n.* offre

big *adj.* beau, grand, gros, massif **big, show, dowdy woman** caouane **extremely big** archigrand **too big for one's britches** trop grand pour ses culottes **anything big or grotesquely out of proportion** zombi

Big *adj.* **Big Dipper** étoile à queue

bigger *adj.* **get bigger** grossir, s'égrandir, égrandir **make bigger** grossir, égrandir

bigmouth *n.* attrape-mouches / attrape à mouches

bilberry *n.* myrtille

bile *n.* bile

bilious *adj.* **be bilious** avoir la bile en mouvement

bill *n.* bec, BILL, billet **legislative bill** mesure

bill *v.* charger

billfold *n.* porte-monnaie, portefeuille

billfull *n.* becquetée

billiard *n.* **billiard ball** pure **billiard cue** queue de billard *pl.* **billiards** billard

billion *n.* billion

bin *n.* **potato bin** pataterie

bind *n.* **caught in a bind** malpris

bind *v.* amarrer, coincer, lier **person who binds or bundles** amarreur

bindweed *n.* **field bindweed** liserine

binge *n.* soûlerie **drinking binge** tchacaillerie

bingo *n.* bingo **bingo hall** bingo **bingo session** bingo **play bingo** bingo

bingo *v.* faire bingo

binoculars *npl.* longue-vue

bird *n.* oiseau, zozo **bird cage** ajoupa, cage à z-oiseau **bird snare** cage **bird trap** cage, filet **bird's claw** griffe **bird of prey** oiseau de grapigne {grapine} **butcher bird** mangeur moqueur, moqueur français {muet / sauvage / d'hiver}, pirate **cuckoo bird** coucou, longue queue **frigate bird** carencro de mer, frégate **man-o'-war bird** carencro de mer **marsh bird** râle **odd bird** abricot, abricotier **rain bird** oiseau de pluie **a bird in the hand is worth two in the bush** un oiseau dans la main en vaut deux dans une talle **flip the bird** montrer le doigt **any long-legged bird with a spatula-shaped beak** spatule **kill a bird in flight or on the wing** tuer un oiseau au vol *pl.* **birds of a feather flock together** chien mord chien **covey of birds** volière **flock of birds in flight** volier, volée

bird's-eye *n.* **bird's-eye cloth** ouvré

birdcall *n.* moque

birdhouse *n.* maison à z-oiseau

birth *n.* naissance **birth certificate** baptistaire **birth control** empêchement de famille **birth place** pays de naissance **give birth** accoucher, faire la culbute, rendre au monde **practice birth control** empêcher la famille **help give birth** délivrer **be on the verge of giving birth** remouiller

birthday *n.* fête de naissance, fête

birthmark *n.* dartre, signe de beauté, signe **cause to have a birthmark** marquer

biscuit *n.* biscuit, gonfleau **sea biscuit** gâteau **unsuccessful biscuit** mailloche

bishop *n.* évêque **bishop's residence** évêché **title of a bishop, a governor, etc.** votre excellence

bishopric *n.* évêché

bison *n.* **American bison** bœuf sauvage

bisque *n.* bisque **crawfish bisque** bisque d'écrevisses

bit *n.* bosse, bridon, escalin, frein, grignote, morceau, mèche, once, peu, picaillon, tierlambèche, vrille, bout, mors **bit or piece** grillot **dock bit** écluse **drill bit** DRILL **little bit** goûtée, peu **tiny bit** idée **drill bit for metal** mèche en fer **drill bit for wood** mèche en bois **a little bit** un petit brin **a tiny bit** un tout petit peu **bite the bit** prendre le mors aux dents **not one bit** pas un foutre **quite a bit** joliment **a little bit of** un peu de *pl.* **bits** babiche, des petits boutailles **to bits** en cannelles

bite *n.* mordure

bite *v.* mordre **bite again** remordre **bite at** chicoter **bite the bit** prendre le mors aux dents

biting *adj.* grappilleux

biting *n.* mordure

bitter *adj.* amer comme du fiel, amer

bittern *n.* **American bittern** biorque, butor, cape-cape, couac-soleil, couac, garde-soleil **least bittern** cap-cap doré

bitterness *n.* rancœur

bitterweed *n.* absinthe, herbe amère

bizarre *adj.* baroque, bizarre, suspect **look strange or bizarre** faire drôle

blabber *n.* bagueulard

blabber *v.* bagueuler

black *adj.* noir comme du charbon {de la suit / l'as de pique / un fond de chaudière}, noiron, négrite **black child** négrillon **black eye** nioque **black man** noiron **black person** bossal, carencro, congo, macaque, noir, négrillon, nègre, tête à raisins **black woman** noirette, négresse **black person who speaks Cajun or Creole** nègre créole {français} **black person who speaks French or Creole** Créole **black person who does not speak Creole or Cajun** nègre américain **dark black** congo **turn black** noircir, se noircir **dark-skinned black man** corbeau **make black and blue** bleusir **give a black eye** casser un œil (à qqn), donner un BLACK-EYE **have some black ancestry** avoir un ravet dans la poche **in the manner of black people** nègre **person who has one black and three white grandparents** quarteron **term used to refer to black people collectively** négraille

black *n.* noir **lamp black** noir de lampe

blackberry *n.* mûre d'éronce / mûre de ronces hautes / mûre douce {haute}, mûre **blackberry bush** talle d'éronces, éronce **go blackberry picking** aller aux mûres

blackbird *n.* merle, pape choc, tchoc, étourneau **red-winged blackbird** caporal, étourneau **redwing blackbird** tchoc aux ailes rouges / choc aile rouge, z-aile rouge

blackboard *n.* ardoise, tableau

blacken *v.* noircir

blackhaw *n.* alisier

blackhead *n.* suppuron

blackish *adj.* noiret, noirâtre

blackjack *n.* **blackjack vine** liane noire

blacklisted *adj.* marqué

blackout *v.* BLACKOUT

blacksmith *n.* forgeron, travaillant de forge **blacksmith shop** forge

blacktop *n.* BLACKTOP

bladder *n.* blague **air bladder** blague **gall bladder** fiel **swim bladder** blague **void one's bladder or bowels** faire ses besoins

blade *n.* roulette, brin, lame **blade or runner of a rocking chair** berceuse **ditch-bank blade** volant **plow blade** lame de charrue, oreille de charrue **shoulder blade** clavicule, palette de l'épaule **rocker, blade, runner of a rocking chair** roulette **rocker, blade, or runner of a rocking chair** maille, marchette

blamable *adj.* blâmable, à blâmer

blame *n.* blâme **lay the blame on** passer la blâme sur **deserving of criticism or blame** méprisable

blame *v.* accuser, blâmer, fauter, reprocher **blame o.s.** se blâmer **condemn or blame o.s.** se condamner **reproach or blame o.s.** se reprocher

blameable *adj.* condamnable

blameless *adj.* innocent

blameworthy *adj.* blâmable

blanch *v.* échauder

blanching *n.* échaudage, échaudement

blank *adj.* **blank space** vide

blank *n.* BLANK

blanket *n.* couvert **hand-woven blanket** couverte de pays **saddle blanket** soutadaire *pl.* **cover with blankets** abrier

blaspheme *v.* blasphémer, jurer

blasphemy *n.* blasphème

blaze *n.* flamme

blaze *v.* flamber

bleach *v.* blanchir, déteindre **bleach again** reblanchir **bleach at night** braliner au serein **bleach s.t. in the sun** braliner au soleil **bleach clothes by putting them in direct sunlight** braliner, mettre à la braline

bleaching *n.* blanchissage, blanchissement

bleed *v.* saigner, saigner **bleed to death** saigner à mort **cause to bleed** faire saigner

bleeding *adj.* saignant, saigneux

blemish *n.* tache

blend *v.* mélanger, mêler

bless *v.* bénir, sanctifier

blessed *adj.* béni, heureux, sacré, saint

Blessed *adj.* **the Blessed Virgin** la Sainte Vierge

blessing *n.* bénédiction **blessing of the boats** bénédiction de bateau

blind *adj.* aveugle, BLIND **blind from birth** aveugle de naissance **blind in one eye** borgne

blind *n.* abat-jour, BLIND, jalousie **hunter's blind** but, talle **outside blind** abat-jour **Venetian blind** abat-jour, jalousie, persienne

blind *v.* aveugler, embrouiller, éblouir, éborgner **blind o.s.** s'aveugler, s'éborgner

blinder *npl.* **blinders** garde-yeux, masque

blindfold *n.* masque

blindfold *v.* masquer les yeux

blindfolded *adj.* masqué

blinding *adj.* aveuglant, éblouissant

blinding *n.* éblouissement

blink *v.* paupiller, quéloëter

blinker *npl.* **blinkers** garde-yeux

blinking *n.* quéloëtement

blissful *adj.* **be blissful** raser

blister *n.* ampoule, blessure, cloche d'eau, cloche, mâchure **fever blister** bobo de fièvre, bouton de fièvre

blister *v.* ampouler, clocher **cause to blister** faire ampouler
blistered *adj.* ampoulé **get blistered** s'ampouler
block *n.* barre, bloc, cale, carreau, pilier de maison, carré **block and tackle** poulie **butcher's block** bloc **city block** bloc, îlet **support block** pilier **a chip off the old block** bon chien tient de race
block *v.* barrer, bloquer
blockade *v.* barreauter, barrer
blockage *n.* blocage **free of a blockage** dégoter
blocked *adj.* **get blocked up, constipated** se bloquer
blocking *n.* barrage
blond *adj.* baille, blanco, blond **blond person** baillonne **pale blond** gouère
blood *n.* sang **blood clot** caillou de sang **blood pressure** pression de sang **blood sausage** boudin rouge **mixed blood** sang mêlé **acid blood condition** sang hâcre **high blood pressure** sang (trop) haut / sang trop fort **low blood pressure** sang (trop) bas **loss of blood** perte de sang **make bad blood** se faire du mauvais sang **offspring of mixed blood** bâtard **person of mixed blood or impure race** sang-mêlé **of mixed breed, mixed blood** abâtardi **person of mixed white and African-American blood** bleu, quarteron **person of mixed white, Native American, and/or African-American blood** Sabine
bloodhound *n.* chien taïaut, taïaut
bloodweed *n.* bon-bout, herbe du {à} sang, herbe à bâton
bloody *adj.* saignant, saigneux
bloom *n.* fleur **in bloom** fleuri
bloom *v.* faire des fleurs, fleurir, monter en fleurs **bloom again** refleurir
blooming *adj.* fleuri
blossom *v.* fleurir
blotter *n.* brouillard
blotting *n.* **blotting paper** pompier
blouse *n.* corsage **old-fashioned child's blouse to which trousers are buttoned** matelote
blow *n.* coup, poque, secousse, élance, secouée **blow with a stick** coup de bâton **finishing blow** coup de grâce **fist blow** poque **mortal blow** coup mortel **deliver a blow** flanquer un coup **deal a blow with the foot / the elbow / the fist / the head, etc.** foutre un coup de pied {coude / poing / tête, etc.} *pl.* **series of blows** saboulée **shower of blows** ramasse, saboulée **volley of blows** trempée **a series of blows or slaps** claquée
blow *v.* souffler, corner **blow out** souffler **blow a horn** corner **blow a conch shell horn** bourgonner **wipe or blow the nose** moucher
blowfly *n.* mouche à ver
blowgun *n.* sarboucane
blowing *n.* **blowing of the nose** mouchage
blowpipe *n.* sarboucane
blubber *v.* gueuler
blue *adj.* bleu **dark blue** bleu foncé / gros bleu **pale blue** bleu pâle / bleu Sainte Vierge **make black and blue** bleusir
blue *npl.* **the blues** hongas **have the blues** avoir le cul rouge, avoir les zinzins
blue *v.* bleusir
blueberry *n.* myrtille
bluebird *n.* oiseau bleu
bluejay *n.* geai
blueness *n.* bleu
blueprint *n.* plan
bluestem *n.* **bushy bluestem** paille jaune
bluff *n.* bloff **man who is a bluff** homme de paille
bluff *v.* bloffer
bluffer *n.* bloffeur
bluing *n.* bleu à laver, bleu
bluish *adj.* bleuzâtre
blunder *n.* canicroche, échappe
blur *v.* brouiller
blurred *adj.* brouillé
blurry *adj.* embrouillé
blush *v.* rougir
blusher *n.* rouge
boar *n.* bella, verrat **wild boar** cochon de garde, cochon farouche
board *n.* BOARD, comité, conseil, pieu, planche, lanière **board fence** barrière à {de} pieux **administrative board** commission **ironing board** planche à repasser **on board** à bord de **running board** marche-pied **school board** commission scolaire **sign board** affiche **upright board** pieu deboute, planche deboute **church board of trustees** comité d'église **command to a person to encourage him/her to get in line, get on board, get with the program** 'poteau, Caillette'!
board *v.* aborder, embarquer, pensionner **board a vehicle** s'embarquer
boarder *n.* pensionnaire, pensionné
boarding *n.* **boarding house** pensionnat **boarding school** pensionnat
boardwalk *n.* banquette
boast *n.* vanterie
boast *v.* se vanter, vanter
boaster *n.* vanteur
boastful *adj.* fier, vanteur **boastful person** blanc-bec
boasting *n.* vaillantise, vanterie
boat *n.* barque, bateau, BOAT, chabec, gnole, navire, vaisseau **by boat** en {par} bateau **dredge boat** grète-boat **fishing boat** canotte, goélette **flat-bottom boat** péniche **flat boat** bateau **freight boat** bateau à fret **gravy boat** moque, saucière **oyster boat** bateau à-z-huîtres **shrimp boat** bateau de chevrette **slow boat** PUTTPUTT **toy boat** BOAT **tug boat** TUG **butterfly net boat** paupiéreur **wing net boat** paupiéreur **bring into or onto a boat** embarquer
boatbuilder *n.* faiseur de bateaux

boathouse *n.* hangar à bateau
bobber *n.* bouchon **fishing-line bobber** PLUG
bobbin *n.* bobine, navette
bobcat *n.* chat-tigre, chat sauvage, pichou
bobolink *n.* ortolan
bobwhite *n.* perdrix
bodice *n.* corsage
bodily *adj.* corporel
bodkin *n.* passe-galon
bodock *n.* bois d'arc
body *n.* corps **dead body** carcasse **official body** collège **uncover one's body** se découvrir
bog *v.* **bog down** embourber, s'embourber
bogged *adj.* **get bogged down in mud** abouer
boggy *adj.* **boggy area** pétrin
bohemian *n.* gipsie
boil *n.* bouilli, carbone, crapaud, humeur **crawfish boil** bouilli d'écrevisses **shrimp boil** bouilliture de chevrettes **core of an abscess or boil** mèche
boil *v.* bouillir, faire bouillir **boil again** rebouillir **boil briskly** bouillir à gros bouillons **boil down to the same thing** revenir au même
boiler *n.* bouilloir, siau **double boiler** chaudière d'eau **steam boiler** bouilloire **one who fires a boiler or furnace** chauffeur *pl.* **battery of pots and boilers used in processing sugar** équipage
boiling *adj.* bouillant
boiling *n.* bouillage
boisterous *adj.* brigand, carnassier **boisterous, rowdy child** barbot **disorderly, boisterous person** carnageur
boisterousness *n.* carnageries
bold *adj.* audacieux, hardi
boldness *n.* audace, organe, assurance
boll *n.* gosse, grabot **boll weevil** BOLL-WEEVE, weev **cotton boll** gosse de coton
bolster *n.* traversin
bolt *n.* boulon, target **lightning bolt** éloise **machine bolt** boulon **tightening of a bolt** boulonnage *pl.* **assembly of bolts** boulonnage
bolt *v.* boulonner **bolt suddenly** partir mors aux dents **bolt together** boulonner
bolting *n.* boulonnage
bomb *n.* bombe **atomic bomb** bombe atomique
bomb *v.* bombarder
bombard *v.* bombarder
bombardier *n.* bombardier
bombardment *n.* bombardement
bond *n.* **put a peace bond on** mettre un empêchement contre *pl.* **break marriage bonds** se démarier
bondage *n.* captivité, esclavage, joug
bone *n.* os, ossaille **fish bone** arête **ham bone** pistolet de jambon, échelon **shin bone** jarret **soup bone** échelon **whale bone** baleine **breast bone of fowl** bréchet *pl.* **bones** ossaille **with bones** osseux
bonito *n.* **Atlantic bonito** bonito
bonkers *adj.* crack
bonnet *n.* bonnet, fourreau
bonus *n.* lagniappe
bony *adj.* osseux
booger *n.* crapaud de nez, crapaud, crèpe
boogeyman *n.* badjo, bébête, christine, croquemitaine, gripette, klou-klouque, loup-garou
book *n.* livre **book sack** cabas **mass book** missel **phone book** livre de téléphone **record book** registre **long drawn-out letter or book** pataraphe *pl.* **keep the books** tenir des livres
bookcase *n.* bibliothèque
booklet *n.* petit livre
boom *interj.* boudoudoume, boum
boom *n.* bôme
boondocks *npl.* fardoche, le finfifond du monde
boor *n.* caïac, dauiaut
boorish *adj.* **rustic, uncultured, uncouth, boorish, ignorant person** gui-gui
boot *n.* botte, malouine **boot strap** STRAP, tire de botte **laced boot** broquin **rubber boot** botte en élastique {gomme} **to boot** par-dessus le marché *pl.* **strap formerly used on boots and shoes** tire
bootie *n.* bouttine
bootleg *adj.* BOOTLEG **bootleg whiskey** BOOTLEG
bootleg *v.* BOOTLEG
bootlegger *n.* BOOTLEG
bootlicker *n.* licheur
booze *n.* boisson
border *n.* bordage, bordure, frontière, bord, quille
border *v.* border **border on** border
bordering *adj.* voisin
bore *n.* CHOKE
bore *v.* abalourdir, achaler, assommer, canuler, DRILL, percer, tanner **one who bores or tires others** assommoir
borecole *n.* chou vert
bored *adj.* **become bored** se tanner
boredom *n.* ennui
borer *n.* drilleur
boring *adj.* canulant, embêtant, ennuyant, tannable **boring person** apostrophe, canule, fatras
born *adj.* **be born** naître **first born** aîné **not yet be born** être sous le caca de vache **that's where I was born** c'est là où mon nombril est enterré
borrow *v.* emprêter, faire un emprunt
borrower *n.* emprunteur
borrowing *n.* emprunt
bosom *n.* jabot, poitrine, sein
boss *n.* BOSS, maître

boss *v.* BULLDOZE

botch *v.* bacher, barboter, barlanguer, bouchonner, gargoter, saganer, sagouiller, saloper

both *pron.* les deux

bother *n.* dérangement, embêtation, embêtement, hariat, trouble **go to the bother** se déranger

bother *v.* abominer, bâdrer, chamailler, couillonner, déranger, embarrasser, embêter, emmerder, emmicher, enquiquiner, gêner, quiquiner, s'embêter, s'emmicher avec, tracasser, troubler, vexer

bothered *adj.* embarrassé **be bothered** avoir un pet accroché, s'embêter

bothering *adj.* **have s.t. bothering one** avoir (qqch) sur le cœur

bothersome *adj.* embarrassant, nuisible, troublant

bots *n.* bottes

bottle *n.* bouteille, fiole, flacon **bottle cap** CAP **baby bottle** biberon, bouteille de bébé / bouteille à {de} lait, bouteille, fiole **water bottle** carafe

bottle *v.* embouteiller

bottlecap *n.* couvert de bouteille, tapon

bottleneck *n.* embouteillage

bottling *n.* embouteillage

bottom *n.* bas, boudoume, dessous, fond, pompon, pountingue, tchu **bony bottom of a chicken** nez du pretre {de l'éveque} **wipe one's bottom** se torcher **from top to bottom** de fond en comble **in or at the bottom of** en bas de

boudin *n.* **rice-based boudin** boudin blanc

bough *npl.* **boughs** branchailles

bouillabaisse *n.* bouillabaisse

bouillon *n.* bouillon, soupe

bounce *n.* bond

bounce *v.* bondir, rebondir **bounce around** ballotter, rebondir

bouncer *n.* constable

bouncy *adj.* rebondissant

bound *v.* bondir

boundary *n.* borne, limite **boundary mark** borne **set boundary marks** borner

bounded *adj.* borné

bouquet *n.* bouquet

bousillage *n.* **prepare bousillage** bousiller **constructed of bousillage** bousillé **amount of bousillage one can hold in two hands** torche **worker who prepares bousillage** tâcheron

bout *n.* **drinking bout** topette

boutique *n.* magasin

bovine *n.* animal, bétaille, bête à corne, bête

bow *n.* arc, devant, rosette, étrave, archet, cocarde

bow *v.* fléchir, se ployer, saluer, se plier **bow down** se baisser

bowed *adj.* cambré

bowel *n.* intestin **bowel movement** selle **have a bowel movement** aller à la selle / avoir une selle, se débloquer *pl.* **bowels** boyau, entrailles **loose bowels** choléra, corps relâché, djarette, dérangement, foire **have loose bowels** avoir la bile en mouvement, avoir la fritche **empty the bowels of** délâcher **void one's bladder or bowels** faire ses besoins

bowfin *n.* choupique

bowing *n.* cambrure

bowl *n.* bol, gamelle, terrine **serving bowl** terrine **soup bowl** assiette creuse, plat creux, soupière **sugar bowl** sucrier **toilet bowl** bol

bowlegged *adj.* cambré

box *n.* boîte, caisse, coffre **box trap** cage, caisse **box or cage submerged in water to store and keep caught fish or crabs alive** vivier **cardboard box** boîte en carton, caisse en carton, carton **carpenter's box** boîte à charpente **ice box** glacière **powder box** poudrière **stuffing box** botton, glande **tobacco box** tabatière **post office box** boîte de poste **put into a box** emboîter **put in a case or box** encaisser

box *v.* boxer, emboîter

boxer *n.* boxeur

boxing *n.* boxe, emboîtement, encaissement **boxing match** boxe

boxwood *n.* buis

boy *n.* garçon, yaïe **altar boy** acolyte, enfant de chœur **little boy** gorgoyo **oh boy** boy, oh (y) yaïe / oh yé yaïe **old boy** vieux nègre **young boy or girl** petit(e) gamin(e) **dear little boy** cher ti nègre *pl.* **boys' room** garçonnière

boy-crazy *adj.* **boy-crazy girl** coureuse

boyfriend *n.* amant, beau, espoir, homme, prétendu

boyhood *n.* vie de garçon

bra *n.* brassière

brace *n.* appui, coin, guette **orthopedic brace** BRACE

brace *v.* guetter

bracelet *n.* bracelet

brackish *adj.* saumâtre

brag *v.* péter à cul cassé, se vanter, vanter

braggart *n.* blanc-bec, casseur de portes ouvertes, défonceur d'une porte ouverte / défonceur de porte(s) ouverte(s), embarrateur, fier-cul, fier, grand parleur et petit faiseur, vanteur

bragging *adj.* **bragging person** vanteur

bragging *n.* vaillantise, vanterie

Brahma *n.* brahma

braid *n.* tchocouette, tresse **braid of hair** couette

braid *v.* tresser, couetter

brain *n.* cervelle *pl.* **brains** cervelle

braise *v.* braiser, étouffer

brake *n.* frein, BRAKE **cane brake** chêneau

bramble *n.* géront, talle d'éronces, éronce *pl.* **pull brambles** éroncer **get covered with brambles or stickers** s'éroncer

bran *n.* **bran and water mixture used as cattle feed** moulée

branch *n.* branche, branche, bras **palm branch** palme **short section of a log or branch** bûche *pl.* **branches** branchage, branchailles **cut branches off** débrancher **cutting off branches** ébranchage **heap of branches placed across a stream to form a makeshift bridge** parieux **planks or branches arranged to permit one to cross running water or a swampy area** pavure **get out from among branches** se débrancher **cut off or strip the branches of** ébrancher

branch *v.* brancher, fourcher **branch off** brancher, fourcher **branch out** brancher

branched *adj.* branchu

branching *adj.* fourchu, fourché

brand *n.* étampe, marque

brand *v.* marquer, étamper

branded *adj.* marqué

branding *n.* **branding iron** fer à marquer, étampe **tool for pressing clothes, branding, soldering, etc.** fer

brandy *n.* brandy, cognac, magnane

brashness *n.* audace

brass *n.* cuivre, tchique **brass knuckles** fer, ferail

brassiere *n.* brassière, corsage de dessous

brat *n.* morveux *pl.* **brats** marmaille

brave *adj.* brave, courageux, vaillant **be brave** s'amarrer le cœur

brave *v.* braver, défier

bravery *n.* braveure, courage

brawl *n.* pique-partout **engage in a brawl** poquer

bray *v.* rechigner

braze *v.* braser, souder

brazen *adj.* effronté

brazenly *adv.* effrontément

brazenness *n.* toupet

brazier *n.* braisier

brazil *n.* **brazil nut** orteil de nègre

breach *n.* bréchure **make a breach or gap** faire brèche

bread *n.* pain **bread crumbs** pain moulé **bread oven** four à pain **bread pudding** pain (de) poudine, poutine de pain, poutine **bread roll** bourrelet **bread that has not risen enough or has cooked too slowly** pain langui **American bread** un LOAF de pain **French bread** pain français **homemade bread** pain de femme {famille / ménage}, pain levé **shortening bread** toteau **toasted bread** pain grillé **wheat bread** pain de froment **chunk of bread** chiffon de pain **piece of bread** crouston **slice of bread** tranche de pain **spread on bread** beurrer **loaf of French bread** flûte de pain, flûte, miche **know where one's bread is buttered** savoir et où son pain est beurré **soft inside part of bread** miette **soft inside part of bread, cake, etc.** mie **long crusty loaf of white bread** pain français

breading *n.* **coat with breading** paner

breadth *n.* largeur, travers **breadth of cloth** laise

break *n.* brisure, cassure, craque

break *v.* battre, briser, casser, craquer, dommager, fragmenter, fêler, amortir, casser, dompter, se casser, se faire **break apart** se dissoudre **break away** s'arracher **break down** casser, défoncer, dégringoler, s'écrouler, écrouler **break even** casser égal **break in** couper, défoncer **break open** défoncer **break out** casser **break up** casser la paille, casser la vaisselle, déchirer la couverture {couverte} (en deux), défropter, faire {avoir} barouche, se casser, se diviser, se quitter **break into bits** cassailler, grémiller **break marriage bonds** se démarier **break of sitting** découvasser, découver **break one's back** se casser en deux **break the sod** fendre la terre **break to pieces** briser, casser en cannelles, fragmenter, égrener **break a Lenten promise** casser sa pénitence **break off a point** épointer **break the back of** éreinter **break the teeth of** édenter **break a chip off of** abroquer **break up a household or marriage** casser le ménage **break up a relationship or marriage** casser la patte **break, cut, or chop into pieces** écharpiller **break a promise not to indulge in s.t.** casser le petit bâton **dislocate or break one's hip** s'éhancher **hurt or break one's back** s'éreinter **dislocate or break the hip of** éhancher **spurn, reject, or break up with a suitor** donner son {un} capot (à qqn) **it's time to break up the party or conversation** c'est l'heure qu'on casse le rond **one who tends to break things** brise-fer, briseur, casse-brise **day is breaking** le jour est après se faire **child that breaks everything** casse-tout **all hell broke loose** le diable s'en a mêlé

breakable *adj.* cassable, cassant, casvel, fragile

breakage *n.* cassage

breakdown *n.* écroulement

breakfast *n.* déjeuner **eat breakfast** déjeuner

breaking *n.* cassage, cassement, cassée **breaking down** défonçage **breaking in** défonçage **breaking into** défonçage **breaking up** cassement

breast *n.* mamelle, poitrail, poitrine, sein, téton, tête **breast chain** BREAST-CHAIN **breast collar** bricole **breast yoke** BREAST-YOKE **breast bone of fowl** bréchet **breast of a horse** poitrail **woman's breast** estomac **expose the chest or breast** se dépoitrailler

breastfeeding *n.* tétée

breath *n.* haleine, respire, souffle **draw breath** prendre son respire **take breath away** couper le souffle (à qqn) **catch one's breath** prendre son respire **lose one's breath** pâmer, se pâmer **out of breath** essoufflé **hold one's breath until blue in the face** pâmer, se pâmer **be out of breath** manquer de souffle **breathe one's last breath** expirer **get out of breath** s'essoufler **cause to be out of breath** essouffler

breathe *v.* respirer, souffler **breathe in** aspirer **breathe one's last breath** expirer **breathe with whistling or a rattle in the throat** siller

breathing *n.* respiration

breathlessness *n.* essoufflement

Breaux Bridge *n.* Pont Breaux

bred *adj.* **bred to fight** gaïme

breech *npl.* **knee breeches** brayette
breeching *n.* acculoire, reculoire
breed *n.* race **of mixed breed, mixed blood** abâtardi
breed *v.* engendrer, faire servir
breeder *n.* éleveur **breeder or trainer of racehorses** coursier **horse breeder or trainer** maquillon
breeding *n.* vacherie, élevage **good breeding** politesse
breeze *n.* brise **cool breeze** fraîche **in the cool breeze** à la fraîche **take advantage of a cool breeze** attraper la fraîche, prendre la fraîche
Brer Rabbit *n.* Lapin
briar *n.* géront, éronce **saw briar** liane de skine *pl.* **clump of bushes, briars, or shrubs** talle
bribe *n.* **accept a bribe** se graisser la patte
bribe *v.* acheter, graisser la main {les poches}, se graisser la patte
bric-a-brac *n.* artifailles, artifaux **cheap bric-a-brac** tchincaillerie
brick *n.* brique **brick kiln** briquerie **crushed brick used to scour floors** brique **spread powdered brick on floors to scour and clean them** briquer *pl.* **cover with bricks** briqueter **hit s.o. like a ton of bricks** cogner qqn comme une bol de merde
brick *v.* briqueter
brick-making *n.* briquerie
brickfield *n.* briquerie
bricklayer *n.* maçon, maçonneur
brickmason *n.* maçon
bridal *adj.* **bridal wreath plant** couronne de mariée
bride *n.* marié, époux
bride-to-be *n.* prétende-femme
bridegroom *n.* époux
bridge *n.* pont **bridge railing** garde-fou **heap of branches placed across a stream to form a makeshift bridge** parieux
bridle *n.* bride, bridon, frein **hackamore bridle** bossal
bridle *v.* brider, gréer
brief *adj.* bref, court
brief *npl.* **briefs** caleçon
briefcase *n.* portefeuille
brigand *n.* brigand
brigandage *n.* brigandage
bright *adj.* brillant, clair, voyant **not bright** mal en train
brightness *n.* brillance, clair
brilliance *n.* brillance, béluette
brilliant *adj.* éclatant
brilliantine *n.* brillantine
brim *n.* bec, faît **to the brim** à (la) rase, à la rasée **fill to the brim** aufaîter **full to the brim** plein à déborder, à ras
brimming *adj.* plein à déborder
brimstone *n.* soufre
brindled *adj.* alizon
brine *n.* saumure
bring *v.* amener, apporter, emmener, hurler, mener, porter **bring about** occasionner **bring along** s'amener **bring back** ramener, rapporter, rentrer, reporter **bring closer** rapprocher **bring forth** produire **bring frequently** apportailler **bring in** pomper, rentrer **bring o.s.** s'amener **bring out** faire ressortir, ressortir, sortir, sourdre **bring together** assembler **bring up** monter **bring back together** réunir **bring closer together** rapprocher **bring back and forth** apportailler **bring back to life** ressusciter **bring into or onto a boat** embarquer **bring into or under a shelter** abrier
brisket *n.* bréchet
bristle *v.* regricher **bristle up** regricher les cheveux, regricher, se regricher
broad *adj.* large
broadcast *n.* émission, programme
broadcast *v.* publier, faire assavoir
broadcloth *n.* drap
broaden *v.* rélargir
broadening *n.* élargissement
broccoli *n.* broccoli
brogue *n.* rametien
broil *v.* rôtir
broke *adj.* BROKE, cassé **be broke** être à la hache **completely broke** cassé à la souche {chousse} **financially broke** à plate
broken *adj.* baroque, cassé, craqué, dompte **broken with age or illness** abîmé **in a broken, mixed way** baroque
brokenhearted *adj.* **be brokenhearted** se désoler
broker *n.* BROKER
bronchitis *n.* bronchite
bronchus *n.* bronche
bronco *n.* potre
broncobuster *n.* maquillon
brooch *n.* épinglette
brood *n.* nigée, élève
brood *v.* couver, faire des jonglements
brood-hen *n.* éleveuse
brooder *n.* éleveuse
brooding *n.* jonglement
brook *n.* coulée
broom *n.* balai **broom straw** mie de balai **broom made of palmetto leaves or coarse prairie grass** balai acadien {cadien} **a new broom sweeps clean** tout nouveau, tout beau **hit with a broom** donner un coup de balai
broomstick *n.* manche à balai
broth *n.* bouillon, jus, soupe **broth with roux** soupe maigre
brothel *n.* bordel
brother *n.* frère, frère **half brother** demi-frère
brother-in-law *n.* beau-frère
brotherhood *n.* fraternité
brow *n.* front **unknit one's brow** défroncer le front

browbeat *v.* BULLDOZE
brown *adj.* châtain, marron, brun **golden brown** jaune **make brown** brunesir **reddish brown or yellowish brown** alizon
brown *v.* brunesir, faire jaunir, rôtir, écuisser
brownish *adj.* brunâtre, châtain
bruise *n.* bleu, mâchure, nioque **bruise or spot on skin** placard
bruise *v.* bleusir, mâcher, mâchurer
brunette *n.* brune, brunette
brush *n.* brosse **brush for scrubbing the floor** fourbissoir **clothes brush** brosse à habits {linge} **shaving brush** pinceau, savonnette **shoe brush** brosse à souliers **clear of trees and brush** déboiser
brush *v.* brosser, rifler **brush o.s.** se brosser **brush with a card** mousser **card, comb or brush** carder
brushing *n.* brossage
brushwood *n.* fardoche
brusque *adj.* **correct in a brusque way** ramasser
Brussels *n.* **Brussels sprouts** choux de Bruxelles
brutal *adj.* brutal, violent
brutality *n.* brutalité
brutalize *v.* brutaliser
brutally *adv.* brut
brute *n.* animal
brutish *adj.* brut **rough, brutish person** animal, casseur de portes ouvertes, défonceur d'une porte ouverte / défonceur de porte(s) ouverte(s)
bubble *n.* écume
bubbling *n.* glou-glou
buck *v.* corcobiller
bucket *n.* baille, baquet, bokette, chaudron, siau
bucking *n.* corcobiage
buckle *n.* boucle, bouclet
buckle *v.* boucler **buckle o.s., one's belt** se boucler
buckshot *n.* postes
bud *n.* bourgeon, formance, bouton **flower bud** bouton de fleur
bud *v.* bourgeonner
budding *n.* bourgeonnement
buddy *n.* camarade, compagnon, padna, vieux chien, vieux corps
budge *v.* **budge again** regrouiller
buff *v.* **one who rubs, buffs or polishes** frotteur
buffalo *n.* bœuf sauvage, buffalo
buffet *n.* buffet
buffoon *n.* bouffon, paillasse
buffoonery *n.* bouffonnerie
bug *n.* bébête, bétaille, bête, insecte, loulou **bug or worm that curls up when touched** tortue **chinch bug** punaise de champ {clos} **corn bug** punaise de champ {clos} **frightening bug** tataille **June bug** barbot, bête à chandelle, hanneton **lightning bug** bétaille à feu **love bug** 'tit carencro, besson **May bug** barbot, bête à Guillaume, hanneton **pill bug** rouleau **stink bug** punaise **larva of the tiger beetle or pill bug** loulou
bugaboo *n.* loup-garou
buggy *n.* boghei, bourrinque, charrette **marsh buggy** boghei de boue, boghei de plairie, traîneau **one-seat buggy** boghei **two-seat buggy** HACK **two-wheeled horse-drawn buggy** carriole **body of a buggy** caisse
bugle *n.* cornet
build *v.* allonger, bâtir, construire, monter, ériger, passer **build a nest** nicher **build on pillars** bloquer **build o.s. a home** se bâtir **build a protective enclosure around** cager **build larger quarters for o.s.** s'égrandir **build o.s. a barn, a store** se bâtir un magasin **build o.s. a home or business** s'établir
builder *n.* bâtisseur, constructeur **house builder** monteur de maisons
building *n.* bâtiment, bâtisse, cambuse, construction, édifice, établissement **capitol building** capitale **school building** école **crude wooden building** baraque **big, usually delapidated or poorly constructed building** chabraque
built *adj.* membré **well built** bien corporé, bien membré
bulb *n.* bulbe **light bulb** globe électrique / globe de lampe, globe
bulk *n.* **in bulk** en gros
bull *n.* bœuf, bétaille, bête, taureau **bull in a china shop** brisefer, briseur **bull too old to breed** caïac **wild bull** beson **tell a cock and bull story** chanter des midis à quatorze heures **name commonly given to a bull of mottled, grayish-blue with red spots** pivelé
bullbat *n.* crapaud volant, engoulevent, feursie, piejègue, pigeon maringouin
bulldog *n.* bouledogue
bulldoze *v.* BULLDOZE
bulldozer *n.* BULLDOZER
bullet *n.* balle
bullfrog *n.* ouaouaron
bullheadedness *n.* obstination
bullwhip *n.* couarte, fouet à bœuf
bully *n.* bouledou, boulet, bourreau, taureau du bois
bully *v.* brutaliser, BULLDOZE
bulrush *n.* jonc **giant bulrush** jonc rond
bum *n.* bidet, couac-soleil, câlin, filandrin, flâneur, racatcha, TRAMP, traînard, traîneur
bumblebee *n.* bourdon de terre, bourdon
bump *n.* bosse, nioque, nocoyau, boussole, nioque **bump on the skin of an alligator** bouton **raise a bump** embosser *pl.* **goose bumps** peau de canard **provoke or cause bumps or swelling of skin** louper
bump *v.* aborder, camper, cogner **bump into** cogner, s'aborder contre **bump o.s.** se cogner **bump into each other** s'aborder
bumper *n.* FENDER

bumpkin *n.* **country bumpkin** bitaco
bumpy *adj.* raboteux **be bumpy** raboter
bun *n.* brioche, catogan, choque, huppe, tchique, tignon, tortillon, roulon
bunch *n.* bataclan, grappe, lot, massacre, régime, séquelle, tallée, tas, trallée, troupe **a bunch** hourra **the bunch** tout le sacré bataclan **the whole damn bunch** toute la sacrée séquelle
bunched *adj.* **bunched up** raccoquillé
bundle *n.* chiffon, gerbe, paquet, patatras, botte, bouillée **rolled or wrapped bundle** rouleau
bundle *v.* botteler, SHOCK **person who binds or bundles** amarreur
bundling *n.* empaquetage
bung *n.* cheville, bouchon **barrel bung** bombe
bungle *v.* barboter, barlanguer, bouchonner, saganer, sagouiller
bunion *n.* racatcha, éperon
bunk *n.* calembour
bunny *n.* **dust bunny** duvet
bunting *n.* petit pape **black-throated bunting** ortolan **painted bunting** pape rouge {vert / doré}, pape
bur *n.* racatcha
burden *n.* fardeau, poids **bear the burden of one's problems** porter sa croix
bureau *n.* bureau
burglary *n.* vol
burial *n.* enterrement **burial vault** tombeau **prepare for burial** ensevelir
buried *adj.* **be buried** s'enterrer
burlap *n.* pite **peat, gunny, or burlap sack** sac de pitre
burly *adj.* un coquin de
burn *n.* brûlure
burn *v.* brûler, cautériser **burn o.s.** se brûler **burn the candle at both ends** brûler la chandelle aux deux bouts
burnable *adj.* brûlable
burned *adj.* **be burned** brûler **get o.s. burned** se faire brûler
burner *n.* bobèche **burner rack** mèche **lamp burner** desse, tête de lampe
burning *adj.* ardent **burning sensation** brûlement **burning log or stick** tison
burning *n.* brûlage **burning of the stomach** pimenterie
burnt *adj.* **burnt part of a wood or forest** brûlé
burst *n.* éclat
burst *v.* boster, casser, s'éclater, éclabousser, éclater, aboutir **burst open** crâler, défoncer **burst into tears** se désoler **burst out laughing** se fendre à rire **cause to burst** éclater
bury *v.* enterrer **bury o.s. or each other** s'enterrer
bus *n.* BUS, transfert **school bus** transfert d'école, TRUCK d'école **horse-drawn school bus** transfert
bush *n.* **blackberry bush** talle d'éronces, éronce **prickle bush** éronce **sticker bush** éronce **thorn bush** garofier **Chickasaw rose bush** chéroquis **not beat around the bush** pas aller les quatre chemins **take the shape of a bush** taller **a bird in the hand is worth two in the bush** un oiseau dans la main en vaut deux dans une talle *pl.* **clump of bushes, briars, or shrubs** talle
bush *v.* **bush out** taller
bushel *n.* boisseau, bouchelle, manne **bushel basket** boisseau, manne
bushy *adj.* fournu
business *n.* affaire, business, compagnie, occupation **do business** faire (un/une) barguine (avec) **shrimp business** affaire de chevrette {de drill / de nutria / de piège / de pêche / de trôle / d'huile (etc.)} **do business with** patroniser **have no business** avoir pas d'affaire à (faire qqch) **the fishing business** pêche **be the business of** regarder **small cheap business or place of amusement** tchouflangue **do a good business** monter en grade **get down to business** s'attabler **mind one's own business** s'occuper de sa tambouille à soi-même, s'occuper de ses affaires {oignons}, s'occuper de ses affaires **mind your own business** va brasser dans tes chaudières **it's none of your business** c'est pas de tes affaires **build o.s. a home or business** s'établir
businessman *n.* homme d'affaires
bust *n.* jabot **large bust** armeuil
bust *v.* boster
bustle *n.* commerce, commérage, GRECIAN BEND, maquignonnage
busy *adj.* actif, occupé
busy *v.* **busy o.s.** s'occuper
busybody *n.* espionneur, fouillailleur, fouillard, fouille-merde, fouille-merdeur, fouille-nez, fouilleur, fourgailleur, fourre-nez, reluqueuse, roufian, roufianeur
but *adv.* seulement
but *conj.* BUT, mais, par exemple
but *npl.* **there's no ifs, ands or buts** il y a pas de catherine
butane *n.* **butane tank** TANK à butane
butcher *n.* boucher, tueur **butcher bird** mangeur moqueur, moqueur français {muet / sauvage / d'hiver} **butcher knife** couteau de boucherie, grand couteau, poignard **butcher shop** halle **butcher's block** bloc
butcher *v.* faire boucherie, plumer
butchering *n.* boucherie
butt *n.* fesse, gogo, tchu, troufignon, croupion
butt *v.* cornailler, foncer **butt in** fourrer son nez, roufianer, s'emmêler, se mêler dans
butter *n.* beurre **butter churn** moulin à beurre **peanut butter** peanut-beurre
butter *v.* beurrer **butter up** embeurrer, licher
buttered *adj.* **know where one's bread is buttered** savoir et où son pain est beurré
butterfly *n.* papillon
buttermilk *n.* lait de beurre

buttock *n.* croupe, fesse *pl.* **buttocks** pompon **said when s.o.'s underpants have crawled up and become stuck between the buttocks** il y a un cabri dans le maïs

button *n.* bouton, bouton **bachelor's button** vieux garçon **belly button** bourrique, cabri, nombril **collar button** bouton de col **press a button** peser (sur) un bouton **take a button from one dress to put on another** dégréer Saint Paul pour gréer Saint Pierre

button *v.* boutonner, se boutonner **button again** reboutonner

buttonbush *n.* bois-bouton, bois de marais

buttonhole *n.* boutonnière

buttonwood *n.* cotonnier, langue de femme

buy *v.* acheter avec, acheter **buy again** racheter **buy back** racheter **buy retail** acheter en détail **buy by weight** acheter au poids **buy for o.s.** s'acheter **buy on credit** acheter à crédit **buy on a whim** acheter à l'œil **buy a round of drinks** payer la traite **buy little at a time** acheter à la tchiquette **buy a lottery or raffle ticket** prendre une mise **buy hastily and without thorough examination** acheter à l'œil **what one could buy for two and a half cents** quarti

buyer *n.* acheteur

buying *n.* achat

buzz *n.* bourdonnement

buzz *v.* bourdonner, siller

buzzard *n.* **turkey buzzard** carencro tête-rouge, carencro

buzzing *n.* bourdonnement, silement

by *prep.* auprès de, de, en, par, à

bye-bye *n.* **say bye-bye** faire BYE-BYE

C

cab *n.* chartil

cabal *v.* cabaler

cabbage *n.* chou **cabbage plant** plant de chou **cabbage seedling** plant de chou **head of cabbage** pomme de chou, tête de chou

cabin *n.* cabanasse, cabane, cabaneau, CAMP, cabanage, cabine **ramshackle cabin** ajoupa

cabinet *n.* cabinet **cabinet maker** meublier **kitchen cabinet** garde-manger

cable *n.* cordeau, câble **cable television** câble **stern cable** reculoire

caboose *n.* cabousse

cacao *n.* coco

cache *n.* cache

cackle *v.* cacasser, closser

cactus *n.* raquette **prickly pear cactus** raquette

cadaver *n.* cadavre

cafe *n.* café

café *n.* bar, BARROOM, restaurant **café brûlot** café (au) brûlot

cage *n.* cage **bird cage** ajoupa, cage à z-oiseau **crab cage** carrelet **hen cage** pondoire **box or cage submerged in water to store and keep caught fish or crabs alive** vivier **put in a cage** encager

cage *v.* encager

caging *n.* encaissage

cajole *v.* manioler, miauler

cajoler *n.* emmioleur

cajolery *n.* mialement

Cajun *adj.* acadien, cadien **Cajun French** cadien, français cadien **person of any origin who speaks Cajun French** Cadien

Cajun *n.* Cadien **lazy Cajun** Cadien ventre jaune **insulting name for an African-American, a mulatto, or a Cajun** bougali

cake *n.* galette, gâteau, tourtière, toteau **cake pan** assiette à gâteau(x), plaque à gateau **cake made of brown sugar or molasses and nuts** colle **crab cake** boulette de crabe **plain cake** mâche-pain **shrimp cake** boulette de chevrette **yeast cake** galette, YEASTCAKE **layer of a cake** galette, mâche-pain **sweetened fried rice cake** cala **deep fried corn or wheat cake** beigne **soft inside part of bread, cake, etc.** mie **biscuit dough cooked in the shape of a flat cake** tcheck

calamity *n.* calamité

calcified *adj.* **calcified mass in the body** gravelle

calcify *v.* calciner

calculate *v.* calculer, figurer, additionner **one who calculates numbers** carculeur

calculation *n.* calcul

calculus *n.* pierre

calendar *n.* almanach, calendrier, compteur de mois

calf *n.* gras de jambe, musse, veau, mollet **calf pen** parc à veaux {vaches} **calf weaner** museau **fatted calf** veau engraissé **stomach of an unweaned calf** grillade à la chique {Chine}

calibrate *v.* calibrer

calico *n.* calicot **printed calico** indienne

calinda *n.* calinda

caliper *npl.* **calipers** compas

call *n.* appel, langage, visite **call for chickens** quiquitte **duck call** appeleur, cornet, moque à canards / moque-canard, moque, sifflet de canard **have a close call** rifler **produce its customary call** chanter

call *v.* appeler, hucher, hurler, moquer **call again** rappeler **call back** rappeler **call ducks** moquer un canard / moquer des canards **call on** appeler sur {dessus}, visiter **call out** appeler, crier après (qqn), crier **call upon** appeler sur {dessus} **call a fool** traiter de fou **call bad names** appeler des {les} noms **call by whistling** siffler après **call out for** crier après (qqn) **call by crying out** hucher **call on the phone** téléphoner

called *adj.* **be called** s'appeler, se nommer

caller *n.* visiteur, appeleur *pl.* **callers** compagnie

calling *n.* profession, vocation

callus *n.* durillon

calm *adj.* calme, dull, sage, tranquille, vitré **become calm** se calmer **fall calm** accalmir, s'accalmir

calm *n.* paix, tranquillité

calm *v.* accalmir, apaiser, calmer, emmioler, tranquilliser **calm down** accalmir, calmer, laissez un bloque en bas de la maison!, mettre de l'eau dans son vin, s'accalmir, s'apaiser, se calmer, se tranquilliser

calomel *n.* calomel

calumny *n.* calomnie

Calvary *n.* calvaire

camaraderie *n.* camaraderie

cambric *n.* **cambric cloth** batiste

camel *n.* chameau

camellia *n.* **camellia flower** camélia **camellia shrub** camélia **camellia tree** camélia

camera *n.* caméra, kodak

camisole *n.* chemise de dessous

camouflage *n.* camouflage

camp *n.* campement **camp bed** couchette **workers camp, quarters** camp

camp *v.* cabaner, CAMP, camper, faire chaudière, se camper, tenter

campaign *n.* campagne **military campaign** campagne

campaign *v.* cabaler

camphor *n.* camphre **camphor tree** camphrier

camphorate *v.* camphrer

camphorated *adj.* camphré

camping *n.* **camping trip** camperie

campsite *n.* cabanage

can *n.* boîte, CAN, pinte **can opener** ouvreur de canne **aluminum can** CAN d'aluminum, pinte **coffee can** cafetière **oil can** huilier **tin can** CAN, pinte **watering can** arrosoir **dented or crumpled pan or can** bassin bossu {cabossu}

can *v.* CAN, encanner **it can be** il y a moyen

Canada *n.* Canada

Canadian *adj.* canadien

Canadian *n.* Canadien

canal *n.* canal **passage, trail, path, or canal** trace

Canal *n.* **Intercoastal Canal** INTERCOASTAL

cancel *v.* annuler

cancer *n.* cancer, chancre

cancerous *adj.* cancéreux

candidacy *n.* **announce one's candidacy** s'annoncer

candidate *n.* candidat **political candidate who resorts to corrupt campaign methods** cabaleur **be a candidate** courir **be a candidate for a position** galoper

candle *n.* chandelle **candle holder** chandelier **roman candle** fusée **burn the candle at both ends** brûler la chandelle aux deux bouts **snuff out the candle** tuer la chandelle

candle *v.* rayer

candlestick *n.* chandelier

candy *n.* bonbon, candi, douceur, doudouces, suce, dragée **candy bar** barre de candi **candy cane** candi barré **peppermint candy** candi barré **store-bought or fancy cookie or candy** friandise

cane *n.* canne, roseau **cane brake** chêneau **cane cutter** sabreur **cane cutting** coupage de canne **cane harvest** coupage de canne **cane knife** couteau à {de} canne, sabre à canne, sabre **cane reed** cannette **cane shaver** raseuse **cane syrup** sirop de batterie **cane cutting machine** coupeuse à {de} cannes **candy cane** candi barré **hog cane** canne des cochons **plant cane** plant de canne **quill cane** canne de cochon **river cane** jonc **seed cane** plant de canne **sugar cane** canne à sucre, canne **windrow cane** mettre les cannes en matelas **sugar cane factory** sucrerie **sugar cane field** champ de canne **sugar cane stubble** chicot de canne **wild cane reed** canne farouche, canne à fuseau, canne à pêche {pêcher} **thick cane syrup drawn just before the syrup crystallizes into sugar** cuite **cut the cane at the end of summer so that it will resprout** raser les cannes **top of sugar cane stalk** faît de canne à sucre **crush and grind sugar cane** rouler les cannes **first- / second- / third-year sugar cane stubble** premier / deuxième / troisième chicot

canecrusher *n.* rolle

canecutter *n.* machine à canne

canister *n.* **coffee canister** cafetière

canned *adj.* en CAN

canner *n.* canneur

cannery *n.* cannerie

cannibal *n.* cannibale, carrencaouai

canning *n.* **canning jar** bocal, flacon, pobon

cannon *n.* canon

cannonball *n.* **do a cannonball dive** casser la vaisselle, plonger à casser la vaisselle

canoe *n.* **dugout canoe** pirogue

canonize *v.* canoniser

canopy *n.* dais **canopy bed** lit à ciel **bed canopy** ciel de lit

cantaloupe *n.* melon (en) français / melon de France, melon d'eau, melon musqué

canticle *n.* cantique

canvas *n.* toile

canvass *v.* **canvass a neighborhood** faire la côte

cap *n.* bonnet, CAP, capsule, casque, casquette, couvert **cap pistol** pétard **baseball cap** CAP, casque à bec, casque, casquette **bottle cap** CAP **cradle cap** chapeau **firing cap** capsule **knee cap** boulotte de genou **pistol cap** CAP **skull cap** capuchon **put a cap on a bottle** CAP **old hat or cap** bidon, capuchon

cap *v.* CAP

capable *adj.* capable, compétent, habile, adroit
capacity *n.* capacité, pouvoir
capaiba *n.* capahu
cape *n.* cape, pointe de terre
caper *npl.* **cut capers** faire des canicroches, faire des corcobiages
caper *v.* regimber
capital *adj.* capital **capital sin** péché capital
capital *n.* capitale
capitalist *n.* capitaliste
capitol *n.* **capitol building** capitale
capon *n.* chapon
caponize *v.* chaponner
caprice *n.* caprice, ravigaud
capricious *adj.* capricieux
capsize *v.* capoter, chavirer
capsule *n.* pastille, pilule, capsule
captain *n.* Capitaine Souris, capitaine, capitaine
captivity *n.* captivité
capture *v.* attraper, empoigner
car *n.* automobile, char, voiture **car jack** JACK **car lock** étrier **baggage car** char à bagages **by car** en {par} char **freight car** char à fret **old car** bastringue, chabraque **passenger car** char à passagers **train car** traîneau **old junky car** char-à-banc **get into a car or train** monter dans un char
carafe *n.* carafe
caramel *n.* caramel
carapace *n.* écale, écorce
carbine *n.* carabine
carbolic *adj.* carbolique **carbolic acid** acide carbolique
carbolic *n.* **carbolic acid ointment** onguent à ver
carbuncle *n.* anthrax, carbone, crapaud, nique de guêpe
carburetor *n.* corporel
carcass *n.* carcasse **carcass of an animal** charogne
card *n.* carte, carde **card game** bataille, bourre, casino, charbon, gro-blo, POKENO, solitaire **Christmas card** carte de Christmas **greeting card** carte **playing card** carte **trump card** atout, tourne **do card readings** tirer des cartes **brush with a card** mousser *pl.* **play cards for money** gambler **draw cards from a deck** piocher **club for playing cards** cantique
card *v.* mousser **card, comb or brush** carder
cardboard *n.* carton, en carton **cardboard box** boîte en carton, caisse en carton, carton **made of cardboard** en carton
cardinal *adj.* cardinal
cardinal *n.* cardinau, cardinal
care *n.* cure, diligence, garde, précaution, soin **with care** avec soin **take care of** garder, guetter, prendre en soin, s'occuper, soigner, surveiller **take care of o.s.** s'entretenir, se soigner **do with care** se donner de la peine **dress with great care** se gréer **adopted or placed in foster care** placé
care *v.* **care for** protecter, soigner, tenir de, tenir à **not care** s'en foutre (pas mal), se ficher, se sacrer
cared *adj.* **cared for** soigné
careening *n.* virage
carefree *adj.* bambara, sans souci la rose **lackadaisical, carefree person** menfoutbin **in a carefree way** larigobil
careful *adj.* attentionné, prudent, précautioneux, prévoyant, rangeux **be careful** faire attention, LOOK OUT, prendre garde, prendre précaution, veille voir **overly careful of details** nigeant
carefully *adv.* aisé, avec soin, bien, précieusement
careless *adj.* menfoutbin, négligent **careless or imprudent act** imprudence **be careless about** négliger
carelessly *adv.* machinalement, à la menfoutbin **rapidly and carelessly** (à) (la) bride abattue, à la bride molle
carelessness *n.* mal soin, manque d'attention, négligence
caress *n.* caresse, faire minouche, minouche
caress *v.* caresser **caress each other** se caresser
cargo *n.* LOAD **without cargo** allège
caricature *n.* caricature
carmelized *adj.* **carmelized sugar** brûlot
carnation *n.* narcisse
carnaval *n.* **name of the carnaval queen** Dorothée
Carnaval *n.* **masked Carnaval reveller** christine
carnival *n.* carnaval
Carnival *n.* carnaval
carousal *n.* boumlala
carouse *v.* bambocher, faire (le) rougarou, pintocher
carouser *n.* bambocheur, bervocheur, pintocheur
carp *n.* carpe **blue carp** carpe bleue **white carp** carpe blanche **yellow carp** carpe jaune
carpenter *n.* charpenteur, charpentier, ouvrier **carpenter's box** boîte à charpente **carpenter's plane** varlope **carpenter's saw** scie à bois **carpenter's square** pied-de-roi / pied-du-roi, équerre **carpenter's folding ruler** pied-de-roi / pied-du-roi
carpenter *v.* charpenter
carpentry *n.* charpente **do carpentry** faire la charpente, travailler à la charpente, charpenter
carpet *n.* tapis
carping *adj.* babillard
carport *adj.* porte cochère
carport *n.* garage postiche, porte cochère
carriage *n.* berlingue, voiture **carriage house** remise **carriage shaft** menoir **carriage step** marchette **baby carriage** boghei **fancy carriage** calèche, carrosse **two-seat carriage** barouche **high class carriage** carrosse
carried *adj.* **carried away** emporté **get carried away** s'emporter
carrier *n.* porteur **mail carrier** postillon
carrion *n.* charogne **carrion crow** carencro
carrot *n.* carotte
carry *v.* abouler, apporter, charrier, charroyer, emmener, emporter, entraîner, portailler, porter, voyager **carry back** reporter

carry on emmener, mener **carry out** accomplir, conduire, mener **carry tales** cancaner, porter des paquets **carry up** monter **carry a child** porter un enfant **carry a load** faire un voyage **carry a message** faire une commission **carry on noisily** brigander **carry on a racket** amener un tapage {du train} **carry s.o. on one's shoulders** faire le carcan **carry one's belongings on one's back** être comme la tortue

carrying *n.* halage **carrying on** carnageries

cart *n.* bourrinque, diable, wagonnette **four-wheel cart** char-à-banc **ox cart** charrette à bœufs **two-wheeled cart** bouleton, charrette, waguine **hand-propelled railroad cart** char-à-bras **put the cart before the horse** mettre le bogui avant le cheval

cartilage *n.* croquant

cartload *n.* charretée

cartomancy *n.* **practice cartomancy** tirer des cartes

carton *n.* carton

cartridge *n.* cartouche

carve *v.* couper, découper, tailler, trancher **carve down** détailler **carve up** débiter **tool used to carve out pirogues** tille ronde

carving *n.* découpage, sculpture

case *n.* caisse, cas **glass case** vitrière **in case** en cas que, en tout cas (que), en tout cas **legal case** cas **misery case** pratique à chagrin **in case that** par cas que **in any case** dans tous les cas, en tout cas, n'importe comment, n'importe, toujours **in that case** d'abord, dans ce cas-là, tant qu'à faire **just in case** en tout cas **put in a case or box** encaisser

cash *n.* argent comptant, CASH, fonds **cash register** régistre **pay cash** acheter au CASH

cash *v.* CASH

cashew *n.* acajou

cashmere *n.* cachemire

casino *n.* casino

cask *npl.* **put into casks or barrels** enformer

cassabanana *n.* brésil, casse-banane, cocobanane

cassava *n.* **cassava tree** arbre (à) volaille, manioc

casserole *n.* casserole, daube **casserole dish** casserole

cassette *n.* cassette

cassock *n.* soutane

cast *adj.* **cast net** carrelet

cast *v.* tirer, mouler **cast aside** jeter à côté **cast lots** tirer au sort **cast off** se démettre, semer **cast a glance** tirer un œil **cast a spell** mettre {faire} un gris-gris, passer un coundja (à qqn) **cast a spell on** donner un coundja à, faire un condjo contre, gris-gris, mettre un condjo sur **one who casts spells** candjateur, ouangateur

cast-net *n.* épervier

caster *n.* roulette

casting *n.* moulage

castle *n.* château **a man's house is his castle** charbonnier est maître chez lui

castor *n.* **castor oil** huile de castor, huile de palma christi, huile à purger

castrate *v.* arranger, chaponner, châtrer, couper, opérer, émasculer, marquer **castrate o.s.** s'émasculer

cat *n.* chat, minou, mistigri **cat's cradle** patte de poule **cat's foot** patte de chat **civet cat** civette **female cat** chatte **male cat** chat *pl.* **rain cats and dogs** mouiller des chiens et des chats

catafalque *n.* catafal

catalog *n.* catalogue

catalogne *n.* **strip of material used in making a catalogne** pénille

catalpa *n.* bois puant, catalpa **catalpa tree** atacalpa, bois connu {inconnu}

cataplasm *n.* cataplasme

cataract *n.* cataracte

catastrophe *n.* catastrophe

catch *n.* prise, taquet, attrape **catch of fish** prise de poisson **make a good catch** faire une bonne pêche

catch *v.* attraper, empoigner, poigner, prendre, trapper, attraper, coller **catch again** ressaisir **catch frogs** froguer **catch up** se rattraper **catch a cold** prendre un rhume, s'enrhumer **catch by surprise** poigner **catch up with** attraper, gagner **catch a glimpse of** entr'apercevoir, entrevoir **catch a hold of** se gripper **catch the scent of** éventer **catch with a hook** crocher **catch with a net** seiner **catch with a trawl** trôler **catch shrimp with a trawl** aller aux trôles **hard to catch** filant **be catching a cold** couver un rhume

catch-all *n.* fourre-tout

catcher *n.* **oyster catcher** bec-de-hache

catching *n.* accrochage, attrapage

catechism *n.* catéchisme **teach catechism** montrer le catéchisse **woman who teaches children their catechism in French** montreuse de catéchisme

cater-cornered *adj.* bisquencoin, en coin

caterpillar *n.* chenille **green caterpillar** chenille brûlante *pl.* **act of destroying caterpillars** échenillage **get rid of caterpillars** écheniller

caterwaul *v.* miauler

caterwauling *n.* mialement

catfish *n.* barbote **blue catfish** barbue **bullhead catfish** goujon **channel catfish** barbue, mâchoiron de passe **flathead catfish** barbue à tête plate, goujon caille, goujon jaune, goujon **Gafftopsail catfish** mâchoiron **mud catfish** mâchoiron **Opelousas catfish** mâchoiron **saltwater catfish** mâchoiron **spoonbill catfish** belle-dame, spatule **spotted catfish** mâchoiron **yellow catfish** mâchoiron **black bullhead catfish** palao **blue channel catfish** barbue

cathedral *n.* cathédrale

Catholic *adj.* catholique

Catholic *n.* Catholique **Catholic who ignores many rules of the church** Catholique à gros grain **non-practicing**

Catholic Catholique à gros grain **hypocritical Catholic who makes a show of observing liturgical rites but does not behave morally** Catholique à gros grain **a fervent or fanatical Catholic** Catholique à gros grain

cattail *n.* canne **cattail patch** joncière **cattail plant** jonc de chat {au baril} / jonc plat {matelas}, queue de chat, queue de rat

cattle *n.* **cattle driver** pousseur de bêtes, toucheur de bêtes **cattle guard** pont à craques **cattle ranch** vacherie **cattle tick** pou de bête **head of cattle** tête de bête / tête d'animaux **herd of cattle** vacherie **rearing of cattle** vacherie **round up cattle** faire le tour des bêtes **turn the cattle loose** lâcher les bêtes **cry used to drive cattle or chase cattle away** hoba *pl.* **one who works cattle on horseback** cavalier

caucus *n.* caucus

caught *adj.* **be caught** se faire prendre **get caught** s'accrocher, se faire coller, se prendre **get caught by** attraper **get caught in** attraper **get caught up** se rattraper **get o.s. caught** se faire attraper **having s.t. caught in the throat** égosillé **get jammed or caught** se coincer

caul *n.* toie, voile, voilette **having a veil or caul on one's face at birth** coiffé

cauldron *n.* chaudière à laver, chaudron

cauliflower *n.* chou-fleur

caulk *v.* galféter

caulking *n.* galfétage **caulking knife** couteau de galfat

cause *n.* auteur, cause, occasion, cause **be the cause of** causer

cause *v.* causer, causionner, occasionner **cause sorrow** faire grief **cause a lump** embosser **cause an uproar** faire un carnaval **cause respiratory congestion** oppresser **cause trouble, discord** faire du {un} désordre **cause misery and trouble** brasser mer et larmes **provoke or cause bumps or swelling of skin** louper

causeway *n.* DAM

caustic *adj.* caustique **be caustic in one's speech** avoir la langue comme une vipère **one who makes caustic remarks** passeur de chiques

cauterize *v.* cautériser

caution *v.* précautionner, prévenir

cautious *adj.* prudent **be cautious** prendre précaution, se précautionner

cavalcade *n.* cavaillade

cave *n.* caverne, souterrain

cave *v.* **cave in** débouler, s'écrouler

cavern *n.* caverne, souterrain

caving *n.* **caving in** déboulage, déboulement

cavity *n.* cavité **sinus cavity** cerveau **having a cavity** piqué **fill a dental cavity** boucher une dent **tooth with a cavity** dent creux

cayenne *n.* cayenne **cayenne pepper** cayenne

cease *v.* abandonner, arrêter, cesser, lâcher, quitter

ceaseless *adj.* sans cesse

cedar *n.* cèdre **cedar tree** bois de cèdre, mûrier **red cedar** cyprès **eastern brown cedar** cyprès **eastern red cedar** arbre de cipre **Eastern red cedar** cipre rouge, cèdre rouge

cedarbird *n.* cirier, mûrier

cede *v.* céder, livrer **cede use of land** livrer une terre

ceiling *n.* ceiling, grénit, plafond **ceiling fan** éventail à électricité, éventail électrique **finish the walls or ceiling of** plafonner

celebrant *n.* célébrant

celebrate *v.* célébrer, faire la fête, fêter, célébrer

celebrated *adj.* célèbre, fameux

celebration *n.* célébration, halicasser **Mardi Gras celebration** carnaval

celery *n.* céleri

cell *n.* cachot

cellar *n.* cache-tout, cave

celluloid *n.* caoutchouc

celosia *n.* crête de coq, crête de corusse, crête de guime

cement *n.* ciment

cement *v.* cimenter

cemetery *n.* cimetière

censer *n.* encensoir

censure *v.* blâmer, condamner

census *n.* **census taker** compteur

cent *n.* sou *pl.* **seventy-five cents** six escalins **two and a half cents** quarti **what one could buy for two and a half cents** quarti

center *n.* cœur, centre, milieu, mitan, moyeu **place in center** centrer

center *v.* centraliser, centrer

centipede *n.* bétaille à mille pattes, bête à mille pattes, mille-pattes, ver à mille pattes

central *adj.* central

centralize *v.* centraliser

century *n.* siècle

ceremony *n.* cérémonie **graduation ceremony** graduation **baptize without a church ceremony** endoyer

cereus *n.* **night-blooming cereus** belle de nuit

certain *adj.* assuré, certain, positif, sûr **a certain** tel **not certain** pas sûr **one certain** nommé **imagine o.s. in a certain way** se voir

certainly *adv.* sûr, assuré, assurément, certainement, foutûment, foutrement, obligé, obligément, positivement, sûrement

certainty *n.* assurance, certaineté, certitude, conviction, sûreté **with certainty** à coup sûr

certificate *n.* certificat, document **birth certificate** baptistaire **death certificate** certificat de mortalité **baptism record or certificate** baptistaire

certification *n.* certification

certify *v.* acertainer, certifier

certitude *n.* certitude

cessation *n.* cessation

chafe *v.* limer, échauffer
chafed *adj.* échauffé
chaff *n.* écale **rice chaff** écale de riz
chagrined *adj.* **be chagrined by s.t.** avoir (qqch) sur le cœur
chain *n.* chaîne **chain link** anneau de chaîne **breast chain** BREAST-CHAIN
chain *v.* enchaîner
chaining *n.* enchaînement
chair *n.* chaise, siège, escabie **rocking chair** berce, berceuse, fauteuil **upholstered chair** chaise bourrée **gliding rocking chair** balancine
chairman *n.* président
chaise longue *n.* dormeuse
chalice *n.* calice
chalk *n.* CHALK, craie
challenge *n.* défi
challenge *v.* défendre, défier
challenging *adj.* ROUGH
chamber *n.* **chamber pot** pot de chambre {noce}
chamois *n.* chamois
chamomile *n.* camomine
champ *n.* CHAMP
champagne *n.* champagne **champagne glass** flûte
champion *n.* CHAMP, champion
chance *n.* adonnance, chance, fortune, hasard, opportunité, risque **by chance** d'hasard / par hasard, par adonnance, par hasard **encounter by chance** arriver sur **happen by chance** adonner, s'adonner **have a chance** avoir (une) chance **have the chance** avoir la chance de **miss the chance** manquer le coup **not a chance** pas de chance **take a chance** courir la chance, gambler, prendre une chance / prendre des {ses} chances, risquer, s'aventurer **take a chance with** aventurer **give a second chance** donner une reprise *pl.* **take one's chances** se risquer
change *n.* argent blanc, argent claire, changement, variation, cassée, change, échange **change for the worse** se gâter **give change** échanger **make change** casser, faire (de) l'échange, faire du change
change *v.* changer, modifier, se changer, échanger, changeailler, changeoter **change again** rechanger **change places** changer de place **change residences** décaniller, déloger, déménager **change sides** changer de bord **change course often** vironer **change course suddenly** barder **change one's clothes** se changer, se déchanger, se rechanger **change one's opinions** changer son fusil d'épaule **change often or capriciously** changeailler, changeoter **change the clothes of** déchanger **change the position of** émouver **things change** la roue tourne **cause to change his or her mind** dévirer **spirit which changes its shape** bétaille caille
changeable *adj.* changeable, changeant, fragile, journalier **changeable person** changeoteur
changed *adj.* tourné
changing *adj.* variable
changing *n.* changeage
chanky-chank *n.* tchinqui-tchinque
channel *n.* canal, chenal, manchac, rigolet, station
chant *n.* chant
chap *n.* bougre, gerce, gerçure, JACK
chap *v.* craquer, gercer
chapel *n.* chapelle, oratoire
chaperone *n.* chaperon
chaperoned *adj.* **group being chaperoned** trallée
chaplain *n.* chapelain
chapped *adj.* **be chapped** gercer
chapter *n.* chapitre
character *n.* caractère, nature, personnalité, tempérament **character reference** référence **a character** pétard **unusual character** beau coco **imaginary character in stories designed to frighten children** Madame Grands Doigts **legendary character who brings small gifts to children on New Year's Eve** Petit Bonhomme Janvier **unusual and interesting character** pistolet à deux manches, pistolet **do harm to the character by overindulgence** gâter
characteristic *n.* caractéristique
charade *n.* charade
charcoal *n.* charbon
charge *n.* accusation, charge, cure, frais, garde, tarif **charge account** acompte **assume charge** se charger **in charge** en tête **take charge** prendre charge, se mettre à la tête **have charge of** avoir charge de **in charge of** en charge de **be in charge** être en chef **person in charge** officier **put in charge** rencharger **be in charge of** avoir charge de **bring a charge against** charger, faire {mettre} une charge contre *pl.* **press legal charges against s.o.** mettre une charge contre qqn **shipping and handling charges** fret
charge *v.* accuser, charger, commissionner, encharger, rencharger, charger **charge exorbitant prices** arracher les yeux de la tête
charitable *adj.* charitable
charity *n.* aumône, charité **act of charity** acte de charité **ask for charity** demander la charité, faire {passer} la quête
charivari *n.* charivari
charlatan *n.* charlatan
Charles *n.* **Lake Charles** Lac Charles
charm *n.* berloque, charme, gris-gris, grâce, voudou **magical charm** condjo, ouanga **work like a charm** travailler comme un neuf / travailler comme un papier de musique
charm *v.* charmer, enchanter
charmer *n.* enchanteur
charming *adj.* charmant
charter *n.* charteur **charter flight** charteur
chase *n.* chasse, course
chase *v.* coursailler, courser après, courser, galoper, poursuivre, coursailler, courser **chase away** chasser, décaniller **chase**

off courser, lancer, émousser **chase out** chasser **chase women** rouscailler **chase women or men** coursailler, courser **cry used to drive cattle or chase cattle away** hoba

chasing *n.* **go chasing about at night** faire (le) rougarou

chassis *n.* carcasse

chaste *adj.* chaste, pur

chastity *n.* chasteté, pureté, vertu

chat *n.* causade, causerie, charade

chat *v.* causer, charrer

chatter *n.* barbotage, parlementages, tac-tac

chatter *v.* cacasser, charader, charlanter, jappailler, japper, jarrer, nasiller, parlailler **chatter on** battre sa gueule

chatterbox *n.* attrape-mouches / attrape à mouches, bagueuleur, nénaine, radoteur

chattering *n.* **tiresome chattering** midi à quatorze (heures)

chatting *n.* rametien

chayote *n.* pied de mirliton

cheap *adj.* (à) bon marché **cheap stuff** pacotille **it's not free or cheap** c'est pas merci

cheat *n.* croche, fraudeur

cheat *v.* couillonner, foutre dedans, frauder, graisser ses poches, mettre dedans, planter un piquant, tricher **cheat on** bêtiser, tromper

cheated *adj.* **get cheated** se faire mettre dedans, se faire planter un piquant, se faire prendre **allow o.s. to be cheated** se laisser mettre dedans

cheater *n.* tricheur

cheating *adj.* trompeur

cheating *n.* bloff, couillonade, filouterie, tricherie, tromperie

check *n.* CHECK **social security check** chèque à trous

check *v.* CHECK, passer, CHECK **check on** CHECK sur, voir à

checkered *adj.* carreauté

cheek *n.* bajoue, joue **cheek pouch** abajoue

cheep *v.* piaquer

cheer *v.* **cheer up** débouquer, désennuyer, se débouquer

cheerful *adj.* dégagé, joyeux, rapiqué

cheerfully *adv.* joyeusement

cheese *n.* fromage **cottage cheese** caillé-goutté / caillé-égoutté, caillé, lait égoutté **cream cheese** caillé-goutté / caillé-égoutté **head cheese** gelée de cochon, gelée **hoghead cheese** fromage de cochon, fromage de tête de cochon, fromage de tête **toe cheese** cambouille

cheesecloth *n.* brin, coton à tapisser

chellitis *n.* bride

cherish *v.* chérir

cherished *adj.* chéri

cherry *n.* **black cherry** merise **ground cherry** coqueret **wild cherry** merise **black cherry tree** merisier

chest *n.* boîte, coffre, estomac, jabot, poitrine **chest of drawers** armoire, bureau, commode **chest of a person** poitrail **hope chest** trousseau **ice chest** cooler **with chest exposed** dépoitraillé **bare the chest of** dépoitrailler **expose the chest or breast** se dépoitrailler **suffering from tuberculosis or deep chest congestion** époitriné

chestnut *adj.* châtain

chestnut *n.* **chestnut tree** châtaignier

chew *n.* chique

chew *v.* chicailler, chiquer, mâcher **chew again** remâcher **chew with difficulty** mâchouiller **chew slowly, with pleasure** mâchouiller **one who chews tobacco** chiqueur

chewing *adj.* **chewing gum** gomme **chewing tobacco** tabac à chiquer

chewing *n.* mâchage, mâchement

chewink *n.* grassel, jorée

Chicago *n.* **I don't want to go to Chicago** je n'ai rien perdu à Chicago

chicanery *n.* chicane, chicanerie

chick *n.* petit poulet, poulet *pl.* **remove chicks from nest or incubator twenty-four hours after hatching** mettre par terre **feeding coop for baby chicks** cerne

chicken *n.* poule, volaille, pipi, quiquitte **chicken coop** cage à poules, têt à poules **chicken dropping** crotte de poule **chicken giblet** gésier **chicken gumbo** gombo de poule {volaille} **chicken meat** poulet **chicken pox** grattelle, picote volante / picote de poule / petite picote, picote **chicken roost** perchoir **chicken wire** fil à volaille **chicken yard** basse-cour **chicken nesting place** nichoir **chicken that pecks** picocheur **chicken roost or perch** jouc, jouquoir **bantam chicken** bendé **bob-tailed chicken** chaouinon **dwarf chicken** poule lavanée {lavane} **fried chicken** poule frit {frite}, poulet frit / poulet rôti **leghorn chicken** léguine **roast chicken** poule grillée, poule rôtie, rôtie **shawnee chicken** chaouinon **young chicken** poulet **bony bottom of a chicken** nez du pretre {de l'éveque} *pl.* **call for chickens** quiquitte **don't count your chickens before they hatch** présume pas tes œufs

chickpea *n.* patte de poule

chickweed *n.* cresson

chicory *n.* chicoré, endive

chide *v.* babiller

chief *adj.* premier

chief *n.* chef, tête **chief of police** constable

chifferobe *n.* **section in an armoire or chifferobe for hanging clothing** portemanteau

chiffon *n.* **chiffon fabric** chiffon

chifforobe *n.* chiffonnier

chigger *n.* bête rouge

child *n.* bébé, enfant, gamin, innocent, petit **child that breaks everything** casse-tout **child of a second marriage** enfant du deuxième lit **child who makes a lot of noise while playing** carnageur **female child** fille **only child** seul (d')enfant **young child** petit **second child of a family** cadet **youngest child of a family** bébé **carry a child** porter un enfant **said of a child who struggles or fights** un diable dans un bénitier *pl.* **children's game** carencro-vole, couche-couche caillé **large number of children in a single family** ripopette **imaginary being used to frighten children** croquemitaine

childbirth *n.* accouchage, accouchement, enfantement

childhood *n.* enfance **be in one's second childhood** être en enfance **time of life between childhood and maturity** jeunesse

childish *adj.* enfantile

chill *n.* frisson *pl.* **fever chills** tremble **have chills** avoir le tremble

chill *v.* fraîchir, refroidir

chilly *adj.* frilant, frileux, frète

chime *npl.* **chimes** cordon

chimney *n.* cheminée **chimney built of mud and Spanish moss, or sometimes straw** cheminée bousillée

chin *n.* menton

china *n.* porcelaine

chinaball *n.* **chinaball tree** lilas de Perse, lilas des Indes, lilas parasol, lilas

chinaberry *n.* lilas parasol **chinaberry tree** arbre à chapelets, lilas des Indes, lilas

chinaware *n.* faïence, vaisselle

chine *n.* **pork chine** reintier

Chinese *adj.* chinois **Chinese person** Chinois

chinquapin *n.* **water chinquapin** graine à voler {vallée}, volée

chip *n.* bréchure, brèche, écale **poker chip** jeton **tortilla chip** galette de pain de maïs **wood chip** copeau, éclat, écopeau **a chip off the old block** bon chien tient de race **break a chip off of** abroquer

chip *v.* abroquer, brécher, chacoter

chiropractor *n.* craqueur d'os, crâleur d'os

chisel *n.* ciseau **cold chisel** ciseau à froid **wood chisel** ciseau à bois

chitterling *n.* andouille

chloasma *n.* **afflicted with chloasma** masqué

chloride *n.* **mercuric chloride** calomel

chloroform *n.* chloroforme

chocolate *n.* chocolat, coco

choice *adj.* recherché **choice one** fleur

choice *n.* choix, option, sélection **have the choice** être à même de choisir

choir *n.* chœur

choir-loft *n.* tribune **sing in the choir-loft** chanter dans la tribune

choke *n.* CHOKE **apply the choke** gotter

choke *v.* engoter, gotter, prendre au quiqui, pâmer, s'engoter, s'étouffer, s'étrangler, se gotter, étouffer, étrangler **choke o.s.** s'étrangler **choke up** engorger, engoter **choke with laughter** s'étouffer à {de} rire **choke with sand** s'ensabler **cause to choke** engoter **strangle or choke each other** s'étrangler

choked *adj.* **become choked** s'engorger **get choked** s'engoter

choking *adj.* égosillé

choking *n.* engotement, étouffement, étranglement

cholera *n.* choléra

choose *v.* appointer, choisir, sélecter, trier **choose one's words carefully** placer bien ses mots **be free to choose** être à même de choisir

choosing *n.* triage

chop *n.* bajoue, côtelette **pork chop** côtelette de cochon

chop *v.* bûchailler, chacoter, fendre, hacher, bûcher **chop at** bûchailler **chop down** abattre **chop up** coupailler, découpailler, hachouiller, moudre, mouler **break, cut, or chop into pieces** écharpiller

chore *n.* devoir, ouvrage *pl.* **do daily chores** faire le train **do one's chores** faire ses ouvrages

chorus *n.* **wild hunt, a mysterious racket, din, or chorus that passes through the night sky** chasse-galerie

Christ *n.* Christ **Jesus Christ** Jésus-Christ

Christian *adj.* chrétien

Christian *n.* chrétien

Christianity *n.* christianisme, christianité

Christmas *n.* Christmas, Jour de Noël, Noël **Christmas card** carte de Christmas **Christmas Eve** veille de Christmas, veille de Noël **Christmas tree** arbre de Christmas, arbre de Noël **Father Christmas** christine, Papa Noël

chrome *n.* chrome

chronic *adj.* chronique

chrysanthemum *n.* bouton d'argent, chrysanthème, fleur de la Toussainte, marguerite

chufa *n.* cache-cache

chum *n.* padna

chunk *n.* barre, CHUNK, gobe, gobet, morceau, motte **chunk of bread** chiffon de pain

church *n.* église **church service** office, service **church board of trustees** comité d'église **country church** mission

churchman *n.* écclesiastique

churchwarden *n.* marguiller

churn *n.* baratte, moulin à battre, moulin **butter churn** moulin à beurre

churn *v.* bouliner

ciborium *n.* ciboire

cicada *n.* cigale anglaise {zi-zi}, cigale chanteuse, cigale de nuit, cigale à {de} bois, cigale à chêne, cigale, locuste, ouioui

cigar *n.* cigare

cigarette *n.* cigarette **book of cigarette papers** livre de papiers à cigarette

cinch *n.* senelle **cinch strap** cingle, sangle **be a cinch** être une senelle

cinch *v.* sangler **cinch a saddle onto** cingler

cinder *n.* cendre

cinema *n.* maison de SHOW

cinnamon *n.* cannelle
cinnamon-colored *adj.* cannelle
circle *n.* cercle, rond **form a circle** circuler **in a circle** en rond **make a circle** faire un cercle, faire un tour *pl.* **turn around in circles** bouliner
circle *v.* cercler
circling *n.* cerclage
circular *adj.* circulaire, rond **circular object** rondelle, roulette
circulate *v.* circuler, trafiquer, circuler
circulation *n.* circulation, navigation
circumcision *n.* circoncision
circumstance *n.* circonstance *pl.* **embarrassing circumstances** baribara **set of circumstances** cas **under any circumstances** dans tous les cas
circus *n.* cirque
cistern *n.* citerne, cuve, tonne
citation *n.* citation
cite *v.* citer
citizen *n.* citoyen, national
citric *adj.* **citric acid** acide de citron
citron *n.* **citron plant** citronnier **citron tree** citron
citronella *n.* citronnelle **citronella oil** huile de citronnelle
city *n.* cité, village, ville **city block** bloc, îlet **live in the city** rester en ville **stay in the city** rester en ville **area or district of a city** quartier
civet *n.* **civet cat** civette
civic *adj.* civique
civil *adj.* civil
Civil *adj.* **the Civil War** la Guerre Civile / la Guerre Confédérée / la Guerre des Confédérées
civility *n.* civilité
civilization *n.* civilisation
civilize *v.* civiliser
civilized *adj.* civilisé
clabber *n.* caillé, tape-en-gueule
clabber *v.* cailler
clabbered *adj.* **clabbered milk** lait caillé
clack *onom.* clac
clack *v.* claquer
claim *n.* réclame **lay claim** reclamer
claim *v.* clamer, prétendre, reclamer, soutenir
clairvoyant *n.* devineur
clam *n.* burgau, mouque, palourde **freshwater clam** palourde
clamp *n.* serre-joint
clap *n.* éclat **thunder clap** coup de tonnerre
clap *v.* applaudir, taper
clapboard *n.* **clapboard siding** voliche
clapping *n.* applaudissement, battement
clarify *v.* clarifier
clarifying *n.* **clarifying tank** clarifieuse
clarinet *n.* clarinette
clasp *n.* agrafe **fasten with a clasp** agrafer
class *n.* classe, cours, classe **lower class** cadien **lower class or illiterate Francophone of Louisiana** Cadien **person of low class** drigaille, taïaut
class *v.* classer **class o.s.** se classer
classify *v.* classer **classify o.s.** se classer
classroom *n.* chambre de classe, classe
Claus *n.* **Santa Claus** christine, Papa Noël, SANTA CLAUS
clause *n.* **additional clause** allonge
clavicle *n.* clavicule
clavus *n.* corne, cor
claw *n.* ergot, ongle, pince, ergot **bird's claw** griffe *pl.* **seize with claws or talons** griffer **scratch with the claws** coffrer
claw *v.* coffrer, griffer
clay *n.* terre grasse **clay pigeon** pategau **heavy clay** poutine **constructed of packed clay** pisé
clean *adj.* net, propre **pick o.s. clean** se curer **a new broom sweeps clean** tout nouveau, tout beau
clean *v.* déberner, décombouiller, décrasser, fourbir, laver, nettoyer, propir, propter, éponger **clean carefully** écaler **clean out** défraîchir, purger **clean up** déberner, décrasser, décroûter, propir, propter **clean by picking** curer **clean for cooking** accommoder **clean for o.s.** se propter **clean o.s. up** se déberner, se décrasser, se décrotter, se propter **clean mud off of** débousiller **clean o.s. of filth** se décrasser **clean away mud or filth** décrotter **clean the shells of oysters** décoquiller **clean by picking out foreign particles** dépicoter **clean o.s. of mud or filth** se décrotter **any wad of material used to clean one's bottom** torchon **any wad of material used to dust, clean up, or scrub** torchon
clean-up *n.* proptage
cleaned *adj.* **not cleaned** brut
cleaned-out *adj.* net
cleaner *adj.* **become cleaner** débousiller
cleaner *n.* nettoyeur
cleaning *n.* débarbouillage, fourbissage, nettoyage, proptage
cleanliness *n.* netteté, propreté
cleanse *v.* nettoyer, purifier **cleanse o.s.** se purifier
cleansing *n.* nettoyage, purification
cleanup *n.* nettoyage
clear *adj.* clair, lucide, net, vulière **clear as mud** clair comme de l'eau trouble {de la boue} / clair comme du jus de tabac {chique} **become clear** s'éclaircir **make clear** s'expliquer **as clear as day** clair comme le jour {un miroir}
clear *n.* **in the clear** quitte **be in the clear** être dans le clair
clear *v.* affranchir, déboucher, se dégoter, éclaircir, desservir, débarbouiller, défraîchir, dégréer, désérer, se débarbouiller, se débrouiller **clear off** débarrasser **clear out** débarrasser, dégréer, sacrer le camp, évacuer **clear up** s'arranger, s'éclaircir, se casser, se lever, se refaire, se relever, se réparer **clear out an area** faire grand rond **clear of frost or fog** débrouiller **clear of trees and brush** déboiser **clear**

out weeds or underbrush défraîchir **one who clears land** déséreur

cleared *adj.* désert

clearer *adj.* **become clearer** débousiller

clearing *n.* défraîchi, éclairissage, débarbouillage, défraîchissage, défraîchissement, désérage, éclaircie **clearing away** débarbouillage **clearing off** débourbage **clearing up** éclairissement **clearing in the woods** brûlé **clearing up of the weather** cassée du temps **clearing in the woods or in a marsh** clair

clearly *adv.* clair, clairement, tout en plein, tout à clair

cleat *n.* taquet

cleaver *n.* **meat cleaver** CLEAVE

cleft *adj.* **cleft palate** palais fendu

clematis *n.* clématis

clergy *n.* clergé

clergyman *n.* ministre

clerk *n.* commis **clerk of court** greffier **clerk of court's office** greffe **clerk of the court** commis de jour

clever *adj.* adroit **clever person** canaille

cleverness *n.* adresse

clevis *n.* tête de chat

cliché *n.* cliché

client *n.* client, pratique

clientele *n.* clientèle, patronage, pratique

climate *n.* climat

climb *v.* agripper, engrucher, grimper, grucher, monter, s'engrucher, se hurcher, se jouquer, filer, remonter **climb again** remonter **climb around** montailler **climb down** dégrucher **climb repeatedly** montailler

climbing *adj.* filant, grimpeur

clinch *v.* river, riveter

cling *v.* s'agripper, se coller, se cramponner, se raccrocher

clingy *adj.* collant

clinic *n.* clinique

clip *n.* **at a good clip or pace** raidement **go at a good clip** aller bon train

clip *v.* couper, tailler, tondre

clipper *npl.* **clippers** clips, fauces, pince

clipping *n.* tonnage

clique *n.* bastringue, clique, quinapan

cloak *n.* cape **baby's cloak** carrick, roupe

clock *n.* horloge, montre, pendule, berloque **alarm clock** réveil, réveille

clod *n.* motte, toron **clod of dirt** motte de terre, rabot *pl.* **form clods** motter **form into clods** se motter

clod *v.* motter, se motter

clodhopper *n.* sabot

clog *v.* se gotter, engoter

clogging *n.* bouchage, embouchure

close *adj.* familier, intime, rapproché, près **be close** être grosse affaire

close *adv.* approché, auprès, collé, d'auprès, près, à deux doigts, à touché **close by** au ras, auprès, près, tout près **close to** (à) côté de, au ras (de), auprès de, proche de, près de **close to death** à deux doigts de sa mort **from close** d'auprès **get physically close in a conflict or argument** se souffler dans les narines

close *v.* barrer, fermer, se fermer **close up** se reboucher

close-fitting *adj.* TIGHT

closed *adj.* clos **closed in** enfermé

closeness *n.* justesse

closest *n.* **at the closest** au plus près

closet *n.* boutique, cache-tout, closette, cabinet **junk closet** fourre-tout

closing *n.* clôture

closure *n.* **achieve complete closure** bâcler

clot *n.* caillant, motelon, pelote **blood clot** caillou de sang

clot *v.* calciner

cloth *n.* drogue, fabrique, linge, toile, étoffe **cloth used to scrub the floor** essuie-place **altar cloth** nappe d'autel **bird's-eye cloth** ouvré **cambric cloth** batiste **cotton cloth** coton, linge de coton **damask cloth** damas **guinea cloth** guinée **homespun cloth** cotonnade **household cloth** essuie **Indianhead cloth** indienne **knitted cloth** tricot **thin cloth** brin **dotted cloth of navy cotton** guinée **decorative cloth put underneath the head of a corpse for a funeral** suaire **band of cloth** bande **breadth of cloth** laise **cheap cotton cloth** cotonnade **band of cloth added to a dress or skirt to make it longer** greget **piece of old cloth** guenille **torn piece of cloth** chiffon **triangular piece of cloth** laize **piece or scrap of cloth** carreau

clothe *v.* habiller, vêtir

clothed *adj.* habillé

clothes *npl.* agrès, artifailles, gréement, habillement, habit, linge **clothes peg** épingle à linge **clothes pin** maquillon **clothes rack** portemanteau **dirty clothes** linge **night clothes** pyjamas **ragged clothes** haillonnerie **summer clothes** linge d'été **winter clothes** linge d'hiver **work clothes** linge de travail / linge d'ouvrage **electric clothes dryer** chesseuse **obtain clothes or material** se gréer **bleach clothes by putting them in direct sunlight** braliner, mettre à la braline **adjust one's clothes** s'ajuster **change one's clothes** se changer, se déchanger, se rechanger **put on clothes** se gréer, se mettre du linge **readjust one's clothes** se rajuster **sport fine clothes** farauder **unbutton one's clothes** se déboutonner **wear good clothes** porter du bon linge **change the clothes of** déchanger **lay out clothes on the ground to dry** mettre du linge à la plaille **dress in everyday clothes** s'habiller en tous les jours **fancy or dressy clothes and accessories** farauderie **place for washing clothes or dishes** laverie **tool for pressing clothes, branding, soldering, etc.** fer **put on one's fine clothes** mettre du fond de la malle **take off one's good clothes** déficeler **go to bed with all**

one's clothes on se coucher tout rond **said of one who wears out his clothes quickly** usurier

clothesline *n.* corde à linge, cordelle, ligne à linge, ligne, éparant **take off of a clothesline** décorder

clothespin *n.* bois à linge, maquignon cordelle / maquignon à cheval, pince à linge, épingle à linge **spring clothespin** pinceuse **straight clothespin** cavalier

clothing *n.* agrès, gréement, habillement, harnachement, linge de corps, linge, artifailles **clothing iron** fer à repasser **press clothing** lisser le linge **remove clothing** déshabiller **strange clothing** attriquage, attriquement **surplus clothing** achalage **agitate clothing in a tub of water** sagoter **adjust one's clothing** se rarranger **article of clothing** habillement, habit **change of clothing** change de linge, rechange **piece of clothing** morceau de linge **set of clothing** ensemble **tear one's clothing** se déchirer **dirty item of clothing** soutadaire **remove articles of clothing** se desseller **urinate in one's clothing** se tremper **said of a person who spends much on clothing and little on food** dos brillant et ventre criant

cloud *n.* château, nuage, nué **cloud bank** château **cloud that brings rain** château de pluie, tête de pluie **black cloud** nuage **rain cloud** nuage de pluie, nuage **snow cloud** nuage de neige **squall cloud** grain *pl.* **storm clouds** orage **in the clouds** dans les nuages **be in the clouds** être dans les nués

cloud *v.* **cloud up** brouiller, se troubler, troubler

cloudy *adj.* caille, couvert, embrouillé, nuageux, orageux, boucané, lourd **become cloudy** se couverre, se troubler **get cloudy** brouiller **it's cloudy** le temps est couvert **become cloudy or overcast again** se recouverre

clove *n.* congéror, girofle **clove tree** giroflier **clove of garlic** gosse d'ail **whole clove** clou de girofle

clover *n.* trèfle **four-leaf clover** trèfle à quatre feuilles

clown *n.* bouffon, macaque, paillasse **play the clown** bouffonner **act like a clown** faire le bouffon

clown *v.* bouffonner, faire le bouffon **clown around** bouffonner, carcailler, couillonner, faire le bouffon

clowning *n.* bouffonnerie, couillonnerie

club *n.* CLUB **club for playing cards** cantique *pl.* **clubs** trèfle **jack of clubs** mistchoug, mistigri

clump *n.* groupe **grow into a clump** entaller, taller

clumsily *adv.* palotte

clumsiness *n.* gaucherie

clumsy *adj.* emplâtre, galfat, gauche, maladroit, mazette, pâlot, rabougri **clumsy person** caliberda **clumsy and lazy** gommeux **clumsy, awkward person** bidet **inattentive, clumsy person** galfat **any awkward or clumsy act or utterance** gaucherie

cluster *n.* chiffon, grappe, régime

clutch *n.* couvée, élève

clutter *n.* encombrement

clutter *v.* **clutter up** enfourner

cluttered *adj.* **the place in question is messy, disorganized, cluttered** Caillette pourrait perdre son veau là-dedans

co-heir *n.* cohéritier

co-owner *n.* copropriétaire

co-sign *v.* **co-sign a loan** cautionner

coach *n.* char **railway coach** traîneau

coachman *n.* cocher

coagulate *v.* cailler, calciner

coagulation *n.* caillant

coal *n.* charbon **coal oil** COAL OIL, huile de charbon, huile à {de} lampe **hot coal** braise *pl.* **live coals** braisier **rake over the coals** fourgailler, foutre HELL

coalman *n.* charbonnier

coaltar *n.* goudron

coarse *adj.* brut, gros, malengueulé, racatcha, racheux, ROUGH, vulgaire

coarsely *adv.* brut

coarseness *n.* crudité

coast *n.* côte

Coast *n.* **Coast Guard** Garde de Côte

coat *n.* basque, capot, casaque, gros capot, jaquette, manteau, paletot, renduit, véreuse **coat rack** portemanteau **child's coat** roupe **frock coat** rodingot **having a yellow or golden coat** baillonne **having a golden or tan coat and a white or cream-colored mane and tail** baille

coat *v.* renduire **coat with breading** paner **seal or coat with wax** encirer

coattail *n.* queue de capot

coax *v.* adoucir, cabaler, chouler, chouriner, emmioler, manioler, miauler

coaxing *n.* mialement, cabale

cobalt *n.* cobalt

cobble *v.* **cobble together** emmancher

cobia *n.* limon

cock *n.* coq, corusse **fighting cock** guème gaïme / guime gaïme **fighting cock or hen** gaïme **tell a cock and bull story** chanter des midis à quatorze heures

cock-of-the-walk *n.* taureau du bois

cockerel *n.* **castrated cockerel** chapon

cockeyed *adj.* **be cockeyed** avoir un œil au bois / avoir un œil qui dit merde à l'autre

cockfight *n.* bataille de gaimes

cocking *n.* bracage

cocklebur *n.* herbe coquin

cockroach *n.* ravet

cocoa *n.* cacao

cocograss *n.* coco

coconut *n.* coco

cocoon *n.* coucounne, ver de terre

cod *n.* morue **cod liver oil** huile de foie de morue

coffee *n.* café **coffee bean** graine de café **coffee can** cafetière **coffee canister** cafetière **coffee cup** cope de café, pinte à café, tasse à café **coffee fiend** cafiot **coffee grinder** moulin à café **coffee grounds** marc **coffee jar** cafetière **coffee mill** moulin à café **coffee spoon** cuillère à café **coffee with milk** café au lait **coffee spiked with whiskey** pousse-café **bad coffee** lavure, pissat de chat **black coffee** café fort, café noir **drip coffee** couler le café **dripped coffee** café égoutté **grind coffee** moudre le café, mouler le café **roasted coffee** café grillé **watered-down coffee** cafiau, cholo, clairiasse, piquette **weak coffee** cafiau, cholo, clairiasse, fiou-fiou, piquette, tcharara, toyasse **liquid coffee creamer** crème de lait **wild coffee plant** indigo **take coffee from the pot before it is done brewing** tricher sur la grègue **cup of coffee** tasse de café **sip of coffee** goutte de café **cup of weak coffee** tasse de pissat chaud **pot for serving coffee** cafetière **weak or bad-tasting coffee** tafia **hull of the coffee bean** parchemin **one who drinks a great deal of coffee** cafiot

coffeemaker *n.* grègue

coffeepot *n.* bombe à café, cafetière, grègue à {de} café **drip coffeepot** grègue

coffeeweed *n.* café sauvage

coffer *n.* coffre

coffin *n.* cercueil, coffre

cog *n.* alochon, engrenage, dent

cognac *n.* cognac

coiffed *adj.* coiffé

coiffure *n.* coiffage, coiffure, peignure

coil *n.* ressort, rouleau **metal coil** SPRING

coil *v.* corder, enrouler, rouler, s'entortiller

coin *n.* monnaie **five-cent coin** bleu, cinq-sous, plomb **old coin** picaillon **twelve-and-a-half-cent coin** escalin **five cent coin** nickel **ten cent coin** DIME, dix-sous **twenty-five cent coin** vingt-cinq sous

coincidence *n.* adonnance **by coincidence** par adonnance

colander *n.* coule-macaroni, couloir, crible

cold *adj.* frais, froid, frète **cold one** froide **cold as ice** glacé **be cold** avoir froid, avoir frète **become cold** refroidir **feel cold** avoir frète **keep cold** refroidir **a cold one** 'tite fraide **become cold or colder** frédir, se refroidir **be hot / hungry / cold / thirsty** avoir chaud / faim / froid / soif

cold *n.* frais, froid, rhume **bad cold** grippe **catch cold** attraper du froid **common cold** frais **head cold** rhume de cerveau **catch a cold** prendre un rhume, s'enrhumer **give a cold** enrhumer **have a cold** avoir le rhume **sensitive to cold** frédilleux **be catching a cold** couver un rhume **shiver from the cold** friler, frédiller **feeling or suffering from the cold** frilant, frileux **treat for pneumonia or for a cold by applying mustard plasters** fluxionner **aching or sore muscles associated with having a cold** fraîcheur

cold-natured *adj.* frédilleux

colder *adj.* **become cold or colder** frédir, se refroidir **make cooler or colder** refroidir

coldness *n.* frigidité, froid

cole slaw *n.* choucroute

colic *n.* colique

collapse *n.* débâcle, écroulement

collapse *v.* s'écrouler, écrouler

collar *n.* col, collier **breast collar** bricole **harness collar** bourrure **leather collar** collier en cuir **wooden collar** collier en bois **wooden collar of harness** bois de collier **triangular wooden collar** carcan **remove a wooden collar** décarcaner **take off or unbutton a collar** décarcaner

collarbone *n.* clavicule

collation *n.* collation

colleague *n.* confrère

collect *v.* collecter, ramasser, collecter, toucher **collect payments** collecter **collect a fee** charger **collect for transport** ramasser **collect logs to use as firewood** attraper du bois

collection *n.* ramassage, ramasse, collection **collection basket** quête **collection of funds** quête **collection of a tax** prélèvement d'un impôt **pass a collection plate** faire {passer} la quête, passer la quête **take up a collection** faire {passer} la quête, passer la quête

collector *n.* collecteur **tax collector** collecteur

college *n.* collège

collide *v.* s'aborder **collide with** aborder

collision *n.* abordage

colonade *n.* colonnade

colonel *n.* colonel

colonist *n.* colon

colonize *v.* coloniser

color *n.* teinture **lose color** décolorer, déteindre, se décolorer **drained of color** effacé **man of color** homme de couleur **of one color** uni **people of color** gens de couleur **person of color** nègre congo **cause to lose color** déteindre **remove dye or color** décolorer *pl.* **of many colors** barosse **wear loud colors** s'habiller mardi gras **of many colors or designs** dépareillé

color *v.* couleurer, teindre, teinter **color green** verdir

colored *adj.* **colored man** homme de couleur **colored people** gens de couleur, le monde de couleur **colored woman** femme de couleur **brightly colored** brillant **be brightly colored** briller **yellow or tan colored** barosse

colorful *adj.* **overly colorful or decorative** criard

colorless *adj.* pâle

colossus *n.* colosse

colt *n.* potre, poulain

Columbus *n.* **Knight of Columbus** Chevalier de Colombus

column *n.* colonne **porch column** poteau de galerie

coma *n.* coma, léthargie

comatose *adj.* **in an unconscious or comatose state** en léthergie

comb *n.* crête, démêloir, peigne **comb of a rooster** huppe **large-toothed comb** démêloir

comb *v.* mousser, peigner, étriller **card, comb or brush** carder

combat *n.* bataille, combat
combative *adj.* militant
combed *adj.* **having the hair combed straight back** à la pompadour
combination *n.* combinaison
combine *n.* coupeuse
combine *v.* joindre, s'unir
come *n.* **come and go** va-et-vient
come *v.* arriver, s'en venir, se ranger, sortir de, venir, parvenir, provenir **come across** ressoubler **come after** venir après **come apart** décoller, défiler, se séparer **come back** rentourner, renvenir, retourner, revenez! / reviens! / reviens BACK!, revenir, s'en revenir, s'en revenir / s'en retourner, se rentourner, se retourner, venir BACK **come closer** se rapprocher **come down** descendre **come from** devenir, venir **come get** venir après **come in** entrer, rentrer **come loose** s'arracher, se démancher, se détacher, se dévisser **come near** aborder, approcher, s'approcher, se rater **come off** se retirer **come out** débouquer, sortir de, sortir, sourdre **come together** rassembler, se rassembler **come undone** se défaire **come up** aborder, lever, venir en l'air **come upon** frapper **come and go** naviguer, trafiquer **come back in** rerentrer **come close to** venir (à) un fil de **come down again** redescendre **come into force** venir en force **come on horseback** venir à cheval **come out again** ressortir **come out ahead** sortir l'avant / sortir en avant **come out even** sortir à jeu **come out well** aboutir en bien **come out with** sortir avec **come to mind** venir à l'idée **come to nought** aboutir en rien **come to terms** s'arranger **come up with** comploter **come back to life** ressusciter, revivre **come close to dying** venir un fil {un cheveu / deux cheveux} de sa mort, être venu un cheveu de sa mort **come to a head** aboutir, claquer **come to a standstill** arrêter **come to an end** terminer **come a hair from death** être venu un cheveu de sa mort **come at an opportune time** s'adonner bien **come over for a visit** venir faire une tournée {un tour} **come to a bad end** aboutir en mal **come within a hair of** venir (à) un fil de **come at just the right time** s'adonner bien **come up from under the water** ressourdre **come up out of the water** sourdre **how come** comment (ça) se fait **not come about** tourner en eau de boudin **have come to the end of one's high point** avoir tiré son pétard **plant that comes up spontaneously** plante de bonne aventure
comedy *n.* farce
comet *n.* comète
comfort *n.* aise, bènaise, confort, consolation
comfort *v.* conforter, consoler, reconsoler
comfortable *adj.* confortable **make o.s. comfortable** niquer, se mettre à son aise, se nicher, se niquer
comforter *n.* **eiderdown comforter** édradon
comforting *adj.* consolant
comfy *adj.* douillet
comic *n.* farceur, humoriste
comical *adj.* comique, farce
coming *adj.* **he has it coming to him** ça lui revient **she / he had it coming** c'est bien tapé
coming *n.* arrivée, qui vient *pl.* **goings and comings** va-et-vient
command *n.* ordre **command to a cow to encourage it to get in position for milking** 'poteau, Caillette'!
command *v.* BULLDOZE, ordonner
commandant *n.* commandant
commander *n.* commandant
commandment *n.* commandement
Commandment *npl.* **the Ten Commandments** décalogue, Les Dix Commandements, les Dix Commandements
commemorate *v.* commémorer
commencement *n.* **commencement exercises** graduation
comment *n.* remarque
comment *v.* remarquer
commerce *n.* commerce
commercial *adj.* commercial
commission *n.* commission, commission
commission *v.* commissionner
commissioner *n.* commissionnaire
commit *v.* commettre **commit a sin** faire un péché **commit highway robbery** voler comme dans la forêt des bandits **one who commits suicide** suicide
committee *n.* BOARD, comité **vigilance committee** comité de vigilance **vigilante committee** vigilance **member of a vigilance committee** vigilant
commode *n.* commode
common *adj.* commun, familier, ordinaire
common *n.* **in common** en commun
common-law *n.* **common-law mate** maquereau
commotion *n.* agitation, bacchanale, baribara, berdassement, berdi(s)-berda(s), capotage, commerce, commotion, commérage, haut-le-corps, tchampourra, traillail
communicant *n.* communicant
communicate *v.* communiquer, s'expliquer
communication *n.* communication
communion *n.* communion **communion rail** table sainte **take communion** communier **receive communion during the Easter season** faire ses Pâques **make one's first communion** faire sa première commion **administer the sacrament of communion** communier
communist *adj.* communiste
communist *n.* communiste
community *n.* communauté, commune, société, voisinage, communauté
compact *v.* fouler
compacter *n.* fouleuse
companion *n.* accompagneur, camarade, compagnon, copain **female companion** femelle

company *n.* compagnie, corporation, société, compagnie **insurance company** compagnie d'assurances **keep company** fréquenter, tenir compagnie **oil company** compagnie d'huile **keep company with** se mêlailler
comparable *adj.* comparable
compare *v.* comparer, vérifier
comparison *n.* comparaison
compartment *n.* compartement
compass *n.* boursole, compas
compassion *n.* compassion, miséricorde
compassionate *adj.* compatissant, miséricordieux
compassionately *adv.* miséricordieusement
compatible *adj.* accordant
compel *v.* forcer, obliger
compensate *v.* compenser, récompenser
compensation *n.* compensation, récompense
compete *v.* faire compétition (avec), faire concurrence (avec)
competent *adj.* compétent
competition *n.* compétition, concurrence **sportfishing competition** rodéo **be in competition with** faire compétition (avec)
complacency *n.* complaisance
complain *v.* bougonner, complaindre, grogner, jappailler, pialler, porter plainte, se lamenter, se plaindre **complain incessantly** chiquer du vieux linge **person who constantly whines and complains** pratique à chagrin **one who frequently complains about his health** pot fêlé
complainer *n.* bougonneur, grognard, grogneur, plaignard, plaignoux, pialleur
complaining *adj.* chigneux, gningnin
complaining *n.* piallerie
complaint *n.* charge, lamentation, plainte **lodge a complaint** porter plainte
complete *adj.* absolu, complet, entier, plénière, seul **all is complete** c'est sellé et bridé
complete *v.* accomplir, achever, compléter, finir **complete successfully** passer
completely *adv.* absolument, bien, carrément, complètement, en plein, entièrement, propre, tout net, tout à fait
completion *n.* complétion
complexion *n.* complexion, teint
compliance *n.* obéissance
complicate *v.* compliquer
complicated *adj.* compliqué **become complicated** se compliquer
complication *n.* complication
compliment *n.* compliment **pay a compliment** payer un compliment
compliment *v.* complimenter **compliment each other** se complimenter
comply *v.* se conformer, se soumettre
component *n.* élément
compose *v.* composer, faire des chansons
composed *adj.* aplomb **be composed** consister
composition *n.* composition
compost *n.* **compost heap** pile
composure *n.* aplomb
comprehensible *adj.* comprenable
comprehension *n.* comprenure, compréhension
compress *n.* **cottonseed oil compress** usine
comprise *v.* comprendre
computation *n.* calcul
comrade *n.* compagnon
comradeship *n.* camaraderie
con *n.* trape-sottes **con artist** fraudeur **con game** trape-sottes
con *v.* passer une jambette (à qqn)
concave *adj.* encavé
conceal *v.* cacher, masquer
concealed *adj.* masqué
concede *v.* accorder, admettre
conceit *n.* vanité
conceited *adj.* fier, vain **conceited person** fiéraud
conceivable *adj.* comprenable, concevable
conceive *v.* concevoir, former, concevoir **conceive of** concevoir
concentrate *v.* concentrer **concentrate on** se concentrer
concentrated *adj.* concentré **become concentrated** se concentrer
conception *n.* conception **immaculate conception** immaculée conception **prevent conception** empêcher la famille
Conception *n.* **the Immaculate Conception** l'Immaculée Conception
concern *n.* affaire, business, intérêt **be of concern** s'adresser **it's of no concern to me** ça m'importe pas
concern *v.* chagriner, concerner, regarder, toucher **it doesn't concern you** c'est pas de tes affaires
concerned *adj.* **overly concerned with fairness and detail** observant **as far as he's concerned** tant qu'à pour lui
concerning *adj.* concernant
concerning *prep.* après, pour, sur, à propos de
concert *n.* concert
concession *n.* concession
conclude *v.* achever, conclure, figurer, se figurer, terminer
conclusion *n.* conclusion, fin, finissement, finition (finission) **in conclusion** pour en finir **bring to a final conclusion** bâcler
concoct *v.* inventionner
concoction *n.* décoction
concrete *n.* ciment
concubinage *n.* concubinage
concubine *n.* macorne, maquereau
concur *v.* concourir
condemn *v.* condamner **condemn or blame o.s.** se condamner
condemnable *adj.* condamnable
condemnation *n.* condamnation, conviction

condensed *adj.* concentré
condescend *v.* daigner
condiment *n.* assaisonnement
condition *n.* condition, sort, état, terme **on condition** pourvu **without condition** sans condition **on condition that** sous condition que, à condition que
conditional *adj.* conditionnel
condom *n.* capote, préservative
conduct *n.* comporte, conduite
conduct *v.* conduire, diriger, mener **conduct o.s.** se comporter, se conduire **conduct o.s. in a rowdy or noisy way** emmener
conducted *adj.* emmené
conductor *n.* conducteur
cone *n.* **pine cone** boule de pin, coco de pin, pomme de pin **ice cream cone** cornet de crème, SAY-SO de crème, SAY-SO
coneflower *n.* **prairie coneflower** tétine de négresse
confection *npl.* **confections** douceur
confederate *adj.* confédéré
Confederate *n.* confédéré
confederation *n.* confédération
confer *v.* **confer an honor upon** décorer
conference *n.* conférence **be in conference** cancaner
confess *v.* avouer, confesser, raconter, s'accuser **confess one's sin or guilt** se confesser
confession *n.* confesse, confession **go to confession** se confesser **prayer of confession** confession **hear the confession of and grant absolution** confesser **make the sacrament of confession** confesser
confessional *n.* confessional
confessor *n.* confesseur
confide *v.* fier
confidence *n.* confiance
confident *adj.* assuré
confidently *adv.* brave
confine *v.* carotter, renfermer
confined *adj.* **be confined to one's home** cabaner
confinement *n.* couche
confirm *v.* approuver, confirmer, confirmer
confirmation *n.* confirmation
Confirmation *n.* **sacrament of Confirmation** confirmation **receive the sacrament of Confirmation** confirmer
confirmed *adj.* **be confirmed** confirmer
confiscate *v.* confisquer
conflict *n.* démêlée **start or add to a rumor or conflict by one's words** mettre le feu à la paille {poudre}
confluence *n.* embouchure, fourche
conform *v.* s'adapter, se conformer
conforming *adj.* conforme
conformity *n.* **in conformity** conforme **in conformity with** accordant
confound *v.* confondre, étourdir
confrere *n.* confrère
confront *v.* affronter, confronter, figurer
confrontation *n.* abordage
confuse *v.* bafouer, brouiller, confondre, interboler, mêler, étourdir
confused *adj.* égaré **be confused** s'emmêler **get confused** s'emmêler, se perdre
confusion *n.* cancan, confusion, désordre, embrouille, galimatias, hourra, maquignonnage, pique-partout, bouleverse
congeal *v.* calciner, figer
congest *v.* oppresser
congested *adj.* congesté, oppressé
congestion *n.* congestion **respiratory congestion** oppressement, oppression **cause respiratory congestion** oppresser **having respiratory congestion** oppressé **suffering from tuberculosis or deep chest congestion** époitriné
congo *n.* congo
congratulate *v.* féliciter
congratulation *n.* congratulation, félicitation
congregation *n.* congrégation
congress *n.* congrès, législature
congressman *n.* membre du Congrès
conjecture *n.* conjecture
conjecture *v.* supposer
conjugal *adj.* conjugal
conjunctivitis *n.* maladie de yeux rouges
conjurer *n.* ouangateur
connect *v.* associer, connecter, connecter
connected *adj.* **connected to** connecté avec
connecting *n.* **connecting rod** brimbale
connection *n.* connexion, rapport, relation
conscience *n.* conscience **pang of remorse or conscience** remords de conscience
conscious *adj.* en pleine connaissance
consciousness *n.* connaissance **lose consciousness** BLACKOUT, perdre connaissance, tomber dans les défaillances
conscript *n.* conscrit
conscription *n.* conscription
consecrate *v.* consacrer
consecrated *adj.* sacré
consent *n.* consentement
consent *v.* approuver, consentir
consenting *adj.* consentant
consequence *n.* conséquence, effet, importance, résultat, suite **of little consequence or importance** (ça compte pas plus qu') un pet dans un ouragan *pl.* **suffer the consequences** soufferre les conséquences, subir les conséquences **do s.t. which could have bad consequences** mettre le pied dans la boue
consequential *adj.* important
consequently *adv.* par ainsi
conserve *v.* conserver, préserver, épargner

consider *v.* considérer, contempler, songer, trouver **consider o.s.** se calculer, se compter, se considérer, se croire, se trouver

considerable *adj.* considérable, conséquent

considerate *adj.* attentionné, civil, vaillant

consideration *n.* considération, réflexion

consist *v.* consister

consistency *n.* consistance

consolable *adj.* consolable, reconsolable

consolation *n.* consolation, reconsolation

console *v.* conforter, consoler, reconsoler **console o.s.** se consoler, se reconsoler, se soulager

consoling *adj.* consolant

conspiracy *n.* complot

conspire *v.* comploter

constable *n.* constable

constancy *n.* constance

constantly *adv.* constamment

constipate *v.* barrer, constiper

constipated *adj.* constipé **get blocked up, constipated** se bloquer

constipation *n.* constipation, crotte-au-cul

constituent *n.* constituant

constitution *n.* constitution

construct *v.* bâtir, composer, construire, ériger **construct with bousillage** bousiller

construction *n.* construction, érection **construction with clay** pisé de terre

constructive *adj.* constructive

constructor *n.* constructeur

consult *v.* consulter

consultant *n.* consultant

consultation *n.* consultation, consulte

consume *v.* dépenser, manger, user

consumption *n.* consomption, dépense, tuberculose **be for consumption** se manger

consumptive *adj.* poitrinaire

contact *n.* contact **in contact with** contre

contact *v.* contacter

contagion *n.* infection, pestilence

contagious *adj.* contagieux

contain *v.* contenir, tenir **contain o.s.** se contenir

container *n.* bassin, benne, bouilloir, réservoir, vaisseau **cooking container** chopine **cylindrical container** drum **basket or container** champagne, panier champagne, panier chinois, panier **any metal vessel or container** fer-blanc *pl.* **metal vessels and containers** ferblanterie

contaminate *v.* contaminer, infecter **contaminate o.s.** s'empester

contamination *n.* contamination

contemplate *v.* contempler

contemptuous méprisard

content *adj.* content

content *n.* contenu

contentment *n.* bènaise, contentement

contest *n.* lutte, MATCH **marksmanship contest** pategau **run away from a contest** caler le bouchon

contest *v.* contester

contestable *adj.* contestable, discutable

contestant *n.* **winning contestant in a women's pageant** reine

contiguous *adj.* **be contiguous** attenir, se toucher, toucher

continually *adv.* constamment, continué, à demeure

continuance *n.* continuation

continuation *n.* continuation, extension, prolongation, suite

continue *v.* continuer, GO AHEAD, se continuer

continuous *adj.* perpétuel

contour *n.* contour

contract *n.* contrat **make a contract** contracter **enter into by contract** contracter **hire work done on contract** contracter

contract *v.* contracter, empoigner, raccoquiller

contracted *adj.* raccoquillé

contractor *n.* contracteur

contradict *v.* contrarier, contredire, dédire, démentir, rembarrer **contradict o.s.** se dédire, se démentir **contradict o.s. or each other** se contrarier, se contredire

contradiction *n.* contradiction, contrariété, démenti

contraption *n.* installation

contrariness *n.* contrariété

contrary *adj.* bourru, contrariant, contrarieux **be contrary** avoir un pet en long **be in a contrary mood** avoir le jabot de travers, avoir un coup de lune, avoir un grain

contrary *n.* opposé **contrary to** au contraire de **the contrary** contraire **on the contrary** au contraire, à l'opposé **to the contrary** à l'opposé

contribute *v.* contribuer

contribution *n.* contribution

contrition *n.* **act of contrition** acte de contrition

Contrition *n.* **Act of Contrition** le confesse à Dieu

control *n.* contrôle **birth control** empêchement de famille **practice birth control** empêcher la famille

control *v.* contrôler, dominer, gouverner **control o.s.** se contrôler **hard to control** mal à main

controllable *adj.* contrôlable, gouvernable

conundrum *n.* dévinail

convalesce *v.* se refaire

convene *v.* convoquer

convenience *n.* aise, convénience, facilité

convenient *adj.* commode

convent *n.* couvent

convention *n.* convention

conversation *n.* causade, causerie, charade, conversation, discours, parlement **make conversation** charrer **have a conversation** donner une charade, tenir une conversation **having**

a conversation en parlement **hold a conversation** tenir une conversation **cut into a conversation** couper la conversation {le discours}, prendre la parole **interrupt or correct in conversation** reprendre **it's time to break up the party or conversation** c'est l'heure qu'on casse le rond

converse *v.* causer, charrer, converser, jabloter, se parler

conversion *n.* conversion

convert *n.* converti

convert *v.* convertir, se convertir

converted *adj.* **be converted** se convertir

conveyance *n.* moyen, voiture **connecting conveyance** connexion

conveying *n.* transmission

convict *n.* convict, forcien, prisonnier

conviction *n.* conviction

convince *v.* faire accroire

convinced *adj.* satisfait **be convinced** s'assurer

convocation *n.* convocation

convoke *v.* convoquer

convulsion *n.* attaque, crise

cook *n.* COOK, cuiseur, cuisinier **head cook** chef

cook *v.* cuire, faire cuire, faire la cuisine, rôtir, tambouiller **cook again** recuire **cook down** tarir **cook up** comploter **cook for o.s.** se cuire **cook too long** languir **cook a lot of food** mettre les petits plats dans les gros **cook in a covered pot with little water** étouffer

cooked *adj.* **anything cooked** tambouille **be cooked** se cuire

cooker *n.* **pressure cooker** chaudière à queue

cookery *n.* cuiture

cookie *n.* petit gâteau **cookie hardtack** gâteau **gingerbread cookie** estomac (de) mulâtre **stage plank cookie** estomac (de) mulâtre **store-bought or fancy cookie or candy** friandise

cooking *n.* cuiture, tambouille **cooking container** chopine **cooking grill** gril **cooking oil** huile à cuire, huile **cooking pot** bombe à cuire, bombe, bouille, casserole, chaudière en fer, chaudière noire, chaudière à queue, chaudière, marmite **bad cooking** gargote, ragouillage **bad, unappetizing cooking** ratatouille **do the cooking** cuire, faire la cuisine

cookstove *n.* STOVE

cool *adj.* frais, frète

cool *v.* refroidir **cool off** fraîchir, frédir, rafraîchir, refroidir, se fraîchir, se rafraîchir, se refroidir

cooler *adj.* **get cooler** se fraîchir **make cooler or colder** refroidir

cooler *n.* cooler

cooling *adj.* rafraîchissant

cooling *n.* rafraîchissement

coolness *n.* frais, fraîche, fraîcheur

coonass *n.* COONASS, cul de chaoui

coop *n.* **chicken coop** cage à poules, têt à poules **laying coop** poulailler **feeding coop for baby chicks** cerne

cooped *adj.* **stay cooped up** se cabaner

cooper *n.* **cooper's adze** herminette

cooperation *n.* coopération

cooperative *n.* coopératif

coopful *n.* cagée

coot *n.* poule d'eau

cooter *n.* **Mobile cooter** mobilienne, tortue mobilienne

copper *n.* cuivre

coppered *adj.* cuivré

copperhead *n.* serpent de canne

coppery *adj.* cuivré

copulate *v.* s'accoupler, piquer

copy *n.* copie

copy *v.* copier dessus, copier, imiter, relever, reproduire

coquette *adj.* folâtre

coquette *n.* coquette

coral *n.* **coral bean tree** mamou

cord *n.* corde **blue cord** cordon bleu **length of cord or material used to tie s.t.** amarre **sever the spinal cord** nerfer *pl.* **cords** cordage

cord *v.* corder, écorder

cordage *n.* cordage

corded *adj.* cordé

cordelle *n.* cordelle

cordgrass *n.* **big cordgrass** canne au cochon **smooth cordgrass** herbe d'huître, roseau de cochon

cordial *adj.* cordial

core *n.* cœur **core of an abscess or boil** mèche

coriander *n.* coriance

cork *n.* bouchon, liège

corkscrew *n.* corne de mouton, tire-bouchon, vrille

cormorant *n.* cormoran, z-oie pigeon

corn *n.* cor, corne, durillon, maïs tendre, maïs **corn farmer** faiseur de maïs **corn husk** robe de maïs, robe **corn mill** moulin à maïs **corn shuck** paille à {de} maïs, robe **corn silk** catin, filasse **corn stalks** canne de maïs **corn tassels** barbe de maïs **corn shuck mattress** paillasse **corn grinding or milling** moulage de maïs **corn on the stalk** coton maïs **feed corn** maïs dur **fried corn** maquechou **ground corn** maïs moulé **roasting corn** maïs tendre **smothered corn** maquechou **sweet corn** maïs sucré, maïs tendre **fried corn meal mush** couche-couche **ear of corn** épi de maïs **kernel of corn** grain de maïs **patch of corn** clos de maïs **deep fried corn or wheat cake** beigne **ear of corn with few grains** bougon **stunted ear of corn** épiochon **young ear of corn as it begins to silken** catin **kernel of dried, unripened corn** grillot **stunted, badly formed ear of corn** bougon **thin out sprouts at the roots of corn stalks** bourgeonner

cornbread *n.* pain (de) maïs **baked cornbread** pain levé

corncob *n.* coton-maïs, coton maïs, épi **corncob pipe** pipe en coton de maïs

corncrib *n.* maganière, magasin de {à} maïs

corner *n.* coin, encoignure, racoin **corner post** poteau du coin **loafer's corner** faubourg **turn a corner** tourner **drive into a corner** accointer **put in the corner** cointer **put into a corner** racointer

corner *v.* accointer, cerner, coincer, pousser au creux

cornerstone *n.* pierre angulaire

cornet *n.* cornet

cornfield *n.* clos de maïs

cornflower *n.* vieux garçon

cornice *n.* corniche

cornmeal *n.* farine (de) maïs **steamed, moist cornmeal eaten as a cereal** couche-couche

coroner *n.* coronaire

corporal *adj.* corporel

corporal *n.* caporal

corporation *n.* corporation **civil corporation** corporation

corpse *n.* cadavre, corps

corpulence *n.* corporence

corral *n.* parc, rodaire

corral *v.* parquer

corralling *n.* parcage

correct *adj.* bien, bon, correct, disable, exact, valide

correct *v.* correcter, corriger **correct o.s.** se corriger, se reprendre **correct in a brusque way** ramasser **interrupt or correct in conversation** reprendre

correction *n.* correction

correctly *adv.* correctement, proprement

correspond *v.* correspondre, s'accorder, s'adonner

correspondant *n.* correspondant

correspondence *n.* correspondance

corridor *n.* corridor, passage, passette

corrupt *adj.* croche comme un baril de serpents {d'hameçons} **become corrupt** se débaucher

corrupt *v.* corrupter, débaucher

corrupter *n.* débaucheur

corruption *n.* corruption

corsage *n.* corsage, corsage

corset *n.* corset

cortege *n.* cortège

cosmetic *n.* cosmétique

cost *n.* coût, coûtance, frais, prix **cost of lodging** pension **cost of transportation** fret **at cost** au prix coûtant **at any cost** coûte qui coûte **at no cost** gratis

cost *v.* coûter **cost a fortune** coûter les yeux de la tête **cost what it may** coûte qui coûte

costly *adj.* cher, chérant, coûteux

costume *n.* costume, habit

cot *n.* couchette

cottage *n.* **cottage cheese** caillé-goutté / caillé-égoutté, caillé, lait égoutté

cotton *n.* coton **cotton boll** gosse de coton **cotton cloth** coton, linge de coton **cotton fabric** linge de coton **cotton gin** GIN **cotton goods** cotonnade **cotton mattress** matelas de coton **cotton mill** moulin à coton **cotton picker** ramasseur de coton **cotton picking** ramasse-coton, ramasserie **cotton plant** coton **cotton press** compresse **cotton stalk** bâton de coton **cotton thread** fil de {en} coton **cotton silk fiber** soie de coton **cotton storage shed** cotonnerie **cotton or wool spun to be woven** jeture **gin cotton** passer le coton **yellow cotton** coton jaune **cheap cotton cloth** cotonnade **remove cotton from the bolls** égosser **last cotton left in the fields** graboterie **gathering of cotton** ramasse-coton **pale, unbleached cotton** coton baille **piece of cotton left in the boll after picking** tchie **piece of cotton or wool that has been carded** cardon **device that separates cotton from its seed** hérisson **fabric made of cotton warp and woolen thread** jeture **spool of wool or cotton** cardon **pick unopened bolls of cotton that remain after harvest** graboter **remove pod pieces from harvested cotton** égraboter **bat of carded wool or cotton ready for spinning** écardon **fibrous separation between pods in a cotton boll** oreille de coton

cotton-cloth *n.* **flecked cotton-cloth** guinée

cottonmouth *n.* congo à tête plate / serpent congo, congo, serpent congo

cottonseed *n.* **cottonseed oil compress** usine

cottontail *n.* **cottontail rabbit** lapin à queue blanche

cottonwood *n.* **cottonwood tree** cotonnier **southern cottonwood** liard

couch *n.* sofa

cougar *n.* chat-tigre

cough *n.* toux **cough drop** bonbon à rhume **whooping cough** coqueluche

cough *v.* toussailler, tousser **cough up** tousser

coughing *n.* tousserie

coulee *n.* coulée

council *n.* BOARD, conseil

counsel *n.* conseil **law counsel** conseil

counsel *v.* aviser, conseiller

counselor *n.* aviseur, avocat, conseilleur

count *n.* compte

count *v.* compter, compter **count again** recompter **count on** dépendre dessus {sur} **don't count your chickens before they hatch** présume pas tes œufs **no longer count as important** compter plus z-herbes

counter *n.* bar, comptoir

counterbalance *n.* contrepoids **counterbalance scale** romaine

counterblow *n.* contrecoup

counterfeit *v.* forger

counterfeiter *n.* forgeur

countermark *n.* contremarque

counterpoint *n.* contrepoint

countersign *n.* contresigne

counterweight *n.* contrepoids
counting *n.* calcul
countrified *adj.* cachoupic **uneducated and countrified** cadien
country *n.* campagne, nation, pays **country bumpkin** bitaco **country church** mission **country dweller** campagnard **country home** châlet **country store** boutique de campagne, magasin de campagne **country of origin or birth** pays d'origine **country man who assumes the pose of urban sophistication** fantoche **low country** pays bas **narrow country road** manche **land or country of birth** pays natal
countryside *n.* campagne
county *n.* paroisse **county agent** agent de la paroisse
coup d'état *n.* coup d'état
couple *n.* couple, paire **married couple** ménage **become a couple** s'accoupler **ridiculous or absurd-looking couple** chiquette et berlingue **saying that describes a couple who make a show of affection in public, but who fight frequently in private** c'est un 'cher' ici, 'cher' la-bàs **humorous reference to two poor people who make a couple** la faim et la soif
couple *v.* accoupler, apairer, connecter, s'accoupler
couplet *n.* couplet
coupling *n.* macornage **coupling shaft** fausse-flèche
coupon *n.* coupon, ticket
courage *n.* braveure, cœur, courage, nerf **take courage** s'encourager **take courage again** reprendre courage **mount one's courage, fortitude, determination or resistance** se pomper
courageous *adj.* brave, courageux, vaillant
courgette *n.* cochotte, courgette
courrier *n.* courrier
course *adv.* **of course** bien sûr, naturellement
course *n.* classe, cours, course **change course** avirer **of course** assurément, bien attendu **change course often** vironer **change course suddenly** barder
court *n.* judiciaire, cour **court action** procès **court summons** notice **court of appeal** cour d'appel **court of justice** maison de cour **state court** cour d'état **tennis court** tennis **bring to court** mettre en cour / mettre devant la cour **defend in court** plaider **go to court** aller en cour **file in the clerk of court books** mettre au greffe
court *v.* aller avec, bêtiser, courtiller, courtiser, faire la cour à, faire l'amour (à), fréquenter, se fréquenter **one who courts** courtiseur
courtesy *n.* civilité
courthouse *n.* maison de cour
courting *n.* courtise
courtroom *n.* chambre de cour
courtship *n.* cour, courtise
courtyard *n.* cour
cousin *n.* cousin **cousin through marriage** cousin par alliance **first cousin** cousin germain, premier cousin **first / second / third cousin** premier {deuxième / troisième (etc.)} cousin
cove *n.* anse
cover *n.* couvert, couverture, tapis, couvert **bed cover** couverte **domed cover** cloche **mattress cover** couétil **remove ground cover or mulch** détourer
cover *v.* couverre, plafonner **cover o.s.** s'abrier, se couverre **cover up** s'abrier **cover for protection** abrier **cover in gold** dorer **cover o.s. again** se recouverre **cover the head** coiffer **cover with blankets** abrier **cover with bricks** briqueter **cover with dust** poussiérer **cover with mud** embourber **cover with sand** ensabler **cover with syrup** siroter **cover o.s. in dust** se poudriller, se poussiérer **metal plate used to cover a hole** plaque
covered *adj.* couvert, plein **covered wagon** wagonnette **covered with meal** farineux **completely covered** étouffé **get covered with dust** se poussiérer **get covered with brambles or stickers** s'éroncer
covering *n.* couverture, couette **hard covering** gamelle **head covering** garde-soleil **mattress covering** ensouillure **pillow covering** ensouillure **leather covering of a saddle** corasse **remove a head covering** décoiffer **remove one's head covering** se décoiffer
covey *n.* **covey of birds** volière
cow *n.* animal, bétaille, bête à corne, bête, vache **cow dung** pâté de (merde de) vache **cow herder** vacher **cow patty** pâté de (merde de) vache **cow pie** pâté de (merde de) vache **cow stomach** panse de bête **Hereford cow** vache figure blanche **Jersey cow** jersey **milk cow** laitière, vache à lait **first cow stomach** panse de bête **command to a cow to encourage it to get in position for milking** 'poteau, Caillette'! **name commonly given to a cow** Belle-Feuille, Belle-Jasmine **name commonly given to a light brown cow** Châtine **name commonly given to a spotted milking cow** Caillette *pl.* **malady of cows remedied by cutting off the horns** mal de corne
coward *n.* capon, cavache, vache à lait, ventre jaune
cowardly *adj.* lâche, malva, peureux **act cowardly** caponner **as cowardly as a sheep** capon comme un mouton
cowbird *n.* tchoc à vache
cowboy *n.* cavalier, pousseur de bêtes, toucheur, vacher **cowboy stew** grillades
cower *v.* cailler, niquer
cowlick *n.* tourniquet
cowpath *n.* routine
cowpea *n.* fève à vache
cowpoke *n.* vacher
coxcomb *n.* crête de coq, crête de corusse, crête de guime
coydog *n.* chien farouche
coyote *n.* coyote
coypu *n.* nutria
cozy *adj.* douillet
crab *n.* crabe **crab cage** carrelet **crab cake** boulette de crabe **crab fisherman** pêcheur de {à} crabes {huîtres / chevrettes, etc.} **crab trap** cage à crabe(s) **fiddler crab** tourloulou

sleeping crab crabe (a)dormi **soft-shell crab** crabe molle {moute} **sponge crab** crabe à paquet **Atlantic blue crab** crabe bleue

crabapple *n.* cenellier, pomme haigre, pomme sauvage, pommette **crabapple tree** arbre de pommette

crabbing *n.* **go crabbing** aller aux crabes

crabby *adj.* grichoux

crabgrass *n.* chiendent

crack *n.* cassure, craque, fendasse, fendure, fente, fissure, brisure, crevasse, fêlure

crack *onom.* crac

crack *v.* craquer, crâler, fendre, fêler, plaquer, becqueter, bécher **crack jokes** dire des bêtises {farces} **crack a joke** craquer une farce **crack the whip** flailler le fouet **crack with one's teeth** croquer **crack and peel after hardening** calciner

crackbrained *adj.* **crackbrained person** escouvillon

cracked *adj.* craqué, fendu, fêlé, toqué

cracker *n.* craquette **soda cracker** biscuit soda, biscuit, craquette

crackle *v.* craquer, crâler

crackling *adj.* croquant

crackling *n.* crâlement, graton

crackshot *n.* **be a crackshot** mirer adroit

cradle *n.* berce, branle, berceau **cradle cap** chapeau **cat's cradle** patte de poule

craftiness *n.* finesse

craftsman *n.* artisan

crafty *adj.* affilé, rusé **artful, crafty, sly man** homme d'affût

cram *v.* bourrer, corbier, corder

cramp *n.* crampe **stomach cramp** crampe d'estomac *pl.* **afflicted with cramps** crampeux **subject to cramps** crampeux

crane *n.* grue **blue crane** aigrette câille **whooping crane** grue

cranium *n.* crâne

crank *n.* manivelle

cranky *adj.* **be in a cranky mood** avoir un pet en long

crap *n.* cac, caca, fritche, miche, merde **eat crap!** mange de la merde! **piece of crap** fritche **not be worth a crap** pas valoir une merde

crape *n.* **crape myrtle** arbre Saint-Jean, bois rose, gastronia, laurier rose, myrte rose, myrtille

crappie *n.* sac-à-lait

crash *v.* casser

crass *adj.* crasse

crate *n.* **wooden crate** caisse

craving *n.* appétit

craw *n.* fale, gavion

crawfish *n.* écrevisse **crawfish bisque** bisque d'écrevisses **crawfish boil** bouilli d'écrevisses

crawl *v.* se traîner **crawl silently in or out** se déhaler

crawling *adj.* **be crawling with** pulluler

crayfish *n.* écrevisse

crayon *n.* crayon **oily black crayon used by African-Americans to straighten the hair or beard** cosmétique *pl.* **box of crayons** boîte de couleurs

crazily *adv.* follement

craziness *n.* folerie, folie

crazy *adj.* bête, braqué, coucou, crack, craqué, estropié de la tête / estropié de cervelle, extravagué, fou comme une banane {un bâton / la lune}, fou à baver sus sa chemise / fou à courir les chemins {à manger de l'herbe}, fou à sept cylindres, fou, foulé, fraque, lololle, pas bien plombé, percé, tacalac, timbré, toqué **crazy about** bennêt pour, fou pour **crazy person** fou, toqué **crazy as a goose** bête comme une oie **crazy as a June bug** bête comme une bête à chandelle **act crazy** faire le fou **drive crazy** affoler **go crazy** aller {venir} fou, perdre la canique / perdre ses {les} caniques, perdre la carte, perdre la tête, perdre son {l'} équilibre **half crazy** à demi {moitié} fou **be crazy about** avoir une (graine de) folerie pour **not crazy about** pas fort pour **laugh like crazy** rire comme un fou **love like crazy** aimer à la folerie **not too crazy about** pas trop fou de

creaking *n.* crâlement

cream *n.* crème **cream cheese** caillé-goutté / caillé-égoutté **cream pitcher** crémier, crémière **cream puff** chou-crème, pet de nonne **cream separator** écrémeuse **cream of tartar** crème de tartre **ice cream** crème à la glace / crème glacée, crème **remove cream** écrémer **removing cream** écrémage **whipped cream** crème battue **ice cream cone** cornet de crème, SAY-SO de crème, SAY-SO **ice cream freezer** baratte, FREEZER, sabotière **homemade ice cream** crème de sabotière **served with ice cream** à la mode

creamer *n.* crémier, crémière **powdered creamer** poudre de lait **liquid coffee creamer** crème de lait

creamery *n.* crèmerie

creamy *adj.* crémeux

crease *n.* laize, pli, plissure, pléiure **make a crease in** goder

crease *v.* froncer, goder, plisser

creased *adj.* froncé, plissé

creasing *n.* plissage

create *v.* créer, former **create a disturbance** brigander, tapager **create a ruckus** gambader **create an uproar** faire une quarantaine, tapager **create a big row or fuss** faire un scandale

creation *n.* création

creator *n.* créateur

creature *n.* bétaille, bête, créature, être **imaginary creature used to frighten children into behaving** bébête

credible *adj.* croyable

credit *n.* crédit **extend credit** donner du crédit **have credit** avoir du crédit **buy on credit** acheter à crédit **give o.s. credit** se donner crédit **purchase on credit** achat à crédit **sell on credit** vendre à crédit

credit *v.* créditer

creditor *n.* créditeur **privileged creditor** préférencié

credulous *adj.* crédule

creed *n.* crédo, symbole

Creed *n.* **the Apostles' Creed** le crois en Dieu, le Symbole des Apôtres
creek *n.* coulée
creep *v.* filer
creeper *n.* liane
Creole *adj.* créole **Creole language** nègre **Creole music** la-la **Creole language of Louisiana** créole **Louisiana Creole language** gombo **pertaining to Creole language or culture** créole
creole *n.* créole, patois
Creole *n.* Créole **Louisiana Creole** courivini, créole **speak true Creole** parler gros nègre
Creole-style *adj.* à la créole
creolized *adj.* **creolized language** créole
crepe *n.* crêpe, crêpe **crepe paper** crêpe
cress *n.* cresson
crest *n.* crête, huppe **form a crest** crêter
crested *adj.* crêté, huppé
cretonne *n.* cretonne
crevalle *n.* **crevalle jack** JACK crevalle
crevice *n.* craque, crevasse
crib *n.* berce, crèche
crick *n.* **crick in the neck** torticolis
cricket *n.* criquet, criquette **mole cricket** chien de terre
crier *n.* pleureur
crime *n.* crime, malfait
criminal *adj.* criminel
criminal *n.* bourreau, criminel, malfaisant, malfaiteur
crinoline *n.* malakoff
cripple *v.* affliger, escamoter, escloper, estropier **cripple o.s.** s'estropier
crippled *adj.* affligé, démembré, esclopé, escran, estropié, évergonne
crisis *n.* crise, secousse
crisp *adj.* croquant, crâlant, sec
critical méprisard
critical *adj.* difficile, méprisant, mépriseur **be critical of others** couper avec une hache à deux taillants
criticism *n.* mépris **harsh criticism** compliment **deserving of criticism or blame** méprisable **given to gossip or criticism** méprisant
criticize *v.* critiquer, mépriser, parler mal de, passer des remarques **criticize harshly** bafouer, complimenter **criticize incessantly** couper avec une hache à deux taillants **criticize s.o.** tirer une chique à qqn
critique *v.* passer des remarques
croak *v.* casser la pipe, grogner
croaker *n.* grognard **Atlantic croaker** grognard, meuille noir
crochet *n.* crochet
crochet *v.* crocher
crocheting *n.* crochet
crock *n.* dame-jeanne **earthenware crock** pot de grès
crockery *n.* faïence
crocodile *n.* cocodrie
crook *n.* coquin, croche, filou, pillard, tricheur
crooked *adj.* bisquencoin, chirvauché, cobi, corbin, croche comme un baril de serpents {d'hameçons}, croche, crochu, filou, tordu **crooked as a barrel of snakes** croche comme un baril de serpents {d'hameçons} **make crooked** cobir
crookedness *n.* croche
crookneck *n.* **crookneck squash** cacha, chouquechi, coucroche
crop *n.* fale, plante, récolte **riding crop** couarte **root crop** racinage *pl.* **raise crops** faire récolte **one who grows or cultivates crops** éleveur
crop *v.* racler
cropping *n.* raclage
croquette *n.* boulette
cross *adj.* bourru, grognard, malpatient **become cross** se mettre de travers **be cross or ill-humored, grouchy** être de {en} travers
cross *n.* croix **carry one's cross** porter sa croix **Saint Andrew's cross** herbe à chien **make the sign of the cross** faire la croix, faire le signe de (la) croix **make the sign of the cross over** croiser
Cross *n.* **Red Cross** Croix Rouge **Way of the Cross** chemin de (la) Croix
cross *v.* croiser, traverser **cross again** recroiser, retraverser **cross each other** se croiser **cross quickly or easily** franger **cross by lifting one leg over at a time** enjamber
cross-barred *adj.* barreauté
cross-breed *v.* abâtardir
cross-eyed *adj.* yeux croches **be cross-eyed** avoir un œil qui gagne chez Nonc Pierre, bigler, loucher, regarder croche **look cross-eyed** loucher, regarder croche
cross-tie *n.* CROSS-TIE
crossbred *adj.* abâtardi
crossbreed *v.* croiser
crosscut *n.* **crosscut saw** scie de travers
crossed *adj.* croche
crossing *n.* croison, croisée, traverse
crossroad *n.* chemin de travers(e) *pl.* **crossroads** les quatre manches, quatre-chemins
crosstie *n.* **railroad crosstie** TIE
crosswise *adv.* à travers / en travers (de)
crotch *n.* fourche, fourchon
crouch *v.* niquer, s'accroupiller, s'accroupir
crouched *adj.* accroupi, assodié
crouching *adj.* accroupi
croup *n.* croupe, croup
crouton *n.* croûton
crow *n.* corbeau, corneille **carrion crow** carencro
crowbar *n.* barre à clous, CROWBAR
crowd *n.* bande, dessaim, foule, marmite, ripopette, ripopée,

riquiqui **the whole crowd** toute la chibaigne **be assembled in a crowd** être à rang d'oignons
crowd *v.* poussailler, se fouler **crowd together** s'entasser
crowded *adj.* cordé, foulé **the space in question is crowded** on peut pas y mettre une épingle
crown *n.* calotte, couronne, faît
crown *v.* couronner
crownbeard *n.* herbe à trois quarts {écarts} **Virginia crownbeard** herbe à trois quarts {écarts}
crucifix *n.* crucifix
crucifixion *n.* crucifixion
crucify *v.* crucifier
crud *n.* crasse, encrassement, farcin **remove crud, dirt, or filth** décrasser
cruddy *adj.* crasseux
crude *adj.* commun, rude **crude oil** huile **be crude or ill-mannered** avoir pas de délicatesse
crudeness *n.* grossièreté
crudity *n.* crudité
cruel *adj.* brutal, criminel, cruel, vicieux **cruel act** cruauté **cruel person** criminel, pirate, sans-cœur
cruelly *adv.* brut, cruellement
cruelty *n.* cruauté **act of cruelty** martyr
crumb *n.* crouston, grignote, grillot, grimil, grémille, grémillon *pl.* **bread crumbs** pain moulé
crumble *v.* grémiller, tomber en poudre {poussière}
crumbling *n.* déboulage, déboulement
crumbly *adj.* grémilleux
crunch *v.* croquer, crâler
crunchy *adj.* croquant, crâlant
crupper *n.* bacul, reculoire, sous-queue **crupper strap** croupière
crush *v.* briser, cabaner, mâcher, piler, écramouiller, écraser, émœller, épurer **crush in** encaver **crush the spirits of** défaire **crush and grind sugar cane** rouler les cannes
crushed *adj.* **be crushed** s'écharpiller
crushing *adj.* écrasant
crushing *n.* écrasement
crust *n.* croûte **remove the crust** décroûter **crispy, browned or burnt crust along the bottom of a pot of rice** gratin de riz
crusty *adj.* croûteux **crusty old man** vieux croûteux **disagreeable, crusty old man** caïac
crutch *n.* béquille
cry *n.* cri **cry to stop a horse** ho **cry used to drive cattle or chase cattle away** hoba **cry used to chase away pigs / calves / chickens / dogs / a calf / pigs or chickens** choué / tchiqué / chouche, ouichou / s'en aille / chicaire / shou **cry for calling ducks / calves / cows / horses / pigs / a horse / cows or pigs / a calf into the pen** cani-cani / tchique / tcha / hop / soué, tchoque, choui / co, ho / cho / chicaire **loud cry** gueulée
cry *v.* beugler, brailler, criailler, crier, héler, pialler, pleurer, crier **cry out** crier un cri en l'air, crier, hucher, jeter un cri (en l'air) **cry profusely** brailler comme un petit bébé, brailler à chaudes larmes {haute tête / haute voix}, gueuler **cry out loud** brailler à chaudes larmes {haute tête / haute voix}
crybaby *n.* braillard, brailleur, plaignard, plaignoux
cryer *n.* braillard, brailleur
crying *adj.* criant, gueulard
crying *n.* braille, pleure **loud sobbing and crying** beuglage, beuglement
crystal *n.* cristal
crystallize *v.* tourner en candi
crèche *n.* crèche
cuckold *n.* cocu
cuckoo *n.* **cuckoo bird** coucou, longue queue
cucumber *n.* cocombre **creeping cucumber** citron, cocombre-sent-bon, liane à voico, melon sent-bon **musk cucumber** brésil, casse-banane, cocobanane
cud *n.* chique, ringe **chew cud** ringer **chew one's cud** mâcher sa chique
cuddle *v.* se nicher, se niquer
cudgel *v.* bâtonner
cue *n.* **billiard cue** queue de billard
cuff *n.* poignet **cuff link** bouton de poignet **cuff of trousers** bas de pantalon **shirt cuff** poignet
cull *v.* tâter
cultivate *v.* cultiver, faire, farmer, élever **cultivate vegetables** faire jardin **one who cultivates** cultivateur **one who grows or cultivates crops** éleveur
cultivated *adj.* **not cultivated** sauvage
cultivation *n.* cultivage, culture, élevage **perform the last cultivation on** lâcher
cultivator *n.* grattes, cultivateur **mechanical cultivator** moline
culture *n.* culture, raffinement
culvert *n.* jarre
cunning *adj.* affilé, filou, naré, roué, rusé, SMART **cunning person** filou
cunning *n.* ruse
cup *n.* coupe, CUP, gobelet, moque, tasse, tassée, tchacouelle, demi-tasse **cup of coffee** tasse de café **coffee cup** cope de café, pinte à café, tasse à café **drinking cup** chopine, moque, pinte **measuring cup** mesure, pinte de mesure, tasse à mesure **porcelain cup** tasse à café **tin cup** chopine
cupboard *n.* cabinet
cupcake *n.* petit gâteau à tasse
cupful *n.* tassée
curable *adj.* traitable
curative *adj.* curatif
curative *n.* curative
curb *n.* **curb or restraint for a horse** gourmette

curd *npl.* **curds and whey** couche-couche caillé, tape-en-gueule
curdle *v.* cailler
cure *n.* remède
cure *v.* guérir, passer, rétablir, détourner
curio *n.* bébellerie
curiosity *n.* curiosité
curious *adj.* curieux, fourre-nez
curl *n.* boucle, bouclette, cléclette, frisette *pl.* **in curls** en papillottes
curl *v.* boucler, friser, boucler **curl up** s'enrouler, se racco-quiller **curl the upper lip and show the teeth** rechaner, rechigner
curled *adj.* **curled up** raccoquillé **extremely curly, frizzy, kinky, tightly curled** tchine
curler *n.* **curler paper** tchote **hair curler** papillote *pl.* **in curlers** en papillottes
curlew *n.* **long-billed curlew** corbigeau
curly *adj.* bouclé **extremely curly, frizzy, kinky, tightly curled** tchine
current *adj.* courant
current *n.* bloc, courant **air current** courant d'air **electric current** courant électrique **go against the current** remonter le vent {courant}
curry *v.* étriller
currycomb *n.* étrille
curse *n.* condjo, jurage, jurement, malédiction, voudou *pl.* **curses** sacré diable
curse *v.* blasphémer, jurailler, jurer, maudire, sacrer **curse o.s.** se damner **curse each other** se jurer **one who curses habitually** jurailleur **one who curses or swears** jureur
cursed *adj.* maudit
curt *adj.* bref, prompt
curtain *n.* rideau **window curtain** voile
curuba *n.* brésil, casse-banane, cocobanane
curvature *n.* cambrure
curve *n.* anse, tournure, croche, virage
curve *v.* crochir
curved *adj.* courbé
cushaw *n.* cacha, chouquechi, cou-croche
cushion *n.* coussin
custard *n.* bouillie au lait, bouillie **custard pie** tarte à la bouillie **meringue custard dessert** œufs à la neige, île flottante
custody *n.* emprisonnement, garde **take into custody** ramasser
custom *n.* accoutumance, coutume, habitude, pratique, usage **according to the custom** selon la coutume *pl.* **contemporary customs** mœurs
customarily *adv.* d'habitude, habituellement
customary *adj.* habituel, traditionnel
customer *n.* client, demandant, pratique *pl.* **customers** patronage
cut *adj.* **be cut** se couper **rough cut** massif **be cut into pieces** s'écharpiller
cut *n.* coupe, coupure, inciselage, tranche **cut glass** cristal **cut and placed over a bad road** rolon **cut or opening in land or in a levee for drainage** coupe
cut *v.* couper, entailler, faucher, frendir, inciseler, scigailler, tailler, trancher **cut across** couper en travers **cut again** recouper **cut ahead** couper en avant (de qqn) **cut capers** faire des canicroches, faire des corcobiages **cut completely** couper carré **cut down** couper, jeter **cut easily** trancher **cut in** couper **cut o.s.** se couper **cut off** amputer, couper, découper **cut open** fendre **cut out** couper une fraîche, découper **cut short** couper court, couper le sifflet (à qqn), racler, écourter **cut straight** tailler flèche **cut teeth** couper ses dents, percer ses dents **cut unevenly** chiquenailler **cut unskillfully** cisailler **cut up** bêtiser, carcailler, couillonner, coupacher, coupailler, craquer, débiter, déchiquenailler, découpailler, détailler, faire des bêtises, faire le diable à quatre, faire les quatre cents coups, hacher, malfaire **cut wages** couper les gages **cut a rug** danser la queue raide **cut branches off** débrancher **cut into pieces** débiter, détailler **cut the grass** couper les herbes **cut threads on** tarauder **cut to pieces** coupacher, découpailler **cut a slit into** inciseler **cut down in size** parer **cut down to size** charpenter **cut into a conversation** couper la conversation {le discours}, prendre la parole **cut piece by piece** détailler **cut the throat of** égorger **cut with a saw** scier **cut with a scythe** sabrer **cut apart at the joint** déjointer **cut off the top of** faîter **cut ahead or pass in front** passer en avant **cut or trim the wick of** émécher **cut with a sickle or scythe** sercler **cut off or strip the branches of** ébrancher **cut the tendon of the hind leg** nerfer **cut the cane at the end of summer so that it will resprout** raser les cannes **break, cut, or chop into pieces** écharpiller **it doesn't cut** ça coupe comme une jambe de chien / ça coupe comme la jambe à {de} ma grand-mère / ça coupe aussi bien que mon doigt **group who cuts wood** bûcherie
cut-out *n.* découpage
cute *adj.* joli **cute and small** mignon
cutlet *n.* côtelette **pork cutlet** grillade de cochon
cutter *n.* coupeur **cane cutter** sabreur
cutting *adj.* coupant, mordant **cutting edge** taillant, tranchant
cutting *n.* bouture, coupage, découpage, raclage, taillage, plantard **cutting down** abattage **cutting up** couillonade, couillonnerie, macaquerie **cutting off branches** ébranchage **cutting or flattening** abattage **cane cutting** coupage de canne **ready for cutting** fauchable **close mowing or cutting of grass** raclage d'herbe
cutworm *n.* rouleau
cycle *n.* **lunar cycle** lune
cylinder *n.* cylindre **cylinder oil** huile à cylindre
cypress *n.* cipre **cypress grove** ciprière **cypress knee** boscoyo

de cipre, boscoyo, chicot de cipre **cypress swamp** marécage **cypress vine** chevelure de Vénus **pecky cypress** cipre piqué **choice grain of cypress** cipre frisé

cyst *n.* cyst

D

dabble *v.* tatiner

dad *n.* papa

daddy *n.* papa

dagger *n.* couteau, poignard **Spanish dagger plant** pite **be at dagger's point** être à couteaux tirés

dairy *n.* laiterie

daisy *n.* marguerite

dam *n.* bâtard, DAM, digue

dam *v.* bloquer, boucher

damage *n.* dommage, dédommage, dégât, dévastre, endommagement, faire du dommage, tort **cause damage** faire du degât **do damage** faire du dommage

damage *v.* abîmer, dommager, dédommager, défropter, défroqueter, dégrader, dérater, embêcher, endommager, escamoter, massacrer, porter sur, détamer

damaged *adj.* **badly damaged** abîmé **destroyed or damaged by worms or insects** piqué

damask *n.* **damask cloth** damas

damn *adj.* **damn nut** sacré couillon **damn son-of-a-bitch** sacré fils de garce {putain}

damn *interj.* bordel, bétaille, maudit

damn *n.* **not give a damn** s'en foutre (pas mal), se sacrer

damn *v.* damner, maudire

damnation *n.* damnation

damned *adj.* cerni, damné, maudit, sacré

damned *n.* **the damned** les damnés

damp *adj.* humide, trempe **become damp or moist** s'humecter

dampen *v.* humecter, mouiller

damper *n.* registre, tire

dampness *n.* humidité

damselfly *n.* mamselle

dance *n.* bal, chingding, cotillon, danse, gigue **dance floor** plancher de danse **dance hall** HALL de danse, HALL, salle de danse, salle **dance performed to the sound of the bamboula drum** bamboula **fandango dance** fandango **figured dance** danse ronde **lively dance** valsovienne **masked dance** danse masquée **play-party dance** danse ronde **round dance** danse ronde **square dance** danse carrée, quadrille **traditional Cajun community dance** fais-dodo **wedding ball or dance** bal de noce *pl.* **one who frequents dances** baleur **a series of five dances, traditionally played in order: waltz, polka, waltz in two, two-step, mazurka** ronde de danses

dance *v.* danser, ginguer, jiguer, taper la savate, danser comme une plume **dance about** dansailler, regimber **dance energetically** danser la queue raide **dance smoothly** danser comme une plume **dance vigorously** giguer **dance a jig** giguer **dance a waltz** danser une valse **square dance** danser la quadrille **gathering of neighborhood families, during which people dance** bal de maison

dancer *n.* baleur, danseur

dancing *n.* **go dancing** baler **unaccompanied group singing and dancing event** bazar

dandelion *n.* pissenlit

dandruff *n.* peau morte, son

dandy *n.* candi barré, cul de bonbon

danger *n.* danger, péril **out of danger** sauve

dangerous *adj.* bobo, dangereux **dangerous game** casse-cou **dangerous undertaking** casse-cou **dangerous place noted for leading to injuries** casse-cou **man who pretends to be dangerous but is not** homme de paille

dangerously *adv.* dangereusement

dangle *v.* ballotter, pendre **anything that hangs or dangles** pendrioche

dare *v.* défendre, défier, oser

daring *adj.* téméraire

daring *n.* courage

dark *adj.* foncé, gros, noir, noirâtre, sombre, accablé **be dark** faire noir **become dark** se noircir **get dark** faire brun

dark *n.* noir **in the dark** dans l'obscurité

dark-complexioned *adj.* **dark-complexioned woman** taïque

darken *v.* noircir

darkish *adj.* **darkish hue** noiret

darkness *n.* noir, nuit, obscurité

darling *n.* chou

darn *interj.* bétaille

darn *n.* **not give a darn** se ficher

darn *v.* entreturer, estopper

darned *adj.* cerni, sacré, sapré

darned *adv.* saprement

darning *n.* entretenage, entreturage, raccommodage

dart *n.* dard, dardon, flèche, godet, pince

dart *v.* se lancer **dart out** se darder

dashboard *n.* DASHBOARD, garde-crotte

dasher *n.* palon

date *n.* combien, date, datte, quantième **set a date** amarrer une date **up to date** au courant

date *v.* aller avec, fréquenter, se visiter, sortir avec, dater **date steadily** se fréquenter

dauber *n.* **mud dauber** guêpe noire

daughter *n.* demoiselle, fille **seventh daughter** fleur de lis

youngest daughter yelle **the prettiest daughter** fleur de la famille, la pêche de la bande

daughter-in-law *n.* belle-fille, bru

dawdler *n.* tchicailleur

dawdling *adj.* lambin

dawn *n.* avant-jour, barre du jour, éclair du jour, éclaircie du jour **at dawn** au jour **from dawn to dusk** (de) soleil levant (à) soleil couché

day *n.* jour, journée **day after** lendemain **day before** veille **day after tomorrow** surlendemain **day before yesterday** avant-hier (matin, midi, soir) **day is breaking** le jour est après se faire **all day** toute la journée **be day** faire jour **clear day** belle journée **feast day** fête **good day** bonjour **half day** demi-journée **next day** lendemain **nice day** beau jour, belle journée **slack day** jour ras **from day to day** d'un jour à l'autre, de jour en jour **the day after tomorrow** après-demain **the day before yesterday** avant-hier **light of day** clarté du jour **night and day** nuit et jour **the whole day** toute la journée **time of day** heure **wear every day** porter (qqch) comme la peau **have the day off** débaucher **from one day to the next** d'un jour à l'autre **duration of a day** journée **until this very day** jusqu'à jour d'aujourd'hui **top of the day, from 11 a.m. to 1 p.m.** haut du jour **every dog has his day** chaque chien a son jour **major holiday or holy day** grande fête *pl.* **these days** asteur, au jour d'aujourd'hui, aujourd'hui **two days before** avant-veille **in those days** dans ce temps-là / dans ce temps ça-là / dans ces temps-ça **the old days** le vieux temps / les (bons) vieux temps, le vieux temps passé **the old days** (dans) les autres fois **in the old days** dans le vieux temps **one of these days** un de ces quatre matins **vigil of feast days** vigile **a week, a month, two days ago** ça donne une semaine {un mois / deux jours} que

day-laborer *n.* journalieux

daybreak *n.* avant-jour, barre du jour, piquette du jour, éclair du jour, éclaircie du jour **at daybreak** au jour

daydream *v.* jonglailler, jongler

daydreamer *n.* jongleur

daydreaming *n.* jonglerie

daylight *n.* clarté du jour, jour **be daylight** faire claire **broad daylight** grand jour **in broad daylight** en plein jour

daytime *n.* clarté, jour, journée

daze *v.* étourdir

dazed *adj.* extravagué

dazzle *v.* embrouiller, éblouir

dazzlement *n.* éblouissement

dazzling *adj.* aveuglant, éblouissant

de-ice *v.* dégeler, déglacer

deacon *n.* diacre

dead *adj.* crevé, mort **dead end** cul-de-sac, manche **dead person** mort **play dead** faire le mort **knock s.o. dead** tuer raide **at a dead run** à la pleine course

deaden *v.* amortir

deadly *adj.* mortel

deaf *adj.* sourd comme un poteau {pot / pot de chambre}, sourd **deaf person** sourd **one who is deaf and dumb** sourd-et-muet

deaf-mute *n.* sourd-et-muet, sourd (et) muet

deafen *v.* assourdir

deafening *adj.* assourdissant

deal *n.* barguine, DEAL **big deal** belle affaire!, grosse affaire **good deal** bon barguine **no deal** pas d'affaire! **a great deal** beaucoup, charretée, fameusement, par charretée / à la charretée, pataraphe, un tas dur **make a deal** faire {prendre} des arrangements, faire marché **a great deal of** beaucoup de **make a bad deal** faire un mauvais coup **make a big deal** faire un gros coup **make a good deal** faire un beau {bon} coup **make a big deal out of s.t.** faire toute une histoire (de qqch) **given to making a big deal over nothing** frou-frou **be in the process of making a deal** être en marché

deal *v.* foutre, péter, sacrer, trafiquer, poquer, péter **deal with** manœuvrer **deal with gently, tactfully** prendre en taille douce **deal a blow with the foot / the elbow / the fist / the head, etc.** foutre un coup de pied {coude / poing / tête, etc.} **treat or deal with** traiter

dealer *n.* marchand, trafiqueur

dealing *npl.* **have dealings** avoir affaire (avec)

dear *adj.* cher **dear little boy** cher ti nègre

dear *n.* bien-aimé, catin, cher, chouchoute **my dear** ma négresse, mon cher, mon chéri **poor little dear** chère {pauvre} petite bête

death *n.* fatalité, mort, mortalité **death agony** agonie de la mort, le dernier supplice **death certificate** certificat de mortalité **death place** mouroir **death rattle** le hoquet de la mort, râle de la mort **death struggle** combat de la mort **death throes** agonie de la mort **close to death** à deux doigts de sa mort **put to death** faire mourir **be at death's door** être au grabat, être à la crève **put to death by hanging** pendre **the throes of death** le dernier supplice **at the point of death** mourant **come a hair from death** être venu un cheveu de sa mort **be on the point of death** être sus le mouroir

deathbed *n.* mouroir

debacle *n.* débâcle

debark *v.* écorcher

debarking *n.* écorchement

debase *v.* se dégrader

debasing *adj.* dégradant

debatable *adj.* contestable, discutable, disputable

debauch *v.* chienner, coursailler, courser, débaucher

debaucher *n.* débaucheur

debauchery *n.* chiennerie, coursaillerie, débauchage, débauche

debilitated *adj.* débile

debilitating *adj.* affaiblissant

debility *n.* débilité
debit *v.* débiter
debone *v.* désosser
debris *n.* drigaille, déboulis, débris
debt *n.* dette, endettement, obligation **in debt** endetté **bring into debt** endetter **go into debt** s'endetter **get into debt beyond one's means** endaler **payment of a debt** quittance **he is heavily in debt** il doit à Dieu et ses saints *pl.* **pay one's debts faithfully** être de bonne paye **be overwhelmed with debts** être dans les poux de bois **not paying one's debts** de mauvaise paye
debtor *n.* detteur
debut *n.* début
decade *n.* décade **say a rosary decade** dire une décade {dizaine}
decalog *n.* décalogue
decant *v.* transvider
decanter *n.* carafe, flacon
decay *n.* pourrillon, ruine
decayed *adj.* piqué
deceased *adj.* défunt, pauvre **deceased person** défunt
deceit *n.* canaillerie, duplicité, déception, embêtement, fraude, perfidie, tromperie
deceitful *adj.* par en-dessous, salaud, traître, trompeur **deceitful act** chicane, merde en bouteille **deceitful person** traître **terribly deceitful** traître comme la mort **one who is untrustworthy or deceitful** salaud
deceive *v.* bloffer, BULLDOZE, canailler, chiquer, coquiner, couillonner, embêter, frauder, maquemose, mettre dans le trou, passer la cheville à qqn, piger, tricher, tromper **deceive by flattery** emmioler
deceived *adj.* **be deceived** se faire bloffer **easily deceived** nice
deceiver *n.* bloffeur, enjôleur
December *n.* décembre
decency *n.* décence, propreté
decent *adj.* décent, notable, propre
decently *adv.* proprement
deception *n.* bloff, déception, embêtation, tournure **attempt at deception** routine **one who makes use of intrigue or deception** cabaleur
decide *v.* décider, déterminer, faire son idée, figurer, se décider **decide all at once** se prendre un estampique
decided *adj.* décidé
decipher *v.* déchiffrer
decipherable *adj.* déchiffrable
deciphering *n.* déchiffrage
decision *n.* décision **make a decision** décider
deck *n.* plancher, pont
decked *adj.* **decked out elegantly** en farauderie
declaration *n.* déclaration
Declaration *n.* **the Declaration of Independence** Déclaration d'indépendance
declare *v.* acertainer, affirmer, déclarer, proclamer, raconter **well, I declare** mais jamais
declared *adj.* **be declared** se déclarer
decline *n.* clin, déclin **be on the decline** avoir tiré son pétard
decline *v.* décliner, réduire **decline in health** s'abîmer **decline in price** tomber
decompose *v.* **cause to decompose** décomposer
decorate *v.* décorer, garnir, orner **decorate o.s.** se décorer
decorated *adj.* **decorated elegantly** en farauderie
decoration *n.* bébelle, décoration, fanfreluche, fion, fionnure, garniture **shiny metallic decoration for clothing** brillant **any fancy decoration that can be hung on the wall** accroche-cœur *pl.* **shoddy decorations** affûtiaux **remove ornaments or decorations** dégarnir
decorative *adj.* **overly colorful or decorative** criard
decorous *adj.* disable
decoy *n.* appeau
decrease *n.* réduction
decrease *v.* amoindrir, diminuer, s'amoindrir
decrepit *adj.* **old, decrepit person** cornoyo
decrepitude *n.* **fall into poverty or decrepitude** aller aux brindezingues
dedicate *v.* consacrer, dédier, dévouer, vouer **dedicate o.s.** se consacrer, se dédier
dedicated *adj.* dédiqué
dedication *n.* dédication
deduce *v.* déduire
deduct *v.* ôter
deed *n.* acte, fait, procure **charitable deed** acte de charité **dirty deed** saleté **evil deed** malfait **good deed** bienfait *pl.* **do dirty deeds** faire des saletés
deep *adj.* creux, fond, gros, profond, foncé
deep-fry *v.* rôtir
deepen *v.* creuser, creusir, recreusir
deepened *adj.* **hollow, deepened area** creusement
deeply *adv.* creux
deer *n.* chevreuil
deerfly *n.* frappe d'abord
defacement *n.* barbouillage
defamation *n.* calomnie
defeat *adj.* **suffering defeat** perdant
defeat *v.* écouenner, battre, hacher, herser
defecate *v.* chier, faire caca, faire, salir
defect *n.* défaut, faute
defective *adj.* défectif
defend *v.* défendre, avocasser **defend o.s.** se défendre **defend in court** plaider **side with or defend s.o.** prendre pour qqn
defendant *n.* accusé
defender *n.* défendeur, protecteur
defense *n.* défense
defenseless *adj.* **helpless or defenseless person** gribouille

defensible *adj.* soutenable
defensive *n.* **get on the defensive** se regricher
defer *v.* suspendre
defiance *n.* défi
defiant *adj.* **be defiant of authority** avoir le crin raide
deficient *adj.* **be mentally deficient** pas avoir sa bonne comprenure
defile *v.* profaner, salir
definite *adj.* définitif
definitely *adv.* bien, définiment
definition *n.* définition
definitively *adv.* **definitively and quickly** propre
deflate *v.* dégonfler
defoliate *v.* effeuiller
defoliation *n.* effeuillage
deforest *v.* défraîchir
deforestation *n.* défraîchissement
deforesting *n.* défraîchissage
deform *v.* déformer
deformation *n.* déformation
deformed *adj.* afflictionné, affligé, malformé, tordu
defraud *v.* frauder
defrost *v.* dégeler, déglacer
defunct *adj.* défunt
defy *v.* braver, défier
degenerate *v.* dégénérer
degradation *n.* dégradation
degrade *v.* abaisser, dégrader, se dégrader
degrading *adj.* dégradant
degrease *v.* dégraisser
degree *n.* degré, grade, étage
dehorn *v.* décorner
deign *v.* daigner
deity *n.* dieu, divinité
dejected *adj.* mal en train
delapidated *adj.* **become delapidated** tomber en-val-en-zèle, tomber en doise douale}
delay *n.* retard
delay *v.* détarder, retarder, tarder
delayed *adj.* enretardé **developmentally delayed** en retard
delegate *n.* délégué
delegate *v.* déléguer
delegation *n.* délégation
delerium *n.* pesant
deliberate *v.* délibérer
deliberation *n.* délibération
delicacy *n.* délicatesse, finesse
delicate *adj.* douillet, délicat, fatras, fin, fini
delicatessen *n.* délicatesse
delicious *adj.* bon à la babine, délicieux, goûtable
delight *n.* agrément, délice, enchantement
delight *v.* charmer, enchanter
delightful *adj.* goûtable
delirious *adj.* **be delirious** parler à la berloque, être dans le délire
delirium *n.* délire
deliver *v.* accoucher, délivrer, livrer, rendre au monde, délivrer, sacrer **deliver o.s.** se délivrer **deliver a blow** flanquer un coup **deliver a sermon** faire la prêche
deliverance *n.* délivrance, libération
delivery *n.* délivrée, livraison, accouchage, accouchement, couche, délivrage **delivery man** haleur
deluge *n.* avalasse, déluge
demand *n.* demande, exigence **in demand** en demande **in great demand** recherché
demand *v.* demander, vouloir
demanding *adj.* exigeant, obligeant, particulier **insistently demanding person** tchamandeur
demijohn *n.* dame-jeanne
demitasse *n.* demi-tasse
Democrat *n.* démocrate
demolish *v.* casser, débâtir, démolir, abattre
demon *n.* diable, démon
demonstrate *v.* **validate or demonstrate the worth of** faire valoir
demonstrative *npl.* **particle used with demonstratives** ici
demoralize *v.* démoraliser
den *n.* nid, nique
dengue *n.* dengué
denial *n.* démenti
denounce *v.* déclarer, dénoncer **one who denounces** informeur
dense *adj.* dru, épais
denser *adj.* **become denser** s'épaissir
density *n.* épaisseur
dent *n.* cabossure, cobissure, nioque, cobiche
dent *v.* bosser, cabosser, cobir, encaver **dent in** cabaner
dented *adj.* cobi **get dented** se cabosser
dentist *n.* arracheur de dents, dentiste
denture *npl.* **dentures** râtelier
deny *v.* démentir, dénier, nier **deny o.s.** se priver
depart *v.* braguer, départir, partir, pousser route, quitter, s'en aller
departed *adj.* **departed** défunt **departed person** défunt
departing *adj.* **departing guest** partant
departing *v.* sur une partance
department *n.* département, bureau
departure *n.* départ, partance **on the point of departure** quittable
depend *v.* dépendre dessus {sur}, dépendre **it depends** c'est selon
dependable *adj.* dépendable, fiable
depended *adj.* **person who can be depended upon for help in one's old age** bâton de vieillesse, béquille de vieillesse
dependence *n.* dépendance
dependent *adj.* dépendant **be dependent on** dépendre dessus {sur}

depending *adj.* dépendant
depict *v.* représenter
deplorable *adj.* regrettable
deport *v.* déporter
deportation *n.* déportation, exil
depose *v.* déposer
deposited *adj.* **be deposited or piled up** se ramasser
deposition *n.* déposition **take a deposition** déposer
depot *n.* dépôt, gare
depreciate *v.* déprécier
depressed *adj.* **seem depressed** avoir une mine de chien **be sad or depressed** faire une {la} babine / faire des babines, pendre la babine **state of being depressed** dépit
depression *n.* dépit **economic depression** dépression **a depression used for growing rice** marais **sink or depression in the land** bassière **go into a depression** prendre un dépit / tomber en dépit
Depression *n.* **the Great Depression** dépression
deprive *v.* priver **deprive of goods or property** dégréer
deprived *adj.* **be deprived** pâtir
depth *n.* creuseur, fond **depth to which a plow share penetrates the soil** entrure **depth in the ground corresponding to the length of a spade blade** pique, piquée **extreme depth** finfifond **of less than average depth** bas
deputy *n.* député
derail *v.* dérailler
derailment *n.* déraillement
deranged *adj.* extravagué **be deranged** battre la berloque **mentally deranged** biorqué, estropié de la tête / estropié de cervelle, frappé de la lune, frappé **slightly mentally deranged** pas tout là
derby *n.* **derby hat** bidon
derisive méprisard
derivative *n.* **refined petroleum derivative** huile
derrick *n.* derrick **oil drilling derrick** derrick
derriere *n.* croupion, derrière, fesse, saint-frusquin, tchu, troufignon
descend *v.* descendre, dégrucher **descend or leap the rapids** sauter les rapides
descendant *n.* descendant, enfant
descended *adj.* **be descended** descendre
descent *n.* descente **line of descent** bord
describe *v.* dépeindre **describe or recount in detail** détailler
description *n.* description
desecrate *v.* profaner
desert *n.* désert
desert *v.* abandonner, dégrader, délaisser, déserter
deserter *n.* déserteur, marronneur
desertion *n.* marronnage
deserve *v.* déserver, mériter de, mériter
deserved *adj.* **it is well deserved** c'est bien tapé
deserving *adj.* digne **be deserving of** mériter de
deshell *v.* écouenner
design *n.* dessein, dessin, modèle, plan, propos *pl.* **of many colors or designs** dépareillé
designate *v.* désigner
desirable *adj.* souhaitable, tentable **it is desirable** c'est à souhaiter
desire *n.* aspiration, désir, envie, souhait **satisfy a desire** se donner une bosse **to one's heart's desire** à son contentement
desire *v.* avoir envie de, désirer, souhaiter **desire intensely** en griller (de) **desire strongly** ambitionner pour **desire for o.s.** se souhaiter
desk *n.* bureau, DESK **writing desk** secrétaire
desolate *adj.* désolé **become desolate** se démoraliser
desolation *n.* désolation
despair *n.* désespoir, désespérance **be in despair** avoir le vent debout
despair *v.* désespoirer
despairing *adj.* désespoiré
desperate *adj.* **be desperate or in desperation** être au supplice
desperation *n.* **be desperate or in desperation** être au supplice
despicable *adj.* chéti **despicable person** cœur noir
despise *v.* haïr
dessert *n.* dessert
destiny *n.* destinée, sort
destitute *adj.* misérable **destitute person** misérable **be destitute** être en misère
destitution *n.* abandon, misère
destroy *v.* détruire, exterminer, racler, ruiner **one who destroys** assassineur
destroyed *adj.* **destroyed or damaged by worms or insects** piqué
destroying *n.* **act of destroying caterpillars** échenillage
destruction *n.* destruction, ruine **wanton destruction** sabotage
destructive *adj.* carnassier, destructif
destructively *adv.* **act destructively** carnager
destructiveness *n.* carnageries
detach *v.* décoller, détacher
detail *n.* détail **overly concerned with fairness and detail** observant *pl.* **overly careful of details** nigeant **set out the details** détailler
detail *v.* détailler, formuler
detect *v.* détecter
detection *n.* détection
detective *n.* détective
detergent *n.* **powdered detergent** perline
deteriorate *v.* dégringoler, dégénérer, dépérir, s'abîmer
deterioration *n.* dégringole
determination *n.* détermination, résolution **mount one's courage, fortitude, determination or resistance** se pomper
determine *v.* déterminer, trouver
determined *adj.* déchaîné, décidé, déterminé, entêté, résolu **be determined** s'entêter

detest *v.* abominer, détester
detestable *adj.* détestable, haïssable
detonation *n.* tirage
detour *n.* détour, détourne
detriment *n.* détriment
devastate *v.* dévaster, engloutir, racler, ravager
devastation *n.* dévastation, dévastre
devasted *adj.* **financially devasted** cassé à la maille
develop *v.* développer, formuler, se développer **develop a hole** percer
development *n.* développement, formance, profit, progrès
deviate *v.* dévirer **cause to deviate** faire fourcher
devil *n.* diable, démon **poor devil** pauvre misérable, pauvre vieux chien **the devil** ah, la miche!, Lucifer, Satan **what the devil** que diable (est ça)!, ça par exemple **speak of the devil, see his face** en parlant de la bête, on lui voit la tête
Devil *n.* **the Devil** diable, démon
devilfish *n.* diable
devilish *adj.* diabolique
devilment *n.* le diable et son train
devote *v.* dédier, dévouer **devote o.s.** se dévouer, se dédier
devotedness *n.* dévouement
devotion *n.* dévotion, dévouement
devour *v.* dévorer, friper, soiffer
devout *adj.* pieux, religieux **devout person** pratiqueur, religieux
dew *n.* rosée, serein **dew gathered for washing the eyes** eau de serein **midsummer's day dew** eau de Saint-Jean
dewberry *n.* mûre traînante, mure traînante
dewbill *n.* roupie
dewlap *n.* panne
dexterity *n.* adresse, aplomb
dexterous *adj.* aplomb, tout-mains
diabetes *n.* diabète, maladie de {du} sucre, sang doux
diabolical *adj.* diabolique
diagonal *adj.* bisquencoin, en coin
diagonally *adv.* en biais
dialect *n.* dialecte, patois, rametien
dialogue *n.* dialogue
diameter *n.* diamètre
diamond *n.* diamant, carreau, diamant
diaper *n.* braguet, braguette, couche, drapeau, lange **diaper pin** épingle double, épingle à couche, épingle à linge
diaphragm *n.* toile, toilette
diarrhea *n.* chiasse, chierie, djarette, dérangement, foire, fritche, va-vite **cause diarrhea** déranger le corps **have diarrhea** avoir la fritche, avoir la va-vite **attack of diarrhea** foirée **have dysentery or diarrhea** avoir les boyaux malades
dichondra *n.* patte de cheval, sabot de cheval
dictate *v.* dicter
dictionary *n.* dictionnaire
didapper *n.* plongeon
die *n.* dé
die *v.* cailler la botte, casser la pipe, craquer, crever, disparaître, expirer, faire sa crévation, fumer la pipe, manquer, mourir, paner la botte, passer, périr **die down** tomber **die of hunger** crever de faim **die of laughter** crever de rire **almost die** avoir la vie dans sa main, venir un fil {un cheveu / deux cheveux} de sa mort **cause to die** faire mourir **wilt or die from too much moisture** échauder **live hope and die like an old dog** vivre en espoir et mourir comme un vieux chien **be dying or about to die** être à la crève
diet *n.* diète **on a milk diet** au lait
differ *v.* varier
difference *n.* différence, variation **difference in age** différence **make a difference** faire une différence **it doesn't make any difference** ça fait (pas) rien *pl.* **settle differences** faire ami
different *adj.* différent de, différent **become different** changer
differently *adv.* différent
difficult *adj.* brut, difficile, dur, halant, lourd, malaisé, particulier, pirate, ROUGH, scabreux **be difficult** chauffer, forcer, haler, être de la misère à, être en section **financially difficult** TIGHT **find difficult** être malaisé pour **whiny or difficult child** pienque
difficulty *n.* baribara, damnation, difficulté, embarras, misère, problème, tracas **with difficulty** palotte **chew with difficulty** mâchouiller **have trouble, difficulty** avoir de la misère **period of difficulty** patocaille **have a lot of difficulty doing s.t.** suer des caravelles **have a lot of difficulty dealing with s.o.** avoir du fil à tordre avec qqn *pl.* **have difficulties** avoir du mal **have problems, difficulties** être dans les fardoches
dig *n.* chique
dig *v.* bêcher, fouiller, pelleter, rayer **dig around** fouillailler, fouillarder, fouiller, fourgailler **dig deeper** refouiller **dig out** creuser **dig up** désenterrer, déterrer, exhumer, sourdre **dig a hole** piquer un fossé **dig out a hole** arracher un trou
digest *v.* digérer
digestion *n.* digestion, dégirage **digestion aid** régulateur **regulate one's digestion** se régler
digger *n.* fouilleur, pelleteur **hole digger** terrier **post hole digger** fouilleur de poteau, fouilleur de trous
digging *n.* **digging fork** fourchette
dignitary *n.* dignitaire
dignity *n.* dignité **lower one's dignity or moral standing** s'abaissir
dike *n.* bâtard, DAM, digue, levée **dike or embankment** brûlé
dilapidated *adj.* **be dilapidated** battre la berloque **become dilapidated** tomber en-val-en-zèle / tomber en val et en zèle, tomber en ruine
dilemma *n.* dilemme
diligence *n.* diligence

dilly-dally *v.* berdasser, berlander, dandiner
dilute *v.* baptiser, délayer **dilute the wine** couper le vin
dim *adj.* **grow dim** s'affaiblir
dim-witted *adj.* fafa
dime *n.* DIME, dix-sous
dimension *n.* mesure
diminish *v.* amoindrir, couper, diminuer, réduire, s'amoindrir, se réduire
dimness *n.* obscurité
dimple *n.* grain de beauté
din *n.* bamboula, boulvari, bourilleau, bruit, sabbat **wild hunt, a mysterious racket, din, or chorus that passes through the night sky** chasse-galerie
dine *v.* dîner **dine on** souper
dining *n.* **dining room** salle à manger
dinner *n.* dîner **dinner plate** assiette plate, plat **eat dinner** dîner **gumbo dinner** gombo **have dinner** souper
dint *n.* **by dint of** à force de
diocese *n.* diocèse
dip *n.* **take a dip** plonger
dip *v.* baigner, plonger, tremper, DIP, passer **dip in flour** fariner **dip into sauce** saucer
diphtheria *n.* diphtérie
diploma *n.* diplôme
dipnet *n.* carrelet
dipper *n.* bigote, chopine, CUP, gibote, moque, pinte, poêle **water dipper** tchacouelle
Dipper *n.* **Big Dipper** étoile à queue
direct *adj.* direct, droite
direct *v.* BULLDOZE, courir, directer, diriger, pointer
direction *n.* direction, directive, manière, sens **change direction** rafaler, tourner **reverse direction** BACK **in the direction of** pour, vers **fix a direction for o.s.** se mirer *pl.* **directions** direction **give directions** directer **in all directions** (de) tribord et babord {bâbord}
directive *n.* directive
directly *adv.* carrément, directement, droite, droitement
director *n.* directeur
directory *n.* directoire
dirigible *n.* BALLOON
dirt *n.* crasse, limon, saleté, saloperie, terre friable, terre meuble, terre **dirt thrown to the side of a furrow as the result of plowing** endos **encrusted dirt** farcin **remove dirt** décrotter **bring dirt up** chausser, endosser, raiser, rechausser, renchausser **bringing dirt to crops** endossage **ball of dirt** boule de terre **clod of dirt** motte de terre, rabot **remove top dirt** déchausser **soil with dirt** se bousiller **remove crud, dirt, or filth** décrasser **strip of dirt thrown over by a plow** oreillée **mounding or banking of dirt** buttage
dirtied *adj.* **easily dirtied** salissant
dirtiness *n.* malpropreté, saloperie
dirty *adj.* caca, cochonnier, crasseux, en crottins, malpropre, merdeux, sale, souillon, vilain, cochon, salaud **dirty house** nique à chien **dirty person** salaud **dirty room** nique à chien **dirty woman** soudrillonne **dirty, untidy man** cochon **dirty item of clothing** soutadaire **get dirty** encrasser, plaquer, se salir **any dirty place** parc à cochon(s) **tell dirty stories or coarse jokes** dire des cochonneries {saletés / saloperies} **get o.s. dirty** s'encrasser
dirty *v.* bousiller, cochonner, goudronner, sagouiller, salir, souillonner, pistrailler **dirty up** encrasser
dirtying *adj.* salissant
disabled *adj.* escran
disadvantage *n.* désavantage
disagree *v.* chicoter, désaccorder, se contrarier
disagreeable *adj.* déplaisant, désagréable **disagreeable, crusty old man** caïac **mean, disagreeable person** pichou **be in an uncomfortable or disagreeable situation** être pas aux noces
disagreeableness *n.* désagrément
disagreement *n.* barouche, discorde, désaccord **have a disagreement** faire {avoir} barouche
disappear *v.* caler le bouchon, disparaître, s'esquiver, évanouir **disappear quickly** passer au bleu
disappoint *v.* dérouter, désappointer
disappointing *adj.* foutant
disappointment *n.* désappointement **used to express disappointment when having lost or broken s.t.** BYE-BYE le chaland
disapproval *n.* **express disapproval** faire des gros yeux **show disapproval** pendre la babine **expression of disapproval or reproach** sac à {en} papier **show displeasure or disapproval in one's facial expressions** avoir une figure comme une vache qu'a soif **expression of astonishment, sometimes disapproval** pense donc! **expression of astonishment, pity, or disapproval** pitié
disarm *v.* désarmer
disarrange *v.* pirater **disarrange the hair of** décoiffer, dépeigner
disarray *n.* désordre
disassemble *v.* défaire, dégréer, démancher
disassembling *n.* dégréement
disaster *n.* désastre, échouerie
disavow *v.* renier
disband *v.* disbander
disburse *v.* débourser
disbursement *n.* déboursement
discard *v.* jeter, JUNK
discernment *n.* jugement
discharge *n.* acquittance, acquittement, décharge **nasal discharge** rhume **abnormal discharge of female sex organs** bouillon
discharge *v.* décharger, se décharger, décharger

disciple *n.* disciple
discipline *v.* correcter, corriger
disclose *v.* dévoiler
disclosure *n.* dévoilement
discolor *v.* décolorer, détamer, déteindre, se déteindre
discolored *adj.* **become discolored** se décolorer **become worn, faded, discolored, or tarnished** détamer
discomfort *n.* malaise
disconcert *v.* défaire, dérouter
disconnect *v.* déconnecter, démancher
disconsolate *adj.* inconsolable
discontented *adj.* malcontent **discontented person** malcontent
discontentment *n.* **show discontentment** faire une {la} babine / faire des babines
discontinuation *n.* cessation
discontinue *v.* cesser
discord *n.* barouche, discorde, désaccord, trouble **cause trouble, discord** faire du {un} désordre
discount *n.* acompte, discompte, réduction **give a discount** discompter
discount *v.* discompter
discourage *v.* abattre, décourager
discouraged *adj.* **become discouraged** se décourager
discouragement *n.* découragement
discouraging *adj.* décourageant
discourse *n.* discours
discover *v.* découverre, figurer, frapper, s'apercevoir, trouver, attraper
discovery *n.* découverte, trouvaille, trouve
discretion *n.* prudence
discuss *v.* discuter
discussion *n.* argument, conférence, discussion, parlement
disdain *n.* dédain
disdain *v.* dédaigner
disease *n.* mal, maladie **disease of animals** baves **heart disease** maladie de cœur **skin disease** dartre
disembark *v.* débarquer
disembarking *n.* débarquement, débarque
disengage *v.* déprendre **disengage physically from each other** se décoller
disentangle *v.* dépétrir, désempêtrer
disfigure *v.* défigurer, marquailler, massacrer
disfigured *adj.* défiguré
disfigurement *n.* massacre
disfiguring *adj.* défigurant
disgorge *v.* dégorger
disgrace *n.* disgrace, déshonneur, honte
disgrace *v.* dégrader, déshonorer, éhonter **disgrace o.s.** se dégrader
disgraceful *adj.* disgracieux
disguise *n.* camouflage
disguise *v.* déguiser **disguise o.s.** se déguiser
disgust *n.* dédain, dégoût, répugnance, zire **source of disgust** dégoûtation **used to indicate disgust** hache **used to indicate disgust or irritation** ache **exclamation of surprise, pleasure or disgust** pou-yaille
disgust *v.* acœurer, dégoûter
disgusted *adj.* dégoûté, répugné **be disgusted** avoir zire (de), se dégoûter, être regoulé
disgusting *adj.* dédaignable, dégoûtant, répugnant, révoltant, zirable
disgustingly *adv.* zirablement
dish *n.* bassin, plat **dish made of various meats and rice** galimatias **casserole dish** casserole **fried dish** fricot **soap dish** savonnette **badly prepared dish** ragouillage **highly seasoned dish of rice, beans, and meat** congri *pl.* **dishes** vaisselle **set of dishes** SET de vaisselle **wash the dishes** laver la vaisselle **place for washing clothes or dishes** laverie
dish *v.* **dish out** retirer, tirer
dishcloth *n.* lavette, serviette **dishcloth gourd** torchon
dishearten *v.* abattre
dishevel *v.* dépeigner **dishevel o.s.** s'ébouriffler **dishevel the hair of** ébouriffler, écheveler
disheveled *adj.* chien-fou, effarouché, ébouriffIé, échevelé, épaillé **have disheveled or wild hair** avoir la tête égrichée **person with long, disheveled hair** taïque
dishevelment *n.* ébouriffIage, échevelage
dishonest *adj.* croche, malhonnête, par en-dessous **become dishonest** aller croche
dishonestly *adv.* malhonnêtement
dishonesty *n.* fraude, malhonnêteté, micmac **make use of intrigue and dishonesty in conducting a political campaign** cabaler
dishonor *n.* déshonneur
dishonor *v.* déshonorer, éhonter **dishonor or rape** gâter
dishpan *n.* bassin à vaisselle, plat (à) vaisselle
dishrag *n.* lavette, serviette
dishtowel *n.* essuie-vaisselle, lavette
dishwasher *n.* laveuse de plats {vaisselle}
dishwater *n.* eau grasse / eaux grasses, lavure, savonnure
disinfect *v.* désinfecter, fumiguer
disinfectant *n.* désinfectant
disinfecting *n.* purification
disinherit *v.* déshériter
disinter *v.* déterrer
disinterestedness *n.* désintéressement
disjoin *v.* décoller
disk *n.* **disk harrow** disque, laboureuse, trancheuse **disk plow** trancheuse
dislike *n.* haine *pl.* **have idiosyncratic likes or dislikes** avoir des fions
dislike *v.* haïr
dislocate *v.* démancher, déplacer, éjointer, défaire, déjointer, se

défaire, se déjointer **dislocate or break one's hip** s'éhancher **dislocate a part of one's body** se déranger **dislocate or break the hip of** éhancher
dislodge *v.* décoller
disloyalty *n.* infidélité
dismal *adj.* noir
dismantle *v.* dégréer, démancher, démonter
dismantling *n.* dégréement
dismay *n.* **expression of surprise or dismay** Bon Dieu seigneur {saignable}
dismemberment *n.* démembrement
dismiss *v.* décharger, lâcher **dismiss s.o. rudely** envoyer qqn à la promenade {à la merde}
disobedient *adj.* désobéissant, incrédule **disobedient child** fibi **mischievous, disobedient child** possédé **naughty, disobedient girl** chatte **be willfully disobedient** faire le détestable
disobey *v.* désobéir
disobliging *adj.* mal à main
disorder *n.* berdassement, bouleversement, compassion, confusion, criote, désordre, galimatias, méli-mélange, naufrage, pagaille, tchampourra, trouble, épaillage, éparpillage **great disorder** culbute **in disorder** (de) tribord et babord {bâbord}, effarouché, à la traîne, à la valdrague **in great disorder** par les places
disorderly *adj.* **disorderly woman** yenne **disorderly, boisterous person** carnageur **in a disorderly fashion** pêle-mêle
disorganize *v.* mêlailler
disorganized *adj.* désorganisé **the place in question is messy, disorganized, cluttered** Caillette pourrait perdre son veau là-dedans
disoriented *adj.* **be lost or disoriented** avoir les yeux égarés
disown *v.* répudier
dispatch *v.* expédier
dispensation *n.* dispense
dispense *v.* dispenser
dispersal *n.* épaillage, éparpillage
disperse *v.* disbander, disperser, s'épailler, écarter, épailler, éparer, éparpiller
dispersed *adj.* épaillé
dispersion *n.* dispersion
displace *v.* déplacer
display *n.* exhibition, montrance **window display** vitreau
displease *v.* choquer, déplaire
displeasing *adj.* choquant, offensive
displeasure *n.* **show displeasure or disapproval in one's facial expressions** avoir une figure comme une vache qu'a soif **cause of displeasure** dégoûtation **facial expression of displeasure or sulkiness** babiche
disposal *n.* dispose **at your disposal** à votre dispose
dispose *v.* disposer **man proposes and God disposes** l'homme propose et Dieu dispose
disposed *adj.* disposé **be disposed** se porter à / être porté à **be well disposed** être bien disposé
disposition *n.* attitude, caractère, nature, tempérament **mental disposition** disposition **one of overbearing disposition** bouledou
disputable *adj.* disputable
dispute *n.* argument, dispute, querelle, train **have a dispute** avoir chicane
dispute *v.* **one who wrangles, disputes, fusses** disputeur
disqualify *v.* disqualifier
disquieting *adj.* inquiétant
disregarded *adj.* **be disregarded** chiquer poteau
disrepair *n.* dévaldrague **fall into ruin or disrepair** tomber en doise douale}, tomber en ruine **go to ruin or disrepair** tomber en botte **anything old, in bad shape or disrepair** baraque, chabraque
disreputable *adj.* **disreputable woman** fouine **become disreputable** aller croche
disrespect *n.* irrévérence
disrespectful *adj.* dérespectable, incrédule
disrobe *v.* se déshabiller
dissatisfaction *n.* désatisfaction
dissatisfied *adj.* dessatisfait
dissipate *v.* chienner, coursailler, courser, faire (le) rougarou, traînailler, traînasser, bambocher, gavagner
dissipater *n.* bambocheur, bervocheur
dissipation *n.* chiennerie, coursaillerie
dissoluteness *n.* chiennerie
dissolve *v.* délayer, fondre, se dissoudre, se fondre
dissuade *v.* déconseiller, faire fourcher, virer
distance *n.* distance, trot **a distance** un bout **a good distance** un bon boute **in the distance** au loin **quite a distance** un bon boute **at a distance of** à **place at a distance** éloigner
distance *v.* **distance o.s.** s'éloigner
distant *adj.* lointain **in a distant and unknown place** (là-bas) au diable bouilli
distant *adv.* loin
distaste *n.* dégoût
distasteful *adj.* dégoûtant, désagréable
distill *v.* distiller
distinction *n.* distinction **make a distinction** distinguer, faire une distinction
distinctly *adv.* tout à clair
distinguish *v.* distinguer **distinguish o.s.** se distinguer
distort *v.* déformer
distraction *n.* distraction
distress *n.* **be in need, in distress** être dans le besoin
distress *v.* chagriner, faire le gros cœur à
distressed *adj.* **be badly distressed by s.t.** prendre dur
distressing *adj.* chagrinant
distribute *v.* distribuer, séparer
distribution *n.* distribution, partage

district *n.* territoire **district attorney** avocat (de) district **district within a parish or municipality** district **area or district of a city** quartier

distrust *n.* doute, méfiance

distrust *v.* se méfier

disturb *v.* bousculailler, déranger, désoccuper, giguler, punir, terboliser, troubler

disturbance *n.* agitation, bamboula, baribara, berdas, berdassement, carnage, commotion, dérangement, désordre, fracas, ravaud, sassaquoi, sérail, tapage **create a disturbance** brigander, tapager

disturbed *adj.* **be mentally disturbed** pas avoir (son) idée / pas avoir (sa) bonne idée

disturbing *adj.* cruel, troublant

ditch *n.* canal, fossé **ditch or hole used to prepare bousillage** tâche **drainage ditch** égout **fall into a ditch** prendre le fossé **go into a ditch** prendre le fossé

dither *n.* **be in a dither** être vent-debout

ditty *n.* chansonnette

divan *n.* divan, sofa

dive *n.* plonge, plongée **do a cannonball dive** casser la vaisselle, plonger à casser la vaisselle

dive *v.* plonger **dive in the water** se tirer dans l'eau

diver *n.* plongeur

diversion *n.* banco, distraction, divertissement

diversity *n.* diversité, variété

divert *v.* détourner

divide *v.* diviser, détailler, fourcher, margotter, se diviser, séparer **divide up** partager **divide into rooms** croiser **divide with each other** se partager

diviner *n.* devineur

diving *adj.* plongeur

divining *adj.* **divining rod** devineur

divinity *n.* divinité

divisible *adj.* divisable

division *n.* distribution, division, partage, partition, section **division into portions or shares** dévisage

divorce *n.* divorce

divorce *v.* divorcer, délaisser, démarier, se délaisser, se démarier, se quitter **divorce each other** se divorcer

divorced *adj.* divorcé, quitté, en rabiot **divorced man** divorcé, rabiotte **divorced woman** divorcé, rabiotte **get divorced** se divorcer **be separated or divorced** être quitté de qqn **one who is divorced or separated** délaissé

divvy *v.* **divvy up** distribuer

divvying *n.* **divvying up** dévisage

dizziness *n.* tournement de tête, étourdissement **be subject to attacks of dizziness** voir bleu

dizzy *adj.* soûl, ébahi **get dizzy** se soûler **make dizzy** soûler, étourdir **feel weak, dizzy and likely to faint** avoir des faiblesses, faillir **cause to be dizzy** soûler

do *v.* débattre, faire, foutre **do again** refaire, surfaire **do badly** faire à la six-quatre-deux **do carelessly** barboter **do hurriedly** faire à la bric-brac, friper **do in** achever **do negligently** saloper **do poorly** bouchonner, faire à la six-quatre-deux, gargouiller **do without** se dispenser, se démettre, se passer, se priver **do worse** faire pire **do away with** abolir, défaire, se défaire **do it one's own way** faire à sa manière **do more than the usual** faire des fanferluches **do quickly and not well** faire à tambour battant **do or say s.t. without hesitating or waffling** pas aller les quatre chemins **do things while trying not to be noticed** faire le filou comme un chien basset **make do with** faire avec **go to do nothing** se mettre à rien faire **have to do with** s'agir **let s.o. do s.t.** laisser faire **make or do s.t. carelessly** gargoter **force s.o. to do s.t.** bourlinguer **show how to do s.t.** montrer **swear not to do s.t. again** faire la croix **it is necessary to do without things sometimes** à la guerre comme à la guerre **one has to make do with what one has** quand on a pas de cheval on monte mulet **have a million things to do** avoir quatre cent cinquante mille choses à faire **have nothing one would not do** avoir rien à son épreuve **have too many things to do** brûler la chandelle aux deux bouts **no matter what I say or do** j'ai beau dire et j'ai beau faire **you can't tell me what to do** t'es pas maître ici **one who likes to sit in place and do nothing** raccroupi **don't mention it** il y a pas de quoi **not be doing well** être à l'arnicroche **what are you doing here?** quoi tu grattes ici? **be doing what one likes do** être dans son plat **one who does bad or sloppy work** cochonneur **be doing what one likes to do** être dans sa sauce, être dans son plan **one who does work that requires little effort** dépendeur d'andouille

doable *adj.* faisable

docile *adj.* docile, dompte, gouvernable, à (la) main

dock *n.* écluse **dock bit** écluse **dry dock** WAYS

dock *v.* border la terre

doctor *n.* docteur, médecin, oiseau de malheur **voodoo doctor** ouangateur

doctrine *n.* doctrine

document *n.* document

document *v.* documenter

documentary *n.* documentaire

dodge *v.* barder, esquiver

doer *n.* faiseur **big talker and little doer** défonceur d'une porte ouverte / défonceur de porte(s) ouverte(s)

dog *n.* chien **hunting dog** chien de chasse **mad dog** chien enragé **rabbit dog** briquet, chien à lapins **wild dog** chien farouche **every dog has his day** chaque chien a son jour **brindle cattle dog** chien alison **live hope and die like an old dog** vivre en espoir et mourir comme un vieux chien *pl.* **hunt with dogs** courser **go to the dogs** dégrouler **rain cats and dogs** mouiller des chiens et des chats

dogear *n.* oreille de chien

doggone *adj.* sapré

doggone *adv.* saprement
doggone *interj.* **doggone it** saloperie
doghouse *n.* maison à chien
dogwood *n.* bois cornu, bois de chien, bois de flèche **flowering dogwood** bois-bouton, bois de fer
doing *n.* faisage
doll *n.* catin, poupée, titite **baby doll** catin à viser *pl.* **play with dolls** catiner
doll *v.* **doll o.s. up** se repimper
dollar *n.* gourde, piastre
dolphin *n.* dauphin
dolphinfish *n.* dauphin
dolt *n.* patassa
domain *n.* domaine
domestic *n.* domestique
domesticate *v.* adoucir, apprivoiser, dompter
domesticated *adj.* **able to be domesticated** apprivoisable
domesticating *n.* adoucissage, adoucissement, apprivoisement
domicile *n.* domicile
dominate *v.* dominer
domination *n.* domination
domino *n.* domino **domino game** PITCH
donation *n.* don, donation
done *adj.* **done for** fichu, foutu, rasé **badly done** mal fait **be done** finir, se faire **poorly done** mal fait **it is done** ça y est
donkey *n.* bourriquet, JACK, âne **female donkey** bourrique
doo-doo *n.* dou-dou
doodlebug *n.* tourloulou
doom *v.* **doom o.s.** se damner
door *n.* porte **door lock** serrure **door to door** porte à porte **back door** porte (d')en arrière **communicating door** porte de communication **front door** portage, portale, porte (d') en avant / porte de devant **glass door** porte vitrée **screen door** porte en grille **next door to** voisin (de), à collé de **be at death's door** être au grabat, être à la crève **knock at the door** frapper à la porte
doorbell *n.* cloche
doorjamb *n.* jambage, montant de porte
doorkeeper *n.* portier
doorknob *n.* poigne de (la) porte, poigne **hardware of a doorknob and lock** serrure de porte
doormat *n.* essuie-pieds, essuie-place
doorstep *n.* pas de la porte
doorway *n.* porte
dope *n.* dope, drogue **give dope** doper **take dope** se doper
dope *v.* doper
doped *adj.* **get doped up** se doper
dormer *n.* **dormer window** lucarne
dormitory *n.* dortoir
dormouse *n.* loir
dosage *n.* dosage
dose *n.* dose
dot *n.* picot, point
dot *v.* **dot one's i's** mettre les points sur les i
double *adj.* double
double *n.* double, tocaille
double *v.* **double up** se doubler
double-cross *v.* trahir
double-crosser *n.* salaud
double-faced *adj.* double
doubletree *n.* bacul, palonnier double
doubly *adv.* doublement
doubt *n.* doutance, doute **no doubt** sans doute **without doubt** marquablement, sans doute, sans façon
doubt *v.* douter
doubtful *adj.* disputable, doutable
doubtless *adv.* marquablement
douche *n.* clystère, douche, injection
dough *n.* pâte **fried biscuit dough** toteau **fried bread dough** cala
doughnut *n.* beigne, croquecignole, gonfleau
dove *n.* tourte, tourterelle
dowdy *adj.* **dowdy woman** catchouque **big, show, dowdy woman** caouane
dowel *n.* cheville
dowitcher *n.* bécassine de mer
down *adv.* en bas, par terre **down from** en bas de **down there** là-bas **up and down** de bric et de brac, en haut et en bas
down *n.* duvet, poussant
downdraft *n.* rafalement
downpour *n.* avalasse, averse, bourrasque, ratatouille, rincée
downright *adv.* carrément
downstairs *adv.* en bas
downstream *adv.* en bas
downy *adj.* duveté
dowser *n.* devineur
dowsing *adj.* **dowsing rod** devineur
doze *v.* dormailler, roupiller, singoter, sommeiller **doze off** pêcher, soguer
dozen *n.* douzaine **half dozen** demi-douzaine
draft *n.* courant d'air, tire
draft *v.* courant d'air
drag *n.* DRAG, touche
drag *v.* entraîner, tirer, traîner **drag o.s.** se traîner
dragging *adj.* traînant
dragging *n.* traînage
dragline *n.* DRAG-LINE
dragnet *n.* drague
dragon *n.* dragon
dragonfly *n.* chenaille, cheval de {du} diable / cheval-diable, cigale, hirondelle, mamselle, moiselle, sauterelle
drain *n.* DRAIN, fossé, égout, égouttage d'eau, rigolet *pl.* **drains** travers

drain *v.* chesser, couler, drainer, tarir, vider, égoutter **drain out** couler, tarir **drain by dripping** égoutter

drainage *n.* égout, égouttage **drainage ditch** égout

drama *n.* théâtre

draw *n.* touche

draw *v.* attirailler, attirer, tirer, tracer, traîner, DRAW, haler **draw again** retirer **draw back** rebuter, reculer **draw lots** tirer (à) la courtepaille, tirer au sort **draw near** approcher, s'amener **draw straws** tirer (à) la courtepaille **draw alongside shore** accoster **draw near noon** tirer sur midi **draw each other close** se coller **draw near or nearer** se rapprocher **draw near the end** tirer sur la fin {à sa fin} **draw to the end** tirer sur la fin {à sa fin} **draw cards from a deck** piocher

drawback *n.* désavantage

drawbridge *n.* pont à bascule

drawer *n.* tiroir *pl.* **drawers** caleçon **chest of drawers** armoire, bureau, commode

drawing *n.* dessin, plan **drawing closer** rapprochement

drawl *n.* **speak with a drawl** parler lambin

drawl *v.* parler lambin

dread *n.* crainte, horreur, terreur

dread *v.* craindre

dreadful *adj.* terrible

dreadfully *adv.* affreusement, terriblement

dream *n.* rêve, songe **in a dream world** dans les nuages **quit having a dream** effacer un rêve **be in a dream world** être dans les nués

dream *v.* jongler, rêver

dreamer *n.* barificoteur, rêveur **be a dreamer** barificoter

dreamy *adj.* jongleur

dredge *n.* DRAG-LINE **dredge boat** grète-boat **oyster dredge** drague à main, drague

dredge *v.* fouiller, ouverre **sprinkle or dredge with flour** enfariner

dregs *npl.* marc

drenched *adj.* saucé

dress *adj.* pour propre

dress *n.* cotillon, robe, mimine **dress shoe** soulier fin **dress yoke** fiorelle **long dress** grande robe **uniform dress** costume **wedding dress** robe de noces **loose dress resembling a priest's cassock** romaine **loose dress widely known as a Mother Hubbard** blouse (volante) **peculiar or funny dress** basquine **pride in one's dress** farauderie **skirt of a dress** jupe de robe **having pride in one's dress** faraud

dress *v.* gréer, habiller, se gréer, se préparer, vêtir, accommoder, nettoyer, éventrer **dress again** rhabiller **dress carefully** se repimper **dress down** ramasser **dress elegantly** farauder, se farauder **dress extravagantly** se rafistoler **dress o.s.** s'habiller, se vêtir **dress tackily** s'adrigailler **dress up** farauder, s'habiller, s'éguincher, se casser, se gréer, se préparer **dress warmly** abrier **dress o.s. poorly** s'harnacher **dress with layers** abrier **dress in everyday clothes** s'habiller en tous les jours **dress in poor taste** s'habiller mardi gras **dress to the nines** mettre la malle au soleil **dress up with care** se pimponner **dress with great care** se gréer **dress o.s. in poor taste** s'adrigailler, s'affliger **dress up for a special occasion** mistifriser **dress in a gaudy, flashy, or tacky way** attriquer, s'attriquer **dress o.s. in a strange, gaudy or tacky manner** s'artifailler **gut and dress** débriter

dressed *adj.* attriqué, habillé **dressed tackily** adrigaillé **dressed up** attriqué, rafistolé **dressed in rags** déguénillé **dressed to perfection** tiré à quatre épingles **dressed up smartly** habillé sur le rimpinpin **dressed with taste** quinqué **dressed in poor taste** adrigaillé, dégainé, déguénillé **dressed up like a peacock** faraud comme un paon **badly dressed** affligé, calibossé, dégainé, mal agenclé, mal allianté, mal harnaché **be dressed** être changé **elegantly dressed** faraud, rafistolé **get dressed** s'abrier, s'habiller, se mettre du linge **shabbily dressed** dégainé, mal allianté **well dressed** alingé, bien habillé, faraud, quinqué **badly dressed person** Mardi Gras **get dressed again** se rhabiller **get dressed up** mettre du fond de la malle, mettre la malle au soleil, se casser **be dressed in rags** être en haillons **one dressed in a gaudy or tacky way** Mardi Gras **be improperly dressed** être en dégaine **extremely well dressed** cassé **fancy, elegantly dressed** faquin **be all dressed up** être sur un ratata **crudely or absurdly dressed** mal accoutré **tackily or gaudily dressed** tchifaillé **be not neatly or well dressed** être en dégaine

dresser *n.* chiffonnière, toilette **dresser with drawers and hanging space** chiffonnier **fancy dresser** SPORT

dressing *n.* tannage **dressing table** toilette **rice dressing** far

dressmaker *n.* coudeuse, couturier, couturieuse

dressy *adj.* pour propre

dribbling *adj.* baveur

dried *adj.* sec **dried up** flète

drift *v.* rôdailler

drifter *n.* flottant, rôdailleur

driftwood *adj.* bois dérive

driftwood *n.* bois dérive **driftwood or flotsam** ramassis

drill *n.* DRILL, mèche, rigolet, vrille **drill bit** DRILL **drill bit for metal** mèche en fer **drill bit for wood** mèche en bois

drill *v.* DRILL, percer

driller *n.* drilleur **oil driller** drilleur d'huile

drink *n.* coup, filet, petit filet **drink made of milk poured over carmelized sugar** café au lait **soft drink** pop **give a drink** donner à boire **have a drink** prendre {boire} un filet, prendre la magnane

drink *v.* boire, manier la tapette {topette}, se caler, baba, barboter **drink down** caler **drink excessively** boire comme si on n'avait pas de fond / boire comme un chien {poisson / tablier / trou}, débaucher **drink greedily** soiffer **drink heavily** riboter **drink alcohol again** reboire **drink to excess** boire à l'excès, se mettre à la débauche **drink to**

s.o.'s health boire à la santé de qqn **fit to drink** buvable **one who does not drink alcohol** buveur de lait **one who drinks a great deal of coffee** cafiot

drinkable *adj.* buvable

drinker *n.* **big drinker** bambocheur **habitual drinker** soûlard **heavy drinker** buveur, débauché, pinteur **be a heavy drinker** aimer la bouteille, manier la tapette {topette} **he is a heavy drinker** il crache pas dans la bouteille

drinking *adj.* **not drinking** à jeun

drinking *n.* tchacaillerie **drinking binge** tchacaillerie **drinking bout** topette **drinking cup** chopine, moque, pinte **drinking glass** bocal, gobelet, moque, verre à boire, verre **drinking spree** bamboche, biture, boumlala, guinnegue, topette **drinking straw** canne, cive, tuyau à boire, tuyau **go on a drinking spree** faire {prendre / se foutre} une biture

drip *n.* dégouttation, dégouttement, gouttière

drip *v.* couler, dégoutter, égoutter

drip-dry *v.* ressorer

dripping *n.* dégouttation, égouttage

drive *n.* DRIVE, poussée

drive *v.* courir, DRIVE, ficher, planter, promener, toucher, conduire, guider, manier, pousser, rêner, toucher **drive away** lancer **drive back** reconduire, repousser **drive crazy** affoler **drive down** caler **drive in** enfoncer **drive off** décaniller **drive a stake** planter un piquet {poteau} **drive a wagon** wagonner **drive for hire** toucher **drive in again** renfoncer **drive into a corner** accointer **drive into the ground** masser **drive or lead into a pen** corrailler **cry used to drive cattle or chase cattle away** hoba

drivel *n.* **talk unintelligible drivel** ramancher

driver *n.* cocher, conducteur, haleur, toucheur, chauffeur **cattle driver** pousseur de bêtes, toucheur de bêtes **pile driver** pilon **wagon driver** wagonnier

driving *n.* **driving in** enfoncement

drizzle *n.* brumas, frimas, grainasse, lizerée, mouillasse, mouillasserie

drizzle *v.* brumasser, frimasser, grainasser, grainer, grimacer, mouillasser, pleuvasser

drizzling *n.* petite grimace de pluie

drizzly *adj.* mouillassant, mouillasseux

drool *n.* bave

drool *v.* baver, bavoler

drooling *adj.* baveur

drop *n.* goutte, grain **drop of rain** grain de pluie **cough drop** bonbon à rhume

drop *v.* laisser tomber, larguer, lâcher, quitter tomber, tomber, échapper **drop again** réchapper **drop back** réchapper **drop in uninvited** venir se poquer **drop the handkerchief** cache-mouchoir

dropper *n.* **eye dropper** canne-goutte

dropping *n.* **chicken dropping** crotte de poule *pl.* **hard, rounded animal droppings** crotte

dropsical *adj.* hydropique

dropsy *n.* hydropisie

drought *n.* chesseresse, temps sec **period of rain or drought beginning June 8 and lasting forty days** Saint-Médard

drove *n.* cavaillade

drover *n.* pousseur de bêtes, pousseur, toucheur de bêtes

drown *v.* noyer, noyer **drown o.s.** se faire noyer, se noyer

drowned *adj.* **be drowned** se faire noyer, se noyer

drowse *v.* dormailler

drowsy *adj.* en mort fausse

drubbing *n.* dégelée, pimpette **give a sound drubbing** foutre une ramasse (à qqn)

drug *n.* dope, drogue

druggist *n.* apothécaire, pharmacien

drugstore *n.* apothécaire, pharmacie

drum *n.* tambour **drum made from a joint of bamboo** bamboula **bass drum** basse **black drum** tambour **freshwater drum** casburgot **red drum** poisson rouge **saltwater drum** tambour

drumfish *n.* tambour

drumstick *n.* bâton pilon, bâton, cuisse de poule, jarret

drunk *adj.* bite, camphré, en boisson, gris, ivre, piqué, riboteux, rond, saucé, soûl en farine {patate} / soûl comme un cochon {une grive}, soûl, tchac, TIGHT, toqué **be drunk** avoir une biture, tenir une brique, être dans les brindezingues **dead drunk** mort-ivre **get drunk** faire {prendre / se foutre} une biture, flanquer une pointe, prendre {avoir} une pipine / se tenir une pipine, riboter, se biter, se foutre une bosse, se foutre une cuite, se foutre une ribotte, se piquer une cuite {brosse}, se prendre une cuite, se péter une ribote, se soûler, se tchaquer **get drunk again** se ressoûler **get s.o. drunk** biter, soûler, tchaquer

drunkard *n.* bambocheur, bervocheur, biturier, buveur, cocagne, pintocheur, sac à boisson, soûlard, soiffeur, tafiateur **habitual drunkard** riboteur

drunken *adj.* **drunken spree** ribote **drunken man who makes trouble** taurin

drunkenness *n.* biture, débauchage, débauche

dry *adj.* sec **become dry** séquir **it's dry** il fait sec **run dry** tarir **in a dry, sharp manner** sec **be in a dry area** être à sec

dry *v.* chesser, déchesser, essorer, essuyer, séquir **dry o.s.** s'essuyer, se sécher **dry off** se sécher **dry out** chesser, déchesser, essorer, faire chesser, s'essorer, séquir **dry up** déchesser, flétrir, tarir **dry off again** ressuyer **cause to dry** faire chesser, séquir **hang out to dry** mettre à sécher, éparer, étendre **set out to dry** mettre à la sèche, mettre à sécher **lay out clothes on the ground to dry** mettre du linge à la plaille

dry-goods *npl.* marchandises sèches {secs} **dry-goods store** marchandises sèches {secs}

dryer *n.* chesseuse **electric clothes dryer** chesseuse

drying *adj.* essorant

drying *n.* chessage, chesse, essorage, essuyage, séchade **drying agent** déchessant **floor for drying cotton** gril

duck *n.* canard **duck call** appeleur, cornet, moque à canards / moque-canard, moque, sifflet de canard **duck whistle** sifflet de canard **baldpate duck** zinzin **black duck** canard d'été, canard noir **buffle-head duck** marionnette **canvasback duck** canard cheval **domesticated duck** canard doux **Florida duck** canard des îles, canard noir **gray duck** canard gris **mallard duck** canard français, français, tête-vert **mottled duck** canard français d'été **mule duck** canard mulet **muscovy duck** canard d'Inde **pintail duck** paille-en-queue, paillon **redhead duck** tête rouge **ring-necked duck** canard noir, dos-gris **small duck** caneton **spoon-billed duck** micoine **tame duck** canard doux **wild duck** canard farouche **wood duck** branchu, canard branchu, canard de(s) bois **blue-winged teal duck** sarcelle **fulvous tree duck** mexicain **lesser scaup duck** dos-gris **red head duck** violon **roseate spoonbill duck** spatule **Texas mottled duck** canard des îles, canard noir *pl.* **call ducks** moquer un canard / moquer des canards **lie in wait for ducks as they come in to roost at night** aller {partir} à la passe, aller à la passée

duckling *n.* caneton

duckweed *n.* salade

duct *n.* tuyau

dud *n.* chouchou

due *adj.* dû, payable

due *n.* dû *pl.* **dues** dû

duel *n.* duel, rendez-vous **fight a duel** se battre aux armes

dugout *n.* **dugout canoe** pirogue

dull *adj.* barosse, caille, longis, tannable, dull **dull, slow-witted mind** esprit barosse {rosse} **stupid, dull, heavy person** bûche **become round or dull** s'arrondir

dull *v.* ternir, ébrécher **cause to dull** ternir

dull-witted *adj.* **awkward and dull-witted** pâlot

dumb *adj.* stupide **one who is deaf and dumb** sourd-et-muet

dummy *n.* **dummy hand** mort

dump *n.* **garbage dump** bourrier

dump *v.* capoter, débouler

dumpling *n.* boulette, poutine **blackberry dumpling** poutine de {aux} mûres

dumpy *adj.* courtaud

dung *n.* cac, caca **dung heap** parc à fumier **animal dung** fumier **cow dung** pâté de (merde de) vache

dunk *v.* caler, tremper

dupe *v.* beurrer, bloffer, canailler, coquiner, couillonner, fouler, mettre dans le trou, passer la cheville à qqn, passer un bloff, piger

duped *adj.* **be duped** rester avec la chuille

duping *n.* bloff

duplicate *n.* copie, double

duplicate *v.* copier, reproduire

duplicity *n.* duplicité, fausseté

durability *n.* durabilité, usance

durable *adj.* durable, inusable

duration *n.* durance, durée

during *prep.* dans, dedans, durant, pendant

dusk *n.* brune **at dusk** à la brune **from dawn to dusk** (de) soleil levant (à) soleil couché

dust *n.* nettéyeurs, poussière **dust ball** duvet **dust bunny** duvet **remove dust** époussiérer **cover with dust** poussiérer **cover o.s. in dust** se poudriller, se poussiérer **get covered with dust** se poussiérer

dust *v.* ébrousseter, épousseter, époussiérer **dust o.s.** se poudriller, se poussiérer **dust o.s. off** s'épousseter, s'époussiérer **any wad of material used to dust, clean up, or scrub** torchon

dustbath *n.* **take a dustbath** se poudriller, se poussiérer

duster *n.* époustron **feather duster** plumas, plumeau, plumet, poustron, époussetoir

dusting *n.* époussetage

dustrag *n.* époussetoir

dusty *adj.* poussiéreux **become dusty** se poussiérer **make dusty** poussiérer

Dutch *adj.* **Dutch oven** four de stove, four

duty *n.* devoir, fonction, job, obligation, obligeance **do one's duty** faire son devoir **performance of a duty** quittance **wartime tour of duty** temps de guerre *pl.* **Easter duties** Pâques **household duties** berdas **do one's Easter duties** faire ses Pâques

dwarf *adj.* nain

dwarf *n.* nain

dwell *v.* habiter, rester **dwell in** occuper

dweller *n.* **country dweller** campagnard **rural dweller** habitant

dwelling *n.* demeure, logement, résidence **secondary dwelling** CAMP

dwindle *v.* baisser

dye *n.* teinture **red dye** bachoucta **remove dye or color** décolorer

dye *v.* teindre, teinter, se couleurer, se teindre **dye yellow** jaunir

dyer *n.* teindeur

dying *adj.* mourant **be dying** à la mort

dying *n.* crévation **come close to dying** venir un fil {un cheveu / deux cheveux} de sa mort, être venu un cheveu de sa mort

dynamic *adj.* **person with a dynamic or eccentric personality** pétard

dynamite *n.* dynamite

dynamo *n.* dynamo

dysentery *n.* **have dysentery or diarrhea** avoir les boyaux malades

dyspepsia *n.* dyspépsie

dyspeptic *adj.* dyspéptique

E

each *adj.* chaque, tout **each other** l'un l'autre / l'un à l'autre
each *pron.* chacun, chaque
eager *adj.* anxieux, avide **be eager** ambitionner, avoir le FLAG en l'air **become enthused or eager** s'ambitionner **be ready and eager to go someplace** être dessus le mot de go
eagerness *n.* avidité
eagle *n.* aigle, aiglon **American eagle** aigle à tête blanche **bald eagle** aigle à tête blanche
ear *n.* oreille, épi **by ear** à l'oreille **elephant ear plant** oreille d'éléphant **have a keen ear** attendre clair, avoir les oreilles claires *pl.* **have big ears** avoir des oreilles d'éléphant {de tayaut} / avoir des oreilles comme un pot de chambre / avoir des oreilles comme un taxi avec les deux portes ouvertes
earache *n.* mal d'oreille
eardrop *n.* **eardrop vine** anserine liane
earlier *adv.* plus de bonne heure
early *adj.* matinal, prime
early *adv.* (à / de) bonne heure, tôt **early in the morning** de bon matin **as early as** dès **you don't have to go yet, it's still early** on a plein d'huile dans la lampe
early-maturing *adj.* prime
earn *v.* gagner, mériter, se gagner **earn a living** faire une {sa} vie
earning *n.* gagne, gain
earring *n.* boucle d'oreille, pendrioche **pendant earring set with a solitaire diamond** dormeuse
earth *n.* terre **pack earth** saper
earth *v.* **earth up** butter
earthen *adj.* **earthen jar** jarre en terre, pobon
earthenware *n.* **earthenware crock** pot de grès
earthly *adj.* terrestre
earthquake *n.* tremblement de terre
earthworm *n.* lèche, ver de lèche, ver de terre, ver
ease *n.* aise, bènaise, facilité **at ease** posé **be at one's ease** être à son aise
ease *v.* se déhaler, soulager
easily *adv.* aisé, aisément, couramment, facile, facilement
east *n.* est, trou de la souris
Easter *n.* Pâques **Easter basket** nique de Pâques **Easter duties** Pâques **Easter egg** œuf de lapin **Easter Sunday** Jour de Paques **do one's Easter duties** faire ses Pâques
easy *adj.* aisé, en aise, facile, indulgent, simple **easy to handle** maniable **be easy** être une senelle **not easy** malaisé **make easy or easier** faciliter **that's easy to do** ça aurait pas pris un Yinqui **that's easy to understand.** ça prend pas un avocat **that's easy to understand** ça aurait pas pris un Yinqui **have it easy** ramasser dans les rangs hauts **have things easy** être à son aise **take it easy** paresser, se catiner **have the easy life first** manger le pain blanc en premier
easy-going *adj.* bonasse **nice, easy-going person** SPORT
eat *v.* manger, s'appuyer l'estomac, se nourrir, nanane, niameniame **eat again** remanger **eat away** chicoter, dégobiller **eat greedily** friper, laper, manger à pleine gueule **eat lightly** picocher **eat much** se piquer une bosse **eat noisily** friper **eat quickly** envaler **eat ravenously** dévorer **eat up** dévorer **eat a lot** manger comme quatre / manger comme un cochon {ours / requin} **eat for supper** souper **eat heartily, greedily** manger à ventre déboutonné **eat one's words** renvaler ses paroles **eat a great deal** s'en flanquer une bosse **eat here and there** mangeailler **eat on and off** mangeailler **eat the noon meal** dîner **eat everything on the table** bâcler les plats **eat one thing to the point of disgust** se regouler **one who picks at food or eats lightly** picocheur
eatable *adj.* mangeable
eater *n.* mangeur **heavy eater** goulipiat **be a big eater** avoir des tripes dans les pieds, avoir un bon coup de fourchette
eaves *npl.* corniche, gouttière
ebb *n.* refoule, déclin
eccentric *adj.* **strange or eccentric individual** abricot, abricotier **person with a dynamic or eccentric personality** pétard
ecclesiastic *n.* écclesiastique
echo *n.* écho
eclair *n.* éclair
eclipse *n.* éclipse
economical *adj.* **be economical** picaillonner
economiser *n.* économiseur
economize *v.* ménager, serrer, économiser, épargner
economy *n.* ménagement, économie
eczema *n.* eczéma
eddy *n.* tortillon, tourbillon **water eddy** remous
edge *n.* bord, bordage, linteau, riflette, tranchant, bord, bordure, cant, lisière **edge of the woods** bordure de bois **cutting edge** taillant, tranchant
edging *n.* bordure
edible *adj.* mangeable **be edible** se manger
edible *npl.* **edibles** mangeaille, manger
edict *n.* édit
edification *n.* édification
edifice *n.* édifice
edit *v.* éditer
editor *n.* éditeur
educate *v.* instruire, éduquer **educate o.s.** s'instruire
educated *adj.* informé, instruit, savant **educated to the fingertips, extremely well educated** instruit à la pointe des ongles
education *n.* enseignement, instruction, école, éducation **lacking education** ignorant **get an education** s'instruire
eel *n.* anguille

efface *v.* effacer

effect *n.* effet, résultat **take effect** prendre effet **go into effect** prendre effet **have an effect** agir, faire un effet

effective *adj.* **be effective** faire effet

effeminate *adj.* filleuse **effeminate man** homme de paille, suce-fleur

efficient *adj.* bon à marier

effigy *n.* **grotesque effigy** caricature

effort *n.* débattement, effort, entreprise **effort that is not worth the trouble** raccourci à défunt Pétain / raccourci à Philémon **great effort** compassion **make an effort** s'ambitionner, s'appliquer, se donner la peine **make much effort** faire (le) diable et son train **neighborhood cooperative effort** coup de main **fail in one's effort** chier sur le palonnier **make a great effort** se mettre en trente-quatre {trente-six} **give a great effort to do s.t. and not succeed** chier sa crotte de noces *pl.* **make excessive efforts** se mettre en deux **make great efforts** tirer le diable par la queue **make unnecessary efforts** faire {prendre} des fions **make great efforts to do s.t.** faire de ses pieds et ses mains pour arriver

effortlessly *adv.* normal

effrontery *n.* effronterie, organe, témérité

egg *n.* œuf, coco **egg beater** palette à z-œufs **egg white** blanc d'œuf, glaire **egg yolk** jaune d'œuf **bad egg** calypson, garnement **coddled egg** œuf mollet **Easter egg** œuf de lapin **hard-boiled egg** œuf cam-cam **nest egg** nichoix, nioque **soft-boiled egg** œuf mollet **soft-shelled egg** œuf hardé **tube through which an egg passes before it is laid** pondiaire **any thick viscous substance resembling egg white** glaire *pl.* **knock eggs** bosquer les œufs, pâquer **knocking eggs** pâquage **lay eggs** pondre **setting of eggs** couvée **sit on eggs** couver **cluster of eggs that a female crab carries under her abdominal apron** paquet

eggbeater *n.* batteur d'œuf **hand-held eggbeater** brasseur d'œuf

eggnog *n.* œufs à la neige, eggnog

eggplant *n.* brème

eggshell *n.* coquille d'œuf, écale

egret *n.* héron dos blanc, aigrette **American egret** aigrette noire **blue egret** aigrette bleue **cattle egret** aigrette à vaches **snowy egret** aigrette blanche

eight *n.* huit **about eight** huitaine

eighteen *n.* dix-huit

eighteenth *n.* dix-huitième

eighth *n.* huitième

eightieth *n.* quatre-vingtième

eighty *n.* quatre-vingt

either *adv.* non plus

either *conj.* **either . . . or** soit... ou, soit... soit

eject *v.* mettre (qqn) dehors

eke *v.* **eke out an existence** subsister **try to eke out an existence on poor land** graboter

elapse *v.* se passer, passer

elastic *adj.* rebondissant, élastique

elasticity *n.* élasticité

elbow *n.* coude

elbow *v.* foutre un coup de coude

elder *adj.* aîné

elder *n.* **elder tree, bush, or wood** sureau

elderberry *n.* sureau, herbe à sureau **elderberry plant** pied de sureau

elderly *adj.* âgé **elderly people** vieux monde **be elderly** avoir un bon âge

eldest *adj.* aîné

eldest *n.* premier né

elect *v.* électer, élire

election *n.* élection

electorate *n.* électorat

electric *adj.* électrique **electric light** lampe électrique, lumière électrique **electric line** ligne à lumière **electric wire** fil électrique

electrical *adj.* électrique **electrical line** ligne **electrical outlet** PLUG **electrical wire** fil à l'électricité

electrician *n.* électricien

electricity *n.* électricité

electrify *v.* électrifier

electrocution *n.* électrocution

elegance *n.* élégance **displaying an excessive elegance** faraudé

elegant *adj.* chenaleux, fini, élégant **fancy, elegant clothes** faraud

elegant *n.* chenu

element *n.* élément *pl.* **elements** élément

elementary *adj.* élémentaire

elephant *n.* éléphant **elephant ear plant** oreille d'éléphant

elevate *v.* élever

elevation *n.* butte, élévation

elevator *n.* élévateur

eleven *n.* onze

eleventh *n.* onzième

elf *n.* lutin

eligible *adj.* sujéti

eliminate *v.* abattre, éliminer **eliminate numbness or stiffness** dégourdir

elimination *n.* élimination

elite *n.* élite

elm *n.* orme **Samara elm** bois puant **slippery elm** orme gras **water elm** charmille, châtaignier

eloquence *n.* éloquence

eloquent *adj.* éloquent

else *adv.* **or else** autrement **or else** ou bien

elsewhere *adv.* ailleurs, autre part

elude *v.* esquiver, parer

emaciated *adj.* efflanqué **thin, shriveled, emaciated person** rapapiote

emancipate *v.* affranchir, émanciper

emasculate *v.* émasculer **emasculate o.s.** s'émasculer
embalm *v.* embaumer
embalmer *n.* embaumeur
embankment *n.* DAM, levée, terrasse **dike or embankment** brûlé
embark *v.* s'embarquer
embarkation embarcation
embarking embarcation
embarrass *v.* embarrasser, emberlificoter, gêner, faire honte (à qqn)
embarrassed *adj.* embarrassé, gêné **be embarrassed** avoir honte, se gêner **not be embarrassed to speak** pas avoir la langue dans la poche
embarrassing *adj.* embarrassant, gênant **be in an embarrassing position** tirer le diable par la queue
embarrassment *n.* gêne
embed *v.* engraver
embellish *v.* embellir, siroter
embellishment *n.* embellissement
ember *n.* braise
Ember Days *n.* Quatre-Temps
emblem *n.* emblème
emboss *v.* embosser
embrace *n.* caresse, embrassade **in an embrace** à {en} brasse-corps
embrace *v.* embrasser, s'embrasser, se coller
embracing *n.* embrassement
embroider *v.* broder
embroiderer *n.* brodeur
embroidery *n.* brodage, broderie, brodure **embroidery hoop** tambour
embryo *n.* germe, margot, poussant
emerge *v.* débouquer, sortir
emergency *n.* **emergency baptism** ondoiement **emergency provision** en-tout-cas **anything kept for an emergency** en-tout-cas
emigrant *n.* émigré
emigration *n.* émigration
emissary *n.* émissaire
emotion *n.* émotion *pl.* **bring up feelings or emotions of** émouver
emperor *n.* empereur
emphasis *n.* **used for emphasis** c'est, ti
empire *n.* empire
employ *v.* appliquer, employer, engager, utiliser
employee *n.* commis, employé, engagé **employee of a sugar factory** sucrier **female employee** engagère *pl.* **employees** personnel
employer *n.* BOSS, employeur, engagiste
employment *n.* emploi, job **give employment** employer **take employment** s'engager
empty *adj.* allège, creux, vacant, vide, faux **become empty** se vider **the place is empty** la piste est sèque
empty *v.* vider **empty again** revider **empty the bowels of** délâcher
empty-handed *adj.* allège
emptying *n.* vidage
enamel *n.* grénier, énamelle
enamored *adj.* amoureux, animé
encase *v.* emboîter, empailler, encaisser, envelopper
encasing *n.* emboîtement, encaissage, encaissement
enchain *v.* enchaîner
enchainment *n.* enchaînement
enchant *v.* enchanter
enchanted *adj.* charmant
enchanter *n.* enchanteur
enchantment *n.* enchantement
encircle *v.* cercler, encercler
encirclement *n.* encerclement
encircling *n.* cerclage
enclose *v.* fermer, monter de la barrière, renfermer **enclose with bars** barreauter
enclosed *adj.* clos
enclosure *n.* clôture, corail, entourage, parc **enclosure in which calves are kept separated from cows** chicaire **protective enclosure around a tree or shrub** cage **build a protective enclosure around** cager
encounter *n.* rencontre
encounter *v.* croiser avec, rejoindre, rencontrer **encounter by chance** arriver sur
encourage *v.* ambitionner, encourager **encourage each other** s'encourager
encouragement *n.* encouragement
encouraging *adj.* encourageant
encrust *v.* **encrust with filth** crotter
encumber *v.* enfourner, harnacher
encumbrance *n.* encombrement
end *n.* bout, cesse, complétion, extrémité, fin, finissement, finition (finission), tchu, queue **end to end** boute à boute **end of a loaf of bread** croûte, crouston, nez **back end** derrière **dead end** cul-de-sac, manche **far end** fond **rear end** fesse, gogo **without end** sans cesse **in the end** en dernier, à la fin du compte **stand on end** regricher **at the end of** au bout de **at the end of one's rope** au bout du câble **at the end of the road** au bout du chemin **from one end to the other** d'un boute à l'autre, de bout en blanc **bring to an end** conclure **come to an end** terminer **draw near the end** tirer sur la fin {à sa fin} **draw to the end** tirer sur la fin {à sa fin} **from beginning to end** de fond en comble **have the short end** avoir le boute courte **come to a bad end** aboutir en mal **have come to the end of one's high point** avoir tiré son pétard *pl.* **make ends meet** rapprocher les deux bouts, venir à bout **odds and ends** barrancages, des petits boutailles **do odds and ends** berdasser
end *v.* finir, terminer, barrer, casser, fermer **end up** aboutir, finir par **end a feud** se désembrouiller **end a friendship**

casser la bande **end up with** réchapper **end the day's work** larguer

endearment *n.* **term of endearment** nom doux **ironic term of endearment** ma petite chouette

ending *adj.* **never ending** sans cesse

ending *n.* aboutissage, cesse **a bad beginning, a good ending** mauvaise partance, bonne arrivée

endive *n.* endive

endless *adj.* infini, sans cesse, éternel

endlessly *adv.* à p'us finir, éternellement

endorse *v.* endosser

endorsement *n.* endossement

endorser *n.* endosseur

endowed *adj.* **be well endowed** emmanché

endurable *adj.* endurable

endurance *n.* endurance, tolérance

endure *v.* durer, endurer, STAND, supporter, voir, soufferre **endure intense suffering** voir (du) bleu **endure hardship because of s.o.** avoir du fil à retordre avec qqn

enduring *adj.* endurant

enema *n.* clystère, douche, lavement

enemy *n.* ennemi

energetic *adj.* frais comme un lapin, HOP, élevé sur du vin haigue, énergique

energy *n.* babiche, énergie **exhibit great activity or energy** grouiller *pl.* **save one's energies** se ménager

enervating *adj.* énervant

engage *v.* fiancer **engage in a brawl** poquer **engage in malicious mischief** carnager **engage in political activity** faire de la politique **engage readily or frequently in casual sex** chiennailler, chienner

engaged *adj.* occupé, engagé, fiancé, promis **become engaged** s'engager, se fiancer **become officially engaged** déclarer

engagement *n.* accordement, engagement, fiance **engagement ring** bague d'engagement **set a time for an engagement** citer

engender *v.* engendrer

engine *n.* engin, machine **steam engine** machine à vapeur

engineer *n.* ingénieur

England *n.* Angleterre

English *adj.* américain, anglais **English person** Anglais **English speaker** Anglais **English speaker who is not of French descent** Américain **the English language** américain, anglais **pertaining to the English language** américain

English *n.* américain, anglais **one who speaks English but not French** gueule rouge

English-speaking *adj.* américain

engrave *v.* engraver, frapper, graver

engraved *adj.* **be engraved** se graver

engraving *n.* gravure

engross *v.* préoccuper

engulf *v.* engloutir

enjoy *v.* ENJOY, jouir **enjoy o.s.** se plaire **enjoy or amuse o.s. or each other** s'amuser

enjoyment *n.* jouissance

enlarge *v.* grossir, magnifier, rélargir, s'égrandir, égrandir, élargir **enlarge by addition** rabouter

enlargement *n.* égrandissement

enlarger *n.* égrandisseur

enlarging *n.* élargissement

enlist *v.* enrôler, enregistrer, s'enrôler, s'enregistrer

enlistment *n.* enrôlement

enliven *v.* animer, émouver

enormity *n.* énormité

enormous *adj.* abominable, un coquin de

enormously *adv.* énormément

enough *adv.* assez, à siau **be enough** suffire **have enough** avoir assez, se tanner **it's enough** ça suffit **have eaten enough** avoir la fale pleine **more than enough** de reste **now that's enough** à ça oui

enraged *adj.* **be enraged** se manger de rage **become furious or enraged** s'enrager

enrich *v.* enrichir, fertiliser **enrich o.s.** s'enrichir

enroll *v.* enrôler, s'enrôler

enrollment *n.* enrôlement, enregistrement

ensconce *v.* engraver

entangle *v.* emmêler, empêtrer

entangled *adj.* **become entangled** s'emberner, s'empêtrer **get entangled** s'emmêler

entanglement *n.* embrouille, emmêlement

enter *v.* entrer, pénétrer, rentrer, se fourrer **enter a plea** plaider **enter into by contract** contracter **enter without an invitation or permission** casser **allow to enter** admettre

enterprise *n.* entreprise

enterprising *adj.* **be enterprising** s'entreprendre

entertain *v.* amuser, divertir, entretenir

entertainment *n.* amusement

enthused *adj.* **become enthused or eager** s'ambitionner

enthusiasm *n.* zèle **outburst of enthusiasm** estampique

entice *v.* attirer

enticing *adj.* attirant

entire *adj.* complet, entier, tout

entirely *adv.* absolument, complètement, en plein, entièrement, finiment, tout

entirety *n.* totage

entourage *n.* entourage, fumière

entrail *npl.* **entrails** débris, tripage

entrance *n.* entrance, entrure, entrée, porte **main entrance** portage, portale

entrance *v.* charmer

entrap *v.* attraper

entrench *v.* engraver

entrepreneur *n.* entrepreneur

entrust *v.* confier, fier, rencharger **entrust o.s.** se confier, se livrer à
entry *n.* entrée
envelop *v.* envelopper
envelope *n.* enveloppe
envious envieux
envious *adj.* jaloux
environs *n.* alentours
envoy *n.* émissaire
envy *n.* jalouserie
envy *v.* envier, jalouser
epidemic *n.* épidémie
epilepsy *v.* haut mal
episode *n.* épisode
epistle *n.* épitre
epoch *n.* période, âge, époque
Epsom *n.* **Epsom salt** magnésie **Epsom salts** sel d'epsom, sel à purger
equal *adj.* égal **be equal** être dessus un balan **make equal** égalir, égaliser
equal *n.* MATCH, égal **have no equal** avoir rien à son épreuve **find or provide an equal for** rappareiller
equality *n.* égalité
equalize *v.* égalir, égaliser
equally *adv.* égal
equilibrium *n.* balan, équilibre **lose one's balance or equilibrium** perdre son balan
equip *v.* gréer, équiper **equip o.s.** se gréer **equip a soldier** gréer un soldat
equipment *n.* agrès, gréage, gréement, gréyure, équipage, équipement
equipped *adj.* attelé
equipping *n.* gréage
equisetum *n.* prêle
equivalence *n.* equipollence
era *n.* période, siècle, époque
erase *v.* effacer
eraser *n.* effaceur
erasing *n.* effaçure
erasure *n.* effaçure
erect *v.* dresser, élever, ériger **erect a scaffold** échafauder **erect a fence or barrier around** entourer **erect struts or supports for construction** bloquer
erection *n.* érection **have an erection** bander **lose one's erection** débander
erode *v.* chicoter, dégrader, manger, se laver, se miner
eroded *adj.* **be eroded** se laver
erosion *n.* érosion
err *v.* fauter
errand *n.* commission, course, mission **run an errand** faire une commission *pl.* **be running errands** être en commission
error *n.* erreur, MISTAKE, trompe **in error** en erreur
eruption *n.* **skin eruption** clou
erysipelas *n.* érésipèle
escapade *n.* escapade, tour de lune, échappade
escape *n.* échappe **there's no escape** il y a pas de réchappe **place or means of escape** échappatoire
escape *v.* marronner, partir (en) marron, réchapper, s'escaper, s'échapper, s'évader, se sauver, échapper, évader
escarpment *n.* écore
esophagus *n.* avaloire
especially *adv.* espécialement, particulièrement, spécialement, surtout
espionage *n.* espionnage
essence *n.* extrat
essential *adj.* **main, essential, or basic thing** principal
establish *v.* fonder, établir, monter
establishing *n.* établissement
establishment *n.* établissement
estate *n.* **real estate** propriété
esteem *n.* estime
esteem *v.* apprécier, estimer **esteem o.s.** s'estimer
estimate *v.* estimer
estimation *n.* appréciation, estimation
estranged *adj.* brouillé
estrangement *n.* brouille
etagere *n.* étagère
eternal *adj.* éternel
eternally *adv.* éternellement
eternity *n.* éternité
ether *n.* éther
ethical *adj.* moral
ethnic *adj.* **ethnic group** citoyen, nation
ethnicity *n.* race
etiquette *n.* étiquette
etouffee *n.* étouffée
Eucharist *n.* eucharistie
euchre *n.* youk, euchre
eulogy *n.* récit
Europe *n.* Europe, l'autre bord
European *adj.* européen
European *n.* Européen
evacuate *v.* évacuer
evacuation *n.* évacuation
evade *v.* parer, éviter
evangelize *v.* évangéliser
evaporate *v.* s'évaporer, évanouir, évaporer **cause to evaporate** évaporer
evasion *n.* échappatoire
eve *n.* veille **eve of the eve** avant-veille
Eve *n.* **Christmas Eve** veille de Christmas, veille de Noël **New Year's Eve** veille de l'an
even *adj.* côte à côte, jusqu'à, juste, plange, quitte, rase, uni,

égal **even with** en plan avec, vis-à-vis (de) **getting even** réglement de comptes **make even** plangir, unir, égaler, égalir, égaliser **get even with s.o.** faire manger du calalou (à qqn) **come out even** sortir à jeu

even *adv.* encore, même, seulement **even if** quand même (que) **even so** encore, pourtant, quand même **even though** bien que, quand même (que), quoique

evening *n.* soir, soirée, veillée **evening meal** souper **evening party** soirée, veillée **evening up** effleurage **evening visit** soirée, veillerie, veillée **evening spent with neighbors** veillée **evening spent with family members or friends** banco **good evening** bonsoir **this evening** asoir / à soir / (à) ce soir **tomorrow evening** demain (au) soir **pass an evening** veiller **spend the evening** faire une soirée **late in the evening** sur le tard

evenly *adv.* égal

evenness *n.* égalité

event *n.* épisode, événement **rowdy event** cancan **terrible event** avarie **in the event** en tout cas (que)

eventually *adv.* à la longue

ever *adv.* jamais, rarement, déjà **if ever** si jamais **not ever** pas jamais

everlasting *n.* vulnéraire

every *adj.* chaque, tout

everybody *pron.* tout le monde

everyone *pron.* tous, tout chacun, tout le monde, tout quelqu'un

everything *pron.* tout quelque chose, tout, toute chose **spend everything** se casser à la maille **that beats everything** ça par exemple!

everywhere *adv.* dans les quatre paroisses, partout, tout partout **from everywhere** de toute part

evict *v.* déguerper, déloger

eviction *n.* éviction

evidence *n.* preuve, évidence

evident *adj.* vulière, évident

evidently *adv.* clairement, évidemment

evil *adj.* maudit, mauvais, méchant, vilain **evil deed** malfait **evil person** yeux barrés (comme un cabri) **evil spell** voudou **evil woman** diablesse **with evil intent** malicieusement **wicked, evil, bad, malicious person or thing** maudit, méchant

evil *n.* mal, maudiceté, mauditerie, mauvaiseté, méchanceté **lead into evil** entraîner

evildoer *n.* malfaisant, malfaiteur

ewe *n.* brébis

exact *adj.* définitif, exact, précis **more exact** enfin

exacting *adj.* exigeant, regardant, suspect **exacting in the expectation of payment** regardant **be precise, exacting or meticulous** mettre les points sur les i

exactitude *n.* exactitude

exactly *adv.* droite, exact, exactement, juste, justement, rienquetement

exactness *n.* exactitude

exaggerate *v.* battre la berloque, chanter des midis à quatorze heures, péter à cul cassé **exaggerate badly** déchirer le gingas {ginghat} **one who exaggerates his actions** étouffeur de canards morts

exaggerated *adj.* fort

exaggeration *n.* exagération, menterie

exalted *adj.* noble

exam *n.* **give an exam** passer à l'examen

examination *n.* examen, examination, inspection **succeed in an examination** passer un examen

examine *v.* CHECK, examiner, passer à l'examen **examine o.s.** s'examiner

example *n.* exemple, illustration **for example** comme, par exemple, pour exemple **follow s.o.'s example** prendre exemple dessus {sur / sus} qqn **give a good example** donner le bon exemple **serve as an example** exempler

exceed *v.* dépasser

exceedingly *adv.* comme tout

excellence *n.* excellence

excellent *adj.* carabiné, prime, professionnel

excellently *adv.* fameusement

except *conj.* ebsèpe que, excepté que, réservé que, sauf que pour, sauf que, à part que

except *prep.* dehors, en dehors de, excepté, hormis, sauf

excepting *prep.* excepté

exception *n.* exception, mais **take exception** objecter

excess *n.* excès **in excess** en patate **do to excess** s'en mettre à **drink to excess** boire à l'excès, se mettre à la débauche **work to excess** éreinter **do s.t. in excess** s'en foutre une bosse

excessive *adj.* abusif, carabiné, démesuré, écrasant

excessively *adv.* en patate, trop

exchange *n.* changeage, changeotage, rechange, SWITCH, échange, barguine

exchange *v.* barguiner, brocanter, changeoter, changer, faire (un/une) barguine (avec), se barguiner, échanger, s'échanger **exchange letters** correspondre **exchange punches** poquer

excite *v.* agiter, animer, exciter

excited *adj.* agité, excité, fiévreux **be excited** s'agiter, s'animer, être sur les épingles **become excited** s'exciter **unduly excited** effardé

excitement *n.* excitation, fièvre **wild with excitement** ébourifflé

exclaim *v.* faire des (grands) hélas

exclamation *n.* exclamation

exclusion *n.* exception

excommunicate *v.* excommunier

excommunication *n.* excommunication, excommunion

excrement *n.* cac, caca, excrément, chiure **piece of excrement** étron

excrete *v.* passer

excursion *n.* excursion
excusable *adj.* excusable, pardonnable
excuse *n.* excuse *pl.* **make excuses** se faire des raisons
excuse *v.* excuser, pardonner, s'excuser
execution *n.* exécution
executor *n.* exécuteur
exempt *v.* dispenser, exempter
exempted *adj.* exempti
exemption *n.* exemption, dispense
exercise *n.* exercice *pl.* **commencement exercises** graduation
exercise *v.* exercer, s'exercer
exhale *v.* expirer **inhale and exhale** respirer
exhaust *v.* abîmer, exhausser, fatiguer, tarir
exhausted *adj.* abîmé, efflanqué, mort, éreinté
exhausting *adj.* halant
exhaustion *n.* cuite
exhibit *v.* exposer, montrer **exhibit again** remontrer **exhibit great activity or energy** grouiller
exhibition *n.* exhibition, montrance
exhortation *n.* exhortation
exhumation *n.* exhumation
exhume *v.* désenterrer, exhumer
exigency *n.* exigence
exile *n.* bannissement, exil, exile, exilé **person in exile** exile, exilé
exile *v.* bannir, exiler **exile o.s.** s'exiler
exist *v.* exister
existence *n.* existence **eke out an existence** subsister **try to eke out an existence on poor land** graboter
exit *n.* fourchette
exodus *n.* dérangement
exonerate *v.* absoudre, exonérer
expand *v.* se développer, élargir
expanse *n.* étendue **muddy expanse** vasière **open expanse** large
expect *v.* anticiper, attendre, espérer, expecter, s'attendre **expect with anxiety** appréhenter **not get what one expects** sortir en arrière
expected *adj.* dû
expedition *n.* expédition
expel *v.* bannir, chasser, mettre (qqn) dehors, mettre à la porte
expenditure *n.* déboursement
expense *n.* dépense, frais **free of expense** net *pl.* **incur expenses** faire des dépenses
expensive *adj.* chaud, cher, chérant, coûteux, hors de prix **become more expensive** renchérir
experience *n.* expérience **suffer through a difficult experience** danser la carmagnole
experience *v.* expériencer **experience a strange agitation** faire drôle
experienced *adj.* expériencé
experiment *n.* expériment
experiment *v.* expériencer, expérimenter
experimentation *n.* expérimentation
experimenting *n.* expérimentation
expert *adj.* expert, fin **be expert at, adept at** avoir la main pour
expert *n.* connaisseur, expert, spécialiste
expertise *n.* expertise
expiation *n.* expiation
expiration *n.* expiration
expire *v.* expirer
explain *v.* expliquer, s'expliquer **explain point by point** expliquer point par point
explainable *adj.* explicable
explanation *n.* explication, exposé
explode *v.* crâler, éclater **explode a firecracker** flailler le pétard **explode or pop** éclater
exploit *n.* aventure
exploration *n.* exploration
explore *v.* explorer, sonder
explosion *n.* explosion
explosive *n.* **hidden explosive** mine
export *n.* exportation
export *v.* exporter
exportation *n.* exportation
expose *v.* démasquer, désabrier, dévoiler, exposer **expose o.s.** s'exposer, se mettre au blanc **expose one's intentions** se dévoiler **expose to sunlight** soleiller **expose to full sunlight** mettre au beau soleil **expose the chest or breast** se dépoitrailler **expose the neck and shoulders of** décolleter
exposed *adj.* au blanc, ouvert, à la blanque **be exposed** s'exposer
exposing *n.* dévoilement
exposition *n.* exposition
exposure *n.* blanque
expression *n.* air, expression, parlage **facial expression** expression, figure **pouting expression** babine **facial expression of displeasure or sulkiness** babiche **contorted facial expression** simagris
expressly *adv.* directement, expressément, exprès
expropriate *v.* exproprier
expropriation *n.* expropriation
expulsion *n.* bannissement, éviction **expulsion from Acadia** dérangement **the forcible expulsion of the French-origin population in Acadia by the English in 1755** le Grand Dérangement
extemity *n.* bout
extend *v.* allonger, allongir, continuer, prolonger, rabouter, rallonger, élongir, étendre, courir, s'allonger **extend an afternoon hunt into the early evening** faire une passée
extension *n.* allonge, allongement, extension, hausse, manche, prolongement, rallongement, égrandissement
extensive *adj.* vaste

extent *n.* mesure, étendue **to a great extent** affreux **great in number, size, or extent** majeur
exterminate *v.* détruire, exterminer
extermination *n.* extermination
extinction *n.* extinction
extinguish *v.* éteigner, éteindre
extinguished *adj.* éteint **be extinguished** s'éteindre
extra *adj.* extra **a little something extra received for free** lagniappe
extra *adv.* extra
extra *n.* extra
extract *n.* extrat, parfum, essence **vanilla extract** essence de gâteau, essence de vanille / essence à la vanille, extrat de vanille
extract *v.* arracher, haler
extraction *n.* extraction
extraordinary *adj.* extra, extraordinaire **be extraordinary** être du chenu
extravagance *n.* extravagance
extravagant *adj.* carabiné, décarabiné, extravagué, gaspillard **extravagant or original person** caractère
extreme *adj.* extrême
Extreme *n.* **Extreme Unction** Extrême Onction
extremely *adv.* affreusement, comme tout, diablement, extra, extrêmement, fin, mortel, méchant, sacrément, saprement, terrible, à mort
extremity *n.* extrémité **from one extremity to the other** d'une extrémité à l'autre
extricate *v.* dégager **extricate o.s.** s'en sortir, se démerder, se démêler
exudation *n.* exudation
eye *n.* œil, zyeu **eye dropper** canne-goutte **eye of a needle** chas **eye of a potato** œil de patate **eye of a hook and eye** œillet **black eye** BLACK EYE, nioque **hook and eye closure** agrafe **keep an eye on** guetter, surveiller **with an eye to** en vue de **give a black eye** casser un œil (à qqn), donner un BLACK-EYE **put out one's eye** s'éborgner **white of the eye** blanc d'œil **put out an eye of** éborgner **having a white patch around one eye** lunette *pl.* **eyes** zyeu **sunken eyes** yeux creux **have eyes bigger than one's stomach** avoir les yeux plus grands que le ventre **before one's eyes** dans sa face **have dark eyes** avoir des yeux noirs comme des socos **have bags under one's eyes** avoir les yeux cernés **have rings under one's eyes** avoir les yeux cernés **condition of having red, itchy eyes** air **dew gathered for washing the eyes** eau de serein **see one's life flash before one's eyes** livrer sa carcasse au diable **having a star or white mark between the eyes** lunette
eyeball *n.* canique de l'œil, perle
eyebrow *n.* sourcil
eyedropper *n.* égout
eyeglass *n.* **eyeglass lenses** vitres de lunettes *pl.* **eyeglasses** lunettes, verre
eyelash *n.* paupière
eyelet *n.* œillet
eyelid *n.* paupière *pl.* **bat one's eyelids** battre les yeux
eyesight *n.* vue **lose one's eyesight** perdre la vue
eyetooth *n.* dent d'œil
eyewear *n.* **protective eyewear** garde-yeux
eyewitness *n.* témoin oculaire

F

fable *n.* fable, fiction
fabric *n.* fabrique, linge, étoffe **fabric made of cotton warp and woolen thread** jeture **chiffon fabric** chiffon **cotton fabric** linge de coton **heavy fabric** cretonne
fabricate *v.* bâtir, forger, inventionner, ramancher
fabrication *n.* fabrication
facade *n.* façade
face *n.* binette, face, figure, frimasse, micmac, museau, simagris, visage **face to face** figure à figure, tête à tête, vis-à-vis **face of a clock** cadran **long face** babine longue **large stupid-looking face** baboune **make a face** faire une grimace, se défigurer **show one's face** se montrer le nez {la figure} **wash one's face** se laver la figure **wash one's face with soap** se savonner la figure **find o.s. face to face with** se figurer avec **make a squinting, grinning face** grincher **person with a yellowish-colored face** jaunaca **throw s.t. back in s.o.'s face** retirer qqch dans la figure à qqn **speak of the devil, see his face** en parlant de la bête, on lui voit la tête *pl.* **make faces** grimacer
face *v.* affronter, braver, confronter, donner sur, faire figure **face up** faire figure
facecloth *n.* lavette
facial *adj.* **facial expression** expression, figure **contorted facial expression** simagris
facilitate *v.* faciliter
facility *n.* facilité
facing *adj.* opposé de
fact *n.* fait, réalité **accomplished fact** fait accompli **in fact** de fait, réellement **after the fact** par après **basic law or fact of nature** principe **as a matter of fact** de fait, enfin
faction *n.* faction
factory *n.* fabrique, facterie, facture, manufacture, plante, usine **sugar cane factory** sucrerie **employee of a sugar factory** sucrier
faculty *n.* faculté, faculté
fad *n.* mode, tocate
fade *v.* décolorer, déteindre, en perdre, jaunir, pâlir, se décolorer, se déteindre **cause to fade** décolorer

faded *adj.* fané **become worn, faded, discolored, or tarnished** détamer

fail *v.* FAIL, rater, échouer **fail completely** aboutir en rien **fail in health** manquer, s'écraser, écraser **fail to fire** rater **fail in one's effort** chier sur le palonnier **fail to achieve a goal** manquer

failure *n.* manque **complete failure** fiasco

faint *adj.* faible **become faint** faillir **feel faint** avoir des faiblesses, se sentir faille

faint *v.* tomber dans les fesses à BLACK, tomber en confiture, tomber en défaillance, tomber en soliard, venir faille, évanouir

fainting *n.* **fainting spell** défaillance, évanouissement

faintly *adv.* faiblement

faintness *n.* défaillance, faillitude

fair *adj.* blond, honnête, joli, juste, passable, raisonnable, tchoque-à-bloque, droite **grow white or fair** blondir

fair *adv.* poc à poc

fair *n.* bazar, carnaval, FAIR, festival, tchampourra

fairly *adv.* honnêtement, justement, passablement, plutôt

fairness *n.* justice **overly concerned with fairness and detail** observant

fairy *n.* **tooth fairy** zombi

faith *n.* confiance, croyance, foi **faith healer** toucheur, traiteur **bad faith** mauvaise foi **good faith** bonne foi **have faith** croire **person of no religious faith** créature

faithful *adj.* fidèle, loyal

faithfulness *n.* fidélité, loyauté

fake *adj.* faux

falcon *n.* falcon **peregrine falcon** cossarde, z-aile pointue

fall *n.* automne, capote, saut, plonge, plongée **have a nasty fall** casser la vaisselle **take a bad fall** s'acheter un beau parterre

fall *v.* chuter, tomber, échapper **fall again** retomber **fall apart** tomber en-val-en-zèle / tomber en val et en zèle, tomber en-val-en-zèle, tomber en racaille {racage}, tomber en racaille, tourner en merde, écrouler **fall back** reculer, retomber **fall backwards** tomber à la renverse **fall calm** accalmir, s'accalmir **fall down** aller {faire} boum, capoter, casser la vaisselle, faire boudouboume, se foutre par terre, vacher **fall off** se retirer **fall head first** planter (le) chêne **fall in love** tomber en amour (avec) **fall sick again** chuter, rechuter **fall to pieces** tomber en botte, tomber en racaille {racage}, tomber en racaille **fall back into sin** rechuter **fall in a heap** tomber en racaille {racage}, tomber en racaille **fall into a ditch** prendre le fossé **fall into a swoon** tomber en botte **fall madly in love** s'amouracher **fall on one's stomach** tomber à plate sus le ventre / tomber à plein ventre **fall asleep at the switch** dormir sur un rôti **fall forward on one's head** planter (le) chêne **fall into poverty or decrepitude** aller aux brindezingues **fall into the water with a splash** faire poutchoume **let fall** lâcher **cause to fall** faire tomber **cause to fall apart** se démancher **night has fallen** la brune est arrivée

falling *n.* **falling apart** écroulement **falling out** brouille **falling of leaves** effeuillage **have a falling out** se brouiller

fallow *adj.* **lying fallow** en savane

false *adj.* faux, postiche

falsehood *n.* conte, fabrication, fausseté, menterie **tell a falsehood** déchirer le gingas {ginghat}, faires des contes, tirer une carottc

falsify *v.* fausser, forger

falter *v.* baranquer

fame *n.* gloire, renommée

familial *adj.* familial

familiar *adj.* familier, habitué **be familiar with** être habitué avec

familiarity *n.* familiarité, accointance

family *n.* famille, parentage, famille de riquiqui **family reunion** rassemblée de famille **mainstay of a family** poteau du coin **pertaining to a family** familial **live a happy family life** faire un bon ménage

famine *n.* famine

famished *adj.* affamé

famous *adj.* célèbre, fameux

famously *adv.* fameusement

fan *n.* éventail **ceiling fan** éventail à electricité, éventail électrique **electric fan** éventail électrique **race fan** coursier

fan *v.* venter, éventer **fan o.s.** s'éventer

fan-shaped *adj.* en éventail

fancy *adj.* fin **fancy dresser** SPORT **fancy, elegant clothes** faraud **fancy gadgets are not worth the money one pays for them** pèse bouton, paie couillon

fancy *n.* ravigaud *pl.* **put on frills and fancies** faire {prendre} des fions

fancy *v.* imaginer **fancy o.s.** s'imaginer

fandango *n.* **fandango dance** fandango

fang *n.* dent

fantasy *n.* fantaisie

far *adv.* loin **far away** au loin, loin **far from** loin de **so far** jusque **as far as** jusque **from near and far** de près, de loin

farce *n.* farce, jonglerie

fare *v.* marcher, rouler **fare poorly** aboutir en mal **fare well** aboutir en bien

farewell *n.* adieu

farm *n.* faire l'habitant, ferme, habitation, place **farm animals** animal **farm hand** travaillant de champs {clos} **farm on half** faire récolte à la moitié **produce farm** ferme de produits **tenant farm** rester pour (qqn) **truck farm** ferme de produits **vegetable farm** ferme de produits *pl.* **group of farms or houses** côte

farm *v.* faire récolte, farmer, travailler

farm-related *adj.* agricole

farmer *n.* agriculturiste, cultivateur, cultiveur, fermier, habitant, raboureur, récolteur, récoltier **corn farmer** faiseur de maïs **small farmer** habitant **subsistence farmer** habitant **tenant farmer** tenant **be a farmer** faire l'habitant

fart *n.* pet
fart *v.* lâcher un pet, péter
farthest *adj.* **farthest part** finfifond
farthest *n.* **at the farthest** au plus loin
fascinate *v.* charmer, enchanter
fashion *n.* façon, mode
fashion *v.* façonner
fashioning *n.* façonnage
fast *adj.* avançant, vite, en avant **fast girl** folâtre **pull a fast one on s.o.** passer des crêpes à qqn
fast *adv.* vite, à l'estampique / en estampique
fast *n.* jeûne **Lenten fast** jeûne de Carême
fast *v.* jeûner, s'abstenir
fasten *v.* amarrer, fixer, lier, sangler, loquer **fasten with nails** attacher **fasten with a clasp** agrafer **fasten with a hook** accrocher, barrer
fastener *n.* agrafe
fastening *n.* attache
fastidious *adj.* babillard, fionneur, suspect
fasting *adj.* abstinent, à jeun
fasting *n.* abstinence
fat *adj.* gras, gros **fat person** bidet, bitaco **become fat** s'engraisser **get fat** faire du lard, rengraisser **grow fat** engraisser **get fat again** rengraisser, se rengraisser
fat *n.* graissage, graisse, gras, suif **pork fat** lard **remove fat or grease** dégraisser **strips of pork loin and fat** jambonneau
fatality *n.* fatalité
fate *n.* destinée, sort
father *n.* papa, père, père **my father** mon vieux **like father like son** bon chien tient de race **treat as a father** traiter de père **he is the image of his father** il est le portrait de son père
Father *n.* **Father Christmas** christine, Papa Noël **the almighty Father** le Père tout-puissant
father-in-law *n.* beau-père
fatherland *n.* pays de naissance
fatherless *adj.* orphelin de père
fatigue *n.* cuite, fatigue **cause fatigue** larguer
fatigue *v.* harasser, larguer
fatigued *adj.* fatigué, largue, largué, mal en train
fatiguing *adj.* fatigant
fatso *n.* bidet, bitaco
fatten *v.* engraisser, mettre à l'engrais, rengraisser **fatten up** engraisser, mettre à l'engrais, rengraisser, s'engraisser **fatten up again** rengraisser
fattening *adj.* engraissant
fattening *n.* engraissement **fattening up** engraissement
fatty *adj.* gras **any fatty substance** graissage
faucet *n.* fausset, robinet
fault *n.* défaut, faute **at fault** coupable, fautif **find fault** mépriser, trouver à redire **find fault with** critiquer, mépriser, reprocher
fault-finding *adj.* difficile
favor *n.* bienfait, faveur, grâce, privilège **do a good turn or a favor** faire une belle grâce (à qqn)
favorable *adj.* avantageux, favorable
favorite *adj.* préféré **favorite child** petit gâteau
fawn *n.* bichon
fawn *v.* gourmer
FBI *n.* **FBI agent** fédéral
fear *n.* cache, crainte, frayeur, peur, terreur, épouvante **for fear of** de peur que **for fear that** de peur que **feel fear or apprehension** frémir **out of fear** par la peur **be in great fear** avoir la {une} cache **on account of fear** par la peur
fear *v.* appréhenter, craindre, redouter
fearful *adj.* craignant, craintif, peureux **fearful person** capon
feasible *adj.* faisable
feast *n.* banco, cuite, festin, ramequin **feast day** fête **feast day of obligation** fête d'obligation **the feast of All Saints** Toussaint **vigil of feast days** vigile
Feast *n.* **Feast of the Assumption** assomption
feat *n.* accomplet **feat of strength** coup de force, tour de force
feather *n.* plume **feather duster** plumas, plumeau, plumet, poustron, époussetoir **feather mattress** matelas de plume *pl.* **feathers** plumage **pluck feathers** déplumer, plumer **groom feathers with the beak** s'épivarder, s'épouiller **having feathers along the legs** à grosse arrasse **take the feathers off of** éplumer
feather *v.* plumer
feathering *n.* **tarring and feathering** emplumage
feature *n.* trait
February *n.* février
feces *npl.* excrément, selle **piece of feces** crotte, crottin, étron **step in animal feces** se couper
fed *adj.* **fed up** dégoûté, largué, lasse, répugné **be fed up** avoir assez, se dégoûter, se tanner, être regoulé **be fed up with** avoir le ventre plein, avoir une indigestion de
federal *adj.* fédéral
federation *n.* fédération
fee *n.* **admission fee** admission **miller's fee** moudurage, moulinage **collect a fee** charger
feeble *adj.* chéti, débile, faible
feebly *adv.* faiblement
feed *n.* FEED, nourriture **feed corn** maïs dur **feed slop** ramassis **feed trough** mangeoire **bran and water mixture used as cattle feed** moulée
feed *v.* donner à manger, nourrir, FEED
feeding *n.* nourrissement
feel *v.* ressentir, se sentir, sentir, tatailler, toucher, tâtonner **feel again** ressentir **feel bad** se sentir chéti **feel cold** avoir frète **feel faint** avoir des faiblesses, se sentir faille **feel foolish** se sentir bête, se trouver bête **feel honored** s'honorer **feel lonely** s'ennuyer **feel sick** se sentir foutaise {malade} **feel sorry** plaindre, prendre en pitié **feel up** tripoter, tâter,

tâtonner **feel well** se sentir bien **feel each other up** se tâtonner **feel fear or apprehension** frémir **feel sorry for o.s.** se prendre en pitié **feel underwater for turtles** tâtonner pour des tortues **feel the lack or loss** manquer **feel weak because of hunger** avoir l'estomac faille **feel weak, dizzy and likely to faint** avoir des faiblesses, faillir **not feel well** avoir un pet accroché, être pas (trop) catholique **begin to feel better** rapiquer

feeler *n.* tâton

feeling *adj.* **feeling or suffering from the cold** frilant, frileux

feeling *n.* sensation, sentiment **have a feeling** avoir un à-peu-près *pl.* **bring up feelings or emotions of** émouver

feign *v.* faire semblant (de)

feint *n.* semblant

feisty *adj.* frais comme un lapin

felicitation *n.* félicitation

fell *v.* abattre, bûcher, jeter **fell with a firearm** plomber, plombter **one who fells trees** abatteur

felling *n.* abattage

fellow *adj.* **fellow man** prochain

fellow *n.* bonhomme, bougre, gaillard, JACK, splouque **bad fellow** garnement, mauvais bougre **big fellow** grand {gros} gaillard **good fellow** bon bougre **lazy fellow** bacalet **little fellow** petit bougre **nice fellow** vaillant bougre **old fellow** vieux corps **robust fellow** gaillard **smooth fellow** dard **stupid fellow** patassa **young fellow** petit bougre **big, powerful fellow** caïac **precious little fellow** cher 'tit nègre **tough little fellow** caïacot

felon *n.* félon

female *adj.* femelle

female *n.* femelle

fence *n.* barrière, entourage **barbwire fence** barrière à (fil de fer à) piquants **board fence** barrière à {de} pieux **net fence** barrière à fil de fer et à carreau **high wooden fence** péline **erect a fence or barrier around** entourer **section of fence between two posts** pagée de barrière, pagée **opening in a fence** passe **stretch or length of fence** face de barrière

fence *v.* **fence in** entourer

fencepost *n.* poteau de barrière

fencing *n.* entourage **fencing wire** fil à barrière **rectangular-holed wire fencing** fil de fer à carreau, fil à {de} carreaux

fender *n.* FENDER **flap or fender of a western saddle** basque

fennel *n.* **dog fennel** anis marron

feral *adj.* farouche, marron

ferment *v.* fermenter

fermentation *n.* fermentation

fern *n.* FERN **maidenhair fern** chevelure de Vénus **rattlesnake fern** langue de belle-mère **ribbon fern** langue de serpent

ferocious *adj.* féroce

ferry *n.* FERRY, traverse

fertile *adj.* fertile

fertility *n.* fertilité

fertilize *v.* enrichir, fertiliser, fumer

fertilizer *n.* fumier **fertilizer keep** parc à fumier

ferule *n.* férule

fervent *adj.* ardent, fervent

fervor *n.* ardeur, dévotion, ferveur

festival *n.* festival, tchampourra

festive *adj.* **festive observance** solemnité **festive occasion** tchampourra

fetch *v.* aller après, aller chercher, attraper, hacher, poigner, prendre, s'attraper

feud *n.* haine **end a feud** se désembrouiller

feud *v.* se brouiller

feuding *n.* **quit feuding** débrouiller, se débrouiller

fever *n.* fièvre **fever blister** bobo de fièvre, bouton de fièvre **fever chills** tremble **hay fever** fièvre d'automne, fièvre de foin **high fever** fièvre forte **rabbit fever** fièvre de lapin **scarlet fever** scarlatine **slight fever** fièvre lente **tick fever** fièvre de pou de bois **typhoid fever** fièvre longue / longue fièvre, fièvre typhoïde / grande fièvre, fièvre typhoïde, typhoïde **undulant fever** fièvre de lait **yellow fever** fièvre jaune **have a fever** avoir la fièvre **run a fever** avoir la fièvre

feverish *adj.* fiévreux

few *adj.* peu **a few** quelque

few *pron.* **a few** quelqu'uns, quelques-uns / quelques-unes

fewer *adj.* moins

fiancé *n.* espoir, fiancé, prétend-mari, prétendu

fiancée *n.* espoir, fiancé, prétende-femme, prétendu

fiasco *n.* cancan, fiasco

fib *n.* mensonge, menterie **tell a fib** passer une bleue (à qqn)

fib *v.* conter des menteries, mentir

fibber *n.* conteur de menteries

fiber *n.* **fiber carded in strips** plateau **cotton silk fiber** soie de coton

fibrous *adj.* **tough and fibrous** dur comme du caïac

fickle *adj.* changeable, changeant, en l'air **fickle person** pas bon

fiction *n.* fiction

fictitious *adj.* faux

fiddle *n.* **play second fiddle** seconder

fiddle *v.* **fiddle around** berdasser **one who fiddles around or wastes time** berdasseur

fiddler *n.* violoneux **accompanying fiddler** secondeur **second fiddler** secondeur

fiddling *n.* **fiddling around** berdassement

fidelity *n.* constance, fidélité, loyauté

fidget *v.* fertiller, se basculer

fidgety *adj.* fertillant

field *n.* champ, clos **field glasses** longue-vue **field laborer** travaillant de champs {clos} **oil field** champ d'huile **potato field** clos de patates **rice field** clos de riz **sport field** terrain du jeu **sugar cane field** champ de canne **uncultivated area around a field** chaintre

fiend *n.* **coffee fiend** cafiot
fierce *adj.* bengale, violent
fifteen *n.* quinze **about fifteen** quinzaine
fifteenth *n.* quinzième
fifth *n.* cinquième
fiftieth *n.* cinquantième
fifty *n.* cinquante **about fifty** cinquantaine
fig *n.* figue **fig jam** confiture de figues **fig tree** figue, figuier **Celeste fig** figue céleste **white fig** figue-miel **common purple fig** figue céleste
fight *n.* bataille, chamaille, chamaillerie, chicane, combat, FIGHT, halaillage, halaillement, pique-partout, turlutte **fight in which no one is hurt** bataille à coups de chapeau **pick a fight** picocher **get into a fight** tomber en train **prepare for a fight** enlever sa soutadaire **put up a fight** débattre **be looking for a fight** chicoter pour du tracas, être en chimère **one who provokes or is easily provoked into a fight** piquant
fight *v.* basculer, battre, FIGHT, lutter, se battre, se débattre, se halailler, se hartchiner **fight back** se défendre **fight furiously** débattre comme un chat dans l'eau bénie, se débattre comme le diable dans de l'eau bénite {un bénitier} **fight repeatedly** se batailler **fight a duel** se battre aux armes **fight in play** se batailler **fight with fury** tirer le diable par la queue **fight with mudballs** se sabouler **fight with the fists** boxer **make fight** battre **bred to fight** gaïme **make war or fight** faire la guerre **said of a child who struggles or fights** un diable dans un bénitier
fighter *n.* batailleur
fighting *adj.* **fighting cock** guème gaïme / guime gaïme **fighting cock or hen** gaïme
fighting *n.* **be on the verge of fighting** se souffler dans les narines
figure *n.* figure, forme **figure of speech** expression **have a nice figure** avoir une belle taille
figure *v.* calculer, figurer, se figurer **figure out** déchiffrer, figurer
figuring *n.* calcul
file *n.* affilée, dossier, défilé, lime, rangée **bastard file** briqué, lime-rapé {-râpe} **coarse file** râpe **flat file** lime plate **rattail file** queue de rat **three-sided file** lime à trois quarts **triangular file** tire-point
file *v.* limer, râper **file suit against** mettre en cour / mettre devant la cour **file in the clerk of court books** mettre au greffe
filing *n.* limage
fill *n.* **get one's fill** se rassasier
fill *v.* emboucher, emplir, enfourner, remplir **fill in** boucher **fill o.s.** se remplir **fill out** remplir **fill up** combler, emplir, remplir, s'emplir, se remplir **fill a bottle** embouteiller **fill to overflowing** aufaîter, combler, remplir à déborder **fill a dental cavity** boucher une dent **fill to the brim** aufaîter
filled *adj.* complet, plein, rafalé **become filled** s'emplir
fillet *n.* filet
fillet *v.* filer
filling *adj.* rassasiant
fillip *n.* pichenet
filly *n.* pouliche
film *n.* film, négative, portraits grouillants **roll of film** film
filter *n.* filtre
filter *v.* filtrer
filth *n.* cochonnerie, crasse, encrassement, farcin, saleté, saloperie, ziretté **encrust with filth** crotter **clean o.s. of filth** se décrasser **clean away mud or filth** décrotter **remove crud, dirt, or filth** décrasser **clean o.s. of mud or filth** se décrotter
filthy *adj.* caca, crasseux, en crottins, galeux, sale, salope, souillon, cochon **filthy woman** cochonne **get filthy** s'encrasser **repulsive, filthy, untidy woman** salope
filtration *n.* filtration
filé *n.* filé **filé gumbo** gombo filé **add filé** filer
fin *n.* nageoire
final *adj.* dernier, définitif, final
finally *adv.* au bout du compte, enfin, finalement, pour en finir, une bonne fois, à la fin du compte, à la fin
finance *n.* finance
finance *v.* financer
financially *adv.* **be well-off financially** être bien pour vivre
financier *n.* financier
finch *npl.* **finches** pape
find *n.* découverte, trouvaille
find *v.* détecter, frapper, sourdre, trouver **find again** retrouver **find difficult** être malaisé pour **find o.s.** se trouver **find out** découverre, s'apercevoir, s'aviser, se rendre compte **find out about** se poster **find a way out** s'en sortir **find each other again** se retrouver **find o.s. at the right place** se retrouver à la bonne place **find o.s. face to face with** se figurer avec **find or provide an equal for** rappareiller
fine *adj.* beau, bien, bon, extra, fin, joli, magnifique **be fine** être du chenu **either way is fine** autant à l'ancre qu'à la voile
fine-looking *adj.* regardable
fineness *n.* finesse
finesse *n.* finesse
finger *adj.* **index finger** premier doigt
finger *n.* doigt **finger bandage** doignon, fourreau **finger of whiskey** un doigt de whiskey **index finger** doigt torchant **ring finger** doigt annulaire **give the finger** montrer le doigt **point the finger** pointer le doigt **the thickness of a finger** un doigt d'epais {d'épaisseur} *pl.* **snap one's fingers** flailler les doigts
finger *v.* pointer (qqn) au doigt
fingerless *adj.* **long, fingerless glove** mitaine
fingernail *n.* ongle
fingerstall *n.* doignon
finicky *adj.* difficile, fion-fion, fion **be finicky** avoir des fions
finish *n.* **finish line** ligne **having a smooth finish** glacé

finish *v.* accomplir, achever, compléter, finir, terminer, achever **finish hurriedly** bâcler **finish for the day** débaucher **finish work or school** lâcher **finish first in a contest** gagner **finish laying by the cane crop** larguer le renchaussage **finish the walls or ceiling of** plafonner

finished *adj.* nettement, rasé **it's finished** ça y est

finishing *n.* finissage **finishing blow** coup de grâce

fire *n.* feu **fire guard** garde-feu **fire shield** garde-feu **catch fire** prendre en feu **on fire** enflammé **set fire** foutre le feu (à) **be on fire** brûler **quick, clear fire** braisier **Saint Anthony's fire** érésipèle **remains of a fire** brûlis **trouble spreads like wild fire** le feu est pris dans la paille jaune {grande paille}

fire *v.* craquer, décharger, lâcher, décharger, se décharger, tirer **fire again** retirer **fire a gunshot** sacrer un coup de fusil **fire wildly or aimlessly** tirailler **fail to fire** rater **one who fires a boiler or furnace** chauffeur

firearm *n.* arme à feu **fell with a firearm** plombter

firecracker *n.* fusée, pétard **firecracker that does not explode** chouchou **explode a firecracker** flailler le pétard

firedog *n.* chenet, chevalet

firefly *n.* bétaille à feu, bête à feu, mouche à feu

fireman *n.* pompier

fireplace *n.* cheminée, foyer

firewood *n.* bois de foyer {feu}, bois

fireworks *npl.* feu d'artifice

firing *n.* **firing cap** capsule

firm *adj.* ferme, raide, solide, stable

firmness *n.* détermination, fermeté

first *adj.* germain, premier

first *adv.* d'abord, premier, premièrement **first of all** d'abord **at first** en premier **finish first in a contest** gagner

first *n.* **the first of** le premier de

first-class *adj.* carabiné

first-rate *adj.* fin

firstborn *n.* premier né

fish *n.* poisson **fish bone** arête **fish hook** hameçon **fish patty** boulette **fish pond** vivier **fish stew** courtbouillon **fish that buries itself in the sand** fouille-sable **armored fish** poisson armé **buffalo fish** carpe **bullhead fish** boulehed **carangid fish** caragne **catch fish** empoigner des poissons **flying fish** poisson qui vole **freshwater fish** poisson d'eau douce **salt-water fish** poisson d'eau salée, poisson de mer **sea fish** poisson de mer **sheepshead fish** casbergau d'eau salée **silvery fish** bisquet **catch of fish** prise de poisson **common sheepshead fish** casburgot **silver dollar fish** piastre **stringerful of fish** brochée de poissons **highly seasoned fish stew** bouillabaisse **scale of a fish** écale de poisson **sharp row of teeth of certain fish** peigne

fish *v.* faire la pêche, pêcher **fish with trotlines** pêcher des lignes **fish here and there** pêchailler **fish with a seine** seiner **fish with a butterfly net** paupiérer **fish using a set line or cane pole** pêcher à la ligneguette {ligne} **fish with a square net, cast net or dipnet** carreleter

fisherman *n.* pêcheur **crab fisherman** pêcheur de {à} crabes {huîtres / chevrettes, etc.}

fishhook *n.* alêne

fishing *n.* pêchage, pêche **fishing boat** canotte, goélette **fishing fly** mouche **fishing line** ligne à pêche, ligne **fishing net** drague, NET, varveau **fishing pole** canne à pêche {pêcher}, perche-à-ligne, perche **the fishing business** pêche **have a good fishing trip** faire une bonne pêche

fissure *n.* crevasse, fendasse, fissure

fist *n.* poing **fist blow** poque *pl.* **fight with the fists** boxer

fistfight *n.* bataille à coups de poing **have a fistfight** poquer, se sabouler

fistula *n.* fistule **fistula of withers** mal anglais

fit *adj.* convenable, FIT **fit to wear** mettable **fit to live in** logeable **keep fit** s'entretenir, se tenir en bonne santé

fit *n.* attaque, crise, FIT, secousse **fit of anger** coup de colère **laughing fit** ricane

fit *v.* adapter, aller, FIT, s'adapter **fit together** emmancher, s'adonner **fit glass into** vitrer

fitted *adj.* **badly fitted** malajusté **well fitted out** loqué

fitting *adj.* convenable, FIT **be loose fitting** flagosser

fitting *n.* **fitting together again** raccordement *pl.* **fittings** agrès **fittings for horse or mule** harnais

five *n.* cinq

five-cent *n.* **five-cent coin** plomb

fix *n.* **in a fix** malfoutu **be in a bad fix** danser la carmagnole

fix *v.* accommoder, arranger, installer, ramancher, réparer **fix intently** flamber **fix with a screw** visser **fix a direction for o.s.** se mirer **fix o.s. in a place** se plaquer

fixed *adj.* **get fixed up** s'arranger

fixing *n.* arrangeage, arrangement

flabby *adj.* mou

flag *n.* FLAG

flag *v.* FLAG

flail *n.* flau

flamboyant *adj.* **flamboyant person** candi barré

flame *n.* flamme

flaming *adj.* enflammé

flamingo *n.* flamant

flammable *adj.* enflammant, prime

flank *n.* flanc, plat-côté, rognon, flanc

flannel *n.* flanelle, molleton

flannelette *n.* molleton **made of flannelette** molletonne

flap *n.* **flap or fender of a western saddle** basque **saddle flap** bagari **wooden flap on a diatonic accordion** palette

flap *v.* **flap in the wind** battocher

flapping *n.* **flapping of wings** battement d'ailes

flare *n.* fusée, tenture

flare *v.* flamber

flared *adj.* **flared out** évasé

flash *n.* béluette **flash of lightning** éclair
flash *v.* flamber **see one's life flash before one's eyes** livrer sa carcasse au diable
flashlight *n.* BULL-EYE, FLASH-LIGHT, lumière
flashy *adj.* **dress in a gaudy, flashy, or tacky way** attriquer, s'attriquer
flask *n.* bouteille, fiole, flacon, flasque, topette
flat *adj.* plange, plat comme une merde {planche / punaise}, plate, à plate, FLAT
flat-footed *adj.* **flat-footed person** patte-plate
flatboat *n.* FLAT-BOAT
flatten *v.* afflétrir, aplanir, aplatir, niveler, rabattre, coucher **flatten o.s. out** s'aplatir
flattening *n.* aplatissage **cutting or flattening** abattage
flatter *v.* adoucir, enjôler, flatter **flatter for personal gain** embeurrer, licher **flatter o.s. or each other** se flatter
flatterer *n.* emmioleur, enjôleur, flatteur, licheur
flattery *n.* flatterie
flatulence *n.* gaz
flatware *n.* outils de table
flavor *n.* essence, goût **add flavor** accommoder **have a distinct flavor** goûter
flavor *v.* assaisonner
flaw *n.* défaut
flay *v.* écorcher
flea *n.* puce
fleabane *n.* **daisy fleabane** herbe à vers, vergerolle
flecked *adj.* guiné
flee *v.* fouiner, marronner, échapper, partir (en) marron **flee in order to avoid s.o.** barder
fleece *v.* plumer
flesh *n.* chair **flesh beneath the skin** vif **piece of torn flesh** grillade **tear or mangle one's flesh** s'évianner **tear or mangle the flesh of** évianner
fleshy *adj.* charnu
flexibility *n.* flexibilité
flexible *adj.* ployable, ployant
flick *n.* pichenet
flight *n.* marronnage, vol **charter flight** charteur **in flight** à la vol {vole} **take flight** partir à la vole, prendre des ailes
flighty *adj.* folâtre **restless or flighty person** cerf-volant
flimsy *adj.* escabreux
fling *v.* flanquer, lancer, sacrer **fling o.s.** se lancer
flint *n.* **flint and steel** batte-feu
flip *n.* bascule, culbute **do a flip** cul passe sus la tête **do a flip and land head first** planter (le) chêne
flip *v.* culbuter, se renverser **flip over** capoter **flip the bird** montrer le doigt
flipper *n.* **swimming flipper** nageoire
flirt *n.* coquette, FLIRT
flirt *v.* FLIRT **old man who likes to flirt** vieux rabougri
flirtatious *adj.* folâtre
float *n.* bouchon, flotte, chariot, flotte **parade float** flotte
float *v.* flotter, flotter **float to the top** sourdre
floating *n.* flottage
flock *n.* volière, bande, troupeau **flock of birds in flight** volier, volée **domestic flock** basse-cour
flog *v.* fouetter **flog a person whose hands and feet are tied to four pegs in the ground** fouetter à quatre piquets
flood *n.* déluge, eau haute, fleuve, FLOOD, marée, montage d'eau **flood plain** bassière, batture **flood caused by a break in a levee** crevasse
Flood *n.* **the Great Flood of 1927** grande eau
flood *v.* FLOOD, grande eau, noyer **flood again** re-FLOOD
floodable *adj.* noyable
flooded *adj.* à la flood
floor *n.* plancher, étage, fond **floor beam** lambourde **floor mop** essuie-place **floor for drying cotton** gril **dance floor** plancher de danse **threshing floor** batterie **lay a floor** plancher **on the floor** par terre **take the floor** prendre la parole **cloth used to scrub the floor** essuie-place **puddle of water on the floor** bourbier *pl.* **pace the floors at night** faire son rougarou
floor *v.* aplatir, plancher
flooring *n.* planchage, plancher **apply flooring** plancher **remove flooring** déplanchonner
flop *v.* **flop down** se plaquer
flotsam *n.* **driftwood or flotsam** ramassis
flounce *n.* galand
flounder *n.* flandre **southern flounder** plie
flour *n.* farine **flour made from green corn** farine d'Indien **wheat flour** farine française **dip in flour** fariner **white wheat flour** farine (de) froment **sprinkle with flour or meal** fariner **sprinkle or dredge with flour** enfariner
flour *v.* enfariner, fariner
floured *adj.* farineux
flourish *n.* fion, pataraphe
flow *n.* cours
flow *v.* couler, découler **let water flow** lâcher l'eau
flower *n.* bouquet, fleur **flower bed** banquette, parterre **flower bud** bouton de fleur **flower garden** parterre, verger **flower plant** pied de fleur **flower stand** jardinière **flower trellis** échafaud **flower worn on one's coat lapel** boutonnière **camellia flower** camélia **magnolia flower** magnolia **night-blooming jasmine flower** galant de nuit **sweet pea flower** pois à fleur *pl.* **produce flowers** faire des fleurs **bunch of flowers** bouquet
flower *v.* fleurir
flower-bearing *n.* **flower-bearing plant** bouquet
flower-print *adj.* fleuré
flowered *adj.* **having a flowered print** fleuré
flowerpot *n.* jardinière, pot à fleur
flowing *adj.* coulant
flowing *n.* **flowing back** refoule

flu *n.* dengué, FLU, grippe
fluctuating *adj.* journalier
flue *n.* tuyau **chimney flue** FLUE
fluent *adj.* courant
fluently *adv.* couramment
fluff *v.* éponger **fluff up** brasser
fluffy *adj.* pongeux, sourge, volumé **make fluffy and soft** volumer
flush *adj.* rase, à (la) rase, à la rasée **flush with** en plan avec **making flush** effleurage
flush *n.* flèche
flush *v.* faire sourdre, lever, sauter, enlever
flustered *adj.* épivardé, épouvanté **get flustered** s'épouvanter
flute *n.* flûte
flutter *v.* voltiger **flutter about in the dust** s'effarder
fluttering *n.* voltigement
fly *n.* braguette, mouche, moustique **fly repellant** chasse-mouche **fly speck** chiure de mouche **fly trap** attrape-mouches / attrape à mouches **crane fly** chevrette Alphonse **fishing fly** mouche **green fly** mouche à ver **maggot fly** mouche à ver **Spanish fly** catalique, mouche catalique
fly *v.* voler, voltiger **fly again** revoler **fly around** mouliner **fly away** s'envoler **fly off** partir à la vole, voler **fly into a rage** prendre l'estampique / prendre des estampiques, s'emporter, s'enrager **fly in a triangular formation** voler en pointe **when pigs fly** semaine des quatre jeudis
flycatcher *n.* **scissor-tailed flycatcher** oiseau papillon
flying *adj.* volant
flying *n.* vol, à la vol {vole}
flyswatter *n.* chasse-mouche, palette à mouche(s)
foal *n.* potre, poulain
foam *n.* mer, écume **removing foam** écumage **push aside or remove foam from boiling cane juice** sabler **paddle used to push aside or remove foam from boiling cane juice** sable
foaming *n.* écumage
focused *adj.* **be focused** se comprendre
fodder *n.* foin, fourrage
foe *n.* ennemi
fog *n.* brouillard, brouillasse, serein **clear of frost or fog** débrouiller
fog *v.* **fog up** brouiller, embrouiller, s'embrouiller
foggy *adj.* brouillé, embrouillé **become foggy** s'embrouiller, se brouiller **make foggy** embrouiller
foil *n.* feuille
foil *v.* **foil a plot** avorter un complot
fold *n.* pli
fold *v.* plier, ployer **fold back** replier
folding *n.* ployage
foliage *n.* enfeuillage, feuillage **thick foliage** boisure
folk *n.* **folk healing** traitement *pl.* **folks** gens, peuple **old folks** vieux monde, vieux **old folks' home** maison de vieux
follow *v.* poursuivre, succéder, suivre **follow through** rapporter **follow each other** se suivre **slavishly obey and follow** sauter crapaud (pour qqn)
following *adj.* de suite, suivant
following *adv.* d'après, d'ensuite
following *n.* bastringue, fumière, ripopette, ripopée, traînasse
folly *n.* folerie, folie
fond *adj.* animé, entiché **be fond** s'enticher **become fond of** s'attacher **not fond of** pas fort pour **not too fond of** pas trop fou de
fondle *v.* caresser, tripoter **fondle each other** se caresser
fondly *adv.* tendrement
fondness *n.* affection, attachement
font *n.* **baptismal font or room** baptistaire
fontanel *n.* fontaine
food *n.* aliment, mangeaille, manger, nourrissement, nourriture, nanane, niame-niame **food scraps** ramassis **food store** grosserie, magasin de groceries **fried food** friture **prepared food** plat **raw food** crudité **unappetizing food** lavasse **choice food item** délicatesse **share food with the neighbors** faire le voisinage, voisiner **pick at one's food** picocher **stuff o.s. with food** se bourrer **partially burned piece of food** gratin **one who picks at food or eats lightly** picocheur **stretch a limited amount of food for unexpected company** mettre les petits plats dans les gros **said of a person who spends much on clothing and little on food** dos brillant et ventre criant
food-safe *n.* garde-manger
fool *n.* calebasse, cocodrie, dinde (d'inde), estragot, estronfillau, imbécile, sot **call a fool** traiter de fou **act like a fool** se montrer le tchul {derrière} **treat as a fool** traiter de fou
Fool *n.* **April Fool** poisson d'avril **be tricked on April Fool's Day** manger le poisson d'avril
fool *v.* bloffer, buffalo, BULLDOZE, couillonner, embêter, maquemose, mettre dedans, passer un bloff, poigner, sucrer, youquer **fool around** bêtiser, couillonner, foutumasser, tchincailler **fool with** bêtiser, s'emmicher avec **you're fooling yourself** ta nenaine est caille!
fooled *adj.* **be fooled** rester avec la chuille, se faire tromper **once fooled, twice shy** chat échaudé craint l'eau froide
foolhardiness *n.* audace
fooling *n.* **fooling around** couillonade
foolish *adj.* bête, baroque, biorque, bétasse, codache, couillon comme la lune {un bourriquet / un cheval}, couillon, embarrateur, emplâtre, estropié de la tête / estropié de cervelle, fraque, idiot, imbécile, lolette, sot, tacalac, timbré, écervelé, évargandé **foolish person** andouille, cul plat **foolish thing** couillonade **act foolish** carcailler **be foolish** avoir une calebasse pour sa tête, faire son bête / faire sa bête **feel foolish** se sentir bête, se trouver bête **do foolish things** prendre ses brindezingues **small-minded, foolish person** zozo **silly, foolish, high-strung woman** fraque **say foolish or nonsensical things** lâcher des folies {bêtises}

act foolish in order to reap profit faire l'âne pour avoir l'avoine {le foin} **do s.t. foolish** se jeter à l'eau pour pas se tremper **stupid or foolish person** zinzin **act stupid or foolish** faire le bête **ignorant, uneducated, insignificant or foolish person** cape-cape **one who says silly, foolish things** sottiseux

foolishly *adv.* follement

foolishness *n.* blagaillerie, bêtise, folerie, gnognotte, macaquerie, pacotille **bit of foolishness or nonsense** couillonade

foot *n.* ergot, pagaille, pied, patte **foot ax** hache à pied **foot of the bed** pied de lit **cat's foot** patte de chat **on foot** sus-pied **pig's foot** patte de cochon **presser foot** pied **set foot** mettre le pied **be on foot** être à pied **at the foot of** en bas de *pl.* **flat feet** pieds plats **having large feet** patté **back on one's feet** relevé **webbed foot** nageoire

foot-path *n.* marche-pied

foot-race *n.* bauche

football *n.* FOOTBALL

footbridge *n.* pont à pied

footing *n.* pilier, cale **footing of a house** pilier de maison

footprint *n.* piste, trace

footstool *n.* marche-pied

footwear *n.* **provide footwear** chausser **remove footwear** déchausser **put on footwear** chausser **remove one's footwear** se déchausser **put on or wear footwear** se chausser

fop *n.* pince-minette

for *prep.* pour, à, depuis, pendant, pour

forage *n.* fourrage

forbearance *n.* patience

forbid *v.* défendre, interdire

forbidden *adj.* défendu

force *n.* force, puissance, vigueur **by force** au forçal, par force **by force of** à force de **come into force** venir en force **one who uses excessive force** défonceur d'une porte ouverte / défonceur de porte(s) ouverte(s) *pl.* **armed forces** armée, service militaire, service

force *v.* contrôler, forcer, obliger **force o.s.** s'obliger, se forcer **force out** déloger, faire sortir, lever, sauter **force s.o. to do s.t.** bourlinguer **force s.o. to give in** faire 'poteau, Caillette' à qqn **force s.o. through argument to say or admit s.t.** pousser (qqn) dans les rangs courts **you can't force s.o. against his will** on envoye pas un chien à la chasse à coups de bâton

force-ripen *v.* faire mûrir

forced *adj.* **be forced** être forcé de

fore *n.* devant

forebear *n.* ancêtre

foreboding *n.* apercevance, pressentiment

forecaster *n.* **weather forecaster** prédicateur du temps

foredeck *n.* devant

forefather *n.* ancêtre

forefinger *n.* **between thumb and forefinger** à la pincette

forego *v.* se passer

forehead *n.* front **strike s.o. on the forehead** frapper qqn dans le nom du père

foreign *adj.* étranger **foreign matter** bourrier

foreigner *n.* étranger

forelock *n.* toupet

foreman *n.* BOSS, FOREMAN, écolome

forenoon *n.* avant-midi, matinée

foresee *v.* prévoir

foresight *n.* prévoyance

forest *n.* bois, forêt, grand bois **pine forest** pinière **burnt part of a wood or forest** brûlé

foretell *v.* prédire

forever *adv.* pour toujours, toujours, éternellement

forewarn *v.* avertir d'avance, prévenir

forge *n.* forge

forge *v.* forger

forged *adj.* **be forged** se forger

forger *n.* forgeur

forgery *n.* fabrication

forget *v.* oublier, négliger, s'oublier

forgetful *adj.* oubliard, oublieur

forgetfulness *n.* oubli, oubliance **through forgetfulness** par oubli

forgivable *adj.* pardonnable

forgive *v.* absoudre, pardonner **forgive me** pardon

forgiveness *n.* pardon, absolution, rémission **ask forgiveness** demander pardon

fork *n.* fourche **digging fork** fourchette **garden fork** fourchette **table fork** fourchette

fork *v.* fourcher

forked *adj.* branchu, fourchu, fourché

forkful *n.* fourchettée

forlorn-looking *adj.* défiguré **any bedraggled, forlorn-looking man or boy** juif-errant

form *n.* forme, moule **take form** se former **in good form** bien

form *v.* façonner, former **form again** reformer **form clods** motter **form o.s.** se former **form a circle** circuler **form a crest** crêter **form a head** monter en pomme {tête}, pommer, se pommer **form a scab** cicatriser **form into clods** se motter **form a big ring** faire grand rond

formation *n.* **linear formation** colonne

formed *adj.* **completely formed** bien {tout} formé **badly shaped or formed** malformé

formerly *adv.* anciennement, auparavant, autrefois, d'habitude, habitude

formula *n.* formule

formulate *v.* formuler

fornicate *v.* piquer

forsake *v.* déserter, délaisser

fort *n.* fort

forth *adv.* **and so forth** ainsi de suite

fortieth *adj.* quarantième

fortification *n.* fort, fortification

fortify *v.* assolider, conforter, fortifier

fortifying *adj.* fortifiant

fortitude *n.* endurance, fortitude **mount one's courage, fortitude, determination or resistance** se pomper

fortunate *adj.* bienheureux, chanceux, heureux

fortunately *adv.* heureusement

fortune *n.* bonne aventure, fortune **fortune teller** prédicateur, somnambule, tireur de bonne aventure, tireuse de cartes **good fortune** bonheur **tell fortune** tirer la bonne aventure (à qqn) **cost a fortune** coûter les yeux de la tête **make a fortune** faire (une) fortune **throw away one's fortune** brûler la chandelle aux deux bouts

fortune-teller *n.* devineur

forty *n.* quarante **about forty** quarantaine

forward *adj.* en avancé **forward area** en-avant

forward *adv.* au-devant **step forward** pas avançant **take one step forward and two steps back** faire un pas en avant et deux en arrière

forward *v.* expédier

foster *adj.* **adopted or placed in foster care** placé

foster *v.* cultiver

foul *v.* **foul up** fausser

foul-smelling *adj.* puant

fouled *adj.* **get warped or fouled up** se fausser

found *adj.* **be found** se trouver

found *v.* fonder

foundation *n.* base, fondament, fondation **lay the foundation of** fonder

foundry *n.* fonderie

fountain *n.* fontaine, jeu d'eau

four *n.* quatre **four aces** quatre-z-as **four o'clock plant** belle de nuit, quatre heures *pl.* **on all fours** à quatre pattes

four-by-four *n.* quatre-par-quatre

four-by-six *n.* quatre-par-six

four-wheel *n.* **four-wheel cart** char-à-banc

fourteen *n.* quatorze

fourteenth *n.* quatorzième

fourth *n.* quatrième **fourth part** quartier **one fourth** quart **in the fourth place** quatrièmement

fourthly *adv.* quatrièmement

fowl *n.* **guinea fowl** pintale **collection of roosting fowl** jouquée

fox *n.* renard **sly as a fox** filou comme un renard

fracas *n.* fracas, hourra, mêlée, obstination

fraction *n.* fraction

fracture *n.* cassure

fragile *adj.* cassant, casvel, fragile, frêle

fragment *n.* brisure, fragment, morceau, picaillon, pièce *pl.* **remove fragments** dérocher **be reduced to fragments** s'écharpiller

fragment *v.* fragmenter

fragmentation *n.* fragmentation

fragrance *n.* parfine

frail *adj.* fragile, frêle

frame *n.* carré, encadrement, FRAME, moule, cadre **frame of mind** disposition **bed frame** carré de lit **quilting frame** cadre **basic frame of a house** carré de maison

frame *v.* cadrer

framework *n.* carré

framing *n.* encadrement

franc *n.* **French franc** franc

France *n.* France

Francophone *n.* **lower class or illiterate Francophone of Louisiana** Cadien

frank *adj.* franc

frankly *adv.* en termes, franchement

fraternity *n.* fraternité

fraternize *v.* fraterniser **term formerly used by some to refer to a white person who fraternized with black people** négrier

fratricide *n.* fratricide

fraud *n.* embêtement, fraude, tromperie

fraudulently *adv.* en fraude, par fraude

fray *n.* démêlée

fray *v.* défiler

frazzled *adj.* haillonné

freckle *n.* basane, basanure, cocodinde, picodinde

freckled *adj.* basaneux, basané, caille, picassé

free *adj.* dégagé, exempti, gratis, libre, quitte **free rein** passe-droit **set free** affranchir, délivrer, déprendre, relâcher, émanciper **be free to choose** être à même de choisir **get free from mud** se débourber **it's not free or cheap** c'est pas merci

free *v.* affranchir, donner la liberté, décoincer, dégager, libérer, exempter **free o.s.** se décoincer, se dégager, se déprendre **free from mud** débourber **free of a blockage** dégoter

free-for-all *n.* pique-partout **free-for-all fight** mêlée

free-thinker *n.* ventre-rouge

freedom *n.* liberté **give freedom** donner la liberté

freemason *n.* franc-maçon

freemasonry *n.* franc-maçonnerie

freeze *v.* geler, glacer

freezer *n.* DEEP FREEZE, FREEZER, glacière **ice cream freezer** baratte, FREEZER, sabotière

freezing *adj.* glaçant

freight *n.* fret **freight boat** bateau à fret **freight car** char à fret **freight train** char à fret, fret

French *adj.* français **real French people** les vrais Français **the French language** français **loaf of French bread** miche

French *n.* français **Acadian French** acadien **Cajun French** cadien, français cadien **Louisiana French** français **Standard French** le vrai français **speak French badly** parler français comme un Chinois **the real French** le vrai français **one who speaks English but not French** gueule rouge **one who tries unsuccessfully to speak standard French** javion **person of any origin who speaks Cajun French** Cadien

French-speaking *adj.* **French-speaking Louisianan** Français

Frenchman *n.* Français **low class Frenchman** gascon pieds-pus
frenum *n.* filet
frequent *v.* bêtiser, fréquenter **frequent prostitutes** putainer **frequent dances, balls, etc.** baler **one who frequents dances** baleur
frequentation *n.* fréquentation
frequenting *n.* fréquentation
frequently *adv.* souvent de(s) fois / souventefois, souvent, à tout moment
fresh *adj.* doux, frais
freshen *v.* regaincher **freshen up** se lavailler
freshly *adv.* frais, fraîchement
freshness *n.* frais
fret *v.* s'inquiéter, se chagriner, se tracasser
fretful *adj.* agité
fretting *n.* jonglement
friable *adj.* **make friable** ameublir
fricassee *n.* fricassée
friction *n.* friction, frottage, frottement
Friday *n.* vendredi **Good Friday** Vendredi Saint
fried *adj.* frit **deep fried** farci
friend *n.* ami, camarade, copain, padna, vieux corps, vieux nègre **female friend** amille, amise **my friend** ma vieille, mon vieux, vieux nègre **old friend** vieux chien, vieux nègre *pl.* **become friends** faire camarades **make friends** faire ami **become friends again** faire camarades **be good friends** être bon ami
friendly *adj.* amiable, amicable, cordial, vaillant **be friendly** être grosse affaire **in a friendly way** amicablement
friendship *n.* amitié, camaraderie **end a friendship** casser la bande
frigate *n.* frégate **frigate bird** carencro de mer, frégate
fright *n.* alarme, frayeur, horreur, panique, peur, épouvantaille, épouvante
frighten *v.* donner une pourgale, effaroucher, effrayer, faire peur (à), foutre une pourgale (à), intimider, terrifier, épeurer, épivarder, épouvanter **frighten away** épivarder, évader **imaginary being used to frighten children** badjo, croquemitaine **imaginary creature used to frighten children into behaving** bébête **imaginary character in stories designed to frighten children** Madame Grands Doigts
frightened *adj.* effarouché, épivardé, épouvanté **be frightened** avoir peur à mort, s'effaroucher, s'effrayer **become frightened** s'épouvanter
frightening *adj.* effarouchant, effrayant, redoutable, épouvantable
frightful *adj.* affreux, effroyable, horrible
frigidity *n.* frigidité
frill *n.* falbana, fanfreluche, fion, flafla, frange, frou-frou *pl.* **put on frills** faire des frou-frou **put on frills and fancies** faire {prendre} des fions
fringe *n.* frange *pl.* **apply fringes** franger
fringe *v.* franger
fringed *adj.* à franges
frisk *v.* fouiller, fourgailler, fringuer **frisk about** gambader
frisky *adj.* fertillant, fringant
fritter *n.* beigne, beignet, crêpe, friture, gonfleau **fritter, fried pastry dough sometimes dipped in syrup** oreille de cochon
frizz *v.* friser
frizzy *adj.* tchine **extremely curly, frizzy, kinky, tightly curled** tchine
frock *n.* **frock coat** rodingot
froe *n.* freau
frog *n.* ouaouaron, raine **green frog** grenouille, rainette **rain frog** bébête de marais **medium-sized frog found along ditches** creux-creux **dark frog with a white belly** bébête *pl.* **catch frogs** froguer **frogs' legs** cuisses de ouaouaron
frogfruit *n.* cailleau
frogging *n.* **go frogging** froguer
frolic *v.* ginguer
from *prep.* avec, côté, dans, de, depuis, à travers / en travers (de), à prendre de
front *adj.* **front door** portage, portale **front porch** galerie en avant **front room** chambre de devant, chambre en avant **front yard** cour (de) devant {(d')en avant}
front *n.* (d')en avant, devant, devanture, en-avant, face, façade, figure **seabreeze front** grain **shirt front** jabot **in front of** au-devant, devant, en avant de **from in front** par devant / par en avant, par devant **located in front** (d')en avant **right in front** droite devant
frontage *n.* devanture
frontier *n.* frontière
frost *n.* gelée, verglas **clear of frost or fog** débrouiller **there is frost on the ground** les boulangeries se sont battues
froth *n.* mer, écume
frown *n.* frimousse, grimace
frown *v.* faire une frimousse, frimousser, grimacer
frozen *adj.* glacé
frugal *adj.* **be frugal** ménager
fruit *n.* fruit **fruit jar** pobon **fruit orchard** verger **fruit stand** fruit-stand **fruit tree** arbre à fruit, bois de fruit **fruit of the date palm** datte **bear fruit** donner, fruiter, monter en fruit, rapporter **produce fruit** rapporter **yield fruit** rendre *pl.* **fruits and vegetables** produit
fruitfulness *n.* fertilité
frustrate *v.* affoler
frustrated *adj.* **become frustrated** s'affoler
fry *v.* faire frire, frire, rôtir
fryer *n.* poulet
frying *n.* friture **frying pan** chaudière à frire, four, poêle en fer, poêle luminum, poêle, poêlon
fugitive *adj.* marron

fugitive *n.* marron, marronneur
fulcrum *n.* pivot
fulfillment *n.* exécution
full *adj.* complet, entier, gonfle, plein, plénière, propre, tchoque-à-bloque, criblé, foulé, germain, gonfle, plein **full of** bourré de **be full** avoir la fale pleine **become full** profiter **completely full** tout plein **pack full** corbier, corder **be full of hot air** flafla
fully *adv.* en plein, entièrement, largement
fumigate *v.* boucaner, fumiguer
fumigation *n.* fumigation
fun *adj.* amusant
fun *n.* agrément, amusement, divertissement, FUN, jeu, plaisir **have fun** avoir du FUN, avoir du plaisir, jouer, s'amuser, se divertir, se mettre en gingue **make fun** moquer, se foutre **make fun of** faire FUN de **poke fun at** ridiculer, se moquer **make fun of s.o. by imitation** faire des macaqueries dessus qqn **it's not fun and games** ça c'est pas baptême catin **fond of making fun of others** moqueur
function *n.* fonction, office **upset the accurate and proper function of** dérégler
function *v.* agiter, courir, galoper, marcher, travailler
functioning *n.* opération
fund *npl.* **funds** fonds, ressource **collection of funds** quête
fundraiser *n.* bénéfice
fundraising *n.* **gaming event for fundraising purposes** banco
funeral *n.* **funeral procession** enterrement **funeral service** enterrement, service
fungus *n.* champignon **fungus collected for kindling** tondre
funnel *n.* entonnoir, tonneau, boudinière, bourreuse
funnel *v.* entonner
funny *adj.* amusant, chatouillant, comique, drôle de, drôle, farce, risible, SPORT **funny person** couillon **funny or silly person** macaque
funny-looking *adj.* **ugly, funny-looking person** macaque
fur *n.* **soft, fuzzy fur of young animals** duvet
furious *adj.* enragé **become furious or enraged** s'enrager
furnace *n.* four, fourneau **one who fires a boiler or furnace** chauffeur
furnish *v.* donner, fournir, gréer, meubler
furnished *adj.* fourni
furnishing *npl.* **furnishings** fourniture
furniture *n.* butin, fourniture, garniture, gréement, ménage **furniture maker** meublier **piece of furniture** fourniture, meuble, morceau de ménage {butin}
furred *adj.* fourré
furrow *n.* bas de rang, sillon, raie **furrow or trench for planting seeds** rigolet *pl.* **make furrows** endosser, raiser
furrow *v.* sillonner
furry *adj.* fourré **material that is plush, velvety, or furry** peluche
further *adv.* davantage
furthermore *adv.* puis
fury *n.* fureur **fight with fury** tirer le diable par la queue
fuscata *n.* **magnolia fuscata** calicantuce
fuse *n.* mèche
fusillade *n.* fusillade
fusion *n.* fusion
fuss *n.* chamaille, chamaillerie, difficulté, dispute, querelle, train **make a fuss** se quereller **create a big row or fuss** faire un scandale
fuss *v.* bombarder, chamailler, jappailler, querellailler, quereller, se chicaner, se contrarier **fuss at** gronder, obstiner, se disputer **fuss with each other** se chamailler **one who wrangles, disputes, fusses** disputeur
fussiness *n.* **given to much fussiness over nothing** frou-frou
fussing *n.* babillage
fussy *adj.* babillard, difficile, délicat, grognard **be fussy** avoir des fions
futile *adj.* en vain
future *adj.* **future wife** prétende-femme
future *n.* avenir, futur **in the future** à l'avenir **have a good future** avoir une bonne avenir **one who predicts the future** prédicateur
fuzz *n.* **peach fuzz** duvet
fuzzy *adj.* duveté

G-string *n.* branle-bas
gab *n.* **have the gift of gab** avoir le palais bien fendu
gab *v.* bavarder, parlailler, radoter
gabardine *n.* gabardine
gabber *n.* radoteur
gabbing *n.* radotage, radote
gable *n.* pignon
gad *v.* **gad about** courailler les rues, fiander, flâner, fringuer, fronder, roulailler
gadabout *n.* flâneur
gadding *n.* **gadding about** à la fringue
gadget *n.* installation *pl.* **fancy gadgets are not worth the money one pays for them** pèse bouton, paie couillon
gadwall *n.* canard gris
gaff *n.* gaffe
gaffle *n.* gaffe
Gafftopsail *n.* mâchoiron de passe
gager *n.* pompeur
gaiety *n.* gaieté

gain *n.* bénéfice, gagne, gain, profit, rapport **flatter for personal gain** embeurrer, licher

gain *v.* gagner, profiter, bénéficier **gain on** gagner **gain the advantage over** engagner

gainsay *v.* contredire, dédire

gait *n.* marche, pas **having a rough gait** patteux, patté

gall *n.* bile, effronterie, fiel, galle **gall bladder** fiel **plant gall** poreau

gallant *adj.* galant

gallantry *n.* braveure

gallinule *n.* **Florida gallinule** poule d'eau de marais **purple gallinule** râle bleu(e) / râle d'eau

gallivant *v.* courailler les rues, coursailler, fiander, rôdailler, rôder, roulailler, rouler, traînailler, traînasser, traîner les rues, traîner **one who gallivants or runs around** rôdailleur, rôdeur

gallivanter *n.* traînard

gallon *n.* gallon

gallop *n.* galop **fast gallop** grand galop **slow gallop** petit galop

gallop *v.* galoper

galloping *n.* galopade

gallstone *n.* pierre

galvanize *v.* galvaniser

gamble *n.* gamblage

gamble *v.* gambler

gambler *n.* gambleur, parieur

gambling *n.* gamblage **gambling joint** cantique

gambol *v.* ginguer

game *n.* game, jeu, partie, gibier, viande farouche **game bag** carnassière, carrelet, havresac **game of baseball** pelote **game of tag** TAG **game of stealing bases** calinda **game in which the players have to catch an object thrown into the middle of their circle** grippe et grappe **game in which the player who gets the ball tries to hit any of the other players with it** pique-partout **game played by little girls in which they spin around so quickly that their skirts take the shape of a bell** fromages **game in which two boys each take one leg and one arm of another and swing him back and forth so that his buttocks strike the buttocks of another who is leaning over** passer à la bascule **ball game** game de pelote **card game** bataille, bourre, casino, charbon, gro-blo, POKENO, solitaire **children's game** carencro-vole, couche-couche caillé **dangerous game** casse-cou **domino game** PITCH **guessing game** devinette, dévinage **traditional word game** calembour **punishment or game in which a person is swung by the arms and legs** bascule **traditional children's game in which players raise an index finger if an animal or object named in the game can fly** pigeon-vole *pl.* **it's not fun and games** ça c'est pas baptême catin

gamecock *n.* bataillon, corusse

gander *n.* mâle z-oie

gang *n.* broque, bande, batelée, gang, ripopée, séquelle **the whole gang** tout la broque, toute la chibaigne

gangrene *n.* gangrène **turn into gangrene** gangrener

gangrenous *adj.* **become gangrenous** gangrener, se gangrener

gangster *n.* brigand

gap *n.* espace, manque, ouverture, trou **make a breach or gap** faire brèche

gape *v.* bâiller

gaper *n.* bâilleur

gar *n.* **alligator gar** poisson armé **spotted gar** poisson armé

garage *n.* garage, remise

garb *n.* habit

garbage *n.* drigaille **garbage dump** bourrier

garble *v.* ramancher

garden *n.* jardin **garden fork** fourchette **garden produce** jardinage **garden seeds** grainage **garden shears** pince **garden sprinkler** arrosoir **flower garden** parterre, verger **vegetable garden** jardin **raise a garden** faire jardin

garden *v.* faire le jardin

gardener *n.* jardinier

gardenia *n.* jasmin

gardening *n.* ouvrage de cour **do the gardening** faire le jardin

garfish *n.* michouéron, poisson armé **alligator garfish** poisson armé **long-nosed or needle-nosed garfish** bec-fin

gargle *v.* gargaliser

garlic *n.* ail **garlic greens** queues d'ail **clove of garlic** gosse d'ail **string of garlic** tresse d'ail **stuff with garlic** piquer à l'ail **stuffed with garlic** piqué à l'ail **bulb or head of garlic** tête d'ail

garment *n.* **old, ragged garment** babiche *pl.* **wedding garments and accessories** agrès de noces

garnish *v.* coincer

garret *n.* grénit

garrison *v.* garnir

garrulous *adj.* bavard, bavardeur, charrant, charreur

garter *n.* altière, jarretière

gas *n.* GASOLINE, gaz **gas pump** pompe à gaz **gas station** station d'huile, station de gaz **gas tank** TANK à gaz **natural gas** gaz **step on the gas** agiter

gash *n.* inciselage

gash *v.* écharpiller

gasoline *n.* essence, GASOLINE, gaz, huile frète

gasp *n.* soupir

gasp *v.* soupirer

gaspergou *n.* casburgot

gate *n.* porte, clayon **farm gate** clayon **field gate** porte de clos **yard gate** clayon, petite porte de jardin, porte de cour **salt water barrier gate** lock

gather *npl.* **remove pleats or gathers** défroncer

gather *v.* assembler, collecter, cueillir, entasser, froncer, ramasser, rassembler, s'assembler, se joindre, se mettre ensemble **gather together** rassembler **gather up** ramasser

gathered *adj.* froncé

gatherer *n.* ramasseur

gathering *n.* assemblage, meeting, passée, ramassage, rassemblée, réunion, assemblée **gathering of cotton** ramasse-coton **gathering of neighborhood families, during which people dance** bal de maison **noisy gathering** taoubas **social gathering** papaille, partie **social gathering for removing cotton from the bolls** égosserie **social gathering at which a suckling pig is roasted** cochon de lait **social gathering at which meat is cooked on an outdoor pit** barbecue

gaudily *adv.* **tackily or gaudily dressed** tchifaillé

gaudy *adj.* barosse, mardi gras, catchouque **dress in a gaudy, flashy, or tacky way** attriquer, s'attriquer **dress o.s. in a strange, gaudy or tacky manner** s'artifailler

gauge *n.* mesure

gaunt *adj.* égaré

gauze *n.* brin, gaze

gawker *n.* miron

gay *adj.* dégagé, gai

gaze *n.* **fix one's gaze on** fixer avec les yeux

gaze *v.* reluquer

gazette *n.* gazette

gear *n.* engrenage, équipage, équipement, arrochon

gear-wheel *n.* **tooth of a gear-wheel** alochon

gearshift *n.* **gearshift lever** bâton pour transmission

gee *interj.* boy, gee

gel *n.* **hair gel** pommade

gel *v.* geler

gelatin *n.* gelée, gélatine

gem *n.* bijou

gender *n.* sexe

genealogy *n.* généalogie, héritage

general *adj.* général

general *n.* général **attorney general** avocat général **vicar general** vicaire général

generally *adv.* généralement

generate *v.* générer

generation *n.* génération **the old generation** le vieux monde **the young generation** le jeune monde

generosity *n.* générosité, largesse

generous *adj.* (de) bon cœur, donneur, généreux

genitalia *n.* **female genitalia** tête de caouène

genitals *npl.* affaire **female genitals** caouane, cocotte, galette, grenouille, monouque, pacane, pistache, pétchotte

genius *n.* génie

gentle *adj.* docile, doux comme (le doux dans) le miel, NICE, doux **become gentle** s'adoucir

gentle *v.* adoucir, dompter

gentleman *n.* galant, gentilhomme, GENTLEMAN, monsieur

gentleness *n.* douceur

gentling *n.* adoucissage, adoucissement

gently *adv.* doucement, poliment

genuflection *n.* génuflexion

genuine *adj.* vrai

geographic *adj.* **geographic area or region** district

geography *n.* géographie

geology *n.* géologie

geranium *n.* géronium **red geranium** cire rouge **sweet geranium** géronium à la rose

germ *n.* germe, margot, poussant **germ of a potato** œil de patate

German *adj.* allemand **the German language** allemand

German *n.* Allemand, allemand

Germany *n.* Allemagne

germinate *v.* germer

germination *n.* germination

gesticulate *v.* gesticuler

gesture *n.* geste, signe **unnecessarily showy gesture** fion *pl.* **make gestures** gesticuler **ritual words or gestures used by a folk healer during a treatment** simagris

get *v.* attraper, hacher, obtenir, poigner, prendre, recevoir, s'attraper, s'obtenir, faire, se faire **get after** rentrer derrière, tomber derrière (qqn) **get again** ravoir **get along** rouler, s'en haler de **get around** naviguer **get away** fendre l'air, haler son gratin, passez!, s'échapper **get back** ravoir, se remettre, se réoccuper **get between** se glisser entre **get by** s'arracher, se débarrasser, se débattre, se défendre, se démerder, se démêler **get in** aborder, monter, rentrer **get into** rentrer **get o.s.** se fourrer **get off** descendre, débarquer, débaucher **get on** aborder, monter, s'embarquer **get out** descendre, filer, foutre le camp, foutre le champ, péter son camp, se dégager **get together** se mettre ensemble, se rejoindre **get up** se soulever **get away with** s'esquiver **get back into** rembarquer **get back together** se reprendre **get by with** faire avec **get for o.s.** se prendre **get in again** rembarquer **get o.s. out** se décoincer, se démerder **get out of** s'arracher **get out quickly** se dégager **get up again** se relever **get on a horse** monter à cheval **get out of here** va péter à Lacassine **get along with each other** s'accorder, s'adonner **get along as man and wife** faire un bon ménage **get off of or out of** débarquer **come get** venir après **go get** aller après, aller chercher **not get along** avoir de la différence, s'adonner comme chien et chat **don't get your hopes up on that** fais-toi pas une gomme avec ça **not get or not have any of s.t.** s'en passer au bout du bec **be out to get s.o.** être derrière qqn **you take what you can get** si on peut pas téter maman, il faut téter mémère **the more it goes, the worse it gets** le plus ça va, le pire c'est

get-together *n.* **get-together on Candelmas** tournerie de crêpes **get-together where people gather to sing, usually at Christmas time** ratatouille

getaway *n.* **make a getaway** fendre l'air, lever la queue

getting *n.* **getting off of or out of** débarquement
ghost *n.* christine, feu follet, lutin, revenant, vision, zombi
giant *n.* colosse, géant
gibberish *n.* bagoul **talk gibberish** baranquer
giblet *n.* **chicken giblet** gésier *pl.* **giblets** débris **pork giblets in sauce** débris du cochon
gift *n.* cadeau, don, donation, offrande **New Year's gift** étrenne
gigantic *adj.* géant
giggle *npl.* **the giggles** riquiqui
giggle *v.* hennir
giggly *adj.* effardé
gigolo *n.* gigolo
gild *v.* dorer
gill *n.* ouie
gillnet *n.* seine
gimlet *n.* vrille
gin *n.* GIN, moulin à coton **cotton gin** GIN **pass through a gin** mouliner
gin *v.* mouliner
ginger *n.* gingembre
gingerbread *n.* **gingerbread cookie** estomac (de) mulâtre
gingerbreading *n.* accroche-cœur
gingham *n.* gingas, guingan
gingiva *n.* gencive
ginning *n.* moulinage
giraffe *n.* girafe
girdle *n.* ceinture, corset, écharpe **band or girdle of elastic material** corselette
girdle *v.* cercler, cerner
girl *n.* demoiselle, femelle, fille **little girl** 'tite fille, chouchoute, criquette, fillette, fillotte **my girl** ma négresse **little brunette girl** faquetaïque **plump, fat girl** molène **the prettiest girl** la pêche de la bande **young boy or girl** petit(e) gamin(e)
girlfriend *n.* amant, belle, blonde, espoir, femelle, GIRLFRIEND, négresse, prétendu
girth *n.* sangle
give *v.* accorder, donner, fournir, dévouer, foutre **give back** redonner, rendre, rentourner **give in** céder, fléchir, plier, s'abandonner à, se plier, se soumettre **give out** craquer **give over** livrer **give repeatedly** donnailler **give up** abandonner, caler le bouchon, laisser aller la baratte, lâcher la baratte, lâcher la patate, lâcher, renoncer, résigner, sacrifier, se décourager **give o.s. away** se dévoiler **give o.s. up** s'abandonner à, se délivrer, se livrer à, se livrer **give up on** décompter **give here and there** donnailler **give to various people** donnailler **give up in the middle of an undertaking** dételer le wagon au milieu du marais / dételer le mulet des rangs **don't give up** lâche pas la patate **I give up** au diable la boutique **make s.o. give in** amener au bercail, amener qqn au bercail **force s.o. to give in** faire 'poteau, Caillette' à qqn
given *adj.* certain
gizzard *n.* gésier
glad *adj.* content
gladly *adv.* bien, de bon cœur
gladness *n.* joie
glair *n.* glaire
glance *n.* regard **cast a glance** tirer un œil **take a quick glance** jeter un coup d'œil
glance *v.* jeter la vue
gland *n.* glande **packing gland** glande **swollen gland under the arm** crois-sein
glanders *npl.* égourbes
glare *n.* lueur
glare *v.* flamber **glare at** flamber
glaring *adj.* aveuglant
glass *n.* bocal, verre, vitre **champagne glass** flûte **cut glass** cristal **drinking glass** bocal, gobelet, moque, verre à boire, verre **lamp glass** cheminée de lampe, cheminée **like glass** vitré **magnifying glass** pierre à feu **fit glass into** vitrer **pane of glass** vitrage, vitre **shard of glass** verre-bouteille **fragment of broken glass** verre-bouteille **made with fitted glass** vitré **the contents of a glass** verrée *pl.* **glasses** verre **field glasses** longue-vue
glassful *n.* verrée
glassy *adj.* vitré
glaze *v.* peinturer, vernir, vitrer
glazed *adj.* glacé, vitré
gleam *v.* étinceler
glean *v.* glainer
glee *n.* gaieté
glide *v.* planer
glimpse *n.* coup d'œil **catch a glimpse of** entr'apercevoir, entrevoir
glimpse *v.* entr'apercevoir, entrevoir
glitter *v.* briller
glittering *adj.* brillant, éclatant
globe *n.* globe **lamp globe** cheminée de lampe, cheminée
gloomy *adj.* sombre
glorification *n.* glorification
glorify *v.* glorifier
glorious *adj.* glorieux
glory *n.* gloire **morning glory** belle de jour, liane à marteau, livrier **morning glory vine** gloire du matin **wild morning glory** liserine
glossy *adj.* poli
glove *n.* gant **long, fingerless glove** mitaine *pl.* **put gloves on s.o.** ganter **put on gloves** se ganter **remove one's gloves** se déganter
glue *n.* colle, glue, goudron **stick with glue** coller **smear o.s. with glue, tar, or a similar substance** se goudronner **smear with tar or glue** goudronner
glue *v.* coller

gluey *adj.* collant, siroté
gluing *n.* collage
glutton *n.* galfat, goulipiat **be a glutton** avoir un bon coup de fourchette
gluttonous *adj.* avare, friponneur, galfat, gourmand, gros yeux / gros-yeux, safre
gluttonously *adv.* safrement
gluttony *n.* gourmandise, licherie, safreté
gnash *v.* grincher
gnashing *n.* grinchement
gnat *n.* brûlot, moustique
gnaw *v.* ronger
go *n.* **no go** pienque **come and go** va-et-vient **on the go** à la traîne **be on the go** avoir la queue sur le dos, être en rode **be constantly on the go** trapinailler
go *v.* aller, galoper, GONE, passer, se mettre, naviguer **go after** aller après, aller chercher, partir après **go against** regricher, se regricher contre **go ahead** GO AHEAD, marcher **go around** entourer, faire le tour **go astray** aller croche, s'égarer, s'éloigner, se débaucher, se perdre **go away** aller au large, déloger, départir, foutre le camp, foutre le champ, péter son camp, s'en aller, s'éloigner, va péter à Lacassine **go back** retourner, revirer, se rentourner, se retourner **go backwards** aller en reculons **go before** précéder **go beyond** dépasser, surpasser **go by** dépasser, passer, se passer **go crazy** perdre la canique / perdre ses {les} caniques **go down** baisser, descendre **go fast** agiter, SPEED **go in** entrer, rentrer **go obliquely** biaiser **go off** craquer, se décharger **go on** aller de l'avant, continuer, pousser route, se continuer **go on!** va donc! **go out** s'éteindre, sortir **go outside** aller dehors **go poof** faire pouf **go quickly** couper une fraîche, faire une fraîche, se pas **go slowly** aller (à) petit train, aller le train **go smoothly** travailler comme un neuf / travailler comme un papier de musique **go through** pénétrer **go up** monter, remonter **go upwards** aller en remontant **go well** ballotter **go with** s'adonner **go wrong** aller WRONG, aller à travers **go across diagonally** biaiser **go after s.o.** aller par derrière qqn **go away again** repartir **go back over** recourir **go down again** redescendre **go down into** s'enfoncer **go heavy on** forcer **go out again** ressortir **go out with** fréquenter, sortir avec **go over again** repasser **go steady with** aller avec **go up again** remonter **go back and forth** tournailler, trafiquer **go deep or far down** encaver, se caler **go around the exterior of a house** faire le tour de la maison **go slowly and carefully, in the manner of old folks** aller au train des vieux **let go** décharger, laisser tomber, échapper **let go of** larguer, lâcher **make go away** passer **oh, go on** va te cacher / va te faire cacher à Lafayette **let's go to work** allons s'y mettre **come and go** naviguer, trafiquer **cause to let go** décramponner **it's time to go** c'est l'heure qu'on lève la paille **I don't want to go to Chicago** je n'ai rien perdu à Chicago **you don't have to go yet, it's still early** on a plein d'huile dans la lampe **know how far one can go** connaître où cabri porte la queue, savoir où cabri porte la queue **be going** aller, être parti **how's it going?** comment les affaires?, comment ça ballotte?, comment ça se brasse? **it's going well** ça va sur des roulettes **it goes without saying** ça va sans dire **things are going well** mieux que ça et les prêtres seraient jaloux / mieux que ça serait de la gourmandise {une bêtise} **nothing has been going right** cuisses cailles a passé **said of one who goes to bed early** calibossé **the more it goes, the worse it gets** le plus ça va, le pire c'est **one who goes to unnecessary trouble or tries too hard** fionneur
goad *n.* arguinil, panquet, piquion
goal *n.* but
goat *n.* cabri **female goat** bique
goatee *n.* barbiche, barbichet, bouquin, mentonnière
goatsucker *n.* mangeur maringouins, piejègue, pigeon maringouin
goatweed *n.* herbe à cabri {mouton}
gobble *v.* dévorer, gober
gobbler *n.* dindon
goblet *n.* bocal, gobelet
god *n.* dieu
God *n.* dieu, le Bon Dieu **almighty God** Dieu tout-puissant **thank God** grâce à Dieu, merci Bon Dieu **for God's sake** pour l'amour de Dieu / pour l'amour du Bon Dieu **pertaining to God** dominicale **man proposes and God disposes** l'homme propose et Dieu dispose **for the love of God** pour l'amour de Dieu / pour l'amour du Bon Dieu
God-forsaken *adj.* **in some God-forsaken place** (là-bas) au diable bouilli
godchild *n.* **female godchild** fillette, filleule **male godchild** filleul
goddaughter *n.* fillette, filleule
godfather *n.* parrain
godforsaken *adj.* **godforsaken place** pays perdu
godliness *n.* piété
godmother *n.* marraine, nénaine
godson *n.* filleul
goggle *npl.* **goggles** conserve, lunettes
goggle-eye *n.* patassa à grande gueule
going *n.* **going over s.t. again** repassage **get going** se mettre en mouvement *pl.* **goings on** allure, commerce, commérage **goings and comings** va-et-vient
goiter *n.* goitre, grosse-gorge
gold *n.* or **of gold** d'or / en or **cover in gold** dorer
golden *adj.* d'or / en or, baille
goldenrod *n.* barre d'or, herbe à bâton, saint-jean, verge d'or
golf *n.* golf
gone *adj.* GONE
goner *n.* **be a goner** livrer sa carcasse au diable
gonorrhea *n.* chaude-pisse, coulante
good *adj.* (de) bon cœur, bien, bon cœur, bon comme la vie,

bon, FIT, pur, vaillant, valide, bon comme son père {un ange} **good at** fort pour **good sense** raison **good for use** servable **exceedingly good** bon comme la vie **look good** avoir bonne mine **make good** réparer **not good** pas fameux **pretty good** assez bien **stand good** se mettre bon pour **terribly good** méchant **a good while** un bon bout de temps **contrary to good sense** à la rebours du bon sens **in a good mood** (de / en) bonne humeur, gai comme un fou **be as good as anyone else** être pas plus chien que boule **do a good turn or a favor** faire une belle grâce (à qqn) **especially or particularly good** extra

good *n.* bien **do good** faire du bien **your good** ton bonheur **take the good with the bad** manger les grillots avec le tactac

good-bye *n.* adieu, au revoir, bonjour, BYE-BYE **good-bye for now** on va se revoir

good-for-nothing *adj.* faignant, pas bon, pimbêche, propre à rien **good-for-nothing person** fatras, hariat, raclin **good-for-nothing woman** bonne-à-rienne **worthless, good-for-nothing, lazy girl** bringue

good-for-nothing *n.* beau tchoc, bidet, bon-à-rien, foutraille, guinche, ingrandjin, monstre, rôquelaure, saloperie, traînailleur, vaurien

good-looking *adj.* joli, vaillant

good-natured *adj.* bonasse **a good or good-natured person** la barbue du bon Dieu

goodhearted *adj.* bon cœur

goodness *interj.* monde

goodness *n.* bonté, zenfants **great goodness** chien salé **my goodness** en conscience, tonibas **for goodness sake** bonté ti possible **the essence of goodness** la barbue du bon Dieu

goods *npl.* butin, gréyure, marchandise **canned goods** cannage **cotton goods** cotonnade **shoddy goods** pacotille, tchincaillerie **deprive of goods or property** dégréer

goody *n.* bonbon, friandise

goody-goody *adj.* bonasse

goof *v.* **goof off** bêtiser

goofish *n.* casburgot

goofy *adj.* bétasse

goose *n.* oie **goose bumps** peau de canard **goose whistle** sifflet à z-oie **blue goose** oie aigle, z-oie bleu(e) **Canada goose** Canada, oie canadienne / z-oie canadien, outarde **Canadian goose** oie canadienne / z-oie canadien **domestic goose** z-oie câille, z-oie de cour **eagle goose** oie aigle **laying goose** oie couvasse **snow goose** oie, z-oie blanc {blanche} **white-fronted goose** oie nonnette, z-oie câille **wild goose** z-oie marron

gooseberry *n.* piquanier

gooseflesh *n.* peau de canard

gore *n.* laize, circulaire

gore *v.* coffrer, foncer

gospel *n.* évangile **teach the gospel** évangéliser

gossip *n.* bagueulage, cancanage, cancanailles, charade, jacasserie, mauvaise langue, mépris, parlement, parlementages, radotage, radotement, rametien, rapporteur **mischievous gossip** cancan **nasty, vicious gossip** vilain parlement **given to gossip or criticism** méprisant **the unknown source of a third-hand story or piece of gossip** l'homme qu'a vu l'homme qu'a vu l'ours

gossip *v.* cancaner, faire des parlements, jacasser, nasiller, parlailler, parler, porter des paquets, radoter, tchiper **gossip about** médire, mépriser **gossip maliciously** mépriser **one who gossips** bagueuleur

gossiper *n.* cancaneur, grande langue, radoteur **old gossiper** catachrèse

gossipmonger *n.* radoteur

gossipy *adj.* **gossipy woman** jacasse

gouge *n.* coche

gouge *v.* crever

gourd *n.* calebasse **dishcloth gourd** torchon **nub of the stem of a gourd plant** tchique

gourmet *n.* gourmet

gout *n.* goitre, gâte

govern *v.* contrôler, gouverner

governable *adj.* gouvernable

government *n.* gouvernement **federal government** gouvernement fédéral **form of government** régime

governor *n.* gouverneur **title of a bishop, a governor, etc.** votre excellence

gown *n.* blouse, robe

grab *v.* agripper, attraper, empoigner, gaffer, gripper, poigner, prendre, s'agripper, saisir **grab again** ressaisir **grab between thumb and forefinger** attraper à la pincette **grab hold of each other** s'attraper

grace *n.* grâce **sanctifying grace** grâce sanctifiante

gracefulness *n.* grâce

gracious *interj.* en conscience, monde

gradation *n.* gradation

grade *n.* degré, grade, grade, livre, marque

grade *v.* correcter

grading *n.* gradation

gradually *adv.* petite à petite, à fur et à mesure

graduate *n.* gradué

graduate *v.* graduer **graduate from** graduer

graduation *n.* **graduation ceremony** graduation

grafitti *n.* marcaillage

graft *n.* greffe

graft *v.* greffer

grafter *n.* greffeur

grafting *n.* **slip for transplanting or grafting** bouture

grain *n.* grain **grain of salt** grain de sel **grain of dust or cinder** béluette **balls of grain** grainage **veining or grain** veine *pl.* **remove grains** égrener

grammar *n.* grammaire

Grand *adj.* **inhabitant of Grand Isle** grandîlier

grandchild *n.* petit-enfant
granddaughter *n.* petite-fille
grandfather *n.* grand-père, pépère, vieux-pape
grandma *n.* nénaine, vieux-mame
grandmother *n.* grand-maman, grand-mère, mémère, nénaine, vieux-mame
grandnephew *n.* petit-neveu
grandniece *n.* petite-nièce
grandpa *n.* grandpa, vieux-pape
grandparent *npl.* **grandparents** grands-parents **person who has one black and three white grandparents** quarteron
grandson *n.* petit-fils
granite *n.* granite
grant *n.* concession
grant *v.* accorder, donner
grape *n.* raisin **muscat grape** muscat **southern fox grape** soco *pl.* **bunch of grapes** grappe de raisin, paquet de raisins
grapefruit *n.* chadègue, pamplemousse
grapevine *n.* vigne de raisin
grappling *n.* **grappling hook** grappin
Gras *n.* **Mardi Gras** Mardi Gras **Mardi Gras celebration** carnaval **Mardi Gras king** roi **Mardi Gras runner** coureur de Mardi Gras **masked person who is celebrating Mardi Gras** Mardi Gras **take part in a costumed Mardi Gras run** courir Mardi Gras
grasp *n.* grippe, poigne, prise **get a good grasp or grip** prendre une bonne prise
grasp *v.* agripper, empoigner, gaffer, gripper, poigner, s'agripper, saisir **grasp each other** s'empoigner
grass *n.* herbe **grass widow** veuve délaissée **grass or other plants for feeding livestock** pâturage **barnyard grass** queue de chaqui **Bermuda grass** BLUE GRASS, chiendent **blue grass** BLUE GRASS **carpet grass** petit gazon **chestnut grass** herbe à fer **couch grass** chiendent **dallis grass** chiendent **Dallis grass** gros gazon **feather grass** paille jaune **foxtail grass** herbe de timitée **lawn grass** gazon **marsh grass** canne des cochons, paille fine **needle grass** paille chat-tigre **nut grass** coco **pampas grass** vétiver **panic grass** herbe ronde **ribbon grass** jarretière de la Sainte Vierge **rye grass** RYE GRASS **sorrel grass** caca matelot **sour grass** caca matelot **star grass** herbe à trois quarts {écarts} **swamp grass** herbe de marais **sweetheart grass** jarretière de la Sainte Vierge **switch grass** canuche, chiendent, paille jaune **tall grass** gazon **three-cornered grass** herbe à trois coins, jonc au trois quarts {à trois écartes} **wild grass** riz de l'âne {de long}, riz farouche {sauvage} **blade of grass** brin d'herbe **clump of grass** talle d'herbe **cut the grass** couper les herbes **stalk of grass** pied d'herbe **tufted perennial grass** vétiver **yellow nut grass** cache-cache **stubble and grass in a field after harvesting** glaine **amount of grass or hay cut with one swing of the blade or scythe** fauchée **salt water marsh grass** paillette
grasshopper *n.* chevalet, cigale, criquet, locuste, sauterelle **lubber grasshopper** cheval-carotte / cheval-carosse, cheval de {du} diable / cheval-diable, sauterelle cheval **marsh grasshopper** sauterelle de maiche
grassland *n.* savane, prairie
grate *n.* gril
grate *v.* grincher, râper
grateful *adj.* reconnaissant **be grateful** reconnaître
gratefulness *n.* gratitude
grater *n.* rate, râpe, râpeuse
gratification *n.* gratification
gratify *v.* contenter, satisfaire
grating *n.* râpage
gratis *adj.* gratis
gratitude *n.* gratitude, reconnaissance
gratuity *n.* TIP
grave *adj.* grave, sérieux
grave *n.* fosse, tombe, tombeau **grave marker** remarque de tombe
gravel *n.* gravois, gravail **piece of gravel** caillou, gravelle
gravely *adv.* gravement
graveyard *n.* cimetière
gravity *n.* gravité, gravité
gravy *n.* sauce **gravy boat** moque, saucière **brown gravy** sauce rouillée **cream gravy** sauce blanche **greasy gravy** graisse
gray *adj.* gris
gray-haired *adj.* gris
grayish *adj.* caillematchal, pivelé
graze *v.* rifler, écorcher **lick, scrape or graze one's skin** se friper
grazing *n.* **grazing land** pâturage **fenced-in area for grazing** savane
grease *n.* graisse **apply grease** se graisser **axle grease** graisse à charette **remove fat or grease** dégraisser
grease *v.* graisser **grease o.s.** se graisser
greasing *n.* graissage
greasy *adj.* gras
great *adj.* grand, magnifique, merveilleux, noble **look great** faire un effet bœuf
great-grandfather *n.* arrière-grand-père, grand-grand-père
great-grandmother *n.* arrière-grand-mère, grand-grand-mère
great-grandparent *npl.* **great-grandparents** grands-grands-parents
great-nephew *n.* petit-neveu, petit neveu
great-niece *n.* petite-nièce
greater *adj.* meilleur **greater than usual or expected** haut
greatly *adv.* très
greatness *n.* grandeur
grebe *n.* grèbe **pied-billed grebe** culotte, macreuse, plongeon, sac-à-plomb
greed *n.* avarice, avidité, friponnerie
greedily *adv.* safrement, à pleine bouche {gueule}

greediness *n.* friponnerie, licherie

greedy *adj.* avide, friponneur, gourmand comme un chien {cochon}, gourmand, gros yeux / gros-yeux, rapiat, rasoir, regardant, safre **greedy person** galfat, goulipiat, rafalé **be greedy** avoir les yeux plus grands que le ventre

Greek *adj.* grec **Greek language** grec

green *adj.* vert, vert **green as grass** vert comme de l'herbe {des herbes} **green in color** vert comme de l'herbe {des herbes} **become green** verdir **color green** verdir **make green** verdir **turn green** verdir **become green again** reverdir

green *n.* **Paris green** vert de Paris *pl.* **greens** verdage, verdure **beet greens** queues de betteraves **edible greens** verdage, verdure **garlic greens** queues d'ail **mustard greens** moutarde **turnip greens** queues de navet

greenery *n.* verdure, vert

greenhorn *n.* blanc-bec

greenness *n.* verdure

greet *v.* dire (le) bonjour, faire BYE-BYE, saluer **expression used to greet a visitor one hasn't seen for a long time** est-ce que t'amènes la pluie?

greeting *n.* salut **greeting card** carte

grenade *n.* grenade **hand grenade** grenade à main

grenadier *n.* grenadier

grid *n.* **grid iron** gril

griddle *n.* plaque

grief *n.* chagrin, douleur, désolation

grief-stricken *adj.* désolé

grieve *v.* chagriner, faire de la peine, gémir, se chagriner **it grieves me** ça me fait de la peine

grieved *adj.* chagrin

grieving *adj.* en peine, peineux

grill *n.* grille, rôtisserie **cooking grill** gril

grill *v.* griller

grimace *n.* binette, frimasse, frimousse, grimace, micmac, simagris

grimace *v.* avoir une figure comme une vache qu'a soif, faire une frimousse, frimousser, grimacer, se défigurer

grin *n.* sourire

grin *v.* grincher, sourire

grind *v.* grainer, moudre, mouler, critcher, égrener **crush and grind sugar cane** rouler les cannes

grinder *n.* moulin **coffee grinder** moulin à café **meat grinder** moulin à viande

grinding *adj.* **make a grinding sound** grincher

grinding *n.* moudurage **grinding or milling** moudage, moulage **grinding of sugar cane** roulage **corn grinding or milling** moulage de maïs

grindle *n.* choupique

grindstone *n.* meule, mulon **put one's shoulder to the grindstone** mettre l'épaule à la roue

grinning *adj.* **make a squinting, grinning face** grincher

grip *n.* manche, poigne, prise **loosen one's grip** décramponner **get a good grasp or grip** prendre une bonne prise

grip *v.* agripper, pincer

gripe *v.* se lamenter, se plaindre

griper *n.* plaignard, plaignoux

grist *n.* **grist mill** moulin à gru

grit *npl.* **grits** gru

grit *v.* critcher

groan *v.* grogner, gémir

grocer *n.* grossier

grocery *n.* **grocery basket** panier de grosseries **grocery store** boutique, grosserie, magasin de groceries *pl.* **groceries** commission, grosserie

grog *n.* todie

groin *n.* aingue

groom *n.* marié

groom *v.* **groom feathers with the beak** s'épivarder, s'épouiller

groomed *adj.* soigné **poorly groomed** déguénillé **look badly groomed** avoir une mine de chien

groove *n.* coulisse, encoche **groove of a tongue-and-groove coupling** rainure **tongue and groove lumber** ceiling

groove *v.* encocher

grope *v.* se tâtonner, tatailler, tâter, tâtonner

gross *adj.* commun, crasse

grouchy *adj.* babillard, bourru, grognard **be grouchy** regricher **mean, grouchy, ill-tempered person** bourreau **be cross or ill-humored, grouchy** être de {en} travers

ground *adj.* **finely ground** fin

ground *n.* terrain, terre **ground auger** mèche-terrière **ground ways** WAYS **high ground** butte, terre haute **lose ground** en perdre **remove ground cover or mulch** détourer **high ground not subject to flooding** écore **on the ground** par terre, à terre **onto the ground** à terre **paw the ground** piocher **to the ground** par terre **drive into the ground** masser **hole in the ground supposedly made by an enraged bull** trou de taureau *pl.* **coffee grounds** marc

groundhog *n.* chien de terre

group *n.* armée, bande, bastringue, batelée, clique, commune, faction, lot, riquiqui, troupe, gang, groupe **group being chaperoned** trallée **group of closely related species** famille **ethnic group** citoyen, nation **large number or group** trallée **member of a group or society** membre **member of a group organized in Saint Martinsville in the early 1880s to restore white rule** régulateur

grove *n.* île **grove of pine trees in the open prairie** île de pins **grove or stand of oak trees in an otherwise treeless swamp** chênière **cypress grove** ciprière **oak grove** chêneau, chênerie, chênière **pecan grove** pacanière **pine grove** pinière **willow grove** saulière

grow *v.* faire, grandir, pousser, profiter, s'augmenter, se développer, élever, élever **grow again** repousser **grow back** repousser, reprendre **grow dim** s'affaiblir **grow fast** pousser à vue d'œil **grow fat** engraisser **grow lukewarm** quédir **grow old** vieillir **grow pale** pâlir **grow soft** se ramollir **grow**

strong se fortifier **grow stronger** renforcir, se renforcir **grow thin** fondre **grow up** grandir, grossir **grow weary** lasser, se larguer **grow up quickly** grandir comme un pied de chou **grow into a clump** entaller, taller **grow white or fair** blondir **one who grows or cultivates crops** éleveur
growl *n.* grognement
growl *v.* gourgousser, grincher, râler, brasser
growling *adj.* grognard
growling *n.* grinchement
grown *adj.* **grown up** grand **grown or produced in Louisiana** créole **full grown** bien {tout} formé **child who tries to act grown up** péteur
grownup *npl.* **grownups** le grand monde
growth *n.* développement, pousse, profit **new growth** repousse **remove growth** éclaircir **a greenish grassy growth appearing on wood or on the ground after a rain** limon **make a new spurt of growth** prendre une nouvelle sève
grudge *n.* **bear a grudge** porter une rancune **have a grudge** avoir un piment contre, avoir une dent contre qqn **hold a grudge** en vouloir à, soigner un petit chien {veau} (pour qqn)
grumble *v.* bombarder, babiller, bougonner, grogner, nasonner, se plaindre, gargouiller
grumbler *n.* bougonneur, grognard, grogneur
grumbling *adj.* grognard
grumbling *n.* bougonnement, grognement
grunt *v.* grogner
guarantee *n.* caution, garantie **collateral guarantee** sécurité
guarantee *v.* assurer, certifier, garantir
guard *n.* garde, WATCHMAN **cattle guard** pont à craques **fire guard** garde-feu **keeping guard** garde **mud guard** garde-boue **national guard** milice **be on one's guard** s'observer, se méfier *pl.* **guards** garde
Guard *n.* **Coast Guard** Garde de Côte
guard *v.* protecter, protéger **guard against** se préserver
guardian *n.* garde, gardien, protecteur, tuteur **guardian angel** ange gardien
guardsman *n.* garde
guess *v.* deviner
guessing *n.* **guessing game** devinette, dévinage
guest *n.* invité **departing guest** partant **inopportune guest** juif-errant *pl.* **group of guests** compagnie
guidance *n.* guidance
guide *n.* guide, guideur, pilote, tuteur
guide *v.* directer, gouverner, guider, mener, piloter **guide with reins** rêner
guileless *adj.* naïve
guilelessness *n.* naïveté
guilt *n.* blâme **admit guilt** s'accuser **admission of guilt** admission
guiltless *adj.* ignorant, pur
guilty *adj.* coupable, fautif **have a guilty look on one's face** faire le filou comme un chien basset
guinea *n.* **guinea cloth** guinée **guinea fowl** pintale **guinea hen** pintale **guinea pig** cochon guinée **marsh guinea** râle bleu(e) / râle d'eau
guitar *n.* guitare
gulf *n.* golfe
Gulf *n.* golfe **Gulf of Mexico** Golfe du Mexique **the Gulf of Mexico** la grande mer
gully *n.* coulée
gulp *v.* gober **gulp down** engueuler, envaler, gober
gum *n.* gomme **gum arabic** gomme arabique **gum tree** copal **chewing gum** gomme **sea gum** gomme de mer **sweet gum tree** copal **tupelo gum tree** olivier **remove gum or any gummy substance** dégommer **ball of gum** boule de gomme **stick of gum** galette de gomme, palette de gomme, palette **fruit of the tupelo gum tree** boule d'olivier *pl.* **gums** gencive
gum *v.* mâchouiller **gum up** engommer
gumbo *n.* gombo, terre grasse **gumbo dinner** gombo **gumbo made with greens and cured meat** gombo z'herbes **chicken gumbo** gombo de poule {volaille} **filé gumbo** gombo filé **okra gumbo** gombo févi **seafood gumbo** gombo de fruit de mer
gummy *adj.* gommeux **become gummy** s'engommer
gun *n.* fusil **gun barrel** canon de fusil **gun hammer** marteau **gun handle** manche **gun shell** cartouche **gun sight** mire **cocked gun** pistolet braqué
gunner *n.* fusillier
gunny *n.* pite **peat, gunny, or burlap sack** sac de pitre
gunpowder *n.* poudre à fusil, poudre
gunshot *n.* coup de fusil, tirage **fire a gunshot** sacrer un coup de fusil
gurgling *n.* glou-glou
gush *v.* pisser, voler
gust *n.* **gust of wind** bouffée de vent, rafale **sudden gust of wind** coup de vent
gust *v.* rafaler
gut *npl.* **guts** entrailles, tripe
gut *v.* étriper, éventrer **gut and dress** débriter
gutter *n.* dégouttière, gouttière **roof gutter** dalle
guy *n.* bougre, gaillard, splouque **tough guy** péteur, taureau, tonnerre **wise guy** dard
gypsy *n.* fideleine, gipsie
gyration *n.* giration

habit *n.* accoutumance, coutume, habitude **break one's habit** se déshabituer **be in the habit** avoir (la) coutume (de), être habitué avec **break of a habit of** déshabituer

habitable *adj.* habitable, logeable, vivable
habitual *adj.* habituel
habitually *adv.* habitude, habituellement
hack *n.* HACK
hack *v.* cisailler, gober, écharpiller **hack at** chacoter **hack up** chiquenailler, coupailler, hachouiller
hackamore *n.* **hackamore bridle** bossal
hackberry *n.* bois de cogné / bois inconnu **hackberry tree** bois connu {inconnu}
hacksaw *n.* scie à fer
had *adj.* **be had** rester avec la chuille
hag *n.* garce
haggard *adj.* échiné
haggard-looking *adj.* abattu, égaré
haggle *v.* barguiner, chicaner, rapigner **one who bargains or haggles** barguineur
haha *onom.* quiaque-quiaque
hail *n.* grêle
hail *v.* grêler, saluer, parvenir **hail for a ride** FLAG
hair *n.* cheveu **hair curler** papillote **hair gel** pommade **hair pin** épingle à cheveux **hair grown long at the ears** bagari **bleach hair** blondir les cheveux **body hair** poil **long hair** grands cheveux **tearing hair out** échevelage **shed hair or skin** déplumer **fine hair on the body of humans** duvet **one hair that sticks up and refuses to lie in place** mauvaiseté **bleach one's hair** se blondir **braid of hair** couette **brush one's hair** se brosser les cheveux **coarse animal hair** crin **comb one's hair** se peigner les cheveux, se peigner **curl one's hair** se boucler **having disheveled hair** ébouriffé **head of hair** chevelure, crignasse, tête **lock of hair** pince de cheveux, tchocouette **part one's hair** trier les cheveux **tease one's hair** se tiser les cheveux **twist of hair** cagouette **disarrange the hair of** décoiffer, dépeigner **dishevel the hair of** ébouriffler, écheveler **come a hair from death** être venu un cheveu de sa mort **get one's hair messed up** se décoiffer **line where hair is parted** partage **have one's hair all matted up** avoir sa crignasse en lutine **having the hair combed straight back** à la pompadour **mess up one's hair** s'ébouriffler **come within a hair of** venir (à) un fil de **mess up the hair of** ébouriffler, écheveler **have disheveled or wild hair** avoir la tête égrichée **manner of styling the hair** coiffage, coiffure, peignure **messing up of the hair** ébouriffage **person with long, disheveled hair** taïque **roll, twist, or knot of hair worn at the back of the head** catogan, choque, tchique, tignon
hairbrush *n.* brosse à cheveux {de tête}
haircut *n.* coupe (de cheveux)
hairdo *n.* coiffage, coiffure, peignure, toupet **having a type of hairdo** coiffé
hairdresser *n.* coiffeur
hairless *adj.* chauve
hairpiece *n.* toupet
hairy *adj.* duveté, poileux, poilu
Haitian *n.* haïtien
half *adj.* demi
half *n.* demi, moitié **half and half** moitié-moitié **half of any spherical object** gamelle **in half** en moitié **farm on half** faire récolte à la moitié **two and a half cents** quarti **what one could buy for two and a half cents** quarti *pl.* **sharecrop on halves** travailler à la moitié
half *prefix.* mi-
half-boot *n.* broquin
half-breed *adj.* abâtardi
half-breed *n.* binacle, sang-mêlé
half-crazy *adj.* à moitié fou
half-cup *n.* demi-tasse
half-pint *n.* chacta
halfway *adv.* moitié, à moitié route
hall *n.* HALL, salle **bingo hall** bingo **dance hall** HALL de danse, HALL, salle de danse, salle
Halloween *n.* veille de la Toussaint
hallucination *n.* hallucination
hallway *n.* corridor, HALL, passette
halt *interj.* halt
halt *n.* arrêt
halt *v.* arrêter, s'arrêter **halt overnight** faire chaudière
halter *n.* bossal **put a halter on an animal** amarrer **part of rigging on halter** anneau
ham *n.* jambon, jarret **ham bone** pistolet de jambon, échelon
hame *n.* haulier, hème
hammer *n.* marteau **gun hammer** marteau **gun hammer and trigger** chien de fusil
hammer *v.* fouler
hammock *n.* hamac
hamper *n.* manne, panier
hamper *v.* mettre des bâtons dans la roue {les roues}
hand *n.* griffe, main, aiguille **hand adze** tille **hand grenade** grenade à main **hand loom** métier **hand pump** pompe à la main, pompe **hand towel** essuie-mains **hand truck** diable **at hand** à portée **dummy hand** mort **farm hand** travaillant de champs {clos} **helping hand** coup de main, touche **hired hand** engagé **little hand** mainette **lend a hand** donner la {une} main, mettre la main **sew by hand** coudre au doigt, coudre à la main **sew by hand over** surjeter **get the upper hand** prendre le dessus **have the upper hand** emmancher **lend a helping hand** donner un coup de main **palm of the hand** paume **stretch out one's hand** allonger la main **a bird in the hand is worth two in the bush** un oiseau dans la main en vaut deux dans une talle **strike with the side of the hand** sacrer un coup de main *pl.* **shake hands** se donner la main, secouer la main **win hands down** roqueter **shake hands upon concluding a bargain** se donner la palmée **wash one's hands** se laver les mains **get one's hands on** coller, escolter **have one's hands tied** être amenotté **walk**

on one's hands planter (le) chêne **washing of the priest's hands at mass** lavabo

hand *v.* passer **hand down** passer **hand over** dégainer, livrer

handbag *n.* porte-monnaie

handball *n.* pelote à la main

handbasin *n.* bassin à mains / bassin lave mains, cuvette

handcart *n.* charrette à bras

handcuff *n.* manoque, menotte *pl.* **put handcuffs on s.o.** manoquer

handcuff *v.* amenotter

handful *n.* magnée, maintée, pleine main, poigne, poignée

handicap *n.* HANDICAP

handicapped *adj.* affictionné, affligé **be mentally handicapped** pas avoir sa bonne comprenure, pas avoir (son) idée / pas avoir (sa) bonne idée

handkerchief *n.* mouche-nez, mouchoir **drop the handkerchief** cache-mouchoir

handle *n.* manche, manivelle, poignet, prise **gun handle** manche **pump handle** bras de pompe **round handle** rondin **wooden handle of a butter churn** palon **refit a handle** ramancher **put a handle on a tool** emmancher **loosen or remove a handle** démancher

handle *v.* manœuvrer, manier, ménager, toucher **handle again** remanier **handle o.s.** se manier **handle roughly** hartchiner, maganer, manier

handler *n.* manieur

handmade *adj.* fait à la main

handsome *adj.* beau, vaillant **handsome man** bel homme **become more beautiful or more handsome** se bellesir

handwinch *n.* vireveau

handwriting *n.* main, écriture **illegible handwriting** pataraphe

handy *adj.* adroit, bon à marier, commode, à (la) main, à toutes mains **not handy** mal à main

handy *adv.* à portée

handyman *n.* bedeau

hang *v.* accrocher, engrucher, pendre, se raccrocher, suspendre **hang around** gavagner, traîner **hang o.s.** se pendre **hang up** accrocher, pendre, suspendre **hang in there** lâche pas la patate **hang on hinges** pendre **hang out to dry** mettre à sécher, éparer, étendre **hang up on s.o.** raccrocher sus qqn **hang wallpaper or tapestry** tapisser **put or hang in the sun** mettre au soleil **anything that hangs or dangles** pendrioche **any part of a woman's apparel that hangs or is out of place** guiguiches

hangar *n.* hangar

hanger *n.* **paper hanger** tapisseur

hanging *adj.* traînant, à la pendille {pendriole} **hanging thread** filasse **leave s.o. hanging** laisser (qqn) suspendu

hanging *n.* accrochage **put to death by hanging** pendre

hangnail *n.* belle-mère, fouille-fouille, herculant, mangeur d'ongle, tour d'ongle

hangout *n.* **hangout for loafers** faubourg

hangover *n.* **have a hangover** être à soguer

hank *n.* **wind into a hank or skein** travouiller

hanker *v.* **hanker after** ambitionner pour

happen *v.* adonner, arriver, avoir lieu, prendre place, s'adonner, se faire, se passer **happen advantageously** tomber dans le panneau **happen quickly** passer comme une balle **happen to** devenir **happen upon** croiser avec **happen by chance** adonner, s'adonner **happen at a bad time** s'adonner mal **just so happen** s'adonner **what's happening?** qui ça dit?, quoi (c'est) qui se brasse (là)?, quoi ça dit? **that happened a long time ago** ça date de l'an quarante

happening *n.* épisode, événement *pl.* **happenings** allure

happily *adv.* heureusement

happiness *n.* bonheur, félicité, gaieté, joie

happy *adj.* bienheureux, bènaise, content, fier, gai comme un fou, gai, heureux comme un poisson {les poissons} dans l'eau, heureux, joyeux **be happy** raser

happy-go-lucky *adj.* **happy-go-lucky person** JACK-A-DON'T-CARE

harass *v.* faire (de) la misère (à qqn), harasser

harassing *n.* harassement

harassment *n.* harassement

harbor *n.* port

harbor *v.* entretenir

hard *adj.* difficile, dur comme du caillou {du fer / la brique / la pierre, dur, halant, lourd **hard person** sans-cœur **hard times** patocaille **become hard** durcir **times are hard** les affaires se brassent mal **have a hard time** misérer **make things hard for o.s.** rabourer à travers les rangs **do things the hard way** rabourer à travers les rangs **suffer misery or a hard time with** passer du bleu de ciel avec qqn, soufferre du bleu de ciel avec

hard *adv.* dur, fort, raide, rudement **one who goes to unnecessary trouble or tries too hard** fionneur

hard-hearted *adj.* dur

hard-surfaced *adj.* pavé

hard-working *adj.* **hard-working man** bon travailleur

harden *v.* affermir, durcir, endurcir, figer, se rendurcir **harden again** rendurcir

hardened *adj.* **become hardened** s'endurcir

hardening *n.* durcissement, endurcissement **hardening of the arteries** endurcissement des artères

hardhead *n.* tête de caouène

hardheaded *adj.* obstineux, obstiné, tête dûre, têtu **hardheaded person** caouane, tête dûre

hardly *adv.* guère, pas guère, à peine

hardness *n.* dureté

hardship *n.* **endure hardship because of s.o.** avoir du fil à retordre avec qqn **have a lot of trouble and hardship in life** manger de la misère, passer de la misère *pl.* **live through hardships** passer de la misère

hardtack *n.* **cookie hardtack** gâteau

hardware *n.* **hardware store** magasin à ferraille
hardworking *adj.* travaillant
hardy *adj.* gaillard, hardi
hare *n.* lapin, lièvre
harlot *n.* bonne-à-rienne, bordel, popotte, prostituée
harm *n.* dommage, dédommage, tort **do harm to the character by overindulgence** gâter **free of harm** sauve
harm *v.* dommager, dédommager, faire (de / du) tort **said of someone who has harmed you and against whom you seek revenge** je lui garde chien de ma chienne
harmful *adj.* criminel
harmonica *n.* casse-babine, fend-gueule, flûte à bouche, flûte à gueule, flûte, musique à babines {bouche / gueule}
harmonize *v.* correspondre
harness *n.* agrès, attelage, harnais, haulier **harness collar** bourrure **harness lines** guide **harness rigging** attelle, trait de chaîne **set of harness** jeu
harness *v.* amarrer, harnacher, atteler
harnessing *n.* agrès, attelle, harnachement
harp *n.* harpe **Jew's harp** trompe
harping *n.* cassement de tête
harpoon *n.* harpon
harpoon *v.* darder
harrass *v.* chicoter
harrier *n.* cossarde
harrow *n.* herse **harrow tine** dent de herse **harrow tooth** dent de herse **disk harrow** disque, laboureuse, trancheuse
harrow *v.* herser
harrowing *n.* hersage
harsh *adj.* sévère, sec **harsh words** paroles blessantes
harshly *adv.* rudement
harvest *n.* cueillette, moisson, moissonage, ramasse, récolte, ramasserie **cane harvest** coupage de canne **communal harvest** ramassage **sugar cane harvest** roulaison **work in the sugar cane harvest** rouler
harvest *v.* casser, faire récolte, ramasser, récolter, sauver
harvester *n.* casseur, ramasseur, ramasseuse
harvesting *n.* ramasse, cassage **harvesting machine** coupeuse **harvesting of the last cotton** grabotage **cotton harvesting machine** ramasseuse à coton **go through harvesting a crop** faire une passée
hash *n.* **make a stew or hash with** ragouiller
hassle *n.* trouble
haste *n.* presse **make haste** s'appresser, se presser
hasten *v.* s'emparer
hastily *adv.* à la mistanflute
hat *n.* chapeau, fourreau **derby hat** bidon **felt hat** chapeau de laine **odd-looking hat** turlututu **old hat** cala **panama hat** panama **straw hat** chapeau de paille **top hat** bidon **ugly hat** carabas **old hat or cap** bidon, capuchon **tall, pointed hat** capuchon **upper part of a hat** calotte **bend in or out with a hat** cabaner
hatch *v.* bécher, croquetter, éclore **don't count your chickens before they hatch** présume pas tes œufs
hatchet *n.* casse-tête, hache à main, hache
hatching *n.* couvage
hate *n.* haine **full of hate** haineux
hate *v.* abominer, détester, haïr **one who hates** haïsseur
hateful *adj.* criminel, détestable, haïssable **hateful or mean person** vache habillée en zinc
hater *n.* haïsseur
hating *adj.* haineux
hatred *n.* haine
haughtily *adv.* fièrement
haughtiness *n.* gloire
haughty *adj.* fier, noble, suspect **haughty person** fiéraud **be haughty, vain** s'en croire **act in a pretentious, haughty or affected way** fionner
haul *v.* haler, traîner **haul a house** traîner une maison
hauler *n.* haleur
hauling *n.* halage, traînage **rice hauling** halage de riz
haunt *v.* **if you speak ill of others, it comes back to haunt you** crache dans l'air, ça tombe sur le (bout du) nez
have *v.* avoir, faire, se faire, être, faire **have again** ravoir **have better** avoir intérêt de, avoir plus quitte **have just** sortir de, venir **have to** avoir pour, devoir, falloir **have it in for** en vouloir à, s'en prendre après (qqn) **not have to** pas avoir la peine **you don't have to go yet, it's still early** on a plein d'huile dans la lampe **not get or not have any of s.t.** s'en passer au bout du bec **every dog has his day** chaque chien a son jour
havoc *n.* dégât, dévastation, naufrage, ravage **cause havoc** ravager **wreak havoc** carnassier **wreak havoc on** dévaster
haw *interj.* ha
haw *n.* cenelle, pommette bleue **haw tree** cenellier
hawk *n.* faucon, mangeur (de) poules / mangeur de poulet **chicken hawk** hibou de paille, tchacalata, z-aile rond(e) **Cooper's hawk** aiglon, z-aile rond(e) **duck hawk** cossarde, z-aile pointue **marsh hawk** chocolatière, cossarde **mosquito hawk** chenaille, cheval de {du} diable / cheval-diable, cigale, hirondelle, mamselle, mangeur maringouins, mastoc, moiselle, sauterelle **prairie hawk** chocolatière, cossarde **red-tailed hawk** cossarde **sparrow hawk** cliclique, cossarde, hibou, mangeur (de) poules / mangeur de poulet, émerillon, épervier
hawthorn *n.* cenellier, pommier
hay *n.* foin, fourrage **hay barn** magasin de {à} foin **hay fever** fièvre d'automne, fièvre de foin **hay loft** grénit **hay rack** crèche, râtelier **mowed hay** andain **bale of hay** botte de foin **amount of grass or hay cut with one swing of the blade or scythe** fauchée
haystack *n.* berge, muleron, mulon, paille de riz
hazard *n.* danger, hasard, risque
hazardous *adj.* risqué
hazardously *adv.* dangereusement

haze *n.* brouillard
hazy *adj.* boucané, embrouillé
he *pron.* il, lui, ça
he-mule *n.* mulet
head *n.* caboche, cagouette, calebasse, caloque, caloquinte, calotte, caouane, capitaine, casaquin, coco, coyoche, créneure, en tête, premier, tête, pomme **head cheese** gelée de cochon, gelée **head cold** rhume de cerveau **head covering** garde-soleil **head start** partance **head of the bed** tête de lit **head waters of a bayou** marais **arrow head** pierre de sauvage **fall head first** planter (le) chêne **cover the head** coiffer **form a head** monter en pomme {tête}, pommer, se pommer **lower one's head** baisser la tête **remove a head covering** décoiffer **remove one's head covering** se décoiffer **be at the head** être à la tête **be over one's head** être dans (qqch) par dessus la tête **come to a head** aboutir, claquer **coming to a head** aboutissage **stand on one's head** planter (le) chêne **strike on the head** décoxer **rap on the head with the knuckles** calotte **fall forward on one's head** planter (le) chêne **get in over one's head** s'empêtrer **go up to one's head** monter à la tête **soft spot on the top of an infant's head** fontaine
head *v.* gagner vers, gagner, pommer, prendre pour, se diriger, se pommer **head for** pousser route **head off** débagager, détourner **head for or towards** donner la tête vers **head for the open** donner au large
headache *n.* mal de tête, migraine **give a headache** entêter
headboard *n.* **headboard of a bed** barre du lit
headed *adj.* pommé **be headed** être en grappe
heading *n.* titre
headlamp *n.* BULL-EYE
headland *n.* allée de clos, chemin de travers(e), allée, chaintre, chemin de charrette, HEADLAND, routine à la volonté, tournage, tournaille, tournant, tourne, tournure, virée
headlight *n.* fanal
headline *n.* titre
headman *n.* BOSS
headpiece *n.* coiffure
headscarf *n.* tignon
headstrong *adj.* braqué **be headstrong** faire à sa tête
headway *n.* avance
heal *v.* guérir
healer *n.* **healer who lifts the uvula when it has fallen** leveur de (la) luette **faith healer** toucheur, traiteur **traditional healer** traiteur
healing *adj.* curatif, soulageant
healing *n.* **folk healing** traitement
health *n.* portement, santé **decline in health** s'abîmer **fail in health** manquer, s'écraser, écraser **improve in health** se refaire **in bad health** en mauvaise santé **in good health** bien portant, bien, en bonne santé, FIT, gaillard **in poor health** abîmé **lose one's health** s'écraser **recover one's health** se rétablir **to your health** à votre santé **be in good health** se porter bien **drink to s.o.'s health** boire à la santé de qqn **one who frequently complains about his health** pot fêlé
healthful *adj.* fortifiant
healthy *adj.* bien portant, gaillard, sain, vaillant
heap *n.* butte, entassement, masse, pile, pilot, ramasse, tapée, tas **compost heap** pile **dung heap** parc à fumier **trash heap** bourrier **fall in a heap** tomber en racaille {racage}, tomber en racaille *pl.* **heaps** en masse et en pile
heap *v.* entasser **heap up** amasser, mettre en tas
hear *v.* attendre **hear about** attendre parler de **hear of** attendre parler de **hear each other** s'attendre **hear the confession of and grant absolution** confesser
hearer *n.* auditeur
hearing *n.* audition **be hard of hearing** attendre dur, attendre haut
hearse *n.* corbillard
heart *n.* cœur, courage, cœur **heart attack** attaque de cœur **heart disease** maladie de cœur **heart trouble** mal de cœur, maladie de cœur **lose heart** se décourager **take heart** prendre courage, s'encourager **break one's heart** casser le cœur **break s.o.'s heart** casser le cœur à qqn, crever le cœur à qqn **learn by heart** apprendre par cœur **open one's heart** ouvrir son cœur **wear one's heart on one's sleeve** avoir le cœur sur ses bras **have a heavy heart** avoir un cœur lourd **with a good heart** de bon cœur **with all my heart** de tout mon cœur **I don't have the heart** j'ai pas le cœur
heartache *n.* chagrin, point dans le cœur
heartbeat *n.* battement de cœur
heartbreaking *adj.* chagrinant
heartbroken *adj.* désolé **be heartbroken in love** avoir une boule sus le cœur
heartburn *n.* brûlement d'estomac, brûlement
hearted *n.* **good hearted** (de) bon cœur
heartening *adj.* encourageant
hearth *n.* foyer
heartless *adj.* sans cœur, vicieux **heartless person** sans-cœur
heartrending *adj.* pénible
heartworm *n.* ver de cœur
heat *n.* chaleur, chaud **heat development** réchauffement **heat lightning** éloise **heat rash** échauboulure, échauffure **heat of the day** fumée de midi **in heat** en chaleur, en galope, en rougarou, en saison **prickly heat** échauboulure, échauffure **suffering from the heat** achalé
heat *v.* chauffer, réchauffer, échauder **heat one's residence** se chauffer
heater *n.* réchaud, STOVE **kerosene heater** réchaud à coloïe **wood heater** réchaud à {en} bois
heathen *adj.* païen
heathen *n.* païen
heating *n.* chauffage, chauffe **combustible material used for heating** chauffage

heave *v.* **heave a sigh** pousser un soupir

heaven *n.* ciel, paradis **for heaven's sake** mais enfin!, tonnerre de foutre *pl.* **good heavens** chien salé, sacré bleu, tonibas

heavily *adv.* raide

heavy *adj.* lourd, massif, pâlot, fourni **be heavy** peser **make heavy** alourdir **stupid, dull, heavy person** bûche

Hebrew *adj.* hébreu

heck *interj.* **heck no** foutre non! **oh heck** chia

heck *n.* **heck of a thing** belle gratte **one heck of a** un bébé de

hedge *n.* buis, haie **Cherokee hedge** haie de chéroquie

hedgerow *n.* haie

heed *n.* attention

heel *n.* croûte, crouston, talon **wear down the heel of** aculer *pl.* **press one's heels into** talonner

heifer *n.* taure

height *n.* altitude, grandeur, hauteur **height of a room** arasement **height of the ceiling** arasement **height of a shovel or spade** creuseur **of a certain height** haut **former unit of height equaling approximately six feet** toise

heir *n.* héritier

helicopter *n.* HELICOPTER

heliotrope *n.* **Indian heliotrope** herbe à chenille

hell *interj.* bordel, bordelation, bétaille **hell no** fichtre non

hell *n.* enfer **raise hell** faire le diable à quatre, faire un scandale, malfaire **all hell broke loose** le diable s'en a mêlé **the hell, you say** belle affaire! **go to hell** ton cul!, tourner en merde, va te cacher / va te faire cacher à Lafayette, va te coucher, va te faire foutre!, va à la merde **go to hell!** mange de la merde! **sure as hell** foutrement **what the hell** sacré misère! **get the hell out** couper une fraîche **that's a hell of a thing!** ça c'est une affaire, oui! **raise all kinds of hell** faire les quatre-cents coups, faire les quatre cents coups **tell s.o. to go to hell** envoyer qqn à la promenade {à la merde}, envoyer se cacher / envoyer se faire foutre

hello *n.* allô **say hello** dire (le) bonjour

help *n.* aide, assistance, coup de main, secours **offer one's help** s'offrir **person who can be depended upon for help in one's old age** bâton de vieillesse, béquille de vieillesse

help *v.* aider, assister, donner la {une} main, donner un coup d'épaule, donner un coup de main, secourir **help o.s.** faire une passée, se prendre **help out** assister **help each other** s'assister **help give birth** délivrer **help o.s. or each other** s'aider **help s.o. start a venture** donner une partence (à qqn)

helper *n.* aide, aideur, assistant

helpful *adj.* utile, vaillant

helping *n.* bosse

helpless *adj.* sans défense **helpless or defenseless person** gribouille **be helpless** être au supplice **poor helpless person** gueux

helter-skelter *n.* (de) tribord et babord {bâbord}

hem *n.* ourlet, surjet **rolled hem** rabat **make a rolled hem** rabattre

hem *v.* ourler, border **hem in** cerner, entourer

hemline *n.* ourlet

hemorrhage *n.* hémorragie, perte de sang

hemorrhoid *npl.* **hemorrhoids** hémorroïdes

hemp *n.* manila **Indian hemp** herbe à serpent **southern water hemp** belle-dame

hemstitch *v.* picouer

hemstitching *n.* picot

hen *n.* cocotte, poule **hen cage** pondoire **hen house** poulailler **hen that sometimes lays its eggs in the field instead of in the henhouse** poulet d'herbe **bantam hen** poule pita **broody hen** couvasse, couveuse **Cornish hen** poule béneé, poule bénée **guinea hen** pintale, poule guinée **laying hen** pondeuse **marsh hen** râle bleu(e) / râle d'eau, râle **setting hen** couvasse, couveuse **speckled hen** poule gingas **wet hen** poule mouillée **young hen** poulette **fat hen or pullet** poularde **marsh water hen** râle poule d'eau **remove a hen from its roost** déjouquer **fighting cock or hen** gaïme

hence *adv.* donc, par conséquence

henceforth *adv.* à l'avenir

henhouse *n.* pondoire

hepatic *adj.* hépatique

her *poss.* le, son

her *pron.* elle, le, ça **of her** en **to her** le, lui

herb *n.* herbe *pl.* **aromatic herbs** herbages, herbailles

herbicide *n.* poison **treat with pesticide or herbicide** empoisonner

Hercules *n.* hercule

herd *n.* pied de bêtes, troupeau de bêtes, troupeau **herd of cattle** vacherie

herd *v.* pousser, toucher, parquer

herder *n.* pousseur de bêtes **cow herder** vacher **stock herder** toucheur

here *adv.* ici dans {dedans}, ici **here are** voici **here is** voici **here and there** bord ici bord là, de bric et de brac, ici et là **around here** ici, par ici **from here** d'ici **in here** ici dans {dedans}, ici dedans **over here** ici **right here** droite ici **I'm out of here** au diable la boutique **no one is here** la piste est sèque

here *interj.* tiens

hereabout *adv.* autour

hereditary *adj.* héréditaire

heredity *n.* hérédité

Hereford *n.* **Hereford cow** vache figure blanche

heresy *n.* hérésie

heretic *n.* hérétique

heritage *n.* succession, héritage

hermit *n.* ermite

hernia *n.* descente, effort, hernie

hero *n.* héros

heroine *n.* héroïne

heron *n.* héron **blue heron** héron bleu **great heron** grand héron **green-backed heron** cape-cape **Louisiana heron** aigrette câille **night heron** gros-bec, grosbec **great blue heron** grand héron, sans-joie **little green heron** cape-cape

herpes *n.* dartre

herpes zoster *n.* ceinture

hers *poss.* sien

herself *pron.* se, soi-même

hesitant *adj.* au {en} balan / sur le {un} balan

hesitate *v.* berlander, hésiter

hesitation *n.* hésitation

hex *n.* gris-gris **put a hex on s.o.** mettre {faire} un gris-gris

hey *interj.* hourra

hibiscus *n.* guimauve, étoile de Texas

hiccup *n.* hoquet *pl.* **hiccups** hoquet

hiccup *v.* hoquer

hick *n.* bitaco

hickory *n.* bois connu {inconnu}, hickory **hickory tree** noyer **water hickory** pacane amère **water hickory tree** pacanier amer

hidden *adj.* secret **hidden away from civilization** renfouillé **something that is hidden** cache

hide *n.* couenne, peau

hide *v.* cacher, s'ouacher, se cacher **hide the whip** cacher-fouet

hide-and-seek *n.* cachette, fête-à-cacher, raspaille

hide-and-seek *v.* cache-cache Nicolas, cache-est-faite / cache-et-faite / cache-fette / cachez-fête / caché-fête, cacher-fouet

hide-the-ring *v.* cache-cache (bin) la bague

hiding *n.* **hiding place** cachette

high *adj.* haut, fort **high noon** grand midi **high season** saison haute **high society** les grandes gens **high tide** haute marée **way up high** dans l'air du temps **get on one's high horse** monter sur ses grands chevaux

high *adv.* en l'air, haut **high up** en l'air, l'air du temps

high-paying *adj.* payant

high-strung *adj.* fraque **silly, foolish, high-strung woman** fraque

highest *adj.* **highest part** haut **the highest point of a pitched roof** pignon

highly *adv.* **think too highly of o.s.** se croire

highway *n.* chemin, grand chemin, routine à volonté **main highway** altère

hill *n.* butte, côte, côteau, colline, taille

hillbilly *n.* **loud, jazzy hillbilly music** tchinqui-tchinque

him *pron.* le, li, lui, ça **of him** en **to him** le, lui

himself *pron.* lui-même, se, soi-même

hind *n.* (d')en arrière

hinder *v.* empêcher

hindquarter *n.* cuisse, jarret *pl.* **hindquarters of a horse** croupe

hindrance *n.* accroche-cœur, canicroche, empêche, empêchement, enfarge, obstacle

hinge *n.* couplet, penture, pivot

hint *v.* **hint or suggest** mettre la puce à l'oreille (à qqn)

hip *n.* hanche **dislocate one's hip** déhancher **dislocate or break one's hip** s'éhancher **dislocate or break the hip of** éhancher

hire *n.* **drive for hire** toucher

hire *v.* engager **hire o.s. out** s'engager **hire work done on contract** contracter

hirer *n.* engagiste

his *poss.* le, sien, son

hiss *v.* siffler, siller

history *n.* histoire

hit *adj.* frappé

hit *n.* coup **lucky hit** trouve

hit *v.* aborder, assaper, battre, bosquer, coffrer, cogner, craquer une tape, flanquer un coup, frapper, maquemose, nioquer, roquer, sacrer, sangler, saquer, talocher, taper, tapocher, toquer, noquecer **hit o.s.** se cogner **hit together** nioquer **hit the road** prendre le chemin **hit with a broom** donner un coup de balai **hit s.o. like a ton of bricks** cogner qqn comme une bol de merde

hitch *n.* canicroche

hitch *v.* accrocher, atteler **hitch up** accrocher

hitched *adj.* **get hitched** s'emmancher

hitching-rack *n.* râtelier

hitting *n.* frappement

hive *n.* ruche **bee hive** caisse à mouches, chouce de miel, cloche, ruche *pl.* **hives** échauboulure

hoard *v.* amasser, entasser

hoarse *adj.* enroué, oppressé, égorgé **be hoarse** avoir la pépie **grow hoarse** s'enrouer **make hoarse** enrouer

hoarseness *n.* oppressement, oppression

hobble *n.* talbot, enfarge *pl.* **remove hobbles** désempêtrer

hobble *v.* empêtrer, talboter, enfarger

hobby *n.* passe-temps

hobo *n.* gipsie, hobo, TRAMP, traînard, vagabond **wander about as a hobo** traînailler les chemins

hockey *n.* hockey

hodgepodge *n.* gombo, jambalaya, méli-mélange

hoe *n.* pioche pour rayer, pioche à coton, pioche

hoe *v.* piocher

hoeing *n.* piochage

hoer *n.* piocheur

hog *n.* cochon, porc **hog lard** graisse (de) cochon **hog pen** parc à cochon(s) **hog wire** fil de fer à carreau, fil à {de} carreaux

hoghead *n.* **hoghead cheese** fromage de cochon, fromage de tête de cochon, fromage de tête

hogshead *n.* boucaut

hogwash *n.* gnognotte

hoist *n.* poulie, élévateur

hoist *v.* hisser **hoist o.s.** se hisser

hold *n.* grippe, prise, cale **catch hold of** gaffer **get hold of** accaparer, coller, escolter, s'atteler **grab hold of** cramponner **grab hold of each other** s'attraper **loosen one's hold** décramponner **catch a hold of** se gripper

hold *v.* contenir, tchambo, tenir **hold back** tenir **hold fast** cramponner, se cramponner, tenir bon **hold o.s.** se tenir **hold on** rester avec, tenir bon **hold onto** tenir **hold out** tenir **hold together** tenir ensemble **hold up** soutenir, tenir en l'air **hold a conversation** tenir une conversation **hold a grudge** en vouloir à, soigner un petit chien {veau} (pour qqn) **hold in regard** regarder **hold o.s. back** se retenir **hold o.s. up** se soutenir **hold out against** résister **hold s.t. against** avoir une dent contre qqn **hold on tightly to one another** se tenir comme un gris-gris **hold one's breath until blue in the face** pâmer, se pâmer **ability to hold** poigne **keep a vigil or hold a wake over** veiller

holder *n.* **candle holder** chandelier

hole *n.* ouverture, trou, troufignon **hole digger** terrier **hole in the ground supposedly made by an enraged bull** trou de taureau **mud hole** bourbier, bourbière **post hole digger** fouilleur de poteau, fouilleur de trous **develop a hole** percer **dig a hole** piquer un fossé **get a hole** percer **ditch or hole used to prepare bousillage** tâche **dig out a hole** arracher un trou *pl.* **get holes** se percer **having holes** troué **full of holes** criblé **pierce full of holes** cribler

holey *adj.* troué

holiday *n.* fête **major holiday or holy day** grande fête

holier-than-thou *adj.* **holier-than-thou person** sainte nitouche

holler *v.* crier, hurler

hollow *adj.* creux **hollow, deepened area** creusement

hollow *n.* **hollow in a prairie** trou de taureau

hollow *v.* **hollow out** creuser **hollow out again** recreusir

holy *adj.* béni, sacré, saint **holy land** terre sainte **holy oil** sainte huile **holy orders** ordre **holy picture** portrait saint

homage *n.* hommage

home *n.* casse, demeure, domicile, maison, résidence **home management** ménagerie **at home** à la maison **country home** châlet **leave home** déloger **nursing home** maison de santé, maison de vieux **reach home** se rendre chez soi **retirement home** maison de vieux **return home** se ranger **at one's home** chez soi **go back home** se renvoyer **old folks' home** maison de vieux **rebuild one's home** se rebâtir **stay at home** cabaner, rester chez soi, se cabaner **make one's home in a new place** se ranger **build o.s. a home** se bâtir **build o.s. a home or business** s'établir **spend the winter in one's seasonal home** camper

homebody *n.* **be a homebody** cabaner

homemade *adj.* de {du} pays

homesick *adj.* ennuyeux

homespun *adj.* fait au métier

homestead *n.* place

hominy *n.* sagamité

homosexual *n.* suceur

hon *n.* cher

honest *adj.* droite, franc, honnête, sincère

honest-to-god *adj.* positif

honestly *adv.* droitement, honnêtement

honesty *n.* honnêteté, propreté

honey *n.* miel, cher

honeybee *n.* abeille, mouche à miel

honeydew *n.* **honeydew melon** melon doux

honeyed *adj.* mielleux

honeymoon *n.* lune de miel

honeysuckle *n.* chèvrefeuille **bush honeysuckle** chèvrefeuille de France

honk *v.* corner

honor *n.* distinction, hommage, honneur **word of honor** parole d'honneur **confer an honor upon** décorer

honor *v.* glorifier, honorer **honor o.s.** s'honorer

honorable *adj.* d'honneur, honorable

honored *adj.* **feel honored** s'honorer

hood *n.* masque, top

hoodlum *n.* **hoodlum who breaks up dances by starting fights** casseur de bal

hoof *n.* ergot, sabot **hoof of a horse** sabot de cheval

hook *n.* accroche, accrochoire, anse, croc, crochet, hameçon, pendrioche, taquet **hook and eye closure** agrafe **fish hook** hameçon **grappling hook** grappin **snap hook** cobbe **stringer hook** alêne **catch with a hook** crocher **fasten with a hook** accrocher, barrer **place on a hook** engrucher **take down from a hook** décrocher

hook *v.* accrocher, agrafer, crocher, engrucher **hook on again** se raccrocher

hooked *adj.* accrochi, accroché après, corbin **get hooked** s'accrocher, s'addicter

hooker *n.* putain

hooking *n.* accrochage

hoop *n.* cercle **hoop skirt** malakoff **barrel hoop** frette **embroidery hoop** tambour **wooden or iron hoop that children roll with a stick** roulette

hoopnet *n.* carrelet

hooray *interj.* hourra

hoot *n.* **hoot owl** chouette

hop *v.* sautailler

hope *n.* espoir, espérance **hope chest** trousseau **beyond hope** fichu, foutu **lose hope** désespoirer **without hope** désespoiré, foutu comme Henri IV sur le Pont Neuf **live hope and die like an old dog** vivre en espoir et mourir comme un vieux chien **give up hope** décompter **there's no hope of recovery or recuperation** il y a pas de réchappe **cause to lose hope** désespoirer *pl.* **don't get your hopes up on that** fais-toi pas une gomme avec ça

hope *v.* avoir espoir (de), espérer, souhaiter

hoped *adj.* **it is to be hoped** c'est à souhaiter

hopelessness *n.* **expression of surprise, impatience, or hopelessness** sapristi

hopping *n.* sautaillement

hopscotch *n.* barène, marenne, pouscaille

horizon *n.* horizon

horn *n.* bourgo, cornet, trompette, corne, cornet **hollow horn** corne creuse **musical horn** cornet **blow a horn** corner **blow a conch shell horn** bourgonner *pl.* **horns** encornure **set of horns, antlers** panage **strike with the horns** cornailler

hornet *n.* guêpe, hornette **hornet's nest** potiche **veil surrounding a hornet's nest** robe **mean as a wasp or hornet** mauvaise comme une guêpe

horoscope *n.* horoscope

horrible *adj.* affreux, détestable, horrible, épouvantable

horror *n.* abomination, horreur

horse *n.* cheval, dada, yéya **horse race** course de chevaux **horse rider** cavalier **horse swapper** changeur de chevaux **horse breeder or trainer** maquillon **horse that paces or racks** racca **horse that is liable to kick** cheval traître **horse on the left in a draft team** gaucher **horse on the right in a draft team** droitier **balky horse** cheval rétif **bay horse** cheval bai **draft horse** cheval de tire, cheval normand **female horse** jument **midget horse** chacta **nonthoroughbred horse** cheval créole **race horse** cheval de course **runt horse** craquelin **saddle horse** cheval de selle **sluggish horse** cheval rosse **stud horse** égaron **ride a horse** RIDE à cheval **scrawny, underfed horse** raclin **fittings for horse or mule** harnais **ankle of a horse** joint **get on a horse** monter à cheval **get on one's high horse** monter sur ses grands chevaux **wild, untamed or unbroken horse** potre **don't look a gift horse in the mouth** cheval donné, regarde pas la bride **put the cart before the horse** mettre le bogui avant le cheval **person who is passionate about horse racing** coursier *pl.* **herd of horses** manade

horse *v.* **horse around** faire son couillon

horseback *n.* **come on horseback** venir à cheval **go on horseback** aller à cheval **ride on horseback** RIDE à cheval **travel on horseback** monter à cheval **go on horseback again** remonter à cheval

horsefly *n.* taon

horsehair *n.* **horsehair rope** cabresse

horseman *n.* cavalier, maquillon

horseplay *n.* jeu de chien

horseradish *n.* chou-navet

horseshoe *n.* fer à cheval {chevaux}, fer, plaque, sabot, soulier de cheval

horsetail *n.* prêle

hosanna *interj.* hosanna

hose *n.* **hose nozzle** arrosoir **water hose** pompe

hospital *n.* hôpital

hospitality *n.* **show hospitality** recevoir

host *n.* hostie

hostelry *n.* hôtellerie

hot *adj.* bouillant, chaud, enragé **hot sauce** sauce piquante **be hot** avoir chaud, faire chaud **burning hot** brûlant **stiflingly hot** achalant **be hot / hungry / cold / thirsty** avoir chaud / faim / froid / soif **get too hot** rôtir **excessively warm or hot** achalé **make uncomfortably warm or hot** achaler

hot-tempered *adj.* coléreux

hotel *n.* hôtel

hound *n.* taïaut **basset hound** chien basset

hound *v.* prêcher

hour *n.* heure **half hour** demi-heure **miles per hour** milles à l'heure **quarter of an hour** quart d'heure *pl.* **at all hours** à toutes heures

house *n.* cambuse, habitation, maison debout, maison **house builder** monteur de maisons **house moving** traînage de maison **house plan** plan de maison **house servant** domestique **house shoe** soulier de maison **house slipper** slip, soulier de maison **auction house** encan **boarding house** pensionnat **carriage house** remise **clean house** faire le ménage, nettoyer la maison **dirty house** nique à chien **hen house** poulailler **ice house** glacière **keep house** tenir (la) maison **laying house** pondoire **modest house** CAMP **muskrat house** butte à rat / butte de rat musqué **play house** jouer (à la) madame **potato house** pataterie **school house** maison d'école **isolated house in the prairie** cassine **at the house** sur la place (de) **haul a house** traîner une maison **large fine house** château **large, old house** bastringue **lock the house** encler la maison **move a house** traîner une maison **at the house of** (à) côté de, côté, chez **a man's house is his castle** charbonnier est maître chez lui **footing of a house** pilier de maison **layout of a house** plan de maison **add on to one's house** s'égrandir **get out of the house** découver **induce to leave the house** découver **go around the exterior of a house** faire le tour de la maison **a man is master of his own house** charbonnier est maître chez lui *pl.* **block of houses** bloc **group of farms or houses** côte

house *v.* loger

housecoat *n.* josé

housefly *n.* mouche

household *n.* ménage **household belongings** butin **household cloth** essuie **household duties** berdas **household projects** berdassement **break up a household or marriage** casser le ménage

housekeeper *n.* ménagère

housekeeping *n.* ménage, ménagerie

housepainter *n.* peintureur

housework *n.* berdas

hover *v.* planer, voltiger

how *adv.* comme, comment, que **how about that** comment tu crois? **how are things?** comment les haricots?, comment ça boulotte?, comment ça se brasse?, comment ça se plume? **how are you?** (comment) ça va?, comment les haricots?, comment vous êtes?, comment ça boulotte?, comment ça se brasse?, comment ça se plume?, comment ça va? **how's it going?** comment les affaires?, comment ça ballotte?, comment ça se brasse?, qui ça dit?, quoi ça dit? **how can it be** comment ça se peut **how in the world** comment dans le monde! **how are you? how are things?** comment le cabri apporte sa queue? **how are you?, how are things?** comment c'est / comment les cannes sont / comment les haricots?

however *adv.* cependant, par exemple, pour (de) même, pour même, pourtant, seulement

howl *n.* aboiement, hurlement

howl *v.* hurlailler, hurler, pialler, aboyer

howling *n.* aboiement, hurlement

hub *n.* moyeu **hub of a wheel** moyeu

Hubbard *n.* **loose dress widely known as a Mother Hubbard** blouse (volante)

hubbub *n.* bouri-boura, carnage, commerce, commérage, maquignonnage, sassaquoi

huddle *v.* niquer, s'amasser, se raccoquiller **huddle up** se raccoquiller

hug *n.* caresse, embrassade

hug *v.* embrasser **hug each other** s'embrasser, se caresser

huge archigrand

huge *adj.* abominable, falbana de, immense, monstre, un coquin de, vaste

hugeness *n.* énormité

hugging *n.* embrassement

huh *interj.* **huh?** hein

hull *n.* gosse, écorce, épelure, cale

hull *v.* savaner, écorcher **hull in a mortar** piler

hullabaloo *n.* baribara

hulling *n.* écorchement **hulling mill** moulin à piles

hum *n.* bourdonnement

hum *v.* bourdonner, chantonnier, ronfler, turluter

human *adj.* humain

human *n.* **any crude representation of a human figure** bonhomme

humanity *n.* humanité

humble *v.* abattre **humble o.s.** s'abaisser

humbug *n.* pacotille

humid *adj.* humide, lourd

humidity *n.* humidité

humiliate *v.* abaisser, humilier, mortifier, éhonter **humiliate o.s.** s'humilier

humiliating *adj.* humiliant

humiliation *n.* humiliation

humility *n.* humilité

humming *n.* bourdonnement, ronflement

hummingbird *n.* baron, colibri, kildi, oiseau-mouche / oiseau-à-mouche, oiseau de fleurs / z-oiseau-fleur /zozo-fleur, suce-fleur **ruby-throated hummingbird** oiseau de fleurs / z-oiseau-fleur /zozo-fleur

humor *n.* humeur, veine **in a good humor** rapiqué **person who is in a bad humor** bâton merdeux

humorist *n.* humoriste

humorous *adj.* farce

humus *n.* **patch of vegetation and humus that has not yet stabilized** flottant

hunchbacked *adj.* bossu, boscot

hunched *adj.* **hunched over** raccoquillé

hundred *n.* cent **about a hundred** centaine

hundredth *n.* **one hundredth** centième

hunger *n.* appétit, faim **die of hunger** crever de faim **satisfy one's hunger** s'appuyer l'estomac, se rassasier

hungry *adj.* **be hungry** affamer, avoir faim comme un chien, avoir faim, avoir la fale basse, avoir la fale creuse **go hungry** pâtir **make hungry** affamer **I got hungry** la faim m'a pris **cause to be hungry** affamer **be hot / hungry / cold / thirsty** avoir chaud / faim / froid / soif **one who is always hungry** crève-faim

hunt *n.* chasse **hunt at dusk or at night** guette **night hunt** passée **wild hunt, a mysterious racket, din, or chorus that passes through the night sky** chasse-galerie **late evening hunt** passée **go on a hunt** aller à la chasse **extend an afternoon hunt into the early evening** faire une passée **go on a late evening hunt** aller à la volée

hunt *v.* chasser, coucher, faire la chasse **hunt with dogs** courser **hunt at night with a light** chasser au flambeau **hunt at night with the aid of a powerful light** BULL-EYE

hunter *n.* chasseur **hunter's blind** but, talle **recreational hunter** SPORT *pl.* **group of hunters** piquet

hunting *n.* **hunting bag** carnassière, carrelet **hunting dog** chien de chasse **hunting season** chasse **go hunting** aller à la chasse **go hunting at dusk or at night** aller {partir} à la guette, faire la guette **go alligator hunting** aller aux caïmans **go squirrel hunting** aller aux écureuils

hurl *v.* lancer **hurl insults** tirer des chiques {une chique} **hurl o.s.** se darder

hurling *n.* lancement

hurricane *n.* cyclone, ouragan **hurricane lamp** lampe à globe

hurried *adj.* pressé

hurry *n.* dépêche, presse **in a hurry** hourri-hourra, pressé, à la dépêche, à la presse **leave in a hurry** haler ses caniques **one is impatient, anxious, in a hurry** le temps dure (à qqn de faire qqch)

hurry *v.* dépêcher, galoper, grouiller, mousser, s'appresser, s'emparer, se dégager, se grouiller, se hâter, se presser **hurry up** dépêche-toi!, grouille ton casaquin {tchu}, hourra, s'appresser, se dépêcher, se presser

hurt *adj.* **get hurt** attraper du mal

hurt *n.* blessure, bobo, tort

hurt *v.* avoir du mal, blesser, défroqueter, faire (du) bobo, faire (du) mal **hurt o.s.** s'abîmer, se blesser, se faire (du) mal **hurt o.s. badly** se massacrer **hurt or break one's back** s'éreinter

hurtful *adj.* offensive

hurting *adj.* escran

husband *n.* homme, mari, vieux, époux **future husband** prétend-mari, prétendu **legal husband** légitime **my husband** mon vieux

hush *v.* faire poteau, taire

husk *n.* gosse, paille à {de} maïs, paille, épelure **corn husk** robe de maïs, robe

husk *v.* écaler, effeuiller

husked *adj.* **be shucked, husked, peeled** s'écaler

husky *adj.* membré comme une tortue de rosée

hut *n.* ajoupa, cabanage, maison d'arbres

hyacinth *n.* hyacinthe **water hyacinth** herbe du bayou, jacinthe d'eau, lilé

hybrid *adj.* bâtard, abâtardi

hybridize *v.* abâtardir

hydrangea *n.* hortensia

hydrogen *n.* hydrogène

hydrophobia *n.* hydrophobie, rage

Hyena *n.* Bouki

hymn *n.* cantique

hyperactive *adj.* **be mischievous or hyperactive** avoir le diable au corps

hypnotist *n.* magnatiseur

hypnotize *v.* hypnotiser, magnatiser

hypocrisy *n.* hypocrisie

hypocrite *n.* couteau à deux tranchants, hypocrite, sainte nitouche **hypocrite who appears virtuous** pain de sucre

hypocritical *adj.* en dessous, par en-dessous

hypodermic *adj.* **hypodermic needle** aiguille

hyponotize *v.* charmer

hysteria *n.* hystérie

hysterical *adj.* hystérique

I

i *npl.* **dot one's i's** mettre les points sur les i

I *pron.* je, moi **I spy** raspaille

ibis *n.* croche **white ibis** bec-croche

ice *n.* glace **ice box** glacière **ice chest** cooler **ice cream** crème à la glace / crème glacée, crème **ice house** glacière **ice pick** pique **ice tongs** pinces à glace **ice cream cone** cornet de crème, SAY-SO de crème, SAY-SO **ice cream freezer** baratte, FREEZER, sabotière **homemade ice cream** crème de sabotière **put on ice** glacer **served with ice cream** à la mode **thick layer of ice over a body of water** pont de glace

ice *v.* glacer, blanchir

icicle *n.* chandelle de glace

icy *adj.* glacé, glaçant

idea *n.* avis, idée, opinion, pensée, sentiment **foolish idea** chimère **sudden idea or whim** estampique **unrealistic idea or plan** rêve de poule **get the idea** prendre idée **have an idea** se faire une idée

ideal *adj.* idéal

identical *adj.* même, pareil comme, pareil

identify *v.* identifier, placer

identity *n.* identité

idiosyncrasy *n.* arnicrot

idiot *n.* attrape-mouches / attrape à mouches, biorque, calebasse, couillon d'eau douce, couillon, embêté, idiot, imbécile, sot, tchu

idiotic *adj.* coucou, idiot, imbécile

idle *adj.* **be idle** flânailler, flâner, LOAF, être à rien faire

idle *v.* lingir, paresser

idler *n.* câlin

if *conj.* en cas que, qui, si c'est que, si **if ever** si jamais **if only** si seulement **if there's a way** s'il y a moyen **as if** comme si **what if** aussi bien que

if *npl.* **there's no ifs, ands or buts** il y a pas de catherine

ignis fatuus *n.* feu follet

ignite *v.* prendre en feu, s'allumer

ignorance *n.* ignorance **used to express ignorance** ha

ignorant *adj.* ignorant, malinstruit **ignorant, uneducated, insignificant or foolish person** cape-cape **rustic, uncultured, uncouth, boorish, ignorant person** gui-gui

ill *adj.* malade **ill will** malveillance **ill at ease** mal à son aise **become ill** prendre le lit **look ill** avoir une mine de chien **extreme ill will** rancune **speak ill of** parler mal de **sick, ill, unhealthy person** malade **woman of ill repute** bordel, pas-bonne **if you speak ill of others, it comes back to haunt you** crache dans l'air, ça tombe sur le (bout du) nez

ill-advised *adj.* maladvisé

ill-bred *adj.* mal élevé / malélevé

ill-humored *adj.* **be ill-humored** être dans ses feurdaines **be cross or ill-humored, grouchy** être de {en} travers

ill-intended *adj.* malintentionné

ill-intentioned *adj.* malintentionné

ill-mannered *adj.* mal élevé / malélevé, malinstruit **rough, ill-mannered person** cheval habillé (en zinc) **vulgar, ill-mannered person** bitaco **be crude or ill-mannered** avoir pas de délicatesse

ill-natured *adj.* grognard

ill-tempered *adj.* grichoux, grognard, malpatient, malému, suspect **ill-tempered girl** picouette **mean, grouchy, ill-tempered person** bourreau **obnoxious or ill-tempered person** crotte

illegal *adj.* défendu, BOOTLEG

illegitimate *adj.* **illegitimate child** œuf de caïman {carencro}, bâtard, enfant inconnu, poulet d'herbe

illiterate *adj.* illettré
illness *n.* mal, maladie
illuminate *v.* éclairer
illuminated *adj.* éclairé
illumination *n.* éclairage
illustration *n.* illustration
image *n.* image, portrait **he is the image of his father** il est le portrait de son père
imaginable *adj.* imaginable
imagination *n.* fantaisie, imagination
imagine *v.* figurer, imaginer, inventionner, s'imaginer, se faire une idée, se figurer **imagine o.s. in a certain way** se voir **can you imagine it?** tonnerre de foutre
imbecile *n.* couillon d'eau douce, couillon, dinde (d'inde), estragot, idiot, imbécile, luron, riquiqui
imitate *v.* copier, imiter, moquer
imitation *n.* imitation
immaculate *adj.* **immaculate conception** immaculée conception
Immaculate *adj.* **the Immaculate Conception** l'Immaculée Conception
immediately aussitôt
immediately *adv.* carrément, directement, droite, droitement, immédiatement, raide, tout de suite / toutesuite, tout de suite, tout droite
immense *adj.* falbana de, immense
immerse *v.* caler, plonger **immerse in disinfectant solution** baigner
immersion *n.* immersion **immersion school** école d'immersion
immigrant *n.* immigrant
immigrate *v.* immigrer
immigration *n.* immigration
immodest *adj.* impur **do nasty things or immodest acts** faire des vilaines choses
immoral *adj.* sale **immoral person** saloperie **immoral or indecent act** cochonnerie
immorality *n.* malpropreté, saloperie **commit immorality** faire des saletés
immortal *adj.* immortel
immortality *n.* immortalité
impair *v.* gâter
impassable *adj.* impassable
impasse *n.* manche
impatience *n.* impatienterie **expression of surprise, impatience, or hopelessness** sapristi
impatient *adj.* impatient, impatienté, malpatient **be impatient** manquer un pain dans sa fournaise **make impatient** patienter **one is impatient, anxious, in a hurry** le temps dure (à qqn de faire qqch)
impede *v.* gêner, mettre des bâtons dans la roue {les roues}
impediment *n.* accroche-cœur, canicroche, empêche, enfarge *pl.* **put impediments or obstacles in the way of one's success** mettre des bâtons dans la roue {les roues}
imperfect *adj.* imparfait
impetigo *n.* feu sauvage
implement *n.* outil *pl.* **implements** équipage, équipement
implore *v.* prier, prêcher, supplier
impolite *adj.* impoli, mal élevé / malélevé, mal élevé
import *v.* importer
importance *n.* conséquence, importance **be of importance** compter **man of importance** homme de conséquence **person of importance or renown** personnage **it's of no importance** peu importe **of little consequence or importance** (ça compte pas plus qu') un pet dans un ouragan **person of wealth or importance** BIG BOY
important *adj.* grand, grave, gros, important, notable **important person** gros chat, gros chien **act important** faire le {son} grand / faire la grande **most important** principal **rich or important person** gros dos **no longer count as important** compter plus z-herbes **act as if one is more important than one really is** faire le {son} grand / faire la grande
impose *v.* abuser, imposer, sangler, faire un abus (à qqn)
imposing *adj.* redoutable **imposing, officious person** bouledou **imposing and noisy person** sassaquoi
impossible *adj.* impossible **it's impossible** il y a pas (de) moyen de {pour}
imposter *n.* imposteur
impotent *adj.* clair
impoverish *v.* appauvrir, empauvrir
impoverished *adj.* pauvre, à plate **become impoverished** s'empauvrir **one who is impoverished** pauvre
impregnate *v.* embêter, remplir
impress *v.* impressionner
impression *n.* impression **make an impression on** impressionner **give a bad impression** faire mauvaise mine **give an odd impression** faire drôle **make a certain impression** se présenter **give a particular impression when heard** sonner **do s.t. in order to make a good impression** faire des ricracs
impressive *adj.* impressionnant
imprint *n.* impression, étampe
imprint *v.* graver, imprimer, étamper
imprinting *n.* étampage
imprison *v.* emprisonner
imprisonment *n.* emprisonnement
improper *adj.* indisable, mal-à-propos, mal à propos **be improper, out of the way, uncalled for** avoir pas de place
improperly *adv.* mal
improve *v.* abonnir, bonifier, improuver, perfectionner, réformer, s'abonnir, raugmenter, se refaire **improve o.s.** se bonifier, se perfectionner **improve in health** se refaire
improvement *n.* improuvement, progrès
improvise *v.* patenter, ramancher

imprudence *n.* imprudence
imprudent *adj.* risqueux **careless or imprudent act** imprudence
impudence *n.* effronterie, organe
impudent *adj.* effronté **be impudent** rebiffer **you are impudent** tu crois (que) t'as de la barbe et des crochets **you are acting too impudent** c'est l'heure de voir à couper tes culottes
impudently *adv.* effrontément
impulse *n.* caprice
impulsive *adj.* capricieux, prime
impure *adj.* hâcre, impur **person of mixed blood or impure race** sang-mêlé
in *adv.* dedans
in *prep.* après, dans, dedans, en dedans, en, à, dans, dedans, en, à
in-law *npl.* **in-laws** beaux-parents
inappropriate *adj.* mal-à-propos, mal à propos
inasmuch *conj.* **inasmuch as** puisque
inattention *n.* manque d'attention
inattentive *adj.* galfat **inattentive, clumsy person** galfat
incapable *adj.* incapable **incapable or incompetent person** zéro
incarcerate *v.* emprisonner
incense *n.* encens **perfume with incense** encenser
incense *v.* encenser
incensing *n.* encensement
incentive *n.* encouragement
incessantly *adv.* à p'us finir
inch *n.* pouce *pl.* **twelve inches** pied
incision *n.* coupure **make an incision in** inciseler
incite *v.* assaisonner, enticher, instiguer, provoquer
incitement *n.* instigation
inclination *n.* gré, penchant, tendance, tournure **have a bad bent or inclination** avoir une mauvaise tournure
incline *n.* pente
incline *v.* pencher
inclined *adj.* assodié, disposé, en pente, à pic
include *v.* comprendre, compter, includer
included *adj.* compris, enrabatan **be included in** transférer
income *n.* rente, revenu
incompetent *adj.* **incapable or incompetent person** zéro
incomprehensible *adj.* incomprenable
inconsequential *adj.* pouilleux
inconsistently *adv.* (de) tribord et babord {bâbord}
inconsolable *adj.* désolé **be inconsolable** se désoler
inconstant *adj.* changeable, changeant
inconvenience *v.* embarrasser
inconvenienced *adj.* embarrassé
inconvenient *adj.* malcommode, à (la) désamain / à la démain / au désamain **be inconvenient** s'adonner mal
incorporate *v.* incorporer
incorrect *adj.* mauvais, croche
incorrigible *adj.* détestable, pirate **incorrigible person** enfant terrible
increase *n.* augmentation
increase *v.* augmenter, hausser, monter, raugmenter, s'augmenter, se refaire **increase one's production** forcer **increase the noise of by accelerating** fronner
incredible *adj.* incroyable
incubate *v.* couver
incubating *n.* couvage
incubator *n.* couveuse
incur *v.* contracter **incur expenses** faire des dépenses
incurable *adj.* engravé, inguérissable
indebt *v.* endetter **indebt o.s.** s'endetter
indebted *adj.* endetté
indebtedness *n.* endettement
indecency *n.* saloperie
indecent *adj.* sale **indecent person** saloperie **indecent act or utterance** coquaillerie **do indecent things** faire des saloperies **immoral or indecent act** cochonnerie
indecently *adv.* cochon
indecision *n.* hésitation
indecisive *adj.* folâtre
indeed *adv.* bien, foutûment, voir
indented *adj.* encavé
independence *n.* indépendance
Independence *n.* **the Declaration of Independence** Déclaration d'indépendance
independent *adj.* indépendant **independent person** DON'T-CARE
index *n.* index **index finger** doigt torchant
Indian *adj.* **Indian summer** été des Indiens
Indian *n.* **Indian territory** territoire des Indiens **American Indian** indien, Indien, sauvage **Cherokee Indian** chéroquis **half Indian** à moitié sauvage
Indianhead *n.* **Indianhead cloth** indienne
indicate *v.* faire signe, indiquer, montrer
indication *n.* apercevance, indication, signe, symptôme, marque
indictment *n.* charge
indifferent *adj.* bambara **be indifferent** s'en fricasser
indigence *n.* pauvreté, pauvrie
indigestion *n.* indigestion
indigo *adj.* indigo
indigo *n.* **indigo plant** café sauvage
indiscreet *adj.* bagueulard
indiscrete *adj.* indisable
indiscretion *n.* imprudence
individual *adj.* personnel
individual *n.* chrétien, individu, individuel, monde, paroissien, personne **strange or eccentric individual** abricot
indolent *adj.* en mort fausse
induce *v.* **induce to leave the house** découver

induct *v.* installer
indulge *v.* catiner **indulge in** s'en mettre à **indulge a passion** se donner une bosse **indulge freely in** faire abus de **indulge in reveries** jongler
indulgence *n.* indulgence
indulgent *adj.* indulgent
industrial *adj.* industriel
industrious *adj.* travaillant
industry *n.* industrie
inebriated *adj.* camphré **be inebriated** être dans son vinaigre **slightly inebriated** tchac
inept *adj.* **inept at** malpris à
inexpensive *adj.* (à) bon marché
inexperienced *adj.* vert
infallible *adj.* infaillible
infamy *n.* honte
infancy *n.* enfance
infant *n.* bébé, enfant, poupon
infantile *adj.* enfantile **infantile paralysis** fièvre à vingt-quatre heures
infantry *n.* infanterie
infatuated *adj.* entiché **become infatuated** s'amouracher, s'enticher
infatuation *n.* entichement, tocate
infect *v.* infecter
infected *adj.* **become infected** s'empester
infection *n.* gangrène, humeur, infection, pourriture
infectious *adj.* contagieux
infer *v.* déduire
inferior *adj.* chacta
infernal *adj.* infernal
infest *v.* empester, infester
infested *adj.* criblé
infidelity *n.* infidélité
infinite *adj.* infini
infirm *adj.* esclopé
inflamed *adj.* enflammé **be inflamed** se enflammer
inflammation *n.* enflammation, inflammation **inflammation of the edge of the eyelid** cire
inflammatory *adj.* enflammant
inflate *v.* gonfler, pomper, souffler **inflate o.s.** se souffler
inflation *n.* gonflage
influence *n.* influence
influence *v.* affecter, influencer, porter sur **attempt to influence** cabaler
influenced *adj.* **easily influenced person** toutout
influenza *n.* FLU
inform *v.* avertir, faire acconnaître, informer, renseigner **inform beforehand** avertir d'avance **inform o.s.** se renseigner
informality *n.* informalité
information *n.* avertissement, information, renseignement **get information** prendre des informations, s'aviser **new information** nouvelle **useful bit of information** TIP
informed *adj.* au courant, informé **well informed** posté **be informed of** savoir **be wise, informed** avoir le nez long
informer *n.* informeur
infringe *v.* casser
infuriate *v.* partir son feu
ingenious *adj.* inventeur
ingest *v.* prendre
ingrain *v.* engraver
ingredient *n.* ingrédient
inhabitable *adj.* habitable, vivable
inhabitant *n.* habitant
inhalation *n.* inspiration
inhale *v.* aspirer, inspirer **inhale and exhale** respirer
inhaling *n.* **take by inhaling** renifler
inherit *v.* hériter
inheritance *n.* héritage, héritance, héritation
initiate *v.* baptiser **initiate a process** faire des démarches
inject *v.* injecter
injection *n.* injection, SHOT
injure *v.* blesser, défroqueter, faire (du) bobo, émecter **injure o.s.** s'abîmer **injure the testicles of** écouiller **shoot, injure, or kill by shooting** tirer
injury *n.* blessure, détriment
injustice *n.* crime, injustice
ink *n.* encre **ink pot** encrier **ink spot** barbot **ink well** encrier
inlet *n.* anse, manchac, raccroc
inmate *n.* forcien
inn *n.* hôtellerie
innards *npl.* dedans, débris, fressures
inning *n.* manche
innocence *n.* innocence, pureté
innocent *adj.* ignorant, innocent, pur, vert **one who is innocent** innocent **one who pretends to be innocent** sainte nitouche
inoculate *v.* vacciner
inquire *v.* demander, questionner, s'informer, s'émoyer, se renseigner
inquirer *n.* questionneur
inquisitiveness *n.* curiosité
insane *adj.* coucou, extravagué, fou **insane person** fou **become insane** perdre la carte
insanity *n.* folie
inscription *n.* inscription
insect *n.* bébête, bétaille, bête, insecte, loulou *pl.* **destroyed or damaged by worms or insects** piqué
insecticide *n.* poison
inseparable *adj.* inséparable
insert *v.* **insert upright** caler
inside *adv.* dedans, là-dedans
inside *n.* dedans **inside out** à l'envers / à renvers **from the inside** par endedans *pl.* **insides** dedans
inside *prep.* dans, dedans, en dedans
insignificant *adj.* **insignificant person** pienque, péteur,

tchacafané **insignificant thing** pet sec **insignificant person or thing** pacotille **become insignificant** tourner en eau de boudin **rather insignificant person** queue de la comète **ignorant, uneducated, insignificant or foolish person** cape-cape

insist *v.* insister, obstiner **insist on firmly** obstiner

insistence *n.* insistance

insistent *adj.* demandant

insolence *n.* insolence

insolent *adj.* insolent

inspect *v.* CHECK, examiner, inspecter

inspection *n.* inspection **official visitation or inspection** visitation

inspector *n.* inspecteur

inspiration *n.* inspiration, édification

inspire *v.* inspirer

instable *adj.* **instable person** changeoteur

install *v.* installer **install o.s.** s'installer **install the wooden struts in a wall** bâtonner

installation *n.* installation

installment *n.* acompte, installation, installement

instance *n.* **for instance** comme

instant *n.* instant, moment **this instant** à l'instant

instantly *adv.* raide, tout droite, à l'instant

instead *adv.* **instead of** ailleurs de, au lieu (de), place de, plutôt que {de} / plutôt de, à la place de

instigate *v.* instiguer, provoquer

instigation *n.* instigation

instigator *n.* instigateur

instinct *n.* instinct

instinctive *adj.* instinctif

instinctively *adv.* machinalement

institute *n.* institution

institution *n.* institution **financial institution** banque

instruct *v.* enseigner, instruire, rencharger

instruction *n.* direction, instruction **catechetical instruction** catéchisme

instructor *n.* enseignant, enseigneur, instructeur

instrument *n.* instrument **musical instrument** instrument, musique, tchinqui-tchinque **percussive instrument** bastringue **musical instrument used to keep time** baloche **sharp or pointed instrument** dard

insufferable *adj.* insouffrable, maudit, pénible **insufferable child** pirate

insulate *v.* INSULATE

insulation *n.* insulation

insult *n.* affront, bagueulage, injure, insulte, outrage **veiled insult** chique *pl.* **hurl insults** tirer des chiques {une chique} **used to construct insults** espèce

insult *v.* abuser, affronter, agoniser, apostropher, insulter, outrager

insulting *adj.* abusif, insultant, offensive, outrageux

insurable *adj.* assurable

insurance *n.* assurance **insurance company** compagnie d'assurances **insurance policy** police **insurance or public assistance** bénéfice

insure *v.* assurer

insured *adj.* **insured party** assuré

insurer *n.* assureur

integrity *n.* honneur, honnêteté

intellect *n.* intelligence

intelligence *n.* intelligence

intelligent *adj.* intelligent, smatte comme une fève plate, smatte comme une tomate **be intelligent** avoir (une) bonne idée **not intelligent** pas bien développé, smatte comme une fève plate **be not intelligent** être peu intelligent **insult used for s.o. arrogant or not intelligent** c'est pas toi qu'es le taureau du côteau

intend *v.* avoir idée de, vouloir

intended *adj.* à **made or intended esp. for a given purpose** exprès

intense *adj.* gros

intensify *v.* **used to intensify or qualify another noun** un coquin de

intensity *n.* force

intent *n.* intention **with evil intent** malicieusement

intention *n.* dessein, idée, intention, plan **have the intention** PLAN **state one's mind or intention** se déclarer *pl.* **expose one's intentions** se dévoiler

intentionally *adv.* par exprès

intentioned *adj.* intentionné

inter *v.* enterrer

interbreed *v.* croiser

intercede *v.* intercéder

Intercoastal *n.* **Intercoastal Canal** INTERCOASTAL

intercourse *n.* **sexual intercourse** coquage **have intercourse with** piquer **have sexual intercourse** avoir des relations

interdict *n.* interdit

interdiction *n.* interdiction

interest *n.* intérêt **interest rates** intérêt **bear interest** rapporter **take interest** s'intéresser **yield interest** rapporter **take a keen interest** s'ambitionner *pl.* **know where one's interests lie** savoir et où son pain est beurré

interest *v.* intéresser, tenter

interested *adj.* intéressé **be interested** s'intéresser **no longer interested** dégoûté

interesting *adj.* intéressant, intéressé **unusual and interesting character** pistolet à deux manches, pistolet

interfere *v.* mettre son nez dans le bol, mettre son nez dans son bol, méler son grain de sel, pignocher **interfere in** se mêler dans

interior *n.* dedans, intérieur

intermarriage *n.* entremariage

interment *n.* enterrement

intermingle *v.* mêler, s'entremêler

international *adj.* international

internode *n.* **internode of sugar cane** jointure de canne
interpret *v.* interpréter, traduire
interpreter *n.* interpréteur, interprète
interrogate *v.* bûcher
interrogative *adj.* **sentence-initial interrogative marker** est-ce que
interrupt *v.* couper la conversation {le discours}, rembarrer, désoccuper **interrupt or correct in conversation** reprendre
intersection *n.* quatre-chemins, croisée
interval *n.* intervalle
interview *n.* interview
intestate *adj.* intestat
intestine *n.* intestin **large intestine** la tripe du nord **pig's intestine** chaudin *pl.* **intestines** boyau, tripe **intestines used as food** tripe
intimate *adj.* familier, intime **be intimate** se coller sur
intimidate *v.* BULLDOZE, intimider
into *prep.* dans, en
intolerable *adj.* insouffrable
intoxicate *v.* soûler, tchaquer
intoxicated *adj.* bite, camphré, piqué, tchac, TIGHT **become intoxicated** prendre une guinguette
intoxicating *adj.* soûlant
intractable *adj.* pirate
intrigue *n.* micmac **make use of intrigue and dishonesty in conducting a political campaign** cabaler **one who makes use of intrigue or deception** cabaleur
intrigued *adj.* intrigué
introduce *v.* introduire, pomper, présenter, baptiser **introduce o.s.** s'introduire, se présenter
introduction *n.* introduction, présentation
intrude *v.* se fourrer
invent *v.* créer, forger, inventer, inventionner, patenter, ramancher, se forger
invention *n.* invention
inventive *adj.* inventeur
inventor *n.* créateur, forgeur
inventory *n.* inventaire
invest *v.* invester
investigate *v.* explorer, investiguer **investigate carefully** passer au peigne fin
investigation *n.* investigation, recherche
investigator *n.* **federal investigator** fédéral
invigorate *v.* émouver
invigorated *adj.* frais comme un lapin
invisible *adj.* invisible **invisible person** homme invisible
invitation *n.* invitation, TREAT **enter without an invitation or permission** casser
invite *v.* inviter **invite again** rinviter **invite each other** s'inviter
inviting *adj.* invitant
invocation *n.* invocation
invoice *n.* BILL
invoke *v.* invoquer
involve *v.* embourber
involved *adj.* **involved in** connecté avec **be involved in** être emmêlé dans **get involved with** s'occuper avec **get deeply involved** s'empêtrer **be deeply involved in** être embourbé dans **get o.s. deeply involved** s'embarrasser, s'emberner
iodine *n.* iodine **tincture of iodine** teinture
iris *n.* **Louisiana iris** glaie **wild iris** glaie
irk *v.* brûler
iron *n.* fer **branding iron** fer à marquer, étampe **cast iron** fonte **clothing iron** fer à repasser **grid iron** gril **pressing iron** fer à repasser **scrap iron** ferail **soldering iron** fer à souder **made of iron** en fer **piece of iron** ferrement **galvanized or corrugated iron** zinc **piece of junk iron** ferail *pl.* **have too many irons in the fire** avoir trop de fers au feu
iron *v.* lisser le linge, repasser **iron out wrinkles** défroncer
ironclad *adj.* ferré
ironic *adj.* **ironic or affectionate term for a person** coco
ironing *n.* repassage **ironing board** planche à repasser
ironweed *n.* tête de femme
irremediable *adj.* engravé
irresponsible *adj.* frou-frou
irreverence *n.* irrévérence
irreverent *adj.* irrévérent
irrigate *v.* arroser, pomper
irritable *adj.* chacta, chocatif
irritate *v.* achaler, agacer, brûler, chicoter, envelimer, foutumasser, irriter, tchincailler, échauffer, énerver
irritated *adj.* achalé, bouqué **get irritated** s'énerver
irritating *adj.* achalant, agaçant, enrageant, énervant
irritation *n.* agacerie **cause irritation in** irriter **having an irritation of the skin** échauffé **used to indicate disgust or irritation** ache **expression used to show surprise, irritation or anger** fils de chien {garce / putain} / fils de putain de bordel {garce}, fils de monstre {pistache / poteau} / fils de poteau de barrière
ischuria *n.* tranchement d'urine
isinglass *n.* caoutchouc
island *n.* île, îlette
isle *n.* île
Isle *n.* **inhabitant of Grand Isle** grandîlier
isolate *v.* quarantiner
isolated *adj.* renfouillé
issue *n.* copie, question
it *n.* **it in children's games** cornoyo
it *pron.* alle, il, le, li, lui, ça, il **it's time** c'est temps **from it** en **of it** en **on it** là-dessus **that's it** c'est justement, c'est ça, ça y est **to it** le, lui
Italian *adj.* **the Italian language** italien
Italian *n.* italien
itch *n.* démangeaison, gale, grattelle *pl.* **get itches** prendre des démangeaisons
itch *v.* démanger
itchy *adj.* galeux

item *n.* article *pl.* **cheap items** bagatelle
its *poss.* le, son
itself *pron.* lui-même, se, soi-même
ivy *n.* **poison ivy** herbe à la puce

J

jab *v.* jaquer **jab with an elbow** foutre un coup de coude
jabber *v.* cacasser, charlanter, jacasser
jabot *n.* jabot
jack *n.* levier, JACK, valet **jack of clubs** mistchoug, mistigri **car jack** JACK **crevalle jack** JACK crevalle **one-eyed jack** mistigri **rope jack** tarabi **lift with a jack** JACK
jack *v.* JACK
jack-plane *n.* varlope
jackass *n.* bourriquet, âne
jacket *n.* capot, jaquette, josé **yellow jacket** guêpe rouge, guêpe **loose outer jacket** JUMPER
jackfish *n.* JACK crevalle
jackpot *n.* pot
jackrabbit *n.* lièvre du Texas
jackstone *n.* JACK
jaguar *n.* jaguar
jail *n.* prison, calabousse **put in jail** emprisonner, mettre en prison
jalopy *n.* chabraque, tchacara
jam *n.* confiture **fig jam** confiture de figues **toe jam** cambouille **traffic jam** embouteillage
jam *v.* coincer
jamb *n.* encadrement, quille
jambalaya *n.* jambalaya
jammed *adj.* cordé **get jammed or caught** se coincer
jamming *n.* coincement
janitor *n.* balayeur
January *n.* janvier
Japan *n.* Japon
Japanese *adj.* japonais **Japanese person** Japon
jar *n.* cruche, jarre **canning jar** bocal, flacon, pobon **coffee jar** cafetière **earthen jar** dame-jeanne, jarre en terre **fruit jar** pobon **preserve jar** flacon **preserving jar** pobon **preserving jar rubber** élastique **pot or jar from which syrup or honey is served** compotier *pl.* **put into jars** enjarrer
jargon *n.* argot, jargon
jasmine *n.* jasmin **Cape jasmine** jasmin **night-blooming jasmine** jasmin de nuit **night-blooming jasmine flower** galant de nuit **night-blooming jasmine plant** galant de nuit
jaundice *n.* jaunisse
jaw *n.* mâchoire **lower jaw** jaboune
jawbone *n.* mâchoire
jawbreaker *n.* JAW-BREAK
jay *n.* geai
jaybird *n.* geai, pienque
jazz *n.* jazz **jazz band** JAZZ BAND
jealous *adj.* jaloux, envieux **be jealous** jalouser
jealousy *n.* jalouserie
jeer *v.* **jeer at** se moquer
jell *v.* figer
jello *n.* gélatine
jelly *n.* confiture, gelée, glue, marmalade **jelly bean** crotte de poule
jellyfish *n.* glue, quatre-z-yeux **stinging jellyfish** glue-qui-brûle
jenny *n.* âne
Jeremiad *n.* jérémiade
jerk *n.* champignon
jerk *v.* ballotter
jersey *n.* jersey
Jersey *n.* **Jersey cow** jersey
jessamine *n.* **orange jessamine** jasmin d'orange
Jesuit *adj.* jésuite
Jesuit *n.* Jésuite
Jesus *n.* Jésus-Christ **Jesus Christ** Jésus-Christ
jet *n.* jet
Jew *n.* Juif **Jew's harp** trompe **wandering Jew** juif-errant **Wandering Jew** Juif errant
jewel *n.* bijou
jeweler *n.* horloger
jewelry *n.* bijouterie **jewelry shop** boutique de bijouterie **jewelry store** bijouterie **piece of jewelry** dorure
Jewish *adj.* hébreu, juif **Jewish Passover** Pâques **Jewish person** Juif
jig *n.* gigue, valsovienne **dance a jig** giguer
jig *v.* giguer
jiggle *v.* actionner
jingle *n.* **jingle bell** cloche
jinx *n.* condjo, guigne **have a jinx** avoir la guigne
jinx *v.* donner un coundja à, faire un condjo contre, mettre un condjo sur
jittery *adj.* nerveux
job *n.* devoir, fonction, job, métier, ouvrage, position, travail, tâche **job done badly or carelessly** bachoucta d'ouvrage **messy job** débauchage **do a good job** faire un bon job **do a shitty job** faire fritche **loaf on the job** gournoter **sleep on the job** dormir sur un rôti **it will do the job** ça va faire l'affaire **move from one place or job to another** transférer **it will do the trick, do the job** ça va faire l'affaire *pl.* **work odd jobs** jober **one who does odd jobs** jobeur
jockey *n.* cavalier, kêtch, maquillon, toucheur de cheval, toucheur
jockey *v.* maquillonner
John *n.* **Saint John the Baptist** St. Jean Baptiste

johns *npl.* **long johns** longues-jambes

join *v.* joindre, s'associer, marier **join together** macorner, s'unir, unir **join in pairs** accoupler **join end to end** abouter, henter, rabouter **join in a pair** apairer

joint *n.* henture, joint, jointure, maille, nocoyau, joint, nœud **gambling joint** cantique **scarf joint** henture **soldered joint** soudure *pl.* **having stiff or sore muscles or joints** escran

jointed *adj.* jointé

joist *n.* lambourde, madrier, solive, soliveau

joke *n.* blague, bêtise, couillonade, farce, histoire farce, jeu, JOKE, malice, niche **joke teller** farceur **practical joke** coup, niche **crack a joke** craquer une farce **play a joke, trick, or prank** faire {jouer} une malice **play a practical joke** faire des canicroches *pl.* **crack jokes** dire des bêtises {farces} **play jokes** faire des bêtises **tell jokes** bêtiser, faire des farces **tell dirty jokes** dire des cochonneries **tell dirty stories or coarse jokes** dire des cochonneries {saletés / saloperies}

joke *v.* badiner, blaguer, bêtiser, craquer, JOKE, moquer **joke around** JOKE

joker *n.* couillon, maudit, mistchoug, mistigri, mouche **practical joker** bêtiseur, canaille

jokester *n.* blagueur, farceur

joking *n.* couillonade, couillonnerie, folerie, menterie

jolt *n.* secouage, secouement, secousse

jolt *v.* secouer

jolting *n.* secouage, secouement

jostle *v.* bousculer **jostle each other** se bousculer

jostled *adj.* **get jostled around noisily** se berdasser

jostling *n.* bousculade, poussade

journal *n.* journal

journey *n.* route, tournée, voyage **take a long journey** faire une grande route

journey *v.* voyager

journeyman *n.* journalieux

jowl *n.* bajoue

joy *n.* agrément, joie, jouissance, joyeuseté **joy of life** joie de vivre

joyful *adj.* joyeux

joyfully *adv.* joyeusement

joyfulness *n.* joyeuseté

judge *n.* juge

judge *v.* juger **judge again** rejuger

judgment *n.* jugement **use one's judgment** user son jugement **not have good judgment** avoir pas plus d'à peu près qu'une truie aux socos

Judgment *n.* **Judgment Day** le jour du jugement **Final Judgment** jugement du Bon Dieu

judiciary *adj.* judiciaire

jug *n.* cruche, JUG

juice *n.* jus, vin **berry juice** vin de mûre **squeeze juice** épurer **sugar cane juice** jus, vin de canne

juice *v.* juter

juicy *adj.* juteux

jukebox *n.* piano

July *n.* juillet

jumble *n.* jambalaya, mélange, méli-mélange, éparpillage

jumble *v.* mêlailler

jump *n.* bond, saut, sautaillement **jump rope** corde à sauter

jump *v.* corcobiller, foncer, gigailler, ginguer, jumper, regimber, sauter, se tirer, faire ressourdre, faire sourdre **jump about** sautailler **jump again** ressauter **jump around** corcobiller **jump over** sauter **jump on s.o.** sauter sur le casaquin de qqn **jump over again** ressauter **jump out of surprise** ressauter **jump on s.o. with both feet** monter dessus à pieds joints

jumper *n.* JUMPER, sauteur

jumping *n.* sautaillement **jumping around** corcobiage, sautaillage, sautaillement

jumpsuit *n.* JUMPER

jumpy *adj.* poltron

junction *n.* jonction

juncture *n.* jointure, jonction

June *n.* juin

junk *n.* bagatelle, crapule, drigaille, fatras, gargote, ingrandjin, pacotille, tchincaillerie, vauriennerie, artifailles **junk closet** fourre-tout **old junk** vieillerie **piece of junk iron** ferail **piece of junk or trash** cochonnerie

jurisdiction *n.* jurisdiction

jurisprudence *n.* loi

juror *n.* membre du jury **be a juror** être du jury

jury *n.* jury **be on the jury** être du jury **member of the jury** membre du jury

Jury *n.* **Police Jury** Jury de Police

jury-rig *v.* harnacher

just *adj.* droite, juste, raisonnable, rien que / yanque / yienque / yinque

just *adv.* juste, justement

justice *n.* droiture, juge, justice **justice of the peace** juge de paix **justice is not always immediate, but it will prevail in the end** le Bon Dieu descend pas pour bûcher **give justice** donner justice **render justice** rendre justice **court of justice** maison de cour

justifiable *adj.* justifiable

justification *n.* justification

justify *v.* justifier **justify or vindicate o.s.** se justifier

justly *adv.* droitement, justement

kale *n.* **curled kale** chou vert

kayak *n.* kayak

kee *onom.* qui

keel *n.* quille

keenness *n.* **mental keenness** pénétration

keep *n.* **fertilizer keep** parc à fumier

keep *v.* garder, préserver, quitter, sauver, se conserver, tenir, garder, soigner **keep away** rester à côté, se bouquer après, se mettre à côté, se tenir à côté **keep back** retenir, réserver **keep cold** refroidir **keep fit** s'entretenir, se tenir en bonne santé **keep from** aider **keep o.s.** se garder, se tenir **keep silent** pas siffler, se taire **keep up** entretenir, soutenir **keep from perishing** préserver **keep o.s. regular** se régler **keep the books** tenir des livres **keep the peace** tenir la paix **keep up with** suivre **keep an eye on** guetter, surveiller **keep watch over the sick** veiller les malades {un malade} **keep a vigil or hold a wake over** veiller

keeper *n.* garde, teneur

keeping *n.* **in keeping with** accordant

keepsake *n.* souvenir

keg *n.* keg

kennel *n.* cabane de chien, niche

keno *n.* kino

kept *adj.* **kept woman** femme tenue

kerchief *n.* tignon

kernel *n.* noyau **kernel of corn** grain de maïs **kernel of unpopped popcorn** grillot **kernel of dried, unripened corn** grillot

kerosene *n.* COAL OIL, huile de charbon, huile à {de} lampe **kerosene heater** réchaud à coloïe **kerosene lamp** lampe à globe

kestrel *n.* **American kestrel** cossarde

kettle *n.* bombe, bouille, bouilloire, teakettle **second kettle in a battery** flambeau **third kettle in a battery** sirop *pl.* **kettles used in the preparation of cane sugar** batterie

key *n.* clef **bass key** second

keyed *adj.* **keyed up** excité

khaki *adj.* jaune, khaki

khaki *n.* khaki

kick *n.* coup de pied

kick *v.* coupdepiéter, passer à coup de pied, regimber, sacrer un coup de pied, toquer un coup de pied, tirer des coups de pied **kick out** mettre (qqn) dehors, mettre à la porte

kid *n.* gamin

kid *v.* bêtiser

kidding *n.* **no kidding!** pas de bêtise!

kidnap *v.* enlever, kidnap, voler

kidnapper *n.* kidnapper

kidney *n.* kidney, pierre, pigueroin, rognon, pigueroin **kidney stew** étouffée de rognons **kidney stone** pierre *pl.* **have weak kidneys** avoir la pipi

kill *v.* abattre, achever, tuer **kill o.s.** se tuer **kill by bleeding** saigner **kill by shooting** plomber **kill o.s. working** se tuer à travailler **kill a bird in flight or on the wing** tuer un oiseau au vol **shoot, injure, or kill by shooting** tirer

killdeer *n.* colibri, piaillard, pluvier doré

killer *n.* tueur

killing *n.* meurtre

kiln *n.* **brick kiln** briquerie

kilter *n.* **get out of kilter** se déranger

kin *adj.* parent

kin *n.* famille, monde, parent, parenté

kind *adj.* (de) bon cœur, amicable, bon, charitable, indulgent, vaillant

kind *n.* espèce, genre, grade, qualité, sorte, variété **kind of** manière **three of a kind** trois de la même qualité **they are two of a kind** ça chie dans le même sac *pl.* **different kinds of** différentes qualités de / différent de qualités de

kindling *n.* allume-feu **piece of kindling** copeau, éclat, écopeau **fungus collected for kindling** tondre **bundle of sticks used for kindling** fagot

kindly *adj.* charrant

kindness *n.* bienfait, bonté, douceur, tendresse **have the kindness** avoir (de) la bonté de

kinfolk *n.* monde

king *n.* roi, roi **Mardi Gras king** roi

kingbird *n.* corneille fouetteur

kingfisher *n.* martin-plongeur

kinky *adj.* crotté **extremely curly, frizzy, kinky, tightly curled** tchine

kinship *n.* parenté

kiss *n.* bec, caresse, embrassade, bo

kiss *v.* becquer, embrasser, bo **kiss each other** s'embrasser, se becquer

kisser *n.* bec

kissing *n.* embrassement

kitchen *n.* cuisine, salle à manger **kitchen cabinet** garde-manger **kitchen sink** lavier, SINK, zinc **kitchen utensils** artifailles **set of kitchen utensils** batterie de cuisine

kite *n.* balan, cerf-volant

kitten *n.* minou

kitty *n.* pot, minou **here kitty** mine mine (mini mini)

Klansman *n.* klou-klouque

klutz *n.* caliberda

knack *n.* **have the knack** connaître la tune

knead *v.* pétriner, pétrir

kneading *n.* pétrissage

knee *n.* genou **knee breeches** brayette **knee cap** boulotte de genou **cypress knee** boscoyo de cipre, boscoyo, chicot de cipre *pl.* **put s.o. on his knees** mettre (qqn) sur {dessus} ses genoux

knee-deep *adv.* à pieds joints

kneecap *n.* boulette de genou

kneel *v.* se mettre à genoux {d'à genoux / sur les genoux} **make s.o. kneel** mettre (qqn) sur {dessus} ses genoux, mettre à genoux

kneeler *n.* prie-Dieu

kneeling *n.* à genoux

knicknack *n.* bébelle, bébellerie *pl.* **knickknacks** artifailles, artifaux

knife *n.* couteau **knife sharpener** effile, lime **butcher knife** couteau de boucherie, grand couteau, poignard **cane knife** couteau à {de} canne, sabre à canne, sabre **caulking knife** couteau de galfat **draw knife** couteau à deux manches **oyster knife** couteau à z-huîtres **pocket knife** ganif **round knife** couteau rond **table knife** couteau de table **stick with a knife** engarocher un couteau

knight *n.* cavalier, chevalier

Knight *n.* **Knight of Columbus** Chevalier de Colombus

knit *n.* tricot

knit *v.* brocher, tricoter, froncer

knob *n.* poigne, poignet

knock *n.* frappage

knock *v.* cogner, frapper, taper **knock again** refrapper **knock down** abattre, capoter, foutre par terre **knock eggs** bosquer les œufs, pâquer **knock o.s.** se cogner **knock off** larguer **knock out** knock-out **knock over** capoter, foutre par terre, jeter **knock up** embêter **knock o.s. out** s'étourdir **knock s.o. dead** tuer raide **knock at the door** frapper à la porte **knock flat on the ground** aplatir

knock-out *n.* knock-out

knocked *adj.* frappé **be knocked down** éclapoutir

knocking *n.* frappage, frappement **knocking eggs** pâquage

knot *n.* nœud, maille, nocoyau **knot on a tree** boscoyo **undo a knot in** démarrer **get a knot on one's head** se cabosser la tête **roll, twist, or knot of hair worn at the back of the head** catogan, choque, tchique, tignon

knot *v.* nouer

knotted *adj.* **get knotted up** se nouer

knotting *n.* amarrage

know *v.* savoir, connaître **know better** savoir mieux **know everything** avoir le nez long **know how** connaître comment, connaître **know well** être habitué avec **know each other** se connaître **know what's happening** connaître la tune **know what to believe** connaître où cabri porte la queue **know where one's interests lie** savoir et où son pain est beurré **know how far one can go** connaître où cabri porte la queue, savoir où cabri porte la queue **let know** donner à connaître **you know** tu {vous} connais / vous connaissez **not know what one is talking about** être pas aux noces **I don't know** ça me BEAT **let s.o. know** donner à connaître, laisser connaître **as far as I know** à {de} ma connaissance **it takes one to know one** chien mord chien **one who knows everything** savant

know-how *n.* savoir-faire

know-it-all *n.* avocat (de) district, avocat, maîtresse d'école

knowledge *n.* connaissance, information, savoir **practical knowledge** savoir-faire **to my knowledge** à {de} ma connaissance

knowledgeable *adj.* savant **be knowledgeable** connaître ses oignons

known *adj.* **make known** faire acconnaître, faire assavoir **widely known** familier **become well known** se distinguer **let it be known** faire dire

knuckle *n.* nocoyau *pl.* **brass knuckles** fer, ferail **rubbing of the knuckles on s.o.'s head** critché

Kodak *n.* kodak

kohlrabi *n.* chou-navet

Ku Klux Klan *n.* klan, klou-klouque

kumquat *n.* **sour kumquat** petite orange haigre **sweet kumquat** petite orange douce

L

label *n.* colle, ticket

labor *n.* œuvre, ouvrage, travail **labor union** union **do hard manual labor** halailler

labor *v.* travailler **labor hard** s'ambitionner

laborer *n.* laboureux, travaillant, travailleur **field laborer** travaillant de champs {clos} **hired laborer** engagé

lace *n.* babiche, dentelle

lack *n.* absence, manque **lack of attention** manque d'attention **lack of good manners** manque de retenue **for lack of** faute de **feel the lack or loss** manquer

lack *v.* manquer

lackadaisical *adj.* **lackadaisical, carefree person** menfoutbin

lacking *adj.* **be lacking** manquer

ladder *n.* escabeau, échelle

ladle *n.* bigote, cuillère à lait, cuillère à soupe, gibote, moque, pinte, poêle

lady *n.* dame **young lady** demoiselle, mademoiselle, mamselle *pl.* **ladies' man** courtisaud, maquereau, splouque, suceur-de-fleurs

Lady *n.* **Our Lady** Notre Dame

ladyfish *n.* banane, mamselle, poisson à femme

Lafitte *n.* **Lafitte skiff** lafitte

Lafourche *n.* **person from Lafourche Parish** Fourchon **of or from Lafourche Parish** lafourchais

lag *v.* **lag behind** rester en arrière **lag behind in one's work** traîner les savates

lake *n.* lac

Lake *n.* **Lake Arthur** Lac Arthur **Lake Charles** Lac Charles

lakeshore *n.* bord du lac

lamb *n.* agneau, mouton, viande de mouton

lame *adj.* boiteux, démembré, escran, estropié **be lame** boiter **one who is lame** bo

lament *n.* lamentation

lament *v.* gémir, se lamenter

lamentable *adj.* lamentable

lamentation *n.* lamentation **repeated lamentation** jérémiade
laminate *v.* laminer
lamp *n.* lampe, lumière **lamp black** noir de lampe **lamp burner** desse, tête de lampe **lamp glass** cheminée de lampe, cheminée **lamp globe** cheminée de lampe, cheminée **hurricane lamp** lampe à globe **kerosene lamp** lampe à globe **oil lamp** lampe à {de} coal oil, lampe
lampas *n.* ampas
lampblack *n.* suie
lampshade *n.* SHADE, voile de lampe
land *n.* domaine, terre **land that doesn't flood** côteau **land or country of birth** pays natal **land that has been cleared by burning** brûlis **land that has not been cleared of its timber** bois debout **bottom land** platin **cleared land** défraîchi, désert **grazing land** pâturage **holy land** terre sainte **level land** terre niveau, terre égale **native land** pays natal **uncultivated land** savane **flat land along a waterway** batture **swampy land between prairies and swamps** prairie tremblante **flat, level land** terre plange **low, marshy land** platin **parcel of land** champ **piece of land** morceau de terre **plot of land** terrain **point of land** pointe **parcel of land measuring 640 acres** section **piece of land that has sunk** maraille **area of land partially enclosed by woodland** anse **piece of land that has been cleared** défraîchissement **newly cleared land that has not yet been cultivated** terre neuf **cede use of land** livrer une terre **low area of land** bassin **one who clears land** déséreur **rectangular parcel of land** mouchoir **plot or patch of land in a field** carreau
land *v.* border la terre, aborder
land-holder *n.* **large land-holder** gros blanc
landing *adj.* **landing place** débarque
landing-stage *n.* dépôt
landlord *n.* bourgeois, propriétaire
landowner *n.* bourgeois
landslide *n.* déboulement de terre
lane *n.* manche
language *n.* langage, langue, parlure **language of the Acadians** acadien **Arabic language** Arabique **Creole language** nègre **creolized language** créole **Greek language** grec **Polish language** polonais **Russian language** russien **Creole language of Louisiana** créole **Louisiana Creole language** gombo **the English language** américain, anglais **the French language** français **the German language** allemand **the Italian language** italien **the Spanish language** espagnol
languid *adj.* cagou
languish *v.* languir
lanky *adj.* élingué
lantana *n.* cailleau
lantern *n.* fanal, jabloroc, lanterne
lap *n.* joint
lap *v.* laper
lard *n.* béquine, graisse douce, graisse, lard **hog lard** graisse (de) cochon
large *adj.* abominable, beau, bien corporé, grand, gros, large **at large** en vacances, LOOSE
largely *adv.* largement
largess *n.* largesse
lariat *n.* ariate, lasse
lark *n.* escapade **field lark** alouette, caille de clos, caille de prairie
larkspur *n.* patte d'alouette
larva *n.* **mosquito larva** lève-queue, tourne-queue, vire-cul, vire-de-bord, vire-vire
larynx *n.* gargoton
lash *n.* babiche, fouet, gland
lashing *n.* amarrage
lasso *n.* ariate, lasse **remove a lasso** délasser
lasso *v.* lasser, LASSO
lassoing *n.* lassage
last *adj.* dernier, final **last one** dernier **last rites** Extrême Onction **last in rank** dernier **at last** enfin, finalement **next to last** avant-dernier **second to last** avant-dernier
last *v.* durer, tenir, durer
last-born *adj.* **last-born child in a family** nichoix, nioque
lasting *adj.* durable, inusable
latch *n.* crochet, loquet, taquet, target
latch *v.* accrocher, attaquer, loquer, taquer
late *adj.* défunt, pauvre
late *adv.* au tard, en retard, enretardé, tard **late in the evening** sur le tard **be late** tarder, être tard **make late** tarder **of late** dernièrement **too late** le docteur après la mort!, trop tard **it's too late now** Baille a couru **one who is late for every and any occasion** queue de la comète
lately *adv.* dernièrement, nouvellement
later *adv.* plus tard, puis **see you later** on va se revoir **sooner or later** tôt ou tard, tantôt-bétôt
latest *n.* **at the latest** au plus tard
lath *n.* douelle, latte, couvre-joint
lathe *n.* **shape or turn on a lathe** tourner
lathering *n.* savonnure
Latin *adj.* latin
Latin *n.* latin
Laud *n.* **oh Laud** LORD
laudanum *n.* laudanum
laugh *n.* rire
laugh *v.* ricaner, rire **laugh at** rire après {de}, se moquer **laugh excessively** s'étouffer à {de} rire **laugh heartily** quiaquer, rire comme un fou, rire à se foutre par terre, s'étouffer à {de} rire, se fendre la gueule à rire **laugh loudly** ricaner **laugh like crazy** rire comme un fou **laugh to o.s.** rire dans sa barbe **laugh in a condescending or mocking way** ricaner
laughable *adj.* chatouillant, risible
laughing *adj.* **always laughing** ricaneur
laughing *n.* **laughing fit** ricane **burst out laughing** se fendre à rire **split one's sides laughing** se fendre les côtés à rire

laughingstock *n.* risée **make a laughingstock of o.s.** faire une risée de soi-même

laughter *n.* ricanement, rire **loud laughter** ricanement **choke with laughter** s'étouffer à {de} rire **die of laughter** crever de rire **easily given to laughter** ricaneur

launch *v.* entamer

launching *n.* lancement

laundromat *n.* laundry

laundry *n.* laundry, lavage, lessive, linge **do laundry** faire le {un / son} lavage, laver le linge (sale), laver **do the laundry** faire la lessive **do a load of laundry** faire une lessive **room or building used as a pantry, mudroom, laundry room, etc.** dépense

laurel *n.* **laurel tree** laurier, olivier **cherry laurel tree** laurier amande {mande}

lavatory *n.* bassin

lavish *v.* **lavish inordinate affection on** gâter

law *n.* loi, législation, ordonnance, règle **law counsel** conseil **civil law** loi **the law** loi **basic law or fact of nature** principe **against the law** défendu **seize by law** saisir **lay down the law to s.o.** lire un catéchisse à qqn, lire un chapître à qqn

lawful *adj.* légal, légitime

lawn *n.* lawn **lawn mower** coupe-paille, coupeuse d'herbes, faucheuse, lawn-mower, machine à z-herbe **lawn sprinkler** arrosoir **mow the lawn** couper les herbes

lawsuit *n.* poursuite, procès

lawyer *n.* avocat, conseil

lax *adj.* lâche

laxative *n.* purge, régulateur **take a laxative** se purger

lay *v.* passer **lay down** dégrucher, déposer **lay eggs** pondre **lay off** décharger, lay-off, lâcher **lay out** ensevelir, étendre **lay a floor** plancher **lay explosive mines** miner **lay the blame on** passer la blâme sur **lay the foundation of** fonder **lay down the law to s.o.** lire un catéchisse à qqn, lire un chapître à qqn **lay out clothes on the ground to dry** mettre du linge à la plaille

layer *n.* couche, lit, pondeuse, renduit **layer of a cake** galette, mâche-pain **outer layer** vernis **top layer** pardessus **thick layer of ice over a body of water** pont de glace *pl.* **dress with layers** abrier

layette *n.* trousseau de bébé

laying *n.* **laying coop** poulailler **laying hen** pondeuse **laying house** pondoire **laying rack or nest** nichoir **laying by of sugar cane crop** renchaussage **finish laying by the cane crop** larguer le renchaussage

layout *n.* aises **layout of a house** plan de maison

laziness *n.* cagne, faignanterie, paresse **be afflicted with laziness** attraper un coup de lilas

lazy *adj.* barosse, câlin, doucement, faignant, paresseux, pimbêche **lazy person** couique, loafer **act lazy** faire le paresseux **be lazy** attraper un coup de lilas, avoir les côtes en long, flânailler, flâner, paresser **clumsy and lazy** gommeux **worthless, good-for-nothing, lazy girl** bringue

lazybones *npl.* bidet, câlin, filandrin

lead *n.* plomb **take the lead** prendre la tête **be in the lead** avoir le devant

lead *v.* conduire, guider, mener, amener, galoper **lead astray** égarer **lead away** emmener **lead back** ramener, reconduire **lead to** gagner **lead a life** mener la {une} vie **lead into evil** entraîner **lead a dissolute life** fouiner **lead an indecent life** saloper **drive or lead into a pen** corrailler

leaded *adj.* plombé

leader *n.* capitaine, chef, leader, premier, tête **team leader** Capitaine Souris, capitaine **the leader** le taureau sur le côteau {la butte} **be the leader** être en chef

leadership *n.* **highest point of leadership or authority** tête

leaf *n.* feuillage, feuille **bay leaf** laurier *pl.* **beet leaves** queues de betteraves **outer leaves** paille **shed leaves** s'effeuiller **strip leaves off of** effeuiller **falling of leaves** effeuillage **bunch of tobacco leaves** manoque

leak *n.* dégouttation, dégouttement, gouttière

leak *v.* couler **leak out** couler

lean *adj.* maigre, élingué **get lean** maigrir

lean *v.* appuyer, camper, carguer, cointer, pencher, s'appuyer, se carguer, se pencher **lean back** carguer, recarguer, se carguer, se recarguer **lean over** baisser, se pencher

lean-to *n.* cabildeau

leaning *n.* penchant

leanness *n.* maigreur

leap *n.* bond, saut

leap *v.* foncer, sautailler, sauter, se lancer **leap over** franger **descend or leap the rapids** sauter les rapides

learn *v.* apprendre, découverre, ramasser **learn about** se poster **learn how** apprendre à **learn by heart** apprendre par cœur **learn quickly or easily** apprendre par cœur comme un perroquet

learned *adj.* **learned person** savant

learning *n.* savoir, science

lease *n.* **lease on land** droit de la terre

lease *v.* louer

least *adj.* moindre

least *adv.* **at least** au moins, bien, du moins **the least** le moins **in the least** moindrement

leather *n.* cuir, peau **leather punch** perce-cuir **uncured leather** peau **tie or leather strap for tying two oxen together by the horns** macorne

leathersmith *n.* gréyeur

leave *n.* **take leave of one another** se laisser **take French leave** partir (en) marron

leave *v.* aller au large, braguer, décamper, départir, ficher le {son} camp, flanquer son camp, GONE, laisser, lever le pied, partir, pousser route, QUIT, quitter, sacrer le camp, s'arracher, s'en aller, sortir de, quitter **leave abruptly** haler son gratin

leave again repartir **leave alone** quitter tranquille **leave be** laisser tranquille **leave behind** laisser **leave out** manquer, sauter **leave quickly** haler ses fesses {ses frètes / son frète} **leave each other** se laisser **leave in peace** quitter tranquille **leave lying about** laisser à la traîne **leave me alone** va te cacher / va te faire cacher à Lafayette **leave room between** espacer **leave s.o. hanging** laisser (qqn) suspendu **leave space between** espacer **leave tracks on** pistrailler **leave behind on purpose** dégrader **leave hurriedly, without explanation** partir sous une superstition **leave in a hurry** haler ses caniques **leave on one's own** livrer qqn à soi-même **leave s.o. in suspense** laisser (qqn) suspendu **leave without informing anyone** partir (en) marron **leave to one's own devices** livrer qqn à soi-même **about to leave** en partance / sur sa partance **ready to leave** quittable **induce to leave the house** découver **if you leave, someone else will usurp your place** chien qui va à la chasse perd sa place **be ready to leave** avoir la couarte sus l'épaule **pack up and leave** faire son paquet **go away and leave me alone** va te coucher **said of visitors who leave when others arrive** faire sauvage **be leaving** être parti **I'm leaving** au diable la boutique

leaven *n.* ferment, levain

leaving *adj.* **those leaving** sortant

leaving *n.* restant **leaving work** débauchage, débauche

lecture *n.* colle, lecture

ledge *n.* corniche

leech *n.* sangsue

leek *n.* poireau

left *adj.* gauche **left over** de reste **be left** rester **something left behind or abandoned** quittage **be left in the lurch somewhere** être cargué dans une place

left *n.* gauche **horse on the left in a draft team** gaucher

left-handed *adj.* gaucher **left-handed person** gaucheux

leftover *adj.* **leftover part** drigaille

leftover *n.* **leftover part** restant *pl.* **leftovers** ramasserie

leg *n.* cuisse, jambe, patte, pilier, quille, canon, pied **scaly leg** patrique **trouser leg** cuissière **wooden leg** jambe de liège **back of leg** gras de jambe **cross by lifting one leg over at a time** enjamber **give s.o. an advantage, a leg up** donner un pied (à qqn) *pl.* **frogs' legs** cuisses de ouaouaron **thin legs** jambes de quiquisse **have big legs** avoir des jambes comme des globes de lampe **have shapely legs** avoir des jambes comme des globes de lampe **have thin legs** avoir des jambes de baguettes / avoir des jambes comme des baguettes de coton {des baguettes de fusil / des pattes de moqueur} **spread one's legs** s'éjarer **have one's legs spread** être éjarré / se tenir éjarré **pull the legs off of** élinguer **having feathers along the legs** à grosse arrasse **stand up on hind legs again** se remater **split apart by pulling on the legs of** écuisser

legal *adj.* légal

legality *n.* légalité

legalize *v.* légaliser

legally *adv.* légitime

legging *n.* léguine **Indian legging** mitasse

leghorn *n.* **leghorn chicken** léguine

legible *adj.* lisable

legion *n.* légion

legislation *n.* législation **piece of legislation** loi

legislator *n.* législateur

legislature *n.* législature

legitimate *adj.* légitime

legitimately *adv.* légitime

lemon *n.* citron, limon **lemon tree** limonier

lemonade *n.* limonade

lemonfish *n.* limon, poisson limon

lemongrass *n.* citronnelle

lend *v.* avancer, laisser avoir, prêter **lend a hand** donner la {une} main, mettre la main **lend a helping hand** donner un coup de main

lendable *adj.* prêtable

lender *n.* prêteur

length *n.* longueur

lengthen *v.* allonger, allongir, prolonger, rabouter, rallonger, élongir, étendre

lengthening *n.* allongement, rallongement

lens *n.* vitre *pl.* **eyeglass lenses** vitres de lunettes

Lent *n.* Carême **observe Lent** faire le Carême

Lenten *adj.* **Lenten fast** jeûne de Carême

leper *n.* lépreux

leprosy *n.* lèpre

less *adv.* moins **less than** moins que **less and less** en moins à moins **even less** encore moins **still less** encore moins **more or less** dans un approchant, manière, plus ou moins **by so much less** autant moins **neither more nor less** ni plus ni moins, ni plus, ni moins

less *prep.* moins

lessen *v.* affaiblir, amoindrir

lesser *adj.* moindre

lesson *n.* leçon **need to be taught a lesson** avoir besoin du manila trempe *pl.* **give lessons** faire l'école

let *v.* laisser faire, laisser, louer, permettre, quitter **let's** allons **let alone** laisser tranquille **let be** laisser faire **let down** baisser, détrousser **let fall** lâcher **let in** admettre **let know** donner à connaître **let loose** larguer **let o.s.** se laisser **let rise** éponger **let's go** allons **let's start** allons s'y mettre **let go of** lâcher **let s.o. know** donner à connaître, laisser connaître **let water flow** lâcher l'eau **let's suppose that** supposant **let air out of** dégonfler **let s.o. do s.t.** laisser faire **let's go to work** allons s'y mettre **let slip a bad word** échapper une mauvaise parole

letter *n.* lettre, postillon, épitre, lettre **long drawn-out letter or book** pataraphe *pl.* **exchange letters** correspondre **exchange of letters** correspondance

lettuce *n.* laitue, salade **wild lettuce** laitue **head of lettuce** tête de laitue

leucorrhoea *n.* perles blanches

levee *n.* batture, levée, élevée

level *adj.* au niveau, de niveau, plange, plate, uni **level with** en plan avec **make level** unir

level *n.* étage, niveau **surveyor's level** niveleur

level *v.* aplanir, niveler, plangir, égaler, égalir, égaliser, braquer, niveler

leveling *n.* aplanissement, effleurage

lever *n.* levier, rance **gearshift lever** bâton pour transmission

liable *adj.* sujet, assujetti

liar *n.* conteur de menteries, diseur de menteries, menteur

liberate *v.* décharger, déprendre, libérer

liberation *n.* libération

libertine *adj.* pas bon

liberty *n.* liberté

library *n.* bibliothèque, librairie, library

lice *n.* **beggar's lice** arcollant

license *n.* licence, permis **license number** numéro de licence **license plate** licence **vehicle license** bavette

lichen *n.* polipot

lick *v.* licher **lick o.s.** se licher **lick one's lips** se licher les babines **lick, scrape or graze one's skin** se friper

lid *n.* couvert

lie *n.* fabrication, mensonge, menterie **big lie** grosse menterie **white lie** menterie blanche **a big lie** une belle bleue **tell a lie** passer une menterie, pousser une menterie *pl.* **lies** accroires **tell lies** conter des menteries, mentir

lie *v.* mentir **lie down** niquer, s'allonger **lie down again** se recoucher **lie in ambush** faire l'embuscade **lie in wait** faire la guette **lie through one's teeth** mentir comme un arracheur de dents / mentir comme un dentist, être menteur comme un arracheur de dents **lie in wait for ducks as they come in to roost at night** aller {partir} à la passe, aller à la passée **know where one's interests lie** savoir et où son pain est beurré

lieutenant *n.* lieutenant

life *n.* vie, durée **life story** vie **bachelor life** vie de garçon **joy of life** joie de vivre **lead a life** mener la {une} vie **live one's life** vivre sa vie **never in life** jamais de la vie **one's entire life** tout(e) sa vie **see one's life flash before one's eyes** livrer sa carcasse au diable **bring back to life** ressusciter **come back to life** ressusciter, revivre **have a hard life** tirer la courte paille **have a miserable life** vivre en espoir et mourir comme un vieux chien **lead a dissolute life** fouiner **lead an indecent life** saloper **take one's own life** se prendre la vie **have the easy life first** manger le pain blanc en premier **give new strength or life** ravioter **live a happy family life** faire un bon ménage **take on new strength or new life** ravigorer

lifeless *adj.* longis

lifestyle *n.* vie

lifetime *n.* vie, vivant **during one's lifetime** la vie durante **for one's lifetime** la vie durante **not marry in one's lifetime** rester pour graine

lift *n.* élévateur **give a lift** ramasser

lift *v.* enlever, hausser, lever, soulever **lift up** élever **lift o.s. up** se hausser **lift up again** relever **lift with a jack** JACK **raise or lift o.s. up** se lever

lifting *n.* levée, soulèvement **used when lifting a baby in the air** houppala

light *adj.* clair, leste, léger, sourge **be light** faire claire

light *n.* clair, clarté, lampe, lumière **light bulb** globe électrique / globe de lampe, globe **light of day** clarté du jour **electric light** lampe électrique, lumière électrique **provide light for o.s.** s'éclairer **in the light** à la clarté **turn on the light** ouvrir la lumière

light *v.* éclairer, allumer **light up** petiller

light-colored *adj.* gouère

lightbulb *n.* bulbe, lumière

lighted *adj.* éclairé

lighten *v.* alléger, éloiser

lighting *n.* éclairage

lightly *adv.* léger

lightness *n.* légèreté

lightning *n.* éclair, électricité, éloise **lightning bolt** éloise **lightning rod** paratonnerre **heat lightning** éloise **sheet lightning** éloise **flash of lightning** éclair

like *adj.* pareil **like that** pareil

like *adv.* manière

like *npl.* **the likes of that** pareil **have idiosyncratic likes or dislikes** avoir des fions

like *prep.* comme, pareil comme **just like** pareil comme, tel comme

like *v.* aimer, tenir de, tenir à **like more** aimer mieux **like very much** aimer comme cochon aime la boue {la lavure / le maïs} **how do you like that?** comment tu crois? **how do you like that** comment tu crois? **be doing what one likes do** être dans son plat **be doing what one likes to do** être dans son plan

likeable *adj.* aimable, avenant, vaillant

likelihood *n.* probabilité

likely *adj.* capable, probable, sujet **not likely** pas d'apparence **more than likely** plus de prouvable, plus que probable

likely *adv.* probablement, prouvable

likeness *n.* ressemblance, semblance

likewise *adv.* aussi, pareillement

liking *n.* **have a liking** tenir de, tenir à

lilac *n.* lilas

lily *n.* lis **canna lily** langue de {du} bœuf **day lily** lys jaune **Easter lily** lys blanc, lys de la Sainte Vierge, lys de Saint-Joseph **mariposa lily** roseau d'Egypte **surprise lily** surprise **swamp lily** herbe à malo **common water lily** herbe du bayou **Saint Joseph lily** lys de Saint-Joseph **yellow water lily** herbe au coeur

limb *n.* membre, branche **small tree limb** rolon **be left out on a limb** chiquer poteau

limber *v.* **limber up** dégourdir, se dégourdir

lime *n.* chaux, limon **lime tree** limonier **whitewash with lime** chauter

limeade *n.* limonade

limit *n.* borne, limite **at the limit** rendu **set a limit on** limiter *pl.* **set limits** borner **test the limits of** mettre à l'épreuve

limit *v.* limiter **limit o.s.** se limiter

limitation *n.* restriction

limited *adj.* borné

limousine *n.* limousine

limp *v.* boitailler

limp *n.* **have a bad limp** boiter tout bas

limp *v.* boiter **one who limps** bo

limping *adj.* boiteux

limping *n.* boitement, boiterie

linden *n.* tilleul

line *n.* affilée, file, ligne, rangée, défilé **line of descent** bord **line of work** ouvrage **line where hair is parted** partage **electric line** ligne à lumière **electrical line** ligne **finish line** ligne **fishing line** ligne à pêche, ligne **in line** en ligne **plumb line** plombant **power line** ligne à lumière **property line** ligne **set line** ligneguette **straight line** ligne droite **telephone line** ligne **trawl line** trôle **in line with** vis-à-vis (de) **get into line** s'aligner **in a line** affilé **out of line** bisquencoin **put in line** aligner **fish using a set line or cane pole** pêcher à la ligneguette {ligne} **be warped or out of line** faire bassin **the point of an outside wall created by the roof line** pignon **command to a person to encourage him/her to get in line, get on board, get with the program** 'poteau, Caillette'! *pl.* **harness lines** guide

line *v.* doubler, redoubler **line up** aligner, corder, s'aligner, se corder

lineage *n.* branche, chicot

linear *adj.* **linear formation** colonne

lined *adj.* **lined up** en ligne

linen *n.* toile *pl.* **bed linens** linge

linger *v.* traînailler

lingerie *n.* lingerie

lingo *n.* jargon

liniment *n.* **gray liniment** longuent-graisse

lining *n.* doubleur, doublage, doublure, redoublage **lining of the intestine** raclure **add lining** doubler, redoubler **take out the lining** dédoubler

link *n.* anneau, connexion, maille **chain link** anneau de chaîne **cuff link** bouton de poignet

link *v.* connecter

linseed *n.* **linseed oil** huile de lin

lint *n.* volume

lion *n.* lion

lip *n.* lèvre, babine **lip of a plant** margot **large lip** babine **big, thick lip** babinot **curl the upper lip and show the teeth** rechaner, rechigner *pl.* **lick one's lips** se licher les babines

liqueur *n.* liqueur **absinthe liqueur** absinthe

liquid *n.* liquide **in liquid form** en liquide **set in liquid** mettre à la trempe

liquify *v.* fondre

liquor *n.* boisson, liqueur **shot of liquor** todie

list *n.* catalogue, liste, lis

listen *v.* écouter

listener *n.* écouteur, auditeur

listless *adj.* cagou, caille, traînassant

lit *adj.* éclairé **well lit** clair

litany *n.* litanie

liter *n.* litre

literate *adj.* savant

literature *n.* littérature

lithe *adj.* leste

litter *n.* wagon, portée

little *adj.* petit, tout petit

little *adv.* pas MUCH, peu **little by little** petite à petite, poc à poc, tout doucement!, à fur et à mesure, à mesure

little *n.* idée **a little** manière, un peu

livable vivable

livable *adj.* habitable, logeable

live *adj.* en direct

live *v.* demeurer, loger, vivre, rester **live alone** rester seul **live long** résister **live on** rester pour (qqn) **live poorly** vivocher **live together** s'accoler, s'accoupler, s'adopter, s'emmancher, sauter le (manche à) balai, se macorner, se placer **live through hardships** passer de la misère **live in a tent** tenter **live in the city** rester en ville **live a happy family life** faire un bon ménage **live together as a couple** se prendre **live together out of wedlock** macorner avec, vivre en désordre **live hope and die like an old dog** vivre en espoir et mourir comme un vieux chien **fit to live in** logeable **man who lives with another man's wife** maquereau **woman who lives with a man, though not married to him** femme placée

livelihood *n.* vie

lively *adj.* animé, HOP, leste, prime, requinquiné, vif, vigoureux, vivant, élevé sur du vin haigue **become lively** s'animer

liven *v.* **liven up** assaisonner

liver *n.* foie noir, foie **liver stew** étouffée de foie **cod liver oil** huile de foie de morue **abuse one's liver** s'insulter les foies **covered with liver spots** masqué

liverwurst *n.* foie gras

livestock *n.* bétaille, animal **raise livestock** élever des bêtes **grass or other plants for feeding livestock** pâturage

livid *adj.* livide

living *adj.* en vie, vivant **living being** vivant **living together** accolé, emmanché, macorné, placé

living *n.* vie **living quarters** logement, place, quartier **living room** chambre de devant, chambre en avant, parloir, salon **living together** amarrage, emmanchement, jouqué, macornage **one's living** pain **earn a living** faire une {sa} vie **for a living** pour une vie **zest for living** joie de vivre **work for one's living** faire une {sa} vie **work hard for a living** gagner son pain par la sueur de son front

lizard *n.* lézard

load *n.* charge, charretée, fardeau, LOAD, poids, voyage **load of any vehicle** bargée **carry a load** faire un voyage

load *v.* armer, charger **load again** recharger **load into a vehicle** charger

loaded *adj.* fourni **loaded with** bourré de

loaf *n.* LOAF **loaf of French bread** flûte de pain, flûte **long crusty loaf of white bread** pain français **end of a loaf of bread** croûte, crouston, nez

loaf *v.* berlander, flânailler, flâner, gavagner, lingir, LOAF, paresser, soguer, tchincailler, vernailler **loaf on the job** gournoter

loafer *n.* filandrin, flâneur, loafer, tchicailleur, traînailleur, traîneur **loafer's corner** faubourg *pl.* **hangout for loafers** faubourg

loan *n.* emprunt, prêt, prête **co-sign a loan** cautionner **get a loan** faire un emprunt

loan *v.* prêter

loathing *n.* répugnance

loathsome *adj.* répugnant

lobby *n.* vestibule

lobster *n.* homard, lobster

local *adj.* local

locality *n.* endroit

locally *adv.* localement

located *adj.* **be located** se trouver, situer, siéger

location *n.* location, place **place o.s. in a location** se braquer

lock *n.* boucle, bouclette, cadenas, lock, mèche, écluse **lock of hair** pince de cheveux **car lock** étrier **door lock** serrure **hardware of a doorknob and lock** serrure de porte

lock *v.* barrer, cléter, embarrer, encler, mettre en clef, mettre enclé, taquer **lock in** rembarrer **lock o.s.** se barrer **lock up** encler, enfermer, rembarrer **lock o.s. up** se renfermer **lock the house** encler la maison **lock with a bar** barrer

locked *adj.* **become locked** se barrer

locking *n.* barrage

lockjaw *n.* tétanos

locomotive *n.* locomotive, train **dummy locomotive** charabouche **one who operates a locomotive or steamboat engine** ingénieur

locust *n.* cigale, locuste **black locust** arkansia **flowering locust** arkansia **honey locust** bois d'amourette, garofier, piquant mourette / piquant (d')amourette / piquant mort raide **seven-year locust** cigale à chêne **seventeen-year locust** cigale à {de} bois, locuste **sweet locust** garofier **honey locust tree** acacia, févier **spring locust tree** garofier **flowering black locust tree** acacia

lodge *v.* loger **lodge a complaint** porter plainte

lodger *n.* locataire, pensionné

lodging *n.* logement, pension **lodging for farm stock** têt **provide lodging** accommoder **build o.s. lodging** se loger **cost of lodging** pension **take up lodging** se loger *pl.* **move to new lodgings** reloger, se reloger

loft *n.* grénit **hay loft** grénit

log *n.* log **rounded log** rolon **squared log** plançon **burning log or stick** tison **cut log from a tree** bille de bois **section of a log** bille **short section of a log or branch** bûche *pl.* **collect logs to use as firewood** attraper du bois

loin *n.* **backstrap loin** reintier **strips of pork loin and fat** jambonneau

loiter *v.* traîner **loiter about** traînailler

loiterer *n.* traînailleur

lollipop *n.* sucette

loneliness *n.* ennui

lonely *adj.* ennuyant **become lonely** s'ennuyer **feel lonely** s'ennuyer

lonesome *adj.* ennuyeux **be lonesome** s'ennuyer **get lonesome** s'ennuyer

long *adj.* grand, long **long johns** longues-jambes **so long** tant **person with long, disheveled hair** taïque

long *adv.* long **before long** bientôt **how long** combien longtemps / comment longtemps, comment longtemps **so long** au revoir **as long as** partant que, tant que

long *v.* désirer

long-legged *adj.* **thin, long-legged man** quinze-côtes

long-lived *adj.* éternel **be long-lived** avoir les foies blancs

longer *adv.* davantage **no longer** pus

longing *n.* aspiration, désir, ennui, envie

loofah *n.* torchon

look *n.* air, allure, mine, regard **bad look** mauvaise mine **have a blank look** avoir les yeux gouaires **have a violent, passionate look** flamber des {les} yeux *pl.* **recover one's former good looks** se refaire

look *v.* regarder, reluquer **look after** garder, s'occuper **look alike** s'imiter **look around** chercher **look at** guetter, LOOK OUT, regarder **look bad** avoir mauvaise mine **look cross-eyed** loucher, regarder croche **look for** chercher après, chercher pour, chercher, fouiller après {pour}, regarder pour **look good** avoir bonne mine **look great** faire un effet bœuf **look here** tiens **look ill** avoir une mine de chien **look like** avoir des faux airs avec, donner des faux airs à qqn, ressembler (pareil) comme {à}, ressembler **look out** faire attention, LOOK OUT **look over** inspecter **look sad** avoir une mine de chien **look terrible** ressembler le diable avant jour **look at o.s.** se regarder **look at repeatedly** regardailler **look badly groomed** avoir une mine de chien **look for again** rechercher **look for trouble** chercher (une) chique

look at each other se regarder **look for each other** se chercher **look like one another** se ressembler **look strange or bizarre** faire drôle **now look here** à ça oui **don't look a gift horse in the mouth** cheval donné, regarde pas la bride **be looking for trouble** chicoter pour du tracas **be looking for a fight** chicoter pour du tracas, être en chimère **be looking for a quarrel** babiller

looking *adj.* **sickly looking** cagou, égaré **unhealthy looking** chéti **become better looking** se refaire

lookout *n.* garde, guette **be on the lookout** avoir l'œil sec

loom *n.* **hand loom** métier

loon *n.* grand plongeon

loose mouvant

loose *adj.* LOOSE, lâche **loose woman** chiennailleur, coursailleur, courseur, traîneuse **become loose** déclouer, se détendre **come loose** s'arracher, se démancher, se détacher, se dévisser **coming loose** démoyé **get loose** se déprendre, se détacher, échapper **let loose** larguer **turn loose** lâcher **woman of loose morals** fouine, jument de brancard **all hell broke loose** le diable s'en a mêlé **sloppy, slovenly, or morally loose woman** truie

loose *v.* déprendre

loosen *v.* ameublir, desserrer, décoincer, démancher, démarrer, lâcher, détendre **loosen the reins of** dérêner

looseness *n.* jeu

loosestrife *n.* herbe à bale

loot *v.* piller

looter *n.* pillard

looting *n.* pillage, pillerie

lope *n.* petit galop

loquat *n.* mispilusse

lord *n.* seigneur

Lord *n.* **Lord's prayer** oraison dominicale **oh Lord** LORD **the Good Lord** le Bon Dieu

lose *v.* caler, perdre, sortir en arrière, écarter, égarer, perdre **lose again** reperdre **lose by miscarriage** perdre **lose one's marbles** perdre la canique / perdre ses {les} caniques **lose one's balance or equilibrium** perdre son balan **lose one's way or direction** se perdre **cause to lose color** déteindre **cause to lose hope** désespoirer **make s.o. lose his temper** faire pouf **you snooze you lose** chien qui va à la chasse perd sa place

loser *n.* bon-à-rien, perdant, vaurien

losing *adj.* perdant

loss *n.* dommage, perte **at a loss** perdant **what a loss** quelle perte **be at a loss** être malaisé pour **feel the lack or loss** manquer *pl.* **recover one's losses** se rattraper

lost *adj.* écarté **get lost** faire bagasse, s'écarter, s'écartiller, s'égarer, s'éloigner, se perdre, va aux crèpes!, va te cacher / va te faire cacher à Lafayette **be lost or disoriented** avoir les yeux égarés **all is lost** c'est bernique **cause to be lost** égarer **one who is lost** poisson à terre sèque **animal that has been deliberately lost and is wandering the streets** corde échappée

lot *n.* bataclan, champ, lot, ramasse, sort, tallée, terrain **a lot** beaucoup, en masse de, en masse, gros, hourra, joliment, pataraphe, plein, tapée, tas, un tas, à tire-larigot, énormément **whole lot** massacre **a lot of** beaucoup de, plein de, un tas de **there's a whole lot of it** il y en a en masse et en pile *pl.* **lots** courtepaille, en masse et en pile **cast lots** tirer au sort **draw lots** tirer (à) la courtepaille, tirer au sort **sell in large lots** vendre en gros

lottery *n.* loterie, raffle **lottery ticket** mise **buy a lottery or raffle ticket** prendre une mise

lotto *n.* kino

lotus *n.* **American lotus** volée **American nelumbo yellow lotus** volée

loud *adj.* criard, fort **out loud** à haute tête, à pleine tête

loud *adv.* à pleine tête

loudly *adv.* fort, à pleine tête

Louisiana *n.* Louisiane **Louisiana, for a Texas Cajun** le vieux pays **from Louisiana** louisianais **of Louisiana** louisianais **native to Louisiana** créole **person from Louisiana** Louisianais **Creole language of Louisiana** créole **grown or produced in Louisiana** créole **lower class or illiterate Francophone of Louisiana** Cadien

Louisianan *n.* **French-speaking Louisianan** Français **any Louisianan who speaks a local variety of French** Créole

lounge *v.* flânailler, flâner **lounge around** berlander

louse *n.* pou, puce **chicken louse** pou de poule **crab louse** crabe **head louse** pou de tête *pl.* **remove lice** épouiller **infested with lice** pouilleux

lout *n.* caïac

louver *n.* louvre

love *n.* amitié, amour **in love** amouraché, amoureux, en amour **make love** faire des amours à, faire l'amour (à) **deeply in love** amoureux comme une puce **fall in love** tomber en amour (avec) **for the love of God** pour l'amour de Dieu / pour l'amour du Bon Dieu **for the love of Pete** pitié d'amour **fall madly in love** s'amouracher

love *v.* aimer **love tenderly** chérir **love like crazy** aimer à la folerie **love o.s. or each other** s'aimer

lovely *adj.* fin

lover *n.* amant, amoureux, maquereau

low *adj.* bas, basse-classe **person of low class** drigaille

low *v.* beugler, treller

low-class *adj.* **low-class people** bas monde, crapule, crasse **low-class person** crapule

low-cut *adj.* décolleté

low-fat *adj.* maigre

low-lying *adj.* **low-lying area susceptible to flooding** crevasse

lowdown *adj.* **lowdown act** crasse

lower *v.* baisser, abaisser **lower again** rabaisser, rebaisser

lower o.s. s'abaisser **lower one's dignity or moral standing** s'abaissir
lowering *n.* rabaissement
lowest *adj.* dernier
lowland *n.* bassière, crevasse, platin d'eau **lowland where rainwater collects and stands** coulée **pond lowland** bas-d'eau
lowlife *n.* crapule *pl.* **lowlives** chierie, criote
lowly *adj.* pouilleux
loyal *adj.* loyal
loyalty *n.* fidélité, loyauté **loyalty to a party or group** partisanerie
lozenge *n.* pastille
lubricate *v.* graisser, huiler
lubricating *n.* graissage
lucid *adj.* lucide **be lucid** se comprendre
Lucifer *n.* Lucifer
luck *n.* chance, fortune, LUCK **bad luck** BAD LUCK, guignasse, guigne, malchance, malheur **good luck** bonne chance **be bad luck** être la nenaine (à qqn) **out of luck** flambé **stroke of luck** coup d'accroc, coup de chance **stroke of bad luck** pipine d'eau douce, un BAD LUCK **one who has no luck** poisson à terre sèque **have a run of bad luck** avoir la guigne
luckily *adv.* chanceusement, une chance (que) / chance
lucky *adj.* avantagé, chanceux, heureux **lucky hit** trouve **strike it lucky** faire un beau {bon} coup
luggage *n.* bagage
lugger *n.* canotte, lougre **Louisiana lugger** canotte
lukewarm *adj.* quède **grow lukewarm** quédir **make lukewarm** attiédir, quédir
lukewarmness *n.* quiédeur
lumbar *n.* **lumbar region** rein
lumber *n.* bois, matérielle **rough cut lumber** bois massif **six by eight lumber** six par huit **six by six lumber** six par six **tongue and groove lumber** ceiling
lumberjack *n.* abatteur, bûcheur
lump *n.* boscoyo, bosse, motelon, pelote, tumeur **lump of sugar** bosse de sucre **hard lump** caillou **hard lump on or under the skin** durillon **cause a lump** embosser
lunar *adj.* **lunar cycle** lune
lunch *n.* dîner, LUNCH **lunch pail** bassin d'école **have lunch** dîner
lung *n.* bronche, poumon, foie blanc *pl.* **at the top of one's lungs** à pleine tête
lunge *v.* foncer, se darder
lure *n.* appât
lure *v.* attirer
lust *n.* luxure
lye *n.* caustique
lying *adj.* **be lying flat** être à plate **leave lying about** laisser à la traîne
lynch *v.* LYNCH
lynx *n.* pichou

M

machete *n.* machette
machine *n.* engin, machine **machine bolt** boulon **baling machine** emballeuse **harvesting machine** coupeuse **mowing machine** faucheuse **planting machine** planteur **reaping machine** ramasseuse **sewing machine** coudeuse, machine à coudre **thrashing machine** moulin à battre **threshing machine** batteuse **washing machine** laveuse **welding machine** soudeuse **sewing machine treadle** marchette **cane cutting machine** coupeuse à {de} cannes **cotton harvesting machine** ramasseuse à coton **rice cutting machine** coupeuse de riz **old, worn out tool or machine** fatras
machine-made *adj.* fait à la machine
machinery *n.* machinerie **one who operates heavy machinery** ingénieur
machinist *n.* ingénieur
mackerel *n.* maquereau **king mackerel** gros macriau, roi **yellow mackerel** maquereau
mad *adj.* chaud, fâché **get mad** s'embrouiller, se chauffer **get mad again** rebouquer **get angry, mad, upset** se choquer
madam *n.* madame, mame
maddening *adj.* enrageant
made *adj.* **made of** de, en **made or intended esp. for a given purpose** exprès **badly made** mal fait, malattriqué **ready made** tout fait
madhouse *n.* déboulis
madly *adv.* follement
madness *n.* folerie, folie
magazine *n.* magazine
magic *n.* **magic spell** ouanga
magical *adj.* charmant, magique **magical charm** ouanga
magician *n.* sorcier
magnesia *n.* magnésie **milk of magnesia** lait de magnésie
magnet *n.* aimant
magnetize *v.* magnatiser
magnificent *adj.* carabiné, magnifique
magnificently *adv.* magnifiquement
magnify *v.* magnifier
magnifying *n.* **magnifying glass** pierre à feu
magnitude *n.* grandeur
magnolia *n.* arbre à rameau, bois de rameaux, grand laurier **magnolia flower** magnolia **magnolia fuscata** calicantuce **magnolia tree** magnolia, rameau **banana magnolia** friscata **sweet bay magnolia** petit laurier **branch of a magnolia blessed by a priest on Palm Sunday** rameau
magus *n.* mage
mahogany *n.* acajou
maid *n.* domestique, servant **old maid** VALENTINE, vieille fille **remain an old maid** monter en grain(e), rester pour graine

maiden *n.* mademoiselle **having the maiden name of** née
maidenhair *n.* capillaire
mail *n.* MAIL, malle, poste **mail carrier** postillon
mail *v.* poster
mailbox *n.* boîte de poste, boîte à malle
mailman *n.* postillon
maim *v.* affliger, estropier **maim o.s.** s'estropier
maimed *adj.* démembré
main *adj.* cardinal, central, premier, principal **main entrance** portage, portale **main street** grande {grand'} rue, grande rue / grand'rue **main, essential, or basic thing** principal
mainly *adv.* principalement
mainstay *n.* **mainstay of a family** poteau du coin
maintain *v.* clamer, entretenir, garder, préserver, reclamer, soutenir, quitter, tenir
maintenance *n.* entretenue, entretien, entretiennement, maintien, support
maize *n.* maïs
majority *n.* la majeur partie, majorité, plupart **of the age of majority** grand, maître et majeur
make *v.* bâtir, composer, créer, faire, façonner, foutre, ramancher, se faire, percer **make up** comploter, débrouiller, faire camarades, forger, ramancher, se débrouiller, se forger, se réconcilier **make as if** faire comme si **make for o.s.** se faire **make up for** compenser **make up with** se refaire à **make up one's mind** se décider **make or do s.t. carelessly** gargoter **one who makes a big show of doing s.t. that is not really difficult** casseur de portes ouvertes
make-up *n.* **woman wearing too much make-up** Mardi Gras
maker *n.* auteur, faiseur **maker of a promissory note** prometteur **barrel maker** faiseur de baril **cabinet maker** meublier **furniture maker** meublier **quilt maker** quilteuse **sausage maker** saucisseur **trawlnet maker** découpeur
making *n.* faisage
maladjusted *adj.* **maladjusted person** malajusté
malady *n.* **malady of cows remedied by cutting off the horns** mal de corne
malaria *n.* fièvre longue / longue fièvre, fièvre malarienne, fièvre marélia, malaria
malcontent *n.* malcontent
male *adj.* mâle
male *n.* mâle
malediction *n.* malédiction
malfeasance *n.* malfaisance
malformation *n.* déformation
malice *n.* malice, malveillance, rancune **out of malice** par rancune
malicious *adj.* malicieux, malintentionné, malédictieux, mauvais, MEAN, méchant **malicious person** langue de serpent **wicked, evil, bad, malicious person or thing** maudit, méchant
maliciously *adv.* malicieusement
mallard *n.* **northern black mallard** canard noir du nord
mallet *n.* maillet
mallow *n.* mauve **false mallow** herbe à serpent **Indian mallow** herbe à serpent **crimson-eye rose mallow** guimauve
maltreat *v.* crucifier
mama *n.* maman, mame
mamou *n.* **mamou tea** thé de mamou
man *n.* bonhomme, bougre, homme, oh (y) yaïe / oh yé yaïe, yaïe, vieux chien **big man** gaillard, gros bétaille **delivery man** haleur **good man** vaillant bougre **my man** mon homme, mon nègre **nice man** vaillant bougre **old man** vieillard, vieux croûton, vieux nègre, vieux **one-eyed man** borgne **strong man** hercule **weak man** vache à lait **a man's house is his castle** charbonnier est maître chez lui **a man is master of his own house** charbonnier est maître chez lui **country man who assumes the pose of urban sophistication** fantoche **big, strapping man** boulet **heavy, stout man** patassa **short, stumpy man** crapaud **tough old man** boscoyo **burly, large, strong man** taupin **be a yes man for s.o.** sauter crapaud (pour qqn) **huge and strong man or animal** colosse **be a strong, powerful man** être homme **be one's right hand man** être le bras droite *pl.* **chase women or men** coursailler, courser
man-chaser *n.* chiennailleur, coursailleur, courseur
man-o'-war *n.* **man-o'-war bird** carencro de mer
manage *v.* arriver, faire galoper, galoper, manœuvrer, ménager, opérer, s'arracher, s'en haler de, se débarrasser, se débattre, se défendre, se démerder, se démêler, courir, manier
manageable *adj.* maniable, à (la) main
management *n.* administration, gouvernement, ménagement **home management** ménagerie
manager *n.* directeur, gérant, ménageur **manager on a plantation** écolome **female manager** ménagère
manatee *n.* vache de mer
mane *n.* crignasse, crin, crinière **having a golden or tan coat and a white or cream-colored mane and tail** baille
maneuver *v.* manœuvrer
maneuvering *n.* manigance
mange *n.* gale **as bad as the mange** maudit comme une gale
manger *n.* crèche, mangeoire
mangle *v.* **mangle o.s.** se massacrer **tear or mangle one's flesh** s'évianner **tear or mangle the flesh of** évianner
mangrove *n.* **mangrove tree** manglier
mangy *adj.* galeux
manhandle *v.* hartchiner
manihot *n.* arbre (à) volaille
manipulate *v.* manier
mankind *n.* monde
manner *n.* façon, manière *pl.* **manners** mœurs, manière **good manners** usage, étiquette **have bad manners** avoir des vilaines manières **lack of good manners** manque de retenue **person with affected manners** fionneur **person with stiff manners** pain de sucre

mannered *adj.* **overly mannered** fion-fion **well mannered** bien élevé, civil
mansion *n.* château
mantel *n.* corniche
mantelpiece *n.* boisure de cheminée, corniche
mantis *n.* **praying mantis** bâton, cheval de {du} diable / cheval-diable, diable
mantle *n.* cape, globe
mantlepiece *n.* cheminée **mantlepiece scarf** arbriquin
manufacture *n.* fabrication
manufacture *v.* fabriquer, manufacturer
manufactured *adj.* **be manufactured** se fabriquer
manufacturer *n.* manufactureur
manure *n.* fumier
many *adj.* beaucoup de, en masse de, un tas de, énormément **as many** autant de **so many** assez de, autant de
many *pron.* fièrement, hourra, joliment, plein de, plein **great many** chouinque **how many** combien **however many** n'importe combien **not many** pas grand, peu **so many** si tant, si tellement, tant **as many as** jusqu'à
manyplies *n.* feuillet
map *n.* carte, map
maple *n.* érable **maple tree** plaine **maple wood** plaine
mar *v.* **mar the appearance of** défigurer
marble *n.* cristal, marbre **marble made of agate** grillot **playing marble** canique, marbre, pure, stchoune *pl.* **lose one's marbles** perdre la canique / perdre ses {les} caniques
marbleized *adj.* marbré
march *n.* marche
March *n.* mars
Mardi *n.* **Mardi Gras** Mardi Gras **Mardi Gras celebration** carnaval **Mardi Gras king** roi **Mardi Gras runner** coureur de Mardi Gras **masked person who is celebrating Mardi Gras** Mardi Gras **take part in a costumed Mardi Gras run** courir Mardi Gras
mare *n.* jument, potresse, éleveuse **young mare** pouliche **wild, unbroken mare** potresse
margarine *n.* margarine
margin *n.* bordage, bord
Maria *n.* **Santa Maria** camomine sauvage
marigold *n.* œillet d'Inde / œillet de dinde / œillet français **bur marigold** fourchette **swamp marigold** fourchette
marinade *n.* marinade
marinate *v.* amariner
marinated *adj.* amariné
marinating *n.* amarinage
mariner *n.* **mariner's needle** boursole
marionette *n.* marionnette
mark *n.* but, impression, indication, marque, piste, remarque, signe, grade **mark left by fist** poque **beauty mark** signe postiche, signe **bench mark** borne **boundary mark** borne **having a star or white mark between the eyes** lunette
mark *v.* marquer, étamper **mark again** remarquer **mark up** marquailler **mark for identification** marquer
marked *adj.* marqué
marker *n.* **grave marker** remarque de tombe
market *n.* marché **meat market** halle **stock market** marché
marketplace *n.* marché
marksman *n.* tireur
marksmanship *n.* **marksmanship contest** pategau
marmalade *n.* marmalade
marriage *n.* mariage, noce **by marriage** par alliance **break marriage bonds** se démarier **perform the marriage ceremony of** marier **perform a marriage ceremony for again** remarier **announce an intended marriage** publier les bans **break up a household or marriage** casser le ménage **break up a relationship or marriage** casser la patte
married *adj.* **married couple** ménage **get married** faire chaudière ensemble, marier, s'emmancher, s'épouser, se casser le cou, se marier
marrow *n.* moelle
marrowy *adj.* moelleux
marry *v.* marier, épouser **marry again** se remarier **marry each other** s'épouser **never marry** monter en grain(e) **not marry in one's lifetime** rester pour graine **a woman who marries must accommodate herself to her husband's habits, family, etc.** qui prend mari, prend pays
marsh *n.* marais, mèche, platin, plérion, prés humides **marsh buggy** boghei de boue, boghei de plairie, traîneau **freshwater marsh** prairie **sea marsh** grande mèche **trembling marsh** maîche tremblant **treeless brackish or saltwater marsh** prairie (tremblante) **area in a salt marsh governed by the tides** mare
marshall *n.* **town marshall** constable
marshland *n.* **marshland that has been reclaimed by draining** dessèchement **alluvial marshland** prairie molle, prairie tremblante
marshmallow *n.* guimauve
marten *n.* fouine
martin *n.* **bee martin** corneille fouetteur **king martin** martin-plongeur **purple martin** hirondelle, oiseau de pluie *pl.* **any of a variety of swallows or martins** martinet
Martin *n.* **northern part of Saint Martin Parish** par en haut
martingale *n.* martingale
Martinsville *n.* **member of a group organized in Saint Martinsville in the early 1880s to restore white rule** régulateur
martyr *n.* martyr
martyr *v.* martyriser
martyrdom *n.* martyr
marvel *n.* merveille, miracle
marvelous *adj.* admirable, merveilleux
Mary *n.* **the Virgin Mary** Notre Dame
mash *n.* purée

mash *v.* mâcher, écraser, se mâcher

mask *n.* masque **wear a mask** se masquer **put on a mask** se masquer **take off one's mask** se démasquer

mask *v.* masquer

masked *adj.* masqué **masked person** masque

masking *n.* mascarade

mason *n.* maçon, maçonneur **mason's trowel** douelle

masonry *n.* maçonne, maçonnerie, maçonnage, maçonne **tear down masonry** démaçonner

masquerade *n.* mascarade

mass *n.* masse, volume **mass book** missel **have a mass said** recommander une messe

Mass *n.* messe **High Mass** grande messe **Low Mass** messe basse **Unsung Mass** messe basse **irreverent parody of the Catholic Mass** messe noire **prayers, singing, reading, etc., offered by lay people in lieu of actual Mass** messe blanche {sec}

massacre *n.* massacre, tuerie

massacre *v.* massacrer

massage *n.* massage

massage *v.* frotter

massaging *n.* frottage, frottement

masseur *n.* frotteur

masseuse *n.* frotteur

mast *n.* mât

master *n.* BOSS, maître **a man is master of his own house** charbonnier est maître chez lui

mastery *n.* mâtrissage

mastic *n.* mastic

masticate *v.* mâcher

mastication *n.* mâchage, mâchement

mastitis *n.* pis enflammé

masturbate *v.* s'abuser, tirer une poignette

masturbation *n.* masturbation, poignette

match *n.* allumette, MATCH, tournoi **boxing match** boxe **wrestling match** basculage, lutte **have no match** avoir rien à son épreuve **meet one's match** trouver son maître

match *v.* accorder, correspondre, rappareiller, s'accorder, s'adonner **match up** accorder, rappareiller **match up s.o. of quality with s.o. much less worthy or attractive** donner de la confiture aux cochons

mate *n.* **common-law mate** maquereau **deceased mate or spouse** son défunt / sa défunte

mate *v.* accoupler, s'accoupler

material *n.* matière, matérielle, étoffe **sealing material for walls** plafonnage **combustible material used for heating** chauffage **any stringy material** filasse **strip of material used in making a catalogne** pénille **fine net material used for mosquito bars, veils, etc.** bobinette **obtain clothes or material** se gréer **any wad of material used to clean one's bottom** torchon **any wad of material used to dust, clean up, or scrub** torchon **uneven thread in woven material** motelon **length of cord or material used to tie s.t.** amarre *pl.* **materials** matériaux **building materials** matériaux **collection of materials used for a specific task, occupation, etc.** gréement

maternity *n.* maternité

mathematician *n.* carculeur

mathematics *n.* mathématique

mating *n.* **take a cow to the bull for mating** pousser en parcage

matrix *n.* matrice

matted *adj.* **have one's hair all matted up** avoir sa crignasse en lutine

matter *n.* affaire, matière, question **foreign matter** bourrier **reading matter** littérature **no matter what I say or do** j'ai beau dire et j'ai beau faire **what's the matter?** qui il y a / qui y a / qui i-n-a / qui il a, quoi (il) y a? / quoi i-n-a? **as a matter of fact** enfin **skim floating matter from the surface of** écrémer

matter *v.* compter quelque chose, compter **it doesn't matter** n'importe, ça fait (pas) rien **it doesn't matter to me** autant à l'ancre qu'à la voile

mattress *n.* matelas **mattress cover** couétil **mattress covering** ensouillure **mattress ticking** couette de matelas, couétil **cotton mattress** matelas de coton **feather mattress** matelas de plume **moss mattress** matelas de mousse **shuck mattress** matelas de paille {paillasse} **straw mattress** matelas de paille {paillasse}, paillasse **corn shuck mattress** paillasse **contents of a straw mattress** paillassée

maturation *n.* meurizon

mature *adj.* bien {tout} formé, fort, mature

mature *v.* mûrir

maturity *n.* maturité, meurizon **time of life between childhood and maturity** jeunesse

maul *n.* masse

mauve *adj.* mauve

maw *n.* fale

maxim *n.* dicton

May *n.* mai

maybe *adv.* peut-être que, peut-être, possiblement

mayhaw *n.* pomme de mai, pommette **mayhaw tree** pommetier, pommette, pommier

mayonnaise *n.* mayonnaise

mayor *n.* maire de ville, maire

maypop *n.* liane de grenade, grenade

mazurka *n.* mazurka **a series of five dances, traditionally played in order: waltz, polka, waltz in two, two-step, mazurka** ronde de danses

me *pron.* me, moi **for me** moi **to me** dans moi {toi, eux, etc.}, me, moi **according to me** pour moi

meadow *n.* prairie, savane

meager *adj.* chéti

meal *n.* farine, repas **meal with guests** fricot **evening meal**

souper **light meal** collation **self-service meal** buffet **badly prepared meal** hoi **covered with meal** farineux **the noon meal** dîner **fried corn meal mush** couche-couche **eat the noon meal** dîner **sandwich or small meal** LUNCH **sprinkle with flour or meal** fariner

mealy *adj.* grémilleux

mean *adj.* bas, bengale, carnassier, chacta, espiègle, maudit, mauvais, MEAN, méchant, pichou **mean person** palais bleu, pirate **mean, disagreeable person** pichou **mean as a wasp** méchant comme une guêpe **mean, grouchy, ill-tempered person** bourreau **mean as a wasp or hornet** mauvaise comme une guêpe **say s.t. mean** passer une chique (à qqn) **hateful or mean person** vache habillée en zinc **in a bad, mean way** mauvais

mean *npl.* **means** instrument, manière, moyen, pousse-pousse, ressource **have means** avoir les {des} moyens, être en moyen **by means of** en, par **by no means** nullement

mean *v.* MEAN, vouloir dire

meander *v.* serpenter

meaning *n.* signification

meanly *adv.* chétiment

meanness *n.* maudiceté, mauditerie, mauvaiseté

meantime *n.* **in the meantime** dans l'intrevalle / dans les intrevalles

meanwhile *adv.* en attendant

measles *npl.* rougelles, rougeole **German measles** roséole

measurable *adj.* mesurable

measure *n.* mesure **dry measure** baril **in measure of** par

measure *v.* mesurer

measurement *n.* mesure, mesurement **measurement six feet in length** compas

measuring *adj.* **measuring cup** mesure **measuring spoon** mesure **measuring tape** mesure **twelve-inch rule or measuring stick** pied-de-roi / pied-du-roi

measuring *n.* mesurement **measuring cup** pinte de mesure, tasse à mesure **measuring tape** TAPE

meat *n.* bête, chair, viande, nanane **meat cleaver** CLEAVE **meat grinder** moulin à viande **meat market** halle **meat pie** pâté **meat sliced and pickled** grillade amarinée {à la marinée} **meat cooked on a barbecue pit** barbecue **ground meat** viande hachée, viande moulue **organ meat** viandes d'endedans **salted meat** viande salée **smoked meat** viande fumée **organ meat stew** grillades **roast meat over hot coals** barbecue **shank meat for stew or soup** jarret **portion of meat** rôti **prepared without meat** maigre **side of meat** plat-côté **pork organ meat stew** fricassée de cochon **pieces of meat that have been marinated, salted and peppered** grillades **abstain from eating meat** faire maigre **slice of salted meat** landrine **hard, tough, sinewy meat of poor grade** tiraille **parcel out cuts of meat** débiter **slice or cube of meat** grillade *pl.* **dish made of various meats and rice** galimatias **a share of assorted meats from community slaughtering** rôti

meatball *n.* boulette

meatless *adj.* maigre

mechanic *n.* artisan, mécanicien **mechanic work** mécanique **mechanic's shop** garage *pl.* **mechanics** mécanique

mechanically *adv.* machinalement

medal *n.* médaille

meddle *v.* fourrer le doigt partout, fourrer son nez, mettre son nez dans le bol, méler son grain de sel, pignocher, roufianer **repeatedly and obnoxiously meddle in other people's business** fouillailler

meddler *n.* roufian, roufianeur

meddlesome *adj.* **meddlesome person** pique-partout

meddling *adj.* fouillard

medical *adj.* médical **one who is under medical care or treatment** patient

medicament *n.* médicament

medicate *v.* médeciner **medicate o.s.** se médeciner

medication *n.* médecine

medicinal *adj.* médicinal

medicine *n.* médecine, médicament, remède **medicine tablet** tablette **take medicine** se médeciner **treat with medicine** médeciner

mediocre *adj.* quède

meditate *v.* jongler

meditation *n.* méditation

medium moyen

medlar *n.* **medlar tree** mispilusse, néfrier

meek *adj.* craintif

meekness *n.* humilité

meet *v.* joindre, rejoindre, rencontrer, s'assembler, se joindre, se réunir, s'accointer **meet accidentally** buter **meet with** joindre **meet each other** se rejoindre, se rencontrer **meet up with** rejoindre **meet each other again** se revoir **make ends meet** venir à bout

meeting *n.* appointement, assemblée, meeting, rencontre, réunion, rendez-vous **meeting place** rendez-vous **meeting of women for the purpose of carding cotton or wool** écarderie

melee *n.* mêlée

mellow *adj.* sage **make mellow** ameublir

melodious *adj.* mélodieux

melody *n.* chant, mélodie, TUNE

melon *n.* caloquinte, melon **honeydew melon** melon doux

melonette *n.* melon sent-bon, citron, cocombre-sent-bon

melt *v.* défiger, fondre, se fondre **cause to melt** défiger

melting *n.* fondage **reduce by melting** rendre

member *n.* membre **member of the jury** membre du jury **member of a body of officials** siège **member of a group or society** membre **member of a group organized in Saint Martinsville in the early 1880s to restore white rule** régulateur **become a member of** joindre

membrane *n.* membrane

memoir *n.* mémoire

memorable *adj.* mémorable
memory *n.* idée, mémoire, souvenance **have a good memory** avoir une tête **have a poor memory** avoir une tête de poule
menace *n.* menace
menace *v.* menacer
menacing *adj.* menaçant
menagerie *n.* ménagerie
mend *v.* arranger, entreturer, estopper, piéceter, raccommoder, rafistoler, rapiécer, rarranger, réparer **mend one's ways** se corriger, se réformer
mendable *adj.* raccommodable, réparable
mended *adj.* rafistolé
mendicant *n.* bégueur, tchamandeur
mending *n.* arrangement, raccommodage, rafistolage, rapiécement, rapiéçage, réparage, entretenage, entreturage
menhaden *n.* loche
meningitis *n.* **spinal meningitis** fièvre à vingt-quatre heures
menopause *n.* changement d'age, changement de vie, ménopause **go through menopause** avoir {faire} le tour d'âge, avoir le retour d'âge, changer de vie **she has reached menopause** son âge l'a passé
menses *n.* règle
menstruate *v.* avoir la marguerite, avoir le FLAG, avoir une semaine, régler, voir
mental *adj.* **of a normal mental state** naturel
mention *n.* mention **make mention** faire mention
mention *v.* mentionner, nommer **don't mention it** il y a pas de quoi
meow *n.* miaou
meow *v.* miauler
merchandise *n.* butin, marchanderie, marchandise **inferior merchandise** gargote
merchant *n.* marchand, trafiqueur, vendeur **pack merchant** marchand (de) paquet **wholesale merchant** grossier
merciful *adj.* miséricordieux
mercifully *adv.* miséricordieusement
mercurochrome *n.* MONKEY BLOOD
mercury *n.* mercure, vif-argent
mercy *interj.* tristesse
mercy *n.* compassion, merci, miséricorde **be at the mercy of** être à le merci de
mere *adj.* simple
merely *adv.* bonnement, justement
merganser *n.* **American merganser** bec-scie
meringue *n.* meringue **meringue custard dessert** œufs à la neige, île flottante
merit *n.* mérite, valeur
merit *v.* déserver, mériter
merry *adj.* gai, joyeux
merry-go-round *n.* carrousel, FLY-HORSE
mesh *n.* maillage **mesh wire** fil à volaille **make mesh** mailler
mesmerize *v.* magnatiser
mesquite *n.* mousquite
mess *n.* barbouillage, bastringue, compassion, criote, culbute, débauchage, dégât, galimatias, jambalaya, mélanage, méli-mélange, naufrage, pagaille, patasserie, pillage, pétrin, ratatin, tchampourra, échouerie, épaillage, éparpillage **make a mess** carnager, faire du {un} désordre, faire du degât, faire un jambalaya (de) **make a mess of** culbuter, dévaliser, massacrer
mess *v.* **mess around** couillonner, faire son couillon, foutumasser, s'embêter **mess up** barboter, barbouiller, bouchonner, bousiller, cochonner, culbuter, défropter, défroqueter, gargoter, goudronner, gâcher, lâcher la patate, pirater, pondre un œuf, soursoubler **mess things up** brasser mer et larmes **mess up one's hair** s'ébouriffler **mess up the hair of** ébouriffler, écheveler **one who messes up writing, painting, etc.** barbouilleur
message *n.* communication, message, commission **written message** lettre, note **carry a message** faire une commission **send a message** laisser connaître
messed *adj.* **messed up** dévergondé, malfoutu **get one's hair messed up** se décoiffer
messenger *n.* commissionnaire, courrier, messager
messing *n.* **messing up of the hair** ébouriffiage
messy *adj.* **the place in question is messy, disorganized, cluttered** Caillette pourrait perdre son veau là-dedans
metal *n.* métal **made of stainless metal or aluminum** brillant **any brightly colored rust-resistant metal** fer-blanc **thin, straight cylindrical piece or bar of metal or wood** barreau *pl.* **any of a variety of metals** zinc
meteorite *n.* pierre à tonnerre
method *n.* pratique, procès
Methodist *adj.* méthodiste
meticulous *adj.* rangeux, suspect **be precise, exacting or meticulous** mettre les points sur les i
mew *n.* miaou
mew *v.* miauler
mewing *n.* mialement
Mexican *adj.* mexicain
Mexican *n.* Mexicain
Mexico *n.* **Gulf of Mexico** Golfe du Mexique **the Gulf of Mexico** la grande mer
microphone *n.* microphone
mid *prefix.* mi-
mid-forties *n.* mi-quarante
Mid-Lent *prefix.* mi-carême
midday *n.* mi-jour, midi
middle *n.* centre, milieu, mitan **in the middle** au milieu **right in the middle** au beau milieu / droite dans le milieu **right in the middle of** droite au ras de
middle-sized moyen
middle. *n.* **in the middle.** au beau milieu
middling *adj.* quède
midget *n.* chacta

midnight *n.* minuit
midriff *n.* ceinture
midsummer *n.* **midsummer's day dew** eau de Saint-Jean
midway *adv.* en mi-route
midwife *n.* accoucheuse, chasse-femme, femme sage
might *n.* pouvoir **with all one's might** à tout décarabiné
might *v.* **one might as well say** (vaut) autant dire
mighty *adj.* puissant
migraine *n.* migraine
migratory *adj.* voyageur
mil *n.* millième
milder *adj.* **become milder** s'amollir
mildew *n.* moisi, moisissure
mildew *v.* moisir, cramoisir
mildewed *adj.* moisi **become mildewed** se moisir
mile *n.* mille **half mile** demi-mille *pl.* **miles per hour** milles à l'heure
mileage *n.* millage
militant *adj.* militant
military *n.* militaire, service **military officer** officier **military service** service **military tank** TANK **do one's military service** faire son service **military service** service militaire
militia *n.* milice
milk *n.* lait, lolo **milk cow** laitière, vache à lait **milk pail** bassin à lait **milk praline** praline au lait **milk strainer** passe-lait **milk tooth** caquisse **milk of magnesia** lait de magnésie **milk left in a cow's udder for the calf after milking** lampogne, renvoyure **clabbered milk** lait caillé **low-fat milk** lait bleu **skim milk** lait bleu **coffee with milk** café au lait **pitcher of milk** pot de lait **on a milk diet** au lait **drink made of milk poured over carmelized sugar** café au lait
milk *v.* tirer, traire **milk again** retirer
milked *v.* **get into position to be milked** se pier
milker *n.* laitier
milking *n.* tirage
milking-pail *n.* tire-vache
milkmaid *n.* laitière
milkman *n.* laitier
milkweed *n.* herbe à houatte, laitereau, petit pourpier **common milkweed** mal-nommée
Milky *adj.* **the Milky Way** poussinière
mill *n.* usine, moulin **coffee mill** moulin à café **corn mill** moulin à maïs **cotton mill** moulin à coton **grist mill** moulin à gru **hulling mill** moulin à piles **rice mill** moulin à riz **sugar mill** moulin à sucre, sucrerie **syrup mill** sucrerie **horse-operated mill of five pestles** moulin à piles **sugar cane mill** moulin à canne
mill *v.* moudre, piler, mouler **mill around** marchailler, mouliner, tournailler
miller *n.* moudeur, moulinier **miller payment** moudurage, moulinage **miller's fee** moudurage, moulinage
millet *n.* mil, millet **broomcorn millet** herbe à balai
milliner *n.* modiste
milling *n.* pilage **milling around** moulinage **grinding or milling** moudage, moulage **corn grinding or milling** moulage de maïs
million *n.* million *pl.* **millions** des milles
millionaire *n.* millionnaire
millipede *n.* bétaille à mille pattes, bête à mille pattes, mille-pattes
mimic *v.* imiter, moquer
mimosa *n.* mimosa **mimosa tree** gloire d'Asie, loucou
mince *v.* hacher, moudre, mouler **not mince words** pas mettre des gants
mind *n.* esprit, idée, intention, tête **in mind** à (la) main **bear in mind** retiendre en mémoire **change one's mind** changer son idée, se dégoûter **change s.o.'s mind** dégoûter **come to mind** venir à l'idée **dull, slow-witted mind** esprit barosse {rosse} **frame of mind** disposition **lose one's mind** perdre la carte, perdre la raison, perdre son idée **presence of mind** présence d'esprit **speak one's mind** parler français **state one's mind or intention** se déclarer **in one's right mind** en connaissance **make up one's mind** faire son idée, se décider **talk out of one's mind** baranquer **totally out of one's mind** fou à baver sus sa chemise / fou à courir les chemins {à manger de l'herbe} **not be in one's right mind** pas avoir (son) idée / pas avoir (sa) bonne idée **cause to change his or her mind** dévirer
mind *v.* **mind one's own business** s'occuper de sa tambouille à soi-même, s'occuper de ses affaires {oignons}, s'occuper de ses affaires **mind your own business** va brasser dans tes chaudières **never mind** n'importe
mine *n.* mine *pl.* **lay explosive mines** miner
mine *poss.* mien
mine *v.* miner, miner
miner *n.* mineur
mineral *n.* minéral
mingle *v.* se mêler, se faufiler
mini-blind *n.* BLIND
minister *n.* ministre, prêcheur *pl.* **title in addressing certain ministers, Catholic monks or brothers** frère
ministry *n.* ministère
mink *n.* belette
minnow *n.* loche, mini, truite
minor *adj.* véniel
minor *n.* mineur
mint *n.* baume tranquille, baume, menthe
minus *prep.* moins
minute *n.* minute **in a minute** bientôt, à la minute
miracle *n.* miracle
miraculous *adj.* miraculeux
mire *n.* boue **stick in the mire** embourber
mirliton *n.* **mirliton plant** pied de mirliton
mirror *n.* miroir

mirrored *adj.* **be reflected or mirrored** réflecter
misbehave *v.* brigander, faire des brigandages, faire des corcobiages, mener
misbehavior *n.* brigandage
miscarriage *n.* fausse-couche, fausse accouchement, fausse-couche, perte **have a miscarriage** perdre **lose by miscarriage** perdre
miscarry *v.* avorter, perdre
mischief *n.* canaillerie, malfaisance, malice **make mischief** brigander, canailler **malicious mischief** carnage **full of mischief** damné **engage in malicious mischief** carnager
mischief-maker *n.* malicieux **old mischief-maker** vieux damné
mischievous *adj.* brigand, canaille, carnassier, damné, fibi, indigne, malfaisant, malicieux, maudit, méchant, nigeant, par en-dessous, réveillé **mischievous child** brigand **mischievous person** canaille, macaque, malicieux, maudit, rogoyo **mischievous, disobedient child** possédé **be mischievous** faire des macaqueries **naughty, mischievous female** pichouette **be mischievous or hyperactive** avoir le diable au corps
mischievously *adv.* **act mischievously** faire les quatre cents coups
mischievousness *n.* canaillerie, macaquerie, malice
misdeal *n.* MISDEAL
miser *n.* avare, chiche
miserable *adj.* misérable, pouillasse, ratché **miserable person** misérable **be miserable** misérer **be in a miserable position** tirer le diable par la queue
miserably *adv.* misérablement, tristement
miserliness *n.* chicheresse, chichetesse, chicheté
miserly *adj.* chiche, juif, TIGHT
misery *n.* misère, mortel, pouillasserie **misery case** pratique à chagrin **deal misery** faire (de) la misère (à qqn) **cause misery and trouble** brasser mer et larmes **suffer misery or a hard time with** passer du bleu de ciel avec qqn, soufferre du bleu de ciel avec **state of misery** débine
misfire *v.* rater, manquer
misfit *n.* malajusté, rebut
misfortune *n.* calamité, malchance, malheur, misère, tragédie **constant misfortune** guigne
misgiving *n.* apercevance
mishandle *v.* maltraiter
mishap *n.* accident, malchance, malheur
misjudge *v.* maljuger
mislead *v.* égarer
misleading *adj.* trompeur
misled *adj.* maladvisé
mismatched *adj.* dépareillé
misplace *v.* déplacer, écarter
misplaced *adj.* écarté
miss *n.* demoiselle, mademoiselle, mamselle
miss *v.* manquer, regretter, s'ennuyer **miss the chance** manquer le coup **miss by a narrow margin** se rater
missal *n.* missel
misshape *v.* déformer
misshapen *adj.* malformé
missing *adj.* **nothing is missing** c'est sellé et bridé **be or go missing** manquer
mission *n.* mission
missionary *n.* missionnaire **series of sermons by a missionary lasting three to seven days** mission
Mississippi *n.* **Mississippi River** fleuve
missive *n.* lettre
mist *n.* brouillard, nuage, serein **fine mist** petite pluie fine **there is a mist or vapor rising from the ground** les pierres sont après brûler
mist *v.* brumasser, grimacer
mistake *n.* erreur, faute, MISTAKE, trompe, échappe **foolish mistake** bêtise **make a mistake** fauter, se tromper **make a big mistake** chier sur le palonnier, faire une coche mal taillée
mistake *v.* **mistake s.o. or s.t. for s.o. or s.t. else** prendre qqn/qqch pour qqn/qqch
mistaken *adj.* en erreur **be mistaken** faire une coche mal taillée, se tromper
mister *n.* monsieur
mistflower *n.* herbe à crapaud blanche
mistletoe *n.* **bunch of mistletoe** couronne de chêne
mistreat *v.* abuser, abîmer, basculer, bourlinguer, bourrasser, brutaliser, maganer, maltraiter
mistreatment *n.* bourlingue, brutalité
mistress *n.* maîtresse, poupoune
mistrust *n.* méfiance
misty *adj.* boucané, brouillé, brumassant, embrouillé
misunderstanding *n.* brouille, difficulté, malcompris, malentendu, méli-mélange
misunderstood *adj.* mal compris
misuse *n.* abus
mite *n.* mite
miter *n.* mitre
mitten *n.* mitaine, mitasse, ménotte
mix *n.* assemblage
mix *v.* démêler, mélanger, mêlailler, mêler, mêlzir, s'entremêler, se faufiler, se mêler, abâtardir, brasser, s'enfaufiler **mix again** remêler **mix up** mêlailler, ramancher **mix with** se mêlailler **mix with a utensil** battre
mix-up *n.* mélanage
mixed *adj.* assorti, bâtard, varié, abâtardi, baroque **mixed blood** sang mêlé **not mixed** STRAIGHT **be mixed up** s'emmêler **get mixed up with** se mêler dans **offspring of mixed blood** bâtard **person of mixed blood or impure race** sang-mêlé **person of mixed white and African-American blood** bleu, quarteron **woman of mixed Caucasian and American Indian descent** vénus **person of mixed white, Native**

American, and/or African-American blood Sabine **in a broken, mixed way** baroque

mixing *n.* brassage, brassement

mixture *n.* amalgame, assemblage, décoction, galimatias, gombo, mélange **mixture of all sorts of things** jambalaya **mixture of mud and Spanish moss used in the construction of houses and chimneys** bousillage

moan *v.* gémir, se lamenter

moaning *n.* beuglage, beuglement

mob *n.* ripopée

moccasin *n.* choupèque, quantier, soulier sauvage **water moccasin** congo à tête plate / serpent congo, congo, serpent congo, serpent d'eau, serpent à tête plate

mock *v.* moquer, se moquer

mockery *n.* moquerie

mocking *adj.* moqueur

mockingbird *n.* moqueur, tcharatte **French mockingbird** moqueur français {muet / sauvage / d'hiver}

model *n.* exemple, modèle, patron

moderate *v.* adoucir, modérer, se modérer

modest *adj.* modeste

modestly *adv.* modestement

modesty *n.* modestie

modify *v.* modifier

moist *adj.* humide, souple **become damp or moist** s'humecter

moisten *v.* détremper, humecter, tremper

moistness *n.* humidité

moisture *n.* humidité

molar *n.* molaire

molasses *n.* BLACK JOE, melasse

mold *n.* champignon, moisi, moisissure, moule, moule

mold *v.* mouler, pétriner

moldboard *n.* oreille

molding *n.* moulage, moule, moulure, quille

moldy *adj.* moisi **get moldy** se moisir

mole *n.* signe de beauté, signe, dartre, taupe **mole tunnel** souterrain **false mole** signe postiche

molest *v.* **sexually molest** affronter

molt *v.* dumer

mom *n.* maman, mame

moment *n.* heure, instant, moment, secousse, temps, point **any moment** n'importe quand **at the moment** pour le moment, sur le moment **from the moment** dès que / desque / drès que **in a moment** dans un (tit) élan, dans un instant, dans un moment **right this moment** pour le moment *pl.* **moments ago** juste, justement

monastery *n.* monastère

Monday *n.* lundi

money *n.* argent, monnaie, pousse-pousse **earn money** se faire de l'argent, se gagner de l'argent **make money** se faire de l'argent **save money** ménager, économiser **silver money** argent blanc, argent claire **waste money** gaspiller de l'argent **withdraw money** retirer de l'argent **have no money** être à la hache **sack of money** bourse **waster of money** gavagneur **not save money in a bank** cacher son argent dans des cornes à bœuf **ride competitively or for money** toucher **make a lot of money by questionable means** se graisser la patte

money-box *n.* banque

mongrel *adj.* abâtardi

mongrel *n.* bâtard, taïaut

mongrelized *adj.* **be mongrelized** s'abâtardir

mongrelizing *n.* abâtardissage, abâtardissement

monk *n.* religieux *pl.* **title in addressing certain ministers, Catholic monks or brothers** frère

monkey *n.* macaque **monkey wrench** clef anglaise

Monkey *n.* **Parrot and Monkey brand baking powder** YEAST macaque

monkeyshine *npl.* **monkeyshines** canicroche, macaquerie

mons pubis *n.* bosse

Monsignor *n.* monseigneur

monster *n.* bétaille, monstre, tataille

month *n.* mois **every month** tous les mois **last month** le mois passé **next month** le mois prochain / le mois qui vient **a week, a month, two days ago** ça donne une semaine {un mois / deux jours} que *pl.* **in two months** dans deux mois

monthly *adv.* tous les mois

monument *n.* monument

moo *v.* beugler

mood *n.* disposition, humeur, veine **bad mood** humeur furvoyante **subject to mood swings** journalier **in a bad mood** de {en} mauvaise humeur, enflé, mal en train **in a good mood** (de / en) bonne humeur, gai comme un fou **be in a bad mood** avoir un pet accroché, avoir une croche (d') accrochée, babiller, regricher, être dans les brindezingues, être dans ses feurdaines, être de {en} travers, être en chimère **be in a contrary mood** avoir le jabot de travers, avoir un coup de lune, avoir un grain, avoir un tour de lune **be in a cranky mood** avoir un pet en long

moody *adj.* bourru, journalier **moody person** journalieux

moon *n.* lune **full moon** plein de (la) lune, pleine lune **new moon** nouveau de lune **phase of the moon** quartier **waning of the moon** clin de lune

moonlight *n.* clair de lune

moonstruck *adj.* frappé de la lune

moor *v.* amarrer

mop *n.* MOP, vadrouille **floor mop** essuie-place

mop *v.* fourbir, MOP, passer **one who scrubs or mops** fourbisseur

mopping *n.* fourbissage

moral *adj.* chaste, moral

moral *npl.* **morals** mœurs **of weak morals** basse-classe **woman of loose morals** fouine, jument de brancard **woman of questionable morals** poupoune

more *adj.* d'autre

more *adv.* davantage, encore, mieux, plus, plutôt **more than** au-dessus (de), par-dessus **more and more** de plus en plus **more or less** dans un approchant, manière, plus ou moins **even more** encore plus **much more** bien plus **no more** pus **once more** de nouveau **still more** encore plus **not more than** juste **neither more nor less** ni plus ni moins, ni plus, ni moins **no more than that** pas plus que ça **use more than usual** forcer **do more than the usual** faire des fanferluches **the more it goes, the worse it gets** le plus ça va, le pire c'est **all the more** d'autant plus **so much more** d'autant plus

more *prefix.* re-

moreover *adv.* aussi bien

moreover *conj.* bien que

morning *n.* avant-midi, matin, matinée **morning glory** belle de jour, liane à marteau, livrier **morning glory vine** gloire du matin **good morning** bonjour **this morning** (à) ce matin, à (ce) matin / ce matin **wild morning glory** liserine **early in the morning** de bon matin

moron *n.* biorque, emplâtre, espingouin, estronfillau

morose *adj.* paisé

morrow *n.* lendemain

morsel *n.* écale **tasty morsel** nanane

mortal *adj.* mortel **mortal blow** coup mortel **mortal sin** péché mortel

mortality *n.* mortalité

mortally *adv.* mortellement

mortar *n.* mortier, pile **mortar and pestle** pile et pilon

mortar-mix *n.* mortier

mortarful *n.* pilée

mortgage *n.* hypothèque

mortgage *v.* hypothéquer

mortify *v.* mortifier **mortify o.s.** se mortifier

mortifying *adj.* mortifiant

mortise *n.* mortaise

mortise *v.* mortaiser

mortising *n.* mortaisage

mosquito *n.* cousin, maringouin, moustique **mosquito bar** bère, drap à maringoins, moustiquaire **mosquito larva** lève-queue, tourne-queue **mosquito net** bère, drap à maringoins, moustiquaire

moss *n.* mousse **moss mattress** matelas de mousse **remove moss** émousser **rose moss** pourpier **Spanish moss** barbe espagnole, mousse espagnole, mousse **removal of moss** émoussage **mixture of mud and Spanish moss used in the construction of houses and chimneys** bousillage

most *n.* plupart **at most** tout au plus **the most** plus **at the most** tout au plus

mostly *adv.* plussement, surtout

motel *n.* motel

moth *n.* mite

moth-eaten *adj.* mangeaillé, miteux, mité, piqué

mothball *adj.* boule de carbolique

mother *n.* maman, mère **mother superior** mère **my mother** ma vieille

Mother *n.* **loose dress widely known as a Mother Hubbard** blouse (volante)

mother-in-law *n.* belle-mère

mother-of-pearl *n.* nacre

motherhood *n.* maternité

motherless *adj.* orphelin de mère

motion *n.* geste, grouillement, motion, mouvement **swinging motion** balan

motivate *v.* émouver

motley *adj.* barosse

motor *n.* engin, machine **inboard motor** PUTTPUTT

mottled *adj.* pivelé

mound *n.* butte, côteau, taille **mound of potatoes covered with dirt for storage** pataterie **pimple mound** huppe **make a mound of** embutter *pl.* **store in mounds** butter

mound *v.* embutter

mount *v.* grimper, monter **mount one's courage, fortitude, determination or resistance** se pomper **stuff and mount** usiner

mountain *n.* montagne

mounting *n.* **mounting or putting together** gréement

mourner *n.* pleureur

mourning *n.* deuil **in mourning** en deuil **partial mourning** demi-deuil **wear mourning** porter le deuil **in deep mourning** en gros deuil

mouse *n.* souris

mousetrap *n.* attrape à souris, trappe à souris

mouth *n.* attrape-mouches / attrape à mouches, babiche, balafre, bec, bouche, grabot, gueule **mouth of the river** bouche de la rivière **mouth sore in an infant** mal blanc **mouth of a river or bayou** engueulement **big mouth** grosse babiche **shut one's mouth** fermer sa bouche, fermer son grabot **make the mouth water** faire la bouche couler **cause the mouth to pucker** barrer la bouche **not open one's mouth** pas siffler

mouthful *n.* chique, gobe, gorgée, gueulée, bouchée **big mouthful** gobet

movable *adj.* transportable

move *n.* délogement **wrestling move in which a wrestler places one leg behind his opponent's legs and pulls him backwards to the mat** jambette **any sudden move or spurt** estampique **one who is always on the move** rôdeur

move *v.* braguer, charrier, charroyer, décaniller, déloger, déménager, grouiller, manier, mouver, remuer, se grouiller, se haler, se remuer, émouver, déménager **move about** gigailler, ginguer, mouver **move again** regrouiller **move ahead** s'avancer **move along** tirailler **move around** grouiller, mouliner **move away** débagager, se déloger **move back** BACK, reculer, se reculer **move forward** avancer **move in** se loger **move o.s.** se décaniller, se déniquer, se haler, se transplanter **move on** débagager **move out** décamper **move toward** se diriger **move up** avancer **move a house** traîner une maison **move s.o. to sadness** crever le cœur à qqn **move to new lodgings** reloger, se reloger **move by means of rollers** rouler **move o.s. out of the way** se pousser **move from one place or job to another** transférer **cause to move out** déniquer **one who moves around a lot** navigueur **one who is always moving around** cerf-volant

movement *n.* grouillement, mouvement, remuage, remuement **bowel movement** selle **rocking movement** bercement **vigilante movement** vigilance **have a bowel movement** aller à la selle / avoir une selle, se débloquer

movie *n.* film, portrait, portraits grouillants, SHOW **movie theater** maison de SHOW, SHOW *pl.* **movies** portrait, SHOW

moving mouvant

moving *n.* déménagement, remuage **moving around** moulinage **house moving** traînage de maison **wooden roller used for moving buildings** rance

mow *v.* faucher **mow the lawn** couper les herbes

mower *n.* **lawn mower** coupe-paille, coupeuse d'herbes, faucheuse, lawn-mower, machine à z-herbe **sickle bar mower** raseuse

mowing *n.* fauchage **mowing machine** faucheuse **close mowing or cutting of grass** raclage d'herbe **ready for mowing** fauchable

Mrs. *n.* madame, mame

much *adj.* beaucoup de, en masse de

much *adv.* affreux, beaucoup, fameusement, fièrement, foutûment, gros, joliment, MUCH, plein de, plein, très, à mort, énormément **as much** autant de, autant **how much** combien, comme, comment **how much?** comment gros de **not much** pas grand, pas grand'chose, pas grande affaire, pas MUCH, peu **so much** assez de, autant de, autant, si tant, si tellement, tant, tellement, à force (que) **too much** de trop, trop **as much as** tant que **as much as one wishes** à son contentement **not too much** pas de trop **twice as much** double

much *n.* un tas de, un tas **so much for that** adieu la calèche! **have too much** en avoir par dessus la tête

mucus *n.* flegme, morve, morviat, rhume, roupille **dried mucus** crapaud de nez, crapaud, crèpe

mud *n.* boue, limon **mud dauber** guêpe noire **mud guard** garde-boue **mud hole** bourbier, bourbière **mud puddle** bourbier **wet mud** vase **clean mud off of** débousiller **cover with mud** embourber **free from mud** débourber **clean away mud or filth** décrotter **mixture of mud and Spanish moss used in the construction of houses and chimneys** bousillage **get free from mud** se débourber **pull from the mud** débourber **stuck in the mud** embourbé **clean o.s. of mud or filth** se décrotter **get bogged down in mud** abouer **get stuck in the mud** embourber, s'embourber **walk around in the mud** patrouiller

mudball *n.* **mudball placed on a stick and thrown at a distance** boule à nana {nénaine} *pl.* **fight with mudballs** se sabouler

mudboat *n.* bateau de boue

muddle *n.* embrouille, jambalaya

muddy *adj.* bourbeux, bourbé, bousilleux, bousillé, embourbé, vaseux, trouble **muddy expanse** vasière **get muddy** se bourber **get o.s. muddy** s'embourber

muddy *v.* embarbouiller, embourber, saganer

mudfish *n.* choupique, meuille

mudhole *n.* pétrin

mudroom *n.* **room or building used as a pantry, mudroom, laundry room, etc.** dépense

mug *n.* gobelet, moque **shaving mug** savonnette

muggy *adj.* lourd

mulatto *n.* mulâtre, mêlé **light-colored mulatto** passé-blanc **light-skinned mulatto, usually with predominantly Caucasian features** quarteron **insulting name for an African-American, a mulatto, or a Cajun** bougali

mulberry *n.* mûre d'arbre **mulberry tree** mûrier **French mulberry** chassepareille

mulch *n.* **remove ground cover or mulch** détourer

mule *n.* bourriquet, bourrique, mule, muloche, mulet **stud mule** JACK **fittings for horse or mule** harnais

mullein *n.* **common mullein** molène **turkey mullein plant** molène

mullet *n.* meuille **striped mullet** meuille

mullion *n.* **window mullion** montant

multicolored *adj.* caille

multiplier *n.* **multiplier onion** échalote

multitude *n.* foule

mumble *v.* barboter, jargonner, mâchouiller ses mots, rabâcher, ramancher

mumbling *n.* baribara, jargon

mumps *npl.* jobe

municipal *adj.* municipal

munition *n.* munition

murder *n.* assassin, assassinat, assassination, meurtre

murder *v.* assassiner

murderer *n.* assassin, assassineur, tueur

murky *adj.* trouble

murmur *v.* susurrer

muscadine *n.* liane de soco, muscat, soco **muscadine vine** soco **white muscadine** soco blanc

muscat *n.* **muscat grape** muscat **muscat wine** muscat

muscatel *n.* muscatel

muscle *n.* muscle, nerf **pulled muscle** nerf halé *pl.* **having stiff or sore muscles or joints** escran

muscular *adj.* bien membré, membré comme une tortue de rosée

muser *n.* jongleur

museum *n.* musée

mush *n.* moche **fried corn meal mush** couche-couche
mushroom *n.* champignon, maison de crapaud
music *n.* musique **Creole music** la-la **zydeco music** zaricot **piece of music** pièce de musique **loud, jazzy hillbilly music** tchinqui-tchinque **traditional Acadian Cajun/ Creole music** musique française
musician *n.* joueur de musique, musicien
musing *adj.* jongleur
musked *adj.* musqué
musket *n.* musqette **open-hammered musket** fusil à piston
muskmelon *n.* melon (en) français / melon de France, melon musqué
muskrat *n.* rat musqué, rat **muskrat house** butte à rat / butte de rat musqué
musky *adj.* musqué
mussel *n.* palourde
mussing *n.* échevelage
must *v.* devoir, être obligé, devoir
mustache *n.* moustache
mustard *n.* moutarde **mustard greens** moutarde **mustard plaster** sinapisse
mustiness *n.* moisi, moisissure
mute *adj.* muet
mutt *n.* taïaut
mutter *v.* gourgousser, ramancher
muttering *n.* baribara
mutton *n.* mouton, viande de mouton **mutton suet** graisse de mouton **leg of mutton** gigot
muzzle *n.* bonnet, bossal, bossard, bouche-gueule, museau, panier
my *poss.* le, mon
myopic *adj.* myope
myrtle *n.* **myrtle tree** gastronia **crape myrtle** arbre Saint-Jean, bois rose, gastronia, laurier rose, myrte rose, myrtille **sea myrtle** manglier **wax myrtle** cirier
myself *pron.* me, moi-même **myself, yourself, ourselves, etc.** entre moi-même {toi-même, nous-mêmes, etc.}
mysterious *adj.* mystérieux
mystery *n.* mystère
mystic *n.* devineur
mystify *v.* mystifailler, mystifier

N

naïve *adj.* naïve, vert comme de l'herbe
naïveté *n.* naïveté
nacre *n.* nacre
nag *n.* attineur, picocheur
nag *v.* attiner, faire (de) la misère (à qqn), obstiner, picocher, pourgaler, querellailler, picocher, prêcher **torment or nag s.o.** être derrière qqn **one who picks at or nags** picocheur
nagging *n.* babillage, cassement de tête
nail *n.* carvelle, clou de marteau, clou, ongle, accrochoire
nail *v.* attacher, clouer
nailing *n.* attachage, clouage
naked *adj.* nu **buck naked** nu tchu **get naked** se mettre (tout) nu **completely or stark naked** nu comme un ver / tout nu
nakedness *n.* nudité
namby-pamby *n.* toutout
name *n.* nom **Christian name** premier nom **first name** premier nom **given name** nom donné, premier nom **last name** nom de famille / dernier nom **pet name** sobriquet **in name only** à gros grain **perpetuate the name** relever le nom (de) **having the maiden name of** née *pl.* **call bad names** appeler des {les} noms
name *v.* appeler, appointer, mentionner, nommer
named *adj.* **be named** s'appeler **one named** nommé
namesake *n.* tocaille
naming *n.* appointement
nap *n.* NAP, somme **take a nap** faire {prendre} un somme, faire singo, prendre un NAP, sommeiller, être après {à} singo **take a cat nap** soguer **take a good nap** cogner un bon somme
nape *n.* **nape of the neck** barre du cou, cagouette
napkin *n.* serviette **sanitary napkin** braguette, linge
narrate *v.* conter, raconter, ramancher
narration *n.* raconte
narrow *adj.* juste, étroit **small or narrow** large comme deux doigts / large comme mes deux fesses
nastiness *n.* cochonnerie
nasty *adj.* cochon, dédaignable, méchant, vilain, zirable, vilain **do nasty things** faire des cochonneries **say nasty things** dire des cochonneries {saletés / saloperies}, dire des cochonneries **do nasty things or immodest acts** faire des vilaines choses **in an ugly or nasty way** vilain
nation *n.* nation
Nation *npl.* **the United Nations** les Nations Unies
national *adj.* national **national guard** milice
national *n.* national
nationality *n.* nationale, nationalité
native *adj.* native, originaire **native land** pays natal **native to Louisiana** créole
native *n.* native
nativity *n.* nativité **nativity scene** crèche
natural *adj.* naturel, naturel **natural gas** gaz
naturally *adv.* comme de juste, naturel, naturellement, normal
nature *n.* nature
naught *n.* zéro **turn to naught** tomber en poudre {poussière}
naughty *adj.* brigand, espiègle **naughty, disobedient girl** chatte **naughty, mischievous female** pichouette

nausea *n.* mal au cœur, vomissement
nauseate *v.* acœurer
navel *n.* bourrique, cabri, nombril
navigable *adj.* navigable
navigate *v.* naviguer
navigation *n.* navigation
navigator *n.* navigateur, navigueur
nay *adv.* non
near *adj.* rapproché
near *adv.* (à) côté de, alentour (de) / à l'entour (de), alentour, approché, au ras (de), auprès de, auprès, autour (de), collé à {après / de}, collé, environ, proche de, près de, près, à touché **be near** toucher à **from near and far** de près, de loin
near-at-hand *adj.* à (la) main
nearby *adv.* alentour, au ras, dans les parages, près, tout près, à portée, à touché
nearing *adj.* **be nearing** donner sur
nearly *adv.* approchant, bien proche, en approchant, environ, manière, presque, proche que, proche, près de, quasiment, manquer de, vouloir
nearsighted *adj.* myope
neat *adj.* net, propre
neatness *n.* netteté, propreté
necessarily *adv.* nécessairement, obligé, obligément
necessary *adj.* nécessaire **be necessary** falloir **it is necessary to do without things sometimes** à la guerre comme à la guerre
necessity *n.* besoin, nécessité, obligeance **of necessity** nécessairement
neck *n.* cou **stiff neck** torticolis **break one's neck** se casser le cou **wring the neck of** étourdir **bare one's neck and shoulders** se décolleter **expose the neck and shoulders of** décolleter **back of the neck** cagouette **crick in the neck** torticolis **nape of the neck** barre du cou, cagouette **baring of the neck, shoulders, etc.** décolletage
necklace *n.* collier
neckline *n.* **low neckline** décolletage **having a low neckline** décolleté
necktie *n.* cravate
need *n.* besoin, nécessité **be in need, in distress** être dans le besoin
need *v.* avoir besoin (de), avoir de besoin (de) **need to be taught a lesson** avoir besoin du manila trempe **not need** pas avoir la peine
needed *adj.* **be needed** être de besoin
needle *n.* aiguille **needle for making mesh** aiguille à mailler **hypodermic needle** aiguille **mariner's needle** boursole **sewing needle** aiguille à fil **eye of a needle** chas *pl.* **be on pins and needles** être sur les épingles
needlefish *n.* aiguille, crayon
needlework *n.* couture
needy *adj.* collant
ne'er-do-well *n.* fatras
negative *n.* négative
negatively *adv.* négative
neglect *n.* mal soin, négligeation, négligence
neglect *v.* négliger **neglect o.s.** s'abandonner, se négliger
neglected *adj.* **neglected child** enfant à la traîne **neglected condition** dévaldrague
neglectful *adj.* négligent
negligence *n.* négligeation, négligence
negligent *adj.* négligent **be negligent in doing s.t.** faire à la six-quatre-deux
negligible *adj.* négligeable
negotiate *v.* **negotiate the terms of** amarrer
negotiation *npl.* **in negotiations** en parlement
negro *n.* nègre
negro-town *n.* faubourg
neigh *v.* hennir, rechigner
neighbor *n.* prochain, voisin *pl.* **the neighbors** voisinage **visit one's neighbors** se voisiner **evening spent with neighbors** veillée **sell to one's neighbors** vendre à la côte **share food with the neighbors** faire le voisinage, voisiner
neighborhood *n.* alentours, côte, canton, district, entourage, environs, voisinage **neighborhood cooperative effort** coup de main **communal neighborhood slaughter or butchering event** boucherie de bloque {de quartier} **in the neighborhood** dans les parages
neighboring *adj.* voisin
neighborly *adj.* **be neighborly** voisiner
neither *adv.* non plus
neither *conj.* ni (l')un (et) ni l'autre, ni **neither one** ni (l')un (et) ni l'autre **neither . . . nor** ni... ni
nelumbo *n.* graine à voler {vallée}
nephew *n.* neveu
nerve *n.* audace, effronterie, fiel, nerf, tchique, toupet **have the nerve** avoir le {du} toupet **have a lot of nerve** avoir le {du} toupet
nerveracking *adj.* énervant
nervous *adj.* hors de moi-même {toi-même, etc.}, nerveux, poltron **nervous system** système nerveux **become nervous** s'agiter, s'énerver **extremely nervous or agitated** nerfé
nervure *n.* bâton
nervy *adj.* effronté
nest *n.* nid, nique **nest egg** nichoix, nioque **nest of rats** nique à rats **hornet's nest** potiche **wasp nest** nique de guêpe **build a nest** nicher **laying rack or nest** nichoir **remove from a nest** dénicher, déniquer **take out of a nest** déniquer **veil surrounding a hornet's nest** robe
nest *v.* nicher, niquer, se niquer
nestful *n.* nigée
nesting *n.* **chicken nesting place** nichoir
nestle *v.* se nicher, se niquer
net *adj.* net

net *n.* filet, seine **net fence** barrière à fil de fer et à carreau **butterfly net** paupière **cast net** carrelet **fishing net** drague, NET, varveau **gill net** tramail **mosquito net** bère, drap à maringoins, moustiquaire **three-panel net** tramail **throw net** carrelet **trawl net** trôle **fine net material used for mosquito bars, veils, etc.** bobinette **monofilament fishing net** seine à poisson **panel of net** maille **seine fishing net** seine **catch with a net** seiner **ring on a net through which a rope is threaded** organeau **bag of a trawl net** sac du trawl **tighten the mesh links of a trawl net** serrer les nœuds

netting *n.* filet, maillage **netting used to make a mosquito bar** brin à bère

nettle *n.* **horse nettle** cocombre zombi **stinging nettle** ortie

neuralgia *n.* névralgie **facial neuralgia** tic douloureux / tic St. Honoré

neutral *adj.* neutre

never *adv.* jamais, pas jamais **but never** mais jamais

nevertheless *adv.* cependant, pour (de) même, pour même, pourtant, tout de même

new *adj.* neuf, nouveau, original **brand new** tout neuf **what's new?** quoi {qui} ça dit?, quoi il y a de nouveau?, quoi ça dit?

New *adj.* **New Year's Day** Jour de l'An **New Year's Eve** veille de l'an **New Year's gift** étrenne

newborn *adj.* naissant, nouveau-né

newcomer *n.* nouveau arrivé

newly *adv.* frais, fraîchement, nouvellement

newness *n.* nouveauté

news *n.* information, mot, nouvelle, renseignement **news reporter** rapporteur **bring news** porter des nouvelles **send news** laisser connaître **piece of news** nouvelle **what's the news?** quelle nouvelle? **pass the word or news** donner le mot

newspaper *n.* gazette, journal, papier-nouvelles, papier

next *adj.* prochain, suivant, voisin **next to** (à) côté de, approché, au ras (de), auprès de, côté, collé à {après / de}, sur le côté de, voisin (de) **what next?** et ensuite?

next *adv.* après, d'après, d'ensuite, ensuite, puis, qui vient

next *n.* prochain

nibble *v.* chicoter, grignoter, mangeailler **nibble at** mangeailler

nibbling *n.* grignotage

nice *adj.* agréable, avenant, beau, bon, joli, NICE, plaisant, vaillant, joli **nice people** du vaillant monde **nice, easy-going person** SPORT **be nice** faire bonne mine

nicely *adv.* en grâce

nicety *n.* raffinement

nick *n.* bréchure, cobiche, coche, brèche

nick *v.* abroquer, brécher, cocher, ébrécher, érifler

nickel *n.* bleu, cinq-sous, nickel, plomb, nickel

nickelodeon *n.* piano

nickname *n.* nom donné, petit nom, sobriquet, tit-nom **give a nickname** sobriquer

nickname *v.* sobriquer

nicotine *n.* nicotine

niece *n.* nièce

night *n.* nuit, soir **night clothes** pyjamas **night shirt** chemise de nuit **night and day** nuit et jour **night before last** avant-hier soir **night has fallen** la brune est arrivée **be night** faire noir **good night** bonsoir **last night** hier (au) soir **tomorrow night** demain (au) soir **spend the night** coucher, faire la veillée **hunt at night with the aid of a powerful light** BULL-EYE **spend a sleepless night** passer une nuit à la plaille **with the intention of spending the night** à la veille

Night *n.* **Night Rider** Chevalier de Nuit

nightcap *n.* capuchon

nightclothes *npl.* linge à dormir {de nuit}

nightclub *n.* CLUB **nightclub where one dances to Cajun music** salle de danse

nightfall *n.* **at nightfall** sur le tard, à la nuit

nightgown *n.* blouse de nuit, blouse, camisole, jupe de nuit, robe de nuit

nighthawk *n.* crapaud volant, engoulevent, feursie, mangeur maringouins, piejègue, pigeon maringouin **Florida nighthawk** engoulevent

nightjar *n.* mangeur maringouins

nightmare *n.* cauchemar, pesant

nightshade *n.* **plant of the nightshade family** morelle

nine *n.* neuf *pl.* **nines** des neufs **dress to the nines** mettre la malle au soleil

nineteen *n.* dix-neuf

nineteenth *n.* dix-neuvième

ninetieth *n.* quatre-vingt-dixième

ninety *n.* quatre-vingt-dix

ninth *n.* neuvième

nipple *n.* bouboune, tétine, tété **nipple of a bottle** sucette **nipple of a baby bottle** biberon, suceron **human nipple** mamelon

nitpicker *n.* chipoteur

nitrite *n.* **sodium nitrite** salpêtre

nitwit *n.* attrape-mouches / attrape à mouches, couillon d'eau douce, couillon, espingouin, estragot, luron, riquiqui, robio

no *adj.* aucun

no *adv.* ne, non, pas **no way** jamais de la vie **but no** mais non **oh no** jamais de la vie

no-no *adv.* non-non

Noah *n.* **Noah's ark** arche

noble *adj.* noble

nobody *pron.* pas... personne, personne, péteur

nod *v.* **nod off** pêcher **nod off while avoiding sleep** cogner des clous **said when s.o. is nodding off to sleep** le bouchon est après caler

node *n.* maille, nœud

noggin *n.* caboche, calebasse, caloque, caloquinte, caouane, casaquin

noise *n.* bacchanale, berdas, berdassement, berdi(s)-berda(s), boulvari, bourilleau, bruit, carnage, faïouque, hourra, hélas, jargon, pataraphe, potin, sabbat, sassaquoi, sérail, tapage, tatamage, traillail, train, trimage **noise of moving heavy objects** berdassement **great noise** bouri-boura **loud noise** turlutte **make noise** amener un tapage {du train}, faire du potin, faire du train, faire un carnaval, râler, tapager **make noise by shaking or moving around** berdasser **increase the noise of by accelerating** fronner **make a lot of noise** faire l'artillerie, faire les quatre cents coups, ferrailler **one who makes unnecessary noise** berdassier **make a great deal of noise** berdasser **child who makes a lot of noise while playing** carnageur *pl.* **make throaty noises** gourgousser

noisy *adj.* criard, carnassier **noisy, unruly person** tonnerre à la voile **imposing and noisy person** sassaquoi **bunch of noisy or annoying children** ripopée

nominate *v.* nommer

nomination *n.* appointement, nomination

non-conformist *n.* ventre-rouge

nonbeliever *n.* créature

none *adv.* pas

none *pron.* aucun

nonsense *n.* bêtasserie, bibillote, bêtise, calembour, flafla, foutaise, gnognotte, macaquerie, pacotille, ripopée, va te cacher / va te faire cacher à Lafayette **talk nonsense** baranquer, déparler **utter nonsense** lâcher des folies {bêtises} **bit of foolishness or nonsense** couillonade

nonsensical *adj.* **say foolish or nonsensical things** lâcher des folies {bêtises}

nook *n.* niche, racoin

noon *n.* midi **high noon** grand midi **the noon meal** dîner **draw near noon** tirer sur midi **stroke of noon** coup de midi **eat the noon meal** dîner

nor *conj.* ni **neither . . . nor** ni ... ni **neither more nor less** ni plus ni moins

normal *adj.* naturel, normal

normally *adv.* normal

Norman *adj.* normand

north *n.* nord **north side** bord du nord

North *n.* **person from the North** gueule rouge

northeast *n.* nord-est

Northerner *n.* Yankee

northwest *n.* noroît

nose *n.* museau, nez **blow one's nose** se moucher **stick one's nose in** fourrer son nez **stick one's nose in other people's affairs** méler son grain de sel **blowing of the nose** mouchage **have a big nose** avoir une quille **running at the nose** morveux **have a long, pointed nose** avoir un nez comme un bec (à lancette / blanc), avoir un nez de manche de pompe **wipe or blow the nose** moucher

nose *v.* **nose around** fouille-merder, fouiller, fourgailler, foutumasser

nostalgia *n.* ennui

nostril *n.* cerveau, narine

nosy *adj.* curieux, fouillard, fourre-nez **nosy person** fouillailleur, fouillard, fouille-merde, fouille-merdeur, fouille-nez, fouilleur, fourgailleur, fourre-nez

not *adv.* ne, ni, non, pas, point **not ever** pas jamais **not only** non seulement **certainly not** fichtre non

notable *adj.* notable

notary *n.* notaire **notary public** notaire publique

notch *n.* bréchure, brèche, coche, encoche, picot

notch *v.* cocher, encocher

note *n.* mot, note, un mot d'écrit **monetary note** BILL, billet **promissory note** billet, contrat **take note** noter **maker of a promissory note** prometteur

notebook *n.* cahier

nothing *n.* ouinque, pas... pacane, pas rien, rien **nothing anymore** plus . . . rien **nothing doing** nullement, pas d'affaire!, pas de chance, pienque **nothing at all** (pas) rien du tout, pas un foutre **nothing has been going right** cuisses cailles a passé **do nothing** être à rien faire **it's nothing** c'est (pas) rien **say nothing** pas dire coinque {pacane}, pas dire coinque **there's nothing left to say** halez la planche **have nothing one would not do** avoir rien à son épreuve **there's nothing more to talk about** au boute le boute **go to do nothing** se mettre à rien faire **much ado about nothing** une grande estampique pour rien **talk much about nothing** en flanquer **given to making a big deal over nothing** frou-frou **one who likes to sit in place and do nothing** raccroupi

notice *n.* attention, note, notice **give notice** donner notice, notifier **public notice** affiche **give notice of** afficher **take notice of** LOOK OUT

notice *v.* apercevoir, noter, observer, remarquer, s'apercevoir

noticeable *adj.* apercevable, observable, remarquable

notification *n.* avertissement, notice

notify *v.* avertir, noticer, notifier

notion *n.* ravigaud **get the notion** prendre idée **have a notion** avoir un à-peu-près **take a notion** s'inventionner de {à}

nought *n.* **come to nought** aboutir en rien

nourish *v.* nourrir **nourish o.s.** se nourrir

nourishing *adj.* nourrissant, consistant

nourishment *n.* aliment, nourriture

nouveau riche *n.* parvenu

novel *n.* roman

novelty *n.* nouveauté

November *n.* novembre

novena *n.* neuvaine, novène

novice *n.* blanc-bec, novice

novitiate *n.* noviciat

now *adv.* asteur, maintenant, à present **just now** juste, justement **right now** asteur, droite asteur, pour le moment **until now** jusqu'à jour d'aujourd'hui

nowadays *adv.* asteur, aujourd'hui, maintenant, à present

nowhere *adv.* (en) nulle part, nulle place **place in the middle of nowhere** fardoche

nozzle *n.* **hose nozzle** arrosoir
nub *n.* **nub of the stem of a gourd plant** tchique
nude *adj.* nu **swim nude** se baigner à la plie
nudity *n.* nudité
nuisance *n.* désagrément, embêtement, nuisance, pest **talkative nuisance** nénaine **be a nuisance** nuire
numb *adj.* engourdi **get numb** s'engourdir **render numb** engourdir
numb *v.* engourdir
number *n.* chiffre, figure, nombre, numéro **large number** quantité **license number** numéro de licence **phone number** numéro de téléphone **greatest number or amount** majorité **large number or group** trallée **in sufficient number** grandement **great in number, size, or extent** majeur *pl.* **one who calculates numbers** carculeur
number *v.* numéroter
numbering *n.* numérotage
numbing *adj.* engourdissant
numbing *n.* engourdissement
numbness *n.* engourdissement **eliminate numbness or stiffness** dégourdir
numerous *adj.* abondant, affreux
nun *n.* religieux, sœur
nunnery *n.* couvent
nuptial *adj.* nuptial
nurse *n.* garde-malade, infirmière, soigneur **practical nurse** soigneuse de malade
nurse *v.* donner à téter, faire téter, nourrir, téter
nursery *n.* parc aux petits **nursery rhyme** comptine
nursing *adj.* **nursing home** maison de santé, maison de vieux
nursing *n.* tétée
nurture *v.* nourrir
nut *n.* abricot, abricotier, beau coco, coucou, couillon, noix, noix, virole **brazil nut** orteil de nègre **wing nut** noix avec des ailes / noix-z-oreilles, noix
nutcracker *n.* casse-noix, casse-pacane
nutmeg *n.* maniguette, muscade, noix-muscade **nutmeg tree** muscadier
nutria *n.* nutria
nutritious *adj.* nourrissant
nuts *adj.* crack, percé
nutty *adj.* craqué, fêlé **nutty person** coucou

oak *n.* chêne **oak grove** chêneau, chênerie, chênière **cow oak** chêne à vache **poison oak** chêne poison **red oak** chêne rouge **water oak** chêne gris **white oak** chêne blanc, chêne vert **southern live oak** chêne blanc, chêne vert **swamp chestnut oak** chêne à vache **row of planted oak trees** chênière **grove or stand of oak trees in an otherwise treeless swamp** chênière
oar *n.* pagaille, rame
oarlock *n.* encaille
oat *npl.* **oats** avoine **sow wild oats** chienner
oath *n.* serment **false oath** faux-serment **mild oath to express surprise, regret or discontent** batiscan **take an oath** sermenter
oatmeal *n.* farine d'avoine
obedience *n.* obéissance
obedient *adj.* obéissant
obese *adj.* **obese or overweight person** paillasse
obey *n.* **make s.o. obey** faire 'poteau, Caillette' à qqn
obey *v.* obéir, écouter, observer **slavishly obey and follow** sauter crapaud (pour qqn) **make s.o. obey** amener au bercail, amener qqn au bercail
object *n.* objet **old object of little value** antiquité *pl.* **useless or worthless objects** tchincaillerie
object *v.* mettre empêchement, objecter, opposer, trouver à redire
objection *n.* objection
objective *n.* but, fin
obligated *adj.* assujetti **be obligated** avoir pour **be obligated to** avoir pour
obligation *n.* devoir, obligation **feast day of obligation** fête d'obligation
oblige *v.* accommoder, obliger, forcer **oblige o.s.** se forcer
obliged *adj.* assujetti **be obliged** devoir, être obligé
obliging *adj.* complaisant, obligeant
oblique *adj.* biais
obliquely *adv.* en biais
obnoxious *adj.* merdeux, nuisible **obnoxious or ill-tempered person** crotte
obscurity *n.* obscurité
observable *adj.* observable
observance *n.* observance **festive observance** solemnité
observant *adj.* observeur
observation *n.* observation
observe *v.* guetter, noter, observer, regarder **observe each other** s'observer
obsessed *adj.* braqué **be obsessed by** se braquer sur
obstacle *n.* accroche-cœur, canicroche, difficulté, empêche, empêchement, obstacle *pl.* **put impediments or obstacles in the way of one's success** mettre des bâtons dans la roue {les roues}
obstinacy *n.* entêtement, obstination
obstinate *adj.* entêté, obstiné, têtu **be obstinate** avoir une tête de caïman, obstiner **become obstinate** s'entêter
obstruct *v.* bloquer, boucher, CAP, engorger, engoter, mettre des bâtons dans la roue {les roues}, nuire
obstructed *adj.* **become obstructed** s'engorger

obstruction *n.* blocage, encombrement, engotement, obstruction, embarras
obtain *v.* obtenir, prendre **obtain for o.s.** s'obtenir **obtain clothes or material** se gréer
obvious *adj.* clair, vulière, évident **that's obvious** ça crève les yeux, ça prend pas un avocat
obviously *adv.* clairement, comme de juste, naturellement, évidemment
occasion *n.* coup, fois, occasion
occasion *v.* causionner
occasional *adj.* occasionnel
occasionally *adv.* (de) temps en temps, quelquefois
occupant *n.* occupant
occupation *n.* business, emploi, occupation, ouvrage, travail
occupied *adj.* occupé **be up to, occupied with** brasser, brèter
occupy *v.* occuper **occupy again** réoccuper **occupy o.s.** s'occuper **occupy a position** camper **occupy a seat as a member of a body of officials** siéger
occur *v.* arriver, se passer, taper **occur to s.o.** frapper
occurrence *n.* événement
ocean *n.* mer, océan **Atlantic ocean** atlantique **the ocean** la grande mer
ocelot *n.* chat-tigre
octagon *n.* octagon
October *n.* octobre
octopus *n.* poulpe
odd *adj.* curieux, drôle de, drôle, original, étrange **odd bird** abricotier **one who does odd jobs** jobeur
odd *npl.* **odds and ends** barrancages
oddball *n.* beau coco
odds *npl.* **odds and ends** des petits boutailles **at odds** divorcé **do odds and ends** berdasser **be at odds** être fâché **get at odds** se brouiller **be on bad terms or at odds** être en divorce
odor *n.* odeur, senteur **odor of stagnant water** hydroforme **bad odor** puanteur, puantise **have an odor** sentir
of *prep.* de, à
off *adj.* OFF
off *prep.* dehors **off of** dehors
off-bar *v.* décacher
offal *n.* débris, tripage
offend *v.* affronter, blesser, choquer, déplaire, mortifier, offenser **offend each other** s'offenser
offended *adj.* **be offended** se choquer **easily offended** regardant, suspect
offense *n.* blessure, crime, injure, offense **take offense** s'offenser, se choquer
offensive *adj.* choquant, offensive
offer *n.* offre, TREAT **make an offer or proposal** faire un(e) offre
offer *v.* offère, proposer, présenter **offer no resistance** faire play **offer to o.s.** s'offrir
offering *n.* donation, offrande **take up an offering** faire {passer} la quête
offertory *n.* offertoire
office *n.* office **office of records** greffe **post office** malle, office, POST-OFFICE, poste **small office** cabinette **post office box** boîte de poste **place in office** installer **run for office** galoper
officer *n.* officier **military officer** officier **police officer** constable, officier de police, officier, police **presiding officer** président
official *adj.* officiel
official *n.* chargé, officiel **government official** chargé d'affaires *pl.* **member of a body of officials** siège
officially *adv.* officiellement
officiant *n.* officiant
officiate *v.* officier
officious *adj.* **imposing, officious person** bouledou
offshore *adj.* au large
offspring *n.* enfant, petit **offspring born out of wedlock** bâtard **man not able to produce offspring** homme clair
often *adv.* souvent de(s) fois / souventefois, souvent, à tout moment **so often** tant **every so often** toutes les distances
ogle *v.* reluquer, rincer ses yeux
oh *interj.* ah, ayayaie, ko, mais jamais, oh **oh boy** boy, oh (y) yaïe / oh yé yaïe **oh heck** chia **oh Laud** LORD **oh Lord** LORD **oh no** jamais de la vie **oh shucks** chia **oh, go on** va te cacher / va te faire cacher à Lafayette
oil *n.* graisse, pétrole, huile **oil can** huilier **oil company** compagnie d'huile **oil driller** drilleur d'huile **oil field** champ d'huile **oil lamp** lampe à {de} coal oil, lampe **oil refinery** raffinerie d'huile **oil rig** puits d'huile, RIG **oil well** puits **oil drilling derrick** derrick **castor oil** huile de castor, huile de palma christi, huile à purger **citronella oil** huile de citronnelle **coal oil** COAL OIL, huile de charbon, huile à {de} lampe **cooking oil** huile à cuire, huile **crude oil** huile **cylinder oil** huile à cylindre **holy oil** sainte huile **linseed oil** huile de lin **olive oil** huile d'olive, huile douce, huile fine **vegetable oil** huile **cottonseed oil compress** usine **cod liver oil** huile de foie de morue **pine tar oil** huile de goudron **forty gallon oil barrel** baril **place where oil is pressed out of seeds** usine
oil *v.* huiler
oilcloth *n.* tapis de table, toile cirée
oiler *n.* huilier
oilfield *n.* clos d'huile
oilworker *npl.* **oilworkers** gens d'huile / le monde de l'huile
oily *adj.* huileux
ointment *n.* onguent **carbolic acid ointment** onguent à ver
okay *adj.* c'est bien, correct **it's okay** ça fait (pas) rien **it's okay by me** ça m'est égal
okay *interj.* ALL RIGHT
okra *n.* corne grecque, févi, gombo de jardin, gombo filé,

gombo, gombo févi **okra gumbo** gombo févi **cooked okra** gombo filé

old *adj.* ancien, d'âge, hors d'âge, racatcha, vieux, âgé, éternel **old enough to be responsible for one's own actions** maître et majeur **anything old** pourrillon **extremely old** hors d'âge **grow old** vieillir **how old** comment fort **be old and unmarried** avoir les talons jaunes **anything old or beat up** hariat **anything old and in bad condition** racatcha **anything old, in bad shape or disrepair** baraque, chabraque **it is old** ça date de l'an quarante **it is very old** ça date du temps d'Artaguette **you're never too old** la mort n'a pas de fin

Old *n.* **the Old World** l'autre bord

old-fashioned *adj.* à la vieille mode

oleander *n.* laurana **white oleander** laurier blanc

olive *n.* olive **olive oil** huile d'olive, huile douce, huile fine **olive tree** olivier **sweet-scented olive** olivier de la Chine, olivier

omasum *n.* feuillet

omelet *n.* omelette d'œufs, omelette

omission *n.* omission **sin of omission** péché d'omission

omit *v.* manquer

omnipotence *n.* omnipotence

omnipotent *adj.* omnipotent

on *prep.* après, dessus, en haut (de), sur

once *adv.* un coup que, une fois que **once again** encore une fois, une autre fois **once more** encore une fois **once and for all** tout bonnement, une bonne fois **once, twice, three times a year, day, week, month** une {deux, trois} fois par an {jour, semaine, mois} **at once** aussitôt, directement, immédiatement, tout droite **all at once** tout d'un(e) secousse

one *adj.* nommé, un

one *pron.* aucun, on, tel, un **one another** l'un l'autre / l'un à l'autre, un et l'autre **one by one** un par un **each one** chacun, chaque **either one** n'importe quel **next one** prochain **no one** pas... personne, personne **not one** aucun **that one** celui-là / celui-là-là / celui-là-ici, ça-là(-là) **the one** celui **this one** celui-ci / celui-ici, celui-là / celui-là-là / celui-là-ici, ça-ici(-là) / ça-icitte(-là), ça-là(-là) **which one** quel **whichever one** n'importe quel **any one any** n'importe quel **no one else** personne d'autre **the one that** celui que, celui qui, elle qui {que} **the one who** celui que, celui qui, elle qui {que} **each one for himself** chacun pour lui-même **not a single one** pas un seul

one-eyed *adj.* **one-eyed jack** mistigri

one-half *n.* **give one-half** donner la moitié

one-seat *n.* **one-seat buggy** boghei

one-step *n.* pas de un {deux, etc.}

one-testicled *adj.* **one-testicled animal** ronquouin

oneness *n.* unité

ones *pron.* **the ones** celui

oneself *pron.* se, soi-même **by oneself** tout seul

onion *n.* oignon, tête d'oignon, échalote **onion ring** rondelle d'oignon **onion top** faît d'oignon, échalote **onion tops** queues d'oignon **green onion** oignon vert **Indian onion** oignon chauvage **multiplier onion** échalote *pl.* **green onions** haut des oignons, queues d'oignon

onlooker *n.* miron

only *adj.* seul, unique

only *adv.* juste, justement, rienquetement, seulement **if only** plutôt, si seulement **not only** non seulement

only *conj.* que, rien que / yanque / yienque / yinque

onto *prep.* sur

ooze *v.* suppurer

opaque *adj.* foulé

Opelousas *n.* Opelousas

open *adj.* ouvert **burst open** crâler **wide open** au blanc

open *n.* **head for the open** donner au large **out in the open** au blanc, à bic-à-blanc, à la blanque **bring out into the open** mettre au clair

open *v.* débarrer, débloquer, déboucher, ouverre, s'ouverre, ouverre **open onto** frapper **open wide** carrisser **open for o.s.** s'ouverre **not open one's mouth** pas siffler

opener *n.* ouvreur **can opener** ouvreur de canne

opening *n.* ouvertation, ouverture, trou **opening in a fence** passe **square opening** écarrure **any opening in a building** ouverture **cut or opening in land or in a levee for drainage** coupe

openly *adv.* ouvertement

openness *n.* blanque

operate *v.* courir, faire galoper, galoper, manœuvrer, operater, travailler, manier, opérer **operate on** opérer **one who operates heavy machinery** ingénieur **one who operates a locomotive or steamboat engine** ingénieur

operating *n.* **operating table** table d'opération

operation *n.* opération **perform a medical operation on** opérer

operator *n.* opérateur

opinion *n.* avis, croyance, opinion, pensée, sentiment **change one's opinion** virer de bord **in my opinion** pour moi, à mon opinion **in the opinion of** d'après **be of an opinion** penser **be of the opinion** être d'opinion *pl.* **change one's opinions** changer son fusil d'épaule

opossum *n.* rat de bois

opponent *n.* opponent

opportune *adj.* favorable

opportunity *n.* chance, occasion, opportunité **missed opportunity** chouchou **have an opportunity** avoir (une) chance **have the opportunity to** avoir la chance de

oppose *v.* contrarier, contredire, mettre opposition à, opposer, résister, se regricher contre, se remater

opposed *adj.* **opposed to** contre **be opposed** objecter, s'opposer **those opposed** opposition

opposite *adj.* en face de, opposé de **turn the opposite side out** revirer

opposite *n.* opposé, rebours
opposition *n.* opposition **in opposition** contre
oppress *v.* fouler sur (qqn), accabler
oppressed *adj.* **heavily oppressed** achalé
oppression *n.* oppression
oppressive *adj.* accablant
option *n.* option
or *conj.* ou bien, ou **or else** ou bien **or rather** enfin **either . . . or** soit... ou, soit... soit **whether . . . or** soit que... ou que
orange *adj.* orange
orange *n.* orange **orange tree** oranger **flowering orange** jasmin d'orange **mock orange** bois d'arc **osage orange** bois d'arc
orator *n.* orateur
oratory *n.* oratoire
orbit *n.* cours
orchard *n.* verger **fruit orchard** verger **pecan orchard** pacanière
orchestra *n.* BAND, orchestre
ordain *v.* ordonner
order *n.* classe, commandement, ordre, règle, commande **in order** rangé **in order that** pour que **in order to** pour, à **religious order or society** communauté **arrange in order** classer **put in order** arrimer, mettre en ordre, organiser, ramasser **set in order** arranger **effectively put in order** rafistoler **put a restraining order on s.o.** mettre un empêchement contre **put one's affairs in order** régler ses affaires **put out of working order** déralinguer *pl.* **holy orders** ordre
order *v.* encharger, ordonner, régler, commander, recommander
orderly *adj.* rangeux **orderly condition** ordre
ordinance *n.* ordonnance
ordinarily *adv.* ordinaire, ordinairement
ordinary *adj.* commun, ordinaire, quède, simple
ordinary *n.* **do s.t. out of the ordinary** perdre son {l'} équilibre
ordination *n.* ordre, ordination
ore *n.* minéral
organ *n.* glande, organe, orgue **organ meat stew** grillades, sauce de débris **pipe organ** orgue **pork organ meat stew** fricassée de cochon *pl.* **internal organs** fressures **various edible organs** débris
organist *n.* organiste
organization *n.* organisation, société **charitable organization** charité
organize *v.* organiser, organiser **organize o.s.** s'organiser **organize into a group** s'organiser **organize one's resources efficiently** se ménager
organized *adj.* **get organized** s'organiser
orgy *n.* pique-partout
origin *n.* cause, origine, provenance, racine, source
original *adj.* original, originel **original sin** pêché originel **extravagant or original person** caractère
originally *adv.* originalement, originellement
originate *v.* devenir, originer, provenir
oriole *n.* petit pape **Baltimore oriole** pape de bois, petit pape
ornament *n.* bébelle, fionnure, ornement **gold ornament** dorure **any spherical ornament** boulouque *pl.* **remove ornaments or decorations** dégarnir
ornament *v.* orner
ornery *adj.* contrariant
orphan *n.* orphelin
orphanage *n.* orphelinat
orphanhood *n.* orphelinage
oscillation *n.* ballottement
osteomelitis *n.* enflure blanche
other *adj.* autre **other than** autre que, en dehors de
other *pron.* **each other** l'un l'autre / l'un à l'autre, un et l'autre **one thing and the other** un et l'autre **one is as bad as the other** caca pour merde
others *pron.* autrui
otherwise *adv.* autrement de {que} ça, autrement, à part de ça
otter *n.* loutre
ouch *interj.* ayayaie
ounce *n.* once
our *poss.* notre
ours *poss.* nôtre
ourselves *pron.* nous-autres-mêmes, nous-mêmes, nous, se **myself, yourself, ourselves, etc.** entre moi-même {toi-même, nous-mêmes, etc.} **between us or ourselves** entre nous
out *adj.* éteint
out *adv.* en dehors **out of** (à) côté de, dans, hors **out of sorts** cagou **all out** à pieds joints **be out to do s.t.** chercher
out *npl.* **on the outs** en querelle, en sérail **be on the outs** être fâché
out-of-sorts *adj.* foutaise
outbreak *n.* explosion
outburst *n.* explosion **outburst of enthusiasm** estampique **outburst of anger or rage** emportement
outcast *n.* rebut
outcome *n.* aboutissage, résultat **ultimate outcome** retour
outdo *v.* surmonter, surpasser **outdo o.s.** se mettre en trente-quatre {trente-six} **outdo o.s. or each other** se surmonter
outdoors *adv.* dehors, en pleine air
outfit *n.* **hand-sewn wedding outfit made for one's daughter** amour-de-maman
outfit *v.* parer, équiper **outfit completely** gréer
outgoing *n.* **the outgoing** sortant
outhouse *n.* cabane, cabine en dehors, cabinet, commode, lieu **go to the outhouse or toilet** aller dehors
outing *n.* excursion, promenade
outlaw *n.* brigand, félon
outlet *n.* manchac **electrical outlet** PLUG
outline *n.* contour, silhouette
outperform *v.* **one who outperforms one's peers** capitaine
outpost *n.* garde
output *n.* production

outrage *n.* brutalité, outrage
outrage *v.* outrager
outrageous *adj.* bétaille, outrageux
outright *adv.* carrément
outset *n.* début
outside *adv.* dehors, en dehors, hors
outside *n.* dehors
outsider *n.* étranger
outspoken *adj.* **be outspoken** pas avoir la langue dans la poche
outstanding *adj.* remarquable **show o.s. as outstanding or superior** gagner le sucre
outwardly *adv.* ouvertement
ovary *n.* ovaire
oven *n.* bas du STOVE, bassine, boîte à pain, four, fourneau, OVEN **bread oven** four à pain **Dutch oven** four de stove, four **remove from the oven** défourner
over *adj.* nettement **get over** se refaire à **it's over with** au boute le boute **it's over and done with** caca pour merde **it's all over** Baille a couru, c'est bernique
over *adv.* **over and above** par-dessus le marché **from all over** de toute part
over *prep.* au-dessus (de), en dessus, par-dessus, sur
overbearing *adj.* écrasant **one of overbearing disposition** bouledou
overblouse *n.* josé
overcast *adj.* caille, couvert, nuageux **become overcast** s'amarrer, se baisser, se charger, se couverre **become cloudy or overcast again** se recouverre
overcharge *v.* **overcharge for goods** arracher les yeux de la tête
overcoat *n.* capot, gros capot, manteau, OVERCOAT, pardessus
overcome *v.* accabler, bâcler, surmonter
overcook *v.* trop pousser
overdo *v.* **one who overdoes things** étouffeur de canards morts
overexcited *adj.* épouvanté
overflow *n.* débord, débordage, débordement
overflow *v.* déborder
overflowing *adj.* à déborder
overflowing *n.* débord, débordage, débordement **fill to overflowing** aufaîter, combler, remplir à déborder
overgarment *n.* casaque
overhead *adv.* par-dessus
overheat *v.* achaler, échauffer
overheated *adj.* achalé, échauffé **become overheated** échauffer **get overheated** s'échauffer
overindulge *v.* **overindulge in** faire abus de
overlap *v.* croiser
overlook *v.* sauter
overpower *v.* bâcler
overpriced *adj.* chérant
overreact *v.* faire toute une histoire (de qqch)
overrun *adj.* **be overrun with** pulluler
overrun *v.* empester
overseer *n.* écolome
overshoe *npl.* **overshoes** soulier en élastique
oversight *n.* omission, oubli, oubliance **by oversight** par oubliance
overstay *v.* **one who overstays his or her welcome** pâté
overtake *v.* attraper, rattraper
overthrow *n.* capotage
overture *npl.* **make overtures** faire des avances
overturn *v.* bouleverser, bousculailler, bousculer, renverser, éclapoutir
overturning *n.* bouleversement, bousculade
overweight *adj.* **obese or overweight person** paillasse
overwhelm *v.* accabler, prendre
overwhelmed *adj.* achalé, criblé **be overwhelmed** être empêtré
overwork *v.* escrimer **overwork o.s.** s'escrimer
owe *v.* devoir **owe more** redevoir **still owe** redevoir
owl *n.* coucoua, hibou **barred owl** hibou grosse tête **hoot owl** chouette, hibou grosse tête **night owl** hibou grosse tête **screech owl** chat-huant, chouette **great horned owl** hibou à cornes
own *adj.* propre
own *n.* **our own** à nous-autres-mêmes **your own** tien **hold one's own** se défendre **take as one's own** adopter
own *v.* appartenir, avoir, OWN **own up** admettre, déclarer, s'accuser
owner *n.* BOSS, maître, maîtresse, propriétaire **joint owner** copropriétaire **plantation owner** planteur
ox *n.* **ox cart** charrette à bœufs **draft ox** bœuf de tire, bœuf
ox-fly *n.* taon
oxalis *n.* trèfle salé
oyster *n.* huître **oyster bed** banc d'huîtres **oyster boat** bateau à-z-huîtres **oyster catcher** bec-de-hache **oyster dredge** drague à main, drague **oyster knife** couteau à z-huîtres **oyster shell** coquille d'huître **oyster skiff** skiff à z-huîtres **oyster tongs** gaffe à main, gaffe **vegetable oyster** certifis *pl.* **tong oysters using a gaffe** gaffer des huîtres **clean the shells of oysters** découquiller
oyster-grower *n.* huîtreur
oysterbed *n.* grève

pace *n.* deux-chemin, pas, train **go at a slow pace** aller petit trotte **at a good clip or pace** raidement
pace *v.* aller le {à} deux-chemin, aller le racca {rack}, aller

les deux chemins, aller le train **pace back and forth** marchailler **pace the floors at night** faire son rougarou

pacifier *n.* chique, sucette

pacifying *n.* apaisement

pacing *n.* deux-chemin

pack *n.* paquet, bande, troupeau **pack merchant** marchand (de) paquet

pack *v.* emballer, encaisser, enfourner, fouler, paqueter, pilonner, se fouler **pack down** assaper, fouler, plaquer **pack full** corbier, corder **pack up** empaqueter, paqueter **pack up and leave** faire son paquet **pack down with the feet** piloter

package *n.* paquet

package *v.* emballer, paqueter

packaging *n.* emballage, empaquetage, enveloppement

packed *adj.* cordé **packed in** serré **become packed** se fouler **tightly packed** tchoque-à-bloque

packing *n.* bourrage, emballage, empaquetage, foulage **packing gland** glande

pad *n.* braguette, coussin, matelas **pad to put on a bed to protect it against bedwetting** pissenlit, pissou **collar pad** paillasson **saddle pad** soutadaire **writing pad** tablette

pad *v.* bourrer

padding *n.* doublure **padding used under a saddle** dossière

paddle *n.* pagaille, palette **paddle used to push aside or remove foam from boiling cane juice** sable

paddle *v.* pagailler, partir à la pagaille, pagailler

paddlefish *n.* belle-dame, spatule

paddler *n.* pagailleur

paddling *n.* **by means of paddling** à la pagaille

padlock *n.* cadenas

pagan *adj.* païen

pagan *n.* païen

page *n.* page

paid *adj.* **paid up** quitte

pail *n.* baquet à boire, baquet, siau **lunch pail** bassin d'école **milk pail** bassin à lait

pain *n.* douleur, mal, peine, souffrance **in pain** douleureux **sharp pain** barre, point **shooting pain** lancement, lancée **throbbing pain** lancement, lancée **sharp pain of pneumonia** point de pneumonie **lower back pain** mal aux reins **twinge of pain in one's back** point de côté **expression of anger, pain, or surprise** (que le) tonnerre m'écrase!, tonnerre, mes chiens **unable to stand pain or sickness** ganache **one who is sensitive to physical pain** cœur de poule *pl.* **take unnecessary pains** faire {prendre} des fions

pain *v.* faire (du) mal

painful *adj.* **be painful** faire grief

painstaking *adj.* nigeant

paint *n.* peinture **coat of paint** couche

paint *v.* peindre, renduire, peinturer **paint yellow** jaunir

paintbrush *n.* brosse, pinceau

painter *n.* peintureur, peintre

painting *n.* peinturage, portrait **messy writing or painting** barbouillage

pair *n.* couple, paire, TEAM, paire **join in a pair** apairer *pl.* **in pairs** deux par deux **join in pairs** accoupler

pair *v.* **pair off** rappareiller **pair up** s'accoupler

pal *n.* camarade, padna

palace *n.* château, palais

palatable *adj.* mangeable

palate *n.* palais **cleft palate** palais fendu **soft palate** luette

pale *adj.* effacé, pâle, pâlot **become pale** pâlir **grow pale** pâlir **sickly pale** blême **turn pale** blêmir

pale *v.* blanchir

palisade *n.* péline

pall *n.* **pall bearer** apporteur, porteur

pallet *n.* palette

palm *n.* palme **palm branch** palme **palm tree** palmier **palm of the hand** paume **swamp palm** latanier

Palm *n.* **Palm Sunday** petites Pâques

palmetto *n.* latanier, palmier

paltry *adj.* **puny, paltry, rickety person** bougon

pamper *v.* catiner **pamper o.s.** se catiner

pamphlet *n.* pamphlet, petit livre

pan *n.* **baking pan** casse, plateau **cake pan** assiette à gâteau(x), plaque à gateau **frying pan** chaudière à frire, four, poêle en fer, poêle luminum, poêle, poêlon **pie pan** assiette à gâteau(x) **roasting pan** carrière, plateau **square baking pan** cabaret **dented or crumpled pan or can** bassin bossu {cabossu}

panama *n.* **panama hat** panama

pancake *n.* **pancake turner** palette **thin pancake** crêpe

pandemonium *n.* halicasser

pane *n.* **pane of glass** vitrage, vitre **window pane** carreau de chassis, carreau, châssis, vitre de châssis, vitre

panel *n.* pagée

paneling *n.* plafonnage

panful *n.* fer-blanc, poêlée

pang *n.* **pang of remorse or conscience** remords de conscience

panic *n.* panique

panic *v.* paniquer

panic-stricken *adj.* épivardé

pansy *n.* pensée

panther *n.* panthère

pantie *npl.* **panties** caleçon, pantelettes

pantless *adj.* déculotté, en queue de chemise

pantry *n.* cave, dépense **pantry** garde-manger **room or building used as a pantry, mudroom, laundry room, etc.** dépense

pants *npl.* culotte, pantalon **short pants** demi, pantalons courts **remove one's pants** se déculotter **remove the pants of** déculotter **she wears the pants** elle porte les culottes

papa *n.* papa

paper *n.* papier **paper bag** paquet, sac à {en} papier **paper hanger** tapisseur **blotting paper** pompier **crepe paper** crêpe **curler paper** tchote **silver paper** brillant *pl.* **book of cigarette papers** livre de papiers à cigarette

papier-mâché *n.* papier-mâché

par *n.* **up to par** HOP

parachute *n.* parachute

parade *n.* parade, procession **parade float** flotte

parade *v.* parader **parade o.s.** se parader

paradise *n.* paradis

paraffin *n.* paraffine

paragraph *n.* paragraphe

parallel *adj.* côte à côte

paralysis *n.* paralysie **infantile paralysis** fièvre à vingt-quatre heures

paralyze *v.* paralyser

parapet *n.* parapet

parasite *n.* parasite

parasitic *adj.* abuseur

parasol *n.* ombrelle, parapluie, parasol

parcel *n.* paquet, parcelle

parcel *v.* **parcel out** distribuer, partager, rationner **parcel out cuts of meat** débiter

parch *v.* déchesser, graler, griller

pardon *interj.* **pardon?** hein, est-il

pardon *n.* pardon **ask pardon** s'excuser

pardon *v.* absoudre, pardonner

pardonable *adj.* excusable, pardonnable

paregoric *n.* parégorique

parent *n.* parent

parent-in-law *npl.* **parents-in-law** beaux-parents

parentage *n.* sang

parentless *adj.* orphelin de père et de mère

paring *n.* épelure

Paris *n.* **Paris green** vert de Paris **plaster of Paris** blanc de Paris, plâtre de Paris

parish *adj.* paroissial

parish *n.* **church parish** paroisse **civil parish** paroisse **up the parish** par en haut *pl.* **parishes along the Mississippi** paroisses du fleuve

Parish *n.* **Avoyelles Parish** Avoyelles *pl.* **Florida Parishes** paroisses floridiennes

parishioner *n.* paroissien

Parisian *adj.* parisien

Parisian *n.* parisien

park *n.* parc

park *v.* parquer, PARK, se parquer

parlor *n.* parloir, salon

parochial *adj.* paroissial

parody *n.* **irreverent parody of the Catholic Mass** messe noire

parrafin *n.* blanc de baleine

parrot *n.* perroquet

Parrot *n.* **Parrot and Monkey brand baking powder** YEAST macaque

parry *v.* parer, détourner

parsimony *n.* chicheresse, chichetesse, chicheté

parsley *n.* persil

part *n.* devant, morceau, part, partage, partie, portion, triure **farthest part** finfifond **greatest part** plupart **highest part** haut **in part** partiellement **leftover part** restant **take part** faire part, participer, prendre part **be part of** transférer **take part in a race** tirer une course **for my part** de mon bord **left over part** balance **the greater part** la majeure partie **be a part of** faire part **for the most part** la majeure partie, pour la plupart, pour la plus grande partie *pl.* **inedible waste parts** débris **inedible or waste parts of a plant** débris

part *v.* se séparer, séparer

parted *adj.* **line where hair is parted** partage

partial *adj.* partiel

partially *adv.* moitié, par-dessus les buttes

participate *v.* participer

participation *n.* participation

particle *n.* grain

particular *adj.* certain, difficile, espécial, fionneur, particulier, regardant, spécial **treat o.s. or each other in a particular way** se traiter

particularly *adv.* particulièrement

partier *n.* riboteur

partisan *n.* **be a partisan of** supporter

partition *n.* barrage, cloison, division, mur, partition, séparation

partition *v.* croiser, diviser

partly *adv.* partiellement

partner *n.* associé, padna **female dancing partner** joueuse

partnership *n.* association, compagnie **in partnership** de société

partridge *n.* perdrix **young partridge** perdreau, perdriole

party *n.* bord, crasé, faction, papaille, partie, PARTY **party spirit** partisanerie **evening party** soirée, veillée **insured party** assuré **political party** parti **quilting party** piquerie **roofing party** piquerie **shingling party** piquerie **supper party** fricot **wedding party** partie de noce **wild party** bamboula **be party to** faire part **large noisy party** halicasser **young people's party** bal de maison **give an evening party** faire une soirée **it's time to break up the party or conversation** c'est l'heure qu'on casse le rond

party *v.* fêter

paspalum *n.* **tall paspalum** chiendent

pass *n.* lettre de passe, manchac, passe

pass *v.* dépasser, passer en grade, passer, adopter, approuver, passer **pass around** entourer **pass away** passer **pass by** affranchir, fronner **pass on** passer **pass out** tomber en soliard **pass over** sauter **pass a test** passer un examen **pass an evening** veiller **pass by again** repasser **pass a collection plate** faire {passer} la quête, passer la quête **pass a sentence on** prononcer **pass by each other** se croiser **pass through a gin** mouliner **pass the word or news** donner le mot **pass under or over without coming in contact** affranchir **cause to pass** passer **cut ahead or pass in front** passer en avant

passable *adj.* navigable, passable

passably *adv.* passablement

passage *n.* marche-pied, passage, RIDE, verset **passage on public transportation** passage **passage through a barrier** passe **passage, trail, path, or canal** trace **cleared area for passage** chenal

passageway *n.* passage

passenger *n.* passager **passenger car** char à passagers **passenger train** char à passagers

passer-by *n.* passant

passing *n.* passage **passing again** repassage **passing on** transmission

passion *n.* **indulge a passion** se donner une bosse

passionflower *n.* liane de grenade **yellow passionflower** liane à vipère

Passover *n.* **Jewish Passover** Pâques

passport *n.* passeport

past *adj.* dépassé, passé

past *n.* passé **the past** (dans) les autres fois **in the past** autrefois, d'habitude, en arrière, habitude, il y plusieurs temps passés

pasta *n.* macaroni

paste *n.* colle **canned tomato paste** conserve

pastime *n.* banco, passe-temps

pastor *n.* curé, pasteur **assistant pastor** vicaire

pastry *n.* pastru

pasturage *n.* pâturage

pasture *n.* pâturage, savane, vacherie **in the pasture** au large **out to pasture** au large **putting out to pasture** pâturage **put a horse to pasture** mettre un cheval à l'herbe

pasturing *n.* pâturage

pat *v.* **pat down** fouiller, fourgailler

patch *n.* taille, carreau, pièce **clear patch** défraîchi **having a white patch around one eye** lunette

patch *v.* piéceter, rabouter, raccommoder, rapiécer **patch up** rabouter, raccommoder, rafistoler, rapiécer, regaincher

patched *adj.* **patched up** rafistolé

patching *n.* raboutage, raccommodage, rafistolage, rapiécement, rapiéçage **patching up** rapiécement, rapiéçage

patent *n.* patente

patent *v.* patenter

path *n.* allée, chemin, cours, passe, routine, TRACK **path of a saw** chemin de scie **blind path leading only to a house or farm** manche

pathetic *adj.* triste **be pathetic** faire pitié

pathway *n.* **pathway through a field** passe

patience *n.* patience **have patience** patienter **lose one's patience** s'impatienter **at the end of one's patience** au bout de patience

patient *adj.* endurant, patient **be patient** patienter

patient *n.* patient, pratique

patois *n.* patois, rametien

patron *n.* patron **patron saint** patron

patronage *n.* patronage

patronize *v.* acheter avec, patroniser

pattern *n.* modèle, moule, patron

patty *n.* **cow patty** pâté de (merde de) vache **fish patty** boulette

Paul *n.* **rob Peter to pay Paul** dégreer Saint-Pierre pour gréer Saint-Paul

paunch *n.* bedaine, panse

pause *v.* couper

pave *v.* BLACKTOP **pave with asphalt or tar** goudronner

paved *adj.* pavé

pavement *n.* pavage, PAVE

paving *n.* pavage

paw *n.* griffe, main, patte, pied

paw *v.* tatailler, tâter, tâtonner **paw the ground** piocher

pawpaw *n.* jasmine **pawpaw fruit** assimine **pawpaw tree** assiminier, jasminier

pay *n.* paye **group of people who do certain work together without pay** personniers

pay *v.* payer, se payer, payer, se payer **pay again** repayer **pay back** repayer **pay expenses** payer les frais **pay o.s.** se payer **pay off** acquitter, s'acquitter **pay out** débourser **pay a compliment** payer un compliment **pay a visit** payer une visite **pay the cost** payer les frais **pay a short visit** faire une passée **pay by the month** payer par {au} mois **pay for a drink** payer la traite **pay one's debts faithfully** être de bonne paye **pay or settle one's accounts** payer ses comptes, régler ses comptes **rob Peter to pay Paul** dégreer Saint-Pierre pour gréer Saint-Paul

payable *adj.* payable

payer *n.* payant

paying *adj.* payant

payment *n.* acquittance, acquittement **payment of a debt** quittance **miller payment** moudurage, moulinage **partial payment** acompte, installation, installement **exacting in the expectation of payment** regardant *pl.* **collect payments** collecter

pea *n.* fève **black-eyed pea** BLACK EYE, fève (à) z-yeux noir, fève au cœur noir, fève nombouril noir **crowder pea** fève cordée **dwarf pea** fève nain {nine} **field pea** fève de clos **gray pea** fève grise **green pea** petit pois, pois doux {rond}, pois **lady-finger pea** patte de poule **sweet pea** petit pois, pois doux {rond}, pois **sweet pea flower** pois à fleur *pl.* **like two peas in a pod** comme des patates et des puces

be alike as two peas in a pod se ressembler comme deux gouttes d'eau

peace *n.* agrément, paix **keep the peace** tenir la paix **leave in peace** quitter tranquille **justice of the peace** juge de paix

peacefully *adv.* tranquillement

peach *n.* pêche **peach fuzz** duvet **peach tree** pêcher **clingstone peach** pêche à jus **freestone peach** pêche à quitte noyau **wild peach tree** laurier amandé **kernel at the center of a peach pit** amande

peacock *n.* paon **vain as a peacock** faquin comme un paon

peak *n.* faît, faîtage

peanut *n.* pistache de terre, pistache **peanut butter** peanut-beurre **peanut praline** praline aux {à} pistaches **roasted peanut** pistache grillée *pl.* **cream peanuts** pistaches à la crème **salted peanuts** pistaches salées **sugared peanuts** pistaches pralinées

pear *n.* poire **pear tree** poirier **alligator pear** mirliton **balsam pear** mexicain **prickly pear** figue de raquette **vegetable pear** mirliton **vegetable pear vine** liane de mirliton

pearl *n.* perle *pl.* **throw pearls before swine** donner de la confiture aux cochons

pearly everlasting *n.* vulnéraire

peashooter *n.* sarboucane

peat *n.* **peat, gunny, or burlap sack** sac de pitre

pebble *n.* caillou

pecan *n.* pacane **pecan grove** pacanière **pecan orchard** pacanière **pecan tree** pacanier **pecan wood** pacanier **bitter pecan** pacanier amer **wild pecan** pacane à cochon **cultivated pecan tree** pacanier greffé **wild pecan tree** pacanier sauvage {d'aventure} **outer hull of pecan** gosse de pacane, grabot

peck *n.* coup de bec

peck *v.* becquer, becqueter, bécher, picocher, piquer

pecky *adj.* piqué

peculiar *adj.* particulier

pedal *n.* pédale, pagaille, palette **accelerator pedal** marchette **foot pedal** marchette

pedal *v.* pagailler

peddle *v.* pedler

peddler *n.* marchand (à) charrette, pedleur

pedestal *n.* pilier

pedestrian *n.* marcheur

pee *n.* ouioui

pee *v.* faire {tomber} de l'eau

peek *n.* **take a peek** jeter un coup d'œil

peel *n.* pelure, épelure, épluche

peel *v.* écorcher, épelurer, éplucher, déplumer, écaler **peel a scab** écrouter **crack and peel after hardening** calciner

peeled *adj.* **be peeled** s'éplucher **be shucked, husked, peeled** s'écaler

peeler *n.* plucheuse **potato peeler** gratteur

peeling *n.* écorce, écorchement, épelure, épluche, épluchage, épluche

peep *v.* pialler, piaquer

peeping *adj.* **peeping Tom** voyeur

peeved *adj.* bouqué **be peeved** se chagriner **get peeved** se bouquer

peform *v.* ACT

peg *n.* accrochoire, cheville, clou **clothes peg** épingle à linge **take s.o. down a peg or two** mettre de l'eau dans les veines à qqn *pl.* **tool used to insert wooden pegs in construction** clivier

pelican *n.* grand gosier, pélican **brown pelican** pélican

pell-mell *adv.* pêle-mêle

pelt *n.* peau

pelt *v.* canonner, saganer

pen *n.* chicaire, entourage, parc, plume, rodaire, corail **calf pen** parc à veaux {vaches} **hog pen** parc à cochon(s) **sheep pen** bergerie

pen *v.* **pen up** corrailler, emparquer, mettre au parc, parquer, renfermer

penalty *n.* peine, pénalité **under penalty** sous peine

penance *n.* pénitence **do penance** faire pénitence

pencil *n.* crayon **pencil sharpener** chacot à crayon **colored pencil** crayon à {de / en} couleur

pendant *n.* pendrioche

pendulum *n.* balan, balancier

penetrate *v.* pénétrer

penetration *n.* pénétration

penguin *n.* espingouin

penholder *n.* porte-plume

peninsula *n.* pointe de terre

penis *n.* blague, counoute, organe, pine, piraque, racine, bibitte, pinouche, piquant, titisse

penitence *n.* pénitence

penitent *n.* repenti

penitentiary *n.* forçat, pénitencier **state penitentiary** pénitentiaire

penniless *adj.* BROKE, cassé à la maille, cassé

penning *n.* **penning up** parcage

penny *n.* sou *pl.* **pinch pennies** picaillonner

penny-pincher *n.* picaillonneur

pennywort *n.* herbe à parasol

pension *n.* bénéfice, pension **old age pension** rente des vieux

pension *v.* pensionner

pensioned *adj.* **be pensioned** pensionner

pensioner *n.* pensionnaire

pensive *adj.* jongleur

Pentecost *n.* Pentecôte

people *n.* **old people** vieux *pl.* **people** citoyen, gens, monde, on, peuple **other people** autrui **group of people attending a wake** compagnie **these two people are always together** c'est comme Saint Roch et son chien / c'est comme cul et coton de maïs **group of people who do certain work together without pay** personniers **of two things or people** l'un vaut l'autre et l'autre vaut rien / l'un vaut l'autre et les deux vaut rien

pep *v.* **pep s.o. up** remettre

pepper *n.* piment **pepper shaker** poivière, poivrier **banana pepper** piment banane **bell pepper** piment doux, poivron **black pepper** poivre **cayenne pepper** cayenne **hot pepper** piment chaud, piment fort **red pepper** piment fort, piment rouge **sweet pepper** piment doux **water pepper** curage **black pepper plant** poivrier **flavor with pepper** pimenter **hot red or cayenne pepper** piment enragé

pepper *v.* pimenter, poivrer

peppered *adj.* **highly peppered or seasoned** pimenté

peppergrass *n.* cresson

peppermint *n.* peppermint **peppermint candy** candi barré

peppery *adj.* fort

per *prep.* le, par, à

percale *n.* percale

perceivable *adj.* apercevable

perceive *v.* apercevoir

percent *n.* du cent, pour cent, pourcent

percentage *n.* percentage, pourcentage

perceptible *adj.* apercevable

perception *n.* apercevance

perch *n.* ajoupa, brème, perchette **white perch** patassa blanc, sac-à-lait **chicken roost or perch** jouc, jouquoir

perch *v.* jouquer, s'engrucher, se jouquer, se percher, s'asseoir, se poser

percussion *n.* bastringue

perdition *n.* damnation, perdition **go to perdition** tomber en faillance

perfect *adj.* idéal, parfait

perfect *v.* perfectionner

perfection *n.* perfection

perfectly *adv.* finiment

perfidious *adj.* traître

perfidy *n.* perfidie

perforated *adj.* **become perforated** se percer

perform *v.* accomplir, conduire **perform a medical operation on** opérer **perform in a slipshod way** barboter **perform the last cultivation on** lâcher **perform the marriage ceremony of** marier **perform a marriage ceremony for again** remarier

performance *n.* exécution, SHOW **performance of a duty** quittance

performer *n.* joueur

perfume *n.* essence, parfine, parfum **put on perfume** s'essencer

perfume *v.* **perfume with incense** encenser

perhaps *adv.* cependant, peut-être que, peut-être

peril *n.* danger, péril

perilously *adv.* dangereusement

period *n.* point, série, âge, époque, période **period of difficulty** patocaille **menstrual period** règle **short period of time** secousse **short period of intense activity** secousse **have one's menstrual period** voir **having one's menstrual period** gaillard **sleep in for a short period of time** paresser

perish *v.* dépérir, périr

perishing *n.* **keep from perishing** préserver

peritoneum *n.* toilette

periwinkle *n.* bigorneau **trailing periwinkle** bellesivère

perjure *v.* **perjure o.s.** fausser son serment

perjury *v.* faux-serment

permanence *n.* permanence

permanently *adv.* à demeure

permissible *adj.* permettable

permission *n.* permission **enter without an invitation or permission** casser

permit *n.* lettre de passe, licence, permis

permit *v.* autoriser, laisser, permettre, quitter **permit o.s.** se permettre

perpendicular *adj.* aplomb, d'aplomb

perpendicularity *n.* aplomb

perpetrate *v.* commettre

perpetual *adj.* perpétuel

perpetuate *v.* **perpetuate the name** relever le nom (de)

persecute *v.* persécuter

persecution *n.* persécution

persimmon *n.* plaquemine **persimmon tree** plaqueminier **wild persimmon** plaquemine farouche

persist *v.* obstiner, s'entêter

person *n.* aucun, chrétien, gens, individu, individuel, monde, paroissien, personne **person with long hair** dicriche **person with auburn or chestnut-colored hair** châtain **person with a long neck and a small face** gland au bout d'un bâton **hired person** engagé **pot-bellied person** gorgoyo **rich person** gros chien **short person** pichouette, pousse-poussière, souffle-poussière **skinny person** tripe épurée **small person** péquin **undersized person** épiochon **white person** blanc **excessively skinny person** esquelette **heavy, fat person** taupin **small, thin person** titisse **tall, slender person** linguette **very thin person** vermicelle **chubby or fat person** patate **lean, awkwardly built person** filandrin **poor, wretched, ill-clad person** riquiqui **tall, thin, long-legged lanky person** grand tingue-lingue **derisive term applied to a person** ergot **used to describe a short person** deux pouces de jambe et le cul tout de suite

personage *n.* personnage

personal *adj.* personnel

personality *n.* caractère, personnalité **person with a dynamic or eccentric personality** pétard

personally *adv.* personnel

personnel *n.* personnel

perspicacious *adj.* observeur

perspiration *n.* exudation, sueur, transpiration **soaking wet with perspiration** à la nage de sueur

perspire *v.* suer, transpirer
persuade *v.* **persuade not to** virer **persuade s.o. against** dégoûter **try to persuade** chouler, chouriner
persuaded *adj.* satisfait
persuading *n.* **require persuading** berlander
perturb *v.* terboliser
pest *n.* cataplasme, emmicheteur, pestilence
pester *v.* bâdrer, emmerder, enquiquiner, harasser, tracasser **one who annoys, pesters or makes trouble** embarrateur
pestering *n.* harassement
pesticide *n.* **treat with pesticide or herbicide** empoisonner
pestilence *n.* peste, pestilence
pestle *n.* bâton de pile, pilon **mortar and pestle** pile et pilon
pet *n.* **pet name** sobriquet **pet pig** tchounie
pet *v.* caresser, flatter, se tâtonner
Pete *n.* **for the love of Pete** pitié d'amour
Peter *n.* **rob Peter to pay Paul** dégreer Saint-Pierre pour gréer Saint-Paul
petiole *n.* tige
petition *n.* pétition
petition *v.* pétitionner
petrify *v.* pétrifier
petrifying *adj.* pétrifiant
petroleum *n.* huile de charbon, huile **refined petroleum derivative** huile
petticoat *n.* jupe de dessous, jupon, sous-jupe
petty *adj.* observant
pew *n.* banc
phantom *n.* zombi
pharmacist *n.* apothécaire, pharmacien
pharmacy *n.* apothécaire, pharmacie
phase *n.* **phase of the moon** quartier
pheasant *n.* faisan
philander *v.* coursailler, courser, rouscailler **philander with** coursailler, courser
philanderer *n.* coursailleur, courseur, rouscailleur
philandering *adj.* amoureux comme un paon
philandering *n.* coursaillerie
phlegm *n.* flegme, glaire, morviat
phone *n.* **phone book** livre de téléphone **phone number** numéro de téléphone **call on the phone** téléphoner
phone *v.* appeler
phonograph *n.* phonographe
photo *n.* photo
photograph *n.* photo, portrait
photograph *v.* tirer un portrait
photographer *n.* preneur de portraits, tireur de portraits
phrase *n.* phrase
physician *n.* docteur, médecin
piano *n.* piano
picayune *n.* picaillon
pick *n.* pic, pique **ice pick** pique
pick *v.* cueillir, curer, ramasser, casser, picocher, écurder **pick at** mangeailler, picocher **pick on** attiner, chamailler, faire (de) la misère (à qqn), narguer, picasser **pick out** choisir, trier **pick up** prendre, ramasser, ravioter **pick a fight** picocher **pick a quarrel** chercher querelle, faire le ravaud **pick o.s. clean** se curer **pick o.s. up** se soulever **pick one's teeth** s'écurder, se curer les dents **pick at one's food** picocher **pick up with a pitchfork** enfourcher **pick unopened bolls of cotton that remain after harvest** graboter **one who picks at or nags** picocheur **one who picks at food or eats lightly** picocheur
pick-axe *n.* pic
pick-up *n.* **pick-up truck** PICKUP, TRUCK
picker *n.* ramasseur, casseur **cotton picker** ramasseur de coton
pickerelweed *n.* langue de {du} bœuf
picket *n.* pieu
picking *n.* ramassage, passée **cotton picking** ramasse-coton, ramasserie **clean by picking** curer
pickle *n.* cornichon
pickle *v.* amariner
pickled *adj.* en cornichons
pickling *adj.* **pickling solution** marinade, saumure
pickpocket *v.* soulever
picky *adj.* difficile, fion **be picky** avoir le nez fin
picnic *n.* pique-nique
picture *n.* portrait, image **picture of a saint given to a child on the occasion of his or her first communion** image de communion **holy picture** portrait saint **take a picture** tirer un portrait **take s.o.'s picture** prendre qqn en portrait / prendre le portrait de qqn **have one's picture taken** se faire prendre en portrait
picture *v.* dépeindre
piddle *v.* barboter, berdasser, foutumasser, merdailler
piddling *n.* berdassement
pie *n.* PIE, tarte **pie pan** assiette à gâteau(x) **cow pie** pâté de (merde de) vache **custard pie** tarte à la bouillie **meat pie** pâté **sweet potato pie** tarte à la patate douce
piece *n.* bosse, bougillon, CHUNK, fragment, gobe, grain, morceau, parcelle, picaillon, pièce, portion, taillon, écale **piece of anything** boutaille **cut piece by piece** détailler **bit or piece** grillot **by the piece** à la pièce **sell by the piece** vendre à la pièce *pl.* **to pieces** en cannelles **break to pieces** briser, casser en cannelles, fragmenter, égrener **cut into pieces** débiter, détailler **cut to pieces** coupacher, découpailler **fall to pieces** tomber en botte, tomber en racaille {racage}, tomber en racaille **tear to pieces** casser en douelles, écharpiller, étirailler, étriper **break, cut, or chop into pieces** écharpiller
piece *v.* **piece together** rabouter, rajouter, rapiécer
piecing *n.* raboutage
pier *n.* cale, dépôt, pilier **support pier under a house** bloc
pierce *v.* crever, percer, pénétrer **pierce full of holes** cribler **pierce with a pitchfork** enfourcher

pierced *adj.* **pierced with holes** troué
piercing *adj.* perçant
piercing *n.* pénétration
piety *n.* piété
pig *n.* cochon, porc **pig's foot** patte de cochon **pig's intestine** chaudin **female pig** truie **guinea pig** cochon guinée **male pig** verrat **pet pig** tchounie **suckling pig** cochon de lait, tcho-tcho **stuffed pig stomach** gogue, panse bourrée **short, fat pig** petit cochon tonquin **stuffed and baked pig's stomach** chaudin bourré, chaudin *pl.* **when pigs fly** semaine des quatre jeudis
pigeon *n.* pigeon **clay pigeon** pategau **passenger pigeon** pigeon ramier
piglet *n.* goret
pignut *n.* pacane amère
pigpen *n.* cochonnerie, cochonnier, cochonnière, parc à cochon(s), piguerie
pigshed *n.* têt à cochons
pigskin *n.* couenne
pigsty *n.* cochonnerie, cochonnier, cochonnière, parc à cochon(s), piguerie
pigweed *n.* herbe à piquant **spiny pigweed** arroche
pile *n.* butte, entassement, masse, pile, pilot, péline, ramasse, tas, veilloche **pile driver** pilon **pile or stack** quinte **wood pile** bûcher, huche **take apart a pile** décorder *pl.* **piles** hémorroïdes **put in stacks or piles** veillocher
pile *v.* corder **pile together** entasser **pile up** empiler, empiloter, entasser, mettre en tas, piloter, s'entasser, veillocher **pile up wood in the form of a cage** cager du bois
piled *adj.* **be deposited or piled up** se ramasser
pilfer *v.* agrapper
pilfering *n.* coquinerie
pilgrimage *n.* pélerinage
piling *n.* pilier
pill *n.* pastille, pilule
pillage *n.* pillerie
pillage *v.* carnassier
pillar *n.* cale, colonne *pl.* **build on pillars** bloquer
pillow *n.* coussin, oreiller **pillow covering** ensouillure **pillow slip** couverture d'oreiller **pillow ticking** couette d'oreiller **double pillow** traversin
pillowcase *n.* couverture d'oreiller, ensouillure, fourreau, linge à oreiller, oreillon, soucille d'oreiller, soucille, tête d'oreiller
pillowslip *n.* soucille
pilot *n.* pilote
pilot *v.* courir, piloter
pimple *n.* bouton, pustule, suppuron **pimple mound** huppe
pin *n.* épingle, épique **clothes pin** maquillon **diaper pin** épingle double, épingle à couche, épingle à linge **hair pin** épingle à cheveux **rolling pin** rouleau **safety pin** épingle double, épingle à couche, épingle à linge **stick pin** épinglette **straight pin** épingle droite **tie pin** épinglette **attach with a pin** attacher *pl.* **be on pins and needles** être sur les épingles
pin *v.* attacher
pince-nez *n.* pince-nez
pincer *n.* pince
pinch *n.* pince, pincette, pincée **pinch of tobacco** prise de tabac
pinch *v.* pincer **pinch pennies** picaillonner
pine *n.* pin **pine cone** boule de pin, coco de pin, pomme de pin **pine forest** pinière **pine grove** pinière **pine tree** pin **pine tar oil** huile de goudron **pine tree or wood** bois de pin / bois gras **long leaf pine** pin rouge **grove of pine trees in the open prairie** île de pins
pine *v.* languir
pineapple *n.* ananas
pinfeather *n.* poussant
pink *adj.* rose
pink *n.* **Indian pink** chevelure de Vénus
pinkeye *n.* maladie de yeux rouges
pinning *n.* attachage
pintail *n.* **northern pintail** paille-en-queue
pious *adj.* fervent, pieux
piously *adv.* pieusement
pip *n.* pépie
pipe *n.* pipe, tuyau, pipe **pipe organ** orgue **pipe stem** tuyau de pipe **corncob pipe** pipe en coton de maïs **smoking pipe** cachimbo **stove pipe** FLUE **inveterate pipe smoker** pipeur
pipeful *n.* pipée
pipeline *n.* ligne de tuyau, ligne, pipe
piping *n.* pipe
pirate *n.* brigand, pirate *pl.* **pirates** les brigands de Lafitte
pirogue *n.* pirogue **contents of a pirogue** piroguée **ride in a pirogue** se piroguer **transport in a pirogue** piroguer **one who travels by pirogue** pirogueur *pl.* **tool used to carve out pirogues** tille ronde
pirogueful *n.* piroguée
pirouette *n.* giration, pirouette
pirouette *v.* pirouetter
piss *n.* pissat
piss *v.* pisser
pisser *n.* pisseur
pistachio *n.* pistache
pistol *n.* fusil à six coups, pistolet à six coups, pistolet **pistol cap** CAP **cap pistol** pétard
piston *n.* piston
pit *n.* fosse, piqûre, puits, noyau **barbecue pit** barbecue
pitch *n.* pente
pitch *v.* garrocher
pitcher *n.* PITCH, pot, pot d'eau **pitcher of milk** pot de lait **cream pitcher** crémier, crémière
pitchfork *n.* fourche, fourchette de foin **pitchfork for rice** fourche à riz **ten tined pitchfork** fourche à dix dents **pierce**

with a pitchfork enfourcher **pick up with a pitchfork** enfourcher

pitchforkful *n.* fourchée

pith *n.* moelle

pithy *adj.* grémilleux, moelleux

pitiable *adj.* pauvre, pitoyable

pitiful *adj.* lamentable, misérable, pauvre, pitoyable, ratché, triste **be pitiful** faire pitié

pitifully *adv.* tristement

pitiless *adj.* **pitiless person** sans-cœur

pitted *adj.* piqué

pity *n.* compassion, miséricorde, pitié, tristesse **have pity** avoir pitié **take pity** avoir pitié **have pity on** prendre en pitié **it's a pity** c'est dommage **expression of astonishment, pity, or disapproval** pitié

pity *v.* plaindre

pitying *adj.* miséricordieux

pivot *n.* pivot **turn on a pivot** pivoter

pivot *v.* pivoter

placard *n.* placard

place *n.* emplacement, endroit, lieu, location, place, poste **place setting** couvert **place for washing clothes or dishes** laverie **birth place** pays de naissance **death place** mouroir **godforsaken place** pays perdu **hiding place** cachette **take place** arriver, avoir lieu, prendre place, se faire **in place of** au lieu (de), en place de **from place to place** (de) place en place **dangerous place noted for leading to injuries** casse-cou **any dirty place** parc à cochon(s) **in this place** ici dans {dedans} **out of place** mal-à-propos, étrange **put in place** mettre en place **reserve a place** réserver une place **secret hiding place** cache **take the place** prendre la place (de) **go from place to place** faire cerf-volant **all over the place** (de) tribord et babord {bâbord} **get back into place** se replacer **in some God-forsaken place** (là-bas) au diable bouilli **in the first place** premièrement **put back in place** serrer **in a strange place or among strangers** à l'étrange **move from one place or job to another** transférer **fix o.s. in a place** se plaquer **low swampy or marshy place** bassière **throw o.s. out of place** se déranger **put in an undesirable place or situation** enfoncer **remove from a comfortable place or situation** déniquer **small cheap business or place of amusement** tchouflangue **find o.s. at the right place** se retrouver à la bonne place **in a distant and unknown place** (là-bas) au diable bouilli **put s.o. in his or her place** mettre au pas, mettre qqn à sa place **if you leave, someone else will usurp your place** chien qui va à la chasse perd sa place **you need to be put back into your place** c'est l'heure de voir à couper tes culottes *pl.* **change places** changer de place

place *v.* coller, jaquer, placer, poser **place o.s.** braquer, se mettre, se placer **place awkwardly or roughly** plaquer **place on a hook** engrucher **place o.s. in a location** se braquer

placement *n.* emplacement, placement

placing *n.* placement

placket *n.* migaillière

plague *n.* flau, peste, pestilence

plague *v.* tourmenter

plagued *adj.* abattu

plain *adj.* clair, simple

plain *n.* **flood plain** bassière, batture **low coastal plain between marsh and prairie** prairie basse **on the open prairie or plain** au large

plainly *adv.* bonnement, en termes, tout en plein, tout à clair, uniment

plaintiff *n.* plaignant, plaintif

plaintive *adj.* plaintif

plait *v.* tresser

plan *n.* dessein, dessin, intention, plan, programme, projet **house plan** plan de maison **unrealistic idea or plan** rêve de poule *pl.* **make plans** planner **make big, unrealistic plans** barificoter **one who entertains unrealistic plans** barificoteur

plan *v.* combiner, PLAN, planner, prévoir **plan carefully** prendre des proportions

plane *n.* galère, rabot, râpe, varlope **plane with two handles** galère **carpenter's plane** varlope **wood plane** rabot, râpe **take a plane** voler, voltiger

plane *v.* planer, varloper, égalir, galérer, passer (qqch) au rabot

planer *n.* **planer tree** charmille, châtaignier **wood planer** galère **electric wood planer** galère à électricité

planing *n.* aplanissement, galérage, parage

plank *n.* planche **stage plank cookie** estomac (de) mulâtre *pl.* **planks or branches arranged to permit one to cross running water or a swampy area** pavure

plant *n.* pied, plante **plant cane** plant de canne **plant gall** poreau **plant that comes up spontaneously** plante de bonne aventure **plant that creeps or climbs** rameur **arrowhead plant** langue de {du} bœuf **cabbage plant** plant de chou **cattail plant** jonc de chat {au baril} / jonc plat {matelas}, queue de chat, queue de rat **citron plant** citronnier **cotton plant** coton **elderberry plant** pied de sureau **flower-bearing plant** bouquet **flower plant** pied de fleur **indigo plant** café sauvage **industrial plant** plante **mirliton plant** pied de mirliton **smelting plant** fonderie **star-of-Bethlehem plant** étoile de Bethléhem **strawberry plant** fraise **umbrella plant** ombrelle de Japon **volunteer plant** plante de bonne aventure **black pepper plant** poivrier **bridal wreath plant** couronne de mariée **castor bean plant** palma **elephant ear plant** oreille d'éléphant **four o'clock plant** belle de nuit, quatre heures **night-blooming jasmine plant** galant de nuit **Spanish dagger plant** pite **turkey mullein plant** molène **wild coffee plant** indigo **printing shop or plant** imprimerie **layer or division of any plant for propagation** margot **inedible or waste parts of a plant** débris *pl.* **transplant plants** margotter

plant *v.* planter, semer **plant in raised rows** sillonner

plantation *n.* habitation, place **plantation owner** planteur

planter *n.* cultiveur, planteur, récolteur, récoltier, sucrier

planting *n.* plante, plantage **planting machine** planteur

plaque *n.* **commemorative plaque** plaque

plaster *n.* plâtre **plaster of Paris** blanc de Paris, plâtre de Paris **mustard plaster** sinapisse **porous plaster** cirouène **adhesive bandage or plaster** sparadraffe

plastic *n.* caoutchouc, en plastique, plastique **made of plastic** en plastique

plate *n.* assiette, plat, plate **dinner plate** assiette plate, plat **license plate** licence **metal plate used to cover a hole** plaque **pass a collection plate** faire {passer} la quête, passer la quête

plateful *n.* assiettée

platform *n.* plate-forme

platter *n.* cabaret, plat à riz, plat, plateau

plausible *adj.* comprenable, concevable

play *n.* théâtre, jeu **fight in play** se batailler

play *v.* jouer, gratter, jouer **play again** rejouer **play at** faire accroire **play dead** faire le mort **play jokes** faire des bêtises **play noisily** carnager **play possum** faire le mort **play tricks** canailler **play up** gourmer **play a trick** faire des canicroches **play dirty tricks** faire des saloperies **play second fiddle** seconder **play the clown** bouffonner **play with dolls** catiner **play a dirty trick** jouer la patte de cochon, planter un piquant **play a musical accompaniment** accompagner **play a practical joke** faire des canicroches **play cards for money** gambler **play a joke, trick, or prank** faire {jouer} une malice **play around, esp. instead of working** bêtiser **play with in an inappropriate way** bêtiser **play a game of chance for stakes** gambler

playboy *n.* chiennailleur, coursailleur, courseur, potre

player *n.* joueur **accordeon player** accordioniste **ball player** joueur de pelote **record player** graphophone

playground *n.* **school playground** cour d'école, terrain d'école

playing *n.* touche

plaything *n.* amusette, bébelle, joujou

plea *n.* plaiderie **enter a plea** plaider

plead *v.* bourlinguer, intercéder, plaider, se plaider, avocasser, plaider **plead with** prêcher, tomber derrière (qqn)

pleading *n.* plaiderie

pleasant *adj.* accordant, agréable, aimable, beau, charmant, complaisant, conscencieux, consentieux, plaisant, vaillant

please *adv.* voir

please *v.* arranger, contenter, donner du plaisir, je vous en prie, plaire **hard to please** délicat, fionneur, suspect

pleased *adj.* bienheureux, fier, satisfait **be pleased** se contenter

pleasing *adj.* avenant, goûtable

pleasure *n.* agrément, délice, plaisir **pleasure or satisfaction** gloire **give pleasure** donner du plaisir, plaire **take pleasure** prendre plaisir **exclamation of surprise, pleasure or disgust** pou-yaille

pleat *n.* godet, laize, pli, plissure **make a pleat or tuck** faire un godet *pl.* **remove pleats** déplisser **remove pleats or gathers** défroncer

pleat *v.* froncer, goder, plisser

pleated *adj.* froncé, plissé

pleating *n.* plissage

pledge *n.* gage, promesse

pledge *v.* promettre, vouer **pledge o.s.** se vouer

pledged *adj.* promis

plenary *adj.* plénière

plentiful *adj.* abondant, grandement

plenty *adv.* plein

plenty *n.* charretée, par charretée / à la charretée, à siau **plenty of** plein de

pleurisy *n.* pleurésie

pliable *adj.* ployable, ployant

pliers *npl.* pince

plot *n.* combinaison, complot, taille **foil a plot** avorter un complot

plot *v.* combiner, comploter, se combiner

plotting *n.* **secret plotting** machinerie

plover *n.* annonceur, kildi **golden plover** pluvier doré **ring-necked plover** cou-collier **semipalmated plover** cou-blanc **upland plover** papabotte **Wilson plover** collier

plow *n.* charrue **plow blade** lame de charrue, oreille de charrue **disk plow** trancheuse **double plow** BUSTER, charrue double **lister plow** charrue double **middlebuster plow** charrue double **reversible plow** flouque **tractor plow** laboureuse **sharpen a plow** battre une lame de charrue **ridge turned up by plow** endos **depth to which a plow share penetrates the soil** entrure

plow *v.* rabourer, sillonner **plow flat** labourer en planche **plow rows** fendre la terre **plow in rows** labourer en rang

plowing *n.* rabourage

plowman *n.* raboureur

plowshare *n.* lame de charrue **beating of plowshare to sharpen it** battage (de) charrue

plowshoe *n.* **old plowshoe** crocro

pluck *v.* éplumer **pluck feathers** déplumer, plumer

plug *n.* bouchon, cheville, chique, connexion **plug of tobacco** PLUG **plug or twist of chewing tobacco** carotte **spark plug** PLUG

plug *v.* boucher, PLUG, emboucher **plug in** PLUG

plugged *adj.* **plugged up** bouché **be plugged up** se boucher

plum *n.* prune **plum tree** prunier **dried plum** prune sec **Japanese plum** mispilusse, nèfle **Japanese plum tree** néfrier **wild plum tree** prunier sauvage

plumage *n.* plumage

plumb *adj.* aplomb, d'aplomb **plumb line** plombant

plumb *v.* plomber

plumber *n.* homme à pipe

plume *n.* plume
plump *adj.* charnu, rond
plump *v.* éponger
plunder *n.* brigandage, pillerie
plunder *v.* piller
plundering *n.* pillage
plunge *n.* plonge, plongée
plunge *v.* encaver, plonger
plunk *v.* **plunk down** plaquer **plunk o.s. down** se plaquer
plush *adj.* douillet **material that is plush, velvety, or furry** peluche
pneumatophore *n.* boscoyo
pneumonia *n.* fluxion, pneumonie **treat for pneumonia or for a cold by applying mustard plasters** fluxionner
pocket *n.* poche **pocket knife** ganif **pus pocket** dépôt **put in one's pocket** empocher
pocket *v.* empocher
pocketbook *n.* porte-monnaie
pocketful *n.* pochetée, pochée
pocketknife *n.* BARLOW, couteau de poche
pockmark *n.* piqûre
pockmarked *adj.* picassé, piqué, picoté
pod *n.* écale, palette
poem *n.* poème
poet *n.* poète
point *n.* bout, point, point, pointe **point of view** point de vue **point where two bodies of water come together** pointe **explain point by point** expliquer point par point **the point is this** le point est ceci / le point est ça icite **the point of an outside wall created by the roof line** pignon **at this point** à ce point là **have a point** avoir un bon point **at the point of** au point de **make a point of** faire un exprès de **on the point of departure** quittable **put a point on s.t.** épointer **the highest point of a pitched roof** pignon **break off a point** épointer **there is no point in arguing** Taupin vaut Maurin **talk on without getting to the point** se noyer dans son (propre) crachat **have come to the end of one's high point** avoir tiré son pétard
point *v.* pointer, pointer **point at** pointer (qqn) au doigt **point out** désigner, indiquer, pointer (qqn) au doigt **point to** pointer à **point the finger** pointer le doigt **said to point out that s.t. is upside-down** il y a un ouragan dans la Chine
pointed *adj.* pointu **make pointed** appointir
poised *adj.* posé
poison *n.* poison, vénin
poison *v.* empoisonner, envelimer, vénimer **poison o.s. or each other** s'empoisonner
poison-flag *n.* clajeux
poisoning *n.* empoisonnement
poisonous *adj.* poison, vénimeux
poke *v.* attiser, jaquer, tisonner
pokeberry *n.* chou-gras
poker *n.* poker, tison, tisonnier **poker chip** jeton
pokeweed *n.* chou-gras
pole *n.* flèche, perche, pole **fishing pole** canne à pêche {pêcher}, perche-à-ligne, perche **telephone pole** poteau à lumière **fish using a set line or cane pole** pêcher à la ligne-guette {ligne}
polecat *n.* bête puante, civette
police *n.* police **police officer** constable, officier de police, officier, police **the police** loi **chief of police** constable
Police *n.* **Police Jury** Jury de Police
policeman *n.* gendarme, POLICEMAN
policy *n.* police **insurance policy** police
Polish *adj.* polonais **Polish language** polonais
polish *n.* **shoe polish** noir à soulier, SHINE
polish *v.* lisser, polir **one who rubs, buffs or polishes** frotteur
polished *adj.* poli
polite *adj.* bien élevé, civil, civilisé, poli, respectueux
politely *adv.* en grâce, poli, poliment
politeness *n.* civilité, politesse
politic *v.* faire de la politique
politician *n.* politicien **politician who attacks nonexistent issues** défonceur d'une porte ouverte / défonceur de porte(s) ouverte(s)
politics *n.* politique **talk politics** politiquer
polka *n.* **a series of five dances, traditionally played in order: waltz, polka, waltz in two, two-step, mazurka** ronde de danses
polka-dot *n.* picot
poll *n.* POLL **poll supervisor** pollier **poll worker** commissionnaire
polling *n.* **polling place** POLL
pollute *v.* contaminer
pollution *n.* contamination, pollution
pollywog *n.* gorgoyo
pom-pom *n.* pompon
pomegranate *n.* grenade française, grenade **pomegranate tree** grenadier
pommel *n.* plombeau, pommeau
pompano *n.* pompano
pond *n.* bas-d'eau, couline, daigué, marais, platin, trou de taureau, vivier **fish pond** vivier **shallow pond** marais
ponder *v.* calculer, considérer, jonglailler, jongler, réfléchir, songer
pondweed *n.* herbe fine / herbe canard gris
pontoon *n.* ponton
pony *n.* pony **Shetland pony** chacta
ponyfoot *n.* sabot de cheval
poo *n.* dou-dou
poof *interj.* pouf **go poof** faire pouf
pool *n.* billard, marais, piscine, placard, vivier **pool table** table de POOL **natural pool** trou de taureau
poop *n.* dou-dou
poop *v.* caca, dou-dou
poor *adj.* chéti, pauvre comme Job, pauvre **poor dear** pauvre

bête **poor fellow** pauvre bête **poor person** pauvre **poor thing** pauvre bête **poor little thing** chère 'tite bête **poor as a church mouse** pauvre comme un rat (d'église)

poor *n.* **the poor** les pauvres

poorly *adv.* mal, chétiment, moitié, pauvrement, petitement

pop *n.* pop

pop *v.* crâler, plaquer, popper, éclater, graler **explode or pop** éclater

pop-gun *n.* pétard

popcorn *n.* tac-tac **popcorn ball** boule de tactac **popcorn praline** praline au tac-tac **pop popcorn** faire fleurir du tac-tac **kernel of unpopped popcorn** grillot

pope *n.* pape

poplar *n.* **yellow poplar tree** tulipier **tulip tree or yellow poplar** bois-jaune

popping *n.* crâlement

poppy *n.* poppé

popular *adj.* populaire

popularity *n.* popularité

populated *adj.* **heavily populated** populaire

population *n.* population

populous *adj.* populaire

porcelain *n.* porcelain, porcelaine

porch *n.* galerie **front porch** galerie en avant **go out on the porch** prendre la galerie

pore *n.* pore

porgy *n.* **southern porgy** cochon

pork *n.* cochon, porc, viande de cochon **pork chine** reintier **pork chop** côtelette de cochon **pork cutlet** grillade de cochon **pork fat** lard **pork rind** couenne **pork giblets in sauce** débris du cochon **pork organ meat stew** fricassée de cochon **boiled pork** bouilli **side of pork** placôté de porc **strips of pork loin and fat** jambonneau **sliver of marinated pork** grillade amarinée {à la marinée} **stew made from pork stomach** fricassée de la panse **marinated pieces of boneless pork** grillade amarinée {à la marinée} **roasted or grilled slices of pork** grillades

porous *adj.* poreux

porpoise *n.* marsouin

port *n.* port **port side** bord à gauche

Port *n.* **Port Barre** Port Barré

portable *adj.* portable

portage *n.* portage

portage *v.* portager

porter *n.* porteur

portfolio *n.* portefeuille

portion *n.* bosse, fraction, lot, parcelle, part, portion, ration, rationnement **portion of meat** rôti **large portion** ventrée *pl.* **division into portions or shares** dévisage

portion *v.* **portion out** alloquer, apportionner, partager, rationner

portrait *n.* portrait

portulaca *n.* mousse-fleur, pourpier

pose *v.* **pose a difficult problem** tirer une patate chaude (à qqn)

position *n.* office, place, position, situation, STAND, position **change position** grouiller **occupy a position** camper **take one's position** se placer **change the position of** émouver **in an upright position** debout, rapiqué **put back in position** corriger **take up a position** se planter **in a low position, level space or situation** bas

position *v.* **position o.s.** se camper

positive *adj.* positif

positively *adv.* positivement

possess *n.* **possess property** avoir du bien

possess *v.* avoir **possess assets, worth** valoir

possessed *adj.* **possessed person** possédé du diable, possédé **one who is possessed** possédé du diable

possession *n.* possession, propriété **take possession** prendre possession, s'accaparer, s'approprier **take possession of** accaparer, s'emparer **take or retake possession** remparer *pl.* **possessions** bien

possessive *adj.* collant

possibility *n.* possibilité

possible *adj.* possible **not possible** pas d'apparence **it is possible** il y a moyen, ça se peut **if it is possible** s'il y a moyen **is it really possible?** tonnerre est-il {c'est-ti} possible?

possibly *adv.* possiblement

possum *n.* rat de bois **play possum** faire le mort, faire le rat de bois, faire zombi

post *n.* paleron, pieu, pilier, poste, poteau, péline, rance **post office** malle, office, POST-OFFICE, poste **post hole digger** fouilleur de poteau, fouilleur de trous **post office box** boîte de poste **bed post** colonne **corner post** poteau du coin **structural support post** poteau *pl.* **tool to split posts** herminette

post *v.* poster **post again** rafficher **post in order to prevent trespassing** afficher

postage *n.* postage

postal *adj.* postal

postcard *n.* carte postale

poster *n.* affiche, BILL, placard

posterior *n.* boudoume, pountingue

postmaster *n.* agent de poste, postillon

postpone *v.* remettre, retarder, suspendre

posture *n.* **assume an unusual posture** se poster

pot *n.* pot, vase **pot for serving coffee** cafetière **pot with a handle** bomme à tcheue raide **pot or jar from which syrup or honey is served** compotier **chamber pot** pot de chambre {noce} **cooking pot** bombe à cuire, bombe, bouille, casserole, chaudière en fer, chaudière noire, chaudière à queue, chaudière, marmite **ink pot** encrier **iron pot used to boil clothes** potin **cast iron pot** bombe en fer **go to pot** aller à la dégringole, dégringoler, s'en aller au dépit **stirring of a pot** brassage de chaudière **let o.s. go to pot** s'abandonner *pl.* **battery of pots and boilers used in processing sugar** équipage

potash *n.* potasse

potato *n.* patate anglaise, patate, pomme de terre **potato bin** pataterie **potato field** clos de patates **potato house** pataterie **potato peeler** gratteur **potato stew** ragoût de patates **potato vine** liane de patate **Irish potato** patate anglaise, patate ronde, pomme de terre **seed potato** mère patate **sweet potato** igname, patate douce, patate yamme, patate, yam **sweet potato leaf** apénaire **sweet potato pie** tarte à la patate douce **wild potato vine** liserine **yellow-fleshed sweet potato** giraumont patate / patate juraumont **yellow sweet potato** patate jaune **eye of a potato** œil de patate **germ of a potato** œil de patate **short length of potato vine used to grow a new potato plant** margot de patate *pl.* **French fried potatoes** patates frites **mound of potatoes covered with dirt for storage** butte de {à} patates, pataterie

potbelly *n.* bedaine, panse

potful *n.* chaudièrée, fer-blanc, tambouille, gréguée

pottering *n.* berdassement

pottery *n.* potiche

pouch *n.* poche, sac **cheek pouch** abajoue **tobacco pouch** blague, cigalière, parchouesse, tabatière

poultice *n.* cataplasme

poultry *n.* volaille

pound *n.* livre **by the pound** à la livre / par livre

pound *v.* piler, pilonner

pounding *n.* battage, pilage, pilonnage

pour *v.* capoter, couler, verser, vider **pour again** reverser **pour out again** revider **pour using a funnel** entonner **pour from one container into another** transvider

pout *n.* babine longue, babine

pout *v.* avoir {faire} gueule plate, bouder, faire (de) la boude, faire son boudin, faire une {la} babine / faire des babines, pendre du babinot, pendre la babine, prendre une babiche, se bouquer **one who pouts** boudard

pouting *adj.* boudé, bouqué **pouting expression** babine **act in a pouting manner** bouder après (qqn), se bouder **get over a pouting spell** se débouquer

pouting *n.* boude, bouderie

poverty *n.* misère, pauvreté, pauvrie **in poverty** pauvrement **fall into poverty or decrepitude** aller aux brindezingues **be in extreme poverty** être dans la dernière extrémité

powder *n.* poudre **powder box** poudrière **powder puff** mappée, pompon, poudrillon **baking powder** BAKING, soda à pain, YEAST **washing powder** perline, poudre à laver **Parrot and Monkey brand baking powder** YEAST macaque

powder *v.* poudrer **powder o.s.** se poudrer

powdering *n.* poudrage

power *n.* autorité, commission, faculté, force, influence, pouvoir, puissance **power line** ligne à lumière **power saw** scie à électricité **confer power** donner le pouvoir

powerful *adj.* fort, puissant **all powerful** omnipotent, tout-puissant

pox *n.* **chicken pox** grattelle, picote volante / picote de poule / petite picote, picote

practice *n.* clientèle, DRILL, exercice, habitude, pratique, usage **religious practice** dévotion

practice *v.* exercer, pratiquer, s'exercer, se pratiquer, pratiquer, professer **practice birth control** empêcher la famille **make s.o. practice** pratiquer **one who practices his or her religion** pratiqueur

prairie *n.* prairie, savane **natural prairie** prairie marron **trembling prairie** prairie molle **wild prairie** prairie marron **arm of a prairie** anse **hollow in a prairie** trou de taureau **on the open prairie or plain** au large **little wooded area in the middle of the prairie** île d'arbres

praise *v.* applaudir

praline *n.* praline **milk praline** praline au lait **peanut praline** praline aux {à} pistaches **popcorn praline** praline au tac-tac **sesame seed praline** praline au {de} béné

prance *v.* fringuer, se mâter

prank *n.* canaillerie, escapade, malice, niche, tour **play a joke, trick, or prank** faire {jouer} une malice *pl.* **full of pranks** nigeant

prankster *n.* canaille, farceur

prattle *n.* bavardage, charade

prattle *v.* bavarder, cacasser, charader, charlanter, rachanter

prattler *n.* bavard, bavardeur

prawn *n.* lobster

pray *v.* prier

prayer *n.* invocation, oraison, prière **prayer beads** chapelet **prayer of confession** confession **Lord's prayer** oraison dominicale **place of prayer** oratoire *pl.* **prayers, singing, reading, etc., offered by lay people in lieu of actual Mass** messe blanche {sec} **say one's prayers** dire ses prières

praying *n.* **praying mantis** bâton

preach *v.* faire la prêche, prêcher

preacher *n.* prêcheur **preacher's pulpit** baril

preaching *n.* prêchement

precaution *n.* précaution, prévoyance *pl.* **take precautions** prendre des sûretés, se précautionner

precede *v.* précéder

precedent *n.* précédent

precious *adj.* précieux

preciously *adv.* précieusement

precise *adj.* précis **be precise, exacting or meticulous** mettre les points sur les i **be precise in one's work or skill** tirer avec la fine mire

precisely *adv.* exactement, juste, justement

precocious *adj.* prime

predicament *n.* situation

predict *v.* deviner, prédire **one who predicts the future** prédicateur

prediction *n.* prédiction
predictive *adj.* **predictive sign** prédicateur
predictor *n.* prédicateur
preen *v.* se becquer
prefer *v.* aimer mieux, préférer
preferable *adj.* préférable
preference *n.* préférence **in preference to** plutôt que {de} / plutôt de
preferred *adj.* préféré
pregnancy *n.* **in full pregnancy** à {en} pleine ceinture
pregnant *adj.* comme ça, en ceinture, en famille, enceinte, gros, plein, remplie **be pregnant** avoir le CAN, porter un enfant **get pregnant** se mettre en famille, venir en famille **be pregnant with** être en famille pour **become pregnant with** concevoir **become pregnant before getting married** faire Pâques avant Carême **cause to become pregnant** remplir
prejudge *v.* préjuger
prejudice *n.* jugement
prejudice *v.* préjuger
prejudiced *adj.* préjugé **be prejudiced against** avoir un piment contre
premier *n.* premier
premonition *n.* apercevance, avertissement
preoccupation *n.* préoccupation
preoccupy *v.* préoccuper
preparation *n.* préparation *pl.* **make preparations** faire des entrains
prepare *v.* accommoder, disposer, parer, préparer, arranger, éditer **prepare o.s.** s'arranger, se préparer **prepare for burial** ensevelir **prepare for a fight** enlever sa soutadaire **prepare o.s. for a difficult or unpleasant task** s'attabler
prepared *adj.* paré **badly prepared dish** ragouillage
Presbyterian *adj.* presbytérien
Presbyterian *n.* Presbytérien
presbytery *n.* presbytère
prescribe *v.* prescrire
prescription *n.* prescription
presence *n.* assistance, présence **presence of mind** présence d'esprit
present *adj.* courant, présent
present *n.* cadeau, don **at present** asteur, aujourd'hui
present *v.* donner, introduire, produire, présenter **present itself** se présenter **present o.s.** se présenter
presentable *adj.* présentable, regardable
presentation *n.* présentation
presentiment *n.* pressentiment
presently *adv.* bientôt, tantôt
preservation *n.* préservation
preservative *n.* préservative
preserve *n.* **preserve jar** flacon *pl.* **preserves** confiture, conserve, marmalade **berry preserves** confiture aux mûres
preserve *v.* conserver, encanner, garder, préserver **preserve in fat, vinegar or salt** amariner
preserved *adj.* en CAN **be preserved** se conserver
preserving *n.* **preserving jar** pobon
preside *v.* présider, officier
president *n.* président
presiding *n.* **presiding officer** président
press *n.* presse **cotton press** compresse
press *v.* presser, serrer, fouler **press down** rabattre **press a button** peser (sur) un bouton **press one's heels into** talonner **press legal charges against s.o.** mettre une charge contre qqn
pressed *adj.* **place where oil is pressed out of seeds** usine
presser *n.* **presser foot** pied
pressing *adj.* pressant, pressé
pressing *n.* foulage **pressing iron** fer à repasser **tool for pressing clothes, branding, soldering, etc.** fer
pressure *n.* pression **pressure cooker** chaudière à queue **blood pressure** pression de sang **high blood pressure** sang (trop) haut / sang trop fort **low blood pressure** sang (trop) bas **work without pressure** berdasser
presume *v.* présumer
presumptuous *adj.* audacieux
pretend *v.* faire accroire, faire comme si, faire semblant (de), prétendre **pretend to be** se prétendre **pretend to be sick** faire le malade **pretend to be sleeping** faire le congo **one who pretends to be innocent** sainte nitouche **man who pretends to be dangerous but is not** homme de paille
pretense *n.* prétention, semblant **make pretense of doing much** en flanquer
pretension *n.* prétention
pretentious *adj.* prétentieux **pretentious person** pince-minette **act in a pretentious, haughty or affected way** fionner
pretty *adj.* beau, joli
prevail *v.* régner **justice is not always immediate, but it will prevail in the end** le Bon Dieu descend pas pour bûcher
prevaricator *n.* menteur
prevent *v.* empêcher, mettre empêchement, opposer **prevent from wasting** sauver
prevention *n.* prévention
previous *adj.* d'avance, passé
previously *adv.* anciennement, auparavant, déjà
price *n.* coût, coûtance, prix, valeur **price tag** ticket **half price** moitié prix **at half price** à moitié prix **decline in price** tomber **reduce the price** baisser le prix *pl.* **charge exorbitant prices** arracher les yeux de la tête
price *v.* marchander
prick *v.* jaquer, piquer **stick or prick repeatedly** piquailler
prickle *n.* **prickle bush** éronce
prickly *adj.* épineux **prickly heat** échauboulure, échauffure
pride *n.* arrogance, fierté, gloire, glorieuseté, orgueil **pride in one's dress** farauderie **having pride in one's dress** faraud **source of pride** gloire
prie-dieu *n.* prie-Dieu
priest *n.* abbé, curé, oiseau de malheur, prêtre **officiating**

priest officiant **washing of the priest's hands at mass** lavabo **man who studied to be a priest but failed to be ordained** prêtre manqué

primary *adj.* premier, principal **primary school teacher** maîtresse d'école

prime *adj.* prime

primp *v.* pimper, se pimponner, se repimper

primrose *n.* braguette **evening primrose** belle de nuit

prince *n.* prince

princess *n.* prince

principal *adj.* capital, cardinal, central, principal

principal *n.* principal

principally *adv.* principalement

principle *n.* principe

print *n.* **having a flowered print** fleuré

print *v.* frapper, imprimer, publier, étamper

printer *n.* imprimeur

printing *n.* imprimerie **printing shop or plant** imprimerie

priority *n.* priorité

prison *n.* forçat, prison, pénitentiaire **go to prison** envoyer aux fèves

prisoner *n.* prisonnier, pénitencier

prissy *adj.* fion-fion, gningnin **act prissy** faire {prendre} des fions, se flanquer des fions

private *adj.* personnel, privé, secret

privet *n.* buis **swamp privet** bois blanc

privilege *n.* privilège

privileged *adj.* préférencié

privy *n.* **outdoor privy** cabane, cabine en dehors, cabinet

prize *n.* prix

probability *n.* probabilité **used to express a probability** aussi bien que

probable *adj.* probable, prouvable

probably *adv.* probable, probablement, prouvable, prouvablement

probe *n.* tâton

probing *n.* sondage

problem *n.* problème, tracas **problem child** enfant terrible **that's your problem** ça, c'est ta nénaine **pose a difficult problem** tirer une patate chaude (à qqn) *pl.* **have problems, difficulties** être dans les fardoches **bear the burden of one's problems** porter sa croix

procedure *n.* démarche

proceed *v.* pousser route

proceeds *npl.* produit

process *n.* démarche, procès

procession *n.* cortège, procession **funeral procession** enterrement

proclaim *v.* déclarer, proclamer, professer **proclaim o.s.** se proclamer

proclamation *n.* proclamation

procrastinate *v.* dandiner, mouliner la queue du chien, mouliner, tournailler la queue du chien

prod *v.* jaquer

prodigal *adj.* **prodigal son** enfant prodige

prodigy *n.* merveille

produce *n.* produit **produce farm** ferme de produits **garden produce** jardinage

produce *v.* causionner, donner, fabriquer, faire, fournir, générer, produire, sortir avec, produire, rapporter **produce flowers** faire des fleurs **produce results** faire effet **produce its customary call** chanter

produced *adj.* **be produced** se fabriquer **grown or produced in Louisiana** créole

product *n.* production, produit

production *n.* production

profane *v.* jurer, profaner, violer

profanity *n.* jurage, jurement

profess *v.* professer

profession *n.* métier, profession

professional *adj.* professionnel

professional *n.* professionnel **fake professional** charlatan

professor *n.* professeur

profit *n.* bénéfice, commission, gain, produit, profit, rapport, rente, revenu **make a profit** faire du bénéfice, sortir l'avant / sortir en avant **render a profit** donner du {un} retour *pl.* **for a share of the profits** à la part

profit *v.* bénéficier, profiter

profitable *adj.* payant, profitable

profligate *adj.* dévergondé

profound *adj.* gros

program *n.* programme, émission **television program** SHOW **command to a person to encourage him/her to get in line, get on board, get with the program** 'poteau, Caillette'!

progress *n.* avance, développement, pas avançant, progrès

progressive *adj.* progressif

prohibit *v.* défendre, interdire

prohibition *n.* prohibition

project *n.* projet **any difficult project or undertaking** pratique à chagrin *pl.* **household projects** berdassement

prolong *v.* prolonger

prolongation *n.* prolongation, prolongement

prominent *adj.* prononcé

promiscuous *adj.* **be promiscuous** putainer

promise *n.* parole, promesse, vœu **break a promise not to indulge in s.t.** casser le petit bâton **break a Lenten promise** casser sa pénitence *pl.* **unfulfilled promises** accroires

promise *v.* donner sa parole, promettre **one who promises much but accomplishes little** pisseur en l'air

promised *adj.* promis

promissory *adj.* **maker of a promissory note** prometteur

promote *v.* avancer, PROMOTE

promoted *adj.* **be promoted to the next grade in school** passer en grade

promoter *n.* entrepreneur

promotion *n.* avancement, promotion

promptly *adv.* droite
prone *adj.* sujet **be prone to** se porter à / être porté à
pronounce *v.* prononcer
pronounced *adj.* prononcé
pronunciation *n.* prononciation
proof *n.* preuve, épreuve, évidence **furnish proof** documenter **subject to proof** prouvable
prop *n.* appui, guette, support
prop *v.* appuyer, cointer, recarguer **prop o.s.** s'appuyer **prop up** abutter, mâter **prop up with a brace** guetter
propel *v.* **propel with a forked pushpole** fourcher
propeller *n.* palette, PROPEL
proper *adj.* convenable, disable, fini **be proper** convenir
properly *adv.* bien, proprement
property *n.* bien, possession, propriété, terre **property line** ligne **possess property** avoir du bien **acquire property or anything of value** se gagner de quoi **piece of property** morceau de terre **said of landed property that has been expropriated by the state** être domaine **deprive of goods or property** dégréer *pl.* **having healing properties** médicinal
prophecy *n.* prophétie
prophet *n.* astronome, prophète
prophylactic *n.* capote
proportion *n.* proportion **out of proportion** démesuré **anything big or grotesquely out of proportion** zombi
proposal *n.* propos, proposition **make an offer or proposal** faire un(e) offre
propose *v.* proposer **propose a toast** faire un TOAST **man proposes and God disposes** l'homme propose et Dieu dispose
proposer *n.* proposeur
proposition *n.* propos, proposition
proprietor *n.* bourgeois, propriétaire
prosecute *v.* poursuivre
prosecution *n.* poursuite
prosper *v.* prospérer
prosperity *n.* bonheur, prospérité
prosperous *adj.* prospère **be prosperous** boulotter, prospérer
prostitute *n.* catouche, coureuse, coursailleur, femme publique / femme du soir, garce, prostituée, putain, traîneuse **prostitute who holds a professionnal ID card** femme cartée *pl.* **frequent prostitutes** putainer
prostitution *n.* prostitution, putainerie
protect *v.* garder, protecter, protéger
protected *adj.* **protected area for birds, wildlife, etc.** sanctuaire
protection *n.* garde, protection **affording protection** sauve **cover for protection** abrier
protective *adj.* protecteur
protector *n.* protecteur
protest *n.* objection
protest *v.* se mâter contre
Protestant *adj.* protestant
Protestant *n.* Protestant
protraction *n.* prolongation
proud *adj.* faquin comme un paon, fier comme un paon, fier, fiéraud, glorieux, ingrat, orgueilleux, suspect, vanteur **proud person** fanfaron, pétarade **be proud** avoir fier, se croire
proudly *adv.* fièrement
provable *adj.* prouvable
prove *v.* prouver, vérifier, établir
proverb *n.* proverbe
provide *v.* donner, fournir, supporter **provide for o.s.** se fournir, se pourvoir, se provisionner **provide an animal for community slaughter** pousser **find or provide an equal for** rappareiller
provided *conj.* d'abord que, pourvu
providence *n.* providence
provident *adj.* prévoyant
provision *n.* approvisionnement, provision **emergency provision** en-tout-cas *pl.* **provisions** butin, commission **make provisions** prévoir **supply with provisions** provisionner
provoke *v.* agacer, attiner, enticher, irriter, provoquer, siller **provoke or cause bumps or swelling of skin** louper **one who provokes or is easily provoked into a fight** piquant
provoked *adj.* **easily provoked** susceptible **one who provokes or is easily provoked into a fight** piquant
prowl *n.* **be on the prowl** rôder
prowl *v.* rôder **one who roams or prowls around** rôdeur
proximity *n.* **in closest proximity** droite
prudence *n.* prudence, précaution
prudent *adj.* prudent
prudish *adj.* suspect
prune *n.* prune sec, prune
prune *v.* débrancher, tailler, ébrancher
pruning *n.* ébranchage **pruning scissors** sécataire
pry *v.* fouille-merder, fouiller, fourgailler, foutumasser
prying *adj.* fouillard **prying woman** reluqueuse
public *adj.* public
public *n.* public **public notice** affiche **public sale** encan **public school** école publique **in public** en public **notary public** notaire publique **department of public welfare** RELIEF **insurance or public assistance** bénéfice
publication *n.* publication
publicize *v.* publier
publish *v.* publier, éditer
publisher *n.* publieur
pucker *v.* **cause the mouth to pucker** barrer la bouche
pudding *n.* bouillie au lait, bouillie, poutine **bread pudding** pain (de) poudine, poutine de pain, poutine
puddle *n.* placard **puddle of water on the floor** bourbier **mud puddle** bourbier
puff *n.* DRAG **cream puff** chou-crème, pet de nonne **powder puff** mappée, pompon, poudrillon
puff *v.* tirer **puff up** bouffir **puff o.s. up** se gonfler, se souffler
puffed *adj.* **puffed up** enflé **puffed up with pride** joufflu

puffed up in the face joufflu **get puffed up with anger** gourmer
puffy *adj.* gonfle, gonflé
pugnacious *adj.* batailleur
pull *v.* halailler, haler, halocher, tirailler, tirer, haler **pull about** zigonner **pull apart** décrocher, défaire, tiller **pull brambles** éroncer **pull down** déchirer **pull out** arracher **pull tight** étirer **pull together** haler ensemble **pull up** enlever **pull o.s. together** se refaire, se reprendre **pull on persistently** tirailler **pull to shreds** écharpiller **pull from the mud** débourber **pull in all directions** tirailler **pull out of joint** démancher **pull from side to side** zigonner **pull out the shirttail of** déculotter **pull the legs off of** élinguer **pull up by the roots** arracher **pull a fast one on s.o.** passer des crêpes à qqn **pull or shake apart in order to fluff and clean them** tiller **pull or shake apart the strands of in order to fluff and clean them** émousser
pullet *n.* poulette **fat hen or pullet** poularde
pulley *n.* poulie
pulling *n.* **pulling out** arrachage **pulling out of the mud** débourbage **pushing and pulling** halaillement
pulmonary *adj.* poumonique
pulp *n.* nanane, chair
pulpit *n.* chaire **preacher's pulpit** baril
pulsation *n.* battement
pulse *n.* pouls
puma *n.* chat-tigre
pump *n.* pompe **pump handle** bras de pompe **air pump** pompe **gas pump** pompe à gaz **hand pump** pompe à la main, pompe
pump *v.* pomper **pump back** repomper
pumpkin *n.* citrouille, giraumont, PUMPKIN
punch *n.* coup de poing, poque, PUNCH, salade, PUNCH **leather punch** perce-cuir **throw a punch** garrocher un coup de poing, tirer un coup de poing *pl.* **exchange punches** poquer
punch *v.* sacrer un coup de poing, tirer un coup de poing
punctual *adj.* régulier
puncture *n.* piqûre
pungent *adj.* hâcre, piquant
punish *v.* crucifier, punir
punishment *n.* bûchée, correction, peine, punition, touche **punishment or game in which a person is swung by the arms and legs** bascule **physical punishment** douille **put in the corner as punishment** accointer
punk *n.* péteur
puny *adj.* maigréchine **puny, paltry, rickety person** bougon
pupil *n.* écolier, élève
puppet *n.* marionnette, poupée
purchase *n.* achat, ordre **purchase on credit** achat à crédit *pl.* **make purchases on credit** faire un BILL
purchase *v.* acheter **purchase more for o.s.** se racheter
purchaser *n.* acheteur
purchasing *n.* achat
pure *adj.* chaste, pur, STRAIGHT
puree *n.* purée
purely *adv.* purement
purgative *adj.* purgatif
purgative *n.* purgatif, purge
Purgatory *n.* purgatoire
purge *n.* purge
purge *v.* purger **purge o.s.** se purger
purification *n.* purification
purify *v.* désinfecter, purifier **purify o.s.** se purifier
purity *n.* chasteté, pureté
purple *n.* violet
purpose *n.* but, fin, objet, propos **on purpose** exprès, par exprès **do on purpose** faire (par) exprès, faire exprès **for the purpose of** pour **do a task that serves no purpose** mettre de la boucane en sac **made or intended esp. for a given purpose** exprès
purposely *adv.* exprès
purr *v.* ronronner
purring *n.* ronron, ronronnement
purse *n.* bourse, porte-monnaie
purslane *n.* **milk purslane** petit pourpier
pursue *v.* coursailler, courser après, courser, galoper, poursuivre
pursuit *n.* course, poursuite
pus *n.* matière, postume, pourriture **pus pocket** dépôt
push *n.* poussade, pousse, poussée **give a push** donner une pousse
push *v.* poussailler, pousser, péter, se poussailler **push back** repousser **push in** encaver, enfoncer **push on** pousser dessus **push violently** caramboler **push aside or remove foam from boiling cane juice** sabler
pushcart *n.* charrette à bras
pushing *n.* bousculade **pushing and pulling** halaillement
pushpole *n.* fourche **propel with a forked pushpole** fourcher
pustule *n.* pustule
put *v.* jaquer, mettre, placer **put aside** mettre de côté, serrer **put away** mettre de côté, resserrer, sauver, serrer **put back** remettre, replacer **put between** entremettre **put down** dégrucher, déposer, mettre par terre, poser, écraser **put in** additionner, mettre **put o.s.** se mettre **put off** remettre **put on** mettre **put out** fermer, éteigner, éteindre **put together** emmancher, ramancher **put back together** ramancher, remettre **put far away** éloigner **put on again** remettre **put on o.s.** se mettre **put up with** endurer, voir **put back in position** corriger, redressir **put below or under** mettre en bas **put in the corner** cointer **put off until tomorrow** remettre à demain **put one over on** fouler **put out one's eye** s'éborgner **put on hurriedly or carelessly** fourrer, se fourrer **put one over on s.o.** en passer une à qqn **put out an eye of** éborgner **put out of working order** déralinguer **put s.o. in his place** taper ça à qqn / taper sa réponse à qqn **put up with each other** s'endurer **put in the corner as**

punishment accointer **put some more in or on** remettre **put upright bars in a banister** bâtonner **put s.o. in his or her place** mettre au pas, mettre qqn à sa place **put or put back in an upright position** redressir **you need to be put back into your place** c'est l'heure de voir à couper tes culottes

putter *v.* picocher **putter around** tripoter

putting *n.* **putting out to pasture** pâturage **mounting or putting together** gréement

putty *n.* mastic

puzzle *n.* casse-tête, dévinail

puzzle *v.* bafouer

pyjamas *npl.* pyjamas

pyorrhea *n.* escorbut

pâté *n.* tourtière

Q

quack *n.* charlatan

quack *onom.* coinque

quadrille *n.* quadrille

quadroon *n.* griffe, griffien

quail *n.* perdrix, râle **young quail** perdreau

quake *v.* trembler

qualification *n.* qualification *pl.* **having the necessary qualifications** qualifié

qualified *adj.* qualifié

qualify *v.* qualifier **used to intensify or qualify another noun** un coquin de

quality *n.* qualité **of quality** HOP **match up s.o. of quality with s.o. much less worthy or attractive** donner de la confiture aux cochons

quandary *n.* **be in a quandary** être vent-debout

quantity *n.* nombre, quantité **considerable quantity** quantité **large quantity** hourra, massacre, tambouille, tas, trallée **small quantity** poignée **the quantity of oysters, shrimp, etc. held by a "champagne"** champagne **in great quantity** terrible, à tire-larigot **have a large quantity of s.t.** en avoir par dessus la tête

quarantine *n.* quarantine

quarantine *v.* quarantiner **quarantine o.s.** se quarantiner

quarrel *n.* argument, bisbille, chamaille, chamaillerie, chicane, chipote, discorde, dispute, emboulage, obstination, querelle, scandale, scène, train **pick a quarrel** chercher querelle, faire le ravaud **have a quarrel with s.o.** avoir des paroles avec qqn **be looking for a quarrel** babiller

quarrel *v.* avoir des mots (avec qqn), querellailler, quereller, se chipoter, se disputailler, se mêlailler, se quereller **quarrel habitually** s'adonner comme chien et chat **quarrel with** obstiner **quarrel with s.o.** avoir castile avec qqn **quarrel with each other** s'ostiner **they're always quarreling** c'est comme le feu et l'eau / c'est comme chat et chien, c'est comme le feu et l'eau **one who quarrels over trivial matters** chipoteur

quarrelous *adj.* **be quarrelous** être en divorce

quarrelsome *adj.* querelleur

quart *n.* quart de gallon, quart

quarter *n.* quart, quartier, vingt-cinq-sous, vingt-cinq sous, quartier, terme **quarter of an hour** quart d'heure *pl.* **bachelor quarters** garçonnière **living quarters** logement, place, quartier **slave quarters** cabanage, camp **workers camp, quarters** camp **build larger quarters for o.s.** s'égrandir

queen *n.* reine, dame, reine **beauty queen** reine **name of the carnaval queen** Dorothée

queer *adj.* bizarre

quest *n.* recherche

question *n.* demande, question **ask a question** poser une question **be the question** s'agir **point or person in question** sujet

question *v.* demander, questionner **question persistently** pomper

questionable *adj.* doutable

questioner *n.* questionneur

questioning *n.* questionnement

quibble *v.* chicaner, se chicaner

quick *adj.* avançant, court, souple, vif, vite **quick to anger** chocatif

quick *n.* vif

quick-tempered *adj.* prompt

quick-witted *adj.* prompt

quickly *adv.* hourri-hourra, subit, subitement, vite, vitement, vivement **quickly and not very well** à la va vite **definitively and quickly** propre

quickness *n.* vitesse

quicksand *n.* terre tremblante {mouvante}

quicksilver *n.* mercure, vif-argent

quiet *adj.* assogné, calme, dull, paisé, retiré, tranquille **be quiet** bouche ta gueule, paix, toi! / pais-toi! **become quiet** se tranquilliser **keep quiet** rester tranquille

quiet *n.* agrément

quiet *v.* apaiser, tranquilliser **quiet down** laissez un bloque en bas de la maison!, se tranquilliser

quieting *n.* apaisement

quietly *adv.* bas, doucement, tranquillement

quietness *n.* tranquillité

quilt *n.* couverte piquée, quilt, édradon **quilt maker** quilteuse **wedding quilt** quilte d'alliance *pl.* **make quilts** quilter

quilt *v.* quilter

quilted *adj.* piqué

quilter *n.* **female quilter** quilteuse

quilting *n.* **quilting bee** piquerie **quilting frame** cadre **quilting party** piquerie
quinine *n.* quinine
quirk *n.* arnicrot
quit *v.* abandonner, QUIT, quitter
quite *adv.* bien, joliment **not quite** pas tout à fait
quittor *n.* mal de lac
quiver *v.* frémir
quivering *n.* tremblement
quoit *npl.* **game of quoits** galoche
quota *n.* limite, placard **put a quota on s.t.** limiter
quote *v.* citer

R

rabbit *n.* lapin, lièvre **rabbit dog** briquet **rabbit fever** fièvre de lapin **cottontail rabbit** lapin à queue blanche **female rabbit** lapin
rabble *n.* fatras, foutraille, fripaille, marmite, racatcha, ripopée
rabid *adj.* enragé
rabies *n.* hydrophobie, rage **get rabies** s'enrager
raccoon *n.* chaoui, chat **dark-furred raccoon that lives in cypress swamps** chaoui cyprière
race *n.* course, monde, race **race fan** coursier **race track** TRACK **horse race** course de chevaux **run a race** faire une course, tirer une course **the white race** le monde blanc **person of mixed race with a light complexion** Créole de couleur **take part in a race** tirer une course **slow and steady wins the race** petit train va loin **person of mixed blood or impure race** sang-mêlé
race *v.* courir, courser, courir, faire courir **race with** courser
racecourse *n.* course
racehorse *n.* coureur **racehorse rider** kêtch
racer *n.* **blue racer snake** coureuse **southern black racer** fouetteuse
rachitis *n.* maladie d'os
racing *n.* **person who is passionate about horse racing** coursier
racist *n.* raciste
rack *n.* deux-chemin, moule **burner rack** mèche **clothes rack** portemanteau **coat rack** portemanteau **hay rack** crèche, râtelier **laying rack or nest** nichoir **two-wheeled rack to which plows and other field implements are attached** moline **go to rack and ruin** tomber en botte
rack *v.* aller le {à} deux-chemin, aller le racca {rack}, aller les deux chemins
racket *n.* bacchanale, bamboula, berdas, boulvari, bruit, cancan, carnage, faïouque, hourra, sassaquoi, tapage, tatamage, tchampourra, train, raquette **tennis racket** tennis **make a racket** carnager, ferrailler **carry on a racket** amener un tapage {du train} **wild hunt, a mysterious racket, din, or chorus that passes through the night sky** chasse-galerie
radical *n.* ventre-rouge
radio *n.* boîte à musique, radio **radio broadcasting station** station **on the radio** sur {dessus} l'air **speak on the radio** monter sur la radio
radish *n.* radis
radius *n.* ronde
raffle *n.* loterie, raffle **raffle ticket** mise **buy a lottery or raffle ticket** prendre une mise
raffle *v.* raffler **raffle off** raffler
raft *n.* cageux
rafter *n.* chevron, madrier, rance **valley rafter** chevron de vallée
rag *n.* chiffon, guenille, haillon, lambèche, vieux linge **rag left at the door to wipe the feet** essuie-place **rag used to wipe the bottom after a bowel movement** torche *pl.* **rags** chiffonnerie, haillonnerie **in rags** haillonné
ragamuffin *n.* gueux
rage *n.* fureur, rage **fly into a rage** prendre l'estampique / prendre des estampiques, s'emporter, s'enrager
ragged *adj.* dégainé, dévaporé
ragout *n.* fricot, ragoût
ragweed *n.* massicot **giant ragweed** bon-bout, herbe du {à} sang, herbe à bâton **small ragweed** herbe coquin bâtard
raid *n.* **make a raid** faire une passée
rail *n.* râle, rail **clapper rail** râle grise **communion rail** table sainte **king rail** grande râle de prairie **light rail** ranche, ridelle **sora rail** râle masqué
railing *n.* barre de corps, garde-corps, ridelle **bridge railing** garde-fou **stair railing** garde-fou
railroad *n.* chemin de fer **railroad crosstie** TIE **railroad station** dépôt, gare **railroad switch** SWITCH **railroad track** TRACK **hand-propelled railroad cart** char-à-bras **road or railroad spur** branche
railway *n.* **railway coach** traîneau
rain *n.* mouillasse, pluie **rain bird** oiseau de pluie **rain cloud** nuage de pluie, nuage **rain reservoir** digue **rain spout** dalle **drizzling rain** lizerée **heavy rain** avalasse, averse, déluge, ratatouille, saucée **light rain** brumas, frimas **fine rain or snow** poudrin **drop of rain** grain de pluie **spell of rain** série de pluie **period of rain or drought beginning June 8 and lasting forty days** Saint-Médard **fine, gentle, misty rain** grimace
rain *v.* mouiller, pleuvoir, puiter **rain again** remouiller **rain heavily** mouiller des chiens et des chats, mouiller des petits nègres en or / mouiller comme si le Bon Dieu est content, mouiller fort / mouiller par barils {baquets /

bailles}, mouiller jusqu'à les chiens {vaches} buvaient debout / mouiller jusqu'à les vaches beuglent, tomber des petits nègres la tête en bas **rain intermittenly** mouillasser **rain lightly** brumasser, grimacer **rain in torrents** mouiller averse / mouiller à verse **rain cats and dogs** mouiller des chiens et des chats **it's raining** la pluie tombe **it's raining hard** il mouille par siaux **place where it rains a lot** le pot de chambre à Virgile

rainbow *n.* arc-en-ciel

raincoat *n.* capot ciré, capot à pluie, toile cirée, toile

rainshower *n.* orage

rainstorm *n.* mauvaise orage

rainy *adj.* brumassant, mouillasseux, orageux

raise *n.* augmentation

raise *v.* augmenter, dresser, engendrer, faire, farmer, hausser, hisser, lever, rehausser, soulever, élever, raugmenter, renchérir, élever **raise crops** faire récolte **raise o.s.** se hisser **raise up** redresser, regricher, élever **raise a bump** embosser **raise a garden** faire jardin **raise a ruckus** faire un scandale **raise up again** relever **raise the value of** faire valoir **raise all kinds of hell** faire les quatre-cents coups, faire les quatre cents coups **raise or lift o.s. up** se lever

raised *adj.* **badly raised child** pirate

raisin *n.* raisin

raising *n.* levée, soulèvement, vacherie, élevage

rake *n.* gratte, rabasseau, raclée des herbes, raclée, râteau

rake *v.* râtonner **rake up** râtonner **rake over the coals** fourgailler, foutre HELL

ram *n.* bélier, refouloir

ram *v.* bourrer

ramble *v.* **ramble on** radoter

rambler *n.* rôdailleur

rambunctious *adj.* carnassier

ramrod *n.* baguette

ranch *n.* habitation **cattle ranch** vacherie

rancid *adj.* rance **become rancid** rancir

rancor *n.* rancœur, rancune

rancorous *adj.* rancuneux

range *n.* portée

rank *n.* grade

ransack *v.* fourgailler, fureter, ressoubler, soursoubler

rap *n.* apostrophe **rap on the head with the knuckles** calotte

rap *v.* apostropher

rapacious *adj.* rapiat, rasoir

rape *v.* contrôler, violer **dishonor or rape** gâter

rapid *npl.* **descend or leap the rapids** sauter les rapides

rapidly *adv.* **rapidly and carelessly** (à) (la) bride abattue, à la bride molle

rare *adj.* clair, rare, recherché, serré

rarely *adv.* rarement

rarity *n.* rareté

rascal *n.* canaille, crapule, ingrandjin, maudit, monstre, originel, salaud, saloperie, scélérat, tocaille, vaurien, tout-dans-le-monde **you rascal** mon vilain

rascality *n.* bonarienté

rash *adj.* risqueux, téméraire

rash *n.* grattelle, humeur **heat rash** échauboulure, échauffure

rashness *n.* imprudence, témérité

rasp *n.* râpe

rasp *v.* râper, raser

raspberry *n.* framboise

rasping *n.* râpage

rat *n.* rat **female rat** rate *pl.* **nest of rats** nique à rats

rat-tail *n.* **rat-tail file** queue de rat

rate *n.* train **at any rate** dans tous les cas, en tout cas **at the rate of** à *pl.* **interest rates** intérêt

rather *adv.* bien, manière, moyen, plutôt **rather than** plutôt que {de} / plutôt de

rather *conj.* du moins

ratification *n.* confirmation

ratify *v.* approuver, confirmer

ration *n.* ration, rationnement

ration *v.* rationner

rationing *n.* rationnement

ratoon *n.* chicot

rattan *n.* **rattan vine** liane noire

rattle *n.* chichicois, râle, râlement **rattle on and on about s.t.** en faire tout un chapitre **death rattle** le hoquet de la mort, râle de la mort

rattle *v.* interboler **rattle around** se berdasser **rattle in the throat or bronchial tubes** râler

rattle-trap *adj.* **rattle-trap vehicle** tchacara

rattlesnake *n.* serpent (à) sonnette(s), sonnette

ravage *n.* ravage

ravage *v.* dévaster, ravager

ravaging *n.* dévastation

rave *v.* battre la berloque, déparler, parler à la berloque

ravine *n.* coulée

raw *adj.* cru

ray *n.* rayon

razor *n.* rasoir **razor strap** doucine, STRAP **safety razor** pioche

re- *prefix.* re-

re-elect *v.* réélecter, réélire

re-election *n.* réélection

re-embark *v.* rembarquer

re-embarkation *n.* rembarquement

re-employ *v.* remployer, rengager, remployer

re-encase *v.* rencaisser

re-enter *v.* rerentrer

re-establish *v.* rétablir **re-establish o.s.** se réinstaller

re-form *v.* reformer

reaccustom *v.* raccoutumer, réhabituer **reaccustom o.s.** se raccoutumer, se réhabituer

reach *n.* **out of reach** mal à main

reach *v.* atteindre, frapper, se rendre **reach a state** être rendu **reach an agreement** se comprendre, tomber d'accord **reach an understanding** faire {prendre} des arrangements
react *v.* réagir, se mâter contre **quick to react** prime
reaction *n.* réaction
read *v.* lire **read again** relire **enjoyable or easy to read** lisable
readable *adj.* lisable
reader *n.* liseur
reading *adj.* **reading matter** littérature
reading *n.* lecture **prayers, singing, reading, etc., offered by lay people in lieu of actual Mass** messe blanche {sec} *pl.* **do card readings** tirer des cartes
readjust *v.* rajuster **readjust o.s.** se rajuster **readjust one's clothes** se rajuster
readjustment *n.* rajustement
readmit *v.* réadmettre
ready *adj.* paré, prêt **ready to go** frais comme un lapin **ready to leave** quittable **all ready** tout paré **get ready** parer, s'arranger, se propter, se préparer **be ready to go** avoir le FLAG en l'air **be ready to leave** avoir la couarte sus l'épaule **be ready and eager to go someplace** être dessus le mot de go
ready *v.* préparer
real *adj.* franc, vrai, véritable **real estate** propriété
reality *n.* réalité **not paying attention to reality** dans les nuages
realize *v.* réaliser, s'apercevoir
really *adv.* bien, foutûment, franchement, joliment, pour (de) même, pour même, quand même, réellement, terriblement, vrai, vraiment
reap *v.* récolter
reaping *n.* **reaping machine** ramasseuse
reappear *v.* reparaître, ressourdre, réapparaître
reapply *v.* rappliquer
reappoint *v.* rappointer
reapportion *v.* repartager
rear *adj.* **rear end** fesse, gogo
rear *n.* **located in the rear** (d')en arrière
rear *v.* regimber, élever, mâter, se carguer, se mâter **rear back again** se remater
rearing *n.* **rearing of cattle** vacherie
rearm *v.* **rearm o.s.** se réarmer
rearrange *v.* rarranger
reason *n.* cause, raison, raisonnement **the reason why** la raison qui fait **for what reason** pour qui **at the age of reason** fort
reason *v.* raisonner
reasonable *adj.* raisonnable
reasonably *adv.* raisonnablement
reasoning *n.* jugement, raisonnement
reassemble *v.* remettre, se réunir
reassure *v.* rassurer **reassure o.s.** se rassurer
reassured *adj.* **be reassured** se rassurer
reattach *v.* rattacher
rebale *v.* remballer
rebaptize *v.* rebaptiser
rebel *v.* regimber, révolter, se rebuter, se regimber, se remater, se révolter **rebel against** se mâter contre
rebellion *n.* révolte
rebellious *adj.* rebuté
rebend *v.* recrochir, retordre
rebirth *n.* renaissance
rebleach *v.* reblanchir
reblock *v.* reboucher
rebloom *v.* refleurir
reblossom *v.* refleurir
reboil *v.* rebouillir
rebore *v.* repercer
rebound *n.* rebond, rebondissement, ricoche
rebound *v.* bondir, rebondir, ricocher
rebounding *n.* rebondissement
rebox *v.* rencaisser
rebraid *v.* retresser
rebuild *v.* rebâtir, reconstruire, rétablir
rebuilding *n.* reconstruction
rebuke *n.* galop
rebuke *v.* chauffer, ramoner
rebury *v.* renterrer
recall *v.* placer, rappeler, rattraper, se rappeler, se ressouvenir, souvenir
recapture *v.* ressaisir
recaptured *adj.* repris
recatch *v.* rattraper
receipt *n.* quittance, reçu
receive *v.* attraper, prendre, recevoir **receive as payment** collecter **receive the sacrament** communier **receive the sacrament of Confirmation** confirmer **receive communion during the Easter season** faire ses Pâques **receive assistance from department of public welfare** monter sur le RELIEF
recent *adj.* **most recent** dernier
recently *adv.* dernièrement, fraîchement
receptacle *n.* **ash receptacle** cendrier
reception *n.* réception, collation **reception for members of a political party** banco **wedding reception** dessert
recess *n.* RECESS
recharge *v.* recharger
rechew *v.* remâcher
recipe *n.* formule, recette
recitation *n.* récitation **lengthy repetition or recitation** litanie
recite *v.* prononcer, réciter
reckon *v.* se compter
reclad *v.* referrer

recline *v.* capoter, se carguer
reclose *v.* refermer, se reboucher
recognition *n.* reconnaissance
recognizable *adj.* reconnaissable
recognize *v.* reconnaître **recognize each other** se reconnaître
recollection *n.* souvenir
recommend *v.* recommander
recommendable *adj.* recommandable
recommendation *n.* recommandation
recompense *n.* récompense
reconcile *v.* accorder, débouquer, faire camarades, refaire, réconcilier, se rarranger **reconcile with** se refaire à **reconcile o.s. to** se refaire à
reconciled *adj.* **be reconciled** faire ami, refaire ami, se réconcilier **become reconciled** refaire, se rapprocher, se rarranger **become reconciled with** se refaire à **be reconciled after a quarrel** débouquer, se débouquer
reconciliation *n.* rapprochement
reconciling *n.* accordement
reconnect *v.* raccrocher
reconnecting *n.* raccrochage
reconsider *v.* reconsidérer, repenser
reconstitute *v.* reconstituer
reconstruct *v.* reconstruire
reconstruction *n.* reconstruction
recook *v.* recuire
recopy *v.* recopier
record *n.* assiette, compte, disque, dossier, plaque à PHONOGRAPH, plaque, record **record book** registre **record player** graphophone **baptism record or certificate** baptistaire **just for the record** c'est juste pour dire *pl.* **office of records** greffe
record *v.* frapper, récorder, graver
recorder *n.* greffier **tape recorder** récordeur
recork *v.* reboucher
recount *v.* recompter, réciter **recount events in the wrong order** mettre le bogui avant le cheval **recount in a giddy, senseless way** fifoler **describe or recount in detail** détailler
recoup *v.* rattraper
recourse *n.* recours **have recourse** avoir recours(à)
recover *v.* ragaillardir, recouverre, regagner, réchapper, se relever, en gagner, rattraper, ravoir, recouverre, relever, réchapper, se refaire **recover one's losses** se rattraper **recover from the water** ressourdre **recover one's former good looks** se refaire
recovered *adj.* relevé
recovery *n.* rétablissement **there's no hope of recovery or recuperation** il y a pas de réchappe
recreation *n.* banco, divertissement
recross *v.* recroiser, retraverser
recrossing *n.* repassage
rector *n.* curé
rectory *n.* presbytère
rectum *n.* boyau gras
recuperate *v.* ragaillardir, recouverre
recuperation *n.* **there's no hope of recovery or recuperation** il y a pas de réchappe
recur *v.* revenir
recurrence *n.* répétition
recut *v.* recouper, retailler, retrancher
red *adj.* rouge comme une bête rouge / rouge comme une betterave {une écrevisse / une tomate / un piment}, rouge
Red *adj.* **Red Cross** Croix Rouge
redam *v.* reboucher
redbird *n.* cardinau
redbug *n.* bête rouge
redden *v.* rougir
reddish *adj.* rougeâtre **having a reddish coat** rougette
redeem *v.* racheter
redeemer *n.* rédempteur
redemption *n.* rédemption
redesign *v.* refaçonner
redfish *n.* poisson rouge
redig *v.* refouiller
rediscover *v.* retrouver
redivide *v.* repartager
redneck *n.* cou-rouge
redness *n.* rougeur
redo *v.* recourir, refaire, réparer, surfaire
redress *n.* réparation
reduce *v.* couper, dégrossir, rebaisser, réduire, tarir, tomber **reduce by melting** rendre **reduce in size** dégrossir, rapetisser **reduce the price** baisser le prix **reduce the swelling** désenfler
reduced *adj.* **be reduced** se réduire
reduction *n.* réduction
reed *n.* canne, canuche, jonc, roseau, musique **cane reed** cannette **wild cane reed** canne farouche, canne marronne, canne sauvage, canne terre haute, canne à fuseau, canne à pêche {pêcher}
reef *n.* banc
reel *n.* **spool or reel used to put string in skeins** travouil
reel *v.* baranquer
refamiliarize *v.* réhabituer
refashion *v.* refaçonner
refasten *v.* rattacher
refatten *v.* rengraisser
reference *n.* recommandation, référence **character reference** référence
refine *v.* purifier, raffiner
refined *adj.* poli **become refined** se raffiner
refinement *n.* délicatesse, raffinement **lack refinement** avoir pas de délicatesse

refinery *n.* raffinerie **oil refinery** raffinerie d'huile **sugar refinery** raffinerie de sucre, sucrerie
refining *n.* raffinage, raffinement
refish *v.* repêcher
refit *v.* raccorder **refit a handle** ramancher
refitting *n.* raccordement
reflect *v.* guetter, jongler, réflecter, réfléchir, calculer
reflected *adj.* **be reflected or mirrored** réflecter
reflection *n.* jonglage, réflexion
reflood *v.* re-FLOOD
reflux *n.* refoule
refold *v.* replier, reployer
reforge *v.* rebattre, reforger
reform *n.* réforme
reform *v.* réformer **reform o.s.** se réformer
reformation *n.* réformation
refrain *n.* refrain
refrain *v.* s'abstenir, s'empêcher
refresh *v.* rafraîchir
refreshed *adj.* **be refreshed** se rafraîchir
refreshing *adj.* rafraîchissant
refreshing *n.* rafraîchissement
refrigerator *n.* frigidaire, glacière, réfrigerateur
refuge *n.* abri, échappatoire **seek refuge** se ranger **take refuge** se ranger, se réfugier
refugee *n.* réfugié, émigré
refurnish *v.* remeubler
refuse *n.* déboulis, foutraille
refuse *v.* bouquer, refuser **refuse repeatedly** refusailler **refuse to talk** se bouquer après **said when one refuses to repeat o.s.** le prêtre dit pas sa messe deux fois
regain *v.* regagner **regain one's bearings** se retrouver
regard *n.* considération, estime **have regard** regarder, respecter **in regard to** concernant, quant à **with regard to** tant qu'à **hold in regard** regarder
regard *v.* **regard as** considérer
regarding *prep.* dessus
regardless *adj.* dans tous les cas
regime *n.* régime
regiment *n.* **military regiment** régiment
region *n.* pays, région, territoire
register *n.* registre **cash register** régistre
register *v.* enregistrer **register o.s.** s'enregistrer **register to vote** registrer
registrar *n.* commis de jour
registration *n.* enregistrement
registry *n.* greffe **baptismal registry** registre
reglue *v.* recoller
regraft *v.* regreffer
regret *n.* regret
regret *v.* regretter
regretful *adj.* **be regretful** avoir du regret
regrettable *adj.* regrettable
regrind *v.* remoudre
regrowth *n.* repousse
regular *adj.* régulier **keep o.s. regular** se régler
regularly *adv.* réglé, régulier, régulièrement
regulate *v.* ajuster, régler
regulation *n.* ordonnance, régulation
rehandle *v.* remanier
rehang *v.* raccrocher, rependre
rehanging *n.* raccrochage
rehearsal *n.* pratique
rehearse *v.* pratiquer, se pratiquer
reheat *v.* réchauffer
reheating *n.* réchauffage, réchauffement
rehire *v.* remployer, rengager
rehook *v.* raccrocher
rehooked *adj.* **become rehooked** se raccrocher
rehooking *n.* raccrochage
reign *v.* régner
reimbursable *adj.* remboursable
reimburse *v.* rembourser **reimburse o.s.** se payer
reimbursement *n.* remboursement
rein *n.* rêne **rein bar** croix **free rein** passe-droit *pl.* **reins** cordeau, guide **leather reins** cordeau **guide with reins** rêner **loosen the reins of** dérêner **slacken the reins of** dérêner **instrument used to make horse reins out of horse hair** tarabi
rein *v.* rêner
reinflate *v.* regonfler
reinforce *v.* assolider, chausser, enforcir, fortifier, rechausser, renchausser, renforcir **reinforce o.s.** s'enforcir
reinforcement *n.* chandilier, renforcissement, renfort
reinforcing *n.* renforçage
reinstall *v.* réinstaller
reinsure *v.* rassurer
reinsured *adj.* **get reinsured** se rassurer
reinter *v.* renterrer
reinvite *v.* rinviter
reject *n.* rebut
reject *v.* refuser, renier **spurn, reject, or break up with a suitor** donner son {un} capot (à qqn)
rejoin *v.* réunir
rejudge *v.* rejuger
rejuvenate *v.* jeunezir, rajeunir
rekindle *v.* rallumer
rekindled *adj.* **be rekindled** se rallumer
reknead *v.* repétrir
reknot *v.* renouer
relapse *n.* rechute **have a relapse** avoir une rechute, chuter, rechuter
relapse *v.* chuter, rechuter
relate *v.* conter, raconter, rapporter

related *adj.* apparenté, parent, parent de la fesse gauche **related by marriage** parent par alliance
relation *n.* relation *pl.* **relations** parentage **sever relations** casser la paille
relationship *n.* parenté, rapport **have a close relationship** être grosse affaire **be on bad terms in a relationship** être à dos
relative *adj.* **relative to** à propos de
relative *n.* parent **near relative** près-parent *pl.* **relatives** famille, monde, parentage, parenté, race
relax *v.* relâcher, se relâcher, se reposer **relax s.o.** reposer
relaxing *adj.* reposant
relearn *v.* rapprendre
release *n.* délivrance
release *v.* décharger, lâcher, relâcher, échapper, déprendre
relent *v.* s'amollir
reliable *adj.* **be reliable** être de bonne parole, être le bras droite
relic *n.* relique
relief *n.* soulagement
relieve *v.* alléger, délâcher, soulager, ôter
relight *v.* rallumer
relighted *adj.* **be relighted** se rallumer
religion *n.* religion **one who practices his or her religion** pratiqueur
religious *adj.* religieux **religious gathering** prêche
relish *v.* **relish one's own situation** être dans son sirop
reload *v.* rembarquer, recharger
relocate *v.* décaniller, déménager, grouiller, reloger, se reloger
relocation *n.* délogement, déménagement
reluctantly *n.* à contre cœur
rely *v.* compter, dépendre dessus {sur}, se fier, se fonder **don't rely on this happening** fais-toi pas une gomme avec ça
remain *v.* reposer, rester **remain silent** rester bête **remain standing** se tenir debout **remain aloof or apart** rester à part **remain an old maid** monter en grain(e), rester pour graine **remain in one place** végétir
remainder *n.* balance, restant, reste
remaining *adj.* **remaining portion** drigaille
remains *npl.* vestige **remains of a fire** brûlis **funerary remains** reste **human remains** reste
remakc *v.* refaire, refaçonner
remark *n.* remarque **subtly disparaging remark** chique **make a caustic remark** passer une chique (à qqn) *pl.* **make remarks** passer des remarques **make caustic remarks** tirer des chiques {une chique} **temper one's remarks** mettre de l'eau dans son vin **one who makes caustic remarks** passeur de chiques, tireur de chiques
remark *v.* remarquer
remarkable *adj.* remarquable
remarriage *n.* remariage
remarried *adj.* **get remarried** se remarier
remarry *v.* remarier, se remarier
remedy *n.* curative, médecine, médicament, remède, traitement
remelt *v.* refondre
remember *v.* rappeler, se rappeler BACK, se rappeler, se remettre, se ressouvenir, souvenir
remembrance *n.* mémoire, souvenir
remill *v.* remoudre
remind *v.* faire penser, renouveler la mémoire **remind o.s.** se faire penser
reminded *adj.* **be reminded** se faire penser
remission *n.* absolution, remise, rémission
remittance *n.* remise
remix *v.* remêler
remnant *n.* restant, retaille
remoisten *v.* remouiller
remonstrance *n.* remontrance
remorse *n.* remords **pang of remorse or conscience** remords de conscience
remote *adj.* loin, lointain
removal *n.* transfert **removal of moss** émoussage **rust removal** dérouillement
remove *v.* ôter, arracher, emporter, retirer, tirer, éliminer, dégorger **remove o.s.** s'ôter, s'arracher **remove a piece** gober **remove for o.s.** se décrocher **remove from its nest** découvasser, découver **remove from its shell** décoquiller **remove from land intended for cultivation** désérer **remove from a comfortable place or situation** déniquer **remove sticks, leaves, etc., from moss to prepare it for use** écherpiller
removing *n.* **removing cream** écrémage **removing foam** écumage
remunerate *v.* rémunérer
renail *v.* rattacher
rename *v.* renommer
rend *v.* dérater
render *v.* rendre, tourner, rendre **render numb** engourdir **render a profit** donner du {un} retour
rendezvous *n.* rendez-vous
renew *v.* nouveauler, renouveler **renew acquaintances** renouveler les connaissances
renewable *adj.* renouvelable
renewal *n.* renaissance, renouvellement, rénovation
renewed *adj.* **be renewed** se renouveler
renominate *v.* renommer
renounce *v.* abandonner, nier, renoncer
renovate *v.* renouveler
renovation *n.* renouvellement, rénovation
renown *n.* renommée **person of importance or renown** personnage
rent *n.* loyer **be for rent** se louer
rent *v.* louer
renter *n.* locataire
reoccupy *v.* réoccuper **reoccupy o.s.** se réoccuper
reorder *v.* réordonner

reorganization *n.* réorganisation
reorganize *v.* réorganiser **reorganize o.s.** se réorganiser
repack *v.* refouler, remballer, rempaqueter, rencaisser
repackage *v.* rempaqueter
repaint *v.* repeindre, repeinturer
repair *n.* arrangement, raccommodage, réparage, réparation, réparement **beyond repair** hors de service
repair *v.* arranger, harnacher, piéceter, raccommoder, rafistoler, ramancher, rarranger, réparer **repair a shingled roof** piquer une couverture {un toit}
repairable *adj.* raccommodable, réparable
repaired *adj.* rafistolé
repairing *n.* arrangeage, arrangement, rafistolage, réparage
repairman *n.* arrangeur, réparateur **shoe repairman** arrangeur de souliers, cordonnier **watch repairman** horloger
reparable *adj.* arrangeable
reparation *n.* réparation, réparement
repay *v.* rembourser, repayer, récompenser
repayable *adj.* remboursable
repayment *n.* remboursement
repeal *n.* abrogation, annulement
repeal *v.* abolir, révoquer
repeat *v.* redire, répéter **repeat o.s.** se répéter **repeat over and over** rabattre, répétailler **said when one refuses to repeat o.s.** le prêtre dit pas sa messe deux fois
repeatedly *adv.* à tout moment
repel *v.* repousser
repellant *n.* **fly repellant** chasse-mouche
repelled *adj.* **be repelled** avoir zire (de)
repent *v.* se repentir
repentant *adj.* repentant
repentant *n.* repenti
repetition *n.* pratique, répétition **lengthy repetition or recitation** litanie
repierce *v.* repercer
replace *v.* changer, remettre, remplacer, replacer, échanger **replace shoes or stockings** rechausser
replaceable *adj.* remplaçable
replacement *n.* rechange, remplacement, remplaçant, replacement
replacing *n.* replacement
replant *v.* replanter **replant the empty spaces in a row of crops, trees, etc.** recourir les manques
replay *v.* rejouer
repleat *v.* replisser
replica *n.* double
replug *v.* reboucher
reply *n.* réponse
reply *v.* donner réponse, répondre
report *n.* rapport
report *v.* rapporter
reporter *n.* **news reporter** rapporteur
repose *n.* repos
reposed *adj.* reposé
repost *v.* rafficher
repour *v.* reverser
represent *v.* représenter **represent o.s.** se représenter
representation *n.* **any crude representation of a human figure** bonhomme
representative *n.* agent, réprésenteur, représentant **sales representative** commis voyageur **state representative** représenteur de l'état
reprimand *n.* bûchée, cataplasme, galop, pourgale, ratatouille, remontrance, rondinage, saboulée, savonnage, sérénade, touche, gratte **severe reprimand** chauffe
reprimand *v.* babiller, chauffer, disputer, donner des paraboles, faire des remontrances, gronder, lire un catéchisse à qqn, lire un chapître à qqn, pourgaler, ramoner, sabouler, soulever
reprint *v.* réimprimer
reproach *n.* reproche **expression of disapproval or reproach** sac à {en} papier
reproach *v.* faire des reproches, reprocher **reproach or blame o.s.** se reprocher
reproachable *adj.* méprisable, reprochable
reproduce *v.* relever, reproduire
reprove *v.* ramoner
reprune *v.* retailler
republic *n.* république
Republican *n.* républicain
republish *v.* republier
repudiate *v.* nier, renier, renoncer, répudier
repugnance *n.* répugnance **cause repugnance** faire zire
repugnant *adj.* répugnant
repulse *v.* repousser
repulsed *adj.* **be repulsed** avoir dédain de, rebouquer
repulsive *adj.* dégoûtant, haïssable, salope, zirable **repulsive thing** zireté **repulsive, filthy, untidy woman** salope **be repulsive** faire zire
repulsively *adv.* zirablement
repulsiveness *n.* zireté
repurchase *v.* **repurchase for o.s.** se racheter
reputation *n.* renommée, réputation **good reputation** honneur **of good reputation** notable
repute *n.* **woman of ill repute** bordel, pas-bonne
request *n.* demande, pétition **on request** sur application
request *v.* demander
require *v.* demander, obliger, prendre, vouloir
required *adj.* nécessaire, assujetti
reread *v.* relire
rerent *v.* relouer
reroof *v.* recouverre
rerun *v.* recourir
resaw *v.* refendre
rescrape *v.* regratter

rescratch *v.* regratter
rescue *n.* libération
rescue *v.* réchapper, sauver
rescuer *n.* sauveur
reseal *v.* recacheter
research *n.* recherche
research *v.* se poster
reseat *v.* rasseoir
resell *v.* revendre
resemblance *n.* ressemblance, semblance
resemble *v.* avoir des faux airs avec, donner des faux airs à qqn, prendre après {sur}, ressembler (pareil) comme {à}, ressembler, sembler, avoir la coupe de figure de (qqn) **resemble each other** se ressembler **resemble one another** s'imiter **resemble each other closely** se ressembler comme deux gouttes d'eau **person who closely resembles another** tocaille
resembling *adj.* **resembling trait for trait** recopié
reservation *n.* réservation, réserve
reserve *n.* réserve **in reserve** en avant, en réserve **with reserve** avec réserve **without reserve** sans réserve
reserve *v.* réserver **reserve a place** réserver une place
reserved *adj.* réservé, réservé
reservoir *n.* réservoir **rain reservoir** digue
resew *v.* recoudre
resharpen *v.* raffiler, rappointir
reshingle *v.* **reshingle a roof** piquer une couverture {un toit}
reshoe *v.* referrer
reside *v.* demeurer, habiter, loger, rester, vivre
residence *n.* domicile, habitation, résidence **bishop's residence** évêché **change residence** grouiller, mouver **change of residence** délogement **take up residence** s'établir, se fourrer *pl.* **change residences** décaniller, déloger, déménager
resident *n.* résident
residue *n.* **odorous residue between the toes due to uncleanliness** cambouille
resign *v.* résigner, résigner
resigned *adj.* résigné
resilient *adj.* fait du nerf et de la babiche
resin *n.* rosine
resink *v.* renfoncer
resist *v.* résister, se remater
resistance *n.* opposition, résistance **offer no resistance** faire play **yield without resistance** faire play **mount one's courage, fortitude, determination or resistance** se pomper
resistant *adj.* résistant
reslice *v.* retrancher
resoften *v.* ramollir
resole *v.* ressemeler
resoling *n.* ressemelage
resolute *adj.* résolu
resolution *n.* résolution
resolve *v.* déterminer, rarranger
resolved *adj.* décidé, déterminé, résolu
resonance *n.* résonance, résonnement
resonant *adj.* résonnant
resonator *n.* **line with metal resonator hung around a house as part of a traditional prank** rosine
resort *n.* recours
resort *v.* avoir recours(à)
resound *v.* résonner
resounding *adj.* résonnant
resource *n.* ressource *pl.* **organize one's resources efficiently** se ménager
resourcefulness *n.* ressource
respect *n.* considération, respect, vénération **without respect** irrévérent *pl.* **respects** dû
respect *v.* honorer, respecter **respect o.s. or one another** se respecter
respectable *adj.* d'honneur, respectable
respectful *adj.* honorable, respectueux
respiration *n.* respiration
respire *v.* respirer
resplit *v.* refendre
respond *v.* répondre
response *n.* réponse **ready response** bouche-trou **nonsensical response used to avoid answering questions** un petit rien tout neuf
responsibility *n.* responsabilité, responsable **assume responsibility** endosser, se mettre bon pour **take responsibility** se charger *pl.* **one who runs around rather than taking care of responsibilities** rôdailleur
responsible *adj.* responsable **be responsible for** prendre en soin **old enough to be responsible for one's own actions** maître et majeur
rest *n.* repos, restant, reste **take a rest** prendre un repos
rest *v.* reposer, se reposer
restack *v.* recorder
restart *v.* repartir
restaurant *n.* café, restaurant **store or restaurant** gargote
rested *adj.* reposé
restful *adj.* reposant
restitch *v.* recoudre
restless *adj.* brigand **restless or flighty person** cerf-volant **restless or agitated person or animal** loup-garou
restop *v.* reboucher
restoration *n.* restauration, rétablissement
restore *v.* ramener, redonner, rendre, restaurer, rétablir **restore the beauty of** rembellir
restrain *v.* modérer, brider **restrain o.s.** s'empêcher, se contenir, se modérer, se retenir
restraint *n.* frein **without restraint** déchaîné, sans réserve **act without restraint** prendre le mors aux dents **talk without**

restraint avoir le filet coupé **curb or restraint for a horse** gourmette
restricted *adj.* **be restricted** être amenotté
restriction *n.* mais, restriction
restring *v.* raccorder
restroom *n.* cacatoir, commode
result *n.* aboutissage, conséquence, effet, résultat **end result** retour **as a result** par conséquence *pl.* **produce results** faire effet
resurface *v.* ressourdre
resurrection *n.* ressuscitation, résurrection
resuscitate *v.* ressusciter
resuscitation *n.* ressuscitation
reswallow *v.* renvaler
retail *n.* de marchandise, en détail
retailer *n.* **bulk retailer** grossier
retain *v.* retenir, tenir
retake *v.* rattraper, reprendre
retaken *adj.* repris
retame *v.* radoucir
retamp *v.* refouler
retangle *v.* renouer
retard *v.* détarder
retarded *adj.* en retard **retarded person** innocent **mentally retarded** emplâtre, pas bien développé
reteach *v.* remontrer
retell *v.* redire
retention *n.* **urinary retention** tranchement d'urine
rethink *v.* repenser
rethread *v.* renfiler
rethresh *v.* rebattre
reticent *adj.* paisé
retie *v.* ramarrer
retighten *v.* resserrer
retinue *n.* cortège, entourage
retire *v.* prendre sa retraite, RETIRE
retired *adj.* retiré
retirement *n.* retraite **retirement home** maison de vieux
retiring *adj.* retiré
retort *n.* **quick retort** bouche-trou
retouch *v.* retoucher
retrace *v.* retracer
retraction *n.* rétraction
retrain *v.* redresser, raccoutumer, radoucir
retreat *n.* retraite, retraite **make or go on a retreat** faire une retraite
retrieve *v.* rattraper
retriever *n.* chien à canard
retune *v.* raccorder
return *n.* retour **give s.t. in return** donner du {un} retour
return *v.* remettre, rentourner, renvenir, retourner, revenir, s'en revenir, se rentourner, se retourner
returned *adj.* de {en} retour
retwist *v.* retordre
reunion *n.* réunion **family reunion** rassemblée de famille
reunite *v.* réunir, se réunir, se reprendre
reuse *v.* remployer
rev *v.* fronner
reveal *v.* dévoiler **reveal o.s.** se dévoiler
reveler *n.* riboteur
reveller *n.* **masked Carnaval reveller** christine
revenge *n.* **get revenge** se venger
revenge *n.* revenge, vengeance, vindication **get revenge** revenger, se revenger **get one's revenge** prendre sa revenge
revenge *v.* venger
revenue *n.* rente, revenu
revenuer *n.* REVENUE
reverberate *v.* résonner
reverberation *n.* résonnement
revere *v.* vénérer
reverence *n.* révérence, vénération
reverend *adj.* révérend
reverie *n.* jonglage, jonglement, jonglerie *pl.* **indulge in reveries** jongler
reverse *n.* rebours, renverse, revers, envers **in reverse** à (la) rebours, à la renverse
reverse *v.* revirer
review *n.* revue
revision *n.* repassage
revival *n.* renaissance
revive *v.* ravioter, ressusciter, revivre, reprendre
revoke *v.* révoquer
revolt *n.* révolte
revolt *v.* regimber, révolter, se révolter
revolted *adj.* **be revolted** avoir zire (de) **easily revolted** zirou
revolting *adj.* révoltant, zirable
revolution *n.* révolte, révolution, tour
revolutionary *adj.* révolutionnaire
Revolutionary *adj.* **the Revolutionary War** la Guerre de Révolution
reward *n.* compensation, reconnaissance, récompense **unexpected reward** lagniappe
reward *v.* compenser, récompenser, rémunérer
rewarming *n.* réchauffage, réchauffement
rewash *v.* relaver
reweigh *v.* repeser
rewet *v.* remouiller
rewhiten *v.* reblanchir
rewhitewash *v.* reblanchir
rework *v.* retravailler
rewrinkle *v.* replisser
rewrite *v.* récrire
rheumatism *n.* rhumatise, rhumatisme
rhinoceros *n.* rhinocéros

rhyme *n.* rime **nursery rhyme** comptine

rhyme *v.* rimer

rhythm *n.* balan

rib *n.* côte **rib of a boat** courbe *pl.* **side of ribs** rognon

ribbon *n.* cocarde, ribondelle, ruban

ribbonfish *n.* sabre

rice *n.* riz **rice chaff** écale de riz **rice dressing** far **rice field** clos de riz **rice hauling** halage de riz **rice mill** moulin à riz **rice stubble** chaume, chicots de riz **rice cutting machine** coupeuse de riz **rice raised without benefit of irrigation** riz de providence **wild rice** queue de loup **pitchfork for rice** fourche à riz **threshing of rice** battage de riz **sweetened fried rice cake** cala **said of rice when it shoots out from sides instead of only in one cluster** en bottes **red beans and rice** bécassine créole **dish made of various meats and rice** galimatias

rich *adj.* argenté, au dessus de la farine, fertile, riche **rich man** richard **rich or important person** gros dos **get rich** faire (une) fortune, s'enrichir **excessively rich or sweet** accœurant

rich *n.* **newly rich** gueux-parvenu **the rich** les riches **vulgar rich** gueux-parvenu *pl.* **riches** richesse, trésor

richly *adj.* richement

ricket *npl.* **rickets** maladie d'os

rickety *adj.* **puny, paltry, rickety person** bougon

rickrack *n.* ricrac, serpentine

ricochet *n.* ricoche

ricochet *v.* ricocher

rid *adj.* **get rid** se dispenser, se démerder **get rid of** abattre, débarrasser, défaire, passer, se débarrasser, se défaire, se dégréer, se démettre **get rid of caterpillars** écheniller

rid *v.* **rid o.s.** se démerder **rid o.s. of** se défaire

riddance *n.* débarras

riddle *n.* devinette, dévinage, dévinail **opening formula used in telling a riddle** dévine-dévinail

riddle *v.* cribler

riddled *adj.* criblé

ride *n.* RIDE **take a ride** RIDE **go for a ride** se promener **hail for a ride** FLAG **go for a ride on a horse / in a paddled boat such as a pirogue** se promener à cheval {en boghei} / se promener à la pagaille (etc.) **take out for a ride** promener

ride *v.* RIDE, se promener, maquillonner **ride astride** aller à califourchon **ride bare-back** monter à poil **ride side-saddle** aller à dame **ride a horse** RIDE à cheval **ride on horseback** RIDE à cheval **ride in a pirogue** se piroguer **ride competitively or for money** toucher

rider *n.* **horse rider** cavalier **racehorse rider** kêtch *pl.* **group of riders on horseback** cavaillade

Rider *n.* **Night Rider** Chevalier de Nuit

ridge *n.* côteau **ridge row** faîtage **ridge turned up by plow** endos **ridge of sand formed along a river** batture

ridicule *v.* ridiculer, se foutre

ridiculous *adj.* coucou, ridicule, risible

riding *adj.* **riding crop** couarte

ridley *n.* **Atlantic ridley** tortue blanche, tortue de mer ridley

riffraff *n.* chierie, fatras, foutraille, fripaille, racatcha, tchampourra, traînaille

rifle *n.* carabine, tcharabo **twenty-two-caliber rifle** vingt-deux

rift *n.* éclaircie

rig *n.* chevalement, RIG **rig comprising a horse and vehicle** attelage **oil rig** puits d'huile, RIG

rig *v.* **rig out** harnacher **rig up** emmancher

rigging *n.* attelage **harness rigging** attelle, trait de chaîne *pl.* **riggings** agrès

right *adj.* bien, bon, correct, droite, exact, juste, raisonnable **right angle** équerre **all right** ALL RIGHT, correct **be right** avoir raison, avoir un bon point **do right** faire bien **just right** juste bien {bon}, juste comme il faut **that's right** c'est bien, c'est justement **it's all right** c'est correct **be one's right hand man** être le bras droite

right *interj.* **right?** hein

right *n.* dû, droit, droite, justice **the right** à la droite **unlimited right** passe-droit **have the right** avoir le droit **on the right** à droite **to the right** à droite **horse on the right in a draft team** droitier *pl.* **put o.s. to rights** se réparer

right *v.* **right o.s.** se relever

right-hand *adj.* **right-hand side** droite

rightful *adj.* propre

rightly *adv.* droitement

rightness *n.* droiture

rigid *adj.* raide, sévère **make rigid** raidir

riled *adj.* **get riled up** regricher, se regricher

rim *n.* **metal rim** frette

rind *n.* écorce **pork rind** couenne

ring *n.* anneau, bague, organeau, rond, rondelle, roulette, rang **ring finger** doigt annulaire **ring around the neck** collier **ring placed in the nose of a pig** anneau **ring on a net through which a rope is threaded** organeau **engagement ring** bague d'engagement **metal ring** cercle **onion ring** rondelle d'oignon **wedding ring** alliance **iron ring attached to a rope for tying a horse** organeau **form a big ring** faire grand rond *pl.* **have rings under one's eyes** avoir les yeux cernés **any of the rings on a skimmer net through which a rope is passed** organeau

ring *v.* cercler, cerner, sonner, siffler, siller **ring again** ressonner **ring repeatedly** sonnailler

ringer *n.* **bell ringer** sonneur

ringing *n.* sonnerie, silement

ringworm *n.* dartre

rinse *v.* rincer **rinse o.s.** se rincer **rinse out** laver

rinsing *n.* rinçage

rip *n.* accroc, déchirure, raccroc

rip *v.* fendre, érailler, découdre **rip off** arracher **rip open** étriper **rip out** arracher

ripe *adj.* mûr, mature

ripen *v.* mûrir, meurzir

ripening *n.* meurizon

ripped *adj.* éraillé
ripping *n.* déchirage
rise *n.* élévation
rise *v.* augmenter, lever, monter, remonter, s'élever, se soulever **rise up** se regricher, se remater **rise up against** regricher **let rise** éponger
riser *n.* contremarche
rising *adj.* **early rising** matinal
rising *n.* levée, remontage, montage
risk *n.* chance, danger, hasard, risque **run the risk** courir un risque **take a risk** prendre une chance / prendre des {ses} chances **it's not worth the trouble or risk** le jeu (ne) vaut pas la chandelle
risk *v.* aventurer, risquer, s'aventurer **risk o.s.** se risquer
risk-taking *adj.* téméraire
risky *adj.* risqué
rite *npl.* **last rites** extrême-onction, Extrême Onction **practicer of voodoo rites** voudou
rivalry *n.* compétition
river *n.* fleuve, rivière **bend in a river** pointe **mouth of the river** bouche de la rivière **mouth of a river or bayou** engueulement **part of a river with no current** amortie **ridge of sand formed along a river** batture
riverbank *n.* bord
rivet *n.* rivet
rivet *v.* river, riveter
riveter *n.* riveur
rivulet *n.* coulée, rigolet
roach *n.* ravet **wood roach** ravert de bois
road *n.* chemin, manche, route, routine à volonté **road along a fence** chaintre **road or railroad spur** branche **asphalt road** chemin de godron **main road** grand chemin **paved road** BLACKTOP, pavage, PAVE, pavé **side road** allée **along the road** bord du chemin **down the road** bord du chemin **hit the road** prendre le chemin **narrow country road** manche **on the road** en route **yield the road or way** donner le chemin **take the wrong road** prendre le mauvais chemin **be on the wrong road** être mal tourné **set out on the road** prendre le chemin **at the end of the road** au bout du chemin **cut and placed over a bad road** rolon *pl.* **run the roads** courailler les rues, fringuer, rouler les (grands) chemins **running the roads** à la fringue **in the habit of running the roads or gadding about** fringant
roadside *n.* **by the roadside** bord du chemin
roam *v.* courir, rôdailler, rôder, rouler, vagabonder **roam around from place to place** faire le cochon de Saint Antoine **roam the roads at night as a werewolf** courir rougarou **one who roams or prowls around** rôdeur
roamer *n.* rôdailleur
roaming *adj.* **animal or person roaming around at night** loup-garou
roar *v.* grogner, rouler
roast *n.* daube, rôti **community roast** rôti
roast *v.* faire rôtir, farcir, griller, rôtir **roast meat over hot coals** barbecue
roasted *adj.* farci
roaster *n.* poule, rôtisserie
roasting *n.* grillage **roasting pan** carrière, plateau
rob *v.* dégréer, dépouiller, piller, plumer, voler, éplumer **rob Peter to pay Paul** dégreer Saint-Pierre pour gréer Saint-Paul
robber *n.* bandit, brigand, pillard, pirate, voleur
robbery *n.* pillerie, vol **commit highway robbery** voler comme dans la forêt des bandits
robbing *n.* pillage
robe *n.* robe
robin *n.* **American robin** grive **ground robin** grassel
robinia *n.* arkansia
robust *adj.* robuste, résolu, vigoureux
rock *n.* pierre, rocher
rock *v.* bercer **rock contentedly** bercer son âme **rock o.s.** se bercer
rocker *n.* berce, berceuse, fauteuil **rocker, blade, runner of a rocking chair** roulette **rocker, blade, or runner of a rocking chair** maille, marchette
rocket *n.* fusée
rocking *n.* balan **rocking chair** berce, berceuse, fauteuil **rocking movement** bercement **gliding rocking chair** balancine
rod *n.* baguette, bâton **connecting rod** brimbale **divining rod** devineur **dowsing rod** devineur **iron rod** barre de fer **lightning rod** paratonnerre **iron rod for cleaning a stove** baguette de STOVE **staff or rod for surveying or leveling** jalon
rodent *n.* rongeur
rodeo *n.* rodéo
rogation *n.* **rogation days** rogation
rogue *n.* guinche
roll *n.* bourrelet, liste, rouleau, roulon **roll, twist, or knot of hair worn at the back of the head** catogan, choque, tchique, tignon **blackberry roll** bourrelet aux mûres **bread roll** bourrelet
roll *v.* corder, roler, roulailler, rouler, torquer **roll around** roulailler, se rouler **roll down** débouler **roll out** déboulir **roll over** capoter **roll tightly** carotter **roll up** corder, enrouler, retrousser, roler, rouler, s'enrouler, se retrousser **roll o.s. over** se rouler **roll up one's sleeves** enlever sa soutadaire, se desseller
roll-away *n.* **roll-away bed** lit à roulettes
roller *n.* rouleau, roulette **wooden roller used for moving buildings** rance **heavy roller used for crushing sugar cane** rolle *pl.* **move by means of rollers** rouler
rolling *n.* roulage, roulement **rolling over** capotage **rolling pin** rouleau **rolling up** retroussement
roly-poly *n.* rouleau
roman *adj.* **roman candle** fusée
romance *n.* roman
romp *v.* gambader
roof *n.* couverture, faît, toit, top, top **roof gutter** dalle **roof**

stave merrain **roof valley** dalle **roof built over a doorway** rabat **remove the roof** découverre **reshingle a roof** piquerune couverture {un toit} **repair a shingled roof** piquer une couverture {un toit} **the highest point of a pitched roof** pignon **the point of an outside wall created by the roof line** pignon

roof *v.* couverre

roofer *n.* couvreur

roofing *n.* couverture **roofing party** piquerie

room *n.* chambre, espace, pièce, place, salle **boys' room** garçonnière **dining room** salle à manger **dirty room** nique à chien **front room** chambre de devant, chambre en avant **living room** chambre de devant, chambre en avant, parloir, salon **make room** donner de la place, faire de la place **baptismal font or room** baptistaire **there is no more room** on peut pas y mettre une épingle *pl.* **divide into rooms** croiser

roost *n.* ajoupa, engruchade, for, nichoir **chicken roost** perchoir **chicken roost or perch** jouc, jouquoir **get off the roost** déjouquer **any tree in which chickens roost** arbre à {de} poules

roost *v.* jouquer, se jouquer, se percher

rooster *n.* coq, corusse, gaime, rousta **comb of a rooster** huppe

roosting *adj.* **collection of roosting fowl** jouquée

root *n.* racine **root beer** root-bière **root crop** racinage **take root** enraciner, prendre, s'enraciner, végétir **taking root** enracinement *pl.* **having many roots** racineux **bare the roots of** décoller **pull up by the roots** arracher

rooted *adj.* campé comme un as de pique **become rooted** enraciner

rooting *n.* enracinement, racinage

rope *n.* amarrage, amarre, corde, câble, guide, pite **rope jack** tarabi **horsehair rope** cabresse **jump rope** corde à sauter, sauter (à) la corde **skip rope** sauter (à) la corde **strong rope** un (cable de) manila **thick rope** cordeau **weighted rope** ralingue **thick rope used to moor boats** câble **at the end of one's rope** au bout du câble

rope *v.* lasser, LASSO, louper

roping *n.* lassage

ropy *adj.* filant

roquette *n.* roquette

rosa de montana *n.* rose de montagne

rosa montana *n.* liane rose

rosary *n.* chapelet, rosaire **rosary beads** rosaire **blessed rosary beads** chapelet bénit **say the rosary** égrainer le chapelet **say a rosary decade** dire une décade {dizaine} **saying of the rosary beads** égrenage

rose *n.* rose **rose of Sharon** althéa **Cherokee rose** chéroquis **dwarf rose** cinq-sous **moss rose** mousse-fleur **wild rose** chéroquis **Chickasaw rose bush** chéroquis **crimson-eye rose mallow** guimauve

rosebush *n.* rosier **climbing rosebush** rosier filant

rosemary *n.* roumarin

roseola *n.* roséole

rosette *n.* rosette

rosin *n.* rosine

rot *n.* pourriture **black rot** charbon **marked by pocket rot** piqué

rot *v.* dépérir, gâter, pourrir **cause to rot** pourrir

rotate *v.* tourner

rotten *adj.* pourri **become rotten** gâter **in rotten condition** en pourrillon

rottenness *n.* pourriture

rotting *adj.* pourrissant

rouge *n.* rouge

rough *adj.* brut, brutal, malengueulé, raboteux, racheux, ROUGH, rude, scabreux **rough man** pignouf **rough, brutish person** animal, casseur de portes ouvertes, défonceur d'une porte ouverte / défonceur de porte(s) ouverte(s) **rough, ill-mannered person** cheval habillé (en zinc) **be rough** être en section **things are rough** les affaires se brassent mal **having a rough gait** patteux, patté

rough *v.* **rough up** manier

rough-surfaced *adj.* galeux

roughhouse *v.* gambader

roughly *adv.* brut, rudement

roulette *n.* roulette

round *adj.* rond **round slice or section** roulette **make round** rondiner **become round or dull** s'arrondir

round *n.* roulette, viron **make a round** faire un tour

round *v.* arrondir **round off** arrondir **round up cattle** faire le tour des bêtes

roundabout *adj.* **roundabout way** détour

roundness *n.* rondeur

rouse *v.* exciter

rout *n.* débâcle

route *n.* route

routine *n.* routine

roux *n.* roux **broth with roux** soupe maigre

rover *n.* rôdailleur, vagabond

roving *adj.* errant

row *n.* affilée, hariat, obstination, rang, rangée, scandale, scène, ligne **ridge row** faîtage **in a row** à l'affilée / à la filée **create a big row or fuss** faire un scandale *pl.* **plow rows** fendre la terre **plow in rows** labourer en rang **plant in raised rows** sillonner

row *v.* ramer

rowboat *n.* barque, bateau à pagailles, chaloupe, skiff à rames **flat-bottomed rowboat** chaland

rowdy *adj.* brigand **rowdy children** marmaille **boisterous, rowdy child** barbot

rub *v.* frotter **rub o.s.** se frotter **rub with tallow** suiffrer **one who rubs, buffs or polishes** frotteur

rubber *n.* gomme, élastique, caoutchouc **rubber band** élastique **preserving jar rubber** élastique

rubbing *n.* friction, frottage, frottement **rubbing of the knuckles on s.o.'s head** critché **a vigorous rubbing of the scalp in play or in a fight** britchet

rubbish *n.* artifailles, drigaille, déboulis, débris, fardoche, galimatias, ripopée, TRASH

ruby *n.* rubis

ruckus *n.* boulvari, cancan, faïouque, haut-le-corps, ricane, tchampourra **create a ruckus** gambader **make a ruckus** faire (le) rougarou **raise a ruckus** faire un scandale

rudder *n.* gouvernail

rude *adj.* brut, impoli, insolent, mal élevé / malélevé, mal élevé, malengueulé, malinstruit, ROUGH, rude, vilain, vulgaire

rudeness *n.* grossièreté, insolence

ruffian *n.* brigand

ruffle *n.* volant, greget

ruffled *adj.* ébouriff lé **become ruffled** regricher

rug *n.* tapis **rug made of strips** catalogne **rug woven from scraps of cloth** wapi **cut a rug** danser la queue raide

ruin *n.* abandon, dégringole, perdition, ruine, valdrague **go to ruin** aller en ruine, dégringoler, s'en aller au dépit, s'en aller à la perdition, se ruiner, tomber en faillance **fall into ruin or disrepair** tomber en doise douale}, tomber en ruine **go to ruin or disrepair** tomber en botte **go to rack and ruin** tomber en botte *pl.* **be in ruins** battre la berloque

ruin *v.* abîmer, carnassier, défropter, défroqueter, gachiller, gavagner, gâcher, gâchonner, massacrer, ruiner **ruin o.s.** se ruiner

ruined *adj.* abîmé, cassé à la maille, fichu, foutu, hors de service **ruined or worsened state** dépit **financially ruined** cassé à la souche {chousse}

rule *n.* commandement, direction, directive, domination, loi, ordonnance, principe, régulation, règle **twelve-inch rule or measuring stick** pied-de-roi / pied-du-roi

rule *v.* dominer, gouverner, régner

ruler *n.* mesure, règle **carpenter's folding ruler** pied-de-roi / pied-du-roi

rum *n.* tafia

rumble *n.* roulement

rumble *v.* rouler, grogner

rummage *v.* **rummage around** fouillailler, fouillarder, fouiller, fourgailler **rummage through** fourgailler, ressoubler

rummaging *n.* **one fond of rummaging through drawers, closets, etc.** fouillard

rumor *n.* parlement, radotement, rumeur **start or add to a rumor or conflict by one's words** mettre le feu à la paille {poudre}

rump *n.* croupe, croupion, derrière, fesse, nez du pretre {de l'éveque}, saint-frusquin, tchu, troufignon

rumple *v.* chiffonner

run *adj.* **become run down** aller à la dégringole

run *n.* bauche, série, trot **on the run** à la traîne **at a dead run** à la pleine course **in the long run** à la longue **make a short run** faire un petit trotte **take part in a costumed Mardi Gras run** courir Mardi Gras *pl.* **the runs** foirée

run *v.* couler, courir, découler, faire galoper, faire la course, fouiner, galoper, manœuvrer, marcher, opérer, travailler, érailler **run after** courir après (qqn), coursailler, courser, galoper après, galoper **run again** recourir **run aground** s'échouer **run around** courir, coursailler, fiander, fringuer, marronner, rôdailler, rôder, roulailler, rouler, traînailler, traînasser **run away** marronner, partir (en) marron, partir à la course, prendre l'estampique / prendre des estampiques, prendre le mors aux dents, se sauver, tirer une course, échapper **run down** se démonter **run dry** tarir **run into** aborder contre, aborder, arriver sur, buter, cogner, frapper **run off** courser, prendre la course **run over** déborder, fouler sur (qqn), passer sur **run quickly** galoper comme un chat échaudé **run a fever** avoir la fièvre **run a race** faire une course, tirer une course **run an errand** faire une commission **run around on** bêtiser **run for office** galoper **run off track** dérailler **run out of** manquer **run the risk** courir un risque **run the roads** courailler les rues, fringuer, rouler les (grands) chemins **run the streets** traîner les rues **run into each other** s'aborder **run away from a contest** caler le bouchon **run like a scared cat** galoper comme un chat échaudé **be running errands** être en commission **one who gallivants or runs around** rôdailleur, rôdeur **one who runs around rather than taking care of responsibilities** rôdailleur

runaway *adj.* estampique, marron

runaway *n.* marron, marronneur

runner *n.* coureur, liane, berce, coulisse, fil **Mardi Gras runner** coureur de Mardi Gras **blade or runner of a rocking chair** berceuse **rocker, blade, runner of a rocking chair** roulette **rocker, blade, or runner of a rocking chair** maille, marchette

running *adj.* filant **running board** marche-pied

running *n.* course, à la course **running away** marronnage **running the roads** à la fringue **running at the nose** morveux **by running** à la course **start running after** pointer la course par derrière (qqn) **start running fast** baisser à la course **take off running** partir à la course, prendre la course **in the habit of running the roads or gadding about** fringant

runt *n.* avorton, chacta, pichouette, péquin, raboron, raboustin, ragoton, riquiqui, épiochon

rupture *v.* se fendre

ruse *n.* ruse, tournure **clever ruse** coup de malin

rush *n.* déboulis, galope, jonc rond, jonc **Roemer's rush** paille chat-tigre **in a rush** à la galope

rush *v.* se garrocher

Russia *n.* Russie

Russian *adj.* russien **Russian language** russien

rust *n.* rouille **rust removal** dérouillement **remove rust** dérouiller

rust *v.* enrouiller, rouiller, s'enrouiller, se rouiller **cause to rust** enrouiller, rouiller

rustic *adj.* **rustic, uncultured, uncouth, boorish, ignorant person** gui-gui

rustiness *n.* rouillure

rusty *adj.* **rusty spot** rouillure **become rusty** rouiller, s'enrouiller, se rouiller

rut *n.* pente, rainure, rouin **in rut** en rougarou

rutabaga *n.* corne de vache, rutabaga

rye *n.* **rye whiskey** RYE

S

Sabbath *n.* sabbat

saber *n.* sabre

sabotage *n.* sabotage

saboteur *n.* saboteur

sack *n.* sac **sack made of rough cloth** sac de pitre **book sack** cabas **peat, gunny, or burlap sack** sac de pitre

sack *v.* ensaquer

sackful *n.* saquée, pochée

sacking *n.* ensachage

sacrament *n.* sacrement **sacrament of Confirmation** confirmation **receive the sacrament** communier **receive the sacrament of Confirmation** confirmer

sacred *adj.* sacré

sacrifice *n.* quittage, sacrifice

sacrifice *v.* sacrifier **sacrifice o.s., one's time, etc.** se sacrifier

sacrilege *n.* sacrilège

sacristan *n.* sacristain, sacristine

sacristy *n.* sacristie

sad *adj.* chagrin, triste **be sad** avoir un cœur lourd **look sad** avoir une mine de chien **be sad or depressed** faire une {la} babine / faire des babines, pendre la babine **make sad or sorry** faire de la peine **cause to be sad** faire pitié

sadden *v.* chagriner, faire le gros cœur à

saddening *adj.* chagrinant

saddle *n.* bagari, selle **saddle blanket** soutadaire **saddle flap** bagari **saddle pad** soutadaire **saddle sore** mal anglais **saddle tie** bacul, reculoire **saddle tree** fût de selle **cinch a saddle onto** cingler **leather covering of a saddle** corasse **flap or fender of a western saddle** basque

saddle *v.* gréer, harnacher, seller **saddle o.s.** se sangler **saddle up** seller

saddle-break *v.* maquillonner

sadly *adv.* tristement

sadness *n.* chagrin, tristesse **move s.o. to sadness** crever le cœur à qqn

safe *adj.* sauve **safe and sound** sain et sauve

safe *n.* coffre-fort

safeguard *v.* préserver

safety *n.* sûreté, sécurité **safety pin** épingle double, épingle à couche, épingle à linge **safety razor** pioche

sag *n.* **sag in trousers** tchapin

sage *n.* sage **broom sage** paille jaune **wild sage** cailleau

said *adj.* **so said** soi-disant **it is said** soi-disant, ça dit

sail *n.* voile

sailboat *n.* bateau à voiles

sailfish *n.* poisson à voile, voile

sailor *n.* matelot

saint *n.* saint **patron saint** patron **picture of a saint given to a child on the occasion of his or her first communion** image de communion

Saint *n.* **Saint John the Baptist** St. Jean Baptiste *pl.* **All Saints Day** Toussaint **northern part of Saint Martin Parish** par en haut **the feast of All Saints** Toussaint **member of a group organized in Saint Martinsville in the early 1880s to restore white rule** régulateur

saintly *adj.* saint

sake *n.* **your sake** ton bonheur **for God's sake** pour l'amour de Dieu / pour l'amour du Bon Dieu **for heaven's sake** mais enfin!, tonnerre de foutre **for pity's sake** pitié d'amour *pl.* **land sakes** pays

salad *n.* salade **aspic salad** aspic

salamander *n.* chien de terre, sourd

salary *n.* salaire

sale *n.* vendage, vente **public sale** encan **have for sale** tenir **make a sale** contracter *pl.* **sales representative** commis voyageur **sales tax token** brozine

salesman *n.* vendeur **travelling salesman** commis voyageur

salesperson *n.* commis

saliva *n.* crachat, salive **an abnormally increased flow of saliva** salivure

salivation *n.* salivure

sallow *adj.* blême

salmon *n.* saumon

salon *n.* salon

saloon *n.* bar, cabaret, café, saloon

salsify *n.* certifis

salt *n.* sel **salt shaker** salière **Epsom salt** magnésie **not salt** doux, frais **remove salt** dessaler **table salt** sel de table **grain of salt** grain de sel **area in a salt marsh governed by the tides** mare *pl.* **Epsom salts** sel d'epsom, sel à purger

salt *v.* saler

saltpeter *n.* salpêtre

salty *adj.* saumâtre

salutation *n.* salut

salute *n.* salut

salute *v.* saluer

salvation *n.* salut
salve *n.* onguent
salvia *n.* corail
same *adj.* même, uniforme **the same** pareil **the same as** pareil comme **in the same way** tel **amount to the same thing** revenir au même **boil down to the same thing** revenir au même
same *pron.* **the same** le même / la même **all the same** tout de même
sample *n.* SAMPLE, échantillon
sanctify *v.* sanctifier
sanctifying *adj.* sanctifiant **sanctifying grace** grâce sanctifiante
sanctimonious *adj.* **sanctimonious person** pince-minette, sainte nitouche
sanction *n.* confirmation
sanction *v.* autoriser
sanctuary *n.* chœur, sanctuaire
sand *n.* sable **choke with sand** s'ensabler **cover with sand** ensabler **ridge of sand formed along a river** batture
sand *v.* **sand up** ensabler, s'ensabler
sandal *n.* corde, sandale
sanded *adj.* sableux, sablé
sandfly *n.* taon
sandpaper *n.* papier sablé {sableux}
sandpiper *n.* bécassine grosse tête {gros-tête}, papabotte, tchourouc **least sandpiper** pacane **pectoral sandpiper** tchourouc **spotted sandpiper** chevalier de batture
sandwich *n.* sandwich **sandwich or small meal** LUNCH
sandy *adj.* sableux, sablé
sanitary *adj.* **sanitary napkin** braguette, linge
Santa *n.* **Santa Claus** christine, Papa Noël, SANTA CLAUS **Santa Maria** camomine sauvage
sap *n.* alcool de bois, sève **thick milky sap** petit lait
sapwood *n.* aubelle
sarcastic *adj.* grappilleux, mordant
sardine *n.* banane, sardine *pl.* **can of sardines** boîte de sardines
sarsaparilla *n.* chassepareille
sash *n.* ceinture, écharpe, éviale **window sash** châssis
sassafras *n.* sassafras **sassafras tea** thé de sassafras **sassafras tree** bois de filé, bois de gombo, sassafras
sassy *adj.* **act sassy** faire l'effronté
Satan *n.* diable, démon, Satan
sate *v.* rassasier, satisfaire
sated *adj.* rafalé, tanné
sateen *n.* satine
satiate *v.* rassasier **satiate o.s.** s'appuyer l'estomac
satiety *n.* **to satiety** à son contentement
satin *n.* satin
satisfaction *n.* complaisance, contentement, satisfaction **give satisfaction** donner satisfaction **pleasure or satisfaction** gloire
satisfactory *adj.* ALL RIGHT
satisfied *adj.* content, fier, satisfait **be satisfied** se contenter
satisfy *v.* arranger, contenter, donner satisfaction, rassasier, satisfaire **satisfy o.s.** se rassasier **satisfy a desire** se donner une bosse
satisfying *adj.* bien, rassasiant
Saturday *n.* samedi **Holy Saturday** Samedi Saint
sauce *n.* sauce **hot sauce** sauce piquante **seafood sauce** bisque **tomato sauce** sauce aux tomates **dip into sauce** saucer **highly seasoned sauce** sauce piquante
sauced *adj.* saucé
saucepan *n.* bombe, casserole, chaudière à queue
saucer *n.* soucoupe
sauerkraut *n.* choucroute
sausage *n.* saucisse **sausage maker** saucisseur **blood sausage** boudin rouge **Cajun sausage** boudin **flattened sausage** platine **smoked sausage** saucisse boucanée **tripe sausage** andouille **thick, spicy sausage** tchaurisse
savage *adj.* brut, effaré, féroce, sauvage
savage *n.* carrencaouai
save *conj.* ebsèpe que
save *prep.* excepté
save *v.* conserver, esquiver, réchapper, sauver, épargner, serrer **save o.s.** s'épargner, se sauver **save one's energies** se ménager **not save money in a bank** cacher son argent dans des cornes à bœuf
saver *n.* sauveur
savior *n.* rédempteur, sauveur
saw *n.* scie **saw briar** liane de skine **carpenter's saw** scie à bois **circular saw** scie ronde, scie à électricité **crosscut saw** scie de travers **electric saw** scie électrique **hand saw** scie à (la) main, égouine **power saw** scie à électricité **table saw** table à scie **two-handled saw** passe-partout **cut with a saw** scier **path of a saw** chemin de scie
saw *v.* scier, scigailler
sawdust *n.* moulée de scie, moulée, son de scie {bois}, son
sawfish *n.* espadron, poisson à peigne, sabre
sawgrass *n.* jonc coupant, lames d'épée
sawhorse *n.* cheval, chevalet, chevalier, tréteau
sawing *n.* sciage, scierie
sawmill *n.* moulin à scie
sawyer *n.* scieur
say *v.* dire **say again** redire **say bye-bye** faire BYE-BYE **say nothing** pas dire coinque {pacane}, pas dire coinque **say nasty things** dire des cochonneries {saletés / saloperies}, dire des cochonneries **say one's prayers** dire ses prières **say out loud** prononcer **say s.t. bad** planter un piquant **say s.t. mean** passer une chique (à qqn) **say s.t. unbelievable** pondre un œuf **say the beads** égrainer le chapelet **say the rosary** égrainer le chapelet **say to o.s.** se dire en {entre} soi-même **say a rosary decade** dire une décade {dizaine} **say s.t. about s.o.** dire qqch après qqn **say what one thinks** parler français **say foolish or nonsensical things** lâcher des folies {bêtises} **say things that cannot be true** chanter des

midis à quatorze heures **I'll say** r'garde mais donc! **they say** ça dit **not say a word** pas dire coinque {pacane}, pas dire coinque **always say the wrong thing** avoir une gueule comme un vilevaquin **as they say** comme dit l'autre {le bougre} **one would say** on dirait **you don't say** tu me dis pas **do or say s.t. without hesitating or waffling** pas aller les quatre chemins **have s.t. to say** avoir pour dire **it's just to say** c'est juste pour dire **that is to say** c'est-à-dire **that's what you say** ça, c'est ta nénaine **the hell, you say** belle affaire! **what do you say?** quoi {qui} ça dit? **one might as well say** (vaut) autant dire **there's nothing left to say** halez la planche **you might as well say** autant dire **no matter what I say or do** j'ai beau dire et j'ai beau faire **says you** ton cul! **one who says silly, foolish things** sottiseux

saying *n.* dicton, parlage **saying of the rosary beads** égrenage **trite saying** cliché **as the saying goes** comme dit l'autre {le bougre} **it goes without saying** ça va sans dire

scab *n.* cicatrice, corasse, croûte **form a scab** cicatriser **peel a scab** écrouter **remove a scab** décroûter

scabbard *n.* fourreau

scabby *adj.* galeux, croûteux

scabies *n.* grattelle

scaffold *n.* tréteau, échafaud **erect a scaffold** échafauder

scaffold *v.* échafauder

scaffolding *n.* chevalement, échafaud, échafaudage

scald *n.* brûlure

scald *v.* échauder **scald o.s.** s'échauder

scalding *adj.* bouillant

scalding *n.* échaudage, échaudement

scale *n.* balance, pèse, romaine, écale **scale of a fish** écale de poisson **counterbalance scale** romaine **meat or deli scale** romaine à viande

scale *v.* écaler

scaled *adj.* **be scaled** s'écaler

scallion *n.* oignon vert *pl.* **scallions** haut des oignons

scalp *n.* calotte **a vigorous rubbing of the scalp in play or in a fight** britchet

scalping *n.* échevelage

scaly *adj.* galeux **scaly leg** patrique

scamp *n.* bon-à-rien

scan *v.* inspecter

scandal *n.* scandale, tchololo

scandalous *adj.* **prone to slanderous or scandalous talk** mépriseur

scantiness *n.* petitesse

scapula *n.* palette de l'épaule

scapular *n.* scapulaire

scar *n.* cicatrice, marque *pl.* **bearing scars** picassé

scar *v.* cicatriser

scarce *adj.* clair, rare

scarcely *adv.* à peine

scarceness *n.* rareté

scarcity *n.* famine

scare *n.* panique

scare *v.* effaroucher, épouvanter **scare off** épouvanter

scarecrow *n.* bonhomme, épouvantail, épouvantaille

scarf *n.* scarf **scarf joint** henture **mantlepiece scarf** arbriquin

scarlet *adj.* **scarlet fever** scarlatine

scarlet-colored *adj.* rouge comme un écarlate

scary *adj.* effrayant

scat *interj.* chat

scatter *v.* disperser, s'épailler, écarter, épailler, éparer, éparpiller, évader, détasser

scatterbrained *adj.* extravagué, écarté, écervelé

scattered *adj.* par les places, épaillé **things that are scattered or lying around** traînaille, traînasse

scattering *n.* dispersion, épaillage, éparpillage

scaup *n.* **lesser scaup** bec-bleu

scene *n.* scène **make a scene** faire une quarantaine, faire une scène

scent *n.* odeur, parfum, senteur **catch the scent of** éventer

scheme *n.* combinaison, machinerie, manigance

scheme *v.* combiner, se combiner

schemer *n.* cabaleur

scheming *n.* micmac

scholar *n.* étudiant

school *n.* école, bande **school board** commission scolaire **school building** école **school bus** transfert d'école, TRUCK d'école **school house** maison d'école **school playground** cour d'école, terrain d'école **school slate** ardoise **school teacher** maître d'école **attend school** aller à l'école **boarding school** pensionnat **close school** lâcher l'école **immersion school** école d'immersion **public school** école publique **recess school** lâcher l'école **teach school** faire classe, faire l'école, montrer l'école, tenir l'école **horse-drawn school bus** transfert **primary school teacher** maîtresse d'école **English language school** école américain **go to school** aller à l'école **finish work or school** lâcher

schooling *n.* école, éducation

schoolyard *n.* cour d'école

science *n.* science

scientist *n.* scientiste

scissors *npl.* ciseau **pruning scissors** sécataire **pair of scissors** ciseau

scoff *v.* se moquer

scoffing *n.* moquerie

scold *v.* babiller, balbuter, bouleverser, bourlinguer, chamailler, chauffer, disputer, donner des paraboles, engueuler, fourgailler, foutre une chauffe, foutre une pourgale (à), gronder, jurer, lire un catéchisse à qqn, lire un chapître à qqn, passer un cataplâme à qqn, pourgaler, quereller, rentrer derrière, rondiner, sabouler, soulever **scold s.o.** donner un cataplasme à qqn, faire un chapelet à qqn

scolding *n.* babillage, bourlingue, cataplasme, catéchisme, colle, disputage, fourgaille, galop, passée, pourgale, ratatouille, rondinage, savonnage, sérénade **give a scolding, beating** foutre une passée

scoop *n.* pinte

scope *n.* étendue

scorch *v.* brûler, griller **scorch o.s.** se brûler

score *n.* **a score** vingtaine **keep score** tenir compte **settling the score** réglement de comptes

scorn *n.* dédain

scorn *v.* dédaigner

scornful méprisard

scorpion *n.* scorpion

scoundrel *n.* canaille, ingrandjin, monstre, originel, scélérat, vaurien, yeux barrés (comme un cabri)

scourge *n.* flau

scouring-rush *n.* **tall scouring-rush** prêle

scowl *n.* frimousse

scowl *v.* faire une frimousse, frimousser

scowling *adj.* malému

scram *v.* filer, flanquer son camp, se haler, tirer une course

scramble *v.* **scramble down** dégrucher

scrap *n.* boutaille, grignote, lambèche, retaille **piece or scrap of cloth** carreau *pl.* **scraps** ramasserie **food scraps** ramassis

scrape *n.* grafignure

scrape *v.* gratter, racler, râper, râtonner, écorcher, écornifler, écrouter, s'écorcher **scrape off** râtonner **scrape or scratch again** regratter **lick, scrape or graze one's skin** se friper

scraper *n.* gratte, râpe

scraping *n.* grattage, écroutage

scrapper *n.* batailleur

scratch *n.* grafignure, riflure, ériflure **slight scratch** ériflure

scratch *v.* grafigner, gratter, griffer, s'ébrousseter, s'écorcher, se gratter, écornifler, écrouter, érifler **scratch o.s.** se grafigner **scratch slightly** écorcher **scratch with the claws** coffrer **scratch o.s. again or repeatedly** se regratter **scrape or scratch again** regratter

scratching *n.* grattage, écroutage

scrawl *n.* pataraphe

scrawl *v.* grafigner

scrawny *adj.* maigréchine

scream *n.* cri, haut-le-corps

scream *v.* crier, héler, parler à tue-tête / parler à pleine tête

screech *n.* **screech owl** chat-huant, chouette

screen *n.* grille, voile, écran, SCREEN **screen door** porte en grille **fireplace screen** cadre de cheminée

screen *v.* tamiser, voiler

screening *n.* tamisage

screw *n.* vis **flat-head screw** avisse à tête platte **wood screw** vis **Phillips head screw** avisse à quatre coins **fix with a screw** visser

screw *v.* visser, caler **screw s.o. over** foutre le coup à qqn

screwdriver *n.* tournevis

screwed *adj.* foutu comme Henri IV sur le Pont Neuf **be screwed** se visser

screwing *n.* vissage

scribble *v.* grafigner **scribble on** marquailler

scribbling *npl.* **scribblings** grafignure

scripture *n.* **scripture verse** verset

Scripture *npl.* **the Holy Scriptures** Les Saintes Ecritures

scrotum *n.* sac

scrub *v.* brosser, fourbir **any wad of material used to dust, clean up, or scrub** torchon **one who scrubs or mops** fourbisseur

scrubbing *n.* fourbissage

scrubboard *n.* frotteuse, frottoir

scrutinize *v.* tamiser

scuff *v.* écorcher

scuffle *v.* basculer, luttailler

sculpture *n.* sculpture

scum *n.* chierie, criote, mer, écume **remove scum** décombouiller

scup *n.* cochon

scurvy *n.* escorbut

scythe *n.* faucille, faux, fer volant, sabre, volant **cut with a scythe** sabrer **cut with a sickle or scythe** sercler

sea *n.* mer, océan **sea biscuit** gâteau **sea gum** gomme de mer **sea marsh** grande mèche **sea voyage** traverse **out to sea** au large **on the open sea** au large

sea-bob *n.* six-barbes

sea-cow *n.* vache de mer

seabreeze *n.* **seabreeze front** grain

seafood *n.* fruits de (la) mer, manger de mer, marécages, poisson **seafood gumbo** gombo de fruit de mer **seafood sauce** bisque

seagull *n.* goéland, pigeon de mer

seahorse *n.* cheval de mer

seal *n.* estampe

seal *v.* emboucher **seal or coat with wax** encirer

sealed *adj.* clos

sealing *n.* **sealing material for walls** plafonnage

seam *n.* cousure, joint **flat seam** surjet **sewn seam** couture **shoulder seam** épaulette

seamstress *n.* coudeuse, couturieuse, modiste

search *n.* recherche **search warrant** warrant **make a search** chercher

search *v.* chercher, fouillasser, fouiller, fourgailler, tamiser **search for** chercher, fouiller après {pour} **search for again** rechercher **search extensively and exhaustively** chercher à pied et à cheval **search high and low** chercher à pied et à cheval

seashell *n.* coquille de mer, coquille **univalve seashell** calimaçon

seashore *n.* bord de la mer

seasickness *n.* mal de mer

season *n.* saison **high season** saison haute **hunting season** chasse **in season** en saison **trawling season** trôle **weeding season** serclage **spring shrimping season** saison de mai

season *v.* accommoder, amariner, assaisonner **season with vinegar** vinaigrer

seasoned *adj.* amariné **highly seasoned** fort **highly peppered or seasoned** pimenté

seasoning *n.* amarinage, assaisonnement, saisonnage

seat *n.* banc, chaise, siège, fond **have a seat** prendre une chaise **take a seat** s'installer **occupy a seat as a member of a body of officials** siéger **space under the back seat of a skiff** panneau *pl.* **place in seats** asseoir

seat *v.* asseoir **seat o.s.** s'asseoir

seated *adj.* **be seated** asseoir, s'asseoir, être cargué

seatrout *n.* **sand seatrout** fouille-sable

seaweed *n.* du raisin

seclude *v.* **seclude o.s.** se renfermer

seclusion *n.* solitude

second *adj.* **play second fiddle** seconder **in the second place** deuxièmement

second *n.* deuxième, second, seconde, témoin

second *v.* seconder

secondhand *adj.* (de) seconde main, deuxième {seconde} main, seconde {deuxième} main

secondly *adv.* deuxièmement

secret *adj.* secret

secret *n.* secret **in secret** dans le dos, en arrière (de), en secret, à la cachette / en cachette

secretary *n.* secrétaire

secretly *adv.* en arrière (de), en secret, à la cachette / en cachette

section *n.* compartement, partie, section, tranchée

secular *adj.* séculier

secure *adj.* sûr, sauve

security *n.* sûreté, sécurité **social security check** chèque à trous

Security *n.* **Social Security** la patte douce

sedative *n.* calmant, calme

sedge *n.* **broom sedge** queue de chat

seduce *v.* adoucir, beurrer, emmioler, maquemose

seducer *n.* emmioleur

see *v.* apercevoir, voir **see again** revoir **see stars** voir bleu **see you later** on va se revoir **see you soon** talheure **see each other again** se revoir **see o.s. or each other** se voir **see one's life flash before one's eyes** livrer sa carcasse au diable **you see** tu {vous} connais / vous connaissez **speak of angels, see their wings** en parlant des anges, on voit leurs ailes **speak of the devil, see his face** en parlant de la bête, on lui voit la tête

See *n.* **the Holy See** le Saint-Siège

see-saw *n.* balancine

seed *n.* germe, grain, graine, noyau, plant, semence **seed cane** plant de canne **seed potato** mère patate **seed store** magasin de grainage **sesame seed** benné, sésame **go to seed** monter en grain(e) **device that separates cotton from its seed** hérisson *pl.* **seeds** semage **garden seeds** grainage **remove seeds from a pod** dégraboter

seedling *n.* plant **cabbage seedling** plant de chou

seek *v.* chercher, chercher

seem *v.* paraître, regarder, ressembler, sembler **seem depressed** avoir une mine de chien **seem sick** avoir mauvaise mine **seem well** avoir bonne mine **it seems** on dirait **it seems to me** dans mon ressemblant

segment *n.* maille

segregate *v.* quarantiner

seine *n.* seine à poisson, seine, tramail **seine with a pouch** seine à trois mailles **fish with a seine** seiner

seine *v.* seiner

seining *n.* **go seining** aller à la seine

seize *v.* accaparer, attraper, confisquer, empoigner, grappiller, gripper, poigner, prendre, saisir, souquer **seize again** ressaisir **seize by law** saisir **seize for o.s.** s'accaparer **seize with claws or talons** griffer

seizure *n.* crise, tremblement **have an epileptic seizure** tomber d'un mal / tomber du haut mal

seldom *adv.* rarement

select *v.* choisir, sélecter, trier **select randomly** tirer

selection *n.* sélection

self-assurance *n.* aplomb **possess self-assurance** avoir du crin

self-assured *adj.* aplomb

self-confidence *n.* aplomb **have self-confidence** avoir du crin

self-consciousness *n.* gêne

self-denial *n.* **practice self-denial** se mortifier

self-love *n.* amour-propre

self-respect *n.* gloire

self-service *n.* **self-service meal** buffet

selfish *adj.* rapiat

sell *v.* vendre **sell again** revendre **sell illegally** BOOTLEG **sell retail** vendre en détail **sell wholesale** vendre en gros **sell at auction** encanter **sell on credit** vendre à crédit **sell by the piece** vendre à la pièce **sell in large lots** vendre en gros **sell to one's neighbors** vendre à la côte

seller *n.* marchand, vendeur

selling *n.* vendage, vente

selvage *n.* lis

semblance *n.* apparence, semblance

semen *n.* bouillon, décharge, semence

semi *prefix.* mi-

semi-circle *v.* semicercle

semicircular *v.* semicercle

seminarian *n.* séminarien, séminariste

seminary *n.* séminaire

senate *n.* sénat

senator *n.* sénateur

send *v.* envoyer, expédier, ficher, voyer **send away** lâcher, renvoyer **send back** renvoyer **send for** envoyer chercher, voyer pour **send off** envoyer, expédier, renvoyer **send a message** laisser connaître **send a telegram** télégrapher **send away in a hurry** émousser

senile *adj.* égaré **be senile** être en enfance

senna *n.* séné **wild senna** café minote caïac

sensation *n.* sensation **have a peculiar sensation** faire drôle

sense *n.* allure, esprit, idée, raison, sens **common sense** bon sens, à-peu-près, à-propos **good sense** bon sens, esprit, idée, raison **have sense** avoir de l'esprit **make sense** faire de la raison, rimer **lacking common sense** emplâtre **not make sense** avoir pas d'apparence, baranquer, faire pas de rime **contrary to good sense** à la rebours du bon sens **not have good sense** avoir pas plus d'à peu près qu'une truie aux socos *pl.* **take leave of one's senses** se déranger **be out of one's senses with worry** être vent-debout

sensible *adj.* raisonnable **be sensible** avoir de l'esprit

sensibly *adv.* raisonnablement

sensitive *adj.* douillet, délicat, sensible, susceptible, suspect **sensitive to cold** frédilleux **one who is sensitive to physical pain** cœur de poule

sensitivity *n.* délicatesse

sentence *n.* phrase, sentence **pass a sentence on** prononcer

sentiment *n.* sentiment, émotion

separable *adj.* séparable

separate *v.* décoller, décrocher, démêler, détailler, se décoller, se délaisser, se quitter, se séparer, séparer, déchirer la couverture {couverte} (en deux) **device that separates cotton from its seed** hérisson

separated *adj.* en rabiot, quitté **be separated** être séparé (of a couple) **become separated** casser le ménage **be separated or divorced** être quitté de qqn **man separated from his wife** démarié **woman separated from her husband** démarié **one who is divorced or separated** délaissé

separately *adv.* séparément

separation *n.* divorce, séparation, écartement **fibrous separation between pods in a cotton boll** oreille de coton

separator *n.* **cream separator** écrémeuse

September *n.* septembre

sequence *n.* séquence

sequin *n.* brillant

serenade *n.* sérénade

serge *n.* serge

sergeant *n.* sergent

series *n.* série

serious *adj.* grave, sérieux comme une manne de tripes, sérieux

seriously *adv.* gravement, sérieusement, sérieux

seriousness *n.* gravité

sermon *n.* prône, prêche, prêchement, sermon **deliver a sermon** faire la prêche *pl.* **series of sermons by a missionary lasting three to seven days** mission

serpent *n.* serpent

servant *n.* servant **house servant** domestique **male servant** valet

serve *v.* retirer, servir, tirer, délivrer, servir **serve again** resservir **serve o.s.** se servir **serve o.s. again** se resservir **serve as an example** exempler **object destined to serve a particular purpose** préparation **it serves him/her right** c'est bien tapé

service *n.* militaire, service **church service** office, service **funeral service** enterrement, service **military service** service **spiritual service** dévotion **at your service** à votre dispose **be of service** servir **do one's military service** faire son service

serving *n.* **serving bowl** terrine **serving spoon** cuillère à lait **large serving** bosse **excessively large serving of food** cataplasme

sesame *n.* **sesame seed** benné, sésame **sesame seed praline** praline au {de} béné

session *n.* session **bingo session** bingo **period during which a court or a legislative body is in session** siège

set *adj.* **get set up** s'installer

set *n.* service, SET **set line** ligneguette **television set** télévision **forming an incomplete set** dépareillé

set *v.* planter, SET, ajuster, corriger, dresser, ramancher, régler, tendre **set aside** mettre de côté, réserver **set back** retarder **set down** dégrucher, mettre en bas, mettre par terre, poser **set free** affranchir, délivrer, déprendre, relâcher, émanciper **set in** prendre **set limits** borner **set out** partir, prendre pour, étendre **set up** amarrer, arranger, monter **set a date** amarrer une date **set boundary marks** borner **set in liquid** mettre à la trempe **set in order** arranger **set off for** pousser route **set out upon** prendre **set s.o. straight** mettre qqn à sa place **set the table** mettre la table **set a limit on** limiter **set out the details** détailler **set out to dry** mettre à la sèche, mettre à sécher **set out on the road** prendre le chemin **set a time for an engagement** citer

set-up *n.* installation

setback *n.* rechute **have a setback** rechuter

settee *n.* sofa

setting *adj.* couchant

setting *n.* session, couchée, règlement **setting hen** couvasse, couveuse **setting of eggs** couvée **place setting** couvert

settle *v.* décider, fixer, rafficher, s'établir, se comprendre, se fourrer, se ranger, ajuster **settle differences** faire ami **settle in** se planter **settle o.s.** se camper **settle back in** se réinstaller **settle o.s. comfortably** s'ouacher **settle in a spot** camper **settle, often by fighting** régler **pay or settle one's accounts** payer ses comptes, régler ses comptes

settled *adj.* **settled in comfortably** ouaché

settlement *n.* ajustement, arrangement, règlement **settlement**

of workers in some industry camp **settlement of a particular community or ethnic group** côte

settler *n.* colon

settling *n.* **settling the score** réglement de comptes

seven *n.* sept **seven steak** numéro sept

seventeen *n.* dix-sept

seventeenth *n.* dix-septième

seventh *n.* septième

seventieth *n.* soixante-dixième

seventy *n.* soixante-dix

seventy-five *n.* **seventy-five cents** six escalins

sever *v.* **sever relations** casser la paille **sever the spinal cord** nerfer

several *adj.* plusieurs

severe *adj.* strict, sévère

sew *v.* coudre, piquer **sew by hand** coudre au doigt, coudre à la main **sew by hand over** surjeter

sewer *n.* couseur, égouttage d'eau

sewing *n.* cousage, couture **sewing machine** coudeuse, machine à coudre **sewing needle** aiguille à fil **sewing machine treadle** marchette **open-ended sewing thimble** verge

sex *n.* sexe **have sex** caler, coquer, faire l'amour (à), haler un coup, piquer **have sex indiscriminately** piquailler **abnormal discharge of female sex organs** bouillon **engage readily or frequently in casual sex** chiennailler, chienner

sexed *adj.* **highly sexed girl** chatte

sexton *n.* sacristain

sexually *adv.* **said of a person who is still interested and still active sexually** il y a toujours du feu dans la cheminée

sexy *adj.* frayant

shabby *adj.* chéti

shack *n.* cabanasse, cabane, cabaneau, CAMP

shackle *n.* enfarge

shad *n.* sardine

shade *n.* abat-jour, ombrage, ombre, rideau **window shade** abat-jour, SHADE **in the shade** à l'ombrage, à l'ombre / à la lombre / à l'alombre

shade *v.* ombrager **shade o.s.** s'ombrager

shadow *n.* ombrage, ombre

shaft *n.* flèche, pole, brancard **shaft support** étrier **carriage shaft** menoir **coupling shaft** fausse-flèche **horse-drawn shaft for operating machinery** vergue

shaggy *adj.* poileux, poilu

shake *v.* chambranler, frémir, maganer, secouer, trembler, saganer **shake about** se tamiser **shake hands** se donner la main, secouer la main **shake o.s.** se secouer, se tamiser **shake up** ballotter **shake o.s. off** secouer **shake hands upon concluding a bargain** se donner la palmée **shake while dancing in such a way that the whole body trembles** tamiser **cause to shake** chambranler **pull or shake apart in order to fluff and clean them** tiller **pull or shake apart the strands of in order to fluff and clean them** émousser

shaken *adj.* **get emotionally shaken up** regricher

shaker *n.* **shaker made of a gourd filled with seeds** chichicois **pepper shaker** poivière, poivrier **salt shaker** salière

shaking *adj.* tremblant

shaking *n.* secouage, secouement, tremblade, tremblement

shaky *adj.* chambrelant, ébaroui

shallot *n.* sive, échalote **shallot leaves** queues d'oignon

shallow *adj.* bas, plate

shame *n.* disgrace, déshonneur, honte, tristesse, vergogne **put to shame** éhonter

shame *v.* éhonter

shameful *adj.* disgracieux, honteux

shameless *adj.* dévergondé, effronté

shammy *n.* chamois

shampoo *n.* SHAMPOO

shank *n.* jambe

shape *n.* forme, taille **take shape** se former **in bad shape** malfoutu **take the shape of a bush** taller **be in good shape** être bien arrangé **not be in good shape** être à l'arnicroche **anything old, in bad shape or disrepair** chabraque

shape *v.* battre, mouler, travailler **shape or turn on a lathe** tourner

shaped *adj.* **badly shaped or formed** malformé

shapely *adj.* bien corporé, bien taillé

shaping *n.* façonnage

shard *n.* grémille *pl.* **shards** babiche

share *n.* part, portion, ration, rationnement **for a share of the profits** à la part *pl.* **division into portions or shares** dévisage

share *v.* diviser, partager **share with one another** se partager **share food with the neighbors** faire le voisinage, voisiner **share and share alike** part et part égal

sharecrop *v.* travailler à la part, rester pour (qqn) **sharecrop on halves** travailler à la moitié **sharecrop on thirds** travailler au troisième

sharecropper *n.* engagé, tenant, travaillant à la part

shark *n.* requin

sharp *adj.* affilé, coupant, filou, fin, malin, perçant, piquant, pointu, roué, sec, SMART **sharp person** filou **sharp shooter** fusillier **sharp tongue** langue affilée **sharp, wily person** pistolet **be sharp** couper, trancher **extremely sharp** rasant **it is sharp** ça coupe comme la langue de ma grand-mère **it is not sharp** ça coupe comme une jambe de chien / ça coupe comme la jambe à {de} ma grand-mère / ça coupe aussi bien que mon doigt **in a dry, sharp manner** sec

sharpen *v.* aiguiser, appointir, limer, pointiller, pointir, épointer, affiler, chacoter **sharpen a plow** battre une lame de charrue **sharpen by repeated blows** battre

sharpened *adj.* affilé

sharpener *n.* affileur, affileuse, chacot **knife sharpener** effile, lime **pencil sharpener** chacot à crayon

sharpening *adj.* **sharpening stone** pierre à affiler **fine-grain**

sharpening stone meule douce **leather sharpening strop** lime
sharpening *n.* aiguisage, affilage (enfilage)
shatter *v.* briser, grémiller, éclabousser
shave *v.* raser, racler **shave o.s.** se raser
shaven *adj.* rasé
shaver *n.* **cane shaver** raseuse
shaving *n.* rasage **shaving brush** pinceau, savonnette **shaving mug** savonnette **wood shaving** attelle, chacote, copeau, ripe, éclat, écopeau *pl.* **shavings** babiche **wood shavings** ripage, varlopure
shawl *n.* châle
she *pron.* alle, elle, il, ça
she-ass *n.* âne
she-bear *n.* ours
she-devil *n.* diablesse
she-fox *n.* renard
sheaf *n.* gerbe
shear *v.* tondre
shearer *n.* tondeur
shears *npl.* cisaille, fauces, tondeuse **garden shears** pince **tin shears** cisaille
sheath *n.* fourreau
shebang *n.* bataclan **the whole shebang** tout le sacré bataclan, toute la boutique, toute la sacrée séquelle
shed *n.* cabane, cabildeau, hangar, SHED, SHOP **cotton storage shed** cotonnerie
shed *v.* dégainer, verser **shed leaves** s'effeuiller **shed hair or skin** déplumer
sheep *n.* brébis, mouton **sheep pen** bergerie **sheep tallow** suif de mouton
sheep-shearing *n.* tonnage
sheepfold *n.* bergerie
sheepshead *n.* **sheepshead fish** casbergau d'eau salée **common sheepshead fish** casburgot
sheet *n.* drap, feuille, page **sheet lightning** éloise **sign-up sheet** liste
shelf *n.* banc, tablette, étagère **shelf at window for washing dishes** banc-vaisselle **what-not shelf** étagère *pl.* **set of shelves** nonote, étagère
shell *n.* cartouche, gamelle, gosse, écale, écorce, épelure, coquille, écale, écorce **gun shell** cartouche **oyster shell** coquille d'huître **turtle shell** écale de tortue, écale **remove the shell** écouenner
shell *v.* écaler, écosser, épelurer, érober, égrener
shelled *adj.* **be shelled** s'égrainer
sheller *n.* **mechanical sheller** égreneuse, égrenoir
shellfish *n.* calimaçon
shelling *n.* égrenage
shelter *n.* abri, BLIND **shelter for animals** hangar **take shelter** se mettre à l'abri, se réfugier **bring into or under a shelter** abrier
shelter *v.* abrier
shelving *n.* étagère
shepherd *n.* berger
sherbet *n.* sorbet
sheriff *n.* officier, shérif
Shetland *n.* **Shetland pony** chacta
shield *n.* **fire shield** garde-feu
shifting mouvant
shiftless *adj.* **shiftless person** arsouille, péteur
shin *n.* devant de jambe, rasoir **shin bone** jarret
shine *n.* clair
shine *v.* briller, lisser, polir, donner, noircirer
shiner *n.* bisquet
shingle *n.* **wood shingle** bardeau, merrain *pl.* **shingles** ceinture, mal anglais **ax used for trimming of shingles** hache à parer
shingling *n.* **shingling party** piquerie
shining *adj.* brillant, éclatant
shinny *v.* grucher
shiny *adj.* brillant, lissé, poli
ship *n.* bateau, navire, vaisseau
ship *v.* expédier
shipment embarcation
shirk *v.* s'esquiver
shirt *n.* chemise **shirt cuff** poignet **shirt front** jabot **night shirt** chemise de nuit **wool shirt** chemise de laine **wearing only a shirt** en queue de chemise
shirtless *adj.* **shirtless or having one's shirt unbuttoned** dépoitraillé **go shirtless** se dépoitrailler
shirttail *n.* **pull out the shirttail of** déculotter
shirtwaist *n.* josé
shit *n.* merde **turn to shit** tourner en merde
shit *v.* chier
shitty *adj.* merdeux **do a shitty job** faire fritche
shiver *n.* frisson
shiver *v.* frissonner, trembler **shiver from the cold** friler, frédiller
shivering *adj.* tremblant
shivering *n.* frissonnement, tremblement
shock *n.* secousse, SHOCK **shock absorber** chacaça
shock *v.* bousculailler, interboliser, secouer, SHOCK
shocking *adj.* choquant
shod *adj.* ferré
shoddy *adj.* malattriqué **shoddy goods** pacotille, tchincaillerie
shoe *n.* chaussure, soulier, sousouille, toto **shoe brush** brosse à souliers **shoe polish** noir à soulier, SHINE **shoe repairman** arrangeur de souliers, cordonnier **shoe shop** boutique de souliers **shoe size** pointure **dress shoe** soulier fin **house shoe** soulier de maison **old shoe** crocro, quantier **sturdy shoe** boqueteau **tennis shoe** tennis **work shoe** gros soulier **casual slip-on shoe** loafer **heavy work shoe** broquin **old-fashioned high-topped shoe** boubouce **woman's dress**

shoe savate **any heavy, clumsy shoe** sabot **any low top, low quarter, slip-on shoe** savate *pl.* **shoes with laces** souliers amarrés **rubber shoes** soulier en élastique, souliers en caoutchouc **tennis shoes** soulier en élastique **work shoes** souliers d'ouvrage **replace shoes or stockings** rechausser **strap formerly used on boots and shoes** tire

shoe *v.* ferrer

shoe-horn *n.* cuillère à soulier

shoelace *n.* amarre de soulier, corde à soulier, cordon, lacet

shoemaker *n.* arrangeur de souliers, cordonnier

shoestring *n.* corde à soulier, lacet

shoo *interj.* chou

shoo *v.* passez!

shoot *n.* bourgeon, pousse **skeet shoot** pategau **trap shoot** pategau **turkey shoot** pategau

shoot *v.* craquer, flanquer un coup de fusil, plombter, sacrer un coup de fusil, tirailler, tirer, lancer **shoot again** retirer **shoot o.s.** se tirer **shoot repeatedly** saganer **shoot, injure, or kill by shooting** tirer **said of rice when it shoots out from sides instead of only in one cluster** en bottes

shooter *n.* tireur **sharp shooter** fusillier

shooting *n.* tirage **shooting star** comète, étoile filante

shop *n.* atelier, magasin, SHOP, STAND **blacksmith shop** forge **butcher shop** halle **jewelry shop** boutique de bijouterie **mechanic's shop** garage **shoe shop** boutique de souliers **printing shop or plant** imprimerie **retail shop selling clothing, jewelry, crafts or knicknacks** boutique **store or shop** boutique **bull in a china shop** brise-fer, briseur

shop *v.* magasiner, SHOP

shopkeeper *n.* marchand

shopping *n.* **go shopping** magasiner

shore *n.* bord, écore **draw alongside shore** accoster **from the shore** à la terre

shorebird *n.* pivier

short *adj.* bref, court, courtaud, basset, court, petit **short in stature** court sur pattes **be short** être à court **cut short** couper court, couper le sifflet (à qqn)

short *adv.* **in short** enfin

short-legged *adj.* bassette

shortcut *n.* raccourci **supposed shortcut that actually takes longer than the normal route** raccourci à défunt Pétain / raccourci à Philémon **take a shortcut** couper au raccourci

shorten *v.* abréger, accourcir, couper court, raccourcir, écourter

shortening *n.* raccourcissement **shortening bread** toteau

shorter *adj.* **become shorter** s'accourcir, se raccourcir **make shorter** abréger, accourcir

shortly *adv.* bientôt, talheure

shorts *npl.* culotte(s) courte(s), pantalons courts

shot *n.* balle, SHOT, SMILE, tirage, élance, coup, filet, plomb **shot of liquor** todie **BB shot** plomb **big shot** BIG BOY, gros chat, gros chien **administer a shot** piquer **take a shot** prendre un SHOT

shotgun *n.* fusil **double-barreled shotgun** fusil à deux canons

shoulder *n.* épaule, épaulière **shoulder blade** clavicule, palette de l'épaule **shoulder seam** épaulette **shoulder strap** bricole, épaulette **shoulder trim** épaulette **strike with one's shoulder** épauler *pl.* **bare one's neck and shoulders** se décolleter **carry s.o. on one's shoulders** faire le carcan **baring of the neck, shoulders, etc.** décolletage **expose the neck and shoulders of** décolleter

shoulder *v.* épauler, endosser

shout *v.* crier, hurler, héler, criailler **shout at** crier après (qqn) **shout loudly** escrimer, s'escrimer **one who yells or shouts** crieur

shouting *n.* hurlement **repeated yelling or shouting** criaillement

shove *n.* poussade, pousse

shove *v.* fourrer, poussailler **shove each other** se poussailler

shovel *n.* chauvelle, pelle-cheuve, pelle croche, pelle droite, pelle plate, pelle, shove **shovel for removing ashes** palette du foyer **square-bladed shovel** pioche **round-edged shovel with holes in the blade** shove à riz **height of a shovel or spade** creuseur

shovel *v.* chauveler, pelleter **one who shovels or spades** pelleteur

shoveler *n.* **northern shoveler** micoine

shovelful *n.* pelletée

shoveling *n.* pelletage

shoving *n.* bousculade

show *adj.* **big, show, dowdy woman** caouane

show *n.* exposition, parade, SHOW **afternoon show** matinée **make a show of o.s.** s'afficher **one who makes a big show of s.t. that is not really difficult** défonceur d'une porte ouverte / défonceur de porte(s) ouverte(s) **one who makes a big show of doing s.t. that is not really difficult** casseur de portes ouvertes

show *v.* donner, dépasser, exposer, marquer, montrer **show again** remontrer **show disapproval** pendre la babine **show o.s.** se montrer **show off** en flanquer, faire le {son} grand / faire la grande, faire son couillon, parader, pour parade, se montrer, se parader, SPORT **show up** paraître, ressourdre, s'amener, s'en venir **show o.s. again** se remontrer **show the way** donner le chemin **show up again** reparaître, réapparaître **show up unexpectedly** sourdre **show how to do s.t.** montrer **show o.s. as outstanding or superior** gagner le sucre **show displeasure or disapproval in one's facial expressions** avoir une figure comme une vache qu'a soif **expression used to show surprise, irritation or anger** fils de chien {garce / putain} / fils de putain de bordel {garce}, fils de monstre {pistache / poteau} / fils de poteau de barrière **curl the upper lip and show the teeth** rechaner, rechigner

show-off *n.* **something done as a show-off act** petit coup de grandeur

showcase *n.* vitreau, vitrière

shower *v.* se baigner
showgirl *n.* circasienne
showing *n.* exhibition, SHOW
showoff *n.* fant-de-tchaque, péteur
showy *adj.* **unnecessarily showy gesture** fion
shred *n.* lambèche *pl.* **pull to shreds** écharpiller
shred *v.* déchirailler, tiller, étirailler
shrew *n.* diablesse
shrewd *adj.* canaille, filou, malin, rusé **shrewd person** canaille, filou
shrewdness *n.* finesse
shrike *n.* moqueur français {muet / sauvage / d'hiver} **loggerhead shrike** pirate
shrill *adj.* perçant
shrimp *n.* chevrette, lobster **shrimp boat** bateau de chevrette **shrimp boil** bouilliture de chevrettes **shrimp business** affaire de chevrette {de drill / de nutria / de piège / de pêche / de trôle / d'huile (etc.)} **shrimp cake** boulette de chevrette **shrimp trap** caisse à chevrette **Brazilian shrimp** brésil **brown shrimp** brésil, chevrette BROWN, chevrette grise **dried shrimp** chevrette sec **fresh shrimp** chevrette verte **jumbo shrimp** chevrette blanche **lake shrimp** chevrette du lac **raw shrimp** chevrette verte **river shrimp** chevrette du fleuve **white shrimp** chevrette blanche **catch shrimp with a trawl** aller aux trôles **unusable pieces of shrimp along with bits of ice in a 210 pound barrel of shrimp** guenille
shrimping *n.* **spring shrimping season** saison de mai
shrink *v.* dégrossir, raccourcir, rapetisser, s'accourcir, se raccourcir, se ratatiner
shrinking *adj.* rapetissant
shrinking *n.* raccourcissement
shrivel *v.* ratatiner **shrivel up** ratatiner, se ratatiner, se rider **cause to shrivel up** ratatiner
shriveled *adj.* **thin, shriveled, emaciated person** rapapiote
Shroud *n.* **the Holy Shroud** Saint suaire
Shrove *n.* **Shrove Tuesday** Mardi Gras
shrub *n.* **camellia shrub** camélia **strawberry shrub** calicantuce *pl.* **clump of bushes, briars, or shrubs** talle
shrubbery *n.* **thick shrubbery or woods** boisure
shrug *v.* carrisser
shrunken *adj.* raccoquillé
shuck *n.* paille **shuck mattress** matelas de paille {paillasse} **corn shuck** paille à {de} maïs, robe **corn shuck mattress** paillasse
shuck *v.* effeuiller, érober
shucked *adj.* **be shucked, husked, peeled** s'écaler
shucking *n.* effeuillage
shucks *interj.* bordelation **oh shucks** chia, saloperie
shudder *v.* frissonner
shuddering *n.* frissonnement
shuffle *v.* brasser, chiffonner, rebrasser
shun *v.* éviter
shut *v.* fermer, se fermer **shut again** refermer **shut down** fermer **shut in** enfermer **shut off** éteindre **shut up** bouche ta gueule, couper le sifflet (à qqn), ferme ta gueule, fermer sa bouche, se boucher, se taire, taire **shut itself again** se refermer **shut o.s. in** se cabaner, se renfermer **shut s.o. up** boucher, faire taire **shut your trap** ferme ta gueule
shutter *n.* abat-jour, persienne **wooden shutter** fenêtre
shuttle *v.* trafiquer
shy *adj.* gêné, honteux, réservé, timide **be timid, shy, bashful** avoir honte **once fooled, twice shy** chat échaudé craint l'eau froide
shyness *n.* honte, timidité **get over one's shyness** se dégêner
sibilant *adj.* **make a sibilant sound in order to attract s.o.'s attention** psiter
sic *v.* siller
sick *adj.* escran, malade comme un carencro {chien}, malade **sick, ill, unhealthy person** malade **feel sick** se sentir foutaise {malade} **get sick** attraper du mal, tomber malade **make sick** barbouiller le cœur, faire (de / du) tort **seem sick** avoir mauvaise mine **take sick** prendre le lit **fall sick again** chuter, rechuter **be sick in bed** être au lit **make o.s. sick** se faire {se rendre} malade, se rendre malade **cause to be sick** rendre malade **pretend to be sick** faire le malade
sick *n.* **anointing of the sick** extrême-onction, Extrême Onction
sicken *v.* acœurer
sickle *n.* faucille, faux **sickle bar mower** raseuse **cut with a sickle or scythe** sercler
sickly *adj.* chéti, douillet, faillotte, fluet, maladif, malfoutu, silliette **sickly looking** cagou, tchiquine **sickly person or animal** crévasse **become sickly** écraser
sickness *n.* mal, maladie **sickness that has no apparent cause** mau de vénure **bout of sickness** attaque de maladie **struck down with sickness** frappé d'une maladie **unable to stand pain or sickness** ganache
side *n.* bord, côté, flanc **side by side** côte à côte, près à près, vis-à-vis (de) **side of the body** plat-côté **side of the story** dicton **side of a flat-bottomed boat** gonelle **back side** derrière **flat side** plate **narrow side** cant **north side** bord du nord **port side** bord à gauche **right side** endroit **on every side** (de) tribord et babord {bâbord} **on the side** à côté **on this side** bord icite **pull from side to side** zigonner **from one side to the other** d'un bord à l'autre **that's his/her side of the story** (ça) c'est son dicton **on the other side** l'autre bord **on the wrong side** à l'envers / à renvers **be on the same side** être du même bord *pl.* **change sides** changer de bord **from all sides** de tous les bords **on all sides** de bric et de brac, de tous les bords **split one's sides laughing** se fendre les côtés à rire
side *v.* **side with or defend s.o.** prendre pour qqn
side-stepping *n.* écart
sideboard *n.* buffet, sideboard
sideburn *n.* prussienne, tempe *pl.* **sideburns** jambon **wear sideburns** se raser à la prussienne

sidewalk *n.* banquette, ciment, trottoir
siding *n.* douelle, voliche **clapboard siding** voliche
siesta *n.* NAP
sieve *n.* couloir, crible, tamis
sift *v.* tamiser
sifter *n.* tamis
sifting *n.* tamisage
sigh *n.* soupir **heave a sigh** pousser un soupir
sigh *v.* soupirer
sight *n.* apercevance, vue **gun sight** mire **in sight** visible **lose sight of** perdre de vue
sight *v.* mirer
sighting *n.* mire
sightly *adj.* regardable
sign *n.* apercevance, BILL, enseigne, geste, indication, marque, remarque, signe, symptôme **sign board** affiche **predictive sign** prédicateur **stop sign** STOP **make a sign to stop** FLAG
sign *v.* endosser, signer
sign-up *adj.* **sign-up sheet** liste
signal *n.* signal
signal *v.* faire signe
signature *n.* signature, signe
significance *n.* signification
significant *adj.* considérable
signify *v.* vouloir dire
silage *n.* ensilage
silence *n.* silence
silence *v.* boucher
silent *adj.* assogné, paisé **be silent** taiser **become silent** taiser **keep silent** pas siffler, se taire **remain silent** rester bête
silhouette *n.* silhouette
silk *n.* soie **corn silk** catin, filasse **cotton silk fiber** soie de coton
silky *adj.* fin
sill *n.* lambourde, madrier, sablière, sole, soliveau, linteau **window sill** linteau de fenêtre, nèche *pl.* **sills** assolement
silliness *n.* bêtise, folie
silly *adj.* bête, baroque, craque-bine, embarrateur, extravagué, fraque, frou-frou, lolette, sot, tacalac, évargandé **silly person** dinde (d'inde) **silly, foolish, high-strung woman** fraque **funny or silly person** macaque **one who says silly, foolish things** sottiseux
silo *n.* **put into a silo** embutter
silt *n.* limon, terre rapportée, vase
silty *adj.* vaseux
silver *n.* argent **silver money** argent blanc, argent claire **silver paper** brillant
silvered *adj.* argenté
silverplate *v.* argenter
silverplated *adj.* argenté
silverware *n.* argent, outils de table
silvery *adj.* argenté
simarouba *n.* simarouba
similar *adj.* pareil, près
simple *adj.* bonasse, naïve, simple, simplement
simple-minded *adj.* bétasse, simple, égaré
simpleton *n.* accroc, couillon d'eau douce, couillon, emplâtre, espingouin, estronfillau, gribouille, robio
simply *adv.* bonnement, justement, modestement, simplement, tout simplement, uniment
sin *n.* péché **sin of omission** péché d'omission **capital sin** péché capital **mortal sin** péché mortel **original sin** péché originel **venial sin** péché véniel **commit a sin** faire un péché **fall back into sin** rechuter
sin *v.* pécher **sin again** repécher
sinapism *n.* sinapisse
since *conj.* d'abord que, depuis (que), en raison que, puisque, à cause que
since *prep.* depuis
sincere *adj.* sincère
sincerely *adv.* sincèrement
sincerity *n.* sincérité
sinew *n.* nerf, tendon
sing *v.* chanter, chanter **sing badly** chanter comme un carencro **sing intermittently** chantailler **sing in the choirloft** chanter dans la tribune **sing softly and repeatedly** chantonnier
singe *v.* brûler, griller
singer *n.* chanteur
singing *n.* chant, chantage **prayers, singing, reading, etc., offered by lay people in lieu of actual Mass** messe blanche {sec} **unaccompanied group singing and dancing event** bazar
single *adj.* seul, simple
singletree *n.* bacul, barconcu, bas-jarret, flèche, palonnier simple, palonnier
sink *n.* lavier, zinc **sink or depression in the land** bassière **kitchen sink** lavier, SINK, zinc
sink *v.* caler, encaver, planter, s'enfoncer, se caler, écaler **sink deeper** se renfoncer **sink to the bottom** caler au fond
sinker *n.* plomb
sinking *n.* **sinking in** enfoncement
sinner *n.* pécheur
sinus *n.* **sinus cavity** cerveau **sinus trouble** mal de cerveau, maladie de cerveau *pl.* **sinuses** cerveau
sip *n.* gorgée **sip of coffee** goutte de café **take a sip** boire une goutte
sir *n.* galant, monsieur
sissified *adj.* filleuse
sister *n.* sœur **half sister** demi-sœur
sister-in-law *n.* belle-sœur
sit *v.* asseoir, prendre une chaise, siéger, sissite **sit astraddle** engarocher **sit astride** se braquer sur **sit down** asseoir, s'asseoir, sissite **sit on** couver **sit back comfortably** se

carguer **sit down again** se rasseoir **sit on eggs** couver **sit up with** veiller les malades {un malade} **sit at the table** se mettre à (la) table **sit on its haunches and beg** faire (sa) belle **stand or sit on its hind legs by itself** faire le beau **one who likes to sit in place and do nothing** raccroupi

site *n.* emplacement

sitting *n.* **break of sitting** découvasser, découver

situate *v.* **situate o.s.** se situer

situation *n.* position, situation **it's a difficult situation** ça c'est pas baptême catin **relish one's own situation** être dans son sirop **be in a difficult situation** être vent-debout **be in a awkward or uncomfortable situation** suer comme un bâtard à une réunion de famille / suer comme un nègre à la messe / suer comme les Ponce **get o.s. out of a difficult situation** se déberner **put in an undesirable place or situation** enfoncer **remove from a comfortable place or situation** dénicher **in a low position, level space or situation** bas **struggle to get out of a bad situation** se débattre comme le diable dans de l'eau bénite {un bénitier} **you have to make the best of a bad situation** si on peut pas téter maman, il faut téter mémère

six *n.* six **six by eight lumber** six par huit **six by six lumber** six par six

six-shooter *n.* fusil à six coups, pistolet à six coups

sixteen *n.* seize

sixteenth *n.* seizième

sixth *n.* sixième

sixtieth *n.* soixantième

sixty *n.* soixante **about sixty** soixantaine

size *n.* grandeur, grosseur, mesure, numéro, taille, volume **shoe size** pointure **reduce in size** dégrossir, rapetisser **great in number, size, or extent** majeur

size *v.* **cut down to size** charpenter

skate *v.* SKATE

skeet *n.* pategau **skeet shoot** pategau **sport of skeet shooting** pategau

skein *n.* **wind into a hank or skein** travouiller

skeleton *n.* esquelette, squelette

sketch *n.* plan

skewer *n.* **spit and skewer** broche

skewer *v.* embrocher

skewering *n.* embrochement

ski *n.* ski

ski *v.* ski

skid *n.* traîneau

skiff *n.* skiff **Lafitte skiff** lafitte **oyster skiff** skiff à z-huîtres **space under the back seat of a skiff** panneau

skill *n.* adresse, art, expertise, industrie

skilled *adj.* **skilled in** fort pour

skillet *n.* poêlon, tchacouelle

skillful *adj.* adroit, aplomb, au fait, fini, habile, à toutes mains

skillfulness *n.* aplomb, habilité

skim *v.* écrémer, écumer **skim floating matter from the surface of** écrémer

skimmer *n.* SKIMMER **black skimmer** bec-à-ciseaux / bec-en-ciseaux

skimming *n.* écrémage, écumage

skin *n.* couenne, membrane, peau, pelure, épluche **skin disease** dartre **skin eruption** clou **shed skin** dumer **on the bare skin** à peau nue **remove the outer skin** écouenner **shed hair or skin** déplumer **bruise or spot on skin** placard **swollen spot on the skin** loupe **lick, scrape or graze one's skin** se friper

skin *v.* plumer, s'ébrousseter, écornifler, écouenner, écrouter, déplumer, écorcher **skin o.s.** s'écorcher **one who skins alligators** écorcheur

skinner *n.* écorcheur

skinning *n.* écorchement, écroutage

skinny *adj.* efflanqué, fini, maigre, maigréchine, méchant, tchiquine **have a skinny behind** avoir des fesses de moiselle

skinny-dip *v.* se baigner à la plie

skip *v.* sauter

skipping *n.* sautaillement

skirmish *n.* accrochage

skirt *n.* jupe, petite robe **skirt of a dress** jupe de robe **hoop skirt** malakoff

skittish *adj.* fraque, poltron

skull *n.* calotte, crâne **skull cap** capuchon

skullcap *n.* caloquinte, calotte

skunk *n.* bête puante, civette, fouine

sky *n.* ciel **up in the sky** dans les nuages **in the air, the sky** l'air du temps

skyline *n.* horizon

slab *n.* plaque, tranche, gobe

slack *adj.* LOOSE **slack day** jour ras

slacken *v.* détendre, lâcher, relâcher, se détendre, se relâcher **slacken the reins of** dérêner

slam *v.* plaquer

slander *n.* calomnie, mépris

slander *v.* bafouer, mépriser

slanderous *adj.* **prone to slanderous or scandalous talk** mépriseur

slang *n.* argot

slant *n.* biais

slanting *adj.* biais

slap *n.* apostrophe, bourlingue, calotte, coup de tape, tape, touche **slap with the back of the hand** vire-tape **give a slap** flailler une tape (à qqn) **give s.o. a slap** foutre une calotte à qqn *pl.* **give several light slaps** tapocher **a series of blows or slaps** claquée

slap *v.* apostropher, calotter, coller une tape, emmancher une tape, engarocher une tape, flanquer une tape, passer à coups de tapes / passer aux tapes, sacrer une tape, souffler une tape, taper, tirer une tape, foutre une ramasse (à qqn), piquer

une tape (à qqn) **slap around** tapocher **slap s.o.** foutre une calotte à qqn, mettre un apostrophe à qqn **slap each other** se taper
slash *n.* inciselage
slash *v.* déchiquenailler, entailler, inciseler
slat *n.* latte
slate *n.* ardoise **school slate** ardoise **writing slate** ardoise
slaughter *n.* boucherie, massacre, tuerie, abattage **communal neighborhood slaughter or butchering event** boucherie de bloque {de quartier}
slaughter *v.* faire boucherie, massacrer, tuer
slaughterer *n.* abatteur
slaughterhouse *n.* boucherie, tuerie
slaughtering *n.* **cooperative slaughtering** boucherie de société
slave *n.* esclave **slave quarters** cabanage, camp *pl.* **freed slaves** gens de couleur libres
slaver *v.* baver
slavery *n.* esclavage
slayer *n.* tueur
sleazy *adj.* basse-classe
sled *n.* traîneau
sledgehammer *n.* masse **big sledgehammer** maillet
sleek *adj.* lissé
sleep *n.* endormitoir, somme, sommeil, dodo **induce sleep in** endormir **go to sleep** faire dodo, s'endormir **put to sleep** endormir **anything that induces sleep** endormitoir **be in deep sleep** être dans le Paris des oies **go back to sleep** se rendormir **put back to sleep** rendormir **go back to sleep for a short period after being awakened** faire une paresse **not get a wink of sleep** passer la nuit blanche **said when s.o. is nodding off to sleep** le bouchon est après caler
sleep *v.* coucher, dormir, se coucher, sommeiller **sleep around** chiennailler, chienner, fêter sa fouine **sleep badly** dormailler **sleep fitfully** dormailler **sleep late** faire la grasse matinée **sleep soundly** dormir comme un caïman {un congo / une caille molle} **sleep well** dormir comme une bûche **sleep away from home** découcher **sleep on the job** dormir sur un rôti **sleep in for a short period of time** paresser **not sleep a wink** pas fermer l'œil **be unable to sleep** avoir l'œil sec
sleepiness *n.* endormitoir
sleeping *adj.* endormi **pretend to be sleeping** faire le congo
sleepless *adj.* **spend a sleepless night** passer la nuit blanche
sleepy *adj.* **sleepy person** dorminique **appear sleepy** avoir les yeux dolents **be sleepy** avoir l'endormitoir, s'endormir
sleepy-head *n.* dorminique
sleet *n.* verglas
sleet *v.* verglacer
sleeve *n.* manche, férule *pl.* **roll up one's sleeves** enlever sa soutadaire, se desseller
sleigh *n.* traîne
slender *adj.* fin, mince, élingué
slenderness *n.* minceur
slice *n.* tartine, tranche, tranchée **slice of bread** tranche de pain **thin slice** galette, lichefrippe
slice *v.* frendir, trancher **slice completely** couper carré
slicer *n.* trancheuse
slick *adj.* filant
slide *n.* glissade
slide *v.* glisser, glisser **slide down** débouler
slider *n.* tortue câille
sliding *n.* déboulage, déboulement, glissade
slight *n.* affront
slight *v.* **slight s.o.** passer le baquet
slightly *adv.* moindrement, un peu
slim *adj.* mince
slim *v.* **slim down** amincir
slime *n.* vase
slimming *n.* amincissement
slimy *adj.* filant, vaseux
sling *v.* garrocher
slingshot *n.* archer, NIGGER-SHOOT
slip *n.* canicroche, jupe de dessous, jupe, jupon, slip, sous-jupe, échappe, camisole, slip **slip for transplanting or grafting** bouture **pillow slip** couverture d'oreiller
slip *v.* glisser, se déhaler, glisser, échapper **slip into quietly** se glisser **slip off unnoticed** s'exiler **let slip** échapper **let slip a bad word** échapper une mauvaise parole
slip-knot *n.* lasse
slip-on *n.* **casual slip-on shoe** loafer
slipper *n.* savate de chambre {maison}, savate, slip, soulier de chambre, soulier de maison **bath slipper** soulier de bain **bedroom slipper** savate, slip, soulier de maison **house slipper** slip, soulier de maison
slippery *adj.* glissant
slipping *n.* glissade, slip
slipshod *adj.* **in a slipshod way** machinalement **do in a slipshod way** barlanguer, bâcler, faire à la bric-brac, haricoter, saganer, sagouiller **perform in a slipshod way** barboter **do s.t. too quickly or in a slipshod way** faire fritche **piece of work done poorly or in a slipshod manner** cochonnerie
slit *n.* fente **cut a slit into** inciseler
sliver *n.* galette
slobber *v.* baver, bavoler
slog *v.* gratter **slog away** gratter
slop *n.* lavure **feed slop** ramassis
slope *n.* pente **downward slope** descente **at a steep slope** à pic
slope *v.* pencher
sloping *adj.* en pente
sloppiness *n.* dégaine
slot *n.* coche, fourreau
sloth *n.* paresse
slothful *adj.* paresseux

slovenliness *n.* dégaine

slovenly *adj.* cochonnier, à la valdrague **slovenly work** pitié d'affaire **be slovenly** se négliger **do in a slovenly way** saloper **work in a slovenly fashion** gargouiller

slow *adj.* barosse, doucement, douillet, lambin, longis, en arrière **become slow** alentir **make slow** alentir **awkward and slow** emplâtre

slow *v.* alentir **slow down** adoucir, calmer, doucement!

slow-moving *adj.* doucement, gningnin, nigeau **awkward and slow-moving person** cataplasme

slow-witted *adj.* **dull, slow-witted mind** esprit barosse {rosse}

slowly *adv.* aisé, doucement comme la lune {un colimaçon / une crabe / une merde / une tortue / Christmas}, doucement, lentement, petite à petite, poc à poc, tout doucement!

slowpoke *n.* vieille tortue

sluggish *adj.* barosse, doucement, gningnin, traînassant

sluggishly *adv.* lentement

slumber *n.* sommeil

slumber *v.* dormir

slurp *v.* friper

slush *n.* verglas

slut *n.* chienne, salope

sly *adj.* filou comme un renard, filou, malin, naré, réveillé **sly person** filou **sly as a fox** filou comme un renard **artful, crafty, sly man** homme d'affût

sly *n.* **on the sly** à la cachette / en cachette

smack *n.* bourlingue

small *adj.* mince, nain, petit, tout petit **small or narrow** large comme deux doigts / large comme mes deux fesses **cute and small** mignon

small-minded *adj.* **small-minded, foolish person** zozo

smaller *adj.* moindre **get smaller** rapetisser **make smaller** rapetisser

smallness *n.* petitesse

smallpox *n.* grosse {mauvaise} picote, picote

smart *adj.* déluré, intelligent, pointu, roué, SMART, vaillant **smart aleck** accroc, fant-de-tchaque, péteur **be smart** avoir une bonne tête **you're not as smart as you think you are** t'es pas proche un avocat

smartened *adj.* **smartened up** requinquiné

smartweed *n.* curage

smash *v.* briser, casser en douelles, écramouiller, égrener, émœller, épurer **smash in** défoncer

smear *n.* balafre, barbouillage

smear *v.* barbouiller, se bousiller, bousiller **smear o.s.** se barboter **smear with tar or glue** goudronner **smear o.s. with glue, tar, or a similar substance** se goudronner

smeared *adj.* bousillé

smell *n.* odeur, senteur **burning smell** brûlé **burnt smell** brûlé **have the smell of** sentir **have a sharp sense of smell** avoir le nez fin

smell *v.* renifler, sentir, éventer **smell again** ressentir **smell bad** puer le tigre {chien}, puer **smell of** puer, sentir

smelting *adj.* **smelting plant** fonderie **smelting works** fonderie

smilax *n.* cantaque

smile *n.* sourire

smile *v.* rire, sourire

smock *n.* blouse

smoke *n.* boucane, fumée **holy smoke** sacré {cré} boucane, sacrée boucane {misère} **make smoke to ward off mosquitoes** faire (de) la boucane

smoke *v.* boucaner, fumer

smoke-dry *v.* boucaner

smoked *adj.* boucané

smokehouse *n.* boucanière

smoker *n.* fumeur **tobacco smoker** fumeur **inveterate pipe smoker** pipeur

smoking *n.* boucanée, boucanage, fumerie **smoking pipe** cachimbo **smoking process for meat** boucanée

smooth *adj.* comme un papier de musique, fin, juste, lissé, uni, égal

smooth *v.* lisser, unir, égaler, égalir, égaliser **smooth out** aplanir **smooth out wrinkles in the skin of** dérider

smoothing *n.* aplanissement, lissage

smoothly *adv.* comme le fil en aiguille, comme un papier de musique, comme une plume, plange

smother *v.* étouffer

smothered *adj.* étouffé **smothered corn** maquechou

smothering *n.* étouffement

smuggler *n.* BOOTLEG

smut *n.* saloperie

snack *n.* collation, goûter

snacking *n.* grignotage

snail *n.* calimaçon, chenille, escargot, snelle **salt water snail** bigorneau

snake *n.* serpent **coachwhip snake** serpent fouetteuse **garter snake** couleuvre, serpent barré(e), serpent cotonnade **grass snake** couleuvre **hognose snake** siffleur **king snake** mangeur {mangeuse} d'œuf(s), serpent mangeur / mangeuse d'œufs **poisonous snake** bâtard sonnette **whip snake** serpent fouetteuse **blue racer snake** coureuse **blue runner snake** serpent fouetteuse **eastern coachwhip snake** fouetteur, fouetteuse **nonvenomous water snake** serpent d'eau **prairie king snake** roi **yellow-bellied water snake** serpent des herbes **yellow chicken snake** mangeur {mangeuse} d'œuf(s), serpent mangeur / mangeuse d'œufs

snake *v.* serpenter

snakebird *n.* bec-à-lancette

snap *n.* agrafe, pichenet, SNAP **snap hook** cobbe

snap *v.* claquer, craquer, plaquer **snap one's fingers** flailler les doigts

snapdragon *n.* gueule de loup

snapper *n.* **red snapper** perche rouge, poisson rouge
snare *n.* attrape, piège, trappe **bird snare** cage **mythical trap or snare against which children were warned** sisi à dents
snare *v.* piéger
snarl *n.* grognement
snarl *v.* grincher, grogner, rechaner
snatch *v.* agrapper, friper, happer, prendre **snatch for o.s.** s'accrocher
sneak *v.* **sneak up** venir en traître
sneakily *adv.* en traître
sneaky *adj.* en dessous, par en-dessous **in a sneaky or stealthy way** à la sourdine
sneer *v.* ricaner
sneeze *n.* éternuement
sneeze *v.* éternuer
sneezing *n.* éternuement
snicker *v.* grincher
sniff *v.* renifler **sniff around** renifler
sniffle *n.* reniflement
sniffle *v.* renifler
sniffling *n.* reniflement
snipe *n.* bécasse de marais, bécasse, bécassine des marais, bécassine, cache-cache, cape-cape **red-breasted snipe** bécassine de mer, carouque, dormeur **sea snipe** dormeur
snitch *n.* porte-paquet, rapporteur
sniveling *adj.* morveux **sniveling person** morveux
snobbish *adj.* noble
snood *n.* roupie
snoop *n.* espionneur, fouillailleur, fouillard, fouille-merde, fouille-merdeur, fouille-nez, fouilleur, fourgailleur, fourre-nez
snoop *v.* fouille-merder, fouiller, fourgailler, foutumasser
snooping *n.* espionnage
snooty *adj.* **be snooty** avoir le nez fin
snooze *v.* soguer **you snooze you lose** chien qui va à la chasse perd sa place
snore *v.* ronfler
snorer *n.* ronfleur
snoring *n.* ronflement **make a snorting sound when snoring** frapper un nœud
snort *v.* renifler, renâcler
snot *n.* morve, morviat, roupille
snotty *adj.* morveux
snout *n.* museau, nez
snow *n.* neige **snow cloud** nuage de neige **melted snow** verglas **fine rain or snow** poudrin
snow *v.* neiger
snowball *n.* boule de neige
snowfall *n.* **light snowfall** poudriaille, poudré de neige
snub *n.* affront
snub *v.* affronter
snuff *n.* chapeau, prise, tabac en poudre **take snuff** priser
snuff *v.* **snuff out the candle** tuer la chandelle
snuff-box *n.* tabatière
snuggle *v.* niquer, se nicher, se niquer
so *adj.* comme ça
so *adv.* ainsi, alors, assez, aussi, donc, enfin, si tant, si tellement, si, tellement, voir, WELL, ça fait **and so** d'abord **like so** astacot
so *conj.* pour que, à force (que) **so that** pour que
so *pron.* **so and so** tel et tel
so-called *adj.* fameux
so-so *adj.* comme ci, comme ça, tchoque-à-bloque
so-so *adv.* poc à poc
soak *v.* assaper, caler, mettre à la trempe, tremper, saucer **put to soak** écaler
soaked *adj.* saucé, trempe **be soaked** se tremper **get soaked** se tremper
soaking *n.* baignage
soap *n.* savon **soap dish** savonnette **soap suds** savonnure **bar of soap** barre de savon, brique de savon **homemade lye soap** savon du pays **wash with soap** savonner **bar of dainty, perfumed soap** savonnette
soap *v.* savonner **soap o.s.** se savonner
soapbox *n.* savonnette
soaping *n.* **soaping up** savonnure
soar *v.* planer
sob *v.* siroter
sobbing *n.* **loud sobbing and crying** beuglage, beuglement
sober *adj.* à jeun
sober *v.* **sober up** dessoûler, se dessoûler **cause to sober up** dessoûler
soccer *n.* pelote au pied
sociable *adj.* sociable
social *adj.* **social security check** chèque à trous
Social *n.* **Social Security** la patte douce
socialize *v.* se fréquenter
socially *adv.* **evening spent socially** veillage
society *n.* association, société **high society** les grandes gens **religious order or society** communauté **member of a group or society** membre
sock *n.* bas, chaussette, chausson **heavy sock** chausson **man's sock** chausson **woman's or child's sock** chaussette
sock *v.* **sock it to s.o.** foutre le coup à qqn
socket *n.* **whip socket** porte-fouet
sod *n.* **break the sod** fendre la terre
soda *n.* pop, soda **soda cracker** biscuit soda, biscuit, craquette **baking soda** soda **strawberry soda** pop rouge
sodium *n.* **sodium nitrite** salpêtre
sofa *n.* longe, sofa
soffit *n.* ceiling
soft *adj.* mollet, mou, pongeux, sourge **soft palate** luette **soft part** mou **soft inside part of bread** miette **soft inside part of bread, cake, etc.** mie **become soft** se ramollir **grow soft** se ramollir **make fluffy and soft** volumer

soften *v.* amollir, attendrir, mollir, ramollir, s'amollir, ameublir
softly *adv.* bas, doucement
softness *n.* tendresse
soil *n.* terre **clay soil** terre grasse **fertile soil** terre forte, terre riche **loose soil** terre friable, terre meuble **poor, unfertile soil** terre pauvre **black, porous, rich soil** terre mourante
soil *v.* beurriner, emberner, embeurriner, emmerder, emmicheter, goudronner, plaquer, salir, souillonner, tacher **soil o.s.** s'emberner, s'emmerder, s'emmicheter, se salir, se tacher **soil with dirt** se bousiller
soiled *adj.* bousillé
soiling *adj.* salissant
sojourn *n.* caravane, séjour
solace *n.* **find solace** se consoler
sold *adj.* **be sold** se vendre
solder *n.* soudure
solder *v.* souder
solderable *adj.* soudable
solderer *n.* soudeur
soldering *n.* soudure **soldering iron** fer à souder **tool for pressing clothes, branding, soldering, etc.** fer
soldier *n.* soldat **Union soldier** Yankee **equip a soldier** gréer un soldat
sole *adj.* unique
sole *n.* semelle
solemn *adj.* solennel
solemnity *n.* solemnité
solicit *v.* cabaler **one who asks or solicits** demandant
soliciting *n.* cabale
solid *adj.* durable, ferme, massif, robuste, solide, stable
solid-colored *adj.* uni
solidity *n.* fermeté
solitaire *n.* solitaire
solitary *adj.* solitaire
solitude *n.* solitude
solution *n.* solution **pickling solution** marinade, saumure
somber *adj.* sombre
some *adj.* plusieurs, quelque **some . . . or another** tel et tel / telle et telle
some *art.* de
some *pron.* quelqu'uns, quelques-uns / quelques-unes
somebody *pron.* un et l'autre
somehow *adv.* manière, quelque manière
someone *pron.* aucun, quelqu'un, tel, un et l'autre **someone else** quelqu'un d'autre **said of someone who has harmed you and against whom you seek revenge** je lui garde chien de ma chienne
somersault *n.* bascule, capotage, carpiche, culbute, pirouette **do a somersault** culbuter
something *n.* de quoi, quelque chose **that's something** ça par exemple!, ça par exemple **unload something undesirable on** caracoler **a little something extra received for free** lagniappe
sometime *adv.* quelque temps
sometimes *adv.* des fois, quelquefois
somewhat *adv.* manière, moyen, par-dessus les buttes
somewhere *adv.* en quelque part, quelque part, quelque place
son *n.* fils, garçon **only son** fils unique **prodigal son** enfant prodige **like father like son** bon chien tient de race
son-in-law *n.* beau-fils, gendre
son-of-a-bitch *n.* enfant de chien, enfant de garce, fils de chien {garce / putain} / fils de putain de bordel {garce} **damn son-of-a-bitch** sacré fils de garce {putain}
son-of-a-gun *n.* enfant de garce, enfant de monstre, fils de monstre {pistache / poteau} / fils de poteau de barrière, maudit, saloperie
song *n.* chanson, chansonnette, chant, chantage **song or musical number to accompany dancing** danse *pl.* **write songs** faire des chansons
songbird *n.* caille
soon *adv.* bientôt, talheure, tantôt, vite **not soon** pas de sitôt **as soon as** aussitôt que, dès que / desque / drès que, dès, sitôt que, une fois que
sooner *adv.* **sooner or later** tôt ou tard, tantôt-bétôt
soot *n.* suie
soothe *v.* soulager
soothing *adj.* adoucissant, soulageant
soothing *n.* soulagement
soothsayer *n.* astronome
soporific *n.* endormitoir
sorceress *n.* sorcier
sordid *adj.* **sordid deed** cochonnerie
sore *adj.* éraillé **be sore** avoir du mal **get sore** se bouquer
sore *n.* bobo, mal, plaie **sore at the corner of the mouth** bridon **saddle sore** mal anglais **mouth sore in an infant** mal blanc
soreness *n.* **soreness from horseback riding** les quatre escalins
sorghum *n.* sorgho
sorrel *adj.* sorrel
sorrel *n.* **wood sorrel** trèfle salé
sorrow *n.* chagrin, douleur, peine, point dans le cœur, regret, remords, tristesse **cause sorrow** faire grief
sorrowful *adj.* en peine, peineux, triste **sorrowful thing** pitié d'affaire
sorrowfully *adv.* tristement
sorry *adj.* **be sorry** avoir du regret, regretter **feel sorry** plaindre, prendre en pitié **I'm sorry** pardon, ça me fait de la peine **feel sorry for o.s.** se prendre en pitié **make sad or sorry** faire de la peine
sorry *interj.* **sorry?** hein, est-il
sort *n.* espèce, genre, qualité, sorte *pl.* **all sorts of things** hourra d'affaires **out of sorts** cagou, mal en train, traînassant **do all sorts of things** faire les quatre cents coups **generally out of sorts** pas être gaillarde

sort *v.* assortir, détailler, trier **sort out** assortir, démêler
sorting *n.* démêlage, triage
sought *adj.* **sought after** recherché
soul *n.* chrétien, âme
sound *adj.* sain, solide **safe and sound** sain et sauve
sound *n.* bruit, son **make a clacking sound** claquer **make a grinding sound** grincher
sound *v.* corner, sonder, sonner
sounding *n.* sondage
soup *n.* potage, soupe **soup bone** échelon **soup bowl** assiette creuse, plat creux, soupière **soup spoon** cuillère à manger, cuillère à table **soup tureen** soupière **soup without meat** soupe maigre **bad soup** lavure
sour *adj.* haigre, hâcre **turn sour** haigrir **turn or make sour** haigrir
sour *v.* haigrir
source *n.* origine, provenance, source **source of disgust** dégoûtation
sourdough *n.* ferment, levain
souring *n.* haigrissement
sourness *n.* haigreur
south *n.* sud
southeast *n.* sud-est
southwest *n.* sud-ouest, suroît
Southwest Louisiana Industrial Institute *n.* Industriel
souvenir *n.* souvenir
sow *n.* tchoune, truie **old sow** vieille truie
sow *v.* planter, semer **sow wild oats** chienner
sowing *n.* **sowing time** semage *pl.* **sowings** semage
soybean *n.* soja, SOYBEAN
space *n.* espace, place **space between a bed and the wall** arouelle, ruette **blank space** vide **in a low position, level space or situation** bas *pl.* **replant the empty spaces in a row of crops, trees, etc.** recourir les manques
space *v.* espacer
spade *n.* bêche, ferrée, pelle plate, pelle, pique **height of a shovel or spade** creuseur *pl.* **spades** pioche **ace of spades** as de pic
spade *v.* bêcher, pelleter **one who shovels or spades** pelleteur
spading *n.* pelletage
spaghetti *n.* spaghetti
Spain *n.* Espagne
span *n.* **span of a step** jambée **span of both arms fully extended** brasse **time span** durée
Spaniard *n.* Espagne, Espagnol
Spanish *adj.* espagnol **Spanish person** Espagne, Espagnol **the Spanish language** espagnol
Spanish *n.* espagnol
spank *v.* fouetter, mouiller
spanking *n.* douille, pile, ratatouille, rincée, roussequette **give a whipping or spanking** piquer le moulin
spare *v.* esquiver, épargner **spare o.s.** se ménager
spark *n.* béluette, étincelle **spark plug** PLUG
spark *v.* étinceler
sparkle *n.* étincelle
sparkle *v.* briller, petiller, étinceler, flamber
sparkling *adj.* brillant, éclatant
sparrow *n.* moineau, pape, petit-moineau, petit pape, petit quiquisse, ti-gris, titisse, yankee
sparse *adj.* clair
sparsely *adv.* à gros grain
spatula *n.* palette
spawn *v.* jeter son lait
spay *v.* arranger
speak *v.* adresser, causer, parler, s'adresser **speak again** reparler **speak coarsely** parler en grosses lettres **speak contemptously** bagueuler **speak diplomatically** dire en taille douce **speak foolishly** lâcher des folies {bêtises} **speak frankly** parler en termes **speak incomprehensibly** bagouler, jargonner **speak incorrectly** parler croche **speak loudly** parler fort **speak rudely** parler en grosses lettres **speak thick** parler gras **speak well** placer bien ses mots **speak badly of** mépriser **speak critically of** écraser **speak French badly** parler français comme un Chinois **speak ill of** parler mal de **speak to s.o.** adresser la parole à qqn **speak true Creole** parler gros nègre **speak banteringly or playfully** bêtiser **speak directly and plainly** pas mettre des gants **speak on the radio** monter sur la radio **speak with a drawl** parler lambin **speak of angels, see their wings** en parlant des anges, on voit leurs ailes **speak in a careful or affected manner** parler en termes **speak of the devil, see his face** en parlant de la bête, on lui voit la tête **so to speak** pour ainsi dire **if you speak ill of others, it comes back to haunt you** crache dans l'air, ça tombe sur le (bout du) nez **be unable to speak because one has forgotten what one wanted to say** se noyer dans son (propre) crachat **not be embarrassed to speak** pas avoir la langue dans la poche **one who tries unsuccessfully to speak standard French** javion **one who speaks English but not French** gueule rouge **person of any origin who speaks Cajun French** Cadien
speaker *n.* orateur, parleur **English speaker** Anglais **English speaker who is not of French descent** Américain
speaking *n.* parole **way of speaking** parlage, parlement **in a manner of speaking** en façon de parler **have a fine style of speaking** avoir beau parlement
spear *v.* darder
special *adj.* espécial, exprès, spécial
specialist *n.* spécialiste
specialize *v.* se spécialiser
specially *adv.* spécialement
specialty *n.* spécialité
species *n.* genre *pl.* **group of closely related species** famille
specific *adj.* particulier
specimen *n.* SAMPLE

speck *n.* bourrier **fly speck** chiure de mouche
speckle *v.* matacher
specklebelly *n.* oie nonnette, z-oie câille
speckled *adj.* barosse, basané, guiné, mataché, pigarlé, taqueté, gingas, pivelé
spectacle *npl.* **spectacles** bernique, lunettes, verre
spectator *npl.* **spectators** audience
speech *n.* adresse, parlage, parlement, parler, parole, raison, voix **incomprehensible speech** bagoul, jargon **figure of speech** expression **manner of speech** raison **uneducated, illiterate speech** cape-cape **make an address or speech** adresser
speed *n.* ardeur, SPEED, train, vitesse **reduce speed** calmer **full speed ahead** tout SPEED **at full speed** (à) (la) bride abattue, à la pleine course **at top speed** la queue raide
speed *v.* SPEED
spell *n.* condjo, gris-gris, ouanga, série, voudou **spell of rain** série de pluie **spell of good weather** série de beau temps **cold spell** frète **dry spell** chesseresse **evil spell** voudou **fainting spell** défaillance, évanouissement **magic spell** ouanga **weak spell** faillitude **cast a spell** mettre {faire} un gris-gris, passer un coundja (à qqn) **cast a spell on** donner un coundja à, faire un condjo contre, gris-gris, mettre un condjo sur **put a spell on s.o.** condjo **have a weak spell** se sentir faille, venir faille **get over a pouting spell** se débouquer *pl.* **one who casts spells** candjateur, ouangateur
spell *v.* espeler
speller *n.* espeleur
spelling *n.* épelage
spend *v.* caler, garrocher, dépenser, mettre, passer, se passer **spend everything** se casser à la maille **spend the evening** faire une soirée **spend the night** coucher, faire la veillée **spend a sleepless night** passer la nuit blanche, passer une nuit à la plaille **spend the winter in one's seasonal home** camper **with the intention of spending the night** à la veille **said of a person who spends much on clothing and little on food** dos brillant et ventre criant
spender *n.* **big spender** haleur d'argent
spendthrift *adj.* gaspillard
spendthrift *n.* dépensier, gavagneur, haleur d'argent
spent *adj.* mort
spice *v.* assaisonner **spice up** assaisonner
spicy *adj.* enragé, fort, piquant
spider *n.* araignée **spider web** fil d'araignée
spike *n.* carvelle
spill *v.* jeter, verser **spill out** débouler, déboulir
spin *v.* bouliner, faire le métier, filer, tournailler **spin on one's toes** pirouetter **spin thread, yarn, or string** filer
spinach *n.* épinard
spinal *adj.* **spinal meningitis** fièvre à vingt-quatre heures **sever the spinal cord** nerfer
spindle *n.* fuseau
spine *n.* rein, reintier, épine, piquant
spineless *adj.* **spineless, weak, wishy-washy person** poule mouillée
spinning *n.* tournement **spinning wheel** métier, roi, rouette
spinster *n.* vieille fille
spiny *adj.* épineux
spirit *n.* courage, feu, lutin, âme, élan, esprit, feu follet **spirit which changes its shape** bétaille caille **evil spirit** gris-gris **party spirit** partisanerie *pl.* **in high spirits** en gingue **crush the spirits of** défaire
Spirit *n.* **Holy Spirit** le Saint Esprit, Saint-Esprit
spirited *adj.* animé, fringant
spiritual *adj.* spirituel
spit *n.* crachat **spit and skewer** broche **put on a spit** embrocher **take off of a spit** débrocher
spit *v.* cracher **spit again** recracher **spit repeatedly** crachailler **spit up** recracher **spit here and there** crachailler **matter that has been spit up** crachis
spite *n.* **in spite of** malgré **in spite of it all** malgré tout **out of spite** par rancune
spiteful *adj.* haïssable, malintentionné, rancuneux
spitful *n.* brochée
spitting *n.* crachement
spittle *n.* crachis, salive
spittoon *n.* crachoir
splash *onom.* ouarjoujoum, poutchoume
splash *v.* éclabousser **splash around in shallow water** patauger
spleen *n.* rate
splendid *adj.* carabiné, magnifique
splendidly *adv.* magnifiquement
splice *v.* laminer
splint *n.* latte **put in a splint** latter
splint *v.* latter
splinter *n.* échappe, écharde, épine
split *adj.* craqué, fendu, fêlé
split *n.* fendasse, fendure
split *v.* craquer, fendre, se diviser, se fendre, tiller **split again** refendre **split up** se délaisser, se séparer **split one's sides laughing** se fendre les côtés à rire **split apart by pulling on the legs of** écuisser **tool to split posts** herminette
spoil *v.* barbouiller, catiner, cochonner, gâcher, gâter, pourrir, ruiner, se gâter **cause to spoil** pourrir
spoilage *n.* pourriture
spoiled *adj.* chéti, gâté, pourri **spoiled by** gâté par (qqn) **act like a spoiled child** faire le gâté
spoiling *n.* gâterie
spoke *n.* rais, ranche
sponge *n.* éponge
sponge *v.* **sponge off** éponger **wipe or sponge** torcher
sponging *adj.* abuseur

spongy *adj.* pongeux
sponsor *n.* parrain
spook *n.* revenant
spool *n.* bobine, fuseau, rouleau **spool or reel used to put string in skeins** travouil
spoon *n.* cuillère, micoine **coffee spoon** cuillère à café **measuring spoon** mesure **serving spoon** cuillère à lait **soup spoon** cuillère à manger, cuillère à table **wooden spoon** micoine **flat wooden spoon** pagaille, palette *pl.* **measuring spoons** cuillères à mésure
spoonful *n.* cuillerée
sport *n.* **sport field** terrain du jeu
sport *v.* **sport around** faire des manigances **sport fine clothes** farauder
sportfishing *n.* **sportfishing competition** rodéo
spot *n.* balafre, placard, place, tache, tache **bald spot** batture **ink spot** barbot **tight spot** pétrin **swollen spot on the skin** loupe **soft spot on the top of an infant's head** fontaine **bruise or spot on skin** placard **put on the spot** tirer une patate chaude (à qqn) **settle in a spot** camper **having a white spot or star on the forehead** luné *pl.* **covered with liver spots** masqué
spot *v.* matacher, se tacher, tacher
spotflower *n.* **creeping spotflower** herbe à crapaud rouge
spotless *adj.* propre
spotted *adj.* barosse, basané, caille, gingas, guiné, mataché, pivelé, taqueté
spouse *n.* légitime, époux **deceased mate or spouse** son défunt / sa défunte
spout *n.* **rain spout** dalle
sprain *n.* foulation, foulure **sprain in the back** forçure
sprain *v.* fouler, refouler, s'éhancher, se fouler
spray *v.* SPRAY, médeciner
sprayer *n.* **pressurized sprayer** pompe
spread *n.* tenture
spread *v.* détasser, pomper, s'épailler, s'éparer, se développer, épailler, éparpiller, étendre, semer, écartiller **spread out** s'étaler, tendre, épailler, éparer, étaler, étrier **spread on bread** beurrer **spread one's legs** s'éjarer **spread the thighs of** écuisser **spread powdered brick on floors to scour and clean them** briquer **trouble spreads like wild fire** le feu est pris dans la paille jaune {grande paille}
spreading *n.* épaillage, écartage, écartillage
spree *n.* pente **drinking spree** bamboche, biture, boumlala, guinnegue, topette **drunken spree** bacchanale, ribote, soûlerie **go on a drinking spree** faire {prendre / se foutre} une biture
spring *n.* fontaine, printemps, ressort, SPRING, source **spring water** eau de source **spring shrimping season** saison de mai **in the spring** au {en} printemps / dans le printemps
spring *v.* **spring back** rebondir
springy *adj.* rebondissant, élastique
sprinkle *v.* mouillasser **sprinkle or dredge with flour** enfariner **sprinkle with any powdery substance** poudrer **sprinkle with flour or meal** fariner
sprinkler *n.* **garden sprinkler** arrosoir **lawn sprinkler** arrosoir
sprinkling *n.* arrosage, arrosement **fine sprinkling** poudrerie
sprite *n.* lutin
sprout *n.* bourgeon, formance, poussant, pousse *pl.* **Brussels sprouts** choux de Bruxelles
sprout *v.* bourgeonner, germer **cause to sprout** faire sourdre
spruce *v.* **spruce up** relever
spruced *adj.* **spruced up** requinquiné
spry *adj.* animé, leste, requinquiné, vif
spryly *adv.* vivement
spur *n.* ergot, racatcha, éperon **road or railroad spur** branche
spur *v.* coffrer, éperonner, piquer aux éperons **spur with the heel** talonner
spurge *n.* **creeping spurge** herbe mal nommée **spotted or blotched spurge** petit pourpier
spurn *v.* **spurn, reject, or break up with a suitor** donner son {un} capot (à qqn)
spurt *n.* **any sudden move or spurt** estampique
spurt *v.* pisser, voler
sputtering *n.* baribara
spy *n.* espion, espionneur
spy *v.* **I spy** raspaille
spying *n.* espionnage
squabble *n.* chamaille, chamaillerie **insignificant squabble over trifles** bataille à coups de chapeau
squabble *v.* chamailler, se chamailler, se disputailler
squalid *adj.* galeux
squall *n.* bourrasque **squall cloud** grain
squander *v.* bambocher, gaspiller, gavagner, saganer, savaner
squanderer *n.* bambocheur
squandering *adj.* gaspillard
squandering *n.* gaspillage, gaspille
square *adj.* carré, carré **make square** équarrer
square *n.* carré **carpenter's square** pied-de-roi / pied-du-roi, équerre
square *v.* équarrer
squash *n.* ciblème **crookneck squash** cacha, chouquechi, coucroche
squash *v.* aplatir, écraser
squashing *n.* écrasement
squat *v.* s'accroupiller, s'accroupir, s'agrouer
squatting *adj.* accroupi
squaw *n.* taïque
squawk *v.* cacasser
squeak *v.* grincher
squeamish *adj.* douillet, zirou
squeeze *v.* pincer, presser, serrer **squeeze juice** épurer **squeeze tightly** souquer
squid *n.* calamar
squint *v.* bicler l'œil, bigler

squinting *adj.* **make a squinting, grinning face** grincher
squirm *v.* débattre comme un chat dans l'eau bénie, fertiller, jigailler, se débattre comme le diable dans de l'eau bénite {un bénitier}
squirrel *n.* écureuil **flying squirrel** écureuil volant **go squirrel hunting** aller aux écureuils
stab *v.* coffrer, couper, engarocher un couteau, nerfer, poignarder
stable *adj.* stable **not mentally stable** pas bien plombé
stable *n.* écurie
stack *n.* berge, pile, pilot, veilloche **pile or stack** quinte *pl.* **put in stacks or piles** veillocher
stack *v.* corder, empiler, empiloter, STACK, mulonner **stack up** veillocher
stacked *adj.* cordé
staff *n.* personnel **staff or rod for surveying or leveling** jalon **bed staff** bâton à {de} lit
stage *n.* degré
stagecoach *n.* diligence
stagger *v.* baranquer, caracoler, gringoler, tricoler, tricoter
staggers *n.* **blind staggers** maladie tournante
stagnant *adj.* mort
stagnate *v.* pourrir
stain *n.* placard, tache *pl.* **causing stains** tachant
stain *v.* se tacher, tacher
staining *adj.* tachant
stainless *adj.* **made of stainless metal or aluminum** brillant
stair *n.* **stair railing** garde-fou *pl.* **stairs** escalier
staircase *n.* escalier
stake *n.* gage, gageure, mise, perche, pique, piquet, poteau, péline, rance, tuteur, rame **drive a stake** planter un piquet {poteau} **support with a stake** ramer **put up as a stake in gambling** gambler *pl.* **play a game of chance for stakes** gambler
stake *v.* abutter, ramer
stale *adj.* rassis
stalk *n.* bâton, coton, pied **stalk of grass** pied d'herbe **cotton stalk** bâton de coton **top of sugar cane stalk** faît de canne à sucre *pl.* **corn stalks** canne de maïs **thin out sprouts at the roots of corn stalks** bourgeonner
stall *n.* écurie
stallion *n.* garrion, potre, égaron, étalon
stalwart *adj.* **stalwart person** poteau du coin
stamina *n.* **have a lot of stamina** avoir pas de rate
stammer *v.* balbuter, barboter, berdouiller, bégayer
stammerer *n.* bégayeur
stammering *adj.* bégayeur
stammering *n.* baribara, bégaiement
stamp *n.* estampe, marque, STAMP, étampe
stamp *v.* pétriner, étamper, piétiner **stamp on** piétiner **stamp with the feet** tapocher **stamp noisily with the feet** talonner
stamping *n.* pilotage, étampage
stance *n.* position
stand *n.* STAND, tréteau, STAND **flower stand** jardinière **fruit stand** fruit-stand **grove or stand of oak trees in an otherwise treeless swamp** chênière
stand *v.* braquer, se mâter, STAND, voir **stand good** se mettre bon pour **stand up** faire (sa) belle, se regricher **stand by o.s.** faire chicot **stand by oneself** faire belle **stand o.s. up** se planter **stand on end** regricher **stand up straight** dresser, mâter, redressir, se redressir **stand up to** regricher **stand in the way** nuire **stand on one's head** planter (le) chêne **stand or go bail** servir de caution {cautionnement / CO-SIGN} **stand s.t. up again** remâter **stand up on hind legs again** se remater **stand or sit on its hind legs by itself** faire le beau **unable to stand pain or sickness** ganache
standing *adj.* debout, sus-pied **standing straight up** grand debout **remain standing** se tenir debout
standing *n.* **lower one's dignity or moral standing** s'abaissir
standstill *n.* **come to a standstill** arrêter
stanza *n.* verset
staple *n.* crampe, piton **wire staple** braquette
star *n.* étoile **shooting star** comète, étoile filante **having a star or white mark between the eyes** lunette **having a white spot or star on the forehead** luné *pl.* **see stars** voir bleu
star-of-Bethlehem *n.* **star-of-Bethlehem plant** étoile de Bethléhem
starboard *n.* bord à droite
starch *n.* amidon, manioc **uncooked starch** manioc
starch *v.* amidonner
starching *n.* amidonnage
stare *v.* **stare at** fixer avec les yeux, louquer, piger, raviser, reluquer **stare intently** flamber des {les} yeux **stare longingly at** rincer ses yeux **woman who stares** reluqueuse
start *n.* commencement, entrain, partance **head start** partance **new start** recommencement **give a start** jumper, ressauter **make a start** faire un entrain, se mettre en train **get a new start** recommencer **make a new start** faire une nouvelle partance
start *v.* commencer, entamer, faire des démarches, faire ressourdre, faire sourdre, monter, originer, ouverre, partir à, partir, prendre, assaisonner **start again** recommencer, reprendre **start up** partir **start out again** repartir **start running after** pointer la course par derrière (qqn) **start up again** repartir **start things off badly** se lever sur le mauvais pied **let's start** allons s'y mettre **help s.o. start a venture** donner une partence (à qqn)
started *adj.* **started again** repris **getting started is the hardest part of a project** cinq sous commencent la piastre
starter *n.* levain, STARTER
starting *prep.* **starting in** à prendre de
startle *v.* interboliser, ébarouir
starve *v.* **starve to death** crever de faim **one who is starving** crève-faim
starving *adj.* affamé

state *n.* condition, état, état **state court** cour d'état **state representative** représenteur de l'état **state of alarm** alarme **reach a state** être rendu

State *npl.* **United States** États-Unis

state *v.* reclamer **state one's mind or intention** se déclarer

statement *n.* déclaration **any official statement by a judge** jugement

station *n.* poste, station **station agent** agent de tickettes {gare} **gas station** station d'huile, station de gaz **railroad station** dépôt, gare **television station** station **radio broadcasting station** station

station *v.* poster **station o.s.** se poster

statue *n.* statue

stature *n.* taille **man of short stature** raboustin, ragoton **person of short stature** raboron, riquiqui **person of small stature** gribouille, grillot

stave *n.* doube **barrel stave** douelle **roof stave** merrain

stay *n.* caravane, séjour

stay *v.* abutter, cadrer, planter (le) chêne, reposer, rester, se coller, se plaquer, tenir **stay alive** rester en vie **stay awake** veiller **stay away** se mettre à côté, se tenir à côté, tenir **stay back** rester en arrière **stay behind** rester en arrière **stay overnight** faire la veillée **stay at home** cabaner, rester chez soi, se cabaner **stay cooped up** se cabaner **stay with it** lâche pas la patate, rester avec **stay in the city** rester en ville **stay out all night** coucher au serein **stay for a long time** camper, se camper **stay up and watch over** veiller **one who stays a long time, esp. one who overstays his or her welcome** campeur

staying *n.* **staying up late** veillerie

steady *adj.* régulier, égal **go steady with** fréquenter

steak *n.* morceau de viande, STEAK **round steak** ROUND STEAK **seven steak** numéro sept

steal *v.* empocher, faire une passée, friper, grappiller, happer, marronner, pirater, s'accrocher, siffler, soulever, voler **steal again** revoler **steal away** s'esquiver **steal from s.o.** mettre le grappin (sur qqn)

stealing *adj.* voleur

stealing *n.* coquinerie, vol **be prone to stealing** avoir des grands doigts

stealthy *adj.* **in a sneaky or stealthy way** à la sourdine

steam *n.* STEAM, vapeur **steam engine** machine à vapeur

steamboat *n.* bateau à vapeur **one who operates a locomotive or steamboat engine** ingénieur

steel *n.* acier **tool steel** acier **flint and steel** batte-feu

steep *adj.* à pic

steeple *n.* clocher, aiguille

steer *n.* bœuf, caïac

steer *v.* courir, diriger, gouverner, guider **steer o.s.** se conduire

steering *n.* **steering wheel** roue

stem *n.* coton, manche, tige, bâton, devant **pipe stem** tuyau de pipe **stub of the stem on a gourd-like plant** coquille

stench *n.* puanteur, puantise

step *n.* démarche, pas, escalier, marche **carriage step** marchette **take one step forward and two steps back** faire un pas en avant et deux en arrière **span of a step** jambée *pl.* **steps** escalier **take steps** faire des démarches

step *v.* marcher, piler **step across** enjamber **step aside** se haler à côté **step forward** pas avançant **step over** enjamber, jamber **step in animal feces** se couper **step on the gas** agiter **step randomly and carelessly** piloter

step-ladder *n.* échelle-double

stepbrother *n.* beau-frère, demi-frère

stepdaughter *n.* belle-fille

stepfather *n.* beau-père, popa d'élève, père levier

stepmother *n.* belle-mère

stepparent *npl.* **stepparents** beaux-parents

stepsister *n.* belle-sœur, demi-sœur

stepson *n.* beau-fils, gendre

sterile *adj.* **sterile man** homme clair

sterilizer *n.* **sterilizer for canning** encanneuse

stern *n.* babord, derrière **stern cable** reculoire

stew *n.* daube, fricadouille, fricassée, fricot, ragoût, étouffée de viande, fricassée **stew made from pork stomach** fricassée de la panse **stew made of Irish potatoes** madeleine **stew made of organ meat** bouilli **beef stew** fricassée de viande **cowboy stew** grillades **fish stew** courtbouillon **kidney stew** étouffée de rognons **liver stew** étouffée de foie **potato stew** ragoût de patates **thick stew** ratatouille **highly seasoned stew** rémoulade, sauce piquante **organ meat stew** grillades, sauce de débris **make a stew or hash with** ragouiller **highly seasoned fish stew** bouillabaisse **pork organ meat stew** fricassée de cochon

stew *v.* fricasser

stewpan *n.* casserole

stick *n.* baguette, bois, bâton **stick pin** épinglette **stick of gum** galette de gomme, palette de gomme, palette **stick used to beat the washing** battoir **walking stick** canne **a stick with a kind of bolt on the end** bâton boulon **stout stick tipped with iron, formerly used as a walking stick** bangala **sharp, pointed stick** pique **beat with a stick** bâtonner, passer à coups de bâton **blow with a stick** coup de bâton **burning log or stick** tison *pl.* **the sticks** fardoche

stick *v.* coller, fourrer, jaquer, piquer, planter, se coller, piquer **stick o.s.** se piquer **stick out** dépasser **stick with** caracoler **stick o.s. with** se planter **stick with glue** coller **stick in the mire** embourber **stick or prick repeatedly** piquailler **stick with a knife** engarocher un couteau **stick with a pointed instrument** darder **stick one's nose in other people's affairs** méler son grain de sel **one hair that sticks up and refuses to lie in place** mauvaiseté

sticker *n.* piquant **sticker bush** éronce *pl.* **get covered with brambles or stickers** s'éroncer

sticky *adj.* collant, gommeux, siroté **become sticky** s'engommer **make sticky** collanter, engommer **any sticky or syrupy material** goudron

sticky-fingered *adj.* filou

stiff *adj.* raide **stiff neck** torticolis **person with stiff manners** pain de sucre

stiffen *v.* raidir

stiffness *n.* **eliminate numbness or stiffness** dégourdir

stifle *v.* pâmer

stifling *adj.* étouffant

stile *n.* jambette

still *adj.* assogné, tranquille **be still** faire poteau

still *adv.* encore, pourtant, toujours

stillborn *adj.* né-mort

stillness *n.* tranquillité

stilt *n.* béquille, échasse **black-necked stilt** avocat, bécasse de marais, bécassine des marais, chien, religieuse, soldat

stimulate *v.* agiter

sting *n.* piqûre

sting *v.* darter, piquailler, piquer

stinger *n.* piquant, dard, dardon, lancette

stinginess *n.* avarice, chicheresse, chichetesse, chicheté

stinging *adj.* piquant

stingray *n.* poisson dardeur, terre **little stingray** raiton

stingy *adj.* avare, chacta, chiche, hardi, intéressé, juif, ratapiot, ratché, regardant, TIGHT **stingy man** ratapiot

stink *n.* puanteur, puantise

stink *v.* puer le tigre {chien}, puer

stinking *adj.* puant

stinkpot *n.* tortue musquée, tortue puante

stinky *adj.* puant

stir *n.* grouillement

stir *v.* brasser, remuer, se remuer, tisonner **stir again** rebrasser **stir up** attiser, exciter, se brasser **stir up trouble** faire le ravaud, merdasser

stirred *adj.* **get stirred up** s'exciter

stirring *n.* brassage, brassement **stirring of a pot** brassage de chaudière

stirrup *n.* étrier **stirrup strap** courroie d'étrieux

stitch *n.* cousure, couture, picot, point, maille, point

stitch *v.* piquer

stock *n.* approvisionnement, chicot, chousse, inventaire, matérielle, provision, race, stock, brancard, croix **stock herder** toucheur **stock market** marché **lodging for farm stock** têt

stock *v.* approvisionner, gréer, provisionner **stock up** s'approvisionner, se provisionner

stocking *n.* bas *pl.* **replace shoes or stockings** rechausser

stocky *adj.* foulé

stoke *v.* attiser

stomach *n.* cafa, estomac, ventre, cœur, fale **stomach cramp** crampe d'estomac **stomach prepared as food** panse **stomach of an unweaned calf** grillade à la chique {Chine} **cow stomach** panse de bête **empty stomach** estomac creuse **sour stomach** estomac haigre **upset stomach** vomissement **fourth stomach of a ruminant or its lining** caillette **first cow stomach** panse de bête **stuffed pig stomach** gogue, panse bourrée **upset the stomach** barbouiller le cœur **stuffed and baked pig's stomach** chaudin bourré, chaudin **have eyes bigger than one's stomach** avoir les yeux plus grands que le ventre

stomachache *n.* crampe d'estomac, mal au {de} ventre, mal d'estomac **have a stomachache** avoir mal au ventre

stomp *v.* piloter, talonner, tapocher

stone *n.* caillou, pierre, gravelle **kidney stone** pierre **sharpening stone** pierre à affiler **whet stone** meule **fine-grain sharpening stone** meule douce **chunk or slab of wood or stone** gobe

stool *v.* taller **stool out** entaller

stoop *v.* se baisser, se pencher

stooped *adj.* courbé, croche

stop *interj.* halt

stop *n.* arrêt **stop sign** STOP

stop *v.* abandonner, arrêter, cesser, empêcher, lâcher, planter (le) chêne, quitter, s'arrêter, STOP **stop by** passer **stop o.s.** se reprendre **stop suddenly** planter (le) chêne **stop up** bloquer, boucher, CAP, engorger, PLUG **stop working temporarily** lay-off **stop up a hole** boucher un trou **stop during a fishing or hunting excursion** faire chaudière **make a sign to stop** FLAG

stop-gap *n.* bouche-trou

stoplight *n.* STOP

stoppage *n.* bouchage, cessation, embouchure, engotement, obstruction

stopped *adj.* **stopped up** bouché

stopper *n.* bouchon, cheville, PLUG

stoppered *adj.* bouché

stopping *n.* **stopping up** engotement

storage *n.* **mound of potatoes covered with dirt for storage** butte de {à} patates

store *n.* magasin, SHOP **store twine** corde à marchand **store window** vitrière **store or restaurant** gargote **store or shop** boutique **country store** boutique de campagne, magasin de campagne **dry-goods store** marchandises sèches {secs} **food store** grosserie, magasin de groceries **grocery store** boutique, grosserie, magasin de groceries **hardware store** magasin à ferraille **jewelry store** bijouterie **seed store** magasin de grainage **build o.s. a barn, a store** se bâtir un magasin

store *v.* resserrer **store in mounds** butter

storehouse *n.* magasin

storekeeper *n.* magasinier, teneur de magasin

storeroom *n.* cache-tout

storm *n.* bourrasque, colonne, coup de temps, coup de vent, ouragan, tempête

story *n.* conte, discours, fable, histoire, plancher, raconte, étage **dirty story** conte cochon **life story** vie **long story** catéchisme **side of the story** dicton **tell a long story** chanter des midis à quatorze heures **tell a cock and bull story** chanter des midis à quatorze heures **that's his/her side of**

the story (ça) c'est son dicton *pl.* **stories often designed to make their teller seem interesting** flafla **tell stories** conter des contes {histoires} **tell dirty stories or coarse jokes** dire des cochonneries {saletés / saloperies}

storyteller *n.* conteur de contes, conteur, raconteur

storytelling *n.* racontage

stoup *n.* bénitier

stout *adj.* bien corporé, foulé **become stout** rengraisser

stove *n.* réchaud, STOVE **stove pipe** FLUE **cast-iron stove** fournette **gas stove** STOVE à gaz **kerosene stove** STOVE à coloïe **portable stove** réchaud **wood stove** réchaud à {en} bois, STOVE à {au} bois

straddle *v.* engarocher, enjamber, jamber, achevaler

straight *adj.* aplomb, direct, droite, STRAIGHT **make straight** décrochir

straight *adv.* droite **straight ahead** à pic **straight to** droite **straight up** à pic

straight *n.* séquence

straightaway *adv.* carrément

straighten *v.* dresser, dressir, raidir, redressir **straighten out** dressir, décrochir **straighten up** raidir, ramasser, redresser, se dresser **straighten up again** rarranger

straightforwardly *adv.* carrément

straightness *n.* droiture

strain *n.* forçure **strain in the back** tour dans le dos **be a strain** chauffer

strain *v.* couler, forcer, haler, se forcer

strainer *n.* couloir, crible, passette, tamis **milk strainer** passe-lait

straining *n.* filtration, coulage

strait *npl.* **be in dire straits** être dans la dernière extrémité

strand *n.* cordon *pl.* **pull or shake apart the strands of in order to fluff and clean them** émousser

strand *v.* s'échouer

strange *adj.* baroque, bizarre, curieux, drôle de, drôle, original, suspect, étrange **strange or eccentric individual** abricot, abricotier **that's strange** ça c'est fort (quand même) **look strange or bizarre** faire drôle **do s.t. strange** perdre son {l'} équilibre **dress o.s. in a strange, gaudy or tacky manner** s'artifailler

strangeness *n.* étrange, dégaine

stranger *n.* étranger *pl.* **in a strange place or among strangers** à l'étrange

strangle *v.* engoter, étrangler **strangle or choke each other** s'étrangler

strangles *n.* gourme

strangling *n.* étranglement

strangulation *n.* étranglement

strap *n.* courroie, STRAP, babiche **strap formerly used on boots and shoes** tire **boot strap** STRAP, tire de botte **cinch strap** cingle, sangle **crupper strap** croupière **razor strap** doucine, STRAP **shoulder strap** bricole, épaulette **stirrup strap** courroie d'étrieux **tie or leather strap for tying two oxen together by the horns** macorne

strap *v.* **strap on** enfiler

straw *n.* mil, paille, brin **straw hat** chapeau de paille **straw mattress** matelas de paille {paillasse}, paillasse **broom straw** mie de balai **drinking straw** canne, cive, tuyau à boire, tuyau **contents of a straw mattress** paillassée *pl.* **draw straws** tirer (à) la courtepaille

strawberry *n.* fraise **strawberry plant** fraise **strawberry shrub** calicantuce **strawberry soda** pop rouge

stray *adj.* écarté

stray *v.* s'écarter, s'écartiller, s'éloigner

straying *n.* écartage **straying to misplace, lose** écartement

streaked *adj.* bousillé, raisé

stream *n.* bayou, couline, coulée, rigolet, rivière **deep water stream** chenal **bank of a stream that has no levee** bordure

street *n.* rue **main street** grande {grand'} rue, grande rue / grand'rue *pl.* **run the streets** traîner les rues

streetcar *n.* char à l'électricité, char électrique

streetlight *n.* lumière de rue

streetwalker *n.* coureuse, coursailleur

strength *n.* force, nerf, puissance, vigueur, énergie, fortitude **gain strength** se renforcir **lack strength** dériver **lose strength** en perdre, s'amortir **feat of strength** coup de force, tour de force **give new strength or life** ravioter **take on new strength or new life** ravigorer

strengthen *v.* affermir, assolider, conforter, enforcir, fortifier, renforcir **strengthen o.s.** se fortifier

strengthening *adj.* fortifiant, renforcissant **strengthening piece** renfort

strengthening *n.* renforcissement, renforçage

stretch *n.* étendue **at a stretch** affilé

stretch *v.* allonger, s'allonger, s'étendre, élongir, étendre, s'allonger **stretch again** retendre **stretch the truth** déchirer le gingas {ginghat} **stretch out one's hand** allonger la main **stretch a limited amount of food for unexpected company** mettre les petits plats dans les gros

stretcher *n.* wagon **wire stretcher** raidissoir, tend-fil, éridisseuse

strict *adj.* dur, strict, sévère

stride *n.* jambée **take a stride** prendre une jambée

strife *n.* combat, débat

strike *n.* coup, STRIKE **go on strike** STRIKE

strike *v.* aborder, assaper, bûcher, battre, bosquer, camper, coffrer, cogner, craquer une tape, emmancher une tape, flanquer un coup, foncer, frapper, maquemose, nioquer, saquer, STRIKE, talocher, taper, tapocher, toquer, cogner, craquer, gratter, sonner **strike again** refrapper **strike a bargain** faire marché **strike it lucky** faire un beau {bon} coup **strike on the head** décoxer **strike with one's shoulder** épauler **strike with the horns** cornailler **strike o.s. or each other**

se frapper **strike s.o. on the forehead** frapper qqn dans le nom du père **strike with the side of the hand** sacrer un coup de main

striker *n.* **striker for triangle** marteau

striking *adj.* impressionnant

striking *n.* frappage, frappement

string *n.* amarre, corde, cordon, ficelle **spin thread, yarn, or string** filer *pl.* **strings** cordage

string *v.* embrocher, enfiler

stringer *n.* broche **stringer hook** alêne **put on a stringer** embrocher **take off of a stringer** débrocher

stringerful *n.* brochée **stringerful of fish** brochée de poissons

stringing *n.* embrochement

stringy *adj.* filant **any stringy material** filasse

strip *n.* lambèche, lichefrippe, lisière, quille, ribondelle *pl.* **tear into strips** ébarbicher

strip *v.* dégréer, dépouiller, se déshabiller **strip o.s.** se dépouiller **strip leaves off of** effeuiller **cut off or strip the branches of** ébrancher

striped *adj.* bariolé, barreauté, à barres

strive *v.* se mettre en deux, se casser en deux

stroke *n.* apoplexie, STROKE **have a stroke** empoigner un STROKE **on the stroke of** sur le coup de (minuit)

stroke *v.* frotter **stroke o.s. or each other** se frotter

stroking *n.* frottage, frottement

stroll *n.* marche **go for a stroll** se promener

stroll *v.* berlander, flânailler, flâner, marchailler

strong *adj.* fort comme un bœuf {le diable / un éléphant / la mort / un mulet / un cheval}, fort, gaillard, hardi, massif, puissant, robuste, solide, un coquin de, vigoureux **grow strong** se fortifier **not yet be strong enough** pas avoir de rein encore

strong-box *n.* coffre-fort

stronger *adj.* **become stronger** renforcir **get stronger** s'enforcir **grow stronger** renforcir, se renforcir **one who thinks he's better or stronger than others** taureau

strongest *adj.* **the strongest or toughest of a group** le taureau sur le côteau {la butte}

strongly *adv.* fort

strop *n.* **leather sharpening strop** lime

struck *adj.* frappé **struck down with sickness** frappé d'une maladie

structure *n.* bâtisse **wooden structure** boisure

struggle *n.* combat, débat, débattement, lutte **death struggle** combat de la mort

struggle *v.* débattre, se débattre **struggle to get out of a bad situation** se débattre comme le diable dans de l'eau bénite {un bénitier} **said of a child who struggles or fights** un diable dans un bénitier

strum *v.* gratter

strut *n.* guette *pl.* **erect struts or supports for construction** bloquer **install the wooden struts in a wall** bâtonner

stub *n.* bougillon

stubble *n.* chicot **stubble and grass in a field after harvesting** glaine **beard stubble** chicot **rice stubble** chaume, chicots de riz **sugar cane stubble** chicot de canne **first- / second- / third-year sugar cane stubble** premier / deuxième / troisième chicot

stubborn *adj.* braqué, buté, entêté, obstineur, obstiné, rétif, tête dûre, têtu **stubborn person** bourrique, caouane, tête dûre **stubborn as a mule** entêté comme un mulet **be stubborn** avoir une tête de caïman, s'entêter **very stubborn** tête dure comme un bourriquet

stubbornly *adv.* **act stupidly or stubbornly** faire la bourrique

stubbornness *n.* entêtement, obstination

stuck *adj.* collé **stuck in one spot** campé comme un as de pique **stuck in the mud** embourbé **stuck like a leech** collé comme un sangsue **be stuck** être fourré **get stuck** caler **be stuck up** avoir le nez rapiqué **be stuck with** être enfoncé avec **get stuck in the mud** embourber, s'embourber

stud *n.* étalon **stud horse** égaron **stud mule** JACK

student *n.* écolier, élève, étudiant

study *n.* étude *pl.* **college or university studies** collège

study *v.* faire des études, étudier **man who studied to be a priest but failed to be ordained** prêtre manqué

stuff *n.* bastringue, matière **cheap stuff** pacotille

stuff *v.* bourrer, corbier, corder, enfourner, farcir, fourrer, bourrer, dauber **stuff and mount** usiner **stuff with garlic** piquer à l'ail **stuff o.s. with food** se bourrer **stuff using a funnel** entonner

stuffed *adj.* farci **stuffed with garlic** piqué à l'ail

stuffiness *n.* oppressement, oppression

stuffing *n.* bourrage, far, bourre, bourrure **stuffing box** botton, glande

stuffy *adj.* accablant, étouffant

stumble *v.* buter, se buter

stumbling *n.* butage

stump *n.* boscoyo, chousse, paleron, chicot, moutchon, moyeu

stump *v.* bafouer

stun *v.* abasourdir, décoctionner, ébarouir, étourdir, détervioler **stun o.s.** s'étourdir

stunned *adj.* épivardé **be stunned after a blow** voir bleu

stunning *adj.* étourdissant

stunning *n.* étourdissement

stunt *n.* tour de force **crazy or bizarre stunt** tour de lune

stupefy *v.* abasourdir

stupid tchu

stupid *adj.* bête, bigot, biorque, braque, bétasse, bête comme ses pieds {un bourriquet / un cabri / un cheval / un chou / un poteau de coin / une bête à cornes / une bête à chandelles / une cruche / une djogue / une z'oie / trente-six chous dans un sac}, bête à coucher dehors {manger de l'herbe / pincer l'herbe}, coucou, couillon comme la lune {un bourriquet / un cheval}, couillon, craque-bine, emplâtre, estropié de la tête / estropié de cervelle, fafa, idiot, imbécile, sot comme un panier percé, sot, stupide, évargandé **stupid fellow** patassa **stupid person** brut, chiqueur de lavettes grasses, sot **stupid thing** couillonade **stupid or foolish person** zinzin **stupid, dull, heavy person** bûche **act stupid or foolish** faire le bête **be as stupid as the moon is high** être aussi bête que la lune est haute **be too stupid to empty a chamber pot** être trop bête pour vider un pot de chambre

stupidity *n.* bêtise

stupidly *adv.* **act stupidly or stubbornly** faire la bourrique

sturdy *adj.* massif, résolu, solide

sturdy *n.* maladie tournante

stutter *v.* balbuter, barboter, berdouiller, bégayer

stutterer *n.* bégayeur

stuttering *adj.* bégayeur

stuttering *n.* baribara, bégaiement

sty *n.* ondure, compère-loriot

style *n.* manière, mode **in style** à la mode **out of style** catchouque **have a fine style of speaking** avoir beau parlement

styling *n.* **manner of styling the hair** coiffage, coiffure, peignure

subdivide *v.* rediviser, subdiviser

subdivision *n.* subdivision

subject *adj.* assujetti, sujet, sujéti

subject *n.* sujet

sublet *v.* relouer

submarine *n.* sous-marin

submerge *v.* caler

submissive *adj.* obéissant **be submissive** se courber

submit *v.* se soumettre **submit an application** mettre une application **submit to authority** fléchir

subscribe *v.* abonner, s'abonner **subscribe to a newspaper** tirer la gazette

subscriber *n.* **become a subscriber** s'abonner

subside *v.* tomber

subsist *v.* exister, subsister, vivre

subsistence *n.* existence **subsistence farmer** habitant

subspecies *n.* race

substance *n.* matière **any fatty substance** graissage **something of value, substance, wealth** de quoi

substantial *adj.* consistant, conséquent

substitute *n.* remplacement, remplaçant

substitute *v.* remplacer

substitution *n.* remplacement

substructure *n.* fondament

subterranean *adj.* souterrain

subtract *v.* débiter

succeed *v.* aboutir, arriver, réussir, se suivre, succéder, suivre **succeed in business** monter en grade **succeed in an examination** passer un examen **give a great effort to do s.t. and not succeed** chier sa crotte de noces

succeeding *n.* **take away s.o.'s chance of succeeding** couper l'herbe à qqn

success *n.* bonheur, prospérité, réussite, succès

successful *adj.* **be successful** réussir

succession *n.* affilée, défilé, succession, suite **in succession** affilé

succomb *v.* craquer

succumb *v.* succomber

such *adj.* **such and such** tel et tel / telle et telle **such as that** pareil **as such** comme tel

such *adv.* si tellement

suck *v.* sucer

sucker *n.* sucette **all-day sucker** suce

suckle *v.* sucer, téter, nourrir

suckling *n.* **suckling pig** cochon de lait, tcho-tcho

sucrose *n.* sucrose

sudden *n.* **all of sudden** tout d'un coup **all of a sudden** tout d'un coup, tout d'un(e) secousse

suddenly *adv.* d'un but en blanc, subit, subitement, tout d'un coup

suds *npl.* **soap suds** savonnure

sue *v.* mettre en cour / mettre devant la cour, poursuivre **sue each other** se poursuivre

suet *n.* **mutton suet** graisse de mouton

suffer *v.* agoniser, misérer, pâtir, soufferre, subir **suffer torments** soufferre des martyres **suffer the consequences** soufferre les conséquences, subir les conséquences **suffer through a difficult experience** danser la carmagnole **suffer misery or a hard time with** passer du bleu de ciel avec qqn, soufferre du bleu de ciel avec **one who suffers in health** pâtira

suffering *adj.* douleureux, esclopé, escran, souffrant **suffering from the heat** achalé **be suffering** tirer le diable par la queue **feeling or suffering from the cold** frilant, frileux

suffering *n.* douleur, souffrance, supplice **experience suffering** voir (du) bleu **endure intense suffering** voir (du) bleu

suffice *v.* faire, suffire **it suffices** suffit que

suffocate *v.* s'asphyxier, étouffer

suffocating *adj.* étouffant

suffocation *n.* étouffement

sugar *n.* sucre **sugar bowl** sucrier **sugar cane** canne **sugar mill** moulin à sucre, sucrerie **sugar refinery** raffinerie de sucre, sucrerie **sugar teat** chique **sugar cane factory** sucrerie **sugar cane field** champ de canne **sugar cane juice** jus, vin de canne **sugar cane mill** moulin à canne **sugar cane stubble** chicot de canne **browned sugar** caramel **carmelized sugar** brûlot **powdered sugar** sucre en poudre **lump of sugar** bosse de sucre **top of sugar cane stalk** faît de canne à sucre **crush and grind sugar cane** rouler les cannes **employee of a sugar factory** sucrier **first- / second- / third-year sugar cane stubble** premier / deuxième / troisième chicot **drink made of milk poured over carmelized sugar** café au lait

sugar *v.* sucrer

sugar-cane-carrier *n.* porteuse

sugarberry *n.* **sugarberry tree** bois connu {inconnu}
sugarcoat *v.* siroter
suggest *v.* proposer **hint or suggest** mettre la puce à l'oreille (à qqn)
suggestion *n.* suggestion
suicide *n.* suicide **commit suicide** se détruire, se prendre la vie, se tuer **one who commits suicide** suicide
suit *n.* ensemble, habit, SUIT **bathing suit** rechange de bain **follow suit** fournir **swimming suit** SUIT à {de} bain / sot-à-bain **file suit against** mettre en cour / mettre devant la cour **light-colored or light-weight summer suit** zinzin
suit *v.* aller, arranger, faire
suitable *adj.* applicable, commode, convenable, disable, FIT **be suitable** convenir
suitcase *n.* cabas, valise
suite *n.* entourage
suitor *n.* cavalier, courtiseur, prétendant, vieux nègre
sulk *v.* bouder, faire la baboune, faire une {la} babine / faire des babines, se bouquer
sulkiness *n.* **facial expression of displeasure or sulkiness** babiche
sulking *adj.* boudé, bouqué
sulking *n.* boude, bouderie
sulky *n.* sulky
sully *v.* saganer, sagouiller
sulphur *n.* soufre
sum *n.* montant, somme
summer *n.* été **Indian summer** été des Indiens **in the summer** en été / dans l'été
summertime *n.* été
summit *n.* faît
summon *v.* appeler **summon by calling** hucher
summons *n.* appel, notice **court summons** notice
sun *n.* soleil **setting sun** soleil baissant **the risen sun** soleil levé / soleil-lever **the rising sun** soleil levant **put or hang in the sun** mettre au soleil
sun *v.* soleiller **sun o.s.** se soleiller
sunbathe *v.* se soleiller, soleiller
sunbonnet *n.* bonnet, garde-soleil
sunburn *n.* coup de soleil
Sunday *n.* dimanche, sabbat **Easter Sunday** Jour de Paques **Palm Sunday** petites Pâques **pertaining to Sunday** dominicale **put on one's Sunday best** se farauder
sunfish *n.* grande gueule **sunfish often locally called perch or sun perch** patassa
sunflower *n.* soleil
sunglasses *npl.* conserve
sunken *adj.* accablé **sunken eyes** yeux creux **sunken in** encavé
sunlight *n.* clarté, soleil **be bright sunlight** faire beau soleil **expose to sunlight** soleiller **expose to full sunlight** mettre au beau soleil
sunny *adj.* beau
sunrise *n.* levée du soleil, soleil levé / soleil-lever **at sunrise** soleil levé / soleil-lever
sunset *n.* soleil couché / soleil-coucher
sunshine *n.* soleil
sunstroke *n.* coup de soleil
sup *v.* souper
superintendent *n.* superintendant
superior *adj.* extra, supérieur **mother superior** mère **show o.s. as outstanding or superior** gagner le sucre
supernatural *adj.* supernaturel
superstition *n.* superstition
superstitious *adj.* superstitieux
supervise *v.* guetter, surveiller **one who supervises or watches** surveillant
supervision *n.* surveillance
supervisor *n.* gérant **poll supervisor** pollier
supper *n.* souper **supper party** fricot **eat supper** souper **eat for supper** souper
supple *adj.* agile, souple **supple in movement** leste
supplejack *n.* liane noire
supplementary *adj.* extra
suppleness *n.* agilité
supplied *adj.* **well supplied** loqué
supply *n.* approvisionnement, provision
supply *v.* approvisionner, fournir **supply o.s.** s'approvisionner **supply with provisions** provisionner
support *n.* accotement, appui, chandilier, soutien, support, tuteur **support beam** solive, soliveau **support block** pilier **support for vining plants** berceau **support pier under a house** bloc **give support** soutenir, supporter **political support** support **shaft support** étrier **structural support post** poteau **means of support** vie *pl.* **erect struts or supports for construction** bloquer
support *v.* abutter, appuyer, BACK, cadrer, caler, encourager, soutenir, supporter, soutenir, supporter **support with a stake** ramer **support o.s. or each other** se soutenir
suppose *adv.* aussi bien que
suppose *v.* figurer, supposer **let's suppose that** supposant
supposed *adj.* fameux **be supposed** être supposé de
supposedly *adv.* soi-disant, supposé
supposing *n.* **supposing that** mettons {mettant} que **supposing it is the case that** supposant
supposition *n.* conjecture
suppurate *v.* suppurer
sure *adj.* assuré, certain, en effet, positif, sûr **sure enough** comme de fait, en effet **sure thing** certaineté **sure as hell** foutrement **be sure** ma foi! **for sure** pour sûr, sûrement **make sure** s'assurer, se rassurer **to be sure** assuré
surely *adv.* sûr, assurément, bien sûr, certainement, positivement, sûrement
surety *n.* sûreté
surface *n.* top, vernis, faît
surface *v.* sourdre

surfeited *adj.* tanné
surgeon *n.* chirurgien
surly *adj.* ROUGH
surmount *v.* surmonter
surname *n.* nom de famille / dernier nom
surpass *v.* battre, BEAT, surmonter, surpasser
surplus *adj.* extra
surprise *n.* surprise, étonnement **by surprise** en traître **catch by surprise** poigner **expression of surprise or dismay** Bon Dieu seigneur {saignable} **exclamation of surprise, pleasure or disgust** pou-yaille **expression of surprise, impatience, or hopelessness** sapristi **expression used to show surprise, irritation or anger** fils de chien {garce / putain} / fils de putain de bordel {garce}, fils de monstre {pistache / poteau} / fils de poteau de barrière **expression of anger, pain, or surprise** (que le) tonnerre m'écrase!, tonnerre, mes chiens
surprise *v.* interboliser, poigner, saisir, surprendre, étonner **surprise o.s.** s'étonner, se surprendre **surprise each other** se surprendre
surprised *adj.* surpris **be surprised** s'étonner
surprising *adj.* surprenant, étonnant
surrender *v.* se délivrer, se livrer
surrey *n.* barouche **fringed surrey** barouche à frange
surround *v.* cerner, encercler, entourer **surround o.s.** s'entourer
surrounding *n.* encerclement, voisinage *pl.* **surroundings** entourage, environs
surveillance *n.* surveillance
survey *v.* arpenter **survey with a toise** toiser
surveying *n.* arpentage **triangular surveying device made of three pieces of wood and measuring six feet at its base, formerly used to survey land in arpents** toise
surveyor *n.* arpenteur, ingénieur civil **surveyor's level** niveleur
survive *v.* survivre, passer
susan *n.* **black-eyed susan** téton de négresse
susceptible *adj.* susceptible
suspect *v.* se douter, se méfier, suspecter
suspended *adj.* à la pendille {pendriole}
suspender *npl.* **suspenders** bretelle, bricole **pair of suspenders** bricole
suspense *n.* **leave s.o. in suspense** laisser (qqn) suspendu
suspicion *n.* doutance, doute
suspicious *adj.* méfiant, suspect **be suspicious of** suspecter **make suspicious by one's words** mettre la puce à l'oreille (à qqn) **person of whom one must be suspicious** soupçonneur
sustain *v.* subir
sustainable *adj.* soutenable
sustaining *adj.* renforcissant
sustenance *n.* pain, soutien
suture *n.* cousure
swallow *n.* gorgée, hirondelle **barn swallow** oiseau de pluie **sea swallow** pigeon de mer *pl.* **any of a variety of swallows or martins** martinet
swallow *v.* caler, envaler **swallow hurriedly** engueuler **swallow up** engloutir
swallowed *adj.* **be swallowed** s'envaler
swallowing *n.* envalage, envalement
swamp *n.* bassière, ciprière, marais, pays bas, platin, rabasilière, SWAMP **cypress swamp** ciprière, marécage **treeless swamp** mèche **elevated land in a swamp** côteau *pl.* **worker in the swamps** swampeur
swampy *adj.* **swampy, woody area that is not easily accessible** portage
swan *n.* cygne **whistling swan** cygne
swap *n.* changeotage
swap *v.* brocanter, changeoter, faire (un/une) barguine (avec), échanger
swapper *n.* **horse swapper** changeur de chevaux
swapping *n.* brocantage
swarm *n.* dessaim, fourmillière
swarm *v.* pulluler
swathe *v.* barligoter
sway *v.* ballotter
swayback *n.* dos-fond
swaybacked *adj.* cargué
swaying *n.* balan
swear *v.* faire serment, jurer, sacrer, sermenter, témoigner **swear at** jurer **swear not to do s.t. again** faire la croix **one who curses or swears** jureur
swearing *n.* serment
sweat *n.* sueur, transpiration, transpire
sweat *v.* suer, transpirer **sweat profusely** suer comme un bâtard à une réunion de famille / suer comme un nègre à la messe / suer comme les Ponce
sweater *n.* jersey, SWEATER, tricot
sweating *n.* transpiration
sweep *n.* **clean sweep** débâcle, raclage **make a clean sweep** bâcler, racler
sweep *v.* balayer **a new broom sweeps clean** tout nouveau, tout beau
sweeper *n.* balayeur **mechanical sweeper** balayeuse
sweeping *n.* balayage **do the sweeping** faire le balayage *pl.* **sweepings** balayures, fatras, nettéyeurs
sweet *adj.* doux comme (le doux dans) le miel, doux, mielleux, NICE **sweet things** douceur **become sweet** s'adoucir **excessively rich or sweet** acœurant
sweet *n.* friandise *pl.* **sweets** douceur, doux
sweetbread *n.* ris
sweeten *v.* adoucir, doucer, sucrer **sweeten again** radoucir
sweetened *adj.* doux
sweetening *adj.* adoucissant

sweetening *n.* adoucissage, adoucissement
sweetgum *n.* **sweetgum tree** arbre à gomme
sweetheart *n.* amant, amoureux, beau, belle, cavalier, chinane, GIRLFRIEND, maouine, catin, chouchoute
sweetness *n.* douceur
sweetshrub *n.* **common sweetshrub** calicantuce
swell *v.* enfler, gonfler, grossir, s'enfler **swell again** regonfler, se regonfler **swell up** bouffir, se gonfler **swell up again** regonfler, se regonfler
swelling *n.* bosse, boussole, enflure, gonflage, gonflure, tumeur **swelling around a fingernail or toenail** poussant **reduce swelling** dégonfler **reduce the swelling** désenfler **provoke or cause bumps or swelling of skin** louper
swerve *n.* virage, écart
swerve *v.* barder, fourcher
swerving *n.* virage, écart
swift *n.* **chimney swift** oiseau (de) cheminée **house swift** oiseau de maison
swig *n.* **take a swig** boire un coup {filet}
swill *n.* ramassis
swim *n.* nage
swim *v.* nager, se baigner **swim nude** se baigner à la plie
swimmer *n.* nageur
swimming *n.* à la nage **swimming flipper** nageoire **swimming suit** SUIT à {de} bain / sot-à-bain **go swimming** baigner
swindle *v.* couillonner, mettre dedans, passer une jambette (à qqn)
swindler *n.* croche, fraudeur
swine *n.* **throw pearls before swine** donner de la confiture aux cochons
swing *n.* balan, balance, galance **swing bar** palonnier *pl.* **subject to mood swings** journalier
swing *v.* ballotter, bercer, galancer, se balancer **swing o.s.** se galancer
swinging *n.* ballottement **swinging motion** balan **walk with arms swinging** marcher démanché
swingle-bar *n.* bacul, barconcu, palonnier
swingletree *n.* palonnier
swingtree *n.* palonnier
swipe *v.* agrapper, friper
swirl *n.* tourbillon
switch *n.* baleine, fausse queue, SWITCH **electric switch** SWITCH **railroad switch** SWITCH
switch *v.* SWITCH **switch off** fermer
switching *n.* switchement
switchman *n.* switcheur
swollen *adj.* enflé, gonfle, gonflé **become swollen** s'enfler **become less swollen** se désenfler
swollenness *n.* nocoyau
swoon *n.* défaillance, évanouissement **fall into a swoon** tomber en botte
swoon *v.* venir faille, évanouir
sword *n.* glaive, sabre **double-edged sword** couteau à deux tranchants
swordfish *n.* espadron
sycamore *n.* cotonnier, langue de femme, liard
symbol *n.* emblème, symbole
sympathetic *adj.* compatissant, sympathique
symptom *n.* signe de maladie, symptôme
synthetic *adj.* **not synthetic** naturel
syphilis *n.* maladie de sang / mauvaise maladie, mauvais sang
syringe *n.* seringue
syrup *n.* melasse, sirop **syrup mill** sucrerie **add syrup** siroter **cane syrup** sirop de batterie **open-kettle syrup** sirop de batterie **thick syrup** toffé **cover with syrup** siroter **thick cane syrup drawn just before the syrup crystallizes into sugar** cuite **crystallized sugar cane syrup** masse-cuite
syrupy *adj.* siroteux **any sticky or syrupy material** goudron
system *n.* système **nervous system** système nerveux

T

Tabasco *n.* Tabasco
tabernacle *n.* tabernacle
table *n.* table **table fork** fourchette **table knife** couteau de table **table salt** sel de table **table saw** table à scie **dressing table** toilette **operating table** table d'opération **pool table** table de POOL **writing table** DESK **set the table** mettre la table **sit at the table** se mettre à (la) table
tablecloth *n.* couvert de table, nappe de table, nappe, nappille, nappillon
tableful *n.* tablée
tablespoon *n.* cuillère à manger, cuillère à table, grand cuillère
tablespoonful *n.* grande cuillerée
tablet *n.* cahier, tablette **medicine tablet** tablette **writing tablet** tablette d'écriture
tableware *n.* vaisselle
taciturn *adj.* taqué
tack *n.* broquette
tack *v.* faufiler
tackily *adv.* **tackily or gaudily dressed** tchifaillé
tackle *n.* **block and tackle** poulie
tacky *adj.* cachoupic, cadien, catchouque, collant, criard, mardi gras, tchinque-tchinque **dress in a gaudy, flashy, or tacky way** attriquer, s'attriquer **dress o.s. in a strange, gaudy or tacky manner** s'artifailler
tactic *n.* tactique
tadpole *n.* gorgoyo, goéland

taffy *n.* candi de maison

tag *n.* TAG, ticket, chatte **price tag** ticket **game of tag** TAG

tail *n.* queue **hollow tail** queue creuse **lizard's tail** herbe à malo **turn tail** fouiner **having a golden or tan coat and a white or cream-colored mane and tail** baille

tailbone *n.* nez du pretre {de l'éveque}

tailor *n.* couturier, tailleur

taint *v.* gâter

take *n.* prise

take *v.* amener, grappiller, poigner, prendre **take after** prendre après {sur}, tenir de **take along** ramasser, s'amener **take apart** défaire, défropter, démancher, démonter, écharpiller **take away** ôter **take back** ramener, reporter, reprendre **take down** descendre **take everything** racler **take in** rapetisser **take o.s.** se prendre **take off** ôter, dégainer, retirer, sacrer le camp, tirer **take on** assumer, prendre **take out** ôter, retirer, sortir **take over** prendre, s'accaparer, s'emparer **take precautions** prendre des sûretés **take stealthily** empocher **take up** enlever, monter **take apart again** redéfaire **take down again** redescendre **take for o.s.** s'approprier, se prendre **take s.t. hard** prendre dur **take up again** reprendre **take up for** soutenir **take apart a pile** décorder **take back and forth** trafiquer **take o.s. out of** s'arracher **take s.o. for s.t.** prendre qqn pour qqch **take up for s.o.** prendre pour qqn **take all the winnings in** roqueter **take out of a nest** dénicher **take part in a race** tirer une course **take coffee from the pot before it is done brewing** tricher sur la grègue **you take what you can get** si on peut pas téter maman, il faut téter mémère **it takes one to know one** chien mord chien

taker *n.* **census taker** compteur

taking *n.* **taking apart** dégréement **taking root** enracinement

tale *n.* conte, fable, histoire, projet, rapport **tale bearer** rapporteur **tall tale** conte, menterie *pl.* **bear tales** rapporter **carry tales** cancaner, porter des paquets **tell tales** conter des contes {histoires} **teller of tall tales** conteur de menteries

tale-bearer *n.* porte-paquet

talebearer *n.* chipoteur

talent *n.* génie

talented *adj.* au fait

talk *n.* adresse, cancanage, causade, causerie, conversation, parlement, parlure **foolish talk** radote **frivolous talk** barbotage **idle talk** charade, charaque, parlementages, radotage, radote, radotement **light-hearted talk** barbotage **private talk** tête à tête **senseless talk** charaque **make idle talk** radoter **foolish, useless, incessant talk** bagueulage **prone to slanderous or scandalous talk** mépriseur

talk *v.* causer, charlanter, charrer, converser, jabloter, parler **talk about** parler de {dessus / après / pour} **talk deliriously** déparler **talk endlessly** parler à l'en plus finir, radoter **talk excessively** bagueuler, battre sa gueule, cacasser **talk excitedly** faire des (grands) hélas **talk idly** ramancher **talk meaninglessly** rachanter **talk much** quiaquer **talk randomly** battre la berloque **talk silly** blaguer, dire des bêtises {farces} **talk unintelligently** baranquer **talk wildly** battre la berloque **talk a lot** charader, flafla, parler un tas, pas avoir la langue dans la poche **talk bad about** médire **talk to o.s.** se parler **talk too much** avoir la langue trop longue, se noyer dans son (propre) crachat **talk unintelligible drivel** ramancher **talk without restraint** avoir le filet coupé **talk behind s.o.'s back** parler en dessous **talk endlessly about s.t.** en faire tout un chapitre **talk much about nothing** en flanquer **talk on and on** chanter des midis à quatorze heures **talk to each other** se parler **talk in a senseless manner** fifoler **talk out of one's mind** baranquer **talk in a rapid, staccato fashion** parler comme du tac-tac **talk to in a soothing way** emmioler **talk at the top of one's voice** parler à tue-tête / parler à pleine tête **talk on without getting to the point** se noyer dans son (propre) crachat **talk loudly and endlessly, the point of being annoying** tapager **refuse to talk** se bouquer après **there's nothing more to talk about** au boute le boute **one who talks a lot** causard **one who talks too much** radoteur **not know what one is talking about** être pas aux noces **one who talks much but does little** grand parleur et petit faiseur

talkative *adj.* bagueulard, bavard, bavardeur, charrant, charreur **talkative nuisance** nénaine **talkative person** bagueulard, bagueuleur, bavard, bavardeur, charreur

talker *n.* bagueulard, causeur, charreur, parleur **big talker** causeur, embarrateur **excessive talker** flafla **sweet talker** gueule douce **big talker and little doer** défonceur d'une porte ouverte / défonceur de porte(s) ouverte(s) **be a big talker** pas avoir la langue d'amarrée

talking *n.* charade **stop talking** fermer sa bouche, fermer son grabot, se boucher

talking-to *n.* **stern talking-to** catéchisme, colle **give a good talking-to** foutre une pourgale (à) **give a stern talking-to** fourgailler

tall *adj.* grand, haut

tallow *n.* graisse de mouton, suif **sheep tallow** suif de mouton **Chinese tallow tree** olivier **full of tallow** suifeux **rub with tallow** suiffrer

tallow *v.* suiffrer

tally *interj.* **tally ho** taïaut

talon *n.* griffe *pl.* **seize with claws or talons** griffer

tame *adj.* docile, dompte, doux, à (la) main **become tame** s'adoucir, s'apprivoiser

tame *v.* adoucir, apprivoiser, dompter

tameable *adj.* apprivoisable

taming *adj.* adoucissant

taming *n.* adoucissage, adoucissement, apprivoisement

tamp *n.* refouloir

tamp *v.* bourrer, fouler, pilonner, éteindre

tamper *n.* pilon, refouloir

tamper *v.* bêtiser

tamping *n.* bourrage, foulage, pilonnage
tan *adj.* **yellow or tan colored** barosse
tan *v.* se brunesir, tanner
tanager *n.* **scarlet tanager** pape Natchitoches
tangle *v.* emmêler, entortiller, nouer **tangle up** mêler **tangle with s.o. or each other** s'accrocher
tangled *adj.* **tangled up in** mêlé dans **get tangled** s'empêtrer, se nouer **get tangled up** s'emmêler, s'entortiller **cause to be tangled up** empêtrer
tangling *n.* entortillage
tank *n.* TANK **butane tank** TANK à butane **clarifying tank** clarifieuse **gas tank** TANK à gaz **military tank** TANK
tanned *adj.* tanné
tannery *n.* tannerie
tanning *n.* tannage
tantrum *n.* crise
tap *n.* apostrophe, fausset, robinet
tap *v.* apostropher, tapocher, tarauder
tape *n.* **tape recorder** récordeur **adhesive tape** plaisse, TAPE **audio tape** ruban, TAPE **bias tape** biais **magnetic tape** ruban **measuring tape** mesure, TAPE **put on tape** mettre sur le TAPE
tape-record *v.* mettre sur le TAPE
tapestry *n.* tapisserie **tapestry worker** tapisseur **hang wallpaper or tapestry** tapisser **hanging wallpaper or tapestry** tapisserie
tapeworm *n.* ver solitaire
tar *n.* BLACKTOP, goudron **pine tar oil** huile de goudron **smear with tar or glue** goudronner **smear o.s. with glue, tar, or a similar substance** se goudronner
tare *n.* liserine
target *n.* but **target in the shape of an animal** pategau
tariff *n.* tarif
tarnish *v.* détamer, se ternir, ternir
tarnished *adj.* **become tarnished** se ternir **become worn, faded, discolored, or tarnished** détamer
tarpaulin *n.* prélat, tarpoline, toile cirée
tarpon *n.* grand-écalle, tarpon
tarragon *n.* estragon
tarring *n.* **tarring and feathering** emplumage
tart *adj.* hâcre
tart *n.* tarte
tartar *n.* **cream of tartar** crème de tartre
task *n.* job, ouvrage, placard, tâche **do a task that serves no purpose** mettre de la boucane en sac **do a task that requires great effort but accomplishes nothing** vider la mer avec un baril défoncé
tassel *n.* frange, gland *pl.* **corn tassels** barbe de maïs
tasseled *adj.* à franges
tasso *n.* tasso
taste *n.* goût, goûtée, penchant **bad taste** mauvais goût **good taste** bon goût **in bad taste** mardi gras **in poor taste** cadien **recover one's taste** se rengoûter **dress in poor taste** s'habiller mardi gras **dressed in poor taste** dégainé, déguénillé *pl.* **person with unrefined or uncouth tastes** dauiaut
taste *v.* goûter **taste like** avoir goût de **taste of** goûter
tasting *adj.* **bad tasting** chéti
tasty *adj.* appétissant, mangeable
tat *v.* tatiner
tatter *n.* ribondelle *pl.* **shreds in tatters** en tierlambèches
tatter *v.* haillonner
tattered *adj.* dévaporé, haillonné, dégainé **become tattered** se défiloper
tatting *n.* tatine **do tatting** tatiner
tattle *v.* dire sur, rapporter
tattler *n.* chipoteur
tattletale *n.* chipoteur, porte-paquet, rapporteur
taunt *v.* narguer
taut *adj.* **get taut** se tendre
tavern *n.* cabaret
taw *n.* joueuse
tax *n.* impôt, tarif, taxe **tax collector** collecteur **sales tax token** brozine **collection of a tax** prélèvement d'un impôt
tax *v.* assesser, taxer
taxable *adj.* taxable
taxi *n.* taxi
taxicab *n.* taxi
taxpayer *n.* payeur de taxes
tea *n.* thé, tisane **herbal tea** thé, tisane **mamou tea** thé de mamou **medicinal tea** thé, tisane **sassafras tea** thé de sassafras **thistle tea** thé de chardon **bay leaf tea** thé de laurier
teacake *n.* petit gâteau sec
teach *v.* apprendre, enseigner, faire l'école, instruire, montrer, remontrer, renseigner, TEACH **teach the gospel** évangéliser **woman who teaches children their catechism in French** montreuse de catéchisme
teacher *n.* enseignant, enseigneur, instructeur, maîtresse, montreur, professeur **school teacher** maître d'école **primary school teacher** maîtresse d'école
teaching *n.* doctrine, enseignement, renseignement
teakettle *n.* casserole, teakettle
teal *n.* sarcelle **blue-winged teal** printanière, sarcelle aile bleue, z-aile bleue **green-winged teal** canard congo, congo, petit congo, sarcelle aile verte, z-aile vert **green-winged teal duck** sarcelle **northern teal / winter teal** sarcelle de nord / sarcelle d'hiver **summer, fall / spring teal** sarcelle d'été / sarcelle automnière / sarcelle printanière
team *n.* TEAM **team leader** Capitaine Souris, capitaine **harnessed team** TEAM **track team** TRACK
teaming *adj.* **be teaming with** bouillir de
tear *n.* accroc, déchirure, larme, raccroc *pl.* **burst into tears** se désoler **be on the verge of tears** avoir un cœur lourd, à contre cœur
tear *v.* déchiquenailler, déchirer, déralinguer, tiller, tirer **tear**

down casser, débâtir, déchirer, défaire, démonter **tear off** arracher, déchirer, dégabiller **tear out** arracher **tear up** déchirer, dérater, haillonner **tear down masonry** démaçonner **tear into strips** ébarbicher **tear one's clothing** se déchirer **tear to pieces** casser en douelles, écharpiller, étirailler, étriper **tear or mangle one's flesh** s'évianner **tear or mangle the flesh of** évianner

tearing *n.* déchirage **tearing out** arrachage **tearing hair out** échevelage

tease *n.* attineur

tease *v.* agacer, appeler des {les} noms, attiner, bêtiser, chamailler, faire (de) la misère (à qqn), narguer, picasser, picocher, pignocher, taquiner, tchincailler, tisonner

teaser *n.* attineur

teasing *adj.* brigand

teasing *n.* taquinerie

teaspoon *n.* cuillère à thé

teaspoonful *n.* petite cuillerée

teat *n.* mamelon, trayon, tétine, téton, tété, tête **sugar teat** chique

teddy *n.* **teddy bear** catin de l'ours

teem *v.* pulluler

teeming *adj.* bouillant, dru

teeth *n.* **brush one's teeth** se brosser les dents

teethe *v.* percer ses dents

teetotaler *n.* buveur de lait

telegram *n.* télégramme **send a telegram** télégrapher

telegraph *n.* télégraphe

telegraph *v.* télégrapher

telephone *n.* téléphone **telephone line** ligne **telephone pole** poteau à lumière **telephone wire** fil de téléphone **answer the telephone** répondre au téléphone

telephone *v.* appeler, téléphoner

television *n.* T.V., télévision **television program** SHOW **television set** télévision **television station** station **cable television** câble

tell *v.* conter, dire, faire acconnaître, raconter, ramancher **tell again** redire **tell jokes** bêtiser, faire des farces **tell lies** conter des menteries, mentir **tell on** dire sur **tell stories** conter des contes {histoires} **tell tales** conter des contes {histoires} **tell dirty jokes** dire des cochonneries **tell s.o. off** donner un cataplasme à qqn, faire un chapelet à qqn, lire un catéchisse à qqn, passer un cataplâme à qqn **tell a cock and bull story** chanter des midis à quatorze heures **tell dirty stories or coarse jokes** dire des cochonneries {saletés / saloperies} **tell s.o. to go to hell** envoyer qqn à la promenade {à la merde}, envoyer se cacher / envoyer se faire foutre **tell s.o. what you think of him or her** mettre au pas **you can't tell me what to do** t'es pas maître ici

teller *n.* diseur **teller of tall tales** conteur de menteries **fortune teller** prédicateur, somnambule, tireur de bonne aventure, tireuse de cartes **joke teller** farceur

temerity *n.* témérité

temper *n.* colère **lose one's temper** regricher **have a bad temper** avoir une colère prime **make s.o. lose his temper** faire pouf

temper *v.* **temper one's remarks** mettre de l'eau dans son vin

temperament *n.* tempérament

temperamental *adj.* **temperamental person** sac à tous grains

temperature *n.* température

tempest *n.* tempête

temple *n.* brancard, bras de lunette, tempe

tempt *v.* tenter

temptation *n.* tentation

tempting *adj.* appétissant, tentable

ten *n.* dix **group of ten** décade **quantity of about ten** dizaine

tenable *adj.* soutenable, tenable

tenant *n.* locataire **tenant farmer** tenant

tend *v.* soigner, galoper **tend to** voir à

tendency *n.* instinct, tendance **have a tendency** se porter à / être porté à

tender *adj.* sensible, tendre

tender-hearted *adj.* **be tender-hearted** avoir le cœur tendre

tenderize *v.* attendrir

tenderly *adv.* tendrement

tenderness *n.* tendresse

tendon *n.* tendon **cut the tendon of the hind leg** nerfer

tendril *n.* vrille

tennis *n.* tennis **tennis ball** tennis **tennis court** tennis **tennis racket** tennis **tennis shoe** tennis **tennis shoes** soulier en élastique

tent *n.* tente **live in a tent** tenter

tenth *n.* dixième

tepid *adj.* quède **become tepid** quédir

tepidity *n.* quiédeur

term *n.* terme, terme *pl.* **come to terms** s'arranger **on friendly terms** bras dessus bras dessous **negotiate the terms of** amarrer **on bad terms with s.o.** en bisbille avec qqn **not on speaking terms** brouillé, divorcé, en querelle **be on bad terms or at odds** être en divorce

terminate *v.* finir, terminer

terminus *n.* dépôt

termite *n.* fromi blanc, termite

tern *n.* **Cabot's tern** pigeon de mer **Forster's tern** pigeon de mer, queue à ciseaux

terrace *n.* terrasse

terrace *v.* terrasser

terrain *n.* terrain

terrapin *n.* **diamondback terrapin** caret, tortue noire

Terrebonne *n.* **person from Terrebonne Parish** Terrebonnier

terrestrial *adj.* terrestre

terrible *adj.* abominable, affreux, condamnable, indigne, terrible, épouvantable **terrible person** criminel **look terrible** ressembler le diable avant jour

terribly *adv.* affreusement, affreux, terriblement
terrified *adj.* épouvanté
terrify *v.* effrayer, terrifier
terrifying *adj.* terrifiant
territory *n.* territoire **Indian territory** territoire des Indiens
terror *n.* frayeur, peur, terreur, épouvantaille, épouvante
test *n.* essai, examen, test, épreuve **pass a test** passer un examen **take a test** passer un examen **put to the test** mettre à l'épreuve
test *v.* expérimenter, faire épreuve, passer à l'examen, sonder, éprouver **test o.s.** s'essayer **test out** expérimenter **test the limits of** mettre à l'épreuve
testament *n.* testament **last will and testament** testament
tester *n.* ciel de lit
testicle *n.* canique, couille, pelote, roupette, testicule *pl.* **testicles** graine **injure the testicles of** écouiller
testify *v.* testifier, témoigner
testimony *n.* déposition, témoignage
testing *n.* essayage, sondage
tetanus *n.* tétanos
Texan *adj.* texien
Texan *n.* Texien
textile *n.* drogue
texture *n.* grain
than *conj.* que
thank *v.* remercier **thank God** grâce à Dieu, merci Bon Dieu **thank you** merci, tata **thank you very much** merci beaucoup
thanks *npl.* remerciement **thanks to** chance à, grâce à **thanks a lot** bien merci **many thanks** bien merci, grand merci, merci bien
thanksgiving *n.* remerciement
Thanksgiving *n.* fête des dindes
Thanksgiving Day *n.* le Jour de Remerciement
that *adj.* ce
that *conj.* que
that *pron.* cela, que, qui, ça-là(-là), ça, celui **that which** ce que, ce qui, ça que, ça qui **that's it** c'est ça, ça y est **about that** là dedans **after that** ensuite, puis **in that** là dedans **on that** là-dessus **it's like that** c'est comme ça **this and that** ci et ça, un et l'autre
thaw *v.* dégeler, déglacer, fondre **thaw out** dégeler, déglacer
the *art.* le
theater *n.* théâtre **movie theater** maison de SHOW, SHOW
theft *n.* vol
their *poss.* eusse, leur, lotre
them *pron.* eux-autres, eux, le, yeux **for them** leur **of them** en **to them** le, leur
themselves *pron.* se
then *adv.* alors, après, d'abord, donc, ensuite, là, puis, voir, ça fait **till then** en attendant **until then** en attendant
there *adv.* là-bas, là, y **there are** il n-a / in'a, il y a / il n-a, il y a, voilà **there is** il n-a / in'a, il y a / il n-a, il y a, voilà **there's no way** il y a pas (de) moyen de {pour} **from there** en **in there** là-dedans, là dedans **on there** là-dessus **over there** là-bas, par là **right there** droite là **under there** là-dessous **well there** mais là! **here and there** bord ici bord là, de bric et de brac, ici et là **out of there** en
there *interj.* tiens
thereafter *adv.* après
therefore *adv.* donc, par conséquence, ça fait
thermometer *n.* thermomètre
these *adj.* ce
these *pron.* celui, ceux-là / ceux-là-là / ceux-là-ici / ceux-ici
they *pron.* eux-autres, eux, ils, on, ça
thick *adj.* dru, épais
thicken *v.* épaissir
thickening *n.* épaississement
thicker *adj.* **become thicker** s'épaissir
thickness *n.* épaisseur
thief *n.* coquin, malhonnête, pillard, voleur **treat as a thief** traiter de voleur
thieve *v.* marronner
thievery *n.* coquinerie, filouterie
thieving *adj.* filou, grappilleux, voleur
thigh *n.* cuisse, hanche, jarret **the thigh of fowl** gros de cuisse *pl.* **spread the thighs of** écuisser
thimble *n.* dé **open-ended sewing thimble** verge
thin *adj.* fin, fini, maigre comme une aigrette {un pique-bois / un tasso} / maigre comme une vieille vache / maigre comme un manche à balai {un poteau de barrière}, maigre, maigréchine, mince, méchant, plate, élingué, clair **thin and weak** fluet, gningnin **thin, long-legged man** quinze-côtes **thin, shriveled, emaciated person** rapapiote **become thin** maigriller, maigrir **grow thin** fondre **wear thin** défiler
thin *v.* amincir, délayer **thin out** amincir, éclaircir **thin out sprouts at the roots of corn stalks** bourgeonner
thing *n.* affaire, chose, machin, machine, maniguette, objet, être **one thing and the other** un et l'autre **be a difficult thing** être une affaire **it's a good thing that** une chance (que) / chance **if it's not one thing, it's another** si c'est pas les maringouins, c'est les chouboulures *pl.* **things change** la roue tourne **old things** vieillerie **do things slowly** calimaçonner **have things easy** être à son aise **mess things up** brasser mer et larmes **of two things or people** l'un vaut l'autre et l'autre vaut rien / l'un vaut l'autre et les deux vaut rien **all kinds of things** toute qualité d'affaires **all sorts of things** hourra d'affaires, toute qualité d'affaires **have a million things to do** avoir quatre cent cinquante mille choses à faire **have too many things to do** brûler la chandelle aux deux bouts **do all sorts of things** faire les quatre cents coups
thingamajig *n.* chose, machin, machine, maniguette
think *v.* croire, jongler, penser, réfléchir **think about** considérer, contempler, guetter, jonglailler, jongler à {après / pour /

sur}, jongler **think again** repenser **think alike** avoir tous leur tête dans le même bonnet **think of** jongler à {après / pour / sur} **think so** penser **think up** imaginer **think of o.s.** se croire **think over again** repenser **think highly of o.s.** se suffire **think much of o.s.** en flanquer **think to myself, yourself, etc.** penser entre moi-même {toi-même, etc.} **think too highly of o.s.** se croire **that's what you think** ta nenaine est caille! **tell s.o. what you think of him or her** mettre au pas **say what one thinks** parler français

thinker *n.* jongleur, penseur **be a good thinker** avoir (une) bonne idée

thinner *adj.* **make appear thinner** amincir

thinness *n.* finesse, maigreur, minceur

thinning *n.* amincissement **thinning out** éclairissage

third *n.* tiers, troisième *pl.* **sharecrop on thirds** travailler au troisième

thirst *n.* soif **provoke thirst in** altérer

thirsty *adj.* altéré, assoiffé **be thirsty** avoir la pépie, avoir soif **make thirsty** altérer **be hot / hungry / cold / thirsty** avoir chaud / faim / froid / soif

thirteen *n.* treize

thirteenth *n.* treizième

thirtieth *n.* trentième

thirty *n.* trente **about thirty** trentaine

this *adj.* ce

this *pron.* ceci, cela, ça-ici(-là) / ça-icitte(-là), ça-là(-là), ça, celui **this and that** ci et ça, un et l'autre **like this** comme ceci

thistle *n.* chardon, garofier **thistle tea** thé de chardon **sow thistle** laitereau

thong *n.* babiche

thorn *n.* dardon, piquant, épine, épique **thorn bush** garofier

thorny *adj.* piquant, épineux

thoroughly *adv.* bien, finiment

those *adj.* ce

those *pron.* celui, ceux-là / ceux-là-là / ceux-là-ici / ceux-ici

though *conj.* donc **even though** malgré que

thought *n.* jonglage, pensée, réflexion **deep thought** jonglerie

thoughtful *adj.* prévoyant

thoughtless *adj.* négligent

thoughtlessness *n.* négligence

thousand *n.* mille, millier **about a thousand** millier

thousandth *n.* millième

thrash *v.* carder, flauber, rincer

thrasher *n.* **brown thrasher** caille de bois, moqueur de canne {bois}, oiseau de cannes

thrashing *n.* brûlée, dandine, douille, dégelée, ramasse, rincée, rinçure, suée, volée **thrashing machine** moulin à battre **give a thrashing** doubler

thread *n.* fil, fil du sept {neuf, douze}, taraud **thread winder** dévideur **thread of white filament sometimes seen floating in the air in spring** fil de la vierge **cotton thread** fil de {en} coton **hanging thread** filasse **loose thread** filasse **spin thread, yarn, or string** filer **uneven thread in woven material** motelon **spool of thread** bobine de fil, fiseau de fil **wool or thread carried by a shuttle** chaîne **roll of wool or cotton thread** rolet **fabric made of cotton warp and woolen thread** jeture *pl.* **threads that cross the warp in a fabric** chaîne **cut threads on** tarauder

thread *v.* renfiler, tarauder, enfaufiler, enfiler

threadbare *adj.* **become threadbare** se défiloper

threat *n.* menace

threaten *v.* menacer

threatening *adj.* menaçant

three *n.* trois **three of a kind** trois de la même qualité

thresh *v.* battre

threshing *n.* battage **threshing floor** batterie **threshing machine** batteuse **threshing of rice** battage de riz

threshold *n.* bas de (la) porte, linteau de porte, passe-porte, soliveau

thrift *n.* ménagement, économie

thrifty *adj.* **be thrifty** serrer, économiser

thriving *adj.* **be thriving** boulotter

throat *n.* gargane, gargoton, gorge, quiqui, gosier **sore throat** mal de gorge **clear one's throat** gratter la gorge, s'excrémer **unclog one's throat** se dégoter **cut the throat of** égorger **take s.o. by the throat** prendre au quiqui **having s.t. caught in the throat** égosillé

throb *v.* battre, lancer

throbbing *n.* battement

throe *npl.* **death throes** agonie de la mort **the throes of death** le dernier supplice

thrombophlebitis *n.* jambe de lait

throne *n.* trône

throttle *v.* étrangler

through *prep.* par, à travers / en travers (de), à travers / en travers (de)

throw *n.* envoyage **throw net** carrelet

throw *v.* envoyer, flanquer, foutre, garrocher, jeter, lancer, sacrer, tirer, voyer **throw away** garrocher, jeter, JUNK **throw down** envaler, foutre, jeter par terre **throw o.s.** s'envoyer, se darder, se flanquer, se garrocher, se jeter, se péter, se tirer **throw on** fourrer, se fourrer **throw out** foutre dehors, jeter à côté, mettre (qqn) dehors **throw quickly** flailler **throw together** garrocher ensemble **throw up** rejeter **throw a punch** garrocher un coup de poing, tirer un coup de poing **throw o.s. down** se jeter par terre **throw away one's fortune** brûler la chandelle aux deux bouts **throw pearls before swine** donner de la confiture aux cochons **throw o.s. out of place** se déranger **throw from one side to another** basculer **throw s.t. back in s.o.'s face** retirer qqch dans la figure à qqn

throwing *n.* lancement

thrush *n.* **speckled thrush** caille pivelée **wood thrush** caille pivelée, coucou, jorée

thrust *n.* élance
thrust *v.* péter
thumb *n.* pouce **between thumb and forefinger** à la pincette
thumbtack *n.* broquette à doigt
thump *n.* pichenet
thunder *n.* orage, tonnerre **thunder clap** coup de tonnerre **holy thunder** sacré tonnerre **roll of thunder** roulement de tonnerre
thunder *v.* tonner
thunderclap *n.* coup de tonnerre
thundershower *n.* grosse orage
thunderstorm *n.* oragan de tonnerre, ouragan, temps bleu
thurible *n.* encensoir
Thursday *n.* jeudi **Holy Thursday** Jeudi Saint
thus *adv.* ainsi, alors, astacot, par ainsi
thwart *v.* **thwart each other** se croiser
thyme *n.* thym
tic *n.* tic
tick *n.* pou **tick fever** fièvre de pou de bois **cattle tick** pou (de) bois, pou de bête **wood tick** pou (de) bois, punaise de bois
tick-tock *n.* tic-tac
ticket *n.* passage, TAG, ticket **lottery ticket** mise **raffle ticket** mise **buy a lottery or raffle ticket** prendre une mise
ticking *n.* couette **mattress ticking** couette de matelas, couétil **pillow ticking** couette d'oreiller
tickle *v.* chatouiller, tatailler
tickling *adj.* chatouillant
tickling *n.* chatouillement
ticklish *adj.* chatouilleux
tidbit *n.* friandise, nanane
tide *n.* bloc, courant, marée **high tide** haute marée *pl.* **area in a salt marsh governed by the tides** mare
tidy *adj.* net, rangé
tidy *v.* **tidy up** propir, ramasser, relever, se décroûter **tidy up again** rarranger
tie *n.* amarrage, amarre, cravate **tie pin** épinglette **tie or leather strap for tying two oxen together by the horns** macorne **saddle tie** bacul, reculoire
tie *v.* amarrer, lier, sortir à jeu **tie on** enfiler **tie up** tortiller
tiger *n.* tigre
tight *adj.* avare, chiche, juste, serré, TIGHT, raide **tight spot** pétrin **get tight** se tendre **pull tight** étirer
tighten *v.* raidir, serrer, tendre **tighten again** resserrer **tighten the mesh links of a trawl net** serrer les nœuds
tightened *adj.* serré
tightening *n.* **tightening of a bolt** boulonnage
tightrope *n.* **tightrope walker** cape-cape
tightwad *n.* avare, chiche
tigress *n.* tigre
tile *n.* **cement tile** ardoise
till *conj.* que
till *prep.* avant, moins, pour
till *v.* cultiver, rabourer
tillable *adj.* arable
tillage *n.* rabourage
timber *n.* bois **heavy timber** gros bois, lambourde, madrier **standing timber** bois debout **undressed timber** log
time *n.* coup, fois, heure, temps **time span** durée **time after time** fois après fois, mainte et mainte fois, à tout moment **time marches on** la roue tourne **time of day** heure **another time** une autre fois **any time** n'importe quand **each time** à chaque coup **in time** à la longue, à temps **it's time** c'est l'heure, c'est temps **kill time** tuer du {le} temps **long time** bel {belle} âge **next time** la prochaine fois **no time** aucun temps **on time** à temps **present time** présent **sowing time** semage **take time** mettre du temps **waste time** badiner, barboter, berdasser, berlander, bêtiser, dandiner, fionner, foutumasser, gournoter, merdailler, siffler dans le vent, soguer, tâtonner **wasting time** berdassement **from time to time** (de) temps en temps, par secousse(s), tous les temps en temps **it's time to go** c'est l'heure qu'on lève la paille **no time at all** aucun temps **it's time to break up the party or conversation** c'est l'heure qu'on casse le rond **a long time** beaucoup de temps, grand-âge, longtemps **all the time** tout le temps, à tout moment **at a time** d'un coup, à la fois **at one time** d'un coup **at that time** dans ce temps-là / dans ce temps ça-là / dans ces temps-ça, en ces temps-là **from the time** dès que / desque / drès que **period of time** élan **rather long time** un bon boute **spend one's time** se passer le temps **take one's time** prendre son temps **waste of time** berdassement **waste one's time** cracher dans le feu, foutumasser son temps, tchincailler **a long time ago** il y a longtemps, il y plusieurs temps passés, longtemps passé **since the time that** du moment que **in no time at all** dans rien de temps **perceive that time moves slowly** trouver le temps long **set a time for an engagement** citer **period of time for a particular activity** saison **at the same time** au même temps **for a long time** il y a longtemps (que) **have a big time** SPORT **have a good time** avoir un {du} bon temps, s'amuser, se chicailler un temps, se coller un temps **have a hard time** avoir un temps dur **in a short time** dans un galop **in my free time** en temps perdu **it is the time** c'est le moment **most of the time** la majeure partie du temps, la moitié du temps, la plupart du temps **short period of time** secousse **take up the time of** occuper **have a hard time of it** haler dessur **have an easy time of it** être à son aise **take a long time doing s.t.** être après manger du patassa **come at an opportune time** s'adonner bien **happen at a bad time** s'adonner mal **it's been a long time** il y a plusieurs temps **not for a long time** pas de sitôt **stay for a long time** camper, se camper **that was a long time ago** ça date du temps d'Artaguette **come at just the right time** s'adonner bien **do s.t. for the first time** avoir son baptême **do s.t. quickly without wasting time** se pas **suffer misery or a hard time**

with passer du bleu de ciel avec qqn, soufferre du bleu de ciel avec **one who stays a long time, esp. one who overstays his or her welcome** campeur **one who fiddles around or wastes time** berdasseur *pl.* **hard times** patocaille **many times** autant comme autant, des fois et des fois, mainte et mainte fois, un tas des fois **the times of abundance are over** le temps à Pascal est fini **at all times** toujours **in olden times** anciennement **so many times** tant de fois

timepiece *n.* horloge

timer *n.* pendule

timid *adj.* craintif, honteux, peureux, timide **be timid** avoir un cœur de poule **be timid, shy, bashful** avoir honte

timidity *n.* timidité

timidness *n.* honte

tincture *n.* **tincture of iodine** teinture

tinder *n.* allume-feu

tine *n.* **harrow tine** dent de herse

tinfoil *n.* brillant

tinker *v.* tripoter

tint *n.* teinture

tint *v.* teindre, teinter

tip *n.* bout, lagniappe, pointe, TIP

tip *v.* **tip over** verser

tipsy *adj.* bite, en boisson, gris, piqué, soûl, tchac, toqué **get tipsy** se tchaquer

tire *n.* TIRE **flat tire** FLAT

tire *v.* abalourdir, achaler, fatiguer, se fatiguer, tanner **tire o.s.** s'échiner **tire out** abîmer, larguer, échiner, éreinter **tire o.s. out** se larguer **one who bores or tires others** assommoir

tired *adj.* fatigué, largue, largué, lasse, terrassé, à bout, échiné, éraillé, impatienté, tanné **tired out** largué, éreinté **appear tired** avoir les yeux égarés **get tired** attraper une touche, larguer, lasser, se donner une touche, se fatiguer, se larguer, se tanner **grow tired** se tanner, tanner **make tired** fatiguer **be tired, asleep on one's feet** dormir debout

tiredness *n.* fatigue

tiresome *adj.* canulant, ennuyant, larguant, lassant **tiresome thing** fatigue **be tiresome** canuler

tiring *adj.* fatigant, larguant, lassant **be tiring** larguer

title *n.* titre **title in addressing certain ministers, Catholic monks or brothers** frère

to *prep.* auprès de, côté, chez, dans, en, envers, pour, vers, à, avant, pour

toad *n.* crapaud

toadfish *n.* crapaud

toadstool *n.* maison de crapaud

toast *n.* pain grillé, TOAST **French toast** pain français, pain perdu **make a toast** trinquer **propose a toast** faire un TOAST

toast *v.* griller

tobacco *n.* chourouque, tabac **tobacco box** tabatière **tobacco pouch** blague, cigalière, parchouesse, tabatière **tobacco smoker** fumeur **tobacco prepared in strips** plateau **chew tobacco** chiquer **chewing tobacco** tabac à chiquer **smoke tobacco** fumer **pinch of tobacco** prise de tabac **plug of tobacco** PLUG **roll of tobacco** torquette **bunch of tobacco leaves** manoque **aromatic black tobacco cultivated in Saint James parish** périque **one who chews tobacco** chiqueur **plug or twist of chewing tobacco** carotte

today *adv.* au jour d'aujourd'hui, aujourd'hui

toddy *n.* todie **hot toddy** todie

toe *n.* orteil **toe cheese** cambouille **toe jam** cambouille **the big toe** le grand {gros} orteil / la grosse orteil *pl.* **spin on one's toes** pirouetter **odorous residue between the toes due to uncleanliness** cambouille

toenail *n.* ongle

toffee *n.* caramel

together *adv.* ensemble **close together** près à près **get together** se mettre ensemble **they are always together** ça porte les mêmes caleçons **these two people are always together** c'est comme Saint Roch et son chien / c'est comme cul et coton de maïs

toil *n.* labeur, travail

toil *v.* travailler

toilet *n.* cabine, cabinet, commode, lieu, toilette **toilet bowl** bol **go to the outhouse or toilet** aller dehors

toise *n.* **survey with a toise** toiser

token *n.* jeton, signe **sales tax token** brozine

tolerable *adj.* passable

tolerate *v.* STAND, supporter **tolerate each other** s'endurer

tolerating *adj.* endurant

toleration *n.* tolérance

Tom *n.* **peeping Tom** voyeur

tomato *n.* tomate **tomato sauce** sauce aux tomates **canned tomato paste** conserve

tomb *n.* tombe, tombeau

tomcat *n.* chat, matou, mâle chat

tomcatting *adj.* **tomcatting man** matou

tomfoolery *n.* canicroche

tomorrow *n.* demain **tomorrow afternoon** demain après-midi **tomorrow evening** demain (au) soir **tomorrow morning** demain matin **tomorrow night** demain (au) soir **day after tomorrow** après demain, surlendemain **a week from tomorrow** demain en huit jours **the day after tomorrow** après-demain

ton *n.* tonne **hit s.o. like a ton of bricks** cogner qqn comme une bol de merde

tonality *n.* clef

tong *npl.* **tongs** pince **fireplace tongs** tire-bbraisesouchon **ice tongs** pinces à glace **oyster tongs** gaffe à main, gaffe

tong *v.* **tong oysters using a gaffe** gaffer des huîtres

tongue *n.* langue, taquet, flèche **tongue of fire** lame de feu **tongue and groove lumber** ceiling **tongue of a tongue-and-groove coupling** languette **coated tongue** langue épais **sharp tongue** langue affilée

tonic *n.* tonique

tonight *n.* asoir / à soir / (à) ce soir

tonnage *n.* tonnage

tonsil *n.* amygdale *pl.* **have one's tonsils removed** faire ôter les amygdales

too *adv.* aussi, itou, trop

tool *n.* instrument, outil **tool steel** acier **tool to split posts** herminette **tool used to carve out pirogues** tille ronde **tool for pressing clothes, branding, soldering, etc.** fer **tool used to insert wooden pegs in construction** clivier **old, worn out tool or machine** fatras *pl.* **tools** affûtiaux, agrès **any of several boring tools** tarière, virebrequin

toolshed *n.* cabane, SHED

tooth *n.* dent **tooth fairy** zombi **tooth of a gear-wheel** alochon **tooth with a cavity** dent creux **baby tooth** caquisse **broken-off tooth** chicot de dent **harrow tooth** dent de herse **milk tooth** caquisse **wisdom tooth** dent de sagesse *pl.* **cut teeth** couper ses dents, percer ses dents **false teeth** dents fausses {postiches} / fausses dents **several teeth in a row** pagée de dents **pick one's teeth** s'écurder, se curer les dents **set of teeth** dentelure **break the teeth of** édenter **crack with one's teeth** croquer **lie through one's teeth** mentir comme un arracheur de dents / mentir comme un dentist, être menteur comme un arracheur de dents **set of false teeth** râtelier **sharp row of teeth of certain fish** peigne **curl the upper lip and show the teeth** rechaner, rechigner

toothache *n.* mal aux dents

toothbrush *n.* brosse à dents

toothcup *n.* herbe tendre

toothless *adj.* édenté

toothpaste *n.* crème pour les dents

toothpick *n.* cure-dent

top *n.* comble, dessus, faît, haut, moine, pardessus, poque, top, toupie **top hat** bidon **top layer** pardessus **top of sugar cane stalk** faît de canne à sucre **top of the day, from 11 a.m. to 1 p.m.** haut du jour **on top** en dessus, en haut, par-dessus **onion top** faît d'oignon, échalote **spinning top** moine, poque, toupie **on top of** en haut (de), en l'air de, par-dessus, sur **from top to bottom** de fond en comble **over the top** par-dessus **at the top of one's voice** à tue-tète **float to the top** sourdre **cut off the top of** faîter *pl.* **onion tops** queues d'oignon

top-notch *adj.* fini

topple *v.* capoter

torch *n.* flambeau

torment *n.* tourment *pl.* **suffer torments** soufferre des martyres

torment *v.* affliger, emmicher, faire (de) la misère (à qqn), martyriser, tourmenter **torment or nag s.o.** être derrière qqn

tormentor *n.* bourreau

torn *adj.* fendu, haillonné **torn piece** ribondelle

tornado *n.* colonne, cyclone, ouragan, tornado, tourbillon, tourbine

torrefy *v.* griller

torrent *npl.* **rain in torrents** mouiller averse / mouiller à verse

torrid *adj.* brûlant

tortilla *n.* **tortilla chip** galette de pain de maïs

torture *n.* supplice, tourment

torture *v.* martyriser, tourmenter

tortured *adj.* **be tortured** soufferre des martyres

toss *n.* envoyage

toss *v.* envoyer, garrocher, jeter, tirer

total *n.* montant, somme

totality *n.* totage

totter *v.* ballotter, caracoler, tricoler, tricoter

touch *n.* touche *pl.* **final touches** finissage

touch *v.* attenir, contacter, toucher, toucher **touch again** retoucher **touch lightly** rifler **touch up** retoucher **touch o.s. or each other** se toucher

touch-me-not *n.* belsamine, herbe honteuse, sainte nitouche

touch-up *n.* **touch-up artist** brosseur du portrait

touching *adj.* joignant, à touché **be touching** toucher

touching *n.* touche

touchy *adj.* chocatif, susceptible, suspect **untouchable or touchy person** sainte nitouche

tough *adj.* dur, résistant **tough guy** péteur **tough and fibrous** dur comme du caïac **tough old man** boscoyo, vieux caïac **be a tough person** avoir la peau dure comme un cocodrie

toughen *v.* durcir, endurcir

toughening *n.* durcissement, endurcissement

toughest *adj.* **the strongest or toughest of a group** le taureau sur le côteau {la butte}

toughness *n.* dureté

tour *n.* tournée **wartime tour of duty** temps de guerre

tourist *n.* touriste

tournament *n.* tournoi

tousled *adj.* chien-fou

tow *v.* haler

toward *prep.* côté, pour, vers

towards *prep.* envers

towel *n.* essuie-mains, serviette **hand towel** essuie-mains

towheaded *adj.* tête baille

towhee *n.* grassel, jorée

town *n.* cité, commune, village **town marshall** constable **in town** en ville **section of town** canton **incorporated area of a town** corporation

toy *n.* bébelle, fronde, joujou **toy baby** titite **toy boat** BOAT

toy *v.* **toy with** user

trace *n.* piste, trace, vestige, trait

trace *v.* tracer, tracer

track *n.* piste, rouin, trace, TRACK **track team** TRACK **race track** TRACK **railroad track** TRACK **wheel track** pente **keep track of** tenir compte **run off track** dérailler **get back on track** regagner son chemin *pl.* **leave tracks on** pistrailler

track *v.* tracer **track up by walking on** pistrailler

tracker *n.* traceur

tract *n.* cours
tractor *n.* machine, TRACTOR
trade *n.* barguine, commerce, métier, trafic
trade *v.* brocanter, faire (un/une) barguine (avec), se barguiner, trafiquer, traider
trader *n.* brocanteur, barguineur, commerçant
tradesman *n.* commerçant
trading *n.* brocantage
tradition *n.* tradition
traditional *adj.* traditionnel
traffic *n.* navigation, trafic **traffic jam** embouteillage
traffic *v.* trafiquer
tragedy *n.* avarie, tragédie
tragic *adj.* noir
trail *n.* trace, traînasse **passage, trail, path, or canal** trace
trailing *adj.* traînant
trailing *n.* **trailing periwinkle** bellesivère
train *n.* char de chemin de fer, char de haleine, char à vapeur, char, gros char, train **train car** traîneau **freight train** char à fret, fret **passenger train** char à passagers **get into a car or train** monter dans un char
train *v.* pratiquer, dresser
trainer *n.* entraîneur, dompteur **breeder or trainer of racehorses** coursier **horse breeder or trainer** maquillon
training *n.* éducation
traitor *n.* félon, traître
tram *n.* char à l'électricité, char électrique
trammel *n.* tramail
trammel *v.* tramailler
tramp *n.* hobo, TRAMP, vagabond
trample *v.* piler, piloter, piétiner, pétriner, talonner, trapigner, pétriner **trample on** fouler sur (qqn)
trampling *n.* pilotage, piétinage, piétinement
tranquil *adj.* calme, tranquille
tranquility *n.* tranquillité
tranquilize *v.* tranquilliser
tranquilizer *n.* calmant, calme
transfer *n.* transfert
transfer *v.* transférer, transmettre
transgress *v.* pécher, violer
transgression *n.* péché
translate *v.* changer les mots, traduire
translator *n.* traduiseur
transmission *n.* transmission, transmission
transmit *v.* envoyer
transom *n.* transmission, transom
transparent *adj.* clair
transplant *v.* transplanter **transplant o.s.** se transplanter **transplant plants** margotter
transplanted *adj.* **be transplanted** se transplanter
transplanting *n.* **slip for transplanting or grafting** bouture
transport *n.* halage, portage **collect for transport** ramasser
transport *v.* charreter, charrier, charroyer, haler, naviguer, transférer, transporter, voyager, amener **transport by waterway** flotter **transport in a pirogue** piroguer
transportable *adj.* transportable
transportation *n.* charroyage, RIDE, transportation **cost of transportation** fret **have no transportation** être à pied **means of transportation** embarcation **mode of transportation** moyen
transporting *n.* roulage
transpose *v.* transposer
transversal *adj.* **transversal bar in rowboats** barre
trap *n.* attrape-mouches / attrape à mouches, attrape, piège, trappe **trap shoot** pategau **bird trap** cage, filet **box trap** cage, caisse **crab trap** cage à crabe(s) **fly trap** attrape-mouches / attrape à mouches **shrimp trap** caisse à chevrette **spring trap** tribuchet **special trap used in seafood fishing** cage **mythical trap or snare against which children were warned** sisi à dents **homemade bird trap** tribuchet **shut your trap** ferme ta gueule **get taken in a trap** se prendre **trigger of a bird trap** bois-malin **tripping device on a trap** marchette
trap *v.* attraper, piéger, prendre, trapper
trapeze *n.* trapèze
trapper *n.* piégeur, trappeur
trapping *n.* attrapage, piégeage, piège **go trapping** aller au piège *pl.* **trappings** harnachement
trash *n.* brouille, broussailles, crapule, drigaille, débris, fardoche, fatras, foutraille, guenille, hariat, tchincaillerie, TRASH, vauriennerie **trash heap** bourrier **pile of trash** ramassis **piece of junk or trash** cochonnerie
travel *n.* navigation **travel bag** cabas
travel *v.* faire route, naviguer, parcourir, trafiquer, voyager, voyager **travel around** traîner **travel on** pousser route **travel by water** flotter **travel on horseback** monter à cheval **travel a great deal** rôdailler, rôder **one who travels by pirogue** pirogueur
traveler *n.* navigueur, voyageur
traveling *adj.* voyageur
travelling *n.* **travelling salesman** commis voyageur
traverse *v.* croiser, parcourir, traverser
trawl *n.* trôle **trawl line** trôle **trawl net** trôle **catch with a trawl** trôler **bag of a trawl net** sac du trawl **tighten the mesh links of a trawl net** serrer les nœuds
trawl *v.* trôler
trawler *n.* bateau de trawl, biloxi, floridien, lafitte, trôleur
trawling *n.* trôle **trawling season** trôle **go trawling** aller aux trôles
trawlnet *n.* **trawlnet maker** découpeur **certain place on a trawlnet where the mesh comes together** tête
tray *n.* cabaret, plat, plateau
treacherous *adj.* traître
treacherously *adv.* en traître

treachery *n.* perfidie
tread *v.* marcher **tread down** aculer, crochir
treadle *n.* pédale **sewing machine treadle** marchette
treasure *n.* trésor
treasurer *n.* trésorier
treat *n.* délicatesse, TREAT **give o.s. a treat** prendre un bossal
treat *v.* médeciner, traiter, traiter, triter **treat cruelly** crimer **treat differently** faire une distinction **treat effectively** détourner **treat medically** traiter **treat harshly, cruelly** faire des duretés à **treat o.s. to** s'offrir **treat with medicine** médeciner **treat as a father** traiter de père **treat as a fool** traiter de fou **treat as a thief** traiter de voleur **treat or deal with** traiter **treat with pesticide or herbicide** empoisonner **treat o.s. or each other in a particular way** se traiter **treat for pneumonia or for a cold by applying mustard plasters** fluxionner
treatable *adj.* traitable
treatment *n.* traitement **one who is under medical care or treatment** patient
treaty *n.* convention
tree *n.* arbre, bois **apple tree** pommier **apricot tree** abricotier **banana tree** bananier **bay tree** laurier **bayonet tree** baïonnette **beech tree** hêtre **camellia tree** camélia **camphor tree** camphrier **cassava tree** arbre (à) volaille, manioc **catalpa tree** atacalpa, bois connu {inconnu} **cedar tree** bois de cèdre, mûrier **chestnut tree** châtaignier **chinaball tree** lilas de Perse, lilas des Indes, lilas parasol, lilas **chinaberry tree** arbre à chapelets, lilas des Indes, lilas **Christmas tree** arbre de Christmas, arbre de Noël **citron tree** citron **clove tree** giroflier **cottonwood tree** cotonnier **crabapple tree** arbre de pommette **fig tree** figue, figuier **fruit tree** arbre à fruit, bois de fruit **gum tree** copal **hackberry tree** bois connu {inconnu} **haw tree** cenellier **hickory tree** noyer **laurel tree** laurier, olivier **lemon tree** limonier **lime tree** limonier **magnolia tree** magnolia, rameau **mangrove tree** manglier **maple tree** plaine **mayhaw tree** pommetier, pommette, pommier **medlar tree** mispilusse, néfrier **mimosa tree** gloire d'Asie, loucou **mulberry tree** mûrier **myrtle tree** gastronia **nutmeg tree** muscadier **olive tree** olivier **orange tree** oranger **palm tree** palmier **pawpaw tree** assiminier, jasminier **peach tree** pêcher **pear tree** poirier **pecan tree** pacanier **persimmon tree** plaqueminier **pine tree** pin **planer tree** charmille, châtaignier **plum tree** prunier **pomegranate tree** grenadier **saddle tree** fût de selle **sassafras tree** bois de filé, bois de gombo, sassafras **sugarberry tree** bois connu {inconnu} **sweetgum tree** arbre à gomme **walnut tree** nogalier **willow tree** saule, saulier **winterberry tree** cenellier **felled tree trunk** log **small tree limb** rolon **pine tree or wood** bois de pin / bois gras **tulip tree or yellow poplar** bois-jaune **any tree in which chickens roost** arbre à {de} poules **black cherry tree** merisier **black walnut tree** noyer **cherry laurel tree** laurier amande {mande} **Chinese tallow tree** olivier **coral bean tree** mamou **cultivated pecan tree** pacanier greffé **honey locust tree** acacia, févier **Japanese plum tree** néfrier **red bay tree** petit laurier **spring locust tree** garofier **sweet bay tree** laurier doux **sweet gum tree** copal **tupelo gum tree** olivier **water hickory tree** pacanier amer **weeping willow tree** saule pleurant **wild peach tree** laurier amandé **wild pecan tree** pacanier sauvage {d'aventure} **wild plum tree** prunier sauvage **yellow poplar tree** tulipier **flowering black locust tree** acacia **knot on a tree** boscoyo **fruit of the tupelo gum tree** boule d'olivier *pl.* **clear of trees and brush** déboiser **one who fells trees** abatteur **grove of pine trees in the open prairie** île de pins **row of planted oak trees** chênière **grove or stand of oak trees in an otherwise treeless swamp** chênière
treetop *n.* faîtage
trelease *n.* liane noire
trellis *n.* trille **bean trellis** berceau de fèves **flower trellis** échafaud **vine trellis** échafaud
tremble *v.* frémir, trembler
trembling *adj.* tremblant
trembling *n.* tremblade, tremblement
tremendously *adv.* énormément
tremor *n.* tremblement de terre
trench *n.* fossé, rigolet **furrow or trench for planting seeds** rigolet
tress *n.* tresse
trestle *n.* cheval, chevalet, tréteau
trial *n.* essai, procès, épreuve
triangle *n.* 'tit-fer, bastringue, petit fer / ti-fer, triangle, fer **striker for triangle** marteau
triangular *adj.* **triangular piece of cloth** laize
tribe *n.* tribu
tribulation *n.* tribulation
trick *n.* attrape, embêtation, jonglerie, malice, manigance, niche, routine, tour, tournure, pli, tallée **dirty trick** crasse **mischievous trick** canaillerie **sly trick** coup de malin **play a trick** faire des canicroches **play a dirty trick** jouer la patte de cochon, planter un piquant **play a joke, trick, or prank** faire {jouer} une malice **it will do the trick, do the job** ça va faire l'affaire *pl.* **play tricks** canailler **play dirty tricks** faire des saloperies **do fancy acrobatic tricks** faire des papillotes
trick *v.* attraper, embêter, fouler, passer des crêpes à qqn, passer un bloff, sucrer, tricher, youquer, coquiner **trick s.o.** passer la cheville à qqn
tricked *adj.* **be tricked** prendre un bloff **be tricked on April Fool's Day** manger le poisson d'avril
trickery *n.* filouterie, macaquerie
trickle *n.* dégouttation, dégouttement
trickle *v.* découler, dégoutter
trickster *n.* canaille

tricky *adj.* canaille, malin

tricycle *n.* TRICYCLE

trifle *n.* babiole, fiferlin, picaillon, rien *pl.* **wrangle over trifles** chicoter

trifling *adj.* négligeable

trigger *n.* gâchette **trigger of a bird trap** bois-malin **gun hammer and trigger** chien de fusil

trim *n.* accroche-cœur, moule, moulure, ornement **shoulder trim** épaulette

trim *v.* charpenter, découper, garnir, parer, tailler, ébrancher **trim evenly** tailler flèche **cut or trim the wick of** émécher

trimming *n.* appliqué, fion, fionnure, garniture, taillage, ébranchage

trinity *n.* trinité

Trinity *n.* **Holy Trinity** Sainte Trinité

trinket *n.* berloque, bébelle, bébellerie, mirlifiche *pl.* **trinkets** artifailles, artifaux

trip *n.* excursion, promenade, tour, tournée, voyage **camping trip** camperie **take a trip** faire un voyage, se promener, voyager **have a nice trip** bon voyage **take a short trip** faire une petite course **have a good fishing trip** faire une bonne pêche

trip *v.* buter, rebuter **trip s.o.** donner une jambette, foutre une jambette à qqn **using one's own leg to trip s.o. else** jambette

tripe *n.* panse de bête, panse **tripe sausage** andouille **traditional dish of veal tripe** tripes à la chique

triple *v.* tripler

tripod *n.* trois-pieds, tréteau

tripping *n.* **tripping device on a trap** marchette **form of tripping** jambette

triumph *n.* triomphe

trombone *n.* trombone

troop *n.* troupe

trot *n.* galop, trot

trot *v.* trotter, trotter

trotline *n.* drague, ligne, palangre *pl.* **fish with trotlines** pêcher des lignes

trotter *n.* trotteur

trotting *adj.* trotteur

trouble *n.* baribara, cancan, charade, damnation, discorde, embarras, misère, mortel, peine, potin, pouille, ravaud, tracas, train, tribulation, trouble, difficulté **trouble spreads like wild fire** le feu est pris dans la paille jaune {grande paille} **avoid trouble** faire le tour **bring trouble** amener du tracas **cause trouble** amener du tracas, embarrasser, faire du tracas, faire du trouble, semer de la merde **give trouble** donner du tracas, faire (de) la misère (à qqn), faire danser, faire des embarras, gêner **have trouble** avoir (du) tracas, avoir chicane, avoir de la peine à, avoir du mal **heart trouble** mal de cœur, maladie de cœur **in trouble** malfoutu, malpris **make trouble** amener du tracas, faire danser, faire du tracas **sinus trouble** mal de cerveau, maladie de cerveau **start trouble** partir de la misère **cause trouble, discord** faire du {un} désordre **have trouble, difficulty** avoir de la misère **be in trouble** être dans le noir **get into trouble** rentrer dans le tracas, se faire froguer, se mettre en tracas / se mettre dans le tracas **headed for trouble** mal braqué **look for trouble** chercher (une) chique **stir up trouble** faire le ravaud, merdasser **take the trouble** prendre la peine, prendre le tracas, s'embarrasser, se donner de la misère, se donner du tracas, se donner la peine, se donner le trouble / se prendre le trouble, se donner le trouble, se déranger **now the trouble has really begun** là, la merde est pris, ça c'est (de la) merde chez Pierre **a lot of trouble** embarrassement **be looking for trouble** chicoter pour du tracas **cause misery and trouble** brasser mer et larmes **go to great trouble** faire des fanferluches **it's not worth the trouble or risk** le jeu (ne) vaut pas la chandelle **have a lot of trouble and hardship in life** manger de la misère, passer de la misère **be in a peck of trouble** danser comme un dinde dans la cendre chaude **one who goes to unnecessary trouble or tries too hard** fionneur **one who annoys, pesters or makes trouble** embarrateur *pl.* **endless troubles** mille misères

trouble *v.* affliger, troubler **annoy or trouble persistently** persécuter

trouble-maker *n.* agaceur

troubled *adj.* embarrassé, trouble

troublemaker *n.* carnageur, casseur de bal, désordeur, faiseur d'embarras, tchicailleur, tonnerre

troublesome *adj.* embarrassant, embarrateur, emmerdant, fâchant, gênant, malcommode, tracassant

troubling *adj.* troublant

trough *n.* auge, pétrin **feed trough** mangeoire **watering trough** abreuvoir, bac **one half of a barrel used as a washtub, water trough, etc.** barrique

trouser *adj.* **trouser leg** cuissière

trousers *npl.* culotte, pantalon **short trousers** brayette **cuff of trousers** bas de pantalon **sag in trousers** tchapin

trousseau *n.* trousseau

trout *n.* perche, truite **cypress trout** choupique **sea trout** truite de mer, truite **speckled trout** truite grise, truite **white trout** fouille-sable, truite blanche **sand sea trout** truite blanche **spotted sea trout** truite grise

trowel *n.* truelle **mason's trowel** douelle

truck *n.* TRUCK **truck farm** ferme de produits **hand truck** diable **pick-up truck** PICKUP, TRUCK

truckload *n.* voyage

true *adj.* droite, franc, juste, vrai, véritable, propre **say things that cannot be true** chanter des midis à quatorze heures

truly *adv.* pour (de) même, pour même, réellement, vrai, vraiment

trump *n.* atout **trump card** atout, tourne

trump *v.* couper, ficher
trumpet *n.* trompette
trundle *n.* **trundle bed** lit à roulettes, roulette
trunk *n.* malle, corps, trompe, tronc **trunk of a car** malle **felled tree trunk** log
trust *n.* confiance **worthy of trust** dépendable **betray the trust of** tromper
trust *v.* fier, s'affier, se fier **not trust banks** cacher son argent dans des cornes à bœuf
trustee *npl.* **church board of trustees** comité d'église
trustworthy *adj.* fiable, fidèle, solide
truth *n.* vrai, vérité **stretch the truth** déchirer le gingas {ginghat} **tell the truth** pour bien {ainsi} dire, pour vrai dire **the honest truth** la franche vérité
truthful *adj.* honnête
truthfully *adv.* franchement, honnêtement
try *n.* entreprise, essai
try *v.* entreprendre, essayer, tenter, éprouver, juger **try o.s.** s'essayer **try out** faire épreuve, éprouver **try to persuade** chouler, chouriner **try to eke out an existence on poor land** graboter **try to do things that are beyond one's social or financial means** péter plus haut que son nez {cul} **one who tries unsuccessfully to speak standard French** javion **one who goes to unnecessary trouble or tries too hard** fionneur
trying *adj.* pénible
trying *n.* essayage
trysting *n.* **trysting place** rendez-vous
tub *n.* baille, bassine, bassinet **foot tub** baille, bassin, petite baille **wooden tub** bac **old-fashioned tub for bathing** baille à bain {baigner}
tube *n.* tuyau **tube through which an egg passes before it is laid** pondiaire
tuber *n.* **any tuber** patate
tubercular *adj.* poitrinaire
tuberculosis *n.* consomption, maladie de poitrine, tuberculose **afflicted with tuberculosis** poitrinaire **suffering from tuberculosis or deep chest congestion** époitriné **one who is afflicted with tuberculosis** poitrinaire
tuberose *n.* tibereuse
tuck *n.* godet, pince **make a pleat or tuck** faire un godet *pl.* **make tucks in** goder
tuck *v.* **tuck in** replier, roler **tuck up** se retrousser
Tuesday *n.* mardi **Shrove Tuesday** Mardi Gras
tuff *v.* bourrer
tuft *n.* bouillée, huppe, pompon
tufted *adj.* huppé
tug *n.* **tug boat** TUG
tug *v.* haler, halocher, halailler
tularemia *n.* fièvre de lapin
tulip *n.* **tulip tree or yellow poplar** bois-jaune
tumble *n.* capote
tumble *v.* **tumble down** débouler, dégrouler **tumble out** débouler, déboulir
tumblebug *n.* fouille-merde
tumbling *n.* dégringolage **tumbling down** dégringolage
tumor *n.* tumeur **cancerous tumor in horses** mal de marais
tuna *n.* bordeau
tune *n.* air, mélodie, TUNE
tune *v.* accorder, raccorder
tuneful *adj.* mélodieux
tunnel *n.* **mole tunnel** souterrain
tupelo *n.* olivier **tupelo gum tree** olivier **fruit of the tupelo gum tree** boule d'olivier
turban *n.* tignon
turbulence *n.* halicasser
turd *n.* crotte, crottin
tureen *n.* turine **soup tureen** soupière
turkey *n.* **turkey buzzard** carencro **turkey shoot** pategau **female turkey** dinde (d'inde) **male turkey** dinde (d'inde), dindon **tom turkey** dinde (d'inde), dindon **water turkey** bec-à-lancette
turkey-hen *n.* dinde (d'inde)
turn *n.* tour, tournure, virement, anse, tour **good turn** bienfait **each his turn** chacun (à) son tour **each in turn** chacun (à) son tour **take one's turn** prendre son tour **do a good turn or a favor** faire une belle grâce (à qqn) *pl.* **by turns** par tours
turn *v.* boulotter, faire, se tourner, se virer, tournailler, tourner, virer, brancher **turn around** revirer, se revirer de bord, se tourner, se virer de bord, se virer, tourner de bord, tourner, virer de bord **turn aside** dévirer, fourcher **turn back** revirer **turn black** noircir, se noircir **turn down** refuser **turn green** verdir **turn into** tourner, virer **turn loose** lâcher **turn off** ôter, débarquer, fermer, éteindre **turn on** allumer, mettre ON, mettre **turn out** déguerper, larguer, tourner **turn over** basculer, capoter, chavirer, retourner, se renverser, tourner bout pour bout **turn pale** blêmir **turn quickly** pirouetter **turn sour** haigrir **turn topsy-turvy** bouleverser, bousculer, dévaliser, soursoubler **turn up** retrousser **turn upside-down** basculer, bousculer, renverser **turn white** blanchir **turn a corner** tourner **turn completely around** tourner bout pour bout **turn inside out** virer à l'envers **turn into gangrene** gangrener **turn o.s. around** se retourner de bord **turn o.s. in** se livrer à **turn o.s. over** se rouler **turn on again** remettre **turn one's back** tourner le dos **turn to shit** tourner en merde **turn around and around** tournailler **turn around in circles** bouliner **turn on a pivot** pivoter **turn on the light** ouvrir la lumière **turn or make sour** haigrir **turn s.o. away from** virer **turn ten years old** faire dix {vingt, etc.} ans **turn the cattle loose** lâcher les bêtes **turn over in an incubator** raiser **turn the opposite side out** revirer **shape or turn on a lathe** tourner
turnaround *n.* tournage

turned *adj.* tourné **turned around** tourné **turned on** dessus
turner *n.* **pancake turner** palette
turning *n.* tournement, virage, virement
turnip *n.* navet **turnip greens** queues de navet **Indian turnip** navet chauvage, oignon d'ali {d'alié}
turnover *n.* tarte couvert
turnrow *n.* allée de clos, allée, chaintre, chemin de charrette, chemin de travers(e), HEADLAND, routine à la volonté, tournage, tournaille, tournant, tourne, tournure, virée
turpentine *n.* térébenthine
turtle *n.* mobilienne, tortue mobilienne, tortue **turtle shell** écale de tortue, écale **green turtle** mobilienne, tortue mobilienne, tortue verte **loggerhead turtle** trois-rangs **map turtle** tortue de cyprière, tortue de lac **mud turtle** caret, tortue de boue **musk turtle** tortue musquée, tortue puante **sea turtle** tortue de mer **snapping turtle** trois-rangs **softshell turtle** caille-molle, tortue molle / tortue écaille molle / tortue caille molle **stripe-necked turtle** tortue cou barré **yellow-bellied turtle** tortue ventre jaune, ventre jaune **loggerhead snapping turtle** tortue caïman, tortue caouenne, tortue cocodril, tortue de cyprière **alligator snapping turtle** caouane, caouenne à trois rangs, tortue caïman, tortue caouenne, tortue cocodril, tortue de cyprière **common snapping turtle** caouenne galeuse, tortue caouenne, tortue double-porte **green sea turtle** tortue de mer verte **hawksbill sea turtle** tortue perroquet **leatherback sea turtle** tortue molle / tortue écaille molle / tortue caille molle **three-toed box turtle** tortue de canne, tortue de rosée **freshwater loggerhead snapping turtle** caouane, caouenne à trois rangs *pl.* **feel underwater for turtles** tâtonner pour des tortues
tusk *n.* crochet, accroc **elephant's tusk** défense d'éléphant
tussle *v.* se halailler
tutor *n.* tuteur
tweezers *npl.* arracheur de piquants, pincette
twelfth *n.* douzième
twelve *n.* douze
twentieth *n.* vingtième
twenty *n.* vingt **about twenty** vingtaine
twenty-two-caliber *n.* **twenty-two-caliber rifle** vingt-deux
twice *adv.* double **twice as many** une fois (de) plus **twice as much** une fois (de) plus
twin *n.* besson, jumeau, touine
twine *n.* ficelle **store twine** corde à marchand
twinge *n.* **twinge of pain in one's back** point de côté
twirl *v.* tortiller
twist *n.* forçure **twist of hair** cagouette **roll, twist, or knot of hair worn at the back of the head** catogan, choque, tchique, tignon **plug or twist of chewing tobacco** carotte
twist *v.* cobir, entortiller, tordre, torquer, tortiller, refouler **twist around** tortiller **twist o.s.** se tordre
twist-loaf *n.* pain tressé
twisted *adj.* cobi, courbé, tordu
twisting *n.* entortillage **twisting of the back** tour de reins
twitch *n.* tic
two *n.* deux **two weeks** quinze jours **two by two** deux par deux **two and a half cents** quarti **there's no two ways about it** il y a pas de catherine **they are two of a kind** ça chie dans le même sac **what one could buy for two and a half cents** quarti **a bird in the hand is worth two in the bush** un oiseau dans la main en vaut deux dans une talle
two-by-four *n.* deux-par-quatre, deux-par-quatre
two-faced *adj.* en dessous **two-faced person** couteau à deux tranchants
two-seat *n.* **two-seat buggy** HACK
two-step *n.* deux-pas, TWO-STEP **a series of five dances, traditionally played in order: waltz, polka, waltz in two, two-step, mazurka** ronde de danses
two-wheeled *adj.* **two-wheeled cart** bouleton
tying *n.* amarrage
type *n.* classe, espèce, grade, qualité, sorte, variété
typewriter *n.* machine à écrire, TYPEWRITER
typhoid *n.* fièvre typhoïde, typhoïde **typhoid fever** fièvre longue / longue fièvre, fièvre typhoïde / grande fièvre, fièvre typhoïde, typhoïde
typhus *n.* fièvre de rat
tyrannize *v.* BULLDOZE
tyranny *n.* oppression
tyrant *n.* bourreau
tête-à-tête *n.* **have a tête-à-tête** cancaner

U

udder *n.* mamelle, pair, pis
uglier *adj.* **make or become ugly or uglier** laidir
ugliness *n.* laideur
ugly *adj.* laid comme un bouki {macaque} / laid comme un coin de banquette {les sept péchés capitaux}, laid, maudit comme un péché mortel, vilain comme un coin de banquette / vilain comme un péché {un macaque / le diable}, vilain **ugly person** vilain **ugly woman** fouine, taïque **ugly, funny-looking person** macaque **become ugly** enlaidir **be ugly as sin** avoir une figure de pot de chambre craquée **in an ugly way** laidement **in an ugly or nasty way** vilain **in an ugly or unkind way** vilainement **make or become ugly or uglier** laidir
ulcer *n.* chancre, ulcère
ulcerate *v.* ulcérer
ulcerated *adj.* **become ulcerated** s'ulcérer, ulcérer

ultimate *adj.* dernier, extrême, final
umbrella *n.* ombrelle, parapluie, parasol **umbrella plant** ombrelle de Japon
unable *adj.* **be unable** être malaisé pour
unaccompanied *adj.* **person unaccompanied by his or her partner** veuve
unadulterated *adj.* pur
unattractive *adj.* **tall, thin and unattractive man** fanal
unaware *adj.* ignorant
unbale *v.* déballer
unbaling *n.* déballage
unbaste *v.* défaufiler
unbearable *adj.* insouffrable
unbeatable *adj.* imbattable
unbecoming *adj.* **act in an unbecoming manner** prendre ses brindezingues
unbelievable *adj.* fort, incomprenable, incroyable **say s.t. unbelievable** pondre un œuf
unbelieving *adj.* méfiant
unbend *v.* déployer
unbending *adj.* raide
unbind *v.* décoincer
unblock *v.* débloquer
unblocking *n.* déblocage, débloquement
unbolt *v.* déboulonner, dévisser
unbolted *adj.* **become unbolted** se dévisser
unbuckle *v.* déboucler
unbutton *v.* déboutonner **unbutton one's clothes** se déboutonner
uncalled *adj.* **be improper, out of the way, uncalled for** avoir pas de place
uncared-for *adj.* **uncared-for child** enfant à la traîne
unceremoniously *adv.* uniment
uncertain *adj.* doutable
uncertainty *n.* doutance, doute
unchain *v.* déchaîner
unchained *adj.* déchaîné
unchecked *adj.* démesuré
uncivilized *adj.* sauvage
unclasp *v.* dégrafer
uncle *n.* oncle
unclean *adj.* malpropre
unclog *v.* débloquer, déboucher, débourrer, dégoter
unclogged *adj.* **become unclogged** se dégoter
unclogging *n.* déblocage, débloquement
uncock *v.* débraquer, désarmer
uncomb *v.* dépeigner
uncomfortable *adj.* mal à son aise, malcommode **be in an uncomfortable or disagreeable situation** être pas aux noces **be in a awkward or uncomfortable situation** suer comme un bâtard à une réunion de famille / suer comme un nègre à la messe / suer comme les Ponce
uncommon *adj.* extraordinaire, rare
unconcerned *adj.* **be unconcerned** s'en fricasser
unconscious *adj.* insensible, sans connaissance **in an unconscious or comatose state** en léthergie
unconsolable *adj.* inconsolable
uncontrollable *adj.* **be uncontrollable** prendre le mors aux dents
uncontrolled *adj.* démesuré
uncooperative *adj.* contrariant
uncork *v.* déboucher
uncouple *v.* découpler
uncouth *adj.* malinstruit **uncouth man** pignouf **rustic, uncultured, uncouth, boorish, ignorant person** gui-gui **person with unrefined or uncouth tastes** dauiaut
uncover *v.* découverre, désabrier **uncover o.s.** se désabrier
uncovered *adj.* à l'air
unction *n.* onction **extreme unction** extrême-onction
Unction *n.* **Extreme Unction** Extrême Onction
uncultivated *adj.* farouche
uncultured *adj.* **rustic, uncultured, uncouth, boorish, ignorant person** gui-gui
uncurl *v.* déboucler
undecided *adj.* au {en} balan / sur le {un} balan **be undecided** hésiter
under *adv.* bas, en bas de, en bas, en dessous, par-dessous
under *prep.* dessous, en dessous (de), par-dessous, sous
underbelly *n.* bas-ventre
underbrush *n.* fardoche **clear out weeds or underbrush** défraîchir
underclothes *npl.* linge de dessous / linge d'en-dessous
undercurrent *n.* remous
undergo *v.* subir
underground *adj.* souterrain
underhand *adj.* **underhand work** machinerie
underhanded *adj.* filou, par en-dessous
underneath *adv.* en bas de, en bas, en dessous, là-dessous, par-dessous
underneath *prep.* au-dessous, dessous, en dessous (de), par-dessous
underpants *npl.* caleçon **woman's underpants** step-in **said when s.o.'s underpants have crawled up and become stuck between the buttocks** il y a un cabri dans le maïs
underpinning *n.* fondament, assolement
undershirt *n.* chemise de peau **man's undershirt** chemise de dessous
undershorts *npl.* caleçon
underside *n.* bas, dessous, fond
undersize *adj.* nain
underskirt *n.* jupe
understand *v.* comprendre, savoir, voir **understand o.s. or each other** se comprendre **make understand** donner à comprendre **bring to understand definitely** rencharger

understand *v.* **that's easy to understand** ça prend pas un avocat
understandable *adj.* comprenable
understanding *n.* comprenure, compréhension, entendement **reach an understanding** faire {prendre} des arrangements
understood *adj.* attendu, compris
undertake *v.* débattre, entamer, entreprendre, tenter
undertaking *n.* entreprise **dangerous undertaking** casse-cou **any difficult project or undertaking** pratique à chagrin **give up in the middle of an undertaking** dételer le wagon au milieu du marais / dételer le mulet des rangs
underwear *n.* linge de dessous / linge d'en-dessous **women's underwear** pantelettes
underwrite *v.* cautionner
undiluted *adj.* STRAIGHT
undisciplined *adj.* **unmanageable, undisciplined, unruly child** brigand
undo *v.* défaire, défropter, déprendre **undo again** redéfaire **undo a knot in** démarrer
undomesticated *adj.* brut, marron, sauvage
undone *adj.* **come undone** se défaire
undress *v.* déshabiller **undress o.s.** se dépouiller, se déshabiller
undressed *adj.* **get undressed** se dégréer
undulant *adj.* **undulant fever** fièvre de lait
unearth *v.* désenterrer, déterrer, ressoubler
uneasiness *n.* anxiété, malaise
uneasy *adj.* anxieux, inquiet
uneducated *adj.* malinstruit **uneducated and countrified** cadien **ignorant, uneducated, insignificant or foolish person** cape-cape
uneven *adj.* mal égal, raboteux
unevenness *n.* rabot
unexpectedly *adv.* à la sourdine
unfamiliar *adj.* étranger
unfasten *v.* dégrafer, démarrer, détacher
unfavorably *adv.* mal
unfertilized *adj.* clair
unfetter *v.* désenferger
unfold *v.* déployer, développer
unfortunate *adj.* fâchant, malchanceux, malheureux, misérable, regrettable
unfortunately *adv.* malheureusement
ungainly *adj.* **ungainly person** rabougri
ungirth *v.* dessangler
unglove *v.* déganter
unglue *v.* décoller **unglue o.s.** se décoller
unglued *adj.* **become unglued** se décoller
ungracious *adj.* malému
unhappily *adv.* malheureusement
unhappiness *n.* malheur
unhappy *adj.* chagrin, malcontent, malheureux
unharness *v.* déjouquer, dételer
unharnessing *n.* dételage
unhealthy *adj.* malade, maladif, malsain **sick, ill, unhealthy person** malade
unhem *v.* détrousser
unhitch *v.* démarrer, dételer
unhitching *n.* dételage
unhook *v.* décrocher, dégrafer, détaquer **unhook o.s.** se décrocher **one who unhooks s.t.** dépendeur
unhurt *adj.* sauve
uniform *adj.* uniforme
uniform *n.* habit **uniform dress** costume
unimportant *adj.* négligeable **unimportant thing** babiole
unintelligent *adj.* smatte comme la tomate à Firin du Marais Plate **unintelligent person** corde échappée
uninvited *adj.* **drop in uninvited** venir se poquer
union *n.* union **labor union** union
Union *n.* **Union soldier** Yankee
unique *adj.* unique
unite *v.* joindre, s'unir, se mettre ensemble, unir
united *adj.* uni
United *adj.* **United States** États-Unis **the United Nations** les Nations Unies
unity *n.* unité
universe *n.* univers
university *n.* collège, université
unkempt *adj.* effaré
unkemptness *n.* ébouriffage
unkind *adj.* dur, haïssable **unkind action** canaillerie **unkind person** pirate **unpleasant, unkind person** bordel **in an ugly or unkind way** vilainement
unknowing *adj.* ignorant
unknown *adj.* **in a distant and unknown place** (là-bas) au diable bouilli
unlace *v.* délacer
unlatch *v.* débarrer, décrocher, détaquer
unleash *v.* lâcher
unless *conj.* autrement que, hormis que, sans (que), sauf que, à moins (que)
unlevel *adj.* **make unlevel** déniveler
unlikable *adj.* mal à main
unlikely *adj.* **be unlikely** avoir pas d'apparence
unload *v.* décharger, débarquer **unload something undesirable on** caracoler
unloading *n.* décharge, déchargeage, déchargement, débarquement
unlock *v.* débarrer, décler
unlucky *adj.* guignard, malchanceux **be unlucky** avoir autant de chance qu'un rat dans un tuyau de pipe, avoir pas plus de chance qu'une sauterelle dans un parc de dindes
unmanageable *adj.* **unmanageable, undisciplined, unruly child** brigand

unmarried *adj.* seul **unmarried man** bachelier **young, unmarried woman known for having a wild side** bougresse **be old and unmarried** avoir les talons jaunes
unmask *v.* démasquer
unmatched *adj.* dépareillé
unmixed *adj.* pur
unnail *v.* déclouer, détacher
unnailed *adj.* **become unnailed** déclouer, se déclouer
unnerve *v.* énerver
unnerved *adj.* **become unnerved** s'énerver
unnoticed *adj.* **slip off unnoticed** s'exiler
unpack *v.* déballer
unpacking *n.* déballage
unpaired *adj.* dépareillé
unpin *v.* détacher
unpleasant *adj.* choquant, déplaisant, désagréable, malcommode **unpleasant person** gribouille **unpleasant, unkind person** bordel
unpleasantness *n.* désagrément
unpleat *v.* défroncer, déplisser
unplug *v.* déconnecter
unpretentious *adj.* retiré
unprocessed *adj.* naturel
unravel *v.* défiler, dénouer, désentortiller, détordre, détortiller, s'effiloper, se détordre, se détortiller, écharpiller, érailler
unraveled *adj.* éraillé **become unraveled** s'effiloper **become unraveled or untwisted** se détordre **become untwisted or unraveled** se détortiller
unreal *adj.* fort
unrefined *adj.* racatcha **person with unrefined or uncouth tastes** dauiaut
unrelenting *adj.* déchaîné
unreliable *adj.* **unreliable person** girouette
unreserved *adj.* fringant
unrestrained *adj.* décarabiné, dégagé
unrestrainedly *adv.* à tout décarabiné
unrig *v.* dégréer
unripe *adj.* vert
unroll *v.* dérouler, défiler, détrousser
unrolled *adj.* **become unrolled** se dérouler
unroof *v.* découverre
unruly *adj.* brigand, canaille, déchaîné **unruly child** morveux **noisy, unruly person** tonnerre à la voile **unmanageable, undisciplined, unruly child** brigand
unsaddle *v.* desseller
unscrew *v.* dévisser
unscrewed *adj.* **become unscrewed** se dévisser
unscrewing *n.* dévissage
unseal *v.* décacheter
unseen *adj.* invisible
unsettled *adj.* trouble, fragile
unsew *v.* découdre
unsewn *adj.* **become unsewn** découdre, se découdre
unshoe *v.* déferrer
unsnap *v.* dégrafer
unsolder *v.* dessouder
unsoldered *adj.* **become unsoldered** se dessouder
unspoil *v.* dégâter
unspoiled *adj.* **become unspoiled** se dégâter
unstable *adj.* folâtre **mentally unstable** pas balancé
unsteady *adj.* chambrelant, journalier, variable
unstick *v.* décoller
unstop *v.* déboucher, dégoter
unstring *v.* débrocher
unsuccessful *adj.* **be unsuccessful** échouer
unsure *adj.* doutable
unswerving *adj.* déchaîné
untack *v.* défaufiler
untamed *adj.* farouche, sauvage, potre
untangle *v.* démêler, dénouer, désentortiller, étrier **untangle o.s.** se démêler
untangling *n.* démêlage
unthread *v.* défiler
untidiness *n.* malpropreté
untidy *adj.* déguénillé, dévergondé, malpropre, salope, ébouriffé **dirty, untidy man** cochon **repulsive, filthy, untidy woman** salope
untie *v.* défaire, démarrer, délacer
untighten *v.* desserrer
until *conj.* dès que / desque / drès que, jusqu'à que, jusqu'à tant (que), jusqu'à temps, que
until *prep.* jusqu'à, jusque, pour
untouchable *adj.* **untouchable or touchy person** sainte nitouche
untrue *adj.* faux
untrustworthy *adj.* comme un(e) serpent à sonnette, salaud **one who is untrustworthy or deceitful** salaud
untucked *adj.* déculotté
untune *v.* désaccorder
untwist *v.* désentortiller, détordre, détortiller
untwisted *adj.* **become untwisted or unraveled** se détortiller **become unraveled or untwisted** se détordre
unusual *adj.* drôle, extraordinaire **unusual and interesting character** pistolet à deux manches, pistolet
unveil *v.* dévoiler
unveiling *n.* dévoilement
unwax *v.* décirer
unwedge *v.* décoincer
unwelcome *adj.* **person who hangs around unwelcome** cataplasme
unwillingly *n.* à contre cœur
unwind *v.* détravouiller **unwind itself** se démonter
unwound *adj.* démonté
unwrap *v.* développer

unwrapped *adj.* **become unwrapped** se développer
unwrinkle *v.* défroncer, déplisser
unyoke *v.* déjouquer
up *adj.* **get up** se lever, se relever
up *adv.* en haut, en l'air **up there** en haut, là-haut **up to** jusqu'à **up and down** de bric et de brac, en haut et en bas **it's up to** ça reste à (qqn) **pack up and leave** faire son paquet **be up to, occupied with** brasser, brèter **give s.o. an advantage, a leg up** donner un pied (à qqn)
up *prep.* en haut (de)
up-to-date *adj.* déluré
upbraid *v.* fourgailler, jurer
upbraiding *n.* fourgaille
upbringing *adj.* **person of modest upbringing and little education** badjo
upcoming *adj.* prochain, qui vient
upend *v.* chavirer, culbuter, mâter
uphold *v.* supporter
upholster *v.* bourrer
upholsterer *n.* tapisseur
upkeep *n.* entretenue, entretien, entretiennement, maintien, soutien, support
upon *prep.* dessus, en haut (de), sur
upper *adj.* haut **upper part** dessus **get the upper hand** prendre le dessus **have the upper hand** emmancher **curl the upper lip and show the teeth** rechigner
upright *adj.* debout, droite **upright board** pieu deboute, planche deboute **fully upright** grand debout **in an upright position** debout **put or put back in an upright position** redressir
uproar *n.* bamboula, berdas, hourra, ricane, sabbat, sassaquoi, sérail, tapage, tatamage, tchololo, trimage **cause an uproar** faire un carnaval **create an uproar** faire une quarantaine, tapager
uproot *v.* arracher, déraciner, déchousser
uprooting *n.* arrachage
upset *adj.* **upset stomach** vomissement **become upset** se démoraliser **get angry, mad, upset** se choquer
upset *n.* capotage
upset *v.* basculer, bouleverser, bousculailler, bousculer, défaire, enrager, mettre en bouleverse, pirater, terboliser **upset the stomach** barbouiller le cœur **upset the order or arrangement of** berdasser **upset the accurate and proper function of** dérégler
upsetting *adj.* enrageant
upside-down *adj.* en bas **said to point out that s.t. is upside-down** il y a un ouragan dans la Chine
upstairs *adv.* en haut, en l'air, là-haut
upstart *n.* gueux-parvenu, parvenu
upstream *adv.* en haut
urge *v.* encourager **urge on** mousser **urge to attack** siller
urgency *n.* presse
urgent *adj.* pressant, pressé **be urgent** presser
urinal *n.* pissoir
urinary *n.* **urinary retention** tranchement d'urine
urinate *v.* faire {tomber} de l'eau, jeter de l'eau, pisser, tomber de l'eau, uriner, faire pipi **urinate involuntarily** se retremper **urinate in one's clothing** se tremper
urine *n.* pipi, pissat, urine, ouioui
us *pron.* nous-autres, nous-mêmes, nous **to us** nous **between us or ourselves** entre nous **all of us** nous tous
usable *adj.* servable, usable
usage *n.* accoutumance, pratique, usage, utilité
use *n.* dépense, usage, usance, use, utilité **in use** en service, servable **make use of** appliquer, faire usage de, utiliser **cede use of land** livrer une terre **there's no use** c'est pas la peine / ça vaut pas la peine **wear for everyday use** traîner
use *v.* dépenser, employer, faire usage de, prendre, se servir, user, passer **use up** dépenser, tarir, user **use more than usual** forcer **which uses much** usurier **which uses up quickly** usurier **one who uses excessive force** défonceur d'une porte ouverte / défonceur de porte(s) ouverte(s)
used *adj.* (de) seconde main, deuxième {seconde} main, seconde {deuxième} main, usé **used up** usé **be used** être servi **be used again** resservir **be used to** avoir habitude (de), être habitué avec **get used to** s'accoutumer, s'adonner, s'habituer **get used to again** se réhabituer **cause to get used to** accoutumer
useful *adj.* utile **be useful again** resservir **make o.s. useful** se rendre utile
usefulness *n.* utilité
useless *adj.* en vain, hors de service **do s.t. useless** cracher dans le feu, siffler dans le vent
usher *n.* bedeau
usual *adj.* commun, habituel, naturel, ordinaire **as usual** comme (d')habitude
usually *adv.* comme (d')habitude, d'habitude, habitude, habitudement, habituellement, ordinaire, ordinairement, plussement
usufruct *n.* usufruit
usurp *v.* **if you leave, someone else will usurp your place** chien qui va à la chasse perd sa place
usury *n.* usure
utensil *npl.* **kitchen utensils** artifailles **set of kitchen utensils** batterie de cuisine
utility *n.* utilité
utilize *v.* utiliser
utmost *adj.* extrême
utter *adj.* seul
utter *v.* souffler **utter incoherently** cacasser **utter violent abuse** bagueuler **not utter a word** pas coinquer
uvula *n.* loi, luette **healer who lifts the uvula when it has fallen** leveur de (la) luette

V

vacant *adj.* vacant, vide
vacation *n.* vacance **on vacation** en vacances **take a vacation** lay-off
vaccinate *v.* vacciner **one who vaccinates** vaccineur
vaccination *n.* vaccination
vaccine *n.* vaccin, vaccine
vagabond *n.* flottant, gipsie, hobo, juif-errant, rôdailleur, TRAMP, traîné, vagabond
vagrant *adj.* errant
vagrant *n.* vagabond
vain *adj.* faquin, fier comme un paon, fier, fiéraud, glorieux, noble, orgueilleux, vain **vain person** fiéraud, pince-minette **vain as a peacock** faquin comme un paon **be vain** se croire **be haughty, vain** s'en croire
vain *n.* **in vain** en vain
vainglory *n.* gloire
valence *n.* valence
valentine *n.* VALENTINE
valiant *adj.* vaillant
valid *adj.* valide
validate *v.* **validate or demonstrate the worth of** faire valoir
validity *n.* validité
valise *n.* cabas
valley *n.* **valley rafter** chevron de vallée **roof valley** dalle
valuable *adj.* précieux
value *n.* mérite, valeur **lose value** déprécier **raise the value of** faire valoir **something of value, substance, wealth** de quoi **that is of little value** ça compte pas plus qu'un pet dans un ouragan {la poussière}, ça craque pas fort **thing of little or no value** fiferlin
value *v.* apprécier **value greatly** chérir
valve *n.* soupape
vandal *n.* brigand, carnageur
vandalism *n.* brigandage, carnageries, sabotage
vanilla *n.* vanille **vanilla extract** essence de gâteau, essence de vanille / essence à la vanille, extrat de vanille
vanish *v.* disparaître, passer au bleu
vanity *n.* fierté, gloire, glorieuseté, orgueil, vanité
vapor *n.* vapeur **there is a mist or vapor rising from the ground** les pierres sont après brûler
vaporize *v.* vaporiser
variable *adj.* variable
variance *n.* **be at variance** désaccorder
variation *n.* changement, variation
varicella *n.* picote
varied *adj.* assorti, varié
variety *n.* diversité, qualité, variété
various *adj.* différent de
varnish *n.* vernis
varnish *v.* vernir
varnishing *n.* vernissage
vary *v.* courir, varier
vase *n.* gobelet, pot, vase
Vaseline *n.* vaséline **apply Vaseline** vaséliner
vast *adj.* vaste
vat *n.* **dipping vat for livestock** dip **wooden vat for feeding lifestock** bac
Vatican *n.* Vatican
vault *n.* **burial vault** caveau, four, tombeau
vaulter *n.* sauteur
veal *n.* veau, viande de veau **traditional dish of veal tripe** tripes à la chique
veer *v.* barder, vironer
vegetable *n.* légume, végétable **vegetable farm** ferme de produits **vegetable garden** jardin **vegetable oil** huile **vegetable pear vine** liane de mirliton *pl.* **cultivate vegetables** faire jardin **fresh vegetables** jardinage **green vegetables** verdage, verdure **fruits and vegetables** produit
vegetation *n.* **patch of vegetation and humus that has not yet stabilized** flottant
vehicle embarcation
vehicle *n.* moyen, voiture **vehicle license** bavette **any old vehicle** bastringue **board a vehicle** s'embarquer **get into a vehicle** embarquer **load into a vehicle** charger
veil *n.* voile, voilette **veil surrounding a hornet's nest** robe **bridal veil assembly with wreath attached** couronne **wear a veil** se voiler **having a veil or caul on one's face at birth** coiffé
veil *v.* voiler
vein *n.* veine *pl.* **veins** bâton **varicose veins** jambe de lait
veined *adj.* marbré
veining *n.* **veining or grain** veine
velocity *n.* vitesse
velvet *n.* velours
velvety *adj.* **material that is plush, velvety, or furry** peluche
vena cava *n.* veine de sang
venerate *v.* vénérer
veneration *n.* vénération
vengeance *n.* vengeance, vindication **vengeance never evens out a wrong** le sirop et biscuits cassent pas égal
venial *adj.* véniel **venial sin** péché véniel
venison *n.* viande de chevreuil
venom *n.* vénin
venomous *adj.* poison, poisonné
vent *n.* registre **air vent** registre
ventilate *v.* airer
venture *n.* **help s.o. start a venture** donner une partence (à qqn)
venture *v.* aventurer, oser, risquer, s'aventurer

Venus *n.* vénus
veranda *n.* galerie
verbal *adj.* de bouche
verbally *adv.* de bouche
verbatim *adv.* mot pour mot
verbena *n.* admirable, caillot, verveine
verdict *n.* sentence
verdigris *n.* vert de gris
verge *n.* **on the verge of** au point de **be on the verge of fighting** se souffler dans les narines
verifiable *adj.* vérifiable
verify *v.* acertainer, se rendre compte, vérifier
veritable *adj.* franc, vrai, véritable
vermicelli *n.* vermicelle
vermifuge *n.* vermifuge
Vermilion *n.* **area off of Highway 14 between Kaplan and Gueydan in Vermilion Parish** mèche
vermin *n.* vermine
versatile *adj.* tout-mains
verse *n.* vers **scripture verse** verset
version *n.* dicton, version
vertebra *n.* maille du dos, nœud **any of the individual vertebra making up the backbone** nœud de rein
vertical *adj.* vertical
verve *n.* élan
very *adv.* affreusement, affreux, assez, beaucoup, bien, comme tout, extra, fichu, fin, fort, joliment, méchant, même, plein, sacrément, saprement, terrible, très
vesicular stomatitis *n.* bales
vessel *n.* navire, vaisseau **winnowing vessel** vanne **any vessel of tin or aluminum** bassin **any metal vessel or container** fer-blanc *pl.* **metal vessels and containers** ferblanterie
vest *n.* gilet, veste
vestibule *n.* HALL, vestibule
vestige *n.* vestige
vetch *n.* liserine
veteran *n.* vétéran
veterinarian *n.* docteur d'animaux, vaccineur, vétérinaire **veterinarian for horses** marichal
veterinary *adj.* vétérinaire
vex *v.* agoniser, tourmenter, vexer **vex again** recroiser
vexed *adj.* abattu **vexed with** pas satisfait après
vexing *adj.* foutant, vexant
vibration *n.* vibration
vicar *n.* vicaire **vicar general** vicaire général
vice *n.* vice
vice-president *n.* vice-président
vicinity *n.* environs, voisinage **in the vicinity of** autour (de)
vicious *adj.* bobo, carnassier, malva, traître, vicieux
victim *n.* victime
victory *n.* triomphe, victoire
victual *npl.* **victuals** mangeaille
vie *v.* faire concurrence (avec)
view *n.* apercevance, opinion, vue **in view** au blanc **in view of** en vue de **in full view** à la blanque **point of view** point de vue
view *v.* regarder
vigil *n.* vigile **vigil of feast days** vigile **keep a vigil or hold a wake over** veiller
vigilance *n.* vigilance **vigilance committee** comité de vigilance **member of a vigilance committee** vigilant
vigilant *adj.* vigilant
vigilante *n.* vigilant **vigilante committee** vigilance **vigilante movement** vigilance
vigor *n.* vigueur, énergie **lacking vigor** longis
vigorous *adj.* vaillant, vigoureux, énergique
vile *adj.* bas
villain *n.* scélérat
vindicate *v.* justifier **justify or vindicate o.s.** se justifier
vindication *n.* justification
vine *n.* fil, liane, vigne **vine trellis** échafaud **blackjack vine** liane noire **cypress vine** chevelure de Vénus **eardrop vine** anserine liane **muscadine vine** soco **potato vine** liane de patate **rattan vine** liane noire **morning glory vine** gloire du matin **vegetable pear vine** liane de mirliton **wild potato vine** liserine **short length of potato vine used to grow a new potato plant** margot de patate
vinegar *n.* vinaigre **season with vinegar** vinaigrer
vining *adj.* filant
violate *v.* violer, casser
violence *n.* violence
violent *adj.* violent
violet *n.* violet, violette **wild violet** violette marronne {farouche / sauvage}
violin *n.* violon
violinist *n.* violoneux
viper *n.* aspic, vipère
vireo *n.* **red-eyed vireo** caille de laurier
virgin *n.* vierge
Virgin *n.* **the Virgin Mary** Notre Dame **the Blessed Virgin** la Sainte Vierge
virginal *adj.* pur
virginity *n.* virginité
virtue *n.* vertu
virtuous *adj.* vertueux
visage *n.* visage
vise *n.* étau
visible *adj.* visible **highly visible** voyant
visibly *adj.* à vue d'œil
vision *n.* vue
visit *n.* promenade, tour, tournée, visite **evening visit** soirée, veillerie, veillée **short visit** saucée **spiritual visit** avertissement **pay a visit** payer une visite **go for a visit** se promener **make a long visit** camper, se camper **make a short**

visit faire un tour, faire une (petite) saucée **make an evening visit** aller à la veille, faire la veillée, faire une veillée **pay a short visit** faire une passée **pay an evening visit** veiller **come over for a visit** venir faire une tournée {un tour}

visit *v.* fréquenter, payer une visite, visiter, voir **visit quickly** tirer un saut **visit each other** se visiter **visit one another** se fréquenter **visit one's neighbors** se voisiner

visitation *n.* visitation **official visitation or inspection** visitation

visiting *n.* **go visiting** visiter

visitor *n.* visiteur **frequent visitor** juif-errant *pl.* **visitors** compagnie **said of visitors who leave when others arrive** faire sauvage

visor *n.* bec

vitamin *n.* vitamine

vixen *n.* renard

vocalization *n.* langage

vocation *n.* profession, vocation

voice *n.* voix **at the top of one's voice** à tue-tète

void *adj.* vide

void *n.* vide

void *v.* annuler **void one's bladder or bowels** faire ses besoins

voile *n.* lawn

volume *n.* volume, volume

volunteer *adj.* volontaire

volunteer *n.* volontaire **volunteer plant** plante de bonne aventure

volunteer *v.* **a woman who volunteers often at church** grenouille de bénitier

vomit *n.* dégobillage, vomissage, vomissement, vomit

vomit *v.* rejeter, vomir **vomit again** revomir

vomited *adj.* **vomited substance** vomissage, vomit

vomiting *n.* vomissage, vomissement

voodoo *n.* voudou **voodoo doctor** ouangateur **practicer of voodoo rites** voudou **of or pertaining to voodooism or a voodoo** voudou

voodooism *n.* **of or pertaining to voodooism or a voodoo** voudou

voracious vorace

vote *n.* voix, vote

vote *v.* voter **register to vote** registrer

voter *n.* votant, voteur **voter who can be bought** flottant

vouch *v.* cautionner, garantir, servir de caution {cautionnement / CO-SIGN}

voucher *n.* ticket

vow *n.* vœu *pl.* **taking of vows** profession

vow *v.* vouer **vow o.s.** se vouer

voyage *n.* navigation, voyage **sea voyage** traverse

voyeur *n.* voyeur

vulgar *adj.* malpropre, racatcha, vulgaire **vulgar woman** guinche **vulgar, ill-mannered person** bitaco **in a vulgar way** cochon

vulgarity *n.* grossièreté

vulture *n.* **black vulture** carencro tête noire, carencro *pl.* **like vultures around carrion** comme des carencros autour d'une charogne

wacko *n.* coucou

wad *n.* chiffon, bouchon, bourre, chique

wadding *n.* bourrage **remove the wadding** débourrer

waddle *v.* marcher en macreuse

wade *v.* **wade or walk around in water or mud** patauger

wading *n.* pataugeage

wage *n.* gage *pl.* **wages** engagement, paye, salaire **cut wages** couper les gages

wager *n.* gageure, pari

wager *v.* gager, gambler, parier

wagerer *n.* gageur, parieur

wagon *n.* wagonnette **wagon driver** wagonnier **covered wagon** wagonnette **four-wheeled wagon** wagon **spring wagon** waguine **wooden wagon** wagon **drive a wagon** wagonner **on the wagon** à jeun **long piece of wood by means of which a pair of horses or mules is attached to a wagon** flèche

wagoner *n.* wagonnier

wagonful *n.* charretée

wagonload *n.* cargaison, voyage

wainscot *n.* boisure

wainscoting *n.* boisure, plafonnage

waist *n.* ceinture, taille **around the waist** à {en} brasse-corps **walk together holding each other by the waist** marcher à la crochette

wait *n.* **lie in wait** faire la guette **lie in wait for ducks as they come in to roost at night** aller {partir} à la passe, aller à la passée

wait *v.* arrêter, attendre, espérer, veille voir **wait on** servir **I can hardly wait** le temps me dure (de / que) **be unable to wait any longer** (ne) pouvoir plus durer

wake *n.* ensevelissement **keep a vigil or hold a wake over** veiller

wake *v.* **wake up** réveiller, s'éveiller, se réveiller

waking *n.* réveil

walk *n.* marche, viron **go for a walk** faire {prendre} une marche, se promener à pied, se promener

walk *v.* aller à pied, marcher **walk around** marchailler, mouliner **walk back** remarcher **walk unsteadily** gringoler **walk all over** fouler sur (qqn) **walk back and forth** trapigner **walk on one's hands** planter (le) chêne **walk with arms swinging** marcher démanché **walk around in the mud** patrouiller **walk together holding each other by the waist** marcher à la crochette **wade or walk around in water or mud** patauger

walker *n.* marcheur **tightrope walker** cape-cape

walking *n.* marchage **walking around** moulinage **walking stick** canne **walking in mud or shallow water** pataugeage **track up by walking on** pistrailler

wall *n.* barrage, entourage, lattage, mur, muraille, plafonnage, cloison *pl.* **finish the walls or ceiling of** plafonner

wall *v.* **wall in** entourer

wallet *n.* porte-monnaie, portefeuille **steal s.o.'s wallet** soulager (qqn) de sa porte-monnaie

wallflower *n.* **be a wallflower** galérer les bancs

wallpaper *n.* papier, tapisserie **hang wallpaper or tapestry** tapisser **hanging wallpaper or tapestry** tapisserie

wallpaper *v.* papier, papiéter, tapisser

wallpapering *n.* tapisserie

walnut *n.* **walnut tree** nogalier **black walnut** orteil de nègre **black walnut tree** noyer

waltz *n.* valse **waltz with two variant beats** valse à deux-temps **dance a waltz** danser une valse **a series of five dances, traditionally played in order: waltz, polka, waltz in two, two-step, mazurka** ronde de danses

waltz *v.* danser une valse, valser

wander *v.* rôdailler **wander aimlessly** vernailler **wander around** traîner, vagabonder **wander away** s'écarter **wander about as a hobo** traînailler les chemins **one who wanders about** juif-errant

wanderer *n.* rôdailleur, roulailleur, rouleur

wandering *adj.* errant

wandering *n.* **wandering Jew** juif-errant

Wandering *n.* **Wandering Jew** Juif errant

wane *v.* décliner

waning *n.* déclin **waning of the moon** clin de lune

want *n.* manque, nécessité

want *v.* avoir pour, pâtir, souhaiter, vouloir **not want s.t.** vouloir pas de **I don't want to go to Chicago** je n'ai rien perdu à Chicago

war *n.* guerre **make war or fight** faire la guerre

War *n.* **World War I** la Première Guerre Mondiale **World War II** la Guerre Numéro Deux **the Civil War** la Guerre Civile / la Guerre Confédérée / la Guerre des Confédérées **the Revolutionary War** la Guerre de Révolution

warbler *n.* **yellow-rumped warbler** foufou

ward *n.* gardien

ward *v.* **ward off** détourner, parer

wardrobe *n.* armoire, boutique **possessing a large wardrobe** alingé

ware *npl.* **wares** marchandise

warehouse *n.* magasin

warm *adj.* **get warm** se réchauffer **uncomfortably warm** achalant **excessively warm or hot** achalé **make uncomfortably warm or hot** achaler

warm *v.* réchauffer **warm o.s.** se chauffer, se réchauffer **warm slightly** attiédir **warm up** se réchauffer

warmer *adj.* **get warmer** se réchauffer

warming *n.* réchauffage

warmly *adv.* chaudement

warmth *n.* chaleur, chaud

warn *v.* avertir, précautionner, prévenir **warn subtly about a danger** mettre la puce à l'oreille (à qqn)

warning *n.* avertissement, prévenir

warp *v.* couétir, crochir, fausser **cause to warp** couétir

warped *adj.* **become warped** couétir **get warped or fouled up** se fausser **be warped or out of line** faire bassin **become bent or warped** se crochir

warrant *n.* commission, warrant **arrest warrant** warrant **search warrant** warrant

warrant *v.* garantir

warranty *n.* garantie

wart *n.* dartre, poreau, verrue

wartime *n.* **wartime tour of duty** temps de guerre

wash *n.* laundry, lavage **do the wash** laver

wash *v.* débarbouiller, fourbir, laver, éponger **wash again** relaver **wash away** dégrader, laver, se miner **wash o.s.** se débarbouiller, se décroûter, se laver **wash out** laver **wash over** laver **wash up** décroûter, se décrasser, se décrotter **wash o.s. partially** se lavailler **wash one's hands** se laver les mains **wash the dishes** laver la vaisselle **wash with soap** savonner **wash one's face with soap** se savonner la figure

washbasin *n.* bassin à mains / bassin lave mains, bassin à vaisselle, bol de lavabo, bol à mains, bol, lavabo

washboard *n.* battoir, frotteuse, frottoir, WASHBOARD

washbowl *n.* bassine

washed *adj.* **get washed away** se laver

washer *n.* laveuse, roulette, WASHER, rondelle

washerwoman *n.* laveuse

washhouse *n.* cabane à laver, hangar à laver, laverie

washing *n.* débarbouillage, lavage, lavement, laverie **washing machine** laveuse **washing powder** perline, poudre à laver **washing away of mud** débourbage **washing of the priest's hands at mass** lavabo **any washing device** laveuse **place for washing clothes or dishes** laverie **stick used to beat the washing** battoir

washrag *n.* lavette

washstand *n.* lavabo

washtub *n.* bac, baille à laver, bassine **washtub full** bassinée **one half of a barrel used as a washtub, water trough, etc.** barrique

wasp *n.* bourdon, guêpe **wasp nest** nique de guêpe **mud wasp** guêpe noire **paper wasp** guêpe anglaise **mean as a wasp** méchant comme une guêpe **mean as a wasp or hornet** mauvaise comme une guêpe

waste *n.* gargotage, gaspillage, gaspille, perdition, perte **waste of time** berdassement **yard waste** herbages, herbailles **inedible waste parts** débris **go to waste** s'en aller à la perdition **what a waste** quelle perte

waste *v.* gaspiller, gavagner, saganer, savaner **waste away** dépérir, misérer, s'abîmer **one who fiddles around or wastes time** berdasseur

wasteful *adj.* dépensier, gaspillard, gaspilleur **wasteful person** gavagneur

waster *n.* **waster of money** gavagneur

wasting *n.* gaspillage, gaspille **wasting away** patrique **wasting time** berdassement **prevent from wasting** sauver **do s.t. quickly without wasting time** se pas

watch *n.* berloque, guette, montre **watch repairman** horloger **keep watch** faire la fatrouille, veiller **keeping watch** garde **keep watch over the sick** veiller les malades {un malade} **be on the watch** LOOK OUT

watch *v.* guetter, regarder **watch closely** guetter comme un détectif **watch out** guetter, hourra, prendre garde, s'en guetter, veille voir **watch over** surveiller **watch each other** s'observer **stay up and watch over** veiller **one who supervises or watches** surveillant

watchdog *n.* chien de garde

watchful *adj.* vigilant

watchfulness *n.* vigilance

watching *n.* guettage

watchmaker *n.* horloger

watchman *n.* WATCHMAN

water *n.* eau, baba **water bottle** carafe **water moccasin** congo à tête plate / serpent congo, congo, serpent congo, serpent d'eau, serpent à tête plate **water intentionally left out at night and later used for washing the eyes** eau de serein **cold water** eau fraîche **cool water** eau fraîche **dirty water** lessive **draw water** tirer de l'eau **fresh water** eau douce, eau fraîche **high water** montage d'eau **holy water** eau bénite {bénie} **salt water** eau salée {saumâtre} **soapy water** savonnure **spring water** eau de source **stagnant water** eau morte **sweetened water** tchompète **let water flow** lâcher l'eau **body of water** mer **cup of water** pinte d'eau **go under water** caler **puddle of water on the floor** bourbier **odor of stagnant water** hydroforme **fall into the water with a splash** faire poutchoume *pl.* **head waters of a bayou** marais

water *v.* arroser, pomper **water down** baptiser **water the animals** faire boire **make the mouth water** faire la bouche couler

water-flag *n.* clajeux

water-hole *n.* vivier

waterbed *n.* lit d'eau

watercraft *n.* **watercraft used for crossing a bayou or other body of water** traverse

watercress *n.* cresson

watering *n.* arrosage, arrosement **watering can** arrosoir **watering trough** abreuvoir, bac

watermelon *n.* melon d'eau, melon doux, melon vert, melon

waterspout *n.* tourbillon

waterway *n.* **transport by waterway** flotter

waterwheel *n.* **waterwheel used for draining land to be reclaimed** dessèchement

wattle *n.* jabot

wave *n.* flot, onde, lame **cold wave** coup de nord **permanent wave** cléclette, WAVE **tidal wave** raz de marée *pl.* **set waves** WAVE

wave *v.* voyager, WAVE **wave at** faire BYE-BYE

waver *v.* tricoler, tricoter **cause to waver** chavirer

wavering *adj.* **in a wavering fashion** (de) tribord et babord {bâbord}

wax *n.* cire **remove wax** décirer **seal or coat with wax** encirer **device to catch dripping wax of a candle** bobèche

wax *v.* cirer, encirer, profiter, ciroper, se refaire

waxberry *n.* **small waxberry** cirier

waxing *n.* cirage, profitant

waxwing *n.* **cedar waxwing** cirier, mûrier, ortolan

way *interj.* **no way** jamais de la vie

way *n.* chemin, façon, habitude, manière, moyen, route **way of speaking** parlement **either way** n'importe **make way** donner le chemin **no way** pas d'affaire! **roundabout way** détour **that way** par là **this way** comme ceci, par ici **by way of** par **either way is fine** autant à l'ancre qu'à la voile **this way and that** comme ci, comme ça **the way it really is** la franche vérité **feel one's way** tâtonner **in a way** dans {d'} une manière **in any way** n'importe comment **in no way** nullement **in one's way** dans son chemin **in the way** nuisible **in this way** ainsi, astacot **in what way** comment **it's this way** c'est comme ça **show the way** donner le chemin **that's his way** c'est sa manière **there's no way** il y a pas (de) moyen de {pour} **find a way out** s'en sortir **the other way around** contraire **there's no way out** il y a pas de réchappe **in one way or another** (d')une manière ou une {l'} autre **go a long way** faire une grande route **if there's a way** s'il y a moyen **in a small way** petitement **in such a way** si tellement **in the same way** pareillement **stand in the way** nuire **do it one's own way** faire à sa manière **get out of the way** se décaniller, se déniquer, se reculer, sortir du chemin **yield the road or way** donner le chemin **don't go out of your way** fais pas un exprès **move o.s. out of the way** se pousser **be improper, out of the way, uncalled for** avoir pas de place *pl.* **ways** mœurs, WAYS **a ways** un bout **ground ways** WAYS **mend one's ways** se corriger, se réformer **there's no two ways about it** il y a pas de catherine

Way *n.* **Way of the Cross** chemin de (la) Croix **the Milky Way** poussinière

we *pron.* nous-autres, nous, on

weak *adj.* chéti, douillet, débile, escabreux, faible, faillard, faille, fatras, fragile, frêle, ganache, ébahi, ébaroui **be weak** dériver **become weak or weaker** s'affaiblir **spineless, weak, wishy-washy person** poule mouillée **feel weak because of hunger** avoir l'estomac faille **feel weak, dizzy and likely to faint** avoir des faiblesses, faillir **thin and weak** fluet, gningnin **person of weak character** gouère

weaken *v.* affaiblir, décliner, fadir, s'affaiblir, s'amollir, s'amortir

weakening *adj.* affaiblissant

weakening *n.* affaiblissement

weaker *adj.* **become weak or weaker** s'affaiblir

weakling *n.* **be a weakling** avoir un cœur de poisson

weakly *adv.* faiblement

weakness *n.* débilité, défaillance, faiblesse, faillitude

wealth *n.* richesse, trésor **ill-gotten wealth** farine du diable **person of wealth or importance** BIG BOY **something of value, substance, wealth** de quoi

wealthy *adj.* argenté, emmanché, fort, riche comme Crésus, riche **be wealthy** avoir du foin dans ses bottes, avoir la poche pleine, avoir l'argent tambour battant, pas être à pied **become wealthy** s'enrichir **be abundantly wealthy so that one can afford excess and foolishness** amarrer ses chiens avec des saucisses

wealthy *n.* **the wealthy** les riches

wean *v.* ôter dessus la bouteille, sevrer

weaner *n.* **calf weaner** museau

weaning *n.* sevrage

weapon *n.* arme

wear *v.* mettre, porter **wear away** chicoter, défiler, dégrader **wear down** harasser **wear out** défiler, s'user, se démancher, user, échiner **wear sideburns** se raser à la prussienne **wear thin** défiler **wear a mask** se masquer **wear a veil** se voiler **wear every day** porter (qqch) comme la peau **wear good clothes** porter du bon linge **wear loud colors** s'habiller mardi gras **wear o.s. out** s'escrimer, s'esquinter, se donner une touche **wear for everyday use** traîner **wear down the heel of** aculer **wear one's heart on one's sleeve** avoir le cœur sur ses bras **fit to wear** mettable **put on or wear footwear** se chausser **that will not wear out** inusable **she wears the pants** elle porte les culottes **said of one who wears out his clothes quickly** usurier

wearable *adj.* mettable, portable

weariness *n.* fatigue

wearisome *adj.* larguant **wearisome thing** fatigue

weary *adj.* fatigué, largue, largué, lasse, tanné **grow weary** lasser, se larguer

weary *v.* abalourdir, achaler

weasel *n.* belette, fouine

weather *n.* temps, élément **weather forecaster** prédicateur du temps **bad weather** coup de temps, mauvais temps **hazy weather** temps boucané **warm weather** chaud **the weather is spoiling** le temps est après se gâter **be bad weather** faire mauvais temps, faire mauvais **be good weather** faire beau temps **cloudy, overcast weather** temps couvert **gloomy, overcast weather** temps boucané **have good weather** avoir du bon {beau} temps **it's rainy weather** le temps est à la pluie **spell of good weather** série de beau temps **clearing up of the weather** cassée du temps

weatherboard *n.* voliche **apply weatherboard** volicher

weatherboard *v.* volicher

weatherboarding *n.* volichage **remove weatherboarding** détourer **process of weatherboarding a house** volichage

weatherman *n.* prédicateur du temps

weathervane *n.* air de vent, girouette

weave *v.* faire le métier, frapper au métier **weave in and out** tricoter

weaving *n.* frappage **thick weaving made of strips of used cloth, often used for rugs** lirette

web *n.* **spider web** fil d'araignée

wed *v.* marier, épouser

wedding *n.* mariage, noce, nuptial **wedding dress** robe de noces **wedding party** partie de noce **wedding quilt** quilte d'alliance **wedding reception** dessert **wedding ring** alliance **wedding ball or dance** bal de noce **wedding garments and accessories** agrès de noces **hand-sewn wedding outfit made for one's daughter** amour-de-maman

wedge *n.* coin de fer, coin

wedge *v.* coincer

wedging *n.* coincement

Wednesday *n.* mercredi **Ash Wednesday** Mercredi des Cendres

weed *n.* herbe farouche, herbe **alligator weed** herbe à cocodrie {de batture} **camphor weed** baume (de) sauvage **cypress weed** anis marron **indigo weed** indigo **jimson weed** cornard **Yankee weed** anis sauvage *pl.* **weeds** grandes herbes, herbages, herbailles **tall weeds** fardoche **clear out weeds or underbrush** défraîchir

weed *v.* sercler

weeder *n.* herse, sercleur

weeding *n.* serclage **weeding season** serclage

week *n.* semaine **last week** la semaine passée **next week** la semaine prochaine, la semaine qui vient **per week** par semaine **a week, a month, two days ago** ça donne une semaine {un mois / deux jours} que *pl.* **two weeks** quinze jours

Week *n.* **Holy Week** la semaine sainte

weekday *n.* jour de semaine

weekend *n.* fin de semaine, WEEKEND

weekly *adv.* par semaine

weep *v.* beugler, brailler, crier, pleurer **weep profusely** se désoler
weeper *n.* pleureur
weeping *n.* braille, pleure
weevil *n.* mite **boll weevil** BOLL-WEEVE, weev *pl.* **full of weevils** miteux, mité
weevily *adj.* miteux, mité
weigh *v.* peser, peser **weigh o.s.** se peser
weighing *n.* pesage
weight *n.* pesanteur, poids **add weight** alourdir **gain weight** faire du corps, gagner du poids, gagner **lead weight** panneau, plomb **lose weight** fondre, maigrir, perdre du poids, se faire maigrir **regain weight** rengraisser, reprendre du poids, se rengraisser **buy by weight** acheter au poids **put on weight** engraisser **lead ball attached along the bottom of a trawl net to serve as a weight** balle de plomb
weight *v.* **weight with lead** plomber
weighted *adj.* plombé **weighted rope** ralingue
weir *n.* varveau
weird *adj.* drôle de
weirdo *n.* beau coco
welcome *adj.* **you're welcome** de rien, il y a pas de quoi
welcome *n.* **overstay one's welcome** se camper
welcome *v.* recevoir
weld *n.* soudure
weld *v.* souder
weldable *adj.* soudable
welder *n.* soudeur
welding *n.* **welding machine** soudeuse
welfare *n.* salut, WELFARE **department of public welfare** RELIEF
well *adv.* ALL RIGHT, bien portant, bien, comme le fil en aiguille, comme un papier de musique, comme une plume, enfin, et bien, fameusement, gaillard, WELL **well enough** assez bien **as well** aussi bien, enrabatan, itou **be well** se porter bien, être bien **darn well** sacrément **feel well** se sentir bien **get well** guérir, ragaillardir, se rétablir **not well** chéti, traînassant **oh well** aussi bien que **seem well** avoir bonne mine **very well** bien bien **just as well** autant {tant} quitte, autant quitte **might as well** autant {tant} quitte **not be well** être pas (trop) catholique **not feel well** avoir un pet accroché **not so well** poc à poc **quickly and not very well** à la va vite
well *conj.* mais
well *interj.* ben, ma foi!, r'garde mais donc!, tiens **well then** ben **well, I declare** mais jamais
well *n.* puits **ink well** encrier **oil well** puits d'huile, puits **water well** puits à {d'} eau
well-advised *adj.* bien avisé
well-behaved *adj.* bon
well-being *n.* bien-être
well-dressed *adj.* **well-dressed person** faraud
well-to-do *adj.* argenté, fort
welt *n.* loupe
wench *n.* belle-dame
weredog *n.* loup-garou
werewolf *n.* chien-loup, loup-garou **roam the roads at night as a werewolf** courir rougarou
west *n.* ouest
wet *adj.* humide, souple, trempe **get wet** s'humecter, se tremper **get wet again** se retremper **soaking wet with perspiration** à la nage de sueur **cause to be wet** tremper
wet *v.* humecter, mouiller, tremper, saucer **wet again** retremper **wet o.s.** se retremper, se tremper **wet the bed** retremper le lit, tremper le lit
wetness *n.* humidité
whale *n.* baleine **whale bone** baleine
wharf *n.* dépôt, port
what *adj.* quel
what *pron.* ce que, ce qui, ou qui ou quoi, qu'est-ce que, qui ce que / qui c'est que, qui ce qui / qui c'est qui, qui, quoi ce (que) / quoi c'est (que), quoi ce qui / quoi c'est qui, quoi, quèque, ça par exemple!, ça que, ça qui **what?** ça **what** qué **what?** est-il **what are** qui ce que / qui c'est que, quoi ce (que) / quoi c'est (que) **what else** qui d'autre **what if** mettons {mettant} que **what is** qui ce que / qui c'est que, quoi ce (que) / quoi c'est (que) **what's happening?** qui ça dit? **what's new?** qui ça dit? **what's up?** qui ça dit?, quoi ça dit? **what is it** qui il y a / qui y a / qui i-n-a / qui il a **what's the matter?** quoi (il) y a? / quoi i-n-a? **for what** pour qui **no matter what** qu'importe
what-not *n.* nonote **what-not shelf** étagère
what's-his-name *n.* chose
whatchamacallit *n.* chose
whatever *pron.* n'importe qui, n'importe quoi, qu'importe
wheat *n.* blé, froment **wheat bread** pain de froment **wheat flour** farine française **deep fried corn or wheat cake** beigne
wheedle *v.* emmioler, miauler
wheedling *n.* mialement
wheel *n.* roue **wheel track** pente **fifth wheel** cinquième roue **spinning wheel** métier, roi, rouette **steering wheel** roue **hub of a wheel** moyeu
wheelbarrow *n.* berouette
wheelbarrowful *n.* berouettée
wheelchair *n.* chaise à roues
wheeze *v.* siller sur l'estomac, siller
wheezing *n.* silement
whelk *n.* calimaçon
when *adv.* comme, du temps que, dès que / desque / drès que, quand, que, un coup que **even when** quand même (que)
whenever *adv.* n'importe quand, n'importe qui temps, quand
where *adv.* ayoù ce que / iousque / ousque / oùsque, ayoù, là où / là vou, que
wherever *adv.* n'importe ayoù, partout
wherewithal *n.* pousse-pousse

whet *n.* **whet stone** meule
whether *conj.* que **whether . . . or** soit que... ou que **whether . . . or not** quand même que… ou non
whey *n.* petit-lait, petit lait **curds and whey** couche-couche caillé, tape-en-gueule
which *adj.* quel
which *pron.* que, quel, qui, quoi **about which** dont, que **of which** dont, que
whichever *adj.* n'importe quel
whiff *n.* **get a whiff of** éventer
whiffletree *n.* bacul, barconcu
while *conj.* du temps que, en, pendant (que), tandis que, tandis, tant que
while *n.* **a while** élan **a good while** un bon bout de temps, un bon élan **after a while** talheure **quite a while** un bon boute, un bon élan **take a while** mettre du temps **a short while ago** talheure **once in a while** (de) temps en temps **every once in a while** tous les tremblements de terre
whim *n.* caprice, ravigaud, tocate **buy on a whim** acheter à l'œil **sudden idea or whim** estampique *pl.* **full of whims** capricieux
whine *v.* pialler **person who constantly whines and complains** pratique à chagrin
whiner *n.* plaignard, plaignoux, pialleur
whining *adj.* chigneux, gningnin
whining *n.* piallerie
whinny *v.* hennir
whiny *adj.* gueulard **whiny or difficult child** pienque
whip *n.* coursaillère, fouet, SWITCH, toucheron, baleine **whip socket** porte-fouet **buggy whip** fouet de boghei **leather whip** fouet de peau **short whip made of plaited thongs** couarte **crack one's whip** claquer son fouet **crack the whip** flailler le fouet **hide the whip** cacher-fouet **snap one's whip** claquer son fouet **tip of a whip** tchicadence **leather tip of a whip** mèche
whip *v.* abominer, assaper, bûcher, baleiner, carder, doubler, esquinter, flailler, flauber, fouetter, hacher, herser, louper, racler, rincer, roquer, roucheter, roustailler, tailler, tiller, épiauler, étriper, bûchailler, couarter **whip s.o.** passer à la baleine
whipping *n.* bûcherie, bûchée, brûlée, dandine, douille, décoction, pile, raclure, raclée, ramasse, ratatouille, rincée, rinçure, roussequette, rousseture, roussetée, suée, trempe, volée **give a whipping** plumer le dinde, sacrer une raclée, tailler **give a whipping or spanking** piquer le moulin **give a good whipping** donner une volée
whir *v.* ronfler
whirl *v.* bouliner, tournailler **whirl around** turluter
whirligig *n.* pirouette
whirlpool *n.* tortillon, vire-vire
whirlwind *n.* tourbillon
whisk *v.* passer à la baleine
whisker *n.* chicot *pl.* **whiskers** barbe, moustache **side whiskers** bagari, jambon, platine, prussienne
whiskey *n.* whisky **bootleg whiskey** BOOTLEG **camphorated whiskey** whisky camphré **rye whiskey** RYE **finger of whiskey** un doigt de whiskey
whisper *v.* chuchoter, susurrer
whispering *n.* chuchotement
whistle *n.* coup de sifflet, sifflet **duck whistle** sifflet de canard **goose whistle** sifflet à z-oie
whistle *v.* siffler, soubler, siller **whistle at** siffler après
whistler *n.* siffleur
whistling *adj.* sifflant
whistling *n.* sifflage, sifflement **call by whistling** siffler après
white *adj.* blanc comme du coton {du lait / la neige / un champignon / un linge}, blanc **white lie** menterie blanche **white people** le monde blanc **make white** blanchir **turn white** blanchir **the white race** le monde blanc **grow white or fair** blondir **predominantly white in color** blanchette **person who has one black and three white grandparents** quarteron **term formerly used by some to refer to a white person who fraternized with black people** négrier
white *n.* **white of the eye** blanc d'œil **egg white** blanc d'œuf, glaire **upper-class white** gros blanc **any thick viscous substance resembling egg white** glaire
whiten *v.* blanchir **whiten again** reblanchir
whiteness *n.* blancheur
whitening *n.* blanchissage, blanchissement
whitewash *v.* blanchir **whitewash again** reblanchir **whitewash with lime** chauter
whitewashing *n.* blanchissage, blanchissement
whiting *n.* robal
whitish *adj.* blanchâtre
whitlow *n.* fouillou, panaris, tour d'ongle, tourniole
whittle *v.* chacoter, chicoter, écharpiller **whittle down** dégobiller, dégrossir, détailler
whiz *v.* ronfler, siller **whiz by** fronner
who *pron.* quel, qui ce que / qui c'est que, qui ce qui / qui c'est qui, qui **who are** qui ce que / qui c'est que **who else** qui d'autre **who is** qui ce que / qui c'est que
whole *adj.* complet, entier, tout rond, tout
wholesale *adj.* au prix coûtant, en gros
wholesale *n.* **buy wholesale** acheter en gros **sell wholesale** vendre en gros
wholly *adv.* complètement, entièrement, tout
whom *pron.* que, quel, qui ce que / qui c'est que, qui **about whom** dont, que **of whom** dont
whooping *n.* **whooping cough** coqueluche
whore *n.* bordel, chienne, garce, prostituée, putain, salope
whore *v.* **whore around** fêter sa fouine, putainer
whorehouse *n.* bordel, maison de putain
whose *poss.* que, dont

why *adv.* comment (ça) se fait, pour qui, pourqui, pourquoi que, pourquoi, quoi faire **that's why** c'est pour ça

wick *n.* mèche **charred part of lamp wick** chapeau **cut or trim the wick of** émécher

wicked *adj.* malva, mauvais, MEAN, méchant **wicked, evil, bad, malicious person or thing** maudit, méchant **be wicked** avoir un cœur noir

wickedness *n.* canaillerie, mauvaiseté, méchanceté

wide *adj.* grand, large

widely *adv.* large

widen *v.* rélargir, s'élargir, élargir

widening *n.* élargissement

wider *adj.* **become wider** s'élargir **make wider** élargir

widgeon *n.* **American widgeon** zinzin

widow *n.* veuve **grass widow** veuve délaissée **act like a widow** faire la veuve

widowed *adj.* veuve

widower *n.* veuve

width *n.* laise, largeur, travers

wife *n.* dame, femme, vieux, époux **future wife** prétende-femme, prétendu **legal wife** légitime **my wife** ma vieille

wig *n.* perruque

wiggle-tail *n.* lève-queue, vire-cul, vire-de-bord, vire-vire

wigwam *n.* cabane sauvage

wild *adj.* brut, déchaîné, effaré, farouche, foulé, fringant, féroce, marron, sauvage, bronque **wild girl** folâtre **wild card with a value between 10 and the jack** mouche **have disheveled or wild hair** avoir la tête égrichée

wild *n.* **gone back to the wild** marron

wilderness *n.* désert, pays perdu

wildflower *n.* **wildflower with a showy yellow flower** pissenlit

wile *n.* ruse

will *n.* courage, gré, volonté, vouloir **ill will** malveillance **last will and testament** testament **extreme ill will** rancune **you can't force s.o. against his will** on envoye pas un chien à la chasse à coups de bâton

will *v.* vouloir

will-o'-the-wisp *n.* feu follet

willet *n.* **western willet** vire-vire

willfulness *n.* entêtement

willing *adj.* consentant, volontaire

willingly *adv.* de bon cœur

willingness *n.* consentement

willow *n.* **willow grove** saulière **willow tree** saule, saulier **weeping willow tree** saule pleurant

willpower *n.* vouloir

willy nilly *adv.* bon gré, mal gré

wilt *v.* afflétrir, faner, flétrir **wilt or die from too much moisture** échauder

wilted *adj.* fané, flète

wily *adj.* rusé **sharp, wily person** pistolet

win *n.* **big win in which one takes the entire pot** raclage

win *v.* gagner, se gagner **win again** regagner **win back** regagner **win hands down** roqueter **slow and steady wins the race** petit train va loin

wind *n.* haleine, souffle, vent **wind from the ocean** vent du large **break wind** lâcher un pet **heavy wind** gros vent **north wind** vent de nord **pass wind** craquer du vent **southwest wind** vent du large **strong wind** vent à décorner un bœuf **nippy wind coming from several directions** vent fringant **northwest wind that heralds good weather** balai du ciel **gust of wind** bouffée de vent, rafale **a cold northeast wind** vent des Lantier **flap in the wind** battocher **go against the wind** remonter le vent {courant} **helpful or welcome wind** vent de grâce *pl.* **March winds** vents de Carême **strong spring winds** vents de Carême

wind *v.* enrouler, entortiller, essouffler, monter, rouler, serpenter, tortiller, tourner **wind up** terminer **wind up again** remonter **wind into a hank or skein** travouiller

windbag *n.* flafla

winded *adj.* **become winded** s'essoufler

winder *n.* **thread winder** dévideur

windfall *n.* lagniappe, trouve

winding *n.* entortillage

windlass *n.* vireveau

windmill *n.* moulin à vent

window *n.* châssis, fenêtre, vitrage, vitre **window curtain** voile **window display** vitreau **window mullion** montant **window pane** carreau de chassis, carreau, châssis, vitre de châssis, vitre **window sash** châssis **window shade** abat-jour, SHADE **window sill** linteau de fenêtre, nèche **dormer window** lucarne **store window** vitrière **paneless, sashless window** fenêtre **plate glass window** vitre **stained glass window** vitrage, vitreau

windpipe *n.* gargoton

windrow *n.* matelas

windrow *v.* windrow

windy *adj.* venteux **be windy** venter

wine *n.* vin **bitter wine** vin hâcre **dry wine** vin hâcre **home-made wine** vin **muscat wine** muscat **sparkling wine** champagne **strong wine** vin à vingt batailles au gallon **dilute the wine** couper le vin

wing *n.* aile **wing nut** noix avec des ailes / noix-z-oreilles, noix *pl.* **flapping of wings** battement d'ailes **speak of angels, see their wings** en parlant des anges, on voit leurs ailes

wingstem *n.* herbe à trois quarts {écarts}

wink *n.* clin d'œil, clin **not sleep a wink** pas fermer l'œil

wink *v.* quéloëter

winking *n.* quéloëtement

winnable *adj.* gagnable

winner *n.* gagnant, gagneur **winner at cards** haleur d'argent

winning *adj.* gagnant

winning *npl.* **take all the winnings in** roqueter

winnow *v.* vanner, évanner
winnowing *adj.* **winnowing vessel** vanne
winnowing *n.* vannage
winter *n.* hiver **in winter** dans (l')hiver / en hiver **spend the winter in one's seasonal home** camper
winterberry *n.* **winterberry tree** cenellier
wipe *v.* essuyer, torcher **wipe down** passer **wipe o.s.** s'essuyer **wipe off again** ressuyer **wipe or sponge** torcher **wipe or blow the nose** moucher **rag used to wipe the bottom after a bowel movement** torche
wiping *n.* essuyage
wire *n.* fil de fer, fil **wire stretcher** raidissoir, tend-fil, éridisseuse **baling wire** fil d'alton **barbed wire** fil de fer à piquant, fil de fer, fil à piquants **chicken wire** fil à volaille **electric wire** fil électrique **electrical wire** fil à l'électricité **fencing wire** fil à barrière **hog wire** fil de fer à carreau, fil à {de} carreaux **mesh wire** fil à volaille **telephone wire** fil de téléphone **rectangular-holed wire fencing** fil de fer à carreau, fil à {de} carreaux **thin brass or iron tie wire** fil d'alton
wire *v.* enfiler
wirecutter *n.* pince
wisdom *n.* sagesse **wisdom tooth** dent de sagesse
wise *adj.* déluré **wise man** mage **wise person** sage, savant **be wise, informed** avoir le nez long **be wise to s.o.'s tricks** être dans le panneau à qqn
wish *n.* désir, envie, gré, souhait, volonté
wish *v.* avoir envie de, désirer, souhaiter, vouloir **wish for o.s.** se souhaiter, se vouloir **wish to be** se vouloir **if you wish** si tu veux **as much as one wishes** à son contentement
wishy-washy *adj.* **wishy-washy person** lavette **spineless, weak, wishy-washy person** poule mouillée
wisteria *n.* glycine, liane blanche
witch *n.* sorcier
with *n.* **fight with each other** se piguenocher
with *prep.* avec, à, après, auprès de, à **not with it** pas bien plombé
withdraw *v.* s'éloigner, se retirer, retirer
withdrawal *n.* retraite
withdrawn *adj.* taqué
wither *v.* déchesser, dépérir, faner, flétrir, misérer
withered *adj.* fané, flète
withers *npl.* garrot **fistula of withers** mal anglais
withhold *v.* retenir
without *conj.* sans (que)
without *prep.* avec pas, sans
witness *n.* témoin **bear witness** testifier, témoigner **false witness** faux témoignage
wizard *n.* sorcier
wobble *v.* ballotter, caracoler, voiler
wobbly *adj.* escrampé
wolf *n.* loup, loulou **prairie wolf** coyote **red wolf** loup rouge
wolfdog *n.* chien-loup
woman *n.* femelle, femme, torquette, négresse **woman confined for childbirth** accouchée **woman whose husband has left her** veuve rabiotte **woman of mixed Caucasian and American Indian descent** vénus **beautiful woman** beauté **big woman** colosse, domboune **brown-haired woman** brune, brunette **Indian woman** taïque **old woman** vieille bique, vieux **a woman who marries must accommodate herself to her husband's habits, family, etc.** qui prend mari, prend pays **short, heavyset woman** balloune **short, stout woman** tamponne *pl.* **chase women** rouscailler **chase women or men** coursailler, courser **meeting of women for the purpose of carding cotton or wool** écarderie
woman-chaser *n.* bambocheur, bervocheur, chiennailleur, coursailleur, courseur, potre, rouscailleur
womanizer *n.* chiennailleur, coursailleur, courseur
womanizing *adj.* amoureux comme un paon, amoureux comme une puce
womb *n.* entrailles, matrice
wonder *n.* merveille, étonnement
wonder *v.* se demander **wonder at** s'étonner
wonderful *adj.* admirable, magnifique, merveilleux
wonderfully *adv.* magnifiquement
woo *v.* courtiller, courtiser, faire la cour à, faire l'amour (à)
wood *n.* bois **wood pile** bûcher, huche **light wood** liège **maple wood** plaine **pecan wood** pacanier **rough wood** gros bois **stove wood** bois de STOVE **armful of wood** brassée de bois **cord of wood** corde de bois **piece of wood** rondin **rank of wood** corde de bois **armful of wood put into a fire** attisée **pile up wood in the form of a cage** cager du bois **chimney or fireplace wood** bois de cheminée **group who cuts wood** bûcherie **heavy piece of wood** bille **pine tree or wood** bois de pin / bois gras **long piece of wood by means of which a pair of horses or mules is attached to a wagon** flèche **burnt part of a wood or forest** brûlé **chunk or slab of wood or stone** gobe **piece of rough or knotty wood** boscoyo **thin, straight cylindrical piece or bar of metal or wood** barreau *pl.* **woods** bois, grand bois **thick woods** forêt **piney woods of north and west Louisiana** pinière **point of woods** pointe de bois, pointe **edge of the woods** bordure de bois **thick shrubbery or woods** boisure
woodcock *n.* bécasse de nuit, bécasse
woodcutter *n.* bûcheur de bois, bûcheur, déséreur
wooded *adj.* **little wooded area in the middle of the prairie** île d'arbres
wooden *adj.* **wooden leg** jambe de liège
woodland *n.* terre de bois **area of land partially enclosed by woodland** anse
woodpecker *n.* pique-bois **golden woodpecker** pique-bois doré {jaune} **ivory-billed woodpecker** grande pique-bois,

poule de bois **red-headed woodpecker** pique-bois tête rouge **wryneck woodpecker** torcou

woodsman *n.* déséreur

woodwork *n.* boisure, boiture d'encadrement

woody *adj.* **swampy, woody area that is not easily accessible** portage

wooer *n.* prétendant

wool *n.* laine **wool carded in strips** PLUG **wool or thread carried by a shuttle** chaîne **spool of wool or cotton** cardon **cotton or wool spun to be woven** jeture **bat of carded wool or cotton ready for spinning** écardon **piece of cotton or wool that has been carded** cardon

word *n.* mot, parole, terme **word for word** mot pour mot **word of honor** parole d'honneur **bad word** vilain mot **dirty word** vilain mot **send word** envoyer dire, faire dire **traditional word game** calembour **give one's word** donner sa parole **in a word** enfin **keep one's word** tenir à sa parole **not a word** ouinque **pass the word or news** donner le mot **let slip a bad word** échapper une mauvaise parole **person of his or her word** personne de parole *pl.* **harsh words** paroles blessantes **ritual words or gestures used by a folk healer during a treatment** simagris **eat one's words** renvaler ses paroles **in other words** c'est-à-dire, en autres mots **not mince words** pas mettre des gants **choose one's words carefully** placer bien ses mots **use s.o.'s words against him or her** retirer qqch dans la figure à qqn **have a way with words** avoir le palais bien fendu

Word *n.* **the Word** parole

work *n.* œuvre, job, labeur, occupation, ouvrage, travail **work bench** établi **work of art** œuvre **badly-done work** barbouillage **good work** bonne œuvre **leaving work** débauchage, débauche **mechanic work** mécanique **slovenly work** pitié d'affaire **underhand work** machinerie **underhanded work** croche **written work** écrit **yard work** ouvrage de cour **finish work or school** lâcher **be off work** débaucher **careless, sloppy work** barbotage **do inferior work** berdasser **do light work** berdasser **get to work** mettre l'épaule à la roue **go to work** embaucher, prendre l'ouvrage, se mettre à l'ouvrage **line of work** ouvrage **piece of work** job **spoil one's work** broucheter **line of work or activity** ligne **piece of work done poorly or in a slipshod manner** cochonnerie **end the day's work** larguer **let's go to work** allons s'y mettre **long, hard, steady work** sainte-hale-ça **one who does work that requires little effort** dépendeur d'andouille **lag behind in one's work** traîner les savates **one who does bad or sloppy work** cochonneur **that's not in my line of work** c'est pas ma ligne **group of people who do certain work together without pay** personniers *pl.* **smelting works** fonderie

work *v.* boulotter, courir, marcher, opérer, travailler, pratiquer **work again** retravailler **work at** travailler **work faster** faire plus d'avance **work hard** gratter, haler, misérer **work lightly** picocher **work tirelessly** se déchaîner **work together** haler ensemble **work well** travailler comme un neuf / travailler comme un papier de musique **work odd jobs** jober **work to excess** éreinter **work too hurriedly** broucheter **work without pressure** berdasser **work by the day** jober, travailler par jour, travailler à la journée **work by the week** travailler par semaine **work for one's living** faire une {sa} vie **work hard at s.t.** s'esquinter **work hard without stopping** HIGH **work like a charm** travailler comme un neuf / travailler comme un papier de musique **work o.s. to excess** s'éreinter **work as a day laborer** travailler à la journée **work hard for a living** gagner son pain par la sueur de son front **work in a slovenly fashion** gargouiller **work for a share of profits** travailler à la part **work in the sugar cane harvest** rouler **work by the job, task, or piece** travailler à la tâche **not work** pas casser la rate **one who works cattle on horseback** cavalier **one who works in a careless or slipshod way** barboteur

workable *adj.* maniable

worked *adj.* **get emotionally worked up** s'épouvanter

worker *n.* travaillant, travailleur **worker in the swamps** swampeur **worker who prepares bousillage** tâcheron **good worker** bon travailleur **hard worker** cheval de bataille, haleur d'ouvrage **poll worker** commissionnaire **tapestry worker** tapisseur *pl.* **workers camp, quarters** camp **settlement of workers in some industry** camp

working *adj.* **working man or woman** travaillant

working *n.* opération **begin working** embaucher **stop working temporarily** lay-off **kill o.s. working** se tuer à travailler **in proper working condition** correct

workmanship *n.* travail **product of workmanship** apprêtement

workroom *n.* SHOP

workshop *n.* atelier, SHOP

world *n.* monde, terre, univers **the world** création **the whole world** tout le monde entier **bring into the world** amener (un enfant) au monde, rendre au monde **how in the world** comment dans le monde! **in a dream world** dans les nuages **be in a dream world** être dans les nués

World *n.* **World War I** la Première Guerre Mondiale **World War II** la Guerre Numéro Deux **the Old World** l'autre bord

worldly *adj.* séculier

worm *n.* bétaille, ver **grub worm** ver blanc **span worm** arpenteuse **surveyor worm** arpenteuse **woodeating worm** ver de bois **bug or worm that curls up when touched** tortue *pl.* **destroyed or damaged by worms or insects** piqué

worm-eaten *adj.* piqué

wormhole *n.* piqûre

wormwood *n.* absinthe, herbe sainte, herbe à vers

worn *adj.* racatcha, rasé **worn out** abîmé, efflanqué, fatras, malfoutu, mort, racatcha, usé, à bout, échiné, éraillé **get**

worn out attraper une touche, se donner une touche **become worn, faded, discolored, or tarnished** détamer

worried *adj.* anxieux, inquiet, trouble **be worried** avoir le vent debout, être tracassé **be extremely worried** être vent-debout

worrisome *adj.* agaçant, inquiétant, tracassant

worry *n.* tracas **be out of one's senses with worry** être vent-debout *pl.* **have worries over** s'emmicher avec

worry *v.* agacer, emmicher, giguler, jongler, occuper, s'inquiéter, se tracasser, tourmenter, tracasser, user **worry about** jongler, s'emmicher avec **cause to worry** giguler, occuper, tourmenter, tracasser

worrying *adj.* tracassant

worse *adj.* pire **worse and worse** (de) pire en pire **get worse** empirer, engraver, rempirer, s'en aller au dépit, s'engraver **make worse** engraver, rempirer **from bad to worse** de mal en pire **so much the worse** tant pire **go from bad to worse** dégrouler **take a turn for the worse** empirer **the more it goes, the worse it gets** le plus ça va, le pire c'est

worse *adv.* plus mal

worsen *v.* décliner, dégénérer, engraver, rempirer, s'engraver

worsened *adj.* **ruined or worsened state** dépit

worship *n.* adoration

worship *v.* adorer

worshipper *n.* adorateur

worst *adj.* pire

worth *adj.* **be worth** valoir **it's worth as much** c'est tant quitte **it's not worth it** c'est pas la peine / ça vaut pas la peine **it's not worth much** ça craque pas fort **neither is worth much** l'un vaut l'autre et l'autre vaut rien / l'un vaut l'autre et les deux vaut rien **not be worth a crap** pas valoir une merde **it's not worth the trouble or risk** le jeu (ne) vaut pas la chandelle **fancy gadgets are not worth the money one pays for them** pèse bouton, paie couillon

worth *n.* mérite, valeur **validate or demonstrate the worth of** faire valoir

worthless *adj.* fatras, pas assez bon pour faire du savon **worthless fellow** racatcha **worthless man** couac-soleil, haricot fleur, vaurien **worthless person** foutraille, TRASH **worthless thing** cochonnerie, fatras, fritche **worthless idea or thing** foutaise **worthless person or animal** drigaille **worthless thing or person** farbana, vauriennerie **worthless, good-for-nothing, lazy girl** bringue **worthless person who thinks a lot of himself** petit couteau

worthlessness *n.* bonarienté, faignanterie

worthwhile *adj.* **be worthwhile** compter quelque chose

worthy *adj.* digne

would *v.* **would that** plutôt

wound *adj.* **wound down** démonté **get wound up as one begins talking** monter sa manivelle

wound *n.* blessure, bobo, plaie **slight wound** grafignure

wound *v.* blesser **wound o.s.** se blesser

woven *adj.* **loosely woven** poreux

wow *interj.* boy, oh (y) yaïe / oh yé yaïe

wow *n.* yaïe

wrangle *v.* chamailler, se chamailler, se disputailler **wrangle over trifles** chicoter **one who wrangles, disputes, fusses** disputeur

wrangling *n.* halaillement

wrap *v.* bander, bourrer, envelopper, tortiller **wrap up** bourrer **wrap o.s. around** s'entortiller **wrap o.s. up** s'envelopper

wrapper *n.* enveloppe

wrapping *n.* enveloppement

wrathful *adj.* en fantaisie

wreath *n.* couronne **bridal wreath plant** couronne de mariée

wreck *n.* abordage **have a wreck** planter (le) chêne

wren *n.* bénéri, roi Bertaud, roitelet **Carolina wren** prie-Dieu

wrench *n.* clef anglaise, clef, WRENCH **wrench in the back** tour de reins **monkey wrench** clef anglaise **any big wrench** macorenche

wrenching *n.* détour

wrestle *v.* colletailler, luttailler, lutter **arm wrestle** coucher au poignet **wrist wrestle** coucher au poignet

wrestler *n.* lutteur

wrestling *adj.* **wrestling move in which a wrestler places one leg behind his opponent's legs and pulls him backwards to the mat** jambette

wrestling *n.* **wrestling match** basculage, lutte

wretch *n.* misérable

wretched *adj.* pouillasse, ratché

wretched-looking *adj.* raponneau

wretchedness *n.* pouillasserie

wriggle *v.* fertiller, tortiller

wring *v.* se tordre **wring out** tordre **wring out again** retordre **wring the neck of** étourdir

wrinkle *n.* gerce, gerçure, pli, plissure, ride *pl.* **iron out wrinkles** défroncer **smooth out wrinkles in the skin of** dérider

wrinkle *v.* chiffonner, froncer, plisser, rider

wrinkled *adj.* frisé, froncé, ridé, plissé **become wrinkled** se rider

wrinkling *n.* plissage

wrist *n.* poignet **wrist wrestle** coucher au poignet **dislocated wrist** poignet ouvert **sprained wrist** poignet ouvert

write *v.* écrire **write again** récrire **write back** récrire **write down** documenter **write songs** faire des chansons **write in response** récrire **write to each other** s'écrire

writer *n.* auteur, écrivain

writing *n.* écrit, écritage, écriture **messy writing or painting** barbouillage

wrong *adj.* croche, mauvais, méchant, WRONG **wrong side** revers **be wrong** avoir tort, se tromper **what's wrong?** qui il y a / qui y a / qui i-n-a / qui il a **have s.t. wrong** y avoir qqch de WRONG **always say the wrong thing** avoir une gueule comme un vilevaquin

wrong *n.* injure, mal, offense, tort **do wrong** faire (de / du) tort, malfaire **in the wrong** en tort / dans le tort **be in the wrong** avoir tort **vengeance never evens out a wrong** le sirop et biscuits cassent pas égal

wrong *v.* **wrong by abusing one's rights** faire un passe-droit

wrongly *adv.* mal

Y

yam *n.* igname, patate douce, yam **yellow yam** patate giraumont

Yankee *n.* gueule rouge, Yankee

yap *v.* jappailler, japper

yapping *n.* jappement

yard *n.* corail, cour, yard **yard waste** herbages, herbailles **yard work** ouvrage de cour **yard behind a house** large **back yard** cour (d')en arrière **chicken yard** basse-cour **front yard** cour (de) devant {(d')en avant}

yardstick *n.* mesure

yarn *n.* fil **spin thread, yarn, or string** filer

yaupon cassinier

yawl *n.* gnole

yawn *n.* bâille, bâillement

yawn *v.* bâiller, faire son mulet

yawner *n.* bâilleur

yawning *n.* bâillement

yeah *adv.* oui

year *n.* an, année **last year** l'année passée **next year** l'année prochaine / l'année qui vient **this year** cette année (c't' année / est'année), cette année *pl.* **many years ago** des années **be ten years old** avoir dix {vingt, etc.} ans **turn ten years old** faire dix {vingt, etc.} ans

Year *n.* **New Year's Day** Jour de l'An **New Year's Eve** veille de l'an **New Year's gift** étrenne

yearly *adj.* annuel

yearning *n.* aspiration

yeast *n.* ferment, levain, YEAST **yeast cake** galette, YEASTCAKE

yell *n.* cri, haut-le-corps, hurlement

yell *v.* bagueuler, criailler, crier, hurler, héler, pousser un cri **yell at** crier après (qqn) **yell obnoxiously** hurlailler **yell out again** recrier **one who yells** criard **one who yells or shouts** crieur

yelling *n.* hurlement **repeated yelling or shouting** criaillement

yellow *adj.* jaune **yellow fever** fièvre jaune **yellow or tan colored** barosse **become yellow** jaunir **dye yellow** jaunir **make yellow** jaunir **paint yellow** jaunir

yellow *v.* jaunir

yellow-belly *n.* ventre jaune

yellow-legs *n.* patte jaune **greater yellow-legs** clouclouque

yellowish *adj.* jaunâtre

yellowish-colored *adj.* **person with a yellowish-colored face** jaunaca

yellowtail *n.* mademoiselle

yelp *v.* jappailler, japper

yelping *n.* jappement

yes *adv.* oui, vouiche **but yes** mais oui

yes *interj.* ain-hein **yes, indeed** foutûment oui **heck yes** fichtre oui **hell yes** fichtre oui

yes *n.* **be a yes man for s.o.** sauter crapaud (pour qqn)

yesterday *n.* hier **yesterday morning** hier matin **yesterday noon** hier midi **day before yesterday** avant-hier (matin, midi, soir) **the day before yesterday** avant-hier

yet *adv.* cependant, pourtant **not yet** pas encore

yield *v.* cailler, céder, fournir, obéir, plier, produire, rapporter, s'abandonner à, se soumettre, succomber, rendre **yield without resistance** faire play **yield the road or way** donner le chemin

yoke *n.* joug, youque **breast yoke** BREAST-YOKE **dress yoke** fiorelle **round yoke** fiorelle

yoke *v.* accoupler, ajouquer, macorner, youquer

yoking *n.* macornage

yolk *n.* **egg yolk** jaune d'œuf

you *pron.* te, toi-même, toi, tu (t'), vous-autres, vous-même, vous **you all** vous-autres **you know** tu {vous} connais / vous connaissez **you see** tu {vous} connais / vous connaissez **you yourselves** vous-autres même **for you** te, toi, vous **to you** te, vous

young *adj.* jeune, petit **young man** jeune gens **young people** jeunesse **young person** jeune, jeunesse **young woman** créature, fille **young, unmarried woman known for having a wild side** bougresse **the young generation** le jeune monde

young *n.* **the young** le jeune monde

younger *adj.* petit **get younger** rajeunir **grow younger** jeunezir **trying to act like a younger person** rapiqué

your *poss.* le, ton, votre **your own** tien

yours *poss.* eusse tiennes, te le tien, tien, ton tien, vôtre

yourself *pron.* te, toi-même, toi, vous-même, vous **for yourself** toi **myself, yourself, ourselves, etc.** entre moi-même {toi-même, nous-mêmes, etc.}

yourselves *pron.* vous **you yourselves** vous-autres même

youth *n.* jeune, jeunesse

youthfulness *n.* jeunesse

yoyo *n.* yoyo

yucca *n.* pique

Z

zeal *n.* zèle
zebra *n.* ZEBRA
zero *n.* zéro
zest *n.* **zest for living** joie de vivre
zestful *adj.* animé
zigzag *n.* zigzag
zigzag *v.* zigzaguer
zinnia *n.* vieux garçon
zipper *n.* zip, braguette
zoo *n.* zoo
zucchini *n.* cochotte, courgette
zydeco *n.* **zydeco music** zaricot